BUCKSCH-REPRINT

Herbert Bucksch

Wörterbuch für
Ingenieurbau und Baumaschinen

*

Dictionary of
Civil Engineering and Construction
Machinery and Equipment

Band I Volume
Deutsch · Englisch / German · English

Volume II Band
English · German / Englisch · Deutsch

BAUVERLAG GMBH · WIESBADEN AND BERLIN

CIP-Kurztitelaufnahme der Deutschen Bibliothek

Bucksch, Herbert:
Wörterbuch für Ingenieurbau und Baumaschinen = Dictionary of civil engineering and construction, machinery and equipment / Herbert Bucksch. – Unveränd. Nachdr. d. 3. Aufl., 2. Nachdr. – Wiesbaden; Berlin: Bauverlag, 1987.
   (Bucksch-Reprint)
   Nebent.: Wörterbuch Bau. – Enth.: Bd. 1. Deutschenglisch. Vol 2. English German
   ISBN 3-7625-2553-6

NE: HST; NT

BUCKSCH-REPRINT
Unveränderter Nachdruck der 3. Auflage 1965
Unchanged reprint of the third edition 1965

1. Nachdruck / 1st reprint 1981
2. Nachdruck / 1nd reprint 1987

Das Werk ist urheberrechtlich geschützt.
Die dadurch begründeten Rechte, insbesondere die der Übersetzung, des Nachdruckes, der Entnahme von Abbildungen, der Funksendung, der Wiedergabe auf fotomechanischem oder ähnlichem Wege (Fotokopie, Mikrokopie) und der Speicherung in Datenverarbeitungsanlagen, bleiben, auch bei nur auszugsweiser Verwertung vorbehalten.

© 1981 by Bauverlag GmbH · Wiesbaden und Berlin
Druck: Hans Meister KG, Kassel

ISBN 3-7625-2553-6

VORWORT DES VERLAGES ZUM NACHDRUCK

Von Herbert Bucksch gibt es bereits eine Reihe von bewährten Fachwörterbüchern im technischen Bereich. Einmalig in ihrer Vollständigkeit und weltweit verbreitet sind die beiden großen Ausgaben

- Wörterbuch für Bautechnik und Baumaschinen
  (zwei Bände mit zusammen etwa 2 400 Seiten)
- Wörterbuch für Architektur, Hochbau und Baustoffe
  (zwei Bände mit zusammen etwa 2 100 Seiten)

die je Band bzw. pro Sprache nahezu 70 000 Stichwörter, z. T. mit ergänzenden lexigraphischen Erläuterungen, nachweisen!

Unternehmen, Institutionen, Planungs- und Projektierungsbüros, Auslandsbaustellen und -Niederlassungen, Übersetzer, Dolmetscher und Bibliotheken sollten die Bucksch-Wörterbücher auch nur in diesen ausführlichen, aktuellen Ausgaben verwenden.

Verständlicherweise hat dieser umfassende Wörterbuchnachweis seinen Preis, der vor allem für manchen Privatinteressenten bzw. Studenten nur sehr schwer aufzubringen ist. Um deshalb möglichst breiten Kreisen der international interessierten bzw. vielleicht nur gelegentlich in diesem Bereich tätigen Baufachwelt ein für diese Ansprüche ausreichendes Bau-Fachwörterbuch in besonders preisgünstiger Form zugänglich zu machen, wurde das vorliegende

- Wörterbuch Bau – Building Dictionary
  Deutsch-Englisch/Englisch-Deutsch

in einem Band mit zusammen etwa 850 Seiten herausgegeben. Es handelt sich hierbei um den unveränderten Nachdruck der dritten Auflage 1965 des zweibändigen „Wörterbuches für Ingenieurbau und Baumaschinen" von Herbert Bucksch. Immerhin enthielt diese Ausgabe schon damals pro Sprache rund 25 000 Stichwörter aus dem Gesamtbereich der Bautechnik.

Wiesbaden   Bauverlag GmbH

VORWORT ZUR ERSTEN AUFLAGE

Unsere heutige Zivilisation ist ohne den modernen Ingenieurbau nicht mehr denkbar. Durch ihn werden die Bauten zur Ausnützung der Wasserkräfte, wie Talsperren und Wasserkraftwerke, die Verkehrsverbindungen, wie Straßen, Brücken, Kanäle, Eisenbahnlinien und Flugplätze, die Bewässerungs- und Entwässerungsanlagen für die Gewinnung neuer Kulturflächen, die menschlichen Siedlungen in der Vielfalt ihrer Formen usw. geschaffen. Der Mensch verändert die Oberfläche der Erde.

Obwohl bereits im Altertum imposante Bauwerke geschaffen worden sind, wofür die Chinesische Mauer und die Sieben Weltwunder als die bekanntesten Beispiele dienen mögen, brach für den Ingenieurbau jedoch erst mit dem Zeitalter der Erfindungen eine neue Epoche an. Die Lokomotive erforderte Schienenstränge, das Auto verlangte nach Straßen, und für das Flugzeug mußten geeignete Flächen zum Starten und Landen geschaffen werden. Die stetige Verbesserung der Erfindungen bedingte eine Ausweitung der von diesen Erfindungen benötigten Anlagen, und der Ingenieurbau mußte sich zur Erfüllung der ihm in immer rascherem Tempo gestellten Aufgaben eine Reihe von Wissensgebieten erschließen. Systematische Forschung wurde unumgänglich, und bald stellte sich die Notwendigkeit einer Dokumentation der Ergebnisse heraus.

Die Interessen und Ziele der Bauingenieure aller Völker sind die gleichen; sie wollen mit ihren Bauwerken dem Wohl der Menschheit dienen. Daraus ergibt sich die Forderung zu internationaler Zusammenarbeit.

Die heute zur Vertiefung des Wissens auf den einzelnen Teilgebieten des Ingenieurbaues auf internationaler Ebene abgehaltenen Konferenzen sind der Grundstein für diese Zusammenarbeit. Die persönliche Fühlungnahme führt zur Beseitigung des Trennenden und des Mißtrauens. Zwischenstaatliche Bindungen werden jedoch auch auf andere Art und Weise geknüpft. So ist z. B. die „Deutsche Gesellschaft für Erd- und Grundbau" mit der diesbezüglichen Fachorganisation der USA, „ASCE Soil Mechanics and Foundations Division", übereingekommen, einen gegenseitigen Austausch des Wissens auf ihrem Fachgebiet durchzuführen. Als Korrespondenzsprachen wurden Englisch und Deutsch bestimmt.

Die internationale Zusammenarbeit auf dem Gebiete des Ingenieurbaues lenkt nun auch demzufolge das Augenmerk auf die Fachterminologie in bezug auf eine Gegenüberstellung der Begriffe in den verschiedenen Sprachen.

Die heutigen Sprachen erleben täglich die Geburt neuer Wörter. Der Ingenieurbau mit seinen Ausläufern in die verschiedenartigsten Wissensgebiete hat daran, wie überhaupt die Technik, erheblichen Anteil. Hier ergibt sich nun die Forderung nach technischen Wörterbüchern.

Die Zusammenstellung eines technischen Wörterbuches ist wegen der schon in der eigenen Sprache oft unklaren Begriffsbestimmung eines einzelnen technischen Wortes schwierig, und bei der Auswahl des meistens dem gleichen Gesetz verschiedener Definitionsmöglichkeiten unterliegenden fremdsprachlichen Wortes ist daher größte Vorsicht geboten. Selbst wenn technische Wörter frei von jeder Zweideutigkeit in bezug auf ihre Definition sind, ist bei einer Gegenüberstellung mit dem fremdsprachlichen Wort stets zu prüfen, ob sich die Definitionen in beiden Sprachen vom technischen Standpunkt aus decken.

Das vorliegende Wörterbuch wurde mit dem Ziel zusammengestellt, die internationale Zusammenarbeit auf dem Gebiete des Ingenieurbaues zu fördern. Bei der Bearbeitung wurden die neuesten Quellen erschöpft. Viele Begriffe sind hier zum ersten Male lexikographisch erfaßt.

Verlag und Verfasser hoffen, mit der Vorlage dieses Wörterbuches einem Bedürfnis der Kreise des Ingenieurbaues entsprochen zu haben.

Köln, im Februar 1955   H. Bucksch

VORWORT ZUR ZWEITEN AUFLAGE

Diese Auflage erscheint in wesentlich größerem Umfang als die erste. Die Eintragungen wurden noch einmal überprüft und die Terminologie wurde auf den neuesten Stand gebracht. Eine Aufteilung in zwei Bände ist bei dieser Ausgabe als zweckmäßig erachtet worden. Verlag und Verfasser hoffen, daß diese Auflage ebenso den Beifall der Fachkreise findet, der der ersten Auflage zuteil geworden ist. Anregungen aus Benutzerkreisen werden stets dankbar entgegengenommen.

Köln, im Mai 1958   H. Bucksch

PUBLISHERS PREFACE

Herbert Bucksch has already published several widely approved technical dictionaries in the field of engineering. Unique in the comprehensive nature of their coverage are:

Dictionary of Civil Engineering and Construction Machinery and Equipment
(2 volumes, approx. 2 400 pp)

Dictionary of Architecture, Building Construction and Materials
(2 volumes, approx. 2 100 pp)

These two dictionaries each contain approx. 70 000 entries for each language, in some cases with additional lexicographic explanation.

Construction firms, institutions, planning offices, overseas construction undertaking libraries, and translators and interpreters will naturally continue to require the comprehensive original editions. However, we also wished to make available at a lower price a dictionary that would appeal to students, and private individuals throughout the world, whether professionally engaged in the field or only requiring a work for occassional reference. We are therefore publishing

Bauwörterbuch − Building Dictionary
German-English/English-German

This is a one. volume reprint (approx. 850 pages) taken from the 1965 third edition of the Dictionary of Civil Engineering and Construction Machinery and Equipment (2 volumes). Some 25 000 entries in each language covering the field of civil engineering.

Wiesbaden   Bauverlag GmbH

PREFACE TO THE FIRST EDITION

Our present civilisation is hardly conceivable without the achievements of modern civil engineering. The "use and convenience" to man of all these activities can scarcely be denied. Civil engineers had certainly left their mark on the face of Nature, damming great lakes and constructing hydro-electric plants, highways, bridges, canals, railway lines, airports, towns, etc.

Although remarkable structures have been erected in ancient times, e. g. the Great Wall of China and the Seven Ancient Wonders of the World, it was not until the last century that civil engineering entered upon a new era. The steam locomotive required trackings, the automobile called for high-quality roads and the aircraft for suitable landing, taking off and servicing facilities. Steady improvements of these inventions brought about a further development of these facilities and civil engineering spread itself over a wide range of scientific fields in order to meet the ever increasing demands. Systematic research became imperative with detailed documentation of the results obtained.

As civil engineers of all countries work towards the same aim of "directing the great sources of power in Nature to the use and convenience of man," international co-operation becomes inevitable.

The foundations of this international co-operation are the many conferences convened by the individual civil engineering organisations in which the experience is pooled for the benefit of all concerned. Civil engineers of all nations thus get into touch with each other and this personal contact soon removes any reserve or sense of mistrust. International connections between civil engineers can be initiated in many ways. For instance, the "Deutsche Gesellschaft für Erd- und Grundbau" (German Society for Soil and Foundation Engineering) and the "ASCE Soil Mechanics and Foundations Division" exchange their knowledge in their relevant field by correspondence in English and German.

This international partnership naturally draws attention to the terminology involved and the selection of equivalent terms in the various languages.

To-day's languages frequently experience the introduction of new words and the field of civil engineering with its widespread ramifications into various other related fields contributes to a considerable extent to this phenomenon. Thus, technical dictionaries are required.

The compilation of a technical dictionary is already difficult because the scope of meaning of a single word in one language is not always clearly defined, and when selecting the appropriate term in the foreign language, which might also not be subject to precise definition, great care must be exercised. Even if technical terms are free from any ambiguity as to their meaning, it must always be borne in mind, that the selected relative foreign words must cover the same range of technical definition.

This dictionary has been compiled in an attempt to foster the harmony of international partnership in Civil Engineering, and the latest relevant literature has been searched for its compilation. It contains a multitude of definitions not yet incorporated into any other dictionary available to-day.

It is hoped by the publisher as well as the author, that this dictionary will fill the gap felt in the past.

Cologne, February 1955   H. Bucksch

PREFACE TO THE SECOND EDITION

This edition is considerably larger than the first one. The entries have been checked again and new words were added. It was considered to be advisable to split this edition up into two tomes. The publisher and the author hope that this edition will be as welcomed by all engineering circles as was the first edition. Suggestions from readers are invited.

Cologne, May 1958   H. Bucksch

EINFÜHRUNG

Die Wörter sind alphabetisch geordnet. Zum Zwecke einer Darstellung nach technischen Gesichtspunkten sind bei manchen Begriffen weitere außerhalb der alphabetischen Reihenfolge aufgeführt. Beispiel:

Fahrzeuge *npl* **für den Transport** *m* **von Boden** *m* **und Steinbaustoffen** *mpl*
   geländegängiger luftbereifter Erdtransportwagen *m*, gummibereiftes Erdbau-Lastfahrzeug *n*, geländegängiger Förderwagen *m* in Kraftwagen-Bauart *f*, Muldenkipper *m*, Groß-Förderwagen *m*, gleisloser Förderwagen *m*, Motorkipper, Erdtransportfahrzeug für Fremdbeladung

      Halbanhänger *m* mit Bodenentleerung *f* durch Klappen *fpl*, aufsattelbarer Bodenentleerer *m*, aufgesattelter Erdtransportwagen mit Bodenentleerung, Fabrikat THE EUCLID ROAD MACHINERY COMPANY, CLEVELAND 17, OHIO, USA
                                        usw.

Kohle *f*
   Abfall ~
   Anthrazit *m*
   Back ~, siehe: weiche ~
   Braun ~
   Erbs ~, siehe: Grieß ~
   erdige Stein ~
                         usw.

Anwendung der Klammern:
a) eckige Klammern:
   1. Definition eines Wortes, z. B.

   2. Bestimmung des Sachgebietes, z. B.

b) runde Klammern:
   3. Auslassungen, z. B.

   4. Abkürzungen, z. B.

(earth and rock) hauling equipment
   rubber-tired (US)/rubber-tyred (Brit.) off-(the-)highway hauling unit (or earth-moving vehicle)

      EUCLID bottom-dump wagon

coal
   waste ~
   anthracite (~)
   brown ~

   earthy ~, smut

Bodendruck *m*, Bodenpressung *f*, Flächenpressung *f*, Flächendruck [*z. B.* einer Gleiskette *f* auf den Untergrund *m*]

Fertigbehandlung *f*, Endbearbeitung *f* [*Beton m*]

Doppel(rohr)tunnel *m* = Doppelrohrtunnel, Doppeltunnel
     oder
(Beton)Dichtungsmittel *n* = Dichtungsmittel, Betondichtungsmittel *n*

(Geol.) = Geologie
(Min.) = Mineralogie
(Brit.) = Großbritannien
(US) = USA

Die Tilde ~ *tritt an die Stelle des zu wiederholenden Wortes, z. B.* Halde f, Vorrats~, Material~ = Halde f, Vorratshalde, Materialhalde

Die Tilde ~ *im Fettdruck tritt an die Stelle des darüber befindlichen Wortes oder des zu wiederholenden Wortteiles, welcher vor dem Strich steht, z. B.*

Krone f
~ f = Krone f
Abbinde|verzögerer m
~**wärme** f = Abbindewärme f

Das Komma teilt Wörter gleicher Definition.
Das Semikolon teilt Wörter gleicher Definition, die aber einerseits in den USA und andererseits in Großbritannien gebräuchlich sind.

Das Geschlecht der deutschen Wörter ist wie folgt angegeben:

> m = *männlich*
> f = *weiblich*
> n = *sächlich*
> mpl = *das betreffende Wort ist in der Pluralform angegeben, wobei die Einzahlform männlich ist. Dementsprechend sind* fpl *und* npl *zu verstehen.*

Wörter, deren Gebrauch vom Public Works Industry Committee [Großbritannien] für den betreffenden Begriff nicht mehr empfohlen werden und deshalb besser nicht mehr angewandt werden sollen, sind durch das ihnen vorangestellte oder nachgestellte Wort [deprecated] gekennzeichnet.

„TRADEMARK" gibt an, daß es sich bei dem betreffenden Begriff um eine Schutzmarke handelt.

Das Sternchen (*) bedeutet, daß im Deutsch-Englischen Teil weitere in Beziehung zu dem betreffenden Begriff stehende Wörter gegeben sind. Dieses (*) erscheint also nur im Englisch-Deutschen Teil.

INTRODUCTION

The terms are compiled in alphabetical order. Certain terms, however, forming subject titles from a technical point of view are accompanied by a sub-section giving other words relevant to the subject. Example:

Fahrzeuge *npl* **für den Transport** *m* **von Boden** *m* **und Steinbaustoffen** *mpl*
    geländegängiger luftbereifter Erdtransportwagen *m*, gummibereiftes Erdbau-Lastfahrzeug *n*, geländegängiger Förderwagen *m* in Kraftwagen-Bauart *f*, Muldenkipper *m*, Groß-Förderwagen *m*, gleisloser Förderwagen *m*, Motorkipper, Erdtransportfahrzeug für Fremdbeladung

    Halbanhänger *m* mit Bodenentleerung *f* durch Klappen *fpl*, aufsattelbarer Bodenentleerer *m*, aufgesattelter Erdtransportwagen mit Bodenentleerung, Fabrikat THE EUCLID ROAD MACHINERY COMPANY, CLEVELAND 17, OHIO, USA
                                etc.

Kohle *f*
    Abfall~
    Anthrazit *m*
    Back~, siehe: weiche ~
    Braun~
    Erbs~, siehe: Grieß~
    erdige Stein~
                                    etc.

Brackets are used:
a) Square Brackets:
    (1) to define a term, e.g.

    (2) to denote the particular field, e.g.

b) Round Brackets:
    (3) for terms or part of terms which can be omitted, e.g.

    (4) for abbreviations, e.g.

(earth and rock) hauling equipment

    rubber-tired (US)/rubber-tyred (Brit.) off-(the-)highway hauling unit (or earth-moving vehicle)

    EUCLID bottom-dump wagon

coal
    waste~
    anthracite (~)

    brown~

    earthy~, smut

Bodendruck *m*, Bodenpressung *f*, Flächenpressung *f*, Flächendruck [z. B. *einer Gleiskette f auf den Untergrund m*]
Fertigbehandlung *f*, Endbearbeitung *f* [*Beton m*]

Doppel(rohr)tunnel *m* = Doppelrohrtunnel, Doppeltunnel
            or
(Beton)Dichtungsmittel *n* = Dichtungsmittel, Betondichtungsmittel
(Geol.) = Geology
(Min.) = Mineralogy
(Brit.) = Great Britain
(US) = USA

The Tilde ~ *substitutes the word to be repeated, e. g.*
Halde *f*, Vorrats~, Material~ = Halde *f*, Vorratshalde, Materialhalde

The Tilde ~ *substitutes the preceding word or the part of the preceding word printed before the sign* | *and to be repeated in the following one, e.g.*

Krone *f*
~ *f* = Krone *f*
Abbinde|regler *m*
~**verzögerer** = Abbindeverzögerer *m*

The Comma separates equivalent definitions.
The Semicolon separates equivalent definitions but alternatively used either in the USA or Great Britain.

The gender of the German words is indicated by:

> *m* = *masculine*
> *f* = *feminine*
> *n* = *neuter*
> *mpl* = *the term is given in its plural form with the singular being masculine; fpl and npl apply accordingly.*

Where the Public Works Industrie Committee [Great Britain] is of the opinion that the particular use of a term is incorrect and should preferably be discontinued, it is preceded, or followed, by the word [deprecated].

"TRADEMARK" indicates that a word is a proprietary name owned by a particular company and valued by it as identifying its product.

The asterisk (*) denotes that the term is accompanied in the German-English part by further words. It therefore appears in the English-German part only.

The German letter «β» means «sz».

BAND I

VOLUME I

*

DEUTSCH - ENGLISCH

GERMAN - ENGLISH

A

Abart *f*, Spielart = variety

Abbau *m*, Demontage *f*, Ausbau = dismantling

~ [*organische Stoffe in lufthaltigem Wasser*] = decomposition, digestion

~ **von Förderhalden**, ~ ~ Bergehalden = bank reclamation

Abbau(en) *m*, (*n*) [*Steinbruch m*] = quarrying

Abbau(en) *m*, (*n*), Abdecken *n*, Abräumen *n* [*ausbeutbare oder nicht ausbeutbare Schichten fpl*] = stripping [*overburden or thin layers of pay material*]

abbauen, siehe: demontieren

~, gewinnen [*Bergwerk n*] = to win, to work

abbaufähige Menge *f*, abbauwürdige ~ = pay(ing) quantity

abbaufähiges Material *n*, abbauwürdiges ~ = pay(ing) material

Abbau|hammer *m*, (Kohlen)Pickhammer, Förderhammer = coal picker, ~ pick hammer

~**meißel** *m*, siehe: Bohrmeißel

~**stempel** *m* **aus Stahl** *m* **für Bergbau** *m* = steel mine prop

(~)**Wand** *f*, Abtragwand [*Steinbruch m*] = (working-)face

abbauwürdige Schicht *f*, abbaufähige ~ = pay(ing) formation

Abbinde|beschleuniger *m*, Abbindezeitbeschleuniger [*Zement m*] = accelerator, accelerating agent (or admixture)

~**beschleunigung** *f*, Erstarrungsbeschleunigung, Hydra(ta)tionsbeschleunigung [*Zement m*] = acceleration of setting (Brit.); ~~ set

~**geschwindigkeit** *f* [*Zement m*] = rate of setting (Brit.); ~ ~ set

~**geschwindigkeit** *f* [*Verschnittbitumen n*] = rate of cure

~**kraft** *f* [*Zement m*] = setting power (Brit.); set ~

~**kurve** *f* [*Zement m*] = curve of setting (Brit.); ~ ~ set

~**mechanismus** *m* [*Zement m*] = mechanism of setting (Brit.); ~ ~ set

abbinden, erstarren [*Zement m*] = to set, to hydrate

~ [*Verschnittbitumen n*] = to cure

~, zulegen [*Holzkonstruktion f*] = to join, to trim

Abbinden *n*, Abbindung *f*, Erstarrung *f*, Erstarren *n*, Hydra(ta)tion *f* [*Zement m*] = setting (Brit.); set, hydrating, (cement) hydration

~, Abbindung *f* [*Verschnittbitumen n*] = curing

Abbinde|prüfgerät *n* [*Zement m*] = setting tester (Brit.); set ~

~**prüfung** *f*, Prüfung des Erstarrens, Erstarrungsprüfung [*Zement m*] = setting test (Brit.); set ~, (cement) hydration ~

~**regler** *m*, Abbindezeitregler [*Zement m*] = setting-time controlling agent (Brit.); set-time ~ ~

~**temperatur** *f*, Erstarrungstemperatur, Hydra(ta)tionstemperatur = temperature of setting (Brit.); ~ ~ set, ~ ~ (cement) hydration

~**verhalten** *n* [*Zement m*] = setting behaviour (Brit.); set behavior (US)

~**verzögerer** *m* [*Zement m*] = retarding admix(ture), retarder (of set)

~**wärme** *f*, Hydra(ta)tionswärme, Erstarrungswärme [*Zement m*] = heat of hydration (US); ~ ~ setting (Brit.); ~ generated while taking initial set

~**wert** *m* [*Zement m*] = setting value (Brit.); set ~

Abbinde|zeit *f*, Erstarrungszeit, Hydra(ta)tionszeit = setting time (or period) (Brit.); set ~ (~ ~)
~zeit *f* [*Verschnittbitumen n*] = curing time
~zeitbeschleuniger *m*, siehe: Abbindebeschleuniger
~zeitregler *m*, siehe: Abbinderegler
Abbindung *f*, siehe: Abbinden *n* [*Zement m*]
~, siehe: Abbinden *n* [*Verschnittbitumen n*]
Abbindungs-Schrumpfung *f*, Erstarrungs-Schrumpfung, Hydra(ta)tionsschrumpfung [*Zement m*] = setting shrinkage (Brit.); set ~
Abblasung *f* (Geol.), siehe: Deflation *f*
Abblättern *n*, Abblätterung *f*, Abschuppen *n*, Abschuppung = scaling
Abblend|schalter *m* = dip(ping) switch, dipper
~vorrichtung *f* = anti-dazzle device
Abbolzung *f*, siehe: Abspreizung *f*
(ab)böschen = to slope
Abbrand *m* von Legierungsbestandteilen *mpl* = loss of alloying elements during deposition
Abbrausen *n* [*Gesteinsaufbereitung f*] = rinsing
abbrechen, abreißen [*Gebäude n*] = to demolish, to pull down, to take down
(ab)bremsen, anziehen die Bremse = to brake, to apply the brake
Abbremsfläche *f*, Abbremsplatz *m* [*Fläche zum Abbremsen der Flugzeuge nach Warmlaufen der Motoren*] = warming up pad, warm(ing)-up apron, warmup pad
Abbrennen *n* alter Ölfarbenanstriche *mpl*, Flammstrahlreinigung *f* = blowlamp treatment of old coats of oil paint
~ von Basaltpflaster *n*, thermische Aufrauhung *f* = heat treatment of basalt paving setts
abbrennstumpfschweißen = to flash weld
Abbrennstumpfschweißung *f*, Abbrennstumpfschweißen *n* = flash welding
Abbröckeln *n*, Abbröck(e)lung *f* [*Straßendecke f*] = fretting; [*deprecated: (un-)ravel(ling)* *break up of the road surface because of binder failure*]

(ab)bröckeln = to crumble away
Abbruch *m*, Abbrucharbeit(en) *f*, (*fpl*), Abtragung *f*, Abtrag *m* = wrecking, demolition work, pulling down, taking down
~hammer *m* = demolition pick (hammer)
~ufer *n*, Prallufer = eroding bank, washing ~
~werkzeug *n* = demolition tool
~zone *f* (Geol.) = fault(ed) zone
ABC-Verfahren *n* = ABC-process [*alum, blood, coal process*]
Abdachung *f*, Böschung *f*, Ausbiß *m* (Geol.) = scarp, escarpment
Abdachungs|fluß *m* = consequent river
~tal *n* = consequent valley
Abdämmung *f*, Absperrung = damming
~, Isolierung *f* = insulation
~ durch Moränen *fpl* = morainal damming
~ durch Sandsäcke *mpl*, Sandsackabdämmung, Abdämmung mit Sandsäcken, Sandsackabsperrung = sand bag damming
Abdämmungs|becken *n* (Geol.) = basin due to damming
~see *m*, Stausee (Geol.) = obstruction lake, ponded ~
~stufe *f* (Geol.) = step due to ponding
Abdampf *m* = exhaust steam
~schale *f* = evaporating dish
Abdampfung *f*, siehe: nasse Destillation *f*
Abdecken *n*, siehe: Abbau(en) *m*, (*n*)
~, siehe: Absplitten *n*
abdecken, siehe: auszwicken
~, bedecken = to cover
~, freimachen = to uncover
(Ab)Deck|haube *f* = hood
~platte *f* = cover(ing) slab, ~ plate
~rost *m*, Abdeckgitter(rost) *n*, (*m*) = (cover) grating, (~) grate
~splitt *m* = cover aggregate (for seal), cover stone, gritting material; blotter (material) (for bituminous prime coat) (US); surface dressing chipping(s) (Brit.)
~stein *m* [*Mauerkrone f*] = coping stone
Abdeckung *f*; siehe unter „Nachbehandlung *f* [*Beton m*]"

Abdeckung *f*, Zudeckung = covering
(ab)dichten = to seal, to pack
Abdicht|platte *f* **für Hydraulik** *f* = gland
~ring *m* = packing ring
Abdichtung *f* [*Rohr n, Ventil n*] = sealing (off), packing
~, siehe: Feuchtigkeitsisolierung *f*
~, Grundwasser~ = waterproofing
(Ab)Dichtungs|graben *m*, Verherdung *f* [*Talsperre f*] = cut-off trench
~lage *f*, siehe: Sperrschicht *f*
~mauer *f*, Abdichtungssporn *m*, Herdmauer, Fußmauer [*Talsperre f*] = (toe) cut-off wall
~schleier *m*, Injektionsschleier, (Ab)Dichtungsschirm *m*, (Ab)Dichtungsgürtel *m*, Einpreßschürze *f*, Injektionsschirm, Schleierdichtung, Schleierverpressung = grouted cut-off wall
~sporn *m*. siehe: Abdichtungsmauer *f*
~technik *f* = waterproofing technique
~teppich *m*, siehe: (Dichtungs)Schürze *f*
(ab)drosseln = to throttle (down)
Abdrückversuch *m* **für Nahtschweißungen** *{pl}* = pillow test; burst ~ (US)
Abessinierbrunnen *m* [*jetzt soll nur noch der Ausdruck ,,Rammbrunnen" verwendet werden*] = Abyssinian well, hollow ram pump
Abfall *m*, Abfallstoff *m* = waste, refuse
~beize *f* = waste pickling liquor
~beseitigung *f* [*durch Ortsentwässerung f und Müllabfuhr f*] = refuse disposal
Abfälle *f* **(oder Abfall** *m***) aus gewerblichen Betrieben** *mpl* = industrial refuse
abfallen [*Kurve f*] = to drop, to descend
abfallende Verwerfung *f* (Geol.) = fault dipping against the beds
abfallender Ast *m*, absteigender ~ = descending branch
~ Strand *m* = shelving beach
abfallendes Gelände *n* = sloping ground
~ Ufer *n* = shelving shore
~ Vorland *n* = piedmont slope
Abfall|erz *n* = waste ore, tailings
~erzeugnis *n*, Abfallprodukt *n* = waste product
~gummi *m* = waste rubber
~kohle *f* = waste coal

~-Lauge *f*, Ablauge = spent lye, waste liquor
~rohr *n*, siehe: Abflußrohr
~rohr *n*, Fallrohr, Abfluß *m* [*an Gebäudewand senkrecht herabgeführter Rohrstrang, durch den das von den Aborten, Ausgüssen, Bädern oder dem Dach kommende Wasser der Grundleitung zufließt*] = soil stack
~säure *f* = waste acid, spent ~
~stoff *m*, Abfall *m* = refuse, waste
Abfaltung *f* (Geol.) = downfolding
Abfang|graben *m*, Sammelgraben, Auffanggraben, (Abfang)Sammler *m* = intercepting ditch, catch-water ~
~graben *m* [*Rieselfeld n*] = pick-up carrier
~stoffe *mpl*; siehe unter ,,Abwasserwesen *n*"
~straße *f*, Entlastungsstraße = alternative side-street
Abfangung *f* = interception
abfasen [*abschrägen rechteckiger Kanten durch Fräsen, Schleifen oder Brennschneiden*] = to chamfer
Abfegen *n*, siehe: Abkehren *n*
(ab)feilen *f* = to file off
abflachen [*Böschung f*] = to flatten [*slope*]
Abflachung *f* **einer Krümmung** *f* = easing of a bend
abflauen [*Wind m*] = to abate
abfließen = to flow off
abfluchten, ausfluchten, einfluchten = to range into line, ~ ~ out
Abfluchtung *f*, siehe: Ausfluchtung
Abfluß *m* = flow
~ [*eines Niederschlagsgebietes n*] = run-off
~, Vorflut *f* = discharge
~, siehe: Abflußmenge *f*
~beiwert *m*, siehe: Abflußkoeffizient *m*
~gebiet *n*, Niederschlag(s)gebiet, Einzuggebiet, Sammelgebiet = watershed (US); catchment area, drainage basin, drainage area, catchment-basin, gathering-ground (Brit.)
~geschwindigkeit *f* = velocity of flow, discharge speed
~graben *m*, offener Graben = (open) ditch, field ~, drainage ~

Abfluß|hahn m, siehe: Ablaßhahn
~kanal m; siehe unter „Talsperre f"
~kanal m [*Kanalisierung f*] = sewer
~koeffizient m, Abflußbeiwert m, Abflußverhältnis n [*Verhältniszahl zwischen Abflußhöhe und Niederschlagshöhe*] = coefficient of runoff [*of a catchment area*]
~koeffizient m, Abflußbeiwert m [*Ungleichförmigkeit eines Wasserlaufes*] = discharge coefficient (Brit.); coefficient of discharge (US)
~kurve f, siehe: Abflußmengenkurve
~leitung f; siehe unter „Talsperre f"
~menge f, Abfluß(wassermenge) m, (f) [*Wasser, das in der Sekunde einen Querschnitt durchfließt*] = river discharge, flow
~menge f, Regen~ [*eines Niederschlagsgebietes* n] = runoff
~menge f **bei Mittelwasser** n, MQ = average flow, mean ~
~menge f **bei niedrigstem Niedrigwasser** n, NNQ = low flow record
~menge f **bei Niedrigwasser** n, NQ = low flow
~(mengen)kurve f [*Fluß* m] = hydrograph of flow, flow hydrograph, discharge curve, hydrograph curve of discharges
~(mengen)kurve f, Regen~ [*Niederschlagsgebiet* n] = runoff hydrograph
~querschnitt m, Durchflußquerschnitt, benetzter Querschnitt, durchströmter Querschnitt [*von dem abfließenden Wasser erfüllter Querschnitt*] = discharge section, cross-section of stream discharge
~rohr n = discharge pipe
~rohr n [*Waschbecken* n] = wastepipe
~rohr n, Regenrohr, Abfallrohr, Fallrohr [*am Haus* n] = downpipe, downcomer, downspout, fall pipe
~spende f = yield factor (of a catchment)
~verhältnis n, siehe: Abflußkoeffizient m
~vermögen n [*Meeresarm* m] = tidal capacity [*arm of the sea*]
~wassermenge f, siehe: Abflußmenge
abfräsen = to mill, to grind

Abfuhr f **überschüssiger Bodenmassen**, ~ **auf Kippe** = surplus cartage
~fahrzeug n, Abtransportfahrzeug = haul-away vehicle
~schute f, siehe: Baggerschute
Abfüllpumpe f, Faßpumpe = barrelpump, barrel exhausting pump
Abgänge mpl, menschliche ~, menschliche Abgangsstoffe mpl = (human) excreta
Abgas n = waste gas, exhaust ~
(ab)geböscht = sloped
abgeflachtes Rundeisen n = flattened round bar
abgekürzte Verkehrsprüfung f = accelerated traffic test
~ Wetterbeständigkeitsprobe f, Bewitterungskurzprüfung f, Bewitterungsschnellprüfung f = accelerated weathering test
abgekürztes Verfahren n, Schnellverfahren = accelerated procedure
abgelegene Baustelle f = isolated site
abgenutzter Teil m, abgenutztes Teil n = worn part
abgeriegeltes Tal n = blocked-up valley, obstructed ~
abgerundete Fugenkante f = bull-nose, bull's nose
abgerundetes Stahlprofil n = rounded steel section
abgerutschte Bodenmasse f = slipping mass
abgesackte Kehlnaht f = fillet weld with vertical leg unintentionally shorter than the horizontal leg
abgescherter Erdkeil m = slipping soil wedge
abgeschwemmter Laterit m = low-level laterite
abgesenkter Grundwasserspiegel m = lowered ground-water table
abgesetzte Fugen fpl [*verschieden gefärbte Stoß- und Lagerfugen* fpl] = masonry joints of different colo(u)rs
abgespannter Mast m = guyed mast
abgesplittet = gritted, grit-blinded
abgestufte Betonmauer f = stepped concrete wall
abgestufter Filter m, abgestuftes Filter n = graded filter

abgestuftes Material n, gesiebtes ~ = graded material, screened ~, ~ aggregate

abgetopptes Öl n = reduced oil

~ russisches (Roh)Erdöl n, Masut n = mazut, masut

abgetreppte Wangenmauer f = stepped side wall

abgewalzte Schüttung f, Walzdamm m = rolled fill

~ Stärke f, **~ Dicke** f = rolled thickness

abgewandelt = modified

(Ab)Glätten n = smoothing

Abgleichbohle f, Abstreichbohle, Abziehbohle [*Betondeckenfertiger m*] = strike-off (screed), screeding beam, level(l)ing beam, level(l)ing screed, front screed

Abgleichen n, Abstreichen n, Abziehen n = level(l)ing, striking off, strike-off

abgleichen [*Zementvermörtelung f*] = to shape

~, (ab)schürfen, abziehen [*Erdbau m*] = to skim

Abgleitung f (Geol.), siehe: Bodenkriechen n

Abgliederungs|halbinsel f = detached peninsula

~insel f = detached island

abgraten = to trimm, to burr

Abgratwerkzeug n = trimming tool

(Ab)Hang m = flank of a hill, hillside, slope

Abheben n [*Brückenlager n*] = lifting

~ der Schwimmschicht f [*Klärbecken n*] = skimming

~ von Rasen m **und Humus** m = clearing, stripping

Abhebung f (Geol.), siehe: Deflation f

Abhilfe(maßnahme) f, Behebung f = remedial measure, cure

Abhitze f, Abwärme f = waste heat

~rückgewinnung f, siehe: Abwärmerückgewinnung

abhobeln = to plane

Abholort m = point of collection

Abholung f = collection

Abholzung f = cutting down of a forest

Abietinsäure f = abietic acid

abkanten = to edge

~ [*Bleche npl*] = to fold

Abkantung f [*Treppe f*] = splaying, chamfering, splayed jointing

Abkehren n, Abfegen n = brooming, sweeping, brushing

Abkehrfluß m = obsequent river

Abkeilen n [*Gestein n*] = wedging

(Ab)Klopfer m, Abklopfhammer = chipper, scaling hammer, chipping hammer

abkreiden, abschnüren [*Baumstamm m*] = to chalk-line

Abkreuzung f, siehe: Andreaskreuz n

Ablade|anlage f, Ausladeanlage, Entladeanlage = unloading installation, off-loading ~

~gleis n, Ausladegleis, Entladegleis = unloading (side) track, ~ sidiag, off-loading (~) ~

~kosten f, Ausladekosten, Entladekosten = cost of unloading, ~ ~ off-loading

~kran m, Ausladekran, Entladekran = unloading crane, off-loading ~

Abladen n, siehe: Ausladen n

ablagern [*Holz n*] = to season

Ablagerung f, Akkumulation f, Ablagerungsvorgang m (Geol.) = deposition (process), sedimentation (~)

~ [*als abgelagerter Stoff*] = sediment, deposit

Ablagerungs|gestein n, siehe: Schichtgestein

~gürtel m = belt of deposit(ion)

~landschaft f = depositional topography

~medium n = depositing medium

~ort m (Geol.) = locus of deposition, site ~ ~

~periode f = period of deposition

~riß m = deposit crack

~struktur f = deposition structure

~tätigkeit f = depositional activity, ~ work

~vorgang m, siehe: Ablagerung f

~zone f = zone of deposition, ~ ~ sedimentation, sedimentation zone

~zyklus m = sedimentary cycle

ablandiger Wind m = off-shore wind, land breeze, land wind

ablängen = to cut to precise length

Ablassen n; siehe unter „Talsperre f"

Ablaß m, siehe: Auslaß m

~düker m = regulating siphon

Ablaß|hahn *m*, Abflußhahn, Entleerungshahn = drain cock
~rohr *n* = outlet pipe
~schieber *m* = outlet valve
~stollen *m* = outlet tunnel
~stopfen *m* = drain plug
~ventil *n*, Auslaßventil = outlet valve
~verschluß *m* = outlet gate
Ablation *f*; siehe unter „Gletscher *m*"
Ablauf *m*; siehe unter „Talsperre *f*"
~ [*Säule f*] = throat, cavetto
~berg *m*, Eselsrücken *m* = hump, double incline
ablaufen lassen [*Wasser n von einer Fläche f*] = to shed
Ablauf|(ge)rinne *f*, (*n*) = drain, gutter, channel, grip, flume
~geschwindigkeit *f* [*Stapellauf m*] = launching speed
~ventil *n* [*Waschbecken n*] = (waste) plug
Ablauge *f*, Abfall-Lauge = waste liquor, spent lye
ableiten [*Wasser in einen Fluß*] = to discharge [*water into a river*]
Ableitung *f* [*Formel f*] = derivation
~ großer Wassermengen, einen Fluß für die ~ ~ ~ umbauen = regulation of a river for high discharge capacity
Ableitungsstollen *m*; siehe unter „Talsperre *f*"
Ablenkplatte *f*, Prallblech *n*, Leitblech, Ablenkblech = deflecting plate
Ablenkungs|knie *n* [*Fluß m*] = elbow of capture
~schlucht *f* [*Fluß m*] = gorge of diverted river, ~ ~ diverting
Ablesen *n*, Ablesung *f* = reading off
ablesen = to read off, to take readings
Ableuchtlampe *f* = inspection lamp
(ab)löschen [*Kalk m*] = to slake
Ablösung *f*, Ablösen *n* [*flüssiges Bindemittel n*] = stripping
~ des Strahles *m*; siehe unter „Talsperre *f*"
Ablösungs|anzeiger *m* [*Haftfestigkeit zwischen bit. Bindemittel und Mineralmasse*] = displacement indicator
~versuch *m* = stripping test
~widerstand *m* = stripping resistance

abloten, siehe: absenken
Abluft *f* = exhaust (or used, or outgoing, or waste) air
~filter *m*, *n* = waste air filter
Abmarkung *f* **der Uferlinie** *f* = marking of the bank line, staking out the bank line
Abmaß *n*, Maßabweichung *f*, Toleranz *f* = deviation, off-size, margin, permissible variation, tolerance
Abmessung *f*, siehe: Dosierung *f*
Abmessungen *fpl*; siehe unter „Baumaschinen *fpl* und Baugeräte *npl*"
Abmeß|anlage *f* **für Betonzuschlagstoffe** *mpl*, Zuschlagsiloanlage *f*, Großbunkeranlage *f*, Reihensiloanlage *f*, Siloabmeßanlage, Dosieranlage für Zuschlagstoffe, ~ ~ Zuschläge = (central aggregate) batch(ing) plant, proportioning ~, measuring ~, batcher ~, dry-batch(ing) ~
~anlage *f* **mit einmaligem Halten** *n* **der Fahrzeuge** *npl* = one-stop batch plant
~ ~ zweimaligem ~ ~ ~ = two-stop batch plant
~ ~ dreimaligem ~ ~ ~ = three-stop batch plant
~kiste *f*, Zumeßkiste *f*, Meßgefäß *n* = batch box, ga(u)ge ~
~schnecke *f*, Dosierschnecke, Zuteilschnecke, Zumeßschnecke = proportioning worm conveyor, ~ screw
~vorrichtung *f*, Dosiervorrichtung, Zuteilvorrichtung, Zumeßvorrichtung = proportioning device, ga(u)ging ~, measuring ~, batching ~
Abminderungsbeiwert *m* = reduction factor
abmontieren, siehe: demontieren
Abnahme *f* [*die Übernahme der Bauleistung nach Fertigstellung*] = acceptance
~bescheinigung *f* = certificate of acceptance
~prüfung *f* = acceptance test
~verweigerung *f* = rejection
~vorschriften *fpl*, Normalien *f*, Abnahmebedingungen *fpl* = (contract) specifications, specs
Abnutzung *f*, Verschleiß *m*, Abnützung *f* = wear and tear

Abnutzungsversuch m (oder **Abnützungsprobe** f) **durch Reibung** f [*Härte* f] = attrition test [*hardness*]

~ (~ ~) im Trommelverfahren n **durch Stahlkugeln** fpl [*Härte* f] = (Los Angeles) rattler test [*hardness*]

Abnützungswert m [*Straßenbaugestein* n] = aggregate abrasion value

Abortgrube f, Fäkaliengrube, Latrinengrube, Senkgrube = feces pit, privy

abpfählen, abstecken, abpflocken = to peg out, ~ set ~, ~ stake ~

Abputzhammer m = waller's hammer, walling ~

abrammen = to ram, to tamp

Abrammen n, Stoßverdichtung f, Stampfen n = (compaction by) ramming, tamping, punning, compacting; [*deprecated: beating*]

Abrams'scher (Feinheits) Modul m, F_m = Abrams fineness modulus, F. M.

Abrasionsbucht f, Abschleifungsbucht = abrasion embayment, corrosion ~

Abraum m, Überlagerung f, Deckschutt m, Deckgebirge n, Abraumschicht f (Geol.) = overburden, shelf, overlay, uncallow, topspit; tir [*in Scotland*]

Abräumen n, siehe: Abbau(en) m, (n)

Abraum|förderbrücke f = overburden transporter (or conveyor) bridge

~förderwagen m = wagon for the removal of overburden

~halde f, siehe: Aussatzhalde f

~-Hochlöffel(bagger) m, Großlöffel-Abraumbagger m = stripper, (long-boom) stripping shovel (Ward-)Leonard-Schaltung f = Ward-Leonard system of variable voltage control

~lok(omotive) f **für den Tagebau** m = loco(motive) for open-cast mining (operations)

~schicht f, siehe: Abraum m

~seilbahn f = overburden ropeway

Abrechnungsmenge f = pay(able) quantity

Abreiben n, siehe: Abschleifung f

Abreißen n [*automatischer Syphon* m] = un-priming (Brit.); stop siphoning (US)

Abrichthobel m, Schrupphobel, Schropphobel = jack plane

Abrieb m, Abschleifen n, Abschleifung f, Abreiben n, Abreibung f, Abschliff m = abrasion

~festigkeit f, Widerstandsvermögen n gegen Abschleifen n, Abschliffestigkeit, Abschleifwiderstand m = abrasion resistance

Abrißpunkt m, Festpunkt, Fixpunkt = bench mark

Abrollen n **von Glasuren** fpl = crawling of glazes

Abrollgerät n **für Bitumen-Fertigbahnen** fpl = P.B.S. laying machine, lick roller, stamp licker

Abrundungskoeffizient m [*Kies* m] = roundness index

Abrüsten n, siehe: Ausrüsten n

Abrutschung f (Geol.), siehe: Bodenkriechen n

Absack|maschine f, Einsackmaschine, Abfüllmaschine für Säcke = bagging machine, bag packing machine, bag packer

~waage f, siehe: Einsackwaage

absägen, siehe: abtrummen

Absanden n, Absandung f = sanding, sand dressing, sand spreading

Absatz|boden m, Kolluvialboden = transported soil, colluvial ~

~gestein n, siehe: Schichtgestein

~möglichkeit f = marketing opportunity

absatzweise arbeitende Mischanlage f; siehe unter „Makadam-Maschinenanlage f"

absatzweises Wiegen n = intermittent weighing

Absäuern n = acid washing, ~ etching

Abschabspachtel m, f = flexible knife

abschälen, entrinden, (ent)schälen, abborken = to disbark, to peel, to strip the bark

Abscheider m [*Staub* m] = precipitator

~, Fang m, **Traps** m = separator; trap (Brit.); interceptor (US)

(Ab)Scher|beanspruchung f = shear(ing) stress

~bolzen m, **(Ab)Scherstift** m = shear(ing) pin

~festigkeit f = shear(ing) strength

Abscherung f, **Abscheren** n = shear(ing) (action)

Abschiebung — Absenkungstrichter

Abschiebung f (Geol.), siehe: Verwerfung f
Abschirmung f = shielding
Abschirmwand f, Abschirmmauer f = curtain wall
Abschlagen n [Steine mpl] = napping
Abschlagzahlung f, Akontozahlung = payment on account, instalment payment
abschlämmen, (sich) absetzen, ausschlämmen = to settle (out)
Abschlämmgeschwindigkeit f, siehe: Sinkgeschwindigkeit
abschleifen = to abrade
Abschleifen n, siehe: Abschleifung f
Abschleif|probe f, siehe: Abschleifversuch m
~prüfung f, siehe: Abschleifversuch m
Abschleifung f, Abschleifen n, Abrieb m, Abreiben n, Abreibung, Abschliff m = abrasion
Abschleifungs|bucht f, siehe: Abrasionsbucht
~verlust m = abrasion loss
Abschleif|versuch m, Abschleifprüfung f, Abriebprobe f, Abreibungsversuch m, Abschleifprobe f = abrasion test
~widerstand m, Abriebfestigkeit f, Widerstandsvermögen n gegen Abschleifen, Abschliffestigkeit f = abrasion resistance
~wirkung f, Schleifwirkung [z. B. von Sand m] = abrasiveness [e. g. of sand]
Abschleppen n [Erdbau m] = dragging
~ [Fahrzeug n] = towing
Abschlepp|-Fahrzeug n, Abschleppkran m, Fahrzeugrettungskran = recovery vehicle, breakdown van, crash truck
~-Seil n, Schlepptau n = towing rope
abschlichten [Holz n] = to clean, to finish off
Abschließung f eines Meeresarmes m = closing of an arm of the sea
Abschließungsküste f = concordant coast
Abschliff m, siehe: Abschleifung f
Abschluß|damm m der Spülfläche f = surrounding embankment (of a spoil ground) (Brit.); retaining dike, retaining level (US)
~organ n, Absperrverschluß m, Absperrorgan = shutoff unit
~schütz(e) m, (f); siehe unter „Talsperre f"
~wand f, Trennmauer f = cut-off wall

Abschmelzung f (Geol.); siehe unter „Gletscher m"
Abschmieren n, Abschmierung f = lubrication
Abschmier|fahrzeug n = greasing and lubricating service vehicle (or rig)
~-LKW m = greasing and lubricating truck
Abschneiden n einer Krümmung f = cutting out of a bend, ~ ~ ~ ~ curve
~ von Pfählen mpl **und Spundwänden** fpl **unter Wasser** n = cutting of piles and sheet piling under water
Abschneider m, Ziegel~ = (brick) cutter
~draht m, Abschneidedraht, Ziegel~ = (brick) cutting wire
Abschnitt m, Teilstrecke f, Teilstück n = section
abschnüren, siehe: abkreiden
~ [Wasser n] = to impound
abschrägen = to bevel, to chamfer
Abschräghobel m = shooting plane
Abschrägung f, Druckschlag m [Gewölbe n] = splaying, bevel
Abschrecken n = quenching
abschrecken = to quench
Abschreckofen m = quenching furnace
abschreiben = to depreciate
Abschreibung f, Absetzung f für Abnutzung f = write-off (or writing-off) of depreciations
~ im Rechnungswesen n = depreciation accounting
Abschuppung f (Geol.) = exfoliation, spalling, desquamation, scaling (off)
(ab)schürfen, abziehen, abgleichen [Erdbau m] = to skim
(Ab)Schürfen n, siehe: Abziehen n
Absendeort m, Versandort = point of shipping
absenkeln, abloten = to plumb
Absenken n des Auslegers m = lowering of the jib (Brit.); ~ ~ ~ boom (US)
Absenkinsel f = artificial island, sand ~
Absenkung f; siehe unter „Talsperre f"
~ (Geol.), siehe: Verwerfung f
Absenkungs|fläche f = area of depression, zone ~ ~
~trichter m = cone of depression, drawdown cone

Absetzanlage — Abspülungsfaden

Absetz|anlage *f*, siehe: Bandabsetzer *m*
~band *n*, siehe: Absetzförderband
~becken *n*; s. unter „Abwasserwesen *n*"
Absetzen *n* [*Aushuberde f längs der Ausschachtung f*] = sidecasting [*piling spoil alongside the excavation from which it is taken*]
~, siehe: Absetzvorgang *m*
~ von Paraffin = deposition of paraffin
absetzen, siehe: abschlämmen
Absetzer *m*, siehe: Band **~**
Absetz|(förder)band *n*, Auslegerförderband = stacker belt, **~** conveyor
~geschwindigkeit *f* = rate of settling
~gestein *n*, siehe: Schichtgestein
~glas *n* [*dient zur Bestimmung der Raummenge der während gewisser Zeit absetzbaren Schwebestoffe in cm^3/l*] = settling cone, **~** glass
~grad *m* **von Markierungsfarbe** *f* = degree of settling of traffic paint
~klärung *f*; siehe unter „Abwasserwesen *n*"
~kurve *f* = sedimentation curve
~probe *f*, Probe *f* auf Reinheit *f* [*Betonzuschlag m*] = test for silt, silt content test for fine aggregate
~raum *m* = sedimentation chamber
Absetzung *f*, siehe: Rutschung *f*
~ für Abnützung *f*, siehe: Abschreibung *f*
Absetz|versuch *m*, Sedimentierprobe *f*, Sedimentierversuch *m*, Schlämmanalyse *f*, Aräometeranalyse = decantation test (US); sedimentation **~**, hydrometer **~** (or analysis)
~vorgang *m*, Absetzen *n* [*zum Trennen von leichteren und schwereren Stoffen*] = settling process, sedimentation **~**
Absiebung *f*, Absieben *n*, Klassierungssiebung *f* = screening, size separation
absoluter Ausdehnungsbeiwert *m* = absolute coefficient of expansion
Absonderungsform *f* (Geol.) = structure, parting, jointing
absorbieren = to absorb
absorbierender Boden *m* = absorptive soil
Absorption *f*, Aufzehrung *f* [*Einsaugen eines Stoffes in das Innere eines anderen ohne chemische Vereinigung*] = absorption

Absorptions|gefäß *n* = absorption vessel, **~** tube
~mittel *n* = absorbent
~-Naturgasolin *n* = absorption gasoline
~öl *n* = scrubbing oil
~rohr *n* [*Chlorungsapparatur f*] = absorption tower
~spektrum *n* = absorption spectrum
~turm *m*, Trockenturm [*DIN 12500*] = absorption tube with bottom outlet
~vermögen *n*, Absorptionsfähigkeit *f* = absorptive capacity, absorption **~**, **~** property
Abspaltung *f* [*Magma n*] = differentiation
~ [*Gebirgsbildung f*] = rift building, rifting
Abspanndraht *m* = stay wire
Abspanner *m*, Reduziertransformator *m* = step-down transformer
Abspannseil *n*, siehe: Trosse *f*
Abspannung *f* (oder **Abspannen** *n*) **mit Seilen** *npl*, siehe: Trossenabspannung
absperren [*Förderbohrung f*] = to close in [*producing well*]
Absperr|hahn *n*, siehe: Abstellhahn
~organ *n*, Abschlußorgan, Absperrverschluß *m* = shutoff unit
~schieber *m* = gate valve, sluice **~**
Absperrung *f* [*Straße f*] = barricading, barrier
~ = blocking, damming
Absperr|ventil *n* = shut-off valve, closing **~**, stop **~**
~verschluß *m*, siehe: Abschlußorgan *n*
Absplitten *n*, Abdecken *n* = gritting, chipping, grit blinding; [*deprecated*: blinding, dressing]
Absplittern *n*, Absplitterung *f* = chipping, spalling, splintering
Abspreizung *f*, Verspreizung, Bölzung, Abbolzung = propping (up)
Abspießen *n*, Absprießung *f*, Verstreben, Verstrebung, Aussprießen, Aussprießung = strutting
Abspießwinde *f* = strut jack
Abspulen *n*, Abwickeln *n* = coiling
Abspülungsfaden *m* (Geol.) = rain rill, wet-weather **~**

Abstand m = spacing
Abstand(s)halter m = distance-piece, spacer
abstecken, abpfählen, abpflocken, verpflocken = to peg out, ~ stake ~, ~ set ~
Abstecken n, siehe: Absteckung(sarbeiten) f, (fpl)
~ **von Übergangsbögen** mpl **in Klothoidenform** f = setting-out of clothoid transition curves
Absteck)Pflock m, Absteckpfahl m = setting-out peg, ~ stake
Absteckung(sarbeiten) f, (fpl), Abstecken n, Verpflockung f, Verpflocken n = pegging out (work), stake out
abstehender Schenkel m [Winkelstahl m] = outstanding flange
absteifen, aussteifen = to brace
Absteifung f, Aussteifung f = bracing
~, Versteifung f [Gebäude n] = horizontal shoring, flying ~
absteigender Ast m, siehe: abfallender ~
Abstell|fläche f, Standplatz m = (hard-) standing, hardstand
~**gleis** n = storage track
~**hahn** m, Absperrhahn = shut off cock
(ab)stocken, faulen [Holz n] = to rot
Abstrebung f [Gebäude n] = raking shoring
Abstreich|bohle f, siehe: Abgleichbohle
~**vorrichtung** f [Abheben der Schwimmschicht eines Klärbeckens] = skimmer
Abstreichen n, siehe: Abgleichen
Abstreifer m, Schwimmstoff~ = scum-collector
~**gut** n = skimmings
Abstufung f [Mineralmasse f] = gradation, grading
~ [Steuer f] = graduation (of tax)
Abstufungsschichtung f (Geol.) = graded bedding
Abstumpfung f, Anrauhung [Straßendecke f] = skidproofing
Abstützung f [Gebäude n] = shoring
Abstützungsgestell n, Abstützungsrahmen m = shoring frame
Abszisse f, Auftraglinie f = abscissa
Abszissen|achse f = axis of abscissa
~**element** n = element measured along axis of x

Abteilungsleiter m = department head
abteufen = to sink
Abteufen n = sinking
Abteuf|hammer m = sinker
~**lüfter** m, Grubenlüfter, Schachtventilator m = pit ventilator
~**rohr** n = sinking tube
abtorfen = to dig peat
Abtrag m, Einschnitt m, Abtragung f [Bodenentnahme über zukünftigem Planum] = cut(ting)
~, siehe: Abbruch m
Abtragen n, Abtragarbeit(en) $f(pl)$ [Boden m] = cutting
Abtrag|material n = cut(ting)
~**station** f [Förderband n] = idler set
Abtragung f (Geol.); siehe unter „Denudation f"
~ **durch Wind** m, siehe: Deflation f
Abtragungs|gebirge n = mountain of erosion
~**küste** f = abrasion coast
~**terrasse** f, Denudationsterasse f (Geol.) = denudation terrace, structural rock bench
Abtragwand f siehe: Abbauwand
Abtreppen n, Terrassieren n = stepping, benching; notching (Brit.)
Abtreppungsriß m [Bauwerkssenkung f] = oblique crack
Abtretungsurkunde f = deed of conveyance
Abtropfstein m, Stalaktit m = stalactite
abtrummen, absägen = to saw up
Abtun n; siehe unter „1. Schießen n; 2. Sprengen n"
Abwalzen n, Druckverdichtung f, Walzverdichtung, Walzkompression f = (compaction by) rolling
~ **mit Gummiwalzen** fpl; siehe unter „Walze f"
~ **mit Stahlmantelwalzen** fpl; siehe unter „Walze f"
Abwärmerückgewinnung f, Abhitzerückgewinnung = waste heat reclamation, ~ ~ recovery
Abwärts|förderung f = downward conveying
~**lüftung** f = downcast ventilation
Abwasserlast f [Fluß m] = (river) pollution, sewage pollution of a river

Abwasserwesen

Abwasserwesen n [*Gesamtheit der mit dem Abwasser zusammenhängenden Aufgaben. Das Abwasserwesen umfaßt Abwassertechnik, Abwasserwirtschaft, Abwasserchemie, Abwasserbiologie, Abwasserhygiene und Abwasserrecht*] — sewerage and sewage disposal

Abfanggraben m [*Rieselfeld n*] — pick-up carrier
Abfangsammler m, siehe: Hauptkanalisationsrohr n
Abfangstoffe mpl [*am Rechen*] — screenings
Abfangung f — interception
Abfluß m, Vorflut f — discharge
Abfluß m [*von einer Fläche f*] — runoff
ablassen [*Schlamm m*] — to draw-off
Ablaufkanal m — effluent conduit, ~ channel
Ablaufseite f [*Becken n*] — discharge side [*tank*]
Abortgrube f, Senkgrube — privy pit, feces pit
absetzbarer Stoff m, ~ Schwebestoff — settleable solid
Absetzbecken n, Absitzbecken, Klärbecken — settling basin, sedimentation ~, subsidence ~
  Bamag-Becken — Bamag tank, ~ basin
  Dorr-Becken — Dorr tank, ~ basin
  Dortmund-Becken — Dortmund tank, ~ basin
  Leipziger Becken — Leipzig tank, ~ basin
  Neustädter Becken — Neustädter tank, ~ basin
Absetzgeschwindigkeit f, Absitzgeschwindigkeit, Klärgeschwindigkeit — settling velocity, rate of settling
Absetzklärung f, Absitzklärung — sedimentation, settling
Absetzraum m, Absitzraum, Klärraum — settling compartment, sedimentation chamber
Absetzteich m, siehe: Klärteich
Absetzvorgang m, Absitzvorgang, Klärvorgang — settling process, sedimentation (~), subsidence
Abwasser n, Abwässer npl — sewage, foul water, sewage effluent, liquid waste
Abwasseranfall m — sewage flow
Abwasseranlagen fpl — sewerage works
Abwasser-Auslauf m ins Meer — ocean outfall
Abwasserbehandlung f, Abwasserreinigung f, Abwasserklärung f — sewage treatment, ~ purification
Abwasserbeseitigung f — sewage disposal
Abwasserbeseitigungsanlage f — sewage disposal works
Abwasserchlorung f [*Entkeimung von rohem oder gereinigtem Abwasser durch Einführen von Chlor*] — sewage chlorination
Abwasserfaulraum m, siehe: Schlammfaulraum
Abwasserinstallation f [*Hausabwasser n*] — soil stack installation
Abwasserkanal m — sewer
Abwasserkanalreinigung f — sewer cleaning

Abwasserkanaltunnel m, Kanalisationstunnel — sewer tunnel
Abwasserklärung f, siehe: Abwasserbehandlung f
Abwasserleitung f — disposal line, foul water line, sewer line, sewage pipe line

Abwasserpilz m — sewage fungus
Abwasserrechen m — screen
  Feinrechen m — fine screen
  Grobrechen m — coarse screen, rack
Abwasserreinigung f, siehe: Abwasserbehandlung
Abwasserreinigungsanlage f, Kläranlage — sewage (purification) works, ~ (treatment)plant

Abwasserstoß m — sewage dose
Abwassertechnik f, Kanalisationstechnik — sewage engineering
Abwasserverrieselung f — broad irrigation of sewage
Abwässer-Verteilung f — sewage diffusion
aktivierter Schlamm m, siehe: belebter Schlamm
anaerober Abbau m, siehe: Schlammfaulung f
Auflandungsteich m, siehe: Klärteich
Ausfaulung f, siehe: Schlammfaulung
Ausräumer m, Schlamm~ — sludge scraper
Bandkratzer m — sludge collector
behandelter Schlamm m — secondary (sewage) sludge
Beizereiabwasser n — waste pickling liquor, spent pickle liquor

belebter Schlamm m [*die Ausdrücke Belebtschlamm und aktivierter Schlamm sollen nicht mehr verwendet werden (DIN 4045)*] — activated (sewage) sludge
Belebungsanlage f — activated-sludge plant
Belebungsbecken n — aeration tank
Belebungsverfahren n [*die Ausdrücke Belebtschlammverfahren und Schlammbelebungsverfahren sollen nicht mehr verwendet werden (DIN 4045)*] — activated-sludge method

Belüfter m — aerator
Bevölkerungsdichte f — population density
Bewässerung f mit Abwasser — land treatment, sewage irrigation
Bio-Filter m, n, biologischer Körper m — bio-filter, bacteria bed, bacteria filter
Bio-Filteranlage f — biofiltration plant
biologische Reinigung f, ~ Abwasserbehandlung, ~ Nachbehandlung [*Abbau der Stoffe durch Kleinlebewesen*] — bacteria treatment, biological purification
biologischer Körper m, siehe: Bio-Filter n, m

Abwasserwesen

biologischer Rasen m [eines Tropfkörpers m]	surface film, biological slime
Blähschlamm m	bulking sludge
Bodenlysimeter m	soil lysimeter
Bürstenbelüftung f	brush aeration
Bürstenwalze f	brush-aerator [activated sludge process]
chemische Ausfällung f, ~ Klärung	chemical precipitation
chemische Behandlung f	chemical treatment
chemische Schlammbehandlung f	conditioning, seasoning
DORR-Klärer m	DORR (sewage) clarifier
dünnes Abwasser n	weak sewage
Dunstrohr n [einer Kläranlage f]	vent [of a sewage plant]
Durchflußbehandlung f [metallhaltige Industrieabwässer]	flow-through treatment [metal industry wastes]
eiförmiger Sammler m, Eikanal m, eiförmiges Kanalrohr n, Eiprofilrohr	egg-shaped sewer (pipe)
Einzugsgebiet n	tributary drainage area
Emscher Brunnen m, ~ Absetzbrunnen, ~ Klärbrunnen, Imhoffbrunnen	Emscher tank, Imhoff ~, ~ basin
Fabrikabwässer f, siehe: Industrieabwasser n	
Fällmittel n, siehe: Fällungschemikal n	
Fällungschemikal n, Fällmittel n	chemical precipitant
Faulbehälter m, siehe: Schlammfaulraum m	
Faulgas n [das bei der geruchlosen alkalischen Faulung (Methangärung) von Abwasserschlamm entstehende Gas]	sewage gas, sludge ~, digestor ~
Fäulnis f	putrefaction, digestion, septicity
Fäulnisfähigkeit f, Faulfähigkeit	putrescibility, digestibility
Faulraumanlage f	septic treatment plant
Faulraumheizung f [zur Beschleunigung des Faulvorganges im getrennten Schlammfaulraum]	digester heating
Faulschlamm m	digested (sewage) sludge
Faulung f, siehe: Schlamm ~	
Faulvorgang m, siehe: Schlammfaulung	
Faulwasser n	septic sewage
Faulzeit f	digestion period
Fein(abwasser)rechen m	fine screen
feste Gasdecke f [Schlammfaulraum m]	fixed cover [digestion tank]
Filterplatte f für Belüftungszwecke mpl	diffuser plate, air diffusor, filtros plate
Flockenbildung f	floc formation
Flockenschlamm m	flocculated (sewage) sludge
flüssiger Schlamm m	liquid (sewage) sludge
Frischschlamm m [unzersetzter Schlamm, wie er z. B. in Absetzbecken anfällt]	green (sewage) sludge, fresh (~) ~, primary (~) ~
Furchenbecken n für Schlammbelebung f	aeration tank of the longitudinal furrow system

Abwasserwesen

Furchensystem n [Abwasserverrieselung f]	ridge-and-furrow method of sewage irrigation
Gärfaulverfahren n	fermentation-septization process
gärungserregend	fermentative
Gärungserreger m	ferment
Gär(ungs)fähigkeit f	fermentability
gärungshemmend	anti-fermentative
Gasdecke f [eines Schlammfaulraumes m]	tank cover
gechlortes Abwasser n	chlorinated sewage
gewerbliches Abwasser n	commercial sewage, trade waste, trade sewage
Giftigkeit f	toxicity
Grabenmethode f der Schlammbeseitigung f	burying method of sludge disposal
Grob(abwasser)rechen m	coarse (bar) screen, (trash) rack
Hauptkanalisationsrohr n, Hauptsammler m, Abfangsammler, Abwassersammler, Hauptableitungskanal m, Schmutzwasser(abfang)sammler	trunk sewer, main ∼, outfall ∼, intercepting ∼, interceptor
Hausabwasser n, Kommunalabwässer	domestic sewage, ∼ waste
hintereinander geschaltete Becken npl	series-flow basins
horizontal durchflossenes Becken n, siehe: waagerecht ∼ ∼	
humusbildender Schlamm m, Humusschlamm	humus sludge
hydraulischer Radius m	hydraulic radius
Imhoffbrunnen m, s.: Emscher Brunnen	
Impfen n von Abwasserschlamm [verhütet die saure Gärung des Frischschlamms und leitet unmittelbar seine Methangärung ein]	mixing the fresh and ripe (sewage) sludge, seeding green (sewage) sludge with ripe (sewage) sludge
Impfschlamm m [in Methangärung befindlicher Faulschlamm]	ripe (sewage) sludge
Industrieabwasser n, Fabrikabwässer f, industrielle Abwässer	industrial waste (water), factory effluent, industrial sewage
Kanal(isations)rohrnetz n, Abwassernetz	sewer (pipe) system
Kanalisationstechnik f, Abwassertechnik	sewage engineering
Kanalisationstunnel m, Abwasserkanaltunnel	sewer tunnel
Kläranlage f, siehe: Abwasserreinigungsanlage	
Klärbecken n, siehe: Absetzbecken	
Klärbrunnen m	sedimentation tank
Klärgeschwindigkeit f, Absetzgeschwindigkeit, Absitzgeschwindigkeit	settling velocity
Klärgrube f	cesspool, cesspit
Klärraum m, siehe: Absetzraum	
Klärschlamm m	(sewage) sludge

Abwasserwesen

Klärteich *m*, Absetzteich, Auflandungsteich [*vom Abwasser sehr langsam durchflossenes Absetzbecken einfachster Art (Erdbecken, Sickerbecken), in dem der Schlamm dauernd liegenbleiben kann*] — settling pond, ~ lagoon

Klärvorgang *m*, siehe: Absetzvorgang

Kleinlebewesen *n* — micro-organism

Koagulationsbecken *n* — coagulation basin, flocculation ~

Kokereiabwasser *n* — coke oven waste

Kommunalabwässer *f*, siehe: Hausabwasser

Küchenabwasser *n* — scullery waste

Lachenbildung *f* auf Tropfkörpern *mpl* — ponding

landwirtschaftliche Abwasserverwertung *f* — agricultural utilization of sewage

lotrecht durchflossenes Becken *n*, siehe: senkrecht ~ ~

Mälzereiabwasser *n* — malt house waste

Manchester-Becken *n* — Hurd tank

Mischkanalisation *f*, Mischsystem *n* — combined system (of sewerage)

Mischwasser *n* — combined water [*sewage and storm water combined*]

Mischwasserkanal *m* — combined (water) sewer

Molkereiabwasser *n* — creamery waste, dairy ~, milk (plant) ~

Nachfaulraum *m* — second-stage digestion tank

Nachklärbecken *n* — final-settling basin, ~ tank, secondary clarification ~

Nachklärbecken *n* einer Tropfköperanlage *f* — humus tank

Nachklärung *f*, Nachklären *n* — secondary settling, ~ sedimentation, final ~, final clarification

Nährlösung *f* — broth

Naßschlamm *m* — wet sludge

nebeneinander geschaltete Becken *npl* — parallel-flow basins

Nebensammler *m* — sewer lateral, lateral sewer

Niederschlagsbecken *n* — coagulation basin, flocculation ~

Oberflächenbelüftung *f* — surface aeration

Paddelradbelüftung *f* — paddle-wheel aeration

pendelndes Belüftungsrohr *n* [*eines Tauchkörpers m*] — swinging air pipe, swing diffuser

phenolhaltiges Abwasser *n* — phenolic waste

Preßkuchen *m* [*Schlammentwässerung f*] — filter cake

Psychodafliege *f*, siehe: Schmetterlingsfliege

Rechengut *n*, Rechenrückstände *mpl* — screenings, rakings

Regendauer *f* — time of rainfall, duration of precipitation, duration of rainfall

Regenhäufigkeit *f* — frequency of precipitation, storm frequency

Regenleistung *f* — rainfall per second

Regenmeßstelle f	rain(fall) ga(u)ge, rain-ga(u)ging station
Regenspende f	rainfall per second per hectar
Regenstärke f	intensity-time relationship
Regenstärkelinie f	intensity-duration curve, rainfall time-intensity curve
Regenumlaufkanal m	rain-water by-pass
Regenwasser n	rain water, storm water, storm sewage
Regenwasser(aufhalte)becken n	storm-water tank
Regenwasserkanal m	storm(-water) sewer, storm drain, surface water sewer
rohes Abwasser n	crude sewage
Rohschlamm m	raw sludge, crude ~, fresh ~
Rücklaufschlamm m, Rücknahmeschlamm	return-sludge
Ruhebetrieb m, Sedimentation f im ~	quiescent settling, sedimentation on the fill-and-draw principle
Rührwerkbecken n mit Zusatzluft f	aeration chamber, ~ tank
Sammler m für die getrennte Entwässerung, Schmutzwasserkanal	separate sewer, sanitary sewer
Sammler m für die Mischentwässerung	combined (storm and sanitary) sewer
saure Gärung f	acid-ripening stage, acid stage, acid fermentation
schales Abwasser n	stale sewage
Schlammablagerung f	deposition of sludge
Schlammablaßrohr n	sludge (draw-off) pipe
Schlammablaßventil n	sludge valve
Schlammauslaugung f, Schlammwaschen n	elutriation of sludge
Schlammausräumer m, Schlammkratzer	sludge scraper
Schlammbelebungsverfahren, siehe: Belebungsverfahren	
Schlammbrunnen m	sludge well
Schlammeindicker m	sludge thickener, densifier
Schlammentwässerung f	de-watering of sludge
Schlammfaulraum m, Faulbehälter m, Abwasserfaulraum	sludge-digestion chamber, ~ compartment, (sludge) digester, digester tank, digestion tank
Schlammfaulturm m	digestion tower
Schlammfaulung f, Ausfaulung, Faulvorgang m, Faulung, anaerober Abbau m	(sewage) sludge digestion, (sludge) digestion (process)
Schlammfladen m	flake of sludge
Schlammindex m	sludge index
Schlammkratzer m, siehe: Schlammausräumer	
Schlammkuchen m	sludge cake
Schlammpresse f	sludge press
Schlammrinne f	sludge channel, ~ trough
Schlammrückführung f	sludge return
Schlammschleuder f	sludge centrifuge

Abwasserwesen

Schlammschleuse *f*	sludge gate
Schlammschlitz *m*	sludge slot
Schlammsumpf *m*	sludge sump
Schlammteich *m*	sludge lagoon
(Schlamm)Trockenbeet *n*	(sewage) sludge bed, sewage treatment bed, drying bed, sludge draining bed
Schlammtrocknung *f*	(sewage) sludge drying, de-watering of sludge
Schlammverbrennung *f*	incineration of sludge
Schlammverwertung *f*	utilization of sludge
Schlammwasser *n*	sludge liquor
Schlammwasser *n* bei der Schlammeindickung *f*	supernatant (sludge)
Schlammwasserabflußrohr *n* einer Eindickanlage *f*	supernatant draw-off pipe
Schlammzersetzung *f*	decomposition of sludge
Schlammzylinder *m*	sludge cylinder
Schlitztrommel *f*	cutting screen
Schlitztrommel *f*, Fabrikat CHICAGO PUMP COMPANY	CHICAGO PUMP COMPANY comminutor
Schmetterlingsfliege *f*, Psychodafliege	moth fly, filter ~, sewage ~
Schmutzwasser *n*	sewage without storm water
Schmutzwasserkanal *m*, siehe: Sammler für die getrennte Entwässerung	
senkrecht durchflossenes Becken *n*, lotrecht ~ ~, vertikal ~ ~	vertical-flow basin, ~ tank
städtisches Abwasser *n*	town sewage, city ~
Torfbreiklärschlamm *m*	peat clarified sludge
Trennkanalisation *f*, Trennsystem *n*	separate system
Trockenbeet *n*, siehe: Schlamm ~	
Tropfkörper *m*	trickling filter, percolating ~, sprinkling ~
hochbelasteter ~, Hochleistungs ~	high-rate ~ ~, high-capacity ~ ~
schwachbelasteter ~	low-rate ~ ~, low-capacity ~ ~
Verbindungssammler *m* zwischen Hauptsammler und Nebensammler	submain, branch sewer
Verteilerscheibe *f* [*Schlammfaulraum m*]	sludge distributor
Verteilung *f* flüssigen Faulschlammes auf Felder durch Pumpen	pumping to agricultural land
Verteilungssprinkler *m*, siehe: Wandersprenger *m*	
vertikal durchflossenes Becken *n*, siehe: senkrecht ~ ~	
Vorabsetzklärung *f*, Vorabsitzklärung	primary sedimentation, ~ settling
Vorkammer *f* einer Klärbeckenanlage *f*	receiving chamber
Vorklärbecken *n*	preliminary clarification tank, ~ ~ basin
Vorklärung *f*	preliminary clarification, presedimentation
waagerecht durchflossenes Becken *n*, horizontal ~ ~	horizontal-flow basin, ~ tank

Wandersprenger m, Verteilungssprinkler m [*Verteilung von Abwasser auf Tropfkörpern*] — travelling distributor
Wäschereiabwasser n — laundry waste water
zusitzendes Grundwasser n — groundwater entering sewers
zweistöckiges Absetzbecken n, ~ Absitzbecken, ~ Klärbecken — two-storey tank, ~ basin

---

Abweis|mittel n = repellent
~stein m, siehe: Prellstein
Abweisungsblech n, Prallblech [*im Fangkessel m beim Druckluftbetonförderer m*] = (central) baffle
Abwicklung f **der Wölbungsleibung** f = development of soffit
Abwicklungslänge f = developed length
Abwinkelung f **des (Förder)Bandes** n = superelevation of the belt
Abwitterung f; siehe unter „Denudation f"
Abwitterungs|hang m = erosion slope
~produkte npl, siehe: Verwitterungskruste f
Abwölbung f (Geol.) = downward bowing
Abwurf|band n, Abwurfförderband = discharge conveyor (belt), ~ belt
~höhe f, Ausschütthöhe = dumping height
~schurre f, Austragschurre, Austragungsschurre, Auslaufschurre = swivel chute, discharge ~
~vorrichtung f, siehe: Ausschüttvorrichtung
Abwürgen n [*Motor* m] = stalling [*engine*]
abyssisch, plutonisch, grundlos (Geol.) [*in der Tiefe, besonders in der Tiefsee* f *gebildet*] = abyssal, abysmal
abyssisches Gestein n, Tiefengestein, plutonisches Gestein, Plutonit m, subkrustales Gestein, Intrusivgestein = abysmal rock
Abzapf|brunnen m, Entlastungsbrunnen [*in artesisch gespanntem Grundwasser* n] = bleeder well
~hahn m = drawing-off cock
~vorrichtung f = drawing-off device
Abzieh|band n **im Haldentunnel** m = tunnel conveyor (belt)
~bohle f, siehe: Abgleichbohle
~eisen n = steel straightedge

~element n, siehe: Einbauelement
Abziehen n, siehe: Abgleichen n
~, Subtraktion f = subtraction
~, (Ab)Schürfen n = skimming [*the removal of the top layer or of the irregularities in the ground surface*]
abziehen [*von einem Silo* m] = to withdraw
~, subtrahieren = to subtract
~, siehe: abgleichen
Abzieher m, Abziehvorrichtung f = puller
Abzieh|latte f = smoothing board, screed(ing) ~, level(l)ing ~
~schraube f = withdrawing screw (Brit.); pulling (-off) ~ (US)
~silo m = live storage bin
~stein m = bench stone
~verteilgerät n, zweiachsiger Erdhobel m mit Eigenantrieb m = maintainer (scraper), blade maintainer, (road) patrol, road maintainer, autopatrol (grader), motor patrol, maintainer grader
~vorrichtung f, Abzieher m = puller
Abzug|band n = delivery conveyor (belt)
~kanal m, siehe: Durchlaß m
~rinne f [*Abziehen von einem Silo* m] = withdrawing conveyor
~röhre f, Entwässerungskanal m [*Brückenentwässerung* f] = drain pipe, drainage conduit
~schieber m, siehe: Schieberschütz(e)
Abzweig|leitung f = branch line
~rohr n = branch pipe
~stück n = tee-branch
Abzweigung f **eines Kanals** m = arm of a canal, branch ~ ~ ~
Abzweigventil n = branch valve
abzwerchen, abzwirchen = to plane timber across the grain
Achat|mörser m = agate mortar
~schwüle f = thunder egg
Achse f [*Mathematik* f] = axis

Achse — Affinität

Achse *f*, **Rad** ~
  Vorder ~
  Hinter ~
  Lauf ~
  (An)Triebs ~ Treib ~
  gefedert
  Trag ~
Achsstand *m*, Achs(en)abstand
Achslast *f*, Achsdruck *m*, Achsbelastung *f*
  Lenk ~, Leit ~
  Schwing ~
Achslager *n*
Achszapfen *m*, Achsstumpf *m*, Achsstummel *m*, Achs(en)hals *m* [*Teil der Achse, der im Lager ruht*]

axle
  front ~
  rear ~
  free ~
  drive ~, driving ~, live ~, power ~
  spring-mounted
  bearing ~
  axle base, axle spacing
  axle-load
  steering ~
  oscillating ~
  ~ bearing
  journal

Achselzapfen *m*; siehe unter „Holzverbindung *f*"
Achsenkreuz *n*, Achsensystem *n*, Koordinatensystem, Koordinatenkreuz = coordinate axis, ~ system (of axes)
achsrechter Schub *m*, Axialschub, Seitenschub = side thrust, lateral shear
achtfacher Hammerseilzug *m* = eight-part hammer line
Achtflach *n*, Achtflächner *m* = octahedron
Acht-Stunden-Tag *m* = eight-hour day
Achtwertigkeit *f* = octavalence
Ackerbulldog *m*, siehe: Ackerschlepper *m*
ackerfähig, kultivierbar, anbaufähig, urbar, kulturfähig, anbauwürdig [*Boden m*] = arable
Acker|(gleis)kettenschlepper *m*, Ackerbulldog *m* auf (Gleis)Ketten = agricat (tractor) (US)
~krume *f* = agricultural topsoil
~schlepper *m*, Ackerbulldog *m*, Ackertrecker *m*, Ackertraktor *m* = farm tractor
~straußgras *n* = windle straw
~trespe *f* = brome (grass)
~walze *f* = land roller
~wiese *f* = arable meadow
~winde *f* = bindweed, small morningglory
Adamellit *m* (Geol.) = adamellite
Addition *f* **von Kräften**, Zusammenzählung *f* ~ ~ = summation of forces
Ader|gneis *m*, Arterit *m* = vein gneiss

~mahagoni *n* = veined mahogany
Adhäsion *f*, scheinbare Haftfestigkeit *f*, Grenzflächenkraft *f* = adhesion, adhesiveness
adhäsionsfördernder Zusatzstoff *m*, siehe: Netzhaftmittel *n*
Adhäsions|verbesserer *m*, siehe: Netzhaftmittel *n*
~wasser *n* = cohesive water
adiabatische Linie *f*, Druck-Volumenkurve *f*, Adiabate *f*, adiabatische Kurve *f* = adiabatic line
Adinol *m* (Geol.) = adinole
Adlerzange *f* = stone lifting tongs
Adsorption *f* = adsorption
Adsorptions|druck *m* = adsorption pressure
~kraft *f* = adsorption power
~wärme *f* = heat of adsorption
~wasser *n*, äußeres Haftwasser, adsorptiv gebundenes Wasser [*Boden m*] = adsorbed (soil) water
Advance-Dieselmotorwalze *f* = advance diesel road roller
Advektionsnebel *m*, Mischungsnebel = advection fog
Adventivkegel *m* = adventive cone
AEROCRET-Gasbeton *m* [*Trademark*] = AEROCRETE
Aerolith *m* = aerolite
Affe *m*, Erdwinde *f*, Handkabelwinde = windlass
Affinität *f*, Verbindungsstreben *n* = affinity, liking

Affinitätsachse f = axis of affinity
Agalmatolith m (Geol.), siehe: Bildstein m
Agens n = agent
Agglomerat n (Geol.) = agglomerate
Aggregat n, Maschinen~ = rig, outfit
~, Stromerzeugungs~, Stromerzeuger~ [*besteht aus Antriebsmaschine mit gekuppeltem Generator*] = generating set, electric generator (set), generator, electric set
Aggressivbeständigkeit f [*Beton* m] = resistance to disintegrating effects, ~ ~ aggressive influence
Aggressivität f = aggressive action
Ägirin m (Min.) = aegirine, aegirite
A-Horizont m, Auslaugungshorizont m, Auslaugungsschicht f, Eluvialhorizont = A horizon, zone of removal
Ahorn m = maple
Akkord|arbeit f = piece work, task ~
~**lohn** m = piece wage
~**satz** m = piece rate
Akkumulation f, siehe: Ablagerung f
Akku(mulatoren)|batterie f, Speicherbatterie, Sammler m, Akku(mulator) m = accumulator battery, storage ~
~**lok(omotive)** f = (storage-)battery loco(motive), accumulator loco(motive)
~**-Triebwagen** m = battery railcar
Akmittrachyt m = acmite trachyte
Akontozahlung f, Abschlagzahlung = payment on account, instalment payment
Aktinolith n (Min.) = actinolite
Aktionsradius m, siehe: Bereich m
aktiver Erddruck m, angreifender ~ ~ = active lateral earth pressure
aktivierter Kalkmörtel m **für Außenputz** = activated lime mortar
Aktivkohle f, aktive Kohle f, a-Kohle f = active (or activated) carbon (or charcoal, or coal)
Akustikplatte f = acoustical slab, ~ board
akustisches Echolot n = sound-ranging altimeter, sonic ~, echo sounder
~ **Signal** n = audible signal
akzessorisches Mineral n, Übergemengteil m, n = accessory mineral
Alabandin n (Min.), siehe: Glanzblende f
Alabaster m, feinkörniger Gips m, körnigkristallinischer Gips = alabaster

~**gips** m, siehe: Marmorgips
Alaun|erde f = alum coal
~**gips** m, siehe: Marmorgips
~**schiefer** m = alum slate
~**schieferton** m = alum shale
ALBARET-Schaffußwalze f; siehe unter „Walze f"
Albertit m = albertite, Albert coal, Albert shale
Albertschlag m; siehe unter „Drahtseil n"
Albino-Bitumen n, helles Bitumen n = albino asphalt (US); ~ bitumen (Brit.)
Albit m (Min.) = albite, white schorl
~**-Chloritschiefer** m = albitite
Alginsäure f, Algensäure f = alginic acid
Algorithmus m = algorithm
Alhidade f = alidade, sight rule
Alkali n = alkali
~**augit** m = soda pyroxene
alkaliempfindliche Betonzuschläge mpl = reactive materials in concrete
Alkali|feldspat m = alkali(c) fel(d)spar
~**granit** m = alkali-granite
~**hornblende** f = soda amphibole
~**kalkbasalt** m = calc-alkali basalt
~**kalkgestein** n = calc-alkali(ne) rock
~**metall** m = alkali metal
alkalisch = alkaline
alkalische Anregung f = alkaline activation
~ **Lösung** f = alkaline solution
~ **Reaktion** f **der Zuschläge** mpl **mit dem Zement** m, Alkali-Zuschlagstoff-Reaktion = alkali-aggregate reaction (or expansion)
~ **Salmiakfumarole** f = alkaline ammoniacal fumarole
alkalischer Boden m = alkaline soil
Alkalität f, Alkalinität, laugensalzige Eigenschaft f = alkalinity
Alkali-Zuschlagstoff-Reaktion f, alkalische Reaktion f der Zuschläge mpl mit dem Zement m = alkali-aggregate reaction (or expansion)
Alkydharz n = alkyd resin
Allein|druck m, reiner Druck m = direct compression
~**vertretung** f = sole agency
Allemontit m (Min.), siehe: Arsenantimon n

allgemeine Lagekarte f = general location map

Allgemeine Ortskrankenkasse f = Local Health Insurance Society

Allgemeiner Deutscher Automobilclub m, A. D. A. C. = General Automobile Club of Germany

Allgemeinheit f = general public

allmähliche Erweiterung f **eines Flusses** m = progressive widening of a river

~ **Verengung** f **eines Flusses** m = progressive narrowing of a river, ~ contracting ~ ~

allotriomorph = allotriomorphic, anhedral

allotriomorphes Kristall n = anhedron, allotriomorphic crystal

allotriomorph-körnig = allotriomorphic-granular, granitic, granitoid, xenomorphic-granular

Allotrop m = allotrope

Allotyp m = allotype

All-Rad|-Antrieb m = all-wheel drive

~-**Druckluftbremse** f = all-wheel air brake

~-**Lenkung** f, siehe: All-Rad-Steuerung f

~-**Räumer** m = all-wheel drive dozer

~-**Schlepper** m, All-Rad-Traktor m, All-Rad-Trecker m = all-wheel drive tractor

~-**Steuerung** f, All-Rad-Lenkung f = all-wheel steer(ing)

~-**Traktor** m, siehe: All-Rad-Schlepper m

alluvialer Verwitterungsschutt m = alluvial mantle rock

Alluvial|fächerschutt m = alluvial fan (accumulations)

~**kegel** m = alluvial cone

Alluvium n, Anlandung f, Anschütte f, Verlandung f (Geol.) = alluvium, alluvial deposit

~, **Nacheiszeit** f = postglacial period

alluviumbedeckt = alluvium-covered

All-Wetter-Straße f = all-weather road

Allzweck-Gerät n; siehe unter „Baumaschinen fpl und Baugeräte npl"

Alpen|erle f, Grünerle = green alder

~**gneis** m (protogene gneiss, protogenic ~, protogin (e gneiss)

~**granit** m = Alpine granite

~**kalk(stein)** m = Alpine limestone

~**see** m = Alpine lake

~**tunnel** m = Alpine tunnel

~**vorland** n = Alpine piedmont

Alstonit m, Bariumaragonit m (Min.) = alstonite

Altarm m, siehe: Altwasser n

Alterung f, Alterungsprozeß m = ageing

~, siehe: Rekristallisation f [Schraube f, Niet m]

Alterungsbeständigkeit f = durability

Alt|material n = salvage, arisings

~**reifengummi** m = scrap tyre rubber (Brit.); ~ tire ~ (US)

~**sand** m, gebrauchter Formsand m = used mo(u)lding sand

~**schnee** m = old snow

~**stadtsanierung** f = city clearance

~**wasser** n, toter Arm m, Altarm = oxbow (lake); bayou (US)

~**wert** m = salvage value

Aluminium n = aluminium (Brit.); aluminum (US)

~**arsenat** n = alumin(i)um arsenate

~**-Aussichtswagen** m = alumin(i)um dome car

~**oxyd** n, Tonerde f, Al_2O_3 = alumina

~**schmelzwerk** n = alumin(i)um smelting plant

~**seifenfett** n **von glänzendem Aussehen** n **und hoher Transparenz** f = lucid compound

~**silikat** n = alumin(i)um silicate

~**sprengkapsel** f; siehe unter „1. Schießen n; 2. Sprengen n"

Alunit m [tonerdereicher Alaunschiefer] = alunite, alumstone

Alveolinenkalk(stein) m = alveolina limestone

Amaranthholz n, Luftholz, Purpurholz = amaranth wood, purple ~

Amazonenstein m (Min.) = amazonstone, amazonite

Amboinaholz n = amboina wood

Amboß m = anvil

Ambursen-Staumauer f; siehe unter „Talsperre f"

Ameisensäure f, Formylsäure = formic acid

amerikanische Silbertanne f = noble silver fir

amerikanisches Pfeilergerät n [Brücke f] = Standard Unit Steel Trestles

Amethyst m (Min.) = amethyst
Amiant m (Min.), siehe: Asbest m
Amiesit m = Amiesite [*is a cold-laid plant-mix usually placed in two courses*]
Ammoniak-Drucklaugung f = ammonia leaching pressure process
Ammonium|hydroxyd n = spirits of hartshorn, NH_4OH
~sulfat n = ammonium sulphate (Brit.); ~ sulfate (US)
Ammonsalpetersprengstoff m; siehe unter „1. Schießen n; 2. Sprengen n"
Amöbenruhr f = amoebic dysentery
amorph [*ist der Gegensatz zu kristallin*] = amorpho(u)s
amorpher Quarz m, Kieselsäure-Glas n = vitreous silica
Amortisierung f, Amortisation f = capital depreciation
Amosit (asbest) m (Min.) = Amosite [*this name embodies the initials of the company exploiting this material in the Transvaal, viz. the «Asbestos Mines of South Africa»*]
amperometrische Titration f = amperometric titration
Amphibol|asbest m (Min.), siehe: Hornblendeasbest
~gruppe f = amphibole group
Amphibolit m = amphibolite
Amphibolmagnetit m = amphibole magnetite
Amplitude f, Schwing(ungs)weite f, Ausschlag(weite) m, (f) = amplitude
Anaglyphenbild n = anaglyph
Analogie-Rechenmaschine f = analogy computor
Analysensiebapparat m = testing (or test) sieve vibrator with sieves
Analzim m (Min.) = analcite, analcime
Anatas m (Min.) = anatase
Anatexis f, Palingenese f, Einschmelzungsmetamorphose f = palingenesis
anbaufähig, siehe: ackerfähig
Anbau|geräte npl (oder Zusatzvorrichtungen fpl) **für (Gleis)Kettenschlepper mpl** = crawler tractor attachments
~streuer m; siehe unter „Streugerät n für den Winterdienst m"

~-Verteilerkasten m = tail gate spreader box
anbauwürdig, siehe: ackerfähig
Anbohr|meißel m; siehe unter „Bohrmeißel"
~stahl m = starter steel, starting ~
anböschen = to bank against, to fill and grade
Anbruchsgebiet n = region where an avalanche starts
Andalusit m, Al_2SiO_5 (Min.) = andalusite
Änderung f der Stromrichtung f = change of direction of the current
Andesin n (Min.) = andesine
Andesit m (Geol.) = andesite
~asche f = andesite ash
Andreaskreuz n, Kreuzstreben fpl, Kreuzband n, Abkreuzung f = diagonal struts, St. Andrew's cross, saltier cross bars, cross stays
Andrehkurbel f, Anwerfkurbel, Startkurbel, Anwurfkurbel, Anlaßkurbel = starting crank
Anemometer n, Wind(stärke)messer m = anemometer, wind ga(u)ge
Aneroidbarometer n, Dosenbarometer, Federbarometer, Luftdruckhöhenmesser m, Aneroid n = aneroid barometer
Anfahrkraft f = tractive force
Anfahrtsdalbe f = guiding dolphin
anfällig = vulnerable
Anfall|gespärre n, Anfallgebinde n = hip rafters
~punkt m [Dach n] = hip ridge
~stelle f = source of supply
Anfänger|stein m [Pflaster n] = starter
~(ziegel) m, siehe: Kämpfer(stein) m
Anfangs|festigkeit f = initial strength, early ~
~gehalt n = commencing salary
~schwindung f [Beton m] = initial shrinkage
Anflugwinkel m; siehe unter „Flugplatz m"
Anfressung f, Korrosion f, Anfressen n, Angreifen n = corrosion
Anfuhr f, Anlieferung f = shipment, delivery
~weg m [zur Baustelle f] = haul road, construction ~

Angebot — angesäte Böschung 35

Angebot *n*
  Absprache *f* unter Bietern *mpl*, Preisabsprache ~
  Alternativ ~
  ~ für Entwurf und Bau
  Angebotsblankett *n*
  Angebotsgegenüberstellung *f*
  Angebotseröffnungstermin *m*, Submissionstermin

  Angebotseinholung *f*, Ausschreibung *f*

  Angebotssumme *f*, Angebotspreis *m*
  Auftragserteilung *f*, Vergabe *f*

  Auftraggeber *m*, Bauherr *m*, Bauherrschaft *f*
  Auftragsschreiben *n*
  Auftragnehmer *m*
  beschränkte Ausschreibung *f*

  Bieter *m*
  Gegen~ *n*
  Haupt~
  Leistungsbeschreibung *f*
  Leistungsverzeichnis *n*
    kostenvergütete Position *f*, Leistungsposition

  Massenverzeichnis *n*, Mengenverzeichnis
  Mindestfordernder *m*
  öffentliche Ausschreibung *f*
  Submission *f*
  unterbieten
  Vertragsunterlagen *fpl*
  Zuschlags~ *n*
  zusätzlich

1. bid; 2. proposal (US); tender, offer (Brit.)
  combining to eliminate competition, price fixing
  alternative ~, alternate ~
  "turn-key" bid, all-in tender
  form (of tender)
  summary (or schedule) of ~s
  opening date, submission date, tendering date, date set for the opening of tenders
  competitive tender(ing) action, bidding procedure; adjudication (US)
  ~ sum
  contract award, award (or letting) of contract, contract-letting
  promoter, purchaser, owner, sponsor, employer, client
  letter (or notice) of award
  successful bidder, ~ tenderer
  limited submission, ~ public tender action (or tendering)
  bidder, tenderer
  competitive ~
  base ~
  specification
  schedule of prices
    pay item

  bill of quantities
  lowest bidder (or tenderer)
  open tendering
  submission (of competitive tenders)
  to undercut
  contract documents
  winning bid (US); ~ tender (Brit.)
  "extra over"

---

angefault [*Holz n*] = partially putrid
angefaultes Abwasser *n* = fouled sewage
angeflanscht = flange mounted
angefressen [*Chemie f*] = corroded
angefügte Ebene *f* = tied plain
angegliederte Halbinsel *f*, Angliederungshalbinsel = attached peninsula, tied ~
~ Insel *f*, Angliederungsinsel = attached island, tied ~
angegriffenes Fossil *n*, angelöstes ~ = corroded fossil, partly dissolved ~

angehauenes Widerlager *n* = reduced abutment
angehren = to mitre
angelöstes Fossil *n*, siehe: angegriffenes ~
angelsächsisches Gewölbe *n*, normannisches ~, Fächergewölbe, Trichtergewölbe = fan vaulting
angenommene Belastung *f*, Belastungsannahme *f* = assumed load
angesäte Böschung *f*, eingesäte ~ = seeded slope

angesäuertes Wasser n = acidulated water, acidulous ~

angeschlossene Bevölkerung f = contributary population

angeschwemmte Sandinsel f, Sandbank f, Sandbarre f [*Sandanschwemmung vor Flußmündungen in das Meer*] = sandhead, off-shore bar, (sand)bar, coastal bar

angeschwemmter Seetang m = cast-up seaweed

(an)gespannter Grundwasserspiegel m = perched (or false) (ground-) water table

angespülter Flußschutt m = river wash

angewandte Geologie f = applied geology

angewittert (Geol.) = weathered

angewitterter Geschiebelehm m = mesotil

angezogen [*Schraube* f] = tight

Anglesit m, Vitrolbleierz n, PbSO$_4$ (Min.) = anglesite

Angliederungs|halbinsel f, angegliederte Halbinsel = tied peninsula, attached ~

~insel f, angegliederte Insel = tied island, attached ~

angreifend = aggressive

~ [*im Sinne von korrosiv*] = corrosive

angreifender Erddruck m, siehe: aktiver ~

Angriffsmoment n = applied moment

Angulatensandstein m = Angulatus sandstone

Anhänge|bürstenwalze f, Schleppbürstenwalze, Anhängebesenwalze, Schleppbesenwalze, Anhängekehrwalze, Schleppkehrwalze = trailer (type road) brush

~chassis n, Anhängechassis, Schleppfahrgestell n, Anhängefahrgestell n, Anhänger-Fahrgestell = trailer chassis

~-Erdhobel m, siehe: Anhänge-Straßenhobel

~fahrzeug n, Anhänger m = towed vehicle, trailer

~-Fegemaschine f, siehe: Anhänge-Straßenkehrmaschine

~gerät n = trailer-type unit

~grabgerät n = trailer-type (excavator) digger

~-Kehrmaschine f, siehe: Anhänge-Straßenkehrmaschine

~kehrwalze f, siehe: Anhängebürstenwalze

~kupplung f, Anhängerkupplung = trailer coupling

~mischer m = trailer mixer

Anhänger m, Anhängefahrzeug n = trailer, towed vehicle

~ als Prüfwagen für Straßenbrücken = deadweight trailer for testing road bridges

~ mit Bodenentleerung, Bodenentleerer (-Anhänger) m [*schleppergezogen*] = trailer-bottom dump, bottom-dump tractor truck, tractor-drawn bottom-dump trailer, bottom-dump tractor-trailer

~bagger m = trailer excavator

~-Chassis n, Anhängechassis, Schleppfahrgestell n, Anhängefahrgestell, Anhänger-Fahrgestell = trailer chassis

~kran m = trailer crane

~kupplung f, Anhängekupplung = trailer coupling

Anhänge|-Schürf(kübel)wagen m; siehe unter „Radschrapper m"

~-Schwingungswalze f; siehe unter „Walze"

~-Straßenaufreißer m = towed-type road ripper, trailer-type ~ ~

~-Straßenhobel m, geschleppter Erdhobel, Anhänge-Wegehobel, Anhänge-Erdhobel, Anhängestraßenhobel, Schleppwegehobel, Schlepperdhobel = towed-type (or pull) grader

~-Straßenkehrmaschine f, Anhänge-Fegemaschine f, Anhänge-Kehrmaschine f, Schleppstraßenkehrmaschine, Schleppstraßenfegemaschine = traction-driven (or trailer-type) rotary sweeper (or scavenging machine, or road sweeper, or mechanical sweeper, or road sweeping machine), towed-type road sweeper

~streuer m; siehe unter: „Streugerät n für den Winterdienst m"

Anhängewagen m [*Erdbau* m]

~ mit Niederdruckgummibereifung f

tractor wagon, trailer ~

wheel type ~ ~ having low-pressure tyres (Brit.)/tires (US)

Anhängewagen — Ankerstrom

(Gleis)Ketten-~, Raupenwagen, Großraumlore *f* auf (Gleis)Ketten *fpl*

~ ~ with track type equipment, caterpillar tread wagon

Anhänge-Wegehobel *m*, siehe: Anhänge-Straßenhobel
(An)Hebespindel *f*, **Hebebock** *m* = jack
anhydrisch, wasserfrei = anhydrous, anhydric
Anhydrisierungsmittel *n* = dehydrating agent
Anhydrit *m*, wasserfreier Gips *m*, wasserfreies Kalziumsulfat *n* = anhydrite
~**gruppe** *f* = Middle Muschelkalk
~**knolle** *f* = anhydritic concretion, concretion of anhydrite
~**putz** *m*, Anhydritbinder *m*, DIN 4208 = anhydrite plaster [*no more manufactured in Great Britain since 1952*]
~**region** *f* = anhydrite zone
~**schnur** *f* = anhydrite band
Anilin|farbe *f* = aniline dye
~**punkt** *m* [*Kohlenwasserstoff-Lösungsmittel n*] = aniline point
~**rot** *n* = aniline red, anileine, tyraline
~**schwarz** *m* = aniline black
~**sulfat** *n*, schwefelsaures Anilin *n* = aniline sulphate, anilic ~
~**violett** *n* = aniline violett, regina purple
Anion *n* = anion
Anisholz *n* = aniseed wood, anise-seed ~
Anisoklinalfalte *f* = anisoclinal fold
anisotropes Mineral *n* = anisotropic mineral
Anker *m* [*elektrische Maschine f, Magnet m*] = armature
~ = impulse starter
~ [*Relais n*] = tongue
~ [*Verankerung f, Uhr f, Schiff n*] = anchor
~ [*elektrischer Leitungsbaum m*] = guy, stay
~, siehe: Ankerstab *m*
~ **mit Sternschaltung** *f* = star-connected armature
~**ausbau** *m*; siehe unter „Tunnelbau"
~**block** *m*, siehe: Ankerklotz *m*
~**bock** *m* [*Hängebrücke f*] = chain chair, ~ standard
~**bohrung** *f* [*Elektrotechnik*] = armature bore

~**boje** *f* = mooring buoy
~**bolzen** *m* = anchor bolt, holding down ~, tie ~, foundation ~
~**flansch** *m* [*Elektrotechnik f*] = armature flange, core haed
~**fluß** *m*, Ankerkraftfluß = armature flux
~**holm** *m* = cross-beam
~**kammer** *f* [*Hängebrücke f*] = anchorage chamber
~**kette** *f*, Spannkette [*Hängebrücke f*] = tension chain, tightening ~, anchorage ~
~**klotz** *m*, Ankerblock *m*, Verankerungsklotz, Verankerungsblock = stay block
~**kurzschlußbremse** *f* = armature short circuiting brake
~**loch-Bohrgerät** *n* = roof-pinning rock drill
~**luftspalt** *m* [*Elektrotechnik*] = armature gap
~**mutter** *f* = tie nut
~**nut** *f* [*Elektrotechnik*] = armature slot
~**pfahl** *m* = anchor pile
~**pfeiler** *m*, Verankerungspfeiler = anchorage pier
~**platte** *f*, Verankerungsplatte = anchor plate, tie ~
~**platz** *m* = anchorage
~**riegel** *m*, Ankersplint *m* = tie cotter
~**schacht** *m* [*Hängebrücke f*] = anchorage shaft
~**scheibe** *f* = anchor ring (Brit.); form anchor (US)
~**schelle** *f* = clamp, guy ~
~**schiene** *f* = tie bar
~**schrägpfahl** *m* = battered anchor pile
~**schraube** *f*, Fundamentschraube = anchor bolt, tie ~, holding down ~
~**seil** *n*, siehe: Trosse *f*
~**spannschraube** *f* [*Leitungsmast m*] = stay tightener, swivel; slack puller (US)
~**splint** *m*, Ankerriegel *m* = tie cotter
~**spule** *f* [*Elektrotechnik*] = armature coil
~**stab** *m*, (Zug)Anker *m*, Zugstange *f* = anchor bar, holding down rod
~**strom** *m* = armature current

Ankerwinde *f*, Schiffswinde = anchor hoist
ankörnen = to mark, to centre, to punch
Ankündigungsschild *n* [*Autobahn f*] = advance direction notice
Anlage *f*, Einrichtung *f*, Betriebsanlage = facility, installation, plant
~ [*Brief m*] = enclosure
~**kapital** *n*, Investitionskapital *n* = invested capital
~**kosten** *f*, Kostenaufwand *m* = capital costs (or expenditure, or outlay)
Anlandebrücke *f* = landing stage
Anlandung *f*, siehe: Alluvium *n*
Anlasser *m*, Starter *m*, Anlaßvorrichtung *f* = starter, accelerator, starting apparatus
Anlaß|kraftstoff *m* = priming fuel
~**kurbel** *f*, siehe: Andrehkurbel
~**motor** *m*, siehe: Anwurfmotor
~**schalter** *m* = starter switch
~**verdichter** *m*, Anlaßkompressor *m* = starting (or auxiliary) compressor
~**-Vorrichtung** *f*, siehe: Anlasser *m*
~**wert** *m* [*Suspension f*] = yield value
Anlauf *m*, siehe: Anzug *m*
~**zeit** *f* = lead time
Anlege|aufzug *m*, Anlegebauaufzug = lean-to builders' hoist
~**-Plattform** *f* **für Schiffe** *npl* = berthing beam
~**vorrichtung** *f*, siehe: Schiffshaltevorrichtung
Anlernen *n*, Ausbildung *f* = training
Anlieferung *f*, Anfuhr *f* = shipment, delivery
Anlieger *m* [*an einer Straße f*] = resident [*alongside a road*]
~**grundstück** *n* [*Straße f*] = marginal property
~**rechtwasser** *n*, siehe: garantiertes Brauchwasser *n*
~**straße** *f* = service road
anmachen [*Mörtel m*] = to mix
Anmach(e)wasser *n*, Mischwasser = mix(ing) water, ga(u)ging ~, batch ~
anmontiert = attached
anmooriger Boden *m*, siehe: Moorerde *f*
Annabergit *m*, Nickelblüte *f* (Min.) = annabergite, nickel-bloom
(An)Näherungs|höhe *f* = spot level
~**probe(stück)** *f*, (*n*) = spot sample

~**rechnung** *f*, Berechnung *f* der (An-)Näherungswerte *mpl*, (An)Näherungsverfahren *n*, (an)näherungsweise Berechnung = approximation, approximate method
Anordnung *f* [*z. B. von Maschinen*] = arrangement
~ [*z. B. Tankstellen fpl an einer Straße f*] = siting
anorganische Säure *f* = inorganic acid
anorganischer Binder *m* = inorganic cement
Anorthit *m*, Kalkfeldspat *m*, $CaAl_2Si_2O_8$ (Min.) = anorthite, indianite, limefeldspar, lime-felspar
An-Ort-Mischverfahren *n*, siehe: Bodenmischverfahren
Anpassungsfähigkeit *f* = flexibility
Anpreßdruck *m* [*z. B. Eimerleiter f beim Grabenbagger m*] = crowd pressure
Anrampung *f* = ramp
Anrauhung *f*, siehe: Abstumpfung
Anreger *m* [*Zement m*] = activator
Anreicherung *f* = accumulation
~**shorizont** *m*, siehe: B-Horizont
~**smittel** *n* = enriching medium
anreißen = to trace, to mark
Anreißen *n* = marking, tracing
Ansäen *n*, Besamung *f*, Ansaat *f*, Besämung, Säen *n* = seeding, sowing
Ansatz *m*, Kessel~ = (boiler) scale
~**feile** *f* = flat file
~**flansch** *m* = connecting flange
~**muffe** *f* = connecting socket
~**ring** *m* [*Zementbrennen n*] = clinker ring
~**rohr** *n* = extension pipe
Ansaugemenge *f* [*Kompressor m*] = actual volume of the cylinder
Ansaugen *n*, Ansaugung *f* = priming, suction
(An)Saug|filter *m*, *n* = suction filter
~**luft** *f* = suction air
~**rohr** *n*, siehe: Saugrohr
Anschaffungskosten *f* = initial cost(s), first ~
anscheren, spleißen = to splice
(An)Schiftung *f*; siehe unter „Holzverbindung *f*"
Anschlag *m*, (Kosten)(Vor)~ = estimate of costs

Anschlag = stop
~bund n = stop collar
~schalter m, Begrenzungsschalter, Endschalter = limit switch, stop ~
~schraube f = stop screw
Anschluß m = connection
~blech n = connection plate
~gleis n, Gleisanschluß m, Stichgleis n = spur track; rail(way) spur (Brit.); rail(road) ~ (US)
~leitung f = connection line
~niet m = connecting rivet
~punkt m, Anschlußstelle f, Zufahrtstelle f [Autobahn f] = acces point, interconnecting roadway, interchange
~rampe f [Autobahn f] = access ramp, interchange
~wert m [Elektrotechnik f] = connected load, connection ~
~winkel m, Befestigungswinkel = clip angle, (angle) cleat, angle bracket, (end) connection angle
Anschütte f (Geol.)., siehe: Alluvium n
Anschwemmung f, siehe: Auflandung f
Anschwemmungsküste f = alluvial coast
Ansicht f, Aufriß m, Vertikalprojektion f = elevation, profile
~ im Aufriß m und Schnitt m = sectional elevation, ~ view
~ ~ Grundriß m = plan view
~ ~ Seitenriß m = side elevation, ~ view
Anspannen n der Vorspannglieder npl = stressing of the tension members
Ansprechen n [Schaltung f] = response
Anspring|nase f [automatischer Siphon m] = priming nose (Brit.); sealing bucket (US)
~-Wasserspiegel m [automatischer Siphon m] = priming level
Anstauung f, Stau m, Spiegelerhebung f = banked up water level, damming
Ansteckdeichsel f = detachable tow-bar
anstehend = in-place, in-situ
anstehender Boden m = in-situ soil, site ~, in-place ~
anstehendes Gestein n, gewachsener Fels m, Kernfels, Sprengfels, Felsuntergrund m, anstehender Fels, anstehendes Felsgestein n = ledge rock, outcropping ~, underlying ~, bed ~, country ~, solid ~

ansteigende Straße f = road with rising gradient
Anstreicher m, Maler m = painter
Anstrich m = coat, painting
~film m = surface coating film
~fläche f = painting surface
~-Markierungsstreifen m = paint stripe
~stoff-Kunstharz n = coating resin
~wert m = painting value
Anteil m = rate
~ [z. B. Boden m] = fraction
Anthrazenöl n = anthracene oil, green ~
Antigorit m, Blätterserpentin m (Min.) = antigorite
Antiklinale f, siehe: Sattel m der Faltung f
Antikline f, siehe: Sattel m der Faltung f
Antimon|arsen n (Min.), siehe: Arsenantimon n
~blei n = antimonial lead, hard ~
~blende f, Kermesit m (Min.) = kermesite, pyrostibnite
~blüte f, Valentinit m (Min.) = valentinite, Sb_2O_3
~glanz m, Antimonit m (Min.) = antimonite; antimony glance [absolete term]
~nickelglanz m, Ullmanit m (Min.) = ullmanite, nickel antimony glance, NiSbS
~silberblende f, dunkles Rotgültigerz n, Pyrargyrit m, Ag_3SbS_3 (Min.) = pyrargyrite, ruby silver ore, darkred silver ore
ANTI-PETROL-Schlämme f [Trademark] = ANTIPETROL slurry [fuel-resistant Oberbach slurry]
Anti|schaummittel n, siehe: Schaumverhütungsmittel
~schmiermittel n = antilubricating agent
antiseptisch = antiseptic
Antizyklon m, Hoch(druckgebiet) n = anticyclone, high
Antragsformular n = form of application, application form, application blank
Antransport m = hauling operations
antransportieren mit LKW m = to truck to (US); to transport to with lorries (Brit.)
Antriebs|aggregat n = drive unit
~art f = kind of drive
~kette f, Treibkette f, Triebkette = driving chain, drive chain; propel (drive) chain (US)

Antriebs|kettenrad n, Antriebsturas m = driving sprocket, drive ~, propel ~
~kraft f, Triebkraft, Treibkraft = driving (or motive) power (or force)
~mechanismus m; siehe unter „Baumaschinen fpl und Baugeräte npl"
~rad n, Triebrad n, Treibrad n = driving wheel, drive ~, traction ~
~riemen m = drive belt, driving ~
~ritzel n, siehe: Triebling m
~teil m, n = driving part, drive section
~turas m, Antriebskettenrad n = drive sprocket, propel ~, driving ~
~vorgelege n = drive back gear
~welle f, Triebwelle = driveshaft, driving shaft
Anwachsufer n = accreting bank, deposition bluff
Anweisung f für den Bau von Betonfahrbahndecken fpl, ABB = Obligatory Specification for the Construction of Concrete Surfacings
~ ~ ~ ~ ~ bituminösen Fahrbahndecken fpl = Obligatory Specification for the Construction of Bituminous Surfacings
~ ~ ~ ~ ~ Pflasterdecken fpl = Obligatory Specification for the Construction of Sett-pavings
~ ~ die Abnahme von Betonfahrbahndecken fpl der Reichsautobahnen fpl, AAB = Obligatory Specification for the Acceptance of Concrete Surfacings on the Motor Roads
Anwendungs|gebiet n, Anwendungsbereich m = field of use, ~ ~ application, scope
~möglichkeit f, Anwendbarkeit f = applicability
~temperatur f = application temperature
Anwerfkurbel f, siehe: Andrehkurbel
anwuchsverhindernde Schiffsanstrichfarbe f, Schiffsbodenfarbe = antifouling
Anwurfmotor m, Anlaß(hilfs)motor, Anwerfmotor, Startmotor = starting engine
Anwürgen n; siehe unter: „1. Schießen n; 2. Sprengen n"
Anzapfdampfmaschine f, Anzapfdampfmotor m = bleeder (type) steam engine

Anzapfen n = bleeding
Anzeige|gerät n, Anzeiger m = indicator, indicating instrument
~vorrichtung f für Bunkerfüllungen fpl, siehe: Bunkerstandanzeiger m
Anziehen n [Bremse f] = application [brake]
~ [Mörtel m] = initial hardening
anziehen [Mutter f] = to snug [nut]
Anziehungskraft f [z. B. des Mondes m] = gravitational attraction
~ der Moleküle npl = molecular attraction
Anzug m, Anlauf m [Mauer f] = batter, battice [wall]
Anzugsmoment n, Anlauf(dreh)moment [Motor m] = starting torque
äolisch, aërisch (Geol.) [durch Wind gebildet] = eolian
äolische Abtragung f, siehe: Deflation f
äolischer Staub m (Geol.) = windblown dust
Apatit m (Min.) = apatite
Apfelsinenschalengreif(er)korb m = orange-peel grab, fourbladed circular bucket (or grab)
Aplit m = (h)aplite
Apophyse f (Geol.) [ein von einer größeren subkrustalen Masse f abzweigender Gang m] = apophysis [a veinlike offshoot from an igneous intrusion]
Aprolith m; siehe unter „Vulkan m"
Aquädukt m, Wasserleitungsbrücke f = aqueduct, water conduit bridge
aquatisches Sedimentgestein n = waterborne sediment
äquatoriales Klima n = equatorial climate
äquivalenter Verdichtungsdruck m [nach Hvorslev] = equivalent pressure
äquiviskose Temperatur f, Equiviskositätstemperatur f [Vergleichstemperatur bei der Teer eine Viskosität von 50 Sekunden hat] = equi-viscous temperature [abbrev. E. V. T.]
arabische Ziffer f = Arabic numeral
Aragonit m (Min.) = aragonite
Aräometer m, siehe: hydrostatische Senkwaage f
~analyse f, siehe: Absetzversuch m
„Arbeiten" n [Beton m] = expansion and contraction

Arbeiterlager — Armierung

Arbeiter|lager n, siehe: Baustellenlager
~stunde f = man-hour
Arbeitgeberverband m **des Baugewerbes** n = Building Trades Employers Association
Arbeitnehmer m = employe(e)
Arbeits|amt n = labo(u)r office
~ausschuß m = working committee
~ausschuß m **Flugplatzbefestigung** = airfield runways committee
~bereich m = operational range
~breite f = working width
~bühne f = working platform
~bühne f; siehe unter „Fertigbehandlung f"
~einsatz m, siehe: Einsatz
~einstellung f, siehe: Arbeitsunterbrechung f
~element n; siehe unter „Baumaschinen fpl und Baugeräte npl"
~ersparnis f = labo(u)r saving
~fortschritt m, Baufortschritt, Arbeitstempo n, Bautempo = progress of works
~gang m = operation, process, pass
~gang m = working speed
~gemeinschaft f, **Arge** f = contracting combine, bidding combination, contractor combination, amalgamation of contractors, partnership, jointventure (firm) federführende Firma f = sponsor (US); pilot firm, lead firm
~gemeinschaft f **der Bitumenindustrie** f, ARBIT = German Bitumen Industry Association
~gerät n [*Universalbagger* m] = front-end attachment
~geschwindigkeit f [*im Gegensatz zur Transportgeschwindigkeit einer Baumaschine*] = operating speed, working ~, on-the-job travel ~ [*construction machinery*]
~höhe f = working height
~hygiene f = occupational hygiene
~kräfte f = labo(u)r force
Einsatz m = employment
~losigkeit f = unemployment
~maschine f = machine
~plan m, siehe: Bau(zeit)plan
~prinzip n [*Baumaschine* f] = operating principle

~schacht m = working shaft
~schutz(be)kleidung f = protective clothing
~schutzdach n; siehe unter „Fertigbehandlung f"
~silo m = surge bin, ~ hopper
~spiel n [*Maschine* f] = work(ing) cycle
~studie f, siehe: Arbeitsuntersuchung f
~tag m = working day
~tempo n, siehe: Arbeitsfortschritt m
~trupp m, siehe: Kolonne f
~umfang m = scope of work
~unterbrechung f, Arbeitseinstellung f = stoppage
~untersuchung f, Arbeitsstudie f [*Maschine* f] = equipment production study [*machine*]
~vermögen n = energy
~weise f [*Maschine* f] = mode of operation
~woche f = working-week
~zeichnung f, Ausführungszeichnung = working drawing
~zeit n; siehe unter „Fertigbehandlung f"
~zug m (**von Großgerät** n) = equipment train
~zylinder m = working cylinder
Architektengebühr f = architect's compensation
architektonische Gestaltung f = architectural design
Arge f, siehe: Arbeitsgemeinschaft f
Argentit m, Silberglanz m (Min.) = argentite, silver glance
Argillit m [*natürlich entwässerter Tonschiefer* m] = argillite
Arkose f, Arkosesandstein m, Feldspatsand m = arkose (sandstone), arkosic grit
arktisches Spermacetiöl n, siehe: Döglingtran m
Armatur f, (Rohr)Formstück n = fitting, pipe ~
  grobe ~ = rough (or large) ~
  feine ~ = fine (or small) ~
Armaturen|beleuchtung f = dash lamp
~brett n = instrument board, ~ panel
armes Erz n = low grade ore, poor ~
Armgas n [*von Gasolin n befreites Erdgas*] = residue gas, stripped ~
Armierung f, Bewehrung f, Beton ~, Stahleinlagen fpl = reinforcement

armorikanisches Gebirge n = Armorican mountain range
aromatisches Lösungsmittel n = aromatic solvent
Arretierung f [*Laufgewichtswaage* f] = beam lifters
Arsen|antimon n, Antimonarsen n, Allemonit m (Min.) = allemontite
~**blüte** f, Arsenolith m, As$_2$O$_3$ (Min.) = arsenolite
~**kies** m, Mißpickel m, FeAsS (Min.) = arsenical pyrite, arsenopyrite, mispickel
~-**Nickelkies** m, Gersdorffit m (Min.) = gersdorffite
~**olith** m (Min.), siehe: Arsenblüte f
Arterit m, siehe: Adergneis m
artesische Druckhöhe f, artesischer Spiegel m = artesian head
~ **Quelle** f, artesischer Brunnen m, Überlaufbrunnen, frei ausfließende Wasserbohrung f [*Bohrbrunnen, dessen Wasser durch eigenen Überdruck zur Oberfläche gelangt*] = artesian spring, ~ well
artesisches (Grund)Wasser n, artesisch gespanntes (Grund)Wasser [*Grundwasser, das mit artesischem Brunnen gewonnen werden kann. Das artesische Wasser ist eine Sonderform des gespannten Grundwassers*] = artesian (ground-) water
Arzneischleuse f; siehe unter „pneumatische Gründung f"
ärztliche Fürsorge f (**oder Betreuung** f) = medical attention (or attendance)
~ **Hilfe** f = medical assistance
Asbest m (Min.) [*in Italien, Griechenland, Frankreich und dem Orient wird für Asbest auch der Name „Amiant" gebraucht; amianthus = Amiant, Strahlsteinasbest*] = asbestos; amianthus [*a fine, silky asbestos*]
~**gewebe** n = asbestos textile
~**grube** f = asbestos mine
Asbestosis f, Asbestose f = asbestosis [*disease of the lungs due to inhalation of asbestos particles*]
Asbestschiefer m = asbestos slate
Asbestzement m = asbestos cement
~**platte** f **zur Mauerverkleidung** f = asbestos cement siding shingle
~**platten** fpl = asbestos cement sheeting
Asbolan m (Min.), siehe: Kobaltschwärze f
Asche f = ashes
Aschen|bahn f = cinder track
~**schieferton** m = ashy shale
~**tonschiefer** m = ash slate
~**tuff** m = vitric tuff
Asphalt m [*mit Mineralien durchsetzte Bitumina im engeren Sinne, wie die natürlichen Asphaltgesteine und die künstlichen Bitumen-Mineralgemische*] = mineral-filled asphalt (US); asphalt (Brit.) [*natural or mechanical mixture in which bitumen (Brit.)/ asphalt (US) is associated with inert mineral matter*]
~**aufbereitungsanlage** f; siehe unter „Makadam-Maschinenanlage f"
~**auskleidung** f = asphaltic lining
~**belageinbaumasse** f, Asphaltdeckenmischung f = asphalt paving mixture
~**beton** m = asphalt(ic) concrete; bituminous concrete (US); high stone content asphalt containing up to 65 per cent of stone, stone filled asphalt
~**betonplatte** f = asphaltic concrete (or paving) slab
~**binder** m, Asphaltbinderschicht f = asphaltic binder
(~) **Bitumenemulsion** f; siehe unter „Bitumen n im engeren Sinne"
~**bordstein** m = asphalt curb
~**brot** n = asphalt loave, ~ cake, ~ block [*deprecated*]; mastic block
~**dach** n, Bitumenpappdach = asphalt built-up roof
~**decke** f = asphalt pavement (or surfacing)
~**deckenerhitzer** m = asphalt surface heater (US); road heater (or burner) (Brit.)
~**deckenmischung** f, siehe: Asphaltbelageinbaumasse f
~**eingußdecke** f, siehe: Walzschottergußasphalt m
~**emulsion** f; siehe unter „Bitumen n im engeren Sinne"
Asphalten n = asphalten
Asphalteur m, Gußasphaltstreicher m = spreader (Brit.)

Asphalt|feinbeton m = fine (-graded) asphalt(ic) concrete; fine-aggregate bituminous concrete (US)
~**(fuß)boden** m = asphalt flooring
~**gestein** n, Bergasphalt m = asphalt(ic) rock, bituminous rock, rock asphalt
~**grobbeton** m = coarse (-graded) asphalt(ic) concrete; coarse-aggregate bituminous concrete (US)
Asphaltit m = asphaltite
Asphalt|kaltbeton m, siehe: Dammanasphalt m
~**lack** m [*säurefester, rasch trocknender, glänzender Anstrichstoff zu Isolierungen und zum Rostschutz von Eisen*] = asphalt varnish, black Japan
~**lager** n, Asphaltvorkommen n, Asphaltvorkommnis n, Asphaltlagerstätte f = asphalt deposit
~**makadam** m bituminöser Makadam, Bitumenmakadam = bituminous (or bitumen) macadam, macadam with bitumen binder (Brit.); asphalt ~ (US)
~**mastix** m = bituminous mastic, asphalt ~
~**-Mastixmatte** f = bituminous mastic mattress, asphalt ~
~**matte** f = asphalt mattress [*mesh-reinforced*]
~**mehl** n, Asphaltrohmehl = asphalt powder, ~ meal
~**mischmakadam** m, Steinschlagasphalt m = bitumen macadam, bituminous ~ (Brit.); asphalt ~ (US)
~**mörtel** m [*in Dtschld. Gemisch aus Sand und Steinmehl mit mindestens 12 Gew.% Bitumen, Erweichungspunkt Ring und Kugel 50—85 Grad*] = asphaltic mortar
~**öl** n = asphaltic oil
~**platte** f = asphalt (paving) block (or tile)
~**plattenpflaster** n = asphalt block paving/pavement (US)
~**rohmehl** n, siehe: Asphaltmehl
~**säge** f = asphalt cutting saw
~**sand** m = sand asphalt (US); asphalt(ic) sand
~**sandstein** m, bituminöser Sandstein m = bituminous sandstone, asphalt(ic) ~
~**schiff** n = asphalt-mattress laying vessel
~**schindel** f = asphalt shingle (US)
~**schotter-Versuchsstrecke** f [*Eisenbahn f*] = asphalt ballast section
~**see** m, Pechsee = asphalt lake pitch ~
~**splitt** m, Bitumensplitt = asphaltic bitumen-coated chip(ping)s (Brit.); asphalt-coated ~ (US)
~**splittdecke** f, Bitumensplittdecke f = bitumen macadam carpet (Brit.); asphalt ~ ~ (US)
~**straße** f = bituminous road
~**tränkmakadam** m = asphalt macadam (penetration method), asphalt penetration macadam, bituminous macadam, asphalt-grouted macadam (US); bitumen-grouted stone, asphalt(ic) macadam (Brit.)
~**vorkommen** n, siehe: Asphaltlager n
Ästelzaun m, Spalierzaun m = lattice fence
Astfäule f [*Holz n*] = rot of the branches
Asynchronmotor m **für Drehstrom** m, Induktionsmotor, Drehstrommotor = asynchronous motor, polyphase induction ~
Atacamit m, Salzkupfererz n (Min.) = atacamite
Atemschutzgerät n, Atmungsgerät = respiratory device, breathing apparatus
Äthan n, siehe: Dimethyl n
Äthylen n, C_2H_4 = ethylene
Atlas|erz n (Min.) = fibrous malachite
~**zeder** f, Silberzeder f = silver cedar, mount Atlas cedar of Algeria
Atmosphärenüberdruck m, atü = pounds per square inch gauge, psig
Atmosphärilien f [*Bestandteile der Luft*] = natural weathering agencies
atmosphärischer Niederschlag m = atmospheric precipitation
Atmungsgerät n, Atemschutzgerät = breathing apparatus, respiratory device
Atoll n, Ringriff n = atoll
Atom|explosion f = atomic blast
~**kraftwerk** n, Atomenergieanlage f, Kernkraftwerk, Atom-Elektrizitätswerk = atomic power station, nuclear power plant
Atramentstein m (Min.) = inkstone, native copperas

Atterberg'sche Konsistenzgrenzen *fpl*, siehe: Konsistenzgrenzen nach Atterberg

Ätzkali *n*, siehe: Kaliumhydroxyd *n*

~lösung *f*, Kalilauge *f* = solution of caustic potash, (caustic) potash lye

Ätz|kalk *m*, Kalziumhydroxyd *n* = caustic lime

~natron *n*, kaustische Soda *f*, kaustisches Soda *n*, Natriumhydroxyd *n* = caustic soda

~natronprobe *f*, Ätznatronprüfung *f* [*Betonzuschlag m*] = organic test for fine aggregate, test for organic matter, Abrams' test, extraction with caustic soda, colorimetric test

Auboden *m* = river marsh soil

Auelehm *m*, siehe: Silt *m*

Auenebene *f*, Flußaue *f*, Hochflutebene *f* = flood plain

Aufbau *m*, Montage *f* = erection, construction

~bagger *m*; siehe unter „Autobagger"

~-Grabenbagger *m* = truck-mounted ditcher (US); lorry-mounted ~ (Brit.)

~kran *m*, schnellfahrender Autokran, Last(kraft)wagenkran, Autokran auf Chassis mit Eigenantrieb = truck crane

~wert *m* **nach Jahn** = granulometric composition value

Aufbereitungsanlage *f* **für Mischmakadam** *m* **und Walzasphalt** *m*; siehe unter „Makadam-Maschinenanlage *f* zur Herstellung *f* von bituminösen Straßenbelagsmassen *fpl*"

~ ~ Zuschlagstoffe *mpl* = aggregate(s) (preparation) plant (or installation)

Aufbereitungs|empfindlichkeit *f* = temperature susceptibility [*bituminous binder*]

~maschinen *fpl*, Verarbeitungsmaschinen = process(ing) machinery, ~ equipment

~prozeß *m*, Aufbereitungsvorgang *m* = processing procedure

aufblasbarer Gummischlauch *m* **für Kanäle** *mpl* **im Beton** *m* = ductube, inflatable rubber core

aufbrechen, aufhacken = to pick, to break up

Aufbringen *n* [*z. B. Bindemittel n oder Splitt m*] = application

Aufbringungsrate *f* [*Straßenoberflächenbehandlung f*] = rate of spread, ~ ~ application

Aufbruch|hammer *m*, siehe: Straßenaufbruchhammer

~massen *f*, Aufbruch(material) *m*, (*n*) [*z. B. Straßendecke*] = scarified material(s)

Aufenthaltsraum *m* = rest room

Auffahrt *f*, siehe: Rampe *f*

Auffahrunfall *m* = running-up accident

Auffang|becken *n* [*Oberflächenwasserabführung f*] = catch basin (structure)

~kessel *m*, Fangkessel, Rohrfänger *m* [*Druckluftbetonförderer m*] = discharge box

~rinne *f*, Hangrinne *f* = intercepting gutter, ~ channel

auffinden = to locate

Aufforstung *f* = (af)forestation

(Auf)Füllboden *m*, Schüttmaterial *n*, Schüttmasse *f*, Auftragmaterial *n* = fill earth, fill(ing), fill material

Auffüllböschung *f*, siehe: Dammböschung

Auffüllung *f*, siehe: (Auf)Schüttung *f*

Aufgabe *f*, Beschickung *f*, Material~, Beschicken *n* = feed, material(s) ~

~apparat *m*, siehe: Speiser *m*

~becherwerk *n*, Beschickungsbecherwerk, Aufgabeelevator *m* = feed (bucket) elevator, feeding ~

~behälter *m*, siehe: Aufgabetrichter *m*

~gut *n* = feed material

~plattenband *n*, siehe: Plattenbandspeiser *m*

~schuh *m* = feed boot

~schurre *f*, Beschickungsschurre = feed chute

~trichter *m*, Beschickungssilo *m*, Beschickungsbehälter *m*, Aufgabesilo, Aufgabebehälter *m* = feed hopper

~vorrichtung *f* **für Zuschlagstoffe** *mpl* = aggregate feeder

Aufgeber *m*, siehe: Speiser *m*

aufgeblähte Hochofenschlacke *f*, siehe: Hochofenschaumschlacke

aufgeblähter Schiefer *m*, siehe: Blähschiefer

~ Ton *m*, siehe: Blähton

aufgebrachte Last *f*, siehe: Belastung *f*

aufgefülltes Gelände — aufpumpen

aufgefülltes Gelände n, aufgeschüttetes ~ = filled ground, made ~
aufgehängte Fahrbahn f = suspended deck
aufgeklautes Holz n; siehe unter „Holzverbindung f"
aufgelöste Staumauer f; siehe unter „Talsperre f"
aufgesattelt [Fahrzeug n] = semi-trailer type, gooseneck ~
aufgesattelter Anhänger m, siehe: Halbanhänger
~ **Kippanhänger** m = dump semi-trailer
aufgeschüttetes Erdplanum n = artificial subgrade
~ **Gelände** n, aufgefülltes ~ = filled ground, made ~
aufgezwungene Schwingung f, siehe: erzwungene ~
Aufgleisen n = rerailing
aufhacken, siehe: aufbrechen
Aufhacken n = picking
Aufhänge|-Fender m = suspended fender
~**stange** f = hanger rod
Aufheizung f **von bituminösen Bindemitteln** npl = heating of pumpable bituminous material
aufhellen = to relieve the dark appearance
Aufkipp-Bauweise f, Richtaufbauweise f = tilt-up method, ~ construction
aufklauen; siehe unter „Holzverbindung f"
aufkohlen = to carburize
Auflader m, Aufladekompressor m, Aufladegebläse n, Vorverdichter m = supercharger
(Auf)Lader m, siehe: Lademaschine f
~ **für Schüttgut** n, siehe: Becher(werk)auflader m
Aufladung f [Motor m] = supercharging
Auflager n = bearing
~**bank** f [Brückenpfeiler m] = bridge seat [bridge pier]
~**bedingung** f = condition of support
~**druck** m, Auflagerkraft f, Lagerdruck, Stützenwiderstand m, Stützendruck, Gegendruck, Stützkraft f, Auflagerreaktion f, Auflagerwiderstand m = bearing pressure, pressure on bearing surface, reaction at support
~**fläche** f = bearing area
~**konsole** f = bearing bracket

~**kraft** f, siehe: Auflagerdruck m
~**mitte** f = centre of support (Brit); center ~ ~ (US)
~**platte** f = bearing plate, bed ~
~**punkt** m = point of support
~**reaktion** f, siehe: Auflagerdruck m
~**widerstand** m, siehe: Auflagerdruck m
Auf|landung f, Anschwemmung f, Aufschwemmung f, Aufschlickung f, natürliche Kolmotion f (Geol.) = filling up, silting up, accreation through alluvium, aggradation
~**last** f, siehe: Belastung f
~**laufbremse** f = over-run breaking gear, over-run controlled brake
~**lichtmikroskop** n = reflecting microscope
~**lieger** m, siehe: Halbanhänger m
~**lieger-Mulden-Erdbaufahrzeug** n = semi-trailer dump wagon
~**lockerung** f = loosening
~**lockerungsgrad** m = degree of loosening
~**lockerungsschnecke** f [Schwarzbelageinbaumaschine f] = agitator
~**lösung** f, Zerfall m, Zerrüttung f = disintegration
~**lötflansch** m = soldered flange, brazed ~
~**maß** n = measurement (of quantities), site measuring
gemeinsames ~ = joint ~
aufmauern = to brick up
Aufnahme f **von natürlichen Baustoffvorkommen** npl **für den Straßenbau** m = highway materials survey
~**band** n = receiving conveyor (belt)
~**becherwerk** n = bucket elevator
~**bunker** m, siehe: Baustellensilo m
~**mischen** n, Aufnahmemischverfahren n = travel plant mixing, travel(l)ing plant method
~**mischer** m; siehe unter „Bodenvermörtelungsmaschine f"
~**mischverfahren** n, siehe: Aufnahmemischen n
~**trichter** m, Fülltrichter = receiving hopper, (feed) ~, charging ~
aufnehmen von Profilen = to profile
Aufnehmer m, siehe: Becher(werk)auflader m
aufpumpen = to inflate

(Auf)Quellen n, Quellung f, Schwellbewegung f, Schwellung f, Schwellen n, Aufquellung = swelling

Aufrauhen n, Aufrauhung f = roughening (treatment)

aufrauhen = to roughen

Aufrauhgerät n, Aufrauhmaschine f = roughening machine

Aufrauhung f, Aufrauhen n = roughening (treatment)

Aufreißen n [*Straßendecke f*] = scarification, scarifying

Aufreißer m = ripper [*large cultivator of heavier construction throughout and having only about half the number of tynes* (Brit.)/*tines* (US)]

~vorrichtung f [*z. B. an einer Walze f*] = scarifier (attachment)

~zahn m, Aufreißzahn = tyne (Brit.); scrarifler tine (US)

Aufreiß|hammer m, siehe: Straßenaufbruchhammer

Aufriß m, Ansicht f, Vertikalprojektion f = elevation, profile

Aufsattelanhänger m, siehe: Halbanhänger

Aufsatz|schlüssel m = socket wrench

~teil m, drehbarer Oberteil [*Autobagger m*] = shovel revolving unit

Aufsaugung f = imbibition

Aufschlämmung f, grobe Suspension f = cement suspension

Aufschleppe f, siehe: Schiffs~

Aufschlickung f, siehe: Auflandung

aufschließen, erschließen = to link up

Aufschluß m, Ausgehende n, Ausstreichende n (Geol.) = (rock) outcrop

~bohrung f, Suchbohrung, Prospektionsbohrung, Pionierbohrung, Aufschließungsbohrung = scouting; wild cat (US)

~methode f, Aufschluß(verfahren) m, (n) = exploration method, investigation method

(Auf)Schüttung f, Auftrag m, Auffüllung f, Dammaufschüttung bis zukünftiges Planum n = fill(ing)

Aufschüttungslage f, Schüttlage = fill lift

Aufschwemmung f, siehe: Auflandung f

~, Suspension f = suspension

Aufschwimmklassierer m, siehe: Zyklonnaßklassierer

Aufsetzwinkel m = bottom bracket

Aufsichtspersonal n = supervising staff, supervisory personnel

aufspachteln, verstreichen = to float

Aufspanner m, Aufspann-Transformator m = step-up transformer

Aufspannfutter n, Klemmfutter = chuck

(Auf)Speicherung f; siehe unter „Talsperre f"

Aufspülung f, hydraulische Auffüllung f, Spülkippe f = hydraulic fill

Aufstandsfläche f, Rad~ = (tyre) contact area (Brit.); (tire) ~ ~, tire-pavement ~ ~ (US)

aufstapeln, siehe: stapeln

aufstauen = to retain, to impound

Aufstell|bock m = frame

~geräte npl **für Turmdrehkrane** mpl = erecting devices for (mono-) tower cranes

Aufstellungsplatz m **für Baustelleneinrichtung** f = site for mechanical plant

Aufstemmen n, Übersichbrechen n (Geol.) = overhead stoping

Aufstieg m [*einer Fahrbahn f*] = rise [*of a carriageway*]

Aufstocken n **des Kopfstückes** n [*Kletter-Turmdrehkran* m] = mounting of the crane head

Aufstrich-Klebemasse f, siehe: Klebemasse

auftauen = to thaw (out)

(Auf)Tausalz n [*früher: Streusalz*] = de-icing salt, ice-control ~

Auftrag m, siehe: (Auf)Schüttung f

auftragen [*auf eine Karte f*] = to plot

Auftrag|erteilung f; siehe unter „Angebot n"

~geber m; siehe unter „Angebot n"

~linie f, siehe: Abszisse f

~material f, siehe: (Auf)Füllboden m

~nehmer m; siehe unter „Angebot n"

~schreiben n; siehe unter „Angebot n"

~wert m = contract price

Auf|trieb m = buoyancy

~trieb m, Sohlenwasserdruck m [*Talsperre f*] = uplift, foundation water pressure

~tropfstein m, Stalagmit m = stalagmite

~vulkanisieren n **eines neuen Laufstreifens** m, siehe: Besohlung f

~walzen n **einer neuen Decklage** f [*Straße f*] = resurfacing

Aufwalzflansch — Ausfallstraße

Aufwalzflansch m = expanded flange, rolled-on ~
aufwickeln = to spool
Auf|wickeltrommel f = winding drum
~windvorrichtung f = jacking equipment
~wölbung f (Geol.) = uplift
~zehrung f, siehe: Absorption f
Aufzug m = lift
~ = hoist
~, siehe: Bauaufzug m
Aufzugs|kasten m; siehe unter „Betonmischer m"
~kasten m = skip with bottom discharge
~-Klein(beton)mischer m; siehe unter „Betonmischer m"
~kübel m; siehe unter „Betonmischer"
~schienen fpl [Betonmischer m] = trackway for skip rollers
~winde f = hoist winch
Augen|bolzen m, Augbolzen, Schraubenbolzen mit Ring, Ringbolzen, Ösenbolzen = eye bolt
~gneis m = eye gneiss, augen-gneiss
~höhe f, Augenpunkt m = eye level, height of eye
~kohle f, = eye coal, birdseye ~, circular ~, curley cannel
~scheinnahme f = visual inspection

~stab m = eye bar
Augit m (Min.) = augite
~-Granit m = augite-granite
Augitit m = augitite
Ausbau m, Demontage f, Abbau m = dismantling
~ einer Flußmündung f **in See** f = prolongation of a river mouth seawards
~geschwindigkeit f, Berechnungsgeschwindigkeit [Straße f] =design speed
~programm n, Ausbauplan m, Entwicklungsplan = development program(me)
~stufe f, Bauabschnitt m, Baustadium n = stage
Ausbesserung f [Straße], siehe: Ausflicken n
Ausbeulen n = buckling
ausbeuten = to exploit
Ausbildung f, siehe: Anlernen n
Ausbildungs|lehrgang m = training course
~stätte f = training centre (Brit.); ~ center (US)
Ausbiß m (Geol.), siehe: Abdachung f
Ausblasevorrichtung f [Bindemittelspritzmaschine f] = air scavenging gear, pneumatic ~ ~
Ausblühung(en) f [Beton m] =efflorescence
Ausbreittisch m nach DIN 1164 = flow table of DIN 1164

Ausbreit(ungs)versuch m, Setzprobe f, Ausbreitprobe
   Ausbreitmaß n, Fließmaß
   Setzbecher m

slump test (for consistency)

   slump
   mo(u)ld, conical shell, slump cone

Ausbruch m; siehe unter „Tunnelbau m"
Ausbruchsgestein n, siehe: Ergußgestein
Ausbruchstelle f; siehe unter „Tunnelbau m"
Ausdehnungs|gefäß n = expansion vessel
~koeffizient m = coefficient of expansion
Ausdornen n = broaching
auseinander|nehmen, siehe: demontieren
~schrauben [Bohrgestänge n] = to break the joint
~ziehen = to telescope
Ausfachung f [Fachwerk n] = web members, ~ bracing
Ausfachungsstab m = stay rod

ausfahrbare Stütze f, Seitenstütze [z. B. Autobagger m] = outrigger
Ausfahrgleis n = departure track
Ausfahrt(stelle) f [Autobahn f]= exit point, egress ~
Ausfall m [Baumaschine f] = breakdown
~korngemisch n = discontinuously-graded aggregate, omitted-size fraction
~körnung f, Auslaßkörnung, unstetige Kornabstufung, diskontinuierliche ~ = discontinuous grading, gap ~, discontinuous granulometry
~straße f = outward-bound road, exit~, driveway

Ausfällung f, Ausfällen n = precipitation
~, Sinkstoff m = sediment, deposit
Ausfiltern n [Verkehr m] = filtration
Ausflicken n, Flickverfahren n, Flickarbeit f, Ausbesserung f [Straße f] = patch(ing) work, mending, patching
ausflocken, dispergieren, entflocken = to deflocculate
Ausflockung f, Entflockung, Dispergierung = deflocculation
~, Koagulation, Gerinnung f = coagulation [the precipitation of colloids from solutions]
ausfluchten, siehe: abfluchten
Ausfluchtung f, Bauflucht f, Abfluchtung, Einfluchtung = alignment; alinement (US)
Neuausfluchtung f = re-~
Fluchtpfahl m = ~ stake
Ausflügler m = excursionist
Ausfluß-Viskosimeter n, Auslaufviskosimeter = orifice visco(si)meter
ausfugen, verfugen = to point
Ausfugung f, Ausfugen n, Verfugen = pointing
Ausführungs|art f, Bauart [Baumaschine f] = construction
~garantie f = completion bond, performance ~
~zeichnung f, Arbeitszeichnung = working drawing
Ausfüllen n [Pflasterdecke f] = feeding, jointing (of sett paving)
Ausgabebeleg m = issue voucher
Ausgangs|bitumen n, Grundbitumen = base asphalt (US); ~ asphaltic bitumen (Brit.)
~gestein n = parent rock
~material n für Krack-Prozesse mpl = cracking stock
ausgebrannt [z. B. Schiff n] = firegutted
ausgefahren [Straße f] = rutted, worn into ruts, worn down
ausgelastet sein [z. B. Maschine f, Fahrzeug n] = to be given a full work-out
Ausgleich|becken n; siehe unter „Talsperre f"
~behälter m; siehe unter „Talsperre f"
ausgleichen [Unebenheit f] = to average out, to correct

Ausgleicher m = balancing group
Ausgleich|feder f, siehe: Spannfeder
~getriebe n, siehe: Differentialgetriebe
~gewicht n = bascule weight
~halde f = surge pile
~kolben m, Entlastungskolben = dummy piston [piston to balance out-of-line moments]
~rahmen m = equalizer frame
~schicht f, Ausgleichlage f [Straßenbau m] = leve(l)ing course (or underlay), regulating ~
~ventil n = relief valve
ausglühbare Bestandteile mpl [Boden m] = organic matter (present), ~ impurity
ausglühen, tempern = to anneal
Ausgrabungsfund m = article of antiquity
aushärtbare Aluminiumlegierung f = heat-treatable alumin(i)um alloy
Aushub m, Erdaushub, Ausschachtung f, Baggerung, Bodenaushub, Trockenbaggerung, Trockenbaggerei f = (common) excavation, earth ~, digging, excavating
~ in gewachsenem Boden m = primary excavation [digging in undisturbed soil, as distinguished from rehandling stockpiles]
~(boden) m, Aushuberde f, Bodenaushub m, Erdaushub [durch Trockenbaggerung gewonnener Baustoff oder Aussatzmaterial] = excavated earth, muck; spoil [Aussatzmaterial]
~böschung f = excavation slope
~gerät n, Aushubmaschine f = (excavator) digger
auskeilen = to provide with wedges
~ (Geol.) = to die away, ~ ~ out, to end off, to peter out, to pinch (out), to taper out, to thin out, to wedge out, to thin away
auskeilende Wechsellagerung f (Geol.) = dovetailing, interdigitation, interfingering
~ Zwischenlage f (Geol.) = interfingering member
Auskleidung f, Verkleidung, Futter n = lining
Auskleidungsmaschine f = lining machine

ausklingende Falte *f* (Geol.) = lessening fold
~ **vulkanische Tätigkeit** *f* = declining volcanic activity
ausklinken = to release, to disengage
~ [*Flansch m*] = to notch [*flange*]
Ausklinkmaschine *f* [*Flanschen mpl*] = notching machine
Ausklinkung *f* [*Flansch m*] = notch(ing)
ausknicken, einknicken = to buckle, to yield to axial compression
Auskofferung *f*, siehe: Planums~
auskolkbarer Boden *m* = erodible soil, ~ material, erosive ~
(aus)kolken, siehe: auswaschen
(Aus)Kolkung *f*, Unterspülung *f*, Unterwaschung, Wegspülung, Kolk *m*, Auswaschung = scour(ing), undermining, underwashing, subsurface erosion
~ **durch Eis** = exaration, glacial scour
auskragen, vorkragen = to corbel outwards, to cantilever, to project
auskragender Fußweg *m*, vorkragender ~, auslagender ~ = cantilever(ed) footway
Auskragung *f* **der Schichten** *fpl* [*Gewölbe n*] = projection of courses
~ **des Gesimses** = projection of cornice
auskreuzen [*Nietkopf m*] = to cut out the rivet head with a cross-cut chisel
auskristallisieren (Min.) = to cristallize out
~ [*trockenes Klima n*] = to effloresce
Auslade|gleis *n*, siehe: Abladegleis
~**kran** *m*, siehe: Abladekran
Ausladen *n*, Abladen, Entladen = unloading, off-loading
Ausladung *f*, Reichweite *f* [*Drehkran m*] = working radius, outreach
Auslandstätigkeit *f* = out-of-the-country job
Auslaß *m*, Ablaß = outlet, discharge
~**körnung** *f*, siehe: Ausfallkörnung
Auslauf *m*, freier ~ [*Erdöl n*] = natural flow
~**bauwerk** *n* = outlet (or outfall) structure (or headwork, or works)
~**bauwerk** *n*; siehe unter „Talsperre *f*"
Ausläufer *m* [*Gebirge n*] = spur
~ [*Wetterkarte f*] = extension
Auslauf|kanal *m* = outlet channel

~**kasten** *m* = discharge box
~**quelle** *f* = descending spring
~**regulierungsbauwerk** *n* = escape regulator
~**schurre** *f*, Austrag(ungs)schurre, Abwurfschurre = discharge chute, swivel~
~**stollen** *m*; siehe unter „Talsperre *f*"
~**versuch** *m*, Bremsversuch [*Bestimmung des Reibungsbeiwertes auf der Straße*] = braking test, stopping distance ~
~**viskosimeter** *n*, siehe: Ausfluß-Viskosimeter
Auslaugung *f* [*Boden m*] = leaching
Auslaugungs|horizont *m*, siehe: A-Horizont
~**see** *m* = sink (hole) lake
~**stoffe** *mpl* = dissolved material
~**tasche** *f* = solution pocket
~**trümmer** *f* = leaching residue
~**wässer** *npl* = leaching waters
~**zone** *f* = leached zone
Ausleger *m* [*Kran m, Bagger m*] = boom (US); (inclined) jib (Brit.)
~, siehe: Baggerleiterrahmen *m*
~**anlenkpunkt** *m* = fulcrum of the jib (Brit.); ~ ~ ~ boom (US)
~**ansatz** *m* = jib boom (US)
~**balkenträger** *m*, siehe: Auslegerträger
~**-Bohrwagen** *m*, siehe: Bohrjumbo *m*
~**brücke** *f* = cantilever bridge
~**-Dachbinder** *m* = cantilevered roof truss
~**-Drehkran** *m*, siehe: Schwenkkran
~**endschalter** *m* = jib limit switch (Brit.); boom ~ ~ (US)
~**-Förderband** *n*, Absetz(förder)band = stacker belt
~**fuß** *m* = lower end of the jib (Brit.); ~ ~ ~ ~ boom (US)
~**-Hubseil** *n* = boom (derricking) cable (US); jib (~) ~ (Brit.)
~**-Hubzylinder** *m* = boom lift cylinder (US); jib ~ ~ (Brit.)
~**kopf** *m* = boom point (US); jib ~ (Brit.)
~**kopf** *m* **mit Festpunkt** *m* = boom point with fixed point (US); jib ~ ~ ~ ~ (Brit.)
~**kratzer** *m* = boom scraper
~**laufkran** *m* = (cantilever) tower transporter

Ausleger|schrapper m **mit Ladewagen für den Streckenvortrieb,** Fabrikat HASENCLEVER A. G., DÜSSELDORF, DEUTSCHLAND = crawler-mounted scraper and loader

~**seil** n = boom cable (US); jib ~ (Brit.)
~**spitze** f = tip of the jib (Brit.); ~ ~ ~ boom
~**stellung** f = jib position (Brit.); boom ~ (US)
~**stiel** m, siehe: Löffelstiel
~**träger** m, Auslegerbalkenträger, Kragbalken(träger) m = cantilever girder
~**trommel** f = boom drum (US); jib ~ (Brit.)
~**verstellseile** npl = jib raising and lowering cables (Brit.); boom ~ ~ ~ ~ (US)
~**verstellwerk** n = jib raising and lowering gear (Brit.); boom ~ ~ ~ (US)
~**verstellwinde** f = jib raising and lowering hoist (Brit.); boom ~ ~ ~ ~ (US)
~**winde** f, Baggerwindwerk n = boom hoist (US); jib ~ (Brit.)

Auslöse|haken m = detaching hook
~**hebel** m = disengaging lever
~**knagge** f = disengaging tappet
~**magnet** m = release magnet, releasing ~
~**mechanismus** m = trip mechanism

Auslöser m, Sperrklinke f = detent, catch, pawl

Auslösespule f = trip coil

Auslösung f [für zusätzliche Nebenkosten] = subsistence allowance, cost of living allowance (Brit.); subsistence, living allowance (US); separation allowance

Auslösungsbeben n = simultaneous earthquake

Ausmauerung f = brick lining

ausmittig, siehe: außermittig

~ **gedrückte Stahlbetonsäule** f = eccentrically loaded reinforced concrete column

ausmörteln = to fill the voids with mortar

Ausmündung f **eines Kanals** m **in einen Fluß** = outlet of a canal into a river

ausnagen, siehe: erodieren

Ausnutzung f [Baumaschine f] = work-out

auspressen, einpressen, injizieren, verpressen = to inject, to grout under pressure

~, ausquetschen = to squeeze out

Auspressung f, siehe: Injektion f

Auspreß|eigenschaft f, siehe: Strangpreßeigenschaft

~**verfahren** n, siehe: Einpreßverfahren

Auspuff|gas n = exhaust gas
~**hub** m, Auspufftakt m = exhaust stroke, scavenging ~
~**krümmer** m = exhaust manifold
~**pfeife** f = exhaust whistle
~**rohr** n = exhaust pipe
~**schelle** f = exhaust clamp
~**schlitz** m = exhaust port
~**seite** f = exhaust side
~**takt** m, Auspuffhub m = exhaust stroke, scavenging ~
~**topf** m, Schalldämpfer m = silencer (Brit.); exhaust muffler
~**ventil** n = exhaust valve
~**ventilfeder** f = exhaust valve spring
~**ventilkipphebel** m = exhaust valve rocker arm

auspumpen, trockenlegen, leerpumpen = to dewater, to unwater

ausquetschen, auspressen = to squeeze out

ausräumende Tätigkeit f **der Wellen** fpl = quarrying action of the waves

(Aus)Rollgrenze f; siehe unter „Konsistenzgrenzen fpl nach Atterberg"

Ausrück|hebel m, Auskupplungshebel = throw-out lever, disengaging ~
~**klaue** f = clutch coupling box
~**kupplung** f = disengaging clutch
~**welle** f = disengaging arbor

Ausrundungshalbmesser m, Ausrundungsradius m = radius of curvature

Ausrüsten n, Abrüsten n = striking [the releasing or lowering of centering or other temporary support]

ausrüsten, ausstatten = to fit out

Ausrüstung f, Ausstattung = equipment

Ausrüstungskai m, Ausrüstungskaje f = fitting out quay

Aussatz|halde f, Abraumhalde = waste pile
~**kippe** f = spoil dump, spoil deposit, waste site, waste area, spoil area, spoil bank, (spoil) tip, shoot; [deprecated: chute]

Ausschachtung f, siehe: Aushub m

ausschalen = to strip
Ausschalen n = stripping, form ~
Ausschaltdruck m **eines Kompressors** m = cutting out pressure of a compressor
ausschalten [*Elektrotechnik f*] = to switch off, to disconnect ,to cut out, to put out of circuit, to break the circuit
Ausschaltstellung f, Nullstellung = open position, neutral ~, (switch-)off ~
Ausscheidungs|lagerstätte f = precipitated deposit
~sedimentgestein n, siehe: chemisches Sedimentgestein
ausscheuern (Geol.) = to scour out
Ausschlachten n [*Maschine f*] = cannibalizing
Ausschlag m [*Magnetnadel f*] = deflection, deflexion
Ausschlag(weite) m, (f), Schwingungsweite, Amplitude f = amplitude
ausschlämmen, siehe: abschlämmen
Ausschlichthammer m = planishing hammer
Ausschnitt m, Kreissektor m = sector
Ausschöpfen n einer Quelle f = draining of a spring
Ausschreibung f; siehe unter ,,Angebot n"
Ausschütt|höhe f, siehe: Abwurfhöhe
~vorrichtung f, Abwurfvorrichtung = dumping device
~vorrichtung f für Torladewagen m, Abwurfvorrichtung ~ ~ = straddle dump device, dumping device for straddle carrier
(Aus)Schwitzen n, siehe: Bluten n
Aussetz|-Naßbagger m, Aussetz-Schwimmbagger [*Schwimmbagger, der im Aussetzbetrieb mit einem einzigen Grabwerkzeug arbeitet, das in regelmäßigem Arbeitsspiel gräbt, fördert und entleert*] = intermittent dredger (Brit.); ~ dredge (US)
~-Trockenbagger m = intermittent excavator
Aussichtsturm m = observation tower
Aussickerung f = seepage
aussintern = to sinter
aussommern [*Kunststein m*] = to season during the sommer [*artificial stone*]

Ausspalten n [*Pflasterstein m*] = cleaving
Aussparung f = recess, blockout, embrasure
Aussprießen n, Verstrebung f, Verstreben n, Abspießen n = strutting
Ausstaken n **der Fachwerkwand** f = nogging of the half-timbered wall with sticks
ausstatten, ausrüsten = to fit out
aussteifen, absteifen = to brace
Aussteifung f, Absteifung = bracing
~ des Bogens m, Bogenaussteifung = arch stiffening, ~ stiffener
Aussteifungs|träger m = stiffener
~winkel m = angle iron stiffener, stiffening angle, stiffener angle
Aussteigzarge f [*Dachöffnung f*] = trap door frame
Ausstellung f **von technischem Bedarf für die chemische und Mineralölindustrie** = chemical and petroleum engineering exhibition
Ausstellungs|datum n = date of origination
~palast m = exhibition palace
Ausstoß m [*Produktion f*] = output
Ausstrahlung f **in Abhängigkeit** f **vom Ausstrahlungswinkel** m = angular emissivity
ausstreichen, ausgehen (Geol.) = to crop out, to outcrop
Ausströmen n **von Dampf** m = exhaustion of steam
austauschbare Ionen npl, auswechselbare ~ ~ = exchangeable ions
Austauschbarkeit f, Auswechselbarkeit = interchangeability
Austausch|fähigkeit f [*die Menge der austauschbaren Kationen in einem Boden*] = exchange capacity [*the quantity of exchangeable cations in a soil*]
~motor m = interchangeable power unit
austiefen = to deepen
Austiefung f = deepening
Austiefungssee m = erosion lake, lake due to erosion
Austragsmischer m; siehe unter ,,Betonmischer"
Austrag(ungs)schurre f, Auslaufschurre, Abwurfschurre = swivel chute, discharge ~

Austragungsschurre *f*; siehe unter „Betonmischer *m*"
Austritts|gefälle *n* = exit gradient
~stelle *f* [*Wasser n*] = point of escape, ~ ~ exit, ~ ~ issue
Auswahl *f* = selection
Auswasch|delta *n* = outwash delta
~ebene *f* = outwash plain, (over)wash ~
auswaschen, unterspülen, (aus)kolken = to scour, to underwash
~ aus = to wash out of
Auswasch|fächer *m* = outwash fan
~probe *f* [*Beton m*] = washing test [*concrete*]
~schotter *m* = (glacial) outwash gravel
Auswaschungs|boden *m*, siehe: Eluvialboden
~tasche *f*, Auswaschungstrichter *m* = sink
auswechselbar, austauschbar = interchangeable
Auswechselbarkeit *f*, Austauschbarkeit = interchangeability
auswehen (Geol.) = to deflate
Auswehung *f* (Geol.) = deflation
Ausweich|gleis *n* = passing track
~stelle *f*, Kreuzungsstelle [*Hafen m*] = layby, passing place
ausweiten = to widen
Auswertung *f*, Bewertung *f* = evaluation
~ von Meißelschäden *mpl* = drill bit evaluation
Auswitterung *f*; siehe unter „Denudation *f*"
Auswuchten *n*, Auswuchtung *f* = balancing
auswuchten = to balance the weights
Auswuchtmaschine *f* = balancing machine
Außen|ansicht *f* = exterior view
~anstrichfarbe *f* = exterior paint
~backenbremse *f* = external cheek brake
~böschung *f* = outside slope
~dock *n* = open dock
~druck *m* = external pressure
~gerüst *n*, siehe: Außenrüstung *f*
~gewindezahn *m* = male thread, external screw thread

~hafen *m* = open basin, outer harbo(u)r
~kante *f* = outer edge
~luft *f* = outside air
~mantel *m* = outer jacket
~mantel *m* [*Erdkruste f*] = litosphere
~mauer *f* = external wall
~meer *n* [*Atoll n*] = open ocean
~öffnung *f* [*Brücke f*] = end span
~putz *m* = external rendering
~rüstung *f*, Außengerüst *n* = outside scaffold(ing), external ~
~rüttler *m*, Außenvibrator *m* = external vibrator
~rüttlung *f*, Außenvibration *f* = external vibration
~strand *m* = outer shore
~taster *m* = outside (thread) caliper
~temperatur *f* = outside temperature, external ~, outdoor ~
~temperaturfühler *m* = outdoor temperature sensing device, outside ~ ~ ~, external ~ ~ ~
~vibrator *m*, siehe: Außenrüttler *m*
~vorspannung *f* = outer pre-stress
~wange *f*, Wandwange [*Treppe f*] = outer string, wall ~
~zone *f* = outer zone
äußeres Haftwasser *n*, siehe: Adsorptionswasser
außermittig, ausmittig, exzentrisch = off-center (US); off-centre (Brit.); eccentric
außermittiger Anschluß *m* = eccentric connection
~ Lastangriff *m* = eccentric application of load, ~ loading
außermittiges Knicken *n* = eccentric buckling
ausziehbar, verlängerbar = telescopic
Auszieh|gleis *n*, siehe: Sortiergleis
~leiter *f* = extending ladder
~schacht *m* = upcast (shaft), discharge (air shaft)
auszwicken, verzwicken, abdecken [*Packe f*] = to chink, to choke, to blind, to key
autallotriomorph (Geol.), siehe: panidiomorphkörnig
Autoanhänger-Einachs-Mischer *m*, siehe: (luftbereifter) Einachs(-Schnell)mischer

Autobagger *m*, **Pneubagger** *m*, gummibereifter selbstfahrbarer Universal-Bagger, Universal-Autobagger *m*, Automobilbagger, Universal-Autokran *m*, Fahrzeugbagger [*wenn mit Vollgummibereifung, dann sind die Ausdrücke „Pneubagger" und „pneumatic-tired" natürlich nicht anwendbar*]

pneumatic-tired shovel-crane, rubber-mounted (shovel-)crane (US); pneumatic-tyred mechanical shovel, rubber-mounted mechanical shovel (Brit.); excavator-crane

    Autobagger mit Selbstfahrwerk *n*, langsamfahrender Autobagger (oder Autokran *m*) [*ca. 12—15 km/h.*]

mobile ~ ~, self-propelled ~ ~, one-engine ~ ~, wheel-mounted one-engine shovel-crane (or mechanical shovel), single-engine rubber-mounted shovel-crane (or mechanical shovel), wagon crane, carrier crane, transit-crane

        Selbstfahrwerk *n*, Straßenräder-Unterwagen *m*, Radwagen [*Baggermotor m gleichzeitig Antriebsmotor des Fahrwerks n*]

rubber-tire (or rubber-tyre) carrier propelled by turntable engine, pneumatic-tired (or pneumatic-tyred) chassis propelled by turntable engine

    Autobagger auf Chassis *n* mit Eigenantrieb *m*, Last(kraft)wagenbagger *m*, schnellfahrender Autobagger, Aufbaubagger [*ca. 30—35 km/h.*]

truck (-mounted) (pneumatic-tired) shovel(-crane) (US); lorry-mounted pneumatic-tyred mechanical shovel (Brit.); shovel mounted on standard truck chassis, truck mounted shovel, truck-mounted excavator

        Eigenantrieb Autofahrwerk *n*, Eigenantrieb-Unterwagen *m*, Lastwagenfahrgestell *n*

rubber-tire (or rubber-tyre) carrier (or chassis) with its own engine and automotive-type drive

        Oberwagen *m*, Baggeroberwagen, Oberteil *m*

superstructure

    Autobagger auf Chassis *n* mit Eigenantrieb *m*, Fabrikat THE THEW SHOVEL CO., LORAIN, OHIO, USA

(rubber-tire)MOTO-CRANE[*a registered trade-mark of the THEW SHOVEL CO., identifying a complete, integral THEW-built rubber-tire machine — of turntable and carrier — with the carrier designed and built exclusively for a shovel-crane mounting*]

    einmotoriger Pneubagger, Fabrikat KOEHRING CO., MILWAUKEE 16, WIS., USA

CRUISER-CRANE [*Trademark*]

    Autobagger mit Dreiachsfahrgestell *n* und zwei Motoren *mpl*, Dreiachslast(kraft)wagenbagger *m*

three-axle truck shovel

    ausfahrbare Stütze *f*, Seitenstütze

outrigger

Autobahn *f*, Autostraße *f*, Nurkraftwagenstraße *f* = motorway, autobahn, motor road

~ mit Mittelstreifen *m* = dual (or double) carriageway motor road

~ mit vier Spuren *fpl* **ohne Mittelstreifen** *m* = four-lane single-carriageway motor road

~ ohne Mittelstreifen *m* = single-carriageway motor road

Autobahn|-Betonmischer m, siehe Brückenmischer
~brückenmischer m, siehe: Brückenmischer
~meisterei f = motorway breakdown and repair depot
~randstreifen m [in *Dtschld.*] = hardened outside verge
Autobus m, (Omni)Bus = bus, passenger service vehicle
~bahnhof m, (Omni)Busbahnhof m = bus terminal (or station, or terminus) oberirdischer ~ = surface ~ ~
~haltestelle f = bus halt, ~ stop
Autodrehscheibe f = driveway turntable
autogenes Schneiden n = autogenous cutting
~ Schneid- und Schweißgerät n = autogenous cutting and welding apparatus
~ Tal n = autogenous valley
Auto-Greifer m = rubber-mounted grab(bing crane)
Auto-Kino n = drive-in-theatre
Autoklav m, Dampfdruckerhitzer m = autoclave
~gips m = autoclaved gypsum
~prüfung f [*Zement* m] = autoclave test
Auto|kolonne f = motorcade (US); convoy (Brit.)
~kran m = truck(-mounted) crane
automatische Ausschüttwaage f = automatic dumping batcher scale
~ Beschickung f, **~ (Material)Aufgabe** f = auto-feed
~ Waage f, **(Ver)Wiegeautomat** m = automatic scale
automatischer Schwimmer m = automatic float
automatisches Nivellierinstrument n = automatic level
~ (Straßen)Verkehrszählgerät n = automatic traffic counter

Automatisierung f = automation (process)
Automobil|bagger m, siehe: Autobagger
~motor m = automobile engine
~-Sprengwagen m, siehe: Bitumen-Sprengwagen
~steinbrecher m, Autosteinbrecher = pneumatic-tired crusher (US); rubber-mounted ~, self-propelled crushing plant
Auto-Montagefabrik f = automotive assembly plant
automorph = euhedral
(Auto)Parkplatz m = parking place, car park, parking lot
~rennbahn f = car racing track
~scheinwerfer m = auto headlight
~schrapper m **mit 2-Rad-Schlepper** m, siehe: Einachs-Motorschrapper
~schrapper m **mit 4-Rad-Schlepper** m = tractor scraper, motor(ised) ~ (with 4-wheel traction)
~schütter m, Vorderkipper m, Motorkübelwagen m, Kopfschütter m, Vorkopf-Schütter m, Frontkipper m, Motorkipper = dumper, shuttle ~, front tipper
~steinbrecher m, Automobilsteinbrecher = self-propelled crushing plant, rubber-mounted crusher; pneumatic-tired crusher (US)
~waschplatz m = car wash, (vehicle) washdown
Auwald m = lowland forest
Aventurin|feldspat m, Sonnenstein m (Min.) = sunstone, aventurine fel(d)spar
~quarz m (Min.) = aventurine quartz
axiales (Erd)Beben n = linear earthquake
Axial|gebläse n = axial blower
~schub m, achsrechter Schub, Seitenschub = lateral shear, side thrust
~ventilator m = axial fan
Axinit m (Min.) = axinite

Azbe-Schachtofen m
Schnitt m durch den Ofen m
Höhe f
Materialaufzug m
Stein m
Koks m

Azbe vertical lime kiln
section through kiln
elevation
skip hoist
stone
coke

Azbe-Schachtofen — Backen(stein)brecher

Aufgabebehälter *m* — charging bin
verstellbare Klappen *fpl* — adjustable gates
Aufgabevorrichtungen *fpl* — feeders
Vorwärmzone *f* — preheating zone
Brennzone *f*, Kalzinierzone *f* — calcining zone, burning zone
Kühlzone *f* — cooling zone
Ventilatorbühne *f* — fan floor
Arbeitsbühne *f* — operating floor
Abgasventilator *m* — exhaust fan
Luftventilator *m* — air fan
primäres Abgas *n* — primary exhaust
sekundäres Abgas *n* — secondary exhaust
Abnahmestelle *f* für Gasumlauf *m* — recirculation off-take
seitliche Öffnung *f* für Gasumlauf *m* — side recirculation
untere Öffnung *f* für Gasumlauf *m* — lower recirculation
zentrale Öffnung *f* für Gasumlauf *m* — center recirculation (US); centre ~ (Brit.)
Schieber-Einrichtung *f* — stroke adjustment
Entleerungsvorrichtungen *fpl* — reciprocating discharge feeders
unterteilter Kalkbehälter *m* — sectioned lime storage hopper
Kamin *m* — stack
Kamin *m* für eventuelle Verwendung natürlichen Zuges *m* — alternate stacks for natural draft (US)/draught (Brit.) only

---

Azetat *n*, essigsaures Salz *n* = acetate
Azetylen|entwickler *m* = acetylene generator
~-Flammstrahlbrenner *m* zum Aufrauhen von Basaltpflaster = acetylene heat sett treatment unit
~flasche *f* = acetylene cylinder, ~ bottle
~(gas) *n* = acetylene (gas)
~sauerstoff(schneid)brenner *m* = oxyacetylene burner

Azidität *f*, Säuregehalt *m*, Neutralisationszahl *f*, Säuregrad *m* = acidity, acidic content
Azimut *n*, *m*, Scheitelkreis *m* = azimuth
Azohumussäure *f* = azo-humic acid
Azurit *m*, Kupferglasur *f* (Min.) = azurite, chessylite

B

Bach|geröll(e) *n* = rolled pebbles
~wacke *f* = river boulder
Backenbremse *f* = shoe brake

Backen(stein)brecher *m* [*früher: Backenquetsche f*] — jaw (type rock) crusher (or breaker)
Arbeitsorgan *n*, Arbeitselement *n* — working element
Austragsspaltweite *f*, siehe: (untere Brech)Spaltweite
Austrittsöffnung *f*, Austragsspalt *m*, Entleerungsspalt, Entleerungsöffnung — discharge opening, ~ point, outlet ~
~ mit geradlinigen Backenplatten *fpl* — straight plate ~ ~
~ mit Rollenlagerung *f* — roller bearing ~ ~
~ mit unten befestigter Schwingenbrechbacke *f* — Dodge ~ ~
Backenplatte *f* — jaw (crushing) plate

bewegliche Brechbacke *f*, siehe: Schwingenbrechbacke	
Blake'scher (Doppel-)Kniehebelbackenbrecher *m*, siehe: Doppelkniehebelbrecher	
Brechbacke *f*, Brechbacken *m*	crushing jaw
Brechelement *n*, Brechorgan *n*	crushing member
Brecherrahmen *m*, Brecherkörper *m*	base, (main) frame, crusher ~
Brechfläche *f*	crushing surface [*crushing jaw*]
Brechmaul *n*	feed opening, receiving ~, crusher ~, mouth
Brechraum *m*	crushing chamber
Doppel~, Doppelschwingenbrecher, Zweischwingenbrecher	twin ~ ~, two movable ~ ~, double movable ~ ~
Doppelkniehebelbrecher *m*, Zweipendelbackenbrecher, Blake'scher (Doppel-)Kniehebelbackenbrecher [*erfunden von dem Amerikaner Blake im Jahre 1858*]	Blake (type jaw) crusher (or breaker); double toggle crusher, compound toggle lever stone breaker (Brit.); swing jaw crusher
dreiteilige Druckplatte *f*, ~ Kniehebelplatte	three-piece toggle plate
Druckplatte *f*, siehe: Kniehebelplatte	
Einschwingenbrecher *m*	(Dalton) overhead eccentric (type jaw) crusher, single toggle jaw crusher
Einschwingen-Granulator *m*, Granulator-Splittbrecher *m*	single-toggle granulator, single-toggle type jaw granulator, chipping(s) breaker
Einstellzahn *m*	adjusting sprocket
Einzugswinkel *m*	angle of nip
Entleerungsspalt *m*, siehe: Austrittsöffnung *f*	
Exzenterlager *n* der Zugstange *f*, Zugstangenlager	pitman eccentric bearing
Exzenter(welle) *m*, (*f*), Antriebswelle	(overhead) eccentric (shaft), swing jaw shaft
Exzenterwellenlager *n*	eccentric shaft bearing
Fein~, Nach~	secondary ~ ~, reduction ~ ~, fine ~ ~
Festbacken *m*, siehe: Stirnwandbrechbacke *f*	
Festbackenplatte *f*	fixed jaw (crushing) plate, front crushing plate
Flachriemen-Antriebsscheibe *f*, Schwungscheibe für Flachriemen(an)trieb *m*	flywheel crowned for flat belt
geradlinige Backenplatte *f* [*Grobbackenbrecher m*]	straight jaw (crushing) plate
gewölbte Backenplatte *f* [*Feinbackenbrecher m*]	curved jaw (crushing) plate
Gleitklotz *m* [*Blake-Brecher m*]	sliding wedge block
Granulator-Splittbrecher *m*, siehe: Einschwingen-Granulator *m*	
Groß~	(large) primary ~ ~

Herausspringen n des Brechgutes n aus dem Brechmaul n	belching
Hub m	stroke
Keilriemen-Antriebsscheibe f, Schwungscheibe f für Keilriemenantrieb m	flywheel grooved for V-belt
Kniehebelplatte f, Druckplatte	toggle plate
Maulbreite f	opening across the width of the jaws
Maulweite f [Spaltweite der Eintrittsöffnung f]	jaw opening [distance between the jaws at the top of the crusher opening]
Nach~, siehe: Fein~	
(Nach)Stellkeil m, verstellbarer Keil	adjusting wedge, push ~, pull ~
oberer Seitenkeil m	upper cheek plate
reibender Brechvorgang m	rubbing action
Schwingachse f [Blake-Brecher m]	swing jaw shaft
Schwingbackenplatte f	swing jaw (crushing) plate
Schwinge f [Einschwingenbrecher m]	pitman
Schwingenbrechbacke f, Schwingbacken m, bewegliche Brechbacke	swing(ing) jaw, movable ~, moving ~
Schwingenlager n [Einschwingenbrecher m]	pitman eccentric bearing
Schwungrad n, Schwungscheibe f	flywheel
Stauung f	packing, choking
Stellkeil m, siehe: Nach~	
Stirnwandbrechbacke f, Festbacken m	stationary jaw
(untere Brech)Spaltweite f, Spaltweite der Austrittsöffnung f, Austragsspaltweite	jaw setting, clearance [distance between the jaws at the discharge point at the bottom of the crushing chamber]
unterer Seitenkeil m	lower cheek plate
verstellbarer Keil m, siehe: (Nach)Stellkeil	
Zugstange f [Blake-Brecher m]	pitman
Zugstangenlager n, siehe: Exzenterlager n der Zugstange f	
Zugstangenwelle f [Blake-Brecher m]	pitman shaft
Zweipendel~, siehe: Doppelkniehebelbrecher	
Zweischwingerbrecher m, siehe: Doppel~	

Backkohle f; siehe unter „Kohle f"
Backstein m, Ziegel(stein) m, Vollziegel m [früher: Mauerziegel m] = (building) brick, solid ~
~**brecher** m, siehe: Ziegelbrecher
~**ton** m, Töpferton, Ballton = ball clay, potters' ~
Baculitenkalk m = Baculites limestone
Badestrand m = bathing beach
Bagger m, Trockenbagger = excavator
~, Naßbagger, Schwimmbagger = dredger (Brit.); dredge (US)
~**eimer** m, Baggerbecher m [beim Naßbagger m] = dredge(r) bucket
~**eimer** m, Baggerbecher m [beim Trockenbagger m] = excavator bucket
~**führer** m [Löffelbagger m] = shovel(l)er
~**gleis** n = excavator track
~**greifer** m, siehe: Baggerkorb m
~**greifer** m, siehe: Greif(er)bagger m

Bagger|korb *m*, Greif(er)korb *m*, Bagger-Greif(er)korb *m*, Baggergreifer *m* = grab (bucket), grapple, grabbing bucket
~kran *m*, Kranbagger *m* = shovel crane, crane-excavator, excavator crane
~leiter *f*; siehe unter „Grabenbagger *m* mit Eimern"
~leiter *f*; siehe unter „Naßbagger *m*"
~leiterrahmen *m*, Eimerleiterrahmen, Ausleger *m* = ladder frame
(~) Löffel *m*, Grablöffel, Grabgefäß *n* = bucket, dipper, shovel, shovel dipper, excavator bucket
~maschinen *fpl* = excavating and dredging machinery

~pumpe *f*, Förderpumpe = dredging pump, dredge(r) ~
~rost *m*, Matratze *f* = excavator (supporting) mat, platform, pontoon
~sand *m* = dredged river sand
~schute *f*, (Abfuhr)Schute = hopper barge (Brit.); scow (US)
~schutenwinde *f* = scow winding gear (US); hopper barge winding gear (Brit.)
~schwelle *f* = sleeper for crane navvy (Brit.); tie for power shovel (US)
~seil *n* = excavator cable

Bagger-Senkkastengründung *f*
  Absenkung(svorgang) *f*, (*m*)
  Außenseitenrahmenviereck *n*
  Außenseitenwandrahmen *m*
  Baggerschacht *m*, Baggerbrunnen *m*
  Bauglied *n*
  Betonpfropfen *m*
  Fach *n*
  Fachspitze *f*
  Führungspferch *m*
  Grundform *f* an der Unterkante *f*
  Innenseitenscheidewandrahmen *m*
  Kastenträgerwand *f*
  Längsscheidewand *f*
  Ordinate — 91
  Querscheidewand *f*
  Rahmenzwischenraum *m*
  Schneid(e)kammer *f*
  Schneid(e)kante *f*
  Schneid(e)kantenträger *m*
  verspannte Stahlplattenwand *f*
  Versteifungs-Kastenträger-Scheidewand *f*
  Verteilungsblock *m*
  Wandfläche *f*
  Zwischenwandrahmen *m*

open-dredged caisson method
  caisson-sinking, spotting
  outside-frame square
  outside wall frame
  dredge(r) well
  structural shape
  tremie-seal concrete
  panel
  panel point
  guide pen
  plan size at cutting edge
  inside-diaphragm frame
  box-girder wall
  longitudinal diaphragm
  El. — 91
  transverse diaphragm
  frame spacing
  cutting-edge chamber
  cutting-edge
  cutting-edge girder
  braced steel-plate wall
  inside stiffening box-girder diaphragm

  distributing block
  wall face
  diaphragm frame

Bagger|stampfer *m*, siehe: Freifall-Kranstampfer
~stelle *f*, Grabstelle = digging site, ~ point
~torf *m* = dredged peat

~-Transportwagen *m* = excavator low-loader
Baggerung *f*, siehe: Aushub *m*
Baggerwindwerk *n*, Auslegerwinde *f* = boom hoist (US); jib ~ (Brit.)

Bahn|damm *m*, Eisen~ = railway embankment (Brit.); railroad ~ (US)
~körper *m* = railway right-of-way (Brit.); railroad ~ (US)
~meisterwagen *m*, siehe: Draisine *f*
~schotter *m*, siehe: Eisenbahnschotter
~steig *m* [*Untergrundbahnhof m*] = station floor
~steig *m* = station platform
~steigkarre(n) *f*, (*m*) = baggage truck
~übergang *m*, siehe: niveaugleicher ~
bahnverladbar = suitable for rail transport
Bahnversand *m*, Eisen~ = rail shipment
Bai *f*, Bucht *f*, Einbuchtung = bay
Bairdienschiefer *m* (Geol.) = Bairdia shale
Bake *f*, Zwischenzeichen *n* [*Autobahn f*] = warning sign
Balancierdampfmaschine *f* = beam (steam) engine
Balken *m*, Träger *m*, Balkenträger = girder (Brit.); beam
~anker *m* = beam (tie) bar
~auflager *n* **im Ziegelmauerwerk** *n* = beam pocket in brickwork
~biegepresse *f*, siehe: Trägerbiegepresse
~brause *f* [*Schweiz*]; siehe: Sprengrampe *f*
~formmaschine *f*, Hohlbalkenmaschine = (precast) concrete joist machine, lintel machine
~kopf *m* = beam head
~kopfschalung *f* = end form(s)
~lehrgerüst *n* = beam centering (US); ~ centring (Brit.)
~rüttler *m* = (precast) concrete joist shaker (or shaking machine)
~träger *m*, siehe: Balken *m*
~(träger)biegepresse *f*, siehe: Trägerbiegepresse
~(träger)rostdecke *f*, siehe: Trägerrostdecke
~untersicht *f* = beam bottom
~waage *f* = (weigh) beam scale
Ballast *m* = ballast
~gewicht *n* = ballast weight
~kasten *m* [*Baudrehkran m*] = ballast frame

~wasser *n* = ballast water
Ballon|methode *f*, siehe: Gummiblasenmethode
~reifen *m* = balloon tyre (Brit.); ~ tire (US)
Ballton *m*, siehe: Backsteinton
Balme *f* (Geol.) = overhang
Balsam|kolophonium *n* = gum rosin
~tanne *f* = balsam fir
Banatit *m* (Geol.) = banatite
Band|abmeßanlage *f* = belt type proportioning unit
~absetzer *m*, (Schwenk)Absetzer. Bandabwurfgerät *n*, Absetzer für Hoch-, Tief- und Dammschüttung *f*, Absetzanlage *f* = stacker
   Dammschütter-~ *m*, Hochabsetzer = ~ for building up embankments
   Tiefschütter-~ *m* = ~ for filling below track level
~abzug *m*; siehe unter „Fertigbehandlung *f*"
~abzug *m* [*aus einem Silo m*] = withdrawing by belt
bandagiertes Druckrohr *n* = ring-reinforced pressure pipe (or conduit)
Band|aufgeber *m*, siehe: Bandspeiser *m*
~(auf)lader *m* (mit Höheneinstellung *f*) = elevating belt conveyor, conveyor loader, belt ~, belt elevator (with adjustable elevation gear)
~bebauung *f* = ribbon building, ~ development
~beschicker *m*, Bandspeiser *m*, Bandaufgeber *m*, Aufgabeband *n*, Beschickungsband = belt feeder
~bremse *f* = band brake
~brücke *f* = belt conveyor bridge
~eisen *n* (Min.) = taenite
~eisen *n*, Bandstahl *m* = hoop-iron, hoops, hoop steel, hooping, band steel, strap steel, strip (steel), steel strip
Bänder|gneis *m* = banded gneiss, ribbon ~
~ton *m*, dünngeschichteter Ton = varve(d) (glacial) clay, pellodite, banded clay, leaf clay, book clay, ribbon clay
~ton *m* **mit Jahresringen** *mpl* = seasonally banded clay, ~ stratified ~

Bandförderer m, Förderband n, Gurtförderer, Gurtförderband — belt conveyor, band ~

Ablenktrommel f	snub(bing) pulley, snubber ~
Abstreicher m, Abstreifer m	belt wiper, scraper
Abwurfende n	discharge end
Abwurfwagen m	travel(l)ing tripper
Antriebstrommel f	drive pulley, motorized ~
ausziehbar	extendible
Bandbelag m	belt cover, band ~
Bandbrücke f	conveyor belt frame
Banddecke f	cover
Bandförderung f, Bandtransport m	belt conveying, ~ conveyance
Bandmulde f	belt trough
Bandrücklaufrolle f	return idler
Bandspannung f, Straffung f	tension
Bandstraße f, Transport-~	sectional ground conveyor
Bandtragrahmen m	carryable belt conveyor frame
Bandtrommel f, siehe: Trommel	
(Band)Umlenkrolle f, siehe: Trommel f	
Baumwollband n, Baumwollgurt m	cotton fabric duck belt (or band), ~ reinforced belt (or band)
(belastete) Tragrolle f	carrier (idler), supporting roller
Cordband n	rayon cord (or fabric) belt(ing)
dreiteilige Rollenstation f	three-roller idler set, troughed idler, three-pulley idler, 3-spindle troughing idler
dünne Gummischicht f	skin
einteilige Tragrolle f	flat idler
Eintrommelantrieb m mit Ablenktrommel f	snub(bing) pulley drive, snubber ~ ~
Eintrommel-Kopfantrieb m	head pulley drive
(End)Trommel f, siehe: Trommel	
fahrbarer Gurtförderer m, Fahrband n Schwenkradsatz m	portable belt (or band) conveyor swivel wheels
Ferntransportband n, Langstreckenförderbandanlage f zum Transport m von Gesteinen npl, Streckenband	"rock road"
Flachband n, Flachgurt m	flat belt, ~ band
flache Tragrolle f	flat idler, ~ roller
Förderbandrolle f	(conveyor) idler, (idler) roller
Förderband n zur Bodenentladung f von Güterwagen mpl	belt type car unloader
Förderband-Tragwerk n	conveyor gantry
Führungs- und Tragrolle f	guidler, training idler, self-aligning (guide) idler
Gewichtsspannvorrichtung f	gravity takeup
Glasrollenförderband n	belt conveyor with glass idlers
Gummibelag m	rubber cover
Gummi(förder)gurt m, Gummi(förder)band n	rubber (conveyor) belt(ing) (or band)

Bandförderer — Bandschelle

Klaubeband n, siehe: Leseband	
Kopfantriebstrommel f	motorized (or drive) head pulley, head drive pulley
Kopftrommel f	head pulley
Langstreckenbandförderanlage f zum Transport m von Gesteinen npl, Ferntransportband n, Streckenband	"rock road"
Leseband n, Klaubeband	picking belt (or band) conveyor
Muldenband n, siehe: Trogband	
Muldenbandrolle f	belt troughing roller
Muldengurtförderband n	trough belt (or band) conveyor
oberer Strang m, Tragseite f, Obergurt m	carrier side, upper strand, carrying strand
Rollenstation f	idler set
rotierende Bürste f	brush outfit for cleaning carrier side
scharfkantiges Fördergut n	abrasive material
schmiegsame Tragrolle f	flexible (belt) conveyor idler, limberoller
Schüttbeanspruchung f	loading impact
Schwanztrommel f	tail pulley, return ~
Spannrolle f, Spanntrommel f	takeup pulley
Spannstation f, Spannvorrichtung f	takeup (set)
Straffung f, Bandspannung f	tension
Stückgut ~	package (~) ~
stückiges Schüttgut n	lumpy material
Textilband n, Textilgurt m	fabric carcass belt
Tragrolle f, siehe: belastete ~	
Tragrollenstation f	carrier idler set
Transportbandanlage f	fixed conveyor
Transport-Bandstraße f, siehe: Bandstraße	
Trogband n, Muldenband, Troggurt m, Muldengurt	trough belt, ~ band
Trommel f, Endtrommel, Bandtrommel, (Band) Umlenkrolle f, Endumlenktrommel	pulley
Trommelelektromotor m	pulley (electric) motor
Umlenkrolle f, siehe: Trommel f	
Umspannungsbogen m	arc of contact
unbelastete Tragrolle f	return idler, belt return roller
unbelasteter Strang m, unterer ~, Untergurt m	lower strand, return ~
Zweitrommelantrieb m	two-pulley drive, tandem ~
Zwischenlage f	ply

Band|(förder)schnecke f = open-spiral worm conveyor, antifriction ~ ~
~kabel n = flat cable
~kanal m, siehe: Haldentunnel m
~kühlsystem n, Kühlbandanlage f = cooling belt system
~kupplung f = rim clutch (coupling)
~lader m, siehe: Band(auf)lader
~maß n, Meßband n = measuring tape
~porphyr m = banded porphyry
~säge f; siehe unter „Säge f"
~schelle f = ribbon clip

Band|schleifmaschine f = (flexible) belt sander, (~) ~ sanding machine
~schnecke f. siehe: Band(förder)schnecke
~-Selbstauflader m = belt type bucket elevator loader, self-loading tractor bucket elevator
~speiser m, Bandbeschicker m, Bandaufgeber m, Aufgabeband n, Beschickungsband = belt feeder
~stahl m, siehe: Bandeisen n
~straße f; siehe unter „Bandförderer m"
~strömung f, laminare Strömung f = streamline flow
~waage f = conveyor type scale
~zuteilung f = proportioning by conveyor belt
Bankett n, siehe: Berme f
~mischer m = wheel-mounted concrete mixer with discharge belt
Bank|hobel m = jointer plane
~schere f = bench shear
Bankungsspalte f (Geol.) = bedding joint
Banse f [Förderturm m] = muck (or skiploading) bin (or hopper)
Bär m; siehe unter „Rammanlage f"
Baracke f = hut
Barackenlager n = hut camp
Barertrag m = cash (or net) proceeds
Bariumaragonit m (Min.), siehe: Alstonit m
Barometerstand m = barometric height
barometrische Höhenbestimmung f, ~ Höhenaufnahme f, ~ Höhenmessung f = barometric level(l)ing
Barrièreeis n = Barrier ice
Baryt m (Min.), siehe: Schwerspat m
~feldspat m, Hyalophan m (Min.) = hyalophane
~(o)salpeter m (Min.) = nitrobarite
Basal|konglomerat n = base (or basal) conglomerate
~sandstein m = basal sandstone
~scholle f (Geol.) = overridden mass
Basalt m = basalt
~eisenerz n = basaltic iron ore
~lava f, Lungstein m = basaltic lava
~pflasterstein m = basalt (paving) sett
~schutt m = basaltic débris, ~ scree
~tuff m, Trapptuff m = basaltic tuff, trap ~
~wacke f = basaltic wacke

Basalzement m (Geol.) = basal matrix, ~ cement(ing material)
Basen|austausch m = base exchange
~grad m = basicity factor
Basisbruch m = toe failure
basischer Diorit m = basic diorite
~ Porphyrit m = basic porphyrites
basisches kohlensaures Blei n, siehe: Bleiweiß n
~ Kupferazetat n, siehe: Grünspan m
Bastion f (Geol.) = ledge
Bastit m, siehe: Schillerspat m
Bast|kohle f = bast coal
~matte f = bast mat
~rüster f, siehe: Flatterrüster
Batholith m, Riesenstock m, Liegendkörper m (Geol.) = batholith, bathylith
bathyale Zone f (Geol.) = bathyal zone
batterie-elektrisch = battery-electric
Batterie|kasten m = battery box
~ladegeräte npl = battery charging equipment
Bau|abschnitt m, Ausbaustufe f, Baustadium n = stage (of construction)
~achse f, siehe: Bau(werk)achse
~arbeiten f = building works, construction ~
~art f, Ausführungsart [Baumaschine f] = construction
~aufseher m = building inspector, superintendent
~aufsicht f, Bauüberwachung f = supervision of works
(~)Aufzug m = (contractors') hoist, builders' ~
~austrocknungsofen m, siehe: Kokskorb m
~behörde f = building authority
~bestimmungen f, Bauvorschriften f = building regulations
~betrieb m = construction management
~betrieb m = construction operations
~betriebsforschung f = construction management research
~betriebsplan m, siehe: Bau(zeit)plan
~betriebsunfall m mit tödlichem Ausgang = fatal construction mishap (or accident)
~bude f, Leutebude f = workmen's shelter
~büro n, Baustellenbüro = site office, job ~
~diesellok(omotive) f; siehe unter „Feldbahnanlage f"

Bau-Dokumentation — Baugrundverbesserung

Bau|-Dokumentation *f* = documentation of building topics
~-Drehkran *m* = tower building crane
~einrichtung *f*, s.: Baustelleneinrichtung
~eisenwaren *f* = iron mongery for building trades
~element *n* = construction medium
baufällig = delipidated, ramshackle
Bau|fehler *m* = building fault
~firma *f* = construction company, ~ firm, building ~
~flucht *f*, siehe: Ausfluchtung *f*
~fluchtlinie *f* [*Straße f*] = building line
~fortschritt *m*, siehe: Arbeitsfortschritt
~fortschrittsplan *m*, siehe: Bau(zeit)plan
~frist *f*, Bauzeit *f* = completion period (or time), construction ~ (~ ~)
~fristenplan *m*, siehe: Bau(zeit)plan *m*
~führer *m* = supervisor
~gemeinkosten *f* = general construction costs
~genossenschaft *f* = cooperative (or benefit) building society
~gerätemietsatzliste *f*, Gerätemietsatzliste = list of hiring charges for building plant and contractors' equipment, schedule of rates for the hire of contractors' equipment and building plant; equipment rental compilation (US)

~gewerbe *n*, siehe: Bauhandwerk *n*
~gewerkschaft *f* = building trades counsel union
~gips *m*, gebrannter Gips *m* [*jeder für Bauzwecke geeignete gebrannte Gipsstein m*] = calcined gypsum, gypsum plaster for building purposes
~glas *n* = construction(al) glass
~grube *f* = excavation, building pit, open cut
~grubenaufzug *m*, Grubenaufzug = building pit hoist, foundation ~
~grubenauskleidung *f* = open cut lining
~grubenaussteifung *f*, Baugrubenabsteifung *f* = open cut bracing, braced open cut
~grund *m*, Untergrund *m* = subsoil, foundation soil
~grund(ab)dichtung *f* = waterproofing of foundation, subsoil waterproofing, foundation soil waterproofing
~grundkarte *f*, siehe: Bodenkarte *f*
~grundmechanik *f*, siehe: Bodenmechanik
~gruntersuchung *f*, siehe: Bodenuntersuchung

Baugrundverbesserung *f*, **Baugrundverfestigung** *f*, **Bodenstabilisierung** *f*, **Bodenstabilisation** *f*, **Bodenverbesserung** *f*
   Tiefstabilisierung *f*, (Boden)Verfestigung *f* von Tiefgründungen *fpl*, Untergrunddichtung *f*
      Zementmörteleinpressung *f*, Zementmörteleinspritzung *f*, Zementmörtelinjektion *f*, Zementmörtelunterpressung *f*, Zementmörtelauspressung *f*
      Poreninjektion *f*
      Zementmilcheinpressung *f*

   chemische Baugrundverbesserung *f*, chemische Injektion *f*
   Kluftinjektion *f*, Felsinjektion, Gesteinsauspressung *f*

artificial (or soil, or ground) cementation (or solidification, or stabilization, or stabilisation)
   sub-soil ~, subsurface ~

      cement mortar grouting, subsurface grouting with cement mortar

      soil injection
      subsurface grouting with cement water grout
   artificial method of cementation by the injection of chemicals
   cementation of rock fissures, rock sealing

Joosten-Verfahren *n*, Tiefkälteverfahren, chemische Verfestigung nach Joosten, Chemikalverfahren *n* nach Dr. Joosten [*Jahr 1926*]	Joosten process, Joosten chemical solidification process
Gefriergründung *f*, Baugrundvereisung *f*; Gefrierverfahren *n* [*Bergbau m*]	freezing process
Poetsch-Verfahren *n* [*Jahr 1883*]	Poetsch (freezing) process
Dehottay-Verfahren *n* [*Jahr 1931*]	Dehottay process
Rodio-Verfahren *n* [*Jahr 1935*]	Rodio process
elektro-osmotische Baugrundverbesserung *f*	electro-osmotic solidification, electrical ~, ~ stabilization
Oberflächenstabilisation *f*, Bodenvermörtelung *f*, Bodenverfestigung der Oberfläche *f*	soil cementation (or stabilization) on the surface, (surface) soil stabilization (or solidification)
Teervermörtelung *f*, Teerverfestigung	soil stabilization with tar, tar soil stabilization
Bitumenvermörtelung *f*, bituminöse Bodenvermörtelung *f*, Bitumenverfestigung	soil stabilization with asphaltic bitumen (Brit.); soil asphalt (US)
Vermörtelung mit künstlichen Harzen *npl*	soil stabilization with artificial resins
Salzvermörtelung *f*, Salzverfestigung	salt stabilization
Bodenbeton *m*, Erdbeton, Bodenzement *m*, Zementtonbeton	soil-cement
Bodenvermörtelung *f* mit Stabilisatorbeigabe *f*	additive soil stabilisation
mechanische Bodenverfestigung *f*, Tonbeton *m*	mechanical (or granular) (soil) stabilisation
Zementvermörtelung *f*, Bodenvermörtelung *f* mit Zement *m*	cement-soil stabilisation

---

Bau|grundverdichtung *f*, natürliche ~ = subsoil consolidation, ground ~
~**grundvereisung** *f*; siehe unter „Baugrundverbesserung *f*"
~**(hand)karren** *m*, Bau(hand)karre *f* = builder's hand cart
~**handwerk** *n*, Baugewerbe *n* = building trade(s), trowel ~, construction ~
~**handwerker** *m* = building trade worker
~**herr(schaft)** *m*, (*f*); siehe unter „Angebot *n*"
~**hilfsgeräte** *npl* = auxiliary building (or construction) equipment
~**hof** *m*, Gerätepark *m* = plant depot, contractor's yard, equipment repair yard, equipment pool
~**hofreparatur** *f* [*Baumaschine f*] = depot repair, plant ~ ~
~**höhe** *f* = height of construction
~**holz** *n*, siehe: Baunutzholz
~**industrie** *f*, Bauwirtschaft *f* = construction (or building, or contracting, or civil-engineering) industry
~**ingenieur** *m* = construction engineer, civil ~
~**ingenieurwesen** *n*, Ingenieurbau *m* = civil engineering and building construction
~**kalk** *m* = building lime, construction ~
~**kalkhydrat** *n* = trowel trades hydrated lime
~**kantine** *f*, siehe: Bau(stellen)kantine

Baukarre(n) — Baumaschinen und Baugeräte

Bau|karre(n) *f*, (*m*), s.: Bau(hand)karre(n)
~kastenprinzip *n* = sectional system
~kasten-System-Anlage *f*, halbstationäre Anlage *f* [*Makadam-Maschinen-Anlage f*] = sectional type plant
~kaufmann *m* = purchasing clerk
baukeramische Industrie *f* = structural clay industry
baukeramischer Ton *m*, Ziegelton = building clay, structural ~
baukeramisches Erzeugnis *n* = structural clay product (or body), heavy clay product (~ ~)
Bau|klammer *f* = dog
~klinker *m* = clinker, klinker, construction ~
~kompressor *m*, Bauluftverdichter *m*, Bau-Druckluiterzeuger *m* = contractors' (air) compressor

~körper *m*, Bauwerk *n*, Kunstkörper = structure
~kostenaufgliederung *f* = construction-cost breakdown
~kraftwerk *n* = site power plant (or station)
~kran *m*, Hochbaukran = building crane
~kran *m* = construction-site crane
~landbeschaffung *f*, Grunderwerb *m* [*in Österreich: Grundeinlösung f*] = acquisition of land, land purchase
~leiter *m* = engineer's-agent, project manager
bauliche Durchbildung *f*, ~ Gestaltung *f* = design and construction
Bau|lok(omotive) *f*; siehe unter „Feldbahnanlage *f*"
~los *n* = contract section
~luftverdichter *m*, siehe: Baukompressor *m*

Baumaschinen *fpl* **und Baugeräte** *npl*	construction machinery, construction equipment, contractors' plant and machinery, constructional plant, building and civil engineering plant, public works equipment, contracting plant, contractor equipment
abgenutzter Teil *m*, abgenutztes ~ *n*	worn part
Abholort *m*	point of collection
Abholung *f*	collection
Abladekosten *f*, Entladekosten *f*, Ausladekosten	cost of unloading
Abmessungen *fpl*	dimensions, size
Abmessungen *fpl* und Leistung *f*	size and rate of working
Abschreibung *f*, Absetzung *f* für Abnutzung *f*	write-off (or writing-off) of depreciations
Absendeort *m*, Versandort *m*	point of shipping, ~ ~ shipment
Allzweck-Gerät *n*	jack-of-all-trades rig
Anbaugerät *n*, Zusatzvorrichtung *f*	attachment
Antriebsgruppe *f*	power unit
Antriebsmechanismus *m*	driving mechanism
Antriebsteil *m*, *n*	driving part, drive section
Anwendungsgebiet *n*, Einsatzbereich *m*	field of application, ~ ~ use
Arbeitselement *n*, Betriebsteil *m*, *n*, Arbeitsaggregat *n*, Arbeitsorgan *n*	working part
Arbeitsgeschwindigkeit *f*	on-the-job travel speed, working ~, operating ~
Arbeitsprinzip *n*	operating principle
Arbeitsspiel *n*	work(ing) cycle, operating ~
Arbeitsuntersuchung *f*, Arbeitsstudie *f*	equipment production study
Ausfall *m*, Geräte~	breakdown equipment ~
Ausführungsart *f*, Bauart *f*	construction

Baumaschinen und Baugeräte

Ausnutzung f, Auslastung	work-out
Auswechselbarkeit f, Austauschbarkeit f	interchangeability
Bauart f, siehe: Ausführungsart	
Bauhof m, siehe: Gerätepark m	
Baumaschinen-Fibel f	construction machinery and equipment primer
Baumaschinenindustrie f	construction machinery and equipment industry
Baumaschineningenieur m	construction machinery and equipment engineer
Baumuster n	type, model
Baustelleneinsatz m	construction-site service
Bedienungselement n, Steuerorgan n, Schaltorgan	(operating) control
Bedienungsmann m, siehe: (Geräte-)Bediener m	
Bestimmungsort m	destination
Betriebsfähigkeit f, betriebsfähiger Zustand m	operating condition (or order), running ~ (~ ~)
Betriebskosten f	operating costs
Betriebssicherheit f	operating safety
Betriebsstundenzähler m	hour meter
Betriebsteil m, n, siehe: Arbeitselement n	
Daten, siehe: (technische) Daten f	
Druckknopfsteuerung f, Fingerdrucksteuerung	push-button (or press-button) control
Eigengewicht n	dead weight
Einmannbedienung f	one-man operation, ~ control
Einsatzbereich m, Anwendungsgebiet n	field of application, ~ ~ use
Einstellbarkeit f, Verstellbarkeit f	adjustability
Einzelgerät n, Geräteeinheit f	equipment item, piece of equipment, plant item, equipment unit
Einzelteil m, n	individual part
elektrische Betätigung f	electric operation
Empfangsort m	receiving point
Entwurf m, zeichnerische Ausarbeitung f	design
Ersatzteil m, n	replacement part, spare (part)
Ersatzteildienst m	replacement parts service, spare ~ ~
Fabrikat n	make
Fahrstellung f	travel position
Freibeweglichkeit f, Manövrierfähigkeit	manoeuvrability (Brit.); maneuverability (US)
gebrochener Teil m, gebrochenes ~ n	broken part
Gehäuse n	housing, casing
(Geräte)Ausfall m	(equipment) breakdown
(Geräte)Bediener m, Maschinenführer m, Bedienungsmann m	(plant) operator, driver, equipment operator, plant hand; operative (Brit.)
Gerätebestand m, Maschinenpark m, Gerätepark	equipment inventory
Geräteeinheit f, siehe: Einzelgerät n	

Baumaschinen und Baugeräte

Geräteeinsatz m	employment of plant, disposition of equipment, equipment utilization
Geräteliste f	list of equipment, plant register
(Geräte)Mietkosten f, Gerätemiete f	hire charge, equipment rental
(Geräte)Mietsatz m	equipment rental rate, plant-hire rate
Gerätemietsatzliste f, Baugerätemietsatzliste f	equipment rental compilation (US); list of hiring charges for building plant and contractors' equipment, schedule of rates for the hire of contractors' equipment and building plant
Gerätepark m, Bauhof m	plant depot, contractor's yard, equipment repair yard, equipment pool
Gerätepark m, siehe: Gerätebestand m	
Gerätestunden fpl	machine-hours worked by plant
Geräteträger m, Grundgerät n	basic unit, ~ tool
Gerätevermietung f	equipment renting
Gerätezug m	train of plant items, equipment train
Großgerät n	heavy plant, high-powered equipment, heavy duty construction equipment, major equipment, capital equipment
Grundgerät n, Geräteträger m	basic unit, ~ tool
Handbedienung f, Handbetätigung f	manual operation
hydraulische Betätigung f	hydraulic operation
in der Leistung f übertreffen	to outperform (US); to outdo (Brit.)
in der Praxis f bewährt	field proven, field tested, job-proved
Kauf-Mietvertrag m	(equipment) rental contract with purchase option
Konstruktionsmerkmal n	construction(al) feature
Kraftabnahme f	power take-off
Kraftbedarf m, Energiebedarf	(horse)power requirement
Leistung f, Arbeitsleistung	performance, output, capacity
Leistungsreserve f	undeveloped potential of production power, reserve power
Leistungtabelle f	performance table
Luxusausführung f	de luxe model
Maschinenführer m, siehe: (Geräte-)Bediener m	
maßstabgerechtes Modell n	scale model
mechanische Betätigung f	mechanical operation
Mieter m	lessee
Mietsatz m, siehe: (Geräte)Mietsatz	
Mietvertrag m	rental contract
Mietzeit f	rental period
mittelschwer	medium-duty
Neuentwicklung f	novelty
niedrige Schwerpunktlage f	low centre of gravity (Brit.); ~ center ~ ~ (US)
Nutzungsdauer f, Lebensdauer	working life, service(able) life
Ölbadschmierung f	oil-bath lubrication
ortsbeweglich, fahrbar	portable, mobile

Baumaschinen und Baugeräte

Ortsbeweglichkeit *f*	portability
Ortswechsel *m*, siehe: Transport *m* von Baustelle *f* zu Baustelle	
Prüfstand *m*	test stand
Reisegeschwindigkeit *f*	travel speed
robust	rugged, robust
Rücklieferung *f*	return shipment
Rückwärtsgeschwindigkeit *f*	reverse speed
Schaltorgan *n*, s.: Bedienungselement *n*	
Schmierstelle *f*	lubrication point
schwere Ausführung *f*	heavy duty type
Schwerpunktlage *f*	centre of gravity (Brit.); center ~ ~ (US)
Schwerpunktverlagerung *f*	displacement of centre of gravity (Brit.); ~ ~ center ~ ~ (US)
Steuerorgan *n*, s.: Bedienungselement *n*	
störungsfreier Betrieb *m*	trouble-free operation
(technische) Daten *f*	specifications
Transport *m* von Baustelle *f* zu Baustelle, Ortswechsel *m*	job-to-job hauling (or transport)
Transportstellung *f*	transporting position
Transportzeit *f*	moving time between jobs
Überholung *f*, Überholen *n*	overhaul
umbauen	to convert
unvermeidliche Verlustzeit *f*	lost-time, unavoidable delay factor
(Ver)Fahren *n*	travel(l)ing
Verkehrswert *m*, Zeitwert *m*	present value, trade-in value
vermeidbare Verlustzeit *f*	downtime
Vermieter *m*	lessor
Versandgewicht *n*	shipping weight
Verschleißteil *m*, *n*	wearing part
Verstellbarkeit *f*, siehe: Einstellbarkeit	
vielseitiges Gerät *n*	versatile equipment item
Mehrzweckgerät *n* [*z. B. Turmdrehkran m*]	multi-purpose equipment item
Umbaugerät *n* [*z. B. Raupenbagger m*]	conversion ~ ~
Kombinationsgerät *n* [*z. B. Diesel-Kompressorschlepper m*]	combination ~ ~
Austauschgerät *n* [*Auswechseln eines vollständigen Geräteteils, nicht einer Zusatzeinrichtung, z. B. Dieselmotor durch Elektromotor bei Mischern*]	interchangeable ~ ~
Wiederverwendungsgerät *n* [*z. B. eiserne Schalung f*]	multi-use ~ ~
Vielseitigkeit *f*	versatility
Vorwärtsgeschwindigkeit *f*	forward speed
Wartezeit *f*, Stehzeit	stand-by time
wahlweiser Zusatzteil *m*, wahlweises ~ *n*	optional attachment
zeichnerische Ausarbeitung *f*, siehe: Entwurf *m*	

Baumaschinen und Baugeräte — Bausteinverwitterung

Zeitwert *m*, siehe: Verkehrswert
Zubehör *m, n* — accessories
Zubehörteil *m, n* — accessory part
Zugänglichkeit *f* — accessibility
Zusatzeinrichtung *f*, Anbaugerät *n* — attachment

Baumeister *m* = master builder
Baumfallsäge *f*, siehe: Kettensäge mit Benzinmotor *m*

Baumgrenze *f* (Geol.) = timber line

Baumischbelag *m* — road mix surface
~ mit dicht abgestuftem Korngemenge, dichter ~ — graded aggregate type ~ ~ ~, dense-graded ~ ~ ~
~ von der Art des Makadam, offener ~, hohlraumreicher ~ — macadam aggregate type ~ ~ ~, open-graded ~ ~ ~

Baumischer *m* = construction mixer
Baumischverfahren *n* **mit bituminösen Bindemitteln ausgeführt mit Straßenhobel** = road mix process with bituminous binders by means of a grader
baumkantig, waldkantig [*Holz n*] = dull edged, rough ~
Baumkluppe *f* = tree ga(u)ge
Baumkran *m* = logging crane
Baumkübel *m* = shrub tub
Baumkunde *f*. siehe: Dendrologie *f*
Baummörtel *m*, siehe: Mauermörtel
Baumrost *m*, siehe: Drahthose *f*
Baumschere *f* = pruning shear
Baumschieber *m*; siehe unter „Bulldozer *m*"
Baumschule *f* = (tree) nursery
Baumstamm *m* = tree trunk
Baumstein *m*, Dendrit *m* = dendrite
Baumstock *m*, siehe: Baumstumpf *m*
Baumstumpf *m*, Baumstock *m*, Stumpf, Stubben *m* [*in Österreich: Strunk m*] = (tree) stump
~zieher *m*, siehe: Wurzelzieher
Baumuster *n* = model, type
Baum|wollsaatöl *n* = cotton oil
~wüste *f* = arboreal desert
~zucht *f* = arboriculture
Bau|nebenleistungen *f* = ancillary works
~nivellier(instrument) *m*, (*n*) = builders' level
~(nutz)holz *n* = lumber, timber [*timber is lumber that is 5 inches or larger in its smallest diameter*]
~papier *n* = building paper

~plan *m*, siehe: Bau(zeit)plan
~planung *f* = project planning
~platte *f* = building board (or slab)
~platten *fpl* = sheet building materials
~polizeibestimmungen *fpl* = Building Code Provisions
~praktiker *m*, siehe: Bautechniker *m*
~praxis *f* = building practice
~preisverordnung *f* = Building Prices Order
~programm *n*, siehe: Bau(zeit)plan *m*
(~)Projekt *n*, Bauvorhaben *n* = construction(al) project, (building) ~
~-Radschlepper *m* = contractor-type wheel tractor
~saison *f* = construction season, building ~
~sand *m* = building sand
~schraubenwinde *f*, Lehrgerüstspindel *f* = contractor's jack screw
~schreinerei *f* = Bautischlerei *f*
~schule *f* = school of building
~schutt *m* = rubbish
~sparkasse *f* = building and loan association
~stadium *n*, siehe: Bauabschnitt *m*
~stahl *m* = structural steel, constructional ~
~stahlgewebe *n* [*punktgeschweißt*] = steel fabric (mat), welded fabric [*spotwelded*]
~statik *f* = statics for structural engineering
~stein *m* = (building) stone
~stein *m* [*im Sinne von Ziegel(stein) m*] = (building)brick
~steinverwitterung *f* = building stone weathering

Baustelle f = site (of works), building site, job-site, project site. construction site
~ **des Hochbaues** m = building site for multi-storey buildings
~ ~ **Ingenieurbaues** m = engineering building site
Baustellen|(auf)räumung f = job cleanup, cleanup and move out
~**büro** n, Baubüro = job office, site ~
~**dampfwinde** f, Baudampfwinde = contractor's steam hoist
~**einrichtung** f. Baueinrichtung = (job-) site installations, site facilities, site plant, constructional plant
~**einsatz** m = construction-site service
~-**Flachbodenselbstentlader** m = narrow ga(u)ge flat dump car
~**gleis** n; siehe unter „Feldbahnanlage f"

Baustellensilo m, (Sorten)-Zwischen(lade)- bunker m, Aufnahmebunker m, Aufnahmesilo m — (storage) bin, overhead hopper, receiving ~

ortsfester ~ mit Waage f — fixed batching unit

fahrbarer ~ mit zwei Taschen fpl und Waage f — two-bin portable batcher

Arbeitssilo m, Arbeitsbunker m — surge bin, surge hopper

Baustellen|stoß m [Stahlbau m] = field connection, ~ joint, site ~
~**straße** f, Baustellenweg m = builders' road, site ~
~**überwachung** f = field supervision, site ~
~**verkehr** m, Bauverkehr = construction(al) traffic
~**versuch** m = works test
~-**Verteilungstafel** f, Baustellenverteiler = distribution board (or panel) for construction sites
Baustoff m = building material, construction ~
~-**Fabrikant** m = building (or construction) materials producer
~-**Fachmann** m = construction materials engineer
~**händler** m = building (or construction) material(s) dealer (or merchant)
~**maschine** f = building (or construction) material(s) machine
~**prüfmaschine** f = building (or construction) materials testing machine

~-**Instandsetzungs-Werkstatt** f = field workshop
~**kantine** f, Baukantine = site canteen
~**labor(atorium)** n = field lab(oratory), on-job ~
~**lager** n, Unterkunftslager n, Lagerunterkünfte fpl, Arbeiterlager = contractor's construction camp, workers' ~
~**mischer** m = on-site mixer
~**montage** f = erection on the site
~**niet** m = field rivet, site ~
~**organisation** f = job "housekeeping" (US); site organization
~**prüfung** f = site test
~**räumung** f, s. Baustellen(auf)räumung
~**schweißung** f = site welding
~-**Selbstentlader** m = narrow ga(u)ge dump car

~**prüfung** f = building materials testing, construction ~ ~
Bau|stollen m = construction adit
~**tafel** f = building panel
~**tagebuch** n = job record
~**technik** f [als betriebstechnische Anwendung f] = construction technique
~**technik** f [als Wissenschaft f] = construction engineering
~**techniker** m. Baupraktiker m = building technican
Bautechnische Auskunftsstelle f = Building Information Centre
bautechnische Bodenkunde f, siehe: Bodenmechanik f
Bauteil m, n = building unit, structural part, ~ member
Bautenschutz m = preservation of buildings
~**mittel** n = building preservative
Bautischlerei f, Bauschreinerei f = building trade joinery
Bauüberwachung f, Bauaufsicht f = supervision of works

Bau- und Montageverfahren n = construction and erection method
Bauunternehmer m = (public works) contractor, construction ~
~verband m = general contractors association
Bau|unternehmung f, **Bauunternehmen** n = (public works) contracting firm
~verkehr m, siehe: Baustellenverkehr
~vorhaben n, siehe: (Bau)Projekt n
~vorhaben n **der öffentlichen Hand** = public works project
~vorschrift f = building regulation
~weiche f = narrow-ga(u)ge track switch
Bauweise f = construction(al) method, method of construction
~ Hoyer f, Stahlsaitenbeton m = Hoyer method, prestressed concrete with thin wires
~ f **mit maßeinheitlichen Bauteilen** mpl, npl = modular method
Bauwelt f = construction world
Bauwerk n, Kunstkörper m, Baukörper m = structure
~abdichtung f **gegen Bodenfeuchte** f, Feuchtigkeitsisolierung f = damp-proofing
~abdichtung f **gegen Grundwasser** n = waterproofing
~achse f, Bauachse, Symmetrieachse = centre line (Brit.); center ~ (US)
~eisen n = constructional iron, structural ~
Bauwerks|fuge f = structural joint
~last f = load of structure
~setzung f = settlement of structure, structural settlement
Bauwerkzeug n = construction tool, contractors' ~
Bau|wesenversicherung f = all risks erection insurance
~winde f = (contractors') winch, builders' ~
~wirtschaft f, siehe: Bauindustrie f
Bauxit m, Tonerdehydrat n, Beauxit, $Al(OH)_3$ (Min.) = bauxite, beauxite
Bau|zeit f, siehe: Baufrist f
~zeithochwasser n; siehe unter „Talsperre f"

~(zeit)plan m, Arbeitsplan m, Baufristenplan m, Baubetriebsplan m, Bauprogramm n, Baufortschrittsplan m = construction (or work, or time) schedule, schedule of construction operations. job plan, job schedule, phasing, (phased) program(me) of works, (programme &) progress chart, progress schedule
~ziegel(stein) m = building brick
Bayonetthaken m = bayonet hook
Beanspruchbarkeit f, zulässige Spannung f = permissible stress, allowable ~
Beanspruchung f = stress
bearbeitete Naht f, nach~ ~ = flush weld, weld machined flush
Beaufschlagung f [*Turbine* f] = admission
Bebakung f = beaconing
Becher m, Eimer m [*Becherwerk* n] = conveyor bucket
~auflader m, siehe: Becherwerkauflader
~befestigungsschiene f, Eimerbefestigungsschiene = rail for fixing elevator buckets
~(be)lademaschine f, siehe: Becher(werk)auflader m
~(be)lademaschine f **mit Schneckenbeschickung** f = screw feed type bucket elevator loader
(~)Elevator m, siehe: Becherwerk n
~glas n = beaker
~-Gummiband n, Eimer-Gummiband = bucket elevator rubber belt
~gurt m, siehe: Becherwerkgurt
~kette f, Eimerkette = ladder chain carrying the buckets, bucket elevator chain
~koralle f = corallite, cup coral
~lademaschine f, siehe: Becher(werk)auflader m
~lademaschine f **mit Schneckenbeschickung** f, Becherbelademaschine ~ ~ = screw feed type bucket elevator loader
~leiter f, Eimerleiter = bucket ladder
~rad n, Schöpfrad, Eimerrad [*Waschmaschine* f] = dewatering wheel
~reihe f, siehe: Becherstrang m
~strang m, Eimerstrang, Becherreihe f, Eimerreihe = line of buckets, bucket line

Becherwerk *n*, Eimerketten-Aufzug *m*, (Becher-) Elevator *m*, Aufnahmebecherwerk *n*, Aufnahmeelevator, Becherwerkförderer = (bucket) (type) elevator, scoopflight conveyor

Becher(werk)auflader *m*, (Eimerketten-) Fahrlader, Selbstauflader, (Auf)Lader für Schüttgut, Aufnehmer, selbstaufnehmendes Förderband *n*, Becherwerks-(fahr)lader, Becher(be)lademaschine *f*, Becherwerk-Ladeschaufler *m*, Fahrlade-Gerät *n*, Motor-Selbstlader für Schüttgüter = bucket elevator loader, portable loader, multi-bucket loader, conveyor type bucket loader

~ **auf (Gleis)Ketten** *fpl*, ~ ~ Raupen *fpl* = crawler bucket (elevator) loader, track-laying type ~ (~) ~, caterpillar type ~ (~) ~, creeper-mounted ~ (~) ~

~ **mit Band** *n* = multi-bucket loader with belt conveyor discharge arrangement

Becher|werkförderer *m*, siehe: Becherwerk *n*

~**werkfuß** *m* = bucket (elevator) boot

~**werkfußtrommel** *f* = boot pulley

~**(werk)gurt** *m* = elevator belt(ing), ~ conveyor belt

~**werk-Ladeschaufler** *m*, siehe: Becher-(werk)auflader *m*

~**werks(fahr)lader** *m*, siehe: Becher(werk)-auflader

~**werkskopf** *m* = bucket elevator head

~**werkslader** *m*, siehe: Becher(werk)auflader

Becken *n* = basin

~**bildung** *f* (Geol.) = basining

~**landschaft** *f* (Geol.) = basin topography

~**urinal** *n* = pedestal urinal

~**verfahren** *n*, Checksystem *n*, Überstaubewässerung *f* = basin system irrigation, check irrigation

~**wüste** *f* = basin desert

bedachen = to roof

Bedachung *f* = roofing

Bedarfs|haltestelle *f* = request stop

~**spitze** *f*, siehe: Belastungsspitze

bedecken, abdecken = to cover

bedielen = to plank, to board

Bediener *m*, siehe: Bedienungsmann *m*

Bedienungs|element *n*; siehe unter „Baumaschinen und Baugeräte"

~**fehler** *m* = operating error, ~ mistake

~**hebel** *m*, Betätigungshebel, Steuerhebel, Schalthebel = operating lever

~**kabine** *f*, siehe: Führerkabine

~**kette** *f* = operating chain

~**knopf** *m*, Druckknopf = push-button

~**knopfschalter** *m*, Fingerdruckschalter, Druckknopfschalter = push-button switch

~**mann** *m*, Maschinenführer *m*, (Geräte-)Bediener *m* = (plant) operator, driver, equipment operator, plant hand; operative (Brit.)

~**personal** *n* = service personnel

~**podest** *n*, siehe: Bedienungsstand *m*

~**sitz** *m*, Führersitz, Fahr itz = driver's seat

~**stand** *m*, Steuerstand, Bedienungspodest *n* = operator's platform, control ~, control station

~**vorrichtung** *f* = operating device

Beetschlacke *f* = bank slag

Befähigungs|nachweis *m* = experience record

~**schreiben** *n* = letter of capacity

befahrbar = runnable

befahrbare Schachtabdeckung *f* = carriageway cover

befestigter Radspurstreifen *m*, Spurstreifenstraße *f* = strip(e) road, creteway, trackways

Befestigung *f*, Straßenbefestigung = pavement [*a general term for a paved surface*]

~ **von Böschungen** *fpl* = stabilization of slopes

Befestigungs|bolzen *m* = fixing bolt

~**schraube** *f* = fastening screw

Befeuchtungs-Elektroabscheider *m* = wet type electric precipitator

beflogene Route *f*, ~ Strecke *f* = airway

Beförderung *f* = transportation, conveyance, conveying

~ **von Stückgütern** *npl* = package handling

Befragungsmethode *f* **von Haus** *n* **zu Haus**, Verkehrsbefragung *f* ~ ~ ~ ~ = dwelling unit interview method, internal (type of O & D) survey, home-interview method

Befragungsmethode durch Postkarten *fpl*, Postkartenzählung *f* = motor driver postal card method, post-card survey
~ auf der Straße *f*, Verkehrsbefragung ~ ~ ~ = external (type of O & D) survey, roadside interview method
beginnender Bruch *m* = incipient failure
Begleitbruch *m* (Geol.) = auxiliary fracture
Begleiterstraße *f* [*einer Stadtautobahn f*] = frontage road
Begleitverwerfer *m*, Nebenverwerfung *f* (Geol.) = auxiliary fault, branch ~, minor ~, companion ~
Begrenzungs|linie *f* = limiting line
~schalter *m*, Anschlagschalter, Endschalter = limit switch, stop ~
~stein *m* = border stone
Begriffsbezeichnung *f* = definition
begrünen, siehe: berasen
Behälter *m*, Transportgefäß *n*, Transportbehälter = container
~, Zisterne *f*, Tank *m*, Flüssigkeitsbehälter *m*, Sammelbehälter = container (for liquids), (storage) tank, cistern
~ für „Haus-zu-Haus-Verkehr" *m* = traffic container
~bau *m* = tank construction
~kuppel *f* = tank dome
~-Straßenfahrzeug *n*, Silofahrzeug = container road carrier
~waage *f*, Gefäßwaage = bucket scale, hopper ~
(~) Wickelmaschine *f* = (tank) winding machine
Behandeln *n*, Behandlung *f* = treatment, processing
Beharrung *f*, Aufrechterhaltung *f* des Widerstandes *m* [*Gummi-Bitumen-Mischung f*] = tenacity
Beharrungsvermögen *n*, Trägheitsvermögen, Trägheit *f*, Trägheitskraft *f* = inertia
behauen [*Stein m*] = to scabble
Behebung *f*, siehe: Abhilfe(maßnahme) *f*
Behelfs|bauten *f* = temporary structures (or works)
~-Hochwasserentlastungsanlage *f*; siehe unter „Talsperre *f*"
behelfsmäßiger Flachbagger *m*, siehe: (Front-)Ladeschaufel *f*

Behelfsmethode *f* = makeshift method
Behörde *f*, Regierungsdienststelle *f* = authority; governmental agency (US)
Beilegering *m* = spacing collar, spacer
Beimischung *f*, Zumischung *f*, Zusatzstoff *m* = admixture, addition, additive
Beitel *m*, Handmeißel *m*, Handsetzeisen *n* = (wood) chisel
Beiwert *m*, Modul *m*, Kennziffer *f* = modulus (Brit.); module (US)
~ der wirksamen Kohäsion *f*, siehe: Kohäsionsfaktor *m*
~ vom Zustand des Bodens abhängig [*Hochwasser n*] = coefficient of run-off which is dependent on the nature of the catchment
Beiwinkel *m* = lug angle
Beizen *n* [*Holz n*] = staining
~ = pickling
Bekämpfung *f* = control
Bekohlungs|kran *m*, Kohlenkran = coaling crane
~schiff *n* = coaling vessel, ~ craft
Belademaschine *f*, siehe: Lademaschine
beladende (Geräte)Einheit *f* = loading unit
Belagsgut *n*, siehe: Straßenbelageinbaumasse *f*
belastbar [*Walze f*] = ballastable
Belastung *f*, Auflast *f*, aufgebrachte Last *f* = (super)imposed load, surcharge, loading, additional load
~ des Überlaufes *m*; siehe unter „Talsperre *f*"
Belastungs|annahme *f* = assumed load
~fall *m* = case of loading
~messer *m*, Lastenmesser = load(o)meter
~meßdose *f* = load cell
~metamorphose *f* (Geol.) = load metamorphism
~probe *f*, Belastungsversuch *m* = load(ing) test, bearing ~
~-Setzungsdiagramm *n*, Lastsenkungskurve *f*, Lastsetzungskurve = load-settlement curve
~spitze *f*, Bedarfsspitze *f* = peak demand (time)
~stempel *m* = load piston
~versuch *m*, siehe: Belastungsprobe *f*
~vorrichtung *f* [*Baugrunduntersuchung f*] = ground-testing rig

belebter Boden m = organic soil
~ Schlamm m = activated sludge
Belegschaft f, Personal n = staff, personnel, working force
Belemnit m = belemnite
Belemnitellenkreide f = belemnitella chalk
Beleuchtungsmast m, Lichtmast, Leuchtmast, Straßenlampensäule f = (street) lighting column, lighting standard
Belonit m (Min.) = acicular bismuth

belüfteter Beton m; siehe unter „Beton"
~ Überfallstrahl m; siehe unter „Talsperre f"
Belüftungs|leitung f, Luftventil n = air-intake (Brit.); aeration conduit [*automatic siphon*]
~messer m, Luftmengenmesser m, Luftgehalts-Prüfgerät n, Luftmeßgerät n [*Beton* m] = air (entrainment) meter, entrained air indicator

---

Belüftungsmittel n, Betonbelüfter m, Lufteinschlußmittel n, LP-Zusatz m, luftporenbildender Zusatzstoff m, LP-Stoff, Luftporenerzeuger m
    VINSOL RESIN [*ein Destillationsprodukt* n *des Holzteeröles*] [*Trademark*]

    DAREX AEA [*ein TriäthoIaminsalz* n *eines sulfonierten Kohlenwasserstoffes* m] [*Trademark*]

air-entraining agent, air entrainment agent, air-entraining admixture for concrete, air-entraining compound, AEA

    VINSOL RESIN [*Trademark*] [*consists substantially of the petroleum-hydrocarbon extract of pine wood*]
    DAREX AEA [*Trademark*] [*is substantially a triethanolamine salt of a sulfonated hydrocarbon*]

Bemessung f, Dimensionsbestimmung f, Dimensionierung f = dimensioning
~ von Betonquerschnitten mpl **mit Biegung** f **und Längskraft** f = dimensional design of concrete cross-sections for bending and axial load
~ ~ Maschinenleistungen fpl = rating
Bemessungstafel f = design table
benachbartes Bauwerk n = adjacent structure
Benetzbarkeit f = wettability
Benetzen n, Umhüllen n [*mit Bindemittel* n] = coating, wetting; wet mixing (US)
benetzter Querschnitt m = wetted cross section (Brit.); area of waterway (US)
~ Umfang m **des Querschnittes** = wetted perimeter
Benetzungs|mittel n = coating agent, wetting ~
~wasser n, siehe: hygroskopisches Wasser
Benitoit m = benitoite
Benne f [*in der Schweiz*], siehe: Schiebkarre(n) f, (m)
bestmögliche Verdichtung f = optimum compaction

Bentonit m [*ist ein an feinsten Teilchen* $< 0,001$ *mm reicher Kolloid-Ton* m] = bentonite, bentonitic clay
Benutzer m = user
Benzin n, Motoren~, Otto-Kraftstoff m = gas(oline) (or gasolene) (naphtha) (US); petrol (Brit.); Otto type fuel
~abscheider m, Benzinfang m = petrol trap (Brit.); gas(olene) (or gasoline) interceptor (US)
benzin|betrieben = gasoline-driven (US); petrol-driven (Brit.)
~elektrischer Antrieb m = petrol-electric drive (Brit.); gas-electric ~ (US)
Benzin|-Hochfrequenzinnenrüttler m = petrol-driven high frequency immersion concrete vibrator (Brit.); gas(oline) (or gasolene) ~ ~ (US)
~-Hubkarre(n) f, (m) = gas(olene)-powered lift truck (US); petrol-powered ~ ~ (Brit.)
~kanister m = jerrycan, petrol can (Brit.); gasoline (storage) can (US)
~lager n = petrol dump (Brit.)

Benzinmotor — Bergungsschiff

Benzin|motor m, Vergasermotor m, Otto-(Vergaser)motor = gas(oline) engine, gasolene ~ (US); petrol ~ (Brit.); Otto cycle engine
~rüttelstampfer m = petrol engine (operated) vibratory tamper (Brit.); gasoline (or gas(olene)) ~ ~ (US)
~rüttler m, Benzinvibrator m = petrol vibrator (Brit.); gasolene ~ (US)
~stampfer m = petrol-powered rammer (Brit.); gas(olene) (or gasoline) ~ (US)
~stromerzeuger m = petrol-driven generator, ~ generating set (Brit.); gasolene-driven ~, gas(oline)-driven ~ (US)
Benzol n = benzene
~-Unlösliches n = insoluble in benzene, benzene insolubles, extrinsic insolubles
Beobachtungs|stollen m; siehe unter „Talsperre f"
~strecke f, siehe: Versuchsstrecke
~turm m = lookout tower, watch ~
Bepflanzung f = planting
Berapp m, siehe: Rapputz m
berasen, begrünen = to grass down, to sow down to grass
beratender Ingenieur m = consulting engineer
berechnetes Gefälle n, berechnete Fallhöhe f = theoretical height of fall
Berechnung f = computation, calculation
~ der Annäherungswerte mpl, siehe: (An-)Näherungsberechnung f
~ von durchlaufenden Balken mpl = dimensional design of continuous beams
Berechnungs|formel f = formula of computation
~grundlage f = base of calculation
~regen m = design storm
~tafel f, Rechentafel f = chart
~weise f **im Stahlbetonbau** m = design method for reinforced concrete construction
Bereich m, Aktionsradius m, Reichweite f = range, reach
Bereifung f = formation of hoar frost ~ = tire(s) (US); tyre(s) (Brit.)
Bereifungsluftkühler m = air cooler with metal frost depositing surfaces
Berg m, taubes Gestein n = gangue
bergab = downgrade, downhill

Berg|ahorn m, Ur(l)e f, Ehre f, gemeiner Ahorn m, stumpfblättriger Ahorn = sycamore, greater maple
~akademie f = mining academy, school of mines
~asphalt m, siehe: Asphaltgestein n
bergauf = upgrade, uphill
Berg|butter f (Min.) = rock-butter
~fett n = mineral fat [*ozokerite*], ~ tallow [*hatchettite*], mountain tallow [*hatchettite*]
bergfeuchtes Gestein n = fresh rock
Berg|föhre f, siehe: Bergkiefer f
~gipfel m = mountain summit
~grün n = mountain green
~gut n, Fossil n = fossil
~halde f = pit heap, mine-waste ~
~hang m, siehe: Berglehne f
~hang-Entwässerung f = mountain slope drainage
~ingenieur m = mining engineer
~kiefer f, Bergföhre f, Legföhre = mountain pine
~kiesel m = rock flint
~lehne f, Berghang m = mountain slope
~milch f = agaric mineral, rock milk
~öl n = mountain oil
~rüster f, Bergulme f, Haselrüster f = mountain elm, Scotch ~, wych ~
~schaden m = mining damage
~schlag m, Steinschlag m = popping rock, rock fall
~schraffen fpl [*Karte* f] = hill hachures
~see m = mountain lake, (~) tarn
~seife f = mountain soap, rock ~
~senkungsgebiet n, bergbauliches Senkungsgebiet = mining subsidence region
~steiger m = mountain climber
~sturz m, Felsabbruch m, Felssturz m = débris-slide, rock avalanche
~sturzsee m (Geol.) = rock-slide lake
~teer m = mineral tar [*maltha*]
~tobel m (Geol.) = mountain gulch
~tunnel m, siehe: Felstunnel
~ufer n [*Fluß* m] = cliff bank
~ulme f, siehe: Bergrüster f
Bergungs|arbeiten f = salvage works
~geräte npl = salvage appliances
~kran m, siehe: Unfallkran
~schiff n = salvage ship

Berg(werk)halde f = pit heap, mine-waste ~
Bergwerkschacht m, siehe: Grubenschacht
Bergwirtschaft f = mineral industry
berieseln = to sprinkle
Beries(e)lungs|anlage f [*Straßenwalze f*] = water sprinkler tank

~rohr n, siehe: Sprengrohr
Berliner Ring m [*Autobahnring m um Berlin*] = Berlin Orbital Ring Road
Berme f, (Sicherheits)Bankett n = bench (ing) (Brit.); berm
Bermen-Profiliermaschine f = berm shaper, ~ shaping machine

Bernoulli-Satz m

Lagenenergie f, potentielle Energie, Energie f der Lage f

Bewegungsenergie f kinetische Energie f, Energie f der Bewegung f

Bernoulli's theorem, ~ equation

potential energy

kinetic energy

Bernstein m = amber, succinite
~säure f = succinic acid
Berufs|ausbildung f = professional training
~genossenschaft f = trade federation
~krankheit f = vocational disease, professional ~
~praxis f = professional practice
berufs|ständische Vertretung f = corporate (occupational) representation
~widrig = unprofessional
Beruhigungs|becken n; siehe unter „Talsperre f"
Berührungs|überhitzer m = contact superheater
~umprägung f, siehe: Kontaktmetamorphose f
Beryll m (Min.) = beryl
Besamung f, siehe: Ansäen n
Beschaffenheit f, Zustand m = condition
Beschäftigungsverhältnis n = employment
Beschickervorrichtung f, Aufgabevorrichtung = feeding device
Beschickung f, siehe: Aufgabe f
Beschickungs|apparat m, siehe: Speiser m
~aufzug m = feeder skip hoist
~becherwerk n, siehe: Aufgabebecherwerk n
~bunker m, Aufgabebunker = feed tank
~schnecke f, siehe: Schneckenspeiser m
~schurre f, siehe: Aufgabeschurre
~trichter m, Aufgabetrichter = feed hopper
~vorgang m, Aufgabevorgang = feed process

Beschilderung f, Straßensignalisierung f = provision of road signs, sign-posting, signing
Beschleunigungs|bogen m = acceleration curve
~spur f = acceleration lane
Beschneiden n [*Blech n, Träger m*] = shearing
beschottern = to rubble, to ballast
Beschotterung f, Beschottern n = metalling (Brit.); rubble work
beschränkte Ausschreibung f; siehe unter „Angebot n"
~ Platzverhältnisse f = confined quarters
Beschriftung f, Beschriften n = lettering
Beschürfung f, siehe: Schürfen n
Beseitigen n, Beseitigung f = removal
Besenschleppe f = broom drag
besiedeln = to populate
Besohlung f, Aufvulkanisieren n eines neuen Laufstreifens m = topcap
Besprengen n, Berieseln n, Beries(e)lung f = sprinkling
Beständigkeit f [*Emulsion f*] = stability
Beständigkeitsprüfung f, Haltbarkeitsprüfung f, Dauerhaftigkeitsprüfung = durability test
Bestandsaufnahme f = stock-taking
Bestimmung f des Alkoholgehaltes m von Alkohol-Wasser-Mischungen f pl = alkoholometry
Bestimmungsort m = destination
Betanken n = (re-)fuelling
Betätigungshebel m, Bedienungshebel, Steuerhebel = operating lever

Beton

Beton, Zementbeton *m* — concrete, cement ~
  AEA-~, siehe: belüfteter ~
  AEROKRET-Gas~ — AEROCRETE [*Trademark*]
  antiseptischer ~ — antiseptic ~
  Auf~, Ober~ — top (course) ~
  Baustellen~ — field ~, job-mix ~
  Bauwerks-~, siehe: Konstruktions~
  belüfteter ~, AEA-~, Luftporen~, Bläschen~ — air-entrained ~, air-entraining ~
  ~ mit leichten Zuschlagstoffen *mpl* — lightweight aggregate ~
  Bims~ — pumice ~
  Bläschen~, siehe: belüfteter ~
  Bruchstein~, siehe: Zyklopen~
  Dampfgas~ — steam-cured gas-formed ~
  Decken~, siehe: Straßendecken~
  Einkorn~ — short range aggregate ~
  Eis~ — ice ~
  entfeinter ~, Schütt~ — no-fines ~ (Brit.); popcorn ~ (US)
  erdfeuchter ~, steifer ~ — no-slump ~, "dry" ~, stiff ~
  erhärteter ~, Fest~ — hardened ~
  Fertig~, siehe: Transport~
  Fest~, erhärteter ~ — hardened ~
  flüssiger ~, siehe: Guß~
  Frisch~, unabgebundener ~ — fresh(ly-mixed) ~, unset ~
  frühstandfester ~ — ~ with high early stability
  frühtragfester ~ — ~ with high early strength, high-early-strength ~
  Füll~, siehe: Mager ~
  Fundament~ — foundation ~
  Gas~ — gas-formed ~, (chemically) aerated ~, aerated cement
  Gefälle~ — sloping ~
  gering beanspruchter ~ — non-stressed ~
  gerissener ~ — cracked ~
  gewöhnlicher ~, siehe: Schwer~
  Glas~ — glazed reinforced ~
  Grob~ — coarse ~
  Großkorn~ — ~ with large aggregate
  grüner ~, siehe: junger ~
  Guß~, Rinnen~, flüssiger ~ — chuted ~
  handgemischter ~ — hand-mixed ~
  Hochbau~ — building ~
  Hochofenschlacken~ — slag ~
  Holz(faser)~, Holzwolle~ — wood fibre ~ (Brit.); ~ fiber ~ (US)
  Holzmehl~, Sägemehl~ — sawdust ~
  Isolier~ — insulating ~
  junger ~, grüner ~ — green ~
  Kesselschlacken~, Lösch(e)~ — (boilerhouse) cinder ~, ashes ~; (boiler) clinker ~ (Brit.)
  Kies~ — ~ made from natural aggregates

Beton

Kokslösch(e)~	breeze ~
Konstruktions~, Bauwerks~	structural ~
Kontraktor~	tremie ~, fixed ~ ~
Kunstharz~	~ with artifical resin admixture
Leicht~ [in Deutschland Raumgewichte von 250 bis 1800 kg/m³]	light(-weight) ~
Luftporen~, siehe: belüfteter ~	
Mager~, Füll~, Spar~, zementarmer ~	lean(-mixed) ~
maschinell gemischter ~	machine-mixed ~
Massen~	mass ~, bulk ~, concrete-in-mass
nagelbarer ~, Nagel~	nailing ~
Ober~, Auf~	top (course) concrete
Ort~	cast-in-place ~, ~ cast in position, ~ cast in situ, poured-in-place ~
Poren~, siehe: Zellen~	
Portlandzement~	Portland cement ~, P. C. C.
Prepakt~, vorgepackter ~, Schlämm ~, Skelett~	Prepakt ~, prepacked ~, grout-intruded ~
Pump(kret)~	pumping ~, pumped ~, pumpcrete
Rinnen~, siehe: Guß~	
rißbewehrter ~	crack-reinforced ~
Rüttel~, Vibrations~	vibrated ~
Rüttelgrob~	vibrated coarse ~
Sack~ unter Wasser	underwater ~ filled in bags
Sägemehl~, siehe: Holzmehl~	
Sand~ [1. im Zuschlagstoff kein oder nur wenig grobes Korn > 7 mm; 2. Zement-Sand-Gemisch mit einem Mischungsverhältnis von 1:4 bis 1:20]	sand ~ [1. concrete with no or little coarse aggregate > 7 mm; 2. cement-sand mixture from 1:4 up 1:20]
Saug~, siehe: Vakuum~	
Schalstocher~	rodded ~, puddled ~
Schaum~ [Poren fpl mit Luft f gefüllt]	foam(ed) ~, ~ areated with foam
Schill~ [Seemuschelschalen als Zuschlagstoff]	oyster-shell ~
Schlämm~, siehe: Prepakt~	
Schleuder~	centrifugally cast ~, spun ~
Schock~, Stoß~ [250 Schläge/min.]	concrete compacted by jolting
Schotter~	ballast ~
Schraub~	screwcrete
Schütt~, siehe: entfeinter ~	
Schwer~, ~ mit geschlossenem Gefüge n, gewöhnlicher ~ [in Deutschland Raumgewichte von 1800 bis 2750 kg/m³]	heavy ~, high-density ~
Schwerst~ m [in Deutschland Raumgewichte von 2750 bis 5000 kg/m³]	super-heavy ~
Sicht~	exposed ~
Skelett, siehe: Prepakt~	
Spann~, siehe: vorgespannter ~	
Spar~, siehe: Mager~	

Beton — Betonbau

Splitt~ | ~ made from natural and broken aggregates

Spritz~, Torkret~ | jetcrete, gun-applied concrete, air-placed concrete, shotcrete, gunite, pneumatically placed ~, gunned ~

Stahl~ [*früher: Eisen*~] | (steel) reinforced ~; [*deprecated: ferroconcrete*]

statisch bewehrter ~ | statically reinforced ~
steifer ~, siehe: erdfeuchter ~
Stoß~, siehe: Schock~
(Straßen)Decken~ | pavement ~; paving ~ (US)
Transport~, Fertig~ | ready-mixed ~
  Nachmischen n | agitating
  Trocken- und Naßmischen n während der Fahrt f | truck mixing
  Naßmischen n während der Fahrt f | shrink-mixing, partial mixing
Transportmischer~ | transit-mix(ed) ~, truck-mixed ~
Trichter~ | tremie(d)~, tremie(d) grout
unabgebundener ~, siehe: Frisch~
unbewehrter~ | non-reinforced ~, unreinforced ~, plain ~

Unter~ | rough ~, sub-~, base course ~
Unterwasser~ | underwater ~
Vakuum~, Saug~ | VACUUM CONCRETE [*Trademark*]
vorgepackter ~, siehe: Prepakt~
vorgespannter ~, Spann~ | pre-stressed ~
Vorsatz~ | face ~
Walz~ | rolled ~
wasserdichter ~ | watertight ~
Weich~ | high-slump ~, plastic(ised) ~, buttery ~

Zellen~, Poren~, aufgeblähter ~ | cellular-expanded ~
Ziegelsplitt~, Trümmerschutt~ | crushed (clay) brick ~, crushed brick aggregate ~

Ziegelsplitt-Schütt~, Trümmerschutt-~, Schütt~ | crushed (clay) brick aggregate no-fines concrete
Zier~ | ornamental ~, decorative ~
Zyklopen~, Bruchstein~ | cyclopean ~, rubble ~

Beton|ablauf(ge)rinne f, (n) = concrete dish, ~ catch-gutter, ~ surface channel
~abwasserrohr n = concrete sewer pipe
betonaggressiv = aggressive to concrete
Beton|anlieferung f = concrete delivery
~arbeiten f = concrete work(s)
~armierung f, siehe: Bewehrung f
~(auf)bereitung f = concrete fabrication
~aufbruchhammer m = concrete breaker
~aufbruchstahl m = concrete breaker point, ~ ~ steel
~aufzug m = concrete hoist
~ausbesserung f = concrete reintegration
~auskleidung f = concrete lining
~automat m; siehe unter „Betonmischer m"
~bahnautomat m, Fabrikat ABG = concrete vibrator and finisher with rotating (or rotary) grading screed, revolving paddle finisher
~bau m = concrete constructional work, ~ construction

Beton|bauer *m* = concretor
~baumaschinen *fpl* = concrete machinery
~beanspruchung *f* = stressing of concrete
~belüfter *m*, siehe: Belüftungsmittel *n*
~belüftungsmesser *m*, siehe: Belüftungsmesser
~bereitung *f*, siehe: Betonaufbereitung
~bestandteil *m*, Betonkomponente *f* = concrete ingredient
~bewehrung *f*, siehe: Bewehrung
~block *m* = concrete block
~blockbuhne *f* = concrete block groyne (Brit.); ~ ~ groin (US)
~blockmaschine *f*, siehe: Beton(form)steinmaschine
~-Bogengewichts(stau)mauer *f*; siehe unter „Talsperre *f*"
~bogenrippe *f* = concrete arch rib
~bohle *f* = concrete plank

~bordsteingerät *n* = concrete curb-stone building machine; ~ kerb(stone) ~ ~, ~ kirb(stone) ~ ~ (Brit.)
~brecher *m* = concrete breaker
~brechsand *m*; siehe unter „(Beton-)Zuschlagstoffe *mpl*"
(~)Brunnenring *m* = concrete cylinder
~büchse *f*, Betonlöffel *m* [*Tiefbohrtechnik f*] = dump bailer
~-Bürgersteigplatte *f* = concrete sidewalk slab (US); ~ footpath ~ (Brit.)
~dachplatte *f* = concrete roof slab
~dachstein *m* = concrete roofing tile, cement roof tile
~dachsteinautomat *m*, Zementdachsteinautomat *m* = automatic concrete roofing tile machine
~decke *f* = concrete floor

Betondecke *f*, Betonbelag *m*, Zement~
einschichtig einbauen
zweischichtig einbauen
zweischichtig naß auf naß einbauen

Messung *f* der Stärke *f* von Betondecken *fpl* mittels dynamischer Verfahren *npl*

(cement) concrete pavement
to pour in one lift
to pour in two lifts
to place the top layer in position before the initial set of the bottom layer
measurement of the thickness of concrete pavements by dynamic methods

---

Betondecken|balken *m* = precast concrete joist
~fertiger *m*, siehe: Beton(fahrbahn)fertiger
~geräte *npl* = concrete paving equipment
~hebegeräte *npl* = concrete slab raising equipment
(Beton)Deckenhebeverfahren *n* durch Einpressen von einem aus Feinsand, Mo,

Schluff und Kolloidmaterial als Zuschlag, Zement als Bindemittel und Wasser als Verflüssiger bestehendem Gemisch bei Setzung von Betonfahrbahnplatten, Mud-Jack-Verfahren = mud-jack(ing) (of pavements slabs), mud-jack treatment

Betondecken|innenrüttler *m*; siehe unter „Betonrüttelgeräte *npl*"
~überzug *m* = concrete resurfacing

Beton(decken)verteiler *m*, Betonstraßenverteiler
~ mit Rand-Tauchvibratoren *mpl*
Stetig(beton)verteiler *m*

(Beton)Schneckenverteiler *m*
(Beton)Schneckenverteiler *m*, Fabrikat JAEGER
Schnecken(beton)verteiler *m* mit Glättelement *n*

concrete spreader, ~ spreading machine, ~ distributor, ~ pavement spreader
~ ~ with side form vibrators
continuous type (concrete) distributor (or spreader, or spreading machine)
screw spreader
JAEGER spreader

combination screw-screed spreader

Beton(decken)verteiler — Betonfang(e)damm

Betonverteiler *m* mit hin- und hergehender Verteilerschaufel *f* (oder Schrapperschaufel, oder Wendeschaufel), Schaufelverteiler *m*, Fabrikat BLAW-KNOX COMPANY, PITTSBURGH, USA = BLAW-KNOX spreader-vibrator

Schaufel(beton)verteiler *m*, Schild(beton)verteiler = transverse spreading blade concrete spreader, reciprocating blade spreading machine, blade spreader, blade-type spreading machine

Betonverteilungswagen *m*, (Beton-)Querverteiler *m* = trough-type concrete distributor, hopper spreader, box spreading machine, box (type) (concrete) spreader, box hopper distributor, hopper-type spreading machine

~ ohne Bodenplatte *f* = open-bottomed ~ ~ ~, spreading machine without bottom doors

Betonverteilungswagen mit Bodenplatte *f* = controlled-discharge door ~ ~ ~, spreading machine fitted with bottom doors

(Beton)|Dichtungsmittel *n*, siehe: Dichtungsmittel

~diele *f* = precast slab floor

~dosierwaage *f*, Betonmischwaage = concrete batcher scale

~druckfestigkeit *f* = concrete compressive strength

~druckrohr *n* = concrete pressure pipe

~ebner *m* = straight edge

~einbau *m*, Betoneinbringung *f* = placement (or pouring, or depositing, or placing) of concrete, concrete pour

~einbringung *f* durch Pumpen *n* = pumpcrete placement

~einpreßmaschine *f* = concrete grouter, ~ pressure grouting machine

~einrüttelgeräte *npl*, siehe: Betonrüttelgeräte

~(ein)rüttlung *f*; siehe unter „Betonrüttelgeräte *npl*"

~eisenbiegemaschine *f*, s.: Biegemaschine

~eisenbieger *m* = reinforcement bar-bender, rod bender

~eisenhandbieger *m* = hand operated bar-bender

~eisen(hand)schneider *m* = hand operated bar cutter, bar cutter, bar cutting shears, reinforcement bar shear cutter, rod shear

~eisenschere *f* (oder Betonstahlschneidemaschine *f*) mit elektrischem Antrieb *m* = electric reinforcement bar cutting machine

~emulsion *f* = concrete emulsion

~fabrik *f*, Großbetonanlage *f* = concrete mixing plant, concrete central-mix plant, central batching and mixing station, central weigh batching and mixing plant, wet and dry batch concrete plant, automatic batch plant

~fabrik *f* als Reihenanlage *f* = concrete mixing plant with belt conveying

~fabrik *f* als Turmanlage *f*, siehe: Turmbetonzentrale *f*

~fabrik *f* System JOHNSON, siehe: JOHNSON-Turm *m*

~(fahrbahn)fertiger *m*, Betondeckenfertiger *m* = concrete (pavement) finisher, concrete finishing machine

~(fahrbahn)platte *f*, Straßenbetonfeld *n*, Straßenbetonplatte = concrete (road) slab, paving~, highway~, road-way~, road bay, road panel, road slab

~(fahrbahn)platte *f* mit nachträglichem Verbund *m* = post-tensioned highway slab

~fang(e)damm *m* = concrete cofferdam

Beton|fassadenplatte f, Betonwerksteinplatte = concrete facing slab
~**feinsand** m; siehe unter „(Beton)Zuschlagstoffe mpl"
~**feld** n, Betonplatte f, Feld n = concrete bay, ~ (pavement) slab
(~)**Fertigbehandlung** f = finishing operations
~**fertiger** m, siehe: Beton(fahrbahn)fertiger
(~)**Fertigteil** m, n, Formling m, Fertigbetonteil = precast (concrete) unit, prefabricated (~) ~, precast structural element
~**festigkeit** f = concrete strength
~**fibel** f = concrete primer
~**förderapparat** m = concrete placing machine, ~ placer, ~ handling machine
~**förderleitung** f = concrete discharge pipe
~**förderung** f = concrete placement, ~ placing
~**formöl** n = concrete mo(u)ld oil
~**formstahl** m = deformed (concrete) (reinforcing) bar
~**(form)steinmaschine** f, Betonblockmaschine f, Steinfertiger m, Steinformmaschine f, Stein(fertigungs)maschine = (concrete) block (-making) machine, (~) block-forming ~, (~) building block ~
~**(form)steinprüfpresse** f = (concrete) ~ block testing machine
~**(form)steinwerk** n, Betonsteinbetrieb m = (concrete) block plant, blockyard, concrete brick plant
(~)**Fugenschleifgerät** n; siehe unter „Fuge f"
(~)**Fugenschneider** m; siehe unter „Fuge f"
~**fugenunterhaltung** f = concrete pavement joint maintenance
~**füllung** f = concrete filling
~**gefüge** n = concrete texture
~**-Gewichts(stau)mauer** f = concrete gravity dam
(~)**Gießmast** m = concrete chuting (or placing) mast, gin pole type concrete spouting plant
(~)**Gießrinne** f = concrete chute
(~)**Gießrinnenanlage** f = concrete spouting plant
(~)**Gießrohr** n Betonhosenrohr n = concrete placing tube
(~)**Gießturm** m = concrete chuting (or placing) tower, elevator tower, cage type concrete spouting plant, tower concrete spouting plant
~**glätter** m = float
~**grobsand** m; siehe unter „(Beton)Zuschlagstoffe mpl"
~**härtemittel** n, Härtungsmittel n, Betonhartstoff m = concrete hardening agent, ~ hardener, integral floor hardener, surface ~
~**hebeanlage** f, Betonhebewerk n = concrete-elevating plant (or gear)
~**hinterfüllung** f, siehe: Betonummantelung f
(~)**Hohlblockstein** m, siehe: Hohlblockstein
~**hosenrohr** n, siehe: (Beton)Gießrohr
Betonier|aggregat n = concrete paving machine
~**anlage** f = concreting plant
~**bandturm** m = concrete belt type placing tower
~**bett** n = casting bed
~**bettform** f = casting bed mo(u)ld
~**brücke** f **mit Gleßrinnen** fpl = concrete distribution service gantry with chutes (Brit.); ~ ~ trestle ~ ~ (US)
~**bühne** f = concrete placing (or pouring, or placement) platform

---

Betonieren n, **Betonier(ungs)arbeiten** f = concreting
~ unter Wasser n = under-water ~
einbetonieren = to concrete in
~ bei Frost m = cold weather concreting
Betonierabschnitt m = ~ section

Betonierkolonne — Betonmischer

Betonierkolonne *f* = concreting gang
Betonierungsplatz *m*, Herstellungsplatz = casting yard
Betonierzug *m* = concreting train; paving ~ (US)
Beton|karre(n) *f*, *(m)*, siehe: Beton(rund)kipper *m*
~**kern** *m*; siehe unter „Talsperre *f*"
~**kernbohrmaschine** *f*, siehe: Kernbohrgerät *n*
~**kerndamm** *m*; siehe unter „Talsperre *f*"
~**kies** *m*; siehe unter „(Beton)Zuschlagstoffe *mpl*"
~**kipper** *m*, siehe: Beton(rund)kipper
(~) **Kippkübel** *m* [*Bauaufzug m*] = tipover (concrete) bucket, concrete tipping skip, concrete tipping hopper

~**klotz** *m* = concrete block
~**kolben** *m* [*die in die Rohrleitung eingeschobene Kesselfüllung eines Druckluftbetonförderers*] = batch
~**komponente** *f*, Betonbestandteil *m* = concrete ingredient
~**kriechen** *n* = creep of concrete
~**kübel** *m*, siehe: Betonschuttkübel
~**labor(atorium)** *n* = concrete lab(oratory)
~**lieferwerk** *n* = commercial ready-mix plant, ~ concrete ~
~**löffel** *m*, siehe: Betonbüchse *f*
~**mantel** *m* [*Tunnel m*] = concrete lining
~**mauerung** *f*, Stollen(aus)betonierung *f* = in-situ concrete facing (or lining), tunnel concreting
~**mauerwerk** *n* = concrete masonry

Betonmischer *m*, **Betonmischmaschine** *f*
Aufzugskasten *m*, (Schräg)Aufzugskübel *m*, Kippkübel *m*, Vorfüllkasten *m*, Mischer(beschickungs)kübel, Beschikkerkübel, Beschickeraufzug *m*, Beschickerkasten *m*
Aufzugs-Klein(beton)mischer *m*

Aufzugskübelrahmen *m*, (Schräg-)Aufzugsschienen *fpl*
Aufzugskübelwaage *f*, Mischer(beschickungs)kübelwaage
Austragsmischer *m*, siehe: Durchlaufmischer *m*
Austragung *f*
Austragungsschurre *f*
Betonautomat *m*, siehe: Durchlauf-(Beton)Zwangsmischer *m*
Betonmischer *m* mit Handschrapperbeschickung *f* des Aufzugskübels *m*

Betontransportwagen *m* mit aufgebautem Rührwerk(smischer) *n*, *(m)*, siehe: Nachmischer *m*
Betonzwangsmischer, siehe: Zwangsmischer
Chargen-Beton-Zwangsmischer *m*
Chargenmischer *m*, siehe: Periodenmischer *m*
Doppel-Konus-Kipptrommelmischer *m*
Doppeltrommel(beton)mischer

concrete mixer, concrete mixing machine (loading) skip, mixer hopper, open-end skip, folding weigher, power-operated skip, side-loader, (loading) hopper

small-capacity (concrete) mixer with winch
inclined guides, trackway for skip rollers

hopper scale

discharge
discharge chute, pouring chute

concrete mixer fitted with mechanical skip loader attachment, scraper-fed concrete mixer

batch-type concrete pug-mill (mixer)

duo-cone tilting type mixer
double-drum (concrete) mixer

Betonmischer

Durchlaufmischer *m*, Mischer *m* mit Schurrenaustragung *f*, Austragsmischer, Freifall-Durchlaufmischer — closed drum (concrete) mixer with tipping chute discharge

Durchlauf-(Beton-)Zwangsmischer *m*, Stetig(beton)zwangsmischer *m*, kontinuierlicher (Beton-)Zwangsmischer *m*, Betonautomat *m*, Konti-Mischer — constant-flow (or continuous) (concrete) pug mill mixer

Einseilaufzug *m* — single rope (or cable) hoist

Eintrog-Zwangsmischer mit vertikalem Rührwerk *n* — single-shaft pug(-)mill mixer

Freifall-Chargen-Kipptrommelmischer [*ortsfest*], Fabrikat THE T. L. SMITH COMPANY, MILWAUKEE 45, WISCONSIN, USA — SMITH TILTER [*Trademark*]

Freifallchargenmischer *m* — free fall (type) batch mixer, gravity batch ~, rotary batch mixer

Freifall-Durchlaufmischer *m*, siehe: Durchlaufmischer

Freifallmischer *m*, siehe: Trommelmischer

Freifallmischer mit Umkehraustragung *f*, siehe: Umkehr(trommel)(beton)-mischer

Freifallmischung *f*, Freifallmischen *n* — lifting, dropping and turning mixing action

Gegenstrom-Schnellmischer *m*, Tellermischer — counter-current revolving-pan mixer

Großbetonmischer — volume-production concrete mixer

Kippkübel *m*, siehe: Aufzugskasten *m*

Kipptrommelmischer *m* — tilting (drum) mixer, tilt(-drum) mixer

Knetmischer *m*, siehe: Zwangsbetonmischer mit vertikalem Rührwerk *n*

kombinierter Nach- und Liefermischer *m*, Fabrikat THE T. L. SMITH COMPANY, MILWAUKEE 45, WISCONSIN, USA [*als „Liefermischer" mit der Anlage für die Wasserzugabe*] — SMITH MOBILE [*Trademark*]

Konti-Mischer, siehe: Durchlauf-(Beton-)Zwangsmischer

kontinuierlicher (Beton)Zwangsmischer *m*, siehe: Durchlauf-(Beton-)Zwangsmischer

Kübelaufzugsmischer — elevating hopper mixer

Mischer mit 280 Liter Fassungsvermögen für ungemischtes Material und 195 Liter Leistung in fertiger Mischung — mixer 10/7 [*capacity is ten cubic feet unmixed and seven cubic feet mixed*]

Mischerführer *m* — mixer driver

Mischer *m* mit Schurrenaustragung *f*, siehe: Durchlaufmischer

Mischschaufel *f* — mixing (or helical, or baffle) blade

Betonmischer — Betonmischwaage 85

Nachmischer *m*, Betontransportwagen *m* mit aufgebautem Rührwerk(smischer) *n*, (*m*) [*zentrale Betonaufbereitung f*]	agitating (or agitator) conveyor (or truck), truck agitator (US); agitating lorry; agitator [*deprecated*] (Brit.)
Nachmischer *m* [*ohne Fahrzeug n*]	agitator, remixer
Periodenmischer *m*, Chargenmischer, Stoßmischer, absatzweise arbeitender Mischer	batch mixer
Reibradbetonmischer *m*	friction wheel-drive concrete mixer
Sackaufschneider *m*	bag cutter
Seelemann-Regulus-Mischer *m*, REGULUS-Beton-Mischautomat *m* [*Bindemittel n und Zuschlagstoffe f laufend im Mischungsverhältnis n zugeteilt*]	Seelemann-Regulus mixer [*aggregate and cement is measured by means of feed screws, giving a continuous output of concrete*]
Stetig(beton)zwangsmischer *m*, siehe: Durchlauf-(Beton-)Zwangsmischer	
Stoßmischer *m*, siehe: Periodenmischer	
Straßen(beton)mischer *m*, Straßenbetoniermaschine *f*	rotating drum paver mixer, travel(l)ing (concrete) mixer (plant), combined mixing and paving machine, (combined) paver, paving mixer, (concrete) paver
Tellermischer, siehe: Gegenstrom-Schnellmischer	
Trogmischer *m*	open-pan mixer
Trommelmischer *m*, Freifallmischer	rotary (drum) mixer, rotary type mixer, (revolving) druem (typ) mixer
Umkehr(trommel)(beton)mischer *m*, Freifallmischer mit Umkehraustragung *f*, Mischer mit Reversier-Mischtrommel *f*, Chargen-Betonmischer mit Wendetrommel	closed drum (concrete) mixer with reverse discharge, (free fall type) non-tilt(ing) (drum) mixer, N. T. mixer
Vakuum~	vacuum~
Vorfüllkasten *m*, siehe: Aufzugskasten	
Wasserbehälter *m*	water (measuring) tank
Wasseruhr *f*, Wasserzähler *m*, Wasserdosierungsapparat *m*	sight ga(u)ge
Zwangsbetonmischer *m* mit vertikalem Rührwerk *n*, Kneter *m*, Knetmischer *m*	pug(-)mill (mixer)
Zwangsbetonmischer *m* mit horizontalem Rührwerk *n*	pan type concrete mixer
Zwangsmischung *f*, Zwangsmischen *n*	rolling and kneading mixing action, non-lift mixing action
Zweitrog-Zwangsbetonmischer mit vertikalem Rührwerk *n*	two-shaft pug(-)mill concrete mixer

---

Beton|mischplatz *m* = concrete mixing site

~mischturm *m*, Turmbetonzentrale *f*, Betonfabrik *f* als Turmanlage *f* = concrete mixing tower

~mischung *f* = concrete mix(ture)

~mischungsverhältnis *n* = concrete proportion

~mischwaage *f*, Betondosierwaage = concrete batcher scale

Beton|montagebau m = precast (concrete) building
~ortpfahl m; siehe unter „Gründungspfahl m"
~packlage f, Kleinschlag m aus Betonbrocken mpl, Betonschotter m = (aggregate of) broken concrete, concrete hardcore
~pfahl m; siehe unter „Gründungspfahl m"
~pfahlwerk n = concrete pile making plant
~pflasterstein m = concrete paving sett
~pfropfen m, Betonplombe f = concrete plug
~pfropfen m; siehe unter „Bagger-Senkkastengründung f"
~platte f, siehe: Betonfeld n
~platte f = concrete tile
~plattenfundament n, großflächiges Fundament n, Fundamentplatte f = raft foundation, mat foundation, foundation raft
~plattenheben n, Plattenheben = raising of sunken (concrete) slabs
~plattenpresse f = concrete tile press
~platten-Stampfmaschine f, Stampfmaschine für Betonplattenherstellung f = concrete tile tamping machine
~plombe f, siehe: Betonpfropfen m
~polier m = concrete foreman
~probe f, Betonversuch m = concrete test
~probewürfel m, siehe: Betonwürfel
~prüfhammer m = concrete test hammer
~prüfpresse f, siehe: Prüfpresse

~pumpe f = concrete pump, pumpcrete machine
~pumpe f System **TORKRET**, Torkretpumpe f [*Trademark*] = TORKRET concrete pump
~querverteiler m, siehe: Betonverteilungswagen m
~rinnstein m = concrete channel
~rohrform f, siehe: Zementrohrform
~rohrherstellung f in Rohrgräben mpl = pipe-casting in trenches
~rohrmaschine f, (Beton)Rohrfertigungsmaschine = concrete pipe making machine
~rohrpresse f, Presse f für Betonrohrherstellung f = concrete pipe press
~rohrprüfpresse f = concrete pipe compression tester
~rohrschale f, Betonschale = concrete split duct
~rohrstampfmaschine f, siehe: Zementrohrstampfmaschine
~rohr-Vibriermaschine f, Betonrohr-Vibrator m, Vibiermaschine f für Betonrohre npl, Vibrationsrohrmaschine, Betonrohrvibrationsmaschine = concrete pipe vibrating machine
~rundbehälter m = concrete circular tank
~rundkipper m, Japaner(karren) m, Japaner-(Kipp)Karre f, (Kipp)-Betonkarre(n) = concrete buggy, hand concrete-cart, rocker-dump hand cart
~(rund)kipper m, Betonschüsselwagen m [*als Schienenfahrzeug* n] = concrete tip wagon (Brit); ~narrow-gage railcar (US)

Betonrüttelgeräte npl, **Betoneinrüttelgeräte**, **Betonrüttler** mpl, **Betonvibratoren** mpl

Außenrüttler m, Außenvibrator m
Betondeckeninnenrüttler(-Fertiger) m, Tauchrüttler-Betonstraßen-Fertiger m

Beton(ein)rüttlung f
Druckluftrüttler m, Preßluftrüttler
Elektro-Innenrüttler m
Elektrorüttler m, Elektrovibrator m, Magnetrüttler m, Magnetvibrator m

concrete vibrating equipment, concreting vibrating plant

external vibrator
full depth internal concrete pavement (or paving/US) vibrator, full depth internal slab vibrator; paving vibrator (US); internal vibrating machine (Brit.)
concrete vibration
pneumatic vibrator, air ~
electric poker vibrator
electric vibrator, electro-magnet ~

Betonrüttelgeräte

handgeführter elektrischer Oberflächenrüttler *m*	electro-powered hand-operated surface vibrator
Hochfrequenz-Schwingverdichter *m*	high-frequency concrete compacting and finishing machine
Hochfrequenzfertiger *m*	
(Innen)Rüttelflasche *f*	vibrating cylinder, ~ head
Innenrüttler *m*, Tauchrüttler, Tiefenrüttler, Innenvibrator *m*, Beton~	internal vibrator, immersion ~, concrete mass ~, (concrete) poker ~, needle ~, pervibrator, concrete vibrator for mass work, spud vibrator for concrete
Innenrüttler *m* (oder Innenvibrator *m*) mit biegsamer Welle *f*, Innenrüttler mit Biegeweller-Motorantrieb *m*	flexible shaft (drive) poker type (concrete) vibrator, flexible shaft internal vibrator
Innenrüttler *m* mit starrer Welle *f*	stiff-shaft vibrator
Magnetrüttler, siehe: Elektrorüttler	
Oberflächenrüttlung *f*	surface vibration
Plattenvibrator *m*, siehe: Rüttelplatte *f*	
Preßlufttrüttler *m*, siehe: Druckluftrüttler	
Rüttler *m* mit Explosionsmotorantrieb *m*	gasoline (or gasolene) vibrator (US); petrol ~ (Brit.)
Rüttelbohle *f*, Vibrierbohle, Vibratorbohle, Verdichtungsbohle	vibrating beam
Rüttel(bohlen)fertiger *m*, schienengeführter Oberflächenrüttler *m* [*mit Glättelement n*]	power-propelled surface vibrating and finishing machine, vibratory finishing machine for concrete pavements, concrete finishing road vibrator, vibratory concrete compacting and finishing machine, road vibrating and finishing machine
Rüttel(bohlen)fertiger *m* ohne Glättelement *n*	road vibrating machine [*the finishing screed is omitted*]
Rüttelflasche *f*, siehe: Innenrüttelflasche	
Rüttelplatte *f*, Plattenvibrator *m*, Plattenrüttler *m*, Vibratonplatte *f*, Schwingungsplatte, Vibrationsplatte	vibrating plate (or pan), pan vibrator, vibration slab, plate vibrator, vibratory baseplate, vibratory base plate compactor, vibrating plate compactor
Rütteltisch *m*, Tischrüttler *m*	shaking table, shaker table
Schalungsrüttler *m*, Beton~	(concrete) form vibrator
Schwingtisch *m*, siehe: Vibriertisch	
Seitenschalungsinnenrüttler *m*	side form vibrator
Stabrüttler *m*, Stabvibrator *m*	internal vibrator with handle
Tauchrüttler, siehe: Innenrüttler	
Tiefenrüttler, siehe: Innenrüttler	
Tischrüttler *m*, siehe: Rütteltisch	
Verdichtungsbohle, siehe: Rüttelbohle	
Vibrationsglätter *m*	vibrating float
Vibrationsmaschine *f* [*Herstellung f von Betonbauelementen npl*]	vibrating mo(u)lding machine
Vibrationsnadel *f*	(immersion) poker, ~ needle

Betonrüttelgeräte — Betonsteinwerk

Vibrationsplatte *f*, siehe: Rüttelplatte
Vibrator-Glättbohle *f* mit Fahrwerk *n* System SAGER & WOERNER, Sa-Woe-Bohle *f* — vibrating screed with travel(l)ing gear
Vibrierbohle *f*, siehe: Rüttelbohle
Vibriertisch *m*, Schwingtisch — (precast concreting) vibration table (or table vibrator, or vibrating table)

Beton|rüttelstampfer *m* [*Straßenbeton m*] = (road) vibrating tamper, concrete tamping and screed board vibrator
~**säge** *f* = concrete saw
~**sägeblatt** *n* = concrete sawing blade
~**sand** *m*; siehe unter „(Beton)Zuschlagstoffe *mpl*"
~**schale** *f*, Betonrohrschale = concrete split duct
~**schale** *f* = concrete shell
~**schalplattenbauweise** *f* = construction with concrete slabs used as formwork
(~) **Schalung** *f*, siehe: Schalung
(~) **Schalungsschiene** *f*, siehe: Seitenschalung *f*
(~) **Schlämmschicht** *f*, siehe: Zementmilch *f*
(~) **Schleifmaschine** *f* mit Biegewelle *f* = flexible grinder, ~ shaft concrete grinding machine
(~) **Schneckenverteiler** *m* = (concrete) screw spreader
~**schneidscheibe** *f* = concrete sawing blade
~**schotter** *m*, siehe: Betonpacklage *f*
~**schürze** *f* = concrete apron
~**schüsselwagen** *m*, siehe: Beton(rund)kipper *m* [*als Schienenfahrzeug n*]
~(**schütt**)**kübel** *m*, Kabelkrankübel *m*, Betontransportkübel = concrete bucket, ~ placing skip
~**schwimmdock** *n* = floating concrete (dry) dock
~**skelett** *n* = concrete frame
~**spannung** *f* = concrete stress
~**sperre** *f*; siehe unter „Talsperre *f*"
~**splitt** *m*; siehe unter „(Beton)Zuschlagstoffe *mpl*"
~**spritzmaschine** *f*, (Torkret-)Zement(mörtel)kanone *f*, Torkretbeton-Spritzmaschine *f*, Druckluft-Spritzgerät *n*, Zementmörtel-Spritzapparat *m* nach dem Torkretverfahren *n* Tektor *m*, Torkretkanone *f* = (pneumatic) concrete gun, cement concrete gunite machine, air placing machine, concrete placing gun, jetcrete gun, Boulder Pneumatic Concretor
~**spritzverfahren** *n*, siehe: Torkretverfahren
~**stahl** *m*, siehe: Bewehrungseisen *n*
~**stahlbiegemaschine** *f*, siehe: Biegemaschine
~**stahlschneidemaschine** *f*, siehe: Betoneisenschere *f*
~**stampfer** *m* = concrete tamper, ~ rammer
Betonstein *m* = (precast) concrete block
~**automat** *m*, Vollautomat, Steinautomat = automatic block(-making) machine
~**betrieb** *m*, siehe: Beton(form)steinwerk *n*
~**form** *f* = concrete block mo(u)ld
~**herstellung** *f* = block making
~**industrie** *f* = concrete block industry, precast products ~
~**-Jahrbuch** *n* = Precast Concrete Year Book
~**maschine** *f*, siehe: Beton(form)steinmaschine
~**presse** *f* = concrete block press, ~ brick ~
~**prüfpresse** *f*, siehe: Beton(form)steinprüfpresse
~**-Rüttelstampfmaschine** *f* = concrete block shaking and tamping machine
~**schlag** *m*; siehe unter „(Beton)Zuschlagstoffe *mpl*"
~**stampfmaschine** *f*, siehe: Stampfmaschine
~**werk** *n*, siehe: Beton(form)steinwerk

Betonstraßenbau — Betonverteiler

Betonstraßenbau m — concrete road construction; concrete road paving (US)

Baustelleneinrichtung f und Arbeitsfolge f mit zentraler Mischanlage f — organizational setup for central batching and mixing
provisorische Zufahrtstraße f zur Materialanlieferung f — temporary road for delivery of materials
Haldenschüttung f — stockpiling
Greifer(kran) m, Greifbagger m, Greifkran m, Greiferbagger m, Baggergreifer m — bucket crane, grab, grabbing crane, grab excavator, grab bucket crane
Becherwerk n, Elevator m — elevator
Zwischenlade-Bunker m für Zuschlagstoffe mpl — aggregate bin
Dosierung f, Abmessung, Zuteilung — batching
Mischen n — mixing
Transport m zur Einbaustelle f — haulage to working face (or laying site)
Planumfertiger m — subgrader
Setzen n von Schalungsschienen fpl — form laying, form setting
Unterlagspapier n, Papierunterlage f, Straßenbaupapier — concreting paper, underlay ~, concrete subgrade ~, sub-soil ~, road lining
Verteiler m — spreader
Fertiger m — finisher, finishing machine
Fugenherstellung f — joint finishing
Sonnenschutzdächer npl — curing tents
Sandabdeckung f, Sandnachbehandlung f — sand curing
Fugenverguß m, Fugenvergußarbeiten f — joint sealing (works)
Einbaubetrieb m — paving run (US)

Beton|straßen(bohlen)fertiger m, Brückenfertiger = concrete road finisher (or finishing machine)
~straßenverteiler m, siehe: Beton(decken)verteiler
~streifen m = concrete strip, ~ lane Pilot~, Richt~ = pilot ~ ~ Zwischen~ = intermediate ~ ~
~tabelle f = concrete table
~technologie f = concrete technology
~transportfahrzeug n = concrete hauler, ~ hauling unit
~transportkübel m, siehe: Beton(schütt)kübel
~transportwagen m mit aufgebautem Rührwerk (smischer) n, (m), Nachmischer m, Rührwagen m [zentrale Betonaufbereitung f] = agitating (or agitator) conveyor (or truck), truck agitator (US); agitating lorry; agitator [deprecated] (Brit.)
~transportwagen m mit Schüttrinne f, Fabrikat MAXON CONSTRUCTION CO., DAYTON, OHIO, USA = DUMPCRETE [Trademark]
~trichter m = concrete placement funnel
~ummantelung f, Betonhinterfüllung f = concrete envelope, ~ haunching
~verdichtung f = concrete compaction
~verdichtungsgerät n = concrete compactor
~verflüssiger m, Plastifizierungsmittel n, plastifizierendes Betonzusatzmittel, BV-Stoff m, Weichmacher m = plasticizer, workability agent; wetting agent (Brit.)
~-Verschlußschwelle f = concrete gate sill
~versuch m, Betonprobe f = concrete test
~verteiler m, siehe: Betondeckenverteiler

Beton|verteilungswagen *m.* (Beton-)Querverteiler *m* = trough-type concrete distributor, hopper spreader, box spreading machine, box (type) (concrete) spreader, box hopper distributor, hopper-type spreading machine
~**vibrator** *m,* Betonrüttler *m* = concrete vibrator
~-**Vorfertigungsstelle** *f,* bewegliches Montagebetonwerk *n* = precast concrete manufacturing yard
~**wandschale** *f* = concrete wall shell
~**ware** *f* = concrete products, precast wares
~**warenfertigung** *f,* Betonwarenherstellung *f* = concrete products manufacture, ~ ~ manufacturing
~**warenform** *f,* siehe: Zementwarenform
~**werk** *n* = concrete products plant, ~ works
~**werk-Bauelement** *n* = concrete masonry unit
~**werkstein** *m* = concrete ashlar, cast stone, artificial stone
~**werksteinplatte** *f,* Betonfassadenplatte = concrete facing slab

---

Betonwirkstoff *m*, Betonzusatzmittel *n* [*wird dem Beton beigegeben*]	additive for concrete; concrete admix (US); admixture
Abbindebeschleuniger *m*	accelerating agent
Abbindeverzögerer *m*	retarding admix(ture)
Blähmittel *n*	gas-forming agent
Dichtungsmittel *n*	damp-proofing and permeability reducing agent
Luftporenerzeuger *m*	air-entraining agent
Mörtelzusatz *m*	grouting agent
Plastifizierungsmittel *n*	workability agent
Puzzolan *n*	pozzolan
Schutzmittel *n* gegen alkaliempfindliche Zuschlagstoffe *mpl*	alkali-aggregate expansion inhibitor
zementartiger Stoff *m*	cementitious material

Betonwürfel *m*, Betonprobewürfel *m*	concrete test cube
Prüfungsalter *m*	age at test
Druckfestigkeit *f,* Würfelfestigkeit *f*	compressive strength, cube ~, crushing ~
Würfelform *f*	cube mo(u)ld
Druckpresse *f,* (Beton)Würfelpresse *f,* Prüfpresse *f*	compression machine

---

Beton|zerrüttung *f* = concrete disintegration
~-**Zertrümmerungsmaschine** *f* = concrete pavement shattering machine

~**zusammensetzung** *f* = concrete composition
~**zusatzmittel** *n,* siehe: Betonwirkstoff *m*

(Beton)Zuschlagstoffe *mpl*, (Beton-)Zuschläge *mpl*	(cement) (concrete) aggregate
natürliche Stoffe *mpl*, Naturmaterial *n*	natural aggregate
natürlicher Feinzuschlag *m*, Betonsand *m* [*Durchgang durch das Rundlochsieb 7 nach DIN 1170*]	natural fine aggregate, natural sand [*this term shall mean an aggregate mainly passing a 3/16 in. B. S. test sieve*]

(Beton)Zuschlagstoffe — Betriebswasserstollen

natürlicher Grobzuschlag m, Betonkies m [*Rückstand auf dem Rundlochsieb 7 nach DIN 1170*]

zerkleinerte Stoffe mpl, gebrochenes Material n
  zerkleinerter Feinzuschlag m, Betonbrechsand m
    Betonfeinsand m [< *1 mm*]
    Betongrobsand m [*3/7 mm*]
  zerkleinerter Grobzuschlag m
    Betonsplitt m [*7/30 mm*]
    Betonsteinschlag m [*30/70 mm*]
  Betonzuschlag(stoff) m nicht größer als 37 mm
  einkörniges Material n

künstliche Stoffe mpl

natural coarse aggregate, natural gravel [*this term shall mean an aggregate mainly retained on a 3/16 in. B. S. test sieve*]
crushed aggregates
  crushed fine aggregate

    crushed stone sand
    crushed gravel sand
  crushed coarse aggregate
    crushed gravel
    crushed stone
  concrete ballast (Brit.) [*containing nothing larger than $1^1/_2$ in.*]
  single-size material [*material a major proportion of whose particles are of sizes lying between narrow limits*]
artificial aggregates

Betonzwangsmischer m; siehe unter „Betonmischer"
Betrieb m = management
(Betriebs)|Anlage f, Einrichtung f = facility, installation, plant
~**anlagen** fpl = service facilities, plant ~
~**anlagen** fpl für den Schwerkraftverkehr m = roadside engineering works to meet the operating requirements of heavy motor traffic
~**auslaß** m, Auslaufbauwerk n [*Talsperre* f] = river outlet, reservoir ~ (works)
~**bereitschaft** f, Betriebsfähigkeit f, betriebsfähiger Zustand m = operating order, running ~, ~ condition
~**dauer** f eines Filters, Betriebsperiode f ~ ~, Betriebszeit f ~ ~ = filter run
~**druck** m, Arbeitsdruck = operating pressure
~**druck** m im **Verteilungsnetz** n = service pressure
~**einnahme** f = operating income
~**erfahrung** f = managerial experience
~**fähigkeit** f, siehe: Betriebsbereitschaft f
~**fehler** m = operating fault
~**ingenieur** m = operating engineer
~**ingenieur** m [*Schweiz*], betriebswissenschaftlich ausgebildeter Ingenieur = industrial engineer

~**kapital** n = working capital
~**kontrolle** f, Betriebsüberwachung f = operation control
~**kosten** fpl, Betriebsausgaben fpl = operating costs, costs of operation, operating expenses
~**mangel** m = operating failure
~**schwierigkeiten** fpl = operating troubles
~**sicherheit** f = operating safety
~**spannung** f = operating voltage
~**spitzenstunde** f [*Straße* f] = peak hour of usage
~**stoff** m, Treibstoff, Kraftstoff = driving fuel, power ~
~**störung** f = break-down
~**studie** f = management study
~**stundenzähler** m = hour meter
~**teil** m, n, Arbeitselement n, Arbeitsaggregat n, Arbeitsorgan n = working part
~**überwachung** f mit **Fernsehgerät** n = TV control of operations
~**umstellung** f = operational change over
~**verhältnisse** npl = operating conditions, working ~
~**verschluß** m; siehe unter „Talsperre f"
~**wasserstollen** m; siehe unter „Talsperre f"

Betriebs|wirtschaftlichkeit f = operating economy

~wissenschaft f = business and management

betriebswissenschaftlich ausgebildeter Ingenieur m [*in der Schweiz: Betriebsingenieur*] = industrial engineer

Betriebszeit f = operating time

~ eines Filters m, n = filter run

Bett|ausfüllung f [*Fluß m*] = gorge fill

~erhöhung f [*Fluß m*] = aggradation of the channel

~schicht f, (Unter)Bettungsschicht = bed(ding course), underlay, cushion (course); sub-crust (Brit.)

Bettungs|reiniger m, Bettungsreinigungsmaschine f [*Eisenbahnbau m*] = ballast cleaner

~schicht f, siehe: Bettschicht

~ziffer f, Druck-Setzungs-Quotient m, Planumsmodul m, Bodenziffer f nach Westergaard = subgrade modulus K, modulus of subgrade reaction K, modulus of soil reaction K

~ziffer f = bedding value

~ziffer f = coefficient of soil (or subgrade) reaction

Bett|vereng(er)ung f [*Fluß m*] = constriction of the channel

~verlust m = loss of level reach water

Beulen n = plate buckling, local ~

Beul|sicherheit f = safety against plate buckling

~spannung f = plate buckling stress

Be- und Entlüftungsstein m [*aus Beton m*] = ventilating block

Bevölkerungsdichte f = density of population

Bevorratung f, siehe: Lagerhaltung f

bewachsener Boden m = vegetated soil

Bewachsung f = vegetation

bewaldet = forested

Bewässerung f mit Abwasser n; siehe unter „Abwasserwesen n"

Bewässerungs|anlagen fpl = irrigation works

~kanal m = irrigation canal

~nebenkanal m, Bewässerungsseitenkanal = irrigation lateral (canal)

~nebenkanal m für eine Farm f = farm lateral

~speicher(becken) m, (n) = irrigation pool

~speicherung f = irrigation storage

bewegliche Brücke f = movable bridge

~ Last f = moving load

~ Schalung f = moving form(s), ~ formwork

~ Sohle f [*Fluß m*] = shifting bed

bewegliches Auflager n = expansion bearing

~ Montagebetonwerk n, Beton-Vorfertigungsstelle f = precast concrete manufacturing yard

bewegte Moräne f = moving moraine

Bewegungs|energie f; siehe unter „Bernoulli-Satz m"

~fortpflanzung f = communication of motion

~lehre f, Kinematik f = kinematics

~metamorphose f = dynamic(al) metamorphism, dynamo-metamorphism

~übertragung f = transmission of motion

~umkehr f = reversal, return of motion

~verdichtung f, siehe: Vibrationsverdichtung

~-Zeit-Analyse f = motion-time analysis

bewehrtes Kabel n, armiertes ~, Panzerkabel = armo(u)red cable

~ Mauerwerk n, armiertes ~ = reinforced brickwork

Bewehrung f, Armierung, Beton~ = (concrete) reinforcement

Bewehrungs|eisen n, Bewehrungsstahl m, Armierungseisen, Armierungsstahl [*früher: Moniereisen*] = (steel) reinforcing bar, reinforcing steel, re-bar, reinforcing rod, concrete ~ ~

~käfig m, Armierungskäfig = reinforcing cage

~kolonne f, Armierungskolonne = barfixing gang (or team, or crew, or party)

~matte f in Rautenform f = diamond-shaped reinforcing mesh, ~ mesh reinforcement, ~ fabric reinforcement

~mattenauslegemaschine f für Gerinneauskleidungen fpl = mesh laying jumbo

~mattenverlegegerät n [*Betonstraßenbau m*] = fabric layer

~stoß m, Armierungsstoß = splice

Bewerbungsschreiben — Biegung

Bewerbungsschreiben n = application letter
Bewertungsverfahren n, Auswertungsverfahren = evaluating method
Bewetterung f; siehe unter „Tunnelbau m"
Bewirtschaftung f, Zwangs~ = rationing
Bewitterungs|kurzprüfung f, siehe: abgekürzte Wetterbeständigkeitsprobe f
~prüfung f = weathering test
bezahlter Urlaub m = paid vacation
Bezeichnungsschild n, Typenschild = name-plate
Bezettelungsmethode f = windshield card method, two-cordon ~
bezogene Verformung f = unit deformation
Bezugs|ebene f, Bezugsfläche f = datum (plane), ~ surface
~horizont m, Leithorizont (Geol.) = datum horizon, key ~, "marker"
~punkt m = referring object, reference mark, reference point
~zeichnung f = reference drawing
B-Horizont m, Anreicherungshorizont, Anreicherungsschicht f, Illuvialhorizont, Einschwemmungshorizont [*Bodenkunde f*] = B-horizon, zone of concentration, zone of illuviation
Biberschwanz(ziegel) m = plain tile

Biege|achse f [*Balken m*] = neutral axis
~balken m, Probebalken = flexure test beam
~beanspruchung f = bending stress, transverse ~, flexural rigidity
~drillknicken n = torsional-flexural buckling
~druckspannung f = compressive stress due to bending
~ebene f = plane of bending
~elastizität f = bending elasticity
biegefest, starr, biegesteif = rigid
Biege|festigkeit f = bending strength
~größe f = bending coefficient
~halbmesser m = bend radius
~knickung f = flexural bending
~maschine f, Profileisen~, Betoneisen~, Betonstahl~, Profilstahl~ = reinforcement (bar-)bending machine, power-operated bar-bender, powered bender, powered rod bender
~moment n = bending moment
~plan m = bending schedule, bar-bending list
~platz m [*Betonbau m*] = steel-bending yard
~presse f = bending press
~spannung f = flexural stress, bending ~

Biegeversuch m, **Biegeprobe** f | bending test
Hin- und Her-~ | alternating ~ ~, test by bending in opposite directions
Schlag~ | shock ~ ~, blow ~ ~
Kerb~ | notch ~ ~
Einkerbhin- und -her~ | alternating notch ~ ~
Kerbschlag~ | notch shock test, shock test with notched test piece
Abschreck~, Härtungs~ | ~ ~ in tempered (or quenched) state
Kalt~ | cold~ ~
Warm~ | warm ~ ~

Biegewelle f, Schlauchwelle = flexible shaft
Biegezug|festigkeit f = flexure strength, flexural ~, tensile (or tension) strength in bending
~festigkeit f [*Betonbalken m*] = beam-tensile strength
~festigkeitsmodul m = modulus-of-rupture (in bending), modulus of rupture in flexure, extreme fibre stress in tension
~festigkeitsprüfung f = tensile bending test
~spannung f = bending tensile stress
Biegung f, **Biegen** n = bending

Biegung f mit Längskraft f = combined bending and axial stress, ~ axial and flexural stress

biegungsfreie Schale f = thin curved shell not subjected to bending

Bienenwabenverband m, Pflasterverband, gabbroider Verband, granoblastischer Verband, Mosaikverband (Geol.) = granoblastic texture

Bieter m = bidder, tenderer

Bietungsgarantie f = bid bond (US)

Bild|samkeit f, siehe: Plastizität f

~stein m, Agalmatolith m (Geol.) = pagodite, agalmatolite

billige Straße f = low-cost road

Billner'sches Vakuumverfahren n, Unterdruck-Oberflächenbehandlung f frischen Betons m, Saugbetonverfahren = VACUUM CONCRETE process

Bims m = pumice

~kies m = pumice gravel

~stein m = pumice stone

binär, aus zwei Elementen npl bestehend = binary

Binde|blech n [Stahlbau m] = batten (plate), stay ~, tie ~

~draht m = binding wire

~erde f, Bodenmörtel m, haftendes Lockergestein n, Bodenbinder m, Binderton m = binder soil, soil mortar, clay (binder), soil matrix, soil binder

~mittel n, Binder m, Straßenbauhilfsstoff m = matrix (Brit.); binder

~mittel n, verkittende Zwischensubstanz f [Beton m, Gestein n] = matrix, cement, cementing material

~mittel n aus Eisen n (Geol.) = ferruginous cement(ing material)

~mittel n aus Kalk m (Geol.) = calcareous cementing material (or cement)

~mitteldosierapparat m = binder-batcher

~mitteldosierung f = binder batching

~mittelhaut f = binder film

~mittelkocher m, Kocher m, Schmelzkessel m = heater, heating kettle, melting tank; boiler [deprecated]

~mittel n mit Haftanreger m = doped binder

~mittel-Sprengrohr n = distributor bar

~mittel-Spritzmaschine f, Bindemittelverteiler m = binder spraying machine, ~ distributor, bitumen ~, bituminous ~, tar/bitumen (Brit.)/asphalt (US) ~, maintenance distributor

~mittelwaage f, Zement(silo)waage = cement weigh(ing) batcher, ~ batcher scale

~mittelwaage f; siehe unter „Mabadam-Maschinenanlage f"

~mittelwabe f = circular cement compartment

~mittel-Zuteilschnecke f, siehe: Zement-Abmeßschnecke

Binder m, siehe: ~schicht f

~, siehe: Bindemittel n

~, Dachbinder = truss

~abstand m = spacing of trusses

~gespärre n, Bundgespärre = principal rafters

~material n = binder course material

~schicht f [Straße f] = (surface) base course, base-course (of the surfacing) (Brit.); binder course, base coat, binding course, bottom coat, bottom course; [deprecated: black base] [the layer or layers of surfacing other than the wearing course]

~sparren m = common rafter, principal ~

~ton m, siehe: Bindeerde f

~ziegel(stein) m, Binderstein m = bonder bondstone, header

~(ziegel)schicht f, Binder(Ziegel)steinschicht = heading course, header ~

Binde|schicht f [Straße f] = binder coat, tack coat

~schichtanspritzung f = tack coating

~schicht-Spritzapparat m = tack-coater

~wert m unter Wassereinwirkung f, BWW = binding value under the action of water [bituminous binder]

~zeitregler m = setting time controlling agent

bindig, kohäsiv = cohesive, plastic

bindige Beimengung f = cohesive matter

Bindigkeit f, siehe: Kohäsion f

Binnen|düne f, siehe: Winddüne

~eisdecke f, Eismantel m (Geol.) = continental ice sheet

Binnengewässer — Bitumen 95

Binnen|gewässer n = inland water
~gewässerfahrzeug n = inland craft
~schiffahrt f = inland navigation

~schiffahrtkanal m, künstliche Wasserstraße f = inland (navigation) canal, artifical navigation ~, barge ~

Binnenschiffahrtschleuse f, Sperrschleuse — navigation lock, inland ~
Durchschleusen n, Schleusung f — lockage, locking
Einzelschleuse f — single ~ ~
Hubtor n — vertical lift gate
Kammerschleuse f — chamber ~ ~, lift ~ ~
Kanalschleuse f — canal ~ ~
Klapptor n — trap gate
lichte Duchfahrtshöhe f — craft clearance height
Obertor n — head gate
Schachtschleuse f — shaft ~ ~
Schleppzugschleuse f, Schiffezugschleuse — multiple ~ ~
Schleusengefälle n, Fallhöhe f — lift of a lock
Schleusentor n — lock gate
Schleusentreppe f — staircase flights, staircase locks, chain of locks, stairway of locks
Schleusenwärter m, Schleusenmeister m — lockkeeper
Schwelle f — mitre sill, clap sill, lock sill
Stemmtor n — mitre(d) gate
Umlauf m — culvert
Untertor n — tail gate, lower gate
Verschluß m, Schütz(e) n, (f) — sluice, gate, sluice gate
Zylinderschütz(e) m, (f) — cylindrical sluice (or gate, or sluice gate)

Binnen|see m = inland lake
~wasserstraße f, Binnenschiffahrtstraße f = inland waterway
~wasserstraßentransport m = inland waterway transportation
Binsenmatte f = rush mat
Bio-Filter n, m; siehe unter „Abwasserwesen"
Biotit m (Min.) = biotite
~granit m [*früher: Granitit* m] = biotitegranite, granitite
Bischofsmütze f, siehe: Gehrung f
Bismit m, Wismutocker m, Bi_2O_3 (Min.) = bismuth ochre, bismite

Bismuthin m, Wismutglanz m, Bi_2S_3 (Min.) = bismuthinite, bismuth glance
Bitter|erde f, siehe: Magnesiumoxyd n
~kalk m, magnesiahaltiger Kalkstein m, magnesiahaltiger hydraulischer Kalk m, Dolomitkalk m, dolomitischer Kalkstein m = magnesian limestone, dolomitic limestone, dolomite [*a limestone containing not less than 5 nor more than 40 per cent of magnesium carbonate*]
~salz n, Magnesiumsulfat n = Epsom salt, magnesium sulphate, sulphate of magnesium

---

Bitumen n [*alle natürlich vorkommenden oder durch einfache (nicht destruktive) Destillation aus Naturstoffen hergestellten flüssigen oder festen schmelzbaren oder löslichen Kohlenwasserstoffgemische, in*

bitumen [*a generic term applied to native substances of variable color, hardness and volatility; composed principally of hydrocarbons, substantially free from oxygenated bodies; sometimes associated with mine-*

denen Sauerstoffverbindungen mehr oder weniger, mineralische Stoffe dagegen nur in untergeordnetem Maße enthalten sein können. Definition von H. Mallison 1944]

Bitumen, größtenteils unlöslich in Schwefelkohlenstoff m und größtenteils unverseifbar

ral matter, the non-mineral constituents being fusible and largely soluble in carbon disulfide, yielding water-insoluble sulfonation products. Definition from "ASPHALTS AND ALLIED SUBSTANCES, FIFTH EDITION 1944"]
(asphaltic) pyrobitumen

Bitumen|-Anhänger m = asphalt trailer (US); asphaltic bitumen ∼ (Brit.)

∼-Auskleidung f **für Gerinne** npl = asphaltic canal lining (US); bitumen ∼ ∼ (Brit.)

∼dachpappe f **mit breitem Überlappungsstreifen** m = wide selvage (or selvedge) asphalt roofing (US)

∼decke f = asphalt pavement (US); asphaltic bitumen ∼ (Brit.)

∼-Dichtungshaut f = waterproofing membrane; asphalt ∼ (US); (asphaltic) bitumen membrane (Brit.)

∼-Einspritzregelventil n = asphalt injection control valve (US); asphaltic bitumen ∼ ∼ ∼ (Brit.)

∼emulsion f; siehe unter „Bitumen n im engeren Sinne"

∼-Facharbeiter m = asphalt workman

∼farbe f = asphalt paint (US); asphaltic bitumen ∼ (Brit.)

∼-Fertigauskleidung f **für Gerinne** npl = prefabricated asphalt canal lining (US); ∼ (asphaltic) bitumen ∼ ∼ (Brit.)

∼-Fertigbahn f, **Bitumengewebebahn** = prefabricated bituminous surfacing, P. B. S., prefabricated bituminized hessian surfacing, bituminized jute hessian cloth

∼-Fugenvergußmaterial n = asphalt filler (US)

bitumengetränkt = asphalt-saturated (US); (asphaltic) bitumen-impregnated (Brit.)

bitumengetränkte Dämmplatte f = (asphaltic) bitumen-impregnated insulating board (Brit.); asphalt saturated ∼ ∼ (US)

Bitumengewebebahn f, siehe: Bitumen-Fertigbahn

Bitumen n **im engeren Sinne** [*halbfeste, zähe bis feste, springharte und schmelzbare Produkte von schwarzer Farbe, die bei der Aufarbeitung von Erdölen als Destillationsrückstände gewonnen werden sowie das in Schwefelkohlenstoff lösliche der Naturasphalte. Der handelsübliche Begriff „Bitumen" umfaßt jedoch nur die ersterwähnten Destillationsrückstände*]

dampfraffiniert
geblasen, oxydiert
gekrackt
kerosingefluxt
Verschnittbitumen

schnellabbindend

asphaltic bitumen (Brit.); **asphalt** (US) [*is normally derived from the distillation of selected asphaltic base crude oils*]

steam refined
(air-)blown, oxidized
cracked
kerosine-fluxed
cut-back (∼ ∼) [*the flux used is a distillate*]
 rapid-curing

Bitumen im engeren Sinne — Bitumenpenetration

mittelschnellabbindend	medium-curing
langsamabbindend	slow-curing
Sammelbegriff für Verschnittbitumen und Straßenöle	liquid asphalts, liquid asphaltic materials (US)
Schnellbinder *m*	Rapid Curing Liquid Asphaltic Materials
Mittelbinder *m*	Medium Curing Liquid Asphaltic Materials
Langsambinder *m*	Slow Curing Liquid Asphaltic Materials
Straßenöl *n*	road oil, dust-laying oil
(Asphalt)Bitumenemulsion *f*, Asphaltemulsion *f*, Kaltasphalt *m*	asphaltic emulsion, emulsified asphalt (US); bitumen emulsion, cold (bitumen) emulsion, asphaltic bitumen road emulsion (Brit.); cold asphalt
schnellbrechend, unstabil, labil	rapid setting, labile, quick-breaking
mittelschnellbrechend, halbstabil	medium setting, normal setting, semistable, medium-breaking
langsambrechend, stabil	slow setting, stable, slow-breaking
Zerfall *m*, Brechen *n*	breaking, breakdown
Emulgator *m*, Stabilisator *m*, Schutzkolloid *n*	emulsifying agent, emulsifier, emulsion stabilizer, emulsion stabilizing agent
emulgieren	to emulsify
Emulgation *f*, Emulgieren *n*	emulsification
Schwebezustand *m*	suspension
feinstverteiltes Bitumen *n*	minute globules of bituminous material
Destillationsbitumen *n*	residual asphalt (US); ~ asphaltic bitumen (Brit.)
Straßenbaubitumen *n*, Asphaltzement *m*	asphalt(ic) cement, penetration grade, paving(-grade) asphalt, road asphalt (US); penetration grade bitumen (Brit.) [*a fluxed or unfluxed asphalt specially prepared as to quality and consistency for direct use in the manufacture of bituminous pavements, and having a penetration at 25 w. (77 F.) of between 5 and 300, under a load of 100 g. applied for 5 sec.*]
Kriechen *n*	volume flow

Bitumen|kanone *f* [*Bitumenunterpressung f*] = asphalt gun (US); bitumen ~ (Brit.)

~-Kesselwagen-Erhitzer *m* = asphalt tank car heater (US); asphaltic bitumen ~ ~ ~ (Brit.)

~kocher *m*, siehe: Teer- und Bitumenkocher

~lack = bituminous varnish

~makadam *m*, siehe: Asphaltmakadam

~-Mineralgemisch *n*, bituminöse Mineralmasse *f* = asphaltic bitumen-aggregate mixture (Brit.); asphaltic-aggregate ~ (US)

~penetration *f* = asphalt penetration (US); asphaltic bitumen ~ (Brit.)

Bitumen|pumpe f = asphalt pump (US); asphaltic bitumen ~ (Brit.)
~**schlämme** f = bituminous slurry (Brit.); asphalt(ic) ~ (US)
~**splitt** m, siehe: Asphaltsplitt
~-**Splittdecke** f, siehe: Asphaltsplittdecke
~-**Sprengwagen** m, Druckverteiler m, Tankspritzmaschine f, Großspritzgerät n, Automobil-Sprengwagen m, Drucksprengwagen m, Drucktankwagen, Motor-Spritzwagen m, Rampen-Tankspritzmaschine f, Automobil-Spritzwagen m = bulk bitumen distributor, pressure tank lorry, pressure spray tanker (Brit.); pressure distributor truck, asphalt truck distributor (US); pressure tanker, truck mounted distributor, road oil distributor tanker
~-**Straßenbau** m = asphalt paving (US)
~-**Straßenbaugeräte** npl, Schwarzstraßenbaugeräte, Asphalt- und Teerstraßenbaugeräte = asphalt (paving) equipment (US); machinery for bituminous construction
~-**Umschlaganlage** f = bulk (asphaltic) bitumen installation, bulk (asphaltic) bitumen reception facility (Brit.); ~ asphalt ~ ~ (US)
~-**Umwälz-Erhitzer** m = circulating heater (for heating and unloading tanks of asphalt (US)/asphaltic bitumen (Brit.)
~- **und Teerkocher** m = asphalt and tar (melting) kettle (US); asphaltic bitumen and tar (melting) kettle (Brit.)
~-**Unterpressung** f = asphalt underseal(ing), ~ subseal(ing) (US); asphaltic bitumen ~ (Brit.)
~**vermörtelung** f; siehe unter „Baugrundverbesserung f"
~**verteiler** m = asphalt distributor (US); asphaltic bitumen ~ (Brit.)
bituminiert = bituminized, bituminised
bituminös = bituminous
bituminöse Bauwerkabdichtung f = bituminous damp-proofing and waterproofing
~ **Binderschicht** f, bituminöser Binder m [Straßenbau m] = bituminous binder
~ **Bodenvermörtelung** f; siehe unter „Baugrundverbesserung f"
~ **Decke** f nach dem **Makadamprinzip** n = macadam-aggregate type bituminous pavement
~ **Mineralmasse** f, siehe: Bitumen-Mineralgemisch n
~ **Mischanlage** f = bituminous mixing plant
~ **Mischdecke** f = plant-mixed bituminous pavement
~ **Tragschicht** f [Straßenbau m] = bituminous base course, black base
bituminöser Kalkstein m, Stinkkalk m = bituminous limestone, stinkstone
~ **Makadam** m, siehe: Asphaltmakadam
(~) **Ölschiefer** m = bituminous oil shale, (asphaltic) pyrobituminous ~
~ **Sandstein** m, siehe: Asphaltsandstein
~ **Schutzanstrich** m = bituminous protective coating
~ **Teppich(belag)** m = bituminous (or bitumen) carpet (or mat) (Brit.); asphalt ~ (~ ~) (US)
bituminöses Holz n, siehe: Lignit m
Blähen n [Ton m] = bloating [clay]
Bläh|mittel n, siehe: Metalltreibmittel n
~**pore** f = bubble-hole
~**schiefer** m, aufgeblähter Schiefer m = expanded shale
~**ton** m, aufgeblähter Ton m = expanded clay; bloating clay (Brit.); lightweight aggregate (US)
 Drehofen-Blähton m = rotary kiln expanded clay (Brit.); HAYDITE, FEATHERLITE, ROCKLITE, SOLITE (US) [Trademarks]
 Sinter-Blähton m = sintered expanded clay
Blake'scher Doppelkniehebelbackenbrecher m; siehe unter „Backenbrecher"
blanke Schraube f = turned bolt, finished ~
Blankglühen n = bright annealing
Blase f [Gußasphalt m] = blister
Blasebalg m = (forge-)bellow(s)
blasende Wetterführung f = pressure air supply, forced ~ ~
Blasenkupfer n = blister copper
Blasevorrichtung f, siehe: Luftspülvorrichtung
Blaskopf m, Spülluftkopf [Bohrhammer m] = puff blowing head

Blasversetzen n = pneumatic stowing
Blättchenstruktur f = laminated structure
Blatterde f = leaf mould
Blätter|kohle f = laminated coal, leaf ~
~**schiefer** m = leaf shale
~**serpentin** m (Min.), siehe: Antigorit m
~**ton** m = foliated clay
~**siedestein** m (Min.), siehe: Heulandit m
Blätterung f (Geol.) = foliation
Blatt|feder f = laminated (or flat, or leaf, or blade, or plate) spring
~**silber** n = leaf silver
~**stoß** m, Laschung f = scarf (joint)
~**verdunstung** f, Interzeption f = evaporation from the leaves of plants
Blau|asbest m, Kapasbest m (Min.) = blue asbestos, Cape~
~**brenner** m, Bunsenbrenner = Bunsen (gas) burner
~**eisenerde** f, Blaueisenerz n, Vivianit m (Min.) = (earthy) vivianite
blaues Öl n = blue oil, pressed distillate
Blau|pause f = blue print
~**salz** n, $K_3Fe(CN_6)$ = potassium ferrocyanide
~**säure** f, Zyanwasserstoff m, HCN = hydrocyanic acid

~**ton** m = blue clay
Blech n, Tafel~, Eisen~ = metal sheet, sheet metal, sheet iron
  dickes ~ = plate
  dünnes ~ = tin sheet
~**biegemaschine** f = plate bending machine, sheet metal folding machine
~**bogen** m = plate arch
~**bördelmaschine** f = plate-flanging machine, sheet-bordering ~
~**dichtungsstreifen** m = sheet-metal water stop
~**dicke** f = plate thickness, ga(u)ge of sheet
~**falzmaschine** f = seaming machine
~**gliederband** n, siehe: Plattenband-(förderer) n, (m)
~**haut** f = skin plate
~**kanister** m = sheet metal can
~**kante** f = edge of plate, ~ ~ sheet
~**lehre** f = sheet (or plate) ga(u)ge
~**lochsieb** n = perforated plate sieve, ~ metal screen
~**paket** n = stack of sheets
~**richtmaschine** f = plate straightening machine, sheet metal ~ ~
~**rohrleitung** f = sheet-metal conduit

Blechträger m, **Vollwandträger**   (steel) plate girder; girder (US)
  verminderter Querschnitt m net sectional area
  Gurtplatte f plate
  Stoß m splice
  Versteifung f stiffener
  Steg m, Stegblech n web (plate)
  Flansch m, Flanschblech n flange (plate)
  Futter n packing
  Flanschwinkel m, Winkel   (flange) angle

Blechzylinder m [*Walzenverschluß* m] = plate-steel (roller) gate cylinder
Blei|antimonglanz m, Zinckenit m, PbS × Sb_2S_3 (Min.) = zinkenite
~**arsenat** n = lead arsenate
~**azetat** n, siehe: Bleizucker m
~**azid** n = lead azide
~**benzin** n = leaded petrol (Brit.)
Bleich|erde f, Bleichton m = active earth, bleaching ~

~**kalk** m, siehe: Chlorkalk
~**pulver** n, siehe: Chlorkalk m
~**ton** m, siehe: Bleicherde f
Blei|erz n = lead ore
~**farbe** f = lead paint
~**glanz** m, Galenit m, PbS = galena, lead glance
~**glas** n = lead glass
~ **(hochofen)schlacke** f = lead slag
~**hornerz** n, siehe: Phosgenit m (Min.)

Blei|hydrokarbonat n, siehe: Bleiweiß n
~lasur f, Linarit m, PbSO$_4$ × Cu(OH)$_2$ (Min.) = linarite
~lot n, siehe: Schnurlot
~mennige f (Min.) = minium
~mennige f [*Chemie* f] = red lead
~schere f = soft metal snip
~schlacke f, siehe: Bleihochofenschlacke
~spat m, Weißbleierz n, Kohlenbleispat m, Zerussit m, PbCO$_3$ (Min.) = cerussite, white lead ore
~speise f = lead speiss
~tetraäthyl n, BTÄ, Pb(C$_2$H$_5$)$_4$ = tetra ethyl lead, TEL
~vergiftung f = lead poisoning
~weiß n, Bleihydrokarbonat n, basisches kohlensaures Blei n, Pb$_3$(CO$_3$)$_2$ (OH)$_2$ = white lead, basic lead carbonate
~wolle f = lead wool
~zucker m, Bleiazetat n, Pb(C$_2$H$_3$O$_2$) × 3H$_2$O = lead acetate, acetate of lead, sugar lead
blendehaltig [*Mineral* n] = blendous
blendfrei [*Straße* f] = glare-free, nonglare
Blend|freiheit f = absence of glare
~schutzhecke f = anti-dazzle hedge
Blendung f = dazzle (glare)
Blicksilber n = lightened silver
Blindflansch m, Deckelflansch = blank flange, blind ~
Blinkfeuer n, Blinklicht n [*allgemein*] = intermittent light (or beacon)
~, Blinklicht n [*Lichtdauer* f größer als *Dunkeldauer* f] = occulting light (or beacon) [*a light regularly eclipsed in which the duration of the light is greater than the duration of darkness*]
~, Blinklicht n [*Lichtdauer* f kürzer als *Dunkeldauer* f] = flashing light (or beacon) [*a light regularly eclipsed in which the duration of light is shorter than the duration of darkness*]
Blinklampe f = flash lamp
Blitz|röhre f, siehe: Fulgurit m
~-Rohrzange f = grip wrench
Block m [*nach Fischer und Udluft (Jahr 1936), nach Niggli (Jahr 1938), nach Gallwitz (Jahr 1939) und nach Grengg (Jahr 1942); heißt hier "grobsteiniger Boden"*] 2000 bis 200 mm] = boulder [*2000 to 300 mm*]

~ [*Seilzug* m], siehe: Flasche f
~gletscher m = rock glacier, ~ train, talus train
~gründung f [*Wellenbrecher* m] = "pellmell" concrete blocks (Brit.)
~haus n = log house
Blockieren n [*Rad* n] = locking
Block|lava f; siehe unter „Vulkan m"
~steinformat n = block form
~strand m = shingle beach
~strom m = rock flow, ~ stream
~winde f, siehe: Flaschenzug m
Blume f, (Gesteins)Staub m, Steinmehl n, Gesteinsmehl = flour, stone dust
Blumenesche f, Mannaesche = manna ash, flowering ~
Bluten n, (Aus)Schwitzen n [*Überfluß* m *an Bindemittel* n *bei Schwarzdecken* fpl] = bleeding, ponding, fatting (-up)
~, Wasserabstoßen n, Wasserabsonderung f [*Beton* m] = bleeding, sweating, water gain
Blutregen m = blood rain
Bö f = squall
Bock|dalbe m = raker dolphin
~-Derrick(kran) m = stiff-leg derrick (crane) (US); Scotch ~ (~) (Brit.)
~gerüst n = trestle work
~kran m, Gerüstkran = frame crane
~strebenkonstruktion f = framework of struts and braces
~winde f, Kanalwinde f, Wellbaum m = (hand) crab
Boden m, Erdstoff m, Lockergestein n = dirt (US); soil, earth
~abdichtung f = soil (or earth) waterproofing
~analyse f = soil analysis
~andeckung f = soil (or earth) covering, soiling
~andeckung f von Seitenböschungen fpl = soiling side slopes
~anteil m = soil fraction
~aufschluß m = exploratory work
~aushub m, siehe: Aushub
~belag, siehe: Fußbodenbelag
~beton m, Erdbeton m, Bodenzement m, Zementtonboden m = soil-cement
~bewachsung f, siehe: Pflanzenbewuchs m
(~)Bewässerung f = (soil) irrigation

Boden|bewegung f, Bodenverlagerung f = earth movement, soil ~

~**binder** m, siehe: Bindeerde f

~**druck** m, Bodenpressung f, Flächenpressung f, Flächendruck m [z. B. einer Gleiskette f auf den Untergrund m] = ground pressure, bearing load, road pressure, ground-bearing ~

~**druck(meß)dose** f, Erddruck(meß)dose = soil pressure cell, earth-pressure (measuring) cell

~**eigenschaft** f = soil property
ingenieurbautechnische ~ = engineering ~ ~

~-**Einschnitt** m = soil cutting

bodenentleerender Erdtransportwagen m; siehe unter „Fahrzeuge npl für den Transport m von Boden m und Steinbaustoffen mpl"

Boden|entleerer m [Schachtfördergefäß n] = skip, skep, dumping shaft ~

~**entleerer** m; siehe unter „Fahrzeuge npl für den Transport m von Boden m und Steinbaustoffen mpl"

~**entleerung** f = bottom dump discharge, bottom-dumping

~**entleerungsventil** n = bottom drain valve

(~)**Entnahmestelle** f, Gewinnungsstelle f = borrow source

~**entwässerung** f; siehe unter „Entwässerung f"

~**entwicklungsprozeß** m = soil-building process, soil-forming ~

~**erhaltung** f = soil conservation

~**feuchte** f, Bodenfeuchtigkeit f, Bodennässe f = soil moisture, ground ~

~**fließen** n, Erdfließen n, Fließrutschung f, Murgang m = soil-flow, solifluction, earth flow, solifluxion

~**fördergerät** n, siehe: Erdbewegungsgroßgerät

~**förderung** f **mit Pferd** n **und Wagen** m = leading, teaming (Brit.)

~**förderung** f **mit Schubkarren** mpl = wheeling (Brit.)

~**form** f, Geländeform f = land form

~**fräse** f = rotavator, rotary hoe, rotary tiller, soil pulverizer

~**freiheit** f = ground clearance

~**frost** m = ground frost

~**gare** f = tilth

~**gehbelag** m, siehe: Fußbodenbelag

~**gemisch** n, Bodenmischung f = soil mix(ture), ~ aggregate

~**geologie** f = agrogeology

~**güte** f **in ländlichen Gegenden** fpl = orographical features of the ground in rural areas

~**hebung** f = land upheaval

~**ingenieur** m, siehe: Bodenmechaniker m

~**kabel** n, Erdkabel = underground cable

~**karte** f, Baugrundkarte f = soil map

~**kennzeichnung** f = identification of soils

~**kern** m, siehe: Bodenprobekern

~**klappe** f [Fahrzeug n] = bottom-dump hatch

~**klassifizierung** f = soil classification

~**kolloid** n, Bodenquellstoff m [0,002 bis 0,00002 mm] = (soil) colloid, soil colloidal particle

~**korrosion** f [Rohr n] = underground corrosion

~**kriechen** n, Gekriech n = soil-creep

~**krümel** m, Erdkrümel = soil crumb

(~)**Kultivator** m = (agricultural) cultivator, field ~

~**kunde** f, Pedologie f = pedology

bodenkundliche Vorarbeiten fpl = preliminary soil investigations

bodenlos, ohne Boden = bottomless

Boden|markierung f [Schweiz]; siehe: Straßenmarkierung f

~**masse** f, Erdmasse f = soil mass, earth mass

~**mechanik** f, Erdstoffmechanik f, Baugrundmechanik, Erdbaumechanik, Grundbaumechanik, bautechnische Bodenkunde f = soil mechanics

~**mechaniker** m, Bodeningenieur m = soils engineer

~**mischer** m, Mehrwellen-Boden-Zwangsmischer, Bodenmischmaschine f = non-elevating road-mixer, pulverizing mixer, rotary (speed) mixer, soil-mixer, soil mixing machine, mix-in-travel plant, mix-in-place machine, mix-in-place travel(l)ing plant, rotary soil mixer

~**mischung** f, siehe: Bodengemisch n

Bodenmischverfahren — Bodenvermörtelung

Boden|mischverfahren n, An-Ort-Mischverfahren = mix(ed)-in-place (method), site mixing in place
~**mörtel** m, siehe: Bindeerde f
~**müdigkeit** f = soil sickness
~**nässe** f, siehe: Bodenfeuchte f
~**nebel** m = ground fog
~**öffnung** f = bottom opening
~**physik** f = soil physics
bodenphysikalische Grundlage f = soil physics basis
Boden|platte f, siehe: Fuß~
~**platte** f **mit Doppel(winkel)greifern** mpl = double grouser (track) shoe
~**pressung** f, siehe: Bodendruck m
~**probe** f, Bodenprobestück n = soil sample, ~ specimen, earth ~
~**probe(ent)nahme** f = soil sampling
~**(probe)kern** m = soil core, core of soil
~**(probe)kernnehmer** m = core cutter
~**probenahmegerät** n **mit Metallfolie** f = metal foil sampler
~**profil** n **bei ingenieurgeologischer Untersuchung** f = soil section
~**profil** n **in der landwirtschaftlichen Bodenkunde** f = soil profile
~**prüfung** f = soil test
~**quelle** f = spring of intermediate depth
~**quellstoff** m, siehe: Bodenkolloid n
~**rückstrahler** m = cat's eye
~**satz** m = bottom sediment
~**satzgestein** n, siehe: Schichtgestein
~**satzprobe** f [*Leuchtpetroleum* n] = flock test
~**saugvermögen** n = soil suction
~-**Scherspannungsmeßdose** f = shear cell
~**schichtenverzeichnis** n = soil section sheet (or diagram)
~**schnellvermörtelung** f **für militärische Zwecke** = expeditious military soil stabilization
~**scholle** f, Erdscholle = soil clod
~**schwelle** f, Grundschwelle, Sohlschwelle, Stauschwelle, Unterschwelle [*niederdeutsch: Süll* m, n] = (ground) sill
~**schwingungsrüttler** m = soil vibrator, vibratory (soil) compactor
~**skelett** n = soil skeleton
~**sonde** f, Sondenbohrer m = probing staff, pricker ~

~**spekulation** f = land speculation
~**stabilisation** f, siehe: Baugrundverbesserung f
~**stabilisator** m = soil stabilizer
~**stabilisierung** f, siehe: Baugrundverbesserung f
~**standfestigkeit** f = soil stability
~**struktur** f = soil texture
~**teilchen** n = soil grain (or particle)
~**unebenheit** f = ground irregularity
~**untersuchung** f **an der Oberfläche** f = surface reconnaissance
~**untersuchung** f, Voruntersuchung f **des Baugrundes** m, Untergrundforschung f, Baugrunduntersuchung f = soil investigation, ~ exploration, subsurface ~ (or reconnaissance), foundation exploration (work), soil study, foundation testing, site exploration, sub-soil investigation
~**untersuchung** f **mit Spülstangengerät** n = jet probing, rod sounding
~**untersuchungsbohrung** f = boring for soil investigation
~**verbesserung** f, siehe: Baugrundverbesserung
~**verdichter** m, Bodenverdichtungsgerät n = soil (or earth) compacting machine
~**verdichtung** f, künstliche ~ = soil (or earth) compaction (or densification)
~**verdichtung** f, natürliche ~, Eigensetzung f, Eigenverfestigung f, Konsolidation f, Konsolidierung f = (soil) (or earth) consolidation

(~**verdichtung** f **durch) Einschlämmen** n, siehe: Einspülen n
~**verdichtungsgerät** n, siehe: Bodenverdichter m
~**verfestigung** f= soil solidification, earth ~
~**verfestigung** f **der Oberfläche** f; siehe unter „Baugrundverbesserung f"
~**verlagerung** f, siehe: Bodenbewegung f
~**verluste** mpl [*Elektrolyse* f]=losses in soil
~**vermörtelung** f; siehe unter „Baugrundverbesserung f"
~**vermörtelung** f **mit Salz** n = salt-soil stabilisation (or stabilization)
~**vermörtelung** f **mit Zement** m, Zementvermörtelung = cement-soil stabilisation (or stabilization)

Bodenvermörtelungsmaschine — Bogenfeld

Bodenvermörtelungsmaschine *f*, **Bodenvermörtelungsgerät** *n*	soil stabilizing machine, soil stabilizer, road mixer, soil stabilisation machine
Bodenmischmaschine *f*, Bodenmischer *m*, Mehrwellen-Bodenzwangsmischer	non-elevating road mixer, pulverizing mixer, rotary (speed) mixer, soil mixing machine, mix-in-travel plant, mix-in-place machine, mix-in-place travel(l)ing plant, (rotary) soil mixer
Bodenmischmaschine SAWOE, Raupen-Schneckenfräse *f* [*Hersteller: LINNHOFF, BERLIN*]	SAWOE single-pass machine
Raupenschlepper *m*	caterpillar tracks for propulsion
Fräse *f*	tined rotor
Mischschnecke *f*	gathering rotor
Verteilerschnecke *f*	spreading rotor
Vibratorschleppe *f*	vibrating screed board
Bodenmischmaschine VOEGELE	VOEGELE three-tined rotor machine
Bodenmischmaschine STRABAG	STRABAG single-pass mix-in-place machine
Verteiler *m*	tamping beam
Dreiwellenmischer *m*	three mixing rotors
Bodenmischmaschine SONTHOFEN	SONTHOFEN mix-in-place machine
Vertikal-Zwangsmischer *m*	four vertical shaft rotors
Ein-Gang-Mischer (oder Ein-Gang-Bodenvermört(e)ler *m*) HARNISCHFEGER	SINGLE PASS SOIL STABILIZER
Bodenmischmaschine, Fabrikat ROTARY HOES LTD.	HOWARD SINGLE-PASS EQUIPMENT
Mehrgang(boden)mischer SEAMAN	SEAMAN MIXER
Aufnahmemischer, Aufnehmermischer, Bodenvermörtelungsmaschine mit hochliegendem Zwangsmischer	windrow-type travel(l)ing (or travel) (asphalt) (or road) plant, elevating roadmixer, travel(l)ing (mixing) plant, travel(l)ing mixer for soil stabilisation, road pug travel-mix plant
Aufnahmemischer REISER	REISER travel-mix soil-stabilisation machine
Aufnahmemischer WOOD	WOOD road-mixer
Aufnahmemischer BARBER-GREENE	BARBER-GREENE travel mixing plant

---

Boden|wasser *n* = subsurface water
~**welle** *f* = undulation of ground
~**wind** *m* = surface wind, ground ~
~**zement** *m*, siehe: Bodenbeton *m*
~**-Zement-Gemisch** *n* = soil-cement mixture
~**ziffer** *f*, siehe: Bettungsziffer
Böen|front *f* = squally front
~**gewitter** *n* = line squall
~**kragen** *m* = storm collar
~**regen** *m* = squally rain, ~ shower
~**staffel** *f* = secondary squall front
Boetonasphalt *m* = buton asphalt
Bogen|achse *f* = axis or arch
~**art** *f* = type of arch
~**aussteifung** *f* = arch stiffening
~**balken(träger)** *m*, siehe: Bogenträger
~**brücke** *f* = arch bridge
~**düne** *f*, Sicheldüne *f* = barchan, crescent-shaped dune, barkhan
~**fachwerk** *n* = arch truss
~**feld** *n* = arch panel

Bogen|form *f* = form of arch
~gewichtssperre *f*; siehe unter „Talsperre *f*"
~gewichts(stau)mauer *f*; siehe unter „Talsperre *f*"
~gleis *n* = curved track
~gurt(ung) *m*, (*f*) = arched boom
~gurt(ungs)winkeleisen *n* = arched boom angle iron
~hintermauerung *f*, siehe: Bogenzwickel *m*
~höhe *f* = height of arch
~kämpfer *m*, siehe: Kämpferstein *m*
~küste *f* = curving beach
~lager *n* = arch bearing
~lehrgerüst *n* = arch centering (US); ~ centring (Brit.)
~leibung *f* = intrados, soffit
~linie *f*, Bogenprofil *n* = outline of arch
~mauer *f*; siehe unter „Talsperre *f*"
Bogen *m* mit aufgeständerter Fahrbahn *f* = spandrel braced arch
~ ~ **ausgesteiften Zwickeln** *mpl* = arch with braced spandrels
~ ~ **eingespannten Enden** *npl* = arch with fixed ends, fixed arch
~ ~ **Kämpfergelenken** *npl*, Zweigelenkbogen *m* = two-hinged arch, double-hinged ~, arch hinged at the (a)butments
Bogen|moräne *f* = crescentic moraine
~pfeil *m*, Stich *m* = rise (of arch), upward camber, versed sine
~pfeiler(stau)mauer *f*; siehe unter „Talsperre *f*"
~profil *n*, siehe: Bogenlinie *f*
~rippe *f* = arch rib
~rohr *n* = bend
~rücken *m*, äußere Bogenfläche *f* = extrados, back of arch
~schalung *f* = arch form
~scheitel *m*, Scheitelpunkt *m* = crown, vertex, apex, key, top
~schenkel *m* = haunch
~schub *m* = tangential thrust, thrust of arch
~schütz(e) *m*, (*f*), Segmentschütz(e) Segmentverschluß *m*, Segmentwehr *n* = segment shaped sluice, segmental sluice gate, taintor (or tainter) gate, radial gate

~sehnenträger *m* = polygonal bowstring girder, segmental ~ ~
~sperre *f*; siehe unter „Talsperre *f*"
~sperrmauer *f*; siehe unter „Talsperre *f*"
~stab *m* = bar of arch
~(stau)mauer *f*; siehe unter „Talsperre *f*"
~träger *m*, Bogenbalken(träger) *m* = arched girder (Brit.); curved beam
~träger *m* mit aufgehobenem Horizontalschub *m* = arched girder with balanced horizontal thrust, ~ ~ without horizontal thrust
~träger *m* mit aufgeständerter Fahrbahn *f* = spandrel-braced arch
~träger *m* mit Durchzug *m* = arched girder with intermediate tie
~träger *m* mit gebrochenen Linien *fpl* = arched girder with polygonal outlines
~träger *m* mit Zugband *n* = tied arch; bowstring girder (Brit.); bowstring beam
~überlauf *m* = arch spillway
~verankerung *f* = grappling of arch
~verband *m* = arch bond
~weite *f* = span of arch
~widerlager *n* = arch abutment
~wirkung *f*, Gewölbewirkung [*Erddruckverteilung f*] = arching effect
~zirkel *m* = wing divider
~zwickel *m*, Bogenhintermauerung *f* = spandrel
Bohle *f*, Holz~ = (wood) plank
~ *f*, siehe: Abgleichbohle
~ *f*, siehe: Stampfbohle
Bohlen|belag *m* = plank covering, planking
~fußboden *m* = plank floor
~rost *m* = plank foundation platform
~weg *m* = plank road
Bohr|abteilung *f* = drilling department
~anlage *f* = drilling rig
~arbeiten *fpl* = drilling operations, ~ work
~ausrüstung *f* = drilling equipment, ~ outfit
~brunnen *m* = drilled well, bore-well, tube well
~diamanten *mpl*, schwarze Diamanten = carbon(ado)s, black diamonds, drilling diamonds

Bohrdraube — Bohrmeister

Bohr|draube *f*, siehe: Bohrwinde *f*
~**druck** *m* [*auf dem Meißel lastendes Gewicht des Gestänges*] = weight on the bit
~**druckdiagramm** *n* = weight indicator chart
~**druckmesser** *m*, Bohrdruckmeßgerät *n*, Drillometer *n* = weight indicator, drilling ~, drillometer
~**druckregulierung** *f* = drilling control
bohren = to drill, to bore
Bohren *n* = drilling, boring
~ **mit Verkehrspülung** *f* = counterflush drilling, drilling with reversed circulation
~ **ohne geologische Vorstudien** *fpl* = blind drilling
Bohrer|schneide *f*; siehe unter „Bohrmeißel *m*"

Bohrhammer *m*, Gesteinsbohrhammer

~ in Hochfrequenzausführung *f*
Bohrhammerstütze *f*, Bohrknecht *m*, Bohr(er)stütze *f*, Vorschubstütze *f*
Elektro-~
Hartstein-~
Hochleistungs-~
Normal-~
Schnell-~
Preßluft-~, Druckluft-~
Universal-~
mit Handumsatz *m*

Bohr|jumbo *m*, Ausleger-Bohrwagen *m*, Groß-Bohrwagen [*schwerer Bohrwagen auf Gleis mit schweren Bohrhämmern mpl*] = (tunnel) jumbo, drilling jumbo
~**käfer** *m* = borer
~**kern** *m*, siehe: Probekern
(~)**Kernentnahme** *f*, (Bohr)Kerngewinnung *f* = core recovery, ~ extraction
~**kernprüfung** *f* = core test
~**knarre** *f* = ratchet brace, ~ drill
~**knarrenbohrer** *m* = ratchet brace bit
~**knecht** *m*, Bohr(er)stütze *f*, Bohrhammerstütze *f*, Vorschubstütze *f* = pneumatic feed leg for rock drill, air leg
~**krone** *f*, siehe: Bohrmeißel *m*
~**lafette** *f* [*Bohrwagen m*] = mast, guide shell [*drill wagon*]

~**stütze** *f*, siehe: Bohrknecht *m*
~**vorschubbereich** *m* = feeding range (US)
Bohr|feld *n*, Bohrgelände *n* = drilling field
~**flüssigkeit** *f* = drilling fluid
~**fortschritt** *m* = drilling progress, ~ rate, rate of drilling progress
~**fortschrittsdiagramm** *n*, Bohrfortschrittsschaubild *n* = drilling progress chart
~**gelände** *n*, siehe: Bohrfeld *n*
~**gestänge** *n* = (string of) drill pipe
~**gestängeanschlußstück** *n* = substitute
~**gestängefett** *n* = drill pipe thread dope
~**gestängezapfen** *m* = drill pipe pin
~**grat** *m* = burr
~**greifer** *m* = hammer grab
~**gut** *n*, siehe: Bohrschmant *m*

(hand) hammer (rock) drill, (rock) drill hammer

high-frequency (~) ~ (~) ~
pneumatic feed leg for rock drill, air leg

electric (~) ~ (~) ~
hard rock (~) ~ (~) ~
high-capacity (~) ~ (~) ~
standard type (~) ~ (~) ~
rapid (~) ~ (~) ~
pneumatic (~) ~ (~) ~
a.c./d.c. (~) ~ (~) ~
arranged for turning by hand

~**leier** *f* = brace
~**loch** *n* = borehole, bore, boring
~**lochanordnung** *f* **für Felssprengung** *f* = hole (or bore-hole) placement for rock blasting
~**lochbesatzstoff** *m*, Sprenglochbesatzstoff = stemming material, tamping ~
~**lochdistanz** *f* = borehole spacing
~**lochfutterrohr** *n*, Brunnenmantel *m* = well casing
~**lochkamera** *f* = bore-hole camera
~**lochkopfgas** *n* = casing-head gas
~**maschine** *f* = drilling machine
~**mehl** *n*, siehe: Bohrschmant *m*
~**meister** *m* = foreman-driller

Bohrmeißel

Bohrmeißel m, **Bohrkrone** f, **Abbaumeißel** m, **Gesteinsbohrerkrone** f
    rock(-drill) bit, rock cutter bit, (drill) bit, drilling bit, boring bit, cutting bit

Anbohrmeißel
    starting bit, starter bit

(Bohr)Schneide f, (Bohr)Meißelschneide, Bohrerschneide
    (drill) bit (cutting) edge, drill point, chisel-type bit cutting edge

Diskenmeißel, Scheibenmeißel
    disc bit

Doppel-Meißelschneide f
    two-point chisel type bit cutting edge

Drehbohrmeißel, Rotarybohrmeißel
    rotary bit

Düsenmeißel
    jet bit

Erweiterungsmeißel, Erweiterungskrone
    enlarginc bit

Exzentermeißel
    eccentric bit

festgewordener Meißel
    stuck bit

Fischschwanzmeißel
    fish-tail bit

Flügelkrone f
    soft formation cutter head

Flügelmeißel
    bit with wings

Gleitbohrmeißel
    sliding drill bit

Glückshaken m, siehe: Meißelfanghaken

Hartmetallmeißel, Hartmetallkrone
    (tungsten) carbide (tipped drill) bit (or steel), drill bit with tungsten carbide insert (or tip)

Hartmetallschneide f
    carbide (drill) bit cutting edge

Kegelmeißel, Konusmeißel
    cone bit

Kernbohrkrone f
    (rock) core bit, core shoe, cutter head

Konusmeißel m, siehe: Kegelmeißel

Kreuzmeißel
    cross bit, cross auger

Kreuzschneide f
    cross bit (or cross auger) cutting edge

Kronennippel m
    core bit connection

Kronenschneide f
    crowned (drill) bit cutting edge, crowned drill point

Meißelblatt n
    bit blade

Meißelfanghaken m, Glückshaken
    bit hook, wall hook

Meißelschaft m
    bit shank

Meißelzapfen m
    bit pin

Meißelprobe f [an Meißel haftende Gesteinsprobe f]
    bit sample

Meißelschneide f, siehe: (Bohr)Schneide

Nachnehmer m, Nachnehmebohrmeißel, Räumer m
    reamer, reaming bit

Rollenmeißel
    roller bit

Rotarybohrmeißel, siehe: Drehbohrmeißel

Scheibenmeißel, siehe: Diskenmeißel

Schlagbohrmeißel
    cable drilling bit

Schneide f, siehe: Bohrschneide

Schrot(bohr)krone
    (chilled) shot-bit

Spatenmeißel
    drag bit, spudding bit

Spiralmeißel
    spiral bit

Spitzmeißel
    diamond point(ed) bit, rotary drilling bit with pointed cutting edge

Bohrmeißel — Bordstein

Spüllöcher *npl* im Bohrmeißel	holes (or perforations) in the (drilling) bit, openings in the sides of the cutting bit
Sternmeißel	star bit
Stufenmeißel	step bit, pilot bit
Zylinderrollenmeißel	Reed roller bit

Bohr|pfahl *m*; siehe unter „Gründungspfahl"
~**protokoll** *n* = boring report, ~ record sheet, ~ log
~**punkt** *m* [*Tiefbohrtechnik f*] = well location
~**register** *n* = drilling log
~**schlamm** *m* = drilling mud, rotary ~
~**schlammaufbereitung** *f* [*Rotary-Bohrverfahren n*] = mud conditioning
~**schlammdichte** *f*, Bohrschlammgewicht *n* [*Rotary-Bohrverfahren n*] = density of the drilling mud, weight ~ ~ ~ ~
~**schlammischer** *m* [*Rotary-Bohrverfahren n*] = mud mixer
~**schmant** *m*, Bohrgut *n*, Bohrmehl *n* = well cuttings, drill ~, rock ~, drillings
~**schneide** *f*; siehe unter „Bohrmeißel *m*"
~**schwamm** *m* = boring sponge
~**seil** *n* = drilling cable, ~ rope, ~ line
~**spindel** *f* = drill spindle
~**spitze** *f* = tip
~**stahl** *m* [*Drucklufthammer m*] = jumper
~**stange** *f* = drill rod, boring ~, drilling ~, bore ~, ~ bar
~**stange** *f* [*Rotary-Bohrverfahren n*] = auger stem, one length of drill pipe
~**stütze** *f*; siehe unter „Bohrhammer *m*"
~**technik** *f* = drilling engineering
~**tisch** *m*, Drehtisch, Rotarytisch *m* = rotary table, turn table
~**turm** *m* = drill tower, drilling derrick
~**turmbühne** *f* = derrick platform
~**(turm)flur** *m* = derrick floor
~**turmgalgen** *m* = gin-pole of a derrick
~**turmkranz** *m* = derrick cornice
~**turmrost** *m* = derrick grillage
~**turmsteiger** *m* = derrick man
Bohrungen *fpl* **mit Luftspülung** *fpl* **bei Prospektierungen** *fpl* = prospect sampling by airflush drill

Bohr|unternehmung *f*, Bohrunternehmen *n*, Bohrfirma *f* = drilling firm
~**unterwagen** *m* = drill carriage
~**verfahren** *n* = drilling method, boring ~
~**vorrichtung** *f* = drill jig
~**wagen** *m*, Leichtbohrwagen, Bohrwagen mit Lafette *f* = wagon drill
~**werkzeug** *n* = drilling tool
~**winde** *f*, Bohrdraube *f* = bit brace, plain ~, sleeve ~
~**winde** *f* = boring winch
~**wurm** *m*, siehe: Schiffswurm
Boje *f* = buoy
Bol(us) *m*, Boluserde *f* [*stark eisenschüssiger, z. T. kalkführender brauner Ton m*] = bolus, bole
Bolzen|(ab)schneider *m* = bolt clipper
~**gelenk** *n* = pin joint
~**loch** *n* = pin hole
~**schießgerät** *n* = cartridge-powered tool, powder-actuated ~, bolt driving gun
~**schweißpistole** *f* = stud welding gun
~**schweißung** *f* = stud welding
~**setzer** *m* = stud driver, ~ setter
Bölzung *f*, siehe: Abspreizung *f*
Bomben(ab)wurfplatz *m* = bombing base
bombensicher = bomb-resistant, bomb proof
Bombentrichter *m* = bomb crater
Boots|anlegestelle *f* = boat landing
~**hafen** *m* = boat harbo(u)r
Borax|kalk *m* = calcium borate
~**see** *m* = borax lake
Borazit *m* (Min.) = boracite
Bördel|mutter *f* = knurled nut
~**nietung** *f*; siehe unter „Niet *m*"
~**probe** *f* = flanging test
Bord|schwelle *f*, (Hoch)Bordstein *m*, Schrammbord *n* = curb(stone); kerb(stone), kirb(stone) (Brit.)
~**stein** *m*, siehe: Kantenstein
~**stein** *m*, siehe: Bordschwelle *f*

Bord|steinführung f = kerb(stone) (or kirb, or kirbstone) alignment (Brit.); curb-(stone) ~
~steinparken n = curb parking
Borkenkäfer m = bark boring beetle
Bornit m, Buntkupferkies m, Cu_5FeS_4 (Min.) = bornite, erubescite, horseflesh ore, peacock ore, variegated copper ore
Borosilikat n = borosilicate
Borsäure f, H_3BO_3 = bor(ac)ic acid
borsaurer Kalk m = borate of lime
BOSCH-Bau- und Installationshammer m, Fabrikat ROBERT BOSCH G. m. b. H., STUTTGART, DEUTSCHLAND = BOSCH builder's hammer
böschen, siehe: ab~
Böschung f = slope
~ (Geol.), siehe: Abdachung f
~ im Abtrag m, Einschnittböschung f, Böschung im Einschnitt = slope of cutting, cutting slope
~ im Auftrag m, siehe: Dammböschung f
Böschungs|auskleidungsmaschine f = (single) slope (canal) lining machine (or liner)
~befestigung f = slope stabilization
~betoniermaschine f = (single) slope (canal) concrete paver
~hobel m, Hang-Kippschar f = backsloper, slope grader
~kopf m = embankment crown retainer
~mauer f = toe wall
~neigung f = inclination of slope
~pfahl m, Böschungspflock m = slope stake, ~ peg
~pflaster n = slope sett paving
~planiermaschine f = (single) slope (canal) trimmer (or trimming machine)
~planier- und -verdichtungsmaschine f = embankment shaping and compaction machine
~profil n = profile of slope
~rutschung f, Gleitflächenbruch m = failure by spreading, lateral slide
~schutz m = slope protection
~standfestigkeit f = slope stability
~verkleidung f = revetment

~verkleidungsstein m = embankment face stone
~waage f, siehe: Gefällmesser m
~walze f = embankment (or slope) roller
~winkel m = angle of slope
~ziehen n [*mit Straßenhobel* m] = bank-sloping job
Bossenwerk n, Bossage f = bossage
Bottnischer Meerbusen m = Gulf of Bothnia
Boucherieverfahren n [*Holzschutzbehandlung* f] = Boucherie process
Boutellienstein m = moldavite
Brachland n, Brachacker m = fallow land, ~ ground
brackig = brackish, saltish
Brackwasser n = brackish water
~kalk m = brackish water limestone
Brand|bekämpfung f, Feuerlöschen n = fire fighting
~gefahr f, Feuergefahr = fire risk
~graben m [*Wald* m] = fire lane
~herd m = seat of a fire
~mauer f = fire-resisting wall
~schiefer m = oil shale
~schutz m, Feuerschutz = fire protection, fire proofing
Brandung f = surf
Brandungs|boot n = surf boat
~breccie f [*diese Schreibweise ist zu vermeiden*], Brandungsbrekzie f = surf breccia
~ebene f = abrasion plain
~gebilde n = wave-cut topography
~kehle f = notch
~kluft f = wave-cut chasm
~schutt m = wave-worn material
Branntkalk m, gebrannter Kalk, Brennkalk m = (quick)lime, anhydrous lime, common lime, calcined calcium carbonate
Brauchwasser n, siehe: Leitungswasser
Brauneisen n (Min.) = brown haematite
~erz n, Limonit m (Min.) = limonite, brown iron ore, limonitic (iron) ore
Braunfleckigkeit f [*Mörtelfuge* f] = brown staining [*mortar joint*]
Braunit m (Min.) = braunite
Braunkohlen|grube f = soft-coal mine
~sandstein m = brown-coal grit

Braunkohlen|schwelkoks m = brown-coal low temperature coke
~tagebau m = brown-coal opencast mining
Braunquarzsandstein m = brownstone
Braun'sche Röhre f = cathode-ray tube
Braunstein m, Weichmanganerz n (Min.) = pyrolusite (with manganite)
Breccie f [*dieser Ausdruck sollte vermieden werden*], Brekzie f, „Naturbeton" m, Bretschie f = breccia
Brech|anlage f, Steinbrecheranlage f = breaking plant, stone-breaking ~, crushing ~, stone-crushing ~, rock crushing ~, rock breaking ~, crushed stone ~
~barkeitsprüfung f **mit Splitt** m = breaking time test with chippings [*asphalt emulsion* (US)]
~barkeitsprüfung f **nach Caroselli** = breaking time test of Caroselli [*asphalt emulsion* (US)]
~eisen n, siehe: Brechstange f
Brechen n; siehe unter „Hartzerkleinerung f"
Brecher m, Grobzerkleinerungsmaschine f = crusher, breaking machine
~anlage f, siehe: Brechanlage
~aufgeber m, Brecherspeiser m = rock feeder, crusher ~
~schlacke f = crushed slag, broken ~
~trommel f = breaking drum, crushing ~
Brech|kies m = crushed gravel
~mantel m = crushing mantle
~platte f, Abscherplatte = shear plate
~punkt m [*Bitumen* n] = brittle point
~ring m = breaking ring, crushing ~
~sand m [*umfaßt in den USA den Kornstufenbereich 0—4,76 mm*] = screening(s), stone ~ crusher ~, artificial sand, manufactured sand, stone sand, crushed stone sand
~stange f, Brecheisen n, Hebebaum m = dwang (Brit.); crowbar
~-Temperatur f **nach Fraas**, Brechpunkt m ~ ~ = Fraas brittle temperature, ~ breaking point, Fraas bend-brittle point
Brech- und Siebanlage f = crushing and screening plant, ~ ~ installation

Brechungsindex m, Brechungsexponent m [*Optik* f] = refractive index, refraction ~
Brechwalzwerk n, siehe: Walzwerk
Brechweinstein m = tartar emetic
Brei m = slip, paste
Breit|beil n = block bill, broad axe
~eisen n = broad-tool, bolster
Breiten|grad m = degree of latitude
~komplement n = colatitude
~kreis m = parallel of latitude
~streuung f = dispersion in breadth, ~ ~ direction
Breit|flachstahl m = universal plate
~flanschträger(balken) m, Breitflanschbalken(träger) m, Breitflanschprofil n = H-girder, broad flange girder, wide flange girder (Brit.); broad flange beam, H-beam, wide flange beam, wide flange section
~fußschiene f = flat bottom rail, flange ~; girder rail (US)
~hacke f, Breithaue f = (cross) mattock
~holz n = halfround wood
Brekzie f, siehe: Breccie
Brems|abdeckblech n = drum plate
~ausgleich m = brake cross
~backe f = brake shoe
~band n = brake band
~bandbelag m = brake band lining
~bandkloben m = brake band block
~bandspanner m = brake band tightener
~beiwert m = braking force coefficient
~belag m = brake lining, ~ facing, ~ covering
~belagsatz m = lining service group
~bereich m = braking range
~berg m = self-acting incline(d plane), double-acting incline(d plane), jig haulage installation on the slope
~bergwinde f, Bremsberghaspel m, f = winch for jig haulage on the slope
~betätigung f = brake operation
~druckleitung f = brake pressure line
~druckventil n = brake pressure valve
~eindruck m, siehe: Bremsspur f
~einstellwinde f = brake adjusting jack
Bremse f **mit Reserve** f = oversize brake
bremsen, siehe: ab~

Bremsentlüftung *f* = bleeding of the brake
Bremserhäuschen *n* = brakeman's box, car rider's ~
Brems|flüssigkeitsbehälter *m* = brake fluid supply tank
~**fußhebel** *m*, siehe: Bremspedal *n*
~**gestänge** *n* = brake rods, ~ linkage, ~ rigging
~**handgriff** *m*, siehe: Bremshebelgriff
~**handhebel** *m* = brake hand lever
~**hauptzylinder** *m* = master cylinder
~**hebel** *m* = brake lever, ~ operating ~
~**hebelgriff** *m*, Bremshandgriff = brake handle
~**hebelkette** *f* [*Rotary-Bohrverfahren n*] = brake lever chain
~**klotz** *m*, Bremsschuh *m* = brake shoe, ~ block, slipper
~**klotz** *m* [*Tiefbohrtechnik f*] = scotch
~**klotzdruck** *m* [*Eisenbahn f*] = percentage of brake power
~**kraft** *f* = braking force
~**leitung** *f* = brake piping, ~ pipe
~**licht** *n* = stop light
~**manschette** *f* = brake sealing cup
~**pedal** *n*, Bremsfußhebel *m* = brake pedal
~**reibung** *f* = braking friction
~**ring** *m* = brake ring
~**sand** *m* = track sand
~**schacht** *m* [*Bergbau m*] = brake shaft
~**scheibe** *f* = brake pulley, ~ disc, ~ disk
~**schlauch** *m* = brake hose
~**schlüssel** *m* = brake spanner
~**schuh** *m*, siehe: Bremsklotz *m*
~**seil** *n*, Bremskabel *n* = brake cable
~**sektor** *m*, Bremszahnbogen *m* = brake pinion, ~ sector
~**spur** *f*, Bremseindruck *m* = braking impression, brake ~
~**stand** *m*, Prüfstand = test stand, ~ bench, ~ bed; torque stand (US)
~**träger** *m* = girder to resist braking
~**trommel** *f* = brake drum
~**verband** *m* = braking bracing
~**verlustzeit** *f* = brake lag
~**weg** *m* = braking distance
~**welle** *f* = brake shaft, ~ axle
~**wellenhebel** *m* = brake toggle lever
~**wirkung** *f* = braking effect
~**zahnsegment** *n* = brake ratchet
~**zugstange** *f* = brake (pull) bar, ~ rod, ~ lever connecting rod, tension rod
Brennbereich *m* = firing range, burning ~
Brennen *n* **von Ziegeln** *mpl*, Ziegelbrennen = firing of bricks, burning ~ ~
Brenner *m* = burner
~ **nach dem Selbstvergasungsprinzip** *n* = torch-generating type burner
~**gebläse** *n* = burner blower
~**mundstück** *n* = burner nozzle
Brenn|kalk *m*, siehe: Branntkalk
~**kammer** *f* = combustion chamber
~**kapsel** *f* [*Keramik f*] = saggar
Brennkraft|-Handramme *f*, Hand-Explosionsramme, Explosions(stampf)ramme = internal combustion (engine powered) rammer, explosion type tamper
~**motor** *m*, siehe: Verbrennungsmotor
Brenn|ofen *m* = calcining kiln, burning ~
~**öl** *n*, siehe: Petroleum *n*
~**punkt** *m* [*Prüfversuch m*] = fire point; [*deprecated: ignition point*]
~**schneiden** *n* = flame cutting, torch ~, torch burning
~**schwindung** *f* = shrinkage in firing
~**spiritus** *m* = industrial methylated spirit, fuel alcohol
~**spirituskocher** *m* = primus stove (Brit.)
~**stoffausnutzung** *f* = fuel efficiency
~**stoffbehälter** *m*, Brennstofftank *m* = fuel tank
~**stoffdüse** *f* [*Vergaser m*] = fuel jet
~**stoffeinspritzpumpe** *f*; siehe unter „Pumpe"
~**stoffersparnis** *f*, Brennstoffeinsparung *f* = fuel economy, saving in fuel
~**stoffhahn** *m* = fuel cock
~**stoff-Luftgemisch** *n* = fuel-air mixture
~**stoffmotor** *m* = engine
~**stoffnadelventil** *n* = carburet(t)or needle valve, carburet(t)er
~**stoffnocken** *m* = fuel cam
~**stoffpumpengehäuse** *n* = fuel pump housing
~**stoffreiniger** *m*, Kraftstoffilter *m*, *n* = fuel strainer, ~ filter
~**stoffstand** *m* = fuel level

Brenn|temperatur f [*Kalk* m] = temperature of calcination
~trommel f [*für Zement* m] = calcining drum
~zone f; siehe unter ,,Azbe-Schachtofen m"
Bresche f, siehe: Bruch m
Breschmauer f, entlastete Futtermauer = counter-arched revetment
Bretter|dach n = board roof
~fußboden m = boarded floor(ing)
~lager n = timber store
~stoß m = stack of boards
Brikettpresse f, Brikettierpresse = briquetting press
Brillenflansch m = tongued flange
Brinell|-Härtezahl f = B. H. N. [*Brinell Hardness Number*]
~-Probe f = Brinell hardness test
Bringungsweg m [*in Österreich*]; siehe: Förderweite f
Britisches Normalprofil n = British Standard Section
Brock m; siehe unter ,,Grobkies m"
Bröckel|torf m = crumbling peat

~tuff m, Puzzolanerde f = pozzuolana, pozzolana, puzzolano, puzzolana
Brockenmergel m = clastic marl
Brodel-Luftanschluß m [*Druckluftbetonförderer* m] = booster air pipe
Bromgold n = bromide of gold
Bronze|gelenk n = bronze hinge, ~ joint
~lack m = bronze varnish
~lager = gun-metal bushed bearing, bronze bush, bronze bearing
Bronzit m (Min.) = bronzite
Brown'sche Bewegung f = Brownian movement
Bruch m (Geol.), siehe: Verwerfung f
~, Bresche f [*z. B. Deich* m] = breach
~, Fenn n, Fehn n = fen, marshy ground
~, Brucherscheinung f = failure
~belastung f, siehe: Bruchlast f
~dehnung f = failure strain, strain at failure
~ebene f = plane of rupture
~festigkeit f = breaking strength, ultimate ~
~festigkeit f **in sprödem Zustand** m, Sprödbruch m = brittle fracture

Bruchflächenbeschaffenheit f von Zuschlagstoffen mpl	surface texture of aggregates
glasig	glassy
glatt	smooth
körnig	granular
rauh	rough
kristallin	crystalline
porös	porous

Bruch|fuge f (Geol.) = crack (Brit.); fracture
~gebirge n = faulted mountains
~gestein n = quarry rock
~last f, Bruchbelastung f, Grenzbelastung, Grenzlast = failure load, ultimate ~
~linie f [*Mohr'scher (Spannungs)Kreis* m] = envelope of failure, line of rupture, Mohr's envelope, strength envelope, envelope of rupture
~linie f, Verwerfungslinie = fault line
~liniental n = fault line valley

~rechnung f = fractions
~sattel m (Geol.) = fault saddle
~schleppung f (Geol.) = fault drag
~see m = fault basin lake
~sicherheitsnachweis m [*Stahlbeton* m] = determination of the ultimate bearing capacity [*reinforced concrete*]
~spaltenbildung f (Geol.) = rifting
~spannung f = failure stress, ultimate ~, breaking ~
~stein m = quarry stone, ~ block
~steinmauerwerk n = snecked rubble walling

Bruch|stein(stau)mauer *f* in Bogenform; siehe unter „Talsperre"
~stückgestein *n*, siehe: klastisches Sediment(gestein) *n*
~tal *n* = fault(-zone) valley
~torf *m* = fen peat [*richer in mineral content than moor peat*]
~wand *f*; siehe unter „Steinbruch *m*"
~zone *f* (Geol.), siehe: Sprödigkeitszone
Brucit *m* (Min.) = brucite

Brücke *f*	**bridge**
Abbau *m*	dismantling
Abroll~, Rollklapp~, Schaukel~	roller bascule ~
Abspanngerüst *n*, Hilfsgerüst *n*	erection tower
Amerikanisches Pfeilergerät *n*	Standard Unit Steel Trestles
Aquädukt *m*, siehe: Wasserleitungs~	
Auflager *n*	bearing
Auflagerquader *m* [*Brückenpfeiler m*]	bearing pad [*bridge pier*]
Aufstellgerüst *n*	erecting stage
Ausleger~, Gerber~	cantilever ~
Ausleger-Fußgänger~	cantilever foot (or pedestrian) ~
Balken~, Träger~, Balkenträger~	girder ~ (Brit.); beam ~
Belastungslänge *f*	loaded length
Besichtigungswagen *m* mit Antriebsmotor *m*	motorised inspection troll(e)y
Betonbalken~	concrete girder ~
Betonfahrbahn *f*	concrete floor
Betonfahrbahnplatte *f*	concrete decking
bewegliche ~	movable ~
bewegliches Auflager *n*	expansion bearing
Bewegungsfuge *f*	movement joint in bridge-deck
bituminöser Brückenbelag *m*	bituminous surfacing for bridge decks
Blechträger~, Vollwandträger~	(steel) plate girder ~; girder ~ (US)
Blechträgertrog~	trough plate girder span
Bogen~, gewölbte ~	arch(ed) ~
horizontale Scheitelverschiebung *f*	horizontal displacement of crown
oberer Gewölbering *m*	upper arch barrel
Querschnitt *m* im Gewölbeviertel *n*	cross section in $^1/_4$ span
Scheitelquerschnitt *m*	section through crown
Brückenbau *m*	bridge construction
Brückenbaufirma *f*	bridge-building firm
Brückenbauingenieur *m*	bridge (construction) engineer
Brückenbetriebseinrichtung *f*	bridge operating mechanism
Brückeneinweihung *f*	bridge dedication
Brückengeländer *n*	bridge parapet
Brückengradiente *f*	gradient of ~
Brückenjoch *n*	~ bent
Brückenpfeiler *m*	~ pier
Brückenrampe *f*, Brückenzufahrt *f*	~ approach
Brückenrost *m*	~ grating, grating for bridge deck
Brückenschiff *n*	~ pontoon
Brückenseil *n*	suspension bridge strand
Brückentafel *f*, (Fahrbahn)Tafel	decking, bridge ~

Brücke

~ ohne Gebührenabgabe *f* — free ~
Dauer~ — permanent ~
Dauerbehelfs~ — semi-permanent ~
Deck~, Brücke mit oben liegender Fahrbahn *f* — deck ~
Doppel~ — twin ~
Doppeldreh~ — double swing (-span) ~
doppelgleisige Eisenbahn~ — double track railway ~ (Brit.); ~ ~ railroad ~ (US)
Doppelzug~ — double draw ~
Dreh~ — swing ~
  gleicharmig — symmetrical
  ungleicharmig — dissymmetrical
Dreh~ mit Wasserauftrieb *m* — hydrostatic swing ~
drei nebeneinander liegende Brückenzüge *mpl* — three adjacent single bridges
erhöhter Randstreifen *m* — raised margin
Endrahmen *m*, Portal(verband) *n*, (*m*) — portal bracing
Etagen~ — double-deck ~
Fächer~ — radiating ~
Fachwerk(balken)~, Sprengwerk~ — truss(ed) ~
Fachwerkbogen~ — braced arch(ed) ~
Fachwerkhänge~ — lattice suspension ~
Fahrbahn *f* — roadway, carriageway
Fahrbahnblech *n* — roadway (or carriageway) deck plate
Fahrbahndecke *f* — roadway flooring, ~ surfacing
Fahrbahnrost *m* — roadway grating
Fahrbahntafel *f*, siehe: Brückentafel
Fähr~, Schwebefähre *f* — aerial ferry
Fahrzeug~ — vehicular ~
Falt~ — folding ~
Feldmitte *f* — midspan
festes Auflager *n* — fixed bearing
flachgesprengte Bogen~ — flat-trussed arch(ed) ~
Floß~ — raft ~
Flut~ — flood ~
freier Vorbau *m*, Freivorbauweise *f*, Freivorbau *m* — cantilever method (of construction), construction without falsework
Fußgänger~ — foot ~, pedestrian ~
Gebühren-~ — toll bridge
gerade — right ~
Gerber~, siehe: Ausleger~
Gerüst~ — scaffold ~
Gesamtkabelzug *m* — total cable stress
geschlossene ~ — ~ with wind ties
Gestaltung *f* — aesthetic design
gewölbte ~, Bogen~ — arch(ed) ~
Gitter~ — trellis ~
Hafen~ — dock ~
Halbtauch~ — semi-high level ~

Hänge~	suspension ~
in sich verankerte ~	self-anchored ~ ~
erdverankerte ~	~ ~ with shore anchorages
Hänge~ mit Versteifungsträger *m*	suspension ~ with horizontal tie
Hängestrebe *f*	suspension strut
Hängewerk~	hanging truss ~
Hauptöffnung *f*, Hauptfeld *n*, Mittelöffnung, Mittelfeld	main span, centre span
Hilfsgerüst *n*, Abspanngerüst	erection tower
Hoch~	high-level ~
Holzbrückentafel *f*	timber decking
Holzpfahlrost *m*	timber falsework piles, timber underwater falsework platform
Hub~	(vertical) lift ~
Hubstütze *f*	jacking pier
Joch~	trestle ~, trestle bridging
Kabel~	cable ~
Kabel~ mit Versteifungsbalken *m*	stiffened cable suspension ~
Kämpferdruck *m*	pressure on abutment
Kanal~	canal ~ (or aqueduct)
Kettenhänge~	chain suspension ~
Klapp~, Wipp~	bascule ~, balance ~
Kurven~	curved ~
Landpfeiler *m*	land pier, shore pier
Längsvorspannung *f* durch Stützenbewegungen *fpl*	longitudinal prestressing produced by altering the levels of the points of support
Leichtfahrbahn *f*, orthotrope Platte *f* [*„orthotrop" ist eine Abkürzung für „orthogonal-anisotrop" und besagt, daß die Steifigkeit der Platte längs und quer zur Brückenachse verschieden ist*]	light gauge carriageway, orthotropic(al) plate, fine meshed carriageway grid, light gauge decking
lichte Weite *f*	clear span
Mittelöffnung *f*, Hauptöffnung, Mittelfeld, Hauptfeld *n*	main span, centre span
Mittelpfeiler *m*	central pier, centre support
Mittelträger~	middle support ~
Montage *f*	erection
Montagespannung *f*	tensile stress in the cable
nicht mehr standfeste ~	under-strength ~
Not~	emergency ~
oben offene Fachwerk~	pony-truss ~
Öffnung *f*, Feld *n*	span
orthotrope Platte *f*, siehe: Leichtfahrbahn *f*	
patentverschlossenes Seil *n*	locked-wire strand cable
Pendelstütze *f*, Pendelpfeiler *m*	rocking pier, hinged pier
Pfeilerverbreiterung *f*	pier widening
Ponton~	pontoon ~, floating ~ ~
Pontondreh~	pontoon swing ~

Brücke

Portal(verband) n, (m), Endrahmen m	portal bracing
Prahmgerüst n	erecting pontoon stage
Pylonenkopf m	pylone head, tower head
Randträger m	outside girder
Rohrleitungs~	pipeline ~
Roll~, Schiebe~	roller ~
Rollklapp~, Abroll~, Schaukel~	roller bascule ~
Schiebe~, Roll~	roller ~
schiefe ~	skew(ed) ~
Schiffahrtsöffnung f	ship channel
Schleppträger m	bridge seating girder
Schlingerverband m	sway bracing
schräge Stahlbeton-Rahmen~	reinforced concrete skewed rigid frame ~
Schwebefähre f, siehe: Fährbrücke	
Schwimm~	floating ~
Schwingung f infolge Winddruck m	wind vibration
Seildurchhang m	cable sag
Seillage f	layer of strands, strand layer
Seitenöffnung f, Seitenfeld n	side-span
Sicherheitsstreifen m	safety strip
Sinusoidenzug~	sinusoidal draw ~
Sohlplatte f	base grid
Spannbeton~	prestressed ~
Sprengkammer f	demolition chamber, blast chamber
Sprengwerk~, Fachwerk(balken)~	truss(ed) ~
Stahlbetonfahrbahntafel f	reinforced concrete deck (slabs)
Stahlbetonfertigträger~	precast reinforced concrete beam ~
Stahlgeländer n	steel-rail parapet
Stahlplattenfahrbahn f	steel plate roadway
Stahlsohlplatte f, Stahllagerplatte, Stahlsohlblech n	steel sole plate, ~ bed ~
Stahlüberbau m	steel superstructure
Standardbrückensystem n	unit-construction bridge system
Steifrahmen~	rigid frame ~
Stein~	masonry ~
Straßen~	road ~, highway ~
Straßen- und Eisenbahn~	road-rail ~
Strompfeiler m	water pier, river pier
Stromseite f	channel side
Stütze f	support
Stützenhebung f	raising of the supports
Stützensenkung f	lowering of supports
Tafelplatte f	decking slab
Tal~, Viadukt n	viaduct
Tauch~, überflutbare ~	submersible ~, causeway
Träger~, siehe: Balken ~	
Trägeranschluß m	girder connection
Trägerfeldstück n	individual girder part
Tragkabel n	suspender cable

Tragkette f	suspension chain
Transport~, Verlade~	transporter ~
Trog~, Brücke mit unten liegender Fahrbahn f, offene ~	trough ~, open ~
Turmpfeiler m	tower pier
Überbau m	superstructure
überflutbare ~, Tauch~	submersible ~, causeway
Überroll~	roller ~ sliding over the fixed part
Überziehen n [Brückenseil n]	pulling to place
Uferseite f	shore side
Unterbau m	substructure
Unterroll~	roller ~ sliding under the fixed part
Verankerungspfeiler m, Ankerpfeiler	anchorage pier
Verbundbauweise f zwischen dem Stahltragwerk n und der Stahlbetonfahrbahnplatte f	composite concrete-steel girders
Verlade~, Transport~	transporter ~
Vermessungsmast m	sighting tower
Versteifungsträger m	stiffening girder
Vollwandträger~, siehe: Blechträger~	
Vorbau-Derrick-Kran m	erecting derrick (crane); erecting derricking jib crane (Brit.); erecting derricking boom crane (US)
Vorbauspitze f	projecting end
Wälzklapp~	rolling lift
Wasserleitungs~, Aquädukt m	water conduit ~, aqueduct
weitgespannt	wide span
Widerlager n	abutment
Wipp~, Klapp~	bascule ~, balance ~
Zufahrt f	approach
Zug~	draw ~
Zweigelenkbogenscheiben~	two-pinned arch ~

Brücken|fertiger m, siehe: Betonstraßen(bohlen)fertiger
~kran m = goliath crane (Brit.); gantry ~ (US)
~laufkran m = travel(l)ing bridge crane
~mischer m, Autobahn-Betonmischer m, RAB-Brückenmischer, Autobahnbrückenmischer = bridge(-type travelling concrete) mixer, bridge type travelling mixer plant, superhighway-bridge-mixer
~straße f, siehe: Hochstraße
~waage f = weighbridge, platform weighing machine
Brüden m, Wrasen m, Schwaden m = water vapo(u)r
Brunnen m **im Kreidefelsen** m = chalk wel

~bau m = construction of wells, well construction
~bohren n = well drilling, ~ boring
~bohrgerät n = well drill(ing rig)
~gräber m = well-digger, well-sinker, pitman
~greifer m = hammer grab
~gründung f, (Senk)Brunnenfundation f = well(-sunk) foundation, sunk well ~, caisson ~
~kandelaber m, Laternenpfahl m mit Brunnen m = lamp post fountain
~mantel m, Bohrlochfutterrohr n = well casing
~pumpe f = well pump
~reihe f = row of wells

Brunnen|ring *m*, Beton~ = concrete cylinder
~rohr *n* [*Elektroosmose f*] = well electrode
Brust *f*, siehe unter „Tunnelbau *m*"
~leier *f*, Handbohrer *m* = breast drill, hand ~
~schild *n*; siehe unter „Bulldozer *m*"
Brüstung(smauer) *f* = parapet (wall)
Brustzapfen *m*; siehe unter „Holzverbindung *f*"
Bruttoquerschnitt *n* = gross section(al area)
Buchse *f* = bushing
Bucht *f* (Geol.) = bight, inlet

Buckelblech *n*, geknickte Platte *f* = buckled plate
~spundwand *f* = buckled plate sheet piling
Buckelschweißung *f* = projection welding
Bude *f*, Schuppen *m* = shed
Bügel *m* [*Bewehrung f*] = stirrup
~ = bail
~bewehrung *f*, Bügelarmierung *f* = longitudinal bar and lateral tie reinforcement
~eisen *n* = (asphalt) smoothing iron
Buhne *f* = groyne (Brit.); groin (US)
Buhnenbau *m* = groyning (Brit.); groining (US)

Bulldozer *m*, **Frontraumer** *m*, **Schürfschlepper** *m*, **Planierschlepper**

    Bulldozer auf Luftreifen *mpl*, Radschlepper-Bulldozer *m*, Reifentrecker *m* mit Planierschild *n*, Radschlepper *m* mit Planierschild, gummibereifter Bulldozer, Planierreifenschlepper

    Bulldozer auf Raupen, Planierraupe *f*, Bulldozer auf Gleisketten *fpl* [*die Ausdrücke „Raupen" sowie „Planierraupe" sollten nicht mehr verwendet werden, dafür „Gleisketten" und „Planier-Gleiskettengerät"*]

    Planier-Gleiskettengerät *n* [*früher: Planierraupe f*] für Stubbenrodearbeiten

    Stubbenrodeschild *n*

    Planier-Gleiskettengerät [*früher: Planierraupe*] für Baumfällarbeiten, Baumschieber *m*

    Baumfällschild *n*, dreiseitiges Stoßschild, dreiseitiges Streichschild

    Schubstange *f*; Stoßbarren *m* [*Österreich*]

    Planier-Gleiskettengerät [*früher: Planierraupe*] mit (Unterholz-) Roderechen *m*

    Planier-Gleiskettengerät [*früher: Planierraupe*] mit schneepflugartiger Anordnung des Planierschildes, Trassenschäler *m*, Planier-Gleiskettengerät mit Schwenkschild *n*, Seitenräumer *m*

(bull)dozer(-equipped tractor), tractordozer

    pneumatic-tired ~ (US); pneumatic-tyred ~ (Brit.); bulldozer fitted to wheel tractor, wheeled ~

    (bull)dozer fitted to track-laying (type) tractor, caterpillar bulldozer, crawler tractor with bulldozer, bulldozer-equipped track-type tractor

    rootdozer

    dozer blade for rooting work
    treedozer

    dozer blade for tree felling work; stumper; three-sided bulldozer; three-sided moldboard (US)
    pusher bar

    caterpillar bulldozer with brush rake (or clearing rake)

    roadbuilder, trailbuilder, gradebuilder, angledozer, bulldozer with angling blade, sidedozer, crawler tractor fitted with hydraulic angledozer, angle-blade dozer, bullgrader [*the word "angledozer" is also used for the equipment which, when mounted on a tractor, constitutes a complete machine*]

Erdschürftransport m	bulldozing
Seitenräumer-Planierschild n, Schwenkschild, winkelbares Schild, Schrägschild, Winkel-Planierschild	angledozer, angling blade
hydraulisch gesteuert (oder betätigt)	hydraulically operated
seilgesteuert, seilmechanisch betätigt, kabelbetätigt	cable-operated, cable-controlled
Planierschild n, Brustschild, Fronträumer-Planierschild, Vorbau-Brustschild	dozer blade; pusher-blade (Brit.); dozer apron, bulldozer (blade); straight pusher-blade (Brit.)
Bulldozer(-Lade)schaufel f, Bulldozer-Schaufellader m	(bull)dózer-shovel, dozer-loader
Querschild-Abstützung f	bulldozer stabilizer
Felsrechen m, Steinharke f	rock rake
Bulldozer(-Lade)schaufeleinrichtung f	shovel dozer attachment
Heckaufreißer m	rear scarifier attachment
Querschild n, festes Schild, Gerad-Schild	bulldozer [*the word "bulldozer" is also used for the equipment which, when mounted on a tractor, constitutes a complete machine*]

Bund|axt f = carpenters' axe
~balken m = joining ba(u)lk
Bündel|bewehrung f, Bündelarmierung f = bundled reinforcement
~dalbe m = dolphin with parallel piles
bundesstaatliche Wasserkraft-Politik f = federal hydro policy
Bundes|straße f = Federal highway, ~ road
~verband m **der Deutschen Industrie** f = Federal Union of German Industry
~verkehrsministerium n = Federal Ministry of Transport, ~ MOT
~wasserstraße f = Federal navigable water course
Bund|flansch = union flange, coupling ~
~gespärre n, siehe: Bindergespärre
bündig mit, niveaueben = flush to, flush with, dead level
Bund|lager n = collar end bearing
~mutter f = flange nut, collar ~
~mutter-Verankerung f = collar-nut anchorage, flange-nut ~
~schraube f = collar screw
BUNGARTZ-Handfräse f, Fabrikat BUNGARTZ & CO., MÜNCHEN, DEUTSCHLAND = BUNGARTZ rotary tiller
Bunker m, Materialbunker, Taschensilo m = (materials) bunker

~abzugsorgan n = bin withdrawing device
~grube f, Erdbunker m [*Materiallagerung f*] = storage pit
~rüttler m, siehe: Haftvibrator m
~stand m, Füll(ungs)grad m, Füllstand m = material level (in bin)
~standanzeiger m, Anzeigevorrichtung f für Bunkerfüllungen fpl, Silo-Füllstandanzeiger m = (bin) level indicator, material-level ~
~standanzeiger m **mit umlaufendem Flügel** m = rotating-paddle type of material-level indicator
~tasche f, Silotasche, Bunkerwabe f, Silowabe = bin compartment
~tasche f [*Kohlenbunker* m] = bunker pocket
~vibrator m, siehe: Haftvibrator
~wabe f, siehe: Bunkertasche f
Bunsenbrenner m, siehe: Blaubrenner
bunter Verband m (Geol.) = poikiloblastic texture
buntknochiger Bernstein m = mottled osseous amber
Bunt|kupferkies m (Min.), siehe: Bornit m
~sandstein m = variegated sandstone (Brit.); mottled ~, bunter ~
~wacke f = sparagmite

Burette — chemisches Sedimentgestein

Burette *f* = buret(te)
Bürgersteig *m*, Gehsteig *m*, Gehweg *m*, Fußweg *m* = sidewalk (US); footpath, footway, foot pavement (Brit.); [*deprecated: pathway, pavement*]
~ **aus Betonplatten** *fpl* = concrete flagged footpath (Brit.)
~ ~ **Platten** *fpl* = flagged footpath (Brit.)
~**betonplatte** *f* = concrete flag
Burgunderpech *n* = Burgundy pitch
Büro|gebäude *n*, Bürohaus *n* = office building
~**wagen** *m* = mobile site office
Bürstenwalze *f*; siehe unter „Straßenkehrmaschine *f*"
Busch|packwerk *n*, siehe: Faschinat *n*
~**schneider** *m*, Buschpflüger *m* = brush cutter
Buttersäure *f* = butyric acid
Butylalkohol *m* = butyl alcohol
Butylen *n*, C_4H_8 = butylene
BV-Stoff *m*, siehe: Betonverflüssiger *m*
Bytownit *m* (Min.) = bytownite

C

Caisson *n*, Senkkasten *m* = caisson; well monolith (US)
~**gründung** *f*, Senkkastengründung *f* = caisson foundation
~**krankheit** *f*, Preßluftkrankheit, Drucklufterkrankung *f*, Senkkastenkrankheit = compressed-air sickness, caisson disease, compressed air illness, bends
Caliche *f*, siehe: erdiges Rohsalz *n*
Calyx-Bohrer *m* = calyx core drill
CBR-Verfahren *n* = California Bearing Ratio (and Expansion) Test
Centipoise *f* = centipoise
Ceratitenkalk *m* = ceratite limestone
Cermet *n* **auf Carbidbasis** *f* = carbide-base cermet
Chabasit *m*, Würfelsiedestein *m* (Min.) = chabazite
Chalzedon *m* (Min.) = chalcedony
~**schwüle** *f* = chalcedony nodule
Chalkopyrit *m*, siehe: Kupferkies *m*
Charge *f* = batch, charge
Chargen|messer *m*, siehe: Chargen-Zählvorrichtung *f*

~**mischanlage** *f*, absatzweise arbeitende Mischanlage *f* = batch (-mix) type plant, intermittent weighbatch (mixing) plant, batch (mixing) plant, batching and mixing plant
~**mischer** *m*, siehe: Periodenmischer
~**mischzeitmesser** *m* = batchmeter
~**registriergerät** *n*, siehe: Chargenzählvorrichtung *f*
~**silo** *m* = batch holding hopper
~**-Zählvorrichtung** *f*, Chargenzähler *m*, Chargenmesser *m*, Chargenregistriergerät *n* = batch counter, ~ recorder
~**zusammensetzung** *f* = composition of batch
~**zwangsmischer** *m* = batch pugmill
Chargierbunker *m* = batch bin
Chassis *n* = chassis
Chausseepappel *f*, siehe: Pyramidenpappel
Chaussierung *f*, wassergebundene Schotterdecke *f*, wassergebundener Makadam *m* = water-bound macadam; [*deprecated: mud-bound* ~]
Checksystem *n*, siehe: Beckenverfahren *n*
Chefingenieur *m* = chief engineer
Chemiekalk *m* = chemical lime
~**hydrat** *n* = chemical industry hydrated lime
Chemikal *n* = chemical
~**injektion** *f*, chemische Injektion *f*, ~ Auspressung *f*, ~ Verpressung, ~ Einpressung = injection of chemicals
chemisch gebundener Wasserstoff *m* = chemically combined hydrogen, fixed ~
chemische Baugrundverbesserung *f*; siehe unter „Baugrundverbesserung"
~ **Ökologie** *f* = chemical ecology
~ **Verfestigung** *f* **nach Joosten**; siehe unter „Baugrundverbesserung *f*"
~ **Zusammensetzung** *f* = chemical composition
chemischer Angriff *m* = chemical attack
~ **Vorgang** *m* = chemical process
chemisches Sedimentgestein *n*, Fällungsgestein *n*, Präzipitatgestein, Ausscheidungssediment(gestein) *n*, chemisches Absatzgestein *n* = chemically deposited sedimentary rock, ~ formed rock

chemische Verwitterung *f*, Gesteinszersetzung *f*, chemische Gesteinsauflösung *f* = chemical weathering

Chilesalpeter *m*, Natriumnitrat *n*, Natronsalpeter *m*, $NaNO_3$ = soda nitre, Chile salpetre, sodium nitrate, Chile nitre, nitrate of soda, Chile saltpeter, Chili saltpetre

Chinesische Mauer *f* = Great Wall of China

chinesisches Holzöl *n*, Tungöl *n* = Chinese wood oil, tung ~, China wood ~

Chloanthit *m*, Weißnickelkies *m* (Min.) = chloanthite, white nickel

Chlor *n* = chlorine

Chloratit *n*; siehe unter „1. Schießen *n*; 2. Sprengen *n*"

Chlordosierung *f* = chlorine dosing

Chloridsalz *n* = chloride salt

Chlorit *m* (Min.) = chlorite, green earth

~**bildung** *f* = chloritization

~**schiefer** *m* = chlorite-schist

Chloritoidschiefer *m* = chloritoid schist

Chlor|kalk *m*, Bleichkalk *m*, Bleichpulver *n* = chlorinated lime, bleaching powder, chloride of lime

~**kautschukfarbe** *f* = chlorinated rubber paint

~**magnesium** *n*, Magnesiumchlorid *n*, $MgCl_2$ = magnesium chloride

~**methyl** *n*, siehe: Methylchlorid *n*

~**silber** *n*, AgCl = silver chloride

Chlorung *f* **von Abwasser** *n*; siehe unter „Abwasserwesen *n*"

Chlorwasserstoffsäure *f*, Salzsäure *f*, HCl = muriatic acid, hydrochloric ~

Cholesterin *n* = cholesterol

C-Horizont *m* = C horizon

chromatographische Fraktionierung *f* = chromatographic fractionation

Chrom|eisenerz *n*, siehe: Chromit *m* (Min.)

~**erzstein** *m* = ferrochrome brick

~**glimmer** *m*, Fuchsit *m* (Min.) = fuchsite

Chromit *m*, Chromeisenerz *n*, $FeOCr_2O_3$ (Min.) = chromite, chrome iron ore

Chrom|magnesitstein *m* = chrome-magnesite brick

~**stahl** *m* = chrome steel

~**stein** *m* = chrome brick

Chrysolith *m* (Min.) = chrysolite

Chrysotilasbest *m*, Kanadaasbest, $H_4Mg_3Si_2O_9$ (Min.) = Canadian asbestos, chrysotile

Cif-Wert *m* **Maschinen** = landed cost of plant and equipment

Cipolino *m*, siehe: Kalkglimmerschiefer *m*

Claisenkolben *m* = claisen flask

Cobaltin *n*, siehe: Glanzkobalt *m*

Code-Leuchtfeuer *n* = code beacon

Colcrete-Mischer *m*, siehe: Zement-Sand-Schlämme-Mischer

COLES-Kranwagen *m* = COLES lorry-mounted crane (Brit.) [*Trademark*]

Cordband *n* = cord belt

Cornwallkessel *m*, Einflammrohrkessel *m* = Cornish boiler

Cotton|ölpech *n* = cotton-oil pitch

~**pech** *n* = cotton pitch

~**stearinpech** *n* = cotton-stearin pitch

Coulomb'sches Bruchprisma *n* = Coulomb soil-failure prism

Coulomb'sche Theorie *f* = Coulomb's theory, wedge ~, Coulomb's sliding-wedge analysis

Cristobalit *m* (Min.) = christobalite

CRYPTO-System *n* [*schwedisches Ölbrennverfahren für Ring- und Zickzacköfen mpl*] [*Trademark*] = Swedish impulse oil-firing system [*brick manufacture*]

Culman-Verfahren *n* = Culman's method

Cuprit *m*, Rotkupfererz *n*, Cu_2O (Min.) = cuprite

Cutter(saug)bagger *m*; siehe unter „Naßbagger *m*"

Cycling-Anlage *f* = cycle plant

D

Dach *n* = roof

~**antenne** *f* = overhouse aerial

~**aufsatz** *m* = skylight turret, ridge ~

~**ausmittlung** *f*, Dachzerlegung *f*, Dachentwurf *m* = roof design

~**aussteigluke** *f* = trap door on roof

~**balken** *m* = roof beam, ~ tree, beam of the roof

~**binder** *m* = roof truss

~**binderauflager** *n* = roof truss bearing

~**binderbalken** *m* = chief beam

~**binderfuß** *m* = roof truss shoe

Dach|deckung f, Dacheindeckung = roofing, roof covering, roof sheathing
~**deckungsstoff** m, Dacheindeckungsmaterial n = roof (decking) material
~**element** n, siehe: Dachtafel f
~**entwässerung** f = roof drainage
~**entwurf** m, siehe: Dachausmittlung f
~**erker** m, Dachnase f = attic gabled dormer window
~**fenster** n = dormer window
~**filz** m = roofing felt
~**first** m, Dachförste f = ridge
~**fläche** f, Dachseite f = pane of a roof
~**garten** m = roof garden
~**gebinde** n = roof course
~**gebirge** n [Bergbau m] = roof rock
~**geschoß** n = attic floor, garret ~, loft
~**gesims** n = string course, cornice of a roof, eaves mouldings
~**gesparre** n = timber work of a roof, rafters
~**grat** m = arris

~**haken** m, Dachknappe m = roof hook, slater's ~
~**haube** f, siehe: Dachkappe f
~**haut** f = roof membrane, ~ sheating
~**kammer** f = garret
~**kappe** f, Dachreiter m, Dachhaube f = lantern light, ridge turret
~**kehle** f, Einkehle = channel of a roof, gutter between two slopes
~**knappe** m, Dachhaken m = roof hook slater's ~
~**konstruktion** f = roof structure
~**kühler** m, Scheitel-Kühler [Motor m] = cabane radiator; saddle ~ (US)
~**laterne** f, Aufdach n, Überdach = open roof, lantern light
~**latte** f = roof batten
~**lattung** f = roof battens, ~ lathing
~**lüfter** m = roof ventilator
~**nase** f, siehe: Dacherker m
~**neigung** f = roof pitch, slope of roof, roof slope, pitch of roof

---

Dachpappenfertigungsanlage f
Rohpappenrolle f, Abwickelvorrichtung f für Rohdachpappe f
Vorratshang m
Vortränker m, Vorimprägnierer m
Tränkpfanne f, Tränkungstank m
Hänge f, Feuchtläufer m
Belagsmasse-Vorrat m
Belagswalzen fpl
Streuer m
reine einfarbige Bestreuung f
gemischte Farbbestreuung f
Mischer m für farbige Streumittel npl
Streumittel-Vorrat m
Becherwerk n
Talkum n
wassergekühlte Trommeln fpl
Zugbeanspruchung f
Preß- und Zugwalzen fpl
Walze f zum Einpressen n einer Markierung f
Gewichtsprüfer m
Kühlhänge f, Kühlhang m
Abschneidemesser n
Wickelvorrichtung f
angetriebene Zubringerrollen fpl

roll roofing plant
jumbo roll dry felt

dry looper
presaturator
saturator tank
wet looper
asphalt coating storage
coating rolls
granule hopper
solid colo(u)rs
mixed colo(u)rs
baffled mixer
granule storage
spill
talc
water cooled drums
tension
pressure-rolls
texturing roll

weighometer
cooling looper
cut off knife
roll roofing winding mandrel
driven feeder rolls

Dachpappenfertigungsanlage — Dammbalken(stau)wehr

Förderband n	conveyor
Gegendruckrolle f	mandrel pressure roll
Schindelschneider m	universal shingle cutter
Rundmesser n zur Aufteilung f in der Längsrichtung f	circular roll with knife
Rollen-Abtransport-Förderband n	roller conveyor
abgekieste Rolle f	grit roll

Dach|pfanne f = pantile, flemish tile
~**pfette** f = purlin
~**pflegemittel** n = roof preservative
~**platte** f, siehe: Dachtafel f
~**profil** n; siehe unter „Straßenquerschnittausbildung f"
~**reiter** m, siehe: Dachkappe f
~**rinne** f = gutter (dripping) eaves
~**schalung** f, äußere ~ = roof boarding
~**schiefer** m = roof(ing) slate
~**schifter** m = hip rafter
~**schindel** f = shindle (US); shingle, shide (Brit.)
~**seite** f, Dachfläche f = pane of a roof
~**sparren** m = rafter
~**sparrenfalte** f (Geol.) = chevron fold
~**sprosse** f **für Glasdächer** npl = trellis for glass roofs

~**stein** m, siehe: Dachziegel m
~**steinaufzug** m, Dachziegelaufzug = roof(ing) tile hoist
~**steinmaschine** f, Dachziegelmaschine = roof(ing) tile machine
~**tafel** f, Dachelement n, Dachplatte f = roof panel, ~ slab
~**träger** m = roof girder
~**zerlegung** f, siehe: Dachausmittlung f
~**ziegel** m, Dachstein m = roof(ing) tile
~**ziegelaufzug** m, Dachsteinaufzug = roof(ing) tile hoist
Daimler-Motor m = Daimler engine
Dalbe m, Pfahlbündel n, Duckdalbe = dolphin, pile cluster
Dalben|kopf m = dolphin head
~**pfahl** m = dolphin pile

Damm m	embankment
Erd~	earth(-fill) ~
Fuß m	toe, foot
(Rampen)Schüttung f, Dammschüttung	fill (construction), embankment fill
Sohle f, Basis f	base
Dammbau m	embanking
Dammbaustoff m	1. embankment fill material; 2. dam fill material [*earth dam*]
Krone f	crown
Schulter f, Rand m	edge
Mitte f, Kern m	body
Verkehrs~	~ for traffic facilities

Dammanasphalt m, Essener Asphalt, Es-As, Asphaltkaltbeton m = Damman cold asphalt; fine cold asphalt, cold fine asphalt (carpet) (Brit.)
Damm|aufschüttung f **bis zukünftiges Planum** n, Auftrag m, (Auf)Schüttung f, Auffüllung f = fill(ing)

~**balken** m, Staubalken = stop log
~**balkennut** f, Staubalkennut = stop-log groove
~**balkenverschluß** m, Staubalkenverschluß = stop-log gate
~**balken(stau)wehr** n, Staubalkenwehr = stop log weir

Damm|böschung f, Böschung f im Auftrag m, Auffüllböschung = slope of embankment, embankment slope, fill slope

~erde f, Oberboden m, Mutterboden, Krume f = top soil

~herstellung f = formation of embankment

~höhe f [*Talsperre f*] = dam height

~höhe f = embankment height

~kern m; siehe unter „Talsperre f"

~kernmauer f; siehe unter „Talsperre f"

Dämm|platte f, Isolierplatte = insulating slab

~schicht f = insulating course, ~ layer

Dammschütter-Bandabsetzer m, Hochabsetzer m = stacker for building up embankments

Dämmstoff m, Isolierstoff = insulating material

Dammstraße f = causeway

Dämmwandplatte f, Isolierwandplatte = insulating wall board

Dampf|auslegerkran m = steam jib crane (Brit.); ~ boom ~ (US)

~bagger m auf (Gleis) Ketten fpl = crawler steam excavator

~bär m; siehe unter „Rammanlage f"

~bereiter m, siehe: Dampferzeuger m

~blase f = steam bubble

~bohranlage f = steam drilling rig

~boot n = steam boat

~bremse f = steam brake

~diagramm n, Dampfdruckdiagramm = steam diagram, ~ pressure ~

~dichte f = density of steam

~dichtemesser m = condenser ga(u)ge

~dom m, Kesseldom = steam dome

~druckerhitzer m, Autoklav m = autoclave

~druckminderer m = steam pressure reducer

~erhärtung f [*Beton m*] = steam curing

~erzeuger m, Dampfbereiter m = vapor generator (US); steam ~ (Brit.)

~erzeuger m, Kesselwagenerhitzer m = tank car heater, booster ~

~hammer m; siehe unter „Rammanlage f"

~härtekessel m = steam curing vessel

~härtungsschuppen m = steam curing shed

~(hoch)löffel(bagger) m = steam navvy (Brit.); ~ shovel

~-Holzaufbringungswinde f = steam logging hoist

~kammer f [*Betonsteinfertigung f*] = curing chamber, ~ room

(~) Kessel m = (steam) boiler

~kesselüberwachungsverein m = Steam Boiler Supervising Association

~kraftwerk n = steam (power) plant, ~ electric generating plant, steam-electric station

~leitung f = steam line

~löffel(bagger) m, siehe: Dampfhochlöffel(bagger)

~luftpumpe f = steam air pump

~mantelrohr n = steam-jacketed pipe

~mantelzylinder m = jacketed cylinder

~maschine f, siehe: Dampfmotor

~maschinenregulator m = steam engine governor

~molkerei f = steam dairy

~motor m, Dampfmaschine f = steam engine

~nietmaschine f = steam riveting machine

~öler m = steam lubricator

~pfeife f = steam whistle

~pflug m = steam plough (Brit.); ~ plow (US)

~pochwerk n, Dampfstampfmühle f = steam stamp

~quelle f (Geol.) = steam vent

~(ramm)bär m; siehe unter „Rammanlage f"

~(ramm)hammer m; siehe unter „Rammanlage f"

~rammwinde f = steam pile-driving hoist

~reduzierventil n = steam reducing valve

~reibungsarbeit f = steam friction work

~reinigungssieb n = steam strainer

~reserve f, Dampfvorrat m = steam reserve

~rohr n = steam pipe

~sack m = steam pocket

~sägewerk n = steam saw mill

~sammler m = steam collector

~-Schienengreifer(kran) m, Greifer (-kran) m auf Schienen fpl mit Dampfantrieb m = rail-mounted steam grab(bing crane), ~ ~ (grab) bucket crane

Dampf|schiffahrt *f* = steam navigation
~schlange *f* = steam coil
~schlauch *m* = steam hose
~schleierfeuerung *f* = steam-fan furnace, furnace with steam jets above grate
~schleife *f*, Wasserkreislauf *m* = automatic return of water
~schlepper *m*, Schleppdampfer *m* = steam tug (boat), ~ towboat
~schmierapparat *m* = steam lubrication apparatus, duplex plunger lubricator
~schmierung *f* = steam lubrication
~sirene *f* = steam siren
~stampfmühle *f*, Dampfpochwerk *n* = steam stamp
~strahl *m* = steam jet
~strahlgebläse *n* = steam jet blower
~strahlpumpe *f* = injector
~strahlreiniger *m*, Dampfstrahlgerät *n* = steam cleaner
~strahlrührgebläse *n* = steam mixing jet
~trockenheit *f* = dryness of the steam
~turbine *f* = steam turbine
~turbinenkraftwerk *n* = steam turbine power station

~turbinen-Lok(omotive) *f* **mit elektrischer Leistungsübertragung** *f* = steam-turbine-electric locomotive
~überdruck *m* = effective steam pressure, steam pressure above atmospheric pressure
~überhitzer *m* = steam superheater
~überhitzung *f* = steam superheating
Dämpfung *f* = damping
Dämpfungs|effekt *m* = damping effect
~feder *f* = cushioning spring
Dampf|universalbagger *m* = steam universal excavator
~verteilung *f* = steam distribution
~vorrat *m*, Dampfreserve *f* = steam reserve
~vulkanisator *m* = steam vulcanizer
~walze *f* = steam roller
~winde *f* **mit geneigten Zylindern** *mpl* = diagonal (steam) winch
~zähler *m* = steam meter, ~ counter
~zerstäubungsbrenner *m* = steam atomizing oil burner
~zuleitungsrohr *n* = steam supply pipe

Dampfzylinderöl *n*	**steam cylinder oil**
leicht gefettet	lightly compounded
mittel gefettet	medium compounded
stark gefettet	heavily compounded

Darcy-Gesetz *n*, d'Arcy'sches (Filter-) Gesetz *n* = d'Arcy's law, Darcy's ~
Darre *f*, Röstplatte *f* = hot plate
Darrprobe *f* [*Betonzuschlag(stoff)* *m*] = test for aggregate moisture
Daten *f*; siehe unter „Baumaschinen" *fpl* und Baugeräte *npl*"
Daube *f*, siehe: Holz~
Daubenrohr *n* = stave pipe
Dauer|beanspruchung *f* = repetition of stress
~belastung *f* = continuous load(ing)
~betrieb *m* [*Maschine f*] = continuous operation
~biegeversuch *m* = fatigue bend test
~brennprobe *f* = long burning test
~bruch *m* = endurance failure, fatigue ~

~festigkeit *f* = fatigue life, endurance limit, fatigue limit, fatigue strength
~festigkeitsprüfung *f*, siehe: Dauerversuch *m*
~fettschmierung *f* = permanent grease lubrication
~förderer *m*, siehe: Stetigförderer
~frost *m* = permafrost
~haftigkeitsprüfung *f*, siehe: Beständigkeitsprüfung
Dauerkurve *f* = duration curve
~ *f* **der Abflußmengen** *fpl*, Durchflußdauerkurve *f* = rating curve of flow, graph of flow (Brit.); rating (or flow) curve, flow-duration curve (US)
dauernd gefrorener Boden *m*, ewiggefrorener ~ = permafrost soil

Dauer|parker *m* = day parker
~schalung *f* = re-usable shuttering
~schlagbiegeversuch *m* = repeated impact bending test
~schlagprobe *f* = continuous impact test
~versuch *m*, Dauerfestigkeitsprüfung *f* = endurance test, fatigue ~
~zugversuch *m* = repeated tensile test
Daumen|sprung *m* = thumb jump
~welle *f*, Nockenwelle = cam shaft
Dazit *m* (Geol.) = dacite
Dechenit *m* (Min.) = dechenite
Deck|anstrich *m* = top coat, finishing ~
~brücke *f* = deck bridge
Decke *f*, siehe: Straßendecke
~ [*Hochbau m*] = floor, ceiling
Deckel *m* = lid
~dole *f*; siehe unter „Durchlaß *m*"
~flansch *m*, siehe: Blindflansch
Decken|balken *m* = floor joist, ceiling ~
~bau *m*, Straßen~ = paving works (or operations) (US); surfacing work (Brit.)
~belastung *f* [*Hochbau m*] = floor load(ing)
~einbaugerät *n*, Deckeneinbaumaschine *f*, Straßendeckeneinbaugerät, Straßendeckeneinbaumaschine = (highway) paver; paving tool (US)
~einbaumaterial *n* [*Straße f*] = surfacing material
~einbauzug *m* = paving train (US)
~fertiger *m*, (Straßen)Fertiger *m* = (road) finisher, finishing machine
~füllkörper *m*, siehe: Füllkörper
Deck(en)gebirge *n* = overthrust mountain
Decken|granit *m* = mantle granite
~heizung *f*, siehe: Strahlungs~
~hohlkörper *m*, siehe: Füllkörper
~hohlstein *m* = hollow filler tile
~putz *m* = ceiling plaster
~schaden *m* [*Straßendecke f*] = pavement distress
~schalung *f* = floor slab form
~schluß *m*; siehe unter „Fertigbehandlung *f*"
~schlußbohle *f*, siehe: Glättbohle
~schlußübergang *m* = finishing pass
~stütze *f* = steel shore
~tafel *f* = ceiling panel
~träger *m* = floor beam

~verteiler *m* = paving spreader (US)
Deck|gebirge *n*, siehe: Abraum *m*
~kraft *f* [*Farbe f*] = covering power
~kran *m* = deck crane
~lage [*Bitumendachpappe f*] = cap sheet
~lage *f*, siehe: Verschleißschicht *f*
~lasche *f* = butt-trap (Brit.); coverplate (US); splice plate
~material *n* = wearing course material
~platte *f* = cover plate
~schute *f* = deck barge; ~ scow (US)
~schutt *m*, siehe: Abraum *m*
~werk *n* = rubble slope, sloping rubble wall
~werksetzer *m* = waller
Deflation *f*, Abblasung *f*, Abtragung *f* durch Wind *m*, Abhebung *f*, Winderosion *f*, Windabtragung, äolische Abtragung (Geol.) = (wind) deflation
Deformationsmesser *m*, Verformungsmesser *m*, Deformator *m* = deformometer, deformability meter
Deformator-Klinograph Galileo *m* = Galileo slide-ga(u)ge
DEGEBO, Deutsche Gesellschaft für Bodenforschung = German Research Society for Soil Mechanics, German Soil Mechanics Research Association
~-Schwingungsmaschine *f* = two-mass oscillator
dehnbarer Boden *m* = dilative soil, dilatable
dehnbares Gußeisen *n* = ductile cast-ron
Dehnbarkeit *f*, siehe: Streckbarkeit *f*
Dehnungsfuge *f*; siehe unter „Fuge"
(Dehnungs)Fugenvergußmasse *f*; siehe unter „Fuge *f*"
Dehnungs|geber SR-4 *n*, siehe: elektrisches Spannungsgerät SR-4 *n*
~messung *f* = strain control
~schreiber *m* = tension meter
~zahl *f* = coefficient of expansion
Dehnweg *m* = trajectory of strain
Dehottay-Verfahren *n*; siehe unter „Baugrundverbesserung *f*"
De-Hydrierung *f*, siehe: Wasserentziehung *f*
Deich *m* = dike, dyke
~(ein)bruch *m* = dyke breach, dike ~
~hauptmann *m* = dike-master
~land *n* = dykeland, innings

Deichsel *f* = tow-bar
Dekantierventil *n* = decanting valve
deklinante Buhne *f* = groyne (Brit.)/groin (US) pointing slightly downstream
Delerit *m* = coarse-grained basalt
Delle *f* = dell, birdbath
DELMAG-Stampfer *m* [*Trademark*], siehe: Frosch *m*
Delta *n*, Mündungskegel *m* = delta
~aufschüttung *f*, Deltabildung *f* = delta building (or fill)
~damm *m* = deltaic embankment
~niederung *f* = delta flats
Demontage *f*, Abbau *m* = dismantling
demontieren, abbauen, auseinandernehmen, abmontieren = to disassemble, to strip down, to dismantle
denaturiertes Salz *n* = denaturated salt
Dendritenbildung *f* = dendritic formation
Dentrituff *m* = dendritic tufa
Dendrologie *f*, Baumkunde *f* = dendrology
Dendrometer *m* = dendrograph

Denudation *f*

Verwitterung *f*, Abwitterung *f*
  chemische Verwitterung *f*, Gesteinszersetzung, chemische Gesteinsauflösung *f*
    Einwitterung *f*
    Auswitterung *f*
  mechanische Verwitterung *f*, physikalische ~, Gesteinszerfall *m*
Erosion *f*, (flächenhafte) Ausnagung *f*, Abtragung *f*
Transport *m*, Verfrachtung *f*

denudation (Brit.); abrasion [*the making bare of the surface of the earth*]
weathering, process of rock wastage
  chemical weathering

    weathering from top to bottom
    weathering from bottom to top
  mechanical weathering, physical ~, rock disintegration
erosion, geological erosion

transport

Denudations|ebene *f*, Fastebene, Rumpffläche *f* = denudation plain, peneplain, peneplane
~terrasse *f* (Geol.), siehe: Abtragungsterrasse

Deponie *f*, siehe: Haldenschüttung *f*
Derbyshire-Basalt *m* = toadstone

Derrick-Kran *m*, Mastenkran, Ladebaum *m*

A-~
Bock-~ [*Schwenkwinkel auf etwa 280° beschränkt*]
  Bockstrebe *f*
Derrickwinde *f*
Eisenbahn-~

Gitter-~
Holz-~
hydraulischer ~
Montage-Derrick-Kran; Vorbau-Derrick Kran [*im Brückenbau m*]

derricking jib crane (Brit.); ~ boom ~ (US); derrick (crane) [*invented by Henderson in 1845*]
A-~ ~ ~, jinniwink
stiff-leg ~ ~ ~(US); Scotch ~ ~ ~ (Brit.)
  back-stay, stiff-leg
derrick winch
railway car ~ ~ ~ (Brit.); railroad car ~ ~ ~ (US)
lattice(d) ~ ~ ~
wood ~ ~ ~, timber ~ ~ ~
hydraulic ~ ~ ~
erecting ~ ~ ~

Derrick-Kran — dichtbewaldet

nahtloser ~ — weldless ~ ~ ~
Scheren-~ ohne Ausleger m — shears ~ ~ ~
Schwergut-~ — heavy ~ ~ ~
Schwimm-~, Derrick-Ponton m — floating (or barge) ~ ~ ~
Trossen-~ [*Ausleger m mit 360° Schwenkwinkel m*] — guy ~ ~ ~
Trossen-~ ohne Ausleger m, Hebezeug-Mast m — gin pole (derrick) (crane) [*guyed derrick pole* (or *mast*) *used in conjuction with either pulley-blocks or a winch*]
Unfall-~ — auto wrecking ~ ~ ~

Descloizit m (Min.) = descloizite
Desintegrator m; siehe unter „Mühle f"
Destillat n = distillate
Destillations|benzin n = straight-run gasolene (or gasoline) (US)
~**bitumen** n; siehe unter „Bitumen n im engeren Sinne"
~**kolben** m = distillation flask
Destillatpech n = straight run pitch
Detailentwurf m, Detailkonstruktion f = part design
detonierende Zündschnur f; siehe unter „1. Schießen n; 2. Sprengen n"
(deutsche) Asphalteingußdecke f, siehe: Walzschottergußasphalt m
Deutsche Gesellschaft für Bodenforschung f, siehe: DEGEBO
Deutscher Ausschuß m **für Stahlbeton** = German Reinforced Concrete Association
~ **Betonverein** m = German Concrete Association
~ **Straßenbauverband** m = German Road Building Association
Deutscher Verband für Wohnungswesen, Städtebau und Raumplanung = German Association for Housing, Town Building and Planning
deutsches Weidelgras n = common rye grass
Deutzmotor m = Deutz engine
Deval-|Probe f = Deval test
~**Trommelmühle** f, Deval-Abnutzungstrommel f = Deval attrition (or testing) machine
Dewargefäß n, Weinholdgefäß = Dewar flask
Dezentrationszone f [*Boden m*] = zone of removal

Dezimalklassifikation f = decimal index system
Diabas m = diabase
~-**Mandelstein** m = amygdaloidal diabase
~**tuff** m, Grünsteintuff = diabasic (or greenstone) tuff
Diagenese f = diagenesis
Diagonal|bohlenfertiger m, Betondeckenfertiger m mit Diagonal-Glättbohle f = diagonal screed finisher
~**stab** m = diagonal member
~**steife** f = diagonal stiffener
~**strebe** f = diagonal brace, ~ strut
Diagramm n, graphische Darstellung f, Schaubild n = diagram, graphic representation, diagrammatic representation, graph
Diaklase f (Geol.) = diaclase
Diallag m (Mir.) = diallage
Diamant|bohrer m = diamond drill
~**bohrung** f = diamond drill boring
~**kernbohren** n = diamond coring, ~ core drilling
~**kernbohrer** m = diamond core drill
~**sägeblatt** n = diamond saw blade
Diaphthorese f (Geol.), siehe: rückläufige Metamorphose f
Diapositiv n = slide
Diaspor m (Min.) = diaspore
Diatomee f, Kieselalge f, Stabalge f = diatom
Diatomeen|erde f, Diatomit n, Kieselalgenerde f, Kieselgur f = diatom(aceous) earth, diatomite, Kieselgur
~**schlamm** m, Kiesel(algen)schlamm, Diatomeenschlick m = diatom ooze
dicht, hohlraumarm, geschlossen (abgestuft) = dense(-graded)
dichtbewaldet = heavily forested

Dichte — Diesel-Schmalspurlok(omotive)

Dichte *f* [*z. B. Gas n*] = specific gravity
Dichtemesser *m*, siehe: hydrostatische Senkwaage *f*
dichter Gips *m* = massive gypsum
~ Kalkstein *m* = compact limestone, mountain ~
~ polierbarer Kalkstein *m*, siehe: technischer Marmor *m*
~ Sandasphalt *m*, heißer ~ = sheet asphalt
dichtes Gestein *n*, siehe: kompaktes ~
Dichtigkeits-Prüfgerät *n* = density control unit [*for checking asphaltic concrete during construction*]
Dichtungs|gürtel *m*; siehe unter „Talsperre *f*"
~haut *f* = damp-proof membrane
~manschette *f* = gasket, packing, sealing member
~mittel *n*, Sperrzusatz *m*, wasserabweisendes Mittel *n* [*Beton m*] = water-proofer, concrete waterproofing compound, water-repellent, water-repelling agent, densifier, densifying agent, dampproofing and permeability reducing agent
~muffe *f* = jointing sleeve, sleeve joint
~packung *f* = packing set
~schirm *m*; siehe unter „Talsperre *f*"
~schleier *m*; siehe unter „Talsperre *f*"
(~) Schürze *f*, Dichtungsvorlage *f*, Dichtungsteppich *m*, Abdichtungsteppich = (waterproof) blanket, impervious ~
~strick *m* = sealing rope
~vorlage *f*, siehe: Dichtungsschürze *f*
Dickicht *n* = thicket
Dickenhobelmaschine *f* = timber sizer
diebessicher = pilfer-proof, thief-proof
Dielektrizitätskonstante *f* = specific inductive capacity, S.I.C., dielectric constant
Dienst|brücke *f*; siehe unter „Talsperre *f*"
~fahrzeug *n* = service vehicle
~gewicht *n* = service weight, working ~
Diesel|aggregat *n* **mit Generator** *m*, Diesel-Stromerzeuger *m*, Diesel-Elektro-Gruppe *f*, Dieselelektro-Aggregat *n* = diesel generating set, diesel motor-generator-set

~antrieb *m* = Diesel drive
~-Autoschütter *m* = diesel (shuttle) dumper
~bär *m*; siehe unter „Rammanlage *f*"
~-Einachs-Räumer *m* = diesel-driven hand-guided two-wheel dozer
diesel-elektrische Lok(omotive) *f* = diesel-electric loco(motive)
diesel-elektrischer Antrieb *m*, Verbundantrieb = diesel-electric drive
Diesel|fahrzeug *n* = diesel engine vehicle
~feldbahnlok(omotive) *f*; siehe unter „Feldbahnanlage *f*"
~-Gleisbaukran *m* = diesel-driven track laying crane
~hammer *m*; siehe unter „Rammanlage *f*"
diesel-hydraulische Lok(omotive) *f* = diesel-hydraulic loco(motive)
Diesel|karre(n) *f*, (*m*) = diesel truck
~-Kompressoranlage *f*, Diesel-Preßluftanlage, Diesel-Druckluftanlage = diesel (air) compressor
~kompressorschlepper *m* = diesel universal compressor tractor, diesel tractor-compressor
~-Kraftstoff *m* = diesel fuel (Brit.); (diesel fuel oil (US)
~-Lok(omotive) *f* = diesel loco(-motive)
~motor *m* = diesel engine
~motor *m* **mit Aufladung** *f* = supercharged diesel engine, turbodiesel (engine), turbocharged diesel engine
~pfahlramme *f*; siehe unter „Rammanlage *f*"
~pfahlzieher *m* = diesel pile-puller, ~ pile extractor
~-Radschlepper *m* = diesel wheel-type tractor, ~ wheeled ~
~-Raupengreifer(kran) *m*, Greifer(kran) auf Gleisketten *fpl* mit Dieselantrieb *m* = caterpillar (or tracklaying) diesel-driven grab(bing crane) ~ (~ ~) ~ (grab) bucket crane
~-Schienengreifer(kran) *m*, Greifer(kran) auf Schienen mit Dieselantrieb *m* = rail-mounted diesel-driven grab(bing crane), ~ ~ (grab) bucket crane
~-Schlepper-Kran *m* = diesel tractor crane
~-Schmalspurlok(omotive) *f*; siehe unter „Feldbahnanlage *f*"

Diesel-Schmieröl — dolomitisches Kalkgestein

Diesel|-Schmieröl n = diesel engine oil
~**schwimmsaugbagger** m, Dieselnaßsaugbagger = diesel suction dredge(r)
~**-Triebwagen** m = (self-propelled) diesel railcar
~**universalbagger** m = diesel universal excavator
~**-Zylinderlaufbuchse** f = diesel liner
Differential|-Flaschenzug m = differential pulley block
~**-Getriebe** n, siehe: Umlaufgetriebe
~**-Rechnung** f = differential calculus
~**sperre** f = differential pawl
~**trieb** m = differential drive
Differenzenmethode f [*Berechnung von Tragwerken mit veränderlichen Trägheitsmomenten npl*] = constant segment method [*analysis of non-uniform structural members*]
Dihydrat n, Rohgips m, $CaSO_4 \times 2H_2O$ [*Ausgangsmaterial n für gebrannten Gips m*] = raw gypsum
Dimensionierung f, Bemessung f, Dimensionsbestimmung f = dimensioning
Dimethyl n, Äthan n, C_2H_6 = dimethyl ethane
DIN = German Standard Specification
Dinarische Alpen f = Dinaric Alps
Dinasstein m [*veraltete Bezeichnung*]; Silikastein m, Quarzitstein, Quarzkalkziegel m = silica brick
dioktaedrischer Glimmer m = dioctahedral mica
Dioptas m (Min.) = dioptase, emerald copper
Diorit m = diorite
Diplomingenieur m = diploma engineer
Dipyrschiefer m, Schmelzsteinschiefer m = dipyre (or dipyrite, or mizzonite) slate
direkte Dehnung f = direct strain
direkter Antrieb m = direct drive
~ **Auslaufstollen** m; s. unter „Talsperre f"
~ **Scherversuch** m = direct shear test
direkt wirkende Ramme f; siehe unter „Rammanlage f"
~ **wirkender Rammbär** m; siehe unter „Rammanlage f"
Dischinger-Vorspannsystem n [*Vorspannung f durch hydraulische Pressen fpl*] = Dischinger pre-stressing method [*pre-tension produced by hydraulic jacks*]

Diskenmeißel m; siehe unter „Bohrmeißel"
diskontinuierliche Kornabstufung f, siehe: Ausfallkörnung f
Diskusegge f, siehe: (Teller)Scheibenegge
Dislokationsbeben n; siehe unter „Erdbeben n"
dispergieren, ausflocken = to deflocculate
Dispergierungsmittel n, Dispergenz f, Dispersionsmittel = defloculation agent, dispersing ~
Dispersion f = dispersion
Distanz|ring m = spacer
~**stück** n = separator
Disthen m, Zyanit m (Min.) = disthene, kyanite
Ditroit m = ditroite
divergentstrahlig-körnige Struktur f (oder Textur f), ophitische ~ (~ ~), Intersertalstruktur, Intersertaltextur = ophitic texture
Dock|anlage f = dock installation
~**hafen** m = dock harbo(u)r
~**schleuse** f, Trocken~, Einfahrt-Schleuse = entrance lock, lock entrance
~**- und Hafenbau** m = dock and harbo(u)r construction (or works)
Doggerbank f = Dogger Bank
Döglingtran m, Entenwaltran m, arktisches Spermacetiöl n = bottlenose oil
DOLBERG-Kleinbagger m [*Trademark*] = DOLBERG midget excavator
Doleneinlauf m = inlet of sewer, surface water gull(e)y
Dolerit m = dolerite
Doline f, Karsttrichter m = doline, dolina
Dolomit m, siehe: Dolomitgestein n
~, Perlspat m, Dolomitspat (Min.) = pearl spar, (pearly) dolomite
~**asche** f, Dolomitsand m = earthy dolomite
Dolomiten f = The Dolomites
Dolomitgestein n, Dolomit(fels) m = dolomite (rock) [*a limestone containing in excess of 40 per cent of magnesium carbonate as the dolomite molecule*]
dolomitischer Kalkstein m, siehe: Bitterkalk m
dolomitisches Kalkgestein n, siehe: Bitterkalk m

Dolomit|kalk m, siehe: Bitterkalk
~**kalk-Mörtel** m = dolomitic lime putty
~**marmor** m = dolomite marble [*a crystalline variety of limestone, containing in excess of 40 per cent of magnesium carbonate as the dolomite molecule*]
~**marmor** m mit zwischen 5—40% **Magnesiumkarbonat** n = dolomitic marble, magnesian marble
~**sand** m, siehe: Dolomitasche f
~**spat** m, siehe: Dolomit m
~**stein** m = dolomite brick
~**-Zerfall** m **bei thermischem Gleichgewicht** n = equilibrium thermal decomposition of dolomite

Domgebirge n = dome(d) mountains
donlägiger Schacht m, tonnlägiger ~ = sloping shaft
Doppel|backenbrecher m; siehe unter „Backenbrecher m"
~**backenbremse** f = double-shoe brake
~**(bau)aufzug** m = double (contractors') (or builders') hoist
~**bereifung** f = dual tyres (Brit.); ~ tires (US)
~**blatt** n; siehe unter „Holzverbindung f"
~**bogen(stau)mauer** f; siehe unter „Talsperre f"
~**bohlenfertiger** m = twin-screed finisher, two-screed ~, double screed ~
~**brechung** f (Min.) = double refraction
~**brücke** f = twin bridge
~**chlorid** n = bichloride, dichloride
~**decker** m, Doppelstufensieb n, Sieb n mit zwei Siebfeldern *npl*, Zweidecker m, zweistufiges Sieb n = double deck screen, DD screen
~**elektromotoren-Spillwinde** f = two-motor hoist
~**ender(kessel)** m **mit gemeinsamer Flammkammer** f = double ended boiler with common combustion chamber
~**falzziegel** m, Pfannenziegel = single Roman tile
~**gefäß(förder)pumpe** f = dual-tank type pump, ~ pneumatic conveying system
~**generator** m = double current generator

doppelgleisige Bahnlinie f = double-track line
Doppel|hammerbrecher m = double hammer breaker (or crusher)
~**hammermühle** f = two-shaft hammer mill
~**hydrat** n, siehe: Rohgips m
~**kniehebelbrecher** m; siehe unter „Backenbrecher m"
~**konus-Kipptrommelmischer** m; siehe unter „Betonmischer m"
~**kopfschiene** f, Stuhlschiene = double headed rail
~**laschenkettenbecherwerk** n = bucket elevator with double roller type chains
~**laschennietung** f; siehe unter „Niet m"
~**mäkler** m; siehe unter „Rammanlage f"
~**(material)umschlag** m = double-handling
~**meißelschneide** f = two-point chisel type bit cutting edge
~**nutmotor** m = double squirrel-cage induction motor
~**pentagon-Winkelprisma** n = double prism optical square
~**-Querbohlen(beton)fertiger** m = double-screed transverse finisher
~**rad** n, Zwillingsrad = dual wheel
~**radlenkbock** m = dual wheel steering gear
~**(rohr)tunnel** m, siehe: Doppeltunnel
~**-Rotoren-Prallbrecher** m, Zweiwalzen-Prallbrecher, Prallbrecher mit zwei Rotoren = double impeller impact breaker
~**sackbohrer** m = two-pocket bore
~**schaufellader** m = twin rocker shovel
~**schichtenbetrieb** m = double-shifts operation
~**schlagbohlenfertiger** m, Doppelstampfbohlenfertiger = double tamping beam finisher
~**schlüssel** m, doppelmäuliger Schraubenschlüssel m = double-ended spanner (Brit.); double head wrench
~**-Schmelzkessel** m [*Fugenvergußmasse f*] = double-boiler kettle
~**schwenkkran** m, siehe: Duplexkran
~**-Schwertwäsche** f = double-log washer

Doppelschwingenbrecher — Drahtglas

Doppel|schwingenbrecher *m*; siehe unter „Backenbrecher *m*"

~seilgreifer *m*, siehe: Zweiseilgreif(er)korb *m*

~-skisprung-Überfall *m* über die Krafthausdecke *f*; siehe unter „Talsperre *f*"

~spat *m* = double refraction calcspar

~spitzhacke *f*, Doppelspitzpickel *m*, Zweispitz *m* = (clay) pick [pointed at both ends]

~spurkranzrad *n* = double-flanged wheel

~stampfbohlenfertiger *m*, Doppelschlagbohlenfertiger = double tamping beam finisher

~stegblechträger *m* = double-webbed girder

~stufensieb *n*, siehe: Doppeldecker *m*

~taschen-Baustellensilo *m* = bin with twin hoppers

doppelte Oberflächenbehandlung *f* [Straße *f*] = double surface treatment, armo(u)r coat, two-pass surface treatment, inverted penetration surface treatment, multiple-lift treatment

doppelte Stegverlaschung *f* = double-strab web joint

~ Versatzung *f*; siehe unter „Holzverbindung *f*"

doppeltes Dreieckfachwerk *n* = double triangular truss, ~ Warren ~

~ Hängewerk *n*, doppelter Hängebock *m* = queen (post) truss, queen-post roof, queen posts

doppeltkohlensaurer Kalk *m*, $CaH_2(CO_3)_2$ = calcium bicarbonate

Doppel-T|-Profil *n* = I-beam section

~-Stahl *m* = I-steel

Doppel|trommelbetoniermaschine *f*; siehe unter „Straßen(beton)mischer *m*"

~trommel(beton)straßenmischer *m*; siehe unter „Straßen(beton)mischer *m*"

~trommelrammwinde *f* = double-drum pile driving winch

~trommel(seil)winde *f* = double drum (rope) (or cable) winch

~tunnel *m*, Zwillingstunnel, Doppelrohrtunnel = twin(-bore) tunnel

~walzwerk *n*, Doppelwalzenbrecher *m* = four-roll crusher

doppelwandiger Spundwandfang(e)damm *m*, doppeltes Spundwandbauwerk *n* = double-wall(ed) sheetpile cofferdam

Doppelwellen|sieb *n* = twin shaft screen

~zwangsmischer *m*; siehe unter „Makadam-Maschinenanlage *f*"

Dorfstraße *f* = village road

Dorry-Härte *f* = Dorry hardness

Dortmunder Brunnen *m*; siehe unter „Abwasserwesen *n*"

Dosen|barometer *n*, siehe: Aneroidbarometer

~sextant *m* = box sextant

Dosieranlage *f* für Zement *m*, Zementsilo *m* mit Dosierung *f* = cement batch(ing) plant

~ *f* für Zuschlagstoffe *mpl* = aggregate batching plant, proportioning ~

Dosier|apparat *m*, Zuteilapparat, Zumeßapparat [Zuschlag(stoffe) m(pl), Zement *m*] = batcher, apportioning gear

~apparat *m* [Schwarzdeckenmischanlage *f*] = multi-compartment aggregate feeder

~apparat *m* nach Raumteilen *mpl* = volume(tric) batcher

~apparatwaage *f* = batcher scale

~bandwaage *f* = proportioning weight-feeder-conveyor

~silo *m* = batch bin, batching ~

Dosierung *f*, Zuteilung *f*, Zumessung *f*, Abmessung *f* = proportioning, batching, ga(u)ging, measuring

Dosier|vorrichtung *f*, siehe: Abmeßvorrichtung

~waage *f*, Wiegetrichter *m* = weigh batcher (Brit.); weighing batcher (with scale) (US); weigh hopper

Douglasie *f*, Harzkiefer *f*, Terpentinkiefer *f* = Douglas fir, Oregon pine, pitch pine

Dowsongas *n*, Mischgas, Stadtgas = Dowson gas

Draht|anker *m* = wire tie

~bündel *n* = group of wires

~bürste *f* = wire brush

~gewebe *n*, Drahtgeflecht *n* = wire mesh, ~ fabric, netting wire, woven ~, wire cloth

~glas *n* = wire(d) glass

Drahtgurtvollelevator — (Draht)Seil(schwebe)bahn

Draht|gurtvollelevator m = continuous wire-belt elevator
~haspel m, f = wire reel
~hose f, Schutzgitter n, Baumrost m = tree-guard
~kabel n, siehe: Drahtseil n
~klemme f = wire grip
~litze f; siehe unter „Drahtseil n"
~schere f = wire cutter, shear ~
~seele f = core

Drahtseil n, **Drahtkabel** n, **Stahl(draht)seil** [*erfunden von dem Deutschen W. A. Julius Albert*] — (steel) wire rope, (steel) cable

Albertschlag m, Längsschlag, Gleichschlag, Parallelschlag	Lang lay
Doppelflachlitze f	double flattened strand
(Draht)Litze f	strand
Drahtseil mit Rolle f	cable and reel
Drahtseilnetz n	wire rope grid
Flach(draht)litze f, Litze f mit dreieckigem Querschnitt m, Dreikantlitze	flattened strand
Gleichschlag m, siehe: Albertschlag	
Hanfseele f	fibre core (Brit.); fiber core (US); hemp core
herumlegen, umschlagen	to twist
Kreuzschlag m	regular lay, standard lay, right lay, cross lay
Längsschlag m, siehe: Albertschlag	
Litze f, siehe: Drahtlitze	
Litze f mit dreieckigem Querschnitt, siehe: Flach(draht)litze	
Parallelschlag m, siehe: Albertschlag	
patentverschlossenes Drahtseil n	locked-wire strand cable
Rund(draht)litze f	round strand
Schlinge f	sling
Seilfett n	cable grease, rope grease
Stahlseele f	steel core
umschlagen, herumlegen	to twist
vorgeformt	pre-formed
vorgeformtes drallarmes Drahtseil	TRU-LAY-ROPE [*Trademark*]
24-ädriges Kabel n	24-wire cable

(Draht)Seil(schwebe)bahn f, **(Luft)Seilbahn**, **Drahtseilhängebahn** — aerial (or cable) ropeway (or tramway); ~ (~ ~) railroad (US)

Ein-~, Einseil(schwebe)bahn f [*sogenannte englische Bauart f; erfunden 1644 von Adam Wybe, von den Engländern Robinson und Hodgson um 1856—1870 weiterentwickelt*] — single rope ~ ~, monocable ~ ~, single ropeway

Doppel-~, Zwei-Seil(schwebe)bahn f [*sogenannte deutsche Bauart f*] — double rope ~ ~, bi-cable ~ ~, double ropeway

Feldweite f — span

(Draht) Seil (schwebe) bahn — Drehschlagbohren

Pendelbetrieb m — "to and fro" system, jig-back system
Skilift m, Schneeschuhläuferaufzug m — ski-hoist
Tragseil n — carrying rope, rail ~
Tragseil n in verschlossener Form — locked coil carrying rope
Wagen m — carrier
Zugseil n — hauling rope

Drahtseil-Standbahn f, siehe: Seil-Standbahnanlage f
Drahtzaun m = cable fence
drahtumwundenes Betonrohr n **mit Vorspannung** f = pre-stressed concrete spun pipe
Draht|verhau m = wire entanglement
~**widerstandsmeßgerät** n = strain ga(u)ge
~**zange** f = pliers, cutting plier
Draisine f, Eisenbahndraisine, Bahnmeisterwagen m = trackmotor car (US); platelayers' troll(e)y (Brit.)
Drall m = twist
drallfreies Seil n = non-spinning rope
Dränabstand m; siehe unter „Entwässerung f"
Dränage f, (Röhren)Dränung f, Drainage f [dieser Ausdruck sollte nicht mehr verwendet werden]; siehe unter „Entwässerung f"
~ **des Bodens durch Anwendung eines elektrischen Potentials**, siehe: Elektro-Osmose f
Dränbewässerung f, Untergrundbewässerung f = subterraneous irrigation
Drängraben m = drainage trench
~**aushub** m = drainage trenching
(Drän-) Grabenfräser m, siehe: Grabkettenbagger m
Drän|maschine f = Kjellmann-Franki machine
~**rohr** n; siehe unter „Entwässerung f"
~**schicht** f, siehe: Filterschicht
~**spaten** m, Stechspaten m = grafting tool
Dränung f; siehe unter „Entwässerung f"
Dränwerkzeug n = drainage tool
Draufsicht f = tope side view
Dreh|aufreißer m = revolving ripper
~**ausleger** m = swivelling jib (Brit.); swiveling boom (US)
~**bank** f = lathe

drehbare Laufrolle f = caster (wheel) castor (~)
Dreh|bohrer m = rotary drill
~**bohrmaschine** f = rotating (or rotary) drilling machine
~**bohrmeißel** m; siehe unter „Bohrmeißel"
~**bohrung** f, Drehbohren n = rotary drilling
~**bühne** f = rotating deck
~**feuer** n = rotating beacon
~**gasgriff** m = twist grip throttle control
~**gelenk** n = swivel joint
~**gestell** n = bogie (truck)
~**griff** m = turning handle
~**kappe** f = rotocap
~**kopfbolzen** m = swivel pin
~**kopfkugel** f = swivel ball
~**kran** m, siehe: Schwenkkran
~**kranz** m = circular pathway
Drehmoment n = torque
~-**Abscherung** f = rotational shear
~**messer** m = torquemeter
~-**Wandler** m = torque converter
Dreh|ofen m, Rotierofen m = rotary kiln
~**pflug** m = one-way plough (Brit.); ~ plow (US)
~**punkt** m = fulcrum
~**radius** m [Bagger m] = rotating deck radius
~**rahmen** m = revolving frame
~**rohrofen** m = tubular rotary kiln
~**säule** f, siehe: Kranmast m
~**scheibe** f = turntable
~**scheibenkipper** m = turntable tip
~**schemel** m = pivoted bogie
~**schemelkurvenfahrwerk** n = travelling gear with pivoted bogie for running on curved rails
~**schieber** m [Zement(silo)waage f] = rotary valve [cement weigh(ing) batcher]
~**schlagbohren** n = percussive-rotary drilling

Dreh|schurre f = swivel(ling)chute, ~ spout
~strom-Generator m = polyphase generator, three-phase ~, polyphase alternator
~strommotor m = three-phase motor, polyphase ~
~trommel f zur Tonkügelchenherstellung f = drum pelletizer
~verwerfung f (Geol.) = pivotal (or rotary, or tension) fault
~waage f = rotary scale
~werkbremse f [Bagger m] = swing brake, slewing gear ~
~winkel m = angle of rotation
~zahl f, minutliche Umlaufzahl f = revolutions per minute, speed
~zapfen m = pivot, fulcrum pin, trunnion
Dreiachs|autokran m = three-axle truck-crane
~-Druckversuch m, Dreiachsialversuch = triaxial (compression) test
~-Fahrgestell n, Dreiachs-Unterwagen m [Bagger m] = three-axle carrier
~-Fahrzeug n = three-axle vehicle
~-Hinterkipper m = three-axle rear-dump truck; ~ ~ lorry (Brit.)
~last(kraft)wagenbagger m; siehe unter Autobagger m"
~-Lkw m = three-axle truck; ~ lorry (Brit.)
dreiaxiale Druckzelle f, siehe: Triaxialgerät n
Dreiaxialversuch m, siehe: Dreiachs-Druckversuch
Drei|baum m, Montage-~ = shear-legs, tripod, sheer-legs, sheers
~decker(sieb) m, (n) = triple-deck vibrating screen
dreidimensionale Rohrleitung f, siehe: räumlich verlegte ~
Dreieck|anordnung f; siehe: Dreiecksystem n
~diagramm n = triangular diagram
~gitterkonstruktion f = triangular latticed construction
~kastenkonstruktion f = triangular construction
~last f = triangular load(ing)
~(meß)wehr n = V-shaped notch

~schaltung f = delta connection
~sprengwerk n = triangulated truss, triangular ~
~system n, Dreieckanordnung f = triangular system, triangulated ~
~träger m = triangulated girder, triangular ~
~verband m = triangulated bracing, triangular ~
~wehr n, siehe: Dreieckmeßwehr
dreietagig, dreistöckig, dreigeschossig = three-floored
dreietagige Kreuzung f, dreistöckige ~, dreigeschossige ~ = triple-deck grade separation structure, three-level ~ ~ ~
dreifach sichere Auslegerwinde f [Bagger m] = triple-safe boom hoist (US); ~ jib ~ (Brit.)
dreifaches Hausteinfenster n = threefold window in work(ed) stone
Drei|fachsilo m, Drei-Wabensilo, Drei-Taschensilo = three-compartment bin
~fachwellblech n, Tripelwellblech = triple corrugated (sheet) iron
~farbenschreiber m = three-colo(u)r recorder
~füllungstür f = three-panelled door
~fuß m = tripod
~fußblock m = tetrapod (concrete) block
~fuß-Grabenramme f = three-legged (or triplex (backfill) tamper (or rammer)
~ganggetriebe n = three-speed gear
~gelenkbogen m = three-hinged arch, arch with three hinges
~gelenk-Fachwerkbogen m = three-hinged braced arch, trussed arch with three hinges
~gelenkrahmen m = three-hinged frame
dreigeschossig, dreistöckig, dreietagig = three-floored
Drei|kammer(hohlblock)stein m = three hole hollow block
~kantangelfeile f = three-square file with tang
~kanteisen n = triangular bar, ~ iron
~kanter m (Geol.) = dreikanter, ventifact, glyptolith, gibber
~kantlitze f; siehe unter „Drahtseil n"
~kantlitzen(draht)seil n, Flachlitzen-(draht)seil = flattened strand cable

Drei|klanghorn n = triple tone horn
~leiterkabel n = three-conductor cable, triple ~
~-Momente-Satz m = theory of three moments
~motoren-Elektrobagger m = three-motor all-electric shovel
~motoren-Laufkran m [*für elektrischen Betrieb* m] = three-motor travel(l)ing crane
dreimotoriger Elektroantrieb m = three-motor drive
Drei|punkt-Aufhängung f = three-point suspension (mounting)
~quartier n, Dreiviertelstein m = three quarters
~rad n = tricycle
~rad-Bohrwagen m **mit Lafette** f = three-wheel(ed) wagon drill
~rad-Walze f; siehe unter „Walze"
~schlauchbrenner m [*Schweißen* n] = double oxygen-hose cutting torch
~-Seil-Schrapper m, Schleppschrapperanlage f mit 3-Seil-Anordnung f = rapid shifting drag scraper machine, rapid-shifter
~seitenentleerung f = three-way dump discharge
~seiten-Kipper m = three-way tipper
dreispurige Straße f = undivided two-way road with three lanes altogether
dreistöckig, dreietagig, dreigeschossig = three-floored
Drei|-Taschensilo m, siehe: Dreifachsilo
dreiteilig ausgebildeter Rahmen m = three-section framing bent
Drei|trommel(seil)winde f, Dreitrommelhaspel f, m = three-drum hoist
~viertel(elliptik)feder f = three quarter elliptic spring
~viertelsäule f, eingebundene Säule = imbedded column
~viertelstein m, Dreiquartier n = three quarters
~-Wabensilo m, siehe: Dreifachsilo
~walzenbrecher m; siehe unter „Walzwerk n"
~wegausgleichventil n = three-way compensating valve
~wegehahn m = three-way cock

~wegeschalter m = three-way switch
~wegeverschraubung f = three-way cornection
~zonenbauweise f, österreichische Bauweise = (English-)Austrian method
~zylinder(dampf)maschine f, Drillings-(dampf)maschine = triple (cylinder) steam engine
Drempel m = sill
~wand f, Kniestockwand, Versenkungswand = jamb wall
Driftströmung f = drift current
Drillings|bogen m = triforium
~fenster n = triple lancet window
Drillknickung f, Torsionsknickung = torsional buckling
Drillometer n, Bohrdruckmesser m = drillometer, weight indicator, drilling indicator
Drillung f, siehe: Torsion f
Drillungssteife f, siehe: Torsionssteifigkeit f
Drillwiderstand m, Torsionswiderstand = torsional resistance
Drittel|dach n = roof with pitch of 1:3
~punkt m = third point
Drossel|gestänge n = throttle linkage
~klappe f = butterfly valve
~klappe f **mit Fallgewichtsantrieb** m, siehe: Fallgewichtsdrosselklappe
~klappe f **mit hydraulischem Antrieb** m = hydraulically operated butterfly valve
~klappenhebel m = throttle lever
~klappenkörper m = circular leaf
~schieber m = throttle slide (valve)
~turbine f = throttling turbine
~ventil n = throttle valve
~welle f = butterfly spindle
Druck|abfall m, Druckabnahme f = pressure drop
~abnahme f, siehe: Druckabfall m
~anstieg m, Druckzunahme f = pressure rise
~armierung f, siehe: Druckbewehrung
~aufbau-Versuch m = pressure build-up test
~ausgleich m = equalization of pressure
~auswaschung f = pressure washing operation
~beanspruchung f = compressive strain
~behälter m, Druckgefäß n, Druckkessel m = pressure vessel, ~ tank

Druck|bewehrung f, **Druckarmierung** f [*Stahleinlagen in auf Druck beanspruchten Betonteilen*] = compressive reinforcement
~**bolzen** m = thrust bolt, pin pusher
~**bolzen** m [*Kupplung* f] = clutch fork ball support
~**diagonale** f [*Fachwerk* n] = compression diagonal
~**dislokation** f (Geol.) = pressure fault
~**dose** f, siehe: (Boden)Druck(meß)dose
~**einspritzung** f [*Dieselmaschine* f] = injection under pressure
~**entlastung** f = decompression
~**entlastungsventil** n = pressure relief valve
~**erhöhungs(pumpen)anlage** f, siehe: Druckverstärker(pumpen)anlage
~**faltung** f (Geol.) = compressional folding
~**faser** f [*Träger* m] = compressive fibre (Brit.); ~ fiber (US)
~**feder** f = compression spring
~**festigkeit** f [*Beton* m] = compressive strength, crushing ~
~**festigkeitsstreuung** f = distribution of compressive strength
~**filter** m, n = pressure filter
~**fläche** f = surface under pressure, ~ taking up pressure, area of pressure, pressure area
~**flüssigkeit** f = pressure liquid
~**gärung** f = fermentation under pressure
~**gas** n, Preßgas = compressed gas
~**gasförderverfahren** n, Preßgasförderverfahren [*Druckförderung von Flüssigkeiten mit Hilfe von Erdgas*] = gas lift
~**gebläse** n = pressure blower
~**gefälle** n, siehe: Druckhöhe f
~**gefäß** n, siehe: Druckbehälter m
~**gerät** n, siehe: Oedometer m
~**glied** n = compression member
~**gurt** m [*Träger* m] = compression flange
~**gurt** m [*Fachwerk* n] = compression chord
~**haltung** f = maintenance of pressure, pressure maintenance
~**hebel** m = lever acting by pressure
~**höhe** f, Wassersäule f, Wassersäulenhöhe, Druckgefälle n, Fallhöhe = (water) head, pressure ~

~**höhenverlust** m = loss of (water) head, ~ ~ pressure head
~**hydrierung** f **von Kohle** f = coal hydrogenation process
~**kessel** m, siehe: Druckbehälter m
~**kessel** m, siehe: Treibkessel
~**kluft** f (Geol.) = pressure joint
~**knopfanlasser** m = push-button starter
druckknopfgesteuerter Materialzufluß m = push-button bulk flow
Druck|knopfschalter m, Fingerdruckschalter, Bedienungsknopfschalter = push-button (or press-button) switch
~**knopfsteuerung** f, Fingerdrucksteuerung = push-button (or press-button) control
~**kraft** f = compressive force
~**kristallisation** f = piezocrystallisation
~**kugellager** n = thrust ball bearing
~**lager** n = thrust bearing
~**leitung** f; siehe unter „Talsperre f"
~**leitung** f = pressure line
~**linie** f, Mittelkraftlinie, Stützlinie = pressure line
~**lok(omotive)** f = train-pushing engine
Druckluft f, Preßluft, komprimierte Luft = compressed air
~-**Abbauhammer** m, Druckluft-(Kohlen)-Pickhammer, Druckluft-Förderhammer = pneumatic (or air) coal picker (or pick hammer)
~**abteufung** f = pneumatic shaft sinking
~**anlasser** m = (compressed) air starter
~**antrieb** m = (compressed) air drive, pneumatic drive
~-**Aufbruchhammer** m, siehe: Druckluft-Aufreißhammer
~-**Aufreißhammer** m, Druckluft-Aufbruchhammer, Druckluftthammer für Aufreißarbeiten = pneumatic (or air) (pavement) breaker, air hammer, pneumatic pick
~**ausgleich** m = air pressure compensation
~-**Außenrüttler** m, Druckluft-Außenvibrator m = pneumatic external vibrator
~**axt** f, Preßluftaxt = air-driven (or pneumatic) axe (or pointer)
~**becken** n = diffused-air tank

Druckluft|behälter *m*, Druckluftkessel *m*, Windkessel, Druckluftspeicher *m*, Speicherkessel = (compressed) air vessel, air receiver

~belüftung *f* = diffused air aeration [*activated sludge process*]

druckluftbetätigt = (compressed) air operated

Druckluft|-Betonförderer *m*, pneumatisches Betonfördergerät *n*, (Druckluft-)Betonförderanlage *f*, Druckluft-Fördereinrichtung *f* für Beton = (pneumatic) concrete placer

~betonförderung *f*, pneumatischer Betontransport *m*, pneumatische Betonförderung, Preßluft-Betonförderung = pneumatic concrete placing

druckluftbetriebene Fettpresse *f* = air-operated grease unit

Druckluft|-Bodenramme *f* = pneumatic (or air) soil (or earth) rammer

~bohrhammer *m*, siehe: Druckluftgesteinsbohrhammer

~bremse *f*, Luftdruckbremse = air brake, compressed ~ ~

~-Drehkolben-Drehbohrmaschine *f* = pneumatic rotary piston rotating (or rotary) drilling machine

~einpreßgerät *n*, Injektor *m* = pressure grouting machine, (pneumatic) grouter, (cement) grout pump, grout ejector, power pump for grouting

~einspritzung *f* = air injection

~erkrankung *f*, Preßluftkrankheit *f*, Caissonkrankheit = compressed-air sickness, caisson disease, compressed air illness, bends

~erzeuger *m*, Luftverdichter *m*, Kompressor *m* = (air) compressor

~-Felsbohrhammer *m*, siehe: Druckluft-(gesteins)bohrhammer

~-Fernsteuerung *f*, Druckluft-Fernbedienung *f*, Druckluft-Fernbetätigung *f* = pneumatic remote control

~feuerung *f* = furnace with forced draught (Brit.); ~ ~ ~ draft (US)

~förderer *m*, Druckluftförderanlage *f* = pressure (or blast) pneumatic conveyor (or conveying system)

~-Förderhammer *m*, siehe: Druckluft-Abbauhammer

~-Förderrinne *f*, Luftförderrinne, pneumatische Förderrinne, Luft-Rutsche *f*, Gebläseluft-Förderrinne = airslide

~förderung *f*, siehe: pneumatische Förderung

~-Gegenhalter *m*, Druckluftvorhalter = pneumatic dolly, ~ holder-up

~gerät *n*, Druckluftwerkzeug *n* = compressed air tool

~geräte *npl* = compressed air equipment

~(gesteins)bohrhammer *m*, Druckluft-Felsbohrhammer = hammer-type pneumatic hand-held drill

druckluftgesteuert = pneumatically controlled

Druckluft|-Glättbohle *f* = pneumatic vibrated (finishing) screed (or smoother)

~gründung *f*, pneumatische Gründung = pneumatic foundation work, foundation work under compressed air

~hammer *m*; siehe unter „Rammanlage *f*"

~hammer *m* für Aufreißarbeiten *fpl*, siehe: Druckluft-Aufreißhammer

~hebebock *m*, Druckluftpresse *f*, Druckluftwinde *f*, Druckluft-Hubspindel *f*, Druckluft-Wagenheber *m*, Preßluft-Hebebock, Preßluftwinde *f* = air jack

~heber *m* = compressed-air ejector, air-jet lift

~hebezeug *n*, Preßlufthebezeug = pneumatic lifting device

~-Holzbohrer *m*, Preßluft-Holzbohrer = air auger, ~ wood borer

~horn *n* = air pressure horn

~-Hubspindel *f*, siehe: Druckluft-hebebock *m*

~-Innenrüttler *m*, Druckluft-Innenvibrator *m* = pneumatic internal vibrator

~kammer *f*, Preßluftsenkkasten *m*, Druckluftsenkkasten = air caisson, pneumatic ~ [*open at the bottom and shut at the top*]

~kessel *m*, siehe: Druckluftbehälter *m*

~-kesselsteinabklopfer *m*, pneumatischer Kesselsteinabklopfer = pneumatic scaling hammer, ~ ~ chipper

~kipper *m* = pneumatic tip(ping) wagon

Druckluft|-(Kohlen)Pickhammer m, siehe: Druckluft-Abbauhammer

~-Krankenschleuse f; siehe unter „pneumatische Gründung f"

~kühlung f = forced-draught cooling

~lader m, pneumatischer Lader = pneumatic loader

~leitung f = compressed air line

~lok(omotive) f; siehe unter „Feldbahnanlage f"

~-Maulschlüssel m = pneumatic wrench, air ~

~meißel m, Preßluftmeißel = pneumatic chipping hammer

~motor m, Preßluftmotor = compressed air motor
= (compressed-)air riveter, air riveting

~-Niethammer m, Preßluft-Niethammer hammer, pneumatic riveting hammer

~nietung f, Preßluftnietung = pneumatic riveting

~öler m, Preßluftöler = air lubricator

~(pfahl)ramme f; siehe unter „Rammanlage f"

~pfeife f, Preßluftpfeife = compressed air whistle

~pflasterramme f, Preßluftpflasterramme = pneumatic (sett) paving rammer

~-Pickhammer m, siehe: Druckluft-Abbauhammer

~pistole f, Preßluftpistole = compressed air gun

~presse f, Drucklufthebebock m, Druckluftwinde f, Druckluft-Hubspindel f, Druckluft-Wagenheber m = air jack

~pumpe f = air lift pump, compressed air ~

~ramme f, Preßluftramme [für Verdichtungsarbeiten] = pneumatic rammer

~ramme f; siehe unter „Rammanlage f"

~rüttler m; siehe unter „Beton(ein)rüttelgeräte npl"

~säge f, Preßluftsäge = air(-operated) saw, air-powered ~

~säulenschwenkkran m = pneumatic pillar crane

~schaltung f, Drucklufteuerung, Preßluftschaltung, Preßluftsteuerung = = pneumatic control, compressed-air ~

~schlauch m, Preßluftschlauch, Kompressorschlauch = air hose, flexible air line

(Druck)Luftschleuse f, Preßluftschleuse = (pressed) air-lock

Druckluft|senkkasten m, siehe: Druckluftkammer f

~spanndorn m = pneumatic expanding mandrel

~spannung f = air chucking

~spatenhammer m, Preßluftspatenhammer = pneumatic (clay) digger, ~ (~) spade, ~ spader, ~ spade hammer, air (-operated clay) spade

~speicher m, siehe: Druckluftbehälter m

~spritzgerät n, siehe: Betonspritzmaschine f

~stampfer m, Preßluftstampfer = pneumatic tamper

~steuerung f, siehe: Druckluftschaltung f

~-Überkopf-(Schaufel)Lader m, siehe: Druckluftwurfschaufellader

~-Verputzgerät n = pneumatic plasterthrowing machine, ~ plastering machine

~-Wagenheber m, siehe: Druckluftpresse f

~werkzeug n, Preßluftwerkzeug, Druckluftgerät n, Preßluftgerät = pneumatic tool, (compressed-) air ~

~winde f, siehe: Druckluftpresse f

~wurfschaufellader m, Druckluft-Überkopf-(Schaufel)Lader = pneumatic rocker (type) shovel (loader), ~ overshot loader, ~ overhead loader, ~ flipover bucket loader, ~ overloader

~-Zahnrad-Drehbohrmaschine f = pneumatic gear rotary (or rotating) drilling machine

~zementtransport m, Druckluftzementförderung f = pneumatic cement handling

~zug m = air hoist, pneumatic ~

~zylinder m = pneumatic cylinder

Druck|messer m = pressure ga(u)ge

~(meß)dose f = pressure cell, ~ capsule

~minderventil n = pressure reducing valve, ~ relief ~

~mutter f = thrust nut

~öl n = pressurized oil, hydraulic pressure ~

~ölbehälter m = hydraulic pressure oil vessel, pressurized oil ~

~öler m = force feed oiler

druckölgesteuert — Druckverteiler 139

druckölgesteuert = controlled by pressurized oil
Druck|öllenkung *f* = pressurized oil steer(ing)
~ölung *f* = pressure feed lubrication, forced ~ ~
~pfahl *m*; siehe unter „Gründungspfahl"
~pfosten *m* = strut
~-Porenziffer-Diagramm *n* = pressure-voids ratio diagram
~-Porenziffer-Verhältnis *n* = pressure voids-ratio ratio
~probe *f*, Druckprüfung *f* = compression (strength) test
~prüfpresse *f* = compression tester, ~ machine
~prüfung *f*, Druckprobe *f* = compression (strength) test
~prüfung *f* [*Gestein n*] = crushing (or compressive) (strength) test (on rock specimens)
~prüfungswert *m* [*Straßenbaugestein n*] = aggregate crushing value
~pumpe *f* = force pump
~querschnitt *m*, gedrückter Querschnitt = cross section under compression
~regulierventil *n* = pressure regulating valve
~ring *m* = thrust collar, ~ washer
~rohr *n* = pressure pipe
~rohrleitung *f* = pressure pipe line, ~ conduit
(~)Rüttler *m*, Schwinggerät *n* [*Rütteldruckverfahren n*] = vibroflot (machine)
~säule *f* [*Dammbalkenwehr n*] = holding down beam
~schacht *m*, Druckleitungsschacht, Fallschacht = penstock shaft, pressure ~
~schlag *m*, Abschrägung *f* [*Gewölbe n*] = bevel, splaying
~schlauchfilter *m, n* = pressure (type) cloth filter dust collector
~schräge *f*, Druckdiagonale *f*, gedrückte Diagonale = diagonal strut, ~ in compression, compression diagonal
~schütz(e) *m, (f)* = sluice valve with bottom release
~schwimmer *m* [*Motor m*] = pressure float
~-Setzungs-Quotient *m*, siehe: Bettungsziffer *f*

~setzungsversuch *m*, siehe: Kompressionsversuch
~spannung *f* = compressive stress, intensity of ~ ~
~spannungstextur *f* (Geol.) = shear structure
~spirale *f* [*Vorspannung f*] = spiral duct
~sprengwagen *m*, siehe: Bitumen-Sprengwagen
~stab *m*, Druckglied *n* [*Fachwerk n*] = compression(al) member, ~ bar
~stange *f* [*Motor m*] = push rod
~stange *f* = forcing lever
~stollen *m*; siehe unter „Talsperre *f*"
~störung *f* = pressure disturbance
~strahl *m* = jet of water
~strahlbagger *m*, Hydromonitor *m* = monitor, giant
~strahlbaggerung *f* = hydraulicking
~struktur *f* (Geol.) = pressure structure
~stufe *f* = pressure stage
~stütze *f* = compression column
~tankwagen *m*, siehe: Bitumen-Sprengwagen
~textur *f* (Geol.) = granulitic structure
~tränkung *f*, Holzimprägnierung *f* nach dem Kesseldruckverfahren *n*, Holztränkung unter Druck = pressure treatment, impregnating timber by ~ ~
~turbine *f* **mit Geschwindigkeitsstufen** *fpl* = impulse turbine with velocity stages
~umformer *m* = pressure transformer
~umlaufschmierung *f*, zwangsläufige Schmierung = force-feed lubrication
~ *m* **und Zug** *m* = compression and tension
~verdichtung *f*, siehe: Abwalzen *n*
~verstärkerpumpe *f* = booster pump
~verstärker(pumpen)anlage *f*, Druckverstärkerstation *f*, Verstärkungspumpenanlage, Druckerhöhungs(pumpen)anlage = booster station, ~ plant, boosting ~
~versuch *m*, Druckfestigkeitsprüfung *f* = compression test
~versuch *m* **bei seitlich unbehinderter Ausdehnung** *f* = unconfined compression test
~verteller *m*, siehe: Bitumen-Sprengwagen *m*

Druck|verteilung f [im Baugrund m] = stress distribution [through soils]
~**verteilung** f = distribution of pressure
~**verteilungsschicht** f, siehe: Sauberkeitsschicht
~**-Volumenkurve** f, adiabatische Linie f = adiabatic line
~**wassernietmaschine** f = hydraulic riveting machine
~**wasserreaktor** m = pressurised water reactor
~**(wasser)stollen** m; siehe unter „Talsperre"
~**welle** f [im Bohrloch n] = pressure surge
~**wiederaufbau** m = pressure restoration, ~ replacement
~**zerkleinerung** f = compression reduction
~**zerstäubungsbrenner** m = mechanical atomizing oil burner
~**zone** f [Balken m] = compression zone
~**zug** m = forced draught (Brit.); ~ draft (US)
~**zwiebel** f, Spannungsdiagramm n nach Boussinesq = bulb of pressure, pressure bulb
Drum(lin) m, Drümmel m, Rückenberg m (Geol.) = drumlin
Drusentextur f (Geol.) = drusy structure
Dübel m = dowel
~**bohrer** m, kurzer Schlangenbohrer mit zylindrischem Schaft = dowel bit, auger bit with short straight shank
~**bohrer** m **mit Gewindeschaft** = screw shank dowel bit
~**stein** m = dowel brick
Duckdalbe m, siehe: Dalbe
Düker m, Duker m = dip pipe
~, Duker m = inverted siphon; siphon culvert [deprecated]
Duktilität f, siehe: Streckbarkeit f
Düllspaten m = socket spade
Düne f, Sand~ = dune, sand dune, down
Dünge|kalk m = aglime, agricultural lime, agstone, liming material
~**mittelfabrik** f, Düngemittelwerk n = fertilizer plant
Dunglege f = dung dump
Dunit m (Geol.) = dunite, olivine-rock
dunkles Rotgültigerz n (Min.), siehe: Antimonsilberblende f

dünner Balken m = slender beam
dünn|plattige Spaltung f (Geol.) = slaty cleavage
~**schalige Kalotte** f = thin-shell dome
Dünnschliff m, Gesteinsplättchen n von etwa 0,02—0,03 mm = rock slice
dünn|viskoses Schmieröl n = spindle oil
~**wandiger Stahlzylinder** m **zur Bodenproben(ent)nahme** f = thin-walled tubing
~**wandiges Rohr** n = thin-walled pipe
Dünung f = swell waves
Duplex|kette f = duplex chain
~**kran** m, Doppelschwenkkran = duplex crane
~**-Rollenkette** f = double strand roller chain
DUPRA-Brecher m [Trademark], Fabrikat KLÖCKNER - HUMBOLDT - DEUTZ, KÖLN, DEUTSCHLAND = DUPRA double impeller impact breaker [Trademark]
Duraluminium n = duralumin
Durch|biegung f = deflection
~**biegungsmesser** m = deflectometer
~**bruch** m = break-through
~**bruchgestein** n, siehe: Ergußgestein
Durchfahrts|höhe f = headroom
~**portal** n = portal type gantry arranged to allow passage of rolling stock
durchfeuchten = to soak
Durchfluß|dauerkurve f, siehe: Dauerkurve der Abflußmengen fpl
~**(mengen)messer** m = flow meter
~**messer** m [Fluß m] = current meter
durchführbar = feasible
Durchführungsverordnung f = regulation
Durchgangs|bahnhof m = through station
~**gewindebohrer** m = through hole tap
~**sieb** n = limiting screen
~**straße** f, siehe: Ortsdurchfahrt f
~**verkehr** m = through traffic
durchgehende Schweißnaht f = continuous weld
Durch|hang m = sag(ging)
~**körner** m = pin punch
~**kreuzungs-Zwilling** m = cruciform twin group [mineralogy]
~**lässigkeit** f, Wasser~ = permeability
Durchlässigkeitsbeiwert m = coefficient of permeability, transmission constant, permeability coefficient

Durchlässigkeitsgerät n **mit abnehmender Wasserhöhe** f (oder abnehmendem Wasserdruck m) = falling head permeameter
~ ~ **gleichbleibender Wasserhöhe** f (oder gleichbleibendem Wasserdruck m) = constant head permeameter

Durchlässigkeitsversuch m **mit abnehmendem Wasserdruck** m = falling-head permeability test
~ ~ **gleichbleibendem Wasserdruck** m = constant-head permeability test

---

Durchlaß m, **Abzugkanal** m
Bogen~, überwölbter ~
Betonrohr~
Dreiröhren~
~ mit Parallelflügeln mpl
Endmauer f
Flügel(stirn)mauer f
gekuppelter Platten~
Kasten~
Platten~, gedeckter ~, Deckeldole f
Röhren~
Stirnmauer f
Treppen~, Kaskaden~
umwölbter ~
Zweiröhren~
Vielfach~

(drainage) culvert, drainage duct
arch(ed) (~) ~
concrete pipe (~) ~
triple (~) ~, three-barrel ~
(~) ~ with parallel wings
end wall
wing (head)wall, return wall
twin slab (~) ~
box (~) ~
slab (~) ~
pipe (~) ~, pipe cross drain
headwall
cascade (~) ~
English (~) ~
double (~) ~, twin type pipe (~) ~
multiple-opening (~) ~

Durchlauf-(Beton-)Zwangsmischer m; siehe unter „Betonmischer m"
durchlaufende Ankerwand f = anchor wall
durchlaufender Balken m, ~ **Träger** m, ~ **Balkenträger** m = continuous beam; ~ girder (Brit.)
~ **Hängeträger(balken)** m, siehe: Girlanden(balken)träger m
~ **Rahmen** m = continuous frame
durchlaufenes Kolbenvolumen n, Hubvolumen [Kompressor m] = swept volume, piston displacement
Durchlauf|mahlung f; siehe unter „Mühle f"
~**messer** m = flow meter
~**mischer** m, Mischer m mit Schurrenaustragung f, Austragsmischer, Freifall-Durchlaufmischer m = closed drum (concrete) mixer with tipping chute discharge
~**pfette** f = continuous purlin
~**träger** m = continuous beam
~**waschmaschine** f, Durchlaufwäsche f = flow washer (or washing machine)
~**-Zwangsmischer** m; siehe unter „Betonmischer m"

Durch|leuchtung f = trans-illumination
~**licht** n = transmitted light
~**lüftung** f [Boden m] = aeration
~**messer** m = diameter
~**satz** m [Material n] = throughput
~**schlagsröhre** f, vulkanischer Schlot m, Eruptionskanal m, vulkanischer Neck m, Esse f = (volcanic) neck, pipe(-like conduit)
~**schlagsspannung** f [Kabelvergußmasse f] = breakdown voltage [electrical filling compound]
durchschleusen = to lock
Durch|sickerung f, Versickerung f = percolation
~**steckschraube** f, Bolzen m mit Kopf m und Mutter f = bolt and nut
~**stich** m = cut
~**teufung** f = sinking through
~**tränken** n, Durchtränkung f, Imprägnieren n = impregnation
~**weichen** n = soaking
~**wurf(sieb)** m, (n) = riddle
Dürrständer m = dead standing tree
Düse f = jet

Düsen|bohren *n*, siehe: Feuerstrahlbohren
~**(flug)motor-Luftdruck** *m* = jet exhaust blast
~**(flug)motor-Treibstoff** *m* = jet(-turbine) fuel
~**meißel** *m*; siehe unter „Bohrmeißel"
~**öffnung** *f*, Düsenmundstück *n* = nozzle
~**schieber** *m* = jet valve
~**strang** *m*, siehe: Sprengrampe *f*
düsentreibstoffeste Fugenvergußmasse *f* = jet and fuel resisting joint sealing compound, JFR compound
Düsenverkehrsflugzeug *n* = jet liner
Dy *m* [*vollständig zersetzter Torf*] = dy
Dyassandstein *m* = dyas sandstone
dynamische Belastung *f* = dynamic load
~ **Bettungsziffer** *f* = dynamic modulus of subgrade reaction
~ **Geologie** *f* = physical geology
~ **Viskosität** *f* = absolute viscosity
dynamischer Eindringungswiderstand *m* = dynamic penetration
Dynamit *n*, *m* = dynamite
Dynamometamorphose *f*, Pressungsumwandlung *f*, Pressungsumprägung *f* = dynamic metamorphism
Dynamometer *n* = dynamometer
~**versuch** *m* = dynamometer test

E

Ebbe *f* = ebb tide
~**marke** *f*, Ebbelinie *f* = low water mark
~**rinne** *f* = ebb(-tide) channel
Ebb(e)strom *m*, Ebb(e)strömung *f* = ebb stream, ebb current, ebb-tide current
Ebbe- und Flut-Zone *f*, Litoral *n* = littoral zone
Ebbewassermenge *f* = volume of water discharging on the ebb-tide, volume of the ebb
Ebene *f* (Geol.) = plain
~ = plane
ebene Deformation *f* = plane strain
ebenerdige Kreuzung *f*, siehe: plangleiche ~
ebener Rahmen *m* **mit starren Ecken** *fpl* = rigid-jointed plane framework
ebenes Fachwerk *n*, ~ **Tragwerk** *n* = plane frame(work), ~ truss

Ebenflächigkeit *f*, Ebenheit *f*, Planebenheit *f* = evenness
Eberesche *f* = mountain ash
Ebner *m*; siehe unter „Fertigbehandlung *f*"
Echolot *n* = absolute altimeter
echte Tonfliese *f*, ~ keramische ~ = real clay tile
echter Hausschwamm *m*, siehe: tränender ~
~ **Löß** *m*, siehe: Urlöß
~ **Obsidian** *m* = true obsidian, Iceland agate
Eck|(absperr)ventil *n* = angle (shut-off) valve
~**aussteifung** *f* [*Kastenträger m*] = corner truss
~**blech** *n* = knee bracket
~**förmigkeit** *f*, Winkeligkeit, Kantigkeit [*z. B. Brekzie f*] = angularity [*e. g. breccia*]
eckiges Bruchstück *n* (Geol.) = angular fragment
Eck|leiste *f* **für Decken** *fpl* = cove
~**naht** *f* = corner weld, ~ joint
~**pfosten** *m* [*Fachwerkbrücke f*] = hip vertical
~**stein** *m* = quoin
~**überblattung** *f* **mit schrägem Schnitt** *m*; siehe unter „Holzverbindung *f*"
~**verkämmung** *f* **mit schrägem Kamm** *m*; siehe unter „Holzverbindung *f*"
~**versteifung** *f* = corner bracing
Edel|metall *n* = noble metal, precious ~
~**splitt** *m* = double broken and double screened chip(ping)s
~**tanne** *f*, siehe: Weißtanne
Effe *f*, siehe: Rüster *f*
effektive Pferdestärke *f*, nutzbare ~ = brake horsepower
effektiver Schub *m* = effective shear
Effusivgestein *n*, siehe: Ergußgestein
Ehre *f*, siehe: Bergahorn *m*
Eich|öl *n* = reference fuel
~**substanz** *f* = standard substance for calibration
~**tabelle** *f* = calibration chart
Eichung *f* = calibration
Eigenfahrbahn-System *n* = transit system with own right-of-way

Eigen|fahrwerk n = self-propelled travelling gear
~feuchtigkeit f = inherent moisture
~frequenz f = natural frequency
eigengestaltig, idiomorph [*Mineral* n] = idiomorphic
Eigen|gewicht n = dead (or fixed) weight (or load)
~konsolidation f, siehe: Konsolidierung f
~setzung f, siehe: Konsolidierung f
~spannung f = residual stress
~tumswohnung f = horizontal property
~verfestigung f, siehe: Konsolidierung f
Eignungsprüfung f = suitability test, preliminary ~
Eikanal m, eiförmiger Sammler m, eiförmiges Kanalrohr n, Eiprofilrohr n = egg-shaped sewer (pipe)
Eimer m = bucket
~, Becher m [*Becherwerk* n] = conveyor bucket
~kette f, Becherkette = ladder chain carrying the buckets, bucket elevator chain
Eimerketten|aufzug m, siehe: Becherwerk n
~fahrlader m, siehe: Becher(werk)auflader m
~fahrlader m **mit Drehabsatzband** n = swivel conveyor bucket loader
~grabenbagger m; siehe unter „Grabenbagger m mit Eimern mpl"
~-Hochbagger m = face bucket ladder excavator
~naßbagger m; siehe unter „Naßbagger m"
~raupenbagger m = crawler bucket ladder excavator
~schwimmbagger m; siehe unter „Naßbagger m"
~-Tiefbagger m = bucket ladder excavator working below ground level
~trockenbagger m, Eimertrockenbagger m = bucket ladder excavator, dredger excavator, chain bucket excavator, continuous land bucket dredger, multi-bucket excavator
Eimer|latrine f = bucket latrine
~leiter f; siehe unter „Naßbagger m"
~leiter f, Becherleiter = bucket ladder

~leitergrabenbagger m; siehe unter „Grabenbagger m mit Eimern mpl"
~leiterrahmen m, siehe: Baggerleiterrahmen
~rad n, Kreiseimerleiter f [*Grabenbagger* m] = digging wheel
~rad n, Schöpfrad, Becherrad [*Waschmaschine* f] = dewatering wheel
~reihe f, siehe: Eimerstrang m
~seilbagger m, siehe: Schürfkübelbagger m
~seilkübel m, siehe: Schleppschaufel f
~seil-Schreitbagger m, siehe: Schleppschaufel-Schreitbagger
~strang m, Becherstrang, Eimerreihe f, Becherreihe = line of buckets
~trockenbagger m, siehe: Eimerkettentrockenbagger
Einachs-Anhänger m = single-axle trailer
Einachser m = single-axle unit, two-wheel ~
Einachs|fahrwerk n = single-axle travel(l)ing gear, ~ undercarriage
~-Gußasphaltkocher m = semi-trailer type mastic asphalt boiler (or cooker)
einachsige Spannung f = uniaxial stress
einachsiger Erdtransportwagen m **mit Einachs-Radschlepper** m = motor wagon
Einachs|-Luftverdichter m = trailer compressor
~mischer m, siehe: (luftbereifter) Einachs(-Schnell)mischer
~-Motor-Schrapper m, Autoschrapper m mit 2-Rad-Schlepper m, Schrapper m mit gummibereiftem Einachs-Traktor m, Motor-Schürf(kübel)wagen m mit Einachs-Schlepper m, motorisierter Schürfkübel m mit Einachs-Traktor m [*z. B. Fabrikate CATERPILAR und Le TOURNEAU TOURNAPULL*] = tractor-scraper, motor(ized) scraper, motor scraper (with two-wheel traction)
~räumer m = hand-guided two-wheel dozer
~-Reifen-Sattelschlepper m, siehe: (Zweirad-)Vorspänner m
~schlepper m, Einachsradschlepper, Zweirad-Schlepper, Einachszugwagen m, Zweirad-Trecker m = two-wheel(ed) tractor

Einachs-Schlepperkran m, **Einachs-Krananhänger** m
Einachs-Schlepperkran m, Fabrikat LeTOURNEAU-WESTINGHOUSE COMPANY, PEORIA, ILLINOIS, USA

tractor-drawn crane, lift-and-carry ~

TOURNACRANE, LeTOURNEAU portable crane [*Trademark*]

Einachs-Zugwagen m, siehe: (Zweirad-) Vorspänner m
Einankerumformer m = synchronous converter
Ein-Arbeitsgang-Verfahren n [*Bodenvermörtelung f*] = single-pass mixing
Einbahn|straße f = one-way road
~straßenpaar n = one-way pair
Einbau m, Schütterbeiten f = (fill) placing (operations), placement
~-Dieselmotor m = built-in diesel engine
~element n, Abziehelement n [*Schwarzdeckenfertiger* m] = floating screed
~fähigkeit f [*Beton* m] = placeability
~gerät n [*Straße* f] = laying machine
~gerät n für Gerinne-Auskleidungen *fpl*; siehe unter „Kanalbaumaschinen *fpl*"
~kolonne f [*Straßenbau* m] = laying (or spreading) gang (or team, or crew, or party)
~kosten f [*Straßendecke* f] = laying costs, costs of laying
~kosten f [*Bodenvermörtelung* f] = processing costs
~leistung f [*Straßenfertiger* m] = laydown rate [*road finisher*]
~maschine f, siehe: Deckeneinbaugerät n
~- oder Verteil-Gerät n für Splitt, Schotter und bituminöses Mischgut = paverspreader
(~)Schicht f = lift, layer, course, pour
~stelle f, Vortriebsstelle f [*Straßenbau* m] = spreading site, placing point, laying ~, placement ~; working face (Brit.)
~streifen m [*Straßenbau* m] = paving lane (US); pavement ~
~streuer m; siehe unter „Streugerät n für den Winterdienst m"
~temperatur f [*Straßenbelag* m] = laying temperature
~wassergehalt m = placement moisture (or water) content

einbetonierte Stahlkonstruktion f = concrete-encased steel construction
einbetonierter Träger m = cased beam
Einbinden n = connecting to existing work
einbinden [*Straße f in die Landschaft*] = to fit [*the road into the landscape*]
~ = to feather [*to blend the edge of new material smoothly into the old surface*]
Einbruchscaldera m = engulfment caldera
einbuchtendes Ufer n, Konkave f eines Flusses = concave bank
Einbuchtung f = embayment
Eindecker m, Einstufensieb n = single deck screen
eindeichen = to bank in
Eindicker m = thickener
~ mit Kratzer-Klassierer m = spiral rake thickener, ~ scraper ~, classifier for fine separations
Eindrehmaschine f [*Herstellung f von Geschirrporzellan n*] = jigger
Eindring|mörtel m, siehe: Einpreßmörtel m
~öl n = penetrating oil
Eindringung f, Penetration f = penetration
Eindring(ungs)messer m, Penetrometer n, Eindringgerät n = penetrometer
Eindruck-Scherfestigkeits-Prüfung f = punching shear stability test
einebnen, einplanieren, verebnen = to spread and level
Einebnungspflug m, siehe: Planierpflug m
Einfach-Abmeßeinrichtung f = single-material batcher
~ mit Waage f = single-material scale batcher
Einfach-Bereifung f = single tyre (Brit.); ~ tire (US)
einfache Ausfachung f = single system of triangulation
~ Biegung f = simple flexure
~ Gewichts(stau)mauer f; siehe unter „Talsperre f"

einfache Vergitterung f [*Stütze f*] = single lacing
einfacher (Erz) Gang m = vein
~ **Heizröhrenkessel** m = single cylinder multitubular boiler
~ **Träger m auf zwei Stützen** fpl = simple beam
einfaches Blatt; siehe unter „Holzverbindung f"
~ **Deckenvorgelege** n, einfache Vorlegewelle f = jack shaft
~ **Dreieckfachwerk** n = single-web system truss
~ **Hängewerk** n, einsäuliges ~ = king (post) truss
~ **Sprengwerk** n = simple truss
Einfach-(Gesteins) Waage f = single weighbatcher
~-**Gewölbesperre** f; siehe unter „Talsperre f"
~-**Spurkranzrad** n = single-flanged wheel
einfachwirkend = single-acting
Einfäd(e)lungs|länge f; siehe unter „Verkehr m"
~**raum** m; siehe unter „Verkehr m"

Einfahr|gleis n [*Verschiebebahnhof m*] = receiving track
~**pulver** n = bon ami powder, break-in ~
Einfahrt|schleuse f, siehe: Dockschleuse
~**tor** n zur gebührenpflichtigen Autobahn f = toll gate
Einfamilienhaus n = single-family house
Einfeldrahmen m = frame of one bay
Einflammrohrkessel m, siehe: Cornwallkessel
einfluchten, siehe: abfluchten
Einfluchtung f, siehe: Ausfluchtung
Einfluß|fläche f = influence diagram
~**linie** f = line of influence
Einfriedigung f, **Einzäunung** f, **Umzäunung** f = fencing, boundary fence
einfüllen, verfüllen [*z. B. Graben m*] = to backfill, to fill in, to re-fill
Einfüll|stelle f = filling point
~**trichter** m = receiving hopper
Ein-Gang-Mischer m = single pass soil mixer (or stabilizer), single-pass travel mixer, single-pass rotary tiller and spreader

---

Ein-Gang-Mischer m, **Ein-Gang-Bodenvermörteler** m, **Fabrikat HARNISCHFEGER CORPORATION, MILWAUKEE, USA**

Single Pass Soil Stabilizer

Abgleichbohle f, Endklappe f	tail gate
Anzapfen n	bleeding
Bedienungshebel m	control lever
Bitumenmesser m	asphalt meter (US); asphaltic bitumen ~ (Brit.)
Bitumenpumpe f	asphalt pump
Deichsel f	push bar
Deichselaufhängung f	push bar support
Doppelwellenzwangsmischer m	pug mill
Einspritzdüse f	spray nozzle
Endklappe f, Abgleichbohle f	tail gate
Filtersieb n	strainer
Flüssigkeitswagen m	liquid truck
gegenläufige Rotoren mpl	contra-rotating rotors
Hubzylinder m	hoisting cylinder, lifting ~
Kimme f	rear sight
Kippzylinder m	tilting cylinder
Korn n	front sight
Lenkbremse f	steering brake
Mischerantrieb m	mixer drive

Ein-Gang-Mischer — einkammeriges Druckgefäß

Mischschaufel *f*	(pug mill) paddle
Richtpflock *m*	guide stake
Rücklaufleitung *f*	return line
rückwärts fahren	to back up
Schneidwelle *f*, Welle mit festen Schlägern	cutting rotor, front rotor
Seitenblech *n*	side angle
Spritzventil *n*	spray valve
Spülen *n*	flushing
Spur *f*, Bahn *f*, Streifen *m*	lane
Startgraben *m*	header
Überlappung *f*	lap
Umführungsventil *n*	by-pass valve
Umstellhebel *m*	shift lever
Vermörteln *n*, Verfestigen *n*	processing
Vermörtelungskammer *f*, Arbeitskammer	processing chamber, mixing box
Verriegelungseinrichtung *f*	NoRol [*Trademark*]
Visiervorrichtung *f*	guide sights
Wassermesser *m*	water meter

---

eingebaut = built-in, inbuilt
eingedeicht = diked
eingeeist = icebound
eingefallener Kraterrand *m* = broken-down rim (of the crater)
Ein-Gefäß|(förder)pumpe *f* = single-tank type pump, ~ pneumatic conveying system
~trockenbagger *m* = single-bucket excavator
eingeführte Luft *f*, siehe: eingeschlossene ~
eingefurchter Kegel (Geol.) = trenched cone
Eingemeindung *f* = annexation
(ein)gesackter Zement *m*, Sackzement = bagged cement
eingeschlossene Luft *f*, eingeführte ~ [*Beton m*] = entrained air
eingeschlossener Konstruktionsteil *m* = enclosed structural member
eingeschneit, verschneit = snowed-up, snow-bound
eingeschobene Treppe *f*, Leitertreppe = stairs with treads between strings
eingeschossiger Bau *m*, einstöckiger ~, eingeschossiges Gebäude *n*, einstöckiges ~, einetagiger Bau *m*, einetagiges Gebäude = single-stor(e)y building, single-floored ~

eingespannt [*z. B. Säule f*] = restrained
eingespannter Träger *m*, ~ Balken *m* = fixed beam, girder with fixed ends
eingestemmte Treppe *f* = stairs mortised into strings
eingesumpfter Kalk *m*, siehe: Kalkteig *m*
eingleisige Brücke *f* = single line bridge, ~ track ~
eingleisiger Tunnel *m* = single line tunnel, ~ track ~
Einhandstein *m* = one-hand block
einhängiges Dach *n*, Pultdach, Flugdach, Halbdach, Schleppdach = lean-to roof, pent ~, shed
Einhebelbedienung *f*, Einhebelsteuerung, Einhebelbetätigung = single lever control (or operation)
einheimisches Bau(nutz)holz *n* = home-grown timber, native ~
einheitlich gebauter Vulkan *m* = monogenic volcano
Einheits|last *f* = unit load
~preis *m* = unit price, rate
~vektor *m* = unit vector
einhüftiger Bogen *m*, steigender ~ = inclined arch, rising ~, rampant ~
einkammeriges Druckgefäß *n*, siehe: Treibkessel *m*

Einkaufsabteilung — Einpreßmörtel 147

Einkaufs|abteilung *f* = purchasing department
~**viertel** *n* = shopping center (US); ~ centre (Brit.)
Einkehrfluß *m* = resequent river
Einketten|-Baggerkorb *m* = single chain digging grab
~**-Greifbagger** *m* = single chain grab excavator
~**-Raupe(nfahrwerk)** *f*, (*n*) = single crawler unit
Einkieselung *f* = silicification
Einkipphöhe *f* [*Baustellensilo m*] = bin feeding height
einknicken, ausknicken = to buckle, to yield to axial compression
einkörniges Material *n*; siehe unter „(Beton-)Zuschlagstoffe *mpl*"
Einkurbelpumpe *f* = single throw pump
Einlage *f*, Zwischenlegscheibe *f* = shim
Einlagerung *f* (Geol.), siehe: Einschluß *m*
einlagiger Betoneinbau *m* = full-course (construction) work
~**Bitumenteppich** *m* = single-coat asphalt (Brit.)
Einlaß|bauwerk *n* **zum Kraftwerk** *n*; siehe unter „Talsperre *f*"
~**bauwerk** *n*, siehe: Einlauf(bauwerk) *m*, (*n*)
~**hebel** *m*, Einlaßventil-Steuerhebel *m* = inlet cam roller lever
~**rohr** *n*, Einlaufrohr = inlet pipe, intake ~
~**schacht** *m*, Einlaufschacht = intake shaft, inlet ~
~**schieber** *m* = inlet (slide) valve
~**turm** *m*; siehe unter „Talsperre *f*"
~**verschluß** *m*; siehe unter „Talsperre *f*"
Einlauf *m* = inlet
~**(bauwerk)** *m*, (*n*), Einlaßbauwerk, Entnahmebauwerk = intake (structure), inlet (~) (or works), head works
~**becken** *n* = inlet reservoir
~**becken** *n* [*Oberflächenwasserversorgung f*] = intake basin
~**(ge)rinne** *f*, (*n*), siehe: Einlaufkanal *m*
~**kanal** *m*, Einlauf(ge)rinne *f*, (*n*), Zulauf(ge)rinne = inlet channel
~**kasten** *m* = feed box
~**leitung** *f* = intake line

~**rechenreiniger** *m* = trashrack rake
~**regulierungsbauwerk** *n* = inlet regulator
~**rohr**, Einlaßrohr = inlet pipe, intake ~
~**rost** *m* = inlet grating, ~ grate
~**schacht** *m*, Einlaßschacht = intake shaft, inlet ~
~**schmieröl** *n* = running-in compound
~**schütz(e)** *m*, (*f*) = inlet sluice
~**schwelle** *f* = inlet sill
~**trichter** *m* = inlet funnel
~**trommel** *f* [*Kugel(mahl)mühle f*] = drum feeder
~**trommel** *f* **mit Schöpfschnecke** *f* [*Kugel(mahl)mühle f*] = drum-and-scoop feeder
~**trompete** *f*; siehe unter „Talsperre *f*"
~**turm** *m*; siehe unter „Talsperre *f*"
~**ventil** *n* = inlet valve
Einmann|bedienung *f*; siehe unter „Baumaschinen *fpl* und Baugeräte *npl*"
~**-Handschrapper** *m* = one-man scraper
~**säge** *f*, Waldsteifsäge = one-man crossout saw
~**wagen** *m* = one-man car
Einmotoren|bagger *m* = one-power unit excavator
~**greiferhubwerk** *n* = grab(bing) hoisting gear with one power unit
einmotoriger Pneubagger *m*, Fabrikat KOEHRING CO., MILWAUKEE 10, USA; siehe unter „Autobagger"
Ein-Motor-Kran *m* **mit Dieselantrieb** *m* = single diesel engine crane
~ ~ **elektrischem Antrieb** *m* = single motor crane
Einmündung *f* [*Straße f*] = junction
Einplanieren *n* [*mechanisch*] = planing
einplanieren, einebnen, verebnen = to spread and level
einpressen, auspressen, injizieren, verpressen = to inject, to grout under pressure
Einpreß|druck *m*, Auspreßdruck, Injektionsdruck, Verpreßdruck = grouting pressure
~**gas** *n* = input gas
~**loch** *n*, Auspreßloch, Injektionsloch, Verpreßloch = grout hole
~**mörtel** *m*, Eindringmörtel, Auspreßmörtel, Injektionsmörtel, Verpreßmörtel = intrusion mortar

Einpreß|schürze *f*; siehe unter „Talsperre *f*"

~verfahren *n*, Injektionsverfahren, Auspreßverfahren, Verpreßverfahren = pressure grouting (or injection) process, (grout) injection

Einrad|-Fahrvorrichtung *f* = single-wheel(ed) troll(e)y

~-Wagenschieber *m* = railway-wagon shifter

Einrammen *n* [*Pfahl m*] = pile driving

einreihige Nietung *f* = single (row) rivet(ed) joint

Einrichtung *f*. (Betriebs)Anlage *f* = facility, installation, plant

Einrollenlager *n* = single-roller bearing

Einrückhebel *m* = engaging lever

Einrütteln *n*, Einrüttlung *f* = vibrating

Einrüttlung *f*, Einrütteln *n* = vibrating

Einrüttlungsverdichtung *f*, siehe: Vibrationsverdichtung

Einsacken *n*, Absacken *n* = bagging, sacking(-off)

Einsack|maschine *f*, Absackmaschine, Abfüllmaschine für Säcke = bagging machine, bag-packing ~, bag packer

~waage *f*, Absackwaage = bagging scale

Einsanden *n* [*Pflasterfuge f*] = feeding, rejointing of sett paving

Einsatz *m*, Arbeits~ = employment

~ = insert

~ für Hydraulikpumpe *f* bzw. **Aufladegebläse** *n* = cartridge

~bereich *m*, *n*; siehe unter „Baumaschinen *fpl* und Baugeräte *npl*"

~flugplatz *m*; siehe unter „Flugplatz"

~stück *n*, Distanzstück = insert

einsäuliges Hängewerk *n*, siehe: einfaches ~

Einschaler *m* = form setter

Einschaltmineral *n* = released mineral

Einschalung *f*, siehe: Schalung

Einscharungsmoräne *f*; siehe unter „Gletscher *m*"

Ein-Schaufelwellenmischer *m*, Einwellen-Knetmischer, Einwellen-Zwangsmischer = single shaft pug mill, long ~ ~

Einscheiben|antrieb *m* = single-speed drive, constant-speed ~

~drehbank *f* = single pulley lathe

~trockenkupplung *f* = single plate dry clutch

einschichtiger Betrieb *m* = single-shift work, ~ operation

Einschienen|bahn *f* zum Betontransport *m*, Transport-Einschienenbahn = monorail (concrete) transporter (or conveyor), single rail (~) ~ (~ ~)

~-Hängebahn *f* = overhead monorail

~laufkatze *f*, Einschienenlastkatze = single rail troll(e)y

Einschließstand *m* [*Militärflugplatz m*] = firing-in butt

einschlafen [*Wind m*] = to die down

einschlämmen mit Wasser *n* = to flush with water

~ ~ ~ [*wassergebundene Schotterdecke f*] = to wash in the fines by sluincig [*waterbound macadam*]

Einschlämmen *n*, Bodenverdichtung *f* durch Einschlämmen, Einspülen *n*, Einspülverfahren *n*, Spülspritzverfahren, Spülkipperverfahren, Wasserstrahlverfahren = sluicing

~ [*Straßenbau m*] = flushing

Einschleifpaste *f* = grinding compound

Einschluß *m*, Einlagerung *f* (Geol.) [*Sonderbildung f in Mineralien oder Gesteinen*] = inclusion, inlier

Einschmelzungsmetamorphose *f*, Palingenese *f*, Anatexis *f* [*Reaktivierung f vorher erstarrter Schmelzen fpl*] (Geol.) = palingenesis

Einschnitt *m*, Abtrag *m* = cut(ting)

~ und Damm *m*, Abtrag *m* und Auftrag *m* (oder Aufschüttung *f*) = cut(ting) and fill

~aushub *m* = excavation of cutting

~böschung *f*, siehe: Böschung im Abtrag

einschnittige Verbindung *f*, einschnittiges Gelenk *n* [*Stahlbau m*] = single lap joint, single-shear joint

Einschnürung *f* = contraction, neck-down, necking

Einschwemmungshorizont *m*, B-Horizont, Anreicherungshorizont, Anreicherungsschicht *f*, Illuvialhorizont = B-horizon, zone of concentration, zone of illuviation

einschwimmen = to float into position (or place)

Einschwingen|brecher *m*; siehe unter „Backenbrecher"

~-Granulator *m*, Granulator-Splittbrecher *m* = single-toggle granulator, ~ type jaw ~, chipping(s) breaker

Einseil|-Greifkorb *m*, Einseil-Baggergreifer *m* = single-line bucket

~haken *m* = single-line hook

~-Schrapper *m* = single-rope scraper

~(schwebe)bahn *f*; siehe unter „Drahtseilschwebebahn"

einseitig einfallender Bergkamm *m*, ~ ~ Felsrücken *m* = hogback

~ zusammengesetztes Faltengebirge *n* = unilaterally compound folded mountains

einseitiger Korbbogen *m* = single-centred compound curve

~ Querschnitt *m*, siehe: Überhöhung *f*

Einspannbedienung *f* = end condition

Einspannung *f* = restraint, fixity

Einspann(ungs)moment *n* = end moment, restraint ~, fixed end moment

Einsparung *f*, Ersparnis *f* = saving

einspringender Winkel *m* = re-entering angle

einspringendes Widerlager *n* = re-entering abutment

Einspritzpumpengestänge *n* = rack setting arm

Einspülen *n*, Einspülverfahren *n*, (Bodenverdichtung *f* durch) Einschlämmen *n*, Spülspritzverfahren, Spülkippverfahren, Wasserstrahlverfahren = sluicing

~, Einbringen *n* mit Spülhilfe *f* [*Pfahl m*] = water jetting, pile-sinking with the water-jet, water-jet driving, pile jetting

(Ein)Spülrohr *n* [*Pfahl m*] = jetting pipe

Einspundung *f* = closed sheeting

Einständerfahrgestell *n* = single-pole travelling gear

Einstau *m*, Wasser~; siehe unter „Talsperre *f*"

~filter *n*, *m* = contact bed, ~ filter

Einsteig(e)|luke *f* = hatch(way)

~schacht *m*, siehe: Mannloch *n*

einstellbarer Kontakt *m* = adjustable contact

Einstell|barkeit *f*; siehe unter „Baumaschinen *fpl* und Baugeräte *npl*"

~bereich *m* = range of adjustment

~gewicht *n*, Laufgewicht = poise weight, sliding ~, jockey ~, moving poise

einstellige Zahl *f* = number with one digit

Einstell|kompaß *m*, siehe: Regelkompaß

~mutter *f* = adjusting nut

einstemmen = to mortise in

einstöckiger Bau *m*, siehe: eingeschossiger ~

einstrahlender Verkehr *m* = city-bound traffic

Einstreichfeile *f*, Schraubenkopffeile = screw-head file, slitting ~, feather-edge(d) ~

Einstreudecke *f*, Streumakadam *m* = dry penetration surfacing, ~ process penetration macadam

Ein-Stufen-Destillation *f* [*Erdölaufbereitung f*] = single-flash distillation

Einstufensieb *n*, Eindecker *m* = single deck screen

einstufige Druckturbine *f* = single-stage impulse turbine

~ Mahlung *f*, Einstufenmahlung = one-stage grinding, single-passage ~

~ Verdichtung *f* [*Kompressor m*] = single-stage compression

Einsturz *m*, Nachfall *m* = cave(-in)

~beben *n* = subsidence earthquake

~becken *n* = subsidence basin

~doline *f* = collapse dolina, ~ doline

einstürzen [*z. B. Brücke f*] = to collapse [*e. g. bridge*]

Einsturzsee *m* = sink lake

Einsumpfen *n*, Einsümpfen = ponding

~, siehe: Naßlöschverfahren *n*

Eintafelschütz(e) *m*, (*f*) = single leaf (sluice) gate

Eintags|fliege *f* = may fly

~probe(stück) *f*, (*n*) = day-old specimen

Eintauch|lötung *f*, Eintauchlöten *n* = dip soldering

~rohr *n* = immersion pipe

~schmierung *f* = flood lubrication

einteiliges Lagergehäuse *n* = solid housing

Einteilung *f* **der Gesteine** *npl* **in Handelsgruppen** *fpl* = trade grouping of rocks

eintouriger Elektromotor *m* = constant speed motor

eintouriges Schloß *n* = single turn lock

eintrocknender See *m* = evanescent lake

Eintrommel|-Seilwinde f = single drum rope winch
~straßen(beton)mischer m; siehe unter „Straßen(beton)mischer"
~winde f = single-drum winch
eintrümiger Schacht m = undivided shaft, single ~
eintrümiges Seil n = one-side(d) rope
Ein-und Ausrückkupplung f, siehe: Schaltkupplung
(Ein)Visieren n = sighting, boning(-in)
Einwalzen-Prallbrecher m, Prallbrecher mit einer Schlagwalze = single impeller impact breaker
einwandfrei [in bezug auf Güte] = sound
einwandiger Blechbogen m = single-webbed plate arch
~ Obergurt m = top boom with single web
Einweihungsfeier f = dedication ceremony
Einweisen n [LKW m] = spotting
Einweiser m [beim Abkippen n] = spotter, dumperman
Einwellen-Zwangsmischer m, Einwellen-Knetmischer, Ein-Schaufelwellenmischer = single shaft pug mill, long ~ ~
einwirken auf = to act upon
Einwirkung = action
Einwitterung f; siehe unter „Denudation f"
Einwohnergleichwert m = population equivalent
Einwölbung f **auf Kuf** = barrel vaulting
~ ~ Schwalbenschwanz = dovetail vaulting
Einwurftrichter m = hopper
Einzahn-Gewindestrehler m = single-tooth chaser
Einzäunung f, Einfriedigung, Umzäunung = boundary fence, fencing
Einzel|antrieb m = direct motor drive
~aufhängung f = individual suspension
~bedienung f = individual operation
~brenner m [Schweißen n] = torch with non-variable head, non-variable (head) torch
~druckknopfsteuerung f = single push-button control
~fundament n = spot footing, isolated ~, independent ~
~gipfel m (Geol.) = solitary peak
~ketten-Entladegreifer m = single chain unloading (grab) bucket
~korn n, Gesteinskorn, Partikelchen n, Einzelteilchen n, Körnchen n = particle, grain
~kreuzung f, Kreuzung von zwei Straßen fpl = crossing
~kristall n = unit crystal
~last f, einzeln wirkende Last, einzeln konzentrierte Last = concentrated load, single ~, load concentrated at a point; point load (US)
~prämiensystem n = single incentive bonus scheme
~schuß m [Pfahl m, Rohr n] = section
~-Silo m **mit Waage** f = batching unit
~vulkan m = central volcano, solitary ~
einziehbares Fahrgestell n = retractable undercarriage [airplane]
Einzieh|kran m = luffing crane, level ~ ~
~schacht m = downcast air shaft
~werk n [Kran m] = (level) luffing gear
Einzonenbauweise f, siehe: englische Bauweise
Einzuggebiet n; siehe unter „Entwässerung f"
Einzweckstraße f = single-purpose road
Eiprofilrohr n, siehe: Eikanal m
Eis|barre f = ice-barrage, ice-dam
~berg m = iceberg
~bildung f = ice formation, ~ segregation, segregation of ice, formation of ice
~blink m = iceblink
~brecher m = ice-breaker [ship]
~brecher m = ice guard
~brechpflug m = ice-breaking ram of the vessel
~druck m = ice pressure
Eisenalaun m (Min.) = iron alum, halotrichite
Eisenbahn|damm m, siehe: Bahndamm
~draisine f, siehe: Draisine
~fähre f = train ferry
~-Kesselwagen m = rail-tanker, tanker wagon (Brit.); railroad tank car (US)
~oberbau m = permanent way [abbrev. p. w.]
~schiene f = railway rail (Brit.); railroad ~ (US)

Eisenbahn|schotter *m*, Gleisschotter *m*, Bettungsschotter *m*, Bahnschotter = (railway) (track) ballast (Brit.); railroad (~) ~ (US); treck ~

~-Unfallkran *m* = breakdown crane, accident ~, permanent way crane (Brit.); wrecking ~ (US)

Eisen|band *n* = metal strap, iron ~

~becher *m*, siehe: Eisenelevatorbecher

eisenbereiftes Fahrzeug *n* = iron-tyred vehicle (Brit.); iron-tired ~ (US)

Eisen|blech *n*, siehe: Blech

~chlorür *n*, Ferrochlorid *n*, $FeCl_2 + 4H_2O$ = ferrous chloride

~(elevator)becher *m* = iron elevator bucket

~flechter *m* = steel fixer

~frischflammofen *m* = puddling furnace

~glas *n*, Fe_2SiO_4 (Min.) = fayalite, iron-olivine

~glimmerschiefer *m* (Geol.) = itabaryte, itabarite

~graupen *f* (Min.) = granular bog iron ore

eisenhaltiges Wasser *n* = ferruginous water

Eisen|hochofen-Stückschlacke *f*, siehe: Hochofenschlacke

~hüttenschlacke *f*, siehe: Metall(hütten)-schlacke

~hydroxid *n*, $Fe(OH)_3$ = ferric hydrate

~lebererz *n* (Min.) = hepatic iron ore

~mennige *f* = iron ochre

~nickelkies *m* (Min.) = nicopyrite, pentlandite

~ölseife *f* = iron oleate

~oolith *m*, siehe: Eisenrogenstein *m*

~oxyd *n*, Fe_2O_3 = ferric oxide, iron ~

~oxydgelb *n* = yellow iron oxide

~oxydhydrat *n* = hydrous ferric oxide

~oxydul *n* = ferrosoferic oxide

~rad *n*, eisenbereiftes Rad *n* = metal wheel, steel-rimmed ~

~rogenstein *m*, Eisenoolith *m* = oolitic iron ore

~sandstein *m*; siehe unter „Sandstein *m*"

~schere *f* = iron cutters

~schwamm-Herstellung *f* im Tunnelofen *m* = tunnel kiln sponge iron process

~selenür *n* = ferrous selenide

~sinter *m* = iron dross, pitticite

~spat *m*, Siderit *m* (Min.) = chalybite, siderite, spathic iron

~spinell *m*, Hercynit *m*, $FeAl_2O_4$ (Min.) = iron spinel, hercynite

~sulfat *n* = ferrous sulphate, iron ~, sulphate of iron, copperas

~sulfatchlorid *n* = chlorinated copperas

~ton *m*, Toneisenstein *m* = clay ironstone, iron clay

~tongranat *m* = iron-aluminium garnet

~vitriol *m*, *n*, Melanterit *m* (Min.) = green vitriol, melanterite

~zinkblende *f* (Min.) = marmatite

eiserner Baustellensilo *m* für Zuschlagstoffe *mpl*, Kiessilo *m* = steel gravel (storage) bin

Eis|feld *n* = ice field, ice-floe, ice-pack, ice-jam

~gang *m* = embacle

~gischt *f* = freezing sprays

~glätte *f* = silver frost

~klappe *f* = ice gate

~kluft *f* [Holz *n*] = frost cleft (or shake)

~klüftigkeit *f* = cracking (or splitting) by frost

~lawine *f*; siehe unter „Gletscher *m*"

~linse *f* = ice lens

~mantel *m*, siehe: Binneneisdecke *f* (Geol.)

~räumung *f* = ice removal

~-Schmelzvorgang *m* = melting of ice

~scholle *f* = ice flow, block of ice

~schranke *f* = ice barrier

~schrumpfung *f* = glacial shrinkage

~sohle *f* = ice sole

~spat *m* = ice spar

~sprengung *f*, Eissprengen *n* = breaking up of the ice by explosives

~stein *m*, siehe: Kryolith *m* (Min.)

~stopfung *f* = packing of ice

Eiseinkalk *m*, siehe: oolithischer Kalkstein *m*

Eis|tisch *m*; siehe unter „Gletscher *m*"

~tor *n* = ice cave

~verbreitungszentrum *n* = center of ice dispersal (US); centre ~ ~ ~ (Brit.)

~wall *m* = ice rampart

~wüste *f* = ice desert

eiszapfenförmig = icicle shaped

Eiweißstickstoff *m* = albuminoid nitrogen

Eklogit *m* = eclogite

Elaeolith *m*, Ölstein *m* (Min.) = elaeolite
~**syenit** *m* = elaeolite-syenite
Elastikreifen *m*, Vollgummireifen = solid tire (US); ~ tyre (Brit.); hard-rubber ~
elastische Dehnung *f* = elastic strain
~ **Durchbiegung** *f* = deflection
~ **Leitung** *f*, siehe: Schlauch *m*
~ **Linie** *f* = elastic curve
~ **Platte** *f* = elastic slab
~ **Verformung** *f* = elastic deformation
~ **Verformungsarbeit** *f* = resilience
elastischer Baugrund *m* = elastic foundation
~ **Bereich** *m* = elastic range
~ **Gleichgewichtszustand** *m* = elastic equilibrium
~ **Schwerpunkt** *m* = elastic center of gravity (US); ~ centre ~ ~ (Brit.)
elastisches Erdharz *n*, siehe: Elaterit *m*
~ **Verfahren** *n*; siehe unter „geophysikalische Baugrunduntersuchung *f*"
~ **Verhalten** *n* = elastic behavio(u)r
elastisch-isotroper Halbraum *m* = semi-infinite elastic solid
Elastizität *f* = elasticity
Elastizitäts|gesetz *n* = law of elasticity
~**gleichung** *f* = equation of elasticity, elasticity equation
~**grenze** *f* = limit of elasticity, elastic limit
~**modul** *m*, Elastizitätsmaß *n*, Elastizitätszahl *f*, Modul *m* für Beton *m* nach Young = modulus of elasticity, Young's modulus (Brit.); module of elasticity; Young's module (US)
~**theorie** *f* = theory of elasticity
Elaterit *m*, elastisches Erdharz *n* = elaterite, elastic bitumen, mineral caoutchouc
elektrifiziert = electrified
Elektrifizierung *f* = electrification
~ **mit Industriefrequenz** *f* = industrial-frequency electrification
elektrisch beheiztes Sieb *n* = electrically heated screen
~ **geschweißt** = electrically welded
~ **leitende (Fuß)Bodenfliese** *f* = conductive tile
elektrische Ausrüstung *f* = electrical gear, ~ equipment

~ **Bedienung** *f* **von Erdbaumaschinen** *fpl* = electric control of earthworking machinery
~ **Beheizung** *f* = electrical heating
~ **Bodenverfestigung** *f* = electric (curtain) stabilisation
~ **Durchschlagsfestigkeit** *f* = (di)electric strength
~ **Kraftlenkung** *f* = electric positive power steer(ing)
~ **Laufkatze** *f*, ~ Lastkatze = electric troll(e)y
~ **Sondierung** *f*, siehe: elektrisches Aufschlußverfahren *n*
~ **Stumpfschweißmaschine** *f* = electric butt welding apparatus
~ **(Trommel)Seilwinde** *f*, elektrisches (Trommel)Seilwindwerk *n* = electrical (rope, or cable) winch
elektrischer Anlasser *m* = electric starter
~ **Flammbogen** *m* = electric arc
~ **Laufkran** *m* = electric travel(l)ing crane
~ **Mehrmotorenkran** *m* = multiple motor crane
~ **Porenwasserdruckmesser** *m*, siehe: elektrisches Porenwasserdruck-Meßgerät *n*
~ **Strom** *m* = electric current
~ **Thermometer** *m*, Thermoelement *n*, elekrisches Thermometer *n* = electrical thermometer, electrothermic ga(u)ge
~ **Verleimapparat** *m* = electric glueing unit
~ **Widerstandsofen** *m* = electric furnace with resistors
~ **Zünder** *m*; siehe unter „1. Schießen *n*; 2. Sprengen *n*"
~ **Zündschnurzünder** *m*; siehe unter 1. Schießen *n*; 2. Sprengen *n*"
elektrisches Aufschlußverfahren *n*, geoelektrische Baugrunduntersuchung *f*, elektrische Sondierung *f* = electrical exploration method
~ **Porenwasserdruck-Meßgerät** *n*, elektrischer Porenwasserdruckmesser *m* = electrical(ly operating) pore water pressure cell (or gauge)
~ **Schweißen** *n*; siehe unter „Schweißen"
~ **Spannungsgerät SR-4** *n*, resistiver Dehnungsmesser SR-4 *m* = electric SR-4 ga(u)ge, strain ga(u)ge SR-4, (electrical-) resistance strain ga(u)ge SR-4

Elektrizitäts|gesellschaft *f* = electricity supply company
~werk *n* = electric power station
Elektro|abscheider *m*, Elektrofilter *n*, *m* = electrical dust collector, electric precipitator
~antrieb *m* = electric drive

~-Außenrüttler *m*, Elektro-Außenvibrator *m* = electric external vibrator
~-Bohrhammer *m* = electric (hand) hammer (rock) drill, ~ (rock) drill hammer
elektrochemische Verfestigung *f* **von Ton** *m* = electrochemical solidification (or hardening) of clay

---

Elektrode *f*
 dünngetauchte ~
 Flußmittel-Tauch-~
 nichtumhüllte ~
 Tauch~
 umhüllte ~, Mantel~, ummantelte ~, umwickelte ~

electrode
 washed ~
 fluxed ~
 bare ~, plain ~
 dipped ~
 covered ~, coated ~

---

elektrodynamisches Verfahren *n* = electrodynamic method
Elektro|-(Einschienen)hängebahn *f* = telpher
~(end)osmose *f* = electro-osmosis, electrical endosmose
~fahrzeug *n* = electric vehicle
~filter *n*, *m*, siehe: Elektroabscheider *m*
~-Flanschmotor *m* = flange motor
~(flaschen)zug *m* = electric hoist (or pulley) block
~(flaschen)zug-Laufkran *m* = travel(l)ing crane with electric hoist (or pulley) block
~flurfördermittel *n*, siehe: Elektrokarre(n) *f*, (*m*)
~-Fußmotor *m* = foot-type motor
~gabelstapler *m* = electric fork lift truck
~-Gesteins-Drehbohrmaschine *f* = electric rotating (or rotary) rock drilling machine
~gleisstopfer *m*, Elektroschotterstopfer = electric tie tamper (US); ~ track ~ (Brit.)
~hammer *m* = electric (impact) hammer
~-Handblechschere *f* = electric tinners' snip
~-Handbohrmaschine *f* = electric hand drill
~-Handhobelmaschine *f* = electric hand planer (or planing machine)

~-Hochfrequenz-Innenrüttler *m* = electric high frequency immersion (concrete) vibrator
~-Hochlöffel(bagger) *m* = electric shovel, electric-operated excavator
~-Innenrüttler *m* = electric internal vibrator
~kabel *n* = electric power cable
~karre(n) *f*, (*m*), Elektroflurfördermittel *n* = electrical industrial truck, electric freight truck
~karre(n) *f*, (*m*) **für Zementblocksteine** *mpl* = electric block truck
~karrenanhänger *m* = electric industrial truck (or freight) trailer
~karrenkran *m* = electric (industrial) truck crane
~-Kleinwerkzeug *n* = electric hand tool
~kran *m* = electric crane
~-Lasthebemagnet *m* = electric lifting magnet
~-Lenkmotor *m* = electric steering motor
~lötkolben *m* = electric soldering iron
elektromagnetisch = electro-magnetic
elektromagnetischer Förderer *m* = electromagnet conveyor
~ Haftvibrator *m* = electromagnetic bin vibrator
~ Vibrator *m*, ~ Schwingungsrüttler *m*, ~ Schwingungserzeuger *m* = pulsating electromagnet

elektromagnetischer Walzenscheider m = rotor type magnetic separator
Elektromotor m = motor, electric ~
Elektronen-Tastenrechenmaschine f = electronic digital computor
elektronisch gesteuerte Betondosierung f = electronic concrete batching
elektronische Rechenmaschine f, Elektronen-Rechenmaschine = electronic calculator, ~ computing machine
~ **Trocknung** f = electronic drying
~ **Waage** f = electronic scale
elektronisches Durchbiegungsmeßgerät n = electronic deflection-measuring unit
Elektroofen m = electric furnace
Elektro-Osmose f, Dränage des Bodens durch Anwendung eines elektrischen Potentials, Elektro(-Osmose-)Entwässerung f = electro-osmosis, electro-osmotic drainage, subsoil drainage by the electro-osmotic method
   elektrisches Potential n = electric(al) potential
   Filterbrunnen m mit Kathodenspannung f = wellpoint cathode, brass ~
   Ladungsteilchen n = charge
   Minuspol = negative pole
   Rohr n mit Anodenspannung f = pipe anode, iron ~
   Zwei-Leiter-System n [bei kapillar gehaltenem Wasser haftet eine dünne Wasserschicht an der Wandung des Kapillarröhrchens während sich innerhalb des dadurch gebildeten Wasserröhrchens eine Restmenge Wasser bewegen kann] = double layer [in a cylindrical capillary tube filled with water, we must distinguish between the free water and a boundary film of water adjacent to the capillary wall. This explanation was given by Helmholtz in 1879]
elektro-osmotische Baugrundverbesserung f; siehe unter „Baugrundverbesserung f"
Elektro|phorese f = electrophoresis
~**-Plattformkarre(n)** f, (m) = electric platform truck
~**punktschweißmaschine** f = electric spot welding machine
~**ramme** f; siehe unter „Rammanlage f"
~**rohr** n = conduit
~**rührer** m = electric stirrer
~**rüttelbohle** f, Elektro-Vibratorbohle = electric vibrating beam
~**rüttelplatte** f = electric vibrating plate
~**rüttelstampfbohle** f = vibrating tamper with electrically operated units, electric vibrating tamper
~**rüttelstampfer** m = electric vibrating tamper
~**rüttler** m; siehe unter „Betonrüttelgeräte npl"
~**-Schienenbohrmaschine** f = electric rail drilling machine
~**-Schienengreifer(kran)** m, Greifer(kran) auf Schienen fpl mit Elektroantrieb m = rail-mounted electric grab(bing crane), ~ ~ (grab) bucket crane
~**-Schienensägemaschine** f = electric rail sawing machine
~**-Schienenstoßhobelmaschine** f = electric rail joint planing machine
~**schotterstopfer** m, siehe: Elektrogleisstopfer
~**schraubenzieher** m = electric screwdriver
~**schweißaggregat** n = electric welding set
~**schweißmaschine** f = electric welding machine
~**-Schweißtransformator** m = electric welding transformer
~**schweißung** f = electric welding
~**-Schwenkmotor** m [Bagger m] = electric slewing motor
~**schwimmsaugbagger** m, Elektronaßsaugbagger = electric suction dredge(r)
~**sieb** n = electrically vibrated screen, electric vibrating ~
~**stahl** m = electric steel
~**-Stampfer** m = electric rammer, ~ tamper
~**stapler** m = electric lift truck
~**-Universalbagger** m **auf Gleisketten** fpl = electric caterpillar shovel
~**vibrator** m; siehe unter „Betonrüttelgeräte npl"
~**-Vibratorbohle** f, Elektrorüttelbohle = electric vibrating beam
~**werkzeug** n = electric tool
~**winde** f = electric hoist
~**zug** m = electric block

elementarer Kohlenstoff — englischer Quarzit

elementarer Kohlenstoff m = uncombined carbon
Elendsviertel n = slum
~**sanierung** f = slum clearance, ~ rehabilitation
Elevator m, siehe: Becherwerk n
~**ausleger** m = bucket elevator boom
~**becher** m = elevator bucket
~**gurtband** n = bucket elevator belt
Eller f, **Erle** f, **Else** f = alder, alnus
Ellipsen-Schwingsieb n = elliptical-motion screen, screen having elliptical vibratory action
elliptisches Integral n = elliptic integral
Ellira-Schweißung f = union melt welding, submerged arch ~
Ellis-Verfahren n [*technisches Spaltverfahren*] = tube and tank process
Elmsfeuer n = St. Elmo's fire, Saint Elmo's fire
Elsbeerbaum m = sorb, service tree
Else f, siehe: Eller f
Eluvial|boden m, Verwitterungsboden, Verwitterungslockergestein n, Auswaschungsboden = residual soil (or earth)
~**horizont** m, siehe: Auslaugungshorizont
Eluviationszone f = zone of eluviation
Emaillier|ofen m = enamel(l)ing furnace
~**ton** m = enamel(l)ing clay
Emissionsspektrographie f = emission spectrographic method
Empfangsgebäude n = reception building
Emplektit m, Kupferwismutglanz m, $CuBiS_2$ (Min.) = emplectite
Emscher Brunnen m; siehe unter „Abwasserwesen n"
Emulgation f = emulsification
Emulgator m, siehe: Stabilisator m
emulgieren = to emulsify
Emulsionsanstrich m = emulsion coating
End|auflager n [*frei drehbar*] = end support [*pin-jointed*]
~**ausschalter** m für Hubhöhe f [*Turmdrehkran* n] = height cut-out
~**aussteifung** f [*Blechträger* m] = end stiffener
~**bearbeitung** f, siehe: Fertigbehandlung f [*Beton* m]
~**bindeblech** n [*Stütze* f] = end tie-plate

~**diagonale** f, Endstrebe f [*Fachwerkbrücke* f] = end raker, (inclined) end post
~**feld** n = end panel
~**festigkeit** f = final strength
endloser Förderer m = endless conveyor
End|moräne f; siehe unter „Gletscher m"
~**produkt-Förderband** n [*Brech- und Siebanlage* f] = finished product (or material, or grade) conveyor
~**punkt** m, Endstation f [*mitunter ist damit ein Bahnhof verbunden*] = terminal, terminus
~**rahmen** m, siehe: Portal(verband) n, (m)
~**schalter** m, Begrenzungsschalter, Anschlagschalter = limit switch, stop ~
~**schwelle** f = end sill
~**steife** f [*Blechträger* m] = end stiffener, end stiffening angle
~**stück** n für Planiermesser n = end bit
~**träger** m = terminal beam
endverankert = end-anchored
Endverschiebung f [*Fachwerk* n] = end restraint
Energie f, Kraft f = power
~**bedarf** m, Kraftbedarf = (horse-) power requirement
Energie f **der Bewegung** f; siehe unter „Bernoulli-Satz m"
~**erzeugung** f, Krafterzeugung f = power generation, ~ generating, ~ production
~**kapazität** f = generating capacity
~**netz** n = national grid
~**projekt** n = power scheme
~**quelle** f = source of power
~**vernichter** m; siehe unter „Talsperre f"
~**vernichtung** f des Überfall(e)s m = dissipation of energy of the fall
~**versorgung** f, Kraftversorgung, Stromversorgung = power supply
~**verzehrung** f [*Wehr* n] = stilling
Engbohrloch n, Vorbohrloch mit engem Durchmesser m = slim hole
englische Bauweise f, Einzonenbauweise f [*Tunnelbau* m] = English method, ~ system of timbering
~ **Seil(schwebe)bahn** f; siehe unter „Drahtseilschwebebahn f"
englischer Quarzit m = gannister (Brit.); ganister (US)

englischer Schraubenschlüssel m, Franzose m = agricultural wrench
~ **Tripel** m = rottenstone
englisches Raigras n = perennial rye grass
Engobe f, **Engobierer** n = slip coating, engobe
Engobeton m = coating clay
Engobiermaschine f = slip coating machine
Engpaß m = bottleneck, deadline
Enstatit m, MgSiO₃ (Min.) = enstatite
Entemulgierbarkeit f = demulsibility
Entenwaltran m, siehe: Döglingtran
entfeuchten = to dehumidify
Ent|flockung f, Ausflockung = deflocculation
~**gasung** f, trockene Destillation f, Zersetzungsdestillation f = destructive distillation, dry ~ [sometimes referred to as "pyrolysis"]
entgegenwirken = to counteract
Entglasung f = devitrification
entgleisen = to derail
Enthärtung f; siehe unter „Wasserreinigung f"
Entlade|anlage f = unloader, unloading installation
~**gleis** n, siehe: Abladegleis
~**kran** m, siehe: Abladekran
Entladen n, siehe: Ausladen n
Entladeschaufel f, Kraftschaufel f, Waggonschrapper m, Waggonschaufel für Schüttgüter npl = hand scraper (for unloading railway cars), manually-guided drag skip (~ ~ ~ ~)
Entlastungs|brunnen m, siehe: Abzapfbrunnen in artesisch gespanntem Grundwasser n
~**brunnen** m = relief well
~**-Dränageloch** n, siehe: Entwässerungsschlitz m
~**methode** f [Sprengen n weicher Baugrundmassen fpl] = relief method, ~ blasting
~**platte** f = relieving platform
~**stollen** m; siehe unter „Talsperre f"
~**straße** f, siehe: Umgehungsstraße
Entleeröffnung f = discharge opening
Entleerungs|schieber m = discharge gate
~**ventil** n = drain valve
Entlüfter m = breather

Entlüftungsschacht m, Luftschacht, Wetterschacht = ventilation shaft, air ~, ventilating ~
Entminung f = mine removal
Entmischung f = segregation
Entnahme|bauwerk n; siehe unter „Talsperre f"
~**boden** m = borrow soil
~**büchse** f [Bodenprobe f] = sampling tin
~**einschnitt** m = borrow cut(ting)
~**gerät** n für Bodenproben fpl = soil sampler, sampling tool
~**grube** f = borrow pit
~**kubatur** f = borrow yardage
~**material** n = borrow excavation material
~**sand** m = sandy borrow
~**schacht** m = offtake shaft
~**stelle** f, Gewinnungsstelle f = borrow source
~**tunnel** m, siehe: Haldentunnel
entrinden, siehe: abschälen
Entrostung f = removal of rust
Entschalungsöl n, Schalöl n = form oil, mo(u)ld ~
Entschlammen n [Abwasserwesen n] = desludging
Entschlämmungsapparat m, Schlämmapparat [Materialaufbereitung f] = desiltor
Entschwef(e)lung f = desulfurization
entspannen = to destress
Entspannungs|-Spaltanlage f = flashing plant
~**-Verfahren** n [technisches Spaltverfahren] = flashing process
entspringen [Fluß m] = to rise
Entstaubungsanlage f, Staubabsaugungsanlage f, Staubsammleranlage f = dust collection plant, ~ exhaust ~
Entstehungs|material n [Boden m] = parent material
~**temperatur** f = original temperature
Enttrümmerung(sarbeiten) f, Schutträumung(sarbeiten) f, Trümmerräumung(sarbeiten) f = blitzed site clearance
Entwaldung f = deforestation
entwässerbar = drainable
Entwässern n [Sandaufbereitung f] = dewatering
entwässerter Scherversuch m = drained shear(ing) test

Entwässerung

Entwässerung *f*, **Trockenlegung** *f* — **drainage**

Abfanggraben *m*	intercepting ditch, catch-water ditch
Abfangsammler *m*, siehe: Sammler	
Auffangbecken *n* [*Oberflächenwasserabführung f*]	catch basin (structure)
Auslaufbauwerk *n*	outlet (or outfall) structure (Brit.); outlet (or outfall) headwork (US)
befestigter offener Entwässerungsgraben *m*	paved ditch
Betonablauf(ge)rinne *f*, (*n*)	concrete catch-gutter, concrete dish, concrete surface channel
Bodenentwässerung, siehe: Untergrundentwässerung	
Dränabstand *m*, Saugerabstand	distance between branch drains
Dränage *f*, (Röhren)Dränung *f*	pipe drainage
Dränage in Rechteckform *f*	gridiron drainage
Drän *m*	drain
Drängrabenaushub *m*	drainage trenching
Dränrohr *n*	drain(age) pipe
dränieren	to drain
Durchsickerung *f*, Versickerung *f*	percolation [*the passage of water through pervious material*]
Einlauf *m*	inlet
Einlaufrost *m*	inlet grate, inlet grating
Einzuggebiet *n*, siehe: Niederschlagsgebiet	
Entwässerungsmulde *f* [*30 m breit und 8 cm tief*]	earth saucer drain (Brit.)
Ergiebigkeit *f*	intensity of rainfall
Filterdrän *m*, siehe: Sickerdrän	
Filterfüllung *f*, siehe: Sickerfüllung	
Fischgrätendränage *f*	herringbone drainage, lateral drainage; mitre drainage (Brit.); miter drainage (US)
Flutdrän *m*	storm(-water) sewer, storm drain
geschlagener Wechsel *m*	punched drain pipe bend
Hauptdrän *m*	leader drain, main drain
Kastendrän *m*	box drain
Landdrän *m*	land drain, field drain, agricultural pipe drain
Maulwurfdrän *m*	mole drain
Niederschlag *m*	precipitation, rainfall
Niederschlagsgebiet *n*, Einzuggebiet, Sammelgebiet, Abflußgebiet	watershed (US); catchment area, drainage basin, drainage area, catchment-basin, gathering-ground (Brit.)
Oberflächenabfluß *m*	overland flow
Oberflächenentwässerung *f*	surface drainage, storm drainage
Oberflächenentwässerung durch offene Gräben *mpl*	open surface (or storm) drainage

Entwässerung

Oberflächenentwässerung durch Dränung *f*	sub-drain type surface (or storm) drainage
Oberflächenwasser *n*, siehe: Tag(es)wasser	
offener Graben *m*, Abflußgraben	(open) ditch, field ditch, drainage ditch
Planumsdrän *m*	subgrade drain
Rasendrän *m*	turf drain
Regenabflußmenge *f*	run-off
Röhrendränung *f*, siehe: Dränage *f*	
Rohr(sicker)drän *m*	pipe drain, subdrain, subsoil drain, stone-filled trench with pipe, pipe subdrain
Rohrdrän *m* mit offenen Stößen	open (joint) (sub-soil) drain
Rosteinlauf *m*	grated inlet
Rückstauwasser *n*	backwater
Sammelgebiet *n*, siehe: Niederschlagsgebiet	
Sammelrinne *f*	collecting channel
Sammler *m*, Abfangsammler *m*	outfall drain, drain outfall, interceptor, collecting drain, intercepting drain, catch(-water) drain
Sauger *m*	branch drain, subsidiary drain, feeder drain
Saugerabstand *m*, siehe: Dränabstand	
Schlammfang *m*	trap
Sickerdrän *m*, Steindrän, Steinrigole *f*, Filterdrän	rubble drain, blind drain, spall drain, stone drain, stone-filled trench, French drain, filter drain
Sickerfüllung *f*, Filterfüllung	porous backfill(ing)
Sickergrube *f*	soakage pit, soaking pit, soakaway; [*in Scotland: rummel*]
Steindrän *m*, siehe: Sickerdrän	
Stichgraben *m*	off-set ditch
Tag(es)wasser *n*, Oberflächenwasser	surface water
Untergrundentwässerung *f*, Bodenentwässerung, Tiefenentwässerung	(sub)soil (or subsurface) drainage, underdrainage, subdrainage, ground water drainage
Elektro(-Osmose)-Entwässerung *f*	subsoil drainage by the electro-osmosis method, electroosmotic drainage
Thermo-Osmose *f*	thermo-osmosis
Grundwasser(ab)senkungsanlage *f*	ground water lowering installation, dewatering installation
Grundwasser(ab)senkung *f* mit geschlitzten Filterrohren *npl*	ground water lowering by filter wells
Grundwasser(ab)senkungsanlage mit Filterbrunnen *mpl*	well-point (dewatering) installation (or system)
Versickerung *f*, siehe: Durchsickerung	
Vorfluter *m* [*Gewässer n das die Abflußmenge eines anderen aufnimmt*]	outfall (ditch), main outfall, outfall drain, drain outfall, receiving stream
verrohren	to pipe

Entwässerungs|apparat m [*Materialaufbereitung f*] = dewatering unit, dewaterer, dehydrator
~kammer f [*Waschmaschine f*] = drain bin
~prüfung f [*Bitumenemulsion f*] = dehydration test
~schlitz m, Sickerschlitz m, Entlastungs-Dränageloch n = weep hole, weeper, drainage opening, drainage hole
~schürze f; siehe unter „Talsperre f"
~stollen m = drainage gallery, ~ tunnel
~teppich m = drainage blanket
Entwicklungs|richtung f = trend of development
~stadium n = development stage
Entwurf m, zeichnerische Ausarbeitung f, zeichnerische Konstruktion f = design
~betriebsbedingung f = operating design condition
~merkmal n = design standard
~richtlinien fpl = design specifications

~strecke f = design section
Entwurf|- und Bauauftrag m = "turn-key" type of contract
~- und Konstruktionsausstellung f = design engineering show
Entzündbarkeit f, Feuergefährlichkeit f, Schwerentflammbarmachung f = inflammability
Epidiorit m = epidiorite
Epidot m $HCA_2(Al, Fe_3)Si_3O_{13}$ (Min.) = epidote
EPRA-Brecher m [*Trademark*], Fabrikat KLÖCKNER-HUMBOLDT-DEUTZ, KÖLN, DEUTSCHLAND = EPRA single impeller impact breaker [*Trademark*]
Equiviskositätstemperatur f, siehe: äquiviskose Temperatur
Erbsenstein m, Pisolith m = pisolite, pisolitic limestone
Erbs|kies m, siehe: Perlkies
~kohle f; siehe unter „Kohle f"
Erdachse f = axis of the earth

Erdarbeiten f, **Erdbau** m
Massenberechnung f
Massenausgleich m

Umrißverfahren n, Lageplan-Massenermittlung f [*bei dem die Erdmassen aus dem Lageplan ermittelt werden*]
Massenplan m, Transportplan

earthwork(s)
computing quantities of ~
balancing quantities, balanced excavation, earthwork balance
contour method of grade design and earthwork calculation

haul (mass) diagram, mass haul ~, haul and mass ~

Erd|arbeiter m = navvy (Brit.)
~aufschüttung f = earth fill
(~)Aushub m, siehe: Aushub
Erdbau m, siehe: Erdarbeiten f
~firma f = earthmoving contracting firm
~geräte npl = earthworking machinery, ~ equipment

~labor(atorium) n = soils lab(oratory), earth materials ~, soil mechanics ~, soil testing ~
~-Lastfahrzeug n; siehe unter „Fahrzeuge npl für den Transport m von Boden m und Steinbaustoffen mpl"
~mechanik f, siehe: Bodenmechanik
~werk n = earth structure
~wesen n = earthwork engineering

Erdbeben n
~flutwellen fpl, Tsunanis
Dislokations~, tektonisches ~
Epizentrum n

earthquake
seismic sea waves, tsunanis
tectonic ~
epicentre

erdbebensicher ~-resistant, quake-prof, aseismic
Oberflächenwelle *f* surface wave
Hypozentrum *n*, Erdbebenherd *m* focus, origin
vulkanisches ~ volcanic ~
See ~ submarine ~
~kunde *f*, Seismik *f*, Seismologie *f* seismology
Erdstoß *m* earth shock

Erd|beton *m*, siehe: Bodenbeton
~bewegungen *f* = dirtmoving (US); earthmoving, soil shifting operations
~bewegungsgroßgerät *n*, Bodenfördergerät *n*, Erdbewegungsmaschine *f* = dirtmover (US); earthmoving gear (Brit.); earthmover
~bildungskunde *f*, siehe: Geologie *f*
~boden *m* [*als Fläche*] = ground
~bogen *m*, siehe: Gegenbogen
~bohrer *m* [*Bodensonde f zur Entnahme von Proben bis etwa 1,50 m Tiefe*] = earth borer
~bohrgerät *n*, Erdbohrmaschine *f* = earth boring machine, soil ~ ~, earth drill, soil drill
~böschung *f* = bank [*an earth slope formed or trimmed to shape*]
~bunker *m*, siehe: Bunkergrube *f*
~damm *m* [*als Verkehrsdamm*] = earth embankment, soil ~
~damm *m*, (Erdschüttungs)Staudamm *m* = earth dam, ~ fill ~, earth-work
~drehung *f* = rotation of the earth
Erddruck *m* = lateral earth (or soil) pressure
~berechnung *f* = earth pressure calculation, soil ~ ~
~messung *f* = measurement of earth pressure
~meßdose *f*, siehe: Bodendruck(meß)dose
erden = to ground
Erd|falte *f* = nappe, earth fold
~fang(e)damm *m*, Lockergesteinsfang(e)damm = earth(work) cofferdam
~fließen *n*, siehe: Bodenkriechen
~gas *n*, Naturgas = natural gas, rock ~
~gasometer *m*, Erd-Gassammler *m*, Erd-Gasbehälter *m*, unterirdischer Gasspeicher *m* = underground gas-holder, ~ gas-tank, ~ gasometer

~gassonde *f*, siehe: produzierende ~
~geschoßfußboden *m* = bottom floor(ing)
~hobel *m*, siehe: Straßenhobel
erdige Steinkohle *f*; siehe unter „Kohle"
erdiger Gips *m*, erdiges Gipsgestein *n*, feinporiges Gipsgestein = gypsite, earthy gypsum, friable gypsum
erdiges Rohsalz *n*, Caliche *f* = caliche
Erd|kabel *n*, siehe: Bodenkabel
~kippe *f*, siehe: Kippe
~kobalt *m* (Min.), siehe: Kobaltschwärze *f*
~kratzer *m*, Schrapper *m* = scraper
~kruste *f*, siehe: Erdrinde *f*
Erdöl *n*, Roh(erd)öl *n*, Rohpetroleum *n* = crude oil (petroleum), crude naphtha, petroleum, rock oil
~benzin = naphtha (US)
~bitumen *n*, Erdölpech *n* = petroleum asphalt, oil ~ ~ (US); petroleum asphaltic bitumen (Brit.)
~destillat *n* = petroleum distillate
~fraktion *f* = petroleum fraction
erdölfündige Bohrung *f*, siehe: Ölbrunnen *m*
Erd|ölgallerte *f*, siehe: Vaselin *n*
~pech *n*, siehe: Erdölbitumen *n*
~zement *m* = oil well cement
Erd|pech *n*, siehe: Naturasphalt *m*
(~)Planum *n*, siehe: Untergrund *m*
(~)Planumfertiger *m* = concrete bay subgrader (Brit.); subgrade planer, subgrading machine (US); (power) finegrader, (precision) subgrader, mechanical fine-grader, formgrader
  Schneidmesser *n*, Hobelmeser = cutter bar
  Kratzerkette *f* = transverse conveyor
  Abgleichbohle *f* = strike-off (screed)
(~)Planumherstellung *f* = subgrading, subgrade preparation (US); formation work (Brit.)

Erd|rinde *f*, Erdkruste *f*, Lithosphäre *f* = lithosphere, crust of the earth
    äußerer Gesteinsmantel *m* = outer rocky earth shell
    Sima *n* = sima
    S(i)al *n* = sial
~rutsch *m* [*in kleinem Umfang*] = slip, earth ~
~rutschung *f*, siehe: Rutschung
~sauganlage *f* zu Lande, landgängige Erdsauganlage = dry-land suction dredging plant
~schürftransport *m* = (bull)dozing
(Erdschüttungs) Staudamm *m*; siehe unter „Talsperre *f*"
Erd|schutzwall *m* = earth traverse
~stoff *m*, siehe: Boden *m*
~stoffmechanik *f*, siehe: Bodenmechanik
~straße *f* = earth road (Brit.); dirt ~ (US); soil ~
    vermörtelt, verfestigt = stabilised
~transportwagen *m*; siehe unter „Fahrzeuge *npl* für den Transport *m* von Boden *m* und Steinbaustoffen *mpl*"
~- und Grundbau *m* = soil (and foundation) engineering
erdverlegte Rohrleitung *f* = buried pipework
Erd|wachs *n*, siehe: Ozokerit *m*
~wärmeentlüftung *f* = removal of terrestrial (or ground) heat by ventilation
~widerstand *m*, passiver Erddruck *m* = passive lateral earth (or soil) pressure
~winde *f*, siehe: Affe *m*

Erfahrung *f*
    praktische ~
    Erfahrungsschatz *m*
    Erfahrungsformel *f*, empirische Formel *f*
    Erfahrungsziffer *f*, Erfahrungswert *m*

experience
    actual ~, practical ~
    accumulated and recorded ~
    empirical formula
    empirical coefficient, factor of value

---

ergänzte Einflußlinie *f* = complementary influence line
Ergänzungswinkel *m*, Komplementwinkel = complementary angle
Ergiebigkeit *f* = yield
~ = intensity of rainfall
Erguß**gestein** *n*, vulkanisches Gestein, Durchbruchgestein, Effusivgestein, Ausbruchgestein, Extrusivgestein, Oberflächengestein, suprakrustales Erstarrungsgestein, Vulkanit *m* = lava flow, extrusive rock, (igneous) volcanic rock [*cooled on the Earth's surface*]
Erhärtung *f*, Erhärten *n* = hardening
~ des Betons *m* ohne Nachbehandlung *f* durch Feuchthalten *n* = self-curing
Erhärtungs|geschwindigkeit *f* [*Beton m*] = rate of hardening
~mechanismus *m* [*Beton m*] = mechanics of hardening [*concrete*]
~schwindung *f*, Trocknungs-Schrumpfung *f* [*Beton*] = drying shrinkage [*concrete*]
~zeit *f* = hardening time, ~ period

Erhitzer *m*, Vorwärmer *m* = (pre-)heater
~schlange *f*, Heizschlange, Wärmeschlange = heating coil
Erhöhung *f*; siehe unter „Talsperre *f*"
Erkundung *f* = reconnaissance
Erle *f*, siehe: Eller *f*
Erlenmeyer-Kolben *m* = Erlenmeyer flask
Ermittlung *f* = determination
Ermüdungs|beiwert *m* = coefficient of fatigue
~bruch *m* = fatigue failure
erodieren, ausnagen = to erode
Erosion *f*; siehe unter „Denudation *f*"
~ im engeren Sinne = river erosion
Erosions|kraft *f* = erosive power
~topf *m*; siehe unter „Gletscher *m*"
Erprobungsstraße *f* = test track
erratischer Block *m*, siehe: Findling(s-stein) *m*
~ Sandsteinblock *m* = graywether, sarsen stone, Saracen's stone
Erregerkraft *f* = exciting force
Ersatz|mittel *n* = substitute
~rad *n* = spare wheel

Ersatz|teil m; siehe unter „Baumaschinen fpl und Baugeräte npl"
~teilhaltung f = keeping spare parts
erschließen, siehe: aufschließen
Erschließungsstollen m = exploratory drift
Erschütterungsbeständigkeit f = impact and vibration resistance
Erschwernis f = aggravating condition
Erstarrung f [Zement m], siehe: Abbinden n
Erstarrungs|gestein n, Massengestein, Glutflußgestein = igneous rock, primary ~
~niveau n [Magma n] = level of solidification
~punkt m = congealing point, solidification ~
~punkt m [Bitumen n] = finger-nail hardness point
~vorgang m (Geol.) = magmatic differentiation
~wärme f = heat of solidification
Erstdampf m, Primärdampf = primary steam
erster Bauabschnitt m, erste Ausbaustufe f = first-stage development
~ Gang m [Motor m] = first gear
„Erster Spatenstich" m = ground breaking ceremony
Erstickungsgefahr f = asphyxiation risk
Erstsprengung f = primary (drilling and) blasting
ertrunkener Fluß m = drowned river
Eruptions|kanal m, siehe: Durchschlagsröhre f
~kopf m [Tiefbohrtechnik f] = control casing head
~krater m einer Bohrung f, Ausbruchskrater ~ ~ = well crater
~kreuz n [Tiefbohrtechnik f] = cristmas tree
Eruptiv|gestein n, magmatisches Gestein = magmatic rock, eruptive ~
~gesteinstafel f = eruptive sheet
~sonde f, frei ausfließende Bohrung f = flowing well, well producing by flow
~stock m = eruptive stock
Erweichung f der Kristallmitte f [Natronkalkfeldspat m] = kernel-decomposition [plagioclase]
Erweichungspunkt m, siehe: Schmelzpunkt
~ [Segerkegel m] = squatting temperature

Erweiterungs|bohrer m = post hole digger
~krone f; siehe unter „Bohrmeißel m"
~meißel m; siehe unter „Bohrmeißel m"
~-Spiralbohrer m = post (soil) auger
Erzeugerwerk n, siehe: Lieferwerk
Erz|abbau-Tagebetrieb m = open-cast ore mining
~bergwerk n = ore mine
~brecher m = ore crusher
~fall m = ore shoot
~formation f = ore formation
~frachtschiff n = ore carrier
~gallapfel m = French gall nut
~gang m, siehe: Erztrum m
~klauber m = ore picker
~körper m = ore-body
~lagerstätte f, Erzvorkommen n = ore deposit, mineral ~
~lineal n = elongated lens, pod
~magma n = ore magma
~schlacke f = ore slag
~schlauch m = ore chimney, ~ pipe
~trum n, Erzgang m = metalliferous vein, (ore) lode
~umschlaganlage f = ore handling plant, ~ ~ installation
~verhüttung f = metallurgical working of ores
~verladebrücke f = ore bridge
~vorkommen n, Erzlagerstätte f. Erzvorkommnis n = ore deposit, mineral ~
~weg m = ore channel
erzwungene Schwingung f, aufgezwungene ~ = forced vibration
Eschenahorn m = ash-leaved maple
ESCH-MAGNETA-Sieb n [Trademark], Fabrikat ESCH-WERKE K.-G., DUISBURG, DEUTSCHLAND = armature-type electro-magnetic vibrating screen
Eselsrücken m, siehe: Ablaufberg m
~bogen m, Karniesbogen = ogee arch
Eskaladierfalte f (Geol.) = overlapping fold
Espe f, Zitterpappel f = aspen
Esse f, siehe: Durchschlagsröhre f
Essener Asphalt m, siehe: Dammanasphalt
Essenszeit f = meal-time
Essexit m (Geol.) = essexite
Essigsäure f = acetic acid

Essigsäureanhydrid n = acetic anhydride
essigsaures Salz n, siehe: Azetat n
Estobitumen n = esto-bitumen, esto-asphalt
estländischer Brennschiefer m, Kukersit m = kukersit

Estrichgips m = flooring plaster, tiling ~, hard(-finish) ~
Estrich-Glättmaschine f = trowel(l)ing machine, mechanical trowel, power trowel, rotary finisher
Etagenkessel m = multiple stage boiler

EUCLID-Lademaschine f, Förderband-Anhängeschürfwagen m, Schürfwagen mit Förderbandausleger m, EUCLID-Lader m, Fabrikat THE EUCLID ROAD MACHINERY CO., CLEVELAND 17, OHIO, USA	**EUCLID LOADER** [*Trademark*]
Böschungsarbeiten f	slope work
Förderbahnleisten fpl	skirts
Förderband n	belt
gelenkige Brückenkonstruktion f, Pivotverbindung f	pivot connection
Kopfrolle f, obere Umlenktrommel f	head pulley
Lader m	conveyor
Pflugschar f	mold board plow
Schnittiefe f, Schnitt-Tiefe	depth of cut
Schnittwinkel m	angle of cut
Schürfschneide f	cutting edge, ~ blade
Schwanzrolle f, untere Umlenktrommel f	tail pulley
Traktorführer m, Schlepperfahrer m	tractor operator
Zugraupe f, (Gleis)Kettenschlepper m	puller (crawler) tractor, towing caterpillar tractor

---

Euler'sche Formel f = Euler's formula
eupelagische Meeresablagerung f, Tiefseeschlamm m = pelagic deposit, deep-sea ~, deep-sea ooze, ozeanic deposit, thalassic deposit
eutektoidische Struktur f = eutectoid texture
Evolute f = evolute
Evolutionstheorie f = theory of evolution
Evolvente f = involute
Evolventen|rad n = involute gear
~verzahnung f = involute toothing
Eversionsbecken n = eversion basin, basin due to evorsion
ewiggefrorener Boden m, siehe: dauernd gefrorener ~
Exaration f = glacial denudation, ~ erosion
Exerzierplatz m = parade ground

Exhalationslagerstätte f = exhalation deposit
Exhaustor m = exhaust fan
Expansions|bandbremse f = expanding band brake
~hub m, Arbeitshub, Ausdehnungshub = expansion stroke, firing ~, working ~, power ~
Experimentalverfahren n, siehe: Versuchsmethode f
explosibles Gemisch n = explosive mixture
Explosion f [*Bergwerk* n] = fire damp ~ = explosion
Explosions|caldera m = caldera of subsidence
~graben m (Geol.) = explosion fissure, ~ trench
~hub m = explosion stroke, expansion ~

Explosions|motor m = internal combustion engine, I. C. ~
~ramme f, siehe: Brennkraft-Handramme f
~raum m = explosion chamber
~röhre f, Explosionsöffnung f (Geol.) = (explosion) pipe, (~) vent
~stampfer m, Hand-~ = heavy-duty internal combustion tamper
~stampframme f, siehe: Brennkraft-Handramme
Explosiv|stoff m, Sprengstoff = explosive
~verbrennung f = combustion by explosion
Export|ausschuß m der Bauindustrie f = Export Group for the Constructional Industries
~verpackung f = export packing
Exsikkator m, Trockenapparat m = desiccator
Extraktions|apparat m, Extraktor m = extractor
~kolben m = extraction flask
Extrusiv|gestein n, siehe: Ergußgestein
~masse f = extrusive (mass)
Exzenter m = eccentric
~anlauf m = eccentric catch
~antrieb m = eccentric drive
~meißel m = eccentric bit
~presse f = eccentric press
~ring m = eccentric strap
~-Schwingsieb n, Exzenterschwinger m, Exzenterwellen-(Vibrations-Plan-)sieb, Schwingsieb mit Exzenterantrieb = mechanically vibrated eccentric type screen, eccentric type vibrating screen
~stange f = eccentric rod
~welle f = eccentric shaft
exzentrisch, siehe: außermittig
exzentrische Last f = eccentric load
Exzentrizität f, Außermittigkeit f, Ausmitte f = eccentricity

F

Fabrikat n = make
Fabrikations|anlagen fpl, Fabrikationsbetrieb m = manufacturing facilities, ~ plant
~forschung f = manufacturing research

Fabrik|esse f, siehe: Fabrikkamin m
~fenster n, Werkstattfenster = factory window
~gebäude n, Werkgebäude = factory building
~gelände n, Werkgelände = factory ground
~halle f, Industriehalle, Werkhalle = factory hangar
~kamin m, Fabrikschornstein m, Fabrikesse f, Fabrikschlot m = factory chimney
~lader m, siehe: Industrielader
Facettengeschiebe n, siehe: Pyramidalgeröll(e) n
Fach|arbeiter m, Spezialarbeiter = skilled worker
~dolmetscher m, technischer ~ = technical interpreter
Fächer|brücke f = radiating bridge
~einbruch m [*Tunnelbau* m] = fan cut
fächerförmig spleißen = to fan out
Fächer|gewölbe n, Trichtergewölbe, angelsächsisches Gewölbe, normannisches Gewölbe, Palmengewölbe, Strahlengewölbe = fan vaulting
~pflaster(decke) n, (f), Kleinpflaster(decke) in Fächerform f = fanwise paving, circular ~, DURAX ~, radial sett ~, random ~
Fach|literatur f = professional literature
~mann m = expert
~simpelei f = shop talk
fachsimpeln = to talk shop,
Fach|übersetzer m, technischer ~ = technical translator
~wand f = panel wall
~weite f [*Fachwerk* n] = panel length
Fachwerk n = framework, latticework, truss
~, siehe Fachwerkträger m
~ mit genieteten Knoten mpl = rivetted truss
~balken m, siehe: Fachwerk(träger)
~balkenbrücke f, siehe: Fachwerkbrücke
~berechnung f = computation of (trusses in) latticework
~binder m = roof truss
~bogen m = braced arch, trussed ~, arch in trellis work

Fachwerk|brücke f, Fachwerkbalkenbrücke, Gitterbrücke [*die Hauptträger bestehen aus Fachwerkträgern*] = truss bridge, lattice ~
~-Deckbrücke f = deck truss span
~ecke f, Ecke des Fachwerkes n = corner of framework
~hängebrücke f = lattice suspension bridge
~hängeträger m = latticed suspension girder
~pfette f = lattice purlin
~sichelbogen m = sickle-shaped trussed arch
~stab m = truss member, frame ~
~stütze f = lattice column
~system n = framed system
~(träger) n, (m), gegliederter (Balken-)Träger, Fachwerkbalken m, Tragwerk n, Fachwerkbalkenträger, Gitterbalken(träger), Gitterträger = truss(ed) girder, lattice ~
~-Trogbrücke f = trough truss span
~turm m = latticed construction tower
~verbundträger m = lattice-type composite beam
~versteifungsträger m = stiffening truss
Fachzeitschrift f = trade journal
Faden|klee m = hop trefoil
~kreuz n = cross(ed) threads, ~ hairs, ~ wires
~pilz m = filamentous fungus
~visiervorrichtung f, Fadendiopter m = cross wire sight; ~ hair diopter (US)
~ziehvermögen n, siehe: Streckbarkeit f
Fahlerz n, siehe: Graugültigerz
Fahlunit m = fahlunite
Fahrantrieb m = travel drive
Fahrbahn f [*Straße* f] = carriageway; [*deprecated: road, road-way, road surface*]
~ [*Brücke* f] = platform
~aufhängung f [*Brücke* f] = platform suspension
~belag m, Fahrbahndecke f = carriageway surfacing
~belastung f [*Brücke* f] = load on platform
~markierung f [*in der Schweiz: Bodenmarkierung*] = carriageway marking

~markierungsmaschine f [*in der Schweiz: Bodenmarkierungsmaschine*] = carriageway marking machine
~platte f = carriageway slab [*e. g. asphaltic concrete slab*]
~platte f [*Brücke* f] = floor slab, ~ plate
~reibung f = road friction
~rost m [*Brücke* f] = floor system; ~ grid (US)
~tafel f; siehe unter „Brücke f"
Fahrband n; siehe unter „Bandförderer m"
fahrbar, ortsbeweglich = mobile, portable
fahrbare (oder ortsbewegliche) Gesteinsaufbereitungsanlage f (oder Brech- und Siebanlage) = portable (or mobile) crushing and screening plant
~ Hängewaage f = travel(l)ing type suspended weighbatcher
~ Laderampe f = travelramp
~ Siebanlage f = portable (or mobile) screening plant
~ Wagenunterkunft f = caravan
fahrbarer Drehkran m, siehe: Fahrkran
~ Gurtförderer m; siehe unter „Bandförderer"
~ Kompressor m, ~ Luftverdichter m, ~ Drucklufterzeuger m = portable compressor
~ Kran m, siehe: Fahrkran
~ Mischer m, fahrbare Mischmaschine f, Fahrmischer = portable mixer, mobile ~
~ (Schwenk)Kran m, siehe: Fahrkran
~ Silo m, Fahrsilo [*für Baustellen fpl*] = portable bin
fahrbares Montagegerüst n = traveler (US)
Fahrbremse f = travel(l)ing brake
Fähr|brücke f, Schwebefähre = aerial ferry, ferry bridge
~dampfer m, Dampffähre f = steam ferry
(Fahr)|Deichsel f = tow-bar
~draht m, Oberleitungsdraht, Fahrleitung f = contact wire, trolley ~
~eigenschaft f [*Straße* f] = riding quality
Fahrer|beanspruchung f = strain of driving, driver tension
~flucht f = "hit and run" offence
~gewohnheit f = driver habit

Fahrer|haus n, Führerhaus, Fahrerkabine f, Führerkabine = driver's cab(in), operator's control ~
~**sicht** f = driver vision
Fahr|fußhebel m, Gashebel = accelerator pedal, foot throttle
~**gastabfertigung** f = passenger handling
~**gasthafen** m = passenger berth
~**gastverkehr** m, Personenverkehr = passenger traffic
~**gastzähler** m = passenger counter
~**gelderhebung** f = fare collection
~**geschwindigkeit** f ~ travel(l)ing speed
~**gestell** n, Untergestell, Chassis n = carrier, chassis
~**gestellrahmen** m = chassis frame
~**gestelltragfähigkeit** f = useful load of chassis
~**gleis** n = rail track
~**karte** f = ticket
~**kran** m, fahrbarer Drehkran, fahrbarer (Schwenk)Kran = mobile crane
~**lade-Gerät** n, Fahrlader m = loader
~**lade-Gerät** n, siehe: (Front-)Ladeschaufel f
~**lade-Gerät** n, siehe: Becher(werk)auflader m
~**lader** m, Fahrlade-Gerät n = loader
~**lader** m, siehe: Becher(werk)auflader m
~**lader** m, siehe: (Front-)Ladeschaufel f
~**lehrer** m = driving instructor
~**leitung** f = contact line
~**leitung** f, siehe: Fahrdraht m
~**mischer** m, siehe: fahrbarer Mischer
~**motor** m, Fahrzeugmotor = travel(l)ing engine, vehicle
~**oberfläche** f = running surface
~**rad** n = pedal cycle, (bi)cycle
~**radbereifung** f = pneumatic (bi)cycle tires (US)/tyres (Brit.)
~**radfelge** f = (bi)cycle felloe (or rim), pedal cycle ~ (~ ~)
~**radspeiche** f = (bi)cycle spoke, pedal cycle ~
~**radstand** m = (bi)cycle stand, pedal cycle ~
~**radweg** m, Rad(fahr)weg = (bi)cycle track, pedal cycle ~
~**radzubehör** m, n = (bi)cycle accessories, pedal cycle ~

~**richtung** f, Fahrtrichtung = direction of travel
~**rinne** f, Spurstreifen m, Radeindruck m, Radspur f = wheelers [in an earth road]
~**rinne** f, Fahrwasser n, Fahrt f = ship channel, fairway, passage (of harbours)
~**schalter** m = controller
~**schalter** m **für konstantes Drehmoment** n = continuous torque controller
~**schalterkontakt** m = controller contact
~**schiene** f = running rail
Fährschiff n = ferry-boat
Fahr|schrapper m; siehe unter ,,Seilförderanlage f"
~**schüler** m = driving pupil
~**silo** m, fahrbarer Silo [für Baustellen fpl] = portable bin
~**sprenger** m [Abwasserverteilung f auf Tropfkörpern mpl] = travel(l)ing distributor
(~)**Spur** f, Verkehrsspur = (traffic) lane
~ **am Mittelstreifen** m = median (traffic) lane
~ ~ **Randstreifen** m = shoulder (traffic) lane
Fahrstuhl|aufzug m, siehe: Turmgerüstaufzug
~**gerüst** n = lift frame
Fahrt f = trip
~, siehe: Fahrrinne f
~, Übergang m [z. B. mit einer Walze f] = pass
Fahrtenbuch n = log book
(Fahrt)End(aus)schalter m = limit switch
Fährtensandstein m = Chiroterium sandstone
Fahrtreppe f, siehe: Rolltreppe
Fahr(t)richtung f = direction of travel
Fahr|wasser n, siehe: Fahrrinne f
~**werk** n = travel(l)ing gear, undercarriage
~**werk** n [Tiefladewagen m] = dolly
~**werkbremse** f = travel(l)ing gear brake
~**zeit** f = journey time
Fahrzeug n = vehicle
~ **für den Bodentransport** m, Erdbaufahrzeug = vehicle for transport of earth
~**art** f = type of vehicle

Fahrzeug-Dieselmotor — Fahrzeuge für den Transport von Boden

Fahrzeug|-Dieselmotor *m* = vehicle diesel engine

~(dreh)kran *m*, Fahrzeugschwenkkran, Autokran, gummibereifter selbstfahrbarer Universalkran *[kann Luftbereifung f oder Vollgummibereifung haben]* = rubber-mounted revolver crane, ~ revolving ~, ~ slewing ~; ~ swing-jib ~ (Brit.); ~ swing(-boom) ~ (US)

Fahrzeuge *npl* **für den Transport** *m* **von Boden** *m* **und Steinbaustoffen** *mpl*	**(earth and rock) hauling equipment**
geländegängiger luftbereifter Erdtransportwagen *m*, gummibereiftes Erdbau-Lastfahrzeug *n*, geländegängiger Förderwagen *m* in Kraftwagen-Bauart *f*, Muldenkipper *m*, Groß-Förderwagen *m*, gleisloser Förderwagen *m*, Motorkipper, Erdtransportfahrzeug für Fremdbeladung	rubber-tired (US)/rubber-tyred (Brit.) off-(the-)higway hauling unit (or earth-moving vehicle)
Halbanhänger *m* mit Bodenentleerung *f* durch Klappen *fpl*, aufsattelbarer Bodenentleerer *m*, aufgesattelter Erdtransportwagen mit Bodenentleerung, Fabrikat THE EUCLID ROAD MACHINERY COMPANY, CLEVELAND, 17 OHIO, USA	EUCLID bottom-dump wagon
Bodenklappe *f*, Bodentür *f*	trailer door
Selbstfahrer-Rückwärtskipper *m*, Selbstfahrer-Hinterkipper, Fabrikat EUCLID	EUCLID rear-dump wagon, EUCLID end-dump truck
Halbanhänger-Seitenkipper *m*, aufgesattelter Seitenkipper, Fabrikat EUCLID	EUCLID side-dump wagon
Erdtransportwagen *m*, Fabrikat KOEHRING COMPANY, MILWAUKEE 10, USA	DUMPTOR [*Trademark*]
Autoschüttler *m*, Vorderkipper *m*, Motorkübelwagen *m*, Kopfschütter *m*, Fabrikat ZETTELMEYER, KONZ bei TRIER, DEUTSCHLAND	(shuttle) dumper, front tipper
rückwärtskippender Erdtransportwagen *m*, Gelenkwagen-Hinterkipper *m*, Fabrikat Le TOURNEAU-WESTINGHOUSE COMPANY, PEORIA, ILLINOIS, USA	TOURNAROCKER [*Trademark*], 16.5 cubic yard rear dump rock wagon
bodenentleerender Erdtransportwagen *m*, Gelenkwagen-Bodenentleerer *m*, Fabrikat Le TOURNEAU	TOURNAHOPPER [*Trademark*], 15 cubic yard bottom-dump wagon
Gelenkwagen mit Entleerung durch Verschieben der Wannenwände auf dem feststehenden Wannenboden, Fabrikat Le TOURNEAU	TOURNATRAILER [*Trademark*]

luftbereifter Muldenkipper *m*, Fabrikat WILLIAM JONES LTD.
    DOBBIN wagon

Großraumlore *f* auf (Gleis)Ketten *fpl*, Raupen(anhänger)wagen *m*, Großraumraupenwagen *m*
    caterpillar tread wagon, track-type wagon

Großraumraupenwagen *m*, Fabrikat ATHEY PRODUCTS CORPORATION, CHICAGO 38, USA
    ATHEY two-way dump trailer, ATHEY wagon, ATHEY universal dump trailer

MENCK-Raupenwagen *m* [*Trademark*], Fabrikat MENCK & HAMBROCK, HAMBURG-ALTONA, DEUTSCHLAND
    MENCK caterpillar tread wagon

Muldenkipper *m*, Feldbahnlore *f*, (Mulden)Kipplore *f*, Stahlmuldenkipper, Muldenwagen
    steel tip wagon, side tipping wagon, (rocker) dump car, jubilee wagon, skip, jubilee skip (Brit.); industrial rail car (US)

Holzkastenkipper *m*
    wood tip wagon, wood skip, track wheel wood dump wagon

Kipperkarre(n) *f*, (*m*)
    buggy [*triangular shaped iron handcart*]

Förderung *f*, Transport *m*
    hauling, haulage

Förderweite *f*, Transportweite
    haul(age distance) (US); lead, run (Brit.)

Muldenkipper *m*, Muldentransporter *m*, Muldenkipper-LKW *m*
    dump truck

Mulden-Erdbaufahrzeug *n*
    dump wagon

Fahrzeug|kolonne *f* = caravan of vehicles
~**kran** *m*, siehe: Fahrzeugdrehkran
~**panne** *f* = vehicular breakdown
~**rad** *n* = vehicle wheel
~**rettungskran** *m*, siehe: Abschlepp-Fahrzeug *n*
~**schwenkkran** *m*, siehe: Fahrzeug(dreh)kran
~**stoß** *m* [*Anlegebrücke f*] = docking load, ~ stress
~**strom** *m* = vehicle traffic stream
~**(trommel)winde** *f* = drum winch mounted on a vehicle
~**tunnel** *m* = vehicle tunnel
~**unfall** *m* = vehicular accident
~**verkehr** *m* = vehicular traffic
~**waage** *f* = vehicle scale
~**winde** *f*, siehe: Fahrzeugtrommelwinde
Fahrzielanzeiger *m* [*beim Autobus m*] = destination indicator
Fäkalien *f* = feces, faeces
~**abfuhr** *f* = scavenging service
~**grube** *f*, Abortgrube = feces pit, faeces ~

Fäkalstoffe *mpl* = fecal matter
Falle *f*, siehe: Schütz(e) *n*, (*f*)
~ = trap
fällen [*Bäume mpl*] = to fell
~ [*Chemie f*] = to precipitate
fallen, ein~ (Geol.) = to dip, to fall
Fallenwehr *n* = (vertical) leaf gate
Fall|gewichtsdrosselklappe *f*, Drosselklappe mit Fallgewichtsantrieb *m* = fallingweight (type) butterfly valve
~**hammer** *m*; siehe unter „Rammanlage *f*"
~**höhe** *f*, siehe: Druckhöhe
~**höhenverlust** *m*, Druckhöhenverlust = head loss, loss of head
~**klappe** *f* = drop gate
Fällmittel *n*, Fällungsmittel = precipitant, coagulant
Fall|plattenkran *m*, siehe: Freifallkranstampfer *m*
~**rohr** *n* [*für Schmutzwasser n*] = soil-pipe
~**rohr** *n* [*für Regenwasser n*] = rainwater down pipe
~**schacht** *m*; siehe unter „Talsperre *f*"

Fall|schacht m [*Tunnelbau* m] = downhole
~schirm m = parachute
~-Stampfverdichtungsmaschine f = dropping-weight compaction machine, ~ compactor
~stromvergaser m = down-draught carburettor, ~ carburettor (Brit.); downdraft carburetor (US)
~tür f = trap door
Fällungs|chemikal n; siehe unter „Abwasserwesen n"
~gestein n, siehe: chemisches Sedimentgestein) n
~mittel n, Fällmittel = precipitant, coagulant
Fall|-Viskosimeter n = sinker visco(si)meter
~wasser n [*Zuckerfabrik* f] = vacuum-pan water [*beet-sugar factory*]
~wind m = down wind, katabatic ~, fall ~
falsches Abbinden n, vorzeitiges ~, falsche Abbindung f, vorzeitige Abbindung = false set; ~ setting (Brit.)
Falschluft f = false air
Falt|balg m, Membran(e)balg m = membrane bellows
~brücke f = folding bridge
Falten|gebirge n = folded mountain(s)
~rohrbogen f = creased pipe bend
Faltung f (Geol.) = folding, bending
Falz|fräser m = notching cutter
~ziegel m, Falzstein m = interlocking roofing tile
Familie f (Geol.) = clan
Fang m, siehe: Abscheider m
Fang(e)damm m = cofferdam, bulkhead
~ aus Holzstapeln mpl = timber-crib type cofferdam
~-Spundwandzelle f = cofferdam cell
~wand f = cofferdam skin
Fängerglocke f [*Ventil* n] = valve guard
Fang|haken m [*Bohrgerät* n] = extractor, grapple
~vorrichtung f = intercepting device
Farbbindemittel n = vehicle, cold water paint cement, paint vehicle
Färben n = colo(u)ring
Farbhaut f, siehe: Farbüberzug m

farbiger Belag m, Farbbelag = colo(u)red surfacing
Farb|lichtsignal n = colour-light signal
~pigment n = paint pigment
~spritzpistole f = paint spray gun
~stoff m = colo(u)ring material, ~ matter
~strichziehmaschine f, siehe: Gerät n zum Anzeichnen n der Verkehrslinien
~ton m = paint clay
~tönung f = shade
~überzug m, Farbhaut f = paint coat
Färbversuch m = disco(u)loration test
Farm-zum-Markt-Straße f = (farm-to-)market road
Farn m = fern
Faschinat n, Packfaschinat, Packwerk n, Faschinenpackwerk, Faschinenlage f, Buschpackwerk = fascine mattresses weighted with rubble
Faschine f, Strauchwerkbündel n = fascine, faggot, bundle of brushwood, brushwood fascine
Faschinen|damm m = fascine dike
~floß n, siehe: Sinkstück n
~matte f = fascine mattress
~packwerk n, siehe: Faschinat n
~wehr n = weir of fascines
(~) Wippe f, Faschinenwurst f = wipped fascine, saucisse, saucisson
Faser|fett n = fibre grease (Brit.); fiber ~ (US)
~gips m, spätiger Gips = fibrous gypsum, satin spar
~kalk m = fibrous calcite
~kiesel m, Sillimanit m, Fibrolith m (Min.) = fibrolite, sillimanite
~platte f, Fasertafel f = fibreboard (Brit.); fiberboard (US)
~siedestein m, Spreustein m (Min.) = fibrous zeolite
~stoffänger m [*Zellstoffindustrie* f] = catch-all, save-all
~torf m, filziger Torf, Wurzeltorf = fibrous peat
Fassaden|klinker m, Fassadenstein m = facing clinker (brick)
~verkleidung f = facing
Fassoneisen n, Profileisen n, Formeisen n, Profilstahl m, Stahlprofil n = section iron, steel section

Fassungsvermögen — Fein(erd)planum

Fassungsvermögen n, Stauraum m, Speicherfähigkeit f = storage capacity [*reservoir*]
~, Inhalt m = capacity
Fastebeue f, siehe: Denudationsebene
Faß|aufzug m = barrel hoist
~**bitumen** n = barreled asphalt (US); barreled asphaltic bitumen (Brit.)
~**daube** f, siehe: (Holz)Daube
~**erhitzer** m = barrel heater
~**pech** n = cooper's pitch, pitch in casks
~**pumpe** f, Abfüllpumpe = barrel pump
~**reifenprinzip** n = wooden barrel principle
~**reinigungsanlage** f, Faßwaschanlage = barrel washing device
~**sprenger** m = hand-operated sprayer (or spraying machine) for drawing direct from drums or barrels, direct from drum type sprayer
~**spritzer** m für Kaltasphalt m = hand-operated cold emulsion spraying machine (or sprayer) for drawing direct from drums or barrels, direct from drum type cold emulsion sprayer (or spraying machine)
~**wärmeschrank** m = barrel heating pocket
Fata Morgana f, Luftspiegelung f = mirage
faulen, siehe: (ab)stocken [*Holz* n]
Faulen n **der erhärteten Zementmörtelung** f = rotting of soil cement
faules Gestein n, fauler Fels m, faules Felsgestein n = soft rock
Faulgas n = 1.) sewer gas, 2.) digester ~
Fäulnis f, Fävle f [*Holz* n] = rot
~**fähigkeit** f = putrescibility
Faulschlamm m; siehe unter „Abwasserwesen n"
Faustregel f, Faustformel f, empirische Regel = rule of thumb
Fayalit m, Eisenglas n (Min.) = fayalite, iron-olivine
Fazies f (Geol.) = facies
Feder|bandkupplung f = spring band coupling
~**bandstahl** m = spring-steel cross-bands
~**bolzen-Bolzen** m = bolt for spring bolt
~**drucksonde** f = spring-pressure sounding apparatus
~**egge** f, siehe: Federzahnegge
~**erz** n, Jamesonit m (Min.) = jamesonite, feather ore
federführende Firma f = sponsor (US); pilot firm, "lead" firm
Federgras n = feather grass
federnde Formänderung f, elastische ~, ~Deformation f [*Beton* m] = elastic deformation and elastic recovery [*concrete*]
Feder|puffer m, Federpufferung f = spring buffer
~**ring** m, Federscheibe f, federnde Unterlegscheibe = lock washer, spring ~
~**spannung** f = spring tension
~**stahl** m = spring steel
~**stahlbohrer** m = flat steel drill
Federung f, Ab~ = springing, spring suspension
Feder(zahn)egge f = spring-tooth harrow
Fegemaschine f, siehe: Straßenkehrmaschine
Fehl|anzeige f = nil return, ~ report
~**bedarf** m = deficiency
~**brand** m, siehe: Kalkkern m
Fehler|dreieck n = triangle of error
~**grenze** f = limit of error
Fehl|schlag m, Versagen n = failure
~**schuß** m; siehe unter „1. Schießen n; 2. Sprengen n"
~**stelle** f = crack, defect
Fehn n, siehe: Bruch m
Fein|backenbrecher m = fine jaw crusher
~**brechen** n; siehe unter „Hartzerkleinerung f"
~**brecher** m, Feinsteinbrecher, Nachbrecher = fine crusher, reduction ~, secondary ~
~**(brech)walzwerk** n = fine tertiary crusher with rolls
~**bruch** m; siehe unter „Hartzerkleinerung f"
~**dreheinrichtung** f [*Kran* m] = slewing device
~**druckmesser** m, Mikromanometer n = micro-pressure ga(u)ge
~**einstellung** f, Justierung f = fine adjustment, precise ~
~**(erd)planum** n = planed subgrade (US); formation (Brit.); subgrade [*deprecated*]

Fein(erd)planumhöhe — Feintrennung

Fein|(erd)planumhöhe *f* = formation level (Brit.); planed subgrade level (US)

feine Rißbildung *f*; siehe unter „Riß *m*"

feiner Mo *m*; siehe unter „Mehlsand *m*"

feines Siebkorn IVa, siehe: Mittelsand *m*

feingemahlener vulkanischer Tuffstein *m*, siehe: Traß *m*

Feingips *m*, **Feingut** *n* = finely-ground gypsum, land plaster

feingriffig = fine-gripping [*surfacing*]

Fein|hammerbrecher *m* = split hammer rotary granulator, swing ~ ~ ~

~heitsmodul *m*, Körnungsmodul = fineness modulus (Brit); ~ module (US)

~kegelbrecher *m* **mit segmentförmigem Brechkopf** *m* = fine gyrasphere crusher

feinkeramischer Ofen *m* = pottery kiln

Fein|kies *m* [*nach DIN 1179 7—3 mm; nach DIN 4022, Deutsche Geologische Landesanstalt, Degebo und Dienemann 5—2 mm; nach DIN 4220 7—2 mm; nach Fischer und Udluft 5—2 mm (heißt hier „kleiner Graup"); nach Niggli 20 bis 2 mm*] = fine gravel [*A.S.E.E. fraction 9.52 mm to 2.00 mm*]

~korn *n* = fine grain

~kornanteil *m* [*Boden m*] = fine fraction of the soil

feinkörnig = fine-grained

~-dicht, felsitisch = felsitic

Feinkreiselbrecher *m*, **Feinkegelbrecher** *m*, **Fein-Rundbrecher** = fine reduction gyratory (crusher), fine reduction cone crusher

feinkristallin, kryptokristallin = cryptocrystalline

Fein|mahlung *f*; siehe unter „Mühle *f*"

~maschensieb *n* = fine wire screen

~material *n*, Feinstoffe *mpl* = fines

~mehlsand *m*; siehe unter „Mehlsand"

feinplanieren = to fine-grade

Fein|planieren *n* = final grading, fine-grading

~planum *n*, siehe: Fein(erd)planum *n*

feinporiges Gipsgestein *n*, siehe: erdiger Gips *m*

Feinrechen *m*; siehe unter „Abwasserwesen *n*"

Feinsand *m* [*nach Niggli (Jahr 1938) und International Society of Soil Science (here called "fine sand") 0,2—0,02 mm*] = fine sand and coarse silt (Brit.)

~, Staubsand *m* [*nach DIN 4022 0,2 bis 0,1 mm; nach Atterberg 0,2—0,02 mm; nach Fischer und Udluft (Jahr 1936) 0,2—0,02 mm (heißt hier „Silt")*] = fine sand [*Division of Soil Survey (US) 0.25—0.05 mm; A.S.E.E. fraction 0.25 bis 0.074 mm; British Standard 0.2 bis 0.06 mm*]; fine sand and coarse silt (Brit.) [*0.2—0.02 mm*]

~klassierung *f* = classification of fine sand

Feinschlämme *f*, Zementmilch *f* = laitance

Feinschluff *m* [*nach Deutsche Geologische Landesanstalt 0,005—0,002 mm, nach Degebo und Terzaghi 0,006—0,002 mm; nach Fischer und Udluft (Jahr 1936) 0,005—0,002 mm*] = fine silt [*British Standard 0.006 to 0.002 mm*]

~ [*nach Niggli (Jahr 1938) 0,002 bis 0,0002 mm; dieselbe Korngröße heißt nach Grengg (Jahr 1942) „Schlamm", nach Fischer und Udluft „Sink", nach Terzaghi „Kolloidschlamm", im übrigen meistens „(Roh)Ton"*] = clay

Fein|schotter *m* = 1½ inch size broken stone

~schotterboden *m*; siehe unter „Kies *m*"

~senkbremse *f* [*Kran m*] = lowering brake

~sieben *n*, Feinsiebung *f* = fine screening

Feinstbestandteile *mpl* [*Betonmischung f*] = fine aggregate dust [*concrete mix*]

Fein(stein)brecher *m*, Nachbrecher = reduction crusher, fine ~, secondary ~

Feinste(s) *n* [*nach Grengg (Jahr 1942) Bodenteilchen kleiner als 0,0002 mm*] = clay

Feinst|korntechnik *f* [*Betonbau m*] = technical use of ultra-fine aggregate particles

~mahlung *f* = pulverizing

feinstzerteilter Feststoff *m* = finely divided solid

Feintrennung *f* [*Siebung f*] = fine separation

Fein|waage *f* = sensitive balance
~zerkleinerung *f*, Mahlen *n*, Mahlung *f*; siehe unter „Hartzerkleinerung *f*"
~zerkleinerungsmaschine *f*, siehe: Mühle *f*
Feld *n* [*Fachwerk n*] = panel

~ *n*, Beton**~**, Beton(decken)platte *f* = (road) panel, (road) bay, concrete bay, concrete (pavement) slab
~ahorn *m*, siehe: Maßholder *f*
~arbeiten *f* = field work

Feldbahn(anlage) *f*

light railroad system, narrow gage railroad (US); Jubilee track system, light railway system, field railway system (Brit.); narrow-ga(u)ge track system

Baustellengleis *n*, Schmalspurgleis *n*, Feldbahngleis	jubilee track(ing) (Brit.); industrial ~ (US); narrow-ga(u)ge ~
Dachschwelle *f*	roof-type sleeper (Brit.); ~ tie (US) turntable
Drehscheibe *f*	
Feldbahnlore *f* aus Stahl, Muldenkipper *m*, Stahlmuldenkipper, Stahlkipplore, Stahlbaustellenlore, Stahl-Feldbahnlore, (Mulden)Kipplore *f*, Baustellenlore aus Stahl	industrial railcar (US); jubilee wagon (or skip), steel tip wagon, tipping truck, side tipping wagon, skip (Brit.)
Feldbahnlok(omotive) *f*, Bau(stellen)-lok(omotive) *f*	field loco(motive)
Motorlok(omotive) *f*	motor loco(motive)
Schmalspurlok(omotive) *f*, Fabrikat DECAUVILLE	DECAUVILLE motor tractor
Verbrennungslok(omotive) *f*	petrol loco(motive) (Brit.); gasolene ~, gasoline ~ (US)
Druckluftlok(omotive) *f*, Preßluftlok(omotive)	compressed air loco(motive)
elektrische Lok(omotive)	electric loco(motive)
feuerlose (Dampf)Lok(omotive) *f*	fireless steam loco(motive)
Dampflok(omotive) *f*	steam loco(motive)
Akku(mulatoren)lok(omotive) *f*	(storage) battery loco(motive), accumulator ~
Schlepplok(omotive) *f*	towing loco(motive)
Dieselfeldbahnlok(omotive) *f*, Diesel-Schmalspurlok(omotive) *f*, Baudiesellok(omotive) *f*	diesel field loco(motive)
Feldbahnschiene *f*	field rail
Klemmplatte *f*	base plate, sleeper clamping plate, tie clamping plate
Klemmplattenschraube *f*	plate clamping bolt
Kletterzungenweiche *f*	climbing tongue switch
Laschenbolzen *m*	fish(-plate) bolt
Rahmengleis *n*	tracking complete with sleepers (Brit.); ~ ~ ~ ties (US)
Rillenschwelle *f*	grooved sleeper (Brit.); ~ tie (US)
Schienenbieger *m*	jim crow (Brit.); rail bender
Schienenfuß *m*	bottom flange
Schienenkopf *m*	top flange, railhead

Feldbahn(anlage) — Felsschüttungsstaudamm

Schienennagelhammer m   track layer's hammer, ~ ~ mallet, trackmen's adze

Schienensteg m   web

Schienennagel m   rail fixing nail, rail spike, dog spike, track spike

---

Feld|buch n [*Kettenvermessung f*] = field book, chain ~

~effe f, siehe: Feldulme f

~-Feuchtigkeits-Äquivalent n [*ist derjenige Wassergehalt, Wassergewicht geteilt durch Gewicht der Festmasse, bei dem ein Tropfen Wasser auf der ebenen Oberfläche des Bodens nicht sogleich absorbiert wird, sondern sich ausbreitet und der Oberfläche ein glänzendes Aussehen verleiht*] = field moisture equivalent [*is defined as the minimum moisture content, expressed as a percentage of the weight of the ovendried soil, at which a drop of water placed on a smooth surface of the soil will not immediately be absorbed by the soil, but will spread out over the surface and give it a shiny appearance, abbrev. FME, symbol W_{fme}*]

~mitte f [*Brücke f, Träger m*] = midspan

~moment n = moment at midspan

~ofen m, Feldbrandofen, Meiler m [*Ziegelherstellung f*] = clamp

~rüster f, siehe: Feldulme f

~schmiede f = field forge, bottom blast ~, portable ~

~spat m = fel(d)spar

~spatbasalt m = fel(d)spathoidal basalt

~spatsand m, siehe: Arkose f

~spatvertreter m = fel(d)spathoid mineral

~stecher m, siehe: Fernglas n

~stein m = field stone

~telefon n = field telephone

~ulme f, Feldrüster f, Feldeffe f = common elm, small-leaved elm

~ und Industriebahngerät n = light railway material

Feld|verdichtung f (von Boden m) = field compaction (of soil)

~versuch m, siehe: Freifeldprüfung f

~weg m = field path

~weite f = panel length

Felge f, Rad ~ = rim

Fels m, Gestein n, Felsgestein, Festgestein = rock

~abbruch m, Felssturz m, Bergsturz = débris-slide, rock avalanche

~abtrag m, siehe: Felseinschnitt m

~aushub m für das Planum = rock cutting in formation

~baggerung f, Felsaushub m, Felsausbruch m = (solid) rock excavation

Felsblock m, Steinblock = block of rock

~-Greifkorb m = stone grapple, rock ~, stone grab

Fels|bohren n, siehe: Gesteinsbohren

~bohrer m, Gesteinsbohrer = rock drill

~brecher m; siehe unter „Naßbagger m"

~einschnitt m, Felsabtrag m = rock cut

Felsen|alaun m = rock alum

~riff n = rocky ledge

~schaufel f [*Schürflader m*] = rock bucket

Fels|(förder)kübel m = stone skip

(~) Geröll(e) n, Gesteinstrümmer f, Gesteinsschutt m, Felstrümmer f, Trümmermaterial n = rock débris, ~ waste rubble (Geol.)

~gestein n, siehe: Fels m

~grat m = high rocky ridge

~gründung f = foundation in rock

~injektion f, siehe: Gesteinsauspressung f

Felsit m = felsite [*obsolete term: felstone*]

felsitisch, feinkörnig-dicht = felsitic

Felsitporphyr m = felsitic porphyry

Fels|kübel n, siehe: Felsförderkübel

~löffel m = rock dipper

~massen f = rock masses

~mechanik f, Geomechanik f = rock mechanics

~rechen m, Steinharke f = rock rake

~ritze f = crevice

~schicht f, Gesteinsschicht = rock formation

~schüttungsstaudamm m; siehe unter „Talsperre f"

Fels|sprengung f = rock blasting
~sturz m, siehe: Felsabbruch m
~transport-Kippmulde f [*Erdbau-Lastfahrzeug n*] = rock-type dump body
~trümmer f, Trümmermaterial n (Geol.) = rock waste
~tunnel m, Bergtunnel m, Gebirgstunnel = rock tunnel
~trümmer f, siehe: (Fels)Geröll(e)n (Geol.)
~untergrund m, siehe: anstehendes Gestein n
~wand f = rock face
Fender m = bumper, fender
Fenn n, siehe: Bruch m
Fenster|bank f = window sill
~dichtungsstrick m = window sealing rope
~geschoß n [*z. B. von Kirchen fpl*] = clerestory
~glas n = window glass
~stollen m, siehe: Zugangsstollen
Fern|anzeige f = remote indication
~bedienung f, siehe: Fernsteuerung f
~betätigung f, siehe Fernsteuerung f
Ferner m, siehe: Gletscher m
Fernfahrer m = long-distance driver
ferngesteuert = remotely controlled
Fern|glas n, Feldstecher m = binoculars, field glasses
~heizung f = district heating (system)

~heizwerk n = central heating station
~meldeturm m = telephone tower
~registriergerät n = remote recorder
~schreiber m = teleprinter
~schwimmer m = remotely controlled float
~sehturm m = TV tower
~sehverkehrslenkung f = television monitoring
~steuerung f, Fernbedienung f, Fernbetätigung = remote control
~thermometer n = remote-reading thermometer
~transport m = long-distance haulage work
~transportband n, siehe: Langstreckenförderbandanlage f zum Transport m von Gesteinen npl
~verkehr m = long-distance traffic
~verkehrsbeschilderung f = long-distance signing
~verkehrsstraße f = trunkline road, trunk road [*deprecated: arterial road*]
Ferrit m = ferrite, soft pure iron
Ferrochlorid n, siehe: Eisenchlorür n
ferroelektrisches Kristall n = ferroelectric crystal
Ferro|oxalat n = ferrous oxalate
~silizium n = ferro-silicon
fertig eingebaut = complete in place
Fertigbauweise f = precast construction

Fertigbehandlung f, Endbearbeitung f [*Beton m*]	(surface) finishing operations
Arbeitsbühne f	(trowel(l)ing) bridge, joint finishing bridge, float bridge, finisher's bridge
Ebner m, Richtscheit n, Setzlatte f, Richtlatte, Wiegelatte	straight edge
Deckenschluß m	finish
Bandabzug m	finishing by belt
Glätter m	float
Kantenbrecher m	rounding tool, edging tool for rounding concrete arrises, jointing tool, bullnose trowel, arris trowel, arrissing tool
Handarbeit f	hand finishing
geriffelter Deckenschluß m	ridged finish
glatter Deckenschluß m	smooth finish
Piassavabesen m	bass broom
Abziehlatte f	smoothing board, screed(ing) board, levelling board

Zementmilch *f* = laitance
rauher Deckenschluß *m* = rough finish
Arbeitsschutzdach *n*, Arbeitszelt *n* = concrete finishing tent
Fugenmaurer *m* = finisher
gebrochene Fugenkante *f* = arris [*the rounded edge of the concrete slab at a joint*]

Fertigbeton|-Doppelwandtafel *f* = precast concrete sandwich panel
~**pfahl** *m*; siehe unter „Gründungspfahl"
~**platte** *f* = precast slab
~**teil** *m, n*, siehe: (Beton)Fertigteil
~**wandplatte** *f* = concrete wall panel
Fertigdecke *f* = precast floor
fertige Bitumendachpappe *f* = ready roofing
Fertiger *m*, siehe: Deckenfertiger *m*
~ **mit fester Arbeitsbreite** *f* = fixed width finisher
~ ~ **selbstverstellbarer Arbeitsbreite** *f* = self-widening finisher
~**bohle** *f*; siehe unter „Schwarzbelageinbaumaschine *f*"
Fertig|erzeugnis *n* = finished product
~**stellungstermin** *m* = completion date, target ~
~**teil** *m, n*, siehe: (Beton)Fertigteil
Fesselballon *m* = captive balloon
Festbettverfahren *n* [*technisches Spaltverfahren*] = fixed bed process
feste Kupplung *f* = (solid) coupling
fester Grund *m* = firm bottom
~ **Körper** *m* = solid body
festes Auflager *n* = fixed bearing
~ **Schmiermittel** *n* = solid lubricant
festgelagerter Sand *m* = compact sand
Festgestein *n*, siehe: Fels *m*
festgewordener Meißel *m*; siehe unter „Bohrmeißel"
Festigkeit *f*, Material~ = (material) strength
Festigkeits|prüfung *f* = strength test
~**wert** *m* = mechanical property
Fest|landsdüne *f*, Winddüne = inland dune [*deposition by wind*]
~**mörtel** *m* = hardened mortar
~**-Paraffin** *n* = paraffin

~**preis** *m* = fixed price
~**preisvertrag** *m* = lump-sum contract, firm price~, fixed price ~
~**punkt** *m*, siehe: Abrißpunkt
~**sieb** *n* = fixed screen
~**stellbremse** *f* = parking brake
~**stoff** *m* = solid matter
~**werden** *n* [*Rohr n oder Bohrzeug n im Bohrloch n*] = freezing
fette Mischung *f* = rich mix
fetter Lehm *m* = heavy loam
~ **Mörtel** *m* = fatty mortar
~ **Ton** *m* = heavy clay
Fett|fang *m*, Fettabscheider *m* = grease trap (Brit.); ~ interceptor (US)
~**gas** *n*, siehe: Ölgas
~**kalk** *m*, siehe: Weißkalk
~**pech** *n* = fatty(-acid) pitch
~**presse** *f* = grease unit, ~ gun
~**preßbüchse** *f*, Staufferbüchse = stuffing box, grease cup
feuchtes Bohrlochkopfgas *n*, siehe: Reichnaturgas
~ **Naturgas** *n*, siehe: Reichnaturgas
Feuchthaltung *f* [*Beton m*] = moist curing [*concrete*]
Feuchtigkeits|gehalt *m*, siehe: Wassergehalt
~**isolierung** *f*, Abdichtung *f* [*Bauwerk n gegen Bodenfeuchte f*] = damp-proofing
~**kammer** *f*, Feuchtraum *m* = humidity chamber
~**korrosion** *f* = aqueous corrosion
~**meßdose** *f* = moisture cell
Feuerberg *m*, siehe: Vulkan *m*
~**tuff** *m*, siehe: vulkanischer Tuff
feuerbeständig = fire-proof
Feuer|beton *m* = castable refractory
~**braunkohle** *f* = fuel brown coal [*incorrectly termed "non-bituminous brown coal"*]

feuerfest [*in bezug auf Festgesteine und Tone zur Herstellung feuerfester Produkte, Schmelztemperatur oberhalb 1600 Grad Celsius*] = refractory
   halbfeuerfest [*Schmelztemp. zwischen 1500 und 1600 Grad Celsius*] = semi-refractory
   hochfeuerfest [*Schmelztemp. über 1800 Grad Celsius*] = high-refractory

---

feuerfeste Faser *f* = refractory fiber (US); ~ fibre (Brit.)
feuerfester Beton *m* = refractory concrete
~ **Isolierstein** *m* = insulating fire brick
~ **Ton** *m*, siehe: Schamotte *f*
~ **Tonerde-Kieselsäure-Stein** *m* = alumina-silica refractory
feuerfestes Erzeugnis *n* = refractory
~ **Oxyd** *n* = refractory oxide
Feuer|fortschritt *m* [*Ziegelofen m*] = fire travel
~**gas** *n*, Rauchgas, Verbrennungsgas = flue gas
~**gefahr** *f*, siehe: Brandgefahr
~**gefährlichkeit** *f*, siehe: Entzündbarkeit *f*
feuerhemmende Farbe *f* = fire-retardant paint
feuerhemmendes Holz *n* = fire-retardant wood
Feuer|kugelstein *m*, Meteorit *m* = meteorite
~**löschprüfung** *f* = fire-fighting test
~**löschpumpe** *f*, Feuerspritze *f* = fire pump
feuerlose (Dampf)Lok(omotive) *f*; siehe unter „Feldbahnanlage *f*"
Feuer|meldeanlage *f* = fire alarm system
~**opal** *m* (Min.) = fire opal
~**röhrenkessel** *m*, siehe: Heizröhrenkessel
~**rost** *m*, (Kessel)Rost *m* = grate, boiler ~
~**roststab** *m*, (Kessel)Roststab = grate bar, fire ~
~**schiff** *n* = lightship, light-vessel
~**schutz** *m*, siehe: Brandschutz
~**schutzfarbe** *f*, Flammschutzfarbe, Brandschutzfarbe = fire protection paint
feuersicher = fire-safe
Feuerspritze *f*, Feuerlöschpumpe *f* = fire pump

Feuerstein *m*, siehe: Flint *m*
~**knollen** *m*, Flintknollen *m* = flint pebble
Feuerstrahlbohren *n*, Strahlbohrung *f*, Düsenbohren [*früher: Schmelzbohren*] = jet-piercing, heat drilling
Feuerung *f* [*Kessel m*] = furnace
~, Feuern *n* = firing
Feuer|(ungs)raum *m*, Heizkammer *f* = fire box
~**wehrschlauch** *m* = fire hose
Fibel *f* = primer
Fibrolith *m* (Min.), siehe: Faserkiesel *m*
Filter|becken *n* = filtering basin
~**brunnenstaffel** *f*, Filterrohrbrunnenstaffel = wellpoint system
~**drän** *m*, siehe unter „Entwässerung *f*"
~**füllung** *f*; siehe unter „Entwässerung *f*"
~**kies** *m* = filter gravel
~**kuchen** *m* = filter cake
~**patrone** *f* = filter cartridge
~**preßplatte** *f* = filter press plate
~**sand** *m* = filter sand
~**schicht** *f*, Dränschicht *f* = filter layer
~**schlauch** *m* = filter hose
~**sieb** *n*, Saugkorb *m*, Seiher *m* = filtering screen, strainer
~**stein** *m* [*Luftrutsche f*] = porous block
~**stein** *m* = porous stone dise [*triaxial-compression test chamber*]
~**stein** *m* = filter stone
~**stoffgewebe** *n* = filter cloth
~**wasser** *n* [*gefiltertes Sickerwasser*] = filtered infiltration water
~**wasser** *n* = filtered water
~**zone** *f* = filter zone
Filtrationsbeschleuniger *m* [*Paraffin n*] = wax modifier
filtriertes Rückstandsöl *n* = filtered stock
Filz *m* = felt

Findling(sstein) *m*, erratischer Block *m* Erratiker *m* [*in den Alpen auch „Geißberger" genannt*] = erratic block

Fingerdruck|schalter *m*, siehe: Druckknopfschalter

~**steuerung** *f* = finger tip control

Fingerpier *m* = finger pier

Finsterwalder-Vorspannsystem *n* [*Vorspannung durch das Eigengewicht der Brücke f selbst*] = Finsterwalder prestressing method [*the dead load produces pretension in the reinforcement*]

Fioringras *n*, siehe: weißes Straußgras

Firmen|bauleiter *m* = contractor's agent

~**zeitschrift** *f* = house magazin

Firn *m* (Geol.) = névé, firn

First *m* = ridge

~**pfette** *f* = ridge purlin

~**ziegel** *m* = ridge tile

Fisch *m* [*im Bohrloch verlorener Eisenteil*] = fish

fischbauchförmig = fish-bellied

Fischbauchträger *m*, Linsenträger = fish-beam

Fischereihafen *m* = fish harbo(u)r

Fisch|grätendränage *f*; siehe unter „Entwässerung *f*"

~**leim** *m* = fish glue

~**paß** *m*, siehe: Fischtreppe *f*

~**schuppen** *m* = fishscale

~**schwanzmeißel** *m*; siehe unter „Bohrmeißel"

~**sterben** *n*, Fischsterblichkeit *f* = fish mortality, kill-out of fish

~**teich** *m* = stock pond

~**treppe** *f*, Fischpaß *m* = fish way, fish ladder, fish-pass

Fitschenbeitel *m* = plugging chisel

fixer Kohlenstoff *m* = fixed carbon

Fixiersalz *n*, Natriumthiosulfat *n*, unterschwefligsaures Natrium *n* = sodium thiosulfate

Fixpunkt *m*, siehe: Abrißpunkt

Fjord *m* = fjord, flord

Flach|bagger *m* = surface digging machine

~**bagger-Lader** *m*, siehe: Pflugbagger *m*

~**baggerung** *f*, Flachbaggern *n* = surface excavation, surface digging, shallow cut digging, shallow grading

~**band** *n*; siehe unter „Bandförderer *m*"

~**blech** *n* = flat (stele) plate

~**boden-Kippritsche** *f* [*LKW m*] = combination dump and platform body

~**bodenselbstentlader** *m* = track wheel flat dump car

~**brunnen** *m* = shallow well

~**draht** *m* = flat wire

~**(draht)litze** *f*; siehe unter „Drahtseil *n*"

flache Hochebene *f* = tableland

Flacheisengitterwerk *n* = flat lacing, ~ trellis work

Flächen|blitz *m* = sheet lightning

~**fundament** *n* = footing

flächenhafte Ausnagung *f*; siehe unter „Denudation *f*"

Flächen|last *f* = area load

~**leistung** *f* = yardage

~**messer** *m*, Planimeter *n* = planimeter

~**pressung** *f*, siehe: Bodendruck *m*

~**rüttler** *m*, Ober~ = surface vibrator, ~ vibrating machine

~**tragwerk** *n* = plane (load-)bearing structure, load-bearing slab

flacher Bogen *m*, siehe: Stichbogen

~ **Einschnitt** *m* = shallow cut(ting)

flache Tragrolle *f*; siehe unter „Bandförderer *m*"

Flachfeile *f*, gewöhnliche Feile = flat file

flach(gängig)es Gewinde *n*, Flachgewinde = square thread

Flach|glas *n* = flat glass

~**gründung** *f*, Flachfundation *f* = shallow foundation

~**kolben** *m* = flat-topped piston

~**kopfniet** *m* = flat-head rivet

~**küste** *f* = flat low-lying coast

~**land** *n* = plain country, level ~

~**landfluß** *m* = plain river

~**litze** *f*; siehe unter „Drahtseil *n*"

~**löffelbagger** *m*; siehe: Planierbagger

Flachmoor *n*, Nieder(ungs)moor = shallow moor, lowland ~

~**torf** *m* = bottom peat

Flach|pfanne *f* = grooved tile, gutter ~

~**-Probe(ent)nahmeapparat** *m* = shallow sampler, ~ sample taker

~**riemen** *m* = flat belt

~**riemenscheibe** *f* = flat belt pulley

Flachschieber *m* = flat slide valve

Flach|schiebersiloverschluß *m* = sliding type bin door
~schürfbohrung *f* = shallow sampling
~schüttung *f* = dumping in thin layers, thin-layer fill
flachseitiges Ziegel(stein)pflaster *n* = flat brick paving
Flach|sieb *n*, Plansieb = flat screen
~spitzraspel *f* = flat rasp
~spundbohle *f* = flat-web sheet pile
~stab *m* = flat bar
~-Stangen(transport)rost *m*, Flachstangenaufgeber *m* = flat (or level) bar screen, ~ (~ ~) screen of bars, ~ (~ ~) grizzly
~wulststahl *m* = flat bulb iron
~wurzel *f* = spread root
~zange *f* = flat pliers
~zellen-Fang(e)damm *m* = flat-shaped cell cofferdam
Fladenlava *f*; siehe unter „Vulkan *m*"
Flammbrenner *m* = flame type burner
Flammenphotometer *n* = hydrogen flame photometer
Flammentrostung *f* = flame descaling, ~ cleaning
Flammpunkt *m* = flash point
~prüfer *m* = flash-point apparatus
Flammrohr|doppelkessel *m*, Zwillingkessel *m* = twin Cornish boiler
~kessel *m* = flue boiler
Flamm|ruß *m* = carbon block
~schmelzofen *m*, Reverberierofen = reverberatory furnace
~schutzfarbe *f*, siehe: Feuerschutzfarbe
Flansch *m* = flange
~-Elektromotor *m*, Elektro-Flanschmotor = flanged motor
Flanschen|absperrschieber *m* = sluice valve with flanged ends
~dichtungsmanschette *f* = flange gasket
~rohr *n* = flanged pipe
~(rohr)formstück *n* = flanged fitting
Flansch|neigung *f* = flange slope
~schraube *f* = flange bolt
~verbindung *f* = flange(d) (pipe) joint
~wulsteisen *n* = bulb rail iron
Flasche *f*, Block *m*, Kloben *m*, Seilflasche Seilkloben, Unterflasche [*Seilzug m*] = block

Flaschengas *n* = cylinder gas
flaschengrün [*Mineral n*] = bottle green [*mineral*]
Flaschen|hebebock *m*, Flaschenwinde *f* = bottle jack
~zug *m*, Seilzug, Blockwinde *f*, Seilzug *m*; Talje *f* [*seemännischer Ausdruck*] = (block and) tackle, (rope) pulley block, lifting block, hoist block, rigging with blocks
~zugblock *m* = travelling block
~zugseilführung *f* = wire line guide
Flattergras *n* = millet (grass)
flatternde Betondecke *f* = flexing concrete pavement
Flatter|rüster *f*, Bastrüster *f*, Bastulme *f* = soft-leaved elm
flaue Brise *f* = light wind, breeze
Flechtwerk *n* = wicker-work, wattle work, basket work
~zaun *m*, Flechtzaun, Flechtwerk *n*, Schlickzaun = wicker (work) fence
Fleurometer *n* = flourometer
Flick|arbeit *f*, siehe: Ausflicken *n*
~mörtel *m* = patching mortar, repair ~
~stelle *f* [*Straße f*] = patch
~verfahren *n*, siehe: Ausflicken *n*
fliegend gelagert = taper bore mounted
Flieger *m* = extension flight conveyor, swivel ~ ~, thrower belt unit ~ *m*, siehe: Gegengewichtrinne *f*
~horst *m*; siehe unter „Flugplatz *m*"
Flieger *m* **mit Einlauftrichter** *m* = swivelpiler [*thrower belt unit with hopper*]
Fliehgewicht *n* = spider
~ = centrifugal weight
Fliehkraft|abscheider *m*, siehe: Zyklon *m*
~antrieb *m* = centrifugal drive
~(naß)klassierer *m* = centrifugal classifier
~regler *m*, Zentrifugalregulator *m* = centrifugal governor
~zyklon *m*, siehe: Zyklon
Fliesen|fußboden *m* = tile floor(ing)
~legerarbeiten *fpl* = tile layers' work
Fließ|bild *n* = flow diagram, ~ sheet
~dehnung *f* = yield strain
~eigenschaft *f* = flow property
Fließen *n* (Geol.) = rock flowage
fließen [*Metall n*] = to yield
Fließförderer *m*, siehe: Stetigförderer *m*

Fließ|formel f = formula of flow
~gefüge n, siehe: Fluidalgefüge
~grenze f, unterer Plastizitätszustand m, w_f [Boden m] = liquid limit [symbol w_L]
~grenze f [Stahl m] = yield point
~grenzengerät n, siehe: Gerät n zur Bestimmung der Fließgrenze f
~maß n, Setzmaß, Ausbreitmaß, Sackmaß [Beton m] = slump
~probe f = flow test
~punkt m [Kälteverhalten n von Dieselkraftstoff m] = pour point
~rutschung f, siehe: Bodenkriechen n
~sicherheit f von Vollwand-Verbundkonstruktionen fpl = yield safety of solid-web composite structures
~spannung f [Metall n] = yield stress
~ton m, siehe: Quickton
~tracht f, siehe: Fluidalgefüge n
~widerstand m = resistance to flow
Flint m, Feuerstein m = flint
Flinzgraphit m = flake graphite
Flocken|schlamm m; siehe unter „Abwasserwesen n"
~stein m, Krokydolith m (Min.) = krokidolite, crocidolite
flößen f = to raft
Floß|kanal m = canal for rafting wood
~rinne f, Floßgasse f = log chute
~schleuse f = log sluice
Flotation f, Schwimmaufbereitung f = flotation
Flotationsapparat m = flotation machine

FLOTTAIR [Trademark] [fahrbarer luftgekühlter Kompressor m], Fabrikat FLOTTMANN G. m. b. H., HERNE/ WESTFALEN, DEUTSCHLAND = FLOTTAIR towed air-cooled (air) compressor [Trademark]
flözleerer Sandstein m = farewell-rock
Flucht|pfahl m; siehe unter „Ausfluchtung f"
~stange f, Fluchtstab m = ranging pole, ~ rod
Fluder m, Holz(ge)rinne f, (n) = wood flume, timber ~
Flug|asche f, Kessel~ = fly-ash, flue dust
~benzintankanlage f, siehe unter „Flugzeugtreibstofftankanlage f"
Flügel|anzeigedämpfer m, Flügelzeigerdämpfer = paddle dampening device
~füßlerschlamm m, Pteropodenschlamm m = pteropod ooze
~krone f; siehe unter „Bohrmeißel m"
~mauer f, Flügelstirnmauer f [Durchlaß m] = wing (head)wall, return wall
~meißel m; siehe unter „Bohrmeißel m"
~mutter f, Flügelschraubenmutter = (butter)fly (screw) nut, wing (~) ~
~ (rad) m, (n) [Bunkerstandanzeiger m] = rotating paddle
~schiene f = wing rail
~sonde f = vane apparatus, ~ penetrometer, ~ shear tester
~stirnmauer f, siehe: Flügelmauer
Fluglinie f, Luft(verkehrs)linie = air line, ~ route

Flugplatz m	**airfield**
Abbremsplatz m	warm(ing)-up apron (or pad)
Abfertigungsgebäude n	terminal building
Abstellfläche f, Standplatz m	hardstand, (hard)standing, parking apron
Abwurfgebiet n	dropping zone [an area in which parachute troops or supplies are dropped]
Anflugsektor m, Einflugschneise f	approach funnel (Brit.); approach zone (US); flying gap [this term is used in India]
Anflugsektorbezugsfläche f	approach surface
Anflugwinkel m	angle of glied
Auffangflugplatz m	layback [a term used in India for a satelite in rear of an operational area for use upon withdrawal]

Flugplatz

Aufsetzpunkt m [Landung f]	touchdown point
Auslauf m, Stoppfläche f	over-run, stopway
Ausweichflughafen m	alternate aerodrome
barometrische Höhe f	density altitude
Befeuerung f	lighting
Abstandsfeuer n, Entfernungsfeuer	distance marking light
Anflugfeuer n	approach light
Drehleuchtfeuer n	rotating beacon
Entfernungsfeuer n, siehe: Abstandsfeuer	
Festfeuer	fixed light
Feuer n, Luftfahrtfeuer n, Leuchte f	(aeronautical) light
Gefahrenfeuer	hazard beacon
Hindernisfeuer n, Hindernislicht n	obstruction light, aviation ~ ~, aircraft warning light
Hochleistungsfeuer n	high-intensity light
Horizontfeuer n	horizon light
Kennfeuer n	identification beacon
Leuchte f, siehe: Feuer n	
Leuchtfeuer n	beacon
Linearfeuer	linear light
Punktfeuer	point light
Leuchtpfad m, Landepfad m	flare path
Randfeuer n, Umrandungsfeuer	boundary light
Rollwegfeuer n, Zu(roll)wegfeuer, Rollweglampe f	taxi-way light
Schwebungsfeuer n	oscillating beacon
Schwellenfeuer n	threshold light
Stahlturm m mit Hindernisleuchten fpl	illumination tower
Start- und Landebahnbefeuerung f	runway lighting
Verdichtungsfeuer n	range light
Zu(roll)wegfeuer n, s.: Rollwegfeuer	
Bereitstellungsfläche f	alert platform, marshalling area, assembly area, readiness area, taxi holding position, alert apron
Betankungsfeld n	refuel(l)ing apron
Betriebsfläche f	operational area
Boden(abfertigungs)anlagen fpl	ground installations, ground facilities, ground-handling facilities
Bodensicht f	ground visibility
Bodenwind m	ground wind, surface wind
Einflugschneise f, siehe: Anflugsektor m	
Einflugschneisenbeleuchtung f	approach lighting system
Einsatzflugplatz m	combat airfield
Einzelabstellfläche f	dispersal, dispersed (hard)standing
Feldflugplatz m	advanced landing ground, A. L. G.
Feuermeldeanlage f	fire alarm system
Fliegerhorst m	(air-)base (US); RAF-Station (Brit.)
Flughafenbezugspunkt m, Rollfeldbezugspunkt m	aerodrome reference point

Flugplatz

Flughafenerkennungszeichen n, Flughafenkennzeichen	aerodrome identification sign
Flughafen m	aerodrome, airdrome [*an all-weather airfield equipped with facilities for shelter, supply and maintenance of aircraft. The term is no longer authorized officially, but is still widely used in technical reports. "Airdrome" is frequently employed for "Airfield" in American publications*]
Flugleitung(sgebäude) f, (n), FS-Kontrollturm m, Flugleitungsturm	flying control (Brit.); base operations (US); control tower
Flugsicherungsdienst m	air traffic control service
Flugverkehr m	air traffic
(Flugzeug)Halle f	hangar, aeroplane ~
kleine ~	hangarette [*a term used in India for a lightly roofed hangar of not more than 70 feet span*]
Freihandelszone f	customs-free trade zone
Flugzeugtreibstofftankanlage f	(bulk) aviation fuel installation, multitank aviation fuel installation
Frontflugplatz m	forward airfield
Grasnarbenlandefläche f	grass landing ground
(Hallen)Vorfeld n	apron
Haltepunkt m	taxi-holding position
Instrumenten-Landebahn f	instrument runway
Instrumenten-Wasserlandebahn f	instrument channel
Kegelbezugsfläche f	concial surface
Landekreuz n	landing cross, landing "T"
Landerichtungsanzeiger m	landing direction indicator
Landestreifen m	landing strip
Leuchtfeuer n	beacon
Luftstraße f	airway
Nebenflugplatz m	satellite airfield, auxiliary ~
Notlandestreifen m	emergency landing strip
Nur-Landebahn f	landing runway
Nur-Startbahn f	take-off runway
Piste f, siehe: Start- und Landebahn f	
Randmarkierungen fpl, Randkennzeichen n	boundary markers
Rollfeld n	manoeuvring area
(Roll)Feldhütte f	crew hut, dispersal ~
Rollfeldbezugspunkt m, siehe: Flughafenbezugspunkt	
Rollfläche f	movement area
Schlechtwetterbedingungen f	IFR (weather) conditions
Schwebungsfeuer n	oscillating beacon
Scheinflugplatz m	dummy airfield
seitliche Übergangsbezugsfläche f	transitional surface
Sichtzeichen n	marker

Flugplatz — Flugzeugtreibstofftankanlage

Splitterschutzboxe *f*	aircraft pen (Brit.); ~ revetment (US)
Standplatz *m*, siehe: Abstellfläche *f*	
Start- und Landebahn *f*, Piste *f*	runway
Start- und Landebahnfeuer *n*	contact light
Start- und Landestreifen *m*	air strip
Uhrenanlage *f*	clock system
Umrandungsfeuer *n*, Randfeuer	boundary light
Verdichtungsfeuer *n*	range light
Verkehrsflughafen *m*	(commercial) airport
Wasserlandebahn *f*	channel
Wasserlandebahnfeuer *n*	channel light
Wasserlandebahn-Grundlänge *f*	channel selected basic length
Wasser-Rollweg *m*	taxi - channel
Wendebecken *n*	turning basin
Werft *f*	tech(nical) hangar, maintenance ~
Windrose *f*	windrose
Windsack *m*	wind cone, wind sock, sleeve
zollfreier Flughafen *m*, Freiflughafen	customs-free aerodrome
Zubahn *f*, Rollweg *m*, Rollfeldringstraße *f*, (Zu)Rollbahn *f*	taxi-track, taxi-way (US); perimeter (track) (Brit.); taxiing strip
Abzweig-~	branch ~
Haupt-~	main ~

Flugplatzbauschalung *f* = airport forms
Flugsand *m* = wind-blown sand, blow(n)~
Flugstaub *m* = airborne dust
~abscheidung *f* **durch Ultraschall** *m* **(oder Überschall)** = ultrasonic (or supersonic) flue dust elimination

Flugzeugschleppwinde *f* = airplane handling winch

Flugzeugtreibstofftankanlage *f* — **(bulk) aviation fuel installation, multi-tank ~ ~ ~**

Anzeigegerät *n* für explosive Dünste *mpl*	explosive vapo(u)r indicating instrument, vapo(u)r indicator
Atmungsgerät *n*	breathing apparatus, respiratory apparatus
Auslitern *n*	dipping
Behälter *m*, Flüssigkeitsbehälter *m*, Tank *m*, Zisterne *f*, Sammelbehälter *m*	(storage) tank, cistern, container (for liquids)
Benzinfang *m*	interceptor, trap
Be- und Entlüftung *f*	ventilation and aeration
Blasenabscheider *m*	air bubble eliminator
Bleibenzin *n*	leaded petrol (Brit.)
Domdeckel *m*	inspection cover
Domschacht *m*	inspection chamber
Durchlaufmesser *m*	flow meter
eichen, auslitern	to dip, to calibrate
Eichtabelle *f*	calibration chart

Einatmen n	inhalation
Einfüllstelle f	filling point
Eisenbahn-Kesselwagen m	rail tanker, tanker wagon (Brit.); railroad tank car (US)
Exhaustor m	tank fumes extract fan
Explosionsfähigkeit f	explosibility, explosiveness
elektrisch verbunden	electrically blonded
Flanschendichtung f mit Feder f und Nut m	flanged joint with tongue and groove
Flanschendichtung f mit eingelegtem Ring m	flanged joint with conical ring
Flugbenzin n	aviation petrol, ~ spirit (Brit.); aviation gasoline, avgas (US)
Flugbenzintankanlage f	multi-tank aviation spirit installation (Brit.); ~ aviation gasoline ~ (US)
Flüssigkeitsbehälter m, siehe: Behälter	
Fußventil n	foot valve
Gel m	gel
Gesichtsmaske f mit Atmungsschlauch m	face mask with breathing tube
Lufttrockner m	air drier
Peilstab m	dipstick, dip rod
Probe(ent)nahmerohr n	sampling pipe
Rückschlagklappe f	flap valve
Saugrohr n	suction pipe
Schlamm m	sludge
Schnellschlußventil n	rapid-closing valve, quick-closing ~
Schutzbekleidung f	protective clothing
Schwergewichtsentleerung f	gravity discharge
Sicherheitsbestimmung f	safety regulation
Straßentankwagen m	raod tanker, bowser (Brit.); tank truck (US)
Tank m, siehe: Behälter m	
Umspülleitung f	circulation piping
Wasserzapfleitung f	water draw-off piping
Zapfeinrichtung f	draw-off unit
Zapfstelle f	dispense point, refuel(l)ing hydrant

Fluidalgefüge n, Fließgefüge, fluidale Textur f, Fluidaltextur, Fließtracht f, Flußgefüge, Fluktationsgefüge = fluidal arrangement, fluxion structure, flow structure

Fluor n [*chemisches Element F, Atomgewicht 19*] = fluorine

Fluoreszenz-Indikator m = fluorescent indicator

Fluorid n = fluoride

fluorieren = to fluoridate

Fluorit m, Flußspat m, CaF_2 = fluor(-spar), fluorite, calcium fluoride, fluoride of calcium

Fluor|kalzium n, siehe: Kalziumfluorid n
~kohlenwasserstoff m = fluorcarbon
~natrium n = sodium fluoride
~salz n = fluoride
~wasserstoffsäure f, Flußsäure = hydrofluoric acid, fluorhydric ~

Flurofen m [*Ziegelherstellung f*] = horizontal brick kiln

Flur|schaden *m* = surface and trespass damage, damage to crops, injury done to the fields
flüssige Phase *f* = liquid phase
~ Vaseline *f* = liquid petrolatum
flüssiger Binder *m*, siehe: flüssiges Bindemittel
~ Brennstoff *m* = liquid fuel
~ Sauerstoff *m* = liquid oxygen (explosive)
~ Treibstoff *m* [*Heizöle npl und Treibstoffe mpl*] = liquid fuel
~ Zustand *m* = liquid state, ~ condition
flüssiges Bindemittel *n*, flüssiger Binder *m* = fluid (or liquid) binder (or binding agent)
Flüssigkeits|behälter *m*, siehe: Behälter
~bremse *f*, hydraulische Bremse = hydraulic brake, hydromatic ~
~dämpfung *f* = liquid dampening
~dichtemesser *m*, siehe: hydrostatische Senkwaage *f*
~druck *m*, hydrostatischer Druck = hydrostatic pressure
~kreislauf *m* = liquid cycle
~mechanik *f* = fluid mechanics
~reibung *f* = fluid friction
~säule *f* = liquid column
~spiegel *m* = fluid surface, surface of liquid
~stand *m* = fluid level, level of liquid
~strömung *f* = fluid flow
~-Transportfahrzeug *n*, Flüssigkeits-Transporter *m*, Straßentanker *m*, Straßentankwagen *m*, Straßentransporter *m* für flüssiges Gut, Straßen-Flüssigkeitstransporter [*selbstfahrend*] = liquid hauler, ~ hauling truck
~verlust *m* = fluid loss
Flüstergewölbe *n* = whispering dome
Fluß *m* **mit Sandboden** *m* = sand-bed river
~ablagerung *f*, Flußsediment *n*, fluviatiles Sediment = river deposit, fluvial ~, ~ outwash
~abschnitt *m* = reach of the river
flußabwärts, stromabwärts = downstream, down river
Fluß|amt *n* = rivers board

~anzapfung *f*, Flußenthauptung = betrunking of rivers, river beheading
~arm *m* = river arm, ~ branch
~aue *f*, siehe: Auenebene *f*
flußaufwärts, stromaufwärts = up river, up-stream
Fluß|bagger *m*; siehe unter „Naßbagger"
~bank *f* = river bar
~bau *m* = river construction, ~ engineering
~bauarbeiten *fpl* = river works
~bauingenieur *m* = river conservancy engineer
~baustein *m* = river construction stone
~bauwerk *n* = river structure
~bett *n*, Flußschlauch *m* = river bed
~bett-Abflachung *f* = river bed degradation
~brücke *f* = river bridge
Flüßchen *n* = riverlet, rivulet, streamlet
Fluß|deich *m*, siehe: (Fluß)Uferdamm *m*
~eisen *n* = mild steel, soft ~
~fall *m* = river fall
~fisch *m* = fresh water fish, sweet ~ ~
~gefüge *n*, siehe: Fluidalgefüge
~geschiebe *n*, siehe: Geschiebe(masse) *n*, (*f*)
~gold *n* = alluvial gold, placer ~, river ~
~hafen *m* **mit Betriebsanlagen** *fpl* = river port
~haltung *f* = reach of river
~kabel *n* = river cable
~kies *m* = river gravel
~kiesel *m* = river pebble of quartz
~korrektion *f*, siehe: Flußregulierung *f*
~kraftwerk *n*, siehe: Laufkraftwerk
~krümmung *f* = bend of a river, river bend
~kunde *f* = fluviology, potamology
~kurve *f* = river curve
~lauf *m* = river course, course of a river
~lauf-Talsperre *f* = river dam
~laufveränderung *f* = channel modification
~leitwerk *n*, Parallelwerk = river (training) wall
~löß *m* = river loess
~mäander *m*, Flußschlinge *f*, Mäander = meander

Fluß|messung *f* = river ga(u)ging
~mündung *f* = mouth of the river, river mouth, estuary
~mündung *f* **ohne Gezeiteneinwirkung** *f* = non-tidal estuary
~naßbagger *m*; siehe unter „Naßbagger"
~oase *f* = river oasis
~oberlauf *m*, Oberlauf = upper course of the river
~pegel *m* = fluviometer, river ga(u)ge
~pegelstation *f* = river ga(u)ging station
~regulierung *f*, Flußreg(e)lung *f*, Flußkorrektion *f* = (artificial) river regulation, stream straightening, river rectification, river improvement
~sand *m*, Schwemmsand [*alluvial*] = river sand
~säure *f*, Fluorwasserstoffsäure = hydrofluoric acid, fluorhydric ~
~säureflasche *f* [*Bohrlochneigungsmessung f*] = acid bottle
~schiffahrt *f* = river traffic, ~ navigation
~schlamm *m* = river mud
~schlauch *m*, Flußbett *n* = river bed
~schleuse *f* = river (navigation) lock
~schlick *m* = clay containing river silt
~schlinge *f*, siehe: Flußmäander *m*
~schnellen *fpl* = river rapids
~schotter *m*, siehe: Geschiebe *n*
~schutt *m* = river wash
~schwerspat *m*, Barytflußspat = fluor-spar of baryte
~sediment *n*, siehe: Flußablagerung *f*
~sohle *f* = river floor, ~ bottom
~spaltung *f* = divarication of a river, branching ~ ~ ~, diffluent [*converse of confluent*]
~spat *m*, Fluorit *m*, CaF_2 = fluor-spar, fluorite
~stadium *n* = riverhood
~stahl *m* = medium carbonsteel; high ~ ~
~strömung *f* = river flow
~terrasse *f* = terrace of the river, alluvial (river) bench, alluvial terrace
~terrassenseife *f* = bench placer
~übergang *m* = river crossing
~übergang *m* = place where the current passes from one bank to the other
~überschwemmung *f* = river inundation

Flußufer *n*, Ufer = bank of the river river bank
~damm *m*, Uferdamm, Flußdeich *m* = river shore embankment
~linie *f*, Uferlinie = bank line, river ~ ~
Fluß|umleitdurchlaß *m* = river diversion culvert
~umleitung *f* = river diversion
~unterlauf *m*, Unterlauf = lower course of the river
~untertunnelung *f* = tunnel under river
~vermessung *f* = river survey
~vermischung *f* = bifurcation
~verunreinigung *f* [*durch Einleitung ungeklärter Abwässer*] = river pollution
~wasser *n* = river water
~wasserspiegel *m* = river water table
~wasserstand *m* = river stage
~wehr *n* = river weir
~wiese *f* = river meadow
~zinn *n* = river tin
Flut *f*, Tideflut, aufsteigende Flut, Tidestieg *m* [*das Steigen des Wassers vom Tideniedrigwasser zum folgenden Tidehochwasser*] = high tide of water, flood tide, flowing tide
~, Hochwasser *n* = flood, high water, spate
~becken *n*, Gezeitenbecken = tidal basin
~berg *n* = tidal elevation, ~ swelling
~brücke *f* = flood bridge, inundation ~
~drän *m* = storm(-water) sewer
~(ge)rinne *f*, (*n*) = storm channel
~größe *f*, Flutintervall *n*, Tidehub *m*, Gezeitenhub, Thb = range of tide
~hafen *m*, Tidehafen [*offener Hafen im Tidegebiet, der infolge geringer Tiefe nur bei höheren Wasserständen benutzt werden kann*] = tide harbo(u)r, tidal ~
~intervall *n*, siehe: Flutgröße *f*
~kurve *f* = tidal diagram
~lehm *m* = flood loam
~messer *m* [*der die Gezeitenkurve aufzeichnende Pegel*] = tide ga(u)ge, ~ meter, mareograph, mareometer
~mündung *f* = tidal estuary
~öffnung *f* [*Brücke f*] = high-water span, flood ~
~rinne, Flutgerinne *f* = storm channel
~rinne *f* = flood(-tide) channel

Flut|schleuse f = tide lock
~schreiber m, Gezeitenschreiber = registering tide ga(u)ge, marigraph
~(straßen)verkehr m, Verkehr auf Wechselspur f = tidal traffic
~strom m, Flutströmung f = flood (stream), ~ (tide) current
~tor n = flood gate, head ~, crown ~
~tor n, Gezeitentor = tide gate
~ventil n = flooding valve
~verkehr m, siehe: Flut(straßen)verkehr
~vorhersage f = flood forecasting
~wasser n = tide water
~wassermenge f = volume of water entering on the flood-tide, ~ ~ the flood
~wechsel m = turn of the tides
~weg m = floodway
~welle f, siehe: Gezeitenwelle
~wulst f = tidal bulge
~zerreißung f = tidal disruption
fluvial = fluvial
fluviatil = fluviatile
fluviatile Erosion f = fluviatile erosion
fluviatiles Sediment n, siehe: Flußablagerung f
fluvioklastische Gesteine npl = fluvioclastics
fluxen [*durch Beigabe von Fluxmitteln wird der Erweichungspunkt bituminöser Stoffe erniedrigt*] = to flux
Fluxmittel n, Fluxöl n = flux(ing) oil, ~ agent, flux
Fluxpacker m = FLUXO bag packer
Packsilo m = supply bin, ~ tank
Füllstutzen m = filling spout, ~ tube
Föhn m = föhn wind
Föhrde f = inlet, fiard
Föhrdenküste f = fiard type of coastline
Föhre f, siehe: Weißkiefer f
fokussieren = to focus
Folie f = foil
Foraminiferen|-Gattungen fpl **der Kreide** f = cretaceous genera of foraminifera
~-Kalk(stein) m = foraminiferal limestone
~mergel m = foraminiferal marl
~sand m = foraminiferal sand
~-Vergesellschaftung f = foraminiferal assemblage

Förder|anlage f = conveying plant, ~ installation
~band n, siehe: Bandförderer m
~band n, siehe: Fördergurt m
~band-(Anhänge)Schürfwagen m, siehe: Pflugbagger m
~bandrolle f; siehe unter „Bandförderer m"
~bandtrommel f = conveyor pulley
~bohrung f, Fördersonde f, produzierende Bohrung = output well, production ~, paying ~
~brücke f = transporter bridge, conveyor ~, conveying ~
~düse f [*Erdöl* n] = flow nipple, ~ bean
~einrichtungen fpl **für Baustellen** fpl = material handling devices for construction sites
Förderer m, (Material)Fördergerät n = conveyor
Förder|gurt m, Förderband n = conveyor belt(ing), ~ band
~gut n = material to be conveyed
~haken m **für Pumpengestänge** n = sucker rod hook
~hammer m, siehe: Abbauhammer
~karre(n) f, (m), (Transport)Karre(n) = cart
~kessel m, siehe: Treibkessel
~korb m [*Bergwerk* n] = (drawing) cage, hoisting ~, elevator ~
~korb m **mit zwei Etagen** fpl = two-stage drawing cage
~kübel m = skip
~leitung f = conveying line
~maschine f [*Bergwerk* n] = winding engine, drawing ~, hauling ~
fördern, gewinnen [*Bodenschätze* mpl] = to extract, to win
fördernde Gasbohrung f, siehe: (produzierende) Erdgassonde f
Förder|rinne f = trough conveyor, conveyor trough
~rohr n = tubular worm conveyor
~rutsche f, Schurre f = (conveyor) chute, (~) shoot
~schacht m, Treibschacht = main pit, ~ shaft
~schachtseil n, Treibschachtseil = shaft cable

Förder|schnecke f, siehe: Schneckenförderer m
~schwinge f, siehe: Schwing(förder)rinne f
~seil n [*Einseilbahn* f] = haulage rope
~seil n, Schachtseil = winding rope, pit ~, hoisting ~, haulage ~, ~ cable
~sohle f [*Bergwerk* n] = winding level
~sonde f, Förderbohrung f, produzierende Bohrung ~ = output well, production ~, paying ~
~versuch m [*Bohrung* f] = production test
~versuch m durch das Bohrgestänge = drill-stem test
~weite f, Förderstrecke f [*in Österreich:* *Bringungsweite*] [*Bodenförderung* f] = lead, run (Brit.); haul(age distance)
Forellenstein m = troctolite
Forle f, siehe: Weißkiefer f
Form f, Gußform = mo(u)ld
~, Körperform, Gestalt f = shape
~änderungsverfahren n = deformation method
Formations|grenze f (Geol.) = contact between two formations
~grenze f [*Karte* f] = formation(al) boundary, systemic ~
~karte f = formation map

~name m (Geol.) = formation name
~tabelle f (Geol.) = geologic calendar, table of strata
~ und Schichtenkunde f, Stratigraphie f, historische Geologie f = stratigraphy, historical geology, stratigraphical geology
Form|draht m = section wire
~eisen n, siehe: Fassoneisen
~gebung f = shaping
~gebungsverfahren n = method of forming
~gips m, Keramikgips, Formengips = pottery plaster
~kasten m = mo(u)ld box
~lineal n, siehe: Profillehre f
Form|ling m, siehe: (Beton)Fertigteil m
~maschine f = mo(u)lding machine
~platte f, Schaltafel f = form panel
~sand m = mo(u)lding sand
~stahl m = structural shapes
~stück n, siehe: Armatur f
formtreues prismatisches Faltwerk n = undistorted prismatic structure of folded units
Formung f **von Tonkügelchen** npl, Tonkügelchenherstellung f = pellet formation
Forscher m = researcher

Forschung f
Grundlagen~
Fabrikations~
angewandte ~
~ im Außendienst m
Zweck~
Forschungsauftrag m

research
basic~
manufacturing ~
applied ~
field ~
directed ~
~ contract

Forschungsgemeinschaft Bauen und Wohnen, FBW = German Research Association for Building and Housing
Forschungsgesellschaft f = research society (or association)
~ für das Straßenwesen e. V. = German Highway (or Road) Research Association (or Society)
Forschungslabor(atorium) n = research lab(oratory)

Forsterit m, Magnesiumolivin n (Min.) = forsterite
Forst|weg m, Waldweg m = forest track
~wirtschaft f, Waldwirtschaft = forestry
Fort n = fort
~bewegungswiderstand m = resistance to the motion of a vehicle
fortschreitender Bruch m = progressive failure
Fossilienmehl n = fossil meal (or farina, or flour)

Foyait *m* (Geol.) = foyaite
Fracht|aufgeber *m* = freight-forwarder
~brief *m* = freight bill
Frachter *m*, **Frachtschiff** *n* = freighter, cargo vessel
Fracht|kosten *f* = freight costs (or charges)
~zoll *m* = tonnage-fees
Fragment *n*, **Trümmerstück** *n* (Geol.) = fragment
Fraktion *f*, **Schnitt** *m* = cut
~, siehe: Körnung *f*
Fraktionierkolonne *f* = fractionating column
fraktionierte Destillation *f*, stufenweise ~ = fractional distillation
~ Lösung *f* = selective solvation
Fraktionierturm *m* = bubble tower
Fraktionsgröße *f*, siehe: Korngröße
Francis|-Speicherpumpe *f* = Francis type pump-turbine
~-Turbine *f* = Francis water turbine
Frankipfahl *m*; siehe unter „Gründungspfahl *m*"
Franki-Ramme *f* = hammer-tamper
Franzose *m*, siehe: englischer Schraubenschlüssel *m*
französisches Raigras *n* = tall oat grass
Fräs|tiefe *f* [*Bodenvermörtelung f*] = depth of treatment
~vortriebmaschine *f*, siehe: Schräm(vortrieb)maschine *m*
frei aufliegend = simply supported
~ ausgleichendes Differential *n* = differential lock
Frei|ballon *m* = free balloon
~beweglichkeit *f*; siehe unter „Baumaschinen *fpl* und Baugeräte *npl*"
~bord *n*; siehe unter „Talsperre *f*"
freier Kalk *m*, **freies CaO** = free lime
~ Kohlenstoff *m* [*früher: Unlösliches n*] = free carbon [*deprecated*]; toluene insolubles
~ Überfall *m*; siehe unter „Talsperre *f*"
freie Verpflegung *f* und Unterkunft *f* = free board and room
Freifahrung *f* [*Bergbau m*] = freeing
Freifall|bär *m*; siehe unter „Rammanlage" *f*
~bohrer *m* = drop boring tool

~-Bohrverfahren *n* = free fall drilling system
~-Chargenmischer *m*; siehe unter „Betonmischer *m*"
~-Durchlaufmischer *m*; siehe unter „Betonmischer *m*"
~-Kranstampfer *m*, Rammplattenbagger *m*, Baggerstampfer, Stampfbagger, Fallplattenkran *m*, Stampfeinrichtung *f* für Bagger *m*, Baggerstampfgerät *n* = excavator-operated stamper, dropping weight machine, tamping-crane rammer
~mischer *m*; siehe unter „Betonmischer *m*"
~mischer *m* **auf Gleisketten** *fpl* **für Betondeckenbau** *m*; siehe unter „Straßen(beton)mischer *m*"
~mischer *m* **mit Umkehraustragung** *f*; siehe unter „Betonmischer *m*"
~pochwerk *n* = gravity stamp
Freifeldprüfung *f*, Feldversuch *m* = field test
freigeben für den Verkehr *m* = to open to traffic
Freigelände *n* [*Messe f*] = open-air ground, ~ exhibition space
Freihafen *m* = free port
~niederlage *f* = bonded warehouse
Frei|handgeschwindigkeit *f* = hands off speed
~kolbenkompressor *m* = free piston compressor
~kolbenmotor *m* = free piston engine
~lagerplatz *m* = open storage ground, ~ ~ area
~lagerung *f* = outside storage
~landpflanze *f* = open ground plant
~länge *f* [*Kragträger m*] = unsupported length
~laßventil *n*, Freilaufventil, Leerlaufventil = no-load valve
Freilauf *m* = free-wheel(ing system)
~schütz(e) *n*, (*f*), Leerlaufschütz(e) = waste sluice (gate)
~ventil *n*, siehe: Freilaßventil *n*
freilegen = to (lay) bare
Freilegung *f* **von Baugelände** *n*, siehe: Räumung(sarbeiten) *f*
Freileitung *f* [*elektrischer Strom m*] = overhead transmission line

(Frei)Leitungsmast — Frostschutzmittel 189

(Frei)Leitungsmast m = transmission line tower
Freiluft|anlage f = open-air plant, outdoor ~
~lagerung f [*Materialprobe* f] = outdoor exposure
~schaltanlage f; siehe unter „Talsperre f"
~trocknerei f = open-air drying
Freispiegel-Schußstollen m = free flow tail race tunnel
freistehender Pfahl m = free-standing pile
Freistrahl|turbine f = free jet turbine
~überlauf m; siehe unter „Talsperre f"
freitragend = cantilevered
freitragender Balken m = unrestrained beam
~ Rahmen m = cantilever frame
Freiträger m = cantilever beam
Freivorbau m; siehe unter „Brücke f"
Fremden|verkehr m = tourist trade
~verkehrsort m = tourist resort
fremdgestaltig, siehe: xenomorph
Fremd|stoff m = extraneous matter, foreign material
~strom m = outside power
~stromzufuhr f = outside power supply
Freyssinet-Presse f = Freyssinet-type jack
Friedensstand m = peace-time level
Friesische Inseln fpl = Friesian Islands
Friktions|kupplung f, Reib(ungs)kupplung, Rutschkupplung f = friction clutch (coupling)
~winde f, Reibradwinde, Treibscheibenaufzug m = friction hoist
Frisch|beton m; siehe unter „Beton"
~betonprofilometer m = wet surface profilometer
~dampf m = live steam
frische Brise f = fresh wind
Frischluftzufuhr f = admission of fresh air
FRISCH-Schrapperwagen m, FRISCH-(Anhänge-)Schürf(kübel)wagen m = four-wheel(ed) scraper, Make: EISENWERK GEBR. FRISCH K. G., AUGSBURG, DEUTSCHLAND
fristgemäße Fertigstellung f = completion on schedule, ~ in time
Frontalturbine f, Rohrturbine, Stirnturbine = pipe turbine

Front-Fahrlader m **mit (Gleis) Kettenfahrwerk** n, siehe: (Gleis)Kettenschlepper-Frontlader m
Frontkipper m, siehe: Autoschütter m
~ [*allgemeiner Ausdruck* m] = front tipper [*universal term*]
(Front-)Ladeschaufel f, (Front-)Schaufellader m, Frontlader, Hublader, Kübelauflader, Schürflader, behelfsmäßiger Flachbagger m, Planier- und -Ladegerät n, Traktor-Bagger m, Hochladeschaufel f, Fahrlade-Gerät n, Fahrlader m, Front-Fahrlader m = loading shovel, bucket loader, tractor-shovel, front-end (tractor) loader, head-end type tractor-loader
~ mit Kufen fpl, Gleitkufen-Frontlader = skid shovel
~einrichtung f = dozer-shovel unit
Front|platte f = facing slab
~räumer m, siehe: Bulldozer m
(~-)Schaufellader m, siehe: (Front-)Ladeschaufel f
~sitz m = front seat
Frosch m, Klammer f = clip
~ m [*Gleisbau* m] = frog
~ m, DELMAG-Stampfer m, DELMAG-Explosionsramme f, Frosch-Ramme f [*Trademark*] = jumping frog, leaping ~, frog ramming machine, frog type jumping rammer, frog rammer, DELMAG frog tamper [*Trademark*]
Frost|aufgang m, Auftauen n = thaw
~auftritt m = incidence of frost
~beginn m, siehe: Frostschwelle f
frostbeständig, frostsicher [*z. B. Sand* m] = frost-resistant, non-frost-active
Frost|beule f = frost boil
~einwirkung f = frost action
frostempfindlich [*z. B. Schluff* m] = frost-susceptible
Frost|hebung f = frost heaving, ~ heave
~indikator m = ground frost indicator
~kriterium n = frost criterion
~riß m = frost crack
~schutz m = frost protection
~schutzmaßnahme f = frost precaution
Frost|schutzmittel n = antifreeze (mixture), frost protective, anti-freezer, frost-protection agent

Frost|schutzschicht *f*, siehe: Sauberkeitsschicht
~schwelle *f*, Frostbeginn *m* = initiation of freezing
frostsicher, frostbeständig [*z. B.* Sand *m*] = frost-resistant, non-frost-active
Frost|sicherheit *f* = frost resistance
~tiefe *f* = depth of frost penetration, frost-penetration depth
~wetter *n* = frosty weather, freezing ~
~wirkung *f* = frost effect

Fruchtwechsel *m* = rotation of crops
Früh|beetkasten *m* = frame for fencing in vegetable and flower beds
~eiche *f*, Wintereiche *f*, Steineiche *f*, Traubeneiche *f* = Drurmast oak, mountain ~, chestnut ~, sessile-fruited ~
~jahrshochwasser *n* = spring flood
Fuchsit *m*, Chromglimmer *m* (Min.) = fuchsite
Fuchsschwanz *m*, Handsäge *f* = hand saw

Fuge *f*, Beton~	(concrete) joint
abgerundete Fugenkante *f*	bull-nose, arris, bull's nose
angestrichene Dübelhälfte *f*	treated half of the dowel
Anker *m*, Ankereisen *n*	tie bar
Arbeits~, Betonier~	construction ~, stop-end ~
(Aufsteck)Hülse *f* aus Blech, Blechhülse	light metal cap
(Aus)Dehnungs~, Raum~	expansion ~
Betonbrücke *f*	concrete droppings
Dübel *m*, (Beton)Fugendübel	dowel (bar)
durchgehende ~	continuous ~
einfache Verguß~	poured ~ ~
Einschleifen *n* [*Scheinfuge*]	sawing
Falz~ [*in Großbrit. eine verbesserte gespundete Fuge, Erfinder J. H. Walker, patentiert*]	Walker interlocking ~
faserige (Fugen)Einlage *f*	fibrous jointing material
feste Einlage *f*, siehe: Fugeneinlage	
Fugenabstand *m*	distance between joints
Fugenausbildung *f*, Fugenherstellung *f*	joint finishing
Fugenband *n*	joint ribbon
Fugenbläser *m* mit Voranstricheinrichtung *f*	combined air jet and priming unit
Fugeneinbaugerät *n*	joint installing (or placing) machine
Fugeneinlage *f*, feste Einlage *f*, Fugenstreifen *m*	pre-formed (joint) filler, joint sealing strip, (expansion) joint filler, (expansion) joint(ing) strip, pre-mo(u)ded (strip joint) filler, strip of pre-formed filling material
Fugeneisen *n*, Hohlfugeneisen	expansion joint cap strip (US); metal sleeve, metal cap(ping), (metal) capping (strip) (Brit.); joint-forming metal strip
Fugenhalter *m*	supporting device, guard
Fugenherstellung *f*, Fugenausbildung *f*	joint-finishing, ~ construction
Fugenkante *f*	arris
Fugenmaurer *m*	finisher
Fugenprofil *n*	~ profile

Fuge

Fugenpflug m, Fugenräumgerät n mit Pflugstahl m, Schaber m und Drahtbürste f	plough-type raking machine (Brit.) plow-type ~ ~ (US)
Fugenplan m	joint plan
Fugenreinigungsgerät n, Fugenreiniger m	joint cleaner
Fugenreißer m	joint raker
Fugenschleifgerät n [*diese Bezeichnung ist technisch richtiger als die meist übliche „Fugenschneidmaschine f" oder „Fugensäge f" oder „Fugenschneider m"*]	(concrete) joint cutter, joint-cutting machine, (contrection) joint sawing machine, concrete cutter; concrete saw (US)
Fugenschneidgerät n mit Vibriermesser n	joint vibrator, concrete ~ ~, vibrating knife joint cutter
Fugenschneidscheibe f	jointing blade
Fugenschwelle f	sleeper
Fugenspalt m	groove
Fugenstreifen m, siehe: Fugeneinlage f	
(Fugen)Stützkorb m, Stahldrahtkorb	wire chair, metal chair
Fugenverdübelungsgerät n, Fabrikat FLEXIBLE ROAD JOINT MACHINE COMPANY, WARREN, OHIO, USA	FLEX-PLANE dowel machine, FLEX-PLANE mechanical dowel and tie bar installer
Fugenvergußarbeiten f	joint grouting work(s), ~ pouring
Fugenvergußgerät n	joint sealing machine, pouring machine
Fugenvergußkanne f	pouring can (or pot)
(Fugen)Vergußmasse f, Dehn(ungs)-Fugenvergußmasse	(joint-)sealing compound, joint-filling composition, jointing copound, (joint) filler; paving oint sealer (US)
Fugenverwerfung f	joint faulting
Fugenwandung f	joint face
gespundete ~, genutete ~	tongue-and-groove ~, keyed ~
Gummidichtung f	rubber seal
Hand ~	hand-formed ~
Hohlfugeneisen n, siehe: Fugeneisen	
Holz(fugen)einlage f	wooden (~) filler
Hülse f, siehe: (Aufsteck)Hülse aus Blech	
Kantenbrecher m	arris trowel, arrissing tool, bull-nose trowel
Kerbe f	slot
Kunststoff-(Aufsteck)Hülse f	plastics cap
Lastübertragung f	load transfer(ence)
Lastübertragungsmittel n	load transfer device
Längsfuge f	longitudinal ~, lane ~
obere Schein ~	top surface dummy ~
Papp-(Aufsteck)Hülse f	cardboard cap
Preßfuge f	~ which does not allow expansion
Quer ~	transverse ~
Querfugenverdübelung f [*Fugenbrett n, Rundeisendübel m und Baustahlgewebebügel m*]	dowel load-transfer unit

Raum~, (Aus)Dehnungs~, eigentliche ~	expansion ~ (during the day's work), running ~
(Raum~ als) Tagesarbeits~	day's-work ~, expansion ~ at the end of a day's work, end-of-day ~
Schein~	dummy ~, concealed ~, contraction ~, shrinkage ~
Schmelzkessel *m*, siehe: Vergußmassekocher *m*	
Schwellen~ [*eine Fugenart in England wonach ein 60 bis 90 cm breiter Betonbalken unter der Fuge in das verdichtete Planum eingebaut wird*]	sleeper ~ [*it has no value as a loadtransfer device and only reduces by a small amount the intensity of loading on the subgrade at the joint*]
Stahldrahtkorb *m*, (Fugen)Stützkorb	wire chair, metal ~
Stützkorb *m*, siehe: Fugenstützkorb	
Tagesarbeits~, Raum~ als ~	day's-work ~, expansion ~ at the end of a day's work, end-of-day~
untere Schein~	bottom surface dummy ~
verdübelte ~	dowel bar ~, dowelled ~
Vergußmassekocher *m*, Schmelzkessel *m*	heater-mixer
Vergußspalt *m*	sealing groove, groove for sealing compound
versetzte ~	break of ~, breaking ~, staggered ~
verworfene ~	stepped-off ~
vibrationsgeschnittene ~	vibrated ~
Weichholzfugeneinlage *f*	softwood (~) filler
Wieland~	Wieland ~
Wielandfugeneisen *n*	Wieland (jointing) strip, Wieland joint bar, Wieland metal bar

---

Fugen|ausbildung *f* **von Hohlblockstein-Mauerwerk** *n* = jointing in hollow-block masonry	~**stand(s)laufkatze** *f*, Führerstand(s)-lastkatze = man trolley, driver ~, driver-seat crab
~**decke** *f*, siehe: Fugenstraßendecke	**Fuhrgeld** *n*, siehe: Rollgeld
~**kelle** *f* [*Pflasterfuge f*] = sett jointer, ~ feeder	**Führungs|gerüst** *n* = template
~**mörtel** *m*, Baumörtel, Mauermörtel = joint mortar, masonry ~, pointing ~	~**kranz** *m* = guide ring
~**(straßen)decke** *f* [*ausgenommen Beton m*] = paving (Brit.); [*deprecated:* pavement]	~**mast** *m* = guide mast
	~**nut** *f* = guiding groove
	~**rahmen** *m* = guide frame
fühlergesteuert = tracer-controlled	~**ring** *m* = guide ring
Fühlnadel *f* [*Einspritzdüse f*] = feeling pin	~**rippe** *f* = guide rib
Führer|kabine *f*, Führerhaus *n*, Fahrerhaus, Bedienungskabine = driver's cab(in), operator's control ~	~**rolle** *f* = guide roller
	~**rollenbolzen** *m* = guide roller bolt
	~**schiene** *f* = guide rail, lead
~**schein** *m* = driver license	~**schlitten** *m*, Führungsblock *m* = guide block
~**scheinentzug** *m* = suspension of driver license	~**schuh** *m* = guide shoe
	~**stück** *n*, Führung *f* = guide
~**sitz** *m* = driver's seat, driver-seat	~**- und Tragrolle** *f* [*Bandförderer m*] = guidler

Fuhr|unternehmer m, siehe: Transportunternehmer
~**weg** m = cart-path
~**werkverkehr** m, siehe: Gespannverkehr
Fukoidensandstein m = fucoid(al) sandstone
Fulgurit m, Blitzröhre f (Min.) = fulgurite, lightning tube
Füll|boden m, siehe: Auf~
~**eisen** n = plessite
Füller m, Mineral~, Füllstoff m = (mineral) filler, ~ dust
Fuller|erde f = fuller's earth
~**-(Kinyon)Pumpe** f, Zement(staub)pumpe, Fuller-Zementpumpe, Fuller-Entladepumpe = Fuller-Kinyon unloader (pump), F-K (dry) pump
~**kurve** f [*Bindemittel n mit eingeschlossen*] = Fuller's best mix curve
~**parabel** f [*Bindemittel n ausgenommen*] = Fuller's parabola
Füll|(gut)stand m, Behälterstand = bin level
~**körper** m, Decken~, Deckenhohlkörper = filler block, hollow ~ [*floor system*]
~**körper** m [*Abwasserwesen n*] = (fill-and-draw) contact bed, contact filter
~**material** n [*Abwasserwesen n*] = contact material
~**mauerwerk** n = filling-in work
~**splitt** m, siehe: Keilsplitt
~**stab** m, Füllungsstab, Gitterstab, Wandglied n = web member
~**stand** m, siehe: Füllgutstand
(~)**Stundenzeiger** m, Behälter-Standanzeiger, Stand-Meßgerät n = bin level indicator, material ~ ~
~**stutzen** m = filling spout, ~ tube
~**trichter** m, Aufnahmetrichter = (feed) hopper, receiving ~, feeder ~
~**trichter** m **für Flüssigkeiten** fpl = filling funnel
~**trichter-Abzug(s)band** n = hopper conveyor
~**trichter-Waage** f = hopper scale
Füllungs|grad m, siehe: Bunkerstand m
~**stab** m, Füllstab, Wandglied n, Gitterstab [*Fachwerk n*] = web member

Füllverfahren n [*Abwasserreinigung f*] = contract method of sewage treatment
Fundament n = foundation
~**aushub** m = foundation excavation
~**bolzen** m = foundation bolt
~**graben** m = footing trench, foundation ~, ~ ditch
~**höhe** f = foundation level
~**mauer** f, Grundmauer = foundation wall
~**mauerwerk**, n, Grundmauerwerk = foundation brickwork
~**platte** f, siehe: Betonplattenfundament n
~**platte** f, siehe: Grundplatte
~**sohle** f = foundation base
~**verbreiterung** f = extension of the foundation
Fundationskote f, Fundationshöhe f = = level of foundation
Fundbohrung f, Entdeckungsbohrung, Erschließungssonde f = discovery well
Fundierung f, siehe: Gründung
Fündigkeit f **auf Erdöl** n = discovery of petroleum
fünffache Gipskartonplatte f = laminated partition slab (Brit.)
Fünfteldach n = roof with pitch of 1:5
Fünftrommelwinde f, Fünftrommelwindwerk n = five-drum winch
funikulares Wasser n = funicular water
Funk|bake f, Funkfeuer n = wireless beacon, radio ~
~**bake** f, funktelegraphischer Richtungsweiser m = wireless direction indicator
~**haus** n = broadcasting station
~**meßgerät** n = radar device
~**sprechverkehr** m = radio telephone traffic, ~ telephony
funktionelle Gruppe f = functional group
funktionieren = to function
Funkwetterdienst m = meteorological radio service
Furchen|rieselung f = bed irrigation
~**stein** m = furrowed stone
Furfuralharz n = furfural resin
Furnier|holz n = veneer
~**rahmensäge** f = veneer frame saw
~**schälmaschine** f = rotary veneer lathe
Furt f = ford

Fuselöl n, Gärungsamylalkohol m = amylic alcohol, fusel oil
Fusulinellenkalk(stein) m = Fusulinella limestone
Fuß m [*Damm* m] = toe
~**abblendschalter** m = foot operated dimming switch
Fußboden|belag m, (Fuß)Boden(geh)belag = floor topping, ~ surfacing
~**belag** m **aus Ziegeln** mpl **oder Platten** fpl = floor paving
~**einlauf** m = floor drain (US); ~ gull(e)y (Brit.)
~-**Härteprüfgerät** n = floor hardness testing device
~**kitt** m = wooden flooring putty
~**leiste** f, Sockelleiste, Scheuerleiste = skirting board
~**platte** f, Bodenplatte = floor tile, floor(ing) slab; quarry tile (Brit.)
~**rost** m = floor grating, = grate
~**schleifmaschine** f = floor sand-papering machine, sanding ~, floor sander
~**wachs** m = floor wax, ~ polish
Fußbremse f = foot brake
Fußgänger|-Schutzgeländer n = pedestrian guard rail, protection fence, guard fence, safety fence
~-**Schutzinsel** f, Stützinsel für Fußgängerüberweg m = refuge (Brit.); [*deprecated*: *island*]; ~ island, pedestrian island (US)
~**tunnel** m = pedestrian subway, ~ tunnel, underground pedestrian passageway
~**überführung** f = overpass for pedestrians
~**überweg** m = pedestrian crossing, ~ crosswalk
Fuß|gelenk n [*Säule* f] = ball and socket footing
~**mauer** f, siehe: Abdichtungsmauer
~**pedal** n = foot pedal
~**pfette** f, Sparrenschwelle f = inferior purlin
~**platte** f [*Stütze* f] = base plate
~**pumpe** f = foot-pump
~**punkt** m = base
~**punkt** m **der Kraft** f = tracing point of the force

~**punkt** m **einer Senkrechten** f = foot of a perpendicular
~**ringschale** f [*Brückenpfeiler* m] = bottom shell
~**schmiege** f = horizontal cut (of jack rafter)
~**ventil** n = foot valve
~**weg** m, siehe: Bürgersteig m
~**wegausladung** f = cantilever for footway
~**weggerippe** n = footway framing
~**wegkragträger** m = footway cantilever bracket
~**weg-Motorkehrmaschine** f, Motor-Fußwegkehrmaschine = motor footpath brush
~**zapfen** m [*Mast* m] = heel tenon
Futter n, Verkleidung f, Auskleidung = lining
~**automat** n = automatic chucking machine
~**blech** n = lining plate
~**einsäuerungsbehälter** m = sour fodder silo
~**mauer** f, Verkleidungsmauer = revetment wall
~**rahmen** m, Fensterrahmen, Blindrahmen, Blendrahmen = window frame
~**rohr** n = casing pipe, lining tube, guide ~
~**stufe** f, Setzstufe f = riser
~**ziegel(stein)** m, Futterstein = lining brick

G

Gabbro m = gabbro
~**aplit** m = gabbro aplite, beerbachite
~**diorit** m = gabbro-diorite
~**gang** m = gabbroitic dike
gabbroider Verband m (Geol.), siehe: Bienenwabenverband
Gabbro|lagergang m = gabbro sill
~**linse** f = gabbroic lens
~**magma** n = gabbro magma
~**nelsonit** m = gabbro nelsonite
Gabel|anker m = forked tie
~**antrieb** m [*Seilbahn* f] = rope fork drive
~**hebel** m = forked lever
~**kreuzung** f, Straßeneinmündung f Straßengabelung = fork junction

Gabel|lehre *f*, siehe: Rachenlehre
~**schmiege** *f*; siehe unter „Holzverbindung"
~**stange** *f* = fork rod
~**stapler** *m* = fork-lift, fork truck, highlift fork stacking truck, fork lift truck type conveyancer
~**stapler** *m* **mit leichter Lenkbarkeit** *f* = stand-up fork truck
Gab(e)lung *f* = bifurcation
Gabelzinken *m* = prong
Gahnit *m*, Zinkspinell *m*, ZnAl$_2$O$_4$ (Min.) = zinc spinel, gahnite
Gaize *f* = gaize
Galileo-Mikrotelemeter *n* **mit der Methode** *f* **des Bleisenkels** *m* = Galileo microtelemeter with the method of the plumb rule
Gallussäure *f* = gallic acid
galvanische Verzinkung *f* = galvanizing
Galvanisieren = electroplating
Gang|gestein *n* = dike rock, dyke
~**höhe** *f* [*Schraube f*] = pitch
~**reduktion** *f* = gear reduction
~**schalthebel** *m* = gear (shift) lever, change speed lever
(~)**Spill** *n* = capstan
Zahnrad-~ = geared ~
Ganz|decke *f*; siehe unter „Gletscher *m*"
~**metallbehälter** *m* = all-metal container
~**schweiß-Konstruktion** *f* = all-welded construction
~**stahlbauweise** *f*, Vollstahl-Bauweise = all-steel construction
~**stahlkette** *f* = all-steel chain
Garagengebäude *n* = parking garage
garantiertes Brauchwasser *n*, Anliegerrechtwasser = compensation water
Gär|futterbehälter *m* = fermenting container for food
~**kartoffelbehälter** *m* = fermenting container for potatoes
Gartenstadt *f* = greenbelt town
Gas|absaugungsanlage *f* = gas suction plant
~**anzeigegerät** *n* = gas detector set
~**ausbruch** *m* = gas escape
~**behälter** *m*, Gassammler *m*, Gasometer *m* = gas-holder, gas-tank, gasometer
~**benzin** *n*, siehe: Leichtbenzin
Gasbeton *m*; siehe unter „Beton *m*"
~**stein** *m* = aerated cement block
Gas|brenner *m* = gas burner
~-**Chromatographie** *f* = gas chromatography
~**druckregler** *m* = gas pressure regulating governor
~**einpreßbohrung** *f* = gas input well, ~ intake ~
~**einschlüsse** *mpl* = gas occlusions
~**entladungslampe** *f* = vacuum tube lamp, gas discharge ~
~**entwickler** *m* [*Schweißen n*] = gas generator
~**erzeuger** *m*, Generator(ofen) *m* = gas producer
~**flasche** *f* = gas bottle, ~ cylinder
~**gemisch** *n* **mit wenig kondensierbaren Anteilen** *mpl* = dry gas, lean ~
~**horizont** *m* = gas horizon
~**kok(s)** *m* = gas coke
~**lift-Leitungsanschluß** *m* **an der Bohrung** *f* = gas lift hook-up
~**maske** *f* = gas mask, respirator
~**motor** *m* = gas engine
~**öl** *n* **für Absorptionszwecke** *mpl* = straw oil
~**öl** *n*, Solaröl = solar oil (Brit.); gas ~
gasolinfreies Naturgas *n*, siehe: trockenes ~
gasproduzierende Sonde *f* = gas producing well
Gasreinigungswasser *n* = gas liquor
Gas|rohr *n* [*Elektroosmose f*] = rod electrode
~**rohr** *n* = gas tube, ~ tubing
~**rohr-Handlauf** *m* [*Geländer n*] = gas barrel handrail, ~ tubing ~
~**ruß** *m* = gas black
~**sammler** *m*, siehe: Gasbehälter *m*
~**treibverfahren** *n* = gas drive [*oil*]
~**trennung** *f* = separation of gases
Gasse *f*, Gäßchen *n* = lane
Gattersäge *f* = log frame saw
Gattierungswaage *f*, Waage *f* für alle Gemengeteile, Gattierungsgefäßwaage, Gemischwaage, Mischwaage = multiple (-material) (scale) batcher, cumulative (weigh) batcher [*one common hopper for all materials*]

Gauss'sche Normalverteilungskurve f = Gauss normal distribution curve
Gaze f = gauze
geächselter Zapfen m; siehe unter „Holzverbindung f"
Gebäude|anbau m = annex
~anschluß m, Hausanschluß = house connection, building ~
~fundament n = building foundation
~schwingung f = building vibration
~skelett n = building frame
Gebirgs|beschreibung f, Orographie f = orography
~bildung f, Orogenese f, Tektogenese f = mountain building, orogeny
~druck m (Geol.) = pressure of mountain mass
~kette f = chain of mountains
~land n = mountain country
~massiv n = massif
~straße f = mountain road
~tunnel m, = siehe: Felstunnel
~zug m = mountain range
Gebläse n = blower
~luft-Förderrinne f, Luft-Rutsche f, pneumatische Förderrinne, Luftförderrinne = airslide

~luft-Förderrinne f **mit Segeltuch** n = canvas fabric airslide
~luft-Förderrinne f **mit Filtersteinen** mpl = porous block conveyor
~maschine f = mechanical blower
geblasenes Öl n = blown oil
Gebläse|sand m = (sand) blast sand
~wind m = blast (air)
gebleiter Kraftstoff m = leaded fuel
gebleites Benzin n = ethyl gasoline (US); ethylized fuel (Brit.)
gebogener Flansch m = saddle flange
~ Träger m = bow girder
~ ~ mit Zugband n = bowstring girder
geböscht, ab~ = sloped
gebrannter Gips, m siehe: Baugips
~ Kalk m, siehe: Branntkalk
~ Magnesit m, siehe: Magnesiumoxyd n
~ Scherben m = fired earthenware
~ Ton m = fired clay
gebranntes Schieferton-Erzeugnis n = fired shale product
Gebrauch|slast f, siehe: Nutzlast
~spannung f = working stress
gebrauchter Formsand m, siehe: Altsand
gebrochenes Material n; siehe unter „(Beton)Zuschlagstoffe mpl"

Gebührenerhebung f [*Autobahn* f]	toll collection
Abfertigung f	transaction, handling
Ausfahrtstand m	exit booth
Einfahrtstand m	entry booth, entrance booth
Einnahmen fpl	revenue
Fahrt f	vehicle-trip
Fernregistriergerät n	remote recording machine, ~ recorder
Gebührenberechnungsmaschine f	validating machine, validator
Gebührenerhebungsanlage f [*Gesamtkomplex der Gebäude*]	toll station
Gebührenerhebungs- und -prüfanlage f	toll-collection and audit system, interchange equipment
Kartenausgabemaschine f	ticket-issuing machine
Pauschaljahresausweis m	flat-rate annual permit
Plakatausweis m	sticker (on the vehicle)
Photoapparat m	camera
Registrierkasse f	cash totalizer
ständiger Benutzer m	commuter
Wegeabgabe f, (Wege)Gebühr f	toll, fare
Zählschwelle f	treadle

gebührenfrei [*Straße f, Brücke f, Tunnel m*] = toll-free

gebührenpflichtige Autobahn *f*, Zollstraße *f* für Schnellverkehr *m* = toll road, toll (super)highway, (toll) (turn)pike

Gebühren-Verkehrstunnel *m* = toll tunnel

gedeihender Kalk *m*, siehe: ungelöschter gemahlener Kalk *m*

Gedenktafel *f* = memorial tablet

gedoptes Verschnittbitumen *n*, Verschnittbitumen *n* mit Haftanreger *m* = doped cutback

gedrehte Schraube *f* = turned bolt

gedrückt = compressed

Gefahrenstelle *f* = danger point

gefährlicher Querschnitt *m* = critical section

Gefälle *n*, siehe: Niveaudifferenz *f*

~, siehe: Steigung *f*

~ [*Straße f*] = downhill grade

Gefäll|(e)wechsel *m*, Neigungswechsel = slope change

~**messer** *m*, Neigungsmesser, Klinometer *n*, Böschungswaage *f* = (in)clinometer, batter level

~**messer** *m* **zur Fernmessung** *f* = distant-reading (in)clinometer

~**strecke** *f*, Strecke in Gefälle = downhill section, downgrade ~

gefärbtes Schutzglas *n* [*Schweißen n*] = welding glass, filter ~

Gefäß|(förder)pumpe *f* = tank type pump, ~ ~ pneumatic conveying system

~**förderung** *f* [*Bergbau m*] = skip hoisting

~**waage** *f*, siehe: Behälterwaage

gefedert = spring mounted

gefluxtes Bitumen *n* = fluxed asphalt (US); ~ asphaltic bitumen (Brit.) [*the flux used is a residual product*]

Gefrier|gründung *f*, siehe unter „Baugrundverbesserung *f*"

~**punkt** *m* = freezing point

~**punkterniedrigung** *f* [*durch Zusatz von Frostschutzmitteln wird der Gefrierpunkt des Betonanmachewassers etwas herabgesetzt*] = lowering of the freezing point

~**rohr** *n*, Vereisungsrohr = freezing pipe

~**schacht** *m* = freezing shaft

~**schutzmittel** *n*, Frostschutzmittel = anti-freezing compound

~**temperatur** *f* = freezing temperature

~**- und Auftauzyklus** *m*, Tau-Frost-Wechsel *m*, Frost-Tau-Wechsel = freezing and thawing cycle

gefrorener Boden *m*, ~ Untergrund *m* = frozen ground, ~ subsoil

gefugter Dielen(fuß)boden *m* = plain jointed floor

Gegenbogen *m*, Gegenkurve *f*, Gegenkrümmung *f*, S-Kurve = reverse curve

~, Grundbogen, Erdbogen, Konterbogen = inverted arch

Gegen|bürgschaft *f* = counter-security

~**dampf** *m* = counter steam

~**dampfbremse** *f* = counter steam brake

~**diagonale** *f*, Gegenschräge *f*, Wechselstab *m* = counter brace, ~ diagonal

~**drehungskurbeln** *fpl*, Antiparallelkurbeln, gegenläufige Kurbeln = cranks moving in opposite directions, crossed parallelogram

~**druck** *m*, Auflagerdruck, Auflagerkraft *f* = bearing pressure, pressure on bearing surface

~**druck** *m*, Vorlagedruck = back pressure

~**druckarbeit** *f* = work due to back pressure, negative work

~**druck-Dampfmaschine** *f* = back-pressure steam engine

~**druckkolben** *m*, Entlastungskolben, Ausgleichkolben = dummy piston

~**druckregelventil** *n* = back-pressure regulating valve

~**druckturbine** *f* = back-pressure turbine

~**feder** *f* = opposing spring, reacting ~

~**federblatt** *n* = counter leaf

~**feuer** *n*, Rückbrennung *f* = passing of the flames to the front of the furnace

~**gefälle** *n* [*in Längsneigung einer Straße*] = reverse gradient

~**gewicht** *n*, Ausgleichgewicht = counterweight, counterpoise

~**gewichtausleger** *m*, Gegengewichtarm *m* = counterweight jib (Brit.); ~ boom (US)

~**gewichtrinne** *f*, Flieger *m* [*Gußbetoneinrichtung f*] = counter-balanced chute (or spout)

~**gewichtseil** *n* = counterweight rope

Gegen|gewichttrommel f = counterweight drum
~halter m; siehe unter „Niet m"
~hebel m, Winkelhebel mit Wälzflächen fpl = angular lever with rolling surfaces
~induktivität f = mutual inductance
~kette f, Rückhaltekette [Brücke f] = back chain
~kraft f = counter force
~krümmung f, siehe: Gegenbogen m
~kurbel f = crank with drag link
~kurve f, siehe: Gegenbogen m
gegenläufig = contra-rotating
Gegen|laufturbine f = turbine with nozzles and blades rotating in opposite directions
~laufdoppelturbine f = double turbine with blade wheels running in opposite directions
~mutter f, Klemmutter f, Doppelmutter, Kontermutter = lok nut, check ~
~schwingsieb n = opposed-action screen
~spur f [Straße f] = opposing lane
~stab m [Fachwerk n] = counter
Gegenstrom|-Kessel m = counter-current boiler
~-Klassierer m = counter-current classifier
~kondensation f = counter-flow condensation
~kondensator m = counter-current condenser
~-Schnellmischer m; siehe unter „Betonmischer"
~-Sonderschaltung f [Turmdrehkran m] = reverse current lowering connection
~verfahren n = counter-flow process

~waschmaschine f, Gegenstrom-(Trommel)Wäsche f, Gegenstrom-Waschtrommel f = contra-flow washer, ~ washing machine
Gegen|taktschaltung f = push-pull connection, counter-contact ~, push-pull arrangement, push-pull valve operation
~turm m [Kabelkran m] = tail tower
~ufer n [Fluß m] = opposite bank
~verkehr m = opposing traffic
~welle f, Vorgelegewelle = counter shaft
~wind m, Stirnwind = head wind, contrary ~
~winkel m, Wechselwinkel = opposite angle, alternate ~
~zelle f [Akkumulator m] = regulating cell
gegliederter Träger m, siehe: Fachwerk(träger) n, (m)
Gehalt m **an freiem Wasser** n **in Schnee** m = liquid water content of snow
Gehänge|lehm m = slope wash
~schutt m, Schutthalde f (Geol.) = talus material, rubble slope
Gehäuse n = casing, housing
Gehege n = enclosure
Gehlenit m (Min.) = gehlenite
gehobener Strand m = raised beach (Brit.); elevated shore line (US)
Gehölz n = small wood
Gehrung f, Bischofsmütze f = mitreing (Brit.); mitering (US)
Gehrungsstoß m = mitred joint (Brit.); mitered ~ (US)
Geh|steig m, siehe: Bürgersteig m
~weg m, siehe: Bürgersteig m

Gehwegplatte f [entweder künstlich oder natürlich]
  Natur~
  Beton~
Gehwegplattenbelag m

flagstone, paving flag [deprecated: flag]; sidewalk slab (US)
  natural ~
  precast concrete ~
flagging, flag paving, slab paving

Geißberger m, siehe: Findling(sstein) m
gekapselt = clad
geknickte Platte f, Buckelblech n = buckled plate
geknickter (Polygon)Zug m = chain traverse

gekörnte Hochofenschlacke f, siehe: granulierte Hochofenschlacke
Gekriech n, siehe: Bodenkriechen n
gekröpftes Flacheisen n = cranked flat iron
Gekrösestein m = tripestone

gekrümmter Saugschlauch m [*Wasserkraftwerk* n] = elbow (draft) tube (US); ~ (draught) ~ (Brit.)
gekrümmte Schichtungen fpl (Geol.) = contorted strata
~ **Staumauer** f; siehe unter „Talsperre f"
Gelände n = ground, terrain, land
~**auffüllung** f, Geländeaufhöhung f, Geländeaufschüttung = land fill
~**form** f, Geländegestaltung f, Bodenform f = land form, configuration (or conformation) of the ground
geländegängiger Förderwagen m in Kraftwagen-Bauart f; siehe unter „Fahrzeuge npl für den Transport m von Boden m und Steinbaustoffen mpl"
~ **luftbereifter Erdtransportwagen** m; siehe unter „Fahrzeuge npl für den Transport m von Boden m und Steinbaustoffen mpl"
Gelände|gängigkeit f = off-the-highway manoeuvrability (Brit.); ~ maneuverability (US)
~**gefälle** n = natural fall (or slope)
~**höhe** f, Niveau n = ground level
~**oberfläche** f = ground surface
~**oberkante** f, O. K. Terrain, Oberkante Terrain = ground line
~**reifen** m, Reifen mit Geländeprofil n = off-the-highway (or off-the-road ground tire (US); earthmover tyre (Brit.); grip ~; off-road equipment ~
~**streifen** m = strip of ground
Geländerpfosten m = handrail standard
gelatinös-plastische Sprengstoffgemenge npl; siehe unter „1. Schießen n; 2. Sprengen n"
Gelbbleierz n, Wulfenit m, PbMoO$_4$ (Min.) = wulfenite
gelbe Arsenblende f (Min.) = orpiment
Gelbeisenkies m, Schwefelkies m (Min.) = (iron) pyrites, yellow pyrites, fool's gold
Gelbildung f = gel formation, gel development
Gelböl n = straw oil
Geldgeber m = financial backer
Gelenkbolzen m = hinge bolt
~**fachwerk** n = pin-connected truss
gelenkig gelagert = hinged, pin-ended
Gelenk|kette f = sprocket chain

~**-Lok(omotive)** f = articulated loco(motive)
~**pfette** f = articulated purlin
~**rahmen** m = hinged frame
~**schraube** f = swing bolt
~**trägerbrücke** f = hinged girder bridge
~**wagen-Bodenentleerer** m; siehe unter „Fahrzeuge npl für den Transport m von Boden m und Steinbaustoffen mpl"
~**wagen-Hinterkipper** m; siehe unter „Fahrzeuge npl für den Transport m von Boden m und Steinbaustoffen mpl"
~**welle** f = multiple-part shaft, universal joint shaft
gelocht = perforated
gelöschter Kalk m, siehe: Kalziumhydroxid n
Geltungsbereich m [*Norm* f] = scope
gemahlener Branntkalk m, siehe: ungelöschter gemahlener Kalk
~ **massiger Bimstuff** m, siehe: Traß m
gemauerter Reinigungsschacht m, ~ **Einsteig(e)schacht**, gemauertes Mannloch n = brickwork manhole
gemeine Buche f, siehe: Rotbuche
~ **Eberesche** f = rowan
~ **Esche** f = common ash
(~) **Fichte** f, Rottanne f = Norway (or common) spruce
~ **Kiefer** f, siehe: Weißkiefer
gemeines Rispengras n, siehe: rauhes ~
gemeinsames Aufmaß n = joint measurement
Gemengehaus n [*Glasindustrie* f] = glass batch house
Gemengewaage f, siehe: Gesteinswaage
~ **in Laufgewichtsbauart** f = beam and jockey-weight type weigh-batcher (Brit.); beam scale (US)
Gemengteil m [*Gestein* n] = constituent mineral [*rock*]
Gemisch n, siehe: Mischgut n
gemischtbasisches Rohöl n = mixed-base crude petroleum
gemischtes Sedimentgestein n, gemischt mechanisch-chemisches ~ = mixed sedimentary rock
Gemischwaage f, siehe: Gattierungswaage
genagelter Vollwandträger m = nailed timber I-beam

Genauigkeitsgrad — Geologie

Genauigkeitsgrad *m*, siehe: Toleranz *f*
geneigter Tragstiel *m* [*Pfahljoch n*] = raker, batter post
Generalinspekteur *m* für das Straßenwesen *n* = Inspector General of Highway-Engineering
General|unkosten *f* = overhead costs
~unternehmer *m*, Hauptunternehmer = prime contractor, chief ~, general ~
Generator|gas *n* = producer gas
~(ofen) *m*, siehe: Gaserzeuger *m*
Genesungsheim *n* = convalscent home
genietete Stahlträger *mpl* im Verbund *m* mit Stahlbeton-Druckplatten *fpl* = riveted steel joists with reinforced concrete compression flanges
~ Verbindung *f*, genieteter Anschluß *m* = riveted joint, ~ connection
genormt = standardised
genossenschaftliche Gemeinde *f* = cooperative community
Geochemie *f* = geochemistry
geochemische Forschung *f* = geochemical exploration
geochemisches Prospektieren *n* = geochemical prospecting
Geode *f* (Geol.) = geode
geoelektrische Baugrunduntersuchung *f*; siehe unter „geophysikalische ~"
Geologe *m* = geologist
Geologenhacke *f* = geologist's pick, prospector's ~

Geologie *f*
  dynamische ~
  Gesteinskunde *f*, Steinkunde *f*, Petrographie *f*
  Mineralogie *f*
  Formations- und Schichtenkunde *f*, Stratigraphie *f*, historische Geologie *f*
  Paläographie *f*
  geologische Formation *f*
    Neozoikum *n*, Känozoikum, Erdneuzeit *f*
      Alluvium *n* [*Gegenwart*]
      Diluvium *n* [*Eiszeiten*]
      Tertiärformation *f*
        Pliozän *n*
        Miozän *n*
        Oligozän *n*
        Eozän *n*
        Paleozän
    Mesozoikum *n*, Erdmittelalter *n*
      Kreideformation *f*
        Obere ~
        Untere ~
      Juraformation *f*
      Triasformation *f*
    Paläozoikum *n*, Erdaltertum *n*
      Dyasformation *f*, Permformation
      Carbonformation *f*, Steinkohlenformation
        Obere ~
        Untere ~
      Devonformation *f*

geology
  physical ~
  petrology

  mineralogy
  stratigraphy, historical geology, stratigraphical geology

  palaeontology
  formation, system, stage, series
    Neozoic era

      alluvium
      diluvium
      Tertiary System
        Pliocene Period
        Miocene Period
        Oligocene Period
        Eocene Period
        Paleocene Period
    Mesozoic era
      Cretaceous System
        Upper ~ ~
        Lower ~ ~
      Jurassic System
      Triassic System, Trias
    Palaeozoic era
      Dyas, Permian System
      Carboniferous System

        Upper ~ ~
        Lower ~ ~
      Devonian System, Devonic ~

Geologie — geophysikalische Baugrunduntersuchung 201

    Obere ~   Upper ~ ~
    Mittlere ~   Middle ~ ~
    Untere ~   Lower ~ ~
    Silurformation *f*   Silurian System, Siluric ~
    Obere ~   Upper ~ ~
    Untere ~, Ordovikium *n*   Ordovician System
    Cambriumformation *f*   Cambrian System, Cambric ~
    Präkambrium *n*, Erdurzeit *f*   Pre-Cambrian era, Archaean ~, Eozoic ~

---

geologische Aufeinanderfolge *f* = geological succession

~ Karte *f* = geological map

Geomechanik *f*, Felsmechanik = rock mechanics

---

geophysikalische Baugrunduntersuchung *f*

  Schweremessungen *fpl*, gravimetrische Messungen *fpl*

  seismisches Verfahren *n*, seismische Bodenerforschung *f* nach dem Refraktionsverfahren *n*, elastisches Verfahren *n*

    Seismograph *m*, Empfänger *m*

    Erschütterungsstelle *f*
    Erschütterungswelle *f*
    Zweischichtenproblem *n*
    Laufzeitkurve *f*, Wegzeitkurve *f*
    Knickpunkt *m*
    seismisches Gerät *n* mit 6 Empfängern *mpl*
    Ankunftszeit *f*
    gebrochene Welle *f*
    Schallwellenverlauf *m* in zwei Schichten *fpl*

  Widerstandsmessungsverfahren *n*, Verfahren mit galvanischer Elektrodenkopplung *f*, elektrische Widerstandsmessung *f*, geoelektisches Verfahren
    Stromelektrode *f*, Feldelektrode *f*
    Potentialelektrode *f*, Meßelektrode *f*, (Spannungsmeß)Sonde *f*
    Wenner'sche Arbeitsmethode *f*, Wenner'sche Vierpunkt-Methode *f*
    Potentialunterschied *m*, Potentialgefälle *n*
    scheinbar spezifischer (Boden)Widerstand *m*

geophysical field study, ~ investigation, ~ exploration method

  gravimetric investigation

  seismic refraction procedure, refraction survey, seismic survey

    seismometer, pickup, seismic wave receiver
    shot point
    seismic wave
    two(-)layer(ed) problem
    travel time curve
    break point
    six-trace seismograph, six-trace seismic refraction equipment
    arrival time
    refracted wave
    wave front advance in two layers

  electrical resistivity method (or survey), resistivity measurement method, resistivity reconnaissance, resistivity exploration, resistivity survey
    current electrode
    potential electrode

    four electrode system, Wenner method, four-point method
    potential difference, potential drop

    apparent resistivity

geophysikalische Baugrunduntersuchung — Geräte

homogener Baugrund *m* — homogeneous medium
Spieß *m* — current stake
Watson'sche Vierpunkt-Methode *f* — Watson four electrode system method
Äquipotentiallinien *fpl* — equipotential surface
wirklich spezifischer (Boden)Widerstand *m* — actual resistivity
Lee-Methode *f* — Lee method
magnetische Methode *f*, magnetisches Aufschlußverfahren *n* — magnetic method
radioaktives Verfahren *n* — radioactive method
geoelektrische Baugrunduntersuchung *f*, elektrisches Aufschlußverfahren *n*, elektrische Sondierung *f* — electrical exploration method

---

geophysikalischer Prüfungsversuch *m* = geophysical test
Geosynklinale *f*, Senkungstrog *m*, Senkungswanne *f* = geosyncline
geotechnisches Verfahren *n* == geotechnical process
gepackter Steindamm *m*; siehe unter „Talsperre *f*"
Gerade *f* = straight

gerade Endverkämmung *f*; siehe unter „Holzverbindung *f*"
~ **Gewichts(stau)mauer** *f* = straight-gravity dam
gerader **Bogen** *m*, siehe: scheitrechter ~
gerade Zinke *f*; siehe unter „Holzverbindung *f*"

Gerät *n* zur Bestimmung *f* der Fließgrenze *f*, Fließgrenzengerät *n* — (mechanical) liquid limit device, apparatus for plasticity test, casagrande liquid limit machine

Messingschale *f* — brass dish
Nockenwelle *f* — cam
Hartgummiunterlage *f* — hard rubber block
Bodenprobe *f* — soil cake
Furche *f* — groove
Fließkurve *f* — flow curve
semilogarithmisches Netz *n* — semilog plot
Schlag *m* — shock

Gerät *n* zur Bestimmung des Verdichtungsquotienten *m* [*Beton m*] = compacting factor test apparatus
~ ~ ~ **W/Z-Faktors** *m* = concrete mix electric testing apparatus, ratiometer
~ ~ **Messung** *f* der Durchbiegung *f* von nichtstarren Straßendecken *fpl* = leverarm deflection indicator, Benkelman beam (apparatus)

Geräte *npl* für die Material(be)förderung, (Material)Umschlaggeräte *npl* = materials handling machinery (or equipment)
absatzweise arbeitende Fördermittel *npl* = intermittent movement equipment
stetig arbeitende Fördermittel *npl*, Dauerförderer *mpl*, Stetigförderer *mpl* = constant flow equipment, continuous movement equipment

Gerät n **zum Anzeichnen** n **der Verkehrslinien** fpl**, Strichziehmaschine** f**, Straßenmarkierungsmaschine** f**, Farbstrichziehmaschine** f**, Strichziehgerät**

pavement-marking machine, traffic-line marking machine, road-marking machine, safety-line (street) marker, stripe painter, line marker, highway marker, white line machine, carriageway (or highway, or street) marking machine, striping machine, striper

gestrichelte Linie f
ausgezogene Linie f
eine alte gestrichelte Linie unter Synchronisierung f nachziehen
Verkehrs(-Markierungs)farbe f, Straßenmarkierungsfarbe; Signierfarbe [*Schweiz*]

intermittent line
continuous line
to synchronize with the old intermittent line when repainting
traffic(-zoning) paint, zone marking ∼, road-marking ∼, line-marking ∼, road line ∼

Geräte|bediener m = equipment operator, plant ∼, driver; operative (Brit.)
∼bude f = equipment storage hut
∼einheit, Einzelgerät n**, Maschineneinheit, Einzelmaschine** f = equipment unit (or item), piece of equipment, plant item
∼einsatz m = employment of plant, disposition of equipment, equipment utilization
∼liste f = list of equipment, plant register
(∼)Mietkosten f**, Gerätemiete** f = hire charge, equipment rental
(∼)mietsatz m = equipment rental rate, plant-hire rate
∼park m; siehe unter „Baumaschinen fpl und Baugeräte npl"
∼stunden fpl; siehe unter „Baumaschinen fpl und Baugeräte npl"
∼träger m**, Grundgerät** n = basic unit, ∼ tool
∼- und Maschinenunterhaltung f = plant maintenance work
∼vermietung f = equipment renting

∼zug m = train of plant items, equipment train
geräumig = roomy
geräuschlose Kette f = silent chain
Geräuschpegel m**, Lärmpegel** = noise level
Gerbereiabwasser n = tannery waste
Gerbsäure f, siehe: Tannin n
Gerechtsame f**, Servitut** n = easement
geregelte Kreuzung f = controlled crossing
gereinigter Asphalt m = refined natural asphalt, épuré, refined lake asphalt
gerillter Griff m = fluted handle
Gerinne-Auskleidung f**, Kanalauskleidung** = canal lining
überdeckte BitumenDichtungshäute fpl = buried membrane asphalt canal lining (US); ∼ ∼ asphaltic bitumen ∼ ∼ (Brit.)
Gerinnung f, siehe: Ausflockung f
Geröllhalde f (Geol.) = talus, scree
Gersdorffit m (Min.), siehe: Arsen-Nickelkies m
Geruchverschluß m = drain trap, stench ∼

Gerüst n**, Rüstung** f
Bodenplatte f
Halter m
Spindel f, Schraube f, Schraubenspindel
Längsstange f
Pfosten m
Querstange f
Stirnwand f
Rohr n

scaffold(ing)
base plate
lashing
jack, screw ∼
ledger
standard, pole
putlog
wall face
tubing

Gerüstkran *m*, siehe: Bockkran
gerüttelter Steindamm *m*; siehe unter „Talsperre *f*"
Gesamt|belastung *f* = total load
~festigkeit *f* = overall strength
~gewicht *n* der schwimmenden Baulichkeiten *fpl* = buoyancy on the structure
~kerngewinn *m* = over-all core recovery
~programm *n* der Erfordernisse *npl* = total-need program(me)
~spannung *f* = total stress
~starrheit *f* [*Straßenbefestigung f*] = overall rigidity
~tonnage *f* = aggregate tonnage
~volumen *n* = bulk volume, total ~
~wasserhaushalt *m* [*ober- und unterirdisches Wasser n*] = surface flow and underground storage water
Geschäfts|adresse *f* = office (or business) address
~gebiet *n* = business area, central ~ ~, (central) business district
~straße *f* = business thoroughfare
~viertel *n* = business district
geschäumte Hochofenschlacke *f*, siehe: Hochofenschaumschlacke
geschichteter See *m* = stratified lake
Geschiebe|(masse) *n*, (*f*), Flußschotter *m*, Trümmermasse *f*, Flußgeschiebe *n* = shingle, detritus, rubbish
~lehm *m* = glacial loam
~mergel *m* = boulder clay
~rückstand *m* = nappe outlier
~trieb *m* = movement of bed material by river
geschlagener Wechsel *m*; siehe unter „Entwässerung *f*"
geschleifter Spitzbogen *m* = four-centred arch (Brit.); four-centered ~ (US)
geschleppter Erdhobel *m*, siehe: Anhänge-Straßenhobel
geschlitzte Unterlagscheibe *f* = split washer
geschlossen [*Verschleißschicht f*] = close-textured [*wearing course*]
geschlossen abgestufter Asphaltbeton *m* = close-graded aggregate type asphaltic concrete

~ abgestuftes Mineralgemisch *n*, ~ abgestufte Mineralmasse *f* = dense(-graded) (mineral) aggregate, close-graded (~) ~, DGA
geschlossene Ortslage *f*, Ortschaft *f* = built-up area
geschlossener Behälter *m* = box container
geschlossenes Becherwerk *n* mit senkrechter Leiter *f* = totally enclosed vertical elevator
Geschmeidigkeitseigenschaft *f* = plastic quality
geschmiedeter Nagel *m* = spike
~ Stahl *m* = steel forgings
geschraubte Verbindung *f*, Schraubverbindung [*Stahlbau m*] = bolted joint, ~ connection
geschüttete Leichtbetonwand *f* = light-weight no-fines concrete wall
geschütteter Steindamm *m*; siehe unter „Talsperre *f*"
geschüttetes Steindeckwerk *n*, Steinwurf *m*, Rauhwurf *m* = dumped (stone) riprap
Geschützbronze *f* = gunmetal
geschwächter Querschnitt *m* = weakened cross section
geschweißte Rahmenkonstruktion *f* = welded framing
~ Rohrkonstruktion *f* = welded tubular structure
Geschwindigkeits|hebel *m* = speed control lever
~messer *m* = tachometer
~versuchsstrecke *f* = high-speed test track
Gesellschaft *f* Reichsautobahnen = German Motor Road Company
gesenkgeschmiedet = drop-forged
Gesetzmäßigkeit *f* = regularity of features
Gesetzwidrigkeit *f* = anomaly
gesiebtes Material *n*, siehe: abgestuftes ~
gesinterter Zusatzstab *m* = sintered rod
gespannter Grundwasserspiegel *m*, siehe: angespannter ~
Gespannverkehr *m*, Fuhrwerkverkehr, Zugtierverkehr = animal-drawn traffic
Gesperre *n* = pawl and ratchet mechanism
gesprengte Felsmassen *f* = muck
gespülter Damm *m*, siehe: Spüldamm

Gestade *n*, Strand *m* = shore, beach
Gestalt|änderungsenergie *f* = deformation energy
~festigkeit *f* = structural strength
Gestänge|abfangschere *f* = rotary slide tongs
~bruch *m* = breaking of the drill stem
~fahrstuhl *m* = drill pipe elevator
~fett *n* = drill pipe thread dope
~haken *m*, Hakenschlüssel *m*, Drehschlüssel für Bohrgestänge = pipe "hook", ~ wrench

gestängeloses elektrisches Bohrgerät *n* = pipeless electric drill
Gestänge|schlagbohrung *f*, Gestängeschlagbohren *n* = percussive rod boring
~übergang *m* = drill pipe sub
~verbinder *m* = tool joint, drilling ~ ~
gestanztes Loch *n* = punched hole
Gestehungskosten *f* = prime cost, flat ~
Gestein *n*, Fels *m*, Felsgestein *n*, Festgestein = rock

Gesteinsaufbereitungsmaschinen *fpl*	**aggregate production (or producing) equipment**
Zerkleinerungsmaschinen *fpl*	crushing and grinding equipment
Siebemaschinen *fpl*	screening equipment
Waschmaschinen *fpl*	washing equipment

Gesteins|auspressung *f*, Felsinjektion *f*, Kluftinjektion *f* = rock sealing, cementation of rock fissures
~beschreibung *f*, siehe: Petrographie *f*
gesteinsbildendes Mineral *n*, gesteinsbildender Gemengeteil *m* = rock-forming mineral
Gesteins|bindung *f* [*auf bituminösen Verschlußdecken fpl*] = aggregate retention [*on bituminous seal coats*]
~bohren *n*, Felsbohren = rock drilling
~bohrer *m*, Felsbohrer = rock drill
~bohrerkrone *f*, siehe: Bohrmeißel *m*
~bohrhammer *m*, siehe: Bohrhammer
~bohrstahl *m* = rock drill steel
~drehbohren *n*, Felsdrehbohren, Rotations-Gesteinsbohrung *f* = rotary (or rotating) rock drilling
~entstehungslehre *f*, Petrologie *f* = petrology
~festigkeit *f* = rock strength
~gefüge *n* = rock fabric
~gemenge *n*, siehe: Mineralgemisch *n*
~gemengteil *m*, siehe: Gemengteil
~gemisch *n*, siehe: Mineralgemisch
~gerüst *n*, siehe: Mineralgemisch *n*
~hauer *m*, siehe: Mineur *m*
~korn *n*, siehe: Einzelkorn *n*
~masse *f*, siehe: Mineralgemisch *n* [*künstlich*]

~mehl *n*, siehe: Blume *f*
~metamorphose *f*, siehe: Metamorphose
~mikroskopie *f* = petrographie microscopy
~schicht *f*, Felsschicht = rock formation
~silo *m* = aggregate bin
(~) Staub *m*, siehe: Blume *f*
~trockner *m* = rock drier, ~ dryer
~trümmer *f*, Gesteinsschutt *m*, (Fels-) Geröll *n* (Geol.) = rock débris, rubble
~umprägung *f*, siehe: Metamorphose *f*
~waage *f* (mit Wiegesilo *m*), Zuschlagstoffwaage, Gemengewaage = aggregate weigh-batcher (Brit.); aggregate weighing batcher (with scale) (US)
~waschmaschine *f*, Gesteinswäsche *f* = rock washing machine
~zerfall *m*, siehe: physikalische Verwitterung *f*
~zersetzung *f*, siehe: chemische Verwitterung *f*
gesteuerter Überlauf *m* = controlled weir (Brit.); controlled spillway
gestrichelte Linie *f* = intermittent line
Gestück *n*, siehe: Setzpacklageschicht
gestützt = supported
Gesundheits|ingenieur *m* = sanitary engineer
~technik *f* = sanitary engineering
geteertes Segeltuch *n*, siehe: Persenning *f*

geteilte Bodenentleerung f [*Fahrzeug* n] = split-bottom dump

~ Kupplung f = split-second clutch (coupling)

Getreide|elevator m, Schiffselevator = grain elevator

~silo m, Getreidespeicher m = grain silo, granary

~speicherung f = warehousing of grain

~trocknungsanlage f = grain-drying plant

getrennte Lagerung f **von Zuschlagstoffen** mpl **nach Korngrößen** fpl = segregated aggregate stockpiling (or storage)

getrenntes Grundablaßbauwerk n; siehe unter „Talsperre f"

Getriebe|antrieb m = gear drive

~schalthebel m = gear-change lever

Getriebeschaltung f [*als Maschinenteil* m] = gearshift

~ [*als Bedienungstätigkeit* f] = gear shifting

gewachsener Boden m, natürlicher ~ = natural soil, unmade ground

~ Fels m, siehe: Kernfels

Gewächshaus n = greenhouse

gewalzter Damm m; siehe unter „Talsperre f"

gewalztes Flußeisen n = temper-rolled mild steel, ~ soft steel

gewässerkundliches Jahrbuch n = Water Resources Paper

Gewebe|boden m = texture soil [*soil containing a large portion of roots*]

~sieb n = cloth screen

gewendelte Treppe f, siehe: Wendeltreppe

Gewerbesteuer f = occupation tax

gewerblicher Sprengstoff m; siehe unter „1. Schießen n; 2. Sprengen n"

Gewichts|-Abmeßbandspeiser m = constant-weight feeder

~abmessung f, Gewichtsdosierung f, Gewichtszuteilung f, Gewichtsteilmischung f, Gewichtszumessung f, Gewichtsgattierung f, Gewichtszugabe f = gravimetric batching, proportioning by weight, weigh-batching, batching by weight

~mauer f; siehe unter „Talsperre f"

~prozente npl, Gewichtsteile mpl = percentage by weight

Summe f der ~ = cumulative ~ ~

~rückstand m = residue by weight

~sonde f = sounding weight

~sperre f; siehe unter „Talsperre f"

~staumauer f; siehe unter „Talsperre f"

~teilmischung f, siehe: Gewichtsabmessung f

~teilstrich m = weight graduation(mark)

~zuteilung f, siehe: Gewichtsabmessung f

Gewinde n = thread

~bohrer m = tap

~bonrstahl m = threaded drill steel

~loch n = tapped hole

~muffe f = threaded sleeve, screwed socket

~schneideisen n = screw cutting die

~schneidmaschine f = threading machine, screw cutting ~, screwing ~

~spindel f = screw(ed) spindle

gewinnen, abbauen [*Bergwerk* n] = to win, to work

Gewinnung f = winning

Gewinnungsstelle f, siehe: Entnahmestelle f

Gewitter n = thunderstorm

~bö f = thunder-squall

gewobener Gurt m, ~ **Riemen** m = texrope belt

gewöhnliche Feile f, Flachfeile = flat file

Gewölbe n = vault

~-Gewichtssperre f, Bogengewichts(stau)mauer f, Bogengewichtssperre f = arch-gravity dam

gewölbeloser Ziegelofen m = archless brick kiln

Gewölbe|mauer f; siehe unter „Talsperre" f

~mauerwerk n = vaulting masonry, stone arching

~reihen(stau)mauer f; siehe unter „Talsperre f"

~stein m, Wölbstein m = arch stone, voussoir

~wirkung f, siehe: Bogenwirkung f

Geysir m, Geyser m, pulsierende Springquelle f = geyser, gusher

Gezeiten fpl, Tiden fpl = tides

~ablagerung f = tidal mud deposits

~arbeit f, Gezeitenenergie f = tidal power

~berechnung f = tidal calculation

~diagramm n, Gezeitenkurve f, Tidenkurve f = tidal curve, ~ diagram (Brit.); marigram (US)

Gezeiten|einwirkung — Gipskartonplattentafel

Gezeiten|einwirkung f = tide effect
~**energie** f, siehe: Gezeitenarbeit f
~**erscheinung** f, Tideerscheinung = tidal phenomenon
~**feuer** n = tidal light
~**hub** m, Tidehub = range of a tide
~**kraftwerk** n = tidal power plant
~**merkmal** n = tidal feature
~**signal** n = tide-ball
~**spiel** n = tide cycle
~**strand** m = tide beach
~**strömung** f, Tideströmung = tide current, tidal ~
~**strömung** f, starke ~ = race
~**strömung** f in Flußmündungen fpl = estuarine flow
~**überschwemmung** f = tidal inundation
~**verfrühung** f = acceleration, priming [*the shortening of the interval between the time of two high tides*]
~**welle** f, Flutwelle = tide wave, tidal ~
gezogener Bauteil m = tension member
~ **Draht** m = drawn wire
Gichtgas n, siehe: Hochofengas
Giebelstütze f = gable stanchion

Gießerei|drehkran m = foundry (jib) crane (Brit.); ~ (boom) ~ (US)
~**nagel** m = foundry nail
~**roheisen** n = foundry pig-iron
~**sand** m = foundry sand
Gieß|mast m, siehe: (Beton)Gießmast
~**pfannenziegel** m, Pfannenstein m = ladle brick
~**rinnenanlage** f, siehe: (Beton)Gießrinnenanlage
~**ton** m = foundry clay, ladle ~
~**turm** m, siehe: (Beton)Gießturm
~**turmkübel** m, Beton-~ = tower hoist bucket
Giftgehalt m, Giftigkeit f = toxicity
Gilsonitasphalt m, Uintait m = uintaite, gilsonite
Gips m [*Der Gebrauch des Wortes „Gips" ist im Deutschen mehrdeutig. Vielfach wird damit das Gestein, das gebrannte Fertiggut, sowie das Mineral bezeichnet*]
~ (Min.) = gypsum
~**akustikziegel** m = gypsum acoustical tile
~**arbeiter** m, siehe: Putzer m
~**aufbereitungsanlage** f, Gipswerk n = gypsum plant

Gips(bau)platte f, Gipskartonplatte, Rigipsplatte

Tafel f
  einheitliche Dicke f auf ganzer Breite f
  abgeflachter Rand m an den Längskanten fpl
  mit Alu-Folie f auf einer Seite f
Platte f
Brett n, Gipsmembran(e) f

plaster board, gypsum ~

wall board
  square edged
  recessed edged

  with alumin(i)um foil on one side
baseboard
lath, gypsum ~

Gips|(bau)stein m = gypsum precast building block, (precast) gypsum block, cast gypsum block
~**brei** m = gypsum putty, ~ paste
~**brennen** n = gypsum calcination
~**bruch** m = gypsum quarry
~**diele** f = reed-reinforced plaster (or gypsum) board
~ **(dreh)ofen** m = (rotary) calciner
Gipserbeil n = plasterer's hatchet
Gipserde f, Gipsgur f = gypseous soil

Gipserspachtel f, m, Traufel f = wall scraper
Gips|estrich(fuß)boden m = plaster floor(ing)
~**gestein** n = gypsum stone, ~ rock
~**-Hohlstein** m = hollow gypsum tile (US)
~**kalk** m = plaster lime
~ **-Kalk-Putzmörtel** m, siehe: Kalkhydrat-Raschbinder m
~**kartonplatte** f, siehe: Gips(bau)platte
~**kartonplattentafel** f = (plaster) wallboard

Gips|kartonplattenwerk n = plaster-board plant, gypsum wallboard plant
~kocher m, Gipskessel m = calcining kettle, gypsum ~ ~
~lösung f = calcium sulphate solution
~membran(e) f, Brett n [*Gipskartonplatte f*] = (gypsum) lath
~mergel m = gypseous marl
~mörtel m, Gipssandmörtel = gypsum mortar
~ofen m, siehe: Gipsdrehofen
~pfanne f = (gypsum) calcining pan
~platte f, siehe: Gipsbauplatte
~putz m, Putzgips m = gypsum plaster
~sand m = gypseous sand
~sandmörtel m = gypsum-sand mortar
~schlackenzement m; siehe unter „Zement"
~schlackenzement m; siehe unter „Zement"
~sinter m = stalactitical gypsum
~spat m = selenite, sparry gypsum, specular stone, specular gypsum, gypsum spar, gypseous spar
~staub m = raw gypsum dust
~stein m, siehe: Gipsbaustein
~verkleidung f = gypsum sheathing
~werk n, siehe: Gipsaufbereitungsanlage f
Girlanden(balken)träger m, durchlaufender Hängeträger(balken) m = continuous suspension girder (Brit.); ~ ~ beam
Gitter|ausleger m [*Bagger m*] = (steel-) lattice(d) (crane) boom (US)/jib (Brit.)
~balken(träger) m, siehe: Gitterträger
~draht m = fence wire, fencing ~
~konstruktion f = latticed construction
~netzkarte f = gridded map
~pfette f = latticed purlin
~rost m = grid
~sieb n = screen; [*deprecated: riddle*]
~stab m = latticed member
~träger m, Gitterbalken(träger) m = lattice (or braced) girder (Brit.); ~ (~ ~) beam
~trägerdecke f, Gitterbalkendecke, Gitterbalkenträgerdecke = lattice girder floor slab (Brit.); lattice beam ~ ~
~werksmast m = lattice-work mast
Glanz m = lustre

~blende f, Alabandin n, Manganblende f (Min.) = alabandite, mangan-blende
~braunstein m, Schwarzmanganerz n, Hausmannit m (Min.) = hausmannite
~gras n = canary grass
~kobalt m, Kobaltglanz m, Cobaltin n, CoAsS (Min.) = cobalt glance, cobaltite
~kohle f; siehe unter „Kohle f"
~pech n, Maniak n = glance pitch
~ruß m = shining soot
Glasbaustein m = glass block
Glaserkitt m = glazier's putty
Glas|faser f = glass fibre (Brit.); ~ fiber (US)
~füllung f [*Tür f*] = glass panel
~gespinst n = spun glass
~gestein n = glassy rock
Glasieren n = glazing
salzglasiert = salt-glazed
glasiertes Steingut n = glazed whiteware product
glasig [*Grundmasse f*] = glassy, vitreous, hyaline [*ground-mass*]
glasiger Scherben m = vitreous body
Glas|kastenmodell n = glass-sided working model
~ofen m = glass tank
~ofen-Oberbau m = glass-furnace superstructure
~ofen-Regenerator m = glass furnace regenerator
~perlen-Markierungsstreifen m = beaded stripe
~sand m = glass sand
~schneider m = glas cutter
~stein m = glass stone
Glasur f = glaze
Matt~ = mat ~
~binder m = glaze binder
~ für das Einbrandverfahren n = one-fire glaze
~fehler m = glaze defect
~fliese f = glazed tile, face ~
~ziegel m, Glasurstein m, glasierter Ziegelstein = glazed brick
Glas|wanne f = glass tank crown
~wannenofen m = glass tank furnace
~wolle f [*düsengeblasen*] = glass wool
Glätt|band n, Glättriemen m = smoothing belt, finishing ~

Glättbohle — Gleisketten-Fahrlader

Glätt|bohle *f*, **Glättelement** *n*, **Deckenschlußbohle** [*Beton(decken)fertiger m*] = smoothing (or finishing) beam (or screed; or board (Brit.))

~bohlenfertiger *m*, Putzbohlenfertiger = smoothing beam (or screed) finisher (or finishing machine)

Glätte *f*, Schlüpfrigkeit *f* = slipperiness

glatte Schalung *f* = wrought shuttering

Glatteis *n* = glazed ice

~bekämpfung *f* = treatment of icy pavements, highway ice-control

Glätter *m*; siehe unter „Fertigbehandlung *f*"

Glätt|kelle *f*, siehe: Spachtel *m*, *f*

~maschine *f* [*für Beton m*] = mechanical trowel, ~ float

Glattputz *m* = fair faced plaster

Glattrohrbogen *m* = plain pipe bend

Glätt- und Verdichtungsbohle *f* [*Kanalauskleidungsmaschine f*] = ironing-screed [*slip-form canal paver*]

Glaubersalz *n*, $Na_2SO_4 \times 10 H_2O$ = glauber salt, mirabilite, hydrated sodium sulphate

Glaucherz *n* = poor ore

Glaukodot *n* (Min.) = glaucodot(e)

Glaukonit *m* (Min.) = glauconite

glaukonitisch = glauconitic

Glaukonit|kalkstein *m* = glauconitic limestone

~sandstein *m* = glauconitic sandstone

Glaukophan *m* (Min.) = glaucophane

Glazialerosion *f*, Gletschererosion = glaciation

glaziale Flußablagerung *f* = glacial outwash

glaziales und fluvoglaziales Sedimentgestein *n* = ice-borne sediment

Glazialton *m* = glacial clay

Gleichartigkeit *f*, Homogen(e)ität *f* = homogeneity

Gleichdruck|-Axialturbine *f* = axial flow impulse turbine

~-Kondensationsturbine *f* = impulse condensing turbine

gleichförmiger Sand *m* = uniform sand, uniformly graded ~, closely ~ ~

Gleichförmigkeitsbeiwert *m* = homogenising coefficient [*road traffic*]

Gleichgewichts|anzeiger *m*, Gleichgewichtsanzeigeapparat *m* = balance indicator

~bedingung *f* = condition of equilibrium

~zustand *m* = state of equilibrium

gleichmäßig verteilte Belastung *f*, ~ ~ Last *f* = uniformly distributed load

gleichmäßige Kohle *f*; siehe unter „Kohle *f*"

Gleich|richter *m* = rectifier

~schlag *m*; siehe unter „Drahtseil *n*"

Gleichstrom *m* [*Elektrotechnik f*] = dc current, D. C. ~

~verfahren *n* [*Gesteintrockentrommel f*] = parallel-flow process

~waschmaschine *f*, Gleichstromwäsche *f* = uniflow washer (or washing machine)

Gleichwinkel(stau)mauer *f*; siehe unter „Talsperre *f*"

Gleis *n*, Schienenstrang *m*, Schienenweg *m* = rail(way) track (Brit.); rail (road) track (US); tracking, line of rails, two-rail surface track

~anlage *f* = railway trackage (Brit.); railroad ~ (US)

~anschluß *m*, siehe: Anschlußgleis *n*

~arbeiten *f* = railway track-work (Brit.); railroad ~ (US)

~bagger *m*, Schienenbagger = rail-mounted excavator

~bahn *f* = railway train

~baumaschinen *fpl* = track laying machinery

~bremse *f* = car retarder

~fahrzeug *n*, Schienenfahrzeug = rail-mounted (or rail-guided) vehicle

gleisgebunden, schienengeführt, schienengebunden = rail-mounted, rail-guided

Gleis|hebewinde *f* = track (lifting) jack

~kette, siehe: Raupenkette

~kette *f* **für LKW** = truck track

~kette *f* **mit Platten** *fpl* = track group

~kette *f* **ohne Platten** *fpl* = track link assembly

~ketten-Aufstandsfläche *f* = crawler bearing area

gleiskettenfahrbar = crawler-mounted

Gleisketten-Fahrlader *m*, siehe: Gleisketten-Ladeschaufel *f*

Gleisketten-Fahrlader = crawler-mounted bucket (elevator) loader

Gleiskettenfahrwerk n, siehe: Raupenfahrwerk

(Gleis)Kettenfahrzeug n, Raupenfahrzeug = track laying vehicle; tracked ~ [*deprecated*]

Gleis|kettenfertiger m [*früher: Raupenfertiger* m] = caterpillar (or track-laying type) (asphalt) finisher (or paver, or bituminous paving machine, or bituminous spreading-and-finishing machine, or black-top spreader, or asphaltic concrete paver)

~ketten-Frontlader m = front end crawler shovel

~kettengerät n [*früher: Raupengerät* n, *Raupe* f] = caterpillar, tracklayer

~kettengerätfahrer m, Raupenfahrer = cat-jockey

~kettenkran m, Raupenkran = crawler crane

~ketten-Ladeschaufel f, Gleisketten-Schaufellader m, Gleisketten-Fahrlader m [*früher: Raupen-Ladeschaufel* f] = crawler-loader shovel, crawler tractor loader (or shovel)

~kettenrolle f = track roller, tractor ~

~ketten-Schlepper m, siehe: Kettenschlepper m

~kettenschlepper-Frontlader m, Gleiskettenschlepper-Frontladeschaufel f, (Gleis)Ketten-Fahrlader m mit Frontladeschaufel f, Front-Fahrlader m mit (Gleis)Kettenfahrwerk n = crawler tractor (-mounted) front end loader

~ketten-Schlepperwalze f = tracked roller

~kettentraktor(en)kran m, Gleisketten-schlepperkran m, Raupenschlepperkran = crawler tractor crane

~kettenturss m = crawler drive sprocket

~ketten-Wurfschaufellader m, Gleisketten-Über-Kopf-(Schaufel-)Lader m = crawler (or caterpillar, or track-laying type) overhead loader (or overshot loader, or rocker shovel, or flip-over bucket loader, or over-loader)

~ketten-Zugmaschine f, siehe: Kettenschlepper m

gleislos = railless, trackless

gleisloser Baubetrieb m = railless (or trackless) construction operations

~ Erdbau m, **~ Erdtransport** m, gleislose Erdbewegung f = railless earthwork engineering, trackless ~ ~

~ Förderwagen m; siehe unter „Fahrzeuge für den Transport m von Boden und Steinbaustoffen mpl"

gleisloses Fahrzeug n = free-wheeled vehicle

Gleis|rad n = track wheel

~rückmaschine f für absatzweisen Betrieb m = intermittent type track shifting machine

~rückmaschine f für kontinuierlichen Betrieb m = continuous type track shifting machine

~schotter m, siehe: (Eisen)Bahnschotter

~spur f, Spurweite f = track ga(u)ge, rail ~

~stopfer m, Schotterstopfer = tie tamper (US); track ~ (Brit.); ballast ~

~stopfmaschine f = track tamping machine, power ballaster

~verlegung f = track laying

~waage f, Waggonwaage = track-scale, railway-track scale

~zubehör m, n = track accessories

Gleiten n [*metallurgisch*] = slippage, sliding

gleitende Reibung f = sliding friction

Gleit|fläche f [*Stützmauer* f] = plane of rupture

~fläche f [*metallurgisch*] = sliding surface

~flächenbruch m, siehe: Böschungs-rutschung f

~flächenmethode f = method of slices

~flächenrutschung f = landslip due to tectonic movement

~flächenschar f [*Boden* m] = network of slip lines

~geschwindigkeit f = sliding velocity

~kanal m [*Spannbeton* m] = channel, duct, hole

~klausel f = variation clause, fluctuation ~

~körper m [*Bodenmechanik* f] = rupture shear zone

~kreisanalyse f = friction circle analysis

~kufe f [*Frontlader* m] = skid-shoe loader shoe

Gleit|kufen-Frontlader m, siehe: (Front-)Ladeschaufel f mit Kufen fpl
~**lager** n = sliding bearing
~**linie** f = line of sliding
~**modul** m [Stahlbau m] = modulus of rigidity, shearing modulus of elasticity
~**reibung** f = skidding friction
~**reibungsbeiwert** m [Straße f] = kinetic coefficient of friction
~**schalung** f = slip form
~**schalungsfertiger** m = slip form paver, sliding ~ ~, formless paving machine
~**schicht** f (Geol.) = flow sheet (Brit.); sheet of drift (US)
~**schieber-Siloverschluß** m = slide-type fill valve (US)
~**schutz** m [Straße f] = non-skid treatment
Gleitschütz(e) m, (f), = sliding (or slide) gate
~ **mit hydraulischer Steuerung** = high-pressure gate
Gleit|schutzkette f, Schneekette, Schutzkette = non-skid chain, snow ~
~**schutzteppich** m = non-skid carpet (or mat), skid-proof ~
gleitsicher, rutschfest, griffig = non-skid, non-slip, skid-proof
Gleit|theorie f [Stützwand f] = theory of rupture
~**weg** m [metallurgisch] = slip
~**widerstand** m = skid resistance

Gletscher m, **Ferner** m	glacier
Abschmelzung f, Ablation f	wastage, ablation
Endmoräne f	terminal (or end) moraine
~ende n	front, snout
~erosion f, Glazialerosion	glaciation
~kunde f	glaciology
~lawine f, Eislawine	ice-avalanche
~mühle f, ~topf m, ~trichter m	pot-hole, glacier mill
~schnee m	~ snow
~schutt m, Moräne(n)schutt	moraine débris, drift
~see m	lake ponded up by glacier
~sohle f	sole of the ~
~tisch m, Eistisch	~ table
~vorstoß m	forward movement
~zunge f	glacier tongue
Grundmoräne f, Untermoräne	ground moraine
Hänge~	hanging ~, tongue-shaped ~
Hufeisen~	corrie ~, horse-shoe-shaped ~
Innenmoräne f	englacial moraine
Kalben n	calving
Mittelmoräne f, Gufferlinie f	medial moraine
Riesentopf m	giant's kettle
Scheidemoräne f, Einscharungsmoräne f	subglacial moraine
Schmelzwasser n	melt water, melted snow and ice
Seitenmoräne f, Wallmoräne, Randmoräne, Ganzdecke f	lateral moraine
Tal~	valley ~, mountain ~

Glied n = member
Glieder|bandförderer m, siehe: Plattenband(förderer) n, (m)
~**egge** f = chain-and-spike harrow
~**kessel** m, siehe: Sektionalkessel
~**kette** f = link (type) chain

Glieder-Maßstab m, siehe: Zollstock m
Glimmentladung f, Koronaentladung = corona emission
Glimmer m (Min.) = mica
glimmer(halt)ig, glimmerführend = micaceous
Glimmer|plättchen n = mica flake
~**pophyr** m = mica porphyry, micaceous ~
~**sandstein** m = micaceous sandstone
~**schiefer** m = mica-schist, micaceous schist
~**ton** m = shiny clay, illite, hydrous mica
Globigerinenschlamm m = globigerina ooze
Glocken|boje f = bell-buoy
~**ofen** m = bell kiln
~**ventil** n = double beat valve, bell-shaped ~
Glückshaken m; siehe unter „Bohrmeißel m"
Glühen n [Stahl m] = annealing
Glühkopfmotor m, Semi-Diesel m = mixed cycle engine, semi-diesel (~)
~ m, Semi-Dieselmotor m [ein Teil des Verbrennungsraumes m nicht gekühlt] = hot-bulb engine, surface-ignition engine
Glühkopfzündung f = hot-bulb ignition
Glühverlust m [Zement m] = loss on ignition

Glutflußgestein n, siehe: Erstarrungsgestein n
GMC-Chassis n = GMC-chassis
Gneis m = gneiss
~**textur** f = gneissose texture, gneissic ~
Goldbeckdose f, siehe: Luft(-Erddruck)-Meßdose f nach Goldbeck
Goldklee m = hop clover
Golf m, Meerbusen m = gulf
~**strom** m = Gulf Stream
Gooch-Tiegel m = Gooch filter, ~ crucible
Goslarit m, Zinkvitriol n (Min.) = goslarite, white vitriol, white copperas
Graben m, Tiefscholle f, Grabenbruch m, Grabensenke f (Geol.) = graben, trough fault, rift valley
~[mit abgeböschten Wänden fpl] = ditch
~[mit senkrechten Wänden fpl] = trench
Grabenaushub m [angeböschter breiter Graben] = ditching
~ m [schmaler Graben mit senkrechten Wänden] = trenching
~**maschine** f, Grabenbagger m = pipe line excavator (Brit.); trenching plant, trench excavating plant, ditch digger, ditcher, trencher, trench digger, trench excavator, ditching and trenching machine

---

Grabenbagger m mit Eimern mpl

Eimerkettengrabenbagger m, Eimerleitergrabenbagger m

Grabenbagger mit vertikaler Eimerleiter f (oder Eimerkette f)

Grabenbagger mit schräger Eimerleiter f (oder Eimerkette f)

Grabenbagger mit Eimerrad n, Grabenbagger mit Kreiseimerleiter f

Grabenbagger mit Eimerrad, Fabrikat THE CLEVELAND TRENCHER CO., CLEVELAND 17, OHIO, USA

bucket trencher, trenching machine of the bucket elevator type, trenchliner, endless-bucket trencher

boom type trenching machine, boom type ditcher, boom type trencher, ladder ditcher, ladder-type trenching machine

vertical boom type trenching machine, vertical boom ditcher, vertical ladder ditcher

slanting boom type trenching machine, slanting boom ditcher, inclined boom type trench excavator, slanting ladder ditcher

wheel (type) trenching machine, wheel (type) ditcher, wheel (type) trencher, rotary scoop trencher

CLEVELAND trencher

Grabenbagger mit seitlich herauskragendem Eimerrad zur Verbreiterung *f* von Straßen *fpl*
road widener [*wheel type ditcher with the wheel overhanging the chassis so that the machine runs on the carriageway while excavating*]

Grabbecher *m*, Eimerbecher, Grabenbaggereimer *m*
digging bucket, trencher bucket

Grabenbagger auf (Gleis)Ketten *fpl*, ~ auf Raupen *fpl*
track-type trenching machine

Eimerrad *n*, Kreiseimerleiter *f* — digging wheel
Grabbreite *f* — digging width
Baggerleiterantrieb *m* — bucket-line drive
Baggerleiterwinde *f*, Auslegerwinde — boom hoist, ladder ~
Baggerleiter *f*, Ausleger *m*, Eimerleiter — digging ladder, ditcher ladder, bucket flight

Anhänge-Grabenbagger — detachable ditcher
Aufbau-Grabenbagger — truck-mounted ditcher (US); lorry-mounted ditcher (Brit.)

Graben|böschung *f* = bank of ditch
~**bruch** *m* (Geol.), siehe: Graben *m*
~**fräser** *m*, siehe: Grabkettenbagger *m*
~**füllung** *f* = trench backfill
~**greifer** *m* = ditching grab
~**-Methode** *f* [*Sprengen n weicher Baugrundmassen fpl*] = trench method, ~ blasting
~**pflug** *m*, Rigolpflug *m*; Rajolpflug *m* [*dieser Ausdruck sollte nicht mehr angewendet werden*] = plough type ditcher, trench-plough, trenching plough, deep-plough (Brit.) [*US* = *plow*]
~**ramme** *f* = backfill (trench) rammer
~**rand** *m* (Geol.), siehe: Verwerfung *f*
~**reiniger** *m*, Grabenreinigungsmaschine *f* = ditch cleaner, ~ cleaning machine
~**senke** *f* (Geol.), siehe: Graben *m*
~**stampfer** *m* = backfill tamper
~**steife** *f*, siehe: Kanalstrebe *f*
~**verdichter** *m* = backfill compactor
~**vibrationsverdichter** *m* = vibratory backfill compactor, ~ trench ~
~**ziehmaschine** *f* = wire rope-operated trencher

Grab|gabel *f* = digging fork
~**gefäß** *n* = digging bucket
~**gerät** *n* [*Ausleger-Trockenbagger m*] = digging attachment
~**kettenbagger** *m*, (Drän)Grabenfräser *m* = trench cutting machine
~**kraft** *f* [*Bagger m*] = digging power, ~ force
~**naßbagger** *m*; siehe unter „Naßbagger *m*"
~**scheit** *n*, Spaten *m* = spade
~**stelle** *f*, siehe: Baggerstelle
~**trommel** *f* = digging drum
~**werkzeug** *n* = digging tool
Grad *m* **Celsius** = degree Centigrade
Grad *m* **der Störung** *f* = degree of remo(u)lding [*soil mechanics*]

Gradierwerk *n*, **Rieselwerk** *n* — cooler, cooling stack, graduationworks
offenes ~ — open ~ ~
geschlossenes ~ — enclosed ~ ~
Reisig~ — brushwood ~ ~
Latten~ — lattice ~ ~
Ventilator~ — ~ ~ with fan
Gradierfall *m* — graduation, trickling of the brine
Gradierwand *f* — graduating wall, thorn-wall

Grahamitasphalt *m* = grahamite
Grammatit *m* (Min.) = grammatite [*this term is also used as a synonym for tremolite, but this use is undesirable*]
Granat *m* (Min.) = garnet
~fels *m*, **Granatgestein** *n* = garnet rock, garnetyte
Granatit *m* (Min.) = granatite
Grand *m* = gravel of 4—12 mm grain size
Granit *m* = granite
  feinkörniger ~ = fine-grained ~, granitel(le)
  zersetzter ~ = gowan, disintegrated granite
~aplit *m* = granite-(h)aplite
~familie *f* = granite clan
~geröllhalde *f* = granite boulder slope
~gneis *m* = granite gneiss
Granitit *m*, **Biotitgranit** *m* = biotite-granite, granitite
Granit|pflasterstein *m* = granite sett
~porphyr *m* = porphyroid granite, granite-porphyry
~splitt *m*, **Hartsteinsplitt** *m* = granite chip(ping)s
granoblastischer Verband *m* (Geol.), siehe: Bienenwabenverband
Granodiorit *m* = granodiorite
Granophyr *m* = granophyre
Granulator-Splittbrecher *m*, **Einschwingen-Granulator** *m* = single-toggle granulator, single-toggle type jaw granulator, chipping(s) breaker

---

Granulieranlage *f*	nodulizing installation
elektrische Entstaubung *f*	Cotrell Precipitator
gesammelter Staub *m*	collected dust
Staubbehälter *m*	dust surge tank
Becherwerk *n*	bucket elevator
Überlauf *m*	overflow
Aufgabevorrichtung *f*	head box
Aufgabeschnecke *f*	screw feeder
Granuliertrommel *f*	nodulizing drum
Granalien *f*	nodules
Band *n*	belt conveyor
Aufgabeschaufeln *f pl* für Granalien *f*	nodule feed scoops
Ofen *m*	kiln
Kettenabteilung *f*	chain section
Ventilator *m*	fan
staubhaltige Ofengase *n pl*	dusty kiln gases
Tonvorratsbehälter *m*	clay storage tank
Pumpe *f*	pump
Kontrollvorrichtung *f* für Dichte *f*	density controller
Drosselventil *n* und Durchflußkontrolle *f*	pinch valve and flow recorder

---

granulierte Hochofenschlacke *f*, **(künstlicher) Schlackensand** *m*, **gekörnte Hochofenschlacke** *f* = slag sand, granulated blast-furnace slag
Granulierung *f*, **Körnungsverfahren** *n* = granulation (process)
Granulit *m* (Geol.) = granulite, whitestone
Granulometrie *f* = granulometry
graphische Darstellung *f*, siehe: Diagramm *n*
Graphit *m* (Min.) = graphite, plumbago, black lead
Gras|büschel *n* = clump of sod
~mäher *m* = lawn mower
~narbe *f* = grass cover
(~)Sode *f*, **(Rasen)Plagge** *f*, **Rasensode** *f* = (grass) sod, turf ~
Grat *m*, **Bohrgrat** = burr
Grathobel *m* = fillister plane
Gratifikation *f* = bonus

Grat|sparren m = hip rafter, angle ~, angle ridge
~stichbalken m, **Schifter** m, **Schiftersparren** m = jack rafter
~ziegel m = hip tile
kantig = angular
rund = round
gewölbt = bonnet
Graubraunstein m (Min.) = gray manganese(-ore), native manganic hydrate
Grau|erle f, **Weißerle** f = Turkey alder, upland ~
~gültigerz n, **(Kupfer)Fahlerz** = fahl-erz, fahl-ore, grey copper ore, tetrahedrite
~guß m, **Gußeisen** n = (gray) cast iron
~kalk m, **Schwarzkalk** = gray quicklime
~kobalterz n (Min.) = jaipurite, grey cobalt ore
Graup [*nach Fischer und Udluft (Jahr 1936) Boden von 20—2 mm, groß 20 bis 10 mm, mittel 10—5 mm, klein 5—2 mm*] = medium gravel and fine gravel (US) [*25.4 mm to 2.00 mm, "medium" 25.4 to 9.52 mm, "fine" 9.52—2.00*]
Graupelschauer m = graupel shower
Grau|silber n (Min.) = grey silver, carbonate of silver, selbite
~stein m = grey-stone
~wacke f = greywacke, graywacke
~wackenkalk m, **Übergangskalk** m = greywacke limestone, transition-lime
~wackensandstein m = trap sandstone
~wackenschiefer m = greywacke slate
gravimetrische Messungen fpl; siehe unter „geophysikalische Baugrunduntersuchung f"
gravitative Differentiation f (Geol.) = gravitational differentiation
Greifbagger m, **Baggergreifer** m, **Greif(er)kran** m, **Greifer** m, **Greiferbagger** = grab excavator, bucket crane, grab, grabbing crane, (grab) bucket crane
Greifer m, siehe: Greifbagger m
~, Winkel~ [*Gleiskette f*] = grouser
~ausrüstung f [*Kran m*] = grab equipment
~hubwerk n = grab(bing) hoisting gear
Greif(er)kran m, siehe: Greifbagger m

Greiferzahn m = grab(bing) bucket tooth, bucket ~
Greif|korb m, siehe: Baggerkorb
~korb m für allgemeine Bodenbaggerung, Stichboden und Gesteinstrümmer = multi-tine grapple
~kran m, siehe: Greifbagger m
~zange f = grab tongs
Greisen m (Geol.) = greisen
Grenz|fläche f = interface
~flächenkraft f, siehe: Adhäsion f
~flächenspannung f = interfacial tension, interface stress
~flächenwasser n, siehe: hygroskopisches Wasser
~lehre f = limit ga(u)ge
~linie f = limiting line
~sieblinie f, **Siebkennlinie** f = gradation limit, limiting grading curve, particle size (distribution) limit
~stein m, **Begrenzungsstein** = boundary stone
~wert m = limit(ing) value
~wert m für Stützweiten fpl, **Stützweitengrenzwert** m = limiting span
~zone f zwischen Land n und Wasser n = contacting zone of land and water
„**Griechisches Feuer** n" [*igne Vestae*] = "Greek Fire" [*Ignae Vestoe*]
griffig, siehe: gleitsicher
Griffigkeit f [*Straße f*] = non-skid property, road-skid quality, anti-skid property
Griffstange f = handle bar
Griesständer m, **Griessäule** f = sluice pillar
Gritt m [*nach Fischer und Udluft (Jahr 1936) 2,0—0,2 mm, nach Niggli (Jahr 1938) 2,0—0,2 mm (heißt hier „Grobsand"), nach Gallwitz 2,0—0,2 mm (heißt hier „Sand")*] = coarse sand and medium sand (Brit.) [*2.0—0.2 mm*]; coarse sand and medium sand (US) [*2.0—0.25 mm*]
Grob|anteil m = coarse fraction
~blech n, schweres Blech n = heavy (steel) plate
~brecher m, **Schotterbrecher** m = coarse crusher, ~ breaker, (stone) breaker
grobe Suspension f, siehe: Aufschlämmung f

grobes Schlämmkorn Va [*nach Dücker (Jahr 1948) 0,06—0,02 mm*] = coarse silt [*A.S.E.E. fraction 0.074—0.02 mm; British Standard 0.06—0.02 mm*]
~ **Siebkorn** *n*, siehe: Kiesel(stein) *m*
~ **Unkraut** *n* = débris
Grobbrechen *n*; siehe unter „Hartzerkleinerung *f*"
grobgriffig = coarse gripping
Grobkalk *m*, siehe: Pariser Kalkstein *m*
grob|keramische Industrie *f* = heavy-clay industry
~**keramischer Ofen** *m* = heavy clay klin
~**keramisches Erzeugnis** *n* = heavy clay article
Grob|kies *m* [*nach DIN 1179 und DIN 4022 (Jahr 1936) 70—30 mm, nach DIN 4220 70—20 mm, nach DEGEBO 20—ff0 mm, nach Niggli (Jahr 1938) 200—20 mm, nach Dienemann 20—10 mm (heißt hier „Grobschotterboden"), nach Fischer und Udluft (Jahr 1936) 200—20 mm (heißt hier „Brock"), nach Gallwitz (Jahr 1939) 200—20 mm (heißt hier „Schotter")*] = coarse gravel [*A.S.E.E. fraction 76.2 to 25.4 mm*]
~**kegelbrecher** *m* **mit segmentförmigem Brechkopf** *m* = coarse gyrasphere crusher
grobkörnig = coarse-grained
Grob|sand *m*, Schottersand [*nach Atterberg 2,0—0,2 mm, nach Fischer und Udluft (Jahr 1936) 2,0—0,2 mm (heißt hier „Gritt"), nach Niggli (Jahr 1938) 2,0—0,2mm, nach Gallwitz (Jahr 1939) 2,0—0,2 mm (heißt hier „Sand"), nach Dücker (Jahr 1948) 2,0—0,2 mm (heißt hier „mittleres Siebkorn IIIb" 2,0 bis 0,6 mm und „feines Siebkorn IVa" 0,6—0,2 mm, nach DIN 4022 2,0 bis 1,0 mm*] = coarse sand [*International Society of Soil Science 2.0—0.2 mm, A.S.E.E. fraction 2.00—0.59 mm, British Standard 2.0—0.6 mm, Division of Soil Survey (US) 2.0—0.25 mm*]; [*according to Atterberg, Fischer and Udluft, Niggli, Gallwitz, the size from 2.0 to 0.2 mm as classed by them and called by various names as indicated corresponds to the British Standard "coarse sand and medium sand" 2.0—0.2 mm*]

~**schluff** *m* [*nach Niggli (Jahr 1938) 0,02—0,002 mm, dieselbe Korngröße heißt nach Atterberg, Terzaghi, DIN 4022, Fischer und Udluft, Gallwitz und Grengg „Schluff", bei Dücker (Jahr 1948) umfaßt sie „grobes Schlämmkorn Vb" 0,02—0,006 mm und „mittleres Schlämmkorn VI a" 0,006 bis 0,002 mm*] = medium silt and fine silt [*British Standard "medium silt" 0,02 to 0,006 mm and "fine silt" 0,006 to 0,002 mm, "fine silt" A.S.E.E. fraction 0,02 mm to no size limit*]
~**schotter** *m* = coarse crushed stone
~**schotterboden** *m*; siehe unter „Grobkies *m*"
~**sieben** *n*, Grobsiebung *f* = coarse screening
~**sortierrost** *m*, siehe: Stangen(transport)rost
~**spalten** *n* [*Steine mpl mit Keilen mpl*] = blocking, sledging
Grobsplitt *m* = coarse stone chip(ping)
grobsteiniger Boden *m*; siehe unter „Block *m*"
Grob|zerkleinerung *f*; siehe unter „Hartzerkleinerung *f*"
~**zerkleinerungsmaschine** *f*, Brecher *m* = crusher, breaking machine
Groß|baustelle *f* = large-scale project site
~**bauvorhaben** *n*, Großprojekt *n* = large-scale project
~**betonanlage** *f*, siehe: Betonfabrik *f*
großblättrige Linde *f*, siehe: Sommerlinde *f*
Groß|bohrloch(spreng)verfahren *n* = large-diameter hole drilling and blasting, ~ ~ work
~**bohrwagen** *m*, siehe: Bohrjumbo *m*
~**brand** *m*, Großfeuer *n* = multiple-alarm fire
~**brecher** *m* = (large) primary crusher (or breaker), sledger, scalper, stonebreaker (type crusher)
~**bunkeranlage** *f*, siehe: Abmeßanlage für Betonzuschlagstoffe
Größen|analyse *f* = dimensional analysis
~**ordnung** *f* = order
in der ~ von = of the order of
Großerzeugung *f* = production-line method

Großfeuer — Grundierfarbe

Großfeuer *n*, siehe: Großbrand *m*
großflächiges Fundament *n*, siehe: Betonplattenfundament *n*
Groß|-Förderwagen *m*; siehe unter „Fahrzeuge *npl* für den Transport *m* von Boden *m* und Steinbaustoffen *mpl*"
~**formatstein** *m* = large building block
~**gerät** *n* = heavy plant, high-powered equipment, heavy duty construction equipment, major equipment
~**kaliberbohren** *n* = large hole drilling
~**löffel-Abraumbagger** *m*, siehe: Abraum-Hochlöffel(bagger) *m*
~**löffelbagger** *m* = large shovel (type) excavator
~**pflaster(decke)** *n*, (*f*) = large sett paving
~**pflasterstein** *m* = large (paving) sett
~**projekt** *n*, siehe: Großbauvorhaben *n*
~**raumgebiet** *n*, Wirtschaftsgebiet *n* einer großen Stadt *f* = metropolitan region, ~ area
~**raumlore** *f* **auf Gleisketten** *fpl*, Gleisketten(anhänger)wagen *m*, Großraum-Gleiskettenwagen *m*, Raupenanhängerwagen = caterpillar tread wagon, tractor wagon with track type equipment
~**raummischer** *m*, Großraummischmaschine *f* = large-capacity mixer, ~ mixing machine
~**raumschotterverteiler** *m* = large-capacity stone spreader box
~**siedlung** *f* = newtown
~**speicher** *m*; siehe unter „Talsperre *f*"
~**spritzgerät** *n*, siehe: Bitumen-Sprengwagen *m*
~**stadtleben** *n* = metropolitan activity
größte Durchbiegung *f* = maximum deflection
Größtmoment *n* = maximum moment
Groß|turmdrehkran *m* [*ein Portal n läßt den Raum m zwischen den Schienen fpl frei*] = portal-type (mono)tower crane, ~ revolving tower crane, ~ rotating tower crane
~**verbraucher** *m* = wholesale customer
(Groß) Verkehrsader *f*, Hauptfernverkehrsstraße *f* = traffic artery
Großversuch *m* = full-scale experiment, ~ test

großvolumiger Luftreifen *m*, siehe: Riesenluftreifen
Grübchen *n* = pitting
Grube *f* [*über Tage*] = pit
Gruben|aufzug *m*, siehe: Baugrubenaufzug
~**aufzug** *m* = mine hoist
~**aufzugstrommel** *f* = mine hoist drum
~**(förder)wagen** *m*, siehe: Grubenwagen
~**gasabsaugung** *f* = methane drainage
~**holz** *n* = pit props, mine timber
~**kalk** *m*, siehe: Kalkteig *m*
~**kies** *m* = pit gravel
~**lampe** *f* = miner's lamp
~**lok(omotive)** *f* = mine loco(motive), mining ~
~**schacht** *m*, Bergwerksschacht = mine shaft
~**schlacke** *f* = pit slag
~**sohle** *f* = pit floor
~**stempel** *m* = pit prop
~**wagen** *m*, Grubenförderwagen = mine car
~**wand** *f* = pit face
~**wetter** *n* = weather-damp, fire damp
Gruftgewölbe *n* = burial vault
Grünbleierz *n* (Min.), siehe: Pyromorphyt *m*
Grund|ablaß *m*; siehe unter „Talsperre *f*"
~**anlage** *f* = basic plant
~**anstrich** *m*, siehe: Grundierüberzug *m*
~**anstrich** *m* **auf Holz** *n* = filler coat, filling ~, flat ~
~**auslaß** *m*; siehe unter „Talsperre *f*"
~**ausleger** *m* [*Bagger m*] = basic jib (Brit.); ~ boom (US)
~**bagger** *m* = basic shovel
~**baumechanik** *f*, siehe: Bodenmechanik
~**bitumen** *n*, siehe: Ausgangsbitumen
~**bogen** *m*, siehe: Gegenbogen *m*
~**bruch** *m* = breach, subsidence, base failure, shear failure
~**eis** *n* = sponge ice, ground ~, anchor ~
~**erwerb** *m*, siehe: Baulandbeschaffung *f*
~**fläche** *f* = plan area
~**fläche** *f* [*zum Aufstellen n einer Maschine f*] = floor space
~**gerät** *n*, Geräteträger *m* = basic unit, ~ tool
Grundierfarbe *f* = priming paint, primer

Grundierüberzug m, Voranstrich m, Grund(ier)anstrich m = prime coat, priming ~, prime membrane
Grundlagen fpl **und praktische Anwendung** f = principles and practice
grundlegendes Prinzip n = underlying principle
Grund|linie f = base line
~**lohn** m = basic wage
~**luftzone** f = zone of aeration
~**masse** f (Geol.) = groundmass
~**moräne** f; siehe unter „Gletscher m"
~**platte** f = base plate, bed-plate
~**platte** f, Fundamentplatte = base slab, foundation plinth
~**rahmen** m [Sieb n] = base frame [screen]

~**rechtsbreite** f [Straße f] = right-of-way width, width of the road reservation
~**riß** m = (ground-)plan
~**rißsichtweite** f [Straße f] = sight distance in plan
~**schwelle** f, siehe: Bodenschwelle f
~**spannung** f = basic stress
~**stein** m = foundation stone
   den ~ legen = to lay the ~ ~
~**stück** n, siehe: Parzelle f
~**stückseigentümer** m = property owner
~**stücksentwässerungsanlage** f, Abwasserinstallation f = soil stack installation
Gründung f, Fundierung f, Fondation f = foundation
Gründungs|boden m, siehe: Untergrund m
~**fels** m = rock foundation

Gründungspfahl m, Tragpfahl m
  Holz~, Rundholz~
    unbehandelter Holz~
    behandelter Holz~

  Beton~
    Ort(beton)~, Betonort~

    Ort(beton)~ mit permanentem Blechmantel m
    Ortbeton ~ mit konischem Blechmantel m
      Raymond-Betonpfahl m mit konischen teleskopartigen Rohrschüssen mpl, konischer Hülsen-Rammpfahl
      Ortbetonpfahl mit konischem Blechmantel, der zwecks besserer Aufnahme des Außendrucks mit einem wellblechartig geformten Querschnitt im Kaltwalzverfahren hergestellt wird, Fabrikat THE UNION METAL MANUFACTURING CO., CANTON 5, OHIO, USA
        senkrechte Riefelung f
        Rammkern m
    Ort(beton)pfahl mit parallelseitigem Blechmantel m

foundation pile, bearing ~
  wood ~ ~, timber ~ ~
    plain wood ~ ~, plain timber ~ ~
    treated wood ~ ~, treated timber ~ ~
  concrete ~ ~
    cast-in-place ~ ~, cast-in-situ ~ ~, cast-in-the-ground ~ ~, situ-cast ~ ~

    cast-in-place concrete foundation pile with permanent steel shell
    tapered driven shell pile

      Raymond step taper concrete pile, step-tapered Raymond pile

      MONOTUBE foundation pile [*it has a scalloped cross-ssection which is formed by a series of vertical flutings running the full length of the pile. The pile is tapered and is closed at the bottom by a steel boot*] [*Trademark*]

        vertical flutings, internal driving core
    parallel-sided dropped-in-shell pile

Gründungspfahl

(Stahl)Rohrpfahl	(tubular) (steel-)pipe pile
Stahlrohrpfahl mit geschlossenem Ende *n*	closed-end pipe pile
Stahlrohrpfahl mit offenem Ende *n*	open-end pipe pile
Ort(beton)pfahl ohne permanentem Blechmantel	shell-less cast-in-place pile
Klumpfußpfahl *m*	pedestal shell-less pile
Kegelfußpfahl im Absenkverfahren nach Art der bekannten Brunnengründungen hergestellt, Fabrikat RAYMOND CONCRETE PILE CO.	caisson pile, concrete pier, belled-out pier, belled(-out) caisson, bell-bottom caisson
Stahlhülse *f*	steel shell
Stahlschuh *m*	steel boot
Stahldorn *m*	steel mandrel
Stahlrammkern *m*	steel driving core
Pfahl mit Klumpfuß (bzw. Kegelfuß) und ohne pernamentem Stahlmantel *m*	straight-shaft shell-less pile, straight-shaft pier
Fertigbeton~	precast ~ ~
konischer Fertigbeton~	tapered precast ~ ~
parallelseitiger Fertigbeton~, zylindrischer ~	parallel-sided precast ~ ~
Stahlbeton~	reinforced concrete ~ ~
Verbund~	composite (concrete and timber) ~, wood composite ~ ~
Holzpfahl mit Ortbeton	wood pile with cast-in-place concrete
Holzpfahl mit Fertigbeton	wood pile with precast concrete
Stahl~	steel ~ ~
H-Pfahl, Breitflanschträger~	steel H-beam pile
Schraub(en)~	screw ~ ~
Bohr~	drilled ~ ~, bored ~ ~
Druck~	pressure ~ ~
Fertig~	prefabricated ~ ~
Franki-~	Franki ~ ~ (or displacement caisson)
Hohl~	hollow ~ ~
Lot~	vertical ~ ~, plumb ~ ~
Mantel~, Reibungs~	friction(al) ~ ~
Mantelreibung *f*	skin friction, side friction
Pfahlfabrik *f*	~ ~ making plant
Probe~	test ~ ~
Ramm~, gerammter ~	driven ~ ~
Scheiben~	disc ~ ~
Schräg~	batter ~ ~, raking ~ ~
Simplex-~	Simplex ~ ~
Zug~	tension ~ ~
Spitzendruck~, Spitzen(belastungs) ~	point-bearing ~ ~, end-bearing ~ ~
schwebender ~, schwimmender ~	floating ~ ~
Pfahlfuß *m*	pile point

Gründungspfahl — Grüneiche

Pfahlkopf m	pile head
Stoßkoeffizient m	coefficient of restitution
Eindringung f infolge eines Schlages m	penetration of the pile into the soil per blow
Eindringungswiderstand m, Verdrängungswiderstand des Bodens m	penetration resistance, driving resistance
Elastizitätszahl f des Pfahlmaterials n	modulus of elasticity of pile
stehender ~	~ reaching down to load-bearing layer
kappen	to cap
Träger~, Stahlträger~	steel beam ~ ~
Versuchs~, Probe~	test ~ ~
Rammbeanspruchung f	driving stress
Fertigbetonpfahlfabrik f	pile-casting yard
Spülhilfe f	aid of jetting
Pfahlabstand m	pile spacing
Mittenabstand m	center-to-center spacing (US); centre-to-centre ~ (Brit.)
Pfahlgruppe f	pile group
Pfahlgruppierung f	spacing of piles in a group
Versinkungsgrenze f	failure load, ultimate load
Stahldrahtspiralen fpl [Raymondpfahl m]	spiral wire
verlorenes Futterrohr n, verlorener Blechmantel m [Raymondpfahl m]	permanent protective casing (or shell)
Stahlkern m [Raymondpfahl m]	mandrel, pile core
Vortreibrohr n	driving pipe
Franki-Pfahl m mit stählernem Treibkopf m	Frankignoul ~ ~
Spitzenwiderstand m	toe resistance, point resistance
Tragfähigkeit f	carrying capacity, bearing capacity

Gründungs|platte f, Fundamentplatte = foundation slab
~sohle f = foundation level
~tiefe f = depth of foundation
~wesen n, Fundationstechnik f = foundation engineering
Grundwasser n = (under)ground water, phreatic ~
~abdichtung f, siehe: Abdichtung
~(ab)senkungsanlage f; siehe unter „Entwässerung f"
~andrang m, Grundwassereinbruch m, Grundwasserzutritt m = ingress (or inflow, or inrush) of underground (or phreatic) water
~becken n = ground water well
~spiegel m, Grundwasserhorizont m, grundwasserspendende Schicht f = ground water table
~spiegelgefälle n = ground water table gradient
~stand m, Grundwasserhöhe f = ground water (-table) level, ground water elevation, standing water level
~strom m, Grundwasserlauf m = underground stream
~stromsickerung f, Sickerströmung f = (underground) seepage, under-seepage
~strömung f = ground-water flow
~verunreinigung f = ground water pollution
~zutritt m, siehe: Grundwasserandrang m
Grundwerkstoff m [Schweißen n] = base material, parent metal
grüne Ausblühung f, Vanadiumausblühung = green efflorescence
Grüneiche f = holm-oak

Grün|eisenerde *f*, Grüneisenerz *n*, Grüneisenstein *m* (Min.) = dufrenite, green iron ore
~**erle** *f*, siehe: Alpenerle
~**fläche** *f* = green area
~**gürtel** *m* = green belt
~**holz** *n* [*aus Guayana*] = green heart
~**land** *n* = grass land
~**landsmoor** *n* = meadow moor
~**ling** *m* = green product
~**schiefer** *m* = green schist
~**span** *m*, basisches Kupferazetat *n* = copper rust, verdigris
~**stein** *m* = greenstone
~**steintuff** *m*, siehe: Diabastuff
~**streifen** *m*, Rasentrennstreifen *m* [*Straße f*] = landscaped strip, grassy median ~, central grass reserve
Gruppenindexmethode *f* (**für die Dimensionierung von Straßendecken** *fpl*) = group index method (of pavement design)
Gruppierung *f* = grouping
Gufferlinie *f*; siehe unter „Gletscher *m*"
Gummi-Abfederungselement *n* = rubber suspension unit
Gummibehälter *m* **für Flüssigkeiten** *fpl* = rubber tank
gummibereifter Grabenbagger *m* = rubber tired ditcher (US); rubber-tyred ~ (Brit.)
~ **Löffelbagger** *m* = wheel-mounted shovel (-crane)
~ **selbstfahrbarer Universal-Bagger** *m* **(oder Universalkran)**, siehe: Autobagger *m*
gummibereiftes Erdbau-Lastfahrzeug *n*; siehe unter „Fahrzeuge *npl* für den Transport *m* von Boden *m* und Steinbaustoffen *mpl*"
Gummi|-Bitumen-Mineral-Gemisch *n* = rubber-asphalt paving mixture (US)
~**-Bitumen-Mischung** *f* = rubberized asphalt, rubber-asphalt blend (or mixture) (US); rubberized asphaltic bitumen, rubber bitumen mixture (Brit.)
~**blasenmethode** *f*, Ballonmethode [*Nachprüfung f der Verdichtung f*] = (waterfilled) rubber membrane method, rubber balloon ~

~**dichtungsstreifen** *m* = rubber water stop
~ **(-Elevator)becher** *m* = rubber elevator bucket
~**flanschendichtung** *f* = rubber gasket
~ **(förder)gurt** *m*, Gummi(förder)band *n* = rubber (conveyor) belt(ing) (or band)
~**fußboden** *m* = rubberplate (US)
~**lager** *n* = rubber bearing
~**laufkette** *f* = rubber crawler belt
~**masse** *f* = rubber composition, ~ compound
~**-Misch(er)schaufel** *f* = rubber blade, ~ paddle
~**pufferabstützung** *f* [*Erdtransportwagen m*] = rubber cushions
gummireifenfahrbar = rubber-tyre mounted (Brit.); rubber-tire ~ (US)
Gummi|schieber *m*, Schwabber *m* = squeegee
~**schlauch** *m* = rubber tube, rubber hose
~**schnur** *f* = shire
~**straße** *f*, siehe: Kautschuk(-Asphalt)-Straße *f*
gummiverträgliches Schmierfett *n* = rubber compatible grease
Gurt *m*, Gurtung *f* = chord, boom
~ *m*, Band *n* [*Bandförderer m*] = belt
~ [*Träger m*] = flange
~**becherwerk** *n*, Gurtelevator *m*, Bandbecherwerk, Band(becher)elevator = belt(-type bucket) elevator
~**breite** *f* [*Träger m*] = flange width
Gürtelradbodenverdichter *m*; siehe unter „Walze *f*"
Gurt|förderband *n*, siehe: Bandförderer *m*
~**förderer** *m*, siehe: Bandförderer *m*
~**förderer** *m* **mit Seilschrapperkasten** *m* = belt conveyor with cable-hauled bucket
~**lamelle** *f* [*Blechträger m*] = flange plate, cover ~
~**platte** *f* [*Blechträger m*] = cover plate, flange ~
~**plattenstoß** *m* = flange plate joint
~**querschnitt** *m* = flange section, chord ~
~**reihenbecherwerk** *n*, siehe: Gurtvollelevator *m*
~**tragrolle** *f* = carrier idler

Gurtung f, siehe: Gurt m
Gurt(ungs)stab m = boom member, chord ~
Gurt|versteifung f = boom bracing, chord ~, flange stiffening
~vollelevator m, Gurtreihenbecherwerk n, Gurtvollbecherwerk = continuous belt(-type bucket) elevator
~winkel m [*Blechträger* m] = flange angle
Gußasphalt m, Streichasphalt m, Mastixasphalt m = mastic asphalt [*deprecated: floated* ~]
~ausfuhrwagen m = mastic asphalt spreading cart
~decke f, Gußasphaltbelag m = mastic asphalt surfacing
(~-)Einachsmotorkocher m = single-axle mastic cooker with power stirring gear
~-Einbaukocher m = stationary mastic cooker
~fertiger m = mastic asphalt finisher (or finishing machine)
~kocher m, Mastixkocher m = mastic cooker, ~ asphalt mixer
~kocherei f, stationäre Asphaltkochanlage f = stationary mastic cooking plant
~kocher m **mit Dieselmotor** m = mastic cooker with diesel engine-driven stirring gear
~kocher m **mit Elektromotor** m = mastic cooker with electric motor-driven stirring gear
Gußasphalt m **mit Splitt** m = stone-filled mastic asphalt
~motorkocher m, Motorkocher für Gußasphalt m = mastic cooker with power stirring gear
~streicher m, Asphalteur m = spreader (Brit.)
~transportmaschine f, Gußasphalt-Transportwagen m = mastic asphalt mixer (and) transporter
Guß|betoneinrichtungen fpl = concrete spouting equipment
~betonrohr n = cast concrete pipe
~eisen n, siehe: Grauguß m
~eisenpflasterblock m = cast-iron block
~stahldraht m = cast steel wire
~stück n = casting
Gutachten n = report
Güte|klasse f = grade
~prüfung f = soundness test
Güterfernverkehr m = long-haul traffic
Güterichtlinien f, Normen fpl = standard specifications
Güter|nahverkehr m = short-haul traffic
~schuppen m = freight house
~transport m = commercial transport
~wagen m, siehe: Waggon m
Güte|überwachung f = quality control
~wert m [*Profil* n] = mechanical property
Guttaperchazündschnur f, wasserdichte Zündschnur f = white countered guttapercha waterproof fuse

H

haargenaue Einstellung f = hairline adjustment
Haar|kalkmörtel m = hair mortar
~kies m, Millerit m; NiS (Min.) = millerite, capillary pyrite
~nadelkurve f = hair-pin bend (or curve, or turn)
~rohr n, siehe: Kapillarrohr
~röhrchenwasser n, siehe: Kapillarwasser n
Hackboden m [*Erdbau* m]; mildes Gebirge n [*Tunnelbau* m] = hacking (Brit.)
Hacke f = hoe, pick
Hafen m **mit Betriebsanlagen** fpl = port
~anlagen f = harbo(u)r facilities
~bautechnische Gesellschaft e. V. = German Institute of Dock and Harbo(u)r Authorities
~becken n = basin
~brandung f = harbo(u)r surging
~einfahrt f = harbo(u)r entrance
~güterumschlagmittel n = cargo handling appliance (or gear)
~kran m = harbo(u)r crane
~speicher m = cargo warehouse
~stadt f = seaport town, harbo(u)r city (or town)
~technik f = harbo(u)r engineering
~-Wasserstand-Schwankung f = harbour surging (Brit.); harbor ~ (US)

Haff — Haldensand

Haff n = haff
Haftanreger m, siehe: Netzhaftmittel n
haftendes Lockergestein n, siehe: Bindeerde f
Haft|festigkeit f, Haftvermögen n = bond strength
~**festigkeitsmesser** m = adhesion meter
~**festigkeitsverbesserer** m, siehe: Netzhaftmittel n
~**grundmittel** n = wash-primer
~**mittel** n, siehe: Netzhaftmittel
~**pflichtversicherung** f = liability insurance
~**reibung** f = static friction
~**reibungsbeiwert** m = static coefficient of friction
~**spannung** f = bond stress
Haftung f [*Beton* m *an Eisen* n] = bond
Haftvermögen n, Haftfestigkeit f [*Beton an Eisen*] = bond strength
Haftvibrator m, Bunker-Rüttler m = bin vibrator
Hagel|korn n = hailstone
~**schauer** m = hail shower
Hainbuche f, Weißbuche f, Hagebuche f, Hornbaum m = white beach, hornbeam
Haken|blatt n; siehe unter „Holzverbindung f"
~**bolzen** m = hook bolt
~**buhne** f = groyne (Brit.)/groin (US) with short training wall
~**greifer** m, siehe: Motorgreifer(korb) m
~**kette** f = hook chain
~**rolle** f = hook roller
Haken m **und Öse** f = hook and eye
~**zange** f = hooked tongs
Halb|anhänger m, aufgesattelter Anhänger m, Auflieger m, Sattelschlepp-Anhänger m, Aufsattel-Anhänger m = semi-trailer
~**automat** m [*Betonsteinmaschine* f] = semi-automatic block machine
~**chlorschwefel** m = sulphur subchloride
halbautomatische Schweißung f = touch welding
halbes Kleeblatt n [*Anschlußstelle* f] = semi-cloverleaf type junction
halbfest = semi-solid

Halb|freiluft-Kraftwerk n; siehe unter „Talsperre f"
~**holz** n = scantling
~**hydrat(gips)** n, (m), verzögerter ~, $2CaSO_4 \times H_2O$ = retarded hemihydrate gypsum (-plaster)
~**insel** f = peninsula
~**kettenfahrzeug** n = semi-tracked vehicle
halbkontinuierliche Förderanlage f = power and free conveyor
Halbkreisbogen m, Rundbogen m, Zirkelbogen m, voller Bogen m = semicircular arch, round ~
halb|kristallin = hypocrystalline
~-**offen** [*Verschleißschicht* f] = medium-textured [*wearing course*]
Halb|parabelträger m = hog backed girder, semi-parabolic ~
~**portalkran** m, Halbtorkran m = semi-portal (type of pedestal) crane
~**rahmen** m = half frame
~**raum** m = halfspace, semi-infinite space
~**reineisen** n = half pure iron
~**rundstahl** m = half rounds
~**silikastein** m = semi-silica brick
halb|sphärisches Gewölbe n; siehe unter „Talsperre f"
~**stationäre Anlage** f, siehe: Baukasten-System-Anlage
Halb|tagsbeschäftigung f = part-time employment
~**tidebecken** n = half-tide basin
~**torkran** m, siehe: Halbportalkran
~**tränkung** f = semi-grouting (Brit.); semi-penetration treatment
halbversenkt [*Niet* m] = half sunk
Halde f, Vorrats~, Material~ = stockpile, (storage) pile, stock-heap
Halden|abzugsband n = reclaiming conveyor
~**erz** n = waste heap ore
~**lagerung** f, siehe: Haldenschüttung f
~**material** n = (stock-)pile(d) material
~**mischgut** n = stock pile mixture
~**rückverladung** f = stockpile re-handling
~**sand** m [*gekörnte auf die Halde gestürzte Hochofenschlacke* f] = stockpiled granulated blast-furnace slag

Halden|schlacke f = discarded slag
~schüttung f, **Haldenlagerung** f, **Deponie** f = (stock-)piling
~tunnel m, **Vorratstunnel**, **Entnahmetunnel** m, **Bandkanal** m = (stock) reclaiming tunnel, stockpile ~, conveyor ~, recovery ~
~tunnel-Abzugsband n = reclaiming tunnel conveyor
Halle f = hangar
Hälleflinta f (Geol.) = hälleflinta
Hallen|binder m = hall roof truss
~fußboden m = hangar ground floor
Halloysit m (Min.) = halloysite
Haloidsalz n = halide, haloid salt
Hals|lager n = steeve bearing
~niet m [*Blechträger* m] = flange rivet
Haltbar|keitsprüfung f, siehe: Beständigkeitsprüfung
~machung f, **Konservierung** f = preservation
Halte|bucht f **für Omnibusse** mpl = draw-in
~linie f, **Stoplinie** = stop line
~pfahl m = mooring pile
~sichtweite f = stopping distance
~stelle f = halt, stop, stopping-place
~zeichen n = stop sign, halt ~
Haltung f, **Streckenabschnitt** m, **Kanalhaltung**, **Staustrecke** f, **Stauhaltung** [*horizontale oder nahezu horizontale Wasserlaufstrecke im Schiffahrtskanal oder kanalisiertem Strom zwischen zwei Stauanlagen*] = level reach
Hamburger Zimmermann m = journeyman carpenter
Hammer|bohren n = hammer drilling
~brecher m = (swing-)hammer crusher, rotary hammer type breaker
~brecher mit starren Schlägern mpl, **Prallbrecher** = fixed hammer rotary breaker
~fertiger m, siehe: Stampfhammerfertiger
~kessel m = T-shaped boiler
~(kopf)kran m = hammerhead crane, giant cantilever crane
~kopfpfeiler m = hammerhead pier
~lötkolben m = soldering iron with edge, copper bit ~ ~

~(mahl)mühle f; siehe unter „Mühle"
~mühlenschläger m = swing hammer
~nietmaschine f = hammer riveting machine
~nietung f = hammer riveting
hammerrechtes Schicht(en)mauerwerk n = roughly squared coursed rubble masonry, squared rubble walling brought to courses
Hand|antrieb m = hand drive
~arbeit f = hand work, manual ~
~aufgabe f, siehe: Handbeschickung f
~-Auspreßrohr n, siehe: Hand-Einpreßrohr
~bagger m, **Sackbagger** = hand-dredge
~bedienung f; siehe unter „Baumaschinen" fpl und Baugeräte npl"
~beil n = hatchet
~beschickung f, **Handaufgabe** f = hand feed
~betätigung f, **Handbedienung** = manual operation
~betrieb m = hand operation
~blechschere f = hand plate shears, tinner's snip
~-Blockwinde f, siehe: Handflaschenzug m
~bodenfräse f = hand rotary tiller (or rotary hoe, or rotovator, or soil pulverizer)
~bohle f [*Verdichtungsgerät* n] = hand-operated compacting beam
~bohrer m, siehe: Brustleier f
~-Bohrhammer m, siehe: Hand-(Gesteins)Bohrhammer
~bohrmaschine f = hand drilling machine
~bohrung f [*Bohrtechnik*] = hand drilled well
~buch n = manual
~drehbohrung f [*Bodenuntersuchung* f] = auger boring
~-Druckluftrüttelbohle f, **Hand-Preßluftrüttelbohle** = manually operated pneumatic tamper (or tamping beam, or compacting beam)
~eimer m = hand bucket
~einbau m [*Straßendecke* f] = hand spreading, manual laying
~einbau m, **Handverlegung** f [*z. B. Steindeckwerk* n] = hand placement, ~ placing

Hand-Einpreßrohr *n*, Hand-Injektionsrohr *n*, Hand-Auspreßrohr, Hand-Verpreßrohr= injection lance
Handels|dampfer *m* = commercial steamer
~eisen *n*, gewalztes Grobeisen = commercial iron, merchant ~
~güte *f* = commercial quality, ~ grade
~hafen *m* = commercial port
~marine *f* = merchant marine
~metropole *f* = commercial metropolis
Hand|-Explosionsramme *f*, siehe: Brennkraft-Handramme
~fahrgestell *n* = hand-guided carrier
~fahrwerk *n* [*Hängebahnwaage f*] = hand travel(l)ing gear
~fäustel *m* = mash hammer, lump ~
~-Felsbohrhammer *m*, siehe: Hand-(Gesteins)Bohrhammer
~fertiger *m* = hand finisher
~feuerlöscher *m* = fire drencher, ~ extinguisher
~flaschenzug *m*, Hand-Blockwinde *f* = hand-operated hoist block, ~ pulley ~, ~ lifting ~, ~ block (and tackle)
~(förder)karre(n) *f*, (*m*), Handtransportkarr(e)n = hand (push) cart
handgeführt [*z. B. Walze, Stampfer, Gesteinsbohrer, also in Bewegung befindliche Geräte*] = hand-held, hand-operated, manually-operated, hand-guided
handgeführter Rüttelfertiger *m*, Handvibrations(glätt)bohle *f*, Handrüttelfertiger, Handrüttelbohle, handgeführte Rüttelbohle *f*, Handvibratorbohle, Handvibrationsfertiger, Vibrationsfertiger mit Handvorschub *m* = hand-operated (or hand-held, or manually-operated) vibrating finisher (or screed), hand vibrating screed, hand-wheel propelled vibrating concrete finisher
~ Rüttelstampfer *m*, Handrüttelstampfer = hand-guided vibration-and-tamping compaction machine
Hand-(Gesteins)Bohrhammer *m*, Hand-Felsbohrhammer = hand (-held) rock drill, (hand) hammer (rock) drill, (rock) drill hammer, rock drill
handgesteuerte Signalregelung *f*, Handsteuerung von Verkehrssignalen *npl* = manual control of taffic signals

handgesteuertes Verkehrssignal *n* = manually controlled traffic signal
Hand|griff *m* = handle
~habung *f* = manipulation
~hammer *m* = hand hammer
~hebebock *m*, siehe: Handwinde *f*
~hebel *m* = hand lever
~hebelvorschub *m* = hand lever feed
~hubwerk *n* = hand-operated lifting machine, manual hoist
~-Injektionsrohr *n*, Hand-Einpreßrohr, Hand-Auspreßrohr, Hand-Verpreßrohr = injection lance
~kabel(trommel)winde *f*, Handkabel-(trommel)windwerk *n*, Erdwinde *f*, Affe *m*, Hand(seil)winde, mechanische Hand(trommel)winde *f* = hand (steel, or wire, or steel wire) cable winch, hand wire rope winch
~karre(n) *f*, (*m*), Handförderkarre(n), Handtransportkarre(n) = hand (push) cart
~kettenzug *m* = hand-chain block
~kompressor-Spritzmaschine *f* = spraying machine (or sprayer) with hand-operated (air) compressor and hand lance
~kran *m*, handbetriebener Kran = hand-operated crane
~kurbel *f* = hand crank, cranked handle
~lampe *f*, Handleuchte *f* = hand lamp, inspection ~, portable ~
~langerstunde *f*, Hilfsarbeiterstunde = common labourer hour
~laufkatze *f*, Handlastkatze = hand-operated troll(e)y
~leiste *f*, Handlauf *m* [*Geländer n*] = hand rail
~lenkvorrichtung *f* = steering lever
~leuchte *f*, siehe: Handlampe *f*
~loch *n* [*am Dampfkessel m*] = hand hole
~nietmaschine *f* = hand riveting machine
~nietung *f*, Handnieten *n* [*von Hand geschlagene Nietung mit Handdöpper und Hammer*] = riveting by hand, hand riveting
~rad-(Schrauben)Spindel *f* = hand-wheel screw
~ramme *f* = punner (Brit.); hand rammer

Hand|ramme *f*; siehe unter „Rammanlage *f*"
~rohr *n* **mit Düse** *f* [*Handspritzmaschine f*] = spray lance, hand ~
~rührwerk *n*, Handrührer *m* = hand-operated stirring gear
~rüttelbohle *f*, siehe: handgeführter Rüttelfertiger *m*
~rüttelfertiger *m*, siehe: handgeführter Rüttelfertiger
~rüttelstampfer *m*, siehe: handgeführter Rüttelstampfer
~rüttler *m*, Handvibrator *m* = hand vibrator
~säge *f*, siehe: Fuchsschwanz *m*
~schacht *m* = hand(-digged) shaft
~schild *n*, Schweißerschild = face shield, hand screen, hand shield
~schlagnietmaschine *f* **mit Bügel** *m* = pinch bug riveter
~schlauch *m* = hand hose
~schleifmaschine *f* = hand grinder
~schleifmaschine *f* **mit Biegewelle** *f* = flexible shaft hand grinder
~schmierpresse *f* = grease gun
~schneidbrenner *m* = hand flame cutter
~schotter *m* = hand-broken metal
~schrapper *m*, Räumschaufel *f*, Schrapperschaufel = hand scraper, manually guided drag skip
~schrapper-Winde *f* = hand scraper winch
~schürfbohrloch *n* = auger hole
~schweißen *n*, Handschweißung *f* = hand welding, manual ~
~ (seil)winde *f*, siehe: Handkabel(trommel)winde
~siebung *f* = hand sieving
~skizze *f* = free-hand sketch
~sortierung *f* = hand sorting
~speichenrad *n* = hand spoke wheel
~splittstreuer *m*, Splittstreukarre(n) *f*, (*m*), Handsplittverteiler, Handsplittstreugerät *n* = hand-operated chipping(s) spreader, barrow-type ~ ~
~spritzgerät *n*, Handspritzmaschine *f* = small pressure (or hand) sprayer (or distributor)
~stampfbohle *f* **mit Druckluft** *f* = hand-operated pneumatic concrete tamper
~stampfer *m* = hand tamper
~ (strich)ziegel(stein) *m*, Handstrichstein = hand-formed brick, hand-made ~
~stück *n* [*Mineral n*] = hand specimen, ~ sample [*mineral*]
~transportkarre(n) *f*, (*m*), siehe: Handkarre(n)
~verlegung *f*, siehe: Hand-einbau *m*
~-Vibrations(glätt)bohle *f*, siehe: handgeführter Rüttelfertiger *m*
~winde *f*, Handhebebock *m* = hand jack
~winde *f*, siehe: Handkabel(trommel)winde
~ziegel *m*, siehe: Hand(strich)ziegel
Hanf|seele *f*; siehe unter „Drahtseil *n*"
~seil *n* = hemp rope
Hang *m*, siehe: (Ab)Hang *m*
~böschung *f* = hillside slope
Hänge|bahnwaage *f* = suspension rail type travel(l)ing weighbatcher
~birke *f* = drooping birch, weeping ~
~brücke *f*; siehe unter „Brücke *f*"
~decke *f* = hung ceiling, suspended ~
~gefäßwaage *f*, Hängebehälterwaage = suspension hopper scale, ~ bucket ~
~gerüst *n*, siehe: Hängerüstung *f*
~gurtung *f* = suspension boom (or chord)
~konstruktion *f* = hanging system, suspender frame
~leiter *f* = suspension ladder
Hangende *n* (Geol.) = overlying layer, roof
Hangentnahme *f* = hillside borrow
Hänge|rüstung *f*, Hängegerüst *n* = suspended scaffold(ing), hung ~
~säule *f* = 1. king post, broach ~; 2. queen post; 3. truss post [*is either of the two*]
~schiene *f* = suspension rail, overhead ~
~sieb *n* = suspended screen
~sprengwerk *n* = composite truss frame
~stange *f* [*Brücke f*] = suspension rod, suspender
~tal *n* = hanging valley
~waage *f* **mit fester Aufhängung** *f* **unter den Bunkertaschen** *fpl* = weigh-batcher permanently fixed under the bin discharge gates
~werk *n* = suspension structure

Hang|-Kippschar f, siehe: Böschungshobel m
~rampe f = hillside ramp
~rinne f, Auffangrinne f = intercepting gutter, ~ channel
~sickerung f = side-hill seepage
~stollen m = upper gallery, hanging ~
~straße f = (side-)hill road
~tag(es)wasser n = hill-side surface water
Harke f, Rechen m = rake
harmonische Schwingung f = harmonic vibration
Harmotom m (Min.) = harmotome
Harnisch m, siehe: Rutsch ~
Hart|alabaster m, siehe: Marmorgips m
~asphalt m (Geol.) = hard asphalt
~branntstein m, siehe: Vormauerziegel m
Härte|kammer f [Erhärtung f von Betonfertigwaren fpl] = curing chamber
~öl n, siehe: Temperöl

Hart|faserplatte f = hardboard
~gestein n = hard rock, ~ stone
~gußasphalt m = hand-laid stone-filled asphalt
~holz n, Laubholz n = hard wood, leaf ~, deciduous ~
~kobalterz n (Min.) = modumite
~löten n = brazing, hard soldering
~lötlampe f = brazing lamp
~metallbohrung f = steel drill boring
~metallschneide f; siehe unter „Bohrmeißel m"
~papier n = kraft paper, Manila ~
~schicht f (Geol.) = hardpan
~schnee m = hard(-packed) snow
~stahlschöpfkante f = elevator bucket edge made of hard steel
~steinkohlenteerpech n = hard coal-tar pitch
~steinsplitt m, siehe: Granitsplitt
Härtungsmittel n, siehe: Betonhärtemittel

Hartzerkleinerung f

Brechen n, Grobzerkleinerung f, Vorzerkleinerung
  Vorbrechen n
  Grobbrechen n, Grobbruch m

  Feinbrechen n, Nachbrechen n, Feinbruch m, Nachbruch

  Zwischenbrechen n

Mahlen n, Mahlung f, Feinzerkleinerung f
Aufgabegut n
Überlauf m
gleichmäßiges Endprodukt n
kubisches Endprodukt n
Feinstmahlung f

comminution, crushing and grinding
crushing, coarse reduction

  primary crushing
  coarse crushing [discharge at sizes 4 to 6 inch or coarser]
  secondary crushing, fine crushing, reduction [discharge at sizes $1/4$ inch or finer]
  intermediate crushing [discharge at sizes $1/2$ or $3/8$ inch]

grinding, granulation, fine reduction
raw material [rock or ore]
oversize, rejects, tailings, (crusher) waste
uniform product
cubical product
pulverizing, pulverization

Hartzerkleinerungsmaschinen fpl = = crushing and grinding equipment
Harz n = resin
~bitumen n = resinous bitumen (Brit.); ~ asphalt (US)
~gang m [Holz n] = resin duct
~kiefer f, siehe: Terpentinkiefer
~klebemasse f = resin gluing compound

harzmodifiziertes Kunstharz n = rosin-alkyd resin
Harz|öl n, Harznaphtha n, f = resin oil
~pech n = resin pitch
~spiritus m = resin spirit
Haselrüster f, siehe: Bergulme f
Haspel f, m = rope reel

Haspen *m* **und Krampe** *f*, Überwurf *m* = hasp and staple
Haube *f* = hood
Hauer *m* [*Bergbau m*] = hagger, hewer
Häufelpflug *m* = ridging (or double-breasted, or moulding) plough (Brit.)/plow (US)
Haufwerk *n* [*Steinbruch m*] = rock pile
~ ; siehe unter „Tunnelbau *m*"
~**lader** *m* = windrow and stockpile loader
Haupt *n* = head [*e. g. of a dock*]
~**achse** *f* = principal axis
~**drän** *m*; siehe unter „Entwässerung"
~**fernverkehrsstraße** *f*, siehe: (Groß-)Verkehrsader *f*
~**öffnung** *f* [*Brücke f*] = main span
~**pumpe** *f* = main pump
~**schild** *n* [*Autobahnausfahrt f*] = advance direction sign
~**spannung** *f* = principal stress
~**stadtstraße** *f* = major street, ~ highway, arterial (street)
~**straße** *f*, Vorfahrtstraße = major road, ~ highway
~**straßenpaar** *n* = arterial pair
~**strecke** *f* = trunk route
~**strommotor** *m* = series wound motor
~**träger** *m* = main girder
~**verkehrsstromlinie** *f* = major desine line
~**verkehrsstunden** *fpl*, Hauptverkehrszeit *f* = rush hours
(~) **Wasserrohr** *n* = water main casing
Haus|abwasser *n*; siehe unter „Abwasserwesen *n*"
~**anschluß** *m*, Gebäudeanschluß [*z. B. Rohrleitung f*] = house connection, building ~
~**bau** *m* = housing work, house building
Häuserfront *f* = building frontage
Hausmannit *m* (Min.), siehe: Glanzbraunstein *m*
Haustein *m* = dressed stone
Häutchenwasser *n*, siehe: hygroskopisches Wasser
Hauyn (Min.) = hauyne, haüynite
HD-Öl *n*, siehe: Hochdruckschmiermittel *n*
Hebe|baum *m*, siehe: Brechstange *f*

~**bock** *m*, Winde *f*, (An)Hebespindel *f*, Hubspindel = jack
~**bühne** *f* = lifting plattform
Hebel|arm *m* = lever arm
~**bedienung** *f*, Hebelbetätigung = lever control
~**schalter** *m* = knife switch
~**stange** *f* = lever rod
~**wirkung** *f* = leverage action
Heberüberlauf *m*, Saug~ = siphon(ic) spillway
Hebe|transportstapler *m*, siehe: Hubstapler
~**werk** *n*; siehe unter „Schiffshebeanlage *f*"
~**zeug** *n* = elevating plant, lifting appliance, hoisting machine, lifting tackle
~**zwinge** *f*, Hebezwänge *f* = dog, pinch bar, lifting bar, dolly bar, clan bar, wrecking bar
Heckenschneider *m*, Gartenschere *f* = hedge trimmer, garden shears
Heck|motor *m* = rear engine
~**schild** *m* = rear blade
Heft|niet *m* = tack(ing) rivet, stiten ~
~**nieten** *n*, Heftnietung *f* = tack riveting
~**schweißen** *n* = tack welding
Heide *f*, Heideland *n* = heath (land)
~**plagge** *f* = sod of heath
~**sand** *m* = heath sand
Heilquelle *f* = healing spring
Heiß|asphalt *m* = hot asphalt
~ **(einbau-)Teerfeinbeton** *m* = hot-laid fine tar concrete
~ **(einbau-)Teergrobbeton** *m* = hot-laid coarse tar concrete
~**einbau(weise)** *m*, (*f*) [*Straßenbau m*] = hot-laid process, hot-laid method of construction
heißer Sandasphalt *m*, siehe: dichter ~
Heißflurtrocknung *f* [*Ziegel m*] = hot-floor drying [*brick*]
Heißmisch|anlage *f*; siehe unter „Makadäm-Maschinenanlage *f*"
~**makadam** *m* = hot-mixed macadam
Heißmischung *f* [*Straßenbau m*] = hot plant mix
Heißmischverfahren *n* = hot-plant mixing

Heißteer m = hot tar, TH
Heiz|bohle f = hot screed
~element n **aus Zirkonoxyd** n [*elektr. Widerstandsofen* m] = oxide resistor
Heizer m, **Kesselbediener** m, **Kesselwärter** m = fireman, stoker
Heiz|kammer f, **Feuer(ungs)raum** m = fire box
~kanal m = heating duct
~kessel m, siehe: Kocher m
~kessel m = boiler
~körper m = heat-transfer element, heating ~
~mantel m, **Dampfheizmantel** = steam jacket
~mantelrohr n = jacketed pipe
~öl n = burning oil, fuel oil (residue)
~öl n **für Dampferzeugung** f = oil fuel
~röhrenkessel m, **Heizrohrkessel**, **Feuerröhrenkessel** = fire (or smoke) tube boiler, multitubular ~, multitube ~
~schlange f, **Erhitzerschlange**, **Wärmeschlange** = heating coil
~wert m = calorific value
Helge f, siehe: Helling f
Heliotrop m (Min.) = heliotrope, bloodstone
hellbrauner Glimmer m, siehe: Phlogopit m
helles Bitumen n, siehe: Albino-Bitumen
Helling f, **Helge** f = building slip(way)
Helm m, **Sandhalm** m, **Sandhafer** m, **Strandhafer** m = sand-sedge
hemipelagische Meeresablagerung f = continental deposit, hemipelagic ~
Hemmschuh m = skid-pan, wheel block
Herabsetzungsbeiwert m = reduction coefficient
Hercynit m (Min.), siehe: Eisenspinell m
Herdmauer f; siehe unter „Talsperre f"
Herstellung f **benachbarter Plattenfelder in zeitlichem Abstand**, **Wechselfeldeinbau** m [*Betondeckenbau* m] = alternate bay method, ~ (concrete) bay construction
Herstellungs|platz m, **Betonierungsplatz** = casting yard [*precast concrete units*]
~werk n = manufacturing plant
herumlegen, umschlagen; siehe unter „Drahtseil n"

hervorstehend = proud [*of the surface*]
Herzriß m, siehe: Kernriß
Hessonit m (Min.) = hessonite, cinnamon stone
heteromorphes Gestein n = heteromorphous rock
Heulandit m, **Blättersiedestein** m (Min.) = heulandite
hexagonal = hexagonal
HHQ [*größte überhaupt bekannte Abflußmenge* f] = flood intensity
HICO-Schalungsträger mpl [*Trademark*], Fabrikat NORDDEUTSCHE SCHRAUBEN- UND MUTTERN-WERKE A.G., PEINE, DEUTSCHLAND = HICO patent shuttering units, HICO (adjustable horizontal) form supports, HICO steel form supports; HICO centering (US); HICO centring (Brit.); HICO (form-)girders [*Trademark*]
Hiddenit m (Min.) = hiddenite
Hilfs|arbeiter m = unskilled worker, labo(u)rer
~bewehrung f, **Hilfsarmierung** f = secondary reinforcement, subsidiary ~
~buhne f = temporary (or auxiliary) groyne
~fahrwerk n = auxiliary travel(l)ing gear, ~ undercarriage
~polier m = sub-foreman
~quelle f = resource
~schachtmeister m = sub-ganger
Hinter|achse f = rear axle
~achse f **mit Planetengetriebe** n **in den Hinderradnaben** fpl = planetary rear axle
~achsenantrieb m = final drive, rear axle ~
~böschung f = back slope
~deich m = inner dike, ~ dyke
hinterfüllen = to backfill around
Hinter|füllung f = back fill
~kante f = trailing edge [*of the finishing screed*]
~kippentleerung f = end-dumping
~kipper-Last(kraft)wagen m, **Hinter-Kipper(-LKW)** = end-tip(ping)(motor)lorry(Brit.); end-dump truck, rear-dump truck (US)

Hinter|kippung f, Hinterkippen n = rear dumping, end ~
~kippwanne f = rear dump body
~Iand n = hinterland
~mauer(ungs)block m = back-up block
~mauer(ungs)stein m = backing brick, common ~
~preßdruck m = grouting pressure
~radantrieb m = rear wheel drive
~radlenkung f = rear wheel steer(ing)
~spritzkessel m = bougie (Brit.); (pressure) grouting pan, pressure pot
~walze f = rear roll
hin- und hergehende Bewegung f, Rüttelbewegung = reciprocating motion
Hirseneisenstein m, Hirseneisenerz n (Min.) = oölitic hematite
historische Geologie f, siehe: Formations- und Schichtenkunde f
Hitzschlag m = heat apoplexy
Hobelmesser n; siehe: unter „Motor-Straßenhobel m"
Hoch|absetzer m, siehe: Dammschütter-Bandabsetzer m
~baggerung f = excavation of material which has a face
Hochbau m = building construction
~auftrag m = building erection contract
~-Fahrband(förderer) n, (m) = builder's conveyor
~klinker m, siehe: Klinkerziegel m
~kran m; Baukran = building crane
~raupenkran m [dieser Ausdruck ist besser durch „Hochbaugleiskettenkran" zu ersetzen] = track-(laying)type longboom crane (US); ~ long-jib ~ (Brit.)
~wand f = building wall
Hoch|behälter m, siehe: Wasser ~
~bocken n = jacking up
~bordstein m, siehe: Bordschwelle f
~druck-Dampferhärtung f [Betonstein m] = high-pressure steam curing
~druckfett n = high-pressure lubricating grease
~druckfettschmierung f = high-pressure grease lubrication
~(druckgebiet) n, siehe: Antizyklon m
Hochdruck|-Heißwasserheizung f = H.P.H.W. system

~kompressor m, Hochdruck(luft)verdichter m = high-pressure (air) compressor
~-Schlauchleitung f = high-pressure hose line
~schmiermittel n, HD-Öl n = extreme pressure lubricant, EPL
~turbine f = high-pressure turbine
~wasserstrahl m = high pressure water jet
Hoch|ebene f = high plain, plateau
~einbau m [Frostschutzschicht f] = frost blanket laid on old pavement
hochenergetische Strahlung f = high energy radiation
hochfest = high-strength
hochfeste Schraube f = high-strength bolt, high-tensile ~
Hochflutebene f, siehe: Auenebene
Hochfrequenz|fertiger m; siehe unter „Betonrüttelgeräte npl"
~induktionsofen m = high frequency induction furnace
~schwingverdichter m; siehe unter „Betonrüttelgeräte npl"
~-Vibrationstechnik f = high-frequency vibration technique
Hoch|gebirge n = high mountain(s)
~haus n = tall building
~hauskletterkran m = climbing tower crane
~hauskran m = rotary tower crane
hoch|hydraulischer Kalk m = (eminently) hydraulic lime (Brit.); highly hydrated lime, special lime, autoclaved lime, pressure-hydrated lime, hydraulic lime (US)
~kant = on edge
Hoch|kipper m, siehe: Hubkipper
~ladeschaufel f, siehe: (Front-)Ladeschaufel
~leistungsmaschine f, Hochleistungs-Gerät n [z. B. Rüttelstampfmaschine f] = high-capacity machine, high-production ~
~leistungs-Siebmaschine f, Hochleistungssieb n = high-capacity screen
hoch|liegender (Vorrats) Silo m = elevated storage bin
~liegendes Gelände n = high ground
Hochlöffel(bagger) m, siehe: Löffelhochbagger m

Hoch|löffeleinrichtung — hochwertiger Stahl

Hoch|löffeleinrichtung *f*, Löffelhocheinrichtung = face shovel attachment, crowd shovel fitting
~löffelinhalt *m* = (shovel) dipper capacity
~moortorf *m* = hill peat
Hochofen|gas *n*, Gichtgas *n* = top-gases, blast-furnace gas
~schaumschlacke *f*, schaumige Hochofenschlacke, aufgeblähte (oder geschäumte) Hochofenschlacke *f*, Hüttenbims *m*, Kunstbims *m* = foamed (blast-furnace) slag (Brit.); expanded slag (US)
~schlacke *f*, Stückschlacke, Eisenhochofen-Stückschlacke = (iron-ore) blast-furnace slag, lump =
hochraffiniertes aromatenarmes Spindelöl *n* [*mit Rüböl verschnitten*] = mineral colza oil
~ Benzin *n* = normal benzine
hoch|schwefelhaltige Ammonsulfoseife *f* aus Schieferöl *n* = ichthyol
~siedendes Leuchtöl *n*, hochraffiniertes aromatenarmes Solaröl *n* = mineral seal oil
~siedendes Lösungsbenzin *n* = heavy petroleum spirit
Hochspannungsleitung *f* = high voltage line
hochstegig [*Träger n*] = deep webbed
Hochstraße *f*, Brückenstraße *f* = overhead roadway, ~ highway, elevated ~, expressway; skyway (US)
Höchst|achslast *f* = maximum axle load
~geschwindigkeit *f* [*Fahrzeug n*] = maximum speed
~last *f*, siehe: Maximallast
~trockenraumgewicht *n* = maximum dry density
~verkehr *m* = peak traffic
~wasserstand *m* = high water [*abbrev.* H.W.]
höchstzulässige Gradiente *f* = limiting (or ruling) gradient
Hochtemperatur|-Dampferhärtung *f* [*Betonstein m*] = high-temperature steam curing
~verkokung *f* = high-temperature carbonization
Hoch- und Niederdruckturbine *f* **mit entgegengerichteter Dampfströmung** *f* = double-flow turbine

hochviskoses Bindemittel *n* = high-viscosity binder
~ Schmieröl *n* = bright stock, cylinder ~
Hochwasser *n* = flood(water)
~ablagerung *f* = flood plain deposit
~alarmsystem *n*, Hochwasserwarn(ungs)-dienst *m* = flood warning system
~ (auffang)becken *n*, Hochwasserspeicher *m* = flood basin, ~ storage ~, ~ pool, ~ storage reservoir, flood-control reservoir
~bett *n* = major bed
~deich *m*, HW-Schutzdamm *m*, Uferdamm *m* = levee (US); flood bank (Brit.)
~entlastung *f*, Hochwasserabführung *f* = flood relief, ~ discharge
~entlastungsanlage *f*; siehe unter „Talsperre *f*"
~häufigkeit *f* = flood frequency
~katastrophe *f* = flood disaster, ~ calamity
~-Kontrollbauwerk *n* = floodway control structure
~regelung *f* = flood control (operation)
~regulierungsbauwerk *n* = floodway control structure
~regulierungskanal *m* = river flood control channel
~schätzung *f* = flood estimation
~schutz *m*, Hochwasserabwehr *f* = flood protection
~schutzbauten *f* = flood protection works
~schutztalsperre *f*, Hochwasser(auffang)-sperre *f* = flood (control) dam
~speicher *m*, siehe: Hochwasser(auffang)-becken *n*
~speicherung *f*; siehe unter „Talsperre *f*"
~spitze *f* = peak flow, emergency flood flow
~-Sprengdeich *m* = "fuse plug" levee (US); ~ ~ flood bank (Brit.)
~statistik *f* = records of actual floods
~stollen *m*, Überlaufstollen *m* = tunnel type discharge carrier
~überlauf *m*; siehe unter „Talsperre *f*"
~versicherung *f* = flood insurance
~vorhersage *f* = flood prediction
~welle *f* = flood discharge
hochwertiger Stahl *m* = high-grade steel, high-tensile ~

hochwertiges Leuchtöl n = long-time burning oil
Hochwohnhaus(block) n, (m) = high (block of) flats
Höhe f [*über einem Bezugspunkt m*] = elevation, height
~ [*von Trägern mpl usw.*] = depth
~ f über NN, Seehöhe f [*NN = Normal Null = mittlere Seehöhe f*] = altitude above (mean) sea-level
Höhenaufnahme f; siehe unter „Vermessungskunde f"
höhengleiche (oder niveauebene) Straßenkreuzung f **mit Lichtzeichenregelung** f, **signalgesteuerter Knoten** m = signalized street intersection, signal-controlled intersection
Höhen|linie f = contour line
~**linienkarte** f, **Höhenplan** m = contoured plan, contour map, layered map
~**messer** m = altimeter
~**pfahl** m, **Höhenpflock** m = finishing (or grade, or gradient, or level, or fill) peg (or stake)
~**plan** m, siehe: Höhenlinienkarte f
~**unterschied** m = difference in level (or elevation)
hohe Stelle f [*in einer Fläche f*] = bump
hoher Pfahlrost m, siehe: Stelzenunterbau m
höher legierter Stahl m = high alloy steel
höhere Geodäsie f; siehe unter „Vermessungskunde f"
~ **Gewalt** f = Act of God
Hohl|balkenmaschine f, siehe: Balkenformmaschine
~**blockstein** m, **Hohlblockziegel** m = hollow (clay) building (or masonry) block, hollow concrete block, concrete hollow brick; structural hollow tile (US)
~**bohrer** m = hollow drill
~**bohrstange** f = hollow drill (or boring) rod
~**eisen** n, Hohlbeitel m = gouge
hohles baukeramisches Erzeugnis n = hollow ceramic unit for construction
(Hohl)Fugeneisen n = expansion joint cap strip (US); metal sleeve (or capping) (Brit).
~**imprägnierung** f, siehe: Rüping(spar)-verfahren n

~**kammerbereifung** f = pneumatic tyres (Brit.); ~ tires (US)
~**kant** n = hollow chamfer
~**kanteisen** n = fluted bar
~**kastenbauweise** f = box-type construction
~**kehle** f = fillet
~**kolben** m = hollow piston
~**mauer** f, Hohlwand f = cavity wall, hollow ~
~**maueranker** m = cavity-wall tie
~**mauerwerk** n = masonry cavity wall
~**pfahl** m; siehe unter „Gründungspfahl m"
~**profil** n = hollow section
~**querschnitt** m = hollow section
~**raum** m, Pore f = pore, void, interstice
hohlraum|arm, siehe: dicht
~**arme Mischung** f = mix with the least amount of voids
~**frei** = voidless
Hohl|raumminimum n = maximum density
~ **(stau)mauer** f; siehe unter „Talsperre f"
~**stütze** f = hollow stanchion
~**wand** f = carity wall
~**träger** m, Hohlbalken(träger) m = hollow girder (Brit.); ~ beam
~**ziegel** m = hollow brick, cavity brick
~**ziegelmundstücke** npl = dies
HOLDER-Diesel-Einachsräumer m = hand-guided diesel two-wheel dozer, Make: HOLDER G. m. b. H., GRUNBACH bei STUTTGART, DEUTSCHLAND
Höllenstein m, Silbernitrat n = lunar caustic
Holm m = cross (or capping) beam, waling
Holunder m = elder
Holz|abfuhrweg m, Holzaufbringungsstraße f = logging road
~**aufbringungs(trommel)winde** f = logging winch, timber towing ~, logging hoist
~**auskleidung** f = horizontal timber sheeting, lagging
~**axt** f = wood cutter's axe, felling ~
~**balkendecke** f = wooden beam floor
~**bearbeitungsmaschine** f = woodworking machine

Holz|bohrer m = wood borer, auger
~brand m = gangrene
~dalbe f = timber dolphin
(~)Daube f, Faßdaube = (timber) slat, wooden slat, barrel slat, stave
~dreieckleiste f = triangular wooden fillet
hölzerne Pflasterramme f, siehe: Holzstößel m
hölzernes Sprengwerk n = timber truss, wood ~
Holzessig m = pyroligneous acid
Holzfahrbahn f [*Brücke* f] = timber deck(ing), ~ floor
Holzfaser f = grain
~brei m, Holzfasermasse f = wood pulp
~faser-Hartplatte f = wood fiber hardboard
~platte f, poröse ~, Holzfaser-Dämmplatte, Holzfaser-Isolierplatte = wood fibreboard (Brit.); ~ fiberboard (US)
~zuschlag(stoff) m = wood-fiber aggregate (US); wood-fibre ~ (Brit.)
Holz|fender m = timber fender, woodpile ~
~feuerung f = wood-fuel firing
~gasse f; siehe unter „Talsperre f"
~(ge)rinne f, (n), Fluder m = timber flume, wood ~
~gewerbe n = woodworking trade
~greifkorb m, siehe: Rund~
~hammer m = mallet
   schwerer ~ = beetle, mall, maul
~imprägnierung f, siehe: Holztränkung f
~imprägnierung f nach Rüping, siehe: Rüping(spar)verfahren n
~-Kanaldielen fpl = wood sheathing
~kastenkipper m = wood tip wagon, wood skip, track wheel wood dump wagon
~kohle f = charcoal
~kohle-Eisen n = charcoal iron
~kolophonium n = wood rosin
~konservierung f, Holzschutz m = wood preservation
~konstruktion f = timber structure

~kratze(r) f, (m) = wooden scraper
~latte f = wooden slat
~mast m = timber mast
~pfahl m = wooden pile, timber ~
   waldrecht, mit Kopfende nach unten = butt downwards
   zopfrecht, mit Zopfende nach unten = tip downwards
~pflaster(decke) n, (f) = wood paving
~-Plattenband n, Holz-Plattenbandförderer m = wood slat conveyor
~rahmenkonstruktion f = structural wood framing system
~rinde f = wood bark
~rinne f, siehe: Holzgerinne n
~rost m = timber mat
~schal(ungs)platte f, Holzschal(ungs)tafel f = timber form panel, (~) shutter(ing) panel
~schalungsträger m = wooden horizontal form support, ~ concrete ~ ~
~schraube f = wood screw
~schutz m, siehe: Holzkonservierung f
~silo m = timber aggregate bin
~spachtel m, f, Reibebrett n, Streichbrett n [*Gußasphalt* m] = wood float
~spänezuschlag(stoff) m = wood-chip aggregate
~spanplatte f = wood-chip board
~spreize f = timber spreader
~spundwand f; siehe unter „Spundwand"
~steg m [*bei Hochbaustellen fpl*] = wood runway
~stößel m, Stampfe f, hölzerne Pflasterramme f = wooden rammer, ~ tamper, ~ punner
~tafelschalung f = timber panel shuttering, wood ~ ~
~teer m = wood tar
~teerpech n = woodtar pitch
~terpentinöl n = wood turpentine
~tränkung f, Holzimprägnierung f = impregnation of wood
~trockenofen m = seasoning kiln

Holzverbindung f
   Achselzapfen m, geächselter Zapfen
   (An)Schiftung f, Lotschiftung f
   aufgeklautes Holz n
   aufklauen

timber joint, wood ~
   shouldered tenon
   shifting
   V-jointed timber
   to birdsmouth

Holzverbindung — Hopfenlagerhaus

Blattstoß m, Laschung f	scarf (joint)
Brustzapfen m	tusk tenon
Doppelblatt n	table scarf
doppelte Versatzung f	double skew notch
Ecküberlattung f mit schrägem Schnitt m	bevel(l)ed corner halving
Eckverkämmung f mit schrägem Kamm m	corner cogging with oblique cog
einfacher Kamm m	single notch
einfaches Blatt n	half lap
Gabelschmiege f	birdsmouth
Gabelzapfen, siehe: Scherenzapfen	
gerade Endverkämmung f	square end cogging
gerade Zinke f	straight dovetail (groove)
gerades Blatt n	straight halved joint
gerades Blatt n mit Grat m	straight scarf with saddle-backed ends
Hakenblatt n	hooklike halving
Klaue f mit Zapfen m im Nest n	bridle joint
Klauenschiftung f	birdsmouth attachment
Kreuzzapfen m	double halved joint
Laschung f, siehe: Blattstoß m	
Lotschiftung f, siehe: (An)Schiftung	
Nutzzapfen m	tongue and groove joint
Scherenzapfen m, Gabelzapfen	forked mortice and tenon joint
schräger Blattstoß m	oblique scarf
schräger Zapfen m, Schrägzapfen m	tapered tenon
schräges Hakenblatt n mit Keil m	oblique scarf with wedge
schwalbenschwanzförmiges Blatt n mit Brust f	shouldered dovetail halved joint
Seitenzapfen m	side tenon
stumpfe Pfropfung f mit Ring m und Dorn m	butt joint graft with ferrule and dowel
stumpfe Pfropfung f mit Schienen fpl	butt joint graft with fishplates
stumpfer Stoß m mit Laschen fpl	plain butt joint with fishplates
Überblattung f	double notch
Überschneidung f	notching
verborgenes Hakenblatt n	oblique scarf with secret wedge
Verkämmung f	cogging, ca(u)lking, cocking, corking
Verschränkung f	tabled joint
Verzahnung f	indented joint
Verzapfung f	tenon jointing
Verzapfung f mit Grat m	halved scarf with saddle-back ends

Holz|verkleidung f = timber (or wood) lagging (or lining)
~wolle f = wood wool
~wolleleichtbauplatte f = wood-wool slab
~wurm m = wood worm
~zement m = sulfurized coal tar pitch
~-Zuschlag(stoff)silo m = wood panel bin, roadbuilder's wood bin
homogen = homogeneous
Honigstein m, siehe: Melilith m
Hopfen|feld n = hopfield
~lagerhaus n = hop warehouse

Hopperbagger *m*; siehe unter „Naßbagger *m*"
Höppler-Kugelfall-Viskosimeter *n* = rolling sphere instrument, Höppler visco(si)meter, falling ball ~
Hordengestell *n* [*Betonsteinherstellung f*] = curing rack, rack for curing concrete block
Horizontalbohrmaschine *f* = horizontal drilling machine

Horizontal(strom)sichter *m*, **Horizontalgerinne** *n*, **Stromgerinne**
Korntrennung *f* im Naßverfahren *n*
Spitzkasten *m*

Sinkgeschwindigkeit *f*
Restwasser *n* mit dem abschlämmbaren Gut *n*
Aufwasser *n*

Horizontal|-Strömungs-Trockenelektroabscheider *m* = horizontal gas flow dry precipitator
~turbine *f* = horizontal turbine
Hornbaum *m*, siehe: Hainbuche *f*
Hornblende *f* (Min.) = hornblende
~asbest *m*, Amphibolasbest (Min.) = amphibole asbestos
~gneis *m* = amphibolic gneiss, hornblende-gneis
~porphyr *m* = hornblende porphyry
~schiefer *m* = horn(blende)-schist, schistous amphibolite
~silber *n*, Silberhornerz *n*, AgCl (Min.) = cerargyrite, clorargyrite, hornsilver
Hornstein *m* = hornstone
~kies *m* = chert-gravel
Hornfels(gneis) *m* = hornfels
Horst *m* (Geol.) = horst
horstbildender Rotschwingel *m* = shewing fescue
Horstverwerfung *f* (Geol.) = horst fault
Hosenrohr *n* = breeches piece
Hourdis *m*, Tonhohlplatte *f* = segment(al) sewer block (US); hollow gauged brick (Brit.)
Howe-Träger *m*, Howe'scher Binder *m* = Howe truss
Hub|bremse *f* [*Bagger m*] = hoist brake, hoisting gear ~

horizontale Krümmung *f*, ~ Kurve *f* = horizontal curve
horizontales Rührwerk *n* = mixing star
Horizontal|kraft *f* = horizontal force
~schub *m* = horizontal thrust
~sieb *n*, Horizontal-Vibrations-Plansieb = horizontal vibrating screen, level ~ ~
~steife *f* = horizontal stiffener

hydraulic classifier, hydroclassifier

hydraulic classification
cell hopper, classifier pocket, sorting hopper, sorting pocket
settling rate
excess water with the finest slime, overflow ~ ~ ~ ~ ~
swirling water

~höhe *f* = hoisting height
~karre(n) *f*, (*m*), Hubwagen *m* = (industrial) lift truck
~kipper *m*, Hochkipper *m* = (tip and) hoist [*tip which unloads above the level of railway lines*]
~kraft *f* [*Kran m*] = lifting capacity
~lader *m*, siehe: (Front-)Ladeschaufel *f*
~magnet *m*, siehe: Lastmagnet
~platte *f* = lift slab
~schaufel *f*, siehe: Schaufel
Hubschrauber|-Dachflugplatz *m* = roof (top) heliport, roof-top helicopter airport
~flugplatz *m* = heliport
Hub|schütz(e) *n*, (*f*), siehe unter „Talsperre *f*"
~seil *n* = lifting (or hoisting) rope (or cable)
~spindel *f*, siehe: Hebebock *m*
~stapler *m*, Hebetransportstapler *m* = stacker truck
~stapler *m* **mit Ottomotor** *m* = gas lift truck (US); petrol ~ ~ (Brit.)
~trommelwelle *f* = hoisting drum shaft
~wagen *m*, siehe: Hubkarre(n) *f*, (*m*)
~wagen *m* **nach dem Scherenverfahren** *n* = scissor type lift truck
~wehr *n*; siehe unter „Talsperre *f*"
~welle *f* = hoist shaft

Hubwinde f = hoisting winch
hufeisenförmig = horseshoe-shaped
Hufeisental n, siehe: Kahntal
Hügelland n, hügeliges Gelände n = hilly ground, ~ terrain, ~ country, rough ~
Hülse f = sheath, insert
humider Boden m, siehe: Waldboden
humos = humic
Humus m = humus
~**bildung** f = humification
~**boden** m, Humuserde f = humus soil
~**säure** f = humic acid
Hund m, Schutterwagen m, Stollenwagen = skip
Hunt'sche Conveyorkette f = Hunt conveyor
Hütten|bims m, siehe: Hochofenschaumschlacke f
~**kalk** m, siehe: Löschkalk m
~**schlacke** f, siehe: Metall(hütten)schlacke
~**schwemmstein** m [früher: Hochofenschwemmstein] = foamed slag aggregate concrete block
~**stein** m [früher: Hochofenschlackenstein m] = granulated slag aggregate concrete block
HW-Schutzdamm m, siehe: Hochwasserdeich m
Hyalophan m, siehe: Barytfeldspat m
Hyazinth m (Min.) = jacinth, hyacinth
hybrides Gestein n, Mischgestein = hybrid rock
Hydrant m = hydrant
Hydrargillit m, $Al_2O_3 \times 3H_2O$ = gibbsite, hydrargillite
Hydra(ta)tion f, siehe: Abbinden n [Zement m]
Hydra(ta)tionswärme f, siehe: Abbindewärme
Hydratwasser n = water of hydration
Hydraulefaktor m, siehe: Silikatbildner m
Hydraulik f = hydraulics
~**bagger** m = hydraulic excavator
~**-Forschungsinstitut** n = hydraulics research station
~**-Tieflöffel(bagger)** m = all-hydraulic drag-shovel
~**-Universalbagger** m = all-hydraulic crane-excavator
hydraulisch ausfahrbare Stütze f = hydraulic jack out-rigger

hydraulische Arbeitsbühne f = hydraulic working platform
~ **Auffüllung** f, siehe: Aufspülung f
~ **Belastungsvorrichtung** f [Baugrundprüfung f] = hydraulic ground-testing machine
~ **Bördelmaschine** f, ~ Kümpelpresse f = hydraulic flanging machine
~ **Förderung** f = hydraulic transport
~ **Gradiente** f, hydraulisches Gefälle n = hydraulic gradient
~ **Hand-Kippvorrichtung** f = hydraulic hand tipping gear
~ **Hubklappe** f [LKW m] = hydraulic lift tailgate, ~ end loader
~ **Kraftlenkung** f = hydraulic power steer(ing)
~ **Ladeschaufel** f (oder Front-Ladeschaufel, oder hydraulischer Front-Schaufellader m, oder Frontlader, oder Hublader, oder Kübelauflader, oder Schürflader, oder behelfsmäßiger Flachbagger m) = hydraulic loading shovel (or bucket loader, or tractor shovel, or front-end loader, or loader)
~ **Lenkhilfe** f = hydraulic booster steering
~ **Nietmaschine** f = hydraulic riveting machine
~ ~ **mit zwei Bewegungsrichtungen** fpl = two way ram, double acting ~
~ ~ ~ **einer Bewegungsrichtung** f = one way ram, single acting ~
~ **Radbremse** f = hydraulic wheel brake
~ **Rißbildung** f, ~ Rissebildung = hydraulic fracturing process
~ **Rohrbiegemaschine** f = hydraulic pipe bender
~ **Steuerung** f = hydraulic control
~ **Verlegung** f der nicht verwendeten Erdmassen fpl in den Abraum m = open (hydraulic) fill
~ **Vermörtelung** f, siehe: Zementvermörtelung f
~ **Winde** f, siehe: hydraulischer Hebebock m
hydraulischer Grundbruch m = piping by heave, piping failure
~ **Hebebock** m, Preßwasserhebebock, hydraulische Winde f = hydraulic jack

hydraulischer Kalk m [*früher: Zementkalk* m] = semi-hydraulic lime
~ **Mörtel** m = hydraulic mortar
~ **Stoff** m = hydraulic substance, ~ material
~ **Vorschub** m, ~Vorstoß m, hydraulisches Vorstoßen n = hydraulic crowd(ing)
~ **Widder** m; siehe unter „Pumpe *f*"
~ **Zyklon** m, Hydrozyklon m = hydraulic cyclone
hydraulisches Bindemittel n = hydraulic binder, ~ binding medium
~ **Gefälle** n, siehe: hydraulische Gradiente *f*
Hydrierung *f* = hydrogenation
hydrodynamischer Antrieb m = hydrodynamic drive
hydrogeologisch = hydro-geological
Hydro|graphie *f*, Gewässerbeschreibung *f* = hydrography
~**kalkstein** m, siehe: Kunstkalkstein
~**loge** m = hydrologist
~**logie** *f*, Gewässerkunde *f* = hydrology
~**mechanik** *f* = hydromechanics
hydro-mechanische Übertragung *f* = hydro-mechanical transmission
Hydro|mechanisierung *f* = hydraulicking
~**monitor** m, Druckstrahlbagger m = giant, monitor
~**oxygengas** n, siehe: Knallgas n
hydrostatisch = hydrostatic
hydrostatische Senkwaage *f*, Aräometer n, Spindel *f*, Flüssigkeitsdichtemesser m, Aräometer-Spindel = hydrometer, areometer, density meter for liquids, density hydrometer
hydrostatischer Antrieb m = hydrostatic drive
hydrostatisches Lager n, Schwimmlager = hydrostatic (or floating) bearing
Hydrozinkit n, Zinkblüte *f*, $Zn_5[(OH)_3/CO_3]_2$ = hydrozincite, zinc bloom
Hyetograph m = hyetograph
Hygrometer n = teleigrometer
Hygrometrie *f* = hygrometry
hygroskopisches Salz n = hygroscopic salt
~ **Wasser** n, verfestigtes ~, Saugwasser nach Stiny, Grenzflächenwasser, Häutchenwasser, Benetzungswasser = hygroscopic soil water, solidified ~

hypabyssisch = hypabyssal
hyperboloid = hyperbolic
Hypersthen m (Min.) = hypersthene
hypidiomorph = hypidiomorphic
Hypozentrum n; siehe unter „Erdbeben n"
Hysteresisschleife *f*, Hystereseschleife = hysteresis loop, ~ curve

I

Idealsieblinie *f*, Sollsieblinie *f* = good grading curve, type ~ ~, ideal ~ ~
idiomorph, eigengestaltig = idiomorphic
Igelströmit m (Min.) = pyroaurite
Illuvialhorizont m, siehe: B-Horizont
Ilmenit m, $FeTiO_3$ = ilmenite
imitierter Marmor m = simulated marble
Impact-Verfahren n = atomization method
Impfen n; siehe unter „Abwasserwesen n"
Imprägnieranlage *f* = impregnation plant
Impuls m = pulse
inaktiv, träge = inert
indifferentes Gas n = inert gas, indifferent gas
Indigolith m (Min.) = indicolite
indirekt wirkende Ramme *f*; siehe unter „Rammanlage *f*"
Indizieren n **des Druckes** m = obtaining pressure diagrams
Indizierung *f* = indicating
Induktionsmotor m, siehe: Asynchronmotor für Drehstrom m
Industrie|anlage *f* = industrial plant
~**bahnanlage** *f* = industrial railcar system
~**bau** m = industrial construction
~**behälter** m = industrial tank, ~ reservoir
~ **(fuß)boden** m = industrial floor(ing)
~**gebäude** n = industrial building
~**isolierung** *f* = industrial insulation
industrielle Lackierung *f* = industrial coating application
~ **Stiftung** *f* = industrial foundation
~ **Verunreinigung** *f* = industrial pollution
Industrie|lader m, Fabriklader = shovel loader mounted on industrial wheel type tractor, industrial loader
~**messe** *f* = industries fair
~**motor** m = industrial engine
~**ofen** m = industrial kiln

Industrie|papiersack m = industrial paper bag
~**standorte** mpl = industrial location
Infinitesimalrechnung f = infinitesimal calculus
(Infra)Schallbohrwerkzeug n = sonic drill
Infusorienerde f = infusorial earth
Ingenieur m **für Außendienst** m = field engineer
~ ~ **Innendienst** m = office engineer
Ingenieurbau m, siehe: Bauingenieurwesen n
~**firma** f = civil engineering firm, engineer-construction firm
~**klinker(stein)** m, **Ingenieurbauklinkerziegel** m = engineering clinker (brick)
~**werk** n = (civil) engineering structure
~**ziegel(stein)** m = engineering brick
Ingenieur|biologie f = engineering biology
~**geologe** m = engineering geologist
~**geologie** f = engineering geology
~-**Hilfskraft** f = technician (US)
~**holzbau** m = engineered wood construction
~**wirtschaft** f = engineering economics
~**wissenschaft** f, **Technik** f = engineering (science)
~**ziegel** m, **Ingenieurbackstein** m = engineering brick
Inhalt m, **Fassungsvermögen** n = capacity
Injektion f, **Auspressung** f, **Verpressung** f = injection, pressure grouting
Injektions|gut n = grout(ing) material
~**loch** n, siehe: Einpreßloch
~**pumpe** f = injection pump
~**schirm** m = grout curtain
~**schleier** m; siehe unter „Talsperre f"
~**verfahren** n, siehe: Einpreßverfahren
~**wasser** n = water to be injected into
Injektor m, siehe: Druckluifteinpreßgerät n
~**brenner** m = low pressure torch
injizieren, einpressen, auspressen = to inject, to grout under pressure
Injiziergerät n = injecting device
Inkarnatklee m = incarnation clover
inklinante Buhne f = groyne (Brit.)/groin (US) pointing slightly upstream
inkohärent, siehe: nichtbindig
Inländerzeugnis n = home-produced product

Inlands|düne f, siehe: Winddüne
~**markt** m = domestic market, home ~
Innen|ansicht f = interior view
~**anstrichfarbe** f = interior paint
~**ausbau** m [*Haus* n] = internal work
~**flanschlasche** f = side plate
~**fußboden** m = interior floor(ing)
~**kalkputz** m = internal plastering with lime
~**mauerwerk** n = interior masonry
~**moräne** f; siehe unter „Gletscher m"
~**putz** m = internal plastering
~**putz** m **mit Gips** m = internal plastering with plaster
(~)**Rüttelflasche** f = vibrating cylinder, ~ head
~**rüttler** m; siehe unter „Betonrüttelgeräte npl"
~**stadt** f, **Stadtmitte** f = downtown
~**stütze** f = inside column
~**taster** m, **Lochtaster** m = inside calipers
~**vibrator** m, siehe unter „Betonrüttelgeräte npl"
~**vorspannung** f = inner prestress
~**zementputz** m = internal plastering with portland cement
innerbetrieblicher Transport m = intraplant transportation
innere Abscheuerung f = internal scour
~ **Erosion** f = piping
~ **Kraft** f = internal force
innerer Reibungswinkel m = angle of internal friction
Insekten|befall m = insect attack
~**bekämpfungsmittel** n = insecticide
Insolation f = insolation
installierte (Kraft)Leistung f, **Leistungssoll** n = installed (nameplate) capacity
Instand|haltung f, siehe: Unterhaltung f
~**setzung** f, **Reparatur** f, **Ausbesserung** f = rehabilitation, repair (work)
Institut n **für Arbeitswissenschaft** f = Institute for Scientific Labour Studies
~ ~ **Bauforschung** f = Building Research Institute
Integralrechnung f = integral calculus
Internationale Gesellschaft f **für Vorspannung** f = International Federation of Prestressing

Internationale Vereinigung *f* **tür Brückenbau** *m* **und Hochbau** *m* = International Association of Bridge and Structural Engineering

~~~ **hydraulische Forschung** *f* = International Association of Hydraulic Research, IAHR

Intersertalstruktur *f*, siehe: divergentstrahlig-körnige Struktur

Interzeption *f*, siehe: Blattverdunstung *f*

intratellurisch = intratelluric

intrazonaler Boden *m* = intrazonal soil

Intrusion *f* (Geol.) = intrusion

Intrusivlager *n* (Geol.) = intrusive sheet

Investierung *f*, Kapitalanlage *f* = capital investment

Investitionskapital *n*, siehe: Anlagekapital

ionisieren = to ionize

IPRO-Stein *m* [*Trademark*] = IPRO concrete (paving) sett [*manufactured in Holland*]

irländisches Moos *n*, Perlmoos, Knorpeltang *m* = Irish moss, carragheen

Irwin-Schlangenbohrer *m* = long Cuban ring auger

isländischer Doppelspat *m* = Iceland spar

isländisches Moos *n*, siehe: Lungenmoos

Isobare *f* = isobar, line of equal pressure

Isobathenkarte *f*, siehe: Tiefenlinienkarte

Isohyete *f*, siehe: Regengleiche *f*

Isolier|band *n* = electric insulating tape

~**kitt** *m* = electrical insulating putty

~**öl** *n* = (electrical) insulating oil

~**papier** *n* = insulating paper

~**platte** *f*, Dämmplatte = insulating slab

~**stein** *m* = insulating brick

Isolierung *f* [*Rohr n*] = insulation, lagging

Isolierwolle *f* = insulating wool

Isotherme *f* = isotherm, line of equal temperature, isothermal line

Istlinie *f*, Sieblinie des Rohmaterials *n* = actual grading curve

italienische Pappel *f*, siehe: Pyramidenpappel

italienisches Raigras *n* = bearded rye grass, Italian ~ ~

J

Jadeit *m*, Jadestein *m* (Min.) = jadeite

Jahres|betrag *m* = annual rate

~**mittelwert** *m* = average (or mean) annual value

~**niederschlag** *m* = annual rainfall

Jahr(es)ring *m* [*Holz n*] = annual ring

jahreszeitlich = seasonal

Jamesonit *m*, siehe: Federerz *n*

Japaner(karren) *m*, siehe: Betonrundkipper *m*

Jaspopal *m* (Min.) = opal jasper, jasp opal

Jauche|grube *f* = manure dump

~**rinne** *f* = chute for liquid manure

Joch *n*, Pfahl~ = trestle, pile ~ (or bent)

~**bauwerk** *n*, siehe: Pfahl~

~**holm** *m*, Kopfbalken *m* = capsill

Jodsilber *n* = iodide

JOHNSON-(Misch)Turm *m*, Mischturm *m* mit Wabensilo *m*, Fabrikat C. S. JOHNSON COMPANY, CHAMPAIGN, ILLINOIS, USA = JOHNSON automatic batch plant

Joosten-Verfahren *n*; siehe unter „Baugrundverbesserung *f*"

Jörgensen-Mauer *f*; siehe unter „Talsperre *f*"

Judenpech *n* [*Asphalt m aus dem Toten Meer n*] = bitumen judaicum

Jungbaum *m* = sapling

jungfräulicher Boden *m* = virgin earth material

Jura|kalk(stein) *m* = Jurassic limestone

~**phyr** *m* = juraphyre

~**riff** *n* = Jurassic reef

~**sandstein** *m* = Jurrassic sandstone

justieren, einstellen = to adjust

Jute *f* = jute

juvenil, neu entbunden (Geol.) = juvenile

K

Kabel *n* **aus 48 Drähten von 7 mm** ⌀ = cable of 48-7 mm wires

~**formstück** *n*, Kabelformstein *m* = conduit tile (US); (multiple way) cable duct (or conduit, or subway) multitubular slab for cable

~**graben** *m* = cable trench

~**kanal** *m* = cable channel, cable trough

Kabelkran *m*; siehe unter „Seilförderanlage *f*"

~**gegenturm** *m* = tail tower

Kabelkran|kübel m, Beton(schütt)kübel m, Betontransportkübel = concrete bucket, ~ placing skip
~**maschinenturm** m = head tower
Kabel|merkstein m = cable marker
~**schacht** m = cable draw pit
~**schelle** f = cable clamp
~**schmiermittel** n = cable lubricant
~**schranke** f = cable barrier
~**schrapper** m, Seilschrapper m = cable scraper
~**schutzstein** m = cable tile
~**stollen** m = cable tunnel
~**suchgerät** n = cable tracing set, cable detector
~**trommel** f = cable reel
~**vergußmasse** f = electrical filling compound, ~ compound for cable isolations
~**verlegemaschine** f = cable lubricant
~**verlegewinde** f = cable laying hoist, ~ ~ winch
Kabine f = cab(in)
KAELBLE-Planierraupe f = caterpillar bulldozer, Make: CARL KAELBLE G. m. b. H., BACKNANG bei STUTTGART, DEUTSCHLAND
Kahlschlag m = char felling
Kahn|entladebecherwerk n = barge elevator
~**tal** n, Hufeisental n = canoe(-shaped) valley, cigar-shaped ~
Kai|anlagen fpl = quayside appliances, quay accomodations
~**mauer** f, Hafenmauer f = quay wall
Kainit m (Min.) = kainite
Kaiser-Wilhelm-Kanal m, Nord-Ostseekanal m = Baltic Ship Canal, Kiel Canal
Kalfaterhammer m = ca(u)lking mallet
Kalfatern n = caulking, fullering (Brit.); calking (US)
Kali n = protoxide of potassium, prussiate of potash, (anhydrous) potash, potassa
~**alaun** m = potash alum, common alum
~**dünger** m, K_2O = potash manure
~**feldspat** m (Min.) = potash fel(d)spar
kalifornisches Tragfähigkeitsverhältnis n, kalifornischer Index m = California Bearing Ratio, CBR
Kali|lauge f, siehe: Ätzkalilösung f
~**metall** n, siehe: Kalium n

Kali|salpeter m, Kaliumnitrat n, KNO_3 = nitre, (India) salpetre, potassium nitrate, potassic nitrate, saltpeter
~**salz** n = potassic salt, potassium salt
~**seife** f = potash-soap, soft soap
~**silikat** n = potash silicate
~**tonerde** f = aluminate of potash
Kalium n, Kalimetall n = potassium
~**aluminiumsulfat** n, siehe: Alaun m
~**chlorat** n, $KClO_3$ = potassium chlorate
~**hydroxid** n, Kaliumhydrat n, Ätzkali n, $K_2(OH)_2$ = potassium hydroxide, caustic potash, potassium hydrate
~**karbonat** n, siehe: Pottasche f
~**nitrat** n, siehe: Kalisalpeter m
~**oxyd** n, K_2O = potassium monoxide
~**permanganat** n, übermangansaures Kali n, $KMnO_4$ = potassium permanganate
Kalk m = lime
kalkablagernd, kalkabscheidend, kalkausfällend, kalkausscheidend = lime-depositing, lime-precipitating, lime-secreting
Kalk|alabaster m = calcareus alabaster
~**algen** fpl = calcareous algae
~-**Alkaligranit** m = calc-alkali granite
~**anreicherung** f [Boden m] = lime accumulation
~**beton** m = lime concrete
~**bewurf** m = parget of lime
kalkbildend = calcigenous
Kalk|brei m, siehe: Kalkteig m
~**brennen** n = lime burning, ~ calcination
~**brennerei** f = quicklime manufacturing plant
~**chromgranat** m (Min.), siehe: Uwarowit m
~**drehofen** m = rotary lime kiln
~**düngung** f = manuring with lime
~**eisengranat** m (Min.) = calcium iron garnet
~**eisenstein** m = ferruginous limestone, calcareous iron-stone
kalken [Boden m] = to lime
~, siehe: tünchen
Kalk|erde f = calcareous earth
~**fazies** f = calcareous facies, lime-stone ~
~**feldspat** m (Min.), siehe: Anorthit m
kalkgebundener Dinasstein m = English dinas

Kalk|gipsputz *m* = gypsum-lime plaster
~**glimmerschiefer** *m*, Cipolino *m* = green marble, cipolin
~**grube** *f*, Löschgrube *f* = slaking pit
kalk|haltig, kalkig = calcareous, limey
~**haltiger Ton** *m* = calcareous clay
Kalk|harmotom *m* = lime-harmotome, phillipsite, christianite
~**hornfels** *m* = lime silicate rock, calcariferous petrosilex
~**hydrat** *n*, siehe: Löschkalk *m*
~**hydrat-Raschbinder** *m*, Gips-Kalk-Putzmörtel *m* = lime-gypsum plaster, reacted ~
~**kern** *m*, Kalkkrebs *m*, Fehlbrand *m* = cove, unburned lime
~**kies** *m* = calcareous gravel
~**kiesel** *m* (Min.) = calcareous silex
~**kitt** *m* = lime cement
~**krebs** *m*, siehe: Kalkkern *m*
~**krücke** *f* = mortar beater, lime raker
~**licht** *n*, siehe: Knallgaslicht
~**löschtrommel** *f* = lime slaking drum
kalklösende Kohlensäure *f* = aggressive carbonic acid

Kalk|marmor *m* = calcitic marble, limestone ~, crystalline limestone
~**mehl** *n* = flour lime
~**mergel** *m* [75—90% $CaCO_3$] = lime marl, calcareous ~
~**milch** *f*, Tünche *f* = lime milk, cream of lime, whitewash, milk of lime
~**mörtel** *m*, Mauerspeise *f* = lime mortar (L.M.)
~**mühle** *f* = quicklime mill
~**niere** *f*, Kalkschwüle *f* = concretion of lime
~**ofen** *m* = lime kiln
~**oligoklas** *m* = calcic oligoclase
~**onyx** *m*, siehe: Onyxmarmor *m*
~**oolith** *m*, siehe: oolithischer Kalkstein *m*
~**pumpe** *f* = lime paste handling pump
~**putz** *m* = lime plaster
~**rührwerk** *n* = lime agitator
~**salpeter** *m*, salpetersaurer Kalk *m*, Kalziumnitrat *n*, $Ca(NO_3)_2$ = nitrate of lime
~**salz** *n* = calcium salt
~**sand** *m* = calcareous sand, lime ~
Kalksandstein *m*, weißer Mauerstein = sand lime brick, lime-sand ~
~ = sandy limestone, arenaceous ~

Kalkschachtofen *m*
  obere Vorwärmzone *f* und Vorratssilo *m*
  untere Vorwärmzone *f*
  Pufferzone *f* [*neutrale Schicht f*]
  Brennzone *f*
  Kühlzone *f*
  Abzugbühne *f*

vertical lime kiln
  upper preheat and storage zone
  lower preheat zone
  buffer zone
  burning zone
  cooling zone
  draw floor

Kalkschiefer *m*, siehe: Plattenkalk(stein) *m*
~**ton** *m* = calcareous shale
Kalk|schwüle *f*, Kalkniere *f* = concretion of lime
~**silikat** *n* = lime silicate, calcium ~
~**silikatfels** *m* = lime rock
~**sinter** *m* = calcareous sinter, calc-sinter
~**spat** *m*, Kalzit *m* (Min.) = calcite, calcspar
~**spat-Kalkstein** *m* = calcitic limestone
Kalkstein *m*, kohlensaurer Kalk *m*, $CalO_3$ = limestone, calcium carbonate
~**füller** *m* = limestone filler
~**kies** *m* = limestone gravel

~**mastix** *m* = limestone mastic
~**mauerwerk** *n* = limestone masonry
~**schotter** *m* = crushed limestone
~**teermakadam** *m* = limestone tarmacadam
Kalk|stickstoff(-Dünger) *m* = calcium cyanamide, nitrogen manure
~**streuer** *m* = bulk lime spreader
~**suspension** *f* = lime suspension
~**teig** *m*, Kalkbrei *m*, eingesumpfter Kalk *m*, Sumpfkalk, Grubenkalk [*gelöschter Kalk m in nasser Form f*] = lime paste, lime putty, hydrate putty, pit lime
Kalktonerdegestein *n* = cement rock

Kalkton|schiefer m = calcareous slate, limestone ~

~stein m = calcilutyte, lime mud rock

Kalktuff m = tuf aceous limestone (calcareous) tufa, cale tufa

Kalkulationsvordruck m = form for pricing construction works

Kalkulator m = estimator, calculator, quantity surveyor, cost estimator, estimating engineer

Kalkulieren n, Preiskalkulation f = cost estimating

Kalkung f = liming, lime spreading

Kalk|verfahren n, siehe: Naß(sand)verfahren n

~wasser n = lime water

~-Zementmörtel m, siehe: verlängerter Zementmörtel

Kallait m, Türkis m (Min.) = callaite, turquoise

Kalmengürtel m = region of calm, calm belt

Kaltasphalt m; siehe unter „Bitumen n im engeren Sirne"

~-Spritzapparat m = cold emulsion sprayer (or spraying machine)

kalt aufbereitete Mischung f = cold mix

Kalt|bindemittel n = cold binder

~brüchigkeit f = cold shortness

Kältebeständigkeit f = cold resisting property

Kalteinbau|-Asphaltfeinbeton m = cold-laid fine asphaltic concrete

~-Teerfeinbeton m = cold-laid fine tar concrete

~-Teergrobbeton m = cold-laid coarse tar concrete

~(weise) m, (f) [Straßenbau m] = cold-laid process, cold mix method (of construction), cold laying

Kälterückfall m = recurrent cold snap

kaltgereckter Bewehrungsstahl m = cold worked bar

kaltgezogen = cold-drawn

Kalt|lufteinbruch m = influx of cold air

~mischanlage f = cold mix (asphalt) plant (US); bituminous macadam and tarmacadam mixing plant (Brit.)

~mischverfahren n = cold plant mixing

~nieten n = cold riveting

~-Preßschweißung f = cold pressure welding

~start m = cold start

~teer m [ein mit leichten Ölen npl verschnittener Straßenteer m] = cold tar, TC

~verformung f [Metall n] = cold-working

~wasserfarbe f = cold water paint

Kalzinieren n = calcination, calcining

(kalzinierte) Soda f, wasserfreies Natriumkarbonat n, kohlensaures Natrium n, Na_2CO_3 = soda-ash

Kalzit m, **Kalkspat** m (Min.) = calcite, calcspar

Kalzium n = calcium

~bisulfit n, doppelschwefligsaures Kalzium n, Kalziumhydrogensulfit n, saurer schwefligsaurer Kalk m = bisulphite of lime

~chlorid n, Chlorcalcium n, $CaCl_2$ = calcium chloride

~-Harzseife f = calcium rosinate

~hydroxid n, gelöschter Kalk m, $Ca(OH)_2$ = calcium hydroxide, lime hydrate, hydrated lime (powder), slaked lime, calcic hydrate, hydrate of lime

~karbid n, CaC_2 = carbide of calcium, calcium carbide

~nitrat n, siehe: Kalksalpeter m

~ölseife f = calcium oleate

~oxyd n, CaO = calcium exide

~sulfat n **kristallwasserhaltig**, $CaSO_4 \times 2H_2O$ = hydrous crystalline lime sulfate

Kaminkühler m = chimney cooler

Kammer|schleuse f = chamber navigation lock, ~ inland ~, lift ~ ~

~sprengen n; siehe unter „1. Schießen n; 2. Sprengen n"

Kamm|gebirge n = ridge mountain(s)

~gras n = crested dog's-tail

~kies m (Min.) = cock's comb marcasite

Kämpfer|druck m [Brücke f] = pressure on (a)butment

~gelenk n = (a)butment hinge

~linie f = springline, springing line

~punkt m = springing

~randstörung f = disturbance at the springing

~(stein) m, **Anfänger(ziegel)** m, **Bogenkämpfer** m = impost, springer, springring bick, (arch) springing, rein

Kanadaasbest — Kantigkeit

Kanada|asbest *m* (Min.), siehe: Chrysotilasbest
~balsam *m* = Canada balsam
kanadische Fichte *f* = Canadian spruce
Kanal *m*, Leitungs~ = duct, mains subway
~ *m*, künstlicher ~ = canal

~ *m* mit totem Wasserspiegel *m* = sleeping canal, dead ~
~arbeiter *m* [*Abwasser n*] = sewer man
Kanalbau *m* [*Abwasserkanal m*] = sewer construction
~ *m* = canal construction

Kanalbaumaschinen *fpl*

Kanalplaniermaschine *f*
Kanal-Betoniermaschine *f*, Einbaugerät *n* für Gerinneauskleidungen *fpl* in Zementbeton *m*
Einbaugerät *n* für Gerinne-Auskleidungen *fpl*, Kanalauskleidungsmaschine *f*

Kanal-Fugenschleifgerät *n*
Arbeitsgerät *n*, Hilfsgerät

canal trimming and lining equipment, canal building machinery
canal trimmer
canal concrete paver; traveling template form for concrete (US)

canal paver; traveling template form, canal paving rig (US); slip form canal lining machine
canal joint cutter
finishing rig

Kanal|bekleidungsplatte *f* = sewer liner plate
~böschung *f*, Kanalufer *n* = canal bank, ~ slope
~böschungsschutz *m*, siehe: Kanalufersicherung *f*
~brücke *f* = canal aqueduct, ~ bridge
~damm *m* = canal embankment, ~ bank
~dielen *fol* = trench sheeting, ~ piling
~einlaßbauwerk *n* = canal headworks
~gas *n* = sewer gas
~gefälle *n* = canal gradient
~graben *m* = duct trench
~hafen *m* = canal port
~haltung *f*, siehe: Haltung *f*
Kanalisation *f* = sewerage, drainage by sewers, town drainage
Kanalisationsgraben *m* = sewer trench
Kanal(isations)rohr *n* = sewer (pipe)
Kanalisierung *f*, Staureg(e)lung *f* [*Wasserstraße f*] = canalisation
Kanal|klinker(stein) *m*, Kanalklinkerziegel *m* = sewer clinker (brick)
~kraftwerk *n* = diversion type river power plant
~profil *n* = canal section
~pumpwerk *n* = canal pumping station
~querschnitt *m* = canal cross-section

~rohr *n*, siehe: Kanalisationsrohr
~schleuse *f* = canal (navigation) lock
~stein *m* = sewer brick
~strebe *f*, Grabensteife *f*, Kanalspindel *f*, Sprieße *f*; [*in Österreich: Spriessel m*] = trench brace (US); ~ shore, ~ strut, shoring strut (Brit.)
~ufersicherung *f*, Kanalböschungsschutz *m* = canal slope (or bank) protection
~verbreiterung *f* = canal widening
~winde *f*, siehe: Bockwinde
Kandelaber *m* = candelabra
Kanister *m* = can
Kanonenofen *m* = cast iron stove
Kanten|brecher *m*; siehe unter „Fertigbehandlung *f*"
~geröll(e) *n*, siehe : Pyramidalgeröll(e)
~geschiebe *n*, siehe: Pyramidalgeröll *n*
~kiesel *m*, siehe: Pyramidalgeröll(e) *n*
~schutz *m* = edge protection
~stein *m*, Randstein, (Tief-)Bordstein = haunching stone (Brit.); header (US); flush curb(stone)
Kantholz *n* = rectangular timber, squared ~
kantig; siehe unter „Kornform *f*"
Kantigkeit *f*, Winkeligkeit, Eckförmigkeit = angularity

Kaolin *m*, siehe: Porzellanton *m*
Kaolinisierung *f* = kaolinisation
Kaolinit *m* (Min.) = kaolinite
kaolinitischer Ton *m* = kaolin clay
Kaolinsand *m* = kaolin sand
Kap *n* (Geol.) = cape
~**asbest** *m*, siehe: Blauasbest (Min.)
kapazitiver Anzeiger *m* = content indicator
kapillarbrechend = destroying capillary action
Kapillardruck *m* = capillary pressure
Kapillare *f*, siehe: Kapillarrohr *n*
kapillarer Aufstieg *m* = capillary rise
kapillare Sättigung *f* = capillary desaturation
~ **Steighöhe** *f* = capillary elevation
Kapillarimeter *m* = capillary apparatus, capillarimeter
Kapillarität *f*, Rohrsaugkraft *f* = capillarity, capillary attraction
Kapillar|kraft *f* = capillary force
~**potential** *n* = capillary potential
~**rohr** *n*, Haarrohr *n*, Kapillare *f*, Kapillarstrang *m*, Kapillarröhrchen *n* = capillary (tube)
~**röhrchenhohlraum** *m* = capillary bore
~**röhrchenwandung** *f* = capillary wall
~**saugversuch** *m* = capillary water absorption test
~**saum** *m*, Saugsaum *m*, Kapillarzone *f* = capillary fringe
~**spannung** *f* = capillary tension
~**strang** *m*, siehe: Kapillarrohr *n*
~-**Viskosimeter** *n* = capillary visco(si)meter
~**wasser** *n*, Haarröhrchenwasser, Porensaugwasser = capillary water, ~ moisture, water of capillarity
~**zone** *f*, siehe: Kapillarsaum *m*
Kapitalanlage *f*, Investierung *f* = capital investment
Kaplanturbine *f* [*Flügelradturbine f mit verstellbaren Schaufeln fpl*] = Kaplan (water) turbine
Kappenquartz *m* = cap(ped) quartz
Kapsel|gebläse *n* = rotary blower
~**ton** *m*, siehe: Kapillarsaum *m* = sagger clay, saggar ~, seggar~
Kar *m* (Geol.) = corrie, cirque
Karabinerhaken *m* = snap hook
Karawanenpfad *m* = caravan track

Karbolineum *n* = carbolineum, peterlineum, coal tar creosote
Karbol|pech *n*, Kresolharz *n*, Phenolpech *n* = cresol pitch
~**säure** *f*, siehe: Phenol *n*
Karbonat *n*, kohlensaures Salz *n* = carbonate
karbonatisches Gestein *n* = carbonate rock
Karbonisierung *f* = carbonation
Karborund *n*, Siliziumkarbid *n*, SiC = silicon carbide, carbide of silicon, carborundum, carbon silicide
Kardangelenk *n* = (cardan) universal joint
~**welle** *f* = (cardan) universal joint shaft
kardanische Aufhängung *f* = cardanic suspension
Karlsbader Zwilling *m* (Min.) = Carlsbad twinning
Karnallit *m*, $KCl \times MgCl_2 \times 6H_2O$ (Min.) = carnallite
Karosserie *f* = car body
Karpathen *f* = Carpathian Mountains
Karre(n), Förder~, Transport~ *f*, (*m*) = cart
~ **mit Stahlrollen-Plattform** *f* = roller truck
Karrenaufzug *m*, siehe: Plateau-Aufzug
Karrenpfad *m* = wagon trail
Karrenpflug *m* = wheel plough (Brit.); ~ plow (US)
Karst *m* (Geol.) = karst
~**hochfläche** *f* = karst plateau, planina
~**trichter** *m*, Doline *f* = doline, dolina
~**wanne** *f* = karst depression
Karte *f* **mit Höhenlinien** *fpl* = layered map, contour ~
Karten|(gitter)netz *n* = map grid
~**herstellung** *f* = map-making, mapping (work)
~**herstellung** *f* **mit Hilfe von Luftaufnahmen** *fpl* = aerial mapping, mapping by use of aerial photography
~**winkelmesser** *m* = map protractor
Kartondrain *m* = card-board wick
~**loch** *n* = wick hole, cardboard ~ ~
Kascholong *m* (Min.) = cachalong opal
Kasematte *f* = casemate
Kaskade *f* = cascade
Kaskadenfalte *f* (Geol.) = zigzag fold

Kaskadenverdampfer m = cascade evaporator

Kaspisches Meer n = Caspian Sea

Kassettenkonstruktion f = waffle-type construction

kastenartiges Schrappergefäß n; siehe unter „Seilförderanlage f"

Kasten|ausleger m, siehe: vollwandiger Ausleger

~**drän** m; siehe unter „Entwässerung f"

~**fang(e)damm** m = box (type coffer-) dam

~**kipper** m = box type skip, ~~ tip wagon, ~ (~ track wheel) dump wagon

~**querschnitt** m = box-section

~**rahmen** m = box section frame

~**spundbohle** f; siehe unter „Spundwand f"

~**träger** m, Kastenbalken(träger) m = box girder (Brit.); ~ beam

~**verteiler** m, siehe: Verteilerkasten m

Kastoröl n, Rizinusöl n = castor oil

Kataklasit m (Geol.) = cataclastic rock, kataklastic ~

kataklastische Gesteinsform f, Kataklase f = kataklastic structure, cataclastic ~

Katalysator m = catalyst, catalyzer, catalyser, catalytic agent

katalytische Entschwef(e)lung f = catalytic desulfurization

katalytisches Spaltverfahren n = catalytic cracking

~~**mit Natur-Bleicherde als Kontakt** = THERMOPHOR catalytic cracking

~~~ **natürlichem Bauxit als Kontakt und Wasserdampf zur Verminderung der Koksabscheidung** = CYCLOVERSION catalytic cracking

~~~ **Reaktionsraum mit Mischsystem** = fluid catalytic cracking

Katapult m, n = catapult

Kataster|amt n = cadastral office

~**vermessung** f = cadastral survey

Katastrophen|-Hochwasser n = catastrophic flood (Brit.); super flood, flood of record (US)

Kation f = cation

Katzenköpfe mpl [*Pflaster* n] = nigger heads [*rounded cobble stones*]

Kaufhaus n, Warenhaus n = department store

Kauf-Mietvertrag m; siehe unter „Baumaschinen fpl und Baugeräte npl"

kaustisch = caustic

(kaustische) Magnesia f, siehe: Magnesiumoxyd n

Kautschuk|milch f, Kautschuksaft m = latex, rubber ~

~**pulver** n = flocculated latex crumb, rubber powder

~**(-Asphalt)straße** f, Gummistraße f = rubber(-asphalt)road, rubberised ~

Kaverne f = cavern

Kavernenkraftwerk n = underground hydro-electric (power) plant, ~ power station

Keene's Zement m, siehe: Marmorgips m

Kegelbrecher m, Kreiselbrecher, Rundbrecher = cone(-type) crusher, gyratory ~ ~ [*it sizes at the closed side setting*]

Kegelbrecher m, Kreiselbrecher, Rundbrecher = gyratory crusher [*it sizes at the open side setting*]

~ m **mit segmentförmigem Brechkopf** m = gyrasphere crusher

Kegel|drucksonde f = conical penetrometer

~**eindringungsapparat** m, Kegelgerät n, Kegeldruckapparat m [*stabilisierte Mischung* f *mit bituminösem Binder* m] = cone penetrometer, conical ~

~**meißel** m; siehe unter „Bohrmeißel"

~**radgetriebe** n = bevel gear

~**radumlaufgetriebe** n = planetary type bevel gearing

~**schale** f = cone shell

~**schmelzpunktbestimmung** f = cone deformation study

~**stirnrad** n [*Bagger* m] = tapered spurwheel

~**stumpf** m = frustrum of a cone

~**tragfähigkeitsmesser** m = cone bearing (capacity) apparatus

Kehl|(grat)sparren m = valley rafter

~**nahtdicke** f = throat depth

~**ziegel** m = valley tile

Kehrmaschine f, Straßenkehrmaschine, Straßenbesen m, mechanischer Besen, Fegemaschine = mechanical sweeper, road broom, rotary sweeper, rotary road brush, road sweeper, scavenging machine, road sweeping machine

    Kehrwalze f = brush, rotary ~, rotating ~

Kehrmaschine f für Pferdezug m = horse-drawn road sweeper

Keil|anker m = cone anchor

~**einbruch** m [*Stollensprengung f*] = wedge cut

~**klaue** f, Steinwolf m = lewis, stone lifting bolt

~**nutenstoßmaschine** f = push type keyway broaching machine, keyway cutter

~**nutenziehmaschine** f = draw-cut type keyseater

~**riemen(an)trieb** m = texrope drive (US); V(ee)-belt drive (Brit.)

~**schieber** m = paradox gate (US); spectacle-eye sluice valve (Brit.)

~**splitt** m, Füllsplitt m = choke (or intermediate) aggregate (or stone), keystone, filler stone, blinding stone

~**verankerung** f [*Spannbeton m*] = wedge anchoring

~**welle** f = spline(d) shaft

~**wellennut** f, Längsnut = (female) spline

Keimbett n = seed bed

Keller m, Kellergeschoß n = basement, cellar

KELLER-Tiefenrüttler m = KELLER spud vibrator

Kellerüberschwemmung f = flooding of basements

KELLER-Verfahren n, siehe: Rütteldruckverfahren n

Kennwert m = characteristic value

kennzeichnender Punkt m [*Setzungsberechnung f*] = indicator point, point of reference [*settlement calculation*]

Kennziffer f, siehe: Beiwert m

Keramik f = ceramics

Keramikergips m, siehe: Formgips m

keramische Baueinheit f, keramischer Bauteil m = (structural) clay building unit, masonry ~

~ **Erzeugnisse** npl **mit Zellenbildung** f, keramische Leichterzeugnisse = cellulated ceramics

~ **(Fuß)Bodenfliese** f = floor(ing) tile

~ **Masse** f = ceramic body

~**Schutzschicht** f = ceramic coating

~**Trockenanlage** f = ceramic dryer (Brit.); ~ drier (US)

~ **Wandfliese** f, siehe: Wandkeramikplatte f

keramischer Leichtbauteil m = lightweight clay building unit

~ **Rohstoff** m = ceramic raw material

~ **Scherben** m = ceramic body

keramisches Futter n **in Sulfitzellstoffkochern** mpl = ceramic digester linings in sulfide pulp mills

~ **Leichtbauerzeugnis** n = light-weight structural clay product

Keratophyr m (Geol.) = keratophyre

Kerbe f = notch

Kerb|empfindlichkeit f = notch sensitivity

~**nut** f = notch, V-groove

~**stab** m = notched bar

~**tal** n = V-shaped valley

~**wirkung** f = notch effect

Kermesit m, siehe: Antimonblende f (Min.)

Kern m [*Holz n*] = heartwood

~**bohren** n, Kernbohrung f = core boring, ~ drilling, core-drill boring

~**bohrer** m = annular borer

~**bohrgerät** n, Kernbohrmaschine f, Beton~ = (concrete) core (cutting) machine, coring machine, core drill(ing machine), concrete coring drill
Schrot~ = shot ~ ~, shot bit cutter
Diamant~ = diamond ~ ~

~**bohrkrone** f; siehe unter „Bohrmeißel m"

~**büchse** f = core barrel

~**büchsenbohrung** f = tube sample boring

~**damm** m; siehe unter „Talsperre f"

~**entnahme** f, Bohr~, Kerngewinnung f = core recovery, ~ extraction

~**fäule** f [*Holz n*] = rotting of the heart

~**fels** m, gewachsener Fels m, Sprengfels(gestein), anstehendes Gestein n = solid rock, rock to be blasted

~**mauer** f, Damm~ ~ = core wall

~**mauerdamm** m; siehe unter „Talsperre f"

~**reaktor** m = nuclear (power) reactor

~**sand** m = core sand

~**riß** m, Herzriß m [*Holz n*] = heart shake

Kerosin n, siehe: Petroleum n

Kersantit m, Kersanton m = kersantite

Kerzen|teer m = candle tar

~**zündung** f = sparking plug ignition

Kessel m (Geol.) = ca(u)ldron, fault, pit

(**Kessel**)**Ansatz** *m*, Kesselstein *m* = (boiler) scale
~**bediener** *m*, siehe: Heizer *m*
~**bekohlungsanlage** *f* = boiler coaling installation
~**blech** *n* = boiler plate
~**dampfmaschine** *f*, Lokomobile *f* = portable steam engine
~**feuerung** *f* = boiler furnace
(~)**Flugasche** *f* = flue dust, fly-ash, flue ash(es)
~**gips** *m* = kettle-calcined gypsum
~**mantel** *m* = boiler shell
~ **mit Außenfeuerung** *f* = externally fired boiler
~ ~ **Innenfeuerung** *f* = internally fired boiler
Kessel|rost *m*, Feuerrost *m* = (boiler) grate
~**schießen** *n*, Vorkesseln *n* = sprung borehole method
~**schlacke** *f*, Lösch(e) *m*, (*f*) = clinker, furnace ~ (Brit.); (boilerhouse) cinder, breeze
~**schlackenbildung** *f* = clinkering
~**stein** *m*, (Kessel)Ansatz *m* = (boiler) scale
~**steingegenmittel** *n* = boiler fluid, ~ composition
~**stein- und Rostabklopfer** *m* = boiler scale and rust chipper
~**wagenerhitzer** *m*, Dampferzeuger *m* = tank car heater, booster ~
~**wärter** *m*, siehe: Heizer *m*
~**wirkungsgrad** *m* = boiler efficiency
Ketten|(an)trieb *m* = chain drive
~**becherwerk** *n*, Ketten(becher)elevator *m* = chain (type) (bucket) elevator
~**bolzen** *m* = chain pin
~**bruch** *m* [*Mathematik f*] = fractional progression
~**egge** *f* = chain harrow
~**elevator** *m*, siehe: Kettenbecherwerk *n*
~**fahrzeug** *n*, siehe: (Gleis)Kettenfahrzeug
~**förderer** *m* = chain conveyor
~**-Greifer** *m*, Ketten-Greifkorb *m* = chain grab(bing bucket)
~**hebezeug** *n* = chain-hoisting device
~**laufwerk** *n*, siehe: Raupenfahrwerk *n*
~**nietung** *f*; siehe unter „Niet *m*"

~**rad** *n*, (Ketten)Turas *m* = sprocket (wheel)
~**reihenelevator** *m*, siehe: Kettenvollbecherwerk *n*
~**säge** *f* **mit Benzinmotor** *m*, Baumfällsäge *f* = gasoline (or gasolene) chain saw (US)
~**säge** *f* **mit Elektromotor** *m* = electric chain saw
~**schlepper** *m*, Gleisketten-Zugmaschine *f*, Gleisketten-Schlepper *m* [*die Ausdrücke „Raupenschlepper", „Kettenraupe f", „Raupentraktor" und „Raupentrecker" sind nicht mehr anzuwenden*] = crawler(-tread) tractor, (self-laying) track-type (industrial) tractor, caterpillar tractor, tracked tractor, track laying tractor
~**spanner** *m* = chain adjuster, ~ tensioner
~**steinwurf** *m* = chained (breakwater) blocks
~**stollen** *m*, Gleiskettenstollen = dirt grouser
~**strang** *m* [*Becherwerk n*] = endless chain
~**trieb** *m*, siehe: Kettenantrieb
~**trommel** *f* = chain drum
~**turas** *m*, Kettenrad *n*, Turas = sprocket (wheel)
~**vollbecherwerk** *n*, Kettenreihenelevator *m* = continuous chain (type bucket) elevator
~**vorschub** *m*, Kettenvorstoß(en) *m*, (*n*) [*Hochlöffel m*] = chain crowd(ing)
~**zange** *f* = chain tongs
~**zug** *m* = chain hoist, ~ block (and tackle), ~ lifting block, ~ pulley block
Keuper *m* = keuper, copper-bearing shale
~**mergel** *m* = Keuper marl
K-Fachwerk *n* = K-truss
Kiefer *f* = pine
kielholen = to careen
Kiel|stapel *m* = keel block
~**wasser** *n* = wake
Kiene *f*, siehe: Weißkiefer *f*
Kien|holz *n* = resinous wood
~**öl** *n* = pine oil
~**teer** *m* = pine tar
~**teerpech** *n* = pine-tar pitch

Kies *m* [*nach Atterberg, Gallwitz 20 bis 2 mm; nach DIN 4022 70—2 mm; nach Niggli 200—2 mm; nach I. Kopecki größer als 2 mm*] = gravel [*International Society of Soil Science, United States Public Roads Administration, Massachussetts Institute of Technology, British Standard Institution 2—60 mm; A.S.E.E. 76.2—2 mm; Bureau of Reclamation 76.2—4.76 mm; Casagrande (1947) 2000 to 2 mm*]
~**abstreuung** *f* = gravel blotter (US)
~**asphalt** *m*, Kieswalzasphalt *m* = gravel asphalt
~**aufbereitungsanlage** *f*, Kieswerk *n* = gravel plant
~**(auf)schüttung** *f* = gravel fill
~**ballastkasten** *m* = gravel ballast container
~**boden** *m* = gravelly soil
~**deponie** *f* = gravel stockpiling
Kiesel|alge *f*, siehe: Diatomee *f*
~**algenerde** *f*, siehe: Kieselgur *f*
~**breccie** *f* [*dieser Ausdruck sollte nicht mehr verwendet werden*]; Kieselbrekzie *f* = silica breccia
~**chlorid** *n* = silicon chloride
~**gallerte** *f*, Kieselsäuregel *n* = silica gel
~**galmei** *m*, Zinkglas(erz) *n*, Kieselzink(erz) *n* (Min.) = siliceous calamine, willemite
~**gur** *f*, Diatomeenerde *f*, Diatomit *n*, Kieselalgenerde *f* = kieselgur, diatomite, diatom(aceous) earth
kieseliges Bindemittel *n* (Geol.) = siliceous matrix (or cement, or cementing material)
Kiesel|kalk(stein) *m*, kieseliger Kalkstein = siliceous limestone
~**kreide** *f* = chalk flint
~**lage** *f* = pebble bond
~**managan** *n*, Rotbraunstein *m*, Rotspat *m* (Mim.) = rhodonite
~**salz** *n* = silicate
~**sand** *m* = siliceous sand
kieselsauer = silicic
Kieselsäure *f* = silicic acid
kieselsaure Tonerde *f* = hydrous (or hydrated) silicate of aluminum, siliceous earth

Kieselsäure|gel *n*, siehe: Kieselgallerte *f*
~-**Glas** *n*, amorpher Quarz *m* = vitreous silica
kieselsaurer Kalk *m* = silicate of lime
kieselsäurereich = siliceous
Kiesel|schiefer *m*, siehe: Lydit *m*
~**schotter** *m* (Geol.) = siliceous oolite gravels
~**schwamm** *m* = siliceous sponge
~**sinter** *m* = siliceous sinter, geyserite
~**(stein)** *m* [*nach Dücker (Jahr 1948) ,,grobes Siebkorn IIa"* 60—20 *mm und ,,grobes Siebkorn IIb"* 20 *bis* 6 *mm*] = pebble [60—6 mm]
~**substanz** *f* [*Gestein n*] = silica cement
~-**Wolframsäure-Probe** *f* = silico tungstic acid test
Kieserit *m*, $MgSO_4 \times 7H_2O$ (Min.) = kieserite
~**knolle** *f* = kieserite nodule
Kies|feld *n*, Sandfeld = outwash plain
~**filter** *n*, *m* = gravel filter
~**grube** *f* = gravel pit
kiesiger Sand *m* = gravelly sand
~ **Ton** *m* = gravelly clay
Kies|körnung *f* = gravel fraction
~**lager** *n* (Geol.) = gravel deposit
~**naßbagger** *m*, Kiesschwimmbagger = gravel dredge(r)
~**nest** *n*, Steinnest [*Beton m*] = rock pocket
~**pumpe** *f*, siehe: Kolbenbüchse *f*
~**randstreifen** *m*, Kiesstandspur *f* = gravel shoulder
~**schotter** *m*, Steinschotter *m* = ballast
~**schutt** *m* (Geol.) = gravel(l)y detritus, ~ wash
~**schüttung** *f*, siehe: Kiesaufschüttung
~**schüttungsbrunnen** *m* = gravel (-walled) well
~**silo** *m*, eiserner Baustellensilo für Zuschlagstoffe *mpl* = steel gravel (storage) bin
~**standspur** *f*, Kiesrandstreifen *m* = gravel shoulder
~**stock** *m* = pyritic rock
~**straße** *f* = gravel road
~**streugerät** *n* **mit Schleuderverteilung** *f* = spinner type distributor for stone, ~ ~ spreader ~ ~, spinner gritter

Kies|terrasse f = gravel terrace
~trockenbagger m = gravel excavator
~(walz)asphalt m = gravel asphalt [*dense hot-rolled asphalt with gravel as aggregate*]
~wäsche f, Kieswaschmaschine f = gravel washing machine, gravel washer
~werk n, Kiesaufbereitungsanlage f = gravel plant
~wüste f = stony desert
Kilometerstein m = kilometre post
Kilometrierung f = stationing in kilometres
Kiloschlüssel m = torqometer
Kilowattstunde f = Kwhr.
Kimme f, sichtbarer Horizont m = sensible (or apparent, or visible) horizon
Kimmtiefe f, Kimmung f = dip of the horizon, apparent depression of the horizon
kinematische Viskosität f = kinematic viscosity
kinetische Energie f; siehe unter „Bernoulli-Satz m"
Kippanhänger m = dump-body trailer, trailer-dump, tipping trailer
kippbare Ladeschaufel f, Kippwanne f, Kippmulde f [*Frontlader m*] = tilting front end bucket
Kipp-Betonkarre(n) f, (m), siehe: Betonrundkipper m
Kippe f [*Erdbau m*] = tip, shoot, tipple
Kippen n [*z. B. ein Schwimmdock n*] = careening
~pflug m, siehe: Planierpflug
~räumer m, siehe: Planierpflug m
Kipper m, Kipplast(kraft)wagen m, Kipp-LKW m = tipper, dump lorry, tip (motor) lorry, tipping lorry (Brit.); dump truck, tip(ping) truck (US)
~ m [*Wagenkipper m*] = tip
~brücke f mit Kippbühne f = (bridge) transporter with end tipping railway car platform
Kipp|(er)karre(n) f, (m) = buggy
~halde f = dump pile
~kübel m; siehe unter „Betonmischer m"
~kübelaufzug m, Kübel(bau)aufzug m = bucket hoist, skip type (contractors') (or builders') hoist, open-end skip hoist
~löffel m = tilting (dipper) bucket

~lore f; siehe unter „Feldbahnanlage f"
~moment n = overturning moment [*e. g. breakwater*]
~mulde f [*Erdbau-Lastfahrzeug n*] = body
~muldenaufzug m [*am Betonmischer m*] = concrete skip hoist
~ofen m = tilting furnace
Kipppritsche f [*LKW m*] = dump body
Kipppritschenboden m = dump truck body bed (US)
Kipp|schraube f [*Nivellierinstrument n*] = tilting level screw
~sicherheit f = safety against overturning
~tieflader m, siehe: Tieflader m mit Kipp(tief)ladebrücke f
~trommelmischer m; siehe unter „Betonmischer m"
~vorrichtung f, Kippwerk n [*LKW m*] = tipping gear
~weiche f = tilting point
~zapfen m [*Brückenauflager n*] = rocker pin
~zylinder m = tilt cylinder
Kitt m = putty
kittlose Verglasung f = puttyless glazing
Kitt|stoff m = cementing agent, ~ material
~wirkung f, Kittungseigenschaft f = cementitious property
Klammer f = clamp
~ f, siehe: Frosch m
Klangfehlerhaftigkeit f [*Ziegel m*] = dunting
Klanke f = kink
Klappe f, Schieber m = valve
Klappen|gehäuse n, Schiebergehäuse = valve body
~seil n [*Bagger m*] = discharge gate rope
~(stau)wehr n = shutter weir
~ventil n = flap valve
Klapp|schute f = hopper barge (Brit.); hopper scow, bottom-dump scow (US)
~sonde f, Schlämmbüchse f = bailer
Klär|anlage; s. unter „Abwasserwesen n"
~grube f = cesspool, cesspit
~schlamm m; siehe unter „Abwasserwesen n"
~teich m; siehe unter „Abwasserwesen n"
~turm m, Stoffangtrichter m [*Papierfabrik f*] = clarifying tower

Klassierer *m*, Naß~ = classifier
Klassierung(ssiebung) *f* = sizing of the material completely by screening
Klassifizierung *f* = classification
Klassifizierungseigenschaft *f* = index property
klassische Methode *f* = orthodox method, classic ~
klastischer Kalktuff *m* = detrital lime tuff, clastic ~
klastisches Eruptivgestein *n* = clastic eruptive rock
~ **Gestein** *n* = clastic rock
~ **Sedimentgestein** *n* = clastic sedimentary rock
Klatsche *f*, Pritschbläuel *m*, Praker *m*, Patsche *f*, Tatsche *f*, Schlagbrett *n* = muller and plate (Brit.)
Klaubeband *n*, Leseband *n* = picking belt conveyor
Klaue *f* **mit Zapfen** *m* **im Nest** *n*; siehe unter „Holzverbindung *f*"
Klauen|kupplung *f*, Zahnkupplung = jaw clutch (coupling)
~**muffe** *f* = claw collar
~**schiftung** *f*; siehe unter „Holzverbindung *f*"
Klebe|gummi *m* = gum
~**kraft** *f* = agglomerating power
~**masse** *f*, Aufstrichmasse = adhesive, gluing compound
~**schicht** *f* = adhesive coat
klebrige Erle *f*, Schwarzerle *f*, Schwarzeller *f*, Schwarzelse *f* = common alder, black ~
Klebsäule *f* [*Dach n*] = wall stud
Klee|blattkreuzung *f*, Renaissancekreuzung *f* = clover-leaf (flyover) junction, ~ intersection
~**säure** *f*, siehe: Oxalsäure
Klei *m*, Küstenschlick *m* = (clay containing) sea silt
Klein|auflader *m* = small-size bucket (elevator) loader
~**bagger** *m* = midget excavator
~**bahn** *f*, Feldbahn *f* = narrow-gauge railway (Brit.); narrow-gage railroad (US)
~**baustelle** *f* = small-scale (building, or project, or job) site

~**bulldozer** *m* **auf Gleisketten** *fpl*; siehe: Kleinplanierraupe *f*
Kleinchengraphit *m* = colloidal graphite
Kleinelektromotor *m* = small type motor
kleiner Ahorn *m*, siehe: Maßholder *f*
~ **Erdrutsch** *m*, Rutschung *f* = shear slide, (earth) slip
~ **Klee** *m* = lesser yellow trefoil
Kleine'sche (Stahlstein-) Decke *f* = Kleine floor
Klein|foraminiferen *f* = small foraminifera
~**kompressor** *m*, Kleindruckluferzeuger *m*, Kleinluftverdichter *m* [*unter 1 PS*] = fractional horsepower (air) compressor
~**maschine** *f* = small size machine
~**mischer** *m* = small-capacity mixer
~**pflaster** *n* = small stone sett paving
~**pflaster(decke)** *n* (*f*) **in Fächerform** *f* = radial (small stone) sett paving, random ~, durax ~, fanwise ~, circular ~, fanshaped ~
~**pflasterstein** *m* = small (stone) sett
~**planierraupe** *f*, Kleinbulldozer *m* auf Gleisketten *fpl* = baby bulldozer, calfdozer, skipdozer
~**schlag** *m* **aus Betonbrocken** *mpl*, siehe: Betonpacklage *f*
~**schlag** *m* **aus Ziegel(stein)brocken** *mpl*, siehe: Ziegelschotter *m*
~**seilbahn** *f* = light ropeway
Kleinst(elektro)motor *m* = pilot motor, fractional H. P. ~
kleinster Trägheitshalbmesser *m* = least radius of gyration
Klein|tunnelofen *m*, Platten-Tunnelofen = pusher-type kiln
~**verkehrsstraße** *f*, siehe: Nebenstraße
Klemm|backe *f* [*Klemmgriff-Lastenträger m*] = side shoe
~**futter** *n*, Aufspannfutter = chuck
~**griff-Lastenträger** *m*, siehe: Torladewagen *m*
~**kraft** *f* [*von Nieten auf Blechen*] = contact pressure, clamping force
~**schieber** *m* [*Anbaugerät n für palettenlosen Transport*] = push-pull equipment
Kletter|eisen *n*, Steigeisen *n* = pole climbers, climbing irons
~**moor** *n* = climbing bog
~**schalung** *f* = climbing shuttering

Kletter|vermögen n = climbing power
~zungenweiche f; siehe unter „Feldbahnanlage f"
Kliff|hang m (Geol.) = chine
~(küste) n, (f), siehe: Steilküste
~schutt m = undercliff
Klima(tisierungs)anlage f = air conditioning installation (or plant)
    Zuluftanlage f = induction system
    Abluftanlage f = extraction system
    Flatterjalousie f = automatic ventilating louvre
Klingstein m (Geol.) = clinkstone
Klinkenhebel m = ratchet lever
Klinker m, siehe: Klinkerziegel(stein) m
~; siehe unter „Zement m"
~grieß m = clinker grit
~kühler m = clinker cooler
~pflaster n, sieh : Ziegelpflaster
~platte f = clinker slab
~ziegel m, Klinker(stein) m, Hochbau~ m [früher: Mauer~ m] = clinker (brick), klinker (~)
Klino|graph m = clinograph
~meter n, siehe: Gefällmesser m
Klippe f (Geol.) = klippe
Klippenbai f = rocky bay
Kloben m [Seilzug m], siehe: Flasche f
Klopfer m, Ab~ = chipper, scaling hammer
Klopf|festigkeit f = anti-knock performance
klopfhindernder Zusatz m = antiknock agent
Klopfkäfer m = furniture beetle
Klothoide f = spiral (transition) curve, transition spiral, highway spiral
Klothoidentafel f = spiral table for highway design
Klotz m, Block m = block
Kluft f [Holz n] = shake [timber]
~fallwinkel m (Geol.) = fault dip
klüftiger Sandstein m = sandstone containing open seams
Kluft|injektion f; siehe unter „Baugrundverbesserung f"
~quelle f, (Verwerfungs)Spaltenquelle = fracture spring, fissure ~
~wasser n = fissure water, crack ~
Klumpen|bildung f = formation of lumps
~zertrümmerer m, Ringelwalze f = clod crusher
Klumpfußpfahl m; siehe unter „Gründungspfahl m"
klumpig, großstückig = lumpy
Knall|blei n = fulminating lead
~gas n, Hydrooxygengas n = oxyhydrogen (gas)
~gaslicht n, Kalklicht n = limelight
~quecksilber n, Quecksilbercyanat n, Merkuricyanat, Hg(CNO)$_2$ = fulminate (of mercury), mercuric isocyanate
~zündschnur f; siehe unter „1. Schießen n; 2. Sprengen n"
Knäpper m = block of stone drilled for blasting
~bohren n = block holing
~(bohr)hammer m = block holer
~schießen n; siehe unter „1. Schießen n; 2. Sprengen n"
Knappschuß m, Knäpperschuß m = pop shot
Knarre f, Ratsche f = ratchet
Knarrenbohrer m = ratchet drill
Knaulgras n, Knäuelgras n = cocksfoot, orchard grass
Kneifzange f = pincers
Knet|mischer m, Kneter m, Zwangsmischer m mit vertikalem Rührwerk n = pug(-)mill (mixer)
~verdichter m = kneading compactor
~wirkung f, siehe: Verkehrskomprimierung f
Knick|beiwert m = buckling coefficient
~berechnung f = calculation of the buckling strength
~festigkeit f = buckling strength (or resistance), resistance to lateral bending, buckling stability
~länge f [bei Druckstäben mpl] = effective length
~last f = buckling load, collapse ~
~sicherheit f = safety against buckling
~spannung f = buckling stress
Knickung f, Knicken n = buckling
Knick|versuch m = buckling test
~zahl f = buckling coefficient
Kniehebel|nietmaschine f = pneumatic toggle joint riveting machine
~presse f = toggle plate press

Kniestockwand f, siehe: Drempelwand
knirsch stoßen [*Mauerwerk* n] = to be laid touching
Knochen|bett n, Knochenlager n (Geol.) = bonebed
~leim m = bone glue
~öl n = bone-oil, Dippel's oil
~(teer)pech n = bone-tar pitch
Knollen|bildung f [*Zement* m] = lumpiness
~kalk(stein) m = nodular lime(stone), calcareous nodule
Knorpeltang m, siehe: irländisches Moos n
Knorrenloch n [*Holz* n] = knot hole
Knoten|blech n = junction-plate, gusset (-plate), junction gusset
~blechverbindung f = gusseted connection
~dolomit m = knotty dolomite
~(punkt) m [*Fachwerkträger* m] = panel point, system ~, assemblage ~, centre knot
Knüppelweg m, Prügelweg m = corduroy road
Koagulationsindex m = coagulation index [*bitumen emulsion (Brit.)*]

Koagulator m, Koagulationsmittel n = coagulant, flocculating agent
koagulieren = to flocculate
Kobalt|blüte f (Min.) = cobalt bloom, erythrite
~glanz m, Glanzkobalt m (Min.) = cobalt glance, cobaltite
~pulver n = cobalt powder
~schwärze f, Asbolan m, Erdkobalt m (Min.) = asbolane, asbolite
Kocher m, siehe: Bindemittelkocher
~ mit Rührwerk n = heater-mixer
Koch|kessel m = (heating) kettle
~versuch m [*Zement* m] = boiling test [*hydraulic cement*]
Kohäsion f, scheinbare ~, Bindigkeit f [*Boden* m] = cohesion, cohesiveness
Kohäsions|faktor m, Beiwert der wirksamen Kohäsion f = cohesional coefficient
~festigkeit f = cohesive resistance
kohäsionslos, siehe: nichtbindig
kohäsiv, siehe: bindig

Kohle f	**coal**
Abfall ~	waste ~
Anthrazit m	anthracite (~)
Back ~, siehe: weiche ~	
bituminöse ~	bituminous ~
Braun ~	brown ~
Erbs ~, siehe: Grieß ~	
erdige Stein ~	earthy ~, ~ smut
Esse(n) ~, siehe: Schmiede ~	
faserige Braun ~	fibrous brown ~
Fein ~, feinkörnige ~, Kohlenklein n, Kohlengruß m	small ~, slack ~
Fett ~, siehe: weiche ~	
Feuer ~	fuel lignite [*incorrectly termed: non bituminous lignite*]
Förder ~, Roh ~	rough ~, run-of-the mine ~
fossile ~, siehe: Stein ~	
Gas ~, gasreiche ~, Leuchtgas ~	gas ~
gasarme ~	non-gassing ~
gemeine ~, siehe: musch(e)lige Braun ~	
Glanz ~	glance ~, lustrous ~; peacock ~ (US)
gleichmäßige ~	homogeneous ~
Grieß ~, Perl ~, Erbs ~	pea ~
großstückige ~, Stück ~	best ~, large ~

Kohle — kohlensaures Magnesium

Holz~	charcoal
Kannel~	cannel ~
Kohlengruß m, siehe: Feinkohle	
Kohlenklein n, siehe: Feinkohle	
Kohlenstaub m	~ dust, dross
Koks~, siehe: weiche ~	
kuchenbildende ~	caking ~, close burning ~
langflammige ~	candle ~, long flaming ~
Leuchtgas~, siehe: Gas~	
lufttrockene ~	air-dried ~
Mager~, siehe: Sand~	
Matt~	dull ~
Moor(braun)~	moor ~
musch(e)lige Braun~, gemeine ~	common brown ~
Nuß~	(chest)nut ~, nuts
Pech~	pitch ~
Perl~, siehe: Grieß~	
Roh~, siehe: Förder~	
Sand~, magere ~, Mager~, harte ~, kurzflammige ~	non-caking ~, dry burning ~, hard-burning ~, semi-bituminous ~, hard ~; free-ash ~ (US)
Staub~	dust ~, culm
Sinter~	free (or open) burning ~, cherry ~
Schiefer~	slaty ~, foliated ~
Schmiede~, Esse(n)~	smithy ~, forge ~, black-smith ~
Schwarz~, siehe: Stein~	
Schwel~	retort lignite [*incorrectly termed: bituminous lignite*]
Stein~, Schwarz~, fossile ~	black~, fossil ~, pit ~
Stück~, siehe: großstückige ~	
unsortierte ~	unsorted ~
Verkokungs~	coking ~
weiche ~, Back~, backende ~, Fett~, Koks~	caking ~, rich ~, fat ~
Würfel~	cobbles, lump ~, lumps, block coal

Kohle|anode f = carbon anode
~grießwiderstandsofen m = carbon resistance furnace
Kohlen|aufzug m = coal hoist
~bergbaugebiet n = coal mining region
(~)Bleispat m, siehe: Bleispat m (Min.)
~bleivitriolspat m (Min.) = lanarkite
~brecher m = coal-breaker
~bunker m = coal bunker
~eisenstein m, Schwarzstreif m = blackband
~flöz n = coal seam
~förderung f **durch Rohrleitungen** fpl = coal piping, ~ pumping
~greifer m = coal handling bucket
~grießwiderstandsofen m = carbon resistance furnace
~händler m = coal dealer
~kalk(stein) m = carboniferous liemstone
~kipper m = coal tip
~kran m, siehe: Bekohlungskran
~lagerung f = coal storage
~pickhammer m, siehe: Abbauhammer
kohlensaurer Kalk m, siehe: Kalkstein m
kohlensaures Kalium n, siehe: Pottasche f
~ Magnesium n, siehe: Magnesiumkarbonat n

kohlensaures Natron n (oder **Natrium** n), Na₂CO₃ = carbonate of soda
~ **Salz** n, siehe: Karbonat n
Kohlen|schrapper m = coal scraper
~**skipanlage** f = coal skip-winding plant
~**stoff** m = carbon
~**stoffgehalt** m = carbon content
~**stoffstahl** m, unlegierter Stahl = plain carbon steel
~**stoffstein** m, Kohlenstoffziegel m = carbon brick
~**untertagegrube** f = coal mine
~**vergasung** f unter Tage = underground gasification of coal
~**verladebrücke** f = coal(ing) bridge
~**wasserstoff** m = hydrocarbon, carburetted hydrogen
~**wasserstoff-Lösungsmittel** n = hydrocarbon solvent
Kokerei f = coking plant
Kokosmatte f = coconut matting
Koks|korb m, Bauaustrocknungsofen m = (fire) devil, brazier
~**lösch(e)** m, (f) = coke breeze, ~ ashes
Kolben m [Laborgerät n] = flask
~ = piston
~**anzeigedämpfer** m, siehe: Kolbenzeigerdämpfer
~**bohrer** m [Bodenprobenahme f] = piston sampler
~**büchse** f, Kiespumpe f = shell with valve
~**drucklufterzeuger** m, siehe: Kolbenverdichter m
~**gebläse** n = piston blowing engine
~**kompressor** m, siehe: Kolbenverdichter m
~**maschine** f = piston machine
~**pochwerk** n = piston stamp
~**pumpe** f; siehe unter „Pumpe f"
~**verdichter** m, Kolbenkompressor m, Kolbenluftverdichter, Kolbendrucklufterzeuger m = (piston) ring compressor, reciprocating ~
~**zeigerdämpfer** m, Kolbenanzeigedämpfer m = dash pot
Kolk|schutz m = protection against scour, erosion control
~**schutzsperre** f = check dam
~**vertiefung** f = eroded hole (Brit.); scoured ~

Koller(gang) m = pan grinder, grinding mill of the edge runner type
Kollimations|fernrohr n = collimator field glass
~**instrument** n mit fester Basis f und mit 80facher Vergrößerung f = fixed-base 80-magnification collimator
Kollodiumwolle f; siehe unter „1. Schießen n; 2. Sprengen n"
Kolloid n, siehe: Kolloidalzustand m
kolloidale Form f = colloidal form
Kolloidalzustand m, quellstofflicher Zustand m, Kolloid n = colloid(al state) disperse Phase f = disperse phase geschlossene Phase f = dispersion medium
Kolloid|chemie f, Kolloidik f, Kolloidlehre f = colloidal chemistry
~**schlamm** m; siehe unter „Feinschluff m"
Kolluvialboden m, siehe: Absatzboden
kolluvialer Verwitterungsschutt m = colluvial mantle rock
Kolonne f, Trupp m, Arbeits~ = gang, crew, team, party
Kolophonium n = colophonium
Kolorimeter n = chromometer
Kombinationswagen m, siehe: Kombiwagen
Kombinatorik f = combinatorial analysis
kombinierter Förderer m mit Mitnehmern mpl = conveyor and elevator with (scraper) flights
kombinierter Stampfbohlen- und Hammerfertiger m, siehe: (Stampf)Hammerfertiger
kombinierte Saugluft-Druckluft-Förderanlage f, kombinierter pneumatischer Förderer m = combined suction and pressure conveying system, suction-jet ~ ~
~ **Zuschlagstoff-Zement-Dosierwaage** f = combination weighing unit for aggregate and cement, concentric aggregate-cement batcher
Kombi|wagen m, Kombinationswagen = station wagon
~**zange** f = pliers
Kommandogerät n, siehe: Steuertafel f
Kommunalbehörde f = local authority

kommunaler Betrieb — Kontinentalschelf

kommunaler Betrieb m = municipal undertaking
kompaktes Gestein n, dichtes ~, Urgestein, kompakter Fels m = compact rock
Komplementwinkel m, siehe: Ergänzungswinkel m
Kompost m = compost
Kompostieren n = composting
Kompressionsversuch m, Druck-Setzungsversuch m, Zusammendrückversuch m = compression test
Kompressol-Verfahren n = Compressol system
    kegelförmiger Fallstößel m = conical hammer
    Aufzugsgerät n = frame
Kompressor m, Luftverdichter m, Drucklufterzeuger m, Luftkompressor m = (air) compressor
kompressorloser Dieselmotor m = compressor-less injection Diesel (engine)
~ Motor m = solid-injection engine
Kompressor|schlauch m, siehe: Preßluftschlauch
~schlepper m = universal compressor tractor, tractor-compressor
~zylinder m, Verdichterzylinder m = compressor cylinder
Kondensat n = condensate
Kondensationswärme f = heat of condensation
Kondensatrücklaufleitung f = condense return line
Kondens|-Lok(omotive) f = condensing loco(motive)
~topf m = steam trap
~wasser n, Schwitzwasser n, Tauwasser n = condensating water, dripping moisture
Konglomerat n, „Naturbeton" m (Geol.) = conglomerate
Königszapfen m = king pin; center journal (US)
konisch = tapered
konische Handsonde f = manual conical penetrometer
~ Unterlegscheibe f = bevelled washer, tapered ~
konischer Siebzylinder m, siehe: Sortierkonus m

Konkave f **eines Flusses** m, einbuchtendes Ufer n = concave bank
Konservierung f, siehe: Haltbarmachung f
Konservierungsmittel n = preservative
Konsistenz f, Steife f [*Beton* m] = consistency, consistence, fluidity
~beiwert m = coefficient of consisteney
Konsistenzgrenzen fpl **nach Atterberg**, Atterberg'sche Konsistenzgrenzen, Atterberg-Grenzen = consistency limits, Atterberg limits of soil
    Fließgrenze f, W_f = liquid limit, LL [*symbol* w_L]
    (Aus)Rollgrenze, obere Plastizitätsgrenze, W_r = plastic limit, PL [*symbol* w_p]
    Schrumpfgrenze f, W_s = shrinkage limit, SL [*symbol* w_s]
Konsistenzprobe f = consistency test
Konsistometer n = consistometer
Konsole f = bracket
Konsolidierung f, Eigenverfestigung f, Eigensetzung f, Konsolidation f, natürliche Bodenverdichtung f, Eigenkonsolidation f = consolidation, soil ~, earth ~
Konsolkran m, Wandkran = wall crane
Konstrukteur m = designer
Konstruktion f = system
Konstruktions|abteilung f = engineering department
~einzelheit f = design detail
~gewicht n = design weight
~ingenieur m = designing engineer
konstruktionstechnisch = constructional
Konstruktionsteil m, n = structural part, member
konstruktiv = constructive
konstruktiver Ingenieurbau m = structural engineering
Kontakt m (Geol.) = contact influence
~ablagerung f (Geol.) = contact deposit
~gestein n = contact(-altered) rock
~hof m (Geol.) = metamorphic aureole
~metamorphose f, Berührungsumprägung f, Berührungsumwandlung f (Geol.) = contact metamorphism
~zone f (Geol.) = contact
Konti-Mischer m; siehe unter „Betonmischer m"
Kontinentalschelf n = continental shelf

kontinuierliche Dosiereinrichtung f = continuous proportioning plant; [*deprecated: gradation unit*]
kontinuierlicher Mischer m, Stetigmischer m = conutinous mixer, constant-flow ~
Kontraktorverfahren n = fixed tremie pipe (or tube) method
Kontroll|gerät n = cheking device
~-Licht n = warning light
~prüfung f = control test
~rechen m, Profiltaster m = subgrade tester, (subgrade) scratch template, point template
~wehr n = control weir
Kontur f = contour line
Konus|meißel m; siehe unter „Bohrmeißel"
~trommel f = conical-shaped drum
~(zahn)ritzel n = bevel pinion
Konvektor m = convector
Konventionalstrafe f = contract delay penalty, ~ overrun ~
Konzentrat n = concentrate
Konzentrationsfaktor m **nach Fröhlich**, Ordnungszahl f der Spannungsverteilung f = Fröhlich's (stress-) concentration factor
Koog m, siehe: Polder m
Koordimeter n = co-ordimeter
Koordinatenachse f = coordinate axis
koordiniertes Signalisierungssystem n = coordinated control system, linked ~
Kopal m = copal
Kopf|abstand m [*von zwei Fahrzeugen npl*] = headway
~balken m, Jochholm m = capsill
~band n, Strebeband n = strut
~ende n = head-end
~hörer m = headphone
~klee m, Rotklee m = red clover
~leitung f = header (main)
~öl n [*Spermacetiöl* n] = head oil
~platte f [*Säule* f] = cap
~platten-Form f [*zur Herstellung* f *von Kopfplatten*] = cap form
~rasen m = head turf
~(rohr)leitung f = header pipeline, ~ system
~schraube f = cap screw
~schütter m, siehe: Autoschütter m
~schutz m = head protection
~steinpflaster n = cobble stone paving
~verband m [*Mauerwerk* n] = head bond
~wipper m = rotary end tip
Korallen|kalkstein m, Korallen-Riffkalk m = coral limestone
~riff n = coral reef
Korb m [*Greifbagger* m] = bucket
~bogen m = compound curve
~bogen m **mit drei Zentren** npl = three-center(ed) arch (US); three centre(d) ~ (Brit.)
~weide f = osier
Kork|eiche f = cork oak, ~ tree
~isolierung f = cork lagging
Korn|abstufung f = granulometric gradation
~analyse f [*Boden* m] = mechanical analysis
~aufbau m, Kornzusammensetzung f = granulometric composition, granulometry
Körnchen n, siehe: Einzelkorn n

Kornform f, **Korngestalt** f | **particle shape, grain ~**
plattig, flach, scherbig | laminated, flaky
kubisch | cubical shaped, cube-shaped
rund, kugelig, abgerundet | rounded
nadelförmig | elongated
kantig | angular
unregelmäßig | irregular

Korn|gerüst n [*z. B. Sand* m] = granular skeleton
~größe f, Fraktionsgröße = particle size, grain ~
~größenverteilung f = particle-size distribution, grain-size ~, grading
körniger Kalkstein m = granular limestone

Korn|masse *f*, Korngemisch *n*, Körnungsgemisch = aggregate mixture
~trennung *f* **im Naßverfahren** *n*; siehe unter „Horizontal(strom)sichter *m*"
Körnung *f*, Fraktion *f* = nominal size, (size) fraction, size bracket
Körnungs|komponente *f* = soil separate
~modul *m*, siehe: Feinheitsmodul
~verfahren *n*, siehe: Granulierung *f*
Korn-zu-Korn-Druck *m*, wirksame Spannung *f* = effective stress
Kornzusammensetzung *f*, siehe: Kornaufbau *m*
Koronaentladung *f*, siehe: Glimmentladung *f*
körperlicher Kraftaufwand *m* = physical exertion
Korrasion *f*, Sandschliff *m* (Geol.) = corrasion
Korrosion *f*, Anfressung *f* = corrosion
Korrosions|festigkeit *f*, Korrosionsbeständigkeit = corrosion resistance
~schutz *m* = protection against corrosion
Kosten|aufgliederung *f* = breakdown of cost(s), cost(s) breakdown
~aufwand *m*, Anlagekosten *f* = capital expenditure (or costs, or out lay)
~ersparnis *f*, Kosteneinsparung *f* = savings of costs
~überwachung *f* = cost control
kostenvergütete Bodenmassen *fpl* = paydirt (US)
~ Ladung *f* = payload
~ Position *f*; siehe unter „Angebot *n*"
(Kosten) (Vor)Anschlag *m* = estimate (of costs), cost estimate
Kote *f* = level
Krack|-Destillat *n* = cracked distillate
~-Gas *n* = cracking gas, cracker gas
Kraft *f*, Energie *f* = power
~ [*Statik f*] = force
~abnahme *f* = power take-off
kraftangetrieben = power-driven
Kraft|antrieb *m* = power drive
~aufzug *m* = power-operated hoist
~bedarf *m*, siehe: Energiebedarf
kraftbetrieben, kraftgetrieben = power-operated
Kräfte|dreieck *n*, Krafteck *n* = triangle of forces, force triangle

~paar *n* [*Statik f*] = couple (of forces)
Kraft|erzeugung *f*, siehe: Energieerzeugung *f*
~fahrer *m* = chauffeur (US); driver
~fahrerhotel *n*, Hotel für Motorisierte *mpl* = motel (US)
~fahrerverstoß *m* = motoring offence
~fahrzeug *n*, Motorfahrzeug *n* = motor vehicle
~fahrzeugbetriebsstoffsteuer *f*, Betriebsstoffsteuer = motor fuel tax
~fahrzeugtunnel *m* = motor tunnel, automobile traffic ~
~gas *n* = power gas
~hammer *m* = power hammer
~-Handramme *f*, siehe: Kraftstampfer *m*
~haus *n*, Kraftwerksgebäude *n*, Maschinenhaus *n* = power house
~hausüberbau *m* = power house superstructure
~hubwerk *n* = power-operated lifting machine
~karre(n) *f*, (*m*) = power wheelbarrow, mechanical ~
~lenkung *f* = power (-assisted) steer(ing)
~niet *m* = rivet carrying stress
~prüfsieb *n* = power testing screen
~ramme *f*, siehe: Kraftstampfer *m*
~richtung *f* = direction of force
~rührwerk *n* = power-operated stirring gear
~schaufel *f*, siehe: Entladeschaufel
~schluß *m* [*zwischen Fahrbahn f und Fahrzeug n*] = transferable traction power
kraftschlüssiger Antrieb *m* = non-positive drive
Kraftstampfer *m*, Kraft(hand)ramme *f* = power (or mechanical) tamper (or rammer)
Kraftstoff *m*, siehe: Betriebsstoff *m*
~antrieb *m* = fuel drive
~einspritzpumpe *f* = fuel injection pump
Kraftstoff *m* **für Otto-Motor** *m*, (Motoren-) Benzin *n*, Otto-Kraftstoff *m* [*A. S. T. M. D 288—39*] = gas(oline) (or gasolene) (naphtha) (US); petrol (Brit.); Otto type fuel
~harz *n* = gum
~kerosin *n*, Traktorenkraftstoff *m*, Motorenpetroleum *n* = power kerosene, tractor fuel, tractor oil

Kraft|stollen *m*, Wasser ~ = power tunnel, hydro ~, hydro tube
~trommelwinde *f*, Kraft(trommel)windwerk *n* = power(-driven) (drum) winch
~übertragung *f* = power transmission, mechanical transmission of power
~verkehr *m*, Motorfahrzeugverkehr *m* = motor traffic
~versorgung *f*, Energieversorgung, Stromversorgung = power supply
Kraftwerk|anlage *f*, Kraftwerk *n* = power installation (or plant, or station)
~raum *m* = power plant chamber
Kraft|werksgebäude *n*, siehe: Krafthaus *n*
~werkzeug *n* = power-actuated tool
Krag|balken *m*, Kragträger *m*, Kragbalkenträger *m* = cantilevered beam, cantilever, semi-beam, corbel beam, projecting beam; semi-girder (Brit.)
~platte *f* = cantilever
~-Stangen(transport)rost *m*, Krag-Stangenaufgeber *m* = cantilever screen of bars, ~ bar screen, ~ grizzly [*is fixed at one end only, the discharge end being overhung and free to vibrate by the impact of the material on the grizzly*]
Krampe *f*, Krampen *m* = staple
Kran *m* mit Laufkatzenausleger *m* = saddle jib monotower crane (Brit.); ~ boom ~ ~ (US)
Kran|ausleger *m* = crane boom (US); ~ jib (Brit.)
~bagger *m*, siehe: Baggerkran *m*
~förderkübel *m*, siehe: Krankübel *m*
~führer *m* = crane operator
~gleis *n* = crane track(s), ~ tracking
~haken *m* = crane hook
~haus *n*, Kranführerkabine *f*, Kranführerhaus = crane cab(in)
~haus *n* = gantry house
Kranken|auto *n* = motor ambulance
~schleuse *f*; siehe unter „pneumatische Gründung *f*"
~urlaub *m* = sick leave
Kran|kübel *m*, Kranförderkübel = crane skip
~mast *m*, Turm *m*, Drehsäule *f* = (mono-)tower
~oberbau *m* = crane superstructure
~ramme *f*; siehe unter „Rammanlage *f*"

~schiene *f*, Kranbahnschiene = crane rail
~schwerpunktlage *f* **auf abschüssigem Gelände** *n* = crane balance on slope
~träger *m* = crane girder, gantry
~unterbau *m* [*Portalkran m*] = crane pedestal
~unterwagen *m* = crane carrier
~-Zusatzvorrichtung *f* = crane attachment
Krater *m* = crater
Kratz(er)förderer *m*, Kratzertransporteur *m* = drag-chain conveyor
Kratzerkette *f* = drag (chain)
Kreide *f* = chalk
~abbau *m* = chalk quarrying
~boden *m* = chalky soil
~gestein *n* = chalk
~kalkgestein *m* = chalky limestone
~mergel *m* = chalk marl
~schnur *f* = chalk line
Kreis|bogen *m*, Kreiskurve *f* [*Straße f*] = circular arc, ~ curve
~eimerleiter *m*, siehe: Eimerrad *n*
Kreisel|brecher *m*, siehe: Kegelbrecher
~läufer *m* = gyroscope rotor
~pumpe *f*; siehe unter „Pumpe *f*"
~verdichter *m* = centrifugal compressor
~verdichterschaufel *f* = jet blade
kreisendtaumelnde Bewegung *f* [*Kegelbrecher m*] = gyratory movement
kreisfahrbarer Kabelkran *m* **mit einem ortsfesten und einem radial verfahrbarem Turm** *m*; siehe unter „Seilförderanlage *f*"
kreisförmige Krone *f*, Wölbung *f* [*Straße f*] = (barrel) camber; [*deprecated: transverse slope, crossfall*]
Kreis|kipper *m*, siehe: Rundkipper
~kurve *f*, Kreisbogen *m* = circular curve, ~ arc
Kreislauf|prozeß *m*, Kreislaufmahlung *f*, Umlaufmahlung [*Mühle f*] = closed-circuit operation (or grinding)
~vorgang *m*, Zyklus *m* = cycle
Kreis|querschnitt *m* = circular section compressor
~ring *m*, Kreisplatz *m* = (traffic) roundabout (or circle); [*deprecated: gyratory junction, traffic circus*]
~ringplatte *f* = circular floor-plate
~ringscherapparat *m*, siehe: Ringschergerät *n*

Kreis|ringstraße *f*, Kreisplatzstraße = rotary road
~**ringträger** *m* = circular flange beam
~**säge** *f*; siehe unter „Säge *f*"
~**schwing(er)sieb** *n*, siehe: Kreisvibrationssieb
~**seiltrieb** *m* = continuous rope drive
~**sieb** *n* = cylindrical screen
~**stollen** *m* = circular tunnel
~**straße** *f* = district road
~**vibrationssieb** *n*, Kreisschwing(er)sieb *n* = vibrating screen with uniform full circle motion, circle-throw vibrating screen
~**wurf** *m*, Kreisbahn-Siebschwingung *f* = circle(-)throw (gyratory movement)
~**zeigerwaage** *f*, siehe: Zifferblattwaage
~**zelle** *f* = circular cell
~**zellen-Fang(e)damm** *m* = circular cell cofferdam
~**zylinderschale** *f* = circular cylindrical shell
kreiszylindrische Sperre *f*; siehe unter „Talsperre *f*"
Kreosotöl *n* = creosote oil; [*deprecated: creosote*]
Kresolharz *n*, siehe: Karbolpech *n*
Kreuz|band *n*, siehe: Andreaskreuz *n*
~**gelenkkupplung** *f* = universal joint coupling, ~ type ~
~**gewölbe** *n* = groin arch, groined vault, cross vault
~**hacke** *f*, Kreuzpickel *m* = pickaxe [*has one point and one flat end*]
~**kamm** *m* = cross cogging
~**knoten** *m*, Schifferknoten = reef knot
~**libelle** *f* = cross-bubble
~**meißel** *m*; siehe unter „Bohrmeißel"
~**meißel** *m*; siehe unter „Meißel *m*"
~**pickel** *m*, siehe: Kreuzhacke *f*
~**schlag** *m*; siehe unter „Drahtseil *n*"
~**schneide** *f* = cross bit cutting edge, ~ auger ~ ~
~**stake** *f* = herringbone strut
~**stein** *m* (Min.), siehe: Staurolith *m*
~**strebe** *f* = diagonal strut
~**streben** *fpl*, siehe: Andreaskreuz *n*
Kreuzung *f* von zwei Straßen *fpl*, Einzelkreuzung *f* = crossing
Kreuzungs|anlage *f* = interchange

~**bauwerk** *n*, siehe: plankreuzungsfreie Kreuzung *f*
~**rampe** *f* = interchange ramp
~**zufahrt** *f* = intersection approach
kreuzweise bewehrte Decke *f* = two-way slab floor
~ ~ **Platte** *f* = slab spanning in two directions
Kreuzzapfen *m*; siehe unter „Holzverbindung *f*"
~ = cross pin
Kriechdehnung *f* = creep strain
kriechen, wandern [*Schiene f*] = to creep
Kriechen *n* [*Beton m*] = creep, plastic flow, time yield, flow
~ (Geol.) = creep(ing)
~ **von Glasuren** *fpl*, Abrollen *n* ~ ~ = crawling of glazes
Kriechfaser *f* = creep fibre (Brit.); ~ fiber (US)
kriechfreier Stahl *m* = creepless steel
Kriech|gang-Selbstfahrwerk *n* = creeper specd self-propelled carrier
~**geschwindigkeit** *f*, Steiggeschwindigkeit = creep speed
~**raum** *m* unter dem Erdgeschoß *n* von kellerlosen Gebäuden *npl* = crawl space
~**spur** *f* = vehicle climbing lane
Kriegsschiff *n* = man-of-war
Kristall|chemie *f* = crystal chemistry
~**gitter** *n* = crystal structure, ~ lattice
kristalliner Kohlenstoff *m* = crystalline carbon
kristalliner Schiefer *m* = (crystalline) schist
kristallines Gestein *n*, Kristallin *m* = crystalline rock
kristallisierbar = crystallizable
Kristallquarzsand *m* = silica sand, grit
Kristallwasser *n* = crystalline water
Kriterium *n* = criterion
kritische Belastung *f*, ~ **Last** *f* = critical load(ing)
~ **Druckhöhe** *f*, kritisches Gefälle *n* [*Talsperre f*] = critical head
~ **Spannung** *f* = critical stress
kritischer Spanwinkel *m* = critical rake angle
Krone *f* [*Wehr n*] = crest
~ *f*; siehe unter „Straßenquerschnittausbildung *f*"

Krone *f* [*Talsperre f*] = crest; coping, crown (Brit.)
Kronen|mutter *f*, Kronenschraubenmutter = horned (screw) nut, castellated (~) ~
~**nippel** *m*; siehe unter „Bohrmeißel *m*"
~**schneide** *f*; siehe unter „Bohrmeißel *m*"
Krume *f*, siehe: Dammerde *f*
krummer Stahlbetonstab *m* = bent reinforced concrete bar
Krümmer *m*, siehe: Rohrkrümmer
~ [*Wasserkraftwerk n*] = elbow bend, penstock elbow
Krümmung *f* = curvature
Krümmungs|anfangspunkt *m*, Krümmungsendpunkt [*Straße f*] = tangent point
~**grad** *m* [*Straße f*] = degree of curvature
~**halbmesser** *m*, Krümmungsradius *m* [*Straße f*] = radius at bend
~**halbmesser** *m*, Krümmungsradius *m* [*Talsperre f*] = locus of centres (Brit.); line of centers (US)
Kryolith *m*, Eisstein *m*, Na_3AlF_6 (Min.) = cryolite, kryolith, Greenland spar
kryptokristallin, feinkristallin = crypto crystalline
Kubatur *f* = cubic yardage, cubage
Kübel *m* = bucket
~, Schaufel *f*, Ladeschaufel [*Schürflader m*] = bucket, loading ~
Kübelauf|lader *m*, siehe: (Front-)Ladeschaufel *f*
~**zug** *m* [*Betonwerk n*] = skip loader
~**zugswaage** *f* = mixer hopper type weighbatcher
Kübel|(bau)aufzug *m* = skip type (contractor's) (or builders') hoist
~**fettpresse** *f* = volume compressor
kubisch = cubical
kubische Parabel *f* = cubic parabola
kubischer Ausdehnungskoeffizient *m* = cubical coefficient of expansion
kubisches Endkorn *n* [*Brecher m*] = cubical product
Küchenabfälle *f* = garbage, household refuse, kitchen waste
Kufenrahmen *m* = skid frame
Kugel|blitz *m* = ball lightning
~**drucklager** *n* = ball-thrust bearing

~**fallprobe** *f* = dropping-ball (penetration) test
~**fall-Viskosimeter** *n* = falling ball (or sphere) visco(si)meter
~**formtrommel** *f* = drum pelletizer [*clay*]
~**füllung** *f* [*Mühle f*] = ball load
~**härteprüfer** *m* = indentation machine
~**hebel** *m* = ball lever
kugelig; siehe unter „Kornform *f*"
Kugel|kipplager *n*; siehe unter „Lager *n*"
~**(mahl)mühle** *f*; siehe unter „Mühle *f*"
~**mühlenmahlung** *f* = ball milling
~**schaufler** *m*, (Be)Lademaschine *f* mit kugelförmigem Kopf *m* = rotary (headed) excavator
~**schauflerkopf** *m* = rotary head, digging ~
~**schlagprüfung** *f* [*Beton m*] = dynamic ball-impact test method
~**strahlen** *n* = shot peening
~**taster** *m* = ball (or globe) caliper
~**ventil** *n* = ball valve
~**verformtechnik** *f* = pelletizing technique [*clay*]
~**zapfenlager** *n* = ball and socket bearing
Kühlbandanlage *f*, Bandkühlsystem *n* = cooling belt system
Kühler *m* = cooler
~ *m* [*Auto n*] = radiator
Kühl|flüssigkeit *f* = cooling liquid
~**mittel** *n* = coolant, refrigerant
~**mittelrohr** *n* = coolant tube
~**raum** *m* = cold storage room, cooling room, refrigerator room
~**schlange** *f* = cooling coil
~**schwindungsverhalten** *n* = cooling behavio(u)r
~**trommel** *f* = cooling drum
~**turm** *m* = cooling tower
~**vorrichtung** *f* = cooling device
~**wasserstollen** *m*; siehe unter „Talsperre *f*"
Kukersit *m*, estländischer Brennschiefer *m* = kukersit
Kulissenantrieb *m* = link drive
Kulm *m* (Geol.) = culm
Kultivator *m*, Boden~ = (agricultural) cultivator, field ~
kultivierbar, siehe: ackerfähig
Kulturbau *m* = agricultural engineering

Kultur|bauingenieur m = agricultural engineer
~**boden** m = agricultural soil, cultivated ~
~**denkmal** n = ancient monument, historic landmark
~**fläche** f = cultivated area, farmland arable
Kumaronharz n = c(o)umarone resin
Kundendienst m = after-sales service
Kunst|bauwerk n = structure
~**bims** m, siehe: Hochofenschaumschlacke f
~**granitbordstein** m **mit weißem Quarzitkorn** n = precast kerb (Brit.) (or curb) of white granite aggregate
~**harz** n = synthetic resin
~**kalkstein** m, Hydrokalkstein = artifical stone, reconstructed ~
~**körper** m, Bauwerk n, Baukörper m = structure
künstlich (aus)gefällter Kalzit m = artificially precipitated calcite
künstliche Anlandung f [*Strand-Wiederherstellung* f] = nourishment [*beach rehabilitation*]
~ **Bodenverdichtung** f = (soil) (or earth) compaction (or densification), artificial consolidation
künstlicher Anhydrit m, löslicher ~ = artificial anhydrite
(~) **Schlackensand** m, siehe: granulierte Hochofenschlacke f
künstliche Sandinselschüttung f **für Senkkasten** m = sand-island method
~ **Wasserstraße** f, Binnenschiffahrtkanal m = inland (navigation) canal, artificial navigation ~
Kunststoff m = plastic
~-**Kleber** m = plastic adhesive
~-**Markierungsstreifen** m, siehe: plastischer Markierungsstreifen m
~**rohr** n = plastic pipe
Kunstwachs n, siehe: Zeresin(wachs) n
Kupfer|blech n = sheet copper
~**chlorür** n, Cu_2Cl_2 = cuprous chloride
(~) **Fahlerz** n, siehe: Graugültigerz n
~**glanz** m (Min.) = chalcocite, redruthite, copper glance
~**indig** m (Min.) = indigo copper

~**kies** m, Chalkopyrit m, FeCuS (Min.) = copper pyrite, chalcopyrite (Brit.); copper pyrites (US)
~**lasur** f (Min.), siehe: Azurit m
~**nickel** m, siehe: Rotnickelkies m
~**schlacke** f = copper slag
~**schlackenstein** m = cast slag sett, copper ~ ~
~**silberglanz** m (Min.) = stromeyerite
~**sprengkapsel** f; siehe unter „1. Schießen n; 2. Sprengen n"
~**stein** m [*im Flammofen* m] = oxidised copper ores [*in the blast-furnace*]
~**vitriol** n, $CuSO_4 \times 5H_2O$ (Min.) = blue vitriol, chalcanthite, blue stone
~**wismutglanz** m (Min.), siehe: Emplektit m
Kupolschmelzofen m = cupola furnace
Kuppe f = summit
   Wanne f = sag
   Sichtlinie f = sight line, vision ~
   Sichtweg m, Sichtweite f, Sichtlänge f = sight distance, vision distance
Kuppel f, halbsphärisches Gewölbe n = dome, cupola
~ (Geol.), siehe: Lakkolith m
~**gewölbe** n = domical vault
~(**stau**)**mauer** f = dome-shaped dam
Kuppenausrundung f = convex transition between gradients, summit curve
Kuppen- und Wannenausrundungen fpl = transition curves between gradients, ~ radii on ~, vertical curves
Kupplung f **mit Reserve** f = oversize clutch (coupling)
Kupplungs|muffe f = clutch collar
~**scheibe** f = facing
Kurbel|trieb m = crank drive
~- **und Kreuzkopf-Schreitausrüstung** f [*Schreitbagger* m] = crosshead type walking mechanism
~**wannenschutz** m = crankcase guard
~**welle** f = crankshaft
~**zapfen** m = crank pin
Kurort m = health resort
Kurve f **mit kleinstem Halbmesser** m [*Straße* f] = curve of minimum radius
Kurven|abflachung f = curve casement
~**konsistenzmesser** m = curved-trough flow-device

Kurvenlineal *n* = drawing curve
Kurzausleger *m* = short boom (US); ~ jib (Brit.)
kurzfristige Hochwasservorhersage *f* = short-term flood prediction
Kurzlehrgang *m* = short course
kurzschließen = to short-circuit
Kurzschluß(läufer)motor *m* = squirrel cage (type electric) motor, squirrel-cage induction motor
Küste *f* = seaside, sea-coast, seabord
Küsten|bauwerk *n*, Küstenanlage *f* = shore structure
~**bauwesen** *n* = coastal engineering
~**düne** *f*, Stranddüne = coastal (sand) dune, ~ down
~**ebene** *f* = coastal plain
~**erosion** *f* = coast erosion
~**fahrzeug** *n* = coastwise craft
~**funkmeßanlage** *f* = shore radar installation
~**funkmeßgerät** *n* = shore-based radar unit
~**gebiet** *n* = coastal region, ~ territory
~**gebirge** *n* = coastal range, ~ mountain
~**kies** *m* = seashore-gravel, (bench) shingle, gravel without fines
~**land** *n* = coastal land
~**linie** *f*, Meer(es)uferlinie *f* = coastline, shore line
~**sand** *m* = beach sand
~**schiffahrt** *f* = coastal shipping
~**schlick** *m*, siehe: Klei *m*
~**schutz** *m*, Küstensicherung *f*, Küstenerhaltung *f*, Küstenverteidigung *f* = coast protection, sea defence (work), shore protection, coast defence work, coastal protection
~**schutzbauten** *f*, Küstenschutzbauwerke *npl* = coast protection works
~**stadt** *f* = coastal city (or town)
~**strömung** *f*, Küstendrift *f*, Küsten-Meeresströmung = littoral current (or drift), coastal ~, shore ~
~**überschwemmung** *f* = coastal flooding
Kutter *m* = cutter
Kyanisierung *f*, Eintauchverfahren *n* = kyanising

L

labil; siehe unter „Bitumen *n* im engeren Sinne"
labile Dammschüttungsmasse *f* = unstable fill
Labilität *f* = lability; readiness to break
Lability-Test *m* = readiness-to-break test
Laborant *m* = laboratory technician
Labor(atoriums)mischer *m* = laboratory mixer
Labradorit *m* = labradorite
Labyrinthdichtung *f* [*als Dichtungsart f*] = labyrinth seal
~ *f* [*als Material n*] = labyrinth packing
Lachs|paß *m*, Lachstreppe *f* = salmonladder, salmon-stair
Lack|benzin *n*, Testbenzin = painters' naphtha, paint thinner
~**muspapier** *n* = litmus paper
LACOUR-Bär *m*; siehe unter „Rammanlage *f*"
Lade|baum *m*, siehe: Derrick-Kran *m*
~**brücke** *f*, Tiefladebrücke [*Tiefladewagen m*] = deck, platform
~**gewicht** *n* = weight loaded
~**gut** *n* = material to be handled
~**maschine** *f*, (Auf)Lader *m*, Belademaschine, Ladegerät *n*, Verladegerät = (material) loader, mechanical ~
Ladenstraße *f* = retail business street, shopping ~
Lade|platte *f* = pallet
~**profil** *n* = railway clearance (Brit.); railroad ~ (US)
Lader *m* **für Schüttgut** *n*, siehe: Becher(werk)auflader *m*
~ **mit Becherrad** *n* = bucket wheel type loader
Lade|schaufel *f*, siehe: (Front-)Ladeschaufel
~**schaufel** *f*, Schaufel, Kübel *m* [*Schürflader m*] = (loading) bucket
Lage *f* [*Schweißlage*] = layer, pass
Lagen|bauweise *f*, Schichtenbauweise, Lagenschüttung *f* [*Erdbau m*] = layer(ed) construction
~**energie** *f*; siehe unter „Bernoulli-Satz *m*"
~**schüttung** *f*, siehe: Lagenbauweise *f*
~**stärke** *f*, siehe: Schichtstärke

Lageplan — Lagerstuhl mit Bolzen

Lageplan m = lay-out (plan)
~-**Massenermittlung** f; siehe unter „Erdarbeiten fpl"

Lager n, Magazin n = store
~ n, Vorkommen n, Lagerstätte f (Geol.) = deposit

Lager n / bearing
- Achs~ / axle ~
- ausgelaufenes ~ / burnt ~
- Drehzapfen~ / slewing journal ~, king pin ~
- Gleit~ / friction ~, plain ~ ~, plain ~, slidding ~, journal ~
- Kegelrollen~ / taper roller ~ (Brit.); TIMKEN ~ (US) [*Trademark*]
- Kipp~ / rocker ~, tilting ~, pivoting ~
- Kugelkipp~ / rocking ball ~
- Kugel~ / ball ~
- Kugelzapfen~ / ball and socket ~
- Kurbelzapfen~ / crank-pin ~
- Kurbel(wellen)~ / crankshaft ~
- ~bock m / ~ bracket
- ~büchse f / ~ bushing
- ~gehäuse n / ~ housing
- Nadel~ / needle ~
- Pendelrollen~ / self-aligning roller ~, spherical ~ ~
- Radnaben~ / hub ~
- Rillenkugel~ / grooved ball ~
- Ringschmier~ / ~ for ring lubrication
- Ritzelwellen~ / pinion shaft ~
- Rollen~ / roller ~
- Wälz~ / anti-friction ~

Lager|beständigkeit f **der Ottokraftstoffe** mpl = gasoline storage stability
    Punkt m der Druckzeitkurve f = break point
    Induktionszeit f = induction period
    Bombenharzwert m = potential gum
~**deckel** m = bearing cover
~**fuge** f [*Mauerwerk* n] = course joint, horizontal ~
~**gang** m (**oder Sill** m, **oder Intrusivlager** n) **zwischen diskordant aufgelagertem Sediment** n **und seinem Untergrund** m (Geol.) = interformational sill
~**halter** m, siehe: Magazinhalter
~**haltung** f, (Material)Lagerung f, Bevorratung f = (materials) storage, storekeeping, storing
~**haus** n = storehouse
~**hof** m, Lagerplatz m = storage yard
~**hülse** f = bearing jacket
~**luft** f = bearing slackness
~**platte** f, Sohlplatte f = bed plate, sole ~
~**platz** m, Lagerhof m = storage yard
~**ring** m = bearing ring
~**schale** f = bearing case
~**schraube** f = bearing screw
~**schuppen** m = store shed, storage ~, stock ~
~**silo** m, Schachtspeicher m, (Vorrats-)Silo, Silospeicher = silo (warehouse)
~**stätte** f (Geol.), siehe: Lager n
~**stuhl** m = bearing block
~**stuhl** m = pedestal
~**stuhl** m **mit Bolzen** m = shoe

Lagerung *f* = storage
Lagerungsdichte *f* = compactness
Lager|unterkünfte *fpl*, siehe: Baustellenlager *n*
~weißmetall *n* = anti-friction metal, white ~, babbitt ~, Babbitt's ~
~winkel *m* = bearing angle
Lagune *f* = lagoon
Laich|plätze *mpl* = spawning beds
~wanderung *f* = spawn migration
Lakkolith *m*, **Kuppel** *f* (Geol.) = laccolith, laccolite
Lamellen-Fenster *n* = lourred window
laminare Strömung *f*, siehe: Bandströmung *f*
Laminarie *f*, **Riementang** *m* = laminaria
Lamprophyr *m* = lamprophyre
Land|asphalt *m* [*Trinidad*] = land asphalt, land pitch
~drän *m*; siehe unter „Entwässerung *f*"
landeinwärts = inland
Landenge *f*, **Isthmus** *m* = isthmus
Landesplanung *f* = state planning, provincial ~
landgängige Erdsauganlage *f*, siehe: Erdsauganlage *f* zu Lande
Land|gewinnung *f*, **Neu~** *f* = land reclamation, reclamation of land
 ~ durch Eindeichung *f* = ~ by enclosure
 ~ durch Aufschüttung *f* = ~ by filling
landkartenmäßig erfassen = to map
Land|kies *m* = bank gravel
~klima *n* = land-controlled climate
landschaftlicher Ausblick *m*, **schöne Aussicht** *f* = scenic vista
Landschafts|bild *n* = scenery
~gestalter *m* = landscape engineer
~gestaltung *f* = landscaping, landscape treatment (or development)
~gestaltung *f* **an Straßen** *fpl* = roadside improvement
landseitig = landward
Landstraße *f* = (public) highway, rural ~
~, **Provinzstraße** *f* = provincial road
~ **2. Ordnung** *f* = secondary road, county ~
Landungssteg *m*, **Pier** *m*, *f* = pier

Land|verdunstung *f* = evaporation from land surfaces
~zunge *f*, **Nehrung** *f* = spit (of land)
Längeneinheit *f* = unit of length
langfristige Hochwasservorhersage *f* = long-term flood prediction
Langholz *n* = long trunks
~kreissäge *f* = grain wood circular saw
~nachläufer *m* = trailer for timber haulage
~transport *m* = logging
~wagen *m* = log cart
Lang|loch *n* = oblong hole
~lochbohrmaschine *f* = elongated hole drilling machine
~mahd *f*, siehe: Längsreihe *f*
~mahdplanierungsschablone *f*; siehe: Schwadenglätter *m*
~masche *f* [*Sieb n*] = rectangular mesh
langrund = oblong
Längsachse *f* = longitudinal axis
langsam|abbindend [*Verschnittbitumen n*] = slow-curing
~brechend, **stabil** [*Bitumenemulsion f*] = slow-breaking, stable, slow setting
~fahrend = slow-moving
Längs|achse *f* = longitudinal axis
~balken *m*, siehe: Längsträger *m*
~belastung *f* = thrust, axial force
~bewehrung *f*, **Längsarmierung** *f* = longitudinal reinforcement
~bohlenfertiger *m* = longitudinal (or bullfloat) finishing machine, longitudinal floating machine
Largseitenschifter *m* = longitudinal jack rafter
Längs|feld *n* = longitudinal bay
~führung *f* = longitudinal guide
~kraft *f* = longitudinal force
~naht *f* = longitudinal seam
~nut *f*, siehe: Keilwellennut
~preßfuge *f*; siehe unter „Fuge *f*"
~profil *n* = longitudinal profile (or section)
~reihe *f*, **Schwaden** *m*, **Längsmahd** *f*, **Langmahd** *f*, **Streifhaufen** *m* = windrow
~rippe *f* = longitudinal rib
~schlag *m*; siehe unter „Drahtseil *n*"
~schnitt *m* = longitudinal section
~schnitt-Sichtweite *f* = sight distance in profile

Längs|schubkraft f = horizontal shear, longitudinal shear
~steife f [*Kastenträger m*] = longitudinal (web) stiffener
~(tiefen)sicker m = side sub-drain
~träger m, Längsbalken m, Längsträgerbalken, Längsbalkenträger = longitudinal girder (Brit.); ~ beam, stringer
~traverse f = wale
Langstreckenförderbandanlage f zum Transport m von Gesteinen npl, Ferntransportband n = "rock road"
Längs|verband m = longitudinal bracing
~verwerfung f, streichende Verwerfung (Geol.) = strike fault
~werk n [*Meer n*] = sea (protection) wall
~werk n [*Fluß m*] = training wall
Lapilli f = lapilli
Lärche f = larch
Lärmbekämpfung f, Lärmabwehr f = noise abatement
Lasche f = shin, splice piece, fish piece, fish-bar, fishplate
Laschen|bolzen m = fish(-plate) bolt
~nietung f; siehe unter „Niet m"
~stoß m = splice joint
~verbindung f = double butt strap joint
Laschung f, Blattstoß m = scarf (joint)
Last|abfall m = load drop
~angriffspunkt m = point of application of load
~annahme f = design load
~aufbringung f, Lastangriff m = application of load
~bügel m mit zwei Haken mpl = double lifting hooks
Lastenmesser m, siehe: Belastungsmesser
Last|fahrzeug n = freight-carrying vehicle
~fläche f = loaded area
~gabel f = lift fork
~grenze f = safety limit
~haken m = lifting hook
~hebedampfmaschine f = hoisting steam engine
~hebemagnet m, siehe: Lastmagnet
~kahn m = cargo carrying barge
~katze f, Laufkatze f [*Gießerei-Drehkran m*] = jenny (Brit.); troll(e)y

Last(kraft)wagen m, LKW m = lorry (Brit.); (auto) truck (US); road-truck, motor truck
~bagger m; siehe unter „Autobagger"
~fahrer m = trucker
~waage f = (motor-)truck scale (US); lorry ~ (Brit.)
Last|magnet m, Lasthebemagnet, Hubmagnet = (electric) lifting magnet(o), crane ~
~moment n = load moment
~schwankung f = load variation
~senkungskurve f, siehe: Belastungs-Setzungsdiagramm n
~setzungskurve f, siehe: Belastungs-Setzungsdiagramm n
~spiel n = load cycle
~streifen m = load strip
~stufe f = load increment
lasttragende Wand f = (load-)bearing wall
Last|übertragung f = load transfer(ence)
~verteilung f = load distribution, distribution of load, dispersion of load
~verteilungsfundament n = spread foundation, ~ footing
~wechsel m [*Dauerversuch m*] = reversal of stress
~zug m = truck(-trailer) combination (US); lorry-trailer ~ (Brit.)
Lasurspat m (Min.) = lazulite
Lateralerosion f, siehe: Seitenschurf m
Laterit m = laterite
lateritischer Ton m = lateritic clay
Laternen|oberlicht n = lantern light
~pfahl m mit Brunnen m, siehe: Brunnenkandelaber m
Latex m = latex [*plural form: latices*]
Latten|hammer m = carpenters' (roofing) hammer
~kiste f, Lattenverschlag m = crate
~zaun m = paling
Laub|baum m = deciduous tree, broad-leaved ~
~holz n, siehe: Hartholz
~holzteerpech n = hardwood tar pitch
Lauf|achse f = free axle
~bahn f [*Lager n*] = race
~brunnen m = flowing well, running ~
laufende Unterhaltung f, siehe: Wartung f
laufender Meter m = linear metre, Lin. M.

Läufer *m* = runner

~ *m*, Laufrad *n* [*Turbine f; Elektromotor m*] = rotor

~ *m* [*Ziegel m*] = stretcher

~**rute** *f*; siehe unter „Rammanlage *f*"

~**schicht** *f* = stretching course

Lauf|fläche *f* [z. B. Raupe *f*; Rad *n*] = tread

~**gewicht** *n*, Einstellgewicht *n* = poise weight, sliding weight, jockey weight, moving poise

~**gewichtsbalken** *m* = poise beam [*for each material to be weighed*]

~**katze** *f*, siehe: Lastkatze

~**katze** *f* (oder **Lastkatze**) **mit Führerstand** *m* = troll(e)y with operator's cab(in)

~**katze** *f* (oder **Lastkatze**) **mit Greifkorb** *m* = bucket-carrying troll(e)y

~**katzenausleger** *m*, Lastkatzenausleger = saddle jib (Brit.); ~ **boom** (US); jib with crab (Brit.); boom ~ ~ (US)

~**katzenträger** *m*, Lastkatzenträger *m* = overhead troll(e)y beam

~**kraftwerk** *n*, Flußkraftwerk, Laufwasserkraftwerk = river power plant

~**kran** *m* = overhead (travel(l)ing) crane, travel(l)ing ~

~**kranz** *m* = curved roller path

~**rolle** *f* = runner

~**rolle** *f* [*Gleiskette f*] = tread roller

~**rolle** *f* **mit Welle** *f* = roller and shaft

~**rute** *f*; siehe unter „Rammanlage *f*"

(~) **Steg** *m* = catwalk, duckboard, walkway

~**wasserkraftwerk** *n*, siehe: Laufkraftwerk

Laurvikit *m* (Geol.) = la(u)rvikite

Lautarit *m* (Min.) = lautarite

Lava *f* = lava

~**bombe** *f*, vulkanische Bombe = volcanic bomb

~**stromsee** *m* = lake ponded up by lava

Lawine *f* = avalanche

Lawinen|schutt *m* = avalanche débris

~**verbau** *m* = avalanche brake

LBV-Stoff *m*, siehe: luftporenbildender Beton-Verflüssiger *m*

Lebensdauer *f*, Nutzungsdauer = working life, service(able) ~

Leckstelle *f*, undichte Stelle *f* = leak(age)

Leder|handschuh *m* = leather hand pad

~**manschette** *f* = leather guard

Ledigenheim *n* = bachelor quarter

Leergewicht *n*, Taragewicht = tare

Leerlauf *m* [*Maschine f*] = idle run; coasting (Brit.)

~**schütz(e)** *n*, (*f*), siehe: Freilaufschütz(e)

~**stollen** *m* = waste water gallery

~**ventil** *n*, siehe: Freilaßventil *n*

Leerstandanzeiger *m* = low level indicator

Legföhre *f*, Bergkiefer *f*, Bergföhre = mountain-pine

legiertes Motorenöl *n*, HD-Öl, HD-Motorenöl = heavy-duty oil

Lehm *m* = loam

~**heide** *f* = loam heath

~**hütte** *f* = mud hut

~**mergel** *m* = loamy marl

~**schlag** *m* = puddle-clay

~**vorlage** *f* [*Talsperre f*] = puddled loam core

Lehrbuch *n* = instruction book

Lehre *f* = ga(u)ge

Lehr|film *m* = instructional film, training ~

~**gerüst** *n* = cent(e)ring

~**gerüst** *n* **für Plattenbrücke** *f* = deck centering (US); ~ centring (Brit.)

~**gerüst** *n* **mit senkrechter Absteifung** *f* = trestle centering (US); ~ centring (Brit.)

~**gerüstspindel** *f*, Bauschraubenwinde *f* = contractors' jack screw

~**gespärre** *n* = guiding rafters

Lehr|lingsausbildung *f* = apprenticeship training

~**tätigkeit** *f* = teaching activity

Leicht|bau(dreh)kran *m*, Leicht-Turmdrehkran = light (mono)tower crane, ~ rotating tower crane, ~ revolving tower crane

~**bauplatte** *f* = light-weight building board (or slab)

~**benzin** *n*, Gasbenzin, Rohrkopfbenzin, Erdgasbenzin, Naturgasolin *n* = natural gasoline, casing-head ~

~**betonstein** *m* = lightweight concrete block

Leichtbeton-Zuschlag(stoff) *m* = light-weight concrete aggregate

(**Leicht**)**|Bohrwagen** *m* = wagon drill

~**bohrwagen** *m* = wagonette quarry drill

leichte Aufschüttung — Leutebude

leichte Aufschüttung f = lightweight fill
Leichter m = lighter
leichte (Straßen) Decke f = low-type pavement
leichtes Buschwerk n **und grobes Unkraut** n = light brush and débris
leichteste Spaltrichtung f [*Gestein* n] = rift of rock
Leicht|fahrbahn f; siehe unter „Brücke"
~**metallrohrgerüst** n, Leichtmetallrohrrüstung f = light metal tubular scaffold(ing)
~**öl** n = light oil
~**perlit** m = popped perlite
~**perlit-Aufbereitung** f = perlite popping (or processing)
~**petroleumraffinat** n = petroleum leve, light petroleum
~**(pfahl)ramme** f = light-duty (pile) driver
~**trägerdecke** f = lightweight floor(slab)
~**zuschlag(stoff)** m = lightweight aggregate
~**zuschlag(stoff)** m **aus Ton** m = clay aggregate
Leimbauweise f = glued timber construction
Leinöl n = linseed oil
~**firnis** m = linseed oil varnish
~**standöl** n = stand oil
Leinpfad m, Treidelweg m = towpath, towing path
leistenförmig = lath-like [*plagioclase*]
Leistungs|beschreibung f = specification
~**fähigkeit** f = capacity
~**fähigkeit** f **bei voller Sättigung** f [*Straße* f] = saturation capacity
~**lohn** m = productivity wage
~**position** f; siehe unter „Angebot n"
~**reserve** f; siehe unter „Baumaschinen f pl und Baugeräte n pl"
~**soll** n, siehe: installierte (Kraft)Leistung f
~**verzeichnis** n; siehe unter „Angebot"
Leit|bohle f = wale
~**damm** m = longitudinal dyke, training wall, training bank, guide bank
Leiter|gerüst n = ladder scaffold(ing)
~**schacht** m [*Bergbau* m] = footway
Leit|horizont m (Geol.), siehe: Bezugshorizont

~**insel** f = directional island
~**linie** f **am Fahrbahnrand** m = side-of-pavement line
~**pfosten** m = delineator
~**seil** n [*Bagger* m] = tagline
~**spindeldrehbank** f = engine lathe
Leitungs|graben m = service trench
(~) **Kanal** m = duct, mains subway
~**wasser** n, Brauchwasser n = tap water, service ~
Leit|werk n = training work
~**zelle** f, siehe: Tracheide f
Lemniskate f = lemniscate
Lenk|achse f = steering axle
~**bremse** f = steering brake
~**getriebe** n = steering gear
~**kupplung** f = steering clutch (coupling)
~**mechanismus** m = steering mechanism
~**rad** n, Tastrad n = guide wheel
~**rad** n, Steuerrad = steering wheel
Lenkung f = steer(ing)
Lenk|vorrichtung f = steering device
~**walze** f = pony truck
Lenzpumpe f = bilge pump
LEOBA-Spannglied n [*Trademark*] = LEOBA stressing apparatus [*Trademark*]
Leonardschaltung f, Ward-Leonard-Schaltung = Ward-Leonard system of variable voltage control
Lepidokrokit m, Rubinglimmer m [*hieß ursprünglich Goethit* m] = lepidocrocite (Min.)
Lesbarkeitsweite f = legibility distance
Leseband n, Klaubeband n = picking belt conveyor
Letten m = plastic clay
Letterholz n, siehe: Schlangenholz
Leucht|boje f = light buoy, luminous ~
~**bordstein** m = reflectorizing curbstone
~**feuer** n = beacon
~**gas** n = illuminating gas
~**-Inselpfosten** m = illuminated bollard
~**mast** m, siehe: Beleuchtungsmast
~**öl** n, siehe: Petroleum n
~**petroleum** n, siehe: Petroleum
~**turm** m = lighthouse
Leukoxen m, Titanmorphit m (Min.) = leucoxene
Leutebude f, siehe: Baubude

Leuzit m [*früher: weißer Granat* m] = leucite
~basalt m = leucite-basalt
~basanit m = leucite-basanite
~trachit m (Geol.) = amphegenyte
~trephit m = leucite-trephite
Liaston m (Geol.) = Lias(sic) clay
Libanonzeder f = ceder of Lebanon
Libelle f, siehe: Wasserwaage f
Libellensextant m = spirit-level sextant, bubble ~
Libethenit m (Min.) = libethenite
Licht|anlage f = light plant
~bildmeßverfahren n, Photogrammetrie f = photogrammetry, photogrammetric survey(ing)
Lichtbogen|schmelzofen m = arc furnace
~schweißung f; siehe unter „Schweißen n"
~zündung f = arc ignition
lichte Höhe f = headroom, headway
~ Maschenweite f, Sieböffnung f = sieve opening, aperture size; space (US)
~ Weite f, ~ Breite = clear width
lichter Abstand m = clear distance
~ Raum m = clearance
lichtes Graumanganerz n (Min.) = polianite
~ Rotgültigerz n, Proustit m, Ag_3AsS_3 (Min.) = proustite
Licht|hof m = light court
~mast m, siehe: Beleuchtungsmast
~pausapparat m = printing machine, copier, copying machine
~raumhöhe f = clearance height
~raumprofil n = clearance diagram
~reflexion f = light reflectance
~signalsteuerung f = signal control
~weite f [*Balken* m] = effective span [*beam*]
~weite f [*Brücke* f] = clear span
~weite f [*Rohr* n] = internal diameter [*pipe*]
Liderung f = packing
Liefer|industrie f = supply industry
~mischer m, siehe: Transportmischer
liefern und ein(zu)bauen = furnish and install, F & I
Liefer|wagen m [*Automobil* n] = delivery van
~werk n, Erzeugerwerk = producer plant

Liegegebühren f = demurrage (charges)
Liegende n (Geol.) = underlaying
Liegendkörper m (Geol.), siehe: Batolith m
Liegeplatz m [*Kanal* m] = lay bye
~ m [*Schiff* n] = berthing accomodation
Liegezeit f [*Straßendecke* f] = life, service ~, service (time)
Lieschgras n = timothy grass, cat's tail
Lignit m, bituminöses Holz n, Xylit m = lignite
Limburgit m (Geol.) = limburgite
Limnologie f, Seenkunde f = limnology
Limonit m (Min.) = limonite
Linarit m, siehe: Bleilasur f (Min.)
Linderungsmittel n = palliative
Linien|blitz m = forked lightning
~führung f **im Aufriß** m = vertical alignment (Brit.)/alinement (US) of highways
~führung f **im Grundriß** m = horizontal alignment (Brit.)/alinement (US) of highways
~last f, Streckenlast f = line load, linear load, knife-edge load
linsenförmig = lens-shaped, lenticular
Linsen|kopfschraube f = fillister-head screw
~senkniet m = oval head countersunk rivet
Listenpreis m = list price
Lithiumglimmer m (Min.) = lithium mica, lithia ~
Lithographenkalk(stein) m = lithographe stone
Litoral n, Ebbe- und Flutzone f = littoral zone
litorale Meeresablagerung f, landnahe ~= littoral deposit
Litze f; siehe unter „Drahtseil n"
Litzendraht m = strand wire
Lizenzabgabe f = licence tax
LKW m, Last(kraft)wagen m, Straßenkraftwagen m für Lastentransport m = lorry (Brit.); (auto) truck (US); commercial vehicle
~-Anhänger m = truck-trailer (US); lorry trailer (Brit.)
~-Splittstreuer m [*hinten am LKW angebracht*] = lorry tailboard chippings spreader (Brit.); truck ~ ~ ~ (US)

LKW-Transport — Löffelgroßbagger mit Kniehebelvorschubwerk

LKW|-Transport *m*, Straßenanlieferung *f*, Last(kraft)wagentransport = haulage by truck, truck haul(ing) (US); haulage by lorry, lorry haul(ing) (Brit.)
~-(Trommel-)Seilwinde *f* = truck (US)/lorry (Brit.) (cable, or rope) winch
~-Überholspur *f* = truck passing lane (US); lorry ~ ~ (Brit.)
Loch *n* [*Rundlochsieb n*] = gauge (Brit.)
~abstand *m* = pitch
~abzug *m* [*Niet m*] = deduction of rivet holes
~feinblech *n* = perforated (metal) sheet, pierced (metal) sheet
~freßkorrosion *f* = pitting corrosion
~grobblech *n* = perforated metal plate
~karte *f* = punched card, punch-card
~leibungsdruck *m* [*Niet m*] = bearing stress
~leibungsfläche *f* = effective bearing area
~lehre *f* = hole ga(u)ge
~mitte *f* = centre of hole (Brit.); center ~ ~ (US)
~reihe *f* = row of holes, chain ~ ~
~taster *m*, siehe: Innentaster
Lochung *f*, Lochen *n* = perforation, holing
Lochziegel(stein) *m* = perforated brick
Locker|gestein *n*, siehe: Boden *m*
~gesteinsfang(e)damm *m*, siehe: Erdfang(e)damm
Löffel *m* [*Bagger m*] = (shovel) dipper, shovel, bucket, dipper bucket
~bagger *m* = navvy (type) excavator (Brit.); shovel (type) ~, revolving shovel
~bohrer *m*, offene Schappe *f* = spoon-auger

Löffelgroßbagger *m* mit **Kniehebelvorschubwerk** *n*, Fabrikat **MARION POWER SHOVEL COMPANY, MARION, OHIO, USA**	knee action stripping shovel
A-förmiges Gerüst *n*	A-frame, gantry
Alarmsignal *n*	warning signal
Bodenpressung *f*	bearing pressure
Doppelgleiskette *f*	two-belt crawling traction truck
Drehsattel *m*	saddle casting
Führungszylinder *m*	hydraulic jack cylinder
Gleiskettenband *n*	crawler belt
Gleiskettenpaar *n*	pair of crawlers
Hubtrommel *f*	hoisting drum
Hubwerk *n*	hoisting machinery
Königszapfen *m*	center journal (US); king pin
Kurvenfahren *n*	turning
Löffelvorschub *m*	crowding motion
Maschinenhaus *n*	house
Maschinenplattform *f*	machinery deck
Oberwagen *m*	upper frame
Rollenkranz *m*	roller circle, rail ~
Schneidlippe *f*	cast steel lip
Schwenkwerk *n*	rotating machinery
Seitenrahmen *m*	side frame
Stahlgußstück *n* in der Mitte *f*	center casting (US); centre ~ (Brit.)
Stahlgußstück *n* in der Rahmenecke	corner casting
Unterwagenrahmen *m*	lower frame, base structure
Vorschubwerk *n*	crowding machinery

Löffel|hochbagger m, Hochlöffel(bagger) m = power navvy, crane navvy, crowd shovel (Brit.); (face) shovel, power shovel, mechanical shovel, (swing) dipper shovel; luffing-boom shovel (US)
~hocheinrichtung f, siehe: Hochlöffeleinrichtung
~hohlmeißel m = spoon-bit gouge
~inhalt m = (shovel) dipper capacity, dipper shovel ~, (dipper) bucket ~
~klappe f [*Hochlöffel* m] = dipper door (or slide)
~klappenauslöser m = dipper trip [*a device which unlatches the door of a shovel bucket to dump the load*]
~naßbagger m; siehe unter „Naßbagger m"
~stiel m, Auslegerstiel [*Hochlöffel* m] = (dipper) stick (or handle)
~stieltasche f = dipper stick sleeve
~tiefbagger m, Tieflöffel(bagger) m = trench-forming shovel, backacter, backacting shovel (or excavator), dragshovel, trencher, ditcher, trenching hoe, drag bucket (Brit.); (back-)hoe, trenchhoe, pullshovel (US); pullstroke trenching machine, ditching shovel, back digger
~vorderwand f = front wall of dipper
~zahn m = dipper tooth
logarithmisches Wahrscheinlichkeitsgesetz n = log-probability law

Loh|erde f = tan-earth
~gerberei f = tannery, tan-house, tanyard
Lohn|abbau m = wage cutting
~arbeiter m = wage worker
~aufwand m = wage expense
~büro n = staff pay office, payroll section
~empfänger m = wage earner
~faktor m = wage determinant
~festsetzung f = wage determination
~fuhrgewerbe n = carrier's trade
lohngebundene Kosten f = cost incidental to wages
Lohn|höhe f = wage level
~kosten f = payroll costs
~liste f = (wages) payroll
~satz m = wage rate
~steigerung f = wage increase
~tag m = pay day
~tüte f = pay envelope
lokal, örtlich = local
lokales Triangulationsnetz n = local triangulation network
Lokomobile f, Kesseldampfmaschine f = portable steam engine
Lokomobilkessel m = semi-portable boiler
Lokomotiv|drehkran m, Drehkran m auf Normalspur f = locomotive (jib) crane (Brit.); locomotive (boom) crane (US); railway ~ ~ (Brit.); railroad ~ ~ (US)
~kessel m = locomotive (type) boiler

Lokomotivschuppen m	locomotive shed
Rechteckschuppen m	straight shed
Rechteckschuppen mit einem Zugang m	one-ended shed
Rechteckschuppen mit zwei Zugängen mpl	trough shed
Ringschuppen m	round shed
Aufstellgleis n	stabling track
Einzeltoreinfahrtgleis n	radiating track
Drehscheibe f	turntable
Untersuchungsgrube f, Arbeitsgrube	inspection pit
Rauchabführung f	smoke disposal

Lokomotivstrahlgebläse n = locomotive jet blower
Löllingit m, FeAs$_2$ (Min.) = lollingite
Londoner Ton m = London clay

Longitudinalwelle f = longitudinal wave
Lopolith m (Geol.) = lopolith
Lore f = wagon
Lösch(e) m, (f), siehe: Kesselschlacke f

löschen [*Branntkalk m*], siehe: ablöschen
Lösch|grube *f*, siehe: Kalkgrube
~hafen *m* = port of discharge, landing-port
~kalk *m*, Hüttenkalk, Kalkhydrat *n* [*pulverförmig, also trocken gelöschter Kalk m*] = dry hydrate [*high calcium lime slaked as a dry hydrate ground to a powder*]
~kurve *f* [*Kalk m*] = thermal slaking curve
~maschine *f* = slaking machine, hydrator
~pfanne *f* [*Kalk m*] = slaking pan (or vessel)
~schnecke *f* = slaking screw
~verhalten *n* [*Kalk m*] = slaking behavio(u)r
Losdrempel *m*, siehe: Losständer *m*
Lösen *n* [*Erdbau m*] = loosening
loser Zement *m*, unverpackter ~, ungesackter ~ = bulk cement
loskuppeln = to disengage
löslicher Anhydrit *m*, künstlicher ~ = artificial anhydrite
~ Farbstoff *m* = dye(-stuff)
Löslichkeit *f* = solubility
losreißen von = to tear loose from
Losständer *m*, Losdrempel *m*, Setzpfosten *m* = removable sluice pillar
~wehr *n* = sluice weir with removable sluice pillars
Lösung *f* = solution
Lösungs|festigkeit *f* [*Boden m*] = loosening strength
~mittel *n* = solvent, solving agent
lösungsmittelfliehend = lyophobe
Löß *m* = loess, löss [*diluvial deposit of fine loam*]
~ablagerung *f* = deposition of loess
~bildung *f* = loess formation
~haus *n* = loess dwelling
~lehm *m* = loess-clay
~mergel *m* = marl loess
~steilufer *n* = loess bluff
~vorkommen *n* = loess deposit
~wind *m* = loess depositing wind
Loten *n*, Lotung *f* = sounding
Überschall~ = supersonic ~
Löt|kolben *m*, Lötstiel *m*, Löteisen *n* = copper(ing) bit, soldering iron, grozing iron

~lampe *f* = soldering lamp, blowlamp, blowpipe lamp (Brit.); blowtorch (US)
~paste *f* = soldering paste
Lotpfahl *m*; siehe unter „Gründungspfahl *m*"
lotrecht, senkrecht = vertical, perpendicular, plumb
lotrechte Normalspannung *f* [*Baugrund m*] = vertical normal stress
lotrechtes (Schiffs)Hebewerk *n* = non-lock type vertical barge lift
Lotschnur *f*, siehe: Maurerschnur
Lotsen|flagge *f* = pilot flag
~gebühren *f* = pilotage charges
Löt|verbindung *f* = brazed joint
~wasser *n* = chlorate of zinc, monkey
~zange *f* = brazing tongs, soldering tongs, soldering-tweezers, hawk-bill (pliers)
~zinn *n* = solder, plumber's solder, lead-tin solder
LP-Zusatz *m*, siehe: Belüftungsmittel *n*
Lücke *f* = gap
Luft|abschreckungskühler *m* = air-quenching (grate) cooler
~aufnahme *f*, Luftbild *n* = airphoto, aerial photograph, aerial shot
~auftrieb *m* = air buoyancy
luftbereift = pneumatic-tired (US); pneumatic-tyred (Brit.)
(luftbereifter) Einachs(-Schnell)mischer *m*, Autoanhänger-Einachs-Mischer = single-axle trailer mixer
~ Schürflader *m* = rubber-mounted front-end loader
Luft|bildtechnik *f* = aerial engineering
~blase *f* = air bubble
~boje *f* = buoyancy tank
~brücke *f* = air lift
~druck *m* = air blast
~druckimpuls *m* = pulse of air
~durchdringungsmesser *m* = permeameter
~einschluß *m* **in Beton** *m* = air entrainment in concrete
~einschlußmittel *n*, siehe: Belüftungsmittel
~(-Erddruck-)Meßdose *f* **nach Goldbeck**, Goldbeckdose *f* = Goldbeck (pressure)cell
~(-Erddruck-)Meßdose *f* **nach Ritter** = Ritter (pressure) cell

Lufterhärtung — Luftstrahl

Luft|erhärtung *f* [*Betonstein m*] = air curing
~erhitzer *m*, Warmluftgerät *n*, Luftheizapparat *m* = (air) heater, space ~
~feuchtigkeit *f* = air moisture
~förderrinne *f*, siehe: Gebläseluft-Förderrinne
luftförmig = aeriform
Luft|fracht *f* = air freight
~führungskanal *m* [*Luftrutsche f*] = air chamber
~gehalts-Prüfgerät *n*, siehe: Belüftungsmesser *m*
luftgekühlter Dieselmotor *m* = air-cooled diesel engine
luftgetragene Feinststoffe *mpl* = air float fines
luftgetrocknetes Holz *n* = air-seasoned wood
Luft|heber *m* [*Scheidekonus m*] = air lift [*separatory cone*]
~heizapparat *m*, siehe: Lufterhitzer *m*
~holz *n*, siehe: Amaranthholz

lufthydraulisch = hydropneumatic
Luft|insel *f* = still air space
~kabel *n* = overhead electric cable
~kalk *m*, nichthydraulisches Bindemittel *n*, Luftmörtelbildner *m* = non-hydraulic lime, ~ binder
~kanal *m* = air duct
~mengenmesser *m*, siehe: Belüftungsmesser *m*
~meßgerät *n*, siehe: Belüftungsmesser *m*
~mörtel *m* = ordinary lime mortar
Luft|pore *f* = air void
~porenanteil *m*, scheinbare Porosität *f* = air space ratio
~porenbeton *m*; siehe unter „Beton"
luftporenbildender Beton-Verflüssiger *m*, LBV-Stoff *m* = combined plasticizer and air-entraining agent
~ Zusatzstoff *m*, siehe: Belüftungsmittel *n*
Luft|puffer *m* = air cushion
~reifen-Doppelrad *n* = pneumatic dual tired wheel (US); ~ ~ tyred ~ (Brit.)

---

luftreifenfahrbarer Betontransportwagen *m* **mit Mischer** *m*

  Betontransportwagen *m* mit (aufgebautem) Rührwerk(smischer) *n*, (*m*), Nachmischer *m*, Rührwagen [*zentrale Betonmischung f*]

  Transportmischer *m*, Liefermischer *m* [*zentrale Abmessung, Mischen während der Fahrt*]

  Transportmischer mit querliegender Mischtrommel *f*

lorry-mounted mixer (Brit.); motomixer, mixer-type truck, ready-mix (cement) truck (US); transit (concrete) mixer agitator (or agitating) conveyor (or truck), truck agitator (US); agitating lorry; agitator [*deprecated*] (Brit.)

truck mixer, transit-mixer (truck) (US); mixer lorry (Brit.)

side discharge truck paver

Luft|reifenrad *n* = pneumatic-tired wheel (US); pneumatic-tyred ~ (Brit.)
~reifenschlauch *m*, (Reifen)Schlauch = air chamber
~reifenschlepper *m*, Straßenschlepper, Radschlepper = industrial wheel tractor; rubber-tyred tractor (Brit.); pneumatic-tired tractor (US); wheel-type industrial tractor, wheeled tractor
~reiniger *m* = air cleaner
~-Rutsche *f*, siehe: Gebläseluft-Förderrinne *f*
~schacht *m*, siehe: Entlüftungsschacht

~schleuse *f*, Druckluftschleuse, Preßluftschleuse = (pressed) air-lock
~schutzbunker *m* = air-raid shelter
~spiegelung *f*, Fata Morgana *f* = mirage
~spül(bohr)hammer *m* = puff blowing piston rock drill
~spülkolben *m* = puff blowing piston
~spülung *f* [*Bohrhammer m*] = puff blowing
~spülvorrichtung *f*, Blasevorrichtung [*Bohrhammer m*] = puff blowing device
~strahl *m* [*pneumatische Förderanlage f*] = conveying air

Luft|strahl-Prallzerkleinerer m; siehe unter „Mühle f"
~strom-Gebläse n im Zementsilo m = cement blower
~stromsichter m = air classifier to which the product removed from the mill is fed by air
~strömung f, Luftstrom m = air current, stream of air
~temperatur f = atmospheric temperature
lufttrocken [*Holz* n] = air-dry
Luftumschichtung f = air circulation
Lüftungs|maschinen fpl = ventilating equipment
~ziegel m, Lüftungsstein m = air brick
Luft|ventil n = air (relief) valve
~verdichter m, Kompressor m, Drucklufterzeuger m = (air) compressor
~verflüssigung f = liquefaction of air
~vermessung f = aerial surveying, air ~
~verunreinigung f = air pollution
~vorwärmer m = air pre-heater
~waffenbauverwaltung f = Works Directorate of the Air Force
~wäsche f = airwasher
Lungenmoos n, isländisches Moos n = Iceland moss
Lungstein m, siehe: Basaltlava f
Luttenleitung f = air piping, ~ line
Luxusausführung f = de luxe model
Lydit m, Kieselschiefer m = Lydian stone, lydite, touchstone

M

Mäander m, Fluß~, Flußschlinge f = meander
   Prallufer n = cut-off bluff
   Anwachsufer n = deposition bluff, accreting bank
   toter Flußarm m, Altwasser n = deserted channel forming an oxbow lake
Mächtigkeit f (Geol.) = thickness, depth, richness, size, power, substance, width
Magazin n, Lager n = store
~bau m [*Erzgrube* f] = shrinkage stoping
~halter m, Lagerhalter = storekeeper
magere Mischung f = lean mix
Mager|gas n = lean gas
~kalk m = poor quicklime, lean ~
Magma n, Schmelzfluß m, (magmatische) Schmelze f, Schmelzlösung f = magma
~rest m = magmatic residuum
magmatisches Gestein n, siehe: Eruptivgestein
Magnesia f, siehe: Magnesiumoxyd n
magnesiahaltiger hydraulischer Kalk m siehe: Bitterkalk m
~ **Kalkstein** m, siehe: Bitterkalk m
Magnesia|tongranat m = magnesium-aluminium garnet
~-**Treiben** n = action of magnesia, expansion tendency due to magnesia
~zement m = magnesite cement, plastic calcined magnseite, plastic calcines
Magnesit|-Chromstein m = magnesite-chrome brick
~gestein n = magnesite rock
~stein m, Magnesitziegel m = magnesite brick, magnesia ~, ~ refractory
~stein mit 96% MgO = periclase brick
Magnesium|chlorid n, Chlormagnesium n, $MgCl_2$ = magnesium chloride
~hydrosilikat n, wasserhaltiges Mg-Silikat = hydrous silicate of magnesia, ~ magnesium silicate
~karbonat n, kohlensaures Magnesium n, $MgCO_3$ = magnesium carbonate
~olivin n (Min.), siehe: Forsterit m
~oxyd n, kaustische Magnesia f, Bittererde f, gebrannter Magnesit m, MgO = magnesium oxide, magnesia, bitterearth, burnt magnesia, oxide of magnesia
~silikat n, $3\ SiO_3Mg\cdot SH_2O$ = silicate of magnesium, magnesium silicate
~sulfat n, Bittersalz n = sulphate of magnesium, magnesium sulphate, Epsom salt
Magnet|abscheider m, siehe: Magnetscheider
~eisensand m = magnetic ironsand, iserine
~eisenerz n, Magnetit m, Fe_3O_4 (Min.) = magnetite
~greifer m = (electric) lifting magnet(o) with tines (US) / tynes (Brit.); crane ~ ~ ~
magnetischer Bremslüfter m = brake lifting magnet

magnetisches Aufschlußverfahren n; siehe unter „geophysikalische Baugrunduntersuchung f"

Magnetit m, siehe: Magneteisenerz n
Magnetkies m, FeS (Min.) = magnetic pyrite(s), pyrrhotine, pyrrhotite

Magnetkompaß m
magnetischer Nordpol m
Mißweisung f
geographischer Nordpol m

magnetic compass
magnetic North
magnetic declination, ~ variation
geographical North

Magnet|kupplung f = magnetic clutch
~rüttler m; siehe unter „Betonrüttelgeräte npl"
~scheider m, Magnetabscheider m = magnetic separator
~vibrator m; siehe unter „Betonrüttelgeräte npl"
~zündung f = magneto ignition
Mahlbarkeit f = grindability
~prüfer m = grindability machine
Mahlen n; siehe unter „Mühle f"

Mahl|feinheit f = fineness of grinding
~kalk m, siehe: ungelöschter gemahlener Kalk
~kugel f = grinding ball
~mühle f, siehe: Mühle f
~trocknungsanlage f = short tube mill with centrifugal air separator
Mahlung f; siehe unter „Mühle f"
Mahlzusatz m [Zement m] = grinding aid
Maie f, Weißbirke f = common birch

MAIHAK-Bodendruckmeßdose f mit akustischen Schwingungen fpl
Stahlmeßsaite f
Eigenfrequenz f
Deckel m
Elektromagnet m
Empfangsapparatur f
Vergleichssaite f

MAIHAK sonic type cell

vibrating wire
natural frequency
metal membrane surface
electric magnet
acoustic loading control device
unstressed wire

Makadamdecke f, siehe: Schotterdecke

Makadam-Maschinenanlage f zur Herstellung f von bituminösen Straßenbelagsmassen fpl, Trocken- und Mischanlage f zur Herstellung von Mischmakadam m, Aufbereitungsanlage f für Mischmakadam m
Aufbereitungsanlage f für Mischmakadam m und Walzasphalt m, Trocken- und Mischanlage f für Mischmakadam m und Walzasphalt m, Schwarzdeckenmischanlage f, bituminöse Mischanlage, Aufbereitungsanlage für bituminöse Mischdecken

bituminous macadam and tarmacadam mixing plant, coated macadam mixing plant (Brit.); central mixing plant for the preparation of intermediate mixtures, cold mix (asphalt) plant (US)

asphalt and coated macadam mixing plant, dual-purpose mixing plant (or machine) (Brit.); combination hot or cold mix plant (US); (asphalt and) bituminous mixing plant, asphalt and tarmacadam plant, high and low temperature drying and mixing plant, aggregate bituminizing plant, premixing plant

Makadam-Maschinenanlage

Baukasten-System-Anlage *f*, halbstationäre Anlage *f* — sectional type plant

Bedienungsstand *m* — control platform, operator's ~

Benetzen *n*, Umhüllen *n* — coating, wetting; wet mixing (US)

Bindemittel-Eindüsapparatur *f*, Zerstäuber *m* — binder spray nozzle

Bindemittelpumpe *f* — binder (metering) pump (Brit.); bitumen (metering) pump (US)

Bindemittelwaage *f* — binder (weighing) batcher, ~ weigh batcher (Brit.); bitumen (weighing) batcher, ~ weigh batcher (US)

brückenfahrbare Makadamanlage *f* mit Trockentrommel *f*, Mischer *m* und Verteilerkübel *m* — bridge-type travel(l)ing coated macadam plant with drier, mixer and distributor hopper

Chargen-Mischanlage *f*, absatzweise arbeitende Mischanlage *f* — batch(-mix) type plant, intermittent weigh-batch (mixing) plant

Chargen-Mischverfahren *n* — batch mixing, intermittent ~

Doppelwellen-Zwangsmischer *m*, siehe: Zweiwellen-Zwangsmischer

Eindüsrohr *n* — spray tube

einteilige Trocken- und Stetigmischanlage *f* — continous volumetric-type onepiece drying and mixing unit (or plant)

einteilige Trocken- und Mischanlage *f* für Mischmakadam und Walzasphalt — single unit mobile (asphalt and) bituminous mixing plant

Exhaustor *m* — exhaust fan

elektrische Kontrolleinrichtung *f* für die Dauer der Trocken- und Naßmischzeiten *fpl* — electrical time control for the duration of dry and wet mixing

elektrische Startanlage *f* — electric starting system

Einwellen-Zwangsmischer *m*, Einwellen-Knetmischer *m*, Ein-Schaufelwellenmischer — single shaft pug mill, long pug mill, single-shaft mixer

fahrbare Chargen-Mischanlage *f* mit Doppeldecker-Horizontal-Vibratorsieb *n* — portable batch plant with gradation control, mixer-gradation unit

Flickanlage *f* — patch plant, patching machine

Fülleraufgabeelevator *m*, Fülleraufgabebecherwerk *n* — filler (bucket) elevator

Füller(verteiler)schnecke *f* — filler screw

Gesteinswaage *f* (mit Wiegesilo *m*) — aggregate weighbatcher (Brit.); (~) weighing batcher with scale (US)

Heißmischverfahren *n* — hot plant-mixing

Heizmantel *m* — steam jacket

Heizmantelrohr *n* — jacketed pipe

WIMPELLER, WIBAU-Wirbelmischer *m* [*Trademark*] — WIBAU impeller [*Trademark*]

Kaltmischanlage *f* — cold mix (asphalt) plant (US); bituminous macadam and tarmacadam mixing plant (Brit.)

Kaltmischverfahren *n*	cold plant-mixing
(kombinierte) Gleich-Gegenstrom-Trockentrommel *f*	combined contra-flow uniflow drying drum
maschinengemischt	plant-mixed
Maschinenmischung *f*	plant-mix
Mischtemperatur *f*	mixing temperature
ölgefeuert	oil fired
pneumatisches Kommandosystem *n*	pneumatic control system, pneumatic controls
pneumatisch gesteuerte Siloschnauzen *fpl* für das Gestein	pneumatically controlled aggregate bin gates
Schaufelmischer *m*	paddle mixer
Staubabscheider *m*, siehe: Zyklon *m*	
Staub-Sammelschnecke *f*	dust collecting screw
Stetig-Mischanlage *f*, kontinuierliche Mischanlage *f*, Durchlaufmischanlage	continuous volumetric type plant, continuous flow ~, continuous-process ~, continuous mixing ~
Stetig-Mischverfahren *n*, kontinuierliches Mischverfahren *n*	continuous mixing, constant-flow mixing
Trocken- und Mischanlage *f* für Mischmakadam *m* und Walzasphalt *m*, siehe: Aufbereitungsanlage *f* für Mischmakadam und Walzasphalt	
Trockenvormischzeit *f*	dry mixing time
Trommeltrocknungs- und -erwärmungsvorgang *m*	rotary drying and heating process
Walzasphaltanlage *f*, Heißmischanlage *f*, Teerbeton- und Walzasphalt-Mischanlage, Asphaltaufbereitungsanlage	hot-mix (asphalt) plant, central mixing plant for the preparation of high-type hot mixtures (US); asphalt plant
vierzelliger Dosierapparat *m*	four-compartment aggregate feeder
Kaltelevator *m*, Kaltbecherwerk *n*	cold elevator
Trocken-Trommel *f*, Trommel-Trockner, Gesteinstrockner, Straßenbautrockentrommel *f*, Straßenbautrommeltrockner	bituminized aggregate drier (or dryer), revolving (or rotary) drier (for road-making aggregates)
Füller-Rückgewinnung *f*	filler reclamation
Heißelevator *m*, Heißbecherwerk *n*	hot elevator
Mischmaschine *f*, Mischer *m*	mixer
Mischgut-Verladesilo *m*	mixed material storage hopper
Dampferzeuger *m*	steam generator
Bindemittelkocher *m*	binder cooker
zentraler Bedienungsstand *m*	central control platform
Zwangsmischen *n*	pugmill mixing, pressure ~
Zweiwellen-Zwangsmischer *m*, Zweiwellen-Knetmischer *m*, Doppelwellen-Zwangsmischer *m*	twin shaft pug mill, twin-pug-mill mixer, twin-pug mixer, twin pug mill
Zyklon *m*, Fliehkraftabscheider *m*, Zentrifugal-Staubabscheider	(dust collecting) cyclone, cyclone separator, centrifugal dust collector, cyclone type dust collector

Makadamstraße — Maschendraht

Makadamstraße *f*, Steinschlagstraße *f* nach Mac Adam = macadam(ised) road
Mäkler *m*; siehe unter „Rammanlage *f*"
Malachit *m* = malachite
Maler *m*, Anstreicher *m* = painter
~-**Abbrennlampe** *f* = painter's torch
~**eiwerkstatt** *f* = painter's (work)shop
Malm *m* (Geol.) = Malmstone
Malthene *npl* = malthenes

Mangan|blende *f* (Min.), siehe: Glanzblende *f*
~**hartstahl** *m* = manganese steel
~**spat** *m*, Rhodochrosit *m* (Min.) = rhodochrosite, manganese spar
Maniak *n*, siehe: Glanzpech *n*
Manila-Hanfseil *n* = manila hawser
Manipulator *m* **für Schmiedestücke** *npl* = forging manipulator
Mannaesche *f*, siehe: Blumenesche *f*

Mannloch *n*, **Einsteig(e)schacht** *m*, **Reinigungsschacht** *m*	**manhole, inspection pit**
Einfassung *f*	frame
Bügel *m*	crossbar, dog, yoke
Griff *m*	handle, eyebolt
Deckel *m*	cover
verlorener Schacht *m*, verlorenes Mannloch *n*	invisible pit

---

Manometer *n* = pressure ga(u)ge
manövrierunfähig = immobilized
Mansarden|binder *m* = Mansard roof truss
~**dach** *n* **mit durchgehender Firstsäule** *f* = Mansard roof with king post resting on tie beam
~**dach** *n* **mit liegendem Stuhl** *m* **und Versenkung** *f* = Mansard roof with slanted struts and wind filling
~**dach** *n* **mit stehendem Stuhl** *m* **und Versenkung** *f* = Mansard roof with post and parapet
Mantel *m* = jacket [*outer covering*]
~ [*KELLER-Tiefenrüttler m*] = cylinder
~**pfahl** *m*, Reibungspfahl = friction(al) (bearing, or foundation) pile
~**reibung** *f* = skin friction, side ~
Marcus-Wurfförderrinne *f*, siehe: Propellerrinne *f*
Marineleim *m* = marine glue
marine Sedimente *npl* = marine deposits
Markasit *m* (Min.) = marcasite, white iron pyrite, fool's gold
Markierung *f* = marking
Markierungs|farbe *f* = marking paint
~**knopf** *m*, Spurnagel *m*, Verkehrsnagel *m* = traffic stud, street marker, roadstud
~**linie** *f* = marker line

~**maschine** *f* = marking machine
~**streifen** *m* [*Straße f*] = road(way) stripe
~**streifen** *m* **aus heiß aufgebrachter plastischer Masse** *f* = hot-melt plastic stripe
Markstrahl *m* [*Holz m*] = medullary ray
Marmor *m* = marble [*the term strictly applies to a granular crystalline limestone, but in a loose sense it includes any calcareous or other rock of similar hardness that can be polished for decorative purposes*]
~**gips** *m*, Alabastergips *m*, Keene's Zement *m*, Alaungips, Hartalabaster *m* [*früher: Marmorzement m*] = alum-soaked Keene's cement
~**kalkstein** *m*, technischer Marmor *m*, polierbarer dichter Kalkstein = compact polishable limestone
Maronage *f*, siehe: Netzrißbildung *f*
Marsch|kompaß *m*, Prismakompaß *m* = prismatic compass
~**land** *n* = marsh land
~**ton** *m* = sea-clay
Martensit *m* = martensite
Masche *f* [*Maschensieb n*] = aperture, mesh; gauge (Brit.)
Maschen|anordnung *f* = mesh
~**draht** *m* = screen wire

Maschen|sieb *n*, Quadrat(loch)sieb *n* = (square) (mesh) sieve
~sieböffnung *f* = mesh aperture
maschinell = mechanically
~ betriebener Fallhammer *m*; siehe unter „Rammanlage *f*"
maschinelle Ausrüstung *f* = mechanical equipment
maschinell eingebaut = machine-installed
~ ~ [*Straßenbelag m*] = machine-laid, mechanically laid
maschinelle Straßendeckenherstellung *f* = machine-laid work
Maschinen *fpl* **und Geräte** *npl* = plant equipment
(Maschinen-)|Aggregat *n* = rig, outfit
~arbeit *f* = machine operation
~fabrikant *m* = plant maker
~fundament *n* = machine foundation
maschinengemischt = plant mixed, pre-mixed
Maschinen|haus *n*, siehe: Krafthaus *n*
~meister *m* = master mechanic
~mischung *f* = plant mix
~schotter *m* = machine-broken metal (Brit.)
~torf *m* = machine-cut peat
~wesen *n* = mechanical engineering
~ziegel *m*, Schnittziegel *m* = wire-cut brick, machine-made ~
Maschinist *m* = machinist
Maser|holz *n* = veined (or figured) wood
~wuchs *m* [*Holz n*] = wavy fibred growth
Masse *f* = mass
Masseleisen *n*, Roheisen *n* = pig (iron)
Massen|asphalt *m* [*Wasserbau m*] = mass-asphalt
~ausgleich *m*; s. unter „Erdarbeiten *fpl*"
~ausgleich *m* = balancing of masses
~berechnung *f* = computation of quantities
~beschleunigung *f* = acceleration
~entnahme *f* = borrow
~förderer *m*, siehe: Stetigförderer *m*
~gestein *n*, siehe: Erstarrungsgestein *n*
~gut *n*, Schüttgut *n* = bulk material, ~ good
~herstellung *f* = quantity production
~kalkstein *m* = massive limestone
~mittelpunkt *m*, siehe: Schwerpunkt

~plan *m*; siehe unter „Erdarbeiten *fpl*"
~schwungrad *n* = heavy flywheel
~verzeichnis *n*, Mengenverzeichnis = bill of quantities
Massiv|beton(stau)mauer *f*; siehe unter „Talsperre *f*"
~bogen *m* = massive arch
massive Kernmauer *f*; siehe unter „Talsperre *f*"
~ Säule *f* = solid column
massives Wehr *n* = solid weir
Massiv|mauerwerk *n*, Vollmauerwerk = solid brickwork
~-Zwischenwand *f* = solid partition
Mast *m* = mast
Mastenkran *m*, siehe: Derrickkran *m*
Mast|fuß *m* = lower end of the mast
~höhe *f* = height of the mast
Mastix|asphalt *m*, siehe: Gußasphalt
~-Kocher *m*, siehe: Gußasphaltkocher
~-Vergußdecke *f*, Mastixeingußdecke = mastic grouted surfacing (Brit.); mastic penetration pavement
~vergußmasse *f* = mastic filler
Mastverlängerung *f* = mast extension
Masut *n*, abgetopptes russisches (Roh-)Erdöl *n* = masut, mazut
maßeinheitlicher Bauteil *m* = modular building unit
Maßholder *f*, Maßeller *f*, kleiner Ahorn *m*, Feldahorn = common maple, small-leaved ~
mäßige Brise *f* = moderate wind
Maßordnung *f* = modular coordination, ~ measure system
Maßstab-Beziehung *f* = scale relation
maßstabsgerechtes Modell *n* = scale model
Material|anfuhr *f*, Materialanlieferung *f* = material(s) delivery
~aufbereitung *f* = (materials) processing (or dressing, or preparation)
~aufgabe *f*, siehe: Aufgabe
~aufgeber *m*, siehe: Speiser *m*
~aufzug *m* = material(s) elevator
~(be)förderung *f*, Materialumschlag *m* = material(s) handling
Beförderung von Massengütern = handling of bulk materials
Beförderung von Stückgütern = package handling

Materialbehälter — Meeresdenudation

Material|behälter m, Fülltrichter m = (receiving) hopper, feed ~
~beschickung f, siehe: Aufgabe f
(~)Bunker m, Taschensilo m = (materials) bunker
~flußingenieur m = materials handling engineer
(~)Lagerung f, siehe: Lagerhaltung f
~prüfungsanstalt f, Materialprüfungsamt n = material(s) testing laboratory, laboratory for material(s) testing
~schleuse f; siehe unter „pneumatische Gründung f"
(~)Umschlaggeräte npl, Geräte npl für die Material(be)förderung = material(s) handling equipment (or machinery)
~verknappung f, Materialknappheit f = material(s) shortage
Matratze f, siehe: Baggerrost m
Matte f, Asphalt~ = (asphalt) mattress
Mattenbelag m = matting
Mauer|abschnitt m = wall section
~anker m = masonry anchor
~bohrmaschine f = wall drilling machine
~flucht f = wall line
~fräser m = wall milling device
~fraß m = efflorescence of wall
~fuggerät n = (wall-)pointing machine
~gips m, Wandputz m = wall plaster
~klinker m, siehe: Klinker(ziegel) m
~mörtel m, Baumörtel, Fugenmörtel = masonry mortar, joint ~, pointing ~
~nutenfräse f = grooving cutter
~platte f = wall plate
~schuttverwertung f, siehe: Trümmerverwertung
~speise f, siehe: Kalkmörtel m
~verband m = bond
~werk n = masonry
~werk-Schneidscheibe f = masonry-cutting blade
~werksperre f; siehe unter „Talsperre f"
~werk n **über Geländeoberkante** f = above-grade masonry
~werkszement m = masonry cement
~ziegel m, siehe: Backstein m
Maul|eseltransport m = mule-back transportation
~wurfdrän m; siehe unter „Entwässerung f"

~wurf(drän)pflug m, Untergrund-(drän)pflug = mole plough (Brit.); ~ plow (US)
Maurer|hammer m = bricklayer's hammer
~polier m = foreman bricklayer
~schnur f, Lotschnur = plumb-bob cord, plummet ~
Maximal|kontakt m = maximum contact
~last f, Maximalbelastung f, Höchstlast, Höchstbelastung = maximum load(ing)
MBB-Aufnehmer m, Fabrikat MODERNER BAUBEDARF G. M. B. H., STUTTGART, DEUTSCHLAND = ROTOR-LOADER [*Trademark*] [*continuous aggregate loader*]
Mechanik f = mechanics
Mechaniker m = mechanic
mechanische Bodenverfestigung f, Tonbeton m = mechanical (or granular) (soil) stabilisation
~ Eigenschaft f = mechanical property
~ Festigkeit f = mechanical strength
mechanischer Antrieb m = mechanical drive
~ Grabenaushub m = mechanical trenching, ~ cutting of trenches
~ Siebsatz-Schwingungserreger m, siehe: Siebsatzrüttler m
mechanisches Schwingsieb n, mechanischer Schwinger m = mechanically-vibrated screen
~ Sedimentgestein n = mechanically deposited sedimentary rock
mechanische Verfestigung f = stabilized aggregate
(~) Winde f = winch
mechanisch verfestigte Straße f **mit Abdichtung** f **des Planums** n = membrane stabilized soil road
mechanische Verwitterung f, siehe: physikalische ~
Mechanisierung f = mechanisation
Mechanismus m = mechanism
Medizinalöl n, siehe: Paraffinöl
Meerbusen m, Golf m = gulf
Meer(es)arm m = arm of the sea, sea inlet
Meeres|deich m, Seedeich = sea dyke (or dike)
~denudation f = marine denudation

Meeres|grund *m* = sea-bottom
~klima *n* = oceanic climate (US); marine ~ (Brit.)
~kunde *f* = oceanography
~schlamm *m* = ocean ooze
meeresseitig, seewärts = seaward(s)
meeresseitige Böschung *f* = seaward slope
Meeres|spiegel *m*, Seewasserspiegel = sea level
~strömung *f* = marine current (US); ocean ~ (Brit.)
~überschiebung *f* = submergence by sea of land depression (Brit.); marine transgression (US)
Meer(es)|uferlinie *f*, siehe: Küstenlinie
~wasser *n* = seawater
Meer|kies *m* = marine gravel
~schaum *m* (Min.) = sepiolite, meerschaum
~ton *m* = marine clay
Mehl *n*; siehe unter „Mo *m*"
~sand *m*; sieeh unter „Mo *m*"
Mehrachs-Anhänger *m*, Vollanhänger = multi-axle trailer, full ~, multi-wheeler~
Mehrdecker (sieb) *m*, (*n*) = (aggregate) grader, multideck screen
mehr|facher Walzenkessel *m* = multiple cylindrical (or combined) boiler
~faches Fachwerk *n* = multiple-web system truss
Mehr|fachverdampfer *m* = multiple effect evaporator
~fachverflechtung *f* [*Straßenverkehr m*] = multiple weaving
~feldrahmen *m* = multi-bay frame
mehrfeldrige kreuzweise bewehrte Platte *f* = continuous two-way slab
mehrfeldriger Giebelrahmen *m* = multiple span gabled frame
Mehrgang(boden)mischer *m* = multi-pass soil stabiliser
mehr|geschossiger Bau *m* = multiple stor(e)y building
~lagige Dacheindeckung *f* = built-up roof
~lagige Spannbewehrung *f* = multi-layer prestressed reinforcement
~lagige Zwischenwandplatte *f* [*Gipskartonplatte*] = laminated partition slab

~motoriger Elektroantrieb *m* = multiple (electric) motor drive
Mehr|schalengreifer *m*, Mehrschalengreifkorb *m* = multi-bladed circular grab
~scharpflug *m* = gang plough (Brit.); ~ plow (US)
~scheibenkupplung *f* = multi-plate dry clutch
mehrschichtige Einbauweise *f*, Straßenaufbauweise [*Straßenbau m*] = multiple-lift construction, stage ~ (US); multiple-course ~ (Brit.)
mehrschiffig [*Halle f*] = multiple-bay
Mehrseil|greifbagger *m* = multiple rope grab excavator
~-Greifkorb *m*, Mehrseil-Greifer *m* = multiple rope bucket
mehr|spurige Straße *f*, vielspurige ~ = multi-lane highway
~stöckiger Rahmen *m* = tall building frame, multi-stor(e)y ~
~stufige Druckturbine *f*, Druckturbine *f* mit Druckabstufung *f* = multi-stage action turbine, ~ impulse ~, action (or impulse) turbine with pressure stages
~teilige Stütze *f* = built-up column (US); ~ stanchion (Brit.)
~teiliger Druckstab *m* = built-up compression member
~teiliger Querschnitt *m* = built-up section
~teiliger Stab *m* = built-up member
Mehr|wellen-Boden-Zwangsmischer *m*; siehe unter „Bodenvermörtelungsmaschine *f*"
~zellensilo *m* = multi-compartment bin (or silo)
Mehrzweck|bagger *m*, Universalbagger *m*, Umbaubagger *m*, Vielzweckbagger *m* = convertible excavator (Brit.); ~ shovelcrane (US); allpurpose ~, universal ~ Umbaueinrichtung *f* = (convertible) front end attachment, interchangeable ~~~, front end conversion unit, work attachment
~bauwerk *n*, Verbundprojekt *n* [*Talsperre f*] = multi(ple)-purpose structure
~einrichtung *f* = multi-purpose attachment
~fahrzeug *n* = multi-purpose vehicle

Mehrzweck-Industrieschlepper — Meßzylinder

Mehrzweck-Industrieschlepper *m*, siehe: Kompressorschlepper *m*
Meilenstein *m* = milestone
Meiler *m* = charcoal kiln

~, siehe: Feldofen *m*
Meißel *m* [*zur Durchteufung f harter felsiger Schichtenglieder npl*] = auger drill

Meißel *m*	**chisel**
Band~	band ~
Hart~, Maurer~	cold ~
Flach~	flat ~, hand cold ~, chipping ~
Kreuz~	cape (keyseating) ~
Schrot~	blacksmiths' ~
Hand~, Beitel *m*	(wood) ~

Meißel|blatt; siehe unter „Bohrmeißel *m*"
~fanghaken *m*; siehe unter „Bohrmeißel *m*"
meißeln [*mit Handmeißel bearbeiten*] = to chisel
~ [*mit dem Meißel m bohren*] = to drill with a bit
~hammer *m* = chipping hammer
Meißelschaft *m*; siehe unter „Bohrmeißel *m*"
~schneide *f*; siehe unter „Bohrmeißel *m*"
Meißelung *f*, siehe: Schlagbohrverfahren *n*
Meißelzapfen *m*; siehe unter „Bohrmeißel *m*"
Melanglanz *m* (Min.), siehe: Stephanit *m*
Melanterit *m* (Min.), siehe: Eisenvitriol *m,n*
Melaphyr *m*, schwarzer Porphyr *m* = melaphyre, black porphyry
~porphyr *m* = porphyric melaphyre
Melilith *m*, Honigstein *m* = mellite, mellilite
Melioration *f*, Meliorierung *f* = amelioration
Membran(e) *f* = diaphragm, membrane
~balg *m*, Faltbalg = membrane bellows
~-Bunkerstandanzeiger *m* = diaphragm-operated material-level indicator, ~ (bin) ~ ~
MENCK-Bär *m*; siehe unter „Rammanlage *f*"
MENCK-Raupenwagen *m*; siehe unter „Fahrzeuge *npl* für den Transport *m* von Boden und Steinbaustoffen *mpl*"
Mengenverzeichnis *n*, Massenverzeichnis = bill of quantities
Mergel *m* [*40—75% CaCo₃*] = marl

~boden *m* = marly soil
mergeliger Kalkstein *m*, Mergelkalkstein [*90—96% CaCO₃*] = marly limestone
~ Ton *m* [*4—10% CaCO₃*] = marly clay
Mergelschiefer *m*, Schiefermergel *m* = marl slate, slaty marl, margode
Mergelung *f* = marling
Merkblatt *n* = notes, code of practice
Merkuricyanat *n*, siehe: Knallquecksilber
Messer *m*, Zähler *m* = meter
~mischen *n* [*Durchmischen des Bodens mit Straßenhobel m*] = blade mixing
Messing|blech *n* = sheet brass
~lot *n* = brass solder
Messung *f* **von Gezeitenströmungen** *fpl* **in Flußmündungen** *fpl* **während des Mondwechsels** *m* = lunar-cycle measurement of estuarine flows
Meß|band *n*, Bandmaß *n* = measuring tape
~dose *f* = measuring cell
~ergebnis *n* = measuring result
~gefäß *n*, siehe: Abmeßkiste *f*
~kanal *m* = measuring channel
~länge *f* [*Probestab m*] = ga(u)ge length
~latte *f* = measuring rod
~profil *n* = measured profile
~silo *m* = batching silo
~stelle *f* = point of measurement
~tisch *m* = plane table
~tischblatt *n* = plane table sheet
~uhr *f* = dial ga(u)ge
~wehr *n* = measuring weir
~wehr *n* **mit rechtwinkligem Einschnitt** *m* **in U-Form** *f* = notch ga(u)ge
~zylinder *m* = measuring cylinder

Metall|heften n = metal stitching
~(hütten)schlacke f, **(Eisen)Hüttenschlacke** = steel slag, steel-mill ~
~pulver n = metal powder
~schlauch m = flexible metallic tube, metal hose
(~)Treibmittel n, **Blähmittel** n [*Gasbeton m*] = gas-forming agent
~überzug m = metallic coating
metamiktes Zirkon n = metamict zircon
metamorphe Fazies f (Geol.) = metamorphic facies
metamorphes Gestein n, **Umwandlungsgestein**, **Umprägungsgestein** = metamorphic rock, transformed ~
Metamorphose f, **Metamorphismus** m, **Umprägung** f, **Umwandlung** f, **Gesteins~** (Geol.) = metamorphism
Metasomatismus m (Geol.) = metasomatism
Metazentrum n = metacenter (US); metacentre (Brit.)
Meteorit m, siehe: Feuerkugelstein m
Methan n, CH_4 = methane
Methyl|alkohol m = methyl alcohol, wood ~
~äther m, $(CH_3)_2OH$ = methyl(ic) ether
~benzol n, Toluol n, $C_6H_5CH_3$ = toluene, methyl benzene, phenyl-methane
~chlorid n, Chlormethyl n, CH_3Cl = methyl(ic) chloride, chloride of methyl
Metropole f = metropolis
Miet-|Last(kraft)wagen m = for-hire truck (US); ~ lorry (Brit.)
~satz m, Geräte~ = equipment rental rate, plant-hire rate

~wohnhaus n = apartment building
Mikanit n = reconstructed mica, micanite
Mikro|granit m = micro-granite
~klin m, $K_2Al_2Si_6O_{16}$ (Min.) = microcline
~lith m (Geol.) = microlite
~pegmatit m (Geol.) = micro-pegmatite
~pore f = micro-pore
Milch|säure f = lactic acid
~viehweideland n = dairy cattle pasture
milder Tonboden m = mild clay, sandy ~
mildes Gebirge n [*Tunnelbau m*]; **Hackboden** m [*Erdbau m*] = hacking (Brit.)
Militär|bauwesen n = military civil engineering work, infrastructure
~straße f = military road
Millerit m (Min.), siehe: Haarkies m
Millimeterpapier n = millimeter paper
Mimetesit m (Min.) = mimetite, mimetesite
Mindest|abstand m = minimum spacing
~belastung f = minimum load(ing)
~dehnung f = minimum elongation
~dicke f = minimum thickness
~drucklinie f = line of least pressure
~fordernder m; siehe unter „Angebot n"
~querschnitt m = minimum section
Minensuchgerät n = mine detector
Mineral n = mineral
~ader f = mineral vein
~beständigkeitszahl f = mineral stability number [*bitumen emulsion*]
~boden m = mineral soil
~-Fettöl-Gemisch m = compounded oil
(~)Füller m, **Füllstoff** m = (mineral) filler, mineral dust, granular filler, granular dust (filler)

Mineralgemisch n, **Mineralmasse** f, **Gesteinsmasse** f, **Mineralgerüst** n, **Gesteinsgemisch**, **Gesteinsgemenge** n, **Gesteinsgerüst**	(mineral) aggregate, mineral skeleton structure
geschlossen abgestufte(s) ~	dense-graded ~ ~ ~ [*abbrev. DGA*], close-graded ~ ~ ~
offen abgestufte(s) ~	open-graded ~ ~ ~ [*abbrev. OGA*]

Mineralgewinnung f = mineral winning
mineralisches Rizinusöl n = mineral castor oil

Mineralumwandlung f = mineral inversion
Minette f (Geol.) = minette
Mineur m, **Gesteinshauer** m = (rock) driller, hard rock miner

Miniaturtraktor *m*, Miniaturschlepper *m* Miniaturtrecker *m* = pint-size economy tractor

Minimalkontakt *m* = minimum contact

Minimum *n* **der Stahleinlagen** *fpl* **in rechteckigen Stahlbetonquerschnitten** *mpl* **bei beliebigem Lastangriff** *m* = minimum reinforcement for rectangular reinforced concrete sections in eccentric compression for any eccentricity of the compressive force

Ministerium *n* **für öffentliche Arbeiten** *fpl* = Ministry of Public Works

Minium *n*, siehe: Bleimennige *f*

Minus-Temperatur *f* = below-zero temperature

minutliche Umlaufzahl *f*, siehe: Drehzahl

Miozänton *m* = miocene clay

Misch|anilinpunkt *m* [*Kohlenwasserstoff-Lösungsmittel n*] = mixed anilin point

~anlage *f* = mixing plant

~barkeitsprüfung *f* **mit Wasser** *n* = miscibility with water test [*bitumen emulsion*]

~belag *m*, siehe: Mischdecke *f*

~beton-Transportaufbau *m*, Nachmischer *m* = agitator, remixer

~bottich *m* = mixing tank

~bühne *f* = mixing platform

~decke *f*, Mischbelag *m*, Mischanlagendecke, Mischanlagenbelag [*Straße f*] = pre-mix(ed) surfacing, plant-moix pavement

Mischen *n*, Mischprozeß *m*, Mischvorgang *m* = mixing

~ *n* **in Straßenbetonmischern** *mpl* = paver mixing

Mischer *m* **für Teppichbeläge** *mpl* = retread mixer

~führer *m*, (Mischer)Maschinist *m* = mixer driver, ~ operator

Mischer *m* **mit Schurrenaustragung** *f*; siehe unter „Betonmischer *m*"

Misch(er)schaufel *f* = mixer (or mixing) paddle (or blade)

(Mischer-)Segmentteil *m, n* = (mixer) liner segment, sectional liner

Mischer-Stabilitäts-Prüfung *f* = plant mix, test, ~ stability ~

Misch|gas *n*, siehe: Dowsongas

~gestein *n*, hybrides Gestein = hybrid rock

~gut *n*, Mischung *f*, Gemisch *n* = mix(ture)

~gut(-Verlade)silo *m* = mixed material storage hopper

~gutzusammensetzung *f* = mix composition

~kammer *f* = mixing chamber

~kanalisation *f*; siehe unter „Abwasserwesen *n*"

~makadam *m* = (pre-)mixed macadam; coated ~ (Brit.)

Teermakadam *m* = tarmacadam
Asphaltmischmakadam *m*, Steinschlagasphalt *m* = bitumen (or bituminous) macadam (Brit.); asphalt macadam (US) [*While every engineer will be familiar with the term 'Coated Macadam,' there may be a diversity of opinion regarding the range of "black top" materials which are included under this general description. The glossary of Highway Engineering Terms, B.S. 892, describes it as "a road material consisting of coarsely graded mineral aggregate that has been coated with a specified binder, such as road tar, bitumen or the like by a controlled process, having a preponderance of coarse aggregate and a substantial proportion of voids." According to this definition it obviously includes tarmacadam to B.S. 802 and 1242, bitumen macadam to B.S. 1621, cold asphalt to B.S.S. 1960, and similar mixtures.*
On the other hand, manufacturers and suppliers of bituminous surfacing materials, such as members of the Federation of Coated Macadam Industries, regard coated macadam as any materials which can be made in their coating plants at mixing temperatures below about 220 deg. F. irrespective of grading, so materials, such as fine cold asphalt, dense tar surfacing and dense bitumen macadam come within this definition.]

Mischmakadamanlage *f*, siehe: Makadam-Maschinenanlage

Misch|maschine *f*, Mischer *m* = mixer, mixing machine
~maschinist *m*, siehe: Mischerführer *m*
~periode *f*, siehe: Mischzeit *f*
~reihenfolge *f* = mixing sequence
~schleppe *f* = mixing drag
~schnecke *f* = paddle worm conveyor, broken-bladed conveyor
~spiel *n* = mixing cycle
~system *n* [*Dränage f*] = combined system
~teppich(belag) *m*, siehe: Straßenteppich *m*
~trommel *f* mit freier Mischung *f* = free-fall type mixing drum
~turm *m* = mixing tower
~turm *m* für bituminöse Belagsmassen *fpl* = tower-type bituminous mixing plant
Mischung *f*, siehe: Mischgut *n*
Mischungs|entwurf *m* = mix design
~konsistenz *f* = mix consistency
~nebel *m*, Advektionsnebel *m* = advection fog
~tabelle *f* = mixing table
~turbine *f* = mixture turbine
~verhältnis *n* = mix proportions [*ratio of cement (or binder) to aggregate*]
~wirksamkeit *f* = mixing efficiency
Misch|waage *f*, siehe: Gattierungswaage
~wert *m* nach Jekel = Jekel mixing value [*bitumen emulsion (Brit.)*]
~zeit *f*, Mischperiode *f* = mixing time, ~ period, ~ time period
~zug *m* [*Bodenvermörtelung f*] = mixing train [*soil stabilisation*]
mißgriffsicher, siehe: narrensicher
Miß|pickel *m* (Min.), siehe: Arsenkies *m*
~weisung *f* = magnetic declination, ~ variation
mitbestimmender Faktor *m* = contributory factor
Mitnehmer *m*, Mitnehmerschaufel *f* = (scraper) flight
~förderer *m* = flight conveyor
Mittagspause *f* = mid-day break, lunch-break
Mittel|absiebung *f* = medium screening
~bau *m* = central section, ~ building frame
~blech *n* = medium plates

~druckluftverdichter *m*, siehe: zweistufiger Kompressor *m*
~feld *n*, Mittelöffnung *f* [*Brücke f*] = centre span (Brit.); center ~ (US)
mittelfetter Lehm *m* = medium-heavy loam
Mittel|frequenz(beton)fertiger *m* = medium frequency (concrete) finisher
~gebirge *n* = secondary mountain, average mountain
mittelhartes Steinkohlenteerpech *n* = medium-hard coal-tar pitch
Mittel|insel *f* [*Verkehrsinsel f*] = central island
~kies *m* [*nach DIN 1179 30—7 mm; nach DIN 4022 30—5 mm; nach DIN 4220 20—7 mm; nach DEGEBO 10 —5 mm; nach Fischer und Udluft 20—10 mm (heißt hier „großer Graup") und 10—5 mm (heißt hier „mittlerer Graup"); nach Dienemann 10—5 mm*] = medium gravel [*A.S.E.E. fraction 24.5 to 9.52 mm*]
~korn *n* [*Betonzuschlag(stoff) m*] = middle size aggregate
~kraft *f*, siehe: Resultierende *f*
~moräne *f*, siehe unter „Gletscher *m*"
~öffnung *f*, siehe: Mittelfeld *n*
~öl *n* = middle oil, carbolic ~, coal tar
~pfeiler *m* [*Brücke f*] = centre pier (Brit.); center ~ (US)
~sand *m* [*nach DIN 1179 und DIN 4022 1,0—0,2 mm; nach Dücker (Jahr 1948) „feines Siebkorn IV a" 0,6 bis 0,2 mm*] = medium sand [*A.S.E.E. fraction 0.59—0.25 mm; British Standard 0.6—0.2 mm*]
~schifter *m* = intermediate jack rafter
mittelschnellabbindend [*Bitumen n*] = medium-curing
mittelschwere (Straßen-)Decke *f* = intermediate-type pavement
Mittel|spur *f* = median lane [*road*]
~streifen *m* = central reserve, central reservation, central strip, median (strip), medial strip
~streifen-Hochbordstein *m* = median curb(stone)
~trennung *f* [*Siebung f*] = medium separation

Mittelwasser — Moorbruch

Mittel|wasser n = mean water
~zapfenlager n = center pin bearing (US); centre ~ ~ (Brit.)
~zapfenlenkung f = center pin steering (US), centre ~ ~ (Brit.)
mittige Belastung f = axial load(ing)
mittlerer Kraftbedarf m = average power requirement
mittleres Siebkorn IIIa [*nach Dücker 1948*] = granule [6—2 mm]
Mo m [*nach Terzaghi 0,1—0,02 mm; nach DIN 4022 0,1—0,02 mm (heißt hier „Mehlsand"); nach Grengg (Jahr 1942) 0,1—0,02 mm (heißt hier „Mehl")*] = mo [*0.1—0.02 mm*]
Mobil|bagger m = self-propel(l)ed excavator
~drehkran m = mobile (rotary) crane
Modell|ähnlichkeit f = similarity of types
~gips m = mo(u)lding plaster
~haus n = pilot house
~versuch m = model-experiment, model-test
modifiziertes Öl n = treated oil
Modul m, siehe: Beiwert m
~ für Beton nach Young, siehe: Elastizitätsmodul
Mofette f = mofette
Mohnöl n = poppy oil
Mohrscher Spannungskreis m = Mohr's circle (of stress)
  Bruchlinie f = strength envelope, envelope of rupture, envelope of failure, line of rupture, Mohr's envelope
Molasse f = molasses
~fels m (Geol.) = Molasse
Mole f = mole
Molkereiabwasser n = dairy waste
Mollusken-Fauna f = molluscan fauna
Molybdänglanz m (Min.) = molybdenite
Moment n **der inneren Kräfte** fpl = resisting moment
Momenten|ausgleichsverfahren n = moment distribution method
~fläche f = moment diagram
~gleichgewicht n = moment equilibrium
~linie f = moment curve
~nullpunkt m = centre of moments (Brit.; center ~ ~ (US)
~überlagerung f = superposition of moment

Moment|(schraub)zwinge f = quick (action) clamp
~verteilung f = moment distribution
~zünder m; siehe unter „1. Schießen n; 2. Sprengen n"
Monazit m (Min.) = monazite
Moniereisen n, siehe: Bewehrungseisen
monoklines System n = monoclinic system, oblique ~
monoklin kristallisierend = crystallising in the monoclinic system
Monolithbetonbauwerk n = monolithic concrete structure
Monsun m = monsoon
Montage f = assembling, erection
~bau m **mit Betonfertigteilen** mpl = framed building in precast concrete units
~betonwerk n = precast units works, prefabricated ~ ~, precast concrete ~ ~, precast works, precast plant
~bewehrung f = reinforcement for stresses in erection
~decke f = mounted ceiling
~dreibaum m, siehe: Dreibaum
~(-Fließ)band n = assembly line
~kran m = erection crane, erecting ~
~kranausleger m = long steel erector's boom (US)/jib (Brit.)
~mast m = erecting mast
~meister m = erecting supervisor
~plan m = erection schedule
~schraube f = erection bolt
~schweißung f = erection welding
~spannung f = erection stress
~werkstatt f, **Zusammenbauwerkstatt** f = assembly shop
Montan|geologe m = mining geologist
~geologie f [*Ingenieurgeologie* f *des Bergbaues* m] = mining geology
~pech n = montan-tar pitch
Monteur m = fitter
Montmorillonit m = montmorillonite
Monumentalbau m = monumental building (or structure)
Monzonit m = monzonite, syenodiorite
Moor n = bog
~boden m, **reiner Humusboden** m = peaty soil
~bruch m = bog burst

Moor|erde f, anmooriger Boden m [*Gemisch aus Mineralboden mit höchstens 60 Gewichtsteilen organischer Substanz*] = moor soil

~**heide** f = moor land

~**sprengung** f, Schüttsprengverfahren n = bog blasting, peat ~, muck-blasting operation, blasting of peat, swamp shooting method, toe-shooting

~**wasser** n = peaty water

Moosheide f = moss heath

Moräne f; siehe unter „Gletscher m"

~**(n)kies** m = moraine gravel, glacial ~

~**(n)schutt** m, Gletscherschutt = moraine débris

~**(n)schuttboden** m = glacial soil

~**(n)see** m = lake ponded up by moraine material

Morast m = morass

Mörser m [*dient zum Zerstoßen n*] = mortar

Mörtel m = mortar

~**art** f = class of mortar

~**aufbereitung** f = mortar fabrication

~**auskleidung** f, siehe: Mörtelverkleidung f

~**behälter** m [*Mauerfuggerät n*] = mortartank

~**eingußdecke** f [*turbulente Mörtelfertigung f*] = cement-bound surfacing, COLCRETE, colloidal concrete, cement penetration method, cement(-bound) macadam, mortar-bound macadam Zementschotterdecke f zweilagig = sandwich process macadam, COLCRETE constructed in the sandwich process

~**einpressung** f, Mörtelinjektion f = mortar intrusion

~**fuge** f = mortar joint

~**mauerwerk** n = mortar walling

~**mischer** m, Mörtelmischmaschine f = mortar mixer, ~ mixing machine

~**nest** n = mortar pocket

(~)**Putz** m, Putzmörtel m = mortar rendering, ~ plaster

~**schlitten** m = mortar sledge

~**schöpfer** m = mortar scoop

~**spritzmaschine** f, siehe: Betonspritzmaschine f

~**streifen** m = mortar bed

~**trog** m = hod

~**verkleidung** f, Mörtelauskleidung f = mortar lining

~**verteiler** m = mortar spreader

Mosaik|pflaster n = mosaic paving

~**pflasterstein** m = mosaic (paving) sett

~**verband** m (Geol.), siehe: Bienenwabenverband

Motor|-Betonvorderkipper m, Motor-Japaner(karren) m, Motor-Kipp(er-) karre(n) f, (m) = power (concrete) cart (or buggy), motorized buggy, moto-bug

~**bodenfräse** f = self-propelled rotary tiller (or rotary hoe, or rotavator, or soil pulverizer)

~**bootrennstrecke** f = speed boat course

Motoren|benzin n, siehe: Benzin n

~**drehzahl** f = motor speed

~**leistung** f = mechanical output of motor

~**petroleum** n, siehe: Kraftstoffkerosin n

Motor|fahrrad n = motor-assisted pedal cycle

~**fahrzeugverkehr** m, Kraftverkehr m = motor traffic

~**-fegemaschine** f; siehe unter „Straßenkehrmaschine f"

~**-Fußwegkehrmaschine** f, siehe: Fußweg-Motorkehrmaschine f

~**generator** m = motor generator (set)

~**greifer(korb)** m, Hakengreifer m = hook-on bucket

motorisiert = motorised

motorisierter Schürfkübel m mit Einachs-Traktor m, siehe: Einachs-Motor-Schrapper m

Motorisierung f = motorisation

Motor|-Japaner m = power barrow

~**-Kehrmaschine** f = power-driven scavenging machine

~**kipper** m; siehe unter „Fahrzeuge npl für den Transport m von Boden m und Steinbaustoffen mpl"

~**kompressor-Spritzmaschine** f = spraying machine (or sprayer) with power aircompressor and hand lance(s)

~**kraftstoff** m = motor fuel

~**kübelwagen** m, siehe: Autoschütter m

~**lastkahn** m = self-propelling barge, powered ~

~**lok(omotive)** f; siehe unter „Feldbahnanlage f"

Motor m mit Doppelschlußwicklung f = compound-wound motor
Motor m mit mehreren Drehzahlstufen fpl = change-speed motor
~**rad n ohne Beiwagen** m = solo motorcycle
~**roller** m = two-wheeled vehicle with low-powered engine
~**schürf(kübel)wagen** m **mit Einachs-Schlepper** m; siehe: Einachs-Motor-Schrapper m
~**schürf(kübel)wagen** m **mit zusätzlichem Heckantrieb** m; siehe unter „Radschrapper m"
~**schürfzug** m [*Sammelbegriff für einen Radschrapper kombiniert mit entweder Zweiradschlepper m, oder Vierradschlepper oder Raupenschlepper*]; siehe unter „Radschrapper m"
~**schutzschalter** m = protective motor switch
~-**Splittstreumaschine** f, **Motor-Splittstreuer** m = power gritting machine, power chip(ping)s spreader
~-**Spritzmaschine** f [*Verspritzen n durch Pumpe f*] = sprayer (or spraying machine) for hand and power spraying with hand lance(s)
~-**Spritzmaschine** f **kombiniert mit Kocher** m = heater and sprayer (or spraying machine) for hand and power spraying with hand spray unit
~-**Spritzwagen** m, siehe: Bitumen-Sprengwagen m

Motor-Straßenhobel m, **Motor-Wegehobel** m, **Motor-Erdhobel** m, **Motor-Straßenplanierer** m | motor grader, motorized grader, power grader, self-propelled (blade) grader, tractor grader
~ mit schräg verstellbaren Rädern npl | leaning wheel type ~ ~
~ mit Schaufelladeeinrichtung f | ~ ~ fitted with bucket loader
~ mit Planierpflugschild n | ~ ~ fitted with (bull)dozer blade
~ mit Zwillingswalze f | ~ ~ fitted with twin rolls
~ mit Schneepflugeinrichtung f | ~ ~ fitted with snow plough (Brit.)/plow (US) unit
~ mit Aufreißereinrichtung f | ~ ~ fitted with scarifier attachment
Hobelmesser n, (Hobel)Schar f, Hobelblatt n, Planierschar f, Planierschaufel f, Schälmesser n | (planing) blade, grader blade
(Neigungs)Verstellung f | pitch adjustment
Schneide f, Schneidkante f | cutting edge
Drehstuhl m, kreisförmiger Zahnkranz m | circle
Wendekreishalbmesser m | turning radius
Sturz m der Vorderräder npl | wheel lean, front wheel leaning
Anpreßdruck m | blade pressure
Zugstange f | drawbar
Handhebelsteuerung f | hand lever control
Handlenksteuerung f, Handsteuerung f mit Lenkrad n | manual steer(ing)
Schwenkwinkel m | circle reverse
Mechanismus m für Höhenverstellung f des Messers n | lifting mechanism
Verstellbereich n | blade range
zweiachsiger ~, Abziehverteilgerät n | (auto)patrol (grader), motor patrol, blade maintainer, maintainer (scraper), road patrol, road maintainer
Verschwenk-Gestänge n | crank side shift

Motor|-Straßenkehrmaschine *f*; siehe unter „Straßenkehrmaschine *f*"
~**welle** *f* = motor shaft
~**zylinder** *m* [*Kompressor m*] = power cylinder
Mud-Jack-Verfahren *n*, (Beton-)Deckenhebeverfahren *n* durch Einpressen von einem aus Feinsand, Mo, Schluff und Kolloidmaterial als Zuschlag, Zement als Bindemittel und Wasser als Verflüssiger bestehendem Gemisch bei Setzung von Betonfahrbahnplatten = mud-jack(ing) (of pavement slabs) [*i.e. the pressing (by compressed air) of a fluid mixture of cement, clay, fine sand and water under the slabs*]
Muffe *f* = sleeve, socket
Muffen|absperrschieber *m* = sluice valve with socket ends (Brit.); gate valve with bell ends (US)
~**gußrohr** *n* = joint cast iron pipe
~**kitt** *m* = joint cement, sewer joint(ing) compound, pipe joint(ing) compound
~**verbindung** *f* = bell-and-spigot joint, spigot-and-socket ~
~**verbindung** *f* **bei Stoß von Spannbewehrung** *f* = coupler

---

Mühle *f*, **Mahlmühle, Feinzerkleinerungsmaschine** *f*	(grinding) mill, grinder
Abrollen *n* der Mahlkörper *mpl* übereinander	cascading
Aufgabegut *n*	feed material
Doppel-Rotoren-Prall~, Zweiwalzen-Prall~	double impeller impact ~
Durchlaufmahlung *f*	open-circuit operation
einstufige ~	single-stage ~ ~
mehrstufige ~	multi-stage ~ ~
Federkraft~	spring-type ~
Federkraft-Walzen-~, Federrollen-~	spring-type roller ~
	horizontal roller ~
LOESCHE-~, Fabrikat LOESCHE HARTZERKLEINERUNGS- & ZEMENTMASCHINEN KG, DÜSSELDORF, DEUTSCHLAND	LOESCHE ~ ~ ~
Ring(walzen)~, Walzenring ~	ring (roll(er)) ~
Scheiben~	disc ~ (Brit.); disk ~ (US)
Fein~	finishing ~ ~
Feinmahlung *f*, Nachmahlung *f*	fine grinding, finish grinding
Fertiggut *n*	ground product, finished product, discharging material
Fliehkraft~	centrifugal force ~
Pendel~, Fliehkraft~ mit Walzen *fpl*	suspended roller ~
GRIFFIN-(Pendel)~	GRIFFIN centrifugal force roller ~ [*Trademark*]
RAYMOND-Pendel~	RAYMOND roller ~ [*Trademark*]
BRADLEY-~ mit drei Pendelwalzen *fpl*, Dreipendel~	BRADLEY HERCULES three-roll ~ [*Trademark*]
freier Wurf *m*	cataracting
gleichkörniges Produkt *n*	short range product
Hammer~	hammer ~

Mühle

Kolloid ~ | colloid(al) ~
kreisförmige Mahlbahn f, Mahlring m | grinding ring
Mahlfeinheit f | fineness of grinding
mechanische Prall ~, Rotor-Prall ~, Schnelläufer ~ | (impeller) impact ~

Mehrkammerrohr ~ | multi-compartment ~
  Rohr ~, Grieß ~ | tube ~
  Kugel ~ | ball ~
  Siebkugel ~ | screen-discharge ball ~, screen-type ~
  KRUPP- ~ | KRUPP ~
  SMIDTH- ~ | SMIDTH KOMINUTER, F. L. S. KOMINUTER, KOMINUTER mill [*Trademark*]
  (Stahl)Kugelrohr ~ | (steel) ball tube ~
  Trommel ~ | cylindrical batch ~

Naßmahlung f | wet grinding
pneumatische Prall ~, Strahl ~, Luftstrahl-Prallzerkleiner m | jet pulverizer, micronizer, jet mill, reductionizer
Prall ~ | pulvator, impactor, (swing-hammer) pulverizer
satzweise Mahlung f, satzweises Mahlen n | batch grinding, intermittent ~

Schwerkraft ~ | tumbling ~
  Einkammerrohr ~ | single compartment ~
  Flintsteinrohr ~ | flint (stones) tube ~, pebble ~ ~

Sichter ~ | air-separating ~ ~
Sichter ~ mit Schleudersichtung im geschlossenen Kreislauf | air-separating ~ ~ operating with a straight air-current
Sichter ~ mit Stromsichtung im geschlossenen Kreislauf | air-separating ~ ~ with centrifugal separation in a closed circuit
Stiftenschleudermaschine f, Desintegrator m | disintegrating ~, disintegrator
stetige Mahlung f | constant-flow grinding
TRICONE-Kugel ~. Fabrikat HARDINGE CO. | TRICONE ~, three-cone ~

Trockenmahlung f | dry grinding
  Vortrocknung f | pre-dried process (US); pre-dryed process (Brit.)
  Mahltrocknung f | hot-air drying

Umlauflast f | circulating load
Umlaufmahlung f, Kreislaufmahlung, Kreislaufprozeß m | closed-circuit operation (or grinding)
  ~ mit mechanischer Korntrennung f (oder Siebung f) | ~ ~ with screening
  ~ mit pneumatischer Korntrennung f (oder Siebung f) | ~ ~ with air separation
ungleichkörniges Produkt n | long-range product
Vermahlen n | intergrinding
Vormahlen n | raw grinding
Vor ~ | preliminary ~ ~

Walzen~
Zementkugel~
Zwischengut *n*

Mulden|band *n*; siehe unter ,,Bandförderer *m*"
~**bildung** *f* (Geol.) = synclinal formation
~**-Erdbaufahrzeug** *n* = dump wagon
~**falzziegel** *m* = trough gutter tile
~**gewölbe** *n* = trough vault
~**gurtförderband** *n*; siehe unter ,,Bandförderer *m*"
~**gurtförderer** *m*, Muldenbandförderer, Trogbandförderer, Troggurtförderer = trough belt conveyor, ~ band ~
~**kipper** *m*; siehe unter ,,Feldbahnanlage *f*"
~**kipper** *m*; siehe unter ,,Fahrzeuge *npl* für den Transport *m* von Boden *m* und Steinbaustoffen *mpl*"
~**tragbandstation** *f* = carrier idler set for trough belt conveyor
~**tragrolle** *f* = troughing roller
~**wagen** *m* **für Bruchbetrieb** *m* = quarry car
~**wagen** *m* **mit Eigenantrieb** *n* = motor driven, rocker dump car
Müllabladeplatz *m* = refuse tip
Müllast(kraft)wagen *m* = garbage truck (US); refuse wagon (or collector), dustcart (Brit.)
Müll|abfuhr *f* = refuse collection
~**auffüllung** *f* = sanitary landfill
~**eimer** *m*, Müllkübel *m* = dust-bin
Mullit *m*, $3Al_2O_3 \times 2SiO_2$ (Min.) = mullite
~**stein** *m*, siehe: Sillimanitstein
Müllverbrennungsanlage *f* = refuse incinerator, garbage disposal plant, refuse destructor
münden in [*Fluß m*] = to empty into
Mund|loch *n*, Stollen~ = adit opening
~**stück** *n* [*Strangpresse f*] = die
Mündungs|baggerung *f* = esturial dredging
~**hafen** *m*, Stromhafen *m* = estuary harbo(u)r
~**kegel** *m*, Delta *n* = delta

roll(er) (~) ~, roll grinder
preliminator
intermediate material

Munilager *n*, Munitionsdepot *n* = explosives area, bomb dump area, ammunition depot
Munitionsmagazin *n*, Munitionsschuppen *m* = ammunition warehouse
Münster *m* = minster
Murgang *m* = wet land slide
Muschelgestein *n* = shell rock
musch(e)lig = conchoidal, shell-like
musch(e)liger Bruch *m* = conchoidal fracture
Muschel|kalk *m*, Muschelkalkstein *m*, Muschelmarmor *m* = shell(y) limestone, coquina, oyster shell lime
~**kalkformation** *f* = ostracite formation
~**mergel** *m* = shell marl
~**sandstein** *m* = shell(y) sandstone, beach rock
~**schieber** *m* = D slide valve
muschlige Braunkohle *f*; siehe unter ,,Kohle *f*"
Muskovit *m*, K-Al-Glimmer *m*, tonerdereicher Kaliglimmer *m* (Min.) = muscovite, Muscovy glass
~**-Bergbau** *m* = muscovite mining
~**-Biotit-Granit** *m* = muscovite-biotite granite, two mica granite
~**granit** *m* = muscovite granite
Muster-Arbeitsstudie *f* = work sampling study
Mutter *f* = nut
Mutterboden *m*, siehe: Dammerde *f*
~**abhub** *m*, Mutterbodenabtrag *m* = topsoil stripping
~**auftrag** *m*, Mutterbodenandeckung *f* = topsoiling
Mutter|gestein *n* (Geol.) = host rock
~**lauge** *f* = mother liquor, ~ lye
~**pause** *f* = negative, transparency, transparent positive original
~**scheibe** *f* = plain washer
Mylonitisierung *f* = mylonitisation

N

Nabe *f* = nave

Nachbehandlung f [*Beton* m] — curing, after-treatment
Abdeckmatte f — curing blanket
Abdeckpapier n — concrete-curing paper
Abdeckung f — curing overlay
Abdichtungsmittel n — (membrane) curing compound
elektrische Nachbehandlung f — electrical curing
Emulsionsanstrich m, Dichtungshaut f — emulsion coating, concrete curing membrane, curing seal
Nachbehandlungsplatz m — curing yard
Naßhaltung f, Feuchthaltung f — wet job-site~
Sandabdeckung f — sand curing
Sonnen(schutz)dach n — concrete protection tent, curing tent
Sprengwagen m — water sprinkler
Sprinkleranlage f — stationary sprinkling system
Strohmatte f — straw mat
Teichverfahren n, Teichmethode f, Einsumpfen n — ponding

Nach|bestellung f = repeat order
~**brechen** n; siehe unter „Hartzerkleinerung f"
~**brecher** m, Fein(stein)brecher = secondary crusher, reduction ~, fine ~
~**einrütteln** n, Nachvibration f, Nachvibrieren n = re-vibration
~**eiszeit** f, siehe: Alluvium n
~**fall** m, Einsturz m = cave(-in)
~**faulung** f [*Abwasser* n] = secondary digestion
~**gewitter** n = subsequent thunderstorm
nachgiebige Eckverbindung f [*Stahlrahmen* m] = semi-rigid connection
Nachholbedarf m = backlog of needs, inadequacy gap
~ [*Straßenunterhaltung* f] = arrears of road maintenance
Nach|klärbecken n; siehe unter „Abwasserwesen n"
~**klärung** f; siehe unter „Abwasserwesen n„
~**knäppern** n, siehe: Zweitsprengung f mit Bohrlochladung f
~**kühlung** f = after-cooling
~**läufer** m, Anhänger m = trailer
~**löschbunker** m [*Kalk* m] = caving bin
~**mahlung** f; siehe unter „Mühle f"
~**mischen** n [*Transportbeton* m] = agitating

~**mischer** m, siehe: Betontransportwagen m mit (aufgebautem) Rührwerk(smischer) n, (m)
~**mischer** m, Mischbeton-Transportaufbau m [*ohne Fahrzeug* n] = agitator, remixer
~**mittags-Spitzenstunde** f = afternoon peak hour
~**nehmer** m; siehe unter „Bohrmeißel m"
~**rechnung** f = checking
~**schlagebuch** n = reference book
~**schwindungs-Prüfung** f [*feuerfester Stein* m] = reheat test [*fire-brick*]
~**spannen** n [*Spannbeton* m] = secondary tensioning
~**teerung** f = re-tarring
~**trieb** m [*Tunnelbau* m] = secondary heading
Nacht|schicht f = night shift
~**sichtbarkeit** f = night(time) visibility
~**strom** m = night power
~**wächter** m = night watchman
nachverdichten = to recompact
Nach|verdichtung f = final compaction
~**vibration** f, siehe: Nacheinrütteln n
~**weis** m = proof
Nachzahlung f [*Lohn* m, *Gehalt* n] = retroactive pay, back-pay
nackter Boden m = bare ground
Nadelbaum m = coniferous tree, evergreen

Nadel|blende *f*, prismatische ~ (Min.) = red antimony ore
~eindringgerät *n*, Nadeleindringungsmesser *m*, Nadelpenetrometer *m* = needle penetrometer
~eis *n* = needle ice
~eisenstein *m* (Min.) = needle ironstone
~erz *n* (Min.) = needle-ore, belonite, acicular bismuth, aciculite
~(feder)gras *n*, Nadelhafer *m* = rush-leaved feather grass
nadelförmig; siehe unter „Kornform *f*"
Nadel|holz *n*, Weichholz = coniferous wood, pine-wood, soft-wood, resinous wood
~kohle *f* (Min.) = acicular lignite
~penetrometer *m*, siehe: Nadeleindringgerät *n*
~schieber *m* = needle (control) (or regulating) valve
~stein *m* (Min.) = needle-stone, rutilated quartz
~wald *m* = coniferous forest, pine ~
~zinnerz *n* (Min.) = needle-tin
nagelbar = nailable
nagelbarer Ziegel *m* = breeze fixing brick
Nagel|barkeit *f* = nailability
~binder *m* = nailed truss
~bohrer *m* = gim(b)let, piercer, bradawl, nail passer, nail bit, wimble
~erz *n* (Min.) = columnar argillaceous red iron-ore
~fluh *f* = gompholite, nagelfluh
 Bunte ~ = polygenetic ~, variegated ~

~kalk *m* = stylolitic limestone, cone-in-cone ~
~kanone *f* = powder-actuated nailer
~klaue *f* = claw-wrench
~ramme *f* = nail driver
~schleppe *f* = nail drag, spike ~
~schlupf *m* = nail slip
~stift *m* = tack
~zange *f* = nail-nippers
Nah(ablese)kompaß *m* = direct-reading compass
Nahansicht *f* [*z. B. Straßendecke f*] = close-up view
Näherungs|bruch *m* [*Mathem.*] = convergent
~rechnung *f*, siehe: Annäherungsrechnung *f*
~rechnung *f* **nach Cross** = Cross moment distribution method
~wert *m*, An~ = approximate value
Nahkompaß *m*, siehe: Nah(ablese)kompaß
Nahtstelle *f* [*Schwarzdecke f*] = joint
Nakrit *m* (Min.) = nacrite
Naphthalin *n* = naphthalene, naphthalin(e)
~salz *n* = naphthalate
~säure *f* = naphthalic acid
naphthenbasisches Erdöl *n* = naphthene-base crude petroleum
Napoleonit *m* (Min.) = napoleonite
narrensicher, mißgriffsicher = fool-proof
Naßabscheider *m* = water type dust collector
nasse Destillation *f*, Überdampfung *f*, Abdampfung *f* = vaporization, distillation

---

Naßbagger *m*, **Schwimmbagger** *m* | **dredge** (US); **dredger** (Brit.); **dredging craft**

Abfuhrschute *f*, Baggerschute *f*
Baggeraggregat *n*
Baggerpumpe *f*, Förderpumpe
Cutter(saug)bagger *m*, Cuttersauger, (stationärer) Schneidkopf(saug)bagger *m*, (stationärer) Saugbagger mit Schneidkopf
 mechanisch angetriebener Schneidkopf *m*, Fräserkopf *m*, Wühlkopf (-Fräser) *m*

barge (Brit.); scow (US)
dredging appliance
dredge(r) pump, dredging pump
suction-cutter ~, cutter suction ~, cutterhead (pipeline) (hydraulic) ~, clay cutter (suction) ~, hydraulic pipe line ~
 revolving type of cutter head, suction-cutter apparatus, (revolving) cutter, mechanically operated cutter

Schneidkopfwelle f	cutter shaft
den Baggergrund m lösen	to dislodge the material to be excavated
Deckaufbau m	deck house
Schwenkwinde f	swing winch
Drehpunktwirkung f der Pfähle mpl	pivot action of the spuds
Aufnehmvorrichtung f	suction ladder
Schwenkseil n, Seitenwindenseil	swing line
Sauggerät n	suction unit
Aufnahmerohrleitung f, Saugrohr n	suction line
Druck(rohr)leitung f	pressure pipe line
Pfahlseil n	spud rope
Pfahl m	spud
Eimerketten-Schwimmbagger m, Eimer-(ketten)naßbagger	multi-bucket ~, bucket-ladder ~, ladder bucket ~, ladder ~, elevator ~, endless chain ~
Eimerleiter f, Baggerleiter	bucket ladder, digging ladder, dredging ladder, bucket flight
Oberturas m	upper tumbler
Schlitz m im Schiffskörper m	dredging well, ladder well
Baggergut n	dredged material, dredging spoil
Eimerketten-Schwimmbagger mit Förderband n	stacker ~
Eimerketten-Schwimmbagger mit Spülrinne f	sluice ~, flume ~
Felsbrecher m	rock cutter, rock (or chisel) breaker
Flußbagger m	river ~
Grabnaßbagger	digging ~
Greif(er)-Naßbagger m, siehe: Schwimmgreifer m	
Klappschute f	hopper barge (Brit.); hopper scow, bottom-dump scow (US)
Naßbagger mit zwei oder mehreren Typen von Baggeraggregaten npl	compound ~
Naßbaggerung f, Naßbaggerei f	(underwater) dredging, dredge(r) work, underwater excavation
Naßlöffelbagger, Löffelnaßbagger, Schwimmlöffelbagger	dipper (bucket) ~, spoon ~
Pulserbagger, Pulsometerbagger	pulsometer ~
Pumpenbagger mit hydraulischer Bodenlösung f durch Abspritzen n unter hohem Druck m und gleichzeitigem Weiterspülen n, Spüler m, Spülbagger	dustpan (type of hydraulic) ~, hydraulic erosion ~
schwimmend verlegte Leitung f	floating pipeline, floating discharge line, dredge(r) discharge floating line
Absetzstelle f	disposal area, disposal point
Pfahl m	spud
linker Pfahl m, Schreitpfahl	walking spud
rechter Pfahl m, Arbeitspfahl	working spud
Seitenwinde f	swing winch

linkes Seitenwindenseil *n* (oder Schwenkseil)	left (or port) swing line
rechtes Seitenwindenseil *n* (oder Schwenkseil)	right (or starboard) swing line
Saugbagger, Pumpen(naß)bagger	suction ~, (sand-)pump ~, hydraulic (suction) ~
Saugkopf *m*	suction nozzle
Saugkorb *m* mit hydraulischer Lösung *f* des Bodens *m*, Frühling-Saugkopf *m*	draghead with hydraulic jet
Schacht(pumpen)bagger *m*, Hopperbagger *m*	hopper ~
Laderaum *m*	hopper compartment
Schleppsaugkopf *m*	drag suction nozzle
Schute *f* mit festem Deck *n*	decked barge, pontoon flat (Brit.); cargo-box barge (US)
Schute *f* mit festem Boden für Elevatorbetrieb	well barge
Schutensauger *m*	reclamation vessel
schwimmend verlegte Rohrleitung *f*	pipe line floated on pontoons
Schwimmgreifer *m*, Greif(er)-Naßbagger	clamshell (bucket) ~, grab ~, grapple ~
Schwimmlöffelbagger, siehe: Naßlöffelbagger	
Seebagger *m*	marine ~, sea-going ~

Naß|engobierung *f* = wet slip coating
~entstauber *m* = wet-type dust collector
~gas *n*, siehe: Reichnaturgas
(~) Klassierer *m* = classifier
~löschverfahren *n*, Einsumpfen *n* [*Branntkalk m*] = wet slaking process
~(mahl)mühle *f* = wet (grinding) mill
Naßmischen *n*, Naß(Nach-)Mischung *f* [*Zementvermörtelung f*] = moist mixing
~ während der Fahrt *f* [*Transportbeton m*] = shrink-mixing, partial mixing
Naß|pochwerk *n*, Naßstampfmühle *f* = wet stamp
~-Reinigungssieb *n* = wet separating
~(-Sand-)Verfahren *n*, Kalkverfahren *n* = wet-sand process, wet sand-binder construction, (hydrated) lime process, wet-aggregate process, wet sand mix
~setzmaschine *f* = wet type separating device
~-Trennungssiebung *f* = wet classifying
~zyklon *m*, siehe: Zyklonnaßklassierer *m*
Natrium|alginat *n* = sodium alginate
~-Aluminium-Silikat *n* = sodium alumin(i)um silicate
~chlorid *n*, NaCl = sodium chloride
~dampflampe *f* = sodium vapo(u)r lamp
~karbonat *n* = mineral alkali [*old name*], sodium carbonate
~karbonat wasserfrei *n*, siehe: kalzinierte Soda *f*
~nitrat *n*, siehe: Chilesalpeter *m*
~oxyd *n*, Na$_2$O = sodium oxide
~thiosulfat *n*, siehe: Fixiersalz *n*
Natrolith *m* (Min.) = mesotype, natrolite
Natron|feldspat *m* (Min.) = soda fel(d)spar
~glimmer *m* (Min.) = sodium mica
~kalkfeldspat *m*, siehe: Plagioklas *m*
~lauge *f* = lye
~salpeter *m*, siehe: Chilesalpeter
~stein *m* (Min.) = soda zeolite
~wasserglas *n* = soda water glass, soda soluble glass
Naturasphalt *m*, Erdpech *n* = natural asphalt, native ~
~mastix *m* = natural rock asphalt mastic
Naturbenzin-Anlage *f* = natural gasoline plant, ~ gasolene ~ (US)
„Naturbeton" *m*, siehe: Breccie *f*
~, siehe: Konglomerat *n*

Natur|bitumen n = native (or natural) asphalt (US)/asphaltic bitumen (Brit.)
~bordstein m = (natural) stone curb; ~ ~ kerb (or kirb) (Brit.); ~ curbstone
~gas n, siehe: Erdgas
~gasolin n, siehe: Leichtbenzin n
~gasrohrleitung f = natural gas pipeline
~gestein n = natural rock
~hafen m = natural harbo(u)r
~harz n = natural resin
natürliche Bodenverdichtung f, siehe: Konsolidierung f
~ Mineralfaser f = mineral flax
natürlicher Anhydrit m = natural anhydrite
~ Böschungswinkel m, Ruhewinkel = angle of repose
~ Grobzuschlag m; siehe unter „(Beton-) Zuschlagstoffe mpl"
~ Wasserlauf m = natural water course
Natur|material n; siehe unter „(Beton-) Zuschlagstoffe mpl"
~salzsole f = natural brine
(Natur)Stein|bearbeitungsmaschine f = natural stone dressing machine
~-Industrie f = natural stone industry
~mauerwerk n = stone walling, stonework
Naturwerkstein m, siehe: Werkstein
Nebelzerstreuer m = fog disperser, ~ dispeller
Neben|fluß m = affluent (Brit.); tributary
~gleis n = side track, siding
~kanal m, Seitenkanal = lateral canal
~produkt n = by-product
~schlußmotor m = shunt-(wound) motor
~spannung f = secondary stress
~straße f, Seitenstraße, Kleinverkehrsstraße = minor (or subsidiary, or side) road
~verwerfung f, siehe: Begleitverwerfer m
Neftgil n, siehe: Ozokerit m
negative Auflagerkraft f = uplift
Nehrung f, Landzunge f = spit (of land)
neigbares Einrammen n = driving on the rake
neigende Scheinlagerung f (Geol.) = false bedding

Neigung f [*gemessen gegen die Vertikale (oder Lotrechte f)*] = rake, batter; [*deprecated: slope, incline*]
~, siehe: Steigung f
~ [*des Längsprofils n Steigungsverhältnis n*] = gradient, incline; [*deprecated: grade*]
Neigungs|messer m, siehe: Gefällmesser
~winkel m = angle of inclination
Nenn|drehzahl f, Solldrehzahl = rated speed, ~ RPM
~durchmesser m = nominal diameter
~fassungsvermögen n = rated capacity
~last f = nominal load
~leistung f = rated power
~maß n, Sollmaß = nominal size, real measure
~versuch m = rating test
Neonröhre f = neon tube
Nephelin m (Min.) = nepheline, nephelite
~basalt m = nepheline-basalt
Nephelinit m (Min.) = nephelinite
Nephelinsyenit m (Geol.) = nepheline-syenite
nerëitische Sedimente npl = neritic sediments
Nesterbildung f [*Beton*] m = formation of pockets
Netto|preis m = net price
~querschnitt m = net section
Netz n = net(work), netting
~ n, Ordinaten $\sim$ = grid
~angabe f [*Karte f*] = map reference (abbrev. MR), grid ~
~ (anschluß) gerät n = power supply unit (or set)
~armierung f, siehe: Stahlgewebeeinlage f
~ausfall m [*Elektrotechnik f*] = mains failure
~bewehrung f, siehe: Stahlgewebeeinlage f
~gewölbe n, Rautengewölbe = reticulated vaulting
~haftmittel n, Haftanreger m, adhäsionsfördernder Zusatzstoff m, Adhäsionsverbesserer m, Haftmittel n, Haftfestigkeitsverbesserer m = adhesion (promoting) agent, non-stripping agent, antistripping admixture (or additive), dope, bonding additive, activator, antistripping agent

Netz|linie f [Fachwerk n] = working line

~rißbildung f, Maronage f, feine Rißbildung f = (surface) crazing, craze [deprecated: crocodiling] (Brit.); map cracking (US)

~strom m = grid current

~werkkuppel f = network dome

(Neu)Landgewinnung f = land reclamation, reclamation of land

Neumessing n = yellow brass

neuprofilieren = to re-shape

Neu|sand m, ungebrauchter Formsand = unused mo(u)lding sand

~schnee m = new snow

~silber n = German silver

neutrale Achse f, Nullinie f = neutral axis, zero line

Neutralöl n = neutral oil

n-freie Berechnungsweise f = design method not involving the use of the modular ratio

n-freies Traglastverfahren n = ultimate strength design method in which no modular ratio is used

NIA-Freischwinger m [Trademark], Fabrikat HAVER & BOECKER, OELDE/WESTFALEN, DEUTSCHLAND = two-bearing shaft type unbalanced weight screen

NIAGARA-Schwingsieb n [Trademark], Fabrikat HAVER & BOECKER, OELDE/WESTF., DEUTSCHLAND = four-bearing eccentric type vibrating screen, NIAGARA screen

nicht|abspritzendes Öl n = non-fluid oil

~bindig, nichtkohäsiv, inkohärent, kohäsionslos, rollig [Boden m] = non-cohesive, cohesionless, friable, non-plastic, frictional

~gespannte Bewehrung f, siehe: schlaffe ~

~hydraulisches Bindemittel n, siehe: Luftkalk m

~klastisches Sedimentgestein n = non-clastic sedimentary rock

~prismatisches Konstruktionsglied n = non-prismatic member

~-starre Decke f, schmiegsame ~ [Straße f] = flexible pavement, non rigid ~

~tragende (Trenn)Wand f = non-bearing (partition) wall

Nichtüberhol(ungs)strecke f = no-passing zone

nichtunterkellert = basementless

Nickelblüte f, Annabergit m (Min.) = nickel-bloom, annabergite

Nickelin n (Min.), siehe: Rotnickelkies m

Niederdruck|anlage f = low-pressure installation

~-Dampf(er)härtung f [Betonstein m] = low-pressure steam curing

~einpressung f, Niederdruckauspressung f = low-pressure grouting (or injection)

~kompressor m = low-pressure (air) compressor

~reifen m = low-pressure tire (US); ~ tyre (Brit.)

Niederschlag m = precipitation, rainfall

niederschlagen = to precipitate

Niederschlag(s)dauer f, Regendauer f = duration of the storm

~elektrode f [Elektroabscheider m] = collecting electrode

~gebiet n; siehe unter „Entwässerung f"

~koeffizient m = coefficient of rainfall, rainfall coefficient

~messer m = rain-ga(u)ge

~stärke f, Regenstärke [mm/min.] = average rainfall intensity

~statistik f = rainfall record

~wasser n, Regenwasser n = storm water, rain ~

Niederschraubventil n = screw down valve

Niederung f = flat

Niederungsgebiet n [Fluß m] = backswamp area

Nieder(ungs)moor n, siehe: Flachmoor

niedrig gekohlter Stahl m = low carbon steel

~ legierter Stahl m = low alloy steel

niedriges Niedrigwasser n = lower low water

niedrigviskoses Bindemittel n = low-viscosity binder (or matrix)

Niedrigwasser|bett n = minor bed

~reg(e)lung f, Niedrigwasserverbesserung f = low tide regulation, regulation of low water flows

Nieseln n, siehe: Rieselregen m

Niet *m*	**rivet**
~kopf *m*	~ head
~kraft *f*	~ efficiency
~werkstoff *m*	~ material
stauchen	to clench
(ver)nieten	to ~, to close up a ~
zweireihige (oder doppelreihige) Nietung *f*	double ~, double riveted joint
Nieten verstemmen	to ca(u)lk
Kettennietung *f*, Parallelnietung	chain rivet(ed) joint
Versatznietung, Zickzacknietung	staggered (or zigzag) rivet(ed) joint
verjüngte Nietung *f*	lozenge riveting
einschnittiger ~	single-shear ~
Überlappungsnietung *f*	(over)lap riveting
Laschennietung *f*	butt rivet(ed) joint
Doppellaschennietung *f*	double butt strap joint
Bördelnietung *f*	flanged seam riveting
gescheilter Nietkopf *m*	snap head
erhabener Nietkopf *m*	cup head
eckiger Nietkopf *m*, trapezförmiger ~	pan head(ed) ~
spitzer Nietkopf *m*	pointed head, conical head
gehämmerter Nietkopf *m*	hand-made head
runder Nietkopf *m*	ellipsoidal head
Nietteilung *f*, Nietabstand *m* [*Mittenabstand der Niete einer Nietreihe*]	~ pitch, ~ spacing
Hohl~	tubular ~
Heft~	tacking ~
Spreng~	explosive ~
~hammer *m*	~ hammer
schlagen	to drive
(~)Gegenhalter *m*	holder-up, bucker-up, dolly
genietete Verbindung *f*	riveted joint
kopfloser ~	headless ~

Nigrit *m* = nigrite

Nippel *m* = nipple

Nippflut *f*, Nipptide *f*, taube Flut *f* = neap tide, neaps

Nische *f* [*Tunnel m*] = niche

Nitro|benzol *n* = nitrobenzene

~glyzerin *n*; siehe unter „1. Schießen *n*; 2. Sprengen *n*“

~lack *m* = nitrocellulose lacquer

Nitropenta-Sprengschnur *f*; siehe unter „1. Schießen *n*; 2. Sprengen *n*“

Niveau *n*, Geländehöhe *f* = ground level

~differenz *f*, Gefälle *n* [*Wasserkraftwerk n*] = head

niveau|eben, siehe: bündig mit

~gleiche Kreuzung *f*, siehe: plangleiche ~

~gleicher Bahnübergang *m*, schienengleiche Niveaukreuzung *f*, schienengleicher Niveauübergang *m* = level (railway) crossing (Brit.); level (railroad) crossing (US)

Nivellieren *n*; siehe unter „Vermessungskunde *f*“

Nivellier(instrument) *n*; siehe unter „Vermessungskunde *f*“

Nivelliertachymeter *n* = level with compass

Nocken|steuerschalter *m* = camshaft controller

~welle *f*, siehe: Daumenwelle

Nockenwellen-Stampfmaschine f = cam-operated (tamping) (concrete) block machine
Nomogramm n = nomogram
Nord|licht n = Aurora Borealis, Northern Lights
~mannstanne f = Crimean silver fir
~-Ostsee-Kanal m, Kaiser-Wilhelm-Kanal m = Baltic Ship Canal, Kiel Canal
Normal|ausführung f = standard construction
~ausleger m = standard jib (Brit.); ~ boom (US)
~drehzahl f = normal RPM
normale geothermische Tiefenstufe f = normal reciprocal geothermal gradient
~ Stadthauptstraße f, Oberflächen(stadt)hauptstraße = surface artery, ~ arterial
~ Stadtstraße f, Oberflächen(stadt)straße = surface street, ordinary city street
normales Stauziel n; siehe unter „Talsperre f"
Normal|frequenz-Vibrator m = standard frequency vibrator
~güte f = ordinary grade
Normalien f, siehe: Abnahmevorschriften f
Normal|kraft f = normal force
~-Mischungsverhältnis n = nominal mix
~profil(eisen) n = standard section (Brit.); structural shape (US)
~querschnitt m, siehe: Regelquerschnitt
~spannung f = normal stress
~spiegel m; siehe unter „Talsperre f"
~spurgleis n, Regelspurgleis, Vollbahngleis = standard ga(u)ge track
~versuch m = routine test
~ziegel m = standard structural clay tile (US); standard brick
Normen f, Güterichtlinien f = standard specifications
normen = to standardize
Normen|ausschuß m = committee on standardization, standards committee
~eigenschaft f = specification property
~festigkeit f = standard strength, specification ~
~prüfsieb n = standard test sieve
~sand m = specification sand
~tabelle f = specification table
~vorschrift f = standard specification
Normungszahl f = standard figure
Nortonbrunnen m, siehe: Rammbrunnen
Nosean m (Min.) = nosean, noselite
Not|abschließung f = emergency closure
~auslaß m = emergency outlet
~schieber m = emergency valve
~schieberstollen m = emergency valve tunnel
~standsgebiet n = depressed area
~stromaggregat n = standby generating set, emergency current standby generator
~verband m = first aid dressing
~verschluß m = emergency (guard) gate, guard ~
n-stieliger Rahmen m = (portal) frame with n-column
Null|druckfläche f = zone of zero stress
~-Linie f, siehe: neutrale Achse f
~meridian m = Prime Meridian
~punkt m = zero point
numerisch = numerical
Nummernschild n [Auto n] = car registration plate
Nummulitensandstein m = nummulitic sandstone
Nurkraftwagenstraße f, siehe: Autobahn f
Nuten|schleifmaschine f = slot grinder
~stoßmaschine f = slotter
Nut f **und Feder** f [Holz n] = groove and tongue [woodworking]
~ ~ ~ [Maschinenelement n] = slot and key [machine element]
Nutzapfen m; siehe unter „Holzverbindung f"
nutzbare Fahrtiefe f, siehe: Wassertiefe des Fahrwassers n
~ Pferdestärke f, siehe: effektive ~
Nutz|fahrzeug n = commercial vehicle
~last f, Gebrauchslast = live load(ing), incidental superimposed load
~nießer m = beneficiary
~nießung f = usufruct
~querschnitt m [Stab m] = net section
Nutz- und Trinkwasserspeicherbecken n = service reservoir
Nutzungsdauer f; siehe unter „Baumaschinen fpl und Baugeräte npl"

O

oben offene Fachwerkbrücke f = pony truss bridge
Obenöl n = upper cylinder lubricant
Oberbach|-Bitumenschlämme f = Oberbach bituminous slurry (Brit.); ~ asphaltic ~ (US)
~-Teerschlämme f = Oberbach tar slurry
~-Wasserlagerungsprüfung f = Oberbach immersion test
Oberbau m = superstructure
~, Eisenbahn~, Gleis~ = permanent way, p. w.
Oberboden m, siehe: Dammerde f
oberdevonisch (Geol.) = of Upper Devonian age
obere Faser f = top fibre (Brit.); top fiber (US)
oberer Grenzzustand m [*Boden* m] = passive state [*soil*]
~ Windverband m = top lateral bracing
Oberflächen|abdichtungsschicht f = surface membrane
~absieg(e)lung f, siehe: Porenschluß m
~absieg(e)lung f mit Asphaltmastix m = mastic sealing coat
oberflächenaktiv = surface active
Oberflächen|bahn f = ground level railway, surface ~ (Brit); ~~railroad (US)
~behandlung f, OB [*Schwarzdeckenbau* m] = surface treatment, seal coating
~chemie f = surface chemistry
~entwässerung f; siehe unter „Entwässerung f"
~erneuerungsverfahren n, siehe: Retread-Verfahren n
~feinstbehandlung f = super-finish
~frost m, siehe: Spaltenfrost
~gemisch n, Oberflächenmischung f [*Kiesstraße* f] = surface mix(ture)
~gestein n, siehe: Ergußgestein
~härteprüfung f mit einer **Diamant-Pyramide** f = diamond pyramid hardness test
(Ober)Flächen|rüttler m; siehe unter „Betonrüttelgeräte npl"
~rüttlung f; siehe unter „Betonrüttelgeräte npl"

Oberflächen|spannung f = surface tension
~stabilisation f; siehe unter „Baugrundverbesserung f"
~(stadt)straße f, normale Stadtstraße = surface street
~(stadt)straßennetz n = surface street network
~teerung f = surface tarring, ~ dressing with tar
~ton m = surface clay
~verdichter m = surface compactor
~verdichtung f = superficial compaction
~wasser n, Tag(es)wasser n = surface water
Ober|flansch m = top flange
~graben m, siehe: Oberwasserkanal m
~grundwasser n = shallow ground water
Obergurt m = top boom, ~ chord
~ [*Bandförderer* m] = carrier side
~laufkatze f = top-flange troll(e)y
~laufschienen-Elektrohängebahn f = mono-rail telpher
~stab m = upper chord member
~winkel m = top flange angle
oberirdischer Abfluß m = surface runoff (or flow)
oberirdisches Bauwerk n = surface structure
oberirdische Wasserscheide f = surface watershed line, ~ divide
Oberkante f = top level
~ Terrain n, siehe: O.K. Terrain
oberlastig = top-heavy
Ober|lauf-Kettentransporteur m = overhead chain conveyor
~leitungs(omni)bus m = troll(e)y bus, electric troll(e)y; troll(e)y coach (US)
~lichtpfette f = skylight purlin
~putz m = setting coat, skimming ~, set (Brit.); finish coat (US)
~putz-Gips m = finish(ing) plaster
oberschlächtig = overshot
Ober|schwelle f, siehe: Sturz m
~trum m = upper strand
~turas m = head sprocket
~wagen m [*Bagger* m] = superstructure, upper deck
~wagengrundplatte f = deck
Oberwasser n = up-stream water, head ~

Oberwasserkanal m, Obergraben m, Oberkanal m = head race
oberwasserseitig; siehe unter „Talsperre f"
obsequentes Tal n [verläuft in der Richtung f der Abdachung f] = obsequent valley
Obsidian m (Min.) = obsidian
Ochsenkarre(n) f, (m) = bullock cart, oxcart
Ocker m (Min.) = ocher, ochre
OCRAT-Verfahren n [Betonbehandlung f mit gasförmigem Siliziumtetrafluorid n] = OCRAT method
Ödland n = waste land
Oedometer n, Druckgerät n, Verdichtungsapparat m = consolidation (test) apparatus, oedometer
Ofen m **der grobkeramischen Industrie** f = heavy clay kiln
~gebäude n = kiln building
ofengetrocknet [Holz n] = kiln-dried
Ofen|isolierung f = kiln insulation
~ring m = kiln ring
~schaum m = kiln scum
offen [Verschleißschicht f] = open-textured [wearing course]
~ abgestuft = open-graded
~ abgestuftes Mineralgemisch n = open-graded (mineral) aggregate, OGA
offene Mischung f = open mix, coarse ~
offene Schappe f, siehe: Löffelbohrer m
~ Wasserhaltung f = dewatering (or unwatering) by pumping from the building pit
offener Baumischbelag m, Baumischbelag nach Art des Makadam = macadam aggregate type road mix surface
~ Bohrlöffel m = clay auger
~ Entwässerungsgraben m = drainage ditch
~ Graben m = (open) ditch, field ~
~ Güterwagen m, ~ Waggon m = open top railway car (Brit.); ~ ~ railroad ~ (US); gondola car
~ Querschnitt m = open section
~ Senkkasten m = open caisson
~ Tiegel m [Flammpunktprüfung f] = open cup
~ Viersitzer m [PKW] = touring car
~ Zweisitzer m [PKW m] = roadster

offenes Kapillarwasser n = equilibrium moisture content
~ Licht n, **~ Feuer** n = naked light
~ Schrägbecherwerk n = open inclined type bucket elevator
öffentliche Ausschreibung f; siehe unter „Angebot" n
~ Gesundheit f = public health
öffentlicher Massenverkehr m = public transport, ~ service vehicles traffic, mass transportation, mass transit
~ Parkplatz m = public parking place
~ Versorgungsbetrieb m = public utility (undertaking)
öffentliches Bauvorhaben n = public works project
~ Verkehrsfahrzeug n = public service vehicle
Öffnung f [Brücke f, Durchlaufträger m] = span
Oktanzahl f, Oktanziffer f, Klopffestigkeitszahl = octane number
O. K. f **Terrain**, Oberkante f Terrain, Geländeoberkante = ground line
Okular n = eye-piece, eye-glass
~auszug m = eye-piece draw tube
~klemmung f = eye-piece clamping device
~muschel f = eye-piece cup
Ölablaßpfropfen m, Ölablaßstopfen m, Ölablaßschraube f = drain plug for oil sump, oil (pan) drain plug, waste oil screw
Ölabstreifring m, Ölabstreifer m = scraper ring, oil ~ ~
Ölabziehstein m = oil stone
Ölanlasser m = oil cooled starter
Ölansammlung f (Geol.) = entrapment of petroleum
Ölausbeute f = recovery of oil
Ölbad n = oil bath
Ölbadluftfilter n, m = oil-bath air filter
Ölbadschmierung f = oil-bath lubrication
Ölbaum m, Olivenbaum = olive tree
Ölbeize f = oil (base) mordant
Ölbohrgerät n = oil well drill
Ölbohrplattform f **auf See** f = oil drilling island, platform for oil drilling at sea
Ölbohrturm m = oil well derrick
Ölbremse f, siehe: Öldämpfer m
Ölbrenner m = oil burner

Ölbrunnen — Ölzerstäuber

Ölbrunnen *m*, erdölfündige Bohrung *f* = oil well
Öldämpfe *mpl* = oil vapours
Öldämpfer *m*, Ölbremse *f* = oil dash pot, ~ brake, ~ dampe(ne)r
Öldämpfung *f* = oil damping
Oldhamit *m* (Min.) = oldhamite
Öldocht *m* = oil wick
Öldruckbremse *f* = oil brake
Öldruckpresse *f* = oil pressure jack
Öldruckpumpe *f* = oil force pump
öldurchtränkt, siehe: ölgetränkt
Olefin *n* = olefine
Öl(einfüll)stutzen *m* = oil filler (cap)
Ölemulsion *f* = oil emulsion
Ölentziehanlage *f* = oil extracting plant
Öler *m* = oiler, lubricator (nipple)
Ölersatzmethode *f* [*Nachprüfung f der Verdichtung f*] = heavy oil method
Oleum *n*, rauchende Schwefelsäure *f* = fuming sulfuric acid
Ölfalle *f* = oil trap
Ölfang *m* [*an der Radnabe f*] = oil collector
Ölfeld *n* = oil field
Ölfeldwinde *f* = well pulling machine
Ölfeuerung *f* = oil burning, oil-firing
~ = oil fired furnace, ~ burning ~
Ölfilm *m*, Ölhäutchen *n* = film of oil, pellicle ~ ~, oil film
Ölfilter *n*, *m* = oil filter, ~ strainer
Ölfiltertopf *m* = oil filter cartridge
Ölfirnis *m* = oil varnish
Ölfleck(en) *m* = oil stain, stain of oil
ölfleckig = oil-stained
ölfrei, nicht ölführend = barren of oil
Ölgasn, Fettgas, transportables Gas = oil gas
ölgetränkt, ölimprägniert, öldurchtränkt = oil-impregnated
Ölhaut *f*, Ölbatist *m* = oilskin
Ölhäutchen *n*, siehe: Ölfilm *m*
Ölhorizont *m* = oil horizon
Ölhydraulik *f* = pressurized oil system
Oligoklas *m* (Min.) = oligoclase
~ **granit** *m* (Geol.) = miarolyte
oligosaprobe Zone *f* = oligosaprobic zone
Oligosaprobien *fpl* = oligosaprobic organisms
ölimprägniert, siehe: ölgetränkt
Öl-in-Wasser-Emulsion *f* = oil-in-water emulsion

Ölisolator *m* = oil-insulator
Olivenbaum *m*, Ölbaum = olive tree
Olivin *m*, Olivenstein *m* (Min.) = olivine
~ **bombe** *f* (Geol.) = olivine-nodule
~ **fels** *m*, Dunit *m* = dunite, olivine-rock
Ölkabel *n* = oil-filled cable
~ **endverschluß** *m* = oil cable head, ~ ~ end sleeve
Ölkahn *m* = oil barge
Ölkalk(stein) *m* = oil-impregnated limestone
Ölkanne *f* = oilcan, ~ feeder
Ölkännchen *n* = oil can, squirt-oiler
Ölkitt *m* = putty
Ölkuchen *m*, Leinkuchen = oil cake, linseed ~
Ölnut *f* = oil groove
Ölpresse *f* = oil press
Ölquelle *f* = oil well
Ölring *m* = oiling ring
Ölsand *m* = oil sand, "pay" (sand)
Ölsandstein *m* = oil sandstone
Ölschalter *m* **für Warnlicht** *n* = oil switch
Ölschiefer *m*, siehe: bituminöser ~
Ölschlamm *m* = oil mud
Ölschmierpresse *f* = oil gun
Ölschmierpumpe *f* = oil lubricating pump
Ölschutzring *m* = oil catcher, thrower, oil shield
Ölsichtkontrolle *f* = oil sight-feed ga(u)ge
Ölsonde *f* = producing oil well
Ölspritzblech *n* = oil splasher
Ölstandanzeiger *m* = oil level indicator
Ölstein *m* (Min.), siehe: Elaeolith *m*
Ölstelle *f* = oiling point
Ölstutzen *m*, Öleinfüllstutzen = oil filler (cap)
Öltanker *m* = oil tanker
Ölträger *m*, (erd)ölführende Schicht *f* = oil-bearing stratum, petroliferous bed
Öltropfschale *f*, Öltropfenfänger *m* = oil drip pan
Ölumlaufschmierung *f* = oil circulation lubricating system
Ölverteiler *m* = oil manifold
Ölvorrat *m* = oil reserve
Ölwanderung *f* = migration of oil
Ölwanne *f*, Ölsumpf *m* = oil sump
Ölwechsel *m* = oil change
Ölzerstäuber *m* = oil atomizer

Ölzeug *n*, Ölanzug *m* = oil cloth
Ombrometer *n* = ombrometer [*a rainga(u)ge*]
Omnibus *m*, (Auto)Bus = (motor) bus, omnibus
~ mit Oberdeck *n* = double-deck bus
~ ohne Oberdeck *n* = single deck bus
~bahnhof *m*, siehe: (Auto)Busbahnhof
~reise *f*, (Auto)Busreise = bus ride
~werkstatt *f*, (Auto)Buswerkstatt = bus overhaul works
Onyxmarmor *m*, Kalkonyx *m* = onyx marble
oolithischer Kalkstein *m*, Oolithkalk *m*, Kalkoolith *m*, Eisteinkalk = oölitic limestone, oölite
Opalglas *n* = opal glass
Ophikalzit *m* (Geol.) = forsterite-marble, ophicalcite
ophitische Struktur *f*, siehe: divergentstrahlig-körnige ~
optimaler Wassergehalt *m*, ~ Feuchtigkeitsgehalt = optimum moisture content
optisch-akustisches Hilfsmittel *n* = audio visual aid
optische Achsenebene *f* = optical orientation [*mineralogy*]
~ Anzeige *f* = visual observation
optisches Signal *n* = visible signal
Ordnungs|gleis *n* = classification track
~zahl *f* **der Spannungsverteilung** *f*, siehe: Konzentrationsfaktor *m* nach Fröhlich
Organisator *m* = organiser
organisch = organic
organische Verbindung *f* = organic compound
organischer Boden *m* = organic soil
~ Schutt *m* = organic débris
Orgelgebläse = organ bellows
orientalischer Alabaster *m* = oriental alabaster
Orkan *m* = hurricane
Orogenese *f*, siehe: Gebirgsbildung *f*
Orographie *f*, Gebirgsbeschreibung *f* = orography
Orsat-Apparat *m* = Orsat apparatus
Ort|beton *m*; siehe unter „Beton"
~(beton)pfahl *m*; siehe unter „Gründungspfahl"

orthodoxe Erddrucktheorie *f* [*Coulomb, Rankine*] classical earth pressure theory
Orthogneis *m*, Orthogestein *n* = orthogneiss
orthogonales Kurvennetz *n*, rechtwinkliges ~ = orthogonal curve system
Ortho|kieselsäure *f* = orthosilicic acid
~klas *m* (Min.) = orthoclase
~therme *f* (Geol.) = warm spring
orthotrope Platte *f*; siehe unter „Brücke *f*"
örtlich, lokal = local
örtliches Material *n*, lokales ~ = local material, near-by ~
Ortpfahl *m*; siehe unter „Gründungspfahl"
~, Ortpflock *m* [*Bergbau m*] = cornerstake
Orts|beweglichkeit *f*; siehe unter „Baumaschinen *fpl* und Baugeräte *npl*"
(~)Brust *f*; siehe unter „Tunnelbau *m*"
Ortschaft *f*, geschlossene Ortslage *f* = built-up area
Ortsdurchfahrt *f*, Durchgangsstraße *f* = through road, ~ street, town-ship ~
ortsfest, stationär = stationary, static, permanent
Orts|schild *n* = name board, place-name sign
~verkehr *m* = local traffic
Ortungs|bereich *m* [*Funkmeßgerät n*] = radar coverage
~genauigkeit *f* [*Funkmeßgerät n*] = bearing discrimination, ~ accuracy [*radar*]
Os *m*, Esker *m* (Geol.) = esker
Öse *f* = ear, eye, lug
osmotischer Druck *m* = osmotic pressure
österreichische Bauweise *f*, Dreizonenbauweise *f* [*Tunnelbau m*] = (English-)Austrian method
Ostwald-Viskosimeter *n* = U tube visco(si)meter
Otto|-Kraftstoff *m*, siehe: Benzin *n*
~(-Vergaser)motor *m*, siehe: Benzinmotor
Ottrelithschiefer *m* = ottrelite slate
oval-gerippter Draht *m* = oval ribbed wire
Oxalsäure *f*, Kleesäure $(C_2O_2H)_2 \times 2H_2O$ = oxalic acid
Oxychloridzement *m* = oxychloride cement

oxydisches Bleierz n = oxidized lead mineral
Ozeanflug m = transoceanic flight
Ozeanographie f, **Meereskunde** f = oceanographie
Ozokerit m, **Erdwachs** n, **Neftgil** n (Min.) = ozokerite, ozocerite
Ozonisator m = ozoniser

P

Pack|eis n = pack ice
~faschinat n, siehe: Faschinat n
~lage f = allgemeiner Begriff für entweder „Setzpacklage f" oder „Schüttpacke f"
~maschine f [z. B. für Zement m] = packer, packing machine
~silo m [Einsackmaschine f] = supply bin, ~ tank
~vorgang m = packaging operation
~werk n, siehe: Faschinat n
Paketstapeln n [z. B. Ziegel] = packaging
Paläoklima = paleoclimate
Palette f, siehe: Stapelplatte f
Palettenwalze f [Betonbahn-Automat m] = rotating grading screed
Palingenese f, siehe: Anatexis f
Palisadenwand f = palisades
palynologisches Vielkornpräparat n = multi-grain palynological slide
panallotriomorph, siehe: panidiomorphkörnig
Pancakeeis n, **Pfannkuchen** m = pancake ice
panidiomorphkörnig, panallotriomorph, autallotriomorph (Geol.) = panidiomorphic
Panne f = breakdown
Pantograph m, **Storch(en)schnabel** m = pantograph
Panzer|graben m = anti-tank ditch
~kabel n, siehe: bewehrtes Kabel
~platte f = armo(u)r plate
~schießplatz m = tank gunnery range
~übungsgelände n = tank-training area (or ground)
Papier|abrollwagen m = paper spreading machine
~-Brennstoff-Filter m, n = paper-type fuel filter
~-Chromatographie f = paper chromatography
~mühle f = paper mill
~unterlage f, **Unterlagspapier** n, **Straßenbaupapier** = concrete subgrade paper, concreting ~, underlay ~, road lining, sub-soil paper
Papphülse f = cardboard ferrule
Parabelträger m = parabolic girder
parabolisch exzentrisch verlaufende Bewehrung f = parabolic steel excentricity [concrete beam]
parabolischer Obergurt m [Brücke f] = parabolic top chord
Paraffin n = paraffin wax
paraffinbasisches Erdöl n = paraffin-base crude petroleum
Paraffingatsch m = (paraffin) slack wax
paraffinhaltiges Destillat n = paraffin-distillate, wax oil
Paraffin|-Kohlenwasserstoff m = paraffin
~öl n, **Medizinalöl** n = liquid paraffin, medicinal oil
~öl von niedrigem Schmelzpunkt m **zur Imprägnierung** f **von Streichhölzern** npl = match wax
~-Sorption f = paraffin sorption
Paragneis m, **Sedimentgneis**, **Renchgneis**, **Paragestein** n = paragneiss
Paragonit m (Min.) = paragonite
Paraklase f (Geol.), siehe: Verwerfung f
Parallel|flanschträger m = parallel-flanges beam
~schlag m; siehe unter „Drahtseil n"
Parken n = automobile parking
Park|gebäude n [Automobile npl] = parking building
~platz m, **Parkfläche** f, **Auto~** = car park, parking place, parking lot
~raumnot f = street sclerosis (US)
~straße f = park highway, parkway
~streifen m, siehe: Randstreifen
~verbotsschild n = no-parking marker
~zeitmesser m = parking meter
Partialturbine f = partial admission turbine
Partikelchen n, siehe: Einzelkorn n
Parzelle f, **Grundstück** n = plot, land parcel
Passat(wind) m = geostrophic wind

passiver Erddruck *m*, siehe: Erdwiderstand *m*
Paste *f* = paste
Paß *m*, Gebirgs~ = (mountain) pass
~gletscher *m* = through-glacier
~schraube *f* = turned bold, fillet ~
~stück *n* = adapter, flilling piece
~tal *n* = through-valley
pastöse Paraffin-Öl-Emulsion *f* = (sucker-) rod wax
Patent|anmeldung *f* = patent application
~inhaber *m* = patentee
patentverschlossenes Seil *n*; siehe unter „Drahtseil *n*"
Paternoster *m* = paternoster
Pauschal|gebühr *f* = flat-rate tariff
~summe *f* = lump sum
Pause *f*, Lichtpause = print
~ = break
Paus|leinen *n* = tracing cloth
~papier *n* = tracing paper, blue print ~
Pech *n*, Säureharzasphalt *m* = pitch
~blende *f*, siehe: Uranpechblende
~grieß *m* = pitch grit, ~ cake
~harz *n* = pitch resin
~kohle *f*; siehe unter „Kohle *f*"
~mastix *m* = pitch mastic
~schotter *m* = pitch macadam
~see *m*, Asphaltsee = pitch lake, asphalt ~
~stein *m* = pitch-stone
~torf *m* = pitch-peat
Pedalfer *m* = pedalfer
Pedocal *m* = pedocal
Pedologie *f*, Bodenkunde *f* = pedology
Pegel *m*, siehe: Wasserstandsmarke *f*
~meßstelle *f*, Pegel(meß)station *f* = flood measuring post, river ga(u)ging station
Pegmatit *m* = pegmatite
Peilstab *m* [*Tankanlage f*] = dipstick, dip rod
Pektinsäure *f* = pectic acid
pelagische Foraminiferen *fpl* = pelagic foraminifera
Pelton-Rad *n* = Pelton (water) wheel
Pendel *n*, *m* = pendulum
~achse *f* = oscillating axle
~becherwerk *n* = gravity tipping conveyor, tilting bucket ~, swinging bucket elevator

~betrieb *m* = shuttle (service) [*a back and forth motion of a machine which continues to face in one direction*]
~dynamometer *n* = cradle dynamometer
~glätter *m* = reciprocating screed
~kugellager *n* = self-aligning ball bearing
~lenkachse *f* = oscillating steering axle
~lot *n* = pendulum device
~pfeiler *m* = rocking pier, hinged ~
~schlagwerk *m* = pendulum impact tester
~stütze *f* = socketed stanchion
~transport *m* [*z. B. zwischen Bagger m und Kippe f*] = shuttle haul(age)
~verkehr *m* = shuttle traffic
~wagen *m* = shuttle car
~wurfrinne *f*, siehe: Torpedorinne *f*
Pendler *m*, ständiger Benutzer (eines Verkehrsmittels) = commutor
Penetrometer *m*, siehe: Eindring(ungs)messer *m*
Pennin *m* (Min.) = penninite
pennsylvanisches Seilbohren *n*, siehe: Seilschlagbohren *n*
Peptisation *f* = peptisation [*the formation of a sol from a gel*]
Peridotit *m* = peridotite
Periklas *m* (Min.) = periclase
Perimetralfuge *f*; siehe unter „Talsperre *f*"
Periodenmischer *m*; siehe unter „Betonmischer *m*"
periodischer Ofen *m* = intermittent kiln, periodic ~
Perlit-Hochofen *m* = perlite expansion furnace
Perl|kies *m*, Erbskies *m* = pea gravel
~moos *n*, siehe: irländisches Moos
~spat *m* (Min.), siehe: Dolomit *m*
Perowskit *m*, CaTiO$_3$ (Min.) = perovskite
Persenning *f*, geteertes Segeltuch *n*, Presenning *f* = tarp(aulin)
Personal *n*, siehe: Belegschaft *f*
~abbau *m* = cut-down of staff
~kredit *m* = conventional loan (US)
~schwierigkeiten *fpl* = staffing difficulties
Personen|aufzug *m* = passenger hoist (or elevator)
~bahnhof *m* = passenger station

Personen|bandförderer m = passenger conveyor belt
~kraftwagen m, PKW = (passenger) automobile, (passenger) car
~schleuse f; siehe unter: „pneumatische Gründung f"
~verkehr m, Fahrgastverkehr = passenger traffic
Petrographie f, Gesteinsbeschreibung f = petrography
Petroleum n, Leuchtöl n, Leuchtpetroleum, Brennöl, Kerosin n = kerosene, kerosine (US); lighting oil, illuminating oil, paraffin (oil) (Brit.)
Petrolkoks m = petroleum coke
Petrologie f, Gesteinsentstehungslehre f = petrology
Petrol|pech n = petroleum (or oil) pitch
~sand m = petroliferous sand
Pfahl m = pile
~bausiedlung f = lake dwelling
~bockjoch n = double (pile) bent
~bündel n, siehe: Dalbe m
~gründung f = pile(d) foundation

(~) Joch n = (pile) trestle, ~ bent
(~) Jochbauwerk n = trestle-type structure
~kopf m = pile head
~-Kopfplatte f = pile cap
~ramme f; siehe unter „Rammanlage f",
~rammschlauch m = piledriver hose
~rostbauwerk n = pile foundation structure
~rostplatte f = pile platform
~schuh m, Rammspitze f, Pfahlfuß m = drive point, pile shoe, pile point
~wurzel f = tap root
~zieher m, Pfahlausieher = pile extractor, pilepuller, piledrawer
Pfannen|gips m = pan-calcined gypsum
~meer n = transgression sea
~stein m, Gießpfannenziegel m = ladle brick
~ziegel m, siehe: Doppelfalzziegel
Pfannkuchen m, siehe: Pancakeeis n
Pfeiler m = pier, shaft
~bau m [*Bergbau m*] = pillaring

Pfeiler-Bruch-Verfahren n [*Asbesterzabbauverfahren n unter Tage*]	**block-caving method**
Zusammenrutschen n der ungestützten Last f	caving
Randgang m	advance fringe drift
senkrecht aufwärts führender Gang m an der Blockdecke f	corner raise
Sammelpunkt m	grizzly
Grubenrostgang m	grizzly drift
Fördergang m	haulage drift
Förderrutsche f	chute raise

Pfeiler|gewölbe(stau)mauer f; siehe unter „Talsperre f"
~gründung f = pier foundation [*in USA also incorrectly termed "caisson foundation"*]
~gründungshöhe f = pier-base elevation
~kopf(stau)mauer f; siehe unter „Talsperre f"
~kuppel(stau)mauer f; siehe unter „Talsperre f"
~platten(stau)mauer f; siehe unter „Talsperre f"

~schaft m, siehe: Schaftschale f
~(stau)mauer f; siehe unter „Talsperre f"
Pfeil|rädergetriebe n = herringbone gear
~verhältnis n [*Bogen m*] = risespan ratio
~verzahnung f = double helical gearwheels, ~ ~ gearing
Pfennig m (Geol.) = nummulite
Pferde|fleischholz n = horseflesh mahagony
~fuhrwerk n = horse-drawn cart
Pfette f = purlin

Pfettenabstand — Piezometer(rohr)

Pfettenabstand m = purlin spacing
Pflanzen|bewuchs m, Bodenbewachsung f = mantle of vegetation, vegetable cover, vegetation cover
~reste f = plant remains
Pflaster|aufrauhgerät n = sett roughening machine
~bett n = bed
~(decke) n, (f), Steinpflaster n, Pflasterung f = (stone-)sett paving (Brit.); [*in Scotland: causeway*]; block pavement (US)
Pflasterer m, Steinsetzer m = pavior (Brit.); paver (US)
~werkzeug n = paving tool
Pflaster|hammer m = paving hammer
~holz n = wood for paving
~kitt m, Pflastervergußmasse f = sett joint filler (or sealing compound)
~klinker m, siehe: Pflasterziegel m
Pflastern n, Pflasterung f = 1. causeway(ing) [*in Scotland*]; 2. paving with setts
pflastern = to sett pave
Pflaster|platte f = quarry tile
~ramme f = (sett) paving rammer
~rinne f, Rinnstein m = paved gutter, ~ channel, (road) channel
~stampfer m = (sett) paving tamper
~stein m = (paving) sett
~steinherstellung f = sett-making
~steinmaschine f = paving sett making machine
~straße f = sett paved road
~verband m (Geol.), siehe: Bienenwabenverband
~vergußmasse f, Pflasterkitt m = sett joint sealing compound, ~ ~ filler
~ziegel m, Pflasterklinker, Straßenbauklinker m = paving brick, road~
Pflock m = peg, stake
Pflug m = plough (Brit.); plow (US)
~ mit Radstelze f = one-wheel plough (Brit.)/plow (US)
~bagger m (oder **Flachbagger-Lader** m, oder **Schürfbagger**, oder **Förderband-(Anhänge)Schürfwagen** m) **mit kreisförmiger Diskuspflugschar** f (oder **Pflugteller** m) = elevating grader

~bagger m (oder **Flachbagger-Lader** m, oder **Schürfbagger** m) **mit keilförmiger Schar** f = (elevating) loader
Pfosten m, Stange f = post
~ramme f = post driver
~zieher m = post puller
Pfropfen m = plug
Phakolith m (Geol.) = phacolith
Phengit m (Min.) = phengite
Phenol n, Karbolsäure f, Phenylalkohol m, Steinkohlenteerkreosot n, C_6H_5OH = phenol, carbolic acid
phenolharzveredeltes Holz n = phenolic-improved wood
Phenolpech n, siehe: Karbolpech n
Phenylalkohol m, siehe: Phenol n
Phlogopit m, hellbrauner Glimmer m (Min.) = phlogopite, amber mica
Phonolith m (Min.) = phonolite
Phosgenit m, Bleihornerz n (Min.) = phosgenite
Phosphat n = phosphate
~bindung f = phosphate bonding
Phosphorit m (Min.) = phosphorite, rock phosphate
Phosphorpentoxyd n, Phosphorsäureanhydrid n, wasserfreie Phosphorsäure f, P_2O_5 = anhydrous phosphoric acid
Photo|grammetrie f, Lichtbildmeßverfahren n = photogrammetry, photogrammetric survey(ing)
~kopie f = photographic print
Photokopieren n = photo printing
phreatische Linie f = phreatic line
pH-Wert m, Wasserstoffzahl H f, Wasserstoffionenkonzentration f = pH-value, hydrogen-ion concentration
Phyllit m = phyllite
physikalisch-chemische Reaktion f = physico-chemical reaction
physikalische Verwitterung f, Gesteinszerfall m, mechanische Verwitterung f = mechanical weathering, physical ~, rock disintegration
Piassavabesen m = bass broom
Pickhammer m = pick hammer for cutting work
Pier m, f, Landungssteg m = pier
Piezometer(rohr) n = piezometer (pipe), seepage ~

piezometrische Druckhöhe f = piezometric head
Pikrinsäure f = picric acid
Pikrit m = pricite
Pilzdecke(nkonstruktion) f = flat(-)slab (girderless) construction, two-way flat-slab floor
Pinsel|anstrich m = brush painting
~**putz** m = brush plaster
Pionier|bohrung f, siehe: Aufschlußbohrung
~**ramme** f; siehe unter „Rammanlage f"
Pipette f = pipette
Pisolith m, Erbsenstein m = pisolitic limestone, pisolite
Pistazit m (Min.) = pistacite
Piste f; siehe unter „Flugplatz m"
Pistill n = pestle
PKW m, siehe: Personenkraftwagen m
Plagge f, Rasen~, Rasensode f = (turf) sod
Plagioklas m, Natron-Kalkfeldspat m, Schiefspalter m (Min.) = plagioclase, soda-lime fel(d)spar, lime-soda fel(d)spar, plagioclase feldspar, soda-lime plagioclase
planebene Oberfläche f = level plane surface
Planebenheit f, Ebenflächigkeit f, Ebenheit f = evenness
planender Ingenieurbau m, Tiefbau m = civil engineering
Planer m = planner
Pläner Kalk m = Plauen limestone
Planetengetriebe n, siehe: Umlaufgetriebe
~**antrieb** m, Planetenradantrieb = planet power drive
Planetensenkgetriebe n = planetary gear for lowering
plangleiche Kreuzung f, niveaugleiche ~, ebenerdige ~ = grade crossing, intersection at grade, at-grade intersection
Planierbagger m, Flachlöffelbagger = skimmer (shovel)
Planieren n, Planier(ungs)arbeiten f = grading (works), level(l)ing (~), grading operations
  Fein~ ~ = fine ~
  Grob~ ~ = rough ~, coarse ~

Planier|gerät n = planer (Brit.); level-(l)er
~-**Gleiskettengerät** n; siehe unter „Bulldozer m"
~**pflug** m, Kippenräumer m, Gleis-Planierpflug, Einebnungspflug, Kippenpflug = spreader-ditcher
~**raupe** f; siehe unter „Bulldozer m"
~**reifenschlepper** m; siehe unter „Bulldozer m"
~**schar** f; siehe unter „Motor-Straßenhobel m"
~**schild** n; siehe unter „Bulldozer m"
~**schild** n **zum Zuziehen von Gräben** mpl, Verfüllschild, Verfüllvorrichtung f = backfiller attachment
(~) **Schleppe** f = drag
~**schlepper** m, siehe: Bulldozer m
Planier- und -Ladegerät n, siehe: (Front-) Ladeschaufel f
Planier(ungs)arbeiten fpl, siehe: Planieren n
Planimeter n, Flächenmesser m = planimeter
plankreuzungsfreie Kreuzung f, überschneidungsfreie ~, Kreuzungsbauwerk n, niveaufreie Kreuzung = fly over (junction) (Brit.); grade separation structure (US)
Plan|schleifmaschine f = face (or surface) grinder
~**sieb** n, siehe: Flachsieb
Planum n, siehe: Untergrund m
~**arbeiten** fpl = subgrade work
~**aufreißer** m = (sub)grade rooter
~**fertiger** m, siehe: Erdplanumfertiger m
~**herstellung** f = formation work, subgrade preparation, subgrading
(**Planums**)|**Auskofferung** f = subgrade excavation
~**modul** m, siehe: Bettungsziffer f
~**verdichter** m = subgrade compactor
Planungsauftrag m = planning contract
plastifizierend = plasticizing
Plastifizierungsmittel n, siehe: Betonverflüssiger m
plastische Formänderung f [*Beton* m] = plastic recovery [*concrete*]
~ **Straßenmarkierung** f = plastic white line composition

plastischer feuerfester Formling m = plastic refractory
plastischer Markierungsstoff m = plastic marking material
~ **Markierungsstreifen** m, Kunststoff-Markierungsstreifen = plastic roadline, ~ strip
plastisches Bindemittel n = plastic binder
~ **Fließen** n = plastic flow
Plastizität f, Bildsamkeit f = plasticity
Plastizitäts|grenze f; siehe unter „Konsistenzgrenzen fpl nach Atterberg"
~**index** m, Bildsamkeitsindex = plasticity index
~**theorie** f = plastic theory, ductile ~
Plastosphäre f, plastische Zone f, Fließzone (Geol.) = zone of flowage
Plateau-Aufzug m, Plattformaufzug, Karrenaufzug = (tower) platform hoist
Platte f = slab
Plattenbalken m = T-(shaped) beam
~**decke** f = beam and slab construction, slab and beam construction
Plattenband|(förderer) n, (m), Blechgliederband n, Gliederbandförderer m = (plate) apron conveyor
~**speiser** m, Aufgabeplattenband n = apron conveyor feeder, apron type feeder
Platten|belastungsversuch m, Plattendruckversuch m = plate (load) bearing test, "K" ~, plate failure ~
plattenförmige (Gesteins)Absonderung f = platy structure
Platten|fundament n = slab foundation
~**glimmer** m = book mica, sheet mica
~**heben** n, siehe: Beton~
~**kalk(stein)** m, Kalkschiefer m = laminated (or platy, or slabby) limestone
~**leger** m [*Straßenbau*] = street mason [*sometimes wrongly referred to as "mason flagger"*]
~**pflaster** m, Plattenbelag m = slabbing
~**pumpen** n [*Beton* m] = slab pumping, mud-pumping, subgrade erosion, pavement (slab) pumping
~**rüttler** m; siehe unter „Betonrüttelgeräte npl"

~**schalung** f = slab form (work)
~**sperre** f, Pfeilerplatten(stau)mauer f, Plattenpfeiler(stau)mauer, Pfeilerplattensperre = slab and buttress dam
~**streifen** m = wall footing
~**trägerdecke** f = slab beam and girder construction
~**-Tunnelofen** m, Kleintunnelofen = pusher-type kiln
~**vibrator** m; siehe unter „Betonrüttelgeräte npl"
Plattform f = platform
~**-Anhänger** m = platform trailer
~**aufzug** m, siehe: Plateau-Aufzug
~**-Hochhubkarre(n)** f, (m) = high-lift platform truck
~**-Hubkarre(n)** f, (m) = lift platform truck
~**karre(n)** f, (m) = platform track
~**kipper** m [*Waggonkipper* m] = gravity tip
~**-Niederhubkarre(n)** f, (m) = low-lift platform truck
~**-Sattelschlepper** m = flat-top truck trailer
~**waage** f = platform scale
~**wagen** m = platform truck wheel wagon
Platthacke f, Rodehacke f, Rodehaue f = grub(bing) axe, ~ hoe
Platthalm m, Piattrispengras n = Canadian blue grass
Plattieren n = plating
plattierter Stahl m = clad steel
plattiges Gestein n = platy rock
~ **Material** n [*z. B. Betonzuschlag(stoff)* m] = flaky material
Plattigkeit f [*gebrochenes Gestein* n] = slabbiness
pleochroitischer Hof m (Min.) = pleochroic halos
Plexiglas n = plexiglass, perspex
Plus-Minus-Waage f = over-and-under scale
plutonisches Gestein n, Tiefengestein, Plutonit m, subkrustales Gestein = intrusive rock, (igneous) plutonic rock
Pneubagger m, siehe: Autobagger
pneumatische Betonförderung f, siehe: Druckluftbetonförderung f

pneumatische Entstaubung — polierfähig

pneumatische Entstaubung *f* = pneumatic dedusting
~ Förderrinne *f*, siehe: Gebläseluft-Förderrinne

~ Förderung *f*, Druckluftförderung-Preßluftförderung = pneumatic conveying

pneumatische Gründung *f*, Druckluftgründung *f*
  Preßluftsenkkasten *m*, Druckluftsenkkasten *m*, Druckluftkammer *f*
  Schachtrohr *n*
  Materialschleuse *f*
  Personenschleuse *f*
  Krankenschleuse *f*, Druckluft-~
    Vorkammer *f*
    Arzneischleuse *f*
    Krankenkammer *f*
  Rückschlagklappe *f*
  Vertikalschleuse *f*
  Horizontalschleuse *f*
  Arbeitskammer *f*
  (Druck)Luftschleuse *f*, Preßluftschleuse

  Preßluftkrankheit *f*, Druckluftkrankung *f*, Caissonkrankheit, Senkkastenkrankheit
  Dekompression *f*

pneumatic foundation
  air caisson, pneumatic ~

  vertical-air lock tube
  muck-lock, materials-lock
  man-lock
  medical (air-)lock
    antechamber
    food-lock
    medical chamber
  non-return flap
  vertical air-lock
  horizontal air-lock
  working chamber
  (pressed) air-lock, pneumatic excavating air lock
  compressed-air sickness, caisson disease, compressed air illness, bends

  decompression

pneumatische Prall(mahl)mühle *f*; siehe unter „Mühle *f*"
pneumatischer Förderer *m*, pneumatische Förderanlage *f* = pneumatic conveyor, ~ transport system, air activator
~ Getreideheber *m* = pneumatic grain handling unit
pneumatisches Betonfördergerät *n*, pneumatischer Betonförderer *m*, Druckluft-Betonfördergerät, Druckluft-Betonförderer *m* = pneumatic concrete placer
~Förderrohr *n* = air-activated pipe-line
pneumatisch-hydraulisch = pneumo-hydraulic
pneumatisch-hydraulischer Hebebock *m*, pneumatisch-hydraulische Winde *f* = air hydraulic jack
Pneumatolyse *f* = pneumatolysis
Pneurad *n* = pneumatic-tired wheel (US); pneumatic-tyred ~ (Brit.)
Pneuschürflader *m*, Pneu(front)ladeschaufel *f*, Pneuschaufellader *m*, Pneufront-lader, Pneuhublader, Pneukübelauflader = rubber-mounted loading shovel, ~ bucket loader, ~ tractor-shovel, ~ front-end (tractor) loader
Poch|sand *m*, Splittsand *m*, Quetschsand *m* = stamp sand
~werk, siehe: Stampfmühle *f*
Podest *m, n*, siehe: Treppen ~
Podsolboden *m*, siehe: Waldboden
Poetsch-Verfahren *n*; siehe unter „Baugrundverbesserung *f*"
polares Trägheitsmoment *n* = polar moment of inertia
Polarisationsmikroskop *n* = petrographic microscope, polarizing ~
Polarlicht *n* = auroral light
Polder *m*, Ko(o)g *m* = polder
~mühle *f* = wind mill for drainage
Polier *m* = foreman
polierbarer dichter Kalkstein *m*, siehe: technischer Marmor *m*
polierfähig, polierbar = polishable

Polierschiefer *m*, siehe: Tripel *m*
Polizeistreife *f* = police patrol
Poller *m* = bollard
polumschaltbarer Motor *m* = pole-changing motor
Polumschalter *m* = polarity reversing switch
Polygon|mauerwerk *n*, siehe: Vieleckmauerwerk *n*
~zug *m* = traverse
Polypgreifer *m*, Polypgreiferkorb *m* = grabs (US); multi-blade grab (Brit.)
POLYTRAC, vollhydraulisch arbeitendes Mehrzweckgerät *n* mit einem Radschlepper als Grundgerät, Fabrikat BISCHOFF-WERKE K. G., RECKLINGHAUSEN, DEUTSCHLAND = POLYTRAC [*Trademark*] [*all-hydraulic rubber-tired tractor with conversion units, e. g. grab bucket, dozer blade, crane hook, bucket etc.*]
Pontinische Sümpfe *mpl* = Pontine Marshes
Ponton *m* = pontoon
~brücke *f* = pontoon bridge
~kran *m* = pontoon crane
Pore *f*, Hohlraum *m* = void, pore, interstice
Poren|gefüge *n* = pore-structure
~index *m*, siehe: Porenziffer *f*
~injektion *f*; siehe unter „Baugrundverbesserung *f*"
~raum *m*, Porenvolumen *n* = void(s) space, voidage, pore volume, void(s) volume, pore space, total volume of intergranular (soil) space
~-Saugwasser *n*, siehe: Kapillarwasser
~schluß *m*, Oberflächenabsieg(e)lung *f* [*Straße f*] = surface-dressing (treatment), seal(ing) coat; [*deprecated: flush coat, squeegee coat*]
~volumen *n*, siehe: Porenraum *m*
Porenwasser *n* = interstitial water, pore ~
~druck *m* = pore-water pressure
~druckabnahme *f* = pore pressure dissipation
~druckhöhe *f* = pore water head
~druckmeßdose *f* = pore-water pressure cell
~druckmesser *m*, Porenwasserdruck-Meßgerät *n* = pore-water pressure ga(u)ge

~überdruck *m* = neutral stress, hydrostatic excess pressure, excess pore (water) pressure
Poren|zement *m* (Geol.) = pore matrix, ~ cement(ing material)
~ziffer *f*, Porenindex *m* = pore ratio, voids porosity ~, voids index
Porigkeit *f*, Porosität *f* = porosity, apparent density
porös = porous
poröse Masse *f* [*Luftrutsche f*] = porous medium
Porphyr *m* (Geol.) = porphyry
porphyrische Struktur *f* = porphyritic texture
Porphyrit *m* = porphyrite
porphyroblastischer Verband *m* (Geol.) = porphyroblastic texture
Porphyrtuff *m* = porphyritic tuff
Portal|bagger *m*, Torbagger = portal bucket ladder excavator
~kran *m*, siehe: Torkran *m*
~rahmen *m* = portal frame
~(verband) *n*, (*m*), Endrahmen *m* = portal bracing
Portlandstein *m* = Portland stone [*an oolitic freestone*]
Porzellan *n* = chinaware
~emaille *f* = porcelain enamel
~filtertiegel *m* = porcelaine filter
~ton *m*, Porzellanerde *f*, (Roh)Kaolin *m*, Weißerde *f* = kaolin, china clay, porcelain clay, porcelain earth
Position *f*; siehe unter „Angebot *n*"
Postkartenzählung *f*, siehe: Befragungsmethode *f* durch Postkarten *fpl*
potentielle Energie *f*; siehe unter „Bernoulli-Satz *m*"
Potenz *f* = power
~rechnung *f* = involution
Pottasche *f*, Kaliumkarbonat *n*, kohlensaures Kalium *n*, K_2CO_3 = potassium carbonate
Prahm *m* = pram
Praktiker *m* = practitioner, practising engineer
Prallblech *n*, Abweisungsblech [*im Fangkessel beim Druckluftbetonförderer m*] = (central) baffle

Prall|brecher *m* [*früher: Hammerbrecher mit starren Schlägern mpl*] = (impeller) impact (type) breaker (or crusher), impeller impact breaker

~brecher *m* **mit einer Schlagwalze** *f*, Einwalzen-Prallbrecher = single impeller impact breaker

~brecher *m* **mit zwei Rotoren** *mpl*, siehe: Doppel-Rotoren-Prallbrecher

~(mahl)mühle *f*; siehe unter „Mühle *f*"

~platte *f* [*zur Entstaubung und Aufbereitung allerfeinsten Sandkorns*] = impact separator

Pratt-Träger *m* = Pratt truss, Whipple-Murphy truss, Linville ~, N-~

Präzipitatgestein *n*, siehe: chemisches Sedimentgestein *n*

Präzisionsinstrument *n* = precision instrument

Preis|absprache *f* **unter Bietern** *mpl* = collusion among bidders (or tenderers)

~gestehung *f*, Preisermittlung *f* = price-build up, ~ determination, costing

~kalkulation *f*, siehe: Kalkulieren *n*

Prellstein *m*, Abweisstein *m*, Radabweiser *m* = spur post

Presenning *f*, siehe: Persenning

Presse *f* **für Betonrohrherstellung** *f*, siehe: Betonrohrpresse *f*

Pressungsumwandlung *f*, siehe: Dynamometamorphose *f*

Preß|gußrippenrohr *n* = pressed casting ribbed pipe

~kopf *m* [*Betonrohrpresse f*] = concrete pipe press head

~luft *f*, siehe: Druckluft *f*

~torf *m* = pressed peat

~wasserhebebock *m*, siehe: hydraulischer Hebebock

~ziegel *m*, Preßstein *m* = pressed brick

Primär|dampf *m*, siehe: Erstdampf

~löß *m*, siehe: Urlöß

Prismakompaß *m*, Marschkompaß = prismatic compass

prismatische Nadelblende *f* (Min.) = red antimony ore

prismatisch geformte Dachplatte *f* = prismatic roof slab (or panel)

prismatisches Faltwerk *n* = prismatic structure

Prismenfeldstecher *m* = prism binocular glass

Pritsche *f* [*LKW m*] = body

Privat|auto *n* = private automobile

~gewässer *n* = privately owned water

~weg *m* = private street, ~ drive, ~ road, drive way

Probe *f* **auf Reinheit** *f* [*Betonzuschlag-(stoff) m*], Absetzprobe = silt content test for fine aggregate, test for silt

~balken *m*, Biegebalken [*Beton m*] = flexure test beam

~belastung *f* [*Baugrund m*] = ground testing by loading

~belastung *f* = proof load, test ~

~betrieb *m* = test operation

~bohrung *f*, Sondier(ungs)bohrung *f* = exploratory boring

~(ent)nahmeapparat *m*, Probe(ent)nahmegerät *n* = sample taker, sampler

~(ent)nahmestanze *f* = sampling tube

~kern *m*, Bohrkern *m* = (drill) core, test ~

~kern *m* [*Boden m*] = sample core

~körper *m*, Prüfkörper, Probe(stück) *f*, (*n*) = test specimen

~lauf *m*, Probefahrt *f* = test run

~löffel *m*, siehe: Schappe *f*

~mischung *f* = trial mix

~nahme *f*, Probeentnahme *f* = sampling

~stab *m*, Prüfstab = test bar

~strecke *f*, siehe: Versuchsstrecke

~stück *n* = test piece

~würfel *m* = cube test specimen, test cube

~zeit *f* = trial period

~zylinder *m*, zylindrischer Probekörper *m* = control cylinder

Proctor|kurve *f* = dry density/moisture content graph, Proctor compaction curve

~nadel *f*, Proctor'sche Prüfnadel, Proctor'sche Sonde *f*, Proctor'sche Plastizitätsnadel = Proctor (penetration) needle, plasticity ~

~-Prüfung *f*, verbesserter AASHO-Versuch *m*, Proctor-Versuch = Proctor test, standard compaction ~

Produktenölleitung *f* = product line

(produzierende) Erdgassonde *f*, fördernde Gasbohrung *f* = producing gas well

Profil n = profile, sectional shape, section
Profileisen n, siehe: Fassoneisen
(~)Biegemaschine f, siehe: Biegemaschine
~schneider m = section iron cutter
profilgemäß [*Straßenquerschnitt m*] = true to cross-section, line and level (or grade)
Profilhöhe f [*Profilstahl m*] = depth of section
Profilieren n [*Erdbau m*] = shaping, trimming, truing; [*deprecated: regulating*]
Profil|lehre f, Formlineal n = template, templet, camber board
~stahl m, siehe: Fassoneisen n
~stahlrahmen m = structural steel frame
~stein m, siehe: Profilziegel m
~taster m, Kontrollrechen m = subgrade tester, (subgrade) scratch template
~wert m = sectional property
~zeichner m, Profilograph m = profilometer, profilograph [*an instrument for recording the shape of irregularities in a road surface*]
~ziegel m, Profilstein m = purpose-made brick, mo(u)lded ~, profilated ~
Projektbearbeitung f = planning and design work
Promenade f = promenade
Propan(gas) n = propane (gas)
Propeller|rinne f, Marcus-Wurfförderrinne f = Marcus trough conveyor
~turbine f = propeller turbine
Proportionalitätsgrenze f = limit of proportionality, proportional limit
Proportionalstab m = proportional test bar
Prospektionsbohrung f, siehe: Aufschlußbohrung
Proustit m, lichtes Rotgültigerz n, Ag_3AsS_3 (Min.) = proustite
Provinzstraße f, Landstraße f = provincial road
provisorische Umleitung f, zeitweilige ~ = (temporary) diversion
~ Zufahrtsstraße f = temporary access road
Prüf|anstalt f = testing institute
~balkenform f = flexural beam mo(u)ld

Prüfen n **der Kornzusammensetzung** f **durch Siebversuch** m, Siebprobe f = sieve analysis, grading ~, test for ~ ~, test for grading, sieve analysis test, grain size analysis, particle-size analysis
Prüf|körper m, siehe: Probekörper
~maschine f = testing machine
~presse f, Druckpresse f, (Beton-)Würfelpresse f, Betonprüfpresse = compression machine, ~ tester; testing machine for concrete cylinders
~sieb n = test sieve
~stab m, Sondierstab = sounding rod
~stab m, Probestab = test bar
~stand m; siehe unter „Baumaschinen fpl und Baugeräte npl"
Prüfung f **auf Flüchtigkeit** f = volatilization test
~ des Nachschwindens n [*feuerfester Stein m*] = reheat test [*fire-brick*]
~ der Zerstörung f **von Hochofensteinen** mpl **durch Kohlenstoffablagerung** f = carbon disintegration test of blast furnace brick
Prüfungs|alter n = age at test
~zeugnis n = certificate of test
Prüfverfahren n, Prüfmethode f, Versuchsverfahren, Versuchsmethode = test method, testing procedure
Prügelweg m, siehe: Knüppelweg m
Psilomelan m, schwarzer Glaskopf m (Min.) = psilomelane, black iron ore
Psychrometer n = psychrometer, wet and dry bulb hygrometer
Puddeleisen n = puddled iron
Puddingstein m = puddingstone
Puffer m = buffer
Pulp m = pulp
Pulsator m [*Schwingungsprüfung f von Asphaltbelägen mpl auf Stahlplatten fpl*] = pulsating machine
Pulserbagger m; siehe unter „Naßbagger m"
pulsierende Springquelle f, siehe: Geysir m
Pulver|(brannt)kalk m = air-slaked lime, powdered lime, powdered calcium carbonate
~form f = powdery form

Pulverisieren n = pulverizing
pulverisierter Gummi m = powdered rubber
Pulver|kalkstein m = pulverized limestone

~**sprengstoff** m; siehe unter „1. Schießen n; 2. Sprengen n"
~**-Stabilisator** m = powder(ed) stabilizer, solid ~

Pumpe f **pump**

Abessinier~, siehe: Rammrohr~
Abteuf~, Senk~, Bohrloch~   mine ~, shaft-sinking ~
Abwasser~, Schmutzwasser~   sewage handling ~
Ansaugen n priming
Axial~   axial (flow) ~, propeller ~
Baukreisel~   contractors' centrifugal (water) pump
Bau~   contractor's ~
Bohrloch~   bore-hole ~
Brennstoffeinspritz~   fuel injection ~
Dampfdruck~, Pulsometer~   pulsometer ~, steam ~ ~
Dampfstrahl~   air-ejector
Dia-~, siehe: Membran(e)~
Dickstoff~, Schlamm~   solids-handling ~, slush ~, mud ~
Differential~, siehe: Stufenkolben~
Diffusionsluft~, siehe: Quecksilber-Diffusions~
Doppelstiefelhand~   double barrel hand ~
doppelt wirkende ~   double-acting ~
Drehkolben~, Kapsel~, Rotations~   rotary ~
Dreiplunger~   triple throw plunger ~
Drillingseil~   three throw high speed ~
Druck~   (lift and) force ~
Druckluft~, Preßluft~   compressed-air ~, air lift ~
Druckverstärker~, Verstärkungs~   booster ~
Duplex~   duplex ~
Eil~   high-speed ~, express ~
Einpreß~, Injektions~   injection ~
Elektro-Bau~   electric contractors' ~
Entlastungs~   relief ~
Evolventen~   involute ~
Faß~, Abfüll~   barrel exhausting ~, barrel-pump
Flügel~   semi-rotary ~, vane ~, wing ~
Flüssigkeits~   liquid handling ~
Gestängetief ~, siehe: Tiefbrunnenkolben~
Handkolben~   hand operated piston ~
Handspritz~   hand-operated spraying ~
Hub~ mit Rohrkolben m lift(ing) ~ with hollow plunger
Hub~ mit Ventilkolben m lift(ing) ~ with bucket valve piston
Injektions~, siehe: Einpreß~
Kapsel~, siehe: Drehkolben~
Kolben~   piston ~
kombinierte Axial- und Radial~   combined axial and radial flow ~

Kondensat~	condensate ~
Kreisel~, Schleuder~, Zentrifugal~	centrifugal ~
Kreisel~ mit Flügelrad *n*	centrifugal screw (or propeller) ~
Kreisel~ mit spiralförmigen Gehäuse *n*	centrifugal volute ~
Kreisel~ ohne Leitvorrichtung *f*	centrifugal ~ without guide passage
Langhub~	long stroke ~
Lenz~	bilge ~
Maschinen~	mechanically driven ~
Maschinenspritz~	power spraying ~
Membran(e)~, Dia(phragma)-~	diaphragm ~, membrane ~
Motor~	power-operated ~
Perspektiv~	prospecting ~
~ mit gradlinig hin- und hergehendem Kolben *m*	reciprocating piston ~
Pulsometer~, siehe: Dampfdruck~	
~ für Wasserhaltung *f*	dewatering ~, unwatering ~
~ mit Flüssigkeitsgetriebe *n*	fluid-driven pump
Pumpausrüstung *f*	pumping equipment
Pumpen *n*	pumping
Pumpenbock *m*	pumping jack
Pumpendruck *m*	~ pressure
Pumpengehäuse *n*	~ housing
Pump(en)gestänge-(Dreh)Schlüssel *m*	sucker rod wrench
Pump(en)gestängefahrstuhl *m*	sucker rod elevator
Pump(en)gestängehalter *m*	sucker rod hook
Pumpengetriebe *n*	pumping gear
Pumpenkolben *m*	~ piston
Pumpensatz *m*	pumping set
Pumpensaughöhe *f*	pumping lift
Pumpenschuh *m*	sucker
Pumpenschwengel *m*	pumping beam
Pumpenstäbe *mpl*, Pumpengestänge *n*	~ rods, sucker rods
Pumpenstiefel *m*	barrel of a ~
Pumpenventil *n*	~ valve
Quecksilber-Diffusions~, Diffusionsluft~	mercury-vapour ~
Rammrohr~, Abessinier~	hollow ram ~, bored tube ~, Abyssinian ~
Riemen~	belt driven ~
Rohrbrunnen~	artesian well ~
Rohrkolben~	hollow piston ~
Rotations~, siehe: Drehkolben~	
Rundlaufkolben~	runner piston ~, rotating ~ ~
Sandkreisel~	sand sucker
Saugkorb *m*	strainer
Saug~	suction ~, sucking ~
Saug- und Druck~	combined suction and force ~, reciprocating ~
Säure~	acid-handling ~
Schieber~	slide valve ~

Schlamm~, siehe: Dickstoff~
Schmutzwasser~, siehe: Abwasser
Schnecken~ — spindle drag ~
Schraubenkolben~ — ~ with helicoidal piston
selbstansaugend — self-priming
Senk~, siehe: Abteuf~
Sichel~ — crescent ~, sickle ~
Simplex~ — simplex ~
Speise~ — feed ~
Ständer~ — stand ~
Stollen~ — gallery ~
Stoßheber *m*, siehe: Druckwasser~
Strahl~ — jet ~
straßenfahrbare ~ — road ~
Stufenkolben~, Differential~ — differential ~
Stufentauchkolben~ — stage (or differential) plunger ~
Sumpf~ — sump ~
Tauchkolben~, Verdränger~, Plunger~ — plunger ~, ram ~, displacement ~
Tauchkolbenmembran(e)~ — plunger diaphragm ~, plunger membrane ~
Tauch~, siehe: Unterwasser(motor)~
Tiefbrunnenkolben~, Gestängetief~ — deep-well piston~
Topf~, Pitcher~ — pitcher ~
Trag-Kreisel~ — hand-carry centrifugal (water) ~
Transmissions~ — ~ driven by power
Überfüll~ — filling ~
Umwälz~, Umlauf~ — circulating ~
Unterwasser(motor)~, Tauch~ — submersible ~ [*motor sealed against the entry of water*]
Unterwasser(motor)~ mit halbnassem Motor *m* (oder Naßlaufmotor), Tauch~ ~ ~ ~, Unterwasser-Elektro-~ — true submersible pump [*the rotor of the electric motor runs in water*]
Vakuum~ — vacuum ~, evacuator
Ventil~ — valve ~
Verbunddampf~ — compound steam ~
Verbundkreisel~ — two stage centrifugal ~
Verstärkungs~, Druckverstärker~ — booster ~
Walzen~ — drum ~
Wasserstrahl~ — water-operated vacuum ~
Zentrifugal~, siehe: Kreisel~
Zwillings~ — twin ~
Zwillingskolben~ — twin cylinder piston ~

Pump(en)anlage *f* = pumping installation, ~ plant
Pumpen|bewässerung *f* = (power) pump irrigation
~(naß)bagger *m*; siehe unter „Naßbagger *m*"
~sumpf *m* = pump well, sump hole, (pump) sump, sump pit; sump well [*deprecated*]
Pump|fähigkeit *f* [*Beton m*] = pumpability
~kretbetonförderung *f* = hydraulic concrete placing

Pump|speicherkraftwerk n = pumped storage hydropower plant
~speicherung f = pumped storage
Punkt|last f = point load
~schweißmaschine f = spot welding machine
Purpurholz n, siehe: Amarantholz
Putz|aufzug m = plaster hoist
~bohlenfertiger m, siehe: Glättbohlenfertiger
Putzen n, Verputzen = rendering
Putzer m, Gipsarbeiter m, Gipser m = plasterer, pargeter
Putzgips m, Gipsputz m = gypsum plaster

Putz|gipsmörtel m mit guter Haftung f = concrete bonding plaster
~glätter m = electric smoothing trowel
~kelle f = plastering trowel
~(mörtel) m, Mörtelputz m = mortar rendering, plaster
Putz- und Mörtelmischer m = plaster-mortar mixer, plaster and mortar ~
Putz- und Rabitzarbeiten fpl mit **Stuckgips** m = rendering and plastering on metallic lathing with plaster of Paris
Putzwerfer m, Putz-Spritz-Apparat m, Verputzmaschine, Verputzanlage f = plaster-throwing machine, plastering ~
Puzzolanerde f, siehe: Bröckeltuff m

---

puzzolanische Stoffe mpl, **Puzzolane(n)** fpl
  natürliche ~ ~
    Traß m
    vulkanische Aschen fpl
  künstliche ~ ~
    Hochofenschlacke f
    gebrannter Ton m, Terrakotte f; Terrakotta f [*in Österreich*]

pozzolanic materials
  natural ~ ~
    (Rhenish) trass
    volcanic ashes
  artificial ~ ~
    blast-furnace slag
    burnt clay

Pyknometer n = (fruit jar) pycnometer, density bottle, pyknometer
Pylone f = pylon, tower
Pyramidalgeröll(e) n, Kantenkiesel m, Kantengeröll(e) n, Kantengeschiebe n, Facettengeschiebe n = (wind-)faceted pebble(s)
Pyramidenpappel f, italienische Pappel f, Chausseepappel = Lombardy poplar, Italian ~
Pyrargyrit m (Min.), siehe: Antimonsilberblende f
Pyrenäenhalbinsel f = Iberian Peninsula
Pyrogallussäure f, $C_6H_6O_3$ = pyrogallic acid
pyroklastische Gesteine npl (Geol.) = pyroclastic rocks
Pyrometer n = pyrometer
Pyromorphit m, Grünbleierz n (Min.) = pyromorphite
Pyrophyllit m = pyrophyllite
Pyroxen m (Min.) = pyroxene
~granit m = augite granulite
Pyroxenit m (Geol.) = pyroxenite

Q

Quader m, Werkstein m, Quaderstein = dimension stone, cut ~, ashlar
~mauerwerk n, siehe: Werksteinmauerwerk
~sandstein m = upper cretaceous sandstone
~stein m, siehe: Quader m
Quadratloch-Laboratoriumssieb n = laboratory sieve (US)
Quadrat|(loch)sieb n, siehe: Maschensieb n
~stahl m = square bar steel
Qualitätsminderung f = reduction in quality
Quarz m, SiO_2 (Min.) = quartz
~diorit m = quartz-diorte
Quarzit m = quartzite
~stein m, Silikastein m, Quarzkalkziegel m [*früher: Dinasstein* m] = silica brick, ganister ~
Quarz|kies m = quartz(ite) gravel
~porphyr m = quartz-porphyry

Quarz|sand m = quartz(ose) sand, arenaceous ~
~**sandstein** m = silica sandstone
~**schieferton** m = arenaceous shale
~**schmelze** f = siliceous melt
~**trachyt** m = quartz-trachyte
Quecksilber|chlorid n, Sublimat n = corrosive sublimate, mercuric chloride
~**cyanat** n, siehe: Knallquecksilber n
~**dampflampe** f = mercury vapo(u)r (or discharge) lamp
~**hornerz** n (Min.) = horn quicksilver
~**lebererz** n (Min.) = hepatic cinnabar
~**oxydulsalz** n = mercurous salt
Quell|boden m, Schwellboden m = expansive soil, swell ~
~**ergiebigkeit** f [*Straße f*] = effective range of traffic originating in a given area
~**gebiet** n = headwaters
~**punkt** m [*Straßenverkehr m*] = point of origin
quellstofflicher Zustand m, kolloidaler Zustand, Kolloid n = colloid(al state)
Quellteich m = spring-fed pond
Quellung f, siehe: Aufquellen n
Quer|aufschleppe f, siehe: Quer(schiffs)aufschleppe
~**balken** m = joist, transverse beam, cross beam
~**bewehrung** f, Querarmierung f = transverse reinforcement
~**biegeversuch** m = transverse bending test
~**biegung** f = transverse bending
~**bohle** f [*Betondeckenfertiger m*] = transverse screed
~**dehnung** f = lateral strain
~**deich** m = cross dike
~**festigkeit** f = transverse strength
~**gefälle** n = cross fall
~**haupt** n [*Prüfmaschine f*] = cross head
~**kontraktion** f = contraction of area
~**kraft** f [*Statik f*] = (transverse) shear, ~ force
~**kraftfläche** f = shear diagram
~**rahmen** m = bent
~**rahmen** m [*Brücke f*] = cross frame
~**riegel** m, Zwischenriegel, Querschott n, Querschotte f = diaphragm
~**rinne** f [*Straße f*] = water splash
~**ruck** m = radial speed [*road vehicle*]
~**(schiffs)aufschleppe** f = traversing slipway
Querschnitt m = cross-section
~**abnahme** f = reduction of cross section
~**belastung** f |[*Straße f*] = flow
~**-Faktor-Verfahren** n = intersection-factor method
~**fläche** f = cross-sectional area
~**gestaltung** f = shape of section
~**schwächung** f = weakening of cross section
~**wert** m [*Profilstahl m*] = section property, property of section
~**zählung** f = classification count
Quer|schott n, siehe: Querriegel m
~**siederkessel** m = cross tube boiler
~**steife** f = transverse stiffener
~**steifigkeit** f = transverse rigidity
~**straße** f = cross road
~**strebe** f = cross brace
~**stromofen** m für Ölschiefer-Schwelung f = gas-flow oil-shale retort
~**stütze** f [*Bagger m*] = outrigger
~**träger** m, siehe: Unterzug m
~**verband** m = sway bracing
~**verstrebung** f = bracing
~**verteiler** m, siehe: Betonverteilungswagen m
~**vorspannung** f = transverse prestressing
Quetsch|grenze f = compressive yield point
~**sand** m, siehe: Pochsand
Quicksand m = quick sand, running ~
Quickton m, Fließton = quick clay

R

RAB-Brückenmischer m, siehe: Brückenmischer
Rachenlehre f, Gabellehre f = caliper ga(u)ge
Radabweiser m, siehe: Prellstein m
Radar-Geschwindigkeitsmesser m = radar speedmeter [*for measuring the speed of road traffic*]
Radaufreißer m = wheel type ripper

(Rad)Aufstandsfläche — Radschrapper

(Rad)Aufstandsfläche f = (tyre) contact area (Brit.); (tire) ~ ~, tire-pavement ~ ~ (US)

Rad(e)ber f, siehe: Schiebkarre(n) f, (m)

Rädelerz n, Spießglanzbleierz, Schwarzspießglanzerz (Min.) = wheel-ore, bournonite, cog-wheel ore

Räder|tierchenschlamm m, siehe: Radiolarienschlamm

~**vorgelege** n = back gears

~**vorgelege** n mit Fest- und Losscheibe f = spur gearing fitted with fast and loose pulley

Rad-Fahrlader m, Rad-Becherwerk(auf)-lader = rubber-tired bucket (elevator loader

~, Rad-Ladeschaufel f = rubber-tired loading shovel

Rad|(fahr)weg m = (bi)cycle track (or path)

~**fahrwerk** n, Radfahrgestell n, Raduntergestell n = wheel(ed) carrier, ~ chassis, ~ carriage

~**fahrzeug** n = wheeled vehicle

Radialbohrer m = radial drill

radiales Klotz-Gleitlager n = pivoted-pad journal bearing

Radial|gebläse n = radial blower

~**scherung** f = radial shear

~**schnitt** m, Spiegelholz n = radial cut (or conversion)

~**stein** m, Radialziegel m = radial brick

~**straße** f = radial road, ~ highway

~**turbine** f = radial flow turbine

radial verfahrbare Verladebrücke f = radial transporter

~ **verfahrbarer Kabelkran** m; siehe unter „Seilförderanlage f"

Radiator m = radiator

radiatorgekühlt = radiator-cooled

radioaktiv = radio-active

Radiolarienschlamm m, Rädertierchenschlamm, Radiolarienschlick m = radiolaria(n) ooze

Radio-Zeichengeber m = radio indicator

Rad|last f = wheel load
Aufstandsfläche f = contact area

~**lenker** m; siehe unter „Schiene f"

~**nabe** f = hub

~**rennbahn** f = (bi)cycle racing track

Radschlepper m, siehe: Luftreifenschlepper

~-**Bulldozer** m; siehe unter „Bulldozer m"

~-**Frontlader** m, Radschlepper-Frontladeschaufel f = wheel tractor front end loader

~-**Schaufellader** m, Radschlepper-Ladeschaufel f = wheel tractor loader (or shovel)

Radschrapper m — scoop pan self-loading scraper, (wheel) scraper; trailing scoop grader, pan scraper, drag road-scraper (US); buck scraper (Brit.)

Traktor-Schrapper m, Schrapper mit Gleiskettentraktor m, Schürf(kübel)wagenzug m, Motor-Schürfzug m — crawler-scraper rig

Autoschrapper m mit 2-Rad-Schlepper m, Einachs-Motorschrapper m, Schrapper m mit gummibereiftem Einachstraktor, Motorschürf(kübel)wagen mit Einachsschlepper, motorisierter Schürfkübel m mit Einachs-Traktor m, Motor-Schürfzug m, selbstfahrender Schürfwagen m — tractor-scraper, motorized scraper, motor scraper (with two-wheel traction)

Einachs-Motor-Schrapper, Fabrikat Le TOURNEAU-WESTINGHOUSE COMPANY, PEORIA ILLINOIS, USA — TOURNAPULI [*Trademark*]

Radschrapper

Einachs-Motor-Schrapper, Fabrikat WOOLDRIDGE MFG. CO., SUNNYVALE, CALIF. USA	TERRA COBRA [*Trademark*]
Drehpunkt-Hebelwirkung *f*	rear-draft fulcrum leverage
Topfladesystem *n*	boiling bowl loading, boiling action loading
Autoschrapper *m* mit Radschlepper *m*, Motor-Schürfzug *m*, Fabrikat CATERPILLAR TRACTOR CO., PEORIA, ILLINOIS, USA	tractor-scraper, motor(ized) scraper (with 4-wheel traction)
Schrapperwagen *m*, (Anhänge-)Schürf(kübel)wagen *m*	four-wheel(ed) scraper, crawler-tractor-drawn scraper, rubber-mounted tractor-drawn scraper, hauling scraper, pull scraper, pull-type scraper
Schürfkübel *m*, Sattel-Schürfwagen *m*, Schürfkasten *m*	two-wheel(ed) scraper, (tractor-pulled) carrying scraper, wagon-scraper; pan (US)
von 3 Pferden gezogener Radschrapper *m*	fresno scraper (US)
Kübel *m*	bowl, (skimmer) scoop
drehbarer Radschrapper *m*	rotary scraper
gestrichener Inhalt *m*	struck capacity, flush capacity
gehäufter Inhalt *m*	heaped capacity
abgerundete Auswerfvorrichtung *f* (oder Ausstoßplatte *f*)	curved ejector
Schürfzeit *f*	digging time, dig-and-turn time
Schürzenöffnung *f*	apron opening
Transportzeit *f* hin und zurück minus Schürfzeit *f*	in-and-out haul
Rundfahrzeit *f*	round-trip time
Leer-Fahrgeschwindigkeit *f*	empty return speed
Entleeren *n*	dumping (operation)
(Be)Ladezeit *f*	loading time
Schieben *n*	push-loading
Wenden *n*	turning
Schubraupentraktor *m*, Stoßraupe *f*, Schubgleiskettenschlepper *m*, Stoßgleiskettenschlepper, Schubmaschine *f*	crawler push-cat(erpillar), pusher tractor
Schubhilfegerät *n*	pusher, pushloader
Schürfkübel(heck)motor *m*	(wheel) scraper rear engine
kostenvergütete Ladung *f*	pay dirt (US)
dreiteilige Schnittkante *f*	three-piece cutting edge
Motorschürf(kübel)wagen *m* mit zusätzlichem Heckantrieb *m*, doppelmotoriger Radschrapper *m*, Schürfwagen(zug) *m* mit besonderem Schürfkübelmotor, Fabrikat THE EUCLID ROAD MACHINERY CO, CLEVELAND 17, OHIO, USA	EUCLID twin power scraper
Laden *n*	boiling
Schürfen *n*	digging, scraping

Rad|spur *f*, **Radeindruck** *m* [*Straße f*] = rut
~stand *m* = wheelbase
~traktorkran *m*, **Radschlepperkran** = wheeled tractor crane
~überweg *m* = cycle-track crossing
~waschvorrichtung *f* = wheel washer
raffinierende Hydrierung *f* = hydrofining
Rahmen *m* = frame(work)
~bauwerk *n* = framed structure
~ecke *f* = knee (of frame)
~(einzel)teil *m* = frame member
~formel *f* = frame formula
~gleis *n*; siehe unter „Feldbahnanlage *f*"
rahmenloser Ziegelpaket-Transport *m* = palletless package brick transporting
Rahmen|schergerät *n*, siehe: Scherkastengerät *n* nach Casagrande
~ständer *m* = framed stanchion
~stiel *m* = frame leg
Raigras *n* = rye grass
Rajolpflug *m*, siehe: Grabenpflug

Rammanlage *f*, **Ramme** *f* — pile driving plant, piling plant
Auslösehaken *m* — trip hook
Bär *m*, siehe: Rammfallbär
Dieselbär — piling hammer working on the principle of a Diesel engine

    Kolben *m* — piston
    Hebel *m* für Brennstoffpumpe *f* — injection pump lever
    Brennstoffpumpe *f* — injection pump, fuel-oil pump
    Ölspritzdüse *f* — fuel jet in piston head
    Rammjungfer *f* — anvil block
    Hubhöhe *f* — jumping height

Dampfbärramme *f* — pile driving plant (or piling plant) with direct acting steam piling hammer

Dampf(ramm)hammer *m*, Dampf(ramm)bär *m*, (Dampf)Zylinderbär, direkt wirkender Rammbär — direct acting steam piling hammer, steam-engine piston and cylinder in which the piston is the hammer

Dampföler *m* — steam lubricator

Dieselrammanlage *f*, Dieselramme *f* [*bei der DELMAG ist es üblich Ramme und Rammgerüst in der Bezeichnung zu trennen*] — diesel piling plant

direkt wirkende Ramme *f* — direct acting piling plant
Doppelmäkler *m* — lead(er)s
doppelt wirkender (Ramm)Hammer *m*, McKIERNAN-TERRY-Rammhammer *m*, vollautomatischer Schnellschlagbär *m* — double-acting hammer, automatic steam McKIERNAN-TERRY hammer

Dreh(gerüst)ramme *f* — rotary type pile driving plant, ~ ~ piling plant

Druckluftramme *f*, Preßluftramme *f* — (compressed) air (pile) driver
dynamische Rammformel *f* — dynamic pile-driving formula
einfach wirkend — single-acting
Einrammen *n* — driving
Elektro-Ramme *f* — electric driver
Fallgewicht *n*, siehe: Rammfallbär *m* ~ [*Dampframmbär, Dieselbär*] — drop weight
Fallhammer *m*, siehe: Rammfallbär *m*
Fallhöhe *f* — heigth of drop, fall

Rammanlage

Freifallbär m, siehe: Rammfallbär	
Freifallramme f, siehe: indirekt wirkende Ramme	
Gerüstramme f	frame type pile driving plant, ~ ~ piling plant
Handramme f, Pionierramme f	hand-operated driver
hohle Kolbenstange f	hollow piston rod
indirekt wirkende Ramme f, Freifallramme	drop pile hammer plant
Klein(gerüst)ramme f	small frame type pile driving plant (or piling plant)
Kolbenring m	piston ring
Kranramme f	crane type driver, crane pile-driver
LACOUR-Bär m	LACOUR type direct acting steam hammer with steam pipe at the top cylinder
Leicht(gerüst)ramme f	light frame type pile driving plant, ~ ~ ~ piling plant
Mäkler m, Läuferrute f, Laufrute	lead(er), guide rod, guide bar
maschinell betriebener Fallhammer m	mechanically operated drop hammer
Schlagenergie f	energy of blow
Schwenkarm m	spudding arm
Kranmotor m	crane engine
Gummi-Stoßdämpfer m	rubber shock absorber
gummigefederte Seilrolle f	rubber-insulated sheave
Führungsschienen fpl	leads
Schwenkarmantriebsmechanismus m	spudding mechanism
Bohrgerüst n	drilling machinery
Kranführerhaus n	crane cab(in)
Keilriemen m	V-belt
Zahnradgetriebe n	gear assembly
Zahnrad n	spudding gear
Kurbelzapfen m	crank pin
Schubstange f	connecting rod
einscheren [Seil n]	to reeve
hintere Rolle f	heel sheave
Seiltrommel f	cable drum
abstützen	to stabilize
freifallender Rammhammer m	free-falling ram
nach vorn und hinten bis 1:10 und 1:3 neigbar	batter to the lead(er)s adjusted from 1 to 3 backward and 1 to 10 forward
MENCK-Bär m, Fabrikat MENCK & HAMBROCK, HAMBURG-ALTONA, DEUTSCHLAND	MENCK direct acting steam hammer with steam input at the top of the piston rod
neigbares Einrammen n, Schrägrammung f	driving on the rake
Pfahlramme f	foundation pile driving plant
Pionierramme f, siehe: Handramme	
Prellscheibe f	bottom head
Preßlufthammer m, Drucklufthammer	(compressed) air (pile) hammer

Preßluftöler m, Druckluftöler	air lubricator
Preßluftramme f, siehe: Druckluftramme	
Rammbär m, siehe: Rammfallbär	
Ramme f für Holz-Kanaldielen fpl	sheathing hammer
Rammfallbär m, Fallhammer m, Freifallbär, Fallgewicht n, Bär, Rammbär	(tripped) drop hammer, drop pile hammer, winch type hammer, monkey, tup
Rammhaube f	(driving) helmet, ~ cap, cushion bock
Rammformel f	pile driving formula, dynamic ~ ~ ~
Rammgerüst n	pile frame, piling frame
Rammhammer m, siehe: (Schnellschlag-)Rammhammer	
Rammkurve f	pile driving curve
Rammring m	pile ring
Rammprotokoll n	driving record, penetration ~
Rammplatte f	anvil
Rammhammer-Pfahlzieher m, schlagender Pfahlzieher m, Rammbär-Ziehgerät n	double-duty double-acting hammer
Rammvorschrift f	pile driving regulation
Rammwiderstand m	pile driving resistance
Rammwinde f	pile driving hoist
Reihen(gerüst)ramme f	frame type pile driving plant (or piling plant) for driving in row arrangement
Schlagfolge f	succession of blows
Schlagkolben m	percussion piston
Schlagzerstäubung f	kick-atomizing
Schräg(gerüst)ramme f	rake frame type pile driving plant (or piling plant)
Schwimmramme f	floating (pile) driver, marine ~
Schraubenspindel f	jacking screw
(Schnellschlag-)Rammhammer m, Schnellschlagbär m, Schnellschlaghammer	rapid-stroke hammer
Spannschraube f	tie rod nut
Spundwandramme f	sheeting driver
statische Rammformel f	static pile-driving formula
Universal(gerüst)ramme f	universal frame type pile driving plant (or piling plant)
Unterwagen m	undercarriage
Unter-Wasser-Rammhammer m	underwater piling hammer
Vorbauramme f	cantilever type pile driver
Ziehgehänge n	grip
Zylinder m	cylinder
Zylinderbär m, siehe: Dampf(ramm)hammer m	
Zylinderdeckel m	top head
Zylinderkopf m	top cylinder
Zwischenzylinder m	middle cylinder

Rammbrunnen m, Nortonbrunnen [*früher auch „Abessinierbrunnen" genannt*] = drive(n) well
Ramme f, siehe: Rammanlage f
~ f, Stampframme = rammer
Rammjoch n = driven pile trestle
Rammaschine f = mechanical rammer, machine ~
Rammpfahl m; s.unt.„Gründungspfahlm"
~**plattenbagger** m, siehe: Freifall-Kranstampfer m
~**plattenverdichtung** f = dropping weight method of compaction
~**ponton** m = pile-driving barge
~**rohr** n = drive-pipe
~**sonde** f, Schlagsonde = driving rod, drop-penetration sounding apparatus, percussion probe
~**sondierung** f = drop-penetration testing, percussion penetration method, driving test
~**sondierung** f **mit Versuchspfählen** mpl = pre-piling
~**spitze** f, siehe: Pfahlschuh m
Rampe f, Auffahrt f = accomodation ramp, approach ~, raised approach
~ f = ramp
Rampen|schüttung f, Dammschüttung f = embankment fill, fill (construction)
~**-Tankspritzmaschine** f, siehe: Bitumen-Sprengwagen m
Rand|balken m = spandrel beam, fascia
~**bedingung** f = boundary condition
~**einfassung** f = edging
~**gebiet** n = fringe area
~**spannung** f = extreme stress, (edge stress of) extreme fibre stress
~**stein** m, siehe: Kantenstein
~**stein-, Rinnstein- und Gehsteig-Betonier- und -verlegungsmaschine** f, Fabrikat DOTMAR INDUSTRIES INC., KALAMAZOO, MICHIGAN, USA = DOTMAR curb and gutter paver
Randstreifen m = edge strip, marginal ~
~, Standspur f, Parkstreifen = (highway) shoulder, road ~, hardened ~, parking strip, pull-off strip
~**fertiger** m = small finisher used in bankette construction, marginal concrete strip finisher

randverstärkte Betondecke f = thickened edge type concrete pavement
Randwinkel-Messung f = contact angle measurement
Rangier|bahnhof m, siehe: Verschiebebahnhof
~**fahrzeug** n = shunting vehicle, marshalling vehicle
~**gleis** n, Verschiebegleis = shurt rack, yard ~
~**lok(omotive)** f, siehe: Verschiebelok(omotive) f
~**schlepper** m = shunting tractor
Rapakiwi m (Geol.) = Rapakivi Granite
Rapputz m, Rauhputz m, Berapp m = rough cast plastering, pebble-dash ~, rough cast(ing); [*in Scotland: harl*(*ing*)]
Rapsöl n, siehe: Rüböl n
Rasen m = turf
~**ansaat** f = turfing by seeding
~**böschung** f = turf slope
~**drän** m; siehe unter „Entwässerung f"
~**narbe** f = mat of turf
~**schälen** n = turf stripping
(~)**Sode** f, Grassode, (Rasen)Plagge f, Rasenziegel m = (grass) sod, turf ~
~**sodenandeckung** f = turfing by sodding
~**stapel** m = turf sod stockpile
~**trennstreifen** m, siehe: Grünstreifen
~**ziegel** m, siehe: (Rasen)Sode f
Rast|feder f = stop spring
~**haus** n = drive-in restaurant
~**platz** m = lay-by(e), passing place, waiting-bay, halting place (Brit.); roadside rest (US)
Rationalisierung f = rationalization
Ratsche f, Knarre f = ratchet
Rauch|gas n, siehe: Feuergas
~**kammer** f = smoke box
~**quarz** m (Min.) = cairngorm, smoky quartz
~**schutztafel** f [*Brücke* f] = blast plate
~**topas** m = smokestone
Rau(c)hwacke f, Zellendolomitgestein n = crystallized dolomite
Räude f = scabbing [*the loss of aggregate from a surface dressing in patches, leading to exposure of the original road surface*]
Rauhbank f = adjustable iron fore plane

Rauhbelag m [*Straße f*] = roughening course
Rauheit f = rugosity, roughness
rauhe Schalung f = rough shuttering
rauhes (oder gemeines) Rispengras n = rough-stalked meadow grass
Rauh|hartgußasphalt m = rough surfaced hand-laid stone-filled asphalt
~**putz** m, siehe: Rapputz m
~**reif** m = rime frost, hoar-frost
rauhsandig = gritty
Rauhwurf m, siehe: Steinwurf
Raum|beständigkeit f = volume stability
~**dosierung** f, siehe: Volumendosierung
Räumer m, Räumgerät n = remover
~; siehe unter „Bohrmeißel m"
Raum|erhitzer m = space heater
~**fachwerk** n, räumliches Fachwerksystem n = latticework in space, space frame structure
~**fuge** f; siehe unter „Fuge f"
~**gehalt** m = content by volume
~**gewicht** n **der Volumeneinheit** f = volume weight, (bulk) density, bulk specific gravity [*deprecated: box weight*]
~**heizung** f = space heating
~**kurve** f = three-dimensional curve
räumlicher Vier-Säulen-Rahmen m **als Achteckträger** m = octagonal girder four columns space frame

räumlich verlegte Rohrleitung f, dreidimensionale ~ = three-dimensional pipe line
Raumperspektive f = space-perspective
Räumschaufel f, **Schrapperschaufel** [*Arbeitsgerät n beim Handschrapper m*] = drag skip
~, siehe: Handschrapper m
Räumschild n = moldboard (US)
Raumteile mpl = percentage by volume
Raum|teilmischung f, siehe: Volumendosierung f
~**trockner** m = space dryer
Räumung(sarbeiten) f, Freilegung f von Baugelände n [*Entfernen aller Hindernisse pflanzlicher Natur*] = clearing (works) (or operations), land clearing stripping, site-clearing
Raumzumessung f, siehe: Volumendosierung f
Raupe f, Fabrikat CATERPILLAR TRACTOR CO., PEORIA, ILLINOIS, USA = CATERPILLAR [*Trademark*]
~ **mit angebauter nasenförmiger Säge** f = saw-nosed tractor
Raupen|anhängerwagen m, siehe: Großraumlore f auf Gleisketten fpl
~**antriebsrad** n, Raupenantriebsturas m = crawler drive sprocket
~**band** n, siehe: Raupenkette f

Raupen(band)löffelbagger m, Gleisketten-Löffelbagger — crawler-mounted excavator, bucket-excavator mounted on tracks, crawler shovel, track-laying type shovel, caterpillar shovel

Unterwagenrahmen m	lower frame, carbody
Stahlplatten fpl	steel plates
Schwenkgetriebe n	swing gear, slewing ~
Schuhplatten fpl (oder Bodenplatten) der Raupenbänder npl (oder Gleisketten fpl)	crawler shoes, track shoes
Seitenwagen m zur Aufnahme der Raupenfahrgestelle npl (oder Gleiskettenfahrgestelle)	crawler (side) frame
Verbindungsbolzen m	steel link
angeflanscht	flanged
Bodenplattengelenk n, Schuhplattengelenk	crawler shoe link
Ausgleichfeder f, Spannfeder	compensator spring
Unterwagen-Rahmen in X-Rahmenform f	X-frame carbody

Raupen(band)löffelbagger — Raupenfahrzeug

Oberwagenrahmen m	upper frame
Stahlprofilträger m	rolled section
Motor-Generatorsatz m	motor generator set
Hubmotor m	hoist engine
Schwenk- und Fahrmotor m	swing and propel engine
Vorschubmotor m	crowd engine
AMPLIDYNE-Steuerungssystem n zur Veränderung der Erregerspannung f, Fabrikat GENERAL ELECTRIC CO.	AMPLIDYNE [*Trademark*]
ROTOTROL-Steuerungssystem n zur Veränderung der Erregerspannung f, Fabrikat WESTINGHOUSE-ELECTRIC CORP.	ROTOTROL [*Trademark*]
Anortbringen n [*Löffel m*]	spotting [*bucket*]
Auslegerneigung f	boom angle (US); jib ~ (Brit.)
maximale Ausschütthöhe f	maximum dumping height
Ausschütthalbmesser m bei max. Schütthöhe f	dumping radius at maximum height
Ausschütthöhe f bei max. Ausschütthalbmesser m	dumping height at maximum radius
max. Ausschütthalbmesser m	maximum dumping radius
max. Schnitthöhe f	maximum cutting height
Schnitthalbmesser m bei max. Schütthöhe f	cutting radius at maximum height
Schnitthöhe f bei max. Schnitthalbmesser m	cutting height at maximum radius
max. Schnitthalbmesser m	maximum cutting radius
Schwenkkupplung f	swing clutch (coupling)
Hubkupplung f	hoist clutch (coupling)
Lenkkupplung f	steering clutch (coupling)
Baggermotor m	shovel engine
Baggerelektromotor m	shovel motor
Schnitthalbmesser bei 2,4 m über Planum n	cutting radius at 8'—0" elevation
Schnittiefe f unter Planum n	cutting depth below grade
Planierhalbmesser m	radius of clean-up
Schwenkhalbmesser m der Auslegerrolle f	boom point clearance radius (US); jib ~ ~ (Brit.)
Höhenmaß n der Auslegerrolle f	boom point clearance height (US); jib ~ ~ ~ (Brit.)
Bandkupplung f	band clutch (coupling)
Rollenkranz m, Laufrollenring m	roller circle
Leonardschaltung f, Ward-Leonard-Schaltung f	Ward-Leonard system of variable voltage control

raupenfahrbar = crawler-mounted
Raupen|fahrer m, Gleiskettengerätfahrer = cat-jockey
~fahrwerk n, Zweiraupenfahrwerk n, Raupenunterwagen m, (Gleis)Kettenfahrwerk n, (Raupen-)Traktorenlaufwerk n, Kettenlaufwerk, Raupenlaufwerk == creeper undercarriage, crawler unit, crawlers
~fahrzeug n, s.: (Gleis)Kettenfahrzeug n

Raupen|fertiger *m*, siehe: Gleiskettenfertiger

~geräte *npl* = tracked plant, caterpillar equipment, caterpillars, tracklayers

~kette *f*, Raupen(glieder)band *n*, Traktorenkette *f*, Gleiskette *f* = crawler, caterpillar track, (tracklaying) track, crawler track, creeper track, chain track, crawler belt, track chain

~kran *m*, Gleiskettenkran = crawler crane

~ladeschaufel *f*, siehe: Gleisketten-Ladeschaufel

~schlepper *m*, siehe: Kettenschlepper *m*

~schlepper *m* **mit Seitenausleger** *m* = side-boom crawler tractor

~-Schneckenfräse *f*; siehe unter „Bodenvermörtelungsmaschine *f*"

~schuhplatte *f*, Raupenbandschuhplatte = track shoe, crawler ~

~spannen *n* = track tensioning

~speiser *m*, Raupenbeschicker *m* = crawler feeder

~straßen(beton)mischer *m*; siehe unter „Straßen(beton)mischer *m*"

(~-)Traktorenlaufwerk *n*, siehe: Raupenfahrwerk

~unterwagen *m*, siehe: Raupenfahrwerk *n*

~wagen *m*, siehe: Großraumlore *f* auf Gleisketten *fpl*

Raute *f* [*Anschlußstelle f*] = lozange type junction

Rautengewölbe *n*, siehe: Netzgewölbe

Reagenzmittel *n* = reagent

Reaktions|gleichgewicht *n* = reaction equilibrium

~turbine *f*, Rückdruckturbine, Überdruckturbine = reaction (-type) turbine

Realgar *m*, Rotrauschgelb *n* (Min.) = realgar

Rechen *m*, Harke *f* = rake

~ ; siehe unter „Talsperre *f*"

~klassierer *m* = rake-type classifier

~maschine *f* = calculating machine

~schacht *m* = screen well

~schieber *m* = slide rule

~tafel *f*, Berechnungstafel *f* = chart

Rechteckgerinne *n* = rectangular channel

rechtwinklig = rectangular

redaktionseigener Bericht *m* = staff report

Redestillat *n* = re-run oil

Reduktionszirkel *m* = proportional compasses

Reduzier|stück *n*, Staubogen *m* [*Druckluftbetonförderer m*] = adapter bend

~transformator *m*, siehe: Abspanner *m*

Redwood-Viskosimeter I *n* = Redwood visco(si)meter

Redwood-Viskosimeter II *n* = Admiralty visco(si)meter

Reede *f* [*in Österreich und Bayern auch: Rhede f*] = roadsted

reemulgieren = to become reemulsified

reflektierend = reflectorizing, reflecting

Reflexions|horizont *m* = reflecting horizon

~-Strahlungsheizung *f* = reflective radiant conditioning

Reflexstoff *m* = reflectorised material

Reformieren *n* [*Steigerung f der Klopffestigkeit f von Benzin n*] = reforming

Reformierungsverfahren *m* **mit Entschwef(e)lung durch katalytische Druckhydrierung** *f* = hydroforming process

~ Platinkontakt *m* = platforming process

Refraktions-|Intercept *m* = refractivity intercept

~verfahren *n*; siehe unter „geophysikalische Baugrunduntersuchung *f*"

Regel|größe *f* = standard size

~kompaß *m*, Einstellkompaß *m* = adjustment compass

regelmäßiges Schicht(en)mauerwerk *n* = coursed rubble walling

Regel|querschnitt *m*, Normalquerschnitt = typical cross-section

~spurgleis *n*, siehe: Normalspurgleis *n*

~technik *f* = control in mechanical engineering

~ventil *n*, Steuerventil = control valve

Regen|abflußmenge *f*; siehe unter: „Entwässerung *f*"

~dauer *f*, siehe: Niederschlag(s)dauer

~einlauf *m*, Straßeneinlauf *m* = (rainwater) gull(e)y

(~)Einlaufrost *m* = gull(e)y grate (or grating)

Regenerativofen *m* = regenerative furnace

regenerierter Gummi *m* = reclaimed rubber

Regen|erzeugung f = rainmaking
~gleiche f, Isohyete f = isohyetal line (Brit.); line of equal rainfall; isohyetal (US)
~guß m, Sturzregen m = (torrential) downpour
~rohr n, siehe: Abflußrohr
~schatten m = rainless region
~stärke f, siehe: Niederschlag(s)stärke
~wasser n, siehe: Niederschlag(s)wasser
Regie|arbeit(en) f = force(-)account (construction), force-account work
~arbeitskräfte f = direct labour (Brit.); state forces, public ~ (US)
Regionalmetamorphose f, Regionalumprägung f, Versenkungsumprägung = regional metamorphism
Registrier|gerät n, Registrierapparat m = recorder, recording apparatus (or meter)
~kasse f = cash totalizer
~rechenmaschine f = printing calculator
~waage f = recording scale, ~ weighing machine
Regler m = governor
reguläres System n [$Kristall$ n] = cubic system, regular ~
Regulier|hebel m = control lever
~organ n = regulating control
~schieber m, Regulierklappe f = control (or regulating) valve
Regulierungsbauwerk n = headworks (structure), control works, control structure
Regulierverschluß m = regulating (or control) gate
Rehbock'sche Zahnschwelle f = Rehbock dentated sill
Reibahle f = reamer, rimer
Reibebrett n, siehe: Holzspachtel m, f
reibender Brechvorgang m; siehe unter „Backenbrecher m"
Reibepfahl m = fender pile
Reib|kupplung f, siehe: Friktionskupplung
~radwinde f, Friktionswinde, Treibscheibenaufzug m = friction hoist
~rolle f = friction roller
~schale f = porcelain mortar
Reibung f = friction
~ = attrition

Reibungs|beiwert m, Reibungskoeffizient m = frictional coefficient, coefficient of friction
~brekzie f = crush-breccia
~bremse f = friction brake
~korrosion f = fretting corrosion
~kupplung f, siehe: Friktionskupplung
~messer m = skidding machine
~messung f [$Straße$ f] = skidding test, measurement of slipperiness
~pfahl m, siehe: Mantelpfahl
~verankerung f = anchoring by friction
~verlust m [$Hydraulik$ f] = friction head, ~ loss
~widerstand m = frictional resistance
~winkel m, Winkel m der inneren Reibung f = angle of internal friction
Reichnaturgas n, feuchtes Naturgas, feuchtes Bohrlochkopfgas, Naßgas = wet natural (or casing-head) gas, combination ~, natural gas rich in oil vapo(u)rs
Reichsautobahn f, Bundesautobahn = German motorway, German motor road, autobahn
Reichsgemeinschaft f **für Radwegebau e.V.** = German National Society for Cycle Track Construction
Reichsstraße f, Nationalstraße = national road
Reichweite f, siehe: Bereich m
Reifeneindruck m = tyre impression (Brit.); tire ~ (US)
Reifen m **für Erdbaugeräte** npl = earth-mover tire (US)/tyre (Brit.), earth moving ~
~griffigkeit f = tyre grip (Brit.); tire ~ (US)
Reifen m **mit Geländeprofil** n, siehe: Geländereifen m
~luftdruck m = inflation pressure
~panne f = blowout
~profil n = tyre section, ~ tread pattern (Brit.); tire section (US)
~pumpe f = tire pump (US); tyre ~ (Brit.)
~schaden m = tyre failure (Brit.); tire ~ (US)
~schlauch m, siehe: Luft ~

Reifen|(schutz)kette f = tyre chain, driving ~ (Brit.); tire ~ (US)
~trecker m **mit Planierschild** n; siehe unter „Bulldozer m"
Reifeprozeß m [*Beton* m] = curing; [*deprecated: maturing, hardening*]
Reihe f [*Mathematik* f] = progression
Reihen|becherwerk n, **Vollbecherwerk, Vollelevator** m, **Becherwerk in Becheran-Becher-Ausführung** f = continuous (bucket) (type) elevator
~fertigung f, siehe: Serienherstellung f
~haus n = row house
~pflaster n = coursed sett paving, paving in rows, peg top ~, straight course ~, stone sett paving laid in rectilinear pattern
~schlußmotor m = series(-wound) motor
~silo m = rectangular multiple-compartment bin
~siloanlage f, siehe: Abmeßanlage f für Betonzuschlagstoffe mpl
reine Biegung f = simple flexure
~ Fahrzeit f = running time; [*deprecated: travelling time*]
~ Zugfestigkeit f = direct tension (or tensile) strength
reiner Druck m, siehe: Alleindruck m
Reinheitsschicht f, siehe: Sauberkeitsschicht f
Reinigungs|bürste f = cleaning brush
~schacht m, siehe: Mannloch n
~siebung f = separating
Reisig n = faggot-wood
Reiß|brett n = drawing board
~feder f, **Zierfeder** = ruling pen, drawing ~
~kraft f [*Bagger* m] = biting force, break-out ~
~zeug n = drawing instruments
Reiter|libelle f, **Röhrenlibelle** f = main bubble
~sparren m = dormer rafter
Reklameschild n = advertising sign
Rekristallisation f, **Alterung** f [*Schraube* f, *Niet* m] = crystallization
relative Luftfeuchtigkeit f = relative humidity
Reliefmodell n = relief model
Reliktmineral n = relic mineral

Renaissance-Kreuzung f, siehe: Kleeblatt-Kreuzung f
Renchgneis m, **Sedimentgneis** m, **Paragneis** m = paragneiss
Rentabilität f = rentability
Reparatur f, siehe: Instandsetzung f
~dienst m = repair service
~grube f, siehe: Untersuchungsgrube f
~park m = repair depot
Reproduzierbarkeit f = reproducibility
Repulsionsmotor m **mit Dämpferwicklung** f = repulsion motor with damper winding
Reserve|anlage f = stand-by plant
~halde f, Reservematerialhalde = reserve stockpile
~kapazität f = stand-by capacity
resistiver Dehnungsmesser SR-4, siehe: elektrisches Spannungsgerät SR-4 n
Resonanz|förderer m, **Resonanzrinne** f = natural-frequency conveyor
~frequenz f = resonance frequency
~schwingsieb n = spring-supported vibrating screen
~schwingungsverdichter m **(oder Rüttelverdichter** m**) System Professor Lorenz** = BOHN & KÄHLER soil vibrator
Restspannung f = residual stress
Resultierende f, **Resultante** f, **Mittelkraft** f, **resultierende Kraft** f = resultant (of all forces)
Retreadverfahren n, **Oberflächenerneuerungsverfahren** n = retread
Retrometamorphose f, siehe: rückläufige Metamorphose f
Rettungs|arbeiten fpl = rescue work
~boje f = life-buoy
Reverberierofen m, siehe: Flammschmelzofen m
Reversier|getriebe n, **Umkehrgetriebe** n, **Wendegetrieb** ~ = reversing gear
~schaltkupplung f, siehe: Wendeschaltkupplung
~turbine f, sie e: Umkehrturbine
Revolverpresse f = turntable press
Rezeptwähler m [*Betonaufbereitung* f] = mix selection mechanism, mix-selector
reziproker Wert m = inverse value, reversed ~, reciprocal ~
Rhede f, siehe: Reede f

rheologisches Verhalten n = rheological behavio(u)r
Rheopexie f = rheopexy
Rhodochrosit m (Min.), siehe: Manganspat m
Rhodonit m (Min.) = rhodonite
rhombisch = rhombic
Rhyolit m = rhyolite
Richt|aufbauweise f, Aufkipp-Bauweise = tilt-up construction (or method)
~**einbaustreifen** m [Straßenbau m] = pilot (paving) lane (US); ~ pavement ~
~**latte** f, siehe: Wiegelatte
~**linien** fpl **für die optische Führung auf Straßen** fpl = specifications for the lay-out of roads from the point of view of visual requirements
~**pfahl** m = guiding pile, guide ~
~**schacht** m = pilot shaft
~**scheit** n; siehe unter „Fertigbehandlung f"
~**stollen** m, Richtvortrieb m; siehe unter „Tunnelbau m"
Richtungs|gleis n = forwarding track
~**schild** n = advance sign, distant ~
Richtwert m = guide value
Riedgras n [niederdeutsch: Segge f] = sedge
Riegel m [Rahmen m] = center section (US); centre ~ (Brit.)
Riemen m = belt
~**scheiben-Friktionswinde** f = belt hoist
~**tang** m, Laminarie f = laminaria
rieselfähiges Gut n = free-flowing material
Riesel|feld n = irrigated sewage field
~**regen** m, Sprühregen m, Nieseln n = drizzle, drizzling rain
~**schutt** m (Geol.) = fine rolling rock débris
~**werk** n, siehe: Gradierwerk n
Riesen|luftreifen m, großvolumiger Luftreifen = giant (or oversize) pneumatic tire (US)/tyre (Brit.)
~**reifen** m, großvolumiger Reifen = giant (or oversize) tire (US)/tyre (Brit.)
~**senkkasten** m = mammoth caisson
~**stock** m (Geol.), siehe: Batholith m
~**topf** m; siehe unter „Gletscher m"
~**warenhaus** n = mammoth department store
Riff n = reef

riffbildende Koralle f = reef-building coral
Riffelblech n = checkered sheet, ~ plate
Rigipsplatte f, Gipskartonplatte = plaster board, gypsum ~
Rigolpflug m, siehe: Grabenpflug
Rillenlager n = groove bearing
Rindertalg m = beef tallow
Ringel|erz n = ring ore
~**walze** f, Klumpenzertrümmerer m = clod crusher
ringförmiger Querschnitt m, Ringquerschnitt = annular section
Ring|kluft f [Holz n] = cup shake, ring ~, windshake
~**kugellager** n = annular ball bearing
~-**Kugel-Verfahren** n, Ring und Kugelmethode f = Ring-and-Ball test (or method), R. and B. method
~**leitung** f = ring main
~**ofen** m = chamber kiln
~**polygon** n = closed traverse
~**querschnitt** m, ringförmiger Querschnitt = annular section
~**riff** n, Atoll n = atoll
~**rillenlager** n = ring groove bearing
~**rost** m = circular grate
~**schergerät** n, Kreisringscherapparat m = ring shear apparatus
~**schmierlager** n = ring-lubricated bearing
~**spannung** f = hoop stress
~**straße** f = ring road
~**vorspannung** f = circumferential prestressing
Rinne f = channel
~ f [Gußbetonanlage f] = chute, spout
Rinnen|eisen n = trough-shaped iron
~**pflasterstein** m = channel (or gutter) paving sett
Rinnstein m, siehe: Pflasterrinne f
Rinnsteinreinigungsmaschine f **mit Aufladebecherwerk** n = channel scraper and elevator
Rippel(marke) f, Wellenfurche f = ripple marking
Rippendecke f **mit ebener Untersicht** f = ribbed floor with smooth soffit
~ ~ **offener Untersicht** f = ribbed floor with open soffit
Rippenrohr n = gilled tube

Rippen|stahl *m* = multi-rib reinforcing bars
~streckmetall *n* = rib mesh

Riß *m*
  Haar~
  Rißbildung *f*, Rissebildung
  feine Rißbildung *f*, Maronage *f*, Netzrißbildung *f*
  Schwind~, Schwund~
  Ablagerungs~
  Reproduktions~

  Reproduktionsrissebildung *f*

crack
  hair (line) ~
  cracking, formation of cracks
  crazing, craze; [*deprecated: crocodiling (Brit.)*]; map cracking (US)
  shrinkage ~
  deposit ~
  reflection crack [*crack in old concrete pavements reappearing as crack in the asphalt surface*]
  crack reflection, reflection cracking

---

rißbewehrt, rißarmiert [*Beton m*] = crack-reinforced [*concrete*]
Rißfestigkeit *f* [*Beton m*] = resistance to cracking, extensibility [*concrete*]

Ritzhärteprüfer *m* = scratch-hardness tester
Rizinusöl *n*, siehe: Kastoröl *n*

Road-Mix-Verfahren *n* [*ist gewissermaßen eine Abart der „Bodenvermörtelung" und kann ebenfalls nach dem System „mix-in-place" arbeiten*]
  Reinigen *n*
  Grundieren *n* und Oberflächenbehandlung *f*
  Aufbringen *n*
  Fremd-Zuschlagstoff *m*
  Schwaden *m*
  Trocknen *n* der Zuschlagstoffe *mpl*
  Mischen *n*
  Verteilen *n*
  Verdichtung *f*
  Mischen *n* mit Straßenhobel *m*, Schar-Mischung *f*, Messermischen *n*
  An-Ort-Mischverfahren *n*, Mischverfahren *n* ohne Anheben *n* des Mischgutes *n* [*auch mitunter als „Bodenvermörtelung" bezeichnet*]

road-mix (method)

  sweeping
  priming

  aggregate application
  commercial material
  windrow
  aggregate drying
  mixing
  spreading
  compaction
  blade mixing

  mix-in-place (method)

Robinie *f* = locus tree
robust; siehe unter „Baumaschinen *fpl* und Baugeräte *npl*"
Rodehacke *f*, siehe: Platthacke *f*
Rödeldraht *m* = tie wire
Roden *n*, Rodung *f* = uprooting, grubbing up, brush clearing

Roderechen *m*, Unterholz~ = clearing rake, brush rake
Rodio-Verfahren *n*; siehe unter „Baugrundverbesserung *f*"
Rogenstein *m*, Rogenkalk *m* = roestone
Roggenstroh *n* = rye straw
Rohboden *m* = raw soil

Roh|decke *f* = bare floor
~**eisen** *n*, siehe: Masseleisen
~**(erd)öl** *n*, siehe: Erdöl
~**(erd)planum** *n*, siehe: Untergrund *m*
rohe Schraube *f* **mit Mutter** *f*, **schwarze**
~ ~ ~ = black bolt
rohes Spaltbenzin *n* = pressure destillate
Roh|gips *m*, Dihydrat *n*, Doppelhydrat, Rohgipsstein = raw gypsum, dihydrate, natural gypsum
~**humus** *m* = raw humus
~**kaolin** *m*, siehe: Porzellanton *m*
Rohöl *n*, siehe: Erdöl
~-**Emulsion** *f* **mit Wasser** *n* **oder anderen Stoffen** *mpl* = oilfield emulsion
~**leitung** *f* = crude oil line
~**ofen** *m* = still
Roh|perlit-Gestein *n* = perlite ore
~**petroleum** *n*, siehe: Erdöl *n*
~**planum** *n*, siehe: Untergrund *m*
Rohr *n*, siehe: Schilf *n*
~ = pipe
~**anschluß** *m*, siehe: Rohrverbindung *f*
~**aufhängung** *f* = pipe hanger
~**auslegerkran** *m* = pipe-boom crane (US); pipe-jib ~ (Brit.)
~**bogen** *m*, siehe: Rohrkrümmer *m*
~**brunnen** *m* = tube well, tubular ~
~**drän** *m*; siehe unter „Entwässerung *f*"
~**einwalzapparat** *m*, siehe: Siederohrdichtmaschine *f*
Röhren|chassis *n* = tubular chassis
~**destillation** *f* [*Erdölaufbereitung f*] = pipe still distillation
~**dränung** *f*; siehe unter „Entwässerung *f*"
~**geländer** *n* **mit Handlauf** *m* = tubular hand railing
~**libelle** *f*, Reiterlibelle = main bubble
~**ofen** *m* = pipe still, tube still
Rohr|fänger *m*, siehe (Auf)Fangkessel *m*
~**fertigungsmaschine** *f*, siehe: Beton~
(~)**Formstück** *n*, siehe: Armatur *f*
~**geflechtmatte** *f* = woven reed mat
~**gerüst** *n*, Rohrrüstung *f* = tubular scaffold(ing)
~**graben** *m* = pipe trench
~**grabenbau** *m* = pipe trench construction
~**kanal** *m*, siehe: Rohrleitungskanal
~**kern** *m* [*Betonrohrstampfmaschine f*] = steel core
~**kitt** *m* = jointing compound for pipes
~**kompensator** *m*, Rohrausgleicher *m* = pipe expansion bend
~**konstruktion** *f* = tubular structure
~**kopfbenzin** *n*, siehe: Leichtbenzin
~**krümmer** *m*, Rohrbogen *m*, Krümmer *m* = pipe bend
~**legewinde** *f* = pipe-laying winch
~**leitung** *f*, Rohrstrang *m* = pipe line, ~ conduit
~**leitungsbrücke** *f* = pipeline bridge
~**leitungsgrabenaushub** *m* = pipeline trenching
~**(leitungs)kanal** *m* = pipeway
~**lichtweite** *f* = internal pipe dia(meter)
~**mast** *m* = tubular mast
~**muffe** *f* = pipe bell
~**netzlageplan** *m* = pipe network layout (plan)
~**netzsystem** *n* = pipe network system
~**pfahl***m*; siehe unter„Gründungspfahl*m*"
~**profil** *n* = pipe section(al) shape), ~ profile
~**schelle** *f* = pipe clip
~**schiebersteuerung** *f* = tubular slide valve control
~**schlange** *f* = tube coil
~**schlüssel** *m* = pipe wrench
~**schuß** *m* = pipe section
~**schutzanstrich** *m* = pipe coating
~**schwingel** *m* = tall fescue
~**sickerdrän** *m*; siehe unter „Entwässerung *f*"
~**stampfmaschine** *f*, siehe: Zement~
~**stollen** *m* = pipe drift (Brit.); ~ (small-diameter) tunnel, ~ gallery, ~ heading
~**strang** *m*, siehe: Rohrleitung *f*
~**sumpf** *m* = reed swamp
~**turbine** *f*, siehe: Frontalturbine
~**verbindung** *f*, Rohranschluß *m* = pipe connection
~**verlegung** *f* = pipe laying
~**vorschubgerät** *n* = pipe pusher, ~ driver
~**walze** *f*, siehe: Siederohrdichtmaschine *f*
~**wand(ung)** *f* = pipe crust, ~ wall
Roh|schlacke *f* = raw slag
~**splitt** *m* = uncoated chip(ping)s
~**ton** *m*, siehe: Ton

Rohwasser n = raw water
Rollbandpegel m = tape depth-ga(u)ge
Rolle f [*Seilzug* m] = pulley
Rollenbahnweiche f = conveyor switch
rollende Eimerkette f [*Eimerkettenbagger* m] = roller type bucket ladder
Rollen|förderer m = roller conveyor
~**kette** f = roller chain
~**lager** n = roller bearing
~**laufkranz** m = roller race
rollenloser Behälter m = skid container
Rollen|meißel m; siehe unter „Bohrmeißel"
~**station** f [*Bandförderer* m] = idler set
~**station** f = roller seat
Roll|geld n, Fuhrgeld = drayage charges
~**grenze** f; siehe unter „Konsistenzgrenzen fpl nach Atterberg"
rollig, siehe: nichtbindig
Roll|kies m = round gravel
~**maschine** f, siehe: Siederohrdichtmaschine f
~**material** n = rolling stock
~**sand** m = round sand
~**schütz(e)** m, (f), siehe unter „Talsperre f"
~**treppe** f, Fahrtreppe = motorstair, escalator, moving stair(case)
~**widerstand** m = rolling resistance between tyre (Brit.)/tire (US) and road surface
Romankalk m [*früher: (natürlicher) Romanzement* m] = Roman cement, Parker's ~
Romeit m (Min.) = romeite
römischer Ziegel m, siehe: Verblender m
Röntgenographie f = radiography
Roots-Gebläse n = Roots blower
rosa Quarz m (Min.) = rose quartz
Rost m **aus Halbhölzern** npl = foundation platform of half timbers
~, Kessel~, Feuer~ = (boiler) grate
rostbildend = rust-forming
Rost|kitt m = rust cement
~**knolle** f = tubercle, nodule
~**knollenbildung** f = tuberculation, nodulation
~**kühler** m = grate cooler
~**schalung** f = grid-type shuttering
~**schutzanstrich** m = rust-preventative coating
~**schutzfarbe** f = rust protection paint, ~ inhibitive~, anti-rust ~
~**schutzöl** n = slushing oil
~**stab** m = grate bar
Rotarybohrmeißel m; siehe unter „Bohrmeißel"
Rotations|bohrung f **mit Kerngewinnung** f = rotary drilling with core extraction
~-**Gesteins-Bohrung** f, siehe: Gesteinsdrehbohren n
~**kompressor** m, Rotations(luft)verdichter m, Rotations-Drucklufterzeuger m = rotary (air) compressor
~**sonde** f **nach Carlson** = Carlson rotating auger
~**spülbohren** n, Rotationsspülbohrung f = hydraulic rotary drilling (or boring), rotary mud flush boring (or drilling)
~**vibrator** m = rotary type vibrator
~-**(Zylinder-) Viskosimeter** n = rotating cylinder visco(si)meter, rotational visco(si)meter
Rot|braunstein m, siehe: Kieselmangan n
~**buche** f, gemeine Buche f = common beech
~**fäule** f = red rot, pink rot
rotierender Streuteller m; siehe unter „Streugerät n für den Winterdienst m"
Rotierofen m, siehe: Drehofen
Rot|klee m, siehe: Kopfklee
~**kupfererz** n, Cuprit m, Cu_2O (Min.) = cuprite
~**liegendes** n (Geol.) = new-red sandstone
~**nickelkies** m, Kupfernickel m, Nickelin m, NiAs (Min.) = nicolite, copper nickel [*old term: nickeline*]
Rotor m, Schlagwalze f [*Prallbrecher* m] = impeller
~**streuer** m; siehe unter „Streugerät n für den Winterdienst m"
Rot|rauschgelb n (Min.), siehe: Realgar m
~**schwingel** m = red fescue
~**spat** m, siehe: Kieselmangan n
~**tanne** f, siehe: gemeine Fichte f
~**zinkerz** n, Zinkit n, ZnO (Min.) = zincite, red oxide of zinc, spartalite, sterlingite
Rüböl n, Rapsöl n = colza (oil)
Ruchgras n = sweet-scented vernal grass

Rück|blick m [*Nivellieren* n] = backsight
~druckturbine f, siehe: Reaktionsturbine
Rücken|berg m (Geol.), siehe: Drum(lin) m
~öl n [*Spermacetiöl* n] = blubber oil
rückenschlächtiges Wasserrad n = breast water-wheel, back-shot ~
Rück|gewinnung f, Wiedergewinnung f = recovery
~gewinnungsanlage f = reclaiming plant (or installation, or facility)
~haltebecken n; siehe unter „Talsperre f"
~kühlung f = re-cooling, cooling back
rückläufige Metamorphose f, Retrometamorphose f, Diaphthorese f (Geol.) = retrogressive metamorphism
Rück|laufleitung f = return line
~laufsicherung f [*Bauaufzug* m] = device to eliminate "running back"
~laufsperre f [*Bauaufzug* m] = ratchet to eliminate "running back"
~licht n = tail light, rear ~
~nahmefeder f = return spring
~schlag m, Rückstoß m = recoil
rückschreitende Erosion f = backward erosion
rückschreitender Bruch m = retrogressive slide
Rück|standssieb n = retaining screen
~stau m = backflow, afflux
~stauwasser n = backwater
~stoß m, Rückschlag m = recoil
~strahler m = reflector
~stufensieb n = screen for two screening directions
~verladegreifer m = rehandling grab (bing crane)
~verladegreif(er)korb m = rehandling bucket
~verladung f = rehandling
rückwärtige Schutzsperre f; siehe unter „Talsperre f"
Rück|wärts-Aufreiß(er)vorrichtung f = back-ripper
~wärtsentleerung f = rear dump discharge
~wärtsentleerungs-Anhänger m = rear dump trailer
~wärtsfahrt f = reverse run
~wärtsgang m = reverse gear

rückwärtskippender Erdtransportwagen m; siehe unter „Fahrzeuge npl für den Transport m von Boden m und Steinbaustoffen mpl"
Rückzieh|einrichtung f [*Löffelbagger* m] = retract
~kupplung f = retract clutch
~seil n = backhaul rope
Ruderboot n = rowboat
Ruhe|(bei)wert m = at-rest value
~druck m = pressure at-rest
ruhender Boden m = repose soil
~ Tiefengranit m = subjacent body
Ruhe|penetration f [*Schmierfett* n] = unworked penetration
~stellung f, Ruhelage f = stationary position
~winkel m, natürlicher Böschungswinkel = angle of repose
Rühr|arm m = stirring arm
~wagen m, siehe: Betontransportwagen mit (aufgebautem) Rührwerk(smischer) n, (m)
~welle f = stirring shaft
~werk(smischer) n, (m) = agitator, stirrer
~(werk)welle f = agitator shaft
Rumpelkammer f [*Asbesterzabbau* m unter *Tage*] = gloryhole
Rumpffläche f (Geol.), siehe: Denudationsebene f
Rund|behälter m = circular container
~beschicker m, siehe: Tellerspeiser m
~blick m = all-round view
~blick-Führerhaus n, Vollsichtkanzel f = full vision cab(in)
~bogen m, siehe: Halbkreisbogen
~brecher m, siehe: Kegelbrecher m
~draht m = round wire
~(draht)litze f; siehe unter „Drahtseil n"
~eindicker m = circular thickener
~eisen n, Rundstahl m, Beton~ = round bar steel, ~ (~) iron
~erneuerung f von Schulter f zu Schulter f = retreading
~erneuerung f von Wulst f zu Wulst f = remoulding, rebuilding
~herd m [*Sinteranlage* f] = rotary hearth
(Rund)Holzgreifkorb m = (pulp)wood grapple (or grab)

Rundkipper m, Kreiskipper = rotating tip, rotary tippler
~**waage** f = portable tip wagon type concrete batcher scale
Rundkopf|mauer f; siehe unter „Talsperre f"
~**schraube** f = button-head(ed) screw, half-round ~
Rund|korn n = round grain
~**lauf** m = circular track
~**litze** f; siehe unter „Drahtseil n"
~**litzen(draht)seil** n = round strand cable
Rundloch|-Laboratoriumssieb n = (laboratory) screen (US)
~**sieb** n = round-hole screen
Rund|ofen m [*keramische Industrie* f] = circle kiln
~**pfahl** m = round pile
~**schieber** m [*Zuschlagsilo* m] = radial type fill valve
~**stahl** m, siehe: Rundeisen n
(Rund)Wabensilo m = circular multiple-compartment bin
Rungenwagen m, Rungenwaggon m = flat car, platform ~
Runse f, siehe: Felseinschnitt m
Rüping(spar)verfahren f, Hohlimprägnierung f, Teeröltränkung f nach Rüping, Spartränkung f, Holzimprägnierung f nach Rüping = Rüping empty cell process
Rüster f, Ulme f, Effe f = elm
Rüstung f; siehe: Gerüst n
Ruß|gebläse f = soot-blower
~**punkt** m = smoke point
Rutil m, TiO_2 (Min.) = rutile
Rutsche f, Rutschbahn f = shoot
Rutschebene f (Geol.) = plane of sliding
Rutscheindruck m, Rutschspur f = skid mark
rutschfest, siehe: gleitsicher
Rutsch|festigkeit f = resistance to skidding
~**fläche** f [*Böschung* f] = slide-failure surface
~**fließung** f = flow slide
~**gebiet** n, Rutschungsgebiet = slide area; slip ~
~**gefahr** f [*Straßenfahrzeug* n] = skidding risk [*road vehicle*]

(~)**Harnisch** m, Rutschspiegel m = slickenside
~**kupplung** f = slipping clutch
~**pflaster** n = slippery sett paving
~**spiegel** m, siehe: (Rutsch)Harnisch m
~**spur** f, Rutscheindruck m = skid mark
Rutschung f, siehe: kleiner Erdrutsch m
~ f, Erdrutschung, Absetzung f = (land)slide [*earth slip upon a large scale*]
~ (Geol.), siehe: Bodenkriechen n
~ f **durch Verflüssigung** f = liquefaction failure
~ f **infolge dynamischer Einflüsse** mpl, ~ ~ Erschütterung f = landslip due to the effect of earth tremors
~ f ~ **Zunahme** f **der Belastung** f = landslip due to the effect of loading
Rutsch(ungs)gebiet n = slip area; slide ~
Rutsch|weg m [*Fahrzeug* n] = skidding distance
~**zone** f = slip zone; slide zone
Rüttel|bohle f, siehe: Vibrierbohle
~**(bohlen)fertiger** m; siehe unter „Betonrüttelgeräte npl"
~**druckverfahren** n, KELLER-Verfahren = vibrator-jetting deep compaction, vibroflotation (soil-compaction)
~**flasche** f, siehe: Innen~
~**gerät** n, siehe: Vibrator m
~**geräte** npl **zur Materialförderung** f = shaking materials handling equipment
~**platte** f; siehe unter „Betonrüttelgeräte npl"
~**stampfer** m, Vibrationsstampfer = vibrating tamper
~**stampfer** m [*Straßenbeton* m] = (road) vibrating tamper, concrete tamping and screed board vibrator
~**stampfmaschine** f = vibration and mechanical tamping block machine, vibration and tamping (concrete) block machine
~**tisch** m; siehe unter „Betonrüttelgeräte npl"
~**verdichter** m **System Professor Lorenz**, siehe: Resonanzschwingungsverdichter
~ ~ ~

Rüttelverdichtung *f*, siehe: Vibrationsverdichtung *f*
Rüttler *m*; siehe unter „Betonrüttelgeräte *npl*"
~, siehe: Schwinggerät *n*

S

Saatzuchtgut *n* = seed (multiplication) farm
Sach|schaden *m* = property damage
~verständigengebühr *f* = expert fee
Sack|bahnhof *m*, Kopfbahnhof *m* = dead-end station
~bohrer *m* = pocket drill (or bore)
~förderer *m* = bag conveyor
~füllmaschine *f* = sacking apparatus
~gasse *f*, Sackstraße *f* = blind alley, cul-de-sac (street), close [*a local street open at one end only and with special provision for turning around*]
~gasse *f* **ohne Wendemöglichkeit** *f* = dead-end street [*a local street open at one end only without special provision for turning around*]
~maß *n*, siehe: Fließmaß
~schüttung *f* [*Betoneinbringung f*] = depositing underwater concrete in bags
~silo *m* = sack silo
~stapel *m* = bag pile
~stapler *m* = bag lift truck
~straße *f*, siehe: Sackgasse *f*
Sackung *f*, siehe: Senkung *f*
Sack|wall *m* = sack dam
~wendelrutsche *f* = gravity sack shoot
~zement *m* = sacked cement, bagged ~
Safloröl *n* = safflower oil

Säge *f*	saw
Absatz~	fine tooth wood ~
Band~	band ~
Bau-Kreis~	contractors' circular ~
Bogen~	coping ~
Bügel~	framed crosscut ~, hand hacksaw
Fuchsschwanz *m*, Handsäge	hand ~
Gatter~	log frame ~
Gehrungs~	mitre box ~ (Brit.); miter ~ ~ (US)
Hack~	(power) hack ~
Handvorspann~	framed hand ~ with stretchers
Ketten~	chain ~, link tooth ~
Kraft~, Motor~	power ~
Kreis~	circular ~
Laub~	fret ~, compass ~
Richten *n*	setting
Schweif~	turning ~
Spann~	web ~
Streck~	framed hand ~
stumpf	blunt
Vollgatter *n*	gang ~
Sägeblatt *n*	~ blade
Sägebock *m*, Schragen *m*	sawing jack
Sägemehl *n*	sawdust
Sägesand *m*	stone sawing sand
Sägeschnitt *m*	(saw) kerf
Sägewerk *n*, Sägemühle *f*, Schneidemühle	lumber mill (US); saw mill

Salinenwasser n = saline water
Salinität f, Salzhaltigkeit f, Salzgehalt m = salinity, salt content
Salpetersäure f, HNO_3 = nitric acid
salpetersaurer Kalk m, siehe: Kalksalpeter m
salpetrige Säure f = nitrous acid
Salweide f = goat willow, black sallow
Salz|dom m = salt dome
~**gehalt** m, siehe: Salzhaltigkeit f
~**gitterlader** m, Fabrikat A. G. für BERGBAU- und HÜTTENBEDARF, SALZGITTER, DEUTSCHLAND = SALZGITTER mucking shovel
~**glasieren** n = salt glazing
~**glasur** f = salt-glaze
~**haltigkeit** f, Salinität f, Salzgehalt m = salinity, salt content
~**kupfererz** n, Atacamit m = atacamite
~**lagerstätte** f, Salzvorkommen n, Salzvorkommnis n = salt deposit
~**mutter** f = mother of salt
~**säure** f, siehe: Chlorwasserstoffsäure f
salzsaure Kupferchlorürlösung f, Cu_2Cl_2 + HCl + aq = hydrochloric solution of cuprous chloride
Salz|see m = salt lake
~**streuung** f = application of salt
~**sumpf** m = salt swamp
~**vermörtelung** f; siehe unter „Baugrundverbesserung f"
~**vorkommen** n, siehe: Salzlagerstätte f
~**wasserkorrosion** f = salt water corrosion
Sammel|becken n; siehe unter „Talsperre f"
~**behälter** m, siehe: Behälter
~**gebiet** n; siehe unter „Entwässerung f"
~**spur** f [Verkehr m] = storage lane
~**stollen** m = collection gallery
~**trichter** m = collecting hopper
Sammler m; siehe unter „Abwasserwesen n" und „Entwässerung f"
~ **für die Mischentwässerung** f; siehe unter „Abwasserwesen n"
Samum m, Sandsturm m = simoom, sandstorm
Sand m [nach Atterberg, Fischer und Udluft, DIN 4220, International Society of Soil Science 2—0,02 mm; nach DIN 4022, DEGEBO, Terzaghi 2—0,1 mm; nach Casagrande (Jahr 1947), British Standards Institution, Massachusetts Institute of Technology 2—0.06 mm; nach Gallwitz (Jahr 1939) 2—0.2 mm; nach Grengg (Jahr 1942) 2—0,1 mm; nach U.S. Bureau of Soils 2—0.05mm] = sand
~ **mit hellen und dunklen Bestandteilen** mpl = (salt and) pepper sand
~**anteil** m, Sandkörnung f, Sandkorn n = sand fraction
~**anteil-Untersuchungsverfahren** n = sand equivalent test
Sandasphalt m = bitumen sand mix, sand asphalt (Brit.)
~ = sheet asphalt [is a plant mix of asphalt cement with graded sand passing the No. 10 sieve and mineral filler]
~ **im An-Ort-Mischverfahren** n = sand asphalt mixed-in-place construction
~ **mit verteilten Steinen** mpl = stone-filled sheet asphalt, modified Topeka
Sand|aufbereitungsanlage f = sand processing (or dressing, or producing) plant (or installation)
~**aufbruch** m [Grundbruch bei kritischem Gefälle n] = boiling of sand
~**(auf)schüttung** f, Sandauffüllung = sand fill
~**aufspülung** f = hydraulic emplacement of sand, ~ sand filling
~**bank** f = shoal, flat(s), bank in the sea, sandbank
~**barre** f, angeschwemmte Sandinsel f = sand-head, off-shore bar, (sand) bar, coastal bar
~**bett(ung)** n, (f), Sand(unter)bett(ung) = sand underlay, ~ bed(ding course), ~ cushion, ~ blanket
~**boden** m, sandiger Boden = sandy soil
~**böschung** f = sand slope
~**brunnen** n, siehe: vertikale Sanddränage f
~**damm** m = sand embankment
~**drän** m, siehe: vertikale Sanddränage f
~**düne** f, Düne = (sand-)dune, down
~**entwässerungsschnecke** f, Sand(rückgewinnungs)schnecke, Wasserausscheidungsschnecke = sand dewatering screw, ~ dehydrator ~

Sandersatzmethode — Sandstein

Sand|ersatzmethode f [*Nachprüfung* f *der Verdichtung* f] = calibrated sand method
~**fang** m, Sandfänger m = sand trap, ~ catcher
~**fang** m, Sandrückgewinnungsmaschine f = sand reclaiming machine, ~ recovery ~
~**fangbühne** f = sand accretion groyne (Brit.)/groin (US)
~**feld** n, siehe: Kiesfeld
~**feuchtigkeit** f = humidity of the sand
~**filter** n, m = sand filter
~**führung** f [*Fluß* m] = sand transport
~**geröll(e)** n (Geol.) = moving sand débris
sandgeschlämmt = blinded with sand
Sand|grube f = sand pit
~**hafer** m, siehe: Helm m
~**halm** m, siehe: Helm m
~**heide** f = barren, sand heath
~**hose** f = sand-pillar, sand-spout
sandig = sandy, arenaceous
sandiger Kies m = hoggin (Brit.); sandy gravel, path gravel, gravel-sand-clay
~ **Ton** m, magerer ~, Magerton = sandy clay
Sand|inselmethode f, Sandinselschüttung f [*Gründung* f] = sand island method
~**klassieranlage** f = sand classifying installation
~**klassierer** m = sand classifier
~**kohle** f, Magerkohle, magere Kohle, harte Kohle = non-caking coal, dry burning ~, hard ~; free-ash ~ (US)
~**korn** n, Sandteilchen n = sand grain
~**korn** n, siehe: Sandanteil m
~**körnung** f, siehe: Sandanteil m
~**kratzer(kette)** m, (f) = sand drag, dewatering flight conveyor, washbox
~**kreiselpumpe** f = sand sucker
~**lage** f, Sandschicht f = sand layer, ~ course
~**lagerstätte** f, siehe: Sandvorkommen n
~**luzerne** f = variegated alfalfa
~**mergel** m = sandy marl, lime-gravel, clay-grit
~**mühle** f, Sandmahlmühle = sand mill
~**muschel** f = clam
~**naßbaggerei** f, Sandnaßbaggerung f = sand dredging
~**papier** n, Glaspapier = sand paper
~**papieroberfläche** f, Sandpapierrauheit f = sand paper surface, ~ ~ finish [*road surface texture*]
~**pumpe** f [*pennsylvanisches Bohrverfahren* n] = sand pump
~**putzmörtel** n = sanded plaster
~**riedgras** n, siehe: Helm m
~**rückgewinnung** f, Sandwiedergewinnung = sand recovery f, ~ reclamation
~**rückgewinnungsmaschine** f, Sandfang m = sand reclaiming machine, ~ recovery ~
~**rückgewinnungsschnecke** f = sand reclaiming screw
~**sack** m = sand bag
~**sackabdämmung** f, siehe: Abdämmung durch Sandsäcke mpl
~**sackabsperrung** f, siehe: Abdämmung durch Sandsäcke mpl
~**sackwall** m = sand bag embankment
~**schicht** f, Sandlage f = sand layer, ~ course
~**schiefer** m = schistous sandstone, foliated grit(-stone), arenaceous shale
~**schliff** m (Geol.), siehe: Korrosion f
~**schmitze** f, Sandstreifen m = sand streak, streak of sand
~**schnecke** f, Waschschnecke, Spiral-(naß)klassierer m, Schneckenwäsche f = spiral classifier, (spiral) screw washer, screw-type sand classifier, washing screw
~**schüttung** f, siehe: Sandaufschüttung
~**sieb** n = sand screen
~**silo** m = sand bin, ~ silo

Sandstein m
Arkose ~, feldspatreicher ~, Arkose f
Asphaltsand(stein), bituminöser ~

sandstone
arkose (sandstone), arkosic grit'
sand asphalt (US); asphaltic sand (stone), bituminous sandstone

Sandstein — Sand-Ton-Mischung

Bindemittel n, Kitt m [*Zwischenmasse, die dem Sandstein dauernd eine mehr oder minder große Festigkeit verleiht*] — cementing agent
Bunt~ — mottled ~; variegated ~ (Brit.); bunter ~
Eisen~, eisenschüssiger ~ — iron-~, ferrugin(e)ous ~; Hastings sand (Brit.)
feinkörniger ~ — fine-grained ~
Füllmasse f [*Zwischenmasse, die lediglich die Zwischenräume zwischen den Felstrümmern ausfüllt, ohne sie fest und dauernd zu verkitten*] — filling agent having no cementing power
Glaukonit~ — glauconitic ~
Glimmer~ — mica(ceous) ~
grauer ~ — grayband(s)
grobkörniger ~, Kristall~ — coarse-grained ~, gritstone
Kalk~ — calcareous ~, lime-cemented ~
kieselhaltiger ~, verkieselter ~ — siliceous ~
konglomeratischer ~ — conglomeratic ~
Kristall~, siehe: grobkörniger ~
Mergel~ — marly ~
mittelkörniger ~ — medium-grained ~
Muschel~ — shell(y) ~, beach rock
Nummuliten~ — nummulitic ~
ölgesättigter ~ — oil-saturated ~
ölgetränkter ~ — oil-impregnated ~
Quarz~ — silica ~
~block m — ~ boulder
Schiefer~ — shaly ~
streifiger ~ — linsey
~ vom Craig-yr-Hesg Quarry, Pontypridd, England — pennant grit
~schiefer m [*der Porenkitt enthält Glimmer*] — slaty ~
~verkleidung f — ~ masonry facing
Ton~ — argillaceous ~, clayey ~
verkieselter ~, siehe: kieselhaltiger ~

Sand|stoß m = sand face, face of sand
~strahlen n, Sandstrahlbläserei f, Sandstrahlreinigung f, Sandstrahlarbeiten fpl = sand blasting, blast cleaning
~strahlgebläse n = sand blaster, ~ blast(ing) machine; blast generator (US)
~strand m = sand beach
~streifen m, Sandschmitze f = sand streak, streak of sand
~streifenbildung f, Sandschmitzenbildung = sand streaking
~streuen n = sand spreading, sanding
~streuer m, Sandstreugerät n, Sandstreumaschine f = sand spreader
~streu-Nachläufer m = towed-type sand spreader
~sturm m, Samum m = sandstorm, simoom
~teilchen n, Sandkorn n = sand grain
~-Ton-Boden m = sand-clay soil
~-Ton-Mischung f, Sand-Ton-Gemisch n = sand-clay mix(ture)

Sand|-Ton-Straße f = sand-clay road
~topf m [*Gerüst* n] = sand holder
~trockner m = sand drier, ~ dryer
~- und Kieswerk n = sand and gravel plant
~(unter)bett(ung) n, (f), siehe: Sandbett(ung)
~verwehung f, Sandwehe f = sand drift, drift of sand
~vorkommen n, Sandvorkommnis n, Sandlagerstätte f = sand deposit
~waage f = sand scale
~wanderung f = sand migration
~wäsche f, Sandwaschmaschine f = sand washing machine, ~ washer
~wäsche f = sand washing [*filter operation*]; grit ~ [*sewage works operation*]
~wäsche f = grit washing [*sewage works operation*]
~wäscher m = grit washer
~wehe f, Sandverwehung f = drift of sand, sand drift
~wiedergewinnung f, Sandrückgewinnung f = sand recovery, ~ reclamation
~wüste f = sandy desert
~-Zement-Schlämme f, Sand-Zement-Schlempe, Sand-Zement-Schlämpe = sand cement grout
~zunge f = sand-spit
Sanierung f, Stadt~ = clearance, rehabilitation
Sanierungsviertel n = clearance zone, rehabilitation ~
sanitäre Gegenstände mpl = sanitary fittings
Sanitäter m = dresser; aid (US)
Santorinerde f [*nach der griechischen Insel Santorin benannt*] = Santorin earth
Saprobiensystem n = saprobic system
Sapropel m = sapropel
Satellitenstadt f, siehe: Trabantenstadt
Satinholz n, Atlasholz, Seidenholz, Feroleholz = satin wood
Satinweiß n = satin white
Sattdampf m, Naßdampf, gesättigter Dampf = saturated steam
Sattel m **der Faltung** f, Antiklinale f, Antikline f = anticlinal fold, anticline
~anhänger m, Halbanhänger, Sattelschleppanhänger = semi-trailer

~dach n, Giebeldach = saddle (back) roof, couple-close ~, gable ~, double-pitch ~
~holz n = bolster, corbel-piece, head-tree
~lager n = saddle support
~oberlicht n = double-inclined sky-light
~rost m = saddle grate
~schleppanhänger m, siehe: Sattelanhänger
~schlepper m, Zugmaschine f für Halbanhänger mpl = truck tractor for semi-trailers, tractor-truck ~ ~
~schlepperbauart f = semi-trailer type construction
~spalte f (Geol.) = anticlinal fissure
~-Tiefladeanhänger m, Sattel-Tieflader m, Sattel-Tiefbett-Anhänger, Sattel-Tiefladewagen m = semi-low-loader, semi-low-bed trailer, semi-low-load trailer, semi-deck trailer; semi-low-boy (trailer) (US)
~wagen m, Selbstentleerer m mit Sattelboden m = saddle bottomed wagon
Sättigung f = saturation
Sättigungs|druck m = saturation pressure
~grad m = degree of saturation
~linie f = line of saturation, surface ~ ~
~punkt m = saturation point
~zone f = zone of saturation
Satz m **Pläne** = set of plans
satzweise Mahlung f; siehe unter „Mühle" f
Sauberkeitsschicht f, Reinheitsschicht, Frostschutzschicht f, Druckverteilungsschicht, verbesserter Untergrund m [*in Deutschland auch als „Unterbau" bezeichnet, wenn die darüberliegende Schicht „Tragschicht" genannt wird*]; Schüttung f [*in der Schweiz und Österreich; „Schüttung" und „verbesserter Untergrund" ergeben zusammen den „Unterbau"*] = (granular) sub-base (course), frost blanket, foundation (course), antifreeze layer, improved subgrade
Säuberungsmaschine f, Reinigungsmaschine [*für Betonfugen* fpl] = joint cleaner
Sauerstoff|(atmungs)gerät n = oxygen breathing apparatus
~aufnahme f = oxygen uptake, uptake of oxygen

Sauerstoffflasche — Säule

Sauerstoff|flasche f = oxygen cylinder
~**haushalt** m = oxygen economy
~**linie** f = oxygen sag
sauerstofflos, luftlos = anaerobic
Sauerstoff|mangel m, Sauerstoffehlbetrag m = oxygen deficiency
~**salz** n = oxysalt, salt of oxyacid
~**verbrauch** m = oxygen consumption
~**zehrung** f = oxygen depletion
~**zufuhr** f = oxygen supply
Saug|bagger m; siehe unter „Naßbagger"
~**beton** m = vacuum concrete
~**betonverfahren** n, siehe: Billner'sches Vakuumverfahren n
~**brunnen** m = suction well
~**drossel** f [*Elektrotechnik* f] = drainage coil
Sauger m; siehe unter „Entwässerung f"
~, siehe: Saugkorb m
Saug|filter n, m, An~ = suction filter, vacuum ~
~**gas** n, Generatorgas = suction gas, generator ~, producer ~, power ~
~**gebläse** n = suction blower
~**heber** m = siphon
~**heberüberlauf** m; siehe unter „Talsperre f"
~**höhe** f [*Pumpe* f] = suction lift, ~ head
~**hub** m, An~, (An)Saugperiode f = suction stroke
~**korb** m, Seiher m, Sauger m [*Pumpe* f] = strainer
~**lader** m = suction loader
~**leitung** f, Saugrohrleitung = suction line, ~ pipe ~
~**loch** n [*Abteufpumpe* f] = snore-hole
~**luft** f = suction air
~**lüfter** m, siehe: Saugzugventilator m

~**luftförderanlage** f, Saugluftförderer m = suction (or vacuum) pneumatic conveyor (or conveying system), vacuum pump transporter
~**matte** f = vacuum mat
~**napf** m = sucker
~**periode** f, siehe: Saughub m
~**pumpe** f = suction pump
~**raum** m [*Pumpe* f] = inlet chamber
~**raum** m, Kapillarsaum m, Saugsaum = capillary fringe
~**rohr** n, An~ = suction pipe
~**rohr** n [*Pumpe* f] = tail-pipe
~**(rohr)leitung** f = suction line. ~ pipe ~
~**saum** m, siehe: Saugraum
~**schlauch** m = suction hose
~**schlauchfilter** m, n = suction type cloth filter dust collector
~**strahlpumpe** f = sucking jet pump
~-**Straßenkehrmaschine** f = suction scavenger
~**stutzen** m [*Motor* m] = intake
~- **und Druckleitung** f = suction and delivery line
~- **und Druckpumpe** f = combined suction and force pump, reciprocating ~
~**ventil** n [*Kompressor* m] = inlet valve
~**ventil** n = suction valve
~**ventilator** m = suction fan
~**vorrichtung** f **zum Fertigteiltransport** m, Vakuum(an)heber m = vacuum lifter pad
~**wasser** n **nach Stiny**, siehe: hygroskopisches Wasser
~**zug** m = induced draught (Brit.); ~ draft (US)
~**zugventilator** m, Saglüfter m = induced draught fan (Brit.); ~ draft ~ (US)

Säule f [*hat kreisförmigen Querschnitt im Gegensatz zum Pfeiler, der quadratischen oder rechteckigen Querschnitt hat*]	column
Abstand m	interval, intercolumniation
Fundament n	footing
Fuß m, Schuh m	base
Hals m	neck, colarin
Innen~	internal ~
Kapitel n	capital
Knicklänge f	effective column length

Säule — Schachtverzug 341

Kopf m, Knauf m — head
Kopfmoment n — moment at head
Kopfplatte f — head slab
Längsbewehrung f, Längsarmierung — bars
mittig belastete ~ — concentrically (or axially) loaded ~
Muffe f~ — muffle attachment
Pendel~ — ~ with ball and socket seating
Rand~ — external ~
Rippe f — rib
~ von der Höhe eines Stockwerks — ~ of one stor(e)y
Säulenschalung f, Schalungskasten m — ~ box, ~ form
Schaft m — shaft, trunk, body (fust)
Streifen m — strip
Trommel f — drum, disk, tambour
umschnürt — hooped

Säulen|basalt m = columnar basalt
~drehkran m = slewing pillar crane
~gang m = portico
~struktur f = columnar structure
Saumpfad m = bridle-path, bridle-road, bridle-way, driftway, drove(-way), packway
Säure|angriff m = acid attack
~austausch m = acid exchange
~ballon m = acid carboy
~behälter m = acid tank
~behandlung f, Säuren n = acid treatment
~behandlung f, Säuren n = acidation [of oil wells]
~bindungsfähigkeit f, Säurebindungsvermögen n = acid combining capacity
~flasche f = acid bottle
~gehalt m, Azidität f, Säuregrad m, Neutralisationszahl f = acidic content, acidity
~grad m, siehe: Säuregehalt m
~harzasphalt m, Pech n = pitch
~messer m = acidimeter
~rückgewinnungsanlage f = acid recovery plant, ~ reclamation ~, ~ reclaiming ~
saures Gestein n = acid(ic) rock [igneous rock containing over 65% of silica]
Saussuritgabbro m = euphotide
SA-WOE-Bohle f, (FRISCH-)Vibrator-Glättbohle mit Fahrwerk n = SA-WOE vibrating screed with travel(l)ing gear

Schaber m, Kratzer m = scraper
Schablone f = template
Schacht|abteufung f = shaft sinking
~bagger m; siehe unter „Naßbagger"
~bau m = shaft construction
~brunnen m = dug well
~deckel m = manhole cover
~fördergerüst n [Bergbau m] = headframe, headgear, pithead gear
~fördermaschine f = mine winding-engine
~gerüst n, siehe: Turmgerüst
~kabelkasten m = manhole junction box
~kranz m = collar of a shaft
~meister m = ganger
~ofen m = shaft kiln
~ofenkalk m = shaft kiln lime
~ofenklinker m = shaft kiln clinker
~pfeiler m, Bergfeste f = shaft pillar
~(pumpen)bagger m; siehe unter „Naßbagger"
~rohr n = shaft cylinder
~sohle f = shaft bottom
~speicher m, siehe: Lagersilo m
~stein m, Brunnenstein, radialer Formstein, Radialstein, Brunnenziegel(stein), Radialziegel(stein) = radial brick
~teufe f = depth of a shaft
~ventilator m, Grubenlüfter m, Abteuflüfter = mine fan
~verzug m = interval of a shaft, bay ~ ~ ~

Schacht|wandung f = shaft wall
~winde f = shaft hoist
Schadensbehebung f = making good
Schad(en)stelle f = failed area, point of failure
schadhafter Wassermesser m = down water meter
schädliche Ausdehnung f = detrimental expansion
Schädlichkeitsgrenze f = toxic threshold, limiting toxic concentration
Schädlingsbekämpfungsweißöl n = plant spray oil
Schad|stoff m = aggressive substance
~wasser n, aggressives Wasser, angreifendes ~ = aggressive water
Schaffußwalze f; siehe unter „Walze"
Schaftschale f, Pfeilerschaft m = hollow shaft
Schäkel m [mit Bolzen verschließbares U-Eisen] = shackle, clevis
Schälblatt n, Hobelmesser n, Schälmesser, Hobelblatt n, (Hobel)Schar f, Planierschar, Planierschaufel f [Straßenhobel m] = (planing) blade, grader ~
Schalbrett n, Schalungsbrett = shutter(ing) board
Schalen|dach n, Schalenkuppel f = shell roof
~kupplung f [starre Kupplung, bei der zwei Schalenhälften durch 2 bis 5 Schrauben auf jeder Seite auf die Wellenenden so gepreßt werden, daß durch die Reibung allein das Drehmoment übertragen wird] = clamp coupling, split ~
~(stau)mauer f; siehe unter „Talsperre f"
~theorie f = theory of shells
schales Abwasser n = stale sewage
Schal|fett n = form grease
~gerüst n = falsework, lining form
~gerüstpfahl m = falsework pile
~holzreiniger m = timber form cleaning device, wood(en) ~ ~ ~
Schall|bohrwerkzeug n, Infra~ = sonic drill
~dämmung f = sound insulation
~dämpfer m; siehe: Auspufftopf m
~pegel m = sound level
~wand f = baffle board
Schalnagel m = shuttering nail

Schalöl n, siehe: Entschalungsöl
Schalschiene f, siehe: Seitenschalung f
Schaltafel f, Formplatte f, Schalungstafel = form panel, shutter(ing) ~
Schalteröl n = switch oil
Schalt|hebel m, siehe: Bedienungshebel
~kupplung f, Ein- und Ausrückkupplung = clutch (coupling)
~organ n, Steuerorgan, Bedienungselement n = control, operating ~
~schrank m, siehe: Steuertafel f
~tafel f, siehe: Steuertafel
~werksgebäude n = switch building
Schalung f, Betonschalung, Einschalung = formwork, shuttering, forms, concrete forming
Schalungs|anker m = form tie
~auskleidung f = form(work) lining
~brett n, siehe: Schalbrett
~druck m = pressure on the form-work
~einheit f = form section
~kasten m, Säulenschalung f = column box (or form)
~plan m = shutter plan
~rüttler m; siehe unter „Betonrüttelgeräte npl"
~rüttlung f, Schalungsvibration f = (concrete) form vibration
~schiene f, siehe: Seitenschalung f
~tafel f, siehe: Schaltafel f
~träger m = horizontal form support, concrete ~ ~
~unterstützung f = form support
~vibration f, Schalungsrüttlung f = (concrete) form vibration
Schälwerkzeug n = skiving tool
Schamotte f, feuerfester Ton m, Schamotteton m = refractory clay, fireclay, structural clay
~ausmau(e)rung f = refractory lining
~stein m, Schamotteziegel m = refractory clay brick, fire clay brick
Schapf m, siehe: Schöpfkelle f
Schappe f, Probelöffel m = sampling spoon
Schappenbohrer m = shell auger
scharfkantig [Sand m] = angular, sharp
scharfkantiges Plattenwehr n = sharp edged plate weir
Schärfwerkzeug n = sharpening tool

Scharrharz — Scherspannung

Scharrharz n = scrape (US)
Scharriereisen n = bush chisel
Scharrieren n = charring
Scharrierhammer m = bush hammer
Schattenseite f (Geol.) = ubac
Schaubild n, siehe: Diagramm n
Schaufel f, siehe: Schippe f
~ [*Mischer* m] = blade, paddle
~, Kübel m, Ladeschaufel f, Hubschaufel [*Schürflader* m] = bucket, loading ~
~(beton)verteiler m; siehe unter „Beton(decken)verteiler"
~kufe f = skid loader shoe
~lader m, siehe: (Front)Ladeschaufel f
~mischer m = paddle mixer
~rad n [*Bagger* m] = bucket wheel
~radbagger m = bucket wheel(-type) excavator, rotary bucket excavator
~raddampfer m = paddle (wheel) steamer
~radgebläse n = bucket wheel blower
~welle f [*Mischer* m] = paddle shaft
~wellenmischer m = paddle-type mixer
Schauglas n vom Luftfilter n, = jar
Schaum|bildner m, Schaummittel n [*Beton* m] = foaming agent
~bildung f = frothing
~dämpfer m, siehe: Schaumverhütungsmittel n
~feuerlöscher m, siehe: Schaumlöscher
~gummi m = foam rubber
schaumige Hochofenschlacke f, siehe: Hochofenschaumschlacke
Schaum|kalk m, Wellenkalk(stein) m = aragonitic lime(stone)
Schaum|löscher m, Schaumfeuerlöscher = foam type fire extinguisher
~regulierungsmittel n = foam control agent
~ton m = foamclay
~verhütungsmittel n, Antischaummittel, Schaumdämpfer m = antifoam
S(c)heddach n = north-light roof
Scheel|bleierz n, Scheelbleispat m (Min.) = stolzite, scheeletite
~erz n (Min.) = scheelite
Scheelitschwüle f = scheelite spud
Scheiben|egge f, siehe: Tellerscheibenegge
~filter n, m = disc filter
~meißel m; siehe unter „Bohrmeißel"
~nabe f = disc boss

~pfahl m; siehe unter „Gründungspfahl m"
~pflug m = disc plough (Brit.); disk plow (US)
Scheide|konus m = separatory cone
~trichter m = separating funnel
~trommel f = separatory drum
scheinbare Haftfestigkeit f, siehe: Adhäsion f
~ Haftung f [*Umhüllung der Gesteinsoberfläche f durch einen Bitumenfilm m, ohne daß dieser fest haftet*] = coverage
~ Kohäsion f, siehe: Kohäsion
~ Porosität f, siehe: Luftporenanteil m
Schein|fuge f; siehe unter „Fuge"
~werfer m = floodlight, searchlight
Scheitel|gelenk n = crown hinge
~punkt m, Bogenscheitel m = vertex, apex, key, top, crown
Scheitholz n = split firewood
scheitrechter (oder gerader) Bogen m = straight arch, jack ~, flat ~
Schelde f = Scheldt
Schelfeis n = shelf ice
Schellack m = shellac
Schellhammer m = rivet set
Scher|beanspruchung f, Scherspannung f = shear(ing) stress
~belastung f = shear(ing) load
Scherben|index m [*Kies* m] = flakiness index
~kobalt m (Min.) = native arsenic
Scher|büchse f, siehe: Scherkastengerät n nach Casagrande
~dehnung f, siehe: Scherverformung f
Scheren|kreuzung f = scissor junction
~zapfen m; siehe unter „Holzverbindung f"
Scher|festigkeit f = shear(ing) strength
~fläche f = plane of shear
~fläche f [*Niet* m] = shearing section, ~ area
~gerät n = soil shearing test apparatus
~kastengerät n nach Casagrande, Scherapparat m ~ ~, Scherbüchse f, Rahmenschergerät = Casagrande shear test apparatus, box shear apparatus
~kluppe f = shears vice
~kraft f = shearing force
~spannung f, siehe: Scherbeanspruchung f

Scher|verformung *f*, Scherdehnung *f* = shear(ing) strain
~versuch *m* = shearing test
~widerstand *m*, Schubwiderstand = shear(ing) resistance
Scheuerwirkung *f* = scrubbing action
Schicht *f* (Geol.) = bed, stratum
~, Arbeitsschicht *f* = shift
~, Einbau ~ = layer, course, lift
~dicke *f* [*Bodenverfestigung f*] = depth of processing
Schichten|bauweise *f*, siehe: Lagenbauweise
~kunde *f*, siehe: Formations- und Schichtenkunde *f*
~reihe *f* (Geol.) = series of strata
~wasser *n*, Schichtwasser = held water
schichtenweise, lagenweise = in layers
Schicht|gestein *n*, Sedimentgestein, Ablagerungsgestein, Absetzgestein, Absatzgestein, Bodensatzgestein = bedded rock, sedimentary ~
~plattentafel *f*, Tafel *f* aus Beton-Schichtplatten *fpl* = sandwich precast concrete panel
~quelle *f* = gravity spring
~silikat *n*, Tonmineral *n* = clay mineral, layer silicate
~-Silikat-Struktur *f* = layer silicate structure
~stärke *f*, Lagenstärke = thickness of layer
(Schicht) Streichen *n* (Geol.) = strike
Schichtung *f*, Stratifikation *f* (Geol.) = plane of stratification
Schichtwasser *n*, Schichtenwasser = held water
Schiebelehre *f*, siehe: Schieblehre
Schieben *n* [*Walze f*] = shoving [*roller*]
Schieber *m*, Klappe *f* = valve
~gehäuse *n*, siehe: Klappengehäuse

~haus *n* = valve house
~hydrant *m* = sluice valve hydrant
~schütz(e) *m*, (*f*), Abzugschieber *m* = sluice valve
Schiebetor *n* = sliding door
Schieb|karre(n) *f*, (*m*), Schubkarre(n) *f*, (*m*); [*ostdeutsch und mitteldeutsch: Rad(e)ber f; in der Schweiz: Benne f*] = wheel-barrow
~lehre *f*, Schublehre *f*, Schiebelehre = caliper square
Schieds|gericht *n* = arbitration board
~gerichtsbarkeit *f* = arbitration
~gerichtsklausel *f* = arbitration clause
~richter *m* = arbiter
schiefe Biegung *f* = bending in two planes
~ Brücke *f* = skew bridge
~ Ebene *f*, schräge Lahn *f* = inclined plane
~ Straßeneinmündung *f*, ~ Straßengab(e)lung *f* = Y junction
Schiefer *m* = schist
~alaun *m* = feather alum, scissile ~
~gips *m* = foliated gypsum
~kalk(stein) *m* = sparry limestone
~kohle; siehe unter „Kohle *f*"
~kreide *f* = graphitic clay
~mergel *m*, siehe: Mergelschiefer *m*
~niere *f* = reniform slate
~öl *n* = (crude) shale oil
~sandstein *m* = shaly sandstone
~talk *m* = indurated talc
~ton *m* = shale, clay-shale
Schiefer Turm *m* **von Pisa** = Leaning Tower of Pisa
Schieferung *f* (Geol.) = foliation
schiefes Gewölbe *n* = skew(ed) arch
Schiefspalter *m*, siehe: Plagioklas *m*
schiefwinkliger Rahmen *m* = skew(ed) frame

Schiene *f*
  Radlenker *m*, Leitschiene *f*, Zwangsschiene *f*
  Zungen~, Weichen~
  Mutter~, Stamm~
  Zahn~

rail
  check ~, guard ~, safety ~, side ~, rail guard, safeguard
  switch ~, switch blade
  stock ~
  rack ~

Schiene — 1. Schießen; 2. Sprengen

Breitfuß~
Doppelkopf~, Stuhl~
Schienenstoß m

flanged ~, foot~ ~, flat-bottomed ~
bull-head(ed) ~, double headed ~
rail joint

Schienen|bagger m, siehe: Gleisbagger
~band n, Schienenförderband n = rail-mounted (belt) conveyor, shuttle (~) ~
~bieger m = jim crow (Brit.); rail bender
~biege- und -richtmaschine f = rail bending and straightening machine
~bohrknarre f = rail ratchet brace
~bohrmaschine f = rail drilling machine
~bus m, Schienenomnibus = railbus
~fahrzeug n, siehe: Gleisfahrzeug
~(förder)band n = rail-mounted (belt) conveyor, shuttle (~) ~
~fuß m; siehe unter „Feldbahnanlage f"
schienen|geführt, siehe: gleisgebunden
~geführter Oberflächenrüttler m; siehe unter „Betonrüttelgeräte npl"
~gleiche Niveaukreuzung f, niveaugleicher Bahnübergang m = level crossing
Schienen|kopf m; siehe unter „Feldbahnanlage f"
~laufrad n = rail wheel
~nagel m; siehe unter „Feldbahnanlage f"
~nagelhammer m; siehe unter „Feldbahnanlage f"
~oberkante f = top of rail
~(omni)bus m = railbus

~schleifwagen m = rail grinding car
~-Schwarzbelageinbaumaschine f, Schienen-Schwarz(decken)verteiler m, Schienen-Verteilerfertiger m, Schienen-Schwarzdeckenfertiger, Schienen-Schwarzdeckeneinbaumaschine f = rail-mounted (or rail-guided) asphalt finisher (or asphalt paver, or bituminous paving machine, or bituminous spreading-and-finishing machine, or black-top spreader, or asphalt(ic) concrete paver, or bituminous road surfacing finisher, or bituminous paver-finisher or asphalt and coated macadam finisher, or paver-finisher)
~schwelle f = tie (US); sleeper, cross-sill (Brit.); cross-tie
~steg m; siehe unter „Feldbahnanlage f"
~stoß-Schleifmaschine f = rail joint grinding machine
~strang m, siehe: Gleis n
~transport m = rail transport
~weg m, siehe: Gleis n
Schlerlingstanne f = hemlock spruce
Schließbaumwolle f; siehe unter „1. Schießen n; 2. Sprengen n"

---

1. Schießen n; 2. Sprengen n

(Ab)Brenngeschwindigkeit f
Abraumsprengung f
Abtun n
Aluminiumsprengkapsel f

Ammonsalpetersprengstoff m
Anlage f der Schußlöcher npl
Anwürgen n
Anwürgzange f, siehe: Sprengkapselzange
Anzündlitze f
Ausbläser m
Bleiazid n
Bohrlochbesatzstoff m, Sprenglochbesatzstoff
Bohrpatrone f, siehe: Schlagpatrone

1. shooting, 2. blasting

burning speed of fuse
overburden blasting
firing
lead azide alumin(i)um detonator, tetryl-azide detonator
ammonium nitrate (blasting) explosive
spacing and location of holes
crimping

ignitor cord
blown-out shot
lead azide
stemming (or tamping) material

1. Schießen; 2. Sprengen

Brenngeschwindigkeit f, siehe: Abbrenngeschwindigkeit	
Chloratit n, Chlorat-Sprengstoff m	chlorate blasting explosive
Detonation f	detonation
Detonationsgeschwindigkeit f	velocity of detonation
detonierende Zündschnur f, siehe: Knallzündschnur	
detonierender Sprengstoff m, hochbrisanter ~	high (strength) blasting explosive
Drahtschutznetz n	mesh blasting net
Dynamit n	dynamite
Dynamitsprengung f	dynamiting
elektrischer Zünder m	electric detonator
elektrischer Zünder m mit einem Widerstand von 0,9—1,3 Ohm	low tension detonator [*the low-tension fuse-head has a resistance of 0.9 to 1.3 ohms*]
elektrischer Zünder m mit einem Widerstand von 1500—50000 Ohm	high tension detonator [*the high-tension fuse-head has a resistance of 1,500 to 50,000 ohms*]
elektrischer Zündschnurzünder m	electric powder fuse
entzünden	to ignite
Erstsprengung f	primary (drilling and) blasting
Explosivstoff m	explosive
Fehlschuß m	misfired shot
Fehlschußloch n	blow(-out)
Fehlzündung f	misfire, misfiring
flüssige Luft f, Sprengluft f	liquid air
flüssiger Sauerstoff m	liquid oxygen (explosive)
Fortpflanzung f	propagation
gelatinös-plastische Sprengstoffgemenge npl, gelatinöse Ammonsalpetersprengstoffe mpl	gelatinous (blasting) explosives, ammonium nitrate gelatin(e)
gewerblicher Sprengstoff m	commercial explosive
Guttaperchazündschnur f, wasserdichte Zündschnur f	white countered guttapercha waterproof fuse
hochbrisanter Sprengstoff m, detonierender ~	high (strength) blasting explosive
Initialladung f	detonator
Kammersprengen n, Kammersprengverfahren n	coyote tunneling method (US)
Kesselschießen n, Vorkesseln n	sprung bore-hole method
Knallzündschnur f, detonierende Zündschnur f, Nitropentaerythrit-Zündschnur f, Sprengschnur, Nitropenta-Sprengschnur	detonating fuse (or cord), Cordeau
Knäpperschießen n, siehe: Nachknäppern n	
Kollodiumwolle f	collodion cotton
Kondensatorzündmaschine f, Kondensationszündmaschine	condenser discharge (type) blasting machine, CD ~ ~

1. Schießen; 2. Sprengen

Kupfersprengkapsel f	fulminate detonator
Laden n	charging
Leitungsprüfer m	circuit tester
Luftdruck m	air blast
Millisekunden-Verzögerungssprengen n	millisecond delay blasting
Millisekundenzünder m	millisecond delay electric blasting cap (or detonator)
Momentzünder m	instantaneous electric detonator
Nachknäppern n, Knäpperschießen n, Zweitsprengung f mit Bohrlochladung f	pop shooting, secondary drilling and blasting, block-holing, boulder blasting, boulder popping
Nitroglyzerin n, Sprengöl n	nitro-glycerin(e), nitroleum, blasting oil, fulminating oil, explosive oil
Nitropentaerythrit-Zündschnur f, siehe: Knallzündschnur f	
Nitropulver n	nitro-powder
Ohmmeter n	ohmmeter
Pappenzünderhülse f	paper tube
Parallelschaltung f	connection in parallel, parallel series
Pulversprengstoff m, siehe: $\frac{2}{1}$ Schießmittel n	
Pulverzündschnur f	powder fuse
Reihenschaltung f, siehe: Serienschaltung	
Schießbaumwolle f	gun cotton
Schießkabel n, Zündkabel	shot-firing cable
Schießmittel n, Schießstoff m, deflagrierender Sprengstoff m, Pulversprengstoff	low (strength) blasting explosive, powder explosive
Schlagpatrone f, Bohrpatrone	primer cartridge, blasting ∼
schlagwettersichere Zündschnur, Sicherheitszündschnur f	safety fuse
Schnell-Zeitsprengzünder m	short(-period) delay (electric) (blasting) cap, split-second delay cap
Schußloch n, siehe: Sprengloch	
Schwaden m, siehe: Sprenggase npl	
Schwarzpulver n, Sprengpulver	black (blasting) powder, gunpowder
Schwarzpulver n in Pulverform	blasting powder
Schwarzpulver n in Tablettenform f	blasting pellet
Schwarzpulverzündschnur f	black powder fuse
Schwarzpulverzündschnurring m mit Initialladung f	coiled capped fuse
schwergefrierbares Dynamit n, ungefrierbares Dynamit	uncongealable dynamite
Seitenwirkung f	side-shattering effect
Serienschaltung f, Reihenschaltung	connection in series, straight series
Serienschüsse mpl	series firing
Sicherheitszündschnur f, siehe: schlagwettersichere Zündschnur	

Sprengen n von Steinen mpl mit aufgelegter verdämmter Ladung f	plaster shooting (Brit.); mudcapping (US)
Sprenggase npl, Schwaden m	fumes
Sprenggelatine f	blasting gelatine
Sprengkapsel f	blasting cap
Sprengkapselzange f, Würgezange f, Anwürgzange	cap crimper
Sprengladung f	(explosive) charge, bursting ~
Sprengloch n, Schußloch n, Sprengbohrloch	shot-hole, blast-hole
Sprenglochbohrgerät n, Sprenglochbohrmaschine f	blast-hole drill
Sprengluft f, flüssige Luft f	liquid air
Sprengmeister m [früher: Schießmeister]	blasting technician; blaster (US)
Sprengmittel n, siehe: Sprengstoff m	
Sprengöl n, siehe: Nitroglyzerin n	
Sprengpulver n, siehe: Schwarzpulver n	
Sprengschnur f, siehe: Knallzündschnur	
(Spreng)Schuß m	shot
Sprengstoff m, Sprengmittel n	blasting explosive, ~ agent
Sprengstoffmagazin n	explosives magazine
Sprengtrupp m, Sprengkolonne f	firing crew
Sprengung f	explosive blast
Sprengzünder m, elektrischer Momentzünder mit Sprengkapsel f	electric blasting cap, instantaneous cap
Stückung f	fragmentation
Tetryl n	tetryl
Trinitrotoluol n	trinitrotoluene, TNT
Tunnelsprengstoff m	tunnel(l)ing blasting explosive
Unterwasser-Sprenggelatine f	submarine blasting gelatine
Unterwassersprengung f	submarine (or underwater, or subaqueous) blasting
Unterwasserzünder m	submarine detonator
vorgekesseltes Loch n	sprung bore-hole
Vorkesseln n, siehe: Kesselschießen n	
wasserdichte Zündschnur f, siehe: Guttaperchazündschnur f	
Würgezange f, siehe: Sprengkapselzange	
Zeitzünder m	delay detonator
Zeitzündung f	delay action firing
Zünderkopf m	fuse-head
Zündkabel n, Schießkabel	shot-firing cable
Zündmaschine f	(multi-shot) exploder, blasting machine
Zündsatz m	detonating charge, priming compound, primer
Zündschnur f	fuse
Zündschnur f zum Knäpperschießen n [sie brennt 30 cm/sec mit äußerer Flamme]	QUARRYCORD [Trademark]
Zündstrom m	firing current

1. Schießen; 2. Sprengen — Schlackensplittverteilung

Zündung f der Teilladungen fpl mit Verzögerungsintervallen mpl
   decking, deck initiation

Zweitsprengung mit Bohrlochladung f, siehe: Nachknäppern n

Schießplatz m = gunnery base
Schiffahrtbefeuerung f = navigational lightening
Schiffbarkeit f = navigability
Schifferknoten m, siehe: Kreuzknoten
(Schiffs)|Aufschleppe f = (maritime) slipway, slipway for repairs to ships, repairing slipway
~bewuchs m [*Anwuchs m von Balaniden fpl usw.*] = marine fouling

~boden-Farbe f, siehe: anwuchsverhindernde Schiffsanstrichfarbe
~elevator m, siehe: Getreideelevator
~funkmeßgerät n = navigational radar unit
~funkverkehr m = wireless marine navigation
~haltevorrichtung f, Anlegevorrichtung = mooring (device)

Schiffshebeanlage f

Kammerschleuse f
   barge lift
   chamber (or lift) navigation (or inland) lock

(Schiffs)Hebewerk n
   non-lock type barge lift

(Schiffs)Hebewerk für Naßförderung f, Trogschleuse f
   trough lift

(Schiffs)Hebewerk für Trockenförderung
   non-lock type platform barge lift

(Schiffs)Hebewerk mit Gegengewichten npl
   non-lock type counterweight barge lift

Schwimmer(schiffs)hebewerk
   non-lock type float barge lift

lotrechtes (Schiffs)Hebewerk
   non-lock type vertical barge lift

Schiffs|kette f = ship-chain
~tunnel = canal tunnel
(~)Werft f = dockyard, shipbuilding ~
~winde f = ship winch
~wurm m, Bohrwurm = boring worm
Schiftsparren m, Schifter m, Gratstichbalken m = jack rafter
Schiftung f; siehe unter „Holzverbindung f"
Schild|(beton)verteiler m; siehe unter „Beton(decken)verteiler m"
~bogen m, Blendbogen, Nischenbogen, Bogenblende f = shallow arch
Schilf n, Rohr n = reed
~glaserz n (Min.) = freieslebenite
Schill m = oyster shells
Schillerspat m, Bastit m (Min.) = schillerspar, bastite

Schindel f = shingle, shide (Brit.)
Schippe f, Schaufel f, Handschaufel = hand shovel, digging ~
Schipper m, Schüpper m = hand shovel(l)er, hand shovel worker
Schlabberventil n, Überströmventil = overflow valve
Schlachthofhängebahn f = meat conveyor
Schlacken|basalt m = scoriaceous basalt
~halde f = slag pile, ~ stockpile
~mehl n, siehe: Thomasmehl
~ofen m = slag furnace
~pflasterstein m = slag (paving) sett
~puddeln n = pig boiling
~sand m, siehe: granulierte Hochofenschlacke f
~splittverteilung f [*Straße f*] = slagging (Brit.)

Schlacken|stein *m*, Schlackenziegel(stein) *m* = slag brick
~tragschicht *f*, Schlackentragdecke *f* = slag base (course)
~weg *m* = slag track
~wolle *f*, Hochofen~ [*durch hochgespannten Dampf oder in anderer Art verblasene schmelzflüssige, kieselsäurereiche Hochofenschlacke*] = slag wool, mineral ~
~zement *m*; siehe unter „Zement"
~zinn *n* = tin extracted from slag, prillion
Schlafdeich *m* [*Deich, der zwecklos geworden ist*] = safety dike
schlaff bewehrter Teil *m*, ~ bewehrtes ~ *n* = singly reinforced member
schlaffe Bewehrung *f*, ~ Armierung, nichtgespannte ~ = untensioned bar reinforcement, non-prestressed ~
Schlaffseil|-Kabelbagger *m*; siehe unter „Seilförderanlage *f*"
~-Kabelschrapper *m*; siehe unter „Seilförderanlage *f*"
Schlaf|krankheit *f* = sleeping sickness
~-Stadtrandsiedlung *f* = dormitory suburb
~wagen *m* = sleeping car
Schlag *m* [*Drahtseil n*] = lay
schlagartige Zerkleinerung *f*, Schlagzerkleinerung = impact reduction
Schlag|biegeprobe *f* = impact bending test
~bohle *f*, siehe: Stampfbohle
~bohlenfertiger *m*, Stampfbohlenfertiger, Stampfbalkenfertiger = tamping beam finisher, tamper finisher
~bohren *n*, Schlagbohrung *f*, Schlagbohrverfahren *n*, Meißelung *f* = percussive drilling, percussion ~
~bohrmaschine *f* = percussion drilling machine
~bohrmeißel *m*; siehe unter „Bohrmeißel"
~bohrverfahren *n*, siehe: Schlagbohren *n*
~brecher *m* = jaw crusher with inclined crushing chamber
~eisen *n* [*Steinmetzwerkzeug n*] = broad chisel
schlagendes Wetter *n*, siehe: Schlagwetter
Schlag|festigkeit *f*, Stoßwiderstand *m*, Zähigkeit *f* [*Widerstand eines Gesteins gegen Bruch unter Einwirkung von Stößen*] = resistance to impact

~gleisstopfer *m*, Schlagschotterstopfer = percussion-type tie tamper (US); ~ track ~ (Brit.)
~hammer *m* = percussion hammer, ~ breaker
~kolben *m* [*Druckluftthammer m*] = percussion piston
~leiste *f* [*Prallbrecher m*] = impeller bar
~leiste *f*, Beistoß *m* [*Tischlerei f*] = rabbet ledge
~loch *n* = pothole
~lochbildung *f* = potholing
~lochflickgerät *n*, Schlaglochflicker *m* = pot-hole patcher, ~ patching machine
~nietmaschine *f* = percussion riveting machine
~nietung *f*, Schlagnieten *n* = percussion riveting
~patrone *f*; siehe unter „1. Schießen *n*; 2. Sprengen *n*"
~prüfungswert *m* [*Straßenbaugestein n*] = aggregate impact value
~regen *m* = pelting rain, driving ~
~schatten *m* = cast shadow, deep ~
~schere *f*, Rutschschere = (drilling) jars
~schotter *m*, Steinschlag *m* = broken stone, ~ rock
~schotterstopfen *n*, siehe: Schlaggleisstopfen
~sonde *f*, siehe: Rammsonde
~spülbohren *n*, Spülbohrung *f* mit Schnellschlag *m* = percussive hollow rod drilling
~versuch *m*, Stoßversuch = impact test
~walze *f*, Rotor *m* [*Prallbrecher m*] = impeller
~wasser *n* = bilge water
~weite *f*, Funken~, Entladeweite, Funkenstrecke *f* = sparking distance, striking ~, spark gap
~wetter *n*, schlagendes Wetter = explosive atmosphere, fire-damp, weatherdamp; filty (Brit.)
~zahl *f* = number of blows
~zerkleinerung *f*, schlagartige Zerkleinerung = impact reduction
~zündung *f* = percussion priming
Schlamm *m* [*Abwasserwesen n*] = sludge
~; siehe unter „Feinschluff *m*"

Schlamm [*Naßmahlung f*] = slurry [*cement manufacture*]; pulp [*ore dressing*]
~**ablaßventil** n = sludge valve
~**anfall** m = amount of sludge produced
Schlämmapparat m, siehe: Entschlämmungsapparat
Schlamm|(aus)faulung f, anaerober Abbau m = sludge digestion
~**auslaugung** f = elutriation of sludge
~**ausräumer** m = sludge scraper
~**brunnen** m = sludge well
Schlämmbüchse f, siehe: Klappsonde f
~ **mit Klappventil** n = disc valve bailer
~ ~ **Stoßventil** n = dart valve bailer
Schlämmbüchsenprobe f = bailer sample
Schlämme f, Schlempe f, Schlämpe f = slurry, grout
~ **mit emulgiertem Bindemittel** n = bitumen emulsion slurry (Brit.); asphalt ~ ~ (US)
~**mischer** m, Schlempemischer, Schlämpemischer = slurry mixer, grout ~
Schlämmeinrichtung f = elutriator
Schlamm|entwässerung f = dewatering of sludge
~**erhitzer** m, Zement~ = (cement) slurry heater
~**faulraum** m; siehe unter „Abwasserwesen n"
~**faulung** f, Schlammausfaulung, anaerober Abbau m = sludge digestion
~**fladen** m = flake of sludge
~**index** m = sludge index
~**inhibitor** m = detergent, dispersant, antiflocculant
~**kipper(-Muldenwagen)** m = rocker dump car for pasty materials
Schlämm|korn n [*nach Dücker (1948) kleiner als 0,06 mm*] = silt and clay
~**kreide** f, Schlemmkreide = prepared chalk, precipitated ~, whiting
Schlamm|kuchen m = sludge cake
~**leitung** f = discharge pipe [*hydraulic fill*]
~**presse** f = sludge press
~**pumpe** f = sludge pump
~**saugtank** m = mud suction tank
~**schleuder** f = sludge centrifuge
~**stöpsel** m = sludge plug
~**strom** m (Geol.) = mud flow

~**sumpf** m = sludge sump
~**teich** m = sludge lagoon
(~)**Trockenbeet** n = sludge bed, ~ drying ~, ~ draining ~
~**umwälzung** f = sludge stirring
Schlämmung f, Schlämmtrennung f = elutriation
Schlamm|ventil n = sludge valve
~**verbrennung** f = incineration of sludge
Schlämmverfahren n **zur Herstellung von Weichpreßziegeln** = slurry process for making soft-mud brick
Schlamm|verwertung f = utilization of sludge
~**wasser** n = sludge liquor
~**wasser** n [*Eindickung f*] = supernatant (sludge)
Schlämpe f, siehe: Schlämme f
Schlangenholz n, Letterholz = snake wood, letter ~, speckled ~
Schlankheitsgrad m, Schlankheitsverhältnis n [*Beziehung zwischen Stablänge I und Trägheitsmoment J*] = slenderness ratio, ratio of slenderness
Schlauch m, elastische Leitung f = hose, flexible tube
~, siehe: Luftreifen~
~**binder** m = hose clamp
~**boot** n = pneumatic boat, ~ raft, rubber dinghy, inflatable boat
~**filter** m, n, siehe: Trockenfilter
~**haspel** m, f = hose reel
~**leitung** f = hose line
schlauchloser Reifen m = tubeless tire (US); ~ tyre (Brit.)
Schlauch|öler m = hose oiler
~**verschraubung** f = hose coupling
~**welle** f, Biegewelle = hose shaft, flexible ~
schlechte Luft f, verbrauchte ~ = vitiated air
schlechter Fels m, schlechtes (Fels)Gestein n = poor rock
Schlechtwetter n = bad weather, adverse ~, inclement ~
~**-Start- und Landebahn** f; siehe unter „Flugplatz m"
Schleierdichtung f, Injektionsschleier m, Schleierverpressung = grout curtain
Schleife f = loop

schleifenförmiger Rundstahlanker m = anchor(ing) loop of reinforcing steel
Schleif|kontakt m = sliding contact
~**maschine** f **mit Biegewelle** f = flexible shaft grinding machine
~**mittel** n = abradant, abrasive
~**ring** m = slip-ring, collector ring
~**ringläufer** m = slip-ring rotor
~**ringläufer(motor)** m = slip-ring induction motor
~**rohstoff** m = abrasive material
~**sand** m = cutting sand
~**scheibe** f [*Einschleifen* n *von Betonfugen* fpl] = abrasive blade
~**stein** m = grindstone
~**wirkung** f, siehe: Ab~
Schlemmkreide f, siehe: Schlämmkreide
Schlempe f, **Schlämpe** f, **Schlämme** f = grout, slurry
~**mischer** m, Schlämpemischer, Schlämmemischer = grout mixer, slurry ~
Schlepp|anzeige(r)dämpfer m = drag dampening device
~**blech** n [*Brücke* f] = cover plate
~**bürstenwalze** f, siehe: Anhängebürstenwalze
Schleppe f, siehe: Planierschleppe
Schleppen n, **Schlepperei** f [*Kähne mpl*] = towage
Schlepper m, Trecker m, Traktor m = (towing) tractor
~ [*Schiff n; in Österreich: Remorqueur m*] = tug(boat), towboat
~ **mit hydraulischer Greifervorrichtung** f = hydro-clam
~ ~ **Tieflöffel(vorrichtung)** m, (f) = tractor-operated trench hoe
~**(auf)lader** m = tractor-loader
~-**Drehkran** m, Traktor-Drehkran, Trecker-Drehkran, Traktoren-Drehkran, Schlepperkran, Treckerkran, Traktor(en)kran = tractor (revolving) crane
~-**Eimerkettenaufzug** m, Trecker-Eimerkettenaufzug, Traktor-Eimerkettenaufzug, Schlepper-Becherwerk n, Traktor(en)-Becherwerk, Trecker-Becherwerk = tractor elevator
~**führer** m, Treckerführer, Traktorführer = tractor operator
~-**Grabenbagger** m, Trecker-Grabenbagger, Traktor(en)-Grabenbagger = tractor-mounted trench excavator
~**lader** m, Schlepperauflader = tractor-loader
~**motor** m = tractor engine
~**(-Schaufel)lader** m, Trecker(-Schaufel)-lader, Traktor(en)(-Schaufel)lader = tractor-bucket machine
~**seilwinde** f, Schleppertrommelseilwinde, Traktoren(trommel)seilwinde = tractor (cable, or rope) winch
~-**Tieflöffel(bagger)** m = tractor backhoe
Schlepp|kabel n = trailing cable
~**kraft** f [*Fluß m*] = transporting power
~**kurve** f = minimum turning radius
~**löffel** m, siehe: Schleppschaufel f
~**löffelbagger** m, siehe: Schürfkübelbagger
~**lok(omotive)** f; siehe unter „Feldbahnanlage f"
~**netzwinde** f = trawling winch
Schleppflug m = drag plough (Brit.)/plow (US)
Schleppprobe f = elutriation test
Schleppschaufel f, Schlepplöffel m, Eimerseilkübel m, Zugkübel, Eimer m, Schürfkübel, Schleppschaufelkübel = drag(line) bucket, ~ scoop
~**bagger** m, siehe: Schürfkübelbagger m

Schleppschaufel-Schreitbagger m, Eimerseil-Schreitbagger, **Fabrikat MARION POWER SHOVEL COMPANY, MARION, OHIO, USA** | walking dragline, walker
Auslegereinziehmotor m | boom hoist motor (US); jib ~ ~ (Brit.)
Auslegerneigung f | boom angle (US); jib angle (Brit.)
Auslegerseil n | boom hoist cable (US); jib ~ ~ (Brit.)
Ausschüttalbmesser m | dumping radius
Ausschütthöhe f | dumping height

Schleppschaufel-Schreitbagger — Schleudern

Außendurchmesser m	nominal diameter
Eimer-Auskippmaß n	bucket dumping height
Hubmotor m	hoist motor
Hubseil n	hoist cable
Hubtrommel f	hoist drum
kreisförmige Plattform f, Exzenterscheibe f	base, tub
Kurbel- und Gelenk-Schreitausrüstung f (oder -Schreitwerk n)	triangular type travel(l)ing (or walking) mechanism
Maß n der Eimeraufhängung f	bucket carrying clearance
maximaler Seilzug m	maximum pull
rechnerische Tragfläche f	effective bearing area
Rollenstützkreis m	live roller circle
Schreitschuh m	walking (traction) shoe
Schreitwelle f	walking shaft
Schritt m	walking step
Schürfmotor m	drag motor
Schürfseil n	drag cable
Schürfseiltrommel f	drag drum
Schürftiefe f	digging depth
Schwenkmotor m	swing motor
seitlich auspendeln	to tilt sidewise [*shoe*]
Tragrolle f	roller
Trommeldurchmesser m	pitch diameter of drum
Vorderkante f [*Exzenterscheibe f*]	leading edge [*base*]
vor- und rückwärts in der Schreitrichtung f auspendeln	to tilt sidewise [*shoe*]
Wurfweite f des Eimers m	bucket throw

Schlepp|schrapper m; siehe unter „Seilförderanlage f"

~schrapperanlage f **mit 3-Seil-Anordnung** f; siehe unter „Seilförderanlage f"

~seilwinde f, Schlepptrommelseilwinde = towing (cable, or rope) winch

~tau n = hauling rope, drag ~

~-Verdichter m, Anhänge-Verdichter = towed compaction roller

~versuch m [*Straßengriffigkeit f*] = trailer-type method

~verteiler m **auf Kufen** fpl = skid-mounted towed-type spreader

~verteiler m **für Schotter** m, **Teer- und Asphaltbeton** m, ~ für bituminöse Stoffe, Schotter und Splitt m = towed paver (type) aggregate spreader, pull (-type) bituminous concrete and aggregate spreader, finish spreader

~-Vibrationswalze f; siehe unter „Walze"

~winde f = towing winch

~zug m, Schiffszug = train of barges

schlesischer grauer Marmor m = Silesian grey marble

~ Verband m = Silesian bond

Schleuder|band n, Wurf-Transporteur m = jet conveyor

~betonform f = centrifugally cast concrete mo(u)ld

~betonmast m, Betonschleudermast = centrifugally cast concrete mast

~betonrohr n, Betonschleuderrohr = centrifugally cast concrete pipe, spun concrete pipe

~beton-Rohrbalkenträger m = tubular beam of centrifugally cast concrete

~gebläse n = centrifugal blower

~gußrohr n = spun cast-iron pipe

~maschine f, siehe: Schleudervorrichtung f

Schleudern n [*Herstellung f von Betonrohren npl*] = spinning [*manufacture of concrete pipes*]

Schleudersichter m — centrifugal air separator

Schleudersichter m — centrifugal air separator
Streuteller m — distributor plate, distributing plate, lower plate
Mahlgut n — material
Mehl n — finished product
Grieß m — tailings
Ventilator m — fan
Strömungsgeschwindigkeit f — velocity of the air
Einlauftrichter m — feed opening
Kegelräderpaar n — bevel gearing
Ablaufschurre f — tailings spout
Gehäuse n — outer shell, outer casing
Auslauf m — outlet

Schleudervorrichtung f, Schleudermaschine f [*Betonrohrherstellung* f] = spinning unit

Schleuse f [*dieser Begriff umfaßt im Deutschen in weitestem Sinne alle beweglichen Stauvorrichtungen* fpl] = 1. lock; 2. sluice, gate

Schleusen|tor n; siehe unter „Binnenschiffahrtschleuse f"

~**treppe** f; siehe unter „Binnenschiffahrtschleuse f"

Schleuse f **und Kraftwerk** n = station and lock unit

Schlicht|hammer m = smoothing hammer

~**hobel** m, Glatthobel = smooth(ing) plane

Schlick m, schlickiger Ton m, Gezeitenablagerung f, Meer(es)schlamm m = clay containing silt

Schlierenbildung f = streak formation

Schließ|kopf m [*Niet* m] = snap head

~**kraft** f [*Zweischalengreifkorb* m] = closing power [*clamshell bucket*]

~**seil** n = closing rope

~**trommel** f = grab closing drum

Schlingern n [*Eisenbahnzug* m] = train sway, lurching, side sway

Schlitten m = slide, sled runner

~**winde** f, Schlittenhebebock m = sliding jack, traversing ~

Schlitzschweißung f = slot welding

Schloß|eisen n; siehe unter „Spundwand f"

~**reibung** f [*Stahlspundwand* f] = interlock friction

~**schraube** f = carriage bolt

Schlot m; siehe unter „Vulkan m"

Schlotte f (Geol.) = sink

Schlucht f; [*oberdeutsch: Schluft* f] = gorge

Schluchten(stau)mauer f = gorge dam

Schluff m, feinster Staubsand m [*nach Atterberg, Terzaghi, DIN 4022, Fischer und Udluft, Gallwitz, Grengg 0,02 bis 0,002 mm*] = silt, rock flour [*British Standards Institution 0.06—0.002; Massachusetts Institute of Technology 0.06 to 0.002 mm; United States Public Road Administration 0.05—0.005; International Society of Soil Science 0.02—0.002 mm*]

~**ablagerung** f = silt deposition

~**einpreßverfahren** n = silt injection method

schluffig = silty

Schluffkörnung f, Schluffanteil m, Schluff-Komponente f = silt fraction

Schlüpfrigkeit f, siehe: Glätte f

schlüsselfertig = key ready

Schluß|abnahme f = final acceptance

~**übergang** m [*Fertiger, Walze*] = finishing pass

schmale Kuppelbogensperre f **mit waag- und senkrechter Krümmung** f; siehe unter „Talsperre f"

Schmalspur f = narrow ga(u)ge

~**-Dampflok(omotive)** f **mit Ölfeuerung** f = oil-fired metre-ga(u)ge locomotive

~**gleis** n; siehe unter „Feldbahnanlage f"

Schmelz|barkeit f = fusibility

~**bohren** n, siehe: Feuerstrahlbohren

Schmelz|fluß *m* (Geol.), siehe: Magma *n*
~kessel *m*, (Bindemittel)Kocher *m* = heater, heating kettle, melting tank; boiler [*deprecated*]
~kessel *m* **für Fugenvergußmassen** *fpl*, Vergußmasseofen *m* = heating tank for melting joint sealing compounds, melting furnace (or melter) for joint sealers, kettle for heating joint filler, (joint) compound-melting furnace, compound heater
Schmelz|ofen *m* = smelting furnace
~pfropfen *m*, Schmelzstöpsel *m* = fusible plug
~punkt *m*, Erweichungspunkt = softening point, fusion ~, melting ~
~schweißgüte *f*, Schmelzschweißqualität *f* = fusion welding quality
~stein (Min.) = mizzonite, dipyre, dipyrite
~wasser *n*; siehe unter „Gletscher *m*"
~wasserbach *m* = superglacial stream
~zeit *f* [*Glas n*] = founding time
schmiedbarer Eisenguß *m*, siehe: Temperguß
Schmiede|eisen *n* = forging grade steel
~herd *m* = blacksmith's forge
Schmiege *f*, Stellwinkel *m*, Schrägmaß *n* = bevel protractor
schmiegsam, nicht-starr = flexible, non rigid
Schmierdienst *m* = lubricating service
Schmierer *m* = oiler
Schmier|fett *n* = lubricating grease; petroleum ~ (US)
~fettverdickungsmittel *n* = lubricating grease thickener
~film *m* [*Straße f*] = slippery film
~mittel *n* = lubricant
~öl *n* = lubricating oil, lube (oil)
~öl *n* **für bewegliche Maschinenteile** *mpl* = machine(ry) oil
~plan *m* = lubrication plan
~stelle *f* = lubrication point

~tabelle *f* = lubrication chart
Schmirgelleinwand *f* [*in Österreich und Bayern*], Schmergelleinwand *f* [*in Preußen*] = emery cloth
Schmutzwasser *n*; siehe unter „Abwasserwesen *n*"
~(abfang)sammler *m*; siehe unter „Abwasserwesen *n*"
~kanal *m*; siehe unter „Abwasserwesen *n*"
Schnappring *m* = sealing ring
Schnecke *f*, Schneckengang *m* = worm, screw, continuous helical blade, screw flight
Schnecken|(an)trieb *m* = worm drive
~aufgeber *m*, siehe: Schneckenspeiser *m*
~beschickung *f* = worm feed, screw ~
~(beton)verteiler *m* **mit Glättelement** *n*; siehe unter „Beton(decken)verteiler"
~bohrer *m*, Schneidbohrer [*Bodenuntersuchung f*] = worm auger, screw type soil auger
~förderer *m*, Förderschnecke *f*, Transportschnecke = worm (or screw) conveyor, conveyor screw, Archimedean screw ~
~getriebe *n* = worm gear(ing)
~gewölbe *n* = helical barrel vault
~klassierer *m* = classifier using screw principle
~mischer *m* **mit kontinuierlicher Wirkung** *f* = continuous (or constant-flow) screw-type mixer
~speiser *m* Schneckenaufgeber *m*, Speiseschnecke *f*, Beschickungsschnecke *f*, Zubringerschnecke = feed screw, screw feeder
~trieb *m*, siehe: Schneckenantrieb
~trog *m* = worm conveyor trough
~verteiler *m*, siehe: (Beton)Schneckenverteiler *m*
~wäsche *f*, siehe: Sandschnecke *f*
~welle *f* = worm conveyor shaft
~wendegetriebe *n* = worm reversing gear
~winde *f* = worm geared winch

Schneebeseitigungsmaschinen *fpl*, Schneeentfernungsgeräte *npl* [*diese Begriffe umfassen sowohl „Schneeräummaschinen" als auch „Schneepflüge"*]
Fräsmesser *n*

snow clearing machinery, ~ ~ equipment' snow-handling machinery (or equipment)

cutting blade, rotary cutter

Schneebeseitigungsmaschinen — Schneezaun

Hartschnee(räum)maschine *f*	hard snow remover
LINNHOFF-ROLBA-Schneefrässchleuder *f*, Hersteller: EDUARD LINNHOFF MASCHINENFABRIK, BERLIN-TEMPELHOF und NORTHEIM (HAN.)	Linnhoff-Rolba rotary snow plough
Naßschnee *m*	wet snow
ROLBA-Kleinfrässchleuder *f*, Kleinschleuder SNOW-BOY	pedestrian-operated rotary snow plough (Brit.)/plow (US) type SNOW-BOY
Schild(schnee)pflug *m*, Schneepflug mit Frontschar, Einseitenräumer *m*, einseitiger Pflug *m*, Seitenpflug, Einseitenpflug, Schneeräumer-Vorbauschild *n*, Vorbau-Räumschild	blade-type (or straight-blade) snow plough (Brit.)/plow (US), snow plough (Brit.)/plow (US) with angling blade, (reversible) side plough
Schneeauflader *m*	snow loader
Schneebeseitigung *f*, Schneeräumung *f*	snow clearing, ~ removal
Schneebeseitigung *f* von Hand	snow clearance by manual labour
Schneehaufen *m*, Schneewall *m*	snow bank, ~ pile
(Schnee-)Keilpflug *m*, V-Pflug	V-type snow plough (Brit.); ~ ~ plow (US)
(Schnee)Räummaschine *f*	ejecting snow remover
Schneeschleuder *f*	rotary (type) snow plough (Brit.)/plow (US), snow blowing machine, blower-type snow plough (Brit.)/plow (US)
Schnell-Schneekeilpflug *m* an LKW *m* angebaut	speed plough (Brit.); ~ plow (US) [*not equipped with wings*]
schwerer (Schnee)Keilpflug *m* an LKW angebaut	heavy-duty plow (US)/plough (Brit.) [*with and without wings*]
Verdrängungspflug *m*, Schiebepflug	displacement type plow, push plow (US); ~ ~ plough, push plough (Brit.)
verschneite Straße *f*	snow-blocked road
Wurfrad *n*	ejecting rotor
Wurfweite *f*	ejecting distance

Schnee|gestöber *n*, Schneetreiben *n* = driving snow, blowing ~	~**schmelze** *f* = snow melt
~**grenze** *f*, Schneelinie *f* = snow-line	~**schuhläufer-Aufzug** *m*, Ski(schlepp)-lift *m* = ski-hoist
~**kette** *f*, siehe: Gleitschutzkette	~**sturm** *m* = snow storm
~**last** *f*, Schneebelastung *f* = snow load	~**treiben** *n*, siehe: Schneegestöber *n*
~**lawine** *f* = snow-avalanche, snowslide	~**wehe** *f*, Schneeverwehung *f* = snow drift
~**linie** *f*, Schneegrenze *f* = snow-line	

Schneezaun *m*	**snow fence**
Leit-~	leading ~ ~
Rückhalte-~	collecting ~ ~
Horizontallattenzaun	scissors' ~ ~
Vertikallattenzaun	vertical slatted ~
Wirbelbereich *m*	eddy region
Schneezaun aus Papierbahnen *fpl*	paper snow fence

chneidbohrer — Schotteraufbereitungsanlage

Schneid|bohrer *m*, siehe: Schneckenbohrer

~brenner *m* = cutting blow pipe (Brit.); cutting torch, flame cutter (US)

Schneide *f*, Schneidkante *f* = cutting edge

~; siehe unter „Bohrmeißel *m*"

Schneidenlast *f*, Linienlast, Streckenlast = collinear load, line ~

Schneid|flüssigkeit *f* = cutting fluid

~kluppenkörper *m*, Kluppe *f* = stock

~kopf *m* = cutting head

~kopf(saug)bagger *m*; siehe unter „Naßbagger"

~öl *n* = cutting oil

Schnell|(ab)binden *f* = flash setting

~bahnsystem *n* = rapid transit system

~bauaufzug *m* = high-speed building hoist, ~ builders' ~

~bemessung *f*, Schnelldimensionierung = rapid design method

schnellfahrender Autobagger *m*; siehe unter „Autobagger *m*"

Schnell|fahrwerk *n* = speed-mobile carriage

~fahrzeug *n* = fast vehicle

~gang *m* = speed gear

~mischer *m* = speedline mixer

~montagekran *m* = rapid erection crane

~prüfverfahren *n* = rapid control test

~rohrkupplung *f* = quick-acting coupling

~schlagbrecher *m* = rapid action jaw crusher with inclined crushing chamber

(~schlag-)Rammhammer *m*, Schnellschlagbär *m* = rapid-stroke hammer

~schlußventil *n* = rapid-closing valve, quick-closing ~, quick-close ~

~sieb *n* = rapid vibratory motion screen

~spur *f* [*Autobahn f*] = high-speed lane

~transport-(Bindemittel)kocher *m*, Schnelltransport-Schmelzkessel *m*, Fabrikat MAX PIETSCH, HANNOVER, DEUTSCHLAND = single-axle trailer tar and bitumen (Brit.)/ asphalt (US) heater (or heating kettle, or melting tank)

~transport-Spritzmaschine *f* = speedline spraying outfit

~-Triebwagen *m* = rapid transit self-propel(l)ed railcar

~verkehr *m* [*öffentlicher Massenverkehr*] = rapid transit

Schnellverkehrs|(auto)bus *m*, Schnellverkehrsomnibus = express bus

~straße *f* = express road, expressway, express highway

~straße *f* **ohne Zufahrten** *fpl* **zu anliegendem Grundbesitz** *m* = freeway

~strecke *f* [*Bahn f*] = highspeed track

~untergrundbahn *f* = rapid transit subway

Schnell|verschluß *m* [*Rohrleitung f*] = quick-acting coupling

~-Zeitsprengzünder *m*; siehe unter „1. Schießen *n*; 2. Sprengen *n*"

Schnitt *m* = section

~ *m*, Fraktion *f* = cut

~holz *n* = sawn timber

~punkt *m* = intersecting point, point of intersection

~winkel *m* = intersecting angle

~zeichnung *f* = sectional drawing

~ziegel *m*, siehe: Maschinenziegel

Schnitzler *m* = shredder

Schnur|gerüst *n*, siehe: Visiergerüst

~lot *n*, Senkblei *n*, Bleilot *n* = plumb-bob, plummet

schockende Rüttelung *f* [*Rüttelstampfmaschine f*] = jolting

Schocktisch *m* = jolting table

Schollen|eis *n* = floe ice

~lava *f*; siehe unter „Vulkan *m*"

Schoner *m* = schooner

Schönwetter *n* = fair weather, fine ~

~periode *f* = spell of fine weather

Schöpf|becher *m* [*Waschmaschine f*] = dewatering bucket, dredging ~

~becher *m* = scoop

~becherwerk *n*, siehe: Teilbecherwerk

~kelle *f*, Schöpfgefäß *n*; [*oberdeutsch: Schapf m, Schapfe f*] = scoop

~rad *n*, Becherrad [*Waschmaschine f*] = dewatering wheel, dredging ~

Schößling *m* = sapling

Schott *n*, Schotte *f* = bulkhead

~blech *n* [*Kastenträger m*] = transverse diaphragm

Schotter *m* (Geol.); siehe unter „Grobkies *m*"

~ *m*, siehe: Straßen(bau)schotter

~aufbereitungsanlage *f* = rock plant, stone-crushing plant

Schotterbrecher *m*, siehe: Grobbrecher
Schotterdecke *f*, Makadamdecke = macadam surfacing, crushed-rock ~
~ *f* **mit Oberflächenbehandlung** *f* = surface-treated waterbound macadam
Schotter|entlader *m* = ballast unloader
~**gabel** *f*, Stein(schlag)gabel *f* = stone (picker) fork
~**kegel** *m* (Geol.) = alluvial cone
~**-Räummaschine** *f* [*Eisenbahnbau m*] = cribling machine
~**sand** *m*, siehe: Grobsand
~**stopfer** *m*, siehe: Gleisstopfer
~**straße** *f* = metalled road (Brit.); crushed-rock ~, crushed-stone ~
~**tragschicht** *f* = (crushed-stone) macadam base, crushed-rock base, stone macadam type base, stone base (course)
~**- und Splittverteiler** *m*, Schotterverteiler, Makadam-Ausleger *m* = stone spreader, aggregate ~, base paver
~**unterbau** *m* = broken stone bottoming (Brit.); aggregate base (course) (US); brocken stone foundation, macadam foundation
~**werk** *n* = commercial stone-crushing plant
schraffieren = to hatch
schraffiert = hatched
Schräg|aufzug *m* = incline hoist, slope ~
~**aufzugwinde** *f* = incline hoist winch, slope ~ ~
~**bandförderung** *f*; siehe unter „Bandförderer *m*"
~**becherwerk** *n* = inclined bucket elevator
~**bildkamera** *f* = oblique (mapping) camera
~**bodenwagen** *m* = gable bottom car
~**brett** *n* = angle board
~**elevator** *m* = inclined bucket conveyor
Schragen *m*, Sägebock *m* = sawing jack
schräge Zugspannung *f* = diagonal tension
schräges Hakenblatt *n* = oblique scarf
Schräg|maß *n*, siehe: Schmiege *f*
~**pfahl** *m* = raker, batter pile
~**pfahljoch** *n* = tower bent
~**schwerkraftelevator** *m*, Schrägschwerkraftbecherwerk *n* = inclined continuous bucket elevator

~**spreize** *f* = raking shore
~**stempel** *m* = raking prop
Schrägungswinkel *m* = angle of skew
Schräg|verband *m*, Verschwerterung *f* = diagonal bracing
~**verzahnung** *f*, Schraubenverzahnung = helical gearing, helical gear-wheels
~**walzwerk** *n* = oblique rolling mill
~**wand** *f* = battered wall, battering ~
~**wurfsieb** *n* = (mechanical) shaking screen
~**zahnrad** *n*, Schraubenrad *n*, Zahnrad *n* mit Schrägverzahnung *f* = helical gear wheel
~**zugangstollen** *m* = sloping adit
Schräm|kette *f* = cutter chain
~**(vortriebs)maschine** *f*, Fräsvortriebsmaschine = channel(l)ing machine
Schrammbord *n*, siehe: Bordschwelle *f*
Schramme *f* (Geol.) = scar
Schranke *f* = gate
Schränk|eisen *n* = saw set
~**maschine** *f* = saw setting machine
Schrapper *m* [*allgemeiner Ausdruck*] = scraper
~ **mit gummibereiftem Einachs-Traktor** *m*; siehe unter „Radschrapper *m*"
~**anlage** *f*; s. unter „Seilförderanlage *f*"
~**schaufel** *f*, siehe: Räumschaufel
~**wagen** *m*; siehe unter „Radschrapper *m*"
Schrapplader *m* **mit Ausleger** *m*, Fabrikat A.G. für BERGBAU und HÜTTENBEDARF, SALZGITTER, DEUTSCHLAND = boom-type (US)/jib-type (Brit.) cable excavator and loader
Schrauben|anker *m* = mooring screw
~**bolzen** *m* = bolt
~**feder** *f* = helical spring
~**gewinde** *n* = screw thread
~**(hebe)bock** *m*, Schraubenwinde *f*, Schraubenspindel *f*, Spindel = screw jack, jack(ing) screw
~**kopf** *m* = screw head
~**loch** *n* = screw hole
~**mutter** *f*, Mutter = (bolt) nut, screw ~
~**rad** *n*, siehe: Schrägzahnrad
~**schlepper** *m* = screw (propelled) tug
~**schneidwerkzeug** *n* = stock and die
~**spindel** *f*, siehe: Schrauben(hebe)bock *m*

Schraubenverbindung — Schürfkübelbagger

Schrauben|verbindung f, geschraubte Verbindung = bolted connection, ~ joint
~verzahnung f, siehe: Schrägverzahnung
~winde f, siehe: Schrauben(hebe)bock m
~zieher m **mit Holzgriff** m = cabinet screw driver
Schraub|rohrmuffe f = screwed pipe joint
~stock m = bench vice
~zwinge f = screw clamp
Schreibkraft f, Schreiber m = clerk (US)
Schreitbagger m, siehe: Schleppschaufel-Schreitbagger
~ = walking excavator
Schreit|schuh m = walking shoe
~werk n, Schreitausrüstung f = walking mechanism
Schrifterz n (Min.) = sylvanite; graphic tellurium [*this term is obsolete to-day*]
schriftliche Befragungsmethode f = moving vehicle driver postal cards method
schroffes Ufer n = bluff
Schrot m, n = steel shot
~(bohr)krone f; siehe unter „Bohrmeißel m"
~bohrung f, Schrotbohren n = shot drill boring, ~ drilling
~hammer m = spalling hammer
~keil m, Steinspeidel m = spalling wedge
~krone f; siehe unter „Bohrmeißel m"
~säge f = pit saw
Schrott|händler m = metal scrap dealer
~platz m = scrap metal yard
Schrumpfen n [*unabgebundener Beton m*] = contraction
Schrumpf|erzkammer f = shrinkage stope
~grenze f; siehe unter „Konsistenzgrenzen fpl nach Atterberg"
Schrupphobel m = jack plane
Schub m = thrust [*wenn „thrust" und „shear" im gleichen Satz vorkommen, so ist thrust = Horizontalschubkomponente und „shear" = Vertikalschubkomponente; sonst sind beide gleichartig*]
~bewehrung f, Schubarmierung f = thrust reinforcement
~dübel m = shear connector
~dübel m **aus U-Profil** n = channel shear connector

~gleiskettenschlepper m, Stoßgleiskettenschlepper = crawler pushcat(erpillar), pusher tractor
~hilfegerät n; siehe unter „Radschrapper m"
~karre(n) f, (m), siehe: Schiebkarre(n) f, (m)
~karrenfahrer m = wheeler (Brit,)
~laden-Hochdruck-Azetylen-Entwickler m = band case high pressure acetylene generator
~lehre f, siehe: Schieblehre
~raupentraktor m; siehe unter „Radschrapper m"
~stange f = pitman
~stange f; Stoßbarren m [*in Österreich*] = pusher bar [*tree-dozer*]
~widerstand m, Scherwiderstand = shear(ing) resistance
Schubplatte f [*Gleiskette f*] = crawler shoe, track ~
Schulter f [*Eisenbahnbau m und Straßenbau m*] = shoulder (US)
Schulungshalle f = (seat) lecture hall
Schuppen m, Bude f = shed
~blech n = imbricated plate
Schüpper m, siehe: Schipper m
Schurf (des Wassers), siehe: Wassererosion f
Schürfbagger m, siehe: Pflugbagger
Schürf|bohrmaschine f = prospect drilling machine
~bohrung f = sampling, prospect drilling
Schürfen n, Beschürfung f, Schurf m = prospecting
~, siehe: Abziehen n
Schürf|grube f = test pit, trial ~, profile ~, prospect ~
~kasten m; siehe unter „Seilförderanlage f"
~kasten m; siehe unter „Radschrapper m"
~kübel m; siehe unter „Radschrapper m"
~kübel m **für Gabelstapler** m = fork truck scoop
~kübelbagger m, Eimerseilbagger, Schleppschaufelbagger, Schlepplöffelbagger, Zugkübelbagger = dragline (excavator); boom-dragline (US); dragline-type shovel

Schürf|(kübel)raupe *f*, Schürfkübel(gleis)kettenschlepper *m*, MENCK-(BENTELER-) Schürfraupe = scraper-dozer

~(kübel)wagen *m*; siehe unter „Radschrapper *m*"

~kübel-Zugraupe *f*, Schürfkübel-(Gleis-)Kettenfahrzeug *m* = crawler for towing wheel scrapers

~lader *m*, siehe: (Front-)Ladeschaufel *f*

~laderaupe *f*, Schürflade(gleis)kettenfahrzeug *n* = caterpillar type front-end loader, crawler ~ ~ ~

~loch *n* = trial hole, test ~

~raupe *f*, siehe: Schürfkübelraupe

~schacht *m* = prospect shaft

~schlepper *m*, siehe: Bulldozer *m*

~wagen *m*, siehe unter „Radschrapper *m*"

~wagenzug *m*; s. unter „Radschrapper *m*"

Schurre *f* = chute, spout

Schurrenauskleidung *f* = chute lining, spout ~

Schürze *f*, siehe: Dichtungsschürze

~, Scraperfalle *f* = apron

Schürzen|hub *m*, Scraperfallenhub = apron lift

~öffnung *f*; siehe unter „Radschrapper *m*"

Schüssel-Klassierer *m* = bowl classifier

Schuß *m* [*Pfahl m*, *Rohr n*] = section

~(ge)rinne *f*, (*n*) = race, spill channel

~loch *n*; siehe unter „1. Schießen *n*; 2. Sprengen *n*"

~rinne *f*, Schußgerinne *n* = spill channel, race

~schweißung *f* = shot welding

Schute *f*, siehe: Bagger ~

~ = scow (US); barge

~ mit Derrick(kran) *m* = derrick boat; ~ scow (US)

Schutt *m* = rubble, rubbish

~abladeplatz *m* = (rubbish) dump site, (~) ~ ground

Schütt|arbeiten *fpl*, siehe: Einbau *m*

~(beton)bauweise *f* = no-fines concrete construction

~betonschalung *f* = formwork for no-fines concrete

~betonwohnhochhaus *n* = no-fines (concrete) (block of) flats

Schüttel|rinne *f*, siehe: Schwingförderrinne

~rostkühler *m* = shaking grate-type cooler

~-Stangen(transport)rost *m*, Schüttelstangenaufgeber *m* = shaking (bar) grizzly, ~ ~ screen, ~ screen of bars [*mounted on eccentrics so that a forward-and-backward motion is given the entire bar assembly at a speed of 80—100 strokes per minute*]

Schutter *m*; siehe unter „Tunnelbau *m*"

Schutterung *f*, Schuttern *n* = tunnel loading, mucking

Schutterwagen *m*, Hund *m* = skip

Schüttgut *n*, Massengut = bulk material

~entladevorrichtung *f*, Schüttgutentlader *m* = bulk material unloader

~lader *m*, Schüttgutladevorrichtung *f* = bulk material loader

Schutt|halde *f*, siehe: Gehängeschutt *m*

~hang *m* = detrital slope

~haufen *m*, Trümmerhaufen = rubble pile

~kegel *m* (Geol.) = heap of débris

Schütt|körper *m* [*Erdbau m*] = fill

~lage *f*, Aufschüttungslage = fill lift

~masse *f*, siehe: (Auf)Füllboden *m*

~material *n*, siehe: (Auf)Füllboden *m*

~packe *f*, Schüttpacklage *f*, verfestigte ~ = hardcore

Schutträumung(sarbeiten) *f*, siehe: Enttrümmerung(sarbeiten) *f*

Schüttrinne *f* mit Gegengewicht *n* [*Dosiersilo m*] = counterbalanced sub-chute

Schüttsprengverfahren *n*, siehe: Moorsprengung *f*

Schüttung *f*, siehe: (Auf)Schüttung *f*

~ [*in der Schweiz und Österreich*], siehe: Sauberkeitsschicht *f*

Schüttverlust *m* = spillage

Schütz *n* [*Elektrotechnik f*] = contactor

~, siehe Schütz(e)

Schutz|anstrich *m*, Schutzüberzug *m* = protective coat(ing)

~(be)kleidung *f*, Arbeits~ = protective clothing

~blech *n* [*Fahrzeug n*] = mudguard

~brille *f* = (safety) goggles

~dach *n*, siehe: Sonnendach

Schütz(e) *n*, (*f*), Stautafel *f*, Falle *f*, Schützentafel *f* = barrier plate, leaf

Schütz(en)steuerung *f* [*Bagger m*] = contactor control

Schutzfußbekleidung — Schwarzbelageinbaumaschine

Schutz|fußbekleidung *f* = protective footwear
~gasatmosphäre *f* = protective atmosphere
~helm *m* = skullguard
~kappe *f* = grommet
~kette *f*, siehe: Gleitschutzkette
~kleidung *f*, siehe: Schutzbekleidung
~kolloid *n*, siehe: Stabilisator *m*
~maßnahme *f* = precaution
~mittel *n* = preservative
~überzug-Phenolderivat *n* = protective coating intermediate
~werk *n* = protective structure
Schwabber *m*, Gummischieber *m* = squeegee
schwachplastisch = feebly plastic
Schwaden *m*, Wrasen *m*, Brüden *m* = water vapo(u)r

~, siehe: Längsreihe *f*
~beseitiger *m* = windrow eliminator
~glätter *m*, Langmahdplanierungsschablone *f* = windrow evener
Schwalbenschwanz *m* = dovetail, swallow-tail
schwalbenschwanzförmiges Blatt *n* **mit Brust** *f*; siehe unter „Holzverbindung *f*"
Schwalbenschwanz-Überblattung *f* = dovetail halving
Schwallschacht *m*; siehe unter „Talsperre *f*"
Schwamm|fett *n* = sponge-grease
~gummi *m* = sponge rubber
Schwanenhals *m* = gooseneck
~ *m* [*Dränagewerkzeug n*] = swan-necked drainage tool
~-Auslegerkran *m* = gooseneck type crane

Schwarzbelageinbaumaschine *f*, **Schwarz(decken)verteiler** *m*, **Verteilerfertiger** *m*, **Schwarzdeckenfertiger**, **Schwarzdecken-Einbaumaschine**	bituminous road surfacing finisher, asphalt finisher, asphalt paver, bituminous paving machine, bituminous spreading-and-finishing machine, black-top spreader, asphaltic concrete paver, (bituminous) paver-finisher, asphalt and coated macadam finisher, spreader finisher, **black top bituminous paver**
abkippen	to tilt down [*screed*]
Abziehbohle *f*, Glättbohle	screed plate
angezogen [*Bremse f*]	applied
ankippen	to tilt up [*screed*]
Antriebsgehäuse *n*	drive case
Antriebsgruppe *f*	power unit, power plant
Arbeitsgeschwindigkeit *f*	working speed
Ausschlag *m*	deflection
Bedienungsstand *m*	operating deck, ~ platform
Belagsdicke *f*, Schichtdicke	thickness of mat
Betriebsdrehzahlbereich *m*	operating speed range
Bitumen-Mörtelschmiere *f*	"fat"
Bohlenwinkel *m*	screed planing angle
Bremsflüssigkeitsbehälter *m*	brake supply tank
Brenner *m* mit Gebläse *n*	heater and blower unit
Brennerschlauch *m*	burner hose
dauernder Schichtausgleich *m*	continuous course correction
Deckenschluß *m*	finish
Dickeneinstellung *f*	(mat) thickness control
Dickenmesser *m*	thickness ga(u)ge
Drehpunkt *m*	pivot point
Druckring *m*	operating ring

Drückrollen *fpl* für LKW-Räder *npl*, LKW-Schubrollen	bumper rollers
Durchlaßschieber *m*, Mengenregulierschieber	cut-off gate, hopper gate
Einbaustreifen *m*	strip
Einbauteil *m*	(floating) screed
Einbauteil-Hubseil *n*	(floating) screed hoist rope
Einbauvermögen *n*	laying capacity
Einregulierung *f*, Einstellung *f*	adjustment
Einsatzmannschaft *f*	working team
Einspritzdüse *f*	nozzle
Einspritzdüsenhalter *m*	holder type injector
Einstellhandrad *n* für Deckendicke *f*	thickness control handwheel
Einstellorgan *n*	control
Einstellspindel *f*	adjusting screw
elektrische Heizvorrichtung *f* für die Glättbohle	electric screed heater
Exzenter *m*	eccentric
Exzenterstange *f*	eccentric arm
Fahrkupplung *f*	traction clutch
Fahrteil *m*	traction unit
Fahr(t)richtung *f*	direction of travel
Feineinregulierung *f*, Feineinstellung	fine adjustment
Feststellbremse *f*	parking brake
Fettbüchse *f*	screw down cup
gebogene Ablenkungsplatte *f*	curved deflector plate
gelüftet [*Bremse f*]	released
Getriebegang *m*	operating gear
Glättbohle *f*, Abziehbohle	screed plate
Grobfilter *n*, *m*	pre-filter
Größe *f* der Kronenüberhöhung *f*	amount of crown
großer Gang *m*	high speed range
Handradwelle *f* zum Einstellen *n* des Einbauteils *m*	screed lift shaft
Haupteinstellorgan *n*	primary control
Hauptkupplung *f*	master clutch
Hauptlagerdurchmesser *m*	diameter of main journal
Hauptölpumpe *f*	main oil pump
Hinterkante *f* [*Glättbohle f*]	rear edge, back edge
Hinterkipper *m*	tipping truck
Höchstdrehmoment *n*	maximum torque
Höchstdrehzahl *f*	maximum governed speed
Höhe *f*	level
Höhenunterschied *m*	variation in level
Höhenwechsel *m*	change of level
Hupenknopf *m*	horn button
Hydraulikölbehälterentlüfter *m*	hydraulic oil tank breather
klebrige Mischung *f*	tacky mix
kleiner Gang *m*	low speed range
Kontrollschraube *f* [*am Ölbehälter m*]	level plug

Schwarzbelageinbaumaschine

Kraftstoffanlage *f*	fuel system
Kraftstoffeinspritzpumpe *f*	fuel injection pump
Kraftstoffversorgungspumpe *f*	fuel lift pump
Kroneneinstellung *f*	crown control
Kronenüberhöhung *f* im Verhältnis zur Einbaubreite *f*	crown in relation to the width of mat being laid
Lattenrost *m*, Stangenzubringer *m*	(flight) conveyor, bar feeder, bar conveyor
Lattenrostkupplung *f*, Stangenzubringerkupplung	conveyor clutch
Laufsteg *m*	rear platform
Leerlauf *m* [*Hebelstellung f*]	neutral
Lehre *f*	ga(u)ge
lenkbares Vorderrad *n*	front steerable wheel
Lenkbremse *f*	steering brake
Lenkerhebel *m*, Schwenkarm *m*	screed side arm, level(l)ing arm
Lenkhilfe *f*	aid to steering
Lenkkupplungshebel *m*	steering lever
letzte Getriebestufe *f*	final drive
Lichtmaschine *f*	dynamo
LKW-Ladung *f*	truck load
LKW-Schubrollen *fpl*, Drückrollen für LKW-Räder	bumper rollers
Luftfilter *n, m*	air pre-cleaner
Mengenregulierschieber *m*, Durchlaßschieber	hopper gate, cut-off gate
Mindestarbeitsbreite *f*	minimum operating width
Mindestdicke *f*	minimum thickness
Mindestöldruck *m* bei Leerlaufdrehzahl *f*	minimum oil pressure with engine idling
Mischgutbehälter *m*	(receiving) hopper
Mischgutfluß *m*	flow of mix, ~ ~ material
mittlere Dicke *f*	average thickness
Motor-Zweiganggetriebe *n*	two speed gearbox
Nachbarstreifen *m*	adjacent strip
Naht *f*	joint
Nivellierung *f*	levelling
Normalbreite *f*	standard width
normale Motordrehzahl *f* [*Dieselmotor m*]	piston speed
Öldruck *m* bei voller Drehzahl und warmem Motor	oil pressure at full throttle with warm engine
Ölwanneninhalt *m*	wet sump capacity
Pleuellagerdurchmesser *m*	diameter of big end pin journal
Profilregulierung *f*	control of screed
Pumpenleistung *f* pro Minute	pump delivery per minute
Quernaht *f*	transverse joint
Reduzierschuh *m*	cut-off shoe
Regelorgan *n* für den Kraftstoffdruck *m*	fuel pressure control
Reinigungsspritze *f*	spray cleaner
rotierende Auflockerungswalze *f*	agitator (raker bar)

Schauloch n	inspection hatch
Schichtdicke f, Belagsdicke	thickness of mat
Schlagbohle f, Stampfer m, Stampfbohle f	tamper
Schmierölfilter n, m	lubricating oil filter
Schmiertabelle f, Schmierplan m	lubrication timetable
Schräglage f auf der Hinterkante f	riding heel of screed
Schräglage f auf der Vorderkante f	riding toe of screed
Schwenkarm m, Lenkerhebel m	level(l)ing arm, screed side arm
Seitenbegrenzungsblech n	end plate
Seitenblech n des Mischgutbehälters m	hopper side plate
Spannrolle f der Lattenrostkette f, ~ ~ Stangenzubringerkette	conveyor take up roller
Spannschloß n	turnbuckle
Spitzenleistung f bei kurzzeitigem Betrieb m [Motor]	B. H. P. intermittent
Spitzenleistung f bei 12stündigem Dauerbetrieb [Motor]	B. H. P. 12-hr. rating
Stampfbohlenantrieb m	tamper transmission
Stampfer m, Stampfbohle f, Schlagbohle	tamper
Stampferantriebswelle f	tamper drive shaft
Stampferhebel m	tamper lever
Stampfer-Overdrive m	tamper overdrive
Stampferschlagzahl f	tamper speed
Stangenzubringer m, Lattenrost m	bar feeder, (flight) conveyor, bar conveyor
steigen und fallen [Einbauteil m]	to ride up and down
Strebe f	stay bar
Thermosiphon m mit Hilfsflügelradpumpe f	impellor assisted thermo syphon
Turaswelle f	sprocket shaft
Überlappung f	overlap
Umlenkturas m	idler sprocket
Unterbau m, Vorprofil n	base
vergleichmäßigen	to stretch out [the variations in level]
Verlängerungsstück n	extension
Versuchsbelag m	trial mat
Verteilerschnecke f	spreading screw, spreader ~, distributing ~, (cross) auger
Verteilerschneckenkette f	auger chain
verzögernde Wirkung f des Einbauteils m	delayed screed action
Vierganggetriebe n	4-speed gearbox
Visierstange f	guide rod
Vorabstreifer m	tamper shield
Vorderkante f [Glättbohle f]	front edge
Vorderradlenkung f	front steering
Vorgelegekupplung f	transmission clutch
Vorprofil n, Unterbau m	base
Zündknopf m	ignition button

Schwarz|blech n = black sheet iron
~decke f = black top pavement (US); hydrocarbon ~ (Brit.)
~deckenbau m = construction of bituminous surfacings
~deckenfertiger m, siehe: Schwarzbelageinbaumaschine f
~deckenmischanlage f; siehe unter „Makadam-Maschinenanlage f"
~deckenmischgut n, Schwarzdeckeneinbaumasse f, Schwarz(decken)mischung f, Schwarzmaterial = black top paving mixture (US); hydrocarbon pavement ~ (Brit.)
~deckenstraße f = black-top road, ~ highway
schwarzer Glaskopf m (Min.), siehe: Psilomelan m
Schwarz|erle f, siehe: klebrige Erle
~fleckigkeit f = black specking
~föhre f, siehe: Schwarzkiefer f
~kalk m, Graukalk = gray quicklime
~kiefer f, Schwarzföhre f = black pine, Austrian ~
~kupfer n = black copper
~manganerz n, siehe: Glanzbraunstein m (Min.)
~mischung f, siehe: Schwarzdeckenmischgut n
~pappel f = black poplar, ~ populus
~pech n = black pitch
~pulver n; siehe unter „1. Schießen n; 2. Sprengen n"
~spießglanzerz n (Min.), siehe: Rädelerz
~straßenbau m = construction of bituminous roads
~straßenbaugeräte npl, siehe: Bitumen-Straßenbaugeräte npl
~streif m, siehe: Kohleneisenstein m
Schwebe|bahn f = elevated railway (Brit.); ~ railroad (US)
~fähre f, Fahrbrücke f = aerial ferry

~gas-Wärme(aus)tauscher m = suspension type preheater
schwebende Pfahlgründung f, schwimmende ~ = suspended pile(d) foundation, floating ~ ~
schwebendes Grundwasser n, siehe: vadoses Wasser
Schwebstoff m, suspendierter Stoff m = suspended matter
~fracht f = silt load
~stoffführend [$Fluß$ m] = sediment-bearing
schwedisches Verfahren n, schwedische Gleitkreistheorie f [$Bestimmung$ f der $Rutschgefahr$ f $unter$ $Annahme$ f $einer$ $kreisförmigen$ $Rutschfläche$ f ($oder$ $Gleitfläche$)] = Swedish cylindrical-surface method, ~ circular-arc ~
Schwefel|gruppenanalyse f = group sulfur analysis
~kalzium n = calcium sulfide
~karbolsäure f = sulphocarbolic acid
~kies m (Min.), siehe: Gelbeisenkies
~kohlenstoff m, CS_2 = carbon bisulphide, ~ disulphide
~kupfer n, Cu_2S = sulphide of copper
~säure f = sulfuric acid
schwefelsaures Kalzium n, $CaSO_4$ = sulphate of calcium
Schwefel|tellurwismut n (Min.), siehe: Tetradymit m
~trioxyd n = sulphur trioxide
~wasserstoff m, H_2S = hydrogen sulfide
schwefelwasserstoff|freies Erdgas n (oder **Naturgas**) = sweet natural gas
~haltiges Erdgas n (oder **Naturgas**) = sour natural gas
Schwefelzink n, Zinksulfid n, Zinkblende f, ZnS = (zinc) blende, black jack, sphalerite
schweißbares Flußeisen n = malleable mild steel

Schweißen n, **Schweißung** f	welding
Abbrennstumpf~	flash ~
absatzweises Schweißen n	skip ~
Abschmelz~, siehe: Schmelz~	
Aufschweißen n von Bolzen mpl	stud welding
Autogen~	autogenous ~
abwärtsschweißen	to weld down-hand

Bolzenschweißverfahren *n*	stud-~
Bolzenschweißverfahren, wobei nach Einschalten eines sehr kurzen „Vorstromes" vom Bolzen zum Werkstück zur Einleitung einer Ionisation der Hauptstrom eingeschaltet und der Bolzen, der von einer Hülse gehalten wird, durch einen Magneten etwa 1 mm vom Werkstück abgehoben wird	Cyc-Arc-Method
Bördelnaht *f*	butt weld between plates with raised edges
Brennauftrag~	flash ~
Buckel~, Dellen~	projection ~
Dreiblechstoß *m*, Dreiblechnaht *f*	joint between three members
„Drei-Uhr-Schweißung" *f* [*Richtung der Elektrode in Übereinstimmung mit der Stellung eines Stunden-Uhrzeigers*]	three o'clock-~
Durchmischungsgrad *m*	rate of dilution
Ecknaht *f*	corner weld
Einlagen~	single-run ~ (Brit.); single-pass ~ (US)
elektrisches ~, Elektro~	electric ~
Gasentwickler *m*	gas generator
Gas(schmelz)~	gas ~, fusion ~ by means of gas
Hammer~	forge ~
Heftstelle *f*	tack weld
(Hohl)Kehl~	fillet ~
K-Naht *f*	double bevel groove
Kohle~	carbon ~
Kreuzstoß *m*, Kreuznaht *f*	cruciform joint
Laschenstoß *m*	joint with butt strap
Lichtbogen~	(electrical) arc ~, electric arc fusion ~
Lochnaht *f*	plug weld
Nach~	rewelding
Naht~	seam~
Nahtzone *f*	zone adjacent to the weld
Preß~	~ with pressure
Punkt~	spot ~
Sauerstoff-Azetylen-~	oxy-acetylene ~
Schlackenvorlauf *m*	slag flowing ahead of the molten pool
Schlitznaht *f*	slot weld
Schmelz~, Abschmelz~	fusion ~
Schrägstoß *m*	inclined Tee joint
Schuß~	shot ~
Schweißapparat *m*	welder, welding machine
Schweißbrenner *m*	welding burner, ~ torch
Schweißbrille *f*	welding goggles
Schweißdraht *m*, Zusatzwerkstoff *m*	fusion steel wire
Schweißkonstruktion *f*	welded construction
Schweißnaht *f*	welding seam
Schweißstelle *f*	weld

Schweißverbindung f, Schweißstoß m	welded joint
Schweißverformung f	welding distortion
Schweißung in Normallage, Sechs-Uhr-Schweißung	six o'clock-~
Schweißverfahren n mit zwei Metallelektroden unter Pulver, wobei nur die Elektroden unter Spannung stehen; die Steuerung wird aber von der Spannung zwischen Elektroden und Werkstück beeinflußt	Series-Arc-welding method
sichtbare Unterraupe f	penetration bead
Steilflanke f	square edge
Stirnnaht f	edge weld
Stoßnaht f, Stumpfnaht f	butt weld
Stromleiter ~	bond weld
Thermit ~	thermite ~
Tulpennaht f	single U groove with vertical sides
Übergangszone f, Bindezone	weld junction
Überlappungs ~	lap ~
Überkopfschweißen, Zwölf-Uhr-Schweißung	to weld in overhead position
unsymmetrische X-Naht f	asymmetric double Vee groove
Unter-Pulverschweißverfahren n, Maulwurfverfahren, U-P-Verfahren, ELLIRA-Verfahren, Elektro-Linde-Rapid ~	UNIONMELT welding method
Widerstands ~, elektrische Widerstands ~, Widerstandspreß ~	resistance ~
Wurzeleinbrand m	penetration into the root
Y-Naht f	single Vee groove with broad root face
Zickzackpunkt ~	staggered spot ~
Zusatzwerkstoff m, siehe: Schweißdraht m	

Gegenüberstellung der verschiedenen Elektrodentypen

Internationale Elektroden-Symbolisierung		Neue Deutsche Norm DIN 1913	
sauer	(acid)	Es	(erzsaurer Typ)
basisch	(basic)	Kb	(kalkbasischer Typ)
Cellulose	(cellulosic)	Ze	(Zellulose-Typ)
oxydierend	(oxydizing)	Ox	(oxydischer = stark erzsaurer Typ)
Rutil	(rutile) }	Ti	(Titanoxyd-Typ)
Titan	(titania)		
andere Typen	(other types)	So	(Sondertyp)

Schweiß|konstruktion f = welded construction
~ofenschlacke f = puddling cinder, tap ~
~rost m = welded grating, ~ grate
Schwelbraunkohle f = retort brown coal [*incorrectly termed "bituminous brown coal"*]

Schwell|bewegung f, siehe: Schwellung f
~boden m, Quellboden = expansive soil, swell ~
Schwellen|bohrmaschine f = sleeper drilling machine (Brit.); tie ~ ~ (US)
~verlegemaschine f = sleeper laying machine (Brit.); tie ~ ~ (US)
Schwell|fähigkeit f, Schwellvermögen n = expansibility
~rostunterbau m, Schwellrostfundament n = horizontal grillage, ~ grilled foundation
Schwellung f, Schwellen n, Quellung, Quellen, Aufquellen, Schwellbewegung, Aufquellung = bulking, bulkage
~ durch Feuchtigkeit f = bulking, bulkage, moisture expansion
Schwell|vermögen n, Schwellfähigkeit f = expansibility
~zement m, Quellzement, Expansivzement = high-expansion cement, expanding ~, expansive ~
Schwelretortenteer m = retort tar
Schwemm|(land)boden m, Wasserabsatzboden = alluvial soil, transported ~
~landboden m [Tal n] = alluvial floor
~landdoline f = alluvial dolina
~landebene f = alluvial plain, alluvian ~
~sand m, siehe: Flußsand
~theorie f = allochthonous theory [coal formation]
~- und Waschwasser n [Zuckerfabrikation f] = flume water, wheel ~
~verfahren n [Hausmüllbeseitigung f] = water-carrier method [of garbage disposal]
~zeug n, Schwemmgut n, Schwemmstoff m, Schwemmsel n [Fluß m] = floating débris
Schwengel m, Balanzier m = working beam, walking ~, (balance) ~
~bock m [pennsylv. Bohrverfahren n] = sam(p)son post
Schwenk|absetzer m, siehe: Bandabsetzer
~antrieb m = slewing drive
~ausleger m, Schwenkarm m [Kran m] = rotating boom, swing(ing) ~ (US); ~ jib (Brit.)
~bagger m, Schwenktrockenbagger = swing excavator, revolving shovel

schwenkbare Räder npl, Schwenk-Radsatz m = swivel wheels [belt conveyor]
Schwenk|bereich m [Bagger m] = boom swing (US); jib ~ (Brit.)
~bremse f = slewing brake
~bühne f = swinging platform
Schwenken n [Ausleger m] = slewing
Schwenk|-Frontschaufel-Fahrlader m, siehe: Schwenklader
~getriebe n, Schwenkmechanismus m, Schwenkwerk n = slewing mechanism, ~ gear
~kabelkran m; siehe unter „Seilförderanlage f"
~kran m, Drehkran, Auslegerdrehkran = revolving crane, revolver ~, slewing ~; swing-jib ~ (Brit.); swing(-boom) ~ (US)
~kran m [als Bauaufzug m] = crane hoist
~lader m, Schwenkschaufler m, Fahrlader-Schwenkschaufler, Schwenkschaufel(-Fahr)lader, Front-Schwenkschaufler, Schwenk-Frontschaufel-Fahrlader = swing loader, ~ shovel
~mechanismus m, Schwenkgetriebe n, Schwenkwerk n = slewing mechanism, ~ gear
~prisma n = swivelling V-block
~rad n = tumbler gear
~-Radsatz m, schwenkbare Räder npl = swivel wheels [belt conveyor]
~rohr n = swing pipe
~schaufel(-Fahr)lader m, siehe: Schwenklader
~schild n, Seitenräumer-Planierschild, winkelbares Schild, Schrägschild, Winkel-Planierschild = angledozer, angling blade
~tisch m = swivel table
~(trocken)bagger m = swing excavator, revolving shovel
~werk n, siehe: Schwenkmechanismus m
~winkel m, Ver~ [Bagger m] = swing(ing) angle, slewing ~
Schwer|beton-Pflastersteinfertigung f = fabrication of heavy concrete paving setts
~bleierz n (Min.) = plattnerite
Schwere f, Schwerkraft f, Gravitation f = gravity, gravitational force
~anomalie f = gravity anomaly

Schwere|anordnung *f* = gravity arrangement

schwere bituminöse Decke *f*, bituminöser Dauerbelag *m* = high type bituminous pavement

~ Flüssigkeit *f*, Schwerflüssigkeit = liquid of high density, heavy liquid

schwerer Ton *m* = heavy clay

schweres Blech *n*, Grobblech = heavy (steel) plate

~ Erdbeben *n* = sharp (earth)quake

~ Horizontalpendel *n* = heavy horizontal pendulum

~ Wetter *n* = heavy weather

Schwere|klassierung *f* = gravitational classifying

~mangel *m* = gravity defect

~messer *m* [*Meteorologie f*] = barometer

~messungen *fpl*; siehe unter „geophysikalische Baugrunduntersuchung *f*"

~mittelpunkt *m*, Massenmittelpunkt, Schwerpunkt = center of gravity (US); centre ~ ~ (Brit.); centroid

Schwerentflammbarmachung *f*, siehe: Entzündbarkeit *f*

Schwere|potential *n* = gravity potential

~störung *f* = gravity disturbance

~überschuß *m* = gravity surplus

~wert *m* = gravity value

Schwer|fahrzeug *n* = heavy vehicle

~flüssigkeit *f*, schwere Flüssigkeit = heavy liquid, liquid of high density

schwergefrierbares Dynamit *n*; siehe unter „1. Schießen *n*; 2. Sprengen *n*"

Schwergewichts|absackung *f*, Schwergewichtseinsackung = bagging off by gravity

~entleerung *f* = gravity discharge

~kaimauer *f*, Schwergewichtskajenmauer = gravity quay wall

(Schwer)Gewichtsmauer *f*; siehe unter „Talsperre *f*"

Schwergewichts|-Pendelfender *m* = swinging gravity fender

~staumauer *f*; siehe unter „Talsperre *f*"

~-Stützmauer *f* = gravity retaining wall

Schwerkraft *f*, Gravitation *f*, Schwere *f* = gravitational force, gravity, force of gravitation

~aufbereitung *f* [*Mineral n*] = gravity separation

~bahn *f* [*Seilbahn*] = gravity cable(way)

~förderer *m* = gravity conveyor

~komponente *f* = component of gravity

~(rollen)bahn *f*, Schwerkraftrollenförderer *m* = gravity roller runway, ~ ~ conveyor

~verteilung *f* = gravity distribution

Schwer|last *f* = heavy load

~lastausleger *m* = boom for heavy loads (US); jib ~ ~ ~ (Brit.)

~last(kraft)wagen *m*, Schwerlaster *m* = heavy lorry (Brit.); ~ truck (US)

~lastkran *m* = heavy-duty crane

~lastschlepper *m* = heavy-duty tractor

~lastseilbahn *f* = heavy-duty ropeway

~metallseife *f* = heavy-metal soap

~mineral *n* = heavy-weight mineral

~öl *n* = heavy oil

~ölförderpumpe *f* [*Diesel*] = fuel feed pump

~ölmotor *m* = crude oil engine

~punkt *m*, Massenmittelpunkt, Schweremittelpunkt = centroid; center of gravity (US); centre of gravity (Brit.)

~punktlage *f*; siehe unter „Baumaschinen *fpl* und Baugeräte *npl*"

~spat *m*, Baryt *m*, BaSO$_4$ (Min.) = heavy spar, barytes, native barium sulphate, barite

~spatbrekzie *f* = barite breccia

~spatmehl *n*, fein gemahlener Baryt *m* = finely ground barite

~spatzusatz *m* = addition of barytes

~spülung *f* [*Bohren n*] = high weight mud

~stange *f*, Bohrkragen *m* [*Rotary-Bohrverfahren*] = drill collar

~stange *f*, untere ~, Bohrstange [*pennsylv. Bohrverfahren*] = drill stem, auger ~, sinker bar

Schwerst-Verdichter *m*; siehe unter „Walze *f*"

Schwert *n* [*Schwertwäsche f*] = paddle, blade [*log washer*]

Schwertantalerz *n* (Min.) = tantalite

Schwert|gang *m* [*Schwertwäsche f*] = paddle flight, blade ~

~konustrommelwäsche *f* = conical scrubber

Schwert|trommelwäsche *f*, Schwertwaschtrommel *f* = (revolving) (cylindrical) scrubber, rotary scrubber, blade-mill, paddle mill scrubber, stone (and ore) scrubber
~wäsche *f*, Schwertauflöser *m* = log washer
Schwerwelle *f* = (ordinary) wave
Schwibbe *f*, siehe: Windrispe *f*

Schwimm|aufbereitung *f*, Flotation *f*, Schwimmverfahren *n* = flotation
~bagger *m*, siehe: Naßbagger
~band *n* = floating belt conveyor
~decke *f*, Schwimmschicht *f* [*Abwasserwesen n*] = scum, floating cover
~deckenzerstörer *m* [*Abwasserwesen n*] = scum breaker

Schwimmdock *n*
L-förmiges ~
U-förmiges ~

floating (dry) dock
self-docking ~ ~
box ~ ~

Schwimmen *n* [*Pigment n*] = flooding
schwimmende Betonieranlage *f* = floating concrete plant, ~ concreting ~
~ Deckscholle *f* (Geol.) = floating fault block
~ Erdsauganlage *f* = suction dredge(r) without spuds
~ Gasdecke *f* eines Schlammfaulraumes *m* = floating cover of a digestion tank
~ Gründung *f* = floating foundation
~ Insel *f* = exotic block [*overthrust*]
~ Pflanzeninsel *f* = raft of vegetation, river raft
schwimmender Löffelbagger *m*; siehe unter „Naßbagger"
schwimmendes Eisfeld *n* = (sea) floe
Schwimmer *m* = float
~absaugung *f* = floating suction
~armstück *n* = float arm
~gehäuse *n*, Schwimmerkammer *f* = float chamber
~hahn *m* = float cock
~kammer *f*, Schwimmergehäuse *n* = float chamber
~nadel *f* = float needle
~nadelventil *n* = float needle valve
~schalter *m* = float (type) switch
~ (schiffs)hebewerk *n*; siehe unter „Schiffshebeanlage *f*"
~ventil *n* = float valve
Schwimm|-Kahnentladebecherwerk *n* = floating barge elevator, marine leg
~kasten *m* = floating caisson, buoyant box, floating box

~kraft *f*, Auftrieb *m* = buoyant effect, buoyancy
~kran *m* = floating crane
~kruste *f* [*Erdkruste*] = flotation crust
~lager *n*, siehe: hydrostatisches Lager
~löffelbagger *m*; siehe unter „Naßbagger"
~-Moor *n*, Schwimmoor = floating bog
~(pfahl)ramme *f*; siehe unter „Rammanlage *f*"
~ponton *m* mit Steg *m* = floating landing stage
~probe *f* zur Ermittlung der Viskosität *f* nicht zu harter Bitumen *npl* nach A. S. T. M. D. 139—27 = float test
~-Pumpanlage *f* = floating pump station
~ramme *f*; siehe unter „Rammanlage *f*"
~schicht *f*, Schwimmdecke *f* [*Abwasserwesen n*] = scum, floating cover
~schlamm *m* = top sludge, scum
~stoffabstreicher *m* = scum collector
~stoffabweiser *m* = scum board
~tunnel *m* = floating tunnel
~verfahren *n*, siehe: Schwimmaufbereitung *f*
~weste *f*, Korkweste = cork jacket
Schwindbewehrung *f*, Schwindarmierung = shrinkage reinforcement
Schwinden *n*, Schwindung *f* = shrinkage, shrinking
Schwind|riß *m*; siehe unter „Riß"
~rißbildung *f* = contraction cracking
~zugspannung *f* = tensile shrinkage stress
~zugspannungsriß *m* = tensile shrinkage stress crack

Schwing|achse f = oscillating axle
~drahtdehnungsmesser m = vibrating wire strain ga(u)ge
Schwinge f [*Auflager n*] = rocker
~ = rocker-arm, rocking arm
~ [*Backenbrecher m*] = pitman
Schwing|förderrinne f, Schüttelrinne, Förderschwinge f, Schwingrinnenförderer m = shaker conveyor
~förderrohr n, Schwingrohrförderer m = vibrating circular pipe-line
~gerät n, (Druck)Rüttler m [*Rütteldruckverfahren n*] = vibroflot (machine)
~gleisstopfer m, Schwingschotterstopfer = vibrating type tie tamper (US); ~ ~ track ~ (Brit.)
~moor n = quaking bog, trembling ~, quagmire
~rahmen m [*Sieb n*] = vibrating frame
~rinnenförderer m, siehe: Schwingförderrinne f
Schwingsieb, eigentliches ~ n = screen with vibratory action applied through the screen frame, vibrated live frame screen
~ mit elektromagnetischem Antrieb m = electro-magnetic vibrating screen
~ ~ Exzenterantrieb m, siehe: Exzenter-Schwingsieb
~ ~ Massenkraftantrieb m, Unwucht(-Vibrations)sieb n = (mechanically-vibrated) rotating unbalanced (-)weight (type) screen, unbalanced-weight vibrating screen
~ ~ Stahldrahtbespannung f, Harfenvibrator m = vibrating screen with replaceable steel wire bundles
~rahmen m = live (screen) frame, vibrated ~
Schwingtisch m; siehe unter „Betonrüttelgeräte npl"
Schwingungs|becken n; siehe unter „Talsperre f"
~bohle f; siehe: Vibrierbohle
~dämpfer m, Vibrationsdämpfer = vibration absorber, ~ dampener
~(ein)rüttler m, Vibrator m = vibrator
~maschine f = oscillator machine
~platte f; siehe unter „Betonrüttelgeräte npl"

~platte f für Bodenverdichtungen fpl = soil plate vibrator, ~ vibrating plate, ~ vibrating pan, ~ pan vibrator, ~ vibration slab, ~ plate vibrator, ~ vibratory baseplate, ~ vibratory base plate compactor
Schwing(ungs)|verdichter m, siehe: Vibrations-Verdichtungsmaschine f
~verdichtung f, siehe: Vibrationsverdichtung
~walze f; siehe unter „Walze"
~weite f, Vibrationsamplitude f = amplitude
Schwingwascher m = vibratory washing screen
Schwitzen n, Bluten n, Ausschwitzen n [*Schwarzdecke f*] = bleeding, fatting (-up), ponding
Schwitzwasser n, siehe: Kondenswasser
Schwundriß m; siehe unter „Riß m"
Schwung|gewicht n, siehe: Unbalance f
~rad n = flywheel
Scraperfalle f, Schürze f = apron
Sechskant|mutter f = hexagon nut
~schraube f = hexagon bolt
~stahl m = hexagon iron, ~ bar
Sechs-Punkte-Hebevorrichtung f = six-point pickup
Sedimentationsprobe f, siehe: Absetzversuch m
Sediment|gestein n, siehe: Schichtgestein
~gneis m, siehe: Paragneis
~hydraulik f = sediment hydraulics
Sedimentierversuch m, siehe: Absetzversuch
Sedimenttransport m = sediment transport
See f, Meer n = sea
See m = lake
~asphalt m = lake asphalt, ~ pitch
~baggerung f = marine dredging
~bahnhof m = marine terminal
~bau m = marine construction, coastal engineering
~bauingenieur m = coastal engineer
~bauten f = marine works (or structures, or installations)
~beben n; siehe unter „Erdbeben n"
~buhne f, siehe: Strandbuhne f

See|deich m, Meer(es)leich = sea dyke (or dike)
~-Erz n = lake ore
~festung f = seaport fortress
~hafen m mit Betriebsanlagen fpl = (deep-)sea port
~höhe f, Höhe f über NN [NN = Normal Null = mittlere Seehöhe f] = altitude above (mean) sea level, ALT
~kabel n = marine type cable, submarine ~
~kanal m = ship canal
~karte f = sea chart, hydrographic map
~kreide f = lake-marl, bog lime
Seele f [Kabel n] = helix [cable]
Seelemann-Regulus-Mischer m; siehe unter „Betonmischer m"
Seen|ablagerung f = lake deposit, lacustrine ~
~gürtel m = lake-belt
~kette f = chain of lakes
~kunde f, Limnologie f = limnology
See|-Schelde f = Sea-Scheldt
~schiffahrt f = ocean-going shipping
~schutzbauten f = protection works, sea defence ~
~strandkiefer f = maritime pine
~ton m = lacustrine clay
~ufer n = lake shore
seewärts, siehe: meeresseitig
~, seeseitig = lakeward(s)
Seewasserspiegel m, siehe: Meeresspiegel
~ m = lake water level
Seewind m = sea breeze (on-)shore wind
Segeltuch n = canvas
~schlauch m = canvas duct

Segerkegel m = Seger cone, pyrometric ~, fusion ~
Segge f, siehe: Riedgras n
Segment|bogen m, siehe: Stichbogen
~eisen n = half round bar
~schütz(e) n, (f); siehe unter „Talsperre f"
~teil m, n, Mischer ~ = (mixer) liner segment, sectional liner
~verschluß m; siehe unter „Talsperre f"
Sehne f [Mathematik f] = chord
seicht, untief = shallow
Seichtwasserzone f = shallow-water zone
Seidenglimmer m (Min.), siehe: Serizit m
Seifen|gold n = alluvial gold, gulch ~
~-Kohlenwasserstoff-Gel n = soap-hydrocarbon gel
~stein m = soapstone
~zinn n (Min.) = stream tin
Seignettesalz n = Seignette salt, Rochelle ~
Seiher m, Saugkorb m, Filtersieb n = strainer, filtering screen
Seihtuch n, Filtertuch = filter(ing) cloth, ~ fabric
Seil|aufwickler m, Seilführung f = fairlead
~bahn f = rope-way
~bahn-Schleppschrapper m; siehe unter „Seilförderanlage f"
seilbetätigt = cable-operated, cable-powered
Seil|bohrverfahren n = cable-tool (method of) drilling, American system of drilling, cable system
~flasche f, Seilkloben m, Seilblock m = rope block

Seilförderanlage f
    Kabelkran m

        feststehender Kabelkran mit zwei ortsfesten Türmen mpl
        Schwenkkabelkran m, kreisfahrbarer Kabelkran mit einem ortsfesten und einem radial verfahrbaren Turm m, radial verfahrbarer Kabelkran

cable haulage machine
    blondin (Brit.); tautline cableway, (aerial) cableway, cable-crane, overhead cableway
        tautline cableway with two stationary towers, fixed aerial cableway
        tautline cableway with one stationary tower and one radially travel(l)ing tower, radial travel(l)ing cableway

Seilförderanlage

parallelfahrbarer Kabelkran *m*	tautline cableway with both towers travel(l)ing on parallel tracks
schnellaufender Kabelkran *m*	fast cableway
(elektrische) Amplidyne-Steuerung *f*, Fabrikat GENERAL ELECTRIC	G-E amplidyne control
Laufkatzen-Antriebsmotor *m*	carriage drive motor
Tiefen- und Langstreckenförderer *m*	long range excavator-conveyor, long range machine
Schlepperschrapper *m*, (gewöhnlicher) Schrapper	(power) drag scraper (machine), power scraper excavator
Schrapperbühne *f*, Verlade~	loading ramp
Schrapp(er)kübel *m*, Schrapp(er)gefäß *n*	scraper bucket
Reißzähne *mpl*	digging teeth
halbmondartiges Schrappergefäß	crescent scraper bucket
kastenartiges Schrappergefäß, Schürfkasten *m*	box-type scraper bucket
hinteres Kettengehänge *n*, hinterer Kettenzaum *m*	rear bridle chains
vorderes Kettengehänge *n*, vorderer Kettenzaum *m*	front bridle chains
Schrapperseile *npl*	operating cables
Zugseil, Vollseil, Schürfseil	inhaul cable (or line), load ~, pull cable
Rück(hol)seil *n*, Leerseil	outhaul cable (or line), backhaul ~, pull back ~
Schrapperwinde *f*, Schrapperhaspel *f, m*	scraper hoist, drag ~ ~
zweitrommeliger Haspel *m*, Zweitrommel-Schrapperwinde *f*	two-drum scraper hoist
Seiltrommel *f*, Schrapper~	(hoist) drum
Rückzugtrommel *f*	backhaul drum
Zugtrommel *f*	load drum
Kupplung *f*	clutch
Rollenmast *m*	headmast, headpost
Seilumlenkrolle *f*	guide block
Schäkelrolle *f*	guide block with shackle and pins
Zugseilumlenkrolle *f*	load-line guide block
Leerseilumlenkrolle *f*	backhaul-line guide block
Stützweite *f*	(operating) span
Abspannseil *n*, Trosse *f*, Ankerseil *n*	guy cable, guy rope, standing rope, rope guy
Abspannen *n*	guying
Schleppschrapperanlage *f* mit 3-Seil-Anordnung *f*, 3-Seil-Schrapper *m*	rapid shifting drag scraper machine, rapid-shifter
3-Trommel-Schrapperwinde *f*, 3-Trommel-Haspel *f, m*	three-drum rapid shifting hoist
Umlenkstation *f* [*zwei feste Türme mpl*]	bridle towers

Verankerungen *f pl*	log anchors
Laufkatzen-Seil *n*	bridle cable
Umlenkrolle *f*	block
Seil, welches die Laufkatze bewegt	bridle frame shifting cable
Drei-Seil-Anordnung *f*	rapid shifting bridle arrangement
Schleppschrapper mit zwei fahrbaren Türmen, Fabrikat SAUERMAN BROS., INC., CHICAGO 7, ILLINOIS, USA	SAUERMANN tower machine, ~ tower excavator
Kippschrapper *m*	tilting-type drag scraper
Steil-Schleppschrapper *m*	drag scraper with steeply inclined ramp
Schlaffseil-Kabelschrapper *m*, Seilbahn-Schleppschrapper *m*	track cable scraper, slackline (excavator) with bottomless bucket, slackline cableway with bottomless bucket
Tragseil *n*	track cable
Leerseil *n*	tension line
spannen	to tighten
entspannen	to slack off
Gefäß *n* ohne Boden *m*, bodenloses Gefäß	bottomless bucket
Seilflaschenzug *m*	pulley
Schlaffseil-Kabelbagger *m*, Seilbahn-Schwebeschrapper *m*	slackline (cableway) (excavator) with dragline-type bucket
Laufkatze *f*	(wheeled) carrier
Maschinenturm *m*	tower
Tragseil *n*	track cable
Seilanschlag *m*	automatic dump
Gegenturm *m*, hinterer Tragseilmast *m*	tail tower, tail anchor
Schürfstelle *f*	digging point
Entladestelle *f*, Entleerungsstelle	dumping point
Abbau *m*	stripping
Kohlentagebau *m*	open-pit mining
Unterwasserförderung *f*, Naßförderung	digging from underwater
Stapeln *n* von Massengütern *npl*	bulk storage
Haldenschüttung *f*	stockpiling
Schrappen *n* einer Furche *f*	channeling (US); channelling (Brit.)
Schrappweg *m*	bucket path
Stapelgerät *n*	storage machine, drag scraper stockpiler
Abfuhrgleis *n*	railway spur
Windenhaus *n*	hoist house
Ausschachtgerät *n*	excavator
Flußbegradigung *f*	river re-alignment
Kiesgewinnung *f* aus dem Wasser *n*	digging gravel from a river
Haldenrückverladung *f*	handling from storage

Seilförderanlage — Seitenentleerungsanhänger

Schrapperanlage *f*	(drag) scraper installation
Fördergut *n*	material
kompakt gelagertes Gut *n*	hardpacked material
nicht einstürzendes Gut *n*	non-caving material
einstürzendes Gut *n*, nachfallendes Gut	free-caving material
Oberbegriff für Schrapper *m*, Kabelschrapper *m* und Kabelbagger *m*	cable excavator
Pendelschrapper *m*	cable excavator with dragline-type bucket and running-rail type carrier
Schrapplader *m*, Fahrschrapper *m*, Verladeschrapper, Verlade-Fahrschrapper, Fabrikat A. G. für BERGBAU- und HÜTTENBEDARF, SALZGITTER, DEUTSCHLAND	drag scraper and loader, scraper-loader
Straffseil-Kabelbagger *m*, TEKA-Schrapper, Fabrikat KURT VON HAGEN, BLUMROTH ÜBER SOEST, DEUTSCHLAND	cable excavator with bottom-dump bucket and tightened track cable

---

Seilführung *f*, siehe: Seilaufwickler *m*
seilgesteuert = cable-operated, cable-controlled
Seil|-Greifer *m*, Seil-Greifkorb *m* = rope grab(bing) bucket
~**haspel** *m*, *f* = rope reel
~**kloben** *m*, siehe: Seilflasche *f*
~**litze** *f* = (rope) strand
~**scheibe** *f*, Seilrolle *f* = sheave
~**schlag** *m* = rope lay
~**schlagbohren** *n*, pennsylvanisches Seilbohren *n* = churn drilling (or boring), percussive rope ~ (~ ~)
~**schlagbohrgerät** *n* = churn drill, cable ~, well ~
~**schmiermittel** *n* = rope lubricant
~**schrapperkasten** *m* = scraper, cablehauled bucket
~**-Standbahnanlage** *f*, Streckenförderungsanlage *f*, Drahtseil-Standbahn *f* = (endless) rope haulage plant
~**tragrolle** *f* = top pulley
~**trieb** *m* = rope drive
~**trommel** *f* = rope drum
~**umlenkrolle** *f* = guide block
~**vorschub** *m*, Seilvorstoß(en) *m*, (*n*) [*Hochlöffel m*] = rope crowd(ing)

~**winde** *f*, Trommelseilwinde, (Seil)Windwerk *n*, Trommelseilwindwerk = (rope) winch, cable ~
~**winde** *f* hinten am Fahrzeug *n* angebracht, siehe: Trommel~ ~ ~ ~ ~
~**zug** *m*, siehe: Flaschenzug
Seismik *f*, Seismologie *f*, Erdbebenkunde *f* = seismology
seismische Bodenerforschung *f* nach dem **Refraktionsverfahren** *n*; siehe unter „geophysikalische Baugrunduntersuchung *f*"
Seismograph *m* = seismograph
Seiten|anschüttung *f*, Seitenanböschung *f*, Seitenanfüllung *f* = side fill
~**aufriß** *m* = side elevation
~**ausleger-Zusatzvorrichtung** *f* für **Rohrverlegungen** *fpl* = sideboom pipe-laying attachment
~**böschung** *f* = side slope
~**dehnung** *f* = lateral strain
~**druck** *m* = lateral pressure
~**einschnitt** *m* = side cut(ting); [*deprecated:* side long cut]
~**entleerung** *f* = side dump discharge
~**entleerungsanhänger** *m* = side dump trailer

Seiten|entleerungsschaufel *f* [*Frontlader m*] = side dump bucket [*front-end loader*]
~entnahme *f* = side borrow
~führungskraftbeiwert *m* = sideway force coefficient
~graben *m* = side ditch
~hubstapler *m* = side-lift truck
~kanal *m*, siehe: Nebenkanal
~kipper *m* [*Wagen wird um Längsachse um etwa 135—150 Grad gedreht*] = side tippler
~kipper-Anhänger *m* = side-dump trailer, side-tipping dump ~
~kippwaggon *m* = side dump car
~klappenpritsche *f* [*LKW m*] = drop-side body
~kraft *f* = lateral force, side ~
~-Kreiselwipper *m*, Fabrikat STRACHAN & HENSHAW, LTD., BRISTOL 2, ENGLAND = ROTASIDE wagon tippler
~moräne *f*; siehe unter „Gletscher *m*"
~öffnung *f* [*Brücke f*] = side span
~raum *m*, siehe: Seitenstreifen *m*
~räumer *m*; siehe unter „Bulldozer *m*"
~räumschnecke *f* = side delivery auger
~reibung *f* = lateral friction

Seitenschalung *f*, **Straßenbauschalung** *f*, **(Beton)Schalungsschiene** *f*, **Schalschiene**

Fahrschiene *f*
Setzen *n*
Ausschalen *n*
Aussteifungseisen *n*
(Befestigungs)Keil *m*
Pflockstab *m*
LINNHOFF-Fahr- und Schalungsschiene *f*
KRUPP-Schalungsschiene *f*
Pflocktasche *f*
Pflockstabsetzer *m*
Pflockstabeintreiber *m*

(side) form, street form, (concrete) road ~, road-airport ~, track ~; paving ~ (US)
running rail, machine rail
form setting, form laying
stripping
stiffener
wedge
stake, pin
LINNHOFF form [*directly carrying the machines*]
KRUPP form [*integral with rail*]
stake pocket, ~ housing
pin setter, stake setter
pin driver, stake driver [*a paving breaker with a pin-driving fronthead*]

Seiten|schalungsinnenrüttler *m*; siehe unter „Betonrüttelgeräte *npl*"
~schurf *m*, Lateralerosion *f* (Geol.) = lateral erosion by water action
~stampfer *m*, Seitenstößel *m* = thwacker
~steifigkeit *f* = lateral rigidity
~stollen *m*, siehe: Zugangsstollen
~straße *f*, siehe: Nebenstraße
~streifen *m*, Seitenraum *m* [*Straße f*] = verge, margin, roadside waste; [*deprecated: roadside*]
~stütze *f*, siehe: ausfahrbare Stütze
~wand *f* = side wall
seitliche Zufahrt *f* [*zu einer Hauptstraße f*] = marginal access
seitliches Knicken *n* = lateral buckling

Sektionalkessel *m*, Gliederkessel = sectional boiler
Sektor|schütz(e) *n*, (*f*); siehe unter „Talsperre *f*"
~wehr *n*; siehe unter „Talsperre *f*"
selbständige Fahrbahndecke *f* **aus Zement-Ton-Beton** *m*, siehe: Zement-Ton-Betonstraße *f*
selbstansaugend; siehe unter „Pumpe *f*"
selbstansaugender Dieselmotor *m* = naturally aspirated diesel engine
Selbstauflader *m*, siehe: Becher(werk)auflader *m*
selbstaufnehmendes Förderband *n*, siehe: Becher(werk)auflader *m*

Selbstentlader — Setzpacklageschicht

Selbstentlader *m*, Selbstkipper *m* = self unloader
selbstfahrbar, selbstfahrend = self-propelled
selbstfahrbare (oder selbstfahrende) Motor-Spritzmaschine *f* = self-propelled sprayer (or spraying machine) for hand and power spraying with hand lance
Selbst|fahrwerk *n*; siehe unter „Autobagger *m*"
~fahrwerk *n* = self-propeleed carrier
~kipper *m*, Selbstentlader *m* = self unloader
Selbstkosten-Erstattungsvertrag *m* = cost-plus-fee contract, value-cost ~, cost-value ~
~ *m* mit begrenzter Höhe *f* der zuschlagberechtigten Kosten *fpl* = cost-plus-fixed fee contract, cost-plus-profit ~
Selbst|laufrinne *f* [*Hydromechanisierung f*] = flume [*hydraulicking*]
~muldenkipper *m*, Stahlkastenselbstkipper = automatic side tipping wagon
selbst|registrierendes Meßwehr *n* = recorder, recording gauge, recording measuring weir
~tragend = self-supporting
Selen|silber *n* (Min.) = silver selenide
~zelle *f* = selenium cell
Semi-Dieselverfahren *n* = mixed cycle
Senk|bewegung *f* = lowering motion
~blei *n*, siehe: Schnurlot *n*
~bremsensteuerung *f* = lowering brake control
~bremsschaltung *f* = lowering brake connections for cranes in three-phase installations
(~)Brunnengründung *f*, Senkbrunnenfundation *f* = (sunk) well foundation, well-sunk ~, open caisson ~
Senke *f* = swallow
Senk|faschine *f* = brushwood roll with gravel core
~geschwindigkeit *f* [*Bauaufzug m*] = lowering speed
~kasten *m*, Caisson *m* = caisson; well monolith (US)
~kastengründung *f*, siehe: Caissongründung *f*

~kastenkrankheit *f*; siehe unter „pneumatische Gründung *f*"
~niet *m* = counter-sunk rivet
Senkrecht|becherwerk *n* = vertical (bucket) elevator
~schweißung *f* = vertical welding
Senkrücken *m* = saddle-back
Senkung *f*, Setzung *f*, Sackung *f*, Untergrund ~ = (ground) settlement [*downward movements of the soil or of the structure which it supports due to the consolidation of the subsoil*]
Senkungs|betrag *m*, Setzungsbetrag = rate of (ground) settlement
~schutz *m* im Bergbau *m* = protection against mining subsidence
~trog *m*, Senkungswanne *f*, Geosynklinale *f* = geosyncline
Senk|winde *f* = lowering jack
~waage *f*, siehe: hydrostatische ~
Septarienton *m* = septarian clay
Serien|herstellung *f*, Serienfertigung *f*, Reihenfertigung = full scale production, serial fabrication
~muster *n* = production model
~schüsse *mpl*; siehe unter „1. Schießen *n*; 2. Sprengen *n*"
Serizit *m*, Seidenglimmer *m* (Min.) = sericite
~schiefer *m* = sericite schist
Serpentin *m* (Geol.) = serpentine
~asbest *m* (Min.) = serpentine asbestos
Serpentinenstraße *f* = serpentine road
Servitut *n*, Gerechtsame *f* = easement
Setzbecher *m*; siehe unter „Ausbreitversuch *m*"
Setzen *n* von Schalungsschienen *fpl*; siehe unter „Betonstraßenbau *m*"
Setzer *m* = fastener [*for fastening into steel and concrete*]
Setz|kopf *m* [*Niet m*] = die head, set ~
~latte *f*; s. unter „Fertigbehandlung *f*"
~maß *n*, siehe: Fließmaß
Setzpacklageschicht *f*, Gestück *n* = base of stone pitching, (hand-)pitched foundation, hand-set pitching, rough stone pitching, hand-packed bottoming, packed brocken rock soling, hand-pitched stone base, blocking (Brit.); (hand-packed) Telford (type) base (US)

Setzpacklagestein *m*, Vorlagestein *m*, Stückstein *m* = blockstone, handpacked hardcore, pitching stone, pitcher, handpacked stone, hand-placed stone, hand-pitched stone (Brit.); Telford stone, base stone (US)
Setz|pfosten *m*, siehe: Losständer *m*
~probe *f*, siehe: Ausbreit(ungs)versuch *m*
Setzung *f*, siehe: Senkung *f*
Setzungsklassierung *f* **durch flüssige Medien** *npl* = sorting, classifying
~ ~ Luft *f*, Windsichtung *f* = air classification
~ ~ Wasser *n* **oder Luft** *f* = classifying, classification
Setzungsunterschied *m*, siehe: ungleichmäßige Setzung *f*
Sheddach *n*, Scheddach = north light roof
sich absetzen, siehe: abschlämmen
Sicheldüne *f*, siehe: Bogendüne *f*
Sicherheit *f* **gegen Umkippen** *n* = safety against overturning
(Sicherheits)|Bankett *n*, siehe: Berme *f*
~flasche *f* [*Bindemittelrückgewinnungsapparat m*] = water trap

---

Sicherheitsglas *n*
  Verbundglas [*mehrschichtig*]
  vorgespanntes Glas [*einschichtig*]
  Drahtglas

safety glass
  laminated glass
  toughened glass
  wire(d) glass

Sicherheits|-Leitplanke *f* [*Straße f*] = safety fence, guard~, protection ~, guard rail
~spanne *f* = margin of safety
~ventil *n* **mit unmittelbarer Belastung** *f* = dead weight safety valve
~zündschnur *f*, schlagwettersichere Schwarzpulverzündschnur *f* = safety fuse
Sicherungsdraht *m* = lockwire
sichtbarer Horizont *m*, siehe: Kimme *f*
Sichtbarkeit *f* = visibility
Sichten *n* [*Aufbereitung f*] = air sifting
Sichter *m* = separator, air ~, air classifier
Sicht|fläche *f* = face
~höhe *f* [*Kranführer m*] = crane operator's eye level
~linie *f* = sight line, vision ~
~mauerwerk *n* = brick facing
~weite *f*, Sichtlänge *f*, Sichtweg *m* = sight distance, vision ~, visibility ~, seeing ~
Sicker|brunnen *m*, siehe: vertikale Sanddränage *f*
~drän *m*; siehe unter „Entwässerung *f*"
~füllung *f*; siehe unter „Entwässerung *f*"
~grube *f* = soakage pit, soakaway; [*in Scotland:* rummel]
~linie *f* = saturation line (or surface)
~schlitz *m*, siehe: Entwässerungsschlitz
~stollen *m* = filtration gallery
~strömung *f*, siehe: Grundwasserstromsickerung *f*
~verlust *m* = seepage loss, filtration ~
~wasser *n* = infiltration water
Siderit *m* (Min.), siehe: Eisenspat *m*
Sieb|anlage *f* **für (Beton)zuschlagstoffe** *mpl* = concrete aggregate screening plant
~bandrechen *m* = belt screen
~bereich *m* = envelope of grading
~boden *m* = screening medium
~deck *n* = screen(ing) deck
Sieben *n*, siehe: Siebung *f*

Siebextraktionsapparat *m* [*Apparatur für die Schnellanalyse von Straßenproben mit bit. Bindemitteln durch gleichzeitiges Extrahieren und Sieben*]
  Motor *m* mit Getriebe *n*
  Drehpunkt *m* der Schüttelbewegung *f*

sieving extractor

  geared motor unit
  pivot

Hebelklammer *f* — lever clamp
Ring *m* mit 4 Armen *mpl* — clamping ring with 4 legs
Bewegungswinkel *m* — angle of oscillation
Metallhaube *f* mit Preßdeckel *m* — metal head with press cap
Siebsatz *m* — nest of sieves
Ablaßhahn *m* — solution drain valve
Verbindungsstange *f* — connecting rod
Schwungrad *n* — flywheel

Sieb|felnblech *n* = screening sheet
~feld *n* = screening panel
~fläche *f* = screen(ing) surface
~flächenbereich *m* = grading zone
~gewebenummer *f* = mesh number
~grobblech *n* = screening plate
~gut *n* = material(s) to be graded
~kennlinie *f*, siehe: Grenzsieblinie *f*
~kies *m* = screened gravel
~kopf *m* = strainer head
~körper *m* = screen body
~kurve *f*, Sieblinie *f* = (aggregate) grading curve, particle-size distribution curve, grain-size distribution curve
~leistung *f* = screening efficiency
~linie *f*, siehe: Siebkurve *f*
~linie *f* der gewünschten Endprodukte *npl* = nominal grading curve
~linie *f* des Rohmaterials *n*, Ist-Linie = actual grading curve
~löffel *m* [*Sitzventil n*] = atomizer
~maschendrahtgewebe *n* = screen mesh, ~ fabric, ~ cloth
~maschine *f* = screening machine
~normen *fpl* = grading specifications
~öffnung *f*, siehe: lichte Maschenweite *f*
~probe *f*, siehe: Prüfen *n* der Kornzusammensetzung *f* durch Siebversuch *m*
~rahmen *m* = screen frame
Siebsatz *m* = sieve set, set of sieves, nest of sieves
~rüttler *m*, mechanischer Siebsatz-Schwingungserreger *m* = (mechanical) sieve shaker, mechanical vibrator for laboratory test sieves, vibrating test sieve shaker, test sieve vibrator
Siebseide *f* = bolting cloth
Siebstraße *f* mit fallender Masche *f* [am Anfang Grobkornabsiebung und am Ende Feinkornabsiebung f*] = screen surface with decreasing dimension of the clear opening towards the end
~ *f* mit steigender Masche *f* [*am Anfang Feinkornabsiebung f und am Ende Grobkornabsiebung f*] = screen surface with increasing dimension of the clear opening towards the end
Siebtrommel *f*, Sortiertrommel *f*, Trommelsieb *n* = revolving screen, drum screen, rotary screen, trommel
Siebung *f*, Sieben *n*, Sortierung *f*, Sortieren *n* = screening
~ durch spezifisches Gewicht *n* = separating
Sieb|verstopfung *f* = blinding of screen
~zylinder *m* [*Waschtrommel f*] = perforated cylinder
Siede|rohrdichtungsmaschine *f*, Rohreinwalzapparat *m*, Rohrwalze *f*, Rollmaschine = tube beader
~stein *m*, Zeolith *m* (Min.) = zeolite
Siedlung *f* = housing estate
Siedlungsstraße *f* = (housing) estate road
Siemens-Martin-Stahl *m* = Siemens-Martin steel, open-hearth ~
Sierozemboden *m* = Sierozem soil
Sietland *n* [*niederdeutscher Ausdruck*] = low-lying marsh land
Signal|anzeige *f* = aspect
~feld *n* = signal panel
~flagge *f* = jack
signalgesteuerter Knoten *m* = signal-controlled intersection
Signalisierung *f*, siehe: Verkehrssignal-Steuerung *f*
Signalisierungssystem *n* [*Straße f*] = system of controls
Signalreg(e)lung *f*, siehe: Verkehrssignal-Steuerung *f*

Signalschutz m der **Fußgänger** mpl = safe accomodation of pedestrian movements at signal-controlled intersections
Signalsteu(e)rung f, siehe: Verkehrssignal-Steuerung f
Signalwechsel m [*Verkehrssignal-Steuerung* f] = changing of aspect of traffic control signals
Sikkativ n = siccative
Silber|glanz m, Argentit m, Ag_2S (Min.) = argentite, silver glance
~**hornerz** n (Min.), siehe: Hornsilber n
~**lot** n = silver solder
~**nitrat** n, siehe: Höllenstein m
~**pappel** f, Weißpappel f = white poplar, ~ populus, abele
~**tanne** f, amerikanische ~ = noble silver fir
~**vitriol** n = silver sulphate
~**weide** f, Weißweide f = Huntingdon willow, white ~
~**zeder** f, siehe: Atlaszeder f
Silentblock m = cushioning block
Silifizierung f (Geol.) = silicification
Silikagel n = silica gel
Silikastein m, siehe: Quarzitstein m

Silikatbildner m, **Hydraulefaktor** m, **Wasserbindner** m
   Kieselsäure f, Siliziumdioxyd n, SiO_2
   Tonerde f, Aluminiumoxyd n, Al_2O_3
   Eisenoxyd n, Fe_2O_3

matter forming silicates
   silicic acid, silica
   alumina
   ferric oxide, iron oxide

Silikatdecke f, Wasserglasdecke f, Silikatmakadam m = silicated water-bound surfacing, ~ road crust
Silizium|dioxyd n, SiO_2 = silica, dioxide of silicon, silicon dioxide
~**karbid** n, siehe: Karborund n
~**stahl** m = silicon steel
Sillimanit m, siehe: Faserkiesel m
~**stein** m, Mullitstein m = sillimanite brick
Silo m, siehe: Lager ~
~**abmeßanlage** f, siehe: Abmeßanlage für Betonzuschlagstoffe mpl
~**batterie** f = group of bins
~**dosierapparat** m = bin batcher
~**fahrzeug** n, siehe: Behälter-Straßenfahrzeug
~**-Füllstandanzeiger** m, siehe: Bunkerstandanzeiger
siloloser Schwarzdeckenfertiger m = bituminous road surfacing finisher without hopper
Silo|schalung f = silo formwork
~**speicher** m, siehe: Lagersilo m
~**trichter** m, siehe: Silozelle f
~**verschluß** m = 1. bin door fill valve, bin gate [*controls the flow of materials from the storage bin into the batcher hopper*]; 2. discharge gate [*controls the flow of materials into transport vehicle*]
~**waage** f = bin weigh(ing) batcher scale
~**zelle** f, Speicherzelle f, Silotrichter m = silo compartment, ~ hopper
Silt m [*nach Fischer und Udluft (1936) und Gallwitz (1939) 0,2—0,02 mm*], Auelehm m = fine sand and coarse silt [*0.2—0.02 mm, Massachusetts Institute of Technology and British Standard Institution*]
silurisch = siluric, silurian
Simshobel m = rabbet plane, rebateplane
Sink m; siehe unter „Feinschluff m"
~**baum** m = sunken tree
~**geschwindigkeit** f, Abschlämmgeschwindigkeit = settling velocity
~**produkt** n = sink product
~**-Schwimmverfahren** n = sink-float method, heavy-media separation
~**stoff** m, Ausfällung f = sediment
~**stoffablagerung** f = sediment deposition
~**stück** n, Faschinenfloß n = honeycombed fascine raft

Sinnestäuschung f = error of judgment [*road accident*]

Sinter|-Flugasche f = sintered flyash

~metallurgie f = powder metallurgy

Sintern n, **Sinterung** f, beginnendes Schmelzen n = sintering, incipient fusion

Sinter|rost m = sinter(ing) grate, continuous conveyor ~

~tonerde f = sintered alumina

~zone f = sinter(ing) zone

Sintflut f = Deluge of Noah, Noachian Deluge

SIPOREX m [*Trademark*] = eine Gasbetonart [*Erfinderland Schweden*]

Sirene f = siren

Sisalhanf m = sisal hemp

Sitz m **der Setzung** f = seat of settlement

Skala f = scale

Skelett|bau m = skeleton structure

~-Teil m = frame member, skeleton ~

Skikuli m, **Ski-Kurz-Lift** m = small type ski hoist

Ski(schlepp)lift m, siehe: Schneeschuhläuferaufzug m

Skisprung-Überlauf m; siehe unter „Talsperre f"

Skolezit m, Wurmsiedestein m (Min.) = scolecite

S-Kurve f, siehe: Gegenbogen m

Slim-Hole-Bohren n = slim hole drilling

Sockelfundament n = pedestal

Sodastein m, Sodalith m (Min.) = sodalite

Sode f, Plagge f, Grassode, Rasensode f = (grass) sod, turf ~

Sohldruck m, Sohlpressung f = base pressure

Sohle f, Boden m [*als Fläche* f] = bottom ~ [*z. B. Stollen* m] = invert

Sohlenwasserdruck m, Auftrieb m [*Talsperre* f] = uplift, foundation water pressure

Sohl|platte f, Lagerplatte = sole plate, bed ~

~pressung f, siehe: Sohldruck m

~schwelle f, siehe: Bodenschwelle f

~stollen m = bottom drift

Solarisation f = solarization

Solaröl n, siehe: Gasöl n

Soleverdampfer m = brine evaporator

Solfatara f (Geol.) = solfatara

Soll|drehzahl f, Nenndrehzahl = rated speed, ~ RPM

~-Lage f = theoretical location

~maß n, Nennmaß = real measure, nominal size

~sieblinie f, siehe: Idealsieblinie

Solnhofener Schiefer m, ~ Plattenkalk m, ~ Kalkschiefer m = Solnhofen (platy) (lime)stone

solodiziert [*Boden* m] = solodized

Solquelle f = brine spring

Sommer|eiche f, Stieleiche f = common English oak

~ferienverkehr m = summer vacation travel

~linde f, großblättrige Linde f = large-leaved lime-tree

Sonde f = sounding apparatus, soil penetrometer

~ nach Barentsen = coneshaped sounding apparatus

~ nach Künzel = Künzel sounding apparatus

Sonden|bohrer m, Bodensonde f = probing staff, pricker staff

~bohrung f, Sondenpressung f = probing, pricking

~rammung f = driver probing, ~ pricking

Sonder|ausrüstung f = special equipment

~güte f = high grade

~mechanismus m = special mechanism

Sondier|bohrung f, Probebohrung f, Sondierungsbohrung f = exploratory boring

~stab m, Prüfstab = sounding rod

Sondierung f = sounding

Soniskop n = soniscope

Sonnen|dach n, Schutzdach n, Sonnenschutzdach n = concrete protection tent, curing ~

~selte f (Geol.) = adret

~stein m (Min.), siehe: Aventurinfeldspat m

Sorelzement m, Sorel'scher Zement m = Sorel(s) cement, plastic magnesia

Sorten-Zwischen(lade)bunker m, siehe: Baustellensilo m

Sortieren n, siehe: Siebung f

Sortier|gleis n, Zerlegungsgleis, Auszieh-
gleis = sorting track
~konus m, konischer Siebzylinder m =
conical-screen (arrangement), perforated
cone
~trommel f, siehe: Siebtrommel f
Soxhlet-Apparat m = Soxhlet extractor,
~ apparatus
Spachtel f, m, Glättkelle f = float,
smoothing trowel, finishing ~
Spalierzaun m, siehe: Ästelzaun
Spalt|barkeit f, Spaltfähigkeit f =
cleavage (property) [*of rocks and minerals*]
~destillation f = cracking
Spalte f (Geol.) = seam
Spalt|ebene f [*Mineral* n; *Gestein* n] =
cleavage plane, ~ crack [*mineral; rock*]
Spalten|(erd)öl n = crevice oil
~frost m, Oberflächenfrost = frost in the
surfacing
~quelle f, siehe: Kluftquelle
Spalt|festigkeit f = cleavage strength
~keil m = splitting wedge
~sieb n, siehe: Stangen(transport)rost m
spanischer Reiter m = cheveaux de frise
Spann|anker m = anchorage fixture
~armierung f, Spannbewehrung f = prestressing reinforcement
~balken m = prestressed beam
~bahn f, siehe: Spannbett n
~bank f, siehe: Spannbett n
Spannbeton m **mit nachträglichem Verbund** m = post-tensioned prestressed
(reinforced) concrete
~ ~ Verbund m = pre-tensioned prestressed concrete
~behälter m = prestressed concrete
tank
~biegebalken m, Spannbetonprobebalken
= prestressed flexure test beam
~element n, Spannbetonfertigteil m =
precast prestressed concrete unit
~-Gebäuderahmen m = prestressed concrete building frame
~-Hohlblockträger m = prestressed
block-beam
~schienenschwelle f = pre-stressed
concrete sleeper (Brit.)/tie (US)
~stahl m = prestressing steel

~startbahn f = prestressed runway
~straße f = pre-stressed concrete road
~-Straßenbrücke f = prestressed concrete
road bridge
~träger m **ohne Verbund** m = unbonded pre-stressed concrete beam
Spann|bett n, Spannbahn f, Spannbank f
= prestressing bed, ~ rack
~bewehrung f, Spannarmierung f =
prestressing reinforcement
~draht m = prestressing wire
~eisen n [*Straßenspannbeton* m] =
tendon
Spannen n **nach dem Erhärten** n **des Betons** m = tensioning after hardening
of concrete
~ vor dem Erhärten n **des Betons** m =
tensioning prior to the pouring of concrete
Spann|feder f, Ausgleichfeder [*Gleiskette* f]
= compensator spring, equalizer ~
~glied n = prestressing element, tendon
~kabel n [*Spannbeton* m] = tensioned
steel cable
~kanal m = prestressing duct
~kegel m [*Spannbeton* m] = interlocking
cone
~kraft f, Vorspannkraft = prestressing
force
~kraftgefälle n, Vorspannkraftgefälle =
prestressing force gradient
~presse f = jack, puller
~säule f [*Hammerbohrmaschine* f] =
pillar support [*drifter*]
~schloß n = swivel, turnbuckle
~schloß n [*Spannbeton* m] = locking
device
~schraube f = clamp(ing) screw
~schütz(e) n, (f) = pressure sluice (or
shutter)
~spindel f = takeup [*belt conveyor*]
~stahl m = prestressing steel
~station f [*Bandförderer* m] = takeup set
Spannungs|abweichung f, siehe: Span-
nungsunterschied m
~anhäufung f, Druckanhäufung f [*Baugrund* m] = bulb pressure
~anhäufung f, Spannungskonzentration f
= stress concentration
~beanspruchung f = stress application

Spannungs-Dehnungs-Diagramm — Spießglanzbleierz

Spannungs|-Dehnungs-Diagramm n, Spannungs-Dehnungs-Schaubild n = stress-strain diagram
~diagramm n, Druckdiagramm [*Baugrunduntersuchung f*] = pressure diagram
~ermittlung f, Spannungsnachweis m = stress analysis
~konzentration f, Spannungsanhäufung f = stress concentration
~korrosion f = stress corrosion
spannungslose Niveaufläche f (Geol.) = level of no strain
Spannungs|messer m = strain meter
~nachweis m, Spannungsermittlung f = stress analysis
~optik f = photoelasticity
~unterschied m, Sparnungsabweichung f = deviator stress
~verteilung f = stress distribution
~wandler m = voltage transformer, potential ~
~zahl f = stress ratio
~zuwachs m = increase of stress, stress increase
Spann|vorrichtung f = stressing device, tensioning ~
~weite f, Stützweite f = span
Sparren m = rafter
Sparverfahren n [*Holz* n] = empty-cell treatment [*wood*]
Spateisenstein m = spathic iron (ore)
Spatel m, f = spatula
Spaten m, siehe: Grabscheit n
~arbeit f = spade work
~hammer m = clay digger, ~ spade, spader, spade hammer
~meißel m; siehe unter „Bohrmeißel"
spätiger Gips m, siehe: Fasergips
Speckschmierung f = lard lubrication
Specksteinmehl n, siehe: Talkum n
Specularit m (Min.) = specular iron ore
Speichenrad n = spoke-type wheel
Speicher m = warehouse
~; siehe unter „Talsperre f"
~ablaß m; siehe unter „Talsperre f"
~becken n; siehe unter „Talsperre f"
~fähigkeit f, siehe: Fassungsvermögen n
~gestein n, Trägergestein = reservoir rock, container ~

~kessel m, siehe: Druckluftbehälter m
~sperre f; siehe unter „Talsperre f"
Speicherung f, Einstau m, Wassereinstau, Aufspeicherung, Stau, Stauanhebung f = storage, pondage, filling
Speicherzelle f, siehe: Silozelle f
Speisekanal m = feed(er) canal
Speiser m, Beschickungsapparat m, (Material)Aufgeber m, Aufgabeapparat m, Beschickervorrichtung f = feeder, feeding device, charging feeder
Speise|schnecke f, siehe: Schneckenspeiser m
~transformatorenhaus n, Speisetrafohaus n = (electricity) substation
~walze f, Zubringerwalze = roll feeder
~wasser n = feed water
Spermacetiöl n = sperm oil
Sperrad n = ratchet (wheel)
Sperr|ballon m = barrage balloon
~holzplatte f, Sperrholztafel f = plywood panel, ~ sheet
~holzschalung f = plywood slab formwork
~holzunterlage f = plywood base
~klinke f, Sperrzahn m = (locking) pawl
~schicht f, Abdichtungslage f = waterproofing course (or layer)
~schleuse f, siehe: Binnenschiffahrtschleuse
~see m = dam lake
~zahn m, siehe: Sperrklinke f
~zeit f [*Straße*] = block
~zusatz m, siehe: Dichtungsmittel n [*Beton*]
Spesen f = entertainment expenses
Spezial|fahrzeug n = special vehicle
~monteur m = specialist fitter
~profil n = special section
~stahl m = special steel
~transportwagen m = special transporter
Sphärolitgefüge n = spherulitic texture
Spiegel|erhebung f, siehe: Anstauung f
~gefälle n = fall at level (or surface)
~holz n, siehe: Radialschnitt m
spiegeloptisches Verfahren n = optical mirror method
Spiel|raum m = play
~zahl f = number of work cycles
Spießglanzbleierz n, siehe: Rädererz n

Splitt *m* = spilite
Spill *n*, siehe: Gangspill
~winde *f* = hoist
Spilosit *m* (Geol.) = spilosite
Spindel *f*, siehe: Schrauben(hebe)bock *m*
~, siehe: hydrostatische Senkwaage *f*
~ = spindle
~schieber *m* = sluice valve with direct spindle operation
~ventil *n* = spindle valve
Spinell *m* (Min.) = spinel
Spiral|bewehrung *f*, Spiralarmierung *f* = helical reinforcement
~bewehrungsmaschine *f*, Spiralarmierungsmaschine = spiral reinforcing machine
~bohrer *m* = twist drill
~bohrer *m* [*Bodenuntersuchung f*] = (earth) auger, soil ~, ~ boring ~
~bohrerkrone *f* = auger bit
~feder *f* = coil spring
~förderer *m* = spiral (feed) conveyor (or feeder)
spiralförmig angeordnete Mitnehmer-(schaufeln) *mpl*, (*fpl*) = spiral flights
Spiral|konzentrator *m* = spiral concentrator
~kratzer *m* = spiral scraper
~kurve *f* = spiral(l)ed curve
~meißel *m*; siehe unter „Bohrmeißel"
~(naß)klassierer *m*, siehe: Sandschnecke *f*
Spiritus *m*, C$_2$H$_6$O = (methylated) spirit, alcohol
~beize *f* = spirit-based mordant
Spitz|ahorn *m* = Norway maple
~bogen *m* = pointed arch [*abbreviated Ptd.A.*]
Spitzenausleger *m* [*Kran m*] = tip extension
Spitzenbelastung *f* = peak load
~ *f* **am Tage** *m* = peak daytime demand
Spitzen|(belastungs)pfahl *m*; siehe unter „Gründungspfahl *m*"
~drucksonde *f* = car-jack type sounding apparatus
~kraftwerk *n* = peak load power plant
~leistung *f* = peak production
~pfahl *m*; siehe unter „Gründungspfahl *m*"
~spiel *n* [*Zahnräder npl*] = crest clearance

~stunde *f* = peak hour
~zeit *f*, Spitzenperiode *f*, Stoßzeit *f* = peak period
Spitz|meißel *m*; siehe unter „Bohrmeißel"
spleißen, siehe: anscheren
Spleißnadel *f* = splicing needle
Splint *m* = cotter pin
~(holz) *m*, (*n*) = sapwood, alburnum
~fäule *f* = rotting of sapwood
~verbindung *f* = cotter joint
Splitt *m* = chipping, chip(ping)s, stone chips; [*deprecated: screening(s)*]
splittarmer Asphaltfeinbeton *m*, siehe: Topeka *m*
Splitt|brecher *m*; siehe unter „Backenbrecher *m*"
~sand *m*, siehe: Pochsand *m*
~streuer *m*, Splittstreugerät *n*, Splittstreumaschine *f* = chip spreader, chipping(s) machine, chipper, surface dressing chipping distributor
~streuer *m* **mit Schleuderverteilung** *f* = spinner type distributor (or spreader) for chipping(s); spinning (or spinner) gritter
~streukarre(n) *f*, (*m*), Handsplittstreuer *m* = barrow-type chipping(s) spreader, hand-operated ~ ~
Splitt-Teppich *m* = chip(ping)s carpet (or mat)
Splitt und Schotterverteiler *m* = aggregate spreader, stone ~
~verfüllschicht *f* [*Tränkmakadam m*] = choker course (of aggregate)
Spodumen *m* (Min.) = spodumene, triphane
Spore *f* = spore
sporenbildend = spore-forming
Spornrad *n* = individual wheel for road transport of crane
Spratzlava *f*; siehe unter „Vulkan *m*"
Spreitlage *f* = brushwood layer
Spreize *f*, siehe: Steife *f*
Spreiz|holmkurvenfahrwerk *n* = travel(l)ing gear with struts for running on curved rails
~ringkupplung *f* = expanding-band clutch
~träger *m* = spreader truss
Sprengen *n*; siehe unter „1. Schießen *n*; 2. Sprengen *n*"

Spreng|fels *m*, siehe: Kernfels *m*
~gelatine *f*; siehe unter „1. Schießen *n*; 2. Sprengen *n*"
~kammer *f* = demolition chamber, blast ~
~kapsel *f*; siehe unter „1. Schießen *n*; 2. Sprengen *n*"
~loch *n*; siehe unter „1. Schießen *n*; 2. Sprengen *n*"
~lochbohrer *m* = blast-hole drill
~öl *n*, Nitroglyzerin *n* = nitroglycerin(e), nitroleum, blasting oil, explosive oil, fulminating oil
~pulver *n*, Schwarzpulver = black (blasting) powder, gunpowder
~rampe *f*, Düsenstrang *m*, Spritzrampe; Balkenbrause *f* [*Schweiz*]; Spritzbarren *m* [*in Österreich*] [*Motorspritzgerät n*] = spray bar
~ring *m* = circlip
~rohr *n*, Spritzrohr, Beries(e)lungsrohr = spray bar
~schnur *f*; sieeh unter „1. Schießen *n*; 2. Sprengen *n*"
~stelle *f* = blast area
~stofflager *n* = explosives area
~wagen *m* = sprinkler truck (US)
~werkdach *n* = strutted roof
~zünder *m*; siehe unter „1. Schießen *n*; 2. Sprengen *n*"
Spreustein *m* (Min.), siehe: Fasersiedestein
Sprießbrett *n* = poling board
Sprieße *f*, Kanalstrebe *f*; [*in Österreich: Spriessel m*] = shoring strut, trench shore, trench strut (Brit.); trench brace (US)
Spring|flut *f* = spring-tide
~tidenhub *m* = spring range
Spritz|anstrich *m* = spray painting
~auftrag *m* = spray application
~barren *m*, siehe: Sprengrampe *f*
Spritzen *n* mit **Handpumpendruck** *m* und **Handrohr** *n* = hand spraying [*manual pumping and hand lance*]
~ ~ Maschinenpumpendruck *m* und **Handrohr** *n* = power spraying with hand lance
~ ~ Sprengrampe *f* = bar spraying
Spritz|flakon *n*, *m*, siehe: Zerstäuber *m*

~geräte *npl* [*Straßenbau m*] = spraying machinery
~kanone *f*, Monitor *m* = monitor
~pistole *f* = spray gun
~rampe *f*, siehe: Sprengrampe
~rohr *n*, siehe: Sprengrohr
~schlauch *m* = spray hose
Sprödbruch *m*, siehe: Bruchfestigkeit *f* in sprödem Zustand *m*
Sprödigkeitszone *f*, Bruchzone *f*, Zone *f* der Öffnungen *fpl* (Geol.) = zone of fracture
Sprosseneisen *n* = sash bar
Sprudel|quelle *f* = bubbling spring
~stein *m* = flos ferri
Sprüh|brenner *m* = vaporizing burner
~elektrode *f* [*Elektroabscheider m*] = discharge electrode, emitting ~, ionizing ~
~regen *m*, siehe: Rieselregen
Sprung *m* (Geol.), siehe: Verwerfung *f*
~wachs *n* = crackwax
Spül|bagger *m*; siehe unter „Naßbagger *m*"
~behälter *m* = flush tank
~bohren *n*, Spülbohrung *f* = wash boring, jetting, water flush method
~bohren *n* mit **Schnellschlag** *m*, siehe: Schlagspülbohren *n*
~damm *m*, gespülter (Erd)Damm, Vollspüldamm [*Spültransport m und Spüleinbau m*] = hydraulic fill embankment; ~ ~ dam
~einbaudamm *m* [*nur Spüleinbau m*] = semi-hydraulic fill embankment; ~ ~ dam
Spülen *n* [*Pfahl m*], siehe: Einspülen
Spüler *m*; siehe unter „Naßbagger *m*"
Spül|kernbohrung *f* = core wash boring
~kippe *f*, siehe: Aufspülung *f*
~luftkopf *m*, siehe: Blaskopf
~schütz(e) *n*, (*f*) = wash-out gate; flushing gate (US)
~sonde *f* von **Terzaghi** = (Terzaghi) wash-point sounding apparatus, wash, point soil penetrometer
~spritzverfahren *n*, Spülkippverfahren *n* = sluicing
~stange *f* = jetting rod
~stangengerät *n* = jetting cutter rod
Spund|bohle *f* = (sheet) pile
~brett *n* = matchboard

Spundwand f

paarig gerammte ~
Stahlspundbohle f, Spundwandeisen n
LARSSEN-Spundbohle f, LARSSEN-Profil n
Spundwand-Fang(e)damm-Ausbeulung f
Abschluß-Spundwand
fest verankerte ~

Teileinspundung f
Spundwandschloß n, Schloßeisen n
Flachprofil n
Kastenspundbohle f

Buckelblechspundwand f
Spundwandbauwerk n, Spundwandfang(e)damm m

Spundwandramme f
Holzspundwand f
Spundwandzelle f
unverankerte ~
verankerte ~
eingespannte ~
ausgesteifte ~
Spundwandrammung f
Einspundung f, Spundwandumschließung

sheet (pile) wall, sheet piling, sheet pile bulkhead, sheeting
two sheets driven simultaneously
steel sheet pile
LARSSEN (sheet) pile [*Trademark*]

cofferdam boil
bulkhead
sheet (pile) wall encastré at the anchorage
partial sheeting
interlock
straight web
box section (sheet) pile, encased (sheet) pile
buckled plate sheet piling
sheet-pile retaining wall, sheet piling cofferdam; pile dike (US)
sheeting driver
wood sheeting, timber ~
sheet pile cell
free ~ ~
anchored ~ ~
fixed ~
braced ~ ~
sheet pile driving
closed sheeting

Spur f = track(ing) [*depressions worn into the surface of a carriageway*]
~ = ga(u)ge [*railway*]
~, Verkehrs~, Fahr~ = traffic lane
~ [*Fahrspur ohne Vertiefungen*] = track
Spuren-Element n = trace element
Spur|fahren n = tracking
~**haltung** f = keeping to the track
~**kranz** m = (wheel-)flange, wheeled flange
~**kranzrad** n = flanged wheel
~**lager** n = angular bearing
~**nagel** m, siehe: Markierungsknopf m
~**streifen** m, Fahrrinne f [*Erdstraße f*] = wheelers
~**streifenstraße** f, befestigter Radspurstreifen m = strip(e) road, creteway, trackways
~**weite** f, Gleisspur f = track ga(u)ge, rail ~

Stab m [*Stahlbau m*] = member
~**alge** f, siehe: Diatomee f
~**bewehrung** f, Stabarmierung = bar reinforcement
stabil, siehe: langsambrechend
Stabilisator m = stabiliser, stabilising agent
~, Emulgator m, Schutzkolloid n = emulsion stabilizing agent, ~ stabilizer, emulsifier, emulsifying agent
~**flüssigkeit** f = fluid stabilizer, liquid ~
~**pulver-Verteiler** m = powder-spreader, bulk spreader [*a vehicle for distributing stabilisers in powder form*]
Stabilität f, siehe: Standfestigkeit f
Stab|rüttler m; siehe unter „Betonrüttelgeräte npl"
~**stahl** m = bar iron, bar-steel
Stacheldraht m = barbed wire
Stadtautobahn f = urban expressway

Stadt|autobahnnetz n = urban expressway system, ~ ~ net(work)
~bahn f = metropolitan railway (Brit.); ~ railroad (US); urban rapid transit system
~durchgangstunnel m = crosstown tunnel [*a tunnel with no surface connection in the town*]
Städtebau m = municipal engineering
städtebauliche Planung f, siehe: Stadtplanung
Städteplaner m, siehe: Stadtplaner
Städter m, **Stadtbewohner** m = town dweller, city ~
Stadt|gas n, siehe: Dowson gas
~gebiet n = urban area, city ~
~kanalisierung f, **Stadtentwässerung** f = town drainage
~kern m, **Stadtinnere** n, **Stadtmitte** f, **Innenstadt** f = town centre (Brit.); ~ center (US); central district, downtown
~mitte f, siehe: Stadtkern m
~planer m, **Städteplaner** m = city planner, town ~, municipal ~, urban ~
~planung f, **Städteplanung**, **städtebauliche Planung** = city planning, town ~, municipal ~, urban ~
~randsiedlung f = suburb
~straße f = (city) street, municipal road, town ~, urban ~, urban thoroughfare
~straßenausrüstung f = street furniture, ~ equipment
~straßennetz n = (urban) street network, (~) ~ system
~verkehr m = urban traffic
staffelweise arbeiten [z. B. Erdbaugeräte npl] = to work in echelon
stagnierendes Gewässer n = stagnant water
Stahl|anker m = steel tie(-rod)
~aufwand m = amount of steel
Stahlbau m, **Stahlkonstruktion** f = steel construction
~firma f = steel construction firm
Stahlbeton|balken m = reinforced concrete beam
~-Bemessung f = reinforced concrete design
~bestimmungen fpl = Building Code Requirements for Reinforced Concrete
~dammbalken m = reinforced concrete log
~decke f = reinforced concrete floor
~element n, siehe: Stahlbetonfertigteil m
~fachwerk n = reinforced concrete trussed girder
~fertigteil m, **Stahlbetonelement** n = pre-cast reinforced concrete (structural) unit
~-Kernmauer f; siehe unter „Talsperre f"
~kuppel f = reinforced concrete dome
~mauer f = reinforced concrete wall
~pfahl m; siehe unter „Gründungspfahl"
~-Plattenbalken m = reinforced concrete beam and slab
~-Rahmenkonstruktion f, **Stahlbeton-Stabwerk** n = reinforced concrete framed structure
~ringunterlage f = reinforced concrete foundation-ring
~rippendecke f **mit Füllkörpern** mpl = tile-and-joist construction
~rippendecke f **ohne Füllkörper** mpl = slab-and-joist construction, ribbed ~
~rohr n **für Druckleitungen** fpl, **Stahlbeton-Druckrohr** n = reinforced concrete pipe for pressure lines
~-Schalenbauteil m = reinforced concrete shell unit
~schleuderrohr n = centrifugally cast reinforced concrete pipe, spun concrete pipe
~skelett n = reinforced concrete framing (or frame)
~-Stabwerk n, **Stahlbeton-Rahmen-Konstruktion** f = reinforced concrete framed structure
Stahl|blech n = steel sheet
~blech-Druckrohrleitung f = plate steel penstock, steel (power) ~
~(blech)schalung f = metal form(work), steel shuttering, steel form(work)
~blechscheibenrad n = steel sheet disc wheel
~bolzenkette f = steel pin chain
~dalbe m = steel dolphin

Stahl|drahtgeflecht n, Stahldrahtgewebe n = steel mesh, meshwork, grid
~**drahtgurt** m = steel-wire belt
~**drahtseil** n, siehe: Drahtseil
~**druckrohrleitung** f, Stahltriebwasserleitung f = steel penstock
~**gerippe** n, siehe: Stahlskelett n
~**gewebeeinlage** f, Bewehrungsnetz n, Armierungsnetz, Netzarmierung f, Netzbewehrung, Netzgewebeeinlage = reinforcing (road) mesh, mesh reinforcement, fabric reinforcement, reinforcing screen
~**hochbau** m = steel building construction
~**hochbauwerk** n = steel building structure
~**kastenselbstkipper** m, siehe: Selbstmuldenkipper
~**konstruktion** f = (structural) steelwork, steel structure
~**leichtträgerdecke** f **mit Hohlkörpern** mpl = lightweight composite floor of prefabricated steel lattice girders and filler tiles
~**mattenbelag** m = Square Mesh Tracking, SMT [*Trademark*]
~**montage** f = steel erection
~**muldenkipper** m; siehe unter „Fahrzeuge npl für den Transport m von Boden m und Steinbaustoffen mpl"
~**pfahl** m; siehe unter „Gründungspfahl m"
~**platte** f [*Steinformmaschine f*] = steel pallet
~**plattenband(förderer)** n, (m) = steel plate conveyor
~**profil** n, siehe: Fassoneisen n
~**(roh)eisenschlacke** f, siehe: Stahlschlacke
~**rohr(förder)band** n = tubular steel type belt conveyor
~**rohrgerüst** n, Stahlrohrrüstung f = tubular steel scaffold(ing)
~**rohrgitterturm** m = steel tubing lattice tower
~**rohrpfahl** m; siehe unter „Gründungspfahl m"
~**rohrstütze** f = steel tube shore
~**rohrzylinder** m = steel pipe mandrel

~**saitenbeton** m, Bauweise f Hoyer = prestressed concrete with thin wires, Hoyer method
~**schalung** f, siehe: Stahl(blech)schalung f
~**schalungsträger** m = steel horizontal form support
~**scheidewand** f, siehe: Stahltrennwand
~**schiene** f = steel rail
~**schlacke** f, Stahl(roh)eisenschlacke = stahl-eisen slag, slag from pig iron for steel making purposes
~**schrott** m [*Betonzuschlag(stoff) m*] = steel aggregate
~**seele** f; siehe unter „Drahtseil n"
~**seil** n, siehe: Drahtseil
~**skelett** n, Stahlgerippe n = (building) steel frame(work) (or skeleton), steel framing
~**skelettbau** m = steel skeleton construction
~**skelettgebäude** n = steel-frame(d) building
~**spannung** f = steel strain
Stahlspund|bohle f, Spundwandeisen n = steel sheet pile
~**wandzelle** f = steel sheetpile cell
Stahl|stein(geschoß)decke f = floor made up of reinforced brick panels
~**stütze** f = steel column
~**trägerstapel** m = steel cribbing
~**träger-Verbundkonstruktion** f = compound steel beam structure
~**trennwand** f, Stahlscheidewand = steel partition (wall)
~**trümmer** f = steel wreckage
~**werk** n = steel plant
~**wolle** f = steel wool, ~ shaving
Staket n = pale fencing
Stalagmit m, Auftropfstein m = stalagmite
Stalaktit m, Abtropfstein m = stalactite
Stamm m [*entastet*] = log
~**gleis** n = main(-line) track
~**personal** n, Stammbelegschaft f = permanent staff
Stampfasphalt m [*gegebenenfalls mit Bitumen angereichert*] = compressed asphalt
~ **ohne Bitumenzusatz** m = compressed (natural) rock asphalt (surfacing) [*deprecated: powder asphalt, rock asphalt stamped asphalt*]

Stampf|bagger *m*, siehe: Freifall-Kranstampfer *m*
~**balkenfertiger** *m*, siehe: Schlagbohlenfertiger
~**bohle** *f*, Schlagbohle, Stampfbalken *m*, Verdichtungsbohle [*Betondeckenfertiger m*] = tamping beam, tamper ~
~**bohlenfertiger** *m*, siehe: Schlagbohlenfertiger

Stampfe *f*, siehe: Holzstößel *m*
Stampf-Einrichtung *f* **für Bagger**, siehe: Freifall-Kranstampfer *m*
Stampfen *n*, siehe: Abrammen *n*
Stampfer *m* = tamper
~ **für Straßenbauschalung** *f* = form tamper
Stampffertiger *m* = bridge tamper, road tamping machine

(**Stampf**)**Hammerfertiger** *m*, kombinierter **Stampfbohlen- und -hammerfertiger** *m*, **Fabrikat DINGLER-WERKE AG, ZWEIBRÜCKEN / PFALZ, DEUTSCHLAND**	hammer tamping finisher
Abgleichbohle *f*, Abziehbohle *f*	oscillating levelling beam (Brit.); strike-off (US)
Hammerreihe *f*	row of hammers, series of lozenge shaped hammers [*rhomboidal in shape, each weighing about 66 lbs. which fall freely on to the concrete surface*]
Nachstampfbohle *f*	heavy tamping beam, tamper [*delivering 160 blows per minute*]
Schwingungsschleifbalken *m*, Vibrationsschleifbalken *m*	vibrating beam, vibrating smoother

---

Stampfmaschine *f*, Betonstein ~ = tamp(ing) (concrete) (block) machine
~ **für Betonplattenherstellung** *f*, siehe: Betonplatten-Stampfmaschine *f*
~ **für Betonrohrherstellung** *f*, siehe: Zementrohrstampfmaschine *f*
Stampf|mühle *f*, Pochwerk *n* = stamp
~**platte** *f* [*Freifall-Kranstampfer m*] = tamping plate, falling-plate tamping unit
(~)**Ramme** *f* = rammer
Stand|anzeiger *m*, Füll-~, Behälter-Standanzeiger, Stand-Meßgerät *n* = bin level indicator, material ~ ~
~**bahn** *f* **mit Kettenbetrieb** *m* = endless chain haulage plant, tubhaul plant, creeper
Ständerfachwerk *n* = vertical truss
Stand|festigkeit *f*, Standsicherheit *f*, Stabilität *f* = stability
~**geld** *n* = demurrage (charge)
ständiger Benutzer *m*, Pendler *m* = commutor

Stand|kahn *m* = stationary storage barge
~**kessel** *m* = vertical boiler
~**kessel** *m* **mit waagerechten Quersiedern** *mpl*, Lachapellekessel *m* = vertical cross tube boiler
~**-Meßgerät** *n*, siehe: Standanzeiger *m*
~**ort** *n* = location
~**ortbestimmung** *f* = position plotting
~**platz** *m*, siehe: Abstellfläche *f*
~**rohr** *n* = stand pipe, vertical ~
~**sicherheit** *f*, siehe: Standfestigkeit *f*
~**spur** *f* **mit Belag** *m* = paved shoulder
~**spur** *f*, Randstreifen *m*, Parkstreifen = (road) shoulder, highway~, hardened ~, parking strip
~**spurböschung** *f* = shoulder slope
Stange *f*, Pfosten *m* = post
Stangen|aufgeber *m*, siehe: Stangen(transport)rost *m*
~**rostsiebdeck** *n* = grizzly bar deck
~**schlangenbohrer** *m* = hand auger
~**schneckenbohrer** *m* = single twist auger

Stangen|(transport)rost *m*, Stangenaufgeber, Stangensiebrost, Spaltsieb *n*, Grobsortierrost *m* = screen of bars, bar screen, (bar) grizzly, grizzly feeder

~(transport)rost *m* (oder **Stangenaufgeber** *m*) **mit Vibrationsvorrichtung** *f* = grizzly (or screen of bars, or bar screen, or bar grizzly) with vibrating mechanism, vibrating bar grizzly, vibrating rod grizzly

~zinn *n* = bar tin

~zirkel *m* = beam compasses, trammels

Stapel *m* = crib

~ = pile, heap

~abnahmegerät *n* = destacker

~förderer *m*, siehe: Stapler *m*

~gerät *n*; siehe unter „Seilförderanlage *f*"

~lauf *m* = launching ceremony

stapeln, auf~ = to pile (up), to stack

Stapelprüfung *f* **für Asbestspinnfaser** *f* = array test for asbestos spinning fibre (Brit.)/fiber (US)

Stapler *m* = stacker, tiering machine

~, Stapelförderer *m* = piler

starkverdichtete Erdauskleidung *f* = heavy compacted earth lining

starr, biegefest = rigid

starre Decke *f*, **~ Straßendecke** = rigid pavement

~ Knotenverbindung *f* = rigid knot-joint

~ Kreisschwingung *f* = positive circle-throw gyratory movement

starrer Kreisschwinger *m*, **starres Kreisschwingsieb** *n* = positive circle-throw type screen

~ Rahmen *m* = rigid frame, continuous ~

starre Verbindung *f* = fixity at the connection

Starrpunkt *m* [*Bitumen* *n*] = shatter point, brittle ~

Startmotor *m* = starting engine

Start- und Zielort(verkehrs)zählung *f* = origin and destination survey, O-D ~

Statik *f* = statics

stationär, siehe: ortsfest

stationäre Großmischanlage *f*, ortsfeste **~** = central mixing plant

stationärer Strömungszustand *m*, stetiges Fließen *n* = steady state of flow condition

Stationierung *f* = stationing, chainage

statisch bestimmt (oder berechnet) = statically determinate, ~ determined

statische Berechnung *f* = structural analysis

statisches Moment *n* = statical moment

Statisches Tagebuch *n* = Statics Journal

statisch unbestimmt = statically indeterminate

~ unbestimmtes Hauptsystem *n* = statically-indeterminate principal system

statischer Druck *m* = static pressure

Statistiker *m* = statistician

statistische Fehleruntersuchung *f* = statistical control of errors

Stativ *n* = tripod

Statuenmarmor *m* = statuary marble

Stau *m*, siehe: Anstauung *f*

~ [*Straßenverkehr* *m*] = congestion

~anlage *f*, Staustufe *f* = barrage

Staub *m* = dust

~, siehe: Blume *f*

~absaugungsanlage *f*, siehe: Entstaubungsanlage *f*

Staubalkenwehr *n*, Dammbalkenwehr = stop log weir

Staub|ausblasung *f* [*Bohrloch* *n*] = puff-blowing

~bindemittel *n* = dust palliative, ~ preventer

~bindung *f* = dust alleviation, dust (al)laying, alleviation of dust, dust suppression, dust control, abatement of dusting

~(brannt)kalk *m* = pulverized lime

staubdicht = dustproof, dust-tight

Staubecken *n*; siehe unter „Talsperre *f*"

staub|förmiges Schüttgut *n* = pulverulent material

~freier Trockengesteinsbohrer *m* = dustless dry rock(-)drill

Staubgranulierungsverfahren *n* = dust nodulizing process

Staub|kammer *f* = velocity-reducing dust collector

~lawine *f* = loose snow avalanche

~luft *f* = dust-laden air

Staubogen *m*, Reduzierstück *n* [*Druckluftbetonförderer* *m*] = adapter bend

Staubrückgewinnung *f* = dust recovery

Staub|sand *m*, siehe: Feinsand *m*
~schwelung *f* **in der Schwebe** *f* [*Schieferöl n*] = fluidization
~wolke *f* = dust cloud
Stauch|bohrer *m* = percussive drill [*subsurface investigation*]
~temperatur *f* [*Niet m*] = upsetting temperature
Stauchung *f* = pushup
Staudamm *m*; siehe unter „Talsperre *f*"
stauen [*Wasser n*] = to impound, to back up
Stauffer|büchse *f*, Fettpreßbüchse = grease cup, stuffing box
~fett *n* = cup grease
Stau|haltung *f*, siehe: Haltung
~kraftwerk *n* = non-diversion type river power plant
~mauer *f*; siehe unter „Talsperre *f*"
~quelle *f* = contact spring
~raum *m*, siehe: Fassungsvermögen *n*
Staureg(e)lung *f*, siehe: Kanalisierung *f*
Staurolith *m*, Kreuzstein *m* (Min.) = staurolite, staurotide
Stau|schwelle *f*, siehe: Bodenschwelle *f*
~see *m*; siehe unter „Talsperre *f*"
~see *m* (Geol.), unter: Abdämmungssee
~spiegel *m*, siehe: Stauziel *n*
~strecke *f*, siehe: Haltung *f*
~stufe *f*, siehe: Stauanlage *f*
~stufe *f* = fall
~stufenkraftwerk *n* = barrage power station
~tafel *f*, siehe: Schütz(e) *n*, (*f*)
~wand *f* [*Schwerttrommelwäsche f*] = annular dam
~wasserdruck *m* = impounded water pressure
(Stau)Wehr *n*, siehe: Wehr *n*
Stauwerk *n*; siehe unter „Talsperre *f*"
Stauziel *n*, Stauspiegel *m* = level of storage water (Brit.); capacity level, storage level (US); height of the maximum storage
Stearin|pech *n* = stearin pitch
~säure *f* = stearic acid
Stech|heber *m* = plunging siphon
~karre(n) *f*, (*m*) **zum Transport** *m* **über Treppen** *fpl* = stairwalking hand truck
~spaten *m*, siehe: Dränspaten *m*

~uhr *f* = time clock
~zirkel *m* = dividers
Steckbügel *m* = tie
Steg *m*, siehe: Laufsteg *m*
~ [*bei Hochbaustellen fpl*] = runway
Steg(blech) *m*, (*n*) = web (plate)
Stegblech|beule *f* = buckling of the web (plate)
~stoß *m* = web attachment, web (plate) joint
Stegverbindungsstück *n*, Verkupplung *f* = separator
Stehbolzenniethammer *m* = stud riveting hammer
stehendes Wasser *n* [*auf einer Fläche f*] = standing water
Steife *f*, Spreize *f* = stay, shore
~ = stiffener
~, siehe: Konsistenz *f*
steife Brise *f* = strong wind
steifer Anschluß *m* = rigid connection
Steifeziffer *f*, Steifezahl *f* [*Boden m*] = modulus of volume change
Steifheit *f*, Steifigkeit *f* = stiffness, rigidity
steifplastisch = stiff-plastic
Steifrahmen *m* = rigid frame
~brücke *f* = skewed rigid frame bridge
Steig|bö *f* = rising gust
~eisen *n*, siehe: Klettereisen *n*
Steigeschacht *m* = riser shaft, rising ~
Steig|fähigkeit *f* [*Fahrzeug n*] = negotiating capacity, hill climbing ability
~geschwindigkeit *f*, Kriechgeschwindigkeit = creep speed
~spur *f* [*auf Autobahnen fpl für langsamfahrende LKWs bei Steigungen fpl*] = creeper lane, climbing ~
Steigung *f*, Neigung *f*, Gefälle *n* [*Straße f*] = gradient section
Steigungs|strecke *f* = up-grade section, uphill ~
~widerstand *m* = negotiating resistance
Steilförderer *m* = steep-incline conveyor
Steilküste *f*, Steilufer *n*, Kliff *n*, Kliffküste *f* = high coast, bold shore, cliff, cliffed coast(line)
Stein *m* **beim Prepaktbeton** = plum, displacer
~(ab)deckung *f*, siehe: Steindeckwerk *n*

Stein|automat *m*, siehe: Steinfertigungsautomat
~bearbeitungsmaschinen *fpl* = stone working machinery
~bestürzung *f*, siehe: Steindeckwerk *n*
~-Bohrmaschine *f* = natural stone drilling machine

Steinbruch *m*
Abbau *m*
Gruben~
Hang~
Stollen~
abbauen
Wand *f*, (Stein)Bruchwand
stillgelegt
gelernter Steinbrucharbeiter *m*
Steinbruchmaschinen *fpl*
Steinbruchabfall *m*

Stein|bruch(hochlöffel)bagger *m* = quarry shovel, rock ~, heavy duty ~
~buhne *f* = stone built groyne (Brit.); ~ ~ groin (US)
~deckwerk *n*, Stein(ab)deckung *f*, Steinbestürzung *f*, Steinvorlage *f* = (rock) riprap, stone riprap
~drän *m*; siehe unter „Entwässerung *f*"
Steine und Erden-Industrie *f* = Pit and Quarry Industry
Stein|eiche *f*, siehe: Früheiche *f*
~fertiger *m*, siehe: Beton(form)steinmaschine *f*
~(fertigungs)automat *m* = automatic block (making) machine
~(fertigungs)maschine *f*, siehe: Beton(form)steinmaschine
~formmaschine *f*, siehe: Beton(form)steinmaschine
~fräsmaschine *f* = natural stone milling machine
~fülldamm *m*; siehe unter „Talsperre *f*"
~gabel *f*, siehe: Schottergabel *f*
~geschiebe *n* = boulder shingle
~gut *n* [*Tonware f mit porigem Scherben m*] = earthenware
~harke *f*, siehe: Felsrechen *m*
steinhart = rock-hard

(Stein)Brecher *m*, Grobzerkleinerungsmaschine *f* = (rock) crusher, stone ~
Steinbrecheranlage *f*, siehe: Brechanlage *f*
(Stein)Brecher *m* **mit Rollenlagerung** *f* = (rock) crusher with HYDROL bearings (Brit.)

(stone) quarry, rock ~
quarrying
pit ~
hillside ~
mine ~
to strip, to quarry
face
inactive, disused
quarryman, quarry-worker
stone quarrying machinery
grout (US); quarry waste

Stein|holz *n* = magnesium oxychloride
~industrie *f* = rock industry
~-Kastendurchlaß *m* = stone box culvert
~kiefer *f* = stone pine
~kiste *f* = wooden crib filled with riprap
~kistenbau *m* = foundation by timber casing
~kistenwehr *n* = cribwork dry stone weir
~klee *m* = sweet clover, melilot
~knack *m*, Steinschutt *m* = rubble (Brit.)
Steinkohlenteer|kreosot *n*, siehe: Phenol *n*
~pech *n*, Steinkohlenpech = coal-tar pitch
Stein|körnung *f* = nominal size of mineral aggregate, (size) fraction ~ ~ ~, size bracket ~ ~ ~
~-Lehm-Kerndamm *m*; siehe unter „Talsperre *f*"
~maschine *f*, siehe: Beton(form)steinmaschine
~matte *f* = stone matting
Steinmauerwerk *n*, siehe: (Natur-)Steinmauerwerk *n*
~ mit unbearbeiteter Sichtfläche *f* = rubble walling
Stein|mehl *n*, siehe: Blume *f*
~meißel *m* = stone chisel
~metz *m* = mason, stone ~

Stein|mole *f* = rock mole
~nest *n*, siehe: Kiesnest *n*
~packung *f*, siehe: Steinsatz *m*
~pfad *m* = stony track
(~)Pflaster *n*, siehe: Pflasterdecke *f*
~platte *f* = stone slab
~plattenpflaster *n* = stone-block paving
~-Poliermaschine *f* = natural stone polishing machine
~rigole *f*; siehe unter „Entwässerung *f*"
~säge *f* = stone-cutting saw, masonry saw
~salz *n*, Chlornatrium *n*, NaCl = halite, common salt, rock salt
~satz *m*, Steinpackung *f*, vorlageartiges Pflaster *n* = hand placed (stone) riprap, pitched slope
~satzsperre *f*; siehe unter „Talsperre *f*"
Steinschlag *m*, siehe: Bergschlag *m*
~, siehe: Schlagschotter *m*
~asphalt *m*, siehe: Asphaltmischmakadam *m*
~gabel *f*, siehe: Schottergabel
~hammer *m* = stone breakers' hammer
~rinne *f* (Geol.) = bergfall furrow, rock fall ~
~straße *f* **nach Mac Adam**, Makadamstraße *f* = macadam(ised) road
Stein|-Schleifmaschine *f* = natural stone grinding machine
~schotter *m*, siehe: Kiesschotter *m*
~schraube *f* = rag(ged) bolt
~schürze *f* = stone apron
~schutt *m*, siehe: Steinknack *m*
~schüttdamm *m* mit wasserseitiger Betondichtungsdecke *f*; siehe unter „Talsperre *f*"
~setzer *m*, siehe: Pflasterer *m*
~spalthammer *m* = stone sledge, masons' hammer
~speldel *m*, siehe: Schrotkeil *m*
(~)Splitt *m* = (stone) chip(ping)(s)
~splitter *m* = flake, spall, galet, stone splinter
~-Trennsäge *f* = masonry saw, stone-cutting saw
~vorlage *f*, siehe: Steindeckwerk *n*
~wolf *m*, siehe: Keilklaue *f*
~wolle *f* = rock wool
~wolleisolierung *f* = wool batt-type insulation

~wurf *m*, Rauhwurf, geschüttetes Steindeckwerk *n*, geschüttete Stein(ab)deckung *f*, geschüttete Steinbestürzung *f* = truck-dumped (US)/lorry-dumped (Brit.) (stone) riprap, dumped (stone) riprap
~wüste *f* = rocky desert
~zange *f* = stone (lifting) tongs, lifting ~
~zeug *n* [*Tonware f mit verglastem Scherben m*] = stoneware, flint ware
Salzglasur *f* = salt-glaze
verglast = vitrified, vitreous
~zeugrohr *n*, siehe: Tonrohr *n*
Stell|macher *m* = cart-wright, wheelwright
~mutter *f*, Ver~ = adjusting nut
~ring *m*, Ver~ = adjusting ring
~schraube *f*, Ver~ = adjusting screw
Stellung *f* = position
Stelzenunterbau *m*, hoher Pfahlrost *m* = elevated pile foundation grill
Stemm|arbeiten *f* = cutting work(s)
~tor *n*; siehe unter „Binnenschiffahrtschleuse *f*"
Stempel *m* = prop
~ [*CBR-Versuch m*] = penetration piston
~druckfestigkeit *f* [*Bodenbeton m*] = resistance to punching shear
Stephanit *m*, Melanglanz *m* (Min.) = stephanite, brittle silver ore
Steppen|boden *m* = steppe soil
~-Hochebene *f* = barren plateau
Stern|meißel *m*; siehe unter „Bohrmeißel"
~-Standmotor *m* = radial engine
Stetig|(beton)verteiler *m*; siehe unter „Beton(decken)verteiler *m*"
~(beton)zwangsmischer *m*; siehe unter „Betonmischer *m*"
stetiges Fließen *n*, siehe: stationärer Strömungszustand *m*
~ Wiegen *n* = continuous weighing
Stetig|filter *n*, *m* = continuous filter
~förderer *m*, Fließförderer *m*, Massenförderer, Dauerförderer *m* = continuous conveyor
~mischanlage *f* = continuous (mixing) plant
~mischer *m*, siehe: kontinuierlicher Mischer *m*

Stetig|-Trockenbagger m = continuous excavator
~-Zwangsmischer m = constant-flow (or continuous) pug-mill (mixer)
steuerbegünstigt = tax-aided
Steuer|gerät n = controller
~organ n, siehe: Schaltorgan
~rad n, Lenkrad = steering wheel
~stand m, siehe: Bedienungsstand
~tafel f, Steuerungstafel, Kommandogerät n, Schalttafel, Schaltschrank m = control panel
~ventil n, siehe: Regelventil
~welle f = control shaft
Stich m, siehe: Bogenpfeil m
~axt f, Stoßaxt = twybill, mortise axe
~balken m = dragon beam
~bogen m, Segmentbogen m, flacher Bogen m = segmental arch
~flamme f = thin flame, narrow ~, blast ~
~gleis n, siehe: Anschlußgleis
~graben m; siehe unter „Entwässerung f"
~kappe f [*Gewölbe* n] = groin
~kuppel f, Stützkuppel, Hängekuppel, Kugelgewölbe n = spherical dome
~straße f [*Verbindung zwischen Einbahnstraße und Stadtautobahn*] = ramp
~tagsmessung f = random measurement
~torf m = dug peat
Stickstoff m = nitrogen [*former name* "*azote*"]
~oxyd n = oxide of nitrogen
Stiel m [*Rahmen* m] = leg
~eiche f, siehe: Sommereiche f
Stift m = stud
Stiftenschleudermaschine f; siehe unter „Mühle f"
Stift|schlüssel m = fork-wrench, fork spanner
~schraube f = double-ended bolt
Stillegung f = shutdown
Stinkkalk m, siehe: bituminöser Kalkstein m
Stirn|kipper m [*Waggonkipper* m] = end tippler
~mauer f = head wall
~naht f = transverse weld
~turbine f, siehe: Frontalturbine

Stochern n [*Betonverdichtung* f] = rodding, puddling
stocken [*Holz*], siehe: (ab)stocken
Stocken n = stone granulating
Stockpunkt m [*Kälteverhalten* n *von Dieselkraftstoff* m] = setting point
~ [*Öl* n] = pour point [*oil*]
Stockwerk n = stor(e)y
~ (Geol.) = stockwork
Stockwerksgarage f = multistor(e)y parking garage
~ mit beweglichen Rampen fpl = movable-ramp multi-stor(e)y garage
stockwerkshohe Gipsplatte f = big plaster board
Stockwerksrahmen m = multi-stor(e)y portal structure
Stoffangtrichter m, siehe: Klärturm m
Stoffgleitklausel f = materials fluctuation clause
Stollen m; siehe unter „Tunnelbau m"
~ [(*Gleis*)*Kette* f] = grouser, ice and dirt ~
~aufzug m = cherry picker
~lademaschine f, Stollenschaufellader m, Stollenbagger m [*in größerer Ausführung: Tunnelschaufellader* m] = mucking shovel, ~ machine, mechanical muck-loader, mucker, tunnel mucker, tunnel mucking machine, tunnel shovel
~lok(omotive) f = tunnel loco(motive)
~platte f [(*Gleis*)*Kette* f] = grouser-shoe
~vortrieb m; siehe unter „Tunnelbau m"
Stoney-Schütz(e) n, (f); siehe unter „Talsperre f"
Stopfbuchse f [*Kreiselpumpe* f] = gland
Stopp|linie f, siehe: Haltelinie
~straße f = through street, ~ highway
~uhr f = stopwatch
Storch(en)schnabel m, Pantograph m = pantograph
Stör|anfälligkeit f = susceptibility to failures
~faktor m = disturbance factor
~pegel m = level of background noises
Störungs|gewinn m = remo(u)lding gain
~verlust m = remo(u)lding loss
Stoß|axt f, siehe: Stichaxt
~barren m [*in Österreich*], siehe: Schubstange f

Stoß|beanspruchung f = impact stress
~**beiwert** m, Stoßzuschlag m = impact allowance, allowance for impact
~**belastung** f = shock loading
~**(boden)verdichtung** f = soil compaction by impact
~**(boden)verdichtungsgerät** n = impact soil-compaction device
~**bohrmaschine** f = piston drilling machine, drifter (machine)
~**dämpfer** m = shock absorber
~**fuge** f [Mauerwerk n] = vertical joint
~**mischer** m, siehe: Chargenmischer m
~**raupe** f; siehe unter „Radschrapper m"
~**stange** f [Auto n] = bumper, fender
~**versuch** m, Schlagversuch = impact test
stoßweise Balastung f = pulsating load
Stoß|widerstand m [Gestein n], siehe: Schlagfestigkeit f
~**wirkung** f = impact
~**zeit** f, Spitzenzeit f, Spitzenperiode f = peak period
~**ziffer** f, Stoßzahl f = coefficient of impact, impact factor
Strahl|bohrung f, siehe: Feuerstrahlbohren n
~**brenner** m = jet burner
Strahlen|glimmer m (Min.) = striated mica
~**kupfer** n (Min.) = clinoclasite
Strahl|kies m, Markasit m (Min.) = marcasite
~**(mahl)mühle** f; siehe unter „Mühle f"
~**stein** m (Min.), siehe: Aktinolith m
(Strahlungs)|Deckenheizung f = ceiling panel heating
~**fühler** m = radiation detector
~**heizung** f = radiant heating, panel ~
~**kessel** m = radiant heat boiler
~**wärme** f = radiant heat
Strahlwelle f = jet wave, stream ~
Strand m, Gestade n = shore, beach
~**bildung** f = beach building, shore ~
~**buhne** f, Seebuhne f = beach groyne (Brit.); shore jetty (US)
~**düne** f, siehe: Küstendüne
~**hafen** m = dry harbo(u)r, stranding ~
~**hafer** m, siehe: Helm m
~**halde** f (Geol.) = (wave-built) shoreface terrace

~**mauer** f [geneigte Außenfläche f] = sloping sea (protection) wall
~**mauer** f [senkrechte Außenfläche f] = vertical sea (protection) wall
~**terrasse** f, Strandplattform f, Strandleiste f (Geol.) = wave-cut platform
stranggepreßte Bodenplatte f = extruded floor tile
Strang|presse f = extrusion press
~**preßeigenschaft** f, Auspreßeigenschaft [z. B. Schieferton m] = extruding property
~**preßverfahren** n [Ziegelherstellung f] = stiff mud process, wirecut brickmaking
Straße f = road [deprecated: roadway]
~ **mit drei Spuren** fpl je Richtung f = three-lane dual carriageway
~ **ohne Richtungstrennstreifen** m, ungeteilte Straße = undivided two-way road
Straßen|anlieferung f, siehe: LKW-Transport m
~**aufbauweise** f, siehe: mehrschichtige Einbauweise
~**aufbruchhammer** m, Aufbruchhammer, Aufreißhammer = road breaker, pavement breaker, paving breaker; road ripper (Brit.)
~**aufrauhmaschine** f = road grooving machine
~**aufreißer** m = road ripper
~**ausbesserung** f, Straßen-Instandsetzung f, Straßenreparatur f = road repair (work), rehabilitation of road
~**ausrüstung** f = road furniture, ~ equipment
~**bahnblockschiene** f = block rail
~**bahngleise** npl = tram(way) tracks, street railway tracks (Brit.); street car tracks (US)
~**bahnverkehr** m = tram-train traffic
~**bahnwagen** m = streetcar (US); tramcar (Brit.)
~**bahnzug** m = tram-train
Straßenbau m = road construction, roadmaking, road building, highway construction
~**angebot** n = highway contract bid (US)
~**arbeiten** f = roadworks, road construction works
~**ausstellung** f = road show

Straßenbau|behörde f = highway authority
~bindemittel n = paving cement (US); road (engineering) binder
~bitumen n; siehe unter „Bitumen n im engeren Sinne"
~bitumenemulsion f = (bituminous) road emulsion
Straßenbauer m = road builder, roadman
Straßenbau|firma f = road-building firm; paving company (US); road construction company
~forschung f = road research, highway ~
~gestein n, Straßenbelagsgestein = road(making) aggregate, road rock, roadstone
~hilfsstoff m, siehe: Bindemittel n
~industrie f = highway industry
~ingenieur m = road engineer, highway ~
~klinker m, siehe: Pflasterziegel m
~maschinen fpl = road(-building) machinery, ~ equipment, road making plant, mechanical highway equipment
~maschinenfirma f = road-machine firm
~mischer m = mixer for road construction
~papier n, siehe: Papierunterlage f
~platte f = paving slab, road slab [*e. g. asphaltic concrete slab*]
~projekt n = paving project (US); road construction ~
~schalung f, siehe: Seitenschalung f
~-Schaufelmischer m = paddle mixer for road construction

Straßen(bau)schotter m, Schotter = crushed stone (or rock), road stone, macadam; [*deprecated: road metal*]
Straßenbau-Silo- und Dosier-Anlage f, siehe: Trockenbetonfabrik f
Straßenbau|stelle f = road site
~stoff m = road material, highway ~
~technik f [*als betriebstechnische Anwendung f*] = road building technique
~technik f [*als Ingenieurwissenschaft f*] = highway engineering
~trockentrommel f, Straßenbautrommeltrockner m = revolving (or rotary) drier (or dryer) (for roadmaking aggregates), bituminized aggregate drier
~unternehmer m = road contractor, paving ~
Straßen|befestigung f, siehe: Befestigung
~beförderungsmittel n = means of road (or highway) transport
~belageinbaumasse f, Belagsgut n = paving mixture (US); pavement ~
~belagsgestein n, siehe: Straßenbaugestein
~beleuchtung f = street lighting, illumination of streets, public lighting
~benutzer m = highway user, road ~
~bepflanzung f = highway planting, roadside ~
~besen m = road boom, street ~
~betonfeld n, siehe: Beton(fahrbahn)platte f

Straßen(beton)mischer m, **Straßenbetoniermaschine** f

rotating drum paver mixer, travel(l)ing (concrete) mixer (plant), combined mixing and paving machine, (combined) paver, paving mixer, (concrete) paver, concrete mixer-paver, travel(l)ing mixing machine

(RAB-)Brückenmischer m, Autobahnbetonmischer m, Autobahnbrückenmischer m

  bridge(-type) travel(l)ing concrete)mixer, bridge type travel(l)ing mixer (plant), super-highway-bridge mixer

selbstfahrbarer gummibereifter Doppeltrommel-Straßenbetonmischer, Straßenmischer mit Reifenfahrwerk n, Fabrikat KOEHRING, MILWAUKEE, USA

  self-propel(l)ed rubber-mounted twin-batch paver

Straßen(beton)mischer — (Straßen)Deckeneinbaugerät

Raupenstraßen(beton)mischer m, Freifallmischer m auf Gleisketten fpl für Betondeckenbau m
: track-laying track type (combined) paver (Brit.); (concrete) paver (US)

Doppel-Konus-Trommel f
: double-cone-drum

Doppeltrommel(beton)straßenmischer m, Doppeltrommel-Betoniermaschine f, Fabrikat VÖGELE, MANNHEIM, DEUTSCHLAND
: twin-batch paver, twin-drum type (concrete) paver, dual-drum type (concrete) paver, double-drum paver

  Austrag(ungs)schurre f, Entladeschurre
:   discharge chute

  Ausleger m, Schwenkausleger
:   (delivery or distributing) boom

  Ausleger-Kübel m, Betonkübel
:   (self-spreading) bucket, boom bucket, operating bucket

  Beschaufelung f
:   throw-over blades and pick-ups

  (Chargen)Mischspielsteuerung f
:   batchmeter controlled autocycle operation

  (Chargen)Mischzeitmesser m
:   batchmeter

  Doppeltrommel f
:   two-compartment (mixing) drum

  Fertig-Mischkammer f
:   second (mixing) compartment

  Lader m
:   (charging) skip, paver skip

  Laderaufzugswinde f mit gewichtsbelasteter Bremse f
:   combination skip hoist clutch and brake

  Transportschurre f, Überlaufschurre, drehbare Schurre
:   transfer chute

  Vormischkammer f
:   first (mixing) compartment

Doppeltrommel(beton)straßenmischer m, Doppeltrommel-Betoniermaschine f, Fabrikat BLAW-KNOX CO, FOOTE DIVISION, NUNDA, N. Y., USA
: DUOMIX 34 E and DUOMIX 16 E [*Trademark*]

Doppeltrommel(beton)straßenmischer m, Doppeltrommel-Betoniermaschine f, Fabrikat CHAIN BELT COMPANY, MILWAUKEE, WISCONSIN, USA
: REX twinbatch paver

Eintrommelstraßen(beton)mischer m
: single-drum (type) (concrete) paver

Eintrommel(beton)straßenmischer, Fabrikat BLAW-KNOX CO, FOOTE DIVISION, NUNDA, N. Y., USA
: SINGLE MIX MULTIFOOTE PAVER 34 E and SINGLE MIX MULTIFOOTE PAVER 27 E [*Trademark*]

Straßen|betonplatte f, siehe: Beton(fahrbahn)platte

~bewehrungsmatte f, Straßenarmierungsmatte = road mesh, ~ fabric

~blendung f = road glare

~damm m = road embankment, highway ~

(~)Decke f = (road) surfacing (Brit.) [*the top layer or layers, comprising the wearing course and or base-course but no the base*]

(~)Decke f = pavement

(~)Decke f [*alle Einbauschichten fpl zusammen*] = pavement [*a term applied specifically to the whole construction in a road (including any layer strengthened or stabilized in situ by the addition of other material) made to support traffic above the subgrade*]

~deckenbau m, siehe: Deckenbau m

~deckenbauer m = pavior

(~)Deckeneinbaugerät n, Deckeneinbaumaschine f = (highway) paver

Straßen|deckenfertiger *m*, siehe: (Straßen-) Fertiger
~deckenmischung *f* ,Straßendeckenmischgut *n* = road mix(ture)
~einlauf *m*, siehe: Regeneinlauf
~einmündung *f*, Straßengab(e)lung *f*, Gabelkreuzung *f* = fork junction
straßenfahrbare Pumpe *f* = road pump
Straßen|fahrzeug *n* = on-highway vehicle, road ~
~fahrzeugmotor *m* = road vehicle engine
~fegemaschine *f* mit **Kehrichtbehälter** *m* = road sweeper-collector
(~)Fertiger *m*, Deckenfertiger, Straßendeckenfertiger *m* = (road) finisher, finishing machine, laying and finishing machine
~flickarbeiten *f* = patching work, mending

~fräs- und -aufrauhmaschine *f* = road milling and grooving machine
~gab(e)lung*f*,siehe: Straßeneinmündung*f*
~geschwindigkeit *f* = road speed, highway ~
~gestaltung *f* = road design, highway ~
~graben *m* = road(way) ditch, highway ~
(~) Griffigkeit *f* = non-skid property, road-skid quality
~hecke *f* = roadside hedge, live fence
~hobel *m*, Wegehobel *m*, Erdhobel *m*, Straßen-Planierer *m* = (road) grader
~inanspruchnahme *f* = highway load
-Instandsetzung *f*, siehe: Straßenausbesserung *f*
~karte *f* = road map, highway ~

Straßenkehrmaschine *f*, **Fegemaschine**, **Kehrmaschine**

Motor-~
Anhänge-~, Schlepp-~
Bürstenwalze *f*, Kehrwalze *f*
Anhängebürstenwalze *f*, Schleppbürstenwalze

rotary sweeper, scavenging machine, road sweeper, mechanical sweeper, road sweeping machine, street sweeper
power(-driven) ~ ~, engine-driven ~ ~
traction-driven ~ ~, trailer(-type) ~ ~
rotating (or rotary) brush
trailer (type road) brush

Straßen|knoten *m* = intersection
~kocher *m* = road kettle, road maker's heater (US); road cooker (Brit.)
~koffer *m*, Straßenkasten *m*, Straßenbett *n* = roadbed
~körper *m* [*alle über Erdplanum befindlichen Einbauschichten zusammen*] = road structure, pavement
-Kraftwagen *m* für **Lastentransport** *m*, siehe: LKW
~kreuzung *f* = road junction, ~ intersection
~kurve *f* = road curve
~lage *f* [*Fahrzeug n*] = road-holding
~lampensäule *f*, Leuchtmast *m*, Lichtmast, Beleuchtungsmast = (street) lighting column, lighting standard
~landschaft *f* = highway landscape
~laterne *f* = street (lighting) lantern, road ~

~magnetreiniger *m* = magnetic road sweeper
~markierung *f*; Bodenmarkierung *f* [*Schweiz*] = traffic-line marking, traffic-zoning
-Markierungsfarbe *f*, Verkehrs(-Markierungs)farbe *f*; Signierfarbe [*Schweiz*] = traffic(-zoning) paint, zone marking ~, road(-marking) ~, line-marking ~, road-line ~, traffic line
 Bestimmung *f* des Absetzgrades = evaluating degree of settling
 Lichtempfindlichkeit *f* = light sensitivity
 Straßendienstprüfung *f* = road service test
 Trockenzeit *f* bis zur Klebfreiheit *f* = dry to no-pick up time
~markierungsmaschine *f*, siehe: Gerät *n* zum Anzeichnen *n* der Verkehrslinien *fpl*

Straßen|markierungsmaschine *f* für plastische Farbmassen *fpl* = plastic line marking machine
~**meister** *m*, Wegemeister *m* = road overseer
~**meisterei** *f* = highway depot
~**mischer** *m*, siehe: Straßen(beton)mischer *m*

~**namenschild** *n* = street nameplate
~**netz** *n* = road net(work), highway ~, ~ system
~**nutzungsdauer** *f* = road life, highway ~
~**öl** *n*; siehe unter „Bitumen *n* im engeren Sinne"
~**ölung** *f* = (surface) oiling
~**planierer** *m*, siehe: Straßenhobel *m*

Straßenquerschnittausbildung *f*	cross-section of road, profile of road, cross-sectional profile
symmetrische ~ *f*	symmetrical ~ ~ ~
unsymmetrische ~ *f*	unsymmetrical ~ ~ ~
Krone *f*	crown
parabelförmige Krone *f*	parabolic crown, continuous parabolic curve
kreisförmige Krone *f*, Wölbung *f*	camber, barrel camber [*deprecated: transverse slope, cross-fall*]
Dachprofil *n*	straight finish from the shoulder to the centre line, straight crossfalls
Dachprofil *n* mit Firstausrundung *f*	section with two straight lines joined by an easy curve, sloped camber, straight side slopes joined by a central parabolic curve
Quergefälle *n*	crossfall
Längsgefälle *n*, Gradiente *f*	gradient, longitudinal slope
Stich *m*	rise

Straßen|rad *n* = road wheel
~**räder-Unterwagen** *m*; siehe unter „Autobagger *m*"
~**reinigung** *f* = street cleansing
~**reparatur** *f*, siehe: Straßenausbesserung *f*
~**scheitel** *m* = vertex of a road
~**schleifmaschine** *f* = road grinder
~**schlepper** *m*, siehe: Radschlepper *m*
~**schotter** *m*, siehe: Straßenbauschotter *m*
~**seitenschutz** *m* = roadside protection
~**signalisierung** *f*, siehe: Beschilderung *f*
~**sprengwagen** *m* = street flusher, street sprinkler, roadway flusher, street washer
~**tankwagen** *m*, Straßentanker *m* = road tanker; bowser, tank lorry (Brit.); tank truck (US)
~**tankwagen** *m* [*Benzin n*] = (petrol) bowser (Brit.)

~**teer** *m* = road tar [*abbrev. RT*]
~**teerviskosimeter** *n* [*abgek. STV*] = Standard Tar Visco(si)meter [*abbrev. STV*]
~**teppich** *m*, Teppich(belag) *m*, Mischteppich(belag) = road carpet, road mat, (pre-mix(ed)) carpet, mat, carpet-coat, thin surfacing; veneer (Brit.)
~**transport** *m* = road transport, highway ~
~**tunnel** *m*, siehe: Straßen(verkehrs)tunnel *m*
~**übergangsbogen** *m* = highway transition curve
~**umlegung** *f*, siehe: Straßenverlegung *f*
~**unebenheitsmesser** *m* = roughometer, roughness meter [*an instrument for providing a numerical estimate of the irregularity in a road surface*]

Straßenunterbau — Straßenverkehrsunfall

Straßen|unterbau *m* = road foundation
~**unterdükerung** *f* = road siphon
~**verkehr** *m*, siehe: Verkehr *m*
~**verkehrsordnung** *f* = Highway Code
~**verkehrsrecht** *n* = Highway Traffic Law
~**verkehrssicherheit** *f* = highway safety

~**verkehrstechnik** *f* = traffic engineering
  bauliche Maßnahmen *fpl* = engineering
  Verkehrserziehung *f* = education
  polizeiliche Maßnahmen *fpl* = enforcement
~**(verkehrs)tunnel** *m* = vehicular tunnel, road tunnel, vehicular subway

---

Straßenverkehrsunfall *m*
  unmittelbares Auffahren *n* eines Fahrzeuges auf ein stehendes oder vorausfahrendes Fahrzeug oder auf feste Objekte
    seitliches Auffahren *n*
    Auffahren *n*
    zu kurzes Überholen
    schneiden
    Rutschen *n* durch Quergefälle *n*
    doppeltes Überholen *n*
  Schleudern *n* eines Fahrzeuges mit nachfolgendem Sturz, Aufprall oder Abkommen *n*
    Schleudern auf gerader Bahn
    Schleudern in der Kurve
    Schleudern auf glatter Bahn am Waldrand
    Schleudern auf glatter Brückenfahrbahn
    zu weites Überholen
    doppeltes Überholen
  allmähliches Abkommen *n* von der Fahrbahn
    Abkommen infolge Einschlafens am Steuer
    Abdrängen durch Schneiden
    Abgleiten in Gefällstrecken
    Seitenwindeinwirkung
  Zusammenstoß zweier aus Gegenrichtungen oder Querrichtungen kommender Fahrzeuge
    Wenden über den Grünstreifen
    zu weites Überholen
    Überholen bei Gegenverkehr
    Übergang auf Gegenverkehr

road traffic accident
  direct collision of a vehicle with another vehicle which is either stationary or is ahead of the first vehicle, or with a fixed object
    side-swipe
    rear-end collision
    overtaking short
    cutting in
    slide-slip due to crossfall
    double overtaking
  skidding followed by overturning, collision or leaving the road
    skidding on straight section
    skidding on a curve
    skidding or slippery surface at the edge of a forest
    skidding on a slippery surface on a bridge
    overtaking too wide
    double overtaking
  a vehicle leaves the road gradually
    driver falls asleep
    another vehicle cuts in
    skidding on downgrade
    effect of side-wind
  collision between vehicles proceeding in opposite directions or at right angles to each other
    driver makes U-turn across median
    overtaking too wide
    overtaking on section where roadway carries two-way traffic
    collision at point where section with roadway carrying two-way traffic begins

Straßenverkehrsunfall — Streckenabschnitt

    Abkommen auf die Gegenfahrbahn   vehicle crosses median strip
    Überqueren der Fahrbahn an den   vehicle crosses roadway at an interchange
    Anschlußstellen

Straßenverkehrszählgerät n = traffic counter, ~ counting apparatus

---

(Straßen)Verkehrszeichen n road sign, (roadside) traffic (control) sign
  Gefahrenzeichen n, Warnzeichen   danger sign, warning ~
    „Straßenarbeiten"   "Road Works"
    „Rutschgefahr"   "Slippery Carriageway"
    „Straßenverengung"   "Carriageway Narrows"
    „Kreuzung mit einer Straße ohne Vorrang"   "Intersection with a Non-priority Road"
    „Doppelkurve, die erste nach links"   "Double Bend to the Left"
    „Achtung — Kinder"   "Children"
    „Rinne"   "Gutter"
    „unbewachter Bahnübergang"   "Level Crossing without Gates"
  Verbotszeichen n prohibition sign, prohibitory ~
    „Vorrangstraßenkreuzung"   "Priority Road Ahead"
    „Wenden nach links verboten"   "Turning to the Left Prohibited"
    „Überholen verboten"   "Overtaking Prohibited"
  Befehlszeichen, Verpflichtungszeichen, Ordnungszeichen   mandatory sign, regulatory ~
    „Richtung ist einzuhalten"   "Direction to be Followed"
  Hinweiszeichen, Informationszeichen   indication sign, informative ~, guide ~
    „Parken"   "Parking"
    „Krankenhaus"   "Hospital"
    „Station für erste Hilfe"   "First-Aid Station"
    „Tankstelle"   "Filling Station"
    „Ende der Straße mit Vorfahrtsrecht"   "End of Priority"

Straßen|verlegung f, **Straßenumlegung** f = diversion of road
~walze f = road roller
~wärter m = road mender, lengthsman, maintenance man
(~)Zugmaschine f = tractor-truck, truck-tractor (US); motor tractor (Brit.)
stratifizieren (Geol.) = to stratify
Stratigraphie f, siehe: Formations- und Schichtenkunde f
Strauch|egge f, **Buschegge** f = bushharrow
~werk n, **Buschwerk** n = brushwood
~werkbündel n = bundle of brushwood, faggot

Strebe f = brace
~band n, **Kopfband** n = strut
~bogen m = flying buttress, arched ~
Streben|fachwerk n = strut frame, ~ bracing
~fachwerkträger m, **Warren-Tragwerk** n = triangular girder, Warren truss, halflattice girder
Strebe|pfeiler m = buttres
~schwarte f, siehe: Windrispe f
Streck|barkeit f, **Duktilität** f, **Dehnbarkeit**, **Fadenziehvermögen** n = ductility
~barkeitsmesser m = ductility tester
Strecke f, siehe: Abschnitt m
Streckenabschnitt m [*Kanal* m], siehe: Haltung f

Strecken|arbeiter m [*Eisenbahn f*] = platelayer
~band n; siehe unter „Bandförderer m"
~förderungsanlage f, siehe: Seil-Standbahnanlage f
~last f, siehe: Linienlast
~leuchtfeuer n [*Flugverkehr m*] = airway beacon
~vortriebmaschine f [*Tunnelbau m*] = tunnel(l)ing machine
Streck|metall n = expanded metal [*abbrev. XPM*]
~spannung f = yield stress
~zusatz m [*z. B. Farbe f*] = extender
Streich|asphalt m, siehe: Gußasphalt
~balken m = rib(b)and
~brett n, siehe: Holzspachtel m

streichen (Geol.) = to strike, to bear
Streichen n, Schicht~ (Geol.) = strike
streichende Verwerfung f, Längsverwerfung (Geol.) = strike fault
Streich|maß n = back pitch
~torf m = mo(u)lded peat
~wehr n = side weir
Streife f [*Polizei f*] = patrol
Streifen|bildung f [*Pigment n*] = floating
~fundament n = continuous footing, strip foundation
~klee m = soft-knolled trefoil
~last f = strip load
~wagen m [*Polizei f*] = patrol car
Streifhaufen m, siehe: Längsreihe f
Streik m = strike
~posten m = picket
Streitfall m = dispute

Streugerät n für den Winterdienst m	winter (or frost) gritting machine, winter gritter, winter grit spreader
Anhängestreuer m [*mit eigener Laufachse f und eigenem Fahrgestell n*]	towed-type (or trailer) ~ ~ ~
Einbaustreuer m [*ohne eigenes Fahrgestell, feste Verbindung mit LKW*]	built-in bottom (type) ~ ~ ~
Anbaustreuer m [*ohne eigenes Fahrgestell, Verbindung mit LKW nur vorübergehend*]	rear-mounted ~ ~ ~, mechanical gritting attachment; tailgate (vane type) chip spreader, vane type chip spreader; lorry tailboard temporary gritting attachment, attachment (type) gritter (Brit.)
Streuer m mit Spezialaufbau [*an Stelle der üblichen Ladepritsche sitzt dieser Streuer auf dem Fahrgestell des LKW*]	chassis-mounted ~ ~ ~
abstumpfender Stoff m	abrasive
Streugut n	gritting material
rotierender Streuteller m, Rotorstreuer m	spinner, rotary disk type gritter, spinner spreader
Streugutpritsche f [*LKW m*]	bulk gritter body
Walzenstreuer m	hopper type gritter with feed roll

Streu|(last)kraftwagen m = spreader truck (US); ~ lorry (Brit.)
~makadam m, siehe: Einstreudecke f
~salz n, siehe: (Auf)Tausalz n
~salzschaden m = salt scale
Streuung f der Versuchsergebnisse npl = scatter of the test results

Strich|-Punkt-Linie f = dash-dotted line
~regen m = convectional rain
~zeichnung f = line drawing, ~ sketch
~ziehmaschine f, siehe: Gerät n zur Anzeichnung f von Verkehrslinien fpl
Stricklava f; siehe unter „Vulkan m"
Strobe f, siehe: Weymouthkiefer f

Stroh|ballen *m* = straw bale
~matte *f* = straw mat
~seil *n* = straw rope
~stein *m* = carpholite
Strom|angriff *m* = attack by the current
~aufwanderung *f* [*Fisch m*] = upstream migration
~aussteuerung *f* = control current
~bau *m* = stream construction, ~ engineering
~bett *n* = stream bed
~erzeuger *m* = generator, generating set
~erzeuger *m* **für Baustellen** *fpl* = contractors' generator (or generating set)
~erzeugung *f* = generation of electrical power
~erzeugungsaggregat *n*, siehe: Aggregat *n*
~gerinne *n*, siehe: Horizontal(strom)sichter *m*
~hafen *m*, siehe: Mündungshafen *m*
~linienbild *n*, siehe: Strömungsnetz *n*
stromlose Plattierung *f* = electroless plating
Strom|rüttelverfahren *n* **nach Bernatzik** = Bernatzik method of sand compaction by simultaneously applied water injection and vibration
~schnelle *f* = river rapid
~strich *m*, siehe: Talweg *m*
Strömung *f* = current, flow
Strömungs|geometrie *f* = flow geometry
~geschwindigkeit *f* = current velocity
~linie *f* = line of flow, flqw line
~messer *m* = current meter
~netz *n*, Stromlinienbild *n* = flow net
~verhältnisse *npl* **am Meißel** *m* = bit hydraulics
Strom|versorgung *f* = power supply
~zählung *f* = cordon count
Strontianit *m* (Min.) = strontianite
strukturempfindlicher Ton *m* = sensitive clay
Strunk *m*, siehe: Stubben *m*
Stubben *m*, (Baum)Stumpf *m*, Baumstock *m*; Strunk *m* [*in Österreich*] = stump, tree ~
Stubenfliege *f* = housefly
Stuck *m* = stucco
Stückerz *n* = lump ore

Stuckgips *m*, $2\,CaSO_4 \cdot H_2O$ = plaster of Paris
Stück|güter *npl* = piece-goods
~kalk *m*, ungelöschter stückiger Branntkalk *m* = lump lime
~schlacke *f*, Hochofenschlacke = blast-furnace slag, lump ~
~stein *m*, siehe: Setzpacklagestein *m*
~vermessung *f*; siehe unter „Vermessungskunde *f*"
Studiengesellschaft *f* **für Automobilstraßenbau** *m*, STUFA = German Motor Road Research Association
Studienreise *f* = study tour
Stufenbildung *f*, Verwerfung *f* [*Betonplatten fpl*] = stepping-off
stufenlos regelbar = infinitely variable
Stufen|meißel *m*; siehe unter „Bohrmeißel"
~silo *m* = step-by-step bin
~turbine *f* = stage turbine
~waschmaschine *f*, Stufenwäsche *f* = multi-compartement washer (or washing machine)
Stuhlschiene *f*, siehe: Doppelkopfschiene
Stukkatieren *n* = stuccoing
Stumpf *m*, siehe: Stubben *m*
stumpfer Stoß *m* = butt-joint
Stumpfzieher *m*, siehe: Wurzelzieher
Stunden|leistung *f* = hourly output
~lohnarbeiten *f* = daywork
~lohnsatz *m* = rate per working hour, hourly wage rate, daywork rate
~spitzenwert *m* = peak hour value
~verdienst *m* = hourly earning
Sturm *m* = gale
~flut *f* = gale-swept tide
~laterne *f* = road danger lamp
Sturz *m*, Oberschwelle *f* = lintel
~bett *n*; siehe unter „Talsperre *f*"
~regen *m*, Regenguß *m* = (torrential) downpour
~träger *m* = lintel beam
~welle *f* = breaker
Stütze *f* = column
~, Pfosten *m* = stanchion
~ aus legiertem Stahl *m* = alloy-steel leg
Stütz|(en)moment *n* = moment at support, column moment

Stütz|insel f für **Fußgängerüberweg** m, Fußgänger-Schutzinsel = refuge (Brit.) [*deprecated: island*]; refuge island, pedestrian ~ (US)
~**linie** f = line of pressure
~**linienbogen** m = arch thrust line
~**mauer** f, Stützwand f = retaining wall
~**moment** n, siehe: Stützenmoment
~**rahmen** m = supporting frame
~**weite** f, Spannweite f = span
~**weite** f, rechnerische ~ = effective span length
~**zelle** f [Holz n] = open-end cell
Stylolithstruktur f = cone-in-cone structure
subaquatische Rutschung f, Unterwasserrutschung f, Subsolifluktion f = underwater solifluction (or solifluxion, or soil-creep)
subkrustales Gestein n, siehe: plutonisches ~
Sublimat n, siehe: Quecksilberchlorid n
Submission f; siehe unter „Angebot n"
Submissionstermin m; siehe unter „Angebot n"
subtropisch = sub-tropical
Suchbohrung f, siehe: Aufschlußbohrung
Südlicht n = Aurora Australis
Sulfat|bestimmung f nach der Trübungsmessungsmethode f = turbidimetric sulfate determination
~**rückstand** m = sulfated residue
Sulfit|ablauge f = sulphite liquor, ~ lye
~**zellstoffablauge** f = sulfite cellulose liquor
Süll m, n, siehe: Bodenschwelle f
sulphoniertes Rizinusöl n = sulphonated castor oil
Summationskurve f = cumulative curve
Summationskurvenauftrag(ung) m, (f) in logarithmischem Maßstab m = cumulative logarithmic plot
~ in natürlichem Maßstab m = cumulative direct plot
Summenlinie f = cumulative line, cast ~
Summeranlage f = buzzer system
Summier|gerät n = accumulating (traffic) counter

~**wiegen** n = cumulative weighing
Sumpf|ebene f = mud flat
~**eisenerz** n = bog iron ore
sümpfen [*bergmännischer Ausdruck für „entwässern"*] = to drain
Sumpf|gas n = marsh gas
~**(gebiet)** m, (n) = swamp (area)
~**hornklee** m = marsh bird's foot trefoil
~**kalk** m, siehe: Kalkteig m
~**moos** n, Torfmoos n = peat moss, bog ~, Spagnum ~
~**wiese** f = swamp meadow
Supergummiradwalze f; siehe unter „Walze f"
Superposition f von **Wellenflächen** fpl = superposition of wave surfaces
suprakrustales Erstarrungsgestein n, siehe: Ergußgestein n
suspendierter Stoff m, siehe: Schwebstoff m
Suspension f, siehe: Aufschwemmung f
Süßungsprozeß m [Krackbenzin n] = sweetening process
Süßwasser n = fresh water
~**becken** n = fresh-water basin
~**kalk(stein)** m = fresh water limestone
~**schnecke** f = snail
Syenit m = syenite
~**aplit** m = syenite-(h)aplite
Synchron-Getriebe n = constant mesh transmission
Symmetrieachse f, Bau(werk)achse = centre line (Brit.); center ~ (US)
Symons|(kegel)brecher m = (standard type) Symons (cone) crusher
  ununterbrochener Arbeitsgang m = continuous crushing action
  Brechmantel m = mantle
  schlagartige Zerkleinerung f, Schlagzerkleinerung = impact reduction
  geschlossene Hubstellung f = close setting
  Umlaufdruckschmierung f = circulating pressure lubrication
~-**Kegelgranulator** m = short head type (Symons) cone crusher
synchronisiert = synchronized
Synklinale f, Mulde f der Faltung f = syncline
Systemlinie f [Fachwerk] = working line

T

tabellarisch = in tabular form
Tabelle f, **Zahlentafel** f = table
tachymetrische Aufnahme f = tacheometric survey
Tafelblech n, siehe: Blech
tafelig [*Mineral* n] = tabular
Tafel|schalung f = shuttering
~schere f = lever shears
Tagebau m = open pit mining (US); open-cast ~, surface ~, open-cut ~, adit ~ (Brit.)
~grube f = opencast site, ~ mine, surface pit
~-Lok(omotive) f = open-cast mining loco(motive)
Tages|(arbeits)fuge f = day's work joint
~sichtbarkeit f = day visibility
~stollen m, siehe: Zugangsstollen m
Tag(es)wasser n, **Oberflächenwasser** n = surface water

Takelwerk n = rigging
Takt m [*Verbrennungsmaschine* f] = cycle
~arbeit f [*der gleiche zeitlich hintereinander liegende von denselben Handwerkern mpl auszuführende Arbeitsvorgang* m] = piece-work
Tal|brücke f, **Viadukt** n = valley bridge, viaduct
~hang m, **Talflanke** f = valley slope, ~ side
Talje f [*seemännischer Ausdruck für „Flaschenzug"* m] = (block and) tackle, pulley block, lifting block
Talk m (Min.) = talc
~schiefer m = talc schist
Talkum n, **Specksteinmehl** n = talcum powder, powdered talc, French chalk
Tallöl n = tall oil
Tal|löß m = valley loess
~schlucht f = glen
~schotter m = valley gravel
~sohle f = valley bottom, ~ floor

Talsperre f	**dam, hydro ~**
(Ab)Dichtungsgraben m, Verherdung f	cut-off trench
Abflußkanal m, siehe: Unterwasserkanal	
Abflußleitung f	outlet conduit
Abflußmengenkurve f	hydrograph
Ablassen n Entleeren n, Entleerung f, Absenkung f, Absenken n	emptying
Ablaß m auf mittlerer Höhe f	middle-height discharge tunnel
Ablaßregulierschütz(e) n, (f)	outlet control (or regulating) gate
Ablaßrohr n	outlet pipe
Ablaßschieber m, Entleerungsschieber m	outlet valve
Ablaßstollen m, Entleerungsstollen	outlet tunnel
Ablaßverschluß m	emptying gate
Ablauf m, siehe: Unterwasserkanal m	
Ableitungsstollen m, siehe: Unterwasserstollen	
Ablösung f des Strahles m	freeing of the nappe (US); separation of the water layer (Brit.)
Abschlußschütz(e) n, (f), Grundablaßverschluß m	lower gate, ~ sluice, sluice (gate), sluiceway gate
Abschlußwand f, siehe: Herdmauer f	
Absenkung f	drawdown
Absenk(ungs)ziel n	minimum water storage elevation, drawdown level
Ambursen-Staumauer f	Ambursen-type dam

Anzug *m* luftseits, Anlauf *m* ~	downstream batter
Anzug *m* wasserseits, Anlauf *m* ~	upstream batter
aufgelöste Gewichtssperre *f* System Noetzli, Pfeilerkopf(stau)mauer *f*, Rundkopf(stau)mauer von Noetzli, Pfeilerkopfsperre *f*	dam with segmental-headed counterforts (Brit.); round-headed buttress dam
aufgelöste Staumauer *f*, siehe: Pfeiler(stau)mauer *f*	
auf Quote (oder Kote, oder Höhe) 890	at a level of + 890.00 (Brit.); at el. 890 (US)
(Auf)Speicherung *f*, Stau *m*, (Wasser-)Einstau, Stauanhebung *f*	storage, pondage, filling
Aufstockung *f*, Erhöhung *f*, Erhöhen *n*	heightening
Ausgleichbehälter *m*, Ausgleichbecken *n*, Ausgleichweiher *m*	balancing reservoir, compensating reservoir
Auslaufbauwerk *n*, siehe: Betriebsauslaß *m*	
Auslaufstollen *m* [*von Turbine f zum Ableitungstunnel m*]	draft tube tunnel (US); draught ~ ~ (Brit.); discharge branch
Auszugrohr *n*	draft tube (US); draught tube (Brit.)
Baubrücke *f*, siehe: Dienstbrücke	
Baugrube *f*	excavation
Bausteg *m*, siehe: Dienstbrücke *f*	
Bauzeithochwasser *n*, bauzeitliches Hochwasser	construction flood
Becken *n*, siehe: Sammelbecken	
Bedienungsstation *f*	control cabin
Begrenzungsmauer *f* [*Tosbecken n*]	training wall [*stilling basin*]
Behelfs-Hochwasserentlastungsanlage *f*	temporary flood relief works
Belastung *f* des Überlaufes	head on the spillway (US); head of water over spillway (Brit.)
belüfteter Überfallstrahl *m*	aerated nappe (US); aerated sheet of water (Brit.)
Beobachtungsstollen *m*	inspection gallery
bergseitig, oberwasserseitig	upstream
Beruhigungsbecken *n*, Tosbecken	stiling basin, absorption ~ (Brit.); stilling pool (US)
Beton-Bogengewichts(stau)mauer *f*	concrete arch gravity dam
Betonkern *m*, massive Kernmauer *f*	concrete core wall
Beton-Kerndamm *m*, siehe: Kernmauerdamm	
Betonmauer *f*, siehe: (Massiv)Beton(stau)mauer	
Betonpfropfen *m*, Betonplombe *f*	concrete plug
Betonsperre *f*, siehe: Massivbetonmauer *f*	
Beton(stau)mauer *f*, siehe: (Massiv-)Beton(stau)mauer	
Betriebsauslaß *m*, Auslaufbauwerk *n*	river outlet, reservoir outlet (works)
Betriebsverschluß *m*	outlet gate

Betriebswasserstollen m, Druck(wasser)stollen, Triebwasserstollen, Zulaufstollen, (Wasser)Kraftstollen [*Stollen, der im planmäßigen Betrieb voll und unter Scheiteldruck läuft*]	pressure tunnel, tunnel-type penstock, conversion tunnel, pressure gallery, hydro tunnel, hydro tube, power tunnel
Bogenpfeilermauer f, siehe: Gewölbereihen(stau)mauer f	
Bogenschütz(e) n, (f), siehe: Segmentschütz(e)	
Bogen(schwer)gewichts(stau)mauer f, Bogengewichtssperre f, Gewölbe-Gewichtssperre f	arch-gravity dam
Bogensehne f	chord
Bogensperrmauer f, Bogen(stau)mauer f, Bogensperre f, Gewölbe(stau)mauer f, Einfach-Gewölbesperre f	concrete arch(ed) dam
Bogenmauer f mit gleichem Bogenzentriwinkel m, Jörgensen-Mauer f, Gleichwinkel(stau)mauer f, Bogen(stau)mauer mit gleichbleibendem Öffnungswinkel m, Bogen(stau)mauer mit Festwinkel m	constant angle arch dam, variable-radius ~ ~
Kuppel(stau)mauer f	dome-shaped dam
Doppelbogen(stau)mauer f	double arch(ed) dam
Bogen(stau)mauer f mit gleichem Radius m, kreiszylindrische Sperre f	constant radius (arched) dam
Öffnungswinkel m der Krone f	angular width of arch at crest (Brit.); central angle at crest (US)
Querschnitt m im Scheitel m	section at crown of arch (Brit.); section at key (or crown) (US)
Lastaufteilungsverfahren n des Bureau of Reclamation	trial load method of analyzing arch dams
Gewölbering m	arch element
Kragträger m	cantilever element
Radius m der luftseitigen Kronenbegrenzung f	downstream radius of crest (circle)
Scheitelform f wasserseitig	upstream profile at crown of arch (Brit.); ~ ~ of section at key (or crown) (US)
Krümmungsradius m, Krümmungshalbmesser m	locus of centres (Brit.); line of centers (US)
Bogenüberlauf m	arch spillway
Bruchstein(stau)mauer f in Bogenform f	masonry arch gravity dam
Damm aus Felsschüttung f, siehe: Steinfülldamm	
Dammbalkennut f	stop-log groove
Dammkern m; siehe unter „Erd(schüttungsstau)damm m	
Dammkernmauer f, siehe: Kernmauer	

Dichtungsgraben m, siehe: Ab~,
Dichtungskern m; siehe unter „Erd(schüttungsstau)damm m"
Dichtungsschirm m, Dichtungsgürtel m, Injektionsschleier m, Einpreßschürze f, Dichtungsschleier m — grout(ing) curtain, diaphragm
Dichtungsvorlage f, Dichtungsteppich m, Dichtungsschürze f, Ab~, Schürze — (waterproof)blanket, impervious blanket
Dienstbrücke f, Bausteg m, Baubrücke — service gangway (Brit.); distributing bridge, overhead track way, construction trestle (US)

direkter Auslaufstollen m [von Schieberkammer f zum Ableitungstunnel m unter Umgehung des Krafthauses n] — penstock drain, drain(age) tunnel
Doppelbogen(stau)mauer f; siehe unter „Bogensperrmauer f"
Doppel-Skisprung-Überfall m über die Krafthausdecke f — double (or two-jet) ski-jump crossing over the roof of the power house
Druckgefälle n, siehe: Niveaudifferenz f
Druckhöhe f, siehe: Niveaudifferenz f
Druckleitung f, Druckwasserzuleitung — penstock, power penstock
Druckleitungsschacht m, Fallschacht — penstock shaft
Druck(wasser)stollen m, siehe: Betriebswasserstollen
Druckwasserzuleitung f, siehe: Druckleitung
einfache Gewichts(stau)mauer f, siehe: Gewichts(stau)mauer
Einfach-Gewölbesperre f, siehe: Bogensperrmauer f
Einlaßbauwerk n zum Kraftwerk n [als Sperre f ausgebildet] — power plant intake structure, penstock dam
Einlaßturm m, Turmeinlaß m, Einlaufturm, Turmeinlauf — intake tower
Einlaßverschluß m, Einlaufverschluß — head gate, intake ~
Einlaufkanal m, Einlauf(ge)rinne f, (n) Zulauf(ge)rinne f, (n) — inlet channel
Einlauftrompete f, Einlaßtrompete — trumpet inlet
Einpreßschürze f, siehe: Dichtungsschirm m
(Ein)Stau m, Speicherung f, Aufspeicherung — storage, pondage
Energievernichter m — energy dissipator
Energievernichtung f, Energeverzehrung f — energy dissipation
Entenschnäbel-Überlauf m — duck bills type spillway
Entlastungsstollen m — discharge tunnel, ~ outlet
Entlastungsüberlauf m, siehe: Überlauf
Entleerungsstollen m, Ablaßstollen — outlet tunnel

Talsperre

Entnahmebauwerk *n*, Einlaufbauwerk *n*, Einlauf *m*, Einlaßbauwerk	intake (or inlet) works (or structure), head works
Entwässerungsschürze *f*	drainage curtain
Erhöhung *f*, Erhöhen *n*, Aufstockung *f*	heightening
Erd(schüttungs)(stau)damm *m*, Staudamm	earth fill dam, earth(-work) ~
Beton-Fußmauer *f*	concrete cutoff wall
Dränschicht *f*, Filterschicht	pervious shell
(Dichtungs)Kern *m*, Dammkern	(impervious) core, impervious diaphragm
Fußmauer *f*, siehe: Herdmauer	
gespülter (Erd)Damm, (Voll)Spüldamm, gespülter Staudamm	hydraulic fill dam
Randzone *f*	shell
Erddamm *m* mit Querschnittsaufbau *m* in Filterform *f*, ~ ~ symmetrischem Filteraufbau *m*	earth (fill) dam with materials of various permeabilities, zoned earth (fill) dam
eingespülter wasserdichter Kern *m*, Sumpf *m*	core pool
Spüleinbaudamm *m*	semi-hydraulic fill dam
(ab)gewalzter Damm *m*, Walz(stau)damm	rolled earth (fill) dam
Kiesfilter *m, n*	filter blanket of gravel
Einschlämmen *n*, Einspülen *n*	sluicing
Steindeckwerk *n*, Stein(ab)deckung *f*, Steinbestürzung *f*	riprap, rock rip-rap, stone rip-rap
Steinsatz *m*, Steinpackung *f*	hand-placed (stone) riprap, pitched slope
Steinwurf *m*, Rauhwurf, geschüttetes Steindeckwerk *n*, geschüttete Stein(ab)deckung *f*, geschüttete Steinbestürzung *f*	truck-dumped (US)/lorry-dumped (Brit.) riprap, dumped (stone) riprap
Fallhöhe *f*, siehe Niveaudifferenz *f*	
Fallhöhenverlust *m*	head loss
Fallschacht *m*, Druck(leitungs)schacht	penstock shaft
Felsschüttungsstaudamm *m*, siehe: Steinfülldamm	
freier Überfall(strahl) *m*	free nappe (US); free sheet of water (Brit.)
Freistrahlüberlauf *m*	open spillway (US); free waste weir, free spillway
Freibord *n*	freeboard [*the difference in elevation between the top of the dam and the maximum reservoir level that would be attained during the spillway design flood*]
Freiluftschaltanlage *f*	switchyard
Führungswand *f* [*Hochwasserüberfall m*]	training wall
Fuß *m*	toe
Gefälle *n*, siehe: Niveaudifferenz *f*	
Gefällhöhe *f*, siehe: Niveaudifferenz *f*	

Gegenmauer f, Überfallmauer [Tosbecken n]	end wall [stilling basin]
gekrümmte Staumauer f	arch(ed) dam
gekrümmtes Saugrohr n	elbow (draft) tube (US); elbow (draught) tube (Brit.)
gepackter Steindamm m; siehe unter „Steinfülldamm"	
getrenntes Grundablaßbauwerk n	separate sluiceway.structure
Gewichts(stau)mauer f, (massive) Gewichtssperre f, einfache ~, Schwergewichts(stau)mauer	gravity dam
Beton-Gewichts(stau)mauer	concrete gravity dam
Bogen(schwer)gewichts(stau)mauer	arch gravity dam
Bruchstein-Gewichts(stau)mauer	masonry gravity dam
einfaches (oder einschnittiges) Lastaufteilungsverfahren n	simplified (or abridged) trial-load method
gerade Gewichts(stau)mauer	straight-gravity dam
Gleitwiderstand m	sliding resistance
Gleitsicherheitsfaktor m	sliding factor
Scherreibungs-Sicherheitsfaktor m	shear-friction factor
Gewichtsmauer f (oder Schwergewichtssperre f) mit Überfall m	gravity spillway dam (Brit.); gravity type dam spillway (US)
Ausrundung f	ogee curve (Brit.); bucket of ogee (US)
Leitwand f	guide wall (Brit.); training wall (US)
Pfeilerkopf m	up-stream nose, cut-water (Brit.); nose (US)
Pfeilerrücken m	downstream nose (Brit.); downstream pier nosing (US)
Schwelle f	sill (Brit.); gate seat (US)
Überfallrücken m	shaped face, profiled ~ (Brit.); spillway face, profiled face (US)
Gewölbe-Gewichtssperre f, siehe: Bogen(schwer)gewichts(stau)mauer f	
Gewölbemauer f, siehe: Bogensperrmauer f	
Gewölbereihen(stau)mauer f, Vielfachbogensperre f, Bogenpfeiler(stau)mauer f, Pfeilergewölbe(stau)mauer	multiple arch(ed) dam
Gewölbe(stau)mauer f, siehe: Bogensperrmauer	
Gleichgewichtsklappe f	balanced weir (or gate) (Brit.); automatic flap gate
Gleichwinkel(stau)mauer f; siehe unter „Bogensperrmauer f"	
Großspeicher m	large reservoir
Grundablaß m, Grundauslaß m [Auslaß etwa in Höhe der Talsohle oder darunter]	lower (or bottom) discharge tunnel, sluiceway, bottom emptying gallery, bottom outlet, scour outlet
Grundablaßkanal m	sluicing channel
Grundablaßrohr n	bottom outlet pipe

Grundablaßverschluß m, Abschlußschütz(e) n, (f)	sluice (gate), sluiceway gate, lower gate, lower sluice
Grundstrahl m	sluiceway flow
Gründungsfels m	rock foundation
halbdurchlässig	semi-pervious
Halbfreiluft-Kraftwerk n	semioutdoor-type power plant
halbsphärisches Gewölbe n, Kuppel f	dome, cupola
Heberüberlauf m, Saugheberüberlauf	siphon(ic) spillway
Herdmauer f, Fußmauer, (Ab)Dichtungsmauer, (Ab)Dichtungssporn m, Trennmauer, Sporn, Abschlußwand	(toe) cut-off wall
Hochwasserentlastung f, Hochwasserabführung f	flood relief, flood discharge
Hochwasserentlastungsanlage f, siehe: Überlauf m	
Hochwasserentlastungsanlage f vom Stauwerk n getrennt	(side-)channel (type) spillway
Hochwasserentlastungskanal m, Überlaufkanal	spillway channel, ~ chute
Hochwasserschutztalsperre f, Hochwasser(auffang)sperre f	flood (control) dam
Hochwasserspeicherung f	flood control storage, storage of flood
Hochwasserstollen m, siehe: Überlaufstollen	
Hochwasserüberlauf, siehe: Überlauf	
(Hochwasser)Überlauf-Auslaufbauwerk n	spillway outlet structure
(Hochwasser)Überlaufverschluß m	spillway gate
Hohl(stau)mauer f	cavity dam (Brit.); hollow dam (US)
Holzgasse f	logway
Hubschütz(e) n, (f), Hubwehr n	vertical lift gate
hydraulischer Speicher m, siehe: Sammelbecken n	
Injektionsschleier m, siehe: Dichtungsschirm m	
injizieren, einpressen, auspressen	to inject, to grout under pressure
installierte Leistung f, Leistungssoll n	installed (nameplate) capacity
Kavernenkrafthaus n, Kraftwerkskaverne f, Maschinenkaverne	underground power station, ~ hydroelectric (power) plant
Kerndamm m	core-type dam
Kernmauer f, Dammkernmauer	core wall
Kernmauerdamm m, Beton-Kerndamm m	concrete core wall type dam
Kippen n	overturning (Brit.); tilting (US)
Klappe f, Schieber m	valve
Kolkschutz m	protection against scour, erosion control
Kontaktzone f	area of contact
Kote f, Höhe f Quote f	level (Brit.); el. (US)
Krafthaus n, siehe: Maschinenhaus	

Kraftstollen *m*, siehe: Betriebswasserstollen
Kraftwerksgebäude *n*, siehe: Maschinenhaus *n*
Kraftwerkskaverne *f*, siehe: Kavernenkrafthaus *n*
kritische Druckhöhe *f*, kritisches Gefälle *n* — critical head
Krümmer *m* — elbow bend, penstock elbow
Kühlwasserstollen *m* — condensation water tunnel, condensing ~ ~
künstlicher See *m*, siehe: Sammelbecken *n*
Kuppel *f*, halbsphärisches Gewölbe *n* — dome, cupola
Leistungssoll *n*, siehe: installierte Leistung *f*
Maschinenflur *m* — generator floor
Maschinenhaus *n*, Krafthaus *n*, Kraftwerksgebäude *n* [*Gebäude, in dem die Turbinen und die Stromerzeuger oder Arbeitsmaschinen untergebracht sind*] — power house
Maschinenkaverne *f*, Kraftwerkskaverne, Kavernenkrafthaus *n* [*Krafthaus im Innern des Gebirges, bergmännisch oder im Einschnitt mit nachträglicher Überschüttung hergestellt*] — underground power station, ~ hydroelectric (power) plant
(Massiv)Beton(stau)mauer *f*, Betonsperre *f*, Staumauer *f*, Talsperren(stau)mauer, Sperrmauer, Betonsperrmauer — massive concrete dam
massive Kernmauer *f*, siehe: Betonkern *m*
Mauerwerksperre *f*, siehe unter „Steinfülldamm"
Mehrzweckbauwerk *n*, Verbundbauwerk, Vielzweckbauwerk — multi(ple)-purpose structure
Nadelschieber *m* — needle (control) (or regulating) valve
Nebenanlagen *f pl* — appurtenant works, appurtenant structures
Niedrigwasserverbesserung *f*, Niedrigwasserregelung *f* — regulation of low water flows, low tide regulation
Niveaudifferenz *f*, Gefälle *n*, Druckhöhe *f* Druckgefälle, Gefällhöhe, Fallhöhe, Niveauunterschied *m* — head
Normalspiegel *m*, normales Stauziel *n* — normal op(erating) level, normal water storage elevation
Notverschluß *m* — emergency (guard) gate, guard gate
oberwasserseitig, bergseitig — upstream
oberwasserseitige Vorlage *f* — upstream apron
Perimetralfuge *f*, perimetrische Fuge, Umfangsfuge — perimetral joint

Talsperre

Pfeiler(stau)mauer *f*, Pfeilersperre *f*, aufgelöste Staumauer	buttress (type) dam, buttressed dam (US); counterfort (type) dam (Brit.)
Bogenpfeilermauer *f*, Gewölbereihenstaumauer *f*, Vielfachbogensperre *f*, Pfeilergewölbe(stau)mauer	multiple arch(ed) dam
Abstand *m* der Strebepfeilerachsen *fpl*	buttress spacing (US); spacing of counterforts c. to c.
Bogenanfang *m* des Gewölbeinnern *n*	intrados springing line (US); springing of intrados (or soffit) (Brit.)
Bogenanfang *m* des Gewölberückens *m*	extrados springing line (US)
Erzeugende *f*, erzeugende Linie *f*	generators (US); generating line, generatrix (Brit.)
lichter Strebepfeilerabstand *m*, Spannweite *f* des Bogens *m*	clear buttress spacing (US); clear spacing of counterforts, arch span (Brit.)
schiefliegendes Gewölbe *n*	arch barrel (US); inclined barrel arch (Brit.)
Zellen(stau)mauer *f*	cellular dam
Rundkopf(stau)mauer *f* von Noetzli, Pfeilerkopfsperre *f*, Pfeilerkopf(stau)mauer, aufgelöste Gewichtssperre System Noetzli	dam with segmental-headed counterforts (Brit.); round-head(ed) buttress dam
Plattensperre *f*, Plattenpfeiler(stau)mauer *f*, Pfeiler-Plattensperre *f*, Pfeilerplatten(stau)mauer	slab and buttress dam
Pfeilerkuppel(stau)mauer *f*, Vielfach-Kuppelsperre *f*	multiple-dome shaped dam
Pfeiler(stau)mauer *f* mit gelenkiger Aussteifung	articulated buttress dam
Pfeiler(stau)mauer *f* mit starrer Aussteifung *f*	rigid buttress dam
Pfeiler(stau)mauer *f* mit diamantkopfähnlichen Strebepfeilern *mpl*	diamond head buttress dam
Überfallpfeiler *m*	overflow buttress
Pumpspeicher(kraft)werk *n*	pumped-storage hydropower plant
Pumpspeicherung *f*	pumped storage
Rechen *m*	(trash) rack (US); screen (rack), screen grillage (Brit.)
Rechenbauwerk *n*	(trash) rack structure
Rechenquerträger *m*	(trash) rack beam
Rechenreiniger *m*	screen cleaner (Brit.); (trash) rack rake (US)
Rechenstab *m*	trash bar
Regulierungsbauwerk *n*	control works, control structure, headworks (structure)
Ringüberlauf *m*	shaft-and-tunnel spillway, morning-glory spillway, drop-inlet spillway
Ringüberlaufkrone *f*	circular spillway crest
Ringverschluß *m*	ring gate

Rollschütz(e) n, (f)	wheel-mounted gate, fixed-wheel gate, fixed axle gate
Rollschütz(e) n, (f) mit endloser Rollenkette f	roller-mounted leaf gate (or sluice), coaster gate
Rückhaltebecken n	detention basin, detention reservoir [*flood-control reservoir provided with outlet control*]
rückwärtige Schutzsperre f	downstream cofferdam, downstream temporary dam
Rundkopf(stau)mauer f von Noetzli, siehe: aufgelöste Gewichtssperre f System Nötzli	
Sammelbecken n, Staubecken (Speicher)Becken, Speicher(see) m, Stausee m, Talsperrenbecken, hydraulischer Speicher m, künstlicher See m	storage reservoir, (impounding) reservoir, artificial lake, storage pool, accumulation lake
Saugheberüberfall m, siehe: Heberüberfall	
Schalen(stau)mauer f	shell dam, thin arch dam
Schieber m, Klappe f	valve
Schluchten(stau)mauer f	gorge dam
schmale Kuppelbogensperre f mit waag- und senkrechter Krümmung f	dome-shaped thin shell dam with the upstream face having pronounced curvature in both horizontal and vertical planes
Schürze f, siehe: Dichtungsvorlage f	
Schuß(ge)rinne f, (n)	race
Schußstrahl m, siehe: Überfallstrahl	
Schützenbedienungskammer f	gate operating chamber
Schützensteuerorgan n	gate operating control
Schwallschacht m, Wasserschloßschacht m	surge chamber, ~ shaft
(Schwer)Gewichts(stau)mauer f mit dreieckigem Querschnitt m	gravity dam of triangular section
Auftrieb m	uplift
Krone f	coping, crown (Brit.); crest (US)
Luftseite f	downstream face, air-side ~
mittleres Drittel n	middle third
resultierende Kraft f	resultant of all forces
Sohlenwasserdruck m, Auftrieb m	foundation water pressure, uplift
Spitze f des theoretischen Dreiecks n	theoretical apex of the triangle (Brit.); intersection of upstream and downstream faces
Stauhöhe f, Stauziel n	top water level (Brit.); designing ~ ~
Wasserseite f	upstream face, water-side ~
Wellenschlag m	wave action
Segmentschütz(e) n, (f), Segmentverschluß m, Bogenschütz(e), Segmentwehr n	segmental sluice gate, tainter (or taintor) gate, radial gate, segment-shaped sluice
Sektorschütz(e) n, (f), Sektorwehr n	sector (or drum) gate (or sluice)

Talsperre

Skisprung-Überlauf *m*	ski jump spillway
Speicherablaß *m*	reservoir outflow
(Speicher)Becken *n*, siehe: Sammelbecken	
Speichersperre *f*	storage dam
Speicherung *f*, siehe: Stau *m*	
Speicherung *f* zur Energieerzeugung *f*	power storage
Sperrenkörper *m*, Tal~, Stauwerk *n*	(hydro) dam body
Sperrmauer *f*, siehe: (Massiv)Beton(stau)mauer	
Sperrstelle *f*, Talsperrenbaustelle	dam-site
Spiegelschwankung *f*	variation in storage level
Sporn *m*, siehe: Herdmauer *f*	
Spüldamm *m*; siehe unter „Erd(schüttungsstau)damm *m*	
Spülschütz(e) *n*, (*f*)	flushing gate (US); wash-out gate (Brit.)
Stahlbeton-Kernmauer *f*	reinforced concrete core wall
Stau *m*, (Auf)Speicherung *f*, Einstau, Wassereinstau	storage, pondage, filling
Stauanlage *f*, siehe: Staustufe *f*	
Staubecken *n*, siehe: Sammelbecken	
Staudamm *m*, Talsperrendamm	embankment type dam, dam embankment
Staumauer *f*, siehe: Massivbetonmauer *f*	
Staudamm-Staumauer-Kombination *f*	combination type dam
Stausee *m*, siehe: Sammelbecken *n*	
Staustufe *f*, Stauanlage *f*	barrage
Staustufe *f*	fall
Stauwerk *n*, siehe: Sperrenkörper *m*	
Stauwerkskrone *f*, (Tal)Sperrenkrone *f*	dam crest, hydro ~ ~
Stauwerksteil *m* neben der Überfallstrecke *f*	abutment section [*adjoining the (river) overflow (spillway) section*]
Stauziel *n*, Stauspiegel *m*	height of the maximum storage; level of storage water (Brit.); capacity level, storage level (US)
Steinfülldamm *m*, Damm aus Felsschüttung, Felsschüttungsstaudamm, Steinschüttdamm, Staudamm, Steingerüstdamm *m*	rock-fill dam
geschütteter Steindamm *m*	dumped rock-fill dam
Steinschüttdamm mit wasserseitiger Betondichtungsdecke *f*	rock-fill dam with concrete diaphragm on upstream face
Steinschüttdamm mit senkrechtem Erddichtungskern *m*	rock-fill dam with vertical earth core
gerüttelter Steindamm *m*	vibrated rock-fill dam
Mauerwerksperre *f*, Trockenmauerwerksdamm *m*, Steinsatzsperre *f*, gepackter Steindamm *m*	dry masonry dam, rubble ~ ~, dry rubble ~, derrick-and hand-placed stone rock-fill dam
Stein-Ton-Kern *m*	stone-clay core
Stoneyschütz(e) *n*, (*f*)	stoney sluice (or gate)

Sturzbett n [Überlauf m]	(spillway) apron, apron type energy dissipator
Talsperrenbaustelle f, Sperrstelle	dam-site
Talsperrenbecken n, siehe: Sammelbecken	
Talsperrenbeton-Aufbereitungsanlage f	large dam (concrete) plant
Talsperrendamm, siehe: Staudamm	
Talsperrenmauer f, siehe: Massivbetonmauer	
Ton(dichtungs)kern m	clay core
Ton(dichtungs)schürze f	clay blanket
Tonkerndamm m	clay core type embankment (or dam)
Tosbecken n, siehe: Beruhigungsbecken n	
Trennmauer, siehe: Herdmauer	
Triebwasserstollen m, siehe: Betriebswasserstollen	
Trockenmauerwerksdamm; siehe unter „Steinfülldamm"	
Turmeinlaß m, siehe: Einlaßturm m	
Überfall m [Abflußvorgang m beim Überfließen des Wassers über ein Wehr]	overflow
Überfallaufschlagbecken n, siehe: Überfall-Sturzbecken	
überfallfreie Strecke f	nonoverflow section [dam]
Überfallkrone f, Überlaufkrone	overflow crest, spillway crest
Überfall(stau)wehr n, Überlaufwehr	overflow weir, overfall weir, spillway weir, waste-weir, crest-control weir
Überfallstrahl m, überfließender Strahl, Schußstrahl	(overflowing) sheet of water
Überfallstrecke f, Überlaufstrecke	(river) overflow (spillway) section, spillway section
Überfall-Sturzbecken n, Überfallaufschlagbecken n	spillway bucket, roller-bucket type energy dissipator
Überfallwasser n	overflow water
Überjahresspeicherbecken n	conservation (storage) reservoir
Überjahresspeicherung f	conservation storage
Überlauf m, Hochwasserüberlauf, Hochwasserentlastungsanlage f, Überlaufbauwerk n, Entlastungsüberlauf	spillway
Überlaufabführungsanlage f	discharge carrier [is either an open channel or tunnel]
Überlaufen n	overtopping
Überlaufkanal m, Hochwasserentlastungskanal	spillway channel, ~ chute
Überlaufoberfläche f	spillway surface
Überlaufstollen m, Hochwasserstollen	tunnel-type discharge carrier
Überlaufstrecke f, siehe: Überfallstrecke	
Überlauf m über die Stauwerkskrone f	overflow(-type) spillway
Überlaufverschluß m	spillway gate

Talsperre

Überlaufwehr n, siehe: Überfall(stau)wehr	
Umfangsfuge f, siehe: Perimetralfuge	
Umleit(ungs)kanal m	bye-wash, diversion cut, bye-channel, spillway; diversion flume (US)
Umleit(ungs)sperre f zur Bewässerung	diversion dam
Umleit(ungs)stollen m, Umlaufstollen	by-pass tunnel, diversion tunnel
Unterwasseranstieg m	tailwater rise
unterwasserseitig, unterstrom	downstream
Unterwassernotverschluß m	tailgate
Unterwasserkanal m, Ablauf m, Untergraben m, Abflußkanal m	discharge channel, tail race, overflow channel
unterwasserseitige Platte f mit (verkehrt)steigendem Karnies m	ogee downstream slab, cyma $\sim\sim$
unterwasserseitige Vorlage f	downstream apron
Unterwasserstollen m, Ableitungsstollen	tail (race) tunnel
unverschlossener Überlauf m	uncontrolled crest spillway
Verbindungsstollen m der Schützenbedienungskammern fpl	operating gallery
Verbundbauwerk n, siehe: Mehrzweckbauwerk	
Verherdung f, (Ab)Dichtungsgraben m	cut-off trench
Verlandebecken n	silt basin
Verteilerstollen m	penstock manifold, manifold tunnel
verschlossener Überlauf m	gated spillway, gate-controlled spillway, controlled crest spillway
Verzögerungsbecken n	(floodwater) retarding reservoir (or basin), flood detention reservoir, flood-prevention reservoir [*flood-control reservoir provided with uncontrolled outlets*]
Vielfachbogensperre f; siehe unter „Pfeiler(stau)mauer f"	
Vielfachkuppelsperre f; siehe unter „Pfeiler(stau)mauer f"	
Vorsperre f	upstream cofferdam, upstream temporary dam
Walzdamm m; siehe unter „Erd(schüttungsstau)damm m	
(Wasser)Einstau m, (Auf)Speicherung f, Stau m, Stauanhebung f	filling, pondage, storage
Wasserfassung f	water inlets (US); $\sim$ intake (Brit.)
(Wasser)Kraftstollen m, siehe: Betriebswasserstollen	
Wasserkraft-Talsperre f	hydroelectric dam
Wasserschloß n	surge tank
Wasserschloßschacht m, siehe: Schwallschacht m	
wasserseitige Betondichtungsdecke f	impervious concrete diaphragm on the upstream face

Wasserspeicherung *f* — water storage
Wasserumlenkung *f* — river diversion
Wehr *n* (oder Überlauf *m*) mit (verkehrt)steigendem Karnies *m* — ogee weir (or spillway), cyma ~ (~ ~), ogee(-shaped)dam, cyma(-shaped)dam
Widerlagerkissen *n* — saddle

Talweg *m*, Stromstrich *m* (Geol.) [*ist die Verbindungslinie der tiefsten Punkte des Flußlaufes*] = thalweg, valley way, valley line [*the name frequently used for the longitudinal profile of the river, i. e. from source to mouth*]
tandemgetrieben = tandem-driven
Tandemmotor *m* = tandem engine

Tang *m* — seaweed
 Meeresalge *f* — marine algae
 Laminarie *f*, Riementang *m* — laminaria
 Sargossatang *m*, Beerentang *m* — sargassum
 Blasentang *m*, Fukus *m* — bladder wrack, fucus vesiculosus

---

tangentialer Zustrom *m* [*im Fangkessel m beim Druckluftbetonförderer m*] = division of the flow of concrete into two streams by central baffle inside the discharge box which are reunited at the far end of the box
Tangentialkraft *f* = tangential force
Tank *m*, siehe: Behälter *m*
~**anhänger** *m* = tank trailer
Tanker *m*, Tankschiff *n* = tanker (ship)
Tank|spritzmaschine *f*, siehe: Bitumen-Sprengwagen *m*
~**stelle** *f* = filling point, service station; gas(oline) (or gasolene) station (US)
~**wart** *m* = refuel(l)er
Tanne *f* = fir
Tannin *n*, Gerbsäure *f* = tannin, tannic acid, gallo-tannin
Tantal *n* = tantalum
Taragewicht *n*, Leergewicht *n* = tare
Tarier|balken *m* = tare beam
~**waage** *f* = tare balance
Tarif *m* = tariff
Tasche *f*, Abteilung *f* [*Dosierapparat m*] = compartment
Taschen|-Jahrbuch *n* für den Straßenbau *m* = Annual Road Construction Pocket Book
~**silo** *m*, siehe: Bunker *m*
Tasterlehre *f* = snap ga(u)ge

Tastrad *n*, siehe: Lenkrad *n*
Tatsche *f*, siehe: Klatsche *f*
taube Flut *f*, siehe: Nippflut *f*
taubes Gestein *n*, siehe: Berg *m*
Tauchbrücke *f* = low level bridge
Taucher *m* = diver
~**anzug** *m* = diving dress, ~ suit
Tauch|(er)glocke *f* = diving bell
~**gefäß** *n* = immersion vessel
~**rüttler** *m*; siehe unter „Betonrüttelgeräte *npl*"
~**rüttler-Betonstraßen-Fertiger** *m*, Betondeckeninnenrüttler *m*, Tauchvibrationsfertiger *m*, Vibrationsfertiger mit Tauchrüttlern *mpl* = full depth internal concrete pavement (or paving/US) vibrator, ~ ~ ~ slab vibrator; paving vibrator (US); internal vibrating machine (Brit.); internal vibrator type concrete (pavement) finisher
~**schmierung** *f* = splash lubrication
~**verdampfer** *m* = submerged evaporator
~**wägung** *f* = immersion weighing
~**wanne** *f* für Fugeneisen *npl* = immersion kettle for joint-forming metal strips
Tau|-Frostwechsel *m*, siehe: Gefrier- und Auftauzyklus *m*
~**lava** *f*; siehe unter „Vulkan *m*"
~**salz** *n*, siehe: (Auf)Tausalz

Tau|senkung *f* [*Straßendecke f*] = settlement due to thawing out of frost
~**wasser** *n*, siehe: Kondenswasser
Taylor'scher Satz *m* = Taylor's series
Technik *f* [*als betriebstechnische Anwendung f*] = technique, practice
~, Ingenieurwissenschaft *f* = engineering (science)
technisch, betriebstechnisch = technical, practical
Technische Hochschule *f* = Technical College (Brit.); Technological Institute (US)
technische Hydraulik *f* = hydraulics
~ **Messe** *f* = engineering fair
~ **Richtlinien** *fpl* = technical specifications
~ **Strömungslehre** *f* = theory of fluid flow
technischer Beratungsdienst *m* = engineering consultation (or counsel) service
~ **Marmor** *m*, Marmorkalkstein *m*, polierbarer dichter Kalkstein = compact polishable limestone
~ **(Straßen)Überwachungstrupp** *m* = technical (road) patrol
technisches Gas *n* = heating gas
Technische Vorschriften *fpl* **für Erdarbeiten** *f* **bei den Reichsautobahnen** *fpl*, **TVE. RAB** = Technical Specifications for Earthworks for the German Motor Roads
Technologie *f* = technology

Teer *m*
  Absatz~, Absetz~
  Anthrazenöl~
  Archangel~
  aromatisch
  Asphalt~
  Bagasse~
  Baumrinden~
  Bernstein~
  Bienenwachs~
  Birkenholz~
  Bitumenschiefer~, (Öl)Schiefer~
  Blaugas~
  Braunkohlenheizgenerator~
  Braunkohlenkokerei~
  Braunkohlenschwel~
  Braunkohlen~
  Braunkohlenur~
  Buchen(holz)~
  Coalite~
  Del Monte~
  entwässert
  Fettgas~, siehe: Ölgas~
  Fuselölgas~
  Gas(werks)~, Gasanstalts~
  Gummi~
  Hobelspäne~
  Hochofen~
  hochviskoser ~
  Holzabfall~
  Holzdestillation *f*
  Holzsplitter~

tar
  settled ~
  anthracene-oil ~
  Archangel ~
  aromatic
  asphalt ~
  bagasse ~
  wood bark ~
  amber ~
  beeswax ~
  birch wood ~
  shale ~
  blue gas ~
  producer gas brown coal ~
  coke-oven brown coal ~
  retort browncoal ~
  brown-coal ~
  low-temperature brown coal ~
  beech (wood) ~
  coalite ~
  Delmonte ~
  dehydrated

  fusel-oil ~
  gas works coal ~, gas-house coal ~
  rubberized ~
  wood shavings ~
  blast-furnace coal ~
  high-viscosity ~
  wood waste ~
  wood distillation
  wood splittings ~

Horizontal-Retorten ~	horizontal retort ~
Karbokohlen ~	carbocoal ~
Kerzen ~	candle ~
Kien ~	pine ~
Knochen ~	bone ~
Kohlenwassergas ~	dehydrated water-gas ~
Kokerei ~, Zechen ~, Koksofen ~, Steinkohlenkokerei ~	coke oven coal ~
Kork ~	cork ~
Laubholz ~	hardwood ~
Leder ~	leather ~
Lignin ~	lignin ~
Lignit ~	lignite ~
Linoleum ~	linoleum ~
Mond ~	mond ~
Montanwachs ~	montan-wax ~
niedrigviskoser ~	low-viscosity ~
Ölgas ~, Fettgas ~	oil gas ~
Ölschiefer ~, siehe: Bitumenschiefer ~	
Ölwassergas ~	carburetted water gas ~, oil-water-gas ~, fuel-oil gas ~, reformed-gas ~
Roh ~	crude ~ [*deprecated: green ~*]
Rolle-Ofen ~	Rolle-retort browncoal ~
Sägemehl ~	sawdust ~
Schiefer ~, siehe: Bitumenschiefer ~	
Schottischer (Öl)Schiefer ~, Schottischer Bitumenschiefer ~	Scottish shale ~
Schwedischer (Schiffs) ~, siehe: Stockholmer ~	
Schwelretorten ~	retort ~
Steinkohlen ~	(bituminous) coal ~
Steinkohlen(heiz)generator ~	producer-gas coal ~, gas-producer coal ~
Steinkohlenkokerei ~, siehe: Kokerei ~	
Steinkohlen(teer)pech *n*	coal-tar pitch
Stockholmer ~, Schwedischer (Schiffs) ~	Stockholm ~
Strohstoff ~	straw ~
Sulfitzellstoffablauge ~	sulfite cellulose ~, tall oil ~
Tabak ~	tobacco ~
Teerausbeute *f*	yield of ~
Torf-Mondgasgenerator ~	mond gas generator peat ~
Torf-Retortenschwel ~	retort peat ~
Torf-Schwelgenerator ~	producer peat ~
Torf ~	peat ~
Torfur ~	low-temperature peat ~
Vertikal-Retorten ~	vertical retort ~
Vinasse ~	vinasse ~
Wassergas ~	water gas ~

Wetter ~

Zechen ~, siehe: Kokerei ~

high-viscosity product consisting of blown tar, pitch and cut-back with anthracene oil

---

Teerbeton m = tar concrete
~decke f = dense tar surfacing, tar concrete pavement, D. T. S.
~- und Walzasphalt-Mischanlage f, Asphaltaufbereitungsanlage, Walzasphaltanlage, Heißmischanlage = hot-mix (asphalt) plant, central mixing plant for the preparation of high-type hot mixtures (US); asphalt plant
Teer|bitumengemisch n = tar-asphaltic bitumen mixture (Brit.); tar-asphalt ~ (US)
~dach n = tar roof
~eimer m = tar pail
~emulsion f = tar emulsion
~faß n = tar barrel
~feinbeton m, siehe: Heißeinbau-~
teergebunden = tarviated, tar-bound
Teergrobbeton m, siehe: Heißeinbau-~
Teermakadam m = tarmacadam; macadam with tar binder (Brit.)
~-Mischanlage f = tarmacadam mixing plant
Teer|mischanlage f = tar mixing plant
~öltränkung f nach Rüping, siehe: Rüping(spar)verfahren n
~schlauch m = tar hose
~schöpfer m = tar dipping ladle
~schotter m = tarred stone
~schwelerei f = tar distillery
~splitt m = chipping(s) precoated with tar, tarcoated chippings, tarred ~
~spritzgerät n, Teerspritzmaschine f = tarsprayer
~teppich m = tar carpet, ~ mat
~tränkmakadam m [*früher: Teerauſguß-Beschotterung f*] = tar-grouted stone (Brit.); tar penetration macadam, road tar type penetration macadam
Teer- und Bitumen-Kocher m, Teer- und Bitumen-Schmelzkessel m = tar and bitumen (Brit.)/asphalt (US) heater (or heating kettle, or melting tank); ~ ~ ~ boiler [*deprecated*]

Teer- und Bitumen-Vorkocher m = tar and bitumen (Brit.)/asphalt (US), primary heater (or heating kettle, or melting tank); ~ ~ ~ ~ boiler [*deprecated*]
Teerung f = tarring, tarspraying
Teer|vermörtelung f; siehe unter „Baugrundverbesserung f"
~werg n = tarred oakum
Teich|rohr n, Schilfrohr n = (common) reed
~verfahren n; siehe unter „Nachbehandlung f" [*Beton*]
Teil|becherwerk n, Schöpfbecherwerk = spaced (or intermittent, or dredger) bucket (type) elevator
~einspundung f = partial sheeting
~kreis m = pitch circle
~montage f = sub-assembly
~sättigung f = partial saturation
~strecke f, siehe: Abschnitt m
~strich m [*Waage f*] = graduation mark
~strichwaage f = graduated scale
teilweise eingespannter Träger m = partially restrained girder
~ Einspannung f = partial restraint
Tektogenese f, siehe: Gebirgsbildung f
tektonisch = tectonic
tektonischer und topographischer Sattel m (Geol.) = geoanticline
Tektor m, siehe: Betonspritzmaschine f
Telefonzelle f, Telefonhäuschen n = telephone kiosk
Teleskop|-Ausleger m = folding (or telescopic) jib (Brit.); ~ (~ ~) boom (US)
~-Drehsäule f = telescopic (mono-) tower
~kran m = telescopic-armed crane
Teller m [*SEAMAN-Bodenvermörteler* m] = tine plate (US)
~aufgeber m, siehe: Tellerspeiser
~beschicker m, siehe: Tellerspeiser
~bohrer m [*Bodenuntersuchung f*] = disc auger, disk ~

Tellermischer *m*; siehe unter „Betonmischer *m*"

(Teller)Scheibenegge *f*, Diskusegge = disc (or disk) harrow; disk plowing ~ (US)

Teller|speiser *m*, Tellerzuteiler *m*, Telleraufgeber *m*, Tellerbeschicker *m*, Rundbeschicker *m* = disc (or disk) feeder

~ventil *n* = disc (or disk) valve

Tellurblei *n* = lead telluride

Temperatur|anstiegs-Meßverfahren *n* = temperature gradient method

~leitfähigkeit *f* = thermal diffusivity

~meßkurven-Auswertung *f* = interpretation of temperature logs

~spannung *f* = tensile stress due to temperature variations, temperature stress

Temperguß *m*, schmiedbarer Eisenguß *m* annaeled cast-iron, malleable ~

Tempern *n* = tempering, drawing

tempern, ausglühen = to anneal

Temperöl *n*, Härteöl *f* = quenching oil

Tenderlok(omotive) *f* = tender loco(motive), locomotive-car

Teppich(belag) *m*, Straßenteppich *m*, Mischteppich(belag) = carpet-coat, (pre-mix(ed)) carpet, mat, thin surfacing, road carpet, road mat, veneer (Brit.)

~ *m* mit Ölung *f* = oil mat (road) surface

Terpentin|kiefer *f*, Harzkiefer *f*, Douglasie *f* = pitch pine, Oregon ~, Douglas fir, Columbian pine

~öl *n*, $C_{10}H_{16}$ = oil of turpentine, turps

Terrakotta *f* [*in Österreich*]; Terrakotte *f* = terra-cotta

Terrassen|haus *n* = terrace house

~kies *m* (Geol.) = terrace gravel

Terrassieren *n*, siehe: Abtreppen *n*

Terrazzo *m*, Zementmosaik *n* = terrazzo, Venetian mosaic

~schleifmaschine *f* = terrazzo polisher

terrigenes Sediment *n* = terrigenous deposit

Teschenit *m* = teschenite

Testbenzin *n*, siehe: Lackbenzin *n*

~ = white spirit

Tetrachlorkohlenstoff *m*, CCl_4 = carbon tetrachloride

Tetradymit *m*, Schwefeltellurwismut *n*, Bi_2Te_2S (Min.) = tetradymite

Tetrajodkohlenstoff *m* = carbon tetraiodide

Textil|beize *f* = mordant

~gurt *m* [*Becherwerk n*] = canvas belt

Textur *f* [*räumliche Anordnung f der Mineralien fpl sowie die Raumerfüllung*] = texture

T-förmiger Windrichtungsanzeiger *m* = wind Tee

Theodolit *m* = theodolite

theoretischer Endpunkt *m* [*Blechträger m*] = theoretical end

Theralit *m* = theralite

Thermalanalyse *f* = differential thermal analysis

Therme *f*, thermale Quelle *f* = hot spring, thermal ~

thermische Aufrauhung *f*, Abbrennen *n* von Basaltpflaster *n* = heat treatment of basalt paving setts, sett burning

~ Bodenverfestigung *f* = soil stabilisation by heat treatment

~ Ermüdung *f* = thermal fatigue

thermischer Stoß *m* = thermal shock

thermisches Gefälle *n* = thermal gradient

~ Kracken *n* = liquid phase cracking

~ Kraftwerk *n* = thermal (or thermo) power plant (or station)

~ Reformierungsverfahren *n* [*Benzin n*] = thermal reforming process

Thermo|element *n*, elektrisches Thermometer *n* = electric thermometer, electrothermic ga(u)ge

~lumineszenz *f* = thermoluminiscence

Thermo-Osmose *f* = thermo-osmosis

thermophyle Ausfaulung *f* = thermophilic digestion

Thixotropie *f*, Wechselfestigkeit *f* = thixotropy

~effekt *m* = thixotropic hardening

Thomas|mehl *n*, Schlackenmehl *n* Thomasphosphat *n* = Thomal meal, slag flour

~roheisen *n* = basic Bessemer pig-iron

~roheisenschlacke *f* = Thomas pig-iron slag, basic Bessemer pig (iron) slag

~schlacke *f* = basic slag, Thomas ~

Tideerscheinung *f*, siehe: Gezeitenerscheinung

Tide|fluß m = tidal river
~hafen m, siehe: Fluthafen m
~hub m, siehe: Gezeitenhub
~strömung f, siehe: Gezeitenströmung
~wechsel m = tidal range
Tiden fpl, siehe: Gezeiten fpl
Tief|(auf)reißer m = (road) rooter
~baggerung f = deep cut digging
~bau m, planender Ingenieurbau m = civil engineering
~bauarbeiten fpl = below grade construction
~baustelle f = below-grade (construction) site
~bauunternehmer m = civil engineering contractor
~bett-Anhänger m, siehe: Tieflader m
~bordstein m, siehe: Kantenstein m
~brunnen m, Tiefspiegelbrunnen = deep well
~ebene f, siehe: Tiefland n
~einbau m [Frostschutzschicht f] = frost blanket construction with removal of old pavement
tief eingeschnitten [Tal n] = deeply incised
Tiefen|(ein)rüttlung f = deep vibration
~einstellung f = depth control, ~ adjustment
~gestein n, siehe: plutonisches Gestein n
~lehre f = depth ga(u)ge
~linienkarte f, Tiefenkurvenkarte, Isobathenkarte = subsurface contour map
~rüttler m; siehe unter „Betonrüttelgeräte npl"
~rüttler m [Kellerverfahren n, Steuermannverfahren] = spud vibrator
~schwimmer m = loaded float
~sondierung f = deep sounding
~sondierung f mit stufenweiser Belastung f = static penetration testing
~sprengung f [Sprengen n weicher Baugrundmassen fpl] = underfill method, ~ blasting
~stabilisierung f; siehe unter „Baugrundverbesserung f"
~strom m [Ozean m] = bathy current
~stufe f, geothermische ~ = geothermal gradient, geothermic degree

~typ(us) m [Gestein n] = deep-seated type
~- und Langstreckenförderer m; siehe unter „Seilförderanlage f"
~verdichtung f = deep compaction
~verwitterung f = downward weathering
~vulkan m = deep-seated volcano
~wasser n = water at greater depths
~wasser n [Ozean m] = bottom water
~wirkung f = depth effect
~-Zeitkurve f = depth-time curve
Tief|fundation f, siehe: Tiefgründung f
~gang m [Schiff n] = draught (Brit.); draft (US)
~garage f, unterirdische Garage = underground garage
tiefgegründeter Pfeiler m = deep(-water) pier
Tief|gründung f, Tieffundation f = deep foundation
~kälteverfahren n; siehe unter „Baugrundverbesserung f"
~kühlanlage f = intense cooling plant
~ladeanhänger m, siehe: Tieflader
(~)Ladebrücke f [Tiefladewagen m] = deck, platform
~ladelinie f [Schiff n] = (deep) load-line
~lader m, Tiefladeanhänger m, Tiefbett-Anhänger, Tiefladewagen m, Tiefbettlader = low-loader, low-bed trailer, low-load trailer, deck trailer; low boy (trailer) (US)
~lader m mit Kipp(tief)ladebrücke f, Kipptieflader = tilt-deck trailer, tilting platform ~
~ladewagen m [Eisenbahn f] = well wagon
~ladewagen m [Straßenfahrzeug n], siehe: Tieflader m
~land n, Tiefebene f = low-level flat, low-land, bottom land, low-lying land
~landsee m = lowland lake
tiefliegendes Gelände n ~ Land n = low-lying tract of ground, low-level ground, low-lying land
Tieflöffel m, Bagger~, Tiefräumer m = (back)hoe dipper (US); backacter ~ (Brit.)
~-Ausleger m = (back)hoe boom (US); backacter jib (Brit.)

Tieflöffel|-Ausrüstung *f* **für Schwenkschaufler** = swing digger (attachment)
~(bagger) *m*, siehe: Löffeltiefbagger
Tief|ofen *m* = soaking-pit furnace
~ofen *m*, Streichofen [*Hüttenwesen n*] = low furnace
~-Probe(ent)nahmeapparat *m* = deep sampler, ~ sample taker
~pumpenkolben *m* = deep pump piston
~pumpenmanschette *f* = deep pump cup
~reißer *m*, siehe: Tiefaufreißer
~räumer *m*, siehe: Tieflöffel *m*
~scholle *f* (Geol.), siehe: Graben *m*
~schürfbohrung *f* = deep sampling
~schütter-Bandabsetzer *m* = stacker for filling below track level
Tiefsee *f* = deep sea, oceanic abyss
~ablagerung *f*, Tiefseesediment *n* = abysmal deposit, deposit of the deep sea
~ammonit *m* = bathyal ammonite
~graben *m*, Tiefseerinne *f* = trench, depressed trough
~kabel *n* = deep-sea cable
~kern *m* = deep-sea core
~lot *n* = deep-sea lead, ~ sounding apparatus
~lotung *f*, Tiefseemessung = bathymetry, deep sea sounding
~panzer *m* = deep-sea diving outfit
~rinne *f*, Tiefseegraben *m* = depressed trough, trench
~sand *m* = deep-sea sand
~schlamm *m*, siehe: eupelagische Meeresablagerung *f*
~sediment *n*, Tiefseeablagerung *f* = deposit of the deep sea, abysmal deposit
~taucher *m* = deep-sea diver
~thermometer *n* = sounding thermometer, deep sea ~, submarine ~
~ton *m*, roter ~ = red clay
Tief|(spiegel)brunnen *m* = deep well
~straße *f* = depressed highway
~tal *n* = pronounced valley
~terrasse *f* (Geol.) = low-lying terrace
~wasser-Hafenmauer *f* = deep(-water) wharf
~wasserlinie *f* = low-water line
~ziehblech *n* = deep-drawing quality sheet steel

Tiegel|gußstahl *m* = crucible (cast) steel
~ofen *m* = crucible furnace
~stahl *m* = crucible steel
Tierkohle *f*, Knochenkohle, animalische Kohle = animal charcoal, animalic coal
Tiger|auge *n* (Min.) = tiger('s) eye
~sandstein *m* = mottled sandstone
Tilasit *m* = fluoradelite, tilasite
Tillit *m* = tillite
TIMKEN-Lager *n* = TIMKEN roller bearing
Tinguaitgang *m* = tinguaitic dike
Tinkalsee *m* = alkaline lake
Tintometer *n* = tintometer
Tipper *m* **am Vergaser** *m* = carburettor primer, ~ tickler (US)
Tirolergrün *n*, Berggrün = mountain green
Tisch|bohrmaschine *f* [*zur Befestigung an der Werkbank f*] = bench drill(ing machine)
~bohrmaschine *f* = table drilling machine
~bohrmaschine *f* **mit Handhebelvorschub** *m* = sensitive drill press
~drehbank *f* = bench lathe
~drehzahlanzeiger *m* = table speed indicator
~felsen *m* = erosion pillar, rock ~, mushroom rock
~kloben *m*, Bankschraubstock *m* = table vice
~längsweg *m* = longitudinal table traverse
~rüttler *m*; siehe unter „Betonrüttelgeräte *npl*"
~schleifmaschine *f* = bench grinder
~selbstgang *m* [*Werkzeugmaschine f*] = table power traverse
~speiser *m* = table feeder
~steuerhebel *m* = table control lever
Titanat *n* = titanate
Titanit *m*, $CaSiTiO_5$ (Min.) = titanite, sphene
Titanlagerstätte *f*, Titanvorkommen *n*, Titanvorkommnis *n* = titanium deposit
Titanomorphit *m* (Min.), siehe: Leukoxen *n*
Titration *f* = titration

Tochterstadt *f*, siehe: Trabantenstadt
tödlicher Unfall *m*, Unfall mit tödlichem Ausgang *m* = fatal accident
Toleranz *f*, Genauigkeitsgrad *m*, zulässige Maßabweichung = allowance, tolerance
~, Genauigkeitsgrad *m* [*Straßendeckenebenheit f*] = inaccuracy of finish
Toluol *n*, siehe: Methylbenzol *n*
Ton *m*, Rohton [< *0,002 mm*] = clay
~**abbau** *m*, Tongewinnung *f* = getting of clay, clay working
Tonalit *m* (Geol.) = tonalite
Ton|anteil *m*, Tonkomponente *f* = clay fraction
~**aufbereitung** *f* = clay preparation
~**auspressung** *f*, siehe: Toninjektion *f*
~**auswaschebene** *f* = clay outwash plain
~**bagger** *m* = clay excavator
~**band** *n* (Geol.) = clay band
~**bank** *f* = clay bank
~**beton** *m*, mechanische Bodenverfestigung *f* = mechanical (or granular) (soil) stabilisation
~**betonstraße** *f* = mechanically stabilised road, granular ~ ~
~**boden** *m*, Tonerde *f* = clay soil
~**brei** *m* [*Keramik f*] = clay slip
~**dachziegel(stein)** *m*, Tondachstein = clay roof(ing) tile
~(**dichtungs)kern** *m* = clay core
~(**dichtungs)schürze** *f* = clay blanket
~**einpressung** *f*, siehe: Toninjektion *f*
~**eisenstein** *m*, Sphärosiderit *m*, toniger Spateisenstein, Eisenton *m*, Toneisenerz *n* = argillaceous ironstone, clay ~, clay iron ore, iron clay, argillaceous iron ore
~**emulsion** *f* = clay emulsion
~**erde** *f*, Tonboden *m* = clay soil
~**erde** *f* = alumina
~**erdefiltertiegel** *m* = alumina filter
~**erdehydrat** *n*, siehe: Bauxit *m*
~**erde-Kieselsäure-Erzeugnis** *n* = alumina-silica refractory
~**erdenatron** *n* = sodium aluminate
~**erdeschamottestein** *m* = alumina firebrick
~**erde(schmelz)zement** *m*; siehe unter „Zement"

~**erdesilikat** *n*, kieselsaure Tonerde *f* = silicate of alumina
~**erdesulfat** *n*, schwefelsaure Tonerde *f* = alumina sulphate, sulphate of alumina, alum
~**erdeverbindung** *f* = alumina compound
~**erzeugnis** *n*, Tonprodukt *n*, Tonware *f* = clay product
~**fräse** *f* = clay shredder
~**galle** *f* = clay gall, argillaceous ~, marl pellets
~**gehalt** *m* = clay content
~**gestein** *n* = argillaceous rock, clay ~
~**gewinnung** *f*, Tonabbau *m* = getting of clay, clay working
~**gießwulst** *f* [*Rohrverlegung f*] = clay roll
~**gips** *m* = argillaceous gypsum
~**glimmerschiefer** *m* = phyllite
~**grube** *f* = clay pit, ~ quarry
~**gruppe** *f* (Geol.) = allophane group
~**häutchen** *n*, Tonüberzug *m* = clay film
~**hobel** *m* = shale planer
~-**Hohlkügelchen** *n* = clay bubble
~**hohlplatte** *f*, siehe: Hourdis *m*
tonig, tonhaltig = clayey, argillaceous
toniger Boden *m*, tonhaltiger Boden = clayey soil, argillaceous ~
~ **Kalkstein** *m*, tonhaltiger Kalkstein, Tonkalk *m* = clayey limestone, argillaceous ~, argillocalcite
~ **Kies** *m* = clayey gravel, argillaceous ~
~ **Sand** *m*, tonhaltiger Sand = clayey sand, argillaceous ~
Ton|injektion *f*, Toneinpressung *f*, Tonauspressung, Tonverpressung = pressure grouting with clay
~**kalk** *m*, toniger Kalkstein *m*, tonhaltiger Kalkstein = argillaceous limestone, argillocalcite, clayey limestone
~**kern** *m*, Tondichtungskern = clay core
~**kerndamm**; siehe unter „Talsperre *f*"
~**komponente** *f*, Tonanteil *m* = clay fraction
~**konglomerat** *n* = argillaceous conglomerate, clayey ~
~**konkretion** *f* = clay concretion
~**kügelchenherstellung** *f* = pellet formation
~**lage** *f* [*an den Salbändern npl*] = clay course

Ton|lagerstätte *f*, Tonvorkommen *n*, Tonvorkommnis *n* = clay deposit
~lamellen *fpl* = clay laminae
~lehm *m* = clay loam
~linse *f* = lenticle of clay, clay lens
~masse *f* = clay mass
~(mauer)ziegel(stein) *m* = clay brick
~mehl *n* = clay powder, finely ground fire clay
~mergel *m* [10—40% $CaCO_3$] = clay marl, clayey ~, shaley ~
~mineral *n*, Schichtsilikat *n* = clay mineral, layer silicate
~mischer *m*, siehe: Tonschneider *m*
Tonnen|blech *n* = arched plate
~dach *n*, Tonnenflechtwerkdach = barrel roof
~gehalt *m* = tonnage
~gewinn *m* = ton-profit
~gewölbe *n* = barrel vault, wagon ~, tunnel ~
~lager *n* = barrel-shaped roller bearing
~meile *f* = ton-mile
tonnlägige Wassersäulenmaschine *f*, geneigte ~, donlägige ~ = water (pressure) engine with inclined axis
tonnlägiger Schacht *m*, siehe: donlägiger ~ [von 45°—75° Neigung *f*]
Ton|pfeiler *m* (Geol.) = clay pillar
~produkt *n*, siehe: Tonerzeugnis *n*
~reißer *m* = clay shredder
~rohr *n*, Steinzeugrohr = (vitrified) clay pipe (US); stoneware (drain) pipe (Brit.)
Schale *f* = channel (or split) ~ ~ ~
~sand *m* = argillaceous sand, clayey ~
~-Sand-Kies-Mischung *f*, Ton-Sand-Kies-Gemisch *n* = clay-sand-gravel mixture
~sandstein *m* = clayey sandstone, argillaceous ~
~scherbe *f* = clay body
~schiefer *m* = (clay) slate, argillaceous ~, argillite
~schiefer *m* **mit viel Chlorit** *m* = chlorite slate
~schiefernädelchen *n* = slate needle [*rutile*]
~schlamm *m* (Geol.) = clayey mud, argillaceous ~

~schlamm *m* [*Zementindustrie f*] = straight-clay slurry
~schlammgestein *n* = mud rock, clay mudrock
~schlampe *f*, Tonschlämpe, Tonschlämme = clay slurry
~schlick *m* = clayey mud, argillaceous ~
~schneider *m*, Tonmischschneider, Tonmischer *m* [*Ziegelfabrikation f*] = pug mill
~schneider-Anmach(e)wasser *n* = pug mill water
~schneider-Aufbereitung *f* [*deckt sich mit dem Begriff „mit Wasser mischen"*] = pugging
~schneidermesser *n* = pug mill knife
~schnitzler *m* = clay shredder
~schürze *f*, Tondichtungsschürze = clay blanket
~seife *f* = aluminous soap, soap earth
~silo *m* = clay storage bin
~spaten *m* = clay spade
~splitt *m*, siehe: Ziegelsplitt
~splittmauerstein *m*, siehe: Ziegelsplittmauerstein
~spülung *f* [*Bohrtechnik f*] = clay base mud
~stechen *n* = clay digging
~stein *m*, schichtungsloser ~ [*durch Druck und Wasserverlust erhärteter Ton*] = mudstone, clay-stone
~substanz *f* [*Gestein n*] = argillaceous cement, clayey ~
~suspension *f* = clay suspension
~teilchen *n* = clay particle
~tiegel *m*, feuerfester Tiegel = fire clay crucible
~trockner *m* = clay dryer, ~ drier
~trübe *f* = clay detritus held in suspension
~überzug *m*, Tonhäutchen *n* = clay film
Tönung *f*, Farb~ = shade
Ton|verpressung *f*, siehe: Toninjektion *f*
~verteilungsgerät *n* = clay slope revetment spreader
~vorkommen *n*, siehe: Tonlagerstätte *f*
~ware *f*, siehe: Tonerzeugnis *n*
~werk *n* = clay (working) plant, clay work(s)

Ton-Zement-Gemisch — Trägerschere

Ton|-Zement-Gemisch n, Ton-Zement-Mischung f = clay-cement mixture

~ziegel m, Ton(mauer)ziegel(stein) m = clay brick

Topas m (Min.) = topaz

Topeka m, splitterarmer Asphaltfeinbeton m [*Verbunddecke f von Sandasphalt m und Splitt m*] = Topeka (type asphaltic concrete)

Töpferton m, siehe: Backsteinton m

Topographie f = topography

topographische Aufnahme f = topo(graphic) survey

Tor n = gate

~bagger m, siehe: Portalbagger

Torf|bagger m = peat excavator

~einschluß m, Torfnest n = concealed bed of peat, peat pocket

~erde f = peat mo(u)ld

~moos n, siehe: Sumpfmoos n

~mull m, Torfmehl n = peat dust, ~ meal, ~ powder

~nest n, siehe: Torfeinschluß m

~streu f = peat litter

Torkran m, Voll~, (Voll)Portalkran = portal crane, arched pedestal ~

Torkretbeton-Spritzmaschine f, siehe: Betonspritzmaschine

Torkretieren n, siehe: Torkretverfahren n

Torkretmantel m = gunited coating

Torkretpumpe f, Betonpumpe System TORKRET, TORKRET-Betonpumpe = TORKRET concrete pump, ~ pumpcrete machine

Torkretverfahren n, Torkretbeton-Spritzverfahren n, Torkretieren n, Torkretierung f, pneumatische Auftragung f von Putzmörtel m = guniting, cement gun work

(Torkret)Zement(mörtel)kanone f, siehe: Betonspritzmaschine f

Torladewagen m, Klemmgriff-Lastenträger m = straddle carrier (Brit.); ~ truck (US)

Tornister-Spritzgerät n = knapsack sprayer

Torpedorinne f, Wurfförderrinne f mit Pendelantrieb m, Pendelwurfrinne f = torpedo-conveyor

Torsion f, (Ver)Drillung f, Verdrehung f, Verwindung f = torsion

Torsions|-Schwingungsdämpfer m = torsional vibration damper

~spannung f, (Ver)Drillungsspannung, Verdrehungsspannung, Verwindungsspannung = torsional stress

~steifigkeit f, Verdreh(ungs)steifigkeit f, Drillungssteife f = torsional rigidity

~verband m = torsion frame

~viskosimeter n = torsion visco(si)meter

Tosbecken n; siehe unter „Talsperre f"

Totbrennen n [*Gips m*] = dead burning

toter Arm m, Altwasser n = ox bow (lake); bayou (US); mortlake (Brit.)

totgebrannt [*Kalk m*] = overburnt

totgebrannter Gips m, siehe: unlöslicher Anhydrit m

Trabantenstadt f, Tochterstadt, Satellitenstadt n = satellite town, ~ city; satelite community center (US)

Trace f, siehe: Trasse f

Tracheide f, Leitzelle f [*Holz n*] = tracheid

Trachyt m = trachyte

~lava f = trachytic lava

TRAFIC-MOBIL [*Trademark*] [*a road milling and grooving machine*] = Straßenfräs- und Aufrauhmaschine f

Tragband n = carryable belt conveyor

tragbar = carryable

Tragdecke f, siehe: Tragschicht f [*Straße f*]

Trage f = hand barrow

tragender Bauteil m = load-bearing member

Träger m, siehe: Balken m

~anschluß m = girder connection

~biegepresse f, Balken(träger)biegepresse = girder bending press (Brit.); beam ~

~gestein n, siehe: Speichergestein

trägerlose Decke f = flat slab

Träger|rost m = girder grillage, girder grid (Brit.); grillage beams, beam grid

~rostdecke f, Balken(träger)rostdecke = grid-type girder deck (Brit.); two-way beam-and-slab floor

~schere f = joist shears, joist shearing machine, I-iron ~ ~

Trag|fähigkeit *f*, Tragvermögen *n*, Tragleistung *f*, Tragkraft *f*, Tragwiderstand *m* [*Boden m*] = load-carrying (or supporting, or bearing) capacity (or power) [*soil*]
~fähigkeit *f* [*Kran m*] = lifting capacity
~fähigkeitsindex *m* = bearing index
~fähigkeitsmesser *m* = bearing (capacity) apparatus
~fähigkeitsversuch *m* = bearing test
~gewölbe *n* = arch support
Trägheit *f*, siehe: Beharrungsvermögen *n*
Trägheits|ellipse *f* = ellipse of inertia
~kraft *f* = force of inertia
~moment *n* = moment of inertia
~vermögen *n*, siehe: Beharrungsvermögen
Trag|lastverfahren *n* = ultimate load method, ~ ~ design
~pfahl *m* = bearing pile
~ring *m* = bearing ring
~rolle *f*, belastete Rolle = support(ing) roller, carrier (idler)
~rolle *f* [*Gleiskette f*] = carrier roller
~rollenstation *f* = carrier idler set
~schicht *f*, Tragdecke *f* [*in Deutschland auch als "Unterbau" bezeichnet, wenn die darunter liegende Schicht "Sauberkeitsschicht" genannt wird*]; obere und untere Tragschicht [*in der Schweiz und Österreich, beide zusammen mit dem "Belag" werden dann als "Oberbau" bezeichnet*] = base (course)
~schicht *f* aus verfestigtem Material *n* = (stabilised) soil (road) base
~seil *n* [*Seilschwebebahn f*] = rail rope
~tier *n* = pack animal
~werk *n*, siehe: Fachwerk(träger) *n*, (*m*)
~widerstand *m*, siehe: Tragfähigkeit *f*
Trakt *m* = tract
Traktor *m*, siehe: Schlepper *m*
~-Bagger *m*, siehe: (Front-)Ladeschaufel *f*
traktorengezogene Geräte *npl* = tractor-allied (or tractor-drawn) equipment
Traktoren|kette *f*, siehe: Raupenkette
~kraftstoff *m*, siehe: Kraftstoffkerosin *n*
~kran *m*, Schlepperkran, Traktorkran = tractor crane
~(trommel)seilwinde *f*, siehe: Schlepperseilwinde

Traktor-Schrapper *m*; siehe unter „Radschrapper *m*"
tränender Hausschwamm *m*, echter ~ = merulius lacrymans (domesticus), weeping fungus
Tränkdecke *f*, siehe: Tränkmakadam *m*
Tränken *n*, Einguß *m*, Tränkung *f* [*Straßenbau m*] = grouting (Brit.); penetration
tränken [*Straßenbau m*] = to grout (Brit.); to penetrate
Tränk|makadam *m*, Tränkdecke *f*, Tränkmakadamdecke *f* = penetration surfacing (or pavement, or macadam); grouted macadam (or surfacing) (Brit.)
~rinne *f* = horse pond
~tragschicht *f* = penetrated stone base course
Tränkung *f* [*Straße f*] = grouting (Brit.); penetration
Transformatorenöl *n* = (mineral) transformer oil
Transit|lademaß *n* = clearance
~schuppen *m* = transit shed
Transmissionsriemen *m* = transmission belt(ing)
Transpiration *f* [*produktiver Wasserverbrauch m der Pflanze f*] = transpiration
Transport *m* = haulage, transportation, hauling
~, Verfrachtung *f* (Geol.) = transport
transportables Gas *n*, siehe: Ölgas
Transport|bandanlage *f*; siehe unter „Bandförderer *m*"
~bandstraße *f*; siehe unter Bandförderer *m*"
~betonaufbereitungsanlage *f* = ready-mix plant, ready mixed concrete plant
~betonaufbereitungsanlage *f* zur Herstellung *f* von Beton *m* zum Verfahren *n* durch Nachmischer *mpl* = ready-mixed concrete plant of the central mix type
~betonaufbereitungsanlage zur Herstellung *f* von Trockenbeton *m* = transit-mix(ing concrete) plant, ready-mixed concrete plant of the transit-mix type; truck mixer plant (US)
~-Einschienenbahn *f*, siehe: Einschienenbahn zum Betontransport *m*

Transportfahrzeug — Treppe

Transport|fahrzeug n = transporting vehicle, haul(ing) unit, hauler
~**gefäß** n, Behälter m = container
~**karre(n)** f, (m), siehe: Karre(n)
~**mischer** m, Liefermischer m, Fahrmischer [*zentrale Abmessung f, Mischen n während der Fahrt f*] = truck mixer, transit-mixer (truck) (US); mixer lorry (Brit.)
~**plan** m; siehe unter „Erdarbeiten f"
~**schnecke** f, siehe: Schneckenförderer m
~**- und Verteileranhänger** m **mit Bodenentleerung** f = bottom-dump hauling and spreading trailer
~**-unternehmer** m, Fuhrunternehmer m = hauling contractor
~**wagen** m = transporter
trapezförmiges Gerinne n = trapezoidal channel
Trapp m = trap (rock)
~**tuff** m, siehe: Basalttuff m
Traps m, siehe: Abscheider m
Trasse f [*zu vermeiden: Trace f*] = route
Trassen|schäler m, Planier-(Gleis)Kettengerät n mit schneepflugartiger Anordnung des Planierschildes n = roadbuilder, trailbuilder, gradebuilder
~**verbesserung** f = relocation of (line of) route
~**vermessung** f = route surveying
Trassierung f, Trassenwahl f = selection of route, route selection
Trassierungs|grundlagen fpl = principles of alignment
~**merkmal** n = geometric standard
Traß m, feingemahlener vulkanischer Tuffstein m, gemahlener massiger Bimsstuff m = (Rhenish) trass
Traß-Kalk|-Beton m = trass-lime concrete
~**-Mörtel** m, Kalk-Traß-Mörtel m, Traßmörtel m = trass mortar
~**-Zementbeton** m = trass-lime-cement concrete
~**-Zementmörtel** m = trass-lime-cement mortar
Traß-Zement|-Beton m, Zement-Traß-Beton m = trass-cement concrete
~**-Mörtel** m = trass-cement mortar
Traubeneiche f, siehe: Früheiche f

Trauerweide f = weeping willow
Traufel f, Gipserspachtel m, f = wall scraper
Travertin m = travertine
Trecker m, siehe: Schlepper m
Treib|achse f; siehe: unter „Achse f"
~**eis** n = drift(ing) ice, floating ~, flow ~
Treiben n = expansion
Treib|fäustel m = striking hammer, drilling ~
~**kessel** m, Druckkessel, Förderkessel, einkammriges Druckgefäß n = pressure cylinder [*pneumatic concrete placer*]
~**kette** f, siehe: Antriebskette f
~**kraft** f, siehe: Antriebskraft f
~**mittel** n, siehe: Metalltreibmittel n
~**rad** n, siehe: Antriebsrad n
~**sand** m, Triebsand = drift sand
~**scheibenaufzug** m, siehe: Friktionswinde f
~**stoff** m, siehe: Betriebsstoff m
~**stoff-Nachschubbasis** f = fuel-supply base
~**stofftankanlage** f = bulk fuel installation
~**stoffverschüttung** f = fuel spillage
~**zeug** n [*Fluß m*] = flotsam
Treidelweg m, siehe: Leinpfad m
Tremolit m (Min.) = tremolite (asbestos), Italian asbestos
Trenn|insel f = divisional island, separator
~**kanalisation** f; siehe unter „Abwasserwesen n"
~**mauer** f, Abschlußwand f = cutoff wall
~**mauer** f (oder **Trennungsmauer**) **der Schornsteinlängszüge** mpl = withe, mid-feather (wall)
~**schärfe** f [*Sieb n*] = accuracy of sizing
~**streifen** m = dividing strip
~**system** n [*Dränage f*] = separate system
Trennung f **mit schweren Medien** npl = heavy-media separation
Trennungs|sieb n = scalping screen
~**siebung** f [*Entfernen n des Überkorns n oder Unterkorns n*] = scalping
Trennwand f, Scheidewand f = division wall, partition ~
Treppe f [*in einer steilen Böschung f*] = benching

Treppen|giebel *m* = stepped gable
~platte *f* = stair tread
~podest *m, n*, Podest, Treppenabsatz *m* = landing
~steigung *f* = rise
Trias *m*; siehe unter „geologische Formation"
Triaxialgerät *n*, dreiaxiale Druckzelle *f*, triaxiale Scherprüfzelle *f* = triaxial compression cell, ~ ~ test chamber
~ mit fest angeordneter Gummihülle *f* = fixed-sleeve cell
~ mit frei angeordneter Gummihülle = free-sleeve cell
Tribüne *f* = grandstand

Trichter *m* wenn Grundwasser abgesaugt wird = cone of depression
~mörtelmischer *m* = conical mortar mixer
~(naß)klassierer *m* = funnel classifier
~öler *m* = funnel type straight oil cup
Tridymit *m* (Min.) = tridymite
Trieb|kette *f*, siehe: Antriebskette
~kraft *f*, siehe: Antriebskraft *f*
Triebling *m*, Antriebsritzel *n* = driving pinion
Trieb|rad *n*, siehe: Antriebsrad *n*
~sand *m*, Treibsand = drift sand
~satz *m*, siehe: (Zweirad-)Vorspänner *m*
~wagen *m* = self-propel(l)ed railcar

Triebwasserleitung *f*
  Werksgraben *m* mit Rechteckquerschnitt *m*
  Werksgraben *m* mit Trapezquerschnitt *m*
  Triebwasserrohrleitung *f*
  Triebwasserstollen *m*, Betriebswasserstollen, Druck(wasser)stollen, Zulaufstollen, (Wasser-)Kraftstollen [*Stollen, der im planmäßigen Betrieb voll und unter Scheiteldruck läuft*]

penstock
  trench-type ~

  ditch-type ~

  pipe ~
  tunnel-type ~, conversion tunnel, gallery pressure, pressure tunnel

---

triefendnaß = dripping wet
Trift|holz *n* = drift wood
~pfad *m* = drift path, side ~

~wasser *n* = drift water
triklin(isch) = triclinic

Trinidad-Asphaltsee *m*
  Alkalisalz *n*
  Asphaltharz *n*
  asphaltisches Säureanhydrid *n*
  Asphaltogensäure *f*
  Bitumenanteil *m*
  Dispersoid *n*
  durch Bohrung *f* gewonnener flüchtiger Trinidad-Asphalt *m*
  Fullererde *f*
  gereinigter Trinidad-Asphalt *m*

  Gesamtanteil *m* an löslichem Bitumen *n*
  Kohlenstoff-Oleosol *n*
  Landasphalt *m*

Trinidad Pitch Lake
  alkali salt
  asphaltic resin
  asphaltous acid anhydride
  asphaltogenic acid
  bituminous portion
  dispersoid
  Trinaskol

  Fuller's Earth
  Trinidad épuré, ~ refined asphalt, parianite
  total soluble bitumen
  carbon-oleosole
  land asphalt, ~ pitch, shore asphalt

mineralische Asche *f* — mineral ash
organische Schutzhülle *f* — organic matrix
Petroläther *m* — petroleum ether, ~ spirit
rechtsdrehend gegenüber polarisiertem Licht *n* — dextro-rotatory to polarised light
Ringverbindung *f* — ring formation
Schmelzkessel *m* — refiner
Seeasphalt *m* — lake asphalt, ~ pitch
Siedepunkt *m* — boiling point
Tioäther *m* — thio-ether
Trinidad-(Roh)Asphalt *m* — (crude) Trinidad Lake Asphalt
unverseifbar — unsaponifiable
Verbrennung *f* — ignition
verharzen — to resinify
vorhandenes Mineral *n* — adventitous mineral
Weichasphalt *m* — soft asphalt

Trink|brunnen *m* = drinking fountain
~wasser *n* = drinking water, potable ~
~wasserbehälter *m* = drinking water tank, potable ~ ~
Tripel *m*, Polierschiefer *m* = tripoli
Trittschallschutz *m* = sound insulation against structure-borne sounds, structural sound insulation
Trocken|apparat *m*, siehe: Exsikkator *m*
~bagger *m* = excavator
~bagger *m* **für aussetzenden Betrieb** *m* = intermittent-type excavator
~baggerung *f*, Trockenbaggerei *f* = dry-land excavation
~baggerwinde *f* = excavator hoist
~beet *n*; siehe unter „Abwasserwesen *n*"
Trockenbeton *m* [*Gemisch n ohne Wasserzugabe f*] = (dry-)batched aggregate, dry-batch materials, matched ~, batched ~, recombined ~
~fabrik *f*, Straßenbau-Silo- und Dosieranlage *f* = automatic road builders' plant
~-Mischungsverhältnis *n* = cement aggregate ratio
Trockenbohren *n* [*Bodenuntersuchung f*] = dry-sample boring
Trockendock *n* = dry dock, graving ~
~schleuse *f*, siehe: Dockschleuse *f*
trockene Destillation *f*, siehe: Entgasung *f*
~ Kaltluft *f* = cooled and dehumidified air

Trocken|-Elektroabscheider *m* = dry type electric precipitator
~engobierung *f* = dry slip coating
trockenes Naturgas *n*, ~ Bohrlochkopfgas, Trockengas, gasolinfreies Naturgas = dry natural gas, well natural ~, dry casing-head ~
Trocken|fäule *f* = dry rot
~festigkeit *f* = dry strength
~filter *m, n*, Schlauchfilter = cloth filter dust collector, fabric type ~ ~
~gebiet *n* = arid region, ~ area
trocken gelöschter Branntkalk *m*, siehe: Löschkalk
~ gepreßter Hohlziegel *m* = dry press hollow tile
trockene Zwischenwandplatte *f* [*Gipskartonplatte*] = dry partition
Trocken|gewicht *n* = dry weight
~koller(gang) *m* = dry pan
trockenlegen, siehe: auspumpen
~, entwässern = to drain
Trocken|legung *f*, siehe: Entwässerung *f*
~löschverfahren *n* [*Branntkalk m*] = dry slaking process
~mauerwerk *n*, Trockensteinmauer *f* = dry masonry (wall); dyke, dike [*in Scotland*]
~mörtel *m* = dry mortar
~mauerwerksdamm *m*; siehe unter „Talsperre *f*"
~mittel *n* = drier

Trocken|pochwerk *n*, Trockenstampfmühle *f* = dry stamp
~preßverfahren *n* [*Ziegelherstellung f*] = dry press process
~prozeß *m* [*Bauholz n*] = seasoning process
  Lufttrocknung *f* = natural (or air-drying) ~ ~
  Ofentrocknung *f* = artificial (or kiln-drying) ~ ~
  Trockenofen *m* = seasoning kiln
  Wagen *m* zur Holzbeförderung *f* in Trockenöfen *mpl* = carbuck
~raumgewicht *n* = dry (bulk) density
~schrank *m* = drying oven
~siebung *f* = dry mechanical grading
~stampfmühle *f*, Trockenpochwerk *n* = dry stamp
~steinmauer *f*, Trockenmauerwerk *n* = dyke, dike [*in Scotland*]; dry masonry (wall)
~tal *n*, Wadi *m* = wadi [dried-up bed of stream]
~trommel *f*, siehe: Trommeltrockner *m*
~turm *m*, siehe: Absorptionsturm
Trocken- und Mischanlage *f* zur Herstellung von Mischmakadam *m*, siehe: Aufbereitungsanlage *f* für Mischmakadam *m*
Trocken- und Naßmischen *n* während der Fahrt *f* [*Transportbeton m*] = truck mixing
trocknendes Öl *n* [*Farbe f*] = drying oil
Trocknungs-Schrumpfung *f*, Erhärtungsschwindung *f* [*Beton m*] = drying shrinkage
Trog *m*, Wasch-~ [*Schwertwäsche f*] = tub, washer box, trough [*log washer*]
~band *n*; siehe unter „Bandförderer *m*"
~bandförderer *m*, siehe: Muldengurtförderer
~brücke *f* = trough bridge, open ~
~gurtförderer *m*, siehe: Muldengurtförderer
~kettenförderer *m* System Redler = Redler conveyor
~mörtelmischer *m* = trough type mortar mixer
~schleuse *f*; siehe unter „Schiffshebeanlage *f*"
~tal *n*, siehe: U-Tal *n*

Trommel *f* = drum
~; siehe unter „Bandförderer *m*"
~ zur Tonkügelchenherstellung *f* = drum pelletizer
~abscheider *m* = drum separator
~filter *n*, *m* = drum filter
~mischer *m*; siehe unter „Betonmischer *m*"
(~)Seilwinde *f* hinten am Fahrzeug *n* angebracht = rear (cable, or rope) winch
~seilwinde *f*, siehe: Seilwinde
~seilwindwerk *n*, siehe: Seilwinde *f*
~sieb *n*, siehe: Siebtrommel *f*
~trockner *m*, Trockentrommel *f* = revolving (or rotary) drier (or dryer)
~wäsche *f*, siehe: Waschtrommel *f*
~waschsieb *n* = cylindrical washing screen
~welle *f* = drum shaft
~winde *f*, Trommelwindwerk *n* = drum winch
Trompeten-Abzweig *m* = trompet intersection, ~ type junction
Tropenausrüstung *f* = tropical outfit
Tropf|körper *m* = trickling filter, percolating ~
~öler *m* = drip oiler
~punkt *m* = drop(ping) point
tropfwassergeschützt [*Motor m*] = dripproof
Troposphäre *f* = troposphere
Trosse *f*, Abspannseil *n*, Ankerseil *n* = guy-rope, standing rope, guy cable, (rope) guy
Trossen|abspannung *f*, Abspannung *f* (oder Abspannen *n*) mit Seilen *npl* = guying
~derrick-Kran *m* ohne Ausleger *m* = gin pole derrick, gin pole
Trübungs|messer *m* = turbidimeter
~punkt *m* [*Kälteverhalten n von Dieselkraftstoff m*] = cloud point
Trümmer *f* = débris
trümmerhaltiger Sand *m* (Geol.) = detrital sand (Brit.); detritic ~ (US)
Trümmer|haufen *m*, Schutthaufen = rubble pile, pile of rubble
~material *n*, Felstrümmer *f* [*Gesteinsverwitterung f*] = rock waste
~schuttbeton *m*, siehe: Ziegelsplittbeton

Trümmer|stück n (Geol.), siehe: Fragment n
~verwertung f, Mauerschuttverwertung = utilisation of brick rubble
Trupp m, Kolonne f, Arbeits~ = party, crew, gang, team
T-Stück n = Tee, tee-piece
Tuff m; siehe unter „Vulkan m"
~, siehe: Kalk~
~brekzie f = tuff breccia
Tulpenbaum m = tulip tree
Tünche f, siehe: Kalkmilch f
tünchen, weißen, kalken = to whitewash, to limewash
Tundra f = tundra
Tungöl n, chinesisches Holzöl n = tung oil, Chinese wood oil, China wood oil

---

Tunnelbau m	tunnel(l)ing, tunnel work, tunnel construction
Absaugen n des Rauches m	smoke out
Abstiegstollen m, siehe: Zugangsstollen	
Abstützung f	support
Ausbruch m, siehe: Haufwerk n	
Ausbruchprofil n	minimum excavation line
Ausbruchquerschnitt m, gesamtes Querprofil n	full section
Ausbruchstelle f, siehe: Vortriebstelle	
Banse f [*Förderturm m*]	muck bin, skiploading ~ [*headframe*]
belgische Bauweise f, Unterfangungsbauweise	Belgian method
Betonmantel m	concrete lining
Betontransport- und -einbauwagen m	placer
Bewetterung f, Lüftung f	ventilation
Wechsellüftung f, abwechselnde Saug- und Drucklüftung f	plenum method of ventilation, push-pull ventilation
Bohrunterwagen m	drilling carriage
Bohrloch n, Einpreßloch	drilled grout hole
Brust f, siehe: Vortriebstelle f	
Brustschild n, Tunnelschild n, Vortriebsschild n	(tunnel) shield
Schildmantel m	cylindrical steel skin
Druckwasserpresse f	hydraulic ram
Schneidrand m	cutting edge
dauernde Abstützung f	permanent support
Deckgebirge n	surrounding material
Dichtung f, Isolierung f	lagging(s)
Doppel(rohr)tunnel m, siehe: Zwillingstunnel	
Dreizonenbauweise f, siehe: österreichische Bauweise	
Druckstollen m	gallery pressure, pressure tunnel
Einpressung f, Injektion f	pressure grouting, grout injection
Einziehen n von Deckenankern mpl, Ankerausbau m	roof-bolting, roof-bolt installation
Einzonenbauweise f, siehe: englische Bauweise	

Eisenrüstung f, Stahlauszimmerung f, Englische Bauweise f, Einzonenbauweise f	steel tunnel supports (or timbering) English method, English system of timbering
Entwässerungsstollen m	drainage tunnel
Fallschacht m	downhole
Felstunnel m, Bergtunnel, Gebirgstunnel	rock tunnel
Fensterstollen m, siehe: Zugangsstollen	
First m, Decke f	roof
Firstvortrieb m, Firststollen m	top heading
Gebirgsdruck m	earth pressure at great depth, rock pressure, compaction pressure
gesamtes Querprofil n, Ausbruchquerschnitt m	full section
Gewölbe n	soffit, arch
gußeisernes Segment n	cast-iron segment
Haufwerk n, Ausbruch m, Schutter m	muck, excavation, muck pile, trailings
Herstellung eines Tunnels m in offener Baugrube f	open-cut tunnel(l)ing
Hilfsstollen m für den Bau m	construction adit
Holzspreize f	timber spreader
Hund m, Schutterwagen m, Stollenwagen	skip
Injektionsgut n, Einpreßgut n	grout
Kabelstollen m	cable tunnel
Kämpferlinie f	springline
kontinuierliches Stollenbohrgerät n	continuous miner, ~ gallery machine
Kraftfahrzeugtunnel m	motor tunnel, automobile traffic tunnel
Kronbalken m	crown bar
Laden und Schießen n	loading and shooting
Landtunnelbau m	land tunnel(l)ing
Längsentlüftung f	longitudinal ventilation system
lotrechtes Niedertreiben n von Bohrlöchern npl	drown drilling
Luttenleitung f	air line, air piping
Mannschaftsleiter f	manway ladder
Mauerung f, Auskleidung f, Verkleidung f	facing, lining
Mauerwerk n	brickwork
Misch- und Einbauzug m für Tunnelbetonauskleidung f	mixing-placing train for tunnel concreting
Mundloch n	opening
nachträglicher Vollausbruch m	subsequent enlargement to the full section of the tunnel
Nachtrieb m	secondary heading
Nische f	niche
(Orts)Brust f, siehe: Vortriebstelle f	
österreichische Bauweise f, Dreizonenbauweise f	(English-)Austrian Method
Profil n, Querprofil n	section
Quertunnel-Einmündung f	intersection of cross-drift

Richtvortrieb *m*, Richtstollen *m*	pilot heading, pilot tunnel, monkey drift
Rüstung *f*, siehe: Zimmerung *f*	
Schacht *m*, Arbeitsschacht	(working) shaft, construction ~
Schacht *m* für Förderkorb-Gegengewicht *n*	cage counterweight well
Schiebebühne *f*	pass-over
Schiffstunnel *m*	canal tunnel
Schildbauweise *f*, Schildvortrieb *m*	shield tunnel(l)ing
Schutter *m*, siehe: Haufwerk *n*	
Schutterung *f*, Schuttern *n*	tunnel loading, mucking
Schutterwagen *m*, siehe: Hund *m*	
schwimmendes Gebirge *n*	waterlogged ground
Seitenstollen-Gebläse *n*	adit fan
Setzen *n* der Auszimmerung *f*	setting ribs
Sickerpackung *f*	dry packing
Sohle *f*	floor, bottom, invert
Sohlvortrieb *m*, Sohlstollen *m*	bottom heading, floor ~
Sprießung *f*, siehe: Zimmerung	
Stahlauszimmerung *f*, Eisenrüstung *f*	steel timbering (or tunnel supports)
standfestes Gebirge *n*	unsupported ground
Stollen *m* [*unterirdischer Gang auf dem Gebiete des Wasserbaues, der Entwässerung, der Wasserversorgung sowie der Be- und Entlüftung*]	drift (Brit.); (small-diameter) tunnel, gallery, heading
Stollen(aus)betonierung *f*, Betonmauerung *f*	in-situ concrete facing (or lining), tunnel concreting
Stollenbohrgerät *n*	gallery machine, miner
Stollenmund *m*	gallery portal
Stollen- und Tunnelbau *m*	heading and tunnel construction
Stollenvortriebmaschine *f*, Streckenvortriebmaschine *f*	tunnel(l)ing machine
Stollenwagen *m*, siehe: Hund	
Straßen(verkehrs)tunnel *m*	road tunnel, vehicular ~, vehicular subway
(Strecken)Vortrieb *m*	driving, heading, tunnel progress, advance
Tunnel *m* [*Gebirgsdurchstich m im Zuge m von Verkehrswegen mpl*]	tunnel
Tunnelbauer *m*, Tunnelbauingenieur *m*	tunnel(l)er, tunnel(l)ing engineer
Tunnelbau-Geologie *f*	tunnel construction geology
Tunnelbeleuchtung *f*	tunnel lighting (system)
Tunneleingang *m*, Tunnelportal *n*	tunnel portal
Tunnelrinne *f*	tube trench
Unterfangungsbauweise *f*, siehe: belgische Bauweise	
Untergrundbahntunnel *m*	subway (tube)
Unterwassertunnel *m*	underwater tunnel, subaqueous ~
Unterwassertunnelbau *m*	subaqueous tunnel(l)ing, underwater ~
Verkleidung *f*, siehe: Mauerung *f*	

Verlegen n der Schienen fpl des Bohrwagens m	setting jumbo track and wall plate
Versenken n fertiger Tunnelstücke npl oder des ganzen Tunnels m in eine vorher ausgebaggerte Rinne f	trench method of subaqueous tunnel(l)ing, sunken-tube method (or construction)
vierteilige Stahlrippe f	four-piece steel rib
Vollausbruch m	full-circle mining of tunnel heading, full-face work
Vortrieb m	driving, heading
Vortriebstelle f, (Orts)Brust f, Ausbruchstelle f	(working) face
Wand(ung) f	side
wasserdichte Stahlauskleidung f	steel lagging
(Wasser)Kraftstollen m	power tunnel, hydro tunnel, hydro tube
Wasserzutritt m, Wassereinbruch m, Wasserandrang m	ingress of water, inflow of water, inrush of water
Wechsellüftung f; siehe unter „Bewetterung f"	
weiches Gebirge n, mildes ~	soft ground
ziegelgefütterter Tunnel m	brick lined tunnel
Zimmerung f, vorläufiger Ausbau m, Gerüst n, Rüstung f, Stützung f, Sprießung f, Bölzungsrahmen m	temporary supports, timbering, tunnel support
Zugangsstollen m, Fensterstollen, Seitenstollen, Tagesstollen, Abstiegstollen	adit (level), access tunnel, (side) drift
Zwillingstunnel m, Doppel(rohr)tunnel	twin(-bore) tunnel

Tunnelofen m mit **Plattengleitbahn** f = slab kiln, sliding panel tunnel kiln
~**wagen** m = tunnel kiln car
~**wagendecke** f = tunnel kiln car top
Tüpfeltest m = spot test
Turas m = sprocket (wheel)
~, **Kettenrad** n, **Gleiskettenrad** = sprocket (wheel)
Tür|bank f, **Türschwelle** f = door sill, threshold
~**bekleidung** f = door lining
Turbine f mit drei **Gleichdruckstufen** fpl = three-pressure stage turbine
~ ~ **Kondensation** f = condensing turbine
~ ohne **Kondensation** f = non-condensing turbine
Turbinen|bohrer m = turbodrill
~**flurhöhe** f = power house floor level
~**fundament** n = turbine foundation
~**gehäuse** n = turbine casing, ~ cylinder
~**grube** f = turbine pit
~**leitung** f = penstock
~**lok(omotive)** f = turbine loco(motive)
~**reg(e)lung** f = turbine regulation
~**schaufel** f = turbine blade
~**schiff** n = turbine ship
~**spirale** f = scroll case
~**(wasser)messer** m = turbine water meter
Turbo|(auf)lader m [Dieselmotor m] = turbocharger
~**brenner** m = turbo burner
~**generator** m = turbo-generator
~**kupplung** f, hydraulische Kupplung = hydraulic coupling
~**(luft)verdichter** m, **Turbokompressor** m, **Kreisel(luft)verdichter** = turbo-compressor
~**mischer** m = flash mixer
~**satz** m = turbo set
turbulente Grenzschicht f = turbulent boundary layer
turbulentes Fließen n = turbulent flow
Türflügel m = wing of door, leaf ~ ~

Türfutter *n* = lining of door frame
Türkis *m* (Min.), siehe: Kallait *m*
Turm *m* = tower
~, siehe: Kranmast *m*
Turmalin-Granit *m* = tourmaline-granite
Turm|betonzentrale *f*, Betonmischturm *m*, Betonfabrik *f* als Turmanlage *f* = concrete mixing tower
~**biber** *m* = steeple plain tile
~**dach** *n*, Pyramidendach = pyramidal broach roof, polygonal ~ ~, spire roof
~**derrickkran** *m* = tower derrick crane
~**derrickkran-Bühne** *f* = tower derrick crane platform
~**derrickkran-Krone** *f* = tower derrick crane crown
~**derrickkran-Steiger** *m* = tower derrick crane man
~**drehkran** *m* = (mono)tower cra e, rotating ~ ~, revolving ~ ~
~**drehkran-Laufkatze** *f* = traversing saddle
~**einlaß** *m*; siehe unter „Talsperre *f*"
~**falzziegel(stein)** *m*, Turmfalzstein = tower gutter tile
~**garage** *f* **mit Lift** *m*, Autosilo *m* = autosilo [*patented system of Messrs. SICOMATIC, ZÜRICH, SWITZERLAND*]
~**gerüst** *m*, Schachtgerüst [*Bauaufzug m*] = cage, (elevator) tower
~**gerüst(bau)aufzug** *m*, Schachtgerüst-(bau)aufzug, Fahrstuhlaufzug = cage hoist, (elevator) tower hoist
~**gerüstkippkübel** *m*, Schachtgerüstkippkübel = tower (hoist) bucket
~**helm** *m*, Turmspitze *f* = (top of) spire
~**mauer** *f* = tower wall
~**pfeiler** *m* = tower pier
~**uhr** *f* = tower clock
turnusmäßig = in a rotary pattern
Tür|öffnung *f* = door opening
~**rahmen** *m*, Türstock *m*, Türzarge *f*, Türgerüst *n* = door case, ~ frame
TURRIT [*Trademark*] [*in Deutschland hochmikroporöser Leichtkalkbeton m*] = MICROPORITE (US) [*Trademark*]
Typen|drucker *m* = paper roll recorder
~**schild** *n*, Bezeichnungsschild = nameplate
typischer Löß *m*, siehe: Urlöß

U

Ubbelohde-Viskosimeter *n* = suspended level visco(si)meter
Überbau *m* = superstructure
überbeanspruchen = to overstress
Über|beanspruchung *f* = excessive strees
~**blattung** *f*, Blattung, Blatt *n* = halved joint, halving
~**bleibselverband** *m* (Geol.) = palimpsest structure
~**blick** *m* = survey
~**chlorung** *f* = superchlorination
~**dampfung** *f*, siehe: nasse Destillation *f*
~**dosis** *f* [*W.asserreinigung f*] = over-dose
~**druck** *m* = excess pressure
~**druckabblaseventil** *n* = pressure relief valve, "unloader" ~
Überdruckturbine *f*, siehe: Reaktionsturbine
~ **mit Radialdampfströmung** *f* = radial flow reaction turbine
Über|druckventil *n*, Sicherheitsventil = safety valve
~**einanderschichtung** *f*, siehe: Überlagerung *f*
~**fahrung** *f*, siehe: Übergang *m*
~**fall** *m*; siehe unter „Talsperre *f*"
~**fall(stau)wehr** *n*, Überlaufwehr = overflow weir, overfall ~, spillway ~, waste ~, crest control ~
~**fallstrahl** *m*; siehe unter „Talsperre *f*"
~**fallstrecke** *f*, Überlaufstrecke = overflow section
~**fallsturzbecken** *n*; siehe unter „Talsperre *f*"
~**flurhydrant** *m* = pillar hydrant
~**flutung** *f*, siehe: Überschwemmung *f*
~**führung** *f* = overbridge, overpass, overspan bridge, overcrossing
~**gabe** *f* = handing over
~**gang** *m*, Fahrt *f*, Überfahrung *f* [*z. B. mit einer Walze f*] = pass, traverse
Übergangs|boden *m* = transitional soil
~**bogen** *m*, siehe: Übergangskurve *f*
~**bogenlänge** *f* = transition length
~**bogenspirale** *f* = highway transition spiral
~**düse** *f* [*Vergaser m*] = transition jet
~**gebirge** *n* = transition rocks

Übergangs|kalk *m*, siehe: Grauwackenkalk
~kurve *f*, Übergangsbogen *m* = transition curve, easement ~
~lasche *f*, Reduzierlasche = cranked fishplate (Brit.); ~ joint-bar (US)
~periode *f* = change-over period
~schicht *f* = transition bed, bed of passage
~temperatur *f* = transition temperature
~zone *f* (Geol.) = transition zone
~zone *f* [*Schweißen n*] = refined zone
Übergemengteil *m, n*, siehe: akzessorisches Mineral *n*
übergroß = outsize
Überhang *m* = overhang
Überhitzer *m* = superheater
überhöhte Kurve *f* = superelevated turn
überhöhter Träger *m*, ~ Balken(träger), Träger mit Überhöhung = saddle backed girder (Brit.); ~ ~ beam
Über|höhung *f*, einseitiger Querschnitt *m* [*Straßenkurve f*] = superelevation, cant; banking [*deprecated*]
~höhung *f* [*Träger m*] = camber
~holen *n* [*Verkehr m*] = overtaking; passing [*deprecated*]
~holen *n* [*Maschine f*] = overhaul
~holspur *f* = overtaking lane; passing ~ [*deprecated*]
~jahresspeicherbecken *n*; siehe unter „Talsperre *f*"
~kopfgesteinsbohrer *m* = stoper
~kopfladen *n* = overhead loading
~kopfschaufel *f* = overhead bucket
~-Kopf- (Schaufel) Lader *m*, Wurfschaufellader, Überkopf-Fahrlader, Rück(wärts)lader, Überkopfladegerät *n* = rocker (type) shovel (loader), overshot loader, overhead loader, flip-over bucket loader, overloader, overhead shovel
~kopfschweißung *f* = overhead welding
~korn *n* = oversize aggregate
~kragung *f* = projection
~lagerung *f* (Geol.), siehe: Abraum *m*
~lagerung *f*, Auflagerung, Übereinanderschichtung = superposition
~landleitung *f* [*elektr. Strom m*] = transmission line
~landrohrleitung *f* = cross-country pipeline
~landverkehr *m* = interurban traffic
~lappung *f* = overlap
~lappungsnietung *f* = lap riveting
~lappungsschweißung *f* = lap welding
~lappungsstoß *m* = overlap joint
~last(ungs)kupplung *f* = overload clutch (coupling), safety ~ (~)
Überlauf *m*; siehe unter „Talsperre *f*"
~ m [*Sieb n*] = rejects, oversize reject
~quelle *f* = depression spring
~stollen *m*, Hochwasserstollen *m* = tunnel-type discharge carrier
Überleitung *f* [*Wasser von einem Flußgebiet in ein anderes*] = trans-mountain water diversion
übermangansaures Kali *n*, siehe: Kaliumpermanganat *n*
übersättigt = supersaturated
Überschallmethode *f*, siehe: Ultraschallmethode *f*
Überschiebung *f* (Geol.), siehe: Wechsel *m*
über|schläglicher Kostenanschlag *m* = spot estimate
~schneidungsfreie Kreuzung *f*, siehe: plankreuzungsfreie Kreuzung *f*
Überschuß *m* = surplus
überschüssiger Aushub(boden) *m* = spoil, surplus ~, surplus earth (or soil), waste
Überschüttungshöhe *f* [*Betonverteilung f*] = surcharge
überschwemmen = to flood, to inundate
Über|schwemmung *f*, Überflutung *f* = flood(ing), inundation
~setzungsgetriebe *n* = transmission
~sichbrechen *n*, Aufstemmen *n* (Geol.) = overhead stoping
~staubewässerung *f*, siehe: Beckenverfahren *n*
~strömventil *n*, siehe: Schlabberventil *n*
~stunde *f* = overtime hour
~wachung *f* **der Arbeiten** *f* [*z. B. Bodenvermörtelung f*] = field control
~zug(decke) *m*, (*f*) = overlay (pavement); topping, overlay paving (US)
Ufer|angriff *m*, Uferabbruch *m* = erosion of a bank
~ausbesserung *f* [*Fluß m*] = bank reinstatement

Ufer|befestigung *f* = bank stabilization
~damm *m*, HW-Schutzdamm *m*, Hochwasserdeich *m* = levee (US); flood bank (Brit.)
Abbruch *m* = caving in
~erosion *f* = bank erosion
~schutz *m* = bank protection
U-Flugplatz *m* = underground airfield
Uintait *m*, siehe: Gilsonitasphalt *m*
Ullmanit *m* (Min.), siehe: Antimonnickelglanz *m*
Ulme *f*, siehe: Rüster *f*
Ultra|schall *m*, Überschall = ultrasonic sound, ultrasound
~schallimpuls *m* = ultrasonic(sound)pulse
~schallmethode *f*, Überschallmethode *f* = ultrasonic (or supersonic) method
~violett-Spektroskopie *f* = ultraviolet spectrophotometry
Umbau *m* [*Gebäude n*] = structural alteration
~bagger *m*, siehe: Mehrzweckbagger
umbaute Anlage *f* = walled-in plant
umbauter Raum *m* = space enclosed
Umbauvorrichtung *f*; siehe unter „Mehrzweckbagger *m*"
umdrehen [*oberes Ende nach unten bzw. umgekehrt*] = to up-end
Umdrehung *f* = revolution
Umfahrungsstraße *f*, siehe: Umgehungsstraße
Umfangsfuge *f*; siehe unter „Talsperre *f*"
Umfülltankwagen *m* [*als Halbanhänger m*] = semi-trailer type supply tank
Umgehungsstraße *f*, Entlastungsstraße, Umfahrungsstraße = by-pass road, relief ~; [*deprecated: loop road, avoiding road, ring road, detour*]; thruway branch, circumferential route, ~ highway, belt highway (US)
Umgrenzung *f* des lichten Raumes *m* = clearance profile
Umgrenzungslinie *f* = clearance line
Umhüllen *n*, siehe: Benetzen *n*
umhüllter Splitt *m* = coated chip(ping)s; pre-coated ~ [*deprecated*]
Umkehr|getriebe *n*, siehe: Reversiergetriebe *n*
~schaltkupplung *f*, siehe: Wendeschaltkupplung

~(trommel)(beton)mischer *m*; siehe unter „Betonmischer *m*"
~turbine *f*, Umsteuerungsturbine *f*, Reversierturbine *f* = reversing turbine
Umkippen *n* [*fahrbarer Drehkran m*] = tipping
Umkleideraum *m* = locker room
Umlauf|getriebe *n*, Planetengetriebe *n*, Differentialgetriebe = planetary gearing (or gears), differential ~ (~ ~), epicyclic ~ (~ ~)
~heizung *f* = circulation heating
~stollen *m*, siehe: Umleitstollen
~zahl *f* = number of revolutions
Umlegurg *f* [*z. B. Straße f*] = diversion, relocation
Umleit|kanal *m*, Umleitungskanal = by(e)-wash, diversion cut, by(e) channel, spillway; diversion flume (US)
~stollen *m*, Umleitungsstollen, Umlaufstollen = by-pass tunnel, diversion ~
Umleitung *f* = loop road, detour, by-pass; shoofly (US)
Umleitungsbauten *fpl* = (river) diversion works
Umleit(ungs)|kanal *m*; siehe unter „Talsperre *f*"
~sperre *f* zur Bewässerung *f*; siehe unter „Talsperre *f*"
~stollen *m*, Umlaufstollen = diversion tunnel, by-pass ~
~ventil *n* = transflo valve
Umlenkrolle *f* [*Gleiskette f*] = (crawler) idler wheel
~; siehe unter „Bandförderer *m*"
Ummantelung *f* [*Rohr n*] = haunching
Umprägung *f*, Umwandlung *f*, Metamorphose *f* (Geol.) = metamorphism
Umrechnungstabelle *f* = conversion table (or chart)
Umriß|verfahren *n*; siehe unter „Erdarbeiten *fpl*"
~zeichnung *f* = outline drawing
Umschaltventil *n* = cross-over valve
Umschlag|anlage *f* = transfer plant
~kapazität *f* [*Hafen m*] = handling capacity
~kran *m* = materials handling crane
~platz *m* = re-handling point

Umschlingungsfestigkeit f = state of all-round tension, $\sim\sim$ two-dimensional stress equality

umschnürte Säule f = hooped column

Umsetzen n [*Betondeckenfertiger m*] = lane move, moving between lanes, lane change

Umspannstation f = grid substation

Umsteuerungsturbine f, siehe: Umkehrturbine

umwälzen = to circulate

Umwälzpumpe f = circulation pump

Umwandlungsgestein n, siehe: metamorphes Gestein n

Umzäunung f, siehe: Einfriedigung f

Unbalance f, Unwucht f, Schwunggewicht n = out-of-balance weight, unbalance

unbebaut = not built upon

~ [*Acker m*] = uncultivated

unbedeichte Anlandung f = un-embanked alluvial land

unbeschottert, ungeschottert = un-metalled (Brit.)

undichte Stelle f, Leckstelle f = leak(age)

Unebenheit f = unevenness, irregularity
ausgleichen = to true up, to average out

Unelastizität f = inelasticity

Unfall|kran m, Bergungskran = wrecking crane, breakdown $\sim$, accident $\sim$

~rate f = accident toll, $\sim$ rate

unfallsicher = accident-proof

Unfall|situationsplan m = plan of the accident site

~verhütung f = accident prevention

ungebrannter keramischer Scherben m = unfired ceramic body

ungebrauchter Formsand m, siehe: Neusand

ungelernt = unskilled

ungelöschter gemahlener Kalk m, Mahlkalk, gemahlener Branntkalk m, gedeihender Kalk m [*fälschlich als „treibender Kalk" bezeichnet*] = unslaked and ground quicklime

~ stückiger Branntkalk m, Stückkalk m = lump lime

ungesackter Zement m, siehe: loser Zement m

ungeschottert, siehe: unbeschottert

ungesiebter Grubenkies m = pit run gravel

ungesiebtes gebrochenes Material n = crusher-run (stone) (or aggregate)

ungestörte Bodenprobe f = undisturbed (soil) sample

ungeteilte Straße f, Straße ohne Richtungstrennstreifen m = undivided two-way road

Ungewitter n = thunderstorm

ungleichförmiger Sand m = non-uniform sand

Ungleichförmigkeitsgrad m $U = \dfrac{d_{60}}{d_{10}}$ = coefficient of uniformity; uniformity coefficient $C_u = \dfrac{D_{60}}{D_{10}}$

ungleichmäßige Setzung f, $\sim$ Senkung f, Setzungsunterschied m = differential settlement

Universal|-Autobagger m, siehe: Autobagger m

~-Autobagger m **mit Dreiachsfahrgestell** n **und zwei Motoren** mpl; siehe unter „Autobagger m"

~bagger m, siehe: Mehrzweckbagger m

~-Bau(aufzugs)winde f = general purpose hoist

~-Diesel-Auto(mobil)bagger m = rubber-mounted diesel excavator-crane

~-Diesel-Elektro-Raupenbandbagger m, Universal-Diesel-Elektro-Gleiskettenbagger m = convertible diesel-electric caterpillar excavator

~-Diesel-Raupen(band)bagger m = crawler-mounted diesel excavator-crane

~fertiger m = universal finisher

~(Hoch)Baukran m = universal building crane

~-Raupen(band)bagger m = crawler-mounted excavator-crane

~-Schraubenschlüssel m = adjustable spanner

unkartiert = unmapped

Unkraut|abbrennmaschine f = weed burner

~bekämpfung f = weed control

~bekämpfungsmittel n = weed killer, herbicide, weed destroyer

~jäter m = (finger-)weeder

unlöslicher Anhydrit *m*, totgebrannter Gips *m* = deadburnt gypsum
unregelmäßiger Untergrund *m* = erratic subsoil
unregelmäßiges Schicht(en)mauerwerk *n* = unregular rubble walling

unsortierter Branntkalk *m* = run of kiln lime
unstetige Kornabstufung *f*, siehe: diskontinuierliche ~
Unterausschuß *m* = subcommittee
Unterbau *m* = foundation (course)

Unterbau *m* [*Straße*]
  nicht-starr, schmiegsam [*z. B. Kies m*]
  starr [*z. B. Zementbeton m*]
  halb-starr [*z. B. Setzpacke f*]

sub-base
  flexible, non-rigid [*e. g. gravel*]
  rigid [*e. g. cement concrete*]
  half-rigid [*e. g. pitching*]

Unter|betonschicht *f* = bottom concrete layer
~bettungssand *m* = bedding sand
(Unter)Bettungsschicht *f*, Bettschicht = bed(ding) course, underlying course, underlay, cushion course; sub-crust (Brit.)
Unterbringung *f* = housing
Unterdeck *n* [*Sieb n*] = bottom deck
Unterdecke *f* = sub-floor
Unterdruck|bremse *f*, Vakuumbremse *f* = vacuum brake
~-Oberflächenbehandlung *f* frischen Betons *m*, siehe: Billner'sches Vakuumverfahren *n*
~verfahren *n* [*Holztränkung f*] = Boulton process, boiling under vacuum ~
untere Faser *f* = bottom fibre (Brit.); ~ fiber (US)
unterentwickeltes Land *n* = underdeveloped country
unterer Grenzzustand *m* [*Boden m*] = active state [*soil*]
~ Windverband *m* = bottom lateral bracing
Unter|fangen *n*, Unterfangung *f* = underpinning, dead shoring, vertical shoring, needle shoring
~flansch *m* = lower flange
~flasche *f* = bottom-block, return-block, hook-block, fall-block, hoist-block [*deprecated: snatch-block*]
~führung *f* = underbridge, underpass, undercrossing
~füllen *n* von hohlliegenden Betonfahrbahnplatten *fpl* mit Bitumen *n* = (pavement) undersealing, subsealing [*pumping of a low penetration asphalt (US)/asphaltic bitumen (Brit.) under concrete pavement slabs*]
~gestell *n*, Fahrgestell = carrier, underbody
~gleis-Förderschnecke *f* = undertrack screw conveyor
~gleis-Silo *m* = undertrack hopper
Untergrund *m*, Baugrund *m*, Gründungsboden *m* = subsoil, foundation soil
~ *m*, Erdplanum *n*, Planum *n*, Roh(erd)planum *n* = sub-grade, soil ~, earth ~; basement soil (US)
~bahn *f* = underground (or tube) railway (Brit.)/railroad (US)
~bahngleis *n* = tube track (Brit.); subway ~ (US)
~bahntunnel *m* = subway (tube)
~dichtung *f*; siehe unter „Baugrundverbesserung *f*"
~(drän)pflug *m*, siehe: Maulwurf(drän)pflug
~entwässerung *f*; siehe unter „Entwässerung *f*"
~forschung *f*, siehe: Bodenuntersuchung
~probenahme *f* = subsurface sampling
~setzung *f*, (Untergrund)Senkung *f* [*senkrechte Verlagerung f eines Punktes m des Untergrundes m; Senkungserscheinung f am Baugrund m*] = (ground) settlement
~verhältnisse *npl* = subsurface conditions
Untergurt *m*, untere Gurtung *f* [*Fachwerk n*] = bottom (or lower) chord (or boom

Untergurt *m* [*Träger m*] = bottom flange
~laufkatze *f* = bottom-flange troll(e)y
~laufschienen-Elektrohängebahn *f* = bottom flange type telpher, transporter
~stab *m* = bottom boom member, ~ chord ~
~winkel *m* = bottom chord angle, ~ boom ~
Unterhaltung *f*, Instandhaltung *f* = upkeep, maintenance
  laufende ~, Wartung *f* = routine ~
Unterhaltungsarbeiten *f* **im Vergabeverfahren** *n* = contract(-performed) maintenance
Unterholz *n* = underbrush, underwood, undergrowth
(~)Roderechen *m* = brush rake, clearing ~
unter|irdische Erzkammer *f* = sub-level stoping
~irdische Tongewinnung *f* = underground clay mining
~irdisches Bauwerk *n* = underground structure
~kellertes Grundstück *n* = basement site
Unterkellerung *f* = basement (construction)
Unterkorn *n* = undersize (aggregate)
Unterkünfte *fpl* = personnel housing, living quarters
Unterkunftslager *n*, siehe: Baustellenlager *n*
Unterlage *f* [*Steinformmaschine f*] = pallet
Unterlags|brett *n* [*Steinformmaschine f*] = wooden pallet
~papier *n*, siehe: Papierunterlage *f*
Unterlegscheibe *f* = washer
Unterliegerwerk *n* = down stream power plant
Untermoräne *f*; siehe unter „Gletscher *m*"
Unternehmer *m* = contractor
~verband *m* = contractor association
Unterpflasterbahn *f* = cut and cover tramway
Unterpflug *m* = subsoil plough (Brit.); ~ plow, panbreaker, subsoiler (US)
unterpflügen = to plough in (Brit.)
Unterpressen *n* [*Straßendecke f*] = underseal(ing), subseal(ing)

Unterputz *m* = scratch coat
unterschlächtig [*Wasserrad n*] = undershot [*water wheel*]
Unterschneidung *f* [*Planum n*] = undercut(ting), overbreak
Unterschubfeuerung *f* = underfeed stoker
unterschwefligsaures Natrium *n*, siehe: Fixiersalz *n*
Unter|schwelle *f*, siehe: Bodenschwelle *f*
~setzungsgetriebe *n* = reduction gear
~sicht *f* = underside view
unterspannter Betonträger *m* = understressed concrete beam
Unterspülung *f*, siehe: Auskolkung *f*
Untersuchungs|bohrung *f* = prospect boring
~ergebnis *n* = finding
~grube *f*, Reparaturgrube *f* = inspection pit, repair ~
Unter|tagegrube *f* = mine
~tor *n*; siehe unter „Binnenschiffahrtschleuse *f*"
~wagen *m*, Fahrwerk *n* = (travelling) carriage, undercarriage
~waschung *f*, siehe: Auskolkung *f*
Unterwasser *n* = tailwater
~-Düsengrabenzieher *m* = jet-action trencher, jet-type ~
~gründung *f* = subaqueous foundation work
~kanal *m*, Untergraben *m*, Unterkanal, Ablauf *m* = tail race, discharge channel
~kraftwerk *n* = tail water power plant (or installation)
~notverschluß *m* = tailgate
~schallempfänger *m* = submarine sound receiver
~schneidgerät *n* = underwater cutting gear
~sieb *n* = underwater screen
~sprengung *f*; siehe unter „1. Schießen *n*; 2. Sprengen *n*"
~stollen *m*, Ableitungsstollen = tail(race) tunnel
~-Straßen(verkehrs)tunnel *m* = subaqueous vehicular (or road) tunnel
~zünder *m*; siehe unter „1. Schießen *n*; 2. Sprengen *n*"
Unterwindgebläse *n* = undergrate blower

Unterzug — Ventilfeder

Unterzug m, Querträger m = transom, cross beam; cross gilder (Brit.)
untief, seicht = shallow
Untiefe f = shoal
unüberdachter Tribünensitz m = bleacher
unvermeidbare Verlustzeit f = unavoidable delay factor
unverpackter Zement m, siehe: loser Zement m
unverschiebliches Gelenk n = fixed hinge
unverschlossener Überlauf m; siehe unter „Talsperre f"
unverseifbar = unsaponifiable
Unvorhergesehenes n, (Position für) ~ = contingency (item)
Unwucht f, siehe: Unbalance f
~(-Vibrations)sieb n, siehe: Schwingsieb n mit Massenkraftantrieb m
Uranerz n = uranium ore
Uranglimmer m, Kalkuranit m = lime uranite
~, Kupferuranit m = copper uranite, cupro-uranite, tobernite
Uranit m (Min.) = uranite
Uranmineral n = uranium mineral
(Uran)Pechblende f, (Uran)Pecherz n (Min.) = pitchblende
Urboden m, jungfräulicher Boden m = virgin soil, original ~
Ure f, siehe: Bergahorn m
Urgestein n, kompakter Fels m, dichtes Gestein = primitive rock

Urgneis m = fundamental gneiss
Urkalkstein m, echter kristallinischer Marmor m = true marble, recrystallized limestone
Urlaubsmarke f = vacation stamp
Urlöß m, Primärlöß, typischer Löß, echter Löß = true loess
U-Rohr-Viskosimeter n = U-tube visco(si)meter
Urle f, siehe: Bergahorn m
ursprüngliche Kohäsion f = origin cohesion
U-Stahl m, U-Profil n = channel
U-Tal n, Trogtal = U-shaped glaciated valley
Uwarowit m, Kalkchromgranat m, $Ca_3Cr_2Si_3O_{12}$ (Min.) = uwarowite, ouvarovite

V

Vacupreßverfahren n [*Kalkhydratverpackung f*] = vacuum compression method
vadoses Wasser n, schwebendes Grundwasser, kreisendes Wasser = vadose water, suspended subsurface water
Vakuum|anheber m, Saugvorrichtung f zum Fertigteiltransport m = vacuum lifter pad
~bremse f, siehe: Unterdruckbremse
~destillation f = vacuum distillation

Vakuumdruckverfahren n [*Holzschutzbehandlung f*]
  Volldurchtränkung f
  Sparverfahren n [*nur Tränkung der Zellwände fpl*]
  Rüping(spar)verfahren n, Teeröltränkung f nach Rüping, Hohlimprägnierung f

pressure process

  full-cell treatment
  empty-cell treatment

  Rüping empty-cell process

Vakuum-Tonschneider m = vacuum pugmill
Valentinit m (Min.), siehe: Antimonblüte f
Vanadinit m (Min.) = vanadinite
Variante f = variable
Vaselin n, Erdölgallerte f = petrolatum, petroleum jelly

V. D. I. Jahrbuch n = Year Book of the Society of German Engineers
vegetabilisch = vegetable
Ventilationsstollen m = ventilation adit
Ventilator m = fan
Ventil|brunnen m = valve well
~feder f = valve spring

Ventil|sackfüllmaschine f, Ventil(sack)-packmaschine = valve bag filling machine, ~ ~ packer
~steuerung f = valve control
~stößel m = valve push rod
Venturi|-Kanal m = Venturi flume
~-Messer m = Venturi meter
~-Rohr n = Venturi tube
veraltet = outmoded
Verankerung f = anchorage, tieing
Verankerungs|kegel m = anchoring cone
~ring m = anchor loop (Brit.); U-bolt (US)
veranschlagen = to estimate
Veranschlagung f, Veranschlagen n = estimating
Verarbeitbarkeit f, Verarbeitbarkeitsgrad m = workability
Verarbeitungsmaschinen fpl, siehe: Aufbereitungsmaschinen
Verband m [*Tragwerk* n] = bracing
Verbandskasten m = first aid box, ~ ~ kit
verbesserter AASHO-Versuch m, siehe: Proctor-Prüfung f
~ Untergrund m, siehe: Sauberkeitsschicht f
Verbindungsgang m = interconnecting passage
Verblender m, Verblendstein m, römischer Ziegel m [*4,7:9:29 cm*] = facing brick, face ~, Roman ~
Verbrauchssteuer f = excise tax
verbrauchte Luft f, schlechte ~ = vitiated air
Verbreiterung f = widening
Verbrennungs|gas n, siehe: Feuergas
~lok(omotive) f = petrol loco(motive) (Brit.); gasolene loco(motive), gasoline ~ (US)
~luft f = air of combustion
~motor m, Brennkraftmotor = internal combustion engine, I. C. ~
~rückstände f = breeze
Verbund m [*Spannbeton* m] = bond(ing)
~antrieb m, siehe: dieselelektrischer Antrieb m
~bauweise f = composite (method of) construction
~balken m, Verbundträger m, Verbundbalkenträger = flitch(ed) beam, compound ~, sandwich ~; ~ girder (Brit.).
~fachwerkträger m = composite lattice beam
~fundament n = combined footing
~glas n = laminated glass
~körper m = composite member
~pfahl m; siehe unter „Gründungspfahl m"
~projekt n, siehe: Mehrzweckbauwerk n
~querschnitt m = composite section
~sieb n = screen with two screen boxes
~träger m, siehe: Verbundbalken m
~turbine f = compound turbine
~wirkung f **von Decken** fpl **aus Stahlbetonfertigteilen** mpl = bond action in floors of precast reinforced concrete
verchromt = chromium plated, chrome finish
Verdämmen n = stemming
Verdichter m [*Boden* m, *Beton* m] = compactor
~pumpe f [*pneumatische Förderanlage* f] = pneumatic transport pump
~ventil n = compressor valve
~zylinder m, Kompressorzylinder = compressor cylinder
Verdichtung f, künstliche ~ = compaction
~ f, natürliche ~, siehe: Konsolidierung f
Verdichtungs|apparat m, siehe: Oedometer m
~bohle f, siehe: Vibrierbohle
~bohle f, siehe: Stampfbohle
~energie f = compacting energy
~faktor-Prüfung f [*Beton* m] = compacting factor test
~gang m, Verdichtungsübergang = compacting pass
~gerät n = compactor
~pfahl m, Verdrängungspfahl = compacting pile
~setzung f = consolidation settlement
~willigkeit f = compactibility
Verdrängung f = displacement
Verdrängungsbohrer m [*Bodenuntersuchung* f] = displacement auger

Verdrängungspfahl m, Verdichtungspfahl m = compacting pile
verdrehte Schichtungen fpl (Geol.) = twisted strata
Verdreh(ungs)steifigkeit f, siehe: Torsionssteifigkeit f
(Ver)Drillung f, siehe: Torsion f
Verdrückung f = displacement
Verdübelung f = dowel(l)ing
Verdunstung f, siehe: Verflüchtigung f
~ f von freien Wasserspiegeln mpl = evaporation from free-water surfaces
Verdurstungserscheinung f [Zementvermörtelung f] = deficiency of moisture at the surface
Verein m Deutscher Portlandzement-Fabrikanten e. V. = Assiocation of German Portland Cement Manufacturers
~ Zementwerke = Association of German Cement Manufacturers
vereist = icy
Verfahren n = operation, process, method
~ Dischinger [Rahmen m] = prestressing method with rigid tie-rod
verfestigte Schicht f (Geol.) = concretionary horizon
verfestigter Schluffmergel m = silt-stone
verfestigtes Wasser n, siehe: hygroskopisches ~
Verfestigung f **durch Beimischungen** fpl, siehe: Vermörtelung f
~ f von Tiefgründungen fpl; siehe unter „Baugrundverbesserung f"
Verfilzbarkeit f = felting property
verfilzen = to felt
Verflechtungsstrecke f; siehe unter „Verkehr m"
verflüchtigend, flüchtig = volatile
Verflüchtigung f, Verdunstung f = volatilisation, volatility
Verformungs|messer m, siehe: Deformatiorsmesser m
~widerstand m = resistance to deformation
Verfrachtung f, Transport m (Geol.) = transport
verfugen, siehe: ausfugen
Verfüllboden m = back-filling

verfüllen, einfüllen [Graben m] = to re-fill, to backfill, to fill in
Verfüll|gerät n = backfiller
~schicht f [Setzpacke f] = racking course
~vorrichtung f, Planierschild n zum Zuziehen von Gräben = backfiller attachment
Vergabe f; siehe unter „Angebot n"
~verfahren n = contract-awarding procedure
Vergaser m = carburetor (US); carburettor, carburetter
~motor m, siehe: Benzinmotor m
Vergasung f [flüssiger Brennstoff m im Vergaser m] = vaporization, gasification
Vergasungs|gas n = manufactured gas
~mittel n = gasifying agent
Verglasung f = glazing
vergleichende Untersuchung f, Vergleichsstudie f = comparative study
Vergleichs|möglichkeit f = comparability
~spannung f = comparison stress
~versuch m = comparative test
~wert m = comparative value
verglastes Gestein n = vitreous rock
Vergnügungs|dampfer m = pleasure craft
~industrie f = entertainment industry
Vergußmasse f = sealing compound
~; siehe unter „Fuge f"
~ofen m, siehe: Schmelzkessel m für Fugenvergußmassen fpl
Verhalten n = behavio(u)r
Verhältniszahl f = ratio, proportion(ality) factor
Verhältnis n zwischen Belastung f und Durchbiegung f = load-deflection relationship
Verharzung f = resinification
Verharzungsneigung f [Krackbenzin n] = gum forming
Verherdung f; siehe unter „Talsperre f"
Verholzung f = lignification
Verhütungsmaßnahme f = preventive measure
verjüngte Nietung f; siehe unter „Niet m"
Verjüngung f = taper(ing)
Verkämmung f; siehe unter „Holzverbindung f"

Verkehr — Verkehrsmessung

Verkehr m, **Straßen~**
Gegen~
Rund~, Ring~
schwerer ~
Personen~
Kraftwagen~
gemischter ~
Radfahr~
Umgehungs~
Einbahn~
Einbiege~
Schnell~
Zugtier~, Fuhrwerk~, Gespann~
parkender ~
Durchgangs~
Einfäd(e)lungslänge f, Verflechtungslänge
Einfäd(e)lungsraum m, Verflechtungsstrecke f
eisenbereifter ~

traffic, **road ~**, **highway ~**
oncoming ~, opposing ~
gyratory ~, rotary ~
heavy weight ~
passenger ~
vehicular ~
mixed ~
pedal cyclist ~
by-passable ~
one-way ~, uni-directional ~
turning ~
express ~
animal-drawn ~
standing ~
through ~
weaving distance, weaving length

weaving space, weaving area, weaving section
iron-shod wheeled ~

Verkehrs|abwicklung f = traffic handling
~ader f, Groß~, Hauptfernverkehrsstraße f = traffic artery
~ampel f, Verkehrslichtsignal n = traffic (control) (light) signal, traffic light
~anlage f mit Benutzungsgebühr f = toll facility, vehicular toll project
verkehrsarme Zeit f = slack time
Verkehrs|belastung f, siehe: Verkehrslast f
~bewährung f, Verkehrsverhalten n [*eines eingebauten Straßenbaustoffes m*] = road performance, service behavio(u)r
~dichte f [*auf einer bestimmten Streckenlänge f*] = traffic concentration
~entstehung f = traffic generation

~erhebung f, siehe: Verkehrsmessung
~erschütterung f = traffic impact
~erziehung f = training in road sense, traffic safety education
~flughafen m; siehe unter „Flugplatz m"
verkehrsgebundene Schotterdecke f = traffic-bound macadam
Verkehrs|ingenieur m = traffic engineer
~insel f = traffic (island)
~knoten(punkt) m = junction point
~komprimierung f, Knetwirkung f = kneading action of traffic, traffic compaction [*pushes the particles into a closer and more permanent fit*]
~last f, Verkehrsbelastung f = traffic load

Verkehrsleistungsfähigkeit f
theoretische ~, grundlegende ~
mögliche ~
praktische ~

highway capacity, **roadway ~**, **working ~**
basic ~ ~
possible ~ ~
practical ~ ~

Verkehrs|linie f, Verkehrsstrich m = traffic line, white ~
~(-Markierungs)farbe f, siehe: Straßenmarkierungsfarbe f
~menge f, Verkehrsvolumen n = traffic flow, ~ volume

~menge f (oder Verkehrsvolumen n) auf einer bestimmten Breiteneinheit f der Fahrbahn f = traffic flow density
~messung f, Verkehrszählung f, Verkehrserhebung = traffic survey, ~ count, ~ census

Verkehrs|minister m = Minister of Transport
~ministerium n = Ministry of Transport, M.O.T. (Brit.); Transport Ministry
~nagel m, siehe: Markierungsknopf m
~opfer n = traffic victim
~planung f = traffic planning
~polizist m = (traffic) patrolman
~reg(e)lung f = traffic control, regulation of traffic
verkehrsreich = heavily trafficked
Verkehrsschwankung f = traffic fluctuation
(Verkehrs) Signal-Steuerung f, Signalreg(e)lung f, Signalisierung f = signal control, traffic ~ ~
Verkehrssperrung f = block
(Verkehrs) Spur f, Fahrspur f = (traffic) lane
Verkehrs|stockung f, Verkehrsstau m = traffic congestion, ~ jam
~streife f = traffic patrol
~strich m, Verkehrslinie f = traffic line, white ~
~strom m = traffic stream
~stromlinie f = desire line
~sünder m = traffic offender
~toter m = fatality
~übertretung f = traffic offence
~unfall m = traffic accident
~verhalten n, siehe: Verkehrsbewährung f
~volumen n, Verkehrsmenge f = traffic volume, ~ flow
~weg m = (transportation) route
~zählstelle f = observation point, traffic census ~
~zählung f, siehe: Verkehrsmessung f
verkeilen = to wedge, to key
Verkieseln n = silicifying (US); silicating, treatment with silicate (Brit.)
Verkiesung f = gravel filling
verkittende Zwischensubstanz f, siehe: Bindemittel n
Verkittung f [*Gestein* n] = cementation

Verkleidung f, siehe: Auskleidung f
Verknappung f = shortage
Verkokung f = carbonization, coking
Verkokungs|destillat n = coked distillate
~-Spaltanlage f = coking plant
verkoppelte Randbedingung f = linked boundary condition
Verkrustung f = encrustation
Verkupplung f, siehe: Stegverbindungsstück n
Verladeband n = loading belt
Verladebrücke f = (bridge) transporter (crane)
~ mit Drehkran m = (bridge) transporter with revolving crane
~ mit Laufkran m = (bridge) transporter with travel(l)ing crane
Verlade|bühne f = loading platform
~gerät n, siehe: Lademaschine f
~greifer m = loading grab(bing crane), ~ (grab) bucket crane
~greifkorb m = loading bucket
~rampe f = loading ramp
~schrapper m; siehe unter „Seilförderanlage f"
Verlandebecken n; siehe unter „Talsperre f"
Verlandung f, siehe: Alluvium n
~, siehe: Verschlammung f
verlängerter Zementmörtel m, Zementkalkmörtel m, Kalkzementmörtel = lime cement mortar, cement lime ~; gauged ~ (Brit.)
verlaschen = to fishplate
Verlaschen n [*Holz* n] = fishing
verleimter Balken m = glued beam
verlorener Schacht m; siehe unter „Mannloch n"
verlorene Schalung f = sacrifice shuttering, ~ form(work)
Verlustzeit f, Verzögerung f [*Straßenverkehr* m] = stopped time
Vermahlen n; siehe unter „Mühle f"
vermahlen mit = to intergrind with

Vermessungskunde f
Abrißpunkt m, Festpunkt, Fixpunkt
Abschlußfehler m
Aufnahme f, Vermessung f

surveying
bench mark
closing error, error of closure
survey

Vermessungskunde

Dosensextant *m*	box sextant
Eintragen *n*	booking
Feldarbeit *f*	field work
höhere Geodäsie *f*	geodesy, geodetic surveying
Katastervermessung *f*	cadastral survey
Kettenmessung *f*	chain surveying, chaining
Doppelpentagon-Winkelprisma *n*	double prism optical square
einfluchten einer Geraden (aus der Mitte heraus)	to range a straight line (over a fold in the ground)
Feldbuch *n*	field book, chain book
Fluchtstange *f*, Fluchtstab *m*	ranging pole (or rod)
Meßkette *f*	land chain, surveyor's chain
Meßlatte *f*	measuring rod
Metermarke *f*	brass teller
Nadel *f*	arrow
rechtwinklig absetzen	to set out a right angle
Winkelkreuz *n*	cross-staff
Winkelprisma *n*	optical square
Koordinate *f*	co-ordinate
Nivellieren *n*, Höhenaufnahme *f*, Höhenmessung *f*	level(l)ing, survey of heights
Aufnahme *f* der Querprofile *npl*	cross-sectioning, taking cross-sections
barometrisches Nivellieren *n*	barometric level(l)ing
(Ein)Visieren *n*	boning(-in), sighting [*setting out intermediate levels on the straight line joining two given level pegs*]
Höhe *f*	elevation
Längsnivellement *n*	longitudinal section levels
Nivellierlatte *f*	level(l)ing staff
Rückblick *m*	backsight
Vorblick *m*	fore-sight
Visierkreuz *n*	boning rod
Visierscheibe *f*	boning rod with round top piece
Meßtisch *m*	plane table
Nivellierinstrument *n*, Nivellier *n*	level
Nivellier(instrument) *n* mit Ringfernrohr *n*	Y level
Nivellier(instrument) *n* mit Kippschraube *f*	improved ball-and-socket type level
einrichten, justieren	to adjust
Kreuzlibelle *f*	cross-bubble
Nivellier(instrument) mit planparalleler Platte *f*	self-adjusting level
Nivelliertachimeter *n*	level with compass
Objektiv *n*	object-glass
Okular *n*	eye-piece
Präzisionsnivellier(instrument) *n*	precise level
Röhrenlibelle *f*, Reiterlibelle *f*	main bubble
Pantograph *n*, Storchenschnabel *m*	pentagraph, pantograph
Planimeter *n*, Flächenmesser *m*	planimeter

Vermessungskunde — Versandung

Polygon(zug) n, (m)	traverse
Prismakompaß m	prismatic compass
Ausgleichung f	balancing
geknickter Zug m	chain traverse
innerer Winkel m	interior angle
offener Zug m, offenes Polygon n	unclosed traverse
Polygonzug-Aufnahme f	traversing
Ringpolygon n	closed traverse
Winkelfehler m	angular error
Reduktionszirkel m	proportional compasses
Rückwärtseinschneiden n	backsight reading
Stationierung f	stationing, chainage
Stückvermessung f	plane survey(ing)
Tachymetrie f, gleichzeitige Lage- und Höhenmessung f	tacheometry
tachymetrische Aufnahme f	tacheometric survey
Triangulation f, Triangulierung f	triangulation
Vorwärtseinschneiden n	fore-sight reading
Vermessungstrupp m	survey party, surveyor tracing gang
Visiergerüst n, Schnurgerüst	sight rail

Vermiculite|-Erz n = vermiculite ore
~-Gipsputz m = gypsum-vermiculite plaster
~-Putz m = vermiculite plaster
verminderter Querschnitt m [*Blechträger* m] = net sectional area

---

Vermörteln n [*Boden* m]	processing
Zementbeigabe f und Wasserbeigabe und Mischen n	adding and mixing the cement and water
Verdichten n	compacting
Abziehen n	final shaping of the surface
Vermörtelungszug m	stabilizing train

---

vermörtelt [*Straße* f] = stabilized, stabilised
Vermörtelung f, Verfestigung f durch Beimischungen fpl = stabilization, stabilisation, solidification
~ f mit künstlichen Harzen npl; siehe unter „Baugrundverbesserung f"
Vermörtelungskolonne f, Vermörtelungstrupp m = stabilising gang (or team, or crew, or party)
Verpacken n = packaging
Verpflockung f, siehe: Absteckung(sarbeiten) f
Verpressung f, siehe: Injektion f
Verpuffungs|motor m = explosive combustion engine
~-Ölmotor m = explosion oil engine

Verputzen n, Putzen = rendering
Verputzmaschine f, siehe: Putzwerfer m
Verrohren n = piping
verrohrtes Bohrloch n = cased bore hole, lined ~ ~
verrußen = to soot
versagen = to fail
Versagen n, Fehlschlag m = failure
Versand m = shipping, shipment
~benachrichtigung f = notice of dispatch, ~ ~ despatch
~kiste f = shipping box
~silo m [*Zement* m] = packer bin
Versandung f, Versanden n = sand-silting (Brit.); sand filling (US); sanding up

Verschalung *f* = lining, sheeting
Verschiebe|bahnhof *m*, Rangierbahnhof *m* = (freight-)classification yard, marshalling yard, switchyard, shunting station
~einrichtungen *fpl* **für Waggons** *mpl* = marshalling equipment
~gleis *n*, siehe: Rangiergleis *n*
~lok(omotive) *f*, Rangierlok(omotive) *f* = shunting loco(motive), rail shunter
Verschiebungsebene *f* (Geol.) = thrust plane (Brit.); displaced surface (US)
Verschlammung *f*, Verlandung *f* = mud-silting, siltation (Brit.); mud filling (US)
Verschleiß *m*, siehe: Abnützung *f*
~blech *n* = metal wearing plate
~eigenschaft *f* = wearing property
~schicht *f*, Decklage *f* [*Straße f*] = surface course, wearing carpet, wearing course, wearing surface, road surface; top course (US); coat (Brit.); [*deprecated: topping, crust, sheeting, carpet, veneer, top*]
  offen = open-textured
  halb-offen = medium-textured
  geschlossen = close-textured
~schicht *f* **aus Bitumenvermörtelung** *f* = soil-bitumen mix surfacing (Brit.)
~schicht *f* **aus mechanisch verfestigtem Material** *n* = soil surfacing, ~ surface course, earth wearing surface
verschließbar = lockfast, lockable
verschlossener Überlauf *m*; siehe unter „Talsperre *f*"
Verschluß|bauwerk *n* = gate structure
~kammer *f* = gate chamber
~-Konstruktion *f* = gate assembly
Verschmutzung *f* [*Gewässer n, Luft f*] = pollution
Verschneiden *n* = thinning, cutting back
verschneit, eingeschneit = snowed-up, snow-bound
Verschnitt|bitumen *n*; siehe unter „Bitumen *n* im engeren Sinne"
~mittel *n* [*Verschnittbitumen n*] = volatile diluent
~mittel *n* = thinning agent
Verschotterung *f* [*Fluß m*] = choking
Verschränkung *f*; siehe unter „Holzverbindung *f*"

verschrotten = to reduce to scrap
Verschwertung *f*, Schrägverband *m* = diagonal bracing
verseifbar = saponifiable
Verseifung *f* = saponification
Verseifungswert *m* = saponification value
Versenkungsumprägung *f*, siehe: Regionalmetamorphose *f*
Versenkungswand *f*, siehe: Drempelwand
versetzte Kreuzung *f* = staggered junction
Versickerung *f* = infiltration
Versinkungsgrenze *f*; siehe unter „Gründungspfahl *m*"
Versorgungsleitung *f* = supply line
Verspannung *f*, Verzahnung *f* [*Mineralmasse f*] = (aggregate) interlock(ing)
Verspreizung *f*, siehe: Abspreizung *f*
Versprödung *f* = embrittlement
Verstaatlichung *f* = nationalisation
Verstärkerventilator *m* = booster fan
Verstärkungs|bolzen *m* = forcing bolt
~pumpe *f*, Druckverstärkerpumpe = booster pump
~rippe *f*, Versteifungsrippe = stiffening (or reinforcing) rib
Versteifung *f*, siehe: Absteifung *f*
Versteifungs|stab *m* [*Kastenträger m*] = truss bar
~träger *m* **mit Gelenk** *n* = stiffening girder with hinge
Versteinerung *f* = petrifaction
(Ver)Stellmutter *f* = adjusting nut
Verstemmung *f*, Verstemmen *n*, Kalfatern *n* = caulking, fullering (Brit.); calking (US)
Verstopfen *n*, Verstopfung *f* [*Sieb n*] = blinding [*screen*]
verstopft = choked, blocked up
verstrebte Zimmerung *f* = braced timbering
Verstrebung *f*, Aussprießen *n*, Absprießen = strutting
verstreichen, aufspachteln = to float
Versuchs|anstalt *f* = research establishment
~einzelheit *f* = experimental detail, test ~
~feld *n*, Versuchsgelände *n* = test ground, proving ~
~fahrzeug *n* [*z. B. zur Bestimmung f der Bordsteineinführung f*] = design vehicle

Versuchs|methode *f*, Versuchsverfahren *n*, Experimentalverfahren = trial method
~methode *f*, Versuchsverfahren *n*, Prüfverfahren, Prüfmethode = test method, testing procedure
~modell *n* = pilot model
~rad *n* = test wheel
~reihe *f* = test series
~standuntersuchung *f* = trial-test investigation, proving-ground test
~strecke *f*, Probestrecke, Beobachtungsstrecke = experimental (or test) section (or track)
~verfahren *n*, siehe: Versuchsmethode *f*
Versumpfung *f* = formation of marsh (or bog)
Vertau-Boje *f* = can buoy
vertäuen [*Schiff n*] = to tie up
Verteiler *m* = distributor, spreader
~bohle *f* = distributing beam, spreading ~
~fertiger *m*, siehe: Schwarzbelageinbaumaschine *f*
~gurtförderer *m* = distributing belt conveyor
~kasten *m*, Kastenverteiler *m* = spreader box, spreading box, box spreader, spreading hopper, drag (spreader) box, drag spreader
~mundstücke *npl* [*Dosiersilo m*] = breeches chute
~schnecke *f*, Verteilungsschnecke = distributing screw, spreader ~, spreading ~, (cross) auger
~schurre *f* = distributing chute, distribution ~
~stollen *m*; siehe unter „Talsperre *f*"
~ventil *n* = diversion valve
Verteilungsnetz *n* = distribution system
Vertiefung *f* = depression
~ *f* [*Hafen m*] = deepening
vertikale Förderschnecke *f* = (vertical) screw elevator, vertical screw lift
~ Krümmung *f*, **~ Kurve** *f* = vertical curve
~ Sanddränage *f*, lotrechter Sanddrän *m*, Sandbrunnen *m*, Sickerbrunnen *m*, vertikale Sandeinschlämme *f*, Sanddrän *m* = vertical sand drain (or pile)

vertikaler Träger *m* **der Sprießung** *f* = soldier beam
Vertikal|-Förderschnecke *f* = worm elevator, Archimedean screw ~
~klassierer *m* = vertical classifier
~strömungs-Trockenelektroabscheider *m* = vertical gas flow dry precipitator
Vertrags|abschluß *m* = contract agreement
~bedingungen *fpl* = contract provisions
~strafe *f* = contract penalty
Verunreinigung *f* = impurity
Verwerfung *f*, siehe: Stufenbildung *f* [*Betonplatten fpl*]
~ *f*, Bruch *m*, Sprung *m*, Paraklase *f*, Absenkung *f*, Abschiebung *f* [*Grabenrand m*] (Geol.) = fault (plane), geological fault, faulting
Verwerfungs|brekzie *f* = fault breccia
~letten *m* = gouge
~linie *f*, Bruchlinie (Geol.) = fault line
~spaltenquelle *f*, siehe: Kluftquelle
Verwertung *f*, Ausnutzung *f* = utilisation, utilization
Verwindung *f*, siehe: Torsion *f*
verwindungsfest, verwindungssteif = torsion-proof
Verwindungsspannung *f* = torsion(al) stress
Verwitterung *f*; siehe unter „Denudation *f*"
Verwitterungs|boden *m*, siehe: Eluvialboden *m*
~kruste *f*, Abwitterungsprodukte *npl* (Geol.) [*in mächtiger Form als „Rückstandssediment n" bezeichnet*] = residual depoeits [*accumulations of rock waste resulting from disintegration in situ*]
~meßgerät *n* [*Dachpappe f*] = weather-Ometer
~ton *m* = residual clay
verzahnt = indented
Verzahnung *f*, siehe: Verspannung *f*
Verzahnungsstoß *m* = joggle joint
Verzapfung *f*; siehe unter „Holzverbindung *f*"
Verzögerung *f* [*Straßenverkehr m*], siehe: Verlustzeit *f*
Verzögerungs|becken *n*; siehe unter „Talsperre *f*"

Verzögerungs|bogen m = deceleration curve

~spur f = deceleration lane

verzwicken, siehe: auszwicken

Vesuvian m (Min.) = vesuvianite

Viadukt n, Talbrücke f = viaduct, valley bridge

~mauerwerk n, Talbrückenmauerwerk = viaduct masonry, valley bridge ~

Vibrations|amplitude f, Schwingungsweite f = amplitude

~beanspruchung f = vibration(al) stress(ing)

~-Betonsteinmaschine f = vibration (concrete) block machine

~dämpfer m, Schwingungsdämpfer = vibration dampener, ~ absorber

~element n = vibratory member

~erzeuger m = vibrating unit

~fördergerät n, Schwingfördergerät, Vibrationsförderer m, Schwingförderer = vibrating conveying machine

vibrationsfreier Griff m = anti-vibration handle

vibrationsgeschnittene Fuge f = vibrated (concrete) joint

Vibrations|glättbohle f = vibrating smoother, ~ smoothing (or finishing) beam (or screed)

~glätter m = vibrating float

~maschensieb n = square mesh vibrating screen

~maschine f [*Herstellung* f *von Betonbauelementen* npl] = vibrating mo(u)lding machine

~platte f; siehe unter „Betonrüttelgeräte npl"

~rohrmaschine f, siehe: Betonrohr-Vibriermaschine

~sieb n = screen with vibratory action applied direct to the screen cloth

~stampfer m, siehe: Rüttelstampfer

~verdichtung f, Rüttelverdichtung f, dynamische Verdichtung, Schwing(ungs)verdichtung f, Einrüttelungsverdichtung f, Bewegungsverdichtung f = vibrator compaction, vibrating ~, forced vibratory ~, compaction by vibration

~-Verdichtungsmaschine f, Schwing(ungs)verdichter m = vibratory compactor

~viskosimeter n = vibrating-plate visco(si)meter

Vibrator m, Schwingungs(ein)rüttler m, Rüttelgerät n = vibrator

~bohle, siehe: Vibrierbohle

~-Glättbohle f **mit Fahrwerk** n **System SAGER & WOERNER,** FRISCH-Vibrator-Glättbohle, SaWoe-Bohle = vibratory smoothing (or finishing) screed with travel(l)ing gear

~platte f; siehe unter „Betonrüttelgeräte npl"

Vibrier|bohle f, Rüttelbohle, Vibratorbohle, Verdichtungsbohle, Schwingungsbohle = vibrating beam, ~ smoother

~geräte npl **zur Materialförderung** f = vibrating materials handling equipment

~maschine f **für Betonrohre** npl, siehe: Betonrohr-Vibriermaschine f

~tisch m; siehe unter „Betonrüttelgeräte npl"

Vieh|tunnel m = stock subway, cattle creep

~weide f = pasture

Vieleck|mauerwerk n, Polygonmauerwerk n = random rubble masonry

~sprengwerk n = polygonal truss

Vielfach|betonfugenschleifgerät n = multiple blade joint saw

~bogensperre f; siehe unter „Talsperre f"

~brenner m = multi-fuel burner

~kuppelsperre f; siehe unter „Talsperre f"

~-Zuteilgefäß n = multiple batcher hopper

Viel|hebelei f = complicated array of levers

~lingslamellierung f [*Natronkalkfeldspat* m] = lamellar (or banded) twinning [*plagioclase*]

(~)Röhrenkessel m = multitubular boiler

vielspurige Straße f, siehe: mehrspurige ~

vielstegige Brücke f = multi-webbed bridge

vielstöckiges Gebäude n = high-storeyed building

Vielzweckbagger m, siehe: Mehrzweckbagger m

Vier|decker(sieb) m, (n) = four-deck grader, ~ screen

Vier|endeelträger m = Vierendeel girder
~fachsteuergerät n = four-way control box
~furchenpflug m = four-furrow plough (Brit.)/plow (US)
viergehäusige Turbine f = four-cylinder turbine
Vierkant|stahl m = square bar (steel)
~(schrauben)mutter f = square (screw) nut
~welle f [*Schwertwäsche* f] = angle steel log [*log washer*]
Vier|-Momente-Lehrsatz m = four moment theorem
~-Motoren-Laufkran m [*für elektrischen Betrieb* m] = four-motor travel(l)ing crane
~radtrecker m, Zweiachsschlepper m, Vierradschlepper, Vierradtraktor m, Zwei-Achs-Reifen-Sattelschlepper, Zweiachs-Zugwagen m = four-wheel(ed) tractor
~rad-Vorspänner m = four-wheel(ed) prime mover
~takter m = four-stroke cycle engine
~teilung f = quartering
vierzelliger Dosierapparat m = four-material batcher
Visieren n, Ein~ = sighting, boning(-in)
Visier|gerüst n, Schnurgerüst = sight rail, batter board
~linie f = line of sight
Visitenkarte f = calling card, personal ~
visko-elastische Eigenschaft f = viscoelastic property
Viskosimeter n **mit rotierendem Zylinder** m = rotating cylinder visco(si)meter
Viskosimetrie f = viscometry
Viskosität f, Zähflüssigkeit f = viscosity
~-Dichte-Konstante f = viscosity gravity content (or constant)
Vitriolbleierz n, Anglesit m, $PbSO_4$ (Min.) = anglesite
Vivianit m (Min.), siehe: Blaueisenerde f
Volkswirtschaft f = national economy
Voll|anhänger m, siehe: Mehrachsenanhänger
~ausbruch m; siehe unter „Tunnelbau m"
~automatik f = full automatic operation
vollautomatisch = fully automatic

Voll|bahngleis n, siehe: Normalspurgleis
~bahn-Lok(omotive) f = main line loco(motive)
~balken m = solid beam
~balkendecke f = floor made up entirely of beams
~becherwerk n, siehe: Reihenbecherwerk
~-Betonmantelung f [*Rohr* n] = surround
~bohrstahl m = solid drill steel
~dampf m = full steam
~durchtränkung f, Vollimprägnierung [*Holz* n] = Bethell process, full cell ~
~elevator m, siehe: Reihenbecherwerk n
voller Bogen m, siehe: Halbkreisbogen
Voll|förderschnecke f = closed spiral (worm) conveyor
~gatter n = gang saw, multiple blade sawframe
~gummikantenschutz m = edge protection with rubber
~gummireifen m, siehe: Elastikreifen
~hydraulik-Bagger m = all-hydraulic excavator, ~ shovel
~kippanhänger m = wagon [*a full trailer with a dump body*]
~kolben(bohr)hammer m = solid piston rock drill
vollkristallines Erstarrungsgestein n = holocrystalline rock
Voll|-Last f, Vollast = full load
~mauerwerk n, siehe: Massivmauerwerk
~portalkran m, siehe: Torkran
~querschnitt m = gross section(al area)
~scheibe f = solid disc, ~ disk
~schiene f = filled section rail
~sicht f, Rundblick m = all-round view, ~ vision, full ~
~sichtkanzel f, Rundblick-Führerhaus n, Vollsichtkabine f = full-vision cab(in), all-round view ~, all-round vision ~
~stahlbauweise f, Ganzstahl-Bauweise f = all-steel construction
~standanzeiger m = high level indicator
vollständig geschweißt = all-welded
Voll|torkran m, siehe: Torkran
~turbine f = full admission turbine
~wandbogen m = solid-rib arch
~wand-Deckbrücke f = deck plate girder span (US)

vollwandig = solid-webbed
vollwandiger Ausleger *m*, Kastenausleger = box type boom (US); ~ ~ jib (Brit.)
Voll|wandträger *m*, siehe: Blechträger
~wandträger-Trogbrücke *f* = trough plate girder span (US)
~wand-Verbund-Konstruktion *f* = solid web composite structure
~ziegel(stein) *m*, siehe: Backstein
Volumen|dosierung *f*, Raumzumessung, Raumdosierung, Volumenzumessung, Raumteilmischung, Volumenzugabe *f* = (loose-)volume batching, bulk ~, volumetric ~, batching by volume
~vergrößerung *f* **von Sand** *m* = dilatancy of sand
~(wasser)messer *m* = positive (water) meter
~zunahme *f* = volumetric increase
volumetrischer Wirkungsgrad *m* = volumetric efficiency
Vor|alpen *f* = Prealps
~anschlag *m*, siehe: Anschlag
~anstrich *m*, siehe: Grundier-Überzug *m*
~arbeiten *fpl* = preparatory work, preliminary ~
~arbeiter *m* = leading hand
~bau-Harke *f*, Vorbau-Rechen *m* = front rake
~beize *f* = weak mordant
~belüftung *f* = pre-aeration
~berge *mpl*, Vorträge *mpl* [*eines Gebirgszuges m*] = foothills
~blick *m* [*Nivellieren n*] = fore-sight
~bohrer *m* = starter drill, starting ~
~bohrloch *n* **mit kleinem Durchmesser** *m* [*Ölbohrung f*] = rat hole, slim ~
~böschung *f* = fore-slope
~brechen *n*; siehe unter „Hartzerkleinerung *f*"
~brecher *m*, Großbrecher = (large) primary crusher, primary breaker, sledger, scalper, stone-breaker (type crusher), sledging breaker
~chlorung *f* = pre-chlorination
vordere Bohlenkante *f* [*Straßenfertiger m*] = leading edge
Vorder|achsantrieb *m* = front axle drive

~achsaufhängung *f* = front axle suspension
~ansicht *f* = front elevation, ~ view
~grund *m* = fore-ground
~kipper *m*, siehe: Autoschütter *m*
~kipp-(Front)Ladeschaufel *f* = forward-tip(ping) bucket
~radantrieb *m*, Frontantrieb = front wheel drive
Vor|entwurf *m* = preliminary design
~erhitzung *f* = preheating
~fabrikation *f* = pre-fabrication
~fahrtsrecht *n* = right-of-way
~fahrtstraße *f*, Hauptstraße = major road
~finanzierung *f* = initial financing
~flut *f*, Abfluß *m* = discharge
~fluter *m* [*Gewässer n das die Abflußmenge eines anderen aufnimmt*] = outfall (ditch), main outfall, outfall drain, drain outfall, receiving stream, receiving water
~füllkasten *m*; siehe unter „Betonmischer *m*"
~gebirge *n* = front range
vorgeformtes drallarmes Seil *n* = TRU-LAY-ROPE
vorgekesseltes Loch *n*; siehe unter „1. Schießen *n*; 2. Sprengen *n*"
Vorgelege|haspel *m*, *f* = crab winch
~haspel *m*, *f* [*Bergbau m*] = whim with a communicator
~rad *n* = back gear
~welle *f* = countershaft
~welle *f* **zum Fahrwerk** *n* = countershaft for the driving mechanism
~welle *f* **zur Fahrwerklenkung** *f* = countershaft for steering of the driving mechanism
~welle *f* **zur (Gleis)Kettensteuerung** *f* = countershaft for steering of the crawlers
vorgespannte Verbund-Stahlbetonkonstruktion *f* = compound prestressed reinforced concrete structure
vorgespannter Zugring *m* = prestressed tension-ring
vorgespanntes Flächentragwerk *n* = load-bearing prestressed slab
~ Glas *n* = toughened glass

Vor|haltung f [*Baumaschinen* fpl] = furnishing (of machinery and equipment)
~haltung f **von Zuschlagstoffen** mpl = storage of aggregates at the job site
~hersage f = forecasting procedure
~kesseln n, Kesselschießen n = sprungbore hole method
~klärbecken n = preliminary clarification tank (or basin)
~klärung f = preliminary clarification, presedimentation
~kocher m = primary heater, ~ heating kettle, ~ melting tank; ~ boiler [*deprecated*]
~kommen n, Vorkommnis n, Lager(stätte) n, (f) = deposit
~konzentrierung f = preconcentration
~kopf m [*z. B. Schleuse f*] = roundhead
vorkragen, siehe: auskragen
Vorkriegsstand m = prewar level
vorlageartiges Pflaster n, siehe: Steinsatz m
Vorlage f = apron
~stein m, siehe: Setzpacklagestein
Vorland n = foreland
~ n = foreshore
Vorlast f, Vorbelastung f = initial load(ing)
vorläufige Abnahme f = initial acceptance
Vor|laufleitung f = flow line
~mahlen n; siehe unter „Mühle f"
~mauerziegel(stein) m [*früher: Hartbranntstein*] = hard-baked brick
~mischen n **der Betonbestandteile** mpl **vor Einspeisen** n **in den Liefermischer** m [*Transportbeton m*] = pre-shrink mixing
~mischsilo m [*Betonherstellung f*] = prebatching bin
~mischsiloband n = cumulative bin conveyor (belt)
~mischung f, Vormischen n = premixing
~mittagsschicht f = morning shift
~mittags-Spitzenstunde f = morning peak hour
~montage f = pre-assembly
~ort-Omnibus m, Vorort-(Auto)Bus = suburban bus
~ort-Schnellbahn f = system of suburban rail service
~ort-Wohnhaus n = suburban dwelling house
~rat m = stock
vorrätig = carried in stock, on stock
Vorratsbunker m = storage bunker
(Vorrats)|Halde f, Materialhalde = stockpile, (storage) pile, stock-heap
~Silo m, siehe: Lagersilo
~tunnel m, siehe: Haldentunnel
Vor|reiniger m = precleaner
~richtung f = device
~schaltturbine f = primary high-pressure turbine
~schub m, Vorstoß(en) m, (n) [*Hochlöffel(bagger) m*] = crowd(ing(
~schubdistanz f [*Bohrmaschine f*] = feed travel
~schubvorrichtung f [*Bohrmaschine f*] = feed
~schubkupplung f, siehe: Vorstoßkupplung
~schubstütze f; siehe unter „Bohrhammer m"
~schweißflansch m = welded on flange, flange with welded neck
Vorspann m **im (oder mit) Verbund** m = pre-tensioning
~ mit nachträglichem Verbund m = post-tensioning
~ ohne Verbund m = no-bond tensioning
~bündel n = bundle of prestressing tendons
~draht m = prestressing wire
Vorspänner m, siehe: (Zweirad-)Vorspänner m
Vorspann|kabel n = steel prestressing cable
~kraft f, Spannkraft = prestressing force
Vor|spannung f = prestress
~spannung f **von Durchlaufträgern** mpl = continuous prestressing
~spannwagen m, siehe: (Zweirad-)Vorspänner m
~sperre f; siehe unter „Talsperre f"
~stoßkupplung f, Vorschubkupplung = crowd clutch
~stoßseil n, Vorschubseil n [*Hochlöffel(bagger) m*] = crowd rope

Vortrieb *m* [*Tunnelbau m*] = driving, heading
~**geschwindigkeit** *f* [*Betondeckenfertiger m*] = operating speed
~**stelle** *f*, siehe: Einbaustelle *f* [*Straßenbau m*]
~**stelle** *f*; siehe unter „Tunnelbau *m*"
Vor|untersuchung *f* des Baugrundes *m*, siehe: Bodenuntersuchung *f*
~**verbrennung** *f* = precombustion
~**verdichter** *m* = precompactor
~**verdichtung** *f* = initial compaction
~**wärmer** *m*, Erhitzer *m* = (pre-) heater
~**wärmzone** *f* = preheating zone
~**wärtseinschneiden** *n* [*Vermessungskunde f*] = fore-sight reading
~**wegweiser** *m* = advance direction sign
Vorwohlitdecke *f*, siehe: Walzschottergußasphalt *m*
vorzeitiges Abbinden *n*, siehe: falsches ~
Vorzerkleinerung *f*; siehe unter „Hartzerkleinerung"
Vorzündung *f* = pre-ignition
Vouten|balken *m* = haunched beam
~**schräge** *f* = tapered haunch

Vulkan *m*, Feuerberg *m*	volcano
Ausbruch *m*, Eruption *f*	explosion, eruption
Blocklava *f*, Schollenlava, Zackenlava, Aprolith *m*, Spratzlava	block lava, aa (lava)
Einbruchscaldera *m*	engulfment caldera
Schlackenkegel *m*	cinder cone
Explosionscaldera *m*	caldera of subsidence
Halemaumau-Lavasee *m*	Halemaumau fire-pit
Lapilli *f*, vulkanische Steinchen *fpl*	lapilli [*singular: lapillus*]
Lavabombe *f*, vulkanische Bombe	volcanic bomb
Peleische Eruption *f*	Pelean type eruption
Pele's Haar *n*	Pele's hair
Schlot *m*, Esse *f*, Durchschlagsröhre *f*, Neck *m*, Eruptionskanal *m*, Schußröhre *f*, Stielgang *m*, Hals *m*	pipe(-like conduit), (volcanic) neck
Somma *f*	Monte Somma
Stricklava *f*, Fladenlava, Wulstlava, Taulava	ropy lava, pahoehoe lava
tätig	active
vulkanischer Tuff *m*, Feuerbergtuff, Durchbruchgesteintuff	tuff, volcanic tuff, tuffaceous rock
vulkanische Asche *f*, Feuerbergasche	volcanic ash, ~ cinder
vulkanische Brekzie *f*	volcanic breccia
vulkanischer Sand *m*, Feuerbergsand, Kratersand, natürlicher Schlackensand	volcanic sand
vulkanisches Agglomerat *n*	volcanic agglomerate
vulkanische Schlacke *f*	scoria, scoriaceous lava
vulkanisches Gestein *n*, siehe: Ergußgestein *n*	
vulkanisches Glas *n*	volcanic glass
Vulkanit *m*, siehe: Ergußgestein *n*	

---

vulkanisiert = vulcanized

W

Waadt(land) *f (n)* = Vaud
Waage *f* **für alle Gemengeteile** *mpl*, siehe: Gattierungswaage *f*
Waagen-Dosierapparat *m* [*Zuschlagstoffe mpl*] = scale batcher
waagerechte Rollenbahn *f* = level roller runway
waagerechter Ausleger *m* = cantilever jib (Brit.); ∼ boom (US)
∼natürlicher Erddruck *m* **im unberührten Boden** *m* = lateral earth (or soil) pressure at rest, neutral lateral earth pressure, lateral earth pressure at consolidated equilibrium
Waagerechtförderer *m* = horizontal conveyor
Waagscheit *n* = level(l)ing plank
Wabe *f* [*Wabensilo m*] = circular bin compartment
Waben|silo *m*, Rund∼ = circular multiple-compartment bin
∼struktur *f* = honeycombed texture, honeycombing
Wachposten *m* = watchman
Wadi *m*, Trockental *n* = wadi [*dried-up bed of stream*]
Wagen *m* = wagon
∼-Fähranlage *f* = car-ferry terminal
∼fett *n*, Wagenschmiere *f* = sett grease
∼kipper *m*, siehe: Waggonkipper
∼straße *f* = wagon road
∼winde *f*, Wagenheber *m*, Wagenhebebock *m* = car jack
Waggon *m*, Güterwagen *m* = freight car (US); goods van (or wagon), railway wagon (Brit.)

∼ *m* **mit Bodenentleerung** *f*, Bodenentleerer *m* = hopper bottom rail car
∼(band)entlader *m* = (conveyor-type) car unloader
∼entladepumpe *f* = car unloader pump
∼hebeanlage *f* = truck hoist, railway car ∼
∼kipper *m*, Wagenkipper = car dumper, wagon tippler
∼schrapper *m*, siehe: Entladeschaufel *f*
∼verschiebegeräte *npl* = wagon marshalling equipment
∼waage *f*, siehe: Gleiswaage
wahre Kohäsion *f* = true cohesion
Wahrscheinlichkeitsrechnung *f* [*Hochwasser n*] = probability method
waldarm = sparsely wooded
Wald|bestand *m* = forests covering
∼boden *m*, Podsolboden, humider Boden = podzol (soil)
∼hochmoor *n* = high moor forest
∼weg *m*, siehe: Forstweg *m*
∼wirtschaft *f*, Forstwirtschaft *f* = forestry
Walkpenetration *f* [*Schmierfett n*] = worked penetration
Wall *m* = bank
∼abtrag *m* = bank digging
∼moräne *f*; siehe unter „Gletscher *m*"
Walzasphalt *m* = rolled asphalt
∼anlage *f*, siehe unter „Makadam-Maschinenanlage *f*"
∼binderschicht *f* = binder course of rolled asphalt
∼-Chargenmischanlage *f* = asphalt batch(ing) plant
Walzdamm *m*; siehe unter „Talsperre *f*"

Walze *f* | roller
Abwalzen *n* mit Stahlmantelwalzen *fpl* | steel rolling
Abwalzen *n* mit Gummiwalzen *fpl* | pneumatic rolling
Advance-Dieselmotor-(Straßen) ∼ [*Dreirad*∼ *mit Differentialgetriebe n und geteilter Hinterachse f*] | advance diesel (road) ∼
ALBARET-Schaffuß∼; siehe unter „Schaffuß∼"
Anhänge-Schwingungs∼; siehe unter „Vibrations∼"

Walze

Anhänge~, siehe: Schlepp~
belastbar
Benzin~, Ottomotor~

Bodenverfestigungs~, siehe: Verdichtungs~
Dampf(straßen)~
Diesel-Motor-Dreirad-~
Dieselmotor(straßen)~
Dienstgewicht n, Betriebsgewicht

Doppelzylinder~; siehe unter „Schaffuß~"
Dreiachs(-Tandem)~ [*Dreiradwalze mit drei hintereinander liegenden Radsätzen*]
Dreirad~ [*Zweiachswalze mit vorne einem meist geteilten Rad und hinten zwei Rädern, wobei die hinteren Raddurchmesser größer sind als die vorderen*]
Eigengewichts~, siehe: Glatt~
einachsige Gummirad~
Einrad-Motor-~, siehe: handgeführte~ mit Motor m
Einrad~, Einachs~ [*mit und ohne Stützrad n*]
Einrad~ mit Gummireifenfahrwerk n
Fußboden~
Fußweg~, Gehsteig~
Gewicht n der Hinterräder npl von 60 kg je 1 cm linearer Berührungsfläche f
Gitter~
Glatt~, Eigengewichts~, statische ~, statisch wirksame ~

Glattmantel-Schlepp~
Gleisbettungs~
Graben~
Gummi(reifenvielfach)~, Pneu~, Gummi(viel)rad-Verdichtungs~

~ mit nicht oszillierenden Rädern *npl*

~ mit oszillierenden Rädern *npl*

schwingende Gummi(reifenvielfach)~, gummibereifte ~ mit Vibration *f*

ballastable
petrol(-driven) ~ (Brit.); gasoline-driven (or gasolene-driven) ~ (US)

steam (road) ~
diesel engine three-wheel(ed) ~
diesel (road) ~
rolling weight, service ~, working ~, operating ~

three-axle (tandem) ~

macadam ~ (US); three-wheel(ed) (all-purpose) ~, three-roll type machine, three-legged ~, three-roll ~

single-axle compactor

single-wheel(ed) ~

wheeled roller
floor ~
sidewalk ~ (US); footpath ~ (Brit.)
330 pounds per linear inch of tread of rear wheels
grid ~
smooth(-wheeled) ~, static ~, flat-wheel(ed) ~; smooth-tired ~, flat-steel ~ (US)
plain towed ~
permanent way ~
trench ~
pneumatic-tire ~, multi-rubber-tire ~ (US); pneumatic-tyred ~, multi-tyred pneumatic-tyred ~ (Brit.); rubber-tired (US)/-tyred (Brit.) ~, (pneumatic) multiwheel(ed) ~
  straight (or fixed) wheel (pneumatic-tyred) ~
  wobbly (or wobbled) wheel(ed) (pneumatic tire) ~, wobbly:wheel(ed) compactor
vibratory pneumatic-tired (US)/tyred (Brit.) ~; pneumatic-tired vibrating compacting ~ (US)

Walze

~ ~, Fabrikat IOWA MFG. CO., CEDAR RAPIDS, IOWA, USA
   Antriebsmotor *m*
   Vibrator *m*, Rüttler *m*
   Ballastbehälter *m*
   Spiralfeder *f*
   Luftreifen *m*
   Vibrator-Drehzahl *f*
   senkrechte Verdichtungswirkung in der Arbeitsrichtung
   entweichende Luft *f* und Feuchtigkeit *f*
   Überrollung *f*, Walzgang *m*
Gürtelrad~, Gürtelradbodenverdichter *m*
handgeführte ~ mit Motor *m*, Einrad-Motor~, handgeführte kraftgetriebene Einrad ~, Motorhand~
Hand ~ mit variablem Gewicht *n*
Hand ~ mit nicht variablem Gewicht *n*
Hand ~ mit Wasserballast *m*
Hinter~, Hinterwalzrad *n*
Igel ~; siehe unter „Schaffuß ~"
Kleinmotor~
Klumpfuß~; siehe unter „Schaffuß ~"
Kraft~, Motor~
Ottomotor~, siehe: Benzin~
Pneu~, siehe: Gummi(reifenvielfach)~
Rasen~
Raupenschlepper~, (Gleis)Kettenschlepper~
Riesengummi(reifenvielfach)~, Super-Gummirad ~, Schwersverdichter *m*
Riesenschaffuß; siehe unter „Schaffuß~"
Riffel~
Rillen~
Schaffuß~

ALBARET-~, Fabrikat ALBARET, RANTIGNY (OISE), FRANKREICH
~ mit zapfenförmigen Stacheln *mpl*
Schaffuß *m*, Walzen-Stempel *m*
zylindrischer Walzkörper *m*
Doppelzylinder-~ mit gelenkiger Verbindung *f*
Riesen~, Riesenstampf~
in Mehrfachanordnung *f* gezogen
in Einfachanordnung *f* gezogen

CEDARAPIDS COMPACTOR [*Trademark*]
   power unit
   vibrator
   weight box
   coil spring
   pneumatic tire
   vibrating speed
   directional depth penetration

   escaping air and moisture

   pass
~ with movable shoes fixed to the wheels
hand-guided motor ~, power driven single-wheel(ed) ~

ballast type hand ~
fixed weight type hand ~
water ballast hand ~
rear roll, rear roller wheel

light duty power ~

power-driven ~, self-propelled ~

grass ~, lawn ~
tracked ~ [*a tractor with smooth closely-fitting track plates*]
supercompactor

indented ~
disc ~, disk ~
sheeps-foot ~, tamper (~), (sheeps-foot) tamping ~
TOURNEPIEDS [*Trademark*]

peg-foot ~
projecting foot, tamping foot
cylindrical drum
two-unit roll with the units connected together with a pivoting link
giant weight tamper
towed by tractor in multiples
towed by tractor singly

in einer Linie gezogen	towed in line
versetzt gezogen	towed offset
(Schaf)Klumpfuß~	club-foot (type sheepsfoot) ~
(Schaf)Stockfuß~, Igel~, Stachel~, ~ mit konischen Stacheln *mpl*	spiked ~, taper(ed)-foot (type sheepsfoot) ~, pyramid feet ~
Schlepp~, Anhänge~	tractor-drawn ~, towed-type ~
Schieben *n*	shoving
schwere einachsige Gummirad ~	heavy compactor
Schwing(ungs)~, siehe: Vibrations~	
Sportplatztandem~	sports ground type tandem ~
Sportplatz~	sportsfield ~
Stachel~; siehe unter „Schaffuß~"	
Stahlmantel~	steel-faced ~, steel-wheel ~
Stampf~	tamping ~, tamper
statische ~, siehe: Glatt~	
Stockfuß~; siehe unter „Schaffuß~"	
Straßen~	road ~
Tandem~	tandem ~
Verdichtungs~, Bodenverfestigungs~	compaction ~, compactor
schwere ~	heavy-duty ~
Vibrations~, Schwing(ungs)~, Vibrier~, Rüttel~	vibrating ~, vibratory ~
handgeführte kraftbewegte (oder selbstfahrende) ~	hand-guided power-propelled ~ ~
handgezogene ~, von Hand verfahrbare ~	hand-propelled ~ ~
Schlepp~, Anhänge~	trailer (type) ~ ~
Vibrationstandem~ selbstfahrend, selbstfahrende Tandem-Schwing(ungs)~ (oder Tandem-Vibrations~)	self-propelled vibratory tandem ~
Vorder~, Vorderwalzrad *n*	front roll, ~ roller wheel
Waffel~	segmented roll, island roller
Walzbreite *f*	rolling width
Walzenführer *m*, Walzenfahrer *m*, Walzenbediener *m*	rollerman, roller operator
Walze mit gummibereiften Hinterrädern *npl*	portable ~
Walzgrund *m*	surface to be rolled
Walzkompression *f*, Walzverdichtung *f*	compaction by rolling
Walzrad *n*, Walzenzylinder *m*	roller wheel
Wasserballast *m*	water ballast
Wege~	path ~
Wendekreis *m*	turning circel
Zweiachs-(Tandem)~	two axle (tandem) ~
Zweirad-Graben~	dual-compression trench ~

Walzen|ring(mahl)mühle *f*; siehe unter „Mühle"

~(stau)wehr *n*, Walzenverschluß *m* = roller (or rolling) gate (or sluice)

Walz|sand *m* = blinding sand

~schottergußasphalt *m*, (deutsche) Asphalteingußdecke *f* [*früher: Vorwohlitdecke*] = rolled asphaltic macadam

Walz|stahl *m* = rolled steel
~stahl-Schweißkonstruktion *f* = all-welded rolled steel construction
~träger *m* = rolled steel joist (abbrev. RSJ)
~werk *n* = rolling mill

Walzwerk *n*, **Brech~** [*in der Hartzerkleinerungsindustrie Sammelbegriff für Walzenbrecher mpl und Walzen(mahl)mühlen fpl*]

tertiary crusher with rolls [*strictly speaking, the tertiary crusher is the machine used in the third stage of crushing. Often, in large scale operation, the cone crusher is used in this manner. Before the advent of the cone crusher, however, the crushing rolls enjoyed a near monopoly as a tertiary crusher*]

Anpaßfeder *f*, Pufferfeder	compression spring
Beilageeisen *n*	shim
bewegliche Walze *f*	moveable roll
Brechring *m*	(crushing) roll segment
Brechwalze *f*	crushing roll
(Brech)Walzenmantel *m*	(crushing) roll shell
(Brech)Walzenschleifapparat *m*	(crushing) roll grinder
Dreiwalzenbrecher *m*	triple roll crusher
Eisenstücke *npl*	tramp iron
Fremdmaterial *n*	uncrushable material
geriefelte (Brech)Walze *f*	corrugated (crushing) roll
Glattwalzenbrecher *m*	smooth-shell crushing rolls
Körnung *f* des Fertiggutes *n*	product size, size of product
Lagerdruck *m*	thrust of bearing
Manganhartstahl *m*	manganese steel
Manteloberfläche *f*	shell face
Nabe *f*	core
Pufferfeder *f*, siehe: Anpaßfeder	
Pyramidenwalzenbrecher *m*	pyramidal-toothed crushing rolls
Sandwalzenbrecher *m*	crushing rolls for sand production
Spaltweite *f* zwischen den beiden Walzen, Walzenabstand *m*	setting between rolls, feed opening, roll feed
Splittwalzenbrecher *m*	crushing rolls for chippings production
Stahltrommel *f*	steel drum
Stellschraube *f*	adjusting screw
Walzenabstreifer *m*	roll scraper
Walzenbrecher *m* mit Brechplatte *f* und Brechwalze *f*	single roll crusher
Walzenbrecher *m* mit zwei Brechwalzen *fpl*, Zweiwalzenbrecher	crushing rolls, (double) roll crusher, twin roll crusher
Walzen(mahl)mühle *f*	roll(er) (grinding) mill, roll grinder
Zweiwalzenbrecher *m*, siehe: Walzenbrecher *m* mit zwei Brechwalzen *fpl*	

Wand *f* [*Hochbaggerung f*] = face
wandartiger Träger *m* = diaphragm beam
Wandbauplatte *f*, siehe: Wandplatte
Wander|rost *m* = travel(l)ing grate, chain ~
~schalung *f* = travel(l)ing form-(work)
~-Stangen(transport)rost *m*, Wander-Stangenaufgeber *m* = travel(l)ing grizzly feeder, **~-bar** grizzly [*lateral instead of longitudinal bars are used*]

Wanderwelle *f* = travel(l)ing wave

Wand|faserplatte *f* = wallboard

~flächenheizung *f* = wall panel heating

~keramikplatte *f*, keramische Wandfliese *f* = wall tile

~kran *m*, Konsolkran *m* = wall crane

~pfeiler *m* = pilaster

~platte *f*, Wandtafel *f*, Wandelement *n*, Wandbauplatte = wall panel

~putz *m*, Mauergips *m* = wall plaster

~schale *f* = wall shell

~schalung *f* = wall form (work)

~tafel *f*, Wandelement *n*, Wandplatte *f*, Wandbauplatte = wall panel

~verkleidung *f* = wall facing

Wanne *f* [*Maschine f*] = sump

~ *f* = sag [*1. a small valley between ranges of low hills; 2. the hollow or depression formed by the junction of two falling gradients*]

~ *f*, isolierte **~** [*Gebäude n*] = tanking (Brit.) [*refers to all basement construction which is made completely waterproof with asphalt below ground level*]

Wannenausrundung *f* = sag curve, concave transition between gradients

Warenhaus *n*, Kaufhaus *n* = department store

Wärme|abgabe *f* = release of heat

~aufbereitung *f* = pyro-processing

~(aus)dehn(ungs)zahl *f* [*Beton m*] = coefficient of thermal expansion

~(aus)tauscher *m* = heat exchanger

~dämmschicht *f* = heat insulating layer (or course)

~dämmung *f*, Wärmeisolierung *f* = thermal insulation, heat **~**

Warmeinbau *m* [*Straßenbau m*] = warm laying

Wärme|leitfähigkeit *f* = thermal conductivity

~pumpe *f* = heat pump

~schlange *f*, siehe: Heizschlange

~spannungsriß *m* = thermo-fracture

~speicherung *f* = thermal storage

~stoßfestigkeit *f* = thermal shock resistance, **~ ~** behavio(u)r

~strahlungsfühler *m* = heat radiation sensing device

~träger *m*, Wärmeübertragungsmittel *n* = heat transfer medium

~übertragungsmittel *n*, Wärmeträger *m* = heat-transfer medium

~umlauf *m* = heat circulation

~umwandlung *f*, Wärmeumprägung *f*, Wärmemetamorphose *f* (Geol.) = thermal metamorphism

~zufuhr *f* = heat input

warmfester Stahl *m* = high-temperature steel

Warmluftgerät *n*, Lufterhitzer *m* = (air) heater, space **~**

Warmluftheizung *f* = warm-air heating

Warn|hupe *f* = alarm horn

~lampe *f* = warning lamp

~posten *m*, Winkerposten [*Straße f*] = signal man, flagman

~signal *n* = warning signal, alarm **~**

~vorrichtung *f* = warning device

Wartezeit *f* = waiting time

Wartung *f*, laufende Unterhaltung *f*, laufende Instandhaltung *f* = routine maintenance (or upkeep)

Wartungs|anleitung *f* = maintenance guide

~auftrag *m* = term contract for maintenance

Warve *f* = varve

Wasch|benzin *n* mit Siedegrenze *f* zwischen 100 und 200° C = cleaners' naphtha, **~** solvent

~gut *n* = material to be washed

~schnecke *f*, siehe: Sandschnecke

~sieb *n* = rinsing screen

~trog *n*, siehe: Trog

~trommel *f*, Trommelwäsche *f* [*im Gegenstromprinzip n*] = classifying drum, washing **~**

Wasser|absatzboden *m*, siehe: Schwemm-(land)boden *m*

~absonderung *f*, siehe: Wasserabstoßen *n*

~abstoßen *n*, Bluten *n*, Wasserabsonderung *f* [*Beton m*] = bleeding, sweating, water gain

wasserabweisendes Mittel *n*, Dichtungsmittel *n*, Sperrzusatz *m* = water-repellent, water-repelling agent, waterproofer, concrete waterproofing compound

Wasser|abweisung f = water repellency
~affinität f = affinity (or liking) for water
~andrang m, siehe: Wassereinbruch m
~ansammlung f [z. B. auf dem Planum n] = lodgment of water [e. g. on the subgrade]
~aufnahmevermögen n, Wasseraufnahmefähigkeit f [Boden m] = absorptive capacity for water
~auftrieb m = water buoyancy
~ausscheidungsschnecke f, siehe: Sandentwässerungsschnecke
~bad n = water bath
~bad-Druckprüfverfahren n, Wasserlagerungs-Druckfestigkeitsprüfung f = immersioncompression test
~bassin n = water basin
Wasserbau m = hydraulic (or water) engineering (or construction, or works)
   Flußbau m = river construction
   Kanalbau m = canal construction
   Schleusenbau m = lock construction
   Hafenbau m = harbo(u)r construction
   Seebau m = marine construction
   Wasserbauwerk n = hydraulic structure
wasserbauliche Forschungsarbeiten fpl = hydraulic investigations
wasserbeständig = water-resistant, waterproof
Wasser|bindner m, siehe: Silikatbildner m
~brunnen m = water well
~dosierungsapparat m; siehe unter „Betonmischer m"
~druckpresse f [Betonwürfelprüfung f] = hydraulic press
~durchlässigkeit f = permeability
~durchleitungsrecht n = water-piping right
~einbruch m, Wasserzutritt m, Wasserandrang m = ingress of water, inflow ~ ~, in-rush ~ ~
(~)Einstau m; siehe unter „Talsperre f"
~entziehung f, De-Hydrierung f = dehydration
~erosion f, Schurf m (des Wassers) = erosion by water action, geological erosion by stream action
~fall m = waterfall

~fassung f; siehe unter „Talsperre f"
~film m, Wasserhäutchen n = water film, moisture ~
~flughafen m = flying boat base
~flugzeug n = float plane
~flutverfahren n [Ölausbeute f] = water flood method [oil recovery]
wasser|frei, siehe: anhydrisch
~freier Putzgips m = anhydrous gypsum plaster
~führende Bodenschicht f = water bearing soil strata, aquifer, waterbearing formation, aquafer
Wasser n **für gewerbliche Zwecke** mpl = water for industrial use
~gas n = water gas
wassergebundene Schotterdecke f, siehe: Chaussierung f
Wassergehalt m, Feuchtigkeitsgehalt [Boden m] = moisture content, water ~ [soil]
wassergesättigt, wasserdurchsetzt = waterlogged
Wassergewinnung f = water winning
Wasserglas n = water glass, soluble ~
~decke f, siehe: Silikatdecke
wasserhaltiges borsaures Natrium n, $Na_2B_2O_4 \times 10H_2O$ = hydrated sodium borate
~ Magnesia-Tonerde-Silikat n = hydrous iron-magnesium alumin(i)um silicate
~ Mg-Silikat n, siehe: Magnesiumhydrosilikat n
Wasser|haltung f = dewatering, unwatering
~haltungsgeräte npl = de-watering (or unwatering) gears (Brit.); ~ (~ ~) equipment
~haushalt m, Wasserwirtschaft f = water resources
~häutchen n, Wasserfilm m = water film, moisture ~
wasserhelles Hydrier-Leuchtöl n = water white high-grade burning oil
(Wasser) Hochbehälter m = elevated (water) tank, overhead cistern, tower tank
Wasser-in-Öl-Emulsion f, siehe: Kaltasphalt m
Wasserklosett n = WC
Wasserkraft f = hydro power

Wasserkraftanlage — Wasserreinigung

Wasserkraft|anlage f = hydro project
~-Ausbauplan m, **Wasserkraftbauprogramm** n = hydroelectric scheme
~bau m = hydroelectric construction
~kanal m = power canal
~maschine f = hydraulic engine
~nutzung f = utilisation of water power, hydroelectric exploitation
~politik f = hydro policy
(Wasser)|Kraftstollen m, Betriebswasserstollen, Druck(wasser)stollen, Triebwasserstollen, Zulaufstollen [*Stollen. der im planmäßigen Betrieb voll und unter Scheiteldruck läuft*] = power tunnel, hydro tunnel, hydro tube, pressure tunnel, tunnel-type penstock, conversion tunnel, pressure gallery

~kraft-Talsperre f = hydroelectric dam
~kraftwerk n = hydroelectric (power) plant (or work), hydroelectric station
~lauf m = water course
~leitung f, Wasserrohrleitung = water (pipe) line
~ (leitungs)rohr n = waterpipe
wasser|liebend = hydrophibic, waterloving
~lösliches Öl n = emulsifiable oil
Wassermartel m [*Motor m mit Wasserkühlung f*] = water jacket
wassermeidend = hydrophobic, waterhating
Wasser|mörtel m = hydraulic lime mortar
~pore f [*Beton m*] = water void
~recht n = water rights, ~ law

Wasserreinigung f, **Wasseraufbereitung**

Absetzklärung f nach der Behandlung mit Flockungsmitteln npl

Absetzklärung ohne Flockungsmittel
  Schwebestoffe mpl
  Absetzbecken n für kontinuierlichen Betrieb m
  Absetzbecken für aussetzenden Betrieb
  Aufenthaltsdauer f, Durchflußdauer
  Trübe f
  Schlamm m
Algenbekämpfung f
Algenbekämpfungsmittel n
Belüftung f
Beseitigung f übler Geruchs- und Geschmackstoffe mpl
Brackwasseraufbereitung f
Enteisenung f
Entgasung f
  thermischer Entgaser m
  Rieseler m

  Kohlensäure f

Enthärtung f
  Säureimpfung f
  Kalk-Soda-Verfahren n
  Kalkenthärtung f
  Zeolithe npl

water treatment, ~ conditioning, ~ purification

sedimentation [*the process of clarifying water by settling after coagulation by chemical treatment*]

plain sedimentation, ~ subsidence
  suspended matter, ~ solids
  continuous settling basin, ~ subsidence tank
  intermittent settling basin, ~ subsidence tank
  detention period, retention ~
  turbidity
  sludge
algae control, removal of algae
algaecide
aeration
taste and odour removal, ~ ~ ~ control

brackish water conversion
iron removal
deaeration, degassing, degasification
  deaerator, deaerating heater
  tray-type degasifier, spray-type degasifier
  carbonic acid, H_2CO_3, carbon dioxide, CO_2
softening
  acid treatment, ~ injection
  lime soda (softening) process
  lime softening process
  zeolites

Wasserreinigung

Basenaustausch *m*	base exchange, zeolite process
Kesselspeisewasser *n*	boiler feedwater
Entkeimung *f*	disinfection, sterilization
Abkochen *n*	heating
Chlorung *f*	chlorination
direkte Chlorung *f*	gas chlorination
indirekte Chlorung *f*	solution feed chlorination
Hochchlorung *f*	superchlorination
Knickpunktchlorung *f*	break-point chlorination
starker Chlorüberschuß *m*	excessive chlorine residual
Entchlorung *f*	dechlorination
Aktivkohle *f*	active carbon
Oxydationsmittel *n*	oxidizing agent
Chloramin *n*	chloramine
Ultraviolett-Bestrahlung *f*	UV-ray treatment
Entmanganung *f*	manganese removal
Manganbakterien *fpl*	manganese bacteria
Entsäuerung *f*	neutralization, pH-control
Filterung *f*, Filtration *f*	filtration
Langsamfilterung, biologische Filterung	slow sand filtration
Langsamfilter *n*, *m*	slow sand filter
Schnellfilterung, mechanische Filterung	rapid sand filtration
Schnellfilter *n*, *m*	rapid sand filter
geschlossenes Schnellfilter *n*, Druckfilter	pressure filter
Filterspülung *f*	filter backwash
Flockung *f*, Fällung *f*	flocculation, precipitation, coagulation
pH-Wert *m*	pH-value
Flockungsmittel *n*, Fällmittel	coagulant, floccculant
Aluminiumsulfat *n*	(filter) alum, aluminium sulphate
Eisen-II-sulfat *n*	ferrous sulphate
Eisen-III-sulfat *n*	ferric sulphate
Eisenchlorid *n*	ferric chloride
Natriumaluminat *n*	sodium aluminate
Trockendosierung *f*	dry chemical feeding
Flüssigdosierung *f*	solution feeding, liquid chemical feeding
Vermischung *f*	mixing
Wassersprung *m*	hydraulic jump, stationary wave
Flockenbildung *f*	floc formation, flocculation
Kaliumpermanganat *n*	potassium permanganate
Kleinlebewesen *n*	micro-organism
Meereswasseraufbereitung *f*	sea water conversion
Reinwasserbehälter *m*	clear water basin, ~ ~ tank, clear well
Speicherung *f*	storage
Verbrauchsschwankung *f*	fluctuation in demand
Vollentsalzung *f*	demineralization, deionization
Ionenaustausch *m*	ion exchange
Austauschharz *n*	exchange resin

Kationenaustausch *m* — cation exchange
Anionenaustausch *m* — anion exchange
Mischbettaustauschfilter *n, m* — mixed bed exchange unit
Entkieselung *f* — silica removal

Wasser|rohr *n*, Haupt~ = water main casing
~**(rohr)leitung** *f* = water (pipe) line
~**rückhaltevermögen** *n* = water retentivity
~**sackrohr** *n* [*Manometer n*] = siphon
Wassersäulen|höhe *f*, Wassersäule *f*, Druckhöhe, Druckgefälle *n* = (water) head, pressure ~
~**maschine** *f* = water pressure engine
Wasser|scheide *f* = watershed line, (drainage) divide
~**schlag** *m* = water hammer, ~ ram
~**schloß** *n*; siehe unter „Talsperre *f*"
~**schloßschacht** *m*; siehe unter „Talsperre *f*"
~**schöpfwindmühle** *f* = water pump wind mill
~**speicherung** *f*; siehe unter „Talsperre *f*"
~**spiegelschwankung** *f* = variation in water level
~**sprengwagen** *m* = water spraying cart (or wagon)
~**sprung** *m* = hydraulic jump, stationary wave
~**standglas** *n* = water ga(u)ge glass, graduated glass ga(u)ge-tube
~**standsmarke** *f*, Pegel *m* = water mark, ~ post
~**standswechsel** *m* = water level variation
~**stoffionenkonzentration** *f*, siehe: pH-Wert *m*
~**stoffsuperoxydanlage** *f* = hydrogen peroxide plant
~**stoffzahl H** *f*, siehe: pH-Wert *m*
~**strahlpumpe** *f* = waterjet injector
~**strahlverfahren** *n*, Einspülverfahren *n* = sluicing
~**straße** *f* = waterway, water road; barge line (US)
~**straßenbauamt** *n* = river catchment board
~**straßennetz** *n* = waterway system
~**tiefe** *f* **des Fahrwassers** *n*, nutzbare Fahrtiefe = depth of the navigable channel

~**turbine** *f* = water turbine
~**turm** *m* = water tower
~**umlenkung** *f*; siehe unter „Talsperre *f*"
~**uhr** *f*; siehe unter „Betonmischer *m*"
wasserundurchlässige Zone *f* = impervious zone, water barrier
Wasser|undurchlässigkeit *f* = imperviousness to water, impermeability ~ ~, watertightness
~**vernebelung** *f* = atomized water spray
~**versorgung** *f* = water supply
~**versorgungsanlage** *f* = water supply plant, ~ ~ installation
~**versorgungsleitung** *f* = water supplyline
~**waage** *f*, Libelle *f* = (water) level, spirit ~, air ~, hand ~ ~
~**wagen** *m* = water cart (or wagon)
~**wirtschaftspolitik** *f* = water resources policy
~**zähler** *m* = water meter
~**zähler** *m*; siehe unter „Betonmischer *m*"
~**zapfbrunnen** *m*, Hydrantbrunnen = hydrant well (Brit.); combination hydrant and fountain (US)
~**-Zement-Faktor** *m*, Wasser-Zementwert *m* [*Wassergewicht geteilt durch Zementgewicht einer Betonmischung*] = water-cement ratio
~**zutritt** *m*, siehe: Wassereinbruch *m*
wäßrige Lösung *f* = aqueous solution
Wattenmeer *n* = shallow water
Wattgebiet *n* = splash zone
Wattstunde *f* = watt-hour
WC-Becken *n* = pottery closet
Weberknoten *m* = sheet bend
Wechsel *m*, Überschiebung *f* (Geol.) = overthrust fault
~**balken** *m* = trimmer (beam), trimmed joist
~**beanspruchung** *f* = alternating stress
~**beziehung** *f* = correlation
~**feldeinbau** *m*, Herstellung *f* benachbarter Plattenfelder *npl* in zeitlichem Abstand *m* [*Deckenbeton m*] = alternate (concrete) bay construction, ~ bay method

Wechselfestigkeit — Weißbuche

Wechsel|festigkeit *f*, Thixotropie *f* = thixotropy
~lüftung *f*; siehe unter „Tunnelbau *m*"
~spannung *f* = alternating stress
~sparren *m* = valley jack rafter
~stab *m* [*Fachwerk n*] = counter diagonal
~stromerzeuger *m* = alternating-current generator
~(verkehrs)spur *f* = reversible (traffic) lane
Wegbenutzungsrecht *n*, siehe: Wegerecht
Wege|hobel *m*, siehe: Straßenhobel *m*
~meister *m*, siehe: Straßenmeister *m*
~recht *n*, Wegbenutzungsrecht = right-of-way
~recht *n* (oder Wegbenutzungsrecht) **mit Erlaubnis zum Legen von Rohr- und Kabelleitungen** *fpl* = wayleave
Wegräumen *n* = clearing away
Wegspülung *f*, siehe: Auskolkung *f*
Wegweiser *m* = direction post, supplementary direction sign, guide ~; [*deprecated: direction sign, sign-post, finger post*]

Wehr, Stau~ *n*	weir, barrage
festes ~	fixed weir
wasserdurchlässiges ~	permeable weir
massives ~	impermeable weir
aufgelöstes ~	plate weir
gerades ~	rectangular weir
Überlauf~	overflow weir, overfall weir, spillway weir, crest control weir, waste weir
Heber~	siphon(ic) weir
bewegliches ~	movable weir
Hub~, Hubschütz(e) *n*, (*f*)	(vertical) lift gate (or sluice)
Nadel~	needle weir, pin weir
Sektor~	sector weir
Klappen~	shutter weir
Wehrverschluß *m*, Wehr *n*	(weir) gate, penning gate, stop gate, floodgate
überfallender Strahl *m*	nappe
freier überfallender Strahl *m*	free nappe
Schützen~	sluice weir
Walzen~, Walzenverschluß *m*	rolling gate weir (or sluice), roller gate weir (or sluice)
Wehrschwelle *f*	weir sill
Wehrpfeiler *m*	weir pier

Weichasphalt *m* (Geol.) = soft asphalt
weicher Kalkstein *m* = soft limestone
~ machen [*Beton m*] = to butter
Weich|gestein *n* = soft stone
~gummilager *n* = soft rubber bearing
~holz *n*, Nadelholz = softwood, pinewood, coniferous wood, resinous wood
~lot *n* = soft-solder
~löten *n* = soldering
~macher *m*, siehe: Betonverflüssiger *m*
~manganerz *n* (Min.), siehe: Braunstein *m*
weichplastisch = soft-plastic
Weichpreßziegel *m*, Weichschlammziegel = soft-mud brick
Weideland *n* = grazing ground, pasture land
Weiden|geflecht *n* = willow packing
~steckling *m* = withy
Weiher *m*, Teich *m* = pond
Weinfaß *n* = wine barrel
Weinhold-Gefäß *n*, siehe: Dewargefäß
Weiß|birke *f*, Maie *f* = common birch
~bleierz *n* (Min.), siehe: Bleispat *m*
~buche *f*, Hainbuche *f*, Hagebuche *f*, Hornbaum *m* = white beech, hornbeam

weißen — Wendung

weißen, tünchen, kalken = to limewash, to whitewash

weißer Bol(us) *m*, weiße Boluserde *f* = potters' clay, ball ~

Weiß|erde *f*, siehe: Porzellanton *m*

~erle *f*, Grauerle *f* = Turkey alder, upland ~

weißer Mauerstein *m*, siehe: Kalksandstein

weißes Straußgras *n*, Fioringras = bent grass, florin ~, redtop ~

Weiß|kalk *m*, Fettkalk *m* = high-calcium lime, white ~, rich ~, fat ~, pure ~, plastic high-calcium hydrated ~

~kiefer *f*, gemeine Kiefer *f*, Föhre *f*, Fuhre *f*, Kiene *f*, Forle *f* = Scottish pine, white ~, common ~

~klee *m* = white clover, Dutch ~

~nickelkies *m*, Chloanthit *m* (Min.) = c(h)loanthite, white nickel

~ofen *m* = refining furnace

~pappel *f*, Silberpappel *f* = white poplar, ~ populus, abele

weißrandiger Reifen *m*, Weißwand-Reifen = white-wall tire (US)/tyre (Brit.)

Weiß|tanne *f*, Edeltanne *f* = European silver fir

~weide *f*, Silberweide *f* = Huntingdon willow, white ~

weitervergeben [*Bauauftrag m*] = to sub(let), to subcontract, to sub out to

Weizenstroh *n* = wheat straw

Well|asbestzementplatte *f* = corrugated asbestos cement sheet

~baum *m*, Bockwinde *f* = crab, hand ~

~blech *n* = corrugated sheet iron

~blechrohr *n* = corrugated metal pipe

Welle *f* [*Schwertwäsche f*] = log [*log washer*]
~ = shaft

Wellen|auflauf *m* = wave run-up

~berg *m*, Wellenkamm *m* = wave crest

~bildung *f* [*Erdstraße f*] = formation of washboard waves, corrugations, washboarding, corduroy effect; [*deprecated: road waves, deformations, creep*]

~brecher *m* [*Wellenangriff m auf nur einer Seite f*] = bulwark

---

Wellenbrecher *m*	**breakwater**
composite ~
massiver ~ mit Unterbau *m* aus Steinschüttung *f*
~ aus Steinschüttung *f*	(rubble) mound ~
massiver ~	vertical sided ~, wall ~

Wellen|düne *f* = shore dune [*deposition by sea waves*]

~fortpflanzung *f* = wave propagation

~furche *f*, Rippel(marke) *f* = ripple marking

~höhe *f* = wave height

~kalk *m*, Schaumkalk *m* = aragonitic lime(stone)

~kamm *m*, siehe: Wellenberg *m*

~krafttheorie *f* **nach Sainflou** = Sainflou theory (for forces on breakwaters)

~kupplung *f* [*Sammelbegriff*] = coupling

~tal *n* = wave trough

~zapfen *m* = shaft journal

~zug *m* = wave train

Welligkeit *f* = waviness

Wellrohrbogen *m* = corrugated pipe bend

Weltraumrakete *f* = space-rocket

Wende|getriebe *n*, siehe: Reversiergetriebe

~halbmesser *m*, Wenderadius *m* = turning radius

~kreis *m* = turning circle

~kupplung *f* = reverse clutch

Wendel|förderer *m* = vertical magnetic transporter, vibratory spiral elevator

~rollenbahn *f* = roller-fitted spiral (gravity) shoot

~rutsche *f* = helical shoot, spiral (gravity) shoot

~treppe *f*, gewendelte Treppe = helical staircase, helicoidal ~, spiral ~

Wende|platz *m* = turn-around (area)

~radius *m*, siehe: Wendehalbmesser *m*

~schaltkupplung *f*, Reversierschaltkupplung, Umkehrschaltkupplung = reversing clutch (coupling)

~spur *f* = turning path

Wendung *f* = turn

Werft — Widerstandsmoment

Werft *f*, Schiffs~ = dockyard, shipbuilding yard
~**kran** *m* = shipbuilding crane
Werg *n* = oakum
Werk|bank *f* = bench
~**besichtigung** *f* = works visit
~**gelände** *n*, Fabrikgelände = factory ground
~**halle** *f*, siehe: Werkstatthalle
~**kanal** *m*, Werkgraben *m* [*Laufkraftwerk n*] = race
~**stättenausrüstung** *f* = (work)shop equipment
Werkstatt|fertigung *f* = (work)shop manufacture
~**halle** *f*, Werkhalle = (work)shop hangar
~**kran** *m* = (work)shop crane
~**montage** *f* = (work)shop assembly
~**niet** *m* = shop rivet, workshop ~
~**stoß** *m* [*Stahlbau m*] = (work)shop connection
~**wagen** *m* = on-the-job service unit, field service ~
~**zeichnung** *f* = (work)shop drawing
Werkstein *m*, Quader(stein), Naturwerkstein = ashlar, dimension stone, cut stone
~**mauerwerk** *n*, Quader(stein)mauerwerk = ashlar stone walling, ~ stone work
~**verblender** *m* = facing stone
Werks-Transportwagen *m* = plant truck
~**-Kosten** *f* = plant truck operating costs
Werksversuch *m* = (work)shop experiment
Werkzeug|halter *m* = tool holder
~**kasten** *m*, Werkzeugkiste *f* = tool box, ~ chest, ~ kit
~**schrank** *m* = tool cabinet
~**stahl** *m* = tool steel
Wertgegenstand *m* = article of value
wesentlicher Gemengteil *m* = essential mineral
westerwoldisches Raigras *n* = Western Woldicum
Wettbewerbsfähigkeit *f* = competitive position
Wetter *f*, Grubenluft *f* = mine air
~ *n* = weather
~**fahne** *f* = weather vane [*spire*]
~**festigkeit** *f*, Witterungsbeständigkeit = resistance to the action of weather, weather-resistance, weather-proofness
~**leuchten** *n* = summer lightning
~**schacht** *m*, siehe: Entlüftungsschacht *m*
~**seite** *f* = weather side
~**station** *f*, Wetterwarte *f* = weather station, meteorological ~
Weymouthkiefer *f*, Strobe *f* = Weymouth pine, American yellow ~
Wichte *f* = weights
Wickelmaschine *f*, Behälter~ = (tank) winding machine

Widerlager *n*
aufgelöstes ~
blindes ~
geschlossenes ~
abgetrepptes ~
vorspringendes ~
verlorenes ~, unterdrücktes ~
pfahlfundiertes ~
~**kissen** *n*
~**pfeiler** *m*

abutment
hollow ~
blind ~
closed ~
stepped ~
projecting ~
dead ~
pile-supported ~
~ pad
~ pier

Widerstands|beiwert *m* = coefficient of resistance
~**fähigkeit** *f*, siehe: Widerstandsvermögen *n*
~**messungsverfahren** *n*; siehe unter „geophysikalische Baugrunduntersuchung *f*"
~**moment** *n* [*Statik f*] = section modulus, ~ factor

Widerstands|schaltung f = resistive circuit
~schweißung f = resistance welding
~thermometer n = resistance thermometer
~vermögen n, Widerstandsfähigkeit f = capacity of resistance
~vermögen n **gegen Abschleifen** n, Abriebfestigkeit f = abrasion resistance
Wieder|aufbau m = reconstruction
~belastung f, Wiederbelasten n = recharge
~gewinnung f, Rückgewinnung = recovery
~herstellung(sarbeiten) f = remedial works, reconstruction (~), reconditioning
~verwendung f = re-use
~verwendungsmöglichkeit f = reusability
Wiege|balken m = weigh beam
~behälter m, Wiegegefäß n = weighing bucket, weigh box, batcher hopper, weigh(ing) hopper, scale hopper
~gleis n = scale track
~latte f, Richtlatte, Setzlatte, Richtscheit n, Ebner m = straight edge
~meister m = scale master
~schein m = weigh bill
~skala f = weighing dial
~trichter m, siehe: Dosierwaage f
Wiener Kalk m = Vienna lime
Wiesen|beil n = hand turf cutter (or stripper)
~fuchsschwanz m = meadow foxtail
~lieschgras n = cat's tail, timothy
~rispe(ngras) f, (n) = (Kentucky) bluegrass (US); great poa (Brit.); smooth-stalked meadow grass
~schwingel m = meadow fescue, English blue grass
Wildbach m = (mountain) torrent
~verbauung f = control of torrents works
Wildbett n = natural bed
wilde Risse mpl = uncontrolled cracks
„Wildwechsel" m = "Beware of Dear"
Wind|absatzboden m, windtransportierter Boden m = aeolian soil, (wind-)blown ~, wind-borne ~
~abtragung f, siehe: Deflation f
~belastung f, Windlast f = wind load

~druck m = wind pressure
~düne f, Festlandsdüne, Inlandsdüne, Binnendüne = inland dune [deposition by wind]
Winde f, mechanische ~ = winch
~, Hebebock m = jack
Winden|aufzug m = winch hoist
~trommel f = winch drum
Wind|erosion f (Geol.) = (geological) erosion by wind action
~fahne f = wind vane
~geschwindigkeit f = velocity of wind
~hose f = wind spout
~kanal m = wind tunnel
~kessel m, siehe: Druckluftbehälter m
~kluft f [Holz n] = wind crack
~kraftmaschine f = wind power machine
~lampe f = hurricane lamp
~messer m, Anemometer n, Windstärkemesser m = anemometer, wind ga(u)ge
~rispe f, Strebeschwarte f, Schwibbe f = sprocket
~sack m = wind cone, ~ sock, sleeve
~schatten m = wind shield
windschief = twisted
Wind|schutzplane f = windbreak
~schutzscheibe f = windshield
~sedimentgestein n, aeolisches Sedimentgestein = wind-borne deposit, ~ sediment
~sichtung f, Setzungsklassierung f durch Luft = air classification
~stärke f = intensity of wind
~stärkemesser m, siehe: Windmesser
~stille f = calm
~strebe f = wind brace
~strebengurtung f = wind braced boom
~träger m = wind brace
Windung f = loop
Wind|verband m = cross bracing, transverse ~, lateral ~, wind ~
~verbandsstab m = lateral (member) [bridge]
~welle f = wind wave
~werk n, siehe: Seilwinde f
~werkstrommel f = hoisting gear drum
Winkelaufreiber m = angle reamer
Winkel m **der inneren Reibung** f, siehe: Reibungswinkel m

Winkel|eisenpfosten m = angle iron standard

(~) Greifer m [*Gleiskette f*] = grouser

Winkeligkeit f, **Kantigkeit, Eckförmigkeit** = angularity

Winkel|messer m = circular protractor

~**prisma** n = optical square

~**profil** n = angle section

~**schalung** f = L-shaped forms

~**stahl** m = angle-iron

~**stahlrahmen** m = angle iron frame

~**stahlschere** f = angle iron shears

~**stützmauer** f = angular retaining wall

~**verlaschung** f = angle butt strap

~**wulststahl** m = bulb angle iron

Winker m [*Fahrzeug n*] = direction indicator

~**posten** m, siehe: Warnposten

Wintereiche f, siehe: Früheiche f

winterkalte Wüste f = cold desert

Winter|linde f, **kleinblättrige Linde** f = small-leaved lime-tree

~**zelt** n = winterized tent

Wippdrehkran m = level-luffing crane

Wippe f, siehe: Faschinenwippe f

Wippkran m = level-luffing crane

Wirbel|haken m = swivel hook

~**mischer** m = impeller

~**stromkupplung** f = eddy current coupling

~**wind** m = eddy wind, whirlwind

wirkliche Korngröße f = effective grain (or particle) size

wirklichkeitsgetreu = on a lifelike basis

Wirkungsgrad m = efficiency degree

wirtschaftlich = economical

Wirtschaftlichkeit f = economy

Wirtschaftlichkeitsberechnung f = economy calculation

Wirtschafts|gebiet n **einer großen Stadt** f, **Großraumgebiet** n = metropolitan region, ~ area

~**minister** m = Minister for Trade and Commerce

~**weg** m = farm track

Wismut|blende f (Min.) = eulytite, bismuth blende

~**glanz** m, **Bismuthin** m, Bi_2S_3 (Min.) = bismuthinite, bismuth glance

~**nickel(kobalt)kies** m (Min.) = grunauite

~**ocker** m, **Bismit** n, Bi_2O_3 (Min.) = bismuth ochre, bismite

Witherit m (Min.) = witherite

Witterungs|beständigkeit f, **Wetterfestigkeit** = weather-resistance, weatherproofness, resistance to the action of weather

~**einfluß** m = climatic effect, effect of climatic conditions, atmospheric action

Wöhler-Linie f = Wöhler curve

Wohlstand m = financial health

Wohn|baracke f = living hut

~**dichte** f = living density

~**gebiet** n = residential area

~**haus** n = dwelling house

~**hochhaus** n = block of flats, apartment block

~**straße** f = local street

Wohnung f = apartment

Wohnungsbau m = residential construction (or housing), home building

~**projekt** n = housing scheme

Wohn(ungs)raum m = housing volume

Wohn(schlaf)wagen(anhänger) m = accomodation trailer (US); sleeping caravan (Brit.); house trailer

Wölb|linie f = intrados soffit

~**stein** m, siehe: Gewölbestein m

Wölbung f, **kreisförmige Krone** f [*Straße f*] = camber, barrel ~; [*deprecated: transverse slope, crossfall*]

Wolfram n = wolfram, tungsten

Wolframit n (Min.) = wolframite

Wolke f
  Haufen~, Kumulus~
  Schicht~, Stratus~
  Feder~, Zirrus~
  Regen~, Nimbus~
  Schäfchen~, Altokumulus~

cloud
  cumulus, cloud-heap, piled cloud
  stratus (~), cloud-sheet
  cirrus cloud, mare's-tail, paint brush
  nimbus [*low, ragged and shapeless cloud*]
  altocumulus cloud

Gewitter~, Kumulonimbus~ / cumulonimbus, thunder-cloud
Schleier~, Zirrostratus~ / cirrostratus
hohe Schicht~, Altostratus~ / altostratus
Wolkenbank *f* / cloud bank
Wolkenbruch *m* / cloud burst (type storm)
Wolkenscheinwerfer *m* / ceiling projector

Wollastonit *m*, $Ca_3(Si_3O_9)$ (Min.) = wollastonite, tabular spar
Wollfett|-Olein *n* = distilled-grease olein, dégras oil
~-Stearin *n* = dégras stearin
Woll(schweiß)fett *n*, Wollwachs *n* = wool grease, ~ wax, ~ dégras
Wollwäscherei *f* = wool scouring plant
Wolmansalz *n* = Wolman salt
Wrackräumung *f* = wreck clearance
Wrasen *m*, siehe: Schwaden *m*
Wucht|förderer *m* = spring-supported shaker conveyor
Wühltier *n* = burrowing animal
Wulfenit *m*, Gelbbleierz *n*, $PbMoO_4$ (Min.) = wulfenite
Wulst|lava *f*; siehe unter „Vulkan *m*"
~stahl *m* = bulb-tee, bulb-iron
Wünschel|rute *f* = divining rod
~rutengänger *m* = dowser, waterfinder
Wurf *m* [*Sieb n*] = throw, amount of eccentricity
Würfel|erz *n*, Pharmakosiderit *m* (Min.) = pharmacosiderite
~pflasterstein *m* = cube sett
~presse *f*, siehe: Prüfpresse *f*
~siedestein *m*, siehe: Chabasit *m* (Min.)
Wurfförderrinne *f* = reciprocating trough conveyor
~ *f* mit Pendelantrieb *m*, siehe: Torpedorinne *f*
Wurfradschaufel *f* [*Schneeschleuder f*] = rotary blade
Wurfschaufellader *m*, siehe: Über-Kopf-Lader *m*
~ *m* auf Rädern *npl* = transport rocker shovel
Wurftransporteur *m*, Schleuderband *n* = jet conveyor
Würgezange *f*, Sprengkapselzange *f*, Anwürgzange = cap crimper
wurmartig (*Mineral n*) = vermicular, worm-shaped

Wurmsiedestein *m* (Min.), siehe: Skolezit *m*
Wurtzilitbitumen *n* = wurtzilite asphalt (US)/asphaltic bitumen (Brit.); ~ pitch
Wurzel|loch *n*, Wurzelgang *m* = root hole
~stockholz *n* = stump-wood
~torf *m* = fibrous peat
~- und Felsrechen *m* = land-clearing and rock rake, root and rock rake
~zieher *m*, (Baum)Stumpfzieher = stump puller
Wüstensteppe *f* = semidesert

X

xenomorph, fremdgestaltig = xenomorphic
Xenotim *m*, Ytterspat *m*, YPO_4 (Min.) = xenotime
Xylith *m*, siehe: Lignit *m*
Xylol *n* = xylene

Y

YTONG [*Trademark*] = ein kalkgebundener Gasbeton *m*, Leichtstein *m* auf Kalkbasis *f*
Ytterspat *m* (Min.), siehe: Xenotim *m*

Z

Zackenlava *f*; siehe unter „Vulkan *m*"
Zähflüssigkeit *f*, siehe: Viskosität *f*
Zähigkeit *f* [*Gestein n*], siehe: Schlagfestigkeit *f*
~ [*Gummi-Bitumen-Mischung f*] = toughness
Zahlen|tafel *f*, Tabelle *f* = table
~verhältnis *n* = numerial ratio
Zähler *m* [*Mathematik f*] = numerator
Zählposten *m* = observer, checker
Zählung *f* = count

Zählwerk — Zement

Zählwerk n = counter
Zahn|arztgips m = dental plaster
~egge f = tooth harrow
~kupplung f, siehe: Klauenkupplung
~rad-Tenderlok(omotive) f = rack tank loco(motive)
~radwinde f = toothed wheel (hand) crab
~schwelle f = dentated sill
~spitze f = tooth point
~stange f = (toothed) rack
Zahnstangen|bahn f = rack railway (Brit.); ~ railroad (US)
~winde f, Zahnstangenhebebock m = rack-and-pinion jack
Zaun|gewebe n = fence fabric
~pfahl m = fence post
Zebra-Fußgängerübergang m = striped pedestrian crossing
Zechstein m (Geol.) = Zechstein [*the higher of the two series into which the Permian System of Germany is divided. The whole of the English Permian of Durham and Yorkshire is probably of Zechstein age*]
~kalk m = Permian limestone
Zeichen|büro n = drawing office (Brit.); drafting ~ (US)
~erklärung f, Legende f = legend
~tisch m = drawing table
Zeichner m = draughtsman (Brit.); draftsman (US)
zeichnerische Ausarbeitung f, siehe: Entwurf m
Zeiger m = pointer

Zeit|abstand m = time spacing
~aufwand m = expenditure of time
~intervall n = interval of time
~lückenmethode f **nach Greenshields** = Greenshields method [*it is based on the observed "green time requirement" for a single line of passenger cars entering an intersection at minimum headways after starting from standstill*]
~nahme f = timing
~nehmer m = time-keeper
zeitraubend = time-consuming
Zeit|schreiber m = time recorder
~-Schwind-Kurve f = time/shrinkage curve
~-Senkungs-Kurve f, Zeitsetzungskurve = time-settlement curve
~spanne f = period of time, time period, time interval
zeitweilige Umleitung f, siehe: provisorische ~
Zeit|zünder m; siehe unter „1. Schießen n; 2. Sprengen n"
~zündung f; siehe unter „1. Schießen n; 2. Sprengen n"
Zellen|dolomitgestein n, siehe: Rau(c)hwacke f
~fang(e)damm m = cellular cofferdam
~silo m, Zellenspeicher m = (multi-)compartment silo
~(stau)mauer f; siehe unter „Talsperre f"
~turm m **mit Abwiegung** f = combined aggregate and cement weigh batching unit

---

Zement m [*hydraulisches Bindemittel* n]	**(hydraulic) cement, water ~, cement matrix**
Abbinden n, Abbindung f	setting (Brit.); set
Aktivitätsindex m	index of activity
Anreger m	activator
antiseptischer ~	antiseptic ~
Asbest~	asbestos ~
Bauxitland~, Kühl~	b(e)auxite ~
Betonwürfel m im Mischungsverhältnis n von 1 Gewichtsteil m Zement m auf 3 Gewichtsteile mpl Normensand m	3:1 mortar.cube
Brennen n (oder Kalzinieren n) bis mindestens zur Sinterung f	calcining to incipient fusion
brit. Zementart mit maximal 65% Hochofenschlacke f	Portland-blastfurnace ~

Zement

Druckfestigkeit *f*	compressive strength
Druckversuch *m*	compression test
Eisenerz~	iron-ore ~
Eisenportland~ [*abgek. EPZ; max. 30% Schlacke f*]	Eisen-Portland ~, iron Portland ~, German portland slag ~
Expansiv~, siehe: Quell~	
Glühverlust *m*	loss on ignition, ignition loss
Hochofen~ [*abgek. HOZ; max 85% Schlacke*]	Hochofen ~
Hütten~, siehe: Schlacken~	
Hydra(ta)tion *f*	hydration
Kalkfaktor *m*	lime factor
Knollenbildung *f*	lumpiness
Kochversuch *m*	boiling test
Kühl~, Bauxitland~	b(e)auxite ~
Mahlzusatz *m*	grinding aid
Mauerwerks~	masonry ~
Misch~, Natur~ [*in den USA werden Naturzemente durch Brennen unterhalb der Sintergrenze f gewonnen, sie sind also nach der deutschen Auffassung hydraulische Kalke*]	blended ~, natural ~
Nadelgerät *n* nach Gillmore	Gillmore needle
Naßverfahren *n*	wet process
Natur~, siehe: Misch~	
Normensand *m*	standard sand, cement testing sand
Normen~	specification ~, standard ~ ~
Natur~ [*aus Kalkmergel hergestellt*]	natural ~
Oilwell~, Erdöl~, Ölbohr~	oil well ~
Portlandzement-Puzzolangemisch *n*	Portland-pozzolan ~
Portland~ [*abgek. PZ*]	Portland ~
gewöhnlicher ~ [*in Dtschld. Z 225*]	~ ~ for general use, normal ~ ~, ordinary ~ ~; ~ ~ Type I (US)
mäßiger Gipsschlacken ~, ~ Sulfathütten~	moderate sulphate resisting ~; moderate heat of hydration ~; ~ ~ Type II (US)
hochwertiger ~, frühhochfester ~, Schnellerhärter *m* [*in Dtschl. Z 325 und Z 425*]	high early (or initial) strength ~ ~, rapid hardening ~ ~; ~ ~ Type III (US)
~ mit sehr geringer Abbindewärme *f*	low heat of hydration ~, slow hardening ~; ~ ~ Type IV (US)
starker Gipsschlacken~, ~ Sulfathütten~	high sulphate resisting ~ ~, super-sulphate cement; ~ ~ Type V (US)
Luftporen~	air-entraining ~ ~
Prisma *n*	standard briquette
Puzzolan~	pozzolan(ic) ~
Quell~, Expansiv, Schwell~	high-expansion ~, expanding ~, expansive ~
Raumbeständigkeit *f*	volume stability
Rohmischung *f*	raw mixture

Zement — Zementfabrik

Rohschlamm *m* — slurry
Santorin ~ — Santorin ~
Säureindex *m* — index of acidity
Schlacken~, Hütten~ — slag ~, artificial pozzolana ~
Schlämmaschine *f*, Schlämm-Maschine — slurry tank
Schwefelsäureanhydrid *n* — sulphuric anhydride
Tonerde~, Schmelz~, Tonerdeschmelz ~, Aluminos-~ — (high-)alumina ~, aluminous ~, calcium aluminate ~
   Tonerdeschmelzzement *m* aus Jugoslawien — ISTRA-BRAND [*früher: DURAPID*] [*Trademark*]
   ungarischer ~ — CITADUR [*Trademark*]
   Elektro~ — CIMENT DE LA FARGE, CIMENT FONDU [*Trademark*], electric cement

Traß~ — trass ~
Trockenverfahren *n* — dry process
Vicat-Nadelapparat *m* — Vicat needle apparatus, Vicat setting time apparatus

unaufgeschlossener Rückstand *m* — insoluble residue
Zementierungsindex *m* — cementation index
Zementierungswert *m* — cementing value
Zementklinker *m* — cement clinker
   Trikalziumaluminat *n*, aluminatische Schmelze *f*, $3\,CaO \times Al_2O_3$ [*abgek.* C_3A] — tricalcium aluminate
   Trikalziumsilikat *n*, $3\,CaO \times SiO_2$ [*abgek.* C_3S] — tricalcium silicate
   Dikalziumsilikat *n*, Bikalziumsilikat *n*, $2\,CaO \times SiO_2$ [*abgek.* C_2S] — dicalcium silicate
   Tetrakalziumaluminatferrit *n*, Brownmillerit *m*, $4\,CaO \times Al_2O_3 \times Fe_2O_3$ [*abgek.* C_4FA *oder* C_4AF] — tetracalcium aluminoferrite
Zementkuchen *m* — circular-domed pat of cement, cement pat, pat of cement-water paste
Zementteilchen *n* — cement grain

Zement|-Abmeßschnecke *f*, Bindemittel-Zuteilschnecke = cement proportioning screw
~-Anhänger *m* = cement trailer unit
~becherwerk *n* = cement (bucket) elevator
~bedarf *m* = cement requirement
(~)Beton *m*, siehe: Beton *m*
~dachsteinautomat *m*, siehe: Beton-dachsteinautomat *m*
~dosierung *f* = cement batching
~drehofen *m* = rotary cement kiln
~einpressung *f* [*Sammelbegriff für Zementmilcheinpressung und Zementmörteleinpressung*] = injection of cement-water grout or cement mortar
~einpreßmaschine *f*, siehe: Zement-Injektionspumpe *f*
~einspritzapparat *m*, siehe: Zement-Injektionspumpe *f*
~estrich *m* **mit Granitsplitt** *m* = granolithic (floor) surfacing, ~ finish (or surface)
~estrichstreicher *m* = trowel hand
~fabrik *f* = cement mill

Zement|farbe *f*, Färbemittel *n* = co(u)loring admixture

zementgebundene Masse *f* = cement-bonded mass

zementgebundener feuerfester Schamottestein *m* = fireclay grog refractory

Zement|gehalt *m*, Zementfaktor *m* [*Beton m*] = cement content, ~ factor

~-Injektionspumpe *f*, Zementeinpreßmaschine *f*, Zementeinspritzapparat *m*, Zementmilchpumpe *f*, Zementinjektor *m* = cement injection pump

~kalkmörtel *m*, siehe: verlängerter Zementmörtel *m*

~kanone *f*, siehe: Betonspritzmaschine *f*

~kelle *f* = cement trowel

~-Lastkraftwagen *m* = bulk cement truck (US); ~ ~ lorry (Brit.)

~-Leim *m*, Zement-Wassergemisch *n* = cement-water paste

Zementmilch *f*, Feinschlämme *f*, (Beton)Schlämmschicht *f* = laitance

~einpressung *f*; siehe unter „Baugrundverbesserung *f*"

Zementmischprüfung *f* [*Bitumenemulsion f*] = cement mixing test

Zementmörtel *m* = cement mortar

~einpressung *f*; siehe unter „Baugrundverbesserung *f*"

~einspritzgerät *n*, siehe: Zementmörtelinjektor *m*

~einspritzung *f*; siehe unter „Baugrundverbesserung *f*"

~injektion *f*; siehe unter „Baugrundverbesserung *f*"

~-Injektor *m*, Zement-Mörtel-Einspritzgerät *n* = cement mortar injecting device

Zement|(mörtel)kanone *f*, siehe: Beton-Spritzmaschine *f*

~mörtelputz *m*, Zementmörtelputz *m* = cement mortar plaster finish, ~ (~) rendering, ~ plaster rendering, ~ ~ finish

~mörtel-Spritzapparat *m* **nach dem Torkretverfahren** *n*, siehe: Beton-Spritzmaschine *f*

~mosaik *n*, siehe: Terrazzo *m*

~ofen *m* = cement kiln

~paste *f* = cement paste

~prüfung *f* = cement testing

~pumpe *f*, Fuller(-Kinyon)-Pumpe *f*, Fuller-Zementpumpe *f*, Zementstaubpumpe *f* = Fuller-Kinyon unloader (pump), F-K (dry) pump

~putzmörtel *m*, siehe: Zementmörtelputz *m*

~rohrform *f*, Betonrohrform *f* = (concrete) pipe mo(u)ld, (~) ~ form

~rohrstampfmaschine *f*, (Beton)Rohrstampfmaschine *f*, Stampfmaschine *f* für Betonrohrherstellung *f* = concrete pipe tamping machine

~-Rohschlamm *m* = cement slurry

~-Sand-Schlämme *f* = cement-sand grout, sand-cement ~, cement slurry

~-Sand-Schlämme-Mischer *m*, Colcrete-Mischer = Colcrete mixer, cement slurry ~, sand-cement grout ~, cement-sand grout ~

Zement|schachtofen *m* = vertical cement kiln

~-Schlämme *f*, Zementsuspension *f* = (neat) cement-water grout (or mixture), cement grout

~schnecke *f* = cement screw, screw conveyor for bulk cement

~schotterdecke *f* = sandwich process macadam, COLCRETE constructed in the sandwich process

~silo *m*, Bindemittelsilo = bulk cement plant, cement silo

~silo *m* **mit Dosierung** *f*, Dosieranlage *f* für Zement *m* = cement batch(ing) plant

~(silo)waage *f*, Bindemittelwaage = cement batcher scale, ~ weigh(ing) batcher

~spritzschlauch *m* = cement grout discharge hose

~suspension *f*, siehe: Zement-Schlämme *f*

~tanker *m*, Zementtransportfahrzeug *n* = cement tanker, ~ haulage unit, ~ hauler, bulk cement transporter

~tanker *m* **mit Druckluftentladung** *f* = pressurised cement tanker

~tankerlastzug *m* = bulk cement truck-and-trailer unit

~tonbeton *m*, siehe: Bodenbeton

Zement-Ton-Betonstraße — Zerkleinerung

Zement|-Ton-Betonstraße f, selbständige Fahrbahndecke f aus Zement-Ton-Beton m = soil-cement surface course, ~ road
~transportanhänger m **mit Doppelschnecke** f = twin-screw bulk cement trailer
~transportanhänger m **mit Gebläseluft-Förderrinne** f = air-slide bulk cement trailer
~-Traßmörtel m = [cement-trass mortar

Zementumschlaganlage f
  normale Anlage bestehend aus Untergleis-Förderschnecke f, Vertikal-Becherwerk n und großem Vorratssilo m mit Abmeßvorrichtung f
  transportable Anlage mit kleinem Vorratsbehälter m, geneigtem Becherwerk n und Abmeßvorrichtung f

cement handling facility
  conventional plant consisting of an undertrack screw, vertical bucket elevator, storage silo and cement batcher
  inclined bucket elevator plant

Zement|vermörtelung f, hydraulische Vermörtelung f, Bodenvermörtelung f mit Zement m [Straße f] = cement-soil stabilisation (or stabilization)
~verteiler m [Bodenvermörtelung f] = cement spreading machine, cement spreader
~verteilung f **in Säcken** mpl [Zementvermörtelung f] = spreading and spotting cement
~waage f, Bindemittelwaage, Zementsilowaage = cement weigh(ing) batcher, ~ batcher scale
~warenform f, Betonwarenform f = concrete products mo(u)ld
~-Wasser-Verhältnis n [Beton m] = cement water ratio
~zusatzmittel n [wird mit dem Zement zusammen vermahlen] = addition
zentrale Betriebsanlage f = "packaged" plant, central engine ~
zentralisierte Steuerung f, ~ **Bedienung** f = centralized controls
Zentralisierung f = centralization
Zentral|-Reparaturwerkstatt f = central repair (work)shop
~-Steuerstand m = central operating platform
~werkstatt f = central workshop
zentrifugaler Elevator m, zentrifugales Becherwerk n = centrifugal discharge elevator, spaced bucket ~, boot loading ~

~ Schwerkraftelevator m, zentrifugales Schwerkraftbecherwerk n = chain-type spaced bucket elevator with centrifugal gravity discharge
Zentrifugal|-Feuchtigkeits-Äquivalent n = centrifuge moisture equivalent
~moment n = centrifugal moment
~-Pulverkupplung f = powder-type centrifugal coupling
~-Staubabscheider m, siehe: Zyklon m
Zentrifuge f = centrifuge
Zentrifugiermethode f = centrifuge method
zentrisch vorgespannter Betonstab m = gravity centre (Brit.)/center (US) prestressed concrete bar
ZENTROMIX [Trademark], Fabrikat ZENTROMIX G. m. b. H. = concrete aggregate and cement weighbatching installation with centralised oneman control
Zeolith m, Siedestein m = zeolite
Zeresin(wachs) n, Kunstwachs n = ceresine wax
Zerfall m, Zerrüttung f, Auflösung f = disintegration
Zerfallswert-Bestimmung f **nach Weber und Bechler** = breaking time test of Weber and Bechler [bitumen emulsion (Brit.)]
zerfließendes Salz n = deliquescent salt
zerkleinern [Boden m] = to pulverize
Zerkleinerung f, siehe: Hartzerkleinerung

Zerkleinerungsgesetz n nach v. Rittinger [*die aufgewendete Zerkleinerungsarbeit steht in proportionalem Verhältnis zur erzeugten Oberfläche*] = Rittinger's law [*basic law of crushing and pulverizing which states that the work done is in proportion to the area of the new surfaces developed*]
zerklüftetes Gelände n = jagged terrain
Zerlegungsgleis n, Sortiergleis, Ausziehgleis = sorting track
zermürbter Ton m = shattered clay

Zerreißfestigkeit f, siehe: Zugfestigkeit f
zersetzen = to decompose
zersetzter Granit m = decomposed granite, gowan
Zersetzung f = decomposition
Zersetzungsdestillation f, siehe: Entgasung f
Zerstäuber m, Spritzflakon n, m = atomizer
Zerstäubung f = atomisation, atomization
zerstörende Betonprüfung f = destructive testing of concrete

---

zerstörungsfreie Prüfung f **von Beton** m	non-destructive testing of concrete
Ankopplungsmittel n	acoustic coupling agent, couplant
dynamischer Elastizitätsmodul m	dynamic modulus of elasticity
dynamisches Prüfverfahren n	dynamic testing technique
ankoppeln	to couple
Durchlaufzeit f	time of propagation, propagation time, transit time, pulse-transmission time, time of transmittal
Empfangsverstärker m	receiver amplifier
Fortpflanzungsgeschwindigkeit f	velocity of propagation
Geschwindigkeitsmessung f	(longitudinal) ware-velocity method (or measurement), pulse-velocity technique
Gummimembran(e) f	rubber diaphragm
Impulsverfahren n	pulse technique
Kathodenstrahlröhre f	cathode-ray tube
Kugelschlagprüfung f	dynamic ball-impact test method
Laufweglänge f	path length
Knallfunkengeber m	firing-type pulse-velocity measuring device
Longitudinalwelle f	longitudinal ware
mechanisches Hammergerät n	hammer-blow type pulse-velocity measuring device
piezoelektrischer Empfangsschallkopf m	piezoelectric crystal receiving transducer (or head)
piezoelektrischer Sendeschallkopf m	piezoelectric crystal transmitting transducer (or head)
Resonanzfrequenzmessung f	resonant-frequency technique, low-frequency vibration method
Schallkopf m	transducer, pickup
Schallbereich m	sonic range
Schallverfahren n	sonic method
Schallvibration f	sonic vibration
Soniskop n	soniscope
Ultraschall m, Überschall	ultrasonic sound
Ultraschallimpuls m	ultrasonic (sound) pulse

Ultraschallimpuls-Echo-Verfahren n = ultrasonic reflection technique
Ultraschall(impuls)methode f = ultrasonic (pulse) method
Ultraschallbetonprüfgerät n = ultrasonic concrete tester

zerstörungsfreies **Prüfverfahren** n = non-destructive test method
Zertrümmerungs|kugel f = breaking ball
~ramme f = drop hammer for shattering old pavement
Zerussit m (Min.), siehe: Bleispat m
Ziegel m, siehe: Backstein m
~bautechnik f = building methods with brick masonry
~brecher m, Backsteinbrecher = brick crusher
~brennen n = brick burning
~bruch m, siehe: Ziegelschotter m
Ziegelei f = brickworks
~maschinen fpl = brick machinery
Ziegel|fabrikation f, Ziegelherstellung f = brickmaking
~fußboden m = brick floor(ing)
~greifer m, Ziegelsteingreifer = brick gripping device, ~ grab
~gut n, Ziegelton m = brickearth(s), brick clay
~kammerofen m = stationary continuous brick kiln
~mauerwerk n = brick masonry, brickwork
~mehl n = brickdust
~ofen m = brick kiln
~paket n = brick package
~pflaster n, Klinkerpflaster n = brick paving; [*deprecated: brick road*]
~presse f = brick press
~rollenbahn f = roller conveyor for bricks
~rollschicht f = brick-on-edge
~säge f = brick saw
~schleuder f, Ziegelwurfmaschine f; SEEGERS-Steinschleuder f [*Trademark*] = brick-throwing machine
~schotter m, Kleinschlag m aus Ziegel-(stein)brocken mpl, Ziegelbruch m = (aggregate of) broken brick(s), brick rubble, brick hardcore
~splitt m, Tonsplitt = crushed clay brick, burned clay aggregate, clay chippings

~splittbeton m, Trümmerschuttbeton = crushed (clay) brick concrete, crushed brick aggregate ~
~splittmauerstein m, Tonsplittmauerstein = brick of clay chippings
~splitt-Zweikammerstein m = two-hole hollow block of brick-rubble concrete
~stapler m = brick stacker
~stapel m = stacked bricks
~(stein)greifer m = brick grab, ~ gripping device
~ton m, baukeramischer Ton = building clay
~transportwagen m = brick carrier
Zieh|brunnen m = draw well, open bucket well (Brit.); sweep well (US)
~feder f, siehe: Reißfeder
~gerät n = towing unit
~gerät n [*Ziehen von Pfählen und Spundbohlen*] = puller, pulling tool
Zielverkehrszählung f = destination survey
Zielverkehr m zur Innenstadt f = downtown terminal traffic
Zifferblatt|-Abmeßwaage f mit Waagenbehälter m = dial batcher
~waage f, Kreiszeigerwaage = dial type scale
Zimmermanns|polier m = carpenter foreman
~winkel m = carpenter's square
Zinckenit m (Min.), siehe: Bleiantimonglanz m
Zinder m = cinder
Zink|blende f, Zinksulfid n, Schwefelzink n, ZnS = black jack, sphalerite, (zinc) blende, zinc sulphide
~blüte f (Min.), siehe: Hydrozinkit n
~erz n = zinc ore
~glas(erz) n, Kieselzink(erz) n, Kieselgalmei m (Min.) = siliceous calamine, willemite
~grube f = zinc mine

Zinkit *n*, Rotzinkerz *n*, ZnO (Min.) = zincite, red oxide of zinc, spartalite, sterlingite
Zink|seife *f* = zinc soap
~spinell *m* (Min.), siehe: Gahnit *m*
~staubgrundierfarbe *f* = zinc dust primer
~sulfid *n*, siehe: Zinkblende *f*
~vitriol *n*, Goslarit *m* (Min.) = goslarite, white vitriol, white copperas
~weiß *n*, Zinkoxyd *n*, ZnO = zinc white, oxide of zinc
Zinnstein *m*, SnO_2 (Min.) = cassiterite, tin-stone
Zirkel *m* = (pair of) compasses
~bogen *m*, siehe: Halbkreisbogen *m*
Zirkon *m*, $ZrSiO_4$ (Min.) = zircon
~oxyd *n* = zirconia
~silikat *n*, $ZrSiO_4$ = silicate of zirconium
Zirkulations-Sprengrampe *f* = circulating spraybar
Zisterne *f*, siehe: Behälter *m*
Zitronensäure *f* = citric acid
Zitterpappel *f*, siehe: Espe *f*
Zivilluftfahrt *f* = civil aviation
Zoll|stock *m*, Glieder-Maßstab *m* = folding (pocket) rule
~straße *f* **für Schnellverkehr** *m*, siehe: gebührenpflichtige Autobahn *f*
Zone *f* **der Öffnungen** *fpl* (Geol.), siehe: Sprödigkeitszone *f*
Zopfende *n*, Wipfelende [*Pfahl m*] = tip, lower end, tail end
Zubehör *m* = accessories
~teil *m, n* = accessory part
Zubringer|luftlinie *f* = feeder line airline
~schnecke *f*, siehe: Schneckenspeiser *m*
~straße *f* = approach road, feeder ~
~walze *f*, siehe: Speisewalze
Zuckerahorn *m* = sugar maple
Zufahrgleis *n* = approach track
Zufahrt *f* = access way
~rinne *f* [*z. B. zu einem Dock n*] = shipping lane
~stelle *f*, siehe: Anschlußpunkt *m*
Zug *m* = tension
~ = train
Zugänglichkeit *f* = accessibility
Zugangsstollen *m*, Tagesstollen *m*, Fensterstollen *m*, Seitenstollen *m* = adit, access tunnel, side drift, approach adit

Zug|anker *m* = tie rod
~armierung *f*, siehe: Zugbewehrung
~balken *m*, Zug(balken)träger *m* = tie beam; ~ girder (Brit.)
~band *n* = strip, tie (member)
~beanspruchung *f*, Zugspannung *f* = tensile stress, tension
~bewehrung *f*, Zugarmierung *f* = tensile reinforcement
~brücke *f* = draw bridge
~deichsel *f* = draw-bar
~diagonale *f* = tension diagonal
~-Druck-Wechselbeanspruchung *f* = reversed direct stress
~faser *f* = tensile fibre (Brit.); ~ fiber (US)
~feder *f* = tension spring
~festigkeit *f*, Zerreißfestigkeit *f* = tensile strength, tension ~
~glied *n*, Zugstab *m* [*Fachwerk n*] = tension member
~gurt *m* = tension boom, ~ chord, ~ flange
zügige Linienführung *f* = flowing alignment (Brit.)/alinement (US)
Zug|kraft *f* = tensile force
~kraft *f*, Zugleistung *f* = tractive force, ~ effort
~kübelbagger *m*, siehe: Schürfkübelbagger *m*
~maschine *f*, Straßen ~ = tractor-truck, truck-tractor (US); motor tractor (Brit.)
~maschine *f* **mit Kipp-Pritsche** *f* = tipper-tractor
~maschine-Bulldozer *m* = truck tractor bulldozer (US)
~messer *m* = draught gauge (Brit.); draft gage (US)
~raupe *f* = towing caterpillar tractor, puller (crawler) tractor
~riß *m* [*Bauwerkssenkung f*] = vertical crack
~seil *n* = pull rope
~seilwinde *f* = pull-rope winch
~spannung *f*, siehe: Zugbeanspruchung *f*
~stab *m*, Zugglied *n* [*Fachwerk n*] = tension member
~stange *f* = tie rod, tension ~
~tierverkehr *m*, siehe: Gespannverkehr
~versuch *m* = tension test

Zugwagen — Zwanglauf

Zugwagen *m*, Radschrapper-~ = (wheel) scraper tractor

zulässige Last *f*, ~ Belastung *f* = safe load(ing), working ~, allowable ~, permissible ~

~ **Maßabweichung** *f*, Toleranz *f*, Genauigkeitsgrad *m* = tolerance, allowance

~ **Nutzlast** *f* [*LKW m*] = legal payload

~ **Spannung** *f*, Beanspruchbarkeit *f* = permissible stress, allowable ~

Zulassungsgebühr *f* [*Auto n*] = license fee

Zulauf(ge)rinne *f*, (*n*), siehe: Einlaufkanal *m*

zulegen, abbinden [*Holzkonstruktion f*] = to trim, to join

Zuleitungskabel *n* = feed cable

Zulieferant *m* = supplier

zumauern = to brick up

Zumessung *f*, siehe: Dosierung *f*

Zumeß|kiste *f*, siehe: Abmeßkiste *f*

~**vorrichtung** *f*, siehe: Abmeßvorrichtung

Zumischung *f*, siehe: Beimischung *f*

Zündbeschleuniger *m* [*Dieselkraftstoff m*] = dope

Zunder *m* = scale

Zünd|kabel *n*; siehe unter: „1. Schießen *n*; 2. Sprengen *n*"

~**kerze** *f* = spark(ing) plug

~**kerzenprüfgerät** *n* = (spark) plug tester, sparking ~ ~

~**magnet** *m* = ignition magneto

~**papier** *n* = ignition paper

~**schnur** *f*; siehe unter „1. Schießen *n*; 2. Sprengen *n*"

Zungenweiche *f* = tongue(-)switch (turnout)

Zurichten *n* = dressing

zurückschnellen [*Pfahl m*] = to bounce

Zusammenbauwerkstatt *f*, Montagewerkstatt *f* = assembly (work)shop

zusammendrückbar = compressible

Zusammen|drückbarkeit *f* = compressibility

~**drückversuch** *m* mit beschränkter Seitenausdehnung = compression test with confined lateral expansion

~**fluß** *m* [*Flüsse mpl*] = confluence (US); confluent (Brit.); junction

zusammen|geschweißter Stahlmast *m* = tubular welded mast

~**gesetzter (Erz) Gang** *m* = (ore) lode

~**gesetzter Spannbetonbalken(träger)** *m*, ~ Spannbetonträgerbalken *m* = composite prestressed concrete beam; ~ ~ ~ girder (Brit.)

zusammenlegbar = collapsible

Zusammen|setzung *f* = composition

~**wachsung** *f* = concretion

Zusatz|einrichtung *f*, Anbaugerät *n* = attachment

~**spannung** *f* = additional stress

~**stoff** *m*, siehe: Beimischung *f*

~**werkstoff** *m*, Schweißdraht *m* = fusion steel wire

Zuschlagsangebot *n*; siehe unter „Angebot *n*"

Zuschlagsiloanlage *f*, siehe: Abmeßanlage *f* für Betonzuschlagstoffe *mpl*

Zuschlagssilo *m* mit Dosiereinrichtung *f* = bin and batcher plant

~ ~ **Wiegebalken** *m* = (bin and) troll(e)y batcher plant

Zuschlagstoff|abteil *n* [*Chargen-LKW m*] = batch-truck compartment (US); batch-lorry ~ (Brit.)

~-**Becherwerk** *n*, Mineralmasse-Becherwerk *n* = aggregate (bucket) elevator

~**dosierapparat** *m* = aggregate batcher

Zuschlagstoffe *mpl*, siehe: (Beton)Zuschlagstoffe *mpl*

Zuschlagstoff|-Erwärmung *f* = aggregate heating

~**gemenge** *n* = combined aggregate

~**waage** *f*, siehe: Gesteinswaage *f*

zusitzendes Grundwasser *n*; siehe unter „Abwasserwesen *n*"

Zustand *m*, Beschaffenheit *f* = condition

Zustandsänderung *f* **nach Zeit** *f* [*z. B. Geschwindigkeit f, Druck m, Temperatur f*] = rate

Zuteilgefäß *n* = batcher hopper

~**verschluß** *m* = discharge gate

Zuteilschnecke *f* = proportioning screw

Zuteilung *f*, siehe: Dosierung *f*

Zuteilvorrichtung *f*, siehe: Abmeßvorrichtung

Zwanglauf *m* = positive movement

zwangläufige Kupplung f = positive clutch (coupling)

~ **Schmierung** f, siehe: Druck-Umlaufschmierung f

zwangläufiger Exzenterschwinger m = positive throw eccentric type screen

Zwanglauftrieb m = positive drive
 kraftschlüssiger Antrieb m = non-positive drive

Zwangs|auflader m, Lademaschine f mit gegen das Haufwerk fahrender Schaufelkette f und Abwurfband n = force-feed loader

~**auslösung** f = forced release

~**betonmischer** m **mit horizontalem Rührwerk** n = pan type concrete mixer

~**bewirtschaftung** f, siehe: Bewirtschaftung

~**halt** m = compulsory stop

Zwangsmischer m **mit kurzen und langen Mischwerkzeugen** npl = double zone (pug mill) mixer

~ ~ **vertikalem Rührwerk** n, siehe: Knetmischer m

~**schaufel** f = pugmill paddle (or blade)

zwangsgemischt = pugmill-mixed

Zwangsmischung f = rolling and kneading mixing action, non-lift mixing action

Zweck|bindung f = non-diversion

~**dienlichkeit** f = usefulness

~**entfremdung** f = diversion

Zweiachsgestell n, Zweiachsunterwagen m [*Bagger m*] = two-axle carrier

zweiachsiger Erdhobel m, siehe: Abziehverteilergerät n [*mit Eigenantrieb m*]

zweiachsiges Drehgestell n = two-axle bogie

Zweiachsschlepper m, siehe: Vierradtrecker m

Zweiachs-Zugwagen m, siehe: Vierradtrecker m

Zweibahnstraße f = two-way road

Zweibohlenfertiger m = two-screed (or two-beam) finisher (or finishing machine)

Zweidecker m, siehe: Doppeldecker m

zwei-dimensionale Spannung f = two-dimensional stressing

Zweigelenkbogen m = two-hinged arch, arch hinged at the springings
 Zugband n = horizontal tie

Zweiggleis n = branch track

Zweihebelbedienung f = two lever control

Zweikammer(hohlblock)stein m = two-hole hollow block

Zwei-Kraft-Lok(omotive) f = alternative power unit loco(motive), two-power locomotive

Zwei-Lösemittel-Verfahren n [*Schmieröl*] = duo-sol process

Zweimassen|-Schrägwurfsieb n = horizontal counter-balanced action shaking screen

~-**Vibrator** m = two-mass vibrator

Zweimotorengreiferhubwerk n = grab(bing) hoisting gear with two power units

Zweipendelbackenbrecher m; siehe unter „Backenbrecher m"

Zweirad|-Bohrwagen m = two-wheel wagon drill

~**fahrgestell** n = two-wheel carriage

~-**Trecker** m, Einachs-Zugwagen m, Einachs(rad)schlepper m, Zweirad-Schlepper = two-wheel(ed) tractor

(Zweirad-) Vorspänner m, (Zweirad-)Vorspannwagen m, (Zweirad-)Triebsatz m, Zweiradtrecker m, Ein-Achs-Reifen-Sattelschlepper, Einachs-Schlepper, Einachs-Zugwagen n = prime mover

(Zwei)Raupenfahrwerk n, siehe: Raupenfahrwerk n

Zweischalengreifbagger m, Zweischalengreif(er)kran m
 Arbeitsspiel n
  Eingraben n
  Schwenken n
  Entleeren n, Ausschütten n

clamshell(-rigged) crane, clamshell bucket crane
 cycle
  grabbing
  swinging round, slewing
  discharging, dumping

Zweischalen-Greifkorb m, Zweischalen-(bagger)greifer m — clamshell bucket, clamshell basket (US); clamshell grab, pair of half-scoops (Brit.)

Zweischalengreifkorb m für Sand m und Kies m — scraper grab

Zweischalengreifkorb m für Stichboden m und Gesteinstrümmer f — whole-tine grab, tine grab for clay

Zweischalengreifkorb m mit Rammwirkung f — clamshell bucket with pile driver action, impact clam

---

Zweischeiben-Glättmaschine f [Beton m] = double mechanical trowel, ~ ~ float

Zweischwingenbrecher m; siehe unter „Backenbrecher"

Zweiseilgreif(er)korb m, Zweiseilbaggergreifer m, Doppelseilgreifer m = two-line bucket

Zwei-Seil(schwebe)bahn f [sogenannte deutsche Bauart. Erfunden 1861 von Freiherrn J. Dücker] = double ropeway

Zweiseiten-Kippanhänger m = two-way dump trailer

zweiseitiger Korbbogen m = two-centred compound curve

Zweispitz m, siehe: Doppelspitzhacke f

zweispurige Straße f = undivided two-way road with two lanes altogether

zweistegig = double-webbed

zweistieliger symmetrischer Stockwerkrahmen m = symmetrical two-legged multi-storied frame

zweistöckiges Kellergeschoß n = two-stor(e)y basement

Zweistufen-Destillation f [Erdöl n] = double-flash distillation

zweistufiger Backenbrecher m = two-stage jaw crusher

~ **Kompressor** m, ~ Luftverdichter m, ~ Druckluferzeuger m, Mitteldruckkompressor = two-stage (air) compressor

zweistufiges Sieb n, siehe: Doppeldecker m

zweistufige Verdichtung f [Kompressor m] = two-stage compressing

zweisymmetrischer Träger m = bisymmetrical girder

Zweitakt-Dieselmotor m mit Schiebersteuerung f = Schuck-designed diesel engine

~ ~ **Turboaufladung** f = turbo-charged 2-cycle diesel

Zweitaschen-Bunker m, Zweitaschensilo m = two-compartment bin

zweiteiliger Silo(klappen)verschluß m = duplex radial type bin door

Zweitrommelwindwerk n = double-drum hoisting gear

Zweitsprengung f = secondary blasting

~ **mit Bohrlochladung** f; siehe unter „1. Schießen n; 2. Sprengen n"

Zweiwalzen|-Prallbrecher m, siehe: Doppel-Rotoren-Prallbrecher m

~-**Prall(mahl)mühle** f; siehe unter „Mühle f"

Zweiwegeventil n = two-way valve

Zweiwellen-Zwangsmischer m; siehe: unter „Makadam-Maschinenanlage f"

Zweiwellrohrkessel m = Lancashire boiler with corrugated flues

Zwerchhobel m = cross-grain plane

Zwergheide f = ling heath, dwarf shrub

Zwicke f = (rock) spalls

Zwillings|bereifung f = dual tyres (Brit.); ~ tires (US)

~**form** f = twinned form

~**(gleis)kettenschlepper** m = caterpillar twin D 8 tractor

~**kessel** m, siehe: Flammrohrdoppelkessel m

~**lamellierung** f [Natronkalkfeldspat m] = twin lamellae [plagioclase]

~**rad** n, siehe: Doppelrad

~**träger** m = twin girder

Zwischen|bogen m [Spundwand f] = closure arch

~**bunker** m, siehe: Zwischen(lade)bunker

~**durchmesser** m = fractional diameter

~**eiszeit** f = interglacial period

~**fachwerk** n = subdivided-panel truss

~**glied** n = transition link

~**joch** n = intermediate pier

Zwischen|kühler m = inter-cooler
~kühlung f = inter-cooling
~(lade)bunker m, siehe: Baustellensilo m
~lage f [*Förderband* n] = ply
~lage f, Zwischenstellung f = intermediate position
~legscheibe f, Einlage f = shim
~pfette f = middle purlin
~querträger m [*Brücke* f] = intermediate floor beam, ~ cross girder
~querverband m [*Brücke* f] = intermediate transverse frame
~riegel m, Querriegel m, Querschott n = diaphragm
~schicht f = intermediate course
~steife f [*Blechträger* m] = intermediate stiffener
~stellung f, Zwischenlage f = intermediate position
~stufe f = intermediate stage
~stütze f = intermediate column
~tauperiode f = intermediate thaw(ing) period
~transport(last)kraftwagen m = transfer (motor) truck (US); transfer lorry (Brit.)
~zeichen n, Bake f [*Autobahn* f] = warning sign
Zyanit m, siehe: Disthen m
Zyanwasserstoff m, Blausäure f, HCN = hydrocyanic acid
zyklische Kurve f = cyclic(al) curve
~ Symmetrie f = cycle symmetry
~ Veränderung f = cyclic(al) variation
~ Vertauschung f = cyclic(al) permutation
Zyklon m, Fliehkraftabscheider m, Zentrifugal-Staubabscheider m, Fliehkraftzyklon m = cyclone separator, (dust collecting) cyclone, centrifugal dust collector
~naßklassierer m, Naßzyklon m, Aufschwimmklassierer m = cyclone classifier
Zyklopenmauerwerk n = random rubble walling, uncoursed ~ ~, cyclopic ~ ~
Zyklus m, siehe: Kreislaufvorgang m
Zylinderbär m; siehe unter „Rammanlage f"
~bohrung f = cylindrical boring, cylinder bore
~büchse f = cylinder liner
~rollenmeißel m; siehe unter „Bohrmeißel"
~verschluß m = cylindrical gate, cylinder ~
zylindrische Aussenkung f = counterboring
~ Feile f = straight file
zylindrischer Probekörper m, siehe: Probezylinder m
zylindrische Trockentrommel f, zylindrischer Trommeltrockner m = cylindrical drier (or dryer)
zylindrisches Gewinde n = cylindrical thread, straight ~

APPENDIX
ANHANG

Conversion Table Umrechnungstabelle

Multiply by Multipliziere mit	To convert Zur Umwandlung von	To In	
2.54	Inches; Zoll	Centimetres; cm	.39371
30.48	Feet; Fuß	Centimetres; cm	.03281
.03937	Millimetres; mm	Inches; Zoll	
.9144	Yards	Metres; mtr	1.094
1,609.31	Miles; Meilen	Metres; mtr	.000621
3.281	Metres; mtr.	Feet; Fuß	.3048
39.37	Metres; mtr.	Inches; Zoll	
1,853.27	Nautical Miles; Seemeilen	Metres; mtr.	.00054
6.45137	Square inches; Zoll^2	Sq. cms; cm^2	.15501
.093	Square feet; Fuß^2	Sq. metres; m^2	10.7643
.83610	Square yards; Yard^2	Sq. metres; m^2	1.19603
2.58989	Sqare miles; Meile^2	Sq. kilometres; km^2	.38612
16.38618	Cubic inches; Zoll^3	Cub. cms; cm^3	.06103
28.33	Cubic feet; Fuß^3	Litres; Liter	.0353
.02832	Cubic feet; Fuß^3	Cub. metres; m^3	35.31658
6.24	Cubic feet; Fuß^3	Imperial Gallons	.1602
.76451	Cubic yards; Yards^3	Cub. metres; m^3	1.30802
.3732	Pounds (Troy)	Kilogrammes; kg	2.68
31.10	Ounces (Troy)	Grammes; g	.03216
.4536	Pounds (Avoir.)	Kilogrammes; kg	2.2045
7,000.00	Pounds (Avoir.)	Grains (Troy)	.00014
28.35	Ounces (Avoir.)	Grammes; g	.0352
.065	Grains	Grammes; g	15.38
50.80238	Cwt.	Kilogrammes; kg	.01968
.0022	Grammes; g	Pounds (Avoir.)	
1,016.04754	Tons; Tonnen	Kilogrammes; kg	.00098
907.00	Short tons	Kilogrammes; kg	
4.54346	Imperial Gallons	Litres; Liter	.22010
3.785	US Gallons	Litres; Liter	.264
.56793	Pints	Litres; Liter	1.76077
219.97	Cubic metres; m^3	Imperial Gallons	
264.2	Cubic metres; m^3	US Gallons	
61.022	Litres; Liter	Cub. inches; Zoll^3	
3.531	Hektoliter	Cub. feet; Fuß^3	
2.84	Hektoliter	Bushels	
36.34766	Bushels	Litres; Liter	.02751
10.00	Imp. Gall. of water	Pounds	.1
	To obtain Zur Errechnung obiger Einheiten	From von obigen	Multiply by above ist mit obengenanrtem Wert zu multiplizieren

Conversion Table Umrechnungstabelle
Continued Fortsetzung

Multiply by Multipliziere mit	To convert Zur Umwandlung von	To In	
.454	Pounds of water	Litres; Liter	.2202
70.31	Lb. per sq. in. (psi.)	Gm./sq. cms	.01422
.07031	Lb. per sq. in. (psi.)	kg/cm^2	14.22272
4.88241	Lb. per sq. foot; Pfund/Fuß^2	Kilogrammes per sq. metres; kg/m^2	.20482
.00049	Lb. per sq. foot; Pfund/Fuß^2	Kilogrammes per sq. cm; kg/cm^2	2,049.1807
.24803	Lb. per fathom	kg/mtr.	4.0318
1.48816	Lb. per foot; Pfund/Fuß	kg/mtr.	.6719
.49606	Lb. per Yard; Pfund/Yard	kg/mtr.	2.0159
3,333.4784	Tons per foot; Tonne/Fuß	kg/mtr.	.0003
2.3	Lb. per sq. in. (psi.)	Head of water (ft.)	.434
.7	Lb. per sq. in. (psi.)	Head of water (M.)	1.4285
.068	Lb. per sq. in. (psi.)	Atmospheres; Atmosphären	14.7
1.136	Quarts	Litres; Liter	
157.4944	Tons per sq. in.; Tonnen/Zoll^2	kg/cm^2	.0063
1.574944	Tons per sq. in.; Tonnen/Zoll^2	kg/mm^2	.635
10,936.59840	Tons per sq. foot; Tonnen/Fuß^2	kg/mtr^2	.0001
.0361	Gramm/cm^3	lb. per cub. inch; Pfund/Zoll^3	
62.4	Gramm/cm^3	lb. per cub. foot; Pfund/Fuß^3	.016
.593	Lb. per cub. yard; Pfund/Yard^3	kg/mtr^3	1.686
16.02	Lb. per cub. foot; Pfund/Fuß^3	kg/mtr^3 (m^3/kg)	.0624
.4047	Acres	Hektar	2.471
11,960.00	Hektar	Yard^2	
.00155	Sq. mm.; mm^2	Square inch; Zoll^2	
.0998	Lb. per Imp. Gallon	Kgm./litre; kg/Liter	10.02

	To obtain Zur Errechnung obiger Einheiten	From von obigen	Multiply by above ist mit obengenanntem Wert zu multiplizieren

Conversion Table Umrechnungstabelle
Continued Fortsetzung

Multiply by Multipliziere mit	To convert Zur Umwandlung von	To In	
.13825	Foot-lb.; Fuß-Pfund	K'grammetres; mkg	7.2332
.33	Foot-tons	Tonnen-Meter	3.00
309.680	Foot-tons	kilogram-metres	.0032
25.80667	Inch-tons	kilogramm-metres	.0388
41.62314	Inches[4]	cm[4]	.0240
.62138	Kilometre	Miles	1.6092
3,280.8693	Kilometre	Foot; Fuß	
.00453	Imp. Gallons	Cub. metres; mtr[3]	219.98
1.60931	Miles per hour; Meilen pro Stunde	kilometres per hour; km/Stde	.6214
1.467	Miles/h; Meilen/Stde.	Fuß/s	
.869	Miles/h; Meilen/Stde.	Knoten	1.151
1.014	Horse-Power	Force de cheval; Chevaux-vapeur; PS	.9861
746.00	Horse-Power	Watts	.00134
.00136	Watts	PS	
.7373	Watts	Fuß-Pfund/s	
3.415	Wattstunde	B. T. U.	.293
1.36	Kilowatt	PS	
1.341	Kilowatt	HP	
737.3	Kilowatt	Fuß-Pfund/s	
.293	Kilowatt	kcal/s	
.707	H.P.	B.T.U./s	
.178	H.P.	kcal/s	
33,000.00	H.P.	Ft.-lb./min.	
76.00	H.P.	kg-m./sec.	.01316
44.00	Watts	Ft.-lb./min.	.0227
.1	Watts	Kg.-m./sec.	10.00
.948	Kilowatt	B.T.U./s	
860.00	Kilowattstunde (kWh)	kcal	
.447	Pounds per H.P.	Kilogrammes per Cheval-vapeur; kg/PS	2.235
426.9	kcal	kg/m	
3.968	kcal; Kg. Calories	B.T.U.	.252
4.184.00	kcal; Kg. Calories	Joules	.00024

To obtain	From	Multiply by above
Zur Errechnung obiger Einheiten	von obigen	ist mit obengenanntem Wert zu multiplizieren

Conversion Table Umrechnungstabelle
Continued Fortsetzung

Multiply by Multipliziere mit	To convert Zur Umwandlung von	To In	
.738	Joules	Foot-pound	1.356
.1124	kcal/m³	B.T.U./foot³	8.9
1.8	kcal/Kilogramm (kg)	B.T.U./pound	.5556
14.7	Atmospheres	psig, pounds per square inch gauge	.068
2.713	B.T.U./sq. foot	Kg. Calories/m²	.369
1.033	Atmosphären	Kg./cm²	
760.00	Atmosphären	mm Q.-S.	
.293	B.T.U.	Wattstunde	3.415
.0333	Zoll-Quecksilbersäule; Inch-Mercury-Column	atm	
13.6	Zoll-Quecksilbersäule; Inch-Mercury-Column	Zoll-Wassersäule; Inch-Water-Col.	.0735
.49	Zoll-Quecksilbersäule; Inch-Mercury-Column	pound/inch²	
.036	Zoll-Wassersäule; Inch-Water-Column	pound/inch²	
.9	German candles	English candles	1.1111
9.55	Carcels	Candles	.1047
88.00	Miles/hour	Ft./min.	.01134
197.00	Metres/sec.	Ft./min.	.00508
.208	Centipoise	Lb. force sec./sq. ft.	4.8
.54	Kilometre/h	Knoten	
152.4	Tonne/Zoll²	atm	
25,200.00	Therm (= 100000 B.T.U.)	kcal.	
1.093659	Tons per sq. foot; Tonnen/Fuß²	kg/cm²	
5.43	Imp. Gall./sq. yard	Liter/m²	.1845

	To obtain Zur Errechnung obiger Einheiten	From von obigen	Multiply by above ist mit obengenanntem Wert zu multiplizieren

British Weights and Measures

Lineal Measure

4	Inches	make	1 Hand	1 Inch	=	.08	Ft.
9	,,	,,	1 Span		=	.207	Yard
12	,,	,,	1 Foot	1 Link	=	7.92	Inches
3	Feet	,,	1 Yard	1 Foot	=	.333	Yard
5	,,	,,	1 Pace	1 Yard	=	36.00	Inches
6	,,	,	1 Fathom	1 Chain	=	100.00	Links
5.5	Yards	,,	1 Rod, Pole or Perch		=	22.00	Yards
					=	.0125	Miles
4	Poles	,,	1 Chain	1 Furlong	=	220.00	Yards
10	Chains	,,	1 Furlong		=	.125	Miles
8	Furlongs	,,	1 Mile	1 Mile	=	80.00	Chains
3	Miles	,,	1 League		=	1,760.00	Yards
1.151	,,	,,	1 Nautical Mile	A Knot is a speed of 1 Nautical Mile per hour			

Square or Land Measure

144	Sq. Inches	=	1 Sq. Foot
9	Sq. Feet	=	1 Sq. Yard
30.25	Sq. Yards	=	1 Sq. Pole
40	Poles	=	1 Rood
4	Roods	=	1 Acre
640	Acres	=	1 Sq. Mile

An Acre equals 4.840 Square Yards
= .4047 Hectares
1 Sq. Link = 62.75 Sq. Inches (approx.)
1 Sq. Chain = 10,000.00 Sq. Links = 484 Sq. Yards
10 Sq. Chains = 1 Acre = 100,000.0 Sq. Links
= 4,840 Sq. Yards
33 Sq. Yards = 1 Rod of Building = 27.6 Sq. Metre
100 Sq. Feet = Square of Flooring or Roofing
= 9.3 Sq. Metre
272.25 Square Feet = Rod of Bricklayer's Work
= 25.4 Sq. Metre

Cubic or Solid Measure

Cubic Foot = 0.037 cubic yard = 1,728 Cub. Inches = 6.23 Imp. Gall. = 7.48 US-Gallons
= 28,317 Cub. centimetre = .0283 Cub. metre = 28.3 Litres
Cubic Yard = 27 Cub. Feet = 168 Imp. Gall. = 202 US-Gallons = 21.033 Bushels =
.7645 Cubic metre = 764.5 Litres
1 Cubic Inch = 0.00058 Cubic Foot = $16{,}38618 \text{ cm}^3$
Stack of Wood = 108 Cubic Feet = 3.06 Cubic metre
Shipping ton = 40 Cubic Feet of merchandise = 1.13 Cubic metre
Shipping ton = 42 Cubic Feet of timber = 1.18 Cubic metre
One ton or load = 50 Cubic Feet of hewn timber = 1.42 Cubic metre
Ton of displacement of a ship = 35 Cubic Feet = 1.02 Cubic metre

Fluid Memoranda

1 Imp. Gallon of water = 10 lb.
1 Cubic Foot of water = 6.23 Imp. Gall. = 62.3 lb = 7.48 US-Gallons
= .0283 Cub. metre = 1,728.00 Cub. inches
= 28,317.00 Cub. centimetre = .037 Cubic yard
= 28.317 Litres

1 lb. water at 62° F. = .016 Cub. Foot
1 Imp. Gallon = 1.2 US-Gallon = 8 Pints = 277.418 Cub. inches = 4.546 Litres
1 Quart = 2 Pints = .25 Imp. Gall. = 69.35 Cub. inches = 1.136 Litres
1 Pint = 4 Gills = .125 Imp. Gall. = 34.682 Cub. inches = .02 Cub. Ft. = 568.3 Cub. centimetre = .5683 Litres
1 Firkin = 9 Imp. Gall. = 41 Litres
1 Kilderkin = 2 Firkins = 82 Litres
1 British Barrel = 4 Firkins = 36 Imp. Gall. = 1.028 US-Barrel = 288 Pints = .215 Cub. Yard = 5.77 Cub. Ft. = 163.566 Litres
1 Gill = .25 Pint = 8.67 Cub. inches = .142 Litres
1 Inch of Rainfall = 22,622.00 Imp. Gallons per Acre = 100.00 tons (approximately)

Avoirdupois Weight

1 Oz. = 28.35 Grammes = .063 lb. = 16 Drams = 437.5 Grains
1 lb. = 16 Oz. = 453.6 Grammes = .4536 kg = 7,000.00 Grains
1 cwt. (Hundredweight) = 112 lb. = 50.80238 kg
1 Stone = 14 lb. = 6.35 kg
1 Quarter = 28 lb.
1 Butcher Stone = 8 lb.
1 Grain = .0648 Grammes
1 Long ton = 2,240.00 lb. = 1.120 Short ton = 20 cwt. = 1,016.05 kg = 1.01605 Metric tons
1 Short ton = 2,000.00 lb. = .893 Long ton = 907.19 kg = .90719 Metric ton

Miscellaneous

1 US-Gallon = 231 Cub. inches = .1337 Cub. feet = 3.785 Litres = .833 Imp. Gallon
1 US-Pound = 226,8 g
1 PSh = 2512 Btu = 0,986 HPh = 633 kcal = 0,736 kWh
1 kWh = 3415 Btu = 861 kcal = 1,36 PSh
1 Btu (Brit. thermal unit) = 0,252 kcal = 108 mkg = 0,00029 kWh = 0,0004 PSh
1 Imperial Bushel = 36.37 Litres
1 Winchester Bushel (USA) = 35.257 Litres
1 Bale = 205 kg
1 Sack of Cement (USA) = 42.676 kg
1 Acre-foot = 43,560 Cubic feet = 1,232.6 Cubic metre (this unit relates to irrigation computations)
1 US-Barrel = .972 British Barrel = 42 US-Gallons = .208 Cubic Yards = 5.62 Cub. Ft. = 158.98 Litres
1 preußischer Morgen = 2,500.00 Sq. metre = 25 Ar = .25 Hektar = .0025 Sq. kilometre = .61775 Acres
1 Zentner = 50 kg = 110.225 lb.
1 metrisches Pfund = 500 Grammes = 1.1 lb.
1 Cental = .05 Short ton = 45.36 kg
1 Dram = 3 Scruples = 1.77 Grammes
1 morgen-foot = 2,608.847204 Cubic metre (this unit relates to irrigation computations in South Africa)
1 morgen (South-Afrika) = 2.11654 Acres
1 geographische Meile = 4 Seemeilen = 7,240 Kilometer

1 Seemeile (Knoten) = 1,000.00 Faden = 1,852 km
1 preußische Landmeile = 7,532 km
1 Cubic foot/second per 1,000 acres = 0,00708 m³/Sekunde per km²
1 Day-second-foot (dsf.) = 86.400 cu. ft.
1 russische Werst = 1,500.00 Arschinen = 1,06678 km
1 deutsche Quadratmeile = 56,25 Square kilometre (km²)
1 geographische Quadratmeile = 55,06 Square kilometre (km²)
1 russische Quadratwerst = 1,138 km²
1 bbl = 376 pds. = 170,704 kg
1 bbl. = 4 Cubic feet = 0,112 m³
1 mbm (mille feet board measure) = 2,36 m³

Cubic Measures and Weights per Unit of Area
Raummaße und Gewichte pro Flächeneinheit

1 kg/cm² = 14.226 lb./sq. inch (psi) = 2.050 lb/.sq. ft. = 18,450.00 lb./sq. yard = 10 tons/sq. metre
1 kg/m² = .205 lb./sq. ft. = 1.844 lb./sq. yard
1 lb./sq. inch = .0703 kg/cm² = 144 lb./sq. ft.
1 lb./sq. ft. = 9 lb./sq. yard = 4.882 kg/mtr.² = .0069 lb./sq. inch
1 lb./sq. yard = .11 lb./sq. ft. = .542 kg/mtr.²
1 Litre/mtr.² = .020 Imp. Gall./ft.² = .184 Imp. Gall./yard² = .025 US-Gall./ft.² = ,221 US-Gallon/yard²
1 Imp. Gall./ft.² = 9 Imp. Gall./yard² = 48.94 Litres/mtr.²
1 Imp. Gall./yard² = .111 Imp. Gall./ft.² = 5.44 Litres/mtr.²
1 US-Gallon/ft.² = 9 US-Gallons/yard² = 40.77 Litres/mtr.²
1 US-Gallon/yard² = .111 US/Gallon-ft.² = 4.53 Litres/mtr.²
1 Litre/mtr.² = .093 Litre/ft.² = .836 Litre/yard².
1 Litre/ft.² = 9 Liter/yard² = 9.18 Litre/mtr.²
1 Litre/yard² = .111 Litre/ft.² = 1.02 Litre/mtr.²

Velocities Geschwindigkeiten

1 mtr./sec. = 3.6 km/h = 1.093 Yards/sec. = 2.237 Miles/h = 3.281 Ft./sec.
1 km/h = .278 mtr./sec. = .304 Yards/sec. = .622 Miles/h = 0.91178 Ft./sec.
1 Yard/sec. = .915 mtr./sec. = 3.292 km/h = 2.040 Miles/h
1 Mile/h = .447 mtr./sec. = 1.609 km/h = .489 Yards/sec.

Temperatures Temperaturen

Celsius (° C) = 5/9 (° F—32) = 5/4° R
Réaumur (° R) = 4/5° C = 4/9 (° F—32)
Fahrenheit (° F) = 9/5° C + 32 = 9/4° R + 32

°C	°R	°F	°C	°R	°F
— 40	— 32	— 40	+ 60	+ 48	+ 140
— 35	— 28	— 31	+ 65	+ 52	+ 149
— 30	— 24	— 22	+ 70	+ 56	+ 158
— 25	— 20	— 13	+ 75	+ 60	+ 167
— 20	— 16	— 4	+ 80	+ 64	+ 176
— 17.8	— 14.2	0	+ 85	+ 68	+ 185
— 15	— 12	+ 5	+ 90	+ 72	+ 194
— 10	— 8	+ 14	+ 95	+ 76	+ 203
— 5	— 4	+ 23	+ 100	+ 80	+ 212
0	0	+ 32	+ 110	+ 88	+ 230
+ 5	+ 4	+ 41	+ 120	+ 96	+ 248
+ 10	+ 8	+ 50	+ 130	+ 104	+ 266
+ 15	+ 12	+ 59	+ 140	+ 112	+ 284
+ 20	+ 16	+ 68	+ 150	+ 120	+ 302
+ 25	+ 20	+ 77	+ 175	+ 140	+ 347
+ 30	+ 24	+ 86	+ 200	+ 160	+ 392
+ 35	+ 28	+ 95	+ 225	+ 180	+ 437
+ 40	+ 32	+ 104	+ 250	+ 200	+ 482
+ 45	+ 36	+ 113	+ 275	+ 220	+ 527
+ 50	+ 40	+ 122	+ 300	+ 240	+ 572
+ 55	+ 44	+ 131	+ 350	+ 280	+ 662

Schedule of Symbols used in Reinforced Concrete Construction
Übersicht der im Stahlbetonbau gebräuchlichen Bezeichnungen

British
Britisch   German
                                                                          Deutsch

a	= Hebelarm der inneren Kräfte = lever of the resistance moment	z
B	= Breite der Druckzone eines Querschnitts = overall breadth of compressive flange of a beam	b
B_1, B_2	= zulässige Haftspannungen = permissible average and local bond stresses	τ_{1zul}
b	= Stegbreite eines Plattenbalkens = breadth of a rectangular beam or the breadth of the rib of a T- or -L-beam	b_0
c	= zulässige Betonspannung bei reinem Druck = permissible stress in concrete in direct compression	$\varrho_{bd\,zul}$
	= zulässige Stahlspannung bei Säulenlängsbewehrung = permissible compression stress for column bar	$\varrho_{e\,zul}$

British Britisch			German Deutsch
D	=	Durchmesser des Säulenkopfes bei Pilzdecken, Durchmesser eines Längsbewehrungsstabes = diameter of column head supporting flat slab (It is elsewhere used for overall concrete depth, or least lateral dimension of a column)	δ
d	=	Durchmesser eines Querbewehrungsstabes = diameter of one transverse reinforcing bar	δ
h	=	Nutzhöhe einer Stahlbetonplatte = useful height of reinforced concrete slab	h
K	=	Steifheit eines Baugliedes = $\dfrac{J}{L}$ = stiffness of constructional element	
L	=	Länge einer Säule, Lichtweite eines Tragwerks = length of a column or beam between adequate lateral restraints. (In the case of slabs L is the average L_1 and L_2)	h_s bzw. w
L_1, L_2	=	Feldlängen bei Pilzdecken = L_1 (in the case of flat slabs) length of panel in the direction of span L_2 (in the case of flat slabs) width of panel at right angles to direction of span	l_x, l_y
l	=	Spannweite eines Bauteils = effective span of beam or slab or effective height of cloumn	l
		Knicklänge einer Säule	h_k
l_x, l_y	=	Seitenlängen kreuzweise bewehrter Platten = l_x lenght of shorter side of slab spanning in two directions; l_y length of longer side of slab spanning in two directions................................	l_x, l_y
M	=	Biegemomente mit Index nach Bedarf = bending moments (suffixes as required)	M
m	=	Verhältnis der Elastizitätszahlen von Stahl und Beton = modular ratio	n
S	=	Querkraft = total shear across a section	Q
t_b	=	zulässige Stahlspannung in Spiralbewehrung = permissible stress in helical reinforcement	—
u_p	=	Würfelfestigkeit des Betons bei Eignungsprüfungen = cube crushing strength (preliminary test)	W
u_w	=	Würfelfestigkeit des Betons bei Güteprüfungen = cube crushing strength (works test)	W
W	=	Gesamtlast eines Balkens oder einer Platte = total load on beam or slab..	
u˙	=	Gesamtlast je Längen- oder Flächeneinheit = total load per unit area of slab or per unit length of beam	q

U. S. Standard Sieve Data (A. S. T. M.)

Bureau of Standard Sieve Number	Specified sieve opening lichte Maschenweite		Specified wire diameter	
	Inches	Millimeters	Inches	Millimeters
(3/16 in.) 4	—.187	4.76	—.050	1.27
5	—.157	4.00	—.044	1.12
6	—.132	3.36	—.040	1.02
7	—.111	2.83	—.036	—.92
8[1]	—.0937	2.38	—.0331	—.84
10	—.0787	2.00	—.0299	—.76
12	—.0661	1.68	—.0272	—.69
14	—.0555	1.41	—.0240	—.61
16[2]	—.0469	1.19	—.0213	—.54
18	—.0394	1.00	—.0189	—.48
20	—.0331	—.84	—.0165	—.42
25	—.0280	—.71	—.0146	—.37
30[3]	—.0232	—.59	—.0130	—.33
35	—.0197	—.50	—.0114	—.29
40	—.0165	—.42	—.0098	—.25
45	—.0138	—.35	—.0087	—.22
50[4]	—.0117	—.297	—.0074	—.188
60	—.0098	—.250	—.0064	—.162
70	—.0083	—.210	—.0055	—.140
80	—.0070	—.177	—.0047	—.119
100[5]	—.0059	—.149	—.0040	—.102
120	—.0049	—.125	—.0034	—.086
140	—.0041	—.105	—.0029	—.074
170	—.0035	—.088	—.0025	—.063
200	—.0029	—.074	—.0021	—.053
230	—.0024	—.062	—.0018	—.046
270	—.0021	—.053	—.0016	—.041
325	—.0017	—.044	—.0014	—.036

[1] B.S. Sieve No. 7   0.0949 Aperture size (in.)
[2] B.S. Sieve No. 14 0.0474 Aperture size (in.)
[3] B.S. Sieve No. 25 0.0236 Aperture size (in.)
[4] B.S. Sieve No. 52 0.0116 Aperture size (in.)
[5] B.S. Sieve No. 100 0.0060 Aperture size (in.)

Die gebräuchlichsten Siebsysteme mit ihren wichtigsten Daten

Amerikanischer ASTM Maschensiebsatz		Britischer STANDARD Maschensiebsatz		Maschensiebe DIN 1171 Ausgabe 1934			Rundlochsiebe DIN 1170 Ausgabe 1933	
Maschen je Zoll	lichte Maschenweite mm	Maschen je Zoll	lichte Maschenweite mm	Gewebe Nr.	Maschen je cm^2	lichte Maschenweite mm	Lochdurchmesser mm	Umrechnung in lichte Maschenweite mm
—	—	—	—	100	10000	0,060		
200	0,074	200	0,076	80	6400	0,075		
—	—	—	—	70	4900	0,090[2])		
100	0,149	100	0,152	40	1600	0,150		
80	0,177	85	0,178	35[1])	1225	0,177		Umrechnung nach Rotfuchs
70	0,210	72	0,211	30	900	0,200		
60	0,250	60	0,251	24	576	0,250		
50	0,297	52	0,294	20	400	0,300		
—	—	44	0,353	—	—	—		
40	0,420	36	0,422	14	196	0,430		
30	0,590	25	0,599	10	100	0,600		
—	—	—	—	—	—	—	1	0,7
—	—	—	—	8	64	0,750		
20	0,840	18	0,853	—	—	—		
18	1,000	—	—	—	—	1,000		
16	1,190	14	1,200	5	—	1,200		
12	1,680	10	1,676	—	—	—		
10	2,000	8	2,057	—	—	2,000	3	2,3
5	4,000					3	5	3,8
3/16" (4)	4,760	3/16"	4,760			5	7	5,4
1/4"	6,35	1/4"	6,35			6	8	6,2
						8	10	7,8
3/8"	9,52	3/8"	9,52			—	12	9,5
1/2"	12,7	1/2"	12,7			12	15	12
						15	20	16,4
3/4"	19,050	3/4"	19,050			18	25	20,8
1"	25,4	1"	25,4			25	30	25,2
1 1/4"	31,75	1 1/4"	31,75			30	40	34,0
1 1/2"	38,100	1 1/2"	38,100					
2"	50,800							
3"	76,200	3"	76,200					
6"	152,400							

Anmerkung: Unterstrichene Zahlen = Siebe für abgekürzte Siebungen.
[1]) Ergänzungssieb.   [2]) früher 0,088.

Soil Classification Diagram

Classification System	Particle Size Equivalent Diameter MM				British Standard Sieve				
		0.002	0.02		200	72	25	7	3/16 in 3/8 in 3/4 in 1 1/2 in 2 1/2 in
International Society of Soil Science	CLAY	←	SILT		FINE SAND		COARSE SAND		GRAVEL
United States Public Roads Administration	CLAY / COLLOIDS 0.001		SILT	0.005	FINE SAND	0.05	COARSE SAND		GRAVEL
Massachusetts Institute of Technology	CLAY		FINE SILT	MEDIUM SILT	COARSE SILT	FINE SAND	MEDIUM SAND	COARSE SAND	GRAVEL
British Standards Institution	CLAY		FINE SILT	MEDIUM SILT	COARSE SILT	FINE SAND	MEDIUM SAND	COARSE SAND	GRAVEL
Particle Size		0.002	0.006	0.02	0.06	0.2	0.6	2.0	60 MM

499

Übersicht über verschiedene Einteilungsversuche der Lockergesteine (nach Dücker)

Bezeichnung und Korndurchmesser in mm (logar. Einteilung)

Jahr	Vorschläge angewandt durch	200	60	20	6	2,0	0,6	0,2	0,06	0,05/0,02/0,006	0,005	0,002	0,0006 0,0002
ungefähr 1890 bis 95	**U.S. Bureau of Soils** (A. Casagrande 1947)		Gravel				Sand			Silt		Clay	
1905 1913	**A. Atterberg** Internat. Bodenk. Gesellsch.	Steine und Geröll		Kies		Grobsand		Feinsand	Schluff		Ton		
1914 1931	**I. Kopecki**, Mass.-Institute of Technology (M.I.T.) (n. A. Casagrande 1947)			Kies Gravel			Sand			Schluff Silt		Ton Clay	
1925	**K. Terzaghi**					Sand			Mo	Schluff		Kolloid-schlamm	Ultra Ton
1936	**DIN 4022**	Steine		Kies			Sand		Mehl Sand	Schluff		Rohton	
1936	**S. Fischer u. H. Udluft**	Block	Brock	Grand	Graup	Gries	Gritt	Sand		Silt Schluff	Schmand Sink	Schlamm Schweb	
1938	**P. Niggli**	Block	Grobkies		Feinkies		Grobsand	Sand	Feinsand	Grobschluff	Feinschluff	Schlamm Schweb	
1938	**U.S. Depart. of Agriculture** (n.A. Casagrande 1947)			Gravel			Sand			Silt		Clay	
1939	**H. Gallwitz**	Block	Schotter		Kies		Sand			Schluff		Ton	
1942	**R. Grengg**	Grobst. Boden	Grobschotter-Boden	Feinschotter-Boden			Sand		Mehl	Schluff		Schlamm	Fein-stes
1948	**A. Dücker**	Gröbstes Gröbst. I	Siebkorn IIa grobes IIb	IIIa mittleres IIIb	IVa feines IVb			Schlammkorn Va grobes Vb	VIa mittleres VIb		VII feines		

Bauverlag-Wörterbücher

Zement-Wörterbuch / Dictionary of Cement
Herstellung und Technologie
Manufacture and Technology

Von Dipl.-Ing. C. van Amerongen. Deutsch-Englisch/Englisch-Deutsch. 2., neubearbeitete und erweiterte Auflage. 328 Seiten. Format 13,5 x 20,5 cm. Gebunden DM 130,—

Gips-Wörterbuch
Gypsum and Plaster Dictionary
Dictionnaire du gypse et du plâtre
Deutsch — Englisch — Französisch

Von Dipl.-Ing. K.-H. Volkart. 176 Seiten. Rund 3000 Stichwörter. Format 17 x 24 cm. Gebunden DM 85,—

Getriebe-Wörterbuch
Dictionary of Mechanisms

Von H. Bucksch. Deutsch-Englisch/Englisch-Deutsch in einem Band. 286 Seiten mit zahlreichen Zeichnungen. Zusammen rund 16.000 Stichwörter. Format 13,5 x 20,5 cm. Plastik DM 165,—

Preise Stand Dez. '86, Preisänderungen vorbehalten.

Bauverlag·Wiesbaden und Berlin

Bauverlag-Wörterbücher

Wörterbuch für Architektur, Hochbau und Baustoffe
Dictionary of Architecture, Building Construction and Materials

Von H. Bucksch. Format 13,5 x 20,5 cm. Plastik.

Band 1: Deutsch-Englisch. 2. Auflage. 942 Seiten. Rund 65.000 Stichwörter. DM 240,—
Band 2: Englisch-Deutsch. 2. Auflage. 1137 Seiten. Rund 75.000 Stichwörter. DM 240,—

Diese Bände beinhalten nicht nur die alphabetische Folge aller Fachbegriffe, sondern darüber hinaus in allen notwendigen Fällen kurze bis ausführliche Erläuterungen zu den Termini. So erhält das Wörterbuch den zusätzlichen Wert eines Baufachlexikons.

Holz-Wörterbuch
Dictionary of Wood and Woodworking Practice

Von H. Bucksch. Format 13,5 x 17 cm. Gebunden.

Band 1: Deutsch-Englisch. 1. Nachdruck. zur 2. Auflage. 461 Seiten. Rund 20.000 Stichwörter. DM 98,—
Band 2: Englisch-Deutsch. 1. Nachdruck. zur 1. Auflage. 536 Seiten. Rund 20.000 Stichwörter. DM 125,—

Preise Stand Dez. '86, Preisänderungen vorbehalten.

Bauverlag·Wiesbaden und Berlin

Herbert Bucksch

Dictionary of Civil Engineering and Construction Machinery and Equipment

*

Wörterbuch für Ingenieurbau und Baumaschinen

Volume **II** Band

English · German / Englisch · Deutsch

BAUVERLAG GMBH · WIESBADEN AND BERLIN

PREFACE TO THE FIRST EDITION

Our present civilisation is hardly conceivable without the achievements of modern civil engineering. The "use and convenience" to man of all these activities can scarcely be denied. Civil engineers had certainly left their mark on the face of Nature, damming great lakes and constructing hydro-electric plants, highways, bridges, canals, railway lines, airports, towns, etc.

Although remarkable structures have been erected in ancient times, e. g. the Great Wall of China and the Seven Ancient Wonders of the World, it was not until the last century that civil engineering entered upon a new era. The steam locomotive required trackings, the automobile called for high-quality roads and the aircraft for suitable landing, taking off and servicing facilities. Steady improvements of these inventions brought about a further development of these facilities and civil engineering spread itself over a wide range of scientific fields in order to meet the ever increasing demands. Systematic research became imperative with detailed documentation of the results obtained.

As civil engineers of all countries work towards the same aim of "directing the great sources of power in Nature to the use and convenience of man," international co-operation becomes inevitable.

The foundations of this international co-operation are the many conferences convened by the individual civil engineering organisations in which the experience is pooled for the benefit of all concerned. Civil engineers of all nations thus get into touch with each other and this personal contact soon removes any reserve or sense of mistrust. International connections between civil engineers can be initiated in many ways. For instance, the "Deutsche Gesellschaft für Erd- und Grundbau" (German Society for Soil and Foundation Engineering) and the "ASCE Soil Mechanics and Foundations Division" exchange their knowledge in their relevant field by correspondence in English and German.

This international partnership naturally draws attention to the terminology involved and the selection of equivalent terms in the various languages.

To-day's languages frequently experience the introduction of new words and the field of civil engineering with its widespread ramifications into various other related fields contributes to a considerable extent to this phenomenon. Thus, technical dictionaries are required.

The compilation of a technical dictionary is already difficult because the scope of meaning of a single word in one language is not always clearly defined, and when selecting the appropriate term in the foreign language, which might also not be subject to precise definition, great care must be exercised. Even if technical terms are free from any ambiguity as to their meaning, it must always be borne in mind, that the selected relative foreign words must cover the same range of technical definition.

This dictionary has been compiled in an attempt to foster the harmony of international partnership in Civil Engineering, and the latest relevant literature has been searched for its compilation. It contains a multitude of definitions not yet incorporated into any other dictionary available to-day.

It is hoped by the publisher as well as the author, that this dictionary will fill the gap felt in the past.

Cologne, February 1955

H. Bucksch

PREFACE TO THE SECOND EDITION

This edition is considerably larger than the first one. The entries have been checked again and new words were added. It was considered to be advisable to split this edition up into two tomes. The publisher and the author hope that this edition will be as welcomed by all engineering circles as was the first edition. Suggestions from readers are invited.

Cologne, May 1958

H. Bucksch

VORWORT ZUR ERSTEN AUFLAGE

Unsere heutige Zivilisation ist ohne den modernen Ingenieurbau nicht mehr denkbar. Durch ihn werden die Bauten zur Ausnützung der Wasserkräfte, wie Talsperren und Wasserkraftwerke, die Verkehrsverbindungen, wie Straßen, Brücken, Kanäle, Eisenbahnlinien und Flugplätze, die Bewässerungs- und Entwässerungsanlagen für die Gewinnung neuer Kulturflächen, die menschlichen Siedlungen in der Vielfalt ihrer Formen usw. geschaffen. Der Mensch verändert die Oberfläche der Erde.

Obwohl bereits im Altertum imposante Bauwerke geschaffen worden sind, wofür die Chinesische Mauer und die Sieben Weltwunder als die bekanntesten Beispiele dienen mögen, brach für den Ingenieurbau jedoch erst mit dem Zeitalter der Erfindungen eine neue Epoche an. Die Lokomotive erforderte Schienenstränge, das Auto verlangte nach Straßen, und für das Flugzeug mußten geeignete Flächen zum Starten und Landen geschaffen werden. Die stetige Verbesserung der Erfindungen bedingte eine Ausweitung der von diesen Erfindungen benötigten Anlagen, und der Ingenieurbau mußte sich zur Erfüllung der ihm in immer rascherem Tempo gestellten Aufgaben eine Reihe von Wissensgebieten erschließen. Systematische Forschung wurde unumgänglich, und bald stellte sich die Notwendigkeit einer Dokumentation der Ergebnisse heraus.

Die Interessen und Ziele der Bauingenieure aller Völker sind die gleichen; sie wollen mit ihren Bauwerken dem Wohl der Menschheit dienen. Daraus ergibt sich die Forderung zu internationaler Zusammenarbeit.

Die heute zur Vertiefung des Wissens auf den einzelnen Teilgebieten des Ingenieurbaues auf internationaler Ebene abgehaltenen Konferenzen sind der Grundstein für diese Zusammenarbeit. Die persönliche Fühlungnahme führt zur Beseitigung des Trennenden und des Mißtrauens. Zwischenstaatliche Bindungen werden jedoch auch auf andere Art und Weise geknüpft. So ist z. B. die „Deutsche Gesellschaft für Erd- und Grundbau" mit der diesbezüglichen Fachorganisation der USA, „ASCE Soil Mechanics and Foundations Division", übereingekommen, einen gegenseitigen Austausch des Wissens auf ihrem Fachgebiet durchzuführen. Als Korrespondenzsprachen wurden Englisch und Deutsch bestimmt.

Die internationale Zusammenarbeit auf dem Gebiete des Ingenieurbaues lenkt nun auch demzufolge das Augenmerk auf die Fachterminologie in bezug auf eine Gegenüberstellung der Begriffe in den verschiedenen Sprachen.

Die heutigen Sprachen erleben täglich die Geburt neuer Wörter. Der Ingenieurbau mit seinen Ausläufern in die verschiedenartigsten Wissensgebiete hat daran, wie überhaupt die Technik, erheblichen Anteil. Hier ergibt sich nun die Forderung nach technischen Wörterbüchern.

Die Zusammenstellung eines technischen Wörterbuches ist wegen der schon in der eigenen Sprache oft unklaren Begriffsbestimmung eines einzelnen technischen Wortes schwierig, und bei der Auswahl des meistens dem gleichen Gesetz verschiedener Definitionsmöglichkeiten unterliegenden fremdsprachlichen Wortes ist daher größte Vorsicht geboten. Selbst wenn technische Wörter frei von jeder Zweideutigkeit in bezug auf ihre Definition sind, ist bei einer Gegenüberstellung mit dem fremdsprachlichen Wort stets zu prüfen, ob sich die Definitionen in beiden Sprachen vom technischen Standpunkt aus decken.

Das vorliegende Wörterbuch wurde mit dem Ziel zusammengestellt, die internationale Zusammenarbeit auf dem Gebiete des Ingenieurbaues zu fördern. Bei der Bearbeitung wurden die neuesten Quellen erschöpft. Viele Begriffe sind hier zum ersten Male lexikographisch erfaßt.

Verlag und Verfasser hoffen, mit der Vorlage dieses Wörterbuches einem Bedürfnis der Kreise des Ingenieurbaues entsprochen zu haben.

Köln, im Februar 1955
H. Bucksch

VORWORT ZUR ZWEITEN AUFLAGE

Diese Auflage erscheint in wesentlich größerem Umfang als die erste. Die Eintragungen wurden noch einmal überprüft und die Terminologie wurde auf den neuesten Stand gebracht. Eine Aufteilung in zwei Bände ist bei dieser Ausgabe als zweckmäßig erachtet worden. Verlag und Verfasser hoffen, daß diese Auflage ebenso den Beifall der Fachkreise findet, der der ersten Auflage zuteil geworden ist. Anregungen aus Benutzerkreisen werden stets dankbar entgegengenommen.

Köln, im Mai 1958
H. Bucksch

INTRODUCTION

The terms are compiled in alphabetical order. Certain terms, however, forming subject titles from a technical point of view are accompanied in volume I by a sub-section giving other words relevant to the subject. Example:

Fahrzeuge *npl* **für den Transport** *m* **von Boden** *m* **und Steinbaustoffen** *mpl*
   geländegängiger luftbereifter Erdtransportwagen *m*, gummibereiftes Erdbau-Lastfahrzeug *n*, geländegängiger Förderwagen *m* in Kraftwagen-Bauart *f*, Muldenkipper *m*, Groß-Förderwagen *m*, gleisloser Förderwagen *m*, Motorkipper, Erdtransportfahrzeug für Fremdbeladung
     Halbanhänger *m* mit Bodenentleerung *f* durch Klappen *fpl*, aufsattelbarer Bodenentleerer *m*, aufgesattelter Erdtransportwagen mit Bodenentleerung, Fabrikat THE EUCLID ROAD MACHINERY COMPANY, CLEVELAND 17, OHIO, USA
                          etc.

(earth and rock) hauling equipment
   rubber-tired (US)/rubber-tyred (Brit.) off-(the-)highway hauling unit (or earth-moving vehicle)

     EUCLID bottom-dump wagon

Kohle *f*
   Abfall∼
   Anthrazit *m*
   Back∼, siehe: weiche ∼
   Braun∼
   Erbs∼, siehe: Grieß∼
   erdige Stein∼
                   etc.

coal
   waste ∼
   anthracite (∼)

   brown ∼

   earthy ∼, smut

Brackets are used:
a) Square Brackets:
  (1) to define a term, e.g.

  (2) to denote the particular field, e.g.

b) Round Brackets:
  (3) for terms or part of terms which can be omitted, e.g.

  (4) for abbreviations, e.g.

Bodendruck *m*, Bodenpressung *f*, Flächenpressung *f*, Flächendruck [*z. B. einer Gleiskette f auf den Untergrund m*]
Fertigbehandlung *f*, Endbearbeitung *f* [*Beton m*]

Doppel(rohr)tunnel *m* = Doppelrohrtunnel, Doppeltunnel
          or
(Beton)Dichtungsmittel *n* = Dichtungsmittel, Betondichtungsmittel
(Geol.) = Geology
(Min.) = Mineralogy
(Brit.) = Great Britain
(US) = USA

The Tilde ~ substitutes the word to be repeated, e. g.
Halde f, Vorrats~, Material~ = Halde f, Vorratshalde, Materialhalde

The Tilde ~ substitutes the preceding word or the part of the preceding word printed before the sign | and to be repeated in the following one, e.g.

Krone f
~ f = Krone f
Abbinde|regler m
~verzögerer = Abbindeverzögerer m

The Comma separates equivalent definitions.
The Semicolon separates equivalent definitions but alternatively used either in the USA or Great Britain.

The gender of the German words is indicated by:

        m = *masculine*
        f = *feminine*
        n = *neuter*
        mpl = *the term is given in its plural form with the singular being masculine; fpl and npl apply accordingly.*

Where the Public Works Industrie Committee [Great Britain] is of the opinion that the particular use of a term is incorrect and should preferably be discontinued, it is preceded, or followed, by the word [deprecated].

"TRADEMARK" *indicates that a word is a proprietary name owned by a particular company and valued by it as identifying its product.*

The asterisk (*) denotes that the term is accompanied in the German-English part by further words. It therefore appears in the English-German part only.

The German letter «ß» means «sz».

EINFÜHRUNG

Die Wörter sind alphabetisch geordnet. Zum Zwecke einer Darstellung nach technischen Gesichtspunkten sind im Band I bei manchen Begriffen weitere außerhalb der alphabetischen Reihenfolge aufgeführt. Beispiel:

Fahrzeuge *npl* **für den Transport** *m* **von Boden** *m* **und Steinbaustoffen** *mpl*
   geländegängiger luftbereifter Erdtransportwagen *m*, gummibereiftes Erdbau-Lastfahrzeug *n*, geländegängiger Förderwagen *m* in Kraftwagen-Bauart *f*, Muldenkipper *m*, Groß-Förderwagen *m*, gleisloser Förderwagen *m*, Motorkipper, Erdtransportfahrzeug für Fremdbeladung

    Halbanhänger *m* mit Bodenentleerung *f* durch Klappen *fpl*, aufsattelbarer Bodenentleerer *m*, aufgesattelter Erdtransportwagen mit Bodenentleerung, Fabrikat THE EUCLID ROAD MACHINERY COMPANY, CLEVELAND 17, OHIO, USA

                            usw.

Kohle *f*
  Abfall $\sim$
  Anthrazit *m*
  Back $\sim$, siehe: weiche $\sim$
  Braun $\sim$
  Erbs $\sim$, siehe: Grieß $\sim$
  erdige Stein $\sim$

              usw.

Anwendung der Klammern:
a) eckige Klammern:
  1. Definition eines Wortes, z. B.

  2. Bestimmung des Sachgebietes, z. B.

b) runde Klammern:
  3. Auslassungen, z. B.

  4. Abkürzungen, z. B.

(earth and rock) hauling equipment

  rubber-tired (US)/rubber-tyred (Brit.) off-(the-)highway hauling unit (or earth-moving vehicle)

EUCLID bottom-dump wagon

coal
  waste $\sim$
  anthracite ($\sim$)

  brown $\sim$

  earthy $\sim$, smut

Bodendruck *m*, Bodenpressung *f*, Flächenpressung *f*, Flächendruck [*z. B. einer Gleiskette f auf den Untergrund m*]
Fertigbehandlung *f*, Endbearbeitung *f* [*Beton m*]

Doppel(rohr)tunnel *m* = Doppelrohrtunnel, Doppeltunnel
      oder
(Beton)Dichtungsmittel *n* = Dichtungsmittel, Betondichtungsmittel *n*
(Geol.) = Geologie
(Min.) = Mineralogie
(Brit.) = Großbritannien
(US) = USA

Die Tilde ~ *tritt an die Stelle des zu wiederholenden Wortes, z. B.* Halde *f*, Vorrats~, Material~ = Halde *f*, Vorratshalde, Materialhalde

Die Tilde ~ *im Fettdruck tritt an die Stelle des darüber befindlichen Wortes oder des zu wiederholenden Wortteiles, welcher vor dem Strich steht, z. B.*

Krone *f*
~ *f* = Krone *f*
Abbinde|verzögerer *m*
~**wärme** *f* = Abbindewärme *f*

Das Komma teilt Wörter gleicher Definition.
Das Semikolon teilt Wörter gleicher Definition, die aber einerseits in den USA und andererseits in Großbritannien gebräuchlich sind.

Das Geschlecht der deutschen Wörter ist wie folgt angegeben:

>   *m*   = *männlich*
>   *f*   = *weiblich*
>   *n*   = *sächlich*
>   *mpl* = *das betreffende Wort ist in der Pluralform angegeben, wobei die Einzahlform männlich ist. Dementsprechend sind fpl und npl zu verstehen.*

Wörter, deren Gebrauch vom Public Works Industry Committee [Großbritannien] für den betreffenden Begriff nicht mehr empfohlen werden und deshalb besser nicht mehr angewandt werden sollen, sind durch das ihnen vorangestellte oder nachgestellte Wort [deprecated] gekennzeichnet.

„TRADEMARK" gibt an, daß es sich bei dem betreffenden Begriff um eine Schutzmarke handelt.

Das Sternchen (*) bedeutet, daß im Deutsch-Englischen Teil weitere in Beziehung zu dem betreffenden Begriff stehende Wörter gegeben sind. Dieses (*) erscheint also nur im Englisch-Deutschen Teil.

VOLUME II
BAND II

*

ENGLISH - GERMAN
ENGLISCH - DEUTSCH

The asterisk (*) denotes that the term is accompanied in the German-English part by further words.

Das Sternchen (*) bedeutet, daß im Deutsch-Englischen Teil weitere in Beziehung zu dem betreffenden Begriff stehende Wörter gegeben sind.

A

aa (lava) [*Hawaian term*]; block lava = Blocklava *f*, Schollenlava, Zackenlava, Spratzlava, Aprolith *m*

to abandon a well = eine Bohrung *f* aufgeben

to abate = abflauen [*Wind m*]

abatement of dust(ing), alleviation of dust, dust alleviation, dust allaying, dust suppression, dust control = Staubbindung *f*

~ ~ swell = Abschwächung *f* des Seegangs *m*

abattoir, slaughter house = Schlachthof *m*, Schlachthaus *n*

ABC-process = Aluminium-Blut-Kohle-Verfahren *n*

abele, white poplar, abele tree = Silberpappel *f*, Weißpappel

abietic acid = Abietinsäure *f*

ablation, wastage [*glacier*] = Abschmelzung *f*, Ablation *f*

above-grade masonry = Mauerwerk *n* über Geländeoberkante *f*

abradant, abrasive = Schleifmittel *n*
artificial ~ = künstliches ~
natural ~ = natürliches ~

to abrade = abschleifen, abreiben

Abrams' fineness modulus, F. M. = Abrams'scher (Feinheits)Modul *m*, F$_m$

~ test, test for organic matter, organic test for fine aggregate, extraction with caustic soda = Ätznatronprüfung *f*, Ätznatronprobe *f* [*Betonzuschläge mpl*]

*abrasion; denudation (Brit.) = Denudation *f*
~ = Abschleifung *f*, Abschleifen *n*, Abrieb *m*, Abreiben *n*, Abreibung, Abschliff *m*

~ coast = Abtragungsküste *f*

~ embayment, corrosion ~ = Abrasionsbucht *f*, Abschleifungsbucht

~ loss = Abschleif(ungs)verlust *m*, Abriebverlust

~ plain = Brandungsebene *f*

~ resistance = Abschleifwiderstand *m*, Abriebwiderstand, Abriebfestigkeit *f*, Widerstandsvermögen *n* gegen Abschleifen *n*, ~ ~ Abrieb *m*, Abschlifffestigkeit

~ test = Abschleifversuch *m*, Abriebprüfung *f*, Abschleifprüfung, Abriebversuch

abrasive, abradant = Schleifmittel *n*
~, ~ material = abstumpfender Stoff *m* [*Straßenwinterdienst m*]

~ blade = Schleifscheibe *f* [*Einschleifen n von Betonfugen fpl*]

~ cloth, emery ~ = Schleifleinen *n*

~ material = scharfkantiges Fördergut *n*
~ ~ = Schleifrohstoff *m*

abrasiveness [*e. g. of sand*] = (Ab)Schleifwirkung *f*, Abriebwirkung

abrasive paper, emery ~ = Schleifpapier *n*

~ powder = Schleifpulver *n*

~ wear by vehicles [*concrete surface*] = Abriebverschleiß *m* durch Fahrzeuge *npl*

abridged trial-load method — accelerometer

abridged trial-load method, simplified ~ ~ = einfaches Lastaufteilungsverfahren *n*, einschnittiges ~
abscissa = Abszisse *f*, Auftraglinie *f*
absolute altimeter = Echolot *n*
~ **coefficient of expansion** = absoluter Ausdehnungsbeiwert *m*
~ **forest-soil** = absoluter Waldboden *m*
~ **measurement** = Absolutmessung *f*
~**-rest precipitation tank** = Absetzbecken *n* für aussetzenden Betrieb *m*, ~ mit ruhendem Abwasser *n*
absolute strength = absolute Festigkeit *f*
~ **velocity** = absolute Geschwindigkeit *f*
~ **viscosity** = dynamische Viskosität *f*, ~ Zähflüssigkeit *f*
to absorb = absorbieren
absorbent = Absorptionsmittel *n*
absorbing power, see: absorption capacity
absorption = Absorption *f*, Aufzehrung *f* [*Einsaugen eines Stoffes in das Innere eines anderen ohne chemische Vereinigung*]
~ **basin,** stilling ~ (Brit.); stilling pool (US) = Beruhigungsbecken *n*, Tosbecken
~ **capacity,** ~ property, absorptive ~, absorbing power = Absorptionsvermögen *n*, Absorptionsfähigkeit *f*
~ ~ **of a turbine** = Schluckvermögen *n* [*Turbine f*]
~ **filter** = Absorptionsfilter *m, n*
~ **gasoline** = Absorptionsnaturgasolin *n*
~ **oil,** stripping ~, scrubbing ~, wash ~ = Waschöl *n* zur Absorption *f* von Gasolin *n* oder Benzol *n*
~ **spectrum** = Absorptionsspektrum *n*
~ **tower** = Absorptionsturm *m*
~ **type refrigerator** = Absorptionskältemaschine *f*
absorptive capacity, see: absorption ~
~ ~ **for water** = Wasseraufnahmevermögen *n*, Wasseraufnahmefähigkeit *f*
~ **soil** = absorbierender Boden *m*
abundance of seams = Flözreichtum *m*
*abutment = Widerlager *n*
~ **hinge** = Kämpfergelenk *n*
~ **of an arch,** arch abutment = Bogenwiderlager *n*
~ **pad** = Widerlagerkissen *n*

~ **pier** = Widerlagerpfeiler *m*
~ **section** = Stauwerksteil *m* neben der Überfallstrecke *f*
~**stone** = Widerlagerstein *m*
~ **toe wall** (Brit.); rock-fill ~ ~ (US) [*rock-fill dam*] = luftseitige Fußbefestigung *f*
~ **wall** = Stützmauer *f*, Böschungsmauer
abutting = aneinanderstoßend
~ **joint** = stumpfer Stoß *m*
~ **property** = anliegender Grundbesitz *m*
abyssal, abysmal = abyssisch, plutonisch, grundlos (Geol.) [*in der Tiefe, besonders in der Tiefsee f gebildet*]
Abyssinian pump, bored tube ~, hollow ram ~, Abyssinian well = Rammrohrpumpe *f*, Abessinierpumpe
~ **well** = Rammbrunnen *m* [*früher: Abessinierbrunnen*]
acanthite, Ag_2S (Min.) = Akanthit *m*
accelerated procedure = abgekürztes Verfahren *n*, Schnellverfahren
~ **traffic test** = abgekürzte Verkehrsprüfung *f*
~ **weathering test** = abgekürzte Wetterbeständigkeitsprobe *f*, Bewitterungskurzprüfung *f*, Bewitterungsschnellprüfung
accelerating agent, see: accelerator
~ **lane,** see: acceleration ~
acceleration, priming [*the shortening of the interval between the time of two high tides*] = Gezeitenverfrühung *f*
~ **curve** = Beschleunigungsbogen *m*
~ **lane,** accelerating ~ = Beschleunigungsspur *f* [*Straße f*]
~ **of setting** (Brit.); ~ ~ **set** = Abbindebeschleunigung *f*
accelerator, starter, starting apparatus = Anlasser *m*, Starter *m*
~ [*in heating, a centrifugal pump located in the return circuit*] = Rücklaufpumpe *f* [*Zentralheizung f*]
~ [*tanning process*] = Anschärfungsmittel *n*
~**,** accelerating agent, accelerating admixture = Abbindebeschleuniger *m*
~ **pedal,** gas ~ = Gaspedal *n*, Fahrgashebel *m*
accelerometer = Beschleunigungsmesser *m*

acceptance = Abnahme *f* [*die Übernahme der Bauleistung f nach Fertigstellung*]
~ **test** = Abnahmeprüfung *f*
~ **tolerance**, ~ margin, ~ deviation, ~ permissible variation, ~ off-size = Abnahmetoleranz *f*, Abnahme-Maßabweichung *f*, Abnahme-Abmaß *n*
accessibility = Zugänglichkeit *f*
accessories = Zubehör *m*, *n*
accessory mineral = akzessorisches Mineral *n*, Übergemengteil *m*
~ **part** = Zubehörteil *m*, *n*
access point, interconnecting roadway, interchange = Zufahrtstelle *f*, Anschlußpunkt *m*, Anschlußstelle *f* [*Autobahn f*]
~ **ramp**, interchange ~ = Anschlußrampe *f*
~ **shaft** = Zugangschacht *m*
~ **tunnel**, see: adit (level)
~ **way** = Zufahrt *f*
accident crane, see: permanent way ~ (Brit.)
~ ~, wrecking ~, breakdown ~ = Unfallkran *m*, Bergungskran *m*
~ **prevention** = Unfallverhütung *f*
~ **-proof** = unfallsicher
accident toll, ~ rate = Unfallrate *f*
accommodation ramp, approach ~, raised approach = Auffahrt *f*, Rampe *f*
~ **trailer** (US); sleeping caravan (Brit.); house trailer = Wohn(schlaf)wagen(anhänger) *m*
accreting bank, see: deposition bluff
accretion through alluvium, silting up, filling up, aggradation = Auflandung *f*, Anschwemmung *f*, Aufschwemmung *f*, Aufschlickung *f*, natürliche Kolmotion *f* (Geol.)
accumulating counter [*road traffic*] = Summiergerät *n* [*Straßenverkehr m*]
accumulation = Anreicherung *f*
~ **lake**, see: artificial ~
accumulative weighing = Summierwiegen *n*
accumulator battery, storage ~ = Akku(mulatoren)batterie *f*, Speicherbatterie, Sammler *m*, Akku(mulator) *m*
~ **loco(motive)**, (storage) battery ~ = Akku(mulatoren)lok(omotive) *f*
accuracy = Genauigkeit *f*

accuracy of control = Bedienungsgenauigkeit *f*
~ ~ **sizing** = Trennschärfe *f* [*Sieb n*]
a.c./d.c.-(hand) hammer (rock) drill, a.c./d.c.-(rock) drill hammer = Universal-Bohrhammer *m*
acetate = Azetat *n*, essigsaures Salz *n*
~ **of lead**, sugar ~ ~, lead acetate, $Pb(C_2H_3O_2) \times 3\ H_2O$ = Bleizucker *m*, Bleiazetat *n*
acetic acid = Essigsäure *f*
~ **anhydride** = Essigsäureanhydrid *n*
acetylene cylinder (or bottle) = Azetylenflasche *f*
~ **(gas)** = Azetylen(gas) *n*
~ **generator** = Azetylenentwickler *m*
~ **heat sett treatment unit** = Azetylen-Flammstrahlbrenner *m* zum Aufrauhen von Basaltpflaster *n*
~ **sludge** = Azetylenschlamm *m*
achroite (Min.) = Achroit *m*, Mohrenkopf *m*
acicular bismuth (Min.), see: needle-ore
~ **lignite** (Min.) = Nadelkohle *f*
aciculite (Min.), see: needle-ore
acid attack = Säureangriff *m*
~ **combining capacity** = Säurebindungsvermögen *n*
~ **decomposition** = saure Zersetzung *f*
~ **etching**, ~ washing = Absäuern *n*
~ **exchange** = Säureaustausch *m*
~ **fermentation**, ~ (ripening) stage = saure Gärung *f*
~ **firebrick**, see: silica brick
~ **handling pump** = Säurepumpe *f*
~ **heat** = Bildungswärme *f* bei der Säurereaktion *f*
acidic = sauer [*Gestein n*]
acidity, acidic content = Azidität *f*, Säuregrad *m*, Säuregehalt *m*, Neutralisationszahl *f*
acid-proof tank lining = säurefeste Behälterauskleidung *f*
acid recovery plant = Säurerückgewinnungsanlage *f*
~ **(ripening) stage**, see: ~ fermentation
~ **rock**, acidic ~ [*igneous rock containing over 65 per cent of silica*] = saures Gestein *n*
~ **sludge** = Säureteer *m*
~ **solution** = Säurelösung *f*

acid stage, see: ~ fermentation
~ **treatment** = Säurebehandlung *f*
~ **washing**, ~ etching = Absäuern *n*
to acidulate = ansäuern
acidulated water, acidulous ~ = angesäuertes Wasser *n*
acmite, $NaFeSi_2O_6$ (Min.) = Akmit *m*
~ **trachyte** = Akmittrachyt *m*
acoustical material = akustischer Baustoff *m*
~ **plaster** = Akustikputz *m*
~ **slab**, ~ board = Akustikplatte *f*
~ **tile** = Akustikfliese *f*
acoustic coupling agent, couplant = Ankopplungsmittel *n* [*zerstörungsfreie Prüfung f von Beton m*]
acquisition of land, land purchase = Grunderwerb *m*, Baulandbeschaffung *f* [*in Österreich; Grundeinlösung f*]
actinolite (Min.) = Aktinolith *n*
action = Einwirkung *f*
~ **of forces** = Kräftewirkung *f*
~ ~ **magnesia**, expansion tendency due to magnesia = Magnesia-Treiben *n*
~ **turbine**, see: impulse ~
~ ~ **with pressure stages**, impulse ~ ~ ~ ~, multi-stage action turbine, multi-stage impulse turbine = mehrstufige Druckturbine *f*, Druckturbine *f* mit Druckabstufung *f*
to activate = aktivieren
activated aeration = aktivierte Belüftung *f*
~ **carbon**, see: active charcoal
~ **lime mortar** = aktivierter Kalkmörtel *m* für Außenputz *m*
~ **sludge** = Belebtschlamm *m*
activated-sludge method (or process) = Belebtschlammverfahren *n*, Belebungsverfahren
~ **plant** = Belebtschlammanlage *f*
activator = Anreger *m* [*Zement m*]
~, see: dope
active charcoal, ~ carbon, ~ coal, activated carbon = Aktivkohle *f*, aktive Kohle *f*, a-Kohle *f*
~ **earth**, bleaching ~, bleaching clay = Bleicherde *f*, Bleichton *m*
~ **lateral earth pressure** = aktiver Erddruck *m*, angreifender ~
~ **state** [*soil*] = unterer Grenzzustand *m*

Act of God = höhere Gewalt *f*
actual grading curve = Ist-Linie *f*, Sieblinie des Rohmaterials *n*
~ **volume of the cylinder** = Ansaugemenge *f* [*Kompressor m*]
to act upon = einwirken auf
adamellite (Geol.) = Adamellit *m*
adaptor, fitting piece = Paßstück *n*
~ **bend** = Staubogen *m*, Reduzierstück *n* [*Druckluftbetonförderer m*]
added metal, deposited ~ = eingetragenes Schweißgut *n*
addice [*obsolete term*]; adze = Dechsel *f*
addition = Zementzusatzmittel *n* [*wird mit dem Zement m zusammen vermahlen*]
~, see: additive
additional load, see: imposed ~
*****additive**, addition, admixture = Beimischung *f*, Zumischung *f*, Zusatzstoff *m*
~ **for concrete**; concrete admix (US); admixture = Betonzusatzmittel *n*, Betonwirkstoff *m* [*wird dem Beton m beigegeben*]
~ **soil stabilisation (or stabilization)** = Bodenvermörtelung *f* mit Stabilisatorbeigabe *f*
A-derrick (crane), see: jinniwink
adhesion, adhesiveness = Adhäsion *f*, scheinbare Haftfestigkeit *f*, Grenzflächenkraft *f*
~ **agent**, see: dope
~ **meter** = Haftfestigkeitsmesser *m*
adhesive, glu(e)ing compound = Klebemasse *f*, Aufstrich ~
~ **coat** = Klebeschicht *f*
adhesiveness, see: adhesion
adiabatic line, ~ curve = adiabatische Linie *f*, Druck-Volumenkurve *f*, Adiabate *f*
adit, ~ level, access tunnel, (side) drift, construction adit = Zugangsstollen *m*, Tagesstollen, Fensterstollen, Seitenstollen, Abstiegstollen
~ **fan** = Seitenstollen-Gebläse *n*
~ **mining**, open cut ~, surface ~, opencast ~ (Brit.); open-pit ~ (US) = Tagebau *m*
~ **opening** = Mundloch *n*, Stollenloch *n*
adjacent strip = Nachbarstreifen *m*
~ **structure** = benachbartes Bauwerk *n*

adjacent (traffic) lane = Nachbar(verkehrs)spur f
adjudication (US); competitive tender(ing) action, bidding procedure = Ausschreibung f, Angebotseinholung f
adjustability = Einstellbarkeit f, Verstellbarkeit
adjustable flow bean = verstellbare Eruptionsdüse f [*Tiefbohrtechnik*]
~ iron fore plane = Rauhbank f
~ spanner = Universalschraubenschlüssel m
adjusting nut = (Ver)Stellmutter f
~ ring = (Ver)Stellring m
~ screw = (Ver)Stellschraube f
~ ~ = Einstellspindel f [*Schwarzbelageinbaumaschine f*]
~ wedge, push ~ = (Nach)Stellkeil m, verstellbarer Keil [*Backenbrecher m*]
adjustment = Einstellung f, Justierung f, Einregulierung
~ compass = Regelkompaß m, Einstellkompaß
Admiralty visco(si)meter = Redwood-Viskosimeter II n
admission = Beaufschlagung f [*Turbine f*]
~ of fresh air = Frischluftzufuhr f
admixture, see: additive for concrete
*****admixture**, addition, additive = Beimischung f, Zumischung f, Zusatzstoff m
*****ADNUN black top paver** [*Trademark*] = Schwarzbelageinbaumaschine f, Schwarz(decken)verteiler m, Verteilerfertiger m, Fabrikat THE FOOTE COMPANY, NUNDA, NEW YORK, USA
adobe (clay) (US) [*calcareous sandy silts and sandy-silty clays as found in the semiarid regions of the southwestern United States*] = kalkhaltige sandige Schluffe mpl und sandig-schluffige Tone mpl im südwestlichen Teil der USA; entspricht dem Löß m Europas und Asiens
adret (Geol.) = Sonnenseite f
adsorbed (soil) water = Adsorptionswasser n, äußeres Haftwasser, adsorptiv gebundenes Wasser
adsorption [*condensation in the form of a film, of a liquid on the surface of a solid*] = Adsorption f

~ power = Adsorptionskraft f
~ pressure = Adsorptionsdruck m
adularia (Min.) = Adular m
advance diesel road roller = Advance-Dieselmotor(straßen)walze f
~ direction notice = Ankündigungsschild n [*Autobahn f*]
~ ~ sign = Vorwegweiser m
~ ~ ~ = Hauptschild n [*Autobahnausfahrt f*]
advanced landing ground, A. L. G. = Feldflugplatz m
advance payment bond = Vorauszahlungsgarantie f
~ sign, distant ~ = Richtungsschild n
advection fog = Advektionsnebel m, Mischungsnebel
adventive cone (Geol.) = Adventivkegel m
adverse weather, see: inclement ~
advertising sign = Reklameschild n
adz(e) [*axe with the blade rossways to the handle, obsolete term: addice*] = Dechsel f
AEA, see: air-entraining agent
aegirine, aegirite (Min.) = Ägirin m
aeolian rocks (Geol.) = hauptsächlich aus windtransportierten Sandkörnern npl bestehende Gesteine npl
~ soil, (wind-)blown ~, wind-borne ~ = Windabsatzboden m, windtransportierter Boden m
aerated cement, see: ~ concrete
~ ~ block = Gasbetonstein m
~ concrete, ~ cement, chemically ~ ~, gas-formed ~ ~ = Gasbeton m
~ nappe (US); ~ sheet of water (Brit.) = belüfteter Überfallstrahl m
~ skimming tank = belüfteter Fettfang m, Schaumbecken n
aeration [*soil*] = Durchlüftung f [*Boden m*]
~ = Belüftung f
~ chamber, ~ tank = Rührwerkbecken n mit Zusatzluft f, Lüftungsbecken
~ conduit; air-intake (Brit.) [*automatic siphon*] = Belüftungsleitung f, Luftventil n
aerator = Belüftungsanlage f, Belüfter m
~ basin = Belüftungsbecken n
~ pipe = Belüftungsrohr n

AER-Degritter = belüfteter Sandfang m, bei dem die Belüftungsrohre direkt über dem trichterförmigen Sandstapelraum angebracht sind, Fabrikat CHICAGO PUMP CO.

(aerial) cableway; see: blondin (Brit.)

~ car = Wagen m einer Schwebebahn f

~ ~ = Gondel f [*Ballon m*]

~ engineering = Luftbildtechnik f

~ ferry = Schwebefähre f, Fährbrücke f

~ mapping, mapping by use of aerial photography = Kartenherstellung f mit Hilfe von Luftaufnahmen fpl

~ photograph, see: airphoto

*****aerial railroad** (US); see: cable (or aerial) ropeway

*****aerial ropeway,** see: cable ~

~ shot, see: airphoto

*****aerial survey(ing)**, air survey(ing) = Luftvermessung f

*****aerial tramway,** see: cable (or aerial) ropeway

aeriform = luftförmig

aerobe = Aerobier m, luftliebendes Kleinlebewesen n

aerobic = aerob, luftliebend

AEROCRETE [*Trademark*] = AEROKRET-Gasbeton m

aerodrome identification sign = Flughafenerkennungszeichen n

AEROLASTIC [*Trademark: jet-proof joint-sealing compound*] = strahltriebwerkfeste (Fugen)Vergußmasse f

aerolite = Aerolith m

aeronautical light = (Luftfahrt)Feuer n, Leuchte f

aeroplane hangar, aircraft ~ = Flugzeughalle f

AERO-SEALZ [*Trademark*] = vulkanisierter künstlicher Kautschuk m, welcher in heißer, flüssiger Form dem Bitumen beigesetzt wird, Fabrikat UNITED STATES RUBBER INTERNATIONAL, NEW YORK 17, USA

aesthetic design of bridges = Gestaltung f der Brücken fpl

affinity, liking = Affinität f, Verbindungsstreben n

affluent (Brit.); tributary = Nebenfluß m

afflux = Zustrom m

(af)forestation = 1. Aufforstung f; 2. das aufgeforstete Land

after-cooling = Nachkühlung f

afternoon peak hour = Nachmittags-Spitzenstunde f

after-sales service = Kundendienst m

*****after-treatment,** curing [*concrete*] = Nachbehandlung f [*Beton m*]

agalmatolite, pagodite (Min.) = Agalmatolith m

agar = Agar m, n

agaric mineral, see: rock milk

agate mortar = Achatmörser m

age at test = Prüfungsalter n

ageing = Alterung f, Alterungsprozeß m

agent = Agens n

~ ~ = Agent m

agglomerate = Agglomerat n

agglomerating power = Klebekraft f

aggradation, see: accretion through alluvium

~ of the channel = (Fluß)Betterhöhung f

aggravating condition = Erschwernis f

*****aggregate,** concrete ~, cement ~ = (Beton)Zuschlagstoffe mpl, (Beton-) Zuschläge mpl

*****aggregate,** mineral ~, skeleton structure = Mineralgemisch n, Mineralmasse f, Gesteinsmasse f, Gesteinsgemisch n, Gesteinsgemenge n, Gesteinsgerüst n, Mineralgerüst n [*bit. Straßenbau m*]

~ abrasion value = Abnutzungswert n [*Straßenbaugestein n*]

~ batcher = Zuschlagstoffdosierapparat m

(~) batch(ing) plant, (central) (~) ~ ~, proportioning plant, measuring ~, batcher ~, dry-batch(ing) ~ = Abmeßanlage f für Betonzuschlagstoffe mpl, Zuschlagsiloanlage f, Großbunkeranlage f, Reihensiloanlage f, Dosieranlage f für Zuschlagstoffe mpl, Siloabmeßanlage

~ bin = Gesteinssilo m

~ bituminizing plant, see: asphalt and coated macadam mixing plant

~ (bucket) elevator = Zuschlagstoff-Becherwerk n, Mineralmasse-Becherwerk n

~ car storage = Lagerung f von Zuschlagstoffen mpl in Waggons mpl bis zum Verarbeiten n

aggregate crushing value = Druckprüfungswert m [Straßenbaugestein n]
~ **elevator**, see: ~ (bucket) ~
~ **feeder** = Aufgabevorrichtung f für Zuschlagstoffe mpl
~ **grader**, see: multi-deck screen
(~) **grading curve**, particle size distribution ~, grain size distribution ~ = Sieblinie f, Siebkurve f
~ **heating** = Zuschlagstoff-Erwärmung f
~ **impact value** = Schlagprüfungswert m [Straßenbaugestein n]
~ **interlock across the face of the crack** = innige Verklammerung f der Gesteinsteile npl beider Rißufer npl
(~) **interlock(ing)** = Verspannung f, Verzahnung f [Mineralmasse f]
~ **length, total** ~ = Gesamtlänge f
~ **mixture** = Korngemisch n, Körnungsgemisch, Kornmasse f
(~ **of) broken brick(s)**, brick rubble, brick hardcore = Kleinschlag m aus Ziegelsteinbrocken mpl, Ziegelschotter m, Ziegelbruch m
(~ ~) ~ **concrete**, concrete hardcore = Kleinschlag m aus Betonbrocken mpl, Betonpacklage f, Betonschotter m
~ **(or aggregates) preparation plant (or installation)** = Aufbereitungsanlage f für Zuschlagstoffe mpl
*aggregate **production (or producing) equipment** = Gesteinsaufbereitungsmaschinen fpl
~ **railroad** (US); stone supply train (Brit.) = Feldbahn f für Zuschlagstoffe mpl
~ **retention (on bituminous seal coats)** = Gesteinsbindung f (auf bit. Verschlußdecken fpl)
~ **spreader**, stone ~, base paver = Splitt- und Schotterverteiler m, Makadam-Ausleger m
~ **tonnage** = Gesamttonnage f
~ **weigh-batcher** (Brit.); ~ weighing batcher (with scale) (US) = Gesteinswaage f (mit Wiegesilo m), Zuschlagstoffwaage f, Gemengewaage f
aggressive carbonic acid = kalklösende Kohlensäure f
~ **substance** = Schadstoff m

~ **to concrete** = betonaggressiv
~ **water** = Schadwasser n
agitating = Nachmischen n [Transportbeton m]
~ **truck**, see: agitator ~
agitator, remixer = Nachmischer m, Mischbeton-Transportaufbau m [ohne Fahrzeug n]
~, **stirrer** = Rührwerk(smischer) n, (m)
~ [deprecated]; see: agitator (or agitating) truck (or conveyor)
~ = Auflockerungsschnecke f [Schwarzbelageinbaumaschine f]
~ **shaft** = Rühr(werk)welle f
~ **(or agitating) truck (or conveyor)**, truck agitator (US); agitating lorry; agitator [deprecated] (Brit.) = Betontransportwagen m mit (aufgebautem) Rührwerk(smischer) n, (m), Nachmischer m, Rührwagen m, Beton-Transportwagen m mit Nachmischtrommel f [zentrale Betonmischung f]
aglime, see: agricultural lime
agricat (tractor) (US) = Acker(gleis)kettenschlepper m, Ackerbulldog m auf (Gleis)Ketten fpl
agricultural area = landwirtschaftliche Anbaufläche f
(~) **cultivator**, field ~ = (Boden)Kultivator m
~ **engineer** = Kulturbauingenieur m
~ **engineering** = Kulturbau m
~ **lime**, aglime, agstone = Düngekalk m
~ **pipe drain**, see: land ~
~ **soil**, arable ~, cultivated ~ = Kulturboden m
~ **topsoil** = Ackerkrume f
~ **utilization** = landwirtschaftliche Verwertung f
~ **wrench** = englischer Schraubenschlüssel m, Franzose m
agrimotor, see: farm tractor
agrogeology = Bodengeologie f
agsteln = old German name for amber
agstone, see: agricultural lime
A horizon, zone of removal = A-Horizont m, Auslaugungshorizont, Auslaugungsschicht f, Eluvialhorizont m [Bodenkunde f]
aid to steering = Lenkhilfe f

air-activated gravity conveyor = Gebläseluft-Trockenförderer *m* für schwach geneigte Dauerförderung *f*

~ pipeline = pneumatisches Förderrohr *n*

air activator, see: pneumatic conveyor

~ auger, ~ wood borer = Preßluft-Holzbohrer *m*, Druckluft-Holzbohrer

(air-) base (US); RAF-Station (Brit.) = Fliegerhorst *m*, Militär-Flugplatz *m*

air blast = Luftdruck *m*

air-blown asphalt (US); see: blown ~

air-borne dust = Flugstaub *m*

air breaker, see: ~ hammer

~ brick = Lüftungsstein *m*, Lüftungsziegel *m*

~ brake = Druckluftbremse *f*

~ brush = Druckluft-Anstreichgerät *n*, Farbspritzgerät

~ bubble = Luftblase *f*

~ buoyancy = Luftauftrieb *m*

~ caisson, pneumatic ~ = Preßluftsenkkasten *m*, Druckluftsenkkasten, Druckluftkammer *f*, Preßluftkammer

~ chamber = Luftführungskanal *m* [*Luftrutsche f*]

~ ~ = (Luft)(Reifen)Schlauch *m*

~ circulation = Luftumschichtung *f*

~ classification = Setzungsklassierung *f* durch Luft *f*, Windsichtung

~ cleaner, see: ~ filter

~ coal picker, pneumatic ~ ~ = Preßluft-Abbauhammer *m*, Druckluft-Abbauhammer, Preßluft-(Kohlen)Pickhammer, Druckluft-(Kohlen)Pickhammer

(~) compressor = Luftverdichter *m*, Kompressor *m*, Drucklufterzeuger *m*, Luftkompressor

~ conditioning = Luftfeuchtigkeitsreg(e)lung *f*

~ ~ coil odo(u)rs = Betriebsgerüche *mpl* bei Klimaanlagen *fpl*

***air conditioning installation** = Klima-(tisierungs)anlage *f*

~ ~ load = Kühllast *f*

~ control, pneumatic ~ = pneumatische Steuerung *f*, Drucklufsteuerung

air-cooled diesel engine = luftgekühlter Dieselmotor *m*

air cooler with metal frost depositing surfaces = Bereifungsluftkühler *m*

aircraft hangar, aeroplane ~ = Flugzeughalle *f*

~ pen (Brit.); **~ revetment** (US) = Splitterschutzboxe *f*

air curing = Lufterhärtung *f* [*Betonstein m*]

~ current, stream of air = Luftströmung *f*

~ cushion = Luftpuffer *m*

~ diffusion = Druckluftbelüftung *f*

~ drain = Zuluftkanal *m* [*dient zur Zuführung frischer Luft für Fundamentmauerwerk, für Holzbauteile oder zu einer Feuerstätte f*]

~ drill, pneumatic ~ = Druckluftbohrer *m*, Preßluftbohrer

~ -driven (or pneumatic) axe (or pointer) = Preßluftaxt *f*, Druckluftaxt

air-dry [*timber*] = lufttrocken

air duct = Zuluftkanal *m* [*Raumbelüftung, not to be confused with an air drain of masonry*]

air-ejector = Dampfstrahlpumpe *f*

air-entrained concrete, air-entraining ~ = belüfteter Beton *m*, AEA-Beton, Luftporenbeton

air-entraining agent, air-entrainment agent, AEA, air-entraining admixture for concrete, air-entrainment compound = Belüftungsmittel *n*, Betonbelüfter *m*, Lufteinschlußmittel *n*, LP-Zusatz *m*, luftporenbildender Zusatzstoff *m*, LP-Stoff, Luftporenerzeuger *m*

~ concrete, see: air-entrained ~

~ Portland cement = Luftporenzement *m*

air entrainment by flowing water = Wasser-Luft-Mischung *f* bei fließendem Wasser *n*

~ ~ in concrete = Lufteinschluß *m* in Beton *m*

~ (~) meter, concrete ~ (~) ~, entrained air indicator = (Beton-)Luftmengenmesser *m*, Belüftungsmesser *m*, Luftgehaltprüfgerät *n*, Luftmeßgerät *n*

~ fan = Luftventilator *m*

***airfield** = Flugplatz *m*

air filter, ~ cleaner = Luftfilter *n, m*

~ float fines = luftgetragene Feinststoffe *mpl*

Air Force Construction Troops = Luftwaffenbautruppen *fpl*

air freight = Luftfracht *f*
~ grating = Zuluftrost *m* [*Raumbelüftung f*]
~ hammer, see: (compressed-)air (pile) hammer
~ ~, pneumatic breaker, air breaker = Preßlufthammer *m*, Drucklufthammer [*für Aufreißarbeiten fpl*]
(~) heater, space ~ = Lufterhitzer *m*, Warmluftgerät *n*, Luftheizapparat *m*
~ hoist = Druckluftzug *m*, Preßluftzug
~ hose, flexible air line = Preßluftschlauch *m*, Druckluftschlauch, Kompressorschlauch
~ hydraulic jack = pneumatisch-hydraulischer Hebebock *m*, pneumatisch-hydraulische Winde *f*
air-intake (Brit.); see: aeration conduit
~, air inlet = Öffnung *f* für Luftzuführung *f*, Lufteinlaß *m*
air jack = Preßlufthebebock *m*, Drucklufthebebock, Druckluftpresse *f*, Preßluftwinde *f*, Druckluftwinde
~ jet lift = Druckluftheber *m*
~ leg, see: pneumatic feed leg for rock drill
(~) level, spirit ~, water ~ = Wasserwaage *f*, Libelle *f*
~ lift [*an air lift is a water pumping method whereby water may be raised from a well through the medium of compressed air*] = Wasserpumpen *n* mit Druckluft *f*
~ ~ [*separatory cone*] = Luftheber *m* [*Scheidekonus m*]
~ ~ = Luftbrücke *f*
~ ~ pump, compressed-air ~ [*an apparatus for raising water from a well*] = Druckluftpumpe *f*, Preßluftpumpe
~ line, see: air route
~ ~, ~ piping = Luttenleitung *f*
~ lock, (com)pressed ~ ~, pneumatic excavating air lock = Luftschleuse *f*, Druck~, Preß~
~ lubricator = Preßluftöler *m*
~ moisture = Luftfeuchtigkeit *f*
~ of combustion = Verbrennungsluft *f*
air-operated clay spade, see: pneumatic spade
~ grease unit = druckluftbetriebene Fettpresse *f*

~ saw, air-powered ~ air ~ = Preßluftsäge *f*, Druckluftsäge
air-operating company = Luftfahrtgesellschaft *f*
air (pavement) breaker, see: pneumatic (~) ~
~ paving rammer, see: pneumatic ~ ~
airphoto, aerial photograph, aerial shot = Luftaufnahme *f*, Luftbild *n*
air (pile) hammer, see: (compressed-) (~) ~
~ piping, air line = Luttenleitung *f*
air-placed concrete, gun-applied ~, pneumatically placed ~, jetcrete, shotcrete, gunite, gunned concrete = Spritzbeton *m*, Torkretbeton
air placing machine, see: cement gun
airplane handling winch = Flugzeugschleppwinde *f*
air pollution = Luftverunreinigung *f*, Luftverseuchung
airport, commercial ~ = Verkehrsflughafen *m*
(~) apron = (Hallen-)Vorfeld *n*
~ beacon = Flughafen-Leuchtfeuer *n*
~ control tower = Flugleitungsturm *m*, Kontrollturm
~ forms = Flugplatzbauschalung *f*
~ lighting = Flughafen-Befeuerung *f*
~ taxiing strip, see: taxi-track
~ warning light, see: obstruction ~
air-powered saw, see: air-operated ~
air pre-heater = Luftvorwärmer *m*
~ pump, vacuum ~, evacuator = Vakuumpumpe *f*
air-quenching (grate) cooler = Luftabschreckungskühler *m*
air raid shelter = 1.) Luftschutzbunker *m*; 2.) Luftschutzraum *m*
~ rammer, pneumatic ~ ~ = Druckluftramme *f*, Preßluftramme
~ receiver, see: air vessel
~ (relief) valve = Luftventil *n*, Entlüftungsventil
~ riveting hammer, compressed-air riveter = Preßluftniethammer *m*, Druckluftniethammer, pneumatischer Niethammer
~ route, air line = Luftverkehrslinie *f*, Fluglinie
~ saw, see: air-operated ~

air scavenging gear, pneumatic ~ ~ = Ausblasevorrichtung *f* [*Bindemittelspritzmaschine f*]
~ seasoned wood = luftgetrocknetes Holz *n*
air-separating (grinding) mill, grinding air-separating mill = Sichter(mahl)mühle *f*
~ (~) ~ operating with a straight air-current in a closed circuit = Sichter(məhl)mühle *f* mit Stromsichtung *f* in geschlossenem Kreislauf *m*
~ (~) ~ ~ ~ centrifugal separation in a closed circuit = Sichter(mahl)mühle *f* mit Schleudersichtung *f* in geschlossenem Kreislauf *m*
air shaft, ventilating ~, ventilation ~ = Luftschacht *m*, Wetterschacht, Lüftungsschacht, Bewetterungsschacht
air-side face, downstream ~ = Luftseite *f* [*Talsperre f*]
air sifting = Sichten *n* [*Aufbereitung f*]
air siphoning tube = Luftansaugrohr *n*
air-slaked lime, powdered calcium carbonate, powdered lime = Pulver(brannt)kalk *m*
air-slaking = Löschen *n* von Branntkalk *m* an der Luft *f*
airslide = (Gebläse)Luft-Förderrinne *f*, Luft-Rutsche *f*, pneumatische Förderrinne *f*
~ bulk cement trailer = Zementtransport-Anhänger *m* mit (Gebläse)Luft-Förderrinne *f*
air space ratio = scheinbare Porosität *f*, Luftporenanteil *m*
~ spade, see: pneumatic ~
~ stream = Luftstrom *m*
~ strip = Start- und Landestreifen *m* [*Flugplatz m*]
~ surveying, see: aerial ~
~ tamper, see: pneumatic (powered) ~
~ tool, see: pneumatic tool
~ trap = Geruchverschluß *m*
~ valve, ~ relief ~ = Luftventil *n*, Entlüftungsventil
~ vessel, ~ receiver, compressed air vessel = Windkessel *m*, Druckluftkessel *m*, Druckluftbehälter *m*, Druckluftspeicher *m*, Speicherkessel

~ vibration equipment, pneumatic ~ ~ = Preßlufträttelgeräte *npl*, Druckluftrüttelgeräte, Preßluftvibrationsgeräte, Druckluftvibrationsgeräte
~ vibrator, pneumatic ~ = Druckluftrüttler *m*, Preßluftrüttler
~ void = Luftpore *f*
airwasher = Luftwäsche(r) *f*, (*m*)
airway = beflogene Route *f*, ~ Strecke *f*
~ beacon = Streckenleuchtfeuer *n* [*Flugverkehr m*]
air wood borer, see: ~ auger
~ wrench, pneumatic ~ = Druckluft-Maulschlüssel *m*
alabandite, mangan-blende (Min.) = Glanzblende *f*, Alabandin *n*, Manganblende *f*
alabaster = Alabaster *m*, feinkörniger Gips *m*, körnig-kristallinischer Gips
alarm signal, see: warning ~
albertite, Albert coal, Albert shale (Min.) = Albertit *m*
albino asphalt (US); ~ bitumen (Brit.) = Albino-Bitumen *n*, helles Bitumen
albite, white schorl, Na$_2$Al$_2$Si$_6$O$_{16}$ (Min.) = Albit *m*
albitite (Geol.) = Albitit *m*
albumin glue = Albuminleim *m*
albuminoid nitrogen = Albuminoidstickstoff *m*, Eiweißstickstoff
alburnum, see: sapwood
alcoholometry = Bestimmung *f* des Alkoholgehaltes *m* von Alkohol-Wasser-Mischungen *fpl*
alder, alnus = Erle *f*, Eller *f*, Else *f*
alertness = Wachsamkeit *f*
alert platform, marshalling area, assembly area, readiness area, taxi-holding position, alert apron = Bereitstellungsfläche *f* [*Flugplatz m*]
A. L. G., advanced landing ground = Feldflugplatz *m*
alga = Alge *f*
algae control = Algenbekämpfung *f*
~ growth = Algenwachstum *n*
algaecide = Algenbekämpfungsmittel *n*, Algengift *n*
alginic acid = Alginsäure *f*, Algensäure
algorithm = Algorithmus *m*
alidade, sight rule = Alhidade *f*

alignment — all-wheel steer(ing)

*alignment; alinement (US) = 1. Ausfluchtung *f*, Bauflucht *f*; 2. Linienführung *f*
alkali-aggregate expansion inhibitor = Schutzmittel *n* gegen alkaliempfindliche Zuschläge *mpl*
~ **reaction (or expansion)** = Alkali-Zuschlagstoff-Reaktion *f*
alkali(c) fel(d)spar = Alkali-Feldspat *m*
alkali-granite = Alkali-Granit *m*
alkali metal = Alkalimetall *n*
alkaline = alkalisch, laugensalzig
~ **activation** = alkalische Anregung *f*
~ **ammoniacal fumarole** = alkalische Salmiakfumarole *f*
~ **earths** = Erdalkalien *fpl*
~ **lake** = Tinkalsee *m*
~ **soil** = alkalischer Boden *m*
~ **solution** = alkalische Lösung *f*
alkalinity = Alkali(ni)tät *f*, laugensalzige Eigenschaft *f*
alkali-reactive aggregate = alkaliempfindlicher Zuschlag(stoff) *m*
alkyd resin = Alkydharz *n*
allanite, orthite = Allanit *m*, Orthit *m*
allemontite (Min.) = Allemontit *m*, Antimonarsen *n*, Arsenantimon *n*
alleviation of dust, dust alleviation, dust allaying, dust suppression, dust control, abatement of dusting = Staubbindung *f*
all-hydraulic (crane-)excavator, ~ shovel = Hydraulik-Universalbagger *m*, Vollhydraulik-Bagger
~ **dragshovel** = Hydraulik-Tieflöffel-(bagger) *m*
all-in-aggregate [*a term used for both all-in ballast and crusher-run material*], as-raised aggregate (Brit.); total aggregate, naturally mixed aggregates = natürliches Gemisch *n* aller Körnungen *fpl* [*Beton m*]
all-in tender, see: "turn-key" bid
all-metal container = Ganzmetallbehälter *m*
allotriomorphic, anhedral = allotriomorph
~ **crystal,** anhedron = allotriomorphes Kristall *n*
~-**granular,** granitic, granitoid, xenomorphic granular = allotriomorph-körnig

allotrope = Allotrop *m*
allotype = Allotyp *m*
allowable stress, see: permissible ~
allowance, tolerance = Toleranz *f*, Genauigkeitsgrad *m*
~ **for impact,** impact allowance = Stoßzuschlag *m*, Stoßbeiwert *m*
alloy steel = legierter Stahl *m*
~ ~ **leg** = Stütze *f* aus legiertem Stahl *m*
*all-purpose (or convertible, or universal) excavator (or shovel-crane) = Mehrzweckbagger *m*, Universalbagger, Umbaubagger, Vielzweckbagger
all risks erection insurance = Bauwesenversicherung *f*
all-round view, ~ vision = Rundblick *m*, Vollsicht *f*, Rundsicht
all-steel chain = Ganzstahlkette *f*
~ **construction** = Ganzstahl-Bauweise *f*, Vollstahl-Bauweise
~ **frame** = Ganzstahl-Rahmen *m*
alluvial coast = Anschwemmungsküste *f*
~ **cone** (Geol.) = Schotterkegel *m*, Alluvialkegel
~ **deposit,** alluvium = Verlandung *f*, Anschütte *f*, Anlandung *f*, Alluvium *n*, Auflandung *f*
~ **fan (accumulations)** = Alluvialfächerschutt *m*
~ **gold,** gulch ~ = Seifengold *n*
~ **mantle rock** = alluvialer Verwitterungsschutt *m*
~ **matter,** ~ material = Alluvionmaterial *n*
~ **soil** = Schwemm(land)boden *m*, Wasserabsatzboden *m*
alluvium, see: alluvial deposit
~-**covered** = alluviumbedeckt
all-weather road = All-Wetter-Straße *f*
all-welded construction = Ganzschweiß-Konstruktion *f*
~ **rolled steel construction** = Walzstahl-Schweißkonstruktion *f*
all-wheel air brake = Allrad-Druckluftbremse *f*
~ **drive** = All-Rad-Antrieb *m*
~ ~ **dozer** = Allrad-Räumer *m*
~ ~ **tractor** = Allrad-Schlepper *m*
~ **steer(ing)** = All-Rad-Lenkung *f*

almandine, almandite, $Fe_3Al_2(SiO_4)_3$ (Min.) = Almandin *m*

alnus, see: alder

Alpine granite = Alpengranit *m*

~ **lake** = Alpensee *m*

~ **limestone** = Alpenkalk *m*

~ **piedmont** = Alpenvorland *n*

~ **tunnel** = Alpentunnel *m*

~ **valley** = Alpental *n*

alstonite (Min.) = Alstonit *m*, Bariumaragonit *m*

ALT, see: altitude above (mean) sea level

alternate (concrete) bay construction, ~ bay method = Wechselfeldeinbau *m*, Herstellung benachbarter Plattenfelder in zeitlichem Abstand [*Deckenbeton m*]

alternating bending test, test by bending in opposite directions = Hin- und Her-Biegeversuch *m*

alternating-current generator = Wechselstromerzeuger *m*

alternating double filtration = zweistufige Tropfkörperbehandlung *f* mit Wechselbetrieb *m*

~ **notch bending test** = Einkerbhin- und -herbiegeversuch *m*

~ **stress** = Wechselbeanspruchung *f*

alternative power unit loco(motive) = Zwei-Kraft-Lok(omotive) *f*

~ **side-street** = Abfangstraße *f*, Entlastungsstraße

altimeter = Höhenmesser *m*

altitude above (mean) sea-level, ALT = Höhe *f* über NN, Seehöhe *f* [*NN = Normal Null = mittlere Seehöhe f*]

altocumulus cloud = Schäfchenwolke *f*, Altokumuluswolke

alum coal, ~ **earth** = Alaunerde *f*

~ **shale** = Alaunschieferton *m*

~ **slate** = Alaunschiefer *m*

alumina, aluminum oxide Al_2O_3 = Tonerde *f*, Aluminiumoxyd *n*

~ **cement**, see: calcium aluminate ~

~ **filter** = Tonerdefiltertiegel *m*

~ **firebrick**, basic ~ = Tonerdeschamottestein *m*

~ -**silica refractory** = feuerfester Tonerde-Kieselsäure-Stein *m*

aluminate = Tonerdeverbindung *f*, Aluminat *n*

~ **of potash** = Kalitonerde *f*

alumin(i)um arsenate = Aluminiumarsenat *n*

~ **chloride** = Aluminiumchlorid *n*

~ **dome car** = Aluminium-Aussichtswagen *m*

~ **paint** = Aluminiumfarbe *f*

~ **sheet** = Aluminiumblech *n*

~ **smelting work** = Aluminiumschmelzwerk *n*, Aluminiumschmelze *f*

~ **sulphate** = Aluminiumsulfat *n*

aluminoferric = Eisenalaun *m*

aluminous cement, see: calcium aluminate ~

alum-soaked Keene's cement = Marmorgips *m*, Alabastergips *m*, Keene's Zement, Alaungips *m*, Hartalabaster *m* [*früher: Marmorzement m*]

alunite, alumstone = Alunit *m* [*tonreicher Alaunschiefer m*]

Alveolina limestone = Alveolinenkalk(stein) *m*

***amalgamation of contractors**, see: contracting combine

amaranth wood, purple ~ = Amarantholz *n*, Luftholz, Purpurholz

amazonstone, amazonite (Min.) = Amazonenstein *m*

amber, succinite = Bernstein *m*

~ **mica**, phlogopite (Min.) = Phlogopit *m*, hellbrauner Glimmer *m*

~ **tar** = Bernsteinteer *m*

amblygonite (Min.) = Amblygonit *m*

amboina wood = Amboinaholz *n*

Ambursen-type dam = Ambursen-Staumauer *f*, Ambursen-Sperrmauer

amelioration = Melioration *f*

American Municipal Association = Amerikanischer Städtetag *m* [*USA*]

~ **yellow pine**, Weymouth pine = Weymouthkiefer *f*, Strobe *f*

amethyst (Min.) = Amethyst *m*

amianthus (Min.), see: asbestos

amiseite = Amiesit *m*

ammeter, ampere-meter = Amperemesser *m*, Strommesser

ammonia chlorine treatment = Chlorgas-Ammoniakbehandlung *f*

~ **leaching pressure process** = Ammoniak-Drucklaugung *f*

ammonia liquor — angle butt strap

ammonia liquor = Ammoniakwasser *n*
ammonium nitrate (blasting) explosive = Ammonsalpeter-Sprengstoff *m*
~ ~ **gelatine**, gelatinous (blasting) explosives = Ammonsalpetersprengstoff *m*, gelatinös-plastische Sprengstoffgemenge *npl*
ammunition depot, explosives area, bomb dump area = Munitionsdepot *n*, Munilager *n*
~ **warehouse** = Munitionsmagazin *n*, Munitionsschuppen *m*
amoebic dysentery = Amöbenruhr *f*
amorphous = amorph
~ **oxide of aluminum** = Tonerdehydrat *n*
amount of crown = Größe *f* der Kronenüberhöhung *f*
~ ~ **eccentricity**, see: throw
~ ~ **steel** = Stahlaufwand *m*
amperometric titration = amperometrische Titration *f*
amphegenyte (Geol.) = Leuzittrachit *m*
amphibious site = amphibische Baustelle *f*
amphibole asbestos (Min.) = Hornblendeasbest *m*, Amphibolasbest
~ **group** = Amphibolgruppe *f*
~ **magnetite** = Amphibolmagnetit *m*
amphibolic gneiss, hornblende ~ = Hornblendegneis *m*
amphibolite = Amphibolit *m*
amphoteric = amphoter
AMPLIDYNE [*Trademark*] = Amplidyne-Steuerungssystem *n* zur Veränderung der Erregerspannung *f*, Fabrikat GENERAL ELECTRIC CO.
amplitude = Schwing(ungs)weite *f*, Ausschlag(weite) *m*, (*f*), Amplitude *f*
amygdaloidal diabase = Diabas-Mandelstein *m*
anaerobe = Anaerobier *m* [*unter Abschluß von der Luft lebendes Kleinlebewesen*]
anaerobic = sauerstofflos, luftlos, anaerob, unter Abschluß von der Luft lebend
anaglyph = Anaglyphenbild *n*
analcite, analcime (Min.) = Analzim *m*
analogy computor = Analogie-Rechenmaschine *f*
analyser, analyst = Analytiker *m*
anatase (Min.) = Anatas *m*

anchorage = Verankerung *f*
~ [*place where one may anchor*] = Ankerplatz *m*, Ankerstelle *f*
~, roads, roadstead = Reede *f*
~ **fixture** = Spannanker *m*
~ **pier** = Ankerpfeiler *m*, Verankerungspfeiler *m* [*Brücke f*]
anchor bar, holding down rod = Ankerstab *m*
~ **bolt**, holding down ~ = Ankerbolzen *m*
anchored sheet (pile) wall = verankerte Spundwand *f*
anchor hoist = Ankerwinde *f*, Schiffswinde
~ **ice**, see: ground ~
anchoring by friction = Reibungsverankerung *f*
~ **cone** = Verankerungskegel *m*
~ **element** = Verankerungselement *n*
anchor(ing) loop of reinforcing steel = schleifenförmiger Rundstahlanker *m*
anchoring of sheet piling = Spundwandverankerung *f*
anchor loop (Brit.); U-bolt (US) = Verankerungsring *m*
~ **pile** = Ankerpfahl *m*
~ **plate**, tie ~ = Ankerplatte *f*, Verankerungsplatte
~ **ring** (Brit.); form anchor (US) = Ankerscheibe *f*
~ **wall** = durchlaufende Ankerwand *f*
ancient geological gorge = epigenetisches Flußbett *n*
~ **monument**, historic landmark = Kulturdenkmal *n*
andalusite (Min.) = Andalusit *m*
andesine (Min.) = Andesin *n*
andesite (Geol.) = Andesit *m*
andesitic ash = Andesitasche *f*
andradite, $Ca_3Fe_2(SiO_4)_3$ = Andradit *m*, Kalkeisengranat *m*
anemometer, wind ga(u)ge = Wind(stärke)messer *m*, Anemometer *n*, Schalenkreuz *n*
aneroid barometer = Aneroidbarometer *n*, Dosenbarometer
angle block = Winkelendmaß *n*
~ **board** = Schrägbrett *n*
~ **brace**, ~ tie = Kopfband *n*, Kopfbiege *f*
~ **bracket**, corner angle = Eckwinkel *m*
~ **butt strap** = Winkelverlaschung *f*

25

angledozer — annular borer

angledozer, see: roadbuilder
angle-iron frame = Winkelstahlrahmen *m*
angle iron of the chords, boom plate, flange plate = Gurt(ungs)eisen *n*, Gurt(ungs)winkel *m*
~ ~ **shears** = Winkelstahlschere *f*
~ ~ **standard** = Winkeleisenpfosten *m*
~ ~ **stiffener**, stiffening angle = Aussteifungswinkel *m*
~ **lever** = Winkelhebel *m*
~ **of glide** = Gleitwinkel *m*, Anflugwinkel [*Flugzeug n*]
~ ~ **inclination** = Neigungswinkel *m*
~ ~ **internal friction** = Reibungswinkel *m*, Winkel *m* der inneren Reibung *f*
~ ~ **nip** = Einzugswinkel *m* [*Backenbrecher m*]
~ ~ **repose (of the natural slope)** = natürlicher Böschungswinkel *m*, Ruhewinkel
~ ~ **rotation** = Drehwinkel *m*
~ ~ **skew** = Schrägungswinkel *m*
~ ~ **slope** = Böschungswinkel *m*
~ **rafter**, see: hip ~
~ **ridge**, see: hip rafter
anglesite, PbSO$_4$ (Min.) = Anglesit *m*, Vitriolbleierz *n*
angle steel log [*log washer*] = Vierkantwelle *f* [*Schwertwäsche f*]
~ **tie**, see: ~ brace
angling blade, angledozer = Schwenkschild *n*, Seitenräumer-Planierschild, winkelbares Schild, Schrägschild, Winkel-Planierschild
angular, sharp = scharfkantig [*Sand m*]
~ **bearing** = Spurlager *n*
~ **emissivity** = Ausstrahlung *f* in Abhängigkeit vom Ausstrahlungswinkel *m*
~ **error** = Winkelfehler *m* [*Vermessungskunde f*]
~ **fragment** (Geol.) = eckiges Bruchstück *n*
angularity [*e. g. breccia*] = Eckförmigkeit *f*, Wink(e)ligkeit, Kantigkeit [*z. B. Brekzie f*]
angular measurement of arc (Brit.); central angle of arc (US) [*dam*] = Bogenöffnung *f* [*Talsperre f*]
~ **retaining wall** = Winkelstützmauer *f*

~ **(shut-off) valve** = Eck(absperr)ventil *n*
~ **width of arch at crest** (Brit.); central angle at crest (US) = Öffnungswinkel *m* der Krone *f* [*Talsperre f*]
anhedral, see: allotriomorphic
anhedrons, allotriomorphic crystals = allotriomorphe Kristalle *npl*
anhydrite (Min.) = Anhydrit *m*, wasserfreier Gips *m*, wasserfreies Kalziumsulfat *n*
~ **band** = Anhydritschnur *f*
~ **plaster** [*no more manufactured in Great Britain since 1952*] = Anhydritputz *m*, Anhydritbinder *m* DIN 4208
~ **zone** = Anhydritregion *f*
anhydritic concretion, concretion of anhydrite = Anhydritknolle *f*
anhydrous = anhydrisch, wasserfrei
~ **gypsum-plaster** (Brit.) = vollständig entwässerter Gips, der annähernd den deutschen Schachtofengipsen entspricht, wasserfreier Putzgips
~ **lime**, see: quicklime
~ **phosphoric acid** = Phosphorpentoxid *n*, Phosphorsäureanhydrid *n*, wasserfreie Phosphorsäure *f*, P$_2$O$_5$
(~) potash, see: protoxide of potassium
aniline point = Anilinpunkt *m* [*Kohlenwasserstoff-Lösungsmittel n*]
animal-drawn traffic = Zugtierverkehr *m*, Fuhrwerkverkehr, Gespannverkehr
animal glue = Tierleim *m*
anion = Anion *n*
~ **exchanger** = Anionenaustauscher *m*
anionic collector = anionischer Kollektor *m*
anisoclinal fold = Anisoklinalfalte *f*
anisotropic = anisotrop
annabergite, nickel-bloom (Min.) = Annabergit *m*, Nickelblüte *f*
to anneal = glühen, tempern, glühfrischen [*Guß m*]; anlassen, ausglühen [*Stahl m*]
annex = Gebäudeanbau *m*
annexation = Eingemeindung *f*
annual rainfall = Jahresniederschlag *m*, Jahresregenmenge *f*
~ **rate** = Jahresbetrag *m*
~ **ring** = Jahrring *m*, Jahresring [*Holz n*]
annular ball bearing = Ringkugellager *n*
~ **borer** = Kernbohrer *m*

annular dam [*scrubber*] = Stauwand *f* [*Schwerttrommelwäsche f*]
~ **section** = ringförmiger Querschnitt *m*, Ringquerschnitt
anode battery, plate ~ = Anodenbatterie *f*
anodic = anodisch
anorganic = anorganisch
anorthite, indianite, lime-fel(d)spar (Min.) = Kalkfeldspat *m*, Anorthit *m*
anthracene oil, green ~ = Anthrazenöl *n*
~ ~ **tar** = Anthrazenölteer *m*
anthracite (coal) = Anthrazit *m*
anticlinal fissure (Geol.) = Sattelspalte *f*
~ **fold**, anticline (Geol.) = Sattel *m* der Faltung *f*, Antiklinale *f*, Antikline *f*
anti-corrosive coat = Rostschutzanstrich *m*
anticyclone, high = Antizyklon *m*, Hoch(druckgebiet) *n*
anti-dazzle device, dim(med) ~ = Abblendvorrichtung *f*
~ **hedge** = Blendschutzhecke *f*
antifermentative = gärungshemmend
antiflocculant, see: detergent
antifoam, antifoaming agent = Schaumverhütungsmittel *n*, Antischaummittel, Schaumdämpfer *m*
antifouling (composition) = anwuchsverhindernde Schiffsanstrichfarbe *f*, Schiffsbodenfarbe
anti-freeze layer, see: sub-base (course)
~ **(mixture)**, frost protective, anti-freezer, frost-protection agent = Frostschutzmittel *n*
anti-friction bearing = Wälzlager *n*
~ **metal**, white ~, babbitt ~, Babbitt's ~ = Lagerweißmetall *n*
~ **worm conveyor**, open-spiral ~ ~ = Band(förder)schnecke *f*
antigorite (Min.) = Antigorit *m*, Blätterserpentin *m*
anti-knock agent = klopfhindernder Zusatz *m*, Klopfbremse *f*
~ **performance**, ~ property = Klopffestigkeit *f*
antileak ring = Dichtungsring *m*
antilubricating agent = Antischmiermittel *n*
antimonial lead, see: hard ~
antimonite (Min.) = Antimonit *m*, Antimonglanz *m*

anti-rust paint, rust protection ~, rust inhibitive ~ = Rostschutzfarbe *f*
antiseptic cement = antiseptischer Zement *m*
~ **concrete** = antiseptischer Beton *m*
anti-skid property, see: non-skid ~
anti-stripping admixture, see: dope
anti-tank ditch = Panzergraben *m*
anti-vibration handle = vibrationsfreier Griff *m*
anthophyllite (Min.) = Anthophyllit *m*
anvil = Amboß *m*
~ **block** = Amboßstock *m*, Schabotte *f*
apartment = Wohnung *f*
~ **block**, block of flats = Wohnhochhaus *n*
~ **building** = Mietwohnhaus *n*
apatite (Min.) = Apatit *m*
aperture, mesh; gauge (Brit.) = Masche *f* [*Sieb n*]
~ **size**, sieve opening; space (US) = lichte Maschenweite *f*, Sieböffnung *f*
apex, key, top, crown, vertex = Bogenscheitel *m*, Scheitelpunkt *m*
~ **stone**, saddle ~ = Scheitelstein *m*
aphanitic rock = sehr feinkörniger Diabas *m*
aplite (Geol.) = Aplit *m*
apophyllite, fish-eye (Min.) = Apophyllit *m*
apophysis (Geol.) = Apophyse *f*
apparatus for plasticity test, see: liquid limit device
apparent density, see: porosity
~ **depression of the horizon**, see: dip of the horizon
~ **horizon**, sensible ~, visible ~ = Kimme *f*, sichtbarer Horizont *m*
applicability = Anwendbarkeit *f*, Anwendungsmöglichkeit *f*
application [*brake*] = Anzieher *n* [*Bremse f*]
~ = Aufbringen *n* [*z. B. Splitt m*]
~ **form**, ~ blank, form of application = Antragsformular *n*
~ **letter** = Bewerbungsschreiben *n*
~ **of load** = Lastaufbringung *f*, Lastangriff *m*, Kraftangriff
~ ~ **salt** = Salzstreuung *f*
~ **temperature** = Anwendungstemperatur *f*
applied [*brake*] = angezogen [*Bremse f*]

to apportion by weight = nach Gewicht n zuteilen
apportioning gear, see: batcher
apprenticeship training = Lehrlingsausbildung f
approach adit = Zugangstollen m
~ **bank** = Brückenzufahrtrampe f
~ **funnel** (Brit.); ~ **zone** (US); flying gap [*this term is used in India*] = Anflugsektor m, Einflugschneise f
~ **light** = Anflugfeuer n [*Flugplatz m*]
~ **lighting system** = Einflugschneisenbeleuchtung f
~ **ramp**, see: accommodation ramp
~ **road**, feeder ~ = Zubringerstraße f
~ **surface** = Anflugsektorbezugsfläche f
~ **track** = Zufahrgleis n
~ **viaduct** = Zugangsbrücke f
~ **zone**, see: ~ funnel
approximate value = (An)Näherungswert m
approximation, approximate method = Berechnung f der (An)Näherungswerte mpl, (An)Näherungs(be)rechnung f, (An)Näherungsverfahren n
appurtenant works, ~ structures = Nebenanlagen fpl [*Talsperre f*]
apron = Schutzschicht f gegen Unterspülung f, Vorlage f
~ = (Hallen)Vorfeld n [*Flugplatz m*]
~ = Schürze f, Scraperfalle f [*Radschrapper m*]
~, spillway ~, apron type energy dissipator = Sturzbett n [*Überlauf m*]
~ **conveyor**, plate ~ ~ = Plattenband(förderer) n, (m), Blechgliederband n, Gliederband(förderer)
~ **lift** = Schürzenhub m, Scraperfallenhub
~ **opening** = Schürzenöffnung f [*Radschrapper m*]
~ **type feeder**, apron-conveyor feeder = Plattenbandspeiser m, Aufgabeplattenband n
APSCO base paver [*Trademark*] [*a self-powered "dump-truck pushing" paver*] = Eigenantrieb-Verteiler m für bituminöse Stoffe mpl, Schotter m und Splitt m, Fabrikat ALL PURPOSE SPREADER CO., ELYRIA, OHIO, USA

AQUACRETE [*Trademark: a water-repellent cement*] = ein britischer wasserabweisender Zement m
aquafer, see: aquifer
aquatic plant = Wasserpflanze f
~ **vegetation** = Wasserflora f
aqueduct, water conduit bridge = Aquädukt m, Wasserleitungsbrücke f
aqueous corrosion = Feuchtigkeitskorrosion f
~ **solution** = wässerige Lösung f, wäßrige ~
aquifer, water-bearing formation, water-bearing (soil) stratum, aquafer = wasserführende Bodenschicht f, ~ Formation f, Grundwasserleiter m
arabel = ackerfähig, kultivierbar, anbaufähig, urbar, kulturfähig, anbauwürdig
~ **meadow** = Ackerwiese f
~ **soil**, see: agricultural ~
aragonite = Aragonit m
aragonitic lime(stone) = Schaumkalk(stein) m, Wellenkalk(stein)
arbiter = Schiedsrichter m
arbitration = Schiedsgerichtsbarkeit f
~ **board** = Schiedsgericht n
~ **clause** = Schiedsgerichtsklausel f
arboriculture = Baumzucht f
arc furnace = Lichtbogenofen m
arch = Gewölbe n
~ **abutment** = Bogenwiderlager n
Archangel tar = Archangelteer m
arch barrel (US); inclined barrel arch (Brit.) = schiefliegendes Gewölbe n [*Talsperre f*]
~ **bearing** = Bogenlager n
~ **boom** = Bogengurt(ung) m, (f)
~ ~ **angle iron** = Bogengurt(ungs)winkeleisen n
~ **bridge** = Bogenbrücke f, gewölbte Brücke
~ **centering** (US); ~ centring (Brit.) = Bogenlehrgerüst n
~ **culvert**, see: arch(ed) (drainage) ~
arch(ed) bridge = Bogenbrücke f, gewölbte Brücke
arched buttress, see: flying ~
arch(ed) dam = gekrümmte Staumauer f
~ **(drainage) culvert** = Bogendurchlaß m, Bogenabzugkanal m, überwölbter Durchlaß, überwölbter Abzugkanal
~ **girder** (Brit.); see: curved beam

arch(ed) girder with polygonal outlines = Bogenträger *m* mit gebrochenen Linien *fpl*
~ **pedestal crane**, see: portal ~
arch form = Bogenschalung *f*
~**-gravity dam** = Bogengewichts(stau)mauer *f*, Bogengewichtssperre *f*, Gewölbe-Gewichtssperre *f*
Archimedean screw = Archimedes-Schnecke *f*
(~) ~ **conveyor, conveyor screw, worm conveyor** = Förderschnecke *f*, Schneckenförderer *m*, Transportschnecke *f*
arching effect = Bogenwirkung *f*, Gewölbewirkung *f* [*Erddruckverteilung f*]
architect's compensation = Architektengebühr *f*
architectural design = architektonische Gestaltung *f*
~ **metal curtain wall** = Metallaußenwand *f* im Hochbau *m*
archless brick kiln = gewölbeloser Ziegelofen *m*
arch panel = Bogenfeld *n*
~ **rib** = Bogenrippe *f*
~ **span** (Brit.); see: clear buttress spacing (US)
~ **spillway** = Bogenüberlauf *m*
(~) **springing, rein, impost, springer, springing brick** = Bogenkämpfer *m*, Kämpfer(stein) *m*, Anfänger(ziegel) *m*
~ **stiffening** = Bogenaussteifung *f*
~ **stone, voussoir** = Gewölbestein *m*, Wölbstein *m*
~ **support** = Traggewölbe *n*
~ **thrust line** = Stützlinienbogen *m*
~ **truss** = Bogenfachwerk *n*
~ **with braced spandrels** = Bogen *m* mit ausgesteiften Zwickeln *mpl*
~ ~ **fixed ends, fixed arch** = Bogen *m* mit eingespannten Enden *npl*
arc ignition = Lichtbogenzündung *f*
~ **of contact** = Umspannungsbogen *m* [*Bandförderer m*]
~ ~ **swing** = Bogen *m* der Schwenkung *f* [*Bagger m*]
~ **welding**, see: electrical ~ ~
area load = Flächenlast *f*
~ **of depression** = Absenkungsfläche *f*
~ ~ **opening** = Durchlaßfläche *f* [*eines Brunnenfilters m*]
~ ~ **waterway** (US); wetted cross section (Brit.) = benetzter Querschnitt *m*
arenaceous, sandy = sandig
~ **limestone**, sandy ~ = Kalksandstein *m*
~ **sand**, quartz(ose) sand = Quarzsand *m*
~ **shale**, sandy ~ = Quarzschieferton *m*
areometer, see: hydrometer
argentite, silver glance, Ag_2S (Min.) = Silberglanz *m*, Argentit *m*
argillaceous, clayey = tonig
~ **cement** [*rock*] = Tonsubstanz *f*
~ **limestone** = Tonkalk *m*
~ **marl** = Mergelton *m*
~ **rock**, clay ~ = Tongestein *n*
~ **sandstone** = Tonsandstein *m*
~ **slate**, (clay) slate, argillite = Tonschiefer *m*
aridizing = Verfahren bei der Erzeugung von gewerblichem Gips, wobei man durch Einspritzen einer Lösung eines zerfließenden Salzes während des Brennens einen festen Gips von niedriger Konsistenz erhält, dessen Dichte, Wasserhaltevermögen und Erhärtungszeit nicht mehr von Charge zu Charge wechseln
arid region, ~ **area** = Trockengebiet *n*
arisings, salvage = Altmaterial *n*
arkose (sandstone), arkosic grit = Arkose *f*, Arkosesandstein *m*, Feldspatsandstein *m*, feldspatreicher Sandstein
armature slot = Ankernut *f*
arm of the sea, sea inlet = Meer(es)arm *m*
~ ~ = Halterung *f*
~ **of canal**, branch ~ ~ = Kanalabzweigung *f*
armo(u)r coat, double surface treatment, two-pass surface treatment, inverted penetration surface treatment, multiple-lift treatment = doppelte Oberflächenbehandlung *f* [*Straße f*]
armo(u)red cable = bewehrtes Kabel *n*, Panzerkabel *n*
~ **hose** = drahtumflochtener Schlauch *m*
armo(u)r plate = Panzerplatte *f*
~ **wire** = Panzerkabeldraht *m*
aromatic solvent = aromatisches Lösungsmittel *n*

arrangement = Anordnung *f*
array test for asbestos spinning fibre (Brit.)/**fiber** (US) = Stapelprüfung *f* für Asbestspinnfaser *f*
arrears of road maintenance = Nachholbedarf *m* [*Straßenunterhaltung f*]
arris, bull-nose, bull's nose = Fugenkante *f*
arrissing joints, ~ joint edges = Nacharbeiten *n* von Betonfugen *fpl*, Kantenbrechen *n*
~ **tool,** see: bull-nose trowel
arris trowel, see: bull-nose ~
arsenic = Arsen(ik) *n*
arsenical pyrite, arsenopyrite, mispickel, FeAsS (Min.) = Mißpickel *m*, Arsenkies *m*
arsenolite, As$_2$O$_3$ (Min.) = Arsenolith *m*, Arsenblüte *f*
arsenopyrite, see: arsenical pyrite
arterial pair = Stadthauptstraßenpaar *n*
~ **road** [*deprecated*], trunk(line) ~ = Fernverkehrsstraße *f*
~ **(street),** major ~ = Stadthauptstraße *f*
artesian (ground-) water = artesisches (Grund)Wasser *n*, artesisch gespanntes (Grund)Wasser [*ist eine Sonderform des gespannten Grundwassers*]
~ **head** = artesische Druckhöhe *f*, artesischer Spiegel *m*
~ **pressure** = artesischer Druck *m*
~ **spring,** ~ **well** = artesische Quelle *f*, artesischer Brunnen *m*, Überlaufbrunnen, frei ausfließende Wasserbohrung *f* [*Bohrbrunnen, dessen Wasser durch eigenen Überdruck zur Oberfläche gelangt*]
~ **well pump** = Rohrbrunnenpumpe *f*
article of antiquity = Ausgrabungsfund *m*
~ ~ **value** = Wertgegenstand *m*
articulated buttress dam = Pfeiler(stau)mauer *f* mit gelenkiger Aussteifung *f*
~ **loco(motive)** = Gelenk-Lok(omotive) *f*
~ **purlin** = Gelenkpfette *f*
artificial aggregates = künstliche Stoffe *mpl* [*Betonzuschlag(stoff) m*]
~ **anhydrite** = künstlicher Anhydrit *m*, löslicher ~
***artificial (or soil, or ground) cementation (or solidification, or stabilization, or stabilisation)** = Baugrundverbesserung *f*, Baugrundverfestigung *f*, Bodenstabilisierung *f*, Bodenstabilisation *f*, Bodenverbesserung *f*
~ **consolidation,** (soil) (or earth) compaction (or densification) = künstliche Bodenverdichtung *f*
~ **island,** sand ~ = Absenkinsel *f*
~ **lake,** (impounding) reservoir, storage reservoir, storage pool, accumulation lake = Sammelbecken *n*, Staubecken, (Speicher)Becken, Speicher *m*, Stausee *m*, Talsperrenbecken, künstlicher See
~ **limestone,** hydraulic ~ = Kunstkalkstein *m*, Hydrokalkstein
~ **method of cementation by the injection of chemicals** = chemische Baugrundverbesserung *f* (oder Baugrundverfestigung *f*, oder Bodenstabilisation *f*, oder Bodenstabilisation *f*), chemische Injektion *f*
~ **navigation canal,** see: inland canal
~ **peninsula,** man-made ~ = künstliche Halbinsel *f*
~ **pozzolana cement,** see: slag ~
~ **pozzolanic materials** = künstliche puzzolanische Stoffe *mpl*, ~ Puzzolanen *fpl*
~ **river regulation,** stream straightening = Flußregulierung *f*, Flußreg(e)lung *f*
~ **sand,** see: screening(s)
~ **seasoning** = künstliche Holztrocknung *f*
~ **subgrade** = aufgeschüttetes (Erd)Planum *n*
artificially precipitated calcite = künstlich (aus)gefällter Kalzit *m*
asbestos; amianthus [*a fine, silky asbestos*] (Min.) = Asbest *m* [*in Italien, Griechenland, Frankreich und dem Orient wird für Asbest auch der Name „Amiant" gebraucht; amianthus = Amiant, Strahlsteinasbest*]
~ **cement** = Asbestzement *m*
~ ~ **sheeting** = Asbestzementplatten *fpl*
~ ~ **siding shingle** = Asbestzementplatte *f* zur Mauerverkleidung *f*
~ **felt** = Asbestpappe *f* [*Dacheindeckung f*]
~ **mine** = Asbestgrube *f*
~ **mitter** = Asbestfausthandschuh *m*
~ **slate** = Asbestschiefer *m*
~ **textile** = Asbestgewebe *n*

asbolane — asphalt filler

asbolane, asbolite (Min.) = Asbolan *m*, Kobaltschwärze *f*, Erdkobalt *m*
aseismic, quakeproof, earthquake-resistant = erdbebensicher
ashes = Asche *f*
~ **concrete;** (boiler) clinker ~ (Brit.); (boilerhouse) cinder ~ = Kesselschlakkenbeton *m*, Lösch(e)beton
ashlar = Verblendstein *m*
~ **facing** = Steinverblendung *f*
ash-leaved maple = Eschenahorn *m*
ash slate = Aschentonschiefer *m*
ashy shale = Aschenschieferton *m*
Asiatic cholera = asiatische Cholera *f*
as is = mehr oder weniger reparaturbedürftig [*Baumaschine f*]
aspect = Signalanzeige *f*
aspen = Zitterpappel *f*, Espe *f*
*****asphalt** (US); asphaltic bitumen (Brit.); [*deprecated: bitumen*] = Bitumen *n* im engeren Sinne
~ (Brit.); mineral-filled ~ (US) = Asphalt *m*
~ = Asphalt *m* [*als Straßendecke f*]
asphalt-aggregate mixture (US); (asphaltic) bitumen-aggregate ~ (Brit.) = Bitumen-Mineralgemisch *n*, bituminöse Mineralmasse *f*
asphalt and bituminous mixing plant(Brit.), see: ~ and coated macadam mixing plant
~ ~ **coated macadam mixing plant;** asphalt, bituminous macadam and tarmacadam mixing plant; dual-purpose mixing plant (or machine), asphalt and bituminous mixing plant, asphalt and tarmacadam plant, high and low temperature drying and mixing plant (Brit.); combination hot or cold mix plant (US); aggregate bituminizing plant, premixing plant = Trocken- und Mischanlage *f* (oder Aufbereitungsanlage *f*) für Mischmakadam *m* und Walzasphalt *m*, Schwarzdeckenmischanlage *f*, Aufbereitungsanlage für bituminöse Mischdecken, bituminöse Mischanlage
~ ~ **tar (melting) kettle** (US); asphaltic bitumen and tar melting kettle (Brit.) = Bitumen- und Teerkocher *m*

~ **ballast section** = Asphaltschotter-Versuchsstrecke *f* [*Eisenbahn f*]
~**-base crude petroleum** = asphaltbasisches Rohöl *n*
asphalt batch(ing)plant = Walzasphalt-Chargenmischanlage *f*
~, **bituminous macadam and tarmacadam mixing plant** (Brit.), see: asphalt and coated macadam mixing plant
~ **block,** see: ~ cake
~ ~, see: ~ (paving) block (or tile)
~ ~ **paving/pavement** (US) = Asphaltplattenpflaster *n*
~ **built-up roof** = Asphaltdach *n*
~ **cake,** ~ loave, ~ block [*deprecated*]; mastic block = Asphaltbrot *n*
~ **carpet,** ~ mat (US); bituminous (or bitumen) carpet (or mat) (Brit.) = bituminöser Teppich(belag) *m*
~ **cement,** see: asphaltic ~
asphalt-coated (US) = mit Bitumen *n* überzogen
~ **chip(ping)s** (US); asphaltic bitumen-coated ~ (Brit.) = Asphaltsplitt *m*, Bitumensplitt *m*
asphalt coating additive (US) = Haftmittel *n* für Bitumen *n*
~ **color coat** (US) = Oberflächenbehandlung *f* mit Bitumen *n* und Mineralabdeckung *f* mit Farbwirkung *f*
~ **concrete,** see: asphalt(ic) ~
*~ ~ **paver,** see: ~ finisher
~ **curb** = Asphaltbordstein *m*
~ **cutting saw** = Asphaltsäge *f*
~ **deposit** = Asphaltlager *n*, Asphaltvorkommen *n*, Asphaltlagerstätte *f*
~ **dip** = Asphalttauchbad *n*
~ **distributor** (US); asphaltic bitumen ~ (Brit.) = Bitumenverteiler *m*
~ **ductility tester** (US) = Streckbarkeitsmesser *m*
~ **emulsion slurry** (US); bitumen ~ ~ (Brit.) = Schlämme *f* mit emulgiertem Bindemittel *n*
asphalten = Asphalten *n*
asphalt filler (US) = Bitumen-Fugenvergußmaterial *n*

***asphalt finisher,** asphalt paver, bituminous paving machine, bituminous spreading-and-finishing machine, black-top-spreader, asphalt(ic) concrete paver, bituminous road surfacing finisher, (bituminous) paver-finisher, asphalt and coated macadam finisher, spreader finisher, black top bituminous paver = Schwarzbelageinbaumaschine *f*, Schwarz(decken)verteiler *m*, Verteilerfertiger *m*, Schwarzdeckenfertiger *m*, Schwarzdeckeneinbaumaschine *f*

~ **fog coat** (US) = sehr leichte Oberflächenbehandlung *f* mit Bitumen *n* jedoch ohne Mineralabdeckung *f*

asphalt-grouted macadam (US); see: asphalt macadam (penetration method)

asphalt gun (US); bitumen ~ (Brit.) = Bitumenkanone *f* [*Bitumenunterpressung f*]

asphaltic binder = Asphaltbinder *m*, Asphaltbinderschicht *f*

***asphaltic bitumen** (Brit.); see: asphalt (US)

~ ~ **and tar melting kettle** (Brit.); see: asphalt and tar melting kettle (US)

~ **bitumen-coated chip(ping)s** (Brit.); see: asphalt-coated ~

~ **bitumen distributor** (Brit.); see: distributor (US)

~ ~**-impregnated** (Brit.); asphalt-saturated (US) = bitumengetränkt

asphaltic bitumen membrane (Brit.); asphalt ~ (US); waterproofing ~ = Bitumendichtungshaut *f*

~ ~ **penetration** (Brit.); asphalt ~ (US) = Bitumenpenetration *f*

~ ~ **pump** (Brit.) = Bitumenpumpe *f*

~ ~ **road emulsion,** bitumen emulsion, cold (bitumen) ~ (Brit.); emulsion asphalt, asphalt(ic) emulsion (US); cold asphalt = (Asphalt-)Bitumenemulsion *f*, Asphaltemulsion *f*, Kaltasphalt *m*

~ ~ **trailer** (Brit.); see: asphalt ~ (US)

~ ~ **underseal(ing),** ~ ~ subseal(ing) (Brit.); asphalt underseal(ing), ~ subseal(ing) = Bitumen-Unterpressung *f*

~ **canal lining** (US); bitumen ~ ~ (Brit.) = Bitumen-Gerinneauskleidung *f*

asphalt(ic) cement, penetration grade, paving(-grade) asphalt, road asphalt (US); penetration grade bitumen (Brit.) = Straßenbaubitumen *n*

~ **concrete;** bituminous concrete (US); high stone content asphalt containing up to 65 per cent stone, stone filled asphalt = Asphaltbeton *m*

***asphalt(ic) concrete paver,** see: asphalt finisher

~ ~ **slab,** ~ **paving** ~ = Asphaltbetonplatte *f*

asphaltic cutback (US); see: cut-back asphaltic bitumen (Brit.)

~ **emulsion,** asphalt ~ (US); see: asphaltic bitumen road emulsion (Brit.)

~ **limestone,** see: asphalt-impregnated ~

~ **lining** = Asphaltauskleidung *f*

asphalt(ic) macadam (Brit.); see: asphalt macadam (penetration method) (US)

asphaltic mortar = Asphaltmörtel *m* [*in Deutschland: Gemisch aus Sand und Steinmehl mit mind. 12 Gew. % Bitumen, Erweichungspunkt Ring und Kugel 50 bis 85 Grad*]

~ **oil** = Asphaltöl *n*

~ **paving slab,** see: ~ concrete ~

(~) pyrobitumen = Bitumen *n*, größtenteils unlöslich in Schwefelkohlenstoff *m* und größtenteils unverseifbar

(~) pyrobituminous shale, bituminous (oil) ~, oil ~, kerosine coal, paraffin ~, petrolo-shale, pyroschist = (bituminöser) Ölschiefer *m*, Brandschiefer

~ **resin** = Asphaltharz *n*

asphalt(ic) rock, bituminous ~, rock asphalt = Asphaltgestein *n*, Bergasphalt *m*

~ **sand,** sand asphalt (US) = Asphaltsand *m*

~ **sandstone,** see: bituminous ~

~ **slurry** (US); bituminous ~ (Brit.) = Bitumenschlämme *f*

asphalt-impregnated limestone, asphaltic ~, bituminous ~, stinkstone = Asphaltkalkstein *m*, bituminöser Kalkstein, Stinkkalk *m*

asphalt injection control valve (US) = Bitumen-Einspritzregelventil *n*

asphalt insulating siding — asphalt trailer

asphalt insulating siding (US) = Bitumenschindeln *fpl* für Abdichtungszwecke *mpl* für Außenwände *fpl*
asphaltite = Asphaltit *m*
asphalt lake, pitch ~ = Asphaltsee *m*, Pechsee
~ **loave,** see: asphalt cake [*deprecated*]
~ **macadam** (Brit.); see: ~ ~ (penetration method) (US)
~ **macadam** (Brit.); see: ~ ~(penetration method) (US)
~ ~ (US); bitumen (or bituminous) ~, macadam with bitumen binder (Brit.) = Asphaltmakadam *m*, bituminöser Makadam, Bitumenmakadam
~ ~ (US), see: ~ ~ (penetration method)
~ ~ **(penetration method),** ~ penetration macadam, asphalt-grouted macadam, bituminous macadam (US); bitumen-grouted stone, asphalt(ic) macadam, macadam with bitumen binder (Brit.) = Asphalttränkmakadam *m*
~ **mastic,** see: bituminous ~
~ **mat** (US); see: ~ carpet (US)
~ **mattres** [*mesh-reinforced*] = Asphaltmatte *f*
~ **meal,** ~ powder = Asphalt(roh)mehl *n*
~ **membrane** (US); asphaltic bitumen ~ (Brit.); waterproofing ~ = Bitumen-Dichtungshaut *f*
~ **mulch for seeding and protecting roadway areas** = Aufspritzen *n* von Verschnittbitumen *n* zum Schutz *m* von Raseneinsaat *f* und von Straßenrändern *mpl* gegen Erosion *f*
asphaltogenic acid = Asphaltogensäure *f*
asphaltous acid anhydride = asphaltisches Säureanhydrid *n*
asphalt pavement = Asphaltdecke *f*
~ ~ (US) = Bitumendecke *f*
*asphalt paver, see: ~ finisher
~ **paving** (US) = Bitumenstraßenbau *m*
~ **(~) block** (or tile) = Asphaltplatte *f*
~ **(~) equipment** (US); machinery for bituminous construction (Brit.) = Bitumen-Straßenbaugeräte *npl*, Asphalt- und Teerstraßenbaumaschinen *fpl*, Schwarzstraßenbaumaschinen *fpl*
~ ~ **mixture** = Asphaltbelageinbaumasse *f*, Asphaltdeckenmischung *f*

~ **penetration** (US); asphaltic bitumen ~ (Brit.) = Bitumenpenetration *f*
~ ~ **macadam,** see: asphalt macadam (penetration method)
~ **plant,** hot-mix asphalt plant, central mixing plant for the preparation of high-type hot mixtures (US) = Walzasphaltanlage *f*, Heißmischanlage, Teerbeton- und Walzasphalt-Mischanlage *f*, Asphalt-Aufbereitungsanlage
~ **powder,** see: asphalt meal
~ **pump** (US) = Bitumenpumpe *f*
(~ road) heater-planer = Heiß-Planiermaschine *f*
~ **rock,** see: asphalt(ic) ~
~ **roofing surfaced with mineral granules** (US) = Bitumendachpappe *f* mit Mineralkornabstreuung *f*
~ **sandstone,** see: bituminous ~
asphalt-saturated (US); see: asphaltic bitumen-impregnated (Brit.)
~ **and coated asbestos felt** (US) = bitumengetränkte Asbestpappe *f* mit Deckschicht *f*
~ **asbestos felt** (US) = bitumengetränkte Asbestpappe *f*
~ **roofing felt** (US) = bitumengetränkte Dachpappe *f*
asphalt shingle (US) = Asphaltschindel *f*
~ **siding** (US) = Bitumenschindeln *fpl* für Außenwände *fpl*
~ **slurry** (US); see: bituminous ~ (Brit.)
~ **smoothing iron,** see: smoothing iron
~ **spray pump** (US) = Bitumensprengpumpe *f*
~ **(storage) tank** (US) = Bitumenbehälter *m*
~ **subseal(ing)** (US), see: ~ underseal(ing)
~ **surface heater** (US); road heater (or burner) (Brit.) = Asphaltdeckenerhitzer *m*
~ ~ **treatment** (US) = Oberflächenbehandlung *f* mit Bitumen *n*
~ **surfacing** = Asphaltbelag *m*
~ **tank car heater** (US) = Bitumen-Kesselwagen-Erhitzer *m*
~ **tile** = Bitumen-Fußbodenplatte *f*
~ **tar** = Asphaltteer *m*
~ **trailer** (US); asphaltic bitumen ~ (Brit.) = Bitumen-Anhänger *m*

asphalt truck distributor — auger hole

asphalt truck distributor(US); see: pressure tank lorry (Brit.)
~ underseal(ing), ~ subseal(ing) (US); asphaltic bitumen ~ (Brit.) = Bitumen-Unterpressung *f*
~ workman = Bitumen-Facharbeiter *m*
asphyxiation risk = Erstickungsgefahr *f*
as-raised aggregate (Brit.), see: all-in ~
assemblage point, see: centre knot
assembling, erection = Montage *f*, Zusammenbau *m*
assembly area, see: alert platform
~ line = Montage(-Fließ)band *n*, Fließband
~ shop = Zusammenbauwerkstatt *f*, Montagewerkstatt *f*
assignment = übertragene Aufgabe *f*
associated vibration = Begleiterschütterung *f*
Association of German Cement Manufacturers = Verein *m* Deutscher Zementwerke
assumed load = Belastungsannahme *f*
ASTM [*American Society for Testing Materials*] = Amerikanischer Verband *m* für Materialprüfungen [*USA*]
asymetrical = unsymmetrisch
asynchrouous motor, polyphase induction ~ = Asynchronmotor *m* für Drehstrom *m*, Induktionsmotor
atacamite (Min.) = Salzkupfererz *n*, Atacamit *m*
at-grade intersection, see: grade crossing
ATHEY wagon, ATHEY two-way dump trailer, universal dump trailer = Gleiskettenwagen *m*, Raupenwagen *m*, Großraumlore *f* auf Raupen *fpl* (oder Gleisketten *fpl*), Fabrikat ATHEY PRODUCTS CORPORATION, CHICAGO 38, USA
atmospheric actions, see: climatic effects
~ oxygen = Luftsauerstoff *m*
~ pressure = Luftdruck *m*
~ temperature = Lufttemperatur *f* [*Außenluft f*]
atoll = Atoll *n*, Ringriff *n*, ringförmige Koralleninsel
atomic blast = Atom-Explosion *f*
~ hydrogen welding = atomares Lichtbogenschweißen *n*, atomare Wasserstoffschweißung *f*, Arcatom-Schweißung

~ power station, nuclear power plant = Atomkraftwerk *n*, Atomenergieanlage *f*, Kernkraftwerk, Atom-Elektrizitätswerk
atomization = Zerstäubung *f*
~ method = Impact-Verfahren *n*
atomizer = Spritzflakon *n, m*, Zerstäuber *m*
~ = Sieblöffel *m* [*Sitzventil n*]
at-rest value = Ruhedruckwert *m*
attached = anmontiert
~ = beigelegt, beigefügt [*Anlage f zu einem Brief m*]
~ island, tied ~ = angegliederte Insel *f*, Angliederungsinsel
~ peninsula = angegliederte Halbinsel *f*, Angliederungshalbinsel
attachment, rig, front = Zusatzvorrichtung *f*, Anbau-Gerät *n*
~ (type) gritter, see: rear-mounted ~
attack on the coastline [*by the sea*] = Abbruch *m* der Küste *f* [*durch das Meer*]
*Atterberg limits of soil, consistency limits = Konsistenzgrenzen *fpl* nach Atterberg, Atterberg-Grenzen *fpl*, Atterberg'sche Konsistenzgrenzen
attrition = Reibung *f*
~ test [*hardness*] = Abnützungsversuch *m* (oder Abnützungsprobe *f*) durch Reibung *f*
audible signal = akustisches Signal *n*
audio visual aid = optisch-akustisches Hilfsmittel *n*
augen-gneiss (Geol.) = Augengneis *m*
auger, see: (earth) ~
~, see: cross auger
~, wood borer = Holzbohrer *m*
~ bit = Spiralbohrerkrone *f*
~ boring = Handdrehbohrung *f*
~ chain = Verteilerschneckenkette *f*
~ clutch, cross ~ ~ = Verteilerschneckenkupplung *f*
~ drill = Meißel *m* [*zur Durchteufung f harter felsiger Schichtenglieder npl*]
augered hole = Bohrloch *n*
augered-in-place pile, drilled ~, bored ~ = Bohrpfahl *m*
auger extension, cross ~ ~ = Ansatzstück *n* für die Verteilerschnecke *f*
~ hole = Handschürfbohrloch *n*

auger-mining = Kernbohren *n* wobei der Kohlekern durch nachgeschaltete Werkzeuge *npl* weitgehend zerkleinert wird, Großbohrlochverfahren *n*

auger stem, one length of drill pipe = Bohrstange *f* [*Rotary-Bohrverfahren n*]

~ **with valve** = Ventilschappe *f*

augite (Min.) = Augit *m*

augite-granite = Augit-Granit *m*

augite granulite = Pyroxengranulit *m*

augitic greenstone = Augit-Grünstein *m*

augitite = Augitit *m*

Aurora Australis = Südlicht *n*

~ **Borealis**, Northern Lights = Nordlicht *n*

auroral light = Polarlicht *n*

Austrian method, English-Austrian ~ = österreichische Bauweise *f*, Dreizonen-Bauweise *f* [*Tunnelbau m*]

~ **pine**, black ~ = Schwarzkiefer *f*, Schwarzföhre *f*

autobahn, German speedway, German motor road, German motorway = RAB, Reichsautobahn *f*, Bundesautobahn

autoclave = Dampfdruckerhitzer *m*, Autoklav *m*

autoclaved gypsum = Autoklavgips *m*

~ **lime**, pressure-hydrated ~, special ~, highly-hydrated ~, hydraulic ~ (US); (eminently) hydraulic ~ (Brit.) = hochhydraulischer Kalk *m*

autoclave expansion of Portland cement = Ausdehnung *f* von Portlandzement *m* beim Erhitzen *n* unter Druck *m*

auto-feed = automatische Beschickung *f*, ~ (Material)Aufgabe *f*

autogenous cutting = autogenes Schneiden *n*

~ ~ **and welding apparatus** = autogenes Schneid- und Schweißgerät *n*

~ **valley** = autogenes Tal *n*

~ **welding** = Autogenschweißung *f*, Autogenschweißen *n*

auto headlight = Autoscheinwerfer *m*

auto-ignition = Selbstenzündung *f*

automatic batch plant, see: concrete mixing plant

~ **block(making) machine** = Stein(fertigungs)automat *m*, Beton~

~ **chucking machine** = Futterautomat *m*

~ **circuit-breaker** = Schaltautomat *m*

~ **concrete roofing tile machine** = Betondachsteinautomat *m*, Zementdachsteinautomat *m*

~ **dumping batcher scale** = automatische Ausschüttwaage *f*

~ **feed device** = automatische Vorschubvorrichtung *f* [*Bohrmaschine f*]

~ **float** = automatischer Schwimmer *m*

~ **level** = automatisches Nivellierinstrument *n*

~ **road builders plant** = Trockenbetonfabrik *f*, Straßenbau-Silo- und Dosier-Anlage *f*

~ **scale** = automatische Waage *f*, (Ver-)Wiegeautomat *m*

~ **side tipping wagon** = Selbstmuldenkipper *m*, Stahlkastenselbstkipper

~ **steam McKIERNAN-TERRY hammer**, double-acting hammer = doppelt wirkender (Ramm)Hammer *m*, McKIERNAN-TERRY-Rammhammer *m*, Fabrikat McKIERNAN-TERRY CORPORATION, 15 PARK ROW, NEW YORK 7, USA

~ **traffic counter** = automatisches (Straßen)Verkehrszählgerät *n*

automation (process) = Automatisierung *f*

automobile, car, passenger ~ = Personen(kraft)wagen *m*, PKW *m*

~ **jack** = Wagenwinde *f*

~ **parking** = Parken *n*

~ **traffic tunnel**, see: motor ~

automotive assembly plant = Auto-Montagefabrik *f*

~ **(type) steer(ing)** = Lenkradsteuerung *f*

auto parking area = Autoparkplatz *m*

(auto)patrol (grader), see: blade maintainer

autosilo = Turmgarage *f* mit Lift *m*

(auto) truck (US); lorry (Brit.) = Last(kraft)wagen *m*, LKW *m*

~ **wrecking derrick** (crane); ~ ~ derricking jib (Brit.); ~ ~ boom ~ (US) = Unfall-Derrick-Kran *m*

autumn overturn = Herbstzirkulation *f*

autunite (Min.) = Autunit *m*

auxiliary airfield, satellite ~ = Nebenflugplatz *m*

auxiliary building (or construction) equipment = Bauhilfsgeräte npl
~ fault, branch ~, companion ~, minor ~ (Geol.) = Begleitverwerfer m, Nebenverwerfung f
~ fracture (Geol.) = Begleitbruch m
~ travel(l)ing gear, ~ undercarriage = Hilfsfahrwerk n
available chlorine = wirksames Chlor n
~ hydrogen, free ~ = freier Wasserstoff m, disponibler ~
avalanche = Lawine f
~ brake = Lawinenverbau m
~ debris = Lawinenschutt m
aventurine (Min.) = Aventurinquarz m
~ fel(d)spar, sunstone (Min.) = Sonnenstein m, Aventurinfeldspat m
~ quarz = Aventurinquarz m
average (or mean) annual value = Jahresmittelwert m
~ mountain, secondary ~ = Mittelgebirge n
to average out, to correct [*irregularities*] = ausgleichen [*Unebenheiten fpl*]
average power requirement = mittlerer Kraftbedarf m
~ rainfall intensity = Niederschlagsstärke f, Regenstärke [*mm/min.*]
~ thickness = mittlere Dicke f
avgas (US); see: aviation petrol (Brit.)
aviation fuel installation, see: (bulk) ~ ~
~ obstruction light, see: obstruction light
~ petrol (or spirit) (Brit.); aviation gasoline, avgas (US) = Flugbenzin n, Fliegerbenzin
AVUS drying, screening and mixing plant [*Trademark*] = Trocken-, Sieb- und Mischanlage f, Asphaltaufbereitungsanlage, Fabrikat ALFELDER EISENWERKE CARL HEISE K. G., ALFELD/LEINE, DEUTSCHLAND
award of contract, see: contract-letting
axial blower = Axialgebläse n
~ compression = mittiger Druck m
~ fan = Axialventilator m
~ flow impulse turbine = Gleichdruck-Axialturbine f
~ (~) pump, propeller ~ = Axialpumpe f
~ force = Axialkraft f

~ loading = mittige Belastung f
~ stress = mittige Beanspruchung f
axially loaded compression member = mittig belasteter Druckstab m
axinite (Min.) = Axinit m
axis = Achse f [*Mathematik f*]
~ of arch = Bogenachse f
~ ~ rotation = Drehachse f
~ ~ the channel; centre line of channel (Brit.); center ~ ~ ~ (US) = Fahrrinnenachse f
*axle = (Rad)Achse f
~ base, ~ spacing = Achsstand m, Achs(en)abstand
axle-load = Achslast f
azimuth = Azimuth n, m, Scheitelkreis m
azo-humic acid = Azohumussäure f
azote [*the French name for nitrogen, given to it by Lavoisier*] = Stickstoff m
azurite, chessylite, 2 $CuCO_3 \times Cu(OH)_2$ (Min.) = Azurit m, Kupferlasur m

B

babbitt (metal), see: anti-friction ~
baby bulldozer, calfdozer, skipdozer = Klein-Planierraupe f, Klein-Bulldozer m auf Raupen fpl (oder Gleisketten fpl)
baby compressor, small ~ ~ = Klein(luft)verdichter m, Kleinkompressor m, Klein-Drucklufterzeuger
bachelor quarter, ~ house = Ledigenheim n
backacter, back digger, backacting shovel (or excavator), trencher, ditcher, trenchforming shovel (Brit.); (back)hoe, trench hoe, pull-shovel, pull stroke trenching machine, trenching hoe, drag bucket (US) = Tieflöffel(bagger) m, Löffeltiefbagger m
back digger, see: backacter
to back down the forms = auf der Seitenschalung f zurückfahren [*Betondeckenbau m*]
backfill = Hinterfüllung f
to backfill, to fill in, to re-fill = verfüllen, einfüllen [*z. B. Graben m*]
~ ~ around = hinterfüllen
backfill compactor = Grabenverdichter m

backfiller, trenchfiller = Grabenverfüllgerät *n*
backfilling = Verfüllboden *m*
~, re-filling = Verfüllung *f*, Verfüllen *n*
backfill tamper = Grabenstampfer *m*
~ (trench) rammer = Grabenramme *f*
backflow = Rückstau *m*
back gear = Vorgelegerad *n*
backhaul rope [*face shovel*] = Rückziehseil *n* [*Hochlöffel(bagger)* m]
(back)hoe (US); see: backacter (Brit.)
~ dipper (US) = Tieflöffel *m*
backing = Hintermauerung *f*
~ = Hinterfüllung *f* aus Bruchsteinen *mpl*
~ brick, common ~ = Hintermauer(ungs)stein *m*, Hintermauer(ungs)ziegel *m*
~ material = Überzugsmetall *n*
backlash in the gears = totes Spiel *n* im Getriebe *n*
backlog of needs, inadequacy gap; arrears of road maintenance = Nachholbedarf *m*
back of arch, extrados = Bogenrücken *m*, äußere Bogenfläche *f*
back-pay, retroactive pay = Nachzahlung *f* [*Lohn m, Gehalt n*]
back pitch = Lochabstand *m* zweier benachbarter Nietreihen *fpl*
back-pressure steam engine = Gegendruck-Dampfmaschine *f*
~ turbine = Gegendruckturbine *f*
back ripper = Rückwärts-Aufreiß(er)vorrichtung *f*
back-ripping = Aufreißen *n* bei Rückwärtsfahrt *f*
back-shot water wheel, breast ~ ~ = rückenschlächtiges Wasserrad *n*
backsight = Rückblick *m* [*Vermessungskunde f*]
~ reading = Rückwärtseinschneiden *n* [*Vermessungskunde f*]
back siphonage = rückläufige Heberwirkung *f*
backslope = Hinterböschung *f*
backsloper, slope grader = Böschungshobel *m*, Hang-Kippschar *f*
back-swamp area = Niederungsgebiet *n* [*Fluß m*]

back-tracking with the paver = Rückwärtsfahren *n* mit dem Raupenstraßen(beton)mischer *m*
back-up block = Hintermauer(ungs)block *m*
backward erosion = rückschreitende Erosion *f*
backwashing = Filterspülung *f* [*Wasserreinigung f*]
backwash rate = Rückspülgeschwindigkeit *f*
backwater = Rückstauwasser *n*
Baculites limestone = Baculitenkalk(stein) *m*
bad weather, see: inclement ~
baffle, see: central .
~ blade, see: helical ~
~ board = Schallwand *f*
baffled mixer [*roll roofing plant*] = Mischer *m* für farbige Streumittel *npl*
bafflewall (Brit.); see: downstream sill (US)
bagasse tar = Bagasseteer *m*
bag conveyor = Sackförderer *m*
~ cutter = Sackaufschneider *m* [*Betonmischer m*]
baggage truck = Bahnsteigkarre(n) *f*, (*m*)
bagged cement, sacked ~ = Sackzement *m*
bagging, sacking-off = Einsacken *n*
~ machine, see: bag packing ~
~ scale = Einsackwaage *f*, Absackwaage *f*
bag lift truck = Sackstapler *m*
~ (of cement) (US), see: sack (~ ~)
~ (~ ~) (Brit.), see: sack (~ ~)
~ packing machine, ~ packer, bagging machine, bag filling machine = Einsackmaschine *f*, Absackmaschine, Abfüllmaschine für Säcke *mpl*
bail = Bügel *m*
to bail = schöpfen, schlämmen, löffeln
bailer = Schlämmbüchse *f*, Klappsonde *f*
~ sample = Schlämmbüchsenprobe *f*
~ swivel = Schlämmbüchsenwirbel *m*, Schöpfbüchsenwirbel
~ valve = Schlämmbüchsenventil *n*, Schöpfbüchsenventil
bailing drum = Schlämm(seil)trommel *f*, Schöpf(seil)trommel, Löffeltrommel
~ line, ~ rope = Schlämmseil *n*, Schöpfseil, Löffelseil
~ pulley = Schlämm(seil)rolle *f*, Schlämm(seil)scheibe, Schöpf(seil)scheibe *f*

bailing tub = Schöpfbütte *f*
~ **well** = im Schöpfbetrieb *m* fördernde Bohrung *f*, Schöpfsonde *f*
bail of the bailer = Schöpfbüchsenbügel *m*, Schmantlöffelbügel
Bairdia shale = Bairdienschiefer *m*
BAKER TRAVELOADER = Transport-Fahrzeug *n* für Langgut *n* mit Belade- und Entlade-(Stapel-)Vorrichtung *f*, Fabrikat THE BAKER-RAULANG CO., CLEVELAND, OHIO, USA
balance bridge, see: bascule ~
balanced community = Gemeinde *f* mit Wohn- und Arbeitsstätten *fpl* in richtigem Verhältnis angelegt
~ **earthworks** = Erdarbeiten *fpl* mit Massenausgleich *m*
~ **excavation**, see: balancing quantities
balance handle = Schwungkurbel *f*
~ **indicator** = Gleichgewichtsanzeiger *m*, Gleichgewichtsanzeigeapparat *m*
~ **point**, ~ **line** = Kippkante *f* [*Krangleichgewicht n*]
balancing group = Ausgleicher *m*
~ **machine** = Auswuchtmaschine *f*
~ **of masses** = Massenausgleich *m*
~ **quantities**, balanced excavation, earthwork balance = Massenausgleich *m*
~ **reservoir**, compensating ~ = Ausgleichbehälter *m*, Ausgleichbecken *n*
baling hoop = Verpackungsband *n*
balk, see: ba(u)lk
ball and roller bearing = Wälzlager *n*
~ ~ **socket bearing** = Kugelzapfenlager *n*
to ballast, to rubble = beschottern
ballast = Kiesschotter *m*, Steinschotter, Gleisschotter, (Eisen)Bahnschotter
~ = Ballast *m*
ballastable = belastbar [*Walze f*]
ballast box = Ballastkasten *m*
~ **cleaner** = Bettungsreiniger *m*, Bettungsreinigungsmaschine *f*
~ **concrete** = Schotterbeton *m*
~ **frame** = Ballastkasten *m* [*Baudrehkran m*]
~ **tamper**, see: tie ~ (US)
~ **unloader** = Schotterentlader *m*
~ **water** = Ballastwasser *n*
~ **weight** = Ballastgewicht *m*
ball bearing = Kugellager *n*

~ **calliper**, globe ~ = Kugeltaster *m*
~ **clay**, potters' ~, pipe ~ = Töpferton *m*, Backsteinton *m*, Ballton [*Gruppe sedimentärer, hochplastischer, feuerfester Tone. Die Bezeichnung "ball clay" stammt von der alten englischen Praxis der Tongewinnung, bei der der Ton aus den Gruben in Form von Kugeln oder Bällen entnommen wurde, die je 15 kg wogen*]
~ **(grinding) mill** = Kugel(mahl)mühle *f*
~ **lever** = Kugelhebel *m*
~ **lightning** = Kugelblitz *m*
~ **load** = Kugelfüllung *f* [*Mühle f*]
~ **milling** = Kugelmühlenmahlung *f*
balloon tyre (Brit.); ~ **tire** (US) = Ballonreifen *m*
ball-thrust bearing = Kugeldrucklager *n*
ball tube mill, see: (steel) ~ ~ ~
~ **valve** = Kugelventil *n*
balsam fir = Balsamtanne *f*
Baltic Ship Canal, Kiel Canal = Kaiser-Wilhelm-Kanal *m*, Nord-Ostsee-Kanal *m*
banatite (Geol.) = Banatit *m*
band brake = Bandbremse *f*
~ **chisel** = Bandmeißel *m*
~ **clutch** = Bandkupplung *f*
~ **conveyance**, see: belt conveying
~ **conveyor**, see: belt ~
banded clay, see: varve(d) (glacial) clay
~ **coal** = Streifkohle *f*
~ ~ [*formerly called slate coal*] = Schieferkohle *f*
banded-coal type, banded constituent, banded ingredient = Streifenart *f* [*Kohle f*]
banded forms = mit Stahlbändern *npl* umspannte Schalungsformen *fpl*
~ **gneiss**, ribbon ~ = Bändergneis *m*
~ **porphyry** = Bandporphyr *m*
~ **(or lamellar) twinning** [*plagioclase*] = Viellingslamellierung *f*
bandjire [*Malayan term for "torrent"*] = malaiischer Ausdruck für „Wildbach "
band saw = Bandsäge *f*
~ **steel**, see: strap ~
bank [*an earth slope formed or trimmed to shape*] = Erdböschung *f*
~ ~ = Wall *m*

to bank against, to fill and grade = anböschen
bank digging = Wallabtrag *m*
banked up water level = Spiegelerhebung *f*
bank erosion = Ufererosion *f*
~ gravel = Naturkies *m* mit Feinanteilen *npl*
to bank in = eindeichen
banking [*deprecated*]; superelevation, cant = Überhöhung *f* [*Straßenkurve f*]
~ (up) curve = Staulinie *f*, Staukurve *f*
bank line = Uferlinie *f* [*Fluß m*]
~ measure [*volume of soil or rock in its original place in the ground*] = Menge *f* in gewachsenem Zustand *m*
~ of ditch = Grabenböschung *f*
~ ~ the river, river bank = Flußufer *n*
~ protection, river ~ ~ = (Fluß)Uferschutz *m*
~ reclamation = Abbau *m* von Förderhalden *fpl*, ~ ~ Bergehalden
~ reinstatement = Uferausbesserung *f* [*Fluß m*]
~ revetment work, revetting = Uferbefestigung *f* durch Futtermauer *f*
~ right of passage = Uferbetretungsrecht *n*
~ sand = Sand *m* mit 0—12% Ton *m* und Schluff *m*
~ slag = Beetschlacke *f*
~ sloping = Böschungsziehen *n* mit Straßenhobel *m*
~ stabilization = Uferbefestigung *f*
bantam-weight crane = Leichtbauauslegerkran *m*
bar = Stab *m*
~, see: sand-head
~ (Brit.); breaker (US) [*roller of breaking waves*] = Brandungsgürtel *m*
barbed wire = Stacheldraht *m*
bar-bending list, see: bending schedule
BARBER-GREENE tamping level(l)ing finisher = Schwarzbelageinbaumaschine *f*, Raupenfertiger *m*, Gleiskettenfertiger *m*, Fabrikat BARBER-GREENE COMPANY, AURORA, ILLINOIS, USA
barchan, crescent-shaped dune, barkhan = Bogendüne *f*, Sicheldüne *f*
bar cutter, bar cutting shears, hand-operated barcutter, reinforcement bar shear cutter, rod shear = Betoneisen(hand)schneider *m*

~ cutting shears, see: ~ cutter
~ feeder, (flight) conveyor = Stangenzubringer *m*, Lattenrost *m* [*Schwarzbelageinbaumaschine f*]
to bare, to lay ~ = freilegen
bare electrode, plain ~ = nicht umhüllte Elektrode *f*
~ floor = Rohdecke *f*
~ ground = nackter Boden *m*
bar-fixing gang (or team, or crew, or party) = Bewehrungskolonne *f*
to barge = mit Lastkahn *m* transportieren
barge = Lastkahn *m*
~; scow (US) = Schute *f*
~ canal, artificial navigation ~, inland ~, inland navigation ~ = Binnenschiffahrtkanal *m*, künstliche Wasserstraße *f*
~ derricking jib crane (Brit.), see: floating ~ ~ ~
~ elevator = Kahnentladebecherwerk *n*
*~ **lift** = Schiffshebeanlage *f*
~ line (US); see: waterway
~ operation = Schleppbetrieb *m*
~ shipment, boat ~ = Kahnversand *m*
bar grizzly, see: ~ screen
bar-iron = Stabstahl *m*
barite, barytes, heavy spar, native barium sulphate, $BaSO_4$ = Baryt *m*, Schwerspat *m*
bark boring beetle = Borkenkäfer *m*
barkhan, see: barchan
bar of arch = Bogenstab *m*
barometric level(l)ing = barometrische Höhenbestimmung *f*, ~ Höhenaufnahme *f*
*~ **barrage,** weir = (Stau)Wehr *n*
~ ~ = Stauanlage *f*, Staustufe *f*
~ balloon = Sperrballon *m*
~ power station = Staustufenkraftwerk *n*
bar reinforcement = Stabbewehrung *f*, Stabarmierung *f*
(barrel) camber, see: camber
~ controller, ~ switch = Walzenschalter *m* [*Elektrotechnik f*]
barreled asphalt (US) = Faßbitumen *n*
barrel heater = Faßerhitzer *m*
~ heating pocket = Faßwärmeschrank *m*
~ hoist = Faßaufzug *m*
~ of bolt = Schraubenschaft *m*

barrel-pump, barrel exhausting pump = Abfüllpumpe *f*, Faßpumpe
barrel roof = Tonnendach *n*
~ slat, see: timber ~
~ switch, see: ~ controller
~ vault, see: wagon ~
~ washing device = Faßreinigungsanlage *f*, Faßwaschanlage
barren, sand heath = Sandheide *f*
~ plateau = Steppen-Hochebene *f*
barrier, barricading [*a temporary obstruction placed to prevent direct access to a particular area*] = Absperrung *f*
Barrier ice = Barriereeis *n*
barrier plate, leaf = Schütz(e) *n*, (*f*), Stautafel *f*, Falle *f*, Schützentafel
~ reef, encircling ~ = Dammriff *n*
barrow, wheel ~ = Schubkarre(n) *f*, (*m*)
barrow-type chip(ping)s spreader, hand-operated ~ ~ = Splittstreukarre(n) *f*, (*m*), Handsplittstreuer *m*
bar screen, screen of bars, (bar) grizzly, grizzly feeder [*generally used for separating fines from crusher feed*] = Stangen(transport)rost *m*, Stangenaufgeber *m*, Stangensiebrost, Spaltsieb *n*, Grobsortierrost, Siebrost
~ spraying = Spritzen *n* mit Sprengrampe *f*
barytes, see: barite
(basal) cleavage = Spaltbarkeit *f* [*Mineral n*]
~ conglomerate, see: base ~
~ matrix, ~ cement(ing material) (Geol.) = Basalzement *m*
~ sandstone = Basalsandstein *m*
basalt = Basalt *m*
basaltic débris, ~ scree = Basaltschutt *m*
~ iron ore = Basalteisenerz *n*
~ lava = Basaltlava *f*, Lungstein *m*
~ tuff, trap ~ = Basalttuff *m*, Trapptuff
~ wacke = Basaltwacke *f*
basalt (paving) sett = Basaltpflasterstein *m*
bascule bridge, balance ~ = Klappbrücke *f*, Wippbrücke
~ weight = Ausgleichgewicht *n*
base = Fußpunkt *m*
~ = Sohle *f*, Basis *f* [*Damm m*]
~ = Tragschicht *f*, Tragdecke *f*

~, tub = kreisförmige Plattform *f*, Exzenterscheibe *f* [*Schleppschaufel-Schreitbagger m*]
~, air-base (US); RAF-Station (Brit.) = Fliegerhorst *m*, Militär-Flugplatz *m*
~ (Brit.); downstream toe (US) = Basis *f* [(*Schwer*)*Gewichts*(*stau*)*mauer f*]
~ aggregate, ~ material = Material *n* für die Tragschicht *f*
~ bitumen (Brit.); ~ asphalt (US) = Grundbitumen *n*, Ausgangsbitumen *n*
~ coat, see: binder course
~ (or basal) conglomerate = Basalkonglomerat *n*
~ (course) = Tragschicht *f*, Tragdecke *f* [*in Deutschland auch als „Unterbau" bezeichnet, wenn die darunterliegende Schicht „Sauberkeitsschicht" genannt wird*]; obere und untere Tragschicht *f* [*in Schweiz und Österreich: beide zusammen mit dem „Belag" werden dann als „Oberbau" bezeichnet*]
~ ~ concrete, see: rough ~
~ ~ (of the surfacing) (Brit.); see: binder course
~ exchange = Basenaustausch *m*
~ failure, shear ~, breach, subsidence = Grundbruch *m*
~ frame[*screen*] = Grundrahmen *m*[*Sieb n*]
~ line = Grundlinie *f*
~ material, see: ~ aggregate
basement, cellar = Keller *m*, Kellergeschoß *n*
~ (construction) = Unterkellerung *f*
basementless = nichtunterkellert, kellerlos
basement site = unterkellertes Grundstück *n*
~ soil (US), see: subgrade
~ wall = Grundmauer *f*
base-mounted = auf Grundplatte *f* aufgebaut
base of calculation = Berechnungsgrundlage *f*
~ ~ stone pitching, (hand-)pitched foundation, hand-set pitching, rough stone pitching, bottoming, blocking, hand-packing bottoming, hand-pitched stone base, packed broken rock soling (Brit.); (hand-packed) Telford (type) base (US) = Setzpacklageschicht *f*, Gestück *n*

base operations — batch recorder

base operations (US); flying control (Brit.) = Flugleitung(sgebäude) *f*, (*n*)
~ **paver**, aggregate spreader, stone spreader = Schotter- und Splittverteiler *m*, Makadam-Ausleger *m*
~ **plate**, bed-plate = Grundplatte *f* [*Maschine f*]
~ ~ = Fußplatte *f* [*Stütze f*]
~ **pressure** = Sohldruck *m*, Sohlpressung *f*
~ **slab**, foundation plinth = Fundamentplatte *f*, Grundplatte
~ **stone**, see: Telford base
basic Bessemer pig-iron = Thomasroheisen *n*
~ **diorite** = basischer Diorit *m*
~ **firebrick**, alumina ~ = Tonerdeschamottestein *m*
~ **lead carbonate**, see: white lead
~ **plant** = Grundanlage *f*
~ **phorphyrites** = basischer Porphyrit *m*
~ **research** = Grundlagenforschung *f*
~ **rock** [*igneous rock containing less than 52% of silica*] = basisches Gestein *n*
~ **shovel** = Grundbagger *m*
~ **slag**, Thomas ~ = Thomasschlacke *f*, basische Schlacke
~ **stress** = Grundspannung *f*
~ **unit**, ~ **tool** = Grundgerät *n*
~ **wage** = Grundlohn *m*
basicity (factor) = Basengrad *m*
basin = Becken *n*, Bassin *n*
~ **desert** = Beckenwüste *f*
~ **due to damming** = Abdämmungsbecken *n* (Geol.)
basining (Geol.) = Beckenbildung *f*
basin system irrigation, check ~ = Bekkenverfahren *n*, Checksystem *n*, Überstaubewässerung *f*
~ **topography** = Beckenlandschaft *f*
basis of design, design fundamental = Berechnungsgrundlage *f*
basket work, wattle-work, wickerwork = Flechtwerk *n*
bass broom = Piassavabesen *m*
bast coal = Bastkohle *f*
bastite, schillerspar (Min.) = Schillerspat *m*, Bastit *m*
batch, charge = Charge *f*

~ = Beton-Kolben *m* [*die in die Rohrleitung eingeschobene Kesselfüllung eines Druckluftbetonförderers m*]
~ **bin**, batching ~ = Dosiersilo *m*, Chargierbunker *m*
~ **body** = Chargen-(LKW-)Pritsche *f*
~ **box**, ga(u)ge ~ = Zumeßkiste *f*, Abmeßkiste *f*, Meßgefäß *n*
~ **counter** = Chargen-Zählvorrichtung *f*
batched aggregate, see: (dry-)batched aggregate
batcher, apportioning gear = Dosierapparat *m* [*Zuschlagstoffe mpl; Zement m*]
~ **hopper** = Zuteilgefäß *n*
~ ~, see: weighing bucket
~ **plant**, see: (aggregate) batch(ing) plant
~ ~ = die Firma BLAW KNOX LTD. verwendet diesen Ausdruck auch für eine Betonfabrik *f*
~ **scale** = Dosierapparatwaage *f*
batch grinding, intermittent ~ = satzweise Mahlung *f*
~ **holding hopper** = Chargensilo *m*
batching, see: proportioning
~ **and mixing plant**, see: batch(-mix) (type) plant
~ **bin**, see: batch ~
~ **by volume**, see: volume-batching
~ ~ **weight**, see: weigh-batching
~ **device**, see: proportioning ~
~ **plant**, see: (aggregate) batch(ing) plant
~ **silo** = Meßsilo *m* [*Betonaufbereitung f*]
~ **unit** = Einzelsilo *m* mit Waage *f*
batch lorry (Brit.); see: ~ truck (US)
batchmeter = Chargenmischzeitmesser *m*
~ **controlled autocycle operation** = Chargenmischspielsteuerung *f* [*Straßen-(beton)mischer m*]
batch mixer = Chargenmischer *m*, absatzweise arbeitender Mischer, Stoßmischer, Periodenmischer
~ **mixing**, intermittent ~ = Chargen-Mischverfahren *n*
~ **(-mix) (type) plant**, intermittent weigh-batch (mixing) plant, batch mixing plant, batching and mixing plant = Chargenmischanlage *f*, absatzweise arbeitende Mischanlage *f*
batch pugmill = Chargen-Zwangsmischer *m*
~ **recorder** = Chargenregistriergerät *n*

batch truck (US); ~ **lorry** (Brit.) = Last(kraft)wagen *m* zur Aufnahme *f* mehrerer Chargen *fpl*

~-~ compartment (US); batch-lorry ~ (Brit.) = Zuschlagstoffabteil *n* [*Chargen-LKW m*]

batch-type concrete pug-mill (mixer) = Chargen-Beton-Zwangsmischer *m*

batch water, see: ga(u)ging ~

bathing beach = Badestrand *m*

batholith, bathylith (Geol.) = Batholith *m*, Liegendkörper *m*, Riesenstock *m*

bathyal zone (Geol.) = bathyale Zone *f*

batten (plate), tie plate, stay ~ = Bindeblech *n* [*Stahlbau m*]

battened member = Rahmenstab *m*

batter, rake; [*deprecated: slope, incline*] = 1. Neigung *f* [*gemessen gegen die Vertikale*]; 2. künstliche steile Böschung *f*

~, battice [*wall*] = Anzug *m*, Anlauf *m* [*Mauer f*]

~ board, see: sight rail

~ level, see: clinometer

battered anchor pile = Ankerschrägpfahl *m*

~ wall, battering ~ = Schrägwand *f*

batter (foundation, or bearing) pile, raking ~ = Schräg(gründungs)pfahl *m*

~ post, raker = geneigter Tragstiel *m* [*Pfahljoch n*]

battery box = Batteriekasten *m*

~ charging equipment = Batterieladegeräte *npl*

battery-electric = batterie-elektrisch

battery loco(motive), see: accumulator ~

~ plier = Batteriezange *f*

~ railcar = Akkumulator-Triebwagen *m*

battice, see: batter

battle deck floor, battleship deck [*bridge*] = ebene Bleche *npl* die durch daruntergeschweißte parallele Träger *mpl* unterstützt sind, ebene Deckbleche auf Walzträger

Bauer-Leonhardt method [*the prestressing elements consist of high-tensile steel cables, each composed of 7 wires, each 0.12 in. dia and of 255,000 lb./sq.in. strength*] = Bauer-Leonhardt-Verfahren *n*

ba(u)lk = schwerer quadratischer Holzbalken *m*

~ = zwischen zwei Ausschachtungen *fpl* stehengebliebener Boden *m*

bauxite, beauxite, $Al(OH)_3$ = Bauxit *m*

~ cement, beauxite ~ = Kühlzement *m*, Bauxitlandzement

bay = Bai *f*, kleine Bucht *f*

~, concrete ~, panel, concrete (pavement) slab = (Beton)Feld *n*, Betonplatte *f*

~ = Öffnung *f* [*Schützenwehr n*]

bayonet hook = Bajonetthaken *m*

~ joint = Bajonettverschluß *m*

bayou (US), see: ox-bow (lake)

Bazin formula = Bazin-Formel *f*

beach, shore = Strand *m*, Gestade *n*

~ building = Strandbildung *f*

~ groyne (Brit.); shore jetty (US) = Seebuhne *f*, Strandbuhne *f*

~ rock, shell(y) sandstone = Muschelsandstein *m*

~ sand = Küstensand *m*

(~) shingle, see: seashore-gravel

beaching cradle = Fahrgestell *n* (zum Fortbewegen *n*) von Wasserflugzeugen *npl* (auf dem Lande)

beacon = Leuchtfeuer *n*

beaded stripe = Glasperlen-Markierungsstreifen *m*

beam; girder (Brit.) = Balken *m*, Träger *m*, Balkenträger *m*

~, tamping ~ [*concrete finisher*] = (Stampf)Bohle *f* [*Betondeckenfertiger m*]

~ and jockey-weight type weigh-batcher (Brit.); ~ scale, batcher with weigh-beams and balance indicators (US) = Gemengewaage *f* in Laufgewichtsbauart *f*

~ bending press; girder ~ ~ (Brit.) = Trägerbiegepresse *f*, Balken(träger)-biegepresse

~ bottom = Balkenunteransicht *f*

~ bridge, see: girder ~ (Brit.)

~ centering (US); ~ centring (Brit.) = Balkenlehrgerüst *n*

~ compasses, trammels = Stangenzirkel *m*

~ form = Schalungskasten *m* für Stahlbetonbalken *m*

~ grid, see: girder grillage (Brit.)

~ head = Balkenkopf *m*

beam lifters = Arretierung f [*Laufgewichtswaage f*]
~ **of frame**, horizontal member ~ ~ = Rahmenriegel m
~ **pocket in brickwork** = Balkenauflager n im Ziegelmauerwerk n
~ **scale**, weighbeam ~ = Balkenwaage f
~ **(steam) engine** = Balancierdampfmaschine f
~ **tensile strength** = Biegezugfestigkeit f [*Betonbalken m*]
~ **(tie) bar** = Balkenanker m
bearded rye grass, Italian ~ ~ = italienisches Raigras n
***bearing** = Lager n
~ = Auflager n
~ **area** = Auflagerfläche f
~ **axle** = Tragachse f
~ **block** = Lagerstuhl m
~ **bracket** = Auflagerkonsole f
~ **capacity (or power)**, load-carrying ~, supporting ~ [*soil*] = Tragfähigkeit f, Tragvermögen n, Tragkraft f, Tragleistung f, Tragwiderstand m [*Boden m*]
~ **(~) apparatus** = Tragfähigkeitsmesser m
~ **case** = Lagerschale f
~ **cover** = Lagerdeckel m
~ **discrimination**, ~ accuracy [*radar*] = Ortungsgenauigkeit f [*Funkmeßgerät n*]
~ **friction** = Lagerreibung f
~ **index** = Tragfähigkeitsindex m
~ **jacket** = Lagerhülse f
~ **load**, see: ground pressure
~ **pad** [*bridge pier*] = Auflagerquader m [*Brückenpfeiler m*]
***bearing pile**, (foundation) ~ = Tragpfahl m, Gründungspfahl m
~ **plate**, bed ~ = Auflagerplatte f
~ **power**, see: ~ = capacity
~ **pressure**, pressure on bearing surface, reaction at support = Auflagerdruck m, Auflagerkraft f, Lagerdruck, Stützenwiderstand m, Stützendruck, Gegendruck, Stützkraft, Auflagerreaktion f, Auflagerwiderstand
~ **ring** = Tragring m, Lagerring
~ **screw** = Lagerschraube f
~ **slackness** = Lagerluft f
~ **stress** = Lochleibungsdruck m [*Niet m*]

~ **test** [*soil*] = Tragfähigkeitsversuch m [*Boden m*]
~ ~, **load(ing)** ~ = Belastungsversuch m, Belastungsprobe f
~ **value** = Tragfähigkeitswert m
~ **wall**, see: load-~ ~
beating [*deprecated*]; compacting, ramming, tamping, punning = Abrammen n, Stampfen n, Stoßverdichtung f
beautifying = Verschönerung f
bauxite (Min.), see: bauxite
bed = Pflasterbett n
~ = Bett n
~, stratum (Geol.) = Schicht f
bedded rock, sedimentary ~ = Absatzgestein n, Absetzgestein, Ablagerungsgestein, Sediment(ier)gestein, Schichtgestein, Bodensatzgestein
bed(ding course), underlying course, underlay, cushion (course); sub-crust (Brit.) = (Unter)Bettungsschicht f, Bettschicht f
bedding joint (Geol.) = Bankungsspalte f
~ **sand** = Unterbettungssand m
~ **value** = Bettungsziffer f
bed-load transport, transport of detritus = Geschiebeführung f [*Fluß m*]
bed of river, river bed = Flußbett n
bed-plate, see: base plate
~, bearing plate = Auflagerplatte f
~, **sole plate** [*bridge*] = Sohlplatte f, Lagerplatte
bed (or country, or solid, or underlying, or ledge, or outcropping) rock [*any layer of rock underlying soils. Geologically the term denotes material underlying drift deposits*] = anstehendes Gestein n, anstehender Fels m, Felsuntergrund m, gewachsener Fels, Kernfels, Sprengfels
beech (wood) tar = Buchen(holz)teer m
beef cattle pasture = Schlachtviehweideland n
~ **tallow**, ~ dripping = Rindertalg m
beeswax tar = Bienenwachsteer m
beetle, see: maul
behavio(u)r = Verhalten n
beidellite (Min.) = Beidellit m
belching = Herausspringen n des Brechgutes aus dem Brechmaul n
belemnite = Belemnit m

belemnite marl = Belemnitenmergel m
belemnitella chalk = Belemnitellenkreide f
bell, pipe ~ = (Rohr) Muffe f
bell-and-spigot joint = Stemm-Muffenverbindung f
~ **pipe** = Stemm-Muffenrohr n
bell-bottom caisson, see: caisson pile
bell-buoy = Glockenboje f
belled base = knollenförmige Erweiterung f beim Ortpfahl m
belled-out caisson, see: caisson pile
~ **pier**, see: caisson pile
bell kiln = Glockenofen m
bellow(s), forge-bellow(s) = Blasebalg m
bell-shaped ferrule = Glockenzwinge f
~ **valve**, see: double beat ~
belonite (Min.), see: needle-ore
below grade construction = Tiefbauarbeiten fpl
~ ~ ~ **site** = Tiefbaustelle f
~ ~ **military workings** = unterirdische militärische Bauten f
below-zero temperature = Minus-Temperatur f
belt = Riemen m
~ = Gurt m, Band n [Bandförderer m]
~ **(or band) conveying (or conveyance)** = Bandförderung f, Bandtransport m
***belt conveyor, band** ~ = Bandförderer m, Gurtförderer m, Förderband n, Gurtförderband
~ ~ **bridge** = Bandbrücke f
~ ~ **with cable-hauled bucket** = Gurtförderer m mit Seilschrapperkasten m
~ ~ ~ **glass idlers** = Glasrollenförderband n
~ **cover** = Bandbelag m
~ **driven pump** = Riemenpumpe f
~ **elevator**, see: ~ loader
~ ~, see: belt-type bucket elevator
~ **feeder** = Bandbeschicker m, Bandspeiser m, Bandaufgeber m
~ **hoist** = Riemenscheiben-Friktionswinde f
~ **loader, conveyor loader, elevating belt conveyor, belt elevator** (with adjustable elevation gear) = Band(auf)lader m (mit Höheneinstellung f)
~ ~, see: elevating grader
~ **sander,** ~ **sanding machine** = Bandschleifmaschine f

~ **trough** = Bandmulde f
belt-type bucket elevator, belt elevator = Gurtbecherwerk n, Gurtelevator m, Bandbecherwerk, Band(becher)elevator
belt type bucket elevator loader, self-loading tractor bucket elevator = Band-Selbstauflader m
~ ~ **car unloader** = Förderband n zur Bodenentladung f von Güterwagen mpl
~ ~ **proportioning unit** = Bandabmeßanlage f
~ **wiper, scraper** = Abstreicher m, Abstreifer [Bandförderer m]
bench = Werkbank f
~, **benching** (Brit.); **berm** = Berme f, (Sicherheits)Bankett n
~ **anvil** = Bankamboß m
~ **ditch** = Bankettgraben m
~ **drilling machine** = Tischbohrmaschine f
benched foundation = abgetrepptes Fundament n
bench grinder = Tischschleifmaschine f
bench(ing) (Brit.); **berm** [a narrow step or shelf cut in a slope or bank] = Berme f, (Sicherheits)Bankett n
benching, stepping; notching (Brit.) = Abtreppen n, Terrassieren n
~ ~ = Ausrunden n der Ecken fpl von Mannlöchern npl mit Zement m
bench lathe = Tischdrehbank f
~ **mark** = Festpunkt m, Abrißpunkt m, Fixpunkt m, Höhenmarke f
~ **shear** = Bankschere f
~ **stone** = Abziehstein m
~ **type seat** = Sitzbank f
bending, folding (Geol.) = Faltung f
~ = Biegen n, Biegung f
~ **coefficient** = Biegegröße f
~ **elasticity** = Biegeelastizität f
~ **in two planes** = schiefe Biegung f
~ **machine**, see: powered bending machine
~ **moment** = Biegemoment n
~ **oscillation** = Biegeschwingung f
~ **press** = Biegepresse f
~ **radius** = Biegehalbmesser m
~ **schedule, bar-bending list** = Biegeplan m
~ **strength** = Biegefestigkeit f
~ **stress, transverse** ~ = Biegebeanspruchung f, Biegeanstrengung f
~ **tensile stress** = Biegezugspannung f

bending test — bin and batcher plant

*bending test = Biegeversuch m, Biegeprobe f, Biegeprüfung f
bends, see: caisson disease
beneficiation of tungsten ores = Flotation f von Wolframerzen npl
beneficiary = Nutznießer m
benefit building society, see: cooperative ~ ~
benitoite (Min.) = Benitoit m
Benkelman beam (apparatus), lever-arm deflection indicator = Gerät n zur Messung f der Durchbiegung f von nichtstarren Straßendecken fpl
bent, trestle, pile trestle = (Pfahl-)Joch n
~ = Querrahmen m
~ grass, redtop ~, florin ~ = Fioringras n, weißes Straußgras n
~ reinforced concrete bar = krummer Stahlbetonstab m
bentonite, bentonitic clay (Geol.) = Bentonit m
benzene = Benzol n
benzinum purificatum = Raffinat n aus amerikanischem Benzin n
benzol(e), technical benzene = Gemisch n von Benzol n und seinen Homologen Toluol und Xylol
bergfall furrow, rock fall ~ = Steinschlagrinne f
Berlin Orbital Ring Road = Berliner Ring m [Autobahnring m um Berlin]
berm, see: bench(ing) (Brit.)
~ shaper, ~ shaping machine = Bermen-Profiliermaschine f
Bermudez asphalt = Bermudezasphalt m
Bernoulli's theorem (or equation) = Bernoulli-Satz m
berth (or wharf, or jetty) for oil-fuel bunkering = Tankanlage f, Betankungsanlage f
~, dredged ~ [a deepening in front of a tidal quay] = Sohle f [Vertiefung f vor einer Kajenmauer f]
berth(ing accomodation) = Liegeplatz m, Anlegeplatz f, Festmacheplatz [Schiff n]
berthing beam = Anlege-Plattform f für Schiffe npl
Bethell process, see: full cell
bevel, see: splaying
~ gear system = Kegelradgetriebe n

bevel(l)ed corner halving = Ecküberblattung f mit schrägem Schnitt m [Holzverbindung f]
bevel pinion = Konus(zahn)ritzel n
~ protractor = Stellwinkel m, Schmiege f, Schrägmaß n, Anlege(winkel)messer
~ tooth = Schrägzahn m
"BEWARE OF DEAR" = „WILDWECHSEL" m
B horizon, zone of concentration, ~ ~ illuviation = B-Horizont m, Anreicherungshorizont, Anreicherungsschicht f, Illuvialhorizont, Einschwemmungshorizont [Bodenkunde f]
B. H. P. intermittent = Spitzenleistung f bei kurzzeitigem Betrieb m [Motor m]
B. H. P. 12-hr. rating = Spitzenleistung f bei 12-stündigem Dauerbetrieb m [Motor m]
bi-cable aerial (or cable) ropeway, see: double ropeway
bichloride, see: dichloride
(bi)cycle racing track = Radrennbahn f
~ stand = Fahrradstand m
~ track (or path) = Rad(fahr)weg m
*1. bid, 2. proposal (US); tender, offer (Brit.) = Angebot n
~ bond (US) = Bietungsgarantie f
bidder, tenderer = Bieter m
*bidding combination, see: contracting combine
~ procedure, see: adjudication (US)
bid item = Angebotsposition f
~ sum = Angebotssumme f, Angebotspreis m
bifurcation = Gab(e)lung f
"Big Ditch" (US); Panama Canal = Panamakanal m
bight, inlet = Bucht f (Geol.)
big plaster board = stockwerkshohe Gipsplatte f
bilge pump = Lenzpumpe f
bill of quantities = Mengenverzeichnis n, Massenverzeichnis
*bin, storage ~, overhead hopper, receiving bin = Baustellensilo m, Aufnahmebunker m, (Sorten)Zwischen(lade)bunker m
~ and batcher plant = Zuschlagsilo m mit Dosiereinrichtung f

(bin and) trolley batcher plant = Zuschlagsilo *m* mit Wiegebalken *mpl*
binary = binär, binär(isch)
bin batcher = Silodosierapparat *m*
~ compartment = Bunkertasche *f*
binder, matrix, cement = Bindemittel *n*, Binder *m*
~ ; matrix (Brit.) = Bindemittel *n*, Binder *m*, Straßenbauhilfsstoff *m*

binder-batcher = Bindemitteldosierapparat *m*
binder coat, tack ~ = Bindeschicht *f* [*Straßenbau m*]
~ course, base coat, bottom coat, bottom course, binding course; (surface) base course, base-course (of the surfacing) (Brit.) [*deprecated: black base*] = Binder *m*, Binderschicht *f* [*Straßenbau m*]

---

binder distributor, tar/bitumen (Brit.)/asphalt (US) ~, binder spraying machine, bitumen distributor, bituminous distributor, maintenance distributor	**Bindemittelverteiler** *m*, **Bindemittel-Spritzmaschine** *f*
bulk tank sprayer	selbstfahrende Maschine *f* mit geschlossenem Tank *m*
gravity-flow machine	Anhänger-Maschine *f* mit offenem Tank *m*
paper strip test	Papierstreifenprüfung *f* [*Während des Ausspritzens des Bindemittels vorgenommene Prüfung zur Ermittlung der Verteilung desselben auf der Straße, wobei gegenseitig überlappte Papierstreifen ausgelegt und nach Bedeckung mit Bindemittel gewogen werden*]
road tray test	Prüfverfahren für die Messung der Dicke des Bindemittels in der Längsrichtung. Ungefähr 20 × 20 cm große leichte Metallkästen von etwa 5 mm Tiefe werden in der Längsrichtung in der Fahrspur der Spritzmaschine ausgelegt. Nach dem Überfahren werden die Kästen aufgenommen und gewogen
towed-type single-axle binder distributor without binder tank	Nachläufer *m* [*Rampen-Spritzmaschine f ohne Bindemitteltank m, ausgebildet als Einachsfahrzeug n, geeignet zum Anschluß an jeden beliebigen Tankwagen m*], Fabrikat WIBAU G. m. b. H., ROTHENBERGEN/HESSEN, DEUTSCHLAND

---

binder film = Bindemittelhaut *f*
~ (metering) pump (Brit.); bitumen (~) ~ (US) = Bindemittel(abmeß)pumpe *f*
~ soil, soil mortar, clay (binder), soil matrix, soil mortar = Bindeerde *f*, Bodenmörtel *m*, haftendes Lockergestein *n*, Bodenbinder *m*, Binderton *m*

~ spraying machine, see: ~ distributor
~ spray nozzle = Bindemittel-Eindüsapparatur *f*
binding course, see: binder ~
~ wire = Bindedraht *m*
bin door fill valve, bin gate = Siloverschluß *m*

bindweed, small morning-glory = Ackerwinde *f*
bin feeding height = Einkipphöhe *f*
~ gate, ~ door fill valve = Siloverschluß *m*
~ level = Füll(gut)stand *m*, Behälterstand
(~) ~ indicator, material ~ ~ = Bunkerstandanzeiger *m*, Silo-Füllstandanzeiger, Behälter-Standanzeiger, Stand-Meßgerät *n*, (Füll)Standanzeiger
binoculars, field glasses = Feldstecher *m*, Fernglas *n*
bin vibrator = Haftvibrator *m*, Bunkerrüttler *m*
~ weigh(ing) batcher scale = Silowaage *f*
~ withdrawing device = Bunker-Abzugsorgan *n*
~ with twin hoppers = Doppeltaschen-Baustellensilo *m*
biochemical treatment = biologische Reinigung *f* [*Abwasser n*]
biofiltration plant = Bio-Filteranlage *f*
biotite (Min.) = Biotit *m*
~-granite, granitite = Granitit *m*, Biotitgranit *m*
birch wood tar = Birkenholzteer *m*
birdbath, dell [*a concavity in a pavement surface which holds water after a shower or rain*] = Delle *f*
(birds) eye coal = Augenkohle *f*
bird's eye view = Vogelschau *f*, Vogelperspektive *f*
birdsmouth = Gabelschmiege *f*
~ attachment = Klauenschiftung *f*
to birdsmouth = aufklauen
bismuthinite, bismuth glance, Bi$_2$S$_3$ (Min.) = Bismuthin *m*, Wismutglanz *m*
bismuth ochre, bismite, Bi$_2$O$_3$ (Min.) = Wismutocker *m*, Bismit *m*
bistone carpet = Zwei-Mineral-Teppich *m* [*Straßenbau m*]
bisulphite of lime = Kalziumsulfit *n*
bisymmetrical girder = zweisymmetrischer Träger *m*
***bit**, see: rock (drill) ~
~ blade = Meißelblatt *n*
~ brace, plain ~, sleeve ~ = Bohrwinde *f*, Bohrdraube *f*
~ (cutting) edge, see: (drill) ~ (~) ~

~ hook, wall ~ = Meißelfanghaken *m*, Glückshaken
~ hydraulics = Strömungsverhältnisse *npl* am Meißel *m*
~ shank = Meißelschaft *m*
biting force, break-out ~ = Reißkraft *f* [*Bagger m*]
bitter-earth, (burnt) magnesia, magnesium oxide, oxide of magnesia, MgO = Magnesiumoxyd *n*, (kaustische) Magnesia *f*, Bittererde *f*, gebrannter Magnesit *m*
bitulithic (US) = geschlossener Asphaltbeton *m*
***bitumen** = Bitumen *n*
~-aggregate mixture, asphaltic bitumen-aggregate ~ (Brit.); asphalt-aggregate ~ (US) = Bitumen-Mineralgemisch *n*, bituminöse Mineralmasse *f*
bitumen boiler (Brit.) [*deprecated*] = Bitumenkocher *m*
~ canal lining (Brit.), see: asphaltic ~ ~ (US)
~ (or bituminous) carpet (or mat) (Brit.); asphalt carpet (or mat) (US) = bituminöser Teppich(belag) *m*
bitumen-coated chip(ping)s (Brit.); asphalt-coated ~ (US) = bituminierter Splitt *m*
bitumen distributor, see: binder ~
~ emulsion (Brit.), see: asphaltic bitumen road emulsion
~ ~ slurry (Brit.); asphalt ~ ~(US) = Schlämme *f* mit emulgiertem Bindemittel *n*
~-grouted stone(Brit.), see: asphalt macadam (penetration method) (US)
bitumen-impregnated insulating board, asphaltic bitumen-impregnated ~ ~ (Brit.) = bitumengetränkte Dämmplatte *f*
bitumen judaicum = Judenpech *n* [*Asphalt m aus dem Toten Meer n*]
~ (or bituminous) macadam, macadam with bitumen binder (Brit.); asphalt ~ (US) = Asphaltmakadam *m*, bituminöser Makadam, Bitumenmakadam
~ macadam carpet (Brit.); asphalt ~ ~ (US) = Asphaltsplittdecke *f*, Bitumensplittdecke *f*

bitumen (metering) pump (US); binder (~) ~ (Brit.) = Bindemittelpumpe *f*
~ sand mix, sand asphalt (Brit.) = Sandasphalt *m*
bituminized, bituminised = bituminiert
~ aggregate drier (or dryer), revolving (or rotary) drier (for roadmaking aggregates) = Straßenbautrockentrommel *f*, Straßenbautrommeltrockner *m*
bituminized-hessian surfacing, see: prefabricated bituminous surfacing
bituminized jute hessian cloth, see: prefabricated bituminous surfacing
bituminous = bituminös
~ base course, black base = bituminöse Tragschicht *f* [*Straßenbau m*]
~ binder = bituminöse Binderschicht *f* [*Straßenbau m*]
~ brown coal [*deprecated*]; retort ~ ~ = Schwelbraunkohle *f*
~ carpet (Brit.), see: asphalt ~
~ coal = bituminöse Kohle *f*
(~) ~ tar = Steinkohlenteer *m*
~ concrete (US), see: asphalt(ic) ~
~ damp-proofing and waterproofing = bituminöse Bauwerkabdichtung *f*
~ distributor, see: binder ~
~ emulsion (Brit.), see: asphaltic bitumen road emulsion
~ limestone, stinkstone, asphaltic limestone, asphalt-impregnated ~ = bituminöser Kalkstein *m*, Stinkkalk *m*, Asphaltkalkstein
~ macadam (US), see: asphalt macadam (penetration method)
~ macadam (Brit.), see: bitumen ~
*****bituminous macadam and tarmacadam mixing plant**, coated macadam mixing plant (Brit.); central mixing plant for the preparation of intermediate mixtures, cold mix (asphalt) plant (US) = Makadam-Maschinenanlage *f* zur Herstellung *f* von bituminösen Straßenbelagsmassen *fpl*, Trocken- und Mischanlage *f* (oder Aufbereitungsanlage) für Mischmakadam *m*, Mischmakadamanlage *f*, Kaltmischanlage *f*
bituminous mastic, asphalt ~ = Asphaltmastix *m*
~ mat (Brit.); see: asphalt carpet (US)

~ mixer = Mischer *m* für bituminöse Massen *fpl*
~ mixing plant = bituminöse Mischanlage *f*
~ (oil) shale, see: (asphaltic) pyrobituminous shale
~ pavement = bituminöse Decke *f* [*Straße f*]
*****bituminous paver-finisher**, see: asphalt finisher
*****bituminous paving machine**, see: asphalt finisher
~ protective coating = bituminöser Schutzanstrich *m*
~ road, ~ highway = Asphaltstraße *f*
(~) ~ emulsion = Straßenbau(bitumen)-emulsion *f*
*****bituminous road surfacing finisher**, see: asphalt finisher
~ rock, see: asphalt(ic) ~
~ sandstone, asphalt(ic) ~ = Asphaltsandstein *m*, bituminöser Sandstein *m*
~ shale, see: (asphaltic) pyrobituminous ~
~ slurry (Brit.); asphalt(ic) ~ (US) = Bitumenschlämme *f*
*****bituminous spreading-and-finishing machine**, see: asphalt finisher
~ surface course = bituminöse Verschleißschicht *f*
~ surfacing for bridge decks = bituminöser Brückenbelag *m*
~ varnish = Bitumenlack *m*
bitusheet = doppelschichtiger Sandasphalt *m*
bit with wings = Flügelmeißel *m*
black alder, common ~ = klebrige Erle *f*, Schwarzerle, Schwarzeller *f*, Schwarzelse *f*
~ band = Schwarzstreif *m*, Kohleneisenstein *m*
~ base [*deprecated*]; see: binder course
~ ~, bituminous base course = bituminöse Tragschicht *f* [*Straßenbau m*]
~ (blasting) powder, gunpowder = Schwarzpulver *n*, Sprengpulver
~ bolt = rohe Schraube *f* mit Mutter *f*, schwarze ~ ~ ~
~ coal, fossil ~, pit ~ = Steinkohle *f*, Schwarzkohle, fossile Kohle
~ copper = Schwarzkupfer *n*

black cotton soil [*a tropical heavy clay with a 40—50% clay fraction. The parent rock is basalt*] = tropischer schwerer Ton *m* mit 40—50% Tonanteilen *mpl*. Das Ausgangsgestein ist Basalt *m*

~ **diamonds**, drilling ~, carbon(ado)s = Bohrdiamanten *mpl*, schwarze Diamanten

~ **iron ore**, psilomelane (Min.) = Psilomelan *m*, schwarzer Glaskopf *m*

~ **jack**, sphalerite, (zinc) blende, zinc sulphide, ZnS = Zinkblende *f*, Zinksulfid *n*, Schwefelzink *n*

~ **lead**, plumbago, graphite (Min.) = Graphit *m*

~ **oil** = Sammelbegriff *m* für dunkle Öle *npl* mit relativ viel Asphalt *m*

~ **pine**, see: Austrian ~

~ **pitch** = Schwarzpech *n*

~ **poplar** = Schwarzpappel *f*

~ **powder**, see: ~ (blasting) ~

~ ~ **fuse** = Schwarzpulverzündschnur *f*

~ **sallow**, see: goat willow

Black Sea port = Schwarzmeerhafen *m*

black sheet iron = Schwarzblech *n*

blacksmiths' chisel = Schrotmeißel *m*

black specking = Schwarzfleckigkeit *f*

*****black top bituminous paver**, see: asphalt finisher

~ ~ **pavement** (US); hydrocarbon ~ (Brit.) = Schwarzdecke *f*

~ ~ **paver hauler** = Tieflader *m* für Schwarzdeckenfertiger *m*

~ ~ **paving mixture** (US); hydrocarbon pavement ~ (Brit.) = Schwarzdeckenmischgut *n*, Schwarz(decken)mischung *f*, Schwarzdeckeneinbaumasse *f*

~ ~ **road**, ~ highway = Schwarzdeckenstraße *f*

*****black-top spreader**, see: asphalt finisher

bladder wrack, fucus vesicolosus = Blasentang *m*, Fukus *m*

blade, planing ~, grader ~ [*motor grader*] = Hobelmesser *n*, (Hobel)Schar *f*, Hobelblatt *n*, Planierschar *f*, Planierschaufel *f*, Schälmesser *n*

~, paddle = Schaufel *f* [*Mischer m*]

~, see: paddle

~ **grader (self-propelled)**, power grader, motorized ~, motor ~, tractor Motor-Straßenhobel *m*, Motor-Wegehobel *m*, Motor-Erdhobel, Motor-Straßenplanierer *m*

~ **maintainer**, maintainer (scraper), (road) patrol, road maintainer, (auto) patrol (grader), motor patrol, maintainer grader = Abziehverteilgerät *n*, zweiachsiger Erdhobel *m* [*mit Eigenantrieb m*]

~ **mill**, see: scrubber

~ **mixing** = Durchmischen *n* des Bodens *m* mit Straßenhobel *m*, Schar-Mischung *f*, Messermischen *n* [*Bodenmischverfahren n*]

~ **pressure**, planing ~ ~ = Anpreßdruck *m* [*Motor-Straßenhobel m*]

~ **spreader**, reciprocating blade spreading machine, transverse blade concrete pavement spreader, blade-type spreading machine, transverse spreading blade concrete spreader = Schild(beton)verteiler *m*, Schaufel(beton)verteiler *m*

~ **spring**, see: flat ~

blade-type (or straight-blade) snow plough (Brit.)/**plow** (US); snow plough with angling blade, (reversible) side plough = Schild(schnee)pflug *m*, Schneepflug mit Frontschar, Einseitenräumer *m*, einseitiger Pflug, Seitenpflug, Einseitenpflug

blading = Einplanieren *n* mit Straßenhobel *m*

~ **back** = Verteilen *n* des in Längsreihen *fpl* zusammengehäuften Bodens *m* mit Straßenhobel *m*

Blake crusher (or breaker), see: double toggle crusher (Brit.)

blanket, see: impervious ~

~**-grouting** = (Dichtungs)Schürzen-Verpressung *f*

blank flange, see: blind ~

blast (air) = Gebläsewind *m*

~ **area** = Sprengstelle *f*

~ **chamber**, demolition ~ = Sprengkammer *f*

~ **cleaning**, sand blasting = Sandstrahlen *n*, Sandstrahlbläserei *f*, Sandstrahlreinigung *f*

blaster (US); see: blasting technician

blast flame, thin ~, narrow ~ = Stichflamme *f*

blast furnace, iron ~~ = (Eisen)Hochofen *m*
blast-furnace charge = Hochofengicht *f*
~ **coal tar** = Hochofenteer *m*
~ **gas**, top gases = Hochofengas *n*, Gichtgas *n*
~ **slag**, lump ~, iron-ore blast-furnace slag = Hochofenschlacke *f*, (Eisenhochofen-)Stückschlacke
blast generator (US); sand blast(ing) machine, sand blaster = Sandstrahlgebläse *n*, Sandstrahler *m*
blast-hole, bore-hole, shot-hole = Spreng(bohr)loch, Schußloch, Bohrloch
~ **drill**, shot-hole ~, borehole ~ = Sprenglochbohrer *m*, Sprenglochbohrgerät *n*
*****blasting**, shooting = 1. Sprengen *n*; 2. Schießen *n*
~ **cartridge**, primer ~ = Schlagpatrone *f*, Bohrpatrone, Sprengstoffpatrone
~ **explosive**, ~ **agent** = Sprengstoff *m*, Sprengmittel *n*
~ **machine**, (multi-shot) exploder = Zündmaschine *f*
~ **oil**, see: nitro-glycerin(e)
~ **pellet** = Schwarzpulver *n* in Tablettenform *f*
~ **pneumatic conveyor**, see: pressure ~ ~
~ **powder** = Schwarzpulver *n* in Pulverform *f*
~ **technician**; blaster (US) = Sprengmeister *m*
blast plate = Rauchschutztafel *f* [*Brücke f*]
~ **sand**, sand ~ ~ = Gebläsesand *m*
blau-gas = Krackgasgemische *npl* flüchtiger Kohlenwasserstoffe *mpl* mit Wasserstoff *m*
~ **tar** = Blaugasteer *m*
BLAW-KNOX spreader-vibrator = Betonverteiler *m* mit hin- und hergehender Verteilerschaufel *f* (oder Schrapperschaufel, oder Wendeschaufel), Abziehblech *n* und Oberflächenvibrator *m*, Fabrikat BLAW KNOX COMPANY, PITTSBURGH, USA
bleacher = unüberdachter Tribünensitz *m*
bleaching clay, see: active earth
~ **earth**, see: active ~
~ **powder**, chloride of lime, chlorinated lime = Bleichpulver *n*, Chlorkalk *m*, Bleichkalk *m*

bleeder(type) steam engine = Anzapfdampfmaschine *f*
~ **well** = Abzapfbrunnen *m* (oder Entlastungsbrunnen) in artesisch gespanntem Grundwasser *n*
bleeding = Anzapfen *n*
~, **fatting(-up)**, ponding = Bluten *n*, (Aus)Schwitzen *n* [*Überfluß m an Bindemittel n bei Schwarzdecken fpl*]
~, **sweating**, water gain = Bluten *n*, Wasserabstoßen *n*, Wasserabsonderung *f* [*Beton m*]
to blend = zusammensetzen, vermischen
blende, see: black jack
blended cement, natural ~ ~ = Mischzement *m*, Naturzement [*in den USA werden Naturzemente npl durch Brennen n unterhalb der Sintergrenze f gewonnen, sie sind also nach der deutschen Auffassung f hydraulische Kalke mpl*]
blending soils = Zusammensetzen *n* von Bodengemischen *npl*
    surface deposit, roadway soil = Straßenboden *m*
    complementary soil = Zusatzboden
blendous = blendehaltig [*Mineral n*]
to blind, see: to chink
blind abutment = blindes Widerlager *n*
~ **alley**, cul-de-sac (street), close = Sackgasse *f*, Sackstraße *f*
~ **arch** = Blindbogen *m*
~ **drain**, spall ~, stone ~, rubble ~, stone-filled trench, French drain, filter drain = Sickerdrän, Steindrän, Steinrigole *f*, Filterdrän *m*, Sickergraben, Rigole *f*, Sauggraben *m*
~ **drilling** = Bohren *n* ohne geologische Vorstudien *fpl*
blinded with sand = sandgeschlämmt
blind flange, blank ~ = Blindflansch *m*, Deckelflansch
~ **hole thread** = Grundlochgewinde *n*
blinding [*screen*] = Verstopfen *n*, Verstopfung *f* [*Sieb n*]
blinding, dressing [*deprecated*]; gritting, grit blinding, chipping = Absplitten *n*
~, chinking, choking = Auszwicken *n*, Verzwicken *n*, Abdecken *n* [*Packe f*]
blinding sand = Walzsand *m* [*Schotterdecke f*]

blinding (stone), see: choke stone (or aggregate)
blister = Blase *f* [*Gußasphalt m*]
blitzed site clearance = Enttrümmerung(s-arbeiten) *f*, Schutträumung(sarbeiten) *f*, Trümmerräumung(sarbeiten) *f*
bloating [*clay*] = Blähen *n* [*Ton m*]
~ clay (Brit.); lightweight aggregate (US); expanded clay = Blähton *m*
block = Verkehrssperrung *f*
~ = Flasche *f*, Block *m*, Kloben *m* [*Seilzug m*]
~ = Klotz *m*, Block *m*
(~ and) tackle, (rope) pulley block, lifting block, hoist block, rigging with blocks = Flaschenzug *m*, Blockwinde *f*, Seilzug *m*; Talje *f* [*seemännischer Ausdruck*]
~ beam = aus Betonblöcken *mpl* zusammengesetzter Balken *m*
~ bill, broad axe = Breitbeil *n*
*block-caving method = Pfeiler-Bruch-Verfahren *n* [*Asbesterzabbauverfahren n unter Tage*]
block coal = Würfelkohle *f*
blocked up, choked up = verstopft
~ ~ valley, obstructed ~ ~ = abgeriegeltes Tal *n*
block form = Blocksteinformat *n*
block-forming machine, see: (concrete) block(-making) ~
block holer = Knäpper(bohr)hammer *m*
~ holing, see: pop shooting
block-in-course walling = Quadermauerwerk *n*
blocking, sledging = Grobspalten *n* [*Steine mpl mit Keilen mpl*]
~ (Brit.), see: base of stone pitching
~, damming (Geol.) = Absperrung *f*
block lava; aa (~) [*Hawaian term*] = Blocklava *f*, Schollenlava, Zackenlava, Spratzlava, Aprolith *m*
~ making = Betonsteinherstellung *f*
~ (~) machine, see: (concrete) ~ (~) ~
~ mountain = Blockgebirge *n*
~ of flats, apartment block, flat, tenement building = Wohnhochhaus *n*
~ ~ rock, ~ ~ stone = Felsblock *m*
~ ~ stone drilled for blasting = Knäpper *m*
blockout, recess, embrasure = Aussparung *f*

block pavement (US); (stone-)sett paving (Brit.); [*in Scotland: causeway*] = Pflasterdecke *f*, (Stein-)Pflaster *n*, Pflasterung *f*
~ plant, see: (concrete) ~ ~
~ rail = Straßenbahnblockschiene *f*
blocks = Sperrzeiten *fpl*
blockstone (Brit.), see: pitcher
block testing machine, see: (concrete) ~ ~ ~
blockyard, see: (concrete) block plant
blondin (Brit.); tautline cableway, (aerial) cableway, cable-crane, overhead cableway, funicular crane = Kabelkran *m*
blood rain (Geol.) = Blutregen *m*
bloodstone, heliotrope (Min.) = Heliotrop *m*
blotter (material) (for bituminous prime coat) (US); cover aggregate (for seal); cover stone; gritting material; surface dressing chipping(s) (or chips) (Brit.) = Abdecksplitt *m*
blow = Schlag *m*
~, see: blow(-out)
~ bending test, shock ~ ~ = Schlagbiegeversuch *m*
blower = Gebläse *n*
~-type burner = Gebläsebrenner *m*
~-type snow plough (Brit.); see: snow blowing machine
blowing snow = Schneetreiben *n*
~ tunnel ventilation = Druckbewetterung *f*
blow lamp (Brit.); see: blowtorch (US)
blowlamp treatment of old coats of oil paint = Abbrennen *n* alter Ölfarbenanstriche *mpl*, Flammstrahlreinigung *f*
blown asphalt, air-blown ~, oxidized ~ (US)/asphalt(ic) bitumen (Brit.) = geblasenes Bitumen im engeren Sinne, oxydiertes ~ ~ ~ *n*
~ oil = geblasenes Öl *n*
blow(n) sand = wind-blown sand
~ soil, see: aeolian ~
blow(-out) = Fehlschußloch *n*
~ = Reifenpanne *f*
blow(pipe) lamp (Brit.); see: blowtorch (US)
blowtorch (US); soldering lamp, blow-(pipe) lamp (Brit.) = Lötlampe *f*
blubber oil = Rückenöl *n* [*Spermacetiöl n*]

blue asbestos — bolt hole

blue asbestos, Cape ~ (Min.) = Blauasbest *m*, Kapasbest
~ clay = Blauton *m*
blue-grass, Kentucky grass (US); great poa, smooth-stalked meadow grass (Brit.) = Wiesenrispe(ngras) *f*, (*n*)
blue oil, see: pressed distillate
~ print = Blaupause *f*
~ steel plate = Blaublech *n*, Stahlglanzblech *n*, Stahlblech *n* mit graublauer Walzhaut *f*
~ vitriol, chalcanthite, blue stone, $CuSO_4 \times 5 H_2O$ (Min.) = Kupfervitriol *n, m*, Chalkanthit *n*
bluff = schroffes Ufer *n*
blunt file = Stumpffeile *f*
board = Brett *n*
boarded floor(ing) = Bretterfußboden *m*
(board) landing light = Landescheinwerfer *m* [*Flugzeug n*]
boat harbo(u)r = Bootshafen *m*
~ landing = Bootsanlegestelle *f*
~ shipment, barge ~ = Kahnversand *m*
body = Pritsche *f* [*LKW m*]
~ = Kippmulde *f* [*Erdbau-Lastfahrzeug n*]
~ = Körper *m*
~ of weir = Wehrkörper *m*, Wehrmauer *f*
~ stress = Eigenspannung *f*
B. O. E. door sill, see: brick-on-edge ~ ~
bog blasting, peat ~, muck-blasting operation, blasting of peat, swamp-shooting method, toe-shooting = Moorsprengung *f*, Schüttsprengverfahren *n*
~ burst = Moorbruch *m*
~ coal = Sumpfkohle *f*
bogie (truck) = Drehgestell *n*
bog iron ore = Sumpfeisenerz *n*
~ lime, see: lake-marl
~ moss, peat ~, sphagnum ~ = Torfmoos *n*, Sumpfmoos *n*
BOHŃ & KÄHLER soil vibrator (or vibrating-plate compactor) = Rüttelverdichter *m* (oder Resonanzschwingungsverdichter) System Professor Lorenz, Fabrikat BOHŃ & KÄHLER A.G., KIEL, DEUTSCHLAND
boiler, steam ~ = (Dampf)Kessel *m*
~ coaling installation, steam ~ ~ ~ = (Dampf)Kesselbekohlungsanlage *f*
~ composition, see: ~ fluid

~ efficiency, steam ~ ~ = (Dampf-)Kesselwirkungsgrad *m*
~ fluid, ~ composition = (Dampf)Kesselsteingegenmittel *n*
~ furnace = Kesselfeuerung *f*
(~) grate = (Kessel)Rost *m*, Feuerrost *m*
(boilerhouse) cinder, see: clinker
(~) ~ concrete = ashes concrete
boiler plate, steam ~ ~ = (Dampf-)Kesselblech *n*
(~) ~ scale = (Kessel)Ansatz *m*, Kesselstein *m*
~ ~ and rust chipper = Kesselstein- und Rostabklopfer *m*
~ shell, steam ~ ~ = (Dampf)Kesselmantel *m*
boiling [*the movement of the spoil into the bowl of a wheel scraper*] = Laden *n* [*Radschrapper m*]
~ of sand = Sandaufbruch *m* [*Grundbruch m bei kritischem Gefälle n*]
~ test [*hydraulic cement*] = Kochversuch *m*
~ under vacuum process, see: Boulton process
bold shore, high coast, cliff, cliffed coast(line) = Steilküste *f*, Steilufer *n*, Kliff *n*, Kliffküste *f*
bole = Aussparung *f* in einer Wand *f*
~ = Baumstamm *m*
~ = Mineralpigment *n* in Anstrichfarben *fpl*
~, bolus = Bol(us) *m*, Boluserde *f*
bollard = Poller *m*
~ [*a substantial post near the end of a refuge to define its position and to prevent vehicles from over-running the area reserved for pedestrians*] = Inselpfosten *m*
bolster, broad-tool = Breiteisen *n*
~, corbel-piece, head-tree = Sattelholz *n*
bolt = Schraubenbolzen *m*
~ and nut, ~ with ~ = Bolzen *m* mit Kopf *m* und Mutter *f*, Durchsteckschraube *f*
~ clipper = Bolzen(abschneider) *m*
~ driving gun, cartridge-powered tool, powder-actuated tool = Bolzenschießgerät *n*
~ for spring bolt = Federbolzen-Bolzen *m*
~ hole = Schraubenbolzenloch *n*

(bolt) nut — boom point clearance height

(bolt) nut, screw ~ = (Schrauben)Mutter *f*
to bolt on = anbolzen
bolt shank = Schraubenschaft *m*
~ **steel** = Schraubenstahl *m*
~ **stock** = Schraubenmaterial *n*
bolted joint, ~ connection, ~ structural ~ = geschraubte Verbindung *f*, Schraubenverbindung
bolting cloth = Siebseide *f*
bolus, bole = Bol(us) *m*, Boluserde *f*
bomb crater = Bombentrichter *m*
~ **dump area,** see: ammunition depot
bomb-resistant, bomb proof = bombensicher
bombing base = Bomben(ab)wurfplatz *m*
bon ami powder, break-in ~ = Einfahrpulver *n*
bond, masonry ~, brick ~ = Mauerverband *m*
~ = Haftung *f* [*z. B. zwischen Bewehrung f und Beton m*]
~, bonding = Verbund *m* [*Spannbeton m*]
~ **action in floors of precast reinforced concrete** = Verbundwirkung *f* von Decken *fpl* aus Stahlbetonfertigteilen *mpl*
BONDACT method = Verfahren *n* zum einfachen Verputzen *n* von Mauerwerk *n*
BONDACTOR [*Trademark*] = Beton-Spritzmaschine *f*, Fabrik AIR PLACEMENT EQUIPMENT COMPANY, KANSAS CITY 8, MO., USA
bonded girder = Verbundträger *m*
~ **warehouse** = Freihafenniederlage *f*
bond efficiency = Haftwirkung *f* [*z. B. neuer Beton auf altem Beton*]
bonder, bondstone, header = Binderziegel *m*, Binder(ziegel)stein *m*
bond(ing) = Verbund *m* [*Spannbeton m*]
bonding additive, see: dope
bondstone, see: bonder
bond strength = Haftvermögen *n*, Haftfestigkeit *f*
~ **stress** = Haftspannung *f*
bone amber = knochiger Bernstein *m*
~ **coal** = Knabbenkohle *f*
bonebed (Geol.) = Knochenbett *n*, Knochenlager *n*
bone black, ivory ~ = Beinschwarz *n*
~ **glue** = Knochenleim *m*

~ **oil,** Dippel's oil = Knochenöl *n*
~ **-tar pitch** = Knochen(teer)pech *n*
boning(-in), sighting = (Ein)Visieren *n*
boning rod = Visierkreuz *n*
~ ~ **with round top piece** = Visierscheibe *f*
bonus = Gratifikation *f*
book clay, see: varve(d) (glacial) ~
~ **mica,** sheet ~ (Min.) = Plattenglimmer *m*
boom, chord, flange = Gurt(ung) *m*, (*f*)
~, shovel ~ (US); jib, shovel ~ (Brit.) = Ausleger *m* [*Bagger m*]
~, crane ~ (US); jib, inclined jib, crane = jib (Brit.) = Kranausleger *m*
~ **angle** = Auslegerneigung *f*
~ **bracing,** chord ~, flange ~ = Gurtversteifung *f*
~ **brake** (US); jib ~ (Brit.) = Auslegerbremse *f*
~ **cable** (US); jib ~ (Brit.) = Auslegerseil *n* [*Bagger m*]
~ **catch** = Auslegerverriegelung *f*
~ **(derricking) cable** (US); jib (~) ~ (Brit.) = Ausleger-Hubseil *n*
~ **dragline** (US); dragline (excavator), dragline-type shovel = Schürfkübelbagger *m*, Schleppschaufelbagger *m*, Eimerseilbagger *m*, Schlepplöffelbagger, Zugkübelbagger
~ **drum** (US); jib ~ (Brit.) = Auslegertrommel *f*
~ **fall-back** [*backhoe*] = Zurückfallen *n* des Auslegers *m*
~ **foot drum,** ~ ~ **spool** = Auslegerfußtrommel *f*
~ **hoist** (US); jib ~ (Brit.) = Baggerwindwerk *n*, Auslegerwinde *f*
~ ~ **lever** = Hebel *m* für Auslegerwindwerk *n*
~ **lift cylinder** (US); jib ~ ~ (Brit.) = Ausleger-Hubzylinder *m*
~ **line** [*four part*] = Auslegerhalteseil *n* [*vierfach geschert*]
~ **member,** chord ~, flange ~ = Gurt(ungs)stab *m*
~ **plate,** see: angle iron of the chords
~ **point** = Auslegerspitze *f*
~ ~ **clearance height** (US) = Höhenmaß *n* der Auslegerrolle *f* [*Löffelbagger m*]

boom point clearance radius (US) = Schwenkhalbmesser *m* der Auslegerrolle *f* [*Löffelbagger m*]

~ ~ **pin** = Gelenkbolzen *m* der Auslegerspitze *f*

~ ~ **sheave** = Auslegerrolle *f*

~ **scraper** = Auslegerkratzer *m*

~ **side sheave** = Auslegerseitenseilscheibe *f*

~ **swing** (US); jib ~ (Brit.) = Schwenkbereich *m* [*Auslegerbagger m*]

~ **type** (US)/**jib type** (Brit.) **cable excavator and loader** = Schrapplader *m* mit Ausleger *m*, Fabrikat A. G. für BERGBAU-UND HÜTTENBEDARF, SALZGITTER, DEUTSCHLAND

~ ~ **trencher**, ~ **type ditcher, boom type trenching machine, ladder ditcher, ladder-type trenching machine** = Eimerkettengrabenbagger, Eimerleitergrabenbagger *m*

~ **with troll(e)y** (US); jib ~ ~ (Brit.); ~ ~ **crab** = Laufkatzenausleger, Lastkatzenausleger *m*

booming up and down = Anheben *n* und Senken *n* des Auslegers *m*

booster air pipe = Brodel-Luftanschluß *m* [*Druckluftbetonförderer m*]

~ **fan** = Verstärkerventilator *m*

~ **heater** = Kesselwagen-Erhitzer *m* [*Bitumenverflüssigung f*]

~ **pump** = Druckverstärkerpumpe *f*, Verstärkungspumpe

~ **station**, ~ **plant, boosting** ~ ~ = Druckverstärker(pumpen)anlage *f*, Druckverstärker(pumpen)station *f*, Druckerhöhungs(pumpen)anlage, Verstärkungspumpenanlage

boot, bucket (elevator) ~ = Becherwerkfuß *m*, Becherelevatorfuß

~ = Schutzkappe *f*

~ **loading elevator**, see: centrifugal discharge ~

~ **pulley** = Becherwerkfußtrommel *f*

bor(ac)ic acid, H_3BO_3 = Borsäure *f*

boracite (Min.) = Borazit *m*

borate of lime = borsaurer Kalk *m*

borax lake = Boraxsee *m*

bordering tool = Bördeleisen *n*

border stone = Begrenzungsstein *m*, Grenzstein

to bore = bohren

bore, eagre = Seebeben *n*

~ **bar**, see: boring rod

bored caisson, see: drilled-in ~

~ **tube pump**, see: hollow ram ~

bore(hole), boring = Bohrloch *n*

bore-hole, see: blast-hole

~ **camera** = Bohrlochkamera *f*

~ **pump** = Bohrlochpumpe *f*

~ **spacing** = Bohrlochdistanz *f*

~ **tubing**, pipe for lining the bore (or boring) = Bohrlochfutterrohr *n*

borer = Bohrer *m*

~ = Bohrkäfer *m*

bore rod, see: boring ~

bore-well = Bohrbrunnen *m*

boric acid, see: bor(ac)ic ~

boring = Ausdrehen *n*, Aufbohren [*Vergrößern eines Loches*]

~, **bore(hole)** = Bohrloch *n*

~ **bar**, see: ~ rod

*~ **bit**, see: rock(-drill) ~

~ **for soil investigation** = Bodenuntersuchungsbohrung *f*

~ **method**, see: drilling ~

~ **report**, = record sheet, ~ **log** = Bohrprotokoll *n*

~ **rod**, drill ~, drilling ~, bore ~, boring bar, bore bar, drill(ing) bar = Bohrstange *f*

~ **sponge** = Bohrschwamm *m*

~ **winch** = Bohrwinde *f*

~**-worm** = Bohrwurm *m*, Schiffswurm

bornite, erubescite, horse-flesh ore, peacock ore, variegated copper ore, Cu_5FeS_4 (Min.) = Bornit *m*, Buntkupferkies *m*

borosilicate = Borosilikat *n*

borrow = Massenentnahme *f*

~ **cut(ting)** = Entnahmeeinschnitt *m*

~ **excavation**, see: ~ pit

~ ~ **material** = Entnahmematerial *n*

~ **pit**, ~ excavation [*an excavation from which material is taken to a nearby job*] = Entnahmegrube *f*

~ **soil**, borrowed ~, ~ earth; ~ dirt (US) = Entnahmeboden *m*

~ **source** = Entnahmestelle *f*, Gewinnungsstelle *f*

~ **yardage** = Entnahmekubatur *f*

BOSCH lubricating pump = Schmierpumpe f, Fabrikat ROBERT BOSCH GMBH, STUTTGART, DEUTSCHLAND
bossage = Bossenwerk n, Bossage f
Boston caisson foundation, see: Gow ~ ~
bottle brush = Ackerschachtelhalm m
~ **cleaning plant** = Flaschenreinigungsanlage f
~ **green** [*mineral*] = flaschengrün
~ **jack** = Flaschenhebebock m, Flaschenwinde f
bottleneck, deadline = Engpaß m
bottlenose oil = Entenwaltran m, Döglingtran, arktisches Spermacetiöl n
bottling machine = Flaschenfüllmaschine f
bottom = Sohle f
~ = Boden m [*als Fläche* f]
~ **blast forge**, see: field ~
~ **block**, see: fall-block
~ **boom**, ~ chord, ~ flange, lower ~ = Untergurt m, untere Gurtung f
~ **bracket** = Aufsetzwinkel m
~ **coat**, see: binder course
~ **course** = Unterschicht f
~ ~, see: binder course
~ **deck** [*screen*] = Unterdeck n [*Sieb* n]
~ **deposits** = Bodenschlamm m [*Abwasser* n]
~ **discharge tunnel**, see: ~ emptying gallery
~ **drain valve** = Bodenentleerungsventil n
~ **drift** = Sohlstollen m
~ **dump discharge**, bottom-dumping = Bodenentleerung f [*Fahrzeug* n]
bottom-dump hatch = Bodenklappe f [*Fahrzeug* n]
~ **hauling and spreading trailer** = Transport- und Verteileranhänger m mit Bodenentleerung f
~ **scow** (US); see: hopper barge (Brit.)
~ **tractor trailer**, see: trailer-bottom dump
~ ~ **truck**, see: trailer-bottom dump
bottom emptying gallery, scour outlet, bottom outlet, lower discharge tunnel, bottom discharge tunnel, sluiceway, ground outlet = Grundablaß m, Grundauslaß m
~ **fibre** (Brit.); ~ fiber (US) = untere Faser f, ~ Randfaser

~ **flange troll(e)y** = Untergurtlaufkatze f, Untergurtlastkatze
~ ~ **type telpher**, transporter = Untergurtlaufschienen-Elektrohängebahn f
~ **floor(ing)** = Erdgeschoßfußboden m
~ **gate** = Untertor n [*Schleuse* f]
~ **heading**, floor ~ = Sohlvortrieb m, Sohlstollen m
bottoming (Brit.) = Unterbau m
~ (Brit.), see: base of stone pitching
bottomless = ohne Boden m, bodenlos
bottom of the sea, sea bed = Meeresgrund m
~ **opening** = Bodenöffnung f
~ **outlet**, see: ~ emptying gallery
~ ~ **pipe** = Grundablaßrohr n
~ **peat** = Flachmoortorf m
bottoms = Destillationsrückstand m
bottom screen grate = unterer Rostrahmen m mit Roststäben mpl [*Hammerbrecher* m]
~ **section** = unteres Trum n [*Gleiskette* f]
~ **shell** = Fußringschale f [*Brückenpfeiler* m]
~ **surface dummy joint** = untere Scheinfuge f
Boucherie process = Boucherieverfahren n [*Holzschutzbehandlung* f]
bougie (Brit.); (pressure) grouting pan, pressure pot = Hinterspritzkessel m
boulder (Geol.) [2000—300 mm] = Block m [2000—200 mm nach Fischer und Udluft (1936), nach Niggli (1938), nach Gallwitz (1939)]
~ **blasting**, see: pop shooting
~ **clay** [*the stones are not necessarily all of "boulder" size*] = Geschiebemergel m
BOULDER pneumatic concretor [*Trademark*] = Beton-Spritzmaschine f, Fabrikat WINGET LTD., ROCHESTER, ENGLAND
boulder popping, see: pop shooting
~ **shingle** (Geol.) = Steingeschiebe n
boulter cutter = Viertelstabfräser m
Boulton process, boiling under vacuum ~ = Unterdruckverfahren n [*Holztränkung* f]
to bounce = zurückschnellen [*Pfahl* m]
boundary condition = Randbedingung f

boundary fence, fencing = Umzäunung *f*, Einzäunung *f*, Einfriedigung *f*
~ **light** = Randfeuer *n*, Umrandungsfeuer [*Flugplatz m*]
~ **stone** = Grenzstein *m*, Begrenzungsstein
Bourdon ga(u)ge = Bourdonmanometer *n*
bournonite, wheel-ore, cog-wheel ore (Min.) = Rädelerz *n*, Spießglanzbleierz *n*, Schwarzspießglanzerz *n*
bow girder = gebogener Träger *m*
bowl, see: (skimmer) scoop
~ = Staubfangglas *n*
~ = Leuchtenschale *f*
~ **classifier** = Schüsselklassierer *m*
bowser (Brit.); see: tank truck (US)
bowstring girder (Brit.); bowstring beam, tied arch, bowstring arch = Bogenträger *m* mit Zugband *n*
box-annealed sheet = kistengeglühtes Feinblech *n*
box beam; see: ~ girder (Brit.)
~ **container** = geschlossener Behälter *m*
~ **culvert**, see: ~ drainage ~
~ **dam**, see: box type cofferdam
~ **drain** = Kastendrän *m*
~ **(drainage) culvert** = Kastendurchlaß *m*, Kastenabzugkanal *m*
~ **floating dock** = U-förmiges Schwimmdock *n*
~ **girder** (Brit.); ~ beam = Kastenträger *m*, Kastenbalken *m*, Kastenbalkenträger *m*
*****box hopper distributor**, see: trough type concrete distributor
~ **section** = Kastenquerschnitt *m*
~ ~ **frame** = Kastenrahmen *m*
~ ~ **(sheet) pile**, encased (sheet) pile = Kastenspundbohle *f*
~ **sextant** = Dosensextant *m*
~ **shear apparatus**, Casagrande shear test apparatus = Scherapparat *m* nach Casagrande, Scherkastengerät *n*, Scherbüchse *f*
~ **spanner** = Steckschlüssel *m*
~ **spreader**, spreading box, (drag) spreader box, spreading hopper, drag box, drag spreader = Verteilerkasten *m*, Kastenverteiler *m*
*****~, see: trough-type concrete distributor

*****~ **spreading machine**, see: trough-type concrete distributor
~ **type boom** (US)/**jib** (Brit.) = vollwandiger Ausleger *m*, Kastenausleger
~ ~ **cofferdam**, box dam = Kastenfang(e)damm *m*
~ **(~) (concrete) spreader**, see: trough-type concrete distributor
~ ~ **construction** = Hohlkastenbauweise *f*
~ ~ **scraper bucket** = kastenartiges Schrappergefäß *n*, Schürfkasten *m*
~ ~ **skip**, ~ ~ **tip wagon**, ~ ~ **track wheel dump wagon** = Kastenkipper *m*
~ ~ **tip wagon**, ~ ~ **dump** ~ = Kastenkipper *m*
~ **weight** [*deprecated*]; see: volume ~
boxwood = Buchsbaumholz *n*
brace = Strebe *f*, Spriße *f*
~ = Bohrleier *f*
to brace = aussteifen, absteifen
braced arch(ed) bridge = Fachwerkbogenbrücke *f*
~ **beam**, see: lattice girder (Brit.)
~ **girder** (Brit.), see: lattice girder
~ **sheet (pile) wall** = ausgesteifte Spundwand *f*, abgesteifte ~
~ **timbering** = ausgesteifte Zimmerung *f*, abgesteifte ~
bracing = Absteifung *f*, Aussteifung
~ = Verband *m* [*Tragwerk n*]
~ **for road transport** = Transportverstrebung *f*
~ **with verticals**, vertical truss = Ständerfachwerk *n*
bracket = Auflager *n*
~ = Konsole *f*
~ **support** = Kragstütze *f*
brackish, saltish = brackig
~ **water limestone** = Brackwasserkalk(stein) *m*
brad-awl, see: gim(b)let
to brake = (ab)bremsen
BRADLEY HERCULES three-roll mill [*Trademark*] = BRADLEY-Mühle *f* mit drei Pendelwalzen *fpl*
brake band = Bremsband *n*
~ ~ **block** = Bremsbandkloben *m*
~ **block**, see: ~ shoe
~ **disc**, ~ **disk** = Bremsscheibe *f*

brake horsepower = effektive Pferdestärke *f*, nutzbare ~
~ **impression,** braking ~ = Bremsspur *f*, Bremseindruck *m*
~ **lever** = Bremshebel *m*
~ **lifting magnet** = magnetischer Bremslüfter *m*
~ **lining** = Bremsbelag *m*
~ **pulley** = Bremsscheibe *f*
~ **ring** = Bremsring *m*
~ **rods** = Bremsgestänge *n*
~ **shoe,** ~ block, slipper = Bremsklotz *m*, Bremsschuh *m*, Hemmschuh
~ **supply tank** = Bremsflüssigkeitsbehälter *m*
brakesman's box, car rider's ~ = Bremserhäuschen *n*
braking bracing = Bremsverband *m*
~ **distance** = Bremsweg *m*
~ **force** = Bremskraft *f* [*durch das Abbremsen von Fahrzeugen in Höhe der Fahrbahnoberkante angreifende horizontale Kraft bei Brückenbauten*]
~ ~ **coefficient** = Bremsbeiwert *m*
~ **friction** = Bremsreibung *f*
~ **impression,** see: brake ~
~ **range** = Bremsbereich *m*
~ **surface** = Bremsfläche *f*
~ **test,** stopping distance ~ = Auslaufversuch *m*
branch drain, subsidiary ~, feeder ~ = Sauger *m*
~ **fault,** see: auxiliary ~
~ **line** = Abzweigleitung *f*
~ **of canal,** see: arm ~
~ **pipe** = Abzweigrohr *n*
~ **sewer,** submain = Verbindungssammler *m* zwischen Haupt- und Nebensammler [*Abwasser n*]
~ **track** = Zweiggleis *n*
~ **valve** = Abzweigventil *n*
brass and bronze = Buntmetall *n*
~ **bush** = Rotgußbuchse *f*
~ **solder** = Messinglot *n*
~ **tube** = Messingrohr *n*
braunite (Min.) = Braunit *m*
to braze, to solder hard = hartlöten, mit Hartlot *n* löten
brazed flange, soldered ~ = Auflötflansch *m*

~ **joint** = Lötverbindung *f*
brazier, (fire) devil = Kokskorb *m*, Bauaustrocknungsofen *m*
brazing, hard soldering = Hartlöten *n*
~ **lamp** = Hartlötlampe *f*
~ **tongs,** soldering tongs, soldering tweezers, hawk-bill (pliers) = Lötzange *f*
breach, subsidence, base failure, shear failure = Grundbruch *m*
~ = Bruch *m*, Bresche *f* [*z. B. Deich m*]
breakdown = Ausfall *m* [*Baumaschine f*]
~ **crane,** see: permanent way ~ (Brit.)
~, **accident** ~, wrecking ~ = Unfallkran *m*, Bergungskran
~ **of cost(s),** cost(s) breakdown = Kostenaufgliederung *f*
~ **van,** recovery vehicle, crash truck = Abschleppfahrzeug *n*, Abschleppkran *m*
~ **voltage** = Durchschlagsspannung *f* [*Kabelvergußmasse f*]
breaker, breaking wave, surf = Sturzwelle *f*, brandende Welle
~ **(US);** bar (Brit.) [*roller of breaking waves*] = Brandungsgürtel *m*
~ = Unterbrecher *m*
~, stone breaker, coarse crusher, coarse breaker = Grobbrecher *m*, Schotterbrecher
breaking ball = Zertrümmerungskugel *f*
~ **ground** = Einschnittherstellung *f*
~ **joint,** see: break of joint
~ **machine,** crusher, breaker = Brecher *m*, Grobzerkleinerungsmaschine *f*
~ **of waves** = Brandung *f*
~ **plant,** stone-breaking ~, crushing ~, stone-crushing ~, rock crushing ~, rock breaking ~, crushed stone ~ = Brechanlage *f*, (Stein)Brecheranlage
~ **(or ultimate) strength** = Bruchfestigkeit *f*
~ **time test of Caroselli** = Brechbarkeitsprüfung *f* nach Caroselli [*Bitumenemulsion f*]
~ ~ ~ **Weber and Bechler** = Zerfallswert-Bestimmung *f* nach Weber und Bechler [*Bitumenemulsion f*]
~ ~ ~ **with chippings** = Brechbarkeitsprüfung *f* mit Splitt *m* [*Bitumenemulsion f*]

break-in powder, bon ami ~ = Einfahrpulver *n*
break of joint, staggered joint, breaking joint = versetzte Fuge *f*
break-out force, see: biting force
break-through = Durchbruch *m*
to break up, to pick = aufhacken, aufbrechen
*****breakwater** = Wellenbrecher *m*
breast drill, hand ~ = Handbohrer *m*, Brustleier *f*
~ water wheel, see: back-shot ~ ~
breather = Entlüfter *m*
~ tube = Entlüftungsrohr *n*
breathing apparatus, respiratory device = Atmungsgerät *n*, Atemschutzgerät
breccia [*is a conglomerate of sharply angular stones*] = Breccie *f* [*dieser Ausdruck sollte vermieden werden*], Brekzie *f*, „Naturbeton" *m*, Bretschie *f*
breeches chute = Verteilermundstücke *npl* [*Dosiersilo m*]
~ piece = Hosenrohr *n*
breeze [*is a term widely used to cover any type of furnace residues varying from disintegrated clinker to fine, poorly-sintered ashes containing a large proportion of combustible matter*] = Grus *m*
~, see: clinker
~, light wind = flaue Brise *f*
~ fixing brick = nagelbarer Ziegel *m*
brick, see: (building) ~
~ and tile hoisting platform = Steinpritsche *f*
~ burning = Ziegelbrennen *n*
~ carrier = Ziegeltransportwagen *m*
~ clay, see: brickearths
~ crusher, ~ breaker = Ziegelbrecher *m*, Backsteinbrecher
(~) cutter = (Ziegel)Abschneider *m*
(~) cutting wire = Abschneide(r)draht *m*, Ziegel ~
brickdust = Ziegelmehl *n*
brickearths, brickearth, brick clay = Ziegelgut *n*, Ziegelton *m*
brick facing, ~ veneer = Sichtmauerwerk *n*
~ floor(ing) = Ziegel(fuß)boden *m*
~ grab, ~ gripping device = Ziegel(stein)-greifer *m*

~ handling = Ziegeltransport *m* und -handhabung *f*
~ hardcore, see: (aggregate of) broken brick(s)
~ kiln = Ziegelofen *m*
bricklayer = Maurer *m*
bricklayer's hammer = Maurerhammer *m*
brick lined tunnel = ziegelgefütterter Tunnel *m*
~ lining = Ausmau(e)rung *f*
~ machinery = Ziegeleimaschinen *fpl*
~ making = Ziegelfabrikation *f*, Ziegelherstellung *f*
~ masonry, brickwork = Ziegelmauerwerk *n*
~ of clay chippings = Ziegelsplittmauerstein *m*, Tonsplittmauerstein
brick-on-edge (course), upright brick course = Ziegelrollschicht *f*
~ door sill, B. O. E. ~ ~ = Ziegelrollschicht-Türschwelle *f*
~ window sill, B. O. E. ~ ~ = Ziegelrollschicht-Fensterbank *f*
brick package = Ziegelpaket *n*
~ paving; [*deprecated: brick road*] = Ziegelpflaster *n*, Klinkerpflaster
~ press = Ziegelpresse *f*
~ road [*deprecated*], see: brick paving
~ rubble, see: (aggregate of) broken brick(s)
~ saw = Ziegelsäge *f*
~ stacker = Ziegelstapler *m*
~-throwing machine = Ziegelwurfmaschine *f*, Ziegelschleuder *f*; SEEGERS-Steinschleuder *f* [*Trademark*]
to brick up = aufmauern, zumauern
brick veneer, see: ~ facing
brickwork, see: brick masonry
~ manhole = gemauerter Reinigungsschacht *m*, Einsteig(e)schacht aus Mauerwerk *n*
brickworks = Ziegelei *f*, Ziegelfabrik *f*
*****bridge** = Brücke *f*
~ abutment = Brückenwiderlager *n*
~ approach = Brückenrampe *f*, Brückenzufahrt *f*
~ bent, ~ trestle = Brückenjoch *n*
bridge-building firm = Brückenbaufirma *f*
bridge (construction) engineer = Brücken(bau)ingenieur *m*
~ crane = Brückenkran *m*

(bridge) decking — broken-back arrangement of curves 59

(bridge) decking = (Brücken)Tafel *f*, Fahrbahntafel
~ dedication = Brückeneinweihung *f*
~ dismantling = Brückenabbau *m*
~ grating, grating for bridge deck = Brückenrost *m*
~-mixer, see: bridge-(type travel(l)ing concrete) mixer
bridge operating mechanism = Brückenbetriebseinrichtung *f*
bridge-parapet = Brückengeländer *n*
bridge pier = Brückenpfeiler *m*
~ pontoon = Brückenschiff *n*, Brückenboot *n*, Brückenkahn *m*
~ reamer = Nietlochreibahle *f*
~ seating girder = Schleppträger *m*
~ substructure = Brücken-Unterbau *m*
~ superstructure = Brückenüberbau *m*
~ tamper, road tamping machine (Brit.) = Stampffertiger *m*
~ toll = Brückengeld *n*, Brückenzoll *m*, Brückenabgabe *f*
~tramway, see: (**~**) transporter
(~) transporter (crane), **~ tramway** = Verladebrücke *f*
(~) ~ with end tipping railway (Brit.)/railroad (US) car platform = Kipperbrücke *f* mit Kippbühne *f*
(~) ~ ~ revolving crane = Verladebrücke *f* mit Drehkran *m*
(~) ~ ~ travel(l)ing crane = Verladebrücke *f* mit Laufkran *m*
~ truss = Brückenfachwerk *n*
bridge-type travel(l)ing coated macadam plant with drier, mixer and distributor hopper = brückenfahrbare Makadamanlage *f* mit Trockentrommel *f*, Mischer *m* und Verteilerkübel *m*, Fabrikat LINNHOFF, BERLIN-TEMPELHOF
bridge-(type travel(l)ing concrete) mixer, bridge-type travel(l)ing mixer plant, super-highway bridge mixer = Brückenmischer *m*, Autobahn-Betonmischer *m*, Autobahnbrückenmischer, RAB-Brückenmischer
bridge with wind ties = geschlossene Brücke *f*
bridle cable = Laufkatzen-Seil *n* [*Schleppschrapperanlage f mit 3-Seil-Anordnung f*]

~ chains = Kettengehänge *n* [*Seilförderanlage f*]
~ frame shifting cable = Seil, welches die Laufkatze bewegt [*Schleppschrapperanlage f mit 3-Seil-Anordnung f*]
~ joint = Klaue *f* mit Zapfen *m* im Nest *n* [*Holzverbindung f*]
~-path, bridle-road, bridle-way, drift-way, drove, droveway, packway = Saumpfad *m*
bridle towers = Umlenkstation *f* [*zwei feste Türme mpl*]
bright annealing = Blankglühen *n*
brine = Sole *f* [*kochsalzhaltiges Wasser n*]
~ evaporator = Soleverdampfer *m*
~ spring = Solequelle *f*
Brinell Hardness Number, B. H. N. = Brinell-Härte-Zahl *f*
~ hardness test = Brinell-Probe *f*
briquetting press = Brikettpresse *f*
British asphalt = Pech-Gießmasse *f*
~ Standard Section = Britisches Normalprofil *n*
brittle fracture = Bruchfestigkeit *f* im spröden Zustand *m*, Sprödbruch *m* [*z.B. bei Teer m*]
~ point = Brechpunkt *m*
~ ~ ~ = Erstarrungspunkt *m*
~ ~ ~ = Starrpunkt *m* [*Bitumen n*]
~ silver ore (Min.), see: stephanite
broaching = Ausdornen *n*
broach post, king **~ ~** = Hängesäule *f*
broad axe, see: block bill
broadcasting station = Funkhaus *n*, Funkgebäude *n*
broadcast sodding, mulch **~**, topsoil planting = kombinierte Mutterboden- und Rasensodenandeckung *f*
broad flange girder, H-girder, wide flange girder (Brit.); **~ ~ beam**, H-beam, wide flange beam = Breitflanschträger(balken) *m*, Breitflanschbalkenträger
~-leaved tree, see: deciduous **~**
broad-tool, bolster = Breiteisen *n*
brochantite (Min.) = Brochantit *m*
broken-back arrangement of curves = Anordnung von geraden Stücken zwischen gleichsinnig gekrümmten Straßenkurven *fpl*

broken bladed conveyor, see: paddle worm ~
~ **brick(s)**, see: (aggregate of) broken brick(s)
broken-down rim (of the crater) = eingefallener Kraterrand m
broken slag, crushed ~ = Brech(er)schlacke f
~ **stone**, ~ **rock** = Schlagschotter m, Steinschlag m
~ **stone bottoming** (Brit.); see: macadam foundation
~ ~ **foundation**, see: macadam ~
~ ~ **pavement** = Schotterdecke f
brome(grass) = Ackertrespe f
bromide = Bromsilber n
bronzite, (Mg, Fe$_2$) [Si$_2$O$_6$] (Min.) = Bronzit m
brookite, TiO$_2$ (Min.) = Brookit m
broom drag = Besenschleppe f
brooming, sweeping, brushing = Abkehren n, Abfegen n
BROSELEY roofing tile [*Trademark*] = geradlinig geschnittener, gewölbter Biberschwanzbetonstein 260/160 mm, 1,1 kg schwer
broth = Nährlösung f [*Abwasserwesen n*]
brown-coal low temperature coke = Braunkohlenschwelkoks m
~ **opencast mining** = Braunkohlentagebau m
~ **tar** = Braunkohlenteer m
brown coat = mittlere Putzlage f
~ **haematite** (Min.) = Brauneisen n
Brownian movement = Brown'sche Bewegung f
brown staining [*mortar joint*] = Braunfleckigkeit f [*Mörtelfuge f*]
brownstone = Braunquarzsandstein m
brucite, MgOH$_2$ (Min.) = Brucit m
brush aeration = Bürstenbelüftung f [*Belebtschlamm m*]
~ **clearing**, uprooting, grubbing up = Roden n, Rodung f
~ **cutter** = Buschschneider m, Buschpflüger m
~ **gear** = Bürstenapparat m
brushing, see: brooming
brush outfit for cleaning carrier side = rotierende Bürste f [*Bandförderer m*]
~ **painting** = Pinselanstrich m
~ **plaster** = Pinselputz m
~ **rake**, clearing ~ = (Unterholz)Roderechen m
brushwood = Strauchwerk n
~ **cooler (or cooling stack, or graduationworks)** = Reisiggradierwerk n, Reisigrieselwerk
(~) **fascine**, see: fascine
~ **layer** = Spreitlage f
~ **roll with gravel core** = Senkfaschine f
bubble = Blase f [*Libelle f*]
bubble-hole = Blähpore f
bubble sextant, spirit-level = Libellensextant m
~ **tower** = Fraktionierturm m
bubbling spring = Sprudelquelle f
bucker-up, holder-up, dolly = (Niet-)Gegenhalter m
bucket = Eimer m
~ = Kübel m
~ [*wheel ditcher*] = Schaufel f
~, operating ~ = Auslegerkübel m [*Straßenbetoniermaschine f*]
~, dipper, shovel dipper, shovel, dipper bucket, excavator bucket = Löffel m [*Bagger m*]
~ = Korb m, Verladegreifkorb [*Greifbagger m*]
~, loading ~ = (Lade)Schaufel f, Kübel m, Hubschaufel [*Schürflader m*]
~ **arch** = Schleppschaufelbügel m
~ **arm** = Löffelstiel m
bucket-carrying troll(e)y = Laufkatze f (oder Lastkatze) mit Greifkorb m
bucket closing cable socket = Festpunkt m des Greiferhubseils n
~ **conveyor** = Becherwerk n, Eimerkettenaufzug m
~ **crane**, grab, grabbing crane, grab excavator, grab (bucket) crane = Greifer(kran) m, Greifbagger m, Greifkran m, Greiferbagger, Baggergreifer
~ **elevator**, see: (~) (type) elevator
~ ~ **belt** = Elevatorgurtband m
~ ~ **boom** = Elevator-Ausleger m
~ ~ **chain**, ladder chain carrying the buckets = Becherkette f, Eimerkette
~ ~ **head** = Becherwerkskopf m

bucket (elevator) loader, portable ~, conveyor type bucket loader = (Eimerketten)Fahrlader *m*, Becher(werk)auflader *m*, Selbstauflader *m*, Aufnehmer *m*, (Auf-)Lader *m* für Schüttgut *n*, selbstaufnehmendes Förderband *n*, Becherwerkslader *m*, Becherbelademaschine *f*, Becherwerk Ladeschaufler *m*, Fahrladegerät *n*

~ ~ **rubber belt** = Becher-Gummiband *n*

~ ~ **with double roller type chains** = Doppellaschenkettenbecherwerk *n*

~ ~ ~ **fixed buckets** = Becherwerk *n* mit festen Bechern *mpl*

*****bucket-excavator mounted on tracks**, crawler (tractor)-mounted excavator, crawler shovel(-crane), track-laying type shovel, caterpillar shovel, crawler shovel (type) excavator, crawler revolving shovel, caterpillar shovel (type) excavator, caterpillar revolving shovel, track-laying type shovel excavator, track-laying type revolving shovel = Raupen(band)löffelbagger *m*, Gleiskettenlöffelbagger *m*

bucket flight, see: ~ ladder

~ ~, see: digging ladder

~ **hoist**, skip type (contractor'ε) (or builders') hoist = Kübel(bau)aufzug *m*, Kippkübelaufzug *m*

~ **holding cable socket** = Festpunkt *m* des Greiferseils *n*

~ **ladder** = Becherleiter *f*, Eimerleiter

~ ~, digging ~, ladder chain carrying the buckets, bucket flight = Eimerleiter *f*, Baggerleiter [*bei Naßbaggern und Grabenbaggern mit Eimern*]

~ ~ **dredge(r)**, ladder(-bucket) ~, multibucket ~, elevator ~, endless chain ~ = Eimer(ketten)naßbagger *m*, Eimerketten-Schwimmbagger

~ ~ **excavator**, dredger ~, chain bucket ~, continuous land bucket dredger, multi-bucket excavator = Eimerketten-Trockenbagger *m*, Eimertrockenbagger

~ ~ ~ **working below ground level** = Eimerketten-Tiefbagger *m*

~ **latrine** = Eimerlatrine *f*

~ **line**, line of buckets = Becherstrang *m*, Eimerstrang, Becherreihe *f*, Eimerreihe

~ **loader**, see: ~ (elevator) ~

~ ~, see: loading shovel

~ **scale**, hopper ~ = Behälterwaage *f*, Gefäßwaage

~ **sheave** = Löffelflasche *f*

~ ~ **guard** = Löffelseilrollenschutz *m*

~**tooth**, grab(bing) ~ ~ = Greiferzahn *m*

*****bucket trencher**, trenching machine of the bucket elevator type, trenchliner, endless-bucket trencher = Grabenbagger *m* mit Eimern *mpl*

(~) (type) elevator, scoop flight-conveyor [a *device practically the same as a bucket conveyor, except that it is used in a vertical or nearly vertical direction*] = Eimerketten-Aufzug *m*, Becherwerk *n*, Elevator *m*, Becherelevator, Aufnahmebecherwerk

~ **wander** = ungenauer Lauf *m* der Schleppschaufel *f*

~ **wheel**, scoop ~ = Schöpfrad *n*

~ ~ = Schaufelrad *n* [*Bagger m*]

~ ~ **blower** = Schaufelradgebläse *n*

~ **wheel(-type) excavator**, rotary bucket ~ = Schaufelradbagger *m*

~ **wheel type loader** = (Be)Lademaschine *f* mit Becherrad *n* (oder Eimerrad)

to buckle, to yield to axial compression = sich verziehen, sich verwerfen, knicken

buckled plate = geknickte Platte *f*, Buckelblech *n*

~ ~ **sheet piling** = Buckelblechspundwand *f*

buckling = Knickung *f*, Knicken *n*

~ [*shell*] = (Aus)Beulung *f*

~ **coefficient** = Knickbeiwert *m*, Knickzahl *f*

~ **load**, collapse ~ = Knicklast *f*

~ **strength (or resistance)**, resistance to lateral bending, buckling stability = Knickfestigkeit *f*

~ **stress** = Knickspannung *f*

~ **test** = Knickversuch *m*

*****buck scarper** (Brit.); see: trailing scoop grader (US)

buffer = Puffer *m*

BUG 30 [*Trademark*] [*crawler universal excavator*] = Gleisketten-Universalbagger *m*, Fabrikat BÜNGER A. G., DÜSSELDORF, DEUTSCHLAND

buggy — building vibration

buggy = Kipp(er)karre(n) *f*, (*m*)
builders' conveyor = Hochbau-Fahrband-(förderer) *n*, (*m*)
~ **hand cart** = Bau(hand)karre(n) *f*, (*m*)
~ **hoist, contractors'** ~ = (Bau)Aufzug *m*
~ **level** = Bauinvellier(instrument) *m*, (*n*)
~ **road, site** ~ = Baustellenstraße *f*
~ **rotating crane** = Baudrehkran *m*
~ **winch**, see: contractors' ~
***building and civil engineering plant**, see: construction machinery
~ **and loan association,** ~ **society** = Bausparkasse *f*
~ **block machine**, see: (concrete) block(-making) ~
~ **board** = Bauplatte *f*
(~) **brick, solid** ~ = Backstein *m*, Ziegel(stein) *m*, Vollziegel *m*, Bauziegel *m* [*früher: Mauerziegel m*]
~ **clay** = Ziegelton *m*, baukeramischer Ton
Building Code Provisions = Baupolizeibestimmungen *fpl*
~ ~ **Requirements for Reinforced Concrete** = Stahlbetonbestimmungen *fpl*
building concrete = Hochbaubeton *m*
~ **connection**, see: house ~
~ **construction** = Hochbau *m*
~ **contractor** = Bauunternehmer *m*
~ **cost index, construction** ~ ~ = Baukostenindex *m*
~ **crane** = (Hoch)Baukran *m*
~ **erection contract** = Hochbauauftrag *m*
~ **firm, construction firm, construction company** = Baufirma *f*
~ **foundation** = Gebäudefundament *n*
~ **frame** = Gebäudeskelett *n*
~ **frontage** = Hausfront *f*
~ **(or construction, or contracting, or civil-engineering) industry** = Bauindustrie *f*, Bauwirtschaft *f*
Building Information Centre = Bautechnische Auskunftsstelle *f*
building lime, construction ~ = Baukalk *m*
~ **line** = Baufluchtlinie *f* [*Straße f*]
~ **(or construction) material(s) dealer (or merchant)** = Baustoffhändler *m*
~ (~ ~) ~ **machine** = Baustoffmaschine *f*

~ (~ ~) ~ **producer** = Baustoff-Fabrikant *m*
~ (~ ~) ~ **testing machine** = Baustoffprüfmaschine *f*
~ **mortar** = Baumörtel *m*
Building Officials Conference of America = Verband der Baubeamten der USA
building panel = Bautafel *f*
~ **paper** = Baupapier *n*
~ **pit, excavation** = Baugrube *f*
~ ~ **hoist, foundation** ~ = Baugrubenaufzug *m*
~ **practice** = Baupraxis *f*
~ **preservation** = Bautenschutz *m*
~ **preservative** = Bautenschutzmittel *n*
Building Prices Order = Baupreisverordnung *f*
building programme = Bauprogramm *n*
~ **regulations** = Baubestimmungen *fpl*, Bauvorschriften *fpl*
~ **remain** = Mauerrest *m*
Building Research Institute = Institut *n* für Bauforschung *f*
building sand = Bausand *m*
~ **site, site (of work), job-site, project site, construction** ~ = Baustelle *f*
~ ~ **for multi-stor(e)y buildings** = Baustelle *f* des Hochbaues *m*
~ **slip(way)** = Helling *f*, Helge *f*
~ **society,** ~ **and loan association** = Bausparkasse *f*
(~) **steel frame(work) (or skeleton), steel framing** = Stahlskelett *n*
~ **stone** = Baustein *m*
~ ~ **weathering** = Bausteinverwitterung *f*
~ **technician** = Bautechniker *m*, Baupraktiker *m*
~ **trade joinery** = Bautischlerei *f*, Bauschreinerei *f*
~ **trade(s), construction** ~**, trowel** ~ = Bauhandwerk *n*, Baugewerbe *n*
~ **trades counsel union** = Baugewerkschaft *f*
Building Trades Employers Association = Arbeitgeberverband *m* des Baugewerbes *n*
building trade worker = Bauhandwerker *m*
~ **unit, structural part** = Bauteil *m*
~ **vibration** = Gebäudeschwingung *f*

building wall — (bull)dozer shovel

building wall = Hochbauwand *f*
~ **work**, construction ~ = Bauarbeiten *fpl*
built-in, inbuilt = eingebaut
~ **bottom (type) gritter** = Einbaustreuer *m*
~ **diesel engine** = Einbau-Dieselmotor *m*
built-up area = geschlossene Ortslage *f*, Ortschaft *f*
~ **column** (US); ~ **stanchion** (Brit.) = mehrteilige Stütze *f*
~ **compression member** = mehrteiliger Druckstab *m*
~ **girder** = zusammengesetzter Träger *m*
~ **member** = mehrteiliger Stab *m*
~ **roof** = mehrlagige Dacheindeckung *f*
~ **section** = mehrteiliger Querschnitt *m*
bulb angle (iron), bulb-iron = Winkelwulststahl *m*
bulb of pressure, pressure bulb = Druckzwiebel *f*
~ **plate**, flat bulb iron = Flachwulststahl *m*
~ **pressure** = Spannungsanhäufung *f*, Druckanhäufung *f* [*Baugrund m*]
~ **rail iron**, bulb-tee = Flanschwulsteisen *n*
bulk asphaltic bitumen installation (or reception facility) (Brit.), see: bulk bitumen reception facility
*(**bulk) aviation fuel installation**, multitank ~ ~ ~ = Flugzeugtreibstofftankanlage *f*, Flugkraftstofftankanlage
~ **batching**, see: volume ~
~ **bitumen distributor** (Brit.), see: pressure tank lorry
~ ~ **reception facility**, bulk bitumen installation, bulk asphaltic bitumen installation (or reception facility) (Brit.)
~ **asphalt** ~ ~ (US) = Bitumen-Umschlaganlage *f*
~ **cement** = loser (oder unverpackter, oder ungesackter) Zement *m*, Silozement, Behälterzement
~ ~ **plant**, cement silo = Zementsilo *m*, Bindemittelsilo *m*
(~) ~ **transporter**, cement tanker, cement haulage unit, cement hauler = Zementtanker *m*, Zementtransportfahrzeug *n*

(~) ~ **truck** (US); (~) ~ **lorry** (Brit.) = Zement-Lastkraftwagen *m*
~ ~ **truck-and-trailer unit** = Zementtanker-Lastzug *m*
~ **concrete**, mass ~, concrete-in-mass = Massenbeton *m*
(~) **density**, see: volume weight
~ ~, overall ~ [*dry density* + *water*] = Trockengewicht *n* + Wasser *n* [*Boden m*]
~ **fuel installation** = Treibstofftankanlage *f*
~ **good**, see: ~ material
~ **gritter body** = Streugutpritsche *f* [*LKW m*]
bulkhead = Schott *n*, Schotte *f*
~ = Abschluß-Spundwand *f*
~, cofferdam = Fang(e)damm *m*
~ **gate** = Schott(e) *n*, (*f*) zur Ermöglichung *f* der Reparatur *f* eines Segmentwehres *n*
bulking, bulkage = Schwellung *f*, Schwellen *n*, Quellung *f*, Quellen *n*
~, bulkage, moisture expansion = Schwellung *f* durch Feuchtigkeit *f*
bulk lime spreader = Kalkstreuer *m*
~ **material**, ~ **good** = Massengut *n*, Schüttgut *n*
~ ~ **handling** = Schüttgutbewegung *f*
~ ~ **unloader** = Schüttgutentladevorrichtung *f*
~ **specific gravity**, see: volume weight
~ **spreader**, see: powder-spreader
~ **volume**, total ~ = Gesamtvolumen *n*
bull clam shovel = Klapp-Schaufel *f*
bulldozer (blade) = Querschild *n*, festes Schild, Gerad-Schild
*(**bull)dozer(-equipped tractor)**, tractordozer = Bulldozer *m*, Frontträumer *m*, Schürfschlepper *m*, Planierschlepper
(**bull)dozer fitted to track-laying (type) tractor**, caterpillar bulldozer, crawler tractor with bulldozer, bulldozer-equipped track-type tractor = Bulldozer *m* auf Gleisketten *fpl*, Planier-Gleiskettengerät *n*
(**bull)dozer shovel**, dozer-loader = Bulldozer(Lade)schaufel *f*, Bulldozer-Schaufellader *m*

bulldozer stabilizer = Querschild-Abstützung *f*

~ **with angling blade**, see: roadbuilder

(bull)dozing, (bull)dozer digging = Erdschürftransport *m*

bullfloat finishing machine, longitudinal ~ ~ , ~ floating ~ = Längsbohlenfertiger *m*

bull-head(ed) rail, double-headed ~ = Doppelkopfschiene *f*, Stuhlschiene

bull-nose, bull's nose, arris = abgerundete Fugenkante *f*

~ **trowel**, arris trowel, arrissing tool = Kantenbrecher *m*

bullock cart, oxcart = Ochsenkarre(n) *f*, (*m*)

bull wheel, (crawler) driving sprocket, drive sprocket, propel sprocket = Kettenantriebsrad *n*, Antriebskettenrad, Antriebsturas *m*

bulwark = Wellenbrecher *m* [*Angriff m der Wellen fpl auf nur einer Seite f*]

bump = hohe Stelle *f* [*in einer Fläche f*]

bumper, fender = Fender *m*

~ = Stoßstange *f* [*Auto n*]

bumper, fender = 1. Fender *m*; 2. Stoßstange *f* [*Auto n*]

~ **roller** = LKW-Druckrolle *f* [*Schwarzbelageinbaumaschine f*]

bundled reinforcement = Bündelbewehrung *f*, Bündelarmierung *f*

bundle of brushwood, faggot = Strauchwerkbündel *n*

~ ~ **prestressing tendons** = Vorspannbündel *n*

BUNGARTZ two-wheel hand-guided dozer = Einachsräumer *m*, Fabrikat BUNGARTZ & CO., MÜNCHEN 8, DEUTSCHLAND

bungum = Londoner Name für jungen alluvialen Schluff. Im Allgemeinen auf weichen Ton *m* mit oder ohne Schluffanteil *m* angewendet.

bunker, coal ~ = (Kohlen)Bunker *m*

~, **materials** ~ = (Material)Bunker *m*, Taschensilo *m*

~ **pocket** [*coal bunker*] = Bunkertasche *f*

Bunsen (gas) burner = Bunsenbrenner *m*, Blaubrenner *m*

bunter sandstone; mottled ~, variegated ~ (Brit.) = Buntsandstein *m*

buoy = Boje *f*

buoyancy = Auftrieb *m*

~ **on the structure** = Gesamtgewicht *n* der schwimmenden Baulichkeiten *f*

~ **tank** = Luftboje *f*

buoyant box, floating ~, floating caisson = Schwimmkasten *m*

buret(t)e = Bürette *f*

Burgundy pitsch [*sometimes marketed under the name „Vosges pitch". These terms are misnomers, since the material is not a true „pitch", but is readily an oleo-resin*] = Burgunderpech *n*

burial vault = Gruftgewölbe *n*

buried anchorage = unterirdische Verankerung *f*

~ **pipework** = erdverlegte Rohrleitung *f*

burlap = Sackleinen *n* aus Jute *f* oder Hanf *m*

"burned" lime = verbrannter Kalk *m*

burner = Brenner *m*

~ **blower** = Brennergebläse *n*

~ **hose** = Brennerschlauch *m*

burning kiln, calcining ~ = Brennofen *m*

~ **of bricks**, see: firing ~ ~

~ ~ **clinker** = Klinkerbrand *m*

~ **oil** = Brennöl *n*

~ **range**, firing ~ = Brennbereich *m*

~ **zone**, calcining ~ = Brennzone *f* [*Kalkofen m*]

burnt clay = gebrannter Ton *m*, Terrakotte *f* [*in Österreich. Terrakotta*]

~ ~ **aggregate**, see: crushed clay brick

(~) **magnesia**, see: bitter-earth

to burr, to trimm = abgraten

burr = Bohrgrat *m*

burrowing animal = Wühltier *n*

bursting charge, (explosive) ~ = Sprengladung *f*

bus halt, ~ **stop** = (Auto)Bushaltestelle *f*, Omnibushaltestelle

~ **overhaul works** = Omnibus-Werkstatt *f*, (Auto)Bus-Werkstatt

~ **ride** = Omnibusreise *f*, Omnibusfahrt *f*, (Auto)Busreise, (Auto)Busfahrt

bush allowance = Auslösung *f* für Arbeitsaufenthalt im Busch [*z. B. in Afrika*]

~ **chain** = Transmissionskette *f*

~ **chisel** = Scharriereisen *n*

~ **clearing**, de-bushing = Buschräumung *f*

busb hammer = Scharrierhammer *m*
~ harrow = Strauchegge *f*, Buschegge *f*
bushing = Buchse *f*
~ for indoor and outdoor use = Durchführung *f* für Innenraum und Freiluft
business and management = Betriebswissenschaft *f*
~ district, **~ area** = Geschäftsviertel *n*
~ thoroughfare = Geschäftsstraße *f*
bus operation = (Omni)Busbetrieb *m*
BÜSSING lorry (Brit.); **~ truck** (US) = Lastkraft(wagen) *m*, Fabrikat BÜSSING NUTZKRAFTWAGEN GmbH., BRAUNSCHWEIG, DEUTSCHLAND
bus stop, see: **~ halt**
~ terminal (or **station**, or **terminus**) = (Auto)Busbahnhof *m*, Omnibusbahnhof *m*
buton asphalt = Boetonasphalt *m*
to butter = weicher machen [*Beton m*]
(butter)fly (screw) nut, **wing (~) ~** = Flügel(schrauben)mutter *f*
butterfly valve = Drosselklappe *f*
buttery concrete, see: **high-slump ~**
butt joint = stumpfer Stoß *m*
~ ~ graft with ferrule and dowel = stumpfe Pfropfung *f* mit Ring *m* und Dorn *m*
~ ~ ~ fishplates = stumpfe Pfropfung *f* mit Schienen *fpl*
button-head(ed) screw, **half round ~ ~** = Rundkopfschraube *f*
buttress = Strebepfeiler *m*
~ spacing (US); **spacing of counterforts** = Abstand *m* der Strebepfeilerachsen *fpl* [*Talsperre f*]
~ (type) dam, **buttressed ~**, **counterfort (type) dam** = Pfeiler(stau)mauer *f*, Pfeilersperre *f*, aufgelöste Staumauer *f*
butt rivet(ed) joint = Laschennietung *f*
~-strap (Brit.); **coverplate** (US) = Decklasche *f*
butyl alcohol = Butylalkohol *m*, Butanol *n*
butylene, C_4H_8 = Butylen *n*
buzzer system = Summeranlage *f*
bye-channel, see: **bye-wash**

by-pass; **shoofly** (US) = Umleitung *f*
by-passable traffic = Umgehungsverkehr *m*
by-pass road, **~ highway**, **~ street**, **alternate route** [*deprecated: loop road, avoiding ~, ring ~, detour*] = Umgehungsstraße *f*, Umfahrungsstraße *f*
~ tunnel, **diversion ~** = Umleitstollen *m*, Umleitungsstollen [*Talsperre f*]
by-product = Nebenprodukt *n*
bytownite (Min.) = Bytownit *m*
bye-wash, **diversion cut**, **bye-channel**, **spillway**; **diversion flume** (US) = Umleit(ungs)kanal *m*

C

cab(in) = Kabine *f*
cabinet scraper = Ziehklinge *f*
~ screw driver = Schraubenzieher *m* mit Holzgriff *m*
cable, **(steel) wire rope**, **steel cable** = (Stahl)Drahtseil *n*, Drahtkabel *n*, Stahlseil, Stahl(draht)kabel *n*
~ accessories = Kabelzubehör *m*, *n*
~ and reel = Drahtseil *n* mit Rolle *f*
~ barrier = Kabelschranke *f*
~ box = Kabelkasten *m*
~ bridge = Kabelbrücke *f*
~ channel (or **trough**) = Kabelkanal *m*
~ clamp = Kabelschelle *f*
~ control = Seilzug(betätigung) *m*, (*f*)
cable-controlled tractor and bulldozer = seilbetätigter Bulldozer *m*
cable-crane, see: **blondin** (Brit.)
cable detector, **cable tracing set** = Kabelsuchgerät *n*
~ draw pit = Kabelschacht *m*
~ drill, see: **churn ~**
~ drilling bit = Schlagbohrmeißel *m*
~ duct (or **conduit**, or **subway**), **multiple way ~ ~**, **multitubular slab for cable**; **conduit tile** (US) = Kabelformstück *n*, Kabelformstein *m*
~ excavator, **cable-operated ~**, **cable-powered ~**, **cable-controlled** = seilbetätigter Bagger *m*
~ ~ ~ = Oberbegriff *m* für Schrapper *m*, Kabelschrapper *m* und Kabelbagger *m*

cable excavator with bottom-dump bucket and tightened track cable = Straffseil Kabelbagger m, TEKA-Schrapper m, Fabrikat KURT VON HAGEN, BLUMROTH über SOEST, DEUTSCHLAND

~ ~ ~ dragline-type bucket and running-rail type carrier = Pendelschrapper m

~ fence = Drahtseilzaun m

*****cable haulage machine** = Seilförderanlage f

cable-hauled bucket, scraper = Seilschrapperkasten m

cable layer = Kabelverlegemaschine f

~ laying hoist, ~ ~ winch = Kabelverlegewinde f

~ lubricant = Kabelschmiermittel n

~ marker = Kabelmerkstein m

~-operated, cable-powered, cable-controlled = seilbetätigt

~-operated excavator, cable(-powered) ~ = seilbetätigter Bagger m

cable reel = Kabeltrommel f

~ (or aerial) ropeway (or tramway); cable (or aerial) railroad (US) = Drahtseilschwebebahn f

~ sag [*bridge*] = Seildurchhang m

~ scraper = Kabelschrapper m, Seilschrapper m

~ sling = Drahtseilschlinge f

~ spinning = Drahtseilkabelherstellung f

~ stay [*suspension bridge*] = Kabelstrebe f

~ tile = Kabelschutzstein m

~-tool (method of) drilling = Seilbohrverfahren n

cable tramway, see: ~ (or aerial) ropeway

~ trench = Kabelgraben m

~ tunnel = Kabelstollen m

cableway; see: blondin (Brit.)

cable winch, see: (rope) ~

cadastral office = Katasteramt n

~ survey = Katastervermessung f

cage, drawing ~, hoisting ~, elevator ~ = Förderkorb m [*Bergwerk n*]

~ counterweight well = Schacht m für Förderkorb-Gegengewicht n

cage, tower, elevation tower = Schachtgerüst n, Turmgerüst n [*Bauaufzug m*]

~ hoist, (elevator) tower ~ = Schachtgerüstaufzug m, Turmgerüstaufzug, Fahrstuhlaufzug

~ type concrete spouting plant, elevator tower, concrete chuting (or placing) tower = (Beton)Gießturm m

cairngorm, smoky quartz (Min.) = Rauchquarz m

caisson = Senkkasten m, Caisson m

~ disease, compressed-air sickness, compressed air illness, bends = Drucklufterkrankung f, Preßluftkrankheit f, Caissonkrankheit f, Senkkastenkrankheit f

~ foundation = Senkkastengründung f, Caissongründung f

~ ~ (US) [*a misnomer*], pier foundation = Gründung f mit im Absenkverfahren n nach Art der bekannten Brunnengründungen fpl hergestellten Kegelfuß-Ortbetonpfählen mpl ohne permanentem Mantel m

---

caisson pile, concrete pier, belled-out pier, bell bottom caisson, belled-out caisson	Kegelfußpfahl m im Absenkverfahren n nach Art der bekannten Brunnengründungen fpl hergestellt, Fabrikat RAYMOND CONCRETE PILE CO., NEW YORK 6, USA
tripod	Dreibaum m
hoisting apparatus	Hebezeug n
open pier excavation	Absenkverfahren n nach Art der Brunnengründung f
"Chicago method" [*exavation is lined with wooden lagging and with this*	Absenkverfahren nach Art der Brunnengründung mit Holzmantel m,

caisson pile — calcium fluoride

method the pier is usually of constant diameter from top to bottom]

open-pier exavation with precast concrete cylinders, precast concrete-cylinder method, drop-shaft method

wobei der Pfahl im allgemeinen einen konstanten Durchmesser m von unten bis oben aufweist
Absenkverfahren n nach Art der Brunnengründung f mit Brunnenringen mpl

caisson-sinking, spotting = Absenkung-(svorgang) f, (m) [*Senkkasten m*]
caking capacity = Backfähigkeit f
calc-alkali basalt = Alkalikalkbasalt m
~ **granite** = Kalk-Alkaligranit m
~ **(ne) rock** = Alkali-Kalkgestein n
calcareous, limey = kalkhaltig
~ **alabaster** = Kalkalabaster m
~ **algae** = Kalkalgen fpl
~ **cement(ing material)** (Geol.) = Bindemittel n aus Kalk m
~ **clay** = kalkhaltiger Ton m
~ **earth** = Kalkerde f
~ **facies**, see: limestone ~
~ **fel(d)spar** = kalkhaltiger Feldspat m
~ **gravel** = Kalkkies m
~ **iron-stone**, ferruginous limestone = Kalkeisenstein m
~ **marl**, see: lime ~
~ **nodule**, nodular limestone = Knollenkalk m
~ **ore** = kalkiges Erz n
~ **sand**, lime ~ = Kalksand m
~ **sandstone** = Kalksandstein n
~ **shale** = Kalkschieferton m
~ **silex** (Min.) = Kalkkiesel m
~ **sinter**, calc-sinter = Kalksinter m
~ **slate**, limestone ~ = Kalktonschiefer m
~ **tufa**, see: tufaceous limestone
calcariferous petrosilex, lime silicate rock = Kalkhornfels m
calcic hydrate, see: hydrated lime (powder)
~ **marble**, lime ~ = Kalkmarmor m
~ **oligoclase** = Kalkoligoklas m
calcification (US) = Kalkanhäufung f im Boden m
calcigenous = kalkbildend
calcilutyte, lime mud rock = Kalktonstein m
calcination, calcining = Kalzinieren n
calcinator = Kalzinator m
calcined calcium carbonate, see: quicklime

~ **gypsum**, gypsum plaster for building purposes = gebrannter Gips m, Baugips
~ **ore** = Rösterz n
~ **pyrites** = Kiesabbrand m
~ **soda**, Na_2CO_3 = gebrannte Soda f, kalzinierte ~, Natriumkarbonat n
calcining, see: calcination
~ **drum** = Brenntrommel f
~ **kettle**, gypsum ~ ~ = Gipskocher m, Gipskessel m
~ **kiln**, burning ~ = Brennofen m
~ **pan**, gypsum ~ = Gipspfanne f
~ **to incipient fusion** = Brennen n (oder Kalzinieren n) bis mindestens zur Sinterung f [Zement m]
~ **zone**, burning ~ = Brennzone f, Kalzinierzone
CALCIT = internationaler Name für „Kalkspat" m
calcite, calcspar (Min.) = Kalkspat m, Kalzit m
calcitic limestone = Kalkspat-Kalkstein m
~ **marble**, limestone ~, crystalline limestone = Kalkmarmor m
calcium = Kalzium n
~ **aluminate cement**, aluminous ~, (high-)alumina ~ = Tonerdezement m, Schmelzzement, Tonerdeschmelzzement, Aluminous-~
~ **bicarbonate** = doppeltkohlensaurer Kalk m
~ **borate** = Boraxkalk m
~ **carbide**, see: carbide of calcium
~ **carbonate**, whiting, carbonate of lime = Kalziumkarbonat n
~ ~, see: limestone
~ **chloride** = Kalziumchlorid n, Chlorkalzium n
~ **cyanamide**, nitrogen manure = Kalkstickstoff(dünger) m
~ **fluoride**, CaF_2 = Kalziumfluorid n, Fluorkalzium n

calcium-iron garnet (Min.) = Kalkeisengranat m
calcium oleate = Kalzium-Ölseife f
~ oxide = Kalziumoxyd n
~ rosinate = Kalzium-Harzseife f
~ salt = Kalksalz m
~ silicate, lime ~ = Kalziumsilikat n
~ sulfide = Schwefelkalzium n
~ sulfate solution = Gipslösung f
calc-sinter, see: calcareous sinter
calcspar (Min.), see: calcite
(calc) tufa, see: tufaceous limestone
calculated value = Rechenwert m
calculating machine = Rechenmaschine f
calculation of areas = Flächenberechnung f
~ ~ banking (effect) = Stauberechnung f
~ ~ the buckling strength = Knickberechnung f
calculator, (cost) estimator, quantity surveyor, estimating engineer = Kalkulator m
caldera of subsidence = Explosionscaldera m [*Vulkan m*]
calfdozer, see: baby bulldozer
to calibrate = eichen
calibrated accuracy = Eichgenauigkeit f
~ sand method = Sandersatzmethode f [*Nachprüfung f der Verdichtung f*]
calibration = Eichung f
caliche [*a term meaning decomposed limestone containing silt and clay*] = Konglomerat n aus Quarzsand, Kalkstaub und Ton (max. 10%) mit oder ohne Kiesanteilen mpl
~ = erdiges Rohsalz n, Caliche f
California Bearing Ratio, CBR = kalifornisches Tragfähigkeitsverhältnis n, kalifornischer Index m
caliper ga(u)ge = Gabellehre f, Rachenlehre
~ square = Schieblehre f, Schublehre f
calking (US); see: caulking (Brit.)
~, see: cogging
callaite, turquoise (Min.) = Kallait m, Türkis m
calling card, personal **~** = Visitenkarte f

calm = Windstille f
~ belt, region of calm = Kalmengürtel m
calorific value = Heizwert m
calorimetric test = Heizwertversuch m
calp (Brit.) = dunkler, grauer Kalkstein m
calving = Kalben n [*Gletscher m*]
Calyx core drill = Calyx-Bohrer m, Fabrikat INGERSOLL-RAND CO., NEW YORK 4, USA
cam = Daumen m, Knagge f, Nocken m
camber, barrel ~ [*deprecated: transverse slope, crossfall*] = Wölbung f, kreisförmige Krone f [*Straße f*]
~ board, template, templet = Formlineal n, Profillehre f
cam-lifted = durch Nocken angehoben
cam-operated (tamping) (concrete) block machine = Nockenwellen-(Betonstein-)Stampfmaschine f
camshaft = Nockenwelle f, Daumenwelle
~ controller = Nockensteuerschalter m
can = Kanister m
~ buoy = Vertäuboje f
Canada balsam = Kanadabalsam m
Canadian asbestos, chrisotyle, $H_4Mg_3Si_2O_9$ (Min.) = Chrysotilasbest m, Kanadaasbest m
~ blue grass = Platthalm m, Plattrispengras n
~ spruce = kanadische Fichte f
canal bank, see: ~ embankment
~ ~ = Kanalufer n
~ bridge, ~ aqueduct = Kanalbrücke f
~ builder = Kanalbauer m
***canal building machinery**, canal trimming and lining equipment = Kanalbaumaschinen fpl
~ concrete paver; traveling template form for concrete (US) = Kanal-Betoniermaschine f, Einbaugerät n für Gerinne-Auskleidungen fpl in Zementbeton m
~ construction = Kanalbau m
~ cross-section = Kanalquerschnitt m
~ embankment, ~ bank = Kanaldamm m
~ for rafting wood = Floßkanal m
~ headworks = Kanal-Einlaßbauwerk n

canalisation — cap form

canalisation = Karalisierung f, Staureg(e)-lung f [*Wasserstraße f*]
canal joint cutter = Kanal-Fugenschleifgerät n [*Kanalbaumaschine f*]
~ **lining** = Gerinne-Auskleidung f, Kanal-Auskleidung f
buried (membrane) asphalt (US)/asphaltic bitumen (Brit.) canal lining (or membrane) = überdeckte Bitumen-Dichtungshäute fpl für die Auskleidung von Gerinnen npl
~ **(navigation) lock** = Kanalschleuse f
~ **paver**, slip form canal lining machine; canal paving rig (US) = Einbaugerät n für Gerinne-Auskleidungen fpl, Kanalauskleidungsmaschine f
~ ~ **for bituminous mixtures**; traveling template form ~ ~ ~ (US) = Einbaugerät n für Gerinneauskleidungen fpl in bituminösem Mischgut n
~ **port** = Kanalhafen m
~ **pumping station** = Kanalpumpwerk n
~ **section** = Kanalprofil n
~ **slope protection** = Kanalufersicherung f, Kanalböschungsschutz m
~ **trimmer** = Kanalplaniermaschine f
***canal trimming and lining equipment**, see: canal building machinery
~ **tunnel** = Schiffstunnel m
~ **widening** = Kanalverbreiterung f
canary grass = Glanzgras n
candelabra = Kandelaber m
candle tar = Kerzenteer m
cannel coal, lantern ~ = Kennelkohle f
cannibalizing = Ausschlachten n [*Maschine f*]
canoe(-shaped) valley, cigar-shaped ~ = Kahntal n, Hufeisental
cant, superelevation; [*deprecated: banking*] = Überhöhung f, einseitige Querneigung f [*Straßenkurve f*]
to cantilever, to corbel outwards = vorkragen, auskragen
cantilever = Kragplatte f
~, see: cantilevered beam
~ **(arm)** = Kragarm m
~ **bar screen**, see: ~ screen of bars
~ **bridge** = Auslegerbrücke f, Gerberbrücke
cantilevered = frei vorgebaut

~ **beam**, cantilever (beam), semi-beam, corbel beam, projecting beam; semigirder (Brit.) = Kragträger m, Kragbalken m, Kragbalkenträger m, Freiträger
cantilever(ed) column = Stütze f mit einseitigem Kragarm m, Halbrahmen m
~ **footway** = auskragender Fußweg m, vorkragender ~, ausladender ~
~ **roof** = Kragdach n
~ ~ **truss** = Ausleger-Dachbinder m
cantilever foot (or pedestrian) bridge = Ausleger-Fußgängerbrücke f
~ **frame** = freitragender Rahmen m
~ **grizzly**, see: ~ screen of bars
~ **jib** (Brit.); ~ **boom** (US) = waag(e)rechter Ausleger m
~ **method (of construction)**, construction without falsework = Freivorbauweise f, freier Vorbau m, Freivorbau
~ **screen of bars**, ~ bar screen, ~ grizzly = Krag-Stangen(transport)rost m, Krag-Stangenaufgeber m
(~) tower transporter = Auslegerlaufkran m
~ **type pile driver** = Vorbauramme f
canvas = Segeltuch n
~ **belt** = Textilgurt m
~ **duct** = Segeltuchschlauch m
~ **fabric airslide** = (Gebläse)Luft-Förderrinne f mit Segeltuch n
cap = Kopfplatte f [*Säule f*]
~ = Verschlußkappe f
~, driving cap, (driving) helmet, cushion block = Rammhaube f
~ = Aufsteckhülse f [*Raumfugendübel m*]
capacitor motor = Kondensatormotor m
capacity = Leistungsfähigkeit f
~ = Inhalt m, Fassungsvermögen n
~ **level** (US); see: level of storage water (Brit.)
~ **of resistance** = Widerstandsvermögen n, Widerstandsfähigkeit f
cap crimper = Sprengkapselzange f, Würgezange, Anwürgzange
Cape asbestos, see: blue ~ (Min.)
cape (keyseating) chisel = Kreuzmeißel m
cap form = Kopfplatten-Form f [*zur Herstellung f von Kopfplatten fpl*]

capillarimeter, capillary apparatus = Kapillarimeter *n*
capillarity, capillary attraction = Kapillarität *f*, Rohrsaugkraft *f*
capillary, see: ~ tube
~ **apparatus**, capillarimeter = Kapillarimeter *n*
~ **attraction**, see: capillarity
~ **bore** = Kapillarröhrchenhohlraum *m*
~ **constant** = Kapillaritätszahl *f*
~ **depression** = kapillare Absenkung *f*
~ **desaturation** = kapillare Sättigung *f*
~ **elevation** = kapillare Steighöhe *f*
~ **force** = Kapillarkraft *f*
~ **fringe** = Kapillarsaum *m*, Saugsaum, Kapillarzone *f*
~ **moisture**, see: ~ water
~ **potential** = Kapillarpotential *n*
~ **pressure** = Kapillardruck *m*
~ **pyrite** (Min.), see: millerite
~ **rise** = kapillarer Aufstieg *m*
~ **tension** = Kapillarspannung *f*
~ **(tube)** = Kapillarrohr *n*, Haarrohr *n*, Kapillare *f*, Kapillarröhrchen *n*, Kapillarstrang *m*
~ **visco(si)meter** = Kapillar-Viskosimeter *n*
~ **wall** = Kapillarröhrchenwandung *f*
~ **water (or moisture)**, water of capillarity = Kapillarwasser *n*, Haarröhrchenwasser, Porensaugwasser
capital costs, ~ expenditure, ~ outlay = Anlagekosten *f*, Kostenaufwand *m*
~ **depreciation** = Amortisierung *f*, Amortisation *f*
~ **equipment**, see: heavy plant
~ **investment** = Investierung *f*, Kapitalanlage *f*
cap(ped) quartz (Min.) = Kappenquarz *m*
capping beam, cross ~, waling = Holm *m*
~ **stone**, coping ~ = Abdeckstein *m*
~ **(strip)**, metal ~ (~) = Hohlfugeneisen *m*
cap screw = Kopfschraube *f*
~ **sheet** = Decklage *f* [*Bitumendachpappe f*]
capsill = Kopfbalken *m*, Jochholm *m*
capstan = (Gang)Spill *n*

captive balloon = Fesselballon *m*
car, see: automobile
~ = Wagen *m*
caravan = fahrbare Unterkunft *f*
~ **of vehicles** = Fahrzeugkolonne *f*
~ **track** = Karawanenpfad *m*
carbide-base cermet = Cermet *n* auf Carbidbasis *f*
carbide bit, see: (tungsten) carbide (tipped drill) bit
~ **(drill) bit cutting edge** = Hartmetallschneide *f*
~ **of calcium**, calcium carbide, CaC_2 = Kalziumkarbid *n*
~ ~ **silicon**, silicon carbide, carborundum, carbon silicide, SiC = Siliziumkarbid *n*, Karborund *n*
carbocoal tar = Karbokohlenteer *m*
car body = Karosserie *f*
carbody, lower frame = Unterwagen-Rahmen *m* [*Raupenbagger m*]
carbolic acid, phenol, C_6H_5OH = Karbolsäure *f*, Phenol *n*, Steinkohlenteerkreosot *n*, Phenylalkohol *m*
~ **oil**, middle ~, coal tar middle oil = Mittelöl *n*
carbolineum, petrolineum, coal tar creosote = Karbolineum *n*
carbon(ado)s, black diamonds, drilling diamonds = Bohrdiamanten *mpl*, schwarze Diamanten
carbon anode = Kohleanode *f*
~ **arc lamp** = Reinkohlenbogenlampe *f*
carbonate = kohlensaures Salz *n*, Karbonat *n*
~ **of lime**, calcium carbonate, whiting = Kalziumkarbonat *n*
~ ~ **silver**, see: grey silver
~ **of soda**, Na_2CO_3 = kohlensaures Natron *n* (oder Natrium *n*)
~ **rock** = karbonatisches Gestein *n*
carbonation = Karbonisierung *f*
carbon bisulphide, ~ disulphide, CS_2 = Schwefelkohlenstoff *m*
~ **black** = Flammruß *m*
~ **brick** = Kohlenstoffstein *m*
~ **brush** = Kohlenbürste *f*
~ **dioxide**, carbonic acid [*obsolete term: fixed air*] = Kohlensäure *f*
~ ~**-lamp** = Kohlensäure-Lampe *f*

carbon disintegration test of blast furnace brick = Prüfung *f* der Zerstörung *f* von Hochofensteinen *mpl* durch Kohlenstoffablagerung *f*
~ filament lamp = Kohlefadenlampe *f*
carboniferous lime(stone) = Kohlenkalk(stein) *m*
carbonization, coking = Verkokung *f*
carbon resistance furnace = Kohlengrießwiderstandsofen *m*
~ silicide, see: carbide of silicon
~ steel = Kohlenstahl *m*
~ tetrachloride, CCl₄ = Tetrachlorkohlenstoff *m*
~ tetraiodide = Tetrajodkohlenstoff *m*
carborundum, see: carbide of silicon
carburetted hydrogen, see: hydrocarbon
~ water-gas tar, see: oil-water-gas ~
carburettor, carburetter (Brit.); **carburetor** (US) = Vergaser *m*
to carburize = aufkohlen
carcase, carcass, shell (of the building) = Rohbau *m*
cardanic suspension = kardanische Aufhängung *f*
(cardan) universal joint = Kardangelenk *n*
(~) ~ ~ shaft = Kardangelenkwelle *f*
cardboard ferrule = Papphülse *f*
~ wick = Kartondrain *m*
card-controlled batching = lochkartengesteuerte Abmessung *f*, **~ Dosierung**
car dumper, wagon tippler = Waggonkipper *m*, Wagenkipper
to careen = kielholen
careening = Kippen *n* [*z. B. ein Schwimmdock n*]
car-ferry terminal = Wagen-Fähranlage *f*
cargo box barge (US); **decked ~** (Brit.) = Schute *f* mit festem Deck *n*
~ carrying barge = Lastkahn *m*
~ handling appliance (or gear) = Hafengütertransportmittel *n*
~ ~ capacity = Güterumschlagkapazität *f*
~ vessel, freighter = Frachter *m*, Frachtschiff *n*
~ warehouse = Hafenspeicher *m*
car jack = Wagenwinde *f*, Wagenheber *m*, Wagenhebebock *m*

car-jack type sounding apparatus = Spitzendrucksonde *f*
Carlsbad twinning = Karlsbader Zwilling *m* [*Mineralogie f*]
Carlson rotating auger = Rotationssonde *f* nach Carlson
carnallite (Min.) = Karnallit *m*
carnation clover = Inkarnatklee *m*
car park, parking place, parking lot = Parkplatz *m*, Auto~
Carpathian Mountains = Karpaten *f*
carpenter foreman = Zimmermannpolier *m*
carpenters' axe = Bundaxt *f*
~ (roofing) hammer = Latthammer *m*, Spitzhammer
~ square = Zimmermannswinkel *m*
carpet, see: road ~
carpet-coat, see: road carpet
carpholite = Strohstein *m*
car racing track = Autorennbahn *f*
~ registration plate = Nummernschild *n* [*Auto n*]
~ retarder = Gleisbremse *f*
carragheen, see: Irish moss
carriage, travel(l)ing ~ = Unterwagen *m*
~ bolt = Schloßschraube *f*
carriageway [*deprecated: road(way), road surface*] = Fahrbahn *f*
~ cover = befahrbare Schachtabdeckung *f*
~ deck plate, roadway **~ ~** [*bridge*] = Fahrbahnblech *n*
~ haunch(ing) = schmaler Randstreifen *m* zur äußeren Fahrbahneinfassung *f*
~ marking = Fahrbahnmarkierung *f*
~ slab = Fahrbahnplatte *f*
~ surfacing = Fahrbahnbelag *m*
car rider, brakesman = Bremser *m*
carried in stock, on stock = vorrätig
carrier, see: supporting roller
~, underbody = Untergestell *n*, Fahrgestell
~ (idler), (supporting) roller = (belastete) Tragrolle *f* [*Bandförderer m*]
~ ~ set = Tragrollenstation *f*
~ roller = Tragrolle *f* [*Gleiskette f*]
~ side, upper strand, carrying strand = Tragseite *f*, oberer Strang *m*, Obergurt *m* [*Bandförderer m*]

carrier's trade — cast iron sluice valve with round body

carrier's trade = Lohnfuhrgewerbe *n*
carrollite, (Co, Cu)$_3$S$_4$ (Min.) = Carrollit *m*
carryable = tragbar
~ **belt conveyor** = Tragband *n*
~ ~ ~ **frame** = Bandtragrahmen *m*
carrying scraper, two-wheel(ed) ~, wagon-scraper, tractor-pulled ~ ~; pan (US) = Schürfkübel *m*, Sattel-Schürfwagen *m*, Schürfkasten *m*
carry-strain [*DROTT skid-shovel*] = Belastung *f* des Fahrwerkes *n*
car shaker = Waggonentleerer *m*
cart = (Förder)Karre(n) *f*, (*m*), Transportkarre(n)
cart-path = Fuhrweg *m*
cartridge = Patrone *f*
~ = Einsatz *m* für Hydraulikpumpe *f* bzw. Aufladegebläse
cartridge-powered tool, powder-actuated ~, bolt driving gun = Bolzenschießgerät *n*
cart-wright = Stellmacher *m*
car unloader, conveyor-type ~ ~ = Waggon(band)entlader *m*
~ ~ **pump** = Waggonentladepumpe *f*
~ **wash**, (vehicle) washdown = Autowaschplatz *m*
Casagrande liquid limit machine, see: liquid limit device
~ **shear test apparatus**, box shear apparatus = Scherapparat *m* nach Casagrande, Scherkastengerät *n*, Scherbüchse *f*, Rahmenschergerät *n*
cascade = Kaskade *f*
~ **(drainage) culvert** = Treppendurchlaß *m*, Treppenabzugkanal *m*, Kaskadendurchlaß, Kaskadenabzugkanal
~ **evaporator** = Kaskadenverdampfer *m*
cascading = Abrollen *n* der Mahlkörper *mpl* übereinander
cased beam = einbetonierter Balken *m*
~ **borehole**, lined ~ = verrohrtes Bohrloch *n*
case hardened casting = Hartguß *m*
~ **hardening steel** = Einsatzstahl *m*
casein = Kasein *n*
casemate = Kasematte *f*
case of loading = Belastungsfall *m*
casing, pile ~ = Vortreibrohr *n* [*Franki-Pfahl m*]

~, **housing** = Gehäuse *n*
~ = Bohrrohr *n*
~ **clamp** = Bohrrohrschelle *f*
~ **cutter** = Bohrrohrschneider *m*
~ **float** = Bohrrohrschuh-Rückschlagventil *n*
casing-head gas = Bohrlochkopfgas *n*
~ **gasoline**, see: natural ~
casing pipe, lining tube = Futterrohr *n*
~ **protector** = Bohrrohrschutzmuffe *f*, Gummimuffe am Rotary-Bohrgestänge *n*
~ **shoe** = Bohrrohrschuh *m*
~ **swedge** = Bohrrohrtreibebirne *f*
~ **swivel** = Bohrrohrdrehkopf *m*, Bohrrohrwirbel *m*
cassiterite, tin-stone (Min.) = Zinnstein *m*
castable refractory = Feuerbeton *m*
castellated (screw) nut, castle (~) ~, horned (~) ~ = Kronen(schrauben)mutter *f*
caster (wheel), castor (~) = drehbare Laufrolle *f*
cast gypsum block, (precast) gypsum block, gypsum precast building block = Gipsbaustein *m*
casting = Gießen *n* [*in Formen fpl*]
~ = Gußstück *n*
~ **bed** = Betonierbett *n*
~ ~ **mo(u)ld** = Betonierbettform *f*
~ **in sand-lined mo(u)lds** = Sandguß(verfahren) *m*, (*n*)
~ **resin** = Vergußharz *n*
~ **yard** = Betonierungsplatz *m*, Herstellungsplatz
cast-in-place concrete, concrete cast in position, concrete cast in situ, poured-in-place concrete = Ortbeton *m*
~ **(foundation, or bearing) pile**, cast-in-situ pile, cast-in-the-ground pile, situ-cast pile = Ort(beton)pfahl *m*, Betonort(gründungs)pfahl *m*, Ort(beton)tragpfahl
cast iron flanged pipe = gußeisernes Flanschenrohr *n*
~ ~ **pipe** = Gußeisenrohr *n*
~ ~ **segment** = gußeisernes Segment *n* [*Tunnelbau m*]
~ ~ **sluice valve with oval body** = Keil-Ovalschieber *m* aus Gußeisen *n*
~ ~ ~ ~ ~ **round body** = Keil-Rundschieber *m* aus Gußeisen *n*

cast iron socket — catwalk

cast iron socket = Gußeisenmuffe *f*
~ ~ ~ and spigot pressure pipe = Muffendruckrohr *n* aus Gußeisen
~ ~ special casting = Gußeisen-Formstück *n*
~ ~ stove = Kanonenofen *m*
~ light alloy = Leichtmetallguß *m*
~ line, cumulative ~ = Summenlinie *f*
castor oil = Rizinusöl *n*, Kastoröl *n*
~ (wheel), see: caster (wheel)
cast shadow, deep ~ = Schlagschatten *m*
~ slag sett, copper ~ ~ = Kupferschlackenstein *m*
~ steel = Stahlguß *m*, Gußstahl *m*
~ stone, concrete ashlar, artificial stone = Betonwerkstein *m*
~ ~ mo(u)ld = Betonwerksteinform *f*
~ tin bronze = Gußzinnbronze *f*
cast-up seaweed = angeschwemmter (See)Tang *m*
cataclastic rock, kataklastic ~ = Kataklasit *m*
~ structure, kataklastic ~ = kataklastische Gesteinsform *f*, Kataklase *f*
catalyst, catalyzer, catalyser, catalytic agent = Katalysator *m*
catalytic cracking = katalytisches Spaltverfahren *n*
~ desulfurization = katalytische Entschwef(e)lung *f*
catapult = Katapult *m, n*
cataracting = freier Wurf *m* [*Mühle f*]
catastrophic flood (Brit.); super flood, flood of record (US) = Katastrophen-Hochwasser *n*
catch basin (structure) = Auffangbecken *n* [*Oberflächenwasserabführung f*]
catchment area, drainage ~, catchmentbasin, gathering-ground, drainage basin (Brit.); water-shed (US) = Niederschlaggebiet *n*, Einzuggebiet *n*, Sammelgebiet *n*, Abflußgebiet
catch-water ditch, see: intercepting ~
catch(-water) drain, see: interceptor
caterpillar, tracklayer, crawler (machine) = Gleiskettengerät *n*, Raupenkette *f*, Raupe *f* [*der Ausdruck „Gleiskettengerät" ist präziser als „Raupengerät"*]

CATERPILLAR [*Trademark*] = Gleiskettengerät *n*, Raupe *f*, Raupengerät *n*, Fabrikat CATERPILLAR TRACTOR CO., PEORIA, ILLINOIS, USA
~ (or track-laying type, or crawler) (asphalt) finisher (or paver, or bituminous paving machine, or bituminous spreading-and-finishing machine, or blacktop spreader, or asphaltic concrete paver) = Gleiskettenfertiger *m*, Raupenfertiger
~ bulldozer, see: (bull)dozer fitted to track-laying (type) tractor
~ flip-over bucket loader, see: crawler overhead loader
~ overloader, see: crawler overhead loader
~ rocker shovel, see: crawler overhead loader
*caterpillar shovel, see: bucket-excavator mounted on tracks
~ track, see: crawler
~ tracks = (Gleis)Kettenfahrwerk *n*, Raupenfahrwerk
~ tractor, tracked ~, crawler (-tread) ~, track-type (industrial) ~, (self-laying) track-type (industrial) ~, tracklaying ~ = (Gleis)Kettenschlepper *m*, Raupenschlepper *m*, Raupentrecker *m*, Raupentraktor *m*
caterpillar tread wagon, track-type ~, tractor wagon with track type equipment = Großraum-Gleiskettenwagen *m*, Raupen(anhänger)wagen *m*, Großraumlore *f* auf Raupen *fpl*, Großraumraupenwagen *m*
~ twin D 8 tractor = Zwillings(gleis)kettenschlepper *m*, Zwillingsraupenschlepper *m*, Fabrikat PETERSON TRACTOR & EQUIPMENT CO.
~ type front-end loader = Schürfladeraupe *f*, Schürflade(gleis)kettenfahrzeug *n*
cation = Kation *f*
cat-jockey = Gleiskettengerätfahrer *m*, Raupenfahrer *m*
cat's eye = Bodenrückstrahler *m*
~ tail, timothy grass = Wiesenlieschgras *n*
cattle guard = Viehgatter *n*
catwalk, duckboard, walkway = (Lauf-)Steg *m*

ca(u)ldron, fault, pit (Geol.) = Kessel *m*
cauldron (Brit.) = Gußasphaltkocher *m* ohne mechanischem Rührwerk *n*
to ca(u)lk = verstemmen
caulking, fullering (Brit.); calking (US) = Kalfatern *n*
~, see: cogging
~ mallet = Kalfaterhammer *m*
causeway = Dammstraße *f*
~, submersible bridge = überflutbare Brücke *f*, Tauchbrücke
~(ing) [*in Scotland: forming roads of paving stones, or granite setts*] = Pflastern *n*, Pflasterung *f*
caustic = kaustisch
~ lime = Ätzkalk *m*, Kalziumhydroxyd *n*
~ potash, potassium hydroxide, potassium hydrate, $K_2(OH)_2$ = Ätzkali *n*, Kaliumhydroxid *n*, Kaliumhydrat *n*
(~) potash-lye, solution of caustic potash = Kalilauge *f*, Ätzkalilösung *f*
~ soda = Ätznatron *n*, kaustische Soda *f*, kaustisches Soda *n*, Natriumhydroxyd *n*
cave(-in) = Nachfall *m*, Einsturz *m*
cavern = Kaverne *f*
cavetto, throat = Ablauf *m* [*Säule f*]
~ = Hohlkehle *f*
~ vault = Spiegelgewölbe *n*
caving bin = (Kalk)Nachlöschbunker *m*
cavity brick, hollow ~ = Hohlstein *m*, Hohlziegel *m*
~ dam (Brit.); hollow dam (US) = Hohlmauer *f* [*Talsperre f*]
~ fit = eingebauter Filter *m* mit ausgespültem Loch *n* [*Wellpoint-Methode f*]
~ panel = Hohlwandteil *m*
~ wall, hollow ~ = Hohlmauer *f*, Hohlwand *f*
~-wall tie = Hohlmaueranker *m*
CD blasting machine, see: condenser discharge (type) blasting machine
ceiling fitting = Deckenleuchte *f*
~ joist, floor ~, bearer = Deckenbalken *m*
~ panel = Deckentafel *f*
~ ~ heating = (Strahlungs)Deckenheizung *f*
~ plaster = Deckenputz *m*
~ projector = Wolkenscheinwerfer *m*
cellar, basement = Keller *m*, Kellergeschoß *n*

cellular cofferdam = Zellenfang(e)damm *m*
~ dam = Zellenmauer *f* [*Talsperre f*]
~-expanded concrete = Zellenbeton *m*, Porenbeton, aufgeblähter Beton
cellulated ceramics = keramische Erzeugnisse *npl* mit Zellenbildung *f*, keramische Leichterzeugnisse
cement, cementing material, matrix = Bindemittel *n*, verkittende Zwischensubstanz *f*
~, matrix, binder = Bindemittel *n*, Binder *m*
*cement, hydraulic ~, water ~, cement matrix = Zement *m* [*hydraulisches Bindemittel n*]
(~) aggregate, concrete ~ = (Beton-)Zuschlagstoffe *mpl*
~ aggregate ratio = Trockenbeton-Mischungsverhältnis *n*
cementation = Verkittung *f* [*Gestein n*]
~ = Zementieren *n* [*Stahl m*]
~ = Baugrundverbesserung *f*, Baugrundverfestigung *f*
~ of rock fissures, rock sealing = Gesteinsauspressung *f*, Felsinjektion *f*, Kluftinjektion *f*, Gesteinsverpressung
cement batcher = Zementdosierapparat *m*
~ ~ scale, ~ weigh(ing) batcher = Zement(silo)waage *f*, Bindemittelwaage
~ batching = Zementdosierung *f*
~ batch(ing) plant = Zementsilo *m* mit Dosierung *f*, Dosieranlage *f* für Zement *m*
~ blower = Luftstrom-Gebläse *n* im Zementsilo *m*
cement-bonded mass = zementgebundene Masse *f*
*cement(-bound) macadam (or surfacing), see: cement penetration method
cement (bucket) elevator = Zementbecherwerk *n*, Zementelevator *m*
~ burning = Zementbrennen *n*
~ clinker = Zementklinker *m*
~ ~ mineral = Zement-Klinkermineral *n*
*(cement) concrete = (Zement-)Beton *m*
(~) (~) aggregates = (Beton)Zuschlagstoffe *mpl*, (Beton)Zuschläge *mpl*
*(cement) concrete pavement = (Zement-)Betondecke *f*, (Zement)Betonbelag *m*

cement concrete trackway — cement suspension

cement concrete trackway = Zementbeton-Spurstreifenstraße *f*
~ content, ~ factor = Zementgehalt *m*, Zementfaktor *m* [*Beton m*]
~ factor, see: ~ content
~ finish, see: ~ (slab) ~
~ floating = dünner Zementmörtelüberzug *m*
~ grain = Zementteilchen *n*
~ grout, see: cement-water grout (or mixture)
~ ~ discharge hose = Zementspritzschlauch *m*
~ ~ pump, see: pressure grouting machine
~ gun, (pneumatic) concrete gun, gunite machine, air placing machine, concrete placing gun, jetcrete gun; Boulder Pneumatic Concretor = Tektor *m*, (Torkret-)Zement(mörtel)kanone *f*, Torkretbeton-Spritzmaschine *f*, Beton-Spritzmaschine, Druckluftspritzgerät *n*, Zementmörtelspritzapparat *m* nach dem Torkretverfahren *n*, Torkretkanone *f*
cement-gun work, see: guniting
cement handling facility = Zementumschlaganlage *f*
~ haulage unit, see: bulk cement transporter
~ hauler, see: bulk cement transporter
(~) hydration, see: set
~ incorporation = Zementbeigabe *f*, Zementzugabe *f*
cementing agent, ~ material = Kittstoff *m*
~ material (Geol.), see: cement
cement injection = Zementinjektion *f*, Zementeinpressung *f*, Zementauspressung, Zementverpressung
~ injection pump = Zement-Injektionspumpe *f*, Zementeinpreßmaschine *f*, Zementeinspritzapparat *m*, Zementmilchpumpe *f*, Zementinjektor *m*
cementitious property = Kittwirkung *f*, Kittungseigenschaft *f*
cement kiln = Zementofen *m*
~-lime mortar, lime cement ~, gauged ~ = Zementkalkmörtel *m*, verlängerter Zementmörtel, Kalkzementmörtel
*****cement macadam**, see: ~ penetration method
*** ~ matrix**, see: cement

~ mill, ~ works = Zementwerk *n*, Zementfabrik *f*
~ mixing test = Zementmischprüfung *f* [*Bitumenemulsion f*]
~ mortar = Zementmörtel *m*
~ ~ grouting, subsurface grouting with cement mortar = Zementmörteleinpressung *f*, Zementmörteleinspritzung *f*, Zementmörtelinjektion *f*, Zementmörtelunterpressung *f*, Zementmörtelauspressung *f*
~ ~ injecting device = Zementmörtel-Injektor *m*, Zement-Mörtel-Einspritzgerät *n*
~ (~) rendering, ~ ~ plaster finish, ~ plaster rendering, ~ ~ finish = Zementmörtelputz *m*, Zementputzmörtel *m*
~ paste = Zementpaste *f*
~ pat, circular-domed pat of cement, pat of cement-water paste = Zementkuchen *m*
*****cement penetration method, COLCRETE, colloidal concrete, cement(-bound) macadam, mortar-bound macadam, cement-bound surfacing, Hassam pavement** = Mörteleingußdecke *f* [*turbulente Mörtelfertigung f*]
~ proportioning screw = Zement-Abmeß-Schnecke *f*, Bindemittel-Zuteilschnecke *f*
~ rendering, see: ~ mortar
~ rock = Kalktonerdegestein *n*
~ roof tile, see: concrete roofing tile
~-sand grout, sand-cement ~, cement slurry = Zement-Sand-Schlämme *f*
cement screw, screw conveyor for bulk cement = Zementschnecke *f*
~ silo, see: bulk cement plant
~ (slab) finish, ~ floor(ing) = Zementestrich *m*
~ slurry, see: cement-sand grout
~ ~ = Zement-Rohschlamm *m*
~ ~ mixer, see: COLCRETE ~
cement(-soil) stabilisation (or stabilization) = Zementverfestigung *f*, Bodenverfestigung *f* mit Zement *m*
cement spreading machine, ~ spreader = Zementverteiler *m* [*Bodenverfestigung f*]
~ stabilisation, see: cement(-soil) ~
~ suspension = Aufschlämmung *f*, grobe Suspension *f*

cement tanker, see: (bulk) cement transporter

~ **test(ing)** = Zementprüfung f

~ ~ **sand, standard** ~ = Normensand m

~ **trailer unit** = Zement-Anhänger m

cement-trass mortar = Zement-Traß-Mörtel m

cement-treated base = kalifornischer Ausdruck für Unterbau für Betondecken aus verdichtetem Bodenzementbeton aus körnigen Stoffen

cement trowel = Zementkelle f

cement(-water) grout (or mixture), neat ~ ~ = Zementschlämme f, Zementsuspension f

~ **paste** = Zement-Leim m, Zement-Wasser-Gemisch n

cement water ratio = Zement-Wasser-Verhältnis n [Beton m]

~ **weigh(ing) batcher,** ~ batcher scale = Zement(silo)waage f, Bindemittelwaage f

census of fluoridation = Fluoridierungsstatistik f

centering (US); centring (Brit.) = Lehrgerüst n

center journal (US); king pin = Königszapfen m

~ **knot** (US); see: centre ~ (Brit.)

~ **of gravity** (US); centre ~ ~ (Brit.); centroid = Schwerpunkt m, Massenmittelpunkt m

~ **to center spacing** (US); centre to centre ~ (Brit.) = Mittenabstand m

central angle at crest (US); see: angular width of arch at crest (Brit.)

~ ~ **of arc** (US); see: angular measurement of arc (Brit.)

(~) baffle = Prallblech n, Abweisungsblech [im Fangkessel m des Druckluftbetonförderers m]

~ **batching and mixing station,** see: concrete mixing plant

~ **batch(ing) plant,** see: (aggregate) ~ ~

~ **building frame,** ~ section = Mittelbau m

~ **business area,** ~ district, downtown area = zentrales Geschäftsviertel n

~ **control platform** = zentraler Bedienungsstand m, Hauptsteuerand

~ **district;** town centre (Brit.); town center (US) = Stadtkern m, Stadtinneres n

~ **engine plant, "packaged"** ~ = zentrale Betriebsanlage f

~ **grass reserve,** see: grassy median strip

~ **heating station,** ~ ~ plant = Fernheizwerk n

~ **island** = Mittelinsel f [Verkehrsinsel f]

centralized controls = zentralisierte Steuerung f, ~ Bedienung f

centrally symmetrical loading = zentralsymmetrische Belastung f

central mixing plant = stationäre Großmischanlage f, ortsfeste ~

* **central mixing plant for the preparation of intermediate mixtures** (US); see: bituminous macadam and tarmacadam mixing plant (Brit.)

~ ~ ~ ~ ~ ~ **high-type hot mixtures** (US), see: asphalt plant

central-mix-plant = zentrale Mischanlage f

central operating platform = Zentral-Steuerand m

~ **repair (work)shop** = Zentral-Reparaturwerkstatt f

~ **reserve,** ~ reservation, ~ strip, median (stiip), medial strip, dividing strip = Mittelstreifen m

~ **volcano,** solitary ~ = Einzelvulkan m

~ **weigh batching and mixing plant,** see: concrete mixing plant

~ **workshop** = Zentralwerkstatt f

centre flight of the runway = Startbahn-Mittelstück n

~ **knot** (Brit.); center knot (US); system point, assemblage point = Knotenpunkt m

~ **lathe** (Brit.); center ~ (US) = Spitzendrehbank f

~ **line** (Brit.); center ~ (US); C. L. = Bau(werk)achse f, Symmetrieachse

~ **of gravity** (Brit.); see: centroid

~ ~ **ice dispersal** = Eisverbreitungszentrum n

~ ~ **moments** = Momentennullpunkt m

~ **span,** see: train ~

***centrifugal air separator** = Schleudersichter m

~ **blower** = Schleudergebläse n

~ **casting** = Schleuderguß(verfahren) m, (n), Zentrifugalguß(verfahren)

~ **classifier** = Fliehkraft(naß)klassierer m

centrifugal compressor — chain of locks 77

centrifugal compressor = Kreiselverdichter *m*

~ discharge elevator, spaced bucket ~, boot loading ~ = zentrifugaler Elevator *m*, zentrifugales Becherwerk *n*

~ drive = Fliehkraftantrieb *m*

~ dust collector, cyclone separator, (dust collecting) cyclone = Staubabscheider *m*, Zyklon *m*, Fliehkraftabscheider *m*

~ force = Fliehkraft *f*

~ ~ (grinding) mill = Fliehkraft(mahl)-mühle *f*

~ governor = Fliehkraftregler *m*

centrifugally cast concrete, spun ~ = Schleuderbeton *m*

~ ~ ~ mast, spun ~ ~ = Schleuderbetonmast *m*, Betonschleudermast

~ ~ ~ mo(u)ld, spun concrete ~ ~ = Schleuderbetonform *f*

~ ~ ~ pipe, spun ~ ~ = Schleuderbetonrohr *n*, Betonschleuderrohr

~ ~ in metal mo(u)lds = in Metallschleuderformen gegossen

~ ~ sand-lined mo(u)lds = in Sandschleuderformen gegossen

centrifugal pump = Kreiselpumpe *f*, Schleuderpumpe, Zentrifugalpumpe

~ ~ without guide passage = Kreiselpumpe *f* ohne Leitvorrichtung *f*

~ screw (or propeller) pump = Kreiselpumpe *f* mit Flügelrad *n*

~ volute pump = Kreiselpumpe *f* mit spiralförmigem Gehäuse *n*

centrifuge = Zentrifuge *f*

~ method = Zentrifugiermethode *f*

~ moisture equivalent = Zentrifugal-Feuchtigkeits-Äquivalent *n*

centriliner = Maschine *f* zum Auskleiden *n* eiserner Rohrleitungen *fpl* mit Zementmörtel *m*

centring (Brit.); see: centering (US)

centroid; center of gravity (US); centre of gravity (Brit.) = Schwerpunkt *m*, Massenmittelpunkt *m*

ceramic body = keramischer Scherben *m*, keramische Scherbe *f*

~ coating = keramische Schutzschicht *f*

~ digester linings in sulfite pulp mills = keramisches Futter *n* in Sulfitzellstoffkochern *mpl*

~ drier; ~ dryer (Brit.) = keramische Trockenanlage *f*

~ raw material = keramischer Rohstoff *m*

ceramics = Keramik *f*

cerargyrite, chlorargyrite, hornsilver, AgCl (Min.) = Hornsilber *n*, Silberhornerz *n*

ceratite limestone = Ceratitenkalk(stein) *m*

ceresine wax = Zeresin(wachs) *n*, Kunstwachs

cermet [*ceramics and metals*] = Mischung *f* von feuerfesten Metalloxyden *npl* und wärmefesten Metallen *npl*

certificate of acceptance = Abnahmebescheinigung *f*

~ ~ test = Prüfungszeugnis *n*

cerussite, white lead ore (Min.) = (Kohlen)Bleispat *m*, Zerussit *m*, Weißbleierz *n*

cesspool, cesspit = Klärgrube *f*

chabazite (Min.) = Chabasit *m*, Würfelsiedestein *m*

chain adjuster, ~ tensioner = Kettenspanner *m*

chainage, stationing = Stationierung *f*

chain-and-spike harrow = Gliederegge *f*

chain block (and tackle), see: ~ hoist

~ book, field ~ = Feldbuch *n* [*Kettenvermessung f*]

~ bucket elevator, see: ~ (type) (bucket) ~

~ ~ excavator, see: bucket ladder ~

~ conveyor = Kettenförderer *m*

~ crowd(ing) = Kettenvorstoß(en) *m*, (*n*), Kettenvorschub *m* [*Hochlöffel(bagger) m*]

~ drive = Ketten(an)trieb *m*

~ drum = Kettentrommel *f*

chained (breakwater) blocks = Kettensteinwurf *m*

chain elevator, see: chain (type) (bucket) elevator

~ grab(ing bucket) = Ketten-Greifer *m*, Ketten-Greifkorb *m*

~ grate, travel(l)ing ~ = Wanderrost *m*

~ harrow = Kettenegge *f*

~ hoist, block (and tackle), ~ lifting block, ~ pulley block = Kettenzug *m*

chaining, see: chain surveying

chain of lakes = Seenkette *f*

~ ~ locks, stairway of locks, staircase flights, staircase locks = Schleusentreppe *f*

chain of mountains = Gebirgskette *f*
~ **pin** = Kettenbolzen *m*
~ **pulley block**, see: ~ hoist
~ **saw**, link tooth ~ = Kettensäge *f*
~ **steel** = Kettenstahl *m*
~ **surveying**, chaining = Kettenmessung *f*
~ **(suspension) bridge** = Kettenhängebrücke *f*
~ **tensioner**, ~ adjuster = Kettenspanner *m*
~ **tongs** = Kettenzange *f*
~ **track**, see: crawler
~ **traverse** = geknickter (Polygon-)Zug *m* [*Vermessungskunde f*]
~ **(type) (bucket) elevator** = Kettenbecherwerk *n*, Ketten(becher)elevator *m*
chain-type spaced bucket elevator with centrifugal gravity discharge = zentrifugaler Schwerkraftelevator *m*, zentrifugales Schwerkraftbecherwerk *n*
chalcanthite (Min.), see: blue vitriol
chalcedony (Min.) = Chalzedon *m*
~ **nodule** = Chalzedonschwüle *f*
chalcocite, redruthite, copper glance (Min.) = Kupferglanz *m*
chalcopyrite, copper pyrite (Brit.); copper pyrites (US), CuFeS$_2$ (Min.) = Kupferkies *m*, Chalkopyrit *m*
chalk = Kreide *f*
~ = Kreidegestein *n*
~ **cliff** = Kreidefelsen *m*
~ **flint** = Kieselkreide *f*
~ **line** = Kreideschnur *f*
~ ~ = Kreidestrich *m*
~ **marl** = Kreidemergel *m*
~ **quarrying** = Kreideabbau *m*
~ **well** = Brunnen *m* im Kreidefelsen
chalky limestone = Kreidekalkstein *m*
~ **soil** = Kreideboden *m*
chalybite, siderite, spathic iron, FeCO$_3$ (Min.) = Siderit *m*, Eisenspat *m*
chamber kiln = Ringofen *m*
~ **(or lift) navigation (or inland) lock** = Kammerschleuse *f*
to chamfer = abfasen
chamfering, see: splaying
change of curvature = Krümmungsänderung *f*, Krümmungswechsel *m*
~ ~ **level** = Höhenwechsel *m*
change-over period = Übergangsperiode *f*

change-speed motor = Motor *m* mit mehreren Drehzahlstufen *fpl*
changing of aspect of traffic control signals = Signalwechsel *m* [*Verkehrssignalsteu(e)rung f*]
channel, duct, hole = Gleitkanal *m* [*Spannbeton m*]
~, gutter, drain, grip, flume = Ablauf(ge)rinne *f*, (*n*)
~, see: (road) ~
~ = U-Stahl *m*, U-Profil *n*
~ **frame** = U-Eisen-Rahmen *m*
~ **light** = Wasserlandebahn-Feuer *n*
channel(l)ing machine = Schräm(vortriebs)maschine *f*, Fräsvortriebsmaschine
channel paving sett, see: gutter ~ ~
~ **scraper and elevator** = Rinnsteinreinigungsmaschine *f* mit Aufladebecherwerk *n*
~ **shear connector** = Schubdübel *m* aus U-Profil *n*
~ **(or split) stoneware drain pipe** (Brit.); ~ (~ ~) (vitrified) clay pipe (US) = Tonrohrschale *f*, Steinzeugrohrschale *f*
channel-tool = halbrundes Kehlholz *n* [*Handwerkzeug des Asphaltarbeiters*]
channel (type) spillway, see: side-channel (~)~
characteristic of a beacon = Kennung *f*
~ **value** = Kennwert *m*
character light, code ~ = Kennfeuer *n*
charcoal = Holzkohle *f*
~ **iron** = Holzkohle-Eisen *n*
~ **kiln** = Meiler *m*
char felling = Kahlschlag *m*
charge, batch = Charge *f*
~, see: explosive ~
charge-a-paver machine = Maschine *f* für den Umschlag *m* des Trockenbetons zwischen Rad-Transportwagen *m* und dem Straßenbetonmischer *m*
charging bin = Aufgabebehälter *m*
~ **feeder**, see: feeder
~ **hopper**, see: (feed) ~
~ **tank** = geeichter Behälter *m* für Holzschutzbehandlungsmittel *n*
charring = Scharrieren *n*
chart = Berechnungstafel *f*, Rechentafel *f*
chassis, carrier = Chassis *n*, Fahrgestell *n*
~ **frame** = Fahrgestellrahmen *m*

chassis-mounted gritter — chisel

chassis-mounted gritter = Streuer *m* mit Spezialaufbau *m*
to check = nachprüfen
check dam = Kolkschutzsperre *f*
checker, observer = Zählposten *m*
checkered sheet (or plate), chequered ~ (~ ~) = Riffelblech *n*
check irrigation, see: basin system ~
~ nut, lock ~ = Gegenmutter *f*, Klemmmutter *f*
~ rail, guard ~, safety ~, side ~, rail guard, safeguard = Radlenker *m*, Leitschiene *f*, Zwangsschiene *f*
chemical = Chemikal *n*
~ and petroleum engineering exhibition = Ausstellung *f* von technischem Bedarf für die chemische und Mineralölindustrie *f*
~ attack = chemischer Angriff *m*
~ ecology = chemische Ökologie *f*
~ industry hydrated lime = Chemiekalkhydrat *n*
~ lime = Chemiekalk *m*
chemically aerated concrete, see: aerated ~
~ combined hydrogen, fixed ~ = chemisch gebundener Wasserstoff *m*
~ deposited sedimentary rock, ~ formed rock = chemisches Sedimentgestein *n*, Fällungsgestein, Präzipitatgestein, Ausscheidungssedimentgestein, chemisches Absatzgestein
chemical plaster, patented ~ = Edelputz *m*
~ precipitant = Fällungschemikal *n*, Fällmittel *n*
~ precipitation = chemische Ausfällung *f*
~ soil solidification = chemische Bodenverfestigung *f*
~ treatment [*sewage*] = chemische Behandlung *f*
~ weathering = chemische Verwitterung *f*, Gesteinszersetzung *f*, chemische Gesteinsauflösung *f*
cherry picker = Stollenaufzug *m*
chert = Gestein bestehend aus Quarz, Chalcedon oder Opal, bzw. Mischungen dieser Mineralien wobei Chalcedon vorherrscht
chert-gravel = Hornsteinkies *m*
chessylite, see: azurite

chestnut oak, sessile-fruited ~, mountain ~, Drurmast ~ = Traubeneiche *f*, Steineiche, Wintereiche, Früheiche
chevaux de frise = spanischer Reiter *m*
chevron fold (Geol.) = Dachsparrenfalte *f*
chiastolite (Min.) = Chiastolith *m*
Chicago method; see under "caisson pile"
chief contractor, prime ~, general ~ = Generalunternehmer *m*, Hauptunternehmer
Chile nitre, see: soda nitre
~ saltpetre, see: soda nitre
(chilled) shot-bit = Schrot(bohr)krone *f*
chimney cooler = Kühlturm *m*
china clay, kaolin, porcelain clay, porcelain earth = (Roh)Kaolin *m*, Porzellanton *m*, Porzellanerde *f*, Weißerde
chinaware = Porzellan *n*
chine (Geol.) = Kliffhang *m*
Chinese wood oil, see: tung ~
to chink, to choke, to blind, to key = auszwicken, verzwicken, abdecken [*Packe f*]
chinking, see: blinding
chipless thread cutting = Gewindewirbeln *n*
chipped surface = abgesplittete Oberfläche *f*
chipper, see: chip spreader
~, scaling hammer, chipping hammer = (Ab)Klopfer *m*
chipping, see: blinding
~, see: chipping(s)
~ = Absplitten *n*
~, spalling, splintering = Absplittern *n*
~ chisel, hand cold ~, flat ~ = Flachmeißel *m*
~ hammer = Meißelhammer *m*
chipping(s), chips, stone chips; [*deprecated: screening(s)*] = Splitt *m*
~ breaker, see: single-toggle granulator
~ carpet (or mat) = Splitteppich *m*
chip spreader, chipping(s) machine, chipper, surface dressing chipping distributor = Splittstreuer *m*, Splittstreugerät *n*, Splittstreumaschine *f*
to chisel = meißeln [*mit Handmeißel m bearbeiten*]
*****chisel** = Meißel *m*
~, wood ~, firmer ~, mortise ~ = Beitel *m*, Handmeißel *m*

chisel breaker, see: rock cutter
~ shank = Meißelschaft *m*
~ steel = Meißelstahl *m*
~-type bit cutting edge, see: (drill) bit (cutting) edge
c(h)loanthite, white nickel, NiAs$_{2-3}$ (Min.) = Chloanthit *m*, Weißnickelkies *m*
chloramine = Chloramin *n*
chlorargyrite (Min.), see: cerargyrite
chlorate (blasting) explosive = Chloratit *n*, Chlorat-Sprengstoff *m*
~ of zinc, monkey = Lötwasser *n*
chloride of lime, see: bleaching powder
chlorinated lime, see: bleaching powder
~-rubber paint = Chlorkautschukfarbe *f*
chlorinated sewage = gechlortes Abwasser *n*
chlorine = Chlor *n*
~ dosing = Chlordosierung *f*
chlorite, green earth (Min.) = Chlorit *m*
~-schist = Chloritschiefer *m*
chlorite-slate = Tonschiefer *m* mit viel Chlorit *m*
chloritization = Chloritbildung *f*
to choke, see: to chink
choke changing = Düsenwechsel *m* [*Tiefbohren n*]
choked up, blocked up = verstopft
choker course (of aggregate) = Splittverfüllschicht *f* [*Tränkmakadam m*]
choke (or intermediate) stone (or aggregate), keystone, filler stone, blinding (stone) = Keilsplitt *m*, Füllsplitt *m*
choking, seq: blinding
~ of the river course = Verschotterung *f* des Flußlaufes *m*
cholesterol = Cholesterin *n*
chord = Sehne *f* [*Mathematik f*]
~, boom, flange = Gurt(ung) *m*, (*f*)
~ bracing, see: boom ~
~ member, boom **~**, flange **~** = Gurt(ungs)stab *m*
C horizon = C-Horizont *m*
christobalite (Min.) = Cristobalit *m*
chromatographic fractionation = chromatographische Fraktionierung *f*
chrome brick = Chrom(erz)stein *m*
~ iron ore, chromite, FeO . Cr$_2$O$_3$ (Min.) = Chromit *m*, Chromeisenerz *n*
~-magnesite brick = Chrommagnesitstein *m*

~-tungsten steel = Chromwolframstahl *m*
to chromise = inchromieren
chromite, see: chrome iron ore
chromium-plated, chrome-finished = verchromt
chromometer = Kolorimeter *n*
chrysoberyl (Min.) = Chrysoberyll *m*
chrysotile, see: Canadian asbestos
chuck = l(Auf)Spannfutter *n*, Klemmfutter
chucking slide = Spannschieber *m*
churn drill, cable **~**, well **~**, spudding **~** = Seilschlagbohrgerät *n*
~ drilling (or boring), percussive rope **~** (**~ ~**), cable **~** (**~ ~**), well **~** (**~ ~**) = Seilschlagbohren *n*, pennsylvanisches Seilbohren, amerikanisches Seilbohrverfahren *n*
churning and spreading device [*cooling of aggregates*] = Wendeapparat *m* [*Kühlung f von Betonzuschlagstoffen mpl*]
chute, spout; shoot (Brit.) = Schurre *f*
~, spout; shoot (Brit.) = Rinne *f* [*Gußbetonanlage f*]
~, see: log **~**
chuted concrete = Gußbeton *m*, Rinnenbeton, flüssiger Beton
chute for liquid manure = Jaucherinne *f*
cigar-shaped valley, see: canoe(-shaped) **~**
CIMENT DE LA FARGE, **CIMENT FONDU** [*Trademark*], electric cement = Elektroschmelzzement *m*
cinder; see: clinker (Brit.)
~ [*scoriaceous lava from a volcano*] = Schlacke *f*
~ cone = Schlackenkegel *m* [*Vulkan m*]
~ hair = Schlackenwolle *f*
~ track = Aschenbahn *f* [*Sportplatz m*]
cinnamon stone, hessonite (Min.) = Hessonit *m*
cipolin = Kalkglimmerschiefer *m*, Cipolino *m*
circle [*in a grader, the rotary table which supports the blade and regulates its angle*] = Drehstuhl *m*, kreisförmiger Zahnkranz *m*
~ kiln = Rundofen *m* [*keramische Industrie f*]
~ throw, circle-throw gyratory movement = Kreiswurf *m*, Kreisbahn-Siebschwingung *f*

circle-throw (vibrating) screen — clad steel 81

circle-throw (vibrating) screen, vibrating screen with uniform full circle motion = Kreisvibrationssieb n, Kreisschwing(er)sieb n
circle vision cab(in), full-vision ~ = Rundblick-Führerhaus n, Vollsichtkanzel f
circuit analysis = Stabzugberechnungsverfahren n
~ **tester** = Leitungsprüfer m
circular arc, see: ~ curve
~ ~ **analysis**, Swedish cylindrical-surface method, ~ circular-arc ~ = schwedisches Verfahren n, schwedische Gleitkreistheorie f [Bestimmung der Rutschgefahr unter Annahme einer kreisförmigen Rutschfläche (einer Gleitfläche)]
~ **bin compartment** = Wabe f [Wabensilo m]
~ **blank**, round ~ = Ronde f
~ **cell** = Kreiszelle f
~ ~ **cofferdam** = Kreiszellen-Fang(e)damm m
~ **cement compartment** = Bindemittelwabe f [Wabensilo n]
~ **coal**, see: eye ~
~ **container** = Rundbehälter m
~ **curve**, ~ arc = Kreiskurve f, Kreisbogen m [Straße f]
~ **cylindrical shell** = Kreiszylinderschale f
circular-domed pat of cement, see: cement pat
circular flange beam = Kreisringträger m
~ **floor-plate** = Kreisringplatte f
~ **footing** = Kreisfundament n
~ **gallery** = Kreisstollen m
~ **grate** = Ringrost m
~ **horizont curve**, ~ ~ arc = Kreiskurve f im Grundriß, Kreisbogen m ~ ~
~ **leaf** = Drosselklappenkörper m
~ **multiple-compartment bin** = (Rund-)Wabensilo m
~ **paving**, see: fanwise ~
~ **protractor** = Winkelmesser m
~ **saw** = Kreissäge f
~ **section** = Kreisquerschnitt m
~ **spillway crest** = Ringüberlaufkrone f
~ **thickener** = Rundeindicker m
~ **track** = Rundlauf m
~ **tunnel** = Kreistunnel m
to circulate = umwälzen

circulating heater (for heating and unloading tanks of asphalt (US) / asphaltic bitumen (Brit.)) = Bitumen-Umwälz-Erhitzer m
~ **load** = Umlauflast f [Mühle f]
~ **pressure lubrication** = Umlaufdruckschmierung f
~ **pump** = Umwälzpumpe f, Umlaufpumpe
~ **spraybar** = Zirkulations-Sprengrampe f, Zirkulations-Düsenrampe
circulation heating = Umlaufheizung f
~ **with clear water** = Klarwasserspülung f [Rotarybohren n]
~ ~ **mud** = Dickspülung f [Rotarybohren n]
circumferential prestressing = Ringvorspannung f
cirque (Geol.), see: corrie
cirrostratus = Schleierwolke f, Zirrostratuswolke f
cirrus cloud, mare's-tail, paint-brush = Federwolke f, Zirruswolke
cistern, (storage) tank, container (for liquids) = (Flüssigkeits)Behälter m, Tank m, Zisterne f, Sammelbehälter
citric acid = Zitronensäure f
city area, urban ~ = Stadtgebiet n
city-bound traffic = einstrahlender Verkehr m
city dweller, town ~ = Stadtbewohner m, Städter m
~ **government** = Stadtverwaltung f
~ **planner**, town ~, municipal ~ urban ~ = Städteplaner m, Stadtplaner m
(~) **street**, municipal road, town road, urban road, urban street, town street, urban thoroughfare = Stadtstraße f
civil aviation = Zivilluftfahrt f
~ **engineer**, construction ~ = Bauingenieur m
~ **engineering** = Tiefbau m, planender Ingenieurbau m
~ **engineering and building construction** = Ingenieurbau m, Bauingenieurwesen n
~ ~ **equipment** = Baumaschinen fpl und -geräte npl
~ ~ **industry**, see: building ~
clad = gekapselt
~ **steel** = plattierter Stahl m

Claisen flask = Claisenkolben *m*
clam = Sandmuschel *f*
~ (US); see: pair of half-scoops (Brit.)
to clam out = mit Zweischalengreifer *m* ausbaggern
clamp = Feldofen *m*, Feldbrandofen, Meiler *m* [*Ziegelherstellung f*]
~ = Klemme *f*, Schraubzwinge *f*
~ = Klammer *f*
~ **coupling**, split ~ = Schalenkupplung *f*
clamping bolt = Spannbolzen *m*
~ **force**, contact pressure = Klemmkraft *f*, Klemmspannung *f* [*Nietverbindung f*]
~ **nut** = Spannmutter *f*
clamp(ing) screw = Spannschraube *f*
clam(shell bucket) (or basket) (US); see: pair of half-scoops (Brit.)
* ~ ~ **crane**, see: clamshell(-rigged) ~
~ (~) **dredge(r)** = Schwimmgreifer *m* mit Zweischalengreifkorb *m*, Greifnaßbagger *m* ~ ~
~ ~ **with pile driver action**, impact clam = Zweischalengreifkorb *m* mit Rammwirkung *f*
* **clamshell(-rigged) crane**, clamshell bucket crane = Zweischalengreifbagger *m*, Zweischalengreiferkran *m*
clan (Geol.) = Familie *f*
clap sill, see: lock ~
clarain = Clarit *m*
clarification = Klärung *f*
CLARIGESTER = modernisierte Abart des Emscherbrunnens in den USA
clarifying tower = Klärturm *m*, Stoffangtrichter *m* [*Papierfabrik f*]
CLARK 4024 [*Trademark*] = Gabelstapler *m*, Fabrikat RUHR-INTRANS-HUBSTAPLER G. m. b. H., MÜLHEIM-RUHR, DEUTSCHLAND
classical earth pressure theory = orthodoxe Erddrucktheorie *f* [*Coulomb, Rankine*]
classic method, orthodox ~ = klassische Methode *f*
classification = Klassifizierung *f*
~, see: classifying
~ **count** = Querschnittzählung *f*
~ **of fine sand** = Feinsandklassierung *f*
~ ~ **ores** = Erzklassierung *f*
~ **tool** = Klassierapparat *m*
~ **track** = Ordnungsgleis *n*

~ **yard**, see: freight-~ ~
classifier = (Naß)Klassierer *m*
~ **for fine separation**, see: spiral scraper thickener
~ **using screw principle** = Schneckenklassierer *m*
classifying, classification = Setzungsklassierung *f* durch Wasser *n* oder Luft *f*
~, sorting = Setzungsklassierung *f* durch flüssige Medien *npl*
~ **drum**, washing ~ = Waschtrommel *f*, Trommelwäsche *f* [*im Gegenstromprinzip n*]
~ **trough** = (Naß)Klassiertrog *m*
clastic eruptive rock = klastisches Eruptivgestein *n*
~ **lime tuff** = klastischer Kalktuff *m*
~ **marl** = Brockenmergel *m*
~ **(sedimentary) rock**, mechanically deposited (sedimentary) rock = klastisches Sediment(gestein) *n*, mechanisches ~, Trümmergestein, Bruchstückgestein, Trümmersediment(gestein)
claw bar, see: dog
~ **collar** = Klauenmuffe *f*
claw-wrench = Nagelklaue *f*
clay [*United States Public Roads Administration and US Bureau of Soils less than 0.005 mm; otherwise in the USA and in Britain less than 0.002 mm*] = (Roh-)Ton *m*
~ **aggregate** = Leichtzuschlag(stoff) *m* aus Ton *m*
~ **auger** = offener Bohrlöffel *m*
~ **(binder)**, see: binder soil
~ **blanket** = Ton(dichtungs)schürze *f*
~ **body** = Tonscherbe *f*, Tonscherben *m*
~ **brick** = Tonziegel(stein) *m*, Ziegelstein
~ **bubble** = Ton-Hohlkügelchen *n*
~ **building unit**, structural ~ ~ ~, masonry ~ = keramischer Bauteil *m*, keramische Baueinheit *f*
clay-cement = Tonbodenverfestigung *f* mit Zement *m*
clay chip(ping)s, see: crushed clay brick
(~ **containing**) **river silt** = Flußschlick *m*
(~ ~) **sea silt** = Klei *m*, Küstenschlick *m*
~ ~ **silt** = Schlick *m*, schlickiger Ton *m*
~ **core**, ~ ~ **wall** = Ton(dichtungs)kern *m*

clay core type embankment (or dam) = Tonkerndamm *m*

~-cutter (suction) dredge(r), see: suction-cutter ~

clay deposit = Tonlager *n*

~ digger, ~ spade, spader, spade hammer = Spatenhammer *m*

~ digging = Tonstechen *n*

~ emulsion = Tonemulsion *f*

~ excavator = Tonbagger *m*

clayey, argillaceous = tonig

clay-grit, lime-marl, sandy marl = Sandmergel *m*

clay ironstone, iron clay = Eisenton *m*, Toneisenstein *m*

~ marl = Tonmergel *m* [*10—40% CaCO₃*]

~ mill, pug ~ = Tonschneider *m* [*Ziegelherstellung f*]

~ mineral, layer silicate = Tonmineral *n*, Schichtsilikat *n*

(~) pick [*pointed at both ends*] = Doppelspitzhacke *f*, Doppelspitzpickel *n*, Zweispitz *m*

~ pipe, vitrified ~ ~ (US); stoneware drain pipe (Brit.) = Tonrohr *n*, Steinzeugrohr *n*

~ pit = Tongrube *f*

~ plant, see: ~ (working)~

~ preparation = Tonaufbereitung *f*

~ product = Tonerzeugnis *n*

(~) pug-mill = Tonschneider *m*

~ rock, argillaceous ~ = Tongestein *n*

~ roof(ing) tile = Tondachziegel(stein) *m*, Tondachstein

clay-shale, see: shale

clay shredder (device) = Tonfräse *f*, Tonschnitzler *m*

clay slate, see: argillaceous ~

~ slope revetment spreader = Tonverteilungsgerät *n*

~ slurry = Tonschlempe *f*, Tonschlämme *f*, Tonschlämpe

~ spade, see: ~ digger

clay-stone, see: mudstone

clay storage bin = Tonsilo *m*

~ working, getting of clay = Tonabbau *m*, Tongewinnung *f*

~ (~) plant, claywork(s) = Tonwerk *n*

to clean, to finish off = abschlichten [*Holz n*]

cleaners' naphtha (or solvent) = Waschbenzin *n* mit Siedegrenzen *fpl* zwischen 100—200° C.

cleaning brush = Reinigungsbürste *f*

~ tool = Reinigungswerkzeug *n*

clean up and move out, see: job clean-up

clear amber = Klarbernstein *m*

clearance, rehabilitation = Sanierung *f* [*Stadt f*]

~ = lichter Raum *m*

~ = Spiel *n* [*Kolben, Ventil, Lager*]

~, see: jaw setting

~ diagram = Lichtraumprofil *n*

~ height = Lichtraumhöhe *f*

~ line = Umgrenzungslinie *f*

~ profile = Umgrenzung *f* des lichten Raumes *m*

clear buttress spacing (US); clear spacing of counterforts, arch span (Brit.) = lichter Strebepfeilerabstand *m*, Spannweite *f* des Bogens *m* [*Talsperre f*]

~ distance = lichter Abstand *m*

~ drilling (time) break = markanter Bohrfortschrittswechsel *m*

clearing (away) = Wegräumen *n*

~ rake, brush ~ = (Unterholz)Roderechen *m*

~ team = Räumungstrupp *m*

~ (work) (or operations), stripping, land clearing = Räumung(sarbeiten) *f*, *(pl)*, Freilegung *f* von Baugelände *n*

clear spacing of counterforts (Brit.); see: ~ buttress spacing (US)

~ span = lichte Weite *f* [*Brücke f*]

~ width = lichte Breite *f*

cleavage (property) [*of rocks and minerals*] = Spaltbarkeit *f*, Spaltfähigkeit *f*

~ plane, ~ crack = Spaltebene *f*, Spaltfläche *f*

~ strength = Spaltfestigkeit *f*

cleaving = Ausspalten *n* [*Pflasterstein m*]

to clench a rivet = einen Niet *m* stauchen

clerestory = Fenstergeschoß *n* [*z. B. von Kirchen fpl*]

clerk (US) = Schreibkraft *f*, Schreiber *m*

clevis, shackle = Gabel *f*

~ pin = Gabelbolzen *m*

client, see: promoter

cliff, see: bold shore

~ bank = Bergufer *n* [*Fluß m*]

cliffed coast (line), see: bold shore
climatic effects, effects of climatic conditions, atmospheric actions = Witterungseinflüsse *mpl*
climbing bog = Klettermoor *n*
~ irons, pole climbers = Klettereisen *n*, Steigeisen *n*
~ lane, see: creeper ~
~ power = Klettervermögen *n*
~ shuttering = Kletterschalung *f*
~ tongue switch = Kletterzungenweiche *f*
~ tower crane = Kletter-Turmdrehkran *m*, Hochhauskletterkran
clinker, see: cement ~
~, furnace ~ (Brit.); (boilerhouse) cinder [*the final residue from the combustion of coke or coal which has been burnt and re-burnt so as to consume the maximum of combustible matter in it*] = Kesselschlacke *f*, Lösch(e) *m*, (*f*)
~, klinker, construction ~ = Bauklinker *m*
~ (brick), klinker (~) = Klinkerstein *m*, Klinker(ziegel) *m*, Hochbauklinker *m* [*früher: Mauerklinker*]
~ concrete, see: asl es ~
~ cooler = Klinkerkühler *m*
~ grit = Klinkergrieß *m*
~ ring = Ansatzring *m*
clinkering = Kesselschlackenbildung *f*
clinker slab = Klinkerplatte *f*
clinkstone (Geol.) = Klingstein *m*
clinoclasite = Strahlenkupfer *n*
clinometer, inclinometer, batter level = Klinometer *n*, Neigungsmesser, Gefällmesser *m*, Böschungswaage *f*
clip = Klammer *f*, Frosch *m*
cloanthite (Min.), see: chloanthite
clockwise = im Uhrzeigersinn
clod crusher = Ringelwalze *f*, Klumpenzertrümmerer *m*
close, see: blind alley
closed abutment = geschlossenes Widerlager *n*
~-circuit operation, ~ grinding = Kreislaufprozeß *m*, Kreislaufmahlen *n* „Umlaufmahlung *f* [*Mühle f*]
closed-cycle turbine = geschlossene Gasturbine *f*
closed drum (concrete) mixer with reverse discharge, (free fall type) non-tilt(ing) (drum) mixer, N.T. mixer = Umkehr-(trommel)(beton)mischer *m*, Freifallmischer *m* mit Umkehraustragung *f*, Mischer mit Reversier-Mischtrommel *f*, Chargen-Betonmischer mit Wendetrommel

~ ~ (~) ~ ~ tipping chute discharge = Austragsmischer *m*, Freifall-Durchlaufmischer, Mischer *m* mit Schurrenaustragung *f*

closed-end pipe foundation (or bearing) pile = Stahlrohr(gründungs)pfahl *m* mit geschlossenem Ende *n*
closed sheeting = Einspundung *f*, Spundwandumschließung *f*
~ spiral (worm) conveyor = Vollförderschnecke *f*
~ standpipe, pore-pressure measuring device of the closed-standpipe type = geschlossenes Standrohr *n*
~ traverse = Ringpolygon *n* [*Vermessungskunde f*]
close-graded aggregate type asphaltic concrete = geschlossen abgestufter Asphaltbeton *m*
~ (mineral) aggregate, see: dense(-graded) (mineral) ~
to close in [*producing well*] = absperren [*Förderbohrung f*]
closely graded sand, see: uniform ~
close-textured [*wearing course*] = geschlossen [*Verschleißschicht f*]
close-up view = Nahansicht *f*
closing brake = Schließbremse *f* [*Bagger m*]
~ date for receipt of tenders = Abgabetermin *m*
~ error, error of closure = Abschlußfehler *m* [*Vermessungskunde f*]
~ handle = Schießgriff *m*
~ power [*clamshell bucket*] = Schließkraft *f* [*Zweischalengreifkorb m*]
~ rope, digging ~, ~ line [*clamshell excavator*] = Schließseil *n*
~ valve, see: shut-off valve
closure arch [*sheetpiling*] = Zwischenbogen *m* [*Spundwand f*]
~ unit, economy brick (US) = Tonhohlblock $3^1/_2 : 3^1/_2 : 7^1/_2$ Zoll
cloth filter dust collector, fabric type ~ ~ = Trockenfilter *n*, *m*, Schlauchfilter

cloth screen — coarse reduction

cloth screen = Gewebesieb n
clothoid, Euler spiral = Klothoide f
*****cloud** = Wolke f
~ bank = Wolkenbank f
~ burst (type storm) = Wolkenbruch m
cloud-heap, piled cloud, cumulus = Haufenwolke f, Kumuluswolke f
cloud point = Trübungspunkt m [*Kälteverhalten n von Dieselkraftstoff m*]
~ seeding = Bestreuen n von Wolken fpl mit Trockeneis n usw. zur Erzeugung künstlichen Niederschlages m
cloud-sheet, stratus = Schichtwolke f, Stratuswolke f
clover-leaf (flyover) junction, ~ interchange = Kleeblattkreuzung f, Renaissance-Kreuzung f
club-foot (type sheepsfoot) roller = (Schaf-)Klumpfußwalze f
cluster city = Bündelstadt f
clutch collar, see: ~ release sleeve
~ (coupling) = Schaltkupplung f, Ein- und Ausrückkupplung f
~ housing = Kupplungsgehäuse n
~ lining = Kupplungsbelag m
~ operating device, clutching device = Kupplungsgestänge n
~ pedal = Kupplungspedal n
~ ~ clearance = Kupplungsspiel n
~ release sleeve, ~ retainer ring, ~ collar = Kupplungsausrückmuffe f
~ throwout socket = Kupplungsausrückbüchse f
CO$_2$-shielded arc welding = CO$_2$-Schutzgasschweißung f
coach screw = große Holzschraube f mit quadratischem Kopf m
coagulant, flocculating agent, precipitant = Koagulator m, Koagulationsmittel n
coagulation, flocculation = Ausflockung f, Koagulation f, Gerinnung [*Übergang von einem Sol in ein Gel*]
~ index = Koagulationsindex m [*Bitumenemulsion f*]
*****coal** = Kohle f
coal-bearing = kohleführend
coal breaker, ~ crusher = Kohlenbrecher m
~ dealer = Kohlenhändler m
~ handling bucket = Kohlengreifer m
~ hatchet = Kohlenbeil n
~ hoist = Kohlenaufzug m
~ hydrogeration process = Druckhydrierung f von Kohle f
coalification = Inkohlungsprozeß m
coaling = Bekohlung f
~ bridge, coal ~ ~ = Kohlenverladebrücke f
~ craft, ~ vessel = Bekohlungsschiff n
coalite tar = Coaliteteer m
coal mine = Kohlenzeche f
~ mining region = Kohlenbergbaugebiet n
~ oil = Teer n durch Destillation f von Kohle f
~ pebbles = Mugelkohle f
~ picker, ~ pick hammer = Kohlenpickhammer m, Abbauhammer m
~ pumping, ~ piping = Kohlenförderung f durch Rohrleitungen fpl
~ scraper = Kohlenschrapper m
~ seam = Kohlenflöz n
~ skip-winding plant = Kohlenskipanlage f
~ storage = Kohlenlagerung f
~ tar, bituminous ~ ~ = Steinkohlenteer m
~ ~ creosote, see: carbolineum
(~ ~) middle oil, carbolic ~ ~ = Mittelöl n
coal-tar pitch = Steinkohlen(teer)pech n
coal tip = Kohlenkipper m
coarse aggregate bituminous concrete (US); see: coarse(-graded) asphalt(ic) concrete
~ concrete = Grobbeton m
~ crushed stone = Grobschotter m
~ crusher, see: breaker
~ crushing = Grobbrechen n, Grobbruch m
~ fit = Grobpassung f, Grobsitz m
~ fraction = Grobanteil m
~ (-graded) asphalt(ic) concrete; coarse aggregate bituminous concrete (US) = Asphaltgrobbeton m
~ grading (work), see: rough ~ (~)
coarse-grained = grobkörnig
~ sandstone, see: gritstone
coarse gravel = Grobkies m
coarse-gripping [*surfacing*] = grobgriffig
coarse gyrasphere crusher = Grobkegelbrecher m mit segmentförmigem Brechkopf m
~ mix, open ~ ~ = offene Mischung f
~ reduction, crushing = Grobzerkleinerung f, Brechen n, Vorzerkleinerung

*coarse sand = Grobsand *m*, Schottersand *m*

~ screen, rack = Grobrechen *m* [*Abwasserwesen n*]

~ screening = Grobsieben *n*, Grobsiebung *f*

~ silt = grobes Schlämmkorn Va [*nach Dücker (1948)*]

~ stone chip(ping)s = Grobsplitt *m*

(coastal) bar, see: sand-head

~ beach, ~ belt, outlying sands = Nehrung *f*

~ city (or town) = Küstenstadt *f*

~ current, see: shore ~

~ dune, ~ down, ~ sand-dune = Stranddüne *f*, Küstendüne

~ engineer = Seebauingenieur *m*

~ engineering, marine construction = Seebau *m*

~ flooding = Küstenüberschwemmung *f*

~ land = Küstenland *n*

~ mountain, see: coastal range

~ plain = Küstenebene *f*

~ protection, coast protection, coast defence work, sea defence, shore protection = Küstenschutz *m*, Küstensicherung *f*, Küstenerhaltung *f*, Küstenverteidigung *f*

(coastal) range, ~ mountain = Küstengebirge *n*

~ region, ~ territory = Küstengebiet *n*

~ shipping = Küstenschiffahrt *f*

coast defence work, see: coastal protection

coaster gate, see: roller-mounted leaf gate (or sluice)

coasting (Brit.); idle run [*running a bicycle, car, engine without power, as in going downhill*] = Leerlauf *m*

coastline, shoreline = Küstenlinie *f*, Meer(es)uferlinie *f*

coast protection, see: coastal ~

coastwise craft = Küstenfahrzeug *n*

*coat (Brit.); see: wearing course

to coat, to wet = benetzen, umhüllen [*mit Bindemittel n*]

coated chip(ping)s; pre-~ ~ [*deprecated*] = umhüllter Splitt *m*

~ electrode, see: covered ~

*coated macadam (Brit.); (pre-)mixed ~ = Mischmakadam *m*

*coated macadam mixing plant (Brit.); see: bituminous macadam and tarmacadam mixing plant

coating [*deprecated*]; see: surfacing

~, wetting; wet mixing (US) = Benetzen *n*, Umhüllen *n* [*mit Bindemittel n*]

~ clay = Ergobeton *m*

~ resin = Anstrichstoff-Kunstharz *n*

coaxial = gleichachsig

cobalt bloom, erythrite (Min.) = Kobaltblüte *f*

~ glance, cobaltite (Min.) = Kobaltglanz *m*, Glanzkobalt *m*, Cobeltin *n*

~ powder = Kobaltpulver *n*

cobble stone paving = Kopfsteinpflaster *n*

~ (s) [300—60 mm] = Schotter *m* [*nach Gallwitz (1939) 200—20 mm*]

cock = Hahn *m*

cocking, see: cogging

cock's comb marcasite (Min.) = Kammkies *m*

cocks-foot, orchard grass = Knaulgras *n*, Knäuelgras *n*

coconut matting = Kokosmatte *f*

code beacon = Code-Leuchtfeuer *n*

~ of practice, notes = Merkblatt *n*

coefficient of consistency = Konsistenzbeiwert *m*

~ ~ discharge (US); see: discharge coefficient (Brit.)

~ ~ expansion = Ausdehnungskoeffizient *m*

~ ~ fatigue = Ermüdungsbeiwert *m*

~ ~ friction, see: frictional coefficient

~ ~ impact, impact factor = Stoßziffer *f*, Stoßzahl *f*

~ ~ permeability, transmission constant, permeability coefficient = Durchlässigkeitsbeiwert *m*

~ ~ rainfall, rainfall coefficient = Niederschlagskoeffizient *m*

~ ~ restitution = Stoßkoeffizient *m* [*Pfahl m*]

~ ~ runoff = Abflußbeiwert *m*, Abflußverhältnis *n*, Abflußkoeffizient *m* [*Verhältniszahl zwischen Abflußhöhe und Niederschlagshöhe*]

~ ~ soil (or subgrade) reaction = Bettungsziffer *f*

coefficient of thermal expansion — cold storage room

coefficient of thermal expansion = Wärme-(aus-)dehn(ungs)zahl *f* [*Beton m*]

~ ~ **uniformity**, see: uniformity coefficient

cofferdam, bulkhead, coffer dam [*the term "cofferdam" is more often applied to temporary dams in open water*] = Fang(e)damm *m*

~ **boil(s)** = Spundwand-Fang(e)dammausbeulung(en) *f*, (*fpl*)

~ **cell** = Fang(e)damm-Spurdwandzelle *f*

~ **skin** = Fang(e)dammwand *f*

cogging, ca(u)lking, cocking, corking = Verkämmung *f*

cog-wheel ore (Min.), see: bournonite

cohesion, cohesiveness = Kohäsion *f*, Bindigkeit *f*, scheinbare Kohäsion

cohesional coefficient = Kohäsionsfaktor *m*, Beiwert *m* der wirksamen Kohäsion *f*

cohesionless, see: non-cohesive

cohesive = kohäsiv, bindig [*Boden m*]

cohesiveness, see: cohesion

cohesive resistance = Kohäsionsfestigkeit *f*

preparation plant = Koksaufbereitungsanlage *f*

~ **water** = Adhäsionswasser *n*

coil = 1.) Spule *f*; 2.) Wicklung *f*

to coil = aufrollen [*Kabel*]

coiled capped fuse = Schwarzpulverzündschnurring *m* mit Initialladung *f*

coiling = Abspulen *n*, Abwickeln *n*

coil spring = Spiralfeder *f*

coir matting = Kokosmattenbelag *m*

coke-oven brown-coal tar = Braunkohlenkokereiteer *m*

~ **coal tar** = Kokereiteer *m*, Zechenteer *m*, Koksofenteer, Steinkohlenkokereiteer

~ **waste** = Kokereiabwasser *n*

coke picked with a fork = Gabelkoks *m*

coking, see: carbonization

~ **plant** = Kokerei *f*

COLAS, COLD ASPHALT [*Trademark*] = eine Bitumenemulsion *f*

COLASTEX [*Trademark*] = Mischung *f* von 10% Latex mit 90% Bitumen *n* und einer Emulsion *f* [COLAS] von 60% Bitumengehalt *m*

colatitude = Breitenkomplement *n*

*COLCRETE, see: cement penetration method

~ **constructed in the sandwich process**, see: sandwich process macadam

~ **mixer**, cement slurry ~, sand-cement grout ~, cement-sand grout ~ = Colcrete-Mischer *m*, Zement-Sand-Schlämme-Mischer

COLD ASPHALT, COLAS [*Trademark*] = eine Bitumenemulsion *f*

cold asphalt; see: asphaltic bitumen road emulsion (Brit.)

~ **asphalt(ic concrete)** = kaltverarbeitbarer Asphaltbeton *m*

~ **binder** = Kaltbindemittel *n*

~ **(bitumen) emulsion** (Brit.), see: asphaltic bitumen road emulsion

~ **chisel** = Hartmeißel *m*, Maurermeißel

~ **desert** = winterkalte Wüste *f*

~ **emulsion** (Brit.), see: asphaltic bitumen road emulsion

~ ~ **sprayer (or spraying machine)** = Kaltasphalt-Spritzapparat *m*

~ **fine asphalt (carpet)** (Brit.), see: Damman cold asphalt

~ -**laid coarse tar concrete** = Kalteinbau-Teergrobbeton *m*

~ -**laid fine asphaltic concrete** = Kalteinbau-Asphaltfeinbeton *m*

~ -**laid fine tar concrete** = Kalteinbau-Teerfeinbeton *m*

~ -**laid process**, cold mix (method) (of construction), cold laying = Kalteinbau(weise) *m*, (*f*) [*Straße f*]

cold laying, see: cold-laid process

*cold mix (asphalt) plant (US); see: bituminous macadam and tarmacadam mixing plant (Brit.)

~ ~ **(method) (of construction)**, see: cold-laid process

~ **plant-mixing** = Kaltmischverfahren *n*

~ **(pressure) welding** = Kalt-Preßschweißung *f*

~ **resisting property** = Kältebeständigkeit *f*

~ **shortness** = Kaltbrüchigkeit *f*

~ **smoke** = Kraftstoffrauch *m*

~ **start(ing)** = Kaltstart *m*

~ **starting equipment** = Kaltstartanlage *f*

~ **storage room**, cooling ~, refrigerator ~ = Kühlraum *m*

cold tar — column moment

cold tar, TC = Kaltteer *m*
~ **water paint cement,** vehicle, paint vehicle = Farbbindemittel *n*
~ **weather concreting** = Betonieren *n* bei Frost *m*
~ ~ **engine primer pump** = Handeinspritzpumpe *f* für Kaltwetterstart *m*
cold worked bar = kaltgereckter Bewehrungsstab *m*
cold-working = Kaltverformung *f*, Kaltverarbeitung, Kaltrecken *n*
COLES lorry-mounted crane [*Trademark*] = COLES-Kranwagen *m*, Fabrikat STEELS ENGINEERING PRODUCTS LTD., CROWN WORKS, SUNDERLAND, ENGLAND
COLGROUT = kolloidaler Mörtel *m*
COLGUNITE = Naßspritzverfahren *n* mit kolloidalem Mörtel und Beton, hergestellt nach dem COLCRETE-Verfahren
coliform organisms = coliforme Bakterien *fpl*
to collapse [*e. g. bridge*] = einstürzen
collapse dolina = Einsturzdoline *f*
~ **theory** = Bruchtheorie *f*
collapsible = zusammenlegbar
~ **tube** = Tube *f*
~ **water-tank** = zusammenlegbarer Wassertank *m*
collar = Manschette *f*, Halsring *m*
~ ~ = Gießring *m* [*Rohrleitung f*]
~ **beam** = Kehlbalken *m*
~ **end bearing** = Bundlager *n*
collar-nut anchorage = Bundmutter-Verankerung *f*
collar screw = Bundschraube *f*
collecting channel = Sammelkanal *m*
~ **drain,** see: interceptor
~ **electrode** = Niederschlagselektrode *f* [*Elektroabscheider m*]
collection gallery = Sammelstollen *m*
~ **hopper** = Sammeltrichter *m*
collier [*vessel designed to carry coal, also used in carrying ore and other bulk commodities*] = Kohlenschiff *n*, Kohlenfrachter *m*
collimator field glass = Kollimationsfernrohr *n*
collinear load, line ~ = Schneidenlast *f*, Streckenlast, Linienlast

collision accident = Zusammenstoß *m* [*Unfall m*]
collodion cotton = Kollodiumwolle *f*
colloid, see: (soil) colloid(al particle)
~ = Kolloid *n*
colloidal chemistry = Kolloidchemie *f*, Kolloidik *f*, Kolloidlehre *f*
~ **concrete,** see: cement penetration method
~ **form** = kolloidale Form *f*
~ **graphite** = kolloidaler Graphit *m*
~ **mill,** colloid ~ = Kolloid(mahl)mühle *f*
~ **state,** = Kolloidalzustand *m*, quellstofflicher Zustand
 disperse phase = disperse Phase *f*
 dispersion medium = geschlossene Phase *f*
collusion amongst bidders (or tenderers) = Preisabsprache *f* unter Bietern *mpl*
colluvial mantle rock = kolluvialer Verwitterungsschutt *m*
~ **soil,** see: transported ~
COLOCRETE [*Trademark*] = ein brit. Farbzement *m*
colophonium = Kolophonium *n*
colorimetric test, see: test for organic matter
colo(u)r distortion = Farbverzerrung *f*
colo(u)red surfacing = farbiger Belag *m*
colo(u)ring = Färben *n*, Ein~
~ **material** = Farbstoff *m*
colour-light signal = Farblichtsignal *n*
Columbian pine, see: Oregon ~
*column = Säule *f*
~ = Stütze *f*
columnar argillaceous red iron-ore (Min.) = Nagelerz *n*
~ **basalt** = Säulenbasalt *m*
~ **coal** = Stangenkohle *f*
~ **structure** = Säulenstruktur *f*, Stengelgefüge *n*
column bars = Säulenlängsbewehrung *f*
column box (or form) = Schalungskasten *m*, Säulenschalung *f*
~ **capital** = Säulenkapital *n*, Säulenkapitell
~ **clamp** = Säulenzwinge *f*
~ **footing** = Säulenfundament *n*
~ **form,** see: ~ box
~ **formula** = Stützenformel *f*
~ **line** = Stützenreihe *f*
~ **moment,** see: moment at support

colza (oil) — common larch 89

colza (oil) = Rüböl n, Rapsöl
combat airfield = Einsatzflugplatz m
combination bevel = Doppelschmiege f
~ burner tool = Brennerbohrer m
~ dump and platform body = Flachboden-Kipppritsche f [LKW m]
~ equipment item = Kombinationsgerät n
~ hot- or cold-mix plant (US); see: dual-purpose machine (Brit.)
~ hydrant and fountain (US); see: hydrant well (Brit.)
~ pliers = Kombi(nations)zange f
~ screw-screed spreader = Schnecken-(beton)verteiler m mit Glättelement n
~ type dam = Staudamm-Staumauer-Kombination f
~ weighing unit for aggregate and cement, concentric aggregate-cement batcher = kombinierte Zuschlagstoff-Zement-Dosierwaage f
combinatorial analysis = Kombinatorik f
combined aggregate = Zuschlagstoffgemenge n
~ ~ and cement weigh batching unit = Zellenturm m mit Abwiegung f
~ air jet and priming unit = (Beton-)Fugenbläser m mit Voranstrichvorrichtung f
~ axial and radial flow pump = kombinierte Axial- und Radialpumpe f
~ flow turbine, mixed ~ ~ = vereinigte Axial- und Radialturbine f
~ footing = Verbundfundament n
***combined mixing and paving machine**, see: travel(l)ing (concrete) mixer (plant)
~ plasticizer and air-entraining agent = luftporenbildender Betonverflüssiger m, LBV-Stoff m
~ (storm and sanitary) sewer, ~ drain, ~ water sewer = Sammler m für die Mischentwässerung f, Mischwasserkanal m
~ suction and force pump, reciprocating ~ = Saug- und Druckpumpe f
~ ~ ~ pressure conveying system, suction-jet ~ ~ = kombinierte Saugluft-Druckluft-Förderanlage f, kombinierter pneumatischer Förderer m
~ system = Mischkanalisation f, Mischsystem n, Mischentwässerung f

combining to eliminate competition, price fixing = Absprache f unter Bietern mpl
combustion = Verbrennung f
~ chamber = Verbrennungskammer f, Verbrennungsraum m
commencing salary = Anfangsgehalt n
(commercial) airport = Verkehrsflughafen m
~ coating plant = Lieferwerk n für bituminöse Straßenbelagsmassen fpl
~ explosive = gewerblicher Sprengstoff m
~ grade, ~ quality = Handelsgüte f
~ harbo(u)r, ~ (trading) port = Handelshafen m
~ iron, merchant ~ = Handelseisen n
~ material = zusätzlich herangebrachter Boden m zur Verbesserung f des Kornaufbaues m bei der Bodenverfestigung f
~ quality, ~ grade = Handelsgüte f
~ ready-mix plant, ~ concrete ~ = Betonlieferwerk n
~ sewage, trade waste, trade sewage = gewerbliches Abwasser n
~ steamer = Handelsdampfer m
~ transport = Gütertransport m
~ vehicle = Nutzfahrzeug n
~ wood = Handelsholz n
***comminution, crushing and grinding** = Hartzerkleinerung f
comminutor = Schlitztrommel f [Abwasserwesen n]
committee on standardization, standards committee = Normenausschuß m
commodity = Gut n
common alder, see: black ~
~ alum, potash ~ = Kalialaun m
~ ash = gemeine Esche f
~ beech = Rotbuche f, gemeine Buche f
~ birch = Weißbirke f, Maie f
~ brick, see: backing ~
~ elm, small-leaved ~ = Feldulme f, Feldrüster f, Feldeffe f
~ English oak = Stieleiche f, Sommereiche f
(~) excavation, see: digging
~ fel(d)spar, see: orthoclase (Min.)
~ labo(u)rer hour = Handlangerstunde f
~ larch = gemeine Lerche f

common lime, see: anhydrous ~
~ **maple**, small-leaved ~ = Feldahorn m, Maßholder f, Maßeller f, kleiner Ahorn m
~ **pine**, white ~, Scottish ~ = gemeine Kiefer f, Föhre f, Fuhre f, Kiene f, Weißkiefer f
~ **rafter**, principal ~ = Bindersparren m
(~) **reed** = Teichrohr n, Schilfrohr n
~ **rye grass** = deutsches Weidelgras n
~ **salt** (Min.), see: halite
~ **spruce**, Norway ~ = gemeine Fichte f, Rottanne f
communication of motion = Bewegungsfortpflanzung f
community planning = Stadtplanung f
commutator bar = Kollektorstreifen m
~ **motor** = Kollektormotor m
commuter = ständiger Benutzer m, Pendler m
compact apparatus, see: compactor
compacted soil-cement = verdichteter Bodenzementbeton m
compacted thickness = verdichtete Dicke f
compactibility = Verdichtungswilligkeit f
compacting = Zusammenfassen n [der einzelnen Bündel zu einem Drahtkabel]
~ **beam** = Verdichtungsbohle f
~ **energy** = Verdichtungsenergie f
~ **pass** = Verdichtungs(über)gang m
~ **pile** = Verdrängungspfahl m, Verdichtungspfahl
compaction, densification, soil ~, earth ~, artificial consolidation = künstliche Bodenverdichtung f
(~ **by**) **rolling**, roller compaction = Walzkompression f, Walzverdichtung f, Abwalzen, Druckverdichtung
~ ~ **vibration**, see: vibrating compaction
~ **equipment**, compression equipment, ~ plant = Verdichtungsmaschinen fpl und -geräte npl
~ **factor test** = Verdichtungsfaktor-Prüfung f [Beton m]
~ **of cohesionless foundation soil by explosives** = Verdichtung f kohäsionslosen Bodens m mittels Sprengung f
~ **plane near the surface** [soil-cement] = vorverdichtete Stelle f
~ **pressure**, see: rock ~

~ **roller**, compactor = Verdichtungswalze f Bodenverfestigungswalze f
~ **test** = Verdichtungsprüfung f
~ **theory** = Verdichtungstheorie f
compact limestone, mountain ~ = dichter Kalkstein m
compactness = Lagerungsdichte f
compactor, see: compaction roller
~ = Verdichter m [Boden m, Beton m]
~, compact apparatus = Verdichtungsgerät n [Bodenprüfung f]
compact polishable limestone = technischer Marmor m, Marmorkalkstein m, dichter polierbarer Kalkstein m
~ **rock** = kompaktes Gestein n, dichtes ~
companion fault see: auxiliary ~
comparability = Vergleichsmöglichkeit f
comparative study, comparison ~ = vergleichende Untersuchung f, Vergleichsstudie f
~ **test**, comparison ~ = Vergleichsversuch m
~ **value**, comparison ~ = Vergleichswert m
compartment = Abteilung f, Tasche f [Dosierapparat m]
compartmented bin = Wabensilo m
compartment silo, multi-compartment ~ = Zellensilo m, Zellenspeicher m
compass saw, fret ~ = Laubsäge f
compasses, pair of ~ = Zirkel m
compensating reservoir, see: balancing ~
compensation water = garantiertes Brauchwasser n, Anliegerrechtwasser
compensator spring, equalizer ~ = Spannfeder f, Ausgleichfeder [Gleiskette f]
competitive position = Wettbewerbsfähigkeit f
~ **tender** = Gegenangebot n
~ **tender(ing) action**, bidding procedure; adjudication (US) = Ausschreibung f, Angebotseinholung f
complementary influence line = ergänzte Einflußlinie f
~ **soil** = Zusatzboden m
completion bond, performance ~ = Ausführungsgarantie f
~ **date**, target ~ = Fertigstellungstermin m
~ **on schedule**, ~ in time = fristgemäße Fertigstellung f

completion time, ~ period, construction ~ = Baufrist *f*, Bauzeit *f*
complicated array of levers = Vielhebelei *f*
composite beam = Verbundträger *m*
~ **breakwater** = massiver Wellenbrecher *m* mit Unterbau *m* aus Steinschüttung *f*
~ **(concrete and timber) (foundation, or bearing) pile,** wood composite (foundation, or bearing) pile = Verbund(gründungs)pfahl *m*, Verbundtragpfahl
~ **lattice beam** = Verbundfachwerkträger *m*
~ **member** = Verbundkörper *m*
~ **(method of) construction** = Verbundbauweise *f*
~ **prestressed concrete beam;** ~ ~ ~ girder (Brit.) = zusammengesetzter Spannbetonbalken(träger) *m*, ~ Spannbetonträger(balken) *m*
~ **truss frame** = Hängesprengwerk *n*
composition of batch = Chargenzusammensetzung *f*
~ ~ **forces** = Kräftezusammensetzung *f* [*Statik f*]
composting = Kompostieren *n*
compound = Mischung *f*
~ **beam,** see flitch(ed) ~
~ **curve** = Korbbogen *m*
~ **dredge(r)** = Naßbagger *m* mit zwei oder mehreren Typen von Baggeraggregaten *npl*
compounded oil = Mineral-Fettöl-Gemisch *n*
compound-funnel classifier = Drei-Trichter-(Naß)Klassierer *m*, Fabrikat THE DEISTER MACHINE CO., FORT WAYNE 1, IND., USA
compound girder (Brit.); see flitch(ed) beam
~ **heater,** see: heating tank for melting joint sealing compounds
compound-melting furnace, see: heating tank for melting joint sealing compounds
compound prestressed reinforced concrete structure = vorgespannte Verbund-Stahlbetonkonstruktion *f*
~ **steam pump** = Verbunddampfpumpe *f*
~ **steel beam structure** = Stahlträger-Verbundkonstruktion *f*

~ **toggle lever stone breaker** (Brit.), see: double toggle crusher
~ **turbine** = Verbundturbine *f*
~ **-wound motor** = Motor *m* mit Doppelschlußwicklung *f*
compressed air = Druckluft *f*, Preßluft *f*
(~) ~ **control,** pneumatic ~ = Druckluftsteuerung *f*, Preßluftsteuerung, Druckluftschaltung, Preßluftschaltung
~ ~ **gun** = Druckluftpistole *f*, Preßluftpistole
~ ~ **illness,** see: caisson disease
~ ~ **line** = Druckluftleitung *f*, Preßluftleitung
~ ~ **lock,** see: air lock
~ ~ **loco(motive)** = Druckluftlok(omotive) *f*, Preßluftlok(omotive)
~ ~ **motor** = Druckluftmotor *m*, Preßluftmotor
(~) ~ **(pile) driver** = Druckluftramme *f*, Preßluftramme *f*
(compressed-)air (pile) hammer = Preßlufthammer *m*, Druckluſthammer
compressed-air pump, see: air lift ~
~ **riveter,** see: air riveting hammer
~ **sickness,** see: caisson disease
(compressed) air tool, see: pneumatic ~
(compressed) air vessel, air receiver = Druckluftbehälter *m*, Druckluftkessel *m*, Windkessel
~ ~ **whistle** = Druckluftpfeife *f*, Preßluftpfeife
~ **asphalt** = Stampfasphalt *m* [*gegebenenfalls mit Bitumen angereichert*]
~ **member** = gedrückter Bauteil *m*
~ **(natural) rock asphalt (surfacing);** [*deprecated: powder asphalt, rock asphalt, stamped asphalt*] = Stampfasphalt *m* ohne Bitumenzusatz *m*
compressibility = Zusammendrückbarkeit *f*, Verdichtungsfähigkeit
~ **coefficient** = Wert *m* der Zusammendrückbarkeit *f*
compressible = zusammendrückbar
compression = Verdichtung *f* [*Dieselmotor m*]
compressional folding (Geol.) = Druckfaltung *f*
compression and tension = Druck *m* und Zug *m*

compression chord, ~ boom, ~ flange = Druckgurt m [*Fachwerk n*]
~ column = Druckstütze f
~ diagonal, diagonal strut, diagonal in compression = Druckdiagonale f [*Fachwerk n*]
~ equipment, see: compaction ~
~ fibre (Brit.); ~ fiber (US) = Druckfaser f [*Träger m*]
~ flange, see: ~ chord
~ machine, ~ tester; testing machine for concrete cylinders (US) = Betonpresse f, Druckpresse, (Beton)Prüfpresse
~ member = Druckstab m, Druckglied n [*Fachwerk n*]
~ plant = Kompressoranlage f
~ ratio = Verdichtungsverhältnis n, Kompression f [*Dieselmotor m*]
~ roll, drive ~ [*the drive wheel of a steel wheel roller*] = Antriebs-Walzrad n
~ spring = Anpreßfeder f, Pufferfeder [*Walzenbrecher m*]
~ stroke = Kompressionshub m
~ test with confined lateral expansion = Zusammendrückversuch m mit beschränkter Seitenausdehnung f
compressive force = Druckkraft f
~ reinforcement = Druckbewehrung f, Druckarmierung f
~ strength, crushing ~ = Druckfestigkeit f
~ stress = Druckspannung f
~ ~ due to bending = Biege-Druckspannung f
~ yield point = Quetschgrenze f
~ zone = Druckzone f
COMPRESSOL system [*Trademark*] = KOMPRESSOL-Verfahren n
compressor, air ~ = Kompressor m, Luftverdichter m, Drucklufterzeuger m
~ bracket = Konsole f zur Befestigung des Luftpressers am Motor
~ crankcase = Luftpresser-Kurbelgehäuse n
~ cylinder = Verdichterzylinder m, Kompressorzylinder
~ valve = Verdichterventil n
~-less injection diesel (engine) = kompressorloser Dieselmotor m
compulsory stop = Zwangshalt m

concave bank = einbuchtendes Ufer n, Konkave f eines Flusses m
~ transition between gradients, sag curve = Wannenausrundung f
concealed bed of peat, peat pocket = Torfeinschluß m, Torfnest n
~ (concrete) joint, dummy (~) ~, contraction ~, shrinkage ~ = Schein-(beton)fuge f
~ heating, panel ~, radiant ~ = Strahlungsheizung f
concentrate = Konzentrat n
concentrated load, point ~ = Einzellast f, Punktlast
concentric aggregate-cement batcher, see: combination weighing unit for aggregate and cement
conchoidal, shell-like = musch(e)lig
~ fracture = musch(e)liger Bruch m
concordant coast = Abschließungsküste f
*****concrete,** cement ~ = (Zement)Beton m
~ accessories = Betonzubehör m, n
~ admix (US); see: additive for concrete
~ aerated with foam, foam(ed) concrete = Schaumbeton m [*Poren fpl mit Luft f gefüllt*]
*****(concrete) aggregates,** (cement) (~) ~ = (Beton) Zuschlagstoffe mpl, (Beton) Zuschläge mpl
(~) ~ screening plant = Siebanlage f für (Beton)Zuschlagstoffe mpl
(~) air entrainment meter, see: air (entrainment) meter
~ apron = Betonschürze f
~ arch(ed) dam = Bogensperrmauer f, Bogen(stau)mauer, Bogensperre f, Gewölbe(stau)mauer, Einfach-Gewölbesperre f
~ arch gravity dam = Beton-Bogengewichts(stau)mauer f
~ ~ rib = Betonbogenrippe f
~ ashlar, see:. cast stone
~ bagging, ~ filled in bags = Beton m in Säcken mpl als Flußuferschutz m
~ ballast (Brit.) [*containing nothing larger than 1 1/2 inch*] = Betonzuschlag(stoff) m nicht größer als 37 mm
~ batcher scale = Betonmischwaage f, Betondosierwaage f
~ bay, see: bay

concrete bay subgrader (Brit.); (subgrade) planer, subgrading machine (US); power finegrader, (precision) subgrader, mechanical finegrader, form grader = (Erd-)Planumfertiger *m*
~ **beam testing machine** = Balkenbiege-Prüfmaschine *f*
~ **belt type placing tower** = Betonierbandturm *m*
~ **block** = Betonklotz *m*
~ ~ = Betonblock *m*
~ ~, precast ~ ~ = Betonstein *m*
~ ~ **groyne** (Brit.); ~ ~ **groin** (US) = Betonblockbuhne *f*
~ ~ **industry**, precast products ~ ~ = Betonsteinindustrie *f*
(~) **block (-making) machine,** (~) block-forming ~, (~) building block ~ = Betonblockmaschine *f*, Beton(form-)steinmaschine *f*
(~) **block plant,** blockyard, concrete brick plant = Beton(form)steinwerk *n*, Betonsteinbetrieb *m*
~ ~ **press,** ~ **brick** ~ = Betonsteinpresse *f*
~ ~ **shaking and tamping machine** = Betonstein-Rüttelstampfmaschine *f*
(~) ~ **testing machine** = Beton(form-)steinprüfpresse *f*
~ **bonding plaster** = Putzgipsmörtel *m* mit guter Haftung *f*, Putzgips *m* für glatte Betonflächen *fpl*
~ **box** = Betonkasten *m*
~ ~ **(drainage) culvert** = Kastendurchlaß *m* (oder Kastenabzugkanal *m*) aus Beton *m*
~ **breaker** = 1. Betonaufbruchhammer *m*; 2. Betonbrecher *m*
~ ~ **point,** ~ ~ **steel** = Betonaufbruchstahl *m*
~ **breaking machine** = Betonaufbruchmaschine *f*
~ **brick plant,** see: (concrete) block ~
~ ~ **press,** ~ **block** ~ = Betonsteinpresse *f*
~ **bucket,** ~ **placing skip** = Beton(schütt)kübel *m*, Kabelkrankübel *m*
~ **buggy,** (hand) concrete cart, rockerdump hand cart = Betonrundkipper *m*, Japaner(karren) *m*, Japaner-Kipp(er)karre(n) *f*, (*m*), Kipp-Betonkarre(n)

(~) **building block machine,** see: (~) block(-making) machine
~ **cart,** see: ~ buggy
~ **cast in position,** ~ ~ ~ situ, poured-in-place concrete, cast-in-place concrete = Ortbeton *m*
~ **catch gutter,** see: ~ dish
(~) **central-mix-plant,** see: concrete mixing plant
~ **channel** = Betonrinnstein *m*
~ **chute** = (Beton)Gießrinne *f*
~ **chuting (or placing) mast,** see: gin pole type concrete spouting plant
~ ~ (~) **tower,** cage type concrete spouting plant, elevator tower = (Beton)Gießturm *m*
~ **circular tank** = Betonrundbehälter *m*
~ **cofferdam** = Betonfang(e)damm *m*
~ **compacted by jolting** = Schockbeton *m*, Stoßbeton
~ **compaction** = Betonverdichtung *f*
~ **compactor** = Betonverdichtungsgerät *n*
~ **composition** = Betonzusammensetzung *f*
~ **compressive strength,** ~ **crushing** ~ = Betondruckfestigkeit *f*
~ **construction(al work)** = Betonbau *m*
~ **core wall** = Betonkern *m*, massive Kernmauer *f*
~ ~ **wall type embankment (or dam)** = Kernmauerdamm *m*, Betonkerndamm
~ **coring machine,** see: core (cutting) ~
~ **culvert pipe** = Betondurchlaßrohr *n*, Beton-Abzugkanalrohr
~ **curb(stone)** (US & Brit.)/**kerb(stone)** (or **kirb(stone)**) (Brit.) **building machine** = Betonbordsteingerät *n*
~ **curing mat** = Betonabdeckmatte *f*
~ ~ **membrane,** emulsion coating, curing seal = Emulsionsanstrich *m*, Dichtungshaut *f*
~ ~ **solution** = Lösung *f* für Betonnachbehandlung *f*
~ **cutter,** see: joint ~
~ **cylinder** = Brunnenring *m*, Beton ~
~ **decking** = Betonfahrbahnplatte *f* [*Brücke f*]
~ **delivery** = Betonanlieferung *f*
~ **discharge pipe** = Betonförderleitung *f*

concrete dish, ~ catch-gutter, ~ surface channel = Betonablauf(ge)rinne f, (n)
~ **distribution service gantry with chutes** (Brit.); ~ ~ trestle ~ ~ (US) = Betonierbrücke f mit Gießrinnen fpl
* **concrete distributor,** see: ~ spreader
~ **droppings** = Betonbrücke f [*Betonfuge f*[
~**-elevating plant (or gear),** concrete hoist, concrete elevator = Betonhebeanlage f, Betonhebewerk n, Betonaufzug m
concrete emulsion = Betonemulsion f
concrete-encased steel construction = einbetonierte Stahlkonstruktion f
concrete envelope, ~ haunching = Betonummantelung f, Betonhinterfüllung f
~ **fabrication** = Beton(auf)bereitung f
~ **facing slab** = Betonfassadenplatte f, Betonwerksteinplatte
~ **filled in bags,** see: ~ bagging
~ **filling** = Betonfüllung f
~ **finisher,** ~ finishing machine, ~ pavement ~ ~ = Beton(fahrbahn)fertiger m, Betondeckenfertiger m
~ **finishing road vibrator,** vibratory concrete compacting and finishing machine, road vibrating and finishing machine, power-propelled surface vibrating and finishing machine, vibratory finishing machine for concrete pavements = Rüttel(bohlen)fertiger m, schienengeführter Oberflächenrüttler m [*mit Glättelement n*]
~ **finishing tent** = Arbeitsschutzdach n, Arbeitszelt n
~ **flagged footpath** = Bürgersteig m aus Betonplatten fpl
~ **floor** = Betondecke f
~ **foreman** = Betonpolier m
~ **forming,** see: formwork
~ **form support,** horizontal ~ ~ = Schalungsträger m
(~) ~ **vibration** = Schalungsrüttlung f, Schalungsvibration f
(~) ~ **vibrator** = Schalungsrüttler m, Schalungsvibrator m
~ **frame construction with concrete block curtain walls** = Stahlbetonskelettbau m mit Betonblockausmau(e)rung f
~ **gate sill** = Betonverschlußschwelle f

~ **girder bridge** = Betonbalkenbrücke f
~ **gravity dam** = Beton-Gewichts(stau)mauer f
~ **grinder** = Betonschleifmaschine f
~ **grouter,** ~ pressure grouting machine = Betoneinpreßmaschine f
~ **gun,** see: cement gun
~ **handling equipment** = Betonierzubehör m
~ ~ **machine,** see: ~ placing ~
~ **hardcore,** see: (aggregate of) broken concrete
~ **hardener,** ~ hardening agent, integral floor hardener, surface hardener = (Beton)Härtungsmittel n, Betonhärtemittel n, Betonhartstoff m
~ **hauling unit,** ~ hauler = Betontransportfahrzeug n
~ **haunching,** see: ~ envelope
~ **hoist,** see: concrete-elevating plant (or gear)
~ **hollow brick,** see: hollow (clay) building (or masonry) block
to concrete in = einbetonieren
concrete ingredient = Betonbestandteil m, Betonkomponente f
concrete-in-mass, bulk concrete, mass concrete = Massenbeton m
(concrete) joint cutter, see: joint cutter
(~) ~ **sealing machine** = Fugenfüllgerät n
(~) ~ **vibrator,** vibrating knife joint cutter = (Beton)Fugenschneidgerät n mit Vibriermesser n
(~) ~ **with premo(u)lded filler** = Betonfuge f mit fester Einlage f
~ **joist machine,** precast ~ ~ ~, lintel ~ = Balkenformmaschine f, Hohlbalkenmaschine
~ ~ **shaker,** precast ~ ~ ~ (or shaking machine) = Balkenrüttler m, Balkenvibrator m
~ **kerb(stone) (building) machine** (Brit.); see: ~ curb(stone) ~ ~
~ **lab(oratory)** = Betonlabor(atorium) n
~ **lane,** ~ strip = Betonstreifen m
~ **lining** = Betonmantel m [*Tunnel m*]; Betonauskleidung f [*Bewässerungskanal m*]
~ **machinery** = Betonbaumaschinen fpl
~ **masonry** = Betonmauerwerk n

concrete masonry unit = Betonwerk-Bauelement *n*, Betonfertigbauteil *m*

~ **mass vibrator,** pervibrator, internal vibrator, immersion vibrator, (concrete) poker vibrator, needle vibrator, concrete vibrator for mass work = Innenrüttler *m*, Tauchrüttler, Tiefenrüttler, Innenvibrator *m*, Tauchvibrator

~ **mattress** = Betondeckmatte *f*

~ **mix electric testing apparatus,** ratiometer = Gerät *n* zur Bestimmung *f* des W/Z-Faktors *m*

* **concrete mixer,** ~ mixing machine = Betonmischer *m*, Betonmischmaschine *f*

~ **mixer-paver,** see: travel(l)ing (concrete) mixer (plant)

~ **mixer fitted with mechanical skip loader attachment,** scraper-fed concrete mixer = Betonmischer *m* mit Handschrapperbeschickung *f* des Aufzugkübels *m*

~ **mixing plant,** concrete central-mixplant, central batching and mixing station, central weigh batching and mixing plant, wet and dry batch concrete plant = Betonfabrik *f*, Großbetonanlage *f*,

~ ~ ~ **with belt conveying** = Betonfabrik als Reihenanlage *f*

~ ~ **site** = Betonmischplatz *m*

~ ~ **tower** = Turmbetonzentrale *f*, Betonmischturm *m*, Betonturmmischanlage *f*, Betonfabrik als Turmanlage

~ **mix(ture)** = Betonmischung *f*
buttery ~ ~ = weich angemachte ~

~ **mo(u)ld oil** = Betonformöl *n*

~ **narrow-gage railcar** (US); ~ tip wagon (Brit.) = Beton(rund)kipper *m*, Betonschüsselwagen *m* [*als Schienenfahrzeug n*]

~ **ogee spillway** = s-förmiger Betonüberlauf *m*

* **concrete pavement,** cement ~ ~ = Betondecke *f*, Betonbelag *m*, Zement ~

~ ~ **shattering machine** = Beton-Zertrümmerungsmaschine *f*

~ **(pavement) slab,** see: bay

* **concrete pavement spreader,** see: ~ spreader

(~) **paver,** see: travel(l)ing (concrete) mixer (plant)

~ **paving equipment** (US) = Betondeckengeräte *npl*

~ (~) **sett** = Betonpflasterstein *m*

~ **pier,** see: caisson pile

~ **pile making plant** = Betonpfahlwerk *n*

~ **pipe compression tester** = Betonrohrprüfpresse *f*

~ ~ **(drainage) culvert** = Betonrohrdurchlaß *m*, Betonrohrabzugkanal *m*

~ ~ **making machine** = (Beton)Rohrfertigungsmaschine *f*

(~) ~ **mo(u)ld (or form)** = Betonrohrform, Zementrohrform *f*

~ ~ **press** = Betonrohrpresse *f*, Presse *f* für Betonrohrherstellung *f*

~ ~ ~ **head** = Preßkopf *m* [*Betonrohrpresse f*]

~ ~ **tamping machine** = (Beton)Rohrstampfmaschine *f*, Zementrohrstampfmaschine

~ ~ **vibrating machine** = Betonrohr-Vibrator *m*, Betonrohr-Vibriermaschine *f*, Vibriermaschine *f* für Betonrohre *npl*, Vibrationsrohrmaschine, Betonrohrvibrationsmaschine

~ **placement,** ~ placing = 1) Betonförderung *f*; 2) Betoneinbau *m*

~ ~ **funnel** = Betontrichter *m*

~ **placing machine,** ~ placer, ~ handling machine = Betonförderapparat *m*

~ ~ **(or chuting) mast,** see: gin pole type concrete spouting plant

~ ~ **(or pouring, or placement) platform** = Betonierbühne *f*

~ ~ **skip,** see: ~ bucket

~ ~ **tube** = Beton-Gießrohr *n*, Betonhosenrohr *n*

~ **plank** = Betonbohle *f*

~ **plug** = Betonpfropfen *m*, Betonplombe *f*

(~) **poker vibrator,** see: ~ mass ~

~ **pour,** placement (or pouring, or placing) of concrete = Betoneinbringung *f*, Betoneinbau *m*

~ **pressure grouting machine,** see: ~ grouter

~ ~ **pipe** = Betondruckrohr *n*

~ **primer** = Beton-Fibel *f*

~ **products,** precast wares = Betonware *f*

concrete products manufacturing, ~ ~ manufacture = Betonwarenherstellung *f*, Betonwarenfertigung *f*
~ ~ **mo(u)ld** = Zementwarenform *f*, Betonwarenform
~ **plant,** ~ **works** = Betonwerk *n*
~ **proportion** = Betonmischungsverhältnis *n*
~ **protection tent,** curing ~ = Sonnen(schutz)dach *n*, Schutzdach
~ **pump,** pumpcrete machine = Betonpumpe *f*
~ **raft** = großflächiges Betonfundament *n*
(~) **reinforcement,** see: reinforcement
~ **reinforcing bar,** see: reinforcing bar
~ **reintegration** = Betonausbesserung *f*
~ **resurfacing** = Betondeckenüberzug *m*
~ **road,** ~ **highway** = Betonstraße *f*
~ ~ **breaker** = Betonaufbruchhammer *m*
* **concrete road construction;** ~ ~paving (US) = Betonstraßenbau *m*
~ ~ **finisher (or finishing machine)** = Betonstraßen(bohlen)fertiger *m*, Brückenfertiger
(~) ~ **form,** see: side form
~ ~ **slab,** see: bay
~ ~ **vibrator,** vibratory concrete compacting machine, concrete vibrating and finishing machine = Rüttel(bohlen)fertiger *m*, Vibrations(bohlen)fertiger
~ **roof** = Betondach *n*
~ **roofing tile,** cement roof tile = Betondachstein *m*
~ **roof slab** = Betondachplatte *f*
~ **saw** (US); joint cutter = Betonsäge *f* [*in den USA auch auf „Fugenschleifgerät" n angewandt*]
~ **sawing blade** = Betonsägeblatt *n*, Betonschneidscheibe *f*
(~) **screw spreader** = (Beton-)Schneckenverteiler *m*
~ **sewer** = Betonabwasserkanal *m*
~ ~ **cast in place** = Abwasserkanal *m* aus Ortbeton *m*
~ ~ **pipe** = Betonabwasserrohr *n*
~ **shell** = Betonschale *f*
~ ~ **roof** = Betonschalendach *n*
~ **sidewalk slab**(US); ~footpath~ (Brit.) = Beton-Bürgersteigplatte *f*

~ **silt basin** = Beton-Verlandebecken *n* [*Talsperre f*]
~ **skip** = Betonkübel *m*
~ **slab,** see: bay
~ ~, see: road bay
~ ~ **raising equipment** = Betondeckenhebegeräte *npl*
~ **split duct** = Beton(rohr)schale *f*
~ **spouting equipment** = Gußbetoneinrichtungen *fpl*
~ ~ **plant** = (Beton)Gießrinnenanlage *f*
* **concrete spreader,** ~ spreading machine, ~ pavement spreader, ~ distributor = Beton(decken)verteiler *m*, Betonstraßenverteiler *m*
~ ~ **with side form vibrators** = Beton(decken)verteiler *m* mit Rand-Tauchvibratoren *mpl*
concrete-steel bond = Haftung *f* zwischen Bewehrung *f* und Beton *m*
concrete strength = Betonfestigkeit *f*
~ **stress** = Betonspannung *f*
~ **strip,** ~ **lane** = Betonstreifen *m*
~ **subgrade paper,** see: concreting ~
~ **surface channel,** see: ~ dish
~ **table** = Betontabelle *f*
~ **tamper,** = Betonstampfer *m*
~ **tamping and screed board vibrator,** see: vibrating tamper
~ **technologist** = Betontechnologe *m*
~ **test** = Betonversuch *m*, Betonprobe *f*, Betonprüfung *f*
* **concrete test cube** = Beton(probe)würfel *m*
~ ~ **hammer** = Betonprüfhammer *m*
~ **texture** = Betongefüge *n*
~ **tile** = Betonplatte *f*
~ ~ **press** = Betonplattenpresse *f*
~ ~ **tamping machine** = Betonplatten-Stampfmaschine *f*, Stampfmaschine *f* für Betonplattenherstellung *f*
~ **tipping skip,** (~) ~ **hopper,** tip-over (concrete) bucket = (Beton)Kippkübel *m* [*Bauaufzug m*]
~ **tip wagon** (Brit.); ~ **narrow-gage railcar** (US) = Beton(rund)kipper *m*, Betonschüsselwagen *m* [*als Schienenfahrzeug n*]
~ **vibrating and finishing machine,** see: vibratory concrete compacting machine

* **concrete vibrating equipment, ~ ~ plant** = Beton(ein)rüttelgeräte *npl*, Betonvibratoren *mpl*, Betonrüttler *mpl*
~ vibration = Beton(ein)rüttelung *f*
~ vibrator = Betonvibrator *m*, Betonrüttler *m*
~ ~ and finisher with rotating (or rotary) grading screed, revolving paddle finisher = Betonbahn-Automat *m*, Fabrikat ALLGEMEINE BAUMASCHINEN-GESELLSCHAFT, HAMELN/WESER, DEUTSCHLAND rotating (or rotary) grading screed = Palettenwalze *f*, Fräserwalze, schaufelbesetzte Abgleichwalze
~ ~ for mass work, see: concrete mass vibrator
~ wall panel = Fertigbetonwandplatte *f*
~ ~ shell = Betonwandschale *f*
~ waterproofing compound, waterproofer, water-repellent, water-repelling agent, densifier, damp-proofing and permeability reducing agent, densifying agent = (Beton-)Dichtungsmittel *n*, Sperrzusatz *m*, wasserabweisendes Mittel *n*
~ with artificial resin admixture = Kunstharzbeton *m*
~ ~ high early stability = frühstandfester Beton *m*
~ ~ ~ ~ strength = frühtragfester Beton *m*
~ ~ large aggregate = Großkornbeton *m*
~ works, ~ products plant = Betonwerk *n*
~ work = Betonarbeiten *fpl*
concreting = Betonieren *n*, Betonier(ungs)arbeiten *fpl*
~ gang (or team, or party, or crew) = Betonierkolonne *f*
~ paper, underlay **~**, concrete subgrade **~**, road lining, sub-soil paper = Unterlagspapier *n*, Papierunterlage *f*, Straßenbaupapier *n*
~ plant = Betonieranlage *f*
~ section = Betonierabschnitt *m*
~ train; paving **~** (US) = Betonierzug *m*
concretion = Zusammenwachsung *f*
concretionary horizon (Geol.) = verfestigte Schicht *f*

concretion of anhydrite, anhydritic concretion = Anhydritknolle *f*
~ ~ lime = Kalkniere *f*, Kalkschwüle *f*
concretor = Betonbauer *m*
condensate = Kondensat *n*
~ pump = Kondensatpumpe *f*
condensation (or dripping) water (or moisture) = Schwitzwasser *n*, Kondenswasser, Tauwasser
~ water tunnel, condensing **~ ~** = Kühlwasserstollen *m*
condense return line = Kondensatrücklaufleitung *f*
condenser discharge (type) blasting machine, CD **~ ~** = Kondensatorzündmaschine *f*, Kondensationszündmaschine
condensing loco(motive) = Kondens-Lok(omotive) *f*
~ water tunnel, see: condensation **~ ~**
condition = Beschaffenheit *f*, Zustand *m*
~ of support = Auflagerbedingung *f*
conditioning, seasoning [*sewage sludge*] = chemische Schlammbehandlung *f*
conductive tile = elektrisch leitende (Fuß-)Bodenfliese *f*
conduit [*a culvert, drain, sewer, water pipe, gas main, tunnel or duct of most any kind, usually continuous underground*] = Leitung *f*
~ = Elektrorohr *n*
~ tile (US); (multiple way) cable duct (or conduit, or subway), multitubular slab for cable = Kabelformstück *n*, Kabelformstein *m*
cone = Konus *m*, Kegel *m*
~ anchor = Keilanker *m*, Konusanker
~ assy = konisches Lager *n*
~ bearing (capacity) apparatus = Kegeltragfähigkeitsmesser *m*
~ bit = Kegelmeißel *m*, Konusmeißel
~ deformation study = Kegelschmelzpunktbestimmung *f*
cone-in-cone limestone, stylolitic **~** = Nagelkalk *m*
~ structure = Stylolithstruktur *f*
cone of depression = Trichter *m* wenn Grundwasser *n* abgesaugt wird

cone penetration test = Kegeleindringversuch *m*

~ **penetrometer**, see: conical ~

~ **point** = Kegelspitze *f*

~**-shaped earth bunker for concrete aggregate** = kegelförmiger Erdsilo *m* für (Beton)Zuschlagstoffe *mpl*

~**-shaped sounding apparatus** = Sonde *f* nach Barentsen

cone shell = Kegelschale *f*

cone(-type) crusher, gyratory ~ ~ [*it sizes at the closed side setting*] = Kreiselbrecher *m*, Kegelbrecher *m*, Rundbrecher

conferva peat = Conferventorf *m*

configuration (or conformation) of the ground, land form = Geländegestaltung *f*, Geländeform *f*, Bodenform *f*

confined compression test = Ödometerversuch *m*, Zusammendrückungsversuch *m* bei behinderter Seitenausdehnung *f*

~ **quarters** = beschränkte Platzverhältnisse *npl*

confluence, confluent, junction = Zusammenfluß *m* [*Flüsse mpl*]

conformable strata (Geol.) = Parallelschichten *fpl*

conformation of the ground, see: configuration ~ ~ ~

congealing point, solidification ~ = Erstarrungspunkt *m*

congestion, jam = Stau *m*, Stockung *f* [*Straßenverkehr m*]

conglomerate, shingle cemented with sandgrains = Konglomerat *n*, „Naturbeton" *m*

conglomeratic sandstone = konglomeratischer Sandstein *m*

conical head, see: pointed ~

~ **mortar mixer** = Trichtermörtelmischer *m*

~ **(or cone) penetrometer** = Kegeldruckapparat *m*, Kegeleindring(ungs)apparat *m*, Kegelgerät *n* [*stabilisierte Mischung f mit bituminösem Binder m*]

~ ~ = Kegeldrucksonde *f*

~ **roller bearing** = Kegelrollenlager *n*

conical-screen (arrangement) = Sortierkonus *m*

conical scrubber = Schwertkonustrommelwäsche *f*

conical-shaped drum = Konustrommel *f*

conical shell, see: mo(u)ld

coniferous forest, pine ~ = Nadelwald *m*

~ **tree**, evergreen = Nadelbaum *m*

~ **wood**, pinewood, softwood, resinous wood = Nadelholz *n*, Weichholz

connected load, connection ~, wattage = Anschlußwert *m*

connecting cable = Anschlußkabel *n*

~ **flange** = Ansatzflansch *m*

~ **link** = Verbindungsgelenk *n*

~ **rivet** = Anschlußniet *m*

~ **rod** = Pleuelstange *f*, Pleuel *m*

~ ~ **to crank shaft circlip** = Sicherungsring *m* zur Sicherung der Pleuelstange *f* auf Kurbelwelle *f*

~ **socket** = Ansatzmuffe *f*

~ **to existing work** = Einbinden *n*

connection = Anschluß *m*

~ **line** = Anschlußleitung *f*

~ **load**, see: connected load

~ **plate** = Anschlußblech *n*

connector = Verbinder *m*

consequent river = Abdachungsfluß *m*

conservation reservoir, ~ storage ~ = Überjahresspeicherbecken *n*

~ **storage** = Überjahresspeicherung *f*

consideration share = Gratisaktie *f*

consistency, consistence, fluidity = Konsistenz *f*, Steife *f*, Geschmeidigkeit *f* [*Beton m*]

~ **index** [*defines the consistency of the soil in its natural state, as expressed by its natural water content, in respect to its plastic and liquid limits*] = Zustandszahl *f*

*****consistency limits**, see: Atterberg limits of soil

consistometer = Konsistometer *n, m*

consolidation, earth ~, soil ~ ~ = natürliche Bodenverdichtung *f*, Konsolidation *f*, Eigenverfestigung *f*, Eigensetzung *f*, Konsolidierung *f*, Eigenkonsolidation *f*

~ **settlement** = Verdichtungssetzung *f*

consolidation (test) apparatus, oedometer = Verdichtungsapparat *m*, Ödometer *n*, Druckgerät *n*

constancy of volume, volume stability = Raumbeständigkeit f
constant angle arch dam, variable radius ~ ~ = Bogenmauer f mit gleichem Bogenzentriwinkel m, Jörgensen-Mauer f, Gleichwinkelmauer f, Bogenstaumauer mit Festwinkel m, Bogen(stau)mauer mit gleichbleibendem Öffnungswinkel
constant-flow (or continuous) (concrete) pug mill mixer = Durchlauf-(Beton-)Zwangsmischer m, Stetig(beton)-zwangsmischer, kontinuierlicher (Beton-)Zwangsmischer, Betonautomat m, Konti-Mischer
~ **grinding** = stetige Mahlung f
~ **mixer**, see: continuous ~
constant head permeability test = Durchlässigkeitsversuch m mit gleichbleibendem Wasserdruck m
~ ~ **permeameter** = Durchlässigkeitsgerät n mit gleichbleibender Wasserhöhe f
~ **mesh transmission** = Synchron-Getriebe n
~ **radius (arch) dam** = Bogenmauer f mit gleichem Radius m, kreiszylindrische Sperre f
~ **segment method** [*analysis of non-uniform structural members*] = Differenzenmethode f [*Berechnung f von Tragwerken mit veränderlichen Trägheitsmomenten*]
~-**speed drive**, single speed ~ = Einscheibenantrieb m
~-**speed motor** = eintouriger Elektromotor m
constant weight feeder = Gewichts-Abmeßbandspeiser m
constituent material of the concrete = Betonkomponente f, Betonbestandteil m, Einzelbestandteil des Betons
~ **mineral** = (Gesteins)Gemengteil m
constitutional diagram = Zustandsschaubild n
constriction of the channel = (Fluß)Bettverengung f
construction = Ausführungsart f, Bauart f [*Baumaschine f*]
~ **adit** = Hilfsstollen m für den Bau m, Baustollen

constructional = konstruktionstechnisch
~ **engineering** = Maschinenbau m
construction(al) feature = Konstruktionsmerkmal n
~ **glass** = Bauglas n
~ **height** = Bauhöhe f
~ **iron**, structural ~ = Bau(werk)eisen n
~ **literature** = Bauliteratur f
~ **method**, see: method of constrcution
* ~ **plant**, see: construction machinery (or equipment)
~ ~ = Baustelleneinrichtung f
~ **project**, see: (construction) ~
~ **steel**, structural ~ = Baustahl m
~ **traffic** = Bau(stellen)verkehr m
construction and erection method = Bau- und Montageverfahren n
~ **clinker**, see: clinker
~ **company**, see: ~ firm
~ **contractor**, (public works) ~ = Bauunternehmer m
construction-cost breakdown = Baukostenaufgliederung f
construction cost index = Baukostenindex m
~ **day** = Bau(arbeits)tag m
~ **engineer**, civil ~ = Bauingenieur m
~ **engineering** = Bautechnik f
~ **executive**, project ~ (US) = Bauleiter m
~ **firm**, building ~, construction company = Baufirma f
~ **flood** = Bauzeithochwasser n, bauzeitliches Hochwasser
~ **haul road**, see: haul ~
~ **industry**, see: building ~
~ **joint**, ~ concrete ~, stop-end ~ = Arbeitsfuge f, Betonierfuge
~ **lime**, building ~ = Baukalk m
*__construction machinery (or equipment)__, contractors' plant, construction(al) plant, building and civil engineering plant, public works equipment, contracting plant, contractor equipment = Baumaschinen fpl und Baugeräte npl
~ ~ (~ ~) **industry** = Baumaschinenindustrie f
~ **management** = Baubetrieb m
~ **material**, building ~ = Baustoff m

construction material(s) dealer, ~ ~ merchant, see: building ~ ~
~ ~ **engineer, building** ~ ~ = Baustoff-Fachmann *m*
~ ~ **machine,** see: building ~ ~
~ ~ **producer,** see: building ~ ~
~ ~ **testing machine,** see: building ~ ~ ~
~ **medium** = Bauelement *n*
~ **mixer** = Baumischer *m*
~ **of bituminous surfacings** = Schwarzdeckenbau *m*
~ ~ **wells, well construction** = Brunnenbau *m*
~ **operations** = Baubetrieb *m*
~ **period,** see: ~ time
~ **plant,** see: ~ machinery (or equipment)
~ **practice,** see: ~ technique
(~) project, constructional ~ = (Bau-)Projekt *n*, Bauvorhaben *n*
~ **road, haul** ~ = Anfuhrweg *m* [*zur Baustelle f*]
~ **(or work) schedule,** (phased) program(me) of works, phasing, job plan, schedule of construction operations, time schedule, progress chart, progress schedule, job schedule, program(me) and progress chart = Bau(zeit)plan *m*, Arbeitsplan, Baufristenplan
~ **season** = Bausaison *f*
~ **seismograph** = seismisches Gerät *n* für die Baugrunduntersuchung nach dem Refraktionsverfahren *n*
~ **shaft, working** ~ = Arbeitsschacht *m*
~ **site,** see: building ~
~**-site crane** = Bau(stellen)kran *m*
~**-site service** = Baustelleneinsatz *m* [*Baumaschinen fpl*]
construction steel, see: constructional ~
~ **technique,** ~ practice = Bautechnik *f*
~ **time,** ~ period, completion period, completion time = Bauzeit *f*, Baufrist *f*
~ **tool, contractors'** ~ = Bauwerkzeug *n*
~ **trade(s), building** ~, trowel ~ = Baugewerbe *n*, Bauhandwerk *n*
~ **trestle** (US); see: service gangway (Brit.)
~ **with concrete slabs used as formwork** = Betonschalplattenbauweise *f*
~ **work,** see: building ~

~ **world** = Bauwelt *f*
constructive = konstruktiv
consulting engineer = beratender Ingenieur *m*
consumptive use of water = Wasserverbrauch *m*
contact (Geol.) = Kontaktzone *f*
~**(-altered) rock,** contact-metamorphosed ~ = Kontaktgestein *n*
contact angle measurement = Randwinkel-Messung *f*
~ **area; tyre** ~ ~ (Brit.); tire ~ ~ ,tire-pavement ~ ~ (US) = (Rad)Aufstandsfläche *f*
~ **between two formations** (Geol.) = Formationsgrenze *f*
~ **deposit** (Geol.) = Kontaktablagerung *f*
~ **force** = Anpreßkraft *f*
~ **influence** (Geol.) = Kontakt *m*
contacting zone of land and water = Grenzzone *f* zwischen Land *n* und Wasser *n*
contact light = Start- und Landebahnfeuer *n*
~ **metamorphism** = Berührungsumprägung *f*, Kontaktmetamorphose *f*, Berührungsumwandlung *f*, Kontaktumwandlung
contactor = Schütz *n* [*Elektrotechnik f*]
~ **control** = Schütz(en)steuerung *f* [*Bagger m*]
contact pressure, clamping force = Klemmkraft *f* [*Nietverbindung f*]
~ **superheater** = Berührungsüberhitzer *m*
~ **spring** = Stauquelle *f*
container = Behälter *m*, Transportgefäß *n*
~ **(for liquids),** see: cistern
~ **road carrier** = Behälter(-Straßen)fahrzeug *n*, Silofahrzeug
~ **rock, reservoir** ~ = Speichergestein *n*, Trägergestein
content by volume = Raumgehalt *m*
~ **indicator** = kapazitiver Anzeiger *m*
continental deposit, hemipelagic ~ = hemipelagische Meeresablagerung *f*
~ **ice sheet** (Geol.) = Binneneisdecke *f*, Eismantel *m*
~ **shelf** = Kontinentalschelf *n, m*
contingency (item) = (Position *f* für) Unvorhergesehene(s) *n*

continued load — contracting plant 101

continued load = Dauerbelastung *f*
continuous application of sewage = ununterbrochene Beschickung *f* mit Abwasser *n*
~ **beam**; see: ~ girder (Brit.)
~ **belt (type bucket) elevator** = Gurtvollelevator *m*, Gurtreihenbecherwerk *n*, Gurtvollbecherwerk
~ **(bucket) (type) elevator** = Vollelevator *m*, Reihenbecherwerk *n*, Vollbecherwerk, Reihenelevator, Becherwerk (oder Elevator) in Becher-an-Becher-Ausführung *f*
~ **chain (type bucket) elevator** = Kettenvollelevator *m*, Kettenreihenbecherwerk *n*
~ **(concrete) pug mill mixer**, see: constant-flow (~) ~ ~
~ **conveyor** = Stetigförderer *m*, Fließförderer, Massenförderer, Dauerförderer
~ ~ **grate, sinter(ing)** ~ ~ = Sinterrost *m*
~ **course correction** = dauernder Schichtausgleich *m*]*Schwarzbelageinbaumaschine f*]
~ **electrode** = Dauerelektrode *f*
~ **elevator**, see: ~ (bucket) (type) ~
~ **excavator** = Stetig-Trockenbagger *m*
~ **filter** = Stetigfilter *n, m*
~ **footing, strip foundation** = Streifenfundament *n*
~ **frame** = Durchlaufrahmen *m*
~ **gallery machine**, see: ~ miner
~ **girder (Brit.)**; ~ beam = durchlaufender Balken(träger) *m*, ~ Träger(balken) *m*
~ **helical blade**, see: screw
~ **impact test** = Dauerschlagprobe *f*
~ **land bucket dredger**, see: bucket ladder excavator
~ **lavatory range** = Reihenwaschtischanlage *f*
~ **miner**, ~ **gallery machine** = kontinuierliches Stollenbohrgerät *n*
~ **mixer, constant-flow** ~ = Stetigmischer *m*, kontinuierlicher Mischer *m*, kontinuierlich arbeitender Mischer
~ **(mixing) plant**, see: ~ volumetric type plant
~ **operation** = Dauerbetrieb *m*
~ **prestressing** = Vorspannung *f* von Durchlaufträgern *mpl*

~ **purlin** = Durchlaufpfette *f*
~ **rope drive** = Kreisseiltrieb *m*
~ **suspension girder (Brit.)**; ~ ~ **beam** = durchlaufender Hängeträger(balken) *m*, Girlanden(balken)träger
~ **two-way slab** = mehrfeldige kreuzweise bewehrte (oder armierte) Platte *f*
~ **type (concrete) distributor (or spreader, or spreading machine)** = Stetig(beton)verteiler *m*
~ ~ **track shifting machine** = Gleisrückmaschine *f* für kontinuierlichen Betrieb *m*
~ **volumetric type plant**, ~ **(flow)** ~, ~ **mixing** ~, **continuous-process** ~ = Stetigmischanlage *f*, kontinuierliche Mischanlage, Durchlauf-Mischanlage
~ **weighing** = stetiges Wiegen *n*
~ **wire-belt elevator** = Drahtgurtvollelevator *m*, Drahtgurt-Reihenbecherwerk *n*
contorted strata (Geol.) = gekrümmte Schichtungen *fpl*
contour line = Kontur *f*
~ ~ = Höhenlinie *f*
~ **map, layered** ~, **contoured plan** = Höhenlinienkarte *f*, Höhenplan *m*
~ **method of grade design and earthwork calculation** = Umrißverfahren *n* bei dem die Erdmassen aus dem Lageplan *m* ermittelt werden, Massenermittlung *f* im Straßenbau *m* aus dem Lageplan *m*
contract agreement = Vertragsabschluß *m*
~ **award**, see: contract-letting
~ **awarding procedure** = Vergabeverfahren *n*
~ **delay penalty,** ~ **overrun** ~ = Konventionalstrafe *f* bei Fristüberschreitung *f*, Vertragsstrafe ~ =
~ **documents** = Vertragsunterlagen *fpl*
* **contracting combine, bidding combination, contractor combination, amalgamation of contractors, joint(-)venture (firm), partnership** = Arbeitsgemeinschaft *f*, Arge *f*
~ **firm** = Bauunternehmung *f*, Bauunternehmen *n*, Baufirma *f*
~ **industry**, see: building ~
~ **official,** ~ **officer** = Vergabebeamte *m*
~ **plant**, see: construction machinery (or equipment)

contraction = Schrumpfen *n* [*unabgebundener Beton m*]
~, necking, neck-down = Einschnürung *f*
~ coefficient = Verengungszahl *f*
~ cracking = Schwindrißbildung *f*
~ joint, see: concealed (concrete) ~
(~) ~ sawing machine, see: joint cutter
~ of area = Querkontraktion *f*
contract-letting, contract award, award of contract, letting of contract = Vergabe *f*, Auftragserteilung *f*
contractor = Unternehmer *m*
~ association = Unternehmerverband *m*
~ combination, see: contracting combine
* **contractor equipment**, see: construction machinery (or equipment)
contractors' agent = Firmenbauleiter *m*
~ (air) compressor set = Bau(stellen)-kompressor *m*, Bau(stellen)luftverdichter *m*, Bau(stellen)drucklufterzeuger *m*
~ centrifugal (water) pump = Bau(stellen)-Kreiselpumpe *f*
~ circular saw = Bau-Kreissäge *f*
~ construction camp, workers' ~ = Baustellenlager *n*, Lagerunterkünfte *fpl*, Unterkunftslager *n*, Arbeiterlager
~ generator (or generating set) = Stromerzeuger *m* für Baustellen *fpl*
~ hoist, see: builder's ~
~ jack screw = Lehrgerüstspindel *f*, Bauschraubenwinde *f*
* **contractors' plant**, see: construction machinery
~ pump = Bau(stellen)pumpe *f*
~ steam hoist = Bau(stellen)dampfwinde *f*
~ tool, see: construction ~
(~) winch, builders' ~ = Bauwinde *f*
~ yard, plant depot = Bauhof *m*, Gerätepark *m*
contractor-type wheel tractor = Bau-Radschlepper *m*
contract party = Vertragspartei *f*
~ penalty, penalty for breach of contract = Vertragsstrafe *f*, Konventionalstrafe
~ (-performed) maintenance = Unterhaltungsarbeiten *fpl* im Vergabeverfahren *n*
contract price = Auftragswert *m*
~ provisions = Vertragsbedingungen *fpl*

~ section, ~ unit = Baulos *n*
(~) specifications, specs = Abnahmevorschriften *fpl*
contra-flow washer (or washing machine) = Gegenstrom-Durchlaufwaschmaschine, Gegenstrom(trommel)wäsche *f*, Gegenstromwaschtrommel *f*
contra-rotating rotors = gegenläufige Rotoren *mpl*
contributory factor = mitbestimmender Faktor *m*
control = Bekämpfung *f*
~ = Steuerung *f*
~, operating ~ = Schaltorgan *n*, Steuerorgan, Bedienungselement *n*, Einstellorgan
~ cabin [*dam*] = Bedienungsstation *f*
~ current = Stromaussteu(e)rung *f*
~ cylinder = Probezylinder *m*, zylindrischer Probekörper *m*, ~ Prüfkörper
~ equipment = Regelanlage *f*
~ gate, see: regulating ~
~ in mechanical engineering = Regeltechnik *f*
controlled-access road, ~ highway = Straße *f* mit geregelten Zufahrten *fpl*
controlled crest spillway, see: gated ~
~ crossing = geregelte Kreuzung *f*
controlled-discharge door concrete hopper (or trough) spreader, spreading machine fitted with bottom doors = Betonverteilungswagen *m* (oder Betonquerverteiler *m*) mit Bodenplatte *f*
controlled spillway; ~ weir (Brit.) = gesteuerter Überlauf *m*
controller = Steuergerät *n*
control linkage = Lenkgestänge *n*
~ of screed = Profilregulierung *f* [*Schwarzbelageinbaumaschine f*]
~ ~ torrents works = Wildbachverbauung *f*
~ panel = Steuer(ungs)tafel *f*, Kommandogerät *n*, Schaltschrank *m*
~ rod = Bedien(ungs)gestänge *n*
~ shaft = Steuerwelle *f*
~ station, see: operator's platform
~ structure, see: ~ works
~ test = Kontrollprüfung *f*
~ tower = Flugleitungsturm *m*
~ ~ = Einlaufturm *m* [*Talsperre f*]

control valve — copier

control valve, regulating ~ = Regulierschieber *m*, Regulierklappe *f*
~ ~ = Regelventil *n*, Steuerventil, Regulierventil
~ **weir** = Kontrollwehr *n*
~ **works**, ~ structure, headworks (structure) = Regulierungsbauwerk *n*
conurbation = Siedlungsgemeinschaft *f* [*zusammenhängendes und städtisch ausgebautes Gelände in der Umgebung von großen Bevölkerungszentren*]
convalescent-home = Genesungsheim *m*
convectional rain = Strichregen *m*
convector = Konvektor *m*, Wärmeleitplatte *f*
conventional load method = n-Bemessungsverfahren *n*
~ **loan** (US) = Personalkredit *m*
~ **sign** = Sinnbild *n* [*Niet m usw.*]
convergent = Näherungsbruch *m* [*Mathem.*]
conversion (equipment item) = Umbaugerät *n*, Umbausatz *n*
~ (**or converting**) **of logs** = Zertrennen *n* von Stämmen *mpl*
~ **table** = Umrechnungstabelle *f*
~ **tunnel**, see: pressure ~
to convert = umbauen [*Baumaschine f*]
* **convertible excavator**, see: all-purpose ~
convex transition between gradients, summit curve = Kuppenausrundung *f*
conveying air = Luftstrahl *m* [*pneumatische Förderanlage f*]
~ **line** = Förderleitung *f*
~ **plant**, ~ installation = Förderanlage *f*
conveyor = Förderer *m*
~, see: bar feeder
~ **and elevator with (scraper) flights** = kombinierter Förderer *m* mit Mitnehmern *mpl*
~ **belt frame** = Bandbrücke *f* [*Förderband n*]
~ **belt(ing)** (**or band**) = Fördergurt *m*, Förderband *n*
~ **bridge**, transporter ~, conveying ~ = Förderbrücke *f*
~ **bucket** = Becher *m*, Eimer *m* [*Becherwerk n*]
~ **clutch** = Lattenrostkupplung *f*, Stangenzubringerkupplung [*Schwarzbelageinbaumaschine f*]
~ **for pit bottom application** = Förderband *n* für den Füllortbetrieb *m*
~ **gantry** = Förderband-Tragwerk *n*

~ **idler**, see: idler
~ **loader**, see: belt ~
~ **pulley** = Förderbandtrommel *f*
~ **screw**, screw conveyor, worm conveyor, Archimedean screw conveyor = Förderschnecke *f*, Schneckenförderer *m*, Transportschnecke *f*
~ **switch** = Rollenbahnweiche *f*
~ **take up roller** = Spannrolle *f* der Lattenrostkette *f* [*Schwarzbelageinbaumaschine f*]
~ **tunnel**, see: reclaiming ~
(~ **type**) **bucket loader**, see: bucket (elevator) loader
~-**type car unloader**, see: car unloader
~-**type scale** = Bandwaage *f*
cooker, see: heater-mixer
coolant, refrigerant = Kühlmittel *n*
~ **tube** = Kühlmittelrohr *n*
cooled and dehumidified air = trockene Kaltluft *f*
* **cooler**, cooling stack, graduation works = Gradierwerk *n*, Rieselwerk *n*
~ = Kühler *m*
cooling back, re-cooling = Rückkühlung *f*
~ **behavio(u)r** [*structural clay body*] = Kühlschwindungsverhalten *n* [*baukeramisches Erzeugnis n*]
~ **belt system** = Bandkühlsystem *n*, Kühlbandanlage *f* [*Betonzuschlagstoffe mpl*]
~ **coil** = Kühlschlange *f*
~ **device** = Kühlvorrichtung *f*
~ **drum** = Kühltrommel *f*
~ **fin**, ~ rib = Kühlerrippe *f*
~ **liquid** = Kühlflüssigkeit *f*
~ **looper** = Kühlhänge *f* [*Dachpappenfertigungsanlage f*]
~ **rib**, see: ~ fin
~ **tower** = Kühlturm *m*
cooperative (**or benefit**) **building society** = Baugenossenschaft *f*
~ **community** = genossenschaftliche Gemeinde *f*
cooper's pitch, pitch in casks = Faßpech *n*
coordinate axis, ~ system (of axes) = Achsenkreuz *n*, Achsensystem *n*, Koordinatensystem, Koordinatenkreuz
co-ordinated control system, see: linked ~
copier, printing machine, copying machine = Lichtpausapparat *m*

coping — corroded fossil

coping, crown (Brit.); crest = Krone *f* [*Talsperre f*]
~ **saw** = Bogensäge *f*
~ ~ = Laubsäge *f*
~ **stone,** capping ~ = Abdeckstein *m* [*Mauerkrone f*]
copper-bearing shale = Keuper *m*
copper deposit = Kupfer-Lagerstätte *f*
~ **glance** (Min.), see: chalcocite
~ **nickel** (Min.), see: niccolite
~ **pyrite** (Min.), see: chalcopyrite
~ **rust,** verdigris = basisches Kupferazetat *n*, Grünspan *m*
~ **slag** = Kupferschlacke *f*
~ ~ **sett,** cast ~ ~ = Kupferschlackenstein *m*
copying machine, see: copier
copy miller = Schablonenfräsmaschine *f*
coquina, shell(y) limestone, oyster shell lime = Muschelkalk(stein) *m*, Muschelmarmor *m*
coral limestone = Korallenkalkstein *m*, Korallen-Riffkalk *m*
corallite, cup coral = Becherkoralle *f*
coral reef = Korallenriff *n*
corbel beam, see: cantilevered ~
to corbel outwards, to cantilever = vorkragen, auskragen
corbel-piece, see: bolster
cord (Brit.) = Klafter *n, f, m* [*3,584 m³*]
cordage = Faserseil *n*
cord belt = Cordband *n*
Cordeau, see: detonating fuse (or cord)
cordierite, iolite, dichroite (Min.) = Kordierit *m*, Dichroit *m*
corduroy effect, formation of washboard waves, washboarding, corrugations; [*deprecated: road waves, deformations, creep*] = Wellenbildung *f* [*Erdstraße f*]
~ **road** = Knüppelweg *m*, Prügelweg *m*
core = Drahtseele *f*
~ ~ = Nabe *f* [*Walzenbrecher m*]
~ = Kühlereinsatz *m* bzw. Ventileinsatz für Schläuche *mpl*
~, see: impervious ~
~, see: (drill) core
~, **unburned lime** = Kalkkern *m*, Kalkkrebs *m*
~ **barrel** = Kernbüchse *f*
~ **bit,** see: (rock) ~ ~

~ ~ **connection** = Kronennippel *m*
~ **boring,** ~ drilling, core-drill boring = Kernbohren *n*, Kernbohrung *f*
~ **cutter** = Bodenprobekernnehmer *m*
***core (cutting) machine,** (concrete) coring machine, core drill(ing machine), concrete coring drill = Kernbohrgerät *n*, (Beton)Kernbohrmaschine *f*
~ **of soil,** soil core = Boden(probe)kern *m*
~ **pool** = eingespülter wasserdichter Kern *m*, Sumpf *m* [*Erddamm m*]
~ **recovery,** ~ extraction = (Bohr-)Kernentnahme *f*, Kerngewinnung *f*
~ **sample** = Probekern *m*
~ **sand** = Kernsand *m*
~ **shoe,** (rock) core bit
~ **test** = Bohrkernprüfung *f*
core-type embankment (or dam) = Kerndamm *m*
core wall = (Damm)Kernmauer *f*
~ **wash boring** = Spülkernbohrung *f*
* **coring machine,** see: core (cutting) ~
corking, see: cogging
cork lagging = Korkisolierung *f*
~ **oak,** ~ **tree** = Korkeiche *f*
~ **powder** = Korkmehl *n*
~ **tar** = Korkteer *m*
corner angle, see: angle bracket
~ **bracing** = Eckversteifung *f*
~ **cogging with oblique cog** = Eckverkämmung *f* mit schrägem Kamm *m*
~ **truss** = Eckaussteifung *f* [*Kastenträger m*]
Cornish boiler = Einflammrohrkessel *m*, Cornwallkessel *m*
~ **multitubular boiler** = Feuerbüchs(en)kessel *m*
corona emission [*electrical precipitator*] = Glimmentladung *f*, Koronaentladung *f*
corporate (occupational) representation = berufsständische Vertretung *f*
corrasion (Geol.) = Korrasion *f*, Sandschliff *m*
to correct, to average out = ausgleichen [*Unebenheit f*]
correlation = Wechselbeziehung *f*
corrie, cirque (Geol.) = Kar *n*
corroded fossil, partly dissolved ~ = angegriffenes Fossil, angelöstes ~ *n*

corrosion — couple of forces

corrosion = Anfressung f, Korrosion f, Anfressen n, Angreifen n
~ **embayment**, see: abrasion ~
corrosive sublimate, mercuric chloride, HgCl = Sublimat n, Quecksilberchlorid n
corrugated asbestos cement sheet = Wellasbestzementplatte f
~ **(crushing) roll** = geriefelte (Brech-)Walze f
~ **ingot** = Riffelblock m
~ **metal culvert** = Wellblechdurchlaß m, Wellblechrohrabzug(kanal) m
~ ~ **pipe** = Wellblechrohr n
~ ~ **reclaiming tunnel** = Haldentunnel m aus Wellblech
~ **pipe bend** = Wellrohrbogen m
~ **sheet** = Wellblech n
corrugations, see: corduroy effect
~ = Ratterwellen fpl [in Schienen fpl]
corundum brick = Korundstein m
cost estimate, see: estimate (of costs)
~ **estimating** = Kalkulieren n, Preiskalkulation f
(~) **estimator**, see: calculator
costing, see: price build-up
cost of living allowance, see: living allowance
cost-plus-fee contract, value-cost ~, cost-value ~ = Selbstkosten-Erstattungsvertrag m
cost-plus-fixed fee contract, cost-plus-profit ~ = Selbstkosten-Erstattungsvertrag m mit begrenzter Höhe f der zuschlagberechtigten Kosten f
cost-value contract, see: cost-plus-fee ~
cost(s) breakdown, see: breakdown of cost(s)
~ **incidental to wages** = lohngebundene Kosten f
~ **of wages excluding compulsory deduction for social services** = Lohnkosten f ausschließlich der gesetzlichen Aufwendungen fpl
cotter, split pin = Splint m
~ **joint** = Splintverbindung f
cotton fabric duck belt (or band), cotton reinforced belt = Baumwollband n, Baumwollgurt m
~ **oil** = Baumwollsaatöl n

~-~ **pitch** = Cottonölpech n
cotton pitch = Cottonpech n
~-**stearin pitch** = Cottonstearinpech n
cotton waste = Putzwolle f
cottonwood = kanadische Pappel f
Coulomb's sliding-wedge analysis, ~ theory of active earth pressure, wedge theory = Coulomb'sche Theorie f
Coulomb soil-failure prism = Coulomb'sches Bruchprisma n
co(u)loring admixture = Färbemittel n, Zementfarbe f
c(o)umarone resin = Kumaronharz n
count = Zählung f
counter = Zählwerk n
~ = Tresen m
~ **(brace)**, ~ diagonal = Gegenstab m [Fachwerk n]
to counteract = entgegenwirken
counter-balanced cage = Förderkorb m mit Gegengewicht n
~ **chute (or spout)** = Gegengewichtrinne f, Flieger m [Gußbetoneinrichtung f]
~ **sub-chute** = Schüttrinne f mit Gegengewicht n [Dosiersilo m]
counterbalance weight = Gegengewicht n
counterbore for cylinder liner = Versenker m für Zylinderlaufbüchse f
counter-current classifier = Gegenstrom-Klassierer m
~ **revolving-pan mixer** = Gegenstrom-Schnellmischer m, Tellermischer
counter-curve = Gegenkurve f
counter-flow process = Gegenstromverfahren n
counterflush drilling, drilling with reversed circulation = Bohren n mit Verkehrtspülung f
counterfort (type) dam, see: buttress(~) ~
countershaft = Vorgelege(welle) n, (f)
counterweight, counterpoise, counterbalance weight = Gegengewicht n
~ **rope** = Gegengewichtseil n
country rock, see: bed ~
county road, secondary ~ = Landstraße f 2. Ordnung f
couplant, see: acoustic coupling agent
couple = Kräftepaar n [Statik f]
couple-close roof, see: saddle ~
couple of forces = Kräftepaar n

coupler = Muffenverbindung *f* bei Stoß von Spannbewehrung *f*
coupling = Wellenkupplung *f* [*Sammelbegriff*]
~, solid ~ = feste Kupplung *f*
~ flange, union ~ = Bundflansch *m*
course, see: layer
coursed rubble walling = regelmäßiges Schichtmauerwerk *n*
~ sett paving, paving in rows, peg top paving = Reihenpflaster *n*
course joint, horizontal **~** = Lagerfuge *f* [*Mauerwerk n*]
cove = Eckleiste *f* für Decken *fpl*
co-venturer = Argepartner *m*
to cover = bedecken, abdecken
coverage = scheinbare Haftung *f* [*Umhüllung f der Gesteinsoberfläche f durch einen Bitumenfilm m ohne daß dieser fest haftet*]
cover aggregate (for seal); see: blotter (material) (for bituminous prime coat) (US)
covered electrode, coated **~** = umhüllte Elektrode *f*, Mantelelektrode, ummantelte Elektrode, umwickelte **~**
~ hot water floor panel = bedeckte Fußboden-Warmwasserheizfläche *f*
~ market = überdachter Marktplatz *m*
(cover) grating, ~ grate = Abdeck(gitter)rost *m*
covering = Abdeckung *f*, Zudeckung
cover(ing) fill = Abdeck(auf)schüttung *f*
covering of the river banks with slime, mud or stones = Vermurung *f*, Übermurung
~ power, ~ ability = Deckkraft *f*, Deckvermögen *n*
cover(ing) slab, ~ plate = Abdeckplatte *f*
cover-plate (US); see: butt-strap (Brit.)
cover plate = Gurtplatte *f*
~ stone, see: blotter (material) (for bituminous prime coat) (US)
~ strip, narrow strap, top flange plate = Kopfplatte *f*, Deckflacheisen *n*, Lamelle *f*
coving stick = halbrundes Kehlholz *n* [*Asphaltarbeiterwerkzeug n*]
cowl = Haube *f*
cow wheat = Ackerwachtelweizen *m*

coyote tunneling method (US) = Kammersprengverfahren *n*
crab, hand **~** [*a portable winch or windlass*] = Wellbaum *m*, Bockwinde *f*, Kanalwinde
~ travelling winch = Katzfahrwinde *f*, Lastkatzenfahrwinde
~ winch = Vorgelegehaspel *m, f*
* crack = Riß *m*
crack (Brit.); fracture (Geol.) = Bruchfuge *f*
cracked distillate = Krack-Destillat *n*
~ gasolene (or gasoline) (US) = Gasolin *n* (oder Leichtöl *n*) aus dem Krackprozeß *m*
cracker (or cracking) gas = Krackgas *n*
crack formation load = Rißlast *f*
cracking = Spaltdestillation *f*
~ = Rißbildung *f*, Rissebildung *f*
~ (or splitting) by frost = Eisklüftigkeit *f*
~ stock = Ausgangsmaterial *n* für Krackprozesse *mpl*
crack water, see: fissure **~**
crackwax = Sprungwachs *n*
cradle dynamometer = Pendeldynamometer *n*
crane attachment = Kran-Zusatzvorrichtung *f*
~ balance on slope = Kranschwerpunktlage *f* auf abschüssigem Gelände *n*
~ boom (US) = Kranausleger *m*
~ cab(in) = Kranhaus *n*, Krankabine *f*
~ carrier = Kranunterwagen *m*
~ column (US); **~ stanchion** = Kranbahnstütze *f*
crane-excavator, shovel crane, excavator crane = Kranbagger *m*, Baggerkran *m*
crane girder, gantry, crane runway girder = Kranträger *m*
~ grease = Kranschmiere *f*
~ hook, load **~** = Kranhaken *m*
~ jib (Brit.) = Kranausleger *m*
~ magnet(o), see: lifting **~**
~ navvy, power navvy, crowd shovel, (swing) dipper shovel, forward shovel (Brit.); mechanical shovel, (face) shovel, power shovel; luffing boom shovel (US) = Hochlöffel(bagger) *m*, Löffelhochbagger *m*

crane pedestal — crawler track   107

crane pedestal = Kranunterbau *m* [*Portalkran m*]

~ **pile driver**, see: ~ type driver

~ **rail** = Kranschiene *f*, Kranbahnschiene

~ **runway** = Kranbahn *f*

~ ~ **girder**, see: ~ girder

~ **skip** = Kran(förder)kübel *m*

~ **stanchion**; ~ **column** (US) = Kranbahnstütze *f*

~ **superstructure** = Kranoberbau *m*

~ **track(s)**, ~ **tracking** = Krangleis *n*

~ **type driver, crane pile driver** = Kranramme *f*

~ **warning device** = Warnvorrichtung *f* am Kran gegen elektrische Leitungen *fpl*

crankcase = Kurbelwanne *f*

~ **guard** = Kurbelwannenschutz *m*

crank drive = Kurbeltrieb *m*

cranked flat iron = gekröpftes Flacheisen *n*

crank journal = Pleuellagerzapfen *m*

crank pin = Kurbelzapfen *m*

crankshaft = Kurbelwelle *f*

~ **end clearance** = Spiel *n* des Kurbelwellen-Endlagers *n*

crank side shift = Verschwenkgestänge *n* [*Motor-Straßenhobel m*]

crash-barrier = Durchfahrhindernis *n* [*Straße f*]

crash truck, see: breakdown van

crate = Lattenkiste *f*, Lattenverschlag *m*

crater = Krater *m*

~ **compound** = Zahnradfett *n*

crawler, crawler belt, caterpillar track, (tracklaying) track, crawler track, creeper track, chain track, track chain, roller chain track = Gleiskette *f*, Traktorenkette *f*, Raupenkette *f*, Raupen(glieder)band *n*

~ **bearing area** = Gleisketten-Aufstandsfläche *f*

~ **(belt) with rubber grouser** = Gummistollen(gleis)kette *f*

~ **(or track-laying type, or caterpillar type, or creeper-mounted) bucket (elevator) loader** = Becher(werk)auflader *m* auf Gleisketten *fpl*

~ **(~ ~, ~ ~, ~ ~) ladder excavator** = Eimerkettenraupenbagger *m*

~ **crane** = Gleiskettenkran *m*, Raupenkran

~ **drive sprocket** = Gleiskettenantriebsturas *m*, Raupenantriebsrad *n*

~ **flip-over bucket loader**, see: ~ overhead loader

(~) idler wheel = Umlenkrolle *f* [*Gleiskette f*]

crawler-loader shovel, crawler tractor loader (or shovel) = Gleisketten-Ladeschaufel *f*, Gleisketten-Schaufellader *m*, Gleisketten-Fahrlader, Raupenladeschaufel *f*

crawler-mounted = mit Gleiskettenfahrwerk versehen, raupenfahrbar, gleiskettenfahrbar

~ **diesel excavator-crane** = Universal-Diesel-Raupen(band)bagger *m*

* **crawler-mounted excavator**, see: bucket-excavator mounted on tracks

~ **excavator-crane** = Universal-Raupen(band)bagger *m*

~ **scraper and loader** = Auslegerschrapper *m* mit Ladewagen *m* für den Streckenvortrieb *m*, Fabrikat HASENCLEVER A.G., DÜSSELDORF, DEUTSCHLAND

crawler (or caterpillar, or track-laying type) overhead loader (or overshot loader, or rocker shovel, or flip-over bucket loader, or over-loader) = Gleisketten-Wurfschaufellader *m*, Gleisketten-Über-Kopf-(Schaufel-)Lader *m*

~ **push-cat(erpillar), pusher tractor** = Schubgleiskettenschlepper *m*, Stoßgleiskettenschlepper *m*, Schubraupentraktor *m*, Stoßraupe *f*

crawlers, see: crawler unit

crawler-scrape rig, crawler-powered scraper = Traktor-Schrapper *m*, Schrapper *m* mit (Gleis)Kettenschlepper *m*, Schürf-(kübel)wagenzug *m*

crawler shoe, track ~ = Raupen(band)schuhplatte *f*, Bodenplatte

~ ~ **link** = Schuhplattengelenk *n*, Bodenplattengelenk *n* [*Raupe f*]

* **crawler shovel**, see: bucket excavator mounted on tracks

~ **(side) frame** = Seitenwagen *m* zur Aufnahme der Gleiskettenfahrgestelle *npl*

~ **steam excavator** = Dampfbagger *m* auf Gleisketten *fpl*

~ **track**, see: crawler

crawler tractor attachments = Anbaugeräte *npl* (oder Zusatzeinrichtungen *fpl*) für (Gleis)Kettenschlepper *mpl*

~ ~ **crane** = Gleiskettentraktor(en)kran *m*, Gleiskettenschlepperkran, Raupenschlepperkran

~**-tractor drawn scraper**, see: four-wheel(ed) scraper

crawler tractor(-mounted) front end loader = (Gleis)Kettenschlepper-Frontlader *m*, (Gleis)Kettenschlepper-Frontladeschaufel *f*, (Gleis)Ketten-Fahrlader *m* mit Frontladeschaufel *f*, Front-Fahrlader *m* mit (Gleis)Kettenfahrwerk *n*

~ **tractor with bulldozer**, see: bulldozer fitted to track-laying (type) tractor

~ **(-tread) tractor**, see: caterpillar ~

~ **unit**, crawlers, creeper undercarriage = Gleiskettenfahrwerk *n*, Zweiraupenfahrwerk *n*, Raupenunterwagen *m*, Raupenfahrwerk, (Raupen-)Traktorenlaufwerk *n*, Kettenlaufwerk, Raupenlaufwerk

crawling of glazes = Kriechen *n* von Glasuren *fpl*, Abrollen *n* ~ ~

crawl space = Kriechraum *m* unter dem Erdgeschoß *n* von kellerlosen Gebäuden

crazing, surface ~, craze; map cracking (US); [*deprecated: crocodiling*] = feine Rißbildung *f*, Netzrißbildung *f*, Maronage *f* [*Beton m*]

cream of lime, lime milk, whitewash, milk of lime = Kalkmilch *f*, Tünche *f*

creased pipe bend = Faltenrohrbogen *m*

to creep = kriechen, wandern [*Schiene f*]

creep [*deprecated*]; see: corduroy effect

~, creeping (Geol.) = Kriechen *n*

~, (plastic) flow, time yield = Kriechen *n* [*Beton m, Stahl m*]

creeper derrick = Kletter-Derrickkran *m*

~ **lane**, climbing ~ = Steigspur *f*

~ **track**, see: crawler

~ **undercarriage**, see: crawler unit

creep fibre (Brit.); ~ **fiber** (US) = Kriechfaser *f*

creeping, see: creep

creepless steel = kriechfreier Stahl *m*

creep of concrete = Betonkriechen *n*

~ **speed** = Steiggeschwindigkeit *f*, Kriechgeschwindigkeit [*LKW m*]

~ ~ **self-propelled carrier** = Kriechgang-Selbstfahrwerk *n*

creep strain = Kriechdehnung *f*

creosoted wooden post = kreosotgetränkter Holzpfosten *m*

creosote oil; [*deprecated: creosote*] = Kreosotöl *n*

crescentic moraine = Bogenmoräne *f*

crescent pump, sickle ~ = Sichelpumpe *f*

~ **scraper bucket** = halbmondartiges Schrappergefäß *n*

~**-shaped dune**, see: barchan

cresol pitch = Karbolpech *n*, Kresolharz *n*, Phenolpech *n*

crest; coping, crown (Brit.) = Krone *f* [*Talsperre f*]

~**-control weir**, see: waste-weir

crested dog's-tail = Kammgras *n*

crest vertical curve = Kuppe *f* [*Straße f*]

cretaceous genera of foraminifera = Foraminiferen-Gattungen *fpl* der Kreide

CRETEANGLE machine [*Trademark*] = Machine *f* zur Herstellung von Abstandshaltern *mpl* für die Bewehrung

creteway, see: strip(e) road

crevice = Felsritze *f*

~ **oil** = Spalten(erd)öl *n*

crew, gang, team (of workers), party = (Arbeits-)Kolonne *f*, Trupp *m*

~ **hut**, see: dispersal ~

crib = Stapel *m*

cribling machine = Schotterräummaschine *f*

cribwork dry stone weir = Steinkistenwehr *n*

Crimean silver fir = Nordmannstanne *f*

crimping = Anwürgen *n* [*Sprengkapsel f*]

~ **machine** = Krippmaschine *f* für das Drahtweben

cristobalite (Min.) = Cristobalit *m*

criterion = Kriterium *n*

critical head = kritische Druckhöhe *f*, kritisches Gefälle *n* [*Talsperre f*]

~ **load** = kritische Belastung *f*, ~ Last *f*

~ **rake angle** = kritischer Spanwinkel *m*

~ **section** = gefährlicher Querschnitt *m*

~ **stress** = kritische Spannung *f*

crochet file = Gabelfeile *f*

crocodiling [*deprecated*]; (surface) crazing, craze; map cracking (US) = Maronage *f*, feine Rißbildung *f*, Netzrißbildung *f*

croco(is)ite — crowd pressure

croco(is)ite (Min.) = Krokoit *m*
to crop out, to outcrop (Geol.) = ausstreichen, ausgehen
(cross) auger, spreading screw, spreader screw, distributing screw = Verteilerschnecke *f*, Verteilungsschnecke *f* [*Schwarzbelageinbaumaschine f*]
~ ~, see: ~ bit
cross beam, see: capping beam
~ ~; see: cross girder (Brit.).
~ bit, ~ auger = Kreuzmeißel *m*
~ ~ cutting edge = Kreuzschneide *f*, Kreuzmeißelschneide
~ brace = Querstrebe *f*
~ bracing, see: transverse bracing
~-bubble = Kreuzlibelle *f*
cross clamp = Kantenzwinge *f*
~ cogging = Kreuzkamm *m*
cross-country pipeline = Überlandrohrleitung *f*
~ vehicle, off-the-road ~, off-the-highway ~ = geländegängiges Fahrzeug *n*
cross cut hammer = Schrämhammer *m*
crosscut saw = Schrotsäge *f*
cross cutter = Schrämmaschine *f*
cross dike (US); **~ dyke** (Brit.) = Querdeich *m*
crossed threads = Fadenkreuz *n*
crossfall, transverse slope [*deprecated*]; (barrel) camber = Wölbung *f*, kreisförmige Krone *f* [*Straße f*]
~ ~ = Quergefälle *n*
cross frame = Querrahmen *m*
~ girder (Brit.); cross beam, transom = Querträger *m*, Unterzug *m*
~ ~ connection = Querträgeranschluß *m*
cross-grain plane = Zwerchhobel *m*
cross head = Querhaupt *n* [*Prüfmaschine f*]
crosshead type walking mechanism = Kurbel- und Kreuzkopf-Schreitausrüstung *f* [*Schreitbagger m*]
cross hole = Kreuzloch *n*
crossing = Kreuzung *f* von zwei Straßen *fpl*, Einzelkreuzung *f*
~ ~ = Stromübergang *m*
~ file = Vogelzungenfeile *f*
cross lay, see: regular ~
~ link assy = Gestängekulisse *f*, Quergelenk *n*
(~) mattock = Breithacke *f*, Breithaue *f*

Cross moment distribution method = Näherungsrechnung *f* nach Cross, Cross-Verfahren *n*, Momentenausgleichsmethode *f*
cross-over valve = Umschaltventil *n*
cross pin = Kreuzzapfen *m*
~ road = Querstraße *f*
cross-section, transverse section = Querschnitt *m*
~ in $^1/_4$ **span** = Querschnitt *m* im Gewölbeviertel *n* [*Bogenbrücke f*]
~ of stream discharge, see: discharge section
cross sectional area = Querschnittfläche *f*
* cross-sectional profile, see: cross-section of road
cross-sectioning, taking cross-sections = Aufnahme *f* der Querprofile *npl*
* cross-section of road, profile of ~, cross-sectional profile = Straßenquerschnittausbildung *f*
~ shape = Querschnittsform *f*
cross-sill (Brit.); see: sleeper
cross-staff = Winkelkreuz *n*
cross stays, see: diagonal struts
(cross-)tie (US); see: sleeper (Brit.)
crosstown tunnel [*a tunnel with no surface connections in the town*] = Stadtdurchgangstunnel *m*
cross tube boiler = Quersiederkessel *m*
~ vault, see: groin arch
crosswalk, pedestrian crossing = Fußgängerüberweg *m*
crowbar; dwang (Brit.) = Brechstange *f*, Brecheisen *n*, Hebebaum *m*
crowd brake = Vorstoßbremse *f*, Vorschubbremse [*Bagger m*]
~ clutch = Vorstoßkupplung *f*, Vorschubkupplung [*Bagger m*]
crowd(ing) = Vorschub *m*, Vorstoß *m*, Vorstoßen *n* [*Bagger m*]
~ force = Vorschubkraft *f*, Vorstoßkraft **~** [*Hochlöffel(bagger) m*]
~ machinery = Vorschubausrüstung *f*, Vorstoßausrüstung [*Hochlöffel(bagger) m*]
~ rope, ~ line, ~ cable = Vorstoßseil *n*, Vorschubseil *n*
crowd lever = Vorschubhebel *m*, Vorstoßhebel
~ pressure = Anpreßdruck *m* [*z B Eimerleiter f beim Grabenbagger m*]

crowd-retract cable — crushing roll for chippings production

crowd-retract cable = Vorschub-Einzieh-Seil *n*
~ **clutch** = Vorschub-Einzieh-Kupplung *f*
~ **mechanism** = Vorschub-Einzieh-Vorrichtung *f*
crowd shovel (Brit.), see: crane navvy
~ ~ **fitting**, face shovel attachment = Hochlöffeleinrichtung *f*
~ **sprocket** [*shovel*] = Vorstoßturas *m*
crown, see: vertex
~ = Krone *f*
~, see: crest
~ **control** = Straßenkronenregulierung *f* [*Schwarzbelageinbaumaschine f*]
crowned (drill) bit cutting edge, ~ **drill point** = Kronenschneide *f*
crown hinge = Scheitelgelenk *n*
~ **in relation to the width of mat being laid** = Kronenüberhöhung *f* im Verhältnis zur Einbaubreite *f*
crucible furnace = Tiegelofen *m*
~ **steel** = Tiegelstahl *m*
cruciform twin group = Durchkreuzungszwilling *m* [*Mineralogie f*]
crude oil line = Rohölleitung *f*
~ ~ **(petroleum)**, crude naphtha, petroleum, rock oil = Erdöl *n*, Rohöl *n*, Roherdöl *n*, Rohpetroleum *n*
~ **sewage** = rohes Abwasser *n*
(~) shale oil = Schieferöl *n*
~ **tar**; [*deprecated: green* ~] = Rohteer *m*
CRUISER-CRANE [*Trademark*] = Pneubagger *m*, Fabrikat KOEHRING CO., MILWAUKEE 16, WIS., USA
to crumble away = abbröckeln
crumble coal = Formkohle *f*, Feinkohle, Klarkohle, Rieselkohle
crumbling peat, crumble ~ = Bröckeltorf *m*
crush-breccia = Reibungsbrekzie *f*
crushed aggregates = zerkleinerte Stoffe *mpl*, gebrochenes Material *n* [*Betonzuschlag(stoff) m*]
~ **clay brick**, burnt clay aggregate, clay chip(ping)s = Ziegelsplitt *m*, Tonsplitt *m*
~ **(~) aggregate no-fines concrete** = Ziegelsplitt-Schüttbeton *m*, Trümmerschutt-Schüttbeton
~ **(~) concrete**, crushed brick aggregate ~ = Ziegelsplittbeton *m*, Trümmerschuttbeton

~ **coarse aggregate** = zerkleinerter Grobzuschlag(stoff) *m*
~ **coke** = Brechkoks *m*
~ **fine aggregate** = Betonbrechsand *m*, zerkleinerter Feinzuschlag(stoff) *m*
~ **gravel** = Betonsplitt *m* [*7/30 mm*]
~ **gravel** = Brechkies *m*
~ ~ **sand** = Betongrobsand *m* [*3/7 mm*]
~ **limestone** = Kalksteinschotter *m*
~ **rock**, see: ~ stone
~-**rock base**, see: macadam base
~-**rock surfacing**, see: macadam ~
crushed slag, broken ~ = Brecherschlacke *f*
~ **stone** = Betonsteinschlag *m* [*30/70 mm*]
~ ~ **(or rock)**, road stone, macadam [*deprecated: road metal*] = Straßen(bau)schotter *m*, Schotter
~ ~ **macadam base**, see: macadam base
~ ~ **plant**, see: breaking ~
(~) ~-sand, see: sreening(s)
~ **stone sand** = Betonfeinsand *m*
~ **surfacing**, macadam ~ = Schotterdecke *f*
crusher, breaking machine, breaker = Brecher *m*, Grobzerkleinerungsmaschine *f*
(~) base, (~) **(main) frame** = (Brecher-)Rahmen *m*, Brecherkörper *m*
~ **feeder**, see: rock ~
~ **opening**, receiving ~, feed ~, mouth = Brechmaul *n*
~-**run (stone)** = ungesiebtes gebrochenes Gut *n* (oder Material *n*)
crusher screening(s), see: screening(s)
(~) waste, tailings, rejects, oversize (reject) = Überlauf *m*
crushing, see: coarse reduction
* **crushing and grinding**, see: comminution
~ ~ **equipment (or machinery)** = Hartzerkleinerungsmaschinen *fpl*
~ ~ **screening plant (or installation)** = Brech- und Siebanlage *f*
~ **chamber** = Brechraum *m*
~ **jaw** = Brechbacke(n) *f*, (*m*)
~ **mantle** = Brechmantel *m*
~ **plant**, see: breaking ~
~ **roll** = Brechwalze *f*
(~) ~ segment = Brechring *m*
(~) ~ shell = (Brech)Walzenmantel *m*
~ ~ **for chippings production** = Splittwalzenbrecher *m*

crushing roll for sand production — curley-cannel 111

crushing roll for sand production = Sandwalzenbrecher m
~ (or compressive) (strength) test (on rock specimens) = Druckprüfung f
~ surface [*crushing jaw*] = Brechfläche f
cryolite, Greenland spar, kryolith, Na$_3$AlF$_6$ (Min.) = Kryolith m, Eisstein m
cryptocrystalline = kryptokristallin, feinkristallin
crystal chemistry = Kristallchemie f
crystalline basement = kristallines Grundgebirge n
~ carbon = kristalliner Kohlenstoff m
~ limestone, calcitic marble, limestone marble = Kalkmarmor m
~ rock = kristallines Gestein n, Kristallin m
~ schist = kristalliner Schiefer m
crystallizable = kristallisierbar
crystallization [*screw, rivet*] = Rekristallisation f, Alterung f [*Schraube f, Niet n*]
crystallized dolomite = Rau(c)hwacke f, Zellendolomitgestein n
crystal structure, ~ lattice = Kristallgitter n
cubage, see: cubic yardage
cube sett = Würfelpflasterstein m
~ strength, compressive ~, crushing ~ = Würfelfestigkeit f, Druckfestigkeit
~ test = Würfelprobe f
~ ~ specimen, test cube = Probewürfel m
cubical = kubisch
cubic metre of piled wood = Raummeter m [*Holz n*]
~ ~ ~ trunk timber = Festmeter m
~ system, regular ~ = reguläres System n [*Kristall n*]
~ yardage, cubage = Kubatur f
cul-de-sac (street), see: blind alley
culm (Geol.) = Kulm m
Culmann's method = Culmann-Verfahren n
cultivated area, farmland = Kulturfläche f
~ soil, see: agricultural ~
cultivator, agricultural ~, field ~ = (Boden-)Kultivator m
* culvert, drainage ~, drainage duct = Durchlaß m, Abzugkanal m
~ = Umlauf m [*Binnenschiffahrtschleuse f*]
~ pipe = Durchlaßrohr n, Abzugkanalrohr n

cumulative batcher, see: ~ (weigh-)batcher
~ bin conveyor (belt) = Vormischsiloband n
~ curve, cumulating ~ = Summationskurve f, Summenkurve f
~ direct plot = Summationskurvenauftrag(ung) m, (f) in natürlichem Maßstab m
~ line, cast ~ = Summenlinie f
~ logarithmic plot = Summationskurvenauftrag(ung) m, (f) in logarithmischem Maßstab m
~ percentage by weight = Summe f der Gewichtsprozente npl
~ (weigh)batcher, see: multiple ~
cumulonimbus, see: thunder-cloud
cumulus, see: cloud-heap
cup coral, see: corallite
~ grease = Staufferfett n
~ head = erhabener Nietkopf m
cupola furnace = Kupol(schmelz)ofen m
cuprite, Cu$_2$O (Min.) = Cuprit m, Rotkupfererz n
cuprous chloride = Kupferchlorür n
cup shake, ring ~, wind shake = Ringkluft f [*Holz n*]
curb parking = Bordsteinparken n
curb(stone); kerb(stone), kirb(stone) (Brit.) = Bordstein m, Hochbordstein, Bordschwelle f, Schrammbord n
to cure = abbinden [*Verschnittbitumen n*]
cure, remedial measure = Abhilfe(maßnahme) f, Behebung f
curing; [*deprecated: maturing, hardening*] = Reifeprozeß m [*Beton m*]
* curing, see: after-treatment
~ blanket = Abdeckmatte f [*Beton m*]
~ chamber, ~ room = Härtekammer f [*Erhärtung f von Betonfertigwaren fpl*]
~ compound, see: membrane ~
~ overlay = Abdeckung f [*Betonnachbehandlung f*]
~ rack, rack for curing concrete block = Hordengestell n [*Betonsteinherstellung f*]
~ room, see: ~ chamber
~ seal, see: concrete curing membrane
~ temperature, see: setting ~
~ tent, see: concrete protection tent
~ yard = Nachbehandlungsplatz m
curley-cannel, see: eye coal

current, flow = Strömung *f*
~ meter [*hydrographic instrument*] = Strömungsmesser *m*
~ velocity = Strömungsgeschwindigkeit *f*
curtain grouting = Dichtungsschirm-Verpressung *f*
~ wall = Abschirmwand *f*, Abschirmmauer *f*
~ ~ = vorgeblendete Fertigwand *f*
~ ~ method = Verfahren **n** bei dem Beton- und Stahlkonstruktionen außen mit gemauertem Außenwerk *n*, vergossenen Betonteilen *mpl*, Asbest-Zementplatten *fpl* oder Aluminiumverkleidungen *fpl* versehen werden
curvature = Krümmung *f*, Richtungsänderung *f*
curved beam; arched girder (Brit.) = Bogen(balken)träger *m*, Bogenbalken *m*
~ bridge = Kurvenbrücke *f*
~ deflector plate = gebogene Ablenk(ungs)platte *f* [*Schwarzbelageinbaumaschine f*]
~ ejector = abgerundete Auswerfvorrichtung *f* (oder Ausstoßplatte *f*) [*Radschrapper m*]
~ jaw (crushing) plate = gewölbte Backenplatte *f* [*Feinbackenbrecher m*]
~ line = Bogenlinie *f*
~ member = gebogener Bauteil *m*
~ roller = Laufkranz *m*
~ track = Bogengleis *n*
curved-trough flow device = Kurvenkonsistenzmesser *m*
curve of setting (Brit.); **~ ~ set** = Abbindekurve *f*, Erstarrungskurve, Hydra(ta)tionskurve
curving beach = Bogenküste *f*
cusec [*cubic feet per second, as a measure of flow of water*] = 0,0283 m³ pro Sekunde
cushion block, see: helmet
~ (course), see: bed(ding course)
cushioning = Dämpfung *f*
~ block = Silentblock *m*
~ spring = Dämpfungsfeder *f*
cushion valve = Anschlagventil *n*
customs examinations building = Zoll(abfertigungs)gebäude *n*
to cut = schneiden
cut = Abtragmaterial *n*

~, building pit, excavation, cutting, foundation pit = Baugrube *f*
~ ~ = Fraktion *f*, Schnitt *m*
~ ~ = Abtrag *m*, Einschnitt *m*
~ ~ = Durchstich *m*
~, cutting, foundation pit, excavation, building pit = Baugrube *f*
~ and cover tramway = Unterpflasterbahn *f*
~ ~ fill = Einschnitt *m* und Damm *m*, Abtrag *m* und Auftrag *m* (oder Aufschüttung *f*)
~-back (asphaltic bitumen) (Brit.); **~ (asphalt), asphaltic cut-back** (US) [*the flux used is a distillate*] = Verschnittbitumen *n*
cutcha = weicher, schlechter Kalk *m*
cut-down of staff = Personalabbau *m*
cut floor = Einschnittsohle *f*
~ lining = Baugrubenauskleidung *f*
cut-off (Brit.) [*the removal of rainfall by percolation through the soil*] = Versickerung *f* von Niederschlagswasser *n*
~ bluff = Prallufer *n* [*Mäander m*]
~ gate, hopper ~ = Mengenregulierschieber *m*, Durchlaßschieber, Schließblech *n* [*Schwarzbelageinbaumaschine f*]
~ knife = Abschneidemesser *n*
~ shoe = Breiten-Reduzierstück *n* [*Schwarzbelageinbaumaschine f*]
~ side = reduzierte Seite *f* [*Schwarzbelageinbaumaschine f*]
~ trench = Verherdung *f*, Abdichtungsgraben *m*
~ wall = Trennmauer *f*, Abschlußwand *f*
~ ~, toe ~ ~ [*reaching into rock along the bottom of the cut-off trench*] = Herdmauer *f*, Fußmauer, Abdichtungsmauer, Abdichtungssporn *m* [*Talsperre f*]
cutter = Kutter *m*
~ = Schneidkopf *m*
~ bar = Ziehmesser *n* [*Schwarzbelageinbaumaschine f*]
~ head, see: (rock) core bit
~ shaft = Schneidkopfwelle *f* [*Naßbagger m*]
~ (suction) dredge(r), see: suction-cutter ~
cutting, excavation, excavated material = Abtragmaterial *n*
~ = Einschnitt *m*, Abtrag *m*

cutting — dam

cutting, excavation, excavating = Abtragen *n*, Abtragarbeit(en) *f*, (*pl*) [*Boden m*]
~, building pit, excavation, foundation pit, cut = Baugrube *f*
~ **back**, thinning = Verschneiden *n*
~ **bit**, see: bit
~ **blade**, planing ~ [*heater-planer*] = Schneidwerk *n*
~ **blow pipe** (Brit.); cutting torch, flame cutter (US) = Schneidbrenner *m*
~ **compound** = Schneidöl *n*
~ **down of a forest** = Abholzung *f*
~ **edge of a digging machine**, knife = Schneidkante *f*
~ **fluid** = Schneidflüssigkeit *f*
~ **plier**, see: pliers
~ **sand** = Schleifsand *m*
~ **torch** (US); see: ~ blow pipe (Brit.)
~ **wheel**, digging ~ [*wheel ditcher*] = Schaufelrad *n*
~ **work** = Stemmarbeiten *fpl*
to cut to precise length = ablängen
cyanite, disthene = Disthen *m*, Zyanit *m*
cycle = Takt *m* [*Verbrennungsmaschine f*]
~ = Kreislauf *m*, Folge *f*
~ **plant** = Cycling-Anlage *f*
~ (or **bicycle**) **racing track** = Radrennbahn *f*
~ (~ ~) **track** (or **path**) = Rad(fahr)weg *m*
~ (~ ~) ~ (~ ~) **crossing** = Radüberweg *m*
cyclical = zyklisch
~ **variation** = zyklische Veränderung *f*
cyclic symmetry = zyklische Symmetrie *f*
cyclone classification = Zyklonklassierung *f*
~ **classifier** = Naßzyklon *m*, Zyklonnaßklassierer *m*, Aufschwimmklassierer
~ (**separator**), dust collecting cyclone, centrifugal dust collector, cyclone type dust collector (or catcher) = Zyklon *m*, Fliehkraftabscheider *m*, Zentrifugal-Staubabscheider, Fliehkraftzyklon

~ ~ = Waschzyklon *m*, Hydrozyklon
cyclopean aggregate [*fragments weighing more than 100 lb.*] = Zyklopensteine *mpl* [*schwerer als 45,4 kg*]
~ **concrete**, rubble ~ = Zyklopenbeton *m*, Bruchsteinbeton
cyclopie wall = Zyklopenmauerwerk *n*
cylinder = Zylinder *m*
~ = Hydraulikzylinder *m*
~ = Mantel *m* beim Keller-Tiefenrüttler *m*
~ = Mantelrohr *n* [*Ortpfahl m*]
~ **gas** = Flaschengas *n*
~ **head** = Zylinderkopf *m*
~ **liner** = Zylinderlaufbüchse *f*
~ **pressure** = Zylinderinnendruck *m*
~ **wall** = Zylinderwand(ung) *f*
cylindrical batch (**grinding**) **mill** = Trommel(mahl)mühle *f*
~ **bell foundation**, see: ~ foundation
~ **drier** (or **dryer**) = zylindrischer Trommeltrockner *m*, zylindrische Trockentrommel *f*
~ **drum** = zylindrischer Walzkörper *m* [*Walze f*]
~ **foundation**, ~ bell ~ = Ortpfahl *m*, Betongrundpfahl, Bohrpfahl
~ **screen** = Kreissieb *n*
~ **scrubber**, see: scrubber
~ **shell** = Zylinderschale *f*
~ **steel skin** = Schildmantel *m* [*Tunnelbau m*]
~ **washing screen** = Trommelwaschsieb *n*
cyma welr (or **spillway**), see: ogee ~ (~ ~)
cyst = Zyste *f*

D

dacite = Dazit *m*
dairy cattle pasture = Milchviehweideland *n*
~ **waste** = Molkereiabwasser *n*
(**Dalton**) **overhead eccentric** (**type jaw**) **crusher**, single toggle jaw crusher = Einschwingen(backen)brecher *m*

* **dam, hydro ~**
(hydro) dam body
reservoir

(**Tal**) **Sperre** *f*
Stauwerk *n*, (Tal)Sperrenkörper *m*
Staubecken, Speicher(becken) *m*, (*n*)

flood relief works, spillway
bottom discharge works
stilling basin
river outlet, reservoir outlet

Hochwasserentlastungsanlage *f*
Grundablaßanlage *f*
Tosbecken *n*, Beruhigungsbecken *n*
Betriebsauslaß *m*

damage sustained during transit = Transportschaden *m*
dam body, hydro ~ ~ = (Tal)Sperrenkörper *m*, Stauwerk *n*
~ crest, hydro ~ ~ = (Ta`)Sperrenkrone *f*, Stauwerkskrone
~ embankment, see: embankment type dam
~ fill material = Dammbaustoff *m*
~ lake = Talsperrensee *m*
Damman cold asphalt, fine cold asphalt, cold fine asphalt (carpet) (Brit.) = Dammanasphalt *m*, Essener Asphalt *m*, Es-As *m*, Asphaltkaltbeton *m*
damming = Abdämmung *f*, Absperrung
~, blocking (Geol.) = Absperrung *f*
damper = Vibrationsdämpfer *m*
damping effect = Dämpfungseffekt *m*
dampproofing = Feuchtigkeitsisolierung *f*, Abdichtung *f*, Feuchtigkeitssperrung *f* [*Bauwerk n gegen Bodenfeuchte f*]
~ and permeability reducing agent, see: concrete waterproofing compound
damp-proof membrane = Dichtungshaut *f*
dam section = Talsperren-Querschnitt *m*
damsite = Talsperrenbaustelle *f*, Sperrstelle
dam with segmental-headed counterforts (Brit.); round-head(ed) buttress dam = Rundkopfmauer *f* von Noetzli, Pfeilerkopf-Sperre *f*, Pfeilerkopf(stau)mauer *f*
d'Arcy's law, Darcy's ~ = d'Arcy'sches (Filter-)Gesetz *n*, Darcy-Gesetz, Filtergesetz von Darcy
dark-red silver ore, ruby silver ore, pyrargyrite, Ag_3SbS_3 (Min.) = Antimonsilberblende *f*, Pyrargyrit *m*, dunkles Rotgültigerz *n*
dart valve bailer = Schlammbüchse *f* mit Stoßventil *n*
dash-dotted line = Strich-Punkt-Linie *f*
dash lamp, instrument ~ = Armaturenbeleuchtung *f*
~ pot = Kolbenzeigerdämpfer *m*, Kolbenanzeigedämpfer

date of origination = Ausstellungsdatum *n*
~ set for the opening of tenders, submission date, tendering date, opening date = Angebotseröffnungstermin *m*, Submissionstermin *m*
datum horizon, key ~, "marker" (Geol.) = Bezugshorizont *n*, Leithorizont
~ (plane), ~ surface = Bezugsebene *f*, Bezugsfläche *f*
day labo(u)r = Tagelohnarbeit *f*
day-old specimen = Eintagsprobe(stück) *f*, (*n*)
day parker = Dauerparker *m*
day's-work joint, day-to-day ~ = Tages(arbeits)fuge *f*
day visibility = Tagessichtbarkeit *f*
daywork = Stundenlohnarbeit *f*
~ rate, see: hourly wage rate
dazzle (glare) = Blendung *f* [*Autoscheinwerfer m*]
D.C. current, dc ~ = Gleichstrom *m* [*Elektrotechnik f*]
DD screen, see: double deck ~
dead abutment = verlorenes Widerlager *n*, unterdrücktes ~
~ burning = Totbrennen *n* [*Gips m*]
~ canal, sleeping ~ = Kanal *m* mit totem Wasserspiegel *m*
~-end station = Sackbahnhof *m*
~-end street = Sackgasse *f* ohne Wendemöglichkeit *f*
dead level, flush to, flush with = bündig mit, niveaueben, niveaugleich
deadline, see: bottleneck
dead load, dead weight, fixed ~, permanent ~ = Eigengewicht *n*
dead man = Leitfahrzeug *n* [*z. B. ein Kettenschlepper m von dem aus eine Walze auf einer Böschung arbeitet*]
Dead Sea = Totes Meer *n*
dead (or needle, or vertical) shoring, underpinning = Unterfangen *n*, Unterfangung *f*
~ standing tree = Dürrständer *m*

dead weight = Eigengewicht n [*Baumaschine f*]

~ ~, see: dead load

~ ~ **safety valve** = Sicherheitsventil n mit unmittelbarer Belastung f

deadweight trailer for testing road bridges = Anhänger m als Prüfwagen m für Straßenbrücken fpl

débris = Trümmer f

~ = grobes Unkraut n

~ **slide, rock avalanche** = Bergsturz m, Felssturz, Felsabbruch m

debt service = Schuldendienst m

de-bushing, bush clearing = Buschräumung f

debutanized (or stabilized) gasoline (or gasolene) = stabilisiertes Gasolin n

decanting valve = Dekantierventil n

decantation test (US); see: sedimentation ~

decarburizing = Entkohlung f

DECAUVILLE track light railway (system) (Brit.) [*Trademark*] = DECAUVILLE-Feldeisenbahn f

deceleration curve = Verzögerungsbogen m

~ **lane** = Verzögerungsspur f

dechenite (Min.) = Dechenit m

deciduous tree, broad-leaved ~ = Laubbaum m

~ **wood**, leafwood, hardwood = Laubholz n, Hartholz

decimal index system = Dezimalklassifikation f

deck, platform = (Tief)Ladebrücke f [*Tiefladewagen m*]

~ **barge; deck scow** (US) = Deckschute f

~ **bridge** = Deckbrücke f, Brücke f mit oben liegender Fahrbahn f

~ **centering** (US); ~ **centring** (Brit.) = Lehrgerüst n für Plattenbrücke f

~ **crane** = Deckkran m [*Schiff n*]

decking, bridge ~, (bridge) **deck, bridge floor(ing)** = Brückentafel f, (Fahrbahn)Tafel f

~, **deck initiation** = Zündung f der Teilladungen fpl mit Verzögerungsintervallen npl

~ **slab** = Brückentafelplatte f

deck machinery = auf dem Oberwagen m montierte Aggregate npl [*Bagger m*]

~ **structure** = Fahrbahnplatte f [*Brücke f*]

~ **truss span** = Fachwerk-Deckbrücke f

declining volcanic activity = ausklingende vulkanische Tätigkeit f

declutching = Auskuppeln n

to decompose = zersetzen

decomposed granite, gowan = zersetzter Granit m

decomposition = Zersetzung f

decompression = Druckentlastung f

~ **chamber** = Druckentlastungskammer f

decorative concrete, ornamental ~ = Zierbeton m

dedication ceremony = Einweihungsfeier f

deduction of rivet holes = Lochabzug m

deep compaction = Tiefenverdichtung f

~ **cut digging** = Tiefbaggerung f

to deepen = austiefen, vertiefen

deepening = Austiefung f

~ [*harbo(u)r*] = Vertiefung f

deep foundation = Tieffundation f, Tiefgründung f

deeply incised = tief eingeschnitten [*Tal n*]

deep pier, see: deep(-water) ~

~ **sampler**, ~ **sample taker** = Tief-Probe(ent)nahmeapparat m

~ **sampling** = Tiefschürfbohrung f

~ **sand-island caisson** = von künstlicher Sandschüttung f aus niedergebrachter tiefer Senkkasten m

deep-sea cable = Tiefseekabel n

~ **core** = Tiefseekern m

~ **diver** = Tiefseetaucher m

~ **diving outfit** = Tiefseepanzer m

~ **ooze**, ~ **deposit**, pelagic ~ = Tiefseeschlamm m, eupelagische Meeresablagerung f

~ **port**, seaport = Seehafen m mit Betriebsanlagen fpl

deep sounding = Tiefensondierung f

~ ~ **apparatus** = Tiefensondierapparat m

~ **vibration** = Tiefen(ein)rüttlung f

deep(-water) pier = tiefgegründeter Pfeiler m

~ **wharf** = Tiefwasser-Hafenmauer f

deep-webbed = hochstegig [*Träger m*]

deep well = Tiefbrunnen m

~ ~ **piston pump** = Tiefbrunnenkolbenpumpe f, Gestängetiefpumpe

defence method = Abwehrmaßnahme f

deficiency = Fehlbedarf *m*
definition = Begriffsbezeichnung *f*
to deflate (Geol.) = auswehen
deflation, wind ~ = Abtragung *f* durch Wind *m*, Abblasung *f*, Deflation *f*, Auswehung
deflecting plate = Ablenkplatte *f*, Prallblech *n*, Leitblech, Ablenkblech
deflection = Durchbiegung *f*
~ = Ausschlag *m*
deflectometer = Durchbiegungsmesser *m*
deflector; see: downstream sill (US)
~ = Deflektor *m*
to deflocculate = ausflocken, dispergieren
deflocculation = Ausflockung *f*, Entflockung
~ **agent**, dispersing ~ = Dispergierungsmittel *n*, Dispersionsmittel, Dispergenz *f*
deforestation = Entwaldung *f*
deformation = Verformung *f*, Form(ver)änderung *f*, Gestaltänderung
~ **energy** = Gestaltänderungsenergie *f*
~ **method** = Formänderungsverfahren *n*
deformations [*deprecated*]; see: corduroy effect
deformed (concrete reinforcing) bar = Betonformstahl *m*
deformometer, deformability meter = Deformationsmesser *m*, Verformungsmesser *m*, Deformator *m*
dégras oil, see: distilled-grease olein
~ **stearin** = Wollfett-Stearin *n*
degree of curvature = Krümmungsgrad *m* [*Straße f*]
~ ~ **loosening** = Auflockerungsgrad *m*
~ ~ **remo(u)lding** = Grad *m* der Störung *f*
~ ~ **saturation** = Sättigungsgrad *m*
~ ~ **settling of traffic paint** = Absetzgrad *m* von Markierungsfarbe *f*
to dehumidify = entfeuchten
dehydrated tar = entwässerter Teer *m*
~ **water-gas tar** = Kohlenwassergasteer *m*
dehydrating agent = Anhydrisierungsmittel *n*
dehydration = Wasserentziehung *f*, Dehydrierung *f*
~ **test** = Entwässerungsprüfung *f* [*Bitumenemulsion f*]
dehydrator, see: dewatering unit

de-icing salt, ice-control ~ = (Auf-)Tausalz *n* [*früher: Streusalz*]
delay action firing = Zeitzündung *f*
~ **(electric) detonator** = Zeitzünder *m*, elektrischer ~
delineation (US) = Leistungsbeschreibung *f*
delineator; safety post (Brit.) = Leitpfosten *m*
deliquescent salt = zerfließendes Salz *n*
delivery, shipment = Anfuhr *f*, Anlieferung *f*
~ **chute** = Abgabeschurre *f*
~ **valve** = Druckventil *n* [*Kompressor m*]
~ **van** = Lieferwagen *m* [*Auto n*]
dell, see: bird bath
Delmonte tar = Del Monteteer *m*
delph [*a drain behind a sea embankment, on the land side*] = landseitiger Drän *m* hinter einem Seedeich *m*
delta = Delta *n*, Mündungskegel *m*
~ **building (or fill)** = Deltaaufschüttung *f*, Deltabildung
~ **connection** = Dreieckschaltung *f*
~ **flats** = Deltaniederung *f*
deltaic embankment = Deltadamm *m*
Deluge of Noah, Noachian Deluge = Sintflut *f*
de luxe model = Luxusausführung *f*
DEMAG universal excavator = Universal-Bagger *m*, Fabrikat DEMAG AG., DUISBURG, DEUTSCHLAND
to demolish, to pull down, to take down = abbrechen [*Gebäude n*]
demolition chamber, blast ~ = Sprengkammer *f* [*Brücke f*]
~ **pick (hammer)** = Abbruchhammer *m*
~ **tool** = Abbruchwerkzeug *n*
~ **work**, wrecking, pulling down, taking down = Abbrucharbeit(en) *f (pl)*, Abbruch *m*, Abtragung *f*, Abtrag *m*
DEMPSTER-DIGGSTER [*Trademark*] = vollhydraulisch arbeitender Autobagger und -lader, Fabrikat DEMPSTER BROTHERS INC., KNOXVILLE 17, TENNESSEE, USA
demulsibility = Entemulgierbarkeit *f*
demurrage (charge) = Standgeld *n*
~ **(charges)** = Liegegebühren *f*
denaturating agent = Vergällungsmittel *n*
dendritic formation = Dendritenbildung *f*
~ **tufa** = Dendrittuff *m*

dendrograph — derrick girder 117

dendrograph = Dendrometer *n*
dendrology = Dendrologie *f*, Baumkunde *f*
dense(-graded) = dicht, hohlraumarm, geschlossen abgestuft
~ **(mineral) aggregate**, DGA, close-graded (~) ~ = hohlraumarmes (oder geschlossen abgestuftes, oder dichtes) Mineralgemisch *n*, hohlraumarme (oder geschlossen abgestufte, oder dichte) Mineralmasse *f*
~ **road mix surface**, see: graded aggregate type ~ ~ ~
dense tar surfacing, tar concrete pavement, D.T.S. = Teerbetondecke *f*
densification, see: compaction
densifier, see: concrete waterproofing compound
~, sludge thickener = Schlammeindicker *m*, Schlammeindickbehälter *m*
density, see: volume weight
~ **altitude** = barometrische Höhe *f*
~ **bottle**, see: pycnometer
~ **control unit for checking asphaltic concrete during construction** = Dichtigkeitsprüfgerät *n*
~ **currents** = Strömungen *fpl* verschiedener Dichte *f*
~ **meter for liquids**, see: hydrometer
~ **of population** = Bevölkerungsdichte *f*
~ ~ **rainfall** = Regendichte *f*
dental plaster = Zahnarztgips *m*
dentated sill = Zahnschwelle *f*
* **denudation** (Brit.), see: abrasion
~ **plain**, see: peneplain
~ **terrace**, structural rock bench (Geol.) = Denudationsterrasse *f*
deodorant = Geruchbeseitigungsmittel *n*
deodorisation = Geruchbeseitigung *f*
department head = Abteilungsleiter *m*
~ **store** = Kaufhaus *n*, Warenhaus
departure track = Ausfahrtgleis *n*
depolarization = Depolarisation *f*
to depolarize = depolarisieren
deposit (Geol.) = Vorkommen *n*, Vorkommnis *n*, Lager(stätte) *n*, (*f*)
~, sediment = Ablagerung *f* [*als abgelagerter Stoff m*]
~, sediment = Ausfällung *f*, Sinkstoff *m*
~ **crack** = Ablagerungsriß *m*
depositing of concrete, see: placement ~ ~

~ **underwater concrete in bags** = Sackschüttung *f*
deposition, see: sedimentation (process)
depositional topography = Ablagerungslandschaft *f*
deposition bluff, accreting bank = Anwachsufer *n* [*Mäander m*]
deposit welding = Auftragsschweißung *f*
depot repair = Bauhofreparatur *f*
to depreciate = abschreiben
depreciation chargeable in accounts = buchhalterische Abschreibung *f*
depressed area = Notstandsgebiet *n*
~ **highway**, ~ **road** = Tiefstraße *f*
depression = Vertiefung *f*, Mulde *f*, Senkung
~ (US) = Unterdruck *m*
~ **spring** = Überlaufquelle *f*
depth adjustment, ~ **control** = Tiefeneinstellung *f*
~ **effect** = Tiefenwirkung *f*
~ **ga(u)ge** = Tiefenlehre *f*, Tiefenmaß *n*
~ ~ = Pegel *m*
~ **of frost penetration**, frost penetration depth = Frosttiefe *f*
~ ~ **jointing material** = Dichtungstiefe *f* [*Stemm-Muffe f*]
~ ~ **section** = Profilhöhe *f*
~ ~ **the navigable channel** = Wassertiefe *f* des Fahrwassers *n*, nutzbare Fahrtiefe
to derail = entgleisen
derailment = Entgleisen *n*, Entgleisung *f*
derivation = Ableitung *f* [*Formel f*]
derrick, see: derrick crane
~ = Bohrturm *m*
derrick- and hand-placed stone rock-fill dam, see: dry masonry dam
derrick boat; ~ **scow** (US) = Schute *f* mit Derrick(Kran) *m*, Schwimm-Derrick *m*
~ **brace** = Bohrturmstrebe *f*
~ **cellar** = Bohrturmkeller *m*
~ **cornice** = Bohrturmkranz *m*
* **derrick (crane)**; derricking jib ~ (Brit.) = Derrick-Kran *m*, Mastenkran, Ladebaum *m*
~ **crane** = Bohrturmkran *m*
~ **floor** = Bohr(turm)flur *m*
~ **foundation** = (Bohr)Turmfundament *n*
~ ~ **post** = (Bohr)Turmtragpfosten *m*
~ **girder** = (Bohr)Turmquerträger *m*

derrick grillage = (Bohr)Turmrost m
~ leg = (Bohr)Turmmast m, Bohrturmeckpfosten m
~ man = (Bohr)Turmsteiger m
~ ~ = Gestängebühnen-Arbeiter m
~ ~, ~ operator = Derrick-Bediener m
~ platform, working ~ = (Bohr)Turmbühne f, Arbeitsbühne
~ stone = schwerer Stein m [nur mit einem Derrick zu heben]
~ substructure = Bohrturmunterbau m
~ winch = Derrickwinde f
desalting = Entzundern n
descaling = Entzundern n
to descend, to drop = abfallen, absteigen [Kurve f]
descending branch = abfallender Ast m, absteigender ~
~ spring = Auslaufquelle f
descloicite (Min.) = Descloizit m
desiccator = Exsikkator m, Trockenapparat m
design = Entwurf m, zeichnerische Ausarbeitung f (oder Konstruktion f)
~ and construction = bauliche Durchbildung f, ~ Gestaltung f
~ constants = Rechenschema n
~ element, see: ~ standard
~ engineering show = Entwurfs- und Konstruktionsausstellung f
designer = Konstrukteur m
design feature = Konstruktionsmerkmal n
~ fundamentals, basis of design = Berechnungsgrundlage f
designing engineer = Konstruktionsingenieur m
~ water level; top ~ ~ (Brit.) [dam] = Stauhöhe f, Stauziel n
design load = Lastannahme f
~ method for reinforced concrete construction = Berechnungsweise f im Stahlbetonbau n
~ ~ not involving the use of the modular ratio = n-freie Berechnungsweise f
~ specifications = Entwurfsrichtlinien fpl
~ speed = Ausbaugeschwindigkeit f Berechnungsgeschwindigkeit [Straße f]
~ standard, ~ element = Entwurfsmerkmal n

~ storm = Berechnungsregen m
~ table = Bemessungstafel f
~ vehicle = Versuchsfahrzeug n [z. B. für die Bestimmung der Bordsteinführung f]
~ weight = Konstruktionsgewicht n
desiltor = Entschlämmungsapparat m, Schlämmapparat [Materialaufbereitung f]
desilverising of lead bullion = Werkbleientsilberung f
desire line = Verkehrsstromlinie f
desludging = Entschlammen n, Entschlammung f
destacker = Stapelabnahmegerät n
destination = Bestimmungsort m
~ survey = Zielverkehrszählung f
to destress = entspannen
destroying capillary action = kapillarbrechend
destructive distillation, dry ~ [sometimes referred to as "pyrolysis"] = Entgasung f, trockene Destillation f, Zersetzungsdestillation
~ fire = Schadenfeuer n
~ testing of concrete = zerstörende Betonprüfung f
destructor = Verbrennungsofen m [Schlammbeseitigung f durch Verbrennung]
~ station = Kraftwerk n auf Müllverbrennungsbasis f
desulphurisation = Entschwef(e)lung f
detachable bit = auswechselbare (Bohr-)Krone f austauschbare ~
~ ditcher, trailer-type ~, towed-type ~ = Anhänge-Grabenbagger m, Schlepp-Grabenbagger
~ tow-bar = Ansteckdeichsel f
detached house = Einzelhaus n
~ island = Abgliederungsinsel f
~ peninsula = Abgliederungshalbinsel f
detackifier = Zusatzmittel n zur Verhinderung des Zusammenklebens des gemahlenen Gummis
detention basin, ~ reservoir, flood-control reservoir with controlled outlets = Rückhaltebecken n
~ ~ = Rückhaltebecken n [Wasseraufbereitung f]
~ period = Rückhaltedauer f

detention period = Aufenthaltszeit *f*, Durchflußdauer *f* [*Abwasserwesen n*]

detergent [*usually restricted to soap-like substances*], dispersant, anti-flocculant = Schlamminhibitor *m*

deterioration = Verschlechterung *f*, Verschleiß *m*, Anfressung, Abnutzung

determination = Ermittlung *f*, Bestimmung

~ of the ultimate bearing capacity [*reinforced concrete*] = Bruchsicherheitsnachweis *m* [*Stahlbeton m*]

detonating charge, priming compound, primer = Zündsatz *m*

~ fuse (or cord), Cordeau = Knallzündschnur *f*, detonierende Zündschnur, Nitropentaerythrit-Zündschnur, (Nitropenta)Sprengschnur

detonation intensity [*internal combustion engine*] = Detonations-Intensität *f*

detonator = Initialladung *f*, Initialsprengstoff *m*

detrimental expansion = schädliche Ausdehnung *f*

detrital sand (Brit.); detritic sand (US) = trümmerhaltiger Sand *m*

~ slope = Schutthang *m*

detritus, shingle, rubbish = Geschiebe(masse) *n*, (*f*), Flußschotter *m*, Trümmermasse *f*, Flußgeschiebe *n*

~ tank = Sandfang *m*

DEUTZ-DIESEL engine, DD ~ = Dieselmotor *m*, Fabrikat KLÖCKNER-HUMBOLDT-DEUTZ A.G., KÖLN/RHEIN, DEUTSCHLAND

DEUTZ three-cylinder four-stroke (diesel) engine = Deutz-Dreizylinder-Viertakt-Dieselmotor *m*

Deval attrition (or testing) machine = Deval-Trommelmühle *f*, Deval-Abnutzungsmaschine *f*

developed length = Abwick(e)lungslänge *f*

development program(me) = Ausbau-Programm *n*, Ausbauplan *m*

deviance = Summe *f* der Abweichungsquadrate *npl*, Abweichungssumme

deviation, off-size, margin, permissible variation = Abmaß *n*, Maßabweichung *f*

deviator stress = Spannungsunterschied *m*, Spannungsabweichung *f*

device to eliminate "running back" = Rücklaufsicherung *f* [*Bauaufzug m*]

devil, see: fire ~

devitrification = Entglasung *f*

Dewar flask = Dewargefäß *n*, Weinhold-Gefäß

to dewater, to unwater = auspumpen, trockenlegen [*Baugrube f*]

dewaterer, see: dewatering unit

dewatering, unwatering = Wasserhaltung *f* [*Baugrube f*]

~ = Entwässern *n* [*Sandaufbereitung f*]

~ bucket, dredging ~ = Schöpfbecher *m* [*Waschmaschine f*]

~ equipment; ~ gears (Brit.) = Wasserhaltungsgeräte *npl*

~ flight conveyor, see: sand drag

~ installation, ground water lowering installation = Grundwasser(ab)senkungsanlage *f*

~ unit, dewaterer, dehydrator = Entwässerungsapparat *m* [*Materialaufbereitung f*]

~ wheel = Schöpfrad *n*, Becherrad, Eimerrad [*Waschmaschine f*]

dew point = Taupunkt *m*

dextro-rotatory to polarised light = rechtsdrehend gegenüber polarisiertem Licht

DGA, see: dense(-graded) (mineral) aggregate

diabase = Diabas *m*

diabasic tuff, greenstone ~ = Diabastuff *m*, Grünsteintuff *m*

diaclase (Geol.) = Diaklase *f*

diagenesis = Diagenese *f*

diagonal bracing, ~ bond = Verschwerterung *f*, Schrägverband *m*

~ member = Diagonalstab *m* [*Fachwerk n*]

~ rope stay = Diagonal-Drahtseilstrebe *f*

~ screed finisher = Diagonalbohlenfertiger *m*, Betondeckenfertiger mit Diagonal-Glättbohle *f*

~ stiffener = Diagonalsteife *f* [*Blechträger m*]

~ strut, ~ brace, ~ in compression, compression diagonal = Kreuzstrebe *f*, Diagonalstrebe

~ struts, St. Andrew's cross, saltier cross bars, cross stays = Andreaskreuz *n*, Kreuzstreben *fpl*, Kreuzband *n*

~ tension = schräge Zugspannung *f*

diagonal winch, ~ **steam** ~ = Dampfwinde *f* mit geneigten Zylindern *mpl*

diagram, graphic representation, diagrammatic representation, graph = Diagramm *n*, Schaubild *n*, graphische Darstellung *f*

dial batcher = Zifferblatt-Abmeßwaage *f* mit Waagenbehälter *m*, Kreiszeigerwaage

~ **ga(u)ge** = Meßuhr *f*

diallage = Diallag *m*

dial (type) scale = Zifferblattwaage *f*, Kreiszeigerwaage

diameter = Durchmesser *m*

diamond bit = Diamant(bohr)krone *f*

~ **core drill** = Diamant-Kernbohrer *m*

~ **coring,** ~ core drilling = Diamantkernbohrung *f*

~ **drill** = Diamantbohrer *m*

~ ~ **boring,** ~ (system of) drilling = Diamantbohrung *f*

~ **-head buttress dam** = Pfeiler(stau)mauer *f* mit diamantkopfähnlichen Strebepfeilern *mpl*

diamond pyramid hardness test = Oberflächenhärteprüfung *f* mit einer Diamant-Pyramide *f*

~ **saw blade** = Diamant-Sägeblatt *n*

diamond-shaped reinforcing mesh = Bewehrungsmatte *f* in Rautenform *f*, Armierungsmatte ~ ~

diaphragm = Zwischenriegel *m*, Querriegel *m*, Querschott(e) *n*, (*f*)

~, **membrane** = Membran(e) *f*

~ **beam** = wandartiger Träger *m*

~ **frame** = Zwischenwandrahmen *m* [*Bagger-Senkkastengründung f*]

~ **-operated material-level indicator** = Membran(e)-Bunkerstandanzeiger *m*

diaphragm pump, membrane ~ = Membran(e)pumpe *f*, Dia-Pumpe *f*, Diaphragmapumpe

diaspore (Min.) = Diaspor *m*

diatom = Stabalge *f*, Kieselalge *f*. Diatomee *f*

~ **(aceous) earth,** diatomite, Kieselgur (Min.) = Diatomeenerde *f*, Diatomit *n*, Kieselalgenerde *f*, Kieselgur *f*

~ **ooze** = Diatomeenschlamm *m*, Kiesel(algen)schlamm, Diatomeenschlick *m*

diazo reaction = Diazoreaktion *f*

dichloride, bichloride = Doppelchlorid *n*

dichroite (Min.), see: cordierite

die = Mundstück *n* [*Strangpresse f*]

dielectric amplifier = dielektrischer Verstärker *m*

~ **constant,** electric constánt, specific inductive capacity, S.I.C. = Dielektrizitätskonstante *f*

~ **strength,** electric ~ = elektrische Durchschlagfestigkeit *f* [*Bitumen n*]

dies = Hohlziegelmundstücke *npl*

diesel (air) compressor = Diesel-Preßluftanlage *f*, Diesel-Druckluftanlage, Diesel-Kompressoranlage

~ **crawler tractor** = Diesel-(Gleis)Kettenschlepper *m*

diesel-driven, diesel-powered = dieselgetrieben

~ **hand-guided two-wheel dozer** = Diesel-Einachs-Räumer *m*

~ **pump** = Diesel-Pumpe *f*

~ **track laying crane** = Diesel-Gleisbaukran *m*

diesel dumper, ~ shuttle ~, diesel-powered (shuttle) dumper, diesel engine(d) (shuttle) dumper = Diesel-Autoschütter *m*

diesel-electric drive = diesel-elektrischer Antrieb *m*, Verbundantrieb

~ **loco(motive)** = diesel-elektrische Lok(omotive) *f*

~ **set,** see: diesel generating ~

~ **wagon crane** = diesel-elektrischer Autobagger *m* mit Selbstfahrwerk *n*, ~ langsamfahrender Autobagger

diesel engine = Dieselmotor *m*

~ ~ **crane** = Dieselkran *m*

~ **engine(d) dumper,** ~ (shuttle) ~ = Diesel-Autoschütter *m*

~ **engine-driven immersion concrete vibrator** = Diesel-Betoninnenrüttler *m*, Diesel-Betoninnenvibrator *m*

~ **engine lorry** (Brit.); see: ~ truck

~ ~ **oil** = Diesel-Schmieröl *n*

~ ~ **three wheel(ed) roller** = Dieselmotor-Dreiradwalze *f*

~ ~ **vehicle** = Dieselfahrzeug *n*

~ **excavator** = Diesel(trocken)bagger *m*

diesel fuel — diffuser plate 121

diesel fuel = Dieselkraftstoff m
~ (~) **injection system** = Dieseleinspritzanlage f
~ ~ **tax** = Dieselöl-Steuer f
~ **generating set,** ~ motor-generator ~, ~-electric ~ = Diesel-Stromerzeuger m, Diesel-Elektro-Gruppe f, Dieselaggregat n mit Generator m, Dieselelektro-Aggregat n
diesel-hydraulic loco(motive) = dieselhydraulische Lok(omotive) f
diesel injection system, ~ fuel ~ ~ = Dieseleinspritzanlage f
~ **liner** = Diesel-Zylinderlaufbüchse f
~ **loco(motive)** = Diesellok(omotive) f
~ **motor-generator set,** see: ~ generating ~
~ **oil tanker** = Dieselöl-Tankwagen m
~ **operator** = Bediener m eines Dieselmotors m
~ **pile-puller,** ~ pile extractor = Diesel-Pfahlzieher m
~ **piling plant,** ~ pile driver = Dieselrammanlage f, Dieselramme f
diesel-powered, diesel-driven = dieselgetrieben, mit Dieselantrieb m
~ **(shuttle) dumper,** see: diesel dumper
~ **truck,** see: diesel ~
diesel power unit = Diesel-Antriebsgruppe f
~ **railcar** = Dieseltriebwagen m
~ **road roller** = Diesel-Straßenwalze f
~ **shunter,** ~ shunting loco(motive) = Diesel-Rangierlok(omotive) f
~ **(shuttle) dumper,** ~ engine(d) (~) ~, diesel-powered (~) ~ = Diesel-Autoschütter m
~ **spreader-finisher** = Diesel-Verteilerfertiger m
~ **stacking truck** = Dieselstapler m
~ **suction dredge(r)** = Diesel-Schwimmsaugbagger m, Diesel-Naßsaugbagger
~ **tracklayer** = Diesel-(Gleis)Kettengerät n, Diesel-Raupengerät
~ **tractor** = Diesel-Schlepper m, Diesel-Traktor m, Diesel-Trecker m
~ **tractor-compressor,** ~ universal compressor tractor = Dieselkompressorschlepper m
~ **tractor crane** = Dieselschlepper-Kran m

~ **tractor-truck,** ~ truck tractor = Dieselmotor-(Straßen)Zugmaschine f
~ **truck,** diesel-powered ~ = Dieselkarre(n) f, (m)
~ ~, diesel-powered ~; ~ engine lorry (Brit.) = Diesel-LKW m, Diesel-Last(kraft)wagen m
~ **truck-tractor,** ~ tractor-truck = Dieselmotor-(Straßen)Zugmaschine f
~ **universal compressor tractor,** ~ tractor-compressor = Dieselkompressorschlepper m
~ ~ **excavator** = Dieseluniversalbagger m, Diesel-Mehrzweckbagger
~ **wheel-type tractor,** ~ wheeled ~ = Diesel-Radschlepper m, Diesel-Radtrecker m, Diesel-Radtraktor m
difference in level, ~ ~ elevation = Höhenunterschied m
~ **of head** = Gefäll(e)unterschied m [*Turbine f*]
differential calculus = Differentialrechnung f
~ **connection** = Differentialschaltung f
~ **drive** = Differentialtrieb m
~ **galvanometer** = Differentialgalvanometer n
~ **gears (or gearing),** see: planetary ~ (~ ~)
~ **lock** = frei ausgleichendes Differential n
~ **pawl** = Differentialsperre f
~ **plunger pump,** stage ~ ~ = Stufentauchkolbenpumpe f
~ **pulley block** = Differential-Flaschenzug m
~ **pump** = Differentialpumpe f, Stufenkolbenpumpe
~ **settlement** = ungleichmäßige Setzung f, ~ Senkung, Setzungsunterschied m
~ **thermal analysis** = Thermalanalyse f
~ **transformer** = Brückenübertrager m
differentiation = Abspaltung f [*Magma n*]
diffused air aeration = Druckluftbelüftung f [*Schlammbelebungsverfahren n*]
~ ~ **tank** = Druckluftbecken n
diffuser = Luftverteiler m
~ **plate** [*activated sludge process*] = Filterplatte f, Filtros-Platte, Diffuseur m, Belüfterplatte, Verteilerplatte

diffusion cell = Trennzelle *f*, Gas~
dig-and-turn time, digging ~ = Schürfzeit *f* [*Radschrapper m*]
to digest = faulen [*Abwasserwesen n*]
digested sludge = ausgefaulter Schlamm *m* [*Abwasserwesen n*]
digestibility = Fäulnisfähigkeit *f* [*Abwasserwesen n*]
digestion = Faulung *f*, Schlamm~, Aus~, Abbau *m*, Fäulnis *f* [*Abwasserwesen n*]
~ **chamber**, see: digester tank
~ **period** = (Schlamm)Faulzeit *f*
digestor gas = Faulgas *n*
~ **heating** = Faulraumheizung *f*
~ **tank**, (sludge-)digestion chamber (or compartment), (sludge) digestor = (Schlamm)Faulraum *m*
diggable soil = baggerbarer Boden *m*
digger, excavator ~ = Aushubgerät *n*
~ **tooth**, see: digging ~
digging, excavating, earth excavation, (common) excavation = (Erd-)Aushub *m*, Ausschachtung *f*, (Trocken)Baggerung, Trockenbaggerei *f*, Bodenaushub
~ **attachment** = Grabgerät *n* [*Ausleger-Trockenbagger m*]
~ **brake** = Grabbremse *f*
~ **bucket**, trencher ~ = Grabenbaggereimer *m*, Grabbecher *m*, Eimerbecher
~ **cable**, ~ line, ~ rope = Grabseil *n*
~ **drum** = Grabtrommel *f*
~ **force**, ~ power = Grabkraft *f*
~ **fork** = Grabgabel *f*
~ **from the boot** = Schöpfen *n* aus dem Becherwerkfuß *m*
~ **head**, rotary ~ = Kugelschauflerkopf *m*
~ **ladder**, dredging ~, bucket ~ = Eimerleiter *f*, Baggerleiter [*Naßbagger m*]
~ ~, ditcher ~, bucket flight = Eimerleiter *f*, Baggerleiter [*Grabenbagger m*]
~ **lever** [*shovel*] = Grabhebel *m*
~ **line**, ~ cable, ~ rope = Grabseil *n*
~ ~ **boom point sheave** = Grabseilscheibe *f* am Auslegerkopf *m*
~ ~ **drum** = Grabseiltrommel *f*
~ **lock** [*shovel*] = Grabblockierung *f*
~ **motion** = Grabbewegung *f*
~ **point**, ~ site = Grabstelle *f*, Baggerstelle, Aushubstelle

~ **power**, ~ force = Grabkraft *f*
~ **pulls** [*shovel*] = stoßweise Beanspruchung *f* beim Baggern *n*
~ **push** [*shovel*] = Rückdruck *m* beim Baggern *n*
~ **shovel**, hand ~ = Schaufel *f*, Schippe *f*
~ **site**, see: ~ point
~ **time**, dig-and-turn ~ = Schürfzeit *f* [*Radschrapper m*]
~ **tool** = Grabwerkzeug *n*
~ **tooth**, bucket ~, digger ~ = Eimerbecherzahn *m*, Grabbecherzahn
~ **wheel**, cutting ~ = Eimerrad *n*, Kreiseimerleiter *f*, Schaufelrad *n*
dihydrate, raw gypsum, natural gypsum = Rohgips *m*, Dihydrat *n*, Doppelhydrat, $CaSO_4 \cdot 2H_2O$ [*Ausgangsmaterial für gebrannten Gips*]
dike (US); dyke (Brit.) = Deich *m*
~ = großer Graben *m*
~ = Trockensteinmauer *f*, Trockenmauerwerk *n* [*in Schottland*]
~ **land**, innings = Deichland *n*
~ **rock** (US); dyke (Brit.) = Ganggestein *n*
diked, dyked = eingedeicht
dilapidated, ramshackle = baufällig
dilatable soil, dilative ~ = dehnbarer Boden *m*
dilatancy of sand = Volumenvergrößerung *f* von Sand *m*
dilative soil, see: dilatable ~
to dilute = verdünnen
dilution method = Verdünnungsmethode *f*
~ **water** = Verdünnungswasser *n*
dimensional analysis = Größenanalyse *f*
~ **design of concrete cross-sections for bending and axial load** = Bemessung *f* von Betonquerschnitten *mpl* mit Biegung *f* und Längskraft *f*
~ ~ ~ **continuous beams** = Berechnung *f* von durchlaufenden Balken *mpl*
dimensioning = Bemessung *f*, Dimensionierung, Dimensionsbestimmung
dimensions = Abmessungen *fpl*, Baumaße *npl*
dimethyl, ethane, C_2H_6 = Äthan *n*, Dimethyl *n*
dimple (US) = Delle *f* [*kleine Vertiefung im Boden m*]
Dinaric Alps = Dinarische Alpen *f*

dioctahedral mica = dioktaedrischer Glimmer *m*
dioptase, see: emerald copper (Min.)
diorite = Diorit *m*
dioxide of silicon, SiO_2, see: silica
to dip, to fall (Geol.) = (ein)fallen
dip = (Ein)Fallen *n* [*größte Neigung einer Schicht oder eines Ganges gegen die Waag(e)rechte*]
~ **at high angles** = steiles (Ein)Fallen *n*
~ ~ **low angles** = flaches (Ein)Fallen *n*
diploma engineer = Diplomingenieur *m*
dip lubrication = Tauchschmierung *f*
~ **meter**, stratameter = Stratameter *n*
~ **of the horizon**, apparent depression of the horizon = Kimmtiefe *f*, Kimmung *f*
dipped electrode = Tauchelektrode *f*
Dippel's oil, see: bone oil
dipper = Gießlöffel *m* mit langem Stiel *m*
~, see: bucket
~, dip(ping) switch = Abblendschalter *m*
~ **arm**, see: (~) stick
~ **bucket**, see: bucket
~ (~) **dredge(r)**, spoon ~ = Naßlöffelbagger *m*, Löffelnaßbagger, schwimmender Löffelbagger
~ **handle**, see: (~) stick
~ **shovel** = Hochlöffel *m*
(~) **stick**, ~ handle, ~ arm = Löffelstiel *m*, Auslegerstiel
~ ~ **sleeve** = Löffelstieltasche *f*, Auslegerstieltasche
~ **tooth** = Löffelzahn *m*
~ **trip** = Auslösung *f* für Verriegelung *f* der Löffelklappe *f*, Löffelklappenauslöser *m*
dipping bed, inclined ~ (Geol.) = einfallende Schicht *f*
dip(ping) switch, dipper = Abblendschalter *m*
dipping varnish = Tauchlack *m*
dipstick, dip rod = Peilstab *m*
~ = Tauchstab *m* [*Asphaltarbeiterwerkzeug n*]
dipyre, dipyrite, mizzonite (Min.) = Schmelzstein *m*, Dipyr *m*
direct acting = direkt wirkend
~ ~ **piling plant**, ~ ~ pile driving ~ = direkt wirkende Ramme *f*
~ ~ **pump** = schwungradlose Pumpe *f*

~ ~ **steam piling hammer**, steam-engine piston and cylinder in which the piston is the hammer = Dampf(ramm)hammer *m*, Dampf(ramm)bär *m*, (Dampf)Zylinderbär, direkt wirkender Rammbär *m*
~ **compression** = Alleindruck *m*, reiner Druck
~ **current**, d. c. = Gleichstrom *m* [*Elektrizität f*]
~ ~ **generator** = Gleichstromgenerator *m*, Gleichstromdynamo *m*
~ **drive** = direkter Antrieb *m*
directed research = Zweckforschung *f*
~ **well drilling**, see: directional ~ ~
direct from drum type sprayer, hand sprayer (or spraying machine) for drawing direct from drums or barrels = Faßsprenger *m*
directional island = Leitinsel *f*
~ **well drilling**, directed ~ ~ = gerichtetes Bohren *n* [*Bohrgestänge n durch Richtkeile gesteuert*]
direction indicator = Winker *m* [*Fahrzeug n*]
~ **of current** = Stromrichtung *f*
~ ~ **force** = Kraftrichtung *f*
~ ~ **jacking** = Spannrichtung *f* [*Spannbeton m*]
~ ~ **rotation** = Drehsinn *m*, Drehrichtung *f*
~ ~ **the angle of deviation** = Azimut *n*, *m* der Abweichung *f*, Abweichungsrichtung *f*
~ ~ ~ **strike**, bearing of the trend = Streichrichtung *f* (Geol.).
~ ~ **throw** = Hebel-Schaltrichtung *f*
~ ~ **travel** = Fahrtrichtung *f*
~ ~ **welding** = Schweißrichtung *f*
~ **post**, guide ~, supplementary direction sign [*deprecated: direction sign, sign post, finger post*] = Wegweiser *m*
direct labour (Brit.); see: state forces (US)
~ **motor drive** = Einzelantrieb *m*
~-**reading compass** = Nah(ablese)kompaß *m*
director = Direktor *m*
~ = Führungsstück *n*
direct shear test = direkter Scherversuch *m*
~ **strain** = direkte Dehnung *f*
~ **tension (or tensile) strength** = reine Zugfestigkeit *f*

dirt — discharge tunnel

dirt (US); soil, earth = Boden *m*, Erdstoff *m*, Lockergestein *n*
~ grouser = (Gleis)Kettenstollen *m*, Raupenstollen
dirtmover (US); earthmover; earthmoving gear (Brit.) = Erdbewegungsgroßgerät *n*, Bodenfördergerät
dirtmoving (US); earthmoving, soil shifting operations = Erdbewegungen *fpl*
dirt road (US); earth ~ = Erdstraße *f*
to disassemble, to strip down, to dismantle = auseinandernehmen, abbauen, demontieren, abmontieren
to disbark, to peel, to strip the bark = entrinden, abschälen, (ent)schälen, abborken
disc, disk = Scheibe *f*
discarded slag = Haldenschlacke *f*
disc auger = Tellerbohrer *m* [*Bodenuntersuchung f*]
~ bit = Diskenmeißel *m*, Scheibenmeißel
~ boss = Scheibennabe *f*
~ coulter = Scheibensech *n*
~ crusher = Scheibenbrecher *m*
~ feeder = Tellerspeiser *m*, Tellerzuteiler, Telleraufgeber, Tellerbeschicker, Rundbeschicker
~ filter = Scheibenfilter *n, m*
~ (grinding) mill = Scheiben(mahl)mühle *f*
~ harrow; disk plowing harrow (US) = (Teller)Scheibenegge *f*, Diskusegge
~ meter = Scheibenwassermesser *m*
~ mill, ~ grinding ~ = Scheiben(mahl-)mühle *f*
~ plough (Brit.); disk plow (US) = Scheibenpflug *m*, Spatenpflug
~ roller = Rillenwalze *f*
~ screen = Scheibenrechen *m* [*Abwasserwesen n*]
~ turbine = Scheibenturbine *f*
~ valve = Tellerventil *n*
~ ~ bailer = Schlammbüchse *f* mit Klappenventil *n*
~ wheel = Scheibenrad *n*
discharge = Vorflut *f*, Abfluß *m*
~, outlet = Auslaß *m*
to discharge = ableiten [*Wasser in einen Fluß m*]

discharge (air) shaft, upcast ~ = Ausziehschacht *m*
~ basin = Entlastungsbecken *n*
~ belt, ~ conveyor (~) = Abwurf(förder)band *n*
~ box = (Auf)Fangkessel *m*, Rohrfänger *m* [*Druckluftbetonförderer m*]
~ branch; see: draft tube tunnel (US)
~ carrier (channel type spillway) [*is either an open channel or tunnel*] = Überlaufabführungsanlage *f*
~ channel, overflow ~, tail race = Unterwasserkanal *m*, Ablauf *m*, Untergraben *m*, Abflußkanal
~ chute, swivel ~ = Abwurfschurre *f*, Auslaufschurre, Austrag(ungs)schurre
~ coefficient (Brit.); coefficient of discharge (US) = Abflußkoeffizient *m*, Abflußbeiwert *m* [*Ungleichförmigkeit f eines Wasserlaufes m*]
~ conveyor (belt), ~ belt = Abwurf(förder)band *n*
~ curve, see: hydrograph of flow
~ electrode, emitting ~, ionizing ~ = Sprühelektrode *f* [*Elektroabscheider m*]
~ gate = Entleerungsschieber *m*
~ ~ = Zuteilgefäßverschluß *m*
~ ~ rope = Klappenseil *n* [*Baggerlöffel m*]
~ line = Abflußleitung *f*
~ nozzle = Strahldüse *f*
~ opening = Entleeröffnung *f*
~ ~, ~ point, outlet ~ [*jaw crusher*] = Austrittsöffnung *f*, Austragsspalt *m*
~ outlet, ~ tunnel = Entlastungsstollen *m*
~ pipe = Abflußrohr *n*
~ ~ [*hydraulic fill*] = Schlammrohr *n*
~ point, see: ~ opening
~ pressure = Ausflußdruck *m*, Ausströmungsdruck
~ ~ = Einspritzdruck *m* [*Dieselmotor m*]
~ section, cross section of stream discharge = Abflußquerschnitt *m*, Durchflußquerschnitt, benetzter Querschnitt, durchströmter Querschnitt [*von dem abfließenden Wasser erfüllter Querschnitt*]
~ shaft, see: ~ (air) ~
~ speed, see: velocity of flow
~ tunnel, ~ outlet = Entlastungsstollen *m*

discharging material, ground product, finished ~ = Fertiggut n [*Mühle f*]
discolo(u)ration = Verfärbung f
~ test = Färbversuch m
discontinuous grading, gap grading, discontinuous granulometry = diskontinuierliche Kornabstufung f, unstetige ~, Ausfallkörnung f, Auslaßkörnung
~ horizontal member = unterbrochener Riegel m
discontinuously-graded aggregate, omitted-size fraction = Ausfallkorngemisch n
discovery of a deposit = Auffinden n eines Vorkommens n
~ ~ petroleum = Fündigkeit f auf Erdöl n
~ well = Fundbohrung f, Erschließungssonde f
disease germ = Krankheitserreger m, Krankheitskeim m
to disengage = loskuppeln
disengaging clutch, throw-out ~ = Ausrückkupplung f
~ lever, throw-out ~ = Ausrückhebel m, Auskupplungshebel
disinfection dosage of chlorine = Desinfektions-Chlorzusatz m
disintegrated granite, see: gowan
disintegration = Zerfall m, Auflösung f, Zerrüttung f
disintegrator, disintegrating mill = Desintegrator m, Stiftenschleudermaschine f, Schleuder(mahl)mühle f
disk, disc = Scheibe f
~ plowing harrow (US); disc harrow = (Teller)Scheibenegge f, Diskusegge
disking, discing = mit Scheibenegge f bearbeiten
to dismantle, see: to disassemble
dismantling = Demontage f, Abbau m
dispense point, refuel(l)ing hydrant = Zapfstelle f [*Treibstofftankanlage f*]
dispenser = Zapfbehälter m
dispersal, dispersed (hard)standing = Einzelabstellfläche f [*Flugplatz m*]
~ hut, crew ~ = (Roll)Feldhütte f
dispersant, see: detergent
dispersed hydrocarbon system = kolloidal aufgebautes Kohlenwasserstoffsystem n
disperse phase = disperse Phase f

dispersing agent, see: deflocculation ~
dispersion = Dispersion f
~ medium = geschlossene Phase f
dispersoid = Dispersoid n
displaced surface (US); thrust plane (Brit.) (Geol.) = Verschiebungsebene f
displacement = Verdrängung f
~ = Verdrückung f
~, stripping = Bindemittelablösung f
~ auger = Verdrängungsbohrer m [*Bodenuntersuchung f*]
~ indicator, stripping ~ = Ablösungsanzeiger m [*Haftfestigkeit f zwischen bit. Bindemittel n und Mineralmasse f*]
~ of centre of gravity (Brit.); ~ ~ center ~ ~ (US) = Schwerpunktverlagerung f
~ pump, see: plunger ~
displacer, plum = Stein m beim Prepaktbeton m
display panel = Schaufläche f für Ausstellungs- und Verkaufszwecke mpl
disposal area, disposal point = Absetzstelle f [*Naßbagger m*]
~ line, see: foul water line
disposition of equipment, employment of plant, equipment utilization = Geräteeinsatz m
dispute = Streitfall m
distance between branch drains = Dränabstand m, Saugerabstand
~ ~ joints = Fugenabstand m
distance-piece, spacer = Abstandshalter m
distant-reading inclinometer = Neigungsmesser m zur Fernmessung f, Gefäll(e)messer ~ ~
distant sign, advance ~ = Richtungsschild n
disthene, cyanite (Min.) = Disthen m, Zyanit m
distillate = Destillat n
distillation, vaporization = nasse Destillation f, Überdampfung f, Abdampfung f
~ flask = Destillationskolben m
distilled-grease olein, dégras oil = Wollfett-Olein n
distinct bedding = deutliche Schichtung f
distributing beam, spreading ~ = Verteilerbohle f
~ belt conveyor = Verteilergurtförderer m
~ bridge(US); see: service gangway (Brit.)

distributing bucket [*concrete paver*] = Verteilerkübel *m*

~ **chute**, distribution ~ = Verteilerschurre *f*

~ **screw**, spreading ~, spreader ~, (cross) auger = Verteilerschnecke *f*, Verteilungsschnecke [*Schwarzbelageinbaumaschine f*]

distribution board (or panel) for construction sites = Baustellen-Verteilungstafel *f*

~ **of compressive strength** = Druckfestigkeitsstreuung *f*

~ **system** = Verteilungsnetz *n*

distributor, spreader = Verteiler *m*

~ **bar** = Bindemittelsprengrohr *n*

district heating (system) = Fernheizung *f*

~ **road** (Brit.) = Kreisstraße *f*

disturbance at the springing = Kämpferrandstörung *f*

~ **factor** = Störfaktor *m*

ditch = Graben *m* [*mit abgeböschten Wänden fpl*]

~ **cleaner**, ~ cleaning machine = Grabenreiniger *m*, Grabenreinigungsmaschine *f*

~ **cleaning** = Grabenreinigung *f*, Grabensäuberung

~ **digger**, ditcher, trencher, trench digger, trenching plant, trench excavating plant, trench excavator, ditching and trenching machine; pipe line excavator (Brit.) = Grabenbagger *m*, Grabenaushubmaschine *f*

ditcher (Brit.); see: backacter

~, see: ditch digger

~ **ladder**, digging ~ = Grabenbaggerleiter *f*

ditching = Grabenaushub *m* [*abgeböschter breiter Graben m*]

~ **and trenching machine**, see: ditch digger

~ **grab** = Grabengreifer *m*

ditroite (Min.) = Ditroit *m*

diver = Taucher *m*

diversion, temporary ~ [*a temporary detour*] = provisorische Umleitung *f*, zeitweilige ~

~ = Umlegung *f*

~ = Zweckentfremdung *f* [*Haushaltsmittel npl*]

~ **cut**, bye-wash, bye-channel, spillway; diversion flume (US) = Umleit(ungs-)kanal *m* [*Talsperre f*]

~ **dam** = Umleit(ungs)sperre *f* zur Bewässerung *f*

~ **flume** (US); see: ~ cut

~ **tunnel**, by-pass ~ = Umleit(ungs)stollen *m*

~ **type river power plant** = Kanalkraftwerk *n*

~ **valve** = Verteilerventil *n*

~ **works** = Umleitungsbauten *fpl* [*Flußumleitung f*]

divide, see: watershed line

divided highway, ~ road = Straße *f* mit Mittelstreifen *m*

dividers = Stechzirkel *m*

dividing strip = Trennstreifen *m*

diving bell = Tauch(er)glocke *f*

~ **dress**, ~ suit = Taucheranzug *m*

divining rod = Wünschelrute *f*

divisional island, separator = Trenninsel *f*

division wall, partition ~ = Scheidewand *f*, Trennwand

DOBBIN barrow [*Trademark*] (Brit.) = gummibereifte(r) Zweirad-Handkarre(n) *f*, (*m*) (oder Baukarre(n)) mit Vorwärtskippung *f*, Fabrikat WILLIAM JONES LTD.

~ **wagon** (Brit.) = gummibereifter Muldenkipper *m*, Fabrikat WILLIAM JONES LTD.

dock and harbo(u)r construction (or works) = Dock- und Hafenbau *m*

~ **bridge** = Hafenbrücke *f*

~ **entrance** = Dockeinfahrt *f*

~ **floor** = Docksohle *f*

~ **gate** = Docktor *n*

~ ~ **seal** = Docktorverschluß *m*

~ **harbo(u)r** = Dockhafen *m*

docking load, ~ stress = Fahrzeugstoß *m* [*Anlegebrücke f*]

dock installation = Dockanlage *f*

dockyard, shipbuilding yard = (Schiffs-) Werft *f*

documentation of building topics = Bau-Dokumentation *f*

Dodge jaw crusher = Backenbrecher *m* mit unten befestigter Schwingenbrechbacke *f*

dog, pinch bar, dolly bar, lifting bar, wrecking bar, claw bar = Hebezwinge *f*, Hebezwänge *f*
~ = Klinke *f*
Dogger bank = Doggerbank *f*
dog spike, see: track ~
DOLBERG midget excavator = Kleinbagger *m*, Fabrikat DOLBERG-GLASER & PFLAUM G. m. b. H., ESSEN, DEUTSCHLAND
dolerite = Dolerit *m*
dolina, doline = Doline *f*, Karsttrichter *m*
dolly, see: holder-up
~ = Fahrwerk *n* [*Tiefladewagen m*]
~ **bar**, see: dog
dolomite (Min.), see: pearl spar
~, see: grey lime
~ **brick** = Dolomitstein *m*
~ **marble** [*a crystalline variety of limestone, containing in excess of 40 per cent of magnesium carbonate as the dolomite molecule*] = Dolomitmarmor *m*
~ **(rock)** = Dolomitgestein *n*, Dolomit(fels) *m*
dolomitic lime putty = Dolomitkalk-Mörtel *m*
~ **limestone**, magnesian ~ = Bitterkalk *m*, magnesiahaltiges Kalkgestein *n*, magnesiahaltiger hydraulischer Kalk *m*, Dolomitkalk, dolomitisches Kalkgestein
~ **marble**, magnesian marble = Dolomitmarmor *m* mit zwischen 5 bis 40% Magnesiumkarbonat *n*
dolphin, pile cluster, piled dolphin = Dalbe *m*, Pfahlbündel *n*
~ **head** = Dalbenkopf *m*
~ **pile** = Dalbenpfahl *m*
~ **with parallel piles** = Dalbe *m* mit parallelen Pfählen *mpl*
dome, cupola = halbsphärisches Gewölbe *n*, Kuppel *f*
~**(d) mountains** = Domgebirge *n*
dome-shaped dam = Kuppelmauer *f*
domestic heating appliance = Wohnhausheizungsanlage *f*
~ **market**, home ~ = Inlandsmarkt *m*
~ **sewage**, ~ **waste**, house ~ = Hausabwasser *n*
domical vault = Kuppelgewölbe *n*
donkey = Doppelwindenachse *f*

dope, adhesion (promoting) agent, non-stripping agent, anti-stripping admixture (or agent), bonding additive, activator, anti-stripping additive = Haftanreger *m*, (Netz-)Haftmittel *n*, adhäsionsfördernder Zusatzstoff *m*, Adhäsionsverbesserer *m*, Haftfestigkeitsverbesserer *m*
~ = Zündbeschleuniger *m* [*Dieselkraftstoff m*]
doped binder = Bindemittel *n* mit Haftanreger *m*
~ **cutback** = Verschnittbitumen *n* mit Haftanreger *m*, gedoptes Verschnittbitumen *n*
dormer rafter = Reitersparren *m*
dormitory suburb, ~ **area** = Schlaf-Stadtrandsiedlung *f*
Dorry hardness = Dorry-Härte *f* [*Widerstand m von Gesteinen npl gegen Abrieb m*]
Dortmund tank = Dortmunder Brunnen *m*
DOTMAR curb and gutter paver = Randstein-, Rinnstein- und Gehsteig-Betonier- und -verlegungsmaschine *f*, Fabrikat DOTMAR INDUSTRIES INC., KALAMAZOO, MICHIGAN, USA
dotted line = punktierte Linie *f*
double-acting hammer, automatic steam McKIERNAN-TERRY hammer = McKIERNAN-TERRY-Rammhammer *m*, doppelt wirkender (Ramm)Hammer *m*, vollautomatischer Schnellschlagbär *m*, Fabrikat McKIERNAN-TERRY CORPORATION, NEW YORK 7, USA
~ **incline(d plane)**, see: jig haulage installation on the slope
~ **ram**, see: two-way ~
double arch(ed) dam = Doppelbogenmauer *f*
~ **barrel hand pump** = Doppelstiefelhandpumpe *f*
~ **beat valve**, bell-shaped ~ = Glockenventil *n*
~ **bent**, see: ~ pile ~
double-boiler kettle = Doppel-Schmelzkessel *m* [*Fugenvergußmasse f*]
double broken and double screened chip(ping)s = Edelsplitt *m*
~ **butt strap joint** = Doppellaschennietung *f*, zweiseitige Laschennietung

double (or dual) carriageway motor road = Autobahn *f* mit Mittelstreifen *m*

~ -cone drum = Doppel-Konus-Trommel *f* [*Straßenbetoniermaschine f*]

double (contractors') (or builders') hoist = Doppel(bau)aufzug *m*

~ current generator = Doppelgenerator *m*

~ deck bridge = Etagenbrücke *f*

~ ~ screen, DD ~ = Doppeldecker *m*, Doppelstufensieb *n*, Sieb *n* mit zwei Siebfeldern *npl*, Zweidecker *m*, zweistufiges Sieb *n*

~ draw bridge = Doppelzugbrücke *f*

double-drum Colcrete-mixer = Colcrete-Zweitrommelmischer *m*

~ (concrete) mixer = Doppeltrommel(beton)mischer *m*

~ paver, dual-drum type (concrete) paver, twin-drum type (concrete) paver, twin-batch paver = Doppeltrommel(beton)straßenmischer *m*

~ pile driving winch = Doppeltrommelrammwinde *f*

~ (rope) (or cable) winch = Doppeltrommel(seil)winde *f*

double-duty double-acting hammer = Rammhammer-Pfahlzieher *m*, schlagender Pfahlzieher *m*, Rammbär-Ziehgerät *n*

double-ended boiler with common combustion chamber = Doppelender(kessel) *m* mit gemeinsamer Flammkammer *f*

~ spanner (Brit.); double head wrench = Doppelschlüssel *m*, doppelmäuliger Schraubenschlüssel *m*

double fillet weld = zweiseitige Kehlnaht *f*

double-flanged wheel = Doppelspurkranzrad *n*

double-flash distillation = Zweistufen-Destillation *f* [*Erdölaufbereitung f*]

double flattened strand = Doppelflachlitze *f*

double-flow turbine = Hoch- und Niederdruckturbine *f* mit entgegengerichteter Dampfströmung *f*

double grouser (track) shoe = Bodenplatte *f* mit Doppel(winkel)greifern *mpl* [*Gleiskette f*]

~ halved joint = Kreuzzapfen *m*

~ hammer breaker (or crusher) = Doppelhammerbrecher *m*

~ -handling = Doppel(material)umschlag *m*

double-headed rail, bull-head(ed) ~ = Doppelkopfschiene *f*, Stuhlschiene

double helical gear-wheels, ~ ~ gearing = Pfeilverzahnung *f*

~ impeller impact breaker = Doppel-Rotoren-Prallbecher *m*, Zweiwalzen-Prallbrecher, Prallbrecher mit zwei Rotoren *mpl*

~ ~ ~ (grinding) mill = Doppel-Rotoren-Prall(mahl)mühle *f*, Zweiwalzenprall(mahl)mühle *f*

~ incline, see: hump

~ lacing = doppelte Vergitterung *f* [*Stütze f*]

~ lifting hooks, ~ hoist(ing) ~ = Lastbügel *m* mit zwei Haken

~ log washer = Doppelschwertwäsche *f*

~ mechanical trowel, ~ ~ float = Zweischeiben-Glättmaschine *f* für Beton

~ movable jaw crusher (or breaker), see: twin ~ ~ (~ ~)

~ (pile) bent = Pfahlblockjoch *n*

~ pitch roof, see: saddle ~

~ prism optical square = Doppelpentagon-Winkelprisma *n*

~ refraction (Min.) = Doppelbrechung *f*

~ ~ calcspar = Doppelspat *m*

(~) roll crusher, see: roll ~

~ ropeway, double rope (or bi-cable) aerial (or cable) ropeway (or tramway)/railroad (US) = Doppeldrahtseilschwebebahn *f*, Zwei-Seil(schwebe)bahn *f* [*sogenannte deutsche Bauart f*]

double-screed transverse finisher = Doppel-Querbohlen(beton)fertiger *m*

double-shell return flow dryer (or drier) = doppelwandige Trockentrommel *f* mit Rücklauf *m*, doppelwandiger Trommeltrockner *m* ~ ~

double-shifts operation, double-shift work = Doppelschichtenbetrieb *m*

double-shoe brake = Doppelbackenbremse *f*

double skew notch = doppelte Versatzung *f*

~ (or two-jet)ski jump crossing over the roof of the power house = Doppel-Skisprung-Überfall *m* über die Krafthausdecke *f*

double squirrel-cage induction motor — down wind 129

double squirrel-cage induction motor = Doppelnutmotor *m*
~ strand roller chain = Duplex-Rollenkette *f*
double-strap web joint = doppelte Stegverlaschung *f*
double surface treatment, see: armo(u)r coat
~ swing(-span) bridge = Doppeldrehbrücke *f*
~ tamping beam finisher = Doppelstampfbohlenfertiger *m*, Doppelschlagbohlenfertiger
~ toggle crusher, compound toggle lever stone breaker (Brit.); Blake (-type jaw) crusher (or breaker), swing jaw crusher = Blake'scher Doppelkniehebelbackenbrecher *m*, Blake'scher Zweipendelbackenbrecher *m*
~-track line = doppelgleisige Bahnlinie *f*
double triangular truss, ~ Warren ~ = doppeltes Dreieckfachwerk *n*
~ turbine with the blade wheels running in opposite directions = gegenläufige Doppelturbine *f*
~-wall(ed) sheetpile cofferdam = doppelwandiger Spundwandfang(e)damm *m*, doppeltes Spundwandbauwerk *n*
double-webbed = zweistegig, doppelstegig
~ girder = Doppelstegblechträger *m*
double zone (pug mill) mixer = Zwangsmischer *m* mit kurzen und langen Mischwerkzeugen *npl*
Douglas fir, see: Oregon pine
dovetail, swallow-tail = Schwalbenschwanz *m*
~ halving = Schwalbenschwanzüberblattung *f*
dovetailing, interdigitation, interfingering (Geol.) = auskeilende Wechsellagerung *f*
dowel = Dübel *m*
~ bar = (Beton)(Fugen)Dübel *m*
~ ~ joint = verdübelte Fuge *f*
~ bit = Dübelbohrer *m*
~ brick = Dübelstein *m*
~ (l)ing = Verdübelung *f*
dowel load-transfer unit = Querfugenverdübelung *f* [bestehend aus Fugenbrett *n*, Rundeisendübel *m* und Baustahlgewebebügel *m*]

down, (sand-)dune = (Sand)Düne *f*
down-cast air shaft = Einziehschacht *m*
down-draught carburettor, ~ carburetter (Brit.); **down-draft carburetor** (US) = Fallstromvergaser *m*
down drilling = lotrechtes Niedertreiben *n* von Bohrlöchern *npl*
downfolding (Geol.) = Abfaltung *f*
downgrade section, downhill ~ = Gefällstrecke *f*
downhand welding = waag(e)rechtes Schweißen *n*, horizontales ~
down-hole, surface-to-tunnel pipe chute = Fallrohr *n*, Rohr *n* von Erdoberfläche *f* bis zur Tunneldecke *f*
~ = Fallschacht *m* [*Tunnelbau m*]
downpipe, down comer, down spout, fall pipe = Abflußrohr *n*, Regenrohr [*am Haus n*]
downpour, torrential ~ = Regenguß *m*, Sturzregen *m*
downstream = flußabwärts, stromabwärts
~ apron = unterwasserseitige Vorlage *f*
~ baffle (US), see: ~ sill
~ batter = Anzug *m* luftseits [*Talsperre f*]
~ cofferdam, ~ temporary dam = rückwärtige Schutzsperre *f*
~ elevation = Ansicht *f* von unterstrom
~ face, air-side ~ = Luftseite *f* [*Talsperre f*]
~ nose (Brit.); **downstream pier nosing** (US) = Pfeilerrücken *m* [*Talsperre f*]
~ power plant = Unterliegerwerk *n*
~ radius of crest (circle) = Radius *m* der luftseitigen Kronenbegrenzung *f* [*Talsperre f*]
~ sill, downstream baffle (US); baffle-wall (Brit.); deflector, stilling basin baffle = Strahlablenker *m* [*Kolkschutz m einer Talsperre f*]
~ temporary dam, see: ~ cofferdam
~ toe (US); see: base (Brit.)
downtime = vermeidbare Verlustzeit *f* [*Baumaschinen fpl*]
down-town terminal traffic = Zielverkehr *m* zur Innenstadt *f*
downward bowing = Abwölbung *f* (Geol.)
~ conveying = Abwärtsförderung *f*
down wind, katabatic ~ = Fallwind *m*

5

dowser, waterfinder = Wünschelrutengänger *m*
Dowson gas = Dowsongas *n*, Mischgas, Stadtgas
to doze = mit Bulldozer *m* arbeiten
* **dozer**, see: bulldozer
~ **blade**, ~ apron; pusher-blade (Brit.) = (Fronträumer-)Planierschild *n*, Brustschild
~ **blade edge** = Brustschildschneide *f*
~ ~ **for tree felling work;** see: three-sided moldboard (US)
~-**loader**, see: bulldozer-shovel
dozer shovel unit = Frontladeschaufelvorrichtung *f*
dozing, see: bull ~
draft gage (US); draught gauge (Brit.) = Zugmesser *m*
draftsman (US); see: draughtsman (Brit.)
draft tube (US); draught ~ (Brit.) = Auszugrohr *n* [*ein Rohr n im Wasserkraftwerk n*]
~ ~ **tunnel** (US); discharge branch = Auslaufstollen *m* [*von Turbine f zum Ableitungstunnel m*]
drag = Planierschleppe *f*
~ **bit**, see: spudding ~
~ **box**, see: box spreader
~ **brake** = Schürfbremse *f* [*Tieflöffel m*]
~ **bucket** (US); draught ~ (Brit.) = backacter (Brit.)
~ ~, see: dragline ~
~ (**cable**) [*in a pull shovel and a dragline*] = Zugseil *n*, Schürfseil *n*
~ **chain** [*dragline bucket*] = Zugkette *f*, Schürfkette
~ (**chain**) = Kratzerkette *f*
drag(-**chain**) **conveyor** = Kratz(er)förderer *m*, Kratzertransporteur *m*
drag clutch, digging ~ [*backhoe*] = Schürfkupplung *f*
~ **dampening device** = Schleppanzeigedämpfer *m*, Schleppzeigerdämpfer *m*
~ **drum, digging** ~ = Schleppseil-Trommel *f*, Schürftrommel
dragging = Abschleppen *n* [*eine Fläche f*]
drag lever = Schlepphebel *m* [*Bagger m*]
dragline; see: boom dragline (US)
~ **bucket,** ~ scoop, drag ~ = Schleppschaufel *f*, Schlepplöffel *m*, Eimerseilkübel *m*, Zugkübel

~ **yoke**, drag ~ = Seilschloß *n*
drag link = Lenkschubstange *f*
dragon beam = Stichbalken *m*
drag plough (Brit.); ~ plow (US) = Schlepppflug *m*
~ **road-scraper**, see: trailing-scoop grader
~ **rope**, see: hauling ~
~ **scoop**, see: dragline bucket
~ **scraper and loader** = Schrapplader *m*, Fahrschrapper *m*, Verlade-(Fahr-)Schrapper
~ ~ (**machine**), power ~ ~ (~), power scraper excavator = (gewöhnlicher) Schrapper *m*, Schleppschrapper *m*
(~) ~ **hoist** = Schrapperwinde *f*, Schrapperhaspel *m*, *f*
(~) ~ **installation** = Schrapperanlage *f*
~ ~ **stockpiler**, see: storage machine
~ ~ **with steeply inclined ramp** = Steil-Schleppschrapper *m*
dragshovel, see: backacter
dragskip = Schrapperschaufel *f*, Räumschaufel [*Arbeitsgerät n beim Handschrapper m*]
~ (**spreader**) **box**, see: box spreader
~ **yoke**, dragline ~ = Seilschloß *n*
drag-yoke-to-dump-sheave section = Seilstück *n* welches vom Seilschloß zur Kippseilrolle läuft [*Schleppschaufelbagger m*]
drain = Drän *m*
~, see: channel
to drain = dränieren, entwässern
drainable = entwässerbar, dränierbar
* **drainage** = Entwässerung *f*, Trockenlegung *f*
~ **area**, see: catchment ~
~ **basin**, see: catchment area
~ **blanket** = Entwässerungsteppich *m*
* (**drainage**) **culvert**, ~ duct = Durchlaß *m*, Abzugkanal *m*
~ **curtain** = Entwässerungsschürze *f*
~ **ditch**, see: (open) ditch
~ **divide**, see: watershed line
* ~ **duct**, see: (~) culvert
~ **gallery,** ~ tunnel = Entwässerungsstollen *m*
~ **hole**, see: weep hole
~ **opening**, see: weep hole
~ **pipe**, see: drain ~
~ **tool** = Dränwerkzeug *n*
~ **trench** = Drängraben *m*

drainage trenching = Drängrabenaushub *m*
~ **tunnel**, see: penstock drain
~ ~, see: ~ gallery
drain bin = Entwässerungskammer *f* [*Waschmaschine f*]
~ **cock** = Ablaßhahn *m*
drained shear(ing) test = entwässerter Scherversuch *m*
drain outfall, see: interceptor
~ **pipe, drainage** ~ = Dränrohr *n*
~ **plug** = Ablaßstopfen *m*
~ **sluice valve** = Ablaßschieber *m*
~ **trap, stench** ~ = Geruchverschluß *m*
~ **tunnel**, see: penstock drain
~ **valve** = Entleerungsventil *n*
draught (Brit.); **draft** (US) = Tiefgang *m*
~ **gauge** (Brit.); see: draft gage (US)
draughtsman (Brit.); **draftsman** (US) = Zeichner *m*
draught tube (Brit.); see: draft ~ (US)
drawbar = Zugstange *f* [*Motorstraßenhobel m*]
~ = Zugdeichsel *f*
(draw-cut type) keyseater = Keilnutenziehmaschine *f*
drawdown = Absenkung *f* [*Talsperre f*]
~ **level, minimum water storage elevation** = Absenk(ungs)ziel *n*
draw-in = Haltebucht *f* für Omnibusse
drawing board = Reißbrett *n*
~ **curve** = Kurvenlineal *n*
~ **instruments** = Reißzeug *n*
~ **office** (Brit.); **drafting** ~ (US) = Zeichenbüro *n*
~ **pen**, see: ruling ~
~ **table** = Zeichentisch *m*
drawn tube = gezogenes Rohr *n*
draw well, open bucket well (Brit.); **sweep well** (US) = Ziehbrunnen *m*
drayage charges = Rollgeld *n*, Fuhrgeld *n*
* **dredge** (US); **dredger** (Brit.); **dredging craft** = Naßbagger *m*, Schwimmbagger *m*
(dredged) berth [*a deepening in front of a tidal quay*] = Sohle *f* [*Vertiefung f vor einer Kaimauer*]
~ **peat** = Baggertorf *m*
~ **river sand** = Baggersand *m*
dredge(r) bucket = Baggereimer *m* [*beim Naßbagger m*]

~ ~ **(type) elevator, intermittent (or spaced) bucket (type) elevator** = Teilbecherwerk *n*, Schöpfbecherwerk
~ **excavator**, see: bucket ladder ~
dredge(r) hoist = Naßbaggerwinde *f*
~ **well** = Baggerschacht *m*, Baggerbrunnen *m*
dredging, underwater ~, **dredge(r) work, underwater excavation, unterwater digging** = Naßbaggerung *f*, Naßbaggerei *f*
~ **appliance** = Baggeraggregat *n* [*Naßbaggerung f*]
~ **bucket**, see: dewatering ~
~ **ladder, bucket ladder, digging ladder** = Eimerleiter *f*, Baggerleiter [*Naßbagger m*]
~ **pump** = Baggerpumpe *f*
~ **spoil, dredged materials: dredge muck, dredge spoil** (US) = Baggergut *n* [*Naßbagger m*]
~ **well, ladder** ~ = Schlitz *m* im Schiffskörper *m* [*Naßbagger m*]
dreikanter, see: glyptolith
dressed stone = Haustein *m*
dresser = Sanitäter *m*
dressing = Zurichten *n*
~, **blinding** [*deprecated*]; **gritting, grit blinding** = Absplitten *n* [*Verschleißschicht f*]
~, see: processing
~ **hammer, tippler** = Zurichthammer *m*
dried matter = Trockensubstanz *f*, Trockenrückstand *m*
drier, dryer = Trockner *m*
~ = Trockenmittel *n*
drift (US) (Geol.) = Eisdecke *f*
~, see: adit (level)
~ = Gletscherschutt *m*
~ = Dorn *m*
~ (Brit.); (small-diameter) tunnel, gallery, heading = Stollen *m*
to drift = weglaufen [*Frequenz f*]
~ ~ = treiben
drift anchor = Treibanker *m*
~ **canal** = Triftrinne *f*, Triftkanal *m*
~ **conveyor** = Streckenband *n* [*Bergbaum*]
~ **current** = Driftströmung *f*
drifter (machine), piston drilling machine = Stoßbohrmaschine *f*
drifting = Aufreiben *n*, Dornen *n*

drift(ing) ice, floating ~, flow ~, loose ~ = Treibeis *n*
~ net = Treibnetz *n*
~ path, side ~ = Triftpfad *m*
~ water = Triftwasser *n*
drift mine = Tagebaugrube *f*
~ sand = Treibsand *m*, Triebsand
driftway = Abbaustrecke *f* [*Bergbau m*]
~, bridle-path, bridle-road, bridle-way, drove, droveway, packway = Saumpfad *m*
~ winch = Streckenhaspel *m, f*, Streckenwinde *f* [*Bergbau m*]
drift wood = Triftholz *n*, Treibholz
~ ~ peat = Triftholztorf *m*, Treibholztorf
drill barge = Bohrinsel *f*
***(drill) bit,** rock(-drill) bit, drilling bit, boring bit, rock cutter bit = Gesteinsbohrerkrone *f*, Abbaumeißel *m*, Bohrmeißel, Bohrkrone
(~) ~ (cutting) edge, drill point, chisel-type bit cutting edge = (Bohr)Schneide *f*, (Bohr)Meißelschneide, Bohrerschneide
(~) ~ with tungsten carbide insert (or tip), (tungsten) carbide (tipped) (drill) bit = Hartmetallmeißel *m*, Hartmetall-(bohr)krone *f*
~ carriage = Bohrunterwagen *m*
~ collar = Schwerstange *f*
(~) core, test ~ = Bohrkern *m*, Probekern
~ cuttings, well ~, rock ~, drillings = Bohrschmant *m*, Bohrgut *n*, Bohrmehl *n*
drilled grout hole = Bohrloch *n*, Einpreßloch, Verpreßloch, Auspreßloch, Injektionsloch [*Tunnelbau m*]
~-in caisson, bored ~ = [*a type of foundation pier consisting of a heavy steel pipe with a reinforced cutting edge which is driven open end to rock and cleaned out*] = Bohrgründungspfeiler *m*
drilled well = Tief-Bohrbrunnen *m*
driller, rock ~, hard rock miner = Mineur *m*, Gesteinshauer *m*
driller's station = Bohrmeisterstand *m*
drill gauge = Bohrerlehre *f*
***drill hammer,** (hand) hammer (rock)drill, rock drill hammer = Hand-(Gesteins)Bohrhammer *m*, Hand-Felsbohrhammer

~ head = Spindelstock *m* [*Bohrmaschine f*]
~ hole, bore ~ = Bohrloch *n*
drill-hole spacing, bore-hole ~ = Bohrlochanordnung *f*
drilling = Bohren *n*, Aus~
~ and milling machine = Bohr- und Fräsmaschine *f*
~ bar, see: drill rod
* **~ bit,** see: (drill) bit
~ cable, ~ rope, ~ line = Bohrseil *n*
~ campaign = Bohrkampagne *f*
~ capacity, diameter drilled = Bohrdurchmesser *m*
~ control = Bohrdruckregulierung *f*
~ crew = Bohrmannschaft *f*
~ derrick, drill tower = Bohrturm *m*
~ diamonds, black ~, carbon(ado)s = Bohrdiamanten *mpl*, schwarze Diamanten
~ engineering = Bohrtechnik *f*
~ equipment. ~ outfit = Bohrausrüstung *f*
~ field = Bohrfeld *n*, Bohrgelände *n*
~ firm = Bohrunternehmen *n*, Bohrunternehmung *f*, Bohrfirma *f*
~ fluid = Bohrflüssigkeit *f*
~ hammer, striking ~ = Treibfäustel *m*
~ in = Anbohren *n* eines Vorkommens *n*, Anritzen *n* ~ ~
~ indicator, weight ~, drillometer = Drillometer *m*, Bohrdruckmesser *m*, Bohrdruckmeßgerät *n*
~ jaw = Bohrkloben *m* einer Planscheibe *f*
~ jig, drill ~ = Bohrvorrichtung *f*
~ jumbo, (tunnel) jumbo = Bohrjumbo *m*, Ausleger-Bohrwagen *m*, Groß-Bohrwagen
~ line, see: ~ cable
~ machine, boring ~ = Bohrmaschine *f*
~ ~ table = Bohrtisch *m*
~ method, boring ~ = Bohrverfahren *n*
~ mud, rotary ~ = Bohrschlamm *m*
~ operations, ~ work = Bohrarbeiten *fpl*
~ outfit, ~ equipment = Bohrausrüstung *f*
~ pontoon = Bohrponton *m*
~ premium = Bohrprämie *f*
~ progress, ~ rate, rate of drilling progress = Bohrfortschritt *m*
~ ~ chart = Bohrfortschrittsdiagramm *n*, Bohrfortschrittsschaubild *n*
~ range = Bohrbereich *m*
~ rig = Bohranlage *f*

drilling rod — driveway

drilling rod, see: drill ~
~ rope, see: ~ cable
drillings, see: drill cuttings
drilling speed = Bohrgeschwindigkeit *f*
~ tool = Bohrwerkzeug *n*
(~) ~ jont = Gestängeverbinder *m* [*Tiefbohrtechnik f*]
~ with reversed circulation, counterflush drilling = Bohren *n* mit Verkehrtspülung *f*
~ work, see: ~ operations
drill jig, drilling ~ = Bohrvorrichtung *f*
~ pipe = Bohrrohr *n* [*wird nach Beendigung des Bohrens statisch oder dynamisch durch Ziehgerät gezogen*]
~ ~ elevator = Bohrgestängefahrstuhl *m*
~ ~ pin = Bohrgestängezapfen *m*
~ ~ slip = Bohrgestängeabfangkeil *m*
~ ~ sub = Bohrgestängeübergang *m*
~ ~ thread = Bohrgestängegewinde *n*
~ ~ dope = Bohrgestängefett *n*
~ ~ twist-off, breaking of the drill stem = Bohrgestängebruch *m*
~ plough (Brit.); **~ plow** (US) = Rollpflug *m*, Saatpflug, Rillenpflug
~ point, see: (drill) bit (cutting) edge
~ press, upright ~ ~, standard ~ ~ = Säulenbohrmaschine *f*, normale Vertikalbohrmaschine
~ rod, boring ~, drilling ~, bore ~, ~ bar = Bohrstange *f*
drill-runner = Bohrer *m* [*Arbeiter der Bohrlöcher zum Sprengen bohrt*]
drill-sharpening and up-setting machine = Bohrer-Schärf- und -Stauchmaschine *f*
drill speeder (US) = Schnellbohrvorrichtung *f*
~ spindle, drilling ~ = Bohrspindel *f*
~ steel = Bohr(meißel)stahl *m*
~ tower, drilling derrick = Bohrturm *m*
~ wagon = Bohrlafette *f*
to drill with a bit = meißeln [*mit dem Meißel m bohren*]
drinking fountain = Trinkbrunnen *m*
~ water, potable ~ = Trinkwasser *n*
~ ~ supply, potable water ~ = Trinkwasserversorgung *f*
~ ~ tank, potable water ~ = Trinkwasserbehälter *m*
drip oiler = Tropföler *m*

dripping water, see: condensation ~
~ wet = triefend naß
drip-proof = tropfwassergeschützt
drive = Antrieb *m*
to drive = schlagen [*Niet m*]
drive axle, driving ~, live ~, power ~ = Treibachse *f*, (An)Trieb(s)achse
~ back gear = Antriebsvorgelege *n*
~ belt, driving ~ = Antriebsriemen *m*, Treibriemen
~ ~ tightener = Treibriemenspanner *m*
~ bushing = Mitnehmereinsatz *m*
~ case = Antriebsgehäuse *n*
~ chain, driving ~; propel (drive) ~ (US) = Treibkette *f*, Antriebskette *f*, Triebkette
~ clutch = Antriebskupplung *f*
~ end = Antriebsende *n*
~ flange = Antriebsflansch *m*
~ gear = Antriebsmaschine *f*
~ head pulley, see: motorised ~ ~
~-in restaurant = Rasthaus *n*
~-in theatre = Autokino *n*
driven concrete pile = Stahlbetonrammpfahl *m*
drive(n) well = Rammbrunnen *m*, Nortonbrunnen
drive-pipe = Rammrohr *n*
drive point, see: pile shoe
driver, plant hand, (plant) operator, equipment operator; operative (Brit.) = (Geräte-)Bediener *m*, Maschinenführer *m*, Bedienungsmann *m*
~ habit = Fahrergewohnheit *f*
~ probing,**~pricking** = Sondenrammung *f*
driver's cab(in), operator's control ~ = Führerkabine *f*, Führerhaus *n*, Fahrerhaus *n*, Fahrerkabine
~ license = Führerschein *m*
~ seat = Bedienungssitz *m*, Führersitz, Fahrersitz
driver tension, strain of driving = Fahrerbeanspruchung *f*
~ vision = Fahrersicht *f*
drive section, see: driving part
~ shaft, driving shaft = Antriebswelle *f*
~ sprocket, driving ~, propel ~ = Antriebsturas *m*, Antriebskettenrad *n*
~ unit = Antriebsaggregat *n*
driveway, see: private drive

driveway, outward-bound road, exit road = Ausfallstraße *f*
~ **turntable** = Autodrehscheibe *f*
drive wheel, see: driving wheel
driving, pile ~ = Einrammen *n*
~ = Fahren *n*
~, see: tunnel progress
~ **axle**, see: drive ~
~ **belt**, see: drive ~
(~) **cap**, see: helmet
~ **chain**, see: drive chain
~ ~, tyre ~ (Brit.); tire ~ (US) = Reifen(schutz)kette *f*
~ **clutch** = Antriebskupplung *f*
~ **fuel**, power ~ = Betriebsstoff *m*, Treibstoff *m*, Kraftstoff *m*
~ **helmet**, see: helmet
~ **mechanism** = Antriebsmechanismus *m*
~ **on the rake** = neigbares Einrammen *n*, Schrägrammung *f*
~ **part**, drive section = Antriebsteil *m, n*
~ **pinion** = Triebling *m*, Antrieb(s)ritzel *n*
~ **(or motive) power (or force)** = Antriebskraft *f*, Triebkraft, Treibkraft
~ **rain**, pelting ~ = Schlagregen *m*
~ **record**, penetration ~ = Rammprotokoll *n*
~ **resistance** = Rammwiderstand *m*
~ **rod**, drop-penetration sounding apparatus, percussion probe = Rammsonde *f*, Schlagsonde
~ **shaft**, drive ~ = Antriebswelle *f*, Triebwelle
~ **sheave** = Antriebsscheibe *f*
~ **snow** = Schneegestöber *n*, Schneetreiben *n*
~ **speed**, travel(l)ing ~ = Fahrgeschwindigkeit *f*
~ **spring** = Triebfeder *f*
~ **sprocket**, drive ~, propel ~, bull wheel = Antriebskettenrad *n*, Antriebsturas *m*, Kettenantriebsrad
~ **station**, ~ terminal = Antriebsstation *f* [*Seilbahn f*]
~ **test**, drop-penetration testing, percussion penetration method = Rammsondierung *f*
~ **tooth** = Triebzahn *m*
~ **toothed wheel**, ~ cog ~ = Antriebszahnrad *n*

~ **wheel**, drive ~, traction ~ = (An-)Triebsrad *n*, Treibrad
drizzle, drizzling rain = Sprühregen *m*, Rieselregen, Nieseln *n*
dropping birch, weeping ~ = Hängebirke *f*
to drop, to descend = abfallen [*Kurve f*]
drop ball = Fallbär *m* [*zur Zerkleinerung f von Steinblöcken mpl*]
~ **boring tool** = Freifallbohrer *m*
~ **counter** = Tropfenzähler *m*
drop-forged = gesenkgeschmiedet
drop gate = Fallklappe *f*
~ **hammer**, tripped ~ ~, drop pile ~, winch-type ~, monkey, tup = Ramm-(fall)bär *m*, Fallhammer *m*, Freifallbär, Bär, Fallgewicht *n*
~ ~ **for shattering old pavement** = Zertrümmerungsramme *f*
d ~-**inlet spillway**, see: shaft-and-tunnel ~
drop-penetration sounding apparatus, driving rod, percussion probe = Schlagsonde *f*, Rammsonde
~ **testing**, percussion penetration method, driving test = Rammsondierung *f*
drop pile hammer, see: drop hammer
dropping-ball (penetration) test = Kugelfallprobe *f*
dropping-weight compaction machine, ~ compactor = Fall-Stampfverdichtungsmaschine *f*
~ **method of compaction** = Rammplattenverdichtung *f*
drop pipe = Aufsatzrohr *n* [*Brunnen m*]
~ **point** = Tropfpunkt *m*
drop-shaft method; see under "caisson pile"
drop-side body = Seitenklappenpritsche *f* [*LKW m*]
drop type switchboard = Klappenschrank *m*
~ **valve** = hängendes Ventil *n*
~ **weight** = Fallgewicht *n*
DROTT four in one, ~ 4-in-1 = DROTT-Klappschaufellader *m*
drought = Dürre *f*, Trockenheit *f*
drove, see: bridle-path
drowned river = ertrunkener Fluß *m*
drum = Trommel *f*
~ **armature** = Trommelanker *m* [*Elektrotechnik f*]
~ **bench** = Scheibenziehbank *f*

drum brake — dry press hollow tile

drum brake = Trommelbremse *f*
~ circumference = Trommelumfang *m*
~ clutch = Trommelkupplung *f*
~ controller = Walzenschalter *m*
~ filter = Trommelfilter *n, m*
~ gate, see: sector ~
drumlin (Geol.) = Drum(lin) *m*, Drümmel *m*, Rückenberg *m* [*langgestreckter flacher Hügel m aus Moränengeschiebe n*]
drum mixer, see: revolving drum (type) mixer
~ pelletizer = Kugelverformtrommel *f*, Trommel zur Tonkügelchenherstellung *f*
~ pump = Walzenpumpe *f*
~ screen, see: rotary ~
~ separator = Trommelabscheider *m*
~ shaft = Trommelwelle *f*
~ ~ key = Trommelwellenwinkel *m*
~ sluice, see: sector gate
~ starter = Anlaßwalze *f*
~ (type) mixer, see: revolving ~ (~) ~
~ weir = Trommelwehr *n*
~ winch = Trommelwinde *f*, Trommelwindwerk *n*
Drurmast oak, see: chestnut ~
drusy structure (Geol.) = Drusenstruktur *f*
(dry-)batched aggregate, dry-batch materials, matched ~, batched ~, re-combined ~ = Trockenbeton *m* [*Gemisch n ohne Wasserzugabe f*]
dry-batching plant, see: aggregate batching plant
dry choked stone base (course) = trocken verfüllte Schottertragschicht *f*
"dry" concrete, stiff ~, no-slump ~ = erdfeuchter Beton *m*, steifer ~
DRYCRETE [*Trademark*] = ein Betonsperrzusatz *m* in den USA
dry density, dry bulk density [*soil*] = Trockenraumgewicht *n*
~ ~ moisture content graph, see: Proctor compaction curve
~ distillation, see: destructive ~
~ dock, graving dock = Trockendock *n*
dryer, drier = Trockner *m*
dry feed = direkte Dosierung *f*, Trockendosierung
~ ~ chlorination = direkte Chlorung *f*, Chlorung nach dem direkten Verfahren *n*

~ gas, lean gas = Gasgemisch *n* mit wenig kondensierbaren Anteilen *mpl*
~ grinding = Trockenmahlung *f*
~ harbo(u)r, stranding ~ = Strandhafen *m*
~ hydrate = Löschkalk *m*, Hüttenkalk *m*, Kalkhydrat *n*
drying bed, see: sludge ~
~ oil = trocknendes filmbildendes Öl *n*
~ oven = Trockenschrank *m*
~ plant = Trocknungsanlage *f*
~ process = Trocknungsverfahren *n*
~ shrinkage [*concrete*] = Erhärtungsschwindung *f*, Trocknungs-Schrumpfung *f* [*Beton m*]
dry-land excavation = Trockenbaggerung *f*, Trockenbaggerei *f*
~ suction dredging plant = Erdsauganlage *f* zu Lande, landgängige Erdsauganlage
dry masonry (wall) = Trockenmauerwerk *n*, Trockensteinmauer *f*
~ ~ dam, rubble masonry ~, dry rubble ~, derrick- and hand-placed stone rockfill ~ = Mauerwerksperre *f*, Trockenmauerwerksdamm *m*, Steinsatzsperre *f*, gepackter Steindamm *m*
~ mechanical grading = Trockensiebung *f*
~ mortar = Trockenmörtel *m*
~ natural gas, well ~ ~ = trockenes Naturgas *n*, ~ Bohrlochkopfgas *n*
~ packing = Sickerpackung *f* [*Tunnelbau m*]
~ pan grinder = Trockenkollergang *m*
~ partition (Brit.) = Zwischenwandplatte *f* [*zwei Gipskartonplatten fpl von je 10 oder 13 mm Dicke und einem rund 4 cm breiten Zwischenraum der durch quadratische rund 4 cm weite Zellen unterteilt ist*]
~ penetration surfacing, dry process penetration macadam [*a macadam base into which precoated chippings have been rolled*] = Einstreudecke *f*, Streumakadam *m*
~ plate clutch = ₁Trockenscheibenkupplung *f*
~ press hollow tile = trocken gepreßter Hohlziegel *m*, ~ ~ Hohlstein *m*

dry press process = Trockenpreßverfahren n
~ rot = Trockenfäule f
~ rubble dam, see: dry masonry ~
~-sample boring, dry sampling = Trockenbohren n [*Bodenuntersuchung f*]
~ slaking process = Trockenlöschverfahren n [*Branntkalk m*]
~ slip coating = Trockenengobierung f
~ sludge = Trockenschlamm m
~ stamp = Trockenpochwerk n, Trockenstampfmühle f
~ strength = Trockenfestigkeit f
~ type electric precipitator = Trocken-Elektroabscheider m
~ weather flow = Trockenwetterabfluß m
~ weight = Trockengewicht n
D slide valve = Muschelschieber m
D.T.S., see: dense tar surfacing
dual batcher = Dosierbehälter m getrennt für Zuschläge und Zement
~ carriageway motor road, double ~ ~ ~ = Autobahn f mit einem Mittelstreifen m
dual-compression trench roller = Zweirad-Grabenwalze f
dual-drum type concrete paver; see under "travel(l)ing (concrete) mixer (plant)"
dual-dual road = achtspurige Straße f mit vier getrennten doppelspurigen Fahrbahnen fpl und drei Mittelstreifen mpl
dual ignition = Doppelzündung f
dual-purpose machine, asphalt, bituminous macadam and tarmacadam mixing plant (Brit.); combination hotor coldmix plant (US) = Aufbereitungsanlage f (oder Trocken- und Mischanlage f) für Mischmakadam m und Walzasphalt m
dual roller compactor = doppeltwirkende Verdichtungswalze f
dual-tank pneumatic conveying system, ~ type pump = Doppelgefäß(förder)pumpe f
dual tyres (Brit.); ~ tires (US) = Zwillingsbereifung f
dual wheel = Doppelrad n, Zwillingsrad n
~ ~ steering gear = Doppelradlenkbock m
duckbill = Entenschnabel m

duck bills type spillway = Entenschnäbel-Überlauf m
duckboard, see: catwalk
duckling = Miniatur-Entenschnabel m
duck weed = Entenflott n
duct, mains subway = (Leitungs-)Kanal m [*z. B. Telefon n, Heizung f*]
~, hole, channel = Gleitkanal m [*Spannbeton m*]
ductile cast-iron = dehnbares Gußeisen n
~ theory, see: plastic ~
ductility = Duktilität f, Streckbarkeit f, Dehnbarkeit f, Fadenziehvermögen n
~ tester = Streckbarkeitsmesser m
duct trench = (Leitungs)Kanalgraben m
ductube, see: inflatable rubber core
dufrenite, green iron ore (Min.) = Grüneisenerde f, Grüneisenerz n, Grüneisenstein m
dug peat = Stichtorf m
~ well = Schachtbrunnen m
dull bit evaluation = Auswertung f von Meißelschneiden fpl
~ coal, dulls = Mattkohle f
dummy airfield = Scheinflugplatz m
~ (concrete) joint, concealed (~) ~, contraction ~, shrinkage ~ = Schein-(beton)fuge f
~ piston = Ausgleichkolben m, Entlastungskolben
dump bailer = Betonbüchse f, Betonlöffel m [*Tiefbohrtechnik f*]
~ body = Kippprittsche f [*LKW m*]
~ ~ full trailer, see: (tractor) wagon
~ ~ trailer, trailer-dump, tipping trailer = Kippanhänger m
~ cable [*dragline*] = Kippseil n
~ car, see: steel tip wagon
DUMPCRETE [*Trademark*] = Beton-Transportwagen m mit Schüttrinne f, Fabrikat MAXON CONSTRUCTION CO., DAYTON, OHIO, USA
dumped rock-fill dam = geschütteter Steindamm m
~ (stone) riprap, truck-dumped (US)/lorry-dumped (Brit.) riprap = Steinwurf m, Rauhwurf, geschüttetes Steindeckwerk n, geschüttete Stein(ab)deckung f, geschüttete Steinbestürzung

dumper — dust nodulizing process

dumper, shuttle ~, front tipper = Autoschütter *m*, Vorderkipper *m*, Motorkübelwagen *m*, Kopfschütter *m*, Vorkopf-Schütter *m*, Frontkipper, Motorkipper

dumperman, see: spotter

dump ground, see: rubbish dump site

dumping device = Ausschüttvorrichtung *f*, Abwurfvorrichtung

~ ~ for straddle carrier, see: straddle dump device

~ height = Ausschütthöhe *f*, Abwurfhöhe

~ in thin layers, thin-layer fill = Flachschüttung *f*

~ shaft skip, see: skip

dumpling = Bodenklotz *m* [*zwischen Ausschachtungen fpl stehengebliebener Boden m*]

dump lorry, tipper, tip (motor) lorry, tipping lorry (Brit.); dump truck, tip(ping) truck (US) = Kipper *m*, Kipplast(kraft)wagen *m*, Kipp-LKW *m*

~ pile = Kipphalde *f*

~ semi-trailer = aufgesattelter Kippanhänger *m*

~ sheave = Ausschüttrolle *f*, Kippseilflasche *f* [*Schleppschaufelbagger m*]

DUMPTOR [*Trademark*] = Autoschütter *m*, Fabrikat KOEHRING COMPANY, MILWAUKEE 16, USA

    direkt line = gleiche Spurbreite *f* vorn und hinten

    body = Kippmulde *f*

    free-swinging pan = lose Bodenplatte *f*

    off-set pivot on steering axle = außerachsige Schwinglagerung *f* der Vorderachse *f*

dump trailer, see: (tractor) wagon

~ truck (US); see: ~ lorry (Brit.)

~ ~ ~ = Muldentransporter *m*, Muldenkipper(-LKW) *m*

~ ~ body bed (US) = Kipppritschenboden *m* [*LKW*] *m*

~ ~ loader = Ladeschaufel *f* für Kipperlast(kraft)wagen *m*

~ wagon, see: (tractor) wagon

dune, sand ~, down ~ = (Sand)Düne *f*

~ plant = Dünenpflanze *f*

~ sanfd = Dünensand *m*

dung dump = Dunglege *f*

dunite, olivine-rock (Geol) = Dunit *m*, Olivinfels *m*

dunting = Klangfehlerhaftigkeit *f* [*Ziegel(stein) m*]

duo-cone tilting (type) mixer = Doppelkonus-Kipptrommelmischer *m*

DUOMIX 34E and DUOMIX 16E [*Trademark*] = Doppeltrommel(beton)straßenmischer *m*, Fabrikat BLAW KNOX CO., FOOTE DIVISION, NUNDA, N. Y., USA

duo-sol process = Zwei-Lösemittel-Verfahren *n* [*Schmieröl*]

DUO-WAY SCOOP DOZER [*Trademark*] = Aufladegerät *n* mit Räumschild *n*, Fabrikat WAGNERMOBILE, PORTLAND 16, OREGON, USA

duplex chain = Duplexkette *f*

~ pump = Duplexpumpe *f*

~ radial type bin door = zweiteiliger Silo(klappen)verschluß *m*

durability = Alterungsbeständigkeit *f*

~ test = Beständigkeitsprüfung *f*, Haltbarkeitsprüfung *f*, Dauerhaftigkeitsprüfung

durain of the cannel coal = Kanneldurit *m*

duration curve = Dauerkurve *f*

~ of cycle = (Arbeits)Spieldauer *f*

~ ~ the storm = Niederschlagsdauer *f*, Regendauer

DURAX paving, see: fanwise ~

dust alleviation, see: alleviation of dust

~-bin = Mülleimer *m*, Müllkübel *m*

dust cap = Staubdeckel *m*

dust-car, refuse wagon (or collector) (Brit.); garbage truck (US) = Müllast(kraft)wagen *m*

dust collecting cyclone, see: cyclone (separator)

~ (or exhaust) plant = Entstaubungsanlage *f*, Staubabsaugungsanlage *f*, Staubsammleranlage *f*

~ ~ screw = Staubsammelschnecke *f*

~ collector = Entstauber *m*

~ generation = Staubentwicklung *f*

~-laden air, dusty ~ = Staubluft *f*

dust-laying oil, see: road ~

dustless dry rock(-)drill = staubfreier Trockengesteinsbohrer *m*

dust nodulizing process = Staubgranulierungsverfahren *n*

dust palliative, ~ preventer = Staubbindemittel *n*

dustpan (type of hydraulic) dredge(r), hydraulic erosion ~ = Pumpenbagger *m* mit hydraulischer Bodenlösung *f* durch Abspritzen *n* unter hohem Druck *m* und gleichzeitigem Weiterspülen *n*, Spüler *m*

dustproof, dust-tight = staubdicht

dust recovery = Staubrückgewinnung *f*

~ **sickness** = Staubkrankheit *f*

~ **slime** = Staubschlamm *m*

dusty air, dust-laden ~ = Staubluft *f*

Dutch clover, white ~ = Weißklee *m*

dwang (Brit.); see: crowbar

dwarf birch = Zwergbirke *f*

dwarf-shrub heath, ling ~ = Zwergheide *f*

dwelling house = Wohnhaus *n*

~ **unit interview method,** internal type of O & D survey, home-interview method, internal survey [*for O & D study of urban areas*] = Befragungsmethode *f* von Haus *n* zu Haus *n*

dy = Dy *m* [*vollständig zersetzter Torf m*]

dyas sandstone = Dyassandstein *m*

dye(-stuff) = löslicher Farbstoff *m*

dyke (Brit.); dike (US) = Deich *m*

~, dike rock = Ganggestein *n*

~ **breach** = Deich(ein)bruch *m*

~ **land,** innings = Deichland *n*

dynamic ball-impact test method = Kugelschlagprüfung *f*

~ **metamorphism** = Dynamometamorphose *f*, Pressungsumwandlung *f*, Pressungsumprägung *f*, Stauungsmethamorphose *f*

~ **modulus of elasticity** = dynamischer Elastizitätsmodul *m*

~ ~ ~ **subgrade reaction** = dynamische Bettungsziffer *f* [*durch Schwingungsversuch m erhalten*]

~ **penetration** = dynamischer Eindringungswiderstand *m*

~ **pile-driving formula** = dynamische Rammformel *f*

~ **sounding** = dynamische Sondierung *f*

~ **testing technique** = dynamisches Prüfverfahren *n*

dynamite = Dynamit *n, m*

*dynamiting = Dynamitsprengung *f*

dynamo = Lichtmaschine *f*

dynamometer test = Dynamometer-Versuch *m*

E

eagle wood, agaloch = Adlerholz *n*

eagre, bore = Seebeben *n*

ear, eye, lug = Öse *f*

~ **of the groin** = Ohr *n* der Stichkappe *f*

early strength, see: initial ~

earth = Erdkugel *f*

~, soil; dirt (US) = Erdstoff *m*, Boden *m*, Lockergestein *n*

~ **auger,** soil ~, ~ boring ~, ~ drill = Spiralbohrer *m* [*Bodenuntersuchung f*]

~ **balsam** [*a variety of asphalt from Pechelbronn, Alsace*] = Erdbalsam *m*

~ **borer** = Erdbohrer *m* [*Bodensonde f zur Entnahme von Proben bis etwa 1,50 m Tiefe*]

~ **cofferdam,** see: earthwork ~

~ **(or soil) compaction (or densification)**, artificial consolidation = künstliche Bodenverdichtung *f*

~ **(~ ~) consolidation** = natürliche Bodenverdichtung *f*, Konsolidation *f*, Eigenverfestigung *f*, Eigensetzung *f*, Konsolidierung *f*

~ **(~ ~) covering,** soiling = Bodenandeckung *f*

~ **dam,** see: ~ (fill) ~

~ **drill,** see: ~ auger

~ **(or soil) embankment** = Erddamm *m* [*als Verkehrsdamm*]

earthenware = Steingut *n*

earth excavation, see: digging

~ **fill** = Erdaufschüttung *f*

~ **(~) dam,** earthwork dam = (Erdschüttungs)Staudamm *m*, Erddamm, Erdschüttungsdamm

~ **(~) ~ with materials of various permeabilities,** zoned earth (fill) dam = Erddamm *m* mit Querschnittaufbau in Filterform, Erddamm mit symmetrischem Filteraufbau *m*

~ **flow,** see: soil-flow

~ **fold,** nappe (Geol.) = Erdfalte *f*

earth fold (US) (Geol.) = Erdschicht *f*
~ **materials lab(oratory)**, see: soils ~
earth movement, soil ~ (Geol.) = Bodenbewegung *f*, Bodenverlagerung *f*
earthmover; see: dirtmover (US)
~ **tyre** (Brit.); off-the-highway (or off-the-road) tire (US); (ground) grip ~, off-road equipment ~ = Geländereifen *m*, Reifen mit Geländeprofil *n*, Reifen für Erdbaugeräte
earthmoving, soil shifting operations; dirtmoving (US) = Erdbewegungen *fpl*
~ **contracting firm** = Erdbaufirma *f*
~ **gear** (Brit.); see: dirtmover (US)
~ **tyre** (Brit.); ~ **tire** (US) = Erdbaureifen *m*
~ **vehicle** = Erdbaulastfahrzeug *n*
earth pressure = Erddruck *m*
~ ~ **at great depth**, rock pressure, compaction pressure = Gebirgsdruck *m* [*Tunnelbau m*]
~ ~ ~ **rest** = Ruhedruck *m*
~ ~ **calculation** = Erddruckberechnung *f*
earth-pressure (measuring) cell, soil pressure cell = Bodendruck(meß)dose *f*, Erddruck(meß)dose, Bodendruckdose
***earthquake** = Erdbeben *n*
~ **-resistant**, quakeproof, aseismic = erdbebensicher
earth-resistivity = Leitwiderstand *m*
earth road, soil ~; dirt ~ (US) = Erdstraße *f*
~ **saucer drain** (Brit.) = Entwässerungsmulde *f* [*30 cm breit und 8 cm tief*]
~ **shock** = Erdstoß *m*
(~) **slip**, see: slip
~ **solidification**, soil ~ = Bodenverfestigung *f*
~ **structure** = Erdbauwerk *n*
~ **traverse** = Erdschutzwall *m*
~ **(or soil) waterproofing** = Bodenabdichtung *f*
~ **wearing surface**, see: soil surfacing
earthwork balance, balanced excavation, balancing quantities = Massenausgleich *m*
earth (work) cofferdam, earth-fill ~ = Erdfang(e)damm *m*, Lockergesteinsfang(e)damm *m*
earthwork dam, see: earth (fill) dam

~ **engineering** = Erdbauwesen *n*
earthworking machinery, ~ **equipment** = Erdbaugeräte *npl*
***earthwork(s)** = Erdarbeiten *fpl*, Erdbau *m*
earthy dolomite = Dolomitasche *f*
~ **gypsum**, friable ~, gypsite = erdiger Gips *m*, erdiges Gipsgestein, feinporiges Gipsgestein *n*
~ **iron ore** = Eisenmulm *m*
(~) **vivianite** (Min.) = Blaueisenerde *f*, Blauerz *n*, Vivianit *m*
easement = Servitut *n*, Gerechtsame *f*
~ **curve**, transition ~ = Übergangskurve *f*, Übergangsbogen *m*
easing of a bend = Abflachung *f* einer Krümmung *f*
easing-off [*jack*] = Entlastung *f* [*z. B. Hebebock m*]
ebb current, ~ **stream** = Ebb(e)strömung *f*, Ebb(e)strom *m*
~ **tide** = Ebbe *f*
eccentric [*a wheel or cam with an off-centre axis of revolution*] = Exzenter *m*
eccentrically loaded reinforced concrete column = ausmittig gedrückte Stahlbetonsäule *f*
eccentric bit = Exzentermeißel *m*
~ **drive** = Exzenterantrieb *m*
~ **load(ing)**; off-center ~ (US); off-centre ~ (Brit.) = außermittige (oder ausmittige, oder exzentrische) Last *f*, ~ Belastung *f*
~ **shaft** = Exzenterwelle *f*
~ ~ **bearing** = Exzenterwellenlager *n*
~ **type vibrating screen**, see: mechanically-vibrated eccentric type screen
eccentricity = Exzentrizität *f*, Ausmittigkeit *f*, Ausmitte *f*
echelon, to work in ~ = staffelweise arbeiten [*z. B. Erdbaugeräte npl*]
echo sounder, sonic altimeter, sound ranging altimeter = akustisches Echolot *n*
eclogite = Eklogit *m*
economical = wirtschaftlich
economy = Wirtschaftlichkeit *f*
~ **brick** (US); see: closure unit
~ **calculation** = Wirtschaftlichkeitsberechnung *f*
eddy current coupling = Wirbelstrom-Kupplung *f*

eddy field — (electrical) arc welding

eddy field, vortex ~ = Wirbelfeld *n*
eddying, whirling ~ = Wirbelung *f*
eddy wind, whirlwind = Wirbelwind *m*
Edeleanu extract = Extrakt *m* erhalten durch Extraktion *f* von Ölen *npl* mit flüssigem Schwefeldioxyd *n*, Edeleanu-Extrakt *m*
~ **process** = Edeleanu-Verfahren *n*
to edge = abkanten [*z. B. Betonfuge f*]
edge beam = Randträger *m*
~ **disturbance** = Randstörung *f*
edged pincers = Kantenzange *f*
edge protection = Kantenschutz *m*
~ **runner (grinding) mill** = Kollergang *m*
(~ **stress of) extreme fibre stress**, extreme stress = Randspannung *f*
~ **strip**, marginal ~ = Randstreifen *m*
edging = Randeinfassung *f*
~ **tool for rounding concrete arrises**, see: rounding tool
effective bearing area = Lochleibungsfläche *f*
~ **column length** = Knicklänge *f* [*Säule f*]
~ **grain (or particle) size** = wirkliche Korngröße *f*
~ **length** = Knicklänge *f* [*bei einem Druckstab*]
~ **range of traffic originating in a given area** = Quellergiebigkeit *f* [*Straßenverkehr m*]
~ **shear** = effektiver Schub *m*
~ **span (of a beam)** = Lichtweite *f*
~ ~ **length** = rechnerische Stützweite *f*
~ **stress** = wirksame Spannung *f*, Korn-zu-Korn-Druck *m*
effects of climatic conditions, see: climatic effects
efficiency degree = Wirkungsgrad *m*
~ **rating** = wirkungsgradgemäße Einstufung *f*
efflorescence = Ausblühung(en) *f*, (*pl*) [*Beton m*]
egg-shaped sewer (pipe) = Eikanal *m*, eiförmiger Sammler *m*, eiförmiges Kanalrohr *n*, Eiprofilrohr *n*
egress point, see: exit ~
eight-hour day = Acht-Stunden-Tag *m*
eight-part hammer line = 8-facher Hammerseilzug *m*

EIMCO-LOADER = Wurfschaufellader, Über-Kopf-Lader *m*, Fabrikat THE EIMCO CORPORATION, SALT LAKE CITY 10, UTAH, USA
ejecting rotor = Wurfrad *n* [*Schneeschleuder f*]
ejector = Auswerfer *m*
~ = Ejektor *m*, Strahlsauger *m* [*ein durch eine Düse geleiteter Strahl erzeugt seitlich bzw. hinter sich einen Sog, der zum Fördern von Flüssigkeiten oder Gasen verwendet werden kann*]
elaeolite (Min.) = Elaeolith *m*, Ölstein *m*
~-**syenite** = Eläolithsyenit *m*
elastic behavio(u)r = elastisches Verhalten *n*
~ **bitumen**, see: elaterite
~ **center of gravity** (US); ~ **centre** ~ ~ (Brit.) = elastischer Schwerpunkt *m*
~ **circular slab foundation with a load symmetrical about the centre** = zentralsymmetrisch belastetes elastisches Kreisplattenfundament *n*
~ **curve** = elastische Linie *f*
~ **deformation** = elastische Verformung *f*
~ ~ **and elastic recovery** [*concrete*] = federnde Formänderung *f* [*Beton m*]
~ **equilibrium** = elastischer Gleichgewichtszustand *m*
~ **foundation** = elastischer Baugrund *m*
~ **limit** = Elastizitätsgrenze *f*
~ **range** = elastischer Bereich *m*
~ **slab** = elastische Platte *f*
~ **strain** = elastische Dehnung *f*
elasticity equation = Elastizitätsgleichung *f*
elastoplastic = elastisch-plastisch
~ **range** = elastisch-plastischer Bereich *m*
elaterite, elastic bitumen, mineral caoutchouc, elastic mineral pitch (Min.) = Elaterit *m*, elastisches Erdharz *n*, elastisches Erdpech *n*
elbow = Knie *n*
~ **bend**, penstock elbow = Krümmer *m* [*Wasserkraftwerk n*]
~ **(draft) tube** (US); ~ **(draught)** ~ (Brit.) = gekrümmtes Saugrohr *n* [*ein Rohr n im Wasserkrafthaus n*]
~ **of capture** = Ablenkungsknie *n* [*Fluß m*]
elder = Holunder *m*
(electrical) arc welding, electric arc fusion ~ ~ = Lichtbogenschweißung *f*

electrical compound for cable isolation — electric glueing unit   141

electrical compound for cable isolation, see:
~ filling compound
~ curing = elektrische (Beton)Nachbehandlung *f*
~ drainage = Elektroentwässerung *f* [*Entwässerung wenig durchlässiger und daher schwer wasserableitender feindisperser Lockergesteine durch elektrischen Strom, der eine Bewegung des Wassers von einer Elektrode zur anderen erzeugt*]
~ dust collector, ~ precipitator = Elektroabscheider *m*, Elektrofilter *n, m*
~ endosmose, see: electro-osmosis
~ exploration method = geoelektrische Baugrunduntersuchung *f*, elektrisches Aufschlußverfahren *n*, elektrische Sondierung *f*
~ filling compound, ~ compound for cable isolation = Kabelvergußmasse *f*
~ heating = elektrische Beheizung *f*
~ industrial truck, electric (freight) ~ = Elektrokarre(n) *f*, *(m)*, Elektroflurfördermittel *n*
(~) insulating oil = Isolieröl *n*
~ ~ putty = Isolierkitt *m*
electrically-heated concrete = Elektrobeton *m*
~ screen = elektrisch beheiztes Sieb *n*
electrical(ly operating) pore water pressure cell (or ga(u)ge) = elektrisches Porenwasserdruck-Meßgerät *n*, elektrischer Porenwasserdruckmesser *m*
electrically-vibrated screen, electric vibrating ~ = Elektrosieb *n*
(electrical-)resistance strain ga(u)ge SR-4, see: electric SR-4 ga(u)ge
electrical resistivity method (or survey), see: resistivity exploration
~ ~ unit = Widerstandsmessungsgerät *n* [*elektrische Bodenuntersuchung f*]
~ (rope, or cable) winch = elektrische (Trommel)Seilwinde *f*, elektrisches (Trommel)Seilwindwerk *n*
~ solidification, see: electro-osmotic ~
~ switchgear installation = Schaltanlage *f*
~ troll(e)y = elektrische Laufkatze *f*, Elektrolaufkatze, Elektro-Lastkatze
electric arc = elektrischer Flammbogen *m*
~ ~ fusion welding, see: (electrical) arc ~

~ (blasting) cap, instantaneous cap, electric detonting cap, electric explosive cap = Sprengzünder *m*, elektrischer Momentzünder mit Sprengkapsel
~ block = Elektrozug *m* [*ein Hubförderer, den man als elektrisch angetriebene Seilwinde oder als elektromotorisch betriebenen Flaschenzug ansprechen kann*]
~ ~ truck = Elektrokarre(n) *f*, *(m)* für Zementblocksteine *mpl*
~ breaker = Elektro-Aufbruchhammer *m*
~ butt welding apparatus = elektrische Stumpfschweißmaschine *f*
~ caterpillar shovel = Elektro-Universalbagger *m* auf Gleisketten *fpl*
~ cement, CIMENT DE LA FARGE, CIMENT FONDU = Elektroschmelzzement *m*
~ chain saw = Kettensäge *f* mit Elektromotor *m*
~ conductivity = elektrische Leitfähigkeit *f*
~ contractors' pump = Elektro-Bau(stellen)pumpe *f*
~ control of earthworking machinery = elektrische Bedienung *f* von Erdbaumaschinen *fpl*
~ ~ panel = Schalttafel *f*, elektrische ~
~ crane = Elektrokran *m*
~ current = elektrischer Strom *m*
~ (curtain) stabilisation = elektrische Bodenverfestigung *f*
~ derrick (crane) = Elektro-Derrick-(Kran) *m*
~ detonator = (elektrischer) Brückenzünder *m*
~ drive = Elektroantrieb *m*
~ driver, see: ~ pile ~
~ excavator = Elektro(trocken)bagger *m*
~ external vibrator = Elektro-Außenrüttler *m*, Elektro-Außenvibrator *m*
~ fork lift truck = Elektrogabelstapler *m*
~ (freight) truck, see: electrical industrial ~
~ furnace with resistors = elektrischer Widerstandsofen *m*
~ generator (set), generating ~, electric set = (Stromerzeugungs-)Aggregat *n*, Elektro-Generator *m*
~ glueing unit = elektrischer Verleimapparat *m*

electric hammer — electric tool

electric hammer, ~ impact ~ = Elektrohammer *m*
~ **(hand) hammer (rock) drill,** electric (rock) drill hammer = Elektro-Bohrhammer *m*
~ ~ **planer (or planing machine)** = Elektro-Handhobelmaschine *f*
~ ~ **tool** = Elektro-Kleinwerkzeug *n*
~ **high frequency immersion (concrete) vibrator** = Elektro-Hochfrequenz-Innenrüttler *m*, Elektro-Hochfrequenz-Innenvibrator *m*
~ **hoist** = Elektrowinde *f*
~ ~ **motor** = Elektro-Hubmotor *m*
~ **(impact) hammer** = Elektrohammer *m*
~ **insulating tape** = Isolierband *n*
~ **internal vibrator** = Elektroinnenrüttler *m*, Elektroinnenvibrator *m*
(electricity) substation = Speisetransformatorenhaus *n*, Speisetrafohaus *n*
~ **supply company** = Elektrizitätsgesellschaft *f*
(electric) lifting magnet(o), see: lifting ~
(~) ~ ~ with tines (US)/**tynes** (Brit.) = Magnetgreifer *m*
electric lift truck = Elektrostapler *m*
~ **loco(motive)** = Elektro-Lok(omotive) *f*, elektrische Lok(omotive)
~ **motor** = Elektromotor *m*
~ **percussion drill** = Elektro-Schlagbohrer *m*
~ **(pile) driver** = Elektro(pfahl)ramme *f*
~ **platform truck** = Elektro-Plattformkarre(n) *f*, (*m*)
~ **poker vibrator** = Elektro-Innenrüttler *m*, Elektro-Innenvibrator *m*
~ **positive power steer(ing)** = elektrische Kraftlenkung *f*
~ **powder fuse** = elektrischer Zündschnurzünder *m*
~ **power cable** = Elektrokabel *n*
~-**powered hand-operated surface vibrator** = handgeführter elektrischer Oberflächenrüttler *m* (oder Oberflächenvibrator *m*)
electric power station = Elektrizitätswerk *n*
~ **pulley block,** see: ~ hoist ~
~ **rail drilling machine** = Elektro-Schienenbohrmaschine *f*

~ ~ **joint planing machine** = Elektro-Schienenstoßhobelmaschine *f*
~ ~ **sawing machine** = Elektro-Schienensägemaschine *f*
~ **rammer** = Elektro-Stampframme *f* [*Stampfgerät mit elektrischem Antrieb und mit hoher Schlagzahl, ca. 500/Min. zur Bodenverdichtung*]
~ **reinforcement bar-bending machine** = Betoneisen-Biegemaschine *f* mit elektrischem Antrieb
~ ~ **bar cutting machine,** ~ **rod shear** = Betoneisenschere *f* (oder Betonstahlschneidemaschine *f*) mit elektrischem Antrieb *m*
electric-resistivity method = Widerstandsmethode *f* [*Bodenuntersuchung f*]
electric (rock) drill hammer, see: electric (hand) hammer (rock) drill
~ **rod shear,** see: ~ reinforcement bar cutting machine
~ **rotating (or rotary) rock drilling machine** = Elektro-Gesteins-Drehbohrmaschine *f*
~ **set,** see: ~ generator (set)
~ **sheet** = Elektroblech *n*
~ **shovel,** ~-**powered excavator** = Elektro-Hochlöffel(bagger) *m*, Elektro-Löffelhochbagger
~ **smoothing trowel** = Putzglätter *m*
~ **spot welding machine** = Elektropunktschweißmaschine *f*
~ **SR-4 ga(u)ge, strain ga(u)ge SR-4,** (electrical-)resistance strain ga(u)ge SR-4 = elektrisches Spannungsgerät SR-4 *n*, (resistiver) Dehnungsmesser SR-4 *m*
~ **stabilisation,** see: ~ (curtain) ~
~ **starter** = elektrischer Anlasser *m*
~ **steel** = Elektrostahl *m*
~ **steering motor** = Elektro-Lenkmotor *m*
~ **stirrer** = Elektrorührer *m*
~ **tamper** = Elekto-Stampfer *m*
~ **tie tamper** (US); ~ **track** ~ (Brit.) = Elektrogleisstopfer *m*, Elektroschotterstopfer
~ **tinners' snip** = Elektro-Handblechschere *f*
~ **tool** = Elektrowerkzeug *n*

electric travel(l)ing crane = Elektro-Laufkran *m*
~ troll(e)y, troll(e)y bus = Oberleitungsbus *m*, O-Bus
~ ~ = elektrische Laufkatze *f*, Elektrolaufkatze, Elektro-Lastkatze
~ truck, see: electrical industrial ~
~ ~ crane, ~ industrial ~ ~ = Elektrokarrenkran *m*
~ vehicle = Elektrofahrzeug *n*
~ vibrating beam = Elektro-Vibratorbohle *f*, Elektrorüttelbohle
~ ~ plate = Elektrorüttelplatte *f*
~ ~ screen, see: electrically-vibrated ~
~ ~ tamper = Elektrorüttelstampfer *m*
~ vibrator, electro-magnet ~ = Elektrorüttler *m*, Elektrovibrator *m*, Magnetrüttler *m*, Magnetvibrator *m*
~ welding = elektrisches Schweißen *n*, Elektroschweißen
~ ~ machine = Elektroschweißmaschine *f*
~ ~ set = Elektro-Schweißaggregat *n*
~ ~ transformer = Elektro-Schweißtransformator *m*
~ wheel = Elektrorad *n*
electrification = Elektrifizierung *f*
electrified = elektrifiziert
electro-acoustic extensometer = elektroakustischer Dehnungsmesser *m*
electrochemical solidification (or hardening) of clay = elektrochemische Verfestigung *f* von Ton *m*
***electrode** = Elektrode *f*
electrodynamic method = elektrodynamisches Verfahren *n*
electroless plating = stromlose Plattierung *f*
electrolyte level = Säurestand *m*, Säurespiegel *m*
electro-magnet conveyor = elektromagnetischer Förderer *m*
electro-magnetic = elektromagnetisch
~ bin vibrator = elektromagnetischer Haftvibrator *m*, ~ Haftrüttler *m*
~ vibrating screen = Schwingsieb *n* mit elektromagnetischem Antrieb *m*
electro-magnet vibrator, see: electric ~

electromotive = elektromotorisch
electronic batcher = elektronisch gesteuerte Dosiervorrichtung *f*
~ calculator, ~ computing machine = elektronische Rechenmaschine *f*
~ deflection-measuring unit = elektronisches Durchbiegungsmeßgerät *n*
~ digital computor = Elektronen-Tasten-Rechenmaschine *f*
~ drying = elektronische Trocknung *f*
~ scale = elektronische Waage *f*
electron microscope = Elektronenmikroskop *n*
electro-osmosis, electrical endosmose = Elektro(end)osmose *f*
electroösmotic drainage, see: subsoil drainage by the electro-osmosis method
electro-osmotic solidification, electrical ~, ~ stabilization = elektro-osmotische Baugrundverbesserung *f*
electrophoresis = Elektrophorese *f*
electroplating = Galvanisieren *n*
electro-thermic ga(u)ge, electric thermometer = elektrisches Thermometer *n*, Thermoelement *n*
elegrader = 1. Kombination eines normalen Straßenhobels *m* mit einem Schrägförderband *n*; 2. Pflugbagger *m*, Flachbagger-Lader *m*, Schürfbagger *m*, Förderband-Schürfwagen *m*
~ with outrigger = Pflugbagger *m* mit Weitabsetzer *m*
elevated pile foundation grill = Stelzenunterbau *m*, hoher Pfahlrost *m*
~ railway (Brit.); ~ railroad (US) = Schwebebahn *f*
~ roadway, ~ highway, ~ expressway, overhead ~; skyway (US) = Hochstraße *f*, Brückenstraße
~ shore line (US); raised beach (Brit.) = gehobener Strand *m*
~ storage bin = hochliegender (Vorrats-)Silo *m*
~ (water) tank, overhead cistern, tower tank = (Wasser)Hochbehälter *m*
elevating belt conveyor, conveyor loader, belt loader, belt elevator (with adjustable elevation gear) = Band(auf)lader *m* (mit Höheneinstellung *f*)

elevating grader, belt loader [*a disk plow (US)/plough (Brit.) is used for loosening the earth*] = Pflugbagger *m* (oder Flachbagger-Lader *m*, oder Schürfbagger, oder Förderband-Schürfwagen) mit kreisförmiger Diskus-Pflugschar *f* (oder Pflugteller *m*)

~ **hopper mixer** = Kübelaufzugsmischer *m*

~ **plant,** lifting appliance, hoisting machine, lifting tackle = Hebezeug *n*

~ **roadmixer,** see: windrow-type travel(l)ing (asphalt) (or road) plant

~ **tower,** see: concrete chuting (or placing) tower

elevation, profile = Aufriß *m*, Ansicht *f*

~, height = Höhe *f* (über einem Bezugspunkt *m*)

~ **tower,** tower, cage = Schachtgerüst *n*, Turmgerüst *n* [*Bauaufzug m*]

elevator [*a machine that raises material on a belt or a chain of small buckets*] = Elevator *m*

~ **belt(ing),** ~ **conveyor** belt = Becherwerkgurt *m*

~ **boot** = Becherwerkschuh *m*

~ **bucket** = Elevatorbecher *m*

~ ~ **edge made of hard steel** = Hartstahlschöpfkante *f*

~ **dredge(r),** see: bucket ladder ~

~ **tower,** see: concrete chuting (or placing) tower

(~) ~ **hoist,** see: cage ~

elgrader = Kombination eines normalen Straßenhobels *m* mit einem Schrägförderband *n*

ellipse of inertia = Trägheitsellipse *f*

elliptic integral = elliptisches Integral *n*

elliptical arch = Ellipsenbogen *m*

~ **motion screen,** screen having elliptical vibratory action = Ellipsen-Schwingsieb *n*

elm = Ulme *f*, Rüster *f*, Effe *f*

elongated hole drilling machine = Langlochbohrmaschine *f*

~ **lens,** pod = Erzlineal *n*

elongation = Dehnung *f*

elutriation = Schlämmung *f*

~ **test** = Schleppprobe *f*

elutriator = Schlämmeinrichtung *f*

elvan (Brit.) = Quarzporphyr *m* aus Devon und Cornwall

embacle = Eisgang *m*

embanking = Dammbau *m*

***embankment** [*a fill whose top is higher than the adjoining surface*] = Damm *m*

~, see: levee (US)

~, river ~ = (Fluß)Längswerk *n*

~ **face stone** = Böschungsverkleidungsstein *m*

~ **fill,** fill (construction) = (Rampen-)Schüttung *f*, Dammschüttung

~ ~ **material** = Dammbaustoff *m*

~ **for traffic facilities** = Verkehrsdamm *m*

~ **roller,** slope ~ = Böschungswalze *f*

~ **shaping and compaction machine** = Böschungsplanier- und -verdichtungsmaschine *f*

~ **slope,** slope of embankment, fill slope = Dammböschung *f*, Böschung *f* im Auftrag *m*, Auffüllböschung

~ **type dam,** dam embankment = Staudamm *m*, Talsperrendamm

embayment = Einbuchtung *f*

embedded in concrete = in Beton *m* eingebettet, ~ ~ eingebunden

embrasure, recess, blockout = Aussparung *f*

embrittlement = Versprödung *f*

emerald copper, dioptase (Min.) = Dioptas *m*

emergency bridge = Notbrücke *f*

~ **closure** = Notabschließung *f*

~ **current stand-by generator,** standby generating set = Notstromaggregat *n*

~ **flood flow,** see: peak flow

~ **gate,** (~) **guard** ~ = Notverschluß *m*

~ **landing strip** = Notlandestreifen *m*

~ **outlet** = Notauslaß *m* [*Talsperre f*]

~ **valve** = Notschieber *m*

~ ~ **tunnel** = Notschieberstollen *m*

(eminently) hydraulic lime (Brit.); see: autoclaved lime (US)

emission of dust = Staubemission *f*

~ **spectrographic method** = Emissionsspektrographie *f*

emitting electrode, see: discharge ~

empirical = empirisch

emplectite, $CuBiS_2$ (Min.) = Emplektit m, Kupferwismutglanz m
employe(e) = Arbeitnehmer m
employer, see: promoter
employment = Beschäftigungsverhältnis n
~ = (Arbeits)Einsatz m
~ of plant, disposition of equipment, equipment utilization = Geräteeinsatz m
empty-cell treatment = Sparverfahren n [*Holzkonservierung f*]
emptying = Entleeren n
~ = Ablassen n [*Stausee m*]
~ gate = Ablaßverschluß m [*Talsperre f*]
to empty into = münden in [*Fluß m*]
Emscher tank, Imhoff ~ = Emscher Brunnen m
emulsibility = Emulgierbarkeit f
emulsifiable oil = wasserlösliches Öl n, emulgierbares ~
emulsification = Emulgation f, Emulgieren n, Emulgierungsvorgang m
emulsified asphalt (US); see: asphaltic bitumen road emulsion (Brit.)
to emulsify = emulgieren
emulsifying agent, emulsifier, emulsion stabilizer, emulsion stabilizing agent = Emulgator m, Stabilisator, Schutzkolloid n
emulsion [*liquid suspended in liquid*] = Emulsion f
~ coating, see: concrete curing membrane
~ for highway construction, road emulsion = Straßenbauemulsion f
~ of tar, tar emulsion = Teeremulsion f
~ stabilizer, see: emulsifying agent
enamel = Emaille f
enamel(l)ing clay = Emaillerton m
~ furnace = Emaillierofen m
encased (sheet) pile, box section (sheet) ~ = Kastenspundbohle f
encircling reef, barrier ~ = Dammriff n
enclosed cooler (or cooling stack, or graduation-works) = geschlossenes Gradierwerk n, ~ Rieselwerk n
~ structural member = eingeschlossener Konstruktionsteil m

enclosure = Gehege n
~ = Anlage f [*Brief m*]
encrustation = Verkrustung f
end anchorage = Endverankerung f
end-anchored = endverankert
end-bearing (or point-bearing) (foundation, or bearing) pile = Spitzendruckpfahl
end bit = Endstück n für Planiermesser n
~ cap = Verschlußkappe f
~ condition = Einspannbedingung f
(~) connection angle, see: cleat
~ crater = Endkrater m [*Schweißnaht f*]
~ cross-girder, ~ floor beam = Endquerträger m [*Brücke f*]
end-dumping, rear dumping = Hinterkippentleerung f
enddump truck (US); see: end-tip(ping) (motor) lorry (Brit.)
end form(s) = Balkenkopfschalung f
~ frame, portal ~ = Endrahmen m [*Brücke f*]
*endless-bucket trencher, see: bucket ~
endless chain dredge(r), see: bucket ladder ~
~ ~haulage plant, tub-haul plant, creeper = Standbahn f mit Kettenbetrieb m
~ conveyor = endloser Förderer m
(~) rope haulage plant = Seil-Standbahnanlage f, Streckenförderungsanlage f, Drahtseil-Standbahn f
end moment = Einspann(ungs)moment n
~ moraine, terminal ~ = Endmoräne f
end-of-day joint, expansion joint at the end of a day's work = (Raumfuge f als) Tagesarbeitsfuge
end panel = Endfeld n
~ pier = Endpfeiler m
~ plate = Seitenbegrenzungsblech n [*Schwarzbelageinbaumaschine f*]
~ raker, ~ post, inclined end post = Enddiagonale f [*Fachwerk n*]
~ restraint = Endverschiebung f [*Fachwerk n*]
~ sill = Endschwelle f
~ span = Außenöffnung f [*Brücke f*]
~ stiffener, ~ stiffening angle = Endaussteifung f [*Blechträger m*]
~ support (pin-jointed) = Endauflager n (frei drehbar)

end thrust — envelope

end thrust = Enddruck m
~ tie-plate = Endbindeblech n [*Stütze f*]
~ -tip(ping) (motor) lorry (Brit.)/truck (US); end-dump truck, rear-dump = (US) = Hinterkipper-Last(kraft)wagen m, Hinterkipper-LKW m
end tippler = Stirnkipper m
endurance test = Dauerversuch m
endwall = Endmauer f [*Durchlaß m*]
~ [*stilling basin*] = Gegenmauer f, Überfallmauer [*Tosbecken n*]
energy = Arbeitsvermögen n
~ cell = Luftwirbelkammer f
~ dissipation = Energievernichtung f, Energieverzehrung f
~ dissipator = Energievernichter m
~ production = Energieerzeugung f, Energieproduktion f
~ spectrum = Energiespektrum n
engagement = Eingriff m
engaging lever = Einrückhebel m
engine = Brennstoffmotor m
~ block = Brennstoffmotor-Block m
~ clutch = Motorkupplung f
~ controls = Motor-Bedienungsvorrichtungen fpl
engined barge, see: self-propelled ~
engine distillate (US) = ein raffiniertes oder unraffiniertes Petroleumdestillat n, ähnlich Naphtha, von höherem Siedepunkt m
engine-driven rotary sweeper, see: power-(driven) ~ ~
engineer-construction firm, civil engineering firm = Ingenieurbaufirma f
engineered wood construction = Ingenieurholzbau m
engineering, ~ science = Technik f, Ingenieurwissenschaft f
~ biology = Ingenieurbiologie f
~ brick = Ingenieurziegel m, Ingenieurbackstein m
~ building site = Baustelle f des Ingenieurbaues m
~ clinker (brick) = Ingenieurbauklinker(stein) m, Ingenieurbauklinkerziegel m
~ consultation (or counsel, or advisory) service = technischer Beratungsdienst m
~ department = Konstruktionsabteilung f
~ economics = Ingenieurwirtschaft f

~ fair = technische Messe f
~ geologist = Ingenieurgeologe f
~ geology = Ingenieurgeologie f, technische Geologie
Engineering News formula = Engineering News-Formel f [*Rammformel f*]
engineering science, see: engineering
~ structure, civil ~ ~ = Ingenieurbauwerk n
engineer's-agent, project manager = Bauleiter m
engine lathe = Leitspindeldrehbank f
~ oil = Schmieröl n mittlerer Viskosität f, Motorenöl
~ speed = Motor(en)drehzahl f
~ transmission = Getriebe n
englacial moraine = Innenmoräne f
Engler visco(si)meter = Engler-Viskosimeter n
(English-)Austrian method = österreichische Bauweise f, Dreizonen-Bauweise [*Tunnelbau m*]
English blue grass, meadow fescue = Wiesenschwingel m
~ dinas = kalkgebundener Dinasstein m
~ (drainage) culvert = umwölbter Durchlaß m, ~ Abzugkanal m
~ method, ~ system of timbering = englische Bauweise f, Einzonenbauweise [*Tunnelbau m*]
English ton, just ~, long ~ = 1016,05 kg
engobe, see: slip coating
engulfment caldera = Einbruchscaldera m
enlarging bit = Erweiterungsmeißel m, Erweiterungskrone f
enriching medium = Anreicherungsmittel n
enstatite = Enstatit m
entertainment expenses = Spesen f
~ industry = Vergnügungsindustrie f
entrainmed air indicator, see: air (entrainment) meter
entrainment of acid = Mitreißen n von Säure f
entrance lock = Dockschleuse f, Trocken- ~, Einfahrtschleuse
entrapment of petroleum (Geol.) = Ölansammlung f
entry booth, entrance booth = Einfahrtstand m [*Gebührenautobahn f*]
envelope, see: haunching

envelope of failure, line of rupture, Mohr's envelope = Bruchlinie *f* [*Mohr'scher (Spannungs)Kreis m*]
~ ~ **grading** = Siebbereich *m*
eolian = äolisch, aërisch (Geol.)
epicyclic gears (or gearing), planetary ~ (~ ~), differential ~ (~ ~) = Planetengetriebe *n*, Umlaufgetriebe, Differentialgetriebe
epidiorite = Epidiorit *m*
epidote (Min.) = Epidot *m*
EPL, see: extreme pressure lubricant
Epsom salt, magnesium sulphate, sulphate of magnesium = Bittersalz *n*, Magnesiumsulfat *n*
epuré, refined natural asphalt, refined lake asphalt = gereinigter Asphalt *m*
equal angle = gleichschenk(e)liger Winkelstahl *m*
equalizer frame = Ausgleichrahmen *m*
~ **spring,** compensating ~, compensator ~ = Ausgleichfeder *f*, Spannfeder
equation of elasticity = Elastizitätsgleichung *f*
equatorial climate = äquatoriales Klima *n*
equilibrium diagram = Gleichgewichtsschaubild *n*
~ **moisture content** = offenes Kapillarwasser *n*
~ **thermal decomposition of dolomite** = Dolomit-Zerfall *m* bei thermischem Gleichgewicht *n*
equipment = Ausrüstung *f*
~ **breakdown** = Geräteausfall *m*
~ **inventory** = Gerätebestand *m*
~ **item,** piece of equipment, equipment unit, plant item = Einzelgerät *n*, Geräteeinheit *f*
~ **operator,** see: driver
~ **pool,** plant depot, contractor's yard, equipment repair yard = Gerätepark *m*, Bauhof *m*
~ **production study** = Arbeitsuntersuchung *f*, Arbeitsstudie *f* [*Baumaschine f*]
~ **rental,** hire charge = Gerätemiete *f*, (Geräte)Mietkosten *f*
~ ~ **compilation** (US); see: list of hiring charges for building plant and contractor's equipment

(~) ~ **contract with purchase option** = Kauf-Mietvertrag *m*
~ ~ **rate,** plant-hire ~ = (Geräte)Mietsatz *m*
~ **renting** = Gerätevermietung *f*
~ **repair yard,** see: plant depot
~ **storage hut** = Gerätebude *f*
~ **train,** see: train of plant items
~ **unit,** see: ~ item
~ **utilization,** see: employment of plant
equipotential lines = Linien *fpl* gleicher Standrohrspiegel *mpl*
equivalent pressure = äquivalenter Verdichtungsdruck *m* [*nach Hvorslev*]
equi-viscous temperature, E. V. T. = äquiviskose Temperatur *f*, Equiviskositätstemperatur *f*
erecting derrick (crane), ~ derricking jib crane (Brit.); ~ ~ **boom** ~ (US) = Montage-Derrick-Kran *m*, Vorbau-Derrick-Kran [*im Brückenbau m*]
~ **devices for (mono)tower cranes** = Aufstellgeräte *npl* für Turmdrehkrane *mpl*
~ **pontoon stage** [*bridge*] = Prahmgerüst *n*
~ **stage** = Aufstellgerüst *n*
~ **supervisor** = Montagemeister *m*
erection, assembling = Montage *f*
~ **bolt** = Montageschraube *f*
~ **crane,** erecting ~ = Montagekran *m*
~ **crew (or gang, or team, or party)** = Montagekolonne *f*, Montagetrupp *m*
~ **mast** = Montagemast *m*
~ **schedule** = Montageplan *m*
~ **stress** = Montagespannung *f*
~ **tower** [*bridge*] = Hilfsgerüst *n*, Abspanngerüst *n*
~ **welding** = Montageschweißung *f*
Erlenmeyer flask = Erlenmeyerkolben *m*
to erode = erodieren, auskolken, auswaschen
eroded hole (Brit.); scoured ~ = Kolkvertiefung *f*
erodible soil (Brit.); ~ **material** (US); erosive ~ = auskolkbarer Boden *m*
eroding bank, washing ~ = Abbruchufer *n*
erosion, geological ~ [*wear caused by moving water or wind*] = Erosion *f*, (flächenhafte) Ausnagung *f*, Abtragung *f*

erosion by water action, geological erosion by stream action = Schurf *m* (des Wassers), Wassererosion *f*

~ **control**, protection against scour = Kolkschutz *m*

~ **lake**, lake due to erosion = Austiefungssee *m*

~ **of a bank** = Uferangriff *m*, Uferabbruch *m*

~ **slope** = Abwitterungshang *m*

erosive power = Erosionskraft *f*

erratic block = Findling(stein) *m*, erratischer Block *m*, Erratiker *m* [*in den Alpen auch „Geißberger" genannt*]

~ **subsoil** = unregelmäßiger Untergrund *m*

error of closure, see: closing error

~ ~ **judgment** = Sinnestäuschung *f* [*Verkehrsunfall m*]

erubescite (Min.), see: bornite

eruptive rock, magmatic ~ = Eruptivgestein *n*

~ **sheet** = Eruptivgesteinstafel *f*

~ **stock** = Eruptivstock *m*

erythrite (Min.), see: cobalt bloom

escalator [*trademark of Otis Elevator company*]; moving stair(case), motorstair(case), moving stairway = Rolltreppe *f*, Fahrtreppe *f*

escape regulator = Auslaufregulierungsbauwerk *n*

escarpment, scarp (Geol.) = Ausbiß *m*, Abdachung *f*, Böschung *f*

esker (Geol.) = Esker *m*, Os *m*

essential mineral = wesentlicher Gemengteil *m*, wesentliches Mineral *n*

essexite (Geol.) = Essexit *m*

estate road, housing ~ ~ = Siedlungsstraße *f*

ester = Ester *m*

~ **interchange**, double decomposition = Umsalzen *n*, Umestern *n*, Umesterung *f*, Umsalzung

~ **value** = Esterzahl *f*

estimate (of costs), cost estimate = (Kosten)(Vor)Anschlag *m*

estimator, calculator, quantity surveyor, cost estimator, estimating engineer = Kalkulator *m*

esto-bitumen, esto-asphalt = Estobitumen *n*

estuarine flow = Gezeitenströmung *f* in Flußmündungen *fpl*

estuary = Gezeitenflußmündung *f*

~ **harbo(u)r** = Mündungshafen *m*, Stromhafen *m*

ethane = Aethan *n*

ethanol = Aethanol *n*

ether = Äther *m*

ethylene, C_2H_4 = Äthylene *n*

ethylether = Äthyläther *m*

ethyl fluid = Gemisch *n* von Bleitetraäthyl *n*, Äthylendibromid *n* und Äthylenchlorid *n*, Ethylfluid *n*

~ **gasoline**, ethylized fuel = gebleites Benzin *n*

ETTLINGER hand scraper = Handschrapper *m*, Fabrikat ELBA-WERK, ETTLINGEN/BD., DEUTSCHLAND

*****EUCLID LOADER** = Pflugbagger *m* (oder Flachbagger-Lader *m*, oder Förderband-(Anhänge)Schürfwagen *m*) mit gerader Schar *f*, Fabrikat THE EUCLID ROAD MACHINERY CO., CLEVELAND 17, OHIO, USA

~ **twin-power scraper** = Motorschürf(kübel)wagen *m* mit zusätzlichem Heckantrieb *m*, doppelmotoriger Radschrapper *m*, Fabrikat THE EUCLID ROAD MACHINERY CO., CLEVELAND 17, OHIO, USA

euhedral = automorph

eulytite, bismuth blende (Min.) = Wismutblende *f*

euphotide (Geol.) = Saussuritgabbro *m*

European silver fir = Edeltanne *f*, Weißtanne *f*

evacuating = Evakuieren *n* [*Unterdruck erzeugen*]

evacuator, see: vacuum pump

evaluating method = Bewertungsverfahren *n*, Auswertungsverfahren

evanescent lake = eintrocknender See *m*

evaporation from free-water surfaces = Verdunstung *f* von freien Wasserspiegeln

~ ~ **land surfaces** = Landverdunstung *f*

~ ~ **the leaves of plants** = Blattverdunstung *f*, Interzeption *f*

evaporation-precipitation balance = Gleichgewicht *n* zwischen Verdunstung *f* und Niederschlag *m*

even-grained rock = gleichmäßig körniges Gestein n, ~ körniger Fels m
evenness = Ebenflächigkeit f, Ebenheit f, Planebenheit f
evergreen, see: coniferous tree
exaration, glacial scour = (Aus)Kolkung f durch Eis n
excavated earth, muck; spoil [*Aussatzmaterial*] = Aushub(boden) m, Aushuberde f, Bodenaushub, Erdaushub [*durch Trockenbaggerung gewonnener Baustoff oder Aussatzmaterial*]
excavating, see: digging
excavation, building pit = Baugrube f
~, see: digging
~, see: muck
~ **of cutting** = Einschnittaushub m
~ ~ **material which has a face** = Hochbaggerung f
~ **slope** = Aushubböschung f
excavator = Trockenbagger m
~ **bucket** = Baggereimer m [*beim Trockenbagger n*]
(~) ~, (shovel) dipper, shovel, dipper bucket = (Bagger)Löffel m
~ **cable**, ~ line = Baggerseil n
~ **crane**, crane excavator, shovel crane = Kranbagger m, Baggerkran m
~ **(digger)** = Aushubgerät n
~ **hoist** = Trockenbaggerwinde f
~ **line**, see: ~ cable
~ **low-loader** = Bagger-Transportwagen m, Bagger-Tieflader m
~ **mat**, see: (supporting) mat
excavator-operated stamper, tamping-crane rammer = Stampfbagger m, Baggerstampfer m, Freifall-Kranstampfer m, Rammplattenbagger m, Fallplattenkran m, Stampf-Einrichtung f für Bagger m, Baggerstampfgerät n
excavator (supporting) mat, platform, pontoon = Baggerrost m, Matratze f
~ **track** = Baggergleis n
excessive stress = Überbeanspruchung f
excess pore (water) pressure, hydrostatic excess pressure, neutral stress = hydrostatischer Überdruck m, Porenwasser(über)druck m
exchangeable ions = austauschbare Ionen npl

exchange capacity = Austauschfähigkeit f
excise tax = Verbrauchssteuer f
excursionist = Ausflügler m
exfoliation, spalling (Geol.) = Abschuppung f
exhaust air, used ~, outgoing ~, waste ~ = Abluft f
~ **fan**, exhausting ~, exhauster = Exhaustor m
~ **gas** = Auspuffgas n
~ **manifold** = Auspuffkrümmer m
~ **pipe** = Auspuffrohr n
~ **port** = Auspuffschlitz m
~ **stroke**, scavenging ~ = Auspufftakt m, Auspuffhub m
~ **tunnel ventilation** = Saugbewetterung f
~ **valve** = Auspuffventil n
~ ~ **rocker arm** = Auspuffventilkipphebel m
exhibition palace = Ausstellungspalast m
existent gum = Abdampfrückstand m [*DIN 51753 und 51776*]
exit gradient = Austrittsgefälle n
~ **point**, egress ~ = Ausfahrt(stelle) f [*Autobahn*]
~ **road**, outward-bound ~, driveway = Ausfallstraße f
~ **(toll) booth** = Ausfahrtstand m [*Gebührenautobahn f*]
*****expanded clay**; bloating ~ (Brit.); lightweight aggregate (US) = Blähton m, aufgeblähter Ton m
~ **flange**, rolled-on ~ = Aufwalzflansch m
~ **metal**, XPM = Streckmetall n
~ **shale** = Blähschiefer m, aufgeblähter Schiefer m
~ **slag** (US); see: foamed (blastfurnace) slag (Brit.)
expander = Spannvorrichtung f
expanding band = Spreizring m
~ **cement**, high-expansion ~, expansive = Quellzement m
~ **cone** = Spreizkonus m
expansibility = Schwellvermögen n
expansion = Treiben n
~ = Ausdehnung f
~ **bearing** = bewegliches Auflager n
~ **joint** = Raumfuge f, (Aus-)Dehnungsfuge

expansion joint at the end of a day's work, end-of-day joint = (Raumfuge *f* als) Tagesarbeitsfuge

~ ~ **cap strip** (US); metal sleeve, metal capping (Brit.); joint-forming metal strip = (Hohl)Fugeneisen *n*

~ ~ **during the day's work,** running joint = (eigentliche) Raumfuge *f*

~ **jointing compound** = Raumfugenvergußmasse *f*

(~) ~ **filler,** see: pre-formed (joint) ~

(~) ~ **joint(ing) strip,** see: pre-formed (joint) filler

~ **joint sealing groove** = Raumfugenvergußspalt *m*

~ **tendency due to magnesia,** see: action of magnesia

expansion vessel = Ausdehnungsgefäß *n*

expansive soil, swell ~ = Quellboden *m*, Schwellboden

expeditious military soil stabilization = Bodenschnellverfestigung *f* für militärische Zwecke *mpl*

expenditure of time = Zeitaufwand *m*

*experience = Erfahrung *f*

~ **record** = Befähigungsnachweis *m*

experimental (or test) detail = Versuchseinzelheit *f*

~ (~ ~) **roadway (or stretch)** = Straßenversuchsabschnitt *m*

~ (~ ~) **section (or track)** = Versuchsstrecke *f*

expert fee = Sachverständigengebühr *f*

exploder, see: blasting machine

to exploit = ausbeuten

exploration method = Aufschlußverfahren *n*

exploratory boring = Probebohrung *f*, Sondier(ungs)bohrung

~ **drift** = Erschließungsstollen *m*

~ **work** = Bodenaufschluß *m*

explosion oil engine = Verpuffungsölmotor *m*

~ **type rammer,** see: internal combustion (engine powered) rammer

explosive [*a chemical compound that can decompose quickly and violently*] = Explosivstoff *m*

~ **atmosphere,** fire-damp, weather-damp; filty (Brit.) = Schlagwetter *n*

~ **blast** = Sprengung *f*

(~) **charge,** bursting ~ = Sprengladung *f*

~ **combustion engine** = Verpuffungsmotor *m*

~ **limit** = Explosionsgrenze *f*

~ **mixture** = zündfähiges Gemisch *n*

~ **oil,** see: nitro-glycerin(e)

~ **rivet** = Sprengniet *m*

explosives area, see: ammunition depot

~ **magazine** = Sprengstoffmagazin *n*

Export Group for the Constructional Industries = Exportausschuß *m* der Bauindustrie *f*

~ **magazine** = Sprengstoffmagazin *n*

exposed concrete = Sichtbeton *m*

express bus = Schnellverkehrs(auto)bus *m*, Schnellverkehrsomnibus

~ **pump,** see: high-speed ~

~ **road,** expressway, express highway = Schnellverkehrsstraße *f*

~ **traffic** = Schnellverkehr *m*

extender = Streckzusatz *m* [*z. B. Farbe f*]

~ = Kohlenwasserstoffprodukte *npl* oder Chlorparaffine *npl*, welche die Gelierung von PVC mit Weichmachern nicht stören, selbst aber kaum Weichmacherwirkung besitzen

extendible = ausziehbar

extending ladder = Ausziehleiter *f*

extensibility, resistance to cracking [*concrete*] = Rißfestigkeit *f*, Rissefestigkeit

extension = Verlängerungsstück *n*

~ = Ausläufer *m* [*Wetterkarte f*]

~ **flight conveyor,** swivel ~ ~, flight swivel ~ ~, thrower belt unit = Flieger *m* [*Förderband n*]

~ **pipe** = Ansatzrohr *n*

extensometer = Extensometer *n*

extent of a port, port area = Ausdehnung *f* eines Hafens *m*, Hafengebiet *n*

exterior masonry = Außenmauerwerk *n*

~ **paint** = Außenanstrichfarbe *f*

~ **view** = Außenansicht *f*

~ **wall** = Außenmauer *f*

externally fired boiler = Kessel *m* mit Außenfeuerung *f*

(external) rendering = Außenputz *m*

~ **scaffold(ing),** outside ~ = Außenrüstung *f*, Außengerüst *n*

~ **(screw-)thread,** male ~ = Außengewinde *n*, Bolzengewinde

external (or outdoor, or outside) temperature — facing

external (or outdoor, or outside) temperature = Außentemperatur *f*

~ **(type of O & D) survey, road side-interview method** = Befragungsmethode *f* auf der Straße *f*, Verkehrsbefragung *f*

~ ~ ~

~ **vibration** = Außenrüttlung *f*, Außenvibration *f*

~ **vibrator** = Außenrüttler *m*, Außenvibrator *m*

extracting = Extrahieren *n* [*Arbeitsgang der chemischen Industrie*]

extraction solvent = Extraktionsbenzin *n*

~ **with caustic soda**, see: test for organic matter

extractor, grapple = Fanghaken *m* [*Bohrtechnik f*]

~ = Extraktionsapparat *m*

extrados, see: back of arch

~ **spinging line** (US) = Bogenanfang *m* des Gewölberückens *m* [*Talsperre f*]

extra heavy duty truck (US); ~ ~ ~) **lorry** (Brit.) = überschwerer LKW *m*, ~ Lastkraftwagen, ~ Laster *m*

extraneous matter, foreign material = Fremdstoff *m*

"extra over" = zusätzlich [*in Angeboten npl*]

extreme fibre (Brit.); ~ **fiber** (US) = äußerste Faser *f* [*Biegeträger m*]

extreme fibre (Brit.)/**fiber** (US) **stress in tension, modulus-of-rupture (in flexure)** = Biegezugfestigkeitsmodul *m*

~ **pressure lubricant, EPL, extreme pressure oil** = Hochdruckschmiermittel *n*, HD-Öl *n*, EP-Öl

~ **stress, edge stress of extreme fibre stress** = Randspannung *f*

extrinsic insolubles, see: insoluble in benzene

extruded floor tile = stranggepreßte (Fuß-)Bodenplatte *f*

extruding property = Strangpreßeigenschaft *f*, Auspreßeigenschaft [*z. B. Schieferton m*]

extrusion = Strangpreßprofil *n*

~ **press** = Strangpresse *f*

extrusive rock, see: lava flow

eye, see: ear

~ **bar** = Augenstab *m*

~ **bolt** = Aug(en)bolzen *m*, Schraubenbolzen mit Ring, Ringbolzen, Ösenbolzen

~ **coal, birdseye** ~, **circular** ~, **curleycannel** = Augenkohle *f*

~ **gneiss, augen-gneiss** = Augengneis *m*

~ **level, height of eye** = Augenhöhe *f*, Augenpunkt *m*

~ **-piece** = Okular *n*

F

fabric carcass belt = Textilband *n*, Textilgurt *m*

~ **layer** = Bewehrungsmatten-Verlegegerät *n* [*Betonstraßenbau m*]

~ **reinforcement**, see: reinforcing (road) mesh

~ **type dust collector, cloth filter** ~ ~ = Schlauchfilter *n*, *m*, Trockenfilter

face = Wand *f* [*Hochbaggerung f*]

~, **working** ~ = Abbauwand *f*, Abtragwand

~ = Sichtfläche *f*

~, **working** ~ = Vortriebstelle *f*, (Orts-)Brust *f*, Ausbruchstelle [*Tunnelbau m*]

~, **quarry** ~ = (Stein)Bruchwand *f*, Wand

~ **brick**, see: facing ~

~ **bucket ladder excavator** = Eimerketten-Hochbagger *m*

~ **concrete** = Vorsatzbeton *m*

~ **conveyor** = Strebförderer *m*

faced (or facing) brickwork = Verblendmauerwerk *n*, Vormauerwerk

face grinder, surface ~ = Planschleifmaschine *f*

(~) **shovel**, see: crane navvy

~ ~ **attachment, crowd shovel fitting, power** ~ ~, **forward** ~ ~, **mechanical** ~ ~, **(swing) dipper** ~ ~ = Löffelhochvorrichtung *f*, Hochlöffelvorrichtung

~ ~ **bucket** = Baggerlöffel *m*, Hochlöffel

face tile, see: glazed ~

faceted pebble(s), wind-faceted pebble(s) = Kantengeröll *n*, Kantenkiesel *m*, Pyramidalgeröll *n*, Kantengeschiebe *n*, Facettengeschiebe *f*

facies (Geol.) = Fazies *f*

facility, installation, plant = Anlage *f*, Betriebsanlage, Einrichtung *f*

facing = Fassadenverkleidung *f*

facing brick, face ~, Roman ~ = Verblendstein m, Verblender m, römischer Ziegel m [4,7:9:29 cm]
~ brickwork, see: faced ~
~ clinker (brick) = Fassadenklinker m, Fassadenstein m
~ kit, lining service group = Bremsbelagsatz m
~ sand = Modellsand m
~ slab = Frontplatte f
~ stone = Werksteinverblender m
factor of safety = Sicherheitsfaktor m
factory canteen = Werkkantine f
~ ground = Werkgelände n, Fabrikgelände
~ hangar, ~ shed = Fabrikhalle f, Werkhalle, Industriehalle
fag(g)ot, bundle of brushwood = Strauchwerkbündel n
fag(g)ot-wood = Reisig n
fahlerz, fahl-ore, grey copper ore, tetrahedrite (Min.) = (Kupfer)Fahlerz n, Graugültigerz n
to fail = versagen
failed area, point of failure = Schad(en)stelle f [Straßendecke f]
failure = Versagen n, Fehlschlag m
~ = Bruch m, Brucherscheinung f
~ by spreading, lateral slide = Böschungsrutschung f, Gleitflächenbruch m
~ load, ultimate ~ = Bruchlast f, Bruchbelastung f, Grenzbelastung, Grenzlast
~ ~, ultimate ~ = Versinkungsgrenze f [Tragpfahl m]
~ strain, strain at failure = Bruchdehnung f
~ stress, ultimate ~ = Bruchspannung f
fair faced plaster = Glattputz m
fairlead (sheave) = Seilaufwickler m, Seilführung f, Führungsseilrolle f
fairway, ship channel, passage (of harbo(u)rs) = Fahrwasser n, Fahrrinne f, Fahrt f
fair weather = Schönwetter n
fall, slope = Gefälle n
~ = Staustufe f
fall-block, hoist-block, hook-block, return-block, bottom-block; [deprecated: snatch-block] = Unterflasche f, Hakenkloben m
falling ball (or sphere) visco(si)meter = Kugelfall-Viskosimeter n

~ head permeameter = Durchlässigkeitsapparat m mit abnehmender Wasserhöhe f
~ ~ permeability test = Durchlässigkeitsversuch m mit fallendem Wasserdruck m
falling-plate tamping unit, tamping plate = Stampfplatte f[Freifall-Kranstampfer m]
falling-weight (type) butterfly valve = Fallgewichtsdrosselklappe f, Drosselklappe mit Fallgewichtsantrieb m
fallow land (or ground) = Brachland n, Brachacker m
fall pipe, see: downpipe
false bedding (Geol.) = neigende Scheinlagerung f
~ (or perched) (ground-)water table = (an)gespannter Grundwasserspiegel m
~ set, grab ~; false setting (Brit.); premature stiffening = vorzeitiges Abbinden n, vorzeitige Abbindung f, falsches Abbinden, falsche Abbindung [Beton m]
falsework, lining form = Schalgerüst n
~ pile = Schalgerüstpfahl m
fan, ventilating ~ = Ventilator m
~ belt = Ventilatorriemen m
~ blade = Lüfterschaufelblatt n
~ cut = Fächereinbruch m [Stollensprengung f]
~ floor, ventilating ~ ~ = Ventilatorbühne f
to fan out = fächerförmig spleißen
fanwise paving, circular ~, DURAX ~, radial (small stone) sett ~ = Fächerpflaster n
fare collection = Fahrgelderhebung f
farewell-rock = flözleerer Sandstein m
farm building = landwirtschaftliches Gebäude n
farmland, see: cultivated area
farm lateral = Bewässerungs-Seitenkanal m für eine Farm f
~ track = Wirtschaftsweg m
~ tractor, farming ~, agrimotor = Ackerschlepper m, Ackerbulldog m
(farm-to-)market road = Zubringerstraße f für abseits liegendes landwirtschaftlichen Betrieb m
farmyard manure, livestock ~ = Stalldünger m
fascia, spandrel beam = Randbalken m

fascine, brushwood ~ = Faschine f
~ dike (US); **~ dyke** (Brit.) = Faschinendamm m
~ mattress (weighted with rubble) = Faschinenmatte f
~ to be sunk = Senkfaschine f
~ work = (Pack)Faschinat n, Packwerk n, Faschinenpackwerk, Faschinenlage f, Buschpackwerk
fastener [*for fastening into steel and concrete*] = Setzer m
fastening device = Befestigungsvorrichtung f
~ screw = Befestigungsschraube f
fast vehicle = Schnellfahrzeug n
fat [*containing an excess. A fat asphalt mixture is one in which the asphalt cement is in excess and the excess is clearly apparent*] = fett
fatal accident = tödlicher Unfall m, Unfall mit Todesfolge f
~ construction mishap (or accident) = Baubetriebsunfall m mit tödlichem Ausgang m
fatigue-bend test = Dauerbiegeversuch m
fatigue failure (or breakdown), endurance **~ (~ ~)**, repeated stress **~ (~ ~)** = Ermüdungsbruch m, Dauerbruch
~ life, ~ limit, ~ strength, endurance strength, **~ limit** = Dauerfestigkeit f
fat lime, high calcium **~,** white **~,** rich **~,** pure **~,** plastic high calcium hydrated **~** = Fettkalk m, Weißkalk m
fatting(-up), see: bleeding
fatty(-acid) pitch = Fettpech n
fatty alcohol = Fettalkohol m
~ mortar = fetter Mörtel m
~ oil = fettes Öl n
fault, see: **~ (plane)**
~ basin lake = Bruchsee m
~ breccia = Verwerfungsbrekzie f
~ dip = Kluftfallwinkel m
~ dipping against the beds = abfallende Verwerfung f
~ drag = Bruchschleppung f
faulted mountains = Bruchgebirge n
fault(ed) zone = Abbruchzone f
faulting, see: fault (plane)
fault line (Geol.) = Verwerfungslinie f, Bruchlinie

~ ~ valley = Bruchlinientāl n
~ (plane), geological **~**, faulting = Verwerfung f, Bruch m, Sprung m, Paraklase f, Absenkung f, Abschiebung f [*Grabenrand m*]
~ saddle (Geol.) = Bruchsattel m
~ (-zone) valley = Bruchtal n
fayalite, iron-olivine, Fe_2SiO_4 (Min.) = Eisenglas f, Fayalit m
feasible = durchführbar
to feather [*to blend the edge of new material smoothly into the old surface*] = einbinden
feather-alum, scissile alum = Schieferalaun m
feather grass = Federgras n
~ ore, jamesonite (Min.) = Jamesonit m, Federerz n
FEATHERLITE, see: HAYDITE
feces, faeces = Fäkalien f
~ pit = Fäkaliengrube f, Abortgrube, Latrinengrube, Senkgrube
Federal highway, ~ road = Bundesstraße f
~ Ministry of Transport, ~ MOT = Bundesverkehrsministerium n
~ navigable water course = Bundeswasserstraße f
~ Union of German Industry = Bundesverband m der Deutschen Industrie f
feebly plastic = schwachplastisch
feed, material(s) **~** = Beschicken n, (Material)Beschickung f, (Material)Aufgabe f
~ = Vorschubeinrichtung f [*Bohrmaschine f*]
~ boot = Aufgabeschuh m
~ (bucket) elevator, feeding **~** = Aufgabebecherwerk n, Beschickungsbecherwerk, Aufgabeelevator m, Beschickungselevator
~ cable = Zuleitungskabel n
~ canal = Speisekanal m
~ chute; ~ shoot (Brit.) = Aufgabeschurre f, Beschickungsschurre
feeder, feeding device, charging feeder = Speiser m, (Material)Aufgeber m, Beschickungsapparat m, Beschickervorrichtung f, Aufgabeapparat m
~ canal = Speisekanal m
~ drain, see: branch **~**
~ hopper, see: feed **~**
~ line airline = Zubringerluftlinie f

feeder road — fibrous zeolite

feeder road, see: approach ~
~ **skip hoist** = Beschickungsaufzug *m*
(feed) hopper, receiving ~, charging ~, feeder ~ = Fülltrichter *m*, Aufnahmetrichter, Materialbehälter *m*
feeding, jointing (of sett paving) = Ausfüllen *n*, Einsanden *n* [*Pflasterdecke f*]
~ **device**, see: feeder
~ **elevator**, see: feed (bucket) ~
~ **range** (US) = Bohrervorschubbereich *m*
feed process = Beschickungsvorgang *m*, Aufgabevorgang
~ **pump** = Speisepumpe *f*
feed screw, screw feeder, feeding screw = Schneckenspeiser *m*, Speiseschnecke *f*, Schneckenaufgeber *m*, Beschickungsschnecke *f*, Zubringerschnecke
~ **tank** = Beschickungsbunker *m*
~ **travel** = Vorschubdistanz *f* [*Bohrmaschine f*]
~ **water** = Speisewasser *n*
fel(d)spar = Feldspat *m*
feldspathic sandstone = Sandstein *m* mit über 5% Feldspat *m*
fel(d)spathoidal basalt = Feldspatbasalt *m*
fel(d)spathoid mineral = Feldspatvertreter *m*
to fell = fällen
felsite [*obsolete term: felstone*] = Felsit *m*
felsitic = felsitisch, feinkörnig-dicht
~ **porphyry** = Felsitporphyr *m*
felt = Filz *n*, *m*
(female) spline = Keilwellennut *f*, Längsnut
fen, marshy ground = Fehn *n*, Fenn *n*, Bruch *m*
fence fabric = Zaungewebe *n*
~ **post** = Zaunpfahl *m*
~ **wire**, fencing ~ = Gitterdraht *m*, Zaundraht
fencing, see: boundary fence
fender, bumper = Fender *m*
~, bumper = Stoßstange *f* [*Auto n*]
~ **pile** = Reibepfahl *m*
fen peat = Bruchtorf *m*
fermenting container for food = Gärfutterbehälter *m*
~ ~ ~ **potatoes** = Gärkartoffelbehälter *m*
fern = Farn *m*
ferric chloride = Eisenchlorid *n*

~ **hydrate**, $Fe(OH)_3$ = Eisenhydroxid *n*
~ **oxide**, iron ~, Fe_2O_3 = Eisenoxyd *n*
~ **sulphate** = Ferrisulfat *n*
ferro alloy = Ferrolegierung *f*
ferrochrome brick = Chromerzstein *m*
ferro-concrete [*deprecated*]; (steel) reinforced concrete = Stahlbeton *m* [*früher: Eisenbeton m*]
FERROCRETE [*Trademark*] = ein brit. schnell härtender Zement *m*
ferroelectric crystal = ferroelektrisches Kristall *n*
ferro-silicon = Ferrosilizium *n*
ferrosoferric oxide = Eisenoxyduloxyd *n*, Fe_3O_4
ferrous chloride, $FeCl_2 + 4H_2O$ = Ferrochlorid *n*, Eisenchlorür *n*
~ **foundry**, iron ~ = Eisengießerei *f*
~ **selenide** = Eisenselenür *n*
~ **sulphate** = Eisensulfat *n*
ferrugin(e)ous cementing material (or cement) (Geol.) = Bindemittel *n* aus Eisen *n*
~ **limestone**, see: calcareous iron-stone
~ **sandstone**; see: Hastings sand (Brit.)
~ **water** = eisenhaltiges Wasser *n*
to ferry across = mit Fähre *f* übersetzen
ferry-boat = Fährschiff *n*
fertilizer plant = Düngemittelwerk *n*
F & I, furnish and install = liefern und ein(zu)bauen
fibreboard (Brit.); **fiberboard** (US), wood ~ = Holzfaserplatte *f*, poröse ~, Holzfaser-Dämmplatte, Holzfaser-Isolierplatte
fibre core (Brit.); **fiber** ~ (US); hemp ~ = Hanfseele *f* [*Drahtseil n*]
~ **grease** (Brit.); **fiber** ~ (US) = Faserfett *n*
fibrolite, sillimanite (Min.) = Faserkiesel *m*, Sillimanit *m*, Fibrolith *m*
fibrous calcite = Faserkalk *m*
~ **gypsum**, satin spar = spätiger Gips *m*, Fasergips
~ **jointing material** = faserige (Fugen-) Einlage *f*
~ **malachite** (Min.) = Atlaserz *n*
~ **peat** = Fasertorf *m*, Wurzeltorf *m*
~ **zeolite** (Min.) = Fasersiedestein *m*, Spreustein *m*

field — filler

field, in the ~ = im Felde n, auf der Baustelle f
~ **bending** = Biegen n auf der Baustelle f [Bewehrung f]
~ **book,** chain ~ = Feldbuch n [Kettenvermessung f]
~ **brome grass,** brome = Ackertrespe f
~ **capacity** [the moisture-holding capacity of a soil after heavy rain or irrigation] = Wasserhaltevermögen n eines Bodens m nach einem starken Niederschlag m oder nach Bewässerung f
~ **compaction (of soil)** = Feldverdichtung f (von Boden m)
~ **concrete,** job-mix ~ = Baustellenbeton m
~ **connection,** site ~, ~ joint = Baustellenstoß m [Stahlbau m]
~ **control** = Überwachung f der Arbeiten f
~ **crops and forestry in alternation** = Waldfeldbau m
~ **cultivator,** (agricultural) ~ = (Boden-)Kultivator m
~ **ditch,** see: (open)
~ **drag,** planker = Ackerschleife f
~ **drain,** see: land ~
~ **engineer** = Ingenieur m für Außendienst m
FIELDEN-TEKTOR J = Füllgrad-Grenzschalter m, Fabrikat FIELDEN INSTRUMENT DIVISION
field forge, bottom blast ~ = Feldschmiede f
~ **glasses,** see: binoculars
~ **joint,** see: ~ connection
~ **lab(oratory),** on-job ~ = Baustellenlabor(atorium) n
~ **loco(motive)** = Baulok(omotive) f, Feldbahnlok(omotive) f
~ **moisture equivalent** [is defined as the minimum moisture content, expressed as a percentage of the weight of the oven-dried soil, at which a drop of water placed on a smooth surface of the soil will not immediately be absorbed by the soil but will spread out over the surface and give it a shiny appearance; FM~; symbol w/fme] = Feld-Feuchtigkeits-Äquivalent n [ist derjenige Wassergehalt — Wassergewicht geteilt durch Gewicht der Festmasse — bei dem ein Tropfen Wasser auf der ebenen Oberfläche des Bodens nicht sogleich absorbiert wird, sondern sich ausbreitet und der Oberfläche ein glänzendes Aussehen verleiht]
field of application, ~ ~ use = Anwendungsgebiet n, Anwendungsbereich m
~ **painting,** site ~ = Baustellenanstrich m
fieldpath = Feldweg m
field produce = Feldfrucht f
~ **rail** = Feldbahnschiene f
*field railway system (Brit.); see: light railroad ~ (US)
~ **research** = Forschung f im Außendienst m
~ **rivet,** site ~ = Baustellenniet m
~ **service unit,** see: on-the-job service unit
~ **speedwell** = Ackerehrenpreis m
~ **stone** = Feldstein m
~ **supervision,** site ~ = Baustellenüberwachung f
~ **telephone** = Feldtelephon n
~ **test** = Freifeldprüfung f, Feldversuch m
~ **watchman** = Feldhüter m
~ **welded** = auf der Baustelle f geschweißt
~ **work** = Feldarbeiten fpl [Vermessung f]
~ **workshop,** site ~ = Baustellen-Instandsetzungs-Werkstatt f
~ **-wormwood** = Feldbeifuß m
to file off = (ab)feilen
fill, see: fill earth
~, see: fill(ing)
~, see: fill (construction)
~, in ~ = (Auf)Schüttung f, (im) Auftrag m
~ = Schüttkörper m [Erdbau m]
to fill and grade, to bank against = anböschen
fill (construction), see: embankment fill
~ **earth,** fill(ing), fill material = (Auf-)Füllboden m, Schüttmaterial n, Schüttmasse f, Auftragmaterial n
filled asphaltic bitumen (Brit.); ~ asphalt (US) = Bitumen n mit Füller m
~ **ground,** made ~, fill = aufgeschüttetes Gelände n, aufgefülltes ~
filler, mineral ~, mineral dust, granular filler, granular dust (filler) = (Mineral-)Füller m, Füllstoff m
~, see: joint-sealing compound

filler block — fine crushing

filler block, hollow ~ [*floor system*] = (Decken)Füllkörper *m*, Deckenhohlkörper

~ coat, filling ~, flat ~ = Grundanstrich *m* auf Holz *n*

~ screw = Füller(verteiler)schnecke *f*

~ stone, see: choke stone ~

fillet = Hohlkehle *f*, Ausrundung *f*

~ weld = Kehlnaht *f*

~ welding = Kehlnahtschweißung *f*

filleting stick = Kehlholz *n* [*Asphaltarbeiterwerkzeug n*]

to fill in, see: to backfill

fill(ing) = (Auf)Schüttung *f*, Auftrag *m*

~, see: fill earth

filling, pondage ~ = (Wasser)Einstau *m*

~ coat, see: filler ~

~ funnel = Fülltrichter *m* für Flüssigkeiten *fpl*

~ point; gas(oline) station (US); service station = Tankstelle *f*

~ pump = Überfüllpumpe *f*

~ spout, ~ **tube** = Füllstutzen *m*

~ up, see: accretion through alluvium

fillister plane = Grathobel *m*

fill material, fill earth, fill(ing) = Schüttmaterial *n*, Auftragmaterial, Schüttmasse *f*, (Auf)Füllboden *m*

(~) placing (operations), placement = Schüttarbeiten *f*, Einbau *m*

~ slope, embankment ~, slope of embankment = Dammböschung *f*, Auffüllböschung, Böschung im Auftrag *m*

~ stake, grade ~, gradient ~, level ~, finishing ~, ~ peg = Höhenpflock *m*, Höhenpfahl

~ valve, bin door, bin gate [*controls the flow of material from the storage bin into the batcher hopper*] = Siloverschluß *m* [*entleert in Zuteilgefäß n*]

filterability = Filtrierbarkeit *f*

filter cartridge = Filterpatrone *f*

~ cloth, filtering ~ = Filtergewebe *n*

~ drain, see: blind ~

filtered infiltration water = Filterwasser *n* [*im Boden m*]

filtered stock = filtriertes Rückstandsöl *n*

~ water = gefiltertes Wasser *n*, Filterwasser

filter element, kit ~ = Filtereinsatz *m*

~ floor = Filterboden *m*

~ gravel = Filterkies *m*

~ hose = Filterschlauch *m*

filtering basin = Filterbecken *n*

~ cloth, filter ~, ~ fabric = Seihtuch *n*, Filtertuch

~ screen, see: strainer

filter layer = Filterschicht *f*, Dränschicht *f*

~ press plate = Filterpreßplatte *f*

~ sand = Filtersand *m*

~ stone = Filterstein *m*

~ zone = Filterzone *f*

filtration [*traffic*] = Ausfiltern *n*, Sortieren *n*

~ duration = Sortierungsdauer *f*, zeitliches Sortieren *n* [*Verkehr m*]

~ gallery = Sickerstollen *m*

~ loss = Sickerverlust *m*

filty (Brit.); see: explosive atmosphere

final acceptance = Schlußabnahme *f*

~ account = Schlußrechnung *f*

~ annealing = Fertigglühung *f*

~ bituminous surface = bituminöser Deckenabschluß *m* auf einer selbständigen Fahrbahndecke *f* aus Bodenzementbeton *m*

~ boiling point = Siedendpunkt *m*

~ drive = letzte Getriebestufe *f*

~ grading, fine-grading = Feinplanieren *n*

~ -settling basin = Nachklärbecken *n*

final strength = Endfestigkeit *f*

financial health = Wohlstand *m*

financing = Finanzierung *f*, Finanzieren *n*

finding = Untersuchungsergebnis *n*

fine aggregate bituminous concrete (US); see: fine(-graded) asphalt(ic) concrete

~ ~ dust [*concrete mix*] = Feinstbestandteile *mpl* [*Betonmischung f*]

~ asphalt(ic) concrete, see: fine(-graded) ~ ~

fine blading, see: tight ~

~ chip(ping)s, see: ~ (stone) ~

~ cold asphalt (Brit.); see: Damman cold asphalt

~ component of clay soils = Feinkornanteil *m* von Tonböden *mpl*

~ crusher, secondary ~, reduction ~ = Feinbrecher *m*, Nachbrecher

~ crushing, secondary ~, reduction [*discharge at sizes $1/4$ inch or finer*] = Feinbrechen *n*, Nachbrechen, Feinbruch *m*

to fine-grade — fire-damp 157

to fine-grade = feinplanieren
fine(-graded) asphalt(ic) concrete; fine aggregate bituminous concrete (US) = Asphaltfeinbeton *m*
fine-grader, see: concrete bay sub-grader
fine-grading, final grading =Feinplanieren *n*
fine grain = Feinkorn *n*
fine-grained = feinkörnig
~ = bindig [*im Gegensatz zu körnig-granular*]
fine gravel = Feinkies *m*
~ grinding, finish ~ = Feinmahlung *f*, Nachmahlung, Feinmahlen *n*, Nachmahlen
fine-gripping [*surfacing*] = feingriffig
fine gyrasphere crusher = Feinkegelbrecher *m* mit segmentförmigem Brechkopf *m*
~ jaw crusher = Feinbackenbrecher *m*
finely-ground gypsum, land plaster = Feingips *m*, Feingut *n*
fine meshed carriageway grid, see: light ga(u)ge carriageway
fineness modulus (Brit.); ~ module (US) = Feinheitsmodul *m*, Körnungsmodul *m*
~ of grinding = Mahlfeinheit *f*
fine reduction, granulation, grinding = Feinzerkleinerung *f*, Mahlen *n*, Mahlung *f*
~ ~ gyratory (crusher), ~ ~ cone crusher = Feinkreiselbrecher *m*, Feinkegelbrecher *m*
~ rolling rock débris (Geol.) = Rieselschutt *m*
fines = Feinmaterial *n*, Feinstoffe *mpl*
fine sand = Feinsand *m*, Staubsand *m*
~ ~ and coarse silt = Silt *m*, Auelehm *m*
~ screening = Feinsiebung *f*, Feinsieben *n*
~ separation = Feintrennung *f* [*Siebung f*]
~ silt = Feinschluff *m*
~ (stone) chip(ping)s = Feinsplitt *m*
~ tertiary crusher with rolls = Fein(brech)walzwerk *n*
~ tooth web saw = Absatzsäge *f*
~ wire screen = Feinmaschensieb *n*
finger-nail hardness point = Erstarrungspunkt *m* [*Bitumen n*]
finger pier = Fingerpier *m*
~ post [*deprecated*]; see: direction post
~ tip control = Fingerdrucksteuerung *f*
(~-) weeder = Unkrautjäter *m*

finish coat (US); setting ~, skimming coat, set (Brit.) = Oberputz *m*, Feinputz
finished bolt, turned ~ = blanke Schraube *f*, gedrehte ~
~ grade, ~ product, ~ material = Endprodukt *n* [*Siebung f*]
~ product, ~ good = Fertigerzeugnis *n*
~ ~, see: discharging material
~ ~ (or material) conveyor [*crushing and screening plant*] = Endprodukt-Förderband *n*
finisher, road ~, (road) finishing machine, (road) laying and finishing machine = (Straßen)Fertiger *m*, Deckenfertiger, Straßendeckenfertiger
~ = Fugenmaurer *m* [*Betondecke f*]
finisher's bridge, see: float ~
finish grinding, see: fine ~
finishing beam, see: smoothing ~
~ belt, smoothing ~ = Glättband *n*
~ coat, top ~ = Deckanstrich *m*
~ (grinding) mill = Fein(mahl)mühle *f*
~ machine, see: finisher
*finishing (operations), surface ~ (~) = Fertigbehandlung *f*, Endbearbeitung *f* [*Beton m*]
~ pass = Schlußübergang *m* [*Fertiger m, Walze f*]
finish(ing) plaster = Oberputz-Gips *m*
finishing screed, see: smoothing beam
~ stake, see: grade peg
~ trowel, float, smooth(ing) trowel = Glättkelle *f*, Spachtel *m*, *f*
finish spreader, see: towed paver-type aggregate spreader
fiord, fjord = Fjord *m*
florin grass, see: bent ~
fir = Tanne *f*
fire alarm point = Feuermeldestelle *f*
~ ~ system = Feuermeldeanlage *f*
~ bar, grate bar = (Kessel)Roststab *m*
~ box = Feuer(ungs)raum *m*, Heizkammer *f*
~ brigade = Feuerwehr *f*
fireclay, see: refractory clay
~ brick, refractory clay brick = Schamottestein *m*, Schamotteziegel *m*
~ grog refractory = zementgebundener feuerfester Schamottestein *m*
~ mineral = Kaolinit *m*
fire-damp, see: explosive atmosphere

(fire) devil, see: brazier
~ drencher (or extinguisher) = Handfeuerlöscher *m*
fired earthenware = gebrannter Scherben *m*
~ shale product = gebranntes Schieferton-Erzeugnis *n*
fire engine = Feuerlöschspritze *f*
~ fighting = Brandbekämpfung *f*
~ ~ by foam systems = Schaumlöschverfahren *n*
~-~ test = Feuerlöschprüfung *f*
fire-gutted = ausgebrannt [*z. B. Schiff n*]
fire hose = Feuerwehrschlauch *m*
~ lane = Brandgraben *m* [*Wald m*]
fireless steam loco(motive), ~ field ~ = feuerlose (Dampf)Lok(omotive) *f*
fireman, stoker = Heizer *m*, Kesselwärter *m*, Kesselbediener *m*
fire opal (Min.) = Feueropal *m*
fire-pit = Lavasee *m*
fire point; [*deprecated: ignition point*] = Brennpunkt *m* [*Prüfversuch m*]
fire-proof = feuerbeständig
fire proofing, fire protection = Feuerschutz *m*, Brandschutz
~ ~ for steel framing = feuersichere Ummantelung *f* und Abschirmung der Stahlkonstruktion *f*
~ protection paint = Feuerschutzfarbe *f*, Flammschutzfarbe
fire-protective coating = Feuerschutzüberzug *m*
fire pump = Feuerlöschpumpe *f*
fire-resisting wall = Brandmauer *f*, Feuermauer
fire-retardant paint = feuerhemmende Farbe *f*
~ wood = feuerhemmendes Holz *n*
fire risk = Feuergefahr *f*, Brandgefahr
~ travel = Feuerfortschritt *m* [*Ziegelofen m*]
~ tube boiler, smoke ~ ~, multitubular ~, multitube ~ = Heizröhrenkessel *m*, Heizrohrkessel, Feuerröhrenkessel
firing = Abtun *n* [*Schießen n, Sprengen*]
~ crew = Sprengtrupp *m*, Sprengkolonne *f*
~ current, blasting ~ = Zündstrom *m* [*Sprengen n*]
firing-in but = Einschießstand *m* [*Militärflugplatz m*]

firing of bricks, burning ~ ~ = Brennen *n* von Ziegeln *mpl*, Ziegelbrand *m*
~ order = Zündfolge *f*
~ range, burning ~ = Brennbereich *m*
~ type pulse-velocity measuring device = Knallfunkengeber *m*
firm bottom = fester Grund *m*
firmer chisel = Stechbeitel *m*
firm price contract, fixed ~ ~, lump-sum ~ = Festpreisvertrag *m*
firn, névé (Geol.) = Firn
first aid box, ~ ~ kit = Verbandskasten *m*
~ ~ dressing = Notverband *m*
~ cost(s), see: initial ~
~ gear = erster Gang *m* [*Motor m*]
first-stage development = erster Bauabschnitt *m*, erste Ausbaustufe *f*
to fish = fangen, instrumentieren [*Bohrloch n*]
fish-bar, see: fishplate
fish-beam = Fischbauchträger *m*
fish-bellied = fischbauchförmig
fish-bolt, fish-plate ~ = Laschenbolzen *m*
fish-eye (Min.), see: apophyllite
fish glue = Fischleim *m*
~ harbo(u)r, fishery ~, fishing ~ = Fischereihafen *m*
fishing = Verlaschen *n*
~ [*the operation of recovering an object left or dropped in a drill hole*] = Instrumentation *f*, Fangarbeit *f*
~ jars = Fangschere *f*, Fall~
~ tap(er) = Fangdorn *m*
~ tool, ~ instrument = Fanggerät *n* [*Bohrloch n*]
fish-ladder, fishway, fish-pass, fish passage facility = Fischtreppe *f*, Fischpaß *m*
fish mortality, kill-out of fish = Fischsterben *n*, Fischsterblichkeit *f*
fishplate, fish-bar, fish piece, splice piece, shin = Lasche *f*
to ~ = verlaschen
fishplate bolt, fish-bolt = Laschenbolzen *m*
fish-tail bit, two-bladed ~ ~ = Fischschwanzmeißel *m*
fishway, see: fish ladder
fissure spring, see: fracture ~
~ water, crack ~ = Kluftwasser *n*
fitter = Monteur *m*

to fit out — flanged motor 159

to fit out = ausrüsten, ausstatten
to fit the road into the landscape = einbinden [*Straße f in die Landschaft*]
*fitting, pipe ~ = (Rohr)Formstück n, Armatur f
~ out quay = Ausrüstungskai m, Ausrüstungskaje f
~ piece, adaptor = Paßstück n
five-drum winch = Fünftrommelwinde f, Fünftrommelwindwerk n
FIX [*Trademark*] = Druckluft-Hebezeug n, Fabrikat HEINRICH FLOTTMANN G.m.b.H., HERNE, DEUTSCHLAND
fixed = eingespannt
~ aerial cableway, tautline cableway with two stationary towers = feststehender Kabelkran m mit zwei ortsfesten Türmen mpl
~ air [*obsolete term*], see: carbon dioxide
~ arch, arch with fixed ends = Bogen m mit eingespannten Enden npl, eingespannter Bogen
~ axle gate, fixed-wheel ~, wheel-mounted ~ = Rollschütz(e) n, (f)
~ base 80-magnification collimator = Kollimationsinstrument n mit fester Basis f und mit 80-facher Vergrößerung f
~ batching unit = ortsfester Baustellensilo m (oder Zwischenladebunker m) mit Waage f
~ beam = eingespannter Träger m
~ bearing = festes Auflager n
~ bed process = Festbettverfahren n [*technisches Spaltverfahren n*]
~ carbon = fixer Kohlenstoff m
~ column = eingespannte Stütze f
~ conveyor = Transportbandanlage f
~ frame = eingespannter Rahmen m
~ hammer rotary breaker = Hammerbrecher m mit starren Schlägern mpl
~ hydrogen, see: chemically combined ~
~ jaw (crushing) plate, front ~ = Festbackenplatte f
~ load, see: dead ~
~ oil = trocknendes Öl n [*Farbe f*]
~ price = Festpreis m
~ ~ contract, see: firm ~ ~
~ screen = Festsieb n
~ sheet (pile) wall = eingespannte Spundwand f

~-sleeve cell = Triaxialgerät n mit fest angeordneter Gummihülle f
(fixed) tremie concrete = Kontraktorbeton m
~ weir = festes (Stau)Wehr n
~-wheel gate, see: fixed axle ~
fixed width finisher = Fertiger m mit fester Arbeitsbreite f
fixing bolt = Befestigungsbolzen m
fixity, restraint, fixing, end restraint = Einspannung f
fjord, see: flord
flagged footpath = Bürgersteig m aus Platten fpl
flagging, flag paving, slab paving = Gehwegplattenbelag m
flagman, see: signal man
flag paving, see: flagging
flagstaff = Fahnenmast m
flag(stone) (Geol.) = Sedimentgestein n geeignet zur Herstellung f von Gehwegplatten fpl
flagstone, paving flag; [*deprecated: (paving) flag*] = Gehwegplatte f [*entweder künstlich oder natürlich*]
flake, spall, galet, stone splinter = Steinsplitter m
~ = Flocke f
~ graphite = Flinzgraphit m
flakiness index [*gravel*] = Scherbenindex m [*Kies f*]
flaky = flockig
~ material = plattiges Material n [*Betonzuschlag(stoff) m*]
flame cutter (US); see: cutting blow pipe (Brit.)
~ cutting, torch ~, torch burning = Brennschneiden n
~ descaling, ~ cleaning = Brennputzen n
flame-photometer, hydrogen ~ ~ = Flammenphotometer m
flame type burner = Flammbrenner m
flange = Flansch m
~, boom, chord ~ = Gurt(ung) m, (f)
~, wheel-flange = Spurkranz m
~ angle, boom ~, chord ~ =|Gurtwinkel m
~ bolt = Flanschschraube f, Bundbolzen m
flanged fitting = Flanschen(rohr)formstück n
flanged motor = Flansch-(Elektro)motor m, Anbaumotor

flange(d) nut = Bundmutter f
~ pipe = Flanschenrohr n
~ ~ joint = Flanschverbindung f
flanged plate = Bördelblech n, Krempblech n, Kümpelblech
~ rail, foot-rail, flat-bottomed rail, flange rail; girder rail (US) = Breitfußschiene f
~ wheel = Spurkranzrad n
~ joint = Flanschverbindung f
~ motor = Elektro-Flanschmotor m
flange-mounted = angeflanscht
flange plate, see: angle iron of the chords
~ ~ joint = Gurtplattenstoß m
~ rivet = Halsniet m [*Blechträger m*]
~ section, chord ~, boom ~ = Gurtquerschnitt m
~ slope = Flanschneigung f
~ splice = Gurtstoß m
~ stiffening, chord ~, boom ~ = Gurtversteifung f
~ thickness = Flanschdicke f
~ width, boom ~, chord ~ = Gurtbreite f
~ with welded neck, see: welded-on flange
flanging test = Bördelprobe f
flank, see: shoulder (Brit.)
~ of a hill, hillside, slope = (Ab)Hang m
flap valve = Klappenventil n
flare path = Leuchtpfad m, Landepfad [*Flugplatz m*]
flash distillation = Turmdestillation f
flashing = Anschlüsse mpl [*z. B. mit Asbestpappe f*]
~ light (or beacon) [*a light regulary eclipsed in which the duration of light is shorter than the duration of darkness*] = Blinklicht n, Blinkfeuer [*Lichtdauer f kürzer als Dunkeldauer f*]
~ plant = Entspannungsspaltanlage f
~ process = Entspannungsverfahren n [*technisches Spaltverfahren n*]
flash lamp = Blinkanlage f
~ point = Flammpunkt m
~ ~ apparatus = Flammpunktprüfer m
~ ~ c.c. = Flammpunkt m geschlossener Tiegel m
~ ~ o.c. = Flammpunkt m offener Tiegel m
~ setting (Brit.), ~ set = Schnell(ab)binden n
~ smelting = Blitzschmelzen n

~ welding = Brennauftragschweißung f
flask = Kolben m [*Laborgerät n*]
flat = Niederung f
~ arch, see: straight ~
~ band, see: flat belt
~ bar = Flacheisen n
~ (or level) bar screen, ~ (~ ~) screen of bars, ~ (~ ~) grizzly = Flach-Stangen(transport)rost m, Flachstangenaufgeber m, Flachstangen-Siebrost m
flat-base pipe = Rohr n mit flacher Sohle f
flat belt, ~ band = Flachband n, Flachgurt m, Flachriemen m
~-bottomed rail, foot-rail, flange(d) rail; girder rail (US) = Breitfußschiene f
flat brick paving = flachseitiges Ziegel(stein)pflaster n
~ bulb-iron, bulb plate = Flachwulststahl m
~ cable = Bandkabel n
~ car = Rungenwagen m
~ chisel, hand cold ~, chipping ~ = Flachmeißel m
~ coat, see: filler ~
~ cost, see: prime ~
~ glass = Flachglas n
~ grizzly, see: ~ bar screen
~ idler, ~ roller = flache Tragrolle f
~ iron = Flacheisen n
~ lacing, ~ trellis work = Flacheisengitterwerk n
~ lattice bar = Flachstahlvergitterung f [*Stütze f*]
~ low-lying coast = Flachküste f
~ lump hammer = Flächenhammer m
~ plate, see: ~ steel ~
~-plated crawler tractor = (Gleis)Kettenschlepper m mit Flachbandagen fpl
flat pliers = Flachzange f
~ rasp = Flachspitzraspel f
~-rate tariff = Pauschalgebühr f
flat roller, see: ~ idler
~ screen = Flachsieb n, Plansieb
~ ~ of bars, see: ~ bar screen
flat-shaped cell cofferdam = Flachzellen-Fang(e)damm m
flat slab = trägerlose Decke f
~ ~ (girderless) construction, two-way flat-slab floor = Pilzdecke(nkonstruktion) f
~ slide valve = Flachschieber m

flat spring — flight

flat spring, laminated ~, leaf ~, plate ~, blade ~ = Blattfeder *f*
~ steel drill = Federstahlbohrer *m*
~ (~) plate = Flachblech *n*
flat-steel roller (US); see: flat-wheel(ed) ~
to flatten [*slope*] = abflachen
flattened round bar = abgeflachtes Rundeisen *n*
~ strand = Flach(draht)litze *f*, Litze mit dreieckigem Querschnitt, Dreikantlitze
~ ~ cable = Dreikantlitzen(draht)seil *n*
flat-topped piston = Flachkolben *m*
flat-top truck trailer = Plattform-Sattelschlepper *m*
flat trellis work, see: ~ lacing
flat-trussed arch(ed) bridge = flachgesprengte Bogenbrücke *f*
flat turf revetment = Flachrasen *m*
flat-type travel(l)ing mixing machine, non-elevating road mixer, pulverizing mixer, rotary (speed) mixer, soil mixing machine, mix-in-travel plant, mix-in-place machine, mix-in-place travel(l)ing plant, (rotary) soil mixer = Bodenmischmaschine *f*, Bodenmischer *m*, Mehrwellen-Bodenzwangsmischer
flat-web sheet pile = Flachspundbohle *f*
flat-wheel(ed) roller, smooth(-wheeled) ~; flat-steel ~, smooth-tired ~ (US) = Glattwalze *f*, Eigengewichtswalze, statisch wirksame Walze, statische Walze
flat wire = Flachdraht *m*
fletton (Brit.) = zartrötlicher Ziegel(stein) *m* (oder Backstein *m*) aus den Bezirken Peterborough und Bedford in Südostengland
flexibility = Anpassungsfähigkeit *f*
flexible, non-rigid = nicht-starr, schmiegsam
~ airline, air hose = Preßluftschlauch *m*, Druckluftschlauch, Kompressorschlauch
~ bearing surface = bituminöse Decklage *f*
~ (belt) conveyor idler, limberoller = schmiegsame Förderbandtragrolle *f*
~ ~ sander = Bandschleifmaschine *f*
~ culvert = nachgiebiger Durchlaß *m*, ~ Abzugkanal *m*
~ die = offenes Schneideisen *n*
~ drive = Biegewellenantrieb *m*

~ grinder, ~ shaft concrete grinding machine = (Beton)Schleifmaschine *f* mit Biegewelle *f*
~ knife = Abschabspachtel *m*, *f* [*Abschaben alter Ölfarbenanstriche*]
~ metallic tube, metal hose = Metallschlauch *m*
~ pavement, non-rigid ~ = nichtstarre Decke *f*, schmiegsame Decke [*Straße f*]
~ shaft = Biegewelle *f*, Schlauchwelle
~ ~ (drive) poker type (concrete) vibrator, ~ ~ internal vibrator = Innenrüttler *m* (oder Innenvibrator *m*) mit Biegewellen-Motorantrieb *m*
~ ~ grinding machine = Schleifmaschine *f* mit Biegewelle *f*
~ ~ hand grinder = Handschleifmaschine *f* mit Biegewelle *f*
~ steel arch = biegeweicher Stahlbogen *m*
~ ~ conduit = Panzerspannkanal *m* [*Spannbeton m*]
~ tube, hose = elastische Leitung *f*, Schlauch *m*
flexing concrete pavement = flatternde Betondecke *f*
FLEX-PLANE combination broom-traffic liner-spray machine, FLEX-PLANE combination spray-brooming machine = Gerät *n* zur mechanisierten Durchführung *f* der Fertigbehandlung *f* von Betonstraßendecken *fpl*, Fabrikat FLEXIBLE ROAD JOINT MACHINE COMPANY, WARREN, OHIO, USA
FLEX-PLANE dowel machine, FLEX-PLANE mechanical dowel and tie bar installer = Fugenverdübelungsgerät *n*, Fabrikat FLEXIBLE ROAD JOINT MACHINE COMPANY, WARREN, OHIO, USA
flexural beam mo(u)ld = Prüfbalkenform *f*
~ buckling = Biegeknickung *f*
~ member = Biegetragwerk *n*
~ strength, see: flexure ~
~ stress = Biegespannung *f*
flexure strength, flexural ~ = Biegezugfestigkeit *f* [*Beton m*]
~ test beam = Probebalken *m*, Biegebalken, Prüfbalken [*Beton m*]
flight, scraper ~ = Mitnehmer(schaufel) *m*, (*f*)

flight [*the screw thread (helix) of an auger*] = Spirale *f*
~ conveyor = Mitnehmerförderer *m*
~ swivel conveyor, see: extension flight ~
flinger = Wellenschutzhülse *f*
flint = Feuerstein *m*, Flint *m*
~ pebble = Feuersteinknollen *m*, Flintknollen
FLINTSEAL JFR [*jet fuel resistant*] [*Trademark*] = düsentreibstoffeste (Fugen-)Vergußmasse *f*, Fabrikat THE FLINTKOTE COMPANY, NEW YORK 20, N. Y., USA
FLINTSEAL rubber asphalt hot-poured joint sealing compound [*Trademark*] = Fugenvergußmasse *f*, Fabrikat THE FLINTKOTE COMPANY, NEW YORK 20, N. Y., USA
flint (stones) tube (grinding) mill, pebble ~(~) ~ =Flintsteinrohr(mahl)mühle *f*
~ ware, see: stoneware
flip-over bucket loader, see: overhead ~
flitch(ed) beam, sandwich ~, compound ~; ~ girder (Brit.) = Verbundbalken *m*, Verbundträger *m*, Verbundbalkenträger
to float [*mastic asphalt*] = verstreichen, aufspachteln
~ ~ into position (or place) = einschwimmen
float = Schwimmer *m*
~ = Betonglätter *m*
~, smooth(ing) trowel, finishing trowel = Glättkelle *f*, Spachtel *m*, *f*
~ bridge, (trowel(l)ing) ~, joint finishing ~, finisher's ~ = Arbeitsbühne *f* [*Betonfertigbehandlung f*]
~ chamber = Schwimmerkammer *f*
floated asphalt [*deprecated*]; mastic asphalt = Gußasphalt *m*, Streichasphalt *m* [*früher: Mastix-Asphalt m*]
floating = Streifenbildung *f* [*Pigment n*]
~ barge elevator, marine leg = Schwimm-Kahnentladebecherwerk *n*
~ bearing, see: hydrostatic ~
~ (bearing, or foundation) pile = schwebender Pfahl *m*, schwimmender ~
~ belt conveyor = Schwimmband *n*
~ box, see: ~ caisson
~ bridge = Schwimmbrücke *f*

~ caisson, ~ box, buoyant box = Schwimmkasten *m*
~ concrete (dry) dock = Betonschwimmdock *n*
~ concrete (or concreting) plant = schwimmende Betonieranlage *f*
~ crane = Schwimmkran *m*
~ débris = Schwemmzeug *n*, Schwemmgut *n*, Schwemmstoff *m*
~ (or barge) derricking jib crane (Brit.); ~ (~ ~) ~ boom ~ (US); ~ (~ ~) derrick (~), pontoon derrick; derrick boat (US) = Schwimm-Derrick-Kran *m*, Schwimm-Mastenkran *m*, Schwimm-Ladebaum *m*, Derrick-Ponton *m*
~ dock, ~ dry-dock = Schwimmdock *n*
~ drilling plant = schwimmende Bohranlage *f*
~ foundation = schwimmende Gründung *f*
~ ice, see: drift(ing) ~
~ peat = Schwemmtorf *m*
~ (or marine) (pile) driver = Schwimmramme *f*
(~) pontoon bridge = Pontonbrücke *f*
~ pump station = Schwimm-Pumpanlage *f*
~ roof = Schwimmdach *n* [*Benzintank m*]
~ sand processing plant = schwimmende Aufbereitungsanlage *f* für Sand *m*
(~) screed = (frei schwimmender) Einbauteil *m* [*Schwarzbelageinbaumaschine f*]
~ slab foundation = schwimmende Plattengründung *f*
~ suction = Schwimmerabsaugung *f*
~ tunnel = Schwimmtunnel *m*
float plane = Wasserflugzeug *n*
~ test = Schwimmprobe *f* zur Ermittlung *f* der Viskosität *f* nicht zu harter Bitumen *npl* nach A. S. T. M. D 139—27
~ valve = Schwimmerventil *n*
to flocculate = koagulieren
flocculated latex crumb, rubber powder = Kautschukpulver *n*
~ sludge = Flockenschlamm *m*
flocculating agent, see: coagulant
flocculation = Ausflockung *f*
flock test, flocculation ~ = Bodensatzprobe *f* [*Leuchtpetroleum n*]
floe, sea ~ = schwimmendes Eisfeld *n*

floe berg = Eisschollenberg *m*
~ ice = Scholleneis *n*
to flood = fluten
flood, ~ stream, ~ (tide) current = Flutströmung *f*, Flutstrom *m*
~, floodwater = Hochwasser *n*
~, see: flooding
~ bank; see: levee (US)
~ basin, see: ~ (storage) ~
~ bridge = Flutbrücke *f*
~ calamity, see: ~ disaster
~ (control) dam = Hochwasserschutztalsperre *f*, Hochwasserauffangsperre *f*
~ control (operation) = Hochwasserreg(e)lung *f*
~ ~ storage, storage of flood = Hochwasserspeicherung *f*
~ current, see: flood
~ dam, see: ~ (control) ~
~ detention reservoir, see: (floodwater) retarding ~
~ disaster, ~ calamity = Hochwasserkatastrophe *f*
~ discharge = Hochwasserwelle *f*
~ ~, ~ relief = Hochwasserentlastung *f*, Hochwasserabführung *f*
~ district, overflow land = Überschwemmungsgebiet *n*
~ estimation = Hochwasserschätzung *f*
~ forecasting = Flutvorhersage *f*
~ frequency = Hochwasserhäufigkeit *f*
floodgate, see: gate
flooding = Schwimmen *n* [*Pigment n*]
~, inundation, flood = Überschwemmung *f*, Überflutung *f*
~ of basements = Kellerüberschwemmung *f*, Kellerüberflutung
flood intensity = HHQ [*größte überhaupt bekannte Abflußmenge f*]
~ irrigation = Stauries(e)lung *f*
~ level = Hochwasserstand *m*
floodlight, searchlight = Scheinwerfer *m*
flood lubrication = Eintauchschmierung *f*
~ measuring post, river ga(u)ging station = Pegelmeßstelle *f*, Pegel(meß)station *f*
~ of record (US); see: catastrophic flood (Brit.)
~ overflow = Hochwasserüberfall *m*
~ plain = Aueneebene *f*, Flußaue *f*, Hochflutebene *f*

~ ~ deposit = Hochwasserablagerung *f*
~ pool, see: ~ (storage) basin
~ prediction = Hochwasservorhersage *f*
~ prevention reservoir, see: (floodwater) retarding ~
~ protection = Hochwasserschutz *m*
~ ~ works = Hochwasserschutzbauten *f*
~ relief, ~ discharge = Hochwasserentlastung *f*, Hochwasserabführung *f*
~ section = Hochwasserquerschnitt *m*
~ span = Flutöffnung *f*
~ (storage) basin, ~ pool, flood storage reservoir, flood-control reservoir = Hochwasser(auffang)becken *n*, Hochwasserspeicher *m*
~ stream, see: flood
~ tide, flowing ~, high tide of water = (Tide)Flut *f*, aufsteigende Flut, Tidestieg *m*
~ (~) current, see: flood
~ warning system = Hochwasseralarmsystem *n*
floodwater, flood = Hochwasser *n*
(~) retarding reservoir (or basin), flood detention ~, flood prevention ~ = Verzögerungsbecken *n*
~ rise = Hochwasseranschwellung *f*
floodway = Flutweg *m* [*Flußhochwasser n*]
~ control structure = Hochwasserregulierungsbauwerk *n*, Hochwasserkontrollbauwerk
floor, bottom, invert = Sohle *f* [*Tunnel m*]
~, bed = Sohle *f*
~ beam = Deckenträger *m*, Deckenbalken *m*
~ board = Fußbodenbrett *n*
~ boarding = Dielung *f*
~ cloth = Linoleumbelag *m*
~ covering = (Fuß)Bodenbelag *m*
~ drain (US); ~ **gull(e)y** (Brit.) = Fußbodeneinlauf *m*
~ girder, see: ~ joist
~ grating, ~ grate = Fußbodenrost *m*
~ grid (US); ~ **system, ~ grating** = (Brücken)Fahrbahnrost *m*
~ ~ ~ = Rostfußboden *m*
~ gull(e)y (Brit.); see: ~ drain (US)
~ hardness testing device = Fußboden-Härteprüfgerät *n*
~ heading, bottom ~ = Sohlvortrieb *m*, Sohlstollen *m*

flooring adhesive = Fußbodenhaftmittel *n*

~ **plaster, tiling** ~, **hard(-finish)** ~ = Estrichgips *m*

floor(ing) slab; quarry tile (Brit.) = (Fuß)Bodenplatte *f*

~ **tile** = keramische (Fuß)Bodenfliese *f*

floor joist, ceiling ~, **floor girder** = Deckenbalken *m*

~ **load(ing)** = Deckenbelastung *f*

~ **made up entirely of beams** = Vollbalkendecke *f*

~ ~ **of reinforced brick panels** = Stahlstein(geschoß)decke *f*

~ **oil** = Fußbodenöl *n*

~ **paving** = Fußbodenbelag *m* aus Ziegel *mpl* oder Platten *fpl*

~ **plate,** ~ **slab** = (Brücken)Fahrbahnplatte *f*

~ ~ = Bodenplatte *f*

~ **polish** = Bohnerwachs *n*

~ **roller** = Fußbodenwalze *f*

~ **sander,** ~ **sand-papering machine, sanding machine** = Fußbodenschleifmaschine *f*

~ **slab,** see: flooring ~

~ ~, ~ **plate** = (Brücken)Fahrbahnplatte *f*

~ ~ **form** = Deckenschalung *f*

~ **space** = Grundfläche *f* [*zum Aufstellen einer Maschine f*]

~ **surfacing,** see: ~ topping

~ **system,** ~ **grating; floor grid** (US) = (Brücken)Fahrbahnrost *m*

~ **tile,** see: flooring ~

~ **topping,** ~ **surfacing** ~ ~ = (Fuß)Boden(geh)belag *m*, Fußbodenbelag *m*

~ **wax** = Fußbodenwachs *n*

floricin oil = Floricinöl *n*

Florida earth = Floridaerde *f*

flos ferry = Sprudelstein *m*

flotation = Schwimmaufbereitung *f*, Flotation *f*

~ [*the weight supporting ability of a tire, crawler track, or platform on soft ground*] = Tragfähigkeit *f*

~ **machine** = Flotationsapparat *m*

~ **oil** = Öl *n* für Flotation *f*

~ **save-all** = Flotationsstoff-Fänger *m*

flotsam = Treibzeug *n* [*Fluß m*]

FLOTTAIR [*Trademark*] [*portable air-cooled air compressor*] = fahrbarer luftgekühlter Kompressor *m*, Fabrikat HEINRICH FLOTTMANN G. m. b. H., HERNE, DEUTSCHLAND

FLOTTMIX [*Trademark*] [*emulsion mixer*] = Flüssigkeitsmischer *m*, Fabrikat HEINRICH FLOTTMANN G. m. b. H., HERNE, DEUTSCHLAND

flour, stone dust = (Gesteins)Staub *m*, Blume *f*, Steinmehl *n*, Gesteinsmehl

~ **lime** = Kalkmehl *n*

flourometer = Fleurometer *m, n*

flow, see: creep

~, see: river discharge

~ ~ = Durchfluß *m*

~ ~ = Querschnittbelastung *f* [*Straße f*]

~ **area, cross-sectional** ~ ~ = Fließquerschnitt *m*

~ **bean** = Eruptionsdüse *f* [*Tiefbohrtechnik f*]

~ **breccia** = Fließbrekzie *f*

~ **compartment** [*Imhoff tank*] = Durchflußraum *m* [*Emscherbrunnen m*]

~ **diagram,** ~ **sheet,** ~ **scheme** = Fließbild *n*, Strömungsdiagramm *n*, Fließschema *n*

~-**duration curve** (US); see: graph of flow (Brit.)

flowering ash, manna ~ = Blumenesche *f*, Mannaesche

flow hydrograph, see: hydrograph of flow

~ **ice,** see: drift(ing) ~

flowing alignment (Brit.); ~ **alinement** (US) = stetige Linienführung *f*

~ **tide,** see: flood ~

~ **well, running** ~ = Laufbrunnen *m*

~ ~, **well producing by flow** = Eruptivsonde *f*, frei ausfließende Bohrung *f*

flow line = Vorlaufleitung *f*

~ ~, **line of flow** = Strömungslinie *f*

~ **meter** = Durchfluß(mengen)messer *m*

~ **net** = Strömungsnetz *n*, Stromlinienbild *n*

~ **nipple** = Förderdüse *f* [*Erdöl n*]

to flow off = abfließen

flow property = Fließeigenschaft *f*

~ **record** = Abflußmengenmessung *f*

~ **sheet** (Brit.); **sheet of drift** (US) (Geol.) = Gleitschicht *f*

~ ~, see: flow diagram

flow slide — flying chippings

flow slide = Rutschfließung *f*
~ **structure,** see: fluidal arrangement
~ **table** = Ausbreittisch *m*
~ **test** = Fließprobe *f*
~ **through treatment** [*metal industry wastes*] = Durchflußbehandlung *f*
~ **washer,** ~ **washing machine** = Durchlaufwaschmaschine *f*, Durchlaufwäsche *f*
fluate = Fluat *n*
fluctuation clause, variation ~ = Gleitklausel *f*
~ **in demand** = Verbrauchsschwankung *f*
flue ash(es), see: ~ dust
~ **boiler** = Flammrohrkessel *m*
~ **dust,** fly-ash, flue ash(es) = (Kessel-)Flugasche *f*
~ **gas** = Rauchgas *n*, Feuergas *n*, Verbrennungsgas
fluid agent = Verflüssigungsmittel *n*
fluidal arrangement, fluxion structure, flow structure [*rock*] = Fluidalgefüge *n*, Fließgefüge, fluidale Textur *f*, Fluidaltextur, Fließtracht *f*
fluid bed process = Wirbelschichtverfahren *n*
~ **(or liquid) binder (or binding agent)** = flüssiges Bindemittel *n*, flüssiger Binder *m*
~ **catalyst process** = Prozeß *m* mit bewegtem Katalysator *m*, Fließbettverfahren *n*
~ **clutch** = Flüssigkeitskupplung *f*
~ **column** = Wirbelschicht *f* [*Wirbelschichtofen m*]
fluid-driven pump = Pumpe *f* mit Flüssigkeitsgetriebe *n*
fluid flow = Flüssigkeitsströmung *f*
~ **friction** = Flüssigkeitsreibung *f*
~ **heat exchanger** = Flüssigkeits-Wärmeaustauscher *m*
fluidity, see: consistency
fluidization = Staubschwelung *f* in der Schwebe *f* [*Schieferöl n*]
~ **method,** see: fluo-solids method
fluid mechanics = Flüssigkeitsmechanik *f*
~ **slippage** = Schlupf *m* durch die Flüssigkeit
~ **(or liquid) stabilizer** = Stabilisator-Flüssigkeit *f*
flume, see: channel

~ [*hydraulicking*] = Selbstlaufrinne *f* [*Hydromechanisierung f*]
~ **dredge(r),** sluice ~ = Eimerketten-Schwimmbagger *m* mit Spülrinne *f*
fluorcarbon = Fluorkohlenwasserstoff *m*
fluorescence = Fluoreszenz *f*
fluorescent indicator = Fluoreszenz-Indikator *m*
to fluoridate = fluorieren
fluoridation = Fluoridierung *f*
fluor-spar, fluorite, CaF_2 = Flußspat *m*, Fluorit *n*, Fluorkalzium *n*
fluo-solids method, fluidization ~ = Brennen *n* von Kalksteinen *mpl* im Fließverfahren *n*
flush coat [*deprecated*]; see: seal(ing) ~
~ **curbstone;** see: haunching stone (Brit.)
flusher = Straßensprengwagen *m*
flushing = Einschlämmen *n* [*Straßenbau m*]
~ **gate** (US); wash-out gate = Spülschütz(e) *n*, (*f*)
~ **oil** = Spülöl *n*
flush tank = Spülbehälter *m*
flush to, see: dead level
to flush with water, to wash-in the fines by sluicing = einschlämmen mit Wasser *n* [*wassergebundene Schotterdecke f*]
~ ~ ~ ~ = sprengen mit Wasser *n*
fluted bar = Hohlkanteisen *n*
~ **handle** = gerillter Griff *m*
fluvial deposit, river ~, ~ outwash = Flußablagerung *f*
to flux = fluxen
flux = Flußmittel *n*
fluxed asphalt (US); ~ asphaltic bitumen (Brit.) [*the flux used is a residual product*] = gefluxtes Bitumen *n*
~ **electrode** = Flußmittel-Tauch-Elektrode *f*
flux(ing) oil, ~ agent, flux = Fluxmittel *n*, Fluxöl *n*
fluxion structure, see: fluidal arrangement
FLUXO bag packer = Fluxpacker *m*
fly-ash, see: flue dust
fly-away oil = Motorrostschutzmittel *n*
flying boat base = Wasserflughafen *m*
~ **buttress,** arched ~ = Strebebogen *m*
~ **chippings** = Splittablösungen *fpl* [*Oberflächenbehandlung im Straßenbau*]

flying control (Brit.); see: base operations (US)

~ gap; see: approach funnel (Brit.)

~ shoring, horizontal ~ = Absteifung f, Versteifung f [Gebäude n]

fly nut, see: butterfly (screw) ~

fly-off (Brit.) = die Beseitigung von Regenwasser n durch Evaporation f

fly over (junction) (Brit.); grade separation structure (US) = plankreuzungsfreie Kreuzung f, niveaufreie ~, überschneidungsfreie ~, Kreuzungsbauwerk n

flywheel = Schwungrad n

~ housing = Schwungradgehäuse n

F. M., see: Abrams fineness modulus

foamclay = Schaumton m

foam control agent = Schaumregulierungsmittel n

foamed (blastfurnace) slag (Brit.); expanded ~ (US) = Hochofenschaumschlacke f, geschäumte Hochofenschlacke, aufgeblähte Hochofenschlacke, schaumige Hochofenschlacke, Hüttenbims m, Kunstbims

foam(ed) concrete, see: concrete aerated with foam

~ slag aggregate concrete block = Hüttenschwemmstein m [früher: Hochofenschwemmstein]

foaming agent = Schaumbildner m, Schaummittel n [Beton m]

~ tendency = Schaumneigung f

foam inhibitor = Schaumdämpfungsmittel n

~ rubber = Schaumgummi m

~ type fire extinguisher = Schaum(feuer)löscher m

fog disperser, ~ dispeller = Nebelzerstreuer m

föhn wind = Föhn m

foil = Folie f

to fold = falten

~ ~ = abkanten [Bleche npl]

folded mountain(s) = Faltengebirge n

~ plate roof = Faltplattendach n

folding, see: bending

~ (or telescopic) boom (US)/**jib** (Brit.) = Teleskop-Ausleger m [Fahrzeugkran m]

~ bridge = Faltbrücke f

~ elevator = zusammenlegbares Becherwerk n, zusammenlegbarer Elevator m

~ (pocket) rule = Zollstock m, Gliedermaßstab m

~ weigher, see: loading skip

foliated clay = Blätterton m

~ coal, laminated ~ = Blätterkohle f

~ grit-stone, schistous sandstone = Sandschiefer m

~ gypsum = Schiefergips m

foliation (Geol.) = Blätterung f

~ (Geol.) = Schieferung f

food lock = Arzneischleuse f [pneumatische Gründung f]

fool-proof = narrensicher, mißgriffsicher

fool's gold, (iron) pyrites, yellow pyrites, FeS_2 (Min.) = Gelbeisenkies m, Schwefelkies

~ ~, marcasite, white iron pyrite (Min.) = Markasit m

foot, toe = Fuß m [Damm m]

~ = Fuß m [Schaffußwalze f]

~ accelerator = Fußgashebel m

~ basin (Brit.), see: ~ trough

~ brake = Fußbremse f

~ bridge, pedestrian ~ = Fußgängerbrücke f, Fußgängersteg m

~ bucket (Brit.), see: trough

foothills = Vorberge mpl, Vorhügel mpl

footing [a footing is an enlargement of a column or wall in order to reduce the pressure on the soil to the maximum allowable] = Flächenfundament n

~ trench, foundation ~ = Fundamentgraben m

footpath, footway, foot pavement (Brit.); sidewalk (US) [deprecated: pathway, pavement] = Gehweg m, Fußweg m, Gehsteig m, Bürgersteig m

~ roller (Brit.); sidewalk ~ (US) = Fußwegwalze f, Gehsteigwalze

foot pedal = Fußpedal n

footprint = Reifeneindruck m

foot-pump = Fußpumpe f

foot-rail, see: flanged rail

foots oil, sweats = Gemisch n von Paraffin n und Öl n das beim Entparaffinieren n anfällt

foot trough, ~ basin, ~ bucket (Brit.); lower lip (US) = Fußbecken *n*, Auslauf-Vertiefung *f* [*automatischer Syphon m*]
~ **type motor** = Elektro-Fußmotor *m*
footway [*mining*] = Leiterschacht *m* [*Bergbau m*]
~, see: footpath
foraminiferal assemblage = Foraminiferen-Vergesellschaftung *f*
~ **limestone** = Foraminiferen-Kalkstein *m*
force-account work (or construction) = Regiearbeit(en) *f*, (*pl*)
forced-circulation central heating = Pumpenheizung *f*
forced draught (Brit.); ~ **draft** (US) = Druckzug *m*
(~) **vibrating compaction**, see: vibrating compaction
~ **vibration** = erzwungene Schwingung *f*, aufgezwungene ~
force-feed loader = Lademaschine *f* mit gegen das Haufwerk fahrender Schaufelkette *f* und Abwurfband *n*, Zwangsauflader *m*
~ **lubrication** = zwangläufige Schmierung *f*, Druckumlaufschmierung *f*
force of gravity, see: gravitational force
~ ~ **inertia** = Trägheitskraft *f*
~ **parallelogram** = Kräfteparallelogramm *n* [*Statik f*]
~ **polygon** = Krafteck *n*
~ **pump**, lift and ~ ~ = Druckpumpe *f*
~ **triangle**, triangle of forces = Kräftedreieck *n*
forcing bolt = Verstärkungsbolzen *m*
ford = Furt *f*
forecasting = Vorhersage *f*
foreign material, see: extraneous matter
foreland = Vorland *n*
foreman = Polier *m*
~ **bricklayer** = Maurerpolier *m*
~ **-driller** = Bohrmeister *m*
foreshore = Vorland *n*
fore-sight = Vorblick *m* [*Nivellieren n*]
~ **reading** = Vorwärtseinschneiden *n* [*Vermessungskunde f*]
fore-slope = Vorböschung *f*
forestation, see: (af)forestation
forested = bewaldet

forest of foliage = Laubwald *m*
forestry = Forstwirtschaft *f*, Waldwirtschaft *f*
forests covering = Waldbestand *m*
forest track = Waldweg *m*, Forstweg *m*
(forge-)bellow(s) = Blasebalg *m*
forge pontoon = Werkstattponton *m*
forging grade steel = Schmiedeeisen *n*
~ **manipulator** = Manipulator *m* für Schmiedestücke *npl*
for-hire truck (US); ~ **lorry** (Brit.) = Miet-Last(kraft)wagen *m*, Miet-LKW *m*
fork = Gabel *f*
~ = Schaltgabel *f*, Bügel *m*
forked lever = Gabelhebel *m*
~ **lightning** = Linienblitz *m*
~ **mortice and tenon joint** = Scherenzapfen *m*, Gabelzapfen
~ **tie** = Gabelanker *m*
fork junction = Gabelkreuzung *f*, Straßeneinmündung *f*, Straßengab(e)lung *f*
fork-lift, fork truck, high-lift fork stacking truck, fork lift truck type conveyancer = Gabelstapler *m*
fork rod = Gabelstange *f*
~ **truck scoop** = Schürfkübel *m* für Gabelstapler *m*
to form = einschalen
to ~ = bilden
form, see: side ~
~, see: ~ of tender
~ = Formular *n*
~ **anchor** (US); see: anchor ring (Brit.)
*****formation**, system, stage, series (Geol.) = (geologische) Formation *f*
~ (Brit.); planed subgrade (US); subgrade [*deprecated*] = Fein(erd)planum *n*
~ **level** (Brit.) = Fein(erd)planumhöhe *f*
~ **of cracks**, cracking = Rißbildung *f*, Rissebildung *f*
~ ~ **embankment** = Dammherstellung *f*
~ ~ **hoar frost** = Bereifung *f*
~ ~ **ice**, see: ice formation
~ ~ **lumps** = Klumpenbildung *f*
~ ~ **marsh (or bog)** = Versumpfung *f*
~ ~ **pockets** = Nesterbildung *f* [*Beton m*]
~ ~ **washboard waves**, see: corduroy effect

formation work (Brit.); subgrade preparation, subgrading (US) = (Erd)Planumherstellung *f*

form for pricing construction works = Kalkulationsvordruck *m*

~ girder = Schalungsträger *m*

~ grader; see: concrete bay subgrader (Brit.)

~ grease = Schalfett *n*

formic acid = Ameisensäure *f*, Formylsäure

form integral with rail = KRUPP-Schalungsschiene *f* [*Trademark*]

formless paving machine, sliding form paver, slip form paver = Gleitschalungsfertiger *m*

form lining, formwork ~ = Schalungsauskleidung *f*

~ of application, application blank, application form = Antragsformular *n*

~ (of tender) = Angebotsblankett *n*

~ oil, mo(u)ld ~ = Schalöl *n*, Entschalungsöl *n*

~ panel = Schal(ungs)tafel *f*, Formplatte *f*

~ rail = Schalungsschiene *f*

~-riding unit = auf der Schalung *f* laufendes Gerät *n*

forms, see: formwork

form section = Schalungseinheit *f*

~ setter = Einschaler *m*

~ setting = Setzen *n* von Schalungsschienen *fpl*

~ ~ = Einschalen *n*

(~)stripping = Ausschalen *n*

~ support = Schalungsunterstützung *f*

~ tamper = Stampfer *m* für Straßenbauschalung *f*

~ tie = Schalungsanker *m*

formula of computation = Berechnungsformel *f*

~ ~ flow = Fließformel *f*

form vibration, see: (concrete) ~ ~

~ vibrator, see: (concrete) ~ ~

formwork, forms, concrete forming = Einschalung *f*, (Beton-)Schalung *f*

~ for no-fines concrete = Schüttbetonschalung *f*

form(work) lining = Schalungsauskleidung *f*

forsterite (Min.) = Forsterit *m*, Magnesiumolivin *m*

forsterite-marble, ophicalcite (Geol.) = Ophikalzit *m*

fort = Fort *n*

forward airfield = Frontflugplatz *m*

~ shovel (Brit.), see: crane navvy

~ ~ digging = Hochbaggern *n*

~ speed = Vorwärtsgeschwindigkeit *f*

forward-tip(ping) bucket = Vorderkipp-(Front)Ladeschaufel *f*

forwarding track = Richtungsgleis *n*

fossil coal, black ~, pit ~ = Steinkohle *f*, Schwarzkohle, fossile Kohle

~ meal (or farina, or flour) = Fossilienmehl *n*

~ wax, see: ozokerite

foul air duct = Schlechtluft-Absaugkanal *m*

fouled sewage = angefaultes Abwasser *n*

foul water, sewage, liquid waste = Abwasser *n*, Abwässer *f*

~ ~ line, sewer ~, sewage pipe ~, disposal ~ = Abwasserleitung *f*

to found = gründen

foundation = Gründung *f*, Fundierung *f*, Fundation *f*

~ = Fundament *n*

~, see: ~ (course)

~ base = Fundamentsohle *f*

~ boring = Gründungsbohrung *f*

~ brickwork = Grundmauerwerk *n*

~ by timber casing (for stone filling) = Steinkistenbau *m*, Gründung *f* auf Steinkisten *fpl*

~ concrete = Fundamentbeton *m*

~ (course) = Unterbau *m*

~ ditch, see: ~ trench

~ engineering = Gründungswesen *n*, Fundationstechnik *f*

~ excavation = Fundamentaushub *m*

~ exploration (work), see: soil investigation

~ hoist, building pit ~ = Baugrubenaufzug *m*

~ in rock = Felsgründung *f*

~ level = Gründungssohle *f*

*(foundation) pile, (load-)bearing ~ = Gründungspfahl *m*

~ ~ driving plant = Pfahlramme *f*

~ platform of half timbers = Rost *m* aus Halbhölzern *npl*

foundation plinth, base slab = Fundamentplatte *f*, Grundplatte
~ **raft**, see: raft foundation
~ **rock** = Gründungsfels *m*
~ **slab** = Fundamentplatte *f*, Gründungsplatte
~ **soil**, see: subsoil
~ ~ **waterproofing**, waterproofing of foundation, subsoil waterproofing = Baugrund(ab)dichtung *f*
~ **stone** = Grundstein *m*
~ **testing**, see: soil investigation
~ **trench**, footing ~, foundation ditch = Fundamentgraben *m*
~ **wall** = Fundamentmauer *f*
~ **water pressure**, uplift = Sohlenwasserdruck *m*, Auftrieb *m* [*Talsperre f*]
~ **work** = Grundbau *m*, Gründungsarbeit(en) *f*, (*pl*)
~ ~ **under compressed air**, pneumatic foundation work = Druckluftgründung *f*
founding time = Schmelzzeit *f* [*Glas n*]
foundry clay, ladle ~ = Gießton *m*
~ **jib crane** (Brit.); ~ **boom** ~ (US) = Gießerei-Drehkran *m*
~ **pig-iron** = Gießereiroheisen *n*
~ **sand** = Gießereisand *m*
four ball apparatus = Vierkugelapparat *m*
four-bladed circular grab (or bucket), orange-peel grab = Apfelsinenschalengreifkorb *m*
four-centred arch = geschleifter Spitzbogen *m*
four-compartment aggregate feeder = vierzelliger Dosierapparat *m*
four-cylinder turbine = viergehäusige Turbine *f*
four-deck grader = Vierdeckersieb *n*
four-furrow plough (Brit.)/**plow** (US) = Vierfurchenpflug *m*
four-lane single-carriageway motor road = Autobahn *f* mit vier Spuren *fpl* ohne Mittelstreifen *m*
four-material batcher = vierzelliger Dosierapparat *m*
four-moment theorem = Vier-Momente-Lehrsatz *m*
four-motor travel(l)ing crane = Viermotoren-Elektrolaufkran *m*

four-part rigging = Vierfach-Einscherung *f*
four-piece steel rib = vierteilige Stahlrippe *f*
four-pile dolphin = vierpfähliger Dalbe *m*
four-roll crusher, twindual roll ~ = Doppelwalzwerk *n*, Doppelwalzenbrecher *m*
four-stroke cycle engine = Viertakter *m*, Viertaktmotor *m*
four-way control box = Vierfachsteuergerät *n*
four-wheel(ed) prime mover = Vierrad-Vorspänner *m*
~ **scraper**, crawler-tractor drawn ~, rubber-mounted tractor drawn ~, hauling ~, pull ~, pull-type ~, trailer ~, full trailer ~, two-axle ~, full trailer pan, towed four-whee(el)d scraper = Schürf(kübel)wagen *m*, Schrapperwagen *m*, Anhänge-~
~ **tractor** = Vierradschlepper *m*, Vierradtrecker *m*, Vierradtraktor *m*, Zweiachsschlepper, Zweiachs-Reifen-Sattelschlepper
foyaite (Geol.) = Foyait *m*
FPI, fuel pump injection = Förderbeginn *m* der Einspritzpumpe *f*
fraction, see: size bracket
~ = Anteil *m* [*z. B. beim Boden m*]
fractional distillation = Blasendestillation *f*
~ ~ = fraktionierte Destillation *f*
~ **H.P. motor**, see: pilot ~
~ **progression** = Kettenbruch *m*
fractionating column = Fraktionierkolonne *f*
fraction bar = Bruchstrich *m*
fracture; crack (Brit.) (Geol.) = Bruchfuge *f*
~-**chalk** = brüchiger Kalk *m*
fracture spring, fissure ~ = Spaltenquelle *f*, Kluftquelle, Verwerfungsspaltenquelle
fragment (Geol.) = Fragment *n*, Trümmerstück *n*
fragmentation = Stückung *f*
frame, framework = Rahmen *m*
fixed = voll eingespannt
hinged at supports = gelenkig gelagert
~ **crane** = Bockkran *m*, Gerüstkran
framed building in precast concrete units = Montagebau *m* mit Betonfertigteilen *mpl*

framed cross-cut saw, hand hack saw = Bügelsäge f [*Gattungsbegriff*]
~ hand saw = Strecksäge f
~ ~ ~ with stretcher = Handvorspannsäge f, gefaßte Säge
~ stanchion = Rahmenständer m
~ structure = Rahmenbauwerk n
~ system = Fachwerksystem n
frame flange = Rahmenflansch m
~ for fencing in vegetable and flower beds = Frühbeetkasten m
~ formula = Rahmenformel f
~ leg = Rahmenstiel m
~ member, skeleton ~ = Rahmen(einzel)teil m, n
~ of one bay = Einfeldrahmen m
~ plough (Brit.); **~ plow** (US) = Rahmenpflug m
~ type pile driving plant, ~ ~ piling plant = Gerüstramme f
~ ~ ~ ~ ~ (or piling plant) **for driving in row arrangement** = Reihen(gerüst)ramme f
~ with n-column, portal ~ ~ ~ = n-stieliger Rahmen m
framework, see: frame
~, latticework = Fachwerk n
~ of struts and braces = Bockstrebenkonstruktion f
Francis type pump-turbine = Francis-Speicherpumpe f
~ water turbine = Francis-Turbine f
Franki foundation pile, ~ bearing ~, (**~**) **displacement caisson** = Franki-Gründungspfahl m, Franki(-Trag)pfahl
FRANKIGNOUL pile [*Trademark*] = Franki-Pfahl m mit stählernem Treibkopf m
Fraas brittle temperature, ~ breaking point, ~ bend-brittle point = Brechpunkt(-Temperatur) m, (f) nach Fraas
freak value [*data*] = Ausreißer m
free adjudication = freihändige Vergabe f
~ axle = Laufachse f
~ balloon = Freiballon m
freeboard = Freibord n
free board and room = freie Verpflegung f und Unterkunft f
~ bridge = Brücke f ohne Gebührenabgabe f

~-burning coal = Sinterkohle f, Flammkohle
~-burning gas coal = Gasflammkohle f
free carbon [*deprecated*]; **toluene insolubles** = freier Kohlenstoff m [*früher: Unlösliches n*]
~ deviation turbine, see: impulse ~
~ fall drilling system = Freifall-Bohrverfahren n
~ ~ (type) batch mixer, gravity batch ~, rotary **~ ~ ~** = Freifallchargenmischer m
(~ ~ ~) non-tilt(ing) (drum) mixer, see: closed drum (concrete) mixer with reverse discharge
~ floating track system = Drehstabfederung f des (Gleis)Kettenlaufwerkes n
~-flowing material = rieselfähiges Gut n
~ flow tail race tunnel = Freispiegel-Schußstollen m
freehaul [*the maximum distance which excavated material is transported without extra charge*] = maximale Bodentransportweite f ohne Preiszuschlag m
free hydrogen, see: available ~
freeing = Freifahrung f [*Bergbau m*]
~ on the nappe (US); **separation of the water layer** (Brit.) = Ablösung f des Strahles m [*Talsperre f*]
free jet turbine = Freistrahlturbine f
~-lime content = freier Kalkgehalt m [*Beton m*]
freely supported = frei aufliegend
~ ~ liquid = freischwebende Flüssigkeit f
free-piston (air) compressor = Freikolbenkompressor m, Freikolbenverdichter m
~ engine = Freikolbenmotor m
~-turbine tractor = Traktor m (oder Trecker m, oder Schlepper m) mit Gasturbinenantrieb m und Freikolben-Gaserzeuger m
free port = Freihafen m
~ sheet (pile) wall = unverankerte Spundwand f
free-sleeve cell = Triaxialgerät n mit frei angeordneter Gummihülle f
~ spinning = freies Drehen n [*Kabeltrommel f*]
free-standing pile = freistehender Pfahl m
free trade area = Freihandelszone f

freeway — Fröhlich's (stress-)concentration factor 171

freeway = Schnellverkehrsstraße *f* ohne Zufahrten *fpl* zu anliegendem Grundbesitz *m*
free-wheel = Freilauf *m*
free-wheeled vehicle = gleisloses Fahrzeug *n*
freezing and thawing cycle = Gefrier- und Auftau-Zyklus *m*, Tau-Frost-Wechsel *m*
~ **mix(ture)** = Kältemischung *f*
~ **sprays** = Eisgischt *f*
~ **weather**, frosty ~ = Frostwetter *n*
freieslebenite (Min.) = Schilfglaserz *n*
freight bill = Frachtbrief *m*
~ **car** (US); goods wagon, goods van, railway wagon (Brit.) = Güterwagen *m*, Waggon *m*
~ **charges**, see: ~ costs
(~ -)**classification yard**, marshalling yard, switchyard, shunting station = Rangierbahnhof *m*, Verschiebebahnhof
freight costs, ~ charges = Frachtkosten *f*
freighter, cargo vessel = Frachter *m*, Frachtschiff *n*
freight-forwarder = Frachtaufgeber *m*
freight house = Güterschuppen *m*
~ **traffic** = Güterverkehr *m*
French chalk, powdered talc, talcum powder = Talkum *n*, Specksteinmehl *n*
~ **drain**, see: blind ~,
fresh(ly-mixed) concrete, unset ~ = Frischbeton *m*, unabgebundener Beton *m*
fresh rock = bergfeuchtes Gestein *n*
~ **sewage** = frisches Abwasser *n*
~ **sludge**, see: green ~
~ **water** = Süßwasser *n*
~ ~ **basin** = Süßwasserbecken *n*
~ ~ **limestone** = Süßwasserkalk(stein) *m*
~ **wind** = frische Brise *f*
fresno (scraper) (US) = von drei Zugtieren *npl* gezogener Radschrapper *m*
fret saw, compass ~ = Laubsäge *f*
fretting; [*deprecated:* (un)ravel(l)ing] [*breaking up of the road surface because of binder failure*] = Abbröckeln *n*, Abbröck(e)lung *f* [*Straßendecke f*]
~, seizure = Fressen *n* [*Verflüssigung der Metalloberfläche*]
~ **corrosion** = Reibungskorrosion *f*

~ -~ **inhibitor** = Hemmungsmittel *n* der Reibungskorrosion *f*
Freyssinet-type cone = Freyssinet-Kegel *m*
~ **jack** = Freyssinet-Presse *f*
friable, see: noncohesive
~ **gypsum**, see: earthy ~
frictional, see: noncohesive
friction(al) (bearing, or foundation) pile = Mantelpfahl *m*, Reibungspfahl
frictional coefficient, coefficient of friction = Reibungsbeiwert *m*
~ **resistance** = Reibungswiderstand *m*
friction bearing, plain (~) ~, sliding ~ = Gleitlager *n*
~ **brake** = Reibungsbremse *f*
~ **circle analysis** = Gleitkreisanalyse *f*
~ **clutch (coupling)** = Friktionskupplung *f*, Reib(ungs)kupplung
~ **head**, ~ **loss** = Reibungsverlust *m* [*Hydraulik f*]
~ **hoist** = Friktionswinde *f*, Reibradwinde *f*, Treibscheibenaufzug *m*
~ **pile**, see: frictional ~
~ **roller** = Reibrolle *f*
~ -**screw (driven) press** = Friktionsspindelpresse *f*, Reib(trieb)Spindelpresse *f*
friction-wheel drive concrete mixer = Reibrad-Betonmischer *m*
Friesian Islands = Friesische Inseln *fpl*
fringe area = Randgebiet *n*
FRIOPLAST [*Trademark*] = ein schweizerischer Luftporenbildner *m*
FRISCH motor grader = Motor-Straßenhobel *m*, Fabrikat EISENWERK GEBR. FRISCH K. G., AUGSBURG, DEUTSCHLAND
frog [*track laying*] = Frosch *m* [*Gleisbau m*]
~ **rammer**, leaping frog, jumping frog, DELMAG frog tamper, frog ramming machine, frog type jumping rammer = Frosch *m*, DELMAG-Stampfer *m*, Frosch-Ramme *f*, Frosch-Stampfer *m*, Frosch-Explosionsramme *f*, Fabrikat DELMAG MASCHINENFABRIK REINHOLD DORNFELD, ESSSLINGEN/NECKAR, DEUTSCHLAND
Fröhlich's (stress-)concentration factor = Konzentrationsfaktor *m* nach Fröhlich, Ordnungszahl *f* der Spannungsverteilung *f*

front, see: attachment
frontage road = Begleitstraße f [einer Stadtautobahn f]
front axle = Vorderachse f
~ ~ **drive** = Vorderachsenantrieb m
~ **crushing plate**, fixed jaw (~) ~ = Festbackenplatte f [Backenbrecher m]
~ **elevation** = Vorderansicht f
~ **end attachments**, interchangeable ~ ~ ~, convertible ~ ~ ~, front end conversion units, work attachments = Umbaueinrichtungen fpl [Universalbagger m]
~ ~ **crawler shovel** = (Gleis)Ketten-Frontlader m
~-~ **loader**, see: loading shovel
front rake = Vorbau-Harke f, Vorbau-Rechen m
~ **range** = Vorgebirge n
~ **roll**, ~ roller wheel = Vorderwalze f, Vorderwalzrad n
~ **screed**, see: strike-off (~)
~ **steering** = Vorderradlenkung f
~ **tipper**, see: dumper
~ ~ [universal term] = Frontkipper m [allgemeiner Ausdruck m]
~ **wheel drive** = Vorderradantrieb m
frost action = Frosteinwirkung f
~ **blanket**, see: sub-base
~ **boil** = Frostbeule f
~ **cleft (or shake)** = Eiskluft f [Holz n]
~ **crack** = Frostriß m
~ **criterion** = Frostkriterium n
~ **gritting machine**, see: winter ~ ~
~ **heaving**, ~ heave = Frosthebung f
~ **line** [in the soil] = Frostgrenze f [im Boden m]
~ **penetration depth**, depth of frost penetration = Frosttiefe f
~ **precaution** = Frostschutzmaßnahme f
~ **protection** = Frostschutz m
~ **protective**, see: anti-freeze (mixture)
~ **resistance** = Frostsicherheit f
~-**resistant**, non-frost-active = frostbeständig, frostsicher
frost scaling = Frostabblätterung f
~ **shake**, see: ~ cleft
~-**susceptible** = frostempfindlich
frosty weather, see: freezing ~
frothing = Schaumbildung f, Schäumen n

fruit jar pycnometer, see: pycnometer
fuchsite (Min.) = Chromglimmer m, Fuchsit m
FUCHS midget excavator = Kleinbagger m, Fabrikat MASCHINENFABRIK JOHANNES FUCHS K. G., DITZINGEN-STUTTGART, DEUTSCHLAND
fucus vesicolosus, bladder wrack = Blasentang m, Fukus m
fuel-air mixture = Brennstoff-Luftgemisch m
fuel alcohol, industrial methylated spirit = Brennspiritus m
~ **brown coal**; [incorrectly termed "non-bituminous" brown coal] = Feuerbraunkohle f
~ **drive** = Kraftstoffantrieb m
~ **efficiency** = Brennstoffausnutzung f
~ **filter** = Brennstoffilter n, m
~ **injection pump** = Brennstoffeinspritzpumpe f, Kraftstoffeinspritzpumpe
~ **lift pump** = Brennstofförderpumpe f, Kraftstoffversorgungspumpe
fuel(l)ing, re~ = Betanken n
fuel oil, see: ~ residue
~ ~ **gas tar**, see: oil-water-gas ~
~ ~ **(residue)** = Heizöl n
~ **pre-filter** = Brennstoff-Grobfilter n, m
~ **pressure control** = Regelorgan n für den Kraftstoffdruck m
~ **pump** = Brennstoffpumpe f, Treibstoffpumpe, Kraftstoffpumpe
~ ~ **injection**, FPI = Förderbeginn m der Einspritzpumpe f
~ **spillage** = Treibstoffverschüttung f
~ **supply base** = Treibstoff-Nachschubbasis f
~ **system** = Kraftstoffanlage f
~ **tank** = Brennstoffbehälter m
fulcrum = Drehpunkt m
~ **lever** = an zwei Punkten drehbar gelagerter Verstellhebel m
~ **pin**, see: pivot
fulgurite, lightning tube (Min.) = Fulgurit m, Blitzröhre f
full admission turbine = Vollturbine f
~ **automatic operation** = Vollautomatik f
fullcap = Vulkanisieren n eines Laufstreifens m (mit Schulteransatz m) bei verlaufender Kante f

full cell process (or treatment), Bethell ~ (~ ~) = Volldurchtränkung *f*, Vollimprägnierung *f* [*Holz n*]
~-circle mining of tunnel heading, full-face work = Vollausbruch *m*
full-course (construction) work = einlagiger Betoneinbau *m*
full depth internal slab vibrator, ~ ~ ~ concrete pavement (or paving/US) vibrator; internal vibrating machine (Brit.); paving vibrator (US) = Betondeckeninnenrüttler *m*, Tauchrüttler-Betonstraßenfertiger *m*, Vibrationsfertiger *m* mit Tauchrüttlern *mpl*, Tauchvibrationsfertiger
Fuller curve for maximum density = Fuller-Kurve *f*
fullering, see: caulking (Brit.)
Fuller-Kinyon unloader (pump), F-K (dry) pump = Fuller(-Kinyon)-Pumpe *f*, Zement(staub)pumpe *f*, Fullerzementpumpe *f*, Fuller-Entladepumpe *f*
Fuller's earth (Geol.) = Fullererde *f*
Fuller's parabola = Fullerparabel *f* [*Bindemittel n ausgenommen*]
full load = Vollgas *n* bei Belastung *f*
full-scale experiment, ~ test = Großversuch *m*
~ production, serial fabrication = Serienherstellung *f*, Serienfertigung *f*, Reihenfertigung *f*
full section = gesamtes Querprofil *n*
~-~ strength [*steel bar*] = Gesamtquerschnitt-Tragfähigkeit *f*
full time employment = Vollbeschäftigung *f*
(~) trailer, see: multi-axle ~
~ ~ with a dump body, see: (tractor)wagon
~ vision cab(in) = Rundblick-Führerhaus *n*, Vollsichtkanzel *f*
fully-automatic = vollautomatisch
fulminate detonator = Kupfersprengkapsel *f*
~ of mercury, mercuric isocyanate, Hg(ONC)$_2$ = Knallquecksilber *n*, Quecksilbercyanat *n*, Merkuricyanat
fulminating lead = Knallblei *n*
~ oil, see: nitro-glycerin(e)
fumarole (Geol.) = Fumarole *f*
fumes = Sprengschwaden *mpl*

fuming sulphuric acid; [*commercial name "oleum"*] = rauchende Schwefelsäure *f*
~ volcano = dampfender Vulkan *m*
to function = funktionieren
functional group = funktionelle Gruppe *f*
funicular crane; see: blondin (Brit.)
fundamental gneiss = Urgneis *m*
fungicide = Pilzvertilgungsmittel *n*
funnel classifier = Trichter(naß)klassierer *m*
~ type straight oil cup = Trichteröler *m*
furfural resin = Furfuralharz *n*
furnace clinker, see: clinker
furnish and install, F & I = liefern und ein(zu)bauen
furnishing of equipment = Gerätevorhaltung *f*
furniture beetle = Klopfkäfer *m*
fusain = Faserkohle *f*
fuse = Zündschnur *f*
~ = elektrische Sicherung *f*
~-head = Zünderkopf *m*
fusel oil = Fuselöl *n*
~ ~ tar = Fuselölgasteer *m*
fuse plug = Katastrophen-Überlauf *m*
"fuse plug" levee (US) = (Hochwasser) Sprengdeich *m* [*im Gefahrenfall wird der Deich zur Entlastung gesprengt*]
fusibility = Schmelzbarkeit *f*
fusible plug = Schmelzpfropfen *m*, Schmelzstöpsel *m*
fusion cone, see: Seger ~
~ point, melting ~, softening ~ = Schmelzpunkt *m*, Erweichungspunkt *m*
~ steel wire = Schweißdraht *m*, Zusatzwerkstoff *m*
~ welding = (Ab)Schmelzschweißung *f*
~ ~ by means of gas, gas welding = Gas(schmelz)schweißung *f*
FWD motor truck (US)/**lorry** (Brit.) = LKW *m* mit Vierradantrieb *m*

G

gable bottom car = Schrägbodenwagen *m*
~ roof, see: saddle ~
~ stanchion = Giebelstütze *f*
gage (US); **gauge** (Brit.) = 1. Lehre *f*; 2. Pegel *m*; 3. Maß *n*; 4. Spur *f*

gahnite, zinc spinel, $ZnAl_2O_4$ (Min.) = Zink-Spinell *m*, Gahnit *m*

gaize = Gaize *f*

gale = Sturm *m*

galena, lead glance, PbS (Min.) = Bleiglanz *m*, Galenit *m*

gale-swept tide = Sturmflut *f*

galet, see: flake

Galileo-microtelemeter with the method of the plumb rule = Galileo-Mikrotelemeter, *n* mit der Methode des Bleisenkels *m*

Galileo slide-ga(u)ge = Deformator-Klinograph Galileo *m*

gallery; see: drift (Brit.)

~ **machine**, miner = Stollenbohrgerät *n*

~ **portal** = Stollenmund *m*

~ **pump** = Stollenpumpe *f*

gallic acid = Gallussäure *f*

gallo-tannin, see: tannin

galmins [*abbrev. gpm = gallons per minute*] = „Gallonen pro Minute"

galvanizing = Verzinkung *f*

gang, see: crew

ganger = Schachtmeister *m*

gang plough (Brit.); ~ **plow** (US) = Mehrscharfpflug *m*

gangrene = Holzbrand *m*

gang saw = Vollgatter *n*

gangue = taubes Gestein *n*, Berg *m*

gannister (Brit.); **ganister** (US) = englischer Quarzit *m*

~ **brick**, see: silica ~

gantry, crane girder = Kranträger *m*

~ **crane** (US); see: goliath ~ (Brit.)

~ ~ **hoist** (US); goliath ~ ~ (Brit.) = Brückenkranwinde *f*

~ **house** = Kranhaus *n*

gap-graded material = diskontinuierlich (oder unstetig) abgestuftes Material *n*

gap grading, see: discontinuous ~

garbage, household refuse, kitchen waste = Küchenabfälle *f*

~ **disposal plant**, see: refuse incinerator

~ **truck** (US); refuse wagon (Brit.) = Müllast(kraft)wagen *m*

garden shears, hedge-trimmer = Heckenschneider *m*, Gartenschere *f*

GARDNER travel(l)ing mixer [*Trademark*] [*mounted on wheels*] = Aufnahmemischer *m*, Fabrikat GARDNER

garnet (Min.) = Granat *m*

garnet-rock, garnetyte = Granatgestein *n*, Granatfels *m*

gas = Gas *n*

~ = allgemeine Bezeichnung für Gasolin in den USA

~ **analysis** = Gasanalyse *f*

~ **atomizing oil burner** = Luftzerstäubungsbrenner *m*

~ **barrel handrail**, ~ **tubing** ~ = Gasrohr-Handlauf *m* [*Geländer n*]

~ **black** = Gasruß *m*

~ **blow-out**, sudden escape of gas = Gasausbruch *m*

~ **bottle**, ~ **cylinder** = Gasflasche *f*

~ **burner** = Gasbrenner *m*

~ **cap of a structure** = Gaskappe *f* einer Struktur *f*

~ **chromatography** = Gas-Chromatographie *f*

~ **coke** = Gaskok(s) *m*

~ **cylinder** = Gasflasche *f*

~ **detector set** = Gasanzeigegerät *n*

~ **discharge lamp**, see: vacuum tube ~

~ **dome** = Gashaube *f*

~ **drive** = Gastreibverfahren *n* [*Erdöl n*]

gas-electric drive (US); see: petrol-electric ~ (Brit.)

gas engine, see: gas(olene) ~ (US)

~ ~ = Gasmotor *m*, Gaskraftmaschine *f*

~ **escape** = Gasausbruch *m*

~ **field** = Gasfeld *n*

gas-flow oil-shale retort = Querstromofen *m* für Ölschieferschwelung *f*

gas-formed concrete, see: aerated ~

gas-forming agent = Blähmittel *n*, (Metall)Treibmittel *n* [*Beton m*]

gas from low-temperature distillation = Schwelgas *n*

~ **generator** = Gasentwickler *m* [*Schweißen n*]

~ **-holder**, gas-tank, gasometer = Gasbehälter *m*, Gassammler *m*, Gasometer *m*

gas-house coal tar, see: gas works ~ ~

gasification, gasifying = Vergasung *f* [*feste Brennstoffe mpl mit Vergasungsmitteln npl*]

gasification — gate assembly

gasification, vaporization = Vergasung f [*flüssiger Brennstoff m im Vergaser m*]
gasifying, see: gasification
~ agent = Vergasungsmittel n
gas injection valve = Gaseintrittsventil n
~ input line = Gaseinpreßleitung f
~ ~ well, ~ intake ~ = Gaseinpreßbohrung f
gasket, packing, sealing member = Dichtungsmanschette f
gas lift = Druckgasförderverfahren n, Gasliftverfahren
~ ~ hook-up = Gaslift-Leitungsanschluß m [*an der Bohrung f*]
~ ~ truck (US); petrol ~ ~ (Brit.) = Hubstapler m mit Ottomotor m
~ liquor = Gasreinigungswasser n
~ lock = Gaspolster n [*Tiefpumpe f*]
~ mask, respirator = Gasmaske f
~ occlusions = Gaseinschlüsse mpl
~ odo(u)r = Gasgeruch m
~ oil, solar ~ (Brit.) = Gasöl n, Solaröl
~/~ level = Gas/Ölspiegel m [*Spiegel, bei dem die Gaskappe einer Struktur das Öl berührt*]
~/~ ratio of production = Gas/Ölverhältnis n der Förderung f [*pro Faß Öl von etwa 159 Litern mitgeförderte Menge Gas in Kubikfuß*]
gasolene, gasoline (US) = Kraftstoff m für Otto-Motor m
gas(olene) (or gasoline) engine(US); petrol ~ (Brit.); Otto cycle engine = Vergasermotor m, Benzinmotor m, Otto(-Vergaser)motor
~ (~ ~) chain saw (US); petrol ~ ~ (Brit.) = Kettensäge f mit Benzinmotor m, Baumfällsäge f
~ (~ ~) interceptor (US); petrol trap (Brit.) = Benzinabscheider m, Benzinfang m
~ (~ ~) (naphtha) (US); petrol (Brit.); Otto type fuel = (Motoren-)Benzin n, Otto-Kraftstoff m
~ (~ ~) rammer (US); petrol-powered ~ (Brit.) = Benzinstampframme f
~ (~ ~) station (US); see: filling pont
~ (~ ~) (storage) can (US); jerrycan, petrol can (Brit.) = Benzinkanister m

~ (~ ~) ~ stability = Lagerbeständigkeit f der Ottokraftstoffe mpl
break point = Punkt m der Druckzeitkurve f
induction period = Induktionszeit f
potential gum = Bombenharzwert m
gasometer, see: gas-holder
gas-poisoning = Gasvergiftung f
gas-powered lift truck (US) = Benzin-Hubkarre(n) f, (m)
gas pressure = Gasdruck m
~ ~ gauge = Gasdruckmesser m
~ ~ regulating governor = Gasdruckregler m
~ producer = Generator(ofen) m, Gaserzeuger m
~ ~ coal tar, producer-gas ~ ~ = Steinkohlen(heiz)generatorteer m
~ producing well = gasproduzierende Sonde f
~ sand = Gassand m
~ scrubber = Gaswäscher m
~ shale = Gasschiefer m
~ show(ing)s = Gasspuren fpl
~ slippage, by-passing of gas = Gasschlupf m
~ spirit = Gemische npl flüchtiger Kohlenwasserstoffe mpl erhalten z. B. durch Kompression f oder Absorption f bei Verkokung f von Kohlen fpl
~ suction plant = Gasabsaugungsanlage f
gas-tank, see: gas-holder
gas tubing = Gasrohr n
~ ~ handrail, see: ~ barrel ~
gas-volume reading = Gasmengenablesung f
gas welding, fusion welding by means of gas = Gas(schmelz)schweißung f
~ well = Gasbohrung f, Gassonde f, Gasbrunnen m
~ works coal tar, gas-house ~ ~ = Gas(werks)teer m, Gasanstaltsteer
~ yield = Gasausbeute f
gate = Schranke f
~ = Tor n
~, weir ~, penning ~, stop ~, flood ~ = Wehr(verschluß) n, (m)
~ assembly = Verschluß-Konstruktion f

gate chamber = Verschlußkammer *f*
gated spillway, gate-controlled ~, controlled crest spillway = verschlossener Überlauf *m*
gate hoist = Verschlußwindwerk *n*
~ operating chamber = Schützenbedienungskammer *f*
~ ~ control = Schützensteuerorgan *n*
~ structure = Verschlußbauwerk *n*
~ valve = Schieberventil *n*
~ ~ with bell ends (US); sluice valve with socket ends (Brit.) = Muffenabsperrschieber *m*
gathering ground, see: catchment area
gauge (Brit.); see: gage (US)
~ (Brit.) = Loch *n* [*Rundlochsieb n*]
~ (Brit.); aperture, mesh = Masche *f* [*Maschensieb n*]
ga(u)ge box, see: batch ~
ga(u)ged mortar, see: cement-lime ~
ga(u)ging, see: proportioning
~ device, see: proportioning ~
~ water, mixing ~, batch ~, mix ~ = Anmach(e)wasser *n*, Mischwasser
gauze = Gaze *f*
gear = Gang *m*
~ = Zahnrad *n*, Getrieberad
~ backlash = Zahnradspiel *n*
~ box = Getriebegehäuse *n*
gear-change lever = Getriebeschalthebel *m*
gear cutting = Verzahnung *f*
geared motor unit = Motor *m* mit Getriebe *n*
gear grease = Getriebefett *n*
~ housing = Getriebegehäuse *n*
~ luboil = Getriebeöl *n*
~ pump = Zahnradpumpe *f*
~ reduction = (Räder)Untersetzung *f*
gearshift = Getriebeschaltung *f* [*als Maschinenteil m*]
gear shift lever = Gangschalthebel *m*
~ shifting = Getriebeschaltung *f* [*als Bedienungstätigkeit f*]
~ wheel lubrication grease = Zahnradfett *n*
gehlenite (Min.) = Gehlenit *m*
Geiger(-Müller) counter = Geiger-Müller-Zählrohr *n*
gelatinous envelope = Gallerthülle *f*

~ (blasting) explosives, ammonium nitrate = gelatinös-plastische Sprengstoffgemenge *npl*, gelatinöse Ammonsalpetersprengstoffe *mpl*
gel formation (or development) = Gelbildung *f*
general construction costs = Baugemeinkosten *f*
~ contractor, prime ~, chief ~ = Generalunternehmer *m*
General Contractors Association = Bauunternehmerverband *m*
general location map = allgemeine Lagekarte *f*
~ public = Allgemeinheit *f*
~ purpose hoist = Universal-Bau(aufzugs)winde *f*
generating capacity = Energiekapazität *f*
~ plant = Kraftwerk *n*
~ set, see: electric generator (set)
generation of electrical power = Stromerzeugung *f*
~ floor = Maschinenflur *m* [*Kraftwerk n*]
~ gas = Generatorgas *n*
generators (US); generating line, generatrix (Brit.) = Erzeugende *f*, erzeugende Linie *f*
Geneva nomenclature = Genfer Nomenklatur *f* [*Übereinkunft über die Namengebung chemischer Verbindungen*]
geoanticline (Geol.) = tektonischer und topographischer Sattel *m*
geochemical exploration = geochemische Forschung *f*
~ prospecting = geochemisches Prospektieren *n*, geochemische Suche *f*
geochemistry = Geochemie *f*
geode (Geol.) = Geode *f*
geodesy, geodetic surveying = höhere Geodäsie *f*
geological erosion, see: erosion
~ fault, see: fault (plane)
~ investigation, ~ study = geologische Untersuchung *f*
~ map = geologische Karte *f*
~ succession = geologische Aufeinanderfolge *f*
geologist = Geologe *m*
geologist's pick, prospector's ~ = Geologenhacke *f*

*geology = Geologie *f*
geometrical characteristics, ~ **standards** [*road*] = Trassierungselemente *npl* [*Straße f*]
geophysical = geophysikalisch
~ **field study,** ~ **investigation,** ~ **exploration** = geophysikalische Baugrunduntersuchung *f*
geostrophic wind = Passat(wind) *m*
geosyncline = Geosynklinale *f*, Senkungstrog *m*, Senkungswanne *f*
geotechnical process = geotechnisches Verfahren *f*
German Association for Housing, Town Building and Planning = Deutscher Verband *m* für Wohnungswesen, Städtebau und Raumplanung
~ **Concrete Association** = Deutscher Betonverein e. V. *m*
~ **Federal Institute for Road Construction** = Bundesanstalt *f* für Straßenbau
~ **Highway (or Road) Research Association (or Society)** = Forschungsgesellschaft *f* für das Straßenwesen e. V.
~ **Institute of Dock and Harbour Authorities** = Hafenbautechnische Gesellschaft e.V. *f*
~ **motorway,** ~ **motor road, autobahn German speedway** = Reichsautobahn *f* RAB, Bundesautobahn
~ **Reinforced Concrete Association** = Deutscher Ausschuß *m* für Stahlbeton *m*
~ **Research Association for Building and Housing** = Forschungsgemeinschaft *f* Bauen und Wohnen, FBW
~ ~ **Society for Soil Mechanics, German Soil Mechanics Research Association** = DEGEBO, Deutsche Gesellschaft *f* für Bodenforschung *f*
~ **Soil Engineering Society** = Deutsche Gesellschaft *f* für Erd- und Grundbau *m*
~ **speedway,** see: ~ motorway
~ **Union Institute for Hydraulic Engineering** = Bundesanstalt *f* für Wasserbau *m*
germ = Keim *m*
germicidal = keimtötend, bakterizid
germicide = Desinfektionsmittel *n*, Bakteriengift *n*
to germinate = keimen
germination = Keimen *n*, **Keimung** *f*

germinating drum water = Quellwasser *n* [*Mälzerei f*]
gersdorffite, NiAsS (Min.) = Arsennickelkies *m*, Gersdorffit *m*
getting of clay, clay working = Tongewinnung *f*, Tonabbau *m*
geyser, gusher (Geol.) = pulsierende Springquelle *f*, Geysir, Geyser *m*
geyserite, see: siliceous sinter
giant, monitor = Druckstrahlbagger *m*, Hydromonitor *m*
~ **cantilever crane,** see: hammer-head ~
~ **(or oversize) tire** (US); ~ **(**~ ~**) tyre** (Brit.) = Riesenreifen *m*, großvolumiger Reifen
giant's kettle = Riesentopf *m*
giant weight tamper = Riesenstampfwalze *f*, Riesenschaffußwalze *f*
gibbsite, hydrargillite, $Al_2O_3 \times 3H_2O$ (Min.) = Hydrargillit *m*
gilled tube = Rippenrohr *n*
gilsonite, uintaite = Gilsonitasphalt *m*, Uintait *m*
~ **coker distillate** = Verkokungsdestillat *n* aus Gilsonit *m*
gim(b)let, piercer, brad-awl, nail passer, nail kit, wimble = Nagelbohrer *m*
gin pole (derrick) (crane) = Trossen-Derrick-Kran *m* ohne Ausleger *m*, Hebezeug-Mast *m*
~ ~ **of a derrick** = Bohrturmgalgen *m*
~ ~ ~ ~ = Derrickgalgen *m*
~ ~ **type concrete spouting plant, concrete chuting (or placing) mast** = (Beton-)Gießmast *m*
girder (US); **(steel) plate** ~ = Blechträger *m*, Vollwandträger
~ (Brit.); **beam** ~ = Balken *m*, Träger *m*, Balkenträger
~ **bending press** (Brit.); **beam** ~ ~ = Trägerbiegepresse *f*, Balken(träger)-biegepresse *f*
~ **bridge** (US); **plate** ~ ~ = Blechträgerbrücke *f*, Vollwandträgerbrücke
~ **bridge** (Brit.); **beam** ~ ~ = Trägerbrücke *f*, Balken(träger)brücke
~ **grillage, girder grid** (Brit.); **grillage beams, beam grid** = Trägerrost *m*
~ **to resist braking** = Bremsträger *m*
glacial acetic acid = Eisessig *m*

glacial clay = Glazialton m
- ~ **deposit** = glaziale Ablagerung f
- ~ **gravel, moraine** ~ = Moräne(n)kies m
- ~ **loam** = Geschiebelehm m
- ~ **outwash** = glaziale Flußablagerung f
- (~) ~ **gravel** = Auswaschschotter m
- ~ **scour,** exaration = (Aus)Kolkung f durch Eis n
- ~ **shrinkage** = Eisschrumpfung f
- ~ **soil** = Moräne(n)schuttboden m
- ~ **stream** = eiszeitlicher Gletschersee m

glaciation = Glazialerosion f, Gletschererosion

*****glacier** = Gletscher m, Ferner m
- ~ **mill,** pot-hole = Gletschermühle f, Gletschertopf m, Gletschertrichter m
- ~ **tongue** = Gletscherzunge f
- ~ **water** = Gletscherwasser n

glaciology = Gletscherkunde f

glance coal = Glanzkohle f
- ~ **pitch** = Glanzpech n, Maniak n

gland = Stopfbuchse f [*Kreiselpumpe f*]
- ~ ~ = Abdichteplatte f für Hydraulik f
- ~ ~ = Schraubring m [*Schraubmuffe f*]

glare-free, non-glare = blendfrei [*Straßenoberfläche f*]

glass batch house = Gemengehaus n [*Glasindustrie f*]
- ~ **block** = Glasbaustein m, Glasmauerstein
- ~ **cutter** = Glasschneider m
- ~ **fibre** (Brit.); ~, fiber (US) = Glasfaser f
- ~ **furnace regenerator** = Glasofen-Regenerator m
- ~ ~ **superstructure** = Glasofen-Oberbau m

GLASS-KRAFT [*Trademark*] = besteht aus zwei Lagen fpl Kraftpapier n zwischen denen sich eine Schicht f Glasfasern fpl befindet

glass panel = Glasfüllung f [*Tür f*]

glass-sided working model = Glaskastenmodell n

glass silk = Glaswatte f
- ~ **tank** = Glasofen m
- ~ ~ **crown** = Glaswanne f
- ~ **wool** = Glaswolle f

glassy, vitreous, hyaline [*ground mass*] = glasig [*Grundmasse f*]
- ~ **rock** = Glasgestein n

glauberite (Min.) = Glauberit m

glauber salt, mirabilite, hydrated sodium sulphate, $Na_2SO_4 \times 10H_2O$ = Glaubersalz n

glaucodot(e) (Min.) = Glaukodot n

glauconite (Min.) = Glaukonit m

glauconitic = glaukonitisch
- ~ **limestone** = Glaukonitkalkstein m
- ~ **sandstone** = Glaukonitsandstein m

glaucophane (Min.) = Glaukophan m

glaze binder = Glasurbinder m

glazed brick = Glasurziegel m, Glasurstein m, glasierter Ziegel(stein)
- ~ **ice** = Glatteis n
- ~ **reinforced concrete** = Glasbeton m
- ~ **tile,** face ~ = Glasurfliese f
- ~ **whiteware product** = glasiertes Steingut n

glazier's putty = Glaserkitt m, Ölkitt

glazing tees = Verglasungs-T-Stahl m

glen = Talschlucht f

globe caliper, see: ball ~

globigerina ooze = Globigerinenschlamm m

gloryhole = Rumpelkammer f [*Asbestzerabbau m unter Tage*]

glued beam = verleimter Balken m
- ~ **timber construction** = Leimbauweise f

glu(e)ing compound, adhesive = Klebemasse f, Aufstrichklebemasse

glycerol = Glyzerin n

glyptolith, gibber, ventifact, dreikanter [*as it may have more than three sides, the original term "dreikanter" is a misnomer*] = Dreikanter m

gneiss = Gneis m

gneissic texture, gneissose ~ = Gneistextur f

goat willow, black sallow = Salweide f

go devil, see: pig
- ~ ~ = Molch m zur Paraffinbeseitigung f

goggles = Schutzbrille f

Goldbeck (pressure) cell = Luft(-Erddruck-)Meßdose f nach Goldbeck, Goldbeckdose f

gold point = Goldpunkt m der Temperaturskala f

goliath crane (Brit.); gantry crane (US) = Brückenkran m

gompholite, nagelfluh = Nagelfluh f

Gooch crucible, ~ filter = Gooch-Tiegel m

good grading curve, type ~ ~, ideal ~ ~ = Idealsieblinie *f*, Sollsieblinie
goods wagon, ~ van, railway wagon (Brit.); freight car (US) = Güterwagen *m*, Waggon *m*
gooseneck = Schwanenhals *m*
~ type, semi-trailer ~ = aufgesattelt [*Fahrzeug n*]
~ ~ crane = Schwanenhals-Auslegerkran *m*
goosy grass = weiche Trespe *f*
gorge (Geol.) = Schlucht *f* [*oberdeutsch: Schluft f*]
~ dam = Schluchtenmauer *f*
~ fill = (Fluß)Bettausfüllung *f*
~ of diverted river, ~ ~ diverting ~ = Ablenkungsschlucht *f* [*Fluß m*]
gorse = Stachelginster *m*
goslarite, white vitriol, white copperas (Min.) = Goslarit *m*, Zinkvitriol *n*, *m*
gouge = Hohleisen *n*, Hohlbeitel *m*
~ = Verwerfungsletten *m*
gout-weed = Giersch *m*
governmental agency (US); authority = Regierungsdienststelle *f*, Behörde *f*
governor = (Drehzahl)Regler *m*
gowan, decomposed granite, disintegrated granite = zersetzter Granit *m*
Gow caisson foundation, Boston ~ ~ = Brunnengründung *f* Bauart Gow
grab, see: grab(bing crane)
grabbing bucket, see: grab (bucket)
(~) ~ tooth, grab ~ = Greiferzahn *m*
grab(bing crane), bucket crane, grab excavator, grab (bucket) crane = Greifer(Kran) *m*, Greifbagger *m*, Greifkran *m*, Greiferbagger, Baggergreifer *m*
grab(bing) hoisting gear = Greiferhubwerk *n*
grab (bucket), grapple, grabbing bucket = Greif(er)korb *m*, Baggerkorb, Bagger-Greif(er)korb
(grab) bucket crane, see: grab(bing crane)
~ closing drum = Schließtrommel *f*
~ crane, see: grab(bing crane)
~ dredge(r), ~ bucket ~ = Schwimmgreifer *m*, Greifnaßbagger *m*
~ equipment = Greiferausrüstung *f* [*Kran m*]
~ excavator, see: grab(bing crane)

graben (Geol.), see: trough fault
grab operation = Greiferbetrieb *m*
grabs (US); multi-blade grab (Brit.) = Pplypgreifkorb *m*, Polypgreifer *m*
grab set, see: false ~
GRADALL [*Trademark*] = Universal-Erdbearbeitungsmaschine *f*, Fabrikat WARNER & SWASEY, CLEVELAND, OHIO, USA
gradation, grading = Abstufung *f* [*Mineralmasse f*]
~ limit, limiting grading curve, particle-size (distribution) limit, grading limit = Siebkennlinie *f*, Grenzsieblinie *f*
~ unit [*deprecated*]; continuous proportioning plant = kontinuierliche Dosiereinrichtung *f*
grade = Güteklasse *f*
~ [*deprecated*]; see: gradient
~, grain size, particle size = Korngröße *f*
to grade = sieben, durch Siebung *f* in Anteile gleicher Korngröße zerteilen
grade ability = Steigfähigkeit *f* [*Fahrzeug n*]
gradebuilder, see: roadbuilder
grade crossing, intersection at grade, at-grade intersection = plangleiche (oder niveauebene, oder ebenerdige) Kreuzung *f*
graded aggregate, see: ~ material
~ ~ type road mix surface, dense-graded ~ ~ ~ = Baumischbelag *m* mit dicht abgestuftem Korngemenge *n*, dichter Baumischbelag, hohlraumarmer Baumischbelag
~ bedding (Geol.) = Abstufungsschichtung *f*
~ filter = abgestuftes Filter *n*. abgestufter Filter *m*
~ material, screened ~, ~ aggregate = abgestuftes Material *n*, gesiebtes ~
GRADE-MORE slope grader [*Trademark*] = Böschungsplaniervorrichtung *f* an Motor-Straßenhobel *m*, Fabrikat THE GALION IRON WORKS & MFG. CO., GALION, OHIO, USA
grade rooter, subgrade ~ = Planumaufreißer *m*
~ (or gradient, or level, or finishing, or fill) stake (or peg) = Höhenpflock *m*, Höhenpfahl *m*

grade separation structure (US); see: fly over (junction) (Brit.)
grader, road ~ = Straßenhobel m, Wegehobel, Erdhobel, Straßen-Planierer m
~, multi-deck screen, aggregate grader = Mehrdecker(sieb) m, (n)
~ **blade,** see: blade
gradient, incline; [*deprecated: grade*] = Neigung f [*des Längsprofils Steigungsverhältnis*]
~ **curve of a well** = Absenkungskurve f eines Brunnens m
~ **peg,** see: grade ~
~ **section** = Steigung f, Neigung f, Gefälle n [*Straße f*]
grading, particle-size analysis [*the process of determining the proportions of different particle sizes in a granular material by sieving, sedimentation, elutriation or other means*] = Bestimmung f der Korngrößenanteile mpl
grading, grain-size (or particle-size) distribution = Korngrößenverteilung f
~ [*soils*] = Abstufung f
~, see: ~ (works)
~ **analysis,** sieve ~, test for ~ ~, test for grading, sieve analysis test, grain-size analysis = Prüfen n der Kornzusammensetzung f durch Siebversuch m, Siebprobe f
~ **coefficient** = Körnungsziffer f
~ **curve,** aggregate ~ ~, particle-size distribution curve, grain-size ~ ~ = Siebkurve f, Sieblinie f
~ **limit,** see: gradation ~
~ **operations,** see: ~ (works)
~ **specifications** = Siebnormen fpl
~ **surface** = Körnungsfläche f
~ **(work(s)),** level(l)ing ~, ~ operations = Planieren n, Planier(ungs)arbeiten f
rough ~ = Grob-~
fine-~, final ~ = Fein-~
~ **zone** = Sieblinienflächenbereich m
graduated glass ga(u)ge-tube, water-ga(u)ge glass = Wasserstandsglas n
~ **scale** = Teilstrichwaage f
graduation mark = Teilstrich m [*Waage f*]
*****graduation-works,** see: cooler
graft(ing) = Pfropfung f, Aufpfropfen n [*Holzverbindung f*]

grafting tool = Stechspaten m, Dränspaten m
~ **wax** = Baumwachs n
grahamite = Grahamitasphalt m
grain = Holzfaser f
~, particle = Einzelkorn n, Gesteinskorn n, Partikelchen n, Einzelteilchen n, Körnchen n
~**-drying plant** = Getreide-Trocknungsanlage f
grain elevator = Getreideelevator m, Schiffselevator m
~ **growth** = Korngrößenwuchs m
*****grain shape,** see: particle ~
~ **silo,** granary = Getreidesilo m, Getreidespeicher m
~ **size,** particle ~, grade = Korngröße f, Fraktionsgröße
~**-size analysis,** see: grading ~
~**-size distribution,** see: grading
grain wood circular saw = Langholzkreissäge f
granary, grain silo = Getreidespeicher m, Getreidesilo m
granatite (Min..) = Granatit m
grandstand = Tribüne f
granite-aplite, granite-haplite = Granitaplit m
granite-block paving = Granitplattenpflaster n
granite boulder slope = Granitgeröllhalde f
~ **clan** = Granitfamilie f
~ **gneiss** = Granitgneis m
granitel(le), fine-grained granite = feinkörniger Granit m
granite porphyry, porphyroid granite = Granitporphyr m
granitic, see: allotriomorphic-granular
granitite, see: biotite-granite
granitoid, see: allotriomorphic-granular
granoblastic texture = Bienenwabenverband m, Pflasterverband, gabbroider Verband, granoblastischer Verband, Mosaikverband
granodiorite = Granodiorit m
granolithic (floor) surfacing, ~ finish (or surface) = Zementestrich m mit Granitsplitt m
granophyre = Granophyr m

granular bog iron ore (Min.) = Eisengraupen *f*
~ **dust (filler)**, see: filler
~ **skeleton** = Korngerüst *n* [*z. B. Sand m*]
~ **(soil) stabilisation**, see: mechanical (~) ~
~ **stabilised road**, see: mechanically ~ ~
~ ~ **(or mechanically stabilised) surfaces and base courses** = mechanisch verfestigte (oder vermörtelte) Verschleißschichten *fpl* und Tragschichten *fpl*
~ **sub-base**, see: sub-base
to granulate = granulieren
granulated blast-furnace slag, slag sand = gekörnte (oder granulierte) Hochofenschlacke *f*, (künstlicher) Schlackensand *m*
~ **slag aggregate concrete block** = Hüttenstein *m* [*früher: Hochofenschlackenstein*]
granulating hammer = Stockhammer *m*, Kraushammer
granulation, see: fine reduction
~ **(process)** = Granulierung *f*, Körnungsverfahren *n*
granulator = Fein(backen)brecher *m*, Granulator *m*
granule [6—2 mm] = mittleres Siebkorn IIIa *n* [*nach Dücker (1948)*]
granulite, withestone (Geol.) = Granulit *m*
granulitic structure (Geol.) = Drucktextur *f*
granulometric composition, granulometry = Kornaufbau *m*, Kornzusammensetzung *f*
~ ~ **value** = Aufbauwert *m* nach Jahn
~ **gradation** = Kornabstufung *f*
graph, see: diagram
graphic representation, see: diagram
~ **tellurium** [*deprecated*]; sylvanite (Min.) = Schrifterz *n*
graphite, plumbago, black lead (Min.) = Graphit *m*
graphite-inlaid bearing plate = mit Graphit *m* geschmierte Auflagerplatte *f*
graphite lubrication = Graphitschmierung *f*
graphitic clay = Schieferkreide *f*
graph of flow, rating curve of flow (Brit.); rating curve, flow curve, flow duration curve (US) = Dauerkurve *f* der Abflußmengen *fpl*, Durchflußdauerkurve
grapple, multi-bladed (circular) grab; grabs (US) [*a clamshell type bucket having three or more jaws*] = Mehrschalengreifkorb *m*, Mehrschalengreifer *m*
~, see: extractor
~ **dredge(r)**, dredge(r) with multi-bladed (circular) grab; dredge with grabs (US) = Schwimmgreifer *m*, Greifnaßbagger *m*
grappling of arch = Bogenverankerung *f*
grass cover = Grasnarbe *f*
to grass down, to sow down to grass = berasen, begrünen
grass landing ground = Grasnarbenlandefläche *f*
~ **roller**, lawn ~ = Rasenwalze *f*
~ **sod**, (turf) ~ = (Gras)Sode *f*, Rasensode *f*, (Rasen-)Plagge *f*, Rasenziegel *m*
(~) **vegetation** = Grasbewuchs *m*
grassy median strip, landscaped ~, central grass reserve = Grünstreifen *m*, Rasentrennstreifen *m* [*Straße f*]
grate, boiler ~ = (Feuer)Rost *m*, Kesselrost
~, see: grating
~ **bar**, see: fire bar
~ ~ = Roststab *m*
~ **cooler** = Rostkühler *m*
grating, cover ~, (cover) ~ = Abdeck(gitter)rost *m*
~ **for bridge deck**, bridge grating = Brückenrost *m*
graupel shower = Graupelschauer *m*
gravel = Kies *m*
~ **aggregate** = Kieszuschlag(stoff) *m*
~ **asphalt** = Kies(walz)asphalt *m*
~ **blotter** (US) = Kiesabstreuung *f*
~ **deposit** = Kieslager *n*, Kiesvorkommen *n*
~ **detritus**, ~ wash, gravelly ~ (Geol.) = Kiesschutt *m*
~ **dredge(r)** = Kiesnaßbagger *m*, Kiesschwimmbagger
~ **excavator** = Kiestrockenbagger *m*
~ **fill** = Kies(auf)schüttung *f*
~ **filling** = Verkiesung *f*
~ **filter** = Kiesfilter *m, n*
~ **fraction** = Kieskörnung *f*
gravelly = kiesig
gravel pit = Kiesgrube *f*
~ ~ **sand** = aus Kies *m* abgesiebter Sand *m*

gravel plant = Kiesaufbereitungsanlage *f*, Kieswerk *n*
~ **road** = Kiesstraße *f*
~-**sand-clay**; see: hoggin (Brit.)
gravel shoulder = Kiesstandspur *f*, Kiesrandstreifen *m*
~ **stockpiling** = Kiesdeponie *f*
~ **terrace** = Kiesterrasse *f*
gravel(-walled) well = Kiesschüttungsbrunnen *m*
gravel wash, see: ~ detritus
~ **washer**, ~ washing machine = Kieswäsche *f*, Kieswaschmaschine *f*
gravimetric batching, weigh batching = Gewichtsdosierung *f*, Gewichtszuteilung *f*, Gewichtsabmessung *f*, Gewichtszumessung *f*, Gewichtsgattierung *f*
~ **investigation** = Schweremessungen *fpl*, gravimetrische Messungen *fpl* [*geophysikalische Baugrunduntersuchung f*]
graving dock, see: dry ~
gravitational attraction = Anziehungskraft *f*
~ **classifying** = Schwereklassierung *f*
~ **differentiation** = gravitative Differentiation *f*
~ **force**, force of gravity = Schwerkraft *f*, Gravitationskraft *f*
~ **water** = Schwerkraftwasser *n*
gravity batch mixer, see: free fall (type) ~ ~
~ **centre prestressed concrete bar** = zentrisch vorgespannter Betonstab *m*
~ **conveyor** = Schwerkraftförderer *m*
~ **dam of triangular section** = (Schwer-)Gewichts(stau)mauer *f* mit dreieckigem Querschnitt *m*
~ **discharge** = Schwergewichtsentleerung *f*
~ **feed line** = Fallzuleitung *f*
~ **flow-type processing plant** = Aufbereitungsanlage *f* unter Ausnutzung der Schwerkraft *f*
~ **(hydro) dam**, straight ~ (~) ~ = einfache Gewichtsmauer *f*, (Schwer-)Gewichtsmauer *f*, (massive) Gewichtssperre *f*
~ **mixer**, see: free fall type ~
~ **ore loading system** = Erzumschlaganlage *f* nach dem Schwergewichtsfluß *m*

~ **retaining wall** = Schwergewichts-Stützmauer *f*
~ **roller runway**, ~ ~ conveyor = Schwerkraft(rollen)bahn *f*, Schwerkraftrollenförderer *m*
~ **sack shoot** = Sackwendelrutsche *f*
~ **separation** = Schwerkraftaufbereitung *f* [*Mineral n*]
~ **spillway dam** (Brit.); gravity type dam spillway (US) = Gewichtsmauer *f* (oder Schwergewichtssperre *f*) mit Überfall *m*
~ **spring** = Schichtquelle *f*
~ **stamp** = Freifallpochwerk *n*
~ **take-up** = Gewichtsspannvorrichtung *f* [*Bandförderer n*]
~ **tip** = Plattformkipper *m* [*Waggonkipper*]
~ **tipping conveyor**, tilting bucket ~, swinging bucket elevator = Pendelbecherwerk *n*
~ **type dam spillway** (US); see: ~ spillway dam (Brit.)
gray-band(s) = grauer Sandstein *m*
gray cast iron = Grauguß *m*, Gußeisen *n*
~ **manganese(-ore)** (Min.), see: native manganic hydrate
graywacke, see: greywacke
graywether, sarsen stone, Saracen's stone = erratischer Sandsteinblock *m*
grazing ground, pasture land = Weideland *n*
grease cup, stuffing box = Fettpreßbuchse *f*, Staufferbuchse
~ **gun** = Fettpresse *f*
~ **trap** (Brit.); ~ interceptor (US) = Fettfang *m*, Fettabscheider *m*
greasing and lubricating service vehicle (or rig) = Abschmierfahrzeug *n*
greater maple, sycamore = Bergahorn *m*, Ur(l)e *f*, Ehre *f*
great poa, see: blue grass
Great Wall of China = Chinesische Mauer *f*
Greek Fire [*Ignae Vestoe*] = „Griechisches Feuer" *n* [*Igne Vestae*]
green acid = ölunlösliche Sulfosäure *f*
~ **alder** = Grünerle *f*, Alpenerle
~ **area** = Grünfläche *f*
~ **belt** = Grüngürtel *m*
greenbelt town = Gartenstadt *f*

green concrete — grooving cutter

green concrete = junger Beton m, grüner ~
~ earth, see: chlorite
~ efflorescence = grüne Ausblühung f, Vanadiumausblühung
greenheart = Grünholz n [aus Guayana]
greenhouse = Gewächshaus n
green iron ore, see: dufrenite
Greenland spar (Min.), see: cryolite
green lead ore [obsolete term]; pyromorphite (Min.) = Pyromorphit m
~ marble (US) = Handelsbezeichnung f für Serpentin m
~ oil, see: anthracene ~
~ product = Grünling m
greensand = Greensand m
green schist = Grünschiefer m
green sludge, fresh ~ = Frischschlamm m [Abwasserwesen n]
greenstone = Grünstein m [unfrischer Diabas m]
~ tuff, see: diabasic ~
green vitriol, melanterite (Min.) = Melanterit m, Eisenvitriol m, n
greisen (Geol.) = Greisen m
grey cobalt ore (Min.), see: jaipurite
~ copper ore (Min.), see: fahl-erz
~ quick lime = Graukalk m, Schwarzkalk
~ silver, carbonate of silver, selbite (Min.) = Grausilber n
~-stone = Graustein m
greywacke, graywacke = Grauwacke f
~ limestone, transition-lime = Grauwackenkalk m, Übergangskalk
~ slate = Grauwackenschiefer m
grid = Netz n [z. B. auf einer Karte f]
~ = Überlandnetz n [Elektrotechnik f]
~, see: steel mesh
~ current = Netzstrom m
gridded map = Gitternetzkarte f
grid framework = Trägerrost m
gridiron drainage = Dränage f in Rechteckform f
grid-roller = Gitterwalze f
grid structure = Kreuzwerk n
~ substation = Umspannstation f
grid-type girder deck (Brit.); two-way beam-and-slab floor = Trägerrostdecke f, Balken(träger)rostdecke
~ shuttering = Rostschalung f

Griffin centrifugal force roller (grinding) **mill** = Griffin-Pendel(mahl)mühle f
grillage beams; see: girder grillage (Brit.)
grilled foundation = Schwellrostunterbau m
grill foundation pile = Rostpfahl m
grindability = Mahlbarkeit f
~ machine = Mahlbarkeitprüfer m
grinding, see: fine reduction
~ = Schleifen n
~ aid [hydraulic cement] = Mahlzusatz m
~ ball = Mahlkugel f
*** (grinding) mill, grinder** = (Mahl)Mühle f, Feinzerkleinerungsmaschine f
(~) ~ of the edge runner type, pan grinder = Kollergang m
~ oil = Schleiföl n
grindstone = Schleifstein m
grip, see: channel
~ = Ziehgehänge n [Pfahlzieher m]
~ = (Hand)Griff m
~ length = Klemmlänge f [Nietverbindung f]
grit chamber = Sandfang m
~ roll = abgekieste Dachpappenrolle f
gritstone, coarse-grained sandstone = Kristallsandstein m, grobkörniger Sandstein m
gritted, grit blinded = abgesplittet
gritter, gritting machine, grit spreader = Streugerät n
gritting; see: blinding [deprecated]
~ material; see: blotter (material) (for bituminous prime coat) (US)
gritty = rauhsandig
grizzly bar deck = Stangenrostsiebdeck n
grizzly (feeder), see: bar screen
groin = Stichkappe f [Gewölbe n]
~ (US); see: groyne (Brit.)
~ arch, groined vault, cross vault = Kreuzgewölbe n
grommet = Schutzkappe f
~ = Augenring m, Seilring
~-rubber = Gummiring m
groove = Fugenspalt m [Betonfuge f]
~ and tongue = Nut m und Feder f
~ ball bearing = Rillenkugellager n
~ bearing = Rillenlager n
grooved tile, gutter ~ = Flachpfanne f
grooving cutter = Mauernutenfräse f

grooving machine = (Beton)Fugenschleifgerät n
gross calorific value = oberer Heizwert m
GROSS rubber-mounted shovel-crane = Universal-Autobagger m, Fabrikat A. GROSS G.m.b.H., SCHWÄBISCH-GMÜND, DEUTSCHLAND
gross section(al area) = Bruttoquerschnitt m
~ weight = Bruttogewicht n
to ground = erden
ground, terrain, land = Gelände n
~ = Erdboden m [als Fläche f]
~ and bagged lime = gemahlener Sackkalk m
~ bearing pressure, see: ~ pressure
~ breaking ceremony = „Erster Spatenstich" m
*ground cementation, see: artificial ~
~ clearance = Bodenfreiheit f
~ consolidation, see: subsoil ~
~ contact area = Aufstandsfläche f
~ fog = Bodennebel m
~ frost = Bodenfrost m
~ ~ indicator = Frostindikator m
~ grip tire (US)/tyre (Brit.); see: earthmover ~
~ heat, terrestrial ~ = Erdwärme f
~ ice, anchor ~, sponge ~ = Grundeis n
~ irregularity = Bodenunebenheit f
~ level = Geländehöhe f, Niveau n
~ ~ railway, surface ~ = Oberflächenbahn f
~ line = Geländeoberkante f, O.K. Terrain, Oberkante Terrain
groundmass (Geol.) = Grundmasse f
ground moisture, soil ~ = Bodenfeuchte f, Bodenfeuchtigkeit f
~ moraine = Grundmoräne f, Untermoräne
~ outlet, bottom ~ = Grundablaß m
(ground-)plan = Grundriß m
ground pressure, bearing load, road pressure, ground bearing pressure = Bodendruck m, Bodenpressung f, Flächenpressung f, Flächendruck [z. B. einer Gleiskette f auf den Untergrund m]
~ product, see: discharging material
(~) settlement = Untergrundsetzung f, (Untergrund)Senkung f

(~) sill = Bodenschwelle f, Grundschwelle, Sohlschwelle, Unterschwelle, Stauschwelle; [niederdeutsch: Süll m, n]
*~ **solidification**, see: artificial cementation
*~ **stabilization**, see: artificial cementation
~ surface = Geländeoberfläche f
ground-testing rig = Belastungsvorrichtung f [Baugrunduntersuchung f]
ground water, underground ~, phreatic ~ = Grundwasser n
~ ~ bottom = Grundwassersohle f
~ ~ drainage, see: sub-drainage
~ ~ elevation, see: ~ ~ (-table) level
~ ~ entering sewers = zusitzendes Grundwasser n
~ ~ flow = Grundwasserströmung f
~ ~ level, see: ~ ~ (-table) ~
~ ~ lowering by filter wells = Grundwasser(ab)senkung f mit geschlitzten Filterrohren npl
~ ~ ~ installation, see: dewatering ~
~ ~ pollution = Grundwasserverunreinigung f
~ ~ pressure = Grundwasserdruck m
~ ~ table = Grundwasserspiegel m, Grundwasserhorizont m, grundwasserspendende Schicht f
~ ~ (-table) level, ~ ~ elevation, standing water level = Grundwasserstand m, Grundwasserhöhe f
~ ~ well = Grundwasserbecken n
group index method (of pavement design) = Gruppenindexmethode f (für die Dimensionierung von Straßendecken fpl)
grouping = Gruppierung f
group of wires = Drahtbündel n
~ sulfur analysis = Schwefelgruppenanalyse f
grouser = (Winkel)Greifer m, Stollen m, Greifer-Stollen [Gleiskette f]
~ shoe = Stollenplatte f [(Gleis)Kette f]
grout = Schlempe f
~ (US); quarry-waste = Steinbruchabfall m
to grout = tränken
~ ~ under pressure, to inject = injizieren, einpressen, auspressen, verpressen

grout curtain, see: grout(ing) ~
grouted cut-off wall = (Ab)Dichtungsschleier, Injektionsschleier, (Ab)Dichtungsschirm *m*, (Ab)Dichtungsgürtel *m*, Einpreßschürze *f*, Injektionsschirm *m*, Schleierdichtung, Schleierverpressung *f*
~ macadam (or surfacing) (Brit.); penetration ~ (or pavement, or surfacing) = Tränkmakadam *m*, Tränkdecke *f*, Tränkmakadamdecke *f*
grout ejector, see: pressure grouting-machine
grouter, see: pressure grouting machine
grout hole = Einpreßloch *n*, Injektionsloch, Auspreßloch, Verpreßloch
grouting, see: injection process
~ (Brit.); penetration (US) = Tränkung *f*, Tränken *n*, Einguß *m* [*Straße f*]
~ agent = Mörtelzusatz *m*
grout(ing) curtain, diaphragm = Dichtungsschirm *m*, Dichtungsgürtel *m*, Injektionsschleier *m*, Einpreßschürze *f*, Dichtungsschleier *m*, Injektionsschirm *m*
~ material = Injektionsgut *n*
~ mortar = Einpreßmörtel *m*
grouting pan, see: bougie (Brit.)
~ pressure = Einpreßdruck *m*, Auspreßdruck *m*, Verpressungsdruck *m*; Hinterpreßdruck *m* [*Tunnelbau m*]
(grout) injection, see: injection process
~ mixer, slurry ~ = Schlempemischer *m*
~ pump, see: pressure grouting machine
groyne (Brit.); groin (US) = Buhne *f*
~ pointing slightly down-stream = deklinante Buhne *f*
~ ~ ~ up-stream = inklinante Buhne *f*
~ with short training wall = Hakenbuhne *f*
groyning (Brit.); groining (US) = Buhnenbau *m*
grub(bing) axe = Rodehacke *f*, Platthacke
grubbing up, uprooting, brush clearing = Roden *n*, Rodung *f*
grunauite (Min.) = Wismutnickel(kobalt)kies *m*
guard = Schutzblech *n*
~ = Abdeckung *f*
~ fence, safety ~, protection ~, guard rail = 1. Fußgänger-Schutzgeländer *n*; 2. Sicherheits-Leitplanke *f*

~ gate, see: emergency ~
~ rail, see: check ~
~ rail, see: ~ fence
guide = Führung(sstück) *f*, (*n*)
~ = Anschlag *m*
~ bank, see: longitudinal dyke
~ bar = Führungsstange *f*
~ block = Seilumlenkrolle *f*
~ mast = Führungsmast *m*
~ pen = Führungspferch *m* [*Bagger-Senkkastengründung f*]
~ pile, see: guiding ~
~ plate = Führungsplatte *f*
~ post, see: direction ~
~ rail, lead = Führungsschiene *f*
~ rod = Visierstange *f* [*Schwarzbelageinbaumaschine f*]
~ ~ = Führungsstange *f*
~ roller = Führungsrolle *f*, Leitrolle
~ shell, mast = (Bohr)Lafette *f* [*Bohrwagen m*]
~ shoe = Führungsschuh *m*
~ sign, indication ~, informative ~ = Hinweiszeichen *n*, Informationszeichen
~ value = Richtwert *m*
~ wall (Brit.); training wall (US) = Leitwand *f* [*Talsperre f*]
~ wheel = Lenkrad *n*, Tastrad *n*
guiding dolphin = Anfahrtsdalbe *m*
~ groove = Führungsnut *f*
~ pile, guide ~ = Richtpfahl *m*
~ rafters = Lehrgespärre *n*
guidler, training idler, self-aligning (guide) idler = Führungs- und Tragrolle *f* [*Bandförderer m*]
gulch gold, see: alluvial ~
gulf = Meerbusen *m*, Golf *m*
gull(e)y, rainwater ~ = Regeneinlauf *m*, Straßeneinlauf
~ grate, ~ grating = Einlaufrost *m*, Regen~
gully, rain ~ (Geol.) = Runse *f*, Felseinschnitt *m*
gum = Kraftstoffharz *n* [*unlöslicher Rückstand m aus Benzin n beim Lagern n, besonders bei Anwesenheit f von ungesättigten Anteilen mpl, z. B. Krackbenzinen npl*]
~ = Klebegummi *m*
~ = Abdampfrückstand *m*

gumbed (US); see: ozokerite
gumbo = amerikanische Bezeichnung für einen hochplastischen sehr zähen Ton *m*
gum dynamite = explosive Gelatine *f*
~ forming, gumming = Verharzung *f*, Verpichung
~ inhibitor = Stabilisator *m*
~ rosin = Balsamkolophonium *n*
~ test = Abdampfprobe *f*
gun-applied concrete, see: gunite
gun cotton = Schießbaumwolle *f*
gunite, shotcrete, air-placed concrete, gun-applied concrete, jetcrete, pneumatically placed concrete, gunned ~ = Spritzbeton *m*, Torkretbeton
gunite-jacketed steel pipe = torkretiertes Stahlrohr *n*
gunite machine, see: cement gun
gunited coating = Torkretmantel *m*
guniting, cement-gun work = Torkret(betonspritz)verfahren *n*, Torkretieren *n*, pneumatische Auftragung *f* von Putzmörtel *m*, Torkretierung *f*
gunmetal = Geschützbronze *f*
gunned concrete, see: gunite
gunnery base = Schießplatz *m*
gun-perforator, casing gun = Geschoßrohrlocher *m*, Geschoßperforator *m* [*Tiefbohrtechnik f*]
gunpowder, black (blasting) powder = Schwarzpulver *n*, Sprengpulver
gusher, see: geyser (Geol.)
~ = Springer *m* [*Ölförderung f*]
gusset(-plate), junction plate, junction gusset = Knotenblech *n*
gutter, paved ~ = Rinnstein *m*
~, see: channel
gutter-float = halbrundes Kehlreibebrett *n* [*Asphaltarbeiterwerkzeug n*]
gutter paving sett, channel ~ ~ = Rinnen-Pflasterstein *m*
~ tile, grooved ~ = Flachpfanne *f*
guy cable, see: guy(-rope)
~ derrick (crane); ~ derricking jib ~ (Brit.); **~ ~ boom** = (US) = Trossen-Derrick-Kran *m* [*Ausleger m mit 360° Schwenkwinkel m*]
guyed mast = abgespannter Mast *m*
guying = Trossenabspannung *f*, Abspannen *n* (oder Abspannung *f*) mit Seilen *npl*

guy(-rope), standing rope, rope guy, guy cable = Trosse *f*, Abspannseil *n*, Ankerseil *n*, Halteseil, Sturmseil
gypseous marl = Gipsmergel *m*
~ sand = Gipssand *m*
~ soil = Gipserde *f*, Gipsgur *f*
~ spar, see: selenite
gypsite, see: earthy gypsum
Gypstele system (Brit.) = System *n* aus Aluminiumprofilen *npl* mit eingeschobenen Gipsbrettern *npl*
gypsum (Min.) = Gips *m*
~ acoustical tile = Gipsakustikziegel *m*
~ block, see: **~ precast building block**
~ board, plaster ~ = Gipsplatte *f*
~ calcination = Gipsbrennen *n*
(~) calcining kettle = Gipskocher *m*, Gipskessel *m*
(~) ~ pan = Gipspfanne *f*
~ cartilege = Gipsknorpel *m*
~ lath = Gipsmembran(e) *f*, Brett *n* [*bei der Gipskartonplatte*]
~ lime plaster = Kalkgipsputz *m*
~ mortar = Gips(sand)mörtel *m*
~ plant = Gipsaufbereitungsanlage *f*, Gipswerk *n*
~ plaster = Gipsputz *m*, Putzgips *m*
~ ~ for building purposes, calcined gypsum = Baugips *m*, gebrannter Gips
~ precast building block, (precast) gypsum block, cast gypsum block = Gipsbaustein *m*
~ putty, ~ paste = Gipsbrei *m*
~ quarry = Gipsbruch *m*
~-sand mortar = Gipssandmörtel *m*
gypsum sheathing = Gipsverkleidung *f*
~ spar, see: selenite
~ stone, ~ rock = Gipsgestein *n*
~-vermiculite plaster = Vermiculite-Gipsputz *m*
gypsum wallboard plant, plaster board ~ = Gipsplattenwerk *n*
gyrasphere crusher = Kegelbrecher mit segmentförmigem Brechkopf *m*
gyration = Drehung *f*, kreisförmige Bewegung *f*
~ radius, radius of gyration = Trägheitshalbmesser *m*

(gyratory) cone(-type) crusher — hand cart

(gyratory) cone(-type) crusher, see: cone (-type) ~
~ crusher [*it sizes at the open side setting*] = Kegelbrecher m, Kreiselbrecher, Rundbrecher
~ junction [*deprecated*]; see: roundabout
~ movement = kreisendtaumelnde Bewegung f [*Kegelbrecher m*]
~ traffic, rotary ~ = Rundverkehr m, Ringverkehr m
gyroscope rotor = Kreiselläufer m

H

hacking (Brit.) = Hackboden m [*Erdbau m*]
~ = mildes Gebirge n [*Tunnelbau m*]
~ = Aufrauhen n zur Aufnahme f des Putzes m
hack saw, power ~ ~ = Hacksäge f
hagger, hewer = Hauer m [*Bergbau m*]
hail shower = Hagelschauer m
hailstone = Hagelkorn n
hairline adjustment = haargenaue Einstellung f
~ crack, hair ~ = Haarriß m
hair mortar = Haarkalkmörtel m
~-pin bend (or turn, or curve) = Haarnadelkurve f
half-brick wall = halbsteinstarke Wand f
half frame = Halbrahmen m
~ lap = einfaches Blatt n [*Holzverbindung f*]
half-lattice girder, Warren ~, triangular ~, zig-zag ~, Warren truss = Strebenfachwerkträger m, Warren-Tragwerk n
half-pontoon = Halbponton m
half pure iron = Halbreineisen n
~ round bar = Segmenteisen n
~ ~ file = Halbrundfeile f
~ ~ screw, see: button-head(ed) ~
half rounds = Halbrundstahl m
halfspace = Halbraum m
half-sunk = halbversenkt [*Niet*]
half tide = Mitte f der Gezeit f
~-tide basin = Halbtidebecken n
halide, haloid salt = Haloidsalz n
halite, rock salt, common salt, NaCl (Min.) = Steinsalz n

halloysite (Min.) = Halloysit m
hall roof truss = Hallenbinder m
halogenated hydrocarbon = Halogen-Kohlenwasserstoff m
haloid salt, see: halide
halotrichite, iron alum (Min.) = Eisenalaun m
halt, stop, stopping-place = Haltestelle f
halting place, see: layby(e)
halved scarf with saddle-back ends = Verzapfung f mit Grat m
hammer-blow type pulse-velocity measuring device = mechanisches Hammergerät n [*zerstörungsfreie Prüfung f von Beton m*]
hammer crusher, swing-hammer ~, rotary hammer (type) breaker = Hammerbrecher m
*hammer drill, see: (hand) hammer (rock) drill
~ drilling = Hammerbohren n
~ grab = Bohrgreifer m
~ ~ = Brunnengreifer m
hammer-head crane, giant cantilever crane = Hammer(kopf)kran m
~ pier = Hammerkopfpfeiler m
hammer mill = Hammer(mahl)mühle f
*hammer (rock) drill, see: (hand) ~ (~) ~
hammer-tamper = Franki-Ramme f
*hammer tamping finisher = (Stampf-) Hammerfertiger m, kombinierter Stampfbohlen- und Hammerfertiger m, Fabrikat DINGLERWERKE A. G., ZWEIBRÜCKEN/RHEINPFALZ, DEUTSCHLAND
~-type pneumatic hand-held drill = Preßluft(gesteins)bohrhammer m, Druckluft(gesteins)bohrhammer
hand barrow = Trage f
~ brake = Handbremse f
~-broken metal = Handschotter m
hand buggy, see: concrete buggy
hand (cable, or rope) winch = Hand(seil)windwerk n, Handtrommelseilwinde f, Handseilwinde, Handtrommelseilwindwerk
hand-carry centrifugal (water) pump = Trag-Kreiselpumpe f
hand cart, ~ push ~ = Hand(förder)karre(n) f, (m)

hand case high pressure acetylene generator = Schubladen-Hochdruck-Azetylen-Entwickler *m*

~-chain block = Handkettenzug *m*

hand cold chisel, see: chipping ~

~ concrete cart, see: concrete buggy

~ crab, see: crab

~ crank = Handkurbel *f*

~-cut peat = Handtorf *m*

hand distributor, see: ~ sprayer

~ drill, see: breast drill

~ drum winch = Handtrommelwinde *f*, Handtrommelwindwerk *n*

~ feed = Handbeschickung *f*, Hand(material)aufgabe *f*

~ ~ = Handvorschub *m*

~ finisher = Handfertiger *m*

~ flame cutter = Handschneidbrenner *m*

hand-formed brick, hand-made ~ = Hand(strich)ziegel *m*, Handstrichstein *m*

~ joint = Handfuge *f*

hand grinder = Handschleifmaschine *f*

hand-guided carrier = Handfahrgestell *n*

~ motor roller, **~ power-driven single-wheel(ed) roller** = Einrad-Motorwalze *f*, handgeführte kraftgetriebene Einradwalze *f*, handgeführte Walze *f* mit Motor *m*, Motorhandwalze

~ power-propelled vibrating (or vibratory) roller = handgeführte kraftbewegte (oder selbtsfahrende) Vibrationswalze *f* (oder Schwing(ungs)walze)

~ two-wheel dozer = Einachsräumer *m*

~ vibration-and-tamping compaction machine = handgeführter Rüttelstampfer *m*, Handrüttelstampfer *m*

hand hack saw, framed crosscut saw = Bügelsäge *f*

*(hand) hammer (rock) drill, (rock) drill hammer = Hand-(Gesteins)Rohrhammer *m*, Hand-Felsbohrhammer *m*

hand-held, hand-operated, manually-operated = handgeführt [z. B. Walze *f*, Stampfer *m*, Gesteinsbohrer *m*, also in Bewegung befindliche Geräte *npl*]

handing over = Übergabe *f*

hand jack = Handwinde *f*, Handhebebock *m*

hand-laid stone-filled asphalt = Hartgußasphalt *m*

hand lance, see: spray ~

handle = Handgriff *m*, Schaltgriff, Griff, Klinke *f*

~ = Stiel *m*

~ bar = Griffstange *f*

hand level, see: level

handling equipment, materials ~ ~ = (Material)Umschlaggeräte *npl*

~ of bulk materials = Beförderung *f* von Massengütern *npl*

hand-made brick, see: hand-formed ~

~ rivet head = gehämmerter Nietkopf *m*

hand-manipulated vibrator = Handrüttler *m*, Handvibrator *m*

hand-mixed concrete = handgemischter Beton *m*

hand-mixing = Handmischung *f*, Handmischen *n*

hand-operated bar-bender = Betoneisenhandbieger *m*

~ bar-cutter, see: bar cutter

~ chipping(s) spreader, see: barrow-type ~ ~

~ cold emulsion sprayer (or spraying machine) for drawing direct from drums or barrels = Faßspritzer *m* für Kaltasphalt *m*, Faßsprenger *m* ~ ~

~ compacting beam = Handbohle *f* [*Verdichtungsgerät n*]

~ crane = Handkran *m*

~ driver = Handramme *f*, Pionierramme

~ hoist (or pulley, or lifting) block, **~ block (and tackle)** = Handflaschenzug *m*

~ lifting machine = Handhubwerk *n*

~ piston pump = Handkolbenpumpe *f*

~ sprayer (or spraying machine) for drawing direct from drums or barrels, direct from drum type sprayer = Faßsprenger *m*, Faßspritzer *m*

~ spraying pump = Handspritzpumpe *f*

~ stirring gear = Handrührwerk *n*

~ troll(e)y = Handlaufkatze *f*, Handlastkatze

~ vibrating screed (or finisher), hand vibrating screed, hand-wheel propelled vibrating concrete finisher = handgeführter Rüttelfertiger *m*, Handrüttelfertiger *m*, Hand-Vibrationsglättbohle *f*

hand-packed bottoming, see: base of stone pitching

hand-packed stone — hard calcareous slate 189

hand-packed stone, see: pitcher
(~) Telford (type) base (US); see: base of stone pitching (Brit.)
hand-pitched stone base (Brit.), see: base of stone pitching
(hand) (placed) pitching, penning, packed broken rock, soling (Brit.) = Setzpacklage *f*, Setzpacke *f*
hand-placed (stone) riprap, pitched slope = Steinsatz *m*, Steinpackung *f*, vorlageartiges Pflaster *n*
hand placement, ~ placing = Handeinbau *m*, Handverlegung *f*
~ plate shears, tinners' snip = Handblechschere *f*
~ pocket seamer = Deckzange *f*
~ push cart, see: hand cart
handrail standard = Geländerpfosten *m*
hand rammer; punner (Brit.) = Handramme *f*
~ riveting machine = Handnietmaschine *f*
~ rope winch, see: ~ cable ~
~ rotary tiller (or rotary hoe, or rotavator, or soil pulverizer) = Handbodenfräse *f*
~ saw = Handsäge *f*
~ scraper, manually guided drag skip = Handschrapper *m*, Räumschaufel *f*
~ ~ for unloading railway cars, manually guided drag skip ~ ~ ~ ~ ~ = Entlade(kraft)schaufel *f*, Kraftschaufel, Waggonschrapper *m*
~ ~ winch = Handschrapper-Winde *f*
hand-set pitching, see: base of stone pitching
hand shovel, see: digging shovel
~ shovel(l)er, hand-shovel worker = Schipper *m*, Schüpper *m*
~ sieving = Hand(ab)siebung *f*
hands off speed = Freihandgeschwindigkeit *f*
hand soil pulverizer, see: ~ rotary tiller
~ sorting = Handsortierung *f*
~ specimen, ~ sample [*mineral*] = Handstück *n*
~ spoke wheel = Handspeichenrad *n*
~ sprayer, hand distributor, small pressure ~ = Handspritzgerät *n*, Handspritzmaschine *f*, Handspritze *f*

~ spraying [*manual pumping and hand lance*] = Spritzen *n* mit Handpumpendruck *m* und Handrohr *n*
~ spreading, manual laying = Handeinbau *m* [*Straßenbelag m*]
~ steel cable winch, see: ~ wire rope ~
~ support = Handauflage *f*
~ tamper = Handstampfer *m*
hand-tamping beam = Handstampfbohle *f*
hand testing sieve = Hand-Prüfsieb *n*
~ travelling gear = Handfahrwerk *n* [*Hängebahnwaage f*]
~ turf cutter (or stripper) = Wiesenbeil *n*
~ vibrating screed, see: hand-operated ~ ~ (or finisher)
hand-wheel propelled vibrating concrete finisher, see: hand-operated vibrating screed (or finisher)
~ screw = Handrad-(Schrauben)Spindel *f*
hand winch, see: ~ cable ~
~ wire rope winch, hand (steel, or wire, or steel wire) cable winch = Handkabel-(trommel)winde Handkabel(trommel)windwerk *n*
~ work = Handarbeit *f*
hangar = Halle *f*
~ (ground)floor = Hallen(fuß)boden *m*
hanger rod = Aufhängestange *f*
hanging gallery = Hangstollen *m*
~ system = Hängekonstruktion *f*
~ truss bridge = Hängewerkbrücke *f*
~ valley = Hängetal *n*
HANOMAG tractor = Schlepper *m*, Fabrikat HANOMAG, HANNOVER, DEUTSCHLAND
harbo(u)r city (or town), seaport town = Hafenstadt *f*
~ engineering = Hafentechnik *f*
~ entrance = Hafeneinfahrt *f*
~ supervision radar unit = Funkmeßgerät *n* zur Hafenüberwachung *f*
~ surging = Hafenbrandung *f*, Hafen-Wasserstandschwankung *f*
hard asphalt (Geol.) = Hartasphalt *m*
hard-baked brick = Vormauerziegel *m* [*früher: Hartbrandstein m*]
hardboard = Hartfaserplatte *f*
hard calcareous slate = Schiefermarmor *m*

hard coal-tar pitch = Hartsteinkohlenteerpech *n*
hardcore (Brit.) [*a consolidated layer of rubble*] = verfestigte Schüttpacke *f*, ~ Schüttpacklage *f*
hardened concrete = Festbeton *m*
~ shoulder, see: shoulder
hardener, concrete ~ = (Beton-)Härtungsmittel *n*
hardening = Erhärten *n*, Erhärtung *f*
~, maturing [*deprecated*]; curing = Reifeprozeß *m* [*Beton m*]
~, tempering = Härten *n* von Metallen *npl*
~ oil, annealing ~ = Härteöl *n*
hard facing = Hartmetallbesatz *m*
hard(-finish) plaster, see: flooring ~
hard lead, antimonial ~ = Antimonblei *n*
hardness, penetration [*e. g. solid bitumen*] = Penetrationshärtegrad *m*
~ = Härte *f*
hardpan = Hartschicht *f*
hard plaster, see: flooring ~
~ rock, ~ stone = Hartgestein *n*
~ ~ (hand) (hammer) drill, hard rock drill hammer = Hartstein-Bohrhammer *m*, Hartgesteinsbohrer *m*
~ ~ miner, (rock) driller = Mineur *m*, Gesteinshauer *m*
~ rubber tire (US)/**tyre** (Brit.); solid ~ = Vollgummireifen *m*, Elastikreifen
~ shoulder, parking strip, pull-off strip = Standspur *f*, Parkstreifen *m*
~ snow remover, hard-packed ~ ~ = Hartschnee(räum)maschine *f*
~ soldering, brazing = Hartlöten *n*
(~) standing, hardstand, parking apron = Abstellfläche *f*, Standplatz *m*
~ stone, see: ~ rock
hardwood, see: deciduous ~
~ tar = Laubholzteer *m*
~ ~ pitch = Laubholzteerpech *n*
harmonic vibration = harmonische Schwingung *f*
harmotome (Min.) = Harmotom *m*
harsh working mix [*concrete*] = schwer verarbeitbare Mischung *f* [*Beton m*]
hasp and staple = Haspen *m* und Krampe *f*, Überwurf *m*
Hassam pavement, see: cement penetration method

Hastings sand (Brit.); iron-sandstone, ferrugin(e)ous ~ = Eisensandstein *m*, eisenschüssiger Sandstein *m*
to hatch = schraffieren
hatched = schraffiert
hatchet = Handbeil *n*
hatch(way) = Einsteig(e)luke *f*
haulage, transportation = Transport *m*
~ by truck, truck haul(ing) (US); lorry haul(ing), haulage by lorry (Brit.) = LKW-Transport *m*, Straßenanlieferung *f*
haul(age distance); lead, run (Brit.) = Förderweite *f*; Bringungsweg *m* [*in Österreich*] [*Förderung f im Erdbau m*]
haul-away vehicle = Abfuhrfahrzeug *n*
haul diagram, see: ~ (mass) ~
hauler, see: hauling unit
hauling contractor = Transportunternehmer *m*, Fuhrunternehmer
***hauling equipment**, rock and earth ~ ~ = Fahrzeuge *npl* für den Transport *m* von Boden *m* und Steinbaustoffen
~ operations = Antransport *m*
~ rope, drag ~ = Schlepptau *n*
**~ ~ = Zugseil *n* [*Drahtseilschwebebahn f*]
~ scraper, see: four-wheel(ed) ~
~ unit, transporting vehicle, hauler, haul unit = Transportfahrzeug *n*
haul (mass) diagram, mass haul ~ = Massenplan *m*, Transportplan *m* [*Erdbau m*]
~ road, construction ~ = Anfuhrweg *m* [*zur Baustelle f*]
haunch = Bogenschenkel *m*
~, see: shoulder (Brit.)
haunched beam = Voutenbalken *m*
haunching, envelope [*concrete support to the sides of the pipe above the bedding*] = Ummantelung *f* [*Rohr n*]
~ stone (Brit.); header (US); flush curb(stone) = Randstein *m*, Kantenstein, (Tief)Bordstein
hausmannite (Min.) = Glanzbraunstein *m*, Schwarzmanganerz *n*, Hausmannit *m*
haüyne, haüynite (Min.) = Hauyn *m*
hawk-bill (pliers), see: brazing tongs
HAYDITE, FEATHERLITE. ROCKLITE, SOLITE (US) [*Trademark*]; rotary kiln expanded clay (Brit.) = Drehofen-Blähton *m*

"haymaking" (Brit.) = Weitersetzen n von Aushub(boden) m mit einem zweiten Bagger m

hazard beacon = Gefahrenfeuer n [Flugplatz m]

H-beam; see: broad flange girder (Brit.)

head = Niveaudifferenz f, Gefälle n, Druckhöhe f [Talsperre f]

~ [e. g. of a dock] = Haupt n

~, water ~, pressure ~ = Druckhöhe f, Wassersäule f, Wassersäulenhöhe f, Druckgefälle n, Fallhöhe f

~ bond = Kopfverband m [Mauerwerk n]

~ center = Spindelkopfspitze f

~ counterbore = Kopfsenker m

head-end = Kopfende n

~ type tractor-loader, see: loading shovel

header (US); see: bonder

~ = Startgraben m [Bodenverfestigung f]

~ (US); see: haunching stone (Brit.)

~ course, see: heading ~

~ (pipe), ~line = Abflußleitung f, Wasserhauptleitung [Wellpoint-Methode f]

headframe, headgear, pithead gear = Schachtgerüst n [Bergbau m]

head gate = Obertor n [Schleuse f]

~ ~, intake ~ = Einlaßverschluß m

headgear, see: headframe

heading = Vortrieb m

~; see: drift (Brit.)

~, see: tunnel progress

~ and tunnel construction = Stollen- und Tunnelbau m

~ course, header ~ = Binder(ziegel)schicht f, Bindersteinschicht

~ crew (or team, or gang, or party) = Vortriebkolonne f

headless rivet = kopfloser Niet m

head loss, see: loss of head

~ mast, ~ post = Rollenmast m [Seilförderanlage f]

~ oil = Kopföl n [Spermacetiöl n]

head-on crash = Zusammenprall m zweier Fahrzeuge npl von vorn

head on the spillway (US); ~ of water over spillway (Brit.) = Belastung f des Überlaufes m

headphone = Kopfhörer m

head post, see: ~ mast

~ protection = Kopfschutz m

~ pulley = Kopftrommel f [Bandförderer m]

~ ~ drive = Eintrommel-Kopfantrieb m

~ race, see: ~ water canal

headroom, headway = lichte Höhe f

head slab = Kopfplatte f [Säule f]

~ sprocket = Oberturas m

~ tower = Kabelkranmaschinenturm m

head-tree, see: bolster

head turf = Kopfrasen m

headwall = Stirnmauer f [Durchlaß m]

head water canal, ~ race = Ober(wasser)kanal m, Obergraben m

headwaters = Quellgebiet n [Fluß m]

headway, see: headroom

~ = Kopfabstand m [von zwei Fahrzeugen npl]

headworks (structure), control structure, control works = Regulierungsbauwerk n

~, see: intake (or inlet) structure (or works)

health resort = Kurort m

heap of débris (Geol.) = Schuttkegel m

heart cut = Herzschnitt m [Destillatfraktion f mit engen Siedegrenzen fpl]

hearth furnace, open-hearth ~ = Herdofen m

~-refined iron = Herdfrischeisen n

heart shake = Kernriß m, Herzriß m [Holz n]

heartwood = Kern m [Holz n]

heat apoplexy = Hitzschlag m

~ circulation = Wärmeumlauf m

~ drilling, see: jet-piercing

~ engine = Wärmekraftmaschine f

~ equivalent = Wärmeäquivalent n

heater, heating kettle, melting tank; boiler [deprecated] = Schmelzkessel m, (Bindemittel)Kocher m

~, see: air ~

~, pre-~ = Erhitzer m, Vorwärmer m

~ and blower unit = Brenner m mit Gebläse n

~ ~ sprayer (or spraying machine) for hand and power spraying with hand spray unit = Motorspritzmaschine f kombiniert mit Kocher m

heater-mixer, cooker = Kocher m mit Rührwerk n

heater-planer, asphalt road ~ = Heiß-Planiermaschine *f*
heat exchanger = Wärme(aus)tauscher *m*
~ **generated while taking initial set;** ~ **of hydration (US);** ~ **of setting (Brit.)** = Abbindewärme *f*, Hydra(ta)tionswärme *f* [*Beton m*]
heath (land) = Heide *f*, Heideland *n*
~ **sand** = Heidesand *m*
heating coil = Heizschlange *f*, Erhitzerschlange *f*, Wärmeschlange
~ **duct** = Heizkanal *m*
~ **element,** see: heat-transfer ~
~ **gas** = technisches Gas *n*
~ **hood** = Heizhaube *f* [*Heiß-Planiermaschine f*]
(~) **kettle** = Kochkessel *m*
~ **of pumpable bituminous material** = Aufheizung *f* von bit. Bindemitteln *npl*
~ **tank for melting joint sealing compounds,** melting furnace (or melter) for joint sealers, kettle for heating joint filler, (joint) compound-melting furnace, compound heater = Schmelzkessel *m* für Fugenvergußmassen *fpl*, Vergußmasseofen *m*
~ **test** = Erhitzungsprobe *f*
heat input = Wärmezufuhr *f*
~ **insulating layer (or course)** = Wärmedämmschicht *f*
~ **insulation,** thermal ~ = Wärmedämmung *f*, Wärmeisolierung *f*
~ **of adsorption** = Adsorptionswärme *f*
~ ~ **combustion** = Verbrennungswärme *f*
~ ~ **condensation** = Kondensationswärme *f*
~ ~ **fusion** = Schmelzwärme *f*
~ ~ **hydration (US);** see: heat generated while taking initial set
~ ~ **neutralisation** = Neutralisationswärme *f*
~ ~ **setting (Brit.);** see: heat generated while taking initial set
~ ~ **solidification** = Erstarrungswärme *f*
~ ~ **solution** = Lösungswärme *f*
~ **pump** = Wärmepumpe *f*
~ **radiation sensing device** = Wärmestrahlungsfühler *m*
~ **ray** = Wärmestrahl *m*
~ **resistent** = wärmebeständig

~ **transfer** = Wärmeleitung *f*
heat-transfer element, heating element = Heizkörper *m*
~ **medium** = Wärmeträger *m*, Wärmeübertragungsmittel *n*
heat transmission oil = Wärmeübertragungsöl *n*
heat-treatable alumin(i)um alloy = aushärtbare Aluminiumlegierung *f*
heat treatment of basalt paving setts = thermische (Straßen)Aufrauhung *f*, Abbrennen *n* von Basaltpflaster *n*
heavily forested = dichtbewaldet
~ **trafficked** = verkehrsreich
heaving shale = quellender Schieferton *m*
~ **soil** = frostgefährdeter Boden *m*
heavy clay = fetter Ton *m*
~ ~ **article** = grobkeramisches Erzeugnis *n*
~ ~ **industry** = grobkeramische Industrie *f*
~ ~ **kiln** = grobkeramischer Ofen *m*
~ ~ **product,** structural ~ ~, ~ ~ **body** = baukeramisches Erzeugnis *n*
~ **clayworker** = Arbeiter *m* der grobkeramischen Industrie *f*
~ **compacted-earth lining** = starkverdichtete Erdauskleidung *f*
~ **compactor** = schwere einachsige Gummiradwalze *f*
~ **concrete,** high-density ~ = Schwerbeton *m*, gewöhnlicher Beton *m*, Beton mit geschlossenem Gefüge *n*
~ **derrick (crane);** ~ derricking jib ~ (Brit.); ~ ~ **boom** ~ **(US)** = Schwergut-Derrick-Kran *m*, Schwergut-Mastenkran *m*, Schwergut-Ladebaum *m*
heavy-duty construction equipment, see: heavy plant
~ **derrick** = Bohrturm *m* für höchste Beanspruchung *f*
~ **internal combustion tamper** = Explosionsstampfer *m*
~ **oil** = legiertes Motorenöl *n*, HD-Öl, HD-Motorenöl
~ **plow (US)/plough (Brit.)** [*with and without wings*] = schwerer Schneekeilpflug *m* an LKW *m* angebaut
~ **shovel,** see: rock shovel
~ **tractor** = Schwerlastschlepper *m*

heavy ends — hexagonal frame

heavy ends, ~ tails = relativ hochsiedende Anteile *mpl* einer Destillatfraktion *f.* Siedeschwanz *m*
- ~ flywheel = Massenschwungrad *n*
- ~ fuel, masut, mazut = Masut *n*
- ~ ~ (oil) = schweres Heizöl *n*
- ~ load = Schwerlast *f*
- ~ loam = fetter Lehm *m*
- ~ lorry (Brit.); ~ truck (US) = Schwerlast(kraft)wagen *m* Schwerlaster *m*
- ~ media separation, see: sink-float method
- ~-metal soap = Schwermetallseife *f*

heavy naphtha = Schwerbenzin *n*
- ~ oil = Schweröl *n* [*oberhalb des Leuchtöls siedendes Öl n*]
- ~ ~ method = Ölersatzmethode *f* [*Nachprüfung der Verdichtung*]
- ~ petroleum spirit = hochsiedendes Lösungsbenzin *n*
- ~ plant, high-powered equipment, heavyduty construction equipment, major equipment, capital ~ = Großgerät *n*
- ~ plate, ~ steel ~ = Grobblech *n*, schweres Blech
- ~ sea = schwerer Seegang *m*
- ~ spar, see: barite
- ~ steel plate, see: heavy plate
- ~ tails, see: ~ ends
- ~ vehicle = Schwerfahrzeug *n*

hedenbergite, CaFeSi$_2$O$_6$ (Min.) = Hedenbergit *m*
hedge-trimmer, see: garden shears
heel of screed = Bohlenhinterkante *f*
height cut-out = Endausschalter *m* für Hubhöhe *f*
heightening = Erhöhung *f*, Erhöhen *n*. Aufstockung *f* [*Talsperre f*]
height of construction = Bauhöhe *f*
- ~ ~ eye, eye level = Augenhöhe *f*
- ~ ~ the maximum storage; level of storage water (Brit.); capacity level, storage level (US) = Stauziel *n*, Stauspiegel *m*

HELD concrete batching and mixing plant = Zuteil-und Mischanlage *f* für Trockenoder Naßbeton *m*, Fabrikat HANS HELD. MANNHEIM-LUDWIGSHAFEN, DEUTSCHLAND
held water = Schicht(en)wasser *n*
helical barrel vault = Schneckengewölbe *n*

- ~ blade, baffle ~, mixing ~ = Mischschaufel *f* [*Betonmischer m*]
- ~ gearing, helical gear-wheels = Schrägverzahnung *f*, Schraubenverzahnung
- ~ (gear) wheel = Zahnrad *n* mit Schrägverzahnung *f*, Schrägzahnrad *n*, Schraubenrad *n*, schrägverzahntes Getrieberad *n*
- ~ reinforcement = Spiralbewehrung *f*, Spiralarmierung *f*
- ~ shoot, spiral (gravity) ~ = Wendelrutsche *f*
- ~ staircase, spiral ~, helicoidal ~ = Wendeltreppe *f*

heliotrope, see: bloodstone (Min.)
heliport = Hubschrauberflugplatz *m*
helix [*cable*] = Seele *f* [*Kabel n*]
helmet, driving helmet, cap, driving cap, cushion block = Rammhaube *f*
hemlock spruce = Schierlingstanne *f*
hemp core; fibre ~ (Brit.); fiber ~ (US) = Hanfseele *f*, Fasereinlage *f*, Faser(seil)seele *f*, Hanfeinlage
- ~ rope = Hanfseil *n*
- ~ ~ sheave = Hanfseilrolle *f*
- ~ twist = Hanfzopf *m*

HENNE motorised mastic asphalt mixer and heater = Gußasphaltmotorkocher *m*, Fabrikat RICHARD HENNE K. G., HOLZMINDEN, DEUTSCHLAND
hepatic cinnabar (Min.) = Quecksilberlebererz *n*
- ~ iron ore (Min.) = Eisenlebererz *n*

heptane = Heptan *n*
herbicide, see: weed killer
hercynite, iron spinel, FeAl$_2$O$_4$ (Min.) = Hercynit *m*, Eisenspinell *m*
herringbone drainage, mitre ~, lateral ~ = Fischgrätendränage *f*
- ~ gear = Pfeilrädergetriebe *n*
- ~ strut = Kreuzstake *f*

hessian = lose gewebtes Sackleinen *n*
hessonite, see: cinnamon stone
heterogenous = heterogen
heulandite (Min.) = Heulandit *m*, Blättersiedestein *m*
hewer, see: hagger
hewing = Behauen *n*
hexagonal bolt = Sechskantschraube *f*
- ~ frame = sechseckiger Rahmen *m*

hexagonal system = hexagonales System *n* [*Kristall n*]

hexagon iron (or bar) = Sechskantstahl *m*

H-girder (Brit.), see: broad flange ~

~ patent shuttering units, HICO cent(e)ring, HICO (form) girders, HICO (adjustable horizontal) form supports, HICO steel form supports [*Trademark*] = HICO-Schalung(sträger) *f, (mpl)*, Fabrikat NORDDEUTSCHE SCHRAUBEN- UND MUTTERNWERKE A.G., PEINE, DEUTSCHLAND

hiddenite (Min.) = Hiddenit *m*

high, anticyclone = Antizyklon *m*, Hoch(druckgebiet) *n*

high-alloy steel = höher legierter Stahl *m*

(high-) alumina cement, see: calcium aluminate ~

high and low temperature drying and mixing plant, see: asphalt and coated macadam mixing plant

~ (block) of flats = Hochwohnhaus(block) *n, (m)*

~ calcium lime, see: fat lime

~ -capacity machine, high-production ~ = Hochleistungsmaschine *f*, Hochleistungs-Gerät *n* [*z. B. Rüttelstampfmaschine f*]

high carbon steel = hoch gekohlter Stahl *m*

high-density concrete, see: heavy ~

high-early-strength concrete = frühhochfester Beton *m*, frühtragfester ~

high early (or initial) strength Portland cement, rapid hardening ~ ~; high early Portland cement Type III (US) = hochwertiger Zement *m*, frühhochfester ~, Schnellerhärter *m* [*in Deutschland Z 325 und Z 425*]

~ energy radiation = hochenergetische Strahlung *f*

high-expansion cement, expanding ~, expansive ~ = Quellzement *m*, Expansivzement

high-frequency concrete compacting and finishing machine = Hochfrequenz-Schwingverdichter *m*, Hochfrequenzfertiger *m*

~ (hand) hammer (rock) drill, ~ (rock) drill hammer = (Gesteins)Bohrhammer *m* in Hochfrequenzausführung *f*

~ internal vibrator, immersion type high-frequency concrete vibrator, high frequency immersion concrete vibrator = Hochfrequenz(beton)innenrüttler *m*

~ surface vibrating and finishing machine = Hochfrequenzschwingverdichter *m*, Hochfrequenzfertiger *m*

~ vibration technique = Hochfrequenz-Vibrationstechnik *f*

high grade = Sondergüte *f*

~ ~ steel = hochwertiger Stahl *m*

~ ground = hochliegendes Gelände *n*

~ idle = Vollgas *n* bei Leerlauf *m*

~ -intensity arc = hochintensiver Lichtbogen *m*

high-level bridge = Hochbrücke *f*

~ indicator = Vollstandanzeiger *m*

high-lift fork stacking truck, see: fork-lift

~ platform truck = Plattform-Hochhubkarre(n) *f, (m)*

highly hydrated lime, see: autoclaved ~ (US)

high melting wax, solid ~ ~ = Hartparaffin *m*

~ moor forest = Waldhochmoor *n*

~ mountain(s) = Hochgebirge *n*

~ plain, plateau = Hochebene *f*

~ -powered equipment, see: heavy plant

~ -power engine, large gas ~ = Großgasmaschine *f*

high-pressure (air) compressor = Hochdruck-Kompressor *m*, Hochdruck-Luftverdichter *m*

~ gate = Gleitschütz(e) *n, (f)* mit hydraulischer Steuerung *f*

~ grease lubrication = Hochdruckfettschmierung *f*

~ hot water heating system, H. P. H. W. ~ = Hochdruck-Heißwasserheizung *f*

~ lubricating grease = Hochdruckfett *n*

~ steam curing = Hochdruck-Dampferhärtung *f* [*Betonstein m*]

~ turbine = Hochdruckturbine *f*

~ water jet = Hochdruckwasserstrahl *m*

high rocky ridge = Felsgrat *m*

~ slump concrete, plastic(ised) ~, buttery ~ = Weichbeton *m*

high-speed building (or builders') hoist = Schnellbauaufzug *m*

~ lane = Schnellspur *f*

high-speed pump, express ~ = Eilpumpe *f*
~ **range** = großer Gang *m*
~ **test track** = Geschwindigkeitsversuchsstrecke *f*
~ **track** = Schnellverkehrsstrecke *f* [*Bahn f*]
high stone content asphalt containing up to 65 per cent stone, asphalt(ic) concrete; bituminous concrete (US) = Asphaltbeton *m*
high-storeyed building = vielstöckiges Gebäude *n*
high-strength = hochfest
~ **bolt**, high-tensile ~ = hochfeste Schraube *f*
high (strength) blasting explosive = hochbrisanter Sprengstoff *m*, detonierender ~
~ **sulphate resisting Portland cement**, super-sulphate cement; Portland cement Type V (US) = starker Gipsschlackenzement *m*, ~ Sulfathüttenzement
high-temperature carbonization, ~ coking = Hochtemperaturverkokung *f*
~ **stability** = Hitzebeständigkeit *f*
~ **steam curing** = Hochtemperatur-Dampferhärtung *f* [*Betonstein m*]
~ **steel** = warmfester Stahl *m*
high-tensile bolt, high-strength ~ = hochfeste Schraube *f*
~ **steel**, high-grade ~ = hochwertiger Stahl *m*
high tension detonator [*the high tension fuse-head has a resistance of 1,500 to 50,000 ohms*] = elektrischer Zünder *m* mit einem Widerstand *m* von 1500 bis 50000 Ohm
~ **tide of water**, flood tide, flowing tide = (Tide)Flut *f*, Tidestieg *m*, aufsteigende Flut
~-**torqued bolt** = hochverdrillte Schraube *f*
~-**type bituminous pavement** = schwere bituminöse Decke *f*
high-viscosity binder (or binding medium) = hochviskoses Bindemittel *n*, hochviskoser Binder *m*
~ **tar** = hochviskoser Teer *m*
high-void ratio sand = Sand *m* mit viel Haufwerksporen *fpl*

high voltage line = Hochspannungsleitung *f*
~ **water**, H. W. = Höchstwasserstand *m*
highway, public ~, rural ~, road, rural road, public road = Landstraße *f* [*im Gegensatz zur Stadtstraße*]
~, **street** = Stadtstraße *f*
~ **authority** = Straßenbaubehörde *f*
~ **binder**, road ~ = Straßenbaubindemittel *n*, Straßenbaubinder *m*
~ **(border) planting**, see: highway planting
~ **bridge**, road ~ = Straßenbrücke *f*
~ **budget** = Straßenbaubudget *n*, Straßenbauhaushalt *m*
***highway capacity**, roadway ~, working ~ = (Straßen)Verkehrsleistungsfähigkeit *f*
Highway Code = Straßenverkehrsordnung *f*
highway construction, see: road ~
~ **contract bid (US)** = Straßenbauangebot *n*
~ **depot** = Straßenmeisterei *f*
~ **ditch**, road(way) ~ = Straßengraben *m*
~ **embankment**, road ~, ~ fill = Straßendamm *m*
~ **engineer**, road ~ = Straßenbauingenieur *m*
~ **engineering**, road ~ = Straßenbautechnik *f* [*als Ingenieurwissenschaft f*]
~ **fill**, see: ~ embankment
~ **grade separation**, road ~ ~ [*a crossing of highways at different levels*] = niveaufreie Straßenkreuzung *f*
~ **ice control**, treatment of icy pavements = Glatteisbekämpfung *f*
~ **industry**, road ~ = Straßenbauindustrie *f*
~ **investment fund**, road ~ ~ = Straßenbaufonds *m*
~ **landscape** = Straßenlandschaft *f*
~ **load** = Straßeninanspruchnahme *f*
***highway marker**, see: road-marking machine
~ **material(s)**, road ~ = Straßenbaustoff *m*
~ ~ **survey**, road ~ ~ = Aufnahme *f* von natürlichen Baustoffvorkommen *npl* für den Straßenbau *m*
~ **network**, road ~ = Straßennetz *n*

(highway) paver; paving tool (US); laying and finishing machine = (Straßen)Deckeneinbaugerät n, Deckenbaumaschine f, Einbaugerät

highway planting, roadside ~, highway border ~ = Straßen(be)pflanzung f

~ police = Straßenverkehrspolizei f

~ safety, road ~ = Straßenverkehrssicherheit f

~ shoulder, see: shoulder

~ slab, see: road bay

~ speed, road ~ = Straßengeschwindigkeit f

~ spiral, spiral (transition) curve, transition spiral = Klothoide f, Übergangsbogenspirale f

~ structure, road ~ = Kunstbauwerk n

~ system, road ~ = Straßennetz n

*****highway traffic,** road ~ = Straßenverkehr m

Highway Traffic Law = Straßenverkehrsrecht n

highway transition curve = Straßenübergangsbogen m

~ transport, road ~, ~ transportation = Straßentransport m

~ tunnel, road ~ = Straßen(verkehrs)tunnel m

~ user, road ~ = Straßenbenutzer m

~ ~ revenues = Kraftverkehrsbeiträge mpl

hill climbing ability, see: negotiating capacity

~ hachures = Bergschraffen fpl [Karte f]

~ peat = Hochmoortorf m

~ road, see: (side-)hill

hillside, slope, flank of a hill = (Ab)Hang m

~ aggregate bin, ~ ~ silo = Hangsilo m für Zuschlagstoffe mpl, ~ ~ Zuschläge mpl

~ blasting = Hangsprengung f, Hangsprengen n

~ borrow = Hangentnahme f

~ ~ pit = Hangentnahmegrube f

~ ramp = Hangrampe f

~ slope = Hangböschung f

~ surface water = Hangtag(es)wasser n, Hangoberflächenwasser

hilly = hüg(e)lig

~ country = Hügelland n

hinge = Gelenk n

hinged, pin-connected = gelenkig gelagert

~ arch = Gelenkbogen m

~ frame = Gelenkrahmen m

~ girder bridge = Gelenkträgerbrücke f

~ pier, rocking ~ [bridge] = Pendelstütze f, Pendelpfeiler m

hip rafter, angle ~, angle ridge = Gratsparren m

~ rafters = Anfallgespärre n, Anfallgebinde n

*****hip tile** = Gratziegel m

hire charge, equipment rental = (Geräte-)Mietkosten f, Gerätemiete f

historical geology, stratigraphy, stratigraphical geology = Formations- und Schichtenkunde f, Stratigraphie f, historische Geologie f

historic landmark, ancient monument = Kulturdenkmal n

"hit and run" offence = Fahrerflucht f

hitch = Sattel m, Ankupplung f

hoar-frost, rime frost = Rauhreif m

hod, mortar trough, mortar box = Mörteltrog m

hoe = Hacke f

~ (US); see: backacter (Brit.)

~ reeving = Einscherung f des Tieflöffelbaggers m

hoeing plough (Brit.); **~ plow** (US) = Hackpflug m

hogback = einseitig einfallender Bergkamm m, ~ ~ Felsrücken m

hog backed girder, semi-parabolic ~ = Halbparabelträger m

hoggin (Brit.); sandy gravel, path gravel, gravel-sand-clay = sandiger Kies m [mit ton- und/oder kalkhaltigem Binder m]

hog weed = Pfeifenstrauch m

hoist = Aufzug m

~ = Spillwinde f

~-block, see: fall-block

~-block, see: (block and) tackle

hoist brake = Hubbremse f

~ chain = Hubkette f

hoisting cable, ~ rope, lifting ~ = Hubseil n

~ gear = 1. Windwerk n; 2. Hebezeug n

hoist(ing gear) drum = 1. Windwerkstrommel f; 2. Hebezeugtrommel f

hoisting height — hooklike halving

hoisting height = Hubhöhe *f*
~ **line boom point sheave** = Hubseilscheibe *f* am Auslegerkopf *m*
~ ~ **socket** = Hubseilmuffe *f*
~ **machinery**, see: elevating plant
~ **power**, lifting ~ = Hubkraft *f*
~ **rope**, ~ cable, lifting ~ = Hubseil *n*
~ **speed** = Hubgeschwindigkeit *f*
~ **steam engine** = Lasthebedampfmaschine *f*
~ **winch**, hoist ~ = 1. Hubwinde *f*; 2. Aufzugwinde
hoist shaft = Hubwelle *f*
hoist-type dump trailer = Anhänger *m* mit Kippwinde *f*
holder = Düsenhalter *m*
~ **type injector** = Einspritzdüsenhalter *m*
holder-up, dolly, bucker-up = (Niet-)Gegenhalter *m*
holding bolt = Befestigungsschraube *f*
holding-down bolt, tie ~, anchor ~ = Ankerschraube *f*, Fundamentschraube
~ **rod**, anchor bar = Ankerstab *m*
holding line = Greifer-Halteseil *n*
hole, duct, channel = Gleitkanal *m* [*Spannbeton m*]
~ **ga(u)ge** = Lochlehre *f*
~ **(or bore-hole) placement for rock blasting** = Bohrlochanordnung *f* für Felssprengung *f*
hollow abutment = aufgelöstes Widerlager *n*
~ **beam**, ~ girder = Hohlträger *m*, Hohlbalken(träger) *m*
~ **block**, see: filler ~
~ **boring rod**, ~ drill ~ = Hohlbohrstange *f*
~ **brick**, see: cavity ~
~ **ceramics for construction** = hohle baukeramische Erzeugnisse *npl*
~ **chamfer** = Hohlkant *m*
~ **(clay) building (or masonry) block**, hollow concrete block, concrete hollow brick; structural hollow tile (US) = Hohlblockstein *m*, Hohlblockziegel *m*
~ **drill rod**, ~ boring ~ = Hohlbohrstange *f*
~ **filler tile** = Deckenhohlstein *m*
~ **floor slab** = Hohlsteindecke *f*

~ **gauged brick** (Brit.); segment(al) sewer block (US) = Hourdis *m*, Tonhohlplatte *f*
~ **girder**, see: ~ beam
~ **gypsum tile** (US) = Gips-Hohlstein *m*
~ **piston** = Hohlkolben *m*
~ ~ **pump** = Rohrkolbenpumpe *f*
~ **ram pump**, bored tube ~, Abyssinian ~ = Rammrohrpumpe *f*, Abessinierpumpe
~ **section** = Hohlquerschnitt *m*
~ ~ = Hohlprofil *n*
~ **shaft** = Schaftschale *f*, Pfeilerschaft *m*
~ **stanchion** = Hohlstütze *f*
~ **wall**, cavity ~ = Hohlwand *f*, Hohlmauer *f*
holly = Stechpalme *f*
holm oak = Grüneiche *f*
holocrystalline rock = vollkristallines Erstarrungsgestein *n*
home building, residential construction, residential housing = Wohnungsbau *m*
home-grown timber, native ~ = einheimisches Bauholz *n*
home-interview method, dwelling unit interview method, internal type of O & D survey, internal survey [*for O & D study of urban areas*] = Befragungsmethode *f* von Haus zu Haus
home market, domestic ~ = Inlandsmarkt *m*
home-produced product = Inlanderzeugnis *n*
homesite (US) = (Bau)Grundstück *n*
homogeneity = Gleichartigkeit *f*, Homogenität *f*
homogeneous = homogen
homogenising coefficient [*road traffic*] = Gleichförmigkeitsbeiwert *m*
honeycombed fascine raft = Sinkstück *n*, Faschinenfloß *n*
~ **texture**, honeycombing = Wabenstruktur *f*
honing = Honen *n*
hood = Haube *f*
hook and eye = Haken *m* und Öse *f*
~ **-block**, see: fall-block
hook chain = Hakenkette *f*
hooked tongs = Hakenzange *f*
Hooke's law = Hook'sches Gesetz *n*
hooklike halving = Hakenblatt *n*

hook-on bucket = Motorgreifer(korb) *m*, Hakengreifer *m*
hook roller = Hakenrolle *f*
to hook up = anschließen [*z. B. an ein elektrisches Netz n*]
hooped column = umschnürte Säule *f*
hoop-iron, see: strap steel
hoop stress = Ringspannung *f*
hop clover = Goldklee *m*
hopfield = Hopfenfeld *n*
hopper = Zuschlag(stoff)silo *m*
~ [*batcher*] = Zuteiler *m* [*Dosierapparat m*]
~, **receiving** = Mischgutbehälter *m* [*Schwarzbelageinbaumaschine f*]
~, see: feed ~
~ **barge** (Brit.); ~ **scow** (US) = Klappschute *f*
~ **bottom rail car** = Waggon *m* mit Bodenentleerung *f*, Bodenentleerer *m*
~ **compartment** = Laderaum *m* [*Naßbagger m*]
~ **conveyor** = Fülltrichter-Abzugsband *n*
~ **dredge(r)** = Schachtbagger *m*, Hopperbagger *m*
~ **gate**, cut-off ~ = Schließblech *n*, Mengenregulierschieber *m* [*Schwarzbelageinbaumaschine f*]
~ **scale** = Fülltrichterwaage *f*
~ **scow** (US), see: ~ barge (Brit.)
~ **side plate** = Seitenblech *n* des Materialsilos *m* [*Schwarzbelageinbaumaschine f*]
*****hopper spreader**, see: trough-type concrete distributor
~(-**type**) **dump trailer** = Anhänger *m* mit Bodenentleerung *f*
hopper-type spreading machine, see: trough-type concrete distributor
Höppler visco(si)meter, rolling sphere instrument, falling ball ~ = Höppler-Kugelfall-Viskosimeter *n*
hop warehouse = Hopfenlagerhaus *n*
horizon light = Horizontfeuer *n* [*Flugplatz m*]
horizontal alignment (Brit.)/**alinement** (US) **of highways** = Linienführung *f* im Grundriß *m*
~ **component** = Horizontalkomponente *f*
~ **conveyor** = Waagerechttörderer *m*
horizontal counter-balanced action shaking screen = Zweimassen-Schrägwurfsieb *n*

~ **curve** = horizontale Kurve *f*, ~ Krümmung *f*
~ **displacement of crown** = horizontale Scheitelverschiebung *f* [*Bogenbrücke f*]
~ **drilling machine** = Horizontalbohrmaschine *f*
~ **form support**, concrete ~ ~ = Schalungsträger *m*
~ **gas flow dry precipitator** = Horizontalströmungs-Trockenelektroabscheider *m*
~ **grillage**, ~ **grilled foundation** = Schwellrostunterbau *m*
~ **joint**, course ~ = Lagerfuge *f*
~ **member of frame**, beam ~ ~ = Rahmenriegel *m*
~ **property** = Eigentumswohnung *f*
~ **retort tar** = Horizontal-Retortenteer *m*
~ **roller** (**grinding**) **mill** = Federrollen-(mahl)mühle *f*
~ **screen**, level ~ = Horizontalsieb *n*
~ **shoring**, see: flying ~
~ **shear**, longitudinal ~ = Längsschubkraft *f*
~ **stiffener** = Horizontalsteife *f* [*Blechträger m*]
~ **thrust** = Horizontalschub *m*
~ **tie** = Zugband *n* [*Zweigelenkbogen m*]
~ **timber sheeting**, lagging ~ = Holzauskleidung *f*
~ **vibrating screen** = Horizontal(-Vibrations-Plan)sieb *n*
horn = Hupe *f*
hornbeam, white beech = Weißbuche *f*, Hainbuche, Hagebuche, Hornbaum *m*
hornblende (Min.) = Hornblende *f*
~-**gneiss**, see: amphibolic gneiss
horn(blende)-schist, schistous amphibolite = Hornblendeschiefer *m*
horn button = Hupenknopf *m*
horned (**screw**) **nut**, castle ~, castellated ~ = Kronen(schrauben)mutter *f*
hornfels = Hornfels(gneis) *m*
horn quicksilver (Min.) = Quecksilberhornerz *n*
hornsilver (Min.), see: cerargyrite
hornstone (Geol.) = Hornstein *n*
horse-drawn cart = Pferdefuhrwerk *n*
~ **road sweeper** = Kehrmaschine *f* für Pferdezug *m*, Pferde-Kehrmaschine

horse-flesh mahagony — humidity chamber

horse-flesh mahagony = Pferdefleischholz n
~ ore (Min.), see: bornite
horse pond = Pferdeschwemme f
~ ~ = Tränkrinne f [*Betonfertigware f*]
(~) power requirement = Kraftbedarf m, Energiebedarf m
horseshoe-shaped = hufeisenförmig
horst (Geol.) = Horst m
~ fault = Horstverwerfung f
hose, flexible tube = Schlauch m, elastische Leitung f
~ coupling = Schlauchverschraubung f
~ line = Schlauchleitung f
~ oiler = Schlauchöler m
~ shaft = Schlauchwelle f
host rock (Geol.) = Muttergestein n
hot bearing grease = Heißlagerfett n
hot-bulb engine, surface-ignition ~ = Glühkopfmotor m, Semi-Dieselmotor m [*ein Teil des Verbrennungsraumes m nicht gekühlt*]
~ ignition = Glühkopfzündung f
hot floor drying [*brick*] = Heißflurtrocknung f [*Ziegel m*]
hot-galvanized = feuerverzinkt
hot-laid coarse tar concrete = (Heißeinbau-)Teergrobbeton m
~ fine tar concrete = (Heißeinbau-)Teerfeinbeton m
~ process (or method of construction) = Heißeinbau m, Heißeinbauweise f [*Straße f*]
hot-melt plastic stripe = Markierungsstreifen m aus heiß aufgebrachter plastischer Masse f
hot-mix (asphalt) plant, see: asphalt ~
hot neck grease = Heißwalzenfett n
~ plant mix = Heißmischung f
~ plant-mixing = Heißmischverfahren n
~ plate = Darre f, Röstplatte f
~-rolled sheet steel = warmgewalztes Feinblech n
hot screed = Heizbohle f
~ smoke = Ruß m
~ spring, thermal ~ = Therme f, thermale Quelle f
~ tar, TH = Heißteer m
HOTTRIN (Brit.) [*Trademark*] = ein Naturgummimehl n für den bituminösen Straßenbau m

HOUGH PAYLOADER [*Trademark*] = Schürflader m, Pneuladeschaufel f, Fabrikat THE FRANK G. HOUGH CO., LIBERTYVILLE, ILLINOIS, USA
hourly output = Stundenleistung f
~ wage rate, rate per working hour, daywork rate = Stundenlohnsatz m
hour meter = Betriebsstundenzähler m [*Baumaschine f*]
house building, see: housing work
~ connection, building ~ = Hausanschluß m, Gebäudeanschluß
housefly = Stubenfliege f
household refuse, garbage, kitchen waste = Küchenabfälle mpl
house magazine = Firmenzeitschrift f
~ trailer; see: accommodation ~ (US)
housing = Unterbringung f
~, casing = Gehäuse n
~ = Wohnungswesen n
~ estate = Siedlung f
(~) ~ road = Siedlungsstraße f
~ policy = Wohnungsbaupolitik f
~ problem = Wohnungsfrage f, Wohnungsproblem n
~ scheme = Wohnungsbauprojekt n
~ site = Wohnhausbaustelle f
~ volume = Wohn(ungs)raum m
~ work, house building = Hausbau m
HOWARD SINGLE-PASS EQUIPMENT [*Trademark*] = Bodenmischmaschine f, Fabrikat ROTARY HOES LTD., HORNDON, ESSEX, ENGLAND
Howe truss = Howe-Träger m, Howe'scher Binder m
Hoyer method, prestressed concrete with thin wires = Bauweise f Hoyer, Stahlsaitenbeton m
H.P.H.W. heating system, high-pressure hot water ~ ~ = Hochdruck-Heißwasserheizung f
hub = Radnabe f
~ bearing = Radnabenlager n
~ of the (pipe) bell, inside base ~ ~ (~) ~ = Muffengrund m
hull = Schiffsrumpf m, Schiffskörper m
humic = humos
~ acid = Humussäure f
humidity chamber = Feuchtigkeitskammer f, Feuchtraum m [*Erdbaulabor(atorium)n*]

humification = Humusbildung *f*
hump, double incline = Ablaufberg *m*, Ablaufgipfel *m*. Eselsrücken *m*
~ switching = Ablaufberg-Verschiebung *f*
humus = Humus *m*
~ (sewage) sludge = humusbildender Faulschlamm *m*
~ soil = Humusboden *m*, Humuserde *f*
hung ceiling, suspended ~ = Hängedecke *f*
~ scaffold(ing), see: suspended ~
Hunt conveyor = Hunt'sche Conveyorkette *f*
Huntingdon willow, white ~ = Silberweide *f*, Weißweide *f*
hurricane = Orkan *m*
~ lamp = Windlampe *f*
hut = Baracke *f*
~ camp = Barackenlager *n*
Hutchinson visco(si)meter = Viskosimeter *n* nach Hutchinson
HUTHER asphalt paver = Schwarzdecken-Einbaumaschine *f*, Fabrikat HUTHER & CO., BECHTHEIM bei WORMS, DEUTSCHLAND
H.W., high water = Höchstwasserstand *m*
hyaline, see: glassy
hyalophane (Min.) = Barytfeldspat *m*, Hyalophan *m*
hybrid rocks (Geol.) = hybride Gesteine *npl*, Mischgesteine
hydrant stem = Hydrantensäule *f*
~ well (Brit.); combination hydrant and fountain (US) = Wasserzapfbrunnen *m*, Hydrantbrunnen
hydrargillite, see: gibbsite (Min.)
to hydrate, to set = abbinden [*Zement m*]
hydrated lime (powder), lime hydrate, slaked lime, calcic hydrate, hydrate of lime = gelöschter Kalk *m* [*Branntkalk + Wasser*]
(~) ~ process, wet-aggregate ~, wet sand-binder construction, wet-sand process = Naß(-Sand-)Verfahren *n*, Kalkverfahren *n*
~ (or hydrous) silicate of aluminium, siliceous earth = kieselsaure Tonerde *f*
~ sodium borate, $Na_2B_4O_7 \times 10\ H_2O$ = wasserhaltiges borsaures Natrium *n*
~ ~ sulphate, see: glauber salt

hydrate of lime, see: hydrated lime(powder)
~ putty, see: lime paste
hydrating, see: set
hydration, see: set
~ of cement = Zementhydra(ta)tion *f*
hydrator, slaking machine = (Kalk)Löschmaschine *f*
hydraulically operated butterfly valve = Drosselklappe *f* mit hydraulischem Antrieb *m*
hydraulic binder, ~ binding medium = hydraulisches Bindemittel *n*, hydraulischer Binder *m*
~ booster, (~) steering ~ = hydraulischer Kraftverstärker *m* [*Lenkung f*]
~ ~ steering = hydraulische Lenkhilfe *f*, Lenkung *f* mit hydraulischer Kraftverstärkung *f*
~ (bucket) loader, see: ~ loading shovel
*****hydraulic cement,** see: cement
~ classification = Korntrennung *f* im Naßverfahren *n*
*****~ classifier,** hydroclassifier = Horizontal(strom)sichter *m*, Horizontalgerinne *n*, Stromgerinne
~ concrete placing = Pumpkretbetonförderung *f*
~ control = hydraulische Steuerung *f*
~ crowd(ing) = hydraulischer Vorschub *m*, ~ Vorstoß *m*, hydraulisches Vorstoßen *n*
~ cyclone = hydraulischer Zyklon *m*, Hydrozyklon *m*
~ dredge(r), see: suction ~
~ embankment, see: ~ fill
~ emplacement of sand, see: hydraulic sand filling
~ end loader, see: ~ lift tailgate
*****hydraulic engineering (or construction, or works)** = Wasserbau *m*
~ erosion dredge(r), dustpan (type of hydraulic) ~ = Spüler *m*
~ excavator = Hydraulik-(Trocken-)Bagger *m*
~ fill, ~ embankment [*fill moved and placed by running water*] = Spülkippe *f*, Aufspülung *f*, hydraulische Auffüllung *f*
~ ~ dam = (Voll)Spüldamm *m*, gespülter (Erd)Damm [*Erddammbauweise f mit Spültransport m und Spüleinbau m*]

hydraulic fill embankment — hydro-clam 201

hydraulic fill embankment = Vollspüldamm *m*, gespülter (Erd)Damm *m* [*Verkehrsdamm*]
~ **flanging machine** = hydraulische Bördelmaschine *f* (oder Kümpelpresse *f*)
~ **fracturing process** = hydraulische Rissebildung *f*
~ **front-end loader**, see: ~ loading shovel
~ **gear** = Flüssigkeitsgetriebe *n*
~ **gradient** = hydraulisches Gefälle *n*, hydraulische Gradiente *f*
~ **ground-testing machine** = hydraulische Belastungsvorrichtung *f*
~ **hand tipping gear** = hydraulische Hand-Kippvorrichtung *f*
~ **hinge** = hydraulisches Gelenk *n*
~ **hoist** = Hydraulikwinde *f*
~ **investigations** = wasserbauliche Forschungsarbeiten *fpl*
~ **jack** = hydraulischer Hebebock *m*, hydraulische Winde *f*, Hydraulikheber *m*
~ ~ **out-rigger** = hydraulisch ausfahrbare Stütze *f*
~ **jump** = Wassersprung *m*
hydraulicking = Druckstrahlbaggerung *f*
~ ~ = Hydromechanisierung *f*
hydraulic lift tailgate, ~ end loader = hydraulische Hubklappe *f* [*LKW m*]
~ **lime**; see: autoclaved lime (US)
~ ~ **mortar** = Wassermörtel *m*
~ **limestone**, see: artificial ~
~ **loading shovel**, ~ loader, ~ bucket loader, ~ tractor-shovel, ~ front-end loader = hydraulische Ladeschaufel *f*, hydraulischer Schaufellader *m*
~ **material**, ~ substance = hydraulischer Stoff *m*
~ **oil**, (~) pressure ~, pressurized ~ = Drucköl *n*, Hydrauliköl
~ ~ **tank breather** = Hydraulikölbehälterentlüfter *m*
~ **pipe bender** = hydraulische Rohrbiegemaschine *f*
~ ~ **line dredge(r)**, see: suction-cutter ~
~ **power steer(ing)** = hydraulische Kraftlenkung *f*
~ **press** = hydraulische Presse *f*
~ **pressure head** = Wasserdruckhöhe *f*

~ (~) **oil**, pressurized ~, pressure ~ = Drucköl *n*, Hydrauliköl
~ ~ ~ **vessel** = Druckölbehälter *m*
~ **riveting machine** = Hydraulik-Nietmaschine *f*
~ **rotary drilling (or boring)**, rotary mud flush boring (or drilling) = Rotationsspülbohren *n*, Rotationsspülbohrung *f*
hydraulics = (technische) Hydraulik *f*
~ **research station** = Hydraulik-Forschungsinstitut *n*
hydraulic sand filling, ~ emplacement of sand = Sandaufspülung *f*
~ **scraper**, see: ~ wheel ~
~ **semi-dump trailer** = aufgesattelter hydraulischer Kipper *m*
~ **steel construction** = Stahlwasserbau *m*
~ **steering** = hydraulische Lenkung *f*
~ **structure** = Wasserbauwerk *n*
~ **substance**, ~ material = hydraulischer Stoff *m*
~ **(suction) dredge(r)**, pump ~, sandpump ~, suction ~ = Saugbagger *m*, Pumpen(naß)bagger *m*, Sauger *m*
~ **tilting system**, ~ tipping ~ = Kipphydraulik *f*
~ **tractor-shovel**, see: ~ loading shovel
~ **transport** = hydraulische Förderung *f*
~ **tunnel shield jack** = hydraulische Tunnelschildpresse *f*
~ **valve** = hydraulisches Ventil *n*
~ **wheel brake** = hydraulische Radbremse *f*
~ (~) **scraper** = Radschrapper *m* mit Hydraulikvorrichtung *f*
~ **working platform** = hydraulische Arbeitsbühne *f*
hydrocarbon, carburetted hydrogen = Kohlenwasserstoff *m*
~ **group analysis** = Ringanalyse *f*
~ **pavement** (Brit.); black top ~ (US) = Schwarzdecke *f*
~ **solvent** = Kohlenwasserstoff-Lösungsmittel *n*
hydrochloric acid, muriatic ~ = Salzsäure *f*, Chlorwasserstoffsäure
~ **solution of cuprous chloride**, Cu_2Cl_2 + HCl + aq = salzsaure Kupferchlorürlösung *f*
hydro-clam = Schlepper *m* mit hydraulischer Greif(er)vorrichtung *f*

*hydroclassifier, see: hydraulic classifier
hydrocyanic acid, HCN = Blausäure *f,* Zyanwasserstoff *m*
*(hydro) dam = Talsperre *f*
(~) ~ body = (Tal)Sperrenkörper *m,* Stauwerk *n*
(~) ~ crest, see: dam ~
hydrodynamic drive = hydro-dynamischer Antrieb *m*
~ stress = hydrodynamische Spannung *f*
hydrodynamics = Hydrodynamik *f*
hydroelectric dam = Wasserkraft-Talsperre *f*
~ exploitation, utilisation of water power = Wasserkraftnutzung *f*
hydro(-electric power) development = Ausbau *m* der Wasserkraftanlagen *fpl*
hydro-electric scheme = Wasserkraftbauprogramm *n,* Wasserkraft-Ausbauplan *m*
hydrofining = raffinierende Hydrierung *f*
hydroforming process = Reformierungsverfahren *n* mit Entschwef(e)lung *f* durch katalytische Druckhydrierung *f*
hydrogen = Wasserstoff *m*
hydrogenated fat = gehärtetes Fett *n*
hydrogenation = Hydrierung *f*
(hydrogen) flame photometer = Flammenphotometer *m, n*
hydrogen-ion concentration, pH value = Wasserstoffionenkonzentration *f,* Wasserstoffzahl H *f,* pH-Wert *m*
hydrogen peroxide plant = Wasserstoffsuperoxydanlage *f*
~ sulfide, H_2S = Schwefelwasserstoff *m*
hydro-geological = hydrogeologisch
hydrograph of flow, flow hydrograph, discharge curve, hydrograph curve of discharges = Abfluß(mengen)kurve *f*
hydrographic instrument = hydrographisches Instrument *n*
~ map, sea chart = Seekarte *f*
hydrography = Hydrographie *f,* Gewässerbeschreibung *f*
HYDROHOE [*Trademark*] = Hydraulik-Tieflöffel(bagger) *m,* Fabrikat BUCYRUS-ERIE CO., SOUTH MILWAUKEE, WIS., USA
hydrolising tank, septic ~ = Faulraum *m*

hydrologist = Hydrologe *m*
hydrology = Hydrologie *f,* Gewässerkunde *f*
hydro-mechanical transmission = hydromechanische Übertragung *f*
hydromechanics = Hydromechanik *f*
hydrometer, areometer, density meter for liquids, density hydrometer = Aräometer *n,* hydrostatische Senkwaage *f,* Spindel *f,* Flüssigkeitsdichtemesser *m,* Aräometer-Spindel
~ test, see: sedimentation ~
hydrometry = Wassermeßlehre *f*
hydrophane (Min.) = Hydrophan *m,* trüber Edelopal *m*
hydrophibic, water-loving = wasserliebend
hydrophobic, water-hating = wassermeidend
hydropneumatic = lufthydraulisch
hydro policy = Wasserkraftpolitik *f*
~ power = Wasserkraft *f*
~ project = Wasserkraftanlage *f*
hydroseparator = Trenneindicker *m*
hydrosizer = Vertikalstromsichter *m*
hydrosolvent = synthetisches Lösungsmittel *n* erhalten aus Erdölanteilen *mpl* durch spaltende Hydrierung *f* bei hohen Temperaturen *fpl* und niedrigem Druck *m*
hydrostatic (or floating) bearing = hydrostatisches Lager *n,* Schwimmlager
~ drive = hydrostatischer Antrieb *m*
~ excess pressure, see: excess pore (water) pressure
~ load = hydrostatische Last *f*
~ paradox, Pascal's ~ = hydrostatisches Paradoxon *n*
~ pressure = hydrostatischer Druck *m*
~ ~ test = Wasserdruckprüfung *f* [*Rohrleitung f*]
hydrostatics = Hydrostatik *f*
hydrostatic swing bridge = Drehbrücke *f* mit Wasserauftrieb *m*
hydrosulphides = Mercaptane *npl*
hydro tube, see: power tunnel
~ tunnel, see: power ~
hydrous crystalline lime sulfate, $CaSO_4 \times 2H_2O$ = kristallwasserhaltiges Kalziumsulfat *n*

hydrous magnesium silicate — ignitor cord

hydrous magnesium silicate, ~ silicate of magnesia = wasserhaltiges Mg-Silikat n, Magnesiumhydrosilikat
~ mica, see: illite
~ (or hydrated) silicate of aluminium, siliceous earth = kieselsaure Tonerde f
hydrozincite (Min.), see: zinc bloom
hygroscopicity = Hygroskopizität f
hygroscopic salt = hygroskopisches Salz n
~ soil water, solidified ~ = hygroskopisches Wasser n, verfestigtes ~, Saugwasser nach Stiny, Grenzflächenwasser, Benetzungswasser, Häutchenwasser
hypabyssal = hypabyssisch
hyperbolic = hyperboloid
hypersthene, (MgFe)SiO$_3$ (Min) = Hypersthen m
hypidiomorphic = hypidiomorph
hypocrystalline = halbkristallin
hypoid gear = Hypoidgetriebe n
~ (~) oil = Hypoidöl n

I

Iberian Peninsula = Pyrenäenhalbinsel f
IBP, initial boiling point = Siedebeginn m
ice and dirt grouser = (Gleis)Kettenstollen m, (Winkel)Greifer m, Raupenstollen
ice-avalanche = Eislawine f, Gletscherlawine
ice barrier = Eisschranke f
iceberg = Eisberg m
iceblink = Eisblink m
ice-borne sediment = glaziales und fluvoglaziales Sedimentgestein n
icebound = eingeeist
ice-breaker = Eisbrecher m [Schiff n]
ice cave = Eistor n
~ concrete = Eisbeton m
ice-control salt, see: de-icing ~
ice desert = Eiswüste f
~ field = Eisfeld n
~ floe = Eisscholle f
~ formation, formation of ice, ice segregation, segregation of ice = Eisbildung f
~-free = eisfrei
ice-guard = Eisbrecher m
Iceland agate, true obsidian = echter Obsidian m

~ moss = isländisches Moos n, Lungenmoos n
~ spar = isländischer Doppelspat m
ice lens = Eislinse f, Frostlinse
I.C. engine, see: internal combustion ~
ice point = Eispunkt m
~ pressure = Eisdruck m
~ rampart = Eiswall m
~ removal = Eisräumung f
~ segregation, see: ~ formation
~ spar = Eisspat m
ichthyol = hochschwefelhaltige Ammonsulfoseife f aus Schieferöl n
icicle shaped = eiszapfenförmig
icy = vereist
I.D., inside diameter = innerer Durchmesser m
ideal grading curve = Idealsieblinie f
identification beacon = Kennfeuer n [Flugplatz m]
~ of soils = Bodenkennzeichnung f
idiomorphic = idiomorph, eigengestaltig [Mineral n]
to idle = leerlaufen
idle run; see: coasting (Brit.)
idler, conveyor idler, (idler) roller = Förderbandrolle f
~ = Leitrad, Spannrad n, Leerlaufturas m [(Gleis)Kette f]
~ gear = Zwischenzahnrad n
~ pulley = (Riemen)Spannrolle f
~ set = Rollenstation f
~ sprocket, idling ~ = Umlenkturas m
~ wheel, idling ~, crawler ~ ~ = Umlenkrolle f [Gleiskette f]
igneous plutonic rock, see: intrusive ~
~ rock, primary ~ = Massengestein n, Erstarrungsgestein, Glutflußgestein
~ volcanic rock, see: lava flow
ignition = Zündung f
~ accelerator = Zündbeschleuniger m
~ button = Zündknopf m
~ delay = Zündverzug m
~ loss, loss on ignition = Glühverlust m
~ magnet(o) = Zündmagnet m
~ paper = Zündpapier n
~ performance = Zündwilligkeit f
~ point [deprecated]; see: fire ~
ignitor cord = Anzündlitze f

illite, hydrous mica, shiny clay = Glimmerton *m*
illuminated bollard = Leucht-Inselpfosten *m*
illuminating gas = Leuchtgas *n*
~ oil, see: lighting ~
illumination of roads and streets, see: public lighting
ilmenite, FeTiO₃ (Min.) = Ilmenit *m*
imbibition = Aufsaugung *f*
imbricated plate = Schuppenblech *n*
Imhoff tank, Emscher ~ = Emscher-Brunnen *m*
immersion-compression test = Wasserbad-Druckprüfverfahren *n*, Wasserlagerungs-Druckfestigkeitsprüfung *f*
immersion in water = Wasserlagerung *f*
~ kettle for joint-forming metal strips = Tauchwanne *f* für Fugeneisen *npl*
(~) poker, ~ **needle** = Vibrationsnadel *f* [*Innenrüttler m*]
~ type high-frequency concrete vibrator, see: high-frequency internal vibrator
~ vessel = Tauchgefäß *n*
~ vibrator, see: concrete mass ~
~ weighing = Tauchwägung *f*
immobilized = manövrierunfähig
impact = Stoßwirkung *f*
~ allowance, allowance for impact = Stoßbeiwert *m*, Stoßzuschlag *m*
~ and vibration resistance = Erschütterungsbeständigkeit *f*
~ breaker, see: (impeller) impact (type) breaker (or crusher)
~ clam, ~ **clamshell bucket with pile driver action**
~ mill, see: impeller impact grinding mill
IMPACT mixing plant [*Trademark*] = IMPACT-Mischanlage *f*, Fabrikat WIBAU, GELNHAUSEN/ROTHENBERGEN (HESSEN), DEUTSCHLAND
impactor, see: pulverator
impact reduction = schlagartige Zerkleinerung *f*, Schlagzerkleinerung
~ separator = Prallplatte *f* [*zur Entstaubung f und Aufbereitung allerfeinsten Sandkorns n*]
~ soil-compaction device = Stoß(boden)verdichtungsgerät *n*

~ strength = Stoßfestigkeit *f*
~ stress = Stoßbeanspruchung *f*
~ test = Stoßversuch *m*, Schlagversuch *m*
~ (type) breaker (or crusher), see: (impeller) impact (type) breaker (or crusher)
impassable = unpassierbar
impeller = Wirbelmischer *m*
~ = Schlagwalze *f*, Rotor *m* [*Prallbrecher m*]
~ = Schaufelrad *n*
~ = Flügelrad *n* der Wasserpumpe *f*
~ assisted thermo syphon = Thermosyphon *m* mit Hilfsflügelradpumpe *f*
~ bar = Schlagleiste *f* [*Prallbrecher m*]
(~) impact (grinding) mill = (mechanische) Prall(mahl)mühle *f*, Rotor(mahl)mühle, Schnelläufer(mahl)mühle
(~) ~ (type) breaker (or crusher), impeller breaker (or crusher) = Prallbrecher *m*
impermeability to water, see: imperviousness ~ ~
impermeable weir = massives (Stau-)Wehr *n*
(impervious) blanket, waterproof ~ = Dichtungsvorlage *f*, (Ab)Dichtungsteppich *m*, (Dichtungs)Schürze *f*
~ concrete diaphragm on the upstream face = wasserseitige Betondichtungsdecke *f*
(~) core, ~ **diaphragm** = Dammkern *m*, (Dichtungs)Kern
imperviousness to water, impermeability ~ ~, water-tightness = Wasserundurchlässigkeit *f*
impervious zone, water barrier = wasserundurchlässige Zone *f*
imposed load, superimposed ~, surcharge, additional load, loading = aufgebrachte Last *f* (oder Belastung *f*), Auflast *f*
impost, springer, springing brick, springing, rein = Kämpferstein *m*, Anfänger(ziegel) *m*, Bogenkämpfer *m*
impounded water pressure = Stauwasserdruck *m*
(impounding) reservoir, see: artificial lake
impregnated diamond blade = kunststoffgebundene Diamantschleifscheibe *f*
impregnation = Imprägnieren *n*, Durchtränken *n*, Durchtränkung *f*

impregnation of wood — industrial building 205

impregnation of wood = Holztränkung *f*, Holzimprägnierung *f*
improved ball-and-socket type level = Nivellierinstrument *n* mit Kippschraube *f*
~ subgrade = verbesserter Untergrund *m*
impulse condensing turbine = Gleichdruckkondensationsturbine *f*
~ starter = Anker *m*
~ turbine, free deviation ~, action ~ = (Frei)Strahlturbine *f*, (Gleich)Druckturbine, Aktionsturbine
~ ~ with pressure stages, see: action ~ ~ ~ ~
~ ~ with velocity stages = Druckturbine *f* mit Geschwindigkeitsstufen *fpl*
~ wheel = Gleichdruckrad *n* [*Turbine f*]
impure amber = Kunstbernstein *m*
impurity = Verunreinigung *f*
inactive = stillgelegt
inadequacy gap, see: backlog of needs
in-and-out haul [*wheeled scraper*] = Transportlänge *f* hin und zurück minus Schürfzeit *f*
inbuilt, built-in = eingebaut
incarnation clover = Inkarnatklee *m*
incentive bonus payment = Beschleunigungsvergütung *f*
incidence of frost = Frostauftritt *m*
incidental superimposed load, see: live load(ing)
incinerator, refuse ~, garbage disposal plant = Müllverbrennungsanlage *f*
incipient failure = beginnender Bruch *m*
~ fusion, sintering = Sintern *n*, Sinterung *f*, beginnendes Schmelzen *n*
incised meander (Geol.) = eingeschnittener Flußmäander *m*
inclement weather, rough ~, adverse ~, bad ~ = Schlechtwetter *n*
inclination of slope = Böschungsneigung *f*
incline, see: gradient
inclined barrel arch (Brit.); see: arch barrel (US)
~ boom type trench excavator, slanting boom type trenching machine, slanting boom ditcher = Grabenbagger *m* mit schräger Eimerleiter *f*
~ bucket conveyor = Schräg-Elevator *m*
~ ~ elevator plant, ~ ~ ~ cement handling facility = Zementumschlaganlage *f* mit kleinem Vorratsbehälter *m*, geneigtem Becherwerk *n* und Abmeßvorrichtung *f*
~ continuous bucket elevator = Schrägschwerkraftelevator *m*, Schrägschwerkraftbecherwerk *n*
~ guides, trackway for skip rollers = Aufzugskübelrahmen *m*, Schrägaufzugsschienen *fpl* [*Betonmischer m*]
~ plane = schiefe Ebene *f*, schräge Bahn *f*
(~) vane = Eintrittsschaufel *f* [*Vorfilter m, n*]
incline hoist, slope ~ = Schrägaufzug *m*
~ ~ winch, slope ~ ~ = Schrägaufzugwinde *f*
inclinometer, see: clinometer
inclusion, inlier (Geol.) = Einschluß *m*, Einlagerung *f*
incoalation = Inkohlung *f*
incompressibility = Unzusammendrückbarkeit *f*
indentation machine = Kugelhärteprüfer *m*
indented = verzahnt
~ joint = Verzahnung *f* [*Holzverbindung f*]
~ roller = Riffelwalze *f*
indepedent footing, see: isolated ~
index of refraction, refraction index = Refraktionsindex *m*
~ property = Klassifizierungseigenschaft *f*
indianite, see: anorthite
(India) salpetre, see: nitre
indicating = Indizierung *f* [*Dampfmaschine f*]
~ instrument, indicator = Anzeigeinstrument *n*, Anzeiger *m*
indication sign, informative ~, guide ~ = Hinweiszeichen *n*, Informationszeichen
indicator point, see: point of reference
indicolite (Min.) = Indigolith *m*
indifferent gas, see: inert ~
indigo copper (Min.) = Kupferindigo *m*
individual girder part [*bridge*] = Trägerfeldstück *n*
~ operation = Einzelbedienung *f*
indivisible load = unteilbare Last *f*
induced draught fan (Brit.); **~ draft ~** (US) = Saugzugventilator *m*
induction period = Induktionszeit *f*
indurated talc = Schiefertalk *m*
industrial building = Industriegebäude *n*

industrial coating application = industrielle Lackierung f
~ construction = Industriebau m
~ engine = Industriemotor m
~ engineer = betriebswissenschaftlich ausgebildeter Ingenieur m [*in der Schweiz: Betriebsingenieur*]
~ floor(ing) = Industrie(fuß)boden m
~ foundation = industrielle Stiftung f
~-frequency electrification = Elektrifizierung f mit Industriefrequenz f
industrial grade benzene = Lösungsbenzol n
~ insulation = Industrie-Isolierung f
industrialisation = Industrialisierung f
industrialized district = Industriebezirk m
industrial kiln = Industrieofen m
(~) lift truck = Hubkarre(n) f, (m), Hubwagen m
~ loader, shovel loader mounted on industrial wheel type tractor = Fabriklader m, Industrielader
~ location = Industriestandort m
~ loco(motive) = Industriebahnlok(omotive) f
~ methylated spirit, fuel alcohol = Brennspiritus m
~ paper bag = Industrie-Papiersack m
~ pollution = industrielle Verunreinigung f
~ railcar system; narrow gage railroad (US) = Industriebahnanlage f
~ refuse = Abfälle mpl (oder Abfall aus gewerblichen Betrieben mpl)
~ reservoir, ~ tank = Industriebehälter m
~ waste (water) = Industrieabwasser n, Fabrikabwässer npl
~ wheel tractor, rubber tyred ~ (Brit.); pneumatic-tired ~ (US); wheel-type industrial ~, wheeled ~ = Luftreifenschlepper m, Radschlepper, Straßenschlepper
industries fair = Industriemesse f
inelasticity = Unelastizität f
inert = inaktiv, träge
~ gas, indifferent ~ = indifferentes Gas n
inertia = Beharrungsvermögen n, Trägheitsvermögen, Trägheit f

infestation of the water system = Durchbruch m von Wasserorganismen mpl in das Verteilungsnetz
infiltration = Versickerung f
~ water = Sickerwasser n
infinitely variable = stufenlos regelbar
inflammability = Entzündbarkeit f, Feuergefährlichkeit f, Schwerentflammbarmachung f
inflatable rubber core, ductube = aufblasbarer Gummischlauch m für Kanäle mpl im Beton m
inflation pressure = Reifenluftdruck m
to inflate = aufpumpen
inflow of water, see: ingress ~ ~
influence diagram, ~ chart = Einflußdiagramm n
~ line = Einflußlinie f
~ of drink = Alkoholeinfluß m [*Kraftfahrer m*]
influx of cold air = Kaltlufteinbruch m
informative sign, indication ~, guide ~ = Hinweiszeichen n, Informationszeichen
infrastructure, see: military civil engineering work
infusorial earth = Infusorienerde f
ingoing air = Zuluft f
ingress of water, inflow ~ ~, in-rush ~ ~ = Wasserzutritt m, Wassereinbruch m, Wasserandrang m
inhaul [*the line or mechanism by which a cable excavator bucket is pulled toward the dump point*] = 1. Zugseil n, Vollseil, Schürfseil; 2. Zugvorrichtung f, Schürfvorrichtung
inherent moisture = Eigenfeuchtigkeit f
~ strength = Eigenfestigkeit f
initial acceptance = vorläufige Abnahme f
~ boiling point, IBP = Siedebeginn m
~ compaction f = Vorverdichtung f
~ cost(s), first ~ = Anschaffungskosten f
~ financing = Vorfinanzierung f
~ hardening = Anziehen n [*Mörtel m*]
~ load(ing) = Vorlast f, Vorbelastung f
~ shrinkage = Anfangsschwindung f
~ strength, early ~ = Anfangsfestigkeit f
initiation of freezing = Frostschwelle f, Frostbeginn m
to inject, to grout under pressure = injizieren, einpressen, auspressen, verpressen

injected concrete — Inspector General of Highway-Engineering 207

injected concrete = Einpreßbeton m
injecting device = Injiziergerät n
~ gallery = Injektionsstollen m
injection lance = Hand-Injektionsrohr n
~ nozzle = Einspritzdüse f
~ of chemicals = Chemikalinjektion f
~ process, pressure grouting ~, (grout) injection = Injektionsverfahren n, Einpreßverfahren n, Auspreßverfahren, Verpressung f
~ pump = Injektionspumpe f, Einpreßpumpe
~ ~ = Einspritzpumpe f
~ valve = Einspritzventil n
injector = Einspritzer m
~ = Dampfstrahlsauger m
injury accident = Unfall m mit Verletzten mpl
inkstone, native copperas (Min.) = Atramentstein m
inland = landeinwärts
~ canal, artifical navigation ~, inland navigation ~, barge ~ = Binnenschiffahrtkanal m, künstliche Wasserstraße f
~ craft = Binnengewässerfahrzeug n
~ dune [*deposition by wind*] = Festlandsdüne f, Winddüne, Binnendüne, Inlandsdüne
~ lake = Binnensee m
~ lock, see: navigation ~
~ navigation = Binnenschiffahrt f
~ ~ canal, see: ~ canal
~ waters = Binnengewässer npl
~ waterway = Binnenwasserstraße f, Binnenschiffahrtsstraße
inlet = Einlauf m
~, bight = Bucht f
~ channel = Zulauf(ge)rinne f, (n), Einlaufkanal m, Einlauf(ge)rinne f, (n)
~ funnel = Einlauftrichter m
~ grating, ~ grate = Einlaufrost m
~ head = Einlaßdeckel m
~ of sewer, surface water gull(e)y = Doleneinlauf m
~ pipe, intake ~ = Einlaßrohr n, Einlaufrohr
~ regulator = Einlaufregulierungsbauwerk n
~ reservoir = Einlaufbecken n

~ shaft, intake ~ = Einlaufschacht m, Einlaßschacht
~ sill = Einlaufschwelle f
~ sluice = Einlaufschütz(e) n, (f)
~ structure, see: intake (~)
~ valve = Einlaufventil n, Einlaßventil
~ ~ = Saugventil n [*Kompressor m*]
inlier, see: inclusion
inner dike (or dyke) = Hinterdeich m
~ prestress = Innenvorspannung f
innings, see: dike (or dyke) land
inorganic = anorganisch
~ binder = anorganischer Binder m
in-place material, in-situ ~ = anstehendes Material n
~ soil, in-situ ~ = anstehender Boden m
input gas = Einpreßgas n
in-rush of water, see: ingress ~ ~
insect attack = Insektenbefall m
insecticide = Insektenbekämpfungsmittel n
insert, sheath = Hülse f
~ = Einsatzstück n, Einsatz m
~, tip = Bohrspitze f
inside base of the (pipe) bell, hub of the (pipe) bell = Muffengrund m
~ calipers = Lochtaster m, Innentaster
~ column = Innenstütze f
~ stiffening box girder diaphragm = Versteifungs-Kastenträger-Scheidewand f
in-situ, in-place = an Ort m (und Stelle f)
~ concrete facing (or lining), tunnel concreting = Stollen(aus)betonierung f, Betonmauerung f
~ material, see: in-place ~
insolation = Insolation f
insoluble in benzene, extrinsic insolubles, benzene insolubles = Benzol-Unlösliches n
inspection gallery, revision ~ = Beobachtungsstollen m
~ lamp, hand ~, portable ~ = Ableuchtlampe f
~ pit, repair ~ = Untersuchungsgrube f, Reparaturgrube f
*inspection pit, manhole, inspection chamber = Einsteigeschacht m, Mannloch n, Reinigungsschacht m
Inspector General of Highway-Engineering = Generalinspekteur m für das Straßenwesen

installation — interior masonry

installation, plant, facility = (Betriebs-)Anlage *f*, Einrichtung *f*
installed (nameplate) capacity, working ~ = installierte Leistung *f*, Leistungssoll *n*
instalment payment, see: payment on account
instantaneous cap, see: electric (blasting) cap
~ (electric) detonator = (elektrischer) Momentzünder *m*
Institute for Industrial Building and Building Construction = Institut *n* für Industriebauten *fpl* und Baukonstruktionen *fpl*
~ ~ Scientific Labour Studies = Institut *n* für Arbeitswissenschaft *f*
instructional film, training ~ = Lehrfilm *m*
instruction book = Lehrbuch *n*
instrument flight = Schlechtwetterflug *m*
~ runway = Schlechtwetter-Start- und Landebahn *f*
instruments for pit measurements = Meßinstrumente *npl* für den Grubenbetrieb *m*
insulated built-up roof = Dachhaut *f* aus Dachpappe *f* und Dämmplatten *fpl*
insulating brick = Isolierstein *m*
~ concrete = Isolierbeton *m*
~ course, ~ **layer** = Dämmschicht *f*
~ fire brick = feuerfester Isolierstein *m*
~ material = Dämmstoff *m*
~ oil, see: electrical ~ ~
~ paper = Isolierpapier *n*
~ slab = Dämmplatte *f*, Isolierplatte *f*
~ wall board = Dämmwandplatte *f*
~ wool = Isolierwolle *f*
insulation, lagging = Isolierung *f* [Rohr *n*]
intake gate, head ~ = Einlaßverschluß *m*
~ line = Einlaufleitung *f*
~ pipe, inlet ~ = Einlaufrohr *n*, Einlaßrohr
~ shaft, inlet ~ = Einlaßschacht *m*, Einlaufschacht
~ (or inlet) structure (or works), head works = Einlauf(bauwerk) *m*, (*n*), Entnahmebauwerk *n*, Einlaßbauwerk *n*
~ tower = Einlaßturm *m*, Turmeinlaß *m*
integral calculus = Integralrechnung *f*
~ floor hardener, see: concrete hardener
integration technique = Integrationstechnik *f*

intensifier = Verstärker *m*
intensity of rainfall = Ergiebigkeit *f*
~ ~ traffic = Verkehrsdichte *f*
interaction diagram = Zwischenwirkungsdiagramm *n*
interbedded = eingebettet
intercalation of MgO = Einlagerung *f* von MgO
intercepting ditch, catch-water ~, diversion ~ = Abfanggraben *m*, Sammelgraben, Auffanggraben, (Abfang)Sammler *m*
~ gutter, ~ **channel,** catch drain = Hangrinne *f*, Auffangrinne *f*
~ sewer = Sammelabwasserkanal *m*
interceptor (US); see: trap (Brit.)
~, collecting drain, intercepting drain outfall drain, drain outfall, catch(-water) drain = Sammler *m*, Abfang ~
interchange, see: access point
~ equipment, see: toll-collection and audit system
~ ramp, access ~ = Anschlußrampe *f*, Kreuzungsrampe
interchangeability = Auswechselbarkeit *f*, Austauschbarkeit *f*
interchangeable = auswechselbar
interconnecting passage = Verbindungsgang *m*
~ roadway, see: access point
inter-cooler = Zwischenkühler *m*
inter-cooling = Zwischenkühlung *f*
interdigitation, interfingering, dovetailing = auskeilende Wechsellagerung *f* (Geol.)
interface = Grenzfläche *f*
interfacial forces = Grenzflächenkräfte *fpl*
~ tension, interface stress = Grenzflächenspannung *f*
interfingering, see: interdigitation
~ member (Geol.) = auskeilende Zwischenlage *f*
interformational sill (Geol.) = Lagergang *m* (oder Sill *m*, oder Intrusivlager *n*) zwischen diskordant aufgelagertem Sediment *n* und seinem Untergrund *m*
interglacial period = Zwischeneiszeit *f*
to intergrind with = vermahlen mit
interior floor(ing) = Innenfußboden *m*
~ masonry = Innenmauerwerk *n*

interior paint — interstice

interior paint = Innenanstrichfarbe f
~ **view** = Innenansicht f
interlock = Spundwandschloß n, Schloßeisen n
~ **friction** = Schloßreibung f
interlock(ing), see: (aggregate) ~
interlocking cone = Spannkegel m [*Spannbeton m*]
~ **roofing tile** = Falzziegel m, Falzstein m
intermediate course, ~ layer = Zwischenschicht f
~ **crushing** [*discharge at sizes $1/2$ or $3/8$ inch*] = Zwischenbrechen n
~ **igneous rock** = Erstarrungsgestein n mit 55 bis 66% Kieselsäure f
~ **jack rafter** = Mittelschifter m
~ **position** = Zwischenstellung f, Zwischenlage f
~ **shaft** [*a shaft which is driven by one shaft, and drives another*] = Zwischenwelle f
~ **stone**, see: choke ~ (or aggregate)
~ **storage** = Zwischenlagerung f
~ **-type pavement/paving** (US) = mittelschwere (Straßen)Decke f
intermittent beacon, see: ~ light
~ **bucket (type) elevator**, see: dredge(r) bucket (type) ~
~ **grinding, batch ~** = satzweise Mahlung f, satzweises Mahlen n
~ **kiln, periodic ~** = periodischer Ofen m
~ **light (or beacon)** = Blinklicht n, Blinkfeuer n
~ **line** = gestrichelte Linie f
~ **mixing, batch ~** = Chargen-Mischverfahren n
~ **type excavator** = Trockenbagger m für aussetzenden Betrieb m
~ ~ **track shifting machine** = Gleisrückmaschine f für absatzweisen Betrieb m
~ **weigh-batch (mixing) plant**, see: batch (-mix) type plant
~ **weighing** = absatzweises Wiegen n
internal combustion engine, I. C. ~ = Verbrennungsmotor m, Brennkraftmotor m
~ ~ **rammer**, explosion type rammer, internal combustion engine-powered rammer = Hand-Explosionsramme f, Brennkraft-Handramme f, Explosions-(Stampf)ramme f

~ **coolant** = Kühlmittel n [*z. B. Alkohol im Kraftstoff*]
~ **dia(meter)** = Lichtweite f
~ **energy**, see: intrinsic ~
~ **pipe dia(meter)** = Rohrlichtweite f
~ **plant haulage, intraplant transportation** = innerbetrieblicher Transport m
~ **plastering** = Innenputz m
~ ~ **with lime** = Innenkalkputz m
~ ~ ~ **plaster** = Innenputz m mit Gips m
~ ~ ~ **Portland cement** = Innenzementputz m
~ **scour** = innere Abscheuerung f
~ **(type of O & D) survey**, see: dwelling unit interview method
~ **vibrating machine** (Brit.); see: full depth internal slab vibrator
~ **vibrator**, see: concrete mass ~
~ ~ **type concrete (pavement) (or paving** (US)**) finisher** = Tauchrüttler-Betonstraßenfertiger m, Betondeckeninnenrüttler m
~ ~ **with handle** = Stabrüttler m
~ **water pressure, pore ~** = Porenwasserdruck m
internally-clad steel = plattiertes Blech n
International Association of Bridge and Structural Engineering = Internationale Vereinigung f für Brückenbau m und Hochbau m
~ ~ ~ **Hydraulic Research, IAHR** = Internationale Vereinigung f für hydraulische Forschung f
~ **Federation of Prestressing** = Internationale Gesellschaft f für Vorspannung f
interpretation of temperature logs = Temperaturmeßkurven-Auswertung f
intersecting angle = Schnittwinkel m
~ **point** = Schnittpunkt m
intersection = Straßenknoten m
~ **approach** = Kreuzungszufahrt f
~ **at grade**, see: grade crossing
~ **-factor method** = Querschnitt-Faktor-Verfahren n
intersection of cross-drift = Quertunnel-Einmündung f
~ ~ **upstream and down-stream faces; theoretical apex of the triangle** (Brit.) = Spitze f des theoretischen Dreiecks n
interstice, void, pore = Hohlraum m, Pore f

interstitial water, pore ~ = Porenwasser *n*
intrados, soffit [*the upper portion of the internal surface of a drain, sewer, culvert or arch*] = 1. Bogenleibung *f*; 2. Wölblinie *f*
~ springing line (US); springing of intrados (or soffit) (Brit.) = Bogenanfang *m* des Gewölbeinnern *n* [*Talsperre f*]
intraplant transportation, internal plant haulage = innerbetrieblicher Transport *m*
intratelluric = intratellurisch
intrinsic energy, internal ~ = Eigenenergie *f*
~ viscosity = Strukturviskosität *f*
INTRUSION AID [*Trademark*] = Hilfsstoff *m* bei Zementinjektionen *fpl* [*wirkt verflüssigend und hält die feinsten Teilchen npl in Suspension f*]
intrusion grout = Einpreßschlämme *f*
~ mortar = Einpreßmörtel *m*, Eindringmörtel, Injektionsmörtel
intrusive rock, plutonic ~, igneous plutonic ~ [*cooled beneath layers of other rock*] = Tiefengestein *n*, plutonisches Gestein, Plutonit *m*, subkrustales Gestein
~ sheet (Geol.) = Intrusivlager *n*
to inundate, to flood = überschwemmen
inundation, flood(ing) = Überschwemmung *f*, Überflutung *f*
inverse value, see: reversed ~
invert = Sohle *f* [*z. B. Stollen m*]
inverted arch = Grundbogen *m*, Erdbogen, Gegenbogen
~ penetration surface treatment, see: armo(u)r coat
~ siphon; siphon culvert [*deprecated*] = Düker *m*
invested capital = Investitionskapital *n*, Anlagekapital *n*
investigation method, exploration ~ = Aufschlußmethode *f*
invisible pit, ~ manhole = verlorener Schacht *m*, verlorenes Mannloch *n*
involute pump = Evolventenpumpe *f*
involution = Potenzrechnung *f*
iodide = Jodsilber *n*
iodine value, ~ number = Jodzahl *f*
iolite, see: cordierite (Min.)

ion exchanger = Ionenaustauscher *m*
to ionize = ionisieren
ionizing electrode, see: discharge ~
IP petroleum spirit = Lösungsmittel *n* ähnlich Normalbenzin *n*
IP spirit insolubles = Normalbenzin *n* unlösliches
Irish moss, carragheen = irländisches Moos *n*, Perlmoos, Knorpeltang *m*
iron alum, see: halotrichite (Min.)
~-aluminium garnet (Min.) = Eisentongranat *m*
iron clay, see: clay ironstone
~ cutters = Eisenschere *f*
~ dross, see: pitticite
~ elevator bucket = Eisen(elevator)becher *m*
~ foundry, ferrous ~ = Eisengießerei *f*
~ framed bedstead = Feldbett *n*
ironing screed [*slip-form canal paver*] = Glätt- und Verdichtungsbohle *f* [*Kanalauskleidungsmaschine f*]
ironmongery for building trades = Baueisenwaren *fpl*
iron ochre = Eisenmennige *f*
~ oleate = Eisenölseife *f*
~-olivine, see: fayalite (Min.)
iron-ore cement = Eisenerzzement *m*
iron oxide, see: ferric ~
~ Portland cement, Eisen-Portland ~ = Eisenportlandzement *m* [*abgek. EPZ; maximal 30% Schlacke f*]
(~) pyrites, see: fool's gold (Min.)
~-sandstone; see: Hastings sand (Brit.)
iron spinel (Min.), see: hercynite
~-tyred vehicle (Brit.); iron-tired ~ (US) = eisenbereiftes Fahrzeug *n*
to irrigate = bewässern
irrigated farm valley = landwirtschaftlich genutztes Tal *n* mit künstlicher Bewässerung *f*
~ sewage field = Rieselfeld *n*
irrigation, soil ~ = (Boden)Bewässerung *f*
~ canal = Bewässerungskanal *m*
~ dam = Bewässerungs(tal)sperre *f*
~ lateral (canal) = Bewässerungsnebenkanal *m*, Bewässerungsseitenkanal *m*
~ pool = Bewässerungsspeicher(becken) *m*, (*n*)
~ storage = Bewässerungsspeicherung *f*

irrigation works = Bewässerungsanlagen *f pl*
iserine, magnetic iron-sand = Magneteisensand *m*
island [*deprecated*]; see: refuge
~ = Verkehrsinsel *f* [*es gibt zwei Arten von Verkehrsinseln:* 1. *Mittelinsel f*; 2. *Richtungsinsel f*]
~ **roller**, segmented roll = Waffelwalze *f*
isohyetal (US); line of equal rainfall, isohyetal line (Brit.) = Regengleiche *f*, Isohyete *f*
isolated footing, indepedent ~, spot ~ = Einzelfundament *n*
~ **site** = abgelegene Baustelle *f*
isotropic = isotrop
issue voucher = Ausgabebeleg *m*
isthmus = Landenge *f*, Isthmus *m*
itabaryte, itabarite = Eisenglimmerschiefer *m*
Italian asbestos, tremolite (~) (Min.) = Tremolit *m*
~ **poplar**, Lombardy ~ = Pyramidenpappel *f*, italienische Pappel, Chausseepappel
~ **rye grass**, see: bearded ~ ~
item = Position *f*
~ **of plant**, ~ ~ equipment = Geräteeinheit *f*
IWRC, independent wire rope core = unabhängige Stahlseele *f*
IZet road marking machine "MEHRERGIGANT" [*Trademark*] = Straßenmarkierungsmaschine *f*, Fabrikat J. ZINDEL GmbH., STUTTGART-S, DEUTSCHLAND

J

jacinth, hyacinth (Min.) = Hyazinth *m*
jack = Hebebock *m*, Winde *f*, (An-)Hebespindel *f*, Hubspindel
~, puller = Spannpresse *f* [*Spannbeton m*]
~ = Signalflagge *f*
~ [*of a mobile drill barge*] = Hubwerk *n*
to jack = vorschieben mit Winde *f*
~ **arch**, see: straight ~
~ **boom** [*backhoe*] = Hilfsstützbock *m*
jacket [*outer covering*] = Mantel *m*
jacketed pipe = Heizmantelrohr *n*
jacking = Spannen *n* [*Spannbeton m*]

~ **block** = Spannblock *m* [*Spannbeton m*]
~ **equipment** = Aufwindvorrichtung *f*
~ **pier** = Hubstütze *f* [*Brücke f*]
~ **screw**, see: jack ~
~ **travel** = Spannweg *m* [*Spannpresse f*]
~ **up** = Hochbocken *n*
jackknife drilling mast = Klappbohrmast *m*
jack-of-all-road-materials maintenance truck (US) = LKW *m* zur Aufbereitung *f* sämtlicher Mischungen *f pl* für Straßenflickverfahren *npl*
jack-of-all-trades rig, multi-purpose equipment item = Allzweck-Gerät *n*
jack plane = Abrichthobel *m*, Schrupphobel, Schropphobel, Langhobel
~ ~ = Rauhbank *f*
~ **rafter** = Gratstichbalken *m*, Schiftsparren *m*, Schifter *m*
~ **screw**, screw jack, jacking screw = Schrauben(hebe)bock *m*, Schraubenwinde *f*, (Schrauben)Spindel *f*, Hebeschraube *f*
~ **shaft** = einfache Vorgelegewelle *f*
JAEGER Mix-in-Place ROAD BUILDER = Bodenvermörtelungsmaschine *f*, Fabrikat THE JAEGER MACHINE CO., COLUMBUS, OHIO, USA
~ **spreader** = (Beton)Schneckenverteiler *m*, Betondeckenverteiler mit umkehrbaren gegenläufigen Schnecken *f pl*, Fabrikat THE JAEGER MACHINE COMPANY, COLUMBUS 16, OHIO, USA
~ **travel(l)ing plant** [*mounted on tracks*] = Aufnahmemischer *m*, Fabrikat THE JAEGER MACHINE COMPANY, COLUMBUS 16, OHIO, USA
Jäger's increased deflexion value [*calculation of buckling in eccentrically loaded members*] = erhöhte Ausweichzahl *f* von Jäger
jagged terrain = zerklüftetes Gelände *n*
jaipurite, grey cobalt ore (Min.) = Graukobalterz *n*
jamb wall = Drempelwand *f*, Kniestockwand, Versenkungswand
jamesonite, see: feather ore (Min.)
jam nut = Kontermutter *f*, Gegenmutter
jar = Schauglas *n* vom Luftfilter *n*, *m*
jasp opal, opal jasper (Min.) = Jaspopal *m*
jaw brake = Backenbremse *f*

jaw clutch (coupling) = Klauenkupplung *f*, Zahnkupplung

*jaw crusher, ~ breaker, ~ (type rock) ~ = Backen(stein)brecher *m* [*früher: Backenquetsche f*]

~ ~ with inclined crushing chamber = Schlagbrecher *m*

~ (crushing) plate = Backenplatte *f* [*Backenbrecher m*]

~ setting, clearance = (untere Brech-)Spaltweite *f*, Spaltweite der Austrittsöffnung *f*, Austragsspaltweite

Jekel mixing value = Mischwert *m* nach Jekel [*Bitumenemulsion f*]

jenny (Brit.); **troll(e)y** = Lastkatze *f*, Laufkatze [*Gießerei-Drehkran m*]

jerrycan (Brit.), see: gasoline (storage) can (US)

jet-action trencher, jet-type ~ = Unterwasser-Düsengrabenzieher *m*

jet and fuel resisting joint sealing compound, JFR compound = düsentreibstoffeste Fugenvergußmasse *f*

jet bit = Düsenmeißel *m*

~ blade = Kreiselverdichterschaufel *f*

~ burner = Strahlbrenner *m*

~ conveyor = Schleuderband *n*, Wurf-Transporteur *m*

jetcrete, see: gunite

~ gun, see: cement ~

jet exhaust blast = Düsen(flug)motor-Luftdruck *m*

~ fuel, jet-turbine ~ = Düsen(flug)motor-Treibstoff *m*

~ gilsonite = Jet-Gilsonit *m*

~ liner = Düsenverkehrsflugzeug *n*

jet-piercing, heat drilling = Strahlbohrung *f*, Feuerstrahlbohren *n*, Düsenbohren, Flammenstrahlbohren [*früher: Schmelzbohren*]

jet-port = Flugplatz *m* für Düsenflugzeuge *npl*

jet probing, rod sounding = Bodenuntersuchung *f* mit Spülstangengerät *n*

~ pulverizer, micronizer, jet mill, reductionizer = pneumatische Prall(mahl)mühle *f*, Strahl(mahl)mühle, Luftstrahl-Prallzerkleinerer *m*

~ pump = Strahlpumpe *f*

jetting, see: wash boring

~ cutter rod = Spülstangengerät *n*

~ pipe = (Ein)Spülrohr *n* [*Pfahl m*]

~ rod = Spülstange *f*

jet(-turbine) fuel, see: jet ~

jetty, mole = Mole *f*

~, see: jutty

~ caisson = Molenschwimmkasten *m*

~ (or berth, or wharf) for oil fuel bunkering = Tankanlage *f*, Betankungsanlage

jet valve = Düsenschieber *m*

~ wave, stream wave = Strahlwelle *f*

JFR compound, jet and fuel resisting joint sealing compound = düsentreibstoffeste Fugenvergußmasse *f*

jib (Brit.); **boom** (US) = Ausleger *m* [*Bagger m, Kran m*]

~ boom (US) [*an extension piece hinged to the upper end of a crane boom*] = Auslegeransatz *m*, Hilfsausleger *m*

~ (derricking) cable (Brit.); see: boom (~) ~ (US)

~ hoist (Brit.); see: boom ~ (US)

jib type (Brit.)/**boom type** (US) **cable excavator and loader** = Schrapplader *m* mit Ausleger *m*, Fabrikat A.G. für BERGBAU- UND HÜTTENBEDARF, SALZGITTER, DEUTSCHLAND

jig-back system, "to and fro" ~ = Pendelbetrieb *m* [*Drahtseilschwebebahn f*]

jigger = Eindrehmaschine *f* [*Herstellung von Geschirrporzellan*]

jig haulage installation on the slope, self-acting incline(d plane), double-acting incline(d plane) = Bremsberg *m*

jim crow (Brit.), see: rail bender

jinniwink, A-derrick (crane) = A-Derrick-Kran *m*

job clean-up, cleanup and move out = Baustellen(auf)räumung *f*

~ "housekeeping" (US); **site organisation** = Baustellenorganisation *f*

job-mix concrete, field ~ = Baustellenbeton *m*

job office, site ~ = Bau(stellen)büro *n*

~ plan, see: construction (or work) schedule

~ record = Bautagebuch *n*

~ schedule, see: construction (or work) ~

~ site, see: building ~

~-~ installations, site facilities, site plant = Bau(stellen)einrichtung *f*

job-site material [*soil-cement*] = auf der Baustelle *f* anstehendes Material *n*
job-to-job transport (or hauling) = Ortswechsel *m* [*Baumaschine f*]
jockey weight, see: sliding ~
to joggle = kröpfen
joggle joint = Verzahnungsstoß *m*
john citizen = Durchschnittsbürger *m*
JOHNSON automatic batch plant = JOHNSON-(Misch-)Turm *m* mit Wabensilo *m*, Betonfabrik *f*, Fabrikat C. S. JOHNSON COMPANY, CHAMPAIGN, ILLINOIS, USA
to join, to trim = abbinden, zulegen [*Holzkonstruktion f*]
joining ba(u)lk = Bundbalken *m*
joint = Fuge *f*
~ = Nahtstelle *f* [*Schwarzdecke f*]
*****joint**, concrete ~ = (Beton)Fuge *f*
~ **assembly** = Kreuzgelenk *n*, Kardan *n*, Verbindung *f* komplett
~ **cast iron pipe** = Muffengußrohr *n*
~ **cement**, sewer joint compound, pipe joint(ing) compound = Muffenkitt *m*
~ **cleaner** = Fugenreinigungsgerät *n*, Fugenreiniger *m*
~ **compound melting furnace**, see: heating tank for melting joit sealing compounds
~ **concrete** = Fugenbeton *m*
~ **construction**, see: ~ finishing
~ **cutter**, (concrete) ~ ~, joint-cutting machine, (contraction) joint sawing machine, concrete cutter [*in USA also called "concrete saw"*] = Fugenschleifgerät *n* [*diese Bezeichnung ist technisch richtiger als die meist übliche „Fugen-Schneidmaschine" f oder „Fugen-Säge" f, oder „Fugenschneider" m*]
jointer plane = Bankhobel *m*
joint face = Fugenwandung *f*
~ **filler**, see: pre-formed (joint) ~
~ ~, see: joint-sealing compound
joint-filling composition, see: joint-sealing compound
joint finishing, ~ construction = Fugenherstellung *f*, Fugenausbildung *f*
~ ~ **bridge**, see: float ~
~ **grouting work**, ~ pouring = Fugenvergußarbeiten *fpl*

jointing, parting, structure (Geol.) = Absonderungsform *f*
~ **blade** = Fugenschneidscheibe *f*
~ **compound**, see: joint-sealing ~
~ ~ **for pipes** = Rohrkitt *m*
~ **in hollow-block masonry** = Fugenausbildung *f* von Hohlblockstein-Mauerwerk *n*
~ **sleeve**, sleeve joint = Dichtungsmuffe *f*
joint(ing) strip, see: pre-formed (joint) filler
~ **tool**, see: rounding ~
joint in reinforcement = Bewehrungsstoß *m*, Armierungsstoß *m*
~ **installing (or placing) machine** = (Beton)Fugeneinbaugerät *n*
jointless flooring = fugenloser (Fuß)Bodenbelag *m*
joint measurement = gemeinsames Aufmaß *n*
~ **mortar**, masonry ~, pointing ~ = Fugenmörtel *m*, Baumörtel, Mauermörtel
~ **profile** = Fugenprofil *n*
~ **raker** = Fugenreißer *m*
~ **ribbon** = Fugenband *n*
~ **sawing machine**, see: ~ cutter
joint-sealing compound, joint-filling composition, jointing compound, (joint) filler; paving joint sealer (US) = (Dehnungs)Fugenvergußmasse *f*, Vergußmasse, Dehnfugenvergußmasse
~ **machine**, pouring ~ = (Beton-)Fugenvergußgerät *n*
~ **strip**, see: pre-formed (joint) filler
joint slot = Fugenkerbe *f*
~ **spacing** = Fugenabstand *m*
*****joint(-)venture (firm)**, see: contracting combine
joint vibrator, see: (concrete) ~ ~
joist = Querbalken *m*
~ **shears**, joist shearing machine, I-iron ~ ~ ~ = Trägerschere *f*
jolting = schockende Rüttelung *f* [*Rüttelstampfmaschine f*]
~ **table** = Schocktisch *m*
Joosten (chemical solidification) process = Joosten-Verfahren *n*, Tiefkälteverfahren, chemische Verfestigung *f* nach Joosten
Joule effect = Joule-Effekt *m*

journal = Achszapfen *m*, Achsstumpf *m*, Achsstummel *m*, Achs(en)hals *m*, Schenkel *m* [*Teil der Achse, der im Lager ruht*]
~ = (Stütz)Zapfen *m*, Tragzapfen
~ = Lagerzapfen *m*
~ = Zeitschrift *f*
~ **bearing** = Traglager *n*
journeyman carpenter = Hamburger Zimmermann *m*
journey time = Fahrzeit *f*
*****Jubilee track system** (Brit.); see: light railroad system (US)
~ **wagon** (Brit.); see: steel tip wagon
jumbo [*a number of drills mounted on a mobile carriage, and used in tunnels*] = Tunneljumbo *m*
~ **brick** (US) = Tonhohlblock *m*, Blockziegel *m* [*Istmaß* $3^1/_2 : 7^1/_2 : 11^1/_2$ *Zoll, zwei Hohlräume mpl*]
~ **roll dry felt** [*roll roofing plant*] = Rohpappenrolle *f*
~ **utility** (US) = Tonhohlblock *m*, Blockziegel *m* [*Istmaß* $3^1/_2 : 3^1/_2 : 11^1/_2$ *Zoll, drei Hohlräume mpl*]
jumper = Bohrstahl *m* [*Drucklufthammer m*]
jumping frog, see: frog rammer
junction = Einmündung *f* [*Straße f*]
~ **plate**, see: gusset(-plate)
~ **point** = Verkehrsknoten(punkt) *m*
JUNG (shuttle) dumper K 40 = Autoschütter *m*, Fabrikat ARN. JUNG, LOKOMOTIVFABRIK, JUNGENTHAL, DEUTSCHLAND
Jurassic limestone = Jurakalk(stein) *m*
~ **reef** = Jurariff *n*
jute = Jute *f*
jutty, jetty [*a projecting part of a building*] = vorstehender Gebäudeteil *m*

K

KAELBLE truck tractor (US)/**motor tractor** (Brit.) = (Straßen)Zugmaschine *f*, Fabrikat CARL KAELBLE G.m.b.H., BACKNANG bei STUTTGART, DEUTSCHLAND
KAISER concrete pump = Betonpumpe *f*, Fabrikat OTTO KAISER K.G., OBERLAHNSTEIN, DEUTSCHLAND

KANAMITE [*Trademark*] = ein Leichtzuschlagstoff *m* in den USA
KANGO electric hammer [*Trademark*] = Elektro-(Bohr)Hammer *m*, Fabrikat WAGNER & CO., LIMBURG/LAHN, DEUTSCHLAND
kaolin, see: china clay
~ **clay** = kaolinitischer Ton *m*
kaolinisation = Kaolinisierung *f*
kaolinite (Min.) = Kaolinit *m*
Kaplan (water) turbine = Kaplanturbine *f* [*Flügelradturbine f mit verstellbaren Schaufeln fpl*]
Karst = Karst *m* [*Dinarische Alpen bis zum Skutarisee*]
~ **depression** = Karstwanne *f*
katabatic wind, down ~, **fall** ~ = Fallwind *m*
kataklastic rock, cataclastic ~ = Kataklasit *m*
~ **structure, cataclastic** ~ (Geol.) = kataklastische Gesteinsform *f*, Kataklase *f*
kauri butanol value = Kauributanolwert *m*
keel block = Kielstapel *m*
KEENOIL [*Trademark*] = Zinkweiß *n* [*Füllmittel in Kalkseifenfetten*]
keeping spare parts = Ersatzteilhaltung *f*
Kentish Rag (Brit.) = Kalksandstein aus dem Coombe-Bruch, Maidstone
keratophyre (Geol.) = Keratophyr *m*
kerb(stone) (Brit.); see: curb(stone)
kerf, saw ~ = Sägeschnitt *m*
kermesite, pyrostibnite (Min.) = Antimonblende *f*, Kermesit *m*
kernel-decomposition [*plagioclase*] = Erweichung *f* der Kristallmitte *f* [*Natronkalkfeldspat m*]
kerosene, see: lighting oil
kerosine, see: lighting oil
~ **coal**, see: (asphaltic) pyrobituminous ~
kersantite = Kersantit *m*, Kersanton *m*
kettle, heating ~ = Kochkessel *m*
kettle-calcined gypsum = Kesselgips *m*
kettle for heating joint filler, see: heating tank for melting joint sealing compounds
keuper marl = Keupermergel *m*
key, see: apex
~ = Keil *m*
~ = Schlüssel *m*
to key, see: to wedge

to key, see: to chink
keyed joint, tongued-and-groved ~ = gespundete Fuge *f*, genutete ~
key horizon (Geol.). see: datum ~
key ready = schlüsselfertig
~ seat = Keilsitz *m*
keyseater, see: draw-cut type ~
keystone, see: choke stone (or aggregate) ~ = Gewölbestein *m* in der Mitte *f* der Bogenkrone *f*
keyway = Kerbnut *f*, Keilnut *f*
~ cutter, see: push type keyway broaching machine
kibble = Kippkübel *m* [*Schachtfördergefäß n*]
kick-atomizing = Schlagzerstäubung *f* [*Diesel-Pfahlramme f*]
Kiel Canal, see: Baltic Ship Canal
kieselgur, diatomite, diatom(aceous) earth (Min.) = Kieselgur *f*
kieserite (Min.) = Kieserit *m*
~ nodule = Kieseritknolle *f*
KIF [*Trademark*] = Schwalbenschwanzbefestigung *f* auf Betonkonstruktionen *fpl* in den USA
kill-out of fish, fish mortality = Fischsterben *n*, Fischsterblichkeit *f*
kiln = Ofen *m*
seasoning ~ = Holztrocken~
kilndried = ofengetrocknet
~ building = Ofengebäude *n*
~ insulation = Ofenisolierung *f*
~ ring = Ofenring *m*
~ scum = Ofenschaum *m*
kilometre post = Kilometerstein *m*
kindling point = Flammpunkt *m*
kind of drive = Antriebsart *f*
kinematic viscosity = kinematische Viskosität *f*
kinetic coefficient of friction = Gleitreibungsbeiwert *m*
king pin; center journal (US) = Königszapfen *m*
~ ~ bearing, slewing journal ~ = Drehzapfenlager *n*
~ post, broach ~ = Hängesäule *f*
~ (~) truss = einfaches Hängewerk *n*, einsäuliges ~
kink = Klanke *f* [*Seil n*]
kish = Garschaum *m*

~ graphite = Garmschaumgraphit *m*
kit = Ausstattung *f*, Satz *m*
kitchen waste, see: household refuse
Kjellman-Franki machine = Dränmaschine *f*
Kleine floor = Kleine'sche (Stahlstein-) Decke *f*
klinker, see: clinker
klippe (Geol.) = Klippe *f*
knapsack sprayer = Tornister-Spritzgerät *n*
kneading action of traffic, traffic compaction [*pushes the particles into a closer and more permanent fit*] = Verkehrskomprimierung *f*, Knetwirkung *f*
~ compactor = Knetverdichter *m*
*****knee action stripping shovel** = Löffelgroßbagger *m* mit Kniehebelvorschubwerk *n*
~ of frame = Rahmenecke *f*
knife-edge load = Linienlast *f*
knife switch = Hebelschalter *m*
knitting frame oil = Wirkmaschinenöl *n*
knocking = Klopfen *n*
knock meter = Klopfmesser *m*
knot hole = Knorrenloch *n*
knot-joint = Knotenverbindung *f*
knotty dolomite = Knotendolomit *m*
knuckle = Kardandrehzapfen *m*, Knie *n*, Gelenk *n*
knurled nut = Bördelmutter *f*
kraft paper, Manila ~ = Hartpapier *n*
kryolith (Min.), see: cryolite
KSB rotary (air) compressor = Rotationskompressor *m*, Fabrikat KLEIN, SCHANZLIN & BECKER A. G., FRANKENTHAL/Pfalz, DEUTSCHLAND
"K" test, see: plate bearing test
K-truss = K-Fachwerk *n*
kunzite (Min.) = Kunzit *m*
kwhr. = Kilowattstunde *f*
kyanising = Kyanisierung *f*
kyanite, disthene (Min.) = Disthen *m*, Zyanit *m*

L

lab (US); **laboratory** = Labor(atorium) *n*
to label = etikettieren
labile, see: rapid-setting
lability, readiness to break = Labilität *f*

laboratory for materials testing, see: materials testing laboratory
~ mixer = Labor(atoriums)mischer *m*
(~) screen (US) = Rundloch-Labor(atoriums)sieb *n*
~ sieve (US) = Quadratloch-Labor(atoriums)sieb *n*
~ technician = Laborant *m*
labo(u)rer, unskilled worker = Hilfsarbeiter *m*
labo(u)r force = Arbeitskräfte *fpl*
~ office = Arbeitsamt *n*
~ saving = Arbeitsersparnis *f*
~ utilization = Einsatz *m* von Arbeitskräften *fpl*
labyrinth packing = Labyrinthdichtung *f* [*als Material n*]
~ seal = Labyrinthdichtung *f* [*als Dichtungsart f*]
laccolith, laccolite (Geol.) = Lakkolith *m*, Kuppel *f*
lacquer = Lack *m*
lactic acid = Milchsäure *f*
lacustrine clay = Seeton *m*
~ deposit, see: lake ~
ladder(-bucket) dredge(r), see: bucket-ladder ~
ladder chain carrying the buckets, bucket ladder, bucket elevator chain, chain of the (bucket) (type) elevator = Becherkette *f*, Eimerkette
~ ditcher, see: boom type trencher
~ frame = Eimerleiterrahmen *m*, Baggerleiterrahmen, Ausleger *m*
~ hoist = Eimerleiterwinde *f* [*Naßbagger m*]
~ scaffold(ing) = Leitergerüst *n*
~-type trenching machine, boom type trencher, boom type ditcher, boom type trenching machine, ladder ditcher = Eimerkettengrabenbagger *m*, Eimerleitergrabenbagger
ladle brick = Gießpfannenziegel *m*, Pfannenstein *m*
~ clay, see: foundry ~
lagging = Isolieren *n* [*Rohr n*]
~ = Auskleidung *f*, Verkleidung *f* [*Tunnel m*]
~, see: horizontal timber sheeting
lagoon = Lagune *f*

laid-dry bricks = ohne Mörtel *m* verlegte Ziegelsteine *mpl*
laitance = Zementmilch *f*, Feinschlämme *f*, (Beton)Schlämmschicht *f*
lake asphalt, ~ pitch = Seeasphalt *m*
~ belt = Seengürtel *m*
~ deposit, lacustrine ~ = Seenablagerung *f*
~ due to erosion, erosion lake = Austiefungssee *m*
~ dwelling = Pfahlbausiedlung *f*
lake-marl, bog lime = Seekreide *f*
lake ore = See-Erz *n*
~ pitch, see: ~ asphalt
~ ponded up by morainic material = Moräne(n)see *m*
~ ~ ~ ~ glacier = Gletschersee *m*
~ ~ ~ ~ lava = Lavastromsee *m*
~ shore = Seeufer *n*
lakeward(s) = seeseitig, seewärts
lamellar (or banded) twinning [*plagioclase*] = Viellingslamellierung *f*
laminaria = Laminarie *f*, Riementang *m*
laminated coal = Lettenkohle *f*
~, foliated ~ = Blätterkohle *f*
~ glass = Verbundglas *n*
~ insulating (wall) board = mehrlagige Dämmplatte *f*
~ limestone, platy ~, slabby ~ = Plattenkalk(stein) *m*, Kalkschiefer *m*
~ partition slab (Brit.) = 5fache Gipskartonplatte *f*, mehrlagige Zwischenwandplatte
~ sapropelic coal containing numerous animal remains = Plattenkohle *f*
~ shale = Blätterschiefer *m*
~ spring, see: flat ~
~ structure = Blättchenstruktur *f*
lamp black = Lampenruß *m*
~ kerosine = Leuchtpetroleum *n*
~ post fountain = Brunnenkandelaber *m*, Laternenpfahl *m* mit Brunnen *m*
lamprophyre = Lamprophyr *m*
lanarkite (Min.) = Kohlenbleivitriolspat *m*
Lancashire boiler with corrugated flues = Zweiwellrohrkessel *m*
lancet arch = überhöhter Spitzbogen *m*, lanzettförmiger ~
land (or shore) asphalt (or pitch) = Landasphalt *m* [*Trinidadasphalt m*]

land breeze, see: off-shore wind
~ chain, surveyor's ~ = Meßkette *f*
~ clearing, see: clearing (work)
~ ~ and rock rake, root and rock rake = Wurzel- und Felsrechen *m*
~-controlled climate = Landklima *n*
land drain, field ~, agricultural pipe ~ = Landdrän *m*
~ fill = Geländeauffüllung *f*, Geländeverfüllung, Geländeaufhöhung *f*
~ form, see: configuration of the ground
landed cost of plant and equipment = cif-Wert *m* der Maschinen und Geräte
landing = (Treppen)Podest *m, n*, Treppenabsatz *m*
~ cross, ~ "T" = Landekreuz *n* [*Flugplatz m*]
~ direction indicator = Landerichtungsanzeiger *m* [*Flugplatz m*]
landing-port, port of discharge = Löschhafen *m*
landing runway = Nur-Landebahn *f*
~ strip = Landestreifen *m*
land parcel, see: plot
~ pier, shore ~ [*bridge*] = Landpfeiler *m*
~ pitch, see: land asphalt
~ plaster, see: finely-ground gypsum
~ purchase, see: acquisition of land
*land reclamation, reclamation of ~ = (Neu)Landgewinnung *f*
~ roller = Ackerwalze *f*
landscaped strip, see: grassy median ~
landscape engineer = Landschaftsgestalter *m*
landscaping, landscape treatment, landscape development = Landschaftsgestaltung *f*
(land)slide [*earth slip upon a large scale*] (Geol.) = Rutschung *f*, Erdrutschung *f*, Absetzung *f*
landslip due to tectonic movement = Gleitflächenrutschung *f*
~ ~ ~ the effect of earth tremors = Rutschung *f* infolge dynamischer Einflüsse *mpl*, ~ ~ Erschütterung *f*
~ ~ ~ ~ ~ loading = Rutschung *f* infolge Zunahme *f* der Belastung *f*
land speculation = Bodenspekulation *f*
~ upheaval = Bodenhebung *f*
~ use planning = Flächennutzung *f*

landward = landseitig
land wind, see: off-shore ~
lane = Gasse *f*, Gäßchen *n*
~, traffic ~ = (Fahr)Spur *f*, Verkehrsspur
~ joint, see: longitudinal ~
~ marking = (Fahr)Spurmarkierung *f*
~ move, moving between lanes, lane change = Umsetzen *n* [*Betondeckenfertiger m*]
~ pour = Betonstreifeneinbau *m* [*Betonstraße f*]
Lang lay = Gleichschlag *m*, Längsschlag *m*, Albertschlag, Parallelschlag [*Drahtseil n*]
lantern = Laterne *f*
~ coal, cannel ~ = Kennelkohle *f*
~ light = Laternenoberlicht *n*
lap = Überlappung *f*
lapilli [*singular: lapillus*] = Lapilli *f*, vulkanische Steinchen *npl*
lap joint = Überlappungsstoß *m*
~ ~ riveting = Überlappungsnietung *f*
lapped connexion = Stoßüberdeckung *f*
larch = Lärche *f*
lard lubrication = Speckschmierung *f*
large bucket wheel excavator = Großschaufelradbagger *m*
~ building block = Großformatstein *m*
large-capacity mixer, ~ mixing machine = Großraummischer *m*, Großraummischmaschine *f*
~ stone spreader box = Großraumschotterverteiler *m*
large dam (concrete) plant = Talsperrenbeton-Aufbereitungsanlage *f*
large-diameter hole drilling and blasting, ~ ~ work = Großbohrloch(spreng)verfahren *n*
large finisher, ~ finishing machine = Großfertiger *m*
~ gas engine = Großgasmaschine *f*
~ hole drilling = Großkaliberbohren *n*
large-leaved lime tree = großblätt(e)rige Linde *f*, Sommerlinde
large (paving) sett = Großpflasterstein *m*
(~) primary crusher (or breaker), see: stone breaker (type crusher)
~ reservoir = Großspeicher *m* [*Talsperre f*]
~-scale project site = Großbaustelle *f*

large sett paving = Großpflaster(decke) n, (f)
~ shovel (type) excavator = Großlöffelbagger m
LARSSEN (sheet) pile [*Trademark*] = LARSSEN-Spundbohle f, LARSSEN-Profil n
larvicide = Larvenvertilgungsmittel n
larvikite, see: laurvikite
lateral = Sammelstrang m [*z. B. bei einem Sandfilter* m, n]
~ bracing, see: transverse ~
~ buckling = seitliches Knicken n, Kippen n [*Träger* m]
~ canal = Seitenkanal m, Nebenkanal
~ drainage, see: herringbone ~
~ earth (or soil) pressure = Erddruck m
~ ~ (~ ~) ~ at rest, neutral lateral earth pressure, lateral earth pressure at consolidated equilibrium = waag(e)rechter natürlicher Erddruck m im unberührten Boden m
~ friction = Seitenreibung f
~ moraine = Wallmoräne f, Seitenmoräne, Randmoräne, Ganzdecke f
~ rigidity = Seitensteifigkeit f
~ shear, side thrust = achsrechter Schub m, Axialschub, Seitenschub
~ slide, failure by spreading = Böschungsrutschung f, Gleitflächenbruch m
~ spillway = Streichwehr n
~ strain = Seitendehnung f, Querdehnung
~ thrust, side ~ = Seitenschub m, Axialschub, achsrechter Schub
laterally loaded continuous frame = normal zu seiner Ebene belastetes Rahmentragwerk n
laterite = Laterit m [*verwittertes rotes Tongestein* n]
~ road, lateritic ~ = Lateritstraße f
lateritic clay = lateritischer Ton m
latex [*plural form: latices*] = Latex m
lath = Leiste f
lathe = Drehbank f
lath-like [*plagioclase*] = leistenförmig
LATICRETE [*Trademark*] = Gummi-Beton m für Bodenbeläge mpl, Fabrikat UNITED STATES RUBBER CO.
lattice beam; see: ~ girder (Brit.)

~ column = Fachwerkstab m
lattice(d) (crane) jib (Brit.); ~ (crane) boom (US); steel-lattice(d) (~) ~ = Gitterausleger m [*Bagger* m]
~ member = Gitterstab m
~ purlin = Gitterpfette f, Fachwerkpfette
lattice (or braced) girder (Brit.); ~ (or braced) beam = Gitterträger m, Gitterbalken m, Gitterbalkenträger
~ ~ floor slab (Brit.); ~ beam ~ ~ = Gitter(balken)trägerdecke f, Gitterbalkendecke f
~ hoarding = Lattenhorde f
~ purlin = Fachwerkpfette f, Gitterpfette
~ structure = Kristallgitter n
~ ~ = Gitterkonstruktion f
~ suspension bridge = Fachwerkhängebrücke f
lattice-type composite beam = Fachwerkverbundträger m
latticework, framework = Fachwerk n
~ mast = Gitter(werks)mast m
laumontite (Min.) = Laumontit m
launching ceremony = Stapellauf m
~ speed = Ablaufgeschwindigkeit f [*Stapellauf* m]
laundry waste = Wäschereiabwasser n
la(u)rvikite = Laurvikit m
lauterite = Lauterit m (Min.)
lava = Lava f
~ flow, extrusive rock, (igneous) volcanic rock [*cooled on the Earth's surface*] = Ergußgestein n, vulkanisches Gestein, Durchbruchsgestein, Effusivgestein, Ausbruchsgestein, Extrusivgestein, Oberflächengestein, suprakrustales Erstarrungsgestein, Vulkanit m
~ pumice = Bimssteinlava f
lawn mower = Grasmäher m
~ roller, grass ~ = Rasenwalze f
law of elasticity = Elastizitätsgesetz n
lay = Schlag m [*Drahtseil* n]
layback [*a term used in India for a satellite airfield in rear of an operational area for use upon withdrawel*] = Auffangflugplatz m
to (lay) bare = freilegen
lay bye = Liegeplatz m [*Kanal* m]

layby(e), passing place, waiting-bay, halting place (Brit.); roadside rest (US) [*the local widening of a narrow carriageway to enable vehicles to pass each other*] = Rastplatz *m* [*Straße f*]
laydown rate = Einbauleistung *f* [*Straßenfertiger m*]
layer, lift, course, pour = (Einbau)Schicht *f*
~ boundary = Schichtgrenze *f*
layer(ed) construction = Schichtenbauweise *f*, Lagenbauweise, Lagenschüttung *f* [*Erdbau m*]
~ map, see: contour ~
layer of strands, strand layer = Seillage *f* [*Brücke f*]
~ silicate, clay mineral = Schichtsilikat *n*, Tonmineral *n*
~ ~ structure = Schicht-Silikat-Struktur *f*
laying and finishing machine, see: finisher
~ capacity = Einbauvermögen *n* [*Schwarzbelageinbaumaschine f*]
~ (or spreading) gang (or team, or crew, or party) = Einbaukolonne *f*, Einbautrupp *m* [*Straßenbau m*]
~ machine = Einbaugerät *n* [*Straßenbau m*]
~ site, see: spreading ~
~ temperature = Einbautemperatur *f*
lay-out (plan) = Lageplan *m*
lazulite (Min.) = Lasurspat *m*
leaching = Auslaugen *n* [*Boden m*]
lead, run (Brit.); haul(age) (distance) = Förderweite *f*, [*in Österreich: Bringungsweg m*] [*Förderung f im Erdbau m*]
~, guide rail = Führungsschiene *f*
~ acetate, see: acetate of lead
~ arsenate = Bleiarsenat *n*
~ azide = Bleiazid *n*
~ ~ alumin(i)um detonator, tetrylazide ~ = Aluminiumsprengkapsel *f*
~ bronze = Bleibronze *f*
leaded fuel = gebleiter Kraftstoff *m*
~ petrol (Brit.) = Bleibenzin *n*
leader drain, main ~ = Hauptdrän *m*
lead(er)s = Doppelmäkler *m*, Läuferruten *fpl* [*Rammanlage f*]
"lead" firm; see: sponsor (US)
~ glance (Min.), see: galena
~ glass = Bleiglas *n*

leading, teaming (Brit.) = Bodenförderung *f* mit Pferd *n* und Wagen *m*
~ edge = vordere Bohlenkante *f* [*Straßenfertiger m*]
~ hand = Vorarbeiter *m*
lead joint = bleivergossene Stemm-Muffe *f*
~ ore = Bleierz *n*
~ paint = Bleifarbe *f*
~ poisoning = Bleivergiftung *f*
~ seal = Bleiplombe *f*
~ sealing plier = Plombierzange *f*
~ slag = Blei(hochofen)schlacke *f*
~ speiss = Bleispeise *f*
~ susceptibility = Bleiempfindlichkeit *f*
~ telluride = Tellurblei *n*
~ time = Anlaufzeit *f*
~-tin solder, (plumber's) ~, plumber's metal = Lötzinn *n*
lead wool = Bleiwolle *f*
leaf, see: barrier plate
~ = Klappenkörper *m*
~ clay, see: varve(d) (glacial) ~
~ gate, see: vertical ~ ~
~ mould = Blatterde *f*
~ peat = Blättertorf *m*, Laubtorf
~ shale = Blätterschiefer *m*
~ spring, see: flat ~
leafwood, see: deciduous wood
leak(age) = Leckstelle *f*, undichte Stelle *f*
lean coal = Magerkohle *f*
~ gas = Magergas *n*
leaning ram = Hydraulikzylinder *m* zur Sturzverstellung *f* der Vorderräder *npl*
Leaning Tower of Pisa = Schiefer Turm *m* von Pisa
leaning wheel mechanism = Sturzverstellung *f* der Vorderräder *npl* [*Motorstraßenhobel m*]
lean lime, poor ~, ~ quicklime = Magerkalk *m*
~ mix = magere Mischung *f*, mageres Gemisch *n*
~ ~ concrete base = Magerbetontragschicht *f*
~ (-mixed) concrete = Magerbeton *m*, Füllbeton, Sparbeton, zementarmer Beton
lean-to builders' hoist = Anlegeaufzug *m*
leaping frog, see: frog rammer
least radius of gyration = kleinster Trägheitshalbmesser *m*

leather grease = Lederfett *n*
~ **hand pad** = Lederhandschutz *m*
~ **oil** = Lederöl *n*
~ **tar** = Lederteer *m*
lecture hall, see: seat ~ ~
ledge (Geol.) = Bastion *f*
~ **rock**, see: bed ~
Lee-Mc-Call method (or system) (of prestressed concrete construction) [*consists of high-tensile steel bars up to one inch or more in diameter*] = Spannmethode *f* unter Verwendung hochgespannter Stähle *mpl* mit Kreisquerschnitt *m* [*Spannbeton m*]
leg = senkrechter Jochpfahl *m*
~ = Stiel *m* [*Rahmen m*]
legal payload = zulässige Nutzlast *f* [*LKW m*]
legend = Zeichenerklärung *f*
legibility distance = Lesbarkeitsweite *f*
(leg) tripod = Stativ *n*
lemniscate = Lemniskate *f*
lengthsman, road mender, maintenance man = Straßenwärter *m*
lens-shaped, see: lenticular
lenticle of clay = Tonlinse *f*
lenticular, lens-shaped = linsenförmig
LEOBA stressing apparatus [*Trademark*] = LEOBA-Spannglied *n*
lepidocrocite (Min.) = Lepidokrokit *m*, Rubinglimmer *m* [*hieß ursprünglich Goethit*]
lepidomelane (Min.) = Lepidomelan *m*, eisenreicher Biotit *m*
lessee = Mieter *m* [*Baumaschine f*]
lessening fold = ausklingende Falte *f* (Geol.)
lesser yellow trefoil = kleiner Klee *m*
lessor = Vermieter *m* [*Baumaschine f*]
Le TOURNEAU portable crane, TOURNACRANE [*Trademark*] = Einachs-Schlepperkran *m*, Fabrikat Le TOURNEAU-WESTINGHOUSE CO., PEORIA, ILLINOIS, USA
lettering = Beschriften *n*, Beschriftung *f*
letter of award, notice ~ ~ = Auftragsschreiben *n*
~ ~ **capacity** = Befähigungsnachweisschreiben *n*
~ **wood**, snake ~, speckled ~ = Schlangenholz *n*, Letterholz *n*

letting (or award) of contract, contract award = Auftragerteilung *f*, Vergabe *f*
leucite (Min.) = Leuzit *m* [*früher: weißer Granat n*]
leucitite = Leuzitit *m*
leucoxene (Min.) = Leukoxen *m*, Titanomorphit *m*
levee, dike (US); dyke (Brit.); embankment, fill, flood bank = Hochwasserdeich *m*, Uferdamm *m*, HW-Schutzdamm *m*
~ **road** (US) = Hochwasserdeichstraße *f*
level = Geländehöhe *f*, Niveau *n*, Kote *f*
~ = Nivellier(instrument) *n*
~, water ~, spirit ~, air ~, hand ~ ~ = Wasserwaage *f*, Libelle *f*
~ **apron** = waagerechtes Sturzbett *n*
~ **bar screen**, see: flat ~ ~
~ **canal**, ditch ~ = Kanal *m* mit waag(e)rechter Sohle *f*
~ **country**, flat ground = Flachland *n*
~ **crossing**, see: ~ (railway) ~
~ **grizzly**, see: flat bar screen
level(l)er, planer (Brit.) = Planiergerät *n*
level(l)ing, survey of heights = Nivellieren *n*, Höhenaufnahme *f*, Höhenmessung *f*
~, striking-off, strike-off = Abgleichen *n*, Abziehen *n*, Abstreichen *n*
~ **arm**, screed side arm = Schwenkarm *m*, Lenkerhebel *m* [*Schwarzbelageinbaumaschine f*]
~ **beam**, see: strike-off (screed)
~ **control** = automatischer Schichtausgleich *m* [*Schwarzbelageinbaumaschine f*]
~ **(or regulating) course (or underlay)** = Ausgleichschicht *f*, Ausgleichlage *f*
~ **operations**, see: grading (works)
~ **plank** = Waagscheit *n*
~ **screed**, see: strike-off (screed)
~ **staff** = Nivellierlatte *f*
~ **underlay**, see: ~ course
~ **works**, see: grading (~)
(level-)luffing crane = Wippdrehkran *m*
level of background noises = Störpegel *m*
~ ~ **construction work** = Bauhöhe *f* [*Serienfertigung von Schwimmkästen auf beweglichen Plattformen*]
~ ~ **foundation** = Fundationskote *f*, Gründungshöhe *f*

level of no strain (Geol.**)** = spannungslose Niveaufläche *f*
~ ~ solidification = Erstarrungsniveau *n* [*Magma n*]
~ ~ storage water (Brit.); capacity level, storage ~ (US); height of the maximum storage ~ = Stauziel *n*, Stauspiegel *m*
to level out = einebnen
level peg, see: grade ~
~ plane surface = planebene Oberfläche *f*
~ plug = Kontrollschraube *f*
~ (railway) crossing (Brit.); ~ (railroad) ~ (US) = (niveaugleicher) Bahnübergang *m*, schienengleiche Niveaukreuzung *f*, Niveauübergang
~ reach = Haltung *f*, Streckenabschnitt *m*, Kanalhaltung *f*, Staustrecke *f*, Stauhaltung
~ roller runway = waag(e)rechte Rollenbahn *f*
~ screen, horizontal ~ = Horizontalsieb *n*
~ ~ of bars, see: flat bar screen
~ with compass = Nivelliertachymeter *n*
lever arm = Hebelarm *m*
lever-arm deflection indicator, Benkelman beam (apparatus) = Gerät *n* zur Messung *f* der Durchbiegung *f* von Straßendecken *fpl*
lever control = Hebelbedienung *f*, Hebelbetätigung
~ ratchet = Hebelknarre *f*
~ rod = Hebelstange *f*
lewis, stone lifting bolt = Keilklaue *f*, Steinwolf *m*
liability insurance = Haftpflichtversicherung *f*
Lias(sic) formation = Liasformation *f*
license fee = Zulassungsgebühr *f* [*Auto n*]
~ tax = Lizenzabgabe *f*
lick roller, see: P. B. S. laying machine
lid = Deckel *m*
LIEBHERR revolving tower crane = Turmdrehkran *m*, Fabrikat H. LIEBHERR WERK 1, KIRCHDORF/ILLER (WTTBG.), DEUTSCHLAND
life, service ~, service (time) = Liegezeit *f* [*Straßendecke f*]
life-buoy = Rettungsboje *f*
lift = Aufzug *m*
~, layer, pour, course = Einbauschicht *f*

lift-and-carry crane, tractor-drawn ~ = Einachs-Schlepperkran *m*, Einachskrananhänger *m*
(lift and) force pump = Druckpumpe *f*
lift bridge, lifting ~, vertical ~ ~ = Hubbrücke *f*
lifter = Stößel *m*, Ausrückhebel *m*
lift fork = Lastgabel *f*
lifting appliance, see: elevating plant
~ arm = Hubarm *m* [*Frontlader m*]
~ bar, see: dog
~ block, see: (block and) tackle
~ bridge, see: lift ~
~ cable, see: ~ rope
~ chain, hoist(ing) ~ = Hubkette *f*
~ crane = Hubkran *m* [*im Gegensatz zum grabbing crane* = Greiferkran]
~, dropping and turning mixing action = Freifallmischung *f*, Freifallmischen *n*
~ gate, vertical ~ ~ = Hubschütz(e) *n*, (*f*), Hubwehr *n*
~ hook, hoist(ing) ~ = Lasthaken *m*
~ limit switch = Hubendschalter *m*
~ magnet(o), crane ~, electric ~ ~ = Last(hebe)magnet *m*, Hubmagnet
~ platform, hoist(ing) ~ = Hebebühne *f*
lift(ing) pump with bucket valve piston = Hubpumpe *f* mit Ventilkolben *m*
~ ~ ~ hollow plunger = Hubpumpe *f* mit Rohrkolben *m*
lifting rope, ~ cable, hoist(ing) ~ = Hubseil *n*
~ tackle, see: elevating plant
~ tongs, stone (~) ~ = Steinzange *f*
LIFTMOBIL [*Trademark*] = Gabelstapler *m*, Fabrikat MIAG, BRAUNSCHWEIG, DEUTSCHLAND
lift (or chamber) navigation (or inland) lock = Kammerschleuse *f*
~ of a lock = Schleusengefälle *n*, Fallhöhe *f*
~ platform truck = Plattform-Hubkarre(n) *f*, (*m*)
lift slab = Hubplatte *f*
lift-slab method = Verfahren *n* bei dem große Tragflächen *fpl* (Decken *fpl*, Fußböden *mpl*) für die Gesamtfläche des Bauwerkes *n* an Ort und Stelle gegossen und hydraulisch in ihre jeweilige Position *f* gebracht werden

lift truck, see: (industrial) ~ ~
~ winch = Mastwinde *f* [*Kletter-Turmdrehkran m*]
light brush and debris = leichtes Buschwerk *n* und grobes Unkraut *n*
~ buoy, luminous ~ = Leuchtboje *f*
~ concrete, see: light-weight ~
~ court = Lichthof *m*
~ due = Leuchtturmabgabe *f*
light-duty (pile) driver = Leicht(pfahl)ramme *f*
~ power roller = Kleinmotorwalze *f*
lightened silver = Blicksilber *n*
lighter = Leichter *m*
light frame type pile driving plant (or piling plant) = Leicht(gerüst)ramme *f*
light gauge carriageway, orthotropic(al) plate, fine meshed carriageway grid, light gauge decking, orthogonal anisotropic plate = Leichtfahrbahn *f*, orthotrope Platte *f*
~ ~ steel construction = Stahlleichtbau *m*
lighthouse = Leuchtturm *m*
lighting = Beleuchtung *f*
~ = Befeuerung *f* [*Flugplatz m*]
~ column, see: (street) ~ ~
~ oil, illuminating ~, paraffin (oil) (Brit.); kerosine, kerosene = Leuchtöl *n*, (Leucht)Petroleum *n*, Kerosin *n*
~ standard, see: (street) lighting column
light metal cap = Blech(aufsteck)hülse *f* [*Fugendübel m*]
~ ~ tubular scaffold(ing) = Leichtmetallrohrgerüst *n*, Leichtmetallrohrrüstung *f*
~ (mono)tower crane, ~ rotating tower crane, **~** revolving tower crane = Leichtbau(dreh)kran *m*, Leicht-Turmdrehkran
lightning tube, see: fulgurite
light oil = Leichtöl *n*
~ permeability = Lichtdurchlässigkeit *f*
~ petroleum, petroleum leve = Leichtpetroleumraffinat *n*
~ plant = Lichtanlage *f*
***light railroad system,** narrow gage ~ (US); Jubilee track system, light railway system, field railway system (Brit.); narrow ga(u)ge track system = Feldbahnanlage *f*
~ railway material = Feld- und Industriebahngerät·*n*
light-red silver ore (Min.), see: proustite
light reflectance = Lichtreflexion *f*
~ ropeway = Kleinseilbahn *f*
lightship, light-vessel = Feuerschiff *n*
light-traffic road = Straße *f* für leichten Verkehr *m*
light-weight aggregate concrete = Beton *m* mit leichten Zuschlägen *mpl* (oder Zuschlagstoffen *mpl*)
~ bridge deck = Leichtfahrbahn *f*
~ building board (or slab) = Leichtbauplatte *f*
~ ~ unit = Leichtbauteil *m*
~ composite floor of prefabricated steel lattice girders and filler tiles = Stahlleichtträgerdecke *f* mit Hohlkörpern *mpl*
light(-weight) concrete = Leichtbeton *m* [*in Deutschland Raumgewichte von 250 bis 1800 kg/m³*]
lightweight concrete aggregate = Leichtbeton-Zuschlag(stoff) *m*
~ ~ ~ (US); bloating clay (Brit.) = Blähton *m*
~ ~ block = Leichtbetonstein *m*
~ fill = leichte Aufschüttung *f*
~ floor (slab) = Leichtträgerdecke *f*
~ no-fines concrete wall = geschüttete Leichtbetonwand *f*
~ section, light ga(u)ge ~, **~** structural shape = Leichtprofil *n*
~ structural clay product = keramisches Leichtbauerzeugnis *n*
~ ~ shape = Stahlleichtprofil *n*
light wind, breeze = flaue Brise *f*
lignification = Verholzung *f*
lignin tar = Ligninteer *m*
lignite = Lignit *m*, bituminöses Holz *n*, Xylit *m*
~ tar = Lignitteer *m*
lignum vitae = Guajakholz *n*, Pockholz
liking, affinity = Affinität *f*, Verbindungsstreben *n*
limberoller, see: flexible (belt) conveyor idler
limburgite = Limburgit *m*
lime, CaO, see: quicklime

lime = allgemeiner Ausdruck für Kalk *m*
~ accumulation = Kalkanreicherung *f* [*Boden m*]
~ agitator = Kalkrührwerk *n*
~ boil = Schlackenfrischreaktion *f*
~ burning, ~ calcination = Kalkbrennen *n*
~ cement mortar, cement-lime ~
~ concrete = Kalkbeton *m*
~-depositing, lime-precipitating, lime-secreting = kalkablagernd, kalkabscheidend, kalkausfällend
lime-fel(d)spar (Min.), see: anorthite
lime-gravel, see: clay-grit
lime-gypsum plaster, reacted ~ = Kalkhydrat-Raschbinder *m*, Gips-Kalk-Putzmörtel *m*
lime hydrate, see: hydrated lime (powder)
~ kiln = Kalkofen *m*
limelight = Kalklicht *n*, Knallgaslicht
lime lye = Kalklauge *f*
~ marble, calcic ~ = Kalkmarmor *m*
~ marl, calcareous ~ = Kalkmergel *m* [75—90% $CaCO_3$]
~ milk, see: cream of lime
~ mortar, L. M. = Kalkmörtel *m*, Mauerspeise *f*
~ mud rock, see: calcilutyte
~ paste, ~ putty, hydrate putty, pit lime = Kalkbrei *m*, Kalkteig *m*, eingesumpfter Kalk *m*, Sumpfkalk, Grubenkalk
~ ~ handling pump = Kalkpumpe *f*
~ plant = Kalkwerk *n*
~ plaster = Kalkputz *m*
~ process, see: ~ (softening) ~
~ ~, see: hydrated ~ ~
~ putty, see: ~ paste
~ raker, see: mortar beater
~ rock = Kalksilikatfels *m*
~ sand, calcareous ~ = Kalksand *m*
~ ~ brick, sand-lime ~ = Kalksandstein *m*, weißer Mauerstein
~ sandstone = Kalksandstein *m*
~ silicate, calcium ~ = Kalksilikat *m*
~ ~ rock, calcariferous petrosilex = Kalkhornfels *m*
~ slaking drum = Kalklöschtrommel *f*
lime-soda fel(d)spar, plagioclase, soda-lime plagioclase, soda-lime fel(d)spar (Min.) = Plagioklas *m*, Schiefspalter *m*, Natronkalkfeldspat *m*

~ (softening) process = Kalk-Sodaverfahren *n* [*Wasseraufbereitung f*]
lime (softening) process = Kalk-Verfahren *n* [*Wasseraufbereitung f*]
~ spreading, see: liming
lime-stabilized = kalkverfestigt
limestone, calcium carbonate, $CaCO_3$ = Kalkstein *m*, kohlensaurer Kalk *m*
~ (or calcareous) facies = Kalkfazies *f*
~ filler = Kalksteinfüller *m*
~ gravel = Kalksteinkies *m*
~ marble, see: calcitic ~
~ masonry = Kalksteinmauerwerk *n*
~ mastic = Kalksteinmastix *m*
~ rubble = Kalksteinschüttpacke *f*
~ slate, see: calcareous ~
~ tarmacadam = Kalkstein-Teermakadam *m*
~ washing machine, ~ washer = Kalksteinwäsche *f*, Kalksteinwaschmaschine *f*
lime surk(h)i sand mortar = Kalksandmörtel *m* mit Zusatz an gebranntem Ton *m*
~ suspension = Kalksuspension *f*
to limewash, to whitewash = kalken, weißen, tünchen
limey, see: calcareous
liming, lime spreading = Kalkung *f* [*Boden m*]
~ material, see: aglime
limited submission, ~ public tender action, ~ tendering = beschränkte Ausschreibung *f*
limit ga(u)ge = Grenzlehre *f*
limiting gradient, ruling ~ = höchstzulässige Gradiente *f*
~ grading curve, see: gradation limit
~ line = Begrenzungslinie *f*
~ screen = Durchgangssieb *n*
~ span = Stützweitengrenzwert *m*, Grenzwert *m* für Stützweiten *fpl*
~ value, limit ~ = Grenzwert *m*
limit of elasticity, elastic limit = Elastizitätsgrenze *f*
~ switsch, stop ~ = Anschlagschalter *m*, Begrenzungsschalter, Endschalter
limnology = Seenkunde *f*, Limnologie *f*
limonite (Min.) = Limonit *m*
linarite, $PbSO_4 \cdot Cu(OH)_2$ (Min.) = Linarit *m*, Bleilasur *m*

lineal metre — liquid petrolatum

lineal metre, Lin. M. = laufender Meter *m*
linear earthquake = axiales (Erd)Beben *n*
line drawing, ~ sketch = Strichzeichnung *f*
~ load, (col)linear ~, knife-edge ~ = Linienlast *f*, Streckenlast *f*, Schneidenlast
*line marker, see: road-marking machine
~ marking paint, see: traffic(-zoning) ~
~ of buckets, bucket line = Becherreihe *f*, Eimerreihe, Becherstrang *m*, Eimerstrang
~ ~ centers (US); see: locus of centres (Brit.)
~ ~ equal rainfall (Brit.); see: isohyetal (US)
~ ~ flow, flow line = Strömungslinie *f*
~ ~ influence = Einflußlinie *f*
~ ~ least pressure = Mindestdrucklinie *f*
~ ~ pressure = Stützlinie *f*
~ ~ rails; see: rail(way) track (Brit.)
(~ ~) route = Trasse *f*
~ ~ rupture, see: envelope of failure
~ ~ sight = Visierlinie *f*
~ ~ sliding = Gleitlinie *f*
liner = Zylinderlaufbüchse *f*
~ I. D. = innerer Durchmesser *m* der Zylinderlaufbüchse *f*
~ segment, mixer ~ ~, sectional liner ~ = (Mischer-)Segmentteil *m*
line squall = Böengewitter *n*
ling heath, dwarf-shrub ~ = Zwergheide *f*
lining = Verkleidung *f*, Auskleidung *f*
~ = Bremsbackenbelag *m*
~, sheeting = Verschalung *f*
~ brick = Futterziegel *m*, Futterstein *m*
~ form, see: falsework
~ machine = Auskleidungsmaschine *f*
~ service group, facing kit = Bremsbelagsatz *m*
~ tube, casing pipe = Futterrohr *n*
linkage = Gestänge *n*
link assembly = (Gleis)Kettenband *n* ohne Platten *fpl*, Kupplungsglied *n*
~ drive = Kulissenantrieb *m*
linked boundary condition = verkoppelte Randbedingung *f*
~ system, coordinated control system = koordiniertes Signalisierungssystem *n*
link tooth saw, see: chain ~
~ (type) chain = Gliederkette *f*

to link up = aufschließen, erschließen [*ein Gebiet n verkehrsmäßig*]
LINNHOFF drying and mixing plant = Trocken- und Mischanlage *f*, Fabrikat EDUARD LINNHOFF, BERLIN-TEMPELHOF
linoleum tar = Linoleumteer *m*
linseed oil = Leinöl *n*
~ ~ paint = Leinölanstrichfarbe *f*
~ ~ varnish = Leinölfirnis *m*
linsey = streifiger Sandstein *m*
lintel = Sturz *m*, Oberschwelle *f*
~ beam = Sturzträger *m*
~ machine, (precast) concrete joist machine = Balkenformmaschine *f*, Hohlbalkenmaschine
Linville truss, N-~, Pratt ~, Whipple-Murphy ~ = Pratt-Träger *m*
lip = Schneidkante *f* [*Baggerlöffel m*]
liparite, rhyolite = Rhyolith *m*, Liparit *m*
liquefaction failure = Rutschung *f* durch Verflüssigung *f*
~ of air = Luftverflüssigung *f*
liquid air = Sprengluft *f*, flüssige Luft *f*
~ asphalts, asphaltic materials (US) = Sammelbegriff *m* für Verschnittbitumen *npl* und Straßenöle *npl*
liquidated damages for delay in completion = bei Nichteinhaltung *f* der Baufrist *f* zu zahlende Konventionalstrafe *f*
liquid binder, see: fluid ~
~ fuel [*fuel oils and motor fuels*] = Sammelbegriff *m* für Heizöle *npl* und Treibstoffe *mpl*, flüssiger Treibstoff *m*
~ glue = Klärleim *m*
~ handling pump = Flüssigkeitspumpe *f*
~ hauler = Flüssigkeits-Transportfahrzeug *n*
~ limit, LL, [*symbol:* w_L] = Fließgrenze *f*, unterer Plastizitätszustand *m*, W_f [*Boden m*]
*liquid limit device, mechanical ~ ~ ~, apparatus for plasticity test, Casagrande liquid limit machine = Gerät *n* zur Bestimmung *f* der Fließgrenze *f*, Fließgrenzengerät *n*
~ oxygen = flüssiger Sauerstoff *m*
~ paraffin, medicinal ~ = Paraffinöl *n* Medizinalöl
~ petrolatum = flüssige Vaseline *f*

liquid phase cracking — loading shovel

liquid phase cracking = thermisches Kracken *n*
~ rosin, see: tall oil
~ stabilizer, see: fluid ~
~ waste, see: foul water
~ water content of snow = Gehalt *m* an freiem Wasser *n* im Schnee *m*
liquidity index = Fließindex *m*
list of equipment, plant register = Geräteliste *f*
~ of hiring charges for building plant and contractors' equipment, schedule of rates for the hire of contractors' and building plant; equipment rental compilation (US) = Baugerätemietsatzliste *f*
~ price = Listenpreis *m*
lithia mica, lithium ~ (Min.) = Lithiumglimmer *m*
litho-carbon = reines Bitumen *n* aus dem Kalkstein *m* von Uvalde County, Texas, USA
litmus paper = Lackmuspapier *n*
lithographic stone = Lithographen-Kalkstein *m*
*****lithosphere** = Außenmantel *m*
littoral current, see: shore ~
~ deposit = litorale Meeresablagerung *f*
~ drift, see: ~ current
~ zone = Ebbe- und Flutzone *f*, Litoral *n*
live axle, see: drive ~
~ fence, roadside hedge = Straßenhecke *f*
~ load(ing) = Nutzlast *f*, Gebrauchslast
~ (screen) frame, vibrated ~ = Schwingsiebrahmen *m*
~ side of the bucket sheave = bewegliche Seite *f* der Löffelseilrolle *f*
~ steam = Frischdampf *m*
~ storage bin = Abziehsilo *m*
liver peat = Lebertorf *m*
living allowance, subsistence (~), cost of living ~, separation ~ = Auslösung *f*
~ caravan = Wohnwagen *m*
~ density = Wohndichte *f*
~ hut = Wohnbaracke *f*
~ quarters, personnel housing = Unterkünfte *fpl*
load = Last *f*, Belastung *f*
~ application, application of load = Lastaufbringung *f*

load-bearing prestressed slab = vorgespanntes Flächentragwerk *n*
~ slab, plane (load-)bearing structure = Flächentragwerk *n*
~ wall, bearing ~ = lasttragende Wand *f*
load-carrying capacity, see: bearing ~
load cell = Belastungsmeßdose *f*, Lastmeßdose
~ cycle = Lastspiel *n*
load-deflection relationship = Verhältnis *n* zwischen Belastung *f* und Durchbiegung *f*
load distribution, distribution of load, dispersion ~ ~ = Lastverteilung *f*
~ drop = Lastabfall *m*
loaded area = Lastfläche *f*
~ float = Tiefenschwimmer *m*
~ length = Belastungslänge *f* [*Brücke f*]
loader, elevating ~ [*a mo(u)ldboard is used for loosening the earth*] = Pflugbagger *m* (oder Flachbagger-Lader *m*, oder Schürfbagger *m*) mit keilförmiger Schar *f*
~, material ~, mechanical ~ = (Auf-)Lader *m*, (Be)Lademaschine *f* Ladegerät *n*, Verladegerät
~ linkage = Ladegestänge *n*
~ shoe, see: skid-shoe
load increment = Laststufe *f*
loading = Last *f*, Belastung *f*, aufgebrachte Last *f*, Auflast *f*
~ = Beladen *n*, Auflladen, Verladen
~ belt = Verladeband *m*
(~) bucket, see: bucket
~ chute = (Ver)Laderutsche *f*
~ grab(bing crane), ~ (grab) bucket crane = (Ver)Ladegreifer *m*
~ platform = (Ver)Ladebühne *f*
~ ramp = (Ver)Laderampe *f*
~ section = Ladequerschnitt *m* [*Förderband n*]
~ shovel, bucket loader, tractor-shovel, front-end (tractor) loader, (head-end type) tractor-loader, tractor shovel, shovel dozer = (Front-) Ladeschaufel *f*, (Front)Schaufellader *m*, Frontlader *m*, Hublader *m*, Kübelauflader *m*, Schürflader *m*, behelfsmäßiger Flachbagger *m*, Planier- und Ladegerät *n*, Traktor-Bagger *m*, Hochladeschaufel *m*, Fahrlader *m*, Front-Fahrlader

loading skip, (open-end) skip, power-operated skip, folding weigher, side loader, (loading) hopper, mixer hopper = Aufzugkasten m, Aufzugkübel m [Betonmischer m]

~ **test**, load ~, bearing ~ = Belastungsversuch m, Belastungsprobe f

~ **unit** [e. g. a power shovel] = beladende (Geräte)Einheit f [z. B. ein Hochlöffel-(bagger) m]

load lowering [crane] = Lastsenkung f

~ **metamorphism** (Geol.) = Belastungsmetamorphose f

~ **of structure** = Bauwerkslast f

loadometer = Belastungsmesser m, Lastenmesser

load piston = Belastungsstempel m

load-settlement curve = Belastungs-Setzungsdiagramm n, Lastsenkungskurve f, Lastsetzungskurve

load singularity = Belastungssingularität f

~ **stress** = Verkehrsbelastung f [Brücke f]

~ **strip** = Laststreifen m

~ **train** = Lastenzug m [Eisenbahnbrücke f]

~ **transfer(ence)** = Lastübertragung f

~ **variation** = Lastschwankung f

loam = Lehm m

~ **cutter** = Lehmschneider m

~ **heath** = Lehmheide f

~ **mortar** = Lehmmörtel m

loamy marl = Lehmmergel m

local = örtlich

~ **authority** = Kommunalbehörde f

~ **corrosion-promoting cell** = rostförderndes örtliches Element n

Local Health Insurance Society = Allgemeine Ortskrankenkasse f

local material, near-by ~ = örtliches Material n

~ **street** = Wohnhausstraße f

~ **traffic** = Ortsverkehr m

~ **triangulation network** = örtliches Triangulationsnetz n

to locate = auffinden [z. B. brauchbaren Entnahmeboden m]

~ ~ = anordnen [ein Bauwerk n an einer bestimmten Stelle]

location line, route = Trasse f

~ **scheme** = Trassierungsplan m

to lock = durchschleusen

~ ~ = verriegeln

~ ~ = blockieren

lockable, see: lockfast

lockage, locking = Durchschleusen n, Schleusung f

locked coil carrying rope = Tragseil n in verschlossener Form f

locked-wire strand cable, locked cable, locked rope = patentverschlossenes Seil n

locker = Spind m

~ **room** = Umkleideraum m

lockfast, lockable = verschließbar

lock gate = Schleusentor n

locking, see: lockage

~ **device** = Gesperre n

~ ~ = Spannschloß n [Spannbeton m]

(~) pawl = Sperrklinke f, Sperrzahn m

lockkeeper = Schleusenwärter m

lock nut, check ~ = Gegenmutter f, Klemmutter f, Kontermutter

to lock over centre (Brit.)/**center** (US) = sich über der Mittellage f feststellen [Kupplung f]

lock plate = Sicherungsplatte f

~ **screw** = Sicherungsschraube f

~ **sill**, clap ~, mitre ~ = Schleusenschwelle f

~ **wall** = Schleusenwand(ung) f

~ **washer**, spring ~ = Federring m, Federscheibe f, Unterlegscheibe

~ **wire** = Sicherungsdraht m

locomotive boiler, ~ type ~ = Lokomotivkessel m

~**-car**, tender loco(motive) = Tender-Lok(omotive) f

locomotive (jib) crane, railway ~ (Brit.); locomotive (boom) ~, railroad ~ (US); permanent way ~ = Lokomotivdrehkran m, Drehkran m auf Normalspur f

*****locomotive shed** = Lokomotivschuppen m

locus of centres (Brit.); line of centers (US) = Krümmungsradius m [Talsperre f]

locus tree = Robinie f

lode, see: ore ~

lodgment of water = Wasseransammlung f [z. B. auf dem Planum n]

LOESCHE horizontal roller (grinding) mill [*Trademark*] = LOESCHE-(Mahl-)Mühle *f*
loess [*diluvial deposit of fine loam*] = Löß *m*
~ **bluff** = Lößsteilufer *n*
~-**clay** = Lößlehm *m*
loess deposit = Lößvorkommen *n*
~ **depositing wind** = Lößwind *m*
~ **dwelling** = Lößhaus *n*
~ **formation** = Lößbildung *f*
~ **soil** = Lößboden *m*
log = Stamm *m* [*entastet*]
~ = Welle *f* beim Schwertauflöser *m*
logarithmic decrement = logarithmisch ausgedrückte Abnahme *f*
log book = Fahrtenbuch *n*
~ **cart** = Langholzwagen *m*
(~) **chute** = Floßrinne *f*, Floßgasse *f*
~ **frame saw** = Gattersäge *f*
logger = Schlepper *m* für Langholztransport *m*
logging = Langholztransport *m*
~ **crane** = Baumkran *m*, Langholz-Verladekran
~ **hoist** = Holzaufbringungswinde *f*
~ **road** = Holzabfuhrweg *m*, Holzaufbringungsstraße *f*
~ **winch,** (timber) towing ~ = Holzaufbringungs(trommel)winde *f*
log house = Blockhaus *n*
log-probability law = logarithmisches Wahrscheinlichkeitsgesetz *n*
log sluice = Floßschleuse *f*
~ **washer** = Schwertwäsche *f*, Schwertauflöser *m*
logway = Holzgasse *f*
lollingite, FeAs$_2$ (Min.) = Löllingit *m*
Lombardy poplar, see: Italian ~
London clay = Londoner Ton *m*
(long-boom) stripping shovel, stripper = Großlöffelbagger *m*, Abraum-Hochlöffel(bagger) *m*
long burning test = Dauerbrennprobe *f*
~ **Cuban ring auger** = Irwin-Schlangenbohrer *m*
long-distance driver = Fernfahrer *m*
~ **haulage work** = Ferntransport *m*
~ **signing** = Fernverkehrsbeschilderung *f*
~ **traffic** = Fernverkehr *m*

long-feed tunnel drill = Tunnelbohrer *m* mit großem Vorschubbereich *m*
long-haul traffic = Güterfernverkehr *m*
longitudinal axis = Längsachse *f*
~ **bar and lateral tie reinforcement** = Bügelbewehrung *f*, Bügelarmierung *f*
~ **bay** = Längsfeld *n*
~ **beam,** see: stringer
~ **bracing** = Längsverband *m* [*Brücke f*]
~ **diaphragm** = Längsrippe *f* [*Gelenkbogenrahmen m*]
~ **dyke** (Brit.)/**dike** (US), training wall, training bank, guide bank = 1. Leitdamm *m*; 2. Längswerk *n*
~ **finishing machine,** see: bullfloat ~ ~
~ **floating machine,** see: bullfloat finishing machine
~ **force** = Längskraft *f*
~ **girder** (Brit.); see: stringer
~ **guide** = Längsführung *f*
~ **jack rafter** = Langseitenschifter *m*
~ **joint,** lane ~ = Längspreßfuge *f*
~ **profile** (or **section**) = Längsprofil *n*
~ **reinforcement** = Längsbewehrung *f*, Längsarmierung *f*
~ **rib** = Längsrippe *f* [*Blechträger m*]
~ **seam** = Längsnaht *f*
~ **section** = Längsschnitt *m*
~ ~ (or **profile**) = Längsprofil *n*
~ ~ **levels** = Längsnivellement *n*
~ **shear,** horizontal ~ = Längsschubkraft *f*
~ **wave** = Längswelle *f*
~ **web stiffener** = Längssteife *f* [*Kastenträger m*]
long pug mill, see: single shaft ~ ~
~ **range excavator conveyor,** long range machine = Tiefen- und Langstreckenförderer *m*
~ **residuum** = Rückstand *m* von paraffin- oder gemischtbasischen Rohölen *npl* enthaltend alle Schmieröl- und häufig leichtere Fraktionen *fpl*
~ **steel erector's boom** (US)/**jib** (Brit.) = Montageausleger *m* [*Kran m*]
~ **stroke pump** = Langhubpumpe *f*
~-**term flood prediction** = langfristige Hochwasservorhersage *f*
long-time burning oil = hochwertiges Leuchtöl *n*, ~ Brennöl

long-time burning oil for railway use — low-level laterite

long-time burning oil for railway use = Spezialkerosin *n* für Eisenbahnsignallaternen *fpl*
long trunks = Langholz *n*
looking hole, observation ~ = Schauloch *n*
lookout tower, watch ~ = Beobachtungsturm *m*
loom oil = Webstuhlöl *n*
loop = Schleife *f*
~ = Windung *f* [*Behälterwicklung f*]
~ **lifter** = Schlingenheber *m*
looping = Schlingenbildung *f*
loose measure = Aufmaß *n* in unverdichtetem Zustand *m* [*Boden m*]
loosening = Auflockerung *f*
~ = Lösen *n* [*Erdbau m*]
~ **strength** = Lösungsfestigkeit *f* [*Boden m*]
loose snow avalanche = Staublawine *f*
(loose-) volume batching, see: volume batching
lopolith (Geol.) = Lopolith *m*
lorry (Brit.); (auto) truck (US); roadtruck, motor truck = Last(kraft)wagen *m*, LKW *m*
~ **cab** (Brit.); truck ~ (US) = Fahrerhaus *n*
~ **haul(ing)** (Brit.); see: haulage by truck (US)
*lorry-mounted mixer (Brit.); moto-mixer, mixer-type truck, ready-mix (cement) truck (US); transit (concrete) mixer = lufttreifenfahrbarer Betontransportwagen *m* mit Mischer *m*
~ **pneumatic-tyred mechanical shovel** (Brit.); see: truck(-mounted) (pneumatic-tired) shovel (-crane) (US)
lorry passing lane (Brit.); truck ~ ~ (US) = LKW-Überholspur *f*
lorry tailboard temporary gritting attachment (Brit.); see: rear-mounted gritter
lorry-trailer (Brit.); see: truck-trailer (US)
~ **combination** (Brit.); truck-trailer ~ (US) = Lastzug *m*
Los Angeles rattler test, see: rattler ~
loss of head, head loss = Fallhöhenverlust *m* [*Wasserkraftwerk n*]
~ ~ ~ **through filter layer** = nutzbarer Filterwiderstand *m*

~ ~ **level reach water** = Bettverlust *m* [*Kanalhaltung f*]
~ **on ignition,** see: ignition loss
lost gradient = verlorene Steigung *f*
lost-time, unavoidable delay factor = unvermeidliche Verlustzeit *f*
louvred window = Lamellenfenster *n*
low-bed trailer, see: low-loader
low boy (US); see: low-loader
low-cost road = billige Straße *f*
lower (or bottom) chord (or boom, or flange) = Untergurt *m*, untere Gurtung *f*
~ **course of the river** = Flußunterlauf *m*
~ **(or bottom) discharge tunnel,** see: bottom emptying gallery
~ **frame,** see: carbody
~ **gate, tail** ~ = Untertor *n* [*Binnenschiffahrtschleuse f*]
lowered ground-water table = abgesenkter Grundwasserspiegel *m*
lowering brake connections for cranes in three-phase installations = Senkbremsschaltung *f*
~ **jack** = Senkwinde *f*
lower lip (US); see: foot trough (Brit.)
~ **low water** = niedriges Niedrigwasser *n*
~ **strand,** see: return ~
lowest bidder (or tenderer) = Mindestfordernde *m*
low-frequency vibration method, see: resonant-frequency technique
low-grade aggregate [*e. g. slag, limestone*] = Zuschlagstoffe *mpl* geringerer Qualität *f*
~ **iron formation** = niedrigprozentige Eisenformation *f*
~ **ore, poor** ~ = armes Erz *n*
low ground = Niederung *f*
~ **heat of hydration cement,** slow hardening ~; Portland cement Type IV (US) = Zement *m* mit sehr geringer Abbindewärme *f*
~ **idle** = niedrigster Leerlauf *m*
lowland, low-level flat = Tiefland *n*, Tiefebene *f*
~ **moor, shallow** ~ = Nieder(ungs)moor *n*, Flachmoor *n*
low-level bridge = Tauchbrücke *f*
~ **flat,** see: lowland
~ **indicator** = Leerstandanzeiger *m*
~ **laterite** = abgeschwemmter Laterit *m*

low-lift platform truck — lurching

low-lift platform truck = Plattform-Niederhubkarre(n) *f*, (*m*)

low-loader, deck trailer, low-bed trailer, low-load trailer; low-boy (trailer) (US) = Tieflader *m*, Tiefladeanhänger *m*, Tiefbettanhänger, Tiefladewagen *m*

low-lying tract of ground = tiefliegendes Gelände *n*

low-pressure (air) compressor = Niederdruck-Kompressor *m*, Niederdruckluftverdichter *m*

~ **grouting (or injection)** = Niederdruckauspressung *f*, Niederdruckeinpressung, Niederdruckverpressung

~ **installation** = Niederdruckanlage *f*

~ **steam curing** = Niederdruck-Dampf(er)härtung *f* [*Betonstein m*]

~ **tire** (US); ~ **tyre** (Brit.) = Niederdruckreifen *m*

~ **torch** = Injektorbrenner *m*

low speed range = kleiner Gang *m*

~ **(strength) blasting explosive,** powder explosive = Schießmittel *n*, Schießstoff *m*, deflagrierender Sprengstoff, Pulversprengstoff

low-temperature brown-coal tar = Braunkohlenurteer *m*

~ **peat tar** = Torfurteer *m*

low tension detonator [*the low-tension fusehead has a resistance of 0.9 to 1.3 Ohms*] = elektrischer Zünder *m* mit einem Widerstand von 0,9—1,3 Ohm

~ **tide regulation,** regulation of low water flows = Niedrigwasserregulierung *f*, Niedrigwasserverbesserung *f*

low-type pavement/paving (US) = leichte (Straßen)Decke *f*

low-viscosity binder, ~ binding medium = niedrigviskoses Bindemittel *n*, niedrigviskoser Binder *m*

~ **tar** = niedrigviskoser Teer *m*

low water mark = Ebbemarke *f*, Ebbelinie *f*

~ ~ **stand** = Stillstand *m* des Niedrigwassers *n*

lozenge riveting = verjüngte Nietung *f*

~ **type junction** = Raute *f* [*Anschlußstelle f*]

L-shaped forms = Winkelschalung *f*

lubricants = Schmiermittel *npl*

lubricating grease; see: petroleum ~ (US)

~ ~ **thickener** = Schmierfettverdikkungsmittel *n*

~ **oil,** lube ~ = Schmieröl *n*

~ ~ **filter** = Schmierölfilter *n*, *m*

~ **pump** = Schmierpumpe *f*

~ **service** = Schmierdienst *m*

lubrication = Abschmieren *n*, Abschmierung *f*

~ **chart,** ~ time-table, ~ plan = Schmiertabelle *f*, Schmierplan *m*

lucid compound = Aluminiumseifenfett *n* von glänzendem Aussehen *n* und hoher Transparenz *f*

luffing boom shovel (US); see: crane navvy (Brit.)

lug angle, clip ~ [*a short attaching angle that takes a portion of the stress of any member*] = Beiwinkel *m*

~ **bolt** = Nasenbolzen *m*

lumber = Bau(nutz)holz *n*

~ **mill** (US); saw ~ = Sägewerk *n*

luminous buoy, see: light ~

LUMNITE [*Trademark*] = Tonerdeschmelzzement *m*, Fabrikat UNIVERSAL ATLAS PORTLAND CEMENT CO.

lump hammer, mash ~ = Schlägel *m*, Fäustel *m*

lumpiness = Knollenbildung *f* [*Zement m*]

lump lime = Stückkalk *m*, ungelöschter stückiger Kalk *m*

~ **ore** = Stückerz *n*

~ **slag,** (iron-ore) blast-furnace ~ = (Eisenhochofen-)Stückschlacke *f*, Hochofenschlacke

~ **sum** = Pauschalsumme *f*

~ — ~ **contract,** firm price ~, fixed price ~ = Festpreisvertrag *m*

lumpy = klumpig, großstückig

lunar caustic = Höllenstein *m*, Silbernitrat *n*

~ **-cycle measurement of estuarine flows** = Messung *f* von Gezeitenströmungen *fpl* in Flußmündungen *fpl* während des Mondwechsels *m*

lunch-break, mid-day break = Mittagspause *f*

lurching, train sway, side sway = Schlingern *n* [*Eisenbahn f*]

luster = Gefälligkeit *f* des Aussehens *n* [*Schmierfett n*]
lustre = Glanz *m*
Lydian stone, lydite, touchstone = Kieselschiefer *m*, Lydit *m*
lye = Natronlauge *f*
lyophobe = lösungsmittelfliehend

M

macadam-aggregate type bituminous pavement/paving (US) = bituminöse Decke *f* nach dem Makadamprinzip *n*

~ ~ road mix surface, open-graded ~ ~, ~ ~ = Baumischbelag *m* nach Art des Makadams, offener Baumischbelag, hohlraumreicher Baumischbelag

macadam base, crushed stone ~ ~, crushed-rock ~, stone macadam type ~, stone base (course) = Schottertragschicht *f*

~ foundation, broken stone ~; broken stone bottoming (Brit.); aggregate base (course) (US) = Schotterunterbau *m*

~(ised) road = 1. Makadamstraße *f*, Steinschlagstraße *f* nach Mac Adam; 2. Makadamstraße mit Bindemittel *n*

macadam roller (US); three-wheel(ed) (all-purpose) ~, three-roll type machine, three-legged roller, three-roll roller = Dreiradwalze *f*

~ surfacing, crushed-rock ~ = Schotterdecke *f*, Makadamdecke

~ with bitumen binder (Brit.); see: asphalt macadam (US)

~ ~ tar binder (Brit.); see: tarmacadam

machine-broken metal (Brit.) = Maschinenschotter *m*

machine chamber = Maschinenraum *m*

machine-cut peat = Maschinentorf *m*

machine foundation, ~ base, ~ footing = Maschinenfundament *n*

~ grinding = Maschinenschliff *m*

machine-hours worked by plant = Gerätestunden *fpl*

machine-laid, mechanically laid = maschinell eingebaut [*Straßenbelag m*]

machine-made brick, wire-cut ~ = Maschinenziegel *m*, Schnittziegel

machine operation = Maschinenarbeit *f*

~ rammer, see: mechanical ~

machine(ry) oil = Schmieröl *n* für bewegliche Maschinenteile *mpl*

machinery pontoon = Maschinenponton *m*

machinist = Maschinist *m*

made ground, filled ~ ~ = aufgeschüttetes Gelände *n*, aufgefülltes ~

MADSEN (MIX-IN-TRAVEL) ROAD PUG [*Trademark*] = Bodenmischer *m*, Fabrikat MADSEN IRON WORKS INC., LA MIRADA, CALIFORNIA, USA

magma (Geol.) = Magma *n*, Schmelzfluß *m*, (magmatische) Schmelze *f*, Schmelzlösung *f*

magmatic differentiation (Geol.) = Erstarrungsvorgang *m*

~ residuum = Magmarest *m*

~ rock, eruptive ~ = magmatisches Gestein *n*, Eruptivgestein

magnesia brick, see: magnesite ~

~ mica (Min.) = Magnesiaglimmer *m*

magnesian limestone, see: dolomitic ~

~ marble, see: dolomitic ~

magnesite brick, magnesia ~, magnesia refractory = Magnesitstein *m*, Magnesitziegel *m*

~ cement, see: plastic calcined magnesite

~-chrome brick = Magnesit-Chromstein *m*

magnesite rock = Magnesitgestein *n*

magnesium-aluminium garnet (Min.) = Magnesiatongranat *m*

magnesium carbonate, magnesite, carbonate of magnesia, $MgCO_3$ = kohlensaures Magnesium *n*, Magnesiumkarbonat *n*

~ chloride, $MgCl_2$ = Magnesiumchlorid *n*, Chlormagnesium *n*

~ oxide, see: bitter-earth

~ oxychloride = Steinholz *n*

~ sulphate, see: Epsom salt

magnesium-tourmaline (Min.) = Magnesium-Turmalin *m*

magnetic clutch = Magnetkupplung *f*

*****magnetic compass** = Magnetkompaß *m*

~ declination, ~ variation = Mißweisung *f*

~ iron-sand, see: iserine

~ North, M. N. = magnetischer Nordpol *m*

~ pyrite(s), pyrrhotine, pyrrhotite (Min.) = Magnetkies *m*

magnetic road sweeper = Straßenmagnetreiniger m
~ **separator** = Magnet(ab)scheider m
~ **variation**, see: ~ declination
magnetite (Min.) = Magnetit m, Magneteisenerz n
magneto ignition = Magnetzündung f
main = Hauptstrang m
~ **bearing** = Hauptlager n
~ **bubble** = Röhrenlibelle f, Reiterlibelle
~ **drain**, leader ~ = Hauptdrän m
~ **frame** = Hauptrahmen m
~ **girder** = Hauptträger m
~ **journal** = Hauptlagerzapfen m
~ **line loco(motive)** = Vollbahn-Lok(o-motive) f
~ **outfall**, see: outfall (ditch)
~ **pump**, suction ~ [*dredge(r)*] = Baggersaugpumpe f
~ **sewer, trunk** ~ = Hauptabwasserkanal m
mains failure = Netzausfall m [*Elektrotechnik f*]
~ **subway**, see: duct
main span, centre ~ [*bridge*] = Hauptöffnung f, Mittelöffnung, Hauptfeld n, Mittelfeld
~ **track**, main-line ~ = Stammgleis n
maintainer (grader), see: blade maintainer
maintenance, upkeep = Unterhaltung f, Instandhaltung f
~ **distributor**, see: binder ~
~ **guide** = Wartungs-Anleitung f
~ **hangar**, see: technical ~
~ **man**, see: lengthsman
major bed = Hochwasserbett n
~ **desire line** = Hauptverkehrsstromlinie f
~ **equipment**, see: heavy plant
~ **road**, ~ highway (Brit.); preference ~ (US) = Hauptstraße f, Vorfahrtstraße
~ **street** = Hauptstadtstraße f
make = Fabrikat n
makeshift method = Behelfsmethode f
makeup tank = Ausgleichbehälter m
making good = Schadensbehebung f
malachite (Min.) = Malachit m
malaria control = Malariabekämpfung f
male spline = Keil m [*Keilwelle f*]
~ **thread**, see: external (screw) ~
malfunction = fehlerhaftes Funktionieren n

mall, see: maul
mallet = Holzhammer m
Malmstone = Malm m
Maltese cross = Malteserkreuz n
malthenes = Malthene npl
mammoth caisson = Riesensenkkasten m
~ **departement store** = Riesenwarenhaus n
management = Betrieb m
~ **development**, ~ training = Weiter- und Heranbildung f von Betriebsführern mpl
~ **study** = Betriebsstudie f
manager = Betriebsleiter m
managerial experience = Betriebserfahrung f
mandatory sign, regulatory ~ = Befehlszeichen n, Verpflichtungszeichen, Ordnungszeichen
mandrel, pile core = Stahlkern m [*Raymond-Pfahl m*]
~ **pressure roll** [*roll roofing plant*] = Gegendruckrolle f
maneuverability (US) = Freibeweglichkeit f [*Baumaschine f*]
mangan-blende (Min.), see: alabandite
mangan(ese) epidote, piedmontite (Min.) = Piemontit m, Manganepidot m
~ **spar**, rhodochrosite (Min.) = Manganspat m
~ **steel** = Manganhartstahl m
manganite (Min.) = Manganit m
*****manhole**, inspection pit, inspection chamber = Mannloch n, Einsteigeschacht m, Reinigungsschacht m
man-hour = Arbeiterstunde f
manifold = Ansaugstutzen m, Ansaug-Krümmer m
~ ~ = Auspuffstutzen m, Auspuff-Krümmer m
~ **tunnel**, penstock manifold = Verteilerstollen m
manila hawser = Manila-Hanfseil n
~ **paper**, kraft ~ = Hartpapier n
man-lock = Personenschleuse f [*pneumatische Gründung f*]
man-made peninsula, artificial ~ = künstliche Halbinsel f
manna ash, see: flowering ~
manoeuvrability (Brit.); maneuverability (US) = Freibeweglichkeit f

man-of-war = Kriegsschiff n
man-size steel pipe = begehbares Stahlrohr n
mantle granite = Deckengranit m
~ of vegetation, vegetable cover, vegation cover = Pflanzenbewuchs m, Bodenbewachsung f
manual = Handbuch n
~ conical penetrometer = konische Handsonde f
~ control [*street traffic*] = Verkehrsreg(e)lung f durch Zeichengabe f mit Hand f durch Verkehrsschutzmann m
~ ~ of traffic signals = Handsteuerung f von Verkehrssignalen npl, handgesteuerte Signalreg(e)lung f
~ hoist, hand-operated lifting machine = Handhubwerk n
~ laying, see: hand spreading
manually guided drag skip, see: hand scraper
~ operated pneumatic tamper (or tamping beam, or compacting beam) = Hand-Drucklufttrüttelbohle f
manual operation = Handbedienung f, Handbetätigung f
~ vibrating block machine = Hand-Vibrations-Betonsteinmaschine f
~ welding = Handschweißung f
manufactured gas = Vergasungsgas n
~ sand, see: screening(s)
manufacturing facilities, **~ plant** = Fabrikationsanlagen fpl, Fabrikationsbetrieb m
~ plant = Herstellungswerk n
~ research = Fabrikationsforschung f
manure dump = Jauchegrube f
manuring with lime = Kalkdüngung f
manway ladder = Mannschaftsleiter f [*Tunnelbau m*]
to map = landkartenmäßig erfassen
map = (Land)Karte f
~ cracking (US); see: crazing
~ grid = Karten(gitter)netz n
maple = Ahorn m
mapping (work), map-making = Kartenherstellung f
map protractor = Kartenwinkelmesser m
~ reference (abbr. MP), grid ~ = Netzangabe f [*Karte f*]

marble [*metamorphosed limestone*] = Marmor m
marcasite (Min.), see: white iron pyrite
Marcus trough conveyor = Marcus-Wurfförderrinne f, Propellerrinne f
mare's-tail, see: cirrus cloud
margin, see: verge
margin, off-size, deviation, permissible variation = Abmaß n, Maßabweichung f
marginal access = seitliche Zufahrt f [*zu einer Hauptstraße f*]
~ concrete strip finisher, small finisher used in bankette construction = Randstreifenfertiger m
~ property = Anliegergrundstück n
~ strip, see: edge ~
margin of safety = Sicherheitsspanne f
margode, slaty marl, marl-slate = Schiefermergel m, Mergelschiefer m
marigram (US); tidal curve, tidal diagram (Brit.) = Gezeitendiagramm n, Gezeitenkurve f, Tidenkurve f
marine algae = Meeresalge f
~ clay = aus Salzwasserablagerungen stammender Ton m
~ climate (Brit.); see: oceanic ~ (US)
~ construction, coastal engineering = Seebau m
~ current (US); ocean ~ (Brit.) = Meeresströmung f
~ denudation = Meeresdenudation f
~ deposits = marine Sedimente npl
~ diesel fuel = Marinedieselkraftstoff m, Schiffahrtsdieselöl n
~ dredge(r), sea-going ~ = Seebagger m
~ dredging = Seebaggerung f
~ driver, see: floating (pile) ~
~ engine = Schiffsmotor m
~ engineering = Schiffsmaschinenbau m
~ fouling = Schiffsbewuchs m [*Anwuchs von Balaniden usw*]
~ gas turbine = Schiffs-Gasturbine f
~ glue = Marineleim m
~ gravel = Meerkies m
~ installations, see: ~ works
~ leg, see: floating barge elevator
~ oil = Marineöl n
~ (pile) driver, see: floating (~) ~
~ terminal = Seebahnhof m

marine transgression (US); submergence by sea of land depression (Brit.) = Meeresüberschiebung *f*
~ **type cable** = Seekabel *n*
~ **works** (or **structures,** or **installations**) = Seebauten *f*
maritime pine, sea ~ = Seestrandkiefer *f*
~ **slipway,** see: slipway
to mark, to trace = anreißen
"**marker**" (Geol.), see: datum horizon
marker = Absteckzeichen *n*
~ **line** = Markierungslinie *f*
marketing opportunity = Absatzmöglichkeit *f*
market road, see: (farm-to-)market ~
marking machine = Markierungsmaschine *f*
~ (or **staking out**) **of the bank line** = Abmarkung *f* der Uferlinie *f*
~ **paint** = Markierungsfarbe *f*
marl = Mergel *m* [40—75% $CaCO_3$]
marling = Merg(e)lung *f*
marl loess = Lößmergel *m*
marl-slate, see: margode
marly clay = merg(e)liger Ton *m* [*4 bis 10%* $CaCO_3$]
~ **limestone** = merg(e)liger Kalkstein *m*, Mergelkalkstein [90—96% $CaCO_3$]
marmatite (Min.) = Eisenzinkblende *f*
marsh = Marsch *f*
marshalling area, see: alert platform
~ **vehicle, shunting** ~ = Rangierfahrzeug *n*, Verschiebefahrzeug
~ **yard,** switchyard, shunting station, (freight-)classification yard = Verschiebebahnhof *m*, Rangierbahnhof
marsh bird's foot trefoil = Sumpfhornklee *m*
~ **gas** = Sumpfgas *n*
~ **land** = Marschland *n*
marshy ground, see: fen
martensite = Martensit *m*
mash hammer, see: lump ~
mason, stone ~ = Steinmetz *m*
masonry = Mauerwerk *n*
~ **anchor** = Maueranker *m*
~ **arch gravity dam** = Bruchstein(stau)mauer *f* in Bogenform *f*
~ **cavity wall** = Hohlmauerwerk *n*
~ **cement** = Mauerwerkszement *m*

~ **gravity dam** = Bruchstein-Gewichts-(stau)mauer *f*
~ **mortar, joint** ~, **pointing** ~ = Mauermörtel *m*, Baumörtel, Fugenmörtel
~ **saw,** see: stone-cutting ~
~ **unit,** see: clay building ~
masons' hammer, see: stone sledge
mass = Masse *f*
~ **asphalt** = Massenasphalt *m*
~ **concrete,** see: bulk ~
~ ~ **plant** = Groß-Betonaufbereitungsanlage *f*
~ **(haul) diagram, haul** (mass) ~ = Massenplan *m*, Transportplan [*Erdbau m*]
massif = (Gebirgs)Massiv *n*
massive arch = Massivbogen *m*
~ **concrete dam** = Massivbeton(stau)mauer *f*, Betonsperre *f*, Staumauer *f*, Talsperren(stau)mauer
~ **gypsum** = dichter Gips *m*
~ **limestone** = Massenkalkstein *m*
mass transportation, ~ **transit,** public transport, public service vehicles' traffic, municipal transport = öffentlicher (Massen)Verkehr *m*
mast = Mast *m*
master builder = Baumeister *m*
~ **clutch** = Hauptkupplung *f*
~ **mechanic** = Maschinenmeister *m*
~ **pin** = Kettenschlußbolzen *m* [*Gleiskette f*]
mastic (asphalt) [*deprecated: floated* ~] = Gußasphalt *m*, Streichasphalt [*früher: Mastix-Asphalt m*]
~ (~) **finisher** (or **finishing machine**) = Gußasphalt-Fertiger *m*
~ (~) **mixer (and) transporter** = Gußasphalttransportmaschine *f*, Gußasphalttransportwagen *m*
~ (~) **spreading cart** = Gußasphalt-Ausfuhrwagen *m*
~ **block,** see: asphalt cake
~ **cooker,** ~ **asphalt mixer** = Gußasphalt-Kocher *m*, Mastixkocher
~ ~ **with power stirring gear** = Gußasphaltmotorkocher *m*
~ **filler** = Mastixvergußmasse *f*
~ **grouted surfacing** (Brit.); ~ **penetration pavement** = Mastixvergußdecke *f*, Mastixeingußdecke

mastic sealing coat = Oberflächenabsieg(e)-lung *f* mit Asphaltmastix *m*
masut, see: mazut
mat, see: road carpet
~, see: timber ~
matchboard = Spundbrett *n*
matche daggregate, see: (dry-)batched ~
match wax = Paraffin *n* von niedrigem Schmelzpunkt *m* zur Imprägnierung *f* von Streichhölzern *npl*
material = Werkstoff *m,* Material *n*
~ level (in bin) = Bunkerstand *m,* Füllungsgrad *m,* Füllstand *m*
~ ~ indicator, see: (bin) ~ ~
~ loader, see: loader
(material(s)) bunker = (Material)Bunker *m,* Taschensilo *m*
~ delivery = Materialanfuhr *f,* Materialanlieferung *f*
~ elevator = Materialaufzug *m*
~ fluctuation clause, ~ variation ~ = Stoffgleitklausel *f*
***material(s) handling** = Material(be)förderung *f,* Materialumschlag *m*
~ ~ crane = Umschlagkran *m*
~ ~ devices for construction sites = Fördereinrichtungen *fpl* für Baustellen *fpl*
~ ~ engineer = Materialflußingenieur *m*
***~ ~ machinery (or equipment)** = Geräte *npl* für die Material(be)förderung, (Material)Umschlaggeräte
~ loader, see: loader
material(s)-lock, see: muck-lock
(material(s)) processing (or dressing, or preparation) = (Material)Aufbereitung *f*
~ shortage = Materialverknappung *f,* Materialknappheit *f*
(~) storage, storekeeping, storing = Lagerhaltung *f,* (Material)Lagerung *f,* Bevorratung *f*
~ testing laboratory, laboratory for materials testing = Materialprüfungsanstalt *f,* Materialprüfungsamt *n*
~ to be conveyed = Fördergut *n*
~ to be graded = Siebgut *n*
~ to be handled = Ladegut *n*
~ to be washed = Waschgut *n*
mat foundation, see: raft ~
~ of grass = Grasnarbe *f*

~ ~ turf = Rasennarbe *f*
matrix, cement, cementing material = Bindemittel *n,* verkittende Zwischensubstanz *f* [*Gestein n*]
~ (Brit.); binder [*black top road construction*] = Bindemittel *n,* Binder *m,* Straßenbauhilfsstoff *m*
***matter forming silicates** = Silikatbildner *m,* Wasserbildner *m,* Hydraulefaktor *m*
matt glaze = Mattglasur *f*
(mat) thickness control = Dickeneinstellung *f* [*Schwarzbelageinbaumaschine f*]
matting = Mattenbelag *m*
mattock, cross ~ = Breithacke *f,* Breithaue *f*
maturing, hardening [*deprecated*]; **curing** = Reifeprozeß *m* [*Beton m*]
maul, beetle, mall = schwerer Holzhammer *m*
maximum contact = Maximalkontakt *m*
~ deflection = größte Durchbiegung *f*
~ density = Hohlraumminimum *n,* maximale Dichte *f*
~ digging force at the shovel = Grabkraft *f* an der Löffelspitze *f*
~ ~ speed at the shovel = Grabgeschwindigkeit *f* an der Löffelspitze *f*
~ dry density [*soil*] = Höchsttrockenraumgewicht *n* [*Boden m*]
~ governed speed = Höchstdrehzahl *f*
~ load(ing) = Maximalbelastung *f,* Höchstbelastung, Maximallast *f,* Höchstlast
~ moment = Größtmoment *n*
~ speed = Höchstgeschwindigkeit *f*
~ torque = Höchstdrehmoment *n*
mazut, masut, heavy fuel = abgetopptes russisches (Roh)Erdöl *n,* Masut *n*
meadow fescue, see: English blue grass
~ foxtail = Wiesenfuchsschwanz *m*
~ grass = Rispengras *n*
~ moor = Grünlandsmoor *n*
~ peat = Wiesentorf *m*
MEALORUB [*Trademark*] = Kautschukpulver *n* unter Verwendung *f* von leicht vulkanisiertem Latex *m*
meal-time = Essenszeit *f*
mean (or average) annual value = Jahresmittelwert *m*

mean low water springs = mittleres Springniedrigwasser n
~ range = mittlerer Tidenhub m
~ water = Mittelwasser n
meander = (Fluß)Mäander m, Flußschlinge f
means of road (or highway) transport = Straßenbeförderungsmittel n
measured profile = Meßprofil n
measurement of earth pressure = Erddruckmessung f
~ (of quantities), site measuring = Aufmaß n
~ of slipperiness, skidding test = Reibungsmessung f
measuring = Abmessung f, Abmessen n
~, see: proportioning
~ cell = Meßdose f
~ channel = Meßkanal m
~ cylinder = Meßzylinder m
~ device, see: proportioning ~
~ ~ = Meßvorrichtung f
~ plant, see: (aggregate) batching ~
~ result = Meßergebnis n
~ rod = Meßlatte f
~ tape = Meßband n, Bandmaß n
~ weir = Meßwehr n
meat conveyor = Schlachthofhängebahn f
mechanic = Mechaniker m
mechanical analysis = Kornanalyse f, Kornverteilungsbestimmung f
~ blower = Gebläsemaschine f
~ classifier = statischer Klassierapparat m
~ drive = mechanischer Antrieb m
~ engineering = Maschinenwesen n
~ equipment = maschinelle Ausrüstung f
~ finegrader, see: concrete bay subgrader
~ gritting attachment, see: rear-mounted gritter
~ highway equipment, see: roadbuilding machinery
~ joint pipe = Schraubmuffenrohr n
*~ liquid limit device, see: liquid ~ ~
~ loader, see: loader
mechanically deposited sedimentary rock, see: clastic rock
~ driven pump = Maschinenpumpe f
~ laid, see: machine-laid

~ operated barrow-type chipping(s) spreader = Motor-Splittstreukarre(n) f, (m)
~ ~ drop hammer = maschinell betriebener Fallhammer m
~ stabilised road, granular ~ ~ = Tonbetonstraße f
~ vibrated eccentric type screen, eccentric type vibrating screen = Exzenter-Schwingsieb n, Exzenterschwinger m, Exzenterwellen(-Vibrations-Plan)sieb, Schwingsieb mit Exzenterantrieb m
~ vibrated rotating unbalanced(-)weight (type) screen, unbalanced weight vibrating ~ = Unwucht(vibrations)sieb n, Schwingsieb n mit Massenkraftantrieb m
mechanical output of motor = Motorenleistung f
~ plate feeder, reciprocating ~ ~, shaking feeder = Schüttelspeiser m
~ property = Festigkeitswert m
~ rammer, machine ~ = Rammmaschine f
~ ~, power ~ = Kraft(hand)ramme f
(~) shaking screen = Schrägwurfsieb n
~ shovel, see: crane navvy
(~) sieve shaker, mechanical vibrator for laboratory test sieves, vibrating test sieve shaker, test sieve vibrator = Siebsatzrüttler m, mechanischer Siebsatz-Schwingungserreger m
~ (soil) stabilisation, granular (~) ~ [*consists of incorporating other inert soil materials in such proportions that the resultant mixture will have the properties of a stable wellgraded mix. This is compacted at optimum moisture content and sealed*] = mechanische Bodenverfestigung f, Tonbeton m
~ steering with a hydraulic booster = kombinierte mechanisch hydraulische Steuerung f
*mechanical sweeper, see: rotary ~
~ testing = mechanisches Prüfverfahren n
~ transmission of power, see: power transmission
~ trowel, power ~, rotary finisher, trowel(l)ing machine, mechanical float = Estrich-Glättmaschine f
~ vibrator for laboratory test sieves, see: (mechanical) sieve shaker

mechanical weathering, physical ∼, rock disintegration = mechanische Verwitterung *f*, physikalische Verwitterung, Gesteinszerfall *m*

∼ **weeder** = Unkrautjätmaschine *f*

mechanics = Mechanik *f*

∼ **of hardening** [*concrete*] = Erhärtungsmechanismus *m* [*Beton m*]

∼ ∼ **material** = Festigkeitslehre *f*

mechanisation = Mechanisierung *f*

mechanism of setting (Brit.); ∼ ∼ **set** = Abbindemechanismus *m*, Erstarrungsmechanismus, Hydra(ta)tionsmechanismus [*Zement m*]

medial moraine = Mittelmoräne *f*, Gufferlinie *f*

∼ **strip,** see: central reserve

median curb(stone) = Mittelstreifen-Hochbordstein *m*

∼ **lane** = Fahrspur *f* am Mittelstreifen *m*

∼ **(strip) inlet** = Mittelstreifeneinlauf *m* [*Straße f*]

medical (air) lock = Krankenschleuse *f*, Druckluft-∼, Preßluft-∼

∼ **assistance,** ∼ attendance = ärztliche Hilfe *f*

∼ **attention,** ∼ attendance = ärztliche Fürsorge *f*, ∼ Betreuung *f*

medicinal paraffin, see: liquid ∼

Mediterranean seaport = Mittelmeerhafen *m*

medium-breaking, see: medium-setting

medium-curing = mittelschnellabbindend [*Verschnittbitumen n*]

medium-duty = mittelschwer [*Baumaschine f*]

medium frequency (concrete) finisher = Mittelfrequenz(beton)fertiger *m*

∼ **gravel** = Mittelkies *m*

medium-hard coal-tar pitch = mittelhartes Steinkohlenteerpech *n*

medium-heavy loam = mittelfetter Lehm *m*

medium plates = Mittelblech *n*

∼ **screening** = Mittelabsiebung *f*

∼ **separation** = Mitteltrennung *f* [*Siebung f*]

∼-**setting,** normal-setting, semi-stable, medium-breaking = mittelschnellbrechend, halbstabil [*Bitumenemulsion f*]

∼-**textured** [*wearing course*] = halboffen [*Verschleißschicht f*]

medullary ray, wood ∼ = Markstrahl *m*

meerschaum, sepiolite, $Mg_2Si_3O_8 \times 2H_2O$ (Min.) = Meerschaum *m*

melanterite (Min.), see: green vitriol

melaphyre, black porphyry = Melaphyr *m*, schwarzer Porphyr *m*

melilot, sweet clover = Reinklee *m*

mellite, mellilite = Melilith *m*, Honigstein *m*

melted snow and ice, meltwater = Schmelzwasser *n*

melting furnace (or melter) for joint sealers, see: heating tank for melting joint sealing compounds

∼ **of ice** = Eisschmelzvorgang *m*

∼ **point,** see: fusion ∼

member = Stab *m* [*Stahlbau m*]

membrane, diaphragm = Membran(e) *f*

∼ **bellows** = Faltbalg *m*, Membran(e)balg *m*

(∼) curing compound = Abdichtungsmittel *n* [*Betonnachbehandlung f*]

∼ **pump,** diaphragm ∼ = Membran(e)pumpe *f*, Dia-Pumpe

membrane-stabilized soil road = mechanisch verfestigte Straße *f* mit Abdichtung *f* des Planums *n*

memorial tablet = Gedenktafel *f*

menaccanite (Min.) = Menaccanit *m*

MENCK-shovel = MENCK-Hochlöffelbagger *m*, Fabrikat MENCK & HAMBROCK G.m.b.H., HAMBURG-ALTONA, DEUTSCHLAND

mending, see: patching (work)

mercantile marine, merchant ∼ = Handelsmarine *f*, Handelsflotte *f*

merchant iron, see: commercial ∼

∼ **marine** = Handelsmarine *f*

mercuric chloride, see: corrosive sublimate

∼ **isocyanate,** see: fulminate of mercury

mercurous salt = Quecksilberoxydulsalz *n*

mercury, quicksilver (Min.) = Quecksilber *n*

∼ **vapo(u)r (or discharge) lamp** = Quecksilberdampflampe *f*

∼∼-∼ **pump** = Quecksilber-Diffusionspumpe *f*, Diffusionsluftpumpe

meroxene (Min.) = Meroxen *m*

merulius lacrymans (domesticus), weeping fungus = tränender Hausschwamm *m*, echter ~
mesh [*denotes the number of openings per lineal inch measured from centre to centre of parallel wires*] = Maschenzahl *f* pro laufenden Zoll *m*, Maschenanordnung *f*
~, aperture; gauge (Brit.) = Masche *f* [*Sieb n*]
~ aperture = Maschensieböffnung *f*
~ blasting net = Drahtschutznetz *n* [*Sprengen n*]
~ laying jumbo = Bewehrungsmatten-Auslegemaschine *f* für Gerinneauskleidungen *fpl*
~ number = Siebgewebenummer *f*
~ reinforcement, see: reinforcing (road) mesh
(~) sieve, square ~ ~ = Maschensieb *n*, Quadrat(loch)sieb
to mesh with = eingreifen in
meshwork, see: steel mesh
mesotil = angewitterter Geschiebelehm *m*
mesotype, natrolite (Min.) = Natrolith *m*
metacenter (US); **metacentre** (Brit.) = Metazentrum *n*
metacentric height = metazentrische Höhe *f*
(metal) capping (strip) = Hohlfugeneisen *n*
~ chair, wire ~ = (Fugen)Stützkorb *m*, Stahldrahtkorb
~ culvert pipe = Blechdurchlaßrohr *n*
~ foil sampler = Bodenprobenahmegerät *n* mit Metallfolie *f*
~ form(work), steel shuttering, steel form(work) = Stahl(blech)schalung *f*
~ hose, see: flexible metallic tube
metalled road (Brit.); **crushed-stone ~** = Schotterstraße *f*
metallic coating = Metallüberzug *m*
metalling (Brit.); **rubble work** = Beschottern *n*, Beschotterung *f*
metal powder = Metallpulver *n*
~ scrap dealer = Schrotthändler *m*
~ sealing strip = Metallfugeneinlage *f*
*metal sheet, sheet metal, sheet iron = Blech *n*, Tafel~, Eisen~
~ sleeve, see: expansion joint cap strip (US)

~ stitching = Metallheften *n*
~ strap, iron ~ = Eisenband *n*
~ tamper beam, ~ tamping ~ = Metallstampfbohle *f*, Metallverdichtungsbohle, Metallschlagbohle, Metallstampfbalken *m*
~ wearing plate = Verschleißblech *n*
~ wheel, steel-rimmed ~ = Eisenrad *n*, eisenbereiftes Rad
metamict zircon = metamikter Zirkon *m*
metamorphic aureole (Geol.) = Kontakthof *m*
~ facies (Geol.) = metamorphe Fazies *f*
~ rock, transformed ~ = Umwandlungsgestein *n*, metamorphes Gestein *n*, Umprägungsgestein
metamorphism (Geol.) = Umwandlung *f*, Metamorphismus *m*, Metamorphose *f*, Umprägung *f*, Gesteins~
metasilicate = Bisilikat *n*
meteorite = Feuerkugelstein *m*, Meteorit *m*
meter = Messer *m*, Zähler *m*
methane = Methan *n*
~ drainage = Grubengasabsaugung *f*
method, operation, process = Verfahren *n*, Methode *f*
~ of forming = Formgebungsverfahren *n*
~ ~ slices = Gleitflächenmethode *f*
methyl alcohol, wood ~, methanol = Methylalkohol *m*, Methanol *n*, CH_3OH
~ benzene, toluene, phenylmethane, $C_6H_5CH_3$ = Toluol *n*, Methylbenzol *n*
(methylated) spirit, alcohol, C_2H_6O = Spiritus *m*
metropolis = Metropole *f*
metropolitan activity = Großstadtleben *n*
~ railway (Brit.); **~ railroad** (US) = Stadtbahn *f*
~ region, ~ area = Wirtschaftsgebiet *n* einer großen Stadt *f*, Großraumgebiet *n*
mg [*million-gallon*] = Million Gallonen *fpl*
miarolyte (Geol.) = Oligoklasgranit *m*
mica (Min.) = Glimmer *m*
micaceous = glimmer(halt)ig, glimmerführend
mica(ceous) porphyry = Glimmerporphyr *m*
~ sand = glimmer(halt)iger Sand *m*
~ sandstone = Glimmersandstein *m*
~ schist = Glimmerschiefer *m*

mica flake = Glimmerplättchen *n*
micanite, reconstructed mica = Mikanit *n*
microcline (Min.) = Mikroklin *m*
microcrystalline = mikrokristallin
micro-granite = Mikrogranit *m*
microlite (Geol.) = Mikrolith *m*
micronizer, see: jet pulverizer
micro-organism = Kleinlebewesen *n*
micro-pegmatite (Geol.) = Mikropegmatit *m*
MICROPHORITE [*Trademark*] = ein Leichtkalkbeton *m* [*in Deutschland hochmikroporöser TURRIT genannt*]
micro-pore = Mikropore *f*
micro-pressure ga(u)ge = Feindruckmesser *m*, Mikromanometer *m*
mid-day break, lunch break = Mittagspause *f*
middle-height discharge tunnel = Ablaß *m* auf mittlerer Höhe *f* [*Talsperre f*]
middle oil, see: carbolic oil
middleshot wheel = mittelschlächtiges Wasserrad *n*
middle size aggregate = Mittelkorn *n* [*Betonzuschlag(stoff) m*]
~ support bridge = Mittelträgerbrücke *f*
mid-feather (wall), see: withe
midget excavator = Kleinbagger *m*
midspan = Feldmitte *f* [*Brücke f; Balken m*]
~ section = Schnitt *m* in Feldmitte *f*
migration of oil = Ölwanderung *f*
migratory fish = Wanderfisch *m*
mild clay, sandy **~** = milder Tonboden *m*
~ climate (Brit.); temperate **~** = gemäßigtes Klima *n*
~ steel, soft **~** = Flußeisen *n*
milestone = Meilenstein *m*
military base = Stützpunkt *m*
~ civil engineering work, infrastructure = Militärbauwesen *n* [*Flugplätze, Nachschublager usw.*]
~ road = Militärstraße *f*
milk of lime, see: cream **~ ~**
mill, see: grinding **~**
millerite, capillary pyrite, NiS (Min.) = Millerit *m*, Haarkies *m*
millet (grass) = Flattergras *n*
millet-seed sand = windtransportierter kugelförmiger Sand *m*
~ sandstone = Sandstein *m* aus kleinen kugelförmigen Einzelteilchen *npl* kieselsaurer Tonerde *f*

milling beam = Fräskette *f* [*Grabenziehmaschine f*]
millisecond delay blasting = Millisekundenverzögerungssprengen *n*
~ (~) electric (blasting) cap, split-second delay cap = Millisekundenzünder *m*, Schnellzeitsprengzünder *m*
~ ~ firing = Millisekundenzündung *f*
mill (mixer) = Knetmischer *m*, Kneter *m*, Zwangsmischer *m*
millrace = Mühlwasserstrom *m*
~ = Mühlwassergerinne *n*
mill scale = Walzzunder *m*
mine = Untertagegrube *f*
~ air = Wetter *n*, Grubenluft *f*
~ car = Gruben(förder)wagen *m*
~ detector = Minensuchgerät *n*
~ hoist = Grubenaufzug *m*
~ loco(motive), mining **~** = Grubenlok(omotive) *f*
~ pump, shaft-siking **~** = Abteufpumpe *f*, Senkpumpe, Bohrlochpumpe
miner, see: gallery machine
mineral = Mineral *n*
***(mineral) aggregate**, skeleton structure = Mineralmasse *f*, Mineralgemisch *n*, Gesteinsmasse *f*, Mineralgerüst *n*, Gesteinsgerüst, Gesteinsgemisch *n*, Gesteinsgemenge *n* [*Straßenbau m*]
~ alkali [*an old name for sodium carbonate*] = Natriumkarbonat *n*
~ caoutchouc, see: elaterite
~ castor oil = mineralisches Rizinusöl *n*
~ colza oil = hochraffiniertes aromatenarmes Spindelöl *n* [*mit Rüböl verschnitten*]
~ deposit, ore **~** = Erzlagerstätte *f*, Erzvorkommen *n*, Erzvorkommnis *n*
~ fat, see: ozokerite
~-filled asphalt (US); see: asphalt (Brit.)
mineral filler = Mineralfüller *m*
~ flax = natürliche Mineralfaser *f*
~ industry = Bergwirtschaft *f*
~ inversion = Mineralumwandlung *f*
mineralogical composition = mineralogische Zusammensetzung *f*, petrographische **~**
mineralogy = Mineralogie *f*
mineral rubber = mineralischer Gummi *m*, das in der Gummiindustrie *f* verwendete Bitumen

mineral seal oil — mix design

mineral seal oil = hochsiedendes Leuchtöl *n*, hochraffiniertes aromatenarmes Solaröl *n*
~ **stability number** = Mineralbeständigkeitszahl *f* [*Bitumenemulsion f*]
~ **tar** = Bergteer *m*
(~) **transformer oil** = Transformatorenöl *n*
~ **vein** = Mineralader *f*
~ **water** = Mineralwasser *n*
~ **wax** = Mineralwachs *n*
~ **winning** = Mineralgewinnung *f*
~ **wool**, see: slag ~
mine removal = Entminung *f*
(~) **(roof) suspension bolt** = Deckenanker *m*
~ **shaft** = Grubenschacht *m*, Bergwerksschacht
~ **timber, pit props** = Grubenholz *n*
~ **tunnel(l)ing** = Streckenvortrieb *m*
~ **ventilation** = Bewetterung *f*
mine-waste heap, see: pit ~
mine winding-engine = Schachtfördermaschine *f*
minimum contact = Minimalkontakt *m*
~ **elongation** = Mindestdehnung *f*
~ **excavation line** = Ausbruchprofil *n* [*Tunnel m*]
~ **load(ing)** = Mindestlast *f*, Mindestbelastung *f*
~ **oil pressure with engine idling** = Mindestöldruck *m* bei Leerlaufdrehzahl *f*
~ **operating width** = Mindestarbeitsbreite *f*, Mindesteinbaubreite [*Fertiger m*]
~ **reinforcement for rectangular reinforced concrete sections in eccentric compression for any eccentricity of the compressive force** = Minimum *n* der Stahleinlagen *fpl* in rechteckigen Stahlbetonquerschnitten *mpl* bei beliebigem Lastangriff *m*
~ **section** = Mindestquerschnitt *m*
~ **spacing** = Mindestabstand *m*
~ **thickness** = Mindestdicke *f*
~ **turning radius** = Schleppkurve *f* [*Fahrzeug n*]
~ **water storage elevation, draw down level** = Absenk(ungs)ziel *n*
mining academy, school of mines = Bergakademie *f*

mining damage = Bergschaden *m*
~ **engineer** = Bergingenieur *m*
~ **geology** = Montangeologie *f* [*Ingenieurgeologie f des Bergbaues m*]
~ **machinery** = Grubenmaschinen *fpl*
~ **shaft** = Grubenschacht *m*
~ **subsidence region** = Bergsenkungsgebiet *n*, bergbauliches Senkungsgebiet
Minister for Trade and Commerce = Wirtschaftsminister *m*
Ministry of Transport, M.O.T. (Brit.); Transport Ministry = Verkehrsministerium *n*
minium (Min.) = Bleimennige *f*
minor bed = Niedrigwasserbett *n*
~ **fault**, see: auxiliary ~
~ **road, subsidiary ~, side ~** = Nebenstraße *f*, Seitenstraße, Kleinverkehrsstraße
minster = Münster *m*
miocene clay = Miozänton *m*
mirabilite, see: glauber salt
mirage = Fata Morgana *f*, Luftspieg(e)lung *f*
miscibility with water test = Mischbarkeitsprüfung *f* mit Wasser *n* [*Bitumenemulsion f*]
misfire(d shot), misfiring [*failure of all or part of an explosive charge to go off*] = Fehlschuß *m*
mispickel (Min.), see: arsenical pyrite
mist-spray method = Versprühen *n* einer dünnflüssigen Bitumenemulsion *f* mit einem Bindemittelgehalt *m* von 30 bis 35% in einer durchschnittlichen Menge von etwa $^1/_3$ kg/m² unter entsprechendem Druck *m* auf alte ausgemagerte bituminöse Decken *fpl*
mitre box saw (Brit.); miter ~ ~ (US); tenon saw = Gehrungssäge *f*
mitre(d) gate = Stemmtor *n* [*Binnenschiffahrtsschleuse f*]
mitred joint = Gehrungsstoß *m*
mitre drainage (Brit.); see: herringbone ~
mitreing (Brit.): mitering (US) = Gehrung *f*
mitre sill, see: lock sill
mix, see: mix(ture)
~ **composition** = Mischgutzusammensetzung *f*
~ **consistency** = Mischungskonsistenz *f*
~ **design** = Mischungsentwurf *m*

mixed admission turbine = gemischt beaufschlagte Turbine *f*
~ **anilin point** = Mischanilinpunkt *m* [*Kohlenwasserstofflösungsmittel n*]
~-**base crude petroleum** = gemischtbasisches Erdöl *n*
mixed cycle engine, semi-diesel (~) = Glühkopfmotor *m*, Semi-Diesel *m*
~ **flow turbine**, see: combined ~ ~
~ **macadam**, see: pre-mixed ~
~ **material storage hopper** = Mischgut-(Verlade)silo *m*
~ **sedimentary rock** = gemischtes Sedimentgestein *n*, gemischt mechanisch-chemisches ~
mixer = Mischer *m*
~ **driver**, ~ **operator** = Misch(er)maschinist *m*, Mischerführer *m*
~ **for road construction** = Straßenbaumischer *m*
mixer-gradation unit, portable batch plant with gradation control = fahrbare Chargen-Mischanlage *f* mit Doppeldecker-Horizontal-Vibratorsieb *n*
mixer hopper, see: loading skip
~ ~ **type weigh-batcher** = Kübelaufzugwaage *f*
(~) **liner segment**, sectional liner = (Mischer)Segmentteil *m, n*
~ **lorry** (Brit.); see: truck mixer (US)
MIXERMOBILE M-61 [*Trademark*] = luftbereifter selbstfahrbarer Betonmischer *m* mit Betonhebeanlage *f*, Fabrikat WAGNERMOBILE, PORTLAND 16, OREGON, USA
mixer operator, see: ~ driver
***mixer-type truck** (US); see: lorry-mounted mixer (Brit.)
mixing = Mischen *n*, Mischprozeß *m*, Mischvorgang *m*
~ = homogene Vermischung *f* verschiedener Tone *mpl* bzw. Rohstoffe *mpl* in der amerikanischen Ziegelindustrie *f*
~ **blade**, see: ~ paddle
~ ~, see: helical ~
~ **cycle** = Mischspiel *n*
~ **drag** = Mischschleppe *f*
~ **drum** = Mischtrommel *f*
~ **efficiency** = Mischungswirksamkeit *f*
~ **flume**, see: ~ trough

~ **hood** [*rotary speed mixer*] = Mischkammer *f*
~ **(or mixer) paddle (or blade)** = Misch(er)schaufel *f*
mixing-placing train for tunnel concreting = Misch- und Einbauzug *m* für Tunnelbetonauskleidung *f*
mixing plant = Mischanlage *f*
~ **platform** = Mischbühne *f*
~ **screw**, see: mixing worm
~ **sequence** = Mischreihenfolge *f*
~ **star** = horizontales Rührwerk *n*
~ **table** = Mischungstabelle *f*
~ **tank** = Mischbottich *m*
~ **time**, mixing period, mixing time period = Mischzeit *f*, Mischperiode *f*
~ **tower** = Mischturm *m*
~ **train** [*soil stabilisation*] = Mischzug *m*
~ **trough**, ~ flume = Misch(ge)rinne *f*, (*n*)
~ **water**, see: ga(u)ging water
~ **width** = Arbeitsbreite *f* [*Bodenvermörteler m*]
~ **worm**, ~ screw = Mischschnecke *f*
mix(ed)-in-place, site mixing in place = An-Ort-Mischverfahren *n*, Bodenmischverfahren *n*
~ **machine**, (rotary) soil mixer, mix-in-place travel(l)ing plant, non-elevating roadmixer, pulverizing mixer, rotary speed mixer, soil mixing machine, mix-in-travel plant = Bodenmischer *m*, Mehrwellen-Boden-Zwangsmischer *m*
mix proportions = Mischungsverhältnis *n*
~ **selection mechanism**, ~ selector = Rezeptwähler *m* [*Betonaufbereitung f*]
mix(ture) = Gemisch *n*, Mischung *f*, Mischgut *n*
mixture turbine = Mischungsturbine *f*
mix water, see: ga(u)ging ~
mizzonite, see: dipyre
mobile, portable = fahrbar, ortsbeweglich
~ **crane** = Fahrkran *m*
~ **drill barge**, ~ drilling platform = schwimmende Bohrinsel *f*
~ **site office** = Bürowagen *m*
model = Baumuster *m*
~ = Modell *n*
~ **computation** = Modellberechnung *f*
~-**similarity study** = Modellähnlichkeitsstudie *f*

model-test, model-experiment = Modellversuch *m*, Modellprüfung *f*
mode of computing, ~ ~ calculation = Berechnungsweise *f*, Berechnungsverfahren *n*
~ ~ operation = Arbeitsweise *f* [*Maschine f*]
moderate sulphate resisting cement, moderate heat of hydration cement; Portland cement Type II (US) = mäßiger Gipsschlackenzement *m*, ~ Sulfathüttenzement *m*
~ wind = mäßige Brise *f*
modified = abgewandelt
~ aeration = hochbelastete Schlammbelebung *f* [*Abwasser*]
~ soil = verbesserter Boden *m*
~ Topeka, see: stone-filled sheet asphalt
modular building unit = maßeinheitlicher Bauteil *m*
~ coordination, ~ measure system = Maßordnung *f*
~ method = Bauweise *f* mit maßeinheitlichen Bauteilen *mpl*
modulus (Brit.); module (US) = Kennziffer *f*, Modul *m*, Beiwert *m*
~ of elasticity, Young's modulus (Brit.); module (US), Young's module (US) = Elastizitätsmodul *m*, Elastizitätsmaß *n*, Elastizitätszahl *f*, Modul für Beton nach Young
modulus-of-rupture (in flexure), ~ (in bending), extreme fibre stress in tension = Biegezugfestigkeitsmodul *m* [*Beton m*]
modulus of subgrade reaction K, subgrade modulus K, modulus of soil reaction K = Bettungsziffer *f*, Planumsmodul *m*, Druck-Setzungs-Quotient *m*, Bodenziffer *f* [*nach Westergaard*]
~ ~ volume change = Steifezahl *f*, Steifeziffer *f* [*Boden m*]
modumite (Min.) = Hartkobalterz *n*
mofette (Geol.) = Mofette *f* [*trockne Kohlensäureaushauchung f bei einem Vulkan m*]
Mohr's envelope, see: envelope of failure
moist curing [*concrete*] = Feuchthaltung *f* [*Beton m*]
~ mixing = Naßmischen *n*, Naß-Nachmischung *f* [*Zementverfestigung f*]

moisture cell = Feuchtigkeitsmeßdose *f*
~ expansion, see: bulking
~ film, water ~ = Wasserhäutchen *n*, Wasserfilm *m*
Molasse (Geol.) = Molassefels *m*
molasses = Molasse *f*
mold (US) = Probekörperform *f*
moldavite = Bouteillenstein *m*
moldboard (US) = Räumschild *n*
molding (US) = Probekörperherstellung *f* [*z. B. Betonwürfel m*]
mole = Mole *f*
~ = Maulwurf *m*
~ composition = Mol-Zusammensetzung *f*
~ drain = Maulwurfdrän *m*
~ plough (Brit.); mole plow (US) = Maulwurf(drän)pflug *m*, Untergrund(drän)pflug
molluscan fauna = Mollusken-Fauna *f*
molybdenite, MoS_2 (Min.) = Molybdänglanz *m*
molybdenum disulphide = Molybdändisulfid *n*
MOLYKOTE = Schmiermittel *n* auf der Basis *f* von Molybdän-Disulfid (MoS_2)
moment at foot [*column*] = Fußmoment *n*
~ ~ head [*column*] = Kopfmoment *n*
~ ~ support, column moment = Stütz(en)moment *n*
~ curve = Momentenlinie *f*
~ diagram = Momentenfläche *f*
~ distribution = Momentenverteilung *f*
~ ~ method = Momenten-Ausgleichsverfahren *n*
~ equilibrium = Momentengleichgewicht *n*
~ of inertia = Trägheitsmoment *n*
MONARCH Super Blake Crusher [*Trademark*] = Doppelkniehebelbrecher *m*, Fabrikat FREDERICK PARKER LIMITED, LEICESTER, ENGLAND
Mond gas generator peat tar = Torf-Mondgasgeneratorteer *m*
~ tar = Mondteer *m*
monitor, see: giant
monkey, see: drop hammer
~ drift, pilot tunnel, pilot heading = Richtstollen *m*, Richtvortrieb *m*
monobloc = Bohrstange *f* mit eingelöteter Hartmetall-Einfachmeißelschneide *f*

monocable aerial ropeway, see: single ropeway
monoclinic system, oblique ~ = monoklines System n [*Kristall n*]
monogenic volcano = einheitlich gebauter Vulkan m
monolithic concrete structure = Monolithbetonbauwerk n
mono-rail telpher [*the machine travels on a bulb-headed rail secured to the top of an I-beam*] = Obergurtlaufschienen-Elektrohängebahn f
~ transporter (or conveyor), single rail ~ (~ ~) = Einschienenbahn f zum Betontransport m, Transport-Einschienenbahn
(mono)tower = Turm m, Kranmast m, Drehsäule f
~ crane, rotating tower ~, revolving ~ ~ = Turmdrehkran m
MONOTUBE foundation pile [*Trademark*] [*it has a scalloped cross-section which is formed by a series of vertical flutings running the full length of the pile. The pile is tapered and is closed at the bottom by a steel boot*] = Ortbetonpfahl m mit konischem Blechmantel m der zwecks besserer Aufnahme des Außendrucks mit einem wellblechartig geformten Querschnitt im Kaltwalzverfahren hergestellt wird, Fabrikat THE UNION METAL MANUFACTURING CO., CANTON 5, OHIO, USA
montan-tar pitch = Montanpech n
montan-wax tar = Montanwachsteer m
monumental building = Monumentalbau m
monzonite, syenodiorite = Monzonit m
moor coal = Moorkohle f
mooring buoy = Ankerboje f
~ (device) = Anlegevorrichtung f, Schiffshaltevorrichtung
mooring-mast [*strong steel tower to top of which an airship can be moored*] = Luftschiff-Haltemast m
mooring pile = Haltepfahl m
~ screw = Schraubenanker m
moor(land) = Moorheide f
moor peat = Heidetorf m

~ soil = Moorerde f, anmooriger Boden m
morainal damming = Abdämmung f durch Moränen fpl
moraine = Moräne f
~ débris = Moräne(n)schutt m, Gletscherschutt
~ gravel, see: glacial ~
morass = Morast m
mordant = Textilbeize f
Morgan-Gammon water-in-sand estimator = Gerät n zur Bestimmung der Eigenfeuchtigkeit f des Sandes für den kolloidalen Mörtel von Gammon-Morgan
morning glory spillway, see: shaft-and-tunnel ~
~ peak hour = Vormittags-Spitzenstunde f
~ shift = Vormittagsschicht f
morphology (Geol.) = Morphologie f
mortar = Mörtel m
~ ~ = Mörser m
~ beater, lime raker = Kalkkrücke f
~ bed = Mörtelstreifen m
***mortar-bound macadam,** see: cement penetration method
mortar box, see: hod
~ fabrication = Mörtelaufbereitung f
~ intrusion = Mörteleinpressung f, Mörtelinjektion f, Mörtelverpressung
~ joint = Mörtelfuge f
~ lining = Mörtelverkleidung f
~ mixer, ~ mixing machine = Mörtelmischer m, Mörtelmischmaschine f
~ nest, ~ pocket = Mörtelnest n
~ obtained by pure mechanical mixing = mechanischer Mörtel
~ pocket, ~ nest = Mörtelnest n
~ rendering, plaster = Mörtelputz m, Putz(mörtel) m
~ sand = Mörtelsand m
~ scoop = Mörtelschöpfer m
~ sledge = Mörtelschlitten m
~ spreader = Mörtelverteiler m
~ trough, see: hod
~ walling = Mörtelmauerwerk n
mortise axe, twybill = Stoßaxt f, Stichaxt f
mortlake (Brit.); see: ox-bow (lake)
mosaic paving = Mosaikpflaster n
~ (~) sett = Mosaikpflasterstein m

moss heath = Moosheide *f*
~ peat = Moostorf *m*
M.O.T., see: Ministry of Transport
motel (US) = Kraftfahrerhotel *n*, Hotel für Motorisierte *mpl*
mother liquor, ~ lye = Mutterlauge *f*
motion-time-analysis = Bewegungs-Zeit-Analyse *f*
motive (or driving) power (or force) = Antriebskraft *f*, Treibkraft, Triebkraft
moto-bug, see: motorised buggy
*****moto-mixer** (US); see: lorry-mounted mixer (Brit.)
MOTO-PAVER [*Trademark*] [*travel(l)ing bituminous mixer and paver*] = Schwarzdeckenmisch- und -verteilergerät *n*, Fabrikat HETHERINGTON & BERNER INC., INDIANAPOLIS 7, USA
motor, electric **~** = Elektromotor *m*
motor ambulance = Krankenauto *n*
~ armature = Motoranker *m*
~-assisted pedal cycle = Motorfahrrad *n*
(motor) bus = (Kraft)Omnibus *m*, (Auto-)Bus
motorcade (US); convoy (Brit.) = Autokolonne *f*
motorcycle engine = Motorrad-Motor *m*
motor driven hand planer = Elektroabrichtmaschine *f*
~ ~ rocker dump car = Muldenwagen *m* mit Eigenantrieb
motor driver postal card method, see: postcard survey
~ footpath brush = Motor-Fußwegkehrmaschine *f*, Fußweg-Motorkehrmaschine
~ fuel = Motor(en)kraftstoff *m* jeder Art
~ generator (set) = Motorgenerator *m*
*****motor grader**, motorized **~**, power **~**, self-propelled (blade) **~**, tractor **~** = Motorstraßenhobel *m*, Motorwegehobel, Motorerdhobel, Motor-Straßenplanierer *m*
~ ~ push plate = Motorstraßenhobel-Stoßplatte *f*
motoring offence = Kraftfahrerverstoß *m*
motor-in-head vibrator = Rüttler *m* (oder Vibrator *m*) mit eingebautem Motor *m*
motorised Inspection troll(e)y [*bridge*] = Besichtigungswagen *m* mit Antriebsmotor *m*

~ buggy, moto-bug = Motorkipp(er)karre(n) *f*, (*m*)
~ (or drive) head pulley = Kopfantriebstrommel *f* [*stationäres Förderband n*]
*****motor (ized) scraper**, tractor-scraper (with two-wheel traction) = Einachs-Motorschrapper *m*, Autoschrapper mit 2-Rad-Schlepper *m*, Schrapper mit gummibereiftem Einachs-Traktor *m*, Motorschürf(kübel)wagen *m* mit Einachsschlepper, motorisierter Schürfkübel *m* mit Einachstraktor *m*, Motorschürfzug *m*
motor loco(motive) = Motorlok(omotive) *f*
MOTORMULE [*Trademark*] [*crawler tractor carrying loads*] = lasttragender Gleiskettenschlepper *m*, Fabrikat MOTORMULI G.m.b.H., MÜNCHEN, DEUTSCHLAND
motor patrol, see: blade maintainer
~ road, see: motorway
~ spirit = Kraftstoff *m* für Verbrennungsmotoren *mpl* jeder Art, auch gebleit [*Auf Erdölbasis in den USA als „gasoline", in England als „petrol" bezeichnet*]
motorstair(case), see: escalator
motor tractor (Brit.); truck tractor, tractor-truck (US) = (Straßen)Zugmaschine *f*
~ traffic = Kraftverkehr *m*, Motorfahrzeugverkehr *m*
~ truck; see: lorry (Brit.)
~ tunnel, automobile traffic **~** = Kraftfahrzeugtunnel *m*
~ vehicle = Motorfahrzeug *n*, Kraftfahrzeug
~ wagon = einachsiger Erdtransportwagen *m* mit Einachs-Radschlepper *m*
motorway, motor road, autobahn = Autobahn *f*, Autostraße *f*, Nurkraftwagenstraße
~ breakdown and repair depot = Autobahnmeisterei *f*
MOTO-SHOVEL [*Trademark*] = Auto-Hochlöffel(bagger) *m* auf Chassis *n* mit Eigenantrieb *m*, Fabrikat THE THEW SHOVEL CO., LORAIN, OHIO, USA
mottled osseous amber = buntknochiger Bernstein *m*
~ sandstone, see: variegated **~**
mo(u)ld = Form *f*

mo(u)ld, cube ~ = Würfelform *f*
~, conical shell, slump cone = Setzbecher *m*
mo(u)ldboard = Brustschild *n*, Schar *f*, Räumschild *n*
mo(u)ld box = Formkasten *m*
mo(u)lded brick, see: profilated ~
~ **peat** = Streichtorf *m*
mo(u)lding machine = Formmaschine *f*
~ **oil** = Formenöl *n*
~ **plaster** = Modellgips *m*
~ **sand** = Formsand *m*
mo(u)ld oil, see: form ~
mount Atlas cedar of Algeria, see: silver cedar
mountain ash = Eberesche *f*
~ **building**, orogeny = Gebirgsbildung *f*, Orogenese *f*, Tektogenese *f*
~ **climber** = Bergsteiger *m*
~ **country** = Gebirgsland *n*
~ **elm**, Scotch ~, wych ~ = Bergrüster *f*, Bergulme *f*, Haselrüster
~ **gulch** = Bergtobel *m*
~ **lake**, (~) **tarn** = Bergsee *m*
~ **limestone**, see: compact ~
~ **oak**, see: chestnut oak
~ **oil** = Bergöl *n*
mountainous = gebirgig
(mountain) pass = (Gebirgs)Paß *m*
mountain-pine = Legföhre *f*, Bergkiefer *f*, Bergföhre *f*
mountain range = Gebirgszug *m*
~ **road**, ~ **highway** = Gebirgsstraße *f*
~ **slope** = Berglehne *f*, Berghang *m*
~ ~ **drainage** = Berghang-Entwässerung *f*
~ **soap**, rock ~ = Bergseife *f*
~ **stream** = Gebirgsfluß *m*
~ **summit** = Berggipfel *m*
~ **tarn**, see: lake
(~) **torrent** = Wildwasser *n*, Wildbach *m*
mounted ceiling = Montagedecke *f*
mounting unit, see: travel(l)ing gear
mouth of the river, river mouth = Flußmündung *f*
movable bridge = bewegliche Brücke *f*
~ **crushing roll** = bewegliche Brechwalze *f*
~ **jaw**, swing(ing) ~, moving ~ = Schwingen(brech)backe *f*, Schwing(brech)backen *m*

~ **ramp multi-stor(e)y garage** = Stockwerksgarage *f* mit beweglichen Rampen *fpl*
movement joint in bridge-deck = Bewegungsfuge *f* im Brückenbau *m*
~ **of bed material by river** = Geschiebetrieb *m*
moving between lanes, see: lane move
~ **form(s)**, ~ **formwork** = bewegliche Schalung *f*
~ **jaw**, see: movable ~
~ **load** = bewegliche Last *f*
~ **moraine** = bewegte Moräne *f*
~ **poise**, see: sliding weight
~ **sand débris** = Sandgeröll *n*
~ **stair(case)**, see: escalator
~ **time between jobs** = Transportzeit *f* [*Baumaschine f*]
~ **vehicle driver postal cards method** = schriftliche Befragungsmethode *f*
muck, trailings, excavation, muck pile = Haufwerk *n*, Schutter *m*, Ausbruch *m* [*Tunnelbau m*]
muck, see: excavated earth
~, see: muck (soil)
~ **bin** (or **hopper**), skip-loading ~ (~ ~) [*headframe*] = Banse *f* [*Förderturm m*]
muck-blasting operation, see: bog blasting
mucker, see: mucking shovel
mucking, tunnel loading = Schutterung *f*, Schuttern *n*
~ **shovel**, ~ **machine**, (mechanical) muck loader, mucker, tunnel mucker, tunnel mucking machine, tunnel shovel = Stollenlademaschine *f*, Stollenschaufellader *m*, Stollenbagger *m* [*in größerer Ausführung = Tunnelschaufellader*]
muck-lock, materials-lock = Materialschleuse *f* [*pneumatische Gründung f*]
muck pile, see: muck
~ **shifting machinery** = Erdbaumaschinen *fpl*
~ **(soil)** [*is silt mixed with organic material, having a high proportion of water and usually low rate of permeability*] = Schluff *m* mit organischen Anteilen, viel Wasser und von im allgemeinen geringer Durchlässigkeit

mud [*is wet earth with little or no organic material. Normally it is low in sand, high in silt. It may or may not have clay in it*] = nasser Erdstoff *m* mit wenig oder gar keinen organischen Stoffen, im allgemeinen wenig Sand, jedoch viel Schluff, wobei Ton enthalten sein kann

~-bound macadam [*deprecated*]; waterbound macadam = wassergebundene Schotterdecke *f*, Chaussierung *f*

mud cake = Schlammverkleidung *f* des Bohrlochs *n*

mudcapping (US); see: plaster shooting (Brit.)

mud conditioning = Bohrschlammaufbereitung *f* [*Rotary-Bohrverfahren n*]

~ filling (US); see: mud-silting (Brit.)

~ flat = Sumpfebene *f*

~ flow = Schlammstrom *m*

mudgard = Schutzblech *n*

mud hut = Lehmhütte *f*

mud-jack(ing) (of pavement slabs), mudjack treatment = Mud-Jack-Verfahren *n*, (Beton)Deckenhebeverfahren durch Einpressen von einem aus Feinsand, Mo, Schluff und Kolloidmaterial als Zuschlag, Zement als Bindemittel und Wasser als Verflüssiger bestehendem Gemisch bei Setzung von Betonfahrbahnplatten

mud mixer = Bohrschlammischer *m* [*Rotary-Bohrverfahren n*]

~ pump, see: solids-handling ~

mud-pumping, see: pumping

mud pump valve = Schlammpumpenventil *n*

mud-silting, siltation (Brit.); mud filling (US) = Verschlammung *f*, Verlandung *f*

mudstone, clay-stone = durch Druck *m* und Wasserverlust *m* erhärteter Ton *m*, Tonstein *m*

mud suction tank = Schlammsaugtank *m*

muffler, exhaust muffler; silencer (Brit.) = Auspufftopf *m*

MUIR-HILL dumper [*Trademark*] = Erdtransportwagen-Rückwärtskipper *m*, Motorkipper, Fabrikat E. BOYDELL & CO. LTD., MANCHESTER 16, ENGLAND

mulch method = An-Ort-Mischverfahren *n* zur Wiederherstellung *f* einer bestehenden Decke *f* aus verhältnismäßig losem Material *n*

~ sodding, see: broadcast ~

mule-back transportation = Mauleseltransport *m*

muller and plate = Schlagbrett *n*, Tatsche *f*, Praker *m*, Patsche *f*, Pritschbläuel *m*, Klatsche *f*

mullite (Min.) = Mullit *m*

multi-axle trailer, full ~, multi-wheeler ~ = Vollanhänger *m*, Mehrachsanhänger

multi-bay frame, multiple ~ = Mehrfeldrahmen *m*, mehrfeldiger Rahmen

multi blade grab (Brit.) see: grabs (US)

multi-bucket dredge(r), see: bucket ladder dredge(r)

~ excavator, continuous land bucket dredge(r), chain bucket excavator, dredger excavator, bucket ladder excavator = Eimerkettentrockenbagger *m*

~ loader, see: bucket elevator loader

~ ~ with belt conveyor discharge arrangement = Becher(werk)auflader *m* mit Band *n*

multi-cellular hollow section = mehrzelliger Kastenquerschnitt *m*

~ wheel = Mehrzellenrad *n*

multi-compartment aggregate feeder = Dosierapparat *m* [*Schwarzdeckenmischanlage f*]

~ bin (or silo) = Mehrzellensilo *m*, Mehrtaschensilo, Zellensilo, Zellenspeicher *m*

~ (grinding) mill = Mehrkammerrohr-(mahl)mühle *f*

~ (or multiple-compartment) washer (or washing machine) = Stufenwaschmaschine *f*, Stufenwäsche *f*

multi-deck screen, (aggregate) grader = Mehrdecker(sieb) *m*, (*n*)

multiflora rose hedge = Wildrosenhecke *f*

multi-fuel burner = Vielfachbrenner *m*

multi-grain palynological slide = palynologisches Vielkornpräparat *n*

multi-lane highway = mehrspurige Straße *f*, vielspurige ~

multi-layer prestressed reinforcement = mehrlagige Spannbewehrung *f*

multi-level belts = Transportbänder *npl* in Höhenstaff(e)lung *f*

multi-pass soil stabiliser = Mehrgang-(boden)mischer *m*

multi-plate dry clutch = Mehrscheibenkupplung *f*

multiple-alarm fire = Großfeuer *n*, Großbrand *m*

multiple arch(ed) dam = Gewölbereihen-(stau)mauer *f*, Vielfachbogensperre *f*, Bogenpfeiler(stau)mauer *f*, Pfeilergewölbe(stau)mauer *f*

~ batcher, see: ~ weigh-batcher

~ ~ hopper = Vielfach-Zuteilgefäß *n*

multiple-bay = mehrschiffig [*Halle f*]

multiple blade joint saw = Vielfachbetonfugenschleifgerät *n*

~ coil process = Mehrstufenverfahren *n* [*Dehydrierung f von Benzin n*]

~-compartment (or multi-compartment) washer (or washing machine) = Stufenwaschmaschine *f*, Stufenwäsche *f*

multiple-course construction (Brit.); see: multiple-lift ~ (US)

multiple cylindrical boiler, ~ combined ~ = mehrfacher Walzenkessel *m*

~-dome shaped dam = Vielfachkuppelsperre *f*, Pfeilerkuppel(stau)mauer *f*

~ effect evaporator = Mehrfachverdampfer *m*

~ (electric) motor drive = mehrmotoriger Elektroantrieb *m*

~ frame, multi-bay ~ = mehrfeldiger Rahmen *m*, Mehrfeldrahmen

~-fuel engine = Vielstoffmotor *m*

multiple-lift construction, stage ~ (US); multiple-course ~ (Brit.) = mehrschichtige Einbauweise *f*, Straßenaufbauweise

~ treatment, see: armo(u)r coat

multiple(-material) scale batcher, see: multiple weighbatcher

multiple motor crane = elektrischer Mehrmotorenkran *m*

~ navigation (or inland) lock = Schleppzugschleuse *f*, Schiffszugschleuse

multiple-opening (drainage) culvert = Vielfachdurchlaß *m*, Vielfachabzugkanal *m*

multiple-part shaft = Gelenkwelle *f*

multi(ple)-purpose structure = Mehrzweckbauwerk *n*, Verbundprojekt *n* [*Talsperre f*]

multiple rope bucket = Mehrseil-Greifkorb *m* Mehrseil-Greifer *m*

~ ~ grab excavator = Mehrseilgreifbagger *m*

~-seated valve = Etagenventil *n*

multiple span bridge = Brücke *f* mit mehreren Öffnungen *fpl*

~ ~ continuous truss = mehrfeldiger Fachwerk-Durchlaufträger *m*

~ ~ gabled frame = mehrfeldiger Giebelrahmen *m*

~ stage boiler = Etagenkessel *m*

~-stor(e)y building = mehrgeschossiger Bau *m*, mehrstöckiger ~

multiple truss = Mehrfachfachwerk *n*

~ weaving = Mehrfachverflechtung *f*

multiple-web system truss = mehrfaches Fachwerk *n*

multiple (weigh) batcher, multiple(-material) scale batcher, cumulative (weigh-) batcher = Gattierungswaage *f*, Waage *f* für alle Gemengeteile *mpl*, Gattierungsgefäßwaage, Gemischwaage

multi-purpose crawler excavator = Universal-(Gleis)Kettenbagger *m*, Umbau-(Gleis)Kettenbagger

~ attachment = Mehrzweckvorrichtung *f*

~ equipment = Mehrzweckgerät *n*

~ vehicle = Mehrzweckfahrzeug *n*

multi-rib reinforcing bars = Rippenstahl *m*

multi-rubber-tire roller (US), see: pneumatic-tire ~

(multi-shot) exploder, blasting machine = Zündmaschine *f*

multi-stage action turbine, see: action turbine with pressure stages

~ compressor = Mehrstufen(luft)verdichter *m*, Mehrstufenkompressor *m*, Mehrstufendrucklufterzeuger *m*

~ impulse turbine, see: action turbine with pressure stages

~ reaction turbine, reaction turbine with pressure stages = mehrstufige Überdruckturbine *f*, Überdruckturbine *f* mit Druckabstufung *f*

multi-stor(e)y frame, tall building ~ = mehrstöckiger Rahmen *m*, mehrgeschossiger ~

~ parking garage = Stockwerksgarage *f*

multi-stor(e)y portal structure = Stockwerksrahmen *m*
multi-tank aviation spirit installation (Brit.); ~ ~ gasoline (or gasolene) ~ (US) = Flugbenzintankanlage *f*
multi-tine grapple (US); multi-tyne ~ (Brit.) = Greifkorb *m* für allgemeine Bodenbaggerung, Stichboden und Gesteinstrümmer
multitubular boiler, see: fire tube ~
multi-use equipment item = Wiederverwendungsgerät *n*
multi-webbed bridge = vielstegige Brücke *f*
multi-wheeled profilometer = mehrrädiger Profilometer *m*
multiwheeler trailer, see: multi-axle ~
multi-wheel roller; see: pneumatic-tire roller (US)
municipal engineering = Städtebau *m*
~ **planner**, see: town ~
~ **planning**, town ~, city ~, urban ~ = Stadtplanung *f*, Städteplanung, städtebauliche Planung
~ **road**, see: (city) street
~ **sewage** = Kommunalabwasser *n*
~ **transport**, mass transportation, mass transit, public transport, public service vehicles' traffic = öffentlicher (Massen-)Verkehr *m*
muriatic acid, see: hydrochloric ~
muscovite, Muscovy glass (Min.) = Muskovit *m*, K-Al-Glimmer *m*, tonerdereicher Kaliglimmer *m*
~**-biotite granite**, two mica granite = Muskovit-Biotit-Granit *m*
muscovite mining = Muskovit-Bergbau *m*
mushroom valve = Kegelventil *n* mit ebener Unterfläche *f*, Tellerventil *n*
muslin glass = Musselinglas *n*, gemustertes Glas
mylonitisation (Geol.) = Mylonitisierung *f*

N

nacrite (Min.) = Nakrit *m*
nadir = Nadir *m*
nagelfluh, see: gompholite
nailability = Nagelbarkeit *f*
nailable = nagelbar
nail bit, see: gim(b)let

~ **drag**, spike ~ = Nagelschleppe *f*
~ **driver** = Nagelramme *f*
nailed timber I-beam = genagelter Vollwandträger *m*
~ **truss** = Nagelbinder *m*
nailing concrete = nagelbarer Beton *m*
nail nippers = Nagelzange *f*
~ **passer**, see: gim(b)let
~ **slip** = Nagelschlupf *m*
naked = blank [*Draht m*]
~ **light** = offenes Licht *n*, ~ Feuer *n*
name board, place-name sign = Ortsschild *n*
~**-plate** = Typenschild *n*, Bezeichnungsschild
naphtha (US) = Erdölbenzin *n*
naphthalate = Naphthalinsalz *n*
naphthalene, naphthalin(e) = Naphthalin *n*
naphthalic acid = Naphthalinsäure *f*
naphthene-base crude petroleum = naphthenbasisches Erdöl *n*
naphthenic oil = naphthensäurehaltiges Öl *n*
napoleonite (Min.) = Napoleonit *m*
nappe, see: earth fold
~ = untere Fläche *f* des überfallenden Strahles *m*
~ **outlier** (Geol.) = Geschieberückstand *m*
napping = Abschlagen *n* [*Stein m*]
narrow band saw = Tischbandsäge *f*
~ **flame**, thin ~, blast ~ = Stichflamme *f*
*****narrow gage system** (US), see: light railroad ~
narrow ga(u)ge = Schmalspur *f*
narrow-ga(u)ge dump car = Baustellen-Selbstentlader *m*
~ **flat dump car** = Baustellen-Flachbodenselbstentlader *m*
~ **track(ing)**; Jubilee ~ (Brit.); industrial ~ (US) = Schmalspurgleis *n*, Baustellengleis
~ **track switch** = Bauweiche *f*
narrow pillar file = Stiftenfeile *f*
~ **strap**, see: cover strip
national grid = Energienetz *n*
nationalisation = Verstaatlichung *f*
national road = Reichsstraße *f*, Nationalstraße
native arsenic (Min.) = Scherbenkobalt *m*

native asphalt, see: natural ~
~ ~ (US); ~ asphaltic bitumen (Brit.) = Naturbitumen *n*
~ **barium sulphate,** see: barite
~ **copperas** (Min.), see: inkstone
~ **manganic hydrate,** gray manganese (-ore) (Min.) = Graubraunstein *m*
~ **soil,** in-situ ~, natural ~, unmade ground = anstehender Boden *m*, gewachsener ~
~ **timber,** see: home-grown ~
natrolite (Min.), see: mesotype
natural aggregates = natürliche Stoffe *mpl*, Naturmaterial *n* [*Betonzuschlag-(stoff) m*]
~ **anhydrite** = natürlicher Anhydrit *m*
~ **asphalt,** native ~ = Naturasphalt *m*, Erdpech *n*
~ **bar,** billet ~ = Bewehrungsstab *m* aus einem Knüppel hergestellt
~ **bed** = Wildbett *n* [*Fluß m*]
~ **brine** = Natursalzsole *f*
~ **cement,** see: blended ~
~ **coarse aggregate,** ~ gravel = natürlicher Grobzuschlag(stoff) *m*, Betonkies *m*
~ **fall (or slope)** = Geländegefälle *n*
~ **fine aggregate,** ~ sand = natürlicher Feinzuschlag(stoff) *m*, Betonsand *m*
~ **frequency** = Eigenfrequenz *f*
~ **-frequency conveyor** = Resonanzförderer *m*, Resonanzrinne *f*
natural gas, rock ~ = Erdgas *n*, Naturgas
~ **gasoline,** casing-head ~ = Gasbenzin *n*, Rohrkopfbenzin, Leichtbenzin, Erdgasbenzin, Naturgasolin *n*
~ ~ **plant,** ~ gasolene ~ (US) = Naturbenzin-Anlage *f*
~ **gravel,** see: ~ coarse aggregate
~ **gypsum,** see: raw ~
naturally aspirated diesel (engine) = selbstansaugender Diesel(motor) *m*
~ **mixed aggregates;** see: all-in-aggregate (Brit.)
natural opaque ice = Naturtrübeis *n*
~ **resin** = Naturharz *n*
~ **rock** = Naturgestein *n*
~ ~ **asphalt** = Asphaltgestein *n* [*mit Bitumen durchtränktes, natürliches, porenreiches Gestein, durchgängig Kalkstein*]

~ ~ ~ **mastic** = Naturasphaltmastix *m*
~ **rubber** = Naturgummi *m*
~ **sand,** see: ~ fine aggregate
~ **soil,** see: native ~
(~) **stone curb** = Naturbordstein *m*
~ ~ **dressing machine** = (Natur)Steinbearbeitungsmaschine *f*
~ ~ **drilling machine** = (Natur)Steinbohrmaschine *f*
~ ~ **grinding machine** = (Natur)Steinschleifmaschine *f*
~ ~ **milling machine** = (Natur)Steinfräsmaschine *f*
~ ~ **polishing machine** = (Natur)Steinpoliermaschine *f*
~ **stones industry** = Natursteinindustrie *f*
~ **water course** = natürlicher Wasserlauf *m*
~ ~ **loss** = natürlicher Wasserverlust *m* [*Unterschied zwischen Gebietsniederschlag und Abfluß*]
~ **weathering agencies** = Atmosphärilien *f*
navigability = Schiffbarkeit *f*
*****navigation lock,** inland ~ = Binnenschiffahrtschleuse *f*, Sperrschleuse
navigational lighting = Schiffahrtbefeuerung *f*
~ **radar unit** = Schiffsfunkmeßgerät *n*
navvy (Brit.) = Erdarbeiter *m*
~ **excavator** (Brit.); shovel type excavator, revolving shovel = Löffelbagger *m*
neap tide, neaps = Nippflut *f*, Nipptide *f*, taube Flut *f*
near-by material, local ~ = örtliches Material *n*
(neat) cement-water grout (or mixture), see: cement-water grout (or mixture)
neck, pipe, volcanic neck (Geol.) = Durchschlagsröhre *f*, vulkanischer Schlot *m*, Eruptionskanal *m*, vulkanischer Neck *m*
necking, neck-down, contraction = Einschnürung *f*
needle bearing = Nadellager *n*
~ **coal** = Nadelkohle *f*
~ **(control) (or regulating) valve** = Nadelschieber *m*
needle-ore, belonite, acicular bismuth, aciculite (Min.) = Nadelerz *n*

needle penetrometer = Nadeleindringgerät n, Nadeleindringungsmesser m, Nadelpenetrometer n
~ (regulating) valve, see: ~ (control) ~
~ shoring, see: dead ~
~-stone, rutilated quartz = Nadelstein m
needle-tin = Nadelzinnerz n
needle valve = Nadelschieber m
needle vibrator, see: concrete mass ~
~ weir, pin ~ = Nadel(stau)wehr n
negative, transparency, transparent positive original = Mutterpause f
~ reinforcement [*reinforcement so placed as to take tensile stress due to negative bending moment*] = Zugbewehrung f, Zugarmierung
negotiating capacity, hill climbing ability = Steigfähigkeit f [*Fahrzeug n*]
~ resistance = Steigungswiderstand m
neon tube = Neonröhre f
nepheline, nephelite (Min.) = Nephelin m
~-basalt = Nephelinbasalt m
~-syenite = Nephelinsyenit m
nephelinite = Nephelinit m
nephrite (Min.) = Nephrit m
neritic sediments = nerëitische Sedimente npl
nest of sieves, set ~ ~, sieve set = Siebsatz m
net section = Nutzquerschnitt m [*Stab m*]
~ section (al area) = verminderter Querschnitt m, Nettoquerschnitt [*Blechträger m*]
netting wire, woven ~, wire fabric, wire mesh, wire cloth = Drahtgewebe n, Drahtgeflecht n
network of slip lines = Gleitflächenschar f [*Boden m*]
neutral = Leerlauf m [*Hebelstellung f*]
~ axis, zero line = neutrale Achse f, Nullinie f
~ fibre (Brit.); ~ fiber (US) = neutrale Faser f
~ lateral earth (or soil) pressure, see: lateral earth pressure at rest
~ oil = Neutralöl n
~ stress, see: excess pore (water) pressure
névé, firn = Firn m
new-reds andstone (Geol.) = Rotliegende n
new snow = Neuschnee m

Newtonian liquid = Newton'sche Flüssigkeit f
newtown = Großsiedlung f
niccolite, copper nickel, NiAs [*old term: nickeline*] (Min.) = Rotnickelkies m, Nickelin n, Kupfernickel m
niche = Nische f [*Tunnel m*]
nick = Kerbe f
nickel antimony glance (Min.), see: ullmanite
nickel-bloom (Min.), see: annabergite
nickel-plated = vernickelt
nicopyrite, pentlandite (Min.) = Eisennickelkies m
nidger = Reibe- und Drückholz n [*Handwerkzeug des Asphaltarbeiters*]
nigger heads [*rounded cobble stones*] = Katzenköpfe mpl [*Pflaster n*]
night flow = Nachtzufluß m
~ power = Nachtstrom m
~ shift = Nachtschicht f
~ visibility, night-time ~ = Nachtsichtbarkeit f
~ watchman = Nachtwächter m
nigrite (Min.) = Nigrit m
nil return, ~ report = Fehlanzeige f
nipper = Vorschneidezange f
nipple = Nippel m
nitralloy, nitriding steel = Nitrierstahl m
nitrate of lime, $Ca(NO_3)_2$ = Kalksalpeter m, Kalziumnitrat n, salpetersaurer Kalk m
~ ~ mercury = Quecksilbersalpeter m
~ ~ soda, see: soda nitre
nitration = Nitrierung f
nitre, see: potassium nitrate
nitric acid = Salpetersäure f
nitrification = Nitrifikation f
to nitrify = nitrifizieren
nitrobarite = Baryt(o)salpeter m
nitrobenzene = Nitrobenzol n, Mirbanöl n
nitrocellulose lacquer = Nitrolack m
nitrogen = Stickstoff m
~ manure, see: calcium cyanamide
nitro-glycerin(e), nitroleum, blasting oil, fulminating oil, explosive oil = Nitroglyzerin n, Sprengöl n
nitrous acid = salpetrige Säure f
Noachian Deluge, see: Deluge of Noah
noble metal, precious ~ = Edelmetall n

NOBLE Mobile Batching Plant on Wheels = Abmeßanlage *f* für Trockenbeton, NOBLE COMPANY, OAKLAND 20, CALIF., USA

noble silver fir = amerikanische Silbertanne *f*

no-bond tensioning = Vorspannung *f* ohne Verbund *m*

nodular felsite, see: pyromeride

~ limestone, see: calcareous nodule

nodule feed scoops = Aufgabeschaufeln *fpl* für Granalien *f*

nodules = Granalien *f*

nodulizing drum = Granuliertrommel *f*

*****nodulizing installation** = Granulieranlage *f*

no-fines concrete (Brit.); **popcorn ~** (US) = entfeinter Beton *m*, Schüttbeton *m*

~ (~) (block of) flats = Schüttbetonwohnhochhaus *n*

~ ~ construction = Schütt(beton)bauweise *f*

noise abatement = Lärmbekämpfung *f*, Lärmabwehr *f*

~ level = Geräuschpegel *m*

no-load valve = Freilaßventil *n*, Freilaufventil *n*, Leerlaufventil *n*

nominal diameter = Nenndurchmesser *m*

~ grading curve = Sieblinie *f* der gewünschten Endprodukte *npl*

~ load = Nennlast *f*

~ mix = Normal-Mischungsverhältnis *n*

~ size, see: size bracket

~ ~, real measure = Sollmaß *n*, Nennmaß *n*

non-agitating concrete hauler (or hauling unit) = Betontransportfahrzeug *n* ohne Rührwerk *n* oder Mischer *m*

non-aqueous suspension = nichtwäßrige Aufschwemmung *f*

non-bearing (partition) wall = nichttragende (Trenn)Wand *f*

non-blinding screen = sich nicht verstopfendes Sieb *n*, verstopfreies Sieb

non-clastic sedimentary rock = nichtklastisches Sedimentgestein *n*

noncohesive, cohesionless, friable, nonplastic, frictional = nichtbindig, nicht kohäsiv, inkohärent, kohäsionslos, rollig [*Boden m*]

non-continuous grading, see: discontinuous ~

non-deformable = formtreu

*****non-destructive testing of concrete** = zerstörungsfreie Prüfung *f* von Beton *m*

non-diversion = Zweckbindung *f* [*Haushaltsmittel npl*]

~ type river power plant = Staukraftwerk *n*

non-elevating roadmixer, see: mix-in-place machine

non-fluid oil = nichtabspritzendes Öl *n*

non-frost-active, see: frost-resistant

non-glare = glare-free

non heat-treatable alumin(i)um alloy = nicht aushärtbare Aluminiumlegierung *f*

non-hydraulic lime, ~ binder = Luftkalk *m*, nichthydraulisches Bindemittel *n*, Luftmörtelbildner *m*

non-lift mixing action, see: rolling and kneading ~ ~

non-lock type barge lift = (Schiffs)Hebewerk *n*

~ ~ counterweight barge lift = (Schiffs-) Hebewerk *n* mit Gegengewichten *npl*

~ ~ float barge lift = Schwimmer-(schiffs)hebewerk *n*

~ ~ platform barge lift = (Schiffs)Hebewerk *n* für Trockenförderung *f*

~ ~ vertical barge lift = lotrechtes (Schiffs)Hebewerk *n*

non-overflow section [*dam*] = überfallfreie Strecke *f*

non-paved shoulder = Standspur *f* ohne Belag *m*

non-plastic [*soil*], see: noncohesive

non-positive drive = kraftschlüssiger Antrieb *m*

non-prestressed reinforcement, see: untensioned bar ~

non-prismatic member = nichtprismatischer Stab *m*

non-reinforced concrete, unreinforced ~, plain ~ = unbewehrter Beton *m*

non-return flap = Rückschlagklappe *f*

non rigid, see: flexible

non-segregation = Nichtentmischung *f*

non-shrinking = schwindfrei

non-skid, non-slip, skid-proof = gleitsicher, rutschfest, griffig

non-skid carpet, see: skid-proof ~
~ chain, snow ~ = (Gleit)Schutzkette f, Schneekette f
~ property, anti-skid ~, road-skid quality = (Straßen)Griffigkeit f
non-spinning rope = drallfreies Seil n
non-stressed concrete = gering beanspruchter Beton m
non-stripping agent, see: dope
non-tensioned reinforcement = schlaffe Bewehrung f, ~ Armierung
non-tidal estuary = Flußmündung f ohne Gezeiteneinwirkung f
nontrailing suction dredge(r), pump barge = Liegesauger m
non-uniform sand = ungleichförmiger Sand m
non-viscous neutral oil = niedrigviskoses Neutralöl n
no-parking marker (or sign) = Parkverbotsschild n
no-passing zone = Nichtüberholungsstrecke f [Straße f]
norite = Norit m
normal benzine = hochraffiniertes Benzin n
~ chippings, ordinary ~, uncoated ~ = Rohsplitt m
~ force = Normalkraft f
~ full-pool elevation, see: ~ op(erating level
normally aspirated [engine] = normal ansaugend [Motor m]
normal op(erating) level, ~ water storage elevation, normal fullpool elevation = Normalspiegel m, normales Stauziel n [Talsperre f]
~ Portland cement; see: Portland cement Type I (US)
~ reciprocal geothermal gradient = normale geothermische Tiefenstufe f
~ RPM = Normaldrehzahl f
~-setting, see: medium-setting
normal stress = Normalspannung f
Northern Lights, Aurora Borealis = Nordlicht n
north-light roof = S(c)heddach n
Norway maple = Spitzahorn m
~ spruce, see: common ~
nosean, noselite (Min.) = Nosean m
no-slump concrete, see: "dry" ~

not built upon = unbebaut
to notch = ausklinken [Träger m]
notch = Kerbe f
~, V-groove = Kerbnut f
~ (Geol.) = Brandungskehle f
~ bending test = Kerbbiegeversuch m
~ ductile steel = ND-Stahl m
~ effect = Kerbwirkung f
~ gauge = Meßwehr n mit rechtwink(e)ligem Einschnitt m in U-Form f
~ impactstrength = Kerbschlagfestigkeit f
notching (Brit.); see: benching
~ = Überschneidung f [Holzverbindung f]
~ cutter = Falzfräser m
notch sensitivity = Kerbempfindlichkeit f
~ shock test, shock test with notched test piece = Kerbschlagbiegeversuch m
notes, code of practice = Merkblatt n
notice (or letter) of award = Auftragsschreiben n
~ of despatch ~ ~ dispatch = Versandbenachrichtigung f
no-turn overhead and front-end loader = kombinierter Front- und Überkopflader m
nourishment [beach rehabilitation] = künstliche Anlandung f [Strand-Wiederherstellung f]
no(u)vaculite, Arkansas stone = (Ar-) Kansas(wetz)stein m
novelty = Neuentwicklung f [Baumaschine f]
nozzle = Düsenöffnung f, Düsenmundstück n, Düse f
N.T. mixer, see: closed drum (concrete) mixer with reverse discharge
N-truss, see: Linville truss
nuclear energy, ~ power = Atomenergie f, Kernenergie
~ fission = Kernspaltung f
~ (power) plant, see: atomic power station
~ (~) reactor = Kernreaktor m, Atomreaktor
~ shielding, reactor ~ = Reaktor-Strahlungsschutz m
number of blows = Schlagzahl f
~ ~ load cycles, repetitions = Anzahl f der Lastspiele npl
~ ~ revolutions = Umlaufzahl f
~ ~ work cycles = Spielzahl f

number with one digit = einstellige Zahl *f*
numerator = Zähler *m* [*Mathematik f*]
numerical = numerisch
~ ratio = Zahlenverhältnis *n*
nummulite (Geol.) = Pfennig *m*
nummulitic sandstone = Nummulitensandstein *m*
nursery = Baumschule *f*
nut, bolt ~, screw ~ = (Schrauben-) Mutter *f*
~ fatigue testing machine = Gerät *n* zur Dauerprüfung *f* von Schraubenverbindungen *fpl*
nutrient = Nährstoff *m*
~ salt = Nährsalz *n*
~ solution = Nährlösung *f*

O

oakum = Werg *n*, geteerter Hanf *m*
Oberbach immersion test = Oberbach-Wasserlagerungsprüfung *f*
~ slurry = Oberbach-Schlämme *f*
object-glass = Objektiv *n*, Objektträger *m* [*Vermessungskunde f*]
oblique crack = Abtreppungsriß *m* [*Bauwerkssenkung f*]
~ (mapping) camera = Schrägbildkamera *f*
~ rolling mill = Schrägwalzwerk *n*
~ scarf = schräger Blattstoß *m*
~ ~ with secret wedge = verborgenes Hakenblatt *n*
~ ~ with wedge = schräges Hakenblatt *n* mit Keil *m*
~ section = schräger Schnitt *m*
~ system, see: monoclinic ~
oblong = langrund
obscured glass = Milchglas *n*
obsequent river = Abkehrfluß *m*
~ valley = obsequentes Tal *n* [*verläuft in Richtung f der Abdachung f*]
observation point, traffic census point = Verkehrszählstelle *f*
~ tower = Aussichtsturm *m*
~ well = Beobachtungsbrunnen *m*
observer, checker = Zählposten *m*
obsolete = veraltet
obstructed valley, blocked-up ~ = abgeriegeltes Tal *n*

obstruction lake, ponded ~ (Geol.) = Abdämmungssee *m*, Stausee
~ light, aircraft warning ~, aviation obstruction ~ = Hindernisfeuer *n*, Hindernisleuchte *f* [*Flugplatz m*]
obtaining pressure diagrams = Indizieren *n* des Druckes *m*
occulting light (or beacon) [*a light regularly eclipsed in which the duration of light is greater than the duration of darknes*] = Blinkfeuer *n*, Blinklicht *n* [*Lichtdauer f größer als Dunkeldauer f*]
occupational hygiene = Arbeitshygiene *f*
occupation tax = Gewerbesteuer *f*
ocean current (Brit.), see: marine ~ (US)
~-going tanker, see: tanker (ship)
oceanic climate (US); marine ~ (Brit.) = Meeresklima *n*
oceanography = Meereskunde *f*
ocean ooze = Meeresschlamm *m*
~ outfall = Abwasser-Auslauf *m* ins Meer *n*
ocher, ochre (Min.) = Ocker *m*
octagonal girder four columns space frame = räumlicher Vier-Säulen-Rahmen *m* als Achteckträger *m*
octahedron = Achtflach *n*, Achtflächner *m*, Oktaeder *n*, vierseitige Doppelpyramide *f*
octane number = Oktanzahl *f*, Klopffestigkeitszahl
octavalence = Achtwertigkeit *f*
odd-lane road = Straße *f* mit ungleicher Spurenzahl *f*
odo(u)r perception = Geruchwahrnehmung *f*
oedometer, see: consolidation (test) apparatus
off-center (US); off-centre (Brit.); eccentric = ausmittig, exzentrisch
~ laning (US) [*three of the four lanes one way during the morning rush hour into town, and three lanes outbound in the evening are used*] = Wechseln *n* der Verkehrsspurrichtungen *fpl* am Morgen *m* und am Abend *m*
***offer**, see: bid
office address, business ~ = Geschäftsadresse *f*
~ building = Bürogebäude *n*, Bürohaus *n*

office engineer = Ingenieur *m* für Innendienst *m*
off-loading, unloading = Ausladen *n*, Abladen *n*, Entladen *n*
~ **(side) track,** see: unloading (~) ~
off-road performance = Geländegängigkeit *f*
off-set disc harrow = Kultivator *m*
~ **ditch** = Stichgraben *m*
off-shore bar, see: sand-head
~ **dock** = „L"-Dock *n*
~ **wind,** land breeze, land wind = ablandiger Wind *m*
off-size, permissible variation, deviation, margin, tolerance = Abmaß *n*, Maßabweichung *f*, Toleranz *f*
off-street parking = Parken *n* außerhalb der Straßenfläche *f*
off-take shaft = Entnahmeschacht *m*
off-the-highway (or off-the-road) tire (US); earthmover tyre (Brit.); ground grip ~, off-road equipment ~ = Geländereifen *m*, Reifen mit Geländeprofil *n*
~ **vehicle,** see: cross-country ~
OGA, see: open-graded (mineral) aggregate
ogee downstream slab, cyma ~ ~ = unterwasserseitige Platte *f* mit (verkehrt-)steigendem Karnies *n*
~ **weir (or spillway),** cyma ~ (~ ~), ogee(-shaped) dam, cyma (-shaped) dam = Wehr *n* (oder Überlauf *m*) mit (verkehrt)steigendem Karnies *n*
oil barge = Ölkahn *m*
oil-bath air filter (or cleaner) = Ölbadluftfilter *m*, *n*
~ **lubrication** = Ölbadschmierung *f*
oil-bearing stratum, petroliferous bed = Ölträger *f*
oil brake = Öldruckbremse *f*
~ **breather** = Öldampfentlüfter *m*
~ **burner** = Ölbrenner *m*
~ **burning,** ~ firing = Ölfeuerung *f*
~ **cable,** oil-filled ~ = Ölkabel *n*
~ **cake** = Ölkuchen *m*
~ ~ **breaker** = Ölkuchenmühle *f*
~ **can** = Ölkanne *f*
~ **catcher,** ~ deflector = Ölschutz *m*
~ **circulation lubricating system,** ~ circulating lubrication = Ölumlaufschmierung *f*

~ **cup** = Ölbüchse *f*, Öler *m*
~ **dash pot** = Öldämpfer *m*
~ **deflector,** ~ catcher = Ölschutz *m*
~ **dipper rod** = Ölstandmeßstab *m*
~ **drilling island,** platform for oil drilling at sea = Ölbohrplattform *f* auf See *f*
~ **emulsion** = Ölemulsion *f*
~ **engine** = Ölmotor *m*
oiler = Schmierer *m*
~ = Öler *m*
oil field = Ölfeld *n*
oil-field emulsion = Rohöl-Emulsion *f* mit Wasser *n* oder anderen Stoffen *mpl*
oil field going to water = verwässerndes Erdölfeld *n*
~ ~ **winch** = Schlepperwinde *f* für Ölfeldarbeiten *fpl*
oil-fired metre-ga(u)ge loco(motive) = Schmalspur-Dampflok(omotive) *f* mit Ölfeuerung *f*
oil firing, see: ~ burning
~ **force pump** = Öldruckpumpe *f*
~ **gas** = Ölgas *n*, Fettgas, transportables Gas
~ ~ **tar** = Ölgasteer *m*, Fettgasteer
~ **groove** = Ölnut *f*
~ **gun** = Ölungspresse *f*
~ **horizon** = Ölhorizont *m*
oil-impregnated limestone = ölgetränkter Kalkstein *m*
oiling, surface ~ = Straßenölung *f*
~ **hole plug** = Öleinfüllschraube *f*
oil-in-water emulsion = Öl-in-Wasser-Emulsion *f*
oil level indicator, ~ ~ ga(u)ge = Ölstandanzeiger *m*
~ **lubricating pump** = Ölschmierpumpe *f*
~ **manifold** = Ölverteiler *m*
~ **mat (road) surface** = Teppich(belag) *m* mit Ölung *f*
~ **pan** = Ölwanne *f*
~ **pitch,** petroleum ~ = Petrolpech *n*
~ **press** = Ölpresse *f*
~ **pressure** = Öldruck *m*
~ ~ **at full throttle with warm engine** = Öldruck *m* bei voller Drehzahl *f* und warmem Motor *m*
~ ~ **cylinder** = Druckölzylinder *m*
~ ~ **hose** = Öldruckschlauch *m*
~ **removal** = Entölung *f*

oil reserve = Ölvorrat *m*
~ reservoir = Ölbehälter *m*
~ retainer = Ölspritzring *m*
~ sand = Ölsand *m*
~ sandstone = Ölsandstein *m*
~ seasoning = Holztrocknung *f* mit Öl *n*
~ separator = Ölabscheider *m*
~ ~ for steam = Abdampfentöler *m*
~ shale, see: (asphaltic) pyrobituminous shale
~ solvent treatment = verdünnte Ölschutzschicht(behandlung) *f*
~ splash lubrication = Ölspritzschmierung *f*
~ spray = Ölsprühfilm *m*
oil-stone = Öl(abzieh)stein *m*
oil storage and (un)loading terminal = Ölumschlaganlage *f*
~ sump = Ölwanne *f*, Ölsumpf *m*
~ switch, ~ circuit-breaker = Ölschalter *m*
~ tanker = Öltanker *m*
~ trap = Ölfänger *m*
~ ~ = Ölfalle *f* [*Stelle an der sich Erdöl sammelt*]
~ vapours = Öldämpfe *mpl*
~ varnish = Ölfirnis *m*, fetter Firnis
oil-water-gas tar, carburetted water-gas ~, fuel-oil gas ~, reformed-gas ~ = Ölwassergasteer *m*
oil wedge = Ölkeil *m*
~ well = Ölbrunnen *m*, erdölfündige Bohrung *f*, Ölquelle *f*
~ ~ cement = Erdölzement, Ölbohrzement
~ ~ derrick = Ölbohrturm *m*
~ ~ drill = Ölbohrgerät *n*
~ wick = Öldocht *m*
O & K (shuttle) dumper = Autoschütter *m*, Fabrikat ORENSTEIN & KOPPEL UND LÜBECKER MASCHINENBAU A. G., DORTMUND, DEUTSCHLAND
oleaster = wilder Ölbaum *m*
oleic acid = Ölsäure *f*, $C_{18}H_{34}O_2$
Oliensis spot test = qualitative Bestimmung *f* von Bitumen *n* durch Auflösung *f* in heißem Kerosin *n*
oligoclase (Min.) = Oligoklas *m*
oligosaprobic organisms = Oligosaprobien *fpl*

~ zone = oligosaprobe Zone *f*
olivine (Min.) = Olivin *m*, Olivenstein *m*
olivine-nodule (Geol.) = Olivinbombe *f*
olivine-rock, dunite (Geol.) = Dunit *m*, Olivinfels *m*
omitted-size fraction, discontinuously-graded aggregate = Ausfallkorngemisch *n*, Ausfallkornmischung *f*
on a lifelike basis = wirklichkeitsgetreu
once-run benzene = mit Natronlauge *f* und verdünnter Schwefelsäure *f* gewaschenes Redestillat *n*
oncoming traffic, opposing ~ = Gegenverkehr *m*
on edge = hochkant
on-fire glaze = Glasur *f* für das Einbrandverfahren *n*
one-hand block = Einhandstein *m*
one length of drill pipe, auger stem = Bohrstange *f* [*Rotary-Bohrverfahren n*]
one-man operation, ~ control = Einmannbedienung *f*
~ scraper = Einmann-Handschrapper *m*
one-power unit excavator = Einmotorenbagger *m*
one-side(d) rope = eintrümiges Seil *n*
one-stage grinding = einstufige Mahlung *f*
one-stop batch plant = Abmeßanlage *f* mit einmaligem Halten *n* der Fahrzeuge *npl*
one-way pair = Einbahnstraßenpaar *n*
~ plough (Brit.)**/plow** (US) = Drehpflug *m*
~ road = Einbahnstraße *f*
~ traffic, uni-directional ~ = Einbahnverkehr *m*
one-wheel plough (Brit.)**/plow** (US) = Pflug *m* mit Radstelze *f*
on-highway vehicle = Straßenfahrzeug *n*
on-job lab(oratory), field ~ = Baustellenlabor(atorium) *n*
(on)shore wind, sea breeze = Seewind *m*
on-site mixer = Baustellenmischer *m*
on stock, carried in stock = vorrätig
on-the-job service unit, field service unit = Werkstattwagen *m*
~ travel speed, see: working ~
onyx marble = Onyxmarmor *m*, Kalkonyx *m*
oölitic hematite (Min.) = Hirseneisenstein *m*, Hirseneisenerz *n*

oölitic iron ore (Min.) = Eisenrogenstein m, Eisenoolith m
~ limestone, oölite = oolithischer Kalkstein m, Oolithkalk m, Kalkoolith m, Eisteinkalk
opal glass = Opalglas
~ jasper, jasp opal (Min.) = Jaspopal m
open-air drying = Freilufttrocknerei f
~ ground, ~ exhibition space = Freigelände n [Messe f]
~ plant, outdoor ~ = Freiluftanlage f
~ power station = Zentrale f im Freien
open-bottomed concrete trough spreader, ~ ~ hopper, spreading machine without bottom doors = Betonverteilungswagen m (oder Querverteiler m) ohne Bodenplatte f
open bridge, see: trough ~
~ bucket well (Brit.); see: sweep ~ (US)
~ building pit, see: ~ excavation
~ caisson = offener Senkkasten m
~ ~ foundation, see: (sunk) well ~
opencast site, ~ mine = Tagebaugrube f
~ mining loco(motive) = Tagebau-Lok(omotive) f
~ ~ method = Tagebau-Abbauverfahren n
~ ore mining = Erzabbau-Tagebetrieb m
open-circuit operation (or grinding) = Durchlaufmahlung f
open cooler (or cooling stack, or graduation-works) = offenes Gradierwerk n, ~ Rieselwerk
~ cup = offener Tiegel m [Flammpunktprüfung f]
~ cut, see: ~ excavation
open-cut tunnel(l)ing = Herstellung f eines Tunnels m in offener Baugrube f
(open) ditch, field ~, drainage ~ = offener Graben m, Abflußgraben
open dock = Außendock n
*open-dredged caisson method = Bagger-Senkkastengründung f
open-end cell = Stützzelle f [Holz n]
~ pipe foundation (or bearing) pile = Stahlrohr(gründungs)pfahl m mit offenem Ende n
~ skip, see: loading ~
open excavation, ~ cut(ting), ~ building pit = unverkleidete Baugrube f

open-graded (mineral) aggregate, OGA = offen abgestuftes Mineralgemisch n, ~ abgestufte Mineralmasse f
~ road mix surface, see: macadam aggregate type ~ ~ ~
open ground plant = Freilandpflanze f
~-hearth furnace, see: hearth ~
open hill-side duct = Hangkanal m
~ (hydraulic) fill = hydraulische Verlegung f der nicht verwendeten Erdmassen fpl in den Abraum m
~ inclined type bucket elevator = offenes Schrägbecherwerk n, offener Schrägelevator m
~ mix, coarse ~ = offene Mischung f
~ ocean = Außenmeer n [Atoll n]
open-pan mixer = Trogmischer m
open pier excavation; see under "caisson pile"
~ pit coal mining (US); ~ cast ~ ~ (Brit.) = Kohlentagebau m
~ section = offener Querschnitt m
~ spillway (US); free waste weir, free spillway = Freistrahlüberlauf m
~-spiral worm conveyor, anti-friction ~ ~ = Band(förder)schnecke f
open stand pipe, pore-pressure measuring device of the open-standpipe type = offenes Standrohr n
~ storage ground (or area) = Freilagerplatz m
~ surface (or storm) drainage = Oberflächenentwässerung f durch offene Gräben mpl
~ tendering, ~ tender action = öffentliche Ausschreibung f
open-textured [wearing course] = offen [Verschleißschicht f]
open-top railway car (Brit.); ~ railroad (US); gondola car = offener Güterwagen m, ~ Waggon m
open-trench test = Wasserdruckprüfung f bei unverfülltem Rohrgraben m
open-web expanded beam = Vierendeel-Träger m hergestellt aus einem zickzack-förmig aufgeschnittenem I-Profil n
operating brake = Arbeitsbremse f
(~) bucket = Auslegerkübel m [Straßenbetoniermaschine f]
~ chain = Bedienungskette f

operating condition (or order) = Betriebsfähigkeit f, Betriebsbereitschaft f
~ **conditions** = Betriebsverhältnisse npl
(~) **control**, see: control
~ **costs** = Betriebskosten f
~ **deck** = Bedienungsstand m
~ **design condition** = Entwurfbetriebsbedingung f
~ **device** = Bedienungsvorrichtung f
~ **economy** = Betriebswirtschaftlichkeit f
~ **engineer** = Betriebsingenieur m
~ **error**, ~ **mistake** = Bedienungsfehler m
~ **failure** = Betriebsmangel m
~ **fault** = Betriebsfehler m
~ **gallery** = Verbindungsstollen m der Schützenbedienungskammern fpl
~ **gear** = Getriebegang m
~ **handle** = Bedienungsgriff m
~ **instruction** = Bedienungsanweisung f, Betriebsanweisung f
~ **lever** = Bedienungshebel m, Betätigungshebel
~ **order**, see: ~ condition
~ **pressure** = Betriebsdruck m
~ **principle** = Arbeitsprinzip n [*Baumaschine f*]
~ **ring** = Druckring m
~ **safety** = Betriebssicherheit f
(~) **span** = Stützweite f [*Seilförderanlage f*]
~ **speed range** = Betriebsdrehzahlbereich m
~ **weight**, see: service ~
operational area = Betriebsfläche f [*Flugplatz m*]
~ **changeover** = Betriebsumstellung f
~ **range** = Arbeitsbereich m
operative (Brit.); see: driver
operator, see: driver
operator's control cabin, see: driver's ~
~ **platform**, control ~, control station = Bedienungsstand m, Steuerstand
ophicalcite (Geol.), see: forsterite-marble
ophitic texture = divergentstrahlig-körnige (oder ophitische) Struktur f (oder Textur f), Intersertalstruktur, Intersertaltextur
opposed-action screen = Gegenschwingsieb n
opposing lane = Gegen(verkehrs)spur f

~ **traffic**, see: oncoming ~
opposite bank = Gegenufer n [*Fluß m*]
optical mirror method = spiegeloptisches Verfahren n
~ **orientation** [*mineralogy*] = optische Achsenebene f
~ **square** = Winkelprisma n [*Vermessungskunde f*]
optimum compaction = bestmögliche Verdichtung f
~ **moisture content** = optimaler Feuchtigkeitsgehalt m, ~ Wassergehalt
optional attachment = wahlweiser Zusatzteil m [*Baumaschine f*]
orange-peel grab, see: four-bladed circular grab (or bucket)
orchard grass, see: cocks-foot
order = Auftrag m
~ = Größenordnung f
of the ~ of = in der ~ von
ordinary chippings, uncoated ~, normal ~ = Rohsplitt m
ordinary grade = Normalgüte f
~ **lime mortar** = Luftmörtel m
~ **Portland cement**; see: Portland cement Type I (US)
~ **tarmacadam** = kalt verarbeitbarer Teermakadam m
~ **wave** = Schwerwelle f
ore bridge = Erzverladebrücke f
~ **carrier** = Erzfrachtschiff n
~ **channel** = Erzweg m
~ **chimney**, see: ~ pipe
~ **deposit**, mineral ~ = Erzlagerstätte f, Erzvorkommen n, Erzvorkommnis n
~ **deposition** = Erzlagerstättenbildung f
~ **formation** = Erzformation f
Oregon pine, pitch ~, Douglas fir, Columbian pine = Harzkiefer f, Terpentinkiefer, Douglasie f
ore handling plant (or installation) = Erzumschlaganlage f
(~) **lode** = zusammengesetzter (Erz-)Gang m
~ **magma** = Erzmagma n
~ **mine** = Erzbergwerk n
~ **pile** = Erzhalde f
~ **pipe**, ~ **chimney** = Erzschlauch m
~ **scrubber**, see: scrubber
~ **shoot** = Erzfall m

ore slag = Erzschlacke f
organ bellows = Orgelgebläse n
organic débris = organischer Schutt m
~ matter (present), ~ impurity [soil] = ausglühbare Bestandteile mpl [Boden m]
~ soil = organischer Boden m, belebter ~
~ test for fine aggregate, test for organic matter, Abram's test, extraction with caustic soda, colorimetric test = Ätznatronprobe f, Ätznatronprüfung f [Betonzuschlag(stoff) m]
organiser = Organisator m
organization of construction plant and machinery for concrete pavements = Baueinrichtungen fpl und Geräte npl des Betondeckenbaues m
oriental alabaster = orientalischer Alabaster m
oriented diamond bit = Bohrkrone f mit orientiert eingesetztem Diamant m
orifice = Blende f
~ visco(si)meter = Ausfluß-Viskosimeter n, Auslauf-Viskosimeter
origin and destination survey, O-D ~ = Start- und Zielort(verkehrs)zählung f
original temperature = Entstehungstemperatur f
originating traffic = Quellverkehr m
origin cohesion = ursprüngliche Kohäsion f
ornamental concrete, decorative ~ = Zierbeton m
orogeny, see: mountain building
orographical features of the ground in rural areas = Bodengüte f in ländlichen Gegenden fpl
orography = Orographie f, Gebirgsbeschreibung f
orpiment (Min.) = gelbe Arsenblende f
Orsat apparatus = Orsat-Apparat m
orthite (Min.), see: allanite
orthodox method, classic ~ = klassische Methode f
orthogneiss = Orthogneis m, Orthogestein n
orthogonal curve system = orthogonales Kurvennetz n, rechtwinkliges ~
orthosilicate = Orthosilikat n
orthosilicic acid = Orthokieselsäure f

orthotropic(al) plate, see: light gauge carriageway
oscillating axle = Schwingachse f
~ beacon = Schwebungsfeuer n
~ circuit = Schwingkreis m
~ screed = hin- und hergehende Abstreifbohle f
~ smoothing beam = hin- und hergehende Glättbohle f
oscillator machine = Schwingungsmaschine f
osier = Korbweide f
osmosis = Osmose f
ostracite formation = Muschelkalkformation f
Otto cycle engine; gas(olene) (or gasoline) engine (US); petrol engine (Brit.) = Vergasermotor m, Benzinmotor, Otto-(Vergaser)motor
Otto-type fuel = Otto-Kraftstoff m, Otto-Treibstoff
ottrelite slate = Ottrelithschiefer m
out and home ticket = Rückfahrkarte f
outbuilding = Nebengebäude n
outcrop, rock ~ = Aufschluß m (Geol.)
to outcrop, to crop out = ausstreichen, ausgehen (Geol.)
outcropping rock, bed ~, country ~, solid ~, underlying ~, ledge ~ [any layer of rock underlying soils. Geologically the term denotes material underlying drift deposits] = anstehendes Gestein n, gewachsener Fels m, Felsuntergrund m, Kernfels, Sprengfels
to outdo, to outperform = in der Leistung f übertreffen
outdoor exposure = Freiluftlagerung f [Materialprobe f]
~ plant, open-air ~ = Freiluftanlage f
~ swimming pool = Freibad n
~ temperature sensing device = Außentemperaturfühler m
outer chamber = (Schleusen)Vorkammer f
~ harbo(u)r = Außenhafen m
~ jacket = Außenmantel m
~ prestress = Außen-Vorspannung f
~ rail = Außenschiene f
~ shore = Außenstrand m

outer string = (Treppen)Außenwange *f*
~ zone = Außenzone *f*
outfall capacity = Vorflutleistung *f*
~ (ditch), main outfall, outfall drain, drain outfall, receiving stream, receiving water = Vorfluter *m* [*Gewässer n das die Abflußmenge eines anderen aufnimmt*]
~ drain, see: ~ (ditch)
~ drain, interceptor, collecting drain, intercepting drain, drain outfall, catch(water) drain = (Abfang)Sammler *m*
~ headwork, see: outlet structure
~ structure, outlet ~ (Brit.); **~ headwork (US)** = Auslaufbauwerk *n*, Mündungsbauwerk [*Entwässerung f*]
outfit, rig = (Maschinen)Aggregat *n*
outfitting pier = Ausrüstungskai *m*, Ausrüstungskaje *f*
outgoing air, exhaust ~, used ~, waste ~ = Abluft *f*
outlet, discharge = Ablaß *m*, Auslaß
~ channel = Auslaufkanal *m*
~ conduit = Abflußleitung *f*
~ control gate, ~ regulating ~ = Ablaßregulierschütz(e) *n*, (*f*)
~ gate = Betriebsverschluß *m*, Ablaßverschluß
~ headwork, see: ~ structure
~ opening, see: ~ point
~ pipe = Ablaßrohr *n*
~ point, ~ opening, discharge ~ [*jaw crusher*] = Austrittsöffnung *f*, Austragsspalt *m*
~ regulating gate, see: ~ control ~
~ structure, outfall ~ (Brit.); **~ headwork (US)** = Auslaufbauwerk *n*, Mündungsbauwerk [*Entwässerung f*]
~ tunnel = Ablaßstollen *m*
~ valve = Ablaßschieber *m*
~ ~ ~ = Dunstrohr *n*
to outline = skizzieren
outline drawing = Umrißzeichnung *f*, Skizze *f*
~ of arch = Bogenlinie *f*, Bogenprofil *n*
outmoded = veraltet, unmodern
out-of-balance (weight), unbalance = Unbalance *f*, Unwucht *f*, Schwunggewicht *n*
out of service = außer Betrieb

out-of-the country job = Auslandsbauvorhaben *n*
to outperform, to outdo = in der Leistung *f* übertreffen
outport = Vorhafen *m*
output = Ausstoß *m* [*Produktion f*]
~ capacity = Leistungsvermögen *n*
outreach, working radius = Ausladung *f*, Reichweite *f* [*Drehkran m*]
outrigger = ausfahrbare Stütze *f*, Seitenstütze [*z. B. beim Autobagger m*]
outside air = Außenluft *f*
~ diameter = Außendurchmesser *m*
~ power = Fremdstrom *m*, Fremdenergie *f* [*Elektrizität f*]
~ ~ supply = Fremdstromzufuhr *f*, Fremdenergiezufuhr
~ scaffold(ing), external ~ = Außenrüstung *f*, Außengerüst *n*
~ slope = Außenböschung *f*
~ storage = Freilagerung *f*
~ (thread) caliper = Außentaster *m*
~ temperature, external ~, outdoor ~ = Außentemperatur *f*
outsize, oversize = übergroß
~, oversize = Übergröße *f*
outskirts = Außenbezirke *mpl*
outstanding flange = abstehender Schenkel *m* [*Winkelstahl m*]
outward-bound road, exit ~, driveway = Ausfallstraße *f*
outward sweep of the dragline bucket = Auswärtsbewegung *f* der Schleppschaufel *f*
outwash delta = Auswaschdelta *n*
~ fan = Auswaschfächer *m*
~ gravel, glacial ~ ~ = Auswaschschotter *m*
~ plain, (over)wash ~ = Kiesfeld *n*, Sandfeld, Auswaschebene *f*
ouvarovite (Min.), see: uwarowite
oval head countersunk rivet = Linsensenkniet *m*
~ ribbed wire = ovalgerippter Draht *m*
overall core recovery = Gesamtkerngewinn *m*
~ density, bulk ~ [*soil*] = Trockengewicht *n* plus Wasser *m*
~ rigidity = Gesamtstarrheit *f* [*Straßenbefestigung f*]

overall strength = Gesamtfestigkeit *f*

~ weldability, weldability assessed from the effect of mechanical stresses = konstruktiv bedingte Schweißsicherheit *f* [*in der Schweiz: allgemeine Schweißbarkeit f*]

over-and-under scale = Plus-Minus-Waage *f*

overbreak, undercut(ting) = Mehraushub *m* [*Planum n*]

overbridge, overpass, overspan bridge, overcrossing = Überführung *f*

overburden, shelf, overlay, uncallow, topspit; tir [*in Scotland*] = Abraum *m*, Überlagerung *f*, Deckschutt *m*, Deckgebirge *n*, Abraumschicht *f*

~ conveyor bridge, ~ transporter ~ = Abraumförderbrücke *f*

~ loco(motive) = Abraumlok(omotive) *f*

~ pressure = Überlagerungsdruck *m*

~ ropeway = Abraumseilbahn *f*

~ stacker = Abraum-Bandabsetzer *m*

~ stripping, stripping of overburden = Abraumabtrag *m*

~ transport = Abraumtransport *m*, Abraumförderung *f*

~ transporter bridge, ~ conveyor ~ = Abraumförderbrücke *f*

overburnt = totgebrannt *f* [*Kalk m*]

~ particle of limestone, grain in the mortar = Kalkkern *m*, Kalkkrebs *m*, Fehlbrand *m*

overcrossing, see: overbridge

overcrowding = Überbelegung *f*

overcurrent trip = Überstromauslöser *m*

overdeepened = übertieft

overdrive = Schnellgang *m*

overfall weir, waste-weir, overflow weir, spillway weir, crest-control weir = Überfall(stau)wehr *n*, Überlauf(stau)wehr

overfault (Geol) = Übersprung *m*

to overflow = überfallen

overflow = Überfall *m* [*Abflußvorgang m beim Überfließen des Wassers über ein Wehr*]

~ arch dam = Überfallbogen(stau)mauer *f*

~ buttress = Überfallpfeiler *m*

~ channel, discharge ~, tail race = Unterwasserkanal *m*, Ablauf *m*, Untergraben *m*, Abflußkanal *m*

~ crest, spillway ~ = Überfallkrone *f*, Überlaufkrone

~ land, flood district = Überschwemmungsgebiet *n*

~ pipe = Überlaufrohr *n*

~ (spillway) section, river ~ (~) ~, spillway section = Überfallstrecke *f*, Überlaufstrecke

~ (-type) spillway = Überlauf *m* über die Stauwerkskrone

overflow valve = Schlabberventil *n*, Überströmventil

~ water = Überfallwasser *n*

~ weir, see: overfall ~

overgrown with grass = vergrast

overhang (Geol.) = Balme *f*

to ~ = überhängen

overhaul(ing) = Überholung *f*

over-haul [*the distance of the haul in excess of the free haul*] = Zusatztransportweite *f* [*Erdbau m*]

overhead bucket = Überkopf(lade)schaufel *f*, Wurfschaufel

~ cable, electric ~ = Luftkabel *n*

(~) cableway, tautline ~, aerial ~, cable-crane; blondin (Brit.) = Kabelkran *m*

~ chain conveyor = Überlauf-Kettentransporteur *m*

~ cistern, elevated (water) tank, tower tank = (Wasser)Hochbehälter *m*

~ clearance = lichte Höhe *f*, Lichthöhe

~ costs, ~ expenses = Generalunkosten *f*, allgemeine Unkosten

~ crane, (~) travel(l)ing ~ = Laufkran *m*

(~) eccentric (shaft), swing jaw shaft = Exzenter(welle) *m*, (*f*), Antriebswelle [*Backenbrecher m*]

~ ~ (type jaw) crusher, Dalton ~ ~ (~ ~) ~, single toggle jaw crusher = Einschwingen(backen)brecher *m*

~ (electric) cable = Luftkabel *n*

~ expenses, see: ~ costs

~ hopper, receiving bin, (storage) bin = Baustellensilo *m*, Aufnahmebunker *m*, (Sorten)Zwischen(lade)bunker

~ line = Freileitung *f*

overhead loader, overshot ~, rocker shovel, flip-over bucket loader, overloader, overhead shovel = Überkopf(Schaufel)-Lader *m*, Wurfschaufellader, Überkopf-Fahrlader
~ **loading** = Überkopfladen *n*
~ **monorail** = Einschienen-Hängebahn *f*
~ **push-rod operated valve** = hängendes Stößelventil *n*
~ **rail, suspension** ~ = Hängeschiene *f*
~ **roadway,** see: elevated ~
~ **stoping** (Geol.) = Übersichbrechen *n*, Aufstemmen *n*
~ **storage** = Hochlagerung *f*
~ **track way** (US); see: service gangway (Brit.)
~ **transmission line** = Freileitung *f*
(~) travel(l)ing crane, overhead ~ = Laufkran *m*
~ **trolley beam** = Laufkatzenträger *m*
~ **valve** = hängendes Ventil *n*
overlap = Überlappung *f*
~ **joint** = Überlappungsstoß *m*
overlapping fold = Eskaladierfalte *f* (Geol.)
overlay, see: overburden
~ **(pavement);** topping, overlay paving (US) = Überzug(decke) *m*, (*f*)
overload clutch (coupling), safety ~ (~) = Überlast(ungs)kupplung *f*
overloader, see: overhead-loader
overlying layer, roof (Geol.) = Hangende *n*
overpass, see: overbridge
~ **for pedestrians** = Fußgängerüberführung *f*, Fußgängersteg *m*
overridden mass (Geol.) = Basalscholle *f*
overrun, stopway = Auslauf *m* [*Flugplatz m*]
~ **braking gear,** over-run controlled brake = Auflaufbremse *f*
overseas shipment = Überseeversand *m*
overshot [*water-wheel*] = oberschlächtig
~ **loader,** see: overhead loader
oversize, see: (crusher) waste
~ **(aggregate)** = Überkorn *n*
~ **brake** = Bremse *f* mit Reserve *f*
~ **clutch (coupling)** = Kupplung *f* mit Reserve *f*
~ **(or giant) pneumatic tire** (US)/**tyre** (Brit.) = Riesenluftreifen *m*
overspan bridge, see: overbridge

to overstress = überbeanspruchen
overtaking; passing [*deprecated*] = Überholen *n*
~ **lane; passing** ~ [*deprecated*] = Überholspur *f*
over-the-road delivery = Antransport *m* auf Straße *f*
overthrust fault (Geol.) = Wechsel *m*, Überschiebung *f*
~ **mountain** = Deck(en)gebirge *n*
overtime hour = Überstunde *f*
overtopping = Überlaufen *n*
overturning (Brit.); **tilting** (US) = Kippen *n* [*Talsperre f*]
~ **moment** = Kippmoment *n*
(over)wash plain, outwash ~ = Kiesfeld *n*, Sandfeld, Auswaschebene *f*
owner, see: promoter
oxalic acid = Oxalsäure *f*, Kleesäure *f*
ox-bow (lake); bayou (US); mortlake (Brit.) = toter Arm *m*, Altwasser *n*
oxcart, see: bullock cart
oxide of magnesia, see: bitter-earth
~ ~ **nitrogen** = Stickstoffoxyd *n*
oxide resistor = Heizelement *n* aus Zirkonoxyd *n*
~ **structure** = Oxydstruktur *f*
oxidized asphalt (US), see: blown ~
~ **copper ores** [*in the blast-furnace*] = Kupferstein *m*
~ **lead mineral** = oxydisches Bleierz *n*
oxyacetylene cutting torch = Azetylensauerstoff(schneid)brenner *m*
~ **welding** = Sauerstoff-Azetylen-Schweißung *f*
oxychloride cement = Oxychloridzement *m*
oxychromate = Oxychromat *n*
oxygen cylinder = Sauerstoffflasche *f*
oxyhydrogen gas = Knallgas *n*, Hydrooxygengas *n*
oxysalt, salt of oxyacid = Sauerstoffsalz *n*
oyster-shell concrete = Schillbeton *m*
oyster shells = Schill *m*
~ **shell lime,** see: coquina
ozokerite, ozocerite, fossil wax; gumbed (US); mineral fat (Min.) = Ozokerit *n*, Erdwachs *n*, Neftgil *n*
ozoniser = Ozonisator *m*

P

pacing = Abschreiten *n* der Entfernung *f*
package (belt) conveyor, ~ **band** = Stückgutbandförderer *m*
"packaged" plant, central engine ~ = zentrale Betriebsanlage *f*
package handling = Beförderung *f* von Stückgut *n* (oder Stückgütern *npl*)
packaging = Verpacken *n*
~ = Paketstapeln *n* [*z. B. Ziegel*]
pack animal = Tragtier *n*
packed broken rock soling, see: base of stone pitching
packer, see: packing machine
~ **bin** = Versandsilo *m* [*Zement m*]
packer-head (US) = rotierender Kernteil *m* mit Preßflügel *m* [*Betonrohrpresse f*]
pack gravel = Schüttkies *m* [*Kiesschüttungsbrunnen*]
~ **ice** = Packeis *n*
packing, see: gasket
~ = Futter *n* [*Blechträger m*]
~, see: sealing (off)
~ **gland** = Stopfbüchsenpackung *f*, Dichtungssatz *m*
~ **machine,** packer = Packmaschine *f* [*z. B. für Zement m*]
~ **material** = Dichtungsmaterial *n*
~ ~, yarning ~ = Dichtungsstoff *m* [*Stemm-Muffe f*]
~ **ring** = Abdichtring *m*
~ **set** = Dichtungspackung *f*
pack-thread = Bindfaden *m*
packway, see: bridle-path
paddle, blade = Schaufel *f* [*Mischer m*]
~, blade [*log washer*] = Schwert *n*
~ **dampening device** = Flügelanzeigedämpfer *m*, Flügelzeigerdämpfer
~ **flight** [*log washer*] = Schwertgang *m*
~ **mill scrubber,** see: scrubber
~ **mixer** = Schaufelmischer *m*
~ **shaft** = Schaufelwelle *f* [*Mischer m*]
~ **wheel steamer** = Schaufelraddampfer *m*
~ **worm conveyor,** broken bladed ~ = Mischschnecke *f*
paddy field soil = sandiger Lehm *m* mit rund 20% Ton und 40% Sand
pagodite (Min.), see: agalmatolite
pahoehoe lava, see: ropy ~

paid vacation = bezahlter Urlaub *m*
paint = unlösliche Malerfarbe *f*, ~ Anstrichfarbe
~ **brush** = Malerpinsel *m*
~ ~, see: cirrus cloud
~ **clay** = Farbton *m*
painter = Anstreicher *m*
painters' naphtha, paint thinner = Lackbenzin *n*, Testbenzin
~ **torch** = Maler-Abbrennlampe *f*
painter's workshop = Malereiwerkstatt *f*
painting surface = Anstrichfläche *f*
~ **value** = Anstrichwert *m*
paint pigment = Anstrichpigment *n*
~ **spray gun** = Farbspritzpistole *f*
~ **stripe** = Anstrich-Markierungsstreifen *m*
~ **vehicle,** see: cold water paint cement
paired bolts = paarweise angebrachte Bolzen *mpl*
(pair of) compasses = Zirkel *m*
~ ~ **half-scoops** (Brit.); clam(shell) bucket (or basket) (US) = Zweischalen(bagger)greifer *m*, Zweischalengreifkorb *m*
palaeontology = Paläogeographie *f*
pale fencing = Staket *n*
~ **oil** = leicht- oder mittelviskoses Schmieröl *n*, gewöhnlich leicht gefärbtes Neutralöl *n*
paleoclimate = Paläoklima *n*
palimpsest structure (Geol.) = Überbleibselverband *m*
paling = Lattenzaun *m*
palingenesis (Geol.) = Palingenese *f*, Anatexis *f*, Einschmelzungsmetamorphose *f*
palisades = Palisadenwand *f*
pallet = Palette *f*
palletless package brick transporting = rahmenloser Ziegelpaket-Transport *m*
pan (US); see: carrying scraper
~ = Wanne *f*
Panama Canal; "Big Ditch" (US) = Panamakanal *m*
panbreaker (USA); see: subsoil plough (Brit.)
pancake ice = Pancakeeis *n*, Pfannkuchen *m*
pan-calcined gypsum = Pfannengips *m*
panel, see: bay
~ = Feld *n* [*Fachwerk n*]

panel-heated room = flächenbeheizter Raum *m*
panel heating, radiant ~, concealed ~ = Strahlungsheizung *f*
~ length = Feldweite *f*
~ point = Knoten(punkt) *m* [*Fachwerkträger m*]
~ wall = Fachwand *f*
pan grinder, grinding mill of the edge runner type = Kollergang *m*
~ head = eckiger Nietkopf *m*, trapezförmiger ~
panidiomorphic (Geol.) = panidiomorphkörnig, panallotriomorph, autallotriomorph
panning [*snow removal in municipalities*] [*consists of pushing snow into the sewer manholes with large scrapers*] = Schneeräumung *f* mit Schrappern *mpl* durch Schieben *n* der Schneemassen *fpl* in die Straßeneinläufe *mpl*
panoramic sketch = Panoramaskizze *f*
~ view = Panoramaansicht *f*
pantograph = Pantograph *m*, Storch(en)-schnabel *m*
pan type concrete mixer = Zwangsbetonmischer *m* mit horizontalem Rührwerk *n*
~ vibrator, see: plate ~
paper chromatography = Papier-Chromatographie *f*
~ coal = Papierkohle *f*
~ mill = Papiermühle *f*
~ peat = Papiertorf *m*
~ roll recorder = Typendrucker *m*
~ snow fence = Schneezaun *m* aus Papierbahnen *fpl*
~ spreading machine = Papierabrollwagen *m*
~ strip test; see under "binder distributor"
~ type fuel filter = Papier-Brennstofffilter *m, n*
parabola = Parabel *f*
parabolic arch = parabolischer Gewölbebogen *m*
~ girder = Parabelträger *m*
~ steel eccentricity = parabolisch exzentrisch verlaufende Bewehrung *f*
paraclase = Paraklase *f*
paraffin = Paraffin-Kohlenwasserstoff *m*
~ = Fest-Paraffin *n*

~ = in England für „kerosine"
~-base crude petroleum = paraffinbasisches Erdöl *n*
paraffin distillate = paraffinhaltiges Destillat *n*
paraffinic oil = Öl *n* von Paraffinstruktur aus paraffinbasischem Rohöl *n*
paraffin oil = Schmieröldestillat *n* von paraffinischem oder gemischtbasischem Rohöl *n*
~ scale = Rohparaffinrückstand *m* vom Schwitzen *n* von Paraffin-Gatsch *m*
~ shale, see: (asphaltic) pyrobituminous shale
(~) slack wax = Paraffin-Gatsch *m*
~ sorption = Paraffin-Sorption *f*
paraffin wax = Paraffin *n*
paragneiss = Renchgneiss *m*, Sedimentgneis, Paragneis
paragonite (Min.) = Paragonit *m*
parallel-flanged beam = Parallelflanschträger *m*
parallel-flow process = Gleichstromverfahren *n* [*Gesteinstrockentrommel f*]
parallel-sided dropped-in shell foundation (or bearing) pile = Ort(beton)pfahl *m* mit parallelseitigem Blechmantel *m*
parapet (wall) = Brüstung(smauer) *f*
parcel carrier = Kleingutspediteur *m*
parent earth, **~ soil** = Ausgangsboden *m*
~ rock = Ausgangsgestein *n*
pargeter, plasterer = Gipsarbeiter *m*, Gipser *m*, Putzer *m*
parget of lime = Kalkbewurf *m*
Parian cement = entwässerter Gips *m* für Oberputze, der nach dem Herstellungsverfahren am ehesten dem hochgebrannten deutschen Estrichgips entspricht
parianite, Trinidad épuré, Trinidad refined asphalt = gereinigter Trinidadasphalt *m*
Parker's cement, see: Roman ~
park highway, parkway = Parkstraße *f*
parking = Parken *n*
~ apron, see: (hard) standing
~ brake = Feststellbremse *f*
~ building = Parkgebäude *n* [*für Autos*]
~ garage = Abstellgarage *f*
~ meter = Parkzeitmesser *m*
~ place, car park, parking lot = (Auto-)Parkplatz *m*

parking stall = Unterstellraum *m*, Box *f* [*Stockwerksgarage f*]
~ **strip**, pull-off ~, hard shoulder = Standspur *f*, Parkstreifen *m*
part design = Detailkonstruktion *f*, Detailentwurf *m*
partial admission turbine = Partialturbine *f*
partially separate system [*a system of drainage in which the surface water from a portion of the catchment area is conveyed in a separate sewer from that conveying foul water and the surface water from the remainder of the area*] = Teiltrennsystem *n*
partial mixing, shrink ~ = Naßmischen *n* während der Fahrt *f* [*Transportbeton m*]
~ **restraint** = teilweise Einspannung *f*
~ **saturation** = Teilsättigung *f*
~ **sheeting** = Teileinspundung *f*
particle, see: grain
*** particle shape**, grain ~ = Kornform *f*, Korngestalt *f*
~ **size**, grain ~ = Korngröße *f*, Fraktionsgröße
particle-size analysis, see: sieve ~
~ **distribution curve**, see: grading ~
~ **(~) limit**, see: gradation ~
particle velocity = Schallschnelle *f*
parting, jointing, structure = Absonderungsform *f* (Geol.)
partly prestressed = teilweise vorgespannt
*** partnership**, see: contracting combine
parts depot = Ersatzteillager *n*
part swing (dipper) shovel = Löffelbagger *m* mit beschränktem Schwenkbereich *m* [*nicht 360°*]
part-time employment = Halbtagsbeschäftigung *f*
party, see: crew
Pascal's paradox, see: hydrostatic ~
pass, traverse = Übergang *m*, Fahrt *f*, Überfahrung *f* [*z. B. mit einer Walze f*]
passable condition = befahrbarer Zustand *m* [*Straße f*]
passage (of harbo(u)rs), see: fairway
(passenger) automobile, (~) car = Personen(kraft)wagen *m*, PKW *m*
~ **berth** = Fahrgasthafen *m*
~ **conveyor belt** = Personen-Bandförderer *m*

~ **counter** = Fahrgastzähler *m*
~ **handling** = Fahrgastabfertigung *f*
~ **hoist (or elevator)** = Personenaufzug *m*
~ **incline hoist**, ~ slope ~ = Schrägaufzug *m* für Personentransport *m*
~ **service** = Personenverkehr *m*
~ ~ **vehicle** = (Auto)Bus *m*, Omnibus
~ **traffic** = Personenverkehr *m*, Fahrgastverkehr
passing = Durchgang *m* [*Sieb n*]
~ [*deprecated*]; see: overtaking
~ **lane** [*deprecated*]; overtaking ~ = Überholspur *f*
~ **place**, see: layby(e)
~ **track** = Ausweichgleis *n*
passivating agent = Passivierungsmittel *n*
~ **capacity** = passivierende Eigenschaft *f*
passivation effect [*consists in the electro-chemical elimination of local corrosion-promoting cells as they are often found at rivets, screws, fish-plates and other joining elements, and as they can also occur where galvanized and painted steel components are used adjacent to each other*] = Passivierungs-Effekt *m*
passive lateral earth pressure = passiver Erddruck *m*, Erdwiderstand *m*
~ **state** [*soil*] = oberer Grenzzustand *m*
paste = Paste *f*
pasture = Viehweide *f*
patch = Flickstelle *f* [*Straße f*]
patching machine, see: patch plant
~ **mortar**, repair ~ = Flickmörtel *m*
~ **(work)**, mending, patch work = Ausflicken *n*, Flickverfahren *n*, Ausbesserung *f*, Flickarbeit *f* [*Straße f*]
patch plant, patching machine = Flickanlage *f*
patent application = Patentanmeldung *f*
patented plaster, chemical ~ = Edelputz *m*
patentee = Patentinhaber *m*
paternoster = Paternoster *m*
path gravel, see: hoggin
~ **of seepage**, seepage path = Sickerlinie *f*
~ **roller** = Wegewalze *f*
pathway [*deprecated*]; see: footpath
pat of cement-water paste, see: cement pat
patrol = Streife *f* [*Polizei f*]

patrol car = Streifenwagen *m* [*Polizei f*]
~ (grader), see: blade maintainer
patrolman, traffic **~** = Polizist *m* einer Verkehrsstreife *f*
paved ditch = befestigter offener Entwässerungsgraben *m*
~ gutter (or channel), (road) channel = Rinnstein *m*, Pflasterrinne *f*
~ shoulder = Standspur *f* mit Belag *m*
pavement [*a term applied specifically to the whole construction in a road (including any layer strengthened or stabilized in situ by the addition of other material) made to support traffic above the subgrade*] = (Straßen)Decke *f*
pavement [*a general term for a paved surface*] = Befestigung *f*, Straßenbefestigung
~ [*deprecated*]; paving (Brit.) = Fugen(straßen)decke *f* [*ausgenommen Betondecke*]
~ [*deprecated*]; see: footpath
~ breaker, see: road **~**
~ concrete; paving **~** (US) = (Straßen-)Deckenbeton *m*
~ distress = (Straßen)Deckenschaden *m*
~ joint = (Beton)Deckenfuge *f*
~ lane (US); paving **~** (US)
***pavement-marking machine**, see: road-marking **~**
pavement placing = (Straßen)Deckeneinbau *m*
~ slab pumping, see: pumping
~ underseal(ing), see: underseal(ing)
paver (US); paviour (Brit.) = Steinsetzer *m*, Pflasterer *m*
***paver**, see: travel(l)ing (concrete) mixer (plant)
~, see: (highway) **~**
***paver-finisher**, see: asphalt finisher
paver mixing = Mischen *n* in Straßen(beton)mischern *npl*
~ skip, (charging) skip = Lader *m* [*Straßen(beton)mischer m*]
paving = Pflastern *n*
~ (US) = (Straßen)Deckenbau *m*
~ (Brit.); [*deprecated: pavement*] = Fugen(straßen)decke *f* [*ausgenommen Betondecke*]
~ asphalt (US), see: paving(-grade) **~**

~ breaker, see: road **~**
~ brick, road **~** = Pflasterziegel *m*, Pflasterklinker *m*, Straßenbauklinker
~ cement (US); road (engineering) binder = Straßenbaubindemittel *n*
~ company (US); road-building firm = Straßenbaufirma *f*
~ concrete (US); see: pavement **~**
~ contractor, road **~** = Straßenbauunternehmer *m*
~ finisher = Deckenfertiger *m*
~ flag, see: flagstone
***paving form** (US); see: side **~**
~(-grade) asphalt (US); see: asphalt(ic) cement
paving hammer = Pflastererhammer *m*
~ in rows, see: coursed sett paving
~ joint sealer (US); see: joint-sealing compound
~ lane (US); pavement **~** = Einbaustreifen *m* [*Straßenbau m*]
***paving mixer**, see: travel(l)ing (concrete) mixer (plant)
~ mixture (US) = Straßenbelageinbaumasse *f*, Belagsgut *n*
~ operations (US), see: **~ work(s)**
~ project (US) = Straßenbauprojekt *n*
~ rammer, sett **~ ~** = Pflasterramme *f*
~ run (US) = Einbaubetrieb *m* [*Betonstraßenbau m*]
~ sett = Pflasterstein *m*
~ ~ making machine = Pflastersteinmaschine *f*
~ slab (US), see: road bay
~ ~, road slab = Straßenbauplatte *f* [*z. B. Asphaltbetonplatte f*]
~ spreader = Einbau- oder Verteilgerät *n* für Splitt, Schotter und bituminöses Mischgut *n*
~ tamper, sett **~ ~** = Pflasterstampfer *m*
~ tool (US); see: (highway) paver
~ ~ = Pflastererwerkzeug *n*
~ train (US) = Deckeneinbauzug *m*
~ vibrator (US); see: full depth internal slab vibrator
~ with setts = Pflastern *n*, Pflasterung *f*
~ work(s), **~ operations** (US); surfacing work (Brit.) = Deckenbau *m* [*Straße f*]
paviour (Brit.) = Straßendeckenbauer *m*

pavior — to peel

pavior (Brit.); **paver** (US) = Steinsetzer *m*, Pflasterer *m*
pawl, locking ~ = Sperrklinke *f*, Sperrzahn *m*
~ = Ratsche *f*, verzahnter Ring *m*
~ **and ratchet mechanism** = Gesperre *n*
~ **reversing gear** = Klinkenwendegetriebe *n*
pay(able) quantity = Abrechnungsmenge *f*
pay dirt (US) = kostenvergütete Bodenmassen *f* [*Erdbau m*]
~ **envelope** = Lohntüte *f*
~ **formation** = abbauwürdige Schicht *f*
paying quantity = abbaufähige Menge *f*, abbauwürdige ~
pay item = kostenvergütete Position, Leistungsposition
payload = kostenvergütete Ladung *f*
PAYLOADER [*Trademark*]; see: HOUGH ~
pay material = abbaufähiges Material *n*
payment on account, instalment payment = Abschlagzahlung *f*, Akontozahlung
payroll, wages ~ = Lohnliste *f*
~ **costs** = Lohnkosten *f*
P. B. S., see: prefabricated bituminous surfacing
P.B.S. laying machine, lick roller, stamplicker = Abrollgerät *n* für Bitumen-Fertigbahnen *fpl*
peace time level = Friedensstand *m*
peacock ore (Min.), see: bornite
pea gravel = Erbskies *m*, Perlkies
peak daytime demand = Spitzenbelastung *f* am Tage *m*
~ **demand** = Bedarfspitze *f*, Belastungsspitze *f*
~ **flow,** emergency flood flow = Hochwasserspitze *f*
~ **hour** = Spitzenstunde *f*
~ ~ **of usage** = Betriebsspitzenstunde *f*
~ ~ **value** = Stundenspitzenwert *m*
~ **load** = Spitzenbelastung *f*, Spitzenlast *f*
~ ~ **power plant** = Spitzenkraftwerk *n*
~ **period** = Spitzenzeit *f*, Spitzenperiode *f*, Stoßzeit *f*
~ **production** = Spitzenleistung *f*
~ **traffic** = Höchstverkehr *m*
pearl spar, (pearly) dolomite (Min.) = Perlspat *m*, Dolomit *m*, Dolomitspat

peat blasting, see: bog ~
~ **bog** = Torfmoor *n*
~ **clarified sludge** = Torfbreiklärschlamm *m*
~ **coal** = Torfkohle *f*
~ **dust,** ~ meal, ~ powder = Torfmull *m*
~ **excavator** = Torfbagger *m*
~ **formation** = Vertorfung *f*
~ **litter** = Torfstreu *f*
~ **meal,** see: ~ dust
~ **moss,** see: bog ~
~ **mo(u)ld** = Torferde *f*
~ **pocket,** concealed bed of peat = Torfeinschluß *m*, Torfnest *n*
~ **powder,** see: ~ dust
~ **tar** = Torfteer *m*
peaty fibrous coal = Torffaserkohle *f*
~ **pitch coal** = Torfpechkohle *f*
~ **soil** = Moorboden *m*, reiner Humusboden
~ **water** = Moorwasser *n*
pebble [60—6 mm] = Kiesel(stein) *m* [*nach Dücker* [1948] „*grobes Siebkorn IIa*" 60—20 mm und „*grobes Siebkorn IIb*" 20—6 mm]
~ **band** = Kiesellage *f*
~ **-dash plastering,** see: rough cast(ing)
pebble tube (grinding) mill, see: flint ~ (stones) ~ (~) ~
pectic acid = Pektinsäure *f*
pedal cycle, (bi)cycle = Fahrrad *n*
~ **cyclist traffic** = Radfahrverkehr *m*
pedestal = Sockelfundament *n*
~ = Lagerstuhl *m*
~ **bearing** = Stehlager *n*
~ **shell-less foundation (or bearing) pile** = Klumpfuß(gründungs)pfahl *m*
pedestrian crossing, crosswalk = Fußgängerüberweg *m*
~ **guard rail** = Fußgänger-Schutzgeländer *n*
~ **island** (US); see: refuge (Brit.)
~ **subway,** ~ tunnel, underground pedestrian passageway = Fußgängertunnel *m*
pedological identity = bodenkundliche Herkunft *f*
pedology = Pedologie *f*, Bodenkunde *f*
to peel, to disbark, to strip the bark = abschälen, entrinden, (ent)schälen, abborken

peg, stake = Pflock *m*
~ foot roller = (Schaffuß)Walze *f* mit zapfenförmigen Stacheln *mpl*
pegging out (work), stakeout = Absteckung(sarbeiten) *f*, Absteckung *f*, Abstecken *n*, Verpflockung *f*, Verpflocken *n*
pegmatite = Pegmatit *m*
to peg out, to stake ~, to set ~ = abstecken, verpflocken, abpfählen, abpflocken
peg top paving, see: coursed sett ~
pelagic deposit, see: deep sea ooze
~ foraminifera = pelagische Foraminiferen *fpl*
pellet formation = Tonkügelchenherstellung *f*
pelletizing technique = Kugelverformtechnik *f* [*Ton m*]
"pell mell" concrete blocks (Brit.) = Blockgründung *f* [*Wellenbrecher m*]
pellodite, see: varve(d) (glacial) clay
pelting rain, see: driving ~
Pelton water wheel = Pelton-Rad *n*
pendulum = Pendel *n, m*
~ impact tester = Pendelschlagwerk *n*
~ throw = Pendelwurf *m* [*Schleppschaufel f*]

peneplain, denudation plain, peneplane = Denudationsebene *f*, Fastebene, Rumpffläche *f*
penetrated stone base course, penetration base = Tränktragsschicht *f*
penetrating oil = Eindringöl *n*
penetration = Eindringung *f*, Penetration *f*
~ US); grouting (Brit.) = Tränkung *f*, Tränken *n*, Einguß *m* [*Straße f*]
~ grade (US), see: asphalt(ic) cement
~ macadam; see: grouted macadam (Brit.)
~ of the pile into the soil per blow = Eindringung *f* infolge eines Schlages *m* [*Pfahl m*]
~ pavement; see: grouted macadam (Brit.)
~ piston = Stempel *m* [*CBR-Versuch m*]
~ record, see: driving ~
~ resistance = Eindring(ungs)widerstand *m*
~ surfacing; see grouted macadam (Brit.)
penetrometer = Eindring(ungs)messer *m*, Penetrometer *n*, Eindringgerät *n*
peninsula = Halbinsel *f*
pennant grit (Brit.) = Sandstein *m* vom Craig-yr-Hesg Quarry, Pontypridd
penning(Brit.), see: (hand) (placed) pitching
~ gate, see: gate
penninite (Min = Pennin *m*

penstock
conversion tunnel, pressure tunnel, pressure gallery, penstock tunnel, tunnel-type penstock
ditch-type ~

pipe ~
trench-type ~

Triebwasserleitung *f*
Betriebswasserstollen, Druck(wasser)stollen, Triebwasserstollen *m*
Werksgraben *m* mit Trapezquerschnitt *m*
Triebwasserrohrleitung *f*
Werksgraben *m* mit Rechteckquerschnitt *m*

penstock dam, see: power plant intake structure
~ drain, drain tunnel, drainage tunnel = direkter Auslaufstollen *m* [*von Schieberkammer f zum Ableitungstunnel m unter Umgehung f des Kraftwerkes n*]
~ elbow, see: elbow bend
~ manifold, manifold tunnel = Verteilerstollen *m*

~ shaft, pressure ~ = Druck(leitungs)schacht *m*, Fallschacht
pentlandite (Min.); see: nicopyrite
pepper sludge = Suspension *f* von Säureteer *m* im Mineral *n*, das mit Schwefelsäure *f* gesäuert ist, nach Absitzen *n*
peptisation = Peptisation *f* [*Übergang m von Gel n zum Sol n*]
percentage by volume = Raumteile *mpl*, Raumprozente *npl*

percentage by weight — permanent way

***percentage by weight** = Gewichtsprozente *npl*, Gewichtsteile *mpl*
~ cost = anteilige Kosten *f*
perched (ground-)water table, see: false ~ ~
percolating filter, see: trickling ~
~ water = Sickerwasser *n*
percolation [*the passage of water through pervious material*] = Durchsickerung *f*, Versickerung *f*
percussion (or percussive) drilling (or boring) = Schlagbohren *n*, Schlagbohrung *f*, Schlagbohrverfahren *n*, Meißelung *f*
~ drilling machine = Schlagbohrmaschine *f*
~ hammer, ~ breaker = Schlaghammer *m*
~ penetration method, drop-penetration testing, driving test = Rammsondierung *f*
~ piston = Schlagkolben *m*
~ probe, see: driving rod
~ riveting machine = Schlagnietmaschine *f*
percussion-type tie tamper (US); **~ track ~** (Brit.) = Schlaggleisstopfer *m*, Schlagschotterstopfer
percussive drill = Stauchbohrer *m* [*Baugrunduntersuchung f*]
~ hollow rod boring = Schlagspülbohren *n*, Spülbohrung mit Schnellschlag *m*
~ rod boring = Gestängeschlagbohren *n*, Gestängeschlagbohrung *f*
~ ~ drilling (or boring), churn ~ (~ ~) = Seilschlagbohren *n*, pennsylvanisches Seilbohren
~ -rotary drilling = Drehschlagbohren *n*, Drehschlagbohrung *f*
perennial rye grass = englisches Raigras *n*
perfect liquid = reibungsfreie (oder ideale, oder vollkommene) Flüssigkeit *f*
perforated brick = Lochziegel(stein) *m*, Lochstein
~ cone = Sortierkonus *m*, konischer Siebzylinder *m* [*Waschtrommel f*]
~ cylinder = Siebzylinder *m* [*Waschtrommel f*]
~ metal plate = Lochgrobblech *n*
~ ~ sheet = Lochfeinblech *n*

~ plate sieve, ~ metal screen = Blechlochsieb *n*
perforation = Lochung *f*
performance bond, completion ~ = Ausführungsgarantie *f*
~ data = Leistungsangaben *fpl*
~ table = Leistungstabelle *f* [*Baumaschine f*]
pergola = Pergola *f*
periclase (Min.) = Periklas *m*
~ brick = Magnesitstein *m* mit 96% MgO
peridot (Min.) = Peridot *m*
peridotite = Peridotit *m*
perimetral joint = Perimetralfuge *f*, perimetrische Fuge *f*, Umfangsfuge [*Talsperre f*]
periodicity of dosing = Beschickungsturnus *m* [*Tropfkörper m*]
periodic kiln, see: intermittent ~
period of time, time period, time interval = Zeitspanne *f*
peripheral girder = umlaufender Randträger *m*
~ welding = Stumpfschweißung *f*
perlite expansion furnace = Perlit-Hochofen *m*
~ ore = Rohperlit-Gestein *n*
~ popping, ~ processing = Leicht-Perlit-Aufbereitung *f*
permafrost = Dauerfrost *m*
~ soil [*permanently frozen earth*] = dauernd gefrorener Boden *m*, ewiggefrorener Boden *m*
permanent, static, stationary = stationär, ortsfest
~ bridge = Dauerbrücke *f*
~ grease lubrication = Dauerfettschmierung *f*
~ magnetic roll = magnetische Rolle *f* für Rollenbahnen *fpl*
~ plant (facility) = stationäre Anlage *f*
~ protective casing (or shell) = verlorenes Futterrohr *n*, verlorener Blechmantel *m* [*Raymond-Pfahl m*]
~ weight, fixed ~, dead ~, dead load = Eigengewicht *n*
~ staff = Stammbelegschaft *f*, Stammpersonal *n*
~ way, p. w. = (Eisenbahn)Oberbau *m*, Gleisoberbau

permanent way crane, breakdown ~, accident ~ (Brit.); wrecking ~ (US) = Eisenbahn-Unfallkran *m*

~ ~ ~; see: locomotive (jib) crane (Brit.)

~ ~ roller = Gleisbettungswalze *f*

permeability = Wasserdurchlässigkeit *f*

~ coefficient, see: coefficient of permeability

~device for undisturbed sand samples = Gerät *n* zur Bestimmung *f* der Durchlässigkeit *f* von ungestörten Sandproben *fpl*

~ ratio = Durchlässigkeitsziffer *f*

permeameter = Luftdurchdringungsmesser *m*

Permian limestone = Zechsteinkalk *m*

permissible stress, allowable ~ = zulässige Spannung *f*, Beanspruchbarkeit *f*

~ variation, see: off-size

personal card, see: calling ~

~ injury accident = Unfall *m* mit Personenschaden *m*

personnel, staff, working force = Belegschaft *f*, Personal *n*

~ housing, living quarters = Unterkünfte *fpl*

perspex, plexiglass = Plexiglas *n*

perthite (Min.) = Perthit *m*

pervibrator, see: concrete mass vibrator

pervious shell = Dränschicht *f*, Filterschicht

pestle = Pistill *n*

petcock = Kontrollhahn *m*, Ablaßhahn

peterlineum, see: carbolineum

petrifaction (Geol.) = Versteinerung *f*

petrographic microscope, polarizing ~ = Polarisationsmikroskop *n*

~ microscopy = Gesteinsmikroskopie *f*

petrographical method of examination = petrographische Untersuchungsmethode *f*

petrography = Petrographie *f*, Gesteinsbeschreibung *f*

petrol (Brit.); see: gas(oline) naphtha (US)

petrolatum = Petrolatum *n*

(petrol) bowser (Brit.) = Benzin-Straßentanker *m*

~ can (Brit.); see: gasoline (storage) can (US)

~-driven high-frequency immersion concrete vibrator (Brit.) = Benzin-Hochfrequenzinnenrüttler *m*

petrol driver (Brit.) gasolene (or gasoline) ~ (US) = Brennkraftramme *f* [*Ramme zum Einrammen n*]

~ dump (Brit.) = Benzinlager *n*

~-electric drive (Brit.); gas-electric ~ (US) = benzinelektrischer Antrieb *m*

~ engine (Brit.); see: gas(olene) ~ (US)

~ ~ driven immersion vibrator (Brit.) = Innenvibrator *m* (oder Innenrüttler *m*) mit Benzin-Anttieb *m*

~ ~ (operated) vibratory tamper (Brit.) = Benzinrüttelstampfer *m*

petroleum = Bezeichnung für alle festen, flüssigen und gasförmigen Natur-Kohlenwasserstoffe *mpl*

~, see: crude oil (petroleum)

~ asphalt (US); ~ asphaltic bitumen (Brit.) = Erdölbitumen *n*, Erdölpech *n*

~ coke, still coke = Petrolkoks *m*

~ distillate = Erdöldestillat *n*

~ ether = Petroläther *m*

~ fraktion = Erdölfraktion *f*

~ grease (US); lubricating ~ = Schmierfett *n*

~ jelly = Naturvaseline *f*, raffinierte Vaseline

~ leve, see: light petroleum

~ pitch, oil ~ = Petrolpech *n*

~ spirit (Brit.) = sehr leichtes Kohlenwasserstoffgemisch *n* mit einem Flammpunkt *m* unter 0° C

petroliferous sand = Petrolsand *m*

petrol lift truck (Brit.); gas ~ ~ (US) = Hubstapler *m* mit Ottomotor *m*

petrology = Petrologie *f*, Gesteinsentstehungslehre *f*

petrolo-shale, see: (asphaltic) pyrobituminous shale

petrol power unit (Brit.) = Benzin-Antriebsgruppe *f*

petrol-powered rammer (Brit.); gas(olene) (or gasoline) ~ (US) = Benzin(stampf)-ramme *f*

petrol trap (Brit.); gas(olene) (or gasoline) interceptor (US) = Benzinabscheider *m*, Benzinfang *m*

~ vibrator (Brit.) = Benzinrüttler *m*, Benzinvibrator *m*

pharmacosiderite (Min.) = Pharmakosiderit *m*, Würfelerz *n*
(phased) programme of works, see: construction schedule
phengite (Min.) = Phengit *m*
phenol, see: carbolic acid
phenolic-improved wood = phenolharzveredeltes Holz *n*
phenylmethane, see: methyl benzene
phillipsite (Min.) = Philipsit *m*
phlogopite, amber mica (Min.) = Phlogopit *m*, hellbrauner Glimmer *m*
phonolite (Min.) = Phonolith *m*
phosgenite, $PbCl_2 \cdot PbCO_3$ (Min.) = Bleihornerz *n*, Phosgenit *m*
phosphate = Phosphat *n*
~ **bonding** = Phosphatbindung *f*
phosphorite, rock-phosphate = Phosphorit *m*
phosphorus = Phosphor *m*
photoelasticity = Spannungsoptik *f*
photogrammetry, photogrammetric survey(ing) = Photogrammetrie *f*, Lichtbildmeßverfahren *n*
photographic print = Photokopie *f*
photo printing = Photokopieren *n*
phreatic line = phreatische Linie *f*
~ **water**, see: ground ~
pH-value, hydrogen ion concentration = pH-Wert *m*, Wasserstoffzahl H *f*, Wasserstoffionenkonzentration *f*
phyllite (Geol.) = Phyllit *m*
physical exertion = körperlicher Kraftaufwand *m*
~ **geology** = dynamische Geologie *f*
~ **weathering**, see: mechanical ~
physico-chemical reaction = physikalischchemische Reaktion *f*
to pick, clay ~ [*pointed at both ends*] = Doppelspitzhacke *f*, Doppelspitzpickel *m*, Zweispitz *m*
pickaxe [*has one point and one flat cutting end*] = Kreuzhacke *f*, Kreuzpickel *m*
picket = Streikposten *m*
~ = Pfahl *m*
pick hammer for cutting work = Pickhammer *m*
picking = Aufhacken *n*

~ **belt (or band) conveyor** = Leseband *n*, Klaubeband
pick-up carrier = Abfanggraben *m* [*Rieselfeld n*]
~ **(truck) (US)/(lorry) (Brit.)** = leichter LKW *m*
picric acid = Pikrinsäure *f*
picrite = Pikrit *m*
piece-goods = Stückgüter *npl*
piece of equipment, see: equipment item
piece-rate = Akkordsatz *m*
piece wage = Akkordlohn *m*
~-**work**, task work = Akkordarbeit *f*
~ = Taktarbeit *f* [*der gleiche zeitlich hintereinanderliegende von denselben Handwerkern auszuführende Arbeitsvorgang*]
piedmontite (Min.), see: mangan(ese) epidote
piedmont slope = abfallendes Vorland *n*
pier, shaft = Pfeiler *m*
~ = Pylone *f*
~ = Pier *m*, *f*, Landungssteg *m*
~ **arch** = Pfeilerbogen *m*
pier-base elevation = Pfeilergründungshöhe *f*
pier foundation [*in USA also incorrectly termed "caisson foundation"*] = Pfeilergründung *f*
piezocrystallisation = Druckkristallisation *f*
piezometer (pipe), seepage ~ = Piezometer(rohr) *m*
~ **tip** = Piezometer-Meßspitze *f*
piezometric head = piezometrische Druckhöhe *f*
pig, go devil, scraper = Besenschrubber *m* [*wird mit Druckluft vor Inbetriebnahme durch Erdöl- oder Gasleitungen geschossen*]
~ **iron** = Roheisen *n*, Masseleisen *n*
pike, see: toll road
pilaster = Wandpfeiler *m*
to pile (up), to stack = (auf)stapeln
pile, stockpile, storage pile, stock-heap = (Vorrats)Halde *f*, Materialhalde *f*
~ = Pfahl *m*
~ = Spundbohle *f*
***pile, foundation** ~, bearing ~ = Gründungspfahl *m*, Tragpfahl *m*
~ **bent**, (~) **trestle** = (Pfahl)Joch *n*

pile cap = Pfahl-Kopfplatte f, Jochbalken m

~ cluster, dolphin, piled dolphin = Dalbe m, Pfahlbündel n

piled cloud, cloud-heap, cumulus = Haufenwolke f, Kumuluswolke f

~ foundation, see: pile ~

pile dike (US); see: sheetpile retaining wall

~ driver = dieser Ausdruck ist mißverständlich und bedeutet erstens die „Rammanlage" oder die „Ramme" [*sollte besser „pile driving plant" oder „piling plant" heißen*] und zweitens den „Rammbären" [*sollte besser „drop pile hammer" heißen*]

~ ~ hose = Pfahlrammschlauch m

~ ~ operator = Rammaschinist m

~ ~ working on the principle of a Diesel engine = Explosionsbär-Ramme f, Diesel(bär)ramme

pile-driving barge = Rammponton m

~ curve = Rammkurve f

~ formula = Rammformel f

~ hoist = Rammwinde f

***pile driving plant,** piling ~ = Rammanlage f, Ramme f

~ ~ ~ (or piling plant) with direct acting steam piling hammer = Dampfbärramme f

~ ~ regulation = Rammvorschrift f

~ extractor, pilepuller, piledrawer = Pfahl(aus)zieher m

~ foundation, piled ~ = Pfahlgründung f

~ ~ structure = Pfahlrostbauwerk n

~ frame, piling ~ = Rammgerüst n

~ head = Pfahlkopf m

~ jetting, see: water jetting of piles

~ loading test = Pfahlprobebelastungsversuch m

~ materials, stock-piled ~ = Haldenmaterial n

~ of rubble, see: rubble pile

~ platform = Pfahlrostplatte f

~ point, see: ~ shoe

pilepuller, see: pile extractor

piler [*is often an inclined continuous conveyor, though intermittently working vertical hoists are also available, either for hand or power operation and is used for piling bags*] = Stapler m, Stapelförderer m

pile shoe, drive point, pile point = Pfahlschuh m, Rammspitze f, Pfahlfuß m

~-sinking with the water jet, see: water jetting of piles

pile-supported abutment = pfahlfundiertes Widerlager n

(pile) trestle, bent = (Pfahl)Joch n

~ used for the compaction of loose soils = Verdichtungspfahl m

pilfer-proof, thief-proof = diebessicher

piling, stockpiling = Haldenschüttung f, Haldenlagerung f, Deponie f

~ hammer = Rammhammer m

~ ~ working on the principle of a Diesel engine = Dieselbär m

***piling plant,** see: pile driving plant

pillar drill = Säulenbohrmaschine f

pillaring = Pfeilerbau m [*Bergbau m*]

pillar support [*drifter*] = Spannsäule f [*Hammerbohrmaschine f*]

pilotage charge = Lotsengebühr f

pilot bit, see: step ~

~ concrete strip (or lane) = Pilotbetonstreifen m

~ firm; see: sponsor (US)

~ flag = Lotsenflagge f

~ heading, pilot tunnel, monkey drift = Richtvortrieb m, Richtstollen m

~ house = Modellhaus n

~ model = Versuchsmodell n

~ motor, fractional H. P. motor = Kleinst(elektro)motor m

~ (paving) lane (US); ~ pavement ~ = Richteinbaustreifen m [*Straßenbau m*]

~ plant = Versuchsanlage f

~ shaft = Richtschacht m

~ tunnel, see: ~ heading

pincers = Kneifzange f

pinch bar, see: dog

~ bug riveter = Handschlagnietmaschine f mit Bügel m

pin-connected truss = Gelenkbolzenfachwerk n

pine = Kiefer f

~ forest, see: coniferous ~

~ oil = Kienöl n

~ tar = Kienteer m

~ ~ pitch = Kienteerpech n

pinewood, see: coniferous wood

pin connection = Bolzenverbindung f

pin hole — piston displacement

pin hole = Bolzenloch *n*
~ joint = Bolzengelenk *n*
pinion = Ritzel *n*
pinoline = Pinolin *n*, Harzessenz *f*
pint-size economy tractor = Miniaturtraktor *m*, Miniaturschlepper *m*, Miniaturtrecker *m*
pin weir, needle ~ = Nadel(stau)wehr *n*
PIONIER universal excavator [*Trademark*] = Universalbagger *m*, Fabrikat WESERHÜTTE OTTO WOLFF G.m.b.H., BAD OEYNHAUSEN, DEUTSCHLAND
to pipe = verrohren
pipe = Rohr *n*
~, see: volcanic neck
(~) bell = (Rohr)Muffe *f*
(~) end = (Rohr)Muffenende *n*
~ bend = Rohrkrümmer *m*, Rohrbogen *m*, Krümmer *m*
pipe-boom crane (US); pipe-jib ~ (Brit.) = Rohrausleger-Kran *m*
pipe-casting in trenches = Betonrohrherstellung *f* in Rohrgräben *mpl*
pipe clay, see: ball ~
~ clip = Rohrschelle *f*
~ coating = Rohrschutzanstrich *m*
~ conduit, see: pipework
~ connection = Rohrverbindung *f*, Rohranschluß *m*
~ cross-drain, see: ~ culvert
~ crust, ~ **wall** = Rohrwand(ung) *f*
~ culvert, ~ **cross-drain** = Röhrendurchlaß *m*, Röhrenabzugkanal *m*
piped = verrohrt
pipe drain, subdrain, subsoil drain, stonefilled trench with pipe, pipe subdrain = Rohr(sicker)drän *m*
~ drainage = Dränage *f*, Dränung *f*, Röhrendränung *f*, Röhrendränage
~ drift (Brit.); ~ (small-diameter) tunnel, ~ gallery, ~ heading = Rohrstollen *m*
~ driver, see: ~ pusher
~ expansion bend = Rohrkompensator *m*, Rohrausgleicher *m*
*****pipe fitting**, see: fitting
~ flow measurement = Durchflußmessung *f* in Rohrleitungen *fpl*
~ form, see: (concrete) pipe mo(u)ld

~ friction loss = Rohrreibungsverlust *m*
~ gallery; see: ~ drift (Brit.)
~ hanger = Rohraufhängung *f*
~ heading; see: ~ drift (Brit.)
~ joint(ing) compound, see: joint cement
~ laying = Rohrverlegung *f*
pipe-laying winch = Rohrverlegewinde *f*
~ work = Rohrverlegungsarbeiten *f*
pipeless electric drill = gestängeloses elektrisches Bohrgerät *n*
pipe(-like conduit), see: (volcanic) neck
pipe line, see: pipework
~ ~ bridge = Rohrleitungsbrücke *f*
~ ~ excavator (Brit.), see: ditch digger
~ ~ transportation of coal = Rohrförderung *f* von Kohle *f*
~ ~ trenching = Rohrgrabenaushub *m*
~ mo(u)ld, see: concrete ~ ~
~ network layout (plan) = Rohrnetzlageplan *m*
~ ~ system = Rohrnetzsystem *n*
~ pile, see: (tubular) (steel-)pipe pile
~ plug = Rohrstopfen *m*
~ pusher, ~ **driver** = Rohrvorschubgerät *n*
~ section = Rohrschuß *m*
~ section(al shape), ~ **profile** = Rohrprofil *n*
~ still, tube ~ = Röhrenofen *m*
~ ~ distillation = Röhrendestillation *f* [*Erdölaufbereitung f*]
~ subdrain, see: ~ drain
~ summit, ~ **top** = Rohrscheitel *m*
~ trench = Rohrgraben *m*
pipette = Pipette *f*
pipe wall, see: ~ crust
pipeway = Rohr(leitungs)kanal *m*
pipework, piping, pipe line, pipe conduit = Rohrstrang *m*, Rohrleitung *f*
pipe wrench = Rohrschlüssel *m*
piping = Verrohren *n*, Verrohrung *f*
~ = innere Erosion *f*
~, see: pipework
~ by heave, piping failure = hydraulischer Grundbruch *m*
pisolite, pisolitic limestone = Erbsenstein *m*, Pisolith *m*
pistacite (Min.) = Pistazit *m*
piston blowing engine = Kolbengebläse *n*
~ displacement, see: swept volume

piston drilling machine, drifter (machine) = Stoßbohrmaschine *f*
~ **machine** = Kolbenmaschine *f*
~ **meter** = Kolbenwassermesser *m*
~ **pump** = Kolbenpumpe *f*
(~) **ring compressor**, reciprocating compressor = Kolben(luft)verdichter *m*, Kolbenkompressor *m*, Kolben-Drucklufterzeuger *m*
~ **sampler** = Kolbenbohrer *m* [*Bodenprobenahme f*]
~ **speed** = normale Motordrehzahl *f* [*Dieselmotor m*]
~ **stamp** = Kolbenpochwerk *n*
pit = Grube *f* [*über Tage*]
~ **and quarry industry** = Steine und Erden-Industrie *f*
pit ballast, see: ~ gravel
~**-cast pipe** = stehend gegossenes Gußeisenrohr *n*
pitch = Pech *n*, Säureharzasphalt *m*
~ = Ganghöhe *f* [*Schraube f*]
~ = Nietteilung *f*, Nietabstand *m*
pitchblende (Min.) = (Uran)Pechblende *f*, (Uran)Pecherz *n*
pitch circle = Teilkreis *m*
~ **coal** = Pechkohle *f*
pitched foundation, see: base of stone pitching
~ **slope**, see: hand-placed (stone) riprap
pitcher, blockstone, hand-packed stone, hand-placed stone, hand-pitched stone, pitching stone, bottoming, blocking, hand-packed hardcore (Brit.); Telford stone (US) = Setzpacklagestein *m*, Vorlagestein *m*, Stückstein *m*
~ **pump** = Topfpumpe *f*, Pitcherpumpe
pitch grit, ~ **cake** = Pechgrieß *m*
pitching, see: (hand)-(placed) ~
~ **stone**, see: pitcher
pitch lake, asphalt ~ = Asphaltsee *m*, Pechsee
~ **macadam** = Pechschotter *m*
~ **mastic** = Pechmastix *m*
~ **peat** = Pechtorf *m*
~ **pine**, see: Oregon ~
~ **resin** = Pechharz *n*
pitchstone = Pechstein *m*
pit coal, see: black ~
~ **face** = Grubenwand *f*

~ **floor** = Grubensohle *f*
~ **gravel**, ~ **ballast** = Grubenkies *m*
pithead gear, see: headframe
pit heap, mine-waste heap = Berg(werk)halde *f*
~ **lime**, see: lime paste
pitman = Schwinge *f* [*Backenbrecher m*]
~ = Schubstange *f*
~ = Zugstange *f* [*Blake-Brecher m*]
~ **eccentric bearing** = Exzenterlager *n* der Zugstange*f*, Zugstangenlager [*Blake-Brecher m*]
~ ~ ~ = Schwingenlager *n* [*Einschwingenbrecher*]
~ **shaft** = Zugstangenwelle *f* [*Blake-Brecher m*]
~, see: well-digger
pit prop = Grubenstempel *m*
~ **props**, mine timber = Grubenholz *n*
~**-run gravel** = ungesiebter Grubenkies *m*
pit saw = Schrotsäge *f*
~ **slag** = Grubenschlacke *f*
pitticite, iron dross = Eisensinter *m*
pitting = Grübchen *n*
~ **corrosion** = Lochfraßkorrosion *f*
pit ventilator = Abteuflüfter *m*, Grubenlüfter, Schachtventilator *m*
pivot, fulcrum pin = Drehzapfen *m*
pivotal fault, rotary ~, tension ~ (Geol.) = Drehverwerfung *f*
pivoted bogie = Drehschemel *m*
pivoted-pad journal bearing = radiales Klotz-Gleitlager *n*
pivoting bearing, see: tilting ~
pivot point = Drehpunkt *m* [*Schwarzbelageinbaumaschine f*]
placeability = Einbaufähigkeit *f* [*Beton m*]
placement moisture (or water) content = Einbauwassergehalt *m*
~ **(or pouring, or placing, or depositing) of concrete**, concrete pour = Betoneinbau *m*, Betoneinbringung *f*
~ **site**, see: spreading ~
place-name sign, name board = Ortsschild *n*
placer = Betontransport- und -einbauwagen *m* [*Tunnelbau m*]
placing crew, ~ **gang**, ~ **team**, ~ **party** = Einbaukolonne *f*, Einbautrupp *m*
~ **of concrete**, see: placement ~ ~

placing plan = Bewehrungsplan *m*, Armierungsplan
~ point = Einbaustelle *f* [z. B. Beton *m*]
~ train for tunnel concreting = Einbauzug *m* für Tunnelbetonauskleidung *f*
plagioclase, soda-lime fel(d)spar, soda-lime plagioclase, lime-soda fel(d)spar, plagioclase fel(d)spar (Min.) = Plagioklas *m*, Natron-Kalk-Feldspat *m*, Schiefspalter *m*
plain (Geol.) = Ebene *f*, Flachland *n*
~ bar = glatter Stab *m*
~ bearing, see: friction ~
~ brace, see: bit ~
~ butt joint with fishplates = stumpfer Stoß *m* mit Laschen *fpl*
~ carbon steel = Kohlenstoffstahl *m*, unlegierter Stahl *m*
~ concrete = Beton *m* ohne Wirkstoffe *mpl*
~ ~ = unbewehrter Beton *m*, reiner ~
~ contraction joint = unverdübelte Scheinfuge *f*
~ country = Flachland *n*
~ electrode, see: bare ~
~ (friction) bearing, see: friction ~
~ pipe bend = Glattrohrbogen *m*
~ river = Flachlandfluß *m*
~ round bar = glatter Rundstahlstab *m* [*Bewehrung f*]
~ subsidence, ~ sedimentation = Absetzklärung *f* ohne Ausflockungsmittel *n*
~ tile = Biberschwanz(ziegel) *m*
~ towed roller = Glattmantel-Schleppwalze *f*, Glattmantel-Anhängewalze
~ washer = Mutternscheibe *f*
~ web girder, solid ~ ~ = Vollwandträger *m*, vollwandiger Balken *m*
plan, ground ~ = Grundriß *m*
~ area = Grundfläche *f*
plane = Ebene *f*
~ ~ = Hobel *m*
planed asphalt = mit Straßenhobel *m* verteilte und nach Verkehrsübergabe *f* mit Abziehgerät abgezogene Asphaltdecke *f*
~ subgrade (US); see: formation (Brit.)
plane frame(work), ~ truss = ebenes Fachwerk *n*, ~ Tragwerk *n*
~ (load-)bearing structure, load-bearing slab = Flächentragwerk *n*

planeness = Ebenheit *f*
plane of bending = Biegeebene *f*
~ ~ rupture = Bruchebene *f*
~ ~ ~ = Gleitfläche *f* [*Stützmauer f*]
~ ~ shear = Scherfläche *f*
~ ~ sliding (Geol.) = Rutschebene *f*
~ ~ stratification (Geol.) = Schichtungsebene *f*
planer (Brit.); level(l)er = Planiergerät *n*, Planierer *m*
~ (US), see: subgrade ~
plane survey(ing) = Stückvermessung *f*
~ table = Meßtisch *m*
~ ~ sheet = Meßtischblatt *n*
~ tabling = Meßtischaufnahme *f*
planetary drive = Planetenantrieb *m*
~ gears (or gearing), differential ~ ~ (~ ~) epicyclic (~) ~ ~ = Planetengetriebe *n*, Umlaufgetriebe *n*, Differentialgetriebe
~ rear axle = Hinterachse *f* mit Planetengetriebe *n* in den Hinterradnaben *fpl*
~ type bevel gearing = Kegelradumlaufgetriebe *f*
planet power drive = Planetengetriebeantrieb *m*, Planetenradantrieb
plane truss, see: plane frame(work)
planimeter = Planimeter *n*, Flächenmesser *m*
planina, karst plateau = Karsthochfläche *f*
planing = Einplanieren *n* [*mechanisch*]
~ ~ = (Ab)Hobeln *n*
(~) blade, see: blade
~ ~, cutting ~ [*heater-planer*] = Schneidwerk *n*
planishing hammer = Ausschlichthammer *m*, Ausbeulhammer *m*
plank covering, planking = Bohlenbelag *m*
~ foundation platform = Bohlenrost *m*
~ frame = Bohlenzarge *f*
planking, see: plank covering
plank road = Bohlenweg *m*
planned economy = Planwirtschaft *f*
planner = Planer *m*
planning = Planung *f*
~ and design work = Projektbearbeitung *f*
~ commission = Planungskommission *f*
~ contract = Planungsauftrag *m*
plan of the accident site = Unfallsituationsplan *m*

plant, installation, facility = Anlage *f*, Betriebsanlage, Einrichtung *f*
~ **depot,** contractor's yard, equipment repair yard, plant yard = Gerätepark *m*, Bauhof *m*
~ **engineer** = Maschineningenieur *m*
~ **equipment** = Maschinen *fpl* und Geräte *npl*
~ **facilities,** service ~ = Betriebsanlagen *fpl*
~ **hand,** see: driver
~-**hire rate,** see: equipment rental rate
planting = Bepflanzung *f*
plant item, see: equipment ~
~ **maker** = Maschinenfabrikant *m*
plant-maintenance (work) = Geräte- und Maschinenunterhaltung *f*
plant-mix bituminous macadam = maschinengemischter bituminöser Makadam *m*
plant-mixed, premixed = maschinengemischt
plant-mix pavement, see: pre-mix surfacing
plant mix test, ~ stability ~ = Mischer-Stabilitätsprüfung *f*
~ **mixture** = maschinengemischte (Straßen)Belagsmasse *f*
~ **of the manufacturer** = Lieferwerk *n*
~ **operator,** see: driver
~ **register,** see: list of equipment
~ **remains** = Pflanzenreste *mpl*
~ **spray oil** = Schädlingsbekämpfungs-Weißöl *n*
~ **stability test,** see: ~ mix
~ **topsoil** [*shredded grass sod and soil*] = zerfasertes Gras *n* und Boden *m*
~ **truck** = Werks-Transportwagen *m*
~ **yard,** see: ~ depot
PLASPERG [*Trademark*] = mit Furanharz *n* von geringer Viskosität *f* imprägnierter Stuckgips *m*
plaster, mortar rendering = Putz *m*, Putzmörtel *m*, Mörtelputz *m*
~ **and mortar mixer,** plaster-mortar ~ = Putz- und Mörtelmischer *m*
~ **baseboard** = Platte *f* [*Gipskartonplatte f*]
~ **board,** see: gypsum ~
~ ~ **plant,** gypsum wallboard ~ = Gipsplattenwerk *n*
~ **coating** = Gipsüberzug *m*

plasterer, pargeter = Gipsarbeiter *m*, Gipser *m*, Putzer *m*
plasterers' hatchet = Gipserbeil *n*
plaster floor(ing) = Gipsestrich(fuß)boden *m*
~ **hoist** = Putzaufzug *m*
plastering = Innenputz *m*
~ **contractor** = Spezialfirma *f* für Verputzausführungen im Bau- und Gipshandwerk *n*
~ **gun** = Mörtel-Pump- und Spritzanlage *f*
~ **operation** = Verputzvorgang *m*
~ **trowel** = Putzkelle *f*
~ **with gypsum plaster** = Innenputzgips *m*
plaster lime = Gipskalk *m*
~ **machine** = Mörtel-Misch-Pump- und Spritzanlage *f*
~ **of Paris** = Stuckgips *m*
~ **shooting** (Brit.); mudcapping (US) [*explosive cartridges are placed on the material to be blasted*] = Sprengen *n* von Steinen *mpl* mit aufgelegter verdämmter Ladung *f*
plaster-throwing machine, plastering ~ = Putzwerfer *m*, Putz-Spritz-Apparat *m*, Verputzmaschine *f*
plaster wallboard = Gipskartonplattentafel *f*
plastic, see: cohesive [*soil*]
~ **adhesive** = Kunststoffkleber *m*
~ **binder** = plastisches Bindemittel *n*
~ **calcined magnesite,** magnesite cement, plastic calcines = Magnesiazement *m*
~ **clay** = Letten *m*
(~) **flow,** see: creep
~ ~ = plastisches Fließen *n*
~ **high calcium hydrated lime,** see: fat lime
plastic(ised) concrete, see: high-slump ~
plasticity = Plastizität *f*, Bildsamkeit *f*
~ **index,** PI [*symbol I_p*] = Plastizitätsindex *m*, Bildsamkeitsindex [*Boden m*]
~ **needle,** Proctor (penetration) ~, (soil) ~ ~ = Proctor'sche Plastizitätsnadel *f*, Proctor'sche Sonde *f*, Proctor'sche Prüfnadel, Proctornadel
plasticizer, workability agent; wetting agent (Brit.) = Betonverflüssiger *m*, Plastifizierungsmittel *n*, Weichmacher *m*, BV-Stoff *m*, plastifizierendes Betonzusatzmittel

plasticizing = plastifizierend
plastic limit, PL [*symbol* w_p] = (Aus)Rollgrenze *f*, obere Plastizitätsgrenze *f*, Wr [*Boden m*]
~ line marking machine = Straßenmarkierungsmaschine *f* für plastische Farbmassen *fpl*
~ magnesia, see: Sorel('s) cement
~ marking material = plastischer Markierungsstoff *m*
~ quality = Geschmeidigkeitseigenschaft *f*
~ recovery = plastische Formänderung *f* [*Beton m*]
~ refractory = plastischer feuerfester Formling *m*
~ roadline, ~ strip = plastischer Markierungsstreifen *m*, Kunststoff-Markierungsstreifen *m*
~ soil-cement [*a very wet mix employed as a mortar for the construction of linings for ditches, canals and reservoirs*] = plastischer Bodenzementbeton *m*
~ theory, ductile ~ ~ = Plastizitätstheorie *f* [*Stahlbau m*]
~ white line composition = plastische Straßenmarkierung *f*
plastic pipe = Kunststoffrohr *n*
plate = Gurtplatte *f* [*Blechträger m*]
(~) apron conveyor, see: apron ~
~ arch = Blechbogen *m*
plateau, high plain = Hochebene *f*
plate battery, see: anode ~
~ bearing test, ~ load ~ ~, "K" test, plate failure ~ ~ = Platten-Belastungsversuch *m*, Plattendruckversuch *m*
~ bending machine, sheet metal folding machine = Blechbiegemaschine *f*
~ buckling stress = Beulspannung *f*
~ clutch = Scheibenkupplung *f*
~ girder, steel ~ ~; girder (US) = Blechträger *m*, Vollwandträger *m*
~ ~ bridge; girder ~ (US) = Vollwandträgerbrücke *f*, Blechträgerbrücke *f*
~ ~ web = Blechträgersteg *m*
platelayer, railway ~ (Brit.) = Streckenarbeiter *m* [*Eisenbahn f*]
platelayer's troll(e)y (Brit.); track motor car (US) = Draisine *f*, Eisenbahndraisine *f*, Bahnmeisterwagen *m*
plate (load) bearing test, see: ~ bearing ~

~ spring, see: flat ~
plate steel penstock, steel (power) ~ = Stahlblech-Druckrohrleitung *f*
plate-steel (roller) gate cylinder = Blechzylinder *m* [*Walzenverschluß m*]
plate straightening machine, sheet metal ~ ~ = Blechrichtmaschine *f*
~ type clutch = Lamellenkupplung *f*
~ vibrator, vibrating plate (or pan), pan vibrator, vibration slab = Plattenvibrator *m*, Plattenrüttler *m*, Rüttelplatte *f*, Vibratorplatte
plate-webbed arch girder with three hinges = vollwandiger Dreigelenkbogen *m*
plate weir = aufgelöstes (Stau)Wehr *n*
platform = Plattform *f*
~, see: deck
~, see: timber mat
~ hoist, tower ~ ~ = Plateau-Aufzug *m*, Plattform-Aufzug *m*, Karrenaufzug
platforming process = Reformierungsverfahren *n* mit Platinkontakt *m*
platform scale = Plattformwaage *f*
~ track wheel wagon = Plattformwagen *m*
~ trailer = Plattform-Anhänger *m*
~ truck = Plattformkarre(n) *f*, (*m*)
~ weighing machine, weighbridge = Brückenwaage *f*
plating = Plattieren *n*
plattnerite (Min.) = Schwerbleierz *n*
platy limestone, see: laminated ~
~ rock = plattiges Gestein *n*
~ structure = plattenförmige (Gesteins-) Absonderung *f*
Plauen limestone = Plänerkalk *m*
play = Spielraum *m*
pleasure craft = Vergnügungsdampfer *m*
plenum method of ventilation, push-pull ~ = Wechsellüftung *f*, abwechselnde Saug- und Drucklüftung *f* [*Tunnelbau m*]
pleochroic halos (Min.) = pleochroitischer Hof *m*
plexiglass, see: perspex
pliers, cutting plier = Drahtzange *f*
~ = Kombizange *f*
plinth = Säulenplatte *f*
plot, land parcel = Parzelle *f*, Grundstück *n*
to plot = auftragen
plotting = Auftragen *n*

plough (Brit.); see: plow (US)
to plough in (Brit.); to plow in (US) = unterpflügen
plough type ditcher, trench-plough, trenching plough, deep-plough (Brit.) = Grabenpflug *m*, Rigolpflug; Rajolpflug [*dieser Ausdruck sollte nicht mehr verwendet werden*]
~-type raking machine (Brit.); plow-type ~ ~ (US) = Fugenpflug *m*, Fräse *f* zur Entfernung alter Vergußmasse *f*, Fugenaufreißer *m*
plow (US); plough (Brit.) = Pflug *m*
plug = Pfropfen *m*
plugging chisel = Fitschenbeitel *m*
plug tester, spark ~ ~ = Zündkerzenprüfgerät *n*
~ weld = Lochnaht *f* [*Schweißen n*]
plum, see: displacer
to plumb = abloten, absenken
plumbago, black lead, graphite (Min.) = Graphit *m*
plumb-bob, plummet = Schnurlot *n*, Senkblei *n*, Bleilot *n*
~ cord, plummet ~ = Maurerschnur *f*, Lotschnur *f*
plumber's metal, (~) solder, (lead-)tin solder = Lötzinn *n*
plumbic acid = Bleisäure *f*
plumb pile = lotrechter Pfahl *m*
plummet, see: plumb-bob
plunger diaphragm (or membrane) pump = Tauchkolbenmembran(e)pumpe *f*
~ pump, ram ~, displacement ~ = Tauchkolbenpumpe *f*, Verdrängerpumpe, Plungerpumpe
plunging siphon = Stechheber *m*
plurajet shaped blasting = Sprengverfahren *n* durch Anwendung *f* einer in einer Blechschale *f* mit Abdeckplatte *f* untergebrachten Hohlladung *f* die ohne weitere Verdämmung *f* auf die großen Steine *mpl* aufgelegt wird
plutonic rock, see: intrusive ~
pluviometer = Regenmesser *m*
ply = Gewebeeinlage *f*
PLYRON (US) [*Trademark*] = Kombination von Hart- und Sperrholz *n* mit wasserbeständigem Leim *m* verbunden
plywood base = Sperrholzunterlage *f*

~ panel, ~ sheet = Sperrholzplatte *f*, Sperrholztafel *f*
~ slab formwork = Sperrholzschalung *f*
pneumatically controlled = druckluftgesteuert, preßluftgesteuert
~ placed concrete, see: air-placed ~
pneumatic axe, see: air-driven ~
~ boat (or raft), rubber dinghy = Schlauchboot *n*
~ breaker, see: air hammer
~ caisson, see: air ~
~ clay digger, see: ~ spade
~ coal picker, see: air ~ ~
(~) concrete gun, see: cement ~
(~) concrete placer = pneumatisches Betonfördergerät *n*, pneumatischer Betonförderer *m*, Druckluft-Betonfördergerät
~ control system, air ~ ~ = pneumatisches Kommandosystem *n*
~ conveying = pneumatische Förderung *f*
~ conveyor, transport system, air activator = pneumatischer Förderer *m*, pneumatische Förderanlage *f* [*für loses Material n*]
~ cylinder = Preßluftzylinder *m*
~ dedusting = pneumatische Entstaubung *f*
~ (or air) (pavement) breaker = Preßluft-Aufreißhammer *m*, Druckluft-Aufreißhammer, Preßluft-Aufbruchhammer, Druckluft-Aufbruchhammer
~ digger, see: pneumatic spade
~ excavating air lock, see: air lock
~ feed leg for rock drill, air leg = Bohrknecht *m*, Bohr(er)stütze *f*, Bohrhammerstütze, Vorschubstütze
*****pneumatic foundation** = pneumatische Gründung *f*, Druckluftgründung
~ gear rotary (or rotating) drilling machine = Druckluft-Zahnrad-Drehbohrmaschine *f*
~ grain handling unit = pneumatischer Getreideheber *m*
(~) grouter, see: pressure grouting machine
~ hammer drill = Druckluftbohrhammer *m*, Preßluftbohrhammer
~ lifting device = Preßlufthebezeug *n*, Druckhebezeug

pneumatic loader = Preßluftlader m, Druckluftlader

~ **paving rammer,** air ~ ~ = Preßluft-Pflasterramme f, Druckluft-Pflasterramme

~ **pillar crane** = Druckluftsäulenschwenkkran m

~ **plaster-throwing machine,** ~ plastering machine = Druckluft-Verputzgerät n

~ **(powered) tamper,** air tamper = Preßluftstampfer m, Druckluftstampfer

~ **raft,** see: ~ boat

~ **rammer,** air ~ = Druckluftramme f, Preßluftramme

~ **rolling** = Abwalzen n mit Gummiwalzen fpl

~ **rotary piston rotating (or rotary) drilling machine** = Druckluft-Drehkolben-Drehbohrmaschine f

~ **shaft sinking** = Druckluftabteufung f

~ **spade,** ~ clay digger, ~ clay spade, air spade, air-operated clay spade, ~ spader, ~ digger, ~ spade hammer = Preßluft-Spatenhammer m

~ **stower** = pneumatische Versetzmaschine f

~ **tamper,** see: ~ (powered) ~

~ **tip(ping) wagon** = Druckluftkipper m

~ **tire** (US); ~ tyre (Brit.) = Luftreifen m

pneumatic-tired "CATERPILLAR" [Trademark] (US) = Luftreifenschlepper m, Fabrikat CATERPILLAR TRACTOR CO., PEORIA, ILLINOIS, USA

~ **crusher** (US); rubber-mounted ~ = Auto(mobil)steinbrecher m

***pneumatic-tired shovel-crane,** rubber-mounted shovel-crane (US); pneumatic-tyred mechanical shovel, rubber-mounted ~ ~ (Brit.) = Auto(mobil)bagger m, Pneubagger m, gummibereifter selbstfahrbarer Universalbagger, Universal-Autobagger m, Universal-Autokran

~ **tractor** (US); rubber-tyred ~ (Brit.); industrial wheel ~, wheel-type industrial ~, wheeled ~ = Radschlepper m, Straßenschlepper, Luftreifenschlepper

~ **wheel** (US); pneumatic-tyred ~ (Brit.) = Luftreifenrad n

pneumatic-tire roller, multi-rubber-tire ~ (US); pneumatic-tyred ~, multi-tyred ~, pneumatic-tyred ~, rubber-tyred ~ (Brit.); multi-wheel~, pneumatic multi-wheel(ed) ~ = Gummi(reifenvielfach)walze f, Pneuwalze, Gummivielrad-Verdichtungswalze f, Gummiradwalze

pneumatic-tired vibrating compacting roller, see: vibratory pneumatic-tired ~

pneumatic toggle joint riveting machine = pneumatische Kniehebelnietmaschine f

~ **tool,** (compressed-)air ~ = Preßluftwerkzeug n, Druckluftwerkzeug n

~ **transport pump** = Verdichterpumpe f [pneumatische Förderanlage f]

~ **tube conveyor** = pneumatischer Förderer m, pneumatische Förderanlage f [für Material n in kleinen Behältern mpl]

pneumatic-tyred construction plant (Brit.) = luftbereifte Baugeräte npl (oder Baumaschinen fpl)

~ **mechanical shovel** (Brit.); see: pneumatic-tired shovel-crane (US)

pneumatic vibrated (finishing) screed (or smoother) = Druckluft-Glättbohle f, Preßluft-Glättbohle

pneumatic vibrator, air ~ = Druckluftrüttler m, Preßluftrüttler

~ **wrench,** air ~ = Druckluft-Maulschlüssel m, Preßluft-Maulschlüssel

pneumatolytic = pneumatolytisch

pneumo-hydraulic = pneumatisch-pneudraulisch

pocket drill, ~ bore = Sackbohrer m

pod, elongated lens = Erzlineal n

podsolised = podsolisiert

podzolisation = Auslaugung f des Bodens m vom A- nach dem B-Horizont m

podzol (soil) = Waldboden m, Podsolboden, humider Boden, podsoliger Boden

poikiloblastic texture (Geol.) = bunter Verband m

to point = verfugen, ausfugen

point-bearing (or end-bearing) (foundation, or bearing) pile = Spitzendruckpfahl m

pointed arch [abbreviated Ptd.A.] = Spitzbogen m

~ **head,** conical ~ = spitzer Nietkopf m

pointer = Zeiger *m*
pointing = Ausfugen *n*, Ausfugung *f*, Verfugen *n*
~ **machine** = Mauerfuggerät *n*
~ **mortar**, joint ~, masonry ~ = Fugenmörtel *m*, Mauermörtel, Baumörtel
~ **trowel** = Spitzkelle *f*
point load = Punktlast *f*
~ **of application of load** = Lastangriffspunkt *m*, Kraftangriffspunkt
~ ~ **collection** = Abholort *m*
~ ~ **deposit**, laying site = Einbaustelle *f* [*Straßenbau m*]
~ ~ **escape**, ~ ~ **exit**, ~ ~ **issue** = Austrittsstelle *f* [*Wasser n*]
~ ~ **failure**, failed area = Schad(en)stelle *f*
~ ~ **intersection** = Schnittpunkt *m*
~ ~ **measurement** = Meßstelle *f*
~ ~ **reference**, indicator point [*settlement calculation*] = kennzeichnender Punkt *m* [*Setzungsberechnung f*]
~ ~ **shipping** = Absendeort *m*, Versandort
~ ~ **support** = Auflagerpunkt *m*
~ **template**, see: scratch ~
poise beam = Laufgewichtbalken *m*
~ **weight**, sliding weight, jockey weight, moving poise = Laufgewicht, Einstellgewicht
poker vibrator, see: concrete mass ~
P.O.L. [*petrol, oil and lubricants*] = Benzin *n*, Öl *n* und Schmiermittel *npl*
polarity reversing switch = Polumschalter *m*
polarizing microscope, see: petrographic ~
polder = Polder *m*, Koog *m*
pole = Mast *m*
~ = Pol *m*
~ **climbers**, see: climbing irons
polianite (Min.) = lichtes Graumanganerz *n*
police patrol = Polizeistreife *f*
poling board = Spießbrett *n*
polishable = polierfähig, polierbar
pollution, river ~, sewage ~ of a river = Abwasserlast *f* [*Fluß m*]
pollutional organism = Schmutzwasserbewohner *m*, Schmutzwasserorganismus *m*

polygenetic nagelfluh (or gompholite), variegated ~ = bunte Nagelfluh *f*
polygonal bowstring girder, segmental ~ = Bogensehnenträger *m*
~ **truss** = Vielecksprengwerk *n*
polyphase-generator, three-phase generator, polyphase alternator = Drehstromgenerator *m*
polyphase induction motor, see: asynchronous ~
Poncelet wheel = Poncelet'sches Wasserrad *n*
pond = Weiher *m*, Teich *m*
~ = Spülfläche *f* [*Naßbaggerei f*]
pondage, storage, filling = Einstau *m*, Speicherung *f*, Wasser ~
ponded lake, see: obstruction ~
ponderomotive device for protection against overload = Überlastschutzgerät *n*, Pondomat *m*
ponding, see: bleeding
~ = Einsumpfen *n*, Einsümpfen *n* [*Beton m*]
Pontine Marshes = Pontinische Sümpfe *f*
pontoon = Ponton *m*
~, see: timber mat
~ **bridge**, floating ~ ~ = Pontonbrücke *f*
~ **crane** = Pontonkran *m*
~ **derrick**, see: floating (or barge) derricking jib crane
pony-truss bridge = oben offene Fachwerkbrücke *f*
pool [*fish pass*] = Becken *n* [*Fischtreppe f*]
poor lime, see: lean ~
~ **ore** = Glaucherz *n*
~ **rock** = schlechter Fels *m*, schlechtes (Fels)Gestein *n*
popcorn concrete (US); see: no-fines ~ (Brit.)
popped perlite = Leicht-Perlit *m*
popping rock, rock fall = Bergschlag *m*, Steinschlag *m*
pop shooting, secondary (drilling and) blasting, block-holing, boulder poping, boulder blasting = Zweitsprengung *f* mit Bohrlochladung *f*, Knäpperschießen *n*, Nachknäppern *n*
~ **shot** = Knappschuß *m*, Knäpperschuß *m*
to populate = besiedeln
porcelain clay, see: china ~
~ **earth**, see: china clay

porcelain enamel = Porzellanemaille *f*
~ filter = Porzellanfiltertiegel *m*
~ mortar = Reibschale *f*
pore, void, interstice = Hohlraum *m*, Pore *f*
~ matrix, ~ cement(ing material) (Geol.) = Porenzement *m*
~ pressure, internal water ~ = Porenwasserdruck *m*
~ ~ dissipation = Porenwasserdruckabnahme *f*
~ ratio, porosity ~, voids index, voids ratio = Porenziffer *f*, Porenindex *m*
~ space, see: void(s) ~
~ structure = Porengefüge *n*
~ volume, see: void(s) space
~ water, interstitial ~ = Porenwasser *n*
~ ~ head = Porenwasser-Druckhöhe *f*
~ ~ pressure = Porenwasserdruck *m*
~ ~ ~ cell = Porenwasserdruckmeßdose *f*
~ ~ ~ ga(u)ge = Porenwasserdruckmesser *m*
porosity, apparent density = Porigkeit *f*, Porosität *f*
~ ratio, see: pore ~
porous = porös
~ backfill(ing) = Sickerfüllung *f*, Filterfüllung *f*
~ block conveyor = Lufttrutsche *f* (oder Gebläseluft-Förderrinne *f*, oder pneumatischer Förderer *m*) mit Filtersteinen *mpl*
~ disk, ~ disc, ~ stone ~ = Filterstein *m*
~ medium = poröse Masse *f* [*Lufttrutsche f*]
porphyric melaphyre = Melaphyrporphyr *m*
porphyrite = Porphyrit *m*
porphyritic texture = porphyrische Struktur *f*
~ tuff = Porphyrtuff *m*
porphyroblastic (Geol.) = porphyroblastisch
porphyroid granite, granite porphyry = Granitporphyr *m*
porphyry (Geol.) = Porphyr *m*
port [*this term implies both a harbo(u)r and the facilities required for the handling of cargo and the servicing of ships. Ports must have harbo(u)rs*] = Hafen *m* mit Betriebsanlagen *fpl*

portability = Ortsbeweglichkeit *f* [*Baumaschine f*]
portable, mobile = fahrbar, ortsbeweglich
~ batcher, ~ batching bin, ~ ~ silo = fahrbarer Baustellensilo *m* mit Abmeßvorrichtung *f*, straßenfahrbarer Verwiegesilo *m*
~ batch plant with gradation controls, see: mixer-gradation unit
~ belt (or band) conveyor = fahrbarer Gurtförderer *m*, Fahrband *n*
~ crushing and screening plant = fahrbare Brech- und Siebanlage *f*, ~ Gesteinsaufbereitungsanlage *f*
~ roller = Walze *f* mit gummibereiften Hinterrädern *npl*
~ steam engine = Lokomobile *f*, Kesseldampfmaschine *f*
~ tip wagon type concrete batcher scale = Rundkipperwaage *f*
portal = Portal *n*, Eingang *m* [*z. B. Tunnel m*]
~ bracing = Portal(verband) *n*, (*m*), Endrahmen *m*
~ bucket ladder excavator = Portalbagger *m*, Torbagger
~ crane, arched pedestal ~ = (Voll-)Portalkran *m*, (Voll)Torkran *m*
~ frame = Portalrahmen *m*
(~) ~ with n-column = n-stieliger Rahmen *m*
portal-type (mono)tower crane, ~ revolving tower crane, ~ rotating tower crane = Großturmdrehkran *m* [*ein Portal n läßt den Raum zwischen den Schienen fpl frei*]
port area, extent of a port = Hafengebiet *n*, Ausdehnung *f* eines Hafens *m*
Portland-blastfurnace cement (Brit.) = eine brit. Zementart *f* mit maximal 65% Hochofenschlacke *f*
Portland cement concrete, P. C. C. = Portlandzementbeton *m*
~ ~ Type I (US); Portland cement for general use, normal Portland cement, ordinary Portland cement = gewöhnlicher Portlandzement *m* [*in Deutschland Z 225*]
~ ~ ~ II (US); see: moderate sulphate resisting cement

Portland cement Type III (US); see: high early (or initial) strength Portland cement

~ ~ ~ **IV** (US); see: low heat of hydration cement

~ ~ ~ **V** (US); see: high sulphate resisting Portland cement

~ **stone** = Portlandstein *m*

port of discharge, see: landing-port

position = Stellung *f*

~ **of load** = Laststellung *f*

positioner = Stellungsmacher *m*

positive circle-throw gyratory movement = starre Kreisschwingung *f* [*Sieb n*]

~ **clutch (coupling)** = zwangsläufige Kupplung *f*

~ **drive** = zwangsläufiger Antrieb *m*, Zwanglauftrieb *m*

non-~ ~ = kraftschlüssiger Antrieb

positive movement = Zwanglauf *m*

~ **throw eccentric type screen** = zwangsläufiger Exzenterschwinger *m*, zwangläufiges Exzenter-Schwingsieb *n*

post = Pfosten *m*, Stange *f*

post-card survey, motor driver postal card method = Befragungsmethode *f* durch Postkarten *fpl*, Postkartenzählung *f*

post driver = Pfostenramme *f*

postglacial period = Alluvium *n*, Nacheiszeit *f*

post hole digger = Erweiterungsbohrer *m*

POSTONWAY (US) [*Trademark*] = eine Straßenbauweise, bei der als Packlage Blockziegel 8" × 8" × 4" schachbrettartig verlegt werden, die dann mit einer Gußzementschicht als Decklage versehen werden, wobei der Zement gleichzeitig bei Bearbeitung mit einer Vibrationsmaschine die Packlagefugen verschließt

post puller = Pfostenzieher *m*

~ **(soil) auger** = Erweiterungs-Spiralbohrer *m*

post-tensioned highway slab = Betonfahrbahnplatte *f* mit nachträglichem Verbund *m*

~ **prestressed (reinforced) concrete** = Spannbeton *m* mit nachträglichem Verbund *m*

post-tensioning = Vorspann *m* (oder Vorspannung *f*) mit nachträglichem Verbund *m*

potable water, see: drinking ~

potash, see: protoxide of potassium

~ **alum**, see: common ~

~ **fel(d)spar** (Min.) = Kalifeldspat *m*

~ **manure** = Kalidünger *m*

~ **mine waste** = Kaliabwasser *n*

~ **mining** = Kalibergbau *m*

~ **silicate** = Kalisilikat *n*

~ **-soap**, soft soap = Kaliseife *f*

potassa, see: protoxide of potassium

potassic nitrate, see: potassium ~

potassium = Kalium *n*, Kalimetall *n*

~ **aluminium silicate** = Kalium-Tonerde-Silikat *n*, $K_2O \times Al_2O_3 \times 6SiO_2$

~ **carbonate**, K_2CO_3 = Kaliumkarbonat *n*, Pottasche *f*, kohlensaures Kalium *n*

~ **chlorate**, $KClO_3$ = Kaliumchlorat *n*

~ **ferricyanide** = Blausalz *n*

~ **hydrate**, see: caustic potash

~ **hydroxide**, see: caustic potash

~ **iodide** = Jodkalium *n*, Kaliumjodid *n*

~ **(mon)oxide**, K_2O = Kali(umoxyd) *n*

~ **nitrate**, nitre, salpeter, (India) saltpetre, potassic nitrate, KNO_3 = Kalisalpeter *m*, Kaliumnitrat *n*

~ **permanganate** = übermangansaures Kali *n*, Kaliumpermanganat *n*

~ **salt**, potassic salt = Kali(salz) *n*

potential transformer, see: voltage ~

pot-hole, see: glacier mill

~ ~ = Schlagloch *n*

~ **patcher**, ~ **patching machine** = Schlaglochflickgerät *n*, Schlaglochflicker *m*

pot-holing = Schlaglochbildung *f*

potman (Brit.) = Kocher *m* am Standkessel *m* [*Gußasphaltarbeiter m*]

potter's clay, see: ball ~

pottery closet = WC-Becken *n*

~ **kiln** = feinkeramischer Ofen *m*

~ **plaster** = Formgips *m*, Keramikergips, Formengips

poultry house = Geflügelzuchtraum *m*

pounds per square inch gauge, psig = Atmosphärenüberdruck *m*, atü

pour, lift, layer = Einbauschicht *f* [*Beton m*]

poured concrete joint = Betonfuge *f* ohne feste Einlage *f*, einfache Vergußfuge *f*
poured-in-place concrete, see: cast-in-place ~
pouring can, ~ **pot** = Fugenvergußkanne *f*
~ **machine,** see: joint sealing machine
~ **of concrete,** see: placement ~ ~
pour point [*oil*] = Stockpunkt *m* [*Öl n*]
~ ~ = Fließpunkt *m* [*Kälteverhalten n von Dieselkraftstoff m*]
powder-actuated nailer = Nagelkanone *f*
~ **tool,** see: cartridge-powered ~
powder asphalt, rock ~, stamped ~ [*deprecated*]; compressed (natural) rock asphalt (surfacing) = Stampfasphalt *m* ohne Bitumenzusatz *m*
powdered calcium carbonate, see: air-slaked lime
~ **lime,** see: air-slaked ~
~ **stabilizer,** see: powder ~
~ **talc,** see: French chalk
powder explosive, see: low (strength) blasting explosive
~ **fuse** = Pulverzündschnur *f*
~ **metallurgy** = Sintermetallurgie *f*
powder-spreader, bulk spreader [*a vehicle for distributing stabilisers in powder form*] = Stabilisatorpulver-Verteiler *m*
~ **type centrifugal coupling** = Zentrifugal-Pulverkupplung *f*
powdery form = Pulverform *f*
power = Potenz *f*
~ = Energie *f*, Kraft *f*
power-actuated tool = Kraftwerkzeug *n*
power and free conveyors = halbkontinuierliche Förderanlage *f*
~ **axle,** see: drive axle
power-assisted steering = Kraftlenkung *f*
power ballaster, see: track tamping machine
~ **canal** = Wasserkraftkanal *m*
~ **chips spreader** (US); see: ~ gritting machine (Brit.)
~ **(concrete) cart** (or **buggy,** or **barrow**) = Motor-Betonvorderkipper *m*, Motor-Japaner(karren) *m*, Motor-Kipperkarre(n) *f*, (*m*)

~ **cylinder** = Motorzylinder *m* [*Kompressor m*]
~ **dam** = Kraftwerk-Talsperre *f*
~ **drive** = Kraftantrieb *m*
power(-driven) roller, self-propelled ~ = Kraftwalze *f*, Motorwalze *f*
~ **(or engine driven) rotary sweeper** (or **scavenging machine,** or **road sweeper,** or **mechanical sweeper,** or **road sweeping machine,** or **street sweeper**) = Motor-Straßenkehrmaschine *f*, Motor-Fegemaschine *f*
power(-driven) (drum) winch = Krafttrommelwinde *f*, Kraft(trommel)windwerk *n*
powered barge, see: self-propelled ~
~ **(road) bender,** power-operated bar bender, reinforcement (bar-)bending machine = Biegemaschine *f*, Profileisen~, Betoneisen~, Profilstahl~, Betonstahl~
power-feed rock drill = Gesteinsbohrer *m* mit Druckluftstütze *f*
power finegrader; see: concrete bay subgrader (Brit.)
~ **fuel,** see: driving fuel
~ **gas** = Kraftgas *n*
~ **generation,** ~ **generating,** ~ **production** = Energieerzeugung *f*, Krafterzeugung
*****power grader,** see: motor ~
~ **gritting machine** (Brit.); **power chips spreader** (US) = Motor-Splittstreumaschine *f*, Motor-Splittstreuer *m*
(~) hack saw = Hacksäge *f*
~ **hammer** = Krafthammer *m*
~ **house** = Krafthaus *n*, Kraftwerksgebäude *n*, Maschinenhaus *n*
~ ~ **cavern** = (Maschinen)Kaverne *f*
~ ~ **floor level** = Turbinenflurhöhe *f*
~ ~ **superstructure** = Krafthausüberbau *m*
~ **installation,** see: ~ plant
~ **irrigation,** see: pump ~
~ **kerosene,** tractor oil, tractor fuel, power kerosine = Kraftstoffkerosin *n*, Traktorenkraftstoff *m*, Motorenpetroleum *n*, Kraftstoff für Otto-Motore mit Spezialvergasern
~ **navvy** (Brit.); see: crane ~
power-operated = kraftbetrieben
~ **bar bender,** see: powered (rod) bender

power-operated hoist — precast (concrete) unit

power-operated hoist = Kraftaufzug *m*
~ lifting machine = Krafthubwerk *n*
~ stirring gear = Kraftrührwerk *n*
power penstock, see: penstock
~ plant, ~ station, ~ installation = Kraftwerk *n*, Kraftwerkanlage *f*
~ ~ chamber = Kraftwerkraum *m*
~ ~ intake structure, penstock dam = Einlaßbauwerk *n* zum Kraftwerk *n* [*als Sperre f ausgebildet*]
~ production, see: ~ generation
power-propelled surface vibrating and finishing machine, see: concrete finishing road vibrator
power pump for grouting, see: pressure grouting machine
~ road sweeper, see: power(-driven) rotary sweeper
~ saw = Kraftsäge *f*, Motorsäge
~ scheme = Energieprojekt *n*
~ shovel; see: crane navvy (Brit.)
~ spraying pump = Maschinenspritzpumpe *f*
~ ~ with hand lance = Spritzen *n* mit Maschinenpumpendruck *m* und Handrohr *n*
~ station, see: ~ plant
~ steer(ing), power-assisted ~ = Kraftlenkung *f*
~ storage = Speicherung *f* zur Energieerzeugung *f*
~ street sweeper, see: power(-driven) rotary sweeper
~ supply = Kraftversorgung *f*, Energieversorgung *f*, Stromversorgung
~ ~ unit (or set) = Netz(anschluß)gerät *n*
~ take-off = Kraftabnahme *f*
~ ~ group = Zapfwelle *f* komplett
~ (or mechanical) tamper = Kraftstampfer *m*
~ testing screen = Kraftprüfsieb *n*
~ train = Getriebegruppe *f* [*z. B. beim Bagger m*]
~ transmission, mechanical transmission of power = Kraftübertragung *f*
~ trowel, see: mechanical ~
~ tunnel, hydro ~ power tube = (Wasser-)Kraftstollen *m*
~ unit = Antriebsgruppe *f* [*Baumaschine f*]

~ wheelbarrow, mechanical ~ = Kraftkarre(n) *f*, (*m*)
~ winch, see: power(-driven) (drum) ~
pozzolan(ic) cement = Puzzolanzement *m*
*pozzolan(ic) materials = puzzolanische Stoffe *mpl*, Puzzolanen *fpl*
POZZOLITH [*Trademark*] = ein luftporenbildender Zusatzstoff *m* [*eine Mischung von Kalziumligninsulfonat, Laurylnatriumsulfat, Kalziumchlorid und Flugasche*]
   HIGH EARLY ~ [*enthält mehr Kalziumchlorid*]
pozzuolana, pozzolana, puzzolano, puzzolana = Puzzolanerde *f*, Bröckeltuff *m*
practical, technical = (betriebs)technisch
practice, technique = Technik *f* [*als betriebstechnische Anwendung f*]
practitioner, practising engineer = Praktiker *m*
pram = Prahm *m*
Pratt truss, see: Linville ~
Prealps = Voralpen *f*
pre-assembly = Vormontage *f*
pre-automobile days, pre-motor vehicle ~ = Vormotorisierungszeit *f*
prebatching bin = Vormischsilo *m*
preblended rubber = mit Bitumen *n* vermischter Gummi *m*
(precast) concrete block = Betonstein *m*
~ ~ building = Betonmontagebau *m*
~ concrete-cylinder method; see under "caisson pile"
~ concrete industry = Betonsteinindustrie *f*
~ ~ joist = Betondeckenbalken *m*
(~) ~ ~ machine, lintel ~ = Balkenformmaschine *f*, Hohlbalkenmaschine
(~) ~ ~ shaker (or shaking machine) = Balkenrüttler *m*
~ ~ manufacturing yard = bewegliches Montagebetonwerk *n*, Beton-Vorfertigungsstelle *f*
~ ~ sandwich panel = Fertigbeton-Doppelwandtafel *f*
~ (~) unit, pre-fabricated (~) ~, precast structural element = (Beton)Fertigteil *m*, Formling *m*, Fertigbetonteil

Precast Concrete Yearbook = Betonstein-Jahrbuch n
precast construction = Fertigbauweise f
~ **floor** = Fertigdecke f
~ **gypsum block**, see: gypsum (precast building) block
~ **kerb(stone)** (Brit.)/**curb(stone) of white granite aggregate** = Kunstgranitbordstein m mit weißem Quarzitkorn n
~ ~ **vibrating machine** = Vibrations-Bordschwellenmaschine f
~ **prestressed concrete unit** = Spannbetonelement n, Spannbetonfertigteil m
~ **products industry**, see: concrete block ~
~ **reinforced concrete beam bridge** = Stahlbetonfertigträgerbrücke f
~ ~ ~ **(structural) unit** = Stahlbetonfertigteil m, Stahlbetonelement n
~ **slab** = Fertigbetonplatte f
~ ~ **floor** = Betondiele f
~ **structural element**, see: precast (concrete) unit
~ **unit**, see: ~ (concrete) ~
~ **units works**, prefabricated ~ ~, precast concrete ~ ~, precast works, precast plant = Montagebeton-Werk n
~ **wares**, see: concrete products
precaution = Schutzmaßnahme f
precious metal, see: noble ~
precipitant = (Aus)Fäll(ungs)mittel n
to precipitate = niederschlagen
precipitated chalk, see: prepared ~
~ **deposit** = Ausscheidungslagerstätte f
precipitation = Ausfällung f
~, **rainfall** = Niederschlag m
precipitator = Abscheider m [Staub m]
precision instrument = Präzisionsinstrument n
(~) **subgrader**; see: concrete bay ~ (Brit.)
precleaner = Vorreiniger m
~ = Vorabscheider m [Ölbadluftfilter m, n]
precleaning = Vorreinigung f [Staubluft f im Ölbad n]
pre-coated chip(ping)s [deprecated]; see: coated ~
precombustion = Vorverbrennung f
precompactor = Vorverdichter m
preconcentration = Vorkonzentrierung f

prefabricated asphalt canal lining (US); ~ bitumen ~ ~ (Brit.) = Bitumen-Fertigauskleidung f für Gerinne npl
~ **bituminous surfacing**, P. B. S., (prefabricated) bituminized-hessian surfacing, bitumized jute hessian cloth = Bitumen-Fertigbahn f, Bitumengewebebahn
~ **(concrete) unit**, see: precast (~) ~
~ **office block** = vorgefertigtes Bürogebäude n
pre-fabrication = Vorfabrikation f
pre-filter = Grobfilter n, m
pre-formed asphalt joint filler (US) = Fugeneinlage f (oder Fugenstreifen m, oder feste Einlage f) auf Bitumenbasis f
~ **(joint) filler**, joint-sealing strip, (expansion) joint filler, (expansion) joint(ing) strip, premo(u)lded (strip joint) filler, strip of pre-formed filling material = Fugeneinlage f, feste Einlage f, Fugenstreifen m
(pre)heater = Vorwärmer m, Erhitzer m
preheating zone = Vorwärmzone f
PREHY grouter & placer [Trademark] = Druckluftpreßgerät n, Fabrikat THE PREHY CO., NEW YORK 17, USA
pre-ignition = Vorzündung f
preliminary (grinding) mill = Vor(mahl)mühle f
~ **test**, suitability test = Eignungsprüfung f
~ **work**, preparatory ~ = Vorarbeiten fpl
preliminator = Zementkugel(mahl)mühle f
premature stiffening, see: false set
pre-mixed, see: plant-mixed
pre-mix(ed) carpet, see: road carpet
*(**pre-)mixed macadam**; see: coated ~ (Brit.)
pre-mixing = Vormischung f, Vormischen n
~ **plant**; see: asphalt and coated macadam mixing plant (Brit.)
pre-mix(ed) surfacing, plant-mix pavement = Misch(anlagen)decke f, Misch(anlagen)belag m [Straße f]
pre-mo(u)lded (strip joint) filler, see: preformed (joint) filler

prepacked concrete, Prepakt ~, grout-intruded ~ = Prepaktbeton m, vorgepackter Beton, Schlämmbeton, Skelettbeton
preparatory work, preliminary ~ = Vorarbeiten fpl
prepared chalk, whiting, precipitated chalk = Schlämmkreide f, Schlemmkreide
pre-piling = Rammsondierung f mit Versuchspfählen mpl
pre-planning = Vorplanung f
presaturator = Vortränker m [Dachpappenfertigungsanlage f]
present value, trade-in ~ = Verkehrswert m, Zeitwert m [Baumaschine f]
preservation = Haltbarmachung f, Konservierung f
~ of buildings = Bautenschutz m
preservative = Konservierungsmittel n
pre-shrink mixing = Vormischen n der Betonbestandteile mpl (ohne Wasser n) vor Einspeisung f in den Liefermischer m [Transportbeton m]
press-button control, see: push-button ~
(pressed) air lock, see: air lock
pressed brick = Preßstein m, Preßziegel m
~ casting ribbed pipe = Preßgußrippenrohr n
~ distillate, blue oil = Öl n erhalten bei Entparaffinierung f vor der Aufarbeitung f zu Neutralöl, blaues Öl n
~ peat = Preßtorf m
press fit = Preßsitz m
pressure at rest = Ruhedruck m
~ blower = Druckgebläse n
~ build-up test = Druckaufbau-Versuch m
~ bulb, bulb of pressure = Druckzwiebel f
~ cell, ~ capsule = Druckmeßdose f
~ conduit, see: ~ line
~ cylinder = Treibkessel m, Druckkessel, Förderkessel, einkammeriges Druckgefäß n
~ diagram = Druckdiagramm n
~ distillate, PD = Druckdestillat n
~ distributor truck (US); see: pressure tank lorry (Brit.)

~ disturbance = Druckstörung f (Geol.)
~ drop = Druckabfall m
~ fault = Druckdislokation f (Geol.)
~ filter = Druckfilter n, m
~ flow [a method of drainage whereby moisture is impelled to travel up vertical sand drains, the pressure being due to the weight of the overlying embankment] = Entwässerung f durch vertikale Sanddränagen fpl mit Auflast f
~ gallery = Druckstollen m
~ ga(u)ge = Manometer n
~ grouting, see: injection process
~ ~ machine, (pneumatic) grouter, grout pump, cement grout pump, grout ejector, power pump for grouting = Drucklufteinpreßgerät n, Injektor m
~ ~ pan, see: bougie (Brit.)
~ ~ process, injection ~ = Einpreßverfahren n, Injektionsverfahren n, Auspreßverfahren
~ gun fitting = Schmierstelle f
~ head, see: (water) ~
~ -hydrated lime, see: autoclaved ~
pressure joint = Druckkluft f (Geol.)
~ line, ~ conduit = Druckleitung f
~ mixing = Zwangsmischen n, Zwangsmischung f
~ of mountain mass (Geol.) = Gebirgsdruck m
~ on abutment [bridge] = Kämpferdruck m
~ ~ bearing surface, see: bearing pressure
~ ~ the formwork = Schalungsdruck m
~ pipe = Druckrohr n
pressure (or blast) pneumatic conveyor (or conveying system) = Druckluftförderer m, Druckluftförderanlage f
~ pot; see: bougie (Brit.)
~ process = Vakuumdruckverfahren n [Holzschutzbehandlung f]
~ shaft, penstock ~ = Fallschacht m, Druck(leitungs)schacht
~ sluice, ~ shutter = Spannschütz(e) n, (f)
~ structure = Druckstruktur f (Geol.)
~ surge = Druckwelle f [im Bohrloch n]
~ tank, ~ vessel = Druckbehälter m, Druckgefäß n, Druckkessel m

pressure tank lorry — primary crusher (or breaker)

pressure tank lorry, (bulk) bitumen distributor, pressure spray tanker (Brit.); pressure distributor truck, asphalt truck distributor (US); bituminous distributor, pressure tanker, truck mounted distributor, road oil distributor = Großspritzgerät *n*, Druckverteiler *m*, Bitumen-Sprengwagen *m*, Tankspritzmaschine *f*, Automobil-Sprengwagen *m*, Drucksprengwagen *m*, Drucktankwagen *m*, Motorspritzwagen *m*, Rampentank-Spritzmaschine *f*, Motorspritzmaschine *f*, Automobil-Spritzwagen *m*

~-treated timber = druckgetränktes Holz *n*

pressure tunnel, ~ gallery, tunnel-type penstock, conversion tunnel = Betriebswasserstollen *m*, Druck(wasser)stollen, Triebwasserstollen

~ type cloth filter dust collector = Druckschlauchfilter *m, n*

~ vessel, ~ tank = Druckbehälter *m*, Druckgefäß *n*, Druckkessel *m*

~-voids ratio diagram = Druck-Porenziffer-Diagramm *n*

pressure voids-ratio ratio = Druck-Porenziffer-Verhältnis *n*

~ washing operation = Druckauswaschung *f*

pressurised cement tanker = Zementtanker *m* (oder Zementtransportfahrzeug *n*) mit Druckluftentladung *f*

~ oil, hydraulic (pressure) oil = Drucköl *n*

~ ~ system = Ölhydraulik *f*

~ water reactor, PWR = Druckwasser-Reaktor *m*

prestress, pre-stressing = Vorspann(ung) *m*, (*f*)

prestressed beam = Spannbetonbalken *m*

~ block-beam = Spannbeton-Hohlblockträger *m*

~ concrete bridge = Spannbetonbrücke *f*

~ ~ building frame = Spannbeton-Gebäuderahmen *m*

~ ~ element = Spannbetonteil *m*

~ ~ engineer = Spannbetoningenieur *m*

~ ~ road = Spannbetonstraße *f*

~ ~ ~ bridge = Spannbeton-Straßenbrücke *f*

~ ~ sleeper (Brit.); **~ ~ tie** (US) = Spannbetonschienenschwelle *f*

~ ~ spun pipe = drahtumwundenes Betonrohr *n* mit Vorspann(ung) *m*,(*f*)

~ ~ structure = Spannbetonbauwerk *n*

~ ~ tank = Spannbetonbehälter *m*

~ ~ with thin wires, Hoyer method = Stahlsaitenbeton *m*, Bauweise Hoyer *f*

~ flexure test beam = Spannbetonbiegebalken *m*, Spannbetonprobebalken

~ tension ring = vorgespannter Zugring *m*

prestressing bar = (Vor)Spannstab *m*

~ bed, ~ rack = Spannbett *n*, Spannbank *f*, Spannbahn *f*

~ duct = Spannkanal *m*

~ element = Spannglied *n*

~ force = (Vor)Spannkraft *f*

~ instruction = (Vor)Spannanweisung *f*

~ method = (Vor)Spannverfahren *n*

~ ~ with rigid tie rod = Verfahren *n* Dischinger [Rahmen *m*]

~ rack, ~ bed = Spannbahn *f*, Spannbank *f*, Spannbett *n*

~ reinforcement = Spannbewehrung *f*, Spannarmierung, Vor ~

~ steel = Spannbetonstahl *m*

~ wire = Spanndraht *m*

~ work = Spannbetonarbeiten *fpl*

pre-tensioned prestressed concrete = Spannbeton *m* mit Verbund *m*

pre-tensioning = Vorspannung *f* mit Verbund *m*, Vorspann *m* ~ ~

preventer, blowout ~ = Absperrorgan *n* am Bohrloch *n*, Preventer *m*

preventive measure = Verhütungsmaßnahme *f*

prewar level = Vorkriegsstand *m*

price build-up, ~ determination, costing = Preisgestehung *f*, Preisermittlung *f*

price fixing, combining to eliminate competition = Absprache *f* unter Bietern *mpl*

pricker staff, see: probing ~

pricking, probing = Sondenbohrung *f*, Sondenpressung *f*

primary control = Haupt-Steuerorgan *n*, Haupteinstellorgan

~ crusher (or breaker), see: stone breaker (type crusher)

primary (drilling and) blasting = Erstsprengung f
~ **excavation** = Aushub m in gewachsenem Boden m
~ **heater,** ~heating kettle, ~melting tank; ~ boiler [*deprecated*] = Vorkocher m
~ **high-pressure turbine** = Vorschaltturbine f
~ **rock,** see: igneous ~
~ **sludge,** green ~, fresh ~ = Frischschlamm m
prime coat, see: priming ~
~ **contractor,** chief ~, general ~ = Generalunternehmer m
~ **cost,** flat ~ = Gestehungskosten f
~ **membrane,** see: priming coat
~-**membrane canal lining** = aufgespritzte Dichtungshaut f zur Gerinne-Auskleidung f
Prime Meridian = Nullmeridian m
prime mover = Einachs-Zugwagen m [*z. B. Fabrikate CATERPILLAR und LE TOURNEAU (TOURNAPULL)*], Einachs-Schlepper m, Zweiradtrecker m, (Zweirad-)Vorspänner m, (Zweirad-)Vorspannwagen m, (Zweirad-)Triebsatz m, Ein-Achs-Reifen-Sattelschlepper m
~ ~ = Primärantriebsorgan n [*z. B. eine Feldbahnlok(omotive) f*]
~ ~ = Karre(n) f, (m) mit Fahrantrieb m, motorisierter Schubkarre(n) [*die letzte Bezeichnung ist eigentlich unsinnig, denn ein Karren mit Fahrantrieb bedarf nicht mehr des Schubes durch den Bedienungsmann, der nur Karren-Führer ist*]
primer, see: priming paint
~ = Grundiermasse f
~ = Fibel f
~ = Einspritzvorrichtung f, Kaltstartanlage f
~, see: priming compound
~ **cartridge,** blasting ~ = Schlagpatrone f, Bohrpatrone, Sprengstoffpatrone
priming = Anlassen n, Ansaugen n, Ansaugung f [*z. B. Pumpe f*]
~ = Voranstreichen n, Grundieren n
~, see: acceleration
~ **coat,** prime(r) ~, prime membrane = Grundierüberzug m, Voranstrich m, Grund(ier)anstrich m

~ **compound,** detonating charge, primer = Zündsatz m
~ **fuel** = Anlaßkraftstoff m
~ **level** = Anspring-Wasserspiegel m [*automatischer Syphon m*]
~ **nose** (Brit.); sealing bucket (US) = Anspringnase f [*automatischer Syphon m*]
~ **paint,** primer = Grundierfarbe f
primitive rock = Urgestein n, kompakter Fels m, dichtes Gestein, dichter Fels
Primus stove (Brit.) = Brennspirituskocher m
principal rafter, common ~ = Bindersparren m
~ **rafters** = Bindergespärre n, Bundgespärre
~ **stress** = Hauptspannung f
principles and practice = Grundlagen fpl und praktische Anwendung f
print = Pause f
printing calculator = Registrierrechenmaschine f
~ **machine,** see: copier
prismatic compass = Marschkompaß m, Prismakompaß
~ **roof slab (or panel)** = prismatisch geformte Dachplatte f
~ **structure** = prismatisches Faltwerk n
prism binocular glass = Prismenfeldstecher m
prismoidal formula = Prismenformel f [*Massenberechnung f im Erdbau m*]
private automobile = Privatauto n
~ **drive,** ~ road, driveway, private street = Privatweg m
privately owned water = Privatgewässer n
probability method = Wahrscheinlichkeitsrechnung f [*Hochwasser n*]
probing, see: pricking
~ **staff,** pricker ~ = Bodensonde f, Sondenbohrer m
processing, dressing, preparation, materials ~ = (Material)Aufbereitung f
~ ~ = Vermörteln n [*Boden m*]
~ **costs** [*soil-cement*] = Einbaukosten f
~ **machine,** process ~ = Aufbereitungsmaschine f, Verarbeitungsmaschine
process of rock wastage, weathering = Verwitterung f, Auswitterung, Abwitterung

Proctor compaction curve, dry density/ moisture content graph = Proctor-Kurve *f*
~ **(penetration) needle,** see: plasticity ~
~ **test,** standard compaction ~ = Proctor-Prüfung *f,* verbesserter AASHO-Versuch *m,* Proctor-Versuch
producer gas = Generatorgas *n*
~ ~ **brown coal tar** = Braunkohlenheizgeneratorteer *m*
~ ~ **coal tar,** gas-producer ~ ~ = Steinkohlen(heiz)generatorteer *m*
~ **peat tar** = Torf-Schwelgeneratorteer *m*
~ **plant** = Lieferwerk *n,* Erzeugerwerk
producing gas well = (produzierende) Erdgassonde *f,* fördernde Gasbohrung *f*
production-line method = Großerzeugung *f*
production model = Serienmuster *n*
~ **study** [*machine*] = Arbeitsuntersuchung *f* [*Maschine f*]
productivity wage = Leistungslohn *m*
product line = Produktenölleitung *f*
professional disease, see: vocational ~
~ **literature** = Fachliteratur *f*
~ **practice** = Berufspraxis *f*
~ **training** = Berufsausbildung *f*
profilated brick, mo(u)lded ~, purpose-made ~ = Profilstein *m,* Profilziegel *m*
to profile = aufnehmen von Profilen *npl*
profile, section(al shape) = Profil *n*
~, elevation = Aufriß *m,* Ansicht *f,* Vertikalprojektion *f*
*profile of road,** see: cross-section of road
~ ~ **slope** = Böschungsprofil *n*
~ **pit,** see: test pit
profiling = Profilaufnahme *f*
profilometer, profilograph [*an instrument for recording the shape of irregularities in a road surface*] = Profilzeichner *m,* Profilograph *m*
program(me) of works, see: construction schedule
progress chart, see: construction schedule
progression = Reihe *f* [*Mathematik f*]
progressive failure = fortschreitender Bruch *m*
progress of works = Baufortschritt *m,* Arbeitsfortschritt, Arbeitstempo *n,* Bautempo

~ **schedule,** see: construction ~
project = Bauvorhaben *n*
projecting abutment = vorspringendes Widerlager *n*
~ **beam,** see: cantilevered ~
~ **end** = Vorbauspitze *f* [*Brücke f*]
~ **foot,** tamping foot = Schaffuß *m,* Walzen-Stempel *m* [*Schaffußwalze f*]
projection welding = Buckelschweißung *f*
project manager, engineer's-agent = Bauleiter *m*
~ **planning** = Bauplanung *f*
~ **site,** see: building ~
prolongation of a river mouth seawards = Ausbau *m* einer Flußmündung *f* in See *f*
promoter, purchaser, owner, sponsor, employer, client = Auftraggeber *m,* Bauherr *m,* Bauherrschaft *f*
prong = Gabelzinken *m*
prop = Stempel *m*
propane (gas) = Propan(gas) *n*
~ **handling pump** = Propanpumpe *f*
propel chain (US); see: drive ~
propeller pump, see: axial (flow) ~
~ **shaft** = Kardanwelle *f*
propelling torque = Fahr-Drehmoment *n*
propel mechanism = Fahrantrieb *m*
~ **sprocket,** driving ~, drive ~ = Antriebsturas *m,* Antriebskettenrad *n*
property damage = Sachschaden *m*
~ **-owner** = Grundstückseigentümer *m*
property value = Grundstückswert *m*
proportional compasses = Reduktionszirkel *m*
~ **limit,** limit of proportionality = Proportionalitätsgrenze *f*
~ **test bar** = Proportionalstab *m*
proportion(ality) factor, ratio = Verhältniszahl *f*
proportioning, batching, ga(u)ging, measuring = Dosierung *f,* Zuteilung *f,* Zumessung *f,* Abmessung *f*
~ **by conveyor belt** = Bandzuteilung *f*
~ ~ **weight,** see: weigh-batching
~ **device,** batching ~, measuring ~, ga(u)ging ~ = Zumeßvorrichtung *f,* Abmeßvorrichtung, Zuteilvorrichtung, Dosiervorrichtung
~ **plant,** see: (aggregate) batching plant

proportioning screw conveyor, ~ worm ~ = Zuteilschnecke *f*, Abmeßschnecke, Dosierschnecke, Zumeßschnecke

~ weight-feeder-conveyor = Dosierbandwaage *f*

~ worm conveyor, ~ screw ~ = Abmeßschnecke *f*

*proposal, see: bid

propped-cantilever beam = einseitig eingespannter Träger *m*

propping up = Verspreizung *f*, Abspreizung

to prorate = vorgeben

prorated time = Vorgabezeit *f*

prospect boring = Untersuchungsbohrung *f*

~ drilling machine = Schürfbohrmaschine *f*

prospecting = Schürfen *n*, Beschürfung *f*, Schurf *m* [*Suche f nach Bodenschätzen mpl; Bodenuntersuchung f*]

prospector's pick, geologist's ~ = Geologenhacke *f*

prospect pit, see: test ~

~ pump = Perspektivpumpe *f*

~ shaft = Schürfschacht *m*

protection against mining subsidence = Senkungsschutz *m* im Bergbau *m*

~ ~ scour, erosion control = Kolkschutz *m*

~ fence, see: guard ~

~ works, sea defence ~ = Seeschutzbauten *f*

protective atmosphere = Schutzgasatmosphäre *f*

~ clothing = Schutz(be)kleidung *f*, Arbeits~

~ coat(ing) = Schutzanstrich *m*, Schutzüberzug *m*

~ coating intermediate = Schutzüberzug-Phenolderivat *n*

~ footwear = Schutzfußbekleidung *f*

~ motor switsch = Motorschutzschalter *m*

~ structure = Schutzwerk *n*

PROTEX AEA [*Trademark*] = ein Betonbelüftungsmittel *n* in den USA

protogene gneiss, protogenic ~, protogin(e) ~ = Alpengneis *m*

protoxide of potassium, prussiate of potash, (anhydrous) potash, potassa = Kali *n*

protractor, see: circular ~

proud [*of the surface*] = hervorstehend

proustite, ruby silver ore, light-red silver ore, Ag_3AsS_2 (Min.) = Proustit *m*, lichtes Rotgültigerz *n*

provincial planning, see: state ~

~ road = Provinzstraße *f*, Landstraße

proving-ground, test ground = Versuchsgelände *n*, Versuchsfeld *n*, Prüfgelände, Prüffeld

~ test, see: trial-test investigation

provisional sum = Betrag *m* im Angebot *n* für Unvorhergesehenes *n*

provision of road signs, signposting, signing = Beschilderung *f*, Straßensignalisierung *f*

pruning shear = Baumschere *f*

Prussian Blue = Preußisch Blau *n*

prussiate of potash, see: protoxide of potassium

psilomelane, black iron ore (Min.) = schwarzer Glaskopf *m*, Psilomelan *m*

pteropod, sea butterfly = Pteropode *f*, Flügelschnecke *f*

~ ooze = Pteropodenschlamm *m*, Flügelfüßlerschlamm

public bonding requirements = Garantieleistungen *fpl* bei Ausschreibungen *fpl* der öffentlichen Hand *f*

~ forces, see: state ~

~ health = öffentliches Gesundheitswesen *n*

~ highway, (rural) ~, (~) road = Landstraße *f*

~ lighting, illumination of roads and streets = Straßenbeleuchtung *f*

~ parking place = öffentlicher Parkplatz *m*

~ service vehicle = öffentliches Verkehrsfahrzeug *n*

~ ~ vehicles traffic, ~ transport, mass transportation, mass transit = öffentlicher (Massen)Verkehr *m*

~ utility (undertaking) = öffentlicher Versorgungsbetrieb *m*, Versorgungsanlage *f*

(~ works) contractor, construction contractor = Bauunternehmer *m*

*public works equipment, see: construction machinery (or equipment)

~ ~ project = Bauvorhaben *n* der öffentlichen Hand *f*

puck rot, see: red ~
pudding stone = Puddingstein *m*
puddle-clay = Lehmschlag *m*
puddled concrete, see: rodded ~
~ iron = Puddeleisen *n*
puddled loam core = Lehmvorlage *f* [*Talsperre f*]
puddling (US) = Sprengen *n* mit Wasser *n* und unmittelbares Abwalzen *n* einer Chaussierung *f*
~, rodding = Stochern *n* [*Betonverdichtung f*]
~ cinder, tap ~ = Schweißofenschlacke *f*
~ furnace = Eisenfrischflammofen *m*
~ (process) = Puddelverfahren *n*
puff blowing = Staubausblasung *f* [*Bohrloch n*]
~ ~ = Luftspülung *f* [*Bohrhammer m*]
~ ~ device = Luftspülvorrichtung *f*, Blasevorrichtung [*Bohrhammer m*]
~ ~ piston = Luftspülkolben *m* [*Bohrhammer m*]
~ ~ ~ rock drill = Luftspül(bohr)hammer *m*
pugging = Tonschneider-Aufbereitung *f* [*deckt sich mit dem Begriff „mit Wasser mischen"*]
pug mill, clay ~ = Tonschneider *m* [*Ziegelherstellung f*]
~ ~ knife = Tonschneidemesser *n*
pugmill-mixed = zwangsgemischt
pug(-)mill mixer = Knetmischer *m*, Kneter *m*, Zwangsmischer *m* mit vertikalem Rührwerk *n*
pug(-)mill paddle (or blade) = Zwangsmischerscherpaddel *f*
pug(-)mill water = Tonschneider-Anmach(e)wasser *n*
pull = Zugkraft *f*
to pull down, to demolish, to take down = abbrechen [*Gebäude n*]
puller, see: jack
~, pulling tool = Ziehgerät *n*
~ (crawler) tractor, towing caterpillar tractor = Zugraupe *f*
pulley = Riemenscheibe *f*
~ = Rolle *f* [*Seilzug m*]
~ = Trommel *f*, Endtrommel, Bandtrommel, (Band)Umlenkrolle *f*
~ block, see: (block and) tackle

pull grader, see: towed-type grader
pulling down, see: wrecking
pull-off strip, parking ~, hard shoulder = Standspur *f*, Parkstreifen *m*
pull-rope winch = Zugseilwinde *f*
pull scraper, see: four-wheel(ed) ~
pullshovel (US); see: backacter (Brit.)
pull stroke trenching machine (US); see: backacter (Brit.)
~ tow = Schleppkahn *m*
pull-type bituminous concrete and aggregate spreader, see: towed paver-type aggregate spreader
~ scraper, see: four-wheel(ed) ~
~ turf shovel = Zugrasenschaufel *f*
~ winch = Zugwinde *f*
pull wedge, see: push ~
(pulp) wood grapple (or grab) = (Rund-)Holzgreifkorb *m*
pulsating electro-magnet = elektromagnetischer Vibrator *m*, ~ Schwingungsrüttler *m*, ~ Schwingungserzeuger *m*
~ load = stoßweise Last *f*, ~ Belastung *f*
pulse of air = Luftdruckimpuls *m*
~ technique = Impulsverfahren *n*
~-velocity technique, (longitudinal) wave-velocity method (or measurement) = Geschwindigkeitsmessung *f* [*zerstörungsfreie Prüfung f von Beton m*]
pulsometer (pump,) steam ~ (~), aquometer = Dampfdruckpumpe, Pulsometerpumpe
PULVATEX [*Trademark*] = Kautschukpulver *n* mit einem Kautschukgehalt *m* von 60% und 40% Infusorienerde *f*
pulverator, impactor, (swing-hammer) pulverizer = Prall(mahl)mühle
pulverized lime = Staub(brannt)kalk *m*
~ limestone = Pulverkalkstein *m*
pulverizing, pulverization = Zerkleinerung *f* [*Bodenverfestigung f*]
~, pulverization = Pulverisation *f*, Pulverisieren *n*
~, pulverization = Feinstmahlung *f*
~ mixer, see: mix-in-place machine
pulverulent material = staubförmiges Schüttgut *n*
pumice = Bims *m*
~ concrete = Bimsbeton *m*
~ gravel = Bimskies *m*

pumice stone = Bimsstein m
***pump** = Pumpe f
pumpability [*concrete*] = Pumpfähigkeit f
pump barge, nontrailing suction dredge(r) = Liegesauger m
pumpcrete, see: pumping concrete
~ machine, see: concrete pump
pump dredge(r), see: hydraulic (suction) ~
pump driven by power = Transmissionspumpe f
pumped concrete, see: pumping ~
~ storage = Pumpspeicherung f
~ ~ hydropower plant = Pumpspeicher(kraft)werk n
pumping, pavement (slab) ~, slab-~, mud-~, subgrade erosion [*forceful ejection of water-suspended subgrade soil from underneath concrete pavements during the passage of heavy axle loads*] = Plattenpumpen n
~ concrete, pumped concrete, pumpcrete = Pump(kret)beton m
~ gear = Pumpengetriebe n
~ installation = Pump(en)anlage f
~ lift = Pumpensaughöhe f
~ jack = Pumpenbock m
~ only until overflow begins = Pumpen n nur bis zum Einsetzen des Überlaufs [*Hoppersauger m*]
~ piston = Pumpenkolben m
pump(ing) set = Pumpensatz m
pump irrigation, power ~ = Pumpenbewässerung f
(~) sump (pit), pump well, sump hole; sump well [*deprecated*] = Pumpensumpf m
~ with helicoidal piston = Schraubenkolbenpumpe f
punch(ed) card = Lochkarte f
~ drain pipe bend = geschlagener Wechsel m [*Dränrohr n*]
~ hole = gestanztes Loch n
punching shear stability test = Eindruck-Scherfestigkeits-Prüfung f
punner (Brit.), see: hand rammer
punning, see: ramming
purchaser, see: promoter
purchasing authority = Bauherrschaft f, Bauherr m [*in diesem Falle eine Behörde f*]

~ clerk = Baukaufmann m
~ department = Einkaufsabteilung f
pure lime, see: fat ~
~ shear, simple ~ = reine (Ab)Scherung f
purlin = Pfette f
purple wood, see: amaranth ~
purpose-made brick, see: profilated ~
push-button, press-button = Bedienungsknopf m, Druckknopf
~ bulk flow, press-button ~ ~ = druckknopfgesteuerter Materialfluß m
~ control, press-button ~ = Druckknopfsteuerung f, Fingerdrucksteuerung
~ switch, press-button ~ = Bedienungsknopfschalter m, Fingerdruckschalter, Druckknopfschalter
pusher, pushloader = Schubhilfegerät n
~ bar [*tree-dozer*] = Schubstange f; Stoßbarren m [*in Österreich*]
~-blade (Brit.); see: dozer blade
pusher tractor, crawler push cat(erpillar) = Schubraupentraktor m, Stoßraupe f, Schubgleiskettenschlepper m, Stoßgleiskettenschlepper m
pusher-type kiln = Kleintunnelofen m, Platten-Tunnelofen
pushloader, see: pusher
push-loading = Schieben n [*Radschrapper m mit Bulldozer m*]
push-pull equipment = Klemmschieber m [*Anbaugerät n für palettenlosen Transport m*]
~ ventilation, see: plenum method of ventilation
push type keyway broaching machine, keyway cutter = Keilnutenstoßmaschine f
pushup = Stauchung f
push wedge, adjusting ~, pull ~ = (Nach-)Stellkeil m, verstellbarer Keil [*Backenbrecher m*]
putrescibility = Fäulnisfähigkeit f
putrid ooze, rotten slime (Geol.) = Faulschlamm m
putty = Kitt m
puttyless glazing = kittlose Verglasung f
pycnometer, density bottle, pyknometer, fruit jar pycnometer = Pyknometer n [*Meßgerät zur Ermittlung des Luftgehaltes im Beton nach dem Verdrängungsverfahren*]

pylon, tower = Pylone f
pyramidal-toothed crushing rolls = Pyramidenwalzenbrecher m
pyramid feet roller, spiked ~, taper(ed)-foot (type sheepsfoot) ~ = (Schaf-) Stockfußwalze f, Igelwalze, Stachelwalze, Walze mit konischen Stacheln mpl
pyrargyrite, see: dark-red silver ore (Min.)
pyrites (Min.), see: fool's gold
pyritic rock = Kiesstock m
pyroaurite (Min.) = Igelströmit m
pyrobitumen, asphaltic ~ = Bitumen n, größtenteils unlöslich in Schwefelkohlenstoff m und größtenteils unverseifbar
pyrobituminous shale, see: asphaltic ~ ~
pyroclastic rocks (Geol.) = pyroklastische Gesteine npl
pyrogallic acid = Pyrogallussäure f
pyroligneous acid = Holzessig m
pyrolusite (with manganite) (Min.) = Weichmanganerz n, Braunstein m
pyrolysis, see: destructive (or dry) distillation
pyromeride, nodular felsite = Knollenfelsit m
pyrometer = Pyrometer n
pyrometric cone, see: Seger ~
pyromorphite; [obsolete term: green lead ore] (Min.) = Pyromorphit m, Grünbleierz n
pyro-processing = Wärmeaufbereitung f
pyroschist, see: (asphaltic) pyrobituminous shale
pyrostibnite, kermesite (Min.) = Antimonblende f, Kermesit m
pyroxene (Min.) = Pyroxen m
pyroxenite (Geol.) = Pyroxenit m
pyrrhotine (Min.), see: magnetic pyrite(s)
pyrrhotite (Min.), see: magnetic pyrite(s)

Q

quadrant = Viertelkreis m
quake-proof, see: earthquake-resistant
quaking bog, trembling ~, quagmire = Schwingmoor n
quality control = Güteüberwachung f
quantity production = Massenherstellung f
~ surveyor, see: calculator

*****quarry,** stone ~, rock ~ = (Stein)Bruch m
~ body [a dump body with sloped sides] = Steinbruchmulde f
~ car = Muldenwagen m für Bruchbetrieb m
~ face, see: face
quarrying = Abbau m [Steinbruch m]
~ action of the waves = ausräumende Tätigkeit f der Wellen fpl
quarry rock = Bruchgestein n
~ shovel, see: rock ~
~ stone (or block) = Bruchstein m
~ tile (Brit.); floor(ing) slab = (Fuß-) Bodenplatte f
~ ~ = Pflasterplatte f
~-waste; grout (US) = Steinbruchabfall m
QUARRYCORD [Trademark] = Zündschnur f zum Knäpperschießen n [sie brennt 30 cm/sec mit äußerer Flamme]
quarter = Quartier n
~, see: shoulder (Brit.)
quartering = Vierteilung f
quartz (Min.) = Quarz m
~-diorite = Quarzdiorit m
~-dolerite = Quarzdolerit m
quartz gravel, quartzite ~ = Quarzkies m
quartzite = Quarzit m
quartzitic sandstone = Quarzitsandstein m, verkieselter Sandstein m
quartz(ose) sand, see: arenaceous ~
quartz-porphyrite = Quarzporphyrit m
quartz-porphyry = Quarzporphyr m
quartz-trachyte = Quarztrachyt m
quay accomodations, quayside appliances = Kaianlagen fpl
~ wall = Kaimauer f, Hafenmauer
queen post = Hängesäule f
~ (~) truss, ~ posts, queen-post roof = doppeltes Hängewerk n, doppelter Hängebock m
quenching = Abschrecken n, Abschreckung f
~ furnace = Abschreckofen m
quick-acting coupling = Schnellrohrkupplung f, Schnellverschluß m
quick (action) clamp = Moment(schraub)zwinge f, Schnellschraubknecht m
quick-breaking, see: rapid-setting

quick clay = Quickton *m*, Fließton [*thixotropes quicklebendiges Lockergestein n*]
quick-closing valve, see: rapid-closing ~
quicklime, lime, anhydrous lime, common lime, calcined calcium carbonate = Branntkalk *m*, gebrannter Kalk, Brennkalk
~ **manufacturing plant** = Kalkbrennerei *f*
~ **mill** = Kalkmühle *f*
quick sand, running ~ = Quicksand *m*
quicksilver, see: mercury
quiescent water = stilles Wasser *n*
quoin = Eckstein *m*
~ = Gebäu*d*evorsprung *m*
quotation = unverbindliches Preisangebot *n*

R

rabbet plane, rebate-plane = Simshobel *m* [*früher: Gesimshobel*]
~ ~, rebate-plane = Falzhobel *m*
race = Schuß(ge)rinne *f*, (*n*)
~ = Gezeitenströmung *f*
~ = Werkkanal *m*, Werkgraben *m* [*Laufkraftwerk n*]
~ = Laufbahn *f*, Laufring *m* [*Lager n*]
rack, toothed ~ = Zahnstange *f*
~ (US), see: (trash) ~
~ **-and-pinion jack** = Zahnstangenwinde *f*, Zahnstangenhebebock *m*
rack for curing concrete block, see: curing rack
racking course = Verfüllschicht *f* [*Setzpacke f*]
rack rail = Zahnschiene *f*
~ **railway** (Brit.); ~ **railroad** (US) = Zahnstangenbahn *f*
~ **rake** (US); see: screen cleaner (Brit.)
~ **tank loco(motive)** = Zahnrad-Tenderlok(omotive) *f*
radar coverage = Ortungsbereich *m* [*Funkmeßgerät n*]
~ **device** = Funkmeßgerät *n*
radial blower = Radialgebläse *n*
~ **brick** = Radialstein *m*, Radialziegel *m*
~ **cut (or conversion)** = Radialschnitt *m*, Spiegelholz *n*
~ **drill** = Radialbohrer *m*
~ **engine** = Stern-Standmotor *m*

~ **flow reaction turbine** = Überdruckturbine *f* mit Radialdampfströmung *f*
~ ~ **turbine** = Radialturbine *f*
~ **gate**, see: segment shaped sluice
~ **road**, ~ **highway** = Radialstraße *f*
~ **shear** = Radialscherung *f*
~ **(small stone) sett paving**, see: fanwise ~
~ **speed** [*road vehicle*] = Quer-Ruck *m*
~ **stacker** = radial arbeitendes Absetzband *n* [*Zuschlagstofflagerung f*]
~ **transporter** = radialverfahrbare Verladebrücke *f*
~ **travel(l)ing cableway**, tautline cableway with one stationary tower and one radially travel(l)ing tower = radial verfahrbarer Kabelkran, Schwenkkabelkran *m*, kreisfahrbarer Kabelkran mit einem ortsfesten und einem radial verfahrbarem Turm *m*
~ **type fill valve** = Rundschieber *m*
radiant heat = Strahlungswärme *f*
~ ~ **boiler** = Strahlungskessel *m*
~ **heating**, panel ~, concealed ~ = Strahlungsheizung *f*
~ **track** = Einzeltoreinfahrtgleis *n* [*Lokomotivschuppen m*]
radiating bridge = Fächerbrücke *f*
radiation detector = Strahlungsfühler *m*
radiator = Radiator *m*
~ = Kühler *m* [*Auto n*]
~ **-cooled** = radiatorgekühlt
radio-active = radioaktiv
~ **tracer** = radioaktiver Fühler *m*
~ **wastes** = Atommüll *m*
radiography = Röntgenographie *f*
radio indicator = Radio-Zeichengeber *m*
radiolaria(n) ooze = Radiolarienschlamm *m*, Rädertierchenschlamm *m*, Radiolarienschlick *m*
radio telephone traffic, ~ **telephony** = Funksprechverkehr *m*, Sprechfunk *m*
radius at bend = Krümmungshalbmesser *m*
~ **of clean-up** = Planierhalbmesser *m* [*Raupen(band)löffelbagger m*]
~ ~ **curvature** = Ausrundungshalbmesser *m*
~ ~ **gyration**, gyration radius = Trägheitshalbmesser *m*
RAF-Station (Brit.); (air-)base (US) = Fliegerhorst *m*, Militär-Flugplatz *m*

to raft = flößen
raft = Floß n
~ bridge = Floßbrücke f
rafter = Sparren m
raft foundation, mat foundation, foundation raft = großflächiges (Beton)Fundament n, Betonplattenfundament n, Fundamentplatte f
rag(ged) bolt = Steinschraube f
*****rail** = Schiene f
~-and-highway bridge = Eisenbahn- und Straßenbrücke f
rail bender; jim crow (Brit.) = Schienenbieger m
~ bending and straightening machine = Schienenbiege- und -richtmaschine f
railbus = Schienenomnibus m, Schienen-(Auto)Bus m
rail drilling machine = Schienenbohrmaschine f
~-fed = mit Gleisanschluß m versehen
rail fixing nail, see: ~ spike
~ ga(u)ge, track ~ = Spurweite f, Gleisspur f
~ grinding car = Schienenschleifwagen m
~-guard, see: check rail
rail-guided, see: rail-mounted
railhead, top flange = Schienenkopf m
rail joint = Schienenstoß m
~ ~ grinding machine = Schienenstoß-Schleifmaschine f
railles, trackless = gleislos
~ earthwork engineering, trackless ~ ~ = gleisloser Erdbau m, gleislose Erdbewegung f, gleisloser Erdtransport m
rail log, reling log = Relingslog m
rail-mounted, rail-guided = schienengebunden, gleisgebunden, schienengeführt
~ (or rail-guided) asphalt finisher (or asphalt paver, or bituminous paving machine, or bituminous spreading-and-finishing machine, or black-top spreader, or asphalt(ic) concrete paver, or bituminous road surfacing finisher, or bituminous paver-finisher, or asphalt and coated macadam finisher) = Schienen-Schwarzbelageinbaumaschine f, Schienen-Schwarz(decken)verteiler m, Schienen-Verteilerfertiger m, Schienen-Schwarzdeckenfertiger m, Schienen-Schwarzdeckeneinbaumaschine f
~ (belt) conveyor, shuttle (~) ~ = Schienen(förder)band n
~ excavator, rail-guided ~ = Schienenbagger m, Gleisbagger m
~ vehicle, rail-guided ~ = Schienenfahrzeug n, Gleisfahrzeug n
rail plane = Schienenhobel m
~ ratchet brace = Schienenbohrknarre f
railroad (US); **railway** (Brit.) = Eisenbahn f
~ ballast (US); see: railway track ballast (Brit.)
~ (boom) crane (US); see: locomotive (jib) ~ (Brit.)
~ embankment (US); see: railway ~ (Brit.)
railroading (US); **railway construction** (Brit.) = (Eisen)Bahnbau m
rail(road) track (US); see: rail(way) ~ (Brit.)
rail rope = Tragseil n [Seilschwebebahn f]
~ shipment = (Eisen)Bahnversand m
~ shunter, see: shunting loco(motive)
~ spike, rail fixing nail, dog spike, track spike = Schienennagel m
~ steel = Schienenstahl m
~ transport = Schienentransport m
railway (Brit.); **railroad** (US) = Eisenbahn f
~ ballast, see: ~ track ~
~ car hoist (Brit.); **truck ~** = Waggonhebeanlage f
~ clearance (Brit.); **railroad ~** (US) = Ladeprofil n
~ crane (Brit.), see: locomotive (jib) crane
~ embankment (Brit.); **railroad ~** (US); **~ fill** = (Eisen)Bahndamm m
~ rate (Brit.) = Eisenbahnfrachtsatz m
~ right-of-way (Brit.); **railroad ~** (US) = Bahnkörper m
rail(way) spur (Brit.); **spur track** = Anschlußgleis n, Stichgleis, Gleisanschluß m
~ track (Brit.); **rail(road) track** (US); **tracking, line of rails, two-rail surface track** = Schienenstrang m, Gleis n, Schienenweg m

railway trackage (Brit.) = Gleisanlage *f*

(~) (track) ballast (Brit.); railroad (~) (US); track ~, boxing material = Gleisschotter *m*, (Eisen)Bahnschotter

railway-track scale, track-scale = Gleiswaage *f*, Waggonwaage

railway track-work (Brit.); railroad ~ (US) = Gleisarbeiten *fpl*

~ train = Gleisbahn *f*

~ wagon (Brit.); freight car (US); goods wagon, ~ van = Waggon *m*, Güterwagen *m*

~ ~ shifter = Einrad-Wagenschieber *m*

rail-wheel = Schienenrad *n*

raincap = Regenkappe *f*, Regenhaube *f*

rain-day = Regentag *m*

rainfall coefficient, coefficient of rainfall = Niederschlagsbeiwert *m*

~ curve = Niederschlagshöhenkurve *f*

~ record = Niederschlagsstatistik *f*

rain-ga(u)ge = Niederschlagsmesser *m*

(rain) gully (Geol.) = Runse *f*, Felseinschnitt *m*

rainless region = Regenschatten *m*

rainmaking = Regenerzeugung *f*

rain rill, wet-weather ~ = Abspülungsfaden *m* (Geol.)

~ trap = Regenkappe *f*

rainwater gull(e)y, see: gull(e)y

raised approach, see: accomodation ramp

~ beach (Brit.); see: elevated shore line (US)

rake = Rechen *m*, Harke *f*

~, see: batter

~ frame type pile driving plant (or piling plant) = Schräg(gerüst)ramme *f*

raker, see: batter post

~ dolphin = Bockdalbe *m*

rake-type classifier = Rechenklassierer *m*

raking (foundation, or bearing) pile, see: batter (~, ~ ~) ~

~ prop = Schrägstempel *m*

~ shore = Schrägspreize *f*

~ shoring = Abstrebung *f*, Abstreben *n*

ram = Hydraulikzylinder *m*

to ram, to tamp, to stamp = abrammen, stampfen

rammer = (Stampf)Ramme *f*

ramming, tamping, punning, compacting [*deprecated: beating*] = Stampfen *n*, Abrammen *n*, Stoßverdichtung *f*

ramp = Rampe *f*

~ = Anrampung *f*

ramp-type parking garage = rampenförmige Abstellgarage *f*

ram pump, see: plunger ~

ramshackle, dilapidated = baufällig

random cracking = wilde Rißbildung *f*

~ material, ~ mixture = unklassifiziertes Gemisch *n* aus Boden *m* und/oder Gestein *n*

~ measurement = Stichtagsmessung *f*

~ rubble masonry = Polygonmauerwerk *n*, Vieleckmauerwerk

~ ~ walling, uncoursed ~ ~, cyclopic ~ ~ = Zyklopenmauerwerk *n*

range, reach = Aktionsradius *m*, Reichweite *f*, Bereich *m*

~ light = Verdichtungsfeuer *n* [*Flugplatz m*]

~ of a tide = Gezeitenhub *m*, Tidehub *m*

to range out, to range into line = abfluchten, ausfluchten, einfluchten

ranging pole, ~ rod = Fluchtstange *f*, Fluchtstab *m*

rapid = Stromschnelle *f*

~ action jaw crusher with inclined crushing chamber = Schnellschlagbrecher *m*

rapid-closing valve, quick-closing ~, quick-close ~ = Schnellschlußventil *n*

rapid control test = Schnellprüfverfahren *n*

rapid-curing = schnellabbindend [*Verschnittbitumen n*]

rapid design method = Schnellbemessung *f*

~ erection crane = Schnellmontagekran *m*

~ (hand) hammer (rock) drill, rapid (rock) drill hammer, rapid rock drill = Schnellbohrhammer *m*, Schnell-Felsbohrer *m*, Schnell-Gesteinsbohrer

~ hardening Portland cement, see: high early (or initial) strength Portland cement

~ sand filter = Schnell(sand)filter *m, n*

~-setting, labile, quick-breaking = schnellbrechend, unstabil, labil [*Bitumenemulsion f*]

rapid shifting drag scraper machine, rapid shifter = Schleppschrapperanlage *f* mit 3-Seilanordnung *f*
~-stroke hammer = (Schnellschlag-)Rammhammer *m*, Schnellschlagbär *m*, Schnellschlaghammer
rapid transit = Schnellverkehr *m* [*öffentlicher (Massen)Verkehr m*]
~ ~ self-propel(l)ed railcar = Schnell-Triebwagen *m*
~ ~ subway = Schnellverkehrsuntergrundbahn *f*
~ ~ system = Schnellbahnsystem *n*
~ vibratory motion screen = Schnellsieb *n*
ratchet, ~ wheel = Sperrad *n*
~ = Ratsche *f*, Knarre *f*
~ brace, ~ drill = Bohrknarre *f*, Bohrratsche *f*
~ ~ bit = Bohrknarrenbohrer *m*
~ drill = Knarrenbohrer *m*
~ gearing = Sperrgetriebe *n*
~ lever = Knarrenhebel *m*
~ ~ jack = Schrauben(hebe)bock *m* mit Knarrenhebel *m*
~ lock = Sperrblockierung *f*
~ mechanism = Gesperre *n*
~ pipe stock = Knarrenkluppe *f*
~ to eliminate "running back" = Rücklaufsperre *f*
~ (wheel) = Sperrad *n*
rate = Zustandsänderung *f* nach Zeit *f* [*z. B. Geschwindigkeit f, Druck m, Temperatur f*]
~, unit price = Einheitspreis *m*
~ = Anteil *m*
rated capacity = Nennleistung *f*
~ ~ = Nennfassungsvermögen *n*
~ horsepower = Nenn-PS *f*
~ speed, rated RPM = Nenndrehzahl *f*, Solldrehzahl
rate of cure = Abbindegeschwindigkeit *f* [*Verschnittbitumen n*]
(~ ~) drilling progress, drilling rate = Bohrfortschritt *m*
~ ~ (ground) settlement = Senkungsbetrag *m*, Setzungsbetrag
~ ~ hardening = Erhärtungsgeschwindigkeit *f* [*Beton m*]
~ ~ setting (Brit.); **~ ~ set** = Abbindegeschwindigkeit *f*, Hydra(ta)tionsgeschwindigkeit, Erstarrungsgeschwindigkeit
~ ~ spread, ~ ~ application = Aufbringungsrate *f* [*Straßen-Oberflächenbehandlung f*]
~ per working hour, see: hourly wage rate
rating = Bemessung *f* [*von Maschinenleistungen fpl*]
~ curve of flow, see: graph of flow
~ test = Nennversuch *m*
ratio, proportion(ality) factor = Verhältniszahl *f*
ratiometer, concrete mix electric testing apparatus = Gerät *n* zur Bestimmung des W/Z-Faktors *m*
rational design = rechnerischer Entwurf *m*
rationalization = Rationalisierung *f*
rationing = Bewirtschaftung *f*, Zwangs~
rattler test, Los Angeles **~** = Abnützungsversuch *m* (oder Abnützungsprobe *f*) im Trommelverfahren *n* durch Stahlkugeln *fpl*
raveled edge (US) [*road*] = abgebröckelte Kante *f* [*Straße f*]
ravel(l)ing [*deprecated*]; see: fretting
raw clay = Rohton *m*
~ grinding = Vormahlen *n*, Vormahlung *f*
~ gypsum, dihydrate, natural gypsum = Rohgips *m*, Dihydrat *n*, Doppelhydrat, $CaSO_4 \cdot 2H_2O$ [*Ausgangsmaterial für gebrannten Gips*]
~ ~ dust = Gipsstaub *m*
~ humus = Rohhumus *m*
~ mix which has undergone previous decarbonation = vorentsäuertes Rohmehl *n* [*Zementherstellung f*]
~ slag = Rohschlacke *f*
~ soil = Rohboden *m*
~ water = Rohwasser *n*
RAYMOND roller (grinding) mill = RAYMOND-Pendel(mahl)mühle *f*
~ step taper concrete pile, see: step-tapered RAYMOND pile
rayon cord (or fabric) belt(ing) = Cordband *n*
reach, range = Reichweite *f*, Bereich *m*, Aktionsradius *m*
reacted plaster, see: lime-gypsum ~
reaction = Reaktion *f*
~ at support, see: bearing pressure

reaction equilibrium = Reaktionsgleichgewicht *n*

~ **(-type) turbine** = Überdruckturbine *f*, Rückdruckturbine, Reaktionsturbine

reactive materials in concrete, ~ **aggregates** = alkaliempfindliche Betonzuschlagstoffe *mpl*

~ **primer** = reaktives Grundiermittel *n*

reactor shielding, nuclear ~ = Reaktor-Strahlungsschutz *m*

readiness area, see: alert platform

~ **to break, lability** = Labilität *f*

readiness-to-break test = Lability-Test *m*

reading = Ablesen *n*, Ablesung *f*

to read off, to take readings = ablesen

ready-mix (cement) truck (US); see: lorry-mounted mixer (Brit.)

ready-mixed concrete = Transportbeton, Fertigbeton *m*, Lieferbeton

~ ~ **plant, ready-mix** ~ = Transportbetonaufbereitungsanlage *f*

~ ~ ~ **of the central mix type** = Transportbetonaufbereitungsanlage *f* zur Herstellung *f* von Beton zum Verfahren *n* durch Nachmischer *mpl*

~ ~ ~ ~ **transit-mix type**; transit-mix(ing concrete) plant, truck mixer plant (US) = Transportbetonaufbereitungsanlage *f* zur Herstellung *f* von Trockenbeton *m*

~ **pour** = Einbau *m* von Transportbeton *m*

ready roofing = fertige Bitumendachpappe *f*

reagent = Reagenzmittel *n*

real clay tile = echte Tonfliese *f*, ~ keramische Fliese

~ **measure, nominal size** = Sollmaß *n*, Nennmaß

realgar (Min.) = Realgar *m*, Rotrauschgelb *n*

to re-align = neu ausfluchten

reamer, rimer = Reibahle *f*

~, **reaming bit** = Nachnehmer *m*, Nachnehmebohrmeißel *m*, (Auf)Räumer *m*

reaming = (Auf)Reiben *n*, Ausreibarbeit *f* [*Nietloch n*]

rear = Heck *n* [*Baumaschine f*]

~ **axle** = Hinterachse *f*

~ ~ **drive** = Hinterachsantrieb *m*

~ **blade** = Heckschild *n*

~ **(cable, or rope) winch** = (Trommel-)Seilwinde *f* hinten am Fahrzeug *n* angebracht

~ **dump body** = Hinterkipp-Wanne *f* [*LKW m*]

~ ~ **discharge** = Rückwärtsentladung *f*

~ ~ **trailer** = Rückwärtsentladungsanhänger *m*

~-~ **truck** (US); see: end-tip(ping) (motor) lorry (Brit.)

rear dumping, end-dumping = Hinterkippung *f*, Hinterkippentleerung

~ **engine** = Heckmotor *m*

~ **light**, see: tail ~

~-**mounted gritter**, mechanical gritting attachment, attachment (type) gritter; tailgate (vane) type chip spreader, vane type chip spreader; lorry tailboard temporary gritting attachment (Brit.) = Anbaustreuer *m*

rear platform = Laufsteg *m* [*Schwarzbelageinbaumaschine f*]

~ **roll(er)**, ~ roller wheel = Hinterwalze *f*, Heckwalze, Hinterwalzrad *n*

rear-wheel drive = Heckräder-Antrieb *m*, Hinterradantrieb

~ ~ **differential axle** = Hinterradantrieb *m* durch Differential *n*

~ **steer(ing)** = Hinterradlenkung *f*, Heckräder-Lenkung

re-bar, see: reinforcing bar

rebate-plane, see: rabbet plane

reborn city = wiederaufgebaute Stadt *f*

rebuilt = generalüberholt

recalculation = Nachrechnung *f*

recarburizing = Rückkohlung *f* [*Stahl m*]

receiving bin, overhead hopper, (storage) bin = (Sorten)Zwischen(lade)bunker *m*, Aufnahmebunker, Baustellensilo *m*

~ **conveyor (belt)** = Aufnahmeband *n*

(~) **hopper**, see: feed ~

~ ~ = Einfülltrichter *m*

~ **point** = Empfangsort *m*

~ **track** = Einfahrgleis *n*

recent snow = Neuschnee *m*

reception building = Empfangsgebäude *n*

recess, blockout, embrasure = Aussparung *f*

recharge = Wiederbelastung *f*, Wiederbelasten *n*

reciprocal value, see: reversed ~
reciprocating blade spreading machine, see: blade spreader
~ compressor, see: (piston) ring ~
~ motion = hin- und hergehende Bewegung *f*, Rüttelbewegung *f*
~ piston pump = Pumpe *f* mit geradlinig hin- und hergehendem Kolben *m*
~ pump, see: combined suction and force ~
~ screed = Pendelglätter *m*
~ trough conveyor = Wurfförderrinne *f*
reclaimed rubber = regenerierter Gummi *m*
reclaiming conveyor = Haldenabzugsband *n*
~ plant (or installation, or facility) = Rückgewinnungsanlage *f*
~ tunnel, stock ~, stockpile ~, conveyor ~, recovery ~ = Haldentunnel *m*, Entnahmetunnel, Vorratstunnel, Bandkanal *m*
reclamation of land, see: land reclamation
recoil = Rückschlag *m*, Rückstoß *m*
recombined aggregate, see: (dry-)batched ~
to recompact = nachverdichten
reconditioned = wieder instandgesetzt
reconditioning, see: remedial work(s)
reconnaissance = Erkundung *f*
reconstructed mica, micanite = Mikanit *n*
reconstruction = Wiederaufbau *m*
~ (works), see: remedial
re-cooling, cooling back = Rückkühlung *f*
recorder, recording apparatus (or meter) = Registriergerät *n*, Registrierapparat *m*
~, recording ga(u)ge, recording measuring weir = selbstregistrierendes Meßwehr *n*
recording thermal-expansion apparatus = Wärmeausdehnungsschreiber *m*
~ weighing machine, ~ scale = Registrierwaage *f*
records of actual floods = Hochwasserstatistik *f*
recovered acid = Schwefelsäure *f* zurückgewonnen aus Raffinationsabfallsäure *f*
recovery, reclamation = Rückgewinnung *f*, Wiedergewinnung *f*

~ efficiency = Leistung *f* [*Staubsammler m*]
~ tunnel, see: reclaiming ~
~ vehicle, see: breakdown van
~ well = Gewinnungsbohrung *f*
recruitment of labo(u)r = Gestellung *f* von Arbeitskräften *fpl*
recrystallized limestone, see: true marble
rectangular channel = Rechteckgerinne *n*
~ mesh = Langmasche *f* [*Sieb n*]
~ multiple-compartment bin = Reihensilo *m*
~ section = rechtwink(e)liger Querschnitt *m*, rechteckiges Profil *n*
~ timber, squared ~ = Kantholz *n*
rectification of river = Flußbegradigung *f*
recurrence horizon = Grenze *f*
recurrent cold snap = Kälterückfall *m*
red antimony ore (Min.) = prismatische Nadelblende *f*
~ cement mortar [*cement mortar to which a predetermined percentage of surk(h)i is added*] = Zementmörtel *m* mit Zusatz an gebranntem Ton *m*
red clay (Geol.) = (roter) Tiefseeton *m*
~ clover = Rotklee *m*, Kopfklee
~ fescue = Rotschwingel *m*
~ lead = Bleimennige *f* [*Chemie f*]
redevelopment = Neuordnung *f*
REDLER conveyor = Trogkettenförderer *m*, Fabrikat REDLER CONVEYORS LIMITED, DUBRIDGE WORKS, STROUD, GLOS., ENGLAND
red oxide of zinc (Min.), see: zincite
~ rot, puck rot = Rotfäule *f*
redriving = Nachrammen *f*
redruthite (Min.), see: chalcocite
redtop grass, see: bent ~
reduced oil = abgetopptes Öl *n*
to reduce to scrap = verschrotten
reduction, see: fine crushing
~ coefficient, ~ factor = Herabsetzungsbeiwert *m*, Abminderungsbeiwert *m*
~ crusher, secondary ~, fine ~ = Fein(stein)brecher *m*, Nachbrecher
~ gear = Untersetzungsgetriebe *n*
~ in quality = Qualitätsminderung *f*
reductionizer, see: jet pulverizer
Redwood visco(si)meter = Redwood-Viskosimeter I *n*

reed-reinforced plaster (or gypsum) board = Gipsdiele *f*
Reed roller bit = Zylinderrollenmeißel *m*
reed swamp = Rohrsumpf *m*
reeds, rushes = Schilf *n*
reef = Riff *n*
~ = Erzschicht *f* [*Erzgrube f*]
reef-building coral = riffbildende Koralle *f*
reef knof = Kreuzknoten *m*, Schifferknoten
reeling capacity = Seilaufnahmefähigkeit *f*
re-entering angle = einspringender Winkel *m*
reeving = Einscheren *n* der Seile *npl*
to reface = nachschleifen
reference drawing = Bezugszeichnung *f*
~ fuel = Bezugskraftstoff *m*
~ ~ = Substandard-Kraftstoff *m*
referring object, reference mark, reference point = Bezugspunkt *m*
to re-fill, to backfill, to fill in = verfüllen, einfüllen [*Graben m*]
~ ~ = nachfüllen
refined natural asphalt, épuré, refined lake asphalt = gereinigter Asphalt *m*
refiner = Schmelzkessel *m* [*Aufbereitung von gereinigtem Trinidad-Asphalt*]
refinery = Raffinerie *f*
~ gases = Kohlenwasserstoffgase *npl* die bei der Erdölverarbeitung *f* entstehen
refining furnace = Weißofen *m*
~ (process) = Raffination *f*
reflecting horizon = Reflexionshorizont *m*
~ microscope = Auflichtmikroskop *n*
reflective radiant conditioning = Reflexions-Strahlungsheizung *f*
reflectorizing material = Reflexstoff *m*
reflectorizing, reflecting = reflektierend
reformed-gas tar, see: oil-water-gas ~
reforming = Reformieren *n* [*Steigerung der Klopffestigkeit f von Benzin n*]
refraction survey, see: seismic refraction procedure
refractive index = Brechungsindex *m*, Brechungsexponent *m*
refractivity intercept = Refraktions-Intercept *m*
*****refractory** = feuerfest [*in bezug auf Festgesteine und Tone zur Herstellung feuerfester Produkte, Schmelztemperatur oberhalb 1 600 Grad Celsius*]

~ = feuerfestes Erzeugnis *n*
~ clay, fireclay, structural clay = feuerfester Ton *m*, Schamotte(ton) *f*, (*m*)
~ ~ brick, see: fireclay
~ concrete = feuerfester Beton *m*
~ fiber (US); ~ fibre (Brit.) = feuerfeste Faser *f*
~ lining = Schamotteausmauerung *f*
~ oxide = feuerfestes Oxyd *n*
refrigerant, see: coolant
refuel(l)er = Tankwart *m*
(re-)fuel(l)ing = Betanken *n*
~ hydrant, see: dispense point
refuge (Brit.); **~ island**, pedestrian **~** (US); [*deprecated: island*] = Fußgänger-Schutzinsel *f*, Stützinsel *f* für Fußgängerüberweg *m*
refuse = Müll *m*
~, waste = Abfall(stoff) *m*
~ collection = Müllabfuhr *f*
~ incinerator, garbage disposal plant, refuse destructor = Müllverbrennungsanlage *f*
~ tip = Müllabladeplatz *m*
~ wagon (Brit.); see: garbage truck (US)
regenerative furnace = Regenerativofen *m*
regional metamorphism = Regionalmetamorphose *f*, Regionalumprägung *f*, Versenkungsumprägung *f*
region of calm, calm belt = Kalmengürtel *m*
~ where an avalanche starts = Anbruchsgebiet *n*
regularity of features = Gesetzmäßigkeit *f*
regular lay, standard ~, right ~, cross ~ = Kreuzschlag *m* [*Drahtseil n*]
~ system, cubic ~ = reguläres System *n* [*Kristall n*]
regulating control = Regulierorgan *n*
~ course, ~ underlay, level(l)ing ~ = Ausgleichschicht *f*, Ausgleichlage *f*
~ (or control) gate = Regulierverschluß *m*
~ siphon = Ablaßdüker *m*
~ transformer, series ~, variable ~ = Regeltransformator *m*
~ valve, see: control ~
regulation = Durchführungsverordnung *f*
~ of a river for high discharge capacity = einen Fluß *m* für die Ableitung großer Wassermengen umbauen

regulation of low water flows, low tide regulation = Niedrigwasserverbesserung *f*, Niedrigwasserreg(e)lung *f*
~ **of traffic,** see: traffic control
regulatory sign, see: mandatory ~
rehabilitation, repair (work) = Reparatur *f*, Instandsetzung *f*, Ausbesserung *f*
~, **clearance** = Sanierung *f* [*Stadt f*]
rehandling = Rückverladung *f*
re-handling bucket = Rückverladegreifkorb *m*
~ **grab(bing crane),** ~ (grab) bucket crane = Rückverladegreifer *m*
~ **point** = Umschlagplatz *m*
Rehbock dentated sill = Rehbock'sche Zahnschwelle *f*
reheat test [*fire-brick*] = Prüfung *f* des Nachschwindens *n* [*feuerfester Stein m*]
reimulsified, to become ~ = reemulgieren
rein, see: impost
reinforced back strap shovel = Schaufel *f* mit Düllenverstärkung *f*
~ **brick masonry** = bewehrtes (oder armiertes) Ziegelmauerwerk *n*
~ **concrete,** steel ~ ~; ferro-concrete [*deprecated*] = Stahlbeton *m* [*früher: Eisenbeton m*]
~ ~ **arch bridge** = Stahlbetonbogenbrücke *f*
~ ~ **beam** = Stahlbetonbalken *m*
~ ~ ~ **and slab** = Stahlbeton-Plattenbalken *m*
~ ~ **core (wall)** = Stahlbeton-Kernmauer *f*
~ ~ **decking** = Stahlbeton-Brückentafel *f*
~ ~ **design** = Stahlbeton-Bemessung *f*
~ ~ **dome** = Stahlbetonkuppel *f*
~ ~ **engineering** = Stahlbetonbau *m*
~ ~ **floor** = Stahlbetondecke *f*
~ ~ **foundation-ring** = Stahlbetonring-Unterlage *f*
~ ~ **frame(d structure),** ~ ~ framing = Stahlbeton-Stabwerk *n*, Stahlbeton-Rahmenkonstruktion *f*, Stahlbetonskelett *n*
~ ~ **log** = Stahlbetondammbalken *m*
~ ~ **pipe for pressure lines** = Stahlbetonrohr *n* für Druckleitungen *fpl*, Stahlbeton-Druckrohr

~ ~ **reclaiming tunnel** = Haldentunnel *m* aus Stahlbeton *m*
~ ~ **ribbed floor** = Stahlbetonrippendecke *f*
~ ~ **runway** = Stahlbetonstartbahn *f*
~ ~ **shell** = Stahlbetonschale *f*
~ ~ ~ **unit** = Stahlbeton-Schalenbauteil *m*
~ ~ **skewed rigid-frame bridge** = schräge Stahlbeton-Rahmenbrücke *f*
~ ~ **stair** = Stahlbetontreppe *f*
~ ~ **trussed girder** = Stahlbetonfachwerk *n*
~ ~ **wall** = Stahlbetonmauer *f*
~ **seam** = Wulstnaht *f*
reinforcement, concrete ~ = Armierung *f*, Bewehrung *f*, Beton~
~ **bar bender,** rod bender = Betoneisenbieger *m*
~ (~-)**bending machine,** see: powered (rod) bender
~ **bar shear cutter,** hand-operated bar cutter, bar cutter, bar cutting shears = Betoneisen(hand)schneider *m*
~ **for stresses in erection** = Montagebewehrung *f*, Montagearmierung
~ **mat** = Bewehrungsmatte *f*, Armierungsmatte
reinforcing bar, steel ~ ~, re-bar, reinforcing rod, concrete ~ ~ = Bewehrungsstab *m*
~ **cage** = Bewehrungskäfig *m*, Armierungskäfig
~ **(road) mesh,** mesh reinforcement, fabric reinforcement, reinforcing screen = Netzarmierung *f*, Netzbewehrung *f*, Bewehrungsnetz *n*, Armierungsnetz, Stahlgewebeeinlage *f*, Netzgewebeeinlage
~ **rod,** see: ~ bar
~ **screen,** see: ~ (road) mesh
~ **steel** = Betonstahl *m*
rejection = Abnahmeverweigerung *f*
rejects, see: (crusher) waste
relative humidity = relative Luftfeuchtigkeit *f*
relaxation = Entspannung *f* [*auch bei dielektrischer Verschiebung f*]
to release, to disengage = ausklinken
released = gelüftet [*Bremse f*]

released mineral = Einschaltmineral n
release of heat = Wärmeabgabe f
relic mineral = Reliktmineral n
relief channel = Entlastungs(ge)rinne f, (n)
~ **method,** ~ **blasting** = Entlastungsmethode f [*Sprengen n weicher Baugrundmassen fpl*]
~ **model** = Reliefmodell n
~ **outlet** = Entlastungsablaß m
~ **patterned sheet** = Warzenblech n
~ **pump** = Entlastungpumpe f
~ **tunnel** = Entlastungsstollen m
~ **valve** = Ausgleichventil n
to relieve the dark appearance = aufhellen
relieving arch = Entlastungsbogen m
~ **platform** = Entlastungsplatte f
reling log, see: rail ~
relocation, diversion = Umlegung f [*z. B. Straße f*]
~ **of (line of) route** = Trassenverbesserung f
remedial measure, cure = Abhilfe(maßnahme) f, Behebung f
~ **work(s), reconstruction (~), reconditioning** = Wiederherstellung(sarbeiten) f
remixer, agitator = Nachmischer m [*ohne Fahrzeug n*]
remote control = Fernsteuerung f, Fernbedienung f
~ **indication** = Fernanzeige f
remotely controlled = ferngesteuert
~ ~ **float** = Fernschwimmer m
remote-reading thermometer = Fernthermometer n
remote recorder = Fernregistriergerät n
remo(u)lding, rebuilding = Runderneuerung f von Wulst f zu Wulst
~ **gain** = Störungsgewinn m
~ **loss** = Störungsverlust m
removable sluice pillar = Losständer m, Losdrempel m, Setzpfosten m
removal = Beseitigen n, Beseitigung f
remover = Räumer m, Räumgerät n
rendering, external ~ = Außenputz m
~ ~ = (Ver)Putzen n
~ **and plastering on metallic lathing with plaster of Paris** = Putz- und Rabitzarbeiten fpl mit Stuckgips m
renewal = Erneuerung f

reniform slate = Schieferniere f
to rent with purchase option = mit Kaufrecht n mieten
rentability = Rentabilität f
rental contract = Mietvertrag m
~ ~ **with purchase option** = Kauf-Mietvertrag m
~ **period** = Mietzeit f
~ **rate** = Mietsatz m
repair concrete = Flickbeton m
~ **depot** = Reparaturpark m
repairing slipway, see: slipway
repair mortar, patching ~ = Flickmörtel m
~ **pit,** see: inspection pit
~ **service** = Reparaturdienst m
~ **(work),** see: rehabilitation
repeated impact bending test = Dauerschlagbiegeversuch m
~ **tensile test** = Dauerzugversuch m
repeat order = Nachbestellung f
repellent = Abweismittel n
repetitions, see: number of load cycles
replacement part, spare (~) = Ersatzteil m
report = Gutachten n
reporting biotic data = Darstellung f der biologischen Wasserbeschaffenheit f
repose soil = ruhender Boden m
reproducibility = Reproduzierbarkeit f
repulsion motor with damper winding = Repulsionsmotor m mit Dämpferwicklung f
request stop = Bedarfshaltestelle f
rerailing = Aufgleisen n
re-run = Redestillat n
rescission of bid (US); ~ ~ **tender (Brit.)** = Angebotzurücknahme f
rescue squad = Rettungsmannschaft f
~ **work** = Rettungsarbeiten fpl
*****research** = Forschung f
~ **contract** = Forschungsauftrag m
~ **establishment** = Versuchsanstalt f
~ **grant** = Forschungsbeihilfe f
~ **lab(oratory)** = Forschungslabor(atorium) n
~ **society (or association)** = Forschungsgesellschaft f
re-sealing of joints = Nachvergießen n der Fugen fpl

resequent river = Einkehrfluß m
reserve buoyancy = Hilfschwimmkraft f
~ power, undeveloped potential of production power = Leistungsreserve f
~ stockpile = Reservehalde f
reservoir, see: artificial lake
~ lining = Beckenauskleidung f
~ outflow = Speicherablaß m
~ outlet (works), see: river outlet
~ rock, see: container ~
reshaping = Neuprofilieren n
resident = Anlieger m
residential area = Wohngebiet n
~ construction, home building, residential housing = Wohnungsbau m
residual asphalt (US); ~ asphaltic bitumen (Brit.) = unbehandeltes Bitumen n aus der Destillation f von asphaltbasischem Rohöl n, Destillationsbitumen n
~ clay = Verwitterungston m
~ deposits (Geol.) = Abwitterungsprodukte npl, Verwitterungskruste f
~ oil = ölreicher Destillationsrückstand m, das bei der Verarbeitung von Rohöl anfallende mineralische Heizöl¹
~ soil (or earth) = Eluvialboden m, Verwitterungsboden, Verwitterungslockergestein n, Auswaschungsboden
~ stress = Restspannung f
residue by weight = Gewichtsrückstand m
~ gas, stripped ~ = Armgas n [von Gasolin n befreites Erdgas]
residuum = Destillationsrückstand m
resin = Harz n
~ glu(e)ing compound = Harzklebemasse f, Harzaufstrichmasse
resinification = Verharzung f
to resinify = verharzen
resin oil = Harzöl n, Harznaphtha n
resinous = harzig
~ bitumen (Brit.); ~ asphalt (US) = Harzbitumen n
~ wood, see: coniferous ~
resin pitch = Harzpech n
~ spirit = Harzspiritus m
(resistance) strain ga(u)ge SR-4, see: electric SR-4 ga(u)ge
~ thermometer = Widerstandsthermometer n

~ to aggressive influence, ~ ~ disintegrating effects = Aggressivbeständigkeit f [Beton m]
~ ~ cracking, extensibility [concrete] = Rißfestigkeit f, Rissefestigkeit [Beton m]
~ ~ deformation = Verformungswiderstand m
~ ~ disintegrating effects, ~ ~ aggressive influence = Aggressivbeständigkeit f [Beton m]
~ ~ impact [roadstone] = Zähigkeit f, Schlagfestigkeit f, Stoßwiderstand m [Straßenbaugestein n]
~ ~ lateral bending, buckling resistance (or strength) = Knickfestigkeit f
~ ~ punching shear = Stempeldruckfestigkeit f [Bodenbeton m]
~ ~ skidding = Rutschfestigkeit f [Straße f]
~ ~ the action of weather, weather-resistance, weather-proofness = Wetterfestigkeit f, Witterungsbeständigkeit
~ welding = (elektrische) Widerstandsschweißung f, (elektrisches) Widerstandsschweißen n
resisting moment = Moment n der inneren Kräfte fpl
resistive circuit = Widerstandsschaltung f
resistivity exploration, ~ survey, ~ reconnaissance, ~ measurement method, electrical resistivity method (or survey) = Widerstandsmessungsverfahren n, Verfahren n mit galvanischer Elektrodenkopplung f, geoelektrisches Verfahren, elektrische Widerstandsmessung f
resistor = Widerstand m
resolution of forces = Kräftezerlegung f [Statik f]
resonance frequency = Resonanzfrequenz f
resonant-frequency technique, low-frequency vibration method = Resonanzfrequenzmessung f
respiratory device, see: breathing apparatus
response = Ansprechen n [Schaltung f]
restrained = eingespannt [z. B. Säule f]
restraint, see: fixity
~ moment, fixed-end ~ = Einspannmoment n
rest room = Aufenthaltsraum m

resultant (of all forces) = Resultierende *f*, Resultante *f*, Mittelkraft *f*, resultierende Kraft *f*, Ersatzkraft

resurfacing = Aufwalzen *n* einer neuen Decklage *f*

retail business street, shopping ~ = Ladenstraße *f*

retained stability = die Druckfestigkeit der wassergelagerten Proben *fpl* in % der Druckfestigkeit *f* der trocken geprüften Proben *fpl* [*Bitumen-Mineralgemisch n*]

retainer = Halterung *m*, Haltescheibe *f*

retaining basin = Rückhaltebecken *n*

~ screen = Rückstandssieb *n*

~. wall = Stützwand *f*, Stützmauer *f*

retarded hemihydrate gypsum(-plaster), 2 CaSO$_4$ × H$_2$O = verzögerter Halbhydratgips *m*, verzögertes Halbhydrat *n*

retarder (of set), retarding admix(ture) = Abbindeverzögerer *m*

retard ignition = Spätzündung *f*

retarding reservoir (or basin), floodwater ~ (~ ~), flood detention ~ (~ ~), flood-prevention ~ (~ ~) = Verzögerungsbecken *n*

re-tarring = Nachteerung *f*

reticulated vaulting = Rautengewölbe *n*, Netzgewölbe *n*

retort = Schwelretorte *f*

~ brown coal [*incorrectly termed "bituminous brown coal"*] = Schwelbraunkohle *f*

~ ~ ~ tar = Braunkohlenschwelteer *m*

~ coking = Retortenverkokung *f*

~ peat tar = Torf-Retortenschwelteer *m*

retract = Rückziehvorrichtung *f* [*Löffelbagger n*]

retractable undercarriage = einziehbares Fahrgestell *n* [*Flugzeug n*]

retract clutch = Einziehkupplung *f*

~ line = Rückzugseil *n*

retread = Retread-Verfahren *n*, Oberflächenerneuerungsverfahren *n* [*Straße f*]

retread(ing) = Runderneuerung *f* von Schulter *f* zu Schulter *f* [*Gummireifen m*]

retread mixer = Mischer *m* für Teppichbeläge *mpl*

retroactive pay, back-pay = Nachzahlung *f*

retrogressive metamorphism (Geol.) = rückläufige Metamorphose *f*, Retrometamorphose *f*, Diaphthorese *f*

~ slide = rückwärtsschreitender Rutsch *m*

return-block, see: fall-block

return idler = unbelastete Tragrolle *f* (am unteren Strang *m*), Bandrücklaufrolle [*Förderband n*]

~ line = Rücklaufleitung *f*

~ pulley, tail ~ = Schwanztrommel *f* [*Bandförderer m*]

~ shipment = Rücklieferung *f*

~ spring = Rücknahmefeder *f*

~ strand, lower ~ = unterer Strang *m*, unbelasteter ~ [*Bandförderer m*]

~ wall, see: wing (head)wall

reusability = Wiederverwendungsmöglichkeit *f*

re-usable shuttering = Dauerschalung *f*

re-use = Wiederverwendung *f*

reverberatory furnace = Reverberierofen *m*, Flammschmelzofen *m*

reversal = Bewegungsumkehr *f*

~ of stress = Lastwechsel *m* [*Dauerversuch m*]

reverse clutch = Wendekupplung *f*

~ current lowering connection = Gegenstrom-Sonderschaltung *f*

~ curve = Gegenbogen *m*, Gegenkurve *f*, Gegenkrümmung *f*, S-Kurve

reversed direct stress = Zug-Druck-Wechselbeanspruchung *f*

~ value, reciprocal ~, inverse ~ = reziproker Wert *m*, Kehrwert

reverse gear = Rückwärtsgang *m*

~ ~, see: reversing

~ idler shaft = Rücklaufwelle *f*, Leerlaufwelle, Zwischenradwelle

~ run = Rückwärtsfahrt *f*

~ speed = Rückwärtsgeschwindigkeit *f*

reversible = umsteuerbar, umkehrbar

~ side plough (Brit.)/plow (US), see: blade-type snow plough (Brit.)/plow (US)

~ (traffic) lane = Wechsel(verkehrs)spur *f*

reversing clutch (coupling) = Wendeschaltkupplung *f*, Reversierschaltkupplung, Umkehrschaltkupplung

~ friction clutch = Umkehrreibungskupplung *f*

reversing gear, reverse ~ = Reversiergetriebe *n*, Umkehrgetriebe, Wendegetriebe
~ **turbine** = Umkehrturbine *f*, Umsteuerungsturbine, Reversierturbine
revetment = Böschungsverkleidung *f*
~ **wall** = Futtermauer *f*, Verkleidungsmauer *f*
revetting, see: bank revetting work
re-vibration = Nacheinrütteln *n*, Nachvibration *f*, Nachvibrieren *n*
revolution = Umdrehung *f*
revolutions per minute, see: speed
revolving crane, swing ~, slewing ~, revolver ~; swing-jib ~ (Brit.); swing-boom ~ (US) = (Ausleger)Drehkran *m*, Schwenkkran
~ **cylindrical scrubber,** see: scrubber
~ **(or rotary) drier (or dryer)** = Trommeltrockner *m*, Trockentrommel *f*
~ (~ ~) ~ **(for roadmaking aggregates),** bituminized aggregate drier (or dryer) = Straßenbautrockentrommel *f*, Straßenbautrommeltrockner *m*
~ **drum (type) mixer,** rotary (type) mixer, (rotary) drum mixer = Trommelmischer *m*, Freifallmischer
~ **frame** = Drehrahmen *m*
~ **furnace** = Drehofen *m*
~ **paddle finisher,** see: concrete vibrator and finisher with rotating (or rotary) grading screed
~ **ripper** = Dreh-Aufreißer *m*
~ **screen,** see: rotary ~
~ **scrubber,** see: scrubber
~ **shovel** = schwenkbarer Bagger *m*
~ **tower crane,** rotating ~ ~, (mono-)tower ~ = Turmdrehkran *m*
~ **unit,** top ~, upper ~, upper deck, superstructure = Oberwagen *m* [*schwenkbarer Bagger m oder Kran M*]
to re-weld = nachschweißen
REX twinbatch paver = Doppeltrommel-(beton)straßenmischer *m*, Fabrikat CHAIN BELT COMPANY, MILWAUKEE, WISCONSIN, USA
(Rhenish) trass = Traß *m*, fein gemahlener vulkanischer Tuffstein *m*, gemahlener massiger Bimstuff *m*
rheological behaviou(u)r = rheologisches Verhalten *n*

rheology = Fließkunde *f* [*Lehre f von der Verformung f und dem Fließen n der Materie f*]
rhodochrosite, manganese spar, $MnCO_3$ (Min.) = Manganspat *m*, Rhodochrosit *m*
rhodonite (Min.) = Kieselmangan *n*, Rotbraunstein *m*, Rotspat *m*
rhombic = rhombisch
rhyolite, see: liparite
rhyolitic perlite = rhyolitisches Perlite-Gestein *n*
rib(b)and = Streichbalken *m*
ribbed construction, slab-and-joist ~ = Stahlbetonrippendecke *f* ohne Füllkörper *mpl*
~ **dome** = Rippenkuppel *f*
~ **floor with open soffit** ~ = Rippendecke *f* mit offener Untersicht *f*
~ ~ ~ **smooth soffit** = Rippendecke *f* mit ebener Untersicht *f*
~ **oval wire** = gerippter Ovaldraht *m*
ribbon clay, see: varve(d) (glacial) ~
~ **clip** = Bandschelle *f*
~ **development,** ~ **building** = Bandbebauung *f*
~ **gneiss,** see: banded ~
rib mesh = Rippenstreckmetall *n*
RIBMET [*Trademark*] = Rippenstreckmetall *n*
rice cultivation = Reisanbau *m*
rich in precipitate = niederschlagsreich
~ **lime,** see: fat ~
~ **mix** = fette Mischung *f*
riddle [*deprecated*]; screen = Gittersieb *n*
~ = Durchwurf(sieb) *m*, (*n*)
rider platform truck = Fahrer-Plattformkarre(n) *f*, (*m*)
~ **truck** = Fahrerkarre(n) *f*, (*m*) [*Flurfördermittel n*]
to ride up or down = steigen und fallen [*Einbauteil m einer Schwarzbelageinbaumaschine f*]
ridge = First *m*
~ **mountain(s)** = Kammgebirge *n*
~ **purlin** = Firstpfette *f*
~ **roof** = Firstdach *n*
~ **tile** = Firstziegel *m*
riding heel of screed = Schräglage *f* auf der Hinterkante *f* [*Glättbohle f*]

riding quality = Fahreigenschaft *f* [*Straße f*]
~ toe of screed = Schräglage *f* auf der Vorderkante *f* [*Glättbohle f*]
rift of rock = leichteste Spaltrichtung *f* [*Gestein n*]
rifting, rift building (Geol.) = Bruchspaltenbildung *f*, Abspaltung
rift valley, see: trough fault
rig, outfit = (Maschinen)Aggregat *n*
~, see: attachment
rigging with blocks, see: (block and) tackle
right bridge = gerade Brücke *f*
~ lay, see: regular ~
right-of-way = Vorfahrtsrecht *n*
~ = Wegerecht *n*, Wegbenutzungsrecht
~ purchase = Grunderwerb *m* [*z. B. Straße f*]
~ width, width of the road reservation = Grundrechtsbreite *f* [*Straße f*]
rigid = biegefest, starr, biegesteif
~ buttress dam = Pfeiler(stau)mauer *f* mit starrer Aussteifung *f*
~ frame, continuous ~ = starrer Rahmen *m*, Steifrahmen
~ ~ bridge = Steifrahmenbrücke *f*
rigidity, stiffness = Steifigkeit *f*, Steifheit *f*
rigid-jointed plane framework = ebener Rahmen *m* mit starren Ecken *fpl*
~ prismatic structure = steifknotiges Faltwerk *n*
rigid knot-joint = starre Knotenverbindung *f*
~ pavement = starre Decke *f*
rim = (Rad)Felge *f*
~ clutch (coupling) = Bandkupplung *f*
rime frost, hoar-frost = Rauhreif *m*
rimer, see: reamer
Ring-and-Ball test (or method), R. and B. **~ (~ ~)** = Ring-Kugel-Verfahren *n*, Ring- und Kugelmethode *f*
ring compressor, piston ~ ~, reciprocating ~ = Kolben(luft)verdichter *m*, Kolbenkompressor *m*, Kolben-Drucklufterzeuger *m*
~ expander = Ringdehner *m*
~ formation = Ringbildung *f*
~ gap = Ringzwischenraum *m*, Ringstop *m*

~ gate = Ringverschluß *m*
~ groove bearing = Ringrillenlager *n*
~ main = Ringleitung *f*
~ ore = Ringelerz *n*
ring-reinforced pressure pipe (or conduit) = bandagiertes Druckrohr *n*
ring road = Ringstraße *f*
~ (roll(er)) (grinding) mill = Ring-(walzen)(mahl)mühle *f*, Walzenring-(mahl)mühle *f*
~ shake, see: cup ~
~ shear apparatus = Ringschergerät *n*, Kreisringscherapparat *m*
rinsing = Abbrausen *n*
~ screen = Waschsieb *n*
ripper [*large cultivator of heavier construction throughout and having only about half the number of tines*] = Aufreißer *m*
ripple marking = Wellenfurche *f*, Rippelmarke *f*
rip-rap, rock ~, stone ~ = Steindeckwerk *n*, Stein(ab)deckung *f*, Steinbestürzung *f*, Steinvorlage *f*
rise (of arch), upward camber, versed sine = Bogenpfeil *m*, Stich *m*
~ [*of a carriageway*] = Aufstieg *m* [*einer Fahrbahn f*]
riser pipe, wellpoint ~ ~ = Heberleitung *f* [*Wellpoint-Methode f*]
~ shaft, rising ~ = Steigeschacht *m*
rise-span ratio = Pfeilverhältnis *n* [*Bogen m*]
rising gust = Steigbö *f*
Ritter (pressure) cell = Luft-(Erddruck-)Meßdose *f* nach Ritter
Rittinger's law [*basic law of crushing and pulverizing which states that the work done is in proportion to the area of the new surfaces developed*] = Zerkleinerungsgesetz *n* nach v. Rittinger [*die aufgewendete Zerkleinerungsarbeit steht in proportionalem Verhältnis zur erzeugten Oberfläche*]
river = Fluß *m*
~ arm = Flußarm *m*
~ bank, bank of the river = Flußufer *n*
riverbed degradation = Flußbett-Abflachung *f*
river boulder = Bachwacke *f*

river catchment board = Wasserstraßenbauamt n
~ **conservancy engineer** = Flußbauingenieur m
~ **construction (or engineering)** = Flußbau m
~ ~ **stone** = Flußbaustein m
~ **crossing** = Flußübergang m
~ **dam** = Flußlauf-Talsperre f
~ **deposit, fluvial** ~ = Flußablagerung f
~ **discharge, flow** = Abflußmenge f
~ **diversion** = Wasserumlenkung f
~ ~ **culvert** = Flußumleitdurchlaß m
~ **embankment** = (Fluß)Längswerk n
~ **engineering,** see: ~ construction
~ **erosion** = Erosion f im engeren Sinne
~ **flood control channel** = Hochwasserregulierungskanal m
~ **floor** = Flußsohle f
~ **ga(u)ging** = Flußmessung f
~ ~ **station,** see: flood measuring post
~ **gravel** = Flußkies m
~ **lock,** see: ~ (navigation) ~
~ **-marsh soil** = Auboden m
river meadow = Flußwiese f
~ **mouth, mouth of the river** = Flußmündung f
~ **mud** = Flußschlamm m
~ **(navigation) lock** = Flußschleuse f
~ **outlet, reservoir outlet (works)** = Betriebsauslaß m, Auslaufbauwerk n
(~) **overflow (spillway) section, spillway section** = Überfallstrecke f, Überlaufstrecke
~ **pier,** see: water ~
(~) **pollution, sewage pollution of a river** = Abwasserlast f
~ **port** = Flußhafen m mit Betriebsanlagen fpl
~ **power plant** = Lauf(wasser)kraftwerk n, Flußkraftwerk n
~ **rapid** = Stromschnelle f
~ **regulation, artificial river** ~, **stream straightening, river rectification** = Flußregulierung f, Flußreg(e)lung f
~ **sand** = Flußsand m, Schwemmsand
~ **silt,** see: clay containing ~ ~
~ **stage** = Flußwasserstand m

~ **survey** = Flußvermessung f
~ **(training) wall** = (Fluß)Leitwerk n
~ ~ **works** = Leitdämme mpl und Leitwerke npl [Fluß m]
~ **wash** = angespülter Flußschutt m
~ **water table** = Flußwasserspiegel m
~ **weir** = Flußwehr n
~ **work** = Flußbauarbeiten fpl
***rivet** = Niet m
~ **carrying stress** = Kraftniet m
riveted connection, ~ **joint** = genieteter Anschluß m, genietete Verbindung f
~ **steel joists with reinforced concrete compression flanges** = genietete Stahlträger mpl im Verbund m mit Stahlbeton-Druckplatten fpl
rivet hammer = Niethammer m
rivetless chain = splintlose im Gelenk n geschlagene Kette f
rivet pitch, ~ **spacing** = Nietteilung f
~ **truss** = Fachwerk n mit genieteten Knoten mpl
road [*deprecated*]; see: roadway [*deprecated*]
~; [*deprecated: roadway*] = Straße f
~ **aggregate, roadmaking rock, roadmaking aggregate, roadstone** = Straßenbaugestein n, Straßenbelagsgestein n
~ **-airport form,** see: side ~
road asphalt (US), see: asphalt(ic) cement
~ **ballast** = natürliches Gemenge n kleiner Steine mpl, Feinkies m und Sand m mit oder ohne Tonbinder m
road bay, ~ **panel, (concrete) road slab, concrete slab, paving slab, highway slab, road-way slab** = Straßenbetonfeld n, Straßenbetonplatte f, Beton(fahr)bahnplatte
roadbed = Straßenkoffer m, Straßenkasten m, Straßenbett n
road binder, see: ~ (engineering) ~
~ **breaker, paving breaker, pavement breaker, road ripper (Brit.)** = Straßenaufbruchhammer m, Aufreißhammer m
~ **brick,** see: paving
~ **bridge, highway** ~ = Straßenbrücke f
~ **broom, street** ~ = Straßenbesen m
~ **builder, roadman** = Straßenbauer m

roadbuilder, trailbulder, grade-builder, angledozer, bulldozer with angling blade, crawler tractor fitted with hydraulic angledozer = Planiergleiskettengerät *n* mit schneepflugartiger Schräganordnung *f* des Planierschildes *n*, Trassenschäler *m*, Planiergleiskettengerät mit Schwenkschild *n*, Seitenräumer *m*

roadbuilder's wood bin, see: wood panel bin

road-building, see: road construction

~ **firm**, paving company (US); road construction company = Straßenbaufirma *f*, Straßenbauunternehmen *n*

~ **machinery** (or equipment, or plant), road making plant, mechanical highway equipment, road machinery = Straßenbaumaschinen *fpl*

~ **technique** = Straßenbautechnik *f* [*als betriebstechnische Anwendung f*]

road burner (Brit.); see: asphalt surface heater (US)

~ **carpet**, ~ mat, carpet-coat, (premix(ed)) carpet, mat, thin surfacing; veneer (Brit.) = (Straßen)Teppich *m*, Teppichbelag *m*, Mischteppich(belag)

~ **channel**, see: paved gutter

~ **construction**, roadmaking, roadbuilding, highway construction = Straßenbau *m*

~ **contractor**, see: paving ~

~ **curve** = Straßenkurve *f*

~ **danger lamp** = Sturmlaterne *f*

~ **design,** highway ~ = Straßengestaltung *f*

~ **ditch**, see: roadway ~

~ **drill**, see: road breaker

~ **embankment**, highway ~ = Straßendamm *m*

~ **emulsion**, emulsion for highway construction = Straßenbauemulsion *f*

~ **engineer**, see: highway engineer

~ **engineering**, see: highway ~

~ (~) **binder**, paving cement (US) = Straßenbaubindemittel *n*

~ **equipment**, see: ~ furniture

~ **fabric**, see: ~ mesh

(~) **finisher**, see: finishing machine

*road form, see: side ~

~ **foundation** = Straßenunterbau *m*

~ **friction** = Fahrbahnreibung *f*

~ **furniture**, ~ equipment = Straßenausrüstung *f*

~ **glare** = Straßenblendung *f*

(~) **grader** = Straßenhobel *m*, Wegehobel *m*, Erdhobel *m*, Straßen-Planierer *m*

~ **grinder** = Straßenschleifmaschine *f*

~ **grooving machine** = Straßenaufrauhmaschine *f*

~ **gull(e)y**, rainwater ~ = Straßeneinlauf *m*, Regeneinlauf *m*

~ **heater** (Brit.); see: asphalt surface heater (US)

road-holding = Straßenlage *f* [*Fahrzeug n*]

road joint = Straßenfuge *f*

~ **junction**, highway ~ = Straßenkreuzung *f*

~ **kettle**, roadmakers' heater = Straßenkocher *m*

~ **lantern**, see: street (lighting) lantern

~ **life** = Straßennutzungsdauer *f*

~ **line paint**, see: traffic(-zoning) ~

~ **lining**, see: concreting paper

road-machine firm = Straßenbaumaschinenfirma *f*

road machinery, see: road-building ~

(~) **maintainer**, see: blade ~

roadmaking, see: road construction

~ **aggregate**, see: road ~

~ **rock**, see: road aggregate

*road-marking machine**, traffic-line marking machine, pavement marking machine, safety-line (street) marker, stripe painter, line marker, carriageway marking machine, highway marker, striping machine, street marker, withe line machine, striper, striping machine = Gerät *n* zum Anzeichnen *n* der Verkehrslinien *fpl*, Straßenmarkierungsmaschine *f*, Farbstrichziehmaschine *f*, Strichziehgerät *n*

~ **paint**, see: traffic(-zoning) ~

road mat, see: ~ carpet

~ **material**, see: highway ~

~ **mender**, see: lengthsman

~ **mesh**, ~ fabric = Straßenbewehrungsmatte *f*, Straßenarmierungsmatte

~ **metal** [*deprecated*]; see: crushed stone

~ **milling and grooving machine** = Straßenfräs- und -aufrauhmaschine *f*

road-mix (method) = Road-Mix-Verfahren n [*ist gewissermaßen eine Abart der "Bodenverfestigung" und kann ebenfalls nach dem System "mix-in-place" "arbeiten"*]

roadmixer, see: soil-stabilizing machine

road mix surface = Baumischbelag m

~ **mix(ture)** = Straßendeckenmischung f, Straßendeckenmischgut n

~ **net(work)** = Straßennetz n

~ **oil**, dust-laying ~ = Straßenöl n

~ ~ **distributor tanker**; see: pressure tank lorry (Brit.)

~ **overseer** = Straßenmeister m, Wegemeister m

~ **paint**, see: traffic(-zoning) ~

~ **panel**, see: ~ bay

(~) **patrol**, see: blade maintainer

~ **performance**, service behaviou(u)r = Verkehrsverhalten n eines eingebauten Straßenbaustoffes m

~ **pressure**, see: ground ~

~ **pug travel-mix plant**, see: windrow-type travel(l)ing (asphalt) (or road) plant

~ **pump** = straßenfahrbare Pumpe f

~**-rail bridge** = Straßen- und Eisenbahnbrücke f

road repair, rehabilitation of road, road repair work = Straßenausbesserung f, Straßen-Instandsetzung f, Straßenreparatur f

~ ~ **machine** = Straßen-Instandsetzungsmaschine f

~ **research** = Straßenbauforschung f

~ **ripper** = Straßenaufreißer m

~ ~ (Brit.); see: ~ breaker

~ **roller** = Straßenwalze f

(~) **rooter**, see: rooter

~ **service test for traffic paints** = Verkehrsverhalten-Prüfung f für Markierungsfarben fpl

~ **shoulder**, see: shoulder

~ **show** = Straßenbauausstellung f

roads, roadstead, anchorage = Reede f

roadside [*deprecated*]; see: verge ~

~ **ditch** = Straßengraben m

~ **engineering works to meet the operating requirements of heavy motor traffic** = Betriebsanlagen fpl für den Schwer-Kraft(fahrzeug)verkehr m

~ **hedge**, live fence = Straßenhecke f

~ **improvement** = Landschaftsgestaltung f an Straßen fpl

roadside-interview method, see: external (type of O & D) survey

roadside operations = Arbeiten fpl an Banketten npl und Randstreifen mpl

~ **planting**, see: highway ~

~ **protection** = Straßenseitenschutz m

~ **rest** (US); see: layby(e) (Brit.)

~ **restaurant** = Rasthaus n

(~)**traffic (control) sign**, see: traffic (control) sign

~ **waste**, see: verge

*****road sign**, see: traffic (control) sign

~ **siphon** = Straßenunterdükerung f

~ **site** = Straßenbaustelle f

road-skid quality, see: non-skid property

road slab, see: ~ bay

~ ~, **paving slab** = Straßenbauplatte f [*z. B. Asphaltbetonplatte f*]

~ **speed**, highway ~ = Straßengeschwindigkeit f

roadstead, roads, anchorage = Reede f; [*in Österreich und Bayern auch: Rhede f*]

roadster = offener Zweisitzer m, Jagdwagen m [*PKW m*]

roadstone, see: crushed ~

~, see: road aggregate

road stripe, see: road(way) ~

~ **structure**, pavement = Straßenkörper m

roadstud, traffic stud, street marker = Spurnagel m, Markierungsknopf m

road surface [*deprecated*]; see: roadway [*deprecated*]

*****road surface**, see: wearing course

(~) **surfacing** (Brit.), see: surfacing

*****road sweeper** = rotary ~

~-~ **collector** = Straßenfegemaschine f mit Kehrichtbehälter m

*****road sweeping machine**, see: rotary sweeper

~ **tamping machine** (Brit.); see: bridge tamper

~ **tanker**; see: tank truck (US)

road tar, RT = Straßenteer m

~ ~ **type penetration macadam**, see: targrouted stone (Brit.)

*****road traffic**, highway ~ = Straßenverkehr m

road transport, highway ~ = Straßentransport m

~ tray test (Brit.); see under "binder distributor"

road-truck, see: lorry (Brit.)

road tunnel, vehicular ~, vehicular subway = Straßen(verkehrs)tunnel m

~ ~ proper = Straßenraum m eines Tunnels m

~ vehicle engine = Straßenfahrzeugmotor m

~ vibrating and finishing machine, see: concrete finishing road vibrator

~ ~ machine [*the finishing screed is omitted*] = Rüttel(bohlen)fertiger m ohne Glättelement n

(~) vibrating tamper, see: vibrating tamper

road waves [*deprecated*]; see: corduroy effect

roadway [*deprecated*]; road = Straße f

~, road surface, road [*deprecated*]; carriageway = Fahrbahn f

~ capacity, see: highway ~

~ deck plate, carriageway ~ ~ [*bridge*] = Fahrbahnblech n

~ ditch, road ~, highway ~ = Straßengraben m

~ embankment (US) = Straßendamm m

~ flooring, ~ surfacing [*bridge*] = Fahrbahndecke f

~ flusher, street ~, street sprinkler, street washer = Straßensprengwagen m

~ grating = Fahrbahnrost m [*Brücke f*]

~ slab, see: road bay

~ soil = Straßenboden m

road(way) stripe = Markierungsstreifen m [*Straße f*]

roadway surfacing, see: ~ flooring

road wheel = Straßenrad n

~ widener, widener = Grabenbagger m mit seitlich herauskragendem Eimerrad n zur Verbreiterung f von Straßen fpl

~ with rising gradient = ansteigende Straße f

roadworks = Straßenbauarbeiten f

robust, rugged = robust

ROBUSTER [*Trademark*] [*dump truck*] = Muldentransporter m, Fabrikat STOLBERGER MASCHINEN- UND APPARATEBAU G.m.b.H., STOLBERG i. RHLD., DEUTSCHLAND

Rochelle salt, Seignette ~ = Seignettsalz n

rock = Fels m, Gestein n, Felsgestein, Festgestein

~ alum = Felsenalaun m

~ asphalt, see: asphalt(ic) rock

~ ~, stamped ~, powder ~ [*deprecated*]; compressed (natural) rock asphalt (surfacing) = Stampfasphalt m ohne Bitumenzusatz m

~ avalanche, see: débris-slide

*****rock bit**, see: rock(-drill) ~

~ blasting = Felssprengung f

~ breaker, see: ~ cutter

~ breaking plant, see: breaking ~

~ bucket = Felsenschaufel f [*Schürflader m*]

~ cavern = Kaverne f

~ classification = Felsklassifizierung f

(~) core bit, core shoe, cutter head = Kernbohrkrone f

~ crusher, stone ~ = Steinbrecher m

~ crushing plant, see: breaking ~

~ cut = Felseinschnitt m

~ cutter, ~ breaker, chisel breaker = Felsbrecher m

~ ~ bit, see: rock(-drill) ~

~ cutting in formation (Brit.) = Felsaushub m für das Planum

~ cuttings, well ~, drill ~, drillings = Bohrschmant m, Bohrgut n, Bohrmehl n

~ débris, rubble, rock waste (Geol.) = Gesteinstrümer f, Gesteinsschutt m, Geröll(e) n, Felsgeröll(e), Trümmermaterial n, Felstrümmer f

~ dipper = Felslöffel m

~ disintegration, see: mechanical weathering

~ drier, ~ dryer = Gesteinstrockner m

rock drill = Gesteinsbohrer m, Felsbohrer

*****rock(-drill) bit**, rock cutter bit, (drill) bit, drilling bit, boring bit = Gesteinsbohrerkrone f, Abbaumeißel m, Bohrmeißel m, Bohrkrone f

(rock) driller, hard rock miner = Mineur m, Gesteinshauer m

*****(rock) drill hammer**, see: (hand) hammer (rock) drill

rock drilling = Gesteinsbohren n, Felsbohren
~ **drill steel** = Getseinsbohrstahl m
rocker-arm, rocking arm = 1. Schwinge f; 2. Kipphebel m
rocker bearing, tilting ~, pivoting ~ = Kipplager n
~ **cover** = Kipphebeldeckel m
rocker-dump hand cart, see: concrete buggy
rocker pin = Kippzapfen m [*Brückenauflager n*]
~ **shovel**, see: overhead loader
~ **face** = Felswand f
rock fabric = Gesteinsgefüge n
~ **fall**, popping rock = Steinschlag m, Bergschlag
~ ~ **furrow**, see: bergfall ~
~ **feeder**, crusher ~ = Brecheraufgeber m, Brecherspeiser m
rock-fill cofferdam = Steinschüttungs-Fang(e)damm m
~ **dam** = Steinfülldamm m, Steinschüttdamm
~ ~ **with vertical earth core** = Steinschüttdamm m mit senkrechtem Erddichtungskern m
~ **toe wall** (US); see: abutment ~ ~ (Brit.)
rock flint = Bergkiesel m
~ **flour**, see: silt
~ **flow**, ~ stream = Blockstrom m
~ **flowage** (Geol.) = Fließen n
~ **fork** = Felsenforke f
~ **formation** = Felsschicht f, Gesteinsschicht
~ **-forming mineral** = gesteinsbildendes Mineral n, gesteinsbildender Gemengeteil m
rock foundation = Gründungsfels m
~ **gas**, see: natural ~
~ **glacier**, rock train, talus train = Blockgletscher m
rock grab, see: stone grapple
~ **grapple**, see: stone grapple
rock-hard = steinhart
rock industry = Steinindustrie f
rocking arm, see: rocker-arm
~ **ball bearing** = Kugelkipplager n
~ **pier**, hinged ~ = Pendelstütze f, Pendelpfeiler m

ROCKLITE [*Trademark*], see: HAYDITE
rock masses = Felsmassen fpl
~ **mechanics** = Geomechanik f, Felsmechanik
~ **milk**, agaric mineral = Bergmilch f
~ **mole** = Steinmole f
~ **oil**, see: crude oil (petroleum)
(~) **outcrop** (Geol.) = Aufschluß m
~-**phosphate**, see: phosphorite
rock pile = Haufwerk n [*Steinbruch m*]
~ **pinning** = Felsverankerung f mit Dübeln mpl
~ **plant**, stone-crushing ~ = Schotterwerk n, Schotteraufbereitungsanlage f
~ **pocket** = Kiesnest n, Steinnest n [*Beton m*]
~ **pressure**, earth pressure at great depth, compaction pressure = Gebirgsdruck m [*Tunnelbau m*]
*(**rock**) **quarry**, stone ~ = (Stein)Bruch m
rock rake = Felsrechen m, Steinharke f
~ **rip-rap**, see: rip-rap
"**rock road**" = Ferntransportband n, Langstreckenförderbandanlage f zum Transport m von Gesteinen npl, Strekkenband n
rock salt (Min.), see: halite
~ **sealing**, cementation of rock fissures = Felsinjektion f, Gesteinsauspressung f, Kluftinjektion f
~ **shovel**, quarry ~, heavy duty ~ = Steinbruch(hochlöffel)bagger m
~ **slice** = Dünnschliff m, Gesteinsplättchen n von 0,02—0,03 mm
~-**slide lake** = Bergsturzsee m
rock soap, see: mountain ~
(~) **spalls** = Zwicke f
~ **stream**, see: ~ flow
~ **texture** = Gesteinstextur f
~ **to be blasted**, solid rock = Sprengfels(gestein) m, (n), Sprenggestein n, Kernfels m, gewachsener Fels
~ **train**, see: ~ glacier
~ **tunnel** = Felstunnel m, Bergtunnel, Gebirgstunnel
rock-type dump body = Felstransport-Kippmulde f [*Erdbau-Lastfahrzeug n*]
rock washing machine = Gesteinswaschmaschine f, Gesteinswäsche f
~ **waste**, see: débris

rockwool = Steinwolle *f*
rocky bay = Klippenbai *f*
~ desert = Steinwüste *f*
~ ledge = Felsenriff *n*
rod bender, see: reinforcement bar bender
rodded concrete, puddled ~ = Schalstocherbeton *m*
rodding, see: puddling
rod electrode = Gasrohr *n* [*Elektroosmose f*]
~ packing = Kolbenstangenpackung *f*
~ shear, see: bar cutter
~ sounding, see: jet probing
roestone = Rogenstein *m*, Rogenkalk *m*
roll crusher, crushing rolls, double roll crusher, twin roll crusher = Walzenbrecher *m* mit zwei Brechwalzen *fpl*, Zweiwalzenbrecher *m*
rolled asphalt = Walzasphalt *m*
~ asphaltic macadam = Walzschottergußasphalt *m*, (deutsche) Asphalteingußdecke *f*; [*früher: Vorwohlitdecke*]
~ concrete = Walzbeton *m*
~ earth(fill) dam = gewalzter Damm *m*, Walzdamm [*Talsperre f*]
~ fill = abgewalzte Schüttung *f*, Walzdamm *m*
~-on flange, see: expanded ~
rolled pebbles = Bachgeröll(e) *n*
~ section (Brit.); **~ steel shape** = Walzprofil *n*
~ steel = Walzstahl *m*
~ ~ joist, RSJ = Walzträger *m*
~ thickness = abgewalzte Dicke *f*
Rolle retort brown-coal tar = Rolle-Ofenteer *m*
roller, see: (supporting) ~
~, see: idler
*roller = Walze *f*
~ and shaft = Laufrolle *f* mit Welle *f*
~ bascule bridge = Abrollbrücke *f*, Rollklappbrücke, Schaukelbrücke
~ bearing = Rollenlager *n*
~ ~ jaw (type) crusher = Backenbrecher *m* mit Rollenlagerung *f*
~ bit = Rollenmeißel *m*
~ block = Rollenschuh *m*
~ bridge = Rollbrücke *f*, Schiebebrücke
~ ~ sliding over the fixed part = Überrollbrücke *f*

~ ~ ~ under the fixed part = Unterrollbrücke *f*
roller-bucket type energy dissipator, see: spillway bucket
roller chassis for wheel tractor = Walzen-Untersatz *m* für Radschlepper *m*, Walzen-Untergestell *n* ~ ~
~ conveyor = Rollenförderer *m*
~ ~ for bricks = Ziegelrollenbahn *f*
~-fitted spiral (gravity) shoot (Brit.)/**chute** (US) = Wendelrollenbahn *f*
roller (grinding) mill, see: ~ mill
roller mark = Walzradeindruck *m*
~ mill, ~ grinding ~, roll grinder, roll mill = Walzen(mahl)mühle *f*
roller-mounted leaf gate (or sluice), coaster gate = Rollschütz(e) *n*, (*f*) mit endloser Rollenkette *f*
roller operator, rollerman = Walzenführer *m*, Walzenfahrer *m*, Walzenbediener *m*
~ race = Rollenlaufkranz *m*
~ seat = Rollenstation *f*
~ top truck = Karre(n) *f*, (*m*) mit Stahlrollen-Plattform *f*
~ type bucket ladder = rollende Eimerkette *f* [*Eimerkettenbagger m*]
~ wheel = Walzrad *n*, Walzzylinder *m*
~ with movable shoes fixed to the wheels = Gürtelradwalze *f*, Gürtelradbodenverdichter *m*
roll feed, feed opening, setting between rolls = Spaltweite *f* zwischen den beiden Walzen *fpl*, Walzenabstand *m* [*Walzenbrecher m*]
~ feeder = Speisewalze *f*, Zubringerwalze
rolling and kneading mixing action, non-lift mixing action = Zwangsmischung *f*, Zwangsmischen *n*
~ friction = Rollreibung *f*, rollende Reibung
~ lift bridge = Wälzklappbrücke *f*
~ method, Pycnometer ~ = Pyknometer-Verfahren *n*
~ mill = Walzwerk *n*
~ resistance between tyre (Brit.)/**tire** (US) **and road surface, RR** = Rollwiderstand *m*
~ sphere instrument, see: Höppler visco-(si)meter
~ stock = Rollmaterial *n*
~ tubular scaffold(ing) = fahrbare Stahlrohrrüstung *f*

rolling weight, service ~, working ~, operating ~ = Dienstgewicht *n*, Betriebsgewicht [*Walze f*]
~ **width** = Walzbreite *f* [*Walze f*]
***roll roofing plant** = Dachpappenfertigungsanlage *f*
~ ~ **winding mandrel** = Wickelvorrichtung *f* [*Dachpappenfertigungsanlage f*]
~ **scraper** = Walzenabstreifer *m*
Roman brick, see: facing ~
~ ~ **breaking machine** = Maschine *f* zum Zerbrechen *n* von Einloch-Hohlblöcken *mpl* zu Verblendern *mpl*
~ **cement**, Parker's ~ [*The common use of Roman cement in the 18th and last century recalls the fact that it was not actually Roman and had no connection with the builders of classic Rome in any way. The term was coined for a patent cement consisting of septaria nodules discovered and patented by one Parker of London in 1796. Some of the London clay was filled with these nodules which when calcined consisted of 50 per cent. clay, lime 40 per cent. and oxide of 10 per cent. The burned cement weighed about 75 lbs. per trade bushel. It was at first called Parker's cement, the correct term, but 'Roman' was adopted as a trade name. London had the premier deposit but others were discovered at Kimmeridge, Island of Sheppy, Harwich, Glasgow, Giffnock, and Barrhead. Charles Macintosh, of waterproof fame of Crossbasket, near East Kilbridge made Roman cement at Calder Glen, sold as Calderwood Roman Cement at 30s. per barrel. This rich brown cement had a setting action similar to Portland with a much lower tensile strength of course. A good quality Roman cement was burned at Belfast from clay raised in Cromac wood in 1820 called "Irish Roman Cement." It was specially used for chimney building and stucco work and was sold for £1 a barrel. So, Roman cement was British in both basic material and by invention in days long after the decline and fall of the Roman Empire.*] = Romankalk *m* [*früher: (natürlicher) Romanzement m*]
roof = Dach *n*

~ = First *m*, Decke *f* [*Tunnelbau m*]
~, overlying (layer) (Geol.) = Hangende *n*
~ **batten** = Dachlatte *f*
~ **bolt** = Deckenanker *m* [*Tunnelbau m*]
roof-bolting, roof-bolt installation, suspension support installation = Einziehen *n* von Deckenankern *mpl*, Ausbausystem *n* der Verankerung der Schichten im Hangenden, Ankerausbau *m* [*Tunnelbau m*]
~ **work platform** = Arbeitsbühne *f* zum Einziehen *n* von Deckenankern *mpl*
roof covering, ~ **sheathing** = Dacheindeckung *f*
~ **decking material** = Dacheindeckungsmaterial *n*
~ **dome** = Dachkuppel *f*
~ **drainage** = Dachentwässerung *f*
~ **girder** = Dachträger *m*
roofing = Dachdeckung *f*, Dacheindeckung
~ **felt adhesive**, ~ ~ **cement** = Dachpappenklebemasse *f*
~ **material** = Dachdeckungsstoff *m*
~ **slate** = Dachschiefer *m*
roof(ing) tile = Dachziegel *m*, Dachstein *m*
~ ~ **hoist** = Dachziegelaufzug *m*, Dachsteinaufzug
roof membrane = Dachhaut *f*
~ **panel**, ~ **slab** = Dachtafel *f*, Dachelement *n*, Dachplatte *f*
~ **pendant** (Geol.) = Reste des ehemaligen aufgeblätterten Daches, die sofittenartig von oben in tief abgetragene Massen herabgreifen und nach der Tiefe auskeilen
roof-pinning rock drill = Ankerloch-Bohrgerät *n* [*Bohrhammer m zur Herstellung von Bohrlöchern für den Ankerausbau*]
roof pitch = Dachneigung *f*
~ **preservative** = Dachpflegemittel *n*
~ **sheathing**, see: ~ covering
~ **shell** = Dachschale *f*
~ **slab**, see: ~ panel
~ **structure** = Dachkonstruktion *f*
~ **suspension bolt** = Deckenanker *m*
~ **tile**, see: roof(ing) ~
roof(top) heliport, roof-top helicoptor airport = Hubschrauber-Dachflugplatz *m*
roof truss = Dachbinder *m*
~ ~ **bearing** = Dachbinderauflager *n*

roof truss shoe = Dachbinderfuß m
room and pillar system = Kammer-Pfeiler-Bau m
roomy = geräumig
rooter, road ~ [*a massive form of ripper*] = Tief(auf)reißer m
root hole = Wurzelloch n, Wurzelgang m
~ rake = Wurzelrechen m
Roots blower = Rootsgebläse n
rope block = Seilflasche f, Seilkloben m, Seilblock m
~ crowd(ing) [*face shovel*] = Seilvorschub m, Seilvorstoß(en) m, (n) [*Hochlöffel-(bagger)* m]
~ drum = Seiltrommel f
~ grab(bing bucket) = Seil-Greifer m, Seil-Greifkorb m
(~) guy, guy-rope, standing rope, guy cable = Trosse f, Ankerseil n, Abspannseil n
~ lay = Seilschlag m
~ lubricant = Seilschmiermittel n
~ pulley block, see: (block and) tackle
ropeway = Seilbahn f
(rope) winch, cable ~ = (Trommel)Seilwinde f, (Seil)Windwerk n, Trommelseilwindwerk n
ropy lava, pahoehoe ~ = Stricklava f, Fladenlava, Taulava, Wulstlava
~ paint [*paint-work showing lines of brush marks*] = streifiger Anstrich m
roscoelite (Min.) = Roscoelith m
rose quartz (Min.) = rosa Quarz m
rosin-alkyd resin = harzmodifiziertes Kunstharz n
to rot [*timber*] = (ab)stocken, faulen [*Holz n*]
rotary (air) compressor = Rotationsluftverdichter m, Rotations-Drucklufterzeuger m, Rotationskompressor m, Lamellen(luft)kompressor
~ batch mixer, see: free fall (type) batch mixer
~ bit = Drehbohrmeißel m, Rotarybohrmeißel
~ blade = Wurfradschaufel f [*Schneeschleuder f*]
~ blower = Kapselgebläse n
~ broom, see: rotating ~
~ brush tarsprayer = Teerspritzmaschine f mit Bürstenwalze f

~-bucket excavator, bucket wheel(-type) excavator = Schaufelradbagger m
(rotary) calciner = Gips(dreh)ofen m
~ cement kiln = Zementdrehofen m
~ compressor, see: ~ air ~
~ draw works, hoist draw works for rotary = Rotaryhebewerk n, Rotarywindwerk
~ (or revolving) drier (or dryer) = Trommeltrockner m, Trockentrommel f
~ drill = Drehbohrer m
~ drilling = Drehbohren n, Drehbohrung f
~ ~ machine = Drehbohrmaschine f
~ ~ with core extraction = Rotationsbohrung f mit Kerngewinnung f
~ (drum) mixer, see: revolving drum (type) mixer
~ end tip = Kopfwipper m
~ fault, see: pivotal ~
~ finisher, see: mechanical trowel
~ (or rotating) grading screed = schaufelbesetzte Abgleichwalze f, Palettenwalze [*Betonbahnautomat m*]
~ hammer (type) breaker, see: hammer crusher
~ head, digging ~ = Kugelschauflerkopf m
rotary-headed excavator = Kugelschaufler m
rotary hearth = Rundherd m [*Sinteranlage f*]
~ headed excavator = Kugelschaufler m, (Be)Lademaschine f mit kugelförmigem Kopf m
~ hoe, ~ tiller, soil pulverizer, rotavator = Bodenfräse f
~ kiln = Drehofen m, Rotierofen
~ lime kiln = Kalkdrehofen m
~ mixer, see: mix-in-place machine
~ ~, see: revolving drum (type) mixer
~ mud, drilling mud = Bohrschlamm m
~ ~ flush boring (or drilling), see: hydraulic rotary drilling (or boring)
~ pattern, in a ~ ~ = turnusmäßig
~ pump = Drehkolbenpumpe, Kapselpumpe, Rotationspumpe m
~ road = Kreisplatzstraße f
~ rock drill = Gesteinsdrehbohrer m, Felsdrehbohrer

rotary rock drilling — rough 313

rotary rock drilling, rotating ~ ~ = Rotations-Gesteins-Bohrung f, Gesteinsdrehbohren n, Felsdrehbohren
~ **scale** = Drehwaage f
~ **scoop trencher**, see: wheel type ditcher
~ **scraper** = drehbarer Radschrapper m
~ **screen**, revolving ~, drum ~, trommel = Siebtrommel f, Sortiertrommel f, Trommelsieb n
~ **scrubber**, see: scrubber
~ **snow plow (US)/plough (Brit.)** = Stirnradschleuder f, Rotorschneeräumer m, Schneeschleuder
(~) **soil mixer**, see: mix-in-place machine
~ **speed mixer**, see: mix-in-place machine
*~ **sweeper**, road ~, mechanical ~, scavenging machine, road sweeping machine, street sweeper = Straßenkehrmaschine f, Fegemaschine f
~ **tiller**, see: ~ hoe
~ **tippler**, see: rotating tip
~ **traffic**, gyratory ~ = Rundverkehr m, Ringverkehr m
(~) **(type) mixer**, see: revolving drum (type) mixer
~ (~) **pile driving plant (or piling plant)** = Dreh(gerüst)ramme f
~ (~) **snow plough (Brit.)/plow (US)**, snow blowing machine, blower type snow plough (Brit.)/plow (US) = Schneeschleuder f
~ (~) **vibrator** = Rotationsvibrator m, Rotationsrüttler m
~ **valve** [cement weigh(ing) batcher] = Drehschieber m [Zement(silo)waage f]
~ **veneer lathe** = Furnierschälmaschine f
ROTASIDE wagon tippler = Seiten-Kreiselwipper m, Fabr. STRACHAN & HENSHAW, LTD., BRISTOL 2, ENGLAND
rotating beacon = Drehleuchtfeuer n
~ **boom**, swing ~ (US); ~ jib (Brit.) = Schwenkausleger m [Kran m]
~ **(or rotary) brush** = Bürstenwalze f, Kehrwalze
~ **cylinder visco(si)meter**, rotation(al) ~ = Viskosimeter n mit rotierendem Zylinder m, Rotationsviskosimeter
*rotating drum paver mixer, see: travel(l)ing (concrete) mixer (plant)

~ **grading screed**, see: rotary ~ ~
~ **jib (Brit.)**; see: ~ boom (US)
~ **leveller** = Fräserwalze f, Palettenwalze [Betondeckenfertiger m]
~-**paddle type of material-level indicator** = Bunkerstandanzeiger m mit umlaufendem Flügel m
rotating (or runner) piston pump = Rundlauf-Kolbenpumpe f
~ **seat** = Drehsitz m, Schwenksitz
~ **tip**, rotary tippler = Rundkipper m, Kreiskipper [Wagen dreht sich um Längsachse f um 360°]
~ **tower crane**, see: revolving ~ ~
~ **unbalanced (-) weight (type) screen**, see: (mechanically-vibrated) ~ ~ (~) ~
rotational shear = Drehmoment-Abscherung f
~ **visco(si)meter**, rotating cylinder ~, rotation ~ = Viskosimeter n mit rotierendem Zylinder m, Rotationsviskosimeter
rotavator, see: rotary hoe
rotocap = Drehkappe f
rotochamber = Luftzylinder m
rot of the branches = Astfäule f [Holz n]
rotor = Läufer m, Laufrad n [Turbine f; Elektromotor m]
~ = Pumpenschaufel f
ROTOR-LOADER [Trademark] [continuous aggregate loader] = MBB-Aufnehmer m, Fabrikat MODERNER BAUBEDARF G.m.b.H., STUTTGART, DEUTSCHLAND
rotor type magnetic separator = elektromagnetischer Walzenscheider m
ROTOTROL [Trademark] = ROTOTROL-Steuerungssystem n zur Veränderung f der Erregerspannung f, Fabrikat WESTINGHOUSE ELECTRIC CORP. [Raupen(band)löffelbagger m]
rotten slime, putrid ooze = Faulschlamm m
rottenstone = englischer Tripel m
rotting of sap wood = Splintfäule f
~ ~ **soil cement** = Faulen n der erhärteten Zementverfestigung f
~ ~ **the hearth** = Kernfäule f
~ ~ ~ **stem** = Stockfäule f

rough, textured, tractionized = griffig

rough cast(ing), rough cast plastering, pebble-dash plastering; [*in Scotland harl(ing)*] = Rapputz *m*, Rauhputz *m*, Berapp *m*

~ **concrete**, sub-~, base course concrete = Unterbeton *m*

~ **edged** = baumkantig [*Bau(nutz)holz n*]

roughening course = Rauhbelag *m* [*Straße f*]

~ **machine** = Aufrauhgerät *n*, Aufrauhmaschine *f*

~ **(treatment)** = Aufrauhen *n*, Aufrauhung *f*, Abstumpfen *n*

rough formwork, ~ **shuttering** = rauhe Schalung *f*

~ **grading (work), coarse** ~ (~) = Grobplanieren *n*, Grobplanierarbeiten *fpl*

roughly squared coursed rubble masonry, squared rubble walling brought to courses = hammerrechtes Schichtenmauerwerk *n*

roughness, rugosity = Rauheit *f*

roughometer, roughness meter [*an instrument for providing a numerical estimate of the irregularity in a road surface*] = Straßenunebenheitsmesser *m*

rough shuttering, ~ **formwork** = rauhe Schalung *f*

~ ~ **board** = rauhes Schalbrett *n*

~ **-stalked meadow grass** = gemeines Rispengras *n*, rauhes ~

rough stone pitching, see: base of stone pitching

rough surfaced hand-laid stone-filled asphalt = Rauhhartgußasphalt *m*

~ **weather**, adverse ~, inclement ~, bad ~ = Schlechtwetter *n*

roundabout, traffic ~, traffic circle; [*deprecated:gyratory junction, traffic circus*] = Kreisring *m*, Kreisplatz *m*

round arch, semi-circular ~ = Rundbogen *m*, Halbkreisbogen, Zirkelbogen, voller Bogen

~ **bar steel** = Rundstahl *m*, Rundeisen *n*

rounded steel section = abgerundetes Stahlprofil *n*

round gravel = Rollkies *m*

roundhead = Vorkopf *m*

round-head(ed) buttres dam; dam with segmental-headed counterforts (Brit.) = Rundkopf(stau)mauer *f* von Noetzli, Pfeilerkopf-Sperre *f*, Pfeilerkopf(stau)mauer *f*

round-hole screen = Rundlochsieb *n*

rounding tool, edging tool for rounding concrete arrises, joint tool = Kantenbrecher *m*

roundness index [*gravel*] = Abrundungskoeffizient *m* [*Kies m*]

round sand = Rollsand *m*

~ **section** = kreisförmiger Querschnitt *m*

~ **strand** = Rund(draht)litze *f*

~ ~ **cable** = Rundlitzen(draht)seil *n*

round-trip time = Rundfahrzeit *f*

round wire = Runddraht *m*

route, location line = Trasse *f*

~, transportation ~ = Verkehrsweg *m*

~ **selection**, selection of route = Trassierung *f*, Trassenwahl *f*

~ **surveying** = Trassenvermessung *f*

routine maintenance, ~ **upkeep** = Wartung *f*, laufende Unterhaltung *f*, laufende Instandhaltung *f*

~ **test** = Normalversuch *m*

routing bit = Maschinenlöffelbohrer *m*

rowan = gemeine Eberesche *f*

rowboat = Ruderboot *n*

row house = Reihenhaus *n*

~ **of wells** = Brunnenreihe *f*

rubber-asphalt blend (US), see: rubberized asphalt

~ **pavement** (US) = Gummi-Bitumen-Straßendecke *f*

~ **paving mixture** (US) = Gummi-Bitumen-Mineral-Gemisch *n*

rubber(-asphalt) road, rubberised ~ = Gummistraße *f*, Kautschuk(-Asphalt)straße *f*

rubber-balloon method, (water-filled) rubber membrane ~ = Gummiblasenmethode *f*, Ballonmethode [*Nachprüfung der Verdichtung f*]

rubber bearing = Gummilager *n*

~ **belt(ing)**, ~ **conveyor** ~ = Gummi(förder)gurt *m*

~ **bitumen mixture**, rubberized asphaltic bitumen (Brit.); ~ asphalt ~, rubberized asphalt, rubber-asphalt blend (US) = Gummi-Bitummen-Mischung *f*, Gummi-Bitumen-Gemisch *n*

rubber blade, ~ paddle = Gummi-Misch(er)schaufel *f*
~ compatible grease = gummiverträgliches Schmierfett *n*
~ composition, ~ compound = Gummimasse *f*
~ crawler belt = Gummilaufkette *f*
~ cushions = Gummipufferabstützung *f* [*Erdtransportwagen m*]
~ dinghy, pneumatic boat (or raft) = Schlauchboot *n*
~ elevator bucket = Gummi(-Elevator)becher *m*
~ gasket = Gummiflanschendichtung *f*, Gummidichtungsring *m*
~ grouser = Gummistollen *m* [*Gleiskette f*]
~ hose (or tube) = Gummischlauch *m*
rubberized asphalt, rubber-asphalt blend (US); rubberized asphaltic bitumen (Brit.) = Gummi-Bitumen-Mischung *f*
~ road, see: rubber(-asphalt) ~
~ tar = Gummiteer *m*
rubber joint seal = Fugen-Gummidichtung *f*
~ latex = Kautschuksaft *m*, Kautschukmilch *f*
~ membrane method, see: rubber-balloon ~
rubber-mounted crusher; pneumatic-tired ~ (US) = Auto(mobil)steinbrecher *m*
~ diesel excavator-crane = Universal-Diesel-Auto(mobil)bagger *m*
~ grab(bing crane) = Auto-Greifer *m*
~ loading shovel, ~ bucket loader, ~ tractor-shovel, ~ front-end (tractor) loader = luftbereifter Schürflader *m*, Pneuschürflader, Pneu(front)ladeschaufel *f*, Pneuschaufellader, Pneufrontlader, Pneuhublader, Pneukübelauflader
~ revolver crane, ~ revolving crane, ~ slewing ~; ~ swing-jib crane (Brit.); ~ swing(-boom) crane (US) = Fahrzeug(dreh)kran *m*, Fahrzeugschwenkkran, Autokran, gummibereifter selbstfahrbarer Universalkran [*kann Luftbereifung oder Vollgummibereifung haben*]
*****rubber-mounted shovel-crane;** see: pneumatic-tired ~ (US)
~ tractor-drawn scraper, see: four-wheel(ed) ~

rubber paddle, see: ~ blade
rubberplate (US) = Gummi(fuß)boden *m*
rubber powder, flocculated latex crumb = Kautschukpulver *n*
~ rotary hose [*rotary drilling*] = Gummispülschlauch *m*
~ suspension unit = Gummi-Abfederungselement *n*
~ tank = Gummibehälter *m* für Flüssigkeiten *fpl*
~ tire (US); ~ tyre (Brit.) = Gummireifen *m*
rubber-tired ditcher (US) = gummibereifter Grabenbagger *m*
~ off-(the-)highway hauling unit (or earth-moving vehicle) (US) = geländegängiger luftbereifter Erdtransportwagen *m*, gummibereiftes Erdbau-Lastfahrzeug *n*, geländegängiger Förderwagen *m* in Kraftwagen-Bauart *f*, Muldenkipper *m*, Groß-Förderwagen *m*, gleisloser Förderwagen *m*, Motorkipper *m*, Erdtransportfahrzeug für Fremdbeladung *f*
~ roller (US), see: pneumatic-tire ~ (US)
rubber tube (or hose) = Gummischlauch *m*
rubber-tyre mounted (Brit.); rubber-tire ~ (US) = gummireifenfahrbar
rubber water stop = Gummidichtungsstreifen *m*
rubbish, see: detritus
~ dump site, (~) ~ ground = Schuttabladeplatz *m*
to rubble, to ballast = beschottern
rubble (Geol.), see: rock débris
~ (Brit.) = Steinschutt *m*, Steinknack *m*
~ aggregate [*fragments above 6 in. but not weighing more than 100 lb.*] = Betonzuschlag *m* größer als 15 cm und nicht mehr als 45 kg Gewicht
~ concrete, cyclopean ~ = Zyklopenbeton, Bruchsteinbeton *m*
~ drain, see: blind ~
~ masonry dam, dry ~ ~ = Trockenmauerwerksdamm *m*, Mauerwerksperre *f*, Steinsatzsperre *f*, gepackter Steindamm *m*
(~) mound breakwater = Wellenbrecher *m* aus Steinschüttung *f*

rubble pile, pile of rubble = Schutthaufen *m*, Trümmerhaufen
~ slope, sloping rubble wall = Deckwerk *n*
~ ~, talus material (Geol.) = Schutthalde *f*, Gehängeschutt *m*
~ walling = Steinmauerwerk *n* mit unbearbeiteter Sichtfläche *f*
~ work; see: metalling (Brit.)
rubellite (Min.) = Rubellit *m*
ruby silver ore (Min.); see: dark-red silver ore
~ ~ ~ (Min.); see: proustite
rugged, robust = robust
rugosity = Rauheit *f*
ruins = Ruinen *fpl*
rule of thumb = Faustregel *f*
ruling gradient, see: limiting ~
~ pen, drawing ~ = Reißfeder *f*, Ziehfeder
rummel [*Scottish term*]; soakaway, soakage pit = Sickergrube *f*
run, see: lead (Brit.)
runabout ditcher, rubber-tired trenchliner (US); rubber-tyred ~ (Brit.) = Automobil-Grabenbagger *m* (mit Eimern *mpl*)
runnable = befahrbar
runner = Läufer *m*
~ = Laufrolle *f*
~ (or rotating) piston pump = Rundlaufkolbenpumpe *f*
running gear, travel(l)ing ~, undercarriage = Fahrwerk *n*
running-in compound = Einlaufschmieröl *n*
running joint, expansion joint during the day's work = (eigentliche) Raumfuge *f*
~ order, ~ condition = betriebsfähiger Zustand *m*
~ rail = Fahrschiene *f*
~ sand, quicksand = Quicksand *m*
~ surface = Fahroberfläche *f*
~ time; [*deprecated: travel(l)ing time*] = reine Fahrzeit *f* [*Verkehr m*]
running-up accident = Auffahrunfall *m*
running well, see: flowing ~
run-off = Regenabflußmenge *f*
~ = Abfluß *m*
~ hydrograph = Regenabflußmengenkurve *f*

run of kiln lime = unsortierter Branntkalk *m*
runway = Start- und Landebahn *f*, Piste *f*
~ = Steg *m* [*bei Hochbau-Baustellen fpl*]
~ lighting = Start- und Landebahnbefeuerung *f*
Rüping empty cell process = Hohlimprägnierung *f* Rüping(spar)verfahren *n*, Teeröltränkung *f* nach Rüping [*Holz n*]
rupture shear zone = Gleitkörper *m* [*Bodenmechanik f*]
rural expressway = Schnellstraße *f* auf dem Lande *n*
~ highway, see: public ~
rush coal = Schilfkohle *f*
rushes, see: reeds
rush hours = Hauptverkehrsstunden *fpl*, Hauptverkehrszeit *f*
rush-leaved feather grass = Nadel(feder)gras *n*, Nadelhafer *m*
rush mat = Binsenmatte *f*
rust cement = Rostkitt *m*
~-preventative coating = Rostschutzanstrich *m*
rust protection paint, see: anti-rust ~
rut, wheel mark, wheel track = Radspur *f*, Radeindruck *m*
RUTHEMEYER road roller = Straßenwalze *f*, Fabrikat B. RUTHEMEYER, SOEST/WESTFALEN, DEUTSCHLAND
rutilated quartz (Min.); see: needle-stone
rutile (Min.) = Rutil *m*
rutted, worn into ruts, worndown = ausgefahren [*Straße f*]
rye grass = Raigras *n*

S

sack dam = Sackwall *m*
~ (of cement), bag (~ ~) (US) = 94 lbs. = 42,676 kg
~ (~ ~), bag (~ ~) (Brit.) = 112 lbs. = 50,848 kg
sackcloth = Sackleinen *n*
sacked cement, see: bagged ~
sacking apparatus = Sackfüllmaschine *f*
sacking-off, see: bagging
sack silo = Sacksilo *m*

sacrifice shuttering — sand asphalt 317

sacrifice shuttering, ~ form(work) = verlorene Schalung *f*
Sadd El Aali = arabischer Name für den Assuan-Hochdamm in Ägypten
saddle = Sattel *m*
~ = Widerlagerkissen *n* [*Talsperre f*]
~-back = Senkrücken *m*
saddle backed girder (Brit.); ~ ~ beam = überhöhter Träger *m*, ~ Balken(träger) *m*
~ **flange** = gebogener Flansch *m*
~ **jib**(Brit.); ~ boom (US) = Laufkatzenausleger *m*
~ ~ **monotower crane** (Brit.); ~ boom ~ ~ (US) = Kran *m* mit Laufkatzenausleger *m*
~ **roof**, couple-close ~, gable ~, saddleback ~, double-pitch ~ = Satteldach *n*
~ **stone**, apex ~ = Scheitelstein *m*
safeguard, see: check rail
safe-load indicator = Warnvorrichtung *f* für Höchstlast *f*
safety against buckling = Knicksicherheit *f*
~ ~ **plate buckling** = Beulsicherheit *f*
~ ~ **overturning** = Kippsicherheit *f*
~ **clutch (coupling)**, see: overload ~ (~)
~ **fence**, see: guard ~
~ **fuse** = schlagwettersichere Schwarzpulverzündschnur *f*, Sicherheitszündschnur *f*
~ **glass** = Sicherheitsglas *n*
~ **haunch(ing)** = schmaler gerippter Randstreifen *m* zur äußeren Fahrbahneinfassung *f*
*****safety-line (street) marker**, see: roadmarking machine
safety pawl = Sicherheits-Sperrklinke *f*
~ **precaution** = Vorsichtsmaßnahme *f*
~ **rail**, see: check ~
safe (or permissible, or allowable) working load = zulässige Belastung *f*, ~ Last *f*
safflower oil = Safloröl *n*
sag = Wanne *f*, Geländewanne
~, see: sag(ging)
~ **curve**, concave transition between gradients, sag vertical curve = Wannenausrundung *f*, Wanne *f*
sagger clay, saggar ~, seggar ~ = Kapselton *m*

sag(ging) = Durchhang *m*
Sainflou theory (for forces on breakwaters) = Wellenkrafttheorie *f* nach Sainflou
Saint Elmo's fire = Elmsfeuer *n*
sales engineer = Verkaufsingenieur *m*
saline lake, salt ~ = Salzsee *m*
~ **water** = Salinenwasser *n*
salinity = Salzhaltigkeit *f*
salmon ladder, salmon-stair = Lachspaß *m*, Lachstreppe *f*
salt-air corrosion = Salzluftkorrosion *f*
salt dome = Salzdom *m*
~-glaze = Salzglasur *f*
salt glazing = Salzglasieren *n*
saltier cross bars, see: diagonal struts
salt lake, see: saline ~
saltpeter, see: potassium nitrate
salt scale = Streusalzschaden *m* [*Betondecke f*]
salt-soil stabilisation = Bodenverfestigung *f* mit Salz *n*, Salzverfestigung *f*
salt (stabilized) road = salzverfestigte Straße *f*
~ **swamp** = Salzsumpf *m*
~ **water corrosion** = Salzwasserkorrosion *f*
salvage, see: arisings
~ **appliances** = Bergungsgeräte *npl*
~ **ship** = Bergungsschiff *n*
~ **value** = Altwert *m*
~ **work** = Bergungsarbeiten *fpl*
SALZGITTER mucking shovel = Salzgitterlader *m*, Fabrikat SALZGITTER MASCHINEN A. G., SALZGITTER, DEUTSCHLAND
sample core = Probekern *m*
~ **taker**, sampler = Probe(ent)nahmeapparat *m*, Probe(ent)nahmegerät *n*
~ **tin** = Entnahmebüchse *f*
sampling = Probe(ent)nahme *f*
~ = Schürfbohrung *f*
~ **spoon** = Schappe *f*, Probelöffel *m*
~ **tool**, see: soil sampler
~ **tube** = Probe(ent)nahmestanze *f*
sand accretion groyne (Brit.); ~ ~ groin (US) = Sandfangbuhne *f*
~ **asphalt**, bitumen sand mix (Brit.) = Sandasphalt *m*
~ ~ (US); asphaltic sand = Asphaltsand *m*

sand asphalt (US) = 1. heißeingebaute Mischung *f* aus örtlichem Sand *m* und Bitumen *n* ohne besondere Abstufung *f*; 2. Gemisch *n* aus örtlichem Sand und Bitumen mit oder ohne Mineralfüller *m*, entweder im An-Ort-Verfahren oder Aufnahmemischverfahren oder maschinengemischt eingebaut
sand bag dam = Sandsackwall *m*
~-bank, bank in the sea, shoal, flat(s) = Sandbank *f*, Untiefe *f*
(sand) bar, see: sand-head
~ bed, see: sand underlay
~ ~ river = Fluß *m* mit Sandboden *m*
~ blanket, see: ~ underlay
~ blasting, blast cleaning = Sandstrahlen *n*, Sandstrahlbläserei *f*, Sandstrahlreinigung *f*
~ blast(ing) machine, see: blast generator (US)
(~) blast sand = Gebläsesand *m*
~-cement grout, cement-sand ~ = Sand-Zement-Schlämme *f*
sand curing = Sandabdeckung *f* [*Betonnachbehandlung f*]
~ cushion, see: sand underlay
~ deposit = Sandvorkommen *n*
~ dewatering screw, ~ dehydrator ~ = Sandentwässerungsschnecke *f*, Sand(rück)gewinnungsschnecke, Wasserausscheidungsschnecke
~ drag, dewatering flight conveyor, washbox = Sandkratzer(kette) *m*, (*f*)
~ dredging = Sandnaßbaggerei *f*, Sandnaßbaggerung *f*
~ dressing, see: sanding
~ drift, drift of sand = Sandverwehung *f*, Sandwehe *f*
(~) dune, down = (Sand)Düne *f*
sanded plaster = Sandputzmörtel *m*
sand embankment = Sanddamm *m*
~ equivalent test = Sandanteil-Untersuchungsverfahren *n*
~ filled cavity fit = eingebauter Filter *m* in mit Kies ausgefülltem Hohlraum [*Wellpoint-Methode f*]
~ filling (US); see: sand-silting (Brit.)
~ filter = Sandfilter *n*, *m*
~ fraction = Sandkörnung *f*, Sandanteil *m*

~ grain = Sandkorn *n*, Sandteilchen *n*
~ grout = Sandschlämme *f*, Sandschlempe *f*
sand-head, off-shore bar, (sand) bar, coastal bar = angeschwemmte Sandinsel *f*, Sandbank *f*, (Sand)Barre *f*
sand heath, barren = Sandheide *f*
sanding, sand dressing, sand spreading = Absanden *n*, Absandung *f*
~ machine, see: floor sander
~ up; see: sand-silting (Brit.)
sand island, see: artificial ~
sand-island method (of construction) = künstliche Sandinselschüttung *f*
sand-lime brick, see: lime sand ~
sand-lined mo(u)ld = Sandform *f*
sand migration = Sandwanderung *f*
sandpaper surface, ~ finish [*road surface texture*] = Sandpapieroberfläche *f*, Sandpapierrauheit *f*
sand-pillar, sand-spout = Sandhose *f*
sand pit = Sandgrube *f*
~ processing (or **dressing,** or **producing**) **plant** (or **installation**) = Sandaufbereitungsanlage *f*
(sand-)pump dredge(r), see: hydraulic (suction) ~
sand reclaiming machine = Sandrückgewinnungsmaschine *f*
~ ~ screw = Sandrückgewinnungsschnecke *f*
sand sedge = Sandriedgras *n*
sand-silting (Brit.); **sand filling** (US); **sanding up** = Versandung *f*
sand-spit = Sandzunge *f*
sand-spout, sand-pillar = Sandhose *f*
sand spreading, see: sanding
*****sandstone** = Sandstein *m*
~ boulder = Sandsteinblock *m*
~ containing open seams = klüftiger Sandstein *m*
~ masonry facing = Sandsteinverkleidung *f*
~ stratum = Sandsteinschicht *f*
sandstorm, simoom = Sandsturm *m*, Samum *m*
sand streak = Sandstreifen *m* [*Beton m*]
~ streaking [*concrete*] = Sandstreifenbildung *f* [*Beton m*]
~ sucker = Sandkreiselpumpe *f*

sand trap = Sandfang m
~ underlay, ~ bed(ding course), ~ cushion, ~ blanket = Sandbett n, Sandunterbettung f
sandwich beam, flitch(ed) ~; ~ girder (Brit.) = Verbundbalken m, Verbundbalkenträger m, Verbundträger m
~ (precast concrete) panel = Tafel f aus Beton-Schichtplatten fpl, Schichtplattentafel f
~ process macadam, COLCRETE constructed in the sandwich process = Zementschotterdecke f
sandy, arenaceous = sandig
~ borrow = Entnahmesand m
~ clay, see: mild ~
~ gravel, see: hoggin
~ limestone, arenaceous ~ = Kalksandstein m
~ marl, see: clay-grit
sanitarian = Gesundheitstechniker m
sanitary engineer = Gesundheitsingenieur m
~ engineering = Gesundheitstechnik f
~ inspector = Gesundheitsinspektor m
~ landfill = Müllauffüllung f
~ sewer, separate ~ = Schmutzwasserkanal m, Sammler m für die getrennte Entwässerung
Santorin earth = Santorinerde f
sapling = Jungbaum m, Schößling m
saponifiable = verseifbar
saponification = Verseifung f
~ value = Verseifungswert m
sapropel = Sapropel n
sapropelite (coal) = Sapropelkohle f, Sapropelit m
sapwood, alburnum = Splint(holz) m, (n)
sargassum = Sargossatang m, Beerentang
sarsen stone, see: graywether
satellite airfield, see: auxiliary ~
~ town; satellite community center (US) = Trabantenstadt f, Tochterstadt, Satellitenstadt
satin spar, see: fibrous gypsum
~ white = Satinweiß n
saturation = Sättigung f
~ capacity [road] = Leistungsfähigkeit f bei voller Sättigung f

~ line (or surface) = Sättigungslinie f, Sickerlinie f
~ pressure = Sättigungsdruck m
saucisse, saucisson, wipped fascine = (Faschinen)Wippe f, Faschinenwurst f
SAUERMANN tower machine, ~ ~ excavator = Schleppschrapper m mit zwei fahrbaren Türmen, Fabrikat SAUERMAN BROS., INC., CHICAGO 7, USA
saving(s) = Einsparung f, Ersparnis f
~ of costs = Kostenersparnis f, Kosteneinsparung f
*****saw** = Säge f
~ blade = Sägeblatt n
sawdust = Sägemehl n
~ concrete = Holzmehlbeton, Sägemehlbeton m
~ tar = Sägemehlteer m
sawing jack = Sägebock m, Schragen m
(saw) kerf = Sägeschnitt m
saw mill; lumber ~ (US) = Sägemühle f, Sägewerk n
saw-nosed tractor, saw-nose cat(erpillar) ~ = (Gleis)Kettenschlepper m mit angebauter nasenförmiger Säge f
sawn timber = Schnittholz n
saw set = Schränkeisen f
~ setting machine = Schränkmaschine f
~ tooth core drill(ing machine) = Sägezahnkernbohrgerät n, Sägezahnkernbohrmaschine f
to saw up = abtrummen, absägen
scabbing [the loss of aggregate from a surface dressing in patches, leading to exposure of the original road surface] = Räude f
to scabble = behauen [Stein m]
scaffold bridge = Gerüstbrücke f
*****scaffold(ing)** = Gerüst n, Rüstung f
scale = Maßstab m
~ = Skala f
~ = Waage f
~ = Zunder m
~, boiler ~ = (Kessel)Ansatz m
~ batcher = Waagen-Dosierapparat m [Zuschlagstoffe mpl]
~ drawing = Maßskizze f
~ hopper, see: weighing bucket
~ master = Wiegemeister m
~ relation = Maßstab-Beziehung f
~ track = Wiegegleis n

scaling = Abblättern n, Abblätterung f, Abschuppen n, Abschuppung f
~ hammer, chipper = (Ab)Klopfer m
scalper, see: stone breaker (type crusher)
scalping = Trennungssiebung f [Entfernen n des Überkorns n oder Unterkorns n]
~ screen = Trennungssieb n
scantling = Halbholz n, Kreuzholz n
~ (Brit.) = Mauerstein m von mehr als 1,8 m Länge
scar (Geol.) = Schramme f
scarf (joint) = Laschung f, Blattstoß m
scarification, scarifying = Aufreißen n [Straßendecke f]
scarified material(s) = Aufbruchmassen fpl, Aufbruch(material) m, (n) [Straßenaufbruch m]
scarifier (attachment) = Aufreiß(er)vorrichtung f [bei Walze und Wegehobel]
~ tine (US)/**tyne** (Brit.) = Aufreiß(er)zahn m
scarp, escarpment (Geol.) = Abdachung f, Böschung f, Ausbiß m
scatter of the test results = Streuung f der Versuchsergebnisse npl
scavenging air = Spülluft f [Dieselmotor m]
*****scavenging machine**, see: rotary sweeper
~ stroke, see: exhaust ~
scenery = Landschaftsbild n
scenic beauty = Schönheit f der Landschaft f
~ vista = landschaftlicher Ausblick m, schöne Aussicht f
schedule of construction operations, see: construction schedule
~ of prices = Leistungsverzeichnis n
~ of rates for the hire of contractors' and building plant, see: list of hiring charges for building plant and contractors' equipment
scheeletite, stolzite (Min.) = Scheelbleierz n, Scheelbleispat m
scheelite (Min.) = Scheelerz n
~ spud = Scheelitschwüle f
SCHEID pneumatic-tyred (Brit.)/**tired** (US) **roller** = Gummiradwalze f, Fabrikat W. & J. SCHEID, LIMBURG/LAHN, DEUTSCHLAND
Scheldt = Schelde f
schillerspar (Min.), see: bastite

schist, crystalline ~ = kristalliner Schiefer m
schistous amphibolite, see: horn(blende)schist
~ sandstone, see: foliated grit-stone
school of building = Bauschule f
~ ~ mines, see: mining academy
schooner = Schoner m
SCHOPF overhead loader = Wurfschaufellader m, Fabrikat SCHOPF MASCHINENBAU G.m.b.H., STUTTGART-RUIT, DEUTSCHLAND
schorl (Min.) = Schörl m
Schuck-designed diesel engine = Zweitakt-Diesel(motor) m mit Schiebersteuerung f
scissile alum, see: feather-alum
scissor junction = Scherenkreuzung f
~ type lift truck = Hubwagen m nach dem Scherenverfahren n
scissors' fence = Horizontallattenzaun m
scolecite (Min.) = Skolezit m, Wurmsiedestein m
scoop = Schöpfkelle f, Schöpfgefäß n; [oberdeutsch: Schapf m, Schapfe f]
~, skimmer ~, bowl = Kübel m [Radschrapper m]
~-flight conveyor, see: (bucket) (type) elevator
*****scoop pan self-loading scraper**, see: trailing scoop grader
~ wheel, see: bucket wheel
scope = Geltungsbereich m
~ of work = Arbeitsumfang m
scoria, scoriaceous lava = vulkanische Schlacke f
scoriaceous basalt = Schlackenbasalt m
Scotch derrick (crane), ~ derricking jib crane (Brit.); stiff-leg ~ (~), ~ ~ boom crane (US) = Bock-Derrick-Kran m, Bock-Mastenkran m
~ elm, see: mountain ~
Scottish pine, see: common ~
~ shale tar = schottischer (Öl)Schieferteer m, ~ Bitumenschieferteer
scoured hole, see: eroded ~ (Brit.)
scour(ing), undermining, underwashing, subsurface erosion = Unterwaschung f, Unterspülung f, Auskolkung f, Wegspülung f
to scour out = ausscheuern (Geol.)

scour outlet, see: bottom emptying gallery
scouting; wild cat (US) = Aufschlußbohrung f, Suchbohrung, Prospektionsbohrung, Pionierbohrung
scow (US); barge (Brit.) = Schute f, Bagger~, Abfuhr~
~ winding gear (US); barge ~ (Brit.) = (Bagger)Schutenwinde f
scrape (US) = Scharrharz n
scrape-dozer = Schürf(kübel)raupe f
scraper = Schaber m
~; plow (US) = Schabertafel f [Absetzbecken n]
~, belt wiper = Abstreicher m [Bandförderer m]
~ = Schrapper m, Erdkratzer m
~, cable-hauled bucket = Seilschrapperkasten m
*scraper, see: trailing scoop grader
~ bucket = Schrapp(er)-Kübel m, Schrapp(er)gefäß n
scraper-fed concrete mixer, concrete mixer fitted with mechanical skip loader attachment = Betonmischer m mit Handschrapperbeschickung f
(scraper) flight, see: flight
~ grab = Zweischalen-Greifkorb m für Sand m und Kies m
~ hoist, drag ~ ~ = Schrapperwinde f, Schrapperhaspel m, f
~ installation, drag ~ ~ = Schrapperanlage f
~ rope = Schrapperseil n
scrap metal yard = Schrottplatz m
~ tyre rubber (Brit.); ~ tire ~ (US) = Altreifengummi m
scratch coat, first ~ = Unterputz m
~ ga(u)ge = Streichmaß n
scratch-hardness tester = Ritzhärteprüfer m
scratch template, subgrade ~~, subgrade tester, point template = Kontrollrechen m, Profiltaster m
~ work, see: sgraffito
SCR brick (US) [Trademark] = ein Ziegel m der „STRUCTURAL CLAY PRODUCTS RESEARCH FOUNDATION" $2^1/_6":5^1/_2":11^1/_2"$
scree, talus = Geröllhalde f
screed, floating ~ = Einbauteil m [Schwarzbelageinbaumaschine f]

~ extension = Bohlenansatzstück n
~ heating = Bohlenbeheizung f
~ hoist rope = Einbauteil-Hubseil n [Schwarzbelageinbaumaschine f]
screeding beam, see: strike-off (screed)
screed(ing) board, see: smoothing ~
screeding surface of the forms = Oberkante f der Seitenschalung f
screed lift shaft = Handradwelle f zum Einstellen n des Einbauteils m [Schwarzbelageinbaumaschine f]
~ planing angle = Bohlenabziehwinkel m
~ plate = Abziehelement n, Fertigerbohle f, Abziehbohle, Glättbohle [Schwarzbelageinbaumaschine f]
~ side arm, level(l)ing ~ = Schwenkarm m [Schwarzbelageinbaumaschine f]
screen (Brit.); see: (trash) rack (US)
~; [deprecated: riddle] = Gittersieb n
~ (US), see: laboratory ~
~ body = Siebkörper m
~ cleaner (Brit.); (trash) rack rake (US) = Rechenreiniger m
~ cloth, see: ~ fabric
~ deck, screening ~ = Siebdeck n
~-discharge ball (grinding) mill, screentype ~ = Siebkugel(mahl)mühle f
screened gravel = Siebkies m
screen fabric (or mesh, or cloth) = Siebmaschendrahtgewebe n
~ for two screening directions = Rückstufensieb m
~ frame = Siebrahmen m
~ grillage (Brit.); see: (trash) krac (US)
~ grouting = Schleierverpressung f [Talsperrenbau m]
screening (US) = Aufbringen n von Brechsand m
~ = Siebung f, Sieben n, Sortieren n, Sortierung f
~ deck, see: screen ~
~ efficiency = Siebleistung f
~ machine = Siebmaschine f
~ medium = Siebboden m
~ panel = Siebfeld n
~ plant = Siebanlage f
~ plate = Siebgrobblech n
screenings = Abfangstoffe mpl [Abwasserwesen n]

screening(s) [*deprecated*]; chipping(s), chips, stone chips = Splitt *m*
~, **stone** ~, **crusher** ~, **artificial sand, manufactured sand, (crushed) stone sand** = Brechsand *m* [*umfaßt in den USA den Kornstufenbereich von 0 bis 4,76 mm*]
screening sheet = Siebfeinblech *n*
~ **surface, screen** ~ = Siebfläche *f*
screen mesh, see: ~ **fabric**
~ **of bars**, see: **bar screen**
~ **(rack)** (Brit.); see: **(trash) rack** (US)
~ **rejects** = Siebüberlauf *m*
~ **well** = Rechenschacht *m*
~ **wire** = Maschendraht *m*
~ **with two screen boxes** = Verbundsieb *n*
~ ~ **vibratory action applied direct to the screen cloth** = Vibrationssieb *n*
~ ~ ~ ~ ~ ~ **through the screen frame, vibrated live frame screen** = eigentliches Schwingsieb *n*
screw, worm, screw flight, continuous helical blade = Schnecke *f*, Schneckengang *m*
screw caliper, see: ~ **ga(u)ge**
~ **clamp** = Schraubzwinge *f*
~ **(or worm) conveyor, conveyor screw, Archimedean screw conveyor** = Schneckenförderer *m*, Förderschnecke *f*, Transportschnecke *f*
~ **conveyor for bulk cement, cement screw** = Zementschnecke *f*
screwcrete = Schraubbeton *m*
screw cutting die = Gewindeschneideisen *n*
~ ~ **machine**, see: **screwing** ~
~ **down cup** = Fettbüchse *f*
~ ~ **valve** = Niederschraubventil *n*
~ **driver** = Schraubenzieher *m*
screwed pipe joint = Schraubrohrmuffe *f*
~ **spindle** = Gewindespindel *f*
screw elevator, vertical ~ ~, **vertical screw lift** = vertikale Förderschnecke *f*
screw feed, worm ~ = Schneckenbeschickung *f*, Schneckenaufgabe *f*
~ **feeder**, see: **feed screw**
~ **feed type bucket elevator loader** = Becher(be)lademaschine *f* mit Schneckenbeschickung *f*
~ **flight**, see: **screw**
~ **ga(u)ge,** ~ **caliper** = Schraublehre *f*
~ **head file** = Schraubenkopffeile *f*

screwing machine, screw cutting ~, **threading** ~ = Gewindeschneidmaschine *f*, Schraubenschneidmaschine *f*
screw jack, see: **jack screw**
~ **nut, (bolt) nut** = (Schrauben)Mutter *f*
~ **(-propelled) tug** = Schraubenschlepper *m*
screw slot = Schraubennut *f*
~ **spreader**, see: **concrete** ~ ~
~ **steamer** = Schraubendampfer *m*
~ **tug**, see: ~ **(-propelled)** ~
~ **type sand classifier**, see: **spiral classifier**
~ ~ **soil auger**, see: **worm auger**
~ **washer**, see: **spiral classifier**
scroll case = Turbinenspirale *f*
scrubber, (revolving) (cylindrical) scrubber, rotary scrubber, blade-mill, paddle mill scrubber, stone (and ore) scrubber, ore scrubber = Schwerttrommelwäsche *f*, Schwertwaschtrommel *f*
scrubbing action = Scheuerwirkung *f*
scrubbing oil, see: **stripping** ~
scum, top sludge = Schwimmschlamm *m*
seabord, see: **sea-side**
seabottom = Meeresgrund *m*
sea breeze, (on)shore wind = Seewind *m*
~ **chart, hydrographic map** = Seekarte *f*
sea-clay = Marschton *m*
sea-coast, see: **sea-side**
sea defence, see: **coastal protection**
~ ~ **works**, see: **protection** ~
~ **dyke** (Brit.); ~ **dike** (US) = Seedeich *m*, Meer(es)deich *m*
seafarer = Seefahrer *m*
(sea) floe = schwimmendes Eisfeld *n*
sea-going dredge(r), marine ~ = Seebagger *m*, seegehender Bagger
~ **hopper suction dredge(r)** = seegehender Saugbagger *m* mit eigenem Laderaum, Hopperbagger, Hoppersauger [*früher: Schacht-Pumpen-Bagger*]
sea inlet, arm of the sea = Meer(es)arm *m*
~ **level** = Meeresspiegel *m*, Seewasserspiegel *m*
to seal = abdichten
seal coating, see: **surface treatment**
sealed unit = Scheinwerfereinsatz *m*
sealing bucket (US); see: **priming nose** (Brit.)

seal(ing) coat — section

seal(ing) coat, surface dressing (treatment); [*deprecated: flush coat, squeegee coat*] = Porenschluß *m*, Oberflächenabsieg(e)lung *f*

sealing compound = Vergußmasse *f*

~ groove = Vergußspalt *m* [*Betonfuge f*]

~ member, see: gasket

~ (off), packing = Abdichtung *f* [*Rohr n, Ventil n*]

~ ring = Schnappring *m*

~ rope = Dicht(ungs)strick *m*

sealing-wax wood = Siegellackholz *n*

SEALITHOR [*Trademark*] = ein belgischer Gipsschlackenzement *m*

seam = Flöz *n*

~ = Naht *f*

~ = Spalte *f* (Geol.)

SEAMAN SELF-PROPELLED PULVI-MIXER [*Trademark*] = Mehrgang(boden)mischer *m* mit wahlweisem Bindemittel-Meßwerk *n*, Fabrikat SEAMAN MOTORS INC.. MILWAUKEE 3, WISCONSIN, USA

SEAMAN SELF-PROPELLED TRAV-L-PLANT [*Trademark*] = Mehrgang(boden)mischer *m* mit Bindemittel-Meßwerk *n*, Fabrikat SEAMAN MOTORS INC., MILWAUKEE 3, WISCONSIN, USA

sea peat = Meertorf *m*

seaport, deep-sea port = Seehafen *m* mit Betriebsanlagen *fpl*

~ fortress = Seefestung *f*

~ town, harbo(u)r city, harbo(u)r town = Hafenstadt *f*

sea (protection) wall = 'Längswerk *n* [*Meer n*]

searchlight, see: floodlight

sea-sand = Seesand *m*, Meer(es)sand

seashore-gravel, (beach) shingle [*gravel without fines*] = Küstenkies *m*

sea-side, sea-cost, seabord = Küste *f*

sea silt, see: clay containing ~ ~

seasonal = jahreszeitlich

~ deposit (Geol.) = jahreszeitlich bedingte Ablagerung *f*

~ effect = jahreszeitlich bedingter Einfluß *m*

~ movement = jahreszeitlich bedingte Schwankung *f*

seasonally banded (or stratified) clay = Bänderton *m* mit Jahresringen *mpl*

***seasoning process** = Trockenprozeß *m* [*Holz n*]

(seat) lecture hall = Schulungshalle *f*

~ of a fire = Brandherd *m*

~ ~ settlement = Sitz *m* der Setzung *f*

sea wall, see: sea (protection) wall

seaward(s) = meeresseitig, seewärts

seawater = Meer(es)wasser *n*, Seewasser

sea wave = Meereswelle *f*

seaway, deep waterway = Groß-Schiffahrtstraße *f*

***seaweed** = Tang *m*

secondary axis of the oval = kleinere Ovalachse *f*

~ compression = Nachverdichtung *f*

~ control = Neben-Steuerorgan *n*

~ crusher, reduction ~, fine ~ = Nachbrecher *m*, Feinbrecher

~ crushing, see: fine ~

digestion = Nachfaulung *f*

~ (drilling and) blasting, see: pop shooting

~ grouting = Nacheinpressen *n*, Nachverpressen

~ heading = Nachtrieb *m* [*Tunnelbau m*]

~ mountain, average ~ = Mittelgebirge *n*

~ road, county ~ = Landstraße *f* 2. Ordnung

~ settling = Nachklärung *f* [*Abwasser n*]

~ (sewage) sludge = behandelter Schlamm *m*

~ squall front = Böenstaffel *f*

~ stress = Nebenspannung *f*

~ tensioning = Nachspannen *n* [*Spannbeton m*]

~ time effect = sekundärer Setzungseffekt *m*

second drum brake = Reservetrommelbremse *f*

~ ~ clutch = Reservetrommelkupplung *f*

~-stage digestion tank = Nachfaulraum *m*

section = Abschnitt *m*, Strecke *f*, Teilstrecke *f*

~ = Schnitt *m*

~ = Profil *n* [*Tunnelbau m*]

~ = Schuß *m* [*Pfahl m*]

~, see: sectional shape

~ = Schuß *m* [*Rohr n*]

sectional boiler = Sektionalkessel *m*, Gliederkessel *m*
~ **drawing** = Schnittzeichnung *f*
~ **ground conveyor** = (Transport)Bandstraße *f*
~ **iron**, steel section = Fassoneisen *n*, Profileisen, Formeisen, Profilstahl *m*, Stahlprofil *n*
~ **liner**, see: liner segment
~ **property** = Profilwert *m*
section(al shape), profile = Profil *n*
sectional system = Baukastenprinzip *n*
~ **type plant** = Baukasten-System-Anlage *f*, halbstationäre Anlage *f* [*bituminöse Mischanlage f*]
section at crown of arch (Brit.); section at key (or crown) (US) = Querschnitt *m* im Scheitel *m* [*Talsperre f*]
~ **iron cutter** = Profileisenschneider *m*
~ **property**, property of section = Querschnittwert *m* [*Profil n*]
~ **through crown** = Scheitelquerschnitt *m* [*Bogenbrücke f*]
~ **wire** = Formdraht *m*, Fassondraht
sector gate, drum ~, ~ sluice = Sektorschütz(e) *n*, (*f*), Sektorwehr *n*
~ **weir** = Sektor(stau)wehr *n* [*in den USA werden die Sektorwehre unter dem Oberbegriff ,,Trommelwehre" zusammengefaßt. Dies ist eine Bezeichnung nicht in Übereinstimmung mit der deutschen Auffassung, da unter ,,Trommelwehr" im Deutschen etwas anderes verstanden wird*]
sedge = Riedgras *n*; [*niederdeutsch: Segge f*]
sediment, deposit = Sinkstoff *m*, Ausfällung *f*
~, deposit = Ablagerung *f* [*als abgelagerter Stoff m*]
sedimentary cycle = Ablagerungszyklus *m*
~ **rock**, see: bedded ~
sedimentation analysis, see: ~ test
~ **basin**, settling ~, subsidence ~ = Absetzbecken *n*, Absitzbecken, Klärbecken
~ **chamber**, settling ~ = Absetzraum *m*, Klärraum
~ **curve** = Absetzkurve *f*
~ **(process)**, deposition (~) = Ablagerung *f*, Akkumulation *f*, Ablagerungsvorgang *m* (Geol.)

~ **process**, settling ~, subsidence = Absetzvorgang *m*, Absetzen *n* [*zum Trennen von leichteren und schwereren Stoffen mpl*]
~ **tank** = Klärbrunnen *m*
~ **test**, hydrometer test, hydrometer analysis, sedimentation analysis; decantation test (US) = Sedimentierversuch *m*, Absetzversuch, Sedimentationsprobe *f*, Schlämmanalyse *f*, Aräometeranalyse
~ **zone**, zone of sedimentation, deposition zone, zone of deposition = Ablagerungszone *f*
sediment-bearing = schwebstoffführend
sediment deposition = Sinkstoffablagerung *f*
~ **hydraulics** = Sedimenthydraulik *f*
~ **transport** = Sedimenttransport *m*
seed-and-grain-kippler = Schrotmühle *f*
seed bed = Saatbeet *n*
seed-beetle = Samenkäfer *m*
seed collection = Samensortiment *n*
seeded = angesät, eingesät
seeding, sowing (seed) = Ansäen *n*, Besamung *f*, Ansaat *f*, Besämung, Säen
seed-kiln = Saatdarre *f*
seed mixture = Samenmischung *f*
~ **(multiplication) farm** = Saatzuchtgut *n*
seed-pickling machine = Saatgutbeizmaschine *f*
seed trade = Samenhandel *m*
seeing distance, visibility ~, sight ~, vision ~ = Sichtweite *f*, Sichtlänge *f*, Sichtweg *m*
Seelemann-Regulus mixer [*aggregate and cement is measured by means of feed screws, giving a continuous output of concrete*] = Seelemann-Regulus-Mischer *m*
seepage [*the exudation of small quantities of water by percolation*] = Aussickerung *f*
~ **face** = Sickerfläche *f*
~ **failure** = hydraulischer Grundbruch *m*
~ **flow** = Sickerströmung *f*
~ **loss** = Sickerverlust *m*
~ **path**, path of seepage = Sickerlinie *f*
~ **pipe**, see: piezometer (~)
~ **water**, seeping ~ = Sickerwasser *n*

Seger cone, pyrometric ~, fusion ~ = Segerkegel *m*

seggar clay, saggar ~, sagger ~ = Kapselton *m*

segmental arch = Stichbogen *m*, Segmentbogen, flacher Bogen

~ **girder**, see: polygonal bowstring ~

segment(al) sewer block (US); see: hollow gauged brick (Brit.)

segmented roll, island roller = Waffelwalze *f*

segment shaped sluice, segmental sluice gate, taintor (or tainter) gate, radial gate = Bogenschütz(e) *n*, (*f*), Segmentschütz(e), Segmentverschluß *m*, Segmentwehr *n*

segregated aggregate stockpiling (or storage) = getrennte Lagerung *f* nach Korngrößen *fpl*

segregation = Entmischung *f*

~ **of ice**, see: ice formation

Seignette salt, see: Rochelle ~

seismic refraction procedure, refraction survey, seismic survey = seismisches Verfahren *n*, seismische Bodenforschung *f* nach dem Refraktionsverfahren *n*, elastisches Verfahren *n*

~ **resistance** = Widerstandsfähigkeit *f* gegen Erdbebenstöße *npl*

~ **sea waves**, see: tsunanis

seismograph = Seismograph *m*

seismographic exploration = seismische Bodenuntersuchung *f*

seismology = Seismik *f*, Seismologie *f*, Erdbebenkunde *f*

selbite (Min.), see: grey silver'

selection = Auswahl *f*

~ **of route**, route selection = Trassierung *f*, Trassenwahl *f*

selective digging [*separating two or more types of soil while digging them*] = Aushub *m* mit Bodentrennung *f*

~ **solvation** = fraktionierte Lösung *f*

selenite, sparry gypsum, specular stone, specular gypsum, gypsum spar, gypseous spar = Gipsspat *m*

Sélénitza (or **Sélinitza**) **hard asphalt** = Selenizza-Asphalt *m*

selenium cell = Selenzelle *f*

self-acting incline(d plane), see: jig haulage installation on the slope

self-actuated room control from high-speed air = Regelanlage *f* mit Selbstantrieb *m* für höhere Luftgeschwindigkeiten *fpl*

self adjusting level = Nivellierinstrument *n* mit planparalleler Platte *f*

self-aligning ball bearing = Pendelkugellager *n*

~ **(guide) idler**, see: guidler

~ **roller bearing**, spherical ~ ~ = Pendelrollenlager *n*

self-anchored suspension bridge = in sich verankerte Hängebrücke *f*

self-curing = Erhärtung *f* des Betons *m* ohne Nachbehandlung *f* durch Feuchthalten *n*

self-docking floating dock = L-förmiges Schwimmdock *n*

self-erecting = selbstmontierbar

(self-laying) track-type (industrial) tractor, see: caterpillar tractor

self-loading tractor bucket elevator, see: belt type bucket elevator loader

self-priming = selbstansaugend

self-propelled = selbstfahrbar

~ **barge**, powered ~, engined ~ = Motorlastkahn *m*

~ **carrier** = Selbstfahrwerk *n*

~ **crushing plant**, rubber-mounted crusher; pneumatic-tired crusher (US) = Auto(mobil)steinbrecher *m*

~ **excavator** = Mobilbagger *m*

~ **railcar** = Triebwagen *m*

~ **roller**, power-driven ~ = Kraftwalze *f*, Motorwalze

~ **rotary tiller** (or rotary hoe, or rotavator, or soil pulverizer) = Motorbodenfräse *f*

~ **travelling gear** = Eigenfahrwerk *n*

~ **vessel** = Motorschiff *n*

~ **vibratory tandem roller** = Vibrationstandemwalze *f* selbstfahrend, selbstfahrende Tandem-Schwing(ungs)walze (oder Tandem-Vibrationswalze)

self-supporting = selbsttragend

self unloader = Selbstentlader *m*, Selbstkipper *m*

self-widening finisher = (Straßen)Fertiger *m* mit selbstverstellbarer Arbeitsbreite *f*

semi-automatic block machine = Halbautomat *m* [*Betonsteinmaschine f*]

semi-beam, see: cantilevered beam

semi-circular arch, round ~ = Halbkreisbogen *m*, Zirkelbogen, Rundbogen, voller Bogen
semi-cloverleaf type junction = halbe Kleeblattkreuzung *f*
semi-desert = Wüstensteppe *f*
semi-diesel engine, mixed cycle ~ = Glühkopfmotor *m*, Semi-Diesel *m*
semi-flexible = halbschmiegsam
semi-fusain, vitri-fusain, semi-fusite = Halbfusit *m*
semi-girder (Brit.); see: cantilevered beam
semi-grouting (Brit.); semi-penetration treatment = Halbtränkung *f* [*Straße f*]
semi-high level bridge = Halbtauchbrücke *f*
semi-hot tarmacadam = warm verarbeitbarer Teermakadam *m*
semi-hydraulic fill dam; ~ ~ embankment = Spüleinbau-Damm *m* [*nur Spüleinbau m*]
~ lime = hydraulischer Kalk *m* [*früher: Zementkalk m*]
semi-infinite elastic solid, ~ space = elastisch-isotroper Halbraum *m*
semi-low-loader, semi-low-bed trailer, semi-low-load trailer, semi-deck trailer; semi-low-boy (trailer) (US) = Sattel-tiefladeanhänger *m*, Sattel-Tieflader *m*, Sattel-Tiefbettanhänger *m*, Sattel-Tiefladewagen *m*
semi-outdoor-type power plant = Halbfreiluft-Kraftwerk *n*
semi-parabolic girder, hog backed ~ = Halbparabelträger *m*
semi-permanent bridge = Dauerbehelfsbrücke *f*
semi-pervious = halbdurchlässig
semi-portable boiler = Lokomobilkessel *m*
semi-portal (type of pedestal) crane = Halbportalkran *m*, Halbtorkran
semi-rigid = halbstarr
~ connection [*steel framework*] = nachgiebige Eckverbindung *f* [*Stahlrahmen m*]
semi-rotary pump, vane ~, wing ~ = Flügelpumpe *f*
semi-silica brick = Halbsilikastein *m*
semi-solid = halbfest
semi-stable, normal-setting, medium-setting, medium-breaking = mittelschnellbrechend, halbstabil [*Bitumenemulsion f*]
semi-tracked vehicle = Halbkettenfahrzeug *n*
semi-trailer = Halbanhänger *m*, aufgesattelter Anhänger *m*, Auflieger *m*, Sattelschlepper-Anhänger *m*, Aufsattelanhänger *m*
~ combination = Zugmaschine *f* mit Halbanhänger *m*
~ dump wagon = Auflieger-Mulden-Erdbaufahrzeug *n*
~ type, gooseneck type = aufgesattelt [*Fahrzeug n*]
~ ~ construction = Sattelschlepperbauart *f*
~ ~ mastic asphalt boiler = Einachs-Gußasphaltkocher *m*
~ ~ supply tank = Umfülltankwagen *m*
semi-wildcat well = Suchbohrung *f* in einiger Entfernung von einer bereits bekannten Erdöllagerstätte *f*
senarmontite, Sb$_2$O$_3$ (Min.) = Senarmontit *m*
sensible horizon, see: apparent ~
sensitive balance = Feinwaage *f*
~ clay = strukturempfindlicher Ton *m*
separate sewer, see: sanitary ~
~ sluiceway structure = getrenntes Grundablaßbauwerk *n*
~ system = Trennsystem *n*, Trennkanalisation *f* [*Dränage f*]
separating = Reinigungssiebung *f*
~ funnel = Scheidetrichter *m*
separation allowance, see: living ~
~ of gases = Gastrennung *f*
~ ~ the water layer (Brit.); see: freeing of the nappe (US)
~ plant, screening ~ = Siebanlage *f*
~ structure, see: grade ~ ~
separator; see: trap (Brit.)
~, air ~, air classifier = Sichter *m*
~ [*a distance piece, usually of steel or cast-iron, bolted between the webs of parallel side-by-side steel joists to give rigidity and ensure unity of action*] = Stegverbindungsstück *n*, Verkupp(e)lung *f*
~, see: divisional island
~ [*ore separation*] = Sortierer *m*
separatory cone = Scheidekonus *m*

separatory drum = Scheidetrommel *f*
sepiolite (Min.), see: meerschaum
septarian clay = Septarienton *m*
septic tank, hydrolysing ~ = Faulraum *m*
~ **treatment plant** = Faulraumanlage *f*
serial fabrication, full scale production = Serienfertigung *f*, Reihenfertigung, Serienherstellung *f*
sericite (Min.) = Serizit *m*, Seidenglimmer *m*
~ **schist** = Serizitschiefer *m*
series, stage, system, formation = (geologische) Formation *f*
~ **firing** = Serienschüsse *mpl*, Serienzündung *f*, Reihenzündung
~ **of strata** = Schichtenreihe *f* (Geol.)
~ **(-wound) motor** = Reihenschlußmotor *m*, Hauptstrommotor
serpentine (Geol.) = Serpentin *m*
~ **asbestos** (Min.) = Serpentinasbest *m*
~ **road** = Serpentinstraße *f*
serpentinisation (Geol.) = Serpentinisierung *f*
service(able) life, working ~ = Nutzungsdauer *f*, Lebensdauer
service behavio(u)r, see: road performance
~ **facilities**, plant ~ = Betriebsanlagen *fpl*
~ **gangway** (Brit.); distributing bridge, overhead track way, construction trestle (US) = Dienstbrücke *f* [*Talsperrenbau m*]
~ **personnel** = Bedienungspersonal *n*
~ **reservoir** = Nutz- und Trinkwasserspeicherbecken *n*
~ **road** = Anliegerstraße *f*
~ **station**, see: filling point
~ **(time)**, life, service life = Liegezeit *f* [*Straßendecke f*]
~ **tree**, sorb = Elsbeerbaum *m*
~ **trench** = Leitungsgraben *m*
~ **vehicle** = Dienstfahrzeug *n*
~ **water**, tap ~ = Leitungswasser *n*, Brauchwasser
~ **weight**, working ~, operating ~ = Dienstgewicht *n*, Betriebsgewicht
servo-power unit = Servokraft-Zusatzvorrichtung *f*
servo system control = Servobetätigung *f*
sessile-fruited oak, see: chestnut ~
to set, to hydrate = abbinden [*Zement m*]

set; setting (Brit.) = Abbinden *n*, Abbindung *f* [*Zement m*]
~ (Brit.); see: finish coat (US)
~ **of sieves**, see: nest of ~
to set out, see: to peg out
sett, paving ~ = Pflasterstein *m*
~ **burning**, see: heat treatment of setts
~ **feeder**, sett jointer = Fugenkelle *f* [*Pflasterfuge f*]
~ **grease** = Wagenfett *n*, Wagenschmiere *f*
setting = Richten *n* [*Säge f*]
~ (Brit.); see: set
~ **behaviour** (Brit.); set ~ = Abbindeprüfgerät *n*, Hydra(ta)tionsprüfgerät, Erstarrungsprüfgerät
~ **coat** (Brit.); see: finish coat (US)
~ **jumbo track and wall plate** [*tunnel(l)ing*] = Verlegen *n* der Schienen *fpl* des Bohrwagens *m* [*Tunnelbau m*]
setting-out of clothoid transition curves = Abstecken *n* von Übergangsbögen *mpl* in Klothoidenform *f*
~ **peg (or stake)** = Absteckpflock *m*, Absteckpfahl *m*
setting point = Stockpunkt *m* [*Kälteverhalten v von Dieselkraftstoff m*]
~ ~ = Erstarrungspunkt *m* [*Paraffin n*]
~ **power** (Brit.); set ~ = Abbindekraft *f*, Hydra(ta)tionskraft, Erstarrungskraft
~ **shrinkage** (Brit.); set ~ = Abbindungs-Schrumpfung *f*, Erstarrungs-Schrumpfung, Hydra(ta)tionsschrumpfung
~ **temperature**, curing ~ = Abbindetemperatur *f*, Hydra(ta)tionstemperatur, Erstarrungstemperatur
~ **tester** (Brit.); set ~ = Abbindeprüfgerät *n*, Hydra(ta)tionsprüfgerät, Erstarrungsprüfgerät
~ **value** (Brit.); set ~ = Abbindewert *m*, Hydra(ta)tionswert, Erstarrungswert
setting-time controlling agent (Brit.); set-time ~ ~ = Abbinde(zeit)regler *m*, Hydra(ta)tions(zeit)regler, Erstarrungs(zeit)regler
sett joint filler (or sealing compound) = Pflasterkitt *m*, Pflastervergußmasse *f*
settleable solid = absetzbarer Stoff *m*
settled tar = Absatzteer *m*, Absetzteer

settlement, ground ~ [*downward movements of the soil or the structure which it supports due to the consolidation of the subsoil*] = Setzung *f*, Senkung *f* [*die Bezeichnung Setzung wird in der Praxis ganz allgemein für alle Senkungserscheinungen an Bauwerken wie an Baugruben angewendet, nur im Bergbau ist es üblich von Senkungen zu sprechen*]
~ analysis = Setzungsanalyse *f*
~ curve = Setzungskurve *f*
~ due to thawing out of frost = Tausenkung *f* [*Straßendecke f*]
~ joint with interrupted waterproofing membrane and looped bridging strip = Setzungsfuge *f* mit Dichtungsunterbrechung *f* und Dehnungswelle *f*
~ measurement = Setzungsmessung *f*
~ observation = Setzungsbeobachtung *f*
~ plate = Setzungsplatte *f*, Belastungsplatte, Lastplatte
~ relative to structures = Setzung *f* [*senkrechte Verlagerung eines Punktes eines Körpers, eines Bauwerkes. Senkungserscheinung am Bauwerk*]
to settle out = abschlämmen, (sich) absetzen, ausschlämmen
settling basin, see: sedimentation ~
~ chamber, see: sedimentation ~
~ glass = Absetzglas *n*
~ pond, ~ lagoon = Klärteich *m*, Auflandungsteich
~ process, see: sedimentation ~
~ velocity = Sinkgeschwindigkeit *f* [*Teilchen npl in einer Flüssigkeit f*]
sett-making = Pflastersteinherstellung *f*
to sett pave = pflastern
sett paved road = Pflasterstraße *f*
~ paving, stone-sett ~; [*in Scotland: causeway*] = Pflasterdecke *f*, (Stein-)Pflaster *n*, Pflasterung *f*
~ roughening machine = Pflasteraufrauhgerät *n*
sewage, foul water, liquid waste = Abwasser *n*, Abwässer *f*
~ batch, see: ~ dose
~ chlorination = Abwasserchlorung *f*
~ (clarification) plant, ~ treatment ~, ~ works = Kläranlage *f*, Abwasserreinigungsanlage

~ diffusion = Abwasserverteilung *f*
~ disposal = Abwasserbeseitigung *f*
~ ~ works = Abwasserbeseitigungsanlage *f*
~ dose, ~ batch = Beschickungsmenge *f*, Abwasserstoß *m*
~ engineering = Abwassertechnik *f*, Kanalisationstechnik
~ farm = Rieselgut *n*
~ flow = Abwasseranfall *m*
~ fly = Schmetterlingsfliege *f*, Tropfkörperfliege
~ fungus = Abwasserpilz *m*
~ gas, sludge ~, digestor ~ = Faulgas *n*
~ (handling) pump = Abwasserpumpe *f*
~ irrigation, land treatment = Bewässerung *f* mit Abwasser *n*
~ pipe, sewer pipe = Kanal(isations)rohr *n*, Abwasserrohr
~ ~ line, sewer line, disposal line, foul water line = Abwasserrohrleitung *f*
~ plant, ~ treatment ~, ~ works, ~ clarification ~ = Kläranlage *f*, Abwasserreinigungsanlage
~ pollution of a river, (river) pollution = Abwasserlast *f* [*Fluß m*]
~ pump, ~ handling ~ ~ = Abwasserpumpe *f*
~ purification, see: ~ treatment
~ sedimentation plant = Abwasserkläranlage *f*
(~) sludge = Abwasserschlamm *m*, Klärschlamm
~ treatment, ~ purification = Abwasserbehandlung *f*, Abwasserreinigung
~ ~ bed, see: sludge bed
~ works, see: ~ plant
sewer = Abwasserkanal *m*
sewerage, see: ~ works
*sewerage and sewage disposal = Abwasserwesen *n*
~ charge, sewer rental = Kanal(isations)gebühr *f*
~ works, sewerage = Abwasseranlagen *fpl*
sewer bottom = Abwasserkanalsohle *f*
~ brick = Kanalstein *m*
~ cleaning = Kanalreinigung *f*
~ clinker (brick) = Kanalklinker(ziegel) *m*, Kanalklinkerstein *m*
~ flushing = Kanalspülung *f*

sewer gas = Kanalgas n
~ interchange = Zusammenflußanlage f der Abwasserkanäle mpl
~ joint(ing) compound, see: joint cement
~ line, sewage pipe ~, disposal ~ = Abwasserrohrleitung f
~ liner plate = Kanalbekleidungsplatte f
sewer-man = Kanalarbeiter m
sewer pipe, sewage ~ = Kanal(isations)rohr n, Abwasserohr
~ rental, sewerage charge = Kanal(isations)gebühr f
~ trench = Kanal(isations)graben m
~ tunnel = Kanal(isations)tunnel m, Abwasserkanaltunnel
sgraffito, scratch work = Sgraffito m
shackle = Schäkel f
shade = (Farb)Tönung f
shaft = Schacht m
~ = Welle f
~ = Schaft m
~, see: pier
shaft-and-tunnel spillway, morning-glory ~, drop-inlet ~ = Ringüberlauf m
shaft cable = Förderschachtseil n
~ construction = Schachtbau m
~ cylinder = Schachtrohr n
~ for the driving mechanism = Welle f zum Fahrwerk n [Bagger m]
~ ~ swing gear = Welle f zum Schwenkwerk n [Bagger m]
~ hoist = Schachtwinde f
shafting method = Schachtbauweise f
shaft lime kiln = Kalkschachtofen m
~ navigation lock, ~ inland ~ = Schacht-Binnenschiffahrtschleuse f, Schachtschleuse
~ of a column = Säulenschaft m
~ packing = Wellendichtung f
shaft-sinking, mine sinking = Schachtabteufung f
~ pump, mine pump = Abteufpumpe f, Senkpumpe, Bohrlochpumpe
shafts = Deichselgabel f, Doppeldeichsel f
shake [timber] = Kluft f [Holz n]
shaker conveyor = Schüttelrinne f, Förderschwinge f, Schwingförderrinne f, Schwingrinnenförderer m
~ table, see: shaking ~
shaking = Rütteln n

~ (bar) grizzly, ~ bar screen, ~ screen of bars = Schüttelstangen(transport)rost m, Schüttel-Stangenaufgeber m
~ feeder = Schüttelspeiser m
~ grate-type cooler = Schüttelrostkühler m
~ grizzly, see: ~ bar grizzly
~ materials handling equipment = Rüttelgeräte npl zur Materialförderung f
~ screen, mechanical ~ ~ = Schrägwurfsieb n
~ ~ of bars, see: ~ (bar) grizzly
~ table, shaker ~ = Rütteltisch m, Tischrüttler m
shale, clay-shale = Schieferton m, Schieferletten f
~ grease = Rückstand m aus der Leuchtschieferdestillation f
~ oil, see: crude shale ~
~ ~ coker distillate = Verkokungsdestillat n aus Ölschiefer m
~ tar = Bitumenschieferteer m, (Öl-)Schieferteer
shallow = seicht, untief
~ arch = Blendbogen m, Schildbogen
~ cut(ting) = flacher Einschnitt m
~ cut digging, surface ~, surface excavation, shallow grading = Flachbaggern n, Flachbaggerung f
~ foundation = Flachgründung f, Flachfundation f
~ grading, see: ~ cut digging
~ ground water = Obergrundwasser n
~ moor, see: lowland ~
~ sampler, ~ sample taker = Flach-Probe(ent)nahmeapparat m
~ sampling = Flachschürfbohrung f
~ water = Wattenmeer n
~ well = Flachbrunnen m
shaly sandstone = Schiefersandstein m
to shape = abgleichen [z. B. Zementverfestigung f]
shaped face, profiled ~ (Brit.); spillway face, profiled face (US) = Überfallrücken m
shape of particle = Korngestalt f
~ ~ section = Querschnittgestaltung f
shaping, trimming, truing [deprecated: regulating] = Profilieren n [Erdbau m]
~ = Formgebung f

shaping — sheet piling

shaping = Abgleichungsarbeit *f* [*Bodenverfestigung f*]

sharp, angular = scharfkantig [*Sand m*]

~ edged plate weir = scharfkantiges Plattenwehr *n*

sharpening tool = Schärfwerkzeug *n*

shattered clay = zermürbter Ton *m*

shatter-point = Starrpunkt *m* [*Bitumen n*]

shear = Vertikalschub *m* [*wenn „thrust" und „shear" im gleichen Satz vorkommen, so ist „thrust" = Horizontalschubkomponente und „shear" = Vertikalschubkomponente; sonst sind beide gleichartig*]

~, see: shear(ing) (action)

to ~ = abscheren

shear cell = Boden-Scherspannungsmeßdose *f*

~ connector = Schubdübel *m*

~ (or wire) cutter = Drahtschere *f*

~ failure, base **~**, breach, subsidence = Grundbruch *m*

shear(ing) (action) = Abscherung *f*, Abscheren *n*

shearing force = Scherkraft *f*

~ ~ = Querkraft *f*

~ load = Scherbelastung *f*

shear(ing) resistance = Scherwiderstand *m*, Schubwiderstand *m*

~ section, ~ area = Scherfläche *f* [*Niet m*]

~ strain = Scherverformung *f*, Scherdehnung *f*

~ strength = Scherfestigkeit *f*, Schubfestigkeit [*diejenige Kraft, die nötig ist, um die Reibungs-, den Gefüge- und den Haftwiderstand eines Gesteins zu überwinden*]

~ stress = Scherspannung *f*, Scherbeanspruchung *f*, Schubspannung

~ test = Scherversuch *m*

shear-legs, sheer-legs, sheers, tripod = (Montage)Dreibaum *m*

shear pin = Abscherbolzen *m*, Abscherstift *m*

shears derrick (crane); ~ derricking jib ~ (Brit.); **~ ~ boom ~** (US) = Scheren-Derrick-Kran *m* ohne Ausleger *m*

shear slide; see: slip

~ structure = Druckspannungstextur *f* (Geol.)

shears vice = Scherkluppe *f*

sheath, insert = Hülse *f*

sheathing hammer = Ramme *f* für Holz-Kanaldielen *fpl*

sheave = Seilscheibe *f*, Seilrolle *f*

to shed [*water*] = ablaufen lassen [*Wasser n von einer Fläche f*]

shed = Bude *f*, Schuppen *m*

sheep grazing lands = Schafweidegründe *mpl*

sheep(s)-foot roller, tamper **~**, sheep(s)-foot tamping **~**, sheep's-foot **~** = Schaffußwalze *f*

sheers, see: shear-legs

sheet asphalt [*is a plant mix of asphalt cement with graded sand passing the No. 10 sieve and mineral filler*] = Sandasphalt *m*

~ bend = Weberknoten *m*

~ brass = Messingblech *n*

~ buckling = Blechbeulung *f*

~ building materials = Bauplatten *fpl*

~ copper = Kupferblech *n*

~ ga(u)ge = Blechlehre *f*

sheeting, lining = Verkleidung *f*, Auskleidung [*Baugrube f*]

~, see: sheet piling

~ driver = Spundwandramme *f*

sheet iron, sheet metal, metal sheet = (Tafel)Blech *n*, Eisenblech *n*

~ lightning = Flächenblitz *m*

~ metal can = Blechkanister *m*

~ ~ conduit = Blechrohrleitung *f*

~ ~ folding machine, plate bending machine = Blechbiegemaschine *f*

~ ~ straightening machine, see: plate **~ ~**

~ ~ water stop = Blechdichtungsstreifen *m*

sheet mica (Min.), see: book mica

~ of water, overflowing **~ ~ ~** = Überfallstrahl *m*

sheetpile = Spundbohle *f*

~ cell = Spundwandzelle *f*

~ driving = Spundwandrammung *f*

~ retaining wall, sheet piling cofferdam; pile dike (US) = Spundwandbauwerk *n*, Spundwandfang(e)damm *m*

~ wall encastred at the anchorage = fest verankerte Spundwand *f*

sheet piling, sheet pile bulkhead, sheeting, sheet-pile wall, wall of sheet piling, sheet = Spundwand *f*

**sheet piling cofferdam, **sheet-pile retaining wall = Spundwandfang(e)damm *m*, Spundwandbauwerk *n*
**sheetrock **(US) = große Gipsbauplatte *f* in den USA zwischen zwei Lagen *fpl* eines Spezialpapiers *n*
**sheets **= Feinblech *n*
**sheet steel **= Stahlblech *n*
**shelf, **see: overburden
**~ ice **= Schelfeis *n*
**shell **= Randzone *f* [*Erddamm m*]
**shellac **= Schellack *m*
**shell auger **= Schappenbohrer *m*
**~ dam, **thin arch **~ **= Schalen(stau)mauer *f*
**~ face **= Manteloberfläche *f* [*Brechwalze f*]
**~-like, **see: conchoidal
**shell limestone, **see: coquina
**~ marl **= Muschelmergel *m*
**~ (of the building), **see: carcase
**~ rock **= Muschelgestein *n*
**~ roof **= Schalendach *n*, Schalenkuppel *f*
**~ structure **= Schalenbauwerk *n*
**~ with valve **= Kolbenbüchse *f*, Kiespumpe *f*
**shell(y) limestone, **see: coquina
**~ sandstone, **see: beach rock
**shelter **= Schutzraum *m*
**shelving beach **= abfallender Strand *m*
**~ shore **= abfallendes Ufer *n*
**shewing fescue **= horstbildender Rotschwingel *m*
**shide, **shingle (Brit.); shindle (US) = Dachschindel *f*
shield, **see: tunnel **~
**~-driven **= im Schildvortrieb *m* hergestellt
**shielding **= Abschirmung *f*
**~ facility **= Strahlungsschutzanlage *f* [*Reaktor m*]
**shield tunnel(l)ing **= Schildbauweise *f*, Schildvortrieb *m*
**shift **= (Arbeits)Schicht *f*
**shifting **= (An)Schiftung *f*, Lotschiftung *f*
**~ bed **= bewegliche Flußsohle *f*
**shim **= Zwischenlegscheibe *f*, Einlage *f*
**~ **= Beilageeisen *n* [*Walzenbrecher m*]
**shin, **see: fish-plate

**shingle, **shide (Brit.); shindle (US) = Dachschindel *f*
**~, beach ~, **seashore-gravel [*gravel without fines*] = Küstenkies *m*
**~, **see: detritus
**~ beach **= Blockstrand *m*
**shining soot **= Glanzruß *m*
**shiny clay, **illite, hydrous mica = Glimmerton *m*
**shipbuilding crane **= Werftkran *m*
**~ yard, **see: dockyard
**ship canal **= Seekanal *m*
**~ chain **= Schiffskette *f*
**~ channel, **see: fairway
**shipment, **delivery = Anlieferung *f*, Anfuhr *f*
**shipper drum **= Verschiebetrommel *f* [*Hochlöffel(bagger) m*]
**~ shaft **= Verschiebewelle *f* [*Hochlöffel(bagger) m*]
**shipping, **shipment = Versand *m*
**~ box **= Versandkiste *f*
**~ lane **= Zufahrtrinne *f* [*z. B. zu einem Dock n*]
**~ weight **= Versandgewicht *n*
**ship's log **= Schiffslog *n*
**ship winch **= Schiffswinde *f*
**shire **= Gummischnur *f*
**shoal **= Untiefe *f*
**~, **see: sand-bank
**shock **= Erschütterung *f*
**~ absorber **= Stoßdämpfer *m*
~ bending test, **see: blow **~ ~
**~ loading **= Stoßbelastung *f*
**shoe **= Lagerstuhl *m* mit Bolzen *m*
**~, shoe post and crumber **[*wheel ditcher*] = Glättvorrichtung *f*, Grabenglätter *m*
**~ brake **= Backenbremse *f*, Klotzbremse *f*
**shoofly **(US), see: bypass
**shoot, **tip = Kippe *f* [*Erdbau m*]
**~ **(Brit.); chute = Rutsche *f*, Rutschbahn *f*
*****shooting, **see: blasting
**~ plane **= Abschräghobel *m*
**shop assembly **= Werkstattmontage *f*
**~ coat **= Werkstattanstrich *m*
**~ connection **= Werkstattstoß *m* [*Stahlbau m*]
**~ experiment **= Werksversuch *m*
**~ manufacture, **workshop **~ **= Werkstattfertigung *f*

shopping center — shovel cable

shopping center (US); ~ **centre** (Brit.) = Einkaufsviertel n

~ **street**, see: retail business ~

shop rivet = Werkstattniet m

~ **talk** = Fachsimpelei f

shore, beach = Strand m, Gestade n

~ **asphalt**, see: land ~

~**-based radar unit** = Küstenfunkmeßgerät n

shore bulkhead = Fang(e)damm m am Ufer n

~ **current (or drift)**, littoral ~ (~ ~), coastal ~ (~ ~) = Küstenströmung f

~ **dune** [*deposition by sea waves*] = Wellendüne f

~**-face terrace**, see: wave-built ~ ~

shore jetty (US); see: beach groyne (Brit.)

~ **protection**, see: coast defence work

~ **radar installation** = Küstenfunkmeßanlage f

~ **structure** = Küstenbauwerk n, Küstenanlage f

~ **structures** = Küstenbauten f

~ **wind**, see: sea breeze

shoring = Abstützung f [*Gebäude n*]

~ **frame** = Abstützungsgestell n, Abstützungsrahmen m

~ **strut**, trench shore, trench strut (Brit.); trench brace (US) = Kanalstrebe f, Sprieße f, Grabensteife f, Kanalspindel f

short (US); short circuit = Kurzschluß m

shortage = Verknappung f

~ **in weight**, short weight = fehlendes Gewicht n, Mindergewicht

short boom (US); ~ **jib** (Brit.) = Kurzausleger m

to short-circuit = kurzschließen

short circuited, shorted = kurzgeschlossen

short-circuiting switch = Kurzschlußschalter m

short course = Kurzlehrgang m, Schnellkursus m

short-cut test procedure = abgekürztes Prüfverfahren n

short-haul traffic = Güternahverkehr m

short head type (Symons) cone crusher = Symons-Kegelgranulator m

~ **jib** (Brit.); ~ **boom** (US) = Kurzausleger m

~ **link chain** = kurzgliedrige Kette f ohne Steg m

short(-period) delay (electric) (blasting) cap = Schnellzeit(spreng)zünder m

short range aggregate concrete = Einkornbeton m

~ **scarf** = kurzes Hakenblatt n

~ **side of a shaft** = Schachtstoß m

short-term flood prediction = kurzfristige Hochwasservorhersage f

~ **load(ing)** = kurzfristige Lastaufbringung f, ~ Lastenaufbringung

short tube mill with centrifugal air separator = Mahltrocknungsanlage f

~ **turning radius** = großer Einschlag m [*Lenkradsteuerung f*]

~ **weight**, shortage in weight = Mindergewicht n, fehlendes Gewicht

shot = (Spreng)Schuß m

~ = Fettstoß m [*beim Abschmieren n*]

~ **bit**, chilled ~ = Schrot(bohr)krone f

~ ~ **cutter**, see: ~ coring machine

~ **coring machine**, ~ (core) drill, ~ bit cutter = Schrotkernbohrgerät n, Schrotkernbohrmaschine f

shotcrete, see: air-placed concrete

shot drill, see: ~ coring machine

~ ~ **boring**, ~ **drilling** = Schrotbohrung f, Schrotbohren n

~ **firing cable** = Zündkabel n, Schließkabel

shot-hole, blasthole, bore-hole = Spreng(bohr)loch n, Schußloch

shot peening = Kugelstrahlen n

~ **welding** = Schußschweißung f

shoulder, road ~, highway ~, hardened ~, parking strip = Standspur f, Randstreifen m, Parkstreifen m

~, **haunch**, quarter, flank (Brit.) = das äußere Viertel der Fahrbahnbreite f

shouldered tenon = Achselzapfen m, geächselter Zapfen

shoulder lane = Fahrspur f an der Standspur f, ~ am Randstreifen m

~ **pavement** = Standspurdecke f

~ **slope** = Standspurböschung f

shovel; see: crane navvy (Brit.)

~, see: bucket

to shovel = schaufeln

shovel cable = Baggerseil n

shovel control station — side-boom crawler tractor

shovel control station = Baggerbedienungsstand m

shovel-crane, see: crane-excavator

shovel (dipper), see: bucket

~ dozer, see: loading shovel

~ ~ attachment = Bulldozer-Ladeschaufeleinrichtung f

~ engine = Baggermotor m

shovel(l)er = Baggerführer m

shovel loader mounted on industrial wheel type tractor, industrial loader = Industrie-Lader m, Fabriklader

~ motor = Baggerelektromotor m

~ revolving unit = drehbarer Oberteil m, Aufsatzteil [*Autobagger m*]

~ track = Bagger(gleis)kette f, Baggerraupe f

~ type excavator; see: navvy ~ (Brit.)

shoving = Schieben n [*Walze f*]

showcase = Vitrine f

shower of hail = Hagelschauer m

~ ~ rain = Regenschauer m

showers = Abbrausevorrichtung f

shower water = Abbrausewasser n

shredder = Schnitzler m, Schneidewalze f

shrinkage, shrinking = Schwinden n, Schwindung f

~ cavity = Lunker m

~ crack = Schwindriß m, Schwundriß

~ in firing = Brennschwindung f

~ joint, see: concealed (concrete) ~

~ limit = Schwindgrenze f

~ reinforcement = Schwindbewehrung f, Schwindarmierung

~ stope = Schrumpferzkammer f

~ stoping = Magazinbau m [*Erzgrube f*]

shrink-mixing, partial mixing = Naßmischen n während der Fahrt f [*Transportbeton m*]

shunt brake = Nebenschlußbremse f

~ coil = Abzweigspule, Nebenschlußspule

~ current = Nebenschlußstrom m, Zweigstrom

shunting loco(motive), rail shunter, switch(ing) loco(motive), pony engine = Rangierlok(omotive) f, Verschiebelok(omotive)

~ station, see: marshalling yard

~ tractor = Rangierschlepper m, Verschiebetraktor m

~ vehicle, see: marshalling ~

shunt switch = Umgehungsschalter m

~ track, shunting ~, arranging ~ = Rangiergleis n, Verschiebegleis

~ water meter = Partialwassermesser m

~(-wound) motor = Nebenschlußmotor m

shutdown = Stillegung f

shut off cock = Absperrhahn m, Abstellhahn

~-~ unit = Abschlußorgan n, Absperrverschluß m, Absperrorgan

~-~ valve, closing ~ = Absperrventil n

shutter door = Jalousietür f

shuttering = Tafelschalung f

~ board = Schaltbrett n

~ nail = Schalnagel m

~ panel, form ~ = Schal(ungs)tafel f, Formplatte f

~ plan, shutter ~ = (Ein)Schalungsplan m

~ wrought (or planed) on one face = einseitig gehobelte Schalung f

shutter weir = Klappen(stau)wehr n

shuttle car = Pendelwagen m

(~) dumper, see: dumper

~ haul(age) = Pendeltransport m [*z. B. zwischen Bagger und Kippe*]

~ hauler = Pendeltransportgerät n

~ (service) = Pendelbetrieb m

~ traffic = Pendelverkehr m

~ train = Pendelzug m

~ type magneto = Magnetzünder m mit umlaufendem Niederspannungsanker m

siccative, drying oil = Sikkativ n

~, fast drying = schnelltrocknend

~ varnish = Trockenfirnis m

sick leave = Krankenurlaub m

sickle pump, see: crescent ~

~-shaped trussed arch = Fachwerksichelbogen m

side = Seite f

~ ~ = Wand(ung) f [*Tunnelbau m*]

~ aisle, low ~ = Seitenschiff n

~ bend test = Faltversuch m über die Seitenfläche [*Schweiz: Querfaltversuch*]

side-boom crawler tractor = (Gleis)Kettenschlepper m mit Seitenausleger m

side pipe-laying attachment = Seitenausleger-Zusatzvorrichtung f für Rohrverlegungen fpl
side borrow = Seitenentnahme f
~ bow = seitlicher Stromabnehmer m, Seitenbügel m
side-car = Beiwagen m
side-casting = Seitenablage f
(side-)channel (type) spillway = Hochwasserentlastungsanlage f vom Stauwerk n getrennt
side clearance = Seitenspielraum m
~ cut(ting) [*deprecated: side long cut*] = Seiteneinschnitt m
~ delivery auger = Seitenräumschnecke f
~ ditch = Seitengraben m
sidedozer, see: roadbuilder
side drift, see: adit (level)
~ dump bucket = Seitenentleerungsschaufel f [*Frontlader m*]
~ ~ car = Seitenkippwaggon m
~ ~ discharge = Seitenentleerung f
~ ~ loader = Seitenkipper-Frontlader m
~ ~ trailer, side-tipping dump trailer = Seitenkipper-Anhänger m, Seitenentleerungsanhänger
~ elevation = Seitenaufriß m
~ fill = Seitenanböschung f, Seitenanschüttung, Seitenanfüllung
~ force, lateral ~ = Seitenkraft f
*****side-form**, (street) form, (concrete) road form, road-airport form, track form; paving form (US) = (Beton-)Schalungsschiene f, Seitenschalung f, Straßenbauschalung f
~ ~ vibrator = Seitenschalungsinnenrüttler m
~ friction, see: skin ~
(side-)hill road = Hangstraße f
sidehill seepage = Hangsickerung f
side-lift truck = Seitenhubstapler m
side long cut [*deprecated*]; see: side cut(ting)
side-of-pavement line = Leitlinie f am Fahrbahnrand
side path, see: drift ~
~ plate = Innenflanschlasche f
~ plough (Brit.)/**plow** (US), see: blade-type snow plough (Brit.)/plow (US)
~ rail, see: check ~

siderite (Min.), see: chalybite
side road, see: minor road
~ shift motor [*motor grader*] = Hydraulikmotor m für Seitenbewegung f des Drehkranzes m
~ shoe = Klemmbacke f [*Klemmgriff-Lastenträger m*]
~ slope = Seitenböschung f
side-span [*bridge*] = Seitenöffnung f
side sub-drain = Längs(tiefen)sicker m
~ sway, see: lurching
~ tenon = Seitenzapfen m
~ thrust, see: lateral shear
~-tipping dump trailer, see: side-dump trailer
side tipping wagon, see: steel tip ~
~ tippler = Seitenkipper m [*Waggonkipper m*]
~ track, siding = Nebengleis n
sidewalk (US); see: footpath (Brit.)
~ bracket = Fußwegkonsole f
~ railings = Fußweggeländer n
~ roller (US); see: footpath ~ (Brit.)
side wall = Seitenwand f
sideway force coefficient = Seitenführungskraftbeiwert m
side weir = Streichwehr n
siding, side track = Nebengleis n
sieve, (square) (mesh) ~ = Maschensieb n, Quadrat(loch)sieb n
~ analysis, grading ~, test for ~ ~, test for grading, sieve analysis test, grain size analysis, particle size analysis = Prüfen n der Kornzusammensetzung f durch Siebversuch m, Siebprobe f
~ opening, see: aperture size
~ set, see: nest of sieves
~ shaker, see: (mechanical) ~ ~
*****sieving extractor** = Siebextraktionsapparat m
~ test = Siebprüfung f
sight distance, see: seeing ~
~ ~ in plan = Grundriß-Sichtweite f [*Straße f*]
~ ~ in profile = Längsschnitt-Sichtweite f [*Straße f*]
~ ga(u)ge = Wasseruhr f [*Betonmischer m*]
~ rail, batter board = Visiergerüst n, Schnurgerüst
~ rule, see: alidade

sighting — silting up

sighting, boning(-in) = (Ein)Visieren *n*
sightseer = Rundfahrtwagen *m*
Sigma prestressing steel = Sigma-Spannstahl *m*
signal control, traffic ~ ~ = Verkehrssignal-Steuerung *f*, Signalreg(e)lung *f*, Signalsteuerung *f*, Signalisierung *f*, Lichtsignalsteuerung
signalized street intersection, signal-controlled intersection = höhengleiche (oder niveauebene) Straßenkreuzung *f* mit Lichtzeichenreg(e)lung *f*, signalgesteuerter Knoten *m*
signal man, flagman = Warnposten *m*, Winkerposten [*Straße f*]
signing, see: provision of road signs
signpost [*deprecated*], see: direction post
signposting, see: provision of road signs
silencer (Brit.); (exhaust) muffler = Auspufftopf *m*, Schalldämpfer *m*
silent chain = geräuschlose Kette *f*
Silesian bond = schlesischer Verband *m*
~ **grey marble** = schlesischer grauer Marmor *m*
silica, dioxide of silicon, silicon dioxide, SiO_2 = Siliziumdioxyd *n*
~ **breccia** = Kieselbreccie *f* [*dieser Ausdruck sollte nicht mehr verwendet werden*]; Kieselbrekzie *f*
~ **brick,** acid firebrick; gannister ~ (Brit.); ganister ~ (US) = Quarzkalkziegel *m*, Silikastein *m*, Quarzitstein; [*früher: Dinasstein*]
~ **cement** [*rock*] = Kieselsubstanz *f*
~ **gel** = Kieselsäuregel *n*, Kieselgallerte *f*
~ **sand,** grit = Kristallquarzsand *m*
~ **sandstone** = Quarz-Sandstein *m*
silicate = Kieselsalz *n*
silicated water-bound surfacing, silicated road crust = Wasserglasdecke *f*, Silikatdecke, Silikatmakadam *m*
silicate of cotton, see: slag wool
~ ~ **lime** = kieselsaurer Kalk *m*
~ ~ **magnesium,** magnesium silicate = Magnesiumsilikat *n*
silicating (Brit.); see: silicifying (US)
siliceous = kieselsäurereich
~ **calamine,** willemite (Min.) = Kieselzink(erz) *n*, Zinkglas(erz) *n*, Kieselgalmei *m*

~ **earth,** see: hydrous silicate of aluminium
~ **limestone** = Kieselkalk(stein) *m*, kieseliger Kalkstein *m*
~ **matrix (or cement)** (Geol.) = kieseliges Bindemittel *n*
~ **melt** = Quarzschmelze *f*
~ **oolite gravels** (Geol.) = Kieselschotter *m*
~ **sinter,** geyserite = Kieselsinter *m*
~ **sponge** = Kieselschwamm *m*
silicic = kieselsauer
~ **acid** = Kieselsäure *f*
silicon carbide, see: carbide of silicon
~ **chloride** = Kieselchlorid *n*
~ **dioxide,** see: silica
silicification (Geol.) = Silifizierung *f*, Einkieselung
silicifying (US); silicating, treatment with silicate (Brit.) = Verkieseln *n*
silico tungstic acid test = Kiesel-Wolframsäure-Probe *f* [*Nachweisung f von Stickstoffbasen fpl*]
sill, ground ~ = Grundschwelle *f*, Sohlschwelle, Stauschwelle, Bodenschwelle, Unterschwelle; [*niederdeutsch: Süll m,n*]
~ (Geol.) = Lagergang *m*
~, window = Fensterbank *f*
sillimanite (Min.), see: fibrolite
~ **brick** = Sillimanitstein *m*, Mullitstein *m*
sills = Lagengesteine *npl*
silo, silo warehouse = Schachtspeicher *m*, (Vorrats)Silo, Lagersilo *n*, Silospeicher *m*
~ **compartment,** ~ **hopper** = Silozelle *f*, Speicherzelle *f*, Silotrichter *m*
~ **formwork** = Siloschalung *f*
~ **warehouse,** see: silo
silt, rock flour = Schluff *m* [*feinster Staubsand m*]
siltation (Brit.); see: mud-silting
silt basin = Verlandebecken *n*
~ **content test for fine aggregate,** test for silt = Probe *f* auf Reinheit *f*, Absetzprobe *f* [*Betonzuschlag m*]
~ **deposition** = Schluffablagerung *f*
~ **fraction** = Schluffkörnung *f*, Schluffanteil *m*
silting up, see: accreation through alluvium

silt injection method = Schluffeinpreßverfahren *n*
~ load = Schwebstofffracht *f*
siltstone = verfestigter Schluffmergel *m*
silver amalgam (Min.) = Silberamalgam *m*
~ cedar, mount Atlas cedar of Algeria = Atlaszeder *f*, Silberzeder *f*
~ chloride = Chlorsilber *n*
~ frost = Eisglätte *f*
~ glance (Min.), see: argentite
~ selenite (Min.) = Selensilber *n*
~ solder = Silberlot *n*
~ sulphate = Silbervitriol *n*
similarity of types = Modellähnlichkeit *f*
simoom, see: sandstorm
simple beam, simply-supported ~ = einfacher Träger *m* auf zwei Stützen *fpl*
~ flexure = reine Biegung *f*
~ shear, see: pure ~
~ span road (or highway) bridge = Einfeld-Straßenbrücke *f*
~ stress = einachsige Spannung *f*
~ truss = einfaches Sprengwerk *n*
simplex pump = Simplexpumpe *f*
simplified brick construction method [*patented 1934*] = SBC-System *n*
~ (or abridged) trial-load method = einfaches (oder einschnittiges) Lastaufteilungsverfahren *n*
simply supported = frei aufliegend
simulated marble = imitierter Marmor *m*
simultaneous earthquake = Auslösungsbeben *m*
single acting = einfachwirkend
single-axle trailer = Einachs-Anhänger *m*
~ ~ mixer = (luftbereifter) Einachs-(Schnell)mischer *m*, Autoanhänger-Einachs-Mischer *m*
~ travel(l)ing gear, ~ undercarriage = Einachsfahrwerk *n*
~ unit, two-wheel(ed) unit = Einachser *m*
single-bucket excavator = Ein-Gefäßtrockenbagger *m*
single-carriageway motor road = Autobahn *f* ohne Mittelstreifen *m*
single-centred compound curve = einseitiger Korbbogen *m*
single-chain digging grab = Ein-Ketten-Baggerkorb *m*

~ grab excavator = Ein-Ketten-Greifbagger *m*
~ unloading (grab) bucket = Einzelketten-Entladegreifer *m*
single-coat asphalt = einlagiger Bitumenteppich *m*
single compartment (grinding) mill = Einkammerrohr(mahl)mühle *f*
~ crawler unit = Ein-Kettenraupe(nfahrwerk) *f*, (*n*)
~ cylinder multitubular boiler = einfacher Heizröhrenkessel *m*
~ deck screen = Eindecker *m*, Einstufensieb *n*
~ diesel engine crane = Ein-Motor-Kran *m* mit Dieselantrieb *m*
single-drum rope winch = Eintrommelseilwinde *f*
~ (type) (concrete) paver = Eintrommelstraßen(beton)mischer *m*
single-family house = Einfamilienhaus *n*
single-flanged wheel = Einfach-Spurkranzrad *n*
single-flash distillation = Ein-Stufen-Destillation *f*
single impeller impact breaker = Einwalzen-Prallbrecher *m*, Prallbrecher mit einer Schlagwalze *f*
~ incentive bonus scheme = Einzelprämiensystem *n*
~ lacing = einfache Vergitterung *f* [*Stütze f*]
~ lap joint = einschnittige Verbindung *f* [*Stahlbau m*]
~ leaf (sluice) gate = Eintafelschütz(e) *n*, (*f*)
~ lever control (or operation) = Einhebelbedienung *f*, Ein-Hebel-Betätigung
single-line bucket = Einseil-Greifkorb *m*, Einseil-Baggergreifer *m*
~ hook = Einseilhaken *m*
~ traffic = Einspurverkehr *m*
single-material batcher [*each material has its own hopper*] = Einfach-Abmeßeinrichtung *f*
~ scale batcher = Einfach-Abmeßeinrichtung *f* mit Waage *f*
single motor crane = Ein-Motor-Kran *m* mit elektrischem Antrieb *m*

single navigation lock — single-toggle granulator

single navigation lock = Einzelschleuse *f*
~ **notch** = einfacher Kamm *m* [*Holzverbindung f*]
~ **overhead line** = einfache Freileitung *f*
~ **oxygen-hose cutting torch** = Zweischlauchbrenner *m*
single-pass mixing = Ein-Arbeitsgang-Verfahren *n* [*Bodenverfestigung f*]
~ **soil mixer**, ~ ~ **stabilizer**, ~ **travel-mixer**, ~ **rotary tiller and spreader** = Ein-Gang-Mischer *m* [*Bodenverfestigung f*]
*SINGLE PASS SOIL STABILIZER [*Trademark*] = Ein-Gang-Mischer *m*, Ein-Gang-Bodenvermörtelerm,Fabrikat HARNISCHFEGER CORPORATION MILWAUKEE 14, WIS., USA
single-phase, monophase = einphasig
single-piece = einteilig
single-pitch roof = Dach *n* mit einseitigem Gefälle *n*
single plate dry clutch = Einscheibentrockenkupplung *f*
~ **polar dynamo** = Unipolardynamo *m*
single-pole = einpolig
~ **travel(l)ing gear** = Einständer-Fahrgestell *n* [*beim Bandförderer m*]
single pulley lathe = Einscheibendrehbank *f*
single-purpose reservoir = Ein-Zweck-Staubecken *n*
~ **road**, ~ **highway** = Ein-Zweck-Straße *f*
single push-button control = Einzeldruckknopfsteuerung *f*, Einzeldruckknopfbedienung, Einzeldruckknopfbetätigung
~ **rail transporter,** ~ ~ **conveyor**, monorail ~ = Ein-Schienenbahn *f* zum Betontransport *m*, Transport-Einschienenbahn
~ ~ **troll(e)y** = Ein-Schienen-Laufkatze *f*, Ein-Schienen-Lastkatze
~ **roll crusher** = Walzenbrecher *m* mit Brechplatte *f* und Brechwalze *f*
~ **Roman tile** = Doppelfalzziegel(stein)*m*, Pfannenziegel(stein)
~ **rope hoist,** ~ **cable** ~ = Ein-Seilaufzug *m* [*Betonmischer m*]
~ ~ **scraper** = Ein-Seilschrapper *m*
~ **ropeway**, single rope (or monocable) aerial (or cable) ropeway (or tramway)/ railroad (US) = Ein-Drahtseil-Schwebebahn *f*, Ein-Seil(schwebe)bahn [*sogenannte englische Bauart*]
single-seater = Einsitzer *m*
single shaft, undivided ~ = eintrümiger Schacht *m*
~ ~ **pug mill**, long pug mill, single-shaft mixer = Ein-Wellen-Zwangsmischer *m*, Ein-Wellen-Knetmischer
~ ~ ~ ~ **concrete mixer** = Ein-Trog-Zwangsbetonmischer *m* mit vertikalem Rührwerk *n*
single-shear rivet = einschnittiger Niet *m*
single-shift work = einschichtiger Betrieb *m*
single-size material [*material a major proportion of whose particles are of sizes lying between narrow limits*] = einkörniges Material *n*
(single) slope (canal) lining machine (or liner) = Böschungsauskleidungsmaschine *f*
(~) ~ (~) trimming machine (or trimmer) = Böschungsplaniermaschine *f*
(~) ~ concrete paver, see: slope concrete paver
single-spark gap, simple spark gap = Einzelfunkenstrecke *f*
single speed drive, constant-speed ~ = Ein-Scheiben-Antrieb *m*
single-stage compression = einstufige Verdichtung *f* [*Kompressor m*]
~ **impulse turbine** = einstufige Druckturbine *f*
~ **trickling filter** = einstufiger Tropfkörper *m*
single-stor(e)y building = eingeschossiger Bau *m*, einstöckiger ~
single system of triangulation = einfache Ausfachung *f* [*Fachwerk n*]
single-tank type pump, ~ **pneumatic conveying system** = Ein-Gefäß(förder)-pumpe *f*
single-throw pump = Ein-Kurbel-Pumpe *f*
single tire (US); ~ **tyre** (Brit.) = Einfach-Bereifung *f*
single-toggle granulator, ~ **type jaw granulator**, chipping(s) breaker = Einschwingen-Granulator *m*, Granulator-Splittbrecher *m*

single-toggle jaw crusher, Dalton overhead eccentric crusher = Einschwingen-(backen)brecher m

single track bridge = eingleisige Brücke f

~ **twist auger** = Stangenschneckenbohrer m

~ **tyre** (Brit.); ~ **tire** (US) = Einfach-Bereifung f

~ **unit mobile asphalt and bituminous mixing plant** = einteilige Trocken- und Mischanlage f für Mischmakadam m und Walzasphalt m

single-unit truck (US) = zweiachsiger LKW m, ~ Last(kraft)wagen m

single-wall (sheet-pile) cofferdam = einwandiger (Spundwand)Fang(e)damm m

single-webbed plate arch = einwandiger Blechbogen m

single-web system truss = einfaches Dreieckfachwerk n

single weigh batcher = Einfach-(Gesteins-)Waage f

single-wheel(ed) roller = Einradwalze f, Einachswalze

~ **troll(e)y** = Ein-Rad-Fahrvorrichtung f [z. B. für einen Betonvibrator m]

singly reinforced member = schlaff bewehrter Teil m, ~ armierter ~

sink (Geol.) = Schlotte f, Auswaschungstasche f, Auswaschungstrichter m

~, ~ **basin** = Ausguß m, Spültisch m, Ausgußbecken n

to sink = abteufen

sink deck = Spültisch-Einsatz m, Ausguß-Einsatz

sinker = Abteufhammer m

~ **visco(si)meter** = Fall-Viskosimeter n

sink-float method, heavy-method separation = Sink-Schwimmverfahren n

sink hole lake = Auslaugungssee n

sinking = Abteufen n

~ **bucket** = Abteufkübel m

~ **through** = Durchteufung f

~ **trestle** = Abteufgerüst n

~ **tube** = Abteufrohr n

sink product = Sinkprodukt n

sink-stone = Ablaufstein m

sink waste = Spülwasser n, Ausgußwasser

sintered alumina = Sintertonerde f

~ **expanded clay** = Sinter-Blähton m

~ **flyash** = Sinter-Flugasche f

~ **rod** = gesinterter Zusatzstab m

sintering, incipient fusion = Sintern n, Sinterung f, beginnendes Schmelzen n

~ **grate,** sinter ~, continuous conveyor ~ = Sinterrost m

~ **heat** = Sinterhitze f

~ **zone,** sinter ~ = Sinterzone f

sinusoidal draw bridge = Sinusoidenzugbrücke f

siphon = Saugheber m

~ = Wassersackrohr n [*Manometer n*]

~ **barometer** = Heberbarometer n

~ **culvert** [*deprecated*]; see: inverted siphon

siphon(ic) spillway = (Saug)Heberüberlauf m

siphon pipe = Heberrohr n, Heberleitung f

~ **recorder** = Heberschreiber m

siren = Sirene f

sisal hemp = Sisalhanf m

~ **rope** = Sisalhanfseil n

site, see: building ~

~ **canteen** = Bau(stellen)kantine f

site-clearing, stripping, land clearing, clearing (work) (or operations) = Räumung(sarbeiten) f, Freilegung f von Baugelände n

site connection, field ~ = Baustellenstoß m

~ **exploration,** see: soil investigation

site facilities, see: job-site installations

~ **for mechanical plant** = Aufstellungsplatz m für Baustelleneinrichtung f

~ ~ **no-fines concrete construction** = Schüttbetonbaustelle f

~ **measuring,** see: measuring of quantities

~ **mixing in place,** see: mix-in-place

~ **office,** see: job ~

~ **of paver operations** [*paving work*] = Einbaustelle f [*Straßendeckenbau m*]

~ ~ **work,** see: building site

~ **organization;** job "housekeeping" (US) = Baustellenorganisation f

~ **painting,** field ~ = Baustellenanstrich m

~ **power plant,** ~ ~ **station** = Baukraftwerk n

~ **rivet,** field ~ = Baustellenniet m

~ **road,** builder's ~ = Baustellenstraße f

site soil — skip

site soil, in-situ ~ = anstehender Boden *m*
~ **supervision**, field ~ = Baustellenüberwachung *f*
~ **test** = Baustellenprüfung *f*
~ **welding**, field ~ = Baustellenschweißung *f*
siting = Anordnung *f* [*von Bauwerken npl*]
situ-cast (foundation, or bearing) pile, see: cast-in-place (foundation, or bearing) pile
six-point pickup = Sechs-Punkte-Hebevorrichtung *f*
six-trace seismograph (or seismic refraction equipment) = seismisches Gerät *n* mit 6 Empfängern *mpl* [*Baugrunduntersuchung f*]
six wheel drive and steer grader = Dreiachs-Motorstraßenhobel *m* mit Allrad-Antrieb und Allrad-Lenkung, sechsradbetriebener und sechsradgelenkter Motorstraßenhobel
size and rate of working = Abmessungen *fpl* und Leistung *f* [*Baumaschine f*]
~ **bracket, (size) fraction, nominal size** = Körnung *f*, Fraktion *f*
sizing = Größenverhältnis *n*
~ **of the material completely by screening** = Klassierung(ssiebung) *f*
skeleton structure = Skelettbau *m*
skep, see: skip
~ = Bienenkorb *m*
sketch = Skizze *f*
skew angle = schiefer Winkel *m*
skew(ed) arch = schiefes Gewölbe *n*
~ **bridge** = schiefe Brücke *f*
~ **frame** = schiefwink(e)liger Rahmen *m*
~ **rigid frame bridge** = Steifrahmenbrücke *f*
~ **single-span slab** = schiefwinklige Einfeldplatte *f*
~ **slab** = schiefe Deckenplatte *f*
skid = Kufe *f*
~ **container** = rollenloser Behälter *m*
skidding = Schleudern *n* [*Fahrzeug n*]
~ **distance** = Rutschweg *m*
~ **friction** = Gleitreibung *f*
~ **machine** = Reibungsmesser *m*
~ **risk** [*road vehicle*] = Rutschgefahr *f* [*Straßenfahrzeug n*]
~ **test**, see: measurement of slipperiness

skid frame = Kufenrahmen *m*
~ **loader shoe** = Schaufelkufe *f*
~ **mark** = Rutschspur *f*, Rutscheindruck *m*
skid-mounted towed-type spreader = Schleppverteiler *m* auf Kufen *fpl*
skid-pan, wheel block = Hemmschuh *m*
skid-proof, see: non-skid
~ **carpet**, non-skid ~ = Gleitschutzteppich *m*
skid-proofing = Abstumpfung *f*, Anrauhung [*Straßendecke f*]
skid resistance = Griffigkeit *f*
skid-shoe, loader shoe = Gleitkufe *f* [*Frontlader m*]
skid-shovel = Frontlader *m* mit Kufen *fpl*, Gleitkufen-Frontlader *m*, Fabrikat DROTT MANUFACTURING CORP., MILWAUKEE 8, WISCONSIN, USA
~ **transportation** = Verfahren *n* der gefüllten Ladeschaufel *f* auf den Gleitkufen ruhend
ski-hoist = Schneeschuhläufer-Aufzug *m*, Ski(schlepp)lift *m*
ski jump spillway = Skisprung-Überlauf *m* [*Talsperre f*]
to skim = (ab)schürfen, abziehen, abgleichen [*Erdbau m*]
skimmed crude petroleum, see: topped ~~
(skimmer) scoop, bowl = Kübel *m* [*Radschrapper m*]
skimmer (shovel) = Planierbagger *m*, Flachlöffelbagger *m*
skimming [*the removal of the top layer or of the irregularities in the ground surface*] = Abziehen *n*, (Ab)Schürfen *n*
~ **coat** (Brit.); see: finish ~ (US)
skin coulter (Brit.); ~ plow (US) = Vorschäler *m*
~ **friction**, side ~ = Mantelreibung *f* [*Pfahl m*]
~ **plate** = Blechhaut *f*
skip, skep, dumping shaft ~ = Bodenleerer *m* [*Schachtfördergefäß n*]
~ = Förderkübel *m*
~ = Mischerbeschickungskübel *m* [*Betonmischer m*]
~, see: steel tip wagon
~ = Hund *m*, Schutterwagen *m*, Stollenwagen

skipdozer, see: baby bulldozer
skip for tower cranes = Förderkübel *m*
~ loader = Kübelaufzug *m* [*Betonwerk n*]
skip-loading bin (or hopper), see: muck ~ (~ ~)
skip type (contractors') (or builders') hoist, bucket ~ = Kübel(bau)aufzug *m*, Kippkübelaufzug
~ winding = Skipförderung *f*
skiving tool = Schälwerkzeug *n*
skullguard = Schutzhelm *m*
skylight purlin = Oberlichtpfette *f*
skyline = Horizontlinie *f*
skyway (US): see: elevated roadway
slab = Platte *f*
~ and beam construction, beam and slab construction = Plattenbalkendecke *f* [*Stahlbetonplatten fpl mit Stahlbetonbalken mpl*]
~ ~ buttress dam = Pfeilerplatten(stau)mauer *f*, Plattensperre *f*, Plattenpfeiler(stau)mauer, Pfeilerplattensperre
slab-and-joist construction, ribbed ~ = Stahlbetonrippendecke *f* ohne Füllkörper *mpl*
slab beam and girder construction = Plattenträgerdecke *f*
slabbing = Plattenpflaster *n*, Plattenbelag *m*
slabbiness = Plattigkeit *f* [*gebrochenes Gestein n*]
slab bridge = Plattenbrücke *f*
slabby limestone, see: laminated ~
slab (drainage) culvert = Plattendurchlaß *m*, Plattenabzugkanal *m*, gedeckter Durchlaß *m*, Deckeldole *f*
~ form(work) = Plattenschalung *f*
~ foundation = Plattenfundament *n*
~ kiln, sliding panel tunnel kiln = Tunnelofen *n* mit Plattengleitbahn *f*
~ paving, flag ~, flagging = Gehwegplattenbelag *m*
~ pumping, see: pumping
~ spanning in two directions = kreuzweise bewehrte Platte *f*, ~ armierte ~
slack = Durchhang *m*
~ cable = Schlappseil *n*
slackline (excavator) with bottomless bucket, see: track cable scraper

slackline (excavator) with dragline-type bucket, ~ cableway ~ ~ ~ = Schlaffseil-Kabelbagger *m*, Seilbahn-Schwebeschrapper *m*
slack time = verkehrsarme Zeit *f*
~ wax, see: paraffin wax
slag base (course) = Schlackentragschicht *f*
~ cement, artificial pozzolana ~ = Schlackenzement, Hüttenzement *m*
~ concrete = Hochofenschlackenbeton *m*
~ flour, Thomas meal ~ = Schlackenmehl *n*, Thomasmehl *n*, Thomasphosphat *n*
slagging (Brit.) = Schlackensplittverteilung *f* [*Straße f*]
slag (paving) sett = Schlackenpflasterstein *m*
~ pile = Schlackenhalde *f*
~ sand, see: granulated blast-furnace slag
~ track = Schlackenweg *m*
~ wool, mineral ~, silicate of cotton = Schlackenwolle *f*
to slake = (ab)löschen [*Branntkalk m*]
slaked lime, see: hydrated lime (powder)
slaking behavio(u)r = Löschverhalten *n* [*Kalk m*]
~ machine, hydrator = (Kalk)Löschmaschine *f*
~ pan = Löschpfanne *f* [*Kalk m*]
~ pit = Löschgrube *f*, Kalkgrube
~ screw = Löschschnecke *f*
slanting boom type trenching machine, ~ ~ (or ladder) ditcher, inclined boom type trench excavator = Grabenbagger *m* mit schräger Eimerleiter *f*
slat, see: timber ~
slate, see: argillaceous ~
~ coal [*absolete term for banded coal*] = Schieferkohle *f*
slaty cleavage (Geol.) = dünnplattige Spaltung *f*
~ lead (Min.) = Schieferblei *n*
~ marl, see: margode
~ sandstone = Sandsteinschiefer *m*
sledger, see: stone breaker (type crusher)
sledging, see: blocking
~ breaker, see: stone breaker (type crusher)
sled runner = Schlitten *m*

sleeper, cross sill (Brit.); tie (US); cross-tie = Schienenschwelle *f*
~ **for crane navvy** (Brit.); tie for power shovel (US) = Baggerschwelle *f*
~ **laying machine** (Brit.); tie ~ ~ (US) = Schwellenbohrmaschine *f*
~ **laying machine** (Brit.) tie ~ ~ (US) = Schwellenverlegemaschine *f*
sleeping canal, see: dead ~
~ **caravan** (Brit.); see: accommodation trailer (US)
~ **sickness** = Schlafkrankheit *f*
sleeve bearing = Halslager *n*
~ **brace**, see: bit ~
~ **joint**, jointing sleeve = Dichtungsmuffe *f*
~ **socket** = Muffe *f*
slenderness ratio = Schlankheitsgrad *m*, Schlankheitsverhältnis *n*
slewing (operation) = (Ver)Schwenken *n* [*z. B. Bagger m*]
~ **angle** = (Ver)Schwenkwinkel *m*
~ **crane**, see: revolving ~
~ **drive** = Schwenkantrieb *m* [*Bagger m*]
~ **gear**, see: swing ~
~ ~ **brake**, swing ~ = Drehwerkbremse *f*
~ **journal bearing**, king pin ~ = Drehzapfenlager *n*
~ **mechanism**, ~ gear, swing ~ = Schwenkmechanismus *m*, Schwenkgetriebe *n*
~ **motor** = Elektro-Schwenkmotor *m* [*Bagger m*]
~ **ring** = Drehkranz *m*
slickenside = (Rutsch)Harnisch *m*, Rutschspiegel *m*
slide, see: landslide
~ = Diapositiv *n*
~ = Schlitten *m*
slide-correction excavation = Abtrag *m* von Rutschungsmassen *fpl*
slide-failure surface = Rutschfläche *f* [*Böschung f*]
slide (or sliding) gate = Gleitschütz(e) *n,(f)*
~ **rule** = Rechenschieber *m*
~ **type fill valve** (US) = Gleitschieber-Siloverschluß *m*
~, **slippage** = Gleiten *n* [*metallurgisch*]
sliding bearing, see: friction ~
~ **door** = Schiebetor *n*

~ **drill bit** = Gleit-Bohrmeißel *m*
~ **form paver**, see: slip ~ ~
~ **friction** = gleitende Reibung *f*
~ **gate**, see: slide ~
~ **jack**, traversing ~ = Schlittenwinde *f*
~ **panel tunnel kiln**, see: slab kiln
~ **plate** = Gleitblech *n*
~ **shuttering** = Gleitschalung *f*
~ **surface** = Gleitfläche *f* [*metallurgisch*]
~ **type bin door** = Flachschiebersiloverschluß *m*
~ **velocity** = Gleitgeschwindigkeit *f*
~ **wedge block** = Gleitklotz *m* [*Blake-Brecher m*]
~ **weight**, jockey ~, moving poise, poise weight = Laufgewicht *n*, Einstellgewicht
slim hole drilling = Slim-Hole-Bohren *n*
slip, earth ~, shear slide = kleiner Erdrutsch *m*, Rutschung *f*
~ = Brei *m*
~ = Gleitweg *m* [*metallurgisch*]
~ = Schlupf *m*
to ~ = rutschen [*Kupplung f*]
slip area = Rutschungsgebiet *n*
~ **coating**, engobe = Engobe *f*, Engobieren *n*
~ ~ **machine** = Engobiermaschine *f*
~ **form** = Gleitschaltung *f*
~ ~ **canal lining machine**, canal paver, travel(l)ing template form = Einbaugerät *n* für Gerinneauskleidungen *fpl*
~ ~ **paver**, sliding ~ ~, formless-paving machine = Gleitschalungsfertiger *m*
slippage, sliding = Gleiten *n* [*metallurgisch*]
slipper, brake shoe, brake block = Bremsschuh *m*, Bremsklotz *m*
slipperiness = Glätte *f*, Schlüpfrigkeit *f*
slippery film = Schmierfilm *m* [*Straße f*]
~ **sett paving** = Rutschpflaster *n*
slipping mass = abgerutschte Bodenmasse *f*
~ **soil wedge** = abgescherter Erdkeil *m*
slip-ring induction motor = Schleifringläufermotor *m*
slipway, maritime ~, slipway for repairs to ships, repairing slipway = (Schiffs-)Aufschleppe *f*
slip zone = Rutschzone *f*
to slope = (ab)böschen

slope = Böschung f
~, fall = Gefälle n, Niveaudifferenz f
~, hillside, flank of a hill = (Ab)Hang m
~ (canal) lining machine (or liner), see: (single) ~ (~) ~ ~
~ (~) trimming machine, see: (single) ~ (~) ~ ~
~ change = Gefäll(e)wechsel m
~ concrete paver, single ~ ~ ~ = Böschungsbetoniermaschine f
sloped camber [*consists of two straight slopes joined by a parabolic crown*] = Dachprofil n mit Firstausrundung f [*Straßenquerschnittausbildung f*]
slope grader, see: backsloper
~ hoist, see: incline ~
~ ~ winch, see: incline hoist winch
~ lining machine (or liner), see: (single) slope (canal) lining machine
~ of cutting, cutting slope = Einschnittböschung f, Böschung f im Abtrag m, Böschung im Einschnitt m
~ ~ embankment, see: embankment slope
~ ~ roof = Dachneigung f
~ peg, see: ~ stake
~ protection = Böschungsschutz m
~ roller, see: embankment ~
~ sealing = Böschungsdichtung f
~ sett paving = Böschungspflaster n
~ stability = Böschungsstandfestigkeit f
~ stabilization (or stabilisation) = Böschungsbefestigung f
~ stake, ~ peg = Böschungspfahl m, Böschungspflock m
~ trimmer, single ~ ~ ~ = Böschungsplaniermaschine f
~ wash = Gehängelehm m
sloping adit = Schrägzugangsstollen m
~ apron = geneigtes Sturzbett n
~ concrete = Gefällbeton m
~ ground = abfallendes Gelände n
~ rubble wall, see: rubble slope
~ sea (protection) wall = Strandmauer f mit geneigter Außenfläche f
~ shaft = donlägiger Schacht m, tonnlägiger ~
slop wax fraction = Destillationsfraktion f von paraffin- oder gemischtbasischem Rohöl n
slot = Kerbe f

~ and key [*machine element*] = Nut m und Feder f [*Maschinenelement n*]
~ grinder = Nutenschleifmaschine f
slotted hole = Langloch n
slotter = Nutenstoßmaschine f
slot weld = Schlitznaht f [*Schweißen n*]
slow-curing = langsamabbindend [*Verschnittbitumen n*]
slow hardening cement, see: low heat of hydration ~
~ setting, stable, slow-breaking = langsambrechend, stabil [*Bitumenemulsion f*]
sludge = Schlamm m [*Abwasserwesen n*]
~ activation = Schlammbelebung f
~ activity = Abbauleistung f von Belebtschlamm m
~ bed, ~ treatment ~, ~ drying ~, ~ draining ~ = Schlammtrockenbeet n
sludge-blanket filter = schwebendes Schlammfilter n, schwebender Schlammfilter m
sludge boat = Schlammschiff n [*fährt den Schlamm aus den Kläranlagen ins Meer*]
~ cake = Schlammkuchen m
~ centrifuge = Schlammschleuder f
~ channel = Schlammrinne f, Schlammgerinne n
~ collector, ~ scraper = Bandkratzer m, Schlammkratzer, Schlammausräumer m
~ cylinder = Schlammzylinder m
~ decomposition = Schlammzersetzung f
~ demand = stündlicher Sauerstoffbedarf von Belebtschlamm in mg/l bezogen auf die Gewichtseinheit
~ density index = Schlammdichtigkeitsindex m, S. D. I.
~ deposition = Schlammablagerung f
~ dewatering = Schlammentwässerung f
~ digestion = Schlammfaulung f
~ ~ chamber, ~ ~ compartment, (~) digester, digester tank = Schlammfaulraum m
~ ~ tower = Schlammfaulturm m
~ discharge line = Schlammablaufleitung f
~ disposal into the sea = Schlammverschiffung f [*Beseitigung des Abwasserschlammes, besonders des Frischschlammes, indem er mit Tankern aufs Meer gefahren und dort versenkt wird*]

sludge distributor — slurry

sludge distributor [*digestion tank*] = Schlammverteilerscheibe *f*
~ **draining bed,** see: ~ bed
~ **(draw-off) pipe** = Schlammablaßrohr *n*
~ **drying bed,** see: ~ bed
~ ~ **ground** = Schlammtrockenplatz *m*
~ **elutriation** = Schlammauslaugung *f*, Schlammwaschen *n*
~ **excavator** = Schlammbagger *m* [*dient zum Abräumen des lufttrockenen Schlammes*]
~ **flake** = Schlammfladen *m*
~ **gas,** see: sewage ~
~ **gate** = Schlammschleuse *f*
~ **incineration** = Schlammverbrennung *f*
~ **incinerator** = Schlammverbrennungsofen *m*
~ **index** = Schlammindex *m*
~ **lagoon** = Schlammteich *m*
~ **liquor** = Schlammwasser *n*
~ ~ **heating pipe** = Schlammwasserheizrohr *n*
~ **outlet** = Schlammauslaß *m*
~ **pipe,** ~ draw-off ~ = Schlammablaßrohr *n*
~ **plug** = Schlammstöpsel *m*
~ **press** = Schlammpresse *f*, Filterpresse
~ **produced** = Schlammanfall *m*
~ **pump** = Schlammpumpe *f* [*Kreiselpumpe in der Bauart der Spülpumpe oder der Kanalradpumpe*]
~ **reactivation** = Schlammgeneration *f*
~ **removal** = Schlammbeseitigung *f*
~ **remover** = Schlammräumer *m*
~ **return** = Schlammrückführung *f*
~ **scraper,** ~ collector = Schlammkratzer *m*, Schlammausräumer, Bandkratzer
~ **slot** = Schlammschlitz *m*
~ **stirring** = Schlammumwälzung *f*
~ **sump** = Schlammsumpf *m*
~ **thickener,** densifier = Schlammeindicker *m*, Schlammeindickbehälter *m*
~ **thickening** = Schlammeindickung *f*
~ **treatment bed,** see: ~ bed
~ **utilization** = Schlammverwertung *f*
~ **valve** = Schlammventil *n*
~ **well** = Schlammbrunnen *m*
sludging = Entschlammung *f*

to slue about, ~ slew ~, ~ swivel around [*a vertical axis*] = Schwenken *n* [*um eine vertikale Achse f*]
sluice = Schütz(e) *n*, (*f*)
~ = Verschluß *m*
~ **dredge(r),** see: flume ~
~ **for emergency,** emergency sluice = Notverschluß *m*
~ **(gate),** sluiceway ~, lower sluice, lower gate = Grundablaßverschluß *m*, Abschlußschütz(e) *n*, (*f*)
~ **pillar** = Griesständer *m*, Griessäule *f*
~ **valve** = Abzugschieber *m*, Schieberschütz(e) *n*, (*f*)
~ ~ = Absperrschieber *m*, Spindelschieber
~ ~ **hydrant** = Schieberhydrant *m*
~ ~ **with flanged ends** = Flanschenabsperrschieber *m*
~ ~ ~ **socket ends** (Brit.); gate valve with bell ends (US) = Muffenabsperrschieber *m*
sluiceway, see: bottom emptying gallery
~, ~ **opening,** discharge opening = Durchflußöffnung *f* [*Dammbalkenwehr n*]
~, discharge opening, sluiceway opening = Abflußöffnung *f* [*beim Wehr n*]
~ **flow** = Grundstrahl *m*
~ **gate,** see: sluice (gate)
~ **opening,** see: sluiceway
sluice weir with removable sluice pillars = Losständerwehr *n*
~ **with bottom release** = Druckschütz(e) *n*, (*f*)
sluicing = Bodenverdichtung *f* durch Einschlämmen *n*, Einspülverfahren *n*, Spülspritzverfahren, Spülkippverfahren, Wasserstrahlverfahren, Einspülen *n*
~ **channel** = Grundablaßkanal *m*
slum = Elendsviertel *n*
~ **clearance** = Elendsviertelsanierung *f*
slump = Ausbreitmaß *n*, Setzmaß [*Beton*]
~ **cone,** mo(u)ld, conical shell = Setzbecher *m*
*****slump test (for consistency)** = Ausbreit(ungs)versuch *m*, Setzprobe *f*, Ausbreitprobe
slurry = Schlämme *f*, Schlempe *f*, Schlämpe *f*
~ = Rohschlamm *m* [*Zementherstellung f* [

slurry heater — snow blowing machine

slurry heater = Rohrschlammerhitzer *m* [*Zementherstellung f*]

~ mixer, grout ~ = Schlämmemischer *m*

~ process for making soft-mud brick = Schlämmverfahren *n* zur Herstellung *f* von Weichpreßziegeln *mpl*

slushing oil = Rostschutzöl *n*

slush pump, see: solids-handling ~

small-capacity (concrete) mixer with winch = Aufzugs-Klein(beton)mischer *m*

small compressor, see: baby ~

(small-diameter) tunnel; see: drift (Brit.)

small frame type pile driving plant (or piling plant) = Klein(gerüst)ramme *f*

small-leaved elm, see: common ~

~ lime tree = Winterlinde *f*, kleinblätt(e)rige Linde *f*

~ maple, see: common ~

small mixer = Kleinmischer *m*

~ morning-glory, see: bindweed

~ pressure sprayer, see: hand ~

small-scale (building, or project, or job) site = Kleinbaustelle *f*

small-size bucket (elevator) loader = Kleinauflader *m*

~ machine = Kleinmaschine *f*

small (stone) sett = Kleinpflasterstein *m*

~ (~) ~ paving = Kleinpflaster *n*

~ tool = Kleinwerkzeug *n*

~ type motor = Kleinelektromotor *m*

~ ~ ski-hoist = Skikuli *m*, Ski-Kurz-Lift *m*

smaragdite (Min.) = Smaragdit *m*

smelting furnace = Schmelzofen *m*

SMITH-MOBILE = kombinierter Nach- und Liefermischer *m*, Fabrikat THE T. L. SMITH COMPANY, MILWAUKEE 45, WISCONSIN, USA

~ trailer mixer = Anhänger-Liefermischer *m*, Fabrikat T. L. SMITH COMPANY, MILWAUKEE 45, WISCONSIN ,USA

~ with rear engine drive = Liefermischer *m* mit Mischermotor *m*, Fabrikat THE T. L. SMITH COMPANY, MILWAUKEE 45, WISCONSIN, USA

~ with truck engine drive = Liefermischer *m* ohne Mischermotor *m*, Fabrikat THE T. L. SMITH COMPANY, MILWAUKEE, 45, WISCONSIN, USA

SMITH TILTER = Freifall-Chargen-Kipptrommelmischer *m* (ortsfest), Fabrikat THE T. L. SMITH COMPANY, MILWAUKEE 45, WISCONSIN, USA

smoke box = Rauchkammer *f*

~ point = Rußpunkt *m*

smokestone = Rauchtopas *m*

smoke tube boiler, see: fire tube ~

smoky quartz (Min.), see: cairngorm

smoothing (or finishing) beam (or screed; or board (Brit.)) = Glättbohle *f*, Glättelement *n*, Deckenschlußbohle *f*

~ beam (or screed) finisher (or finishing machine) = Putzbohlenfertiger *m*, Glättbohlenfertiger

~ belt, finishing ~ = Glättband *n*, Glättriemen *m*

~ board, screed(ing) ~ = Abziehlatte *f*

~ iron, asphalt ~ ~ = Bügeleisen *n*

smooth(ing) plane = Schlichthobel *m*

smoothing plank = Glättbohle *f* [*Betondeckenfertiger m*]

~ screed, see: ~ beam

~ trowel, float = Glättkelle *f*, Spachtel *m, f*

smooth-shell crushing rolls = Glattwalzenbrecher *m*

smooth-stalked meadow grass (Brit.); see: blue-grass (US)

smooth(-wheeled) roller, see: flat-wheel(ed) ~

shag boat = Räumboot *m*

snail = Süßwasserschnecke *f*

snake wood, see: letter ~

snap ga(u)ge = Tasterlehre *f*

~ (hammer) (Brit.); set (US) = Schelleisen *n*, Döpper *m*, Nietensetzer *m*

~ head, ~ rivet ~ = geschellter Nietkopf *m*

~ hook = Karabinerhaken *m*

snatch-block [*deprecated*]; see: fall block

snecked rubble walling = Bruchsteinmauerwerk *n*

snow-avalanche, see: snowslide

snow bank = Schneehaufen *m*, Schneewall *m*

~ blocked road = verschneite Straße *f*

~ blowing machine; blower-type snow plough (Brit.)/plow (US), rotary (type) snow plough (Brit.)/plow (US) = Schneeschleuder *f*

SNOWCEM [*Trademark*] = eine feine in Pulverform *f* gelieferte Trockenfarbe *f*, die zu etwa 90% aus weißem Portlandzement *m* und zu 10% aus chemischen und Farbzusätzen *mpl* besteht
snow chain, see: non-skid ~
~ **clearing**, ~ **removal** = Schneeräumung *f*, Schneeräumen *n*
*****snow clearing machinery**, snow handling equipment = Schneebeseitigungsmaschinen *fpl*
~ **drift** = Schneewehe *f*, Schneeverwehung *f*
*****snow fence** = Schneezaun *m*
~ **field** = Schneefeld *n*
SNOWCRETE [*Trademark*] = ein britischer weißer Portlandzement *m*
snowed-up, snow-bound = verschneit, eingeschneit
*****snow handling equipment**, see: ~ clearing machinery
snow-line = Schneegrenze *f*, Schneelinie *f*
snow loader = Schneeauflader *m*
snow-melt = Schneeschmelze *f*
snow melting system = Schneeschmelzanlage *f*
~ **plough** (Brit.)/**plow** (US) **with angling blade**, see: blade-type snow plough
~ **removal**, see: ~ clearing
~ **slab** [*avalanche*] = Schneebrett *n*
snowslide, snow-avalanche = Schneelawine *f*
~ **débris** = Lawinenschutt *m*
snow storm = Schneesturm *m*
snub(bing) pulley drive = Eintrommelantrieb *m* mit Ablenktrommel *f*
to snug [*nut*] = anziehen [*Mutter f*]
to soak = durchfeuchten, durchweichen
soakage pit, soakaway, soaking pit [*in Scotland: rummel*] = Sickergrube *f*
soaking = Durchweichen *n*, Durchfeuchtung *f*
soaking-pit furnace = Tiefofen *m*
soap-hydrocarbon gel = Seifen-Kohlenwasserstoff-Gel *n*
soapstone = Seifenstein *m*
soap-thickened oil = seifen-gedicktes Öl *n*
socio-medical = sozialmedizinisch
socio-psychological = sozialpsychologisch
socketed stanchion = Pendelstütze *f*

socket pipe = Muffenrohr *n*
~ **spade** = Düllspaten *m*, Düllgrabscheit *n*
~ **wrench** = Aufsatzschlüssel *m*
sod, see: (grass) sod
soda amphibole = Alkalihornblende *f*
~**ash**, Na_2CO_3 = kalzinierte Soda *f*, wasserfreies Natriumkarbonat *n*
soda fel(d)spar (Min.) = Natronfeldspat *m*
soda-lime fel(d)spar, see: plagioclase (Min.)
~ **plagioclase**, see: plagioclase (Min.)
sodalite (Min.) = Sodalith *m*, Sodastein *m*
soda nitre, Chile saltpeter, sodium nitrate, Chile nitre, nitrate of soda, saltpetre, $NaNO_3$ = Chilesalpeter *m*, Natriumnitrat *n*, Natronsalpeter *m*
~ **pyroxene** = Alkaliaugit *m*
~ **water glass**, ~ **soluble** ~ = Natronwasserglas *n*
~ **zeolite** (Min.) = Natronstein *m*
sodding = Rasensodenarbeiten *fpl*
sodium = Natrium *n*
~ **alginate** = Natriumalginat *n*
~ **aluminate** = Natriumaluminat *n*
~ **chloride**, NaCl = Natriumchlorid *n*
~ **fluoride** = Fluornatrium *n*
~ **mica** (Min.) = Natronglimmer *m*
~ **nitrate**, see: soda nitre
~ **oxide**, Na_2O = Natriumoxyd *n*
~ **phase** = Natriumphase *f*
~ **thiosulfate**, $Na_2S_2O_3 + 5H_2O$ = Natriumthiosulfat *n*, Fixiersalz *n*, unterschwefligsaures Natrium *n*
~ **vapo(u)r lamp** = Natriumdampflampe *f*
sod of heath = Heideplagge *f*
soffit, see: intrados
~ **arch** = Gewölbebogen *m* [*Tunnelbau m*]
soft asphalt (Geol.) = Weichasphalt *m*
soft-coal mine = Braunkohlengrube *f*
softening = Enthärtung *f* [*Wasserreinigung f*]
~ **point**, see: melting ~
soft formation cutter head = Flügelkrone *f*
soft-knolled trefoil = Streifenklee *m*
soft-leaved elm = Flatterrüster *f*, Bastrüster *f*, Flatterulme *f*
soft limestone = weicher Kalkstein *m*
~ **metal snip** = Bleischere *f*

soft-mud brick = Weichpreßziegel *m*, Weichschlammziegel
soft-plastic = weichplastisch
soft rock = faules Gestein *n*, fauler Fels *m*
~ rubber bearing = Weichgummilager *n*
~ soap, see: potash-soap
~-solder = Weichlot *n*
soft steel, mild ~ = Flußeisen *n*
softwood, see: coniferous wood
~ (joint) filler = Weichholzfugeneinlage *f*
soil, earth; dirt (US) = Erdstoff *m*, Boden *m*, Lockergestein *n*
~ aggregate, see: ~ mix(ture)
~ analysis = Bodenanalyse *f*
~ asphalt (US); (surface) soil stabilisation with asphaltic bitumen (Brit.) = Bitumenverfestigung *f*, bituminöse Bodenverfestigung
~ auger, see: earth ~
~ base, see: (stabilized) soil (road) base
~ binder, see: binder soil
soil-bitumen mix surfacing (Brit.) = Verschleißschicht *f* aus Bitumenverfestigung *f*
soil boring auger, see: earth auger
~ building process, soil forming ~ = Bodenentwicklungsprozeß *m*
~ cake = Bodenprobe *f* [*Gerät n zur Bestimmung f der Fließgrenze f*]
~-cement = Bodenbeton *m*, Erdbeton *m*, Bodenzement *m*, Zementverfestigung *f*, Zementtonbeton *m*
*****soil cementation**, see: artificial ~
~ ~ (or stabilization) on the surface, (surface) soil stabilization (or solidification) = Oberflächenstabilisation *f*, Bodenverfestigung *f* (der Oberfläche *f*)
soil-cement mixture = Boden-Zement-Gemisch *n*, Boden-Zement-Mischung *f*
~ paving (US); **~ pavement** = selbständige Fahrbahndecke *f* aus Bodenzementbeton *m*
~ surface course, **~ road** = Zement-Ton-Betonstraße *f*, selbständige Fahrbahndecke *f* aus Zement-Ton-Beton *m*
soil classification = Bodenklassifizierung *f*
~ clod = Bodenscholle *f*, Erdscholle *f*

(~) colloid(al particle) [*0.002 mm — 0.00002 mm*] = Bodenkolloid *n*, Bodenquellstoff *m*
~ (or earth) compacting machine = Bodenverdichtungsgerät *n*
~ (~ ~) compaction (or densification), see: artificial consolidation
~ (~ ~) compaction by impact = Stoß(boden)verdichtung *f*
~ (~ ~) conservation = Bodenerhaltung *f*
~ (~ ~) consolidation = natürliche Bodenverdichtung *f*, Konsolidation *f*, Eigenverfestigung *f*, Eigensetzung *f*, Konsolidierung *f*
~ (~ ~) core, core of soil = Boden(probe)kern *m*
~ (~ ~) covering, soiling = Bodenandeckung *f*
~-creep = Bodenkriechen *n*, Gekriech *n*
soil crumb = Bodenkrümel *m*, Erdkrümel
~ cutting = Bodeneinschnitt *m*
~ drainage, see: subdrainage
~ engineering = Erd- und Grundbau *m*
~ exploration, see: soil investigation
~-flow, solifluction, solifluxion, earth flow = Bodenfließen *n*, Erdfließen *n*, Fließrutschung *f*, (Ab)Rutschung, Abgleitung *f*, Gekriech *n*, Solifluktion *f*, Bodenkriechen *n*
~ forming process, see: ~ building process
~ fraction = Bodenanteil *m*
~ grain, soil particle = Bodenteilchen *n*
soiling side slopes = Bodenandeckung *f* von Seitenböschungen *fpl*
soil injection = Poreninjektion *f*
~ investigation, ~ exploration, subsurface ~ (or reconnaissance), foundation exploration (work), foundation testing, soil study, site exploration, subsoil investigation = Bodenuntersuchung *f*, Voruntersuchung *f* des Baugrundes *m*, Untergrundforschung *f*, Baugrunduntersuchung *f*
~ lysimeter = Bodenlysimeter *m*
~ map = Bodenkarte *f*, Baugrundkarte *f*
~ mass = Bodenmasse *f*
~ matrix, see: binder soil

soil-mechanical investigation = erdbauliche Untersuchung *f*
soil mechanics = Bodenmechanik *f*, Erdstoffmechanik, Baugrundmechanik, Erdbaumechanik, Grundbaumechanik, bautechnische Bodenkunde *f*
~ mechanics lab(oratory), see: soils lab(oratory)
~ mixer, see: mix-in-place machine
~ mix(ture), ~ aggregate = Bodengemisch *n*, Bodenmischung *f*
~ moisture, ground ~ = Bodenfeuchtigkeit *f*, Bodenfeuchte *f*
~ mortar, see: binder soil
~ (or earth) movement (Geol.) = Bodenbewegung *f*, Bodenverlagerung *f*
~ pan vibrator, see: ~ plate ~
~ particle, see: ~ grain
~ penetrometer, see: sounding apparatus
~ physics = Bodenphysik *f*
(~) plasticity needle, see: plasticity needle
~ plate vibrator, ~ vibrating plate, ~ vibrating pan, ~ pan vibrator, ~ vibrating slab, ~ vibrating baseplate, ~ vibratory base plate compactor = Schwingungsplatte *f* für Bodenverdichtungen *fpl*
~ pressure cell, earth-pressure (measuring) cell = Erddruck(meß)dose *f*, Bodendruck(meß)dose, Druck(meß)dose, Bodendruckdose
~ profile [*a term restricted to defining the horizons of the pedological soil, thus embracing the topsoil and subsoil*] = Bodenprofil *n* in der landwirtschaftlichen Bodenkunde *f*
~ property = Bodeneigenschaft *f*
~ pulverizer, see: rotary hoe
~ road, see: earth ~
~ (~) base, see: (stabilized) ~ (~) ~
~ sample, ~ specimen = Bodenprobe *f*, Bodenprobestück *n*
~ sampler, sampling tool = Entnahmegerät *n* für Bodenproben *fpl*
~ sampling = Bodenprobe(ent)nahme *f*
~ section [*the soil profile (not in the pedological sense), being a sectional diagram constructed to show the relationship of soil strata along a given line at a particular site*] = Bodenprofil *n* bei ingenieurgeologischer Untersuchung *f*
~ ~ sheet (or diagram) = Bodenschichtenverzeichnis *n*
soils-engineer = Bodenmechaniker *m*, Bodeningenieur *m*
soil separate = Körnungskomponente *f*
~ shearing test apparatus = Schergerät *n*
~ shifting operations, see: earthmoving
~ skeleton = Bodenskelett *n*
soils lab(oratory), earth materials ~, soil mechanics ~, soil testing ~ = Erdbaulabor(atorium) *n*
*****soil solidification**, see: artificial cementation
~ specimen, ~ sample = Bodenprobe(stück) *f*, (*n*)
~ stability = Bodenstandfestigkeit *f*
***~ stabilization**, see: artificial cementation
~ ~, see: soil cementation (or stabilization) on the surface
~ ~ by heat treatment = thermische Bodenverfestigung *f*
~ stabilizer = Bodenstabilisator *m*
~ ~, see: ~ stabilizing machine
~ stabilizing machine, soil stabilizer, roadmixer, soil-stabilisation machine = Bodenvermörtelungsmaschine *f*, Bodenvermörtelungsgerät *n*
soil-stack installation = Abwasserinstallation *f*, Grundstücksentwässerungsanlage *f* [*Haushaltabwässer npl*]
soil study, see: ~ investigation
~ suction = Bodensaugvermögen *n*
~ surfacing, soil surface course, earth wearing surface = Verschleißschicht *f* aus mechanisch verfestigtem Material *n*
~ survey = Erfassung *f* der Bodenverhältnisse *npl*
~ test = Bodenprüfung *f*
~ texture = Bodenstruktur *f*
~ vibrating plate, see: ~ plate vibrator
~ vibrator, vibratory (soil) compactor = Bodenschwingungsrüttler *m*
~ (or earth) waterproofing = Bodenabdichtung *f*
solarization = Solarisation *f*
solar oil, see: gas ~
solder, see: plumber's metal

soldered flange, see: brazed ~
soldering = Weichlöten *n*, Weichlötung *f*
~ agent = Lötmittel *n*
~ lamp, see: blowtorch
~ paste = Lötpaste *f*, Lötfett *n*
~ tongs, see: brazing ~
~ tweezers, see: brazing tongs
soldier beam = Brustholz *n*
sole agency = Alleinvertretung *f*
~ plate, bed ~ = Sohlplatte *f*, Lagerplatte, Sohlblech *n* [*Brücke f*]
solfatara (Geol.) = Solfatara *f*
solid alcohol = Hartspiritus *m*
~ beam = Vollbalken *m*
~ blasting explosive, ~ ~ agent = fester Sprengstoff *m*
~ brick, see: (building) brick
~ brickwork = massives Mauerwerk *n*, Vollmauerwerk *n*
~ column = massive Säule *f*
~ disc = Vollscheibe *f*
~ fuel = fester Brennstoff *m*
~ housing = einteiliges Gehäuse *n*
solidification, stabilisation, stabilization = Verfestigung *f* durch Beimischungen *fpl*
~ point, congealing ~ = Erstarrungspunkt *m*
solidified water, see: hygroscopic soil ~
solid-injection engine = kompressorloser Motor *m*
solid lubricant = festes Schmiermittel *n*
~ matter = Feststoff *m*
~ partition = Massiv-Zwischenwand *f*
~ piston rock drill = Vollkolben(bohr)hammer *m*
~ rock, rock to be blasted = Kernfels *m*, gewachsener Fels, Sprengfels(gestein) *m*, (*n*)
(~) ~ excavation = Felsbaggerung *f*, Felsaushub *m*
~ rubber tire (US), see: hard ~ ~
solids-displacement method = Verdrängungsmethode *f*
solids-handling pump, slush ~, mud ~ = Dickstoffpumpe *f*, Schlammpumpe
solid stabilizer, see: powder ~
~ tyre (Brit.); ~ tire (US) = Vollgummireifen *m*, Elastikreifen
~ web composite structure = Vollwand-Verbundkonstruktion *f*

~ ~ girder, see: plain ~ ~
~ ~ ~ with arched soffit, ~ ~ ~ ~ ~ bottom flange = Vollwandträger *m* mit gekrümmtem Untergurt *m*
~ ~ hog-backed girder, solid web girder with hog-backed top flange = Vollwandträger *m* mit gekrümmtem Obergurt *m*
~ weir = massives Wehr *n*
solifluction, see: soil-flow
solifluxion, see: soil-flow
soling, see: (hand) (placed) pitching
solitary peak (Geol.) = Einzelgipfel *m*
~ volcano, central ~ = Einzelvulkan *m*
SOLITE, see: HAYDITE [*Trademark*]
solo motorcycle = Motorrad *n* ohne Beiwagen *m*
solubility = Löslichkeit *f*
soluble glass, water ~ = Wasserglas *n*
~ salt = lösliches Salz *n*
solution = Lösung *f*
~-feed process = Naßverfahren *n* [*Wasserreinigung f*]
solution of caustic potash, see: (caustic) potash lye
~ pocket = Auslaugungstasche *f*
solvent = Lösungsmittel *n*
~ naphtha = niedrigsiedender Anteil *m* aus Teer *m*
sonde = Sonde *f*
sone = Einheit *f* für die tatsächlich empfundene Lautheit [*1 Sone = 40 Phon*]
sonic altimeter, see: echo sounder
~ drill = (Infra)Schallbohrwerkzeug *n*
~ method = Schallverfahren *n*
~ type cell = Bodendruckmeßdose *f* mit akustischen Schwingungen *fpl*
~ vibration = Schallvibration *f*
soniscope = Soniskop *n*
SONTHOFENER self-propelled pneumatic-tyred (Brit.)/**pneumatic-tired** (US) **roller** = selbstfahrende Gummiradwalze *f*, Fabrikat BAYERSCHE BERG-, HÜTTEN- UND SALZWERKE A. G., SONTHOFEN, DEUTSCHLAND
to soot = verrußen
soot-blower = Rußgebläse *n*
sooty coal = Rußkohle *f*
sorb, service tree = Elsbeerbaum *m*

Sorel(s) cement, plastic magnesia = Sorelzement m, Sorel'scher Zement
sorting, classifying = Setzungsklassierung f durch flüssige Medien npl
~ track = Sortiergleis n, Zerlegungsgleis, Ausziehgleis
sound [*in respect of quality*] = einwandfrei
sounding = Loten n, Lotung f
~ = Sondierung f
~ apparatus, soil penetrometer = Sonde f
~ rod = Sondierstab m, Prüfstab
~ weight = Gewichtssonde f
sound insulation = Schalldämmung f
~ ~ against structure-borne sounds, structural sound insulation = Trittschallschutz m
~ level = Schallpegel m
soundness test = Güteprüfung f
sound-ranging altimeter, see: echo sounder
sound rock = gesunder Fels m, gesundes Gestein n
~ wave = Schallwelle f
source of supply = Anfallstelle f
sour crude (oil) = Rohöl n mit hohem Schwefelgehalt m
~ natural gas = schwefelwasserstoffhaltiges Erdgas n (oder Naturgas)
to sow down to grass, to grass down = berasen
sowing, see: seeding
Soxhlet extractor (or apparatus) = Soxhlet-Apparat m
space (US): aperture size, sieve opening = lichte Maschenweite f, Sieböffnung f
spaced (or intermittent, or dredger) bucket (type) elevator = Teilbecherwerk n, Schöpfbecherwerk
space dryer = Raumtrockner m
~ enclosed = umbauter Raum m
~ frame structure, latticework in space = räumliches Fachwerksystem n, Raumfachwerk m
~ heater, (air) ~ = Raumerhitzer m
~ heating = Raumheizung f
spacer, distance-piece = Abstandshalter m
~, see: spacing collar
space-rocket = Weltraumrakete f
space standard = Raumnorm f
spacing = Abstand m
~ collar, spacer = Beilegering m

~ diagram = Teildiagramm n
~ of trusses = Binderabstand m
spade = Spaten m, Grabscheit n
~ work = Spatenarbeit f
spall, see: flake
~ drain, see: stone ~
spalling, chipping, splintering = Absplittern n
~ (Geol.), see: exfoliation
~ wedge = Schrotkeil m, Steinspeidel m
spalls, rock **~** = Zwicke f
span = Stützweite f, Spannweite f
spandrel = Bogenzwickel m, Bogenhintermauerung f
~ beam, fascia = Randbalken m
spandrel-braced arch = Bogenträger m mit aufgeständerter Fahrbahn f
span of arch = Bogenweite f
spanner = Spannvorrichtung f
sparagmite = Buntwacke f
spare (part), replacement **~** = Ersatzteil m
~ wheel = Ersatzrad n
spark(ing) plug = Zündkerze f
~ ~ ignition = Kerzenzündung f
~ ~ tester = Zündkerzenprüfgerät n
sparry gypsum, see: selenite
~ limestone = Schieferkalkstein m
sparsely wooded = waldarm
spartalite (Min.), see: zincite
spathic iron (Min.), see: chalybite
spatula = Spatel m, f
spawning bed = Laichplatz m
spawn migration = Laichwanderung f
special authority = Sondergenehmigung f
~ contract provisions = besondere Vertragsbedingungen fpl
specialist fitter = Spezialmonteur m
specialized land clearing team = (Gleis-) Kettenschlepper m mit Rode-Vorbaugerät n und Heck-Zahnaufreißer m
special lime, see: autoclaved **~**
~ mechanism = Sondermechanismus m
~ section = Sonderprofil n, Spezialprofil
~ transporter = Spezialtransportwagen m
~ utility (or purpose) hoist = Spezial(aufzugs)winde f
~ vehicle = Spezialfahrzeug n, Sonderfahrzeug
specification = Leistungsbeschreibung f

specification cement, standard ~ ~ = Normenzement *m*
~ **property** = Normeneigenschaft *f*
~ **sand** = Normensand *m*
specifications, specs, contract ~ ~ = Abnahmevorschriften *fpl*, Normalien *fpl*
~ ~ = technische Daten *f* [*Baumaschine f*]
~ **for the lay-out of roads from the point of view of visual requirements** = Richtlinien *fpl* für die optische Führung *f* auf Straßen *fpl*
specific costs of plant equipment = spezifische Gerätekosten *f*
~ **gravity** = Dichte *f* [*z. B. Gas n*]
~ **inductive capacity,** S.I.C., dielectric constant = Dielektrizitätskonstante *f*
to specify as standard = normen
speckled wood, see: letter ~
specular gypsum, see: selenite
~ **iron ore** (Min.) = Specularit *m*
~ **stone,** see: selenite
speed, revolutions per minute = Drehzahl *f* [*Umdrehungszahl f je Minute f*]
~ **boat course** = Motorbootrennstrecke *f*
~ **control lever** = Geschwindigkeitshebel *m*
speedline mixer = Schnellmischer *m*
~ **spraying outfit** = Schnelltransport-Spritzmaschine *f*
SPEEDLOADER [*Trademark*] = (Be-)Lademaschine *f* mit Eimerkette *f* und Förderband *n*, Fabrikat GEORGE HAISS MFG. CO., INC., NEW YORK 51, USA
speed-mobile carriage = Schnellfahrwerk *n*
speed blow (US); ~ **plough** (Brit.) [*not equipped with wings*] = Schnell-Schneekeilpflug *m* an LKW *m* angebaut
~ **range** = Drehzahlbereich *m*
spell of fine weather = Schönwetterperiode *f*
spent acid, waste ~ = Abfallsäure *f*
~ **lye,** waste liquor = Ablauge *f*, Abfall-Lauge
sperm oil = Spermacetiöl *n*
spessartite, spessartine (Min.) = Spessartin *m*
sphagnum moss, see: bog moss
sphalerite (Min.), see: black jack
sphene (Min.) = Sphen *m*

spherical roller bearing, see: self-aligning ~ ~
spherical shell = Kugelschale *f*
spheroidal shell curved in two directions = doppelt gekrümmte kuppelartige Schale *f*
spherulitic texture = Sphärolitgefüge *n*
spider = Fliehgewicht *n*
spigot = Zapfen *m*
~ (**of the pipe**) = (Rohr)Spitzende *n*
spike = geschmiedeter Nagel *m*
~ **drag,** nail- ~ = Nagelschleppe *f*
spiked roller, see: pyramid feet ~
spilite (Geol.) = Spilit *m*
spillage = Schüttverlust *m*
spill channel = Schußrinne *f*
SPILLING steam engine = Dampfmotor *m*, Fabrikat SPILLINGWERK, MASCHINENFABRIK, HAMBURG 11, DEUTSCHLAND
spillway, flood ~ = Überlauf *m*, Hochwasser-~, Hochwasserentlastungsanlage *f*
~, see: bye-wash
(~) **apron,** apron type energy dissipator = Sturzbett *n* [*Überlauf m*]
~ **bucket,** roller-bucket type energy dissipator = Überfall-Sturzbecken *n*, Überfall-Aufschlagbecken
~ **channel,** ~ **chute** = Überlaufkanal *m*, Hochwasserentlastungskanal
~ **crest,** see: overflow ~
~ **gate** = (Hochwasser)Überlaufverschluß *m*
~ **outlet structure** = (Hochwasser)Überlauf-Auslaufbauwerk *n*
~ **section,** see: (river) overflow ~ ~
~ **weir,** see: waste-weir
spindle = Spindel *f*
~ **drag pump** = Schneckenpumpe *f*
~ **oil** = dünnviskoses Schmieröl *n*
~ **valve** = Spindelventil *n*
spinner spreader = rotierender Streuteller *m*, Rotorstreuer *m*
~ **type distributor (or spreader) for chipping(s),** spinner gritter, spinning gritter = Splittstreugerät *n* mit Schleuderverteilung *f*
~ ~ ~ (~ ~) ~ **stone** = Kiesstreugerät *n* mit Schleuderverteilung *f*

spinning [*manufacture of concrete or cast iron pipes*] = Schleudern *n*

~ **unit** = Schleudervorrichtung *f* [*Betonrohr- oder Gußrohrherstellung f*]

~ **wheel** = Spannrolle *f* [*Hängebrückenbau m*]

to spinn off the drum [*cable*] = von der Trommel *f* ablaufen

spiral bit = Spiralmeißel *m*

~ **chute;** ~ **shoot** (Brit.) = Wendelrutsche *f*

~ **classifier,** (spiral) screw washer, screw-type sand classifier, washing screw = Sandschnecke *f*, Waschschnecke, Spiral-(naß)klassierer *m*, Schneckenwäsche *f*

~ **concentrator** = Spiral-Konzentrator *m*

~ **duct** = Druckspirale *f* [*Vorspannung f*]

~ **(feed) conveyor** (or **feeder**) = Spiralförderer *m*

~ **flights** = spiralförmig angeordnete Mitnehmer(schaufeln) *mpl*, (*fpl*)

~ **flow** = Spiraldurchströmung *f* [*Belebtschlammverfahren n*]

~ ~ **basin** = spiraldurchströmtes Becken *n*

~ **(gravity) shoot,** helical shoot (Brit.) (or chute) = Wendelrutsche *f*

spiral(l)ed curve = Spiralkurve *f*

spiral reinforcing machine = Spiralbewehrungsmaschine *f*, Spiralarmierungsmaschine

~ **scraper thickener,** ~ **rake** ~, classifier for fine separations = Eindicker *m* mit Kratzer-Klassierer *m*

(~) **screw washer,** see: ~ **classifier**

~ **staircase,** see: helical ~'

~ **table for highway design** = Klothoidentafel *f*

~ **(transition) curve,** transition spiral = Klothoide *f*

spiral wire = Stahldrahtspiralen *fpl* [*Raymond-Pfahl m*]

spirit-based mordant = Spiritusbeize *f*

(spirit) level, water ~, air ~ = Wasserwaage *f*, Libelle *f*

spirit-level sextant, bubble sextant = Libellensextant *m*

spirits of hartshorn, NH_4OH = Ammoniumhydroxyd *n*

spit (of land) = Landzunge *f*, Nehrung *f*

splash lubrication = Tauchschmierung *f*

~ **zone** = Wattgebiet *n*

splaying, chamfering, splayed jointing = Abkantung *f* [*Treppe f*]

~, **bevel** = Druckschlag *m*, Abschrägung *f* [*Gewölbe n*]

to splice = anscheren, spleißen

splice = Stoß *m* [*Blechträger m*]

~ = Bewehrungsstoß *m*, Armierungsstoß

~ **piece,** see: fishplate

spline = Fugenbrett *n*

~, **female** ~ = Keilwellennut *f*, Längsnut

spline(d) shaft = Keilwelle *f*

splintering, spalling, chipping = Absplittern *n*

split-bottom dump = geteilte Bodenentleerung *f*

split cable duct = Kabelformsteinschale *f*

~ **coupling,** see: clamp ~

~ **firewood** = Scheitholz *n*

~ **hammer rotary granulator,** swing ~ ~ ~ = Feinhammerbrecher *m*

~ **sampling tube** = geteilte Probe(ent)nahmestanze *f*

split-second clutch (coupling) = geteilte Kupplung *f*

~ **delay cap,** see: millisecond delay electric blasting cap

split spoon = geteilte aufklappbare Entnahmesonde *f*

~ **(or channel) stoneware drain pipe** (Brit.); ~ (~ ~) (vitrified) clay pipe (US) = Tonrohrschale *f*, Steinzeugrohrschale *f*

splitting by frost, see: cracking ~ ~

~ **wedge** = Spaltkeil *m*

split washer = geschlitzte Unterlegscheibe *f*

spodumene, triphane (Min.) = Spodumen *m*

spoil [*dirt (US)/soil or rock which has been removed from its original location*] = ausgehobener Boden *m* oder Fels(gestein) *m*, (*n*)

~, **surplus earth** (or **soil**), surplus spoil, waste = überschüssiger Aushub(boden) *m*

~ **area,** waste area, spoil bank, spoil tip, shoot, spoil deposit, waste site, spoil dump; [*deprecated: chute*] = Aussatzkippe *f*

spoke-type wheel = Speichenrad *n*

sponge-grease — spreading site

sponge-grease = Schwammfett *n*
sponge ice, see: ground ~
~ rubber = Schwammgummi *m*
sponsor, see: promoter
~ (US); pilot firm, "lead" firm = federführende Firma *f*
spool = Kabeltrommel *f*
to spool = aufwickeln [*Windenseil n*]
spool diameter = Aufwickel(ungs)durchmesser *m*
~ drum = Aufwickel(ungs)trommel *f*
spoon-auger = Löffelbohrer *m*, offene Schappe *f*
spoon-bit gouge = Löffelhohlmeißel *m*
spoon dredge(r), see: dipper (bucket) ~
~ sample = Löffelprobe *f*, Sondenprobe *f* [*gestört*]
sportsfield roller = Sportplatzwalze *f*
sports ground type tandem roller = Sportplatztandemwalze *f*
spot estimate = überschläglicher Kostenanschlag *m*
~ footing, see: isolated ~
~ level = Annäherungshöhe *f*
~ sample = (An)Näherungsprobe(stück) *f*, (*n*)
spotter, dumperman = Einweiser *m* [*beim Abkippen n*]
spot test = Tüpfelprobe *f*
spotting [*bucket*] = Anortbringen *n* [*Baggerlöffel m*]
~ = Einweisen *n* [*LKW m*]
~ and spreading cement = Zementverteilung *f* in Säcken *mpl* [*Zementverfestigung f*]
spot welding = Punktschweißung *f*
~ ~ machine = Punktschweißmaschine *f*
spout, chute; shoot (Brit.) = 1. Rinne *f* [*Gußbetonanlage f*]; 2. Schurre *f*
spray application = Spritzauftrag *m*
~ bar = Beries(e)lungsrohr *n*, Sprengrohr *n*, Spritzrohr *n*; Düsenstrang *m*, Sprengrampe *f*, Spritzrampe *f*; Balkenbrause *f* [*Schweiz*]; Spritzbarren *m* [*Österreich*] [*Motorspritzgerät n*]
~ cleaner = Reinigungsspritze *f*
~ coat = Sprühfilm *m*, Spritzfilm
sprayer (or spraying machine) for hand and power spraying with hand lance = Motor-Spritzmaschine *f*

~ (~ ~ ~) with power air compressor and hand lance(s) = Motorkompressor-Spritzmaschine *f*
~ (~ ~ ~) ~ hand operated air compressor and hand lance = Handkompressor-Spritzmaschine *f*
spray gun = Spritzpistole *f*
~ hose = Spritzschlauch *m*
spraying machinery = Spritzgeräte *npl* [*Straßenbau m*]
spray lance, hand ~ = Handrohr *n* mit Düse *f*
SPRAY MASTER [*Trademark*] = Druckverteiler *m*, Fabrikat LITTLEFORD BROS. INC., CINCINNATI 2, OHIO, USA
spray painting = Spritzanstrich *m*
~ tube = Eindüsrohr *n* [*bituminöse Mischanlage f*]
to spread and level = einebnen, verebnen, einplanieren
spreader (Brit.) = Gußasphaltstreicher *m*, Asphalteur *m*
~, see: distributor
~ box, see: box spreader
~ conveyor, see: stacker
~-ditcher = (Gleis-)Planierpflug *m*, Kippenräumer *m*, Einebnungspflug *m*, Kippenpflug
*spreader finisher, see: asphalt ~
~ screw, see: spreading ~
~ truck (US) = Streu-Last(kraft)wagen *m*
~ truss = Spreizträger *m*
spread foundation, ~ footing = Lastverteilungsfundament *n*
spreading and level(l)ing = Einplanieren *n*
~ beam, distributing ~ = Verteilerbohle *f*
~ box, see: box spreader
~ hopper, see: box spreader
~ machine fitted with bottom doors, see: controlled-discharge door concrete hopper (or trough) spreader
~ machine without bottom doors, see: open-bottomed concrete trough spreader
~ screw, distributing ~, spreader screw, (cross) auger = Verteilerschnecke *f*
~ site, laying site, placing point, placement site; working face (Brit.) = Einbaustelle *f*, Vortriebstelle *f* [*Straßenbau m*]

spreading team — squirrel cage (type electric) motor 353

spreading team, see: laying gang
spread root = Flachwurzel f
spring buffer = Federpuffer m
springer, see: impost
spring-fed pond = Quellteich m
spring flood = Frühjahrshochwasser n
springing = Kämpferpunkt m
~ = Federung f
~, see: impost
springline, springing line = Kämpferlinie f
spring-mounted = gefedert
spring of intermediate depth = Bodenquelle f
~ pressure ga(u)ge = Federmanometer n
~ ~ sounding apparatus = Federdrucksonde f
~ range = Springtidenhub m
~ steel = Federstahl m
~ ~ cross-bands = Federbandstahl m
spring-supported shaker conveyor = Wuchtförderer m
~ vibrating screen = Resonanzschwingsieb n
spring tension = Federspannung f
spring-tide = Springflut f
spring-tine cultivator (US) = Federzahnkultivator m
spring-tooth harrow = Feder(zahn)egge f
spring-type roller (grinding) mill = Federkraftwalzen(mahl)mühle f
spring washer, lock ~ = Federring m, Federscheibe f
~ water = Quellwasser n
to sprinkle = berieseln, besprengen
sprinkler truck (US) = Sprengwagen m
sprinkling = Besprengen n, Berieseln n, Beries(e)lung f
sprocket = Strebeschwarte f, Schwibbe f, Windrispe f
~, see: ~ wheel
~ chain = Gelenkkette f
~ shaft = Turaswelle f
~ (wheel) = Kettenrad n, Turas m
sprung bore-hole = vorgekesseltes Loch n
~ ~ method = Kesselschießen n, Vorkesseln n
spud = (Stoß)Pfahl m [Naßbagger m]

spudding bit, drag ~ = Spatenmeißel m
spud hoist = Pfahlwinde f [Naßbagger m]
~ rope = Pfahlseil n [Naßbagger m]
~ vibrator = Tiefenrüttler m [Kellerverfahren n, Steuermannverfahren]
~ ~ for concrete = Betoninnenrüttler m, Betoninnenvibrator m
spun concrete, centrifugally cast ~ = Schleuderbeton m
~ ~ pipe, centrifugally cast ~ ~ = Schleuderbetonrohr n
~ glass = Glasgespinst n
spur = Ausläufer m [Gebirge n]
~ gearing fitted with fast and loose pulley = Rädervorgelege n mit Fest- und Losscheibe f
~ post = Prellstein m, Abweisstein m Radabweiser m
~ track; see: rail(way) spur (Brit.)
~ tunnel = Stichtunnel m
squall = Bö f
squally front = Böenfront f
~ rain (or shower) = Böenregen m
square bar (steel) = Vierkantstahl m
squared rubble walling brought to courses, roughly squared coursed rubble masonry = hammerrechtes Schicht(en)mauerwerk n
~ timber, see: rectangular ~
square end cogging = gerade Endverkämmung f
(~) (mesh) sieve = Maschensieb n, Quadrat(loch)sieb n
~ ~ tracking, S. M. T. = Stahlmattenbelag m
~ ~ vibrating screen = Vibrationsmaschensieb n
~ (screw) nut = Vierkant(schrauben)mutter f
~ thread = flach(gängig)es Gewinde n
squeegee = Schwabber m, Gummischieber m
~ = Räumbalken m [Schlammräumung f von Rechteck-Absetzbecken]
~ coat [deprecated]; see: seal(ing) coat
to squeeze out = ausquetschen, auspressen
squirrel cage (type electric) motor, squirrel-cage induction motor = Kurzschluß(läufer)motor m

S.R.O. [*Special Road Oil, consisting of a creosote cutback bitumen containing a wetting agent, specially prepared for use with the wet sand process*] = Spezial-Straßenöl n

stabilisation, stabilization, solidification = Verfestigung f durch Beimischungen fpl

to stabilise the moisture content of soil = den Wassergehalt m des Bodens m konservieren

stabilised, stabilized = verfestigt [*Straße f*]

~ gasoline, see: debutanized ~

stabilising agent, stabiliser = Stabilisator m

stability = Standsicherheit f, Standfestigkeit f, Stabilität f

~ = Beständigkeit f [*Emulsion f*]

stabilization of slopes = Befestigung f von Böschungen fpl

stabilized aggregate = mechanische Verfestigung f

(~) (or stabilised) soil (road) base = Tragschicht f aus verfestigtem Material n

stabilizer bar = starre Schwinge f [*Zweirad-Hinterradtandem n*]

stabilizing train = Vermörtelungszug m

stabling track = Aufstellgleis n

stack = Kamin m, Schornstein m

stacker, tiering machine = Stapler m

~, spreader conveyor = Bandabsetzer m, (Schwenk)Absetzer, Band-Abwurfgerät n, Absetzer für Hoch-, Tief- und Dammschüttung f Absetzanlage f

~ belt, ~ conveyor = Absetz(förder)band n, Ausleger-Förderband

~ dredge(r) = Eimerketten-Schwimmbagger m mit Förderrinne f

~ for building up embankments = Dammschütter-Bandabsetzer m, Hochabsetzer m

~ ~ filling below track level = Tiefschütter-Bandabsetzer m

~ truck = Hubstapler m, Hebetransportstapler

staff, see: personnel

~ pay office = Lohnbüro n

~ report = redaktionseigener Bericht m

staffing difficulties = Personalschwierigkeiten fpl

stage = Bauabschnitt m, Ausbaustufe f, Baustadium n

~ construction (US); see: multiple lift ~

~ plunger pump, differential plunger ~ = Stufentauchkolbenpumpe f

~ turbine = Stufenturbine f

staggered joint, see: break of joint

~ junction = versetzte Kreuzung f

~ (or zigzag) rivet = Versatznietung f, Zickzacknietung f

~ spot welding = Zickzackpunktschweißung f

stagnant water = stagnierendes Wasser n

stahl-eisen slag, slag from pig-iron for steel making purposes = Stahl(roh)(eisen)-schlacke f

staining = Beizen n [*Holz n*]

stainless = rostfrei

staircase with landing = Podesttreppe f

stair tread = Treppenplatte f

stairwalking hand truck = Stechkarre(n) f, (m) zum Transport über Treppen

stairway of locks, chain of locks, staircase locks, staircase flights = Schleusentreppe f

stacked bricks = Ziegelstapel m

to stake out, see: to peg out

stakeout, see: pegging out (work)

stalactite = Stalaktit m, Abtropfstein m

stalactitical gypsum = Gippsinter m

stalagmite = Stalagmit m, Auftropfstein m

stalling = Abwürgen n [*Motor m*]

stamp, stamper = Pochwerk m, Stampfmühle f

stamped asphalt, see: rock ~

stamp-licker, see: P. B. S. laying machine

stamp sand = Pochsand m, Splittsand, Quetschsand

stanchion = Pfosten m, Stütze f

~ of frame, vertical member ~ ~, vertical leg = Rahmenstiel m

~ section = Stützenquerschnitt m

~ shaft = Stützenschaft m

standard brick; see: ~ structural clay tile (US)

~ briquette = Prisma n [*Zement m*]

~ committee, committee on standardization = Normenausschuß m

~ compaction test, see: Proctor ~

~ figure = Normungszahl f

standard frequency vibrator = Normalfrequenzvibrator m, Normalfrequenzrüttler m

~ (ga(u)ge) track = Normalspurgleis n, Regelspurgleis, Vollbahngleis

standardised, standardized = genormt

to standardize = normen

standard lay, see: regular ~

~ load(ing) = Regellast f, Regelbelastung f

~ method of test for dry to no-pick-up time of traffic paints = Standard-Prüfmethode f der Trockenzeit f von Markierungsfarben fpl bis zur Klebfreiheit f

~ pressure = Normaldruck m

~ sand, cement testing ~ = Normensand m

~ section (Brit.); structural shape (US) = Normalprofil(eisen) n, Regelprofil n

~ size = Regelgröße f [Baumaschine f]

(~) specification cement = Normenzement m

~ specifications = Normen fpl, Güterichtlinien fpl

~ strength = Normenfestigkeit f

~ structural clay tile (US); standard brick = Normalziegel m, Normalstein m

~ substance for calibration = Eichsubstanz f

Standard Tar Visco(si)meter, STV = Straßenteerviskosimeter n, STV

standard test sieve = Normenprüfsieb n

Standard Unit Steel Trestles = Amerikanisches Pfeilergerät n [Brückenbau m]

standard weight = Regelgewicht n

St. Andrew's cross, see: diagonal struts

stand-by capacity = Reservekapazität f

~ generating set, emergency current standby generator = Notstromaggregat n

~ plant = Reserveanlage f

~ time = Wartezeit f [Baumaschine f]

standing, see: hardstanding

~ rope, see: rope (guy)

~ traffic = parkender Verkehr m

~ vehicle [a vehicle stationary upon a highway for reasons other than interruption of traffic] = parkendes Fahrzeug n

~ water = stehendes Wasser n [auf einer Fläche f]

~ ~ level, ground water(-table) level, ground water elevation = Grundwasserstand m, Grundwasserhöhe f

stand oil = Leinölstandöl n

standpipe = Standrohr n

stand pump = Ständerpumpe f

stand-up fork truck = Gabelstapler m mit leichter Lenkbarkeit f

staple = Krampe f, Krampen m

star bit = Sternmeißel m

state of all-round tension, ~ ~ two dimensional stress equality = Umschlingungsfestigkeit f

starter, starting apparatus, accelerator = Anlasser m

~ = Anfängerstein m [Pflaster n]

~ bit, starting ~ = Anbohrmeißel m

~ (drill), starting ~ = Vorbohrer m

~ steel, starting ~ = Anbohrstahl m

starting compressor = Anlaßverdichter m

~ crank = Andrehkurbel f, Anwerfkurbel, Startkurbel, Anwurfkurbel, Anlaßkurbel

~ engine = Anwurfmotor m, Anlaß-(hilfs)motor, Anwerfmotor, Startmotor

~ torque = Anzugsmoment n, Anlauf-(dreh)moment [Motor m]

state forces, public ~ (US); direct labour (Brit.) = Regiearbeitskräfte fpl

~ planning, provincial ~ = Landesplanung f

static, stationary, permanent = stationär, ortsfest

statically determined, ~ determinate = statisch berechnet, ~ bestimmt

~ indeterminate = statisch unbestimmt

~ ~ principal system = statisch unbestimmtes Hauptsystem n

static coefficient of friction = Haftreibungsbeiwert m

~ friction = Haftreibung f

~ penetration testing = Tiefensondierung f mit stufenweiser Belastung f

~ pile driving formula = statische Rammformel f

~ pressure = statischer Druck m

statics = Statik f

~ for structural engineering = Baustatik f

Statics Journal = Statisches Tagebuch n
station = Station f [*Massenplan m*]
~ and lock unit = Schleuse f und Kraftwerk n
stationary, see: static
~ continuous brick kiln = Ziegel-Kammerofen m
~ load = Standlast f
~ mastic cooker with engine-driven stirring gear = Gußasphalt-Einbaukocher m
~ ~ cooking plant = Gußasphaltkocherei f, stationäre Asphaltkochanlage f
~ position = Ruhelage f, Ruhestellung f
~ sprinkling system = Sprinkleranlage f [*Betonnachbehandlung f*]
~ shaft for the driving mechanism = stehende Welle f zum Fahrwerk n
~ ~ ~ reversing gear of the swing mechanism = stehende Welle f zum Drehwerkswendegetriebe n
~ storage barge = Standkahn m
station floor, ~ platform = Bahnsteig m
stationing, chainage = Stationierung f
~ in kilometres = Kilometrierung f
station platform, ~ floor = Bahnsteig m
~ roof = Bahnhofsdach n
~ wagon = Kombi(nations)wagen m
statistical control of errors = statistische Fehleruntersuchung f
~ records = statistische Aufzeichnungen fpl
statistician = Statistiker m
statuary marble = Statuenmarmor m
Stauffer lubricator = Staufferbüchse f
staurolite, staurotide (Min.) = Staurolith m, Kreuzstein m
stave, timber slat, (wooden) slat, barrel ~ = (Holz)Daube f, Faßdaube
~ pipe = Daubenrohr n
stay bar = Strebe f [*Schwarzdeckenfertiger m*]
~ block = Ankerklotz m, Ankerblock m, Verankerungsklotz, Verankerungsblock
~ plate, see: batten (~)
stayputtedness (US) = Schmierfetteigenschaft f wonach das Fett auch bei erhöhten Lagertemperaturen fpl nicht aus dem Lager n abläuft
stay rod = Ausfachungsstab m

~ wire = Abspanndraht m
steady load = gleichmäßig verteilte Last f
~ state of flow condition, ~ flow = stationärer Strömungszustand m, stetiges Fließen n
steam atomizing oil burner = Dampfzerstäubungsbrenner m
(~) boiler = (Dampf)Kessel m
Steam Boiler Supervising Association = Dampfkesselüberwachungsverein m
steam boom crane (US); ~ jib ~ (Brit.) = Dampfauslegerkran m
~ cleaner = Dampfstrahlreiniger m, Dampfstrahlgerät n
~ coal, short flaming ~ = kurzflammige Kohle f
~ coil = Dampfschlange f
~ crane = Dampfkran m
steam-cured gas-formed concrete = Dampfgasbeton m
steam-curing [*concrete*] = Dampfherärtung f [*Beton n*]
~ shed = Dampfhärtungsschuppen m
~ vessel = Dampfhärtekessel m
steam cylinder oil = Dampfzylinderöl n
~ distributing pipe = Dampfverteilungsrohr n
~ dome = Dampfdom m
~ drilling rig = Dampfbohranlage f
~ drive = Dampfantrieb m
~ drum, upper boiler, upper drum = Oberkessel m, Dampfsammler m des kombinierten Kessels m
steamed mechanical wood pulp = Braunschliff m
steam electric generating plant, ~ power plant, steam-electric station = Dampfkraftwerk n
~ engine = Dampfmotor m, Dampfmaschine f
steam-engine piston and cylinder in which the piston is the hammer, direct acting steam piling hammer = Dampf(ramm)hammer m, Dampf(ramm)bär m, (Dampf)Zylinderbär, direkt wirkender Rammbär
steam entrance port = Dampfeinströmungsöffnung f [*Zylinder m*]
~ exhaust port = Dampfaustrittsöffnung f [*Zylinder m*]

steam friction loss — steel cribbing

steam friction loss = Dampfreibungsverlust *m*
~ ~ work = Dampfreibungsarbeit *f*
~ generator; vapor ~ (US) = Dampferzeuger *m*
~ heating coil = Dampfheizschlange *f*
~ hose = Dampfschlauch *m*
~ hydraulic = dampfhydraulisch
~ inlet valve, distributing ~ = Steuerungsventil *n*
~ jacket = (Dampf)Heizmantel *m*
~-jacketed pipe = Dampfmantelrohr *n*
steam jib crane (Brit.); ~ boom ~ (US) = Dampfauslegerkran *m*
~-limit curve = Dampfgrenzkurve *f*
steam line = Dampfleitung *f*
~ logging hoist = Dampf-Holzaufbringungswinde *f*
~ lubricator = Dampföler *m*
~ main = Hauptdampfleitung *f*
~ loco(motive) = Dampflok(omotive) *f*
~ mixing jet = Dampfstrahlrührgebläse *n*
~ navvy (Brit.); ~ shovel = Dampf-(hoch)löffel(bagger) *m*
~ passage = Dampfweg *m*
~ pile-driving hoist = Dampframmwinde *f*
~ piston = Dampfkolben *m*
~ ~ valve = Dampfkolbenventil *n*
~ plough (Brit.); ~ plow (US) = Dampfpflug *m*
~ pocket = Dampfsack *m*
~ power plant, steam-electric station, steam electric generating plant = Dampfkraftwerk *n*
~ pressure diagram = Dampfdruckdiagramm *n*
~ ~ reducer = Dampfdruckminderer *m*
~ ~ regulator = Dampfdruckregler *m*
(~) pulsometer pump = Dampfdruckpumpe *f*, Pulsometerpumpe
~ reducing valve = Dampfreduzierventil *n*
steam-refined asphalt (US); ~ asphaltic bitumen (Brit.) = dampfraffiniertes Bitumen *n* im engeren Sinne
steam (road) roller = Dampf(straßen)walze *f*
~ saw mill = Dampfsägewerk *n*, Dampfsägemühle *f*

~ shovel; ~ navvy (Brit.) = Dampf-(hoch)löffel(bagger) *m*
~ spindle, regulating ~ = Regulierspindel *f*
~ stamp(er) = Dampfpochwerk *n*, Dampfstampfmühle *f*
~ stop cock = Dampfabsperrhahn *m*
~ superheater = Dampfüberhitzer *m*
~ trap = Kondenstopf *m*
~ tug(boat), ~ towboat = Dampfschlepper *m*, Schleppdampfer *m*
~-turbine-electric-loco(motive) = Dampfturbinenlok(omotive) *f* mit elektrischer Leistungsübertragung *f*
steam turbine power plant = Dampfturbinenkraftwerk *n*
~ universal excavator = Dampfuniversalbagger *m*
~ valve = Dampfabsperrventil *n*
~ vent (Geol.) = Dampfquelle *f*
~ vulcanizer = Dampfvulkanisator *m*
~ whistle = Dampfpfeife *f*
~-winch = Dampfwinde *f*
stearic acid = Stearinsäure *f*
stearin pitch = Stearinpech *n*
steel aggregate = Stahlschrott *m* als Betonzuschlag(stoff) *m*
(~) ball tube (grinding) mill = (Stahl-)Kugelrohr(mahl)mühle *f*
~ bed plate, see: ~ sole
~ bending yard = Biegeplatz *m*
~ bridge = Stahlbrücke *f*
~ building construction, ~ structural engineering; ~ frame superstructure = Stahlhochbau *m*
~ ~ structure = Stahlhochbauwerk *n*
~ cable, see: wire rope
~ casting = Stahlformguß *m*
steel-centred silicon carbide blade = Siliziumkarbidschleifscheibe *f* mit Zentrierkern *m* aus Stahl *m*
steel changes = Bohrerlängenstufen *fpl*
~ column = Stahlstütze *f*
~ construction = Stahlbau *m*, Stahlkonstruktion *f*
~ ~ firm = Stahlbaufirma *f*
~ core = Rohrkern *m* [*Betonrohrstampfmachine f*]
~ ~ = Stahlseele *f* [*Drahtseil n*]
~ cribbing = Stahlträgerstapel *m*

steel dolphin, ~ piled ~, ~ pile cluster = Stahldalbe *m*, Stahl-Pfahlbündel *n*
~ drill boring = Hartmetallbohrung *f*
~ erection = Stahlmontage *f*
~ ~ firm = Stahlbaufirma *f*
~ fabric (mat) [*spot-welded*] = Baustahlgewebe *n* [*punktgeschweißt*]
steel-faced roller, steel wheel ~ = Stahlmantelwalze *f*
steel fixer = Eisenflechter *m*
~ fixing = Einbringen *n* der Stahleinlagen *fpl*
~ form(work), see: metal ~
steel-frame(d) building = Stahlskelettgebäude *n*
steel framing, (building) steel frame(work) (or skeleton) = Stahlskelett *n*, Stahlgerippe *n*
~ girder = Stahlträger *m*
~ grade = Stahlsorte *f*
~ gravel (storage) bin = Kiessilo *m*, eiserner Baustellensilo *m*
~ grid = Stahlgitterrost *m*
~ ~ floor = Stahlgitterrostfahrbahn *f* [*Brücke f*]
~ horizontal form support = Stahlschalungsträger *m*
~ hydraulic engineering = Stahlwasserbau *m*
~ lagging = wasserdichte Stahlauskleidung *f* [*Tunnelbau m*]
~ mesh, meshwork, grid = Stahldrahtgeflecht *n*
~ mill slag, see: steel slag
~ mine prop = Abbaustempel *m* aus Stahl *m* für Bergbau *m*
~ pallet = Stahlplatte *f* [*Steinformmaschine f*]
~ partition = Stahltrennwand *f*, Stahlscheidewand
~ penstock, see: plate steel ~
~ pile cluster, see: ~ dolphin
~ pin chain = Stahlbolzenkette *f*
~ pipe mandrel = Stahlrohrzylinder *m*
(~-)pipe pile, see: (tubular) ~ ~
~ plant = Stahlwerk *n*
~ plate conveyor = Stahlplattenband-(förderer) *n*, (*m*)
~ ~ girder, see: plate ~

~ ~ roadway [*bridge*] = Stahlplattenfahrbahn *f*
~ (power) penstock, see: plate steel ~
~ prestressing cable = Vorspannkabel *n*
~ puller = Bohrer-Ziehring *m*
~ rail = Stahlschiene *f*
(~) reinforced concrete; ferro concrete [*deprecated*] = Stahlbeton *m* [*früher: Eisenbeton*]
~ reinforcing bar, see: reinforcing ~
~-rimmed wheel, metal ~ = Eisenrad *n*
~ rolling, ~ wheel ~ = Abwalzen *n* mit Stahlmantelwalzen *fpl*
~ scrap = Stahlschrott *m*
~ section, section iron = Profilstahl *m*, Profileisen *n*, Formeisen *n*, Fassoneisen *n*, Stahlprofil *n*
~ shaft = Stahlwelle *f*
~ shavings, see: ~ wool
~ sheet = Stahlblech *n*
~ ~ disc wheel = Stahlblechscheibenrad *n*
~ ~ pile = Stahl(spund)bohle *f*, Spundwandeisen *n*
~ ~ ~ cell = Stahlspundwandzelle *f*
~ ~ piling, ~ pile wall, ~ sheeting = Stahlspundwand *f*
~ shell = stählernes Mantelrohr *n*
~ shot = Schrot *m, n*
~ shuttering, see: metal form(work)
~ silo = Stahlsilo *m*
~ skeleton construction = Stahlskelettbau *m*
~ slag, ~ mill~ = (Metall)Hüttenschlacke *f*, Eisenhüttenschlacke, Metallschlacke
~ sole plate, ~ bed ~ = Stahlsohlplatte *f* Stahllagerplatte
~ stack = Stahlschornstein *m*
~ straightedge = Abzieheisen *n*
~ strain = Stahlspannung *f*
~ structure, (structural) steelwork = Stahlkonstruktion *f*
~ superstructure = Stahlüberbau *m*
~ tape armouring = Stahlbandarmierung *f*, Stahlbandpanzerung [*Kabel n*]
(~) tendon [*conduit containing prestressing wire*] = Spannkanal *m*, Spanneisen *n*, Spannglied *n*
~ tie-rod = Stahlanker *m*

steel timbering — stepped side wall

steel timbering, ~ tunnel supports = Stahlausimmerung *f*, Eisenrüstung *f*

~ **tip wagon**, (raker) dump car, side tipping ~, jubilee wagon, (jubilee) skip (Brit.); industrial railcar (US) = Feldbahnlore *f*, Muldenkipper, (Mulden-)Kipplore *f*, Stahlmuldenkipper *m*

~ **tube shore** = Stahlrohrstütze *f*

~ **tubing lattice tower** = Stahlrohrgitterturm *m*

~ **tunnel supports**, see: ~ timbering

~ **wheel roller**, see: steel-faced ~

~ (~) **rolling** = Abwalzen *n* mit Stahlmantelwalzen *fpl*

~ **wire** = Stahldraht *m*

~ ~ **belt** = Stahldrahtgurt *m*

(~) ~ **rope**, (steel) cable = (Stahl)Drahtseil *n*, Drahtkabel *n*, Stahlseil

~ **wool**, ~ shavings = Stahlwolle *f*

steelwork, see: steel structure

steel wreckage = Stahltrümmer *f*

steep(-incline) conveyor = Steilförderer *m*

steep water [*malt house*] = Einweichwasser *n* [*Mälzerei f*]

steerability = Lenkfähigkeit *f*

steering axle = Lenkachse *f*

~ ~ **pivot pin** = Lenkachsen-Lagerzapfen *m*

~ **booster**, hydraulic (steering) ~ ~ = hydraulischer Kraftverstärker *m* [*zur Lenkung f*]

~ **brake** = Lenkbremse *f*

~ **clutch (coupling)** = Lenkkupplung *f*

~ **column** = Lenksäule *f*

~ **control valve** = Steuerventil *n*

~ **for driving gear brake** = Steuerung *f* zur Fahrwerksbremse *f*

~ ~ **engine coupling** = Steuerung *f* zur Motorkupplung *f*

~ ~ **hoisting coupling** = Steuerung *f* zur Hubkupplung *f*

~ ~ **reversing gear of driving mechanism** = Steuerung *f* zum Fahrwerkswendegetriebe *n*

~ ~ ~ ~ ~ **the swinging mechanism** = Steuerung *f* zum Schwenkwerkswendegetriebe *n*

~ ~ 2nd **speed** = Steuerung *f* zur 2. Fahrgeschwindigkeit *f*

~ ~ **swing gear reversing clutch** = Steuerung *f* zum Schwenkwerkswendegetriebe *n*

~ ~ ~ ~ **shaft** = Steuerung *f* zur Schwenkbremse *f*

~ **gear** = Lenkgetriebe *n*

~ ~ = Lenkschnecke *f*

~ **jack** = Lenkzylinder *m*

~ **lever** = Lenkkupplungshebel *m*

~ **mechanism** = Lenkmechanismus *m*

~ **of crawlers** = Raupensteuerung *f*, (Gleis)Kettensteuerung

~ **power** = Lenkkraft *f*

~ **ram** [*motor grader*] = Lenk-Hydraulikzylinder *m*

~ **rim** = Steuerkranz *m*

~ **shaft** = Lenkspindel *f* [*Motor-Straßenhobel m*]

~ **wheel** = Steuerrad *n*, Lenkrad

steeve = Klaue *f*

Steffens waste = Melasseabläufe *mpl* [*Zuckerfabrik f*]

St. Elmo's fire = Elmsfeuer *n*

to stem, to tamp, to plug up = verdämmen [*Sprengen n*]

stem = Stengel *m*

~ = Schaft *m*

stemming material, tamping ~ = Bohrlochbesatzstoff *m*, Sprenglochbesatzstoff

stench trap, drain ~ = Geruchverschluß *m*

step aeration = verteilte Abwasserzuführung *f*

~ **bit**, pilot ~ = Stufenmeißel *m*

step-by-step bin = Stufensilo *m*

step-down transformer = Abspanner *m*, Reduziertransformator *m*

step due to ponding (Geol.) = Abdämmungsstufe *f*

stephanite, brittle silver ore (Min.) = Stephanit *m*, Melanglanz *m*

stepless speed modulation = stufenlose Reg(e)lung *f*

stepped abutment = abgetrepptes Widerlager *n*

~ **concrete wall** = abgestufte Betonmauer *f*

~ **expansion joint** = abgetreppte Raumfuge *f*

~ **side wall** = abgetreppte Wangenmauer *f*

stepped turf revetment, headed ~ ~ = Kopfrasen m
steppe-land = Steppe f
steppe-soil = Steppenboden m
stepping, benching; notching (Brit.) = Abtreppen n, Terrassieren n
~-off = Stufenbildung f, Verwerfung f [*Betonplatten fpl*]
step-tapered Raymond pile, Raymond step taper concrete pile = Raymond-Betonpfahl m mit konischen teleskopartigen Rohrschüssen mpl
step-up transformer = Aufspanner m, Aufspann-Transformator m
sterilising agent = Entkeimungsmittel n
~ tower = Sterilisationsturm m [*Ozonbehandlung f*]
sterlingite (Min.), see: zincite
sternbergite (Min.) = Sternbergit m
stern tube luboil = Stevenrohröl n
stick, see: (dipper) ~
sticker [*on a vehicle*] = Plakatausweis m
stick sheave = Löffelstielflasche f, Auslegerstielflasche
sticky = klebrig
~ limit = Klebgrenze f
stiff concrete, see: "dry" ~
stiffened cable suspension bridge = Kabelbrücke f mit Versteifungsbalken
stiffener = Aussteifungsträger m
stiffening angle, see: angle iron stiffener
~ girder with hinge = Versteifungsträger m mit Gelenk n
~ (or reinforcing) rib = Verstärkungsrippe f
~ truss = Fachwerkversteifungsträger m
stiff-fissured clay = steifer geklüfteter Ton m
stiff-leg derrick (crane) (US); Scotch ~ (~) (Brit.) = Bock-Derrickkran m
stiff mud process, wire cut brickmaking = Strangpreßverfahren n [*Ziegelherstellung f*]
stiffness, rigidity = Steifheit f, Steifigkeit f
~ coefficient = Steifezahl f
stiff-plastic = steifplastisch
stiff-shaft vibrator = Innenrüttler m mit starrer Welle f, Innenvibrator m ~ ~ ~
still = Rohölofen m

~ air space = Luftinsel f
~ coke, see: petroleum ~
stilling = Energieverzehrung f [*Wehr n*]
~ basin, absorption ~ (Brit.); stilling pool (US) = Beruhigungsbecken n, Tosbecken n
~ ~ baffle, see: downstream sill
stink coal = Stinkkohle f
stinkstone, see: bituminous limestone
stirrer, see: agitator
stirring arm = Rührarm m
~ shaft = Rührwelle f
stirrup = Bügel m [*Bewehrung f*]
stock = Vorrat m
~ = Schneidkluppenkörper m, Kluppe f
~ and die = Schraubschneidwerkzeug n
stock-heap, see: pile
Stockholm tar = Stockholmer Teer m, schwedischer (Schiffs)Teer
stockist = Lagerhalter m
stock material = Haldenmaterial n
stockpile, see: pile
~ mixture = Haldenmischgut n [*Schwarzdeckenmischgut n*]
~ re-handling = Haldenrückverladung f
~ tunnel, see: reclaiming ~
stockpiling, piling = Haldenschüttung f, Haldenlagerung f, Deponie f
stock pond = Fischteich m
~ rail = Mutterschiene f, Stammschiene
~ reclaiming tunnel, see: reclaiming ~
~ shed, store ~, storage ~ = Lagerschuppen m
stock-taking = Bestandsaufnahme f
stockwork (Geol.) = Stockwerk n
stoker, fireman = Heizer m, Kesselwärter m, Kesselbediener m
Stoke(s) law = Stoke'sches Gesetz n
stolzite, see: scheeletite (Min.)
stone = Stein m
~ (and ore) scrubber, see: scrubber
~ apron = Steinschürze f
~ arching, see: vaulting masonry
~ base (course), see: macadam base
~ blasting, blasting of stones in quarries = Sprengen n im Steinbruch m
~-block paving = Steinplattenpflaster n
stone box culvert = Stein-Kastendurchlaß m, Stein-Abzugkanal m
~ breaker, see: breaker

stone breaker (type crusher), sledger, scalper, (large) primary crusher (or breaker), sledging breaker = Großbrecher *m*, Vorbrecher *m*
~ **breakers' hammer** = Steinschlaghammer *m*
stone-breaking plant, see: breaking ~
stone-built groyne (Brit.)/**groin** (US) = Steinbuhne *f*
stone chisel = Steinmeißel *m*
stone-clay core = Stein-Ton-Kern *m*
stone crusher, rock ~ = Steinbrecher *m*
stone-crushing plant, see: rock plant
stone curb = Naturbordstein *m*
~-**cutting saw, masonry ~** = Stein-Trennsäge *f*
stone drain, rubble ~, blind ~, spall ~ = Sickerdrän *m*, Steindrän, Steinrigole *f*
~ **dust**, see: flour
stone-filled asphalt, see: asphalt(ic) concrete
~ ~ = Hartgußasphalt *m*
~ **mastic asphalt** = Gußasphalt *m* mit Splitt *m*
~ **sand asphalt containing up to about 25 per cent of stone** (Brit.); **Topeka (type asphaltic concrete)** (US) = Topeka *m*, splittarmer Asphaltfeinbeton *m*
~ **sheet asphalt, modified Topeka** = Sandasphalt *m* mit verteilten Steinen *mpl*
~ **trench**, see: blind drain
~ ~ **with pipe**, see: pipe drain
stone granulating = Stocken *n*
~ **(or rock) grapple (or grab)** = Felsblock-Greifkorb *m*
~ **lifting bolt**, see: lewis
~ **(~) tongs**, see: lifting ~
~ **macadam type base**, see: macadam base
~ **matting** = Steinmatte *f*
~ **(picker) fork** = Stein(schlag)gabel *f*, Schottergabel
~ **pine** = Steinkiefer *f*
~ **pitching** = Setzpacke *f*, Setzpacklage *f*
* **(stone) quarry, rock ~** = (Stein-)Bruch *m*
~ **quarrying machinery** = Steinbruchmaschinen *fpl*
~ **riprap**, see: riprap

~-**sand**, see: screening(s)
stone sawing sand = Sägesand *m*
~ **screening(s)**, see: screening(s)
~ **scrubber**, see: scrubber
~ -**sett paving** (Brit.); see: sett ~
stone skip = Fels(förder)kübel *m*
~ **slab** = Steinplatte *f*
~ **sledge, masons' hammer** = Steinspalthammer *m*
~ **splinter**, see: flake
~ **spreader**, see: aggregate ~
~ **supply train** (Brit.); see: aggregate railroad (US)
~ **wall** = Steinwall *m*
~ **walling, stonework** = (Natur)Steinmauerwerk *n*
stoneware, flint ware = Steinzeug *n*
~ **drain pipe** (Brit.); see: clay ~ (US)
stone working machinery = Steinbearbeitungsmaschinen *fpl*
Stoney sluice (or gate) = Stoneyschütz(e) *n*, (*f*)
stony desert = Kieswüste *f*
~ **track** = Steinpfad *m*
stop, see: halt
~ = Anschlag *m*
~ **block** = Anschlagblock *m*
stope filling, stowage = Bergeversatz *m*
stop-end joint = Arbeitsfuge *f*
stoper = Überkopfgesteinsbohrer *m*
stop gate, see: gate
~ **line** = Stoplinie *f*, Haltelinie
~ **log** = Dammbalken *m*
stop-log gate = Dammbalkenverschluß *m*
~ **groove** = Dammbalkennut *f*
~ **weir** = Dammbalkenwehr *n*, Staubalkenwehr
stoppage = Arbeitsunterbrechung *f*, Arbeitseinstellung *f*
~ **place**, see: halt
stopped time = Verlustzeit *f*, Verzögerung *f* [*Verkehr n*]
stopping distance = Haltesichtweite *f*
~ ~ **test**, see: braking ~
stop plate = Anschlagplatte *f*
~ **screw** = Anschlagschraube *f*
~ **sign** = Haltezeichen *n*
~ **siphoning** (US); **un-priming** (Brit.) = Abreißen *n* [*automatischer Syphon m*]
~ **spring** = Rastfeder *f*

stop switch, limit ~ = Begrenzungsschalter *m*, Anschlagschalter, Endschalter
~ **watch** = Stoppuhr *f*
stopway, overrun = Auslauf *m* [*Flugplatz m*]
storage, storing, storekeeping, materials ~ = Lagerhaltung *f*, (Material)Lagerung *f*, Bevorratung *f*
~, pondage = Stau *m*, Speicherung *f*, Einstau
~ **area** (or **ground**) = Lagerfläche *f*, Lagergelände *n*
(~) **battery loco**(**motive**), see: accumulator ~
* (**storage**) **bin**, see: bin
~ **bunker** = Vorratsbunker *m*
~ **capacity** [*reservoir*] = Fassungsvermögen *n*, Stauraum *m*, Speicherfähigkeit *f*
~ **dam** = Speichersperre *f*
~ **lane** = Sammelspur *f*
~ **level**, capacity level (US); level of storage water (Brit.); height of maximum storage = Stauziel *n*, Stauspiegel *m*
~ **machine**, drag scraper stockpiler = = Stapelgerät *n* [*Seilförderanlage f*]
~ **of flood**, flood control storage = Hochwasserspeicherung *f*
(~) **pile**, see: pile
~ **pit** = Bunkergrube *f*, Erdbunker *m*
~ **pool**, see: artificial lake
~ **reservoir**, see: artificial lake
~ (or **store**, or **stock**) **shed** = Lagerschuppen *m*
~ **stability** = Lagerbeständigkeit *f* [*z. B. Zement m*]
(~) **tank**, see: cistern
~ **track** = Abstellgleis *n*
~ **yard** = Lagerhof *m*, Lagerplatz *m*
store = Magazin *n*, Lager *n*
storekeeping, see: storage
stor(e)y = Stockwerk *n*
storing, see: storage
storm channel = Flutrinne *f*
~ **collar** = Böenkragen *m*
~ **drainage**, see: surface ~
~ **water**, rain ~ = Niederschlagswasser *n*, Regenwasser

~ ~ **drainage**, S. W. ~ = Oberflächenwasser-Entwässerung *f*
storm(-**water**) **sewer**, storm drain = Flutdrän *m*
S. T. P., Standard Temperature and Pressure = 0°Celsius und 760 mm Druck
straddle carrier (Brit.); ~ **truck** (US) = Torladewagen *m*, Klemmgriff-Lastenträger *m*
~ **dump device**, dumping device for straddle carrier = Ausschüttvorrichtung *f* für Torladewagen *m*
straddling = rittlings
straight = Gerade *f*
~ **arch**, jack ~, flat ~ = scheitrechter (oder gerader) Bogen *m*
straight-blade snow plough (Brit.)/**plow** (US), see: blade-type ~ ~
straight-blade snow plow (US)/**plough** (Brit.) **mounted on a motor truck** (US)/**lorry** (Brit.) = Schneepflug *m* mit Frontschar *f* an LKW *m* angebaut
straight (**bull**)**dozer blade**, see: (bull)dozer blade
~ **dovetail** (**groove**) = gerade Zinke *f*
~ **drop spillway** = Wehr *n* mit lotrechtem Absturz *m*
~ **edge** = Ebner *m*, Richtscheit *n*, Setzlatte *f*, Richtlatte *f*, Wiegelatte
~ **gravity** (**hydro**) **dam** = gerade Gewichts(stau)mauer *f*
~ **halved joint** = gerades Blatt *n*
~ **jaw** (**crushing**) **plate** = geradlinige Backenplatte *f* [*Grobbackenbrecher m*]
straight-line pitch = geradliniger Nietabstand *m*
straight plate crusher = Backenbrecher *m* mit geradlinigen Backenplatten *fpl*
straight-run gasoline (or **gasolone**) (US) = Benzin *n* aus Erdöl *n* durch direkte Destillation *f* ohne Krackung *f*, Destillationsbenzin *n*
straight scarf with saddle-backed ends = gerades Blatt *n* mit Grat *m*
straight-shaft shell-less foundation (or **bearing**) **pile**, ~ **pier** = Gründungspfahl *m* mit Klumpfuß *m* (bzw. Kegelfuß *m*) und ohne permanentem Stahlmantel *m*

straight wall excavation — stress concentration

straight wall excavation = Aushub m(oder Baugrube f) mit lotrechter Böschung f
~ wheel (pneumatic-tyred) roller = Gummi(reifenvielfach)walze f mit nicht oszillierenden Rädern npl
strain at failure, failure strain = Bruchdehnung f
~ control = Dehnungsmessung f
strainer, filtering screen = Saugkorb m, Seiher m, Filtersieb n
~ = Spanner m, Spannklemme f
strain ga(u)ge SR-4, see: electric SR-4 ga(u)ge
strain meter = Spannungsmesser m
~ of driving, driver tension = Fahrerbeanspruchung f
strand = Litze f, Draht m [Drahtseil n]
stranding harbo(u)r, see: dry ~
strand(ing) wire = Litzendraht m, Seildraht
strap, metal ~ = Eisenband n
~ steel, band ~, hoop-iron, hoops, hoop steel, hooping = Bandstahl m, Bandeisen n
stratification (Geol.) = Schichtung f, Stratifikation f
stratified lake = geschichteter See m
to stratify (Geol.) = stratifizieren
stratigraphy, see: historical geology
stratum, see: bed
stratus, cloud-sheet = Schichtwolke f, Stratuswolke f
straw bale = Strohballen m
~ oil = Handelsbezeichnung f für Gasöl n für Absorptionszwecke mpl, Gelböl
~ rope = Strohseil n
~ tar = Strohstoffteer m
streak formation = Schlierenbildung f
stream carrying material in suspension = schwemmstoffführender Strom m
~ construction, ~ engineering = Strombau m
streamline flow = Bandströmung f, laminare Strömung
stream of air, see: air current
~ pollution = Stromverunreinigung f
~ scour = Flußauskolkung f
~ straightening, see: river regulation
~ tin (Min.) = Seifenzinn n
~ wave, see: jet wave

street, city ~, municipal road, town road, urban street, town street, urban thoroughfare = Stadtstraße f
~ broom, road ~ = Straßenbesen m
~ car (US); tramcar (Brit.) = Straßenbahnwagen m
~ car tracks, ~ railroad ~ (US); tram(way) ~, street railway ~ (Brit.) = Straßenbahngleise npl
~ cleansing = Straßenreinigung f
~ flusher, ~ sprinkler, roadway flusher, street washer = Straßensprengwagen m
***street form**, see: side ~
~ furniture, ~ equipment = Stadtstraßenausrüstung f
~ inlet = Straßenablauf m
~ lighting, illumination of roads and streets, public lighting = Straßenbeleuchtung f
(~) ~ column, lighting standard = Beleuchtungsmast m, Lichtmast m, Leuchtmast, Straßenlampensäule f
~ (~) lantern, road ~ = Straßenlaterne f
~ marker, traffic stud, road stud = Spurnagel m, Markierungsknopf m
~ mason [sometimes wrongly referred to as "mason flagger"] = Plattenleger m [Straßenbau m]
~ nameplate = Straßennamenschild n
~ network, ~ system, urban ~ ~ = Stadtstraßennetz n
~ property line = Straßenfluchtlinie f
~ sclerosis = Parkraumnot f
~ sprinkler, see: flusher
~ sweeper, see: rotary ~
~ system, see: ~ network
~ washer, see: ~ flusher
strengthening [soil] = Verfestigung f [Boden m]
strength of materials = (Material)Festigkeit f
~ test = Festigkeitsprüfung f
stress = Spannung f
~ = Beanspruchung f
~ analysis = Spannungsbestimmung f, Spannungsermittlung
~ application = Spannungsbeanspruchung f
~ concentration = Spannungskonzentration f, Spannungsanhäufung f

stress corrosion = Spannungskorrosion f
~ **distribution** [*through soils*] = Druckverteilung f [*im Baugrund m*]
stressing device, tensioning ~ = Spannvorrichtung f
~ **of concrete** = Beton-Beanspruchung f
~ **of the tension members** = Anspannen n der Vorspannglieder npl
stress level = Spannungsspitze f [*Rohrleitung f*]
~ **meter** = Druckmesser m
~ **method** [*concrete pavement design method in which the pavement is designed so that the most dangerous combined stress is less than the permissible stress in the material*] = Druckmethode f [*Betondecken-Entwurfsmethode f bei der die gefährlichsten Belastungen fpl insgesamt geringer als die zulässigen sind*]
~ **ratio** = Spannungszahl f
~ **redistribution** = Spannungsumlagerung f
stress-relieved = spannungsfrei
stress-strain diagram = Spannungs-Dehnungs-Diagramm n
stretcher = Läufer m [*Ziegel m*]
stretching course = Läuferschicht f
to stretch out [*the variation in level*] = vergleichmäßigen
striated mica (Min.) = Strahlenglimmer m
to strike, to bear (Geol.) = streichen
strike = Streik m
~ (Geol.) = (Schicht)Streichen n
strikebound = bestreikt
strike fault = Längsverwerfung f, streichende Verwerfung
strike-off, see: level(l)ing
~ **(screed)**, screeding beam, level(l)ing beam, level(l)ing screed, front screed = Abstreichbohle f, Abgleichbohle f
striking = Ausrüsten n, Abrüsten n
~ **hammer**, see: drilling ~
~ **off**, see: level(l)ing
(string of) drill pipe = Bohrgestänge n
stringer, longitudinal girder (Brit.) (or beam) = Längs(balken)träger m, Längs(träger)balken m
to strip down, see: to disassemble
~ ~ **the bark**, to disbark, to peel = abschälen, entrinden, (ent)schälen, abborken

strip = Zugband n
~ **(concrete) construction** = Streifeneinbau m [*Deckenbeton m*]
striped pedestrian crossing = Zebra-Fußgängerübergang m
*****stripe painter**, see: road-marking machine
striper, see: road-marking machine
strip(e) road, creteway, trackways = Spurstreifenstraße f, befestigter Radspurstreifen m
strip foundation, continuous footing = Streifenfundament n
striping machine, see: road-marking ~
strip load = Streifenlast f
~ **of ground** = Geländestreifen m
~ ~ **preformed filling material**, see: preformed (joint) filler
stripped gas, see: residue ~
stripper, see: (long-boom) stripping shovel
~ = Seitenturm m, Stripper m
stripping = Ausschalen n
~ = Ablösung f, Ablösen n [*flüssiges Bindemittel n*]
~ = Abdecken n, Abräumen n, Abbau m
~, see: clearing (work)
~ **oil**, scrubbing ~, wash ~, absorption ~ = Waschöl n zur Absorption f von Gasolin n oder Benzol n
~ **resistance** = Ablösungswiderstand m
~ **shovel**, see: long-boom ~ ~
~ **test** = Ablösungsversuch m
stromeyerite (Min.) = Kupfersilberglanz m
strong wind = steife Brise f
structural alteration = Umbau m
~ **analysis** = Baustatik f
~ **clay**, see: refractory ~
(~) clay building unit, masonry unit = keramische Baueinheit f, keramischer Bauteil m
~ ~ **industry** = baukeramische Industrie f
~ ~ **product (or body)**, heavy clay ~ (~ ~) = baukeramisches Erzeugnis n
~ **concrete**, ~ grade ~, ~ ~ mix = Konstruktionsbeton m, Bauwerksbeton
~ **design** = bauliche Durchbildung f
~ **division** [*shovel*] = Hauptteil m
~ **engineering** = konstruktiver Ingenieurbau m
~ **group analysis** = Ringanalyse f

structural hollow tile — sub-drainage

structural hollow tile (US); see: hollow (clay) building (or masonry) block
~ joint = Bauwerksfuge *f*
~ member = Bauglied *n*
~ part, building unit = Bauteil *m*
~ property = bautechnische Eigenschaft *f*
~ rock bench, see: denudation terrace
~ safety measure = bauliche Sicherheitsmaßnahme *f*
~ shape (US); see: standard section (Brit.)
~ sound insulation, sound insulation against structure-borne sounds = Trittschallschutz *m*
~ steel, constructional ~ = Baustahl *m*
~ ~ frame = Profilstahlrahmen *m*
~ ~ member = Stahlbauteil *m*
(~) steelwork, see: steel structure
~ strength = Gestaltfestigkeit *f*
~ stresses in concrete = Gefügespannungen *fpl* im Beton *m*
~ timber = Bauholz *n*
~ wood framing system = Holzrahmenkonstruktion *f*
structure = Baukörper *m*, Bauwerk *n*, Kunstkörper *m*, Kunstbauwerk
~, parting, jointing (Geol.) = Absonderungsform *f*
~ excavation = Fundamentaushub *m* für Kunstbauwerke *npl* einer Straße *f*
strut = Strebeband *n*, Kopfband
~ frame, **~ bracing** = Strebenfachwerk *n*
~ jack = Abspießwinde *f*
strutted roof = Sprengwerkdach *n*
strutting = Verstrebung *f*, Aussprießen *n*, Verstreben *n*, Abspießen, Abspießung, Ausspießung
stucco = Stuck *m*
stuccoing = Stukkatieren *n*
stuck bit = festgewordener Meißel *m*
STUCO [*Trademark*] = eine flüssige Plastikmischung *f* zum Mischen *n* von Gipsmörtel *m* oder Zement *m* an Stelle von Wasser *n*
stud = Stift *m*
~ = Jochsäule *f*
~ bolt = Stiftbolzen *m*
~ driver, **~ setter** = Bolzensetzer *m*
~ riveting hammer = Stehbolzenniethammer *m*

~ welding = Bolzenschweißung *f*
~ ~ gun = Bolzenschweißpistole *f*
study tour = Studienreise *f*
stuffing box, see: grease cup
stump, tree ~ = (Baum)Stumpf *m*, Baumstock *m*, Stubben *m*; Strunk *m* [*in Österreich*]
stumper, see: three-sided moldboard (US)
stump puller = (Baum)Stumpfzieher *m*, Wurzelzieher
stump-wood = Wurzelstockholz *n*
stylolitic limestone, see: cone-in-cone ~
to sub, see: to sublet
sub-agent = Bauleiter *m* [*wenn ein Oberbauleiter vorhanden ist*]
subaqueous foundation (work) = Unterwassergründung *f*
~ tunnel(l)ing, underwater ~ = Unterwassertunnelbau *m*
~ vehicular (or road) tunnel = Unterwasser-Straßen(verkehrs)tunnel *m*
sub-assembly = Teilmontage *f*
sub-base (course), frost blanket, granular subbase, antifreeze layer = Sauberkeitsschicht *f*, Reinheitsschicht, Frostschutzschicht, Druckverteilungsschicht, verbesserter Untergrund *m* [*in Deutschland auch als „Unterbau" bezeichnet, wenn die darüberliegende Schicht „Tragschicht" genannt wird*]; Schüttung *f* [*in der Schweiz und Österreich, „Schüttung" und „verbesserter Untergrund" ergeben zusammen den „Unterbau"*]
subcommittee = Unterausschuß *m*
sub-concrete, see: rough concrete
subcontracting = Einschaltung *f* von Nachunternehmern *mpl*
sub-contractor = Nachunternehmer *m*, Subunternehmer
sub-crust (Brit.); see: bed(ding) course
sub-diagonal = schräger Hilfsstab *m* [*Fachwerk n*]
subdivided-panel truss = Zwischenfachwerk *n*
subdrain, see: pipe drain
sub-drainage, underdrainage, subsurface drainage, (sub-)soil drainage, ground water drainage = Untergrundentwässerung *f*, Bodenentwässerung *f*, Tiefenentwässerung *f*

sub-drain type surface (or storm) drainage = Oberflächenentwässerung *f* durch Dränung *f*
sub-floor = Unterdecke *f*
subglacial moraine = Scheidemoräne *f*, Einscharungsmoräne
subgrade, soil ~, earth ~; basement soil (US) = Untergrund *m*
~ *[deprecated]*; see: formation (Brit.)
~ **compactor** = Planumsverdichter *m*
~ **drain** = Planumsdrän *m*
~ **erosion**, see: pumping
~ **excavation** = (Planum)Auskofferung *f*
subgrade-guided (canal lining) slipform paver (or machine) = auf der Sohle *f* fortbewegter Fertiger *m*
subgrade modulus K, see: modulus of subgrade reaction
(~) planer (US); see: concrete bay subgrader (Brit.)
~ **preparation** (US); see: formation work (Brit.)
~ **rooter**, grade ~ = Planumaufreißer *m*
~ **scratch template**, see: scratch template
~ **tester**, see: scratch template (Brit.)
~ **work** = Planumarbeiten *fpl*
subgrader, see: concrete bay ~ (Brit.)
subgrading (US); see: formation work
~ **machine** (US); see: concrete bay subgrader (Brit.)
subjacent body = ruhender Tiefengranit *m* (Geol.)
to sublet, to subcontract, to sub (out to) = weitervergeben [*Bauauftrag m*]
sublevel stoping = unterirdische Erzkammer *f*
submain, see: branch sewer
submarginal = nicht mehr rentabel, ~ ~ wirtschaftlich, unrentabel, unwirtschaftlich
submarine blasting gelatine = Unterwasser-Sprenggelatine *f*
~ **cable**, marine type cable = Seekabel *n*
~ **detonator**, ~ electric ~ = (elektrischer) Unterwasserzünder *m*
~ **earthquake** = Seebeben *n*
submerged evaporator = Tauchverdampfer *m*
~ **sedimentation tank**, ~ ~ chamber = mehrstöckige Klärgrube *f*, ~ Absetzgrube [*fälschlich als "Frisch-Gerinne" bezeichnet*]
submersible bridge, causeway = Tauchbrücke *f*, überflutbare Brücke
~ **pump** [*motor sealed against the entry of water*] = Unterwasser(motor)pumpe *f*, Tauchpumpe
submission (of competitive tenders) = Submission *f*
subsea(ling), see: underseal(ing)
subsequent enlargement to the full section of the tunnel = nachträglicher Vollausbruch *m*
subsidence, breach, base failure, shear failure [*downward movement of the soil produced by removal or displacement of the underlying strata*] = Grundbruch *m*
~, see: sedimentation process
~ **basin** = Einsturzbecken *n*
~ **basin**, see: sedimentation ~
~ **earthquake** = Einsturzbeben *n*
subsidiary drain, see: branch~
~ **(or secondary) reinforcement** = Hilfsbewehrung *f*, Hilfsarmierung *f*
~ **road**, see: minor ~
subsistence, see: living allowance
subsoil, foundation soil = Untergrund *m*, Baugrund *m*, Gründungsboden *m*
~ **(or subsurface) cementation (or solidification, or stabilisation)** = Tiefenstabilisierung *f*, (Boden)Verfestigung *f* von Tiefgründungen *fpl*, Untergrunddichtung *f*
~ **consolidation**, ground ~ = natürliche Baugrundverdichtung *f*
~ **drain**, see: pipe ~
~ **drainage by the electro-osmosis method**, electroösmotic drainage = Elektro(-Osmose)-Entwässerung *f*
~ **investigation**, see: soil ~
~ **paper**, see: concreting ~
~ **plough** (Brit.); ~ **plow**, pan-breaker, subsoiler (US) = Unterpflug *m*
~ **solidification**, see: ~ cementation
~ **stabilisation**, see: ~ cementation
~ **waterproofing**, see: foundation soil ~
substation, electricity ~ = Speisetransformatorenhaus *n*, Speisetrafohaus *n*
substitute = Ersatzmittel *n*
~ = Bohrgestängeanschlußstück *n*

subsurface cementation, see: subsoil ~
~ conditions = Untergrundverhältnisse *npl*
~ contour map = Tiefenlinienkarte *f*, Tiefenkurvenkarte, Isobathenkarte
~ erosion, see: scour(ing)
~ exploration, see: soil investigation
~ grouting with cement mortar, see: cement mortar grouting
~ ~ ~ ~ water grout = Zementmilcheinpressung *f*
~ investigation, see: soil ~
~ reconnaissance, see: soil investigation
~ sampling = Untergrundprobenahme *f*
~ solidification, see: subsoil cementation
~ stabilisation, see: subsoil cementation
~ water = Bodenwasser *n*
subterranean current = Grundwasserstrom *m*
subterraneous irrigation = Untergrundbewässerung *f*, Dränbewässerung *f*
suburb = Stadtrandsiedlung *f*
suburban bus = Vorort-Omnibus *m*, Vorort-(Auto)Bus
~ dwelling house = Vorort-Wohnhaus *n*
~ residential area = Vorstadtwohngebiet *n*
sub-vertical = senkrechter Hilfsstab *m* [*Fachwerk n*]
subwayite (US) = U-Bahn-Fahrer *m*
subway (tube) = Untergrundbahntunnel *m*
sub-zero temperature = Unter-Null-Temperatur *f*
successful bidder (or tenderer) = Auftragnehmer *m*
succinic acid = Bernsteinsäure *f*
succinite, amber = Bernstein *m*
sucker = Pumpenschuh *m*
~ rod elevator = Pump(en)gestängefahrstuhl *m*
~ rods, pump ~ = Pumpenstäbe *mpl*, Pumpengestänge *n*
(~) rod wax = pastöse Paraffin-Öl-Emulsion *f*
~ ~ wrench = Pump(en)gestänge(-Dreh)-schlüssel *m*
suction, priming ~ = Ansaugen *n*, Ansaugung *f*
~ blower = Sauggebläse *n*

~ casing, ~ shaft (Brit.); lower leg of siphon (US) = Saugleitung *f* [*automatischer Syphon m*]
suction-cutter apparatus, (revolving) cutter = Schneidkopf *m*, Fräserkopf, Wühlkopf(-Fräser) *m* [*Naßbagger m*]
~ dredge(r), cutter suction ~, cutter-(head) (hydraulic) ~, clay-cutter (suction) ~ = Cutter(saug)bagger *m*, Cuttersauger *m*, (stationärer) Schneidkopf-(Saug)Bagger, (stationärer) Saugbagger mit Schneidkopf *m*
suction dredge(r), (sand-)pump ~, hydraulic (suction) ~ = Saugbagger *m*, Pumpen(naß)bagger *m*
~ filter = Ansaugfilter *m, n*
~ head, ~ lift = Saughöhe *f*
suction-jet conveying system, see: combined suction and pressure ~
suction lift, ~ head = Saughöhe *f*
~ line = Saugleitung *f*
~ pipe = (An)Saugrohr *n*
~ (or vacuum) pneumatic conveyor (or conveying system), vacuum pump transporter = Saugluftförderer *m*, Saugluftförderanlage *f*
~ pump, sucking ~ = Saugpumpe *f*
~ scavenger = Saug-Straßenkehrmaschine *f*
~ type cloth filter dust collector = Saugschlauchfilter *m, n*
sugar maple = Zuckerahorn *m*
~ of lead, see: acetate of lead
suitability test, preliminary ~ = Eignungsprüfung *f*
suitable for rail transport = bahnverladbar
sulfated residue = Sulfatrückstand *m*
sulfite cellulose liquor = Sulfitzellstoffablauge *f*
~ ~ tar, tall oil = Sulfitzellstoffablaugeteer *m*
sulfuric acid = Schwefelsäure *f*
sulfurized coal-tar pitch = Holzement *m*
sulphate-bearing water = sulfathaltiges Wasser *n*
sulphate of calcium, calcium sulphate, sulphate of lime = schwefelsaures Kalzium *n*, CaSO$_4$
~ of magnesium, see: Epsom salt

sulphide of copper, CU_2S = Schwefelkupfer n
sulphite liquor (or lye) = Sulfitablauge f
sulphocarbolic acid = Schwefelkarbolsäure f
sulphonated castor oil = sulphoniertes Rizinusöl n
sulphonic acid = Sulfosäure f
sulphuric anhydride = Schwefelsäureanhydrid n
sulphur subchloride = Halbchlorschwefel m
~ trioxide = Schwefeltrioxyd n
sulphuryl chloride = Sulfurylchlorid n
summer lightning = Wetterleuchten n
~ vacation travel = Sommerferienverkehr m
*summit = Kuppe f
~ curve, convex transition between gradients = Kuppenausrundung f
sump = Wanne f [*Maschine f*]
~ hole, see: (pump) sump (pit)
~ pump = Sumpfpumpe f
sunken tree = Sinkbaum m
sunken-tube method, see: trench method of subaqueous tunnel(l)ing
sunk well for foundation purposes, foundation caisson = Gründungsbrunnen m
(~) ~ foundation, open caisson ~, well-sunk ~ = (Senk-)Brunnengründung f, Senkbrunnenfundation f
sunstone (Min.), see: aventurine fel(d)spar
supercharged diesel engine = Dieselmotor m mit Aufladung f
supercharger = Auflader m, Aufladekompressor m, Aufladegebläse n, Vorverdichter m
supercharging = Aufladung f [*Dieselmotor m*]
super-compactor = Riesengummi(reifenvielfach)walze f, Schwerst-Verdichter m, Supergummiradwalze [*Dienstgewicht von 100—200 Tonnen*]
superelevetad turn = überhöhte Kurve f
superelevation, see: cant
~ of the belt = Abwinkelung f des (Förder)Bandes n
superficial compaction = Oberflächenverdichtung f
superfinish = Oberflächenfeinstbehandlung f

super flood (US); see: catastrophic ~ (Brit.)
superglacial stream = Schmelzwasserbach m
superheater = Überhitzer m
super-highway bridge-mixer, see: bridge-(type travel(l)ing concrete) mixer
(super)imposed load, surcharge, loading, additional load = Auflast f, aufgebrachte Belastung f, ~ Last f, Nutzlast [*Decke f*]
superintendent = selbständiger Bauleiter m
SUPERIOR COIL TIE [*Trademark*] = Spiralbindung f für Betonschalungstafeln fpl, Fabrikat SUPERIOR CONCRETE ACCESSORIES, INC., CHICAGO 39, ILLINOIS, USA
superposition of moment = Momentenüberlagerung f
supersaturated = übersättigt
supersonic method, see: ultrasonic ~
~ tunnel = Überschallkanal m
superstructure, upper deck = Oberwagen m [*Bagger m*]
~ = Oberbau m
super-sulphate cement, high sulphate resisting Portland cement; Portland cement Type V (US) = starker Gipsschlackenzement m, ~ Sulfathüttenzement m
supervising staff, supervisory personnel = Aufsichtspersonal n
supervision of works = Bauaufsicht f
supervisor = Bauführer m
supplementary direction sign, see: direction post
supplier = Zulieferant m
to supply downstream interests with water = Brauchwasser n garantieren [*Talsperre f*]
supply industry = Lieferindustrie f
~ line = Versorgungsleitung f
~ tank, ~ bin = Packsilo m [*Einsackmaschine f*]
~ zone = Versorgungszone f
support = Abstützung f
~ = Stiel m
supporting capacity, see: bearing ~
~ frame = Stützrahmen m

supporting material = Stützkörpermaterial n

(~) roller, carrier (idler) = Tragrolle f, belastete ~

~ structure = Tragkonstruktion f

~ ~, ~ body [of an earth dam or rockfill dam] = Stützkörper m

to suppress [electrical appliances] = entstören

suppressor = Entstörer m, Entstörvorrichtung f

surcharge, see: imposed load

~ ~ = Überschüttungshöhe f [Betonverteilung f]

~ lift = Auflastschicht f

surf, see: breaker

surface-active = oberflächenaktiv

surface and trespass damage = Flurschaden m

~ area of the basin = Beckenoberfläche f

~ artery, ~ arterial = normale Stadthauptstraße f, Stadthauptstraße zu ebener Erde

(~) base course (Brit.); see: binder ~

~ chemistry = Oberflächenchemie f

~ coating film = Anstrichfilm m

~ compactor = Oberflächenverdichter m

~ (concrete) slab = Oberbetonplatte f [wenn ein Unterbeton vorhanden ist]

*surface course, see: wearing ~

~ crazing, see: crazing

~ digging, shallow cut ~, surface excavation, shallow grading = Flachbaggern n, Flachbaggerung f

~ digging machine = Flachbagger m

~ drainage, storm ~ = Oberflächenentwässerung f

~ dressing chipping distributor, see: chip spreader

~(-) dressing (treatment), see: seal(ing) coat

surface dressing chipping(s) (Brit.); see: blotter (material) (for bituminous prime coat) (US)

~ ~ with tar, surface tarring = Oberflächenteerung f

~ excavation, see: ~ digging

~ grinder, face ~, ~ grinding machine = Planschleifmaschine f

~ hardener, see: concrete ~

surface-ignition engine, see: hot-bulb ~

surface maintenance costs = Deckenunterhaltungskosten f

~ membrane = Oberflächenabdichtungsschicht f

~ mix(ture) = Oberflächengemisch n, Oberflächenmischung f [Kiesstraße f]

~ pressure, unit ~ = Flächendruck m

~ railway, ground level ~ = Oberflächenbahn f

~ reconnaissance = Bodenuntersuchung f an der Oberfläche f

~ route, see: ~ street

~ run-off, surface flow = oberirdischer Abfluß m

(~) scaling = Abschälen n der Obermörtelschicht f [Betondecke f]

(~) soil stabilization, see: soil stabilization (or cementation) on the surface

~ ~ ~ with artificial resins, ~ ~ ~ ~ synthetic resin bonding agents = Verfestigung f mit künstlichen Harzen npl

~ stop and go driving = Fahren n auf einer Strecke f mit Stopsignalen npl [Gegenteil: non-stop freeway driving]

~ street, ~ route, ~ artery = normale Stadtstraße f, Oberflächen(stadt)straße f

~ ~ network = Oberflächen(stadt)straßennetz n

~ structure = oberirdisches Bauwerk n

~ tarring, ~ dressing with tar = Oberflächenteerung f

*surface texture of aggregates = Bruchflächenbeschaffenheit f von Zuschlagstoffen mpl

surface-to-tunnel pipe chute, downhole = Fallrohr n, Rohr von Erdoberfläche bis zur Tunneldecke f

surface treatment, seal coating = Oberflächenbehandlung f, OB [Arbeitsverfahren n beim Schwarzdeckenbau m]

~ vibrator, surface vibrating machine = (Ober)Flächenrüttler m, (Ober)Flächenvibrator m

~ water = Oberflächenwasser n, Tag(es)wasser n

~ water gull(e)y, inlet of sewer = Doleneinlauf m

~ watershed line, ~ divide = oberirdische Wasserscheide f

surface wind — sweating

surface wind, ground ~ = Bodenwind *m*
surfacing, road ~ (Brit.); [*deprecated: coating, sheeting*] = (Straßen)Decke *f* [*Verschleißschicht und/oder Binder-Schicht, aber Unterbau m ausgeschlossen*]; Belag *m* [*Schweiz und Österreich*]
~ **material** = Deckeneinbaumaterial *n*
surfacing work (Brit.); see: paving work (US)
surf boat = Brandungsboot *n*
~ **breccia** = Brandungsbrekzie *f*
surge bin, ~ hopper = Arbeitssilo *m*
~ **chamber**, ~ shaft = Wasserschloßschacht *m*, Schwallschacht *m*
~ **pile** = Ausgleichhalde *f*
~ **tank** = Wasserschloß *n*
surk(h)i = gebrannter Ton *m* [*in Indien*]
surplus cartage = Abfuhr *f* überschüssiger Bodenmassen *fpl*, ~ auf Kippe *f*
~ **spoil**, see: spoil
surround = Voll-Betonummantelung *f* [*Rohr n*]
surrounding material = Deckgebirge *n* [*Tunnelbau m*]
~ **walls** = Umfassungsmauerwerk *n*
survey = Aufnahme *f*, Vermessung *f*
~ = Überblick *m*
***surveying** = Vermessungskunde *f*
~ **instrument** = Vermessungsgerät *n*
survey of heights, level(l)ing = Nivellieren *n*, Höhenaufnahme *f*, Höhenmessung *f*
surveyor's chain, land ~ = Meßkette *f*
surveyor tracing gang, survey party = Vermessungstrupp *m*
susceptibility to failures = Störanfälligkeit *f*
suspended deck = aufgehängte (Brücken-) Fahrbahn *f*
~ **fender** = Aufhänge-Fender *m*
~ **level visco(si)meter** = Ubbelohde-Viskosimeter *n*
~ **matter** = Schwebstoff *m*
~ **pile(d) foundation**, floating ~ ~ = schwebende Pfahlgründung *f*, schwimmende ~
~ **roller (grinding) mill** = Pendel(mahl)mühle *f*, Fließkraft(mahl)mühle mit Walzen *fpl*
~ **scaffold(ing)**, hung ~ = Hängerüstung *f*, Hängegerüst *n*
~ **screen** = Hängesieb *n*
~ **span** = Einhängeträger *m*
~ **subsurface water**, see: vadose ~
suspender cable [*bridge*] = Tragkabel *n*
~ **connection bracket** = Hängerkonsole *f* [*Brücke f*]
~ **frame**, hanging system = Hängekonstruktion *f*
~ **rope** = Hängeseil *n* [*Brücke f*]
suspension = Aufschwemmung *f*
~ = Aufhängung *f*
~ **bolt** = Deckenanker *m* [*Tunnelbau und Bergbau*]
~ **boom (or chord, or flange)** = Hängegurt(ung) *m*, (*f*)
~ **bridge** = Hängebrücke *f*
~ ~ **strand** = Brückenseil *n*
(~) ~ **tower** = Pylone *f*
~ ~ **with horizontal tie** = Hängebrücke *f* mit Versteifungsträger *m*
~ ~ ~ **shore anchorages** = erdverankerte Hängebrücke *f*
~ **hopper scale**, ~ bucket ~ = Hängegefäßwaage *f*, Hängebehälterwaage *f*
~ **ladder** = Hängeleiter *f*
~ **of driver license** = Führerscheinentzug *m*
~ **rail**, overhead ~ = Hängeschiene *f*
~ ~ **type travel(l)ing weighbatcher** = Hängebahnwaage *f*
~ **rod**, suspender = Hängestange *f* [*Brücke f*]
~ **structure** = Hängewerk *n*
~ **strut** = Hängestrebe *f*
~ **support installation**, see: roof-bolting
~ **type preheater** = Schwebgas-Wärme-(aus)tauscher *m*
swallow = Senke *f*
~-**tail**, dovetail = Schwalbenschwanz *m*
swamp (area) = Sumpf(gebiet) *m*, (*n*)
~ **meadow** = Sumpfwiese *f*
~-**shooting method**, see: bog blasting
swan-neck boom (US); ~ jib (Brit.) = Schwanenhals-Ausleger *m*
swan-necked draining tool = Schwanenhals *m*
sway bracing = Querverband *m*
sweating, bleeding, water gain = Wasserabstoßen *n*, Bluten *n*, Wasserabsonderung *f* [*Beton m*]

sweats, see: foots oil
Swedish cylindrical-surface method, ~ circular-arc ~ = schwedisches Verfahren n, schwedische Gleitkreistheorie f
Swedish impulse oilfiring system [*brick manufacture*] = CRYPTO-System n [*schwedisches Ölbrennverfahren n für Ring- und Zickzacköfen mpl*]
sweep well (US); open bucket ~, draw ~ (Brit.) = Ziehbrunnen m
sweet clover, melilot = Reinklee m
~ natural gas = schwefelwasserstofffreies Erdgas n (oder Naturgas)
~ oil = Öl n mit negativem Doktortest m fast frei von Schwefelwasserstoff m und Mercaptan n
~-scented vernal grass = Ruchgras n
swelling = Aufquellen n, Quellung f, Schwellbewegung, Schwellung, Schwellen
~ resistance = Quellungsbeständigkeit f
swell soil, see: expansive ~
~ waves = Dünung f
swept volume, piston displacement = durchlaufenes Kolbenvolumen n, Hubvolumen [*Kompressor m*]
swinestone [*fetid bituminous limestone*] = Schweinstein m
swing angle = Schwenkwinkel m
~ bolt = Gelenkschraube f
~ boom (US), see: rotating ~
~-boom crane (US); see: revolving ~
swing brake, slewing gear ~ = Drehwerkbremse f [*Bagger m*]
~ bridge = Drehbrücke f
~ clutch (coupling) = Schwenkkupplung f [*Bagger m*]
~ crane, see: revolving ~
~ digger (attachment) = Tieflöffel-Ausrüstung f für Schwenkschaufler m
(~) dipper shovel, (face) ~, power ~, mechanical ~; luffing-boom shovel (US); power navvy, crane ~, crowd shovel (Brit.) = Hochlöffel(bagger) m, Löffelhochbagger
~ excavator = Schwenk(trocken)bagger m
~ gear, slewing ~, swinging ~, slewing mechanism = Schwenkwerk n [*Bagger m*]

~ ~ reversing clutch shaft = Wendegetriebewelle f zum Schwenkwerk n
~ hammer = Hammermühlenschläger m
(swing-)hammer crusher, see: hammer crusher
swing hammer pulverizer, see: pulverator
~ ~ rotary granulator, split ~ ~ ~ = Feinhammerbrecher m
swinging area, turning basin = Wendeplatz m für ein Schiff n
~ bucket elevator, see: gravity tipping conveyor
~ gear, see: swing ~
~ gravity fender = Schwergewichts-Pendelfender m
~ jaw, see: movable ~
~ ~ crusher, see: double toggle ~
~ ~ shaft = Schwingachse f [*Blake-Brecher m*]
~ ~ ~, (overhead) eccentric (shaft) = Exzenter(welle) m, (f), Antriebswelle
swing-jib (Brit.); see: rotating boom (US)
~ crane (Brit.); see: revolving ~
swing lever = Schwenkhebel m
~ loader, ~ shovel = Schwenklader m, Schwenkschaufler m
~ lock = Oberwagen-Blockierung f, Oberwagensperre f
swing-propel shift lever = Schwenk-Fahrt-Schalthebel m
swing scraping = Schwenkschrappen n
~ shaft = Schwenkwelle f
~ throw = Werfen n der Schleppschaufel f während des Schwenkens n
swirl nozzle = Wirbeldüse f
switch = Schalter m
~ blade, see: ~ rail
~ building = Schaltwerksgebäude n
switching = Rangieren n
switch oil = Schalteröl n
~ rail, switch blade = Zungenschiene f, Weichenschiene f
switchyard = Verschiebebahnhof m, Rangierbahnhof
~, switching station = Freiluftschaltanlage f
to swivel around, see: to slue about
swivel ball = Drehkopfkugel f

swivel chute, discharge ~ = Abwurfschurre *f*, Austragschurre, Austragungsschurre, Auslaufschurre

~ **conveyor bucket loader** = Eimerketten-Fahrlader *m* mit Drehabsetzband *n*

~ **coupling** = Drehkupplung *f*

~ **flight conveyor,** see: extension ~ ~

~ **joint** = Drehgelenk *n*

swivel(ling) chute, swivel spout = Drehschurre *f*

swivelpiler [*thrower belt unit with hopper*] = Flieger *m* mit Einlauftrichter *m*

swivel pin = Drehkopfbolzen *m*

~ **spout,** see: swivel(ling) chute

~ **wheels** = Schwenk-Radsatz *m* [*Fahrband n*]

sycamore, see: greater maple

syenite = Syenit *m*

~-**(h)aplite** = Syenitaplit *m*

syenodiorite, see: monzonite

sylvanite (Min.), see: graphic tellurium [*deprecated*]

symmetrical two-legged multi-storied frame = zweistieliger symmetrischer Stockwerkrahmen *m*

*****Symons (cone) crusher,** standard type ~ (~) ~ = Symons(kegel)brecher *m*

~ **intermediate cone crusher** = kombinierter Symons(kegel)brecher und -granulator *m*

synchronized = synchronisiert

synchronous converter = Einankerumformer *m*

synclinal formation (Geol.) = Muldenbildung *f*

syncline = Synklinale *f*, Mulde *f* der Faltung *f*

synthetic resin = Kunstharz *n*

~ **rubber** = synthetischer Kautschuk *m*, ~ Gummi *m*

~ **weir** = Heber(stau)wehr *n*

system, see: series

~ = Konstruktion *f*

~ = System *n*

~ **of controls** = Signalisierungssystem *n* [*Straße f*]

~ ~ **suburban rail service** = Vorort-Schnellbahn *f*

~ **point,** assemblage ~, centre knot = Knotenpunkt *m*

T

table = Tisch *m*

~ = Zahlentafel *f*, Tabelle *f*

tabled joint = Verschränkung *f* [*Holzverbindung f*]

table feeder = Tischspeiser *m*, Tischaufgeber *m*, Tischbeschicker *m*

tableland = flache Hochebene *f*

table scarf = Doppelblatt *n* [*Holzverbindung f*]

~ **vibrator,** see: vibration table

tabular [*mineral*] = tafelig

~ **spar** (Min.), see: wollastonite

tacheometer, tachymeter = Tachymeter *m, n*

tacheometric survey = tachymetrische Aufnahme *f*

tacheometry = Tachymetrie *f*, gleichzeitige Lage- und Höhenmessung *f*

tachometer = Geschwindigkeitsmesser *m*

tachymeter, see: tacheometer

tack = Nagelstift *m*

~ = Anhaftungsvermögen *n*, Klebrigkeit *f* [*Kalk m*]

~ **coat,** see: binder ~

~ **coater** = Bindeschicht-Spritzapparat *m*

~ **coating** = Bindeschichtanspritzung *f*

tacking rivet = Heftniet *m*

tackle, see: (block) and tackle

tack riveting = Heftnieten *n*, Heftnietung *f*

tack welding = Heftschweißen *n*, Heftschweißung *f*

tacky mix = klebrige Mischung *f*, klebriges Mischgut *n*

taenite (Min.) = Bandeisen *n*

"TAG" closed tester = geschlossener Flammpunktprüfer *m* von Tagliabue

tagger = sehr dünnes Feinblech *n*

tagline = Leitseil *n*, Beruhigungsseil [*Bagger m*]

tailboard, tailgate; truck endgate (US) = hintere Klappe *f* am LKW *m*

tailgate, see: tailboard

~ = Unterwassernotverschluß *m*

tail gate, see: lower ~

~ ~ **spreader box** = Anbau-Verteilerkasten *m* [*am hinteren Ende n des LKW's m*]

tail gate (vane type) chip spreader — tangent point

tail gate (vane type) chip spreader, see: rear-mounted gritter
tailings, see: (crusher) waste
~, see: waste ore
~ **pond** = Schlammteich *m* [*Erzaufbereitung f*]
tail light, rear ~ = Rücklicht *n*
~ **pulley, return** ~ = Schwanztrommel *f* [*Bandförderer m*]
~ **race**, see: discharge channel
tail(race) tunnel = Unterwasserstollen *m*, Ableitungsstollen *m*
tall tower = Kabelkrangegenturm *m*
tailwater = Unterwasser *n*
~ **power plant (or installation)** = Unterwasserkraftwerk *n*
~ **rise** = Unterwasseranstieg *m* [*Talsperre f*]
taintor (or tainter) gate, see: segment shaped sluice
to take down, see: to pull ~
take-home pay = Nettoverdienst *m*
take-off runway = Nur-Startbahn *f*
take-up, ~ **set** = Spannvorrichtung *f*, Spannstation *f* [*Bandförderer m*]
~ **pulley** = Spannrolle *f*, Spanntrommel *f*
taking down, see: wrecking
talc (Min.) = Talk *m*
~ **schist** = Talkschiefer *m*
talcum powder, see: French chalk
to talk shop = fachsimpeln
tall building = Hochhaus *n*
~ ~ **frame, multi-stor(e)y** ~ = mehrstöckiger Rahmen *m*
~ **fescue** = Rohrschwingel *m*
~ **oat grass** = französisches Raigras *n*
~ **oil** [*incorrectly termed: liquid resin*] = Tallöl *n*
~ ~ **tar**, see: sulfite cellulose ~
talus, scree (Geol.) = Geröllhalde *f*
~ **material (Geol.)**, see: rubble slope
~ **train**, see: rock glacier
tamper = Stampfer *m*
~, **tamping roller (US)** = Stampfwalze *f* [*in den USA Bezeichnung für Bodenverdichtungswalzen ganz gleich ob Schaffußwalze, Gummiwalze oder Vibrationswalze*]

~, **tamping beam** = Stampfbohle *f*, Schlagbohle, Stampfbalken *m*, Verdichtungsbohle
~ **drive shaft, tamping beam** ~ ~ = Stampfbohlenantriebswelle *f*, Schlagbohlenantriebswelle
~ **extension** = Stampfbohlen-Ansatzstück *n*, Schlagbohlenansatzstück
~ **finisher**, see: tamping beam finisher
~ **overdrive** = Stampfer-Overdrive *m*
~ **shield** = Vorabstreifer *m* [*Schwarzbelageinbaumaschine f*]
~ **speed** = Stampferschlagzahl *f*
~ **transmission** = Stampfbohlenantrieb *m*
tamping, see: ramming
~ **beam, tamper** ~ = Stampfbohle *f*, Schlagbohle, Stampfbalken *m*, Verdichtungsbohle
~ ~ **finisher, tamper finisher** = Stampfbohlenfertiger *m*, Schlagbohlenfertiger, Stampfbalkenfertiger
tamp(ing) (concrete) (block) machine = (Betonstein)Stampfmaschine *f*
tamping-crane rammer, see: excavator-operated stamper
tamping material, see: stemming ~
~ **plate, falling-plate tamping unit** = Stampfplatte *f* [*Freifall-Kranstampfer m*]
~ **roller**, see: tamper (US)
tandem-axle truck (US) = dreiachsiger LKW *m*
tandem drive = Tandemantrieb *m*
~ **roller** = Tandemwalze *f*
~ **saw rig,** ~ **joint cutter** = Tandem(beton)fugenschneider *m*, Tandem(beton)fugenschneidgerät *n*, Fabrikat FELKER MANUFACTURING CO., TORRANCE, CALIF., USA
tan-earth = Loherde *f*
tang = Zapfen *m*
tangent = Gerade *f* [*Linienführung f einer Straße f*]
~ **circles method** = Methode *f* der sich tangierenden Kreise *mpl*
tangential (admission) turbine = Tangentialturbine *f*
~ **thrust** = Bogenschub *m*
tangent point = 1. Krümmungsanfangspunkt *m*; 2. Krümmungsendpunkt [*Straße f*]

tan-house — tarn

tan-house, see: tannery
tank, see: cistern
~ = Panzer *m*
~ **car heater**, booster ~ = Dampferzeuger *m*, Kesselwagenerhitzer *m*
~ **construction** = Behälterbau *m*
~ **dome** = Behälterkuppel *f*
tanker (ship), ocean-going tanker = Tankschiff *n*, Tanker *m*
tank furnace = Glaswannenofen *m*
~ **gunnery range** = Panzerschießplatz *m*
tanking (Brit.) = isolierte Gebäudewanne *f*, Wannenauskleidung *f*
tank lorry (Brit.); see: ~ truck (US)
~ **road** = Panzerstraße *f*
~ **sprayer** = Tanksprengwagen *m*
~ **trailer** = Tankanhänger *m*
tank-training area (or ground) = Panzerübungsgelände *n*
tank truck (US); tank lorry, bowser (Brit.); road tanker = Straßentankwagen *m*, Straßentanker *m*
~ **type pump**, ~ ~ pneumatic conveying system = Gefäß(förder)pumpe *f*
(~) winding machine = (Behälter-)Wickelmaschine *f*
tannery, tan-house, tan-yard = Lohgerberei *f*
~ **waste** = Gerbereiabwasser *n*
tannin, tannic acid, gallo-tannin = Tannin *n*, Gerbsäure *f*
tantalite (Min.) = Schwertantalerz *n*
tantalum = Tantal *n*
tan-yard, see: tannery
tap = Gewindebohrer *m*
~ **cinder**, see: puddling ~
tape depth ga(u)ge = Rollbandpegel *m*
taper, see: tapering
~ **bore mounted** = fliegend gelagert
tapered = konisch
~ **driven shell foundation (or bearing) pile** = Ortbeton(gründungs)pfahl *m* mit konischem Blechmantel *m*
taper(ed)-foot (type sheepsfoot) roller, see: pyramid feet ~
tapered haunch = Voutenschräge *f*
~ **rim** = Flankenneigung *f*
~ **tenon** = Schrägzapfen *m*, schräger Zapfen [*Holzverbindung f*]

tapering, taper = Verjüngung *f*
taper roller bearing (Brit.); TIMKEN ~ [*Trademark*] (US) = Kegelrollenlager *n*
tapped branch pipe sluice valve = Anbohrschieber *m*
~ **hole** = Gewindeloch *n*
tappet = Stößel *m*
~ **clearance** = Stößelspiel *n*
~ **head** = Stößelteller *m*
tap root = Pfahlwurzel *f*
~ **water**, service ~ = Leitungswasser *n*, Brauchwasser
*****tar** = Teer *m*
~ **and bitumen** (Brit.)/**asphalt** (US) **heater (or heating kettle, or melting tank)**; ~ ~ **boiler** [*deprecated*] = Teer- und Bitumen-Kocher *m*, Teer- und Bitumen-Schmelzkessel *m*
~ ~ ~ **primary heater (or heating kettle, or melting tank)**; ~ ~ ~ ~ **boiler** [*deprecated*] = Teer- und Bitumen-Vorkocher *m*
~ **barrel** = Teerfaß *n*
~/**bitumen distributor** (Brit.); see: binder ~
tar-bound, see: tarviated
tar coal = Schwelkohle *f*
tar-coated chipping(s), see: tarred ~
tar concrete pavement, see: dense tar surfacing
~ **destillery** = Teerschwelerei *f*
~ **dipping ladle** = Teerschöpfer *m*
tare = Leergewicht *n*, Taragewicht
~ **balance** = Tarierwaage *f*
~ **beam** = Tarierbalken *m*
tar emulsion = Teeremulsion *f*
tar felt = Teerpappe *f*
target date = Fertigstellungstermin *m*
TARGRANIT (Brit.) [*Trademark*] = geteerter Granitsplitt *m*
tar-grouted stone (Brit.); tar penetration macadam, road tar type penetration macadam = Teertränkmakadam *m* [*früher: Teeraufguß-Beschotterung f*]
tar hose = Teerschlauch *m*
tarmacadam; macadam with tar binder (Brit.) = Teermakadam *m*
tar mixing plant = Teermischanlage *f*
tarn, see: mountain lake

tarp(aulin) = geteertes Segeltuch n, Persenning f, Presenning f
TARPAVING (Brit.) [*Trademark*] = Teermakadam m für Spielplätze mpl und Fußwege mpl
tar penetration macadam; see: tar-grouted stone (Brit.)
tarred chipping(s), tar-coated ~, chipping(s) precoated with tar = Teersplitt m
~ oakum = Teerwerg n
~ stone = Teerschotter m
tarring, tarspraying = Teerung f
tar roof = Teerdach n
~ soil stabilization, soil stabilisation with tar = Teerverfestigung f
~ spray = Teerstreumakadam m
tarsprayer = Teerspritzgerät n, Teerspritzmaschine f
tarspraying, see: tarring
tarviated, tar-bound = teergebunden [*Straße f*]
task work, see: piece ~
tautline cableway; see: blondin (Brit.)
tax-aided = steuerbegünstigt
tax-free = steuerfrei
taxi-holding position, see: alert platform
taxi-track, taxi-way (US); perimeter (track) (Brit.); airport taxiing strip = Zubahn f, Rollweg m, Rollfeldringstraße f, Zurollbahn f
taxi-way light = Rollwegfeuer n, Zu(roll)wegfeuer [*Flugplatz m*]
teachting activity = Lehrtätigkeit f
teaming, see: leading (Brit.)
team (of workers), see: crew
to tear loose from = losreißen von
tearing of mat = Verunstaltung f der Decklage f [*Schwarzstraßenbau m*]
technical, practical = technisch, betriebstechnisch
~ hangar, tech ~, maintenance ~ = Werft f [*Flugplatz m*]
~ (road) patrol = technischer (Straßen-)Überwachungstrupp m
~ specifications = technische Richtlinien fpl
~ use of ultra-fine aggregate particles = Feinstkorntechnik f [*Betonbau m*]
technician (US) = Ingenieur-Hilfskraft f

technique, practice = Technik f [*als betriebstechnische Anwendung f*]
tectonic earthquake = Dislokationsbeben n, tektonisches Beben n
tee-piece, Tee = T-Stück n
telegraph-pole, telephone pole = Telegrafenstange f, Telegrafenmast m
teleigrometer = Hygrometer n
telephone kiosk = Telefonzelle f, Telefonhäuschen n
~ tower = Fernmeldeturm m
~ tunnel = Fernmeldestollen m
teleprinter, telex = Fernschreiber m
to telescope = auseinanderziehen
telescopic = ausziehbar
telescopic-armed crane = Teleskopkran m
telescopic (or folding) boom (US); ~ (~ ~) jib (Brit.) = Teleskopausleger m
~ lift truck = Teleskop-Hubstapler m
~ (mono)tower = Teleskop-Drehsäule f [*Turmdrehkran m*]
television monitoring = Fernsehverkehrslenkung f
Telford base (US); see: base of stone pitching (Brit.)
~ stone (US); see: pitcher (Brit.)
telpher = Elektro(-Einschienen-)hängebahn f
temperature gradient method = Temperaturanstiegs-Meßverfahren n
~ stress = Temperaturspannung f
~ susceptibility = Aufbereitungsempfindlichkeit f [*bit. Bindemittel n*]
~ variation = Temperaturschwankung f
tempering, drawing = Tempern n
temper-rolled mild steel = gewalztes Flußeisen n
template, templet, camber board = Formlineal n, Profillehre f
templet, see: template
(temporary) diversion = provisorische Umleitung f
~ flood relief works = Behelfs-Hochwasserentlastungsanlage f
~ structures (or works) = Behelfsbauten f
tenacity = Beharrung f, Aufrechterhaltung f des Widerstandes m [*Gummi-Bitumen-Mischung f*]
tendency to soot = Rußneigung f

tender, see: bid
- ~ **documents** = Ausschreibungsunterlagen *fpl*, Angebotsunterlagen

tenderer, bidder = Bieter *m*

tendering date, see: date set for the opening of tenders

tender loco(motive), see: locomotive-car

tendon, steel ~ [*conduit containing prestressing wire*] = Spannglied *n*, Spannkanal *m*, Spanneisen *n*

tenon jointing = Verzapfung *f* [*Holzverbindung f*]
- ~ **saw**; see: mitre box saw (Brit.)

tensible = dehnbar

tensile = spannbar
- ~ **bending test** = Biegezugfestigkeitsprüfung *f*
- ~ **force** = Zugkraft *f*
- ~ **reinforcement** = Zugbewehrung *f*, Zugarmierung *f*
- ~ **shrinkage stress** = Schwindzugspannung *f*
- ~ ~ **crack** = Schwindzugspannungsriß *m*
- ~ **splitting test** = Zug-Spalt-Versuch *m*
- ~ **strength**, tension ~ = Zugfestigkeit *f*, Zerreißfestigkeit
- ~ **(or tension) strength in bending**, flexure strength, flexural ~ = Biegezugfestigkeit *f*
- ~ **stress**, tension = Zugspannung *f*, Zugbeanspruchung *f*
- ~ ~ **due to temperature variation** = Temperaturspannung *f*
- ~ ~ **in the concrete** = Beton-Zugspannung *f*

tension = Straffung *f* [*Förderband n*]
- ~, see: tensile stress
- ~ **boom**, ~ chord, ~ flange = Zuggurt *m*
- ~ **fault**, see: pivotal ~
- ~ **flange**, see: ~ boom

tensioning after hardening of concrete = Spannen *n* nach dem Erhärten *n* des Betons *m*
- ~ **device**, stressing ~ = Spannvorrichtung *f*
- ~ **prior to the pouring of concrete** = Spannen *n* vor dem Erhärten *n* des Betons *m*

tension member = Zugstab *m*, zugfester Stab *m*, Zugglied *n* [*Fachwerk n*]

- ~ ~ = gezogener Bauteil *m*
- ~ **meter** = Dehnungsschreiber *m*
- ~ **of spring** = Federspannung *f*
- ~ **spring** = Zugfeder *f*
- ~ **tie** = Zugstrebe *f*

term contract for maintenance = Wartungsauftrag *m*

terminal, terminus = Endstation *f*, Endpunkt *m* [*mitunter ist damit ein Bahnhof m verbunden*]
- ~ **building** = Abfertigungsgebäude *n* [*Flugplatz m*]
- ~ **moraine**, end ~ = Endmoräne *f*
- ~ **well** [*piezometer measurements*] = Meßstation *f*

ternary = aus drei Elementen bestehend, ternär

terrace gravel = Terrassenkies *m*
- ~ **house** = Terrassenhaus *n*
- ~ **of the river** = Flußterrasse *f*

terracing = Terrassieren *n*

terrazzo, Venetian mosaic = Terrazzo *m*, Zementmosaik *n*
- ~ **polisher** = Terrazzoschleifmaschine *f*

terra-cotta = Tarrakotta *f* [*in Österreich*]; Terrakotte *f*

terrain, ground, land = Gelände *n*

terrestrial heat, ground ~ = Erdwärme *f*

terrigenous deposit = terrigenes Sediment *n*

*****tertiary crusher with rolls** = Walzwerk *n*, Brech~

(Terzaghi) wash point sounding apparatus, wash-point soil penetrometer = Spülsonde *f* von Terzaghi

teschenite = Teschenit *m*

test bar = Probestab *m*
- ~ **core**, see: (drill) core
- ~ **cube**, cube test specimen = Probewürfel *m*, Prüfwürfel
- ~ **detail**, see: experimental ~
- ~ **for aggregate moisture** = Darrprobe *f* [*Betonzuschlag(stoff) m*]
- ~ ~ **grading (analysis)**, see: sieve analysis
- ~ ~ **organic matter**, organic test for fine aggregate, Abrams' test, extraction with caustic soda colorimetric test = Ätznatronprüfung *f*, Ätznatronprobe *f*, [*Betonzuschlag(stoff) m*]
- ~ ~ **sieve analysis**, see: sieve analysis

test for silt — thermal power plant

test for silt, silt content test for fine aggregate = Absetzprobe *f*, Probe *f* auf Reinheit *f* [*Betonzuschlag(stoff) m*]

~ ground, proving ~ = Versuchsfeld *n*, Versuchsgelände *n*

~ hole, trial hole = Schürfloch *n*

testing institute, ~ station = Prüfanstalt *f*, Materialprüfungsanstalt

~ machine = Prüfmaschine *f*

~ ~ for concrete cylinders (US); compression machine = Prüfpresse *f*, Druckpresse *f*, Betonpresse *f*, Betonprüfpresse, (Beton)Würfelpresse

~ (or test) sieve vibrator with sieves = Analysensiebapparat *m*

~ station, see: ~ institute

test method, testing procedure = Prüfverfahren *n*, Prüfmethode *f*, Versuchsverfahren, Versuchsmethode

~ operation = Probebetrieb *m*

~ pit, trial ~, profile ~, prospect ~ = Schürfgrube *f*

~ pump = Prüfpumpe *f* [*wird bei der Wellpoint-Methode für das Ansaugen von Einzelbrunnen verwendet*]

~ run = Probelauf *m*, Probefahrt *f*

~ section, ~ track, experimental ~ = Versuchsstrecke *f*, Probestrecke, Beobachtungsstrecke

~ series = Versuchsreihe *f*

~ shell structure = Versuchsschale *f*

~ sieve = Prüfsieb *n*

~ ~ vibrator, see: (mechanical) sieve shaker

~ specimen = Prüfkörper *m*, Probekörper, Probe(stück) *f*, (*n*)

~ stand = Prüfstand *m* [*Baumaschine f*]

~ track, see: ~ section

~ wheel = Versuchsrad *n*

tetracalcium aluminoferrite = Tetrakalziumaluminatferrit *n*, Brownmillerit *m*

tetradymite, Bi_2Te_2S (Min.) = Tetradymit *m*, Schwefeltellurwismut *n*

tetra ethyl lead, TEL = Bleitetraäthyl *n*, Pb $(C_2H_5)_4$, BTÄ

tetragonal system = tetragonales System *n* [*Kristall n*]

tetrahedrite, see: fahlerz (Min.)

tetrapod (concrete) block = Betonkörper *m* aus mehreren Füßen bestehend. Hat gute Verklammerungs- und Durchströmungseigenschaft. Wird zum Molenschutz verwendet.

tetryl = Tetryl *n* [*Hauptladung f einer Sprengkapsel f*]

tetryl-azide detonator, lead azide alumin(i)um detonator = Aluminiumsprengkapsel *f*

texrope drive (US); vee-belt ~ (Brit.) = Keilriemen(an)trieb *m*

texture = Textur *f*

textured, tractionized, rough = griffig [*Straßenoberfläche f*]

~ plaster = oberflächenbehandelter Putz *m*

texture soil [*soil containing a large portion of roots*] = Gewebeboden *m*

texturing = Oberflächenbehandlung *f* zur Erzielung einer Textur *f*

~ roll [*roll roofing plant*] = Walze *f* zum Einpressen *n* einer Markierung *f*

thalweg, valley way, valley line (Geol.) = Talweg *m*, Stromstrich *m*

thaw = Frostaufgang *m*

to thaw out = auftauen

theoretical apex of the triangle (Brit.); intersection of upstream and downstream faces = Spitze *f* des theoretischen Dreiecks *n* [*Talsperre f*]

~ location = Soll-Lage *f*

theory of fluid flow = technische Strömungslehre *f*

~ ~ rupture = Gleittheorie *f* [*Stützwand f*]

~ ~ shells = Schalentheorie *f*

~ ~ three moments = Drei-Momente-Satz *m*

theralite (Geol.) = Theralit *m*

thermal conductivity = Wärmeleitfähigkeit *f*

~ diffusivity = Temperaturleitfähigkeit *f*

~ expansion = Wärmedehnung *f*

~ fatigue = thermische Ermüdung *f*

~ gradient = thermisches Gefälle *n*

~ insulation, heat ~ = Wärmedämmung *f*, Wärmeisolierung *f*

~ metamorphism (Geol.) = Wärmeumwandlung *f*, Wärmeumprägung *f*, Wärmemetamorphose *f*

~ power plant, thermo power station = thermisches Kraftwerk *n*

thermal quality of a building = wärmewirtschaftliche Qualität *f* eines Gebäudes *n*
~ **reforming process** = thermisches Reformierungsverfahren *n* [*Benzin n*]
~ **shock** = thermischer Stoß *m*
~ ~ **resistance** = Wärmestoßfestigkeit *f*
~ **slaking curve** = Löschkurve *f* [*Kalk m*]
~ **spring**, see: hot ~
thermochemistry = Thermochemie *f*
thermo-fracture = Wärmespannungsriß *m*
thermo-osmosis = Thermo-Osmose *f*
thermophilic digestion = thermophyle Ausfaulung *f*
thermo power station, see: thermal power plant
thermostat = Temperaturregler *m*, Thermostat *m*
thickened edge type concrete pavement = randverstärkte Betondecke *f*
thickener = Eindicker *m*
thicket = Dickicht *n*
thickness, depth, richness, size, power, substance, width (Geol.) = Mächtigkeit *f*
~ = Dicke *f*
~ **control hand-wheel** = Einstellhandrad *n* für Deckendicke *f* [*Schwarzbelageinbaumaschine f*]
~ **ga(u)ge** = Dickenmesser *m* [*Schwarzbelageinbaumaschine f*]
thief-proof, see: pilfer-proof
thimble = Kabelschuh *m*, Muffe *f*, (Seil-)Kausche *f*
thin-arch dam, see: shell ~
thin arched slab = dünne gekrümmte Platte *f*
thin curved shell not subjected to bending = biegungsfreie Schale *f*
thin flame, see: narrow ~
thin-layer fill, see: dumping in thin layers
thinning, cutting back = Verschneiden *n*
~ **agent** = Verschnittmittel *n*
thin shell = dünne Schale *f*
~ ~ **dome** = dünnschalige Kalotte *f*
thin surfacing, see: road carpet
thin-walled pipe = dünnwandiges Rohr *n*
third point = Drittelpunkt *m*
thixotropic = thixotrop

~ **hardening** = Thixotropiewirkung *f*
thixotropy = Thixotropie *f*, Wechselfestigkeit *f*
Thomas meal, slag flour, ground basic slag = Thomasmehl *n*, Schlackenmehl, Thomasphosphat *n*
threaded drill steel = Gewinde-Bohrstahl *m*
~ **socket**, screwed sleeve = Gewindemuffe *f*
threading machine, see: screwing ~
three-axle rear dump truck = Dreiachshinterkipper *m*
~ **(tandem) roller** = Dreiachs(-Tandem-)walze *f*
~ **truck**; ~ **lorry** (Brit.) = Dreiachs-LKW *m*, Dreiachslaster *m*, Dreiachs-Lastkraftwagen *m*
~ ~ **crane** = Dreiachsautokran *m*
~ ~ **shovel** = Autobagger *m* mit Dreiachsfahrgestell *n* und zwei Motoren *mpl*, Dreiachslast(kraft)wagenbagger *m*
~ **vehicle** = Dreiachsfahrzeug *n*
three-barrel culvert, triple (drainage) culvert = Dreiröhrendurchlaß *m*, Dreiröhren-Abzugkanal *m*
three-centre(d) arch (Brit.); three-center ~ (US) = Korbbogen *m* mit drei Zentren *npl*
three-coat plaster = Drei-Lagen-Putz *m*
three-colo(u)r recorder = Dreifarbenschreiber *m*, Dreifarben-Registriergerät *n*
three-compartment aggregate feeder = dreizelliger Dosierapparat *m*
~ **bin** = Dreifachsilo *m*
three-conductor cable = Dreileiterkabel *n*
three-dimensional curve, curve in space = Raumkurve *f*
~ **pipe line** = räumlich verlegte Rohrleitung *f*, dreidimensionale ~
three-drum hoist = Dreitrommelwinde *f*
~ **rapid shifting hoist** = Dreitrommel-Schrapperwinde *f*, Dreitrommelhaspel *m, f*
three-floored = dreistöckig
threefold window in work(ed) stone = dreifaches Hausteinfenster *n*
three-hinged arch, arch with three hinges = Dreigelenkbogen *m*

three-hinged braced arch, trussed arch with three hinges = Dreigelenk-Fachwerkbogen m
~ **frame** = Dreigelenkrahmen m
three-hole hollow block = Dreikammer-(hohlblock)stein m
three-lane dual carriageway = Straße f mit drei Spuren fpl je Richtung f
three-legged roller, three-roll type machine, three-wheel(ed) (all-purpose) ~; macadam roller (US) = Dreiradwalze f
~ **(or triplex) (backfill) tamper (or rammer)** = Dreifuß-Grabenramme f
three-level grade separation structure, triple-deck ~ ~ ~ = dreietagiges Kreuzungsbauwerk n
three-motor all-electric shovel = Dreimotoren-Elektrobagger m
~ **drive** = dreimotoriger Elektroantrieb m
~ **travel(l)ing crane** = Dreimotorenlaufkran m [für elektrischen Betrieb m]
~ **workshop overhead travel(l)ing crane** = Dreimotoren-Werkstatt-Elektrolaufkran m
three-panelled door = Dreifüllungstür f
three-phase generator, see: polyphase generator
three-piece toggle plate = dreiteilige Druckplatte f, ~ Kniehebelplatte
three pinned arch-ribbed dome = Dreigelenk-Rippenkuppel f
three-point suspension (mounting) = Dreipunkt-Aufhängung f
three-pressure stage turbine = Turbine f mit drei Gleichdruckstufen fpl
three quarters = Dreiquartier m, Dreiviertelstein m
three-roller idler set, troughed idler, three-pulley idler, 3-spindle troughing idler = dreiteilige Rollenstation f [Bandförderer m]
three-roll type machine, see: three-legged roller
three-section framing bent = dreiteilig ausgebildeter Rahmen m
three-sided moldboard (US); ~ bulldozer, dozer blade for tree-felling work, stumper = dreiseitiges Streichschild n, ~ Stoßschild, Baumfällschild

three-sight range = Nivellierinstrument n für drei Fixpunkte mpl
three-square file with tang = Dreikantangelfeile f
three-stop batch plant = Abmeßanlage f mit dreimaligem Halten n der Fahrzeuge npl
three throw high speed pump = Drillingseilpumpe f
three-way cock = Dreiwegehahn m
~ **compensating valve** = Dreiwege-Ausgleichventil n
~ **tipper,** ~ dump truck; ~ dump lorry (Brit.) = Dreiseitenkipper m
three-wheel(ed) (all-purpose) roller, see: three-legged roller
three-wheel(ed) wagon drill = Dreirad-Bohrwagen m mit Lafette f
threshold light = Schwellenfeuer n [Flugplatz m]
throat = Syphon-Ablenkung f [automatischer Syphon m]
~ **depth** = Kehlnahtdicke f
~ **thickness** = Nahtdicke f [Schweißen n]
throttle = Gashebel m
~ **control** = Drehzahlregulierhebel m
throttling turbine = Drosselturbine f
through-glacier = Paßgletscher m
throughput = Durchsatz m
through station = Durchgangsbahnhof m
~ **street,** ~ **highway** = Stopstraße f
~ **traffic** = Durchgangsverkehr m
through-valley = Paßtal n
throw, amount of eccentricity = Wurf m [Sieb n]
thrower belt unit, see: extension flight conveyor
throw-off carriage [used in overburden removal] = Abwurfwagen m
throw-out lever, disengaging ~ = Ausrückhebel m, Auskupplungshebel
throw-over blades and pickups = Beschaufelung f [Straßen(beton)mischer m]
thrust = Horizontalschub m [wenn „thrust" and „shear" im gleichen Satz vorkommen, so ist thrust = Horizontalschubkomponente und shear = Vertikalschubkomponente; sonst sind beide gleichartig]
~ **bearing** = Drucklager n
~ **bolt** = Druckbolzen m

thrust collar = Druckring *m*
~ nut = Druckmutter *f*
~ of arch = Bogenschub *m*
~ ~ bearing = Lagerdruck *m*
~ plane (Brit.); displaced surface (US) (Geol.) = Verschiebungsebene *f*
~ plate = Stoßplatte *f*
~ washer = Druckscheibe *f*
thumb-filleter = Drückdaumen *m* [*Handwerkzeug des Asphaltarbeiters*]
thumb jump = Daumensprung *m*
thunder-cloud, cumulonimbus = Gewitterwolke *f*, Kumulonimbuswolke *f*
thunder egg = Achatschwüle *f*
thunder-squall = Gewitterbö *f*
thunderstorm = Gewitter *n*
thwacker = Seitenstampfer *m*, Seitenstößel *m*
tidal basin = Flutbecken *n*
~ calculation = Gezeitenberechnung *f*
~ capacity [*arm of the sea*] = Abflußvermögen *n* [*Meeresarm m*]
~ current, see: tide ~
~ curve, see: marigram
~ estuary = Flutmündung *f*
~ feature = Gezeitenmerkmal *n*
~ harbo(u)r, see: tide-harbo(u)r
~ inundation = Gezeitenüberschwemmung *f*
~ light = Gezeitenfeuer *n*
~ marsh = Gezeitenmarsch *f*
~ mud deposits = Gezeitenablagerung *f*
~ phenomenon = Gezeitenerscheinung *f*, Tideerscheinung *f*
~ power = Gezeitenenergie *f*, Gezeitenarbeit *f*
~ ~ plant = Gezeitenkraftwerk *n*
~ range = Tidewechsel *m*
~ river = Tidefluß *m*
~ traffic = Flutverkehr *m*, Verkehr auf Wechselspur [*Straßenverkehr*]
~ wave, tide ~ = Flutwelle *f*, Gezeitenwelle
tide [*the vertical movement of the water — the tide rises and falls*] = Gezeit *f*
tide-ball = Gezeitensignal *n*
tide beach = Gezeitenstrand *m*
~ current, tidal ~ = Gezeitenströmung *f*, Tideströmung
~ cycle = Gezeitenspiel *n*

~ effect = Gezeiteneinwirkung *f*
~ ga(u)ge = Flutmesser *m*
~-harbo(u)r, tidal harbo(u)r = Tidehafen *m*, Fluthafen *m*
tides = Gezeiten *fpl*
tide wave, see: tidal ~
tie (US); sleeper (Brit.) = Schienenschwelle *f*
~ ~ = Steckbügel *m*
~ bar, ~ rod = Anker(eisen) *m*, (*n*) [*Betondeckenfuge f*]
~ ~ = Anker(eisen) *m*, (*n*)
~ beam; ~ girder (Brit.) = Zugbalken(träger) *m*, Zugträger *m*
~ bolt, anchor ~, holding-down ~ = Ankerschraube *f*, Fundamentschraube
tied arch; bowstring girder (Brit.); bowstring beam = Bogenträger *m* mit Zugband *n*
~ island, attached ~ = angegliederte Insel *f*, Angliederungsinsel
~ peninsula, attached ~ = angegliederte Halbinsel *f*, Angliederungshalbinsel
~ plane = angefügte Ebene *f*
tie for power shovel (US); sleeper for crane navvy (Brit.) = Baggerschwelle *f*
tie laying machine (US); sleeper ~ ~ (Brit.) = Schwellenverlegemaschine *f*
~ plate, anchor ~ = Ankerplatte *f*, Verankerungsplatte
~ ~, see: batten (~)
tiering machine, see: stacker
tie rod, see: ~ bar
~ tamper (US); track ~ (Brit.); ballast ~ = Schotterstopfer *m*, Gleisstopfer *m*
to tie up = vertäuen [*Schiff n*]
tie wire = Rödeldraht *m*
tiger's eye (Min.) = Tigerauge *n*
tight blading, fine ~ = Feinplanieren *n* mit Erdhobel *m*
tightening nut = Spannmutter *f*
~ screw = Spannschraube *f*
tile = Fliese *f*
~ [*pipe made of baked clay*] = Tonrohr *n*
tile-and-joist construction = Stahlbetonrippendecke *f* mit Füllkörpern *mpl*
tile floor(ing) = Fliesenfußboden *m*
~ layer's work = Fliesenlegerarbeiten *fpl*
~ making = Dachziegelherstellung *f*
tiling plaster, see: flooring ~

tillite = Tillit *m*
tilt cylinder, tilting ~ = Kippzylinder *m*
tilt(-deck) trailer, tilting platform ~ = Kipptieflader *m*, Tieflader mit Kipp(tief)ladebrücke *f*
to tilt down = abkippen [*sich nach unten neigen*]
tilth = Bodengare *f*
tilting bearing, pivoting ~, rocker ~ = Kipplager *n*
~ **bucket elevator,** see: gravity tipping conveyor
~ **(dipper) bucket** = Kipplöffel *m*
~ **(drum) mixer,** tilt(-drum) mixer = Kipptrommelmischer *m*
~ **front-end bucket** = kippbare Ladeschaufel *f*, Kippwanne *f*, Kippmulde *f* [*Frontlader m*]
~ **furnace** = Kippofen *m*
~ **level screw** = Kippschraube *f* [*Nivellierinstrument n*]
~ **platform trailer,** see: tilt-deck ~
tilt mixer, see: tilting (drum) mixer
to tilt up = ankippen
tilt-up construction, ~ method = Richtaufbauweise *f*, Aufkipp-Bauweise *f*
timber [*is lumber that is 5 inches or larger in its smallest diameter*] = Bau(nutz)holz *n*
~ with two sawn faces = zweiseitig geschnittenes ~
sharp edged = scharfkantig
full edged = fehlkantig
rough edged = baumkantig
~ **aggregate bin** = Holzsilo *m*
timber-crib type cofferdam = Fang(e)damm *m* aus Holzstapeln *mpl*
timber deck(ing), ~ floor = Holzfahrbahn *f* [*Brücke f*]
~ **dolphin** = Holzdalbe *m*
~ **fender,** wood-pile ~, wood ~ = Holzfender *m*
~ **flume,** wood ~ = Fluder *m*, Holz(ge)rinne *f*, (*n*)
~ **fork** = Holzstapelgabel *f*
~ **form cleaning device,** wood(en) ~ ~ ~ = Schalholzreiniger *m*
~ ~ **panel,** see: (~) shutter(ing) panel
~ **gallery** = Holzzimmerungsstollen *m*
timbering [*wood bracing in a tunnel or excavation*] = Zimmerung *f*

*timber joint, wood ~ = Holzverbindung *f*
~ **lagging,** ~ lining, wood ~ = Holzverkleidung *f*
~ **line** (Geol.) = Baumgrenze *f*
~ **mat,** pontoon, platform, (wood) mat [*a wood platform used in sets to support machinery on soft ground*] = Holzrost *m*
~ **panel shuttering,** wood ~ ~ = Holztafelschalung *f*
~ **partition** = Bohlwerk *n* zur Trennung der verschiedenen nebeneinander gelagerten Körnungen *fpl*
~ **(or wood) (bearing, or foundation) pile** = (Rund)Holz(gründungs)pfahl *m*, (Rund)Holz(trag)pfahl
~ **rubbing piece** = Reib(e)holz *n*
(~) **shutter(ing) panel),** timber form panel = Holzschal(ungs)tafel *f*, Holzschal(ungs)platte *f*
~ **sizer** = Dickenhobelmaschine *f*
~ **slat,** (wooden) slat, barrel slat, stave = (Holz)Daube *f*, Faßdaube
~ **spreader** = Holzspreize *f*
~ **structure** = Holzkonstruktion *f*
~ **towing winch,** see: logging ~
~ **truss,** wood ~ = hölzernes Sprengwerk *n*
TIMBER WOLF [*Trademark*] = Torladewagen *m*, Klemmgriff-Lastenträger *m*, Fabrikat BRITISH STRADDLE CARRIER LTD., CAMBRIDGE, ENGLAND
time clock = Stechuhr *f*
~ **consuming** = zeitraubend
timed for port closing = eingestellt für Förderbeginn *m*
timekeeper = Zeitnehmer *m*
time period, ~ interval, period of time = Zeitspanne *f*
timer, machine ~ = Zeit-Zündmaschine *f*, Verzögerungsschalter *m*
time recorder = Zeitschreiber *m*
time-settlement curve = Zeit-Senkungs-Kurve *f*, Zeitsetzungskurve *f*
time/shrinkage curve = Zeit-Schwindkurve *f*
time spacing = Zeitabstand *m*
~ **study** = Zeitstudie *f*
~ **yield,** see: creep

timing = Zeitnahme *f*

~ BTDC, ~ before top dead centre = Einstellung *f* vor oberem Totpunkt *m*

~ gear housing = Stirnräder-Gehäuse *n*

TIMKEN bearing [*Trademark*] (US); see: taper roller ~ (Brit.)

timothy, see: cat's tail

tine plate (US) = Teller *m* [*SEAMAN-Bodenvermörteler m*]

tin mining = Zinnbergbau *m*

tinner's snip, hand plate shears = Handblechschere *f*

tin solder, see: plumber's metal

tin-stone, see: cassiterite (Min.)

tintometer = Tintometer *n*

tip = (Waggon)Kipper *m*

~, insert = Bohrspitze *f*

~, shoot, tipple = Kippe *f* [*Erdbau m*]

(tip and) hoist = Hubkipper *m*, Hochkipper *m*

tip downwards = zopfrecht, mit Zopfende *n* nach unten

tip extension = Spitzenausleger *m*

tip-over (concrete) bucket, concrete tipping skip, (~) ~ hopper = (Beton)Kippkübel *m* [*Bauaufzug m*]

tipper, see: dump lorry (Brit.)

~-tractor = Zugmaschine *f* mit Kipp-Pritsche *f*

tipping = Umkippen *n*

~ full trailer, see: tractor wagon

~ gear = Kippvorrichtung *f*, Kippwerk *n* [*LKW m*]

~ load = Kipplast *f*

tip(ping) (motor) lorry (Brit.), see: dump lorry

tipping trailer, see: dump-body ~

~ truck (US); see: dump lorry (Brit.)

tipple, see: tip

tippler, see: dressing hammer

tir [*Scotland*]; see: overburden

tire (US); tyre (Brit.) = Reifen *m*

~ section (US); tyre ~, ~ tread pattern (Brit.) = Reifenprofil *n*

T-LOCK AMER-PLATE [*Trademark*] = Vinyl-Kunststoffplatte *f* zur Innenverkleidung *f* von Betonkanälen *mpl* und ähnlichen Anlagen *fpl*

TNT, see: trinitrotoluene

toadstone (Brit.) = Derbyshire-Basalt *m*

tobacco tar = Tabakteer *m*

toe, foot = Fuß *m* [*Damm m*]

(~) cut-off wall = Herdmauer *f*, Fußmauer [*Talsperre f*]

~ failure = Basisbruch *m*

~ of screed = Bohlenvorderkante *f*

~ shooting, see: bog blasting

~ wall = Böschungsmauer *f*

toggle breaker, ~ crusher = Kniehebelbrecher *m*

~ plate = Kniehebelplatte *f*, Druckplatte [*Backenbrecher m*]

~ ~ press = Kniehebelpresse *f*

tolerance, allowance = Toleranz *f*, Genauigkeitsgrad *m*

toll = Wegeabgabe *f*, (Wege)Gebühr *f*

~ bridge = Gebühren-Brücke *f*

***toll collection** = Gebührenerhebung *f* [*Autobahn f*]

toll-collection and audit system, interchange equipment = Gebührenerhebungs- und -prüfanlage *f* [*Gebührenautobahn f*]

toll facility, vehicular toll project = Verkehrsanlage *f* mit Benutzungsgebühr *f*

toll-free controlled-access road = gebührenfreie Autostraße *f* mit geregelten Zufahrten *fpl*

toll gate = Einfahrtstor *n* zu einer gebührenpflichtigen Verkehrsanlage *f*

~ road, toll superhighway, turnpike, toll turnpike, pike = gebührenpflichtige Autobahn *f*, Zollstraße *f* für Schnellverkehr *m*

~ station = Gebührenerhebungsanlage *f* [*Gesamtkomplex m der Gebäude npl*]

~ tunnel = Gebühren-Verkehrstunnel *m*

"to and fro" system, see: jig-back ~

toluene, see: methyl benzene

~ insolubles; free carbon [*deprecated*] = freier Kohlenstoff *m* [*früher: Unlösliches n*]

tonalite (Geol.) = Tonalit *m*

tongue and groove joint = Nutzapfen *m*

tongue-and-groove joint, keyed ~ = genutete Fuge *f*, gespundete ~ [*Beton m*]

tongued flange = Brillenflansch *m*

tongue(-)switch (turnout) = Zungenweiche *f*

tool box — torsional oscillation

tool box, ~ **chest,** ~ **kit** = Werkzeugkasten *m*, Werkzeugkiste *f*, Werkzeugsatz *m*
~ **cabinet** = Werkzeugschrank *m*
~ **holder** = Werkzeughalter *m*
~ **joint,** drilling ~ ~ = Gestängeverbinder *m* [*Tiefbohrtechnik f*]
~ **steel** = Werkzeugstahl *m*
tooth angle [*shovel*] = Schneidwinkel *m*
toothed rack, see: rack
~ **rim** = Zahnkranz *m*
tooth harrow = Zahnegge *f*
~ **point** = Zahnspitze *f*
~ **shank** = Zahnschaft *m*
toothed wheel (hand) crab = Zahnradwinde *f*
top, see: vertex
~, ~ **level** = Oberkante *f*
topazolite (Min.) = Topazolith *m*
top boom, ~ **chord,** ~ **flange** = Obergurt *m*
~ ~ **member,** ~ **chord** ~, ~ **flange** ~, upper ~ ~ = Obergurtstab *m*
topcap = Besohlung *f*, Aufvulkanisieren *n* eines neuen Laufstreifens *m*
top coat, finishing ~ = Deckanstrich *m*
~ **concrete,** ~ **course** ~ = Aufbeton *m*, Oberbeton
~ **course** (US); see: wearing ~
~ **drift** = Firststollen *m*
Topeka (type asphaltic concrete) (US); stone-filled sand asphalt containing up to about 25 per cent of stone (Brit.) = Topeka *m*, splittarmer Asphaltfeinbeton *m*
top fibre (Brit.); ~ **fiber** (US) = obere (Rand)Faser *f*
~ **flange,** see: ~ boom
~ ~, rail head = Schienenkopf *m*
~ ~ **angle,** ~ boom ~, ~ chord ~, upper ~ ~ = Obergurtwinkel *m*
~ ~ **plate,** see: cover strip
~ ~ **troll(e)y** = Obergurtlaufkatze *f*, Obergurtlastkatze
~ **gases,** see: blast-furnace gas
~ **gate** [*lock*] = Obertor *n* [*Schleuse f*]
~ **heading** = Firstvortrieb *m*, Firststollen *m*
~-**heavy** = oberlastig
top-hole choke = Eruptionskopf-Düse *f*

top lateral bracing = oberer Windverband *m*
~ **(level)** = Oberkante *f*
topographic survey = topographische Aufnahme *f*
topped crude (petroleum), ~ ~ oil, skimmed ~ ~, reduced ~ ~ = Toprückstand *m*
topping (US); overlay (pavement) = Überzug(decke) *m*, (*f*)
top ring = erster Ring *m*, oberer ~
~ **section** = oberes Trum *n* [*Gleiskette f*]
top side view = Draufsicht *f*
~ **sludge,** scum = Schwimmschlamm *m*
top soil = Mutterboden *m*, Oberboden *m*, Dammerde *f*, Krume *f*
topsoiling = Mutterbodenauftrag *m*, Mutterbodenandeckung *f*
topsoil planting, see: broadcast sodding
~ **stripping** = Mutterbodenabhub *m*, Mutterbodenabtrag *m*
topspit, see: overburden
top surface dummy joint = obere Scheinfuge *f*
~ **unit,** see: revolving ~
~ **water level** (Brit.); designing ~ ~ = Stauhöhe *f*, Stauziel *n*
torch cutting, flame ~, torch burning = Brennschneiden *n*
~-**generating type burner** = Brenner *m* nach dem Selbstvergasungsprinzip *n*
torch peat = Leuchttorf *m*
torpedoeing of oil wells, oil well shooting = Torpedieren *n* von Erdölbohrungen *fpl*
torque = Drehmoment *n*
~ **converter** = Drehmoment-Wandler *m*
torquemeter = Drehmomentmesser *m*
torque wrench = Drehmomentschlüssel *m*
torrent, mountain ~ = Wildbach *m*, Wildwasser *n*
(torrential) downpour = Regenguß *m*, Sturzregen *m*
torsion = Verwindung *f*, Verdrehung *f*, Torsion *f*, (Ver)Drillung *f*
torsional buckling = Drillknickung *f*, Drillknicken *n*
torsional-flexural buckling = Biegedrillknicken *n*, Biegedrillknickung *f*
torsional oscillation = Torsionsschwingung *f*

torsional resistance = Drillwiderstand m
~ **rigidity** = Torsionssteifigkeit f, Verdreh(ungs)steifigkeit, Drillungssteife f
torsion(al) stress = Verwindungsspannung f, Drillspannung, Torsionsspannung
torsional vibration damper = Torsions-Schwingungsdämpfer m
torsion bar suspension = Torsionsfederung f
~ **frame** = Torsionsverband m
torsion-proof = verwindungssteif, verwindungsfest
torsion reinforcement = Drillbewehrung f, Drillarmierung
~ **visco(si)meter** = Torsionsviskosimeter n
total aggregate; see: all-in-aggregate (Brit.)
~ **cable stress** [bridge] = Gesamtkabelzug m
~ **final strength** = Gesamtbruchfestigkeit f
~ **load** = Gesamtlast f, Gesamtbelastung f
totally enclosed = voll gekapselt
~ ~ **vertical elevator** = geschlossenes Becherwerk n mit senkrechter Leiter f
total-need program(me) = Gesamtprogramm n der Erfordernisse npl
total soluble bitumen = Gesamtanteil m an löslichem Bitumen n
~ **stress** = Gesamtspannung f
~ **volume**, see: bulk ~
~ ~ **of intergranular (soil) space**, see: void(s) space
touchstone (Min.), see: Lydian stone
toughened glass = vorgespanntes Glas n
toughness = Zähigkeit f [Gummi-Bitumen-Mischung f]
touring car = offener Viersitzer m [PKW m]
tourist resort = Fremdenverkehrsort m
~ **trade** = Fremdenverkehr m
tourmaline (Min.) = Turmalin m
TOURNACRANE [Trademark], Le TOURNEAU portable crane = Einachs-Schlepperkran m, Einachs-Krananhänger m, Fabrikat Le TOURNEAU-WESTINGHOUSE COMPANY, PEORIA, ILLINOIS, USA
TOURNADOZER [Trademark] = Bulldozer m auf Luftreifen mpl, gummibereifter Schlepper m mit Querschild n, gummibereifter Bulldozer, Reifentrekker m mit Planierschild n, Radschlepper m mit Planierschild n, Planierschlepper m mit Radfahrwerk n, Fabrikat Le TOURNEAU-WESTINGHOUSE COMPANY, PEORIA, ILLINOIS, USA
TOURNAHOPPER [Trademark] = Gelenkwagen-Bodenentleerer m, Fabrikat Le TOURNEAU-WESTINGHOUSE COMPANY, PEORIA, ILLINOIS, USA
TOURNAROCKER [Trademark] = Gelenkwagen-Hinterkipper m, Fabrikat Le TOURNEAU-WESTINGHOUSE COMPANY, PEORIA, ILLINOIS, USA
TOURNATRACTOR [Trademark] = gummibereifter Schlepper m mit Allradantrieb m
TOURNATRAILER [Trademark] = Gelenkwagen m mit Entleerung durch Verschieben der Wannenwände auf dem feststehenden Wannenboden, Fabrikat Le TOURNEAU-WESTINGHOUSE COMPANY, PEORIA, ILLINOIS, USA
TOURNEPIEDS [Trademark] = ALBARET-Schaffußwalze f
towage = Schleppen n, Schlepperei f [Kahn m]
tow-bar = Deichsel f
towboat, tugboat, tug = Schlepper m [Schiff n] [in Österreich: Remorqueur m]
towed carrier, ~ **vehicle**, trailer = Anhänger m
~ **compaction roller** = Schlepp-Verdichter m, Anhänge-Verdichter
towed paver-type aggregate spreader, pull-type bituminous concrete and aggregate spreader, finish spreader = Schleppverteiler m für Schotter, Teer- und Asphaltbeton, Schleppverteiler m für bituminöse Stoffe, Schotter und Splitt

towed-type grader — tracking

towed-type grader, pull grader, trailer-type grader = Anhänge-Straßenhobel m, geschleppter Erdhobel m, Anhänge-Wegehobel, Anhänge-Erdhobel, Schlepp-Straßenhobel, Schlepp-Wegehobel, Schlepp-Erdhobel
~ **gritter**, towed hopper type gritter, trailer type grit and salt spreader, trailer gritter, towed-type gritting machine, trailer grit spreader = Anhängestreuer m, Schleppstreuer
~ **road ripper**, trailer-type ~ ~ = Anhänge-Straßenaufreißer m
~ ~ **sweeper** = Anhänge-Fegemaschine f, Schlepp-Kehrmaschine
~ **roller**, see: tractor-drawn ~
towed vehicle, see: trailer
tower = Turm m
~, see: cage
~, see: pylon
~, see: monotower
~ **bent** = Schrägpfahljoch n
~ **bucket**, ~ hoist ~ = Turmgerüstkippkübel m
~ **building crane** = Baudrehkran m
~ **clock** = Turmuhr f
~ **concrete spouting plant**, cage type ~ ~ ~, concrete chuting tower = (Beton)Gießturm m
~ **crane**, see: (mono)tower crane
~ **derrick crane** = Turmderrickkran m
~ **excavator**, see: SAUERMAN ~ ~
~ **hoist**, see: cage ~
~ ~ **bucket** = Gießturmkübel m
~ (~) = Turmgerüstkippkübel m [*Bauaufzug m*]
tower leg, bridge ~ ~ = Pylon-Stiel m
~ **machine**, see: SAUERMAN ~ ~
TOWERMOBILE CRANE [*Trademark*] = Auto-Turmdrehkran m, Fabrikat WAGNERMOBILE, PORTLAND, OREGON, USA
(tower) platform hoist, see: platform ~
tower saddle = Sattellager n [*Brücke f*]
~ **tank**, see: elevated (water) tank
~ **transporter**, cantilever tower ~ ~ = Auslegerlaufkran m
tower-type bituminous mixing plant = Mischturm m für bituminöse Belagsmassen fpl

towing caterpillar tractor = Zugraupe f, Zug(gleis)kettenschlepper m
~ **path**, towpath = Leinpfad m, Treidelweg m
~ **unit** = Ziehgerät n
~ **winch**, ~ cable ~, ~ rope ~ = Schlepp(trommel)seilwinde f
town dweller, city ~ = Städter m, Stadtbewohner m
~ **planner**, city ~, municipal ~, urban ~ = Städteplaner m, Stadtplaner
~ **road**, see: (city) street
~ **street**, see: (city) ~
towpath, see: towing path
toxicity = Giftigkeit f, Giftgehalt m
to trace, to mark = anreißen
trace element = Spuren-Element n
tracer-controlled = fühlergesteuert
tracheid = Leitzelle f, Tracheide f
trachyte = Trachyt m
trachytic lava = Trachytlava f
tracing cloth = Pausleinen n
~ **paper**, blue print ~ = Pauspapier n
track, see: crawler
~, **tracking** = Gleis n, Schienenstrang m
~ = Spur f [*längliche Vertiefung f in der Straßenoberfläche f*]
~ ~ = Spur f [*Fahrspur ohne Vertiefungen*]
~ **accessories** = Gleiszubehör m, n
~ **ballast**; see: railway (track) ballast (Brit.)
~ **cable scraper**, slackline (excavator) with bottomless bucket, slackline cableway ~ ~ ~ = Schlaffseil-Kabelschrapper m, Seilbahn-Schleppschrapper m
~ **chain**, see: crawler
tracked plant, caterpillar equipment = Raupengeräte npl [*dieser Ausdruck ist zu vermeiden*]; (Gleis)Kettenfahrwerkgeräte npl
~ **roller** = (Gleis)Kettenschlepperwalze f
~ **tractor**, see: caterpillar ~
~ **vehicle** [*deprecated*]; tracklaying ~ = (Gleis)Kettenfahrzeug n
track form, see: side ~
~ **(ga(u)ge**, see: rail ~
~ **group** = (Gleis)Kette f mit Platten fpl
tracking [*the act of driving vehicles one behind another in approximately the same track*] = Spurfahren n

tracking = ausgefahrene Spuren *fpl* auf einer Straße *f*
~; see: rail(way) track (Brit.)
~ **complete with sleepers** (Brit.); ~ ~ ~ **ties** (US) = Rahmengleis *n*
track jack, see: ~ lifting ~
tracklayer, see: caterpillar
~ **chassis** = (Gleis)Kettenfahrwerk *n*, (Gleis)Kettenfahrgestell *n*, (Gleis)Kettenunterwagen *m*
track layer's hammer (or mallet) = Schienennagelhammer *m*
~ **laying** = Gleisverlegung *f*, Gleisbau *m*
track-laying machinery = Gleisbaumaschinen *fpl*
~ **track**, see: crawler ~
~ ~ **type (combined) paver** (Brit.); (concrete) **paver** (US) = Raupenstraßen-(beton)mischer *m*, Freifallmischer *m* auf Raupen *fpl* (oder Gleisketten *fpl*) für Betondeckenbau *m*
~ **type (or caterpillar, or crawler) (asphalt) finisher (or paver, or bituminous paving machine, or bituminous spreading-and-finishing machine, or blacktop spreader)** = Gleiskettenfertiger *m*, Raupenfertiger [*bit. Straßendecken fpl*]
~ ~ **bucket (elevator) loader**, see: crawler ~ (~) ~
~ ~ **flip-over bucket loader**, see: crawler overhead loader
~ ~ **long-boom crane** (US); see: track-type long-boom crane
~ ~ **overhead loader**, see: crawler ~ ~
~ ~ **over-loader**, see: crawler overhead loader
~ ~ **overshot loader**, see: crawler overhead loader
~ ~ **rocker shovel**, see: crawler overhead loader
*****track-laying type shovel (excavator)**, see: bucket-excavator mounted on tracks
~ **vehicle**; tracked ~ [*deprecated*] = (Gleis)Kettenfahrzeug *n*
trackless, railless = gleislos
~ **earthwork engineering**, see: railless ~ ~
track level = (Gleis)Kettenfahrhöhe *f*, Raupenfahrbahn *f*
~ **(lifting) jack** = Gleishebewinde *f*

~ **link assembly** = (Gleis)Kette *f* ohne Platten *fpl*
track motor car (US); see: platelayer's troll(e)y (Brit.)
track roller, tractor ~ = Gleiskettenrolle *f*
~ **sand** = Bremssand *m*
track-scale; railway-track scale (Brit.) = Gleiswaage *f*, Waggonwaage
track shifting machine = Gleisrückmaschine *f*
(~) **shoe**, see: crawler ~
~ **spike**, dog ~, rail ~, rail fixing nail, dogheaded spike = Schienennagel *m*
~ **tamper** (Brit.); tie ~ (US); ballast ~ = Gleisstopfer *m*, Schotterstopfer
~ **tamping machine**, power ballaster = Gleisstopfmaschine *f*
~ **tension** = (Gleis)Kettenspannung *f*
~ **tensioning** = (Gleis)Kettenspannen *n*
track-type (industrial) tractor, see: caterpillar ~
~ **long-boom crane**, track-laying type long-boom crane (US) = Hochbauraupenkran *m*, Hochbaugleiskettenkran
~ **tractor-shovel** = (Gleis)Ketten-Hublader *m*, (Gleis)Ketten-(Front-)Ladeschaufel *f*
~ **trenching machine** = Grabenbagger *m* auf (Gleis)Ketten *fpl*
~ **wagon**, see: caterpillar tread ~
track warping = Gleisverwerfung *f*
trackway for skip rollers, see: inclined guides
trackways, see: strip(e) road
track wheel = Gleisrad *n*
~ ~ **flat dump car** = Flachbodenselbstentlader *m*
~ ~ **wood dump wagon**, wood skip, wood tip wagon = Holzkastenkipper *m*
trackwork = Gleisarbeiten *f*
tract = Trakt *m*
TRACTAIR [*Trademark*] = Kompressorschlepper *m*, Fabrikat LE ROI COMPANY, MILWAUKEE 14, WISCONSIN, USA
traction brake lining = Fahrantrieb-Bremsbelag *m*
~ **braking** = Fahrantrieb-Bremsung *f*
~ **clutch** = Fahrkupplung *f*

traction-driven rotary sweeper — traffic circle

traction-driven (or trailer-type) rotary sweeper (or scavenging machine, or road sweeper, or mechanical sweeper, or road sweeping machine) = Anhänge-Straßenkehrmaschine *f*, Anhänge-Fegemaschine
tractionized, see: textured
traction unit = Fahrteil *m* [*Schwarzbelageinbaumaschine f*]
~ wheel, see: driving ~
tractive effort, ~ force = Zugleistung *f*, Zugkraft *f*, Zugvermögen *n*
tractor = Trecker *m*, Traktor *m*, Schlepper *m*
~-allied (or tractor-drawn) equipment = traktorengezogene Geräte *npl*
tractor (back)hoe (US); ~ backactor (Brit.) = Schlepper-Tieflöffel(bagger) *m*
tractor-bucket machine = Schlepper-Schaufellader *m*
tractor-compressor, see: universal compressor tractor
tractor crane = Traktor(en)kran *m*, Schlepperkran, Treckerkran
tractor-dozer, see: (bull)dozer(-equipped tractor)
(tractor-drawn) bottom-dump trailer, see: trailer-bottom dump
~ crane, lift-and-carry ~ = Einachs-Schlepperkran *m*, Einachs-Krananhänger *m*
~ equipment, see: tractor-allied ~
~ roller, towed(-type) ~ = Schleppwalze *f*, Anhängewalze
~ roller, towed-type ~ = Schleppwalze *f*, Anhängewalze
tractor drill = Schlepper *m* mit aufgebauter Hammerbohrmaschine *f*
~ elevator = Schlepper-Eimerkettenaufzug *m*, Traktor(en)-Becherwerk *n*
~ engine = Schleppermotor *m*
~ equipped with V-plow (US)/V-plough (Brit.) = Schneekeilpflug *m* an Schlepper *m* angebaut
*****tractor grader**, see: motor ~
tractor loader, ~ shovel, shovel dozer [*a tractor equipped with a bucket which can be used to dig, and to elevate to dump at truck height*] = Schürflader *m*
tractor-mounted trench excavator = Schlepper-Grabenbagger *m*

tractor-operated trench hoe = Schlepper *m* mit Tieflöffel(ausrüstung) *m*, (*f*)
(tractor-pulled) carrying scraper, see: carrying ~
tractor revolving crane = Schlepper-Drehkran *m*
~ roller, see: track ~
tractor-scraper (with two-wheel traction), see: motor(ized) scraper
tractor-semi-trailer combination = Zugmaschine *f* mit Halbanhänger *m*
tractor-shovel, see: tractor loader
tractor track = Schlepper-(Gleis)Kette *f*
tractor-truck, truck tractor (US); motor tractor (Brit.) = (Straßen)Zugmaschine *f*
(tractor) wagon, trailer ~, full trailer with a dump body, dump-body full trailer, tipping full trailer, dump wagon, dump (full) trailer = Anhängewagen *m* [*Erdbau m*]
tractor with flat plates, flat-plated crawler tractor = Gleiskette *f* mit Flachbandagen *fpl*, Raupenkette ~ ~
~ winch, ~ cable ~, ~ rope ~ = Schlepper(trommel)seilwinde *f*, Traktoren(trommel)seilwinde
TRACTO-SHOVEL [*Trademark*] = raupenfahrbare (Be)Lademaschine *f*, Fabrikat TRACTOMOTIVE CORPORATION
trade grouping of rocks = Einteilung *f* der Gesteine *npl* in Handelsgruppen *fpl*
trade-in value, see: present ~
trade journal = Fachzeitschrift *f* Fachblatt *n*
trades federation = Berufsgenossenschaft *f*
*****traffic, road ~, highway ~** = Verkehr *m*, Straßen~
~ accident = Verkehrsunfall *m*
~ analysis = Verkehrsanalyse *f*
~ artery = (Groß)Verkehrsader *f*, Hauptfernverkehrsstraße *f*
traffic-bound macadam = verkehrsgebundene Schotterdecke *f*
~ surfacing = Kompressionsbelag *m*
traffic census, see: ~ survey
~ ~ point, observation ~ = Verkehrszählstelle *f*
~ circle, see: roundabout

traffic circus — trailer chassis

traffic circus [*deprecated*]; see: roundabout

~ **compaction**, see: kneading action of traffic

~ **concentration** = Verkehrsdichte *f* [*auf einer bestimmten Streckenlänge f*]

~ **congestion (or jam)** = Verkehrsstokkung *f*, Verkehrsstau *m*

~ **container** = Behälter *m* für „Haus-zu-Haus"-Verkehr *m*

~ **control**, regulation of traffic = Verkehrsreg(e)lung *f*

~ ~ **(light) signal**, traffic signal, traffic light = Verkehrsampel *f*, Verkehrslichtsignal *n*

* ~ **(~) sign**, (roadside) ~ (~) ~, road sign = (Straßen)Verkehrszeichen *n*

~ **count**, see: ~ survey

~ **counter**, ~ counting apparatus = Straßenverkehrszählgerät *n*

~ **development** = Verkehrsausbau *m*

~ **engineer** = Verkehrsingenieur *m*

***traffic engineering** = Straßenverkehrstechnik *f*

~ **flow**, ~ volume (Brit.) = Verkehrsmenge *f* (oder Verkehrsvolumen *n*) auf einer bestimmten Breiteneinheit der Fahrbahn *f* während einer bestimmten Zeit

~ **fluctuation** = Verkehrsschwankung *f*

~ **generation** = Verkehrsentstehung *f*

~ **handling** = Verkehrsabwicklung *f*

~ **impact** = Verkehrserschütterung *f*

(~) **island** = Verkehrsinsel *f*

~ **jam**, see: ~ congestion

~ **lane**, see: lane

~ **light**, ~ signal, ~ control (light) signal = Verkehrsampel *f*, Verkehrslichtsignal *n*

~ **line**, white ~ = Verkehrslinie *f*, Verkehrsstrich *m*

traffic-line marking, traffic-zoning = Straßenmarkierung *f*; Bodenmarkierung *f* [*Schweiz*]

***traffic-line marking machine**, see: road-marking ~

traffic line paint, see: traffic(-zoning) ~

~ **load** = Verkehrslast *f*, Verkehrsbelastung *f*

~ **offence** = Verkehrsübertretung *f*

~ **offender** = Verkehrssünder *m*

~ **paint**, see: traffic(-zoning) ~

~ **patrol** = Verkehrsstreife *f*

(~) **patrolman** = Polizist *m* einer Verkehrsstreife *f*

~ **planning** = Verkehrsplanung *f*

~ **prognosis** = Verkehrsprognose *f*

~ **roundabout**, see: roundabout

~ **safety education**, training in road sense = (Straßen)Verkehrserziehung *f*

~ **sign**, see: ~ control ~

~ **signal**, see: ~ control (light) ~

(~) ~ **control** = Verkehrssignal-Steuerung *f*

~ ~ **setting** = Reg(e)lung *f* von Verkehrssignalen *npl*

~ **stream** = Verkehrsstrom *m*

~ **striping** = Ziehen *n* von Verkehrslinien *fpl*

~ **stud**, see: street marker

~ **survey**, ~ count, ~ census = Verkehrsmessung *f*, Verkehrszählung, Verkehrserhebung

~ **victim** = Verkehrsopfer *n*

~ **volume**, see: ~ flow

~ **(-zoning) paint**, zone marking paint, traffic line paint, road-marking ~, linemarking ~, road line ~ = Verkehrs(Markierungs)farbe *f*, Straßenmarkierungsfarben *f*, Signierfarbe *f* [*Schweiz*]

trail = Weg *m*

trailbuilder, see: roadbuilder

trailer, towed vehicle, towed carrier = Anhänger *m*, Anhängefahrzeug *n*, Nachläufer *m*

~, see: full ~

~-**bottom dump**, bottom-dump tractor truck, tractor-drawn bottom-dump trailer, bottom-dump (tractor-)trailer = schleppergezogener Anhänger *m* mit Bodenentleerung *f*, Bodenentleerer(-Anhänger) *m*

trailer brush, ~ type (road) brush, ~ road brush, towed-type (road) ~ = Anhängebürstenwalze *f*, Schleppbürstenwalze, Anhängebesenwalze, Schleppbesenwalze, Anhängekehrwalze, Schleppkehrwalze

trailer chassis, trailing ~ = Anhänge(r)-Chassis *n*, Schleppfahrgestell *n*, Anhänger-Fahrgestell, Schlepp-Chassis

trailer compressor = Einachs-Luftverdichter m, Einachs-Kompressor m, Einachs-Drucklufterzeuger m
~ **coupling** = Anhänge(r)kupplung f
~ **crane** = Anhängerkran m
~ **door** = Bodenklappe f, Bodentür f [*Bodenentleerer-Anhänger m*]
~-**dump**, see: dump-body trailer
trailer excavator = Anhängerbagger m
~ **for timber haulage** = Langholznachläufer m
~ **gritter**, see: towed-type ~
~ **laboratory** = Anhänge(r)-Labor(atorium) n
~ **mixer** = Anhänge(r)mischer m
~-**type (excavator) digger** = Anhängegrabgerät n
~-**type grit and salt spreader**, see: towed-type gritter
~-**type method** = Schleppversuch m [*Reibungsmessung f auf der Straße f*]
~-**type road ripper**, see: towed-type ~ ~
~-**type rotary sweeper**, see: traction-driven ~ ~
~-**type vibrating roller** = Schlepp-Vibrationswalze f, Anhänge-Schwing(ungs)walze
trailer wagon, see: tractor ~
trailing cable = Schleppkabel n
~ **chassis**, see: trailer ~
~ **edge** [*finishing screed*] = Hinterkante f
***trailing scoop grader**, pan scraper, drag road-scraper, hauling scraper (US); buck scraper (Brit.); (wheel) scraper, scoop pan self-loading scraper = Radschrapper m
~ **spring** = Hinterachsfeder f
~ **suction dredge(r)** = Schleppkopfsauger m [*Naßbagger, der beim Saugen gleichzeitig fährt*]
trailings, see: muck
train ferry = Eisenbahnfähre f
training = Anlernen n, Ausbildung f
~ **centre** (Brit.); ~ **center** (US) = Ausbildungsstätte f
~ **course** = (Ausbildungs)Lehrgang m
~ **film**, instructional ~ = Lehrfilm m
~ **idler**, see: guidler
~ **in road sense**, traffic safety education = (Straßen)Verkehrserziehung f

~ **ship** = Schulschiff n
~ **wall**, river ~ ~ = (Fluß-)Leitwerk n
~ ~ [*stilling basin*] = Begrenzungsmauer f [*Tosbecken n*]
~ ~ = Führungswand f [*Hochwasserüberfall m*]
~ **work** = Leitwerk n
train of barges = Schleppzug m, Schiffszug
~ ~ **fire engine**, fire train = Löschzug m
~ ~ **plant items**, equipment train = Gerätezug m
~ ~ **sway**, see: lurching
trajectory of strain = Dehnweg m
tramcar (Brit.); streetcar (US) = Straßenbahnwagen m
trammels, see: beam compasses
trammel wheel = (zentrisches) Schleifkurbelgetriebe n
tramp iron = Eisenstücke npl [*Brecher m*]
tram rail = Straßenbahnschiene f
~ **route** = Straßenbahnlinie f
~ **track**, tramway ~ (Brit.); street car track (US) = Straßenbahngleis n
~ ~ **removal excavator** = Bagger m (oder Kran m) mit Vorrichtung f zum Ausbau von Straßenbahngleisen
tram-train = Straßenbahnzug m
~ **traffic** = Straßenbahnverkehr m
tramway depot = Straßenbahnhof m, Straßenbahndepot n
~ **system** = Straßenbahnnetz n
tram(way) tracks (Brit.); see: street car ~ (US)
~ **tunnel** = Straßenbahntunnel m
trans-arctic base = transarktischer Stützpunkt m
transatlantic steamer = Überseedampfer m, Transatlantikdampfer
transferable traction power = Kraftschluß m [*zwischen Fahrbahn f und Fahrzeug n*]
transfer caliper, ~ **firm-joint** ~ = Hilfsschenkel-Taster m
~ **(motor) truck** (US); ~ **lorry** (Brit.) = Zwischentransport(lastkraft)wagen m
~ **plant** = Umschlaganlage f
transflo valve = Umleitungsventil n
transformed rock, see: metamorphic ~

transformer oil, see: mineral ~ ~
transgression sea = Pfannenmeer *n*
transient loading = vorübergehende Belastung *f*
trans-illumination = Durchleuchtung *f*
transit = Reisetheodolit *m*, Universalinstrument *n*
~ (concrete) mixer; see: lorry-mounted mixer (Brit.)
transitional soil = Übergangsboden *m*
transition curve, see: easement ~
~ curves between gradients, ~ radii on gradients, vertical curves = Kuppen- und Wannenausrundungen *fpl*
~ length = Übergangsbogenlänge *f*
transition-lime, see: greywacke limestone
transition link = Zwischenglied *n*
~ rocks = Übergangsgebirge *n*
~ slab = Schlepp-Platte *f*
~ spiral, spiral (transition) curve = Klothoide *f*
transit-mix(ed) concrete, truck-mixed ~ = Transportmischerbeton *m*
transit(-)mixer (truck) (US), see: truck mixer
transit-mix(ing concrete) plant, see: ready-mixed concrete plant of the transit-mix type
transit shed = Transitschuppen *m*
~ system with own right-of-way = Eigenfahrbahn-System *n*
transmission = Trieb *m*, Getriebe *n*
~ belt(ing) = Transmissionsriemen *m*
~ clutch = Vorgelegekupplung *f*
~ constant, coefficient of permeability, permeability coefficient = Durchlässigkeitsbeiwert *m*
~ line = Überlandstromleitung *f*
~ ~ tower = Freileitungsmast *m*
transmitted light = Durchlicht *n*
transmitter = Meßwertwandler *m*
trans-mountain water diversion = Überleitung *f* [*Wasser von einem Flußgebiet in ein anderes*]
transoceanic flight = Ozeanflug *m*
transom, see: cross girder (Brit.)
transparency, negative, transparent positive original = Mutterpause *f*
transpiration = Transpiration *f* [*produktiver Wasserverbrauch m der Pflanze f*]

transport (Geol.) = Transport *m*, Verfrachtung *f*
transportation, haulage work = Beförderung *f*, Transport *m*
~ medium = Beförderungsmittel *n*
(~) route = Verkehrsweg *m*
transported soil, colluvial ~ = Absatzboden *m*, Kolluvialboden *m*, Derivatboden, umgelagerter Boden
transporter = Transportwagen *m*
~, bottom flange type telpher = Untergurtlaufschienen-Elektrohängebahn *f*
~, bridge ~, bridge tramway = Verladebrücke *f*
~ bridge, see: conveyor ~
~ crane, bridge ~ ~ = Verladebrücke *f* mit Drehkran *m*
~ with end-tipping railway car platform, bridge ~ ~ ~ ~ ~ ~ = Kipperbrücke *f* mit Kippbühne *f*
~ ~ travel(l)ing crane, bridge ~ ~ ~ ~ = Verladebrücke *f* mit Laufkran *m*
transporting power, transport ~ = Schleppkraft *f* [*Fluß m*]
~ vehicle, see: hauling unit
transport man = Verkehrsfachmann *m*
Transport Ministry, see: Ministry of Transport (Brit.)
transport of detritus, see: bed-load transport
~ power, see: transporting ~
~ rocker shovel = Wurfschaufellader *m* (oder Über-Kopf-Lader) auf Rädern *npl*
transport tricycle = Dreirad *n*
transverse bending = Querbiegung *f*
~ ~ test = Querbiegeversuch *m*
~ bracing, lateral ~, cross ~, wind ~ ~ = Windverband *m*
~ diaphragm = Schottblech *n* [*Kastenträger m*]
~ prestressing = Quervorspannung *f*
~ reinforcement = Querbewehrung *f*, Querarmierung
~ rigidity = Quersteifigkeit *f*
~ screed = Querbohle *f* [*Beton(decken)fertiger m*]
~ section, cross-section = Querschnitt *m*
~ slope [*deprecated*]; see: camber
~ ~ = Quergefälle *n*
~ spreading blade concrete spreader = Schaufel(beton)verteiler *m*

transverse stiffener = Quersteife *f*
~ strength = Querfestigkeit *f*
trap (Brit.); interceptor (US); separator = Traps *m*, Fang *m*, Abscheider *m*
trapezoidal channel = trapezförmiges Gerinne *n*, trapezförmige Rinne *f*
trap gate = Klapptor *n* [*Binnenschiffahrtschleuse f*]
~ (rock) = Trapp *m*
~ sandstone = Grauwackensandstein *m*
~ tuff, see: basaltic ~
trash bar = Rechenstab *m*
(~) rack = screen (rack), screen grillage (Brit.) = Rechen *m*
(~) ~ beam = Rechenquerträger *m*
(~) ~ rake (US); see: screen cleaner (Brit.)
(~) ~ structure = Rechenbauwerk *n*
trass, see: (Rhenish) ~
trass-lime-cement concrete = Trass-Kalk-Zementbeton *m*
travel bituminous mixing plant = Aufnahmemischer *m*
~ brake = Fahrbremse *f*
~ drive = Fahrantrieb *m*
~ engine = Fahrmotor *m*
traveler (US) = fahrbares Montagegerüst *n*
travel(l)ing = (Ver)Fahren *n* [*Fahrzeug n*]
~ bridge = Räumerbrücke *f* [*Absetzbecken n*]
~ ~ crane = Brücken-Laufkran *m*
(~) carriage = Unterwagen *m*
*travel(l)ing (concrete) mixer (plant), concrete mixer-paver, paving mixer, paver, rotating drum paver mixer, combined paver, concrete paver, combined mixing and paving machine = Straßen(beton)mischer *m*, Straßenbetoniermaschine *f*
~ crane, overhead (~) ~ = Laufkran *m*
~ ~ with electric hoist (or pulley) block = Elektro(flaschen)zug-Laufkran *m*
~ distributor = Wandersprenger *m* [*Tropfkörper m*]
~ form (work) = Wanderschalung *f*
~ gantry (or frame) crane = Bockkran *m* (oder Gerüstkran) *m* mit Rädern *npl*
~ gear, undercarriage, running gear, travel unit, mounting unit = Fahrwerk *n*
~ grate, chain ~ = Wanderrost *m*

~ grizzly feeder, ~-bar grizzly = Wander-Stangen(transport)rost *m*, Wander-Stangenaufgeber *m*
~ mixer, see: ~ (concrete) mixer (plant)
~ mixing machine, see: windrow-type travel(l)ing (asphalt) (or road) plant
~ ~ ~, ~ mixer [*this term is sometimes used to include mix-in-place machines and windrow-type plants*] = Wandermischer *m* [*Bodenverfestigung f*]
~ (mixing) plant, see: windrow-type travel(l)ing (asphalt) (or road) plant
~ ~ ~, ~ ~ machine = Straßen(beton)mischer *m*
~ plant method, travel plant mixing = Aufnahmemischverfahren *n*, Aufnahmemischen *n*
traveling template form for bituminous mixtures (US); see: canal paver for ~ ~
~ ~ ~ ~ concrete (US); see: canal concrete paver
travelling time [*deprecated*]; see: running ~
travel(l)ing tripper = Abwurfwagen *m* [*Förderband n*]
~ type suspended weighbatcher = fahrbare Hängewaage *f*
~ wave = Wanderwelle *f*
TRAVELOADER [*Trademark*] = Transport-Fahrzeug *n* für Landgut *n* mit Belade- und Entlade-(Stapel)Vorrichtung *f*
travel path of vehicle = Fahrzeugspur *f*
~ plant mixing, travel(l)ing plant method = Aufnahmemischen *n*, Aufnahmemischverfahren *n*
~ position = Fahrstellung *f*
~ ramp, travelramp = fahrbare Laderampe *f*
~ speed = Reisegeschwindigkeit *f*
~ unit, see: travel(l)ing gear
traverse = Polygonzug *m*, Polygon *n*
~, see: pass
traversing = Polygonzug-Aufnahme *f*
~ jack, see: sliding ~
~ saddle = Turmdrehkran-Laufkatze *f*
~ slip(way) = Quer(schiffs)aufschleppe *f*
travertine = Travertin *m*
trawling winch = Schleppnetzwinde *f*

TRAXCAVATOR SHOVEL [*Trademark*] = Frontladeschaufel *f*, Fabrikat TRACKSON CO.
tread = Lauffläche *f* [*Gleiskette f; Rad n*]
treadle = Zählschwelle *f* [*Gebührenautobahn f*]
tread roller, truck ~ = Laufrolle *f* [*Gleiskette f*]
treated oil = modifiziertes Öl *n*
treater = Emulsionstreater *m* für die Ölreinigung [*kontinuierlich arbeitender Durchlauferhitzer mit Erdgasfeuerung*]
treatment, processing = Behandeln *n*, Behandlung *f*
~ of icy pavements, highway ice control = Glatteisbekämpfung *f*
~ with silicate, silicating (Brit.); silicifying (US) = Verkieseln *n*
tree crusher = Maschine *f* zum Niederbrechen und anschließendem Zerschleißen von Gestrüpp und Bäumen
treedozer, stumper = Planierraupe *f* (oder Planiergleiskettengerät *n*) für Baumfällarbeiten *fpl*, Baumschieber *m*
tree-felling = Bäumefällen *n*
tree-guard = Baumrost *m*, Drahthose *f*, Schutzgitter *n*
tree stinger = Vierrad-Fahrzeug *n* mit Brustschild und Teleskopausleger zum Umegen von Bäumen
~ stump, see: stump
~ trunk = Baumstamm *m*
trellis bridge = Gitterbrücke *f*
trembling bog, see: quaking ~
tremie(d) concrete, ~ grout, fixed ~ ~ = Trichterbeton *m*
tremie pipe, ~ tube = Betonzufuhrrohr *n*
~ ~ (or tube) method, fixed ~ ~ (~ ~) ~ = Kontraktorverfahren *n*
~-seal concrete = Betonpfropfen *m* [*unter Wasser n*]
tremolite (asbestos), Italian asbestos (Min.) = Tremolit *m*
trench = Graben *m* mit senkrechten Wänden *fpl*
~ backfill = Grabenfüllung *f*
~ blasting, see: ~ method
~ brace (US); see: shoring strut (Brit.)
~ cutting machine = (Drän)Grabenfräse(r) *f*, (*m*), Grabkettenbagger *m*

~ digger, see: ditch digger
~ digging, see: trenching
trenched cone (Geol.) = eingefurchter Kegel *m*
trencher, see: ditch digger
~ bucket, digging ~ = Grabenbaggereimer *m*, Grabbecher *m*, Eimerbecher *m*
trench excavating plant, see: ditch digger
~ excavation, see: trenching
~ excavator, see: ditch digger
trenchfiller, backfiller = Grabenverfüllgerät *n*
trench-forming shovel (Brit.), see: backacter
trench hoe (US); see: backacter (Brit.)
trenching, trench digging, trench excavation = Grabenaushub *m* [*schmaler Graben m mit senkrechten Wänden fpl*]
~ hoe (US); see: backacter (Brit.)
***trenching machine of the bucket elevator type**, see: bucket trencher
~ plant, see: ditch digger
***trenchliner**, see: bucket trencher
trench method, ~ blasting = Graben-Methode *f* [*Sprengen n weicher Baugrundmassen fpl*]
~ ~ of subaqueous tunnel(l)ing, sunken-tube method (or construction) = Versenken *n* fertiger Tunnelstücke *npl* oder des ganzen Tunnels *m* in eine vorher ausgebaggerte Rinne *f*
trench roller = Grabenwalze *f*
~ sheeting, trench piling = Kanaldielen *fpl*
~ strut (Brit.), see: shoring ~
trend of development = Entwicklungsrichtung *f*
trepan chisel = Rammeißel *m*
trestle, pile ~, pile bent = (Pfahl)Joch *n*
~ bridge, ~ bridging = Jochbrücke *f*
~ centering (US); ~ centring (Brit.) = Lehrgerüst *n* mit senkrechter Absteifung *f*
~-type structure = (Pfahl)Jochbauwerk *n*
trial hole, test hole = Schürfloch *n*
~ load method of analyzing arch dams = Lastaufteilungsverfahren *n* des Bureau of Reclamation
    arch element = Gewölbering *m*
    cantilever element = Kragträger *m*

trial method = Versuchsverfahren n, Versuchsmethode f, Experimentalverfahren
~ **mix(ture)** = Probemischung f
~ **period** = Probezeit f
~ **pit**, see: test pit
trial-test investigation, proving-ground test = Versuchsstanduntersuchung f
triangle of error = Fehlerdreieck n
~ ~ **forces**, force triangle = Kräftedreieck n
triangular bar, ~ **iron** = Dreikanteisen n
~ **diagram** = Dreieckdiagramm n, Dreieckschaubild n
~ **girder**, see: half-lattice ~
~ **load** = Dreiecklast f
~ **system**, triangulated ~ = Dreieckanordnung f, Dreiecksystem n
~ **type walking mechanism** [*walking dragline*] = Kurbel- und Gelenk-Schreitausrüstung f
~ **wooden fillet** = Holzdreieckleiste f
triangulated bracing = Dreieckverband m
~ **girder** = Dreieckträger m
~ **truss** = Dreiecksprengwerk n
triangulation = Triangulation f
triaxial chart = Dreieck-Berechnungstafel f
~ **compression cell**, ~ ~ **test chamber** = Triaxialgerät n, dreiaxiale Druckzelle f, triaxiale Scherprüfzelle f
    fixed-sleeve cell = ~ mit fest angeordneter Gummihülle f
    free-sleeve cell = ~ mit frei angeordneter Gummihülle f
~ **(compression) test** = dreiachsialer Druckversuch m, Dreiachsialversuch m
tributary; affluent (Brit.) = Nebenfluß m
trickling filter, percolating ~ = Tropfkörper m
triclinic system = triklines System n [*Kristall n*]
tricycle = Dreirad n
tridymite = Tridymit m
to trim, to join = abbinden, zulegen [*Holzkonstruktion f*]
to trimm, to burr = abgraten
trimmer, canal ~ = Kanalprofilmaschine f
~, trimmed joist, trimmer beam = Wechselbalken m

trimming, shaping, truing; [*deprecated: regulating*] = Profilieren n [*Erdbau m*]
~ **tool** = Abgratwerkzeug n
Trinaskol = durch Bohrung f gewonnener flüchtiger Trinidad-Asphalt m
Trinidad épuré, see: parianite
~ **Lake Asphalt**, crude ~ ~ ~ = Trinidad-(Roh)Asphalt m
*****Trinidad Pitch Lake** = Trinidad-Asphaltsee m
~ **refined asphalt**, see: parianite
trinitrotoluene, TNT = Trinitrotoluol n
trip [*traffic*] = Fahrt f
~, release catch = Auslöser m, Auslösemechanismus m
~ **drum** = Löffelklappentrommel f
tripestone = Gekrösestein m
triphane, spodumene (Min.) = Spodumen m
trip hook = Auslösehaken m
triple corrugated (sheet) iron = Dreifachwellblech n
triple-deck grade separation structure, three-level ~ ~ ~ = dreietagiges Kreuzungsbauwerk n
~ **vibrating screen** = Dreideckersieb n, Dreidecker m
triple (drainage) culvert, three-barrel ~ = Dreiröhrendurchlaß m, Dreiröhren-Abzugkanal m
~ **flue boiler** = Dreiflammrohrkessel m
~ **roll crusher** = Dreiwalzenbrecher m
~ **safe boom (US)/jib (Brit.) hoist** = dreifach sichere Auslegerwinde f [*Bagger m*]
~ **throw plunger pump** = Dreiplungerpumpe f
triplex tamper, see: three-legged ~
tripod = Dreifuß m
~, leg = Stativ n
~, see: shear-legs
tripoli = Tripel m, Polierschiefer m
tripped drop hammer, see: drop ~
troll(e)y, see: jenny (Brit.)
~ **batcher plant**, (bin and) ~ ~ ~ = Zuschlagsilo m mit Wiegebalken m
~ **bus**, electric troll(e)y, trackless troll(e)y; troll(e)y coach (US) = Oberleitungsbus m, O-Bus m
~ **track** = Katzfahrbahn f

troll(e)y-train = Oberleitungsbus *m* mit Anhänger *m*
troll(e)y with operator's cab(in) = Laufkatze *f* (oder Lastkatze) mit Führerstand *m*
trommel, see: rotary screen
tropical outfit = Tropenausrüstung *f*
trouble-free operation = störungsfreier Betrieb *m*
trough, see: tub
~ **belt**, ~ **band** = Trogband *n*, Muldenband *n*, Troggurt *m*, Muldengurt
~ ~ **conveyor**, ~ **band** ~ = Muldengurtförderer *m*, Muldenbandförderer, Troggurtförderer, Trogbandförderer
~ **bridge, open** ~ = Trogbrücke *f*, offene Brücke, Brücke mit unten liegender Fahrbahn *f*
~ **conveyor** = Förderrinne *f*
troughed idler, see: three-roller idler set
trough fault, graben, rift valley (Geol.) = Graben *m*, Tiefscholle *f*, Grabenbruch *m*, Grabensenke *f*
~ **gutter tile** = Muldenfalzziegel *m*
~ **in the top of the windrow** = Schwadenmulde *f*
trough lift = (Schiffs)Hebewerk *n* für Naßförderung *f*, Trogschleuse *f*
~ **of the wave** = Wellental *n*
~ **plate girder span** = Blechträgertrogbrücke *f*
trough-shaped iron = Rinneneisen *n*
trough sheet = Trogblech *n*
~-**truss span** = Fachwerk-Trogbrücke *f*
*****trough-type concrete distributor**, hopper spreader, box spreading machine, box (type) (concrete) spreader, box hopper distributor, hopper type spreading machine = Betonverteilungswagen *m*, (Beton) Querverteiler *m*
~ **mortar mixer** = Trogmörtelmischer *m*
trough vault = Muldengewölbe *n*
trowel = Verputzkelle *f*
~ **hand** = Zementestrichstreicher *m*
trowel(l)ing bridge, see: float ~
~ **machine**, see: mechanical trowel
trowel trade(s), construction ~, building ~ = Baugewerbe *n*, Bauhandwerk *n*
~ ~ **hydrated lime** = Baukalkhydrat *n*
truck (US); see: lorry (Brit.)

~ **agitator**, see: agitator (or agitating) truck (or conveyor) (US)
~ **cab** (US); lorry ~ (Brit.) = Fahrerhaus *n*
~ **chassis** = LKW-Fahrgestell *n*
~ **crane** = Aufbaukran *m*, schnellfahrender Autokran, Last(kraft)wagenkran, Autokran auf Chassis mit Eigenantrieb [*auf LKW m aufgebaut*]
~ **endgate** (US); see: tailboard
trucker = Last(kraft)wagenfahrer *m*
truck frame [*crawler shovel*] = Fahrgestell *n*, Fahrgestellrahmen *m*
~ ~ = LKW-Rahmen *m*
~ **haul(ing)** (US), see: haulage by truck
~ **hoe** = Tieflöffel(bagger) *m* auf Chassis mit Eigenantrieb *m*
~ **hoist**; railway car ~ (Brit.) = Waggonhebeanlage *f*
~ **idler** = Leitrad *n* [(*Gleis*)*Kettenfahrwerk n*]
trucking firm (US) = Fuhrbetrieb *m*, Fuhrunternehmen *n*
truck loader = LKW *m* mit Frontladeschaufelvorrichtung *f*
truck-mixed concrete, transit-mix(ed) ~ = Transportmischerbeton *m* [*während der Fahrt trocken und naß gemischter Beton*]
truck mixer, transit(-)mixer (truck) (US); mixer lorry (Brit.) = Transportmischer *m*, Liefermischer *m*, Fahrmischer
~ ~ **plant** (US); see: ready-mixed concrete plant of the transit-mix type
~ **mixing** = Trocken- und Naßmischen *n* während der Fahrt *f* [*Transportbeton m*]
~(-**mounted**) **crane** = Autokran *m*
~-**mounted distributor**, see: pressure tank lorry
~-**mounted excavator** (Brit.); see: truck (-mounted) (pneumatic-tired) shovel (-crane) (US)
truck(-mounted) (pneumatic-tired) shovel (-crane)(US); lorry-mounted pneumatic-tyred mechanical shovel, truck-mounted excavator (Brit.) = Autobagger *m* auf Chassis mit Eigenantrieb, Last(kraft)-wagenbagger, schnellfahrender Autobagger, Aufbaubagger [*ca. 30-55 km/h*]

truck passing lane (US); lorry ~ ~ (Brit.) = LKW-Überholspur *f*
~ plow (US); lorry plough (Brit.) = LKW-Schneepflug *m*
~ roller, see: tread ~
~ scale, motor-truck ~ (US) = Lastkraftwagenwaage *f*
to truck to = antransportieren mit LKW *m*
truck track = Gleiskette *f* für LKW *m*
~ tractor, tractor-truck (US); motor tractor (Brit.) = (Straßen)Zugmaschine *f*
~ ~ bulldozer (US) = Zugmaschine-Bulldozer *m*
truck-trailer (US); lorry-~ (Brit.) = LKW-Anhänger *m*
~ combination, truck ~ (US); lorry-trailer ~ (Brit.) = Lastzug *m*
truck transfer case = LKW-Verteilergetriebe *n*
~ wheel = LKW-Rad *n*
~ ~, ~ roller [*crawler*] = Trägerrolle *f*, Laufrad *n*
truck (US)/**lorry** (Brit.) **(cable, or rope) winch** = LKW-(Trommel-)Seilwinde *f*
true cohesion = wahre Kohäsion *f*
~ loess = echter Löß *m*, typischer ~, Primärlöß, Urlöß
~ marble, recrystallized limestone = echter kristallinischer Marmor *m*, Urkalkstein *m*
~ obsidian, iceland agate = echter Obsidian *m*
~ submersible pump = Unterwasser-(motor)pumpe *f* mit halbnassem Motor *m* (oder Naßlaufmotor), Tauch(motor)-pumpe ~ ~ ~, Unterwasser-Elektro-Pumpe ~ ~ ~
~ to cross-section, line and level (or grade) = profilgemäß [*Straßenquerschnitt m*]
truing, see: shaping
TRU-LAY-ROPE [*Trademark*] = vorgeformtes drallarmes Seil *n*
trumpet intersection = Trompeten-Abzweig(stelle) *m*, (*f*)
trunk (line) road; [*deprecated: arterial road*] = Fernverkehrsstraße *f*
~ route = Hauptstrecke *f*
~ sewer, main ~ = Hauptabwasserkanal *m*
trunnion screw = Zapfenschraube *f*

truss = Fachwerkträger *m*, gegliederter Träger *m*, Fachwerkbalken *m*, Tragwerk *n*
~ analysis = Fachwerkberechnung *f*
~ bar = Versteifungsstab *m* [*Kastenträger m*]
trussed arch = Fachwerkbogen *m*
~ ~ with three hinges, see: three-hinged braced arch
truss(ed) bridge = Sprengwerkbrücke *f*, Fachwerk(balken)brücke
trussed framing = Fachwerkrahmen *m*
truss member = Fachwerkstab *m*, Ausfachungsstab
~ post, king ~ = Hängesäule *f* [*einfacher Hängebock m*]
~ ~, queen ~ = Hängesäule *f* [*doppelter Hängebock m*]
tsunanis, seismic sea waves = Erdbebenflutwellen *fpl*, Tsunanis
tub, see: base
~, washer box, trough [*log washer*] = (Wasch)Trog *m* [*Schwertwäsche f*]
tube and tank process = Ellis-Verfahren *n* [*technisches Spaltverfahren n*]
~ beader = Siederohrdichtmaschine *f*, Rohreinwalzapparat *m*, Rohrwalze *f*, Rollmaschine *f*
~ bender = Röhrenbiegeapparat *m*
~ coil, pipe ~, coiled pipe, serpentine ~ = Rohrschlange *f*
tubeless tire (US)/**tyre** (Brit.) = schlauchloser Reifen *m*
tube level = Röhrenlibelle *f*
~ (or icicle) of calcium carbonate = Tropfstein *m*
    stalactite = Stalaktit *m*, Abtropfstein *m*
    stalagmite = Stalagmit *m*, Auftropfstein *m*
tube railway (Brit.), see: underground ~
~ sample boring = Kernbüchsenbohrung *f*
~ still, see: pipe ~
~ track = Untergrundbahngleis *n*
~ trench = Tunnelrinne *f*
~ well, tubular ~, bore well, drilled well = Rohrbrunnen *m*, Bohrbrunnen
tubular beam of centrifugally cast concrete = Schleuderbeton-Rohrbalkenträger *m*

tubular chassis — tunnel-type penstock

tubular chassis = Röhrenchassis n
~ **frame, frame arch** = Rohrrahmen m [*Motor-Straßenhobel m*]
~ **hand railing** = Röhren-Geländer n mit Handlauf m
~ **mast** = Rohrmast m
~ **member** = Rohrträger m [*der Drehkranzhalter für die Planierschar und die Verbindung vom Vorderradstützbock zum Antriebsfahrgestell sind beim Allis Chalmers motor grader als Rohrträger ausgebildet*]
~ **rivet** = Hohlniet m
~ **rotary kiln** = Drehrohrofen m
~ **shaft** = Hohlwelle f
~ **slide valve control** = Rohrschiebersteuerung f
(~) **(steel-)pipe pile** = (Stahl)Rohr(gründungs)pfahl m, (Stahl)Rohrtragpfahl
~ **steel scaffold(ing)** = Stahlrohrgerüst n, Stahlrohrrüstung f
~ ~ **type belt conveyor** = Stahlrohr(förder)band n
~ **structure** = Rohrkonstruktion f
~ **strut** = Rohrstütze f
~ **welded mast** = zusammengeschweißter Stahlmast m
~ **well,** see: tube ~
~ **worm conveyor** = Förderrohr n
tufa, see: tufaceous limestone
tufaceous limestone, calc(areous) tufa, tufa = Kalktuff m
tuff, volcanic ~, tufaceous rock = vulkanischer Tuff m, Feuerbergtuff, Durchbruchgesteintuff
tufaceous rock, see: tuff
tuff breccia = Tuffbrekzie f
tug(boat), see: towboat
to tug to site = zur Einbaustelle f schleppen [*Schwimmkasten m*]
tulip tree, yellow poplar, white wood tree = Tulpenbaum m
tumbler = Auslöservorrichtung f
tumbling (grinding) mill = Schwerkraft(mahl)mühle f
tundra = Tundra f
tung oil, Chinese wood oil, China wood oil = Tungöl n, chinesisches Holzöl n
(tungsten) carbide = Wolframcarbid n

(~) ~ **(tipped) (drill) bit,** drill bit with tungsten carbide insert (or tip), carbide-insert rock bit = Hartmetallmeißel m, Hartmetallkrone f
tunnel; see: drift (Brit.)
~ = Tunnel m [*Gebirgsdurchstich m im Zuge von Verkehrswegen mpl*]
~ **concreting,** see: in-situ concrete facing (or lining)
~ **conveyor (belt)** = Abziehband n im Haldentunnel m
***tunel(l)ing,** tunnel work, tunnel driving = Tunnelbau m
~ **engineer, tunnel(l)er** = Tunnelbauer m, Tunnelbauingenieur m
~ **explosive** = Tunnelsprengstoff m
~ **machine** = Streckenvortriebmaschine f, Stollenvortriebmaschine
(tunnel) jumbo, drilling jumbo = Bohrjumbo m, Ausleger-Bohrwagen m, Groß-Bohrwagen m
~ **kiln car** = Tunnelofenwagen m
~ ~ ~ **top** = Tunnelofenwagendecke f
~ ~ **plant** = Tunnelofenwerk n
~ ~ **sponge iron process** = Eisenschwamm-Herstellung f im Tunnelofen m
~ **lighting (system)** = Tunnelbeleuchtung f
~ **lining gantry** = Rüstung f zur Stollenausbetonierung (oder Tunnelausbetonierung f)
~ **loading, mucking** = Schutterung f, Schuttern n
~ **loco(motive)** = Stollenlok(omotive) f
~ **mucker,** see: mucking shovel
~ **not under pressure** = Freispiegelstollen m
~ **portal** = Tunneleingang m, Tunnelportal n
~ **progress,** advance, driving, heading = (Strecken)Vortrieb m [*Tunnelbau m*]
~ **ramp** = Tunnelrampe f
(~) **shield,** ~ driving ~ = Brustschild n, Tunnelschild, Vortriebsschild
~ **shovel,** see: mucking
tunnel-type discharge carrier = Überfallstollen m, Überlaufstollen, Hochwasserstollen
~ **penstock,** see: pressure tunnel

tunnel vault — twin rocker shovel

tunnel vault, see: wagon ~
~ work, see: tunnel(l)ing
tup, see: drop hammer
turbidimeter = Trübungsmesser *m*
turbidimetric sulfate determination = Sulfatbestimmung *f* nach der Trübungsmessungsmethode *f*
turbine blade = Turbinenschaufel *f*
~ engine motor car = PKW *m* mit Gasturbinenantrieb *m*
~ pit = Turbinengrube *f*
turbo-charged 2-cycle diesel (engine) = Zweitakt-Diesel(motor) *m* mit Turboaufladung *f*
turbocharger [*diesel engine*] = Turbo(auf)lader *m*
turbocharge tractor = Dieselschlepper *m* mit Turbo(auf)lader *m*
turbo-compressor = Turbo(luft)verdichter *m*
turbodiesel (engine), turbocharged diesel engine = Dieselmotor *m* mit Auflader *m*
turbodrill = Turbinenbohrer *m*
turbo-generator = Turbogenerator *m*
turbulent boundary layer = turbulente Grenzschicht *f*
~ flow = turbulentes Fließen *n*
turf = Rasen *m*
~ cutting plough (Brit.) = Rasenschneider *m*
~ drain = Rasendrän *m*
turfing by seeding = Rasenansaat *f*
~ ~ sodding = Rasensodendeckung *f*
turf knife = Rasenzugmesser *n*
~ peat = Rasentorf *m*
~ sod, see: (grass) ~
~ ~ stockpile = Rasenstapel *m*
~ ~ stripping = Rasenschälen *n*
Turkey alder, upland ~ = Grauerle *f*, Weißerle
turn = Wendung *f*
turn-around (area) = Wendeplatz *m*
turnbuckle = Spannschloß *n*
turned bolt, finished ~ = blanke Schraube *f*, gedrehte ~
turning basin, swinging area = Wendeplatz *m* für ein Schiff *n*
~ circle = Wendekreis *m*
~ handle = Drehgriff *m*
~ path = Wendespur *f*

~ place = Wendeplatz *m*
~ radius = Wendehalbmesser *m*, Wenderadius *m*
~ saw = Schweifsäge *f*
~ traffic = Einbiegeverkehr *m*
"turn-key" bid, all-in tender = Angebot *n* für Entwurf *m* und Bau *m*
"turn-key" type of contract = Entwurf- und Bauauftrag *m*
(turn)pike, see: toll road
turntable = Drehscheibe *f*
~ [*Allis Chalmers motor grader*] = Scharhalter *m*
~ press = Revolverziegelpresse *f*
~ tip = Drehscheibenkipper *m*
turn-wrest plough (Brit.)/**plow** (US) = Kehrpflug *m*
turps, oil of turpentine, $C_{10}H_{16}$ = Terpentinöl *n*
turquoise (Min.), see: callaite
turrelite = Ölschiefer *m* aus Texas
tusk tenon = Brustzapfen *m* [Holzverbindung *f*]
TV control of operations = Betriebsüberwachung *f* mit Fernsehgerät *n*
TV tower = Fernsehturm *m*
twin-batch paver = Doppeltrommel-Betoniermaschine *f*, Doppeltrommel(beton)straßenmischer *m*
twin-bore tunnel, see: twin ~
twin bridge = Doppelbrücke *f*
~ Cornish boiler = Flammrohrdoppelkessel *m*, Zwillingskessel
~ cylinder piston pump = Zwillingskolbenpumpe *f*
twindual roll crusher, four-roll ~ ~ = Doppelwalzenbrecher *m*, Doppelwalzwerk *n*
twin jaw crusher (or breaker), two movable ~ ~ (~ ~), double ~ ~ (~ ~) = Doppelbackenbrecher *m*, Doppelschwingenbrecher, Zweischwingerbrecher
~ lamellae [*plagioclase*] = Zwillingslamellierung *f* [*Natronkalkfeldspat m*]
twinned form = Zwillingsform *f*
twin-power scraper, see: EUCLID ~ ~
twin pug (US); see: twin-shaft paddle mixer (Brit.)
~ pump = Zwillingspumpe *f*
~ rocker shovel = Doppelschaufellader *m*

twin (or double) roll crusher, see: roll crusher

twin-screed (transverse) finisher, two-screed (transverse) finisher = Doppelbohlenfertiger *m*

twin-shaft paddle mixer (Brit.); twin pug (US) = Doppel-Wellen-Zwangsmischer *m*

~ screen = Doppelwellensieb *n*

twin slab (drainage) culvert = gekuppelter Plattendurchlaß *m*, ~ Plattenabzugkanal *m*

~ tunnel, twin-bore ~ = Zwillingstunnel *m*, Doppel(rohr)tunnel

to twist = umschlagen [*Drahtseil n*]

twist = Drall *m*

~ drill = Spiralbohrer *m*

twisted [*wood*] = windschief [*Holz n*]

~ strata (Geol.) = verdrehte Schichtungen *fpl*

twisting stress = Verdrehspannung *f*

two-axle bogie = zweiachsiges Drehgestell *n*

~ carrier = Zweiachsgestell *n*, Zweiachsunterwagen *m* [*Bagger m*]

~ tandem roller = Zweiachs-Tandemwalze *f*

two-beam (or two-screed) finisher (or finishing machine) = Zweibohlen-Fertiger *m*, Doppelbohlenfertiger

two-car diesel train, ~ set = zweiteiliger Dieseltriebwagen *m*

two-centred compound curve = zweiseitiger Korbbogen *m*

two-coat asphalt (Brit.) = zweilagiger Bitumenteppich *m*

two-compartment bin = Zweitaschen-Bunker *m*, Zweitaschen-Silo *m*

two-cordon method, see: windshield-card ~

two-dimensional stressing = zweidimensionale Spannung *f*

two-hinged arch, arch hinged at the springings = Zweigelenkbogen *m*

~ ~ frame = Zweigelenkbogenrahmen *m*

~ frame = Zweigelenkrahmen *m*

two-hole hollow block = Zweikammer(hohlblock)stein *m*

~ ~ ~ of brick rubble concrete = Ziegelsplitt-Zweikammer(hohlblock)stein *m*

two-lane two-way road = Straße *f* mit zwei befestigten Spuren *fpl* in beiden Richtungen *fpl*

two-leaf vertical-lift gate = doppeltes Hubschütz *n*, doppelte Hubschütze *f*
upper leaf = obere Tafel *f*
lower leaf = untere Tafel *f*

two-lever control = Zwei-Hebel-Betätigung *f*, Zwei-Hebel-Bedienung *f*

two-line bucket, ~ grab, ~ grab bucket, ~ grabbing bucket = Zweiseil-Greifkorb *m*, Zweiseilbaggergreifer *m*

two-mass oscillator = (DEGEBO-) Schwingungsmaschine *f*

~ vibrator = Zwei-Massen-Vibrator *m*

two-mica granite, muscovite-biotite granite = Muskovit-Biotit-Granit *m*

two-motor hoist = Doppelelektromotoren-Spillwinde *f*

two movable jaw crusher (or breaker), see: twin ~ ~ (~ ~)

two-panel frame = Zweifeldrahmen *m*

two-pass surface treatment, see: armo(u)r coat

two-pinned arch bridge = Zweigelenkbogenscheibenbrücke *f*

two-pocket bore = Doppelsackbohrer *m*

two-point chisel type bit cutting edge = Doppel-Meißelschneide *f*

two-power locomotive = Zweikraft-Lok(omotive) *f*

two-pulley drive, tandem ~ = Zweitrommelantrieb *m* [*Bandförderer m*]

two-rail surface track; see: rail(way) track (Brit.)

two-screed (transverse) finisher, see: twin-screed (~)

two-shaft hammer mill = Doppelhammer(mahl)mühle *f*

~ pug(-)mill concrete mixer = Zweitrog-Zwangsbetonmischer *m* mit vertikalem Rührwerk *n*

two-speed blower = Zweistufengebläse *n*

~ gearbox = Zweiganggetriebe *n*

two-stage (air) compressor = zweistufiger Kompressor *m*, ~ Luftverdichter *m*, Mitteldruckverdichter, zweistufiger Drucklufterzeuger *m*

~ centrifugal pump = Verbundkreiselpumpe *f*

two-stage compressing = zweistufige Verdichtung *f* [*Kompressor m*]
~ jaw crusher = zweistufiger Backenbrecher *m*
~ trickling filter = zweistufiger Tropfkörper *m*
two-stop batch plant = Abmeßanlage *f* mit zweimaligem Halten *n* der Fahrzeuge *npl*
two-stor(e)y basement = zweistöckiges Kellergeschoß *n*
~ tank = zweistöckiges Absatzbecken *n* [*Abwasserwesen n*]
two-stroke diesel engine = Zweitakt-Diesel(motor) *m*
two-way beam-and-slab floor; grid type girder deck (Brit.) = Trägerrostdecke *f*, Balken(träger)rostdecke
~ dump trailer = Zweiseiten-Kippanhänger *m*
~ flat-slab floor, flat slab (girderless) construction = Pilzdecke(nkonstruktion) *f*
~ inlet = Wechselfalle *f*
~ prestressing = zweiaxiale Vorspannung *f*
~ ram, double acting ~ = doppeltwirkender Hydraulikzylinder *m*
~ road = Zweibahnstraße *f*
~ slab floor = kreuzweise bewehrte Decke *f*, ~ armierte ~
~ valve = Zweiwegeventil *n*
two-wheel(ed) scraper, see: carrying ~
~ tractor = Einachs(rad)schlepper *m*, Zweiradschlepper, Einachszugwagen *m*, Zweirad-Trecker *m*, Zweirad-Traktor *m*
~ unit, see: single-axle ~
~ vehicle with low-powered engine = Motorroller *m*
~ wagon drill = Zweirad-Bohrwagen *m*
twybill, mortise axe = Stichaxt *f*, Stoßaxt
tyne (Brit.); **scarifier tine** (US) = Aufreiß(er)zahn *m*, Aufreiß(er)zinken *m*
typical cross-section = Regelquerschnitt *m*
tyre chain, driving ~ (Brit.); **tire ~** (US) = Reifen(schutz)kette *f*
(~) contact area (Brit.); see: contact area
~ failure (Brit.); **tire ~** (US) = Reifenschaden *m*

~ grip (Brit.); **tire ~** (US) = Reifengriffigkeit *f*
~ impression (Brit.); **tire ~** (US) = Reifeneindruck *m*
~/load/road relationship = Beziehungen *fpl* zwischen Reifen, Belastung und Straße
tyre pump (Brit.); **tire ~** (US) = Reifenpumpe *f*
~ section, ~ tread pattern (Brit.); **tire ~** (US) = Reifenprofil *n*

U

ubac (Geol.) = Schattenseite *f*
Ubbelohde dropping-point = Tropfpunkt *m* nach Ubbelohde
U-cup = Manschette *f*
U-flex oil ring = U-förmiger Ölring *m*
uintaite, see: gilsonite
U-leather = Ledermanschette *f*
ullmanite, nickel antimony glance, NiSbS (Min.) = Ullmanit *m*, Antimonnickelglanz *m*
ultimate flexural analysis = Biege-Bruchfestigkeitsberechnung *f*
~ load, failure ~ = Bruchlast *f*, Bruchbelastung *f*, Grenzbelastung, Grenzlast
~ ~, failure ~ = Versinkungsgrenze *f* [*Tragpfahl m*]
~ ~ method [*concrete pavement design method in which the pavement is designed so as to possess a definite safety factor referred to the ultimate load*] = Bruchfestigkeits-Methode *f* [*Betondecken-Entwurfsmethode f bei der ein bestimmter Sicherheitsfaktor m, der in Beziehung zur Bruchfestigkeit steht, eingesetzt wird*]
~ ~ ~, ~ ~ design = Traglastverfahren *n*
~ strength, see: breaking strength
~ ~ design method in which no modular ratio is used = n-freies Traglastverfahren *n*
~ ~ procedure, ~ ~ design = Traglastverfahren *n*
ultimate stress = Bruchspannung *f*
ultrasonic (or supersonic) concrete tester = Ultraschallbetonprüfgerät *n*

ultrasonic (or supersonic) flue dust elimination = Flugstaubabscheidung f durch Ultraschall m (oder Überschall)
~ **(~) method** = Überschallmethode f, Ultraschallmethode f
~ **reflection technique** = Ultraschallimpuls-Echo-Verfahren n
ultrasonic sound, ultrasound = Ultraschall m, Überschall
~ ~ **control**, ultrasound ~ = Ultraschallsteuerung f, Überschallsteuerung
~ **(sound) pulse** = Ultraschallimpuls m, Überschallimpuls
ultraviolet spectrophotometry = Ultraviolett-Spektroskopie f
unavoidable delay factor, lost-time = unvermeidliche Verlustzeit f [*Baumaschine* f]
unbalance, see: out-of-balance (weight)
unbalanced-weight vibrating screen, (mechanically-vibrated) rotating unbalanced(-)weight (type) screen = Unwucht-Vibrationssieb n, Schwingsieb n mit Massenkraftantrieb m
unbonded prestressed concrete beam = Spannbetonträger m ohne Verbund m
unburned lime, core = Kalkkern m, Kalkkrebs m
uncallow, see: overburden
unclosed traverse = offener Polygonzug m, offenes Polygon n
uncoated = nackt
~ **chip(ping)s**, normal ~, ordinary ~ = Rohsplitt m
uncombined carbon = elementarer Kohlenstoff m
unconfined compression test = Druckversuch m bei seitlich unbehinderter Ausdehnung f
uncongealable dynamite = schwergefrierbares (oder ungefrierbares) Dynamit n
unconserved air conditioning plant = Klimaanlage f ohne Wasserrücknahme f
uncontrolled cracks = wilde Risse mpl
~ **crest spillway** = unverschlossener (Hochwasser)Überlauf m
uncoursed, random = ungeschichtet [*Mauerwerk* n]
to uncover = abdecken, freimachen
uncrushable material = Fremdmaterial n

underbody, see: undercarriage
underbridge, underpass, undercrossing = Unterführung f
underbrush, underwood, undergrowth = Unterholz n
underburnt lime = zu schwach gebrannter Kalk m
undercarriage, travel(l)ing gear, running gear underbody = Fahrwerk n, Unterwagen m
undercliff = Kliffschutt m
undercoat (Brit.) = Unterputz m
undercrossing, see: underbridge
to undercut = unterbieten
underdeveloped country = unterentwickeltes Land n
underdrainage, see: subdrainage
underfeed furnace = Unterschubfeuerung f
~ **stoker** = Unterschubfeuerung f, Rostbeschicker m
underfill-method, underfill blasting = Tiefensprengung f [*Sprengen n weicher Baugrundmassen fpl*]
undergrate blower = Unterwindgebläse n
underground = unterirdisch
~ **airfield** = U-Flugplatz m
~ **cable** = Erdkabel n, Bodenkabel
~ **clay mining** = unterirdische Tongewinnung f
~ **construction equipment** = untertägige Geräte npl
~ **conveying equipment** = Untertage-Förderanlagen fpl
~ **corrosion** = Bodenkorrosion f [*Rohr n*]
~ **gas-holder**, ~ gas- tank, ~ gasometer = Erdgasometer m, Erd-Gassammler m, Erd-Gasbehälter m, unterirdischer Gasspeicher m
~ **gasification of coal** = Kohlenvergasung f unter Tage, Untertagevergasung von Kohle
~ **hydro-electric power plant** underground, power station = Kavernenkraftwerk n, Kavernenzentrale f
~ **(mining) method** = Untertage-Abbauverfahren n
~ **pedestrian passageway**, see: pedestrian subway
~ **(or tube) railway** (Brit.); ~ railroad (US) = Untergrundbahn f

underground stream = Grundwasserstrom m, Grundwasserlauf m
~ **structure** = unterirdisches Bauwerk n
~ **tank** = Erdtank m
~ **train** = Untergrundbahnzug m
~ **turbine house** = Maschinenkaverne f
~ **water**, see: ground ~
undergrowth, see: underbrush
underlay, see: bed(ding course)
~ **paper**, see: concreting ~
underlying course, see: bed(ding ~)
~ **rock**, see: bed rock
undermining, see: scour(ing)
underpass, see: underbridge
underpinning, see: dead shoring
underseal(ing), pavement ~, subseal(ing) = Unterpressen n [Straßendecke f]
under-seepage, (underground) seepage = Sickerströmung f, Grundwasserstromsickerung f
undershot [water-wheel] = unterschlächtig [Wasserrad n]
underside view = Untersicht f
undersize = Untergröße f, Mindermaß n
under-stressed concrete beam = unterspannter Betonträger m
undersize (aggregate) = Unterkorn n
under-strength bridge = nicht mehr standfeste Brücke f
undersurface = Unterseite f
undertrack hopper = Untergleis-Silo m
~ **screw conveyor** = Untergleis-Förderschnecke f
underwashing, see: scour(ing)
underwater ballistics = Unterwasser-Ballistik f
~ **concrete** = Unterwasserbeton m
~ **cutting gear** = Unterwasser-Schneidgerät n
~ **excavating**, dredging (work), underwater dredging = Naßbaggerung f
~ **pile hammer** = Unter-Wasser-Rammhammer m
~ **screen** = Unterwassersieb n
~ **solifluction** (or solifluxion, or soil creep) = subaquatische Rutschung f, Unterwasserrutschung f, Subsolifluktion f
~ **tunnel**, subaqueous ~ = Unterwassertunnel m
underwood, see: underbrush

undeveloped potential of production power, reserve power = Leistungsreserve f [Maschine f]
undistorted prismatic structure of folded units = formtreues prismatisches Faltwerk n
undisturbed (soil) sample = ungestörte (Boden)Probe f
undivided shaft, single ~ = eintrümiger Schacht m
~ **two-way road** = Straße f ohne Richtungstrennstreifen m, ungeteilte Straße
~ ~ ~ **with two lanes altogether** = zweispurige Straße f
~ ~ ~ ~ **three lanes altogether** = dreispurige Straße f
undoped cutback = Verschnittbitumen n ohne Haftanreger m
undulation of ground = Bodenwelle f
un-embanked alluvial land = unbedeichte Anlandung f
unemployment = Arbeitslosigkeit f
unevenness, irregularity = Unebenheit f
unfired ceramic body = ungebrannter keramischer Scherben m
ungraded aggregate = nicht korngestuftes Gestein n
uniaxial stress = einachsige Spannung f
uni-directional traffic, one-way ~ = Einbahnverkehr m
uniflow washer, ~ washing machine = Gleichstromwaschmaschine f, Gleichstromwäsche f
uniformity coefficient, coefficient of uniformity, $C_u = \dfrac{D_{60}}{D_{10}}$ = Ungleichförmigkeitsgrad $U = \dfrac{d_{60}}{d_{10}}$
uniform sand, uniformly graded ~, closely ~ ~ = gleichförmiger Sand m
unilaterally compound folded mountains = einseitig zusammengesetztes Faltengebirge n
union = Anschlußstück n, Verbindung f
~ **flange**, see: coupling ~
UNIONMELT welding method = Unter-Pulverschweißverfahren n, Maulwurfverfahren, U-P-Verfahren, ELLIRA-Verfahren, Elektro-Linde-Rapidschweißung f

unit-construction bridge system = Standardbrückensystem *n*
unit crystal = Einzelkristall *n*
~ deformation = bezogene Verformung *f*
~ load = Einheitslast *f*
~ of atomic power equipment = Reaktoreinheit *f*
~ pressure, surface ~ = Flächendruck *m*
~ price, rate = Einheitspreis *m*
~ water content (US) = erforderliche Wassermenge pro Kubikyard Beton
universal building crane = Universal(Hoch)Baukran *m*
~ compressor tractor, tractor-compressor = Kompressorschlepper *m*, Mehrzweck-Industrieschlepper *m*
~ concrete pile driver = Universalbetonpfahlramme *f*
~ excavator, see: all-purpose ~
~ finisher = Universalfertiger *m*
~ frame type pile driving plant (or piling plant) = Universal(gerüst)ramme *f*
~ joint, cardan ~ ~ = Kardangelenk *n*
~ ~ assy = Kreuzgelenk *n*
~ coupling, ~ type ~ = Kreuzgelenkkupplung *f*
~ ~ shaft = Gelenkwelle *f*
~ plate = Breitflachstahl *m*
~ shingle cutter = Schindelschneider *m* [*Dachpappenfertigungsanlage f*]
unloading crane = Abladekran *m*, Ausladekran, Entladekran
~ installation, unloader = Abladeanlage *f*, Entladeanlage
~ track, off-loading ~ = Entladegleis *n*, Abladegleis, Ausladegleis
unmade ground, see: native soil
unmapped = unkartiert
umetalled (Brit.) = ungeschottert, unbeschottert
unobstracted vision = freie Sicht *f*
unpainted condition = ungestrichener Zustand *m*
un-priming (Brit.); see: stop siphoning (US)
(un)ravelling [*deprecated*], see: fretting
unregular rubble walling = unregelmäßiges Schicht(en)mauerwerk *n*
unreinforced concrete, non-reinforced ~, plain ~ = unbewehrter Beton *m*

unrestrained beam = freitragender Balken *m*
unsaponifiable = unverseifbar
unset concrete, fresh(ly-mixed) ~ = unabgebundener Beton *m*, Frischbeton
unskilled worker, see: labo(u)rer
unslaked and ground quicklime = ungelöschter gemahlener Kalk *m*, gemahlener Branntkalk, gedeihender Kalk, Mahlkalk [*fälschlich als „treibender Kalk" bezeichnet*]
unstable fill = labile Dammschüttungsmasse *f*
~ ground = rolliges Gebirge *n* [*Tunnelbau m*]
unsupported ground = standfestes Gebirge *n* [*Tunnelbau m*]
~ length = Freilänge *f* [*Kragträger m*]
unsurfaced soil base = Lage *f* aus mechanisch verfestigtem Material *n* ohne Verschleißschicht *f*
untensioned bar reinforcement, non-prestressed reinforcement = schlaffe Bewehrung *f* (oder Armierung *f*), nicht gespannte ~
unused mo(u)lding sand = ungebrauchter Formsand *m*, Neusand
to unwater, to dewater = auspumpen, trockenlegen
unwatering, dewatering = Wasserhaltung *f*, Auspumpen *n*
unworked penetration = Ruhpenetration *f* [*Schmierfett n*]
up-arching of the "roof" [*laccolith*] (Geol.) = kuppelförmiges Emporwölben *n* der überlagernden Decke *f*
upcast (shaft), discharge (air) shaft = Ausziehschacht *m*
to up-end = umdrehen [*oberes Ende nach unten bzw. unteres Ende nach oben*]
upgrade section, uphill ~ = Steigungsstrecke *f*
upkeep, see: maintenance
upland alder, see: Turkey ~
uplift (Geol.) = Aufwölbung *f*
~, foundation water pressure = Auftrieb *m*, Sohlenwasserdruck *m* [*Talsperre f*]
~ = negative Auflagerkraft *f*
upper cretaceous sandstone = Quadersandstein *m*

upper cylinder lubricant = Obenöl n
~ ~ lubrication = Obenschmierung f
~ deck, superstructure, upper unit, revolving unit, top unit = Oberwagen m [*Bagger m*]
~ strand = Obertrum m
upright kiln, vertical ~ = Vertikalschachtofen m
up river = flußaufwärts
~ ~ [*part of a river above that part into which the tides comes*] = der nicht den Gezeiten fpl unterliegende Teil des Flusses m
uprooting, see: grubbing up
upsetting temperature = Stauchtemperatur f [*Niet m*]
upset variable = Stauchvariable f
upstream = oberwasserseitig, bergseitig
~ apron = oberwasserseitige Vorlage f
~ batter = Anzug m wasserseits [*Talsperre f*]
~ cofferdam, ~ temporary dam = Vorsperre f
~ face, water-side ~ = Wasserseite f [*Talsperre f*]
~ migration = Stromaufwanderung f [*Fisch m*]
~ nose, cut-water (Brit.); nose (US) = Pfeilerkopf m [*Talsperre f*]
~ profile at crown of arch (Brit.); ~ ~ of section at key (or crown) (US) = Scheitelform f wasserseitig [*Talsperre f*]
~ water = Oberwasser n
upward camber, see: rise (of arch)
uranite (Min.) = Uranit m
uranium mineral = Uraniummineral n
~ ore = Uraniumerz n
urban area, city ~ = Stadtgebiet n
~ dispersal policy = städtische Auflockerungspolitik f
~ expressway = Stadtautobahn f
~ ~ system, ~ ~ net(work) = Stadtautobahnnetz n
~ planner, see: town ~
~ planning, municipal ~, town ~, city ~ = Stadtplanung f, Städteplanung, städtebauliche Planung
~ rapid transit system = Stadtbahn f
~ renewal = städtische Erneuerung f
~ road, see: (city) street

(~) street network, (~) ~ system = Stadtstraßennetz n
*** ~ thoroughfare**, see: (city) street
used air, see: exhaust ~
~ mo(u)lding sand = gebrauchter Formsand m, Altsand
usefulness = Zweckdienlichkeit f
U-shaped glaciated valley = U-Tal n, Trogtal
USKON [*Trademark*] = elektrisch heizbare Gummimatte f zur Erwärmung der Führerstände von Kränen, Lokomotiven usw., Fabrikat UNITED STATES RUBBER CO., NEW YORK 20, USA
usufruct = Nutznießung f
utilisation, utilization = Ausnutzung f, Verwertung
~ of brick rubble = Trümmerverwertung f, Mauerschuttverwertung
~ ~ water power, hydroelectric exploitation = Wasserkraftnutzung f
utility = Versorgungsbetrieb m
~ pole = Leitungsmast m
~ trench = Leitungsgraben m
U tube visco(si)meter = Ostwaldviskosimeter n
uwarowite, ouvarovite (Min.) = Uwarowit m, Kalkchromgranat m

V

vacation stamp = Urlaubsmarke f
vacuum brake = Unterdruckbremse f, Vakuumbremse
~ compression method = Vakupreßverfahren n [*Kalkhydratverpackung f*]
VACUUM CONCRETE [*Trademark*] = Vakuumbeton m, Saugbeton
~ ~ process = Unterdruck-Oberflächenbehandlung f frischen Betons, Billner'sches Vakuumverfahren n, Saugbetonverfahren
vacuum concrete slab = Vakuumbetonplatte f
~ degasification = Vakuum-Entgasung f
~ filtration = Vakuumfiltration f
~ lifter pad = Saugvorrichtung f zum Fertigteiltransport m, Vakuumanheber m
~ mat = Saugmatte f
~ mixer = Vakuummischer m

vacuum pneumatic conveyor, see: suction ~ ~
~ **pug-mill** = Vakuum-Tonschneider *m*
~ **pump**, evacuator, air pump = Vakuumpumpe *f*
~ ~ **oil** = Vakuumpumpenöl *n*
~ ~ **transporter**, see: suction (or vacuum) pneumatic conveyor (or conveying) system
~ **tube lamp**, gas discharge ~ = Gasentladungslampe *f*
vadose water, suspended subsurface ~ = vadoses Wasser *n*, schwebendes Grundwasser, kreisendes Wasser
VAKUMAT [*Trademark*] [*brick extrusion press*] = Ziegelei-Strangpresse *f*, Fabrikat WESERHÜTTE OTTO WOLFF G.m.b.H., BAD OEYNHAUSEN, DEUTSCHLAND
valentinite, Sb_2O_3 (Min.) = Antimonblüte *f*, Valentinit *m*
validator, validating machine = Gebührenberechnungsmaschine *f* [*Gebührenautobahn f*]
valley bottom, ~ floor = Talsohle *f*
~ **bridge**, see: viaduct
~ **flank** = Talflanke *f*
~ **gravel** = Talschotter *m*
~ **jack rafter** = Wechselsparren *m*
~ **line**, see: thalweg
~ **loess** = Tallöß *m*
~ **slope**, ~ side = Talhang *m*, Talflanke *f*
~ **tile** = Kehlziegel *m*
~ **way**, see: thalweg
value-cost contract, see: cost-plus-fee ~
valve = Ventil *n*
~ = Schieber *m*, Klappe *f*
~ **bag filling machine**, ~ ~ packer = Ventilsackfüllmaschine *f*, Ventil(sack)packmaschine
~ **body** = 1. Klappengehäuse *n*, 2. Schiebergehäuse
~ **box** = Schieberkasten *m*
~ **control** = Ventilsteuerung *f*
~ **guard** = Fängerglocke *f* [*Ventil n*]
~ **gumming** = Ventilverpichung *f*
~ **house** = Schieberhaus *n*
~ **pit** = Schieberschacht *m*
~ **recess depth in top of piston** = Ventilausdrehungstiefe *f* im Kolbenboden *m*

~ **spring** = Ventilfeder *f*
~ **tongue** = Schieberzunge *f*
valved section = Schieberstrecke *f*
vane, inclined ~ = Eintrittsschaufel *f* [*Vorfilter m, n*]
~ **apparatus**, ~ penetrometer, shear tester = Flügelsonde *f*
~ **pump**, see: semi-rotary ~
~ **type chip spreader**, see: rear-mounted gritter
vapor generator (US); steam ~ = Dampferzeuger *m*, Dampfbereiter
vaporising burner = Sprühbrenner *m*
vaporization, distillation = nasse Destillation *f*, Überdampfung *f*, Abdampfung *f*
~, see: gasification
vapo(u)r lock = Dampfblasenbildung *f*
variable = Variante *f*
~ **radius arch dam**, see: constant angle ~ ~
variable-speed motor (Brit.); varying speed ~ (US) = Motor *m* mit veränderlicher Drehzahl *f*
~ **transmission system** = Getriebeabstufung *f*
variation clause, fluctuation ~ = Gleitklausel *f*
~ **in storage level** = Spiegelschwankung *f* [*Talsperre f*]
~ ~ **water level** = Wasserspiegelschwankung *f*
variegated alfalfa = Sandluzerne *f*
~ **copper ore** (Min.), see: bornite
~ **sandstone** (Brit.); mottled ~, bunter ~ = Buntsandstein *m*
variety = Abart *f*, Spielart
varnish-maker's and painter's naphtha, V.M.P. Naphtha (US) = Schwerbenzin *n* mit Siedegrenzen *fpl* zwischen 100° und 150° Celsius
varve = Warve *f*
varve(d) (glacial) clay, pellodite, banded clay, leaf clay, book clay, ribbon clay = Bänderton *m*, dünngeschichteter Ton
Vaud = Waadt(land) *f, (n)*
vault = Gewölbe *n*
vaulting masonry, stone arching = Gewölbemauerwerk *n*
vector equation = Vektorgleichung *f*
Vee-belt drive (Brit.); see: texrope ~ (US)

vegetable — vertical magnetic transporter

vegetable = vegetabilisch
~ cover, see: mantle of vegetation
vegetation = Bewachsung *f*
~ cover, see: mantle of vegetation
vehicle = Fahrzeug *n*
~, see: cold water paint cement
~ climbing lane = Kriechspur *f*
~ diesel engine = Fahrzeug-Dieselmotor *m*
~ scale = Fahrzeugwaage *f*
~ traffic stream = Fahrzeugstrom *m*
(~) washdown, see: car wash
~ wheel = Fahrzeugrad *n*
vehicular accident = Fahrzeugunfall *m*
~ breakdown = Fahrzeugpanne *f*
~ bridge = Fahrzeugbrücke *f*
~ subway, see: road tunnel
~ toll project, see: toll facility
~ traffic = Fahrzeugverkehr *m*
~ tunnel, see: road ~
vein = einfacher (Erz)Gang *m*
veined = gemasert [*Holz n*]
vein gneiss = Adergneis *m*, Arterit *m*
velocity of detonation = Detonationsgeschwindigkeit *f*
~ ~ flow, discharge speed = Abflußgeschwindigkeit *f*
~-reducing dust collector = Staubkammer *f*
veneer (Brit.) [*deprecated*]; see: wearing course
~, see: road carpet
~ = Furnierholz *n*
Venetian mosaic, see: terrazzo
ventifact, see: glyptolith
ventilating block = Be- und Entlüftungsstein *m* [*aus Beton m*]
ventilation adit = Bewetterungsstollen *m*
~ duct = Ventilationskanal *m*
~ shaft, see: air ~
ventilator with water spray = Wasserstaublüfter *m*, Wasserstaubventilator *m*
Venturi flume = Venturi-Kanal *m*
~ meter = Venturi-Messer *m*
~ tube = Venturi-Rohr *m*
verdigris, see: copper rust
verge, margin, roadside waste; [*deprecated: roadside*] = Seitenraum *m*, Seitenstreifen *m* [*Straße f*]
vermicular, worm-shaped = wurmartig [*Mineral n*]

vermiculite (Min.) = Vermiculit *m*
to exfoliate = aufblähen
to open into long wormlike threads = wurmartig krümmen
~ ore = Vermiculite-Erz *n*
~ plaster = Vermiculite-Putz *m*
Vernon Shale (Geol.) = rote mittelsilurische lößähnliche Ablagerung *f* im östlichen New York
versatility = Vielseitigkeit *f*
versed sine, see: rise (of arch)
vertex, crown, apex, key, top = Bogenscheitel *m*, Scheitelpunkt *m*
vertical = lotrecht, senkrecht, vertikal
~ air-lock = Vertikalschleuse *f*
~ ~ tube = Schachtrohr *n*
~ alignment (Brit.)/**alinement** (US) **of highways** = Linienführung *f* im Aufriß *m*
~ beds = Kopfgebirge *n*, seigerstehende Schichten *fpl*
~ boiler = Standkessel *m*
~ boom ditcher, ~ ~ type trenching machine, ~ ladder ditcher = Grabenbagger *m* mit vertikaler Eimerleiter *f*
~ (bucket) elevator = Senkrechtbecherwerk *n*, Vertikalbecherwerk *n*
~ cement kiln = Zementschachtofen *m*
~ classifier = Vertikalklassierer *m*
~ clearance = Durchfahrtshöhe *f*
~ crack = Zugriß *m* [*Bauwerkssenkung f*]
~ cross tube boiler = Standkessel *m* mit waag(e)rechten Quersiedern *mpl*, Lachapellekessel
~ curves, see: transition curves between gradients
~ discharge unit heater = vertikal wirkender Lufterhitzer *m*
~ elevator, see: ~ bucket ~
~ joint = Stoßfuge *f* [*Mauerwerk n*]
~ kiln, see: upright ~
(~) leaf gate = Fallenwehr *n*
~ leg, see: ~ member of frame
(~) lift bridge = Hubbrücke *f*
(~) ~ gate = Hubschütz(e) *n*, (*f*), Hubwehr *n*
*****vertical lime kiln** = Kalkschachtofen *m*
~ load(ing) = lotrechte Belastung *f* ~ Last *f*
~ magnetic transporter, vibratory spiral elevator = Wendelförderer *m*

vertical member of frame, ~ leg, stanchion of frame = Rahmenstiel *m*
~ **normal stress** = lotrechte Normalspannung *f* [*Baugrund m*]
~ **retort tar** = Vertikal-Retorten-Teer *m*
(~) **sand drain (or pile, or column)** = vertikaler (oder lotrechter) Sanddrän *m*, Sandbrunnen *m*, Sickerbrunnen *m*, vertikale Sandeinschlämme *f*, Sanddrän *m*, vertikale Sanddränage *f*
~ **screw elevator,** see: screw elevator
~ ~ **lift,** see: screw elevator
~ **sea (protection) wall** = Strandmauer *f* mit senkrechter Außenfläche *f*
~ **shaft** = Richtschacht *m*
~ **shoring,** see: dead shoring
~ **sided breakwater,** wall ~ = massiver Wellenbrecher *m*
~ **slatted fence** = Vertikallattenzaun *m*
~ **truss,** see: bracing with verticals
VfT-High Carbon Coke [*Trademark*] = Spezial-Gießerei-Koks *m* vertrieben von VERKAUFSVEREINIGUNG für TEERERZEUGNISSE (VfT) A.G., ESSEN, DEUTSCHLAND
V-groove, notch = Kerbnut *f*
viaduct, valley bridge = Viadukt *n*, Talbrücke *f*
vibrated coarse concrete = Rüttelgrobbeton *m*, Vibrationsgrobbeton
~ **concrete** = Rüttelbeton *m*, Vibrationsbeton
~ (~) **joint** = vibrationsgeschnittene Fuge *f*
~ **finishing screed,** see: vibrating (or vibrated) ~
~ **frame,** see: live (screen) ~
~ **live frame screen,** see: screen with vibratory action applied direct through the screen frame
~ **pan tamper,** see: pan vibrator
~ **rock fill dam** = gerüttelter Steindamm *m*, ~ Felsschüttungsdamm
~ **screed,** see: vibrating ~
vibrating = (Ein)Rütteln *n*, Vibrieren *n* [*Beton m*]
~ = Vibrieren *n* [*Sieben n*]
~ **backfill (trench) compactor** = Vibrations-Grabenverdichter *m*

~ **bar grizzly,** ~ rod ~, grizzly (or screen of bars, or bar screen, or bar grizzly) with vibrating mechanism = Stangen(transport)rost *m* (oder Stangenaufgeber *m*) mit Vibrationsvorrichtung *f*
~ **beam** = Rüttelbohle *f*, Vibrierbohle, Vibratorbohle, Verdichtungsbohle, Schwingungsbohle
~ **circular pipe-line** = Schwingförderrohr *n*, Schwingrohrförderer *m*
~ **compaction,** vibratory ~, forced ~ ~, compaction by vibration = Schwingverdichtung *f*, Rüttelverdichtung, Vibrationsverdichtung, Schwingungsverdichtung, Einrüttelungsverdichtung, Bewegungsverdichtung, dynamische Verdichtung
~ **conveying machine** = Vibrationsfördergerät *n*, Schwingfördergerät, Vibrationsförderer *m*, Schwingförderer
vibrating cylinder, ~ head = (Innen-)Rüttelflasche *f*
~ **float** = Vibrationsglätter *m*
~ **finishing screed,** see: ~ (or vibrated) ~
~ **frame** = Schwingrahmen *m* [*Sieb n*]
~ **joint-cutter** = Fugenschneider *m* mit Vibriermesser *n*
~ **knife,** blade = Vibriermesser *n*
~ ~ **joint cutter,** see: (concrete) joint vibrator
~ **materials handling equipment** = Vibriergeräte *npl* zur Materialförderung *f*
~ **mo(u)lding machine** = Vibrationsmaschine *f* [*Herstellung f von Betonbauelementen npl*]
~ **plank** = Vibrierbohle *f*, Rüttelbohle, Vibrationsbohle
~ **plate (or pan),** pan vibrator, vibration slab, plate vibrator, vibratory base plate compactor, vibratory base plate, vibrating plate compactor = Rüttelplatte *f*, Plattenvibrator *m*, Plattenrüttler *m*, Vibratorplatte *f*, Schwingungsplatte, Vibrationsplatte
~ **(or vibrated) screed,** ~ (~ ~) smoother, ~ (~ ~) finishing ~ = Vibrations-Glättbohle *f*
~ **screen,** vibrator(y) ~ = Vibrationssieb *n*

vibrating screen, vibrator(y) screen = eigentliches Schwingsieb n
~ ~ with replaceable steel wire bundles = Schwingsieb n mit Stahldrahtbespannung f, Harfenvibrator m
~ ~ ~ uniform full circle motion, circle-throw (vibrating) screen = Kreisvibrationssieb n, Kreisschwing(er)sieb n
~ shuttle smoother = Vibrationspendelglätter m [*Betondeckenfertiger m*]
~ smoother, see: ~ (or vibrated) screed
~ tamper = Rüttelstampfer m, Vibrationsstampfer
~ ~, concrete tamping and screed board vibrator, road vibrating tamper = (Beton)Rüttelstampfer m [*Straßenbeton m*]
~ ~ with electrically-operated units, electric vibrating tamper = Elektro-Rüttelstampfer m
~ test sieve shaker, see: (mechanical) sieve shaker
~ trailer roller, towed-type vibrating roller = Vibrations-Anhängewalze f, Vibrations-Schleppwalze, Anhänge-Vibrationswalze, Anhänge-Schleppwalze
~ type tie tamper (US); ~ ~ track ~ (Brit.) = Schwinggleisstopfer m, Schwingschotterstopfer
~ unit = Vibrationserzeuger m
~ wire strain ga(u)ge = Schwingdrahtdehnungsmesser m
vibration(al) stress(ing) = Vibrationsbeanspruchung f
vibration and mechanical tamping block machine, vibration and tamping (concrete) block machine = Rüttelstampfmaschine f
vibration (concrete) block machine = Vibrations-Betonstein-Maschine f
~ dampener = Vibrationsdämpfer m, Schwingungsdämpfer
~ for placing stone for base course = Rüttelverdichtung f beim Einbau von Schotterunterbau m
~ slab, pan vibrator, vibrating plate (or pan), plate vibrator = Rüttelplatte f, Plattenvibrator m, Plattenrüttler m, Vibratorplatte f
~ stress(ing) = Vibrationsbeanspruchung f

~ table, vibrating ~, table vibrator = Schwingtisch m, Vibriertisch
vibrator = Schwingungs(ein)rüttler m, Vibrator m, Rüttelgerät n
~-jetting deep compaction, vibroflotation (soil-compaction) = Rütteldruckverfahren n, Kellerverfahren
vibratory backfill compactor, ~ trench ~ = Grabenvibrationsverdichter m
~ base plate compactor, see: vibrating plate
~ compaction, see: vibrating ~
~ compactor = Vibrations-Verdichtungsmaschine f, Schwing(ungs)verdichter m
~ ~, soil vibrator, vibratory soil compactor = Bodenschwingungsrüttler m
~ concrete compacting and finishing machine, see: concrete finishing road vibrator
~ earth borer = Vibrations-Erdbohrer m
~ finishing machine for concrete pavements, see: concrete finishing road vibrator
~ (grinding) mill = Schwing(mahl)mühle f
~ member = Vibrationselement n
~ pneumatic-tired (US)/tyred (Brit.) roller, pneumatic-tired vibrating compacting roller = schwingende Gummi(reifenvielfach)walze f, gummibereifte Walze mit Vibration f, Schwing-Gummiradwalze
~ smoothing (or finishing) screed with travel(l)ing gear = Vibrator-Glättbohle f mit Fahrwerk n System SAGER & WOERNER, Sa-Woe-Bohle f
~ soil compactor, see: ~ compactor
~ spiral elevator, see: vertical magnetic transporter
~ washing screen = Schwingwascher m
vibroflot (machine) = (Druck)Rüttler m, Schwinggerät n
vibroflotation (soil-compaction), see: vibrator jetting deep compaction
VIBROMAT [*Trademark*] [*automatic concrete pipe machine*] = automatische (Beton)Rohrfertigungsmaschine f, Fabrikat MASCHINENFABRIK AUGUST HENKE, VLOTHO/WESER, DEUTSCHLAND

Vicat (setting-time) apparatus, ~ needle = Vicat-Nadelapparat *m*
Vienna lime = Wiener Kalk *m*
Vierendeel girder = Vierendeelträger *m*
~ ~ **symmetrical about a horizontal axis** = horizontal-symmetrischer Vierendeelträger *m*
vinasse tar = Vinasseteer *m*
vine terrace on the slope of a hill = Weinbauterrasse *f*, Weinbau(ab)hang *m*
virgin earth material = jungfräulicher Boden *m*
virtual work = virtuelle Arbeit *f*
virus pollution = Virus-Verunreinigung *f*
visco-elastic property = visko-elastische Eigenschaft *f*
visco(si)meter = Viskosimeter *n*
viscosity = Viskosität *f*, Zähflüssigkeit *f*
~ **chart** = Viskogramm *n*
~ **gravity content (or constant)** = Viskositäts-Dichte-Konstante *f*
~ **pole height** = Viskositätspolhöhe *f*
~ **temperature dependency** = Viskositätstemperaturverhalten *n*
visibility = Sichtbarkeit *f*
~ **distance, seeing** ~, **sight** ~, **vision** ~ = Sichtweite *f*, Sichtlänge *f*, Sichtwe *m*
visible horizon, see: apparent ~
~ **signal** = optisches Signal *n*
visual guidance = optische Führung *f* [*Verkehr m*]
~ **observation** = optische Anzeige *f*
~ **inspection** = Augenscheinnahme *f*
vitiated air = verbrauchte Luft *f*, schlechte ~, Schlechtluft
vitreous, glassy [*ground-mass*] = glasig [*Grundmasse f*]
~ **body** = glasiger Scherben *m*, glasige Scherbe *f*
~ **rock** = verglastes Gestein *n*
~ **silica** = amorpher Quarz *m*, Kieselsäure-Glas *n*
vitric tuff = Aschentuff *m*
vitrified, vitreous = verglast
(~) **clay pipe,** see: clay ~
vitri-fusain, semi-fusain = Halbfusit *m*
vitriol peat = Vitrioltorf *m*
vivianite, earthy ~ (Min.) = Blauerz *n*, Vivianit *m*, Blaueisenerde *f*
V-jointed timber = aufgeklautes Holz *n*

vocational disease, professional ~ = Berufskrankheit *f*
VÖGELE asphalt paver = Schwarzdeckenfertiger *m*, Fabrikat JOSEPH VÖGELE AG., MANNHEIM, DEUTSCHLAND
void, see: interstice
voidage, see: void(s) space
voidless = hohlraumfrei
voids-cement ratio = Verhältnis *n* von Luft + Wasser zu Zement *m*
voids ratio, see: pore ~
void(s) space, voidage, void(s) volume, pore volume, pore space, total volume of intergranular (soil) space = Porenraum *m*, Porenvolumen *n*
volatile diluent = Verschnittmittel *n* [*Verschnittbitumen n*]
volatilisation, volatility = Verflüchtigung *f*, Verdunstung *f*
~ **test** = Prüfung *f* auf Flüchtigkeit *f*
volcanic agglomerate (Geol.) = vulkanisches Agglomerat *n*
~ **ash,** ~ **cinder** = vulkanische Asche *f*, Feuerbergasche
~ **bomb** = Lavabombe *f*, vulkanische Bombe
~ **breccia** = vulkanische Brekzie *f*
(~) **glass** = (vulkanisches) Glas *n*
(~) **neck, pipe(-like conduit)** = vulkanischer Schlot *m*, vulkanische Esse *f*, Durchschlagsröhre *f*, Neck *m*, Eruptionskanal *m*, Schußröhre *f*, Stielgang *m*, Hals *m*
~ **rock,** see: lava flow
~ **sand** = vulkanischer Sand *m*, Feuerbergsand, Kratersand, natürlicher Schlackensand
(~) **tuff,** see: tuff
*volcano = Vulkan *m*, Feuerberg *m*
voltage transformer, potential ~ = Spannungswandler *m*
volume batcher, see: volumetric ~
volume-batching, loose-volume batching, bulk batching, volumetric batching, batching by volume = Raumzumessung *f*, Raumdosierung *f*, Volumendosierung *f*, Volumenzumessung *f*, Volumenmischung *f*, Raumteilmischung *f*, Volumenzugabe *f*
volume change = Volumenschwankung *f*

volume compressor — wall plaster

volume compressor = Kübelfettpresse *f*
~ flow = Kriechen *n* [*Bitumen n*]
volume-production concrete mixer = Großbetonmischer *m*
volume stability = Raumbeständigkeit *f*
volumetric batcher, volumen ~ = Dosierapparat *m* nach Raumteilen *mpl*
~ batching, see: volume-batching
~ efficiency = volumetrischer Wirkungsgrad *m*
volume weight, volumetric ~, (bulk) density, bulk specific gravity; [*deprecated: box weight*] = Raumgewicht *n* der Volumeneinheit *f*
vortex motion, whirling ~ = Wirbelbewegung *f*
Vosges = Vogesen *f*
voussoir, see: arch stone
V-plow (US); **V-plough** (Brit.) = Keilpflug *m*
V-shaped notch = Dreieck(meß)wehr *n*
~ valley, V-valley = Kerbtal *n*
V-type snow plough (Brit.)/**plow** (US) = Schnee-Keilpflug *m*
vulcanized = vulkanisiert
vulnerable = anfällig

W

to wade through a pipe = ein Wasserrohr *n* begehen
wader = Wasserstiefel *m*
wadi [*dried-up bed of stream*] = Trockental *n* Wadi *m*
waffle-type construction = Kassettenkonstruktion *f*
wage cutting = Lohnabbau *m*
~ determinant = Lohnfaktor *m*
~ earner = Lohnempfänger *m*
~ expense = Lohnaufwand *m*
~ level = Lohnhöhe *f*
~ rate = Lohnsatz *m*
wages payroll, see: payroll
wage worker = Lohnarbeiter *m*
wagon = Wagen *m*
~ [*a full trailer with a dump body*] = Vollkippanhänger *m*
~ = Lore *f*
~ = Waggon *m*

~ drill = Bohrwagen *m*, Leicht~, Bohrwagen mit Lafette *f*
~ for the removal of overburden = Abraumförderwagen *m*
~ marshalling equipment = Waggon-Verschiebegeräte *npl*
~ road = Wagenstraße *f*
~ scraper, see: carrying ~
~ tippler, car dumper = Waggonkipper *m*
~ trail = Karrenpfad *m*
~ vault, tunnel ~, barrel ~ = Tonnengewölbe *n*
wagonette quarry drill = Leichtbohrwagen *m*
waiting-bay (Brit.); see: layby(e)
wake = Kielwasser *n*
wale(r) = Längstraverse *f*, Leitbohle *f*, Gurt *m* [*Grabenverbau m*]
waling, see: capping beam
walking dragline, walker = Schreitbagger *m* mit Schleppschaufelausrüstung *f*, Schleppschaufel-, Schleppschaufel-Großbagger *m* auf Schreitschuhen *mpl*, Eimerseil-Schreitbagger
~ frame = Schreitrahmen *m*
~ mechanism = Schreitausrüstung *f*, Schreitwerk *n*
~ shoe = Schreitschuh *m*
walking-swing = Schreit-Schwung *m* [*Naßbagger-Schneidkopf m*]
walkway, see: catwalk
wall arch = Wandbogen *m*
wallboard = Wandfaserplatte *f*
~, plaster ~ = Gipskartonplattentafel *f*
wall breakwater, see: vertical sided ~
~ crane = Wandkran *m*, Konsolkran
~ drilling machine = Mauerbohrmaschine *f*
walled-in plant = umbaute Anlage *f*
waller = Deckwerksetzer *m*
wall facing = Wandverkleidung *f*
~ footing = Plattenstreifen *m*
~ form(work) = Wandschalung *f*
~ hook, see: bit ~
~ line = Mauerflucht *f*
~ lining = Wandbelag *m*
~ milling device = Mauerfräser *m*
~ panel = Wandtafel *f*, Wand(bau)platte *f*, Wandelement *n*
~ ~ heating = Wandflächenheizung *f*
~ plaster = Mauergips *m*, Wandputz *m*

wall plate = Mauerlatte *f*
~ pointing machine = Mauerfuggerät *n*
~ scraper = Gipserspachtel *f, m,* Traufel *f*
~ section = Mauerabschnitt *m*
~ shell = Wandschale *f*
~ tile = Wandkeramikplatte *f,* keramische Wandfliese *f*
Ward-Leonard system of variable voltage control = Leonardschaltung *f,* Ward-Leonard-Schaltung
warehouse = Speicher *m*
warehousing of grain = Getreidespeicherung *f*
warm-air heating = Warmluftheizung *f*
warm(ing) up pad, warm(ing)-up apron, warmup pad = Abbremsfläche *f,* Abbremsplatz *m* [*Flugplatz m*]
warm laying = Warmeinbau *m* [*Straßenbau m*]
~ spring = Orthotherme *f*
warning device = Warnvorrichtung *f*
~ lamp = Warnlampe *f*
~ sign = Zwischenzeichen *n,* Bake *f* [*Autobahn f*]
~ signal, alarm ~ = Warnsignal *n*
Warren girder, see: half-lattice ~
~ truss, see: half-lattice girder
washboarding, see: corduroy effect
wash boring, jetting, water-flush method = Spülbohren *n,* Spülbohrung *f*
washbox, see: sand drag
washdown, see: car wash
washed electrode = dünngetauchte Elektrode *f*
washer = Unterlegscheibe *f*
~ box, see: tub
washery slag = Waschberge *mpl*
washholder = Federring *m*
washing and under-water screening machine = Unterwasser-Wasch- und Siebmaschine *f,* Tauch-Wasch- und Siebmaschine
~ bank, eroding ~ = Abbruchufer *n*
~ drum, see: classifying ~
*washing equipment = Waschmaschinen *fpl,* Wäschen *fpl*
~ screen = Waschsieb *n*
~ screw, see: spiral classifier
~ test [*concrete*] = Auswaschprobe *f,* Auswaschprüfung *f*

to wash-in the fines by sluicing, see: to flush with water
wash oil, see: stripping oil
wash-out gate (Brit.); see: flushing gate (US)
wash plain, overwash ~, outwash ~ = Auswaschebene *f,* Kiesfeld *n,* Sandfeld
wash-point soil penetrometer, (Terzaghi) wash point sounding apparatus = Spülsonde *f* von Terzaghi
wash primer = Haftgrundmittel *n*
wash water = Spülwasser *n* [*Filterreinigung f*]
~ ~ trough = Spülwasserrinne *f*
wastage, ablation [*glacier*] = Abschmelzung *f,* Ablation *f*
waste, see: spoil
~, see: crusher waste
~, refuse = Abfall *m,* Abfallstoff *m*
~ acid, spent ~ = Abfallsäure *f*
~ air filter = Abluftfilter *m, n*
~ area, see: spoil ~
~ coal = Abfallkohle *f*
~ gas = Abgas *n*
~-heap ore = Haldenerz *n*
waste heat = Abwärme *f,* Abhitze *f*
~ ~ reclamation = Abwärmerückgewinnung *f,* Abhitzerückgewinnung
~ land = Ödland *n*
~ lime = Abfallkalk *m*
~ liquor, spent lye = Ablauge *f,* Abfall-Lauge
~ ore, tailings = Abfallerz *n*
~ pickling liquor = Abfallbeize *f*
~ pile = Aussatzhalde *f,* Abraumhalde *f*
~ product = Abfallprodukt *n*
~ rubber = Abfallgummi *n*
~ sluice = Freilaufschütz(e) *n, (f),* Leerlaufschütz(e)
~ steam, exhaust ~ = Abdampf *m*
~ water gallery = Leerlaufstollen *m*
waste-weir, overflow weir, spillway weir, overfall weir, crest-control ~ = Überfall(stau)wehr *n,* Überlaufwehr
waste yardage = Aussatzmaterial *n* [*Erdbau m*]
watchman, signal man = Warnposten *m* [*Straßenbau m*]
watch-tower, look-out tower = Beobachtungsturm *m*

water aggressive to concrete = betonschädliches Wasser *n*
~ ballast hand roller = Handwalze *f* **mit Wasserballast** *m*
~ barrier, see: impervious zone
~ bath = Wasserbad *n*
~-bearing rock = wasserführendes Gestein *n*
~ soil stratum, ~ formation, aquifer, aquafer = wasserführende Bodenschicht *f*, **Grundwasserleiter** *m*
water-borne sediment = aquatisches Sedimentgestein *n*
water-bound macadam; see: mud-bound ~ [*deprecated*]
water buoyancy = Wasserauftrieb *m*
~ cart, ~ wagon = Wasserwagen *m*
~ cement, see: cement
~-~ ratio = Wasser-Zement-Faktor *m*, **Wasserzementwert** *m*
water cofferdam = Fang(e)damm *m* **bei Gründungen im Wasser**
~ conduit bridge, see: aqueduct
~ content [*concrete*] **= Wasserzusatz** *m*, **Wassergehalt** *m*
~ ~, see: moisture ~
~-course = Wasserlauf *m*
water drive = Auftrieb *m* **durch Wasserdruck** *m* [*Ölförderung f*]
~ (or hydraulic) engineering (or construction, or works) = Wasserbau *m*
~ ~ lab(oratory) = Wasserbau-Labor(atorium) *n*
water-extraction of asphalt (US)/asphaltic bitumen (Brit.) from rock asphalt = Gewinnung *f* **von Bitumen** *n* **durch Kochen des Gesteins** *n* **mit Wasser**
waterfall = Wasserfall *m*
(water-filled) rubber membrane method, rubber-balloon ~ = Gummiblasenmethode *f*, **Ballonmethode** [*Nachprüfung der Verdichtung*]
water film, moisture ~ = Wasserhäutchen *n*, **Wasserfilm** *m*
waterfinder, see: dowser
water finder = Wasserfindepapier *n*
~ flood method [*oil recovery*] **= Wasserflutverfahren** *n* [*Ölausbeute f*]
~ flow calorimeter = Durchflußkalorimeter *m, n*
water-flush method, see: wash boring

water for industrial use = Wasser *n* **für gewerbliche Zwecke** *mpl*
~ front (US) **= Küstenlinie** *f*
~ gain, see: sweating
~ gas tar = Wassergasteer *m*
~ ga(u)ge glass, graduated glass gaugetube = Wasserstandsglas *n*
~ glass, see: soluble ~
~ hammer, ~ ram = Wasserschlag *m*
~-hating, see: hydrophobic
(water) head, pressure ~ = Wassersäulenhöhe *f*, **Wassersäule** *f*, **Druckhöhe** *f*, **Druckgefälle** *n*, **Fallhöhe** *f*
water inlets (US); **~ intake** (Brit.) **= Wasserfassung** *f* [*Talsperre f*]
~ jacket = Wassermantel *m* [*Motor m mit Wasserkühlung f*]
~ jet injector = Wasserstrahlpumpe *f*
~ jetting of piles, pile-sinking with the water jet, water-jet driving, pile jetting = Einspülen *n* **von Pfählen** *mpl*, **Einbringen** *n* **von Pfählen mit Spülhilfe** *f*
~ law, see: ~ right
(~) level, spirit ~, air ~ = Wasserwaage *f*, **Libelle** *f*
~ ~ = Wasserstand *m*
~ ~ variation = Wasserstandwechsel *m*
~ line, see: ~ pipe
waterlogged [*soil*] **= wassergesättigt, wasserdurchsetzt** [*Boden m*]
water-loving, see: hydrophibic
water main casing = Wasserhauptrohr *n*
~ mark, ~ post = Wasserstandsmarke *f*, **Pegel** *m*
~ masses = Wassermassen *fpl*
~ of capillarity, capillary moisture (or water) = Kapillarwasser *n*, **Haarröhrchenwasser, Porensaugwasser**
~ ~ hydration = Hydratwasser *n*
water-operated vacuum pump = Wasserstrahlpumpe *f*
water paint, cold ~ ~ = Kaltwasserfarbe *f*
water-passing caisson = Senkkasten *m* **mit Wasserdurchlässen** *mpl*
water pier, river ~ [*bridge*] **= Strompfeiler** *m*
~ pipe = Wasser(leitungs)rohr *n*
~ (pipe)line = Wasser(rohr)leitung *f*
~-piping right = Wasserdurchleitungsrecht *n*

water pollution = Wasserverunreinigung *f*
~ pressure engine = Wassersäulenmaschine *f*
(waterproof) blanket, see: impervious ~
waterproofer, see: concrete waterproofing compound
waterproofing = Bauwerkabdichtung *f* gegen Grundwasser *n*, Grundwasserabdichtung *f*, Wassersperrung *f*, wasserdruckhaltende Dichtung *f*
~ course (or layer) = Sperrschicht *f*, Abdichtungslage *f*
~ membrane, asphalt ~ (US); bitumen ~ (Brit.) = Bitumendichtungshaut *f*
~ of foundation, see: foundation soil waterproofing
~ technique = Abdichtungstechnik *f*
waterproof paper, see: concreting ~
water pump wind mill = Wasserschöpfwindmühle *f*
*****water purification** = Wasserreinigung *f*, Wasseraufbereitung *f*
~ ram, see: ~ hammer
water-reducing agent = Mittel *n* zur Herabsetzung *f* der Anmach(e)wassermenge *f*
water repellency = Wasserabweisung *f*
~-repellent, see: concrete waterproofing compound
water resistant binder = wasserbeständiges Bindemittel *n*
~ resources = Wasserhaushalt *m*, Wasserwirtschaft *f*
~ ~ policy commission = Wasserwirtschaftsausschuß *m*
~ retentivity, water-retaining capacity = Wasserhaltevermögen *n* [*Beton m*]
~ right, ~ law = Wasserrecht *n*
~ road, see: waterway
watershed (US); see: catchment area (Brit.)
~ line, (drainage) divide = Wasserscheide *f*
water-side face, see: upstream ~
water splash = Querrinne *f* [*Straße f*]
~ spraying cart (or wagon) = Wassersprengwagen *m*
~ sprinkler tank = Berieselungsanlage *f* [*Straßenwalze f*]
~ storage = Wasserspeicherung *f*

~ supply = Wasserversorgung *f*
~ ~ line = Wasserversorgungsleitung *f*
~ table gradient, ground ~ ~ ~ = Grundwasserspiegelgefälle *n*
~ test = Wasserprüfung *f* [*Verhalten n der Verschnittbitumen npl auf den verschiedenen Gesteinen npl*]
~ ~, hydraulic ~ = Wasserdruckprobe *f*, kalte Druckprobe [*Rohr n, Kessel m*]
watertightness, see: imperviousness to water
water tower = Wasserturm *m*
~ trap = Sicherheitsflasche *f* [*Bindemittelrückgewinnungsapparat m*]
~ type dust collector = Naßabscheider *m*
~ vapo(u)r = Brüden *m*, Wrasen *m*, Schwaden *m*
~ void = Wasserpore *f* [*Beton m*]
~ wagon, see: water cart
waterway, water road; barge line (US) = Wasserstraße *f*
waterways administration = Wasser- und Schiffahrtsverwaltung *f*
water well = Wasserbrunnen *m*
~ white high-grade burning oil = wasserhelles Hydrier-Leuchtöl *n*
~ winning = Wassergewinnung *f*
~ works, see: ~ engineering
~ ~ = Wasserwerk *n*
watt-hour = Wattstunde *f*
wattless current = Blindstrom *m*
wattle-work, see: basket work
wave action = Wellenschlag *m*
~ breaker = Wellenbrecher *m*
(wave-built) shore-face terrace = Strandhalde *f*
wave crest = Wellenberg *m*, Wellenkamm *m*
wave-cut chasm = Brandungskluft *f*
~ platform = Strandterrasse *f*, Strandplattform *f*, Strandleiste *f*
~ topography = Brandungsgebilde *n*
wave front advance in two layers = Schallwellenverlauf *m* in zwei Schichten *fpl* [*seismische Bodenforschung f nach dem Refraktionsverfahren n*]
~ height = Wellenhöhe *f*
~ run-up = Wellenauflauf *m*
~ train = Wellenzug *m*

wave-trap floor (or bed) = wellenbrechende Böschung f
wave trough = Wellental n
~-worn material = Brandungsschutt m
waviness = Welligkeit f [*Erdstraße f*]
wavy fibred growth = Maserwuchs m [*Holz n*]
way leave = Wegerecht n (oder Wegbenutzungsrecht n) mit Erlaubnis zum Legen von Rohr- und Kabelleitungen fpl
wax coal = Wachskohle f
~ modifier = Filtrationsbeschleuniger m [*Paraffin n*]
~ oil, see: paraffin distillate
~ shale = Wachsschiefer m
~ stone = roher Ozokerit mit erdigen Beimengungen fpl
weakened cross-section = geschwächter Querschnitt m
weakening of cross-section = Querschnittschwächung f
wear and tear = Abnützung f, Verschleiß m, Abnutzung f
*****wearing course,** top ~ (US); surface ~, wearing surface, road surface, wearing carpet; coat (Brit.) [*deprecated: top-(ping), crust, sheeting, carpet, veneer*] = Verschleißschicht f, Decklage f [*Straße f*]
~ property = Verschleißeigenschaft f
wear plate = Verschleißblech n
weather = Wetter n
~-damp, see: explosive atmosphere
weathered = angewittert (Geol.)
~ crude petroleum (US) = das Produkt welches aus Rohöl durch den Verlust merklicher Mengen flüchtiger Bestandteile ohne künstliches Zutun bei Lagerung oder Transport entsteht
weathering, process of rock wastage = Verwitterung f, Abwitterung f
~ from bottom to top (Geol.) = Auswitterung f
~ ~ top to bottom (Geol.) = Einwitterung f
~ test = Bewitterungsprüfung f
weather-Ometer = Verwitterungsmeßgerät n [*Dachpappe f*]
weather-proofness, weather-resistance, resistance to the action of weather = Witterungsbeständigkeit f, Wetterfestigkeit f
weather-side = Wetterseite f
weather station, meteorological station = Wetterstation f, Wetterwarte f
~ vane [*spire*] = Wetterfahne f [*Kirchturm m*]
weaving distance (or length) = Einfäd(e)lungslänge f, Verflechtungslänge [*Straßenverkehr m*]
~ space, ~ area, ~ section = Einfäd(e)lungsraum m, Verflechtungsstrecke f [*Straßenverkehr m*]
web member = Füllungsstab m, Wandstab [*Fachwerk n*]
~ members, ~ bracing = Ausfachung f [*Fachwerk n*]
~ of the frame = Riegelsteg m
~ panel = Stegblechfeld n
~ (plate) = Steg(blech) m, (n) [*am Profil n*]
~ saw = Spannsäge f
~ splice, ~ joint = Stegblechstoß m
~ stiffener = Stegblechsteife f
to wedge, to key = verkeilen
wedge anchorage = Keilverankerung f [*Spannbeton m*]
~ cut = Keileinbruch m [*Stollensprengung f*]
wedge theory, see: Coulomb's slidingwedge analysis
wedging = Abkeilen n [*Gestein n*]
weed burner = Unkrautabbrennmaschine f
~ control = Unkrautbekämpfung f
~ killer, herbicide, weed destroyer = Unkrautbekämpfungsmittel n, Unkrautvernichtungsmittel
weekend commuter = Wochenendpendler m
weep hole, weeper, drainage opening, drainage hole = Entwässerungsschlitz m, Sickerschlitz m, Entlastungs-Dränageloch n
weeping birch, see: drooping ~
~ fungus, see: merulius lacrymans (domesticus)
~ willow = Trauerweide f
weigh-batcher (Brit.); weighing batcher (with scale) (US); weigh hopper = Dosierwaage f, Wiegetrichter m

weigh-batching, proportioning by weight, gravimetric batching, batching by weight = Gewichtszumessung *f*, Gewichtsdosierung *f*, Gewichtszuteilung *f*, Gewichtsabmessung *f*, Gewichtsteilmischung *f*, Gewichtszugabe *f*
weigh beam = Wiegebalken *m*
(~) ~ scale = Balkenwaage *f*
weigh bill = Wiegeschein *m*
~ box, see: weighing bucket
weighbridge, see: platform weighing machine
weigh hopper; see: weigh-batcher (Brit.)
weighing batcher with scale (US); see: weigh-batcher (Brit.)
~ bucket, weigh box, weigh(ing) hopper, scale hopper = Wiegebehälter *m*, Wiegegefäß *n*
~ dial = Wiegeskala *f*
weighometer = Gewichtsprüfer *m*
weigh skip = fahrbare Gattierungswaage *f* mit Bodenentleerung *f* zur Beschickung *f* des Aufzugkübels *m*
weight distribution = Gewichtsverteilung *f*
~ graduation (mark) = Gewichtsteilstrich *m*
~ indicator, drilling ~, drillometer = Bohrdruckmesser *m*, Bohrdruckmeßgerät *n*, Drillometer *m*
~ ~ chart = Bohrdruckdiagramm *n*
~ loaded = Ladegewicht *n*
~ on the bit = Bohrdruck *m* [*auf dem Meißel lastendes Gewicht des Gestänges*]
weights = Wichte *f*
*****weir,** barrage = (Stau)Wehr *n*
~ gate, see: gate
~ pier = Wehrpfeiler *m*
~ sill = Wehrschwelle *f*
welded construction = Schweißkonstruktion *f*
~ fabric, steel fabric (mat) = Baustahlgewebe *n* [*punktgeschweißt*]
~ grating, ~ grate = Schweißrost *m*
~ joint = Schweißverbindung *f*, Schweißstoß *m*
~ on flange, flange with welded neck = Vorschweißflansch *m*
~ solid web girder = geschweißter Vollwandträger *m*

~ tubular structure = geschweißte Rohrkonstruktion *f*
welder, welding machine = Schweißapparat *m*
*****welding** = Schweißen *n*, Schweißung *f*
~ burner, ~ torch = Schweißbrenner *m*
~ distortion = Schweißverformung *f*
~ goggles = Schweißbrille *f*
weldless derrick (crane); ~ derricking jib crane (Brit.); **~ ~** boom **~** (US) = nahtloser Derrick-Kran *m*, **~** Mastenkran, **~** Ladebaum *m*
welfare facilities, ~ arrangements = Wohlfahrtseinrichtungen *fpl* [*für Baustellenpersonal n*]
well barge = Schute *f* mit festem Boden *m* für Elevatorbetrieb *m*
~ cuttings, drill ~, rock ~, drillings = Bohrschmant *m*, Bohrgut *n*, Bohrmehl *n*
well-digger, well-sinker, pitman = Brunnengräber *m*
well drill, well drilling rig = Brunnenbohrgerät *n*
~ boring (or drilling) = Brunnenbohren *n*
~ electrode = Brunnenrohr *n* [*Elektroosmose f*]
~ foundation, see: (sunk) ~ ~
~ lining = Brunnenmantel *m*
~ location = Bohrpunkt *m* [*Tiefbohrtechnik f*]
~ natural gas, see: dry ~ ~
wellpoint (dewatering) system (or installation) = Grundwasser(ab)senkungsanlage *f* mit Filterbrunnen *mpl*
~ (~) ~ = Filterbrunnenstaffel *f*
(~) riser pipe = Heberleitung *f*
well production = Brunnenleistung *f*
~ pump = Brunnenpumpe *f*
~ rim = Tiefbettfelge *f*
well-sinker, see: well-digger
well-sunk foundation, see: (sunk) well foundation
WES cell = Bodendruck(meß)dose *f* der Waterways Experiment Station
Western Woldicum = westerwoldisches Raigras *n*
wet-aggregate process, see: wet-sand ~
wet and dry batch concrete plant, see: concrete mixing plant

wet and dry bulb hygrometer, psychrometer = Psychrometer *n*

~ asphaltic bitumen-sand mix process (Brit.); wet asphalt ~ (US) = Naß-(sand)verfahren *n* mit Bitumen *n*

~ classifying = Naß-Trennungssiebung *f*

~ grinding = Naßmahlen *n*, Naßmahlung *f*

~ (~) mill = Naß(mahl)mühle *f*

~ job-site curing (or after-treatment) = Naßhaltung *f*, Feuchthaltung *f* [*Beton m*]

~ land slide = Murgang *m*

~ looper = Feuchtläufer *m*, erste Hänge *f* [*Dachpappenfertigungsanlage f*]

~ mixing (US); see: wetting

~ natural gas, wet casing-head ~, combination ~, natural gas rich in oil vapo(u)rs = feuchtes Naturgas *n*, Reichnaturgas *n*, feuchtes Bohrlochkopfgas, Naßgas

~ process = Naßverfahren *n*

~ ~ rotary cement kiln = Zement-Naßdrehofen *m*

~ rot = Naßfäule *f*

~-sand process, wet sand-binder construction, wet-aggregate process, hydrated lime process, wet sand mix = Naß-(Sand-)Verfahren *n*, Kalkverfahren *n* [*Teer m oder Bitumen n mit nassem Sand m gemischt*]

wet separating = Naß-Reinigungssiebung *f*

~ slaking process = Naßlöschverfahren *n*, Einsumpfen *n* [*Branntkalk m*]

~ slip coating = Naßengobierung *f*

~ soil mix = feuchte bituminöse Bodenvermörtelung *f*

~ stamp(er) = Naßpochwerk *n*, Naßstampfmühle *f*

~ sump capacity = Ölwanneninhalt *m*

~ surface profilometer = Frischbeton-Profilometer *m, n*

wettability = Benetzbarkeit *f*

wetted cross section (Brit.); area of waterway (US) = benetzter Querschnitt *m*

~ perimeter = benetzter Umfang *m* des Querschnitts *m*

wetting, coating; wet mixing (US) = Benetzen *n*, Umhüllen *n* [*mit Bindemittel n*]

~ agent (Brit.); see: plasticizer

~ ~, coating ~ = Benetzungsmittel *n*

~ property, coating ~ = Benetzungseigenschaft *f*

wet type dust collector = Naßentstauber *m*

~ ~ electric precipitator = Befeuchtungs-Elektroabscheider *m*

~ ~ separating device = Naßsetzmaschine *f*

wet-weather rill, rain ~ ~ = Abspülungsfaden *m* (Geol.)

Weymouth pine, see: American yellow ~

wharf (or berth, or jetty) for oil-fuel bunkering = Tankanlage *f*, Betankungsanlage

wheat straw = Weizenstroh *n*

(wheel-)barrow = Schubkarre(n) *f, (m)*, Schiebkarre(n) [*ostdeutsch und mitteldeutsch: Rad(e)ber f; in der Schweiz: Benne f*]

wheel-base = Radstand *m*

wheel block, skid-pan = Hemmschuh *m*

~ ditcher = Schaufelrad-Grabenbagger *m*

wheel(ed) carrier, ~ chassis, ~ carriage = Radfahrwerk *n*, Radfahrgestell *n*, Raduntergestell *n*

(wheeled) carrier = Laufkatze *f* [*Seilförderanlage f*]

(wheeled) flange, wheel-flange = Spurkranz *m*

~ roller = Einradwalze *f* mit Gummireifenfahrwerk *n*

~ tractor crane = Radtraktorkran *m*, Radschlepperkran

~ ~ loader (or shovel) = Radschlepper, Schaufellader *m*, Radschlepper-Ladeschaufel *f*

~ vehicle = Radfahrzeug *n*

wheeler (Brit.) = Schubkarrenfahrer *m*, Schiebkarrenfahrer

wheelers [*in an earth road*] = Fahrrinne *f*, Spurstreifen *m*

wheel frame = Ausleger *m* [*Schaufelrad-Grabenbagger m*]

wheeling (Brit.) = Schubkarrenförderung *f*, Schiebkarrenförderung *f*

wheel load contact area = Radlastaufstandsfläche *f*

~ mark, see: ~ track

wheel-mounted concrete mixer with discharge belt = Bankettmischer *m*

wheel-mounted gate, see: fixed axle ~
~ **shovel(-crane)** = gummibereifter Löffelbagger *m*
wheel-ore (Min.); see: bournonite
wheel plough (Brit.); ~ **plow** (US) = Karrenpflug *m*
(~) **scraper**, see: trailing scoop grader
~ ~ **rear engine** = Schürfkübel(heck)motor *m*
~ ~ **tractor** = (Radschrapper-)Zugwagen *m*
~ **track**, ~ **mark**, **rut** = Radspur *f*, Radeindruck *m*
~ **tractor front end loader** = Radschlepper-Frontlader *m*, Radschlepper-Frontladeschaufel *f*
wheel(-type) ditcher (or **trencher**), **rotary scoop trencher**, **wheel(-type) trenching machine** = Grabenbagger *m* mit Eimerrad *n* (oder Kreiseimerleiter *f*)
wheel-type industrial tractor, see: industrial wheel tractor
~ **ripper** = Radaufreißer *m*
~ **tractor-shovel** = Rad-Hublader *m*, Rad-(Front)Ladeschaufel *f*
wheel washer = Radwaschvorrichtung *f*
Whipple-Murphy truss, see: Linville ~
whirling, see: eddying
whirlwind, see: eddy wind
white beech, **hornbeam** = Weißbuche *f*, Hainbuche *f*, Hagebuche *f*, Hornbaum *m*
~ **bole** = weißer Bolus *m*, weiße Boluserde *f*
~ **cast-in-place concrete** = weißer Ortbeton *m*
~ **cast iron** = Weißguß *m*
~ **clover, Dutch** ~ = Weißklee *m*
~ **concrete** = Weißbeton *m*
~ **copperas** (Min.), see: vitriol ~
~ **countered guttapercha waterproof fuse** = Guttaperchazündschnur *f*, wasserdichte Zündschnur *f*
~ **iron pyrite**, **marcasite**, **fool's gold** (Min.) = Markasit *m*
~ **lead**, **basic lead carbonate**, $Pb_3(CO_3)_2(OH)_2$ = Bleiweiß *n*, Bleihydrokarbonat *n*, basisches kohlensaures Blei *n*
~ ~ **ore**, see: cerussite
~ **lime**, see: fat lime
~ **line, traffic** ~ = Verkehrslinie *f*, Verkehrsstrich *m*

~ ~ **machine**, see: road-marking ~
~ **metal**, see: anti-friction ~
~ **nickel**, **chloanthite** (Min.) = Weißnickelkies *m*, Chloanthit *m*
~ **pine**, see: common ~
~ **poplar**, see: abele
~ **schorl**, see: albite (Min.)
~ **spirit** = Testbenzin *n*
whitestone (Geol.), see: granulite
white vitriol, ~ **copperas**, **goslarite** (Min.) = Goslarit *m*, Zinkvitrol *n*
white-wall tire (US); ~ **tyre** (Brit.) = weißrandiger Reifen *m*, Weißwand-Reifen
to whitewash, **to limewash** = kalken, weißen, tünchen
white willow, Huntingdon ~ = Silberweide *f*, Weißweide *f*
whiting, prepared chalk, precipitated chalk = Schlämmkreide *f*, Schlemmkreide *f*
wholesale customer = Großverbraucher *m*
whole-tine grab, tine grab for clay = Zweischalen-Greifkorb *m* für Stichboden *m* und Gesteinstrümmer *f*
WIBAU binder spraying machine = Rampen-Tank-Spritzmaschine *f*, Fabrikat WIBAU G.m.b.H., ROTHENBERGEN/HESSEN, DEUTSCHLAND
wickerwork, see: basket work
~ **fence, wicker** ~ = Flechtzaun *m*
wick feed lubricator = Dochtöler *m*
~ **hole, cardboard** ~ ~ = Kartondrainloch *n*
wide flange girder (Brit.); see: broad ~ ~
to widen = ausweiten
widened part of duct = Trompete *f* [*Spannbetonkanal m*]
widener, see: road widener
widening = Verbreiterung *f*
~ **spreader** = Schotterverteiler *m* zur Straßenverbreiterung *f*
wide selvage (or **selvedge**) **asphalt roofing** (US) = Bitumendachpappe *f* mit breitem Überlappungsstreifen *m*
width of the road reservation, right-of-way width = Grundrechtsbreite *f* [*Straße f*]
Wieland (concrete) joint = Wieland(beton)fuge *f*
wild cat (US), see: scouting
wildcat well = Suchbohrung *f*

wildcatting campaign = Suchbohrprogramm *n*
wild service tree = Elsbeerbaum *m*
willemite, see: siliceous calamine
willow mattress [*woven of willow trees*] = Weidensteinmatte *f*
~ packing = Weidengeflecht *n*
wimble, see: gim(b)let
to win, to work = abbauen, gewinnen [*Bodenschätze mpl*]
winch, see: (rope) ~
~ drum = Windentrommel *f*
~ for jig haulage on the slope = Bremsbergwinde *f*, Bremsberghaspel *m, f*
~ frame = Windenschild *n* [*Bagger m*]
~ hoist = Windenaufzug *m*
~ type hammer, see: drop ~
wind-blown dust = äolischer Staub *m*
~ sand, blow(n) ~ = Flugsand *m*
wind-borne deposit, ~ sediment = Windsedimentgestein *n*, aeolisches Sedimentgestein
~ soil, see: aeolian ~
wind brace = Windstrebe *f*
~ braced boom = Windstrebengurtung *f*
~ bracing, see: transverse ~
windbreak = Windschutzplane *f*
wind cone, wind-sock, sleeve = Windsack *m*
~ crack = Windkluft *f* [*Holz n*]
(~) deflation (Geol.) = Deflation *f*, Abblasung *f*, Abtragung *f* durch Wind *m*, Windabtragung, äolische Abtragung, Abhebung, Winderosion *f*
wind-faceted pebble(s), see: faceted pebble(s)
wind ga(u)ge, see: anemometer
wind-induced vibration = winderzeugte Schwingung *f*
winding drum = Aufwickeltrommel *f*
~ machine, see: tank ~ ~
~ rope = Aufwickelseil *n*
windlass = Affe *m*, Erdwinde *f*, Handkabelwinde
windle straw = Ackerstraußgras *n*
wind load(ing) = Windbelastung *f*, Windlast *f*
~ mill for drainage = Poldermühle *f*
window glass = Fensterglas *n*
~ sealing rope = Fensterdichtungsstrick *m*
~ sill = Fensterbank *f*
wind power machine = Windkraftmaschine *f*
windrose = Windrose *f*
windrow = Längsreihe *f*, Schwaden *m*, Längsmahd *f*, Streifhaufen *m*, Langmahd *f*
~ and stockpile loader = Haufwerklader *m*
~ eliminator = Schwadenbeseitiger *m* [*Zusatzvorrichtung f am Straßenhobel m*]
~ evener = Schwadenglätter *m*, Langmahdplanierungsschablone *f* [*Zusatzvorrichtung f am Straßenhobel m*]
~-type travel(l)ing (asphalt) (or road) plant, elevating roadmixer, travel(l)ing mixer for soil stabilisation, travel(l)ing (mixing) plant, travel(l)ing mixing machine, road pug travel-mix plant = Aufnahmemischer *m*, Aufnehmermischer, Bodenvermörtelungsmaschine *f* mit hochliegendem Zwangsmischer *m*
windshake, see: cup shake
wind shield = Windschatten *m*
~ ~ = Windschutzscheibe *f*
~ ~ card method, two-cordon ~ = Bezettelungsmethode *f*
wind-sock, see: wind cone
wind spout = Windhose *f*
~ Tee = T-förmiger Windrichtungsanzeiger *m*
~ tunnel = Windkanal *m*
~ vane = Windfahne *f*
~ wave = Windwelle *f*
wine barrel = Weinfaß *n*
wing divider = Bogenzirkel *m*
~ (head) wall, return ~ = Flügel(stirn)mauer *f*
~ nut, see: (butter)fly (screw) nut
~ pump, see: semi-rotary ~
~ rail = Flügelschiene *f*
winning = Gewinnung *f*
~ bid (US); **~ tender** (Brit.) = Zuschlagsangebot *n*
~ design = Ausführungsentwurf *m*
*****winter (or frost) gritting machine, ~(~ ~) gritter** = Streugerät *n* für den Winterdienst *m*
winterized tent = Winterzelt *n*

winter work stoppage = Einstellung *f* der Arbeiten *f* im Winter *m*
wipped fascine, see: saucisse
wire belt = Drahtgurt *m*
~ **cable**, see: ~ rope
~ **cloth**, see: netting wire
~ **cradle**, ~ **chair, metal chair** = Stahldrahtkorb *m* [*Betondeckenfuge f*]
~**-cut brick, machine-made** ~ = Schnittziegel *m*, Maschinenziegel *m*
~**-cut brickmaking**, see: stiff mud process
wire cutter, shear ~ = Drahtschere *f*
wire(d) glass = Drahtglas *n*
wire drawing = Drahtziehen *n*
~ ~ = Fressen *n*, Auswaschen *n* [*des Ventilsitzes m*]
~ ~ **block** = Drahtzug *m*
~ ~ **grease** = Drahtziehfett *n*
~ ~ **machine** = Drahtziehmaschine *f*
~ ~ **plant** = Drahtzieherei *f*
~ **entanglement** = Drahtverhau *m*
~ **fabric**, see: netting wire
wireless beacon = Funkbake *f*
~ **marine navigation** = Schiffsfunkverkehr *m*
wire mesh, see: netting wire
~ **patenting furnace** = Drahtpatentierofen *m*
~ **(or fabric) reinforced silicon carbide blade** = draht- oder gewebeverstärkte Siliziumkarbidschleifscheibe *f*
~ **rope, (steel) cable, steel wire rope** = (Stahl)Drahtseil *n*, Drahtkabel *n*, Stahlseil
~ ~ **core** = Drahtseilseele *f*
~ ~**-operated trencher** = Grabenziehmaschine *f*
~ **tie** = Drahtanker *m*
wirework partition = Drahtflechttrennwand *f*
withdrawing by belt = Bandabzug *m* [*z.B. aus einem Silo m*]
~ **conveyor** = Abzugrinne *f* [*Abziehen n von einem Silo m*]
withe, mid-feather (wall) = Trenn(ungs)mauer *f* der Schornsteinlängszüge *mpl*
witherite, BaCO$_3$ (Min.) = Witherit *m*
withy = Weidensteckling *m*
wobble wheel(ed) compactor, wobbly (or wobbled) wheel(ed) (pneumatic tire) roller = Gummi(reifenvielfach)walze *f* mit oszillierenden Rädern *npl*
WOLFF revolving tower crane = Turmdrehkran *m*, Fabrikat JUL. WOLFF & CO., HEILBRONN/NECKAR, DEUTSCHLAND
wollastonite, tabular spar, Ca$_3$(Si$_3$O$_9$) = Wollastonit *m*
Wolman salts = Wolmansalze *npl*
wood alcohol, methyl ~ = Methylalkohol *m*
~ **bark tar** = Baumrindenteer *m*
~ **borer, auger** = Holzbohrer *m*
wood-chip aggregate = Holzspänezuschlag(stoff) *m*
~ **board** = Holzspanplatte *f*
(wood) chisel = Beitel *m*, Handmeißel *m*
~ **composite (foundation, or bearing) pile**, see: composite (concrete and timber) (foundation, or bearing) pile
~ **cutter's axe, felling axe** = Holzaxt *f*
~ **distillation** = Holzdestillation *f*
wooden barrel principle = Faßreifenprinzip *n*
~ **beam floor** = Holzbalkendecke *f*
~ **crib filled with rip-rap** = Steinkiste *f*
~ **(or wood) form cleaning device, timber** ~ ~ ~ = Schalholzreiniger *m*
~ **(joint) filler** = Holz(fugen)einlage *f*
~ **pallet** = Unterlagsbrett *n* [*Steinformmaschine f*]
~ **pile**, see: timber ~
~ **scraper** = Holzkratze(r) *f*, (*m*)
~ **slat**, see: timber ~
~ **tamper (or rammer)** = Stampfe *f*, Holzstößel *m*, hölzerne Pflasterramme *f*
~ ~ **beam,** ~ **tamping** ~ = Holzstampfbohle *f*, Holzverdichtungsbohle, Holzschlagbohle, Holzstampfbalken *m*
wood-fiber aggregate (US); **wood-fibre** ~ (Brit.) = Holzfaserzuschlag(stoff) *m*
wood fibre (Brit.)/**fiber** (US) **concrete** = Holz(faser)beton *m*, Holzwollebeton
~ ~ **board** = Holzfaserplatte *f*
~ ~ **hardboard** = Holzfaser-Hartplatte *f*
~ **float** = Holzspachtel *m, f*, Streichbrett *n*, Reibebrett *n*
wood flume, timber ~ = Fluder *m*, Holz(ge)rinne *f*, (*n*)
~ **for paving** = Pflasterholz *n*

wood-fuel firing — working stress

wood-fuel firing = Holzfeuerung f
wood grapple, ~ grab, see: pulpwood ~
*wood joint, see: timber ~
(~) mat, see: timber ~
~ opal (Min.) = Holzopal m
~ panel bin, roadbuilders' wood bin = Holzzuschlag(stoff)silo m
~ ~ shuttering, see: timber ~ ~
~ paving = Holzpflasterdecke f, Holzpflaster n
~ peat = Holztorf m
~ pile fender, timber ~ = Holzfender m
~ preservation = Holzkonservierung f, Holzschutz m
~ pulp = Holzfaserbrei m, Holzfasermasse f
WOOD road-mixer = Aufnahmemischer m, Aufnehmermischer m, Fabrikat PETTIBONE WOOD MFG. CO., N. HOLLYWOOD, CALIF., USA
wood rosin = Holzkolophonium n
~ runway = Holzsteg m
~ screw = Holzschraube f
~ shavings tar = Hobelspäneteer m
~ sheathing = Holz-Kanaldielen fpl
~ shuttering cleaning machine = Schalholzreinigungsmaschine f
~ slat conveyor = Holzplattenband(förderer) n, (m)
~ splittings tar = Holzsplitterteer m
~ stave pipe = (Holz)Daubenrohr n
~ tar pitch = Holzteerpech n
~ tip wagon = Holzkastenkipper m
~ truss, timber ~ = hölzernes Sprengwerk n
~ turpentine = Holzterpentinöl n
~ waste tar = Holzabfallteer m
~ wool = Holzwolle f
~ ~ slab = Holzwolleleichtbauplatte f
woodworking = Holzbearbeitung f
~ machine = Holzbearbeitungsmaschine f
~ trade = Holzgewerbe n
wood worm = Holzwurm m
wool batt-type insulation = Steinwolleisolierung f
~ grease, ~ wax, ~ dégras = Woll(schweiß)fett n, Wollwachs n
~ scouring plant, ~ washing ~ = Wollwäscherei f

to work, to win = abbauen, gewinnen [*Bodenschätze mpl*]
workability = Verarbeitbarkeit(sgrad) f, (m)
~ agent, plasticizer; wetting agent (Brit.) = Betonverflüssiger m, Plastifizierungsmittel n, Weichmacher m, BU-Stoff m, plastifizierendes Betonzusatzmittel
work barge (US) = DeLong-Arbeitsinsel f
worked penetration = Walkpenetration f [*Schmierfett n*]
workers' camp, see: contractor's construction camp
working barrel = Tiefpumpenzylinder m
~ (~) valve, travelling ~ = Arbeitsventil n einer Tiefpumpe f
~ capital = Betriebskapital n
~ chamber = Arbeitskammer f
~ committee = Arbeitsausschuß m
~ costs, ~ expenses = Betriebskosten f
~ cycle, work ~ = Arbeitsspiel n
~ cylinder = Arbeitszylinder m
~ day = Arbeitstag m
~ drawing = Arbeitszeichnung f, Ausführungszeichnung
~ element, see: ~ part
~ expenses, ~ costs = Betriebskosten f
(~) face = Abtragwand f, Abbauwand f
(~) ~, see: face
~ force, see: personnel
~ hour = Arbeitsstunde f
~ life, service(able) ~ = Nutzungsdauer f, Lebensdauer
~ line = Netzlinie f, Systemlinie [*Fachwerk n*]
~ part, ~ element = Arbeitselement n, Betriebsteil m, Arbeitsorgan n [*Baumaschine f*]
~ platform = Arbeitsbühne f
~ pressure, operating ~ = Arbeitsdruck m, Betriebsdruck
~ radius, outreach = Ausladung f, Reichweite f [*Drehkran m*]
~ shaft, construction ~ = Arbeitsschacht m
~ speed, on-the-job-travel ~ = Arbeitsgeschwindigkeit f [*Baumaschine f*]
~ stress = Gebrauchsspannung f, Arbeitsspannung

14*

working stroke, expansion ~, firing ~ = Arbeitshub m, Explosionshub
~ week = Arbeitswoche f
~ weight, see: service ~
~ width = Arbeitsbreite f
work item = Leistungsposition f
workmen shelter = Leutebude f
work-out = Ausnutzung f, Auslastung [*Baumaschine f*]
work sampling study = Muster-Arbeitsstudie f
~ schedule, construction ~, (phased) program(me) of works, phasing, job plan, schedule of construction operations, time schedule, progress chart, progress schedule, job schedule, program(me) and progresschart = Bau(zeit)plan m, Arbeitsplan, Baufristenplan
Works Directorate of the Air Force = Luftwaffenbauverwaltung f
(work)shop = Werkstatt f
~ assembly = Werkstattmontage f
~ connection = Werkstattstoß m
~ crane = Werkstattkran m
~ drawing = Werkstattzeichnung f
~ equipment = Werkstattausrüstung f, Werkstättenausrüstung
~ hangar = Werkstatthalle f
~ manufacture = Werkstattfertigung f
works test = Baustellenversuch m
~ visit = Werkbesichtigung f
worm, see: screw
~ auger, screw type soil auger = Schneckenbohrer m, Schneidbohrer [*Bodenuntersuchung f*]
~ conveyor, screw ~, conveyor screw, Archimedean screw conveyor = Förderschnecke f, Schneckenförderer m, Transportschnecke
~ drive = Schnecken(an)trieb m
~ eaten = wurmzerfressen
~ elevator, Archimedean screw elevator = Vertikal-Förderschnecke f, Senkrecht-Förderschnecke
~ feed, screw ~ = Schneckenbeschickung f, Schneckenaufgabe f, Schneckenspeisung
~ geared winch = Schneckenwinde f
~ gear(ing) = Schneckengetriebe n, Schraubengetriebe

~ hole, pipe = Porengang m [*in der Schweiz: Wurmloch n*]
worms' egg = Wurmei n
worm wheel = Schneckenrad n, Schraubenrad
worn, ~ out = abgenutzt
~, ~ out = ausgeschlagen [*Lager n*]
worndown, worn into ruts, rutted = ausgefahren [*Straße f*]
worn tappet head = abgenutzter Stößelkopf m
wortle plate = Ziehlochplatte f
woven cotton fabric = Baumwollgewebe n
~ reed mat = Rohrgeflechtmatte f
~ wire, see: netting ~
wrap = Wickellage f
wrapping = Umwicklung f
~ machine = Wickelmaschine f [*Drahtkabel n*]
~ wire = Wickeldraht n
wreck clearance = Wrackräumung f
wrecking, demolition work, pulling down, taking down = Abbruch(arbeiten) m, (fpl), Abbrucharbeit f, Abtragung f, Abtrag m
~ bar, see: dog
~ crane (US); see: permanent way ~ (Brit.)
~ ~, breakdown ~, accident ~ = Unfallkran m, Bergungskran
wrench = verstellbarer Schraubenschlüssel m
write-off (or writing-off) of depreciations = Abschreibung f, Absetzung für Abnutzung
written instrument = Schriftstück n
wrought shuttering = glatte (Beton-)Schalung f
~ steel = Schweißstahl m
wulfenite, PbMoO$_4$ (Min.) = Wulfenit m, Gelbbleierz n
wych elm, see: mountain ~

X

xenomorphic = xenomorph, fremdgestaltig
~ granular, allotriomorphic-granular, granitic, granitoid = allotriomorphkörnig

xenotime, YPO$_4$ (Min.) = Xenotim *m*, Ytterspat *m*
xerophyte = Trockenpflanze *f*
x-frame carbody = Unterwagen-Rahmen *m* in X-Rahmenform *f* [(*Gleis*)*Kettenbagger m*]
xylene = Xylol *n*

Y

yardage = Flächenleistung *f*
yardstick = Maßstab *m* [*im bildlichen Sinne*]
yard track, shunt ~ = Rangiergleis *n*, Verschiebegleis
yarning material, packing ~ = Dichtungsstoff *m* [*Stemm-Muffe f*]
~ tool = Strickeisen *n* [*Stemm-Muffe f*]
yellow brass = Neumessing *n*
~ iron oxide = Eisenoxydgelb *n*
~ (or iron) pyrites (Min.), see: tool's gold
yield = Ergiebigkeit *f*
~ factor (of a catchment) = Abflußspende *f*
~ point = Streckgrenze *f* [*Stahl m*]
~ safety of solid-web composite structures = Fließsicherheit *f* von Vollwand-Verbundkonstruktionen *fpl*
~ strain = Fließdehnung *f*
~ stress = Streckspannung *f*
~ ~ = Fließspannung *f* [*Stahl m*]
~ value = Anlaßwert *m* [*Suspension f*]
Y junction = schiefe Straßeneinmündung *f*, ~ Straßengab(e)lung *f*
Y level = Nivellierinstrument *n* mit Ringfernrohr *n*
yoke assy = Ausrückgabel *f*
Young's modulus, see: modulus of elasticity

Z

ZEPREX [*Trademark*] = Bezeichnung für den schwedischen Leichtbeton SIPOREX in den USA
zero line, see: neutral axis
zigzag clover = Mittelklee *m*
~ fold (Geol.) = Kaskadenfalte *f*
~ girder, see: half-lattice ~
(zinc) blende, see: black jack
zinc bloom, hydrozincite (Min.) = Hydrozinkit *n*, Zinkblüte *f*
~ dust primer = Zinkstaubgrundierfarbe *f*
zincite, red oxide of zinc, spartalite, sterlingite, ZnO (Min.) = Zinkit *n*, Rotzinkerz *m*
zinc spinel (Min.), see: gahnite
zinkenite, PbS . Sb$_2$S$_3$ (Min.) = Zinkenit *m*, Bleiantimonglanz *m*
zinnwaldite (Min.) = Zinnwaldit *m*
zirconia = Zirkonoxyd *n*
zoisite (Min.) = Zoisit *m*
zonation = Abgrenzung *f* in Zonen *fpl*
zoned earth (fill) dam, see: earth (fill) dam with materials of various permeabilities
zone marking paint, see: traffic-zoning paint
~ of aeration = Grundluftzone *f*
~ ~ concentration, see: B horizon
~ ~ eluviation [*soil*] = Eluviationszone *f*
~ ~ flowage (Geol.) = Plastosphäre *f*, plastische Zone *f*, Fließzone
~ ~ fracture (Geol.) = Zone *f* der Öffnungen *fpl*, Sprödigkeitszone *f*, Bruchzone *f*
~ ~ illuviation, see: B horizon
~ ~ removal, see: A horizon
~ ~ saturation [*the waterlogged strata below the groundwater surface*] = Sättigungszone *f*
~ ~ zero stress = Nulldruckfläche *f*

APPENDIX
ANHANG

Conversion Table Umrechnungstabelle

Multiply by Multipliziere mit	To convert Zur Umwandlung von	To In	
2.54	Inches; Zoll	Centimetres; cm	.39371
30.48	Feet; Fuß	Centimetres; cm	.03281
.03937	Millimetres; mm	Inches; Zoll	
.9144	Yards	Metres; mtr	1.094
1,609.31	Miles; Meilen	Metres; mtr	.000621
3.281	Metres; mtr.	Feet; Fuß	.3048
39.37	Metres; mtr.	Inches; Zoll	
1,853.27	Nautical Miles; Seemeilen	Metres; mtr.	.00054
6.45137	Square inches; Zoll^2	Sq. cms; cm^2	.15501
.093	Square feet; Fuß^2	Sq. metres; m^2	10.7643
.83610	Square yards; Yard^2	Sq. metres; m^2	1.19603
2.58989	Sqare miles; Meile^2	Sq. kilometres; km^2	.38612
16.38618	Cubic inches; Zoll^3	Cub. cms.; cm^3	.06103
28.33	Cubic feet; Fuß^3	Litres; Liter	.0353
.02832	Cubic feet; Fuß^3	Cub. metres; m^3	35.31658
6.24	Cubic feet; Fuß^3	Imperial Gallons	.1602
.76451	Cubic yards; Yards^3	Cub. metres; m^3	1.30802
.3732	Pounds (Troy)	Kilogrammes; kg	2.68
31.10	Ounces (Troy)	Grammes; g	.03216
.4536	Pounds (Avoir.)	Kilogrammes; kg	2.2045
7,000.00	Pounds (Avoir.)	Grains (Troy)	.00014
28.35	Ounces (Avoir.)	Grammes; g	.0352
.065	Grains	Grammes; g	15.38
50.80238	Cwt.	Kilogrammes; kg	.01968
.0022	Grammes; g	Pounds (Avoir.)	
1,016.04754	Tons; Tonnen	Kilogrammes; kg	.00098
907.00	Short tons	Kilogrammes; kg	
4.54346	Imperial Gallons	Litres; Liter	.22010
3.785	US Gallons	Litres; Liter	.264
.56793	Pints	Litres; Liter	1.76077
219.97	Cubic metres; m^3	Imperial Gallons	
264.2	Cubic metres; m^3	US Gallons	
61.022	Litres; Liter	Cub. inches; Zoll^3	
3.531	Hektoliter	Cub. feet; Fuß^3	
2.84	Hektoliter	Bushels	
36.34766	Bushels	Litres; Liter	.02751
10.00	Imp. Gall. of water	Pounds	.1
	To obtain Zur Errechnung obiger Einheiten	From von obigen	Multiply by above ist mit obengenanntem Wert zu multiplizieren

Conversion Table Umrechnungstabelle
Continued Fortsetzung

Multiply by Multipliziere mit	To convert Zur Umwandlung von	To In	
.454	Pounds of water	Litres; Liter	.2202
70.31	Lb. per sq. in. (psi.)	Gm./sq. cms.	.01422
.07031	Lb. per sq. in. (psi.)	kg/cm^2	14.22272
4.88241	Lb. per sq. foot; Pfund/Fuß^2	Kilogrammes per sq. metres; kg/m^2	,20482
.00049	Lb. per sq. foot; Pfund/Fuß^2	Kilogrammes per sq. cm; kg/cm^2	2,049.1807
.24803	Lb. per fathom	kg/mtr.	4.0318
1.48816	Lb. per foot; Pfund/Fuß	kg/mtr.	.6719
.49606	Lb. per Yard; Pfund/Yard	kg/mtr.	2.0159
3,333.4784	Tons per foot; Tonne/Fuß	kg/mtr.	.0003
2.3	Lb. per sq. in. (psi.)	Head of water (ft.)	.434
.7	Lb. per sq. in. (psi.)	Head of water (M.)	1.4285
.068	Lb. per sq. in. (psi.)	Atmospheres; Atmosphären	14.7
1.136	Quarts	Litres; Liter	
157.4944	Tons per sq. in.; Tonnen/Zoll^2	kg/cm^2	.0063
1.574944	Tons per sq. in.; Tonnen/Zoll^2	kg/mm^2	.635
10,936.59840	Tons per sq. foot; Tonnen/Fuß^3	kg/mtr^2	.0001
.0361	Gramm/cm^3	lb. per cub. inch; Pfund/Zoll^3	
62.4	Gramm/cm^3	lb. per cub. foot; Pfund/Fuß^3	.016
.593	Lb. per cub. yard; Pfund/Yard-	kg/mtr-	1.686
16.02	Lb. per cub. foot; Pfund/Fuß^3	kg/mtr^3 (m^3/kg)	.0624
.4047	Acres	Hektar	2.471
11,960.00	Hektar	Yard^2	
.00155	Sq. mm.; mm^2	Square inch; Zoll-	
.0998	Lb. per Imp. Gallon	Kgm./litre; kg/Liter	10.02

To obtain Zur Errechnung obiger Einheiten	From von obigen	Multiply by above ist mit obengenanntem Wert zu multiplizieren

Conversion Table Umrechnungstabelle
Continued Fortsetzung

Multiply by Multipliziere mit	To convert Zur Umwandlung von	To In	
.13825	Foot-lb.; Fuß-Pfund	K'grammetres; mkg	7.2332
.33	Foot-tons	Tonnen-Meter	3.00
309.680	Foot-tons	kilogram-metres	.0032
25.80667	Inch-tons	kilogramm-metres	.0388
41.62314	Inches^4	cm^4	.0240
.62138	Kilometre	Miles	1.6093
3,280.8693	Kilometre	Foot; Fuß	
.00453	Imp. Gallons	Cub. metres; mtr^3	219.98
1.60931	Miles per hour; Meilen pro Stunde	kilometres per hour; km/Stde	.6214
1.467	Miles/h; Meilen/Stde.	Fuß/s	
.869	Miles/h; Meilen/Stde.	Knoten	1.151
1.014	Horse-Power	Force de cheval; Chevaux-vapeur; PS	.9861
746.00	Horse-Power	Watts	.00134
.00136	Watts	PS	
.7373	Watts	Fuß-Pfund/s	
3.415	Wattstunde	B. T. U.	.293
1.36	Kilowatt	PS	
1.341	Kilowatt	HP	
737.3	Kilowatt	Fuß-Pfund/s	
.293	Kilowatt	kcal/s	
.707	H.P.	B.T.U./s	
.178	H.P.	kcal/s	
33,000.00	H.P.	Ft.-lb./min.	
76.00	H.P.	kg-m./sec.	.01316
44.00	Watts	Ft.-lb./min.	.0227
.1	Watts	Kg.-m./sec.	10.00
.948	Kilowatt	B.T.U./s	
860.00	Kilowattstunde (kWh)	kcal	
.447	Pounds per H.P.	Kilogrammes per Cheval-vapeur; kg/PS	2.235
426.9	kcal	kg/m	
3.968	kcal; Kg. Calories	B.T.U.	.252
4,184.00	kcal; Kg. Calories	Joules	.00024

	To obtain Zur Errechnung obiger Einheiten	From von obigen	Multiply by above ist mit obengenanntem Wert zu multiplizieren

Conversion Table Umrechnungstabelle
Continued Fortsetzung

Multiply by Multipliziere mit	To convert Zur Umwandlung von	To In	
.738	Joules	Foot-pound	1.356
.1124	kcal/m³	B.T.U./foot³	8.9
1.8	kcal/Kilogramm (kg)	B.T.U./pound	.5556
14.7	Atmospheres	psig, pounds per square inch gauge	.068
2.713	B.T.U./sq. foot	Kg. Calories/m²	.369
1.033	Atmosphären	Kg./cm²	
760.00	Atmosphären	mm Q.-S.	
.293	B.T.U.	Wattstunde	3.415
.0333	Zoll-Quecksilbersäule; Inch-Mercury-Column	atm	
13.6	Zoll-Quecksilbersäule; Inch-Mercury-Column	Zoll-Wassersäule; Inch-Water-Col.	.0735
.49	Zoll-Quecksilbersäule; Inch-Mercury-Column	pound/inch²	
.036	Zoll-Wassersäule; Inch-Water-Column	pound/inch²	
.9	German candles	English candles	1.1111
9.55	Carcels	Candles	.1047
88.00	Miles/hour	Ft./min.	.01134
197.00	Metres/sec.	Ft./min.	.00508
.208	Centipoise	Lb. force sec./sq. ft.	4.8
.54	Kilometre/h	Knoten	
152.4	Tonne/Zoll²	atm	
25,200.00	Therm (= 100000 B.T.U.)	kcal.	
1.093659	Tons per sq. foot; Tonnen/Fuß²	kg/cm²	
5.43	Imp. Gall./sq. yard	Liter/m²	.1845

To obtain Zur Errechnung obiger Einheiten	From von obigen	Multiply by above ist mit obengenanntem Wert zu multiplizieren

British Weights and Measures

Lineal Measure

4	Inches	make	1 Hand	1 Inch	=	.08 Ft.
9	,,	,,	1 Span		=	.207 Yard
12	,,	,,	1 Foot	1 Link	=	7.92 Inches
3	Feet	,,	1 Yard	1 Foot	=	.333 Yard
5	,,	,,	1 Pace	1 Yard	=	36.00 Inches
6	,,	,,	1 Fathom	1 Chain	=	100.00 Links
5.5	Yards	,,	1 Rod, Pole		=	22.00 Yards
			or Perch		=	.0125 Miles
4	Poles	,,	1 Chain	1 Furlong	=	220.00 Yards
10	Chains	,,	1 Furlong		=	.125 Miles
8	Furlongs	,,	1 Mile	1 Mile	=	80.00 Chains
3	Miles	,,	1 League		=	1,760.00 Yards
1.151	,,	,,	1 Nautical Mile	A Knot is a speed of 1 Nautical Mile per hour

Square or Land Measure

144	Sq. Inches = 1 Sq. Foot	An Acre equals 4.840 Square Yards
9	Sq. Feet = 1 Sq. Yard	= .4047 Hectares
30.25	Sq. Yards = 1 Sq. Pole	1 Sq. Link = 62.75 Sq. Inches (approx.)
40	Poles = 1 Rood	1 Sq. Chain = 10,000.00 Sq. Links = 484 Sq.
4	Roods = 1 Acre	Yards
640	Acres = 1 Sq. Mile	10 Sq. Chains = 1 Acre = 100,000.0 Sq. Links
		= 4,840 Sq. Yards
		33 Sq. Yards = 1 Rod of Building = 27.6 Sq. Metre
		100 Sq. Feet = Square of Flooring or Roofing
		= 9.3 Sq. Metre
		272.25 Square Feet = Rod of Bricklayer's Work
		= 25.4 Sq. Metre

Cubic or Solid Measure

Cubic Foot = 0.037 cubic yard = 1,728 Cub. Inches = 6.23 Imp. Gall. = 7.48 US-Gallons
  = 28,317 Cub. centimetre = .0283 Cub. metre = 28.3 Litres
Cubic Yard = 27 Cub. Feet = 168 Imp. Gall. = 202 US-Gallons = 21.033 Bushels =
  .7645 Cubic metre = 764.5 Litres
1 Cubic Inch = 0.00058 Cubic Foot = 16,38618 cm^3
Stack of Wood = 108 Cubic Feet = 3.06 Cubic metre
Shipping ton = 40 Cubic Feet of merchandise = 1.13 Cubic metre
Shipping ton = 42 Cubic Feet of timber = 1.18 Cubic metre
One ton or load = 50 Cubic Feet of hewn timber = 1.42 Cubic metre
Ton of displacement of a ship = 35 Cubic Feet = 1.02 Cubic metre

Fluid Memoranda

1 Imp. Gallon of water = 10 lb.
1 Cubic Foot of water = 6.23 Imp. Gall. = 62.3 lb = 7.48 US-Gallons
  = .0283 Cub. metre = 1,728.00 Cub. inches
  = 28,317.00 Cub. centimetre = .037 Cubic yard
  = 28.317 Litres

1 lb. water at 62° F. = .016 Cub. Foot
1 Imp. Gallon = 1.2 US-Gallon = 8 Pints = 277.418 Cub. inches = 4.546 Litres
1 Quart = 2 Pints = .25 Imp. Gall. = 69.35 Cub. inches = 1.136 Litres
1 Pint = 4 Gills = .125 Imp. Gall. = 34.682 Cub. inches = .02 Cub. Ft. = 568.3 Cub. centimetre = .5683 Litres
1 Firkin = 9 Imp. Gall. = 41 Litres
1 Kilderkin = 2 Firkins = 82 Litres
1 British Barrel = 4 Firkins = 36 Imp. Gall. = 1.028 US-Barrel = 288 Pints = .215 Cub. Yard = 5.77 Cub. Ft. = 163.566 Litres
1 Gill = .25 Pint = 8.67 Cub. inches = .142 Litres
1 Inch of Rainfall = 22,622.00 Imp. Gallons per Acre = 100.00 tons (approximately)

Avoirdupois Weight

1 Oz. = 28.35 Grammes = .063 lb. = 16 Drams = 437.5 Grains
1 lb. = 16 Oz. = 453.6 Grammes = .4536 kg = 7,000.00 Grains
1 cwt. (Hundredweight) = 112 lb. = 50.80238 kg
1 Stone = 14 lb. = 6.35 kg
1 Quarter = 28 lb.
1 Butcher Stone = 8 lb.
1 Grain = .0648 Grammes
1 Long ton = 2,240.00 lb. = 1.120 Short ton = 20 cwt. = 1,016.05 kg = 1.01605 Metric tons
1 Short ton = 2,000.00 lb. = .893 Long ton = 907.19 kg = .90719 Metric ton

Miscellaneous

1 US-Gallon = 231 Cub. inches = .1337 Cub. feet = 3.785 Litres = .833 Imp. Gallon
1 US-Pound = 226,8 g
1 PSh = 2512 Btu = 0,986 HPh = 633 kcal = 0,736 kWh
1 kWh = 3415 Btu = 861 kcal = 1,36 PSh
1 Btu (Brit. thermal unit) = 0,252 kcal = 108 mkg = 0,00029 kWh = 0,0004 PSh
1 Imperial Bushel = 36.37 Litres
1 Winchester Bushel (USA) = 35.257 Litres
1 Bale = 205 kg
1 Sack of Cement (USA) = 42.676 kg
1 Acre-foot = 43,560 Cubic feet = 1,232.6 Cubic metre (this unit relates to irrigation computations)
1 US-Barrel = .972 British Barrel = 42 US-Gallons = .208 Cubic Yards = 5.62 Cub. Ft. = 158.98 Litres
1 preußischer Morgen = 2,500.00 Sq. metre = 25 Ar = .25 Hektar = .0025 Sq. kilometre = .61775 Acres
1 Zentner = 50 kg = 110.225 lb.
1 metrisches Pfund = 500 Grammes = 1.1 lb.
1 Cental = .05 Short ton = 45.36 kg
1 Dram = 3 Scruples = 1.77 Grammes
1 morgen-foot = 2,608.847204 Cubic metre (this unit relates to irrigation computations in South Africa)
1 morgen (South-Afrika) = 2.11654 Acres
1 geographische Meile = 4 Seemeilen = 7,240 Kilometer

1 Seemeile (Knoten) = 1,000.00 Faden = 1,852 km
1 preußische Landmeile = 7,532 km
1 Cubic foot/second per 1,000 acres = 0,00708 m^3/Sekunde per km^2
1 Day-second-foot (dsf.) = 86.400 cu. ft.
1 russische Werst = 1,500.00 Arschinen = 1,06678 km
1 deutsche Quadratmeile = 56,25 Square kilometre (km^2)
1 geographische Quadratmeile = 55,06 Square kilometre (km^2)
1 russische Quadratwerst = 1,138 km^2
1 bbl = 376 pds. = 170,704 kg
1 bbl. = 4 Cubic feet = 0,112 m^3
1 mbm (mille feet board measure) = 2,36 m^3

Cubic Measures and Weights per Unit of Area
Raummaße und Gewichte pro Flächeneinheit

1 kg/cm^2 = 14.226 lb./sq. inch (psi) = 2.050 lb/.sq. ft. = 18,450.00 lb./sq. yard = 10 tons/sq. metre
1 kg/m^2 = .205 lb./sq. ft. = 1.844 lb./sq. yard
1 lb./sq. inch = .0703 kg/cm^2 = 144 lb./sq. ft.
1 lb./sq. ft. = 9 lb./sq. yard = 4.882 kg/mtr.^{2} = .0069 lb./sq. inch
1 lb./sq. yard = .11 lb./sq. ft. = .542 kg/mtr.^{2}
1 Litre/mtr.^{2} = .020 Imp. Gall./ft.^{2} = .184 Imp. Gall./yard^2 = .025 US-Gall./ft.^{2} = ,221 US-Gallon/yard^2
1 Imp. Gall./ft.^{2} = 9 Imp. Gall./yard^2 = 48.94 Litres/mtr.^{2}
1 Imp. Gall./yard^2 = .111 Imp. Gall./ft.^{2} = 5.44 Litres/mtr.^{2}
1 US-Gallon/ft.^{2} = 9 US-Gallons/yard^2 = 40.77 Litres/mtr.^{2}
1 US-Gallon/yard^2 = .111 US/Gallon-ft.^{2} = 4.53 Litres/mtr.^{2}
1 Litre/mtr.^{2} = .093 Litre/ft.^{2} = .836 Litre/yard^2.
1 Litre/ft.^{2} = 9 Liter/yard^2 = 9.18 Litre/mtr.^{2}
1 Litre/yard^2 = .111 Litre/ft.^{2} = 1.02 Litre/mtr.^{2}

Velocities Geschwindigkeiten

1 mtr./sec. = 3.6 km/h = 1.093 Yards/sec. = 2.237 Miles/h = 3.281 Ft./sec.
1 km/h = .278 mtr./sec. = .304 Yards/sec. = .622 Miles/h = 0.91178 Ft./sec.
1 Yard/sec. = .915 mtr./sec. = 3.292 km/h = 2.040 Miles/h
1 Mile/h = .447 mtr./sec. = 1.609 km/h = .489 Yards/sec.

Temperatures Temperaturen

Celsius (° C)   = 5/9 (° F—32) = 5/4° R
Réaumur (° R)   = 4/5° C   = 4/9 (° F—32)
Fahrenheit (° F) = 9/5° C + 32 = 9/4° R + 32

°C	°R	°F	°C	°R	°F
— 40	— 32	— 40	+ 60	+ 48	+ 140
— 35	— 28	— 31	+ 65	+ 52	+ 149
— 30	— 24	— 22	+ 70	+ 56	+ 158
— 25	— 20	— 13	+ 75	+ 60	+ 167
— 20	— 16	— 4	+ 80	+ 64	+ 176
— 17.8	— 14.2	0	+ 85	+ 68	+ 185
— 15	— 12	+ 5	+ 90	+ 72	+ 194
— 10	— 8	+ 14	+ 95	+ 76	+ 203
— 5	— 4	+ 23	+ 100	+ 80	+ 212
0	0	+ 32	+ 110	+ 88	+ 230
+ 5	+ 4	+ 41	+ 120	+ 96	+ 248
+ 10	+ 8	+ 50	+ 130	+ 104	+ 266
+ 15	+ 12	+ 59	+ 140	+ 112	+ 284
+ 20	+ 16	+ 68	+ 150	+ 120	+ 302
+ 25	+ 20	+ 77	+ 175	+ 140	+ 347
+ 30	+ 24	+ 86	+ 200	+ 160	+ 392
+ 35	+ 28	+ 95	+ 225	+ 180	+ 437
+ 40	+ 32	+ 104	+ 250	+ 200	+ 482
+ 45	+ 36	+ 113	+ 275	+ 220	+ 527
+ 50	+ 40	+ 122	+ 300	+ 240	+ 572
+ 55	+ 44	+ 131	+ 350	+ 280	+ 662

Schedule of Symbols used in Reinforced Concrete Construction
Übersicht der im Stahlbetonbau gebräuchlichen Bezeichnungen

British Britisch			German Deutsch
a	=	Hebelarm der inneren Kräfte = lever of the resistance moment	z
B	=	Breite der Druckzone eines Querschnitts = overall breadth of compressive flange of a beam	b
B_1, B_2	=	zulässige Haftspannungen = permissible average and local bond stresses	τ_{1zul}
b	=	Stegbreite eines Plattenbalkens = breadth of a rectangular beam or the breadth of the rib of a T- or -L-beam	b_0
c	=	zulässige Betonspannung bei reinem Druck = permissible stress in concrete in direct compression	$\varrho_{bd\,zul}$
	=	zulässige Stahlspannung bei Säulenlängsbewehrung = permissible compression stress for column bar	$\varrho_{e\,zul}$

British Britisch			German Deutsch
D	=	Durchmesser des Säulenkopfes bei Pilzdecken, Durchmesser eines Längsbewehrungsstabes = diameter of column head supporting flat slab (It is elsewhere used for overall concrete depth, or least lateral dimension of a column)	δ
d	=	Durchmesser eines Querbewehrungsstabes = diameter of one transverse reinforcing bar	δ
h	=	Nutzhöhe einer Stahlbetonplatte = useful height of reinforced concrete slab	h
K	=	Steifheit eines Baugliedes = $\dfrac{J}{L}$ = stiffness of constructional element	
L	=	Länge einer Säule, Lichtweite eines Tragwerks = length of a column or beam between adequate lateral restraints. (In the case of slabs L is the average L_1 and L_2)	h_s bzw. w
L_1, L_2	=	Feldlängen bei Pilzdecken = L_1 (in the case of flat slabs) length of panel in the direction of span L_2 (in the case of flat slabs) width of panel at right angles to direction of span	l_x, l_y
l	=	Spannweite eines Bauteils = effective span of beam or slab or effective height of cloumn	l
		Knicklänge einer Säule	h_k
l_x, l_y	=	Seitenlängen kreuzweise bewehrter Platten = l_x lenght of shorter side of slab spanning in two directions; l_y length of longer side of slab spanning in two directions	l_x, l_y
M	=	Biegemomente mit Index nach Bedarf = bending moments (suffixes as required)	M
m	=	Verhältnis der Elastizitätszahlen von Stahl und Beton = modular ratio	n
S	=	Querkraft = total shear across a section	Q
t_b	=	zulässige Stahlspannung in Spiralbewehrung = permissible stress in helical reinforcement	—
u_p	=	Würfelfestigkeit des Betons bei Eignungsprüfungen = cube crushing strength (preliminary test)	W
u_w	=	Würfelfestigkeit des Betons bei Güteprüfungen = cube crushing strength (works test)	W
W	=	Gesamtlast eines Balkens oder einer Platte = total load on beam or slab	
u	=	Gesamtlast je Längen- oder Flächeneinheit = total load per unit area of slab or per unit length of beam	q

U. S. Standard Sieve Data (A. S. T. M.)

Bureau of Standard Sieve Number		Specified sieve opening lichte Maschenweite		Specified wire diameter	
		Inches	Millimeters	Inches	Millimeters
(3/16 in.)	4	—.187	4.76	—.050	1.27
	5	—.157	4.00	—.044	1.12
	6	—.132	3.36	—.040	1.02
	7	—.111	2.83	—.036	—.92
	8[1]	—.0937	2.38	—.0331	—.84
	10	—.0787	2.00	—.0299	—.76
	12	—.0661	1.68	—.0272	—.69
	14	—.0555	1.41	—.0240	—.61
	16[2]	—.0469	1.19	—.0213	—.54
	18	—.0394	1.00	—.0189	—.48
	20	—.0331	—.84	—.0165	—.42
	25	—.0280	—.71	—.0146	—.37
	30[3]	—.0232	—.59	—.0130	—.33
	35	—.0197	—.50	—.0114	—.29
	40	—.0165	—.42	—.0098	—.25
	45	—.0138	—.35	—.0087	—.22
	50[4]	—.0117	—.297	—.0074	—.188
	60	—.0098	—.250	—.0064	—.162
	70	—.0083	—.210	—.0055	—.140
	80	—.0070	—.177	—.0047	—.119
	100[5]	—.0059	—.149	—.0040	—.102
	120	—.0049	—.125	—.0034	—.086
	140	—.0041	—.105	—.0029	—.074
	170	—.0035	—.088	—.0025	—.063
	200	—.0029	—.074	—.0021	—.053
	230	—.0024	—.062	—.0018	—.046
	270	—.0021	—.053	—.0016	—.041
	325	—.0017	—.044	—.0014	—.036

[1] B.S. Sieve No. 7   0.0949 Aperture size (in.)
[2] B.S. Sieve No. 14   0.0474 Aperture size (in.)
[3] B.S. Sieve No. 25   0.0236 Aperture size (in.)
[4] B.S. Sieve No. 52   0.0116 Aperture size (in.)
[5] B.S. Sieve No. 100   0.0060 Aperture size (in.)

Die gebräuchlichsten Siebsysteme mit ihren wichtigsten Daten

Amerikanischer ASTM Maschensiebsatz		Britischer STANDARD Maschensiebsatz		Maschensiebe DIN 1171 Ausgabe 1934			Rundlochsiebe DIN 1170 Ausgabe 1933	
Maschen je Zoll	lichte Maschenweite mm	Maschen je Zoll	lichte Maschenweite mm	Gewebe Nr.	Maschen je cm²	lichte Maschenweite mm	Lochdurchmesser mm	Umrechnung in lichte Maschenweite mm
—	—	—	—	100	10000	0,060		
200	0,074	200	0,076	80	6400	0,075		
—	—	—	—	70	4900	0,090[2])		
100	0,149	100	0,152	40	1600	0,150		
80	0,177	85	0,178	35[1])	1225	0,177		
70	0,210	72	0,211	30	900	0,200	Umrechnung nach Rottfuchs	
60	0,250	60	0,251	24	576	0,250		
50	0,297	52	0,294	20	400	0,300		
—	—	44	0,353	—	—	—		
40	0,420	36	0,422	14	196	0,430		
30	0,590	25	0,599	10	100	0,600		
—	—	—	—	—	—	—	1	0,7
—	—	—	—	8	64	0,750		
20	0,840	18	0,853	—	—	—		
18	1,000	—	—	—	—	1,000		
16	1,190	14	1,200	5	—	1,200		
12	1,680	10	1,676	—	—	—		
10	2,000	8	2,057	—	—	2,000	3	2,3
5	4,000					3	5	3,8
3/16″ (4)	4,760	2/16″	4,760			5	7	5,4
1/4″	6,35	1/4″	6,35			6	8	6,2
						8	10	7,8
3/8″	9,52	3/8″	9,52			—	12	9,5
1/2″	12,7	1/2″	12,7			12	15	12
						15	20	16,4
3/4″	19,050	3/4″	19,050			18	25	20,8
1″	25,4	1″	25,4			25	30	25,2
1 1/4″	31,75	1 1/4″	31,75			30	40	34,0
1 1/2″	38,100	1 1/2″	38,100					
2″	50,800							
3″	76,200	3″	76,200					
6″	152,400							

Anmerkung: Unterstrichene Zahlen = Siebe für abgekürzte Siebungen.
[1]) Ergänzungssieb.   [2]) früher 0,088.

Bauverlag-Wörterbücher

Wörterbuch für Baurecht, Grundstücksrecht und Raumordnung
Dictionary of Construction Law, Land Law and Regional Policy

Von H. Bucksch. Format 13,5 x 20,5 cm. Gebunden.

Band 1: Deutsch-Englisch. 1052 Seiten mit rd. 70 000 Stichwörtern. DM 390,–
Band 2: Englisch-Deutsch. 1140 Seiten mit rd. 70 000 Stichwörtern. DM 390,–

Die internationale Zusammenarbeit hat in den letzten Jahren vor allem auch im Baubetrieb einen beträchtlichen Umfang angenommen. Eine einwandfreie sprachliche Verständigung ist ganz entscheidend abhängig von der exakten Kenntnis der englischen Fachbegriffe. Sicherheit bei der Wahl bzw. Übersetzung selbst des speziellsten Fachbegriffes vermittelt dieses umfassendste baurechtliche Wörterbuch.

Wörterbuch für Bautechnik und Baumaschinen
Dictionary of Civil Engineering and Construction Machinery and Equipment

Von H. Bucksch. Format 12,5 x 17 cm.

Band 1: Deutsch-Englisch. 8. Auflage. 1184 Seiten. Rund 68 000 Stichwörter. Plastik DM 180,–
Band 2: Englisch-Deutsch. 8. Auflage. 1219 Seiten. Rund 71 000 Stichwörter. Plastik DM 180,–

Preise Stand Dez. '86, Preisänderungen vorbehalten.

Bauverlag·Wiesbaden und Berlin